THE ALMANAC
OF AMERICAN
POLITICS
1990

The Senators, the Representatives
and the Governors:
Their Records and Election Results,
Their States and Districts

Michael Barone and Grant Ujifusa

National
Journal
Washington, D.C.

Printed in the United States of America by R.R. Donnelley & Sons Company. Composition by Applied Graphics Technologies. Distributed to the trade by Macmillan Publishing Company, 866 Third Avenue, New York, New York 10022. Cover design by Eason Associates.

Photographs by Bruce Reedy, Susan M. Muniak, Day Walters, Stan Barouh, and Richard A. Bloom. For information regarding photographs, contact: National Journal, *1730 M Street N.W., Washington, D.C. 20036. Telephone (202) 857-1400. All rights reserved.*

ISBN 0-89234-043-6 (Cloth)
ISBN 0-89234-044-4 (Paper)

National Journal Inc.
President: John Fox Sullivan
Group Vice President: Roger Kranz
Vice President, Finance: Grace Geisinger
Assistant Publisher: Eleanor D. Evans
Marketing Director: Charles Post
Circulation Director: Gene Sittenfeld

National Journal Inc. is a wholly-owned subsidiary of the Times Mirror Co.

A Times Mirror Company

ALMANAC OF AMERICAN POLITICS 1990

Authors:	Michael Barone, Grant Ujifusa
Editor:	Eleanor D. Evans
Managing Editor:	Gary Cohen
Director of Research and Associate Editor:	John Gallagher
Assistant Editors:	Sarah Orrick, Cathy Newson, Paul Harstad
Research Assistants:	Isobel Ellis, Jane Vermette, Peggie Tuite, David Sobba
Production Manager:	Patrick Sheridan
Production Support:	Lisa Campbell, Gail Reardon
Photographers:	Bruce Reedy, Susan Muniak, Day Walters, Stan Barouh, Richard A. Bloom

Additionally, National Journal Inc. would like to acknowledge the following organizations and people for the services they provided; Tony Black and the National Committee for an Effective Congress; Richard E. Cohen, James A. Barnes and Greta Waller of *National Journal*; Applied Graphics Technologies; Cindy Johns and Eason Associates; U.S. Bureau of the Census; and the Federal Election Commission.

CONTENTS

DISTRICTS AT-A-GLANCE

Districts At-A-Glance is a guide to the geographic area represented by a Member of Congress. Senators will not have a specific location listed next to their name since they represent the entire state.

ALABAMA

Senate		Heflin (D)	
		Shelby (D)	
House	1	Callahan (R)	*Mobile*
	2	Dickinson (R)	*Montgomery*
	3	Browder (D)	*Anniston*
	4	Bevill (D)	*Jasper*
	5	Flippo (D)	*Huntsville*
	6	Erdreich (D)	*Birmingham*
	7	Harris (D)	*Tuscaloosa*

ALASKA

Senate		Stevens (R)	
		Murkowski (R)	
House	1	Young (R)	*At Large*

ARIZONA

Senate		DeConcini (D)	
		McCain (R)	
House	1	Rhodes (R)	*Tempe*
	2	Udall (D)	*Phoenix*
	3	Stump (R)	*Flagstaff*
	4	Kyl (R)	*Scottsdale*
	5	Kolbe (R)	*Tucson*

ARKANSAS

Senate		Bumpers (D)	
		Pryor (D)	
House	1	Alexander (D)	*Jonesboro*
	2	Robinson (D)	*Little Rock*
	3	Hammerschmidt (R)	*Fort Smith*
	4	Anthony (D)	*Pine Bluff*

CALIFORNIA

Senate		Cranston (D)	
		Wilson (R)	
House	1	Bosco (D)	*Santa Rosa*
	2	Herger (R)	*Chico*
	3	Matsui (D)	*Sacramento*
	4	Fazio (D)	*Sacramento*
	5	Pelosi (D)	*San Francisco*
	6	Boxer (D)	*Marin County*
	7	Miller (D)	*Richmond*
	8	Dellums (D)	*Oakland*
	9	Stark (D)	*Hayward*
	10	Edwards (D)	*San Jose*
	11	Lantos (D)	*San Mateo County*
	12	Campbell (R)	*Sunnyvale*
	13	Mineta (D)	*San Jose*
	14	Shumway (R)	*Stockton*
	15	*vacant*	*Modesto*
	16	Panetta (D)	*Monterey*
	17	Pashayan (R)	*Fresno*
	18	Lehman (D)	*Fresno*
	19	Lagomarsino (R)	*Santa Barbara*
	20	Thomas (R)	*Bakersfield*
	21	Gallegly (R)	*Thousand Oaks*
	22	Moorhead (R)	*Pasadena*
	23	Beilenson (D)	*Beverly Hills*
	24	Waxman (D)	*Hollywood*
	25	Roybal (D)	*Los Angeles*
	26	Berman (D)	*Van Nuys*
	27	Levine (D)	*Santa Monica*
	28	Dixon (D)	*Culver City*
	29	Hawkins (D)	*Los Angeles*
	30	Martinez (D)	*El Monte*
	31	Dymally (D)	*Compton*
	32	Anderson (D)	*Long Beach*
	33	Dreier (R)	*Pomona*
	34	Torres (D)	*West Covina*
	35	Lewis (R)	*Redlands*
	36	Brown (D)	*Riverside*
	37	McCandless (R)	*Palm Springs*
	38	Dornan (R)	*Santa Ana*
	39	Dannemeyer (R)	*Anaheim*
	40	Cox (R)	*Newport Beach*
	41	Lowery (R)	*San Diego*
	42	Rohrabacher (R)	*Long Beach*
	43	Packard (R)	*Carlsbad*
	44	Bates (D)	*San Diego*
	45	Hunter (R)	*Coronado*

COLORADO

Senate		Armstrong (R)	
		Wirth (D)	
House	1	Schroeder (D)	*Denver*
	2	Skaggs (D)	*Boulder*
	3	Campbell (D)	*Pueblo*
	4	Brown (R)	*Greeley*
	5	Hefley (R)	*Colorado Springs*
	6	Schaefer (R)	*Lakewood*

CONNECTICUT

Senate		Dodd (D)	
		Lieberman (D)	
House	1	Kennelly (D)	*Hartford*
	2	Gejdenson (D)	*New London*
	3	Morrison (D)	*New Haven*
	4	Shays (R)	*Stamford*
	5	Rowland (R)	*Waterbury*
	6	Johnson (R)	*New Britain*

DELAWARE

Senate		Roth (R)	
		Biden (D)	
House	1	Carper (D)	*At Large*

FLORIDA

Senate		Graham (D)	
		Mack (R)	
House	1	Hutto (D)	*Pensacola*
	2	Grant (R)	*Tallahassee*
	3	Bennett (D)	*Jacksonville*
	4	James (R)	*Daytona Beach*
	5	McCollum (R)	*Orlando*
	6	Stearns (R)	*Ocala*
	7	Gibbons (D)	*Tampa*
	8	Young (R)	*St. Petersburg*
	9	Bilirakis (R)	*Clearwater*
	10	Ireland (R)	*Winter Haven*
	11	Nelson (D)	*Melbourne*
	12	Lewis (R)	*N. Palm Beach*
	13	Goss (R)	*Ft. Myers*
	14	Johnston (D)	*W. Palm Beach*
	15	Shaw (R)	*Ft. Lauderdale*
	16	Smith (D)	*Hollywood*
	17	Lehman (D)	*N. Miami Beach*
	18	*vacant*	*Miami*
	19	Fascell (D)	*Coral Gables*

GEORGIA

Senate		Nunn (D)	
		Fowler (D)	
House	1	Thomas (D)	*Savannah*
	2	Hatcher (D)	*Albany*
	3	Ray (D)	*Columbus*
	4	Jones (D)	*Dunwoody*
	5	Lewis (D)	*Atlanta*
	6	Gingrich (R)	*Carrollton*
	7	Darden (D)	*Marietta*
	8	Rowland (D)	*Macon*
	9	Jenkins (D)	*Dalton*
	10	Barnard (D)	*Augusta*

HAWAII

Senate		Inouye (D)	
		Matsunaga (D)	
House	1	Saiki (R)	*Honolulu*
	2	Akaka (D)	*Outer Islands*

IDAHO

Senate		McClure (R)	
		Symms (R)	
House	1	Craig (R)	*Boise*
	2	Stallings (D)	*Pocatello*

ILLINOIS

Senate		Dixon (D)	
		Simon (D)	
House	1	Hayes (D)	*Chicago*
	2	Savage (D)	*S. Chicago*
	3	Russo (D)	*Oak Lawn*
	4	Sangmeister (D)	*Joliet*
	5	Lipinski (D)	*Chicago*
	6	Hyde (R)	*Wheaton*
	7	Collins (D)	*Chicago*
	8	Rostenkowski (D)	*Chicago*
	9	Yates (D)	*Chicago*
	10	Porter (R)	*Evanston*
	11	Annunzio (D)	*Chicago*
	12	Crane (R)	*Palatine*
	13	Fawell (R)	*Oak Brook*
	14	Hastert (R)	*Elgin*
	15	Madigan (R)	*Bloomington*
	16	Martin (R)	*Rockford*
	17	Evans (D)	*Moline*
	18	Michel (R)	*Peoria*
	19	Bruce (D)	*Danville*
	20	Durbin (D)	*Springfield*
	21	Costello (D)	*East St. Louis*
	22	Poshard (D)	*Carbondale*

INDIANA

Senate	Lugar (R)	
	Coats (R)	
House	1 Visclosky (D)	*Gary*
	2 Sharp (D)	*Muncie*
	3 Hiler (R)	*South Bend*
	4 Long (D)	*Fort Wayne*
	5 Jontz (D)	*Kokomo*
	6 Burton (R)	*Indianapolis*
	7 Myers (R)	*Terre Haute*
	8 McCloskey (D)	*Evansville*
	9 Hamilton (D)	*Bloomington*
	10 Jacobs (D)	*Indianapolis*

IOWA

Senate	Grassley (R)	
	Harkin (D)	
House	1 Leach (R)	*Davenport*
	2 Tauke (R)	*Cedar Rapids*
	3 Nagle (D)	*Waterloo*
	4 Smith (D)	*Des Moines*
	5 Lightfoot (R)	*Council Bluffs*
	6 Grandy (R)	*Sioux City*

KANSAS

Senate	Dole (R)	
	Kassebaum (R)	
House	1 Roberts (R)	*Dodge City*
	2 Slattery (D)	*Topeka*
	3 Meyers (R)	*Kansas City*
	4 Glickman (D)	*Wichita*
	5 Whittaker (R)	*Emporia*

KENTUCKY

Senate	Ford (D)	
	McConnell (R)	
House	1 Hubbard (D)	*Paducah*
	2 Natcher (D)	*Owensboro*
	3 Mazzoli (D)	*Louisville*
	4 Bunning (R)	*Covington*
	5 Rogers (R)	*Somerset*
	6 Hopkins (R)	*Lexington*
	7 Perkins (D)	*Ashland*

LOUISIANA

Senate	Johnston (D)	
	Breaux (D)	
House	1 Livingston (R)	*New Orleans*
	2 Boggs (D)	*New Orleans*
	3 Tauzin (D)	*New Iberia*
	4 McCrery (R)	*Shreveport*
	5 Huckaby (D)	*Monroe*
	6 Baker (R)	*Baton Rouge*
	7 Hayes (D)	*Lafayette*
	8 Holloway (R)	*Alexandria*

MAINE

Senate	Cohen (R)	
	Mitchell (D)	
House	1 Brennan (D)	*Portland*
	2 Snowe (R)	*Bangor*

MARYLAND

Senate	Sarbanes (D)	
	Mikulski (D)	
House	1 Dyson (D)	*Eastern Shore*
	2 Bentley (R)	*Towson*
	3 Cardin (D)	*Baltimore*
	4 McMillen (D)	*Annapolis*
	5 Hoyer (D)	*Landover*
	6 Byron (D)	*Hagerstown*
	7 Mfume (D)	*Baltimore*
	8 Morella (R)	*Montgomery County*

MASSACHUSETTS

Senate	Kennedy, E. (D)	
	Kerry (D)	
House	1 Conte (R)	*Pittsfield*
	2 Neal (D)	*Springfield*
	3 Early (D)	*Worcester*
	4 Frank (D)	*Newton*
	5 Atkins (D)	*Lowell*
	6 Mavroules (D)	*Lynn*
	7 Markey (D)	*Malden*
	8 Kennedy, J. (D)	*Cambridge*
	9 Moakley (D)	*Boston*
	10 Studds (D)	*Cape Cod*
	11 Donnelly (D)	*Boston*

MICHIGAN

Senate	Riegle (D)	
	Levin (D)	
House	1 Conyers (D)	*Detroit*
	2 Pursell (R)	*Ann Arbor*
	3 Wolpe (D)	*Lansing*
	4 Upton (R)	*Benton Harbor*
	5 Henry (R)	*Grand Rapids*
	6 Carr (D)	*Pontiac*
	7 Kildee (D)	*Flint*
	8 Traxler (D)	*Bay City*

	9	Vander Jagt (R)	*Traverse City*
	10	Schuette (R)	*Midland*
	11	Davis (R)	*Upper Peninsula*
	12	Bonior (D)	*Port Huron*
	13	Crockett (D)	*Detroit*
	14	Hertel (D)	*Warren*
	15	Ford (D)	*Wayne*
	16	Dingell (D)	*Dearborn*
	17	Levin (D)	*Southfield*
	18	Broomfield (R)	*Birmingham*

MINNESOTA

Senate		Durenberger (R)	
		Boschwitz (R)	
House	1	Penny (D)	*Rochester*
	2	Weber (R)	*Willmar*
	3	Frenzel (R)	*Bloomington*
	4	Vento (D)	*St. Paul*
	5	Sabo (D)	*Minneapolis*
	6	Sikorski (D)	*Stillwater*
	7	Stangeland (R)	*St. Cloud*
	8	Oberstar (D)	*Duluth*

MISSISSIPPI

Senate		Cochran (R)	
		Lott (R)	
House	1	Whitten (D)	*Oxford*
	2	Espy (D)	*Vicksburg*
	3	Montgomery (D)	*Meridian*
	4	Parker (D)	*Jackson*
	5	Smith (R)	*Pascagoula*

MISSOURI

Senate		Danforth (R)	
		Bond (R)	
House	1	Clay (D)	*St. Louis*
	2	Buechner (R)	*Kirkwood*
	3	Gephardt (D)	*St. Louis*
	4	Skelton (D)	*Jefferson City*
	5	Wheat (D)	*Kansas City*
	6	Coleman (R)	*St. Joseph*
	7	Hancock (R)	*Springfield*
	8	Emerson (R)	*Cape Girardeau*
	9	Volkmer (D)	*Hannibal*

MONTANA

Senate		Baucus (D)	
		Burns (R)	
House	1	Williams (D)	*Helena*
	2	Marlenee (R)	*Billings*

NEBRASKA

Senate		Exon (D)	
		Kerrey (D)	
House	1	Bereuter (R)	*Lincoln*
	2	Hoagland (D)	*Omaha*
	3	Smith (R)	*Grand Island*

NEVADA

Senate		Reid (D)	
		Bryan (D)	
House	1	Bilbray (D)	*Las Vegas*
	2	Vucanovich (R)	*Reno*

NEW HAMPSHIRE

Senate		Humphrey (R)	
		Rudman (R)	
House	1	Smith (R)	*Manchester*
	2	Douglas (R)	*Concord*

NEW JERSEY

Senate		Bradley (D)	
		Lautenberg (D)	
House	1	Florio (D)	*Pine Hill*
	2	Hughes (D)	*Ocean City*
	3	Pallone (D)	*Toms River*
	4	Smith (R)	*Trenton*
	5	Roukema (R)	*Ridgewood*
	6	Dwyer (D)	*Edison*
	7	Rinaldo (R)	*Union*
	8	Roe (D)	*Paterson*
	9	Torricelli (D)	*Hackensack*
	10	Payne (D)	*Newark*
	11	Gallo (R)	*Parsippany*
	12	Courter (R)	*Hackettstown*
	13	Saxton (R)	*Bordentown*
	14	Guarini (D)	*Jersey City*

NEW MEXICO

Senate		Domenici (R)	
		Bingaman (D)	
House	1	Schiff (R)	*Albuquerque*
	2	Skeen (R)	*Picacho*
	3	Richardson (D)	*Santa Fe*

NEW YORK

Senate		Moynihan (D)	
		D'Amato (R)	

House	1	Hochbrueckner (D)	*E. Long Island*
	2	Downey (D)	*Babylon*
	3	Mrazek (D)	*Huntington*
	4	Lent (R)	*E. Rockaway*
	5	McGrath (R)	*Valley Stream*
	6	Flake (D)	*Jamaica*
	7	Ackerman (D)	*Flushing*
	8	Scheuer (D)	*Queens*
	9	Manton (D)	*Astoria*
	10	Schumer (D)	*Flatbush*
	11	Towns (D)	*Brooklyn*
	12	Owens (D)	*Brooklyn*
	13	Solarz (D)	*Brooklyn*
	14	Molinari (R)	*Staten Island*
	15	Green (R)	*Manhattan*
	16	Rangel (D)	*Harlem*
	17	Weiss (D)	*Manhattan*
	18	Garcia (D)	*Bronx*
	19	Engel (D)	*Bronx*
	20	Lowey (D)	*Westchester*
	21	Fish (R)	*Poughkeepsie*
	22	Gilman (R)	*Catskills*
	23	McNulty (D)	*Albany*
	24	Solomon (R)	*Saratoga Springs*
	25	Boehlert (R)	*Utica*
	26	Martin (R)	*Watertown*
	27	Walsh (R)	*Syracuse*
	28	McHugh (D)	*Binghamton*
	29	Horton (R)	*Rochester*
	30	Slaughter (D)	*Rochester*
	31	Paxon (R)	*Buffalo*
	32	LaFalce (D)	*Niagara Falls*
	33	Nowak (D)	*Buffalo*
	34	Houghton (R)	*Corning*

NORTH CAROLINA

Senate		Helms (R)	
		Sanford (D)	
House	1	Jones (D)	*Greenville*
	2	Valentine (D)	*Durham*
	3	Lancaster (D)	*Goldsboro*
	4	Price (D)	*Raleigh*
	5	Neal (D)	*Winston-Salem*
	6	Coble (R)	*Greensboro*
	7	Rose (D)	*Willimington*
	8	Hefner (D)	*Salisbury*
	9	McMillan (R)	*Charlotte*
	10	Ballenger (R)	*Hickory*
	11	Clarke (D)	*Asheville*

NORTH DAKOTA

Senate	Burdick (D)
	Conrad (D)

House	1	Dorgan (D)	*At Large*

OHIO

Senate		Glenn (D)	
		Metzenbaum (D)	
House	1	Luken (D)	*Cincinnati*
	2	Gradison (R)	*Cincinnati*
	3	Hall (D)	*Dayton*
	4	Oxley (R)	*Findlay*
	5	Gillmor (R)	*Bowling Green*
	6	McEwen (R)	*Portsmouth*
	7	DeWine (R)	*Springfield*
	8	Lukens (R)	*Hamilton*
	9	Kaptur (D)	*Toledo*
	10	Miller (R)	*Lancaster*
	11	Eckart (D)	*Cleveland*
	12	Kasich (R)	*Columbus*
	13	Pease (D)	*Oberlin*
	14	Sawyer (D)	*Akron*
	15	Wylie (R)	*Columbus*
	16	Regula (R)	*Canton*
	17	Traficant (D)	*Youngstown*
	18	Applegate (D)	*Steubenville*
	19	Feighan (D)	*Cleveland*
	20	Oakar (D)	*Cleveland*
	21	Stokes (D)	*Cleveland*

OKLAHOMA

Senate		Boren (D)	
		Nickles (R)	
House	1	Inhofe (R)	*Tulsa*
	2	Synar (D)	*Muskogee*
	3	Watkins (D)	*Ada*
	4	McCurdy (D)	*Norman*
	5	Edwards (R)	*Bartlesville*
	6	English (D)	*Oklahoma City*

OREGON

Senate		Hatfield (R)	
		Packwood (R)	
House	1	AuCoin (D)	*Portland*
	2	Smith, R. (R)	*Medford*
	3	Wyden (D)	*Portland*
	4	DeFazio (D)	*Eugene*
	5	Smith, D. (R)	*Salem*

PENNSYLVANIA

Senate		Heinz (R)	
		Specter (R)	
House	1	Foglietta (D)	*Philadelphia*
	2	Gray (D)	*Philadelphia*

3	Borski (D)	*Philadelphia*
4	Kolter (D)	*New Castle*
5	Schulze (R)	*Chester*
6	Yatron (D)	*Reading*
7	Weldon (R)	*Delaware County*
8	Kostmayer (D)	*Bucks County*
9	Shuster (R)	*Altoona*
10	McDade (R)	*Scranton*
11	Kanjorski (D)	*Wilkes Barre*
12	Murtha (D)	*Johnstown*
13	Coughlin (R)	*Villanova*
14	Coyne (D)	*Pittsburgh*
15	Ritter (R)	*Allentown*
16	Walker (R)	*Lancaster*
17	Gekas (R)	*Harrisburg*
18	Walgren (D)	*Pittsburgh*
19	Goodling (R)	*York*
20	Gaydos (D)	*McKeesport*
21	Ridge (R)	*Erie*
22	Murphy (D)	*Monangahela*
23	Clinger (R)	*Warren*

RHODE ISLAND

Senate	Pell (D)	
	Chafee (R)	
House	1 Machtley (R)	*Providence*
	2 Schneider (R)	*Warwick*

SOUTH CAROLINA

Senate	Thurmond (R)	
	Hollings (D)	
House	1 Ravenel (R)	*Charleston*
	2 Spence (R)	*Columbia*
	3 Derrick (D)	*Aiken*
	4 Patterson (D)	*Spartanburg*
	5 Spratt (D)	*Rock Hill*
	6 Tallon (D)	*Florence*

SOUTH DAKOTA

Senate	Pressler (R)	
	Daschle (D)	
House	1 Johnson (D)	*At Large*

TENNESSEE

Senate	Sasser (D)	
	Gore (D)	
House	1 Quillen (R)	*Kingsport*
	2 Duncan (R)	*Knoxville*
	3 Lloyd (D)	*Chattanooga*
	4 Cooper (D)	*Shelbyville*
	5 Clement (D)	*Nashville*
	6 Gordon (D)	*Murfreesboro*
	7 Sundquist (R)	*Memphis*
	8 Tanner (D)	*Jackson*
	9 Ford (D)	*Memphis*

TEXAS

Senate	Bentsen (D)	
	Gramm (R)	
House	1 Chapman (D)	*Texarkana*
	2 Wilson (D)	*Lufkin*
	3 Bartlett (R)	*Dallas*
	4 Hall (D)	*Tyler*
	5 Bryant (D)	*Dallas*
	6 Barton (R)	*Ennis*
	7 Archer (R)	*Houston*
	8 Fields (R)	*Humble*
	9 Brooks (D)	*Beaumont*
	10 Pickle (D)	*Austin*
	11 Leath (D)	*Waco*
	12 *vacant*	*Fort Worth*
	13 Sarpalius (D)	*Amarillo*
	14 Laughlin (D)	*Victoria*
	15 de la Garza (D)	*McAllen*
	16 Coleman (D)	*El Paso*
	17 Stenholm (D)	*Abilene*
	18 Leland (D)	*Houston*
	19 Combest (R)	*Lubbock*
	20 Gonzalez (D)	*San Antonio*
	21 Smith (R)	*Midland*
	22 DeLay (R)	*Houston*
	23 Bustamante (D)	*San Antonio*
	24 Frost (D)	*Dallas*
	25 Andrews (D)	*Houston*
	26 Armey (R)	*Arlington*
	27 Ortiz (D)	*Corpus Christi*

UTAH

Senate	Garn (R)	
	Hatch (R)	
House	1 Hansen (R)	*Ogden*
	2 Owens (D)	*Salt Lake City*
	3 Nielson (R)	*Provo*

VERMONT

Senate	Leahy (D)	
	Jeffords (R)	
House	1 Smith (R)	*At Large*

VIRGINIA

Senate	Warner (R)	
	Robb (D)	

House	1	Bateman (R)	*Newport News*
	2	Pickett (D)	*Norfolk*
	3	Bliley (R)	*Richmond*
	4	Sisisky (D)	*Portsmouth*
	5	Payne (D)	*Danville*
	6	Olin (D)	*Roanoke*
	7	Slaughter (R)	*Charlottesville*
	8	Parris (R)	*Alexandria*
	9	Boucher (D)	*Blacksburg*
	10	Wolf (R)	*Arlington*

WASHINGTON

Senate		Adams (D)	
		Gorton (R)	
House	1	Miller (R)	*Seattle*
	2	Swift (D)	*Everett*
	3	Unsoeld (D)	*Olympia*
	4	Morrison (R)	*Yakima*
	5	Foley (D)	*Spokane*
	6	Dicks (D)	*Tacoma*
	7	McDermott (D)	*Seattle*
	8	Chandler (R)	*Seattle*

WEST VIRGINIA

Senate		Byrd (D)	
		Rockefeller (D)	
House	1	Mollohan (D)	*Wheeling*
	2	Staggers (D)	*Morgantown*
	3	Wise (D)	*Charleston*
	4	Rahall (D)	*Huntington*

WISCONSIN

Senate		Kasten (R)	
		Kohl (D)	
House	1	Aspin (D)	*Kenosha*
	2	Kastenmeier (D)	*Madison*
	3	Gunderson (R)	*Eau Claire*
	4	Kleczka (D)	*Milwaukee*
	5	Moody (D)	*Wauwatosa*
	6	Petri (R)	*Oshkosh*
	7	Obey (D)	*Wausau*
	8	Roth (R)	*Green Bay*
	9	Sensenbrenner (R)	*Sheboygan*

WYOMING

Senate		Wallop (R)	
		Simpson (R)	
House	1	Thomas (R)	*At Large*

GUIDE TO USAGE

The Almanac of American Politics is designed to be self-explanatory. The following guide provides a brief description of each section and a list of sources from which information was derived, both of which serve as a road map to understanding the meaning behind the figures.

The People

Population. All population figures are from the Bureau of the Census, U.S. Department of Commerce, Washington, D.C. 20233, (301) 763-4040. The 1980 Census figures regarding population, education, poverty, ancestry, households and voting age can be found in the following publications: Congressional Districts of the 98th, 99th and 100th Congresses. The 1988 population figures are interim estimates as of December 1, 1988.

Education. The level of higher education is measured by the Census from persons over 25 years of age who have pursued vocational, public, or private forms of college education not necessarily leading to graduation.

Poverty. Poverty level statistics are current as of the 1980 Census. These figures represent the percentage of persons under the poverty level in 1979. Poverty level statistics are updated annually to reflect changes in the Consumer Price Index, but these "poverty thresholds" (published in a Census series called *Current Population Reports*), are arrived at using different analytical methods than those used for the 1980 Census. Comparisons between the two sets of numbers, therefore, have not been made.

Ancestry. For the 1980 Census, the Census Bureau simply asked people what their ancestry was; these figures indicate the percentage that responded that they were members of a particular group and only that group. Those that indicated that their ancestry was of a mixed heritage are not reflected in these figures. The *Almanac* uses the single ancestry statistics because identification with a particular ancestry (Irish, Italian, etc.) is more politically relevant. Only those groups that round up to one percent of the population are listed.

Households. A family consists of a head of household and one or more individuals related by birth, marriage, or adoption to the head of the household. Children are defined as those persons under eighteen years of age that are related to the head of the household by birth, marriage, or adoption. Married couple households are those where the head of the household and spouse are counted as members of the same household. Percentage of housing units rented is determined by relating figures for all owner-occupied housing units to the total amount of housing units. Median house value is determined through usual residence costs, including mortgage payments, deeds or trusts, real estate taxes, fire and hazard insurance, utilities and fuels. Condominiums, mobile homes, trailers, and boats are not included.

Voting Age Population. A tally of persons at least eighteen years of age who are eligible to vote, the voting age population is a measurement of the voter potential in a district. Figures are current as of the 1980 Census. The ethnic breakdown relates to the voting age population only, not to the overall population. The concept of race as defined by the Census Bureau reflects self-identification and not clear-cut biological or scientific definitions.

Registered Voters. The voter registration totals were provided by state Secretaries of State and Boards of Elections. Different states have different cut-off dates for registration—the *Almanac* has tried to list those totals closest to Election Day.

Federal Tax Burden. The federal tax burden is determined by the Tax Foundation, Inc., a non-partisan, non-profit organization located at One Thomas Circle, N.W., Suite 500, Washington, DC 20005, 202-822-9050. The Tax Foundation uses federal-fund taxes (individual, corporate, alcohol, tobacco, etc.) and trust-fund taxes as bases to determine a more accurate picture of the tax burden than Treasury Department tax collection data.

Federal Expenditures. For fiscal year 1988, the Census Bureau compiled statistics on federal expenditures amounting to $884 billion. Not included in these figures are interest on federal debts, international payments and foreign aid, and expenditures for selected federal agencies (i.e. CIA and National Security Agency). *Federal Expenditures by State for Fiscal Year 1988* (March 1989) by the Department of Commerce contains an in-depth discussion of the categories composing the total federal expenditure.

Political Lineup. This block includes the names of top state elected officials as well as a breakdown by party of the State Senate and State House of Representatives. The names of U.S. Senators and a party breakdown of the state's congressional delegation are also provided.

Presidential Vote. The 1984 and 1988 presidential vote is included for each state; the 1988 vote for each congressional district. Presidential vote on the state level was drawn from state election returns. Presidential vote by congressional district was derived from state, county, and precinct results as compiled by staff of the National Committee for an Effective Congress (NCEC), 507 Capitol Ct., N.E., Washington, DC 20002, 202-547-1151. Discrepancies exist between the state and district figures because of inconsistent reporting methods employed by the counties, the states, and the FEC. Results of the presidential primaries were provided by the states.

Biographies. This section lists when each Governor, Senator, and Representative was elected, birth date and birthplace, home, college education (if any), religion, marital status and, if applicable, spouse's name. Also listed is a brief outline of the politician's career, and his or her office addresses and telephone numbers. Committee and subcommittee assignments are provided as well. (Note: On many committees, the chairman and ranking minority member are ex officio members of each subcommittee on which they do not hold a regular assignment.)

Ratings

Rating Groups. The congressional rating statistics of 10 lobby groups are used to provide an idea of a legislator's general ideology and the degree to which the legislator represents different groups' interests. Not just a record of liberal/conservative voting behavior, these ratings come from a range of groups concerned with everything from single issues (environmental concerns) to those that focus on the political interests of a particular group (e.g., consumers). The order of the groups is such that the more "liberal" ones are on the left and the more "conservative" are on the right. Four groups, ACLU, LCV, NTLC and NSI release ratings only once every two years, the duration of one full congressional session. Following is a general description of each organization, its address and telephone number.

ADA   Americans for Democratic Action
1511 K St., N.W., Ste. 941, Washington, DC 20005, 202-638-6447.
   Liberal: Since its founding in 1947, ADA members have pushed for legislation designed to reduce inequality, curtail rising defense spending, prevent encroachments on civil liberties, and

promote international human rights. The ADA uses a broad spectrum of issues for its vote analysis.

ACLU   American Civil Liberties Union
122 Maryland Ave., N.E., Washington, DC 20002, 202-544-1681.

Pro-individual liberties: ACLU seeks to protect individuals from legal, executive, and congressional infringement on basic rights guaranteed by the Bill of Rights. The ACLU ratings are published for every Congress; the 1988 ratings include the years 1987 and 1988.

COPE   Committee on Political Education of the AFL-CIO
815 16th St., N.W., Washington, DC 20006, 202-637-5101.

Liberal-Labor: As the powerful and well-funded arm of the AFL-CIO, COPE is concerned with the economic interests of the American worker. While COPE covers a broad spectrum of issues, it monitors few votes on foreign policy and defense spending.

CFA   Consumer Federation of America
1424 16th St., N.W., Ste. 604, Washington, DC 20036, 202-387-6121.

Pro-Consumer: CFA is a group spawned in the mid-sixties as a pro-consumer counterweight to various business-oriented lobbies. Their voting record concentrates on pocketbook consumer issues and health and safety concerns.

LCV   League of Conservation Voters
1150 Connecticut Ave., N.W., Ste. 201, Washington, DC 20036, 202-785-8683.

Environmental: Formed in 1970, LCV is the national, non-partisan arm of the environmental movement. LCV works to elect pro-environmental candidates to Congress. LCV ratings are based on key votes concerning energy, environment, and natural resource issues, selected by leaders from major national environmental organizations.

ACU   American Conservative Union
38 Ivy St., S.E., Washington, DC 20003, 202-546-6555.

Conservative: Since 1971, the ACU ratings have provided a means of gauging the conservatism of Members of Congress. Foreign policy, social, and budgetary issues are their primary concerns.

NTLC   National Tax-Limitation Committee
201 Massachusetts Ave., N.E., Washington, DC 20002, 202-547-4196

Pro-tax limitation: NTLC was organized in 1975 to seek constitutional and other limits on taxes, spending and deficits at the state and federal levels. Its 500,000 members are actively pursuing a balanced budget/tax limitation amendment to the U. S. Constitution. Their ratings are based on budget issues votes and bills which would have a major impact on long-term taxing and spending programs of the government.

NSI   National Security Index of the American Security Council
499 S. Capitol St., S.W., Ste. 500, Washington, DC 20003, 202-484-1676.

Pro-strong defense: Founded in 1965, the Council feels that American security is best preserved by developing and maintaining large weapons systems to achieve strategic military superiority. The NSI rates members on their support of defense and foreign policy issues that affect the NSI strategy of peace through strength.

COC   Chamber of Commerce of the United States
1615 H Street, N.W., Washington, DC 20062, 202-659-6000.

Pro-business: Founded in 1912 as a voice for organized business, COC represents local, regional, and state chambers of commerce in addition to trade and professional organizations.

CEI   Competitive Enterprise Institute
233 Pennsylvania Ave., S.E., Ste. 200, Washington, DC 20003, 202-547-1010

Pro-free enterprise: Founded in 1984, CEI's purpose is to advance the principles of free enterprise and limited government. CEI focuses primarily on deficit reduction and tax reform, deregulation and privatization, free market approaches to environmental problems, anti-trust reform and international trade.

National Journal Ratings. *National Journal's* rating system establishes a relatively objective method of analyzing congressional voting. A panel of *National Journal* editors and staff initially compiled a list of congressional roll call votes and classified them as either economic, social or foreign policy-related. The Calliope System of Burlington, Vt., provided the computerized roll-call data. The interrelationship of these votes was shown by a statistical procedure called "principal components analysis," which revealed which "yea" votes and which "nay" votes fit a liberal or a conservative pattern. The votes in each of the three subject areas were computer-weighted to reflect the degree they fit the common pattern. All Members of Congress who participated in at least half of the votes in each area received ratings; those who missed more that half the votes were not scored (shown as *). Absences and abstentions were not counted.

Members of Congress were then ranked according to relative liberalism and conservatism. Finally, they were assigned percentiles showing their rank relative to others in their chamber. Percentile scores range from a minimum of 0 to a maximum of 99. Because some Members voted liberal or conservative on every roll call, however, there are ties at the liberal and conservative ends of each scale. For that reason, the maximum percentiles always turn out to be less that 99.

Votes

Key Votes. The Key Votes section is an attempt to illustrate a legislator's stance on important votes where he or she must vote *for* or *against* a national issue. The process grossly oversimplifies the legislative system where months of debate, amendment, pressure, persuasion, and compromise go into a final floor vote. However, the voting record remains the best indication of a member's position on specific issues and his or her general ideological persuasions.

Following is a list of key votes used. A member who was absent, voted present, or who was not in office at the time of a particular vote receives a dash. A vote FOR indicates the member was in favor of the issue; a vote AGN indicates disapproval.

Key votes were drawn from Legi-Slate, a computer system that tracks legislation, voting attendance, committee schedules, etc. For information about Legi-Slate or about their vote recording process, please contact: Legi-Slate, 111 Massachusetts Ave., N.W., Ste. 520, Washington, DC 20002, 202-898-2300.

Senate Votes:

1) **Cut Aged Housing $**   (S 825)   Cut to 25 percent the share of their income that the elderly must pay for federally subsidized rental housing. March 31, 1987. Rejected 43–55. (D:35–18; R:8–37).

2) **Override Hwy Veto**   (HR 2)   Override the veto of the reauthorization of highway and mass transit programs. April 2, 1987. Passed 67–33. (D:54–0; R:13–33).

3) **Kill Plnt Clsng Notice**   (S 1420)   Strike a provision requiring employers to give advance notice of plant closings or mass layoffs. July 9, 1987. Rejected 40–60. (D:4–50; R:36–10).

4) **Min Wage Increase**   (S 837)   Close debate on proposal to increase the minimum wage to $4.55 an hour. September 23, 1988. Rejected 56–35 (60 votes required). (D:48–3; R:8–32).

5) **Bork Nomination** Confirm the nomination of Robert H. Bork as a Supreme Court Justice. October 23, 1987. Rejected 42–58. (D:2–52; R:40–6).

6) **Ban Plastic Guns** (S 9) Table a proposed ban on the manufacture, sale or use of plastic firearms that are difficult to detect. December 4, 1987. Passed 47–42. (D:12–34; R:35–8).

7) **Deny Abortions** (S 557) Allow federally-aided hospitals and schools to refuse to perform abortions or cover them in health plans. January 28, 1988. Passed 56–39. (D:20–32; R:36–7).

8) **Japanese Reparations** (HR 442) Authorize reparations for Japanese Americans interned during World War II. April 20, 1988. Passed 69–27. (D:44–7; R:25–20).

9) **SDI Funding** (S 1174) Table an amendment limiting funds for the Strategic Defense Initiative to $3.7 billion. September 22, 1987. Passed 51–50; the Vice President cast the deciding vote. (D:13–41; R:37–9).

10) **Ban Chem Weaps** (S 1174) Table an amendment barring funds to assemble binary chemical weapons. September 24, 1987. Passed 53–44. (D:19–32; R:34–12).

11) **Aid to Contras** (SJR 243) Provide $36.25 million in military aid to the Nicaraguan contras. February 4, 1988. Passed 51–48. (D:12–41; R:39–7).

12) **Reagan Defense $** (HR 4264) Recommit the conference report on the defense authorization bill to insist on provisions more sympathetic to the Reagan Administration. July 14, 1988. Rejected 35–58. (D:0–49; R:35–9).

House Votes:

1) **Homeless $** (HR 558) Restrict spending for aid to homeless people to the transfer of existing budget authority. March 5, 1987. Rejected 203–207. (D:44–197; R:159–10).

2) **Gephardt Amdt** (HR 3) Impose tariffs or import quotas on nations that have unfair trade practices and also have excessive trade surpluses with the United States [Gephardt Amendment]. April 29, 1987. Passed 218–214. (D:201–55; R:17–159).

3) **Deficit Reduc** (HR 3545) Cut the fiscal 1988 federal deficit by $11.9 billion through a combination of tax increases and spending cuts. October 29, 1987. Passed 206–205. (D:205–41; R:1–164).

4) **Kill Plnt Clsng Notice** (HR 3) Delete the plant-closing notification requirement from the trade bill. April 21, 1988. Rejected 167–253. (D:23–224; R:144–29).

5) **Ban Drug Test** (HR 1827) Strike a provision that would prohibit drug testing of federal employees under a presidential order. April 23, 1987. Rejected 145–242. (D:26–201; R:119–41).

6) **Drug Death Pen** (HR 5210) Permit the death penalty for individuals convicted of a killing while committing a drug felony. September 8, 1988. Passed 299–111. (D:138–102; R:161–9).

7) **Handgun Sales** (HR 5210) Delete the proposed seven-day waiting period for handgun purchases. September 15, 1988. Passed 228–182. (D:101–137; R:127–45).

8) **Ban D.C. Abort $** (HR 4776) Bar the District of Columbia from using its own or federal money to pay for abortions. September 28, 1988. Passed 228–188. (D:88–156; R:140–32).

9) **SDI Research** (HR 1748) Provide $3.6 billion for research on the Strategic Defense Initiative. May 12, 1987. Rejected 207–213. (D:50–196; R:157–17).

10) **Ban Chem Weaps** (HR 1748) Prohibit the spending of funds to assemble binary chemical weapons during fiscal 1988. May 19, 1987. Rejected 191–230. (D:161–86; R:30–144).

11) **Aid to Contras** (HJR 444)   Provide $36.25 million in military aid to the Nicaraguan contras. February 3, 1988. Rejected 211–219. (D:47–207; R:164–12).

12) **Nuclear Testing** (HR 4264)   Bar funds for nuclear tests exceeding one kiloton. April 28, 1988. Passed 214–186. (D:196–38; R:18–148).

Election Results

Election Results. Listed for each member of the House are results of the 1988 general, runoff, and primary elections, as well as the 1986 general elections (results of any special elections are also listed). Gubernatorial and Senatorial results are presented in a like manner. Votes and percentages are included, indicating the margin of victory (due to the process of rounding up and rounding down, some percentages may equal more or less than 100%). Candidates receiving 3% or less of the total vote were not included. Dollar amounts listed to the right of the vote totals are campaign expenditures as reported by the candidate to the Federal Election Commission. Election returns were provided by state Secretaries of State and Boards of Elections.

Campaign Finance

All data are derived from candidates' campaign finance reports and party reports, as well as other official studies available from the Federal Election Commission (FEC), 999 E St., N.W., Washington, DC 20463, 202-376-5140 (toll-free, 1-800-424-9530).

Receipts and disbursement activity covers the period beginning January 1, 1987, and ending December 31, 1988, for House members and Senators elected in 1988. Receipt and disbursement activity for Senators elected in 1984 and 1986 are already stated.

Receipts, Expenditures and Cash-on-Hand/Debt. These three figures give a good overview of a winning candidate's campaign finances for the 1988 elections (primary, runoff and general). Transfer payments from affiliated committees have not been included to avoid double-counting. The data was taken directly from candidate reports.

Receipts. Receipts constitute all incoming funds as reported by the candidate for the 1988 campaign. Candidate committees report all incoming funds either in the form of contributions received from individuals, political parties, PACs, and the candidate themselves, as well as loans, or receipts in the form of earnings on previously received funds (interest, dividends) and rebates (such as the sale of a previously purchased campaign vehicle). These receipts are for the 1987-88 election cycle only.

Expenditures. Expenditures constitute all outgoing funds spent by the candidate committees, including loan repayments and contributions by the committee to other candidates or committees. As in the Receipts category, refunds of contributions have been subtracted from the total.

Cash-on-Hand. Unspent funds refer to a campaign's leftover cash-on-hand, less any reported debts, as of December 31, 1988. In many cases, this figure does not represent the difference between the receipts and expenditures listed. An incumbents campaign report often begins with the Cash-on-Hand (or debt if that is the case) remaining from a previous campaign.

Direct Contributions. These categories do not always equal the total receipts because they do not detail all of the candidates receipts. For example, they do not include income from interest, dividends and rebates.

Individual Contributions. This figure is taken directly from candidate reports for year-end 1987 and 1988 and represents the amount received in personal contributions from individual donors.

Party Contributions. The figure for Party Contributions includes only those organizations that have been registered under the Federal Election Campaign Act. Donations can come either in the form of funds or contributions of goods and services to a campaign. Independent party expenditures spent on behalf of a candidate (*i.e.*, not directly contributed to a candidate committee) are not included in the *Almanac*'s section on Direct Contributions.

Political Action Committees (PACs). PACs are groups that are not affiliated directly with a candidate or political party. PAC figures represent donations of money or in-kind goods and services to a congressional campaign. Total PAC contributions listed are only from those committees registered under the Federal Election Campaign Act.

Candidate Contributions. This figure includes direct candidate contributions, both candidate-secured loans and all other types of loans, and transfers from *other* authorized committees.

ABBREVIATIONS

AA	Administrative Assistant	**C**	Conservative Party (NY)
ACLU	American Civil Liberties Union	**CA**	California
		CA	Carroll Arms Building
ACU	American Conservative Union	**CAB**	Civil Aeronautics Board
		Cand.	Candidate
ADA	Americans for Democratic Action	**CEI**	Competitive Enterprise Institute
Admin.	Administration	**CFA**	Consumer Federation of America
Adv.	Advertising		
Agcy.	Agency	**CG**	Coast Guard
AGN	Against	**Chmn.**	Chairman
Agric.	Agriculture	**CHOB**	Cannon House Office Building
AI	Alaska Independent Party		
AK	Alaska	**Chwmn.**	Chairwoman
AL	Alabama	**CIA**	Central Intelligence Agency
AM., Amer.	American	**Cmtee.**	Committee
AR	Arkansas	**Cncl.**	Council
ARE	Citizens Against Rising Electric Rates (NY)	**Cnty.**	County
		CO	Colorado
Asst.	Assistant	**COC**	Chamber of Commerce of the United States
Atty.	Attorney		
AZ	Arizona	**COH**	Cash-On-Hand
		Col.	College
Bd.	Board	**Comm.**	Commission
Bus.	Business		

COPE	Committee on Political Education (AFL-CIO)	**H**	Capitol Building Room— House side
Corp.	Corporation	**HEW**	Department of Health, Education and Welfare
Crt.	Court		
CT	Connecticut	**HHS**	Department of Health and Human Services
Ctr.	Center		
		HI	Hawaii
		Hlth.	Health
D	Democrat	**HSOB**	Hart Senate Office Building
DC	District of Columbia	**HUD**	Department of Housing and Urban Development
DCCC	Democratic Congressional Campaign Committee		
DE	Delaware	**I, Indep.**	Independent
Dem.	Democratic	**IA**	Iowa
Dept.	Department	**ID**	Idaho
DFL	Democratic–Farmer–Labor Party (MN)	**Ideo.**	Ideological
		IL	Illinois
Dir.	Director	**IN**	Indiana
Dist.	District	**Indiv.**	Individual
DNC	Democratic National Committee	**IR**	Independent-Republican Party (MN)
DOE	Department of Energy		
DOT	Department of Transportation	**IVP**	Independent Voter Party (NY)
Dpty.	Deputy		
DSCC	Democratic Senatorial Campaign Committee	**JBS**	Jobs Party (NY)
		Jnt. Cmtee.	Joint Committee
DSOB	Dirksen Senate Office Building	**KS**	Kansas
		KY	Kentucky
Econ.	Economic	**L**	Liberal Party
ECP	Effective Congress Party	**LA**	Louisiana
EPA	Environmental Protection Agency	**Lbr.**	Labor
		LCV	League of Conservation Voters
Expend.	Expenditure/s		
		Ldr.	Leader
FCC	Federal Communications Commission	**LHOB**	Longworth House Office Building
FCP	Free Congress Political Action Committee	**LIB**	Libertarian Party
		LMV	League of Women Voters
FEC	Federal Election Commission		
Fed.	Federal	**MA**	Massachusetts
FGY	Drug Fighter Party (NY)	**Major.**	Majority
FL	Florida	**MD**	Maryland
FTC	Federal Trade Commission	**ME**	Maine
FTP	Fair Trade Party	**MI**	Michigan
		Minor.	Minority
GA	Georgia	**MN**	Minnesota
GU	Guam	**MO**	Missouri

MS	Mississippi	RI	Rhode Island
MT	Montana	RNC	Republican National Committee
NAP	New Alliance Party (NY)	RSOB	Russell Senate Office Building
NC	North Carolina		
NCPAC	National Conservative PAC	RTL	Right-to-Life
ND	North Dakota		
NE	Nebraska	S	Capitol Building Room— Senate side
NH	New Hampshire		
NJ	New Jersey	SBA	Small Business Administration
NM	New Mexico		
NRCC	National Republican Congressional Committee	SC	South Carolina
		Sch.	School
NRSC	National Republican Senatorial Committee	SD	South Dakota
		Secy.	Secretary
NSC	National Security Council	Sel. Cmtee.	Select Committee
NSI	National Security Index of the American Security Council	Sen.	Senator
		Spec. Cmtee.	Special Committee
		Spkr.	Speaker
NTLC	National Tax-Limitation Committee	St.	State
		Ste.	Suite
NV	Nevada	Subcmtee.	Subcommittee
NY	New York	SWP	Socialist Workers Party
OH	Ohio	TN	Tennessee
OK	Oklahoma	TX	Texas
OMB	Office of Management and Budget	U.	University
OR	Oregon	UDAG	Urban Development Action Grant
PA	Pennsylvania	USAF	United States Air Force
PAC	Political Action Committee	USAFR	United States Air Force Reserve
P & F	Peace & Freedom (CA)		
PBP	People Before Profits	USMC	United States Marine Corps
PJ & J	Peace, Jobs and Justice	USN	United States Navy
POP	Populist Party	UT	Utah
PR	Puerto Rico		
Pres.	President	VA	Veterans Administration
ProL	Pro-Life	VA	Virginia
Prof.	Professional	VCH	Vote Children '88 (NY)
Pub.	Public	VI	Virgin Islands
Publ.	Publisher	VT	Vermont
R, Repub.	Republican	WA	Washington
RC	Rainbow Coalition	WI	Wisconsin
Rep./s	Representative/s	WL	Workers League
RHOB	Rayburn House Office Building	WV	West Virginia
		WY	Wyoming

THE AMERICAN HALF CENTURY

Nearly fifty years ago, Henry Luce, in a February 1941 *Life* magazine editorial, called on his fellow citizens "to create the first great American century." At the time it was far from obvious how this could be done. Hitler and Stalin, allies since their pact of August 1939, and the warlords of Japan with their armies and air forces of 21 million men controlled most of the land mass of Eurasia, while the United States had a military force of only half a million men in arms—the 19th largest in the world. The western economies were still suffering from a dozen years of depression and it was widely assumed that only dictatorships could produce economic growth. The United States, in the words of historian Bradley Smith, "still felt like an isolated, largely self-sufficient and comparatively simple country."

This vision, Luce argued, was too narrow. Culturally, he noted, "there already is an immense American internationalism." American slang, movies and gadgets were popular around the world. More important, Americans—and Americans alone—had the power, if they had the will, to "determine whether a system of free economic enterprise—an economic order compatible with freedom and progress—shall or shall not prevail in this century." Only Americans could provide the "technical and artistic skills" needed to build roads, teach children and cure sick people everywhere. And only Americans could supply "a love of freedom, a feeling for the equality of opportunity, a tradition of self-reliance and independence and also of cooperation."

Luce's vision was derided as grandiose and impractical. Liberals found the phrase "American Century" presumptuous and chauvinistic, in the manner of fifth graders who think it's bragging to vote for themselves in class elections, and Vice President Henry Wallace called instead for a "century of the common man." But as Luce pointed out, the specifics he recommended and the generosity he counseled were all things Wallace and other New Dealers agreed with: this Republican plutocrat was proposing something very much like a global New Deal. Conservative isolationists opposed Luce's vision for that very reason. They thought that his extravagant promises and his martial impulses would foster the large and tyrannical state they feared at home and the standing military force they feared would lead to trouble abroad.

Airily, Luce dismissed these fears. "We are, for a fact, *in* the war," he said—and accurately, since Franklin Roosevelt's naval patrols of the North Atlantic and refusal to sell oil and arms to the Japanese were courting the break that finally came in Pearl Harbor. And this admirer of free enterprise was undaunted at the prospect of a more active government: "We must undertake now to be the Good Samaritan of the entire world."

Luce and the New Dealers who agreed with his ideas, but disliked his label, have been vindicated by the events and accomplishments of the past five decades. The years since 1940 have been the American Half Century. From the time that George Bush set out to fight for his country in war, to the time he was sworn in as commander-in-chief, the American system of market economics, American technical know-how, and American political freedom have swept back the frontiers of totalitarianism, expanded vastly the realm of plenty, and promoted the goals of tolerance and civility abroad and at home. These gains have been won by force of arms, by force of ideas and by force of example.

For a time, none of this seemed apparent. Beginning in the late 1960s, American thinkers and politicians focused on their failure in Vietnam, and got in the habit of comparing their current situation with that of America of 1945—"year zero," as Europeans called it. Then, the argument went, the United States was the predominant military and economic power in the world, with its monopoly of nuclear weapons and its 50% share of the world's gross national product; now, analysts argued in the 1970s and 1980s, America's adversaries were ever more powerful militarily and its economy was shrinking as a percentage of world GNP. A nation which, in 1945, had believed itself successful and good, decided around 1979 (the year of Jimmy Carter's "malaise" speech) that it was unsuccessful and bad. But the comparison was irrelevant. America's position in 1945 was unsustainable, and fortunately so: it was in America's interest for friendly economies to grow and it was beyond America's capacity to prevent unfriendly countries from arming.

By 1989, in any case, the picture of American decline which so many commentators had painted a decade before, no longer makes any sense. The Soviet Union, not the United States, was plainly the victim of "imperial overstretch." It was America's model of a market economy, tempered by welfare state protections, that was proving attractive to the peoples of the world, not the Soviets' (or even Social Democrats') socialism. It was American political freedoms which seemed, sometimes by happy accident and sometimes by force of effort, to be spreading all over the world, not the Soviets' authoritarianism or the dirigisme of Third World dictators. The world was changing in the way the chauvinistic Luce and the dreamy New Dealers wanted. If the 50 years since the United States was poised at the brink of World War II have proved to be an American Half Century, as the 1990s begin, most indications are that the next half century will be more *American* still.

In this American Half Century, America has changed in many ways—and not changed much at all. It has almost doubled in population: a country of 131 million has become a country of 246 million. Its economy has more than quintupled in size, with the gross national product rising from $772.9 billion in 1940 (in constant dollars) to $4,076.5 billion in the first quarter of 1989. The number of working Americans—employed persons plus military personnel—rose from 48 million to 119 million. It has seen per capita incomes more than double. It has seen the number of Americans living in poverty reduced so vastly that the numbers cannot really be calculated, for the living conditions of so many Americans were so different in 1940 than 1990 that the change amounts to moving from third world subsistence agriculture to first world high-tech metropolis.

The changes in where Americans live are most striking, for a new and differently shaped America—the increase in population of 113 million—has been superimposed on the map of the old. Examination of the patterns shows two distinct episodes of growth: the first during the long period of economic growth from 1940 to 1965, the second during the more troubled but in the long run still-growing period from 1965 to 1988 *(see Chart 1)*.

In the first period, from 1940 to 1965, there was still heavy outmigration from the rural South, and rapid growth (often from very low bases) where there was major defense employment. The migration of southern blacks to northern industrial cities, which began quite suddenly around 1940, because of changes wrought by New Deal programs in southern farm economies and because of wartime demand for factory labor, continued until around the time the Civil Rights Act of 1964 was passed and riots started breaking out in northern ghettoes. The West Coast's population more than doubled, increasing by 14.7 million; there was significant growth in Michigan and, reflected mainly in the totals of the suburban areas, in metropolitan New York, Philadelphia, Baltimore and Washington. Growth tended to come where it was directed by the federal government and big corporations.

The growth from 1965 to 1988, the latest year for which census estimates are available, tended to come where it was channeled by small market-driven businesses and by leisure-minded consumers and retirees. Vacationlands boomed—Florida, northern New England and Michigan, southern California, the Ozarks, Arizona and Colorado. There was outmigration from the coal-steel-autos belt, the autos part of which had been a growth area before 1965. Growth practically

Chart 1. STATE POPULATIONS 1940-1988
(in 000s)

State	Population 1988*	Population 1965	1940	Gains or Losses 1940-88		1965-88	1940-65
UNITED STATES	245,810	193,457	132,165	112,748	85%	27%	46%
EAST	**56,535**	**52,354**	**38,727**	**17,808**	**46%**	**8%**	**35%**
Maine	1,206	997	847	359	42%	21%	18%
New Hampshire	1,097	676	492	605	123%	62%	37%
Vermont	556	404	359	197	55%	38%	13%
Massachusetts	5,871	5,502	4,317	1,554	36%	7%	27%
Rhode Island	995	893	713	282	40%	11%	25%
Connecticut	3,241	2,857	1,709	1,532	90%	13%	67%
New York	17,898	17,734	13,479	4,419	33%	1%	32%
New Jersey	7,720	6,767	4,160	3,560	86%	14%	63%
Pennsylvania	12,027	11,620	9,900	2,127	21%	4%	17%
Delaware	660	507	267	393	147%	30%	90%
Maryland	4,644	3,600	1,821	2,823	155%	29%	98%
Dist. Columbia	620	797	663	(43)	-6%	-22%	20%
MIDWEST	**59,894**	**54,224**	**40,144**	**19,750**	**49%**	**10%**	**35%**
Ohio	10,872	10,201	6,908	3,964	57%	7%	48%
Indiana	5,575	4,922	3,428	2,147	63%	13%	44%
Illinois	11,544	10,693	7,897	3,647	46%	8%	35%
Michigan	9,300	8,357	5,256	4,044	77%	11%	59%
Wisconsin	4,858	4,232	3,138	1,720	55%	15%	35%
Minnesota	4,306	3,592	2,792	1,514	54%	20%	29%
Iowa	2,834	2,742	2,538	296	12%	3%	8%
Missouri	5,139	4,467	3,785	1,354	36%	15%	18%
Kansas	2,487	2,206	1,801	686	38%	13%	22%
Nebraska	1,601	1,471	1,316	285	22%	9%	12%
South Dakota	715	692	643	72	11%	3%	8%
North Dakota	663	649	642	21	3%	2%	1%
WEST	**50,425**	**32,204**	**14,378**	**36,047**	**251%**	**57%**	**124%**
Montana	804	706	559	245	44%	14%	26%
Idaho	999	686	525	474	90%	46%	31%
Wyoming	471	332	251	220	88%	42%	32%
Colorado	3,290	1,985	1,123	2,167	193%	66%	77%
New Mexico	1,510	1,012	532	978	184%	49%	90%
Arizona	3,466	1,584	499	2,967	595%	119%	217%
Utah	1,691	991	550	1,141	207%	71%	80%
Nevada	1,060	444	110	950	864%	139%	304%
California	28,168	18,585	6,907	21,261	308%	52%	169%
Oregon	2,741	1,937	1,090	1,651	151%	42%	78%
Washington	4,619	2,967	1,736	2,883	166%	56%	71%
Alaska	513	271	73	440	603%	89%	271%
Hawaii	1,093	704	423	670	158%	55%	66%
SOUTH	**78,956**	**54,675**	**38,916**	**40,040**	**103%**	**44%**	**40%**
West Virginia	1,884	1,786	1,902	(18)	-1%	5%	-6%
Virginia	5,996	4,411	2,678	3,318	124%	36%	65%
North Carolina	6,526	4,863	3,572	2,954	83%	34%	36%
South Carolina	3,493	2,494	1,900	1,593	84%	40%	31%
Georgia	6,401	4,332	3,124	3,277	105%	48%	39%
Florida	12,377	5,954	1,897	10,480	552%	108%	214%
Alabama	4,127	3,443	2,833	1,294	46%	20%	21%
Mississippi	2,627	2,246	2,184	443	20%	17%	3%
Tennessee	4,919	3,798	2,916	2,003	69%	30%	30%
Kentucky	3,721	3,140	2,846	875	31%	19%	10%
Arkansas	2,422	1,894	1,949	473	24%	28%	-3%
Louisiana	4,420	3,496	2,364	2,056	87%	26%	48%
Texas	16,780	10,378	6,415	10,365	162%	62%	62%
Oklahoma	3,263	2,440	2,336	927	40%	34%	4%

*1988 population figures are interim estimates.

stopped in the high-tax metropolitan areas; New York state, which grew 32% in the 25 years before 1965, grew 1% in the 22 years after. Black outmigration from the South stopped, and the Atlantic Coast South and the Oil Patch of Texas and Oklahoma grew faster than average. The West boomed, rising to a population of similar magnitude to those of the East or Midwest, each of which had approximately three times as many people as the West in 1940. Unnoticed at first, cited as a dreadful problem 10 years later, immigration—primarily of Latins and Asians—began to increase around 1965 and, despite low economic growth after the 1973 and 1979 oil shocks, continued to be strong through the 1980s.

For all the changes of the last 50 years, culturally the America of 1940 seems a familiar place. The movies of the 1930s and 1940s were a universal medium watched by everyone; in 1930, when there were 123 million Americans, average weekly movie attendance was 90 million: almost everyone went to the movies every week. These movies were the best popular culture since Dickens, and the ability to speak the language of the 1940s movies, an ability that seems to have come from a native cheeriness and charm, is one of the things that made Ronald Reagan an effective national leader 40 years later. The great popular heroes of that day are, if not household words in every household, still familiar to many millions of Americans who never knew a time when they were not famous: Charles Lindbergh, Joe Louis, Babe Ruth, Clark Gable. In the culturally diverse 1980s, such universally familiar figures and the corny, ingratiating language of the 1940s movies seemed comforting and reassuring. Ronald Reagan, drawing on the idiom that came naturally to him in *Knute Rockne, All American* and *King's Row* almost a half century before, retired in 1989 as one of America's most popular and successful Presidents.

Politically, our world has been turned almost precisely upside down—or has it remained very much the same? In 1940, the presidential candidate of the incumbent party, the party long considered to be a minority in national elections, was nonetheless victorious, winning very large majorities in the South and most of the western states and narrow majorities in the big industrial states of the North. In 1988, the presidential candidate of the incumbent party, a party long considered to be a minority in national elections, was nonetheless victorious, winning very large majorities in the South and most of the western states and narrow majorities in the big industrial states of the North. The only difference is that the winning party in 1940 was the Democrats, and in 1988, the Republicans *(see Chart 2)*.

Both Franklin Roosevelt and George Bush were heavily supported by a hawkish South that backed their assertive foreign policies; both won only 52% in the more prosperous Industrial Belt which had the most to protect. The Farm Belt, with a vested economic interest in inflation and a continuing aversion to foreign military involvement, was the only one of these regions to vote against President Roosevelt and President Bush. The impulse was most accentuated in Iowa, quite possibly the most dovish state in the union, which was the number six Republican state in 1940 and the number two Democratic state in 1988. Only New England, swinging toward the leader who was aiding their British cousins in 1940 and giving a very narrow edge to its home-state governor in 1988, is out of order when these regions are ranked by percentage for the winning candidate.

The symmetry continues. Just as the Republicans, understanding the special appeal of Franklin Roosevelt in the 1930s, hoped that things would go back to what they thought was normal in 1940, so the Democrats, understanding the special appeal of Ronald Reagan in the 1980s, hoped that things would go back to what they thought was normal in 1988. In both cases, their hopes were disappointed. Franklin Roosevelt, it became clear in retrospect, had created a new natural presidential majority for his party. And, as journalist Samuel Lubell pointed out, even when one segment of that coalition became disenchanted, that very disenchantment made him more attractive to another. Given the weakness of party loyalties in the 1980s, it probably goes too far to credit Ronald Reagan with creating a natural presidential majority for his

Republicans. But in the 1988 campaign, the process Lubell described seemed also apparent: as Michael Dukakis made inroads in the culturally liberal but economically market-oriented West Coast, for example, George Bush won the electoral votes of the culturally traditional but economically protectionist-minded factory states of Pennsylvania, Ohio and Michigan. Those who argue that Dukakis could have added a few more points to the 46% of the votes he won by making this or that move in the campaign fail to account for votes he might have lost by such a move. In contrast, George Bush, like Ronald Reagan twice before him, was able to hold together a majority coalition of the economically market-oriented (but culturally often liberal) with the culturally traditional (but economically often protection-minded). The first time, you can say it happened because of Carter's problems. The second time, you can say it was Reagan's smile and feel-good ads. The third time, you—and maybe even some of the Democrats—may conclude that it wasn't just an accident. The Democrats have now lost five of the last six presidential elections. How many times do you have to hit the donkey over the head with a board before you get its attention?

Chart 2. Percentage of Two-Party Vote by Region
For Roosevelt, 1940, and Bush, 1988

	Roosevelt 1940	Bush 1988
UNITED STATES	55%	54%
SOUTH (AL, AS, FL, GA, KY, LA, MS, NC, OK, SC, TN, TX, VA)	73%	59%
WEST (AK*, AZ, CA, CO, HI*, ID, MT, NV, NM, OR, UT, WA, WY)	57%	53%
INDUSTRIAL BELT (DC*, DE, IL, IN, MD, MI, MS, NJ, NY, OH, PA, WV)	52%	52%
FARM BELT (IA, KS, MN, NE, ND, SD, WI)	48%	49.8%
NEW ENGLAND (CT, ME, MA, NH, RI, VT)	53%	50.2%

*1988 only

New Deal Democrats, after 1940, and Reagan Republicans, after 1988, remained a minority in Congress and conspicuously failed to control the governments of the big states. Much of their new constituencies came from volatile new movements—the CIO labor unions, the New Right—which had flared up suddenly and which seemed capable of vanishing suddenly as well. Both groups had vocal support from impassioned intellectuals who felt beleaguered even on their home turf: for we forget that the liberal professors of 1940 were as much in the minority among their articulate peers on campus and off as the conservative professors and think tank associates of 1988 feel they are.

Of course the differences between these majorities are obvious, and have obvious explanations. Franklin Roosevelt wanted to increase the size and scope of the federal government when it was small, representing only 8.2% of the gross national product in 1940, at a time when the unexpected and still not completely explicable collapse of the economy after 1929 left Americans distrustful of econonmic free markets, and as the nation was preparing to go to war—

for war, as the historian William McNeill points out, always results in an increase in government's size and powers. Ronald Reagan and George Bush want to hold down the size and scope of the federal government that they feel has burgeoned in size, representing an exhorbitant amount of the gross national product. This comes at a time when an unexpected and still not completely explicable six-year expansion of the economy has delivered the stable growth and lower energy prices which Keynesian economics and energy price controls conspicuously failed to deliver, and as the nation basks in a long era of peace—for in peacetime, as McNeill suggests, the impetus for and perceived legitimacy of big government tend to decline.

There is another difference as well. In 1940, the United States was in one of the few periods in its history when politics tended to revolve around economics. The politics of economic redistribution created by the Second New Deal of 1935 (steeply progressive taxes, social security, the Wagner labor act) and the rise of the CIO unions in 1937 tended to frame the issues and determine the shape of coalitions of political support in 1940. This was in vivid contrast to the more standard condition of American politics in which cultural differences—regional origin and race, ethnic groups and religions, personal values on issues ranging from Prohibition to slavery and immigration—tended to structure party coalitions. Now in the 1980s—in fact, going back into the early 1960s and even the late 1950s—we have returned in times mostly of peace and mostly of prosperity to a mostly cultural politics. Cultural attitudes and cultural status are far better predictors of political choice than economic status—better predictors than anything but party identification itself.

This makes sense in a country in which, as the University of Michigan longitudinal study shows, economic mobility is the rule rather than the exception, but in which personal values and cultural identity, once established, tend to be fairly permanent. And if the shared experiences of depression and, especially, of war tended to produce a cultural uniformity—a sort of Norman Rockwell, 1940s movies Americanness which prized the average and the normal and scorned and derided the nonconformist and the eccentric—then the extended prosperity and economic growth that (at first, unexpectedly) followed the war produced eventually a flowering of cultural variety, as Americans became able to afford (economically and psychologically) to choose their lifestyle and to give expression to their deepest values.

Voters may continue to treat presidential elections as referenda on the state of the economy and of foreign relations abroad. But the issues that tend to shape political coalitions and to dominate political discourse are very often those that split voters along cultural lines—civil rights, Vietnam, the Watergate scandal that was the culmination of the years when Richard Nixon pitted "the silent majority" against the candidates of "acid, amnesty, and abortion," the Equal Rights Amendment, crime, the Pledge of Allegiance, and prison furloughs. And as doubts increased about the efficacy of government spending and government programs to produce desired change, the demands for such programs became a less vibrant and less decisive part of our politics.

So in 1988, George Bush, the supposedly aristocratic nominee of the party supposedly of the rich, carried every state in the least affluent region of the nation, the South, and the big factory states of the North. Michael Dukakis, from the party supposedly of the poor, carried mostly states where whites shared the culturally liberal values of his native high-income suburb of Brookline. Most voters did not vote by income: the exit polls of the three networks show Dukakis with 60% or more only with one in eight voters with incomes below $12,500 and Bush reaching the 60% level only with one in four voters with incomes above $50,000. In the East, Bush, according to CBS News exit polls, had no advantage no matter how high the income; cultural liberalism there is strong even in the Upper East Side, as Tom Wolfe portrayed in *The Bonfire of the Vanities*. In the West, Bush had no great edge except over the $100,000 line. Only in the South was there anything approaching income-based politics, and it was not purely so: Dukakis's edge among the under-$12,500 voters came from his near-unanimous support from blacks, while

Bush was winning more than 60% beginning at the $25,000 level, which is to say among a substantial majority of the voters. This is the opposite of the model of economic politics that New Dealers cherished, in which a large working class outvotes the selfish but not very numerous rich; here a large and mostly white middle class is outvoting a heavily outnumbered class of blacks and poor.

A better explanation of the election—and of American political choices generally—comes from the polls conducted by The Gallup Organization for Times Mirror Company in 1987 and 1988 which present voters in 10 groups. These are defined not by party identification, but by nine "dimensions," of which four (personal financial pressure, belief in social justice, attitudes toward size of government and attitudes toward business) are primarily economic, and five (religious faith, alienation, degree of tolerance, militant anti-Communism and American exceptionalism) represent cultural values and attitudes. The groups that emerge, as described by Gallup and Times Mirror are, with the percentage they represent of the likely electorate going into November 1988:

Enterprisers.   Affluent, well-educated and predominantly male. This classic Republican group is mainly characterized by its pro-business and anti-government attitudes. Enterprisers are moderate on questions of personal freedom, but oppose increased spending on most social programs. (16%)

Moralists.   Middle-aged and middle-income, this core Republican group is militantly anti-Communist and restrictive on personal freedom issues. (14%)

Upbeats.   Young and optimistic, the members of this group are firm believers in America and in the country's government. Upbeats are moderate in their political attitudes but strongly pro-Reagan. (9%)

Disaffected.   Alienated, pessimistic and financially pressured, this group leans toward the Republicans, but it has historic ties to the Democratic Party. Disaffecteds are skeptical of both big government and big business, but are pro-military. (7%)

Bystanders.   The members of this group are young, predominantly white and poorly educated. They neither participate in politics nor show any interest in current affairs. (0%)

Followers.   Young, poorly educated and disproportionately black. This group shows little interest in politics and is very persuadable and unpredictable. Although they are not critical of government or big business, Followers do not have much faith in America. (4%)

Seculars.   This group is uniquely characterized by its lack of religious belief. In addition, Seculars are strongly committed to personal freedom and are dovish on defense issues. Their level of participation in politics, however, is not as high as one might expect given their education and their political sophistication. (9%)

Sixties Democrats.   This well-educated, heavily female group has a strong belief in social justice, as well as a very low militancy level. These mainstream Democrats are highly tolerant of views and lifestyles they do not share and favor most forms of social spending. (11%)

New Dealers.   Older, blue-collar and religious. The roots of this aging group of traditional Democrats can be traced back to the New Deal. Although supportive of many social spending measures, New Dealers are intolerant on cultural issues and somewhat hawkish on defense. (15%)

God & Country Democrats.   This group is older, poorer and about one-third black, with high numbers concentrated in the South. They have a strong faith in America and are uncritical of its institutions. They favor social spending and are moderately anti-Communist. (6%)

Partisan Poor.   Very low-income, with relatively high proportions of black and poorly educated, this loyal Democratic group has a strong faith in its party's ability to achieve social justice. The Partisan Poor firmly support all levels of social spending, yet they are conservative on some cultural issues. (9%)

Bush's campaign managed to duplicate Reagan's levels of support among Enterprisers, Moralists and Upbeats—no mean feat, given their differences *(see Chart 3)*. Aided undoubtedly by negative attacks on Dukakis, Bush raised his support among Disaffecteds, Followers and New Dealers during the campaign, although he did not equal Reagan's showings among them. But those same tactics, plus Dukakis's own culturally liberal, technocratic posture, held Bush to low percentages from Seculars and Sixties Democrats, voters most likely to be turned off by the use of the Pledge of Allegiance and flag factory visits. Bush's "kinder, gentler" rhetoric evidently helped him improve on Reagan's showing among God & Country Democrats and equal it among the Partisan Poor.

The Gallup-Times Mirror typology was invented for the America of the 1980s; it depends on issues and attitudes which did not exist 20, much less 50, years ago; it is possible only to guess how it might apply to the America Henry Luce was addressing nearly 50 years before. Most likely far larger percentages of voters were New Dealers and Enterprisers, and far fewer were Upbeats or Sixties Democrats—in each case the products of their time as well as their place in society. For voters tend to hold, over their lifetimes, the attitudes and allegiances that guided their first experiences in voting. The young voters of the 1940s were solidly for Franklin Roosevelt: he carried their vote in 1944; as they grew older, the New Dealers cast some of the highest percentages of any age group for Michael Dukakis in 1988. The young voters of the late 1960s and early 1970s carry their almost religious opposition to American military intervention abroad, and their cultural liberalism, into the different and somewhat hostile climate of the 1980s. The young voters of the 1980s, Republican strategists hope, and Democratic strategists fear, will carry their sunny Republicanism into the 2030s and 2040s.

Chart 3. Recalled Vote in 1984 and 1988 Trend in Support for George Bush

	Reagan 1984	May 1988	Sept. 1988	Oct. 1988	Nov. 1988
TOTAL SAMPLE FOR NATION	**58%**	**40%**	**50%**	**50%**	**55%**
Enterprisers	96	83	95	96	98
Moralists	97	82	94	93	96
Upbeats	86	75	85	83	83
Disaffected	81	47	61	60	68
Followers	54	28	39	28	39
Seculars	34	24	17	33	24
Sixties Democrats	25	8	15	10	12
New Dealers	30	14	23	15	27
God & Country Democrats	31	25	20	25	38
Partisan Poor	19	8	9	18	19

So while the political symmetry of the 1940 and 1988 election results reflects some enduring characteristics of American life, it covers over the vast differences between the country that cowered on its side of the ocean, with a wounded economy and an almost nonexistent military, and the country that, in the world's less populous hemisphere, with clamorous conflict over cultural issues and constant crises of confidence, nonetheless has set the example that the rest of the world is hoping to follow.

This *1990 Almanac of American Politics* will look at politics, not just over the past year or two, but will examine, in each state and in many congressional districts, how life and politics have changed over the course of this American Half Century. In many cases, the Almanac will rely on the wonderful *WPA Guides* to the States, prepared in the late 1930s by the Works Progress Administration under the leadership of Harry Hopkins—a set of books which stands as a stern refutation to those who suppose that government is incapable of inspiring works of keen observation and graceful prose.

THE 1988 PRESIDENTIAL CAMPAIGN

Look! We Have Come Through. The 1988 campaign has been widely—maybe universally— criticized. The results were uniformly hailed as unsatisfactory: 46% of the voters did not vote for George Bush, after all, and only 50.1% of those eligible bothered to vote at all. The Democratic nominee, it was said by Democratic Senator Terry Sanford, ran "the worst managed campaign in this century," and he was in any case the choice of only a plurality of Democratic primary voters. George Bush's campaign, many said, was successful because it was more negative and unscrupulous than Michael Dukakis'. All this lamentation sounds plausible. But before the conventional wisdom that 1988 was a dreadful campaign becomes universally accepted, it may be useful to consider some things that the presidential process did not do. It did not select, as either party's nominee, a man who was unacceptable to large parts of his party or who was plainly neurotic or of scurrilous character. It did not, in a nation of great cultural variety, produce open appeals to hatreds and bigotry. It did not end in a result which seemed irrational or inexplicable.

Americans tend to take such blessings for granted. Yet when the 1988 presidential campaign cycle began, they were by no means inevitable. A people mostly uninterested in politics were required to choose from among a dozen or so politicians—about whom they knew little or nothing—the man who would hold, for four and quite possibly eight years, the most important political office in the world. They were asked to choose each party's nominee in a complex and cumbersome process difficult to understand for even dutiful and well-informed citizens, and at a time when the nation's primary means of political communication were the paid media of 30-second television advertisements and the free media of the three commercial TV networks' 22-minute weeknight newscasts. They were required to make this choice, moreover, at a time when no one or two major issues occupied the political landscape or provided a basis for measuring candidates' convictions and capacities. In these circumstances, it is not difficult to imagine how unwise choices could have been made, with consequences that would needlessly complicate the work of government and sap the morale of the nation. Just remember that in April 1987, Gary Hart was far ahead in polls for the Democratic nomination and had big leads in pairings against George Bush and Bob Dole.

In retrospect, it can be argued that the choices were utterly predictable—except that no one predicted all of them. The candidates with the most money and the smoothest organizations won the two parties' nominations. The candidate of the party that could plausibly claim to have delivered peace and prosperity to the nation won the general election. Yet neither result was utterly inevitable, and the contingencies that helped to produce each result tell something about the nation, the contenders and the presidential selection system itself.

On behalf of the system, it can and should be said that its lengthiness and complexity produced nominees who showed the stamina and discipline and organizational ability to run well-financed and well-organized campaigns—talents that have some relationship to those useful in a President. There is no question that the two sons of Norfolk County, Massachusetts, Michael Dukakis and George Bush, created competent organizations and performed ably and with discipline. If neither man outdazzled all his opponents in the campaign season's many debates—and the proliferation of debates was one of the affirmatively good features of this campaign—it is also true that neither was outdazzled or even beaten on points in any primary confrontation. Both showed the capacity to choose the right states to compete in, unlike Bob Dole (who missed his chances to win Missouri and Oklahoma on Super Tuesday) and Dick

Gephardt (who overspent in Florida and Texas on Super Tuesday and missed his chances in Oklahoma and Arkansas). Neither flared up in an outburst of temper that unnerved voters, as Dole did on NBC on New Hampshire primary night ("Stop lying about my record!") or made statements he couldn't substantiate at moments of maximum exposure (as Pat Robertson did in the weeks after his surprise second place finish in Iowa). Voters not fixated on any one issue and not terribly familiar with any candidate seem to have taken a "zero defect" approach into 1988: if they found out anything wrong about any candidate, they scratched his name off the list. After Illinois, on March 15, that left Bush and Dukakis as the only possible choices.

The process itself has its drawbacks. When its caucuses first became prominent in 1976, Iowa was a state in the center of the national spectrum; by 1988, it was far on the nation's left, and was the number two state for Dukakis in November. Its Democratic caucus participants are so uniformly and strongly dovish, that any candidate who does not pass a peacenik's litmus test has no hope of winning *any* support. This may have kept Sam Nunn out of the Democratic race and may have prevented Albert Gore, who tested the waters in Iowa and found them uncongenial, from getting exposure that could have made him a contender outside the South: if Iowa has a veto, it prevents the Democrats from nominating a candidate with a foreign policy acceptable to the 155 electoral votes of the South. Even on the Republican side, Iowa was the number one anti-Reagan state: nowhere else (except in Dole's Kansas) could Bush, as the loyal follower of a mostly successful President, have been held to a pathetic 19% in his own party's contest.

New Hampshire has its biases too. An anti-tax fervor in this New England tax haven caused problems for a mild tax-raiser like Bob Dole, and a preoccupation with a local nuclear power plant among many Democrats guaranteed Michael Dukakis a victory here. But Iowa and New Hampshire and the other early contests produced only one withdrawal, Bruce Babbitt's. So in the 14 weeknight newscasts between New Hampshire and Super Tuesday, the networks were obliged to tell 40% of the primary voters whatever they needed to know about the 12 candidates who were still running. With all that clutter, the number one and two candidates in Iowa, Democrats Dick Gephardt and Paul Simon and Republicans Bob Dole and Pat Robertson, failed utterly to get the momentum that other high Iowa finishers like Jimmy Carter in 1976, George Bush in 1980, and Gary Hart in 1984 got.

The framers of Super Tuesday, southern Democratic legislators, hoped that by bunching all the southern contests on one day they would clinch the nomination for a southern candidate who could win the South's electoral votes in November. They succeeded—except the nomination that was clinched was the Republicans' and the candidate clinching it was George Bush. (Bob Dole stayed on to compete in Illinois a week later, but sent conflicting signals about whether he was in the race and killed his chance to win in what was anyway the most favorable ground for him on the rest of the schedule.) But the Democrat who came out the best on Super Tuesday was the man Bush would refer to in the fall as the "Governor of Massachusetts." True, Albert Gore of Tennessee, after a shrewd and unexpectedly large media buy, finished first in five southern states and second to Jesse Jackson in five more. Yet because the contests were bunched together, and because there was so much clutter, he got little notice. The number one story on the 30-minute Super Tuesday specials and the next night's newscasts was George Bush's sweep of the South. This was followed by Jesse Jackson's victory in five southern states and Michael Dukakis' impressive four-cornered national victory, in Massachusetts, in the Washington state caucuses, and in the Texas and Florida primaries. So the success of Albert Gore, the leading nominatable and electable candidate in 10 of the 50 states, with one-fifth of the nation's population, was dwarfed by the other stories of the night. Like the high Iowa finishers, he found that the clutter prevented him from getting his message across to voters in later contests.

If Illinois—so often the crucial primary—officially ended the Republican race, it effectively ended the Democratic contest, not by giving a decisive victory to Dukakis, but because it was so intensely local. Chicago media have become the most parochial of any major city, concentrating furiously on the mud-wrestling otherwise known as Chicago politics. For them, the Illinois race was a contest between Chicago's Jesse Jackson and Downstate's Paul Simon; Dukakis and Gore got little air time, and finished a dismal third and fourth. That postponed Dukakis's clinching of the nomination and prevented Gore from ever challenging Dukakis in his position as the leading opponent of Jesse Jackson. Jackson's victory in the Michigan caucus convinced the media momentarily that he was winning thousands of white working-class votes (he wasn't: his shrewd organizers flooded thinly-attended caucus sites Outstate, as well as in the Detroit area, with blacks). Gore's endorsement by Mayor Edward Koch in New York made that state look like a real contest (it wasn't: the anti-Jackson majority went overwhelmingly to Dukakis).

It is a characteristic of political markets that they don't work well when a candidate with some significant backing insists on running though he has no chance to win: he is not subject to the discipline of seeking a majority and his opponent is not subject to the discipline of running against someone who can beat him. Jesse Jackson, not because of his race but because of his views, cannot be nominated by the Democrats and, if he were, could not be elected; Americans are not going to choose a man whose response to a military ally of Soviet Russia and a dictator who runs a concentration-camp regime is *Viva Castro!*

1988 was a year of great volatility in the polls. Michael Dukakis led George Bush by double-digit margins in May and June 1988 and then again after the Democratic Convention in July; George Bush was leading by double digits in most polls after the second debate in mid-October and had led other Democrats by similar margins earlier in the year. This volatility was probably less a matter of voters changing their minds on issues than it was of inattention and ignorance: if you know very little about the candidates and don't have intense views on any issues, the lightest breeze can turn you around like a falling leaf. The fact is that for most of the spring both Bush's and Dukakis' advisers were puzzled by the Democrat's big leads, and neither side thought they were sustainable. Where they differed is that Bush's top strategists expected the campaign to go as it did (though they got a bit nervous about it sometimes), while the Dukakis people believed they could win.

Could the Democrats have won? The conventional wisdom, especially among Democrats, is that Dukakis ran "the worst campaign ever." This is nonsense to anyone who remembers the 1972 Democratic National Convention in Miami Beach that put off the candidate's acceptance speech until 3 a.m. and selected Thomas Eagleton for Vice President. Dukakis ran a brilliant convention in Atlanta: he was steely but cordial in his refusal to truckle to Jesse Jackson, and he delivered a wonderfully staged acceptance speech that featured ideas as appealing as possible, considering that peace and prosperity worked for the other side. He stressed his Ellis Island heritage—this was a son of immigrants running in a nation where most people count at least one ancestor from the great 1840–1924 immigration—and he portrayed himself as a man who would use government frugally to solve problems—day care, college costs, home-buying—in a comfortable country where most people are nonetheless nervous about whether they're taking proper care of their children and preparing for the future. He had the nerve to select Lloyd Bentsen as his running mate, despite coolness from Jackson and moans from those who considered him a gray, dull white male. The choice may have had some political downside, by drawing the Democrats into Texas but leaving them still agonizingly short of carrying it. But Bentsen's cool articulateness, his high competence, his mastery of issues, and his stature strengthened the ticket nationwide.

But Dukakis was unable to do in the general election campaign what he did in Atlanta. His organization was strong in the field, and so he decided to run field operations in all 50 states; his fundraising ability was fabulous, so he raised $20 million in soft money most of which went for field work. Aside from California, where his staff was trying to reinvent politics in an almost entirely apolitical Pacific Rim commonwealth, probably most of this money was wasted.

What Dukakis didn't do so well, and hadn't in the primaries, was deliver a few simple messages with enough repetition and discipline to get them across to an electorate actively hostile to any form of political communication. (It was said that any city where a candidate aired a five-minute ad on all local stations experienced a sudden drop in water pressure.) Dukakis's campaign failed to understand that in a presidential campaign you can communicate fewer and less subtle messages than in a seriously contested campaign for senator or governor. They designed advertising—including a notorious set of ads purporting to show Bush campaign advisers planning their ads—which worked against rather than for their cause. At the same time the candidate, by entertaining all manner of questions at press conferences, failed to show the discipline necessary to get his message across on the two- or three-minute segment he would get on the evening newscasts. Dukakis defenders say he was only being open and honest. But you could have said the same of Thomas Jefferson, if he had written slapdash prose, or of Franklin Roosevelt, if he had decided to wing his inaugural or "day of infamy" speeches. A candidate has a duty to adapt his own presentation so that he can communicate effectively with voters over the media of his time.

The Bush campaign was more disciplined in getting its message across and, to be fair to Dukakis, it had an easier message to deliver. Dukakis was running against the party of peace and prosperity, after all; he was not running, as Democrats had anticipated all through the 1980s they would be running, in a year of recession; the Iran-contra scandal did not prove, as Dukakis and many in the media expected, to be another Watergate; the stock market crash of October 1987 did not lead to a downturn in the economy; the Reagan arms control stands led, not to bitter confrontation, but to a treaty to which the Democrats were smugly confident for years the Soviets would never agree. Most importantly, George Bush did not turn out to be a wimp, but instead had, despite the media hubbub over Dan Quayle's selection, as successful a TV convention as Dukakis.

And the Republicans had more ammunition: the furlough issue. On this it is confidently alleged that the Bush campaign lied and that Dukakis should have responded; but in fact the Bush campaign was careful to tell the truth (the more they told it, the more damaging the issue was), and the arguments on the subject that were misleading to the point of falsehood were those made in Dukakis's ads and statements and articles by journalistic shills for the Dukakis campaign. It is alleged that the Bush campaign appealed to racism, although the Bush campaign ads were careful not to use the picture of Willie Horton, but simply to mention that he had been sentenced to jail for life without parole for committing a brutal murder, and that he had been granted weekend furloughs numerous times under a policy Dukakis supported and defended for 11 years and that from one such furlough he did not return but instead went to Maryland where he raped and brutalized a young woman.

Dukakis did have a chance to respond, on April 12, when he was asked about this issue by Albert Gore in a New York debate. At that time Dukakis knew that he would approve a change in the law that allowed life-without-parole prisoners to be furloughed, and he could have taken credit for it. Enough signatures had been gathered to put a referendum on the Massachusetts ballot changing the law, and on March 22, Dukakis had agreed to sign that bill. But then he refused to say that he agreed with the change, grudgingly saying only that the people of Massachusetts and the legislature wanted it, and on April 12, his response to Gore was, "The trouble with you, Al, is that you've never run a criminal justice system." With that bit of arrogance, Dukakis missed his chance to dissociate himself from a position that was politically and morally indefensible. Those who advised him later to respond more aggressively to the furlough issue failed to understand that there is no good argument for the proposition that "life without parole" means "except on Saturdays and Sundays."

The Bush campaign did not originate discussion of the furlough issue. Horton escaped in June 1986 and committed the rape for which he was imprisoned in Maryland in April 1987, a month after Dukakis declared for President. The Horton case and the Dukakis campaign's efforts to hide its record were the subject of a Pulitzer Prize winning series by the Lawrence *Eagle-Tribune*. Liberals had expected Iran-contra or insider trading or the Noriega imbroglio to be the Watergate-type story of executive misconduct and coverup that determined the outcome of the 1988 election; instead Dukakis' coverup of the Willie Horton story was. The July 1988 *Reader's Digest* published an article by Robert James Bidinotto on the case and Dukakis' response, which turned out to be the most influential piece of journalism in the whole campaign.

Bush campaign manager Lee Atwater, who had already heard about the case from research director Jim Pinkerton, went off incognito on the Fourth of July weekend to a motorcyclists' convention in Luray, Virginia. Over the bar, he heard people discussing the *Reader's Digest* article; they were especially angry that Dukakis, while meeting with prisoners' families, refused to meet with the families of Horton's victims. The "revolving door" ad started running that summer and kept running through the campaign; polls showed the effect did not wear off, but continued to hurt Dukakis.

Dukakis backers were infuriated that what they considered a peripheral issue, irrelevant to the presidency, was having such an effect, and some charged that the ads were racist (because Horton is black). But Bush's ads never showed Horton (though an independent committee's ads did), and the prisoners going through the revolving door were mostly white. And anyway, the fact that the ad did work is proof that it was relevant. Advertisements, like any other form of political argument, don't work unless they strike to the quick and say something profound about more than their immediate subject; and the Horton ads did. The episode showed how Dukakis took a sensible and defensible policy (granting furloughs to prisoners scheduled to be released) and carried it to ridiculous extremes (granting furloughs to prisoners sentenced never to be released). It provided a valid basis for an inference that liberal Dukakis appointees would take sensible liberal policies and carry them to ridiculous extremes, with Dukakis's approval—which is exactly what many voters thought happened in the last national Democratic administration. Such an inference was neither racist nor irrational. Dukakis's Massachusetts allows prisoners to vote and his administration sent state officials into prisons to urge them to register and apply for absentee ballots. Horton announced he was for Dukakis, and could have voted for him if Maryland had let him go back to Massachusetts; perhaps he might have been able to if he had applied for an absentee ballot on the ground that he would be unable to return to prison in Massachusetts on election day. The furlough issue, far from being an appeal to racism or a mindless distraction, instead pointed to central defects in Dukakis's candidacy and style of governance.

Can the process be said to work if barely half of those eligible actually voted? 1988 was a year of record low turnout—a record, that is, since 1924, another year of peace and prosperity, when turnout was lower. Yet it's not clear that low turnout affected the result or is evidence of massive discontent with the political system. It's not even clear that turnout now is massively lower than it was in the supposed golden age of turnout in the early 1960s.

The election year did see an effort by activists on the political left to make registration easier and to register more low income voters, in the hopes that they would support liberal and Democratic candidates and policies of economic redistribution. These efforts and those of the Democrats in California had some success. But lowering barriers has only a marginal effect on turnout. The uncomfortable fact is that barriers to voting are lower now than they were 25 years ago, but turnout is down. Moreover, the reservoir of voters is so large that groups of any political views can target and register voters of their beliefs: in 1984, Jesse Jackson sparked efforts to register many blacks in North Carolina, but Jesse Helms registered more conservative Christians and was reelected over Jim Hunt. The only poll to date of all Americans of voting age, by CBS News, suggests that if everyone eligible had voted, George Bush would have won by a larger margin. Evidently he would have gotten big margins from low-informational young people who are upbeat and optimistic about America and did not bother to vote.

You can argue that half of eligible Americans didn't vote because they were disgusted with the system or repelled by the choices. But it seems more likely, given the rather high levels of satisfaction reflected in the polls, that they didn't vote because they didn't feel any raging dissatisfaction or need for change. They may have concluded that things were going well enough that it didn't matter much whether Bush or Dukakis was elected—a proposition for which an intellectually respectable argument can be made.

It should be remembered that the highest turnout under the American flag is not in any long-settled, high-income suburb, not in any stable machine-tended big city precinct, but in the Commonwealth of Puerto Rico. There you will find a politics of enthusiasm: polls show voters have not one good thing to say for the opposition's candidates and not one bad thing to say about their own. On the mainland, polls show that citizens have a more nuanced, sophisticated view of politicians and issues: they admit their own side's shortcomings and concede the other side's strengths. They split tickets habitually and, as Barry Sussman points out in *What Americans Really Think*, they change opinions readily on absorbing even small bits of information. Puerto Rico's enthusiastic partisans march in rallies and surge to the polls in vast numbers; mainland America's sophisticated analysts switch channels when a political broadcast comes on and can't be bothered to vote. Low turnout may be one of the prices of having a population that is not carried away by partisan enthusiasms, and whose view of the society is less clouded by partisan passions and biases than that of many of the political analysts and activists who decry the voters' lack of interest in their business.

But isn't turnout declining at an alarming rate? The figures show a decline, but it's not clear that it's something about which to be alarmed. In presidential elections, and off years since 1972, the percentages of those eligible have jumped about a bit, falling generally but rising in 1982 and 1984, as this series shows *(see Chart 4)*.

Chart 4. Percentage of Voter Turn-out during Presidential and Offyears

	1972	1974	1976	1978	1980	1982	1984	1986	1988
Presidential	55%		54%		53%		53%		50%
Offyear		38%		37%		40%		36%	

You could argue that turnout is falling, or that it is wobbling within a fairly narrow range, from 50% to 55% in presidential elections from 1972 onwards, and 36% to 40% in the off years during that same period. From 1950 to 1972, however, turnout wobbled within consistently higher ranges: 60%–63% in presidential years, 43%–48% in the off years.

Interestingly enough, there was no overlap between 1950–70 and 1972–88 turnout levels. There is an obvious explanation for this sharp difference. The 18-year-old vote, enacted nationally in 1971, vastly increased the number of eligibles but, because 18, 19 and 20-year-olds tend not to be firmly rooted in their communities, not to have a personal stake in election outcomes (and by 1972 the military draft was essentially ended), and not to be as interested in politics as their elders, their inclusion in the potential electorate sharply and permanently reduced overall turnout percentages. Taking into account the effect of the 18-year-old vote, the picture of a sharp and continuing decline in turnout since the 1960s must be modified to show low levels of turnout, with mild declines and occasional upsurges, going back as far as 1950 when Americans, sent hither and yon by World War II, had started to set down their postwar roots.

Fragmented Media.   For more than 50 years, partisans of various stripes have charged—often with some justice—that the media are unfairly biased in favor of one political party and against another. Fifty years ago, there was no doubt that the proprietors of the media were arrayed almost entirely on the Republican side. Henry Luce of *Time* and *Life*, lent the editor of

Fortune to manage Wendell Willkie's campaign; the Cowles brothers of *Look* and the Minneapolis and Des Moines papers, were among his most enthusiastic supporters; Willkie had been featured prominently on one of radio's most popular shows, "Information Please;" and Willkie's mistress was the book editor of the New York *Herald Tribune* which, as the leading moderate Republican newspaper in the nation, would have backed him in any case.

Most other media proprietors were more conservative and far more hostile to Roosevelt and the New Deal. Colonel Robert McCormick of the *Chicago Tribune* was vitriolically anti-Roosevelt: "you have only 88 days," he counted down during the 1936 campaign, "in which to save your country." His cousin, Captain Joseph Patterson of the New York *Daily News*, the nation's biggest circulation newspaper, had supported the New Deal, but by 1940, turned against Roosevelt on foreign policy. William Randolph Hearst, who once hoped for the Democratic presidential nomination himself and threw the California delegation and the nomination to Roosevelt in 1932, was by 1940, bitterly opposed to Roosevelt and the New Deal. Some genteel publishers in the South—the Daniels of Raleigh, the Binghams of Louisville—were faithful Democrats. But no major metropolitan daily supported Roosevelt. The radio commentators who supported him were outnumbered by those opposed. Articulate opinion was hostile. If media hostility and bias and slanting of the news could have defeated a candidate, it would have defeated Roosevelt in 1940. But he won.

If the nation had a natural Democratic majority in presidential elections in years in which the media was biased toward the Republicans and conservatives, a strong case can be made that it has today something approaching a natural Republican majority in presidential elections at a time when most of the media seems biased toward Democrats and liberals. Spokesmen for the major newspapers and television networks jump up and down and swear that they are not biased, and sophisticated members of the press make the much sounder argument that there is a natural bias in news coverage toward the critical and the negative.

An argument of approximately equal sophistication would be that the working levels of the press—the political reporter and the copy editor, the network reporter and the producer—are the products of a generation when the two major stories, from which journalists have reaped professional (and in some cases financial) success and the personal satisfaction that comes from knowing you have done your duty, were Vietnam and Watergate. There is a bias in the profession therefore not so much against Republicans, stewards of the national security establishment, or conservatives, as there is toward treating every story—Iran-contra, stock market insider trading, contra aid—as if it could be another quagmire or scandal. This was certainly evident over the long run of coverage of the 1988 presidential campaign cycle. Much of it took on the tone suggested in the subtitle of Doyle McManus's and Jane Mayer's book on Iran-contra, *Landslide: The Unmaking of a President*—which described not the events which caused the repudiation of the Reagan presidency, but rather events which did not prevent Reagan from achieving a near-record high job rating as he was leaving office and from securing, as no President since Andrew Jackson had, the election of his Vice President to succeed him in office.

As David Broder argues in his book *Behind the Front Page*, reportage is never free from bias, in the sense that it is always undergirded by assumptions—in the case of the best reporters, assumptions based on in-depth knowledge and brilliant instincts—of what the story really is, assumptions that shape where a reporter looks for the story, how he goes about gathering it, and the way he writes it up. In the years around 1940, many working journalists shared the New Deal view of the world, but the demands and assumptions of those who owned the media were Republican, and so was much of the journalistic work product. In the late 1980s, the owners of the major newspapers and broadcast media are in fact not so unrelievedly liberal as their conservative critics suppose, and they exercise far less direct control (if indeed they exercise any at all) over the daily work product of their reporters and editors and producers than their counterparts of 50 years ago. But the guiding assumptions of the working press, and their view of the world, is mostly liberal. For them, the Vietnam war was wrong and spending more money on programs that purport to aid the poor is right; Richard Nixon was wrong in almost everything he did, and affirmative action (a policy, conveniently forgotten by both Nixon's admirers and his critics, which was first adopted in his Administration) is right; assertive American foreign policies are dangerous and harmful to the downtrodden peoples of the Third World, and opposition to any assertion of American power is likely to be right. Media defenders will bridle at accepting the notion, but anyone else will find it silly to disagree, that such notions tended to inform the coverage of politics and public policy in the 1980s in the elite newspapers and on the three major television networks.

There were two key media events in the 1988 campaign. The first was the confrontation between George Bush and Dan Rather on the January 25, 1988, "CBS Evening News." Rather's producers had prepared a six-minute accusatory story suggesting that Bush must have had knowledge of the diversion of funds from the Iran arms deals to the Nicaraguan contras; they played that while Bush, who insisted on appearing live, waited in the studio and then responded in a nine-minute interchange with Rather. It was an electric confrontation: the story was unusually long and harsh in tone, and the unscripted argument was unprecedented; Rather overstepped the bounds of objectivity and talked as one of Bush's opponents might, while Bush (who all along conceded the most damaging charge against him: poor judgment) stunned Rather by asking him if he would like his whole career judged by "those seven minutes that you walked off the set in Miami?" The candidate who had been pictured on the *Newsweek* cover a few weeks before with the caption "the wimp factor" had scored a knockout.

If the adversarial media was unusually visible that night, it became less and less visible to large numbers of voters as the campaign went along. For fewer and fewer people were watching. Just as the audience for metropolitan newspapers had become less than universal many years before because of competition with other media, so in 1988 the audience of network newscasts was growing smaller because of competition from local television broadcasts, from cable channels, from videotape rentals (60% of households had videotape recorders by the end of 1988) and from other forms of entertainment. Political news was obscured by other events—the Reagan-Gorbachev summits in September 1987, the space shuttle launch and the Seoul Olympics in September 1988, the usual baseball playoffs and World Series in October—and many voters got more political news from local stations (there were some 5,000 local television and radio journalists at each national convention) than from the more sophisticated and more adversarial networks.

Even more important, the network audience was seriously diminished by the Hollywood writers' strike, which prevented the networks from broadcasting any new prime time shows until late October. Network viewership in these months was down 4 million, ratings of the most-watched programs were down 9% to 32%, and the overall network share of the audience fell to 68%. Moreover, viewership was highest among downscale people who tend not to vote and the elderly whose political preferences are most firmly rooted. Americans generally, and movable voters in particular, were tuning out the networks which, with their newscasts and commercials on entertainment programs, had become the American public square.

The bad news about this development is that it decreases the amount of political information voters get. The good news is that it reduces the ability, real or perceived, of any small group of media proprietors or producers to sway public opinion. It is consoling in any case to remember that this sway does not amount to control. An overwhelmingly Republican press, often with a bias that would take the breath away from today's media critics, did not prevent the Democrats from winning the presidential elections of 1936, 1940, 1944, 1948 or 1960. A press whose coverage is informed by an adversarial attitude toward many of society's institutions and especially toward American military and foreign policies has not prevented Republicans opposed to those attitudes from winning the presidential elections of 1968, 1972, 1980, 1984 and

1988. Is there some principle of balance working here? Or is this just evidence that voters can make their own judgments about the world around them, filtering out, when they want to, the biases and assumptions of those who provide most of their information?

THE 101st CONGRESS

A Democratic Congress facing a Republican President: in this American Half Century it has come to be almost a norm, with one and usually both houses controlled by the Democrats, while there is a Republican in the White House for 24 of the past 50 years. But "controlled" is a word to be used with caution when speaking of Congress. Despite a tendency in the 1980s toward greater partisanship on the floor and despite the trend toward higher and higher reelection rates, each of the 535 Members of Congress is an independent political actor, with his own political base, responsible to his own particular constituency, possessed of his own political philosophy and political instincts.

What has been interesting about the Congress in the late 1980s is not that it has trouble getting things done—that is an inevitable result of the design of the Constitution—but that it has gotten so many things done, including many which almost all thoughtful people considered impossible. It passed a thoroughgoing tax reform bill. It passed an immigration reform bill. It passed a trade bill that was not irresponsible. It passed a farm bill that ameliorated rather than exacerbated the problem. It passed a catastrophic health care bill with a mechanism to pay for itself. It passed a welfare reform bill that it can call workfare. It has passed budgets and appropriations bills that have sharply cut the federal deficit and, in 1988, even passed them mostly on time. It passed a bill finally providing compensation and an apology for the internment of Japanese Americans in World War II. It passed a fair housing bill. It devised a mechanism for closing down unneeded military bases.

Congress passed all these laws in the 1980s even though the President was inattentive to almost all of them and hostile to some. The Republican candidate for President in 1988 claimed—and got—credit for the nation's prosperity and its increasing strength in the world. The Democratic Congress deserves and, from the looks of the election results in that year, got some credit too.

The Congresses that have produced these results have had some able leaders and many competent followers. For the first six of the Reagan years, the nominal leaders were, to an extent that is unusual, in control of their chambers. Speaker Tip O'Neill, after losing on the Reagan budget and tax cuts in 1981, proved himself a master of long-range political strategy, medium-range legislative tactics, and short-run personal politicking—as strong a Speaker as the House has had since the progressive revolt against "Uncle Joe" Cannon in 1910. Majority Leaders Howard Baker and Robert Dole, after getting over their initial surprise that their party had captured a majority, proved able to rally Republican majorities though they had few votes to spare and many of their charges were inexperienced, temperamental, or thick-headed. Robert Byrd, coming back to the majority leadership in 1987 despite some grumblings by his colleagues, proved he had learned from the success of some of his colleagues, and had many successes even though he announced that in 1988, at age 70, he would give up the leadership to take over as chairman of Appropriations.

But as the 1980s end, both houses have seen more change in or challenge to these effective leaders than they saw during the 1960s and 1970s. From the Kennedy years to the Carter years, the House had only two Speakers, John McCormack and Carl Albert, and the Senate had only one Majority Leader, Mike Mansfield. None of them rode roughshod over the legislative body he nominally led. From 1977 to 1989, the Senate has had four Majority Leaders and the House, two Speakers, one of whom was severely criticized by his fellow Democrats in 1981 and again in 1984, and the other of whom was, in early 1989, under attack on ethics issues and lost his position. For most of the 1980s, the Speakers and Majority Leaders exerted impressive mastery over their houses. But as the decade was ending, Speaker Jim Wright was forced out of office by an ethics investigation, leaving both houses under the leadership of highly competent and presentable men, Senate Majority Leader George Mitchell and Speaker Thomas Foley, who were nonetheless untested in their new positions.

The House: The Embattled Speaker and the Powerful Princes. By November 1990 the leader over most of the legislative work of the 101st Congress will have been Speaker Thomas Foley. Yet a shadow will still probably be cast over its work by his predecessor, Jim Wright, who served as Speaker for only 29 months, but who nonetheless made a legislative record and set a legislative tone which dominates the history of the House in the late 1980s. That the legislative record was substantial and impressive, and that the tone was querulous, resentful and angry, will come as no surprise to those who remember the man after whom Jim Wright seems to have modeled his career and against whom he seems to have measured his success—his fellow Texan, Lyndon Johnson.

There were parallels aplenty between Wright and Johnson. Both were elected to the House from Texas as young men; both had liberal records, especially on economic issues, which made them some enemies back home; both ran in special elections for the Senate before they were 40 and lost: Johnson in 1941 and Wright in 1961; both were respected as legislative tacticians but were not entirely trusted, not by liberals or by conservative Democrats in Washington, not by Texas populists or Tory Democrats back home; and both were hated or deeply distrusted by Republicans. But there were differences. Johnson won his second try for the Senate, in 1948, and his efforts to enrich himself were successful. Wright abandoned his second try for the Senate, in 1966, when he couldn't raise enough money to run a campaign, and his efforts to make money in odd-duck investments and off an unusual book royalty arrangement got him into trouble with the House Ethics Committee—and in 1989 ended his legislative and political career.

Yet Wright was at least as successful a legislator. Johnson was a brilliant Senate Majority Leader but, as Rowland Evans and Robert Novak's superb biography points out, he became less effective after the Democrats won a big liberal majority in 1958, while Wright thrived as leader of the mostly liberal Democratic Caucus in the 1980s. Wright's record as Speaker was substantial. In his first weeks, he quickly passed a clean water bill and a highway bill over President Reagan's veto. He superintended the 1988 trade bill through the House. He took care to get the budget and appropriations bills through, more efficiently than they had been since the glory days of David Stockman. He deserves major credit for the homeless, catastrophic health insurance, and farm credit bills that Congress passed. He took control of the contra aid issue so effectively, in 1987, that he, rather than the Executive Branch, essentially made foreign policy, shutting down support for the contras in 1988 and branding demonstrators seeking political rights from the Sandinistas as tools of the CIA.

In these accomplishments, Wright showed brains, a certain eloquence, discipline and hard work. But he was even less successful than Johnson in establishing trust and affection. Wright's arguments were carefully framed and his oratory was, in an old-fashioned way, eloquent. But even among his closest colleagues, he lacked candor. A loner most of his career and a better talker than a listener, he tried to discipline himself to work with others. But he made major decisions alone, impetuously, even sneakily. Sometimes his initiatives were effective, as on contra aid. But sometimes they worked out badly, as when he announced he was polling members on the 1989 pay increase. And sometimes they made other Democrats nervous, as in 1986, when he announced he favored a tax increase. Wright had solid support from the Democratic Caucus as long as things were going well. But when his ethics problems were looming, he had few solid defenders among his House Democrats, not even among fervent opponents of the contra aid program he killed, not even in the once solidly cohesive Texas delegation.

The specific charges which brought Wright down seem trivial next to the level of his achievements. The amounts he and his wife gained from royalties on his book *Reflections of a Public Man* and from his longtime business partner and benefactor, George Mallick, were not substantial. His defense, that he stayed inside the limits of the rules, was not frivolous. His problem was that, even for those who agreed with his argument, he was at the least pushing the limits and his arguments lacked any patina of frankness. In Lyndon Johnson's day, far more malodorous practices were common and were almost never reported; men like Senator Robert Kerr of Oklahoma would boast how they used public office to make themselves rich. But in the 1980s, even marginal transgressions can trigger an investigation which can lead, by an inexorable process of protracted publicity and public revulsion, to political ruin; and the picture of a man trying to squeeze around the rules was not one that House Democrats would tolerate in a leader. Yet it should be said that even under the terrific pressure of seeing his support dwindle and his arguments greeted with derision, Wright continued to play a powerful and effective role on public policy, notably on Central America. Like a man inexplicably stricken with a fatal illness, he played out his role with a certain grandeur.

The fall of Jim Wright and the abrupt resignation, even as Wright was still pondering his decision, of House Majority Whip Tony Coelho, produced an upheaval in House leadership never before seen in this century except in cases of death in office. The resignation of two of the top three Democratic leaders did not necessarily prove the charge of Republicans like Whip Newt Gingrich that the Democrats were a corrupt liberal welfare-state majority, but it did cast the Democrats—and to some extent the whole House—under a pall that will not easily be dissipated. Disarray seldom works to the benefit of incumbents or leaders—even if, as seemed likely in late May 1989, that disarray was followed by calm, reassuring leadership.

The new Speaker, Thomas Foley, is a man who did not seek the office—he did not even decide to seek his seat in the House until a day before the filing deadline in 1964, and he voted against himself when he was elected House Agriculture Committee chairman in the Democratic caucus after the 1974 election. Foley is almost universally respected for his thoughtfulness and judiciousness; his word and his intellectual honesty are trusted by Republicans as well as Democrats. On his accession, he did not seem likely to be as aggressive a leader as Wright, and certainly not as partisan. But he is head of a body of Democrats who have definite legislative goals and have come to depend upon a Speaker to help get them accomplished. Certainly, he is not likely to be as intrusive in the business of committees and subcommittees—though he will continue to keep a hand in budget proceedings, as he did as Majority Leader. And certainly, he is not as likely to seize control of foreign policy as Wright did—though, as the spokesman for a solid Democratic majority, he may find himself doing just that, even if not entirely intending to. The general expectation in the House is that Foley will not compile as long a legislative record as Wright, but that he will set a less partisan, more conciliatory tone.

But Wright performed contrary to expectations, and Foley may too. The Foley era could turn out to be exceedingly productive, legislatively. They could also turn out to be more acrimonious than expected, if Democrats pursue ethical charges against Gingrich and other Republicans, and Gingrich and other Republicans bring ethical charges, as they have threatened, against another dozen or more Democrats.

In June 1989, House Democrats selected successors to Foley and Coelho. The successful candidate for majority leader was Richard Gephardt, and for whip was William Gray. Both had won positions in the Caucus before, and against some odds: Gephardt squeezed David Obey out for Caucus chairman in 1984, while Gray beat Leon Panetta and others for Budget Committee chairman in 1984 and then beat Mary Rose Oakar and Mike Synar for Caucus chairman in 1988. Within Democratic ranks, Gephardt is a good listener, a coalition builder, a flexible man on policy, who switched from neo-liberal in the early 1980s to a retaliatory position on trade and a believer that "America is in decline" in the late 1980s. He underwent scrutiny as a presidential candidate in 1987 and 1988, and if he did not win much outside the Farm Belt (one place in America that may really be in decline) he did not have any ethical problems. Gephardt defeated Ed Jenkins, a key dealmaker and the chief sponsor of textile trade restrictions on the Ways and Means Committee by a margin of 181–76.

Gray's work on Budget, and his interesting alliance based on support from blacks, from Pennsylvanians and other coal and steel state types and from conservative southerners, made him a favorite for whip. And he has the additional advantage, from most Democrats' point of view, of threatening Jesse Jackson's monopoly of the national spotlight as the only major black politician in America. But Gray had serious competition from David Bonior, a fervent opponent of contra aid appointed by Wright as chief deputy whip, and from Beryl Anthony, Coelho's successor as head of the Democratic Congressional Campaign Committee. He ended up winning with 134 votes to Bonior's 97 and Anthony's 30.

But neither Foley nor his other leaders can run things in the House by themselves. For the House in the 1980s, and even more so in early 1989 as Wright got increasingly distracted by his troubles, has been dominated on many important policy issues by its important committee and subcommittee chairmen. The 1974 reforms which made full committee chairmen elected by the entire Democratic caucus and subcommittee chairmen elected by the Democrats on the full committee have helped to give the House an unusually able and vigorous collection of major chairmen. The days when a doddering elder, an incompetent or a southern conservative, deeply at odds with most northern Democrats, could succeed to a chairmanship are gone, and if that has insured a certain ideological conformity it has also produced a high level of competence. Democratic members don't want to be represented on television by chairmen who will make them look bad.

Of the House's powerful chairmen the foremost are, in alphabetical and seniority order, John Dingell and Dan Rostenkowski. You might call them the Polish princes: they are both of Polish descent; they are the sons of successful politicians, a congressman from Detroit and a Democratic ward committeeman in Chicago; they took office quietly in the 1950s and were held in minimal regard by journalists and liberal critics of the House for many years, Dingell because of his opposition to gun control, Rostenkowski because he was a machine pol. They both inherited the chairmanships of major committees after the 1980 elections and, in those positions, both have performed brilliantly. They are both smart, aggressive and in command, hardworking and, in their different ways, they believe in things—they have convictions about public policy— and make things happen. Also—this sort of thing seems inevitable—they don't much like each other, and each has mused at one time or another about becoming Speaker himself.

The word in the House is that under Dingell, the Energy and Commerce Committee has jurisdiction over everything that isn't a tax, and while Dingell is generous with the spotlight and the credit, supporting his subcommittee chairmen and Investigations and Oversight Subcommittee members, there is no question who sits in which chair. Dingell doesn't always win—Health subcommittee chairman Henry Waxman kept him from lowering clean air standards in the early 1980s—but he usually does, and he is always a tough contender. Dingell believes in government as an active regulator in the securities markets, in telecommunications, in trade relations with countries that in his view don't treat American products fairly, in many environmental matters (though as a Michiganian he thinks current laws unduly burden smokestack industries); and you get the sense that this stems not just from a solicitude for the little guy but also from a sense that everyone should be subject to a stern discipline.

Mr. Dingell, as every Energy and Commerce staffer always calls him, subjects himself to that discipline; as a member seeking votes in his district and a chairman seeking votes in caucus; as an adversary of administrations and interests well able to make their case; and as chairman he subjects witnesses before him to similar discipline. It was his committee and subcommittee that unearthed the $640 toilet seat and the Pentagon-paid kennel fees that made Caspar Weinberger's Pentagon a subject of ridicule; it was they who elicited the testimony which dethroned Anne Burford of EPA and convicted the Reagans' friend Michael Deaver and EPA's Rita Lavelle. Dingell's father, incidentally, was one of the original sponsors of social security, a strong economic liberal who was first elected in 1932 and served until his death in 1955; the 29-year-old Dingell was elected in his place in a district that was then heavily Jewish. He has enough seniority now that one of his former staffers turned congressman is now chairman of a full House committee (John Conyers of Government Operations).

Dan Rostenkowski's father was a ward politician who supported Richard J. Daley against Ben Adamowski in 1955, and lost his place as an alderman in his heavily Polish ward as a result. Daley owed the Rostenkowski family, which is why he indulged the 30-year-old son, after six years in the legislature, in what Daley regarded as his silly idea of seeking a seat in Congress so as to build up seniority when everyone knew real power resided in City Hall in Chicago. Rostenkowski speaks still with the gravelly Chicago accent; he never graduated from college, much less law school; his personal style is that of the big shooter with season tickets to all the games, standing invitations to the golf clubs where the professional athletes play and a regular table at the best local steakhouse. He likes to win, sometimes too much, as on the 1981 tax cut, where he tried to outbid the Reagan Administration on tax breaks to business and failed.

But since then, Rostenkowski has proved a masterful strategist—and one who is steering by the compass of a well thought out philosophy. His great moment—except that it lasted not for a moment, but for months and months of hard work—was the tax reform bill of 1985–86, which he steered to passage in the House through shoals of opposition from right, left and center. Rostenkowski believes that the market economy should be freed from high tax rates and—this was contrary to his institutional interest, as America's chief dispenser of tax breaks— preferences should be eliminated from the tax code. He has a strong conviction, contrary to that of many of his fellow House Democrats, that free trade is in the interest of the United States and that protectionist measures will do more harm to our economy than anyone else's: he, with Senate Finance chairman Lloyd Bentsen, are the two bulwarks against protectionist legislation in the American system as it stands. Congressmen, typically, are responsive to local economic interests, but Rostenkowski's attitudes seem prompted not so much by local interests, as by a view of the economy prompted by the futures markets in Chicago, which now, of course, handle not only pork bellies but stock exchange indexes: in financial markets Chicago has become the headquarters of untramelled, mostly unregulated free enterprise. Yet Rostenkowski also feels an obligation to Democratic Party tradition. When George Bush, a onetime Ways and Means member, talked about cutting the capital gains tax, Rostenkowski's response was to threaten to raise rates on the highest bracket taxpayers.

There are other formidable House committee chairmen as well. Jack Brooks, moving from the chair of Government Operations to Judiciary, is a fearless and tenacious fighter whom no one takes on lightly. Jamie Whitten, senior Member of the House, remains a formidable Appropriations chairman who has adapted himself to the liberal Democratic Caucus and the budget process. Leon Panetta is acknowledged on both sides of the aisle as a genuine expert on the Budget. Morris Udall of Interior and Augustus Hawkins of Education and Labor are in the golden years of their careers as committed liberals. Les Aspin, at risk of vertigo, must balance on a tightrope between his hawkish Armed Services Committee and the dovish House majority. Henry Gonzalez's stubborn integrity helps the House deal with the savings and loan crisis it did so much to create.

But notice should be taken as well of subcommittee chairmen. It is true that more than half of all House Democrats can be addressed as Mr. Chairman, by virtue of chairing some body or other. But with subcommittees, even more than with full committees, it is a truth worth repeating that some are more equal than others. There are six subcommittee chairmen who, because of their jurisdiction and by force of their character and intellect, are likely to stand out in the 101st Congress. One is David Obey, whose Foreign Operations Appropriations subcommittee is the chokepoint for foreign aid, and whose demands for explanations from the Bush Administration on Iran-contra and other issues could raise major issues. A second is John Murtha, the inside operator and Marine veteran who reenlisted and served in Vietnam and who, in 1989, succeeded to the chairmanship of Defense Appropriations, which controls the spigot of federal dollars to the Pentagon. Another is Frank Annunzio, whose Banking subcommittee has jurisdiction over the savings and loan bailout, and who has supported the S&Ls in contrast to full committee chairman Gonzalez. Two come from Energy and Commerce: Henry Waxman, who handles numerous issues through his Health and Environment Subcommittee, and Edward Markey, whose Telecommunications and Finance Subcommittee has a breathtaking jurisdiction that includes the securities and communications industries. Finally, Al Swift's sometimes quiet House Administration Elections Subcommittee will be a cockpit of activity should there be any serious move toward campaign finance reform. Two Ways and Means subcommittee chairmen might be added to the list, but for the fact that they helped to produce two 1988 laws that seem unlikely to be tampered with right away: Pete Stark, who fashioned the catastrophic health insurance bill and the tax to pay for it, and Tom Downey, who overcame what has become the classic obstacle on this issue, liberals who seek too much money, and helped fashion the Family Support Act of 1988.

The House: 1990 and Beyond.   It is commonly said that House Members are insulated from competition, that 98% of them are reelected, that the House is institutionally fated to remain the most liberal branch of government and that it has become an "imperial Congress" disconnected from and unaccountable to the public it is supposed to serve. These sayings are entitled to as much credence as the 1885 rumors of Mark Twain's death—or even less, since Twain did finally die in 1910, while these descriptions of the House, even those that are true now, are reasonably certain to become untrue sometime in the near political future.

To understand why, flash backward some 25 or 30 years, or take down from your shelf James MacGregor Burns's book *The Deadlock of Democracy.* Burns and dozens of journalists and political scientists laid down as law in the days of the Kennedy and Johnson Administrations that the House was the conservative anchor of American government, that its Members, in their various districts and with their perquisites of office, were effectively insulated from competition, and that the ordinary condition of American politics has been conflict between a liberal executive branch run by a president responsive to low-income voters and labor union members and a conservative legislative branch run by elderly congressmen responsive to courthouse square lawyers, small businessmen and large corporation lobbyists. This was a fair description of the way national politics worked at the time and of how it had been working for a decade or two before. But it soon stopped working that way—just about the time the critics had got done laying down iron laws saying it must always do so.

That could be happening again in the 1990s. It is true that the 1986 and 1988 elections saw record numbers of incumbent congressmen returned to office, equalled only in 1968—though the 98% refers to only those who ran for reelection, thus ignoring those Members who retired rather than face certain or possible defeat and understating total turnover. But the reason for the high reelection rate is not that the advantages of incumbency make members unbeatable—they help, but they don't sweep all before them—but that not enough good challengers run. Recent history shows us that when strong challengers, men and women who know how to raise plenty of money and to fashion an attractive platform of their own, run in a year that is at all favorable for their party, many of them will win, and working control of the House can shift as a result. The prime examples are the Democratic sweep of 1974 and the Republican successes of 1980, and there are lesser examples as well. The problem, more recently, is that the issues that motivate young, organizationally competent, elite, ambitious young people who make strong challengers—non-economic issues like Vietnam and Watergate for the Democrats, economic issues like hyperinflation and overtaxation for the Republicans—have simply not been operating in the late 1980s. Culturally liberal Democrats have had to look hard to find signs of oppression in this peaceful, prosperous and tolerant land. Economically conservative Republicans have to squint mightily to find evidence of creeping socialism in the Reagan years. The reason for the high reelection rate is that the system is working—or at least not producing enough motivated malcontents with the political smarts to overcome the considerable, but by no means insuperable, advantages of incumbent congressmen.

That may not be true in the 1990s. The hubbub over the congressional pay raise in early 1989, plus Jim Wright's troubles, created a political environment which seemed more favorable to serious Republican challengers than was the case in 1981, 1983 or 1987. Any hint of economic downturn will prompt some Democrats to believe that opinion will be shifting sharply toward them in the next election. A sourer political environment may stimulate more serious challengers and prove more politically inhospitable to incumbents than the sunnier climes of 1984, 1986 and 1988.

Add to that the effects of redistricting. Looking forward from early 1989, redistricting seems unlikely to give either party the advantage that it gave Democrats in the 1970 and 1980 cycles—in both cases, largely because of the California plans drawn by the late Phillip Burton. As of 1989, control over redistricting in all of the big states, where the lion's share of the malleable boundaries are, was split between the two parties. California, Texas and Florida, the big gainers, all had Republican governors; New York, Pennsylvania, Ohio and Michigan, all likely to lose 2 or 3 seats, had Republican Senates, while Illinois had a Republican governor. Moreover, demographic trends tend to determine the results, for under the one-person-one-vote rule, even the most politically motivated of redistricters is subject to a discipline that limits the political mischief and mayhem he can do. So even if a Democrat should be elected governor of California in 1990, giving Democrats full control over the process there, they will be hard put to draw more than one new Democratic district of the five to seven new seats the state will get. In large states that are losing population, latitude is also limited, partly by the Voting Rights Act, which is universally interpreted to require maximizing the number of majority-black districts—which in turn limits the number of Democratic districts a Democratic redistricter can create. But even if there is a wash between the parties, there will still be increased turnover among individual members, since 20-odd seats will be transferred from one state to another. And the political environment for many incumbents will be more uncertain, and hence more conducive to challengers.

Beyond redistricting, there is no reason to expect that the Democrats' advantage is inevitable, given the system, and there are several reasons to expect that it might disappear some time in the 1992–2000 cycle. In early 1989, the Democrats held 260 seats, 42 over the majority of 218. Their redistricting advantage in the 1982–90 cycle amounted to about 15 seats; that is not likely to be augmented and may be reduced. The tactical advantage the Democrats had, in the skills of their campaign committee chairmen Tony Coelho and Beryl Anthony, were worth perhaps 5 seats an election, or 20 seats from 1982 to 1988; now, with 1984 Reagan campaign manager Ed Rollins installed as the operating head of the Republicans' campaign committee, the Republicans have equalized their position. Finally, there is likely to be continued attrition of Democrats elected in the Watergate year of 1974 and the surrounding years of 1972 and 1976. Many of them represent districts that would otherwise be won by Republicans; many provide much of the leadership and *élan* which have made the Democratic majorities effective. Between 1963 and 1974, the House was transformed from the conservative anchor to the liberal iceboat of American politics. It is possible that it will be transformed again in a similarly brief period, in the other direction, so that the conflict between executive and legislative branches in the late 1990s will be a conflict between President Bill Bradley and Speaker Newt Gingrich.

The Senate in Transition. The Senate, known for years as the world's greatest deliberative body, has not had a particularly distinguished decade: throughout the 1980s, the Senate has been overshadowed in legislative achievement by the House. By a wide margin, the House has had a larger number of talented and creative legislators, sharper political operators and even, arguably, farsighted statesmen than the Senate. Even on foreign policy, usually the province of the Senate because of its treaty-approving responsibilities, control over policy toward Nicaragua was seized from the Republican administration by Speaker Jim Wright and the House, not by any senator. The Senate does have some members who have advanced successful initiatives on major policy—Bill Bradley on tax reform, Daniel Patrick Moynihan on welfare reform, Phil Gramm on budget deficits. But what is notable is that this chamber, a cockpit of presidential ambitions and an incubator of new policies and ideas in the 1950s and 1960s, seems politically so quiescent and intellectually so somnolent.

Part of the reason is the membership. The Republican landslide of 1980 brought into office some senators with not only with minimal political experience but also with only the most rudimentary of political reflexes. The Democrats and Republicans who have won seats in the years since have mostly been men with respectable records in their states but with little special flair for the business. But part of the reason for the comparative torpor of the Senate is the times. The rules and size of the House put a premium on knowledge of detail, preparedness and understanding of the rules: qualities needed to guide policy when no new initiatives are in sight. The rules and size of the Senate put a premium on grandiloquence of vision, venturesomeness of thought and long-range proselytization: qualities that find little opportunity for expression in times when budget deficits and doubts about the efficacy of centralized government action leave little room for policy initiatives like those of the 1960s and early 1970s. The current Senate, if not as dazzling as some Senates past, is nonetheless made up mostly of able people. But it doesn't get as much of a chance as it would like to do much of the kind of work that Senates are best at doing.

It is also a Senate which seems to be undergoing a transition in control—not just of individuals or parties, but of the way in which leadership is exerted. In the 1940s and 1950s, the Senate was controlled by what admiring journalist William S. White called "the Club," an informal group of mostly southern Democrats, politically canny, institutionally cautious and increasingly conservative on public policy. It was in the Club's Senate that Lyndon Johnson, selected for his leadership position by the dominant Club member, Richard Russell of Georgia, exerted masterful control, though for only a few years, from 1955 to 1958, and under peculiar circumstances: a nearly equally divided Democratic Senate combined with a legislatively quiescent Republican President. The 1958 elections brought more than a dozen new senators, most of them liberal Democrats, who set the tone and the agenda of the Senate for the next 20 years. Mike Mansfield, Majority Leader from 1961 to 1977, believed in respecting the prerogatives of individual Senators. That left the liberals, who in numbers, intellectual capacity and political force were far stronger than their adversaries, the opportunity to sculpt new government programs and wage war upon administration policies they disliked.

More than a dozen liberals were defeated in 1978 and 1980; worse than that, the liberals' confidence that they had solutions to the country's problems vanished in those years too. That, and the rather low quality of some of the new members, helped to create a Leaders' Senate in the 1980s. First Howard Baker, then Bob Dole, and finally Robert Byrd, reinstalled as Majority Leader and learning from the successes of those who had displaced him, exercised superintending control over an increasingly partisan Senate by holding their rather slim party majorities together against the depredations of the opposition.

Now the question is whether this will continue under the new Majority Leader, George Mitchell of Maine. He comes to the job from a position more distant from the center of his Party than did Baker, Dole or even Byrd; and while he won the post by an impressive 27–14–14 vote over Daniel Inouye and Bennett Johnston, the core of his support comes from liberals who like to style themselves populists, but whose favored policies have not shown wide popular support in the 1970s and 1980s. His own policy initiatives have been well to the left of the Senate, or even the Democratic Caucus: he was the Finance Committee member who pushed for higher tax rates on upper incomes, in opposition to the central tradeoff of the rate-flattening, preference-cutting tax reform initiated by Bill Bradley. But Mitchell also has strengths as Majority Leader. He speaks easily and well. He has a pleasant temperament, a high degree of civility and a good sense of humor. He knows much about the practicalities of politics as well as its high-flown principles. He won much of his support for Majority Leader as head of the Democratic Senatorial Campaign Committee in 1986, when the Democrats recaptured the Senate; and as leader, the unmarried Mitchell has made a point of traveling to colleagues' states for joint appearances.

Who controls the Senate? George Mitchell and the Democrats do, when they are virtually unanimous on an issue. But often their successes are negative, as when they rejected the nominations of Judge Robert Bork and John Tower (who were replaced by arguably more obdurate conservatives, Judge Anthony Kennedy and Defense Secretary Richard Cheney). Mitchell has put forward a written agenda on which Senate Democrats have agreed, but it is not highly specific nor does it pretend to be all-encompassing. It does not seem likely that Mitchell and the populist liberals around him can pass some of their favorite programs, like higher marginal tax rates for the rich and supply management of farm commodities.

But if the liberals do not control the Senate, neither do old-line or New Rights conservatives. Across-the-board liberals hold about one-quarter of the Senate seats, but old-fashioned, deficit-abhorring Republicans like Bob Dole have even fewer. And however frustrated the liberals may be at their failure to inspire their fellow citizens with their vision, the fiscally conservative Republicans are even more frustrated at seeing their party create the biggest budget deficits in American history. As for the New Right conservatives who were on the offensive in the early 1980s, they are even fewer in number now and some of them—Bill Armstrong and Gordon Humphrey—are retiring in 1990. Successful in some of their causes, clearly blocked on others, they may be a spent force, though Jesse Helms continues to place holds on nominees he doesn't like and to sponsor amendments that attract only a handful of votes.

On issues which their committees handle, powerful chairmen can exert great power. Two of them—Sam Nunn of Armed Services and Lloyd Bentsen of Finance—can, through their expertise, their national reputation, their control of their committees and their stature in the Senate, determine the outcomes of issues pretty much on their own say so. But their power does not necessarily extend far from their ken. And they, like other Senators, can sometimes be frustrated by the Senators who used their mastery of the rules and their stubbornness and willingness to block colleagues to make themselves major negative forces: Howard Metzenbaum on the Democratic left and Jesse Helms on the Republican right. The Senate does have its innovative thinkers—Bradley, Moynihan, Gramm—but in prosaic times, more policy may be effected by competent chairmen who tend to their committee's knitting, as Donald Riegle seems to have done brilliantly on the savings and loan issue. The Senate, as usual, has plenty of presidential candidates (Albert Gore, Bill Bradley, Sam Nunn and maybe Phil Gramm), but it has more members who ran or considered running for President in the past but aren't any more (Bob Dole, Edward Kennedy, Larry Pressler, Dale Bumpers, Alan Cranston, Paul Simon, Terry Sanford, John Glenn and Strom Thurmond). And for the first time in many years, the Senate has some members who are thinking about running for governor. Pete Wilson of California, who in 1988 received more votes for Senator than anyone in American history, has announced he will run for governor of California in 1990; Alfonse D'Amato has hinted that he may run for governor of New York then too. No one has yet volunteered to leave the Senate for the House— though the late Claude Pepper, who made that transition involuntarily and with a 12-year hiatus, became arguably more powerful as a congressman than he had been as a senator. But the

SENATE TERMS
SEAT UP 1990

Democrats (16)

Max Baucus (MT)
Joseph R. Biden, Jr. (DE)
David Lyle Boren (OK)
Bill Bradley (NJ)
James J. Exon (NE)
Albert Gore, Jr. (TN)
Tom Harkin (IA)
Howell Heflin (AL)
J. Bennett Johnston, Jr. (LA)
John F. Kerry (MA)
Carl Levin (MI)
Sam Nunn (GA)
Claiborne Pell (RI)
David Pryor (AR)
John D. (Jay) Rockefeller IV (WV)
Paul Simon (IL)

Republicans (18)

William L. Armstrong (CO)[1]
Rudy Boschwitz (MN)
Daniel R. (Dan) Coats (IN)[2]
Thad Cochran (MS)
William S. Cohen (ME)
Peter V. Domenici (NM)
Phil Gramm (TX)
Mark O. Hatfield (OR)
Jesse A. Helms (NC)
Gordon J. Humphrey (NH)[1]
Nancy L. Kassebaum (KS)
James A. McClure (ID)
Mitch McConnell (KY)
Larry Pressler (SD)
Alan K. Simpson (WY)
Ted Stevens (AK)
Strom Thurmond (SC)
John W. Warner (VA)

SEAT UP 1992

Democrats (20)

Brock Adams (WA)
John B. Breaux (LA)
Dale Bumpers (AR)
Kent Conrad (ND)
Alan Cranston (CA)
Thomas A. Daschle (SD)
Alan J. Dixon (IL)
Christopher J. Dodd (CT)
Wendell H. Ford (KY)
Wyche Fowler (GA)
John Glenn (OH)
Bob Graham (FL)
Ernest F. Hollings (SC)
Daniel K. Inouye (HI)
Patrick J. Leahy (VT)
Barbara A. Mikulski (MD)
Harry Reid (NV)
Terry Sanford (NC)
Richard C. Shelby (AL)
Timothy E. Wirth (CO)

Republicans (14)

Christopher S. (Kit) Bond (MO)
Daniel R. (Dan) Coats (IN)[3]
Alfonse D'Amato (NY)
Robert Dole (KS)
Edwin J. (Jake) Garn (UT)
Charles E. Grassley (IA)
Robert W. Kasten, Jr. (WI)
John McCain (AZ)
Frank H. Murkowski (AK)
Don Nickles (OK)
Robert W. (Bob) Packwood (OR)
Warren Rudman (NH)
Arlen Specter (PA)
Steven D. Symms (ID)

[1] *Retiring*
[2] *Special election to fill the unexpired term of Vice President Dan Quayle.*
[3] *Or winner of 1990 special election.*

SENATE TERMS *(continued)*
SEAT UP 1994

Democrats (19)

Lloyd Bentsen (TX)
Jeff Bingaman (NM)
Richard H. Bryan (NV)
Quentin N. Burdick (ND)
Robert C. Byrd (WV)
Dennis DeConcini (AZ)
Edward M. Kennedy (MA)
Robert Kerrey (NE)
Herbert H. Kohl (WI)
Frank R. Lautenberg (NJ)
Joseph I. Lieberman (CT)
Spark M. Matsunaga (HI)
Howard Metzenbaum (OH)
George Mitchell (ME)
Daniel Patrick Moynihan (NY)
Donald W. Riegle, Jr. (MI)
Charles S. (Chuck) Robb (VA)
Paul S. Sarbanes (MD)
James R. Sasser (TN)

Republicans (14)

Conrad Burns (MT)
John H. Chafee (RI)
John Danforth (MO)
Dave Durenberger (MN)
Slade Gordon (WA)
Orrin G. Hatch (UT)
H. John Heinz III (PA)
James M. Jeffords (VT)
Trent Lott (MS)
Richard Lugar (IN)
Connie Mack III (FL)
William V. Roth, Jr. (DE)
Malcolm Wallop (WY)
Pete Wilson (CA)

Senate, for some politicians at least, is not quite the be-all and end-all it was not so many years ago.

One thing the Senate is more of now is partisan. Senators may socialize across party lines, and there are few of the raging feuds that were once a part of Senate life. But there is no Club now that operates across party lines and tries to run things. The Republicans in the early 1980s sought and won their greatest victories as a united party. The Democrats regained control in 1986 as a united party and, in particular, with victories in the South. The southern Democrats elected in 1986—Terry Sanford of North Carolina, Wyche Fowler of Georgia, Richard Shelby of Alabama, Bob Graham of Florida, John Breaux of Louisiana—see themselves as partisan Democrats, threatened by Republicans, interested in controlling their party to make it behave in ways palatable in their home states (they supported George Mitchell strongly) and uninterested in working with their Senate Republican colleagues.

That means that much is at stake in the 1990 elections. The Republicans profess to have little chance to win control; the Democrats profess to have no hope of making gains: do not believe either side. Senate elections, in a country that does not pay much attention to politics, are highly contingent, and it is possible, as both 1980 and 1986 showed, for the lion's share of close contests to go to one party and give it control. The Republicans have slightly more seats at risk, but as the cycle began, neither party seemed to have an overwhelming advantage.

THE STATES AND REGIONS

More than 50 years ago, when young New Dealers would come to him for advice on how to change life in America, Justice Louis Brandeis, a great crusader for social justice in his time, would begin by saying, "Go home!" His point was that there were too many bright, idealistic young people in the interstices of the Roosevelt Administration and too few in the state governments and, for that matter, in Congress. The states, he felt, should be laboratories of reform. It was impossible to change a geographically huge and culturally and economically diverse country like the United States from a few government offices in its capital city. You had to go out to where things were happening—or to make them happen.

In the 1980s, innovation in government and public policy has come increasingly from outside Washington, indeed from places and sometimes in directions that the liberals of a generation or two ago would have considered unbelievable. State governments have used different strategies to promote growth and economic development. State and local governments have invented educational reforms, while education authorities and lobbyists in Washington, with the conspicuous exception of Reagan Education Secretary William Bennett and sometimes of the American Federation of Teachers, have resisted every change, even as evidence of the evil effects of the programs they have championed accumulates. While members of Congress talk about crime and pass drug bills which may or may not make much difference, state and local prosecutors, judges, legislatures and juries have tripled the population of American prisons from 1976 to 1988.

State governors, in particular, have contributed to the public mood and affected public attitudes toward life in the state far more than Americans' assessment of George Bush in early 1989 seemed to be affecting the public attitude toward life in the nation. Compare the ebullience of Thomas Kean's New Jersey with the cynicism of Edwin Edwards's Louisiana, or reflect on the upbeat mood and economy of James Blanchard's Michigan, which was down in the dumps when he was elected, with the nervousness and uncertainty of Bill Clements's once bullishly confident Texas. Concrete economic conditions contribute to these moods. But government, and political leadership, can make a difference in attitude—a difference which can, in turn, stimulate economic growth that would not otherwise occur or put a damper on an economic expansion that might have occurred. For that reason, the gubernatorial elections typically held in 1990, but in some states held in 1989, 1991 or 1992, could turn out to be just as important in shaping public attitudes and affecting daily life as the presidential elections of 1988 or 1992.

So those interested in government, politics and the tone of American life will watch them for this reason. Those interested in politics and government will watch them for another reason as well: redistricting. In most states, legislatures, limited by the governor's veto, will draw congressional district lines, and the way those lines are drawn in a dozen states could affect the outcome in several dozen House districts in 1992 and in the four elections held thereafter. Both parties are keenly aware of this, and are targetting the state gubernatorial and legislative elections of 1990, and adjacent years in certain states, for particular attention. The following is a list of states where those offices are up, and an indication of who holds them as of 1989.

Gubernatorial Election Cycle

1989, 2 STATES

New Jersey   Virginia

1990, 36 STATES

Alabama	Minnesota
Alaska	**Nebraska**
Arizona	Nevada
Arkansas	**New Hampshire***
California	**New Mexico**
Colorado	New York
Connecticut	Ohio
Florida	**Oklahoma**
Georgia	Oregon
Hawaii	Pennsylvania
Idaho	**Rhode Island**
Illinois	**South Carolina**
Iowa	**South Dakota**
Kansas	Tennessee
Maine	**Texas**
Maryland	Vermont*
Massachusetts	**Wisconsin**
Michigan	Wyoming

1991, 3 STATES

Kentucky   Mississippi
Louisiana

1992, 12 STATES

Delaware	North Dakota
Indiana	**Rhode Island***
Missouri	**Utah**
Montana	Vermont*
New Hampshire*	Washington
North Carolina	West Virginia

---

*States with two-year terms. All others are four-year.
Boldface indicates Republican governor.
Underline indicates governors who may not succeed themselves in the election that year.

ALABAMA

"Moons, red with the dust of barren hills," Carl Carmer wrote in the 1930s in *Stars Fell on Alabama*, "thin pine trunks barring horizons, festering swamps, restless yellow rivers, are all part of a feeling—an emanation of malevolence that threatens to destroy men through dark ways of its own." Against a "background of lazy serenity, of happy-go-lucky ease," Carmer, a Yankee who lived six years in Tuscaloosa, concluded as he witnessed mountain men aim guns at outsiders who might be revenuers, hooded Klansmen burn crosses, and white townspeople lynch a Negro, that "the inevitable reaction to any unusual stimulus was to do something about it, something physical and violent." That violent impulse has been part of life and politics in Alabama since the first Jacksonian farmers replaced the Indians sent west and plowed the steeply inclined red clay hills of the Tennessee Valley and the first plantation owners had hundreds of slaves shipped in to grow cotton on the Black Belt (named for the soil, which grew the cotton that brought the slaves). It was the violent reaction of white Alabamians to desegregation in Tuscaloosa and Freedom Riders in Anniston and schoolchildren on the streets of Birmingham and marchers in Selma that finally gained national backing for the civil rights revolution. Even in Alabama's peaceful economic development there are signs of rawness, in the miners hacking away in the 1880s at the solid-iron rock of Red Mountain to feed the newly cast steel mills glaring in the valley of Birmingham below, in the drivers in the 1980s speeding past the exposed red earth of gouged-out hillsides to interchanges where the small factories and Wal-Mart shopping centers have been sprouting up.

A similar rawness, if not violence, can be seen in Alabama's politics. In tone and often in substance it is as populist as any state, cutting to the bone of deep resentments and yearnings, generous and violent in its impulses. Fifty years ago, Alabama produced some of the most progressive American politicians, crusaders against Wall Street and against the local economic potentates they called the "Big Mules": Hugo Black, senator until he became a Supreme Court Justice in 1937; Lister Hill and John Sparkman, young congressmen who went on to the Senate, sponsors of landmark health and housing legislation; young politicians who as congressmen in the 1950s—Carl Elliott, Albert Rains, Kenneth Roberts, Robert Jones—would give Alabama arguably the nation's most legislatively productive House delegation. On the state level, the foremost populist was Kissin' Jim Folsom, a huge, oratorically overpowering, personally flawed populist who was elected governor (back when consecutive terms were forbidden) in 1946 and 1954 and was a serious candidate again in 1962 when, far into drunkenness, he appeared ridiculous in a late-campaign appearance on the new medium of television, and later watched some of his populist following taken over by his onetime protégé, a young bantam-sized lawyer named George Wallace.

While Wallace was orating in the state Capitol in Montgomery, only a few blocks away at the Dexter Avenue Baptist Church, Martin Luther King, Jr., was leading what turned out to be a civil rights revolution. None of it was planned: seamstress Rosa Parks, tired and footsore, just decided one day in 1955 that she was not going to move to the back of the bus, as Alabama's segregation laws required. King, a 26-year-old minister from Atlanta with a fancy East Coast education, agreed to lead the seemingly hopeless bus boycott and soon found himself the leader of a national movement whose moral force he was one of the few to comprehend. In the standard currency of the time, what King demanded seemed impossible; it was unthinkable that blacks should even vote. In short-run politics, it helped the politician who proclaimed most strongly his opposition. George Wallace, running as a Folsom protégé in the 1958 governor's primary,

ALABAMA — Congressional Districts, Counties, and Selected Places — (7 Districts)

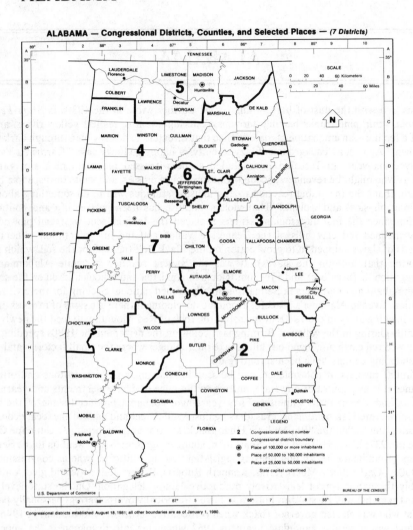

Congressional districts established August 18, 1981; all other boundaries are as of January 1, 1980.

believed he lost because he was "out-segged," and vowed that he never would be again.

He wasn't, and for most of the 24 years from 1962, when he was first elected governor, until he retired in 1986, George Wallace set the tone of public life in Alabama. His feisty populist rhetoric resonated with the state's political tradition and reflected his own political origins—and, together with his own extraordinary intuition for public opinion, made him a national political figure. His first and critical term as governor was not only a failure, but a tragedy. His pledge to stand in the schoolhouse door to prevent desegregation was a charade, its only practical effect being to put others' lives at risk. The violent resistance of Alabama officials—Birmingham commissioner Bull Connor's police dogs and fire hoses in 1963, Sheriff Jim Clark's cordons in Selma in 1965—highlighted, as Martin Luther King sensed they would, the unreason behind the white South's resistance to desegregation and made possible the passage of the Civil Rights Act of 1964 and the Voting Rights Act of 1965.

Yet Wallace's own career prospered. He campaigned effectively in the North in the 1964 and 1972 Democratic presidential primaries, and as a third-party candidate in the 1968 presidential race won 13.5% of the vote. "Send them a message!" Wallace cried, and he shrewdly tailored his own message to local causes and local complaints. Crippled by a gunshot wound in 1972, his force as a national politician was spent by his political defeat by Jimmy Carter in the 1976 Florida primary. But he remained the key figure in Alabama, retiring in 1978 but returning to office in 1982 after his successor, Fob James, proved inept and decided not to seek reelection. In those declining years, he became a sad figure, crippled and unable to hear much, often in dreadful pain, inspiring sympathy by seeking the support of the blacks he had once scorned. "The South has changed," this opportunist who didn't seem to care about race one way or the other said, "and for the better."

Has Alabama? The populism of the 1940s has been transformed, after 40 years of Jim Folsom and George Wallace, into a strident conservatism; a credo that placed Alabama politicians at the fulcrum point of national policy has been shed for one that gives it politicians who stand on the periphery of the national debate. While Atlanta was peacefully desegregating and beginning three decades of vibrant white-collar growth, Birmingham was violently resisting the civil rights movement, only to see the shrinkage of its once substantial blue-collar base—the steel industry—and an outflow of talented people of both races. The rawness of Alabama life seemed to be perpetuating itself.

But during these last 40 years life in Alabama has changed vastly and for the better. For all of Wallace's demagoguery, legal segregation was ended, and Alabama whites have long since accepted integration in schools, on the job, in restaurants, and at the shopping mall. They no longer mind that blacks vote, and since the late 1970s black support has not cost state candidates all white support. Few voters live in the grinding poverty that made the "Big Mules" such inviting targets a half-century ago. But the growth which has transformed so much of the South—the metropolitan expansion as freeways climb over green hills and sprout shopping centers and subdivisions and office complexes—is only beginning to be visible here. Most rural counties, except for a few along the interstates, have been hemorrhaging population slowly in the 1980s; the metro areas have been growing slowly, except for Huntsville with its space and defense facilities. Alabama is a long way from the populist state of the 1930s where most people outside the few cities had no paved roads, electricity, or indoor plumbing, where children walked barefoot to school and many families never saw much cash over the course of a year. But as the 1980s end, Alabama—raw, angry, sometimes conservative and sometimes populist—is not where it wants to be either.

Alabama's politics and politicians have produced state and local government that provides little in the way of services. This was the last state without a full kindergarten program, for example, and the state with the highest infant mortality rate—a fact that has prompted Governor Guy Hunt, a conservative Republican, to support infant and maternal care programs. It is one of the few southern states with no education reform program. Not all of this can be blamed on the politicians—a poor state can only afford so much public spending. But others did better. George Wallace accustomed Alabamians to a politics of rhetoric and little follow-through, of appeals to their prejudices and parochialism and neglect of long-term interests.

Currently, state politics has become a battleground between liberal forces (the Alabama Education Association, other unions, trial lawyers, blacks) and various business interests: the special interests and the "Big Mules," as they still call each other. The state's political cleavages run mostly on corresponding lines, with a Democratic lower income base—black city neighborhoods, smaller white farm counties, especially in the Tennessee Valley Authority in the north—and a Republicans base in the rising affluent class of whites, not only in country club precincts but in donut-shaped circles around urban centers and in the interstate corridors where young families in search of country atmosphere, traditional values, and job opportunities have flocked.

Neither party dominates. Alabama's Democratic base is not firm enough to give the party reliable victories (like those in Tennessee) nor has the affluent sector grown fast enough to make the Republican party label an advantage (as it may be now in South Carolina).

Democratic primaries still attract the lion's share of voters, though not as many as in the past, and Democrats still hold most legislative and minor offices. Liberal-backed candidates may have the edge in the Democratic primary, but seem to be clearly the minority in the higher-turnout general elections at least in the top level races. In 1988 George Bush got 59% of the vote, close to Ronald Reagan's 61% in 1984, and not all that much more than the 56% Guy Hunt won against liberal Democrat Bill Baxley in 1986; Baxley, in turn, was winning almost the same county-by-county percentages as he had in the Democratic runoff. Other offices went simply to candidates with famous names: Lieutenant Governor Jim Folsom, Jr., Treasurer George Wallace, Jr., and his brother-in-law, state Supreme Court Justice Mark Kennedy. Another winner in 1988 was Supreme Court Justice Oscar Adams, who beat a Republican 58%–42%. Adams is black—and ran 2% ahead of George Wallace's son-in-law!

Governor. Alabama, Theodore H. White predicted in 1964, "almost certainly" would be "the first Republican-governed state of the South." Not quite: in 1986 it became one of the last (Mississippi and Georgia still haven't had Republican governors this century). Guy Hunt's victory gave the Republicans their chance, not just to govern the state, but to elect Republicans to state and local offices that have been the preserve of the Democrats for 100 years. Hunt, with the assistance of Republican operative John Grenier—whose success as a young Birmingham lawyer organizing the state for Barry Goldwater prompted White's prediction—is attempting to do that, and may have some success.

Hunt's victory in 1986 still seems improbable. As the Republican nominee in 1978, he won only 26% of the vote; he had held no office higher than Cullman County probate judge; his prospects in 1986 were no better until after Democrats failed to agree who had won their runoff primary. The leading vote-getter was Attorney General Charlie Graddick, running as a supporter of school prayer and the death penalty. But the courts ruled that he used his official powers to let Republican primary voters cast ballots in the Democratic runoff, and the state Democratic party substituted Bill Baxley, the candidate who ended up trailing by 8,756 votes. A tobacco-chewing, high-stakes gambler and late-filing taxpayer, Baxley as attorney general got convictions years later in the 1963 Birmingham Sunday school bombing case and ran for governor as an old-fashioned populist. But he could not overcome the burdens of his liberal reputation and his second-place finish in the runoff.

Hunt is well-positioned to broaden his party's affluent and urban base: he is a lay Primitive Baptist preacher and former Amway salesman who lives on a 140-acre farm on a leafy country road in Holly Pond. Hunt seemed entirely unprepared for the job, yet showed sureness of foot in maneuvering with the legislature and a mastery of communicating with the public through the media. He made a point of making frequent appearances around the state—a contrast with Wallace. He refused to haul down the Confederate Stars and Bars from the Capitol in Montgomery, but argued that it commemorated the sacrifices of many idealistic Alabamians just as the state does in celebrating Martin Luther King Day. He had some limited success in 1988 in getting Republicans elected to probate judgeships or to the county commissions in various parts of the state, defeating about 40 Democratic incumbents; but Democrats still hold all but a few dozen of Alabama's 3,000 or so county offices.

Hunt's prospects for reelection are buoyed by the gradual drop in unemployment and by the more than gradual rise in Republican party identification. One Alabama poll had voters identifying with the Democrats by a 48%–21% margin in 1980 and 42%–35% in 1984, but with Republicans by 40%–39% in 1988. Opponents include Fob James, the plastic barbell entrepreneur who was elected governor in 1978, but chose not to run in 1982 and got only 21% in the 1986 primary; state Senator Charles Bishop; former state Supreme Court chief justice, C. C.

Torbert; and Paul Hubbert, executive director of the Alabama Education Association. Attorney General Don Siegelman, a several-time statewide winner; and Tennessee Valley Congressman Ronnie Flippo, who nearly ran in 1986 are other possible candidates.

Senators. Alabama sends two Democrats to the Senate with similar voting records (they are among the most conservative in their party) but with different personalities and interests. Howell Heflin, elected in 1978 and reelected in 1984, has risen to take a prominent, sometime pivotal, role on national issues—though he has not always cut quite the figure his admirers expected. Richard Shelby, one of the southern Democrats who ousted a 1980 Reagan Republican, Jeremiah Denton, by a narrow margin six years later, has yet to gain the spotlight—or give much sense of how he would perform in it.

"I just try to be the country judge," says Heflin, and in style and temperament that is what he looks to be. Actually, he was a successful trial lawyer in Tuscumbia, in the Tennessee Valley, before he was elected in 1970 as the anti-Wallace chief justice of the state Supreme Court; he got a legal reform referendum passed over Wallace's opposition. When he ran for the Senate in 1978, he expected Wallace to be his opponent; but Wallace declined to run. Heflin beat Congressman Walter Flowers in the primary by running against "the Washington crowd"—a slogan used by Alabama candidates of all political stripes. Heflin has a political pedigree (his uncle, "Cotton Tom" Heflin, was a fierce segregationist who served in the Senate from 1920 to 1931 and once shot a black on a Washington streetcar). Though he is a huge man with the look of a country storekeeper, he prides himself on being a careful lawyer who picks at and tinkers with the rules of law with the delicate touch of a watch repairman. But he also often has a hard time making up his mind.

In 1987, after nearly a decade in the Senate, Heflin suddenly got on camera. On the Iran-contra committee he was expected, as a folksy backcountry southern lawyer, to be another Sam Ervin. Instead he seemed maladroit or off the point, telling reporters that Fawn Hall was putting money in her undergarments and asking how the government persuaded the Sultan of Brunei to give $10 million to the contras. Weeks later in the Judiciary Committee he was a key vote on the nomination of Robert Bork and kept observers guessing how he would vote as he asked Bork why he grew a beard and probed his views on abortion. He ultimately voted against Bork as both too unpredictable and as having a "proclivity for extremism." On other tough issues like immigration and abortion, he has had trouble making up his mind and sometimes missed votes. Heflin has tended to side with liberals and Democrats, voting to override the veto of the Grove City bill, favoring the widely-supported fair housing bill, and voting against confirming a young appointee to a judgeship in Alabama after the man was accused of racial slurs.

On economic issues he shows some of the populism of the Tennessee Valley, supporting subsidies to Alabama farm products on the Agriculture Committee; he champions the economic interests of farmers against environmentalists on pesticides, and he held up the Sipsey wilderness bill in his home turf in a battle with Congressman Ronnie Flippo. On cultural and foreign policy issues his instincts are more conservative. He also chairs on the Senate's Ethics Committee, a thankless chore which he has performed ably.

Electorally Heflin seems strong. He won his first term with no Republican opposition and his second, in 1984, with 63% of the vote against a one-term Birmingham congressman who had been unable to win reelection in 1982. But he did no better than split the white vote against this underfinanced opponent, and the anti-Washington themes that helped him get elected in the first place could undermine what is in most states the asset of incumbency. His likeliest opponent in early 1989 is state Senator Bill Cabaniss. Heflin starts off ahead, but if Guy Hunt's Republicans make the gains they seek in special legislative elections this could end up a closer race than it begins.

Richard Shelby, the junior senator, holds a seat that before his election in 1986 had five occupants in eight years; he hopes to break the jinx. But his victory resulted from negative campaigning and his Senate profile has not been high. He got Don Siegelman to drop out of the primary and attacked his one late-entering primary opponent for his driving record, and with 51% in a five-candidate field barely avoided a runoff against him. In the general election his TV ads attacked Republican incumbent Jeremiah Denton—a Vietnam POW for eight years who blinked out "torture" in Morse code when he was interviewed on TV—not only for voting to cut Social Security but for faking invoices to raise campaign money, voting to raise his pay while cutting veterans' benefits, and driving two Mercedes.

Shelby's political pedigree is conservative: he was a law partner of Walter Flowers, who represented the 7th District before him, and won his critical congressional runoff in 1978 with the support of white conservatives against a black candidate. Despite the large number of blacks in his district, he voted against the Voting Rights Act extension and the Martin Luther King holiday. In the Senate his record is to the right of most Democrats and is especially conservative on foreign policy issues; he refused to provide the party with critical votes on parental leave and the minimum wage. But he did line up with almost all southern Democrats (and with Heflin) against the Bork nomination and with Armed Services Committee Democrats against John Tower's nomination to be Defense secretary. He promised to "put Alabama's needs at the top of his priority list," and seems to concentrate on state issues: keeping a Texas landfill from being dumped in Alabama, making Mobile a Navy homeport, keeping SDI money coming into defense facilities in Huntsville. Shelby also shows a certain decisiveness and takes some original stands on issues—arguing for shareholders' rights and against efforts to insulate corporate managements from takeovers. He has a knack for getting assigned to committees that make big money decisions—House Energy and Commerce, Senate Armed Services and Banking—and could be a critical vote on them in the 1990s.

Presidential politics. In national politics Alabama is on the verge of becoming irrelevant. Sadly, presidential politics in the state is increasingly a matter of race: whites vote overwhelmingly for the Republicans (and for Jesse Jackson's strongest opponent in the Democratic primary) and blacks vote overwhelmingly for Jackson in the primary and the Democrat in the general. After the conventions neither presidential nominee touched down in Alabama, which had to be content with two visits from Dan Quayle.

The single exception in the 1980s was the 1984 Democratic primary, when Alabama gave Walter Mondale a solid win with 35% of the vote, to 21% each for John Glenn and Gary Hart and 20% for Jesse Jackson. But the turnout was only 428,000, as compared to the 940,000 who voted in the Democratic gubernatorial primary in 1986; and this was one of the last times large numbers of blacks, prompted by Joe Reed's Alabama Democratic Conference's and Birmingham Mayor Richard Arrington's backing of Mondale, voted against Jackson. For 1988 the ADC had a new, solidly pro-Jackson competitor, the New South Coalition; and Reed's group endorsed Jackson while pointedly saying that Albert Gore would be a good second choice. In 1988, despite the Super Tuesday hoopla, Democratic turnout was down to 380,000, and Jackson beat Gore 44%–37%. George Bush's big victories that day and in November were expected.

Congressional districting. Alabama's congressional district boundaries haven't been changed much since the mid-1960s. But it might be possible to create near-black-majority (and national Democratic) districts, joining the Black Belt either with Montgomery and or with black parts of the Birmingham area. There's a tantalizing possibility that Republicans and blacks will join to champion some such plan after the 1990 Census, but only a possibility: the Republicans would have to gain a lot of legislative seats in 1990 (and 1989 special elections). Or some such plan could be ordered by the never predictable courts.

The People: Est. Pop. 1988: 4,127,000; Pop. 1980: 3,893,888, up 6.0% 1980–88 and 13.1% 1970–80; 1.68% of U.S. total, 22d largest. 12% with 1–3 yrs. col., 13% with 4+ yrs. col.; 18.9% below poverty level. Single ancestry: 22% English, 6% Irish, 3% German, 1% French. Households (1980): 77% family, 43% with children, 63% married couples; 29.9% housing units rented; median monthly rent: $119; median house value: $33,900. Voting age pop. (1980): 2,731,640; 23% Black, 1% Spanish origin. Registered voters (1988): 2,429,417; no party registration.

1988 Share of Federal Tax Burden: $10,775,000,000; 1.22% of U.S. total, 25th largest.

1988 Share of Federal Expenditures

	Total		Non-Defense		Defense	
Total Expend	$14,354m	(1.62%)	$10,614m	(1.62%)	$4,360m	(1.91%)
St/Lcl Grants	1,721m	(1.50%)	1,718m	(1.50%)	3m	(2.85%)
Salary/Wages	2,665m	(1.98%)	1,182m	(1.76%)	1,483m	(1.76%)
Pymnts to Indiv	7,182m	(1.76%)	6,744m	(1.73%)	438m	(2.35%)
Procurement	2,428m	(1.29%)	620m	(1.33%)	2,428m	(1.29%)
Research/Other	357m	(0.96%)	350m	(0.94%)	8m	(0.94%)

Political Lineup: Governor, Guy Hunt (R); Lt. Gov., Jim Folsom, Jr. (D); Secy. of State, Perry H. Hand (R); Atty. Gen., Don Siegelman (D); Treasurer, George Wallace, Jr. (D); Auditor, Jan Cook (D); State Senate, 35 (28 D, 7 R); State House of Representatives, 105 (86 D, 19 R). Senators, Howell Heflin (D) and Richard C. Shelby (D). Representatives, 7 (5 D and 2 R).

1988 Presidential Vote

Bush (R)	815,576	(59%)
Dukakis (D)	549,506	(40%)

1984 Presidential Vote

Reagan (R)	872,849	(61%)
Mondale (D)	551,899	(38%)

1988 Democratic Presidential Primary

Jackson	176,764	(44%)
Gore	151,739	(37%)
Dukakis	31,306	(8%)
Gephardt	30,214	(7%)
Hart	7,530	(2%)
Simon	3,063	(1%)
Babbitt	2,410	(1%)

1988 Republican Presidential Primary

Bush	137,807	(65%)
Dole	34,733	(16%)
Robertson	29,776	(14%)
Kemp	10,557	(5%)

GOVERNOR

Gov. Guy Hunt (R)

Elected 1986, term expires Jan. 1991; b. June 17, 1933, Holly Pond; home, Holly Pond; Baptist; married (Helen).

Career: Army, 1954–56; Probate Judge, 1964–76; Candidate for Repub. Nomination for Gov., 1978; State Exec. Dir., Agricultural Stabilization and Conservation Service, USDA, 1981–1985.

Office: State Capitol, Montgomery 36130, 205-261-2500.

Election Results

1986 gen.	Guy Hunt (R)	696,203	(56%)
	William J. Baxley (D)	537,163	(44%)
1986 prim.	Guy Hunt (R)	20,823	(60%)
	Doug Carter (R)	8,371	(40%)
1982 gen.	George Wallace (D)	650,538	(58%)
	Emory Folmar (R)	440,815	(39%)

SENATORS
Sen. Howell Heflin (D)

Elected 1978, seat up 1990; b. June 19, 1921, Poulan, GA; home, Tuscumbia; Birmingham-Southern Col., B.A. 1941, U. of AL, J.D. 1948; United Methodist; married (Elizabeth Ann).

Career: USMC, WWII; Practicing atty., 1948–71, 1977–79; Chief Justice, AL Supreme Crt., 1971–77.

Offices: 728 HSOB 20510, 202-224-4124. Also B-29 Fed. Crthse., 15 Lee St., Montgomery 36104, 205-832-7287; P.O. Box 228, Tuscumbia 35674, 205-381-7060; 1800 5th Ave., N., Birmingham 35203, 205-254-1500; and 437 Fed. Crthse. Bldg., Mobile 36602, 205-690-3167.

Committees: *Agriculture, Nutrition, and Forestry* (4th of 10 D). Subcommittees: Rural Development and Rural Electrification (Chairman); Agricultural Production and Stabilization of Prices; Conservation and Forestry. *Energy and Natural Resources* (9th of 10 D). Subcommittees: Energy Research and Development; Mineral Resources Development and Production; Water and Power. *Judiciary* (6th of 8 D). Subcommittees: Antitrust, Monopolies and Business Rights; Courts and Administrative Practice (Chairman); Patents, Copyright and Trademarks. *Select Committee on Ethics* (Chairman).

Group Ratings

	ADA	ACLU	COPE	CFA	LCV	ACU	NTLC	NSI	COC	CEI
1988	30	23	61	67	10	58	36	100	50	29
1987	35	—	61	42	—	46	—	—	50	41

National Journal Ratings

	1988 LIB — 1988 CONS		1987 LIB — 1987 CONS	
Economic	42%	— 57%	59%	— 37%
Social	15%	— 83%	32%	— 65%
Foreign	36%	— 61%	29%	— 68%

Key Votes

1) Cut Aged Housing $	AGN	5) Bork Nomination	AGN	9) SDI Funding	FOR
2) Override Hwy Veto	FOR	6) Ban Plastic Guns	FOR	10) Ban Chem Weaps	FOR
3) Kill Plnt Clsng Notice	AGN	7) Deny Abortions	FOR	11) Aid To Contras	FOR
4) Min Wage Increase	FOR	8) Japanese Reparations	AGN	12) Reagan Defense $	AGN

Election Results

1984 general	Howell Heflin (D)	860,535	(63%)	($2,001,386)
	Albert Lee Smith, Jr. (R)	498,508	(36%)	($574,382)
1984 primary	Howell Heflin (D)	399,817	(83%)	
	Charles Wayne Borden (D)	47,463	(10%)	
	Mrs. Frank Ross Stewart (D)	33,114	(7%)	
1978 general	Howell Heflin (D)	547,054	(94%)	($1,059,113)
	Jerome B. Couch (ProL)	34,951	(6%)	

Sen. Richard C. Shelby (D)

Elected 1986, seat up 1992; b. May 6, 1934, Birmingham; home, Tuscaloosa; U. of AL, B.A. 1957, LL.B. 1963; Presbyterian; married (Annette).

Career: Practicing atty., 1963–78; AL Senate, 1970–78; U.S. House of Reps., 1978–1986.

Offices: 313 HSOB 20510, 202-224-5744. Also 113 St. Joseph Street, 438 U.S. Crthse., Mobile 36602, 205-694-4164; and P.O.Box 2570, Tuscaloosa 35403, 205-759-5047.

Committees: *Armed Services* (10th of 11 D). Subcommittees: Conventional Forces and Alliance Defense; Readiness, Sustainability and Support; Projection Forces and Regional Defense. *Banking, Housing and Urban Affairs* (8th of 12 D). Subcommittees: International Finance and Monetary Policy; Securities. *Special Committee on Aging* (7th of 10 D).

Group Ratings

	ADA	ACLU	COPE	CFA	LCV	ACU	NTLC	NSI	COC	CEI
1988	35	33	79	75	20	60	29	100	57	27
1987	50	—	90	58	—	43	—	—	50	21

National Journal Ratings

	1988 LIB — 1988 CONS		1987 LIB — 1987 CONS	
Economic	37%	61%	74%	0%
Social	33%	66%	32%	65%
Foreign	36%	61%	32%	66%

Key Votes

1) Cut Aged Housing $	FOR	5) Bork Nomination	AGN	9) SDI Funding	FOR
2) Override Hwy Veto	FOR	6) Ban Plastic Guns	FOR	10) Ban Chem Weaps	FOR
3) Kill Plnt Clsng Notice	AGN	7) Deny Abortions	FOR	11) Aid To Contras	FOR
4) Min Wage Increase	AGN	8) Japanese Reparations	AGN	12) Reagan Defense $	AGN

Election Results

1986 general	Richard C. Shelby (D)	609,360	(50%)	($2,259,167)
	Jeremiah Denton (R)	602,537	(50%)	($4,621,163)
1986 primary	Richard C. Shelby (D)	420,155	(51%)	
	Jim Allen, Jr. (D)	294,206	(35%)	
	Four others (D)	114,229	(14%)	
1980 general	Jeremiah Denton (R)	650,362	(50%)	($855,346)
	Jim Folsom, Jr. (D)	617,175	(47%)	($356,647)

FIRST DISTRICT

"Damn the torpedoes! Full speed ahead," cried Admiral David Farragut as, lashed to his mast, he steamed into Mobile, Alabama, in 1864. Mobile, where Alabama's rivers empty into the Gulf of Mexico, is the state's single port, one of the oldest towns on the Gulf Coast. The British governor who took it over from the Spanish in 1763, found "filth, nastiness and brushwood running over the houses" in "the most unhealthy place on the face of the earth." Mobile has mellowed, as it has channeled filth into sewers, insulated houses against rot and mildew, and conquered tropical diseases; British writer Nigel Nicolson in the 1986 found "a southern city as lovely as Charleston or Savannah, lovelier than New Orleans. There is something unmistakably French about it, with a touch of Spain. Great live-oaks rise from perfect lawns, and around them are gathered large houses with double porches, one above the other. Low lights glow from within. Squirrels dance across the lawns. The heat, even after dark, is that of a tropical glasshouse." But, like those other southern ports, this is also an industrial town, with docks and shipyards, separate black and white working-class neighborhoods and the glare of fast food and motel signs on the roads into town.

Mobile is in the center of America's Gulf Coast, a region that was once the southern seaboard of the Confederacy, was long part of the solidly Democratic South, and is now part of the Republican heartland in national elections. From boutique- and stockbroker-thronged Florida retirement towns to the white suburbs of New Orleans to the oil-pumping towns of south Texas, the Gulf has voted solidly Republican for President since the 1960s. In 1988 it was the nation's strongest region for George Bush in contested primaries and one of his strongest in the general. The Mobile area is usually the most Republican part of Alabama and the area most supportive of conservatives in Democratic primaries; blacks vote heavily Democratic, but country club whites are joined in most elections by blue-collar whites whose lives are centered on tradition-minded religions or proud patriotism. The Gulf Coast is probably the most hawkish part of America: Mobile looks south over the steamy Gulf to Castro's Cuba, the Sandinistas' Nicaragua, the guerrillas' Central America, the threatened Panama Canal; threats which seem distant to other Americans seem rather close by here. Farragut's spirit, or that of the Confederates resisting him, inhabits Mobile still.

Mobile forms the heart of Alabama's 1st Congressional District. The district extends to the north, along the lazily flowing Tombigbee and Alabama rivers, near the old forts and mansions and miles of fields that once grew cotton and are more likely now to be producing soybeans or scrub pine and surviving back country settlements of blacks and Cajans (who may or may not be descended from Louisiana Cajuns); and, to the south, along the shores of the Gulf of Mexico, and off the highways and waterways headed there, are the condominiums which are the final homes of thousands of affluent but usually not rich southerners.

The congressman from the 1st District is Sonny Callahan, a Republican with a rags-to-riches biography and a Democrat-to-Republican political history. The oldest boy in a family of nine children whose father died young, Callahan went to work at 12, during World War II; fortunately, the boss was his uncle, who owned a warehouse company. Callahan, after serving in the Navy during Korea, rose to become president of the company at 32 and expanded into real estate and insurance. Like so many outgoing go-getters, he ran for the legislature and was elected at 38. A Democrat, he ran for lieutenant governor and lost the 1982 Democratic primary to Bill Baxley.

At which point 1st District Congressman Jack Edwards told Callahan he was retiring and asked him to run as a Republican in 1984. Edwards was one of the gifts of the Alabama Goldwater landslide to the nation, a surprise winner in 1964 who, as conservatism became more respectable, became a serious and widely respected lawmaker, and eventually ranking Republican on the Defense Appropriations Subcommittee. (So well thought of is Edwards, he was named as one of the co-chairs to the commission that helped pass the military base closing law in 1988.) Callahan's problem was whether to run as a Democrat or Republican, with the party that wins most local Alabama elections or the party which in Congress stands for most of the things he believes in. He chose the Republicans, campaigned lackadaisically, and won just 61% in the Republican primary and only 51% against Democrat Frank McRight.

Callahan has shored himself up by working on local issues: getting the river channels dredged deeper (to help get more traffic for the disappointing Tennessee-Tombigbee Waterway that was completed in 1985); making sure that Mobile gets Navy home port status (bringing in two frigates, two guided missile cruisers, a minesweeper, and their crews and supply contracts). He switched from Public Works and Merchant Marine in his first term—both places where he could help his district—to Energy and Commerce in his second—helpful locally sometimes, but more important on national issues. More of an operator and wheeler-dealer than Edwards, less impartial and disinterested, he is unlikely ever to have his kind of influence; but the qualities that helped thrust him forward in business and the legislature may do the same for him in the House—at least if Republicans ever get close to a majority.

Elected without opposition in 1986, Callahan faced Democrat John Tyson in 1988, a local officeholder and member of a prominent local political family. He was held under 60%. Usually that's a danger sign for an incumbent, but he ran almost even with George Bush, and given the solid voting patterns here, this probably indicates a safe seat.

The People: Est. Pop. 1986: 587,100, up 4.1% 1980–86; Pop. 1980: 563,905, up 14.7% 1970–1980. Households (1980): 78% family, 46% with children, 62% married couples; 29.4% housing units rented; median monthly rent: $127; median house value: $35,600. Voting age pop. (1980): 384,289; 28% Black, 1% Spanish origin, 1% American Indian.

1988 Presidential Vote:

Bush (R) 121,510	(62%)
Dukakis (D). 73,312	(37%)

Rep. H.L. (Sonny) Callahan (R)

Elected 1984; b. Sept. 11, 1932, Mobile; home, Mobile; McGill Institute, U. of AL; Roman Catholic; married (Karen).

Career: Navy, 1952–54; Pres., Finch Co. 1964–85; AL House of Reps., 1970–78; AL Senate, 1978–82.

Offices: 1232 LHOB 20515, 202-225-4931. Also 2970 Cottage Hill Rd., Ste. 126, Mobile 36606, 205-690-2811.

Committees: *Energy and Commerce* (16th of 17 R). Subcommittees: Energy and Power; Transportation, Tourism and Hazardous Materials.

Group Ratings

	ADA	ACLU	COPE	CFA	LCV	ACU	NTLC	NSI	COC	CEI
1988	10	18	21	36	19	96	75	100	93	58
1987	4	—	19	14	—	78	—	—	87	70

National Journal Ratings

	1988 LIB — 1988 CONS		1987 LIB — 1987 CONS	
Economic	21% —	77%	24% —	74%
Social	0% —	95%	10% —	85%
Foreign	0% —	84%	0% —	80%

Key Votes

1) Homeless $	FOR	5) Ban Drug Test	FOR	9) SDI Research	FOR
2) Gephardt Amdt	AGN	6) Drug Death Pen	FOR	10) Ban Chem Weaps	AGN
3) Deficit Reduc	AGN	7) Handgun Sales	FOR	11) Aid to Contras	FOR
4) Kill Plnt Clsng Notice	FOR	8) Ban D.C. Abort $	—	12) Nuclear Testing	AGN

Election Results

1988 general	H.L. (Sonny) Callahan (R)............	115,173	(59%)	($651,127)
	John M. Tyson Jr. (D)................	77,670	(40%)	($125,029)
1988 primary	H.L. (Sonny) Callahan (R), unopposed			
1986 general	H.L. (Sonny) Callahan (R)............	96,469	(100%)	($144,314)

SECOND DISTRICT

A city of less than 200,000, rising from the winding Alabama River on mud flats and greenery-thick and insect-infested Black Belt lowlands, Montgomery, Alabama, has great historic monuments: the Cradle of the Confederacy and the birthplace of the civil rights revolution, the home base in the 1950s of Martin Luther King, Jr., and in the 1960s of George Wallace. Its landmarks include the first Confederate White House and the Dexter Avenue Baptist Church where King in 1955 became spokesman for the bus boycott that began when Rosa Parks was asked to move to the back of a bus and refused. A kind of conclusion was marked in early 1986, when blacks active in the boycott and whites active in opposing it met to commemorate it in a program sponsored by the state department of archives and history, in George Wallace's last year as governor. Some movements do succeed, and some healers do heal. The Stars and Bars of the Confederacy still flies over the Capitol, but the state also honors Martin Luther King Day.

The 2d Congressional District of Alabama covers the southeast corner of the state, including Montgomery, the eastern part of the Black Belt, and the piney woods counties to the south. For all the success of the civil rights revolution, political patterns here are racially polarized: blacks are almost unanimously Democratic, whites very heavily (but no longer unanimously) Republican in national contests or anything that looks like one.

The blacks' preference is rooted in civil rights, specifically in the Kennedy brothers' decision to push for a civil rights bill in 1963. The whites' preference has something to do with race but is also linked with foreign and military policy. This is one of the most hawkish parts of the United States, backing Franklin Roosevelt's interventionism in the 1940s and Lyndon Johnson's in the 1960s. Voters here rejected Jimmy Carter's dovish policies and embraced Ronald Reagan's assertiveness. Cynics would add that the presence of military bases—Montgomery's Maxwell Air Force Base, Fort Rucker near Dothan in the southeast—also made a difference, and certainly they have contributed to the area's economy. But similar changes in attitude took place in parts of the non-metropolitan South with no military presence at all.

The congressman from the 2d District is Bill Dickinson, a Republican elected in an upset in the local Goldwater landslide of 1964 (when few, if any, blacks voted here), reelected sometimes (1972, 1976, 1978, 1982) by tenuous margins, and now one of the most senior and most powerful Republicans in the House. Since 1980 he has been ranking Republican on the House Armed Services Committee. During the first Reagan term, he often dominated and in effect chaired the committee, since the elderly chairman, Mel Price of Illinois, exerted little influence. After the 1984 election, Les Aspin of Wisconsin ousted Price, and took command, depriving Dickinson of some power. But Aspin has generally touched base with, and sometimes allied himself with, Dickinson, who is certainly far more than a cipher.

Armed Services is a difficult committee to dominate. It has a single staff, steeped in expertise and experience, on which members of both parties necessarily rely. The lion's share of the defense budget is driven by previous years' commitments, and the leeway for effective action—for promoting new initiatives or squelching old ones—is limited. Dickinson, sometimes emotional and feisty in the Alabama manner (he flew off the handle after receiving what he considered poor treatment in Bethesda Naval Hospital), is nonetheless well enough informed and clear enough on where he stands to make some impact. He has not been just a rubber stamp for either the Pentagon or the Republican administration, if only because he has institutional interests of his own to assert. He sometimes opposes grandstanding attempts to involve the military in drug law enforcement or to micromanage procurement; he seems more skeptical of the Navy, which he considered favored during the Reagan years, than of the Army and Air Force, which of course have big bases in the 2d District. Dickinson would not be any establishment's choice for his position, but he takes his responsibilities seriously.

Since his tough race against longtime George Wallace press secretary Billy Joe Camp in 1982, Dickinson has had no serious electoral problems. The major threat to him could be redistricting, if the Democratic-controlled state legislature tries to draw a Montgomery-based near-black-majority district for 1992.

The People: Est. Pop. 1986: 574,600, up 4.6% 1980–86; Pop. 1980: 549,505, up 11.7% 1970–80. Households (1980): 76% family, 43% with children, 61% married couples; 31.9% housing units rented; median monthly rent: $110; median house value: $31,700. Voting age pop. (1980): 383,150; 27% Black, 1% Spanish origin.

1988 Presidential Vote:

Bush (R)	118,794	(62%)
Dukakis (D)	71,335	(37%)

Rep. William L. Dickinson (R)

Elected 1964; b. June 5, 1925, Opelika; home, Montgomery; U. of AL, J.D. 1950; United Methodist; married (Barbara).

Career: Navy, WWII; Practicing atty., 1950–63; Judge, Opelika City Crt., 1951–53; Judge, Crt. of Common Pleas, 1953–59; Judge, Lee Cnty. Juvenile Crt., 1953–59; Judge, 5th Judicial Crt. AL, 1959–63; Asst. Vice Pres., Southern Railway System, 1963–64.

Offices: 2406 RHOB 20515, 202-225-2901. Also 301 Fed. Crthse., Montgomery 36104, 205-832-7292; Fed. Bldg., 100 West Troy St., Dothan 36303, 205-794-9680; City Hall, Main St., Opp 36467, 205-493-9253.

Committees: *Armed Services* (Ranking Member of 21 R). Subcommittees: Military Installations and Facilities; Research and Development (Ranking Member). *House Administration* (2d of 8 R). Subcommittees: Office Systems; Personnel and Police.

Group Ratings

	ADA	ACLU	COPE	CFA	LCV	ACU	NTLC	NSI	COC	CEI
1988	20	32	14	27	13	92	66	100	100	59
1987	16	—	13	15	—	76	—	—	86	69

National Journal Ratings

	1988 LIB — 1988 CONS		1987 LIB — 1987 CONS	
Economic	16% —	83%	26% —	73%
Social	28% —	71%	17% —	83%
Foreign	24% —	74%	26% —	73%

Key Votes

1) Homeless $	FOR	5) Ban Drug Test	FOR	9) SDI Research	FOR
2) Gephardt Amdt	AGN	6) Drug Death Pen	FOR	10) Ban Chem Weaps	AGN
3) Deficit Reduc	AGN	7) Handgun Sales	FOR	11) Aid to Contras	FOR
4) Kill Plnt Clsng Notice	FOR	8) Ban D.C. Abort $	AGN	12) Nuclear Testing	AGN

14   ALABAMA

Election Results

1988 general	William L. Dickinson (R)	120,408	(94%)	($234,923)
	Joel Brooke King (L)	7,352	(6%)	
1988 primary	William L. Dickinson, unopposed			
1986 general	William L. Dickinson (R)	115,302	(67%)	($245,555)
	Mercer Stone (D)	57,568	(33%)	($10,015)

THIRD DISTRICT

Across central Alabama, from the Black Belt in the south to the red clay hills in the north, through land that is densely populated but not urbanized, stretches the 3d Congressional District of Alabama. In the south is Tuskegee, a black-majority town in a black-majority county, and the home of Booker T. Washington's Tuskegee Institute. Also in the southern part is Phenix City, a one-time Alabama "sin city" across the Chattahoochee River from Georgia's huge Fort Benning that was cleaned up in the mid-1950s by a young prosecutor, John Patterson, who beat George Wallace in the 1958 governor primary—the one time Wallace let himself be "out-segged." In between is Auburn, home of Auburn University, with its nationally renowned veterinary school and athletic teams (not to mention the fraternity where former first mother Lillian Carter was once a housemother). In the northern part of the district is the small industrial city of Anniston where there is the Army's Fort McClellan. At the western and southern edges of the district are counties increasingly filled up with small subdivisions amid the peanut fields and red hills, inhabited by young families who work at the edges of Birmingham or Montgomery but want to raise their children in an environment that is recognizably country.

In April 1989 this district was the site of one of the nation's more important special elections. It was prompted by the death of Bill Nichols, 3d District congressman for more than 20 years, a severely wounded World War II veteran and onetime Wallace floor leader in the legislature, who as a senior member of the Armed Services Committee and chief House sponsor of the 1986 Goldwater-Nichols Act, strengthened the chairman of the Joint Chiefs of Staff thus simplifying the chain of command; Nichols felt that confusing lines of authority produced the bad decisions that resulted in the deaths in 1983 of 241 Marines when their base in Beirut was penetrated by a car bomb.

The district had voted solidly for George Bush a few months before the special, and Alabama Republicans were hopeful they could capture the seat. They had a plausible candidate, state Senator John Rice, a Gore alternate to the 1988 Democratic convention now turned Republican, a man of such explosive character that he was nicknamed "Hand Grenade" in the state Capitol. The Democrats were running their usual large and in some cases motley field. But the primary winnowed out all but Tuskegee's black Mayor Johnny Ford and Secretary of State Glen Browder, and Browder easily won the runoff. With his "freckle-faced, aw-shucks, Tom Sawyer approach," as one reporter put it, Browder refuted criticism that he was too liberal and a tool of the teachers' unions and the trial lawyers—the two main liberal lobbies in Alabama state politics. He raised more money than Rice and watched as Rice stressed his support of raising the Confederate flag over the state Capitol—not a winning issue here, it turned out, and so presumably not a winning issue in any district in the nation. Browder won impressively, with 65% of the vote, and can be expected to represent this district for a long time, unless he runs for statewide office.

The People: Est. Pop. 1986: 574,800, up 3.5% 1980–86; Pop. 1980: 555,321, up 15.5% 1970–80. Households (1980): 77% family, 43% with children, 62% married couples; 29.6% housing units rented; median monthly rent: $103; median house value: $29,400. Voting age pop. (1980): 390,418; 25% Black, 1% Spanish origin.

1988 Presidential Vote:	Bush (R)	106,069	(60%)
	Dukakis (D)	67,936	(38%)

Rep. Glen Browder (D)

Elected April, 1989; b. January 15, 1943, Sumter, SC; home, Jacksonville; Presbyterian Col., B.A. 1965; Emory U., MA, Ph.D. 1971; United Methodist; married (Sarah).

Career: Public Relations, Presbyterian Col., 1965; Sportswriter, *Alabama Journal*, 1966; Investigator, US Civil Service Commission, 1966–68; Asst. Prof., Jacksonville State U. 1971; AL Secy. of State, 1986–89.

Offices: 1630 LHOB, 20515, 202-225-3261. Also, 7 Fed. Bldg., Opelika 36801, 205-745-6002; and, P.O. Box 2042, Anniston 36202, 205-236-5655

Committees: *Public Works and Transportation* (30th of 30 D). Subcommittees: Water Resources; Economic Development; Investigations and Oversight. *Science, Space and Technology* (30th of 30 D). Subcommittee: Science, Research and Technology.

Group Ratings and Key Votes: Newly Elected

Election Results

1989 special	Glen Browder (D)	47,294	(65%)	($679,297)
	John Rice (R)	25,142	(35%)	($443,927)
1989 runoff	Glen Browder (D)	44,647	(63%)	
	Johnny Ford (D)	26,318	(37%)	
1989 primary	Glen Browder (D)	14,715	(25%)	
	Johnny Ford (D)	14,440	(24%)	
	Jim Preuitt (D)	10,184	(17%)	
	Charles Adams (D)	9,851	(16%)	
	Others	10,443	(17%)	
1988 general	Bill Nichols (D)	117,514	(96%)	($120,303)
	Jerome Shockley (L)	4,793	(4%)	

FOURTH DISTRICT

From central Alabama northeast all the way to New England, the corduroy ridges of the Appalachian mountains divide coastal America from the interior and form the nation's coal-and-steel industrial spine. The mountains cross the great divide between North and South, but there are similarities on both sides. They are apparent when you compare the industrial "black country" of western Pennsylvania around Pittsburgh with the red hill country of northern Alabama around Birmingham that makes up the state's 4th Congressional District. Here are America's two premier steel cities, Pittsburgh and Birmingham; around them is hill country settled by feisty Scotch-Irish farmers in the years between the Revolution and the Civil War; in valley land accessible to railroads are the great steel factories built in the 80 years after the Civil War and the smaller workshops that grew up to serve them in the valleys and on the hillsides. Historically these two regions had different politics: western Pennsylvania was overwhelmingly Republican until the 1930s, while northern Alabama was, except for a few mountain communities that remained loyal to the Union during the Civil War, solidly Democratic through the 1950s. Then both changed. Western Pennsylvania became Democratic in the New Deal, then more Republican on cultural issues, and then with the collapse of the steel industry heavily Democratic again, solidly for Mondale and Dukakis in 1984 and 1988. Northern Alabama left the Democrats over civil rights, voting for Goldwater, Wallace, and Nixon, then supported Jimmy Carter in 1976. Now it is split. Counties close to Birmingham have become Republican in the 1980s, as new people move in seeking a country setting, traditional values, and a job at one of the factories or office centers proliferating along the interstates radiating from the metropolis. Farther out, where textile mills and steel workshops are threatened with closings, the hill counties are still voting heavily for populists running against the "Big Mules."

Alabama's 4th Congressional District covers both areas, from the gritty factory town of Gadsden in the east, across the counties just north of Birmingham, to the hill counties of the west represented by one-time (1937–40) Speaker William Bankhead. The balance is moving toward the Republicans. In 1980 the district went for Jimmy Carter; in 1986 it voted against Democrat Bill Baxley for governor and gave only the barest of margins to Senator Richard Shelby. Yet this almost totally white constituency doesn't totally reject the national Democratic ticket as it did in George Wallace's heyday in the late 1960s: Michael Dukakis got more than 40% here compared to George McGovern's 22% in 1972. These Alabamians seem to be moving closer to straight ticket voting—in some races.

In congressional politics, however, the pattern seems to be, as his campaign pin simply states, "Reelect Our Congressman." It's apparently not necessary to add that that congressman is Tom Bevill, a Democrat first elected in 1966 after serving as one of George Wallace's leaders in the legislature, and one of the last—and most effective—believers in old-fashioned pork barrel politics in the House.

Bevill chairs the Appropriations Subcommittee on Energy and Water Development—a fancy name for public works. He believes that government should spend generously to build dams and public buildings and, in the process, to provide jobs. In northern Alabama 40 years ago, such programs were an unalloyed good: local communities desperately needed the facilities, and local people needed the jobs. Now the need is debatable and the political support less fervent. An example is the Tennessee-Tombigbee Waterway project which passes through western Alabama. Bevill struggled hard to save Tenn-Tom from congressional opponents and had the satisfaction of seeing it open in 1985. At first traffic on the waterway was embarrassingly below projections; it only rose to somewhere near economic levels when the 1988 drought reduced the water level of the Mississippi River. And it has stopped generating construction jobs. Bevill has been fighting rearguard actions to protect his appropriations from blanket cuts and keep alive programs like the Appalachian Regional Commission as well as to start new programs like the super collider. His success has not been total, but is noteworthy in an era when the potential exists for an anti-pork barrel majority coalition of the economizers and environmentalists.

On economic issues Bevill's stands are as close to those of northern Democrats as any member of the Alabama delegation, and with a place in the party's whip organization, he is part of the Democratic leadership rather than an opponent of it. He tends to favor high defense spending and has limited sympathy for liberal positions on most cultural issues. Bevill has had no problems winning reelection since he first won in 1966, replacing a Goldwater Republican who ran unsuccessfully for governor; in fact he has had no serious opposition and seems unlikely to have any.

The People: Est. Pop. 1986: 576,700, up 2.6% 1980–86; Pop. 1980: 562,088, up 19.7% 1970–80. Households (1980): 81% family, 44% with children, 70% married couples; 23.1% housing units rented; median monthly rent: $92; median house value: $28,000. Voting age pop. (1980): 397,076; 6% Black, 1% Spanish origin.

1988 Presidential Vote:

Bush (R)	111,590	(57%)
Dukakis (D)	83,061	(42%)

Rep. Tom Bevill (D)

Elected 1966; b. Mar. 27, 1921, Townley; home, Jasper; U. of AL, B.S. 1943, LL.B. 1948; Baptist; married (Lou).

Career: Army, WWII; Practicing atty., 1948–66; AL House of Reps., 1958–66.

Offices: 2302 RHOB 20515, 202-225-4876. Also 107 Fed. Bldg., Gadsden 35901, 205-546-0201; 1710 Alabama Ave. Rm 247, Federal Bldg., Jasper 35501, 205-221-2310; and 102 Fed. Bldg., Cullman 35055, 205-734-6043.

Committees: *Appropriations* (8th of 35 D). Subcommittees: Energy and Water Development (Chairman); Interior; Military Construction.

Group Ratings

	ADA	ACLU	COPE	CFA	LCV	ACU	NTLC	NSI	COC	CEI
1988	45	50	60	73	25	50	9	100	46	17
1987	40	—	58	54	—	41	—	—	40	14

National Journal Ratings

	1988 LIB — 1988 CONS		1987 LIB — 1987 CONS	
Economic	60% —	37%	61% —	38%
Social	38% —	61%	37% —	62%
Foreign	42% —	57%	35% —	65%

Key Votes

1) Homeless $	AGN	5) Ban Drug Test	FOR	9) SDI Research	FOR
2) Gephardt Amdt	FOR	6) Drug Death Pen	FOR	10) Ban Chem Weaps	AGN
3) Deficit Reduc	AGN	7) Handgun Sales	FOR	11) Aid to Contras	FOR
4) Kill Plnt Clsng Notice	AGN	8) Ban D.C. Abort $	FOR	12) Nuclear Testing	—

Election Results

1988 general	Tom Bevill (D)	131,880	(96%)	($130,642)
	John Sebastian (L)	5,264	(4%)	
1988 primary	Tom Bevill (D), unopposed			
1986 general	Tom Bevill (D)	132,881	(78%)	($149,263)
	Al De Shazo (R)	38,588	(22%)	($10,287)

FIFTH DISTRICT

Few parts of the United States have been more affected by federal government spending than the northernmost slice of Alabama, where the Tennessee River rushes through the red-dirt hills. In 1930 the river was still untamed—unnavigable, with rampaging floods every year—and the hardscrabble farmers and occasional townsmen were poor, without electricity or running water, without shoes or decent nutrition. Then in 1933 the Tennessee Valley Authority (TVA) was created—an idea prompted by the need to do something with the government's World War I munitions plant at Muscle Shoals, and by Nebraska Senator George Norris's and Franklin Roosevelt's desire to promote public power development. TVA dammed the wild river for most of its length, controlled the flooding, produced cheap electric power, and for many years was a proud example of what creative government could do.

Later TVA had its problems: nuclear plants that didn't work, rates that had to be increased, charges that its dams were ruining the environment. In northern Alabama it has long since been taken for granted, much like any local utility. The federal government's big impact now comes from space and defense spending. The Army's Redstone Arsenal has been a major missile development center since the Soviets put up Sputnik in 1957; NASA built its Marshall Space Flight Center in Huntsville in the 1960s. In what had been a quaint courthouse town (1950 population: 14,000) there grew up a scientific and technical community of sufficient competence and critical mass to make this the center in the 1980s for much of the research and development on the Strategic Defense Initiative and one which wants to spend billions on the manned space station.

The Tennessee Valley's political heritage is Democratic: it was first settled by farmers from Tennessee in Andrew Jackson's time. TVA helped make the 5th Congressional District, which includes seven counties along the river at the northern edge of the state, one of the most Democratic districts in the South. But as the fervor for TVA cooled and as the Democrats began seeing technology as a threat and defense and space spending as a waste, the Huntsville area has shifted sharply to the Republicans. The result: the 5th District voted only 40% for Walter Mondale and Michael Dukakis, about their state average.

This trend has so far made little difference in congressional politics. The 5th has a tradition of populist congressmen, from John Sparkman (1937–46), who then spent 32 years in the Senate, through Bob Jones (1947–77), who eventually chaired Public Works, to the current incumbent, Ronnie Flippo. He is an accountant, but not one born with a green eyeshade: his father died falling off a construction platform when Flippo was 7, and while working as an ironworker on a TVA generating plant Flippo fell 55 feet from a construction platform at age 24. His fall was broken by a steel girder and his medical care and education were made possible by workmen's compensation: he has reason to thank providence and government.

One of the few congressmen of his generation with an authentic working class background, Flippo has a liberal record on economic issues and is more moderate on cultural and foreign issues. Flippo is concerned about local issues as well; he was able to double the size of the Sipsey Wilderness Area, making it one of the largest wilderness areas in the Southeast. He passed up chances to run for governor in 1982 and 1986 (when he might well have won), and in early 1989 he was mentioned as a candidate for 1990. 1989 shapes up as a critical year for Flippo, who must try to save the space station from cancellation and decide whether he is willing to take the risks of a gubernatorial race that may mean a tough primary and running against a popular incumbent.

The People: Est. Pop. 1986: 603,400, up 9.7% 1980–86; Pop. 1980: 549,844, up 12.3% 1970–80. Households (1980): 80% family, 46% with children, 68% married couples; 28.0% housing units rented; median monthly rent: $143; median house value: $37,400. Voting age pop. (1980): 385,388; 13% Black, 1% Spanish origin.

1988 Presidential Vote:

Bush (R)	111,763	(59%)
Dukakis (D)	77,172	(40%)

Rep. Ronnie G. Flippo (D)

Elected 1976; b. Aug. 15, 1937, Florence; home, Florence; U. of N. AL, B.S. 1965; U. of AL, M.A. 1966; Church of Christ; married (Faye).

Career: CPA, 1966–77; AL House of Reps., 1971–75; AL Senate, 1975–76.

Offices: 334 RHOB 20515, 202-225-4801. Also 301 N. Seminary St., Florence 35630, 205-766-7692; and Huntsville-Madison Cnty. Jetport, P.O. Box 6065, Huntsville 35806, 205-772-0244.

Committees: *House Administration* (11th of 13 D). Subcommittees: Accounts; Procurement and Printing; Libraries and Memorials; *Ways and Means* (16th of 23 D). Subcommittees: Oversight; Select Revenue Measures.

Group Ratings

	ADA	ACLU	COPE	CFA	LCV	ACU	NTLC	NSI	COC	CEI
1988	45	41	59	64	31	60	25	100	71	25
1987	44	—	57	57	—	26	—	—	47	16

National Journal Ratings

	1988 LIB — 1988 CONS			1987 LIB — 1987 CONS		
Economic	45%	—	55%	57%	—	40%
Social	38%	—	61%	42%	—	57%
Foreign	42%	—	58%	33%	—	65%

Key Votes

1) Homeless $	FOR	5) Ban Drug Test	FOR	9) SDI Research	FOR
2) Gephardt Amdt	FOR	6) Drug Death Pen	FOR	10) Ban Chem Weaps	AGN
3) Deficit Reduc	FOR	7) Handgun Sales	FOR	11) Aid to Contras	FOR
4) Kill Plnt Clsng Notice	FOR	8) Ban D.C. Abort $	FOR	12) Nuclear Testing	AGN

Election Results

1988 general	Ronnie G. Flippo (D)	504,570	(64%)	($504,570)
	Stan McDonald (R)	64,491	(35%)	($145,327)
1988 primary	Ronnie G. Flippo (D), unopposed			
1986 general	Ronnie G. Flippo (D)	125,406	(79%)	($172,356)
	Herb McCarley (R))	33,528	(21%)	

SIXTH DISTRICT

From his perch atop a mountain made entirely of iron ore, the statue of Vulcan, the Roman god of fire and metalworking, looks over the valley that is Birmingham and the city's largest employer—the University of Alabama Medical Center. Vulcan's Red Mountain brought the first steelmakers to Birmingham just after the Civil War; by 1890 it had the South's biggest steel factories; when progress seemed synonymous with industry, Birmingham seemed the most up-to-date and progressive city in the South. But worldwide overcapacity in steel and technological obsolescence at home have sent the American steel industry into long-term decline since the 1950s (although lately steel demand has been strong). Birmingham's violent reaction to civil rights—when police commissioner Bull Connor set dogs and firehoses against peaceful demonstrators and Ku Klux Klansmen bombed a black church and killed four young girls in 1963—was a vivid contrast with Atlanta's quiet desegregation. So Atlanta—the same size as Birmingham in 1950—with its white-collar base has become the cultural and commercial and air transportation capital of the South.

A quarter century later Birmingham has bounced back—though not to Atlanta's levels. Government has helped, making UAB one of the nation's leading medical research complexes, and making the steel companies clean up the valley's once foul and evil-looking air. Health care—with more that 1 in 10 people in the work force—is now the largest sector of employment. Politicians have helped, notably Mayor Richard Arrington, elected in 1979 as Birmingham's first black mayor, who has been a capable political operator (steering critical black votes to Walter Mondale in the 1984 primary) while working with the civic establishment (spending money on culture and the arts and building up the medical services business). In population, Birmingham grew 11% in the 1970s and 6% in 1980–88 after a stagnant 3% in the 1960s; the number of jobs by 1985 topped that of the 1979 pre-recession peak, and kept growing smartly though 1988.

Politically Birmingham has long voted like an affluent, white-collar town, voting consistently against George Wallace and against every Democratic presidential candidate since 1952. In the early days the steel mills were manned mainly by blacks, and even today there is a smaller white working class proportionately than in the big steel manufacturing centers of the North. But as affluent whites continue to move to the area's outer counties, Birmingham and Jefferson County, with their large black populations, are if anything moving slightly left. That pattern was anticipated in congressional races. Republicans held the seat in the 6th District, which includes Birmingham and most of its Jefferson County suburbs, from 1964 to 1982; a Democrat has held it since. The individuals, however, were not really typical. John Buchanan, a minister who started off as a Goldwater Republican, became so liberal on civil rights and other issues that he was defeated in the 1980 primary by Albert Lee Smith; Buchanan later became chairman of Norman Lear's People for the American Way. Smith in turn lost in 1982 to Democrat Ben Erdreich, who has withstood challenges through two Republican presidential years.

Like many younger Democrats, Erdreich started off in local government: as a state legislator he sponsored Alabama's Clean Air Act, and as a county commissioner he became well enough known to be a creditable candidate for Congress. His politics have no roots in the old segregationist South, but neither is he likely to support the kind of big-spending Democratic politics once standard in the North. He is used to assembling a biracial coalition, but in an environment where blacks and whites, voters and activists, are all aware that they cannot get everything they want; he is used to working with business and labor, in an economic setting where both are often desperate to preserve their common stake. He has concentrated heavily on issues of local importance, like the plight of the steel industry, and he has devoted himself heavily to constituency service. He serves on the Banking Committee, where he has worked on the details on housing legislation, and on Government Operations. He has not always been successful; he tried and failed to get a waiver on a local transportation project through the Rules Committee, and he was criticized for objecting to a Justice Department suit against the Teamsters after receiving contributions from the union's PAC.

Politically, Erdreich seems to have made this a safe seat. Republican Jabo Waggoner made a run at him in 1984, but Erdreich won with 60%. The main threat to his career is redistricting. It would be technically possible to draw a black-majority district linking Birmingham's valley precincts with the Black Belt counties to the south, and both blacks and Republicans (who would have a good shot at the remaining Birmingham area seat) have an incentive to push for such a plan. But such a plan has nowhere near enough votes now, and whatever clout Erdreich has will be directed against it.

The People: Est. Pop. 1986: 551,100, dn. 0.6% 1980–86; Pop. 1980: 554,156, up 3.3% 1970–80. Households (1980): 73% family, 39% with children, 56% married couples; 37.8% housing units rented; median monthly rent: $151; median house value: $40,000. Voting age pop. (1980): 404,782; 31% Black, 1% Spanish origin.

1988 Presidential Vote:

Bush (R) 121,126	(57%)
Dukakis (D) 90,465	(43%)

Rep. Ben Erdreich (D)

Elected 1982; b. Dec. 9, 1938, Birmingham; home, Birmingham; Yale U., B.A. 1960; U. of AL, J.D. 1963; Jewish; married (Ellen).

Career: Army, 1963–65; Practicing atty., 1965–71; AL House of Reps., 1970–74; Jefferson Cnty. Comm., 1974–82.

Offices: 439 CHOB 20515, 202-225-4921. Also 105 Fed. Crthse., Birmingham 35203, 205-731-0956.

Committees: *Banking, Finance and Urban Affairs* (16th of 31 D). Subcommittees: Consumer Affairs and Coinage; Financial Institutions Supervision, Regulation and Insurance; Housing and Community Development; Policy Research and Insurance (Chairman). *Government Operations* (17th of 24 D). Subcommittees: Legislation and National Security. *Select Committee on Aging* (21st of 39 D). Subcommittees: Health and Long Term Care.

Group Ratings

	ADA	ACLU	COPE	CFA	LCV	ACU	NTLC	NSI	COC	CEI
1988	50	43	72	91	50	60	34	100	64	28
1987	40	—	71	71	—	30	—	—	53	23

National Journal Ratings

	1988 LIB — 1988 CONS		1987 LIB — 1987 CONS	
Economic	43% —	56%	45% —	55%
Social	38% —	61%	45% —	54%
Foreign	43% —	56%	33% —	65%

Key Votes

1) Homeless $	FOR	5) Ban Drug Test	FOR	9) SDI Research	FOR
2) Gephardt Amdt	FOR	6) Drug Death Pen	FOR	10) Ban Chem Weaps	AGN
3) Deficit Reduc	AGN	7) Handgun Sales	FOR	11) Aid to Contras	FOR
4) Kill Plnt Clsng Notice	FOR	8) Ban D.C. Abort $	FOR	12) Nuclear Testing	AGN

Election Results

1988 general	Ben Erdreich (D)	138,920	(67%)	($159,323)
	Charles Caddis (R)....................	68,788	(33%)	($8,604)
1988 primary	Ben Erdreich, unopposed			
1986 general	Ben Erdreich (D)	139,608	(73%)	($216,526)
	L. Morgan Williams (R)................	51,924	(27%)	($5,534)

SEVENTH DISTRICT

"Tuscaloosa," wrote Carl Carmer in the 1930s in *Stars Fell on Alabama*, "lives a life of its own. Mountains lowering from the north, stagnant marshes sleeping in the south shut it from the world. A malevolent landscape—lush and foreboding—broods over it." Today Tuscaloosa, in the middle of Alabama, seems much less strange: you'll see no Ku Klux Klansmen in their robes, as Carmer did, and witness no lynching, you won't spend an evening listening to fiddlers play simultaneously, each in his own tempo, or visit a cabin a few miles out of town where people have never seen a power line or running water or the inside of a schoolhouse. The bleak poverty and rigid segregation of pre-World War II Alabama are a dim memory now, even in the Black Belt counties south of Tuscaloosa. Southern life may still be distinctive: people still speak in thick accents; blacks and whites, after work and outside public places, still mix very little; and Tuscaloosa is after all the home of the Paul W. "Bear" Bryant Museum and Library. But Alabama no longer seems to a Yankee a foreign country—just a different part of America.

The 7th Congressional District of Alabama, centered on Tuscaloosa, cuts a swath through the state's regions. It includes Selma, the old small city where Sheriff Jim Clark's brutal treatment of blacks seeking to register to vote in 1965 led to the march on Montgomery and passage of the Voting Rights Act and where blacks won a 3–2 majority on the county commission in 1989, and depopulated Black Belt counties where black machine pols pack the rolls with natives who have moved up north. The district spreads north into greater Birmingham and the steel mill suburb of Bessemer. It takes in Shelby County, southeast of Birmingham, which is now the most Republican county in the state. The 7th has a higher black percentage than the state and in 1978 Democrats nearly nominated a black for Congress. But it also contains a sizable Republican base.

This diversity produced a hot race when Richard Shelby, then congressman, ran for the Senate in 1986. Competitors included a black Democrat, a law-and-order Democratic prosecutor, and a Tuscaloosa developer running as a Republican. But the winner was a man who fit the profile of Shelby and the congressman before him, Walter Flowers: a Tuscaloosa lawyer with conservative instincts and strong connections with the well-to-do whites who run local businesses and governments. Claude Harris, as it has turned out, was more in touch with black as well as white constituents, more in line with other Alabama Democrats. After 19 years as a local prosecutor and judge (and service in the Alabama Army National Guard) he had near-unanimous support in Tuscaloosa County and split the Black Belt vote with the blacks. Yet he was attractive enough to affluent whites to win a near-majority in Shelby County. The only threat to his tenure is redistricting. If for 1992, blacks or Republicans create a black-majority district connecting the Black Belt and Birmingham and another Birmingham district heavily tilted toward the affluent, Harris could have trouble. But that's unlikely and Harris in the meantime has demonstrated considerable political strength.

The People: Est. Pop. 1986: 584,900, up 4.7% 1980–86; Pop. 1980: 559,069, up 15.5% 1970–80. Households (1980): 78% family, 45% with children, 62% married couples; 28.8% housing units rented; median monthly rent: $108; median house value: $34,400. Voting age pop. (1980): 386,537; 30% Black, 1% Spanish origin.

1988 Presidential Vote:

Bush (R)	124,724	(59%)
Dukakis (D)	86,225	(41%)

Rep. Claude Harris, Jr. (D)

Elected 1986; b. June 29, 1940, Bessemer; home, Tuscaloosa; U. of AL, B.S. 1962, LL.B. 1965; Baptist; married (Barbara).

Career: Asst. Dist. Atty., Tuscaloosa, 1965–76; Judge, 6th Jud. Circuit 1977–85; Presiding Judge 1980–83; Praticing Atty., 1985–87.

Offices: 1009 LHOB 20515, 202-225-2665. Also Fed. Bldg., Rm. 133, Tuscaloosa 35403, 205-752-3578; 103 Crthse., Bessemer 35020, 205-425-5031; and Fed. Bldg., Selma 36701, 205-872-2684.

Committees: *Agriculture* (20th of 26 D). Subcommittees: Livestock, Dairy and Poultry; Conservation, Credit and Rural Development; Forests, Family Farms and Energy. *Veterans' Affairs* (11th of 21 D). Subcommittees: Hospitals and Health Care; Housing and Memorial Affairs.

Group Ratings

	ADA	ACLU	COPE	CFA	LCV	ACU	NTLC	NSI	COC	CEI
1988	40	50	80	73	50	68	39	100	64	29
1987	36	—	81	57	—	45	—	—	60	27

National Journal Ratings

	1988 LIB — 1988 CONS			1987 LIB — 1987 CONS		
Economic	40%	—	58%	44%	—	55%
Social	38%	—	61%	46%	—	53%
Foreign	40%	—	60%	28%	—	70%

Key Votes

1) Homeless $	FOR	5) Ban Drug Test	FOR	9) SDI Research	FOR
2) Gephardt Amdt	FOR	6) Drug Death Pen	FOR	10) Ban Chem Weaps	AGN
3) Deficit Reduc	AGN	7) Handgun Sales	FOR	11) Aid to Contras	FOR
4) Kill Plnt Clsng Notice	FOR	8) Ban D.C. Abort $	FOR	12) Nuclear Testing	AGN

Election Results

1988 general	Claude Harris, Jr. (D)	136,074	(68%)	($328,296)
	James E. Bacon (R)	63,372	(32%)	($8,737)
1988 primary	Claude Harris, Jr. (D)	70,789	(94%)	
	Wayne Sowell (D)	4,811	(6%)	
1986 general	Claude Harris, Jr. (D)	108,126	(60%)	($485,880)
	Bill McFarland (R)	72,777	(40%)	($299,220)

ALASKA

Half a million of the 245 million Americans living in a gigantic land mass larger than all the Northeastern and Great Lakes states put together, half of them in one metropolitan area, the others scattered in a few small towns and Native settlements over an area so vast that if superimposed on the Lower 48 it would stretch from Florida to Los Angeles to Lake Superior: this is Alaska. Half a century ago it was even emptier, a lonely military outpost in the Northern Pacific, with only 72,000 people sustained by small fishing and lumber industries. Alaska has a boundary on the Soviet Union (in June 1988 Alaskans flew in a 737 jet from Anchorage and Nome to Provideniya and had a pleasant visit with their Siberian neighbors, to whom they are closer geographically and, for Natives, ethnically and culturally than they are with the Lower 48). Alaska is closer to Tokyo than to most of the population centers of the United States and was militarily vulnerable in World War II, and the Japanese held Attu and Kiska in the Aleutians (Congress voted in 1988 to compensate Aleuts who were moved off some of the other islands during the war.)

To defend Alaska in World War II the U.S. Government did more for the territory in four years than it had done since it was purchased from Russia in 1867. The military built the gravel Alcan Highway through Canada so trucks could reach the territory, and they built Alaska's first decent paved roads, an Army fort, and an air base near Anchorage; revived the Alaska Railroad, built by the government in the 1920s to connect the port of Anchorage with Fairbanks in the interior. The military sent in 150,000 servicemen, momentarily tripling Alaska's population. Alaska's population fell back to 99,000 after the war, but as the Cold War intensified the military moved back in, and by 1950 there were 128,000 Americans in Alaska—a handful, by Lower 48 standards, but enough to give life to the demand for statehood that began during the war and was granted finally in 1959.

Three decades later Alaska remains an improbable state—a gigantic land mass at the northern edge of the Pacific Rim, straddling the Arctic Circle, with the tallest mountains in North America and thousands of miles of rugged seacoast. It makes headlines when an Exxon tanker went of the rocks near Valdez early in 1989 and a huge oil spill fouled Prince William Sound. It is on the main airline routes from the United States and even Europe to Japan; Alaskans hope the Anchorage airport will become a world crossroads—but only 7% of Americans have ever been in the state, and most flights are made by small planes that land on unmarked airstrips you can't find on the map or skitter to a stop on one of Alaska's thousands of lakes and inlets. Alaska is also a land where darkness at noon and windchill factors of 60 below zero make daily life in winter a struggle, producing shocking levels of alcoholism and suicide (much higher than reported, as the *Anchorage News* documented). For all the state's economic development and slapdash new construction, nature remains close by: moose nibble shrubbery in suburban Anchorage backyards, and caribou (as George Bush noted in 1988) now breed in record numbers near the Trans-Alaska oil pipeline. But the lone trapper or miner have not been the typical Alaskans since the 1950s; they are young family people in an Anchorage subdivision, or men looking to get ahead (Alaska is still a frontier state in which men still outnumber women) while living in an apartment or trailer park. Alaska is a young state, with a high birth rate and lots of small children; it has a lower proportion of residents over 65 than any other state. However much people may love Alaska, after a while life here is just too rough, and they tend to move back south.

Alaska continues to be frustrated because so many major decisions about its future are made

ALASKA — Congressional District, Boroughs, Census Areas, and Selected Places — *(1 At Large)*

elsewhere. After statehood, it was able to regulate the Seattle salmon fishing companies, but the timber industry was subsidized and run by the U.S. Forest Service and Congress. Oil, discovered in commercial quantities near Anchorage in 1957 and in gigantic amounts in the vast, remote North Slope in 1968, seemed to promise independence. But first Congress had to settle the land ownership questions left open at statehood, which it did in 1971 by passing the Alaska Native Claims Act. The Act set up 12 regional and 220 village Native corporations, gave them $962 million and time to select their own 44 million acres, and ended the Interior Department's freeze that enabled the state to stake claims to mineral-rich acreage.

Alaska also had to get Congress's permission to get the oil out. The only feasible means, a pipeline, was opposed by environmentalists for fear it would destroy the permafrost (land that remains frozen year round except for a few inches at the top) and interfere with caribou migrations. Development-minded Alaskans got a pipeline bill through in 1973, by just a one-vote margin in the Senate, but had to make concessions. The pipeline was built on stilts and passageways left for the caribou, and the North Slope oil couldn't be exported to Japan or the other obvious East Asian markets for Alaska. Finally, the pipeline opened in 1977. Then Congress got to decide which Alaska lands should be set aside as wilderness or otherwise protected from development. Environmentalists from the Lower 48 rallied around the issue, and lobbied the Congress brilliantly; Congress passed, over the objections of Alaska's two senators and in the face of tears from its congressman, the Alaska Lands Act of 1980, which protected 159 million acres.

An argument could be made that things worked out better with outsiders making the decisions. The pipeline came on line just as oil prices were approaching their peak, thus generating maximum revenues to the state which gets 90% of the royalties; the environment was protected more than the oil companies would have done on their own, and at bearable cost; the Natives were left with more autonomy than the non-Native majority of Alaskans would have given them. Meanwhile, the decisions made by Alaskans themselves have not been stellar. The state quickly abolished its sales and income taxes, as oil was providing 85% of its revenue, and voted lavish benefits for its mostly affluent citizens (the cost-of-living differential from the Lower 48 is much less than it used to be and incomes are nearly 50% higher): the oil industry employed one out of ten employed Alaskans; it subsidized mortgage interest so rates were 3% below the market; it made low-interest loans to Alaskan college and graduate students, forgiving half the debt if they return to Alaska for five years; it subsidized housing for old people who have been in Alaska 25 years. In 1974 and 1976 Alaskans voted to move the state capital from tiny, isolated Juneau to a site near Anchorage; but in 1982 they voted not to provide the money for the move, producing a local boom in Juneau, still the capital.

Governor Jay Hammond, a bush pilot elected by narrow margins in 1974 and 1978, trying to make sure that all the money wasn't spent right away, set up a Permanent Fund for most of the oil money (it totalled $8.5 billion by 1988) and insisted that only the interest could be disbursed and only in the form of checks to each Alaska citizen. So in 1988 each Alaskan got a check for $806—and each voter has a stake in preventing legislators from dipping into the Permanent Fund and lowering the states's long-term wealth to meet short-term needs. The need for restraint is apparent from some of the profligate building projects of local and state government. But Governor Steve Cowper, a Democrat elected in 1986, had a point when he argued that the state should establish an endowment for public education rather than just send out checks to citizens—or that if it must send out checks it should impose an income tax to meet public needs. But these arguments evoked no favorable response.

For Alaskans like to think of themselves as free spirits, adventurers and risk-takers, developers of a new country. Their bias is *boomer* rather than *greenie*—Alaskan for *development-minded* and *environmentalist*. Democrats as well as Republicans, union leaders and real estate developers, libertarians as well as advocates of more federal projects here—all favor development and most feel the more untrammeled the better. Zoning is a dirty word, and even Anchorage, which contains 40% of Alaska's people, is a hodgepodge, with businesses and apartments next to single-family houses and trash left outside during the long freezing winter.

Yet Alaskans are not as free as they like to think. State government revenues depend almost entirely on the world price of North Slope oil, which crashed from $36 per barrel in the early 1980s to $13.50 in 1988. Its timber industry depends on federal subsidies and the strength of the dollar versus the yen. Its fishing industry depends on fickle nature. Its transportation infrastructure was built mostly out of military imperative. Its economic future depends heavily on trade with East Asia—and on whether Congress sets up trade barriers.

Alaska now has a multi-billion dollar state government and a local economy with enough tensile strength to show considerable resilience in the face of the collapse of oil prices; the state's population declined from its 1985 peak, but at 537,000 in 1987 it was still far above the 402,000 of 1980 and the 302,000 of pre-pipeline 1970. Congress still is making many of Alaska's decisions, and not always to its satisfaction. The key figure for the state is Senator Ted Stevens, who has more than 20 years seniority and a deep and detailed knowledge of Alaska issues. But against environmentalists, protectionists, and other critics he does not always prevail. He had his achievements in the 100th Congress. One was revision of the law regulating the Native corporations. Some of these unique institutions turned out to be very profitable; others have lost millions. Stevens got the law amended (and got President Reagan to sign it against Interior and Justice Department opposition) to allow profitmaking companies to purchase the Native corporations' losses and use them to reduce their own taxes: this has pumped hundreds of millions into the Native corporations but may cost the Treasury as much as $950 million in revenue. Stevens' bill also extended indefinitely the provision, due to expire in 1991, barring Natives from selling their shares in the corporations and otherwise limiting individual shareholders' rights, unless the corporation votes otherwise. These provisions insulate the Natives, few of whom have shown much commercial acumen, from the cold commercial world, in a worthy attempt to enable them to preserve their culture. But by subsidizing the money-losers and locking in their managements, it tends to give up on the hope that these vehicles could enable the Natives to convert their historic rights in Alaska's land into wealth in the advanced American economy. It should be noted that, despite the resentment of many white voters for the Natives' claims, Stevens and Congressman Don Young followed the consensus view of the Native leaders on these matters.

Another issue Alaska must grapple with is getting permission to export. Stevens won a victory on one such issue in the trade bill, when the House put in a provision requiring that any North Slope oil products refined in Alaska above certain low limits had to be shipped to the Lower 48 before they could be exported elsewhere, even to Canada. Stevens and junior Senator Frank Murkowski promised to vote against the trade bill and to uphold a presidential veto of it, forcing the House to recede from what Stevens argued persuasively was utterly unconstitutional. Alaska also would like to have the Japanese build a natural gas pipeline for exports to Japan, which wants an alternative to expensive oil and dirty coal. Alaska would like to export more timber to East Asia. And it would like to open up the coastal plain of the Arctic National Wildlife Reserve, a big caribou grazing ground, to oil exploration. Complex negotiations went on in the Senate to propitiate the environmentalists, cut the Native corporations into the deal, reduce the state's royalties from the 90% promised in the Statehood Act to 50% (because Congress wants the money to hold down the federal deficit).

Heavily Republican in national elections now, Alaska has elected Democratic governors— and strong rivals—in 1982 and 1986. It has copied Washington State's primary system that allows voters to cross party lines within primaries, choosing one from Column A and one from Column B; it even had a Libertarian party which elected legislators and won 12% for president in 1980 and 15% for governor in 1982, though it has done poorly since. The libertarian impulse that led Alaska to be the first state to decriminalize marijuana is being replaced by a Lower 48-like desire to stamp out crime and drugs—or is this just the equivalent of the sissified town folks throwing the saloonkeepers and gamblers out of the Wild West towns? Some regional partisan patterns persist. Greater Anchorage, with nearly half the state's population, is affluent and tends to be Republican. It is not utterly dependent on oil; its port and airport make it the one place in Alaska where services and amenities are generally available. The smaller settlements in a 200-mile arc around Anchorage are places where boomers from the Lower 48 arrived to seek their fortunes—the Matanuska Valley (one of the few places in Alaska where farming is possible), Seward, the Kenai peninsula, the little port of Valdez at the southern terminus of the pipeline— have been growing more rapidly than any part of the state, attracting people who don't like the big city atmosphere and restrictions of Anchorage; all are heavily Republican. The second largest city, Fairbanks, a pipeline and mineral service center deep in the interior, unprotected from the Arctic winds in winter and fierce crowds of mosquitoes in its brief but hot summer, is mostly Republican, but is also Steve Cowper's home town and base.

The older Alaska and Native Alaska, with far fewer people, are Democratic. The old Alaska, first settled by Russians, can be seen in the fishing towns of the Panhandle and Juneau, located on an inlet of the Pacific up against a steep mountain. Far away to the north and west is the Alaska of the Bush, the villages where Natives—Indians, Aleuts, Eskimos—live, often in poverty. Natives make up 10% of Alaska's population, and 70% in the vast lands north and west of Anchorage and Fairbanks. But they are only 51,000 people living in an area larger than the northeast United States.

Governor. Steve Cowper looks like a governor you'd expect to find in Alaska. Cowper (pronounced *cooper*) has a southern accent, a solid build, a mustache, and a face that looks lived in: he has been married three times, he was a freelance war correspondent in Vietnam, he was an underwater diver. He was one of the legislators who pushed through the Permanent Fund. He extols entrepreneurs, wants to develop a natural gas pipeline and drill in the Arctic National Wildlife Reserve, but he claims not to be indifferent to the environment either. Alaska has built its economy on federal subsidy and the extraction of fish, wood, and oil; Cowper wants it to process these resources too, and to develop its educational system; "new jobs," he says in David Broder's paraphrase, "must be developed from the state's abundant supply of young, well-educated immigrants tuned to trade possibilities with the Pacific Rim." It is a plausible, even inspiring vision. Alaska does have a talented labor supply, important natural resources, and the stability of the U.S. flag off in a corner of the Pacific and in time zones halfway between Washington and Tokyo. But, as Cowper is aware, it could be frustrated if Democrats in Congress build trade barriers across the Pacific.

Cowper won the governorship after a riproaring race in 1986. He beat incumbent Democrat Bill Sheffield, who had beaten him by 260 votes out of 55,000 cast in 1982. In the Republican primary Arliss Sturgulewski beat former Governor (1967–69) and Interior Secretary (1969–70) Walter Hickel after charging him with conflict of interest because he owned stock in a company seeking to build a natural gas pipeline. Cowper narrowly defeated Sturgulewski, and in early 1989 announced he would not seek a second term as governor. Possible candidates include Democratic Lieutenant Governor Steve McAlpine; former governor, Bill Sheffield; former mayor of Anchorage, Tony Knowles; and Republican Senator Frank Murkowski whose Senate seat is not up until 1992.

Senators. Few senators occupy as central a place in their state's public and economic life as Ted Stevens. "They sent me here," Stevens said in one impassioned debate, "to stand up for the state of Alaska." And Alaska's special dependence on the federal government makes Stevens' position more similar to that of an ambassador than a run-of-the-mill legislator. "We ask for special consideration," Stevens is not too shy to say, "because no one else is that far away, no one else has the problems that we have or the potential that we have, and no one else deals with the federal government day in and day out the way we do." Stevens spends plenty of time on national issues, but much of his time and energy are necessarily consumed in dealing with parochial Alaska issues, with which he has been dealing most of his adult lifetime, from his service in the Eisenhower Administration Interior Department and his representation of Native groups as an Anchorage lawyer in the 1950s. He probably knows the details of Alaska legislation better than anyone else. He has been the senior senator almost since he was appointed in 1968 to fill a vacancy created by the death of Bob Bartlett.

Stevens served as Republican whip for four years under Howard Baker, and was one of four candidates to succeed him; he did better than expected, but finally lost 28–25 to Bob Dole. That left him free to concentrate on Alaska issues and on the Defense Appropriations subcommittee he chaired when Republicans had a majority and on which he is now ranking minority member. Stevens has generally been a supporter of higher defense budgets, but has shown independence in his superintendency of the Pentagon budget, and he has not been unwilling to take on the Armed Services Committee when he disagrees with it. This is difficult subject matter, and he is a diligent worker at it, and his opinions are respected. He has long played a constructive role in civil service issues—seeking decent pay for federal employees (a natural position for a man from a state with many federal workers and a high cost of living) but also some restraints. He chaired the Commerce subcommittee on Merchant Marine, and generally supported the subsidies of the maritime industry, though he stoutly resists attempts to boost Seattle at Alaska's expense. He closely follows fishing law—important in Alaska where fishing is the second industry after oil. Stevens' colleagues may sigh as he rises, and wait for another irascible tirade to wear itself out; but they also pay attention to what he says and often line up with him. In the not particularly sympathetic 100th Congress, his record of achievement on Alaska issues—the Native corporations, the Arctic National Wildlife Refuge (ANWR), compensating the Aleuts (and Japanese Americans on the West Coast) for being removed from their homes during World War II—was impressive, even as he was performing ably on national issues.

Stevens seems to have rebounded smartly from his defeat in the leadership race. He still complains and sounds peevish too much to suit his colleagues, but his skills are more sharply honed than ever, and few will denigrate his record of recent accomplishments. At home, he has been reelected by wide margins, and he seems unlikely to face any more serious competition in 1990 than he did in 1972, 1978, or 1984.

Alaska's other senator is Frank Murkowski, a banker from Fairbanks who was first elected in 1980, a Republican who has generally followed Stevens' lead on state and other issues, but who in his second term is showing some initiative of his own. He is for development in Alaska and generally against government interference in the economy; on cultural issues he is a bit more liberal, though law enforcement minded on crime and drugs. He chaired the Veterans Committee in 1985 and 1986, but his most important committee assignment is Energy (the old Interior Committee) where he rather than Stevens took the lead for oil exploration in the ANWR. He is also on Foreign Relations, and is ranking member on the East Asian and Pacific Affairs Subcommittee. He was the leader in banning Alaska stops for Japanese plutonium waste, in seeking reciprocity with Japan in bidding for construction contracts, and in seeking regular air service between Alaska and nearby Siberia. In 1986 he received more spirited opposition than expected, from Glenn Olds, president of Alaska Pacific University. Although criticized in Washington for lacking flashy accomplishments, Murkowski seemed popular in Alaska and was reelected easily. Although his Senate seat is not up until 1992, he may consider running for governor in 1990.

Congressman. Representative Don Young also tends to work well with Stevens. First elected in 1973, after his Democratic opponent Nick Begich was killed in a 1972 plane crash, Young is a Republican from the bush. A former teacher in the winter and riverboat captain in the summer, he is a man of directness, fluent in the salty language in which much of Alaska politics is conducted, fervent in his boomerism and emotional in his appeals. Since 1985 he has been ranking Republican on the Interior Committee; he previously held that position on the subcommittee which handled the Alaska Lands Act. These are frustrating assignments for a congressman of Young's views, for Democratic environmentalists have a comfortable majority on the committee, a solid command of the facts, and a considerable ability to conciliate and influence wavering colleagues. Young, in contrast, tends to be angry, bombastic, even tearful—and often self-defeating. On issues he probably represents Alaska's majority views and he has worked hard to open the Artic National Wildlife Refuge for oil exploration. But his political base has seemed surprisingly weak when he has had significant opposition. In 1978, for example, he won with just 55% of the vote, and in 1984 and 1986, against Pegge Begich, the widow of his predecessor, he won with similarly unimpressive percentages. In 1988, against Peter Gruenstein, a onetime Ralph Nader associate and author of a perceptive 1977 book on Alaska, he won with 62% of the vote.

Presidential politics. In presidential elections Alaska votes Alaska issues, which was not always so: in 1960 and 1968 its vote came eerily close to the national average. After that it voted for development and against the national Democrats: in the year of the Alaska Lands Act it gave only 30% of its votes to Jimmy Carter, and in some places the incumbent President of the United States ran behind Libertarian Ed Clark. But in 1988, it joined the Pacific Rim shift toward the

Democrats. As Steve Cowper noted, Michael Dukakis's free trade views helped him in Alaska, and Dukakis received 36% of the total vote—a distinct uptick from 1984 and 1980.

Alaska has no presidential primary. Its 1988 caucuses in this irreverent state were won by the two reverends who, more than their competitors, could inspire enthusiasts to get out and vote: Pat Robertson and Jesse Jackson.

The People: Est. Pop. 1988: 513,000; Pop. 1980: 401,851, up 27.6% 1980–88 and 32.8% 1970–80; 0.22% of U.S. total, 50th largest. 22% with 1–3 yrs. col., 22% with 4+ yrs. col.; 10.7% below poverty level. Single ancestry: 9% English, 8% German, 4% Irish, 2% Norwegian, French, 1% Swedish, Scottish, Italian, Dutch, Polish. Households (1980): 73% family, 49% with children, 61% married couples; 41.7% housing units rented; median monthly rent: $338; median house value: $75,200. Voting age pop. (1980): 271,106; 14% American Indian, 3% Black, 2% Spanish origin, 2% Asian origin. Registered voters (1988): 296,701; 60,633 D (20%), 61,439 R (21%), 174,629 unaffiliated and minor parties (59%).

1988 Share of Federal Tax Burden: $2,269,000,000; 0.26% of U.S. total, 45th largest.

1988 Share of Federal Expenditures

	Total		Non-Defense		Defense	
Total Expend	$2,664m	(0.30%)	$1,528m	(0.23%)	$1,276m	(0.56%)
St/Lcl Grants	593m	(0.52%)	590m	(0.52%)	2m	(2.06%)
Salary/Wages	1,031m	(0.77%)	377m	(0.56%)	654m	(0.56%)
Pymnts to Indiv	450m	(0.11%)	392m	(0.10%)	58m	(0.31%)
Procurement	561m	(0.30%)	139m	(0.30%)	561m	(0.30%)
Research/Other	30m	(0.08%)	29m	(0.08%)	0m	(0.08%)

Political Lineup: Governor, Steve Cowper (D); Lt. Gov., Stephen McAlpine (D); Atty. Gen., Doug Baily (D); Commissioner of Revenue, Hugh Malone (D). State Senate, 20 (12 R and 8 D); State House of Representatives, 40 (24 D, 16 R).Senators, Ted Stevens (R) and Frank H. Murkowski (R). Representative, 1 R at large.

1988 Presidential Vote

Bush (R) 119,251 (60%)
Dukakis (D). 72,584 (36%)
Others   8,281   (4%)

1984 Presidential Vote

Reagan (R) 138,377 (67%)
Mondale (D) 62,007 (30%)

GOVERNOR

Gov. Steve Cowper (D)

Elected 1986, term expires Dec. 1990; b. August 21, 1938, Petersburg, VA; home, Fairbanks; U. of NC, B.A. 1960, LL.B. 1963; Episcopalian; married (Michael Margaret).

Career: Army, Army Reserve 1959–65; AK Asst. Dist. Atty., 1968–69; Vietnam correspondent (freelance), 1970; Practicing atty., 1971–86; Research diver, 1975–76; AK House of Reps., 1975–78; U.S. House of Reps., 1978–80.

Office: Box A, Juneau 99811, 907-465-3500.

Election Results

1986 gen.	Steve Cowper (D)............	84,943	(47%)
	Arliss Sturgulewski (R)	76,515	(43%)
	Joe Vogler (AI).............	10,013	(6%)
1986 prim.	Steve Cowper (D)............	36,233	(57%)
	William Sheffield (D).........	26,935	(42%)
1982 gen.	William Sheffield (D).........	89,259	(46%)
	Thomas A. Fink (R)..........	71,949	(37%)
	Richard L. Randolph (L)	28,981	(15%)

SENATORS

Sen. Ted Stevens (R)

Appointed Dec. 24, 1968, elected 1970, seat up 1990; b. Nov. 18, 1923, Indianapolis, IN; home, Girdwood; U. of CA at Los Angeles, A.B. 1947, Harvard U., LL.B. 1950; Episcopalian; married (Catherine).

Career: Air Force, WWII; Practicing atty., 1950–53, 1961–68; U.S. Atty., 1953–56; U.S. Dept. of Interior, Legis. counsel, 1956–58, Asst. to the Secy., 1958–60, Solicitor 1960–61; AK House of Reps., 1964–68.

Offices: 522 HSOB 20510, 202-224-3004. Also Fed. Bldg., Box 4, 101 12th Ave., Fairbanks 99701, 907-456-0261; 222 W. 7th Ave., #2, Anchorage 99513, 907-271-5915; Fed. Bldg., Box 149, Juneau 99802, 907-586-7400; 120 Trading Bay Rd., Kenai 99611, 907-283-5808; and 109 Main St., Ketchikan 99901, 907-225-6880.

Committees: *Appropriations* (2d of 13 R). Subcommittees: Commerce, Justice, State, and Judiciary; Defense (Ranking Member); Interior; Labor, Health and Human Services, Education; Military Construction. *Commerce, Science, and Transportation* (4th of 9 R). Subcommittees: Aviation; Communications; Merchant Marine; National Ocean Policy Study (Ranking Member); Science, Technology and Space. *Governmental Affairs* (2d of 6 R). Subcommittees: Federal Services, Post Office and Civil Service (Ranking Member); General Services, Federalism and the District of Columbia; Federal Spending, Budget and Accounting; Investigations; Oversight of Government and Management. *Rules and Administration* (Ranking Member). *Joint Committee on the Library. Joint Committee on Printing.*

Group Ratings

	ADA	ACLU	COPE	CFA	LCV	ACU	NTLC	NSI	COC	CEI
1988	25	41	43	50	40	64	51	100	69	50
1987	25	—	43	33	—	65	—	—	67	39

National Journal Ratings

	1988 LIB — 1988 CONS	1987 LIB — 1987 CONS
Economic	9% — 81%	34% — 65%
Social	48% — 49%	16% — 78%
Foreign	31% — 66%	25% — 73%

Key Votes

1) Cut Aged Housing $	—	5) Bork Nomination	FOR	9) SDI Funding	FOR
2) Override Hwy Veto	AGN	6) Ban Plastic Guns	FOR	10) Ban Chem Weaps	FOR
3) Kill Plnt Clsng Notice	AGN	7) Deny Abortions	FOR	11) Aid To Contras	FOR
4) Min Wage Increase	AGN	8) Japanese Reparations	FOR	12) Reagan Defense $	FOR

Election Results

1984 general	Ted Stevens (R)	146,919	(71%)	($1,323,218)
	John E. Havelock (D)................	58,804	(29%)	($90,685)
1984 primary	Ted Stevens (R)	65,522	(100%)	
1978 general	Ted Stevens (R)	92,783	(76%)	($346,837)
	Donald W. Hobbs (D)................	29,574	(24%)	($21,234)

Sen. Frank H. Murkowski (R)

Elected 1980, seat up 1992; b. Mar. 28, 1933, Seattle, WA; home, Fairbanks; U. of Santa Clara, Seattle U., B.A. 1955; Roman Catholic; married (Nancy).

Career: U. S. Coast Guard, 1955–56; Pacific Bank of Seattle, 1957–58; Natl. Bank of AK, 1959–67; Commissioner, AK Dept. Econ. Devel., 1966–70; Pres., AK Natl. Bank of the North, 1971–80.

Offices: 709 HSOB 20510, 202-224-6665. Also Fed. Bldg, 701 C St., Box 1, Anchorage 99513, 907-271-3735; 101 12th Ave., Fairbanks 99701; and Box 1647 Fed. Bldg, Juneau 99802.

Committees: *Energy and Natural Resources* (5th of 9 R). Subcommittees: Energy Regulation and Conservation; Mineral Resources Development and Production (Ranking Member). *Foreign Relations* (6th of 9 R). Subcommittees: International Economic Policy, Trade, Oceans and Environment; East Asian and Pacific Affairs (Ranking Member); Terrorism, Narcotics and International Communications. *Veterans' Affairs* (Ranking Member). *Select Committee on Indian Affairs* (2d of 3 R). *Select Committee on Intelligence* (3rd of 7 R).

Group Ratings

	ADA	ACLU	COPE	CFA	LCV	ACU	NTLC	NSI	COC	CEI
1988	15	25	24	25	30	79	68	100	85	58
1987	5	—	24	17	—	76	—	—	80	58

National Journal Ratings

	1988 LIB	—	1988 CONS	1987 LIB	—	1987 CONS
Economic	19%	—	80%	32%	—	66%
Social	26%	—	72%	0%	—	94%
Foreign	23%	—	76%	32%	—	66%

Key Votes

1) Cut Aged Housing $	AGN	5) Bork Nomination	FOR	9) SDI Funding	FOR
2) Override Hwy Veto	AGN	6) Ban Plastic Guns	FOR	10) Ban Chem Weaps	FOR
3) Kill Plnt Clsng Notice	FOR	7) Deny Abortions	—	11) Aid To Contras	FOR
4) Min Wage Increase	AGN	8) Japanese Reparations	FOR	12) Reagan Defense $	FOR

Election Results

1986 general	Frank H. Murkowski (R)	97,674	(54%)	($1,389,056)
	Glenn Olds (D)	79,727	(44%)	($412,074)
1986 primary	Frank H. Murkowski (R)	91,705	(100%)	
1980 general	Frank H. Murkowski (R)	84,159	(54%)	($697,387)
	Clark Gruening (D)	72,007	(46%)	($507,445)

REPRESENTATIVE
Rep. Don Young (R)

Elected 1973; b. June 9, 1933, Meridian, CA; home, Fort Yukon; Chico St. Col., B.A. 1958; Episcopalian; married (Lula).

Career: Fort Yukon City Cncl., 1960–64; Mayor, Fort Yukon, 1964–68; AK House of Reps., 1966–70; AK Senate, 1970–73.

Offices: 2331 RHOB, 202-225-5765. Also 222 W. 7th Ave., No. 3, Anchorage 99513, 907-271-5978; 401 Fed. Bldg., Box 1247, Juneau 99802, 907-586-7400; Fed. Bldg., Box 10, 101 12th Ave., Fairbanks 99701, 907-456-0210; and 109 Main St., Ketchikan 99901, 907-225-6880.

Committees: *Interior and Insular Affairs* (Ranking Member of 15 R). Subcommittees: Water, Power and Offshore Energy Resources. *Merchant Marine and Fisheries* (2nd of 17 R). Subcommittees: Coast Guard and Navigation; Fisheries and Wildlife (Ranking Member); Merchant Marine. *Post Office and Civil Service* (4th of 9 R). Subcommittees: Postal Operations and Services; Postal Personnel and Modernization (Ranking Member).

Group Ratings

	ADA	ACLU	COPE	CFA	LCV	ACU	NTLC	NSI	COC	CEI
1988	30	57	44	45	25	63	36	100	69	33
1987	20	—	43	36	—	63	—	—	57	45

National Journal Ratings

	1988 LIB	—	1988 CONS	1987 LIB	—	1987 CONS
Economic	43%	—	57%	31%	—	69%
Social	39%	—	61%	42%	—	57%
Foreign	0%	—	84%	27%	—	72%

Key Votes

1) Homeless $	—	5) Ban Drug Test	AGN	9) SDI Research	FOR
2) Gephardt Amdt	AGN	6) Drug Death Pen	FOR	10) Ban Chem Weaps	AGN
3) Deficit Reduc	—	7) Handgun Sales	FOR	11) Aid to Contras	FOR
4) Kill Plnt Clsng Notice	AGN	8) Ban D.C. Abort $	FOR	12) Nuclear Testing	AGN

Election Results

1988 general	Don Young (R)	120,595	(62%)	($626,377)
	Peter Gruenstein (D).	71,881	(37%)	($402,477)
1988 primary	Don Young (R)	62,803	(91%)	
	George Johnston (R).	6,214	(9%)	
1986 general	Don Young (R)	101,799	(56%)	($487,261)
	Pegge Begich (D)	74,053	(41%)	($269,560)

ARIZONA

"Frontier days are still a living memory," John Gunther reported when he visited Arizona in the 1940s. "People can recall fights with Apaches right around the corner, and the first white child born in Tucson still lives there, aged 77." In 1940, Arizona was sparsely settled, a wide expanse of desert and mountains with only 550,000 people, scattered in dusty crossroads settlements, copper mining company towns, and whistlestop towns on the Santa Fe and Southern Pacific lines. To most Americans at that time Arizona was exotic, the home of the Grand Canyon and the Painted Desert, a place most had never visited but which everyone knew from Western movies—where the cowboys rode out against the Indians over the desert and the sun set behind giant Saguaro cacti.

Then the air conditioner, the jet airliner, and water made possible the affluent urban civilization of 3.3 million that is Arizona today. Air conditioning made life here bearable in the hot summer months. Jets made Arizona accessible first for vacationers and then for businessmen. And water—collected in this almost entirely rainless desert from anything resembling a river and piped in at great expense from the Colorado River—initially made possible Arizona's farm industries and, more important, the vast cities of Phoenix—one of America's fastest-growing major metro area in the 1980s—and Tucson. Three-fourths of Arizonans live today in two cities that are almost entirely the creation of post-World War II America: amid grid streets laid out over deserts, shopping centers and schools clustered where not long ago there was nothing but sagebrush, with water now abundant enough to keep golf courses green and artificial wave machines churning.

For the Midwesterners and Texans who flocked here from the 1940s, the Easterners who started arriving a little later, and the Californians fleeing their own overdevelopment in the 1970s and 1980s, this new Arizona is a fresh start, a chance to build in a desert once owned by Spain and Mexico a quintessentially American civilization. The state is not built on resources: Arizona's copper industry is near exhaustion despite the recent rise in prices and its agriculture is in decline. Instead Arizona lives on technology, which is to say ideas. Phoenix has been attracting high-tech industries since Motorola built a research center for military electronics there in 1948; the dry climate is good for precision manufacturing and the cultural environment attracts well-educated technicians, people who like certainty and order and discipline. That is true also of Arizona's retirees, who tend to be more affluent than average—though they do not form any unusually large percentage of the state's population.

The political and cultural inclinations of the new Arizonans are at the same time untraditional and conservative. There is something vibrant and chaotic and not at all traditional about life in Phoenix—the untramelled growth, the absence of an established order and, sometimes, of established standards of legality and fair play. The establishment occupies a very thin layer atop local society, and except for a few pioneer families most Arizonans are newcomers. Underneath that top layer, there is plenty of money but few standards; plenty of crooked land salesmen, fast-buck artists, and drifters who would have been at home in Raymond Chandler's Los Angeles (though not in the more mature and sophisticated Los Angeles of today). Even so, the new Arizonans see themselves as defenders of old-fashioned free enterprise and traditional moral values, building a new America that, like Disneyland, is a more gleaming and spotless embodiment of old values than the old America ever was.

As Arizona grew, it changed politically, from an old-fashioned, practical-minded Democratic state to a brash, idea-guided Republican one. The old Arizona sent politicians to Washington to funnel government subsidies to the state's dependent economy. So Carl Hayden, Democratic congressman from statehood and Senator from 1927 to 1969, tried to prop up the price of copper and secure water—more precious here than oil—for the cotton, citrus, and cattle farmers. Hayden was the father of the Central Arizona Project enacted after a 21-year fight in 1968; but its original purpose—providing cheap water for farming—has been superseded by the needs of Arizona's thirsty cities. Then, starting with Barry Goldwater's election to the Senate in 1952 (to replace the then Senate Majority Leader, Ernest McFarland), postwar Arizona started sending politicians to Washington to advance their theories and ideas. Goldwater's book *The Conscience of a Conservative* and his big reelection win in otherwise Democratic 1958 made him a national figure and the spiritual leader of Republicans who wanted to roll back the New Deal and pursue, at least in Asia and the Pacific, an aggressive foreign policy. His frank, often blunt and impolitic articulation of his beliefs brought him so much devotion and volunteer support from all over the country that he won the 1964 Republican presidential nomination despite his malapropisms, his modesty, and his evident distaste for running. Goldwater's candidacy turned out to be a harbinger, not a throwback; it did not lead to a repeal of New Deal programs, but did produce a conservative reaction to the Great Society programs that Goldwater's defeat allowed Lyndon Johnson to pass.

Goldwater's conservative ideas had already set the political tone for Arizona. The new Arizonans seeking to root a new American society in desert soil found the state's old "pinto" Democrats unappealing—dusty, rural, old, and more concerned about a few federal dollars when the real growth of the local economy seemed to come from private business. They found the Goldwater Republicans appealing—including some young Arizonans who became prominent in Washington: John Rhodes, Richard Kleindienst, William Rehnquist, Sandra Day O'Connor. Their success is symbolized not only by the fact that Arizona is the only state which has voted Republican in every presidential election since 1948, but by the success of their leaders at the national level: in January 1989, George Bush was sworn in as president by Chief Justice Rehnquist, and Dan Quayle, who spent most of his childhood years growing up next to the Paradise Valley Golf Club, was sworn in as vice president by Justice O'Connor. Who would have thought it in the 1950s, when three of the four were living in Phoenix and the fourth across the desert in Midland, Texas?

Even so, Arizona like other western states elects Democrats here and there; successful and talented Republicans have an innate distaste for government, and few will have anything to do with it. So it was a Democrat, Bruce Babbitt, who dominated state government here for a decade—and set the terms and conditions for Arizona's future growth for decades more. At a cost of some $3.5 billion, the Central Arizona Project diverts Colorado River water up to the Phoenix and Tucson areas, and almost all of it originally was intended for agriculture.

ARIZONA — Congressional Districts, Counties, and Selected Places — *(5 Districts)*

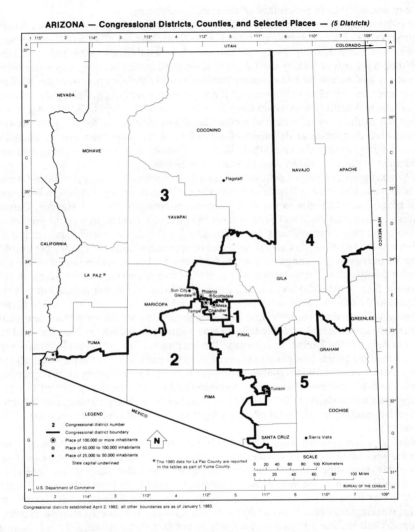

Congressional districts established April 2, 1982; all other boundaries are as of January 1, 1983.

Governor. Bruce Babbitt came to office in 1978 after the resignation of one governor and the death of another to head a minimalist state government: Arizona was the last state in the interstate highway system, the last in the Medicaid program, the last state with a state park system. From an old Flagstaff family, he is an environmentalist who likes to go backpacking, a liberal whose convictions were formed in a summer in Latin America and while working in a U.S. antipoverty program, a Phoenix lawyer who respects the new Arizona that has grown up in the years after World War II. He loved the nuts and bolts of government and used the governor's veto to force the legislature to adopt one program after another. His major achievement was brokering a groundwater compact, reducing water allocations to farmers (who started off using almost 90% of Central Arizona Project water), giving more to cities, and reserving some for the mines, so that groundwater will not be exhausted or polluted by 2025. He also got through the nation's toughest water quality bill, while he subcontracted many social services to flexible, delivery-oriented nonprofit groups. In 1985 he concentrated entirely on children's programs. Babbitt did not seek reelection in 1986, and ran for President instead. His failure to win much support in the Iowa caucuses and New Hampshire primary was attributed to his weaknesses as a television performer and his insistence on the need to raise federal taxes. But for a moment he was on the verge of doing much better in Iowa and if the *Des Moines Register* had endorsed him instead of Paul Simon, he might have emerged as a serious candidate. It was suggested during the campaign that he would make a brilliant OMB Director in a Democratic administration and there may even be tough jobs this man who governed so well in Republican Arizona could even fill admirably in a Republican government.

Arizona has not—this is an understatement—had a governor like him since. In 1986 it had a three-way race between Superintendent of Public Instruction Carolyn Warner, a Democrat who beat Babbitt's choice; Bill Schulz, a Democratic businessman who ran as an independent; and the surprise winner of the Republican primary, Pontiac dealer and onetime legislator Evan Mecham. Mecham won with 40% of the vote, and went on to get himself in terrible political trouble. He rescinded Babbitt's proclamation of Martin Luther King's birthday as a state holiday; a technicality, he said, claims that the governor can't proclaim holidays. He defended the use of the word "pickaninny" in a textbook he endorsed. His education advisor defended parents' right to oppose teaching of evolution in the schools. He called the United States a "Christian nation" at a synagogue breakfast. He hired a man for the revenue department who had not filed his income taxes on time, and a man for the liquor commission who was under investigation in a slaying. The NAACP called for convention-goers to boycott Arizona, and Republican politicians said he was costing the state business and contracts.

Barry Goldwater suggested he resign. Senator John McCain and Congressmen Jim Kolbe, Jay Rhodes, and Jon Kyl did likewise. In December 1986 enough signatures were filed on recall petitions to force an election in May, and Republicans, furious at a politician who reflects their conservatism like a funhouse mirror, started impeachment proceedings in the legislature. Mecham was convicted by the Senate in April, though he was acquitted by a jury later of failure to disclose a $350,000 campaign loan. Secretary of State Rose Mofford, a Democrat from the old mining town of Globe and a veteran of 47 years in state government who wears her silver hair in distinctive beehive, succeeded to office. She survived a bit of controversy when it was charged that her own disclosure forms were not complete. But she recovered and showed mastery over the legislature in 1988. She declares she will run for a full term in 1990 and, while there are sure to be Republicans opposing her, she earned good job ratings in her first two years. If she were not to run, another Democrat who might is Phoenix Mayor Terry Goddard, son of a former governor, head in 1989 of the National League of Cities, and an innovator in city government. Some possible Republicans include Evan Mecham—once again, as well as developer J. Fife Symington (who has received the endorsement of Barry Goldwater) and possibly Jim Kolbe of the 5th District.

Senators. Dennis DeConcini, Arizona's senior senator, is one of those moderate Democrats not from the South but from states that are Republican in national elections—Arizona, Montana, Nebraska, Nevada, North Dakota—whose instincts on many issues are conservative and who often cast swing votes on key legislation. DeConcini has been a key vote especially often because he takes time to make up his mind and sometimes bases his decision on details which other senators have not given much thought to. This was true in his first term on the Panama Canal Treaties, when he insisted on making public his own interpretation that the United States was not pledging to refrain from using military force to keep the canal open in the future—a point the Carter administration and Panama's leaders wanted to fudge, but which seemed worth making when the United States tried to topple Manuel Noriega. In his second term DeConcini cast a critical vote on the Judiciary Committee, after some excruciating and not entirely enlightening questioning, against Judge Robert Bork—a vote that helped make the Bork nomination a party-line issue and doom it in the Democratic Senate. DeConcini came to the Senate with little experience outside Tucson, where his family has been politically prominent for generations, and where he served as county prosecutor. In the Senate he has drawn up and passed an anti-drug bill, and has emphasized aerial patrolling of borders—Tucson is just 64 miles north of Mexico. He also pushed through a revision of trademark law in 1988. On Appropriations he has set his heels in against missile sales in the Middle East and elsewhere. He supports the anti-Communist UNITA group in Angola and champions the Women, Infant and Children (WIC) nutrition program. He does not neglect Arizona issues, working for a new Mount Graham telescope, seeing that the Central Arizona Project money keeps flowing, and supporting transfer of the Indian School land in central Phoenix to developers in return for 108,000 swamp wilderness lands in Florida. He chairs the special committee on Indians that in 1989 uncovered mismanagement by the Bureau of Indian Affairs and kickbacks by contractors to Navajo tribe leaders.

Sometimes DeConcini's positions have caused him problems. He was attacked in 1988 for profits made by buying land and then selling it to the federal government for the CAP or other projects; he claimed that he knew nothing about the government's interest. He was also attacked for bypassing the National Endowment for the Humanities and passing a bill giving $7 million to 94-year-old choreographer Martha Graham to record her ballets, when DeConcini's son-in-law worked for her public relations firm, and for meeting with and accepting campaign money from Arizona-based savings and loan entrepreneur Charles Keating.

These charges and his 12-year-old statement that he would serve only two terms were DeConcini's main electoral problems in 1988. He won his first term in 1976 after the Republicans had a fierce primary that hurt winner Sam Steiger; DeConcini won with 59% in the Democratic year of 1982. In more Republican 1988, he faced Keith DeGreen, a financial planner who sometimes pitched his services on TV—and who also didn't bother to vote in 1982, 1984, or 1986. DeGreen raised little money and made little headway; even so, in Republican Maricopa County—Phoenix and its suburbs, with more than half the state's population, DeConcini ran only barely ahead. He won almost 3–1 in Tucson and Pima County and almost 3–2 in the small counties, however, for a convincing statewide win.

John McCain, was elected to the House only one year and to the Senate only five years after he moved to Arizona—a fast rise even in this migratory state. But, as he says, "the longest place I ever lived in was Hanoi." McCain is one of the very few career military men in Congress, the son and grandson of admirals, a Navy fighter pilot and prisoner of war in North Vietnam for 5½ years. He came to politics with other qualifications as well: he spent his last four years in the Navy as a congressional liaison, and so has been on Capitol Hill for most of the last decade. And he moved to Arizona because it's the home state of his wife. His crucial race was in 1982, when he won a four-way Republican primary to succeed Congressman John Rhodes by a 32%–26% margin. Reelection was easy, and he was strong enough a contender for the Senate (when Goldwater retired in 1986) that he drew no serious Republican primary opposition, while Bruce Babbitt, interested in the White House, declined in March 1985 to make the Senate race.

McCain's greatest asset is his character: he can be pugnacious, but he works hard, says what he believes, and is capable of apologizing—as he did in 1986 for calling the senior citizen development Leisure World "seizure world." His politics is Republican and conservative, but he has not been a down-the-line supporter of the Reagan administration. He was a fierce supporter of contra aid, even when the administration gave up on it, but he spoke against sending Marines to Lebanon; he supported building new aircraft carriers against Navy Secretary John Lehman's critics, but he voted to kill the troubled Bradley fighting vehicle. He has worked with the right-and-left caucus on military reform. He dislikes talking about his years as a prisoner in Vietnam, but spoke out in favor of setting up a U.S. "interest section" there to negotiate on MIAs and Amerasians.

His discovery of problems in Arizona has led him to urge doing more to help Indians, and he thinks Republicans must work hard to earn the votes of Hispanics. He became something of an environmentalist, pushing to passage a bill to ban aircraft flights in the Grand Canyon and supporting the successful fight to stop Cliff Dam.

McCain beat a serious Democrat by a 60%–40% margin in 1986. Mentioned briefly as a vice presidential possibility in 1988, he has the potential of a long and interesting Senate career.

Presidential politics. What Arizona does that is interesting in presidential politics is produce candidates: Barry Goldwater in 1964, Morris Udall in 1976, Bruce Babbitt in 1988. Of different politics and temperament, they are all intellectually honest, personally candid, genuinely engaged in ideas while retaining a lively sense of how the real world works; each has a good sense of humor and is refreshingly unfull of himself; and each lost big.

What Arizona does in presidential elections that is not interesting is vote: it is among the most Republican of states and has not voted for a Democrat since 1948—longer than any other state. Its caucus process produces some interesting results—the defeated head of the Navajo tribe went to Atlanta in 1988 and Evan Mecham went to New Orleans; New York Mayor John Lindsay won his only victory here, far from home, in 1972. Most candidates spend little time in Arizona, and thus miss out on seeing what this newest version of America looks like and understanding how it works.

Congressional districting. Arizona has gained one congressional district in each of the last three censuses, increasing the state's delegation from two districts in the 1950s to five in the 1980s. It will probably rise to six in 1992. After the 1980 Census the Republican legislature drew a plan with one solidly Democratic district, connecting the Hispanic and black neighborhoods of Phoenix and Tucson, and four districts which have turned out to be pretty solidly Republican. It's not clear who will control the post-1990 redistricting, but demography helps the Republicans: the biggest population gaining area is Phoenix where you will find, except for black and Hispanic areas, almost no neighborhoods that regularly support national Democratic candidates.

The People: Est. Pop. 1988: 3,466,000; Pop. 1980: 2,718,215, up 27.5% 1980–88 and 53.1% 1970–80; 1.38% of U.S. total, 25th largest. 21% with 1–3 yrs. col., 17% with 4+ yrs. col.; 13.2% below poverty level. Single ancestry: 10% English, 7% German, 4% Irish, 2% Italian, 1% Polish, French, Swedish, Scottish, Dutch, Norwegian. Households (1980): 74% family, 39% with children, 62% married couples; 31.7% housing units rented; median monthly rent: $228; median house value: $56,600. Voting age pop. (1980): 1,926,728; 13% Spanish origin, 4% American Indian, 3% Black, 1% Asian origin. Registered voters (1988): 1,797,716; 767,716 D (43%), 821,323 R (46%), 209,212 unaffiliated and minor parties (12%).

1988 Share of Federal Tax Burden: $10,964,000,000; 1.24% of U.S. total, 24th largest.

1988 Share of Federal Expenditures

	Total		Non-Defense		Defense	
Total Expend	$12,248m	(1.39%)	$8,238m	(1.26%)	$4,395m	(1.92%)
St/Lcl Grants	1,177m	(1.03%)	1,175m	(1.03%)	2m	(1.38%)
Salary/Wages	1,763m	(1.31%)	892m	(1.33%)	871m	(1.33%)
Pymnts to Indiv	6,019m	(1.47%)	5,540m	(1.42%)	479m	(2.57%)
Procurement	3,034m	(1.61%)	385m	(0.83%)	3,034m	(1.61%)
Research/Other	256m	(0.69%)	246m	(0.66%)	10m	(0.66%)

Political Lineup: Governor, Rose Mofford (D); Secy. of State, James Shumway (D); Atty. Gen., Bob Corbin (R); Treasurer, Ray Rottas (R); Auditor, Douglas Norton (I). State Senate, 30 (17 R and 13 D); State House of Representatives, 60 (34 R and 26 D). Senators, Dennis DeConcini (D) and John McCain (R). Representatives, 5 (4 R and 1 D).

40 ARIZONA

1988 Presidential Vote			1984 Presidential Vote		
Bush (R)	702,541	(60%)	Reagan (R)	681,416	(66%)
Dukakis (D).	454,029	(39%)	Mondale (D)	333,854	(33%)

GOVERNOR

Gov. Rose Mofford (D)

Assumed office April 1988, term expires 1991; b. June 10, 1922, Globe; home, Phoenix; Phoenix Col., U. S. Defense Industrial Col.; Roman Catholic; widowed.

Career: AZ Tax Commissioner 1943–54; Asst. Secy. of State, 1955–75; Asst. Dir., AZ Dept. of Revenue, 1975–77; Secy. of State, 1977–1988.

Office: State Capitol, West Wing, Phoenix 85007, 602-542-4331.

Election Results

1986 gen.	Evan Mecham (R)	343,913	(40%)
	Carolyn Warner (D)	298,986	(34%)
	Bill Schulz (I).	224,085	(26%)
1986 prim.	Evan Mecham (R)	121,614	(54%)
	Burton S. Barr (R)	104,682	(46%)
1982 gen.	Bruce E. Babbitt (D)	455,760	(62%)
	Leo Corbet (R).	236,857	(32%)
	Sam Steiger (I).	36,680	(5%)

SENATORS

Sen. Dennis DeConcini (D)

Elected 1976, seat up 1994; b. May 8, 1937, Tucson; home, Tucson; U. of AZ, B.A. 1959, LL.B. 1963; Roman Catholic; married (Susan).

Career: Army, 1959–60; Practicing atty., 1963–65, 1968–73; Special Counsel, A.A. to Gov. Samuel P. Goddard, 1965–67; Pima Cnty. Atty., 1973–76.

Offices: 328 HSOB 20510, 202-224-4521. Also 700 E. Jefferson, Ste. 200, Phoenix 85034, 602-261-6756; 97 E. Congress, Ste. 120, Tucson 85701, 602-629-6831; and 20 E. Main, Ste. 315, Mesa 85201, 602-261-4998.

Committees: *Appropriations* (8th of 16 D). Subcommittees: Defense; Energy and Water Development; Foreign Operations; Interior; Treasury, Postal Service, and General Government (Chairman). *Judiciary* (4th of 8 D). Subcommittees: Antitrust, Monopolies and Business Rights; Constitution; Patents, Copyrights and Trademarks (Chairman). *Rules and Administration* (5th of 9 D). *Veterans' Affairs* (3d of 6 D). *Select Committee on Indian Affairs* (2d of 5 D). *Select Committee on Intelligence* (6th of 9 D). *Joint Committee on the Library. Joint Committee on Printing.*

Group Ratings

	ADA	ACLU	COPE	CFA	LCV	ACU	NTLC	NSI	COC	CEI
1988	55	44	64	100	50	33	16	40	21	16
1987	60	—	62	75	—	27	—	—	33	26

National Journal Ratings

	1988 LIB — 1988 CONS		1987 LIB — 1987 CONS	
Economic	45% —	54%	44% —	50%
Social	34% —	65%	44% —	55%
Foreign	44% —	54%	45% —	54%

Key Votes

1) Cut Aged Housing $	AGN	5) Bork Nomination	AGN	9) SDI Funding	AGN
2) Override Hwy Veto	FOR	6) Ban Plastic Guns	FOR	10) Ban Chem Weaps	FOR
3) Kill Plnt Clsng Notice	AGN	7) Deny Abortions	FOR	11) Aid To Contras	AGN
4) Min Wage Increase	FOR	8) Japanese Reparations	FOR	12) Reagan Defense $	—

Election Results

1988 general	Dennis DeConcini (D)................	660,403	(57%)	($2,640,650)
	Keith DeGreen (R)..................	478,060	(41%)	($238,369)
1988 primary	Dennis DeConcini (D)................	195,540	(100%)	
1982 general	Dennis DeConcini (D)................	413,951	(59%)	($2,086,401)
	Pete Dunn (R)......................	292,638	(41%)	($884,517)

Sen. John McCain (R)

Elected 1986, seat up 1992; b. Aug. 29, 1936, Panama Canal Zone; home, Phoenix; U.S. Naval Acad., 1958, Natl. War Col., 1973–74; Episcopalian; married (Cindy).

Career: Navy, 1958–80; Dir., Navy Senate Liaison Ofc., 1977–81; U.S. House of Reps., 1982–1986.

Offices: 111 RSOB 20510, 202-224-2235. Also 5353 N. 16th St., Ste. 190, Phoenix 85016, 602-241-2567; 2675 E. Broadway, Tucson 85716, 602-629-6334; and 151 N. Centennial Way, Ste. 1000, Mesa 85201, 602-835-8994.

Committees: *Armed Services* (5th of 9 R). Subcommittees: Conventional Forces and Alliance Defense; Manpower and Personnel (Ranking Member); Projection Forces and Regional Defense. *Commerce, Science and Transportation* (6th of 9 R). Subcommittees: Aviation (Ranking Member); Communications; Consumer. *Select Committee on Indian Affairs* (Vice Chairman of 3 R).

Group Ratings

	ADA	ACLU	COPE	CFA	LCV	ACU	NTLC	NSI	COC	CEI
1988	10	15	17	33	50	80	68	100	64	60
1987	15	—	20	42	—	91	—	—	100	67

National Journal Ratings

	1988 LIB — 1988 CONS		1987 LIB — 1987 CONS	
Economic	27% —	70%	21% —	74%
Social	19% —	78%	13% —	85%
Foreign	0% —	92%	0% —	76%

Key Votes

1) Cut Aged Housing $	FOR	5) Bork Nomination	FOR	9) SDI Funding	FOR
2) Override Hwy Veto	AGN	6) Ban Plastic Guns	FOR	10) Ban Chem Weaps	FOR
3) Kill Plnt Clsng Notice	FOR	7) Deny Abortions	FOR	11) Aid To Contras	FOR
4) Min Wage Increase	AGN	8) Japanese Reparations	AGN	12) Reagan Defense $	—

Election Results

1986 general	John McCain (R)	521,850	(60%)	($2,228,498)
	Richard Kimball (D).................	340,965	(40%)	($657,908)
1986 primary	John McCain (R)	205,965	(100%)	
1980 general	Barry Goldwater (R).................	432,371	(50%)	($949,992)
	Bill Schulz (D)	422,972	(49%)	($2,073,232)

FIRST DISTRICT

Phoenix is the prototypical Sun Belt city, a metropolis that 40 years ago almost no one would have predicted would be one of America's great urban centers. But today it is. It is almost totally the product of the air conditioned years after World War II. In 1940 Phoenix had 65,000 residents; in 1950, 106,000; by 1970 the metropolitan area had nearly one million, in 1980 1.5 million, in 1988 1.9 million. This almost instant metropolis was created not in response to geographical imperative but in spite of it. Neither the copper mines of southern Arizona nor the cotton farms irrigated by the Gila River water needed a city anything like the size of Phoenix, nor is there any thickly populated hinterland in the vast land between the Rio Grande and Los Angeles for which this is the natural commercial center. Nor is Phoenix a giant retirement village. Though there are huge retirement developments northwest of town, Phoenix's economic base has been in research and development and high-tech manufacturing, and its population tends to be young, family-oriented, on the way up from whatever level of society they were born into.

Technologically advanced, with little visual evidence of tradition or heritage beyond the ersatz 1970s Indian and Mexican styled commercial fronts, Phoenix is politically conservative. Not conservative in the Burkean sense, however, here conservatism means devotion to abstract principle, to the ideal of the untrammeled free market, opposition to unionization and minimum wages, abhorrence of government welfare programs. Of all the nation's states, Arizona probably comes closest to this conservative ideal, but it is still an ideal, not a reality. Phoenix, reluctantly, drinks and swims in federally provided water, complains that it has too few 90%-federally-financed freeways, enjoys easy access to federally protected national parks and monuments. But most idealists understand the need to compromise with the practical world. Such abstract politics come naturally, it seems, to engineers and technicians, whose work it is to make unruly nature conform to concrete principle and abstract rule, and to upwardly mobile migrants, who have staked their lives on change and movement and who believe—or want to—that the system works fairly.

The 1st Congressional District of Arizona is the only one wholly within the Phoenix metropolitan area. It includes some of the comfortable neighborhoods east of downtown Phoenix and north of Sky Harbor Airport. The district dips south of the almost-always-dry Salt River and includes some black and low-income neighborhoods, but it also extends to the high-income areas near the Arizona Biltmore and takes in the southern half of high-income Scottsdale. To the south and east it includes two East Valley suburbs, each with more than 100,000 people—Tempe, home of Arizona State University and the Fiesta Bowl, and Mesa, whose central focus is one of the nation's few Mormon temples. To the south is the old desert town of Chandler, which is becoming part of suburbia now that freeways bring it within easy driving distance of Phoenix. This solidly Republican district (it has only a handful of reliably Democratic precincts) has been represented for almost all of the last four decades by members of one family, John Rhodes and his son Jay. John Rhodes, a crew-cut young migrant from Kansas to Mesa, was first elected in the Eisenhower landslide of 1952 and served as House Minority Leader from 1973 to 1980; he stepped down voluntarily and retired from the House in 1982. He was replaced by John McCain, a former Vietnam POW, who was elected Senator in 1986 and was succeeded in the 1st by Jay Rhodes, the winner of a seriously contested four-candidate Republican primary.

Jay Rhodes was not just a name candidate. Like McCain he served in Vietnam—he was the only congressman's son to serve on the ground there. He was active in civic affairs in the Phoenix area and on the board of the Central Arizona Project. In his first term in the House he took a lead role on important issues. As a junior member of Morris Udall's Interior Committee he worked as Udall's "right hand man" on Arizona issues, keeping the money flowing into the Central Arizona Project, and making the tough decision of dropping the environmentally challenged Cliff Dam to do so. He floor managed the bill to swap the government's Indian School in central Phoenix for environmentally unique acreage in Florida. He negotiated an agreement on Salt River-Pima-Maricopa Indian water rights. He was one of the congressmen who urged Governor Evan Mecham to resign, and when it appeared there would be a recall election supported his father's candidacy for governor.

Rhodes also had his moments of passion. In a debate on contra aid, in response to opponents who called for peace in Nicaragua, he noted that the Vietnamese who had been his interpreter and military counterparts were now either slaves or dead. "Yes, peace came to Vietnam," he said. "It was the peace of repression, of poverty, of imprisonment, of death, of slavery." From a district and state where Republicans are clearly the majority, he has been frustrated by being in the minority in the House. He seems to be well thought of in Washington and in his district, and was easily reelected in 1988.

The People: Est. Pop. 1986: 721,800, up 32.7% 1980–86; Pop. 1980: 543,747, up 47.8% 1970–80. Households (1980): 69% family, 35% with children, 58% married couples; 36.0% housing units rented; median monthly rent: $257; median house value: $60,600. Voting age pop. (1980): 399,698; 9% Spanish origin, 3% Black, 1% American Indian, 1% Asian origin.

1988 Presidential Vote: Bush (R) 171,884   (65%)
Dukakis (D). 90,383   (34%)

Rep. John J. Rhodes III (R)

Elected 1986; b. Sept. 8, 1943, Mesa; home, Mesa; Yale U., B.A. 1965, U. of AZ, J.D. 1968; Protestant; married (Ann).

Career: Army, Vietnam; Mesa Bd. of Educ., 1972–76; Practicing atty., 1970–77, 1980–1986.

Offices: 412 CHOB 20515, 202-225-2635. Also 2345 S. Alma School, Mesa 85202, 602-831-6433.

Committees: *Interior and Insular Affairs* (9th of 15 R). Subcommittees: Energy and the Environment; General Oversight and Investigations; National Parks and Public Lands; Water, Power and Offshore Energy Resources. *Small Business* (11th of 17 R). Subcommittees: Exports, Tax Policy and Special Problems; Procurement, Tourism and Rural Development.

Group Ratings

	ADA	ACLU	COPE	CFA	LCV	ACU	NTLC	NSI	COC	CEI
1988	10	17	7	18	13	96	80	100	100	69
1987	4	—	6	14	—	96	—	—	93	77

National Journal Ratings

	1988 LIB — 1988 CONS	1987 LIB — 1987 CONS
Economic	7% — 91%	0% — 89%
Social	13% — 84%	0% — 90%
Foreign	0% — 84%	0% — 80%

Key Votes

1) Homeless $	FOR	5) Ban Drug Test	FOR	9) SDI Research	FOR
2) Gephardt Amdt	AGN	6) Drug Death Pen	FOR	10) Ban Chem Weaps	AGN
3) Deficit Reduc	AGN	7) Handgun Sales	FOR	11) Aid to Contras	FOR
4) Kill Plnt Clsng Notice	FOR	8) Ban D.C. Abort $	FOR	12) Nuclear Testing	AGN

Election Results

1988 general	John J. Rhodes III (R)	184,639	(72%)	($291,961)
	John M. Fillmore (D)	71,388	(28%)	($11,855)
1988 primary	John J. Rhodes III (R)	54,984	(100%)	
1986 general	John J. Rhodes III (R)	127,370	(71%)	($493,182)
	Harry W. Braun III (D)	51,163	(29%)	($31,528)

SECOND DISTRICT

Not far from the skyscrapers of downtown Phoenix and downtown Tucson, across dry river beds and in the shadow of giant outcroppings of mountains, along the railroad tracks that were for decades Arizona's only connection with the rest of the United States, are the dilapidated and shabby neighborhoods. This is where the poor people of Phoenix and Tucson live, with the vacant lots between the small stucco houses and the gaudy roadside establishments that could easily grow back into small patches of desert. These neighborhoods, plus some better-off adjacent areas, form Arizona's 2d Congressional District. It owes its shape to politics: the Republican legislature wanted to concentrate as many of the state's Democratic precincts as possible in this one district, leaving the others largely Republican. Also included is Yuma, 180 miles across the desert southwest of Phoenix, an agricultural center on the Colorado River and on many days of every year the hottest place in the United States. The few towns connecting these three points have mostly been excised from the 2d, leaving a few Indian reservations and a lot of desert. That leaves a district in which 30% of the adults are of Spanish origin, 5% black, and 4% Indian.

Nearly half the district's population is in Phoenix, including the city's downtown and the state Capitol, but it also includes most of Tucson, except for the affluent fringe. Overshadowed demographically by Phoenix, Tucson has always been the more Democratic of the two cities— somewhat more blue-collar, more Mexican-American (the 2d's part of Tucson is 42% Hispanic), less high-tech, not blessed with so many corporate headquarters, with a Democratic Pulitzer rather than a Republican Pulliam newspaper.

Morris Udall, one of the leading and most productive politicians of his generation, is the congressman from the 2d District. First elected to Congress in 1961, to replace his brother Stewart Udall who became Secretary of the Interior, Mo Udall has many legislative accomplishments. One is the 1974 campaign finance law, the source of much carping, but a measure which has substantially improved the political process. Another is the civil service reform of 1978.

Udall labored for years in the dull vineyards of the Post Office and Civil Service Committee; this bill moved, finally, at least a little toward making government employees more accountable. Udall's most noted efforts have been in the environmental field. Since 1977 he has chaired the Interior Committee, which has jurisdiction over national parks, mining and mineral exploration, government land, Indian tribes, and American overseas possessions. He has always been counted as a friend, though not an automatic vote, by environmentalists. During the Carter years, when the committee and the administration were of similar views, he had a number of accomplishments, most notably the 1977 strip mining law and the 1980 Alaska Lands Act. In the Reagan years, Udall got through a nuclear waste act in 1982 and a wilderness act in 1984, and worked at riding herd on the James Watt and Donald Hodel Interior Departments. He led deliberations over the potentially awesome issue of nuclear plant liability, taking a stand between those of the nuclear industry and the environmentalists.

In 1987 and 1988 he spent much time on Arizona issues, including the swap of Phoenix's Indian School for environmentally important wetlands in Florida, the Salt River-Pima-Maricopa Indian water settlement, banning airplanes from beneath the rim of the Grand Canyon, allowing telescopes on Mount Graham. He is alert to Arizona's economic needs, shepherding the Central Arizona Project toward completion and authorizing a Phoenix Outer Loop. Farther afield, he acted to protect the Manassas Battlefield National Park in Virginia from development and to allow an 18-month moratorium on establishing new nuclear waste sites.

Udall has shouldered his responsibilities amid political disappointments and personal tragedies which would crush many others. He ran for President in 1976 and lost to Jimmy Carter, finishing second in six primaries, but never first. In the late 1970s his proposals for public campaign financing languished in the House, and his mining law revision got him into deep trouble—tough challenges in 1978 and 1980—back home. He was stricken with Parkinson's disease in 1980 and late in the decade his vigor was perceptibly diminished. Always known for his jokes and funny stories, he published a book, *Too Funny to be President*, in 1988. But he suffered more tragedy when his wife committed suicide that summer. Yet he remains formidable legislatively in the House and politically in the 2d District. There have also been honors: the westernmost point in Guam was named Udall Point in 1989, a counterpart to the Udall Point named for his brother in St. Croix in 1968: they are the westernmost and easternmost points in the United States.

Electorally, Udall has had an easier time of it since he decided in 1982 to run in this 2d District rather than in the much less Democratic 5th that includes the east side of Tucson and the copper mining country around Bisbee. He has been reelected easily, even in 1986 when he was challenged in the primary by Tucson state Senator Luis Gonzalez. There have been rumors for several years that Udall was about to retire, and if he does he will probably be succeeded by one of the Hispanic legislators from the area. But so far this most productive member of his generation is fighting against hard odds to work on, and winning.

The People: Est. Pop. 1986: 581,300, up 7.4% 1980–86; Pop. 1980: 543,187, up 21.9% 1970–80. Households (1980): 71% family, 42% with children, 56% married couples; 39.8% housing units rented; median monthly rent: $185; median house value: $40,300. Voting age pop. (1980): 372,734; 30% Spanish origin, 5% Black, 4% American Indian, 1% Asian origin.

1988 Presidential Vote: Dukakis (D)...................... 77,493   (55%)

Bush (R) 60,606   (43%)

Rep. Morris K. Udall (D)

Elected 1961; b. June 15, 1922, St. Johns; home, Tucson; U. of AZ, J.D. 1949; Mormon; married (Norma).

Career: Air Force, WWII; Pro basketball player, Denver Nuggets, 1948–49; Practicing atty., 1949–61; Pima Cnty. Atty., 1952–54.

Offices: 235 CHOB 20515, 202-225-4065. Also 373 S. Meyer, Tucson 85701, 602-629-6404; and 522 W. Roosevelt, Phoenix 85003, 602-261-3018.

Committees: *Foreign Affairs* (19th of 28 D). Subcommittees: Arms Control, International Security and Science. *Interior and Insular Affairs* (Chairman of 26 D). Subcommittees: Energy and the Environment (Chairman); Insular and International Affairs; Mining and Natural Resources; Water, Power and Offshore Energy Resources. *Post Office and Civil Service* (14th of 15 D).

Group Ratings

	ADA	ACLU	COPE	CFA	LCV	ACU	NTLC	NSI	COC	CEI
1988	75	80	86	64	81	13	10	0	29	12
1987	82	—	86	79	—	0	—	—	7	9

National Journal Ratings

	1988 LIB — 1988 CONS		1987 LIB — 1987 CONS	
Economic	77% —	22%	73% —	0%
Social	81% —	18%	70% —	28%
Foreign	84% —	0%	81% —	0%

Key Votes

1) Homeless $	AGN	5) Ban Drug Test	AGN	9) SDI Research	AGN
2) Gephardt Amdt	FOR	6) Drug Death Pen	FOR	10) Ban Chem Weaps	FOR
3) Deficit Reduc	FOR	7) Handgun Sales	AGN	11) Aid to Contras	AGN
4) Kill Plnt Clsng Notice	AGN	8) Ban D.C. Abort $	—	12) Nuclear Testing	FOR

Election Results

1988 general	Morris K. Udall (D)	99,895	(73%)	($99,607)
	Joseph D. Sweeney (R)...............	36,309	(27%)	($3,065)
1988 primary	Morris K. Udall (D)	34,350	(100%)	
1986 general	Morris K. Udall (D)	77,239	(73%)	($447,112)
	Sheldon Clark (R)....................	24,522	(23%)	

THIRD DISTRICT

You can still find vestiges of the old Arizona in the state's 3d Congressional District, which takes up most of the western part of the state. Here are old mining towns like Wickenburg, surrounded by dude ranches and flanked by gas stations, and pleasant county seat towns like Prescott that, but for the mountains, look like they were plucked from the Midwest. But in this territory new towns and retirement villages have suddenly sprung up in the desert; here you will find places like Lake Havasu City, proud owner of the transplanted London Bridge. More important demographically, the Phoenix metropolitan area has been moving west and northwest through the desert, so that today 60% of the 3d District's residents live on its eastern edge, in Phoenix and Maricopa County. Here are modest income suburbs like Glendale and the huge retirement community of Sun City just northwest of Phoenix.

This vast influx of people has changed this district from "pinto" (i.e., conservative) Democrat to Republican. Sun City and Lake Havasu City are heavily Republican; these are relatively affluent Midwesterners and others who started voting in many cases in the prosperous 1920s and have not abandoned their party since. The district's part of Phoenix, a strip along the northwest side that is affluent, although not fashionable, and the next-door suburb of Glendale, with nearly 100,000 people, are filled mainly by families with children—a reminder of the suburbia that was so common in the 1950s; similar except for climate to the neighborhoods in which Sun City residents raised their families 30 years ago. Voters here are heavily Republican too. Interestingly, about 13% of the residents of these areas are of Spanish origin: it is a mistake to picture Mexican-Americans in Phoenix as huddled in an impoverished ghetto, for most live in rather pleasant, and diverse, neighborhoods like this.

The congressman from the 3d District, Bob Stump, has a similar political history: he has gone from "pinto" Democrat to Republican himself, literally. He started off as a cotton and grain farmer, in the rich irrigated lands west of Phoenix. He was elected to the state legislature at 31 in 1958, when Democrats were still the majority party there; he was state Senate president in 1975–76, when the 1974 election gave them a majority again. His politics have been solidly conservative; although his farm benefited from subsidized federal water, he has been a foe of government spending generally. When the 3d District's Sam Steiger ran for the Senate in 1976, Stump won a close race for the Democratic nomination and won the general election easily.

In the House, Stump always seemed to belong more with the Republicans than the Democrats, and in 1981 he voted for the Reagan budget and tax plans and for administration policies generally. So that year he decided to switch parties and put on the label that most of his constituency had long since worn. It was a successful move. He won 64% as a Democrat in 1980 and 63% as a Republican in 1982—one of the smoothest party switches of all time. His only possible vulnerability before was in the Democratic primary, and now he was safe from that. Republicans gave him a seat on the Armed Services Committee, where he is one of the most reliable and uncritical supporters of the Pentagon. Generally Stump is a congressman who quietly adds his one vote to the legislative balance, on the side most of his constituents want, and makes few waves, even when he holds a position, which he achieved in 1985, like ranking minority member of the Permanent Select Committee on Intelligence. His fervor seems directed mostly at foreign policy issues. He sponsored a successful amendment to remove restrictions on U.S. aid to the UNITA rebels in Angola. He fervently supports the Nicaraguan contras. He ballyhoos the fight against terrorism and, at home in the national security establishment, he advocates the use of lie detectors.

Stump does not appear to be an original thinker on these matters; his statements are written in a militarese seldom composed outside five-sided buildings. But he does advance with obvious sincerity views which are surely shared by the 3d District which is happy to reelect him overwhelmingly.

The People: Est. Pop. 1986: 665,600, up 22.1% 1980–86; Pop. 1980: 544,870, up 90.8% 1970–80. Households (1980): 78% family, 39% with children, 69% married couples; 24.3% housing units rented; median monthly rent: $222; median house value: $58,300. Voting age pop. (1980): 389,150; 9% Spanish origin, 4% American Indian, 1% Black, 1% Asian origin.

1988 Presidential Vote: Bush (R) 165,706 (64%)
Dukakis (D). 89,460 (35%)

Rep. Bob Stump (R)

Elected 1976; b. April 4, 1927, Phoenix; home, Tolleson; AZ St. U., B.S. 1951; Seventh Day Adventist; divorced.

Career: Navy, WWII; Cotton and grain farmer; AZ House of Reps., 1959–67; AZ Senate, 1967–76, Senate Pres., 1975–76.

Offices: 211 CHOB 20515, 202-225-4576. Also 230 N. First Ave., Rm. 5001, Phoenix 85025, 602-261-6923.

Committees: *Armed Services* (4th of 21 R). Subcommittees: Investigations; Research and Development. *Veterans Affairs* (Ranking Member of 13 R). Subcommittees: Hospitals and Health Care; Oversight and Investigations (Ranking Member).

Group Ratings

	ADA	ACLU	COPE	CFA	LCV	ACU	NTLC	NSI	COC	CEI
1988	0	0	8	18	0	100	99	100	85	93
1987	4	—	9	7	—	100	—	—	100	88

National Journal Ratings

	1988 LIB — 1988 CONS		1987 LIB — 1987 CONS	
Economic	0%	— 93%	0%	— 89%
Social	0%	— 95%	0%	— 90%
Foreign	0%	— 84%	0%	— 80%

Key Votes

1) Homeless $	FOR	5) Ban Drug Test	FOR	9) SDI Research	FOR
2) Gephardt Amdt	AGN	6) Drug Death Pen	FOR	10) Ban Chem Weaps	AGN
3) Deficit Reduc	AGN	7) Handgun Sales	FOR	11) Aid to Contras	FOR
4) Kill Plnt Clsng Notice	FOR	8) Ban D.C. Abort $	FOR	12) Nuclear Testing	AGN

Election Results

1988 general	Bob Stump (R)	174,453	(69%)	($319,690)
	Dave Moss (D)	72,417	(29%)	($26,281)
1988 primary	Bob Stump (R)	58,250	(100%)	
1986 general	Bob Stump (R)	146,462	(100%)	($135,636)

FOURTH DISTRICT

For eight months in 1987 the northbound lane of Pima Road in Scottsdale, Arizona was closed—not for repaving or laying utility pipes, but because of a dispute between local government and Indians, a late skirmish in the 350-year-old war between settlers and Natives. For Pima Road, running straight north and south, separates Scottsdale, one of Phoenix's most affluent suburbs, from the Salt River-Maricopa-Pima Reservation: on one side are condominiums and subdivisions and shopping centers with Western motifs, on the other is vacant land. When the city of Scottsdale paved the Indians' side of Pima Road, which they rented for $7,606 a year, without even asking, the Indians closed their half of the road. Eventually the state came in and raised the rent to $435,000; the Indians agreed to allow the Pima Freeway to be built entirely on their land, if they could build commercial development at interchanges.

Pima Road is, metaphorically at least, the spine of Arizona's 4th Congressional District, which takes in both the affluent neighborhoods in northeast Phoenix and its suburbs and the Indian reservations over the mountains in the far northeast corner of the state. In Phoenix and Scottsdale and Paradise Valley, in the shadow of and behind Camelback Mountain and Squaw Peak, the sunlight falls on the desert with a kind of hush; the careful landscaping of houses and condominiums contrasts with the buff stone of the mountains that punctuate Phoenix's plains and with the brown earth and vagrant cactus plants on the land that has been left undeveloped. Art galleries in shopping centers are full of Western paintings, but inside the houses you can find furniture of just about any period you want. The planting of such a comfortable and secure civilization in such an inhospitable environment—it seldom rains, but when it does anything near a usually dry creek bed can get washed away—is one of the generally unappreciated triumphs of American civilization.

The cultural conflict is matched by political differences. The Navajos have their own turbulent politics, in which Tribal Chairman Peter MacDonald, elected in 1978 and 1986 and defeated by Peterson Zah in 1982, was forced to step down in 1989 because of charges of kickbacks by contractors to his relatives; they have also been voting in increasing numbers, and heavily Democratic, in regular elections. The 4th District's portion of Phoenix and its suburbs is one of the most heavily Republican parts of the country. In between, the 4th hops northeast over the Mazatzal Mountains and the Sierra Ancha to pick up the copper mining towns of Globe and Miami; the Fort Apache Indian Reservation; the dusty Route 66 towns of Holbrook and Winslow, lined with gas stations; and the reservations to the north. This is mixed political terrain, with some Democratic patches. But 79% of the votes are on the Phoenix side of the mountains, and in most elections the 4th District is heavily Republican. There has been serious competition every time no incumbent has been running, and every time the Republican has won. The current congressman is Jon Kyl, son of a former Republican congressman from Iowa—the family's migration matching those of so many constituents—who first won in 1986. He had serious competition in the primary from onetime (1973–77) Congressman John Conlan, who evoked strong opposition not only for his fundamentalist religious beliefs but for what some thought was his untrustworthiness; Kyl, with support from Barry Goldwater and much of the Phoenix business establishment, won 60%–28%. In the general election developer Phil Davis might have given Conlan a tough race, but Kyl won with 65%.

At home Kyl was a lawyer specializing in water law, head of the Phoenix Chamber of Commerce, active in many Republican campaigns: a part of the local establishment. In Washington he is something of a bomb-thrower. On the House Armed Services Committee he emerged in his first term as one of the most active enthusiasts for the Strategic Defense Initiative, opposing the committee's efforts to scale it down and drop the space-based interceptor. At the same time he was one of those congressmen seeking a law to allow the closing down of unnecessary military bases. He has joined with firebrands like Robert Dornan to denounce Jim Wright's actions on Nicaragua. At the same time, he has not neglected local affairs. He was the first Republican House freshman in the 100th Congress to get a bill passed and signed into law, a measure letting the Payson School Board buy 60 acres of government property for a below-market $425,000. Kyl was reelected without difficulty in 1988 and seems to have a safe seat.

The People: Est. Pop. 1986: 670,400, up 23.3% 1980–86; Pop. 1980: 543,493, up 65.9% 1970–80. Households (1980): 76% family, 42% with children, 64% married couples; 27.6% housing units rented; median monthly rent: $267; median house value: $66,200. Voting age pop. (1980): 375,192; 12% American Indian, 4% Spanish origin, 1% Asian origin, 1% Black.

1988 Presidential Vote:

Bush (R)	....	167,264	(65%)
Dukakis (D)	....	88,773	(34%)

Rep. Jon Kyl (R)

Elected 1986; b. April 25, 1942, Oakland, NE; home, Phoenix; U. of AZ, B.A. 1964, LL.B. 1966; Presbyterian; married (Caryll).

Career: Practicing atty., 1966–86; Chmn., Metro. Phoenix Chamber of Commerce, 1985–86.

Offices: 313 CHOB 20515, 202-225-3361. Also 4250 E. Camelback Rd., Phoenix 85018, 602-840-1891.

Committees: *Armed Services* (16th of 21 R). Subcommittees: Research and Development; Investigations. *Government Operations* (8th of 15 R). Subcommittees: Legislation and National Security; Employment and Housing.

Group Ratings

	ADA	ACLU	COPE	CFA	LCV	ACU	NTLC	NSI	COC	CEI
1988	0	9	3	18	19	100	90	100	93	83
1987	0	—	0	7	—	96	—	—	93	86

National Journal Ratings

	1988 LIB — 1988 CONS		1987 LIB — 1987 CONS	
Economic	0%	— 93%	0%	— 89%
Social	0%	— 95%	0%	— 90%
Foreign	29%	— 70%	0%	— 80%

Key Votes

1) Homeless $	FOR	5) Ban Drug Test	FOR	9) SDI Research	FOR
2) Gephardt Amdt	AGN	6) Drug Death Pen	FOR	10) Ban Chem Weaps	AGN
3) Deficit Reduc	AGN	7) Handgun Sales	FOR	11) Aid to Contras	FOR
4) Kill Plnt Clsng Notice	FOR	8) Ban D.C. Abort $	FOR	12) Nuclear Testing	AGN

Election Results

1988 general	Jon Kyl (R)	206,248	(87%)	($316,476)
	Gary Sprunk (L)	30,430	(13%)	
1988 primary	Jon Kyl (R)	51,242	(100%)	
1986 general	Jon Kyl (R)	121,939	(65%)	($1,010,914)
	Philip R. Davis (D)	66,894	(35%)	($822,030)

FIFTH DISTRICT

Arizona's first frontier was in its southeast corner, in the little towns tucked into the valleys just north of the Mexican border. This was the first part of the state to be settled, and for many years the critical part—the site of most of Arizona's copper mines. Copper prices were in a slump for a decade until the late 1980s, and Arizona's mines have had to lay off workers because the market is swamped by lower-cost foreign production. But the pit mines outside Bisbee and Morenci, and the spirited little towns that grew up alongside them and nearby—Tombstone and Douglas, Clifton and even in its early days Tucson—are evidence of the importance of copper to Arizona.

Arizona's 5th Congressional District includes this copper country and, much more populous, the whole east side of the city of Tucson and its suburbs. A new district created after the 1980

Census was intended by the Republican legislature to be a Republican district. It includes the prosperous east side of Tucson and Green Valley to the south, fast-growing Sierra Vista around the Army's Fort Huachuca to the southeast, and a bunch of towns on the road from Tucson to Phoenix. In national politics it is Republican, but it was one of the nation's prime marginal districts in 1982 and 1984; only since 1986 has it been safely Republican.

That is a tribute to Congressman Jim Kolbe, the only Republican ever nominated in the 5th, who lost narrowly to Bisbee Democrat James McNulty in 1982 and then came back and beat him in 1984. Kolbe came to Congress with a reputation as a moderate in the Arizona legislature, spurring Arizona to finally enter the Medicaid program and moving forward ground-water legislation. He won the 5th District with a conservative appeal, campaigning against tax increases, championing the balanced-budget constitutional amendment, and urging a line-item veto.

He still straddles the lines between different kinds of conservatives. His voting record is among the most conservative in the House on economic issues, but mixed on cultural and foreign issues. He is pro-choice on abortion and was one of the Republican Members of Congress to call for the resignation of Governor Evan Mecham. He spoke out against bashing Mexico for not enforcing drug laws, and he thinks cutting the deficit is the nation's number one problem. He takes care to champion some local causes, as when he calls for minting a copper dollar. He won a seat on the Appropriations Committee in his second term, and has had no problems winning reelection in 1986 or 1988.

The People: Est. Pop. 1986: 604,800, up 11.4% 1980–86; Pop. 1980: 542,918, up 55.6% 1970–80. Households (1980): 75% family, 39% with children, 64% married couples; 30.8% housing units rented; median monthly rent: $216; median house value: $57,800. Voting age pop. (1980): 389,954; 14% Spanish origin, 2% Black, 1% Asian origin, 1% American Indian.

1988 Presidential Vote:

Bush (R)	137,081	(55%)
Dukakis (D)	107,920	(44%)

Rep. Jim Kolbe (R)

Elected 1984; b. June 28, 1942, Evanston, IL; home, Tucson; Northwestern U., B.A. 1965, Stanford U., M.B.A. 1967; United Methodist; married (Sarah).

Career: Navy, Vietnam; Asst. to IL Bldg. Authority Architect, 1970–72; Asst. to IL Gov. Ogilvie, 1972–73; Vice Pres., land planning firm; Real estate consultant; AZ Senate, 1977–82.

Offices: 410 CHOB 20515, 202-225-2542. Also 1661 N. Swan, Ste. 112, Tucson 85712, 602-322-3555; and 77 Calle Portal, Ste. B-160, Sierra Vista 85635, 602-459-3115.

Committees: *Appropriations* (21st of 22 R). Subcommittees: Commerce, Justice, State and Judiciary; Military Construction.

Group Ratings

	ADA	ACLU	COPE	CFA	LCV	ACU	NTLC	NSI	COC	CEI
1988	20	22	8	27	31	80	77	100	93	70
1987	8	—	6	21	—	87	—	—	93	73

National Journal Ratings

	1988 LIB	—	1988 CONS		1987 LIB	—	1987 CONS
Economic	0%	—	93%		0%	—	89%
Social	28%	—	71%		23%	—	76%
Foreign	24%	—	74%		25%	—	74%

Key Votes

1) Homeless $	FOR	5) Ban Drug Test	FOR	9) SDI Research	FOR
2) Gephardt Amdt	AGN	6) Drug Death Pen	FOR	10) Ban Chem Weaps	AGN
3) Deficit Reduc	AGN	7) Handgun Sales	FOR	11) Aid to Contras	FOR
4) Kill Plnt Clsng Notice	FOR	8) Ban D.C. Abort $	FOR	12) Nuclear Testing	AGN

Election Results

1988 general	Jim Kolbe (R)....................... 164,462	(68%)	($434,665)
	Judith E. Belcher (D)................. 78,115	(32%)	
1988 primary	Jim Kolbe (R)....................... 38,306	(78%)	
	Al Rodriquez (R) 5,094	(10%)	
	Walt Weber (R) 5,875	(12%)	
1986 general	Jim Kolbe (R)....................... 119,647	(65%)	($619,296)
	Joel Ireland (D)..................... 64,848	(35%)	($31,166)

ARKANSAS

You can see him in Bentonville, a town of 9,000 in the Ozarks, driving a 10-year-old Ford pickup with cages for his bird dogs in the back: Sam Walton, the Arkansan who, in an era of glitzy rich, is America's richest man. The Arkansas Sam Walton started out running dime stores in after World War II was one of the nation's poorest states. The cotton and rice lands of the Mississippi Delta and the hardscrabble hills west of Little Rock had some of the nation's lowest wages and education levels, and so many people were leaving that the state's population declined. But as national growth trickled down to Arkansas, Walton had the intuition that large discount stores in small towns could be immensely profitable, and in 1962 opened his first Wal-Mart 8 miles down the road in Rogers. In 10 years there were 16 Wal-Marts; by 1988 there were more than 1,000, with $12 billion in sales, and Walton's stock ("it's just paper") hovered between $6 to $8 billion. Wal-Mart's success gives a capsule economic history of Arkansas and the rural South and Southwest: after years of stagnation and outmigration, they started growing again in the early 1960s enough to support a downscale retail chain, and by the late 1980s their stronger economies and culturally conservative atmosphere were holding enough young people to make Wal-Mart prosper. Wal-Mart's secrets include friendliness to customers, tough dealing with vendors, ultra-quick distribution, and profit-sharing with its 215,000 employees. At the end of the 1980s the question before Arkansas is whether it can succeed as a state with that same mixture of high competence and country style.

It is a question posed more starkly in Arkansas than in other states. Arkansas begins with fewer resources: in area it's the smallest state between the Mississippi and the Pacific, in population it's the smallest state in the South; it is not blessed with any major industry or great resource. It is the land that was left over when Louisiana and Missouri were carved out of the Louisiana Purchase and what is now Oklahoma was fenced off as Indian Territory. Settled by poor farmers with large families, few slaves, and little cash, it has no Atlanta or Dallas or even

Memphis to be a focus of growth, and though its economy has grown more than the national average in 1940–80, it still hadn't caught up—and as the central core of the Mississippi Valley grew slowly in the 1980s, it fell a little further behind as the nation grew more rapidly.

To increase the state's chances for long-term growth, Governor Bill Clinton, first elected in 1978, has concentrated on trying to upgrade the state's education system, with mixed success. In 1983 he pushed through a reform package that included competency tests not only for new but for working teachers, a teacher pay raise, and a sales tax increase to pay for it. Salaries and achievement levels both rose abruptly, but teachers' groups vociferously opposed the tests, and the sales tax hike did not generate enough money to fulfill Clinton's promises. In 1987 the legislature twice turned down his tax package, to which his angry response was to set up a commission to write an ethics and disclosure bill—the unmistakable implication being that the legislators were bought off by business interests. In 1988 a special session of the legislature again declined to pass Clinton's tax program. As 1988 was ending, Clinton was preparing a bigger education program for 1989: teacher raises of $4,000, merit pay for teachers, more money for Arkansas universities, allowing parents to choose their children's schools, and scholarships and other programs to increase the number of Arkansas high school graduates going on to college. A commission of businessmen led by Sam Walton called for more school consolidations, tougher standards, higher salaries, and more pre-kindergarten programs. Clinton spent the fall of 1988 speaking around the state in favor of his package. But he deferred announcing his tax package until just before the legislature met in January 1989, and the fate of his proposals in that session will be a kind of verdict on his governorship—and a forecast of Arkansas's future. By April 1989, the tax package was soundly defeated by the legislature and Clinton was preparing to once again tour the state with a restructured package.

Clinton wants a higher-skill, higher-wage economy and hopes that higher taxes won't deter investment. With Mississippi's Ray Mabus and Louisiana's Buddy Roemer, Clinton formed a Middle South initiative to attract foreign investment to the Delta lowlands 100 miles on either side of the river. But much of Arkansas's recent growth, especially the retirement boom in the hill country of northern and northwestern Arkansas, builds a constituency that is against increased spending and not much interested in the state's economic future.

Politically, the struggle pits various Democrats against each other. Governor Orval Faubus made Little Rock internationally infamous by provoking a desegregation crisis in 1957; Republican Winthrop Rockefeller replaced him in 1966 and freed the state and the Democrats from segregationist demagoguery and opened the way for a series of new-style Democratic governors—Dale Bumpers, David Pryor, and Clinton. This is perhaps the most safely Democratic of southern states. The Democrats have won most major offices here and by solid margins. It was a target state in 1988 general election for Michael Dukakis, and he got 42% of the two-party vote—winning about as many votes as Walter Mondale, while George Bush ran behind the 1984 Reagan total.

Governor. Bill Clinton, the nation's youngest governor (32) when he was first elected in 1978, is clearly the dominant figure in Arkansas politics, and played a role in 1988 presidential politics. A graduate of Yale Law, a Rhodes Scholar, with a wife who is a lawyer, he was touted quickly for national office. Then he was defeated in 1980 because of local issues—the influx of Cuban refugees at Fort Chaffee (which also cost Jimmy Carter the state) and a rise in license tag fees. By 1982 he seemed more Arkansas: he sported a shorter haircut, his wife started calling herself Hillary Clinton instead of using her maiden name, and he turned down a national platform by declining to run for Democratic national chairman. The combination helped him regain the governorship that year.

Clinton is a good speaker who can rouse Arkansas audiences with both country phrases and inspiring rhetoric, and he speaks often around the state. His skills led many to expect a great speech when he was named the sole nominator of Michael Dukakis in Atlanta. Instead Clinton

ARKANSAS — Congressional Districts, Counties, and Selected Places — *(4 Districts)*

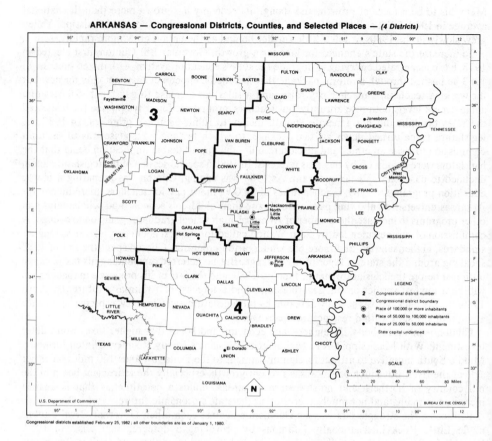

droned on to an inattentive audience and insisted on completing an overlong text to a crowd that just wanted to yell; perhaps he was trying to tone himself down for television. Delegates cheered when Clinton said "In conclusion" and Boston's Billy Bulger told a reporter, "I was a young man when he started." But Clinton gamely turned a disaster into an asset, appearing days later on the "Johnny Carson Show" with some appealing self-deprecating lines, and his standing in Arkansas and national politics seems not to have been diminished. Perhaps he, like George Bush and Dan Quayle, has established usefully low expectations which should be easy to exceed.

Clinton's future depends on whether he can follow up on the success of his 1983 education program and his 1985 jobs program (which focused on upgrading the Arkansas work force) with success on his 1989 education-and-tax package (a higher sales tax, lower taxes on low-incomes and a day care deduction, $200 million more for education) which has already been defeated once by the legislature, though Clinton is sure to try it again. He has said he won't run against Senators David Pryor or Dale Bumpers, who are up in 1990 and 1992, and there is no plausible rationale for him to challenge either of these two likeminded Democrats; he might well run if either retires. Clinton nearly made the 1988 Presidential race, but in July 1987 he decided, after coming to the brink of a candidacy, not to run; it would be too great a strain, he said, on his 7-year-old daughter. Also, with Albert Gore in the race, he was not the sole southerner, making the chances of a Super Tuesday sweep far less likely. He remains a presidential possibility for 1992, more seasoned than when he started out, no longer the first baby boomer national candidate (Quayle and Gore are both younger), widely acceptable, though without a record on national issues.

If Clinton runs for reelection as governor in 1990, he will be the clear favorite. If he doesn't, a gaggle of Democrats—and maybe a serious Republican—will run. Possibilities include Attorney General Steve Clark, Lieutenant Governor Winston Bryant, young state legislator David Matthews, and University of Arkansas President Ray Thornton, a former congressman who is the nephew of Jack and Witt Stephens, the brothers who run a major investment banking operation out of Little Rock and with a fortune of $1 billion are, after Sam Walton, the state's richest men.

Senators. For many years Arkansas has been represented by pairs of senators with contrasting views and temperaments. For 30 years they were John McClellan, a dour conservative and father of the Arkansas River navigation project, and William Fulbright, a quizzical foreign policy expert and skeptic about the Vietnam war. For more than 10 years now the senators have been Dale Bumpers and David Pryor, both from small towns, both having served two terms as governor, both with pro-civil rights records—but each with different stands on issues and different areas of interest.

Dale Bumpers sprang from a small town law practice straight to the governorship and then on to the Senate; there remains much of the small town trial lawyer in him. He is pleasant, fluent, and can speak the language of ordinary people and reduce complicated arguments to simple statements no one could disagree with. But he is also the town iconoclast, with his own idiosyncratic, often unpopular ideas, who nonetheless remains respected and even loved by his peers. The Dale Bumpers who served on a committee that quietly integrated the schools in Charleston, Arkansas, is the same Dale Bumpers who made integration the official policy of the state of Arkansas and who as senator has spoken out loudly against anti-busing amendments. Bumpers was raised a Franklin Roosevelt liberal Democrat; growing up in the 1930s he saw FDR's federal government as the one institution working for the common man. Today he is the southern senator who votes most often with northern Democrats—and the favorite of some for president—but he also has shown a streak of independence and is not a reliable member of any bloc.

As a result he has been a feisty and challenging senator, but not always a successful one. He has not ascended to any major committee positions. He chairs Small Business, the least important of the Senate's standing committees; he has proposed a secondary market for SBA loans and has decried abuses of minority set-aside programs, but the fact is that the SBA hasn't done much more than avoid being zeroed out. He has not stamped his name on any piece of major legislation, although he has taken some interesting stands: he held hearings in 1975 on the danger of aerosol cans to the ozone layer and in 1988 was urging that something be done about global warming and the greenhouse effect; he is one of the Senate's leaders in trying to keep in force the limits of the SALT II treaty even after its expiration date; and he has promoted child immunization programs. In 1988 he made a great to-do about setting up a national commission to plot a course of economic development for on the problems of the impoverished Mississippi Delta counties in Arkansas and other states; but he did not have ready any solutions.

Bumpers has not hesitated to take on losing fights. He battled against decontrol of oil and gas prices from his position on the Senate Energy Committee just behind Louisiana's pro-decontrol Bennett Johnston. He was one of the three senators (Bradley and Hollings were the others) who voted for the 1981 Reagan budget cuts and against the 1981 tax cuts—a set of positions which, if adopted, would have just about eliminated the 1980s deficits. Despite his liberal economic views, he has supported across-the-board budget freezes for half a dozen years and cast a critical vote killing the AFL-CIO's labor law reform bill in the Carter years—for which labor leaders had not forgiven him in 1983 when he was thinking about running for President. He has caustically opposed amending the Constitution to prevent abortions or allow school prayer, and has practically dared opponents to come into Arkansas and fight him on these proposed amendments.

His relish for electoral fights waxes and wanes. In 1980 he was caught a little unawares by the reaction against putting Cuban refugees in Fort Chaffee and was reelected with 59% of the vote—low for him. In 1986, against former U.S. Attorney Asa Hutchinson, an articulate fundamentalist who won fame for leading a raid of a white supremacist group, Bumpers campaigned hard and won solidly. He is expected to run and win easily when his seat comes up in 1992. But he will be 67 then and his days of being mentioned as a Presidential candidate are probably over. He has bowed out twice now, in December 1983 and March 1987, partly because he didn't relish the grueling process and partly because he feared "a total disruption of the closeness my family has cherished."

David Pryor first came to Washington more than 20 years ago and is one of the few Members of Congress to witness—and in his own way reflect—the transition from Lyndon Johnson's Great Society to George Bush's kinder, gentler nation. He was a small town lawyer for only two years before being elected to Congress in 1966, at age 32, from the state's southern district, and made a name for himself as one of the most liberal of southern representatives. At a time when most southerners were segregationists, he voted for civil rights bills and against seating the Mississippi delegation at the 1968 Democratic National Convention, and, at a time when junior members were seldom heard from, held informal hearings in a trailer on nursing home care. But in the Senate in the 1980s, while he has had a more liberal record than most southerners, he has also shown a skepticism toward some aspects of big government, and he won reelection on the slogan "Arkansas comes first."

The transition came in the 1970s. In 1972 he nearly beat 76-year-old Senator John McClellan, leading him in the first primary and losing in the runoff only after McClellan attacked him as labor's candidate. In 1974 he was easily elected governor, and found himself at the head of a state government less in need of reform than of penny-pinching. He won a tough three-candidate primary-and-runoff fight for the Senate in 1978, a year when many of the trends that worked for Republicans nationally in 1980 were already apparent. The Washington he left in 1972 was dominated by liberals who were increasing public spending and even proposing guaranteed annual incomes. The Washington he returned to in 1979 was tightening up on the budget, lowering tax rates, and pondering Soviet and terrorist advances around the world. So in the Senate he has been both more cautious and somewhat more conservative than his House record would suggest.

He has made some waves, however. One of his foremost causes has been to oppose production of nerve gas and the Bigeye nerve gas bomb, even though the Army's main nerve gas facility, the Pine Bluff Arsenal, is in Arkansas. But the other side, arguing that deteriorating U.S. stocks must be replenished to provide some deterrence, has usually prevailed, twice by votes cast by Vice President Bush. Pryor has been one of the senators attacking Pentagon procurement methods, though without winning a big victory. He has crusaded against what he considers "abuses of power" by the Internal Revenue Service, and has sought to require the IRS to pay attorney's fees in cases it loses when it can't show its action was substantially justified. He played some part, but did not take the lead, in the Finance Committee on the 1986 tax reform bill. He has, not surprisingly, championed cotton and rice growers. His greatest success in the Senate so far was getting elected Secretary of the Democratic Conference after the 1988 elections. He was helped when southerners lost races for majority leader and whip, and it remains to be seen how important this position will be. He now also chairs the Senate Aging Committee.

Against as strong a Senate candidate as Arkansas Republicans have ever run, Little Rock area Congressman Ed Bethune, Pryor won reelection with a solid 57% in 1984; he stressed local and farm issues. This was a classic example of how Republicans in the Reagan era were not able to capitalize on the national Democratic record of a southern senator. Pryor is up again in 1990, and the question is whether Arkansas Republicans (Bethune was been party state chairman, but recently moved to Washington, D.C.) will make a serious effort to defeat him, and if so on what grounds.

Presidential politics. Arkansas is a good litmus test for the Democrats: if their national ticket can't win here, it's not likely to win any electoral votes in the South—or to win the election. Jimmy Carter carried the state easily in 1976 and would have again in 1980 but for the furor over the housing of Cuban refugees in Fort Chaffee. Walter Mondale and Michael Dukakis, despite initial hopes, lagged well behind.

In the 1970s almost everyone ignored Arkansas's presidential primary late in the season; its caucus in 1984 was ignored too; in 1987 it voted to join southern Super Tuesday, and was mostly ignored again, as it went for the southern favorites, Albert Gore and George Bush. Arkansas might get a moment in the spotlight if it joins the other Mississippi Valley states and holds a regional primary on a single day. Republican primary turnout, though up, is still the lowest in the South.

Congressional districting. Arkansas's lines have been unchanged since 1982 and little changed since 1962, when the delegation was reduced from six to four seats.

The People: Est. Pop. 1988: 2,422,000; Pop. 1980: 2,286,435, up 5.9% 1980–88 and 18.9% 1970–1980; 0.98% of U.S. total, 33d largest. 11% with 1–3 yrs. col., 10% with 4+ yrs. col.; 19.0% below poverty level. Single ancestry: 18% English, 6% Irish, 4% German, 1% French. Households (1980): 77% family, 41% with children, 65% married couples; 29.5% housing units rented; median monthly rent: $129; median house value: $31,100. Voting age pop. (1980): 1,615,061; 14% Black, 1% Spanish origin. Registered voters (1988): 1,203,016; no party registration.

1988 Share of Federal Tax Burden: $5,852,000,000; 0.66% of U.S. total, 32d largest.

1988 Share of Federal Expenditures

	Total		Non-Defense		Defense	
Total Expend	$7,485m	(0.85%)	$6,142m	(0.94%)	$1,436m	(0.63%)
St/Lcl Grants	1,011m	(0.88%)	1,009m	(0.88%)	2m	(2.08%)
Salary/Wages	822m	(0.61%)	457m	(0.68%)	365m	(0.68%)
Pymnts to Indiv	4,406m	(1.08%)	4,173m	(1.07%)	234m	(1.25%)
Procurement	835m	(0.44%)	93m	(0.20%)	835m	(0.44%)
Research/Other	411m	(1.10%)	410m	(1.11%)	0m	(1.11%)

Political Lineup: Governor, Bill Clinton (D); Lt. Gov., Winston Bryant (D); Secy. of State, Bill McCuen (D); Atty. Gen., Steve Clark (D); Treasurer, Jimmie Lou Fisher (D); Auditor, Julia Hughes Jones (D). State Senate, 35 (31 D and 4 R); State House of Representatives, 100 (88 D and 11 R and 1 I). Senators, Dale Bumpers (D) and David Pryor (D). Representatives, 4 (3 D and 1 R).

1988 Presidential Vote

Bush (R)	466,578	(56%)
Dukakis (D).	349,237	(42%)

1984 Presidential Vote

Reagan (R)	534,774	(60%)
Mondale (D)	338,646	(38%)

1988 Democratic Presidential Primary

Gore.	185,758	(37%)
Dukakis	94,103	(19%)
Jackson	85,003	(17%)
Gephardt..................	59,711	(12%)
Hart......................	18,630	(4%)
Simon	9,020	(2%)
Babbitt	2,614	(1%)
Uncommitted	35,553	(7%)

1988 Republican Presidential Primary

Bush	32,114	(47%)
Dole......................	17,667	(26%)
Robertson	12,918	(19%)
Kemp.....................	3,499	(5%)

GOVERNOR
Gov. Bill Clinton (D)

Elected 1982, term expires Jan. 1991; b. Aug. 19, 1946, Hope; home, Little Rock; Georgetown U., B.S.F.S. 1968, Rhodes Scholar, Oxford U., 1968–70, Yale U., J.D. 1973; Baptist; married (Hillary).

Career: Prof., U. of AR, 1974–76; Dem. Nominee for U.S. House of Reps., 1974; AR Atty. Gen., 1976–78; Gov. of AR, 1978–80; Practicing atty., 1981–82.

Office: State Capitol, Little Rock 72201, 501-682-2345.

Election Results

1986 gen.	Bill Clinton (D)	439,851	(64%)
	Frank White (R)	248,415	(36%)
1986 prim.	Bill Clinton (D)	315,397	(61%)
	Orval E. Faubus (D).........	174,402	(33%)
	W. Dean Goldsby (D)........	30,829	(6%)
1984 gen.	Bill Clinton (D)	554,561	(63%)
	Woody Freeman (R).........	331,987	(37%)

SENATORS
Sen. Dale Bumpers (D)

Elected 1974, seat up 1992; b. Aug. 12, 1925, Charleston; home, Charleston; U. of AR, Northwestern U., LL.B. 1951; Methodist; married (Betty).

Career: USMC, WWII; Practicing atty., 1951–70; Gov. of AR, 1970–74.

Offices: 229 DSOB 20510, 202-224-4843. Also 2527 Fed. Bldg., 700 W. Capitol, Little Rock 72201, 501-378-6286.

Committees: *Appropriations* (9th of 16 D). Subcommittees: Agriculture and Related Agencies; Commerce, Justice, State, and Judiciary; Defense; Interior; Labor, Health and Human Services, Education. *Energy and Natural Resources* (2d of 10 D). Subcommittees: Energy Research and Development; Mineral Resources Development and Production; Public Lands, National Parks and Forests (Chairman). *Small Business* (Chairman of 10 D). Subcommittees: Export and Expansion; Rural Economy and Family Farming.

Group Ratings

	ADA	ACLU	COPE	CFA	LCV	ACU	NTLC	NSI	COC	CEI
1988	80	62	66	91	40	12	16	0	33	16
1987	85	—	65	50	—	8	—	—	35	18

National Journal Ratings

	1988 LIB	—	1988 CONS	1987 LIB	—	1987 CONS
Economic	57%	—	40%	51%	—	45%
Social	73%	—	26%	78%	—	17%
Foreign	76%	—	23%	61%	—	36%

Key Votes

1) Cut Aged Housing $	FOR	5) Bork Nomination	AGN	9) SDI Funding	AGN
2) Override Hwy Veto	FOR	6) Ban Plastic Guns	AGN	10) Ban Chem Weaps	FOR
3) Kill Plnt Clsng Notice	FOR	7) Deny Abortions	AGN	11) Aid To Contras	AGN
4) Min Wage Increase	FOR	8) Japanese Reparations	FOR	12) Reagan Defense $	AGN

Election Results

1986 general	Dale Bumpers (D)...................	433,092	(62%)	($1,672,432)
	Asa Hutchinson (R)	262,300	(38%)	($939,342)
1986 primary	Dale Bumpers (D), unopposed			
1980 general	Dale Bumpers (D)...................	477,905	(59%)	($220,861)
	Bill Clark (R)	330,576	(41%)	($119,196)

Sen. David Pryor (D)

Elected 1978, seat up 1990; b. Aug. 29, 1934, Camden; home, Little Rock; U. of AR, B.A. 1957, LL.B. 1964; Presbyterian; married (Barbara).

Career: Ed. and Publ., *Ouachita Citizen*, Camden, 1957–61; AR House of Reps., 1960–66; Practicing atty., 1964–66; U.S. House of Reps., 1967–72; Cand. for Dem. Nomination for U.S. Senate, 1972; Gov. of AR, 1975–79.

Office: 267 RSOB 20510, 202-224-2353. Also 3030 Fed. Bldg., Little Rock 72201, 501-378-6336.

Committees: *Agriculture, Nutrition, and Forestry* (2d of 10 D). Subcommittees: Agricultural Production and Stabilization of Prices (Chairman); Domestic and Foreign Marketing and Product Promotion; Rural Development and Rural Electrification; Nutrition and Investigations. *Finance* (8th of 11 D). Subcommittees: Medicare and Long-Term Care; Private Retirement and Internal Revenue Service (Chairman); Taxation and Debt Management. *Governmental Affairs* (5th of 8 D). Subcommittees: Federal Services, Post Office and Civil Service (Chairman); Government Management; Investigations. *Select Committee on Ethics* (2d of 3 D). *Special Committee on Aging* (Chairman of 10 D).

Group Ratings

	ADA	ACLU	COPE	CFA	LCV	ACU	NTLC	NSI	COC	CEI
1988	75	56	60	92	30	16	12	10	43	19
1987	75	—	59	50	—	15	—	—	47	24

National Journal Ratings

	1988 LIB — 1988 CONS			1987 LIB — 1987 CONS		
Economic	65%	—	30%	51%	—	45%
Social	62%	—	37%	65%	—	34%
Foreign	70%	—	25%	69%	—	27%

Key Votes

1) Cut Aged Housing $	FOR	5) Bork Nomination	AGN	9) SDI Funding	AGN
2) Override Hwy Veto	FOR	6) Ban Plastic Guns	AGN	10) Ban Chem Weaps	AGN
3) Kill Plnt Clsng Notice	FOR	7) Deny Abortions	AGN	11) Aid To Contras	AGN
4) Min Wage Increase	FOR	8) Japanese Reparations	FOR	12) Reagan Defense $	AGN

Election Results

1984 general	David Pryor (D)	502,341	(57%)	($1,838,352)
	Ed Bethune (R)	373,615	(43%)	($1,072,879)
1984 primary	David Pryor (D), unopposed			
1978 general	David Pryor (D)	395,506	(77%)	($774,824)
	Thomas Kelly, Jr. (R)	84,308	(16%)	($16,208)
	John G. Black (I)	37,211	(7%)	($32,863)

FIRST DISTRICT

In the 1900s and 1910s Arkansas's Mississippi Delta was one of the fast-growing parts of the country, as big landowners drained flat marshlands and, capitalizing on the low-wage economy of the South, brought in poor blacks to tend the cotton and rice and ultimately soybeans. They created successful farm operations and a local population as poor as any in the nation. Around 1940 the Delta began to change, slowly: national minimum wage legislation drew young people out of the Delta and mechanization forced some off the farms. But this land—stretching flat as far as the eye can see past rows of telephone poles and ribbons of asphalt in the shimmering heat—remains poor by national standards and the people undereducated and underemployed.

The Delta forms part of Arkansas's 1st Congressional District; the rest is in the green hill country that begins to rise north of Little Rock and in the cool green Ozarks farther west. The Delta started off heavily Democratic, while some of the hill counties are ancestrally Republican. That changed as partisan preferences oscillated wildly just after the civil rights revolution, but they have returned to the historical norm in the late 1980s: the Delta counties, with their heavy black vote, went for Michael Dukakis in 1988, while the upcountry counties went for George Bush.

The 1st District's congressman, Bill Alexander, has returned to historic norm himself: after a decade as a national Democratic leader, he has, as 1st District congressmen traditionally had, concentrated on local issues and propping up the local economy. First elected in 1968 when he was just 34, Alexander was chosen by Speaker Tip O'Neill and Majority Leader Jim Wright in 1976, when still only a junior member of the Appropriations Committee, to be a deputy whip; in 1980, after Whip John Brademas was defeated, Alexander was picked by O'Neill and Wright to the number four leadership position of chief deputy whip (an appointive post, which became elective in 1982). Though he deviated from party positions occasionally, he became an impassioned opponent of aid to the Nicaraguan contras and spent much time on Latin American affairs. After O'Neill announced that he would retire in 1986, Alexander hoped to move up and succeed Thomas Foley as whip.

But he was short on votes and made a bad mistake. In August 1985, he requisitioned an Air Force plane for a trip to Brazil for what he said would be a delegation of five lawmakers; but he was the only member aboard, and it's not clear that any of the others were ever interested in going. Republicans filmed the almost-empty airliner as it returned to Washington on its $50,000 trip. O'Neill criticized him, and others recalled a 1985 *Wall Street Journal* story depicting him holding an African spear and saying "boogaloo" when a lobbyist came to his office. Alexander said he'd said "Jambo," the Swahili word for hello, but Republicans started calling him "Boogaloo Bill" anyway. He argued that he is a genuine expert on Brazil and gasohol and that his trip had been useful and issued a single-spaced 15-page report on it. All plausible points, perhaps. But nothing is more damaging for a politician than to look ridiculous.

He was hurt worst back home, where Republicans asked 1st District voters to fill out a questionnaire on Alexander's travels and expenses and become eligible for a prize of free air fare for anywhere in the world and where he was receiving spirited primary opposition from conservative Democratic state Senator Jim Wood. "While eastern Arkansas suffered through record high unemployment and recession," a Wood ad said, Alexander "took 19 foreign trips." Wood won 48% of the vote in the May primary, and in early July Alexander left the whip race, saying "the people of the 1st District have sent me a message to work in a different direction. And believe me, I got it loud and clear." He was "no longer a national Democrat, I am an Arkansas Democrat." That may have helped his local standing, and the Republicans, who did so much to raise the junketeering issue against him, had an inexperienced 27-year-old candidate who ended up with barely more than one-third of the vote.

In 1987 and 1988 Alexander still spent some time promoting trade with Latin America, but mainly as a market for Arkansas's agricultural products (he wants to sell rice to Cuba), and denouncing Panama's Manuel Noriega; he remains a promoter of gasohol (he'd like to see an ethanol plant built in the 1st District). He used his seat on Appropriations to channel some money locally and got around the district frequently. When Darrell Glascock, a campaign consultant who had worked for Alexander's Republican opponents (and for 2d District Democrat Tommy Robinson), filed to run in the Democratic primary, local Democrats shrewdly barred him from the ballot and tied him up in a lawsuit for a month; Glascock finally got on the ballot but Alexander won 67%–33%—and had no general election opponent. Alexander was unshrewd enough to say in September 1988 that he'd like to be majority whip. In late April 1989, Alexander filed a complaint with the ethics committee against newly elected Republican Whip Newt Gingrich. As long as Alexander remembers to tend to the needs of the 1st District he seems likely to have a safe seat in a district that, after all, nearly went for Dukakis over Bush.

The People: Est. Pop. 1986: 574,500, up 0.2% 1980–1986; Pop. 1980: 573,551, up 9.5% 1970–80. Households (1980): 78% family, 43% with children, 65% married couples; 32.3% housing units rented; median monthly rent: $99; median house value: $28,000. Voting age pop. (1980): 396,107; 16% Black, 1% Spanish origin.

1988 Presidential Vote:

Bush (R)	95,388	(51%)
Dukakis (D)	89,812	(48%)

Rep. Bill Alexander (D)

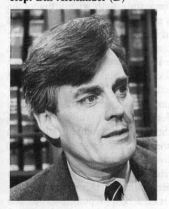

Elected 1968; b. Jan 16, 1934, Memphis, TN; home, Osceola; U. of AR, Southwestern U., B.A. 1957, Vanderbilt U., LL.B. 1960; Episcopalian; divorced.

Career: Army, 1951–53; Law clerk, Fed. Judge Marion Boyd, Memphis, TN, 1960–61; Practicing atty., 1961–68.

Offices: 233 CHOB 20515, 202-225-4076. Also Fed. Bldg., Rm. 211-A, 615 S. Main St., Jonesboro 72401, 501-972-4600; County Cthse. Rm. 3, Forrest City 72335, 501-633-5226; and Fed. Bldg. Rm. 202, Batesville 72501, 501-698-1761.

Committees: *Appropriations* (8th of 35 D). Subcommittees: Commerce, Justice, State, and Judiciary; Military Construction; Treasury, Postal Service and General Government.

Group Ratings

	ADA	ACLU	COPE	CFA	LCV	ACU	NTLC	NSI	COC	CEI
1988	80	82	70	73	44	5	6	44	17	11
1987	68	—	69	71	—	0	—	—	13	8

National Journal Ratings

	1988 LIB — 1988 CONS			1987 LIB — 1987 CONS		
Economic	87%	—	8%	62%	—	35%
Social	70%	—	28%	65%	—	35%
Foreign	64%	—	34%	58%	—	42%

Key Votes

1) Homeless $	FOR	5) Ban Drug Test	AGN	9) SDI Research	AGN
2) Gephardt Amdt	FOR	6) Drug Death Pen	—	10) Ban Chem Weaps	AGN
3) Deficit Reduc	FOR	7) Handgun Sales	FOR	11) Aid to Contras	AGN
4) Kill Plnt Clsng Notice	AGN	8) Ban D.C. Abort $	FOR	12) Nuclear Testing	FOR

Election Results

1988 general	Bill Alexander (D), unopposed			($640,427)
1988 primary	Bill Alexander (D)	94,978	(67%)	
	Darrell Glascock (D).................	46,974	(33%)	
1986 general	Bill Alexander (D)	105,733	(64%)	($703,571)
	Rick Albin (R)	58,937	(36%)	($52,708)

SECOND DISTRICT

Little Rock is the center of Arkansas, geographically and to an even greater extent politically. It sets the tone of the public life of its state as do only a few other state capitals—Boston, Providence, Atlanta, Denver, Honolulu. Little Rock has the state's dominant newspaper, the Democratic *Arkansas Gazette*, and its pesky conservative competitor, *The Arkansas Democrat*. Its television stations reach nearly to the state's boundaries. It has the state government and is the home of the Stephens brothers, two of the nation's richest investment bankers who are politically involved with both parties. Little Rock made for a time an international name for itself forcibly resisting integration of Central High School in 1957; President Eisenhower had to send in federal troops when Governor Orval Faubus refused to enforce a court order. But electorally Little Rock has usually been a progressive force in a state with widely divergent political tendencies. It is not a Republican bastion like some southern cities, and its affluent whites are only beginning to be numerous enough to spread out into the countryside and vastly outnumber the central city blacks.

The 2d Congressional District of Arkansas includes Little Rock, with its large black and affluent white neighborhoods, and North Little Rock, a kind of industrial suburb across the Arkansas River known informally for years as Dog Town, because at the turn of the century Little Rock officials, peeved that North Little Rock was allowed to incorporate separately, dumped all their stray dogs there. The 2d also includes several hill counties to the north and, in the southeast, part of the flat, cotton, rice, and soybean-growing Mississippi plain. It supported Republican Governor Winthrop Rockefeller and his three Democratic successors, Dale Bumpers, David Pryor, and Bill Clinton, and has elected progressive candidates at about every level.

In exception are the last three elections to the House of Representatives, to which it has elected one of the loudest and least predictable of members, nominal Democrat Tommy Robinson. He got his start in public life as a policeman and, with a boost from Governor Bill Clinton, became sheriff of Pulaski County, in which capacity he was quoted as claiming to feed black prisoners "watermelon and chicken." Over television, which has effectively replaced person-to-person campaigning in the Little Rock market, Robinson established himself as a tough-talking good old boy who said what he thought. That reputation, plus an awful lot of money, enabled him to upset Secretary of State Paul Riviere in the 1984 Democratic primary and then to beat Republican Judy Petty (who got national publicity in 1974 when she opposed the then scandal-tarred congressman, Wilbur Mills) narrowly in the general, while a liberal Independent got 11% of the vote.

The money part is troubling. In 1984 he spent over $911,000 in the primary, runoff, and general election races, and spent $441,000 of his own money, all borrowed, to do it. By fall 1986 he had raised $635,000, including $243,000 from political action committees, and spent nearly $500,000 of it to retire his 1984 debt. Loaning a candidate money without commercial collateral is an illegal campaign contribution, and the Federal Election Commission did find violations in Robinson's financing. The FEC did not, however, take any serious enforcement action. So Robinson won his seat with large subventions from a few sources, repaying them eventually with money raised from PACs and Washington political operators—not a pretty picture for a would-be populist.

In Washington Robinson has played on several sides of the street. Jim Wright and Bill Alexander made him part of the whip organization and helped him get a seat on the Armed Services Committee, where he has stoutly supported defense programs they have worked against; his 1984 campaign manager and continuing ally, Darrell Glascock, ran against Alexander in the 1988 primary, and in the fall Robinson taped a radio spot praising Illinois Republican Jack Davis's anti-drug efforts (Davis was beaten by Democrat George Sangmeister anyway). That cost him a seat on Education and Labor. Robinson is an enthusiastic backer of contra aid (he visited the contras in Nicaragua in 1988) and of the MX missile (he told an Arkansas woman who presented him with anti-MX letters to "stick 'em where the sun don't shine"). But he also supported the military base-closing bill (which threatens the Air Force base in Blytheville in Alexander's district) and voted for Jesse Jackson at the 1988 Democratic national convention ("Jackson touched my soul, he pricked my conscience"). He questioned the dispatch of U.S. vessels to the Persian Gulf and made a point of opposing Judge Bork (because a Bork decision upheld imposing the cost of Mississippi's Grand Gulf nuclear plant on Arkansas ratepayers). Robinson has also come under attack for hiring as his administrative assistant the 22-year-old daughter of a major campaign contributor and paying her $60,000 a year without any previous Capitol Hill experience.

Robinson has no particular influence in the House beyond his one often unpredictable vote. But he may have a political future in Arkansas. He had no trouble winning reelection in 1986 or 1988; his 1988 Republican opponent was a man who believed that his North Little Rock trailer was under a radiation attack as part of a conspiracy that extended to President Reagan. Arkansas political observers wonder whether, if Bill Clinton retires in 1990, Robinson will run for governor. He says he will only if there are no other good candidates and adds, "I just don't have the temperament right now to deal with some of the state legislators I'd have to deal with." But that's not a definite no, and anyway Robinson can always change his mind. He is thought to have great appeal in rural counties beyond the 2d District, but it's not clear how that appeal will hold up under sustained scrutiny.

The People: Est. Pop. 1986: 603,600, up 6.1% 1980–1986; Pop. 1980: 569,116, up 24.5% 1970–80. Households (1980): 75% family, 43% with children, 63% married couples; 32.4% housing units rented; median monthly rent: $160; median house value: $37,300. Voting age pop. (1980): 401,104; 15% Black, 1% Spanish origin.

1988 Presidential Vote:

Bush (R)	121,130	(56%)
Dukakis (D)	91,705	(43%)

Rep. Tommy F. Robinson (D)

Elected 1984; b. Mar. 7, 1942, Little Rock; home, Jacksonville; U. of AR at Fayetteville, U. of AR at Little Rock, B.A. 1976; United Methodist; married (Carolyn).

Career: AR St. Police Dept., 1966–68; N. Little Rock Police Dept., 1968–71; U.S. Marshall Srvc., 1971–74; Dir., Public Safety, U. of AR Med. Sciences, Asst. Dir., Public Safety, U. of AR at Fayetteville, 1974–75; Police chief, Jacksonville, 1975–79; AR Dir. of Public Safety, 1979–80; Sheriff, Pulaski Cnty., 1980–84.

Offices: 1541 LHOB 20515, 202-225-2506. Also 1527 Fed. Bldg., 700 W. Capitol, Little Rock 72201, 501-378-5941; 411 N. Spruce St., Searcy 72143, 501-268-4287; and P.O. Box 431, Lonoke Cnty. Crthse., Lonoke 72086, 501-676-6403.

Committees: *Armed Services* (22d of 31 D). Subcommittees: Military Installations and Facilities; Military Personnel and Compensation. *Veterans' Affairs* (9th of 20 D). Subcommittees: Education, Training and Employment; Hospitals and Health Care. *Select Committee On Aging* (28th of 39 D). Subcommittee: Human Services.

Group Ratings

	ADA	ACLU	COPE	CFA	LCV	ACU	NTLC	NSI	COC	CEI
1988	55	70	78	91	50	52	50	100	50	28
1987	52	—	76	50	—	48	—	—	60	32

National Journal Ratings

	1988 LIB — 1988 CONS		1987 LIB — 1987 CONS	
Economic	53%	— 46%	46%	— 52%
Social	46%	— 53%	45%	— 54%
Foreign	38%	— 61%	20%	— 76%

Key Votes

1) Homeless $	FOR	5) Ban Drug Test	AGN	9) SDI Research	FOR
2) Gephardt Amdt	AGN	6) Drug Death Pen	FOR	10) Ban Chem Weaps	AGN
3) Deficit Reduc	AGN	7) Handgun Sales	FOR	11) Aid to Contras	FOR
4) Kill Plnt Clsng Notice	AGN	8) Ban D.C. Abort $	FOR	12) Nuclear Testing	AGN

Election Results

1988 general	Tommy F. Robinson (D)	168,889	(83%)	($459,876)
	Warren Carpenter (R).................	33,475	(17%)	($11,098)
1988 primary	Tommy F. Robinson (D), unopposed			
1986 general	Tommy F. Robinson (D)	128,814	(76%)	($740,921)
	Keith Hamaker (R)...................	11,244	(24%)	($81,863)

THIRD DISTRICT

The Ozarks, green mountains spotted with farmhouses and little towns in northwest Arkansas, have been one of the growth areas in middle America for the last two decades. For long years this was one of the poorest parts of the country, peopled by descendants of original settlers who spoke in old-style dialect and scratched out bare livings from the thin soil of the hills; for better education and decent opportunities young people went elsewhere. But since the mid-1960s the Ozarks' mild climate, scenic mountains, and recreational reservoirs have attracted retirees from big cities and other parts of the Midwest and South, and its low-keyed, tradition-minded lifestyle has attracted or held some younger families. The economy is not rich, but there are signs of vibrancy, from the Bentonville headquarters of Sam Walton, whose Wal-Mart chain has made him America's richest man, to the Springdale home of the Tyson poultry empire. Fort Smith, on the Oklahoma border, and Fayetteville, farther north and the home of the University of Arkansas, are growing comfortably, and prosperity—and, some think, too many people—are spreading over the hills.

The 3d Congressional District covers most of Arkansas's Ozarks and spreads to the east and south. Since the Civil War the hills have harbored many Republicans, and this is the most solidly Republican part of the state today. Fort Smith's Republicanism is anti-government and loyally pro-Reagan; but in the hills, Republicanism is a form of orneriness, rooted in opposition to slavery and secession, hostile to establishments and the lowlands, and welcoming help from the faraway federal government.

The congressman from the 3d District, Arkansas's senior politician these days, is John Paul Hammerschmidt, an ancestral hill Republican. He ran his family's lumber business in Harrison, ran for Congress in 1964 and drew 44% of the vote, then beat the longtime Democrat in 1966. Except for 1974, when he was opposed by a young Arkansas Law School professor named Bill Clinton, he has had no trouble holding onto the seat since.

Hammerschmidt is not very partisan or ideological; he does not contribute often to debate on national issues. His heart seems to be where his roots are, in the hills of Arkansas. On economic issues, Hammerschmidt is a bit more generous than other Republicans with federal spending, representing as he does an historically poor district; on foreign and cultural issues, he is solidly conservative. He is ranking Republican on Public Works and has been ranking member on Veterans' Affairs. On Veterans, the debate, when there is one, is more generational than partisan, with Hammerschmidt mildly inclined to favor his fellow World War II veterans. On Public Works, the question historically is whose district gets the projects, and Hammerschmidt had been effective at getting some for the Arkansas 3d. He does not, however, try hard to be a power to see who gets the rest, though he does oppose efforts by market-minded conservatives to cut pork barrel programs generally. By virtue of his committee position, he was one of the leaders of the successful moves to override President Reagan's vetoes of the water projects and highway bills in 1987.

Hammerschmidt came into the House with George Bush and had been mentioned as a possible Veterans Secretary. He now seems likely to remain in the House, a link with the strengths and weaknesses of the Republican past: with strong roots in his local community and a sense of duty and integrity, but not an aggressive partisan or an active pugilist in the battle of ideas.

The People: Est. Pop. 1986: 616,900, up 7.7% 1980–1986; Pop. 1980: 572,937, up 33.3% 1970–80. Households (1980): 77% family, 39% with children, 68% married couples; 26.0% housing units rented; median monthly rent: $147; median house value: $32,200. Voting age pop. (1980): 414,806; 2% Black, 1% American Indian, 1% Spanish origin.

1988 Presidential Vote:

Bush (R)	....	146,498	(66%)
Dukakis (D)	....	74,413	(33%)

Rep. John Paul Hammerschmidt (R)

Elected 1966; b. May 4, 1922, Harrison; home, Harrison; The Citadel, OK A&M Col., U. of AR; Presbyterian; married (Virginia).

Career: Army Air Corps, WWII; Bd. Chmn., Hammerschmidt Lumber Co.; Chmn., Repub. State Central Cmtee., 1964–66.

Offices: 2110 RHOB 20515, 202-225-4301. Also Main P.O. Bldg., Rm. 248, Ft. Smith 72902, 501-782-7787; and 424, Fed. Bldg., Fayetteville 72701, 501-442-5258.

Committees: *Public Works and Transportation* (Ranking Member of 20 R). *Veterans' Affairs* (2d of 12 R). Subcommittee: Hospitals and Health Care (Ranking Member). *Select Committee on Aging* (2d of 26 R). Subcommittee: Housing and Consumer Interests (Ranking Member).

Group Ratings

	ADA	ACLU	COPE	CFA	LCV	ACU	NTLC	NSI	COC	CEI
1988	10	27	16	45	13	96	65	100	86	56
1987	16	—	15	21	—	68	—	—	87	56

National Journal Ratings

	1988 LIB — 1988 CONS	1987 LIB — 1987 CONS
Economic	24% — 74%	24% — 74%
Social	5% — 91%	36% — 64%
Foreign	0% — 84%	30% — 69%

Key Votes

1) Homeless $	FOR	5) Ban Drug Test	AGN	9) SDI Research	FOR
2) Gephardt Amdt	AGN	6) Drug Death Pen	FOR	10) Ban Chem Weaps	AGN
3) Deficit Reduc	AGN	7) Handgun Sales	FOR	11) Aid to Contras	FOR
4) Kill Plnt Clsng Notice	FOR	8) Ban D.C. Abort $	FOR	12) Nuclear Testing	AGN

Election Results

1988 general	John Paul Hammerschmidt (R)	161,623	(75%)	($159,221)
	David Stewart (D)	54,767	(25%)	($60,054)
1988 primary	John Paul Hammerschmidt (R), unopposed			
1986 general	John Paul Hammerschmidt (R)	115,113	(80%)	($63,341)
	Su Sargent (D)	36,726	(20%)	($11,837)

FOURTH DISTRICT

Southern Arkansas, from the flatlands by the Mississippi to the lowlands on the Texas border, is the part of the state most clearly part of the Deep South. In racial makeup (25% black), economic base (cotton, chickens, oil, rice, soybeans), mores (traditional), and political leanings (solidly Democratic, then pro-Goldwater, Wallace, and Nixon), this is clearly Dixie. Its largest cities are places like El Dorado (pronounced with a long *a*), Pine Bluff, an old agricultural center with a large black population on the flat banks of the Arkansas River, the resort town of Hot Springs, and Texarkana, situated so squarely on the Texas-Arkansas border that the state line runs through City Hall. This is the land that makes up Arkansas's 4th Congressional District.

Politically, the 4th has come most of the way toward rejoining the national Democratic party.

It nearly went for Michael Dukakis in 1988, and its congressman, Beryl Anthony, has become one of his party's effective national leaders. First elected in 1978, Anthony worked quietly and won a seat on Ways and Means. There, on tax and trade bills, he has concentrated on helping local industries like timber (his family is in the business) and poultry industries. He favors lower capital gains tax rates and longer holding periods. But he has also gone along with national Democrats when it counted, as on the 1981 Reagan budget and tax cut votes when he was on Budget. That faithfulness, and his demonstrated ability to raise large sums from PACs for his own campaigns, led Jim Wright to choose him in 1986 to chair the Democratic Congressional Campaign Committee.

Anthony had a tough act to follow and has followed it well. The outgoing chairman Tony Coelho did a brilliant job of raising money from 1981 to 1986, bludgeoning the PACs to give to Democrats and not to Republicans; he erased the Democrats' debt, built a new party headquarters and media center, saw the number of House Democrats rise in the Reagan years, and got himself elected Democratic whip. Anthony followed nimbly in Coelho's footsteps. He made good use of the media center, donated by Averell and Pamela Harriman, which delivers Democratic messages all over the country. He continued to match PACs with Democratic incumbents and challengers who are right on their issues; as a result Democrats outraised Republicans heavily in the 1987–88 cycle. In fact, a single Democratic freshman (Jim Jontz) raised more pre-October money from PACs than all Republican challengers put together. The result was that the Democrats made minor gains in 1988 even when they began with a solid majority of House seats. More incumbents were returned than ever before in American history (98%)—which is just fine with Anthony, since most incumbents are Democrats.

Anthony's only problem is that he may have been too successful. House Republicans, including Leader Robert Michel, are waking up to the fact that their supposed friends, the business PACs, whom they have been protecting against campaign finance reforms, have been transformed by Coelho and Anthony into a Democratic instrument. So some form of PAC limits and public finance, long championed by Democrats, may be in the offing. But Anthony will be in on the framing of any changes, and this national Democrat from Dixie seems likely to continue to be a major force in House elections.

The People: Est. Pop. 1986: 577,200, up 1.1% 1980–1986; Pop. 1980: 570,831, up 11.4% 1970–80. Households (1980): 76% family, 40% with children, 62% married couples; 27.4% housing units rented; median monthly rent: $102; median house value: $26,200. Voting age pop. (1980): 403,044; 25% Black, 1% Spanish origin.

1988 Presidential Vote: Bush (R) 103,562   (52%)
Dukakis (D). 93,307   (46%)

Rep. Beryl F. Anthony, Jr. (D)

Elected 1978; b. Feb. 21, 1938, El Dorado; home, El Dorado; U. of AR, B.S., B.A. 1961, J.D. 1963; Episcopalian; married (Sheila).

Career: Asst. Atty. Gen. of AR, 1964–65; Dpty. Union Cnty. Prosecutor, 1966–70; Prosecuting Atty., 13th Judicial Dist., 1971–76; Legal Counsel, Anthony Forest Products Co., 1977.

Offices: 1117 LHOB 20515, 202-225-3772. Also 206 Fed. Bldg., El Dorado 71730, 501-863-0121; 2521 Fed. Bldg., Pine Bluff 71601, 501-536-3376; and 201 Fed. Bldg., Hot Springs 71901, 501-624-1011.

Committees: *Ways and Means* (14th of 23 D). Subcommittees: Oversight; Health. *Select Committee on Children, Youth, and Families* (7th of 18 D).

Group Ratings

	ADA	ACLU	COPE	CFA	LCV	ACU	NTLC	NSI	COC	CEI
1988	80	65	59	64	31	16	10	11	46	21
1987	68	—	56	57	—	5	—	—	27	8

National Journal Ratings

	1988 LIB — 1988 CONS		1987 LIB — 1987 CONS	
Economic	60%	— 37%	68%	— 27%
Social	66%	— 32%	70%	— 30%
Foreign	64%	— 34%	64%	— 36%

Key Votes

1) Homeless $	AGN	5) Ban Drug Test	AGN	9) SDI Research	AGN
2) Gephardt Amdt	FOR	6) Drug Death Pen	FOR	10) Ban Chem Weaps	AGN
3) Deficit Reduc	FOR	7) Handgun Sales	AGN	11) Aid to Contras	AGN
4) Kill Plnt Clsng Notice	AGN	8) Ban D.C. Abort $	AGN	12) Nuclear Testing	FOR

Election Results

1988 general	Beryl F. Anthony, Jr. (D)	129,508	(69%)	($570,155)
	Roger N. Bell (R)	57,658	(31%)	($21,393)
1988 primary	Beryl F. Anthony, Jr. (D), unopposed			
1986 general	Beryl F. Anthony, Jr. (D)	115,335	(78%)	($179,169)
	Lamar Keels (R)	22,980	(15%)	($23,134)
	Stephen Bitely (I)	10,604	(7%)	

CALIFORNIA

In the days after Pearl Harbor, almost 50 years ago, many Americans thought California would be next. "People stacked sandbags against public buildings to prepare for an aerial attack and glued blackout paper to the windows of their homes in the case of night raids," writes historian John Patrick Diggins. "In Los Angeles and San Francisco civil defense wardens enforced curfews and police followed up rumors of spy networks in Japanese neighborhoods, while at night cars crept without lights along coastal highways. On bluffs and oceanfront rooftops people vigilantly tried to sight the enemy." Rumors flew: the Japanese fleet was 164 miles from Monterey, there were 34 Japanese ships between Los Angeles and San Francisco, periscopes were seen off beaches. A wacky general, John DeWitt, one of those later responsible for forcing Japanese Americans into internment camps, announced breathlessly that Japanese airplanes had flown over San Francisco Bay area on the night of December 8, though they unaccountably didn't drop any bombs.

The fears were mostly baseless. A few balloon-borne bombs landed in an Oregon forest, and later there was some light shelling of the Santa Barbara oil fields. But, as J. Edgar Hoover argued without effect at the time, there was never any evidence of sabotage or disloyalty by Japanese Americans. Unfortunately, in the hysterical months that followed, demands from the Army and from California politicians resulted in their internment—a blight on America's reputation which was assuaged by apology and and redress law of 1988.

This fear and hysteria arose in a part of America that felt disconnected from the rest of the country. "California is an island," Carey McWilliams wrote in the 1940s, America's lightly populated outpost on the Pacific, with only 7 million of the country's 131 million people, thousands of miles across plains, mountains and desert from thickly settled parts of the country and separated from Japan only by the open waters of the Pacific. It was an affluent island in the early 1940s, and one unmistakably American in its culture—yet also a bit bizarre. Farming and oil, extractive industries, were the basis of a still colonial economy: California imported most of its finished goods and lived off its natural resources. Its people, leapfrogging the continent, had come from all over: Yankee stock migrants from the Midwest predominated, southerners (except for the Okies of the late 1930s) were relatively few, European immigrants included the Italian fishermen of San Francisco's North Beach and refugees and expatriate intellectuals like Aldous Huxley and Bertolt Brecht in Los Angeles.

"Sociologically detached from the rest of the country," McWilliams wrote, "California functions in its own right, has its own patterns of political behavior, and exists as a kind of sovereign empire by the western shore." Politically, this empire was ancestrally Republican, ideologically progressive, quickly embracing and quickly discarding nostrums like the End Poverty in California program that made Upton Sinclair the Democratic nominee for governor in 1934 (he lost when FDR among others renounced him), and the "$30 Every Thursday" proposal of a group called Ham and Eggs that got 45% in a 1938 referendum. It voted for Franklin Roosevelt and Harry Truman and at home for progressive Republicans like Hiram Johnson and Earl Warren.

It is a long way from that California to the California of today. The change began explosively in the war, when California became one of the great defense industry states of the nation, making steel and aluminum for the first time, building ships and airplanes by the thousands. Millions of Americans came here, and millions stayed; California's economy was expected to collapse when the big firms shut down after the war; instead, as urbanologist Jane Jacobs points

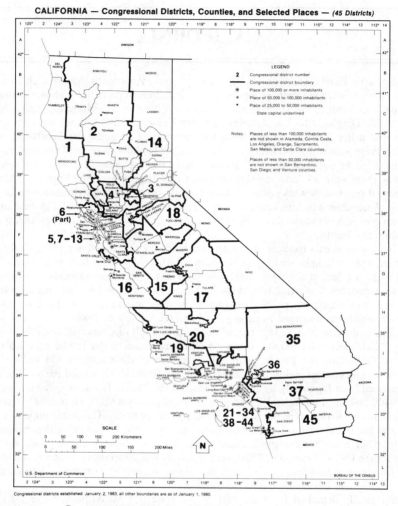

CALIFORNIA — Congressional Districts, Counties, and Selected Places — (45 Districts)

See pages 1443-1448 for additional metropolitan area maps.

out, one-eighth of all the new jobs in the nation in the early postwar years were created in greater Los Angeles. California's growth has had its spurts and pauses, but it was as strong as ever in the 1980s. As the decade ends, California is a nation-state of 27 million people (after the 1990 Census it will account for a larger share of the nation's population than any state has since 1870), with the highest living standards and highest productivity in the world, an economy as technically advanced as any that has ever existed, and a gross domestic product that would be the sixth highest in the world if it were a separate nation.

And in many ways California resembles that separate nation, of similar geographic size and even greater population in the seismically active interstices between ocean and mountains and wasteland, across the Pacific: Japan. Both California and Japan are economically creative, productive, affluent, hard-working: for as Jan Morris wisely observed, "somewhere near the heart of the L.A. ethos there lies, unexpectedly, a layer of solid, old-fashioned, plain hard work.

It suggests to me, unexpectedly, the guild spirit of some medieval town, where workers in iron or lace, the clockmakers and the armorers, competed to give the city the glory of their trades." If the Japanese are known for their fine workmanship, Californians—backup musicians and stagehands, plastic molders and toy designers—pride themselves quietly on being the very best at what they do. There is something bloodless about this competence, an air of nonchalance and unsurprise, but it has made Tokyo and Los Angeles—neither involved in world commerce 150 years ago—the leading trading cities in the world today. But like the great surging cities of the past—like Johnson's or Dickens's London, like Balzac's Paris or Dreiser's New York and Chicago—not the most comfortable. In the metropolitan areas of California, as in Japan, traffic is choking; and if the Japanese live in flimsy houses and cramped apartments, most Californians live in stucco houses in tightly-packed subdivisions or garden apartments on tiny plots of land that a midwesterner would find claustrophobic. California may be more spread out than New York, but there is some of the same surliness and lack of neighborliness in daily life; migrants from the great American interior are surprised when nobody says hi. More than 40% of Los Angeles householders have their phone numbers unlisted.

California, as it moves into the 1990s, also has this in common with Japan: it is a profoundly apolitical commonwealth. Busy in their work, intense in their pursuit of leisure, people on this as on that side of the Pacific Rim take government for granted and have no time for politics. They also take for granted the affluence that seems to flow naturally from the soil and the military security that comes from the resolve of others (for just as American military power defends Japan, so the hawkish American South provides the votes for the arms buildups that defend and enrich sometimes dovish but always defense-industry heavy California). The Los Angeles TV stations run hours of local newscasts each day, but none has a bureau in the state capital of Sacramento; Michael Dukakis, in California to campaign for the primary and at the time quite possibly the next President of the United States, had a hard time making the top four or five stories on the newscast. Viewers are much more interested in the latest drug triple-slaying, the all-day traffic jam on the Santa Monica Freeway, a soap opera actress telling how she has gotten in touch with herself or a reporter speculating on whether Elvis is alive.

Californians, like Japanese, delegate the conduct of their government to a few dull, faceless leaders and a gaggle of factional politicians who provide services to local constituencies but do their real business largely unnoticed in remote government buildings. These officials have created a self-sustaining system in which they routinely receive the renewal of their mandate from a public which is largely indifferent to what they are doing. In California, the liberal voters of the central cities are over-represented by the creative redistricting plans of the late Congressman Phillip Burton, which have given liberal Democrats control of the legislature and the state's congressional delegation. They are also helped because huge sums of money ($2 million in a state Senate race) are needed to reach voters uninterested in, if not actively hostile to, political communication, because almost all political money for state elections comes from lobbyists in Sacramento, and because most successful candidates for the legislature are former staffers who have the contacts and have made the alliances that are necessary to raise that money. And so, unwatched, unnoticed, little monitored, America's most competent state government is run by America's most skillful—but in some cases its most bloodless and cynical—politicians. But there are limits on Sacramento's power. California pioneered initiatives and referenda so voters can pass laws the legislature would never dream of: forcing down property taxes in 1978's Proposition 13, for example, or forcing lower auto insurance rates in 1988's Proposition 103. Affected economic interests spend freely on these issues in such amounts that they overshadow elections for public office. More than $20 million was spent on the 1988 Senate race in California. But $81 million was spent on five insurance ballot propositions.

At this point California ceases to be Japan's doppelganger, and the comparison breaks down. Japan believes in active governmental guidance of investment decisions and of allocating economic growth among existing big corporations, while workers feel great loyalty to the companies that guarantee them lifetime jobs. California believes, inarticulately, that government should provide an infrastructure for economic growth—freeways, huge water supply systems, a fine system of higher and (at least at one time, and maybe in the future) public education and a network of agricultural research. But its growth has come largely from small business units in dozens of industries, with employees moving easily from one job to another, and one of the highest rates of self-employment in the country. Japan believes strongly in racial unity and cultural uniformity. California believes, as much as any place in the world, in racial tolerance and cultural variety, welcoming immigration and cherishing civil liberties. Finally, Japan sees itself as living in a cold corner of a hostile planet, where it must make a living selling things to people who are distant and different. California, naively and perhaps inaccurately, sees itself as the sunny center of the world, as the most American state in a world becoming more and more Americanized. Since so much of the world has come to California—check out the ethnic restaurants on Melrose in Los Angeles or Clement in San Francisco—so California has gone out all over the world. Japan assumes that it is hated and California assumes that it is loved; and if the Japanese assumption has the virtue of being more realistic, its pessimism also has the disadvantage of tending to be self-fulfilling.

The Japanese have also settled on one strategy of government—keeping the status quo liberal Democrats in—while Californians, with a nonchalance that comes from the security of being part of a larger nation, experiment with one form of politics after another. This is the state which anticipated the conservative trend of two decades by electing Ronald Reagan as governor in 1966, when conventional wisdom had it that only pro-welfare state Republicans could win in large states. It is the state that elected in 1974 as his successor the prototypical baby boomer politician, Jerry Brown—scorner of luxury, environmentalist and campaign finance reformer, skeptical about the efficacy of government spending programs and eager to embrace cultural diversity. And it is the state that elected as his successor George Deukmejian in 1982, a colorless and steadfast conservative.

As voters have become less interested in government, support for and opposition to each of these figures has become a way of making a cultural statement or striking a cultural pose, and differences in lifestyles and personal values explain Californians' voting behavior better than anything else. This behavior helps to explain, for example, why the affluent San Francisco media market area produced a 393,000-vote margin for Michael Dukakis, while the equally affluent Los Angeles media market produced a 394,000-vote margin for George Bush; why high-income Beverly Hills and Marin County are heavily Democratic and working-class Norwalk and Bakersfield vote Republican. As it happens, each of California's best-known recent political figures has embodied and represented the cultural values and style of one of the four political regions of the state which, conveniently, each cast about one-quarter of its votes: Los Angeles County, the rest of southern California, the San Francisco Bay area, and the rest of the state.

Personifying southern California is the man who received 63% and 69% of its votes for President, Ronald Reagan. While Los Angeles fills up with immigrants, blacks and singles, the rest of southern California looks more like the Los Angeles of the 1940s: predominantly white, middle-class, midwestern, although its has more Asians and Hispanics than you might think. Essentially, the old Los Angeles has grown out past the freeways into Orange County and the east end of the Los Angeles basin and out into the desert, out past the San Fernando Valley into Ventura County, down south of San Juan Capistrano and Camp Pendleton into northern San Diego County, where it merges with fast-growing San Diego. This is suburbia, but it is also half of the nation's second biggest metropolitan agglomeration, with 14 million people, close to New York's 17 million and far ahead of Chicago's 8 million. It is not farfetched to suppose that early in the 21st century Los Angeles will be the center of the nation's largest concentration of people—the first time in history a nation has ever had its greatest city so far from its center of population.

This urban center developed not because of its location (Los Angeles has no natural harbor and had to build one) or its natural resources (it used to export oil but has had to import it since the 1940s) or its historical eminence (Los Angeles had 102,000 people in 1900). It is a great city because people have wanted it to be, and southern California reflects the optimism, the somewhat innocent confidence, and the know-how of its pioneers. They turned gratefully to Ronald Reagan in the late 1960s, not as someone who veered off the American political spectrum, but as a politician who articulated traditional American values when they seemed under attack from demonstrators on campuses and rioters in ghettos. Further disillusioned in the 1970s, they saw their views vindicated in Reagan's presidency. Their spirit was most vividly represented in the ceremonies of the 1984 Olympics, which Reagan opened in Los Angeles and which for the first time were put on not by a government but by private operators who generated a 33% profit. Here America was triumphant while the Soviet Union dared not let its athletes see the blandishments of southern California, lest they never return: this was not just an artistic triumph for American values but, in retrospect, the first clear admission by the Soviets, even before Gorbachev and perestroika, that they could not compete, that they had lost the Cold War.

Just as the Yankees lost their ancient capital of Boston to a majority of Irish Catholics, so the southern Californians who backed Reagan so strongly saw the center of their metropolis, Los Angeles County, increasingly become the home of people with different backgrounds and different values. By the 1980s, Los Angeles had become the number one immigrant destination in the world, and the central city's population had begun increasing as Mexicans and Koreans, Salvadorans and Vietnamese began doubling up in refurbished houses in central neighborhoods, with whole families working to earn enough to follow so many others out the Hollywood Freeway to the San Fernando Valley or out the Santa Ana Freeway to Orange County. Hispanics and Asians tend to vote for Democrats, but not always and not by large margins; the Vietnamese and Cambodians are pretty solidly Republican. Hollywood and the west side—the generic name for the show-bizzy part of town west of Fairfax—are the centers of one of the nation's largest Jewish populations, with large numbers of singles and gays, as well; these are cultural—not economic—liberals. And California's blacks are concentrated around Watts, in neighborhoods south and southwest of downtown L.A., along the Harbor Freeway and out toward LAX (the only American airport known colloquially by its three-letter code).

Los Angeles County, since the 1970s, has provided the core constituency for the politics of Jerry Brown—although to satisfy party rules he moved his residence to San Francisco in order to be elected state Democratic chairman in early 1989. That was 15 years after he was elected governor, when the balance of electoral power in California seemed to be moving toward the baby boom generation, in an atmosphere of cultural conflict between generations and lifestyles, a conflict mirrored in Brown's rejection of the New Deal politics and cultural conservatism of his own father, who had been elected governor in 1958 and 1962. And Brown's side seemed to be winning: Reagan had been unable to stem the tide of cultural liberation which had produced the de facto legalization of marijuana, abortion, prostitution and pornography, quite unable to persuade most Americans that their country's involvement in Vietnam had been, as he would later say, "a noble cause." Brown proclaimed that "small is beautiful" and that America and California were living in "an era of limits," suggesting that further economic growth was not to be expected, and argued that the United States must accommodate itself to rising movements around the world, by which he meant socialist-minded Third World dictatorships sympathetic or allied to the Soviets. Brown seemed poised to be the politician of the future, extolling the virtues of high-tech and questioning the verities of both welfare state liberals like Hubert Humphrey and free market conservatives like Ronald Reagan.

Yet this view of the world did not pan out very well. One reason is that the cultural conflicts which accounted for much of his support died off; it turned out that there was room enough in California for everyone to live as he pleased. Mexican-American kids can parade their low-slung cars in East L.A., gays can promenade down San Francisco's Castro Street or in the newly incorporated gay-majority West Hollywood, crew cut NCOs can raise large families in Seaside or near Camp Pendleton, elderly ex-Iowans can stroll to the shopping center in Orange—and nobody else minds. A second reason is that voters turned against Brown on some cultural issues. His hesitancy to use pesticides on the 1981 Medfly infestation infuriated many, and his appointee, Chief Justice Rose Bird, who found reasons to overturn every death sentence conviction that came before her, was ousted by a 2 to 1 vote in 1986. A third reason is that California's economy—and America's—performed much better than its critics expected. True, the growth was in large part the product of small business units of the sort Brown championed and it also owed much to government—and had since Earl Warren kept taxes high during World War II to pay for the schools and highways he thought California would need after the war. But growth also produced a yearning for affluence that Brown had little use for, a desire that helps to explain the success of Proposition 13 in 1978. This undid Brown, for in opposing 13 with the same arguments as welfare state liberals, he seemed untrue to his own principles and as cynical as the politicians who rode in the limousines he eschewed. His support collapsed: after winning 59% in California's 1976 Democratic presidential primary, he got only 4% four years later. When he ran for the Senate in 1982, he won only 51% of the primary vote against such giants as novelist Gore Vidal, a state senator from Orange County, and the mayor of Fresno; he lost the general election to the little-known Pete Wilson, then mayor of San Diego, by an unambiguous 52%–45% margin. Brown got himself elected Democratic state chairman in early 1989, prompted by voter-approved campaign finance laws that make the parties the chief conduits of political money in state races; but this was an inside maneuver of the sort he scorned in the past, and there was no indication that his popularity with the voters had recovered.

In state politics the key figure for the 1980s, much to everyone's surprise, turned out to be George Deukmejian, a state senator from Long Beach who was elected attorney general in 1978 against a black congresswoman opposed to the death penalty and who narrowly defeated Los Angeles Mayor Thomas Bradley for the Senate in 1982. In that race the key votes were cast in the quarter of the state outside the Los Angeles, San Diego, and San Francisco media markets— namely the interior valley and mountain regions. This turned out to be California's high-growth area, populated by young families who headed from the smoggy outer reaches of the Los Angeles basin, with its crime-ridden freeways and drug-infested public schools, for the cleaner and culturally more traditional climes of the old Mother Lode country in the foothills of the Sierra, in the growing Sacramento area, and parts of the vast Central Valley. When issues were economic, and when the Democratic nominee was not identified with the cultural liberalism of Hollywood or San Francisco, as in the 1976 presidential race, this non-metropolitan California voted Democratic. But in 1982, against Los Angeles's mayor, and with a gun control referendum on the ballot that brought out many opponents in rural counties, Deukmejian carried the interior of California by a 55%–40% margin. (The coastal counties, filling up with liberals leaving the Bay area and L.A., trended in the other direction and voted 50%–47% for Bradley.)

As for the San Francisco Bay area, it has no better personification than Assembly Speaker Willie Brown, a far more vivid political figure and on occasion a more powerful one in Sacramento than Deukmejian. The Bay area, one of the most affluent parts of the world, is also politically one of the most liberal—if the liberalism in question is cultural rather than economic. For years not just San Francisco, but the East Bay and the Peninsula, and even prosaic-looking suburbs, have attracted those who felt their personal lifestyles were not accepted elsewhere or who relished an atmosphere of revolt—gays and perpetual graduate students, radicals and perennial rebels. The Bay area is environmentalist and dovish, but not much interested in income redistribution or helping the poor. So in 1976, the Bay area had little use for Southern Baptist

Jimmy Carter and almost preferred Betty Ford's husband, voting only 50%–46% Democratic—and costing Carter California's electoral votes. In 1988, while nationally the Democratic ticket was 5% weaker, in the Bay area it was far stronger, as Michael Dukakis led George Bush by a 58%–41% margin. A 58%–40% Bay area margin, plus an edge in the increasingly Bay-influenced coast, helped save Senator Alan Cranston's seat in 1986, as he campaigned primarily as a champion of saving California's environment.

Dukakis's strong showing in the Bay area and the coast (50%–48%), and his carrying of Los Angeles County (52%–47%), were almost enough to enable him to carry California, despite the big margin for Bush in the south outside L.A. County (63%–36%) and the smaller Bush margin in the interior (54%–44%). Overall, Bush carried California by only 51%–48%, less than his national percentage, and one of his weaker showings in a big state. This is evidence that, as the baby boom generation continues to mature, and as Hispanics and Asians produce less-than-unanimous but still significant Democratic margins, national Democrats can hope to carry California, and that California, despite the fact that it has voted Republican in every presidential election since 1964 could be part of a Democratic electoral college majority. But a caution needs to be added. The liberalism that appeals to California is cultural, not economic. The redistributionist policies that may appeal to farmers in Iowa or blacks in Michigan and the trade policies that are thought to appeal to factory workers in Pennsylvania and Ohio are probably vote-losers in California. In the 1940s it was in California where anti-Japanese feeling was strongest, but in 1988 it was the Ohio Dukakis coordinator who produced a TV spot on trade showing the Japanese flag, while the California Dukakis coordinator made darn sure it was not shown in his state. Californians, however liberal, are aware that their affluence depends heavily on commerce and on continued trade with those other nation-states on the other side of the Pacific Rim. Those who look hopefully and with some reason to California as a building block for a new liberal majority must reckon with the differences between its liberalism and that of other states essential to their strategy.

They must remember as well that in the 1980s, as the post-baby boom voters come of age, the Republican Party has grown stronger. The number of registered Republicans has grown from 3.4 million in 1978 to 5.4 million in 1988, while in the same period the number of registered Democrats has increased from 5.7 million to 7.0 million; in other words, Republicans have signed-up more than 60% of net new registrants. Those numbers don't automatically translate into votes, for in the 1970s a lot of registered Democrats had voted Republican already for major office; but they can translate into greater strength in down-the-line contests, and they give the Republicans a body of primary voters that comes closer to representing the broader electorate.

Meanwhile, in this apolitical commonwealth, where political machines were outlawed 75 years ago and media campaigning started 35 years ago, both political parties are trying to reinvent organizational politics, in different ways. The Republicans are relying on money, technology and management techniques to get out their vote, using phone banks to identify their potential voters, mailings to communicate with them, and absentee ballot applications to get them to vote even before anyone goes to the polls. Ironically, it was Democrats who liberalized the registration laws, but Republicans who took advantage of them: Thomas Bradley got a majority of votes cast on election day 1982, but George Deukmejian won because of his big margins among the absentees. The Democrats' strategy is to reinvent the precinct organization. In 1988 the Dukakis campaign and the state Democratic Party hired 500 organizers to recruit precinct chairmen in the 25,000 precincts—they even had ceremonies where they took an oath to finish their quotas—and such efforts are being promised by the new state chairman Jerry Brown. A major target is to register blacks and the Hispanics and Asians who are bound to be a growing percentage of the electorate; such efforts are likely to be more successful than in other big states, since the targets are not those who have failed to vote in the past but those who are new to the area and may be ready to participate. The Democrats' organizational efforts were probably worth a couple of points in 1988. In a state with some excruciatingly close races, Cranston was reelected in 1986 and Deukmejian won his first term as governor in 1982 by 49%–48% margins. Politicians from both parties have an incentive to innovate and organize where they have not before.

A case can be made that California's decline in political interest is a sign of health. Hostilities between different cultural groups produced a politics of enthusiasm and nomination victories for ideological candidates like Barry Goldwater in 1964 and George McGovern in 1972, neither of whom would have been nominated if they had not won California's then winner-take-all presidential primary; as those hostilities have declined, California primaries have produced more moderate winners, like Pete Wilson and Ed Zschau, and general elections have produced divided government, in which Deukmejian is checked by Speaker Willie Brown, while Bradley is balanced by a conservative Los Angeles County Board of Supervisors and Republican Presidents by a supertalented Democratic congressional delegation. The result is a government fiscally restrained and culturally tolerant, but ready at the same time to pump more money into education and to insist on stricter standards for students, sterner restrictions on drug use, and tougher penalties for crime. California, as it approaches the 1990s, after all, is a story of success and not of failure. Its supple and strong economy, its capacity and willingness to welcome newcomers and help them rise, its tolerance of eccentricity but insistence on standards, are all in the best of American traditions. They show what many Americans in the 1960s and 1970s forgot, that America works; and if Californians are less interested in politics and less inclined to call on government than they were in more troubled times, that is perhaps not cause for despair.

Presidential politics. For most of the 1980s California did not seem to count much in presidential politics. Its primary, coming at the end of the season, was pivotal in 1964 and 1972. Since then it has produced such winners as Jerry Brown, Edward Kennedy and Gary Hart for the Democrats, and has been won without serious contest by Ronald Reagan three times. Its 1988 winners were Michael Dukakis and George Bush—after they had already clinched their nominations. It's possible that California could play a critical role in 1992, but unlikely unless it is rescheduled. Otherwise, it's likely to result in the renomination of George Bush and the ratification of whoever has emerged as the leading Democratic opponent of Jesse Jackson—if he decides to run again for President.

In the general election, California may be more pivotal—and could easily have been in 1988 if the national race had gone a little differently. The fact that California ended up Republican by small margins in the close elections of 1960, 1968 and 1976, and that it gave Ronald Reagan two easy victories in 1980 (53%–36%) and 1984 (58%–41%) led many to chalk it up as straight Republican. But its liberal trend on cultural issues made it competitive in 1988 and, though it finally went for George Bush, may already have had its effect on public policy. Republican national chairman and Bush campaign manager Lee Atwater noticed the trend in California during the primary season, and the even stronger trend in Oregon and Washington, both of which Dukakis ultimately carried, and it may have contributed to George Bush's calling for a "kinder, gentler" nation. Certainly the Bush Republicans are not conceding the black, Hispanic, Asian and baby boom voters who are the Democrats' hopes for carrying California.

The 1988 election had one additional result worth noting. Despite the carping of West Coast politicians about the network projections of the election winner, California has usually produced a higher than average percentage for the *loser* of the presidential election, and it did so again in 1988. It's possible that Dukakis won a plurality among West Coast voters who went to the polls on election day, and that Bush's narrow margin was due entirely to absentees.

Governor. At the beginning of the 1980s, few would have picked George Deukmejian as the man who would stand astride California state government for most of the decade; but as the decade was ending there he was, in place and on top. His first victory over Tom Bradley in 1982 was by the narrowest of margins; his second in 1986 was won with a higher percentage than

Ronald Reagan ever got in California. Deukmejian is orderly and aloof, a believer in pomp and ceremony; he is not close to other officials, not even Republicans though he spent four years as attorney general and 16 years in the legislature in Sacramento. He sticks closely to a tight-knit staff and, mostly, to his principles. His first term was marked by his stubbornness and success in sticking to his promise of no new taxes; in his second term, when the state was facing a $1 billion post-tax reform shortfall, he proposed a tax increase in 1988 and then had to back away from it. Critics charged that the state was neglecting education, highways and research, and would pay for it with a weaker economy and slower growth in the 1990s. Deukmejian replies that "we have become the gold at the end of the rainbow."

Deukmejian also made some mistakes. He angered many by abolishing without any notice the state worker health and safety program; organized labor retaliated by pumping crucial money into a close state Senate race and putting the issue on the 1988 ballot and winning. And he was unsuccessful in getting Congressman Dan Lungren confirmed as state treasurer to replace the late Jesse Unruh. Lungren was blocked in the state Senate, largely because he opposed monetary compensation to victims of the Japanese American internment in World War II. Unruh had become a power in the investment world by keeping careful control over the investment of California's pension billions. Probably one of Deukmejian's more notable successes was the defeat of Rose Bird and two other Supreme Court justices in the 1986 election, which gave him new appointments that would make the California Supreme Court, dominated by liberals since 1940, for the first time a bastion of judicial conservatism. And he was proud that the number of prisoners in California, in line with national trends, nearly doubled since he came to office.

These setbacks did not hurt Deukmejian much with the voters, however, and he probably could have been reelected in 1990. But he chose to retire instead. This caused considerable gnashing of teeth among Republicans, who fear that the Democrats will regain the governorship and, with control of the legislature, will control redistricting for the 1990s as Phil Burton did for the 1970s and 1980s. For that reason Senator Pete Wilson was trotted forward by Republican leaders, who were afraid that a little-known candidate couldn't raise the money under the new rules to compete.

The one Democrat clearly in the race in early 1989 was John Van de Kamp, who as attorney general holds an office that is easily portrayed as divorced from politics; a possible contender is Controller Gray Davis, a former top aide to Brown; a bit more colorful and considerably more likely to run is former (1978–87) San Francisco Mayor Dianne Feinstein. All except Feinstein are rather colorless politicians—which seems to be what California has wanted since Ronald Reagan and Jerry Brown left Sacramento. Leo McCarthy is running again for lieutenant governor, and the jockeying for other California statewide offices chould be fierce: Van de Kamp will not be running for reelection as attorney general, Secretary of State March Fong Eu may get a primary opponent, and the new insurance commissioner post set up by Proposition 13 could attract multiple entrants. Treasurer Thomas Hayes is a civil servant type who may be opposed in the primary by Angela (Bay) Buchanan, former Treasurer of the United States and sister of conservative columnist, Pat Buchanan. If he were to win that election he may face Jerry Brown's sister Kathleen. These offices may attract some of the state legislators and so there is likely to be some turnover in the capital.

One who will not be leaving Sacramento, it seems, is Willie Brown. In 1988 he seemed on the ropes, and his prominence in Jesse Jackson's campaign seemed an attempt to make a national political career by a man whose state career seemed in decline. A "Gang of Five" Democratic legislators were prepared to run against him, and Assembly Minority Leader Pat Nolan was hoping to overturn the Democrats' 44–36 majority. But after the election it was Nolan who lost his leadership post and Brown who was stronger than ever. The Democrats increased their lead to 47–33, eliminating the leverage of the Gang of Five (who, one might guess, were assigned office space together in the same broom closet), and reducing downward toward zero the

Republicans' chances of gaining control of the Assembly in 1990. The Democrats also have a strong position (24–15) in the state Senate.

Senators. The Senate majority whip, the winner of the second highest number of popular votes in Senate history, is Alan Cranston of California. After nearly 40 years in California politics, he is clearly a survivor. But he is not quite the power these facts suggest. His most recent victory, in 1986, was actually the biggest upset in the 1986 elections and the product of one of the shrewdest campaigns of recent times. After his humiliating 1984 presidential campaign, he had looked like a goner. He had won nothing more than a victory in a 1983 Wisconsin straw poll—and a $2 million debt. He was 72 on election day 1986 and he looked gaunt and haggard, though he has always been in excellent physical shape, and made himself ridiculous by dying his hair a shade of orange. His views on issues seemed out of line with California: his longtime support of disarmament seemed irrelevant when the contrary policies of Ronald Reagan seemed to be bringing peace, and his longtime support of generous government spending at home seemed foolish to young affluent voters who believe that markets and entrepreneurs, not governments and regulators, produce economic growth. And finally, the Republicans nominated the strongest possible candidate to oppose him, Silicon Valley Representative Ed Zschau, a successful entrepreneur himself, well-financed, tolerant on cultural issues, assertive on foreign policy and market-oriented on economics.

But Cranston was not daunted. In 1984 he set about methodically raising money, phone call by phone call; he eradicated his debt (while Gary Hart and John Glenn, with much better political prospects, could not eradicate theirs) and by 1986 raised another $10 million or so besides. He criss-crossed California's small towns in 1985 and remained on the campaign trail—which these days means in TV studios and raising money personally on the phone and at parties—in 1986. The day after the Republican primary, he had ads on the air attacking Zschau for flip-flopping on issues, and kept a running attack on him through November. At the same time, he used Ansel Adams photographs to identify himself with all the best things in California, and at the last minute sent out 250,000 letters to coastal households on environmental issues. Zschau, a business school graduate who approached campaigning as a management exercise, eventually counterattacked by calling Cranston a liberal and an opponent of the death penalty and tough drug laws. But he never got the footing to get across his own positive message, and Cranston succeeded early in establishing a negative tone. In that environment, turnout was low (8% below 1982), and neither candidate got a majority. But Cranston won 50%–47%.

Cranston started off in public life in the 1930s; as a young journalist he published an unexpurgated version of Hitler's *Mein Kampf*, and in the years after World War II he was a founder of the California Democratic Council, the leading liberal political force in the state. He was elected state controller in 1958 and 1962 and U.S. Senator in 1968, an office to which he has been reelected three times. His career has had its ups and downs: he was defeated for controller in the 1966 Reagan gubernatorial landslide, and he won the Senate seat only when the moderate incumbent, Thomas Kuchel, was defeated in the primary by right-winger Max Rafferty who, despite the revelation that he sat out World War II with an alleged injury and then threw away his crutches on VJ Day, held Cranston to 52%.

Cranston is part dreamy idealist, part shrewd political operator. He got into politics in the 1940s as an advocate of world government and remains more interested in arms control than any other issue. He favors some form of national service, not necessarily military, for young people. But he is also an operator. For 15 years his California colleagues in the Senate were men with rather abstract interests or limited attention spans, and so California constituencies—farmers, aerospace companies, banks and savings and loans, labor unions, the entertainment industry, the new Silicon Valley industries—went to Cranston when they needed help in the Senate. Cranston delivered. When Lockheed needed a federal loan guarantee to stay in business, Cranston produced the critical vote on the floor by persuading a colleague who later admitted to a drinking problem to change his mind. On the Banking Committee for years he looked out for the now beleaguered savings and loans. He also became known as a good vote-counter, cultivating not so much the strongest, best-known Senators as those who are obscure and in some cases of limited talents; and when Robert Byrd moved up to the majority leadership in 1977, Cranston became Democratic whip.

Since his 1984 campaign, his career has been in something of an eclipse. While he was out on the road in 1983 and 1984, he had for the first time a colleague, Pete Wilson, who also looked after the state's economic interests. No longer was Cranston indispensable. In much of 1985 and 1986 he was preoccupied with his campaign. In 1987, when the Democrats regained control of the Senate, Majority Leader Robert Byrd gave him a cold shoulder; he liked to be his own vote counter. In 1989, new Majority Leader George Mitchell seems to be using as his lieutenant South Dakota's Tom Daschle, who is a contemporary and campaign helper to many of the younger Democrats, while most of the men Cranston started off with are gone. Cranston easily beat back opposition from Wendell Ford for the whip post, and he has work that he cares about as chairman of the Veterans Committee.

In California, Cranston has worked hard on registering voters and developing a new Democratic organization with appeal to Hispanics and Asians. Many assume he will quit in 1992 when he turns 78. Cranston says he *is* running; he is a physical fitness buff (a champion sprinter into his seventies) and does not seem disposed to retire. If he is not as much at the center of things as he once was, he retains both his idealistic goals and his insider's skills, and there is more than one tenant in the political graveyard who underestimated his determination and political sense.

The man who has won more votes in a single election than anyone in the history of the United States Congress, could walk down just about any street in Washington or in his home state and not be recognized. He is nonetheless a politician of considerable competence and impressive accomplishments. Pete Wilson grew up in an affluent part of St. Louis, went to Yale, then joined the Marines and went to law school at Boalt Hall in Berkeley; he moved to San Diego, where he was elected assemblyman in 1966 and mayor in 1971. His reputation was as a moderate Republican and an environmentalist, interested in nuts-and-bolts state and local government; he supported Gerald Ford over Ronald Reagan in the 1976 presidential primary (better not bring up his name with Reagan even now), opposed Proposition 13 in 1978, and finished fourth in the Republican gubernatorial primary that year, with 9% of the vote. In 1982, still with the handicap of being well known only in the San Diego media market, which has only 8% of the state's voters, he ran in a 13-candidate primary field for Senator, and finished first, with 38% of the vote, as Pete McCloskey was unable to expand beyond his Bay area base, Barry Goldwater Jr. fizzled, and Robert Dornan and Maureen Reagan never got well enough known to be taken seriously. Wilson was then the beneficiary of the unpopularity of Jerry Brown, and beat him 52%–45%. Six years later, he beat Leo McCarthy, who grew up in the same St. Francis Wood neighborhood of San Francisco as Brown, by the almost identical margin of 53%–44%. In the 10 years between his first and his latest statewide race, Wilson increased his vote total from 230,000 to 5.1 million. In the process, he also broke the jinx that has clung to the seat he holds: no one had been reelected to it since 1952.

How did he do it? His voting record, despite his un-Reaganish past, was mostly pro-Reagan, with dissents on issues like offshore drilling, clean air and highways. On military issues, he has been an enthusiastic supporter of the Reagan defense buildup on the Armed Services Committee and on the floor—which evidently doesn't hurt in California, with its big defense industries—and he was one of those ready to move the military into the fight against drugs. He is an SDI enthusiast and the leading opponent of the Midgetman. In 1985, he showed up in pajamas while recovering from surgery to cast a decisive vote for the balanced budget constitutional amendment. He has worked for research on Alzheimer's disease and AIDS, and wants government to do more about transportation and child care. George Will called him "a rarity: a conservative who understands the discriminating, but vigorous use of government for conservative purposes."

He has spent much time working for California interests and on California issues. On the Agriculture Committee he looks out for California's huge food industry and tries to increase its exports. He was the lead advocate of amendments to the immigration bill allowing in more guestworkers for California growers; he took on the chief sponsor of the immigration bill, Alan Simpson, and won. With less success he tried in 1984 to increase tuna tariffs (the U.S. tuna fleet is based in San Diego). He worked with Cranston and against some Republicans on the California wilderness bill, but broke with him over the Mojave Desert wilderness area; he was one of the leaders against offshore oil drilling off California's coast. Wilson was the chief Senate sponsor of the "wine equity act." He also maintained careful ties with California's entertainment industry, pushing bills to keep the TV networks from sharing syndication profits, to stop foreign pirating of films and videocassettes, and to get favorable transition rules for studios in the 1986 tax reform. And he has been a staunch supporter of Israel.

To all these issues Wilson has brought a strong intellect, a willingness to work hard and master details, and a steely and not terribly pleasant competitiveness. He brought those qualities to campaigning as well. With clockwork precision, he raised a record amount of money, calling in many of the chits he had accumulated, particularly among Los Angeles's usually Democratic west side fundraisers. And he spent his money effectively. His opponent was Leo McCarthy, a similarly quiet but also competent officeholder, a former Assembly speaker and now lieutenant governor, who in California's apolitical environment was scarcely known in any substantive way to the voters. McCarthy made some mistakes in the spring: he attended a fundraiser at which anti-nuclear activist Helen Caldicott called Reagan a lunatic and compared Gorbachev to Jesus Christ (statements which McCarthy did not immediately renounce); he was reluctant to release his income tax returns; he was not endorsed by Dianne Feinstein because he opposed homeporting the battleship Missouri in San Francisco; he was hurt by his opposition to capital punishment and 1986 support of Rose Bird; he was attacked by Wilson for a vote against aid to the elderly in the legislature. Wilson, meanwhile, was running ads saying he didn't send out newsletters but gave the money for research on Alzheimer's disease. In November, Wilson ran slightly better in Los Angeles and the South than he had against Brown, while McCarthy did better than Brown in the Bay area and the Coast. But the overall result was similar, and one Wilson would surely settle for if he runs for governor.

If Wilson is elected governor, he will get to pick the next Senator himself. But Wilson's successor will serve only two years and so will come up for reelection, to a two-year term, in 1992. Alan Cranston's term expires then too, and so it is possible that California will have two Senate races, one with an incumbent with less than two years' service, the other, either with no incumbent or with one who will be 78 years old. The incentive for ambitious politicians to run must be overwhelming, and the potential total cost of those campaigns must be frightening—perhaps as much as the insurance industry spent in this apolitical commonwealth on the referenda of 1988.

Congressional districting. California's House delegation of 45 is the largest since New York had that many districts in the 1940s; it is lopsidedly (27–18) Democratic. That is attributed to the redistricting plans drawn up by the late San Francisco Representative Phillip Burton and Michael Berman, an aide to Representative Henry Waxman and brother of former Assembly majority leader and now U.S. Representative Howard Berman. Republican efforts to forge an alliance with Hispanic legislators failed when Burton figured out how to draw one more Hispanic district than the Republican computers did. The Republicans turned to referenda and won at the polls in 1982, only to have Burton draw another plan before Jerry Brown left office, and the Republican's efforts to create a commission of retired judges to draw the district lines was turned down by the voters in 1984; the final court challenge wasn't dismissed until early 1989. The Burton plan is not quite as unfair as the Republicans claim, however. Any districting plan will tend to understate Republicans' popular vote strength, because so many of their votes are cast in a few high-income, high-turnout areas. And the Republicans' failure to capture majorities in the legislature in the 1980s is due more to their candidates' weaknesses than to the district lines.

In any case, Burton died in 1983, and by 1989 the focus was on what will happen after 1990. The census is expected to give California five or six new seats, to make it the largest state delegation in history. At least two, in southern California, will be Republican no matter who draws the lines: there are no Democratic precincts in this rapidly growing territory. Otherwise, the key is the governor's race in 1990. If the Democrats win, they will probably totally control redistricting, subject only to a court case. If Pete Wilson or another Republican wins, there will be pressure for a compromise. There is, at this point, a good government argument for drawing safe seats for most if not quite all of California's incumbents, since the state has many talented, well-placed and powerful House members, most of them Democrats but some Republicans too. This is rather remarkable because it is hard to be a good legislator if you must fly five hours over three time zones to California on weekends and then take the redeye back to Washington.

The People: Est. Pop. 1988: 28,168,000; Pop. 1980: 23,667,902, up 19% 1980–88 and 18.5% 1970–80; 11.19% of U.S. total, 1st largest. 23% with 1–3 yrs. col., 20% with 4+ yrs. col.; 11.4% below poverty level. Single ancestry: 8% English, 5% German, 3% Irish, 2% Italian, 1% French, Russian, Portuguese, Polish, Swedish, Dutch, Scottish, Norwegian. Households (1980): 69% family, 37% with children, 55% married couples; 44.1% housing units rented; median monthly rent: $253; median house value: $84,700. Voting age pop. (1980): 17,278,944; 16% Spanish origin, 7% Black, 5% Asian origin, 1% American Indian. Registered voters (1988): 14,004,873; 7,052,368 D (50%); 5,406,127 R (39%); 1,546,378 unaffiliated and minor parties (11%).

1988 Share of Federal Tax Burden: $113,203,000,000; 12.80% of U.S. total, largest.

1988 Share of Federal Expenditures

	Total		Non-Defense		Defense	
Total Expend	$102,366m	(11.58%)	$66,020m	(10.07%)	$42,398m	(18.56%)
St/Lcl Grants	11,676m	(10.19%)	11,674m	(10.20%)	2m	(2.16%)
Salary/Wages	16,380m	(12.20%)	6,240m	(9.31%)	10,140m	(9.31%)
Pymnts to Indiv	41,941m	(10.25%)	39,199m	(10.04%)	2,741m	(14.71%)
Procurement	29,457m	(15.61%)	6,052m	(13.02%)	29,457m	(15.61%)
Research/Other	2,913m	(7.80%)	2,855m	(7.70%)	58m	(7.70%)

Political Lineup: Governor, George Deukmejian (R); Lt. Gov., Leo T. McCarthy (D); Secy. of State, March Fong Eu (D); Atty. Gen., John Van de Kamp (D); Treasurer, Thomas Hayes (R); Controller, Gray Davis (D). State Senate, 40 (24 D and 15 R and 1 I); State Assembly, 80 (47 D and 33 R). Senators, Alan Cranston (D) and Pete Wilson (R). Representatives, 45 (27 D and 18 R).

1988 Presidential Vote

Bush (R)	5,054,917	(51%)
Dukakis (D)	4,702,233	(48%)

1984 Presidential Vote

Reagan (R)	5,467,009	(58%)
Mondale (D)	3,922,519	(41%)

1988 Democratic Presidential Primary

Dukakis	1,910,808	(61%)
Jackson	1,102,093	(35%)
Gore	56,645	(2%)
Simon	43,771	(1%)

1988 Republican Presidential Primary

Bush	1,856,273	(83%)
Dole	289,220	(14%)
Robertson	94,779	(4%)

GOVERNOR

Gov. George Deukmejian (R)

Elected 1982, term expires Jan. 1991; b. June 6, 1928, Menands, NY; home, Long Beach; Sienna Col., B.A. 1949, St. Johns U., J.D. 1952; Episcopalian; married (Gloria).

Career: Practicing atty., 1952–53, 1958–62; Army, 1953–55; Atty., Texaco Inc., 1955–58; CA Assembly, 1962–66; CA Senate, 1966–78; CA Atty. Gen., 1978–82.

Office: State Capitol Bldg., Sacramento 95814, 916-445-2841.

Election Results

1986 gen.	George Deukmejian (R)	4,506,601	(61%)
	Tom Bradley (D)	2,781,714	(37%)
1986 prim.	George Deukmejian (R)	1,927,290	(94%)
	William H. R. Clark (R)	132,126	(6%)
1982 gen.	George Deukmejian (R)	3,881,014	(49%)
	Tom Bradley (D)	3,787,669	(48%)

SENATORS

Sen. Alan Cranston (D)

Elected 1968, seat up 1992; b. June 19, 1914, Palo Alto; home, Los Angeles; Pomona Col., U. of Mexico, Stanford U., B.A. 1936; Protestant; separated.

Career: Foreign Correspondent, Intl. News Srvc., 1936–38; Lobbyist, Common Council for American Unity, 1939; Army, WWII; Real estate business, 1947–67; Pres., United World Federalists, 1949–52; CA Controller, 1958–66.

Offices: 112 HSOB 20510, 202-224-3553. Also 1390 Market St., Ste. 918, San Francisco 94102, 415-556-8440; 5757 W. Century Blvd., #620, Los Angeles 90045, 213-215-2186; and 880 Front St., #5S31, San Diego 92188, 619-557-5014.

Committees: *Banking, Housing and Urban Affairs* (2d of 12 D). Subcommittees: Housing and Urban Affairs (Chairman); Securities. *Foreign Relations* (4th of 10 D). Subcommittees: African Affairs; East Asian and Pacific Affairs (Chairman); Western Hemisphere and Peace Corps Affairs. *Veterans' Affairs* (Chairman of 6 D). *Select Committee on Intelligence* (5th of 8 D).

Group Ratings

	ADA	ACLU	COPE	CFA	LCV	ACU	NTLC	NSI	COC	CEI
1988	95	87	91	100	70	0	7	0	29	20
1987	75	—	91	75	—	0	—	—	33	21

National Journal Ratings

	1988 LIB — 1988 CONS		1987 LIB — 1987 CONS	
Economic	71%	— 28%	59%	— 37%
Social	76%	— 23%	88%	— 10%
Foreign	86%	— 0%	74%	— 19%

Key Votes

1) Cut Aged Housing $	AGN	5) Bork Nomination	AGN	9) SDI Funding	AGN
2) Override Hwy Veto	FOR	6) Ban Plastic Guns	AGN	10) Ban Chem Weaps	AGN
3) Kill Plnt Clsng Notice	AGN	7) Deny Abortions	AGN	11) Aid To Contras	AGN
4) Min Wage Increase	FOR	8) Japanese Reparations	FOR	12) Reagan Defense $	AGN

Election Results

1986 general	Alan Cranston (D)	3,646,672	(50%)	($11,037,707)
	Ed Zschau (R)	3,541,804	(47%)	($11,781,316)
1986 primary	Alan Cranston (D)	1,807,244	(81%)	
	Charles Greene (D)	165,594	(7%)	
	John Hancock Abbott (D)	124,218	(6%)	
	Two others (D)	142,193	(6%)	
1980 general	Alan Cranston (D)	4,705,399	(57%)	($2,823,462)
	Paul Gann (R)	3,093,426	(37%)	($1,705,523)

Sen. Pete Wilson (R)

Elected 1982, seat up 1994; b. Aug. 23, 1933, Lake Forest, IL; home, San Diego; Yale U., B.A. 1955, U. of CA at Berkeley, J.D. 1962; Protestant; married (Gayle).

Career: USMC, 1955–58; Practicing atty., 1963–66; CA Assembly, 1966–71, Minor. Whip, 1967–69; Mayor of San Diego, 1971–83.

Offices: 720 HSOB 20510, 202-224-3841. Also 2040 Ferry Bldg., San Francisco 94102, 415-556-4307; 11111 Santa Monica Blvd., #915, Los Angeles 90025, 213-209-6765; Fed. Bldg., 1130 O St., Rm. 4015, Fresno 93721, 209-487-5727; and 401 B St., Ste. 2209, San Diego 92660, 619-557-5257.

Committees: *Agriculture, Nutrition, and Forestry* (8th of 9 R). Subcommittees: Agricultural Production and Stabilization of Prices; Agricultural Research and General Legislation (Ranking Member); Domestic and Foreign Marketing and Production Promotion. *Armed Services* (3rd of 9 R). Subcommittees: Conventional Forces and Alliance Defense (Ranking Member); Manpower and Personnel; Strategic Forces and Nuclear Defense. *Governmental Affairs* (6th of 6 R). Subcommittees: Investigations; Federal Services, Post Office and Civil Service; Oversight of Government Management. *Special Committee on Aging* (5th of 9 R). *Joint Economic Committee.* Subcommittees: Economic Goals and Intergovernmental Policy; Education and Health; National Security and Economics.

Group Ratings

	ADA	ACLU	COPE	CFA	LCV	ACU	NTLC	NSI	COC	CEI
1988	15	46	15	42	70	75	67	100	77	53
1987	30	—	13	42	—	75	—	—	87	62

National Journal Ratings

	1988 LIB — 1988 CONS		1987 LIB — 1987 CONS	
Economic	30% —	69%	29% —	70%
Social	54% —	45%	50% —	49%
Foreign	13% —	84%	0% —	76%

Key Votes

1) Cut Aged Housing $	FOR	5) Bork Nomination	FOR	9) SDI Funding	FOR
2) Override Hwy Veto	FOR	6) Ban Plastic Guns	—	10) Ban Chem Weaps	FOR
3) Kill Plnt Clsng Notice	FOR	7) Deny Abortions	FOR	11) Aid To Contras	FOR
4) Min Wage Increase	—	8) Japanese Reparations	FOR	12) Reagan Defense $	FOR

Election Results

1988 general	Pete Wilson (R).....................	5,143,409	(53%)	($12,969,294)
	Leo T. McCarthy (D)................	4,287,253	(44%)	($6,986,342)
1988 primary	Pete Wilson (R), unopposed			
1982 general	Pete Wilson (R).....................	4,022,565	(52%)	($7,082,651)
	Edmund G. Brown, Jr. (D)...........	3,494,968	(45%)	($5,367,931)

FIRST DISTRICT

The Redwood Empire, the North Coast—50 years ago this seemed an antique, left-behind part of California. "Eureka spreads in checkerboard fashion over an area large enough to accommodate a population several times its present size," wrote the *WPA Guide*. "Its solitary houses are scattered over vast stretches of vacant, weed-grown lots. Along the waterfront are the saloons, cheap hotels and poolrooms of the late 19th century—relics of the days when the tough, flamboyant life of the lonely frontier settlement centered here."

Farther south, back off the foggy coastal valleys in the protected inland flatlands, was agronomist Luther Burbank's laboratory in Santa Rosa, a town that looks middle American enough to have been the setting for dozens of movies. Sealed off from the rest of the country, and in most places from the Pacific itself, by the various ridges of the Coast Range, the north coast of California is a world unto itself. This is wet country, with some of the highest rainfall in the United States—higher as you get toward Oregon—a moist, rainy land of massive trees and rounded mountains, of small towns with filigreed Victorian houses and lumber mills. The Redwood Empire some call it, after the giant trees which grow up and down the coast, is nourished most of the year by drizzle and fog. The first white settlers here were Russians who left little behind them but interesting place names (the Russian River, Fort Ross). They were followed, in the years after the California Gold Rush, by lumbermen and fishermen. By the late 19th century, great fortunes had been made in lumber from the redwoods and Douglas firs, as Eureka's still standing Victorian mansions attest. This Redwood Empire, beginning in the south around Santa Rosa (and, over a hill, in Napa) and continuing all the way up to the Oregon border, forms California's 1st Congressional District.

In the 1970s and 1980s, the North Coast has changed as people have moved here from the San Francisco Bay area. The movement has been heavy in Sonoma County, which is within easy reach of the Golden Gate Bridge on U.S. 101; it has been lighter but more distinctively countercultural in Mendocino County, where the leading cash crop was said to be marijuana. These new North Coasters have brought many of the values and attitudes from the Bay area's liberal and even radical precincts to counties discontented with the sagging fortunes of the lumber industry in a time of national prosperity. The result is that politically, as the country and the interior of California have become more Republican in the 1980s, the Redwood Empire has become more Democratic. In the 1988 presidential election, as in the close 1986 Senate contest, the Redwood Empire counties were solidly Democratic.

Coming along at just the right time for this trend is Congressman Doug Bosco. Throughout his career he has had a gift for being at the right place at the right time. In the 1960s he left New York (which has been losing congressional districts) for school on the West Coast (which has been gaining); in the 1970s he moved to Sonoma County, near the coast north of San Francisco, ran for Congress and lost, and was elected to the Assembly in 1978; in 1982, he ran for Congress just as the 1st District was moving away, after 20 years, from the politics of Republican Representative Don Clausen. He had the good fortune to be running in a recession year, when his support for the lumber and fishing industries was particularly appreciated in the northern part of the district, and when Democrats were ballyhooing the nuclear freeze, a surefire way to enthuse the counterculture migrants in the south.

And he has had the good luck to be serving when environmental issues no longer divided but rather united environmentalist migrants and blue-collar oldtimers. They disagreed bitterly on the California wilderness bill, but that was passed in 1983 with Bosco's support. The big issue now is offshore drilling of oil, which everyone is against, none more so than Bosco. The issue has helped to move the North Coast further toward the Democrats, and got George Bush to agree to a postponement of drilling before the California primary and to oppose it while in office. Apart from stopping oil drilling, Bosco's priority is "seeing that the government provides for the everyday needs of North Coast residents," and he has used his seats on the Public Works and Merchant Marine Committees to see that it does. Among the projects he has supported are the Russian River restoration, Napa River flood control, dredging in Humboldt Bay, improvements on Highway 101 and acquiring a parallel railway right of way, and protecting the Laguna de Santa Rosa marshes. In 1989 he got a seat on Foreign Affairs, and reminded constituents of his support for the nuclear freeze, now forgotten in most of the country. His timing continues to be brilliant: in the last three elections he has won with the biggest percentages of any Redwood Empire congressman in 20 years.

The People: Est. Pop. 1986: 592,800, up 12.7% 1980–86; Pop. 1980: 525,986, up 33.1% 1970–80. Households (1980): 69% family, 35% with children, 57% married couples; 36.4% housing units rented; median monthly rent: $233; median house value: $73,500. Voting age pop. (1980): 390,186; 5% Spanish origin, 2% American Indian, 1% Asian origin, 1% Black.

1988 Presidential Vote:

Dukakis (D)...................	145,811	(55%)
Bush (R)...................	114,103	(43%)

Rep. Douglas H. Bosco (D)

Elected 1982; b. July 28, 1946, New York, NY; home, Occidental; Willamette U., B.A. 1968, J.D. 1971; Roman Catholic; married (Gayle).

Career: Practicing atty., 1971–78; CA Assembly, 1978–82.

Offices: 408 CHOB 20515, 202-225-3311. Also Fed. Bldg., Ste. 329, 777 Sonoma Ave., Santa Rosa 95405, 707-576-1466; and Eureka Inn, Ste. 216, 7th and F Sts., Eureka 95501, 707-445-2055.

Committees: *Foreign Affairs* (26th of 28 D). Subcommittee: Arms Control, International Security and Science. *Merchant Marine and Fisheries* (13th of 21 D). Subcommittee: Fish and Wildlife Conservation and the Environment. *Public Works and Transportation* (10th of 31 D). Subcommittees: Aviation; Investigations and Oversight; Public Buildings and Grounds (Chairman).

Group Ratings

	ADA	ACLU	COPE	CFA	LCV	ACU	NTLC	NSI	COC	CEI
1988	80	74	79	73	56	8	21	20	36	15
1987	68	—	77	57	—	14	—	—	21	16

National Journal Ratings

	1988 LIB — 1988 CONS		1987 LIB — 1987 CONS	
Economic	66% —	33%	46% —	54%
Social	60% —	39%	70% —	28%
Foreign	58% —	41%	61% —	38%

Key Votes

1) Homeless $	AGN	5) Ban Drug Test	AGN	9) SDI Research	AGN
2) Gephardt Amdt	AGN	6) Drug Death Pen	FOR	10) Ban Chem Weaps	AGN
3) Deficit Reduc	FOR	7) Handgun Sales	AGN	11) Aid to Contras	AGN
4) Kill Plnt Clsng Notice	AGN	8) Ban D.C. Abort $	AGN	12) Nuclear Testing	FOR

Election Results

1988 general	Douglas H. Bosco (D).................	159,815	(63%)	($247,779)
	Samuel Vanderbilt (R).................	72,189	(28%)	($7,795)
	Eric Fried (P&F).....................	22,150	(9%)	($7,924)
1988 primary	Douglas H. Bosco (D).................	64,653	(68%)	
	Lionel Gambill (D)...................	13,598	(14%)	
	Neil Bethel Sinclair (D)	11,703	(12%)	
1986 general	Douglas H. Bosco (D).................	138,174	(68%)	($219,608)
	Floyd G. Sampson (R)	54,436	(27%)	
	Elden McFarland (P&F)...............	12,149	(6%)	($9,421)

SECOND DISTRICT

Stretching almost perfectly flat, until purplish or brown mountains (the color changes with the time of day) rise up almost to the horizon, divided by roads and fences as straight as the lines in a geometry text, lies the Sacramento Valley of northern California. Less heavily populated than the Central Valley to the south, the Sacramento Valley cultivates a marvelous variety of crops— rice, plums, almonds, olives. It is blessed with a plentiful supply of California's scarcest resource: water. It is hemmed in on three sides by mountains—the Coast Range on the west, the Sierra Nevada on the east, and the gigantic volcanoes, Mount Lassen and Mount Shasta on the north— which get plenty of the rainfall that drops from the moisture-laden clouds that sweep in from the warm Pacific. From their slopes flow the waters that become the Sacramento River and are distributed over an ingenious set of canals and aqueducts to the Central Valley and the Los Angeles Basin, where they sustain the most productive part of western civilization. The Sacramento Valley has always guarded its water jealously and in the days before one-person-one-vote it had enough seats in the California Senate to veto water decisions it didn't like; today it still retains a plentiful supply for its own use.

This part of California was left behind in the years of metropolitan growth; since the middle 1970s, however, it has been attracting young people who want to be close to the environment and young families who come here to raise their children in a small town atmosphere, where people still go to neighborhood churches and don't have to worry about drugs in the schools. The political result is that an area which used to elect rough and ready Democrats who pulled strings in Sacramento and Washington, now elects abstemious and circumspect Republicans who have solidly conservative voting records and tend to local needs. That is certainly the case in the 2d District of California, which takes in most of the Sacramento Valley, the thinly-populated west and the more thickly populated land that starts sloping gently up toward the Sierras on the east, plus—west over a small range of mountains—part of the wine-growing Napa Valley. The district was represented until 1980 by Democrat Harold "Bizz" Johnson, chairman of the House Public Works Committee, and now by Republican Wally Herger, elected in 1986, a mild-mannered, devout Mormon who has yet to make a major impact in the House.

Herger has deep roots in the southern part of the district, only 20 miles from Sacramento, but represents aptly the values of the new residents of the area. He is a businessman and rancher who was elected to the Assembly in 1980 and was part of the New Right group there. In 1986, when the congressional seat was open, Herger won solid margins over the mayor of Redding in the primary and a Shasta County supervisor in the general. He got a seat on Agriculture and sponsored a successful bill to try to get Japan to let in American farm products. He has also offered floor amendments, trying to eliminate a subsidy for Ted Turner's Goodwill Games and to get the Forest Service to offer wildfire fighting training; on issues generally, he has one of the most conservative records in the California delegation. Against a Democrat who ran more than a perfunctory campaign, he was reelected 59%–39%, and seems to have a reasonably safe seat.

The People: Est. Pop. 1986: 596,600, up 13.4% 1980–86; Pop. 1980: 526,009, up 34.2% 1970–80. Households (1980): 72% family, 37% with children, 62% married couples; 34.7% housing units rented; median monthly rent: $186; median house value: $58,100. Voting age pop. (1980): 384,601; 5% Spanish origin, 2% American Indian, 1% Asian origin, 1% Black.

1988 Presidential Vote:

Bush (R)	138,756	(58%)
Dukakis (D)	96,230	(40%)

Rep. Wally Herger (R)

Elected 1986; b. May 20, 1945, Yuba City; home, Rio Oso; American River Commun. Col., A.A. 1967; CA St. U., 1968–69; Mormon; married (Pamela).

Career: Rancher; Owner, Herger Gas, Inc. 1969–80; CA Assembly, 1980–86.

Offices: 1108 LHOB 20515, 202-225-3076. Also 20 Declaration Dr., Ste. B, Chico 95926, 916-893-8363; 2400 Washington Ave., Ste. 410, Redding 96001, 916-246-5172; and 951 Live Oak Blvd., Ste. 10, Yuba City 95991, 916-673-7182.

Committees: *Agriculture* (15th of 17 R). Subcommittees: Cotton, Rice and Sugar; Domestic Marketing, Consumer Relations, and Nutrition; Forests, Family Farms and Energy. *Merchant Marine and Fisheries* (14th of 17 R). Subcommittees: Oceanography; Fisheries, Wildlife Conservation and the Environment.

Group Ratings

	ADA	ACLU	COPE	CFA	LCV	ACU	NTLC	NSI	COC	CEI
1988	0	17	20	27	0	92	84	100	93	68
1987	8	—	13	14	—	100	—	—	100	77

National Journal Ratings

	1988 LIB — 1988 CONS		1987 LIB — 1987 CONS	
Economic	16% —	83%	0% —	89%
Social	13% —	84%	19% —	78%
Foreign	0% —	84%	0% —	80%

Key Votes

1) Homeless $	FOR	5) Ban Drug Test	FOR	9) SDI Research	FOR
2) Gephardt Amdt	AGN	6) Drug Death Pen	FOR	10) Ban Chem Weaps	AGN
3) Deficit Reduc	AGN	7) Handgun Sales	FOR	11) Aid to Contras	FOR
4) Kill Plnt Clsng Notice	FOR	8) Ban D.C. Abort $	FOR	12) Nuclear Testing	AGN

Election Results

1988 general	Wally Herger (R)	139,010	(59%)	($696,748)
	Wayne Meyer (D)	91,088	(39%)	($193,915)
1988 primary	Wally Herger (R), unopposed			
1986 general	Wally Herger (R)	109,758	(58%)	($628,361)
	Stephen C. Swendiman (D)	74,602	(40%)	($244,097)

THIRD DISTRICT

Sacramento half a century ago was "a calm city of trees, green lawns, and governmental buildings. Along the banks of the river," wrote the *WPA Guide*, "is the oldest part of town, red brick buildings, with tall narrow windows, and tin-roofed awnings projecting over the sidewalk. Curbstones are high, recalling the times when the river flooded its banks. In summer the policemen on traffic duty wear white helmets, like African explorers, for there are three-day cycles of heat when the sun is intense and soft drinks consumption reaches incredible figures. During these spells, Capitol Park, with its 40 acres of tree-shaded lawns, attracts hundreds of steaming citizens."

In 50 years that historic village-capital of 93,000 in the intemperate climate of California's Central Valley has been transformed into the center of a metropolitan area of over one million. Air conditioning has done away with awnings and the need to seek the shade of the Capitol trees; freeways and shopping malls have followed the city as it has grown east and north toward the foothills of the Sierras; affluence has made this one of America's better metropolitan areas and even has people restoring what the WPA writer 50 years ago scorned as "ungainly frame houses with scrollwork twisting from eaves and cornices, left from the effulgent period of the [eighteen] seventies and eighties."

Sacramento has a long history for California; as a frontier outpost it burst suddenly into the American consciousness when gold was discovered at Sutter's mill in 1849. In the Gold Rush, it was the natural choice to be California's capital, halfway between the Mother Lode country in the foothills of the Sierras and San Francisco Bay, and in the middle of California's vast valley. Sacramento has been an important agricultural and food processing center, like the other cities in the valley, but government has been its main business. California's gleaming Capitol is as impressive as any in the nation, just as its state government is as competent as any, though sealed off in Sacramento, far from the big metropolitan areas and little known to a mostly apathetic public, who increasingly view it with cynicism and mistrust. Even so, it keeps growing—despite Ronald Reagan and George Deukmejian. In the 1940s Sacramento was a hangout for a few fabled lobbyists; during the 1980s it became headquarters for a vast army of lobbyists, lawyers, and consultants exceeded in size only by those in Washington, D.C. California's highly competent legislators and their large staffs in effect live year-round in Sacramento, although they usually keep legal residences elsewhere; so good a job do they do in keeping in touch with both constituents and lobbyists that the best way to get elected to the legislature now is to have been a staffer.

Sacramento has become a self-sustaining engine of government. It has also become an upscale, proud city, the site since spring 1987 of a new light-rail system that will reach 18 miles into the suburbs, and the home of a National Basketball League franchise, the Sacramento Kings. In the process, what used to be a Democratic, pro-government, working class bastion has become something very close to an upscale Sun Belt boom town. Sacramento voted against Ronald Reagan for governor in 1966 and 1970, but voted for him for President in 1980 and 1984; the city that spurned Richard Nixon and Gerald Ford voted in 1988 for George Bush. Civil servants and the *Sacramento Bee* once made Sacramento Democratic. But the increasing strength of the private sector here (even though much of it feeds off government), growing affluence, and immigration from elsewhere have helped Republicans.

Most of the city of Sacramento, and its suburbs east of the Sacramento River and south of the American River, form the 3d Congressional District of California. It includes the Capitol, downtown and most of the more affluent parts of the Sacramento area. Historically, it is heavily Democratic; in recent elections, less so. The congressman from the 3d District, Robert Matsui, is a Democrat first elected in a close contest in 1978 and returned easily since then. Matsui is a generally loyal Democrat, but one who has set his own compass on many issues. He is also a sharp practical politician, aware of the needs of California interests, capable of raising money, and receptive to new ideas.

Matsui has served on two of the most powerful committees in the House—Judiciary and Ways and Means—but his greatest accomplishment so far came on another issue, Japanese American reparations. Born in 1941, the infant Matsui and his family were among the West Coast Japanese Americans forced into internment camps in 1942, and although he has no memory of the experience himself, he does remember the silence his family and others maintained about the experience. It was Asian shame, when none of the victims had anything to be ashamed about. He was one of the lead sponsors of the 1988 law which apologized for the internment policy and provided monetary compensation for every survivor of the camps and for so-called voluntary evacuees.

This has not been Matsui's only issue, however. On Ways and Means in 1985 and 1986 he was one of the staunch supporters of rate-lowering, preference-cutting tax reform. He drafted a bill reforming foster care, to help states keep teen mothers and their infants together; he pushed successfully for increased money for job training for migrant workers; he is pushing a package to beef up the supplementary security insurance program. Matsui is one of the Democrats who is trying to redefine liberalism: he has greater respect for market forces than old-fashioned New Dealers, but still believes in government helping the poor; he seems to be moving in just about the same direction as his constituency. In 1987 and 1988 he supported the candidacy of Michael Dukakis—the first House member outside Massachusetts to do so—over the candidacy of his Ways and Means colleague Richard Gephardt, because he found Dukakis's pragmatic, problem-solving approach more congenial than Gephardt's hard line on trade and gloom-and-doom economics.

Matsui, intense and skillful, is well positioned to make useful contributions in the House, but not always in a highly visible way; he still ranks below Chairman Dan Rostenkowski on Ways and Means. He went so far as to explore fundraising possibilities for the 1988 race for Pete Wilson's seat in the Senate, but in July 1987 decided not to run. Matsui was mentioned as a possible candidate for attorney general in 1990 (incumbent John Van de Kamp is running for governor), but he decided to run for reelection to the House, for which he is a formidable favorite.

The People: Est. Pop. 1986: 610,800, up 16.2% 1980–86; Pop. 1980: 525,774, up 21.5% 1970–80. Households (1980): 67% family, 35% with children, 53% married couples; 41.2% housing units rented; median monthly rent: $217; median house value: $67,100. Voting age pop. (1980): 390,354; 8% Spanish origin, 7% Black, 6% Asian origin, 1% American Indian.

1988 Presidential Vote:

Bush (R)	....	132,533	(50%)
Dukakis (D)	....	130,495	(49%)

Rep. Robert T. Matsui (D)

Elected 1978; b. Sept. 17, 1941, Sacramento; home, Sacramento; U. of CA, A.B. 1963, J.D. 1966; United Methodist; married (Doris).

Career: Practicing atty., 1967–78; Sacramento City Cncl., 1971–78.

Offices: 2419 RHOB 20515, 202-225-7163. Also 8058 Fed. Bldg., 650 Capitol Mall, Sacramento 95814, 916-440-3543.

Committees: *Ways and Means* (14th of 23 D). Subcommittees: Human Resources; Trade.

Group Ratings

	ADA	ACLU	COPE	CFA	LCV	ACU	NTLC	NSI	COC	CEI
1988	90	86	88	91	81	4	11	0	36	10
1987	92	—	89	93	—	9	—	—	20	8

National Journal Ratings

	1988 LIB — 1988 CONS		1987 LIB — 1987 CONS	
Economic	67%	— 30%	68%	— 27%
Social	78%	— 20%	78%	— 0%
Foreign	79%	— 16%	81%	— 0%

Key Votes

1) Homeless $	AGN	5) Ban Drug Test	AGN	9) SDI Research	AGN
2) Gephardt Amdt	AGN	6) Drug Death Pen	FOR	10) Ban Chem Weaps	FOR
3) Deficit Reduc	FOR	7) Handgun Sales	AGN	11) Aid to Contras	AGN
4) Kill Plnt Clsng Notice	AGN	8) Ban D.C. Abort $	AGN	12) Nuclear Testing	FOR

Election Results

1988 general	Robert T. Matsui (D)	183,470	(71%)	($638,688)
	Lowell P. Landowski (R)...............	74,296	(29%)	($7,695)
1988 primary	Robert T. Matsui (D), unopposed			
1986 general	Robert T. Matsui (D)	158,709	(76%)	($563,150)
	Lowell Landowski (R)................	50,265	(24%)	($3,043)

FOURTH DISTRICT

The Sacramento Delta, as described by the *WPA Guide* 50 years ago, "is crisscrossed with dikes that hem in winding sloughs, sheltering the lush black-loam farmlands, often far below water level, from floods. It was settled in the early 1850s by disappointed gold seekers who squatted here to raise their own food. In the 1870s, the Chinese coolies who had built the Central Pacific Railroad were put to work reclaiming the Delta region at low wages. Gradually the whole 425,000-acre region of tule marshes was reclaimed by an elaborate system of levees, drainage canals, and pumping plants." By the 1930s, the Delta's incredibly fertile black peat soil was producing most of the nation's asparagus, pears, hops, beans, celery, onions and potatoes. The Delta is the focal point of California's 4th Congressional District, which also includes the residential south side of Sacramento, the city's northern and southern suburbs, and the flat farmlands to the north around Davis. There you can find the University of California branch which started as an agricultural school, became a countercultural haven for a time, and now is quieter again, its paths thronged with bicycles. All of this land is within two hours' drive of San Francisco, but culturally that liberation-minded city is far from these young-family-inhabited farmlands and suburbs.

The 4th District is historically Democratic country, but in national elections it has become somewhat less so. The political influence of San Francisco may be traveling up and down the coast, but it doesn't penetrate inland to the shipyard city of Vallejo, well west of where the Delta, where the waters of the Sacramento and San Joaquin Rivers that have not been diverted toward Los Angeles flow out to the ocean. Industrial Vallejo and West Sacramento remain Democratic; the Sacramento suburbs seem to be shifting from the Democratic preference of the long-dominant *Sacramento Bee* to the Republican politics of the feisty *Sacramento Union*.

This Sacramento area district is represented, appropriately, by a man who is literally a legislator's legislator, and who, in 1986, was voted the best in the 45-member California House delegation in *California* magazine. Vic Fazio used to serve in the California Assembly; before that, he was an Assembly staffer and founder of the estimable *California Journal*. That means that he was learning the legislative business from some of the best teachers in the country, in one of its best schools. He won the 4th District House seat in 1978, when incumbent Robert Leggett prudently retired (it was revealed that he had been maintaining two families for years, and he nearly lost in 1976). Fazio brought to Washington the lessons he learned in Sacramento.

He is in a good position to apply them, as chairman of the Legislative Appropriations Subcommittee which handles Congress's own budget. Some have called him "the mayor of Capitol Hill;" he works to modernize the Capitol Police, to get the scaffolding off the West Front of the Capitol building, to refurbish the Library of Congress. The subcommittee also handles the politically difficult matter of the congressional salary. Fazio stood up stalwartly for the 50% pay raise recommended by the presidential commission in early 1989—and got steamrollered when Speaker Jim Wright flinched and, without consultation, announced he'd polled Members on the subject. Fazio had managed to get smaller raises passed in 1982 and 1987, under the procedure where they go into effect if the House doesn't vote them down; but that seems impossible now, and he may have to start again the Sisyphean task of getting House Members to vote publicly for the raise most of them think privately they need.

On Appropriations, Fazio also serves on the Energy and Water Development Subcommittee—a body more politically useful to him, considering how much water flows into, around, down and under his district, and he attends to Travis Air Force Base and other local problems. He ranks behind Tom Bevill and Lindy Boggs and can hope to become chairman some day. He is respected by colleagues and appreciated as a Member who can and will solve political problems for them, and give them the credit.

Fazio has one other generally not envied committee assignment, on Standards of Official Conduct, universally known as the ethics committee. There he voted to find probable cause that Speaker Jim Wright broke House rules—a vote that must be incredibly uncomfortable for a House insider long interested in leadership positions. Fazio's constituency has forgiven him his position on the pay raise time and again, and he has not had serious competition in elections. The only explanation for his votes is that he thought they were the right thing to do.

But Fazio's power does not come solely from committee positions. He is respected on both sides of the aisle as the House's Mr. Goodwrench, an open and thoughtful politician who understands his colleagues and the world beyond the Hill, who is honest and straightforward and easy to deal with but also a committed partisan and an effective competitor. He has had his disappointments—on the pay raise, and when he was passed over for Democratic Congressional Campaign Committee chairman after the 1986 election (when Tony Coelho moved from that post to majority whip, it would have put too many Californians too high in the leadership, and so Beryl Anthony of Arkansas got the position instead). Fazio did manage Coelho's successful campaign for whip, and he will be the Democrats' lead man on redrawing California's congressional districts after the 1990 Census—a job politicians don't entrust to just anyone.

Fazio has easily survived attacks on the pay raise issue, which is about all the local Republicans raise against him; in 1988 he had no Republican opponent at all.

The People: Est. Pop. 1986: 624,100, up 18.7% 1980–86; Pop. 1980: 525,764, up 34.3% 1970–80. Households (1980): 73% family, 42% with children, 60% married couples; 38.5% housing units rented; median monthly rent: $216; median house value: $64,200. Voting age pop. (1980): 374,278; 10% Spanish origin, 5% Black, 4% Asian origin, 1% American Indian.

1988 Presidential Vote:

Bush (R)	129,477	(51%)
Dukakis (D)	121,847	(48%)

Rep. Vic Fazio (D)

Elected 1978; born Oct. 11, 1942, Winchester, MA; home, West Sacramento; Union Col., B.A. 1965, CA State U.; Episcopalian; married (Judy).

Career: Legis. Consult., 1966–75; Cofounder, *The California Journal*; Consult. and Asst. to CA Assembly Spkr., 1971; CA Assembly, 1975–78.

Offices: 2433 RHOB 20515, 202-225-5716. Also 2525 Natomas Park Dr., Ste. 330, Sacramento 95833, 916-978-4381; and 844B Union Ave., Fairfield 94533, 707-426-4333.

Committees: *Appropriations* (19th of 35 D). Subcommittees: Energy and Water Development; Legislative (Chairman); Military Construction. *Standards of Official Conduct* (2d of 6 D). *Select Committee on Hunger* (5th of 16 D).

Group Ratings

	ADA	ACLU	COPE	CFA	LCV	ACU	NTLC	NSI	COC	CEI
1988	85	100	88	64	69	0	2	20	29	10
1987	80	—	87	79	—	0	—	—	14	7

National Journal Ratings

	1988 LIB — 1988 CONS		1987 LIB — 1987 CONS	
Economic	79% —	17%	73% —	0%
Social	86% —	0%	78% —	0%
Foreign	73% —	26%	66% —	34%

Key Votes

1) Homeless $	AGN	5) Ban Drug Test	AGN	9) SDI Research	AGN
2) Gephardt Amdt	FOR	6) Drug Death Pen	—	10) Ban Chem Weaps	AGN
3) Deficit Reduc	—	7) Handgun Sales	AGN	11) Aid to Contras	AGN
4) Kill Plnt Clsng Notice	AGN	8) Ban D.C. Abort $	AGN	12) Nuclear Testing	FOR

Election Results

1988 general	Vic Fazio (D)	181,184	(99%)	($529,334)
1988 primary	Vic Fazio (D), unopposed			
1986 general	Vic Fazio (D)	128,364	(70%)	($386,346)
	Jack D. Hite (R)	54,596	(30%)	($9,344)

FIFTH DISTRICT

On a sunny day it looks tropical, with brown mountains baking in the sun and light shining off the pastel stucco buildings. On a day when the clouds scud in from the Pacific, it can look sinister, full of dark corners where a private detective's partner might be ambushed by a pretty girl. Its buildings can be majestic, like the monumental Beaux Arts City Hall, or tawdry, like the hotels of the Tenderloin; it is a city that looks exotic at first but which when you look at it closely, could only be American: San Francisco. It grew from nothing to a major city in the single year of 1850, and it is still changing every year. The San Francisco from which American troops sailed into the Pacific during World War II has been transformed today, and not just by gleaming postwar high-rises, but also by the several waves of new migrants and residents who have changed the character of what the *San Francisco Examiner* insists on calling The City.

Its American origins are obvious from the regular grids of streets named after politicians and local developers and laid out over precipitously steep hills. They also are plain from its native literary tradition, which flourished around 1900 when Jack London, Ambrose Bierce and Frank Norris were writing here, and from the home-town artistic traditions of the Arts and Crafts movement of the same era. San Francisco has always been particularly fond of itself and particularly hospitable to outsiders, from the beats of North Beach in the 1950s to the hippies who thronged Haight-Ashbury in 1967 and the gays of Castro Street in the 1970s and 1980s. But San Francisco's taste for the exotic and the arts has always rested on the success of a prosaic, yet booming economy. It is based on everything from food (the Bay Area remains the national outlet for the cornucopia of California's Central Valley) to finance (despite the recent troubles of Bank of America) to high-tech (much of Silicon Valley is financed in San Francisco).

Fifty years ago, San Francisco was a city of 634,000 in a Bay area of 1.6 million; today it is a city of perhaps 744,000 (it peaked at 775,000 in 1950) in a Bay area of 5.6 million. That older San Francisco's economy was still dominated by the port, and this was a burly working-class town with a small but showy upper class: the rich in their mansions in Pacific Heights or their stucco Spanish-style houses out in St. Francis Wood suddenly were heavily outnumbered by the cloth-capped workingmen on the docks and the Irish and Italian and native-stock working families in the little frame houses on streets coming down from the hills. In 1934 it was the scene of a general strike led by Communist sympathizers—perhaps the closest thing to genuine class warfare or the outbreak of a proletarian revolution ever seen in the United States. Politically, San Francisco was a progressive Republican town, the home base of Governor and Senator Hiram Johnson, a strong supporter of Teddy Roosevelt's Progressive candidacy in 1912, always sympathetic to the conservation movement, prone to elect Republican congressmen and legislators with support from labor as well as business. These Progressive Republicans helped to smooth the relations of the rich and the workers, and their political tradition survived into the governorship of Earl Warren; but his last election was in 1950, and by 1958 San Francisco's labor vote was solidly Democratic, and an important part in the Democrats' across-the-board California victory that year.

Today San Francisco's docks are quieter, its factories often torn down for office buildings and hotels, its old working class quarters taken over by new kinds of migrants. It has developed a high-skill service economy, based primarily in its booming downtown. It has seen the successful grandchildren of the general strikers move farther out in the Bay area and has seen all manner of new migrants come in: Chinese and Filipinos and Koreans from East Asia and Hispanics from Mexico and Salvador, in search of a way to move up in the world; medical and law graduates of the nation's elite universities, in search of a job in the city that still remains one of America's favorites; gays and lesbians and survivors of left-wing communes, in search of tolerance of their lifestyle. As San Francisco proper becomes a smaller part of a fast-growing Bay area, San Francisco the city and county (they are one and the same) has become a political jurisdiction in which white non-Hispanic, non-gay, native-born Americans make up only about 25% of the population.

That has inevitably created a new—and distinctive—politics. It is a cultural struggle between two groups which both fall on the Democratic left in the general American political spectrum: homeowners and family householders in the outer parts of the city and members of the business community backing candidates supported by downtown developers versus radicals and gays and blacks backing candidates who want to limit development, impose even stricter rent control and sanction gay marriages. This cultural politics became violent in 1978 when former Supervisor Dan White murdered Mayor George Moscone, a liberal with appeal to both constituencies, and Harvey Milk, the first openly gay member of the Board of Supervisors. The new mayor, Dianne Feinstein, was sympathetic to gays, but vetoed their gay marriage ordinance; she imposed the nation's toughest downtown zoning, limiting high-rises, but deflected lunatic ideas like commercial rent control. Reelected with wide support in 1979 and 1983, Feinstein was runner up to Geraldine Ferraro in Walter Mondale's 1984 vice presidential sweepstakes. Unable to seek a third term as mayor, she retired from office in 1987 and has been moving toward running for governor in 1990.

Her successor is Art Agnos, son of a Greek immigrant bootblack, a social worker who became an assemblyman for 11 years, supported by most of the more leftish blocs in the electorate. Agnos was helped by the weakness of his major opponent, who was unable to add to the homeowning bloc the new Asian immigrants who by no means share all the values of the counterculture, but want to work their way up in the system rather than tear it down. In office Agnos found himself up against tough obstacles. Feinstein left behind a large deficit, forcing this liberal to cut spending 8%. The AIDS epidemic undermined the elan and cut the numbers (5,000 deaths by early 1988) of the gay community, which nonetheless created dozens of mostly volunteer organizations to help AIDS victims. Finally, San Francisco, always dovish on foreign policy, was hard hit by the base closings recommended by the new commission, losing 3,200 of the 8,000 civilian jobs lost nationwide.

The 5th Congressional District of California takes in three-quarters of San Francisco. It includes most of the rich areas of the city: Nob Hill, Russian Hill and Pacific Heights overlooking the Bay; the Marina district down by the water's edge; Presidio Heights with its leafy palms; St. Francis Wood, below Twin Peaks, the home of the city's Catholic elite. It includes the city's middle income Sunset district, with its older houses amid unburied telephone and electric wires, lying on curving hills that were once sand dunes, stretching out toward the ocean. And it includes lower income areas: the sunny Mission District, shielded from the ocean clouds by Twin Peaks; Portrero Hill, with restored houses overlooking downtown; the farther reaches of the city, with their varicolored pastel houses strewn out along grid streets hugging the steep hills. From 1965 to 1983 the politics of this district was dominated by Phillip Burton, an old-fashioned labor-liberal Democrat, an opponent of the Vietnam war from the beginning, who started off on the left wing of the House and ended up the architect of its reforms and who lost the race for House Majority Leader to Jim Wright by only one vote in the Democratic Caucus in 1976. He was succeeded by his wife, Sala, a political force in her own right, who died in 1987 a few days after she endorsed as her successor Nancy Pelosi, who won 35%–31% in an April 1987 primary against Harry Britt, Milk's successor as a gay supervisor.

Pelosi has a fine political pedigree and excellent political instincts. Her father, Thomas D'Alessandro, served in the House from 1939 to 1947 and was mayor of Baltimore for 12 years after that; her brother Thomas D'Alessandro Jr., was mayor from 1967 to 1971; she was California Democratic Party chair in the early 1980s, chaired the Democrats' delegate rules Compliance Review Commission for 1984, and served as the Democratic Senatorial Campaign

Committee's Finance Chair. She has the energy and shrewdness of one who has handled the most delicate political chores and the charm and unflappability of one who has been, at the same time, the parent of five children. Pelosi fit in quickly with the California delegation and has one of the most liberal voting records in Congress—which, with the political legitimacy granted coteries of exotic and solipsistic Hispanic, Asian, and black Maoists and Trotskyites, puts her right about in the middle of the spectrum in San Francisco.

The People: Est. Pop. 1986: 580,200, up 10.3% 1980–86; Pop. 1980: 525,971, dn. 4.8% 1970–80. Households (1980): 48% family, 21% with children, 35% married couples; 63.5% housing units rented; median monthly rent: $264; median house value: $98,900. Voting age pop. (1980): 434,190; 20% Asian origin, 12% Spanish origin, 9% Black.

1988 Presidential Vote:

Dukakis (D)	148,818	(71%)
Bush (R)	57,846	(28%)

Rep. Nancy Pelosi (D)

Elected June 2, 1987; b. March 26, 1940, Baltimore, MD; home, San Francisco; Trinity College, B.A. 1962; Roman Catholic; married (Paul).

Career: CA Dem. Party, Northern Chmn., 1977–81, State Chmn., 1981–83; Fin. Chmn., Dem. Sen. Camp. Cmttee., 1985–86; Pub. rel. exec., Ogilvy and Mather, 1986–87.

Office: 1005 LHOB, 20515, 202-225-4965. Also 450 Golden Gate Ave., #13407, San Francisco 94102, 415-556-4862.

Committees: *Banking, Finance and Urban Affairs* (28th of 31 D). Subcommittee: Housing and Community Development. *Government Operations* (22d of 24 D). Subcommittee: Human Resources and Intergovernmental Relations.

Group Ratings

	ADA	ACLU	COPE	CFA	LCV	ACU	NTLC	NSI	COC	CEI
1988	100	95	96	100	79	0	2	0	21	8
1987	93	—	100	89	—	0	—	—	9	3

National Journal Ratings

	1988 LIB — 1988 CONS		1987 LIB — 1987 CONS	
Economic	87% —	8%	73% —	0%
Social	86% —	0%	78% —	0%
Foreign	84% —	0%	* —	*

Key Votes

1) Homeless $	—	5) Ban Drug Test	—	9) SDI Research	—
2) Gephardt Amdt	—	6) Drug Death Pen	AGN	10) Ban Chem Weaps	—
3) Deficit Reduc	FOR	7) Handgun Sales	AGN	11) Aid to Contras	AGN
4) Kill Plnt Clsng Notice	AGN	8) Ban D.C. Abort $	AGN	12) Nuclear Testing	FOR

Election Results

1988 general	Nancy Pelosi (D)...................	133,530	(76%)	($616,936)
	Bruce M. O'Neill (R)................	33,692	(19%)	($19,245)
1988 primary	Nancy Pelosi (D), unopposed			
1987 special	Nancy Pelosi (D)...................	45,770	(67%)	($1,033,072)
	Harriet Ross (R)...................	22,188	(33%)	($7,547)
1986 general	Sala Burton (D)...................	122,688	(75%)	($388,026)
	Mike Garza (R)	36,039	(22%)	

SIXTH DISTRICT

When the Golden Gate Bridge was opened in 1937, everyone knew San Francisco at its southern end but almost no one had heard of Marin County at the north. Marin then had only 52,000 people, and was known mainly for the redwoods of Muir Woods and the peak of Mount Tamalpais, tourist attractions you could reach before the bridge by taking the ferry to Sausalito, "a strange combination of fishing village, residential suburb, and literary art colony," said the *WPA Guide*. Today Marin, still tucked away between mountains and bay, is a string of affluent suburbs with about 250,000 people, known nationally since the publication of Cyra McFadden's *The Serial* as the epitome of trendiness. Liberated and affluent, it is politically liberal on cultural issues, conservative on economics.

Marin has not, however, turned out to be the harbinger of America's future that many Marinites and others thought, and for many Americans, Marin's combination of personal liberation and economic laissez-faire has come to seem more like self-indulgence and selfishness. In presidential elections, Marin has been almost as perfect an indicator as Maine and Vermont were in 1936. A longtime Republican stronghold, it came within a hairsbreadth of going for George McGovern in 1972. Then it turned around and voted solidly for Gerald Ford in 1976. In 1980 it refused to give Ronald Reagan a majority and gave John Anderson one of his highest percentages in the nation. Against the national trend, it switched and in 1984 and 1988 voted for Walter Mondale and Michael Dukakis. If it starts to swing toward George Bush, he may be in trouble in 1992.

Marin County forms half of California's 6th Congressional District. The other half is a hodgepodge: a bit of southern Sonoma County, the working-class port of Vallejo, and part of San Francisco. But all are strongly Democratic. Southern Sonoma, the bucolic country around Sebastopol, Cotati and Petaluma, seems to be the place where the hippies of yesteryear went when they grew up; not so hemmed in by mountains and bay, stretching out over rolling countryside, it seems to be a somewhat more mellow, less trendy, less affluent Marin. Vallejo is the site of a naval shipyard, the sort of working-class town that Socialists of the Jack London era hoped would be the vanguard of a socialist America. The 6th District's portion of San Francisco includes the mostly black Fillmore and Western Addition areas; Haight-Ashbury, once the bedraggled center of hippiedom and now another gentrifying San Francisco neighborhood; the middle income Richmond area, stretching out north of Golden Gate Park toward the ocean, with its many Chinese residents; and high-income Sea Cliff on the hills overlooking the Golden Gate Bridge. The district was originally drawn, with more grotesque boundaries, for Representative John Burton; but to the surprise of everyone, including his late brother, he announced his retirement before the 1982 elections (he is now back representing San Francisco in the California Assembly).

That led to the victory of the present congresswoman, Barbara Boxer, who is a fitting personification of Marin County politics. Originally from New York, she was elected to the Marin County Board of Supervisors as an environmentalist in 1976. In her first election, the odd makeup of the district helped her. Marin provided most of the votes to give her the 1982 Democratic nomination, while in the general, against a serious (and Marin-based) Republican, she needed the Democratic margins from Vallejo and the Fillmore in order to win. Since then she has won easily.

Contrary to what many House Members must have expected of a Marin County supervisor, Boxer has not proved to be quirky or difficult to get along with. She is a team player, a Member usually loyal to the Democratic leadership, to feminist causes, to caucus groups representing significant constituencies in her district, and a good pol. A prominent member of the congressional military reform caucus, Boxer gained national attention in 1984 for disclosing that the Air Force had paid $7,622 for a coffee pot. She summed up the issue in the offshore oil drilling controversy after Interior Secretary Donald Hodel reneged on his agreement with the California delegation, by saying he was playing a new game, "Let's Break a Deal." Boxer serves on the Budget and Armed Services Committees where she has put some effort into procurement reform and was depressed when San Francisco lost the Presidio on the base closing commission. On Budget, she is one of many Democrats who want to hold defense spending increases down and, because of the deficit, are wary of raising domestic spending very much. This puts her in line with majority opinion in the House and the 6th District. Marin may not be in the national mainstream, but its congresswoman seems to be in the mainstream in the House.

The People: Est. Pop. 1986: 566,900, up 7.8% 1980–86; Pop. 1980: 526,020, up 5.8% 1970–80. Households (1980): 59% family, 30% with children, 46% married couples; 50.4% housing units rented; median monthly rent: $285; median house value: $119,900. Voting age pop. (1980): 409,204; 9% Asian origin, 9% Black, 5% Spanish origin, 1% American Indian.

1988 Presidential Vote:

Dukakis (D)...................	164,296	(64%)
Bush (R)	89,300	(35%)

Rep. Barbara Boxer (D)

Elected 1982; b. Nov. 11, 1940, Brooklyn, NY; home, Greenbrae; Brooklyn Col., B.A. 1962; Jewish; married (Stewart).

Career: Stockbroker, researcher, 1962–65; Journalist, *Pacific Sun*, 1972–74; Dist. aide to U.S. Rep. John Burton, 1974–76; Marin Cnty. Bd. of Spvsrs., 1976–82.

Offices: 307 CHOB 20515, 202-225-5161. Also 450 Golden Gate Ave., San Francisco 94102, 415-556-1333; 3301 Kerner Blvd., Marin 94901 415-457-7272; Sonoma 707-763-6033; and Vallejo 707-552-0720.

Committees: *Budget* (7th of 21 D). Task Force: Urgent Fiscal Issues. *Government Operations* (12th of 24 D). Subcommittees: Legislation and National Security; Government Activities and Transportation. *Select Committee on Children, Youth, and Families* (8th of 18 D).

Group Ratings

	ADA	ACLU	COPE	CFA	LCV	ACU	NTLC	NSI	COC	CEI
1988	80	91	97	82	88	5	8	0	27	-9
1987	92	—	97	79	—	0	—	—	7	6

National Journal Ratings

	1988 LIB — 1988 CONS		1987 LIB — 1987 CONS	
Economic	78% —	22%	73% —	0%
Social	83% —	15%	78% —	0%
Foreign	84% —	0%	81% —	0%

Key Votes

1) Homeless $	AGN	5) Ban Drug Test	AGN	9) SDI Research	AGN
2) Gephardt Amdt	FOR	6) Drug Death Pen	FOR	10) Ban Chem Weaps	FOR
3) Deficit Reduc	FOR	7) Handgun Sales	AGN	11) Aid to Contras	AGN
4) Kill Plnt Clsng Notice	AGN	8) Ban D.C. Abort $	AGN	12) Nuclear Testing	FOR

Election Results

1988 general	Barbara Boxer (D)	176,645	(73%)	($351,687)
	William Steinmetz (R)	64,174	(27%)	($50,532)
1988 primary	Barbara Boxer (D), unopposed			
1986 general	Barbara Boxer (D)	142,946	(74%)	($279,727)
	Franklin Ernst III (R).	50,606	(26%)	($10,171)

SEVENTH DISTRICT

In the days before World War II, not all of the East Bay across from San Francisco was developed. The San Francisco-Oakland Bay Bridge had been finished in 1937, and beyond Oakland and Berkeley there were farms on the level land beneath the mountains of the Diablo Range. To the north, in Contra Costa County, the biggest town was Richmond, with 23,000 people, a deep water harbor and an oil refinery and Ford plant. In World War II Henry J. Kaiser built huge shipyards here which could complete a ship in five days and turned out 20% of the country's merchant ships. The yards employed 91,000, drawn from all over the country. Richmond, with workers jammed into makeshift apartments, saw its population rise to over 100,000, only to sink back to 70,000 after the war, as newly prosperous workers fanned out into more spacious, pleasant surroundings. One place some headed was over San Pablo Ridge to the valley around Concord. This was farming territory in 1940, and Concord had only 1,000 people; today it has over 100,000 and is the urban center of Contra Costa County, with a BART station to whisk commuters across the Bay and affluent suburbs on every side.

Richmond and Concord are the two population centers of the 7th Congressional District of California, one of the four East Bay districts that send senior and talented liberal Democrats to Washington. The 7th includes Contra Costa, which was heavily Democratic when most of its voters lived in Richmond and the industrial towns along the northern arm of the Bay heading to Sacramento. Richmond, now about half black, remains heavily Democratic, but the suburbs around Concord are more Republican, and in 1988 Contra Costa voted only 51% for Michael Dukakis, the lowest of any Bay Area county. But residual Democratic loyalty and personal popularity have combined to make this a safe seat for Congressman George Miller.

Miller was first elected in 1974, but his political lineage goes back before that. His father was a powerful state senator and Miller got his legislative training in Sacramento; in the House he was a protégé and ally of San Francisco's Phillip Burton. Miller is not burdened with the doubts expressed by some Members of the class of 1974 about spending programs; he usually supports them, with some enthusiasm and skill. Like many older Democrats, he regards his duty as keeping the rich from getting too greedy and seeing that the poor and middle-class enjoy economic security and get their share of society's wealth. Physically imposing, with a hearty temper, Miller is a formidable opponent of what he considers ripoffs.

Miller holds important committee positions, not just because of seniority but because of what he does with them. On Interior he is the second-ranking Democrat and often the leading figure as Chairman Morris Udall is weakened by Parkinson's disease; Miller stands to become chairman when Udall retires and could hold that position for many years. Miller has spent much time on water—there is no more important issue in the West—opposing the heavy subsidies farmers in the Central Valley and elsewhere get from the federal government, using the leverage of the long unenforced 1902 limit of 160 acres for subsidized water-users to get them to pay more. This gets him in fights with others in the California delegation, notably Tony Coelho from the Valley, but Miller has operated from a position of strength as chairman of the Water and Power Resources Subcommittee. Yet he is not a dogmatic environmentalist and is open to arguments on the merits of any issue.

Miller is already a committee chairman, as head of the Select Committee on Children, Youth, and Families. Here he was ahead of the curve, squarely facing the problems raised by the fact that we are increasingly a nation of rich adults and poor children. He has pushed for more spending on nutrition programs, more training for child care personnel and more help for adoption. He has scathingly criticized Republicans on some issues but also has worked with them on others. He is not one of those liberals under the illusion that what the poor need is liberation from restraint. He has the perspective of a man who has raised a family himself, not the view of a rebellious teenager within it.

In 1983 Miller took a seat on the Budget Committee and originated the "pay-as-you-go" budget, embraced by House Democrats in 1984 to force budgeters to balance higher spending with cuts in other programs or higher taxes. After the 1988 election, he rotated off Budget and back onto Education and Labor, becoming the fifth ranking Democrat there. That will give him more opportunities to advance legislatively some of the ideas he has been pushing on his select committee, but his chances of rising to the Education and Labor chair any time soon are not good, and he has concentrated more on Interior Committee business for years.

Miller has won reelection by wide margins since 1976. Phil Burton's redistricting plans gave him Richmond, which Ron Dellums of the 8th District also wanted; and different boundaries could make this Contra Costa district considerably more marginal. But Miller seems well positioned to continue to be reelected by wide margins.

The People: Est. Pop. 1986: 585,400, up 11.3% 1980–86; Pop. 1980: 525,990, up 16.9% 1970–80. Households (1980): 72% family, 40% with children, 59% married couples; 34.4% housing units rented; median monthly rent: $261; median house value: $84,600. Voting age pop. (1980): 379,409; 10% Black, 8% Spanish origin, 4% Asian origin, 1% American Indian.

1988 Presidential Vote: Dukakis (D). 136,163   (53%)
                        Bush (R) 116,314   (46%)

Rep. George Miller (D)

Elected 1974; b. May 17, 1945, Richmond; home, Martinez; San Fran. St. Col., B.A. 1968, U. of CA at Davis, J.D. 1972; Roman Catholic; married (Cynthia).

Career: Legis. aide to CA Sen. Major. Ldr., 1969–74; Practicing atty., 1972–74.

Offices: 2228 RHOB 20515, 202-225-2095. Also 367 Civic Dr., Pleasant Hill 94523, 415-687-3260; and 3220 Blume Dr., #218, Richmond 94806, 415-222-4212.

Committees: *Education and Labor* (5th of 22 D). Subcommittees: Elementary, Secondary and Vocational Education; Labor-Management Relations; Postsecondary Education. *Interior and Insular Affairs* (2d of 26 D). Subcommittees: Energy and the Environment; Water, Power and Offshore Energy Resources (Chairman). *Select Committee on Children, Youth, and Families* (Chairman of 18 D).

Group Ratings

	ADA	ACLU	COPE	CFA	LCV	ACU	NTLC	NSI	COC	CEI
1988	95	96	90	100	88	4	16	0	31	16
1987	96	—	89	93	—	13	—	—	20	11

National Journal Ratings

	1988 LIB — 1988 CONS		1987 LIB — 1987 CONS	
Economic	71% —	23%	53% —	46%
Social	86% —	0%	78% —	0%
Foreign	84% —	0%	81% —	0%

Key Votes

1) Homeless $	FOR	5) Ban Drug Test	AGN	9) SDI Research	AGN
2) Gephardt Amdt	AGN	6) Drug Death Pen	AGN	10) Ban Chem Weaps	FOR
3) Deficit Reduc	AGN	7) Handgun Sales	AGN	11) Aid to Contras	AGN
4) Kill Plnt Clsng Notice	AGN	8) Ban D.C. Abort $	AGN	12) Nuclear Testing	FOR

Election Results

1988 general	George Miller (D)...................	170,006	(68%)	($269,887)
	Jean Last (R)	78,478	(32%)	($14,710)
1988 primary	George Miller (D), unopposed			
1986 general	George Miller (D)...................	124,174	(67%)	($312,522)
	Rosemary Thakar (R)................	62,379	(33%)	($92,496)

EIGHTH DISTRICT

The University of California at Berkeley, where half a century ago "the freshmen wears his 'beanie' and smokes only a corncob pipe on campus" and the *WPA Guide* continued, "the other classes give wide berth to sophomore lawn," became the symbol of quite another kind of campus atmosphere a quarter century later, when the so-called Free Speech Movement, protesting an administrator's refusal to let students set up a card table to sign up volunteers for Lyndon Johnson's 1964 campaign, led to months of riots, students strikes and classroom confrontation. That spirit of rebellion no longer animates many students; Berkeley's elite student body, some 30% of them Asian, is studying hard to get ahead in a surging high-tech economy. But the spirit lives on in most adults in Berkeley and in the politics in Berkeley and adjacent parts of the East

Bay. From the hillier parts of the lush Berkeley campus, they can look out over the San Francisco Bay and take in with one gaze one of the most affluent and culturally liberated places in the world. It takes a fevered adolescent imagination to see a land of oppression and poverty. But Berkeley has always attracted the imaginative, and the antics of its often left-dominated city council over the 1970s and 1980s have helped to concentrate, here and in the towns just around, people who want to imagine themselves as part of a virtuous proletariat oppressed by capitalist defense contractors and local landlords. They might be more accurately described, though, as highly educated but underpaid professionals who want to live near stores that stock the right kind of goat cheese.

The 8th Congressional District of California is the Berkeley district, with one-quarter of its residents in Berkeley and the similar suburbs of Albany, Kensington and El Cerrito, about half in Oakland, and another quarter over the Berkeley Hills, in highly affluent suburbs. Like Berkeley, Oakland has poor and middle-income blacks living on the flatlands, and affluent whites—fewer of them left in Oakland—on the curving streets in the hills or in the enclave suburb of Piedmont or in the modest neighborhood where former Attorney General Edwin Meese, son and grandson of Oakland civil servants, grew up. The Contra Costa suburbs over the hills—whether woodsy and rustic like Orinda, Moraga and Lafayette, or full of newly minted subdivisions with pricey houses on treeless streets as in the San Ramon valley—are unsympathetic to anything smacking of radical politics.

Ronald Dellums, the 8th's congressman, is a product of self-consciously radical Berkeley politics, and almost a political antique; he won the seat in 1970, as a radical critic of an incumbent who had one of the most liberal voting records in the House. He continues to infuriate many voters, not all of them Republicans, and for years there was a rock-solid 40% anti-Dellums vote in the district. In 1988, he still lost the Contra Costa suburbs, but he cracked the 60% barrier and won districtwide with 67%—the kind of percentage most incumbents with his seniority win.

Dellums combines the world view of 1960s protesters with the dignity of a senior House subcommittee chairman. He believes, as civil rights marchers did, that American society is infected with racism; he believes, as poverty warriors once did, that government should be much more generous to the poor; he believes, as Vietnam war protesters did, that American military spending is excessive and threatens world peace. His scathing denunciation of the Grenada invasion suggests that he sees virtue in the income-redistribution policies of Socialist countries and no harm in their military connections with the Soviet Union, though certainly he would not endorse their suppressions of civil liberties. He is eloquent in his denunciations of the hideous acts of the South African government, and in June 1986, he was startled when the House adopted by voice vote his amendment placing an embargo on South Africa and ordering all American firms there to leave. The bill ultimately passed by Congress did not have such drastic sanctions, but Dellums's amendment did make vivid the House's disgust with the South African regime and its own willingness to act. Dellums is entitled to satisfaction for having led the way for America to take a stand against injustice.

He is also entitled to some satisfaction for his former stewardship of the Military Construction Subcommittee which he chaired from 1983 until 1989 when he switched to the Research Subcommittee. Though an opponent of many weapons systems, he was also a Marine, and he seems to feel he has a duty to be knowledgeable and scrupulously fair. He has not been a dismantler of military facilities, though he did go against the usual pattern and killed a proposal to make San Francisco (and its heavily black Hunters Point neighborhood) the homeport for the battleship Missouri. Dellums surprised some colleagues in 1986 when he came out vociferously for conservative Marvin Leath for House Armed Services Committee chairman and nominated him in a moving speech before the Democratic Caucus. But this was no departure: like many on the fringes of either party, he supports the seniority system which protects his positions, and he supported elderly Chairman Mel Price in 1984. Moreover, on military and budget issues Dellums and some of his friends had startling success forging joint party positions with Leath and some of his colleagues; such experiences can bond otherwise unlike politicians together. Leath did not win, but Dellums made his point, and in the process established himself as a force to be reckoned with in the caucus. In the meantime, his seniority makes him Chairman of the House District of Columbia Committee, a less important position than it was before the District got home rule in 1973. Dellums' longstanding support of home rule means that he seldom interferes in District matters and opposes the attempts of Congress to rewrite the District's sex discrimination and tax laws. He has agreed with the suggestion, made most recently by Republican Bill Thomas, that D.C. be phased out as a full committee—a nice example of principle taking precedence over self-interest.

The People: Est. Pop. 1986: 550,500, up 4.7% 1980–86; Pop. 1980: 525,646, dn. 1.8% 1970–80. Households (1980): 57% family, 29% with children, 42% married couples; 51.1% housing units rented; median monthly rent: $218; median house value: $107,900. Voting age pop. (1980): 409,168; 24% Black, 8% Asian origin, 6% Spanish origin.

1988 Presidential Vote:
Dukakis (D)	178,961	(70%)
Bush (R)	74,533	(29%)

Rep. Ronald V. Dellums (D)

Elected 1970; b. Nov. 24, 1935, Oakland; home, Oakland; San Fran. St. Col., B.A. 1960, U. of CA, M.S.W. 1962; Protestant; married (Leola).

Career: USMC, 1954–56; Psychiatric social worker, CA Dept. of Mental Hygiene, 1962–64; Prog. Dir., Bayview Community Ctr., 1964–65; Dir., Hunter's Pt. Bayview Youth Opportunity Ctr., 1965–66; Plng. consult., Bay Area Social Plng. Cncl., 1966–67; Dir., San Fran. Econ. Opportunity Empl. Prog., 1967–68; Berkeley City Cncl., 1967–71; Sr. consult., Social Dynamics, Inc., 1968–70.

Offices: 2136 RHOB 20515, 202-225-2661. Also 1720 Oregon St., Rm. 6, Berkeley 94703, 415-548-7767; 201 13th St., Ste. 105, Oakland 94617; and 3730 Mt. Diablo Blvd., Rm. 160, Lafayette 94549, 415-763-0370.

Committees: *Armed Services* (4th of 31 D). Subcommittees: Research and Development (Chairman); Investigations. *District of Columbia* (Chairman of 8 D). Subcommittees: Judiciary and Education; Fiscal Affairs and Health.

Group Ratings

	ADA	ACLU	COPE	CFA	LCV	ACU	NTLC	NSI	COC	CEI
1988	100	100	92	91	94	0	7	0	23	7
1987	100	—	92	100	—	0	—	—	0	3

National Journal Ratings

	1988 LIB — 1988 CONS			1987 LIB — 1987 CONS		
Economic	92%	—	0%	73%	—	0%
Social	86%	—	0%	78%	—	0%
Foreign	68%	—	28%	81%	—	0%

Key Votes

1) Homeless $	AGN	5) Ban Drug Test	AGN	9) SDI Research	AGN
2) Gephardt Amdt	FOR	6) Drug Death Pen	AGN	10) Ban Chem Weaps	FOR
3) Deficit Reduc	FOR	7) Handgun Sales	AGN	11) Aid to Contras	AGN
4) Kill Plnt Clsng Notice	AGN	8) Ban D.C. Abort $	AGN	12) Nuclear Testing	FOR

Election Results

1988 general	Ronald V. Dellums (D)	163,221	(67%)	($1,174,676)
	John J. Cuddihy, Jr. (R)	76,531	(31%)	($7,071)
1988 primary	Ronald V. Dellums (D), unopposed			
1986 general	Ronald V. Dellums (D)	121,790	(60%)	($1,223,490)
	Steven Eigenberg (R)	76,850	(38%)	($74,567)

NINTH DISTRICT

As you look out on the East Bay from the skyscrapers of downtown San Francisco, your eyes go first to the Bay Bridge, then to the big Navy and Army bases and the port of Oakland, up a little to the skyscrapers of Oakland, then over to the left of the Bridge to see if you can make out the towers of the campus in Berkeley. Those are the landmarks: you don't look much to the right, or south, of downtown Oakland, to see the expanse of East Bay neighborhoods and suburbs spreading out down to where the Bay itself spreads out to the width of a miniature sea, spanned by the causeway-like San Mateo Bridge. If you were looking there, though, what you would be seeing is most of the 9th Congressional District of California.

The 9th District includes the old city of Alameda, resolutely middle-class despite its proximity to Navy bases and the Oakland ghetto; it includes some mostly black neighborhoods in Oakland itself; it passes south and includes the modest suburbs of San Leandro (mostly Portuguese-American), San Lorenzo and Hayward, which were cherry grove and dairy farming areas 50 years ago. The terrain here is not much different from other places in the Bay Area; the houses are built of the same materials, mostly stucco; the shopping centers, to outward appearances, are what you see all over. But there are discount chains rather than Saks, bargain drugstores rather than boutiques. Housing prices here are among the most reasonable in the Bay Area, and this is where working people, mostly white but many Mexican-Americans as well, live. Beyond the mountains (you can't see over them from San Francisco) the 9th District includes the upper middle-income suburbs of Pleasanton and Livermore, in a valley outside the Bay Area orbit.

The military is a presence here, from the Oakland waterfront to the Livermore Laboratories, long headed by Edward Teller, which is one of the leading centers for SDI research. But the 9th District votes mostly for Democrats, and usually liberal ones at that. The congressman here is Fortney (Pete) Stark, first elected in 1972 when he beat an elderly incumbent who supported the Vietnam war, and an opponent of SDI, despite Livermore, today. Stark is by nature a kind of insurgent: he started a bank in nearby Walnut Creek and attracted deposits from all over the Bay Area by putting a giant peace symbol atop his headquarters and peace symbol motifs on all the checks. He spent liberally on his own campaign and, reversing what was then the usual practice, got rid of his bank stock before taking a seat on the House Banking Committee.

Now Stark is a senior member of Ways and Means and chairman of one of the most important subcommittees in the House, Health. His path to power came not just through seniority but also through alliance with Chairman Dan Rostenkowski: the Chicago ward committeeman and the West Coast peace banker both went to high school in Wisconsin and get on together just fine. Stark supported Rostenkowski on his big bills, like tax reform; Rostenkowski supports Stark on his. Stark's subcommittee has jurisdiction over Medicare and Medicaid, and the rules it makes affect the whole health care industry—some 12% of the gross national product. Stark has become in effect a technician of America's makeshift welfare state, fixing this and trying to change that so it won't need repair. His biggest achievement was the Medicare Catastrophic Coverage Act of 1988, in which he not only called for new benefits, but provided a new tax—on high-income Social Security recipients—to pay for them. Stark also got passed a bill on the ethics of referrals: he has been trying to crack down on doctors who own labs and order unneeded tests from them, and hospitals that pay doctors a bounty for referring patients. He pushed through bills to provide more in-patient hospital care for the indigent. In 1989, he has a bill that would reduce the use of chlorofluorocarbons by slapping an excise tax on their production. The idea is in line with Stark's philosophy on medical care. He no longer pushes government-supplied national health care, as he once would have reflexively. Instead, he uses taxes and regulations to affect misconduct and provide incentives for economical service, recognizing that government needs not only to promote better care, but must see to it that it doesn't become an unrestrained drain on the Treasury.

Stark has not had many serious political challenges in the 9th District since first winning it in 1972; the closest the Republicans have come was holding him to 55% of the vote in 1980. The American Medical Association's PAC made some $200,000 of independent expenditures against him in 1986, but they failed to help the hapless Republican candidate and reduced rather than increased the AMA's influence on Stark.

The People: Est. Pop. 1986: 581,500, up 10.5% 1980–86; Pop. 1980: 526,234, up 2.8% 1970–80. Households (1984): 71% family, 38% with children, 57% married couples; 40.5% housing units rented; median monthly rent: $258; median house value: $82,800. Voting age pop. (1980): 388,528; 12% Spanish origin, 10% Black, 6% Asian origin, 1% American Indian.

1988 Presidential Vote:

Dukakis (D)	....	124,397	(57%)
Bush (R)	....	91,636	(42%)

Rep. Fortney H. (Pete) Stark (D)

Elected 1972; b. Nov. 11, 1931, Milwaukee, WI; home, Hayward; MIT, B.S. 1953, U. of CA, M.B.A. 1960; Unitarian; married (Carolyn).

Career: Air Force, 1955–57; Founder, Beacon Savings and Loan Assn., 1961; Founder and Pres., Security Natl. Bank, Walnut Creek, 1963–72.

Offices: 1125 LHOB 20515, 202-225-5065. Also 22300 Foothill Blvd., Hayward 94541, 415-635-1092.

Committees: *District of Columbia* (3d of 8 D). Subcommittees: Government Operations and Metropolitan Affairs; Judiciary and Education. *Ways and Means* (5th of 23 D). Subcommittees: Health (Chairman); Select Revenue Measures. *Select Committee on Narcotics Abuse and Control* (3d of 18 D). *Joint Economic Committee.* Subcommittees: Economic Growth, Trade and Taxes; Fiscal and Monetary Policy; Investment, Jobs and Prices.

Group Ratings

	ADA	ACLU	COPE	CFA	LCV	ACU	NTLC	NSI	COC	CEI
1988	90	100	90	82	88	0	14	0	42	16
1987	96	—	90	93	—	13	—	—	20	9

National Journal Ratings

	1988 LIB	—	1988 CONS	1987 LIB	—	1987 CONS
Economic	63%	—	36%	57%	—	40%
Social	*	—	*	78%	—	0%
Foreign	84%	—	0%	81%	—	0%

Key Votes

1) Homeless $	AGN	5) Ban Drug Test	AGN	9) SDI Research	AGN
2) Gephardt Amdt	AGN	6) Drug Death Pen	—	10) Ban Chem Weaps	FOR
3) Deficit Reduc	AGN	7) Handgun Sales	—	11) Aid to Contras	AGN
4) Kill Plnt Clsng Notice	AGN	8) Ban D.C. Abort $	AGN	12) Nuclear Testing	FOR

Election Results

1988 general	Fortney H. (Pete) Stark (D)	152,866	(73%)	($410,540)
	Howard Hertz (R)	56,656	(27%)	($0)
1988 primary	Fortney H. (Pete) Stark (D), unopposed			
1986 general	Fortney H. (Pete) Stark (D)	113,490	(70%)	($533,314)
	David M. Williams (R)	49,300	(30%)	($61,483)

TENTH DISTRICT

Nowhere is the growth of post-World War II America more vividly illustrated than in San Jose, California. Before the war brought so many young Americans to the San Francisco Bay area, San Jose, just beyond the marshlands at the south end of San Francisco Bay and surrounded by lush orchards and fields of crops, was a compact city, "the largest canning and dried-fruit packing center in the world," the *WPA Guide* proclaims, but with only 68,000 people and with the canneries and residential districts just a few blocks from downtown. Few people then anticipated what was about to happen: that San Jose would become the focus of the most massive population growth in the San Francisco Bay Area. Today there are more people in the irregular bounds of San Jose than in the tip of the peninsula that is San Francisco, and there are more people living along the freeways within a few miles of San Jose than there are in San Francisco and the suburbs just below it up to San Bruno Mountain, where the Peninsula suburbs begin. In 1940 San Jose seemed no more likely to become a metropolis than Salinas or Bakersfield. How would people make a living down there?

The answer is: off everything from old-fashioned farming to the most up-to-date high technology. San Jose's growth came from two directions. From the east, people moved down from working-class East Bay neighborhoods, factories were built on vacant land and employees flocked to the new subdivisions nearby. The east side of San Jose is thus largely blue-collar, as are the East Bay suburbs to the north: Fremont, Newark, Union City. In the late 1970s, they came on hard times, as when General Motors closed its Fremont assembly plant. But the 1980s saw revival, as the plant became the site of GM's much ballyhooed joint venture with Toyota. The other stream of migration to San Jose came from the northwest. Here, along U.S. 101 and Interstate 280, is the Silicon Valley, the heart of the nation's microelectronics industry. People here are highly educated and affluent, addicted to Perrier, bicycling, and jogging. The heart of the Silicon Valley is a dozen miles or so up the freeways from downtown San Jose, but the entire area has benefited from the prosperity and growth that the now threatened industry has generated. Santa Clara County, which includes San Jose and many of the Silicon Valley towns, increased in population from 290,000 in 1950 to 1.3 million in 1980.

California's 10th Congressional District consists of eastern and central San Jose, suburban areas nearby, and the East Bay cities just to the north. It spans the southern edge of the Bay from

Hayward to the border between San Jose and Sunnyvale. The 10th has the largest Spanish origin population in the Bay Area (28%), some concentrated in old Mexican neighborhoods in San Jose, but many scattered about the district, as are many products of earlier waves of immigration. This used to be a solidly Democratic district, solid enough to have voted for George McGovern in 1972; rather surprisingly, it voted for Ronald Reagan in 1984 but went comfortably for Michael Dukakis in 1988.

For almost three decades, this part of California has been represented by Democratic Congressman Don Edwards. He has a conservative background: he was once an FBI agent, and he got rich because his family owned the only title company in Santa Clara County during its years of great expansion. When he was elected to Congress in 1962, he started out as one of its most liberal members: one of the early opponents of the Vietnam war and an advocate of abolition of the House Committee on Un-American Activities. Today he continues to be one of the most liberal members of the House, as well as a competent and accomplished legislator.

Oddly, he hasn't risen to the chair of any committee and is still just third on Judiciary and second on Veterans. But he chairs the Civil and Constitutional Rights Subcommittee, which has jurisdiction over civil rights laws and constitutional amendments. In the 1980s Edwards pushed the former to passage and bottled up the latter. He was a leader in reviving the Voting Rights Act in the early 1980s, when support was flagging; he persevered and got the Civil Rights Restoration Act passed in the last Reagan Congress; he was also one of the backers of the 1988 fair housing bill. On all these, Edwards works closely with the civil rights lobby and resists efforts to rewrite or amend the language to which all its groups agree.

He shows even greater stubbornness on constitutional amendments. Proposals to ban abortion, enforce school prayer, require Congress to balance the budget and ban school busing literally do not get a hearing before his subcommittee, on which he has a solid 5 to 3 margin, and he makes no apology for using the rules to the maximum extent to defeat these measures. Similarly, he stands against the death penalty in drug bills and other popular proposals when others fear to do so. He perseveres in the distasteful tasks that fall to Judiciary members, like handling the impeachment of Mississippi federal Judge Walter Nixon after he was convicted of a felony and refused to resign.

On the Veterans' Affairs Committee Edwards has a friendly relationship with Chairman Sonny Montgomery, but sometimes opposes him, as he did in 1986 by pushing to allow veterans to go to court to appeal denial of VA benefits. Together they are patrons of the system of VA hospitals. Edwards has one other important role. He is dean of California's 45-member delegation, the largest in the House and one that has sometimes been fractious. He set up and staffed a delegation office, which monitors legislation for effects on California, and his friendliness and reputation for fairness and candor have made him a leader who has gotten results and sometimes even unity, as on offshore oil drilling.

In the 10th District, Edwards is reelected routinely without significant opposition.

The People: Est. Pop. 1986: 592,800, up 12.7% 1980–86; Pop. 1980: 525,882, up 39.0% 1970–80. Households (1980): 76% family, 48% with children, 61% married couples; 37.7% housing units rented; median monthly rent: $276; median house value: $88,700. Voting age pop. (1980): 360,334; 24% Spanish origin, 10% Asian origin, 5% Black, 1% American Indian.

1988 Presidential Vote:

Dukakis (D)	101,751	(55%)
Bush (R)	80,564	(44%)

Rep. Don Edwards (D)

Elected 1962; b. Jan. 6, 1915, San Jose; home, San Jose; Stanford U., A.B. 1936, J.D. 1938; Unitarian; married (Edith).

Career: FBI Agent, 1940–41; Navy, WWII; Pres., Valley Title Co.

Offices: 2307 RHOB 20515, 202-225-3072. Also 1042 W. Hedding St., Ste. 110, San Jose 95125, 408-247-1711; and 38750 Paseo Padre Pkwy., Fremont 94536, 415-792-5320.

Committees: *Judiciary* (3d of 21 D). Subcommittees: Administrative Law and Governmental Relations; Civil and Constitutional Rights (Chairman); Economic and Commercial Law. *Veterans' Affairs* (2d of 21 D). Subcommittee: Oversight and Investigations.

Group Ratings

	ADA	ACLU	COPE	CFA	LCV	ACU	NTLC	NSI	COC	CEI
1988	100	100	94	100	94	0	8	0	23	7
1987	100	—	94	93	—	0	—	—	0	6

National Journal Ratings

	1988 LIB — 1988 CONS		1987 LIB — 1987 CONS	
Economic	92%	0%	73%	0%
Social	86%	0%	78%	0%
Foreign	79%	16%	81%	0%

Key Votes

1) Homeless $	AGN	5) Ban Drug Test	AGN	9) SDI Research	AGN
2) Gephardt Amdt	FOR	6) Drug Death Pen	AGN	10) Ban Chem Weaps	FOR
3) Deficit Reduc	FOR	7) Handgun Sales	AGN	11) Aid to Contras	AGN
4) Kill Plnt Clsng Notice	AGN	8) Ban D.C. Abort $	AGN	12) Nuclear Testing	FOR

Election Results

1988 general	Don Edwards (D)	142,500	(86%)	($173,537)
	Kennita Watson (Lib)	22,801	(14%)	($0)
1988 primary	Don Edwards (D)	48,276	(83%)	
	Anselmo A. Chavez (D)	9,863	(17%)	
1986 general	Don Edwards (D)	84,240	(71%)	($156,410)
	Michael R. La Crone (R)	31,826	(27%)	

ELEVENTH DISTRICT

In 1940, the Peninsula south of San Francisco was still exotic to city residents. It was reached only by a tortuous route, with its main street passing between a huge bald mountain and a big cement plant, then turning into "a tree-lined boulevard in a country-club domain," passing farther south as a two-lane road through apricot orchards. Almost all of today's Peninsula suburbs already existed, but there was still plenty of vacant land—orchards and tidal waste and hillside—in them. Today the Peninsula suburbs have been filled in, from the bay to the mountain ridge that runs almost on top of the San Andreas Fault, connecting San Francisco and Silicon Valley with an unbroken strip of urban settlement (though the hilltop I-280 runs through park land).

There are two distinct sets of Peninsula suburbs. In the north, adjacent to the city and encircling San Bruno Mountain, are towns that, demographically and politically, are extensions of the city neighborhoods just to the north. Daly City, at the southern extension of the BART lines, has substantial numbers of Mexican-Americans and Asians as well as whites of varying descent; South San Francisco proclaims itself "the industrial city" in big letters on San Bruno Mountain near the Bayshore Freeway; the streets lined with boxy houses in Pacifica and San Bruno wind over sweeping hillsides facing the cemeteries where so many San Franciscans and veterans of Pacific wars have been buried. People in these neighborhoods are mostly from working-class backgrounds, although most are upwardly mobile; they are ancestral Democrats, although they sometimes vote Republican; their orientation is to the urban pace of San Francisco, not the life of the Peninsula suburbs south of the airport.

There the atmosphere is different. The weather is warmer and sunnier, because the mountains protect the towns from the ocean clouds and fogs. The people here are more likely to have white-collar jobs, to be college educated, to be from backgrounds both Protestant and Republican. The weather is perfect for outdoor sports, and there are more jogging and bicycle paths and tennis courts here, in the string of suburbs south from Millbrae to Los Altos, than anywhere else in the United States. Cultural attitudes tend to be liberal; people want to save the environment, oppose Vietnam-like wars, and in some cases even legalize marijuana. On economic issues, however, they are not especially interested in redistributing income nor much concerned with unemployment. The federal government is as much a threat as a source of help.

Most of the Peninsula makes up California's 11th Congressional District, which includes all of the Peninsula from the San Francisco city limits down to Redwood City except the very high-income suburbs of Hillsborough, Woodside, Portola Valley and Atherton. But on a national scale, the 11th is high-income territory; nonetheless, its cultural liberalism almost enabled Walter Mondale to carry it in 1984, and in 1988 it went strongly for Michael Dukakis, whose coattails here may have helped a 27-year-old Democrat, Ted Lempert, capture the ancestrally Republican south Peninsula Assembly district.

The congressman here is Tom Lantos, who for years taught economics at San Francisco State. Lantos is one of the few Members of Congress—ex-POW Senator John McCain is another—who has personal experience living under tyranny. Lantos was born in Hungary and fought as a teenager in the underground against the Nazis; he was one of the Jews saved by the Swedish diplomat Raoul Wallenberg. Lantos devotes much of his attention to his work on the Foreign Affairs Committee. Like almost all the other Democrats there, he has been an opponent of aid to the Nicaraguan contras; but he does not seem to bring to his work the same instinctive mistrust of administration policy or doubts of American good intentions you get from many other post-Watergate Democrats. He made something of a stir in December 1986 when he promised to contribute to Lt. Col. Oliver North's legal defense fund—because, he said, he didn't want North, who wore his Marine uniform and decorations to the committee room where he took the Fifth Amendment, to be a scapegoat for those higher up. Lantos is among the most enthusiastic supporters of Israel, and was the co-sponsor of the measure, which became controversial in the 1984 presidential campaign, to move the U.S. embassy in Israel from Tel Aviv to Jerusalem. He strongly mistrusts the Soviets and in 1982 labored unsuccessfully to persuade the Swedes to use the leverage they gained by trapping a Soviet submarine in their waters to get more information about Wallenberg, who many think has been a Soviet prisoner since 1945. He is proud of being an outspoken backer of Tibetan human rights and invited the Dalai Lama to testify in 1987; he raised the issue in China, at which point Deng Xiaoping called him "ignorant" and "arrogant."

After opposing some Democratic positions on domestic issues early in his tenure, Lantos has voted more with his party lately; he chairs a Government Operations subcommittee and has taken some critical looks at OSHA. In the 101st Congress he is looking into "influence peddling" abuses in HUD by well-connected political consultants.

Lantos won this seat in 1980—one of only four Democrats to replace a Republicans that year—after a bizarre series of events. In late 1978, newly reelected 11th District Congressman Leo Ryan was killed in the Jonestown massacre in Guyana; a Republican experienced in local government won the seat the next spring, after a divisive Democratic primary; then Lantos came in and beat the Republican in 1980 and, spending $1.1 million, again in 1982. He has not had serious competition since.

The People: Est. Pop. 1986: 548,500, up 4.3% 1980–86; Pop. 1980: 525,981, up 5.9% 1970–80. Households (1980): 68% family, 34% with children, 55% married couples; 42.2% housing units rented; median monthly rent: $311; median house value: $117,100. Voting age pop. (1980): 400,549; 12% Spanish origin, 9% Asian origin, 6% Black.

1988 Presidential Vote:	Dukakis (D) 126,351	(58%)
	Bush (R) 89,063	(41%)

Rep. Tom Lantos (D)

Elected 1980; b. Feb. 1, 1928, Budapest, Hungary; home, Burlingame; U. of WA, B.A. 1949, M.A. 1950, U. of CA, Ph.D. 1953; Jewish; married (Annette).

Career: Economist, Bank of America, 1952–53; TV Commentator, San Fran., 1955–63; Dir. of Intl. Programs, CA St. U. system, 1962–71; Econ.-foreign policy adviser to U.S. Sen. Joseph R. Biden Jr., 1978–79; Mbr., Pres. Task Force on Defense and Foreign Policy, 1976; Faculty, San Fran. St. U., 1950–80.

Offices: 1526 LHOB 20515, 202-225-3531. Also 400 El Camino Real, Ste. 800, San Mateo 94402, 415-342-0300.

Committees: *Foreign Affairs* (10th of 28 D). Subcommittees: Asian and Pacific Affairs; Europe and the Middle East; Human Rights and International Organizations. *Government Operations* (10th of 24 D). Subcommittees: Employment and Housing (Chairman); Government Activities and Transportation. *Select Committee on Aging* (15th of 39 D). Subcommittees: Housing and Consumer Interests; Human Services.

Group Ratings

	ADA	ACLU	COPE	CFA	LCV	ACU	NTLC	NSI	COC	CEI
1988	85	73	94	82	94	8	15	20	31	15
1987	84	—	94	79	—	0	—	—	20	6

National Journal Ratings

	1988 LIB — 1988 CONS			1987 LIB — 1987 CONS		
Economic	79%	—	17%	73%	—	0%
Social	66%	—	32%	78%	—	0%
Foreign	60%	—	37%	66%	—	32%

Key Votes

1) Homeless $	AGN	5) Ban Drug Test	AGN	9) SDI Research	AGN
2) Gephardt Amdt	FOR	6) Drug Death Pen	FOR	10) Ban Chem Weaps	FOR
3) Deficit Reduc	FOR	7) Handgun Sales	AGN	11) Aid to Contras	AGN
4) Kill Plnt Clsng Notice	AGN	8) Ban D.C. Abort $	AGN	12) Nuclear Testing	FOR

110   CALIFORNIA

Election Results

1988 general	Tom Lantos (D)....................	145,484	(71%)	($269,510)
	G. M. (Bill) Quraishi (R)..............	50,050	(24%)	($95,575)
1988 primary	Tom Lantos (D), unopposed			
1986 general	Tom Lantos (D)....................	112,380	(74%)	($325,435)
	G. M. (Bill) Quraishi (R)...............	39,315	(26%)	($63,996)

TWELFTH DISTRICT

Half a century ago the writers of the *WPA Guide* could find little to say about Cupertino, California (pop. 2,500). "A crossroads town in flat orchard lands, settled in the 1850s by squatters who banded together when the owner of Rancho Quito tried to chase them off. In the 1880s, several sea captains retired and built prim New England cottages here." Evidently, not much happened in the following 60 years. You would not say that today. In the 1970s, two young men in their twenties set up a computer business in Cupertino they named Apple, and within a few years this collection of stucco subdivisions and low-rise office buildings became the center of what came to be called the Silicon Valley. This, in turn, became the center of America's microchip industry, the premier high-tech region of the country, where computer hackers started new companies and made millions in months. It was where a technology whose potential was unrecognized by America's giant corporations and produced changes in how Americans did business and spent their personal time. The Silicon Valley, in the years since, has had its ups and downs—product revolutions always produce economic losers as well as winners—but it remains prosperous and creative, one of the most important parts of America.

Coinciding with the boundaries of the Silicon Valley to an almost eerie extent is the 12th Congressional District of California. In the north, nearest San Francisco, it includes the center of the Peninsula, taking in Hillsborough, Woodside, Portola Valley and Atherton—the highest income suburbs of San Francisco, where the Silicon Valley's instant millionaires buy houses for sums like "three point four." It includes Palo Alto and the neighboring Menlo Park, the home of Stanford University, of the conservatively inclined Hoover Institution, and of Stanford Research Institute—the places that formulate the theoretical and ideological implications of the microchip revolution. It continues farther south, where Interstate 280 dips below the hills to include the string of towns on the flatlands as well as the high-income hillside suburbs of Los Altos, Saratoga and Monte Sereno, until it reaches Cupertino. It then curves around San Jose, avoiding the city and its east side Mexican-American suburban fringe, and includes part of Santa Cruz County and several agricultural towns south of San Jose, notably Gilroy, the garlic capital of America.

High-tech could start anywhere (Cray builds their supercomputers in Chippewa Falls, Wisconsin); why is so much of it here? Partly because of Stanford, which has encouraged its faculty to experiment with—and profit from—high-tech breakthroughs; partly because early high tech companies, like Hewlett-Packard, are in Palo Alto. Then there is IBM's decision in the 1950s to site a major facility in San Jose. And San Francisco generated a big supply of venturesome venture capital. But high-tech is concentrated in the Silicon Valley largely because this is the kind of place in which smart young innovators like to live. Radical veterans of the counterculture may cluster around the university towns of Berkeley and Santa Cruz; elite law and medical school graduates head to the big central cities where the prestigious jobs are; but techies are free to live in the pleasant, healthy environment beneath the hills that loom over Stanford and San Francisco Bay. While they work in squat rectilinear offices and factories on land that was 50 years ago fertile fruit and vegetable croplands, they can dream of living, when they strike it rich, in the hills where the first settlers here built mills and farmhouses, in stark contemporary houses amid huge live oak and eucalyptus trees. There is a sort of pure Americana here: these communities were rustic but never poor, rural but never bigoted, country-like but still easily accessible to all the luxuries of civilization, culturally interesting but without ethnic discrimination. People here were ahead of the rest of the nation in fighting to preserve the environment, in favoring natural over processed foods, and in indulging in systematic exercise.

The politics here is culturally liberal, concerned about the environment and world peace, and on economics increasingly respectful of free markets. Twenty years ago young liberal Republicans like Pete McCloskey, who won the House seat in a 1967 special against conservative Shirley Temple Black, supposed that the march of progress was toward greater government regulation and provision for the poor. Now moderate Republicans like Ed Zschau, the high-tech entrepreneur who replaced McCloskey in 1982 and who came within 1% of beating Senator Alan Cranston in 1986, think that government is usually a klutz that should stand aside and let entrepreneurs expand the economy so that there is more for almost everyone.

Now the district has another Republican congressman in the same mold, former Stanford Law professor Tom Campbell. But he had a hard struggle and had to beat two tough opponents to win it. The easier one, unexpectedly, was in the primary against Republican incumbent Ernest Konnyu, an assemblyman who won the seat when Zschau ran for the Senate. Konnyu was a misfit for the Silicon Valley: a hardliner on foreign policy (his family fled Communist Hungary), a cultural conservative, an excitable man who had the highest staff turnover of any congressman in 1987. He criticized Corazon Aquino, lost a committee spot by attacking senior Republicans, and according to the *San Jose Mercury News* made unwelcome sexual remarks to a female aide—very much a no-no in these liberated precincts. Against Konnyu, Zschau and high-tech billionaire David Packard backed Campbell, the youngest tenured professor in Stanford history, an economics Ph.D. from the free-market precincts of the University of Chicago, a bureau head in the Reagan Federal Trade Commission, and a moderate on some cultural issues. Campbell beat Konnyu 58%–42%.

Campbell had tougher competition in the general. San Mateo Supervisor Anna Eshoo, winner over Esalen Institute executive Jim Garrison 43%–37% in the Democratic primary, raised over $1 million, positioned herself as a fiscal conservative and a savvy problem-solver, and attacked Campbell for his support of fellow Chicago graduate Robert Bork. Both Campbell and Eshoo ran innovative campaigns, inventing new campaign techniques to go along with television ads (very expensive in this the nation's fourth largest media market) and direct mailings. Campbell assembled an organization that canvassed voters, inviting them to attend town meetings with Campbell and asking what they'd like to know about him; appropriate mailings followed. Eshoo prepared a knockout video, complete with cute graphics attacking "sacred cows," hip music, and a Milan-style desk with an Apple computer, in which she made an extended pitch and said that while places like Iowa or Nebraska or Orange County could make do with an ordinary congressman, the Silicon Valley should have someone special. After she appeared at a rally with Lloyd Bentsen at Stanford, 110,000 copies of the video were distributed, and they seemed to have made a difference. In a district which Campbell had every reason to expect to carry with something like the 63% Zschau won in his first race in 1982, he won by only a 52%–46% margin—one of the nation's closest and most expensive races.

Campbell seems ideally positioned to hold this seat. But Eshoo showed there is a chance for an innovation-minded Democrat in the innovation-minded Silicon Valley.

The People: Est. Pop. 1986: 559,100, up 6.4% 1980–86; Pop. 1980: 525,731, up 13.0% 1970–80. Households (1980): 69% family, 35% with children, 59% married couples; 38.3% housing units rented; median monthly rent: $320; median house value: $150,300. Voting age pop. (1980): 397,900; 8% Spanish origin, 6% Asian origin, 2% Black.

112   CALIFORNIA

1988 Presidential Vote: Bush (R) 133,699   (49%)
Dukakis (D). 132,918   (49%)

Rep. Tom Campbell (R)

Elected 1988; b. Aug. 14, 1952, Chicago, IL; home, Stanford; U. of Chicago, B.A., M.A. 1973, Ph.D. 1980, Harvard U., J.D. 1976; Roman Catholic, married (Susanne).

Career: Law Clerk to Judge George MacKinnon, U.S. Crt. of Appeals, 1976–77; Law Clerk to Justice Byron White, U.S. Supreme Crt., 1977–78; Practicing Atty. 1978–80; White House Fellow, 1980–81; Exec. Asst. to Dpty. U.S. Atty. Gen., 1981; Dir., Bureau of Competition, FTC, 1981–83; Stanford U., Assoc. Prof., 1983–87, Prof., 1987–88.

Offices: 1730 LHOB 20515, 202-225-5411. Also 599 N. Mathilda, Ste. 105, Sunnyvale, 94086, 408-245-4835.

Committees: *Small Business* (16th of 16 R). Subcommittees: SBA, The General Economy and Minority Enterprise Development; Antitrust, Impact of Deregulation and Privatization. *Science, Space and Technology* (19th of 19 R). Subcommittees: Science, Research and Technology; Transportation, Aviation and Materials.

Group Ratings and Key Votes: Newly Elected

Election Results

1988 general	Tom Campbell (R)	136,384	(52%)	($1,440,639)
	Anna G. Eshoo (D)	121,523	(46%)	($1,089,570)
1988 primary	Tom Campbell (R)	41,867	(58%)	
	Ernest L. Konnyu (R)	30,162	(42%)	
1986 general	Ernest L. Konnyu (R)	111,252	(60%)	($950,447)
	Lance T. Weil (D)	69,564	(37%)	($62,377)
	Bill White (L)	6,227	(3%)	

THIRTEENTH DISTRICT

Fifty years ago, most of the acreage around San Jose was vineyards and fruit orchards below the mountains of the Coast Range near San Jose. This was one of the richest agricultural areas in the country, but it was also in the path of some of the most explosive growth the country has ever seen. The city of San Jose, its jagged boundaries expanding up to the limits of other municipalities, increased from 68,000 people in 1940 to 732,000 in 1988; it now has more people than San Francisco, which continues to regard it as a suburb or farm-market town. But San Jose, at the southern end of the Silicon Valley, is something more; its downtown is growing and its historic districts are becoming more urbane: between two mountain ranges, at the southern end of the Bay, it is one of the biggest nodes of development in the Bay area. The 13th Congressional District of California includes about half of San Jose plus some of the adjacent suburbs; the southern and southwestern parts of the city, areas basically suburban and mostly white Anglo. They are farther out than some of the more expensive Silicon Valley suburbs, though similar in outward appearances. Most of the rest of the people in the 13th live in Santa Clara, an old suburban town just west of downtown San Jose, with its own mission and university. The 13th also includes the suburb of Campbell, surrounded by and indistinguishable from San Jose, and Los Gatos, a higher income town going up into the hills.

The congressman from the 13th is Norman Mineta, one of the leaders of the large class of

Democrats first elected in 1974. As mayor Mineta made a name in San Jose in the early 1970s for slowing down development; he was popular enough to succeed a Republican congressman when he retired in 1974 in a district that votes Republican for most other offices. Mineta is now the third ranking member of the Public Works Committee, and chairs the Surface Transportation Subcommittee. He has been one of the government's chief policymakers on aviation issues, from noise regulation to financing airport expansion. He has supported airline deregulation, but has kept a close and critical watch on the FAA's work on safety regulation since.

Mineta is one of those Democrats who gets special assignments. He served three terms on the Budget Committee early in his career, and was one of the key Democrats there in 1981 and 1982, fighting at first unsuccessfully and then with more success against the Reagan budget cuts. More recently he was a member of the Intelligence Committee, where he was critical of former CIA Director William Casey and opposed military or "humanitarian" aid to the Nicaraguan contras. In addition, he is a deputy majority whip, and thus a part of the Democratic leadership.

Mineta's greatest accomplishment, however, was as one of the lead sponsors of the Japanese American redress bill. As a child in World War II, Mineta was shipped off, wearing his cub scout uniform, to one of the internment camps where the government confined West Coast Japanese Americans; his family lost their home and his father's insurance business and for years would not talk about the experience. In the camp in Wyoming, Mineta met Alan Simpson when they were both boys; later he would work with Simpson on the redress bill. It officially apologizes for the internment and provides a $20,000 payment to each survivor of the camps and to so-called voluntary evacuees. Now Mineta is working on making sure enough money is appropriated for the payments.

He is busy on other things as well, including putting pressure on the Japanese to open up their markets to American semiconductors and working to protect artic national wildlife. Mineta has been reelected every two years now without tough competition and, well known in the San Jose area, probably has little reason to worry about redistricting.

The People: Est. Pop. 1986: 575,300, up 9.3% 1980–86; Pop. 1980: 526,281, up 21.6% 1970–80. Households (1980): 71% family, 41% with children, 58% married couples; 39.3% housing units rented; median monthly rent: $331; median house value: $104,900. Voting age pop. (1980): 380,270; 10% Spanish origin, 6% Asian origin, 2% Black, 1% American Indian.

1988 Presidential Vote:

Dukakis (D)	109,830	(49%)
Bush (R)	108,817	(49%)

Rep. Norman Y. Mineta (D)

Elected 1974; b. Nov. 12, 1931, San Jose; home, San Jose; U. of CA at Berkeley, B.S. 1953; United Methodist; separated.

Career: Army, 1953–56; Owner, Mineta Insur. Agcy.; San Jose City Cncl., 1967–71, San Jose Vice Mayor, 1969–71, Mayor, 1971–74.

Offices: 2350 RHOB 20515, 202-225-2631. Also 1245 S. Winchester Blvd., Ste. 310, San Jose 95128, 408-984-6045; and 33 Broadway, Jackson 95642, 209-223-0649.

Committees: *Public Works and Transportation* (3d of 31 D). Subcommittees: Aviation; Investigations and Oversight; Surface Transportation (Chairman). *Science, Space and Technology* (12th of 29 D). Subcommittees: Science, Research and Technology; Space Science and Applications.

Group Ratings

	ADA	ACLU	COPE	CFA	LCV	ACU	NTLC	NSI	COC	CEI
1988	95	90	89	91	81	4	6	0	31	9
1987	88	—	89	79	—	0	—	—	7	7

National Journal Ratings

	1988 LIB — 1988 CONS		1987 LIB — 1987 CONS	
Economic	71%	23%	73%	0%
Social	86%	0%	78%	0%
Foreign	79%	16%	81%	0%

Key Votes

1) Homeless $	AGN	5) Ban Drug Test	AGN	9) SDI Research	AGN
2) Gephardt Amdt	FOR	6) Drug Death Pen	AGN	10) Ban Chem Weaps	FOR
3) Deficit Reduc	FOR	7) Handgun Sales	AGN	11) Aid to Contras	AGN
4) Kill Plnt Clsng Notice	AGN	8) Ban D.C. Abort $	AGN	12) Nuclear Testing	FOR

Election Results

1988 general	Norman Y. Mineta (D)................	143,980	(67%)	($521,674)
	Luke Sommer (R)....................	63,959	(30%)	($25,511)
1988 primary	Norman Y. Mineta (D), unopposed			
1986 general	Norman Y. Mineta (D)...............	107,696	(70%)	($443,822)
	Bob Nash (R)	46,754	(30%)	($33,297)

FOURTEENTH DISTRICT

In the 1970s and 1980s, for the first time in a century, there was steady growth in California's Mother Lode country, where the Central Valley of California begins to slant upward toward the Sierra Nevada. Thousands of Californians—many of them families from smog-filled, middle-class suburbs of the Los Angeles Basin and the San Francisco Bay Area—were looking for a more pleasant, small town, tradition-minded environment—and found it not far away, where the land began to rise. Along the fast-flowing creeks where the '49ers camped and in the forests that still cover most of the ground, they are filling up the old towns whose wonderful names—Placerville, Nevada City, Angels Camp, Poker Flat—recall a way of life made immortal by Mark Twain and Bret Harte, a way of life that abruptly vanished when the ore gave out decades ago. Populations in some counties are rising back up to the levels, never afterwards reached, of the 1850 Census, and old Victorian houses and commercial buildings are being renovated even as new subdivisions are being rebuilt.

Politically, this migration has had the effect of changing territory that was Democratic for many decades into Republican. This became clearly apparent in 1982, when the gun control referendum brought thousands of people to the polls who had not voted before: young fathers in plaid flannel shirts and down-filled jackets, who strongly opposed gun control and provided critical votes for Governor George Deukmejian's narrow first victory, proceeded to vote for Republicans up and down the ballot. The many younger and some older people in California seem to be re-creating in the Sierra foothills the kind of communities their parents or grandparents left behind years ago in the Midwest.

So great has been this growth that in the post-1990 redistricting there will probably be a new congressional district centered in the Mother Lode country. For the moment most of it, from Amador County north to the sparsely populated mountain counties in the northeast corner of the state, is appended to the part of the Central Valley around Stockton and Lodi to make up California's 14th Congressional District. Stockton is the Central Valley's ocean port, with a channel deepened now to 37 feet; Lodi is a smaller town settled almost entirely by North Dakotans.

This is a Republican district designed for Congressman Norman Shumway. Shumway was a member of the board of supervisors in Stockton in 1978 when he beat John McFall, who had been House Democratic whip from 1972 to 1976; McFall made the mistake in 1974 of taking $3,000 from Korean lobbyist Tongsun Park, depositing it in his office account, and using it for personal business. Shumway's reelection since then, in two quite differently-shaped districts, shows the distinct Republican trend in the Mother Lode country. A devout Mormon and firm believer in free enterprise, Shumway has a solid conservative voting record on most issues. He makes a point of voting against the Economic Development Association (EDA) and the Appalachian and Delta regional commissions; however, he is proud of the work he has helped get the government to do on the San Joaquin channel and is an aggressive proponent of the long stalled American River Canyon Dam at Auburn.

Shumway has the opportunity to play a role on a couple of key issues. As a Mormon missionary Shumway spent four years in Japan in the 1950s, speaks the language fluently, and is a staunch advocate of free trade, although he recognizes the difficulties of opening up Japanese markets to American exports. He also points out that American laws prevent us from exporting our oil, natural gas, and raw timber grown on federal land, to Japan and other countries, even though they are in plentiful supply. As the third ranking Republican on the Banking Committee, he has generally supported banks and not savings and loans. But when the giant American Savings & Loan was acquired by the Bass family in the biggest buyout in the industry, he worked to make sure it kept its operations going: it is headquartered in Stockton and is the biggest employer there. He is pushing another measure not so likely to be on the front burner: he wants to name English as our official language, as California did by referendum in 1986.

Shumway's hard-edged but not always clear-minded conservatism has caused him no electoral problems in the 14th District; he is reelected by large margins. The main threat to his tenure will come if the Democrats completely control redistricting, but even then he has enough territory, and the district seems to have grown rapidly enough, that he shouldn't have difficulty finding a safe seat in which to run.

The People: Est. Pop. 1986: 657,200, up 24.9% 1980–86; Pop. 1980: 526,030, up 50.8% 1970–80. Households (1980): 75% family, 39% with children, 65% married couples; 32.1% housing units rented; median monthly rent: $220; median house value: $71,200. Voting age pop. (1980): 381,713; 7% Spanish origin, 2% Asian origin, 1% Black, 1% American Indian.

1988 Presidential Vote: Bush (R) 165,850   (59%)
Dukakis (D). 111,570   (40%)

Rep. Norman D. Shumway (R)

Elected 1978; b. July 28, 1934, Phoenix, AZ; home, Stockton; U. of UT, B.S. 1960, Hastings Col. of Law, J.D. 1963; Mormon; married (Luana).

Career: Practicing atty., 1964–78; San Joaquin Cnty. Bd. of Spvsrs., 1974–78, Chmn., 1978.

Offices: 1203 LHOB 20515, 202-225-2511. Also 1150 W. Robinhood, Ste. 1-A, Stockton 95207, 209-957-7773; and 11899 Edgewood Rd., Ste. B, Auburn 95603, 916-885-3737.

Committees: *Banking, Finance and Urban Affairs* (3d of 20 R). Subcommittees: Economic Stabilization; International Development, Finance, Trade and Monetary Policy; Financial Institutions Supervision, Regulation and Insurance. *Merchant Marine and Fisheries* (4th of 17 R). Subcommittees: Coast Guard and Navigation; Merchant Marine; Oceanography (Ranking Member). *Select Committee on Aging* (4th of 26 R). Subcommittees: Human Services; Retirement Income and Employment.

Group Ratings

	ADA	ACLU	COPE	CFA	LCV	ACU	NTLC	NSI	COC	CEI
1988	0	4	6	27	6	100	90	100	92	91
1987	4	—	7	14	—	96	—	—	100	90

National Journal Ratings

	1988 LIB — 1988 CONS	1987 LIB — 1987 CONS
Economic	0% — 93%	0% — 89%
Social	9% — 89%	0% — 90%
Foreign	0% — 84%	0% — 80%

Key Votes

1) Homeless $	FOR	5) Ban Drug Test	FOR	9) SDI Research	FOR
2) Gephardt Amdt	AGN	6) Drug Death Pen	FOR	10) Ban Chem Weaps	AGN
3) Deficit Reduc	AGN	7) Handgun Sales	FOR	11) Aid to Contras	FOR
4) Kill Plnt Clsng Notice	FOR	8) Ban D.C. Abort $	FOR	12) Nuclear Testing	AGN

Election Results

1988 general	Norman D. Shumway (R)	173,876	(63%)	($492,349)
	Patricia Malberg (D)	103,899	(37%)	($103,678)
1988 primary	Norman D. Shumway (R), unopposed			
1986 general	Norman D. Shumway (R)	146,906	(72%)	($257,431)
	Bill Steele (D)	53,597	(26%)	

FIFTEENTH DISTRICT

The Central Valley, wrote the *WPA Guide* 50 years ago, was "a desert of almost unbelievable fertility under irrigation." The Valley, which had seemed desert to the first white men here, was first farmed by huge landowners before 1900; by 1940 the pattern of Valley agriculture was set. "Farming here is not farming as easterners know it; most of the ranches are food factories, with superintendents and foremen, administrative headquarters and machine sheds. Even the owners of small ranches must concentrate on one crop" and depend on seasonal labor. "The migratory worker, constantly on the move to catch the harvest seasons of one crop after the other—

peaches, walnuts, apricots, grapes, celery—never stays long enough in any area to establish himself as a citizen. He lives apart from other residents, occasionally in barracks behind the fields and orchards, more often in crude shelters of his own devising along the river bottom." Today the Valley is incredibly productive, the nation's leading producer of vegetables and fruits and a major cotton producer as well—the joint creation of man, technology, free enterprise and government.

Nowhere is that more evident than in the 15th Congressional District of California. Here, between Modesto and Fresno, are some of the Valley's most productive farmlands and some of its larger cities. Most of Fresno is in other districts, but some of its suburban fringe and all of its western agricultural region are in the 15th. Here in the flat lands west of Route 99, as it goes from Fresno to Modesto, you can see the Valley's greatest riches, in the Westlands, the real agricultural heart of the Valley. Vast, largely unpopulated, the site of huge corporate farms, they are exceedingly productive and profitable. But they would be worth nothing without the subsidized water which the federal and state governments provide.

Politically, the 15th District remains mostly Democratic in an increasingly Republican Valley. Nearly one-quarter of its residents are of Spanish origin, and about the same number are probably of white southern ancestry; both groups tend to be Democrats on economic issues. But on cultural issues the 15th and the neighboring 17th Districts are also the most family and children-oriented parts of California, except for a couple of suburban Los Angeles districts; the 15th has a higher percentage of children, married couples and families than the national average. In 1988, while the coastal 1st and 16th districts gave Michael Dukakis big majorities, the 15th in the Valley went narrowly for George Bush.

For a little more than 10 years the 15th District was represented in the House by Tony Coelho, who rose rapidly to be one of the most powerful and competent members of the House and then in May 1989 abruptly announced that he would resign. His career was meteoric, even for the post-Watergate House: first elected in 1978, he became the Democrats' campaign committee chairman after the 1980 election, and then moved up to be House Democratic Whip after the 1986 election. Then, dogged by charges of unethical conduct and threatened with the kind of lengthy and acrimonious investigations that beset Jim Wright for months, claiming that he had the support of most Democrats to move up to Majority Leader when Thomas Foley became Speaker, but aware surely that many who pledged their votes had reservations about his elevation, Coelho announced he would quit on June 15, his 47th birthday. Unlike Wright, who clung to office even under humiliating circumstances, Coelho wanted to rise to power his way— or not at all.

This was not the first time Tony Coelho had cut his ties abruptly. Raised on a Valley dairy farm, planning to become a priest, he discovered in college that he had epilepsy—at which point his family shunned him and the Church rejected him for the priesthood. Bob Hope's wife heard about his plight and Hope took Coelho under his arm and suggested that if he couldn't serve the public as a priest he could do so on Capitol Hill instead; and so Coelho got a job with Fresno Representative B. F. Sisk. He stayed with Sisk for 15 years; he learned the politics of agriculture and water at a master's knee, and was elected in his own right when Sisk retired. The obvious thing for Coelho to do in the House was to tend to Valley agricultural interests, and he did, winning seats on the Agriculture and Interior Committees and fighting with Bay Area Democrat George Miller and others over water policy. Coelho also became the chief carpenter of federal dairy subsidy policy.

But he also did far more. More than all but a half dozen other politicians and one or two other Democrats, he shaped the politics of the 1980s. When Coelho took over the campaign committee in 1981, the committee was nearly broke and had been outraised 10-1 by the Republicans; it had a puny direct mail list, relied on a single annual dinner for most of its money, and did little more than funnel a few dollars to incumbents who often didn't need the help. The Republicans had just won the White House and the Senate in stunning upsets and seemed within striking range of winning control of the House. The word was out that the new Reaganites expected Republican-leaning PACs to contribute solely to Republican candidates and free themselves from Democratic control of the House once and for all in 1982. Systematically, as Brooks Jackson describes definitively in *Honest Graft*, a book for which Coelho gave him total access and complete candor, Coelho went about preventing that from happening. He started the long work of building up direct mail fundraising lists and went around the country courting businessmen and entrepreneurs. He provided unprecedented kinds of aid to candidates. Unblushingly, he modeled much of his operation after the successful work of Republicans. Most importantly, he went door to door to PACs all over Washington and let them know he expected them to be bipartisan in their giving—and that if they didn't know of any Democrats they could support, he would be happy to supply them with a list of those who were right on their issue. "Just remember," he would say, "that we control every committee and subcommittee in the House, and we keep score."

His strategy worked. Democrats raised more PAC money than Republicans and campaigned on the social security issue which Tip O'Neill made sure they had a strong position on, and in 1982 they picked up 26 seats. They lost only 15 seats in 1984, while President Reagan won reelection with 59% of the vote. They won a net of five seats in 1986, despite a lack of strong challengers, and lost only a single incumbent. In race after race, even in Republican open seats, Democrats led Republicans in PAC contributions, many of them steered that way by Coelho. The fact that Democrats still had a majority, and a robust working majority, in the House at the end of the 1980s was due primarily to Coelho and O'Neill. Coelho's attention to detail, complete candor, partisan zeal (he managed the ultimately successful but arduous fight to seat Indiana 8th district Democrat Frank McCloskey after disputed results in the 1984 election), and his generosity to colleagues (his own PAC, the Valley Education Fund, contributed $850,000 to colleagues), enabled him to win the whip post by an overwhelming margin over as attractive an opponent as Charles Rangel of New York.

Coelho's first term as whip was successful: he helped Speaker Jim Wright and Majority Leader Thomas Foley compile an impressive legislative record. In his second term he hoped to cleanse himself of his reputation as a sordid fundraiser, committing his party to business interests, by putting together a campaign finance reform package. Behind the scenes he was working not only with colleagues but with leaders of Common Cause on the issue. But the downfall of Jim Wright upset his schedule. Suddenly eyes were on Coelho. He had, after all, solicited big contributions from savings and loan owners in the August 1985 Texas 1st special election and then urged Wright to see them, from which resulted Wright's intercessions with regulators and slowdown of S&L reform measures—and may have helped produce the $100 billion savings and loan crisis. He himself used a Texas S&L owner's Washington yacht for fundraisers without paying for it, for which his committee paid a $50,000 fine. Then it was reported that he had invested in a $100,000 junk bond, under odd circumstances, but probably not in any way which violated House rules and certainly not in any way that violated the law. The *Los Angeles Times* nonetheless reported in May 1989 that he was under criminal investigation. The Republicans' campaign committee ran a telephone poll in the 15th District, asking hypothetical questions about Coelho and the charges.

As Wright was preparing to leave, Wisconsin's David Obey urged longtime Coelho ally Richard Gephardt to run for Majority Leader, and Gephardt made calls sounding out colleagues; he told Coelho the morning of May 26 he was not running, however, and that Coelho had the votes to win. But would the votes stay with him through a protracted investigation? And if elected would he be operating from a position of strength? Coelho evidently concluded that the answers to one or both of these questions were no, and decided to quit the House.

Coelho's successor will presumably be chosen in a special election in which the Democratic nominee will probably be the favorite but which the Republicans, noting that this is a Bush district and that the Valley elects several popular Republican state legislators, may seriously contest.

The People: Est. Pop. 1986: 612,100, up 16.4% 1980–86; Pop. 1980: 525,949, up 30.8% 1970–80. Households (1980): 77% family, 44% with children, 64% married couples; 39.4% housing units rented; median monthly rent: $192; median house value: $57,100. Voting age pop. (1980): 361,570; 20% Spanish origin, 2% Black, 2% Asian origin, 1% American Indian.

1988 Presidential Vote:	Bush (R)	92,471	(52%)
	Dukakis (D)	82,819	(47%)

Rep. Tony L. Coelho (D)

Elected 1978, resigned June, 1989; b. June 15, 1942, Los Banos; home, Merced; Loyola U., L.A., B.A. 1964; Roman Catholic; married (Phyllis).

Career: Staff of U.S. Rep. B. F. Sisk, 1965–78, A. A., 1970–78.

Offices: 403 CHOB 20515, 202-225-6131. Also Fed. Bldg., 415 W. 18th St., Merced 95340, 209-383-4455; 900 H St., Ste. B, Modesto 95354, 209-527-1914; and 419 S. Madera, Kerman 93630, 209-846-7705.

Group Ratings

	ADA	ACLU	COPE	CFA	LCV	ACU	NTLC	NSI	COC	CEI
1988	90	77	87	91	56	12	6	0	23	6
1987	84	—	86	79	—	0	—	—	14	8

National Journal Ratings

	1988 LIB — 1988 CONS		1987 LIB — 1987 CONS	
Economic	92%	— 0%	73%	— 0%
Social	64%	— 34%	78%	— 0%
Foreign	84%	— 0%	76%	— 19%

Key Votes

1) Homeless $	AGN	5) Ban Drug Test	AGN	9) SDI Research	AGN
2) Gephardt Amdt	FOR	6) Drug Death Pen	FOR	10) Ban Chem Weaps	FOR
3) Deficit Reduc	FOR	7) Handgun Sales	FOR	11) Aid to Contras	AGN
4) Kill Plnt Clsng Notice	AGN	8) Ban D.C. Abort $	AGN	12) Nuclear Testing	FOR

Election Results

1988 general	Tony L. Coelho (D)	118,710	(70%)	($972,235)
	Carol Harner (R)	47,957	(28%)	
1988 primary	Tony L. Coelho (D)	50,248	(90%)	
	Gerry Mansell (D)	5,442	(10%)	
1986 general	Tony L. Coelho (D)	93,600	(71%)	($655,211)
	Carol Harner (R)	35,793	(27%)	

SIXTEENTH DISTRICT

In the late 1930s, when John Steinbeck's *Of Mice and Men* and *Cannery Row* were bestsellers, the Monterey in which he grew up had not changed much. "On Saturdays the main street is wide awake," says the *WPA Guide*. "Ranchers and cowboys in blue jeans and high-heeled boots drive in to buy supplies and go to movies; housewives from outlying ranches and truck farms do their week's shopping; tourists and weekenders wander about looking at old adobes, snapping pictures of the fishing fleet, and buying abalone shells; cavalrymen from the post search for amusement; music blares from a few beerhalls; diners in white ties and evening dress sip wine in a resort lodge."

Some of this has changed—Fort Ord has a language school, not cavalry—but much has not. The California coast north and south of Monterey, the state's first capital and "the kernel of California history," still makes a fine living off the land and sea; the fields around Salinas supply much of the nation's lettuce, the fields around Castroville supply almost all of its artichokes, and the vast greenhouses around Watsonville supply a goodly portion of its long-stemmed roses. If the population has been swelled in prosperous decades by people attracted by the Monterey cypresses and the Big Sur mountains, by perhaps the most beautiful coastline in America, there were already many such people 50 years ago in artsy Carmel and the Pebble Beach golf courses and the Del Monte Lodge. The rough working class has mostly vanished—Cannery Row is now refurbished, with one of the nation's finest aquariums—but migrant farmworkers are still here in season, living in conditions most Americans would find intolerable, and the seasonal rhythm of life continues.

The 16th Congressional District of California follows the coastline, from the bare green hills north of Santa Cruz past Monterey and Carmel and down the Big Sur coast past William Randolph Hearst's gaudy San Simeon glaring down at the ocean. The district extends inland as well, into sunny valleys sheltered from the ocean mists, and covers some of the nation's richest farmland. The 16th is a prime example of how, while interior California has become more Republican, the coast has become more Democratic. The older residents—landowners in Salinas and the townspeople who sympathize with them, retirees in Santa Cruz and the Monterey Peninsula—still vote Republican. But population shifts—an influx of liberation-minded young people—have moved the area to the left. The coast seems to attract migrants who, while affluent, subscribe to liberal magazines and buy Sierra Club calendars. Also, the branch of the University of California at Santa Cruz is so liberal (97% for McGovern in 1972) that it changed the political balance of the whole county. (Sometimes the shift has gone too far: the artsy-craftsy ocean village of Carmel, after its mayor and council insisted on banning the sale of ice cream cones, elected conservative movie star Clint Eastwood as mayor in 1986.) Twenty years ago, this area was still solidly Republican, voting against an economic liberal like Hubert Humphrey. Since then, while America has moved right, the coast has moved left, and the 16th District voted 54% for Michael Dukakis in 1988.

That trend has been matched in the career of 16th District Congressman Leon Panetta, who started off as a Republican and is now one of the leading Democrats in Washington, chairman of the House Budget Committee. Panetta first made headlines in 1970, when he was fired as head of the Office of Civil Rights at HEW over policy differences; he switched parties in 1971, returned home and ran for Congress in 1976 against a starchy Republican out of sync with the newcomers to the district. In the House he took on issues reflecting both the old and new preoccupations of the coast. He got a seat on the Agriculture Committee, which allowed him to tend to district interests, as well as to push for more generous nutrition programs and to keep California's rigorous anti-pesticide laws from being superseded by weaker federal standards. He was the House's chief advocate of guestworker amendments to immigration bills, which would provide cheap labor for California's fruit and vegetable growers, and after he got one such amendment through in 1984, over the objections of organized labor and most Democrats, it became clear that the House would not pass an immigration bill without such an amendment. He was the Democrats' lead negotiator in the bipartisan effort of the California delegation to limit offshore oil drilling—stopping drilling in the Reagan years until election pressures got George Bush, as well as Michael Dukakis, to oppose it in 1988.

But it is on the Budget Committee that Panetta has made his most noteworthy contributions. He got a seat there in his second term, just in time for a Democrat—who does not see his primary purpose as increasing government spending programs—to come to grips with the political demands symbolized in California by 1978's Proposition 13 and, nationally, by 1980's Reagan landslide. With Norman Mineta, Richard Gephardt and Timothy Wirth, he was a leader of fiscally cautious northern Democrats—a new breed and one capable of determining the balance on budget issues. Panetta's knowledge of details and political instincts for strategy made him a key player, and in 1984 he tried to become budget chairman. But Panetta was mistrusted by Tip O'Neill, the Democratic caucus wouldn't waive the six-year-limit rule on committee service, and William Gray got the job instead.

Then Panetta got stuck with chairing the task force on the disputed Indiana 8th election. It conducted its own recount, and when it ruled 2 to 1 that Democrat Frank McCloskey had won by four votes, the Republicans were enraged. Panetta was attacked on the floor, and his bipartisan reputation was tarnished. But Panetta stayed busy, working on the immigration bills and providing protections for congressional employees, helping to negotiate the House version of Gramm-Rudman and participating in the 1987 budget summit. After Gray reached the end of the six-year-limit of service on the committee, Panetta was the obvious candidate for Budget chairman. Without significant opposition, he got the job, and will be the House Democrats' point man on budget issues during the Bush term and can serve as chairman for six years. While he focused earlier in the decade on disciplining spending, he now seems more concerned that the big deficits are causing society's resources to dwindle and believes the country needs more public investment.

Panetta's career in the House is an illustration of the new rhythm of House politics: instead of rising slowly over the decades to a position of power, Panetta rose quickly to a national policymaking role because of his talents, then receded after some setbacks and concentrated more on local and committee matters, then rose again. Through it all he has remained extremely popular at home, winning by record margins. His views on issues and his own personal and political roots are an almost perfect fit for the district.

The People: Est. Pop. 1986: 615,800, up 17.0% 1980–86; Pop. 1980: 526,120, up 26.1% 1970–80. Households (1980): 68% family, 36% with children, 56% married couples; 46.1% housing units rented; median monthly rent: $263; median house value: $87,400. Voting age pop. (1980): 391,002; 18% Spanish origin, 5% Asian origin, 4% Black, 1% American Indian.

1988 Presidential Vote: Dukakis (D)....................122,419   (54%)
Bush (R).....................100,293   (44%)

Rep. Leon E. Panetta (D)

Elected 1976; b. June 28, 1938, Monterey; home, Carmel Valley; U. of Santa Clara, B.A. 1960, J.D. 1963; Roman Catholic; married (Sylvia).

Career: Army, 1963–65; Legis. Asst. to U.S. Sen. Thomas Kuchel, 1966–69; Dir., U.S. Ofc. of Civil Rights, Dept. of HEW, 1969–70; Exec. Asst. to Mayor of New York City, 1970–71; Practicing atty., 1971–76.

Offices: 339 CHOB 20515, 202-225-2861. Also 380 Alvarado St., Monterey 93940, 408-649-3555; 100 W. Alisal, Salinas 93901, 408-424-2229; 701 Ocean St., Santa Cruz 95060, 408-429-1976; 1160 Marsh St., San Luis Obispo 93401, 805-541-0143.

Committees: *Agriculture* (6th of 26 D). Subcommittees: Department Operations, Research, and Foreign Agriculture; Forests, Family Farms and Energy; Domestic Marketing, Consumer Relations, and Nutrition. *Budget* (Chairman of 21 D). *House Administration* (3d of 13 D). Subcommittees: Elections; Personnel and Police. *Select Committee on Hunger* (4th of 16 D). Task Force: Domestic Task Force (Chairman).

Group Ratings

	ADA	ACLU	COPE	CFA	LCV	ACU	NTLC	NSI	COC	CEI
1988	90	82	75	82	88	4	11	0	33	17
1987	92	—	73	77	—	0	—	—	20	11

National Journal Ratings

	1988 LIB — 1988 CONS		1987 LIB — 1987 CONS	
Economic	71%	— 23%	68%	— 27%
Social	78%	— 20%	68%	— 31%
Foreign	84%	— 0%	76%	— 19%

Key Votes

1) Homeless $	AGN	5) Ban Drug Test	AGN	9) SDI Research	AGN
2) Gephardt Amdt	FOR	6) Drug Death Pen	FOR	10) Ban Chem Weaps	FOR
3) Deficit Reduc	FOR	7) Handgun Sales	AGN	11) Aid to Contras	AGN
4) Kill Plnt Clsng Notice	AGN	8) Ban D.C. Abort $	AGN	12) Nuclear Testing	FOR

Election Results

1988 general	Leon E. Panetta (D)	177,452	(79%)	($252,336)
	Stanley Monteith (R)	48,375	(21%)	($69,563)
1988 primary	Leon E. Panetta (D)	76,452	(95%)	
	Arthur V. Dunn (D)	4,027	(5%)	
1986 general	Leon E. Panetta (D)	128,151	(78%)	($114,446)
	Louis Darrigo (R)	31,386	(19%)	($9,557)

SEVENTEENTH DISTRICT

Alfalfa, cantaloupes, cotton, grapes, lima beans, olives, peaches, plums, sugar beets, tomatoes, walnuts: these are some of the crops grown in the southern part of the Central Valley, between Fresno and Bakersfield, that makes up California's 17th Congressional District. This is some of the richest agricultural land in the world. Almost all the crops here are produced by very large farming operations that bear little resemblance to the stereotypical family farm: these are serious good-sized businesses. The producers pride themselves on their success through free enterprise but, like most entrepreneurs, they are happy to have the government provide safety nets and helping hands, in the form of crop subsidies, agricultural research, irrigation systems and subsidized water; they want nothing to do with Cesar Chavez's United Farm Workers, whose headquarters is here in Delano, just north of Bakersfield. It's hard to make a theoretical case for such a mixed system—no one would have designed it from scratch—but it works. It has made Central Valley agriculture exceedingly productive; and if it has helped some producers get rich, they can argue they deserve it for the work they do and what they produce.

The congressman from the 17th District is Chip Pashayan, a son of the Fresno area's large and conspicuously successful Armenian-American community and a staunch Republican conservative. Pashayan first won his seat in 1978 by upsetting a Democratic incumbent when the district included more of Fresno than it does now—a harbinger of the conservative victories of the 1980s. Pashayan is a determined and often contentious Republican, of a very different mold from the get-along-go-along Democrats who tended to the Valley's special interests for so many years. Like them, he has tended to district needs, especially on water issues, though he has done much better when he has worked with Democratic whip Tony Coelho (also first elected in 1978 from a district that includes part of Fresno), than when he has worked against him.

In early 1989 Pashayan got a couple of hot seats. Three of the Republicans' four seats on the Rules Committee were vacant, and Pashayan won one of them; he will be regularly outvoted, but can still make a difference on some issues. It's just possible that, if Republicans ever get a majority, Pashayan will be chairman of Rules some time in the 21st century. His other hot seat is on the Ethics Committee, to which he was assigned in 1987. In 1988 and early 1989 that body had the job of investigating Speaker Jim Wright. Some Republicans were afraid that Pashayan would be pressured by Coelho to go easy on Wright, and some conservatives called on him to get tough on Wright regardless of the facts. All this speculation and exhortation turned out to be empty stuff. Shrewd observers know that Ethics Committee members strive for unanimity, and Pashayan voted generally with his fellow Republicans and, on most issues, with the bipartisan majority which found reason to believe Wright violated certain rules. Pashayan was understandably irritated by the suggestions and the pressure, and presumably was prepared to do what sensible politicians do in such cases: do his best to vote on the merits of the issue and then handle the politics.

Pashayan regularly wins reelection with over 70% in presidential years and 60% or under in off years. Redistricting moved his district south, into more Republican territory, for the 1980s; the danger for him would be if redistricting moves it north, to more Democratic territory, for the 1990s. But at this point, Pashayan is well enough placed to help Valley interests that he will be spared any trouble, even by Democratic redrawers, who cannot in any case hurt him badly except by taking away from adjacent Democrats Tony Coelho and Richard Lehman Democratic—precincts they'd like to keep.

The People: Est. Pop. 1986: 607,200, up 15.4% 1980–86; Pop. 1980: 526,033, up 34.6% 1970–80. Households (1980): 79% family, 47% with children, 66% married couples; 36.2% housing units rented; median monthly rent: $189; median house value: $56,800. Voting age pop. (1980): 356,229; 23% Spanish origin, 3% Asian origin, 2% Black, 1% American Indian.

1988 Presidential Vote: Bush (R) 111,250   (59%)
Dukakis (D). 76,021   (40%)

Rep. Charles (Chip) Pashayan, Jr. (R)

Elected 1978; b. Mar. 27, 1941, Fresno; home, Fresno; Pomona Col., B.A. 1963, U. of CA, J.D. 1968, Oxford U., M. Lit. 1977; Congregational; divorced.

Career: Army, 1968–70; Practicing atty., 1969–78; Spec. Asst. to Gen. Counsel, U.S. Dept. of HEW, 1973–75.

Offices: 203 CHOB 20515, 202-225-3341. Also 1702 E. Bullard Ave., #103, Fresno 93710, 209-487-5500; 804 N. Irwin, Hanford 93230, 209-582-2896; 831 W. Center St., Visalia 93291, 209-627-2700; and 201 High St., Delano 93215, 805-725-7371.

Committees: *Rules* (4th of 4 R). Subcommittees: Legislative Process; Rules of the House. *Standards of Official Conduct* (3d of 6 R).

Group Ratings

	ADA	ACLU	COPE	CFA	LCV	ACU	NTLC	NSI	COC	CEI
1988	35	48	34	55	19	64	49	100	57	34
1987	20	—	30	50	—	59	—	—	73	45

National Journal Ratings

	1988 LIB — 1988 CONS	1987 LIB — 1987 CONS
Economic	35% — 64%	33% — 66%
Social	40% — 58%	40% — 60%
Foreign	0% — 84%	20% — 76%

Key Votes

1) Homeless $	FOR	5) Ban Drug Test	AGN	9) SDI Research	FOR
2) Gephardt Amdt	AGN	6) Drug Death Pen	FOR	10) Ban Chem Weaps	AGN
3) Deficit Reduc	AGN	7) Handgun Sales	FOR	11) Aid to Contras	FOR
4) Kill Plnt Clsng Notice	FOR	8) Ban D.C. Abort $	FOR	12) Nuclear Testing	AGN

Election Results

1988 general	Charles (Chip) Pashayan, Jr. (R)	129,568	(72%)	($206,677)
	Vincent Lavery (D)	51,730	(29%)	($5,227)
1988 primary	Charles (Chip) Pashayan, Jr. (R), unopposed			
1986 general	Charles (Chip) Pashayan, Jr. (R)	88,787	(60%)	($304,194)
	John Hartnett (D)	58,682	(40%)	($228,592)

EIGHTEENTH DISTRICT

Fifty years before the California Raisins danced to world fame, Fresno was already the "world's 'raisin center,' " where, according to the *WPA Guide,* "tall modern buildings rise abruptly from the valley floor, surrounded by residential sections planted with trees to provide shade in the sweltering heat of summer." Just outside town "the vineyards radiate in seemingly endless rows, set exactly 10 feet apart"; across the railroad tracks were Spanish movie houses and Japanese shops and, most numerous, the Armenian immigrants who have given Fresno its best known native son, writer William Saroyan, and its special ethnic flavor. In Los Angeles, Fresno—with its middle Americanness, its hot weather, the Raisins— is sometimes the butt of jokes, and unjustly. Fresno is prosperous and rapidly growing, hot in the summer perhaps, but with warm winters, accessible to desert and mountain, and situated squarely in the center of the richest agricultural land in the United States, California's Central Valley. If it is more tradition-minded than California's bigger cities, that is something more and more Americans like, and it has welcomed immigrants, from the Armenians earlier in the century to Mexicans, Vietnamese, and Hmong today. It is a leading competitor for one of the new branches of the University of California planned for the 1990s.

Fresno is the largest component of California's 18th Congressional District, but not exactly its center; in fact, nothing is, since this is one of the most grotesquely-shaped districts in America today. The Fresno portion of the 18th, carefully excised of affluent suburbs, is connected to a similar portion of the smaller Central Valley city of Stockton, 105 miles northwest, by largely uninhabited land on the other side of the Sierra Nevada. Appended to the Fresno end is the agricultural land around the town of Sanger, home of the current congressman, Richard Lehman. The 18th was designed by the late Phillip Burton to accommodate Lehman, one of those young idealistic political maneuverers that the California legislature seems to nurture in such abundance.

Lehman comes from a farming family and has spent most of his adult life in politics. He was part of Jesse Unruh's Robert Kennedy delegation to the 1968 Chicago convention; he was an aide from 1970 to 1976 to a Fresno state senator; he got elected to the Assembly himself in 1976; and he became a congressman, unopposed in his first primary, as soon as this 18th District was created in 1982. Lehman has a liberal voting record on most issues (less so on cultural issues) but is, of course, sensitive to the farming interests in the district. He irritated some farming interests by backing a successful bill to keep several remaining rivers in the mountains undammed, but he also defends strenuously agribusiness' eagerness to import otherwise illegal migrants to work their fields.

Lehman has had some significant legislative accomplishments. On the Interior Committee he worked successfully to get first the Tuolumne and then the Kings River granted wild and scenic river status and created a Mono Basin National Forest Scenic Area. As Phil Burton had figured out when he put together the wilderness bill of 1982, creating parks in your district is the 1980s version of pork barrel politics, and Lehman plays it well. Interior also gives him some sway over questions about water, which is the lifeblood of Valley agriculture. On the Banking Committee, he originated the 1987 Farm Credit Act amendment that created a secondary market for farm real estate loans—the now famous (in some quarters) Freddie Mac. He also fashioned a rural housing prepayment amendment and got it attached to an omnibus housing bill.

Lehman is one of those young Democrats who make politics look easy, and whose skills explain, more than any other single factor, why their party continues to have such large majorities in the House and in most of America's legislatures in the Reagan years of the 1980s. His next goals are a Mid-Valley Canal and a truth-in-savings bill. He has been reelected easily every two years.

The People: Est. Pop. 1986: 642,000, up 22.0% 1980–86; Pop. 1980: 525,990, up 14.2% 1970–80. Households (1980): 70% family, 38% with children, 55% married couples; 42.0% housing units rented; median monthly rent: $186; median house value: $54,500. Voting age pop. (1980): 376,078; 21% Spanish origin, 6% Black, 4% Asian origin, 1% American Indian.

1988 Presidential Vote: Dukakis (D)...................... 101,146   (53%)
                               Bush (R) 88,016   (46%)

Rep. Richard H. Lehman (D)

Elected 1982; b. July 20, 1948, Sanger; home, Sanger; Fresno City Col., CA State U., U. of CA at Santa Cruz, B.A., 1970; Lutheran; married (Patricia).

Career: A. A. to CA St. Sen. George N. Zenovich, 1970–76; CA Assembly, 1976–82.

Offices: 1319 LHOB 20515, 202-225-4540. Also 1900 Mariposa Mall, Ste. 301, Fresno 93721, 209-487-5760; 48 W. Yaney Ave., Sonora 95370, 209-533-1426; and 401 N. San Joaquin St., Ste. 216, Stockton 95202, 209-946-6353.

Committees: *Banking, Finance, and Urban Affairs* (13th of 31 D). Subcommittees: Financial Institutions Supervision, Regulation and Insurance; Housing and Community Development. *Interior and Insular Affairs* (13th of 26 D). Subcommittees: National Parks and Public Lands; Water and Power Resources.

Group Ratings

	ADA	ACLU	COPE	CFA	LCV	ACU	NTLC	NSI	COC	CEI
1988	85	74	93	91	75	9	5	0	25	7
1987	92	—	92	71	—	0	—	—	7	8

National Journal Ratings

	1988 LIB — 1988 CONS		1987 LIB — 1987 CONS	
Economic	92%	0%	73%	0%
Social	73%	25%	78%	0%
Foreign	84%	0%	76%	19%

Key Votes

1) Homeless $	AGN	5) Ban Drug Test	AGN	9) SDI Research	AGN
2) Gephardt Amdt	FOR	6) Drug Death Pen	FOR	10) Ban Chem Weaps	FOR
3) Deficit Reduc	FOR	7) Handgun Sales	AGN	11) Aid to Contras	AGN
4) Kill Plnt Clsng Notice	AGN	8) Ban D.C. Abort $	AGN	12) Nuclear Testing	FOR

Election Results

1988 general	Richard H. Lehman (D)	125,715	(70%)	($193,681)
	David A. Linn (R)	54,034	(30%)	($89,260)
1988 primary	Richard H. Lehman (D), unopposed			
1986 general	Richard H. Lehman (D)	101,480	(71%)	($290,626)
	David C. Crevelt (R)	40,907	(28%)	($32,503)

NINETEENTH DISTRICT

For more than 50 years, Santa Barbara, a Spanish mission town on a thin, sloping stretch of land between the Santa Ynez Mountains and the Pacific Ocean, has been one of the favorite homes and resorts of the American rich. When an earthquake hit in 1925, Santa Barbara took the opportunity to construct many buildings in a style—stucco walls, red tile roofs—aping that of the Mission Santa Barbara; and if commercial frontage, low-income enclaves and the spread of settlement east and west along the coast spoil the perfection of the attempt, this remains a special city nonetheless.

Politically, Santa Barbara is part of coastal California; conservative economically as befits a community full of rich people concerned about preserving capital; liberal culturally as you might expect in a town whose special environment is prized and in which most people have the leisure time and money to indulge their personal tastes. Particular events of the last two decades have symbolized the tension between these two impulses. Santa Barbara hit the national headlines in 1969, when an oil well under the waters of the Pacific blew and the beach was coated with oil; the pictures of the oil slick in the channel and of volunteers trying to wash oil off grounded birds helped to launch the environmental movement of the 1970s. A few years later, Santa Barbara again made headlines as students at the University of California branch near the beach fire-bombed the local branch of the Bank of America, in a spasm of protest against supposedly warmongering big institutions. The 1980s were quieter: Santa Barbara got into the news only when President Ronald Reagan vacationed at his rustic ranch north of the city in the mountains.

The only exception was in 1988, when the House race in the 19th Congressional District of California, of which Santa Barbara is the epicenter, turned out to be the most expensive and one of the most closely contested in the country. It was billed as a test of Reagan's popularity in his home district, because incumbent Republican Robert Lagomarsino had been a supporter of the Administration on most issues, while the Democrat, state Senator Gary K. Hart (no relation to the former Colorado Senator) had been mostly a Reagan critic. But it was not so much a national test as an example of the politics of places that are both upscale and culturally liberal—a small, though not insignificant part of the country. Lagomarsino's political base was not in Santa Barbara anyway, but in Ventura County to the east, where his family has had a big farming operation for years; the verdant farm country, and the small subdivisions and condominiums going up there have long been Republican country, in contrast to the county's largest city, industrial Oxnard. In many ways Lagomarsino has been an adept politician, opposing offshore drilling and working on the Interior Committee to promote the Channel Islands Marine Sanctuary and other local environmental causes (although he was named by Environmental Action as one of its "Dirty Dozen"). He has also worked aggressively on constituency service, proposing tax-free withdrawals from IRAs for first-time homebuyers and, while first winning the seat in a 1974 special election, being careful not to commit himself to opposing the impeachment of Richard Nixon. But he was on the defensive on contra aid, for which he, as a senior Republican on Foreign Affairs, has been a leading advocate.

Hart also has roots in the district—he was a star football player at Santa Barbara high—and has been running for office here for 20 years. He is very much part of the Vietnam-Watergate generation of Democrats, strongly in favor of environmental protection, strongly opposed to American military involvements overseas. As a young teacher he ran for Congress in 1970 and lost 59%–40%; in 1974 he was elected to the California Assembly from Santa Barbara County; in 1982 he was elected to the state Senate from Santa Barbara and Ventura. With strong financial support from Westside Democrats Henry Waxman and Howard Berman, he raised and spent about $1.5 million, as did Lagomarsino, in what turned out to be the single most expensive House race in the country. The Republicans tried to embarrass Hart on some cultural issues, attacking him for opposing the death penalty and bringing up the fact that he turned in his draft card in 1967. But the race went down to the wire, with Lagomarsino winning 50%–49%.

Will there be a rematch in 1990? Hart will have to give up his state senate seat if he runs then, and he might be tempted to wait in the hope that redistricting will pare away the conservative areas around Vandenberg Air Force Base which he lost heavily. Lagomarsino will continue to be active in supporting the Administration on foreign policy and trying to make an attractive record on the environment; he made a lot of noise opposing the pay increase. Hart, as part of the majority in Sacramento, can make a record there. Cross-pressured between its old and new politics, the 19th could be a seriously contested seat again in 1990.

The People: Est. Pop. 1986: 596,500, up 13.4% 1980–86; Pop. 1980: 526,032, up 17.3% 1970–80.

Households (1980): 70% family, 38% with children, 57% married couples; 45.3% housing units rented; median monthly rent: $268; median house value: $88,200. Voting age pop. (1980): 384,025; 21% Spanish origin, 3% Asian origin, 3% Black, 1% American Indian.

1988 Presidential Vote: Bush (R) 123,145   (54%)
                               Dukakis (D). 101,934   (45%)

Rep. Robert J. Lagomarsino (R)

Elected Mar. 5, 1974; b. Sept. 4, 1926, Ventura; home, Ventura; U. of CA at Santa Barbara, B.A. 1950, U. of Santa Clara Law Sch., LL.B. 1953; Roman Catholic; married (Norma Jean).

Career: Navy, WWII; Practicing atty., 1954–74; Ojai City Cncl., 1958, Mayor, 1958–61; CA Senate, 1961–74.

Offices: 2332 RHOB 20515, 202-225-3601. Also 814 State St., Studio 121, Santa Barbara 93101, 805-963-1708; 5740 Ralston, Ste. 101, Ventura 93003, 805-642-2200; and 104 E. Boone St., Ste. E, Santa Maria 93454, 805-922-2131.

Committees: *Foreign Affairs* (3d of 18 R). Subcommittees: Asian and Pacific Affairs; Western Hemisphere Affairs (Ranking Member). *Interior and Insular Affairs* (2d of 15 R). Subcommittees: Insular and International Affairs (Ranking Member); National Parks and Public Lands.

Group Ratings

	ADA	ACLU	COPE	CFA	LCV	ACU	NTLC	NSI	COC	CEI
1988	35	30	13	82	38	80	80	100	93	53
1987	4	—	11	29	—	96	—	—	100	80

National Journal Ratings

	1988 LIB — 1988 CONS	1987 LIB — 1987 CONS
Economic	31% — 67%	0% — 89%
Social	31% — 69%	10% — 85%
Foreign	16% — 78%	0% — 80%

Key Votes

1) Homeless $	FOR	5) Ban Drug Test	FOR	9) SDI Research	FOR
2) Gephardt Amdt	AGN	6) Drug Death Pen	FOR	10) Ban Chem Weaps	AGN
3) Deficit Reduc	AGN	7) Handgun Sales	AGN	11) Aid to Contras	FOR
4) Kill Plnt Clsng Notice	FOR	8) Ban D.C. Abort $	FOR	12) Nuclear Testing	AGN

Election Results

1988 general	Robert J. Lagomarsino (R).	116,026	(50%)	($1,470,674)
	Gary K. Hart (D)	112,033	(49%)	($1,548,193)
1988 primary	Robert J. Lagomarsino (R), unopposed			
1986 general	Robert J. Lagomarsino (R).	122,578	(72%)	($333,464)
	Wayne B. Norris (D).	45,619	(27%)	($16,041)

TWENTIETH DISTRICT

Across the southwest United States on U.S. 66, from the Dust Bowl of Oklahoma and Kansas and Texas they came, in one of the major migrations of the 1930s: the Okies who drove their jalopies laden with all their worldly goods to the Central Valley of California. In a brown decade, the Valley looked green, with its irrigated fields and its eucalyptus-shaded towns. The Okies drove through the Tehachapi Pass, through the mountains that form a semicircle at the south end of the Valley, and headed toward Bakersfield, an oil boom town at the time, in the midst of pastures, vineyards and orchards. Half a century later Bakersfield and Kern County are the part of California with the most southern accents, home of country singers Buck Owens and Merle Haggard; the grievances that the Joads in John Steinbeck's *The Grapes of Wrath* felt toward the farmowners have been replaced by a resentment of Cesar Chavez and his United Farm Workers Union, headquartered in Delano just up the road.

The 20th Congressional District of California includes most of the southern end of the Valley around Bakersfield; to the east it also includes a portion of the desert; to the west it takes in most of San Luis Obispo County all the way to the ocean. Half the district's population, and its center of political gravity, is in the Valley around Bakersfield. The political trends here are pretty much the same as in Oklahoma: it is ancestrally Democratic but, in practice, safely Republican in most elections. Even more Republican is the one-fourth of the district east of Tehachapi, in and around the giant military installations in the desert—the China Lake Naval Weapons Center and Edwards Air Force Base, where most of the space shuttles have landed—and in Lancaster and Palmdale in northern Los Angeles County, where subdivisions and shopping centers are sprouting quickly from the desert around a big Lockheed plant. Political attitudes here are ultraconservative: strongly pro-defense, pro-free market and traditional family values. San Luis Obispo, ranching country for many years, is becoming more liberal but is still the most middle American of California's coastal counties.

The 20th District elects a Republican congressman, Bill Thomas, who is both a professional political scientist and an aggressive political maneuverer. A former college teacher and four-year veteran of the California Assembly, he seems to be one of those people who instinctively knows how to go about being a legislator. He got a seat on the Agriculture Committee in his first term—a plum assignment for a Bakersfield representative—and now sits on Ways and Means. There he mustered minority support for increasing the retirement age in the 1983 social security amendments and supported the 1986 tax reform. Generally conservative, but not a free market theorist, he backed import restrictions on avocados and pushed for the wine equity act.

Thomas, one of his party's leading political tacticians, is the California Republicans' leading strategist on redistricting. He sits on the House Administration Committee, a dull body unless you are interested in serving as a watchdog for your party's interests in campaign finance legislation. He is also the lead Republican sponsor of the measure to impose uniform poll-closing hours across the nation to prevent exit poll results from being broadcast while votes can still be cast on the West Coast. He has a seat on the Budget Committee. He was the Republican on the three-member panel to look into the dispute over the 1984 election result in the 8th District of Indiana, and led a hard and heated charge against the Democrats when they ruled their colleague Frank McCloskey had won by four votes. On that occasion and others he has shown a heated temper. But he is also a good detail man. David Stockman called him "the official cook of the GOP soup kitchen," the man who could tell you what little plums—federal projects, appointments—you needed to give away to win wavering Republicans' votes.

This evidently suits his constituents just fine. Thomas was first elected after the incumbent died suddenly in the summer of 1978; his hardest battle was winning the Republican nomination in a convention. He has won general elections by very impressive margins.

130 CALIFORNIA

The People: Est. Pop. 1986: 654,400, up 24.5% 1980–86; Pop. 1980: 525,750, up 31.9% 1970–80. Households (1980): 75% family, 41% with children, 63% married couples; 36.0% housing units rented; median monthly rent: $215; median house value: $63,600. Voting age pop. (1980): 371,945; 12% Spanish origin, 4% Black, 2% American Indian, 2% Asian origin.

1988 Presidential Vote:

Bush (R)	150,366	(65%)
Dukakis (D)	79,866	(34%)

Rep. William M. Thomas (R)

Elected 1978; b. Dec. 6, 1941, Wallace, ID; home, Bakersfield; San Fran. St. U., B.A. 1963, M.A. 1965; Baptist; married (Sharon).

Career: Prof., Bakersfield Commun. Col., 1965–74; CA Assembly, 1974–78.

Offices: 2402 RHOB 20515, 202-225-2915. Also 4100 Truxtun Ave., #200, Bakersfield 93301, 805-327-3611; 858 W. Jackman St., #115, Lancaster 93534, 805-948-2634; and 1390 Price St., #203, Pismo Beach 93449, 805-773-2533.

Committees: *Budget* (5th of 14 R). Task Forces: Urgent Fiscal Issues; Economic Policy, Projections and Revenues. *House Administration* (Ranking Member of 8 R). Subcommittees: Accounts; Elections (Ranking Member); Office Systems (Ranking Member). *Ways and Means* (7th of 13 R). Subcommittee: Trade.

Group Ratings

	ADA	ACLU	COPE	CFA	LCV	ACU	NTLC	NSI	COC	CEI
1988	25	29	13	45	31	78	71	100	100	57
1987	8	—	10	23	—	70	—	—	92	72

National Journal Ratings

	1988 LIB — 1988 CONS		1987 LIB — 1987 CONS	
Economic	27%	72%	18%	82%
Social	32%	68%	24%	76%
Foreign	0%	84%	20%	76%

Key Votes

1) Homeless $	FOR	5) Ban Drug Test	AGN	9) SDI Research	FOR
2) Gephardt Amdt	AGN	6) Drug Death Pen	FOR	10) Ban Chem Weaps	AGN
3) Deficit Reduc	—	7) Handgun Sales	FOR	11) Aid to Contras	FOR
4) Kill Plnt Clsng Notice	FOR	8) Ban D.C. Abort $	AGN	12) Nuclear Testing	—

Election Results

1988 general	William M. Thomas (R)	162,779	(71%)	($329,354)
	Lita Reid (D)	62,037	(27%)	($15,814)
1988 primary	William M. Thomas (R), unopposed			
1986 general	William M. Thomas (R)	129,989	(73%)	($255,261)
	Jules H. Moquin (D)	49,027	(27%)	($5,573)

TWENTY-FIRST DISTRICT

As greater Los Angeles has grown, it has oozed past the geographic barriers which everyone expected to contain it, filling in not only the plain of the Los Angeles Basin but the flat lands of the San Fernando Valley on the other side of the Cahuenga Pass, then spreading west into the narrow and, 50 years ago, almost entirely unpopulated valleys of Ventura County. Politically, the northern and western fringes of the San Fernando Valley (with boundaries carefully sculpted for political purposes), plus the new Ventura County suburbs connected to it by freeways—Simi Valley, Moorpark, Thousand Oaks (known locally as T.O.) and Camarillo—make up California's 21st Congressional District. This is a unit which in effect has moved west with its constituency. It was located entirely within the San Fernando Valley when it was filled with young families with conservative instincts on cultural issues; now this constituency has moved beyond the Valley, into Ventura County. Following it, interestingly, is the Reagan presidential library, which will be located just west of Simi Valley, after it was turned down by Stanford and failed to find a home on the Westside. In the 1980s, fully 80% of the households in this district are occupied by families, 69% by married couples, and 47% have children—figures well above the national average and exceeded in California only by the predominantly Mexican-American 34th district, on the other side of the Los Angeles Basin. While the divorce rate may be higher here than it was in the Valley 20 years ago, life has probably undergone less change than you would guess judging by outward appearances. Not far away by freeway you are in a California of cultural liberation, ultraconspicuous consumption, and scorn for traditional values. Here you are in California of impressive but not flashy upward mobility, of cultural caution, of salary-earners skeptical of government intervention in the economy, of parents fearful of cultural libertinism yet not eager for interference in their own lives and of patriots admiring an assertive foreign policy but, with the Vietnam example in their minds, worried about the consequences.

The congressman from this 21st District is a Republican experienced in local government, which traditionally in California and still in Ventura County is a nonpartisan, efficient and corruption-free enterprise. Elton Gallegly, a real estate broker and college dropout from a working-class suburb of Los Angeles, was elected at 35 to the Simi Valley city council, became mayor in 1980, and ran for Congress in 1986 when 21st district incumbent Bobbi Fiedler, who got her start as a busing opponent in the San Fernando Valley and beat a Democratic incumbent in 1980, ran for the Senate. Gallegly's main primary opponent was Tony Hope, son of comedian Bob Hope, whose longtime home is in Toluca Lake, in a corner of the Valley; but Tony Hope had spent most of the last decade in Washington and concentrated most of his 90-day campaign in the Valley. Gallegly, who raised more money, won 50%–34%, and had no serious opposition in the general election.

In the House Gallegly won a seat on the Interior Committee, strongly supported Administration policies in general, and SDI and the death penalty for cop killers in particular, and even opposed George Bush's moratorium on offshore oil exploration in his district. In 1988, however, he supported Bush early and, despite NRA contributions, voted for a seven-day waiting period for gun purchasers. His work seemed to pay off. In 1988, Korean-born primary challenger Sang Korman spent $300,000, but Gallegly won 82%–14%. In 1989 Gallegly won a seat on Foreign Affairs.

The People: Est. Pop. 1986: 609,400, up 15.9% 1980–86; Pop. 1980: 525,880, up 41.4% 1970–80. Households (1980): 80% family, 47% with children, 69% married couples; 25.2% housing units rented; median monthly rent: $331; median house value: $114,100. Voting age pop. (1980): 367,604; 9% Spanish origin, 3% Asian origin, 2% Black, 1% American Indian.

| 1988 Presidential Vote: | Bush (R) .... 178,542 | (64%) |
| | Dukakis (D)....................... 95,910 | (35%) |

Rep. Elton Gallegly (R)

Elected 1986; b. Mar. 7, 1944, Huntington Park; home, Simi Valley; L.A. St. Col., 1962–63; Protestant; married (Janice).

Career: Owner and operator of real estate firm; Simi Valley City Cncl., 1979–80; Mayor of Simi Valley, 1980–86.

Offices: 107 CHOB 20515, 202-225-5811. Also 9301 Oakdale Ave., Chatsworth 91311 818-341-2121; and 200 N. Westlake Blvd., Thousand Oaks 91362 805-496-4700.

Committees: *Interior and Insular Affairs* (10th of 15 R). Subcommittees: Insular and International Affairs; National Parks and Public Lands. *Foreign Affairs* (16th of 18 R). Subcommittees: Arms Control, International Security and Science; International Operations.

Group Ratings

	ADA	ACLU	COPE	CFA	LCV	ACU	NTLC	NSI	COC	CEI
1988	15	9	13	27	31	96	83	100	100	74
1987	4	—	6	21	—	96	—	—	100	77

National Journal Ratings

	1988 LIB — 1988 CONS		1987 LIB — 1987 CONS	
Economic	12% —	88%	0% —	89%
Social	12% —	87%	0% —	90%
Foreign	0% —	84%	0% —	80%

Key Votes

1) Homeless $	FOR	5) Ban Drug Test	FOR	9) SDI Research	FOR
2) Gephardt Amdt	AGN	6) Drug Death Pen	FOR	10) Ban Chem Weaps	AGN
3) Deficit Reduc	AGN	7) Handgun Sales	AGN	11) Aid to Contras	FOR
4) Kill Plnt Clsng Notice	FOR	8) Ban D.C. Abort $	FOR	12) Nuclear Testing	AGN

Election Results

1988 general	Elton Gallegly (R) 181,413	(69%)	($465,310)
	Donald E. Stevens (D) 75,739	(29%)	
1988 primary	Elton Gallegly (R) 57,568	(82%)	
	Sang Korman (R)...................... 9,762	(14%)	
1986 general	Elton Gallegly (R) 132,090	(68%)	($591,018)
	Gilbert R. Saldana (D)................ 54,497	(28%)	($65,501)

TWENTY-SECOND DISTRICT

Los Angeles is the only one of America's great metropolitan areas built up against mountains 10,000 feet high—the San Gabriels, whose snow-capped peaks can be seen looming far over the high-rises on smog-free days. The 22d Congressional District of California consists of several parts of the Los Angeles area nestled just below these mountains and their foothills, the Verdugos. One part is Glendale, an old suburb almost directly north of downtown Los Angeles;

elderly Anglos here have been joined in the 1980s by many Iranian immigrants. Just west is Burbank, part of which is in the 22d, and behind the Verdugo Mountains are the suburbs of La Canada and La Crescenta. The 22d includes a string of towns running east from Los Angeles beneath the mountains. These started off as stations on the Santa Fe Railroad line, then became separate little towns, then finally high-income suburbs: Monrovia (starting from the east), Arcadia, Sierra Madre, Temple City, San Marino, half of Pasadena, and South Pasadena. The district also includes the communities of Saugus and Newhall nestled in the mountains north of the San Fernando Valley.

Historically, the political rule in Los Angeles was that the closer to the mountains you got, the more affluent and more Republican the neighborhoods. This is no longer true everywhere—the Hollywood Hills are heavily Democratic—but it still has some validity, for the 22d tends to be heavily Republican. For years these areas were heavily Anglo, peopled by small businessmen and professionals firmly opposed to the Democrats' plans for economic redistribution. Today there are increasing numbers of Iranians and Asians, but the voting habits remain heavily Republican.

The congressman from the 22d is Carlos Moorhead, a Republican with a long history of civic and governmental service. He represented Glendale in the Assembly for 6 years, and when the incumbent retired in 1972 he won a close Republican primary and went to Washington. There he was almost immediately in the spotlight, as one of Richard Nixon's relatively few defenders on the House Judiciary Committee. Moorhead has continued to serve on Judiciary, where he is now the second ranking Republican, and on Energy and Commerce, where he was third in early 1989. His work is the opposite of flashy, and is often devoted to issues like trademark and patent law or reauthorizing federal insurance against nuclear accidents—work that must be done, but not the material for a hot political issue or a direct mail solicitation. He is a hard-working legislative craftsman, probably thought by some Republicans to be too accommodating and by many Democrats to be too conservative; but he perseveres by his own lights.

Moorhead has had almost no trouble winning reelection. In 1982 Phil Burton's redistricting plan put incumbent John Rousselot in the same district with him, but Rousselot, in a rare act of political unselfishness, moved and ran against Democrat Marty Martinez and lost.

The People: Est. Pop. 1986: 572,800, up 8.9% 1980–86; Pop. 1980: 525,939, up 3.3% 1970–80. Households (1980): 66% family, 31% with children, 54% married couples. 43.1% housing units rented; median monthly rent: $267; median house value: $110,100. Voting age pop. (1980): 403,471; 11% Spanish origin, 4% Asian origin, 2% Black, 1% American Indian.

1988 Presidential Vote: Bush (R) 158,823   (64%)
                                Dukakis (D). 86,732   (35%)

Rep. Carlos J. Moorhead (R)

Elected 1972; b. May 5, 1922, Long Beach; home, Glendale; U. of CA at Los Angeles, B.A. 1943, U. of Southern CA, J.D. 1949; Presbyterian; married (Valery).

Career: Army, WWII; Practicing atty.; CA Assembly, 1967–72.

Offices: 2346 RHOB 20515, 202-225-4176. Also 420 N. Brand Blvd., Ste. 304, Glendale 91203, 818-247-8445; and 301 E. Colorado Blvd., #618, Pasadena 91101, 818-792-6168.

Committees: *Energy and Commerce* (3d of 17 R). Subcommittees: Energy and Power (Ranking Member); Telecommunications and Finance. *Judiciary* (2d of 14 R). Subcommittees: Economic and Commercial Law; Courts, Intellectual Property and the Administration of Justice (Ranking Member).

Group Ratings

	ADA	ACLU	COPE	CFA	LCV	ACU	NTLC	NSI	COC	CEI
1988	10	13	7	27	19	96	86	100	100	86
1987	4	—	7	14	—	96	—	—	100	79

National Journal Ratings

	1988 LIB — 1988 CONS		1987 LIB — 1987 CONS	
Economic	0%	93%	0%	89%
Social	0%	95%	0%	90%
Foreign	0%	84%	0%	80%

Key Votes

1) Homeless $	FOR	5) Ban Drug Test	FOR	9) SDI Research	FOR
2) Gephardt Amdt	AGN	6) Drug Death Pen	FOR	10) Ban Chem Weaps	AGN
3) Deficit Reduc	AGN	7) Handgun Sales	FOR	11) Aid to Contras	FOR
4) Kill Plnt Clsng Notice	FOR	8) Ban D.C. Abort $	FOR	12) Nuclear Testing	AGN

Election Results

1988 general	Carlos J. Moorhead (R)	164,699	(70%)	($234,920)
	John G. Simmons (D).................	61,555	(26%)	($18,046)
1988 primary	Carlos J. Moorhead (R)	67,378	(87%)	
	David R. Headrick (R)................	10,314	(13%)	
1986 general	Carlos J. Moorhead (R)	141,096	(74%)	($144,132)
	John G. Simmons (D).................	44,036	(23%)	($26,490)

TWENTY-THIRD DISTRICT

The Westside—it's a term that was not much used 10 years ago, but is now shorthand for what might be the biggest and flashiest concentration of affluence in the world. The boundaries of the Westside are not defined, but it obviously includes most of Los Angeles west of Fairfax Avenue—Beverly Hills, Westwood, Bel Air, Brentwood—and it seems to jump over the Santa Monica Mountains to take in Sherman Oaks and Encino at the southern edge of the San Fernando Valley. This is not just a rich residential area where people buy houses for $1 million, knock down the structure and build something new for another $1 million or so; it is not just a high-priced shopping area, whose Rodeo Drive, a quite ordinary shopping street 20 years ago, is now up there with Fifth Avenue, Bond Street and the Rue Faubourg St. Honore. It is also an office center of great magnitude, headquarters of entertainment companies and of aerospace conglomerates and the home of polo-shirted dealmakers and hot shot entrepreneurs. The Westside is the home of former President Ronald Reagan, who lives in one of the more modest houses in Bel Air, and it is also the center of the second largest Jewish community in the United States—as well as the focus of the 1980s' immigration of Iranians to the United States.

Politically, most of the Westside is included in the 23d Congressional District of California. On the south side of the Santa Monica Mountains, the 23d stretches from the newly incorporated city of West Hollywood, with its gay mayor, through Beverly Hills to the Veterans Home in West Los Angeles and the Pacific Palisades neighborhood where Ronald Reagan lived before 1980. Across the mountains, it includes the hillside communities of Encino and Woodland Hills, and the middle-class Valley neighborhoods of Van Nuys, Reseda and Canoga Park, stretching four and five miles north of Ventura Boulevard on their mile-square grid avenues below. Twenty years ago, these streets were filled with children; now, more often than not, they are quiet. The boundaries at the edge of the district are jagged so as to enclose the maximum number of Democratic votes. You can find plenty of exotic areas here, from Rodeo Drive to Malibu, and in the winter the movie theaters all have signs inviting Academy members in to see nominated films. But the typical neighborhood here is modestly affluent, with many Jewish residents and many professionals—liberal and Democratic in its political tradition—it is willing sometimes these days to consider Republicans.

Anthony Beilenson, who started representing the Westside in the California legislature in 1962 at age 30, is the congressman from the 23d. First elected to the House in 1976 when incumbent Thomas Rees retired, Beilenson is an accomplished legislative strategist and tactician himself, one of the real pros in the House. Yet he is also relatively quiet, more of a loner than a team player, and almost entirely unglitzy. He got the California seat on Rules in 1978 against the wishes of his delegation, and was not happy with the political leanings of the district Phil Burton gave him after the 1980 Census. But he has generally been a leadership man on Rules and has been reelected easily. He has had some specific legislative successes, notably on setting up a Santa Monica Mountains National Recreation Area, but mostly his imprint is hard to see. He ranks third in seniority on Rules today, behind Boston's Joe Moakley and Butler Derrick, so he could conceivably be chairman some day.

Rules is a committee best suited to a legislator willing to remain anonymous; it allows a skilled operator to exert important influence on many different kinds of legislation, but often silently and seldom with any fanfare. Thus, Beilenson has been the House's closest student of the budget process, proposing changes in the early 1980s that were not adopted at that time, but which he advanced later when Gramm-Rudman came up, and he urged the House to prepare a plan to erase the budget deficit by 1989. He is also a leading advocate of full public financing of congressional elections—a lonely cause up through the middle 1980s, but one which is gaining support as problems with the current system accumulate. He never seems afraid to challenge conventional wisdom or to call for solutions that seem politically unacceptable: for 1989 he was urging the phasing in of a 50 cent gas tax increase (we can pay now, he says, or pay OPEC later), and argued that social security should be put on the table in budget negotiations and be subject to cuts. On roll call votes he seems to decide almost entirely on the merits of legislation, without much regard to who is backing or opposing it.

Beilenson has two important new assignments in the 101st Congress. He joined the Budget Committee, where his views may prove a little inconvenient for his fellow Democrats. He also has risen to become chairman of the House Intelligence Committee. His record on foreign policy issues tends to be quite liberal, but he takes his responsibilities seriously and does not sign cynically on to partisan positions without being convinced of their merits. This is Beilenson's last year in his six year rotation on the committee.

The only conceivable threat to Beilenson's tenure is redistricting. Beilenson shares the Westside with two other talented legislators, Henry Waxman and Howard Berman. All three districts have been increased greatly in population in the 1980s and it would be difficult for a Republican-controlled redistricting process to put them in together.

The People: Est. Pop. 1986: 571,700, up 8.7% 1980–86; Pop. 1980: 525,936, up 3.6% 1970–80. Households (1980): 59% family, 26% with children, 47% married couples; 51.8% housing units rented; median monthly rent: $334; median house value: $135,300. Voting age pop. (1980): 422,708; 8% Spanish origin, 3% Asian origin, 3% Black.

1988 Presidential Vote:
Dukakis (D).	138,264	(56%)
Bush (R)	106,610	(43%)

Rep. Anthony C. Beilenson (D)

Elected 1976; b. Oct. 26, 1932, New Rochelle, NY; home, Los Angeles; Harvard Col., A.B. 1954, LL.B. 1957; Jewish; married (Dolores).

Career: Practicing atty., 1957–59; Counsel, CA Assembly Cmtee. on Finance and Insur., 1960; Staff atty., CA Comp. and Insur. Fund, 1961–62; CA Assembly, 1963–66; CA Senate, 1967–77.

Offices: 1025 LHOB 20515, 202-225-5911. Also 11000 Wilshire Blvd., Ste. 14223, Los Angeles 90024, 213-209-7801; and 18401 Burbank Blvd., Ste. 222, Tarzana 91356, 818-345-1560.

Committees: *Budget* (14th of 21 D). Task Forces: Budget Process, Reconciliation and Enforcement; Economic Policy, Projections and Revenues. *Rules* (3d of 9 D). Subcommittee: Rules of the House. *Permanent Select Committee on Intelligence* (Chairman of 12 D). Subcommittee: Program and Budget Authorization (Chairman)

Group Ratings

	ADA	ACLU	COPE	CFA	LCV	ACU	NTLC	NSI	COC	CEI
1988	95	96	75	82	94	8	18	0	50	25
1987	84	—	75	93	—	13	—	—	20	21

National Journal Ratings

	1988 LIB — 1988 CONS		1987 LIB — 1987 CONS	
Economic	52%	— 47%	48%	— 52%
Social	86%	— 0%	62%	— 36%
Foreign	77%	— 21%	81%	— 0%

Key Votes

1) Homeless $	AGN	5) Ban Drug Test	AGN	9) SDI Research	AGN
2) Gephardt Amdt	AGN	6) Drug Death Pen	AGN	10) Ban Chem Weaps	FOR
3) Deficit Reduc	FOR	7) Handgun Sales	AGN	11) Aid to Contras	AGN
4) Kill Plnt Clsng Notice	AGN	8) Ban D.C. Abort $	AGN	12) Nuclear Testing	FOR

Election Results

1988 general	Anthony C. Beilenson (D).............	147,858	(64%)	($140,486)
	Jim Salomon (R).....................	77,184	(33%)	($100,956)
1988 primary	Anthony C. Beilenson (D).............	67,802	(84%)	
	Val Marmillion (D)..................	12,755	(16%)	
1986 general	Anthony C. Beilenson (D).............	121,468	(66%)	($215,076)
	George Woolverton (R)...............	58,746	(32%)	($220,313)

TWENTY-FOURTH DISTRICT

Fifty years ago, the neighborhoods north and west of downtown Los Angeles were mostly standard middle-class territory, populated by families with roots in places like Protestant Iowa and Nebraska, comfortable residential neighborhoods stretching out along the interurban lines and the wide avenues that made Los Angeles one of America's first automobile cities. Many of these neighborhoods were new, and there were still vacant lots and barren hillsides. But this was also Hollywood, the center of America's showbiz industry and, as time went on, newly formed middle-class families moved out along the freeways and settled elsewhere—West Los Angeles on the other side of Beverly Hills, the San Fernando Valley over the Santa Monica Mountains and Orange County far to the southeast on the Santa Ana Freeway. The Fairfax area near Beverly Hills and North Hollywood, off the freeway just over the mountains, became one of Los Angeles's major Jewish neighborhoods. Rich neighborhoods like Hancock Park and Los Feliz kept their tone, but Hollywood itself became seedy, and the Hollywood Hills became the home of the single and the unusual, the soap-opera actress busy finding herself.

Today most signs of decay are being erased as this part of Los Angeles grows—and changes. The fabulous growth of the showbiz industry, fueled by the demand of an economically growing nation (and world) for entertainment, helped to turn around many of even the tackiest parts of Hollywood, and today the boulevards are full of glass and chrome buildings filled with gold-chained and polo-shirted executives, and one previously obscure street after another is now the home of restaurants so chic that their phone numbers are unlisted.

And there are other changes. Along the avenues closer to downtown are less affluent neighborhoods filling up with Latin and Asian immigrants, especially Koreans. They are rising so rapidly in income and seem so thoroughly imbued with respect for order and hard work that they pose little threat to the affluence of the blocks farther west. But there is no question that these latest migrants will play a major role in shaping Los Angeles's future.

This is the land of California's 24th Congressional District, which stretches almost from MacArthur Park and downtown Los Angeles to the limits of Beverly Hills, includes all of Hollywood, Hancock Park and Los Feliz, and goes north over the mountains with the Hollywood sign to take in hill neighborhoods, Universal City and North Hollywood. Politically, these neighborhoods, which were solidly Republican 50 years ago, now form one of the leading liberal constituencies in America. Jewish voters are especially important here, since they tend to turn out when others do not (in off years turnout in Latin and Asian neighborhoods has been close to zero). Gay voters are an important force as well. Someday Mexican-Americans, Korean-Americans and other Asian groups may be large voting blocs here: in 1980 the district's population was 22% Hispanic and 11% Asian, and its children were 44% Hispanic and 15% Asian.

Henry Waxman, congressman from the 24th, is one of the most powerful and skillful legislators in recent American history. He was first elected to the California Assembly in 1968 at age 29, and in his second term chaired the Reapportionment Committee; he went to Congress in 1974 in a district designed, he likes to point out, not by his committee, but by a court. Waxman's big break came after the 1978 election, when he was elected chairman of the Energy and Commerce Committee's Health Subcommittee. This was one of the first times House Democrats decided not to observe seniority in handing out subcommittee chairs, and Waxman's opponent, Richardson Preyer, was popular, competent and widely respected. Nevertheless Waxman argued his case on the issues and also made campaign contributions to other Democrats on the full committee and won the post 15–12.

The campaign contributions were no accident. Waxman and his friends Howard Berman and Mel Levine, now also area congressmen, have built their own political machine in Los Angeles. Its power comes not from patronage but from fund raising and savvy: they raise money from affluent liberals in Los Angeles and put it to good use in campaigns, often managed by Berman's brother Michael and his partner Carl D'Agostino. Their specialty is the targeted direct mail campaign, with hundreds of customized letters sent out to different lists. In the apolitical commonwealth of California, where television advertising is exceedingly expensive and people will do much to avoid politics, Waxman and his machine are credited with electing half a dozen congressmen, at least as many state legislators and several city councilmen, as well as defeating Occidental Petroleum's Armand Hammer and Mayor Tom Bradley on a 1988 ocean dumping ballot issue. They don't always win though. The leaking of a Berman-D'Agostino memo, cynical in its contempt for Bradley and its talk of raising money from rich Jews, embarrassed Councilman Zev Yaroslavsky, who first renounced Berman-D'Agostino and then dropped his 1989 campaign against Bradley.

In the House, Waxman's power comes not so much from political maneuvering, but from his work on substantive issues and his adroit use of procedural tactics. He is now the number three Democrat on Energy and Commerce, the most sought-after committee for Democrats in the 1980s; and he has been an exceptionally productive and knowledgeable legislator. He has dominated all House action on the Clean Air Act since his bravura performance in 1981 and 1982, when he prevented the united forces of the Reagan Administration and Energy and Commerce chairman John Dingell from relaxing the Clean Air Act, delaying action for months while Dingell and allies had a majority, and eventually splitting their forces apart.

Since 1983, he has been trying to put together his own clean air package, but has been blocked by Dingell. Yet on other issues, he has remained a staunch Dingell ally. On health matters, he has led the charge for funding for AIDS research, pushed to passage the law providing damages to children injured by required immunizations, sponsored measures to deal with the problem of adolescent pregnancies, expanded the availability of generic drugs, extended patent protection for drugs during part of the regulatory process. He is now working to legalize the use of heroin to reduce the pain of terminal cancer patients, as he oversees the National Institutes of Health. He has also worked doggedly to expand medicaid coverage, getting an extra $600 million, for example, in the budget scramble for fiscal year 1988, and he plans to expand medicaid further. In 1988, he failed to get Congress to require confidentiality in AIDS testing, but did get an AIDS bill passed with an estimated $1 billion in preventive and treatment programs in addition to the $1.3 billion for research and other programs voted earlier.

Waxman brings to all these tasks an instinct for the legislative process that is second to none, a thorough knowledge of the rules and willingness to exploit every one, and a temperament that is all but unflappable. He considers issues on the merits and sometimes surprises everyone, as he did by opposing the Los Angeles subway on which construction has begun in the district. Short, readily recognizable with his moustache, he makes his arguments calmly and cheerfully, even when opponents are thundering and screaming. Waxman's career shows how the House has changed in the last dozen years. It is more of a meritocracy now; important positions are given not just to senior Members, but to those most capable of using them in the way the majority wants.

At home, Waxman's district seems exceedingly pleased with him: he is probably the first congressman from Los Angeles, and certainly the first liberal congressman from Los Angeles, to be both a legislative power in the House and a political power back home.

The People: Est. Pop. 1986: 589,200, up 12.0% 1980–86; Pop. 1980: 525,918, up 12.8% 1970–80. Households (1980): 47% family, 22% with children, 34% married couples; 76.4% housing units rented; median monthly rent: $235; median house value: $111,700. Voting age pop. (1980): 429,288; 22% Spanish origin, 11% Asian origin, 6% Black.

1988 Presidential Vote:

Dukakis (D)	106,652	(65%)
Bush (R)	55,756	(34%)

Rep. Henry A. Waxman (D)

Elected 1974; b. Sept. 12, 1939, Los Angeles; home, Los Angeles; U. of CA at Los Angeles, B.A. 1961, J.D. 1964; Jewish; married (Janet).

Career: Practicing atty., 1965–68; CA Assembly, 1968–74.

Offices: 2418 RHOB 20515, 202-225-3976. Also 8425 W. 3d St., Ste. 400, Los Angeles 90048, 213-651-1040.

Committees: *Energy and Commerce* (3d of 26 D). Subcommittees: Commerce, Consumer Protection and Competitiveness; Health and the Environment (Chairman). *Government Operations* (4th of 24 D). Subcommittees: Environment, Energy and Natural Resources; Commerce, Consumer and Monetary Affairs; Human Resources and Intergovernmental Relations. *Select Committee on Aging* (10th of 39 D). Subcommittee: Health and Long-Term Care.

Group Ratings

	ADA	ACLU	COPE	CFA	LCV	ACU	NTLC	NSI	COC	CEI
1988	90	100	88	82	88	0	13	0	21	15
1987	92	—	88	93	—	10	—	—	17	12

National Journal Ratings

	1988 LIB — 1988 CONS		1987 LIB — 1987 CONS	
Economic	71% —	23%	66% —	33%
Social	86% —	0%	78% —	0%
Foreign	77% —	21%	75% —	24%

Key Votes

1) Homeless $	AGN	5) Ban Drug Test	—	9) SDI Research	AGN
2) Gephardt Amdt	AGN	6) Drug Death Pen	—	10) Ban Chem Weaps	FOR
3) Deficit Reduc	—	7) Handgun Sales	—	11) Aid to Contras	AGN
4) Kill Plnt Clsng Notice	AGN	8) Ban D.C. Abort $	AGN	12) Nuclear Testing	FOR

Election Results

1988 general	Henry A. Waxman (D)	112,038	(72%)	($191,334)
	John N. Cowles (R)	36,835	(24%)	($15,449)
	Two others	6,198	(4%)	
1988 primary	Henry A. Waxman, unopposed			
1986 general	Henry A. Waxman (D)	103,914	(88%)	($136,807)
	George Abrahams (Lib.)	8,871	(7%)	
	James Green (P&F)	5,388	(5%)	($300)

TWENTY-FIFTH DISTRICT

The site for downtown Los Angeles was originally chosen because it was the only place where the Los Angeles River flowed all year. Fifty years ago, downtown was a modest sight with only its new Mission style Union Station, a 27-story City Hall and the nearby Los Angeles Times building, the Biltmore Hotel across from Pershing Square and a few modest office buildings. Though it has been the subject of derision in the years since, today downtown L.A. is pretty formidable. Huge, charmless high-rises, impressive museums and arts centers, and an Hispanic shopping district on Broadway (the biggest downtown retail operation west of Chicago) jut up impressively through the smog in the bowl of land surrounded by freeways, hills and the now cement-lined river where the center of this pueblo town was established just over 200 years ago. Yet downtown is only one of 18 nodes of office space in greater Los Angeles and has only 4% of the region's jobs.

Downtown Los Angeles is the most prominent, but not the most typical, part of California's 25th Congressional District. Almost all the well-paid downtown workers commute in from elsewhere, glancing at their wristwatches and planning a lane change as they inch ahead on the freeway past the neighborhoods where most of the 25th District's voters live. For this is California's most heavily Hispanic district, and Los Angeles' poorest. It contains, in Boyle Heights just across the Los Angeles River and, farther out, in unincorporated East Los Angeles, the entry points for many migrants from Mexico and parts south; it also contains more pleasant places, like the Highland Park neighborhood, where migrants move as they become more successful, doubling up with relatives and friends from back home to save on rent in the nation's most costly housing market, and saving up to move farther out one of the freeways, to the San Fernando Valley or Orange County. What we are seeing in these areas are not people who are failures but people who are in the process of becoming successes.

These are not ghettos in which Mexican-Americans are indefinitely confined, nor do they have the high crime rates and degree of abandonment of some black ghettos back east. A drive through the area shows not empty storefronts, but busy shops with new signs; not housing riddled with vandalism and neglect, but houses newly painted and with carefully tended gardens. Americans are used to seeing their lowest-income neighborhoods nearly abandoned, but East Los Angeles is thronged with people, and especially with children—although unfortunately many of them are joining gangs when they are in their teens.

Latins are not the only residents of the 25th, it should be added. This is a polyglot district, with all manner of ethnics, from Little Japan in downtown (now a shopping district mostly) to Koreatown on the western district line. There are blacks in the southern end, toward Watts, and in a salient that proceeds north into Pasadena. Politically, it need hardly be added, this is a heavily Democratic district.

For those who take the black (or Irish) experiences as the norm, one of the puzzlers of current politics is why so few Hispanics have won major political office. The 25th District's Congressman, Edward Roybal, is Hispanic to be sure—his parents were from an old New Mexico family and brought him to L.A. as a child—but after he left the Los Angeles Council when he was first elected to Congress in 1962, there were no Hispanics serving there for more than 20 years. They do not even vote much: less than 80,000 residents of the 25th voted for a congressman in 1986, compared to 185,000 in the next-door 22d. For a long time, Mexican-Americans didn't see politics as their way up in the world. There are now two Hispanic council members in Los Angeles, Richard Alatorre and Gloria Molina, both former members of the Assembly and political rivals. But the Hispanic vote is not necessarily leftish: Molina's big issue is her opposition to a new prison in East Los Angeles; in 1986 Mexican-Americans voted to recall Chief Justice Rose Bird and were evenly divided on making English the official state language.

They are not the first ethnic group in America to move up mainly through private sector jobs, largely ignoring politics. Moving up rapidly economically, hobbled less by segregation and discrimination, they don't need as much from government as do blacks.

Roybal is one of California's senior congressmen now, but he has not had the most distinguished record in the House. In 1978, the Ethics Committee recommended that he be censured for having lied about a $1,000 campaign contribution from Tongsun Park which he had converted to his own use. Roybal admitted taking the money, but his supporters, some of whom thought him the victim of discrimination, persuaded the House that he should be reprimanded rather than censured. In 1982 and 1984, he led the opposition to the immigration reform bill of 1986, charging with some passion that the employer sanction provisions would result in discrimination against Hispanic Americans. He failed to persuade the House on employer sanctions, but played a part in stopping the bill in those years. But in 1986 Roybal and other Hispanic congressmen, fearful that a more onerous bill might pass, did not interpose great objections and the Congress finally passed, and the President signed, a bill with employer sanctions, toughened border controls, and a broad exemption for agricultural guestworkers.

Roybal has two important committee assignments. A senior member of Appropriations, he chairs the Treasury, Postal Service, General Government Subcommittee, ordinarily one of the less controversial units, though he has sometimes had problems with his bills on the floor. In 1983, he succeeded Claude Pepper as chairman of the Select Committee on Aging, and he is a co-sponsor of Pepper's long-term health care bill. Roybal is a man of intellectual ability, but sometimes seems cynical. He has a solidly liberal voting record and has no problems winning reelection, though he has had no serious primary opposition for many years. Although past 70, he has shown no sign of retiring. In 1988, his daughter Lucille Roybal-Allard was elected to the California Assembly from a district covering much of the same territory as the 25th.

The People: Est. Pop. 1986: 588,200, up 11.8% 1980–86; Pop. 1980: 526,013, up 9.5% 1970–80. Households (1980): 70% family, 44% with children, 49% married couples; 62.0% housing units rented; median monthly rent: $176; median house value: $65,500. Voting age pop. (1980): 358,659; 57% Spanish origin, 10% Black, 8% Asian origin, 1% American Indian.

1988 Presidential Vote: Dukakis (D)..................... 74,007   (67%)
Bush (R) 34,925   (32%)

Rep. Edward R. Roybal (D)

Elected 1962; b. Feb. 10, 1916, Albuquerque, NM; home, Los Angeles; U. of CA at Los Angeles, Southwestern U.; Roman Catholic; married (Lucille).

Career: Army, WWII; Dir. of Health Educ., L.A. Cnty. Tuberculosis & Health Assn., 1945–49; L.A. City Cncl., 1949–62, Pres. Pro Tem, 1961–62.

Offices: 2211 RHOB 20515, 202-225-6235. Also 300 N. Los Angeles St., Rm. 7106, Los Angeles 90012, 213-894-4870.

Committees: *Appropriations* (6th of 35 D). Subcommittees: Labor, Health and Human Services, and Education; Treasury, Postal Service and General Government (Chairman). *Select Committee on Aging* (Chairman of 39 D). Subcommittee: Retirement Income and Employment (Chairman).

Group Ratings

	ADA	ACLU	COPE	CFA	LCV	ACU	NTLC	NSI	COC	CEI
1988	95	100	93	91	88	0	8	0	23	9
1987	88	—	93	86	—	10	—	—	7	8

National Journal Ratings

	1988 LIB — 1988 CONS		1987 LIB — 1987 CONS	
Economic	79% —	17%	68% —	27%
Social	86% —	0%	78% —	0%
Foreign	84% —	0%	81% —	0%

Key Votes

1) Homeless $	AGN	5) Ban Drug Test	AGN	9) SDI Research	—
2) Gephardt Amdt	AGN	6) Drug Death Pen	AGN	10) Ban Chem Weaps	FOR
3) Deficit Reduc	FOR	7) Handgun Sales	AGN	11) Aid to Contras	AGN
4) Kill Plnt Clsng Notice	AGN	8) Ban D.C. Abort $	AGN	12) Nuclear Testing	FOR

Election Results

1988 general	Edward R. Roybal (D)	85,378	(86%)	($67,957)
	Raul Reyes (P&F)	8,746	(9%)	
	John C. Thie (Lib.)	5,752	(6%)	
1988 primary	Edward R. Roybal, unopposed			
1986 general	Edward R. Roybal (D)	62,692	(76%)	($63,996)
	Gregory L. Hardy (R)	17,588	(21%)	

TWENTY-SIXTH DISTRICT

If you had stood at the crest of the Santa Monica Mountains in 1910—when you would have had to climb on foot to get there—and looked north, you would have seen spread out before you, almost totally empty and barren, 20 miles wide and 12 miles deep, the San Fernando Valley. Its history has been recounted, with surprisingly little distortion, in the movie *Chinatown*. So close to a city that even then was growing explosively, the Valley inspired great plans. Civic leaders like Harry Chandler of the *Los Angeles Times* encouraged city engineer William Mulholland to build a huge aqueduct from the Owens Valley to give Los Angeles water, and got the city to annex most of the Valley, large chunks of which they had, with foresight, already acquired. At the time of World War II, the Valley was only starting to be filled in. In the years afterwards, it was classic suburban territory, filled with *Leave It to Beaver* families: working fathers, homemaker mothers, two or three or four kids walking every day to the local public school, neighborhoods seemingly filled with white Protestants (although actually there were many Catholics and Jews even then). By the 1980s, the Valley had become a rather different place. The land was almost entirely built up, except for the few remaining movie ranches and flood control areas, and the Valley was changing slowly from suburban to urban in character. Today, such parents as there are are often single; such kids as there are (school populations are way down) come home to empty houses; there is a much greater ethnic mix, with many Hispanics and Asians and some blacks as well.

Politically, the Valley changed from being one of California's most marginal constituencies, a battleground between the parties, to becoming rather Democratic; by the 1980s, only the neighborhoods at its fringes were heavily Republican. Demographically, it was large enough to be split among three congressional districts, one of them the 26th—a seat created for and by a particular congressman, Howard Berman. It begins in his political base in the Hollywood Hills, above West Hollywood and Beverly Hills. Here expensive houses are built off the roads that twist up hillsides, nestled under steep overhangs or looking out, from atop a scraped-off hillside, on the whole city. In the early 1960s, the Hollywood Hills were affluent, family-oriented and Republican, voting on economic issues; today they are affluent, single (sometimes gay), and Democratic, thanks to cultural issues. The politician who first perceived and acted on the change was Howard Berman. In 1972, supposedly a terrible year for Democrats, 27 year-old Berman ran for the seat in the Hollywood Hills district represented by the Assembly's Republican leader—and won handily. He became majority leader in the Assembly himself, an active legislator (the chief sculptor of the farm labor law) and, unwilling to wait for his erstwhile ally Leo McCarthy to leave the speakership in two years, challenged him for that office in 1980. The McCarthy forces engineered the election of Willie Brown instead, and Berman, deciding to leave the Assembly, made sure that Phil Burton drew a congressional district for him.

The 26th District created for Berman proceeds directly north from the Hollywood Hills into the heart of the San Fernando Valley. It includes the Democratic middle-class neighborhoods of Van Nuys and Panorama City, goes northwest to take in, within a jagged boundary, the more Democratic parts of Granada Hills, takes in the black neighborhood of Pacoima and the heavily Mexican-American neighborhoods on either side of the Golden State Freeway, and dips a little south to include a carefully selected set of precincts in Burbank. Altogether this is a district with a large, growing and upwardly mobile Mexican-American population, one whose refusal to vote as onesidedly as blacks leaves the 26th district as marginally rather than heavily Democratic in national politics.

Berman has proved to be a powerful and active legislator in the House. Long an ally of Cesar Chavez's United Farm Workers, he opposed Leon Panetta's guestworker amendment to the immigration bill in 1982 and 1984. In 1986, he and Charles Schumer worked up a compromise on the issue, allowing in a large number of guestworkers and opening the way for them to become U.S. citizens. This compromise at first stymied and then, when it was altered, helped to facilitate the passage of the immigration law that year. In 1988 he sponsored the provision allowing 20,000 immigrant visas for migrants without close relatives here, to be selected randomly by computer—"Berman visa applications", they are called by the Irish and others who seek them. On Foreign Affairs, he volunteered to floor manage foreign aid bills; he has always been interested in the Middle East and Mexico (as are many of his constituents), and would like to raise the amount of foreign aid generally. He has taken a hand in crafting anti-apartheid legislation and (with Republican Henry Hyde) a law allowing imposition of arms embargoes on nations that support terrorism; he also wants to stop proliferation of ballistic missile technology, especially to Arab countries. He wants to allow more immigrants in who do not qualify as relatives of current citizens; this would bring in more Hispanics and Asians, which he believes (and Los Angeles today proves) strengthen the economy of the United States.

The same aggressiveness and energy that propel Berman into these legislative issues also helped him to win a seat on the Budget Committee in 1989. Although there were already three California Democrats on it, he waged a year-long campaign and managed to win 23 of 31 votes on the Democratic Steering and Policy Committee. Back in Los Angeles he is known, along with colleague Henry Waxman, as the head of an unusual political machine that raises money in Los Angeles for campaigns there and elsewhere. He has had little trouble getting reelected in the 26th and in 1988, against a Guardian Angel, won 70% of the vote.

The People: Est. Pop. 1986: 573,600, up 9.1% 1980–86; Pop. 1980: 525,995, up 2.4% 1970–80. Households (1980): 68% family, 34% with children, 54% married couples; 44.5% housing units rented; median monthly rent: $282; median house value: $96,200. Voting age pop. (1980): 392,919; 20% Spanish origin, 4% Black, 3% Asian origin, 1% American Indian.

1988 Presidential Vote:
Dukakis (D)	108,660	(55%)
Bush (R)	85,640	(44%)

Rep. Howard L. Berman (D)

Elected 1982; b. Apr. 15, 1941, Los Angeles; home, Sherman Oaks; U. of CA at Los Angeles, B.A. 1962, LL.B. 1965; Jewish; married (Janis).

Career: Practicing atty., 1966–72; CA Assembly, 1973–82, Major. Ldr., 1974–78.

Offices: 137 CHOB 20515, 202-225-4695. Also 14600 Roscoe Blvd., Ste. 506, Panorama City 91402, 818-891-0543.

Committees: *Budget* (18th of 21 D). Task Forces: Budget Process, Reconciliation and Enforcement; Defense, Foreign Policy & Space. *Foreign Affairs* (14th of 28 D). Subcommittees: Arms Control, International Security and Science; International Operations. *Judiciary* (16th of 21 D). Subcommittees: Courts, Intellectual Property and the Administration of Justice; Immigration, Refugees, and International Law.

Group Ratings

	ADA	ACLU	COPE	CFA	LCV	ACU	NTLC	NSI	COC	CEI
1988	95	95	87	100	81	4	12	0	36	14
1987	88	—	88	86	—	0	—	—	13	12

National Journal Ratings

	1988 LIB —	1988 CONS	1987 LIB —	1987 CONS
Economic	60% —	37%	73% —	0%
Social	86% —	0%	78% —	0%
Foreign	84% —	0%	81% —	0%

Key Votes

1) Homeless $	—	5) Ban Drug Test	AGN	9) SDI Research	AGN
2) Gephardt Amdt	FOR	6) Drug Death Pen	AGN	10) Ban Chem Weaps	FOR
3) Deficit Reduc	FOR	7) Handgun Sales	AGN	11) Aid to Contras	AGN
4) Kill Plnt Clsng Notice	AGN	8) Ban D.C. Abort $	AGN	12) Nuclear Testing	FOR

Election Results

1988 general	Howard L. Berman (D) 126,930	(70%)	($409,233)
	G. C. (Brodie) Broderson (R) 53,518	(30%)	
1988 primary	Howard L. Berman, unopposed		
1986 general	Howard L. Berman (D) 98,091	(65%)	($272,956)
	Robert M. Kerns (R) 52,662	(35%)	($10,314)

TWENTY-SEVENTH DISTRICT

In the morning there may be mists, in the winter the air is damp and clammy, even in summers the weather can be chilly, and the water is never very warm and is sometimes polluted; but many southern Californians would never live anywhere except near the beach. Most of them are likely to be found in the 27th Congressional District of California, a long, thin swath of land (plus some odd-shaped salients inland) along the Pacific Coast from Pacific Palisades in the north almost to Palos Verdes in the south. The beach communities are about as diverse as can be imagined. Pacific Palisades, on its cliffs overlooking the ocean and the huge Getty Museum, is residential and more pleasant than grand. Santa Monica and Venice are full of young people living in cheap housing and fearful that they will be expelled for higher-paying tenants or condominium buyers.

They have generated, in Santa Monica's case, an indigenous leftish political movement whose demands seem to be rent control and a slowdown in development, and they regained control of Santa Monica City Hall in 1988. In Venice's case, they back a movement which demands that the last dilapidated canals not have their banks reinforced. Next is Los Angeles International Airport (known by its three letter code, LAX), followed by the beach suburbs of El Segundo (named after Socal's second refinery), Manhattan Beach (more yuppified lately), Hermosa Beach (cramped like Venice, but not as bizarre) and Redondo Beach (with different beachfront and inland sections). The tightly packed frame houses here were originally the homes of elderly retirees; by the 1970s they were inhabited more often by groups of young singles.

Just as the coastal counties of California have become more Democratic and the interior counties more Republican over the years, so it is in the Los Angeles Basin: the Beach towns, once known for their crabbily conservative Republican retirees, are now known for their stylishly radical Democratic baby-boomers. The most active such group is Campaign California, associated with onetime SDS leader and now Assemblyman Tom Hayden; and it is interesting that its major demands seem to amount to the rather conservative project of maintaining Santa Monica in the exact condition it was in around 1978. But neither Campaign California nor the politics of Hayden and his estranged wife Jane Fonda are universal here; the 27th would be a marginal Republican district—as it was before 1982—without the inland territory: odd-shaped fingers of land some four miles inland into a heavily black part of West Los Angeles, half of the prosperous black-majority suburb of Inglewood, the mostly Mexican-American suburbs of Lennox behind the airport and Lawndale behind the South Bay beach towns, and a slice of the mostly-black several-blocks-wide corridor of Los Angeles which connects the port of San Pedro with the rest of the city. These areas, heavily Democratic, have made this a safe district for Representative Mel Levine.

Since his days as valedictorian at Berkeley, Levine has been tabbed as a rising politician through Princeton's Woodrow Wilson School, Harvard Law, seven years of law practice and three terms in the California Assembly. Rich and articulate, pleasant but hard-driving, he has been a political ally of Howard Berman and Henry Waxman since the 1970s. When Phillip Burton's redistricting changed the 27th District from Republican to Democratic, sending fiery conservative Robert Dornan into the 1982 Senate race and ultimately to the 38th district in Orange County, Levine ran for the House and won easily. He was surprised in 1984 to be held to 55% by evangelical Republican (and former Los Angeles Ram) Rob Scribner, who asked supporters to "link arms with us as we literally 'take territory' for our Lord Jesus Christ"; but as Scribner got more exposure, Levine beat him by nearly 2 to 1 in 1986.

Levine is an active legislator who gets involved in issues that go beyond his committee jurisdiction or which he takes beyond them. For example, on the Interior Committee he strongly opposed offshore oil drilling in California; in addition, he was a backer of 1988's Proposition O, which rescinded the Los Angeles law allowing Occidental Petroleum to drill near the ocean. On Foreign Affairs, he argues that it is in our interest to aid Israel, and he has gone beyond that to oppose—and in the process of opposing, modify—arms sales to Kuwait; he is against aiding the Nicaraguan contras, and wrote legislation saying the President could not send troops into combat in Central America without the approval of Congress. He is not on Armed Services, but was active in the Military Reform Caucus, which may not have sat entirely well with the big defense contractors—Hughes, Northrop, Rockwell, TRW—operating in or near the 27th District. On economics he is somewhat less liberal than on other issues, and he has started a group called Rebuild America, which wants generally to improve American competitiveness and specifically to get this country in the vanguard in developing high definition television.

Levine has raised vast sums of money even when, as in 1988, he did not have serious opposition. He took a look at running for the Senate in 1986, but decided against it; he could conceivably do so in 1992 when, if Pete Wilson is elected governor, a seat will be open. His is one of the districts whose political complexion could be sharply altered by just mild changes in redistricting, but at present it appears his friends will be drawing the lines.

The People: Est. Pop. 1986: 564,200, up 7.3% 1980–86; Pop. 1980: 525,929, dn. 4.4% 1970–80. Households (1980): 54% family, 27% with children, 40% married couples; 63.4% housing units rented; median monthly rent: $310; median house value: $121,600. Voting age pop. (1980): 415,975; 12% Spanish origin, 9% Black, 5% Asian origin, 1% American Indian.

1988 Presidential Vote:
Dukakis (D).	126,695	(54%)
Bush (R)	102,897	(44%)

Rep. Mel Levine (D)

Elected 1982; b. June 7, 1943, Los Angeles; home, Los Angeles; U. of CA at Berkeley, A.B. 1964, Princeton U., M.P.A. 1966, Harvard U., J.D. 1969; Jewish; married (Jan).

Career: Practicing atty., 1969–71, 1973–77; Legis. Asst. to U.S. Sen. John V. Tunney, 1971–73; CA Assembly, 1977–82.

Offices: 132 CHOB 20515, 202-225-6451. Also 5250 W. Century Blvd., Ste. 447, Los Angeles 90045, 213-410-9415.

Committees: *Foreign Affairs* (15th of 28 D) Subcommittees: Europe and the Middle East; International Economic Policy and Trade. *Interior and Insular Affairs* (19th of 26 D). Subcommittees: Water, Power and Offshore Energy Resources; National Parks and Public Lands; General Oversight and Investigations. *Select Committee on Narcotics Abuse and Control* (11th of 18 D).

Group Ratings

	ADA	ACLU	COPE	CFA	LCV	ACU	NTLC	NSI	COC	CEI
1988	95	95	89	91	88	4	11	0	36	14
1987	96	—	89	79	—	9	—	—	20	7

National Journal Ratings

	1988 LIB — 1988 CONS		1987 LIB — 1987 CONS	
Economic	57% —	41%	68% —	27%
Social	86% —	0%	78% —	0%
Foreign	79% —	16%	81% —	0%

Key Votes

1) Homeless $	AGN	5) Ban Drug Test	AGN	9) SDI Research	AGN
2) Gephardt Amdt	AGN	6) Drug Death Pen	AGN	10) Ban Chem Weaps	FOR
3) Deficit Reduc	FOR	7) Handgun Sales	AGN	11) Aid to Contras	AGN
4) Kill Plnt Clsng Notice	AGN	8) Ban D.C. Abort $	AGN	12) Nuclear Testing	FOR

Election Results

1988 general	Mel Levin (D).	148,814	(68%)	($398,597)
	Dennis Galbraith (R)	65,307	(30%)	($15,239)
1988 primary	Mel Levin (D).	66,452	(88%)	
	Ralph Cole (D)	8,679	(12%)	
1986 general	Mel Levine (D)	110,403	(64%)	($498,833)
	Robert B. Scribner (R)	59,410	(34%)	($393,860)

TWENTY-EIGHTH DISTRICT

Crenshaw is one of Los Angeles's Art Deco neighborhoods, built in the 1920s and 1930s in vacant flat land near brown hills southwest of downtown Los Angeles. In the years of exceedingly rapid growth after World War II, whole subdivisions—the square mile of Westchester north of Los Angeles International Airport—went up within months. The new homeowners were all white in those days, when it occurred to almost no one that blacks might be interested in buying here. But beginning in the 1950s, Los Angeles area blacks began moving west from the core ghetto area south of downtown, across the nondescript neighborhoods on bent-grid streets south of Wilshire Boulevard and west of the Coliseum where the 1984 Olympic ceremonies were held, out toward Crenshaw and the MGM studios in Culver City and southwest toward the then lightly populated suburb of Inglewood and the unpopulated Fox Hills and Ladera Heights. Today some of the area is all black, but much of it remains racially mixed. A slower, more relaxed pace of change seems to have prevented the wildly fluctuating housing prices and feverish politics often seen in racially changing neighborhoods.

This part of Los Angeles, from downtown to LAX and the Coliseum to Culver City, makes up the 28th Congressional District of California. It has one of the largest numbers of affluent blacks of any district in the United States; it is probably exceeded only by the 5th District of Maryland. Politically, however, they and the 28th District have not trended Republican. Affluent blacks are, if anything, more liberal than poor blacks on economic and certainly on cultural issues, and any affection they have for free market economics is tempered by the knowledge that many of them have profited on the way up by some form of government intervention—a student loan, a public sector job, an affirmative action program. The whites who have remained here seem the type most immune to racial backlash. The result is a constituency which is happy to elect a hard-working, politically savvy, quietly competent black Democrat, Julian Dixon.

Dixon has demonstrated his competence in many ways. In his first term in 1979, he won a seat on the Appropriations Committee. In his second he became chairman of the District of Columbia Appropriations Subcommittee. In his third term he chaired both the Congressional Black Caucus and the Democratic National Convention Rules Committee before which Jesse Jackson made his challenge to the legitimacy of the party rules. In his fourth term Dixon became chairman of the House Ethics Committee. In his fifth term his committee took on the assignment of investigating the Speaker of the House. In his sixth term he took on major responsibilities for setting the entire Pentagon budget. Each assignment he has handled carefully, taking time to learn the facts, and then moving quickly to get what he wants. This is a politician who quietly becomes sure of his ground and then pounces like a tiger.

On District of Columbia matters, for example, he is sympathetic but not sycophantic to the city government and Mayor Marion Barry. While he was on the Appropriations subcommittee on Foreign Operations, he moved early to pressure South Africa to abandon apartheid and to help black African states. As Black Caucus chairman, he declined to push vehemently for a separate Caucus budget resolution, though he did advance one in 1984. As for the Democratic convention, his committee produced a unanimous report which was accepted without demur on the floor.

On Ethics, Dixon proceeded from the beginning, as he did in the case of Speaker Jim Wright, cautiously but not pliantly. He started by issuing new interpretations of House asset reporting requirements, about which many Members complained bitterly, and he made it clear he expected his views to be followed. In some cases the committee found violations but did not recommend punishments, notably in the case of Banking Chairman Fernand St Germain (who was defeated in 1988). In other cases, it has not gotten around to making a decision (Bill Boner of Tennessee was still being investigated when he was elected mayor of Nashville). Dixon's Ethics

Committee does not work as rapidly or punish as severely as some critics would like. But when it does take a stand it does not have to back down.

In the Wright investigation, the committee hired an outside counsel who reportedly did a painstaking job but left the members with difficult judgments to make. Its initial decisions were not unanimous but, importantly on the sole committee with equal numbers of members from both parties, most were bipartisan. Dixon in early 1989 was left in the uncomfortable position of having found probable cause that the Speaker had violated House rules. But any position he took would have been uncomfortable, and Dixon seems to have done what other sensible politicians do in these matters, which is to decide the issue as best he can on the substantive merits and let the political chips fall where they may.

While the Wright investigation was going on, Dixon was switching subcommittees on Appropriations. He retained the D.C. chair, from which he was unsuccessfully defending the D.C. government from amendments overturning its abortion funding and gay rights laws, and he dropped Foreign Operations, and took Defense and Military Construction instead. These two subcommittees together handle the whole Pentagon budget, and Dixon is one of three (Bill Hefner of North Carolina and Norm Dicks of Washington are the other two) who serves on both. Many big defense contractors have operations in or near the 28th District, but as a longtime liberal on foreign policy issues he is likely to be a force for holding down Pentagon spending.

Dixon has not had serious competition at home since he won the seat in the 1978 primary. He was helped then by Henry Waxman and Howard Berman and is considered their ally on many matters.

The People: Est. Pop. 1986: 574,600, up 9.2% 1980–86; Pop. 1980: 525,993, up 6.2% 1970–80. Households: (1980): 60% family, 33% with children, 39% married couples; 67.0% housing units rented; median monthly rent: $198; median house value: $82,600. Voting age pop. (1980): 395,349; 37% Black, 24% Spanish origin, 8% Asian origin.

1988 Presidential Vote:	Dukakis (D)	113,133	(73%)
	Bush (R)	40,680	(26%)

Rep. Julian C. Dixon (D)

Elected 1978; b. Aug. 8, 1934, Washington, D.C.; home, Culver City; CA St. U. at Los Angeles, B.S. 1962, Southwestern U., LL.B. 1967; Episcopalian; married (Betty).

Career: Army, 1957–60; Practicing atty., 1960–73; CA Assembly, 1972–78.

Offices: 2400 RHOB 20515, 202-225-7084. Also 5100 W. Goldleaf Cir., Ste. 208, LA 90056, 213-678-5424.

Committees: *Appropriations* (19th of 35 D). Subcommittees: Defense; District of Columbia (Chairman); Military Construction. *Standards of Official Conduct* (Chairman of 6 D).

Group Ratings

	ADA	ACLU	COPE	CFA	LCV	ACU	NTLC	NSI	COC	CEI
1988	85	100	97	55	81	0	4	0	25	10
1987	96	—	97	71	—	0	—	—	7	5

National Journal Ratings

	1988 LIB	—	1988 CONS	1987 LIB	—	1987 CONS
Economic	84%	—	16%	73%	—	0%
Social	86%	—	0%	78%	—	0%
Foreign	84%	—	0%	81%	—	0%

Key Votes

1) Homeless $	AGN	5) Ban Drug Test	AGN	9) SDI Research	AGN
2) Gephardt Amdt	FOR	6) Drug Death Pen	AGN	10) Ban Chem Weaps	FOR
3) Deficit Reduc	FOR	7) Handgun Sales	AGN	11) Aid to Contras	AGN
4) Kill Plnt Clsng Notice	AGN	8) Ban D.C. Abort $	AGN	12) Nuclear Testing	FOR

Election Results

1988 general	Julian C. Dixon (D)	109,801	(76%)	($114,523)
	George Z. Adams (R).................	28,645	(20%)	
1988 primary	Julian C. Dixon, unopposed			
1986 general	Julian C. Dixon (D)	92,635	(76%)	($103,442)
	George Z. Adams (R).................	25,858	(21%)	($39,341)

TWENTY-NINTH DISTRICT

On East 107th Street in Watts, eight miles straight south of downtown Los Angeles, Símon Rodia had been building his towers for two decades when World War II broke out—erecting a framework of salvaged steel rods, dismantled pipe structures, bed frames and cement, and covering them with glass bottle fragments, ceramic tiles, china plates and thousands of seashells. From 1921 to 1954 he built these Watts Towers, up to 107 feet high, "one of the great works of folk art in the world," writes Richard Saul Wurman in *LA/Access.* Then Rodia abruptly left Los Angeles and, like someone who finishes a crossword puzzle and throws it away, never saw his creation again. He died in 1965, the same year Watts burst into national headlines as the site of one of the first and worst urban riots in the nation.

Blacks first came to Los Angeles in large numbers during World War II, part of the rush of two million war workers, and settled in the old black neighborhood south of downtown. In small frame and stucco bungalows, spread out on the grid streets, black neighborhoods grew, southward and west, but for years never crossed the Southern Pacific tracks and Alameda Street barrier that separated them from white working-class suburbs like South Gate. The Watts riot startled eastern journalists who assumed that all ghettos were full of five-story tenements, like Harlem, and it surprised Los Angeles civic leaders, who had never thought much about the lack of good schools and hospitals, parks and strong community institutions in Watts. In the years since, conditions in Watts have not changed much. But thousands of blacks have moved up from Watts to other places—some all-black, some integrated—and to successful careers. There has been little black migration into Los Angeles since the riot, in contrast to the huge numbers of Latin and Asian immigrants, and in the 1980s, parts of the South Central and Watts neighborhoods have become mostly Mexican-American. With that movement, and with the movement of many blacks to suburbs, blacks are probably a smaller part of the Los Angeles electorate than they used to be. This has had little impact on city elections: Los Angeles's black mayor, Tom Bradley, has won five times with mostly white votes.

Watts is the center of California's 29th Congressional District, which sprawls east, west and north from Watts: east through working-class Huntington Park and South Gate to take in part of white-collar Downey, west toward middle income Inglewood and north toward the Los Angeles Coliseum and the Los Angeles Convention Center. It is still predominantly a black district, but the black population has been falling and since 1970 more than 100,000 Hispanics have moved within its boundaries. As a result, the Democratic percentages here have declined a bit. But this is still California's most Democratic congressional district.

The congressman from the 29th is Augustus Hawkins, chairman of the House Education and Labor Committee, senior member of the Congressional Black Caucus and the senior black legislator in the United States. For 28 years, from 1935 to 1962, he served in the California Assembly, most of the time as its only black member; in 1959 he was nearly elected speaker, and was given, as a consolation prize, a congressional district in the 1962 redistricting. He has been an active member of Education and Labor for many years, and even though he was 76 when he succeeded Carl Perkins as chairman in 1984, he remains in full command of his powers and firm in his convictions—although the climate of opinion has grown more unfavorable to them since he came to Washington.

His convictions are that government programs can help, and have helped, the poor and the middle class; that aid to education has strengthened the nation and helped to make more equal the opportunities open to each child; that federal job programs have made the difference between a productive life and an idle one for hundreds of thousands of Americans; that the government has a responsibility to give jobs to those who cannot find employment in the private sector. His sympathies, it should be added, are by no means confined to blacks, but extend to all whom he considers in economic need. He dismisses arguments that the minimum wage wipes out some low-paying jobs, that higher welfare benefits operate as work disincentives, that the public school systems the federal government has been funding since 1965 have produced less in achievement even as they have gotten more in federal money.

Inevitably, Hawkins has had his disappointments. His name is on the Humphrey-Hawkins Act of 1978, but he was not happy with the contents; he wants a federal job guarantee. He resisted for months and came close to scuttling the 1988 welfare reform bill for months, because he thought benefits should be higher. He wants to raise the minimum wage above $4.65 and opposes a subminimum for young or new workers. As the 1990s begin, there is some reason to think that the climate is becoming more favorable to his ideas. A minimum wage hike was endorsed by George Bush, and there is widespread feeling that something must be done about early childhood education. Hawkins has specific legislation for that, and for many other causes that might turn out to be popular in a kinder, gentler nation. One index is working in his favor. In the Great Society days, a seat on Education and Labor was much sought after; by the middle 1980s some Democratic seats went begging. Now, Hawkins has no trouble filling the committee with mostly like-minded Democrats.

At home, Hawkins is always reelected without difficulty. One possible successor, should he retire, is Assemblywoman Maxine Waters, an articulate and often angry backer of Jesse Jackson. But there will almost surely be a primary battle if Hawkins doesn't run.

The People: Est. Pop. 1986: 582,900, up 10.8% 1980–86; Pop. 1980: 525,938, up 4.9% 1970–80. Households: (1980): 72% family, 47% with children, 43% married couples; 60.0% housing units rented; median monthly rent: $161; median house value: $52,700. Voting age pop. (1980): 339,585; 51% Black, 32% Spanish origin, 1% Asian origin.

1988 Presidential Vote: Dukakis (D)...................... 92,086   (80%)
Bush (R) 22,052   (19%)

Rep. Augustus F. (Gus) Hawkins (D)

Elected 1962; b. Aug. 31, 1907, Shreveport, LA; home, Los Angeles; U. of CA at Los Angeles, A.B. 1931; U. of Southern CA.; United Methodist; married (Elsie).

Career: Real estate business; CA Assembly, 1934–62.

Offices: 2371 RHOB 20515, 202-225-2201. Also 2710 Zoe Ave., Huntington Park 90255, 213-587-0421; and 4509 S. Broadway, Los Angeles 90037, 213-233-0733.

Committees: *Education and Labor* (Chairman of 22 D). Subcommittee: Elementary, Secondary, and Vocational Education (Chairman). *Joint Economic Committee.* Subcommittees: Economic Goals and Intergovernmental Policy; Investment, Jobs and Prices; Education and Health.

Group Ratings

	ADA	ACLU	COPE	CFA	LCV	ACU	NTLC	NSI	COC	CEI
1988	85	100	96	91	75	0	4	10	15	3
1987	92	—	96	71	—	0	—	—	15	4

National Journal Ratings

	1988 LIB — 1988 CONS		1987 LIB — 1987 CONS	
Economic	92%	0%	73%	0%
Social	86%	0%	78%	0%
Foreign	84%	0%	71%	27%

Key Votes

1) Homeless $	AGN	5) Ban Drug Test	AGN	9) SDI Research	AGN
2) Gephardt Amdt	FOR	6) Drug Death Pen	AGN	10) Ban Chem Weaps	FOR
3) Deficit Reduc	FOR	7) Handgun Sales	AGN	11) Aid to Contras	AGN
4) Kill Plnt Clsng Notice	AGN	8) Ban D.C. Abort $	AGN	12) Nuclear Testing	FOR

Election Results

1988 general	Augustus F. Hawkins (D)	88,169	(83%)	($65,833)
	Reuben D. Franco (R)	14,543	(14%)	($4,629)
1988 primary	Augustus F. Hawkins (D)	60,656	(90%)	
	Mervin Evans (D)	6,504	(10%)	
1986 general	Augustus F. Hawkins (D)	78,132	(85%)	($34,061)
	John Van de Brooke (R)	13,432	(15%)	

THIRTIETH DISTRICT

On Atlantic Boulevard, running from South Pasadena down toward the harbor at Long Beach, you can see the future—if not of the United States, then certainly of the Los Angeles Basin. It is, writes the *Washington Post*'s Jay Mathews, "a jarring mosaic of restaurants, car lots, beauty shops, motels, banks, and markets." In territory where the *WPA Guide* 50 years ago found only "gas stations, real estate offices, and roadstands (offering for sale anything from eggs and puppies to firewood and chile con carne)," Mathews now finds suburbs like Monterey Park which are 40% Asian, because a promoter from Hong Kong steered Taiwanese there, and onetime white working-class suburbs like Maywood, Bell, Cudahy and South Gate, where blacks moved in the 1960s and are now moving out and being replaced by Hispanics.

Atlantic Boulevard is one of the thoroughfares that stitches together—or keeps from becoming totally unraveled—the 30th Congressional District of California. It was designed by redistricters to be a Mexican-American district, though most adults are not Hispanic, and Hispanic voters are not just concentrated in a couple of enclosed ghettos, but in fact are dispersed through a wide variety of neighborhoods. As one gets on higher ground, toward the San Gabriel Mountains, income and education levels get higher. In Alhambra, for example, the high school "has become an academic giant," reports Mathews. "Its name is on the lips of college admissions officers and at the top of lists of the leading science and mathematics programs in American education." Sometime in the 21st century, novels will be written describing the by then vanished atmosphere of these suburbs, their immigrant communities and schools, that will almost surely tell more about the human condition than the 1980s minimalist novels, (the aptly named, *Less Than Zero*), about the horrors of growing up rich in Beverly Hills. In the meantime, we can glean hints of what life is like here—its potential and its tawdriness—from its electoral politics.

Long before the Asians and Hispanics came here, these were Democratic areas; but the new migrants, whom some thought would be overwhelmingly Democratic, seem, if anything, to have tilted the district a bit toward the Republicans. Ronald Reagan won a robust majority in the 30th District, carrying Monterey Park and only barely losing working-class Mexican Montebello. George Bush did not carry the area, but ran surprisingly well against the son of an immigrant. Mexicans and Koreans, Salvadorans and Chinese: this generation of immigrants seems more upwardly mobile and more Republican than the white working-class people who lived in the same places 20 and 30 years ago. Working their way upward in small businesses, they are not attracted by a Democratic party that puts its faith in big government; the terrible personal histories of some of these people make them aware of just how decent and secure life in America really is, and they are turned off by a party so many of whose supporters and candidates—not so far away, in Santa Monica and Beverly Hills—seem skeptical or ironic about the virtues of the country they say they want to serve in public office.

The congressman from the 30th District is a Democrat who has had the advantage of being in the right place with the right patrons at the right time. When Marty Martinez, owner of an upholstery company, was elected to the Monterey Park council in 1974, he seemed unlikely to end up in Congress. But in 1980 Howard Berman, running for Assembly speaker, tabbed Martinez to run against an Anglo incumbent, raised money for him, superintended his direct mail campaigning and saw him elected. For the 1982 election, California's master redistricter Phillip Burton wanted to forestall Republicans who were seeking an alliance with Hispanics at the Democrats' expense and, when no one else thought it possible, he created two Hispanic districts, the 30th and 34th. Martinez, financed and scripted by Berman and his ally Henry Waxman, became the Democratic nominee and managed to avoid losing to John Rousselot, a longtime Republican incumbent and onetime John Birch Society organizer, who passed up an easy chance to beat a fellow Republican incumbent, moved into the 30th, and worked hard enough to hold Martinez to a 54%–46% victory.

Since then, Martinez has had opposition from the past and the future. In 1984 Gladys Danielson, wife of former Congressman George Danielson, ran against him in the primary, but Martinez won 75%–25%. He had more trouble in the general, beating Montebello lawyer Richard Gomez by only 52%–43%. Martinez had desultory opposition in 1986. In the 1988 primary, he faced former Monterey Park Mayor Lily Chen, who accused him of putting his "girlfriend" on the payroll and of stating falsely to this *Almanac* and others that he was divorced. But Martinez won again, perhaps as a result of ethnic solidarity, 74%–26%.

Martinez may argue that he is an active legislator and since the 1984 election, has actually chaired an Education and Labor subcommittee. But the fact is that he is close to a zero in terms of activity or influence. This is not out of line with the norm of representatives of immigrant groups in American politics, many of whom turn out to be timeservers. The high school kids who are excelling in math, the parents who are raising families while working double shifts, the immigrants who are saving to bring other relatives over—these are the people building a future in their private lives and in the private sector, while Martinez serves another term in Congress, where the best that can be said of him is that he is an ally of exceedingly talented and creative legislators like Waxman and Berman.

The People: Est. Pop. 1986: 595,000, up 13.1% 1980–86; Pop. 1980: 526,018, up 10.4% 1970–80. Households: (1980): 74% family, 44% with children, 56% married couples; 53.4% housing units rented; median monthly rent: $234; median house value: $73,700. Voting age pop. (1980): 360,738; 48% Spanish origin, 9% Asian origin, 1% Black, 1% American Indian.

1988 Presidential Vote:

Dukakis (D)	66,112	(53%)
Bush (R)	57,754	(46%)

Rep. Matthew G. (Marty) Martinez (D)

Elected 1982; b. Feb. 14, 1929, Walsenburg, CO; home, Monterey Park; Los Angeles Trade Tech. Col., 1950; Roman Catholic; married (Elvira).

Career: USMC, 1947–50; Monterey Park Planning Cmtee., 1971–74; Monterey Park City Cncl., 1974–80; Mayor of Monterey Park, 1976, 1980; CA Assembly, 1980–82.

Offices: 240 CHOB 20515, 202-225-5464. Also 1712 W. Beverly Blvd., Montebello 90640, 213-722-7731; 400 N. Montebello Blvd., Montebello 90640, 213-722-7731.

Committees: *Education and Labor* (9 of 22 D). Subcommittees: Elementary, Secondary, and Vocational Education; Select Education; Employment Opportunities (Chairman). *Government Operations* (20th of 24 D). Subcommittees: Commerce, Consumer and Monetary Affairs; Employment and Housing. *Select Committee on Children, Youth, and Families* (14th of 18 D).

Group Ratings

	ADA	ACLU	COPE	CFA	LCV	ACU	NTLC	NSI	COC	CEI
1988	90	83	99	91	56	0	7	20	23	9
1987	80	—	99	79	—	0	—	—	8	7

National Journal Ratings

	1988 LIB — 1988 CONS		1987 LIB — 1987 CONS	
Economic	92% —	0%	73% —	0%
Social	76% —	24%	78% —	0%
Foreign	79% —	16%	60% —	39%

Key Votes

1) Homeless $	AGN	5) Ban Drug Test	—	9) SDI Research	FOR
2) Gephardt Amdt	FOR	6) Drug Death Pen	—	10) Ban Chem Weaps	AGN
3) Deficit Reduc	FOR	7) Handgun Sales	AGN	11) Aid to Contras	AGN
4) Kill Plnt Clsng Notice	AGN	8) Ban D.C. Abort $	AGN	12) Nuclear Testing	FOR

Election Results

1988 general	Matthew G. Martinez (D)	72,253	(60%)	($460,622)
	Ralph R. Ramirez (R)	43,833	(36%)	($382,111)
1988 primary	Matthew G. Martinez (D)	33,615	(74%)	
	Lily Chen (D)	12,088	(26%)	
1986 general	Matthew G. Martinez (D)	59,369	(63%)	($135,854)
	John W. Almquist (R)................	33,705	(36%)	($70,955)

THIRTY-FIRST DISTRICT

Harbor Gateway is a name invented in 1984 for a part of Los Angeles annexed to the city in 1906—the eight-mile long, four-block wide strip that connects the south central part of Los Angeles with the city's harbor neighborhoods of San Pedro and Wilmington. L.A.'s city fathers thought big and acted on a big scale: they converted what had been a shallow bay with a few marshy inlets into the biggest port on the West Coat, ahead of San Francisco and San Diego with their splendid natural harbors. By the middle 1980s, the harbors of Los Angeles and next-door Long Beach represented the fastest-growing major cargo center in the world, and Harbor Gateway, which for a couple of decades seemed bypassed by L.A.'s growth, was suddenly getting spruced up again.

Harbor Gateway forms the spine of California's 31st Congressional District, patches of towns built up mostly in the 1940s and 1950s and now feeling some growth again. Visually it seems monotonous: neat single-family stucco houses in natural tan or different pastels, often with an above-ground swimming pool and some slightly shabby lawn furniture; fading pink stucco commercial strips of the 1940s and huge defense plants and other factories spread out along the Harbor and San Diego Freeways. But there is more diversity than meets the eye. Harbor Gateway, with no psychic connection to the central city, takes on the character of each of the suburbs it passes through. In the north, it is mostly black, like Watts and the suburbs of Willowbrook and Compton. Just to the south it is Asian, like heavily Japanese American Gardena (also known as the California city which can license poker clubs at which some of the most cutthroat games in the country are played). Farther south, it is heavily Anglo and affluent, like the clientele of the 190th Street shopping centers in Torrance. The 31st also includes some suburbs a little farther afield: Lynwood and Paramount, southeast of Watts, which are more Mexican than black; Bellflower, directly north of Long Beach, still mostly white Anglo; Carson, heavily industrial along the San Diego Freeway.

This part of Los Angeles County has been lower-than-average income and solidly Democratic since the 1930s, when it was almost entirely white. But, like Harbor Gateway, it has seldom seemed a coherent political community. In the 1950s and 1960s, this was the part of California where you could get elected to the legislature by putting up billboards saying "Charles Wilson is a good guy"; in fact, Charles H. Wilson was an assemblyman and (thanks to Speaker Jesse Unruh) a congressman for 18 years until he was beaten after he was shown to have lied about a $600 wedding gift from Korean lobbyist Tongsun Park.

The current representative, former Lieutenant Governor Mervyn Dymally, is a more vivid political figure. He has a distinctive speaking style and accent from his native Trinidad. As lieutenant governor from 1975–79, Dymally liked to say that California would soon have a "Third World majority." True, in the sense that Asians, Latins, and blacks (the smallest group of the three) may become a majority; false, if it means that they share the anti-American reflex of some Third World (and American) politicians.

Dymally serves on the Post Office and Civil Service Subcommittee on Census and Population, and has argued unsuccessfully for the Bureau to make adjustments for undercounting. That would increase the count for places with lots of young black males (by far the most undercounted group) and illegal aliens, like the 31st District, and there are statistically defensible ways of doing it; however, it might be subject to political manipulation by Members of Congress who do not share the integrity Dymally has shown on this issue. He was more successful in getting the Bureau to tabulate subgroups of Asians and Pacific Islanders who, as you can see in the 31st District, are a diverse lot. On Post Office and Civil Service and Foreign Affairs, Dymally generally has a liberal record; he has also taken on some interesting causes, as in his Truth in Auto Rental Act, his bill for stronger enforcement of child support payments, his efforts for civil rights in Micronesia and to give minority firms a share in oil and gas leases on federal lands.

In the past the genial and often non-confrontational Dymally has been criticized for allowing staff, both in Washington and the 31st district, for running ideological agendas (mostly those of the far left) inconsistent with his own views. But Dymally is bright and by no means staff-dependent and has made some organizational changes which seem to have put him on top of the problem. He is reelected every two years by overwhelming margins.

The People: Est. Pop. 1986: 584,700, up 11.2% 1980–86; Pop. 1980: 525,939, up 0.1% 1970–80. Households (1980): 75% family, 47% with children, 54% married couples; 46.6% housing units rented; median monthly rent: $237; median house value: $68,500. Voting age pop. (1980): 354,360; 31% Black, 21% Spanish origin, 8% Asian origin, 1% American Indian.

1988 Presidential Vote:

Dukakis (D)	96,554	(64%)
Bush (R)	51,505	(34%)

Rep. Mervyn M. Dymally (D)

Elected 1980; b. May 12, 1926, Cedros, Trinidad, West Indies; home, Compton; CA St. U., B.A. 1954, M.A. 1969, U.S. Intl. U., Ph.D. 1978; Episcopalian; married (Alice).

Career: Teacher, Los Angeles Schs., 1955–61; Coord., CA Disaster Ofc., 1961–62; CA Assembly, 1962–66; CA Senate, 1966–75; Lt. Gov. of CA, 1975–79.

Offices: 1717 LHOB 20515, 202-225-5425. Also 322 W. Compton Blvd., Ste. 102, Compton 90220, 213-536-6930.

Committees: *District of Columbia* (5th of 8 D). Subcommittees: Fiscal Affairs and Health; Judiciary and Education (Chairman). *Foreign Affairs* (9th of 28 D). Subcommittees: Africa; International Operations (Chairman). *Post Office and Civil Service* (11th of 15 D). Subcommittee: Census and Population.

Group Ratings

	ADA	ACLU	COPE	CFA	LCV	ACU	NTLC	NSI	COC	CEI
1988	90	100	95	100	63	0	4	0	23	8
1987	84	—	94	71	—	0	—	—	0	6

National Journal Ratings

	1988 LIB — 1988 CONS		1987 LIB — 1987 CONS	
Economic	92% —	0%	73% —	0%
Social	86% —	0%	78% —	0%
Foreign	84% —	0%	81% —	0%

Key Votes

1) Homeless $	AGN	5) Ban Drug Test	—	9) SDI Research	AGN
2) Gephardt Amdt	FOR	6) Drug Death Pen	AGN	10) Ban Chem Weaps	FOR
3) Deficit Reduc	FOR	7) Handgun Sales	AGN	11) Aid to Contras	AGN
4) Kill Plnt Clsng Notice	—	8) Ban D.C. Abort $	AGN	12) Nuclear Testing	FOR

Election Results

1988 general	Mervyn M. Dymally (D)...............	100,919	(72%)	($481,799)
	Arnold C. May (R)....................	36,017	(26%)	($10,169)
1988 primary	Mervyn M. Dymally (D)...............	58,806	(85%)	
	Kilpatrick O'Brien (D)	10,037	(15%)	
1986 general	Mervyn M. Dymally (D)...............	77,126	(70%)	($385,063)
	Jack McMurray (R)..................	30,322	(28%)	($41,875)

THIRTY-SECOND DISTRICT

In 1900, when the census-takers showed 102,000 people in Los Angeles, the city fathers decided that they would make their city one of the great metropolises of the world and that they would make its existing swampy and sand-barred harbor into one of the great ports of the world. They succeeded on both counts. By 1909, Los Angeles had annexed the harbor towns of San Pedro and Wilmington; by 1940 the two cities had persuaded the government to dredge channels and build a breakwater and turning basins. Long Beach developed other businesses as well: oil in the 1920s and aircraft in the 1940s. By the 1980s, Los Angeles and Long Beach were the nation's largest ports, bigger than New York, having long since outhustled San Francisco with its complacent merchant class and militant unions perched on the Pacific Rim. The harbor has even acquired a couple of symbols: the Queen Mary, now the biggest tourist attraction of Long Beach, and the Spruce Goose, the huge cargo seaplane that was piloted just once across this harbor by its builder, Howard Hughes. By the time of its centennial celebration in 1988, Long Beach was buzzing with commercial activity. Downtown Long Beach, once full of rundown 1920s buildings and pawn shops, was sprouting $2 billion of construction. Japanese and other Asian businessmen seem comfortable headquartering their U.S. operations, such as Toyota's, in the harbor area or just west in Torrance, near the airport.

The 32d Congressional District of California includes much of this harbor area. Technically, the port is outside the district, a thin land-bridge connecting two disparate Republican areas into a single 42d District and preventing them from contaminating districts which are, like the 32d, Democratic. It includes San Pedro, historically ethnic with Yugoslav and Italian communities, which is now rapidly trending upscale; Long Beach, also upgrading (though its more Republican areas are in the 42d); and, to the northeast, Lakewood (mostly white Anglo) and Hawaiian Gardens (mostly Mexican-American).

The 32d District is ancestrally Democratic, but has been trending Republican in some races as it gets more upscale. In House races, however, it is faithful to Glenn Anderson, a Democrat who has been in politics since the years of Franklin D. Roosevelt. In 1940 he was elected mayor of Hawthorne (home town of the Beach Boys); in 1958 he was elected lieutenant governor of California; in 1966 he lost that office in a Republican year in which he was charged with failing to send in the National Guard promptly when the Watts riot broke out while Governor Pat Brown was out of the state; in 1968 he rebounded and, in a strong Republican year, was elected to the House. Anderson was one of California's more liberal Democrats in the 1950s and 1960s, and today has a generally liberal record, though a 1986 study by *Washington Monthly* showed that the ratings he receives from disparate interest groups add up to the largest total in the House. In other words Anderson—a businessman who has always been close to labor, a liberal who is a practical politician, a pleasant man who is nonetheless hard-working—is good at keeping everybody happy.

Anderson inherited the chairmanship of the House Public Works Committee when James Howard died in March 1988. Anderson was an ally of Howard's and had long been one of the leaders of this Committee which, with its control over highways, water projects and other government building programs, has been one of the chief pork barrel dispensers on Capitol Hill. He helped to increase spending on highways in the 1980s, brought about in large part because of the gas tax increase of 1982; he was the key sponsor of the federal child seat belt law and was a strong supporter of the 21 drinking age and the 55-mile-an-hour speed limit. He has long been one of the leading political enforcers on Public Works, doling out projects to other Members, but making sure they support the committee's bills in return; of course, his position does not hurt the harbor. Some have charged that he has little interest in or knowledge of projects beyond Long Beach and Los Angeles Harbor, and that he let staff handle issues like drug testing. But he nonetheless had the satisfaction of seeing Ronald Reagan, who helped end his career in state government, beaten when the House overrode his vetoes of water and highway bills in early 1987. Back home in the 32d district he usually wins with margins like 1988's 67%–30%.

The People: Est. Pop. 1986: 569,900, up 8.4% 1980–86; Pop. 1980: 525,922, up 0.6% 1970–80. Households (1980): 66% family, 36% with children, 51% married couples; 53.1% housing units rented; median monthly rent: $229; median house value: $78,900. Voting age pop. (1980): 383,383; 19% Spanish origin, 7% Black, 5% Asian origin, 1% American Indian.

1988 Presidential Vote:

Bush (R)	....	89,411	(50%)
Dukakis (D)	....	87,998	(49%)

Rep. Glenn M. Anderson (D)

Elected 1968; b. Feb. 21, 1913, Hawthorne; home, San Pedro; U. of CA at Los Angeles, B.A. 1936; Episcopalian; married (Lee).

Career: Mayor of Hawthorne, 1940–43; CA Assembly, 1943–51; Army, WWII; Lt. Gov. of CA, 1959–67.

Offices: 2329 RHOB 20515, 202-225-6676. Also 300 Long Beach Blvd., Long Beach 90801, 213-437-7665.

Committees: *Public Works and Transportation* (Chairman of 31 D). Subcommittee: Investigations and Oversight (Chairman).

Group Ratings

	ADA	ACLU	COPE	CFA	LCV	ACU	NTLC	NSI	COC	CEI
1988	70	55	83	55	63	10	15	22	0	10
1987	72	—	83	79	—	14	—	—	29	18

National Journal Ratings

	1988 LIB — 1988 CONS		1987 LIB — 1987 CONS	
Economic	77% —	23%	57% —	40%
Social	64% —	36%	51% —	49%
Foreign	68% —	28%	61% —	39%

Key Votes

1) Homeless $	AGN	5) Ban Drug Test	FOR	9) SDI Research	AGN
2) Gephardt Amdt	AGN	6) Drug Death Pen	FOR	10) Ban Chem Weaps	FOR
3) Deficit Reduc	FOR	7) Handgun Sales	AGN	11) Aid to Contras	AGN
4) Kill Plnt Clsng Notice	AGN	8) Ban D.C. Abort $	AGN	12) Nuclear Testing	FOR

Election Results

1988 general	Glenn M. Anderson (D)	114,666	(67%)	($457,410)
	Sanford W. Kahn (R)	50,710	(30%)	($20,608)
1988 primary	Glenn M. Anderson (D), unopposed			
1986 general	Glenn M. Anderson (D)	90,739	(69%)	($417,066)
	Joyce M. Robertson (R)	39,003	(29%)	($11,742)

THIRTY-THIRD DISTRICT

Half a century ago, the thinly settled suburbs of eastern Los Angeles County gathered together in the 12th District of California were represented by New Deal liberal Democrat Jerry Voorhis. California was FDR country, and in these fast-growing suburbs the New Deal seemed like the wave of the future—until after the war Voorhis was beaten by a young lawyer named Richard Nixon. Today's 33d Congressional District of California is the lineal descendant of that 12th District (the change in numbers suggests how California has grown) and contains much of this same territory. It is the eastern end of Los Angeles County, far enough east that the percentage of Mexican-Americans is not much higher than in Nixon's time. One part of the district, with about one-third of its population, is centered around Nixon's home town of Whittier, a onetime Quaker settlement and now a pleasant suburban town with its own civic institutions and colleges, above-average housing prices, and a Mexican-American population of 23%. The other heavily populated part of the district, separated from the Whittier area by the low Puente Hills, is centered on another old college town, Pomona, laid out in the flat lands directly east of Los Angeles, on the last leg of the Santa Fe Railroad on its long trek from Chicago. Just north are the Claremont colleges, which are, among other things, a center for conservative scholarship, and the above-average income suburbs of LaVerne, San Dimas, Covina and Glendora, above the valley floor and not far below the glaring San Gabriel Mountains. Whittier, Pomona and the smaller towns—all were creations of pious Protestants, transplanting their civilization, street grids and their Republican politics from the hardy flatlands of the Midwest to the sunny mountainous land of California.

These colleges have also produced congressmen: Voorhis graduated from Claremont, Nixon from Whittier, and today's 33d District incumbent David Dreier, before he came to Washington, spent most of his adult life on the Claremont campus. Dreier faithfully represents the free market conservatism prevalent at Claremont—but not as effectively as he would probably like. He decries wasteful government spending, but his solutions tend to be gimmicky (a two-thirds vote for raising the debt ceiling, support for the Grace Commission). He is pleased about deregulation of trucking, airlines and natural gas, even as advocates of reregulation are gathering steam. He favors a 15% flat rate income tax, but still found reasons to vote against the 1986 tax reform. He devotes much of his time to the Banking Committee, but he has been out of favor with more practical-minded senior Republicans there.

Dreier can claim credit for some accomplishments, like raising the ceiling on FHA mortgage insurance from $90,000 to $101,250 (Los Angeles County is an expensive housing market). He has the highest-rated environmental record of any California Republican (Eastern Los Angeles County is a high smog zone). He has traveled in Afghanistan and backed support of the Afghan freedom fighters. He has voted for a crackdown on savings and loans even though he comes from a region whose politicians have long been supportive of their greatest excesses. But he has failed to come up with an attractively packaged legislative program that carries his ideas forward, as Jack Kemp and Phil Gramm have.

One thing Dreier has done well is to build up a big campaign treasury. In his first two elections, he beat incumbents—Democrat Jim Lloyd in 1980, Republican Wayne Grisham after he was redistricted with him in 1982—and decided that he never wanted to be pressed for funds again. So while he has been raising plenty of money, he hasn't been spending much—something that takes more self-discipline than one would think—and by March 1988 had more than $1.1 million cash on hand—more than anyone else in Congress. This would give him a head start, though not a huge one, if he should run for the Senate in 1992 when Alan Cranston's and perhaps Pete Wilson's seats will be up. In the meantime, he has a safe seat and a chance to continue serving in a House he must find frustrating.

The People: Est. Pop. 1986: 604,100, up 15.0% 1980–86; Pop. 1980: 525,348, up 15.5% 1970–80. Households (1980): 78% family, 44% with children, 65% married couples; 29.1% housing units rented; median monthly rent: $262; median house value: $86,700. Voting age pop. (1980): 370,470; 16% Spanish origin, 5% Black, 4% Asian origin, 1% American Indian.

1988 Presidential Vote:

Bush (R)	142,335	(62%)
Dukakis (D)	83,319	(36%)

Rep. David Dreier (R)

Elected 1980; b. July 5, 1952, Kansas City, MO; home, La Verne; Claremont McKenna Col., B.A. 1975, M.A. 1976; Christian Scientist; single.

Career: Dir. of Corp. Relations, Claremont McKenna Col., 1975–78; Dir. of Mktg., Industrial Hydrocarbons, 1979–80; Vice Pres., Dreier Develop. Co.

Offices: 411 CHOB 20515, 202-225-2305. Also 112 N. 2d Ave., Covina 91723, 818-339-9078.

Committees: *Banking, Finance and Urban Affairs* (8th of 20 R). Subcommittees: Financial Institutions Supervision, Regulation and Insurance; Housing and Community Development. *Small Business* (6th of 17 R). Subcommittee: Antitrust, Impact of Deregulation and Privatization (Ranking Member).

Group Ratings

	ADA	ACLU	COPE	CFA	LCV	ACU	NTLC	NSI	COC	CEI
1988	5	0	1	27	44	100	94	100	92	94
1987	4	—	1	29	—	96	—	—	100	89

National Journal Ratings

	1988 LIB — 1988 CONS		1987 LIB — 1987 CONS	
Economic	0%	— 93%	0%	— 89%
Social	11%	— 89%	0%	— 90%
Foreign	0%	— 84%	0%	— 80%

Key Votes

1) Homeless $	FOR	5) Ban Drug Test	FOR	9) SDI Research	FOR
2) Gephardt Amdt	AGN	6) Drug Death Pen	FOR	10) Ban Chem Weaps	AGN
3) Deficit Reduc	AGN	7) Handgun Sales	FOR	11) Aid to Contras	FOR
4) Kill Plnt Clsng Notice	FOR	8) Ban D.C. Abort $	FOR	12) Nuclear Testing	AGN

Election Results

1988 general	David Dreier (R).....................	151,704	(69%)	($186,183)
	Nelson Gentry (D)	57,586	(26%)	
1988 primary	David Dreier (R), unopposed			
1986 general	David Dreier (R).....................	118,541	(72%)	($148,242)
	Monty Hempel (D)....................	44,312	(27%)	

THIRTY-FOURTH DISTRICT

In the eastern part of the Los Angeles Basin, where the waters of 10,000-foot Mount San Antonio are drained by the San Gabriel River (rushing torrents when it rains and a dry bed when it doesn't) is one of the industrial zones that has made greater Los Angeles by far the number one manufacturing center in the United States. Along the railroad tracks that parallel and cross the river valley, beneath the roaring east-west freeways, on grid streets just down from stucco garden apartment blocks, are the small smokeless factories (L.A. has the world's strictest air pollution controls) where recent migrants, legal and illegal, and skilled tradesmen work morning and evening shifts. Here, following roughly the diagonal course of the San Gabriel River, is the 34th Congressional District of California. It includes the middle-income suburb of West Covina and the working-class suburbs of Baldwin Park, La Puente and Industry in its northern section, and the basically blue-collar suburbs of Pico Rivera, Santa Fe Springs, South Whittier and Norwalk, all strung out along the Santa Ana Freeway, on the southern section. Connecting them is a narrow corridor through the industrial town of South El Monte.

The 34th district gives a glimpse of the future of California, for it has the largest number of children of any congressional district in the state. The white middle-class children of the 1950s, educated in the schools that burgeoned in every new suburb and finally on the culturally liberal campuses of the University of California, are the adults of California today: technologically capable, relatively high-income, culturally liberal if not liberated. They take affluence and economic growth for granted; they concentrate much of their psychic energy on making life pleasant for themselves. The children of the 34th District, growing up on some of the same terrain, have a different background. Some 48% of them are of Spanish origin. They are part of large families: their parents have the same optimism which produced the large Anglo families of the baby-boom years. Some of them start off speaking little else but Spanish, but most know English, and they are entirely capable of absorbing instruction in it, provided that the political authorities (and Mexican-American lobbying groups) don't keep them confined in classes where the instruction is in a language which will not prepare them for most good jobs.

The 34th District was newly created by Representative Phillip Burton from the results of the 1980 Census. It was Burton's *piece de resistance*. The Republicans had hoped to get crucial Mexican-American votes in the California Assembly and pass a districting plan that had more Mexican-American districts than the Democrats could come up with—and of course more Republican districts as well. But Burton, by creating this district which is 48% Spanish origin, in addition to the 54% Spanish origin 30th and the 64% Spanish origin 25th, did the Republicans one better. From that point on, there was nothing to stop the Democratic legislature and governor from approving Burton's plans.

Nor was there much that anyone could do to stop Democrat Esteban Torres from being elected to Congress. Torres had tried once before, in 1974, against George Danielson in the old 30th District, and fallen short; Mexican-Americans do not invariably vote for Mexican-Americans, presumably because they do not feel deprived of fair representation when they have an Anglo congressman. But Torres does have a positive appeal. He rose from an auto assembly line, through the ranks of the United Auto Workers, to head an antipoverty program in East Los Angeles; in the Carter Administration he was a White House aide and ambassador to UNESCO. He had financial support from the local machine of Henry Waxman and Howard Berman. In 1982, he won a solid primary victory against former Representative Jim Lloyd, whose base is in West Covina, and won the general election by a 57%–43% margin.

Torres has positions on economics you would expect from a UAW veteran; on some cultural issues, such as abortion, his views are more conservative. He represents, after all, the number one family district in Los Angeles, a place where people have committed themselves to family patterns and where their high hopes for the future depend on the progress of their children in schools and in jobs. They are interested in having a secure government safety net, but they seem to believe that their children will get somewhere—as their parents or grandparents emerged from rural Mexico—largely through their own efforts. He has worked particularly hard on hazardous waste laws, has helped preserve the "rule of two" minority set-aside programs and has set new cash reporting requirements for banks to help stop drug traffickers. His current project seems to be improving groundwater quality in the San Gabriel Valley.

Torres's percentage has crept slowly upward to 63% in 1988; this is a district the Republicans are not likely to seriously contest. Redistricting could easily change its political complexion, but because Torres will be protected by Democrats if they are in control, and Republicans don't want to be seen as defeating an Hispanic incumbent, Torres should do fine.

The People: Est. Pop. 1986: 589,700, up 12.0% 1980–86; Pop. 1980: 526,665, up 2.1% 1970–80. Households (1980): 83% family, 53% with children, 68% married couples; 29.3% housing units rented; median monthly rent: $276; median house value: $68,700. Voting age pop. (1980): 348,515; 42% Spanish origin, 4% Asian origin, 2% Black, 1% American Indian.

1988 Presidential Vote:

Bush (R)	73,409	(49%)
Dukakis (D)	76,154	(50%)

Rep. Esteban E. Torres (D)

Elected 1982; b. Jan. 30, 1930, Miami, AZ; home, N. Covina; E. Los Angeles Commun. Col., A.A. 1959, CA State U. at Los Angeles, B.A. 1963, U. of MD, 1965, American U., 1966; No religious affil.; married (Arcy).

Career: Army; Assembly-line worker, Chrysler Corp., 1953–63; Chief Steward, Local 230 UAW, 1961–63; UAW Intl. Rep., Region 6, 1963–64, Inter-Amer. Rep., 1965–68; Dir., E. Los Angeles Commun. Union, 1968–74; Asst. Dir., Intl. Affairs Dept., 1974–77; U.S. Permanent Rep., UNESCO, 1977–79, Special Asst. to Pres. Jimmy Carter, 1979–81; Pres., Intl. Enterprise and Develop. Corp., 1981–82.

Offices: 1740 LHOB 20515, 202-225-5256. Also 8819 Whittier Blvd., Ste. 101, Pico Rivera 90660, 213-695-0702, 818-961-3978.

Committees: *Banking, Finance and Urban Affairs* (18th of 31 D). Subcommittees: Financial Institutions Supervision, Regulation and Insurance; Housing and Community Development. *Small Business* (12th of 27 D). Subcommittees: Procurement, Tourism and Rural Development; Environment and Labor (Chairman).

Group Ratings

	ADA	ACLU	COPE	CFA	LCV	ACU	NTLC	NSI	COC	CEI
1988	90	87	98	91	75	0	7	0	23	9
1987	96	—	97	86	—	0	—	—	7	5

National Journal Ratings

	1988 LIB — 1988 CONS		1987 LIB — 1987 CONS	
Economic	92% —	0%	73% —	0%
Social	72% —	27%	78% —	0%
Foreign	84% —	0%	81% —	0%

Key Votes

1) Homeless $	AGN	5) Ban Drug Test	AGN	9) SDI Research	—
2) Gephardt Amdt	FOR	6) Drug Death Pen	—	10) Ban Chem Weaps	FOR
3) Deficit Reduc	FOR	7) Handgun Sales	AGN	11) Aid to Contras	AGN
4) Kill Plnt Clsng Notice	AGN	8) Ban D.C. Abort $	AGN	12) Nuclear Testing	FOR

Election Results

1988 general	Esteban E. Torres (D)	92,087	(63%)	($227,098)
	Charles M. House (R)	50,954	(35%)	($149,886)
1988 primary	Esteban E. Torres (D)	45,271	(100%)	
1986 general	Esteban E. Torres (D)	66,404	(60%)	($111,685)
	Charles M. House (R)	43,659	(40%)	($81,759)

THIRTY-FIFTH DISTRICT

Half a century ago the desert seemed like the last part of California where people would settle in any numbers, a vast expanse of sagebrush-strewn waste which cars would struggle to get through without overheating before plunging through the narrow mountain road of the Cajon Pass or cruise between two looming mountains through the San Gorgonio Pass into the Los Angeles Basin. Here they would find warm rather than hot weather, towns like Redlands and San Bernardino set out on careful grids, and acres of orange groves and wine vineyards, with U.S. 66, lined with gas stations and auto courts, heading arrow-straight west the last 60 miles to downtown Los Angeles. Today, the eastern end of the Los Angeles Basin and the desert beyond the mountains are the fastest-growing parts of California. Housing prices are relatively low in the towns around San Bernardino and Riverside, partly because the smog accumulates here up against the mountains, and the desert has become a favorite retirement place as most of the oceanfront real estate in California was taken long ago and what is left has been preserved.

The 35th Congressional District of California is one of the three fastest-growing districts in the state—all of them in this same geographic zone. The 35th includes most of San Bernardino County, geographically the largest county in the United States, with ghost towns and weapons testing systems in the desert, tiny towns dominated by huge gas station signs built to catch the eyes of motorists on their five hours' journey across the desert to Las Vegas, mountains and lakes, the Joshua Tree National Monument and the Twenty-nine Palms Marine Corps Base. It has some of the nation's hottest temperatures and some of its lowest rainfall. But only about one-third of its residents live in the desert; the rest are clustered in the eastern end of the Los Angeles Basin. The boundaries there are irregular; the 35th bypasses the heavily Democratic towns and takes in the more affluent towns on the plains and in the foothills: Upland, Montclair and Chino in western San Bernardino County, Redlands, Highland and Loma Linda (a Seventh Day Adventist town) east of the city of San Bernardino.

The congressman from the 35th is one of the leaders of the Republican Party in the House,

Jerry Lewis. A former insurance agent, he served 10 years in the California Assembly and won the House seat without much problem when the incumbent retired in 1978; he is now the chairman of the House Republican Conference, the number three position in the leadership. Lewis rose by something other than the traditional ladder, more as a promoter of ideas than as a parliamentary technician. After the 1984 campaign, he became chairman of the House Republican Research Committee, an informal group that produces policy papers from time to time. Under Lewis it continued to present papers of a high intellectual quality attacking the premises underlying the Democrats' policies. For him and for Republican House Members generally, this is part of an historical progress from debating in the language of home-town Rotaries and Chambers of Commerce to speaking the lingo of OMB bureaucrats and policy mavens, and in the process making the Republicans increasingly the party of ideas. Lewis has had other successes with his colleagues. He beat Bill Thomas for the California seat on the Republican Committee on Committees and has come up with some coups for his fellow Californians. He managed the 1986 drug bill for the Republicans, and after that election, was elected chairman of the House Republican Policy Committee. After the 1988 election, he defeated Lynn Martin of Illinois by four votes for the chairmanship of the House Republican Conference.

In his intra-party councils, Lewis is something of a bridge between the traditional Republicans around Minority Leader Robert Michel and the more aggressive young conservatives typified by Minority Whip Newt Gingrich. But that very mutual acceptability seemed to work against him when the whip position suddenly opened up in March 1989 after the appointment of Richard Cheney as Secretary of Defense. Lewis immediately began running for the job, but he was caught in a squeeze between Gingrich, whose demand that the ethics committee investigate Jim Wright seemed to be jeopardizing his speakership, and Edward Madigan of downstate Illinois, a talented legislative technician on Agriculture and Energy and Commerce who had strong support from oldtimers. When Madigan made it clear he was in the race to stay, opponents of Gingrich forced Lewis out.

That does not consign him to a minor role in the House. He still has his leadership position and the skills which brought him to it. He is also ranking Republican on the Legislative Appropriations Subcommittee, the body which prepares Congress's own budget; there is potential for clout here, particularly since the chairman, Vic Fazio, is also a Californian who is a skilled legislator and easy to get along with. Lewis considered running for lieutenant governor in 1982, a race whose only purpose could have been to position him to run for governor some day; but he decided not to run, and he seems committed to a House career that has been successful far beyond what most would have thought when he ran for the seat a dozen years ago.

The People: Est. Pop. 1986: 671,800, up 27.7% 1980–86; Pop. 1980: 525,956, up 46.3% 1970–80. Households (1980): 77% family, 43% with children, 66% married couples; 29.6% housing units rented; median monthly rent: $235; median house value: $68,000. Voting age pop. (1980): 371,311; 12% Spanish origin, 3% Black, 2% Asian origin, 1% American Indian.

1988 Presidential Vote: Bush (R) 172,872   (65%)
Dukakis (D). 88,126   (33%)

Rep. Jerry Lewis (R)

Elected 1978; b. Oct. 21, 1934, Seattle, WA; home, Redlands; U. of CA at Los Angeles, B.A. 1956; Presbyterian; married (Arlene).

Career: Insur. exec., 1959–78; Field rep. to U.S. Rep. Jerry Pettis, 1968; CA Assembly, 1968–78.

Offices: 2312 RHOB 20515, 202-225-5861. Also 1826 Orange Tree Lane, Ste. 104, Redlands 92374, 714-862-6030.

Committees: *Appropriations* (13th of 22 R). Subcommittees: Foreign Operations, Export Financing and Related Programs; VA, HUD and Independent Agencies; Legislative (Ranking Member).

Group Ratings

	ADA	ACLU	COPE	CFA	LCV	ACU	NTLC	NSI	COC	CEI
1988	5	29	15	30	19	90	60	100	67	54
1987	8	—	14	14	—	83	—	—	93	63

National Journal Ratings

	1988 LIB — 1988 CONS		1987 LIB — 1987 CONS	
Economic	28%	— 71%	19%	— 78%
Social	28%	— 72%	22%	— 77%
Foreign	0%	— 84%	20%	— 76%

Key Votes

1) Homeless $	FOR	5) Ban Drug Test	FOR	9) SDI Research	FOR
2) Gephardt Amdt	AGN	6) Drug Death Pen	FOR	10) Ban Chem Weaps	AGN
3) Deficit Reduc	AGN	7) Handgun Sales	FOR	11) Aid to Contras	FOR
4) Kill Plnt Clsng Notice	FOR	8) Ban D.C. Abort $	FOR	12) Nuclear Testing	—

Election Results

1988 general	Jerry Lewis (R)....................	181,203	(70%)	($337,814)
	Paul Sweeney (D)...................	71,186	(28%)	
1988 primary	Jerry Lewis, unopposed			
1986 general	Jerry Lewis (R)....................	127,235	(77%)	($91,355)
	R. (Sarge) Hall (D).................	38,322	(23%)	

THIRTY-SIXTH DISTRICT

San Bernardino and Riverside, at the far east end of the Los Angeles Basin, where the smog piles up against the mountains, are two cities with their own historical beginnings, more than 50 miles from downtown Los Angeles and the sea. These were originally farm centers. In the orange groves outside Riverside, the navel orange was developed, and the University of California branch located there started off as an agricultural research school. Around San Bernardino there are orange groves, wine vineyards and fruit orchards. Parts of each city, and of several suburbs in the immediate vicinity and to the east, make up the 36th Congressional District of California. The district includes industrial suburbs—Colton, Rialto and Fontana with its once thriving Kaiser Steel plant—and the city of Ontario, west toward Los Angeles, which has its own airport where you can catch a jet to Chicago or Dallas-Fort Worth.

Surrounded by Republican territory, the 36th District is nonetheless Democratic. There is a substantial Mexican-American population in each of these towns, about one-fourth of the district's population; there are a fair number of blacks in each town as well. Union membership is higher in some of these precincts than in most of southern California, and working-class consciousness is perhaps fed by the poor air quality: if you could afford to move to a higher and more expensive area, you probably would.

The 36th District was designed for, and is represented by, a congressman with a long career that has benefited, stage by stage, from redistricting. George Brown was a councilman from Monterey Park, far west of here, when he was first elected to the California Assembly in 1958; he had the good fortune to be placed on the Reapportionment Committee, and when California gained eight House seats in 1962, he was elected to one of them. He ran for the Senate in 1970 and almost beat John Tunney in the primary; if he had, this longtime peacenik—a scientist with a Quaker upbringing who cares deeply about arms control issues—might have beaten George Murphy and made his way to the Senate. Brown found a new district in 1972, here in the eastern part of the valley, and redistricting has altered and shaped it for him.

Brown's committee assignments would seem to be useful ones for the district—Agriculture; Science, Space, and Technology. He supports the Landsat satellites and solar energy (he was named solar congressman of the year in 1988 by the Solar Energy Industries Association), wants to prevent global warming and integrate federal nutrition monitoring. He quit the Intelligence Committee in 1987 because he felt its secrecy requirements were preventing him from mentioning information publicly available elsewhere. He is not quite a power in the House, even yet, but he is a persistent and competent advocate of his own particular and special views, and one determined not to be silenced.

Brown has always had rather marginal districts and his very liberal politics have attracted spirited Republican competition. He was threatened by serious competition when Ronald Reagan's political career began in the middle 1960s and when Reagan's career was ending in the late 1980s. Religious fundamentalist John Paul Stark has run against him four times, holding him to 53%, 54% and 57% in 1980, 1982 and 1984, respectively; in 1986 Brown won 57% against a Colton businessman. In 1988 Stark ran again, won a multi-candidate Republican primary, but lost to Brown 54%–43%. Typically for a Republican challenger, he had far less money than the Democratic incumbent, and his shrill use of the crime issue, such as emphasizing the death penalty for drug dealers, does not seem to have been particularly effective. Brown has one more election to win in the current district lines; for the 1990s he hopes to lose the more Republican precincts in this fast-growing territory and to get a seat he can carry with his liberal, dovish politics for a fourth decade of House elections.

The People: Est. Pop. 1986: 662,700, up 26.0% 1980–86; Pop. 1980: 525,987, up 15.1% 1970–80. Households (1980): 74% family, 44% with children, 59% married couples; 36.5% housing units rented; median monthly rent: $214; median house value: $58,900. Voting age pop. (1980): 362,108; 20% Spanish origin, 7% Black, 1% Asian origin, 1% American Indian.

1988 Presidential Vote:

Bush (R)	100,291	(51%)
Dukakis (D)	92,521	(47%)

Rep. George E. Brown, Jr. (D)

Elected 1972; b. Mar. 6, 1920, Holtville; home, Riverside; U. of CA at Los Angeles, B.A. 1946; United Methodist; widowed.

Career: Army, WWII; Monterey Park City Cncl., 1954–58, Mayor, 1955–56; Personnel, Engineering and Mgt. Consult. for Los Angeles, 1957–61; CA Assembly, 1958–62; U.S. House of Reps., 1962–70.

Offices: 2188 RHOB 20515, 202-225-6161. Also 657 La Cadena Dr., Colton 92324, 714-825-2472; and 3600 Lime St., Ste. 116, Riverside 92501 714-686-8863.

Committees: *Agriculture* (3d of 26 D). Subcommittee: Department Operations, Research and Foreign Agriculture (Chairman). *Science, Space and Technology* (2d of 29 D). Subcommittees: Natural Resources, Agriculture Research and Environment; Science, Research and Technology; International Scientific Cooperation.

Group Ratings

	ADA	ACLU	COPE	CFA	LCV	ACU	NTLC	NSI	COC	CEI
1988	80	100	90	73	75	5	8	20	25	11
1987	76	—	90	57	—	10	—	—	7	10

National Journal Ratings

	1988 LIB — 1988 CONS	1987 LIB — 1987 CONS
Economic	71% — 29%	66% — 33%
Social	86% — 0%	69% — 31%
Foreign	84% — 0%	71% — 27%

Key Votes

1) Homeless $	AGN	5) Ban Drug Test	AGN	9) SDI Research	AGN
2) Gephardt Amdt	AGN	6) Drug Death Pen	AGN	10) Ban Chem Weaps	FOR
3) Deficit Reduc	FOR	7) Handgun Sales	—	11) Aid to Contras	AGN
4) Kill Plnt Clsng Notice	AGN	8) Ban D.C. Abort $	AGN	12) Nuclear Testing	FOR

Election Results

1988 general	George E. Brown, Jr. (D)	103,493	(54%)	($532,897)
	John Paul Stark (R)	81,413	(43%)	($218,696)
1988 primary	George E. Brown, Jr. (D).	48,148	(82%)	
	James D. Sparks (D).	10,450	(18%)	
1986 general	George E. Brown, Jr. (D)	78,118	(57%)	($534,733)
	Bob Henley (R).	58,660	(43%)	($210,003)

THIRTY-SEVENTH DISTRICT

California's desert has become one of the most glamorous and fastest-growing parts of the nation. This was presaged 50 years ago—when the desert was empty land you had to go through in steel-hot Pullmans or about-to-boil-over cars on U.S. 66, on your way to the green valleys and pleasant seacoasts of Los Angeles—by the success of Palm Springs as the *WPA Guide* described as an "ultrasmart winter resort for movie stars and for people who like and can afford to live where and as movie stars live." Demographically, Palm Springs was a dot on the map. But in the 1970s, as the seaside filled up, the clean, dry, roomy desert became more attractive, and by the

1980s what was once just a winter resort had become the year-round home for some half a million people.

Many of them are in the 37th Congressional District, which covers most of Riverside County. West of the desert, it includes a series of geologically fascinating valleys—some rather affluent, some noticeably threadbare—which have large numbers of retirees. To the east, through the San Gorgonio Pass, is the desert proper, where the days are almost always crystal clear, the sky usually blue and cloudless. The desert can be fertile farmland, as it is in the Coachella Valley; almost all of America's dates are produced near Indio, east of Palm Springs. But constant irrigation is necessary for most crops; without daily doses of water, almost any plant will wilt and die in the heat. These towns are quite a contrast with Palm Springs and Palm Desert, which are outposts of affluence (Palm Springs is more showbiz—Sonny Bono is the current mayor, Palm Desert more WASPy). Two Presidents have retired within the confines of the 37th District, Eisenhower in Palm Desert for the winters, Ford in nearby Rancho Mirage—which is also the home of Frank Sinatra and Spiro Agnew. Ronald Reagan has spent every New Year's Eve at the Palm Springs home of Walter Annenberg. The 37th also includes the more affluent and Republican parts of the city of Riverside, plus the towns of Norco and Corona immediately to the east. In the 1980s, this district had the greatest population growth of any in California.

Politically, this is a Republican constituency, although it elects some Democrats to the state legislature. The real contest here, when the district was newly created and without an incumbent in 1982, was in the Republican primary, and the winner, with 25% in a nine-candidate field, was Al McCandless. McCandless is a son of the desert, born in Imperial County; he had a successful auto dealership; he moved upward politically as the desert grew more populous, to a seat on the Riverside County Board of Supervisors in 1970. McCandless is proud of his videotape privacy bill, sponsored after reporters unearthed the video rental records of Judge Robert Bork; he is thinking of advancing a pharmaceutical privacy bill as well. He is also proud of his record of voting against big bills that have widespread support but which, in his view, are bad policy: the plant closing bill, the 1988 trade bill, and the catastrophic health care bill (which, as he pointed out, would be paid for by the affluent social security recipients so numerous in the desert). McCandless has one of the most conservative voting records on Capitol Hill. He has also taken up unusual causes with some success: raising the age of beneficiaries of the foster grandparent plan (to help handicapped adults) and reducing allowable travel costs for federal contractors to levels allowed for federal employees. He is routinely reelected every two years.

The People: Est. Pop. 1986: 700,000, up 33.1% 1980–86; Pop. 1980: 525,938, up 55.8% 1970-80. Households (1980): 74% family, 35% with children, 64% married couples. 29.1% housing units rented; median monthly rent: $235; median house value: $69,300. Voting age pop. (1980): 383,799; 15% Spanish origin, 1% Asian origin, 3% Black, 1% American Indian.

1988 Presidential Vote: Bush (R) 172,644   (61%)
                          Dukakis (D). 108,106   (38%)

Rep. Alfred A. (Al) McCandless (R)

Elected 1982; b. July 23, 1927, Brawley; home, La Quinta; U. of CA at Los Angeles, B.A. 1953; Protestant; married (Gail).

Career: USMC, Korea; Automobile dealer, 1953–75; Riverside Cnty. Spvsr., 1970–82.

Offices: 435 CHOB 20515, 202-225-5330. Also 6529 Riverside Ave., Ste. 165, Riverside 92506, 714-682-7127; and P.O. Box 1495, Palm Desert 92261, 619-340-2900.

Committees: *Banking, Finance and Urban Affairs* (13th of 20 R). Subcommittees: Financial Institutions Supervision, Regulation and Insurance; General Oversight and Investigations; Housing and Community Development; International Development, Finance, Trade and Monetary Policy. *Government Operations* (4th of 15 R). Subcommittee: Government Information, Justice and Agriculture (Ranking Member).

Group Ratings

	ADA	ACLU	COPE	CFA	LCV	ACU	NTLC	NSI	COC	CEI
1988	10	10	2	27	19	95	87	100	92	85
1987	8	—	3	21	—	82	—	—	93	74

National Journal Ratings

	1988 LIB — 1988 CONS	1987 LIB — 1987 CONS
Economic	0% — 93%	18% — 82%
Social	11% — 89%	10% — 85%
Foreign	0% — 84%	0% — 80%

Key Votes

1) Homeless $	FOR	5) Ban Drug Test	FOR	9) SDI Research	FOR
2) Gephardt Amdt	AGN	6) Drug Death Pen	FOR	10) Ban Chem Weaps	AGN
3) Deficit Reduc	AGN	7) Handgun Sales	FOR	11) Aid to Contras	FOR
4) Kill Plnt Clsng Notice	FOR	8) Ban D.C. Abort $	—	12) Nuclear Testing	AGN

Election Results

1988 general	Alfred A. (Al) McCandless (R)	174,284	(64%)	($122,839)
	Johnny Pearson (D)	89,666	(33%)	($13,558)
1988 primary	Alfred A. (Al) McCandless (R)	58,589	(83%)	
	Bud Mathewson (R)	11,897	(17%)	
1986 general	Alfred A. (Al) McCandless (R)	122,416	(64%)	($127,793)
	David E. (Dave) Skinner (D)	69,808	(36%)	($56,185)

THIRTY-EIGHTH DISTRICT

Orange County in those long-ago days before World War II was aptly named: orange groves were planted in neat rows amid the mile-square grid streets laid askew to the barrier lines of ocean and mountains. There were only 130,000 people in this flat, almost vacant land in 1940, while Los Angeles County, an hour or two drive away, had 2.8 million. In the 50 years since, a new America has been created within the Orange County grid, in the most rapid metropolitan growth of the post-World War II era. Orange County had 216,000 people in 1950, 703,000 in 1960, 1.4 million in 1970 and 1.9 million in 1980; since then its growth has been more modest, though it has cleared the two million mark. To its critics, Orange County came to be synonymous with the white middle class and its values, among which were assumed to be racism and callousness toward the poor, a mindless nationalism and hawkishness, and a lamentable taste for middlebrow kitsch, symbolized by Disneyland in Anaheim and Robert Schuller's Crystal Cathedral with its drive-in annex in Garden Grove.

There was some basis for these characterizations as Orange County was growing. It had very few slums and lots of middle-class housing built for families; its cultural attitudes were far less liberated than those in Hollywood or the Westside, and its politics were solidly Republican—especially during the late 1960s, when Governor Ronald Reagan was confronting Watts rioters and Berkeley rebels with his assertions that there was nothing basically wrong with middle class America and its values. But as time went on Orange County turned out to be less homogeneous and more open to change than its critics supposed. Its economy was constantly being transformed by the inevitable upheavals of capitalism: there is no one industry here—not even defense—which undergirds the prosperity of Orange County, and people here must be ready to change and adapt almost as adeptly as the Taiwanese on the other side of the Pacific Rim. Another kind of change is cultural: Orange County in its restrained way has adapted to changes in family life. There has been ethnic change, as well. Orange County always had its Mexican-American community in Santa Ana, but in the 1970s and 1980s, Hispanics and Asians moved out the freeways in large numbers. And as Vietnamese refugees began arriving in large numbers after the fall of Saigon, many headed for the county which had always staunchly supported fighting for their freedom from Communism. The refugees have proved themselves hard workers, with every family member pitching in so that the family can afford to buy one of the stucco houses you see as you zoom by on the freeway or, for the moment, to rent an apartment in one of the many low-rise complexes that you see on the straight streets leading from Disneyland or Knott's Berry Farm to the beaches. The largest concentration of Vietnamese in America today can be found along the Garden Grove and San Diego Freeways in Orange County.

As it happens, this corridor is the center of California's 38th Congressional District, which includes most of Orange County between the Santa Ana and San Diego Freeways, bounded by the Los Angeles County border on the west and the Newport Freeway on the east. Incomes here are somewhat lower than in the rest of the county, and carefully sculpted districts in this area returned Democrats to Congress in the 1960s and 1970s. But the arrival of the Vietnamese changed the political balance here, away from the Democrats who still believe the American presence was harmful to Vietnam. These Vietnamese are not angry that America went there but that it left. This change in political balance was registered in 1984, when this supposedly Democratic district gave Ronald Reagan 69% of its votes and ousted its 10-year Democratic Congressman, Jerry Patterson, for Republican Robert Dornan.

Dornan's aggressiveness, feistiness and tendency to go too far in criticism of his opponents all make sense if you remember that he was a fighter pilot. He volunteered for pilot training while in college and went on active duty in the Air Force in March 1953 during the Korean War; some Democrats attacked him in 1986 for not having served in combat, but he would have if there had not been an armistice three months after he joined. As it was, he was a peacetime fighter pilot until 1958, about as hazardous duty as there is in a peacetime military. Then, with show business connections (his uncle Jack Haley was the Tin Woodsman in *The Wizard of Oz*), he became a TV talk show host in Los Angeles, and flew as a civilian on what he described as "combat missions" in wartime Vietnam. In 1976, when moderate Republican Alphonzo Bell ran for the Senate and opened up his beachfront Los Angeles district, Dornan ran for the House, and against a high-spending Democrat he won narrowly. He was reelected in 1978 and 1980 against an opponent he called "a sick, pompous little ass"; that 1980 race was the most expensive in the country. In all these races, Dornan was working against the local political tide. The Westside was becoming more liberal on cultural issues, opposed to any American military involvement abroad and in favor of abortion and cultural liberation; Dornan, a fervent backer of an active American foreign policy and fervid opponent of abortion, campaigned with bitter invective in a climate rich with hatred and paranoia on all sides.

In Orange County, he has mellowed. He left his old district after the 1982 redistricting made it impossible for him to win (it is now represented by Democrat Mel Levine) and ran for the Senate, raising $1 million from his mailing list but winning only 8% of the primary vote. In 1984, he journeyed down the California coast, got a residence in the 38th District, and took on Democrat Jerry Patterson, a hard-working constituency service politician and advocate for southern California savings and loans on the Banking Committee. Again the tone of the campaign was not elevated: Dornan called Patterson "a sneaky little dirtbag." But with heavy support from the Vietnamese, Dornan won 53%–45%. In 1986, he was a prime target of Democratic campaign chairman Tony Coelho. But Coelho's candidate, former judge and Vietnam veteran David Carter, lost the primary, and the winner, Assemblyman Richard Robinson, though well-known, well-financed and popular, got only 42% of the vote to Dornan's 55%. In 1988, he had weaker opposition and won 60%–36%. The major incident in the campaign came when Dornan's wife, at a public meeting disrupted by gays, asserted (as it turned out inaccurately) that her brother had AIDS. Dornan was under attack for opposing what he considers the promotion of homosexuality as a lifestyle, but has also visited AIDS hospices frequently and supported increased spending on AIDS research and care.

In the House, he continued to act with the fervor that made him known in the 1970s as "B-1 Bob." In 1985, he called Democrat Tom Downey a "draft-dodging wimp" and grabbed his collar and tie. But he also became the first House Member to back George Bush's candidacy, in December 1985, and he vouched for him vociferously to his fellow conservatives. His endorsement was significant, since he was close to Jack Kemp and because he was one of those who were presumed to doubt the sincerity of Bush's conservatism.

Dornan in the past has not been a particularly effective legislator; although the B-1 did survive years of attacks and the federal government no longer funds abortions, those victories were won mostly by others. Still gung-ho about things military, and with as much flying experience as any Member of Congress, he was happy to be assigned to the Armed Services Committee in 1989, though he begins with low seniority 12 years after he entered Congress (only two committee Republicans were in Congress when he was first elected). He got a seat on Intelligence in April 1989, when Richard Cheney became Secretary of Defense. He has bills on some measures widely supported by Republicans (repeal of the War Powers Act, indexing of capital gains) and has had some interesting successes (getting the Fair Housing Act repealed to prevent discrimination against "persons before birth"). He is also chairman of the Republican Study Group. But if he seems hokey or overdramatic to some House colleagues, he is held in high regard in the White House; George Bush is a politician who prizes loyalty and who appreciates Dornan's early support.

The People: Est. Pop. 1986: 582,400, up 10.7% 1980–86; Pop. 1980: 525,919, up 14.2% 1970–80. Households (1980): 77% family, 46% with children, 62% married couples. 42.1% housing units rented; median monthly rent: $299; median house value: $85,100. Voting age pop. (1980): 364,684; 25% Spanish origin, 6% Asian origin, 2% Black, 1% American Indian.

1988 Presidential Vote: Bush (R) 93,697   (61%)
Dukakis (D). 58,068   (38%)

Rep. Robert K. (Bob) Dornan (R)

Elected 1984; b. April 3, 1933, New York, N.Y.; home, Garden Grove; Loyola U.; Roman Catholic; married (Sallie).

Career: Air Force, 1953–58; Broadcast Journalist, 1965-69; Talk show host, 1969–73; CA House of Reps., 1976–82; Cand. for U.S. Senate, 1982.

Offices: 301 CHOB 20515, 202-225-2965. Also 12387 Lewis St., Garden Grove 92640, 714-971-9292.

Committees: *Armed Services* (18th of 21 R). Subcommittees: Research and Development; Readiness. *Permanent Select Committee on Intelligence* (7th of 7 R). Subcommittee: Legislation; *Select Committee on Narcotics Abuse and Control* (6th of 12 R).

Group Ratings

	ADA	ACLU	COPE	CFA	LCV	ACU	NTLC	NSI	COC	CEI
1988	0	5	8	18	13	100	83	100	91	77
1987	0	—	8	14	—	100	—	—	100	84

National Journal Ratings

	1988 LIB — 1988 CONS		1987 LIB — 1987 CONS	
Economic	0%	93%	11%	83%
Social	13%	84%	0%	90%
Foreign	0%	84%	0%	80%

Key Votes

1) Homeless $	FOR	5) Ban Drug Test	FOR	9) SDI Research	FOR
2) Gephardt Amdt	AGN	6) Drug Death Pen	FOR	10) Ban Chem Weaps	AGN
3) Deficit Reduc	AGN	7) Handgun Sales	FOR	11) Aid to Contras	FOR
4) Kill Plnt Clsng Notice	FOR	8) Ban D.C. Abort $	FOR	12) Nuclear Testing	AGN

Election Results

1988 general	Robert K. (Bob) Dornan (R)	87,690	(60%)	($1,755,892)
	Jerry Yudelson (D)	52,399	(36%)	($186,892)
	Two others	7,280	(5%)	
1988 primary	Robert K. (Bob) Dornan, unopposed			
1986 general	Robert K. (Bob) Dornan (R)	66,032	(55%)	($1,174,637)
	Richard Robinson (D)	50,625	(42%)	($581,864)

THIRTY-NINTH DISTRICT

As World War II began, Orange County, California had all the political notoriety of a few thousand acres of citrus trees; today, "Orange County" has become a synonym across the nation, and perhaps the world, for American-style political conservatism. In 1940, there were only 130,000 people living in this prime agricultural real estate; but this southeastern end of the Los Angeles Basin, a mass of flat land surrounded by mountains and sea, was directly in the path of settlement of the most explosively growing metropolitan area in the United States. Population increased ninefold in 30 years: by 1970 there were 1.4 million people there; by the middle 1980s over 2 million. Politically, most of that migration was Republican. For years, Orange County has turned in the highest Republican percentages of any major California county. Ronald Reagan liked to begin and end his campaigns in Orange County and no wonder: it was the county that gave him his largest vote margins—353,000 in 1980 and 428,000 in 1984—in the nation. George Bush's 1988 margin of 317,000 votes was almost as big—and much larger than Michael Dukakis's margin in Los Angeles County. Yet Orange County is not as uniformly affluent or as monolithically conservative and Republican as is supposed. Democrats have been competitive here in many elections, although they are losing ground in the lower-middle income precincts now filling up with anti-Communist Asian-Americans.

The northern section of the heavily populated part of Orange County forms the 39th Congressional District of California, one of three districts wholly within Orange County. It includes Anaheim, home of Disneyland, the amusement park whose opening here in 1955 introduced millions to Orange County, and Anaheim Stadium, where the California Angels and Los Angeles Rams now play (though these landmarks sit just a block outside the district's boundaries). In tiny Yorba Linda, where the subdivisions end and the scrubby hills begin, is the birthplace of Richard Nixon, a man whose career moved back and forth in and out of Orange County for several decades.

What kinds of communities are these? It's a mistake to think of Orange County as just a collection of suburbs, although these communities would not have the economic vitality they do were they not part of a larger metropolitan expanse. In their grid street patterns and square moral outlooks, in their comfortable but far from showy affluence and their industriousness, in their apparent ethnic homogeneity and their adherence to traditional family patterns, they resemble those midwestern towns 40 and 60 miles away from Chicago, which are classified as part of the Chicago metropolitan area by the Census Bureau but in their own residents' minds are places apart. These places also share a strong allegiance to the Republican Party and a conviction that they represent the typical American community—although, in political terms at least, they haven't for many years in post-New Deal, Democrat-majority America. Many of the people here actually come from towns like these in the Midwest and Illinois, at the other end of the Santa Fe Railroad and U.S. 66, and have brought their attitudes with them. If their view of themselves and America is statistically inaccurate, there is a sense in which almost all Americans believe it to be true: this is, for more than Orange Countians, how typical Americans live.

The current congressman, William Dannemeyer, was once, oddly enough, a Democrat; he comes from a working class suburb of Los Angeles, and he was elected as an Orange County Democrat to the California Assembly in 1962 and 1964. But he switched parties when he lost a race for the state Senate, and eventually went back to the Assembly to serve a term as a Republican; and now he seems thoroughly in line with the predilections of the 39th District. There he has been a member of the Health Subcommittee and a frequent antagonist of Chairman Henry Waxman. Dannemeyer is a member of the important Energy and Commerce Committee, where he favors reducing regulation on business, and in 1985 became a member of Judiciary, where he can champion conservative constitutional amendments.

The issue on which Dannemeyer is heard most frequently is AIDS. More than any other Member of Congress, he has been pushing measures to isolate the general population from this disease. Some of his proposals seem no more than common sense and have been widely accepted: closing the bathhouses where the disease has been spread by promiscuous homosexual contacts, testing blood in blood banks for the AIDS virus, barring high-risk persons from donating blood. At other times, he has made statements that turned out to be bizarre. Despite the lack of evidence that the disease is spread except through the blood or sexual contact, Dannemeyer wants to permit hospital personnel to take any steps they want to protect themselves from contact with AIDS patients and to allow parents to keep their children home from schools which AIDS victims attend. He insists that he is only taking a public health approach to the disease, and argues that insisting on confidentiality of test results facilitates the spread of the disease—an opinion that most experts think is wrong, but for which an argument can be made. But though his positions can be defended on neutral grounds—"if we're going to err, let's err on the side of being careful," he says—Dannemeyer insists on raising the issue of whether homosexual conduct is a sin: God's "plan for man," he says, is "Adam and Eve, not Adam and Steve." He opens himself up to charges that he is trying to stir up hatred and persecution of homosexuals; his views that AIDS victims "emit spores" that can spread the disease have received no scientific backing. The fact is that in confronting this disease the country is treading on untested ground, and the likelihood is that those who approach the issue with a morally-based agenda—like Dannemeyer and some of his most fervent opponents—are likely to make some missteps on the way. Dannemeyer insists that his colleagues and administration appointees are not doing the people's will on this issue. Yet his own AIDS ballot initiative was rejected in 1988 by California voters by a 66%–34% margin, and lost in the 39th district 60%–40%.

Dannemeyer was elected the House in 1978 when Charles Wiggins, Richard Nixon's brilliant defender in the House Judiciary Committee impeachment hearings, retired. He has as safe a district as anyone in the House, but he has a reputation even among Republicans for going too far and lost out in 1987 to two freshmen for a seat on the Budget Committee, despite his interest in the subject.

The People: Est. Pop. 1986: 584,500, up 11.2% 1980–86; Pop. 1980: 525,848, up 33.0% 1970-80. Households (1980): 75% family, 41% with children, 63% married couples. 38.1% housing units rented; median monthly rent: $318; median house value: $106,300. Voting age pop. (1980): 380,058; 11% Spanish origin, 3% Asian origin, 1% Black, 1% American Indian.

1988 Presidential Vote:

Bush (R)	167,142	(71%)
Dukakis (D)	66,495	(28%)

Rep. William E. Dannemeyer (R)

Elected 1978; b. Sept. 22., 1929. Los Angeles; home, Fullerton; Valparaiso U., B.A. 1950, U. of CA, Hastings Law Sch., J.D. 1952; Lutheran; married (Evelyn).

Career: Army, Korea; Practicing atty.; Fullerton Dpty. Dist. Atty., 1955–57' Asst. City Atty., Fullerton, 1959–62; CA Assembly, 1963–66, 1976–77.

Offices: 2351 RHOB 20515, 202-225-4111. Also 1235 N. Harbor Blvd., Ste. 100, Fullerton 92632, 714-992-0141.

Committees: *Energy and Commerce* (5th of 17 R). Subcommittees: Health and the Environment; Energy and Power; Commerce, Consumer Protection and Competitiveness. *Judiciary* (8th of 14 R). Subcommittees: Civil and Constitutional Rights; Economic and Commercial Law.

Group Ratings

	ADA	ACLU	COPE	CFA	LCV	ACU	NTLC	NSI	COC	CEI
1988	0	9	5	18	6	100	98	100	92	93
1987	8	—	5	21	—	100	—	—	100	87

National Journal Ratings

	1988 LIB — 1988 CONS			1987 LIB — 1987 CONS		
Economic	0%	—	93%	0%	—	89%
Social	9%	—	89%	19%	—	78%
Foreign	34%	—	66%	0%	—	80%

Key Votes

1) Homeless $	FOR	5) Ban Drug Test	FOR	9) SDI Research	FOR
2) Gephardt Amdt	AGN	6) Drug Death Pen	FOR	10) Ban Chem Weaps	AGN
3) Deficit Reduc	AGN	7) Handgun Sales	FOR	11) Aid to Contras	FOR
4) Kill Plnt Clsng Notice	FOR	8) Ban D.C. Abort $	FOR	12) Nuclear Testing	AGN

Election Results

1988 general	William E. Dannemeyer (R)............	169,360	(74%)	($250,737)
	Don E. Marquis (D)..................	52,162	(23%)	($2,892)
1988 primary	William E. Dannemeyer (R)............	64,862	(85%)	
	John M. Gullixson (R)	11,207	(15%)	
1986 general	William E. Dannemeyer (R)...........	131,603	(75%)	($260,009)
	David C. Vest (D).....................	42,377	(24%)	($7,473)

FORTIETH DISTRICT

Fifty years ago, the land that is now the 40th Congressional District of California, with more than half a million people, was almost entirely vacant: there were perhaps 20,000 people there. Most of it was part of the totally undeveloped Irvine Ranch, a swath of land that extended 10 miles along the Pacific Ocean south from Newport Beach and 22 miles inland, over orange groves and vegetable fields, to the mountains. Now the land is beginning to be filled up, and not just with stucco-housed subdivisions. Near Newport Beach are the 1,000 acres the Irvine developers donated for a local branch of the University of California; at the edge of the property, a once small airstrip has become John Wayne Orange County Airport; just to the east is Coast Mesa's South Costa Plaza, the highest-volume, upscale shopping center in southern California standing in what not too long ago was a lima bean field, so fancy that it has valet parking; and almost everywhere are the gleaming office towers that indicate that here in the city of Irvine, in Newport Beach, even down past where the Santa Ana and San Diego Freeways meet, is one of America's largest office centers. Development here is only spurred by the few remnants of the old days: the artsy settlement on the coast in Laguna Beach, locked in by hills, a few of the older streets in Newport Beach and the Marine Corps air base at El Toro.

This is almost uniformly an affluent area. The subdivisions are walled off from the surrounding roads and freeways, with access limited to a few roads; the old grid street patterns do not provide enough privacy and security for the affluent residents here. The underlying street patterns however, are geometrical, as if people were trying to impose a predictable order on the lush and unpredictable California landscape of mountain, coast and desert. Such attempts do not always succeed, just as the efforts of the conservative Republicans whom voters here inevitably prefer do not always succeed: Richard Nixon retired in disgrace and Ronald Reagan has not been able to completely dismantle the welfare state. But Reagan's themes of traditional values and technological progress remain highly popular in this newest of Americas.

The 40th District has had the sort of representation that unsettled frontier areas get: a member of the John Birch Society, a former county assessor who went to jail and, most recently, an Armed Services Committee member known for his constant travel. He was Robert Badham, first elected in 1976. In 1986 he was opposed in the Republican primary by Nathan Rosenberg, a fringe candidate who is the brother of *est* founder Werner Erhard, and who got 34% in the heart of Orange County nonetheless; in the general election, Badham was held to 61% of the vote—a real rebuke here. Badham prudently chose to retire in 1988.

That left the succession in this most Republican of districts to be determined in the Republican primary. Among the fourteen competitors were Rosenberg, Irvine councilman Dave Baker, and former senior White House counsel Chris Cox. Baker, a 6'8" former basketball player, had Badham's endorsement. But Cox one-upped that with support from such Washington luminaries as Oliver North, who campaigned for him in the district, and Robert Bork, plus Californians of influence in the Reagan Administration such as William French Smith and Arthur Laffer (on whose 1986 Senate primary campaign Cox had served as an adviser). Baker was hurt when someone rose at a candidate forum and questioned his marital fidelity. In the end, Cox raised over one million dollars and won with 31% of the vote, edging out Baker with 29% and Rosenberg with only 18%. The general election was as anticlimactic as expected.

Cox holds joint M.B.A. and J.D. degrees from Harvard, and was a lawyer in Orange County during its boom period before joining the White House staff in 1986. With a seat on Public Works, Cox should be well positioned to work on the many transportation problems that plague Orange County. It's difficult for any Democrat to win this district, and it will be interesting to see whether Cox, after winning a safe seat at age 36, will be a more formidable legislator than his three predecessors.

The People: Est. Pop. 1986: 603,800, up 14.8% 1980–86; Pop. 1980: 525,935, up 58.6% 1970-80. Households (1980): 65% family, 33% with children, 54% married couples; 39.6% housing units rented; median monthly rent: $366; median house value: $130,400. Voting age pop. (1980): 399,759; 7% Spanish origin, 4% Asian origin, 1% Black.

1988 Presidential Vote:

Bush (R)	191,392	(68%)
Dukakis (D)	87,331	(31%)

Rep. C. Christopher Cox (R)

Elected 1988; b. Oct. 16, 1952, St. Paul, MN; home, Newport Beach; U. of Southern CA, B.A. 1973, Harvard U., M.B.A., J.D., 1977; Roman Catholic; single.

Career: Practicing atty., 1978–86; Lecturer, Harvard Bus. Sch., 1982–83; Sr. Assoc. Cnsl., White House, 1986–88.

Offices: 510 CHOB 20515, 202-225-5611. Also 4000 MacArthur Blvd., Ste. 430, Newport Beach 92660, 714-756-2244.

Committees: *Governmental Operations* (14th of 15 R). Subcommittees: Government Activities and Transportation; Commerce, Consumer and Monetary Affairs. *Public Works and Transportation* (19th of 20 R). Economic Development; Public Buildings and Grounds; Surface Transportation; Water Resources.

Group Ratings and Key Votes: Newly Elected

Election Results

1988 general	C. Christopher Cox (R) 181,269	(67%)	($1,110,126)
	Lida Lenney (D)..................... 80,782	(30%)	($47,746)
1988 primary	C. Christopher Cox (R) 30,713	(31%)	
	Dave Baker (R)..................... 29,326	(29%)	
	Nathan Rosenberg (R)................ 17,647	(18%)	
	William Yacobozzi (R)................ 6,290	(6%)	
	Ten others 15,902	(15%)	
1986 general	Robert E. Badham (R).............., 119,829	(60%)	($418,975)
	Bruce W. Sumner (D)................ 75,664	(38%)	($169,872)

FORTY-FIRST DISTRICT

"Life moves at a modulated pace," the *WPA Guide* wrote of San Diego just before World War II, "particularly because of the large number of elderly and retired persons. The city has much of the easygoing spirit of Spanish days, and people live and dress for comfort." San Diego was then a small city of 203,000, with a large part of the Navy and a small tuna fleet anchored in its fine natural harbor. The war that broke out changed San Diego forever. It became the Navy's West Coast headquarters and naval installations proliferated. Later its climate—arguably the most pleasant in the continental United States—made it a not just a favorite retirement place for Navy officers and others, but also brought about the development of a significant industrial base, largely high-skill businesses. By 1980 San Diego had 875,000 residents, and San Diego County, with 1.9 million, was the eighth largest county in the country; it has continued to grow robustly in the 1980s.

San Diego was evenly divided politically before 1945, split between the well-to-do Republican north side and the more modest and sometimes working-class south side. In the years following the war, the heavy immigration gave both the city and county of San Diego a very Republican, conservative complexion. Yet over the years it has also been more raffish and scandal-prone than other California cities. Richard Nixon for years regarded this as his "lucky city"—until the unfolding ITT scandal caused him to cancel plans to have the 1972 Republican National Convention here. Its best-known politician is Pete Wilson, now Senator and candidate for governor, who once served as assemblyman and from 1971 to 1982, as mayor, had a record of honesty and of placing some limits on the city's growth. Not known in any depth statewide, he remains highly popular in San Diego.

California's 41st Congressional District takes in the north side of San Diego where Wilson is most popular, and it is represented by a man who started off as a Wilson protégé, Bill Lowery. The north side includes affluent beach communities (La Jolla, Pacific Beach, Mission Bay) as well as inland, comfortable sections of San Diego. Much of the city's land is still vacant, held that way to some extent by city policies but more by nature: these hillsides are too steep for condominiums, too precipitous for subdivision houses. Although this may seem odd to many, the 41st District has a very small Mexican-American population that is, despite its proximity to Mexico, lower in percentage than those of affluent Los Angeles area districts; the reason seems to be that Mexicans who want to work at San Diego wages can cross the border each day and live more cheaply in Tijuana.

Lowery has solid roots in San Diego; his lifespan coincides almost exactly with San Diego's growth from a provincial Navy town to a major American city. He served in the 1970s as a councilman and then as Pete Wilson's deputy mayor. When Bob Wilson, for 28 years the 41st District's congressman and senior member of the Armed Services Committee, retired in 1980, Lowery ran and edged out two tough candidates, radio station owner Dan MacKinnon in the primary and a Democratic state senator named Bob Wilson in the general. He has been reelected easily ever since, with his toughest challenge coming in the heavily Republican year of 1984.

There are two things San Diego seems interested in having a congressman do. The first is to take care of the military, still the biggest economic force in the city, and the second is to help protect the environment which makes it such an agreeable place to live. Lowery has worked to do both. He failed to get his predecessor's seat on Armed Services in his first term; it went to fellow San Diegoan, Duncan Hunter, instead. But after the 1984 election Lowery got a seat on Appropriations, and on the Military Construction Subcommittee, where he can talk of how there are $227 million in military building projects, and about a study of whether the government should build a second harbor entrance for San Diego. He also works to sweep the Tierrasanta area near San Diego Stadium for World War II shells, one of which killed two local children.

On the environment, Lowery has been the lead Republican in the California House delegation in its long struggle to stop offshore oil drilling. He complained bitterly when Interior Secretary Donald Hodel reneged on an agreement in 1985, and he was pleased when George Bush, during the 1988 campaign and after, moved away from backing the drilling. He also works on other environmental matters, such as getting the federal government to pay for disposal of the raw sewage that comes over the Mexican border and getting $720,000 to help San Diego County protect the least Bell's vireo; this small songbird's inclusion on the endangered species list has held up 90 construction projects in the area.

The People: Est. Pop. 1986: 609,200, up 15.8% 1980–86; Pop. 1980: 526,043, up 30.0% 1970-80. Households (1980): 60% family, 29% with children, 49% married couples. 49.8% housing units rented; median monthly rent: $273; median house value: $106,800. Voting age pop. (1980): 412,731; 6% Spanish origin, 4% Asian origin, 2% Black.

1988 Presidential Vote: Bush (R) 175,588   (58%)

Dukakis (D). 121,278   (40%)

Rep. Bill Lowery (R)

Elected 1980; b. May 2, 1947, San Diego; home, San Diego; San Diego St. U., B.A. 1969, CA Western, J.D. 1970; Roman Catholic; married (Katie).

Career: Pub. rel. 1973–77; San Diego City Cncl., 1977–80; San Diego Dpty. Mayor, 1979–80.

Offices: 2433 RHOB 20515, 202-225-3201. Also 880 Front St., Rm. 6-S-15, San Diego 92188, 619-231-0957.

Committees: *Appropriations* (18th of 22 R). Subcommittees: Interior; Military Construction (Ranking Member); Treasury, Postal Service and General Government.

Group Ratings

	ADA	ACLU	COPE	CFA	LCV	ACU	NTLC	NSI	COC	CEI
1988	15	23	8	18	19	92	67	100	100	59
1987	4	—	7	7	—	87	—	—	73	67

National Journal Ratings

	1988 LIB — 1988 CONS		1987 LIB — 1987 CONS
Economic	10% — 88%		11% — 83%
Social	22% — 77%		10% — 85%
Foreign	0% — 84%		26% — 73%

Key Votes

1) Homeless $	FOR	5) Ban Drug Test	FOR	9) SDI Research	FOR
2) Gephardt Amdt	AGN	6) Drug Death Pen	FOR	10) Ban Chem Weaps	AGN
3) Deficit Reduc	AGN	7) Handgun Sales	AGN	11) Aid to Contras	FOR
4) Kill Plnt Clsng Notice	FOR	8) Ban D.C. Abort $	FOR	12) Nuclear Testing	AGN

Election Results

1988 general	Bill Lowery (R)	187,380	(66%)	($407,025)
	Dan Kripke (D)	88,192	(31%)	($45,311)
1988 primary	Bill Lowery (R)	63,485	(89%)	
	Rick Singer (R)	8,085	(11%)	
1986 general	Bill Lowery (R)	133,566	(68%)	($401,730)
	Dan Kripke (D)	59,816	(30%)	($153,732)

FORTY-SECOND DISTRICT

From the seismically active hills of the Palos Verdes Peninsula, towering over the Pacific, on clear days you can see the port of Los Angeles and Long Beach, thronged with freighters, and the plain of the Los Angeles Basin, filled with freeways and factories, shopping strips and subdivisions, and the mountains far beyond. In the other direction, it is a clear shot to East Asia, the other side of the Pacific Rim. With the harbor booming and Japanese and other Asian firms setting up U.S. headquarters in Torrance and other nearby towns, Palos Verdes, its curving streets and vine-covered front lawns and ranch houses, is now the home of affluent businessmen with a direct stake in free trade.

Palos Verdes and Torrance provide one anchor of the 42nd Congressional District of California. The other is several miles east along the coast, in Orange County: the retirement development of Rossmoor and nearby Seal Beach; the spread-out suburb of Huntington Beach, affluent, but with many renters as well as homeowners; the by now long-settled suburbs of Cypress and Los Alamitos and part of Westminster, with their comfortable stucco houses inhabited increasingly by families who 10 or 15 years ago lived precarious lives in Vietnam. They are connected by a thin land bridge passing along the harbor of Los Angeles and Long Beach, sometimes running only a block inland, sometimes going back a couple of miles to take in Republican Bixby Hills and oil-rig-strewn Signal Hill. The motive for this odd geography is political: redistricter Phillip Burton wanted to keep this Republican territory away from 32d District Democrat Glenn Anderson.

The 42d was one of those districts with a serious contest in 1988, and one in which Oliver North played a minor role. The contest occurred because incumbent Congressman Dan Lungren decided not to run for reelection. He had been nominated for state treasurer by Governor George Deukmejian who, like Lungren, is from Long Beach, even though he was later rejected by the state Senate (largely because he opposed monetary payments in the Japanese American redress bill); he didn't want to stay in Washington and may run for statewide office in 1990. That left a contest for the seat in the Republican primary in this 72% Reagan district.

Initially, the leading contender was Orange County Supervisor Harriet Wieder, who represented nearly half the district. But she was 68 years old and it turned out she had never received the college degree she had been claiming for 25 years in public life; she ended up with 22%, less than what she had been receiving in polls. Another well-known candidate was Stephen Horn, longtime president of California State College-Long Beach. But his Republican ties were with liberals like former Senator Thomas Kuchel, who have no base in the party now; he wound up with 20%. That left the field fairly open for Dana Rohrabacher, a former editorial writer for the *Orange County Register* who had been part of the Reagan speechwriting office. Rohrabacher trumpeted the Reagan connection, argued that he was the most conservative candidate in the field, and brought in Ollie North for a fundraiser. Rohrabacher wound up with 35% of the vote for a relatively easy victory, which he would surely have won without North.

A conservative of libertarian bent, Rohrabacher serves on the Science and Technology and District of Columbia Committees.

The People: Est. Pop. 1986: 570,200, up 8.4% 1980–86; Pop. 1980: 525,909, up 15.0% 1970-80. Households (1980): 67% family, 34% with children, 56% married couples; 40.3% housing units rented; median monthly rent: $336; median house value: $131,500. Voting age pop. (1980): 400,256; 6% Spanish origin, 5% Asian origin, 1% Black, 1% American Indian.

1988 Presidential Vote:

Bush (R)	165,572	(65%)
Dukakis (D)	86,544	(34%)

Rep. Dana Rohrabacher (R)

Elected 1988; b. June 21, 1947, Corona; home, Lomita; Long Beach St. Col. B.A. 1969, U. of Southern CA, M.A. 1971; Baptist; single.

Career: Journalist, 1970–80; Sr. speechwriter and Spec. Asst. to Pres. Ronald Reagan, 1981–88.

Offices: 1017 LHOB 20515, 202-225-2415. Also 2733 Pacific Coast Hwy., Ste. 306, Torrance 90505, 213-325-0668.

Committees: *District of Columbia* (4th of 4 R). Subcommittees: Government Operations and Metropolitan Affairs; Judiciary and Education. *Science, Space and Technology* (17th of 19 R). Subcommittees: Transportation, Aviation and Materials; Space Science and Applications.

Group Ratings and Key Votes: Newly Elected

Election Results

1988 general	Dana Rohrabacher (R)	153,280	(64%)	($494,487)
	Guy C. Kimbrough (D)	78,778	(33%)	($11,889)
1988 primary	Dana Rohrabacher (R)	27,507	(35%)	
	Harriet M. Wieder (R)	17,128	(22%)	
	Steve Horn (R)	15,911	(20%)	
	Andrew J. Littlefair (R)	6,581	(8%)	
	Robert (Bob) Welbourn (R)	4,368	(6%)	
	Three others	6,925	(9%)	
1986 general	Daniel E. Lungren (R)	140,364	(73%)	($215,940)
	Michael P. Blackburn (D)	47,586	(25%)	($17,606)

FORTY-THIRD DISTRICT

Half a century ago north San Diego County, between the Marine Corps's Camp Pendleton and the Del Mar race track down the coast, was mostly uninhabited; there were a few thousand people in the beach towns of Oceanside and Carlsbad and a few thousand more scattered over the dry, brownish hills that rolled inland. Today some 600,000 people live in north San Diego County, in one of America's most comfortable environments. The beach towns have become much built up, while inland what were once little crossroads have become sizable towns or huge condominium developments. Here, amid dry but not desert landscape, you can see miles of rolling hills, with occasional surrealistic trees and sagebrush-like bushes; mountains clump up not in ridges, but here and there, almost at random. Many, but by no means all, of the new residents are retirees; and while some may miss the urbanity and busyness of big cities (or even a metropolitan area like Orange County), most don't. The climate is close to ideal, the air remains clear, there is little fear of crime, and prices are well below those of nearby Orange County. Outside the Los Angeles media market, not frequented by many entertainment celebrities, this area does not have a high profile in the media—which probably suits the modestly successful people who have moved here just fine.

Most of northern San Diego County, plus the southern tip of Orange County (including San Clemente and San Juan Capistrano of Nixon and swallows fame, respectively) form the 43rd Congressional District of California. The people who have moved here are heavily Republican: affluent enough to identify with the party of property, conventional enough in their personal lives to identify with what describes itself as the party of the family, unscarred enough by ethnic differences to identify with the party that fancies it is made up of an unethnic majority. Yet its current congressman won the seat even though he lost the Republican primary. It was a contest that attracted no less than 18 entrants (which made it theoretically possible for a candidate to win with 6%), and its winner, Johnnie Crean, struck most of the other contenders—and many others—as a man who wanted to win the nomination in the worst way, and did. Crean spent some $500,000 of his own money on television advertising that implied that he was the choice of President Reagan, though of course he wasn't, and on direct mail that charged one of his opponents, spuriously, with vote fraud. He won the primary by only 92 votes out of 83,000 cast, and the second place finisher, Carlsbad mayor and dentist Ron Packard, decided to run as a write-in candidate. Packard won in the general: this is a highly literate district, and the Republican Party was encouraging supporters of George Deukmejian to vote by absentee ballots, on which write-ins are easy. Packard had the blessing of most local Republican officials, who were even willing to risk a Democratic victory to stop Crean. The final score: Packard, 37%; Democrat Roy Archer, 32%; Crean, 31%.

Packard has had no serious contests since. He is personable, without previous high-level political experience, a consensus-builder rather than an ideologue in the House, bringing the style of California's nonpartisan, efficiently-minded municipal politics to a chamber and a delegation usually more confrontation-prone. He has compiled a solidly conservative voting record on most issues and has made his own legislative mark—not all that easy to do for a junior Republican—on both a local and a national issue. The local issue was a dispute over that most precious of resources in the West, water; local Indians had been suing for 19 years for treaty water rights in the San Luis Rey River which Uncle Sam had also granted to Vista and Escondido. Packard negotiated with all sides and produced a compromise that passed, granting the Indians new waters from the All-American Canal. Nationally, he sponsored the law requiring airplanes with more than 30 seats to carry electronic collision avoidance systems by the end of 1991.

The People: Est. Pop. 1986: 649,000, up 23.4% 1980–86; Pop. 1980: 525,956, up 99.4% 1970-80. Households (1980): 75% family, 38% with children, 64% married couples. 35.7% housing units rented; median monthly rent: $291; median house value: $109,800. Voting age pop. (1980): 387,050; 11% Spanish origin, 2% Asian origin, 2% Black, 1% American Indian.

1988 Presidential Vote:
Bush (R)	199,744	(68%)
Dukakis (D)	90,746	(31%)

Rep. Ronald C. Packard (R)

Elected 1982; b. Jan. 19, 1931, Meridian, ID; home, Oceanside; Brigham Young U., Portland State U., U. of OR, D.M.D. 1957; Mormon; married (Jean).

Career: Navy, 1957–59; Dentist; Carlsbad Sch. Dist. Bd., 1960–72; Carlsbad City Cncl., 1976–78; Mayor of Carlsbad, 1978–82.

Offices: 316 CHOB 20515, 202-225-3906. Also 2121 Palomar Airport Rd., Ste. 105, Carlsbad 92008, 619-438-0443; and 629 Camino De Los Mares, Ste. 204, San Clemente 92672, 714-496-2343.

Committees: *Public Works and Transportation* (8th of 20 R). Subcommittees: Aviation; Surface Transportation; Water Resources. *Space, Science and Technology* (8th of 18 R). Subcommittees: International Scientific Cooperation (Ranking Member); Space, Science and Applications. *Select Committee on Children, Youth and Families* (4th of 12 R). Task Force: Prevention Strategies.

Group Ratings

	ADA	ACLU	COPE	CFA	LCV	ACU	NTLC	NSI	COC	CEI
1988	5	5	7	18	13	100	78	100	92	74
1987	8	—	5	29	—	86	—	—	93	71

National Journal Ratings

	1988 LIB — 1988 CONS		1987 LIB — 1987 CONS	
Economic	20% —	79%	11% —	83%
Social	0% —	95%	0% —	90%
Foreign	0% —	84%	0% —	80%

Key Votes

1) Homeless $	FOR	5) Ban Drug Test	FOR	9) SDI Research	FOR
2) Gephardt Amdt	AGN	6) Drug Death Pen	—	10) Ban Chem Weaps	AGN
3) Deficit Reduc	AGN	7) Handgun Sales	FOR	11) Aid to Contras	FOR
4) Kill Plnt Clsng Notice	FOR	8) Ban D.C. Abort $	FOR	12) Nuclear Testing	AGN

Election Results

1988 general	Ronald C. Packard (R)	202,478	(72%)	($160,267)
	Howard Greenebaum (D)	72,499	(26%)	($74,087)
1988 primary	Ronald C. Packard, unopposed			
1986 general	Ronald C. Packard (R)	137,341	(73%)	($132,967)
	Joseph Chirra (D)	45,078	(24%)	($26,367)

FORTY-FOURTH DISTRICT

"In the Logan Heights district, south and east of downtown along the curved southern shore," wrote the *WPA Guide* of the less elegant side of San Diego 50 years ago, "sprawl San Diego's Mexican and Negro communities, with Mexican restaurants vending tamales and tacos, and with chicken palaces and big ovens where Negroes barbecue meat." Farther south, toward the Mexican border, "US 101 runs through a dismal stretch of factories, ancient frame buildings and tide flats, and passes among orange and lemon groves and fields of celery operated almost exclusively by Japanese." The south side of San Diego remains the more modest, industrial, if not truly dismal side of town, where today the city's blacks live in neighborhoods stretching east from the gleaming downtown area and where Mexican-Americans are scattered in various parts of the city, from Encanto and Chollas Park in the east, down through the blue-collar suburbs of National City and Chula Vista to the south. They live also, unobtrusively here and there, in mostly Anglo neighborhoods like East San Diego and suburbs like Lemon Grove. Indeed, the Mexican-American percentage here is not as large as most people would guess, given the proximity of Mexico. One reason is that immigrants come to the United States less to get residency and qualify for welfare than they do to get jobs.

This central and southern part of San Diego, enclosed by a jagged line drawn to maximize its Democratic percentage, makes up California's 44th Congressional District. Its boundaries were very carefully sculpted because most of its precincts were in the earlier south side district that surprised everyone and elected a Republican congressman, Duncan Hunter, in 1980. Heavily Republican areas, like the old beach resort of Coronado and the pleasant neighborhood around Balboa Park, were split off and put into a new 45th District, safe for Hunter; the rest, with some new parts added, was made a safe Democratic seat.

This left a district ripe for San Diego County Supervisor Jim Bates. A onetime Republican with 11 years in local government, he was well known for insisting that welfare recipients work, but he was no across-the-board conservative: he first became a Democrat because he opposed the Vietnam war and supported Eugene McCarthy in 1968. In 1982, Bates won both the primary and the general election by wide margins.

In the House he is hard to classify. He was adroit enough to win a seat on the Energy and Commerce Committee in 1983, beating in the process a Los Angeles freshman backed by Health Subcommittee Henry Waxman. But he is regarded by many as erratic and mercurial. He sees himself as an independent thinker, willing to buck the big guys, approaching each issue thoughtfully, ready to advocate unpopular stands like the legalization of some drugs in 1986. But there is a thin boundary between that and being unpredictable and unreliable, and many serious House members think he has crossed that line. In his first years in the House he was criticized bitterly if anonymously for treating his staff capriciously and cruelly; in September 1988 he was accused of sexual harassment of female staff members, in charges that became a centerpiece of the 1988 campaign.

He won that contest 60%–37%, but that is a lower percentage than in his three previous races, and Bates' behavior may invite serious Republican competition or even a primary challenge in 1990. In his behalf it should be said that he has attracted a large core of enthusiastic supporters in San Diego and even his 1988 showing was a solid win. He is a man who has risen far from difficult circumstances, but he needs to discipline himself and focus his talents more steadily if he is to come close to achieving his potential in Congress.

The People: Est. Pop. 1986: 630,200, up 19.8% 1980–86; Pop. 1980: 525,868, up 17.2% 1970-80. Households (1980): 69% family, 41% with children, 52% married couples. 51.9% housing units rented; median monthly rent: $225; median house value: $70,300. Voting age pop. (1980): 379,593; 22% Spanish origin, 13% Black, 7% Asian origin, 1% American Indian.

1988 Presidential Vote: Dukakis (D).   80,893   (51%)
Bush (R)   74,236   (47%)

Rep. Jim Bates (D)

Elected 1982; b. July 21, 1941, Denver, CO; home, San Diego; San Diego State U., B.A. 1974; Congregationalist; married (Marilyn).

Career: USMC, 1959–63; Bank loan officer, 1963–68; Aerospace adminis., 1968–69; San Diego City Cncl., 1971–74; Mbr., San Diego Cnty. Bd. of Spvsrs., 1975–82, Chmn., 1982.

Offices: 244 CHOB 20515, 202-225-5452. Also 3450 College Ave., #220, San Diego 92115, 619-287-8851; and 430 Davidson St., Ste. A, Chula Vista 92010, 619-691-1166.

Committees: *Energy and Commerce* (21st of 26 D). Subcommittees: Energy and Power; Health and the Environment; Transportation and Hazardous Materials. *Government Operations* (24th of 24 D). *House Administration* (8th of 13 D). Procurement and Printing (Chairman); Elections. *Joint Committee on Printing.*

Group Ratings

	ADA	ACLU	COPE	CFA	LCV	ACU	NTLC	NSI	COC	CEI
1988	95	91	83	82	81	8	41	0	46	26
1987	96	—	81	86	—	9	—	—	47	33

National Journal Ratings

	1988 LIB — 1988 CONS		1987 LIB — 1987 CONS	
Economic	54% —	44%	46% —	52%
Social	86% —	0%	78% —	0%
Foreign	84% —	0%	73% —	26%

Key Votes

1) Homeless $	FOR	5) Ban Drug Test	AGN	9) SDI Research	FOR
2) Gephardt Amdt	AGN	6) Drug Death Pen	AGN	10) Ban Chem Weaps	FOR
3) Deficit Reduc	FOR	7) Handgun Sales	AGN	11) Aid to Contras	AGN
4) Kill Plnt Clsng Notice	AGN	8) Ban D.C. Abort $	AGN	12) Nuclear Testing	FOR

Election Results

1988 general	Jim Bates (D)	90,796	(60%)	($480,679)
	Bob Butterfield (R)	55,511	(37%)	($218,388)
1988 primary	Jim Bates (D), unopposed			
1986 general	Jim Bates (D)	70,557	(64%)	($410,133)
	Bill Mitchell (R)	36,359	(33%)	($134,980)

FORTY-FIFTH DISTRICT

San Diego has been one of America's fastest-growing metropolitan areas over the last 50 years; since 1940 San Diego County's population has risen from 289,000 to over two million. As a result, a county represented until 1962 by just one congressman now takes up all or most of four congressional districts. The most recently created of these is California's 45th Congressional District. Although its boundaries seem regular on the map, its population concentrations are oddly dispersed. One is right on the coast: the old beach suburb of Coronado, with its delightful

184   CALIFORNIA

Victorian hotel, the Hotel Del Coronado—the world's largest wooden structure and a favorite of past Presidents—on a narrow peninsula connected by bridge to downtown San Diego and lined at each end by Navy installations.

Another, connected by a land bridge sweeping south through Imperial Beach and the southern edge of the city, runs along the eastern edge of suburban settlement. These are pleasant suburbs nestled between mountains, not terribly high income, but conservative on both economic and cultural issues. The 45th includes the sparsely populated interior of San Diego County, with its small Indian reservations—some of the last traces of the people who populated the state, very lightly, before Junipera Serra set up his missions along the coast. Farther inland, outside San Diego County, is the Imperial Valley, an agricultural area in the desert created entirely by irrigation; the majority of the people here are Mexican, with more huddling in Mexicali, right on the border; the political power is in the hands of the growers.

This is a solidly Republican district, created by Phillip Burton to entice freshman Duncan Hunter out of the otherwise Democratic 44th, most of which he had been representing and which he, alone of San Diego area Republicans, might have won. The strategy worked. Hunter may have had some misgivings: before his election he was a storefront lawyer in a low-income neighborhood, and he was proud of his ability to win votes, often through door-to-door campaigning, among Democrats, including blacks, Hispanics and Asians. But the prospect of having to court a basically contrary constituency indefinitely must have been daunting. So Hunter ran in the 45th and won easily.

Hunter is also a Vietnam veteran and a believer in strong national defense who brings the aggressiveness of a veteran of helicopter combat assaults in Vietnam and the brashness of a poverty lawyer to his work. He went against conventional wisdom by running against 18-year incumbent Lionel Van Deerlin in 1980, when Van Deerlin chaired a subcommittee both important and capable of generating vast campaign contributions. But Hunter outcampaigned the Democrat and won. Once in Washington, he took on his fellow 1980 San Diego freshman Bill Lowery and won a seat on the Armed Services Committee. There he has made some impact on decisions local and national. He is an ardent backer of SDI, of contra aid and of expanding the Navy; however, he led the fight against John Lehman's homeporting plan which would take ships out of San Diego. He was also a lead sponsor of the amendment to use military forces to intercept drug shipments. He pushed through a "return-to-sender" system to intercept sewage flows from across the border in Tijuana and return them to Mexico before sewage can enter the Tijuana River and pollute San Diego beaches.

As chairman of the Republican Research Committee, he is one of the younger, more aggressive Republicans' brokers of ideas; he was also one of the founders of the Conservative Opportunity Society in 1983. Hunter would not claim to be an intellectual, and he is sometimes quite oblivious of institutional barriers and received wisdom. But he is one young Republican whose fervor and backing of ideas whose time seems to have come, have made a difference in the House and seem likely to do so for some years to come.

The People: Est. Pop. 1986: 598,100, up 13.7% 1980–86; Pop. 1980: 525,927, up 43.3% 1970-80. Households (1980): 76% family, 42% with children, 63% married couples. 36.9% housing units rented; median monthly rent: $257; median house value: $88,200. Voting age pop. (1980): 373,038; 14% Spanish origin, 2% Asian origin, 2% Black, 1% American Indian.

1988 Presidential Vote: Bush (R) 153,368   (66%)
Dukakis (D). 76,206   (33%)

Rep. Duncan Hunter (R)

Elected 1980; b. May 31, 1948, Riverside; home, Coronado; Western St. U., B.S.L. 1976, J.D. 1976; Baptist; married (Lynne).

Career: Army, Vietnam; Practicing atty., 1976–80.

Offices: 133 CHOB 20515, 202-225-5672. Also 366 S. Pierce St., El Cajon 932020, 619-579-3001; and 1101 Airport Rd., Imperial 92251, 619-353-5420.

Committees: *Armed Services* (7th of 21 R). Subcommittees: Research and Development; Seapower and Strategic and Critical Materials. *Select Committee on Hunger* (9th of 12 R).

Group Ratings

	ADA	ACLU	COPE	CFA	LCV	ACU	NTLC	NSI	COC	CEI
1988	0	0	21	18	13	100	84	100	77	76
1987	4	—	22	14	—	91	—	—	93	86

National Journal Ratings

	1988 LIB — 1988 CONS	1987 LIB — 1987 CONS
Economic	13% — 85%	11% — 83%
Social	0% — 95%	0% — 90%
Foreign	0% — 84%	0% — 80%

Key Votes

1) Homeless $	FOR	5) Ban Drug Test	FOR	9) SDI Research	FOR
2) Gephardt Amdt	AGN	6) Drug Death Pen	FOR	10) Ban Chem Weaps	AGN
3) Deficit Reduc	AGN	7) Handgun Sales	FOR	11) Aid to Contras	FOR
4) Kill Plnt Clsng Notice	FOR	8) Ban D.C. Abort $	FOR	12) Nuclear Testing	AGN

Election Results

1988 general	Duncan L. Hunter (R)	166,451	(74%)	($489,395)
	Pete Lepiscopo (D)	54,012	(24%)	($8,136)
1988 primary	Duncan L. Hunter (R), unopposed			
1986 general	Duncan L. Hunter (R)	118,900	(77%)	($400,612)
	Hewitt Fitts Ryan (D)................	32,800	(21%)	($21,875)

COLORADO

Colorado 50 years ago was a well-kept secret: its mountains occasionally visited by a few tourists from back east, its mile-high cities still the home of some tuberculosis sufferers, its local establishment the descendants of the rough miners and prospectors who struck it rich in the late 19th century. Denver was affluent and secure in its role as the commercial center, transportation hub, and supply depot for the whole Rocky Mountain area. "Colorado is conservative politically, economically, financially," wrote John Gunther in the 1940s, and Denver "is probably the most self-sufficient, isolated, self-contained and complacent city in the world. [Its] attitude is to hold tight, stand pat, discourage new industry (that might compete), and keep expensive labor out."

For the last several decades, Colorado has been just the opposite. Outside developers started transforming the Denver skyline in the 1940s, winter sports entrepreneurs started building ski resorts and all-year mountain condominiums in the 1950s, young people looking for life in a splendid environment started arriving the 1960s, and oil men from Texas and elsewhere started showing up in the 1970s. Colorado "represented the geography of hope," as one newcomer put it—Dick Lamm, who went on to be elected governor three times. They were attracted by the mountains—the Front Range of the Rockies which rise, suddenly and unforgettably, over the seemingly flat plains that descend imperceptibly downward 1,000 miles to the east, and the hundreds of jutting peaks and ski trails that define the character of of the Western Slope. But the new Coloradans have settled almost entirely along the base of the Front Range, whose population rose from 670,000 in 1940 to 1.3 million in 1960 and 2.3 million in 1980; at the same time the eastern plains dropped from 180,000 to 153,000, while the Western Slope, stagnant at 270,000 from 1940 to 1960, grew to 410,000 in 1980.

Colorado is no longer a secret—and no longer the geography of hope, either. Once a national trendsetter, where experts looked for new lifestyles, new attitudes, and new fads, it has seen its economy devastated in the 1980s. The achievement of building a strip city of millions on parched plains separated by towering mountains from their water supply is awesome. But, as oil prices slumped, Colorado's defense-dependent high-tech industries quit growing, and the state's agricultural sector was battered and the costs began to come due. After decades of growth, in 1986 more people moved out of Colorado than in. The "brown cloud" of depressing smog hanging over the empty new skyscrapers of downtown Denver as dirty slush accumulates in the gutters is not what people came to Colorado for.

As Colorado has boomed and then busted, it has gone through several cycles of political leaders. Back in 1962 it was electing conservative Republicans—a forecast of the Goldwater and Reagan movements to come. In the early 1970s, it sprouted a crop of young, anti-Vietnam war, environment-minded Democrats, whose first victories were electing Congresswoman Pat Schroeder in 1972; in the Watergate year of 1974, electing Dick Lamm governor and Gary Hart U.S. Senator; and, denying state funding for the 1976 Winter Olympics (they went elsewhere). In the late 1970s, Colorado sprouted conservative Republicans who, capitalizing on anger at big government and federal energy regulations, elected majorities in the legislature (their leaders adopted the nickname their adversaries gave them: "the crazies") and elected Senator Bill Armstrong—a preview of Colorado's overwhelming majorities for Ronald Reagan.

By the middle 1980s both groups played out their string. The Democrats won their battles for limiting growth and the Republicans theirs for traditional values, and new issues—the need for growth, the integration of new groups like Hispanics—emerged. Governor Lamm stepped down in 1986, leaving as his parting liberal shot a cry to stop immigration; Gary Hart left the Senate to

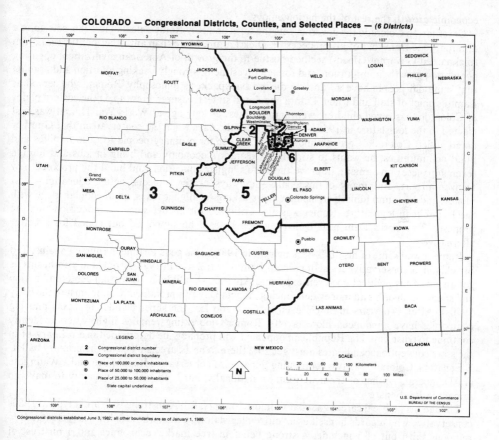

COLORADO — Congressional Districts, Counties, and Selected Places — *(6 Districts)*

make his last, ill-fated run for the Presidency. Republicans like Anne Burford had long since gone to Ronald Reagan's Washington and left government; Congressman Ken Kramer, another "crazy" from the 1970s, ran for the Senate in 1986 and lost. Michael Dukakis made a strong but losing showing in the state, sparking appearances by both candidates in the last weekend of the campaign, and changing Colorado from a state almost as Republican as Arizona to one close to the national average.

This Democratic surge in the late 1980s may represent a repudiation of the conservative Republican philosophy, but it does not amount to an embrace of the environment-minded liberal Democrats. Colorado, one of the first states to legalize abortion, voted 60%–40% against state-financed abortions in 1988, and by a margin of 61%–39% voted to declare English the state's official language, despite the opposition of Governor Roy Romer and other Democrats.

For two decades Colorado voters, unfettered by pressing economic need, with no deep roots in the community, swung wildly from right to left and back again. In the late 1980s Colorado voters, suddenly queasy about the future of their economy and finding themselves with roots in the community, are swinging far less in either direction and opting cautiously for competence and safety. Colorado politics is no longer cultural warfare ("If she wins, we win," Pat Schroeder's buttons read in 1972, "They've had their turn; now it's our turn," ran Gary Hart's slogan in 1974) but just a search by erstwhile trendsetters to figure out how to catch up with the economic growth the rest of the nation enjoys.

Governor. In Colorado the governor sets the tone, and Roy Romer, elected in 1986, sets quite a different tone from that of his predecessor, Dick Lamm. More than any other politician, Lamm (nicknamed Governor Gloom) seemed hostile to the growth of American civilization, opposing population growth, immigration, and foreign investment, strongly backing abortion and arguing that some old people have a "duty to die": a backpacker's philosophy. Romer, who served as Lamm's chief of staff and whom Lamm appointed state Treasurer, grew up on the eastern plains of Colorado, has seven children, went into business as long ago as World War II, and was first elected to the legislature in 1958. He remembers the days when the conservatism that Gunther noted stifled Colorado's growth and made it harder for ordinary people to raise families and build communities; he wants to stimulate Colorado's economy and bring in jobs and foreign (even Japanese) investment, improve the state's higher education, and build the proposed new Denver airport. But many of his goals—highways, water projects, better education—cost money, and he found himself in his first years asking for higher taxes, an unpopular move with the Republican legislature. Romer was also criticized for his decision—or indecision—on the proposed Two Forks Dam near Denver, which he said he supported but hoped for a better alternative.

Romer owed some of his 58%–41% margin in 1986 to his good fortune in running against Ted Strickland, a conservative legislator whom Lamm beat 2 to 1 in 1978. Strickland's enthusiasms got ahead of his political good sense: he said America should be a "Christian-centered" nation and spent much of his ad money denouncing Angela Davis (a prominent Communist in the early 1970s). After two years in office, even as Colorado lost the super collider to Texas and big companies have announced more layoffs, Romer's job rating remains high; voters evidently continue to trust him. His Republican opponent will probably be determined in a primary, or in the state convention; candidates must get 20% there to be assured a place on the primary ballot.

Senators. Colorado has two contrasting Senators, a conservative Republican and a Watergate era Democrat, neither of them well known nationally, but both with the capacity to make an impact in the Senate.

Though his political career goes back almost 30 years, Bill Armstrong is an archetypical 1980s conservative who regards himself as a "citizen legislator," a man whose politics is rooted in deep religious faith but also includes a strong belief in free market economics and a mistrust of government, a successful politician unskilled at political manuevering and willing to retire from the Senate at 53 despite excellent prospects for reelection. He is a businessman who has made his fortune in broadcasting (ironically, a heavily regulated industry) and has spent most of his adult life in public office. He was elected to the Colorado House in 1962, at age 25; to the United States House in 1972, in a new district whose boundaries he helped draw; and to the Senate in 1978. In each case Armstrong came to office just as his party was coming to power and as its ideas seemed to be carrying all before them; in each case there has been a certain disappointment afterwards, as there almost inevitably is in politics.

In the Senate, with seats on Finance and Budget, he has concentrated most on economic issues, and has had notable successes and failures. Typically, they both come when he holds out for something like his ideal position, which gives him great leverage when his vote is needed (to seal a bipartisan compromise or provide a solid Republican front) and no leverage at all when it is not. He was successful in getting income tax indexing into the 1981 tax bill, spurning pleas to hold off until later. It went into effect in 1985 and has become a permanent part of the tax code; it has little immediate effect, but should prevent bracket creep and hold down revenues in times of inflation. On the 1983 social security commission Armstrong made a difference by bridling at an original proposal for tax increases and forcing more cuts in future benefits instead. But by the mid-1980s Armstrong was dismayed by the huge deficits, and found his leverage much reduced. He had little involvement in tax reform or budget issues. After the 1984 election he was elected chairman of the Senate Republican Policy Committee—the only strong conservative to win a leadership position—but spent little time rounding up votes. He did work hard trying to revive the full (and very generous) benefits of the G.I. Bill of Rights, but never quite got it through the Senate. He has also crusaded unsuccessfully to raise the Social Security earnings limit.

Armstrong had more success getting stronger work requirements into Senator Daniel Patrick Moynihan's welfare reform bill in 1988, and he was the Senate's leader on pushing to let tenants buy public housing units. He successfully whittled down William Proxmire's anti-takeover legislation by passing amendments banning golden parachutes, poison pills, and greenmail—making himself the champion of the little shareholder against putatively entrenched management. He was the lead sponsor of the bill to repeal a D.C. law and so permit Georgetown University not to sponsor gay organizations which violate Catholic teachings.

In early 1987 some conservative leaders talked up Armstrong as a Presidential candidate. But he had no stomach for the idea and bowed out quickly. Instead, he spent time on Colorado issues, emphasizing his support for measures to clean up Denver's "brown cloud" (he wants to cut carbon monoxide in half by 1992) and to protect Colorado wilderness. He opposed Timothy Wirth's bill to ban oil shale sales, but he worked with Wirth to put through the Animas-La Plata irrigation project and to settle wilderness water rights.

Yet Armstrong made no move to raise money for reelection and in February 1989 announced he would retire to concentrate on business and religion. Elected by big margins in 1978 and 1984, and still popular, he probably could have won easily. With former Governor Dick Lamm having already taken himself out of the race, neither party will start off with a well known candidate. Entering the race quickly was Republican Congressman Hank Brown, a moderate with an impressive record; other possibilities included conservative state Senator Terry Considine and house majority leader Chris Paulson. Possible Democrats include former state chairman Buie Seawell and Congressmen David Skaggs.

Timothy Wirth is perhaps the archetypical Democrat of the Watergate generation: well-educated, suburban, articulate and hard-working, in line with most of his party's historic traditions but alert to new trends (he was one of the first northern Democrats to oppose oil and gas price controls and was in the middle bloc on the Budget Committee), faintly adversarial to some traditional policies and institutions but at the same time wielding serious governmental responsibilities. Wirth was first elected to the House in 1974, from the suburbs just west of Denver and the university town of Boulder. With a mixed record on economic issues and liberal record on cultural and foreign matters, he was reelected by narrow margins, after expensive and hard-fought campaigns in the 1970s—and with the help of annual Washington seminars for interested constituents, something he apparently invented. He rose quickly on Energy and Commerce—the House's hot committee by the late 1970s—so that after the 1980 election he fell heir to the chair of the Telecommunications, Consumer Protection and Finance Subcommittee. That gave him jurisdiction over TV networks, the telephone industry, and Wall Street—a bonanza for an active policymaker and for an aggressive fundraiser, both of which Wirth is. He was not entirely successful on policy, notably when he lost his AT&T divestiture bill after AT&T got its numerous stockholders to oppose it; but he was one of the most powerful members of the House nonetheless.

Yet in 1986, when Gary Hart declined to run for reelection, Wirth decided to cast that power and seniority aside for what was from the outset a chancy race for the Senate. To be sure, his House seat was not entirely safe either (but the lines were safer in the 1980s than the 1970s); but running in a state which went 63% for Ronald Reagan was anything but a sure thing. Why did he do it? Wirth was perhaps the most overscheduled member of the House, with tough demands on his time from his subcommittee and his marginal seat. And he seems to have wanted to shift subject matter.

Certainly that is what he did once he got to the Senate. He no longer spends much time on

Wall Street or the communications industry. The national—or international—issue Wirth is concentrating on is global warming. More than any other Senator, he has been studying the greenhouse effect and has concluded that the current record warm temperatures indicate a likelihood that we're dangerously heating up the Earth's atmosphere. For that he has a list of solutions: burn less fossil fuel to reduce carbon dioxide emissions (though this may mean more nuclear power as well as solar and other energy sources), promote energy conservation and halt tropical rain forest destruction in other countries as well as here. Wirth does some of this from his seat on the Energy Committee, but as a senator depends less than he did in the House on his committee assignments for a peg. He also serves on Armed Services, Budget, and Banking—three committees juggling with hot potatoes (stabilizing the Pentagon budget, cutting the deficit, bailing out the savings and loans) in 1989 and 1990. And he spends much time on Colorado issues, sometimes working with Bill Armstrong, sometimes against, pushing the Animas-La Plata irrigation project to approval, cutting a compromise on wilderness water rights, calling for a stoppage of the processing of plutonium at the Rocky Flats plant near Denver, and trying to do something about Denver's "brown cloud," which is hard because it is caused by an atmospheric inversion more severe even than in the Los Angeles Basin.

Wirth has no reason to regard his Senate seat as any safer than his House district. His race against Ken Kramer was one of the close contests of 1986, which easily could have gone the other way. Kramer, frizzy-haired, inclined to enthusiasm, tried to make a virtue of his differences in demeanor with the handsome, smooth Wirth by running ads saying he was "not slick, just good." His major issue was the Strategic Defense Initiative, of which he was one of the original boosters, and not just because it is to be deployed in his Colorado Springs home base. Wirth won by carrying the Denver media market and doing well in the Hispanic and northeast farming counties—evidence of the same farm discontent which helped Democrats in 1986 win Senate seats in the Dakotas. Wirth is not up until 1992, too far away for forecasting.

Presidential politics. In the 1988 election Colorado surprised almost everyone by threatening to go Democratic. Michael Dukakis came within a few votes of carrying the Denver metropolitan area, did rather well in the Western Slope and the eastern farm counties, carried the Hispanic areas nicely, and got really trounced only in the strong military town of Colorado Springs. He lost the state by only 8%, far less than the 28%, 24%, 11%, and 28% by which Democrats trailed in the last four elections. One reason is that Dukakis—high-tech, pro-environment, culturally liberal, economically moderate—fit the state better than Walter Mondale, Jimmy Carter, or George McGovern did. Probably more important was Colorado's economic distress.

Colorado has caucuses, dominated by the ideologues—left and right—of both parties. The winners in 1988 were Michael Dukakis (with a margin of 8% over Jesse Jackson) and George Bush (opposed then only by Pat Robertson).

Congressional districting. Colorado's districting plan, imposed by a federal court after Governor Lamm and the legislature deadlocked, is one of the more sensible plans in the country. It places virtually the whole Western Slope in one district (the 3d) and most of the eastern plains in another (the 4th); each is combined with a congenial part of the Front Range. The delegation is now split 3-3, and each incumbent seems to have a safe seat, though that may change as up to three members consider running for Bill Armstrong's Senate seat. Lagging population growth means that Colorado probably won't gain a new seat from the 1990 Census, as it did in 1970 and 1980.

The People: Est. Pop. 1988: 3,290,000; Pop. 1980: 2,889,964, up 13.8% 1980–88 and 30.8% 1970–80; 1.36% of U.S. total, 27th largest. 21% with 1–3 yrs. col., 23% with 4+ yrs. col.; 10.1% below poverty level. Single ancestry: 11% German, 9% English, 4% Irish, 2% Italian, 1% Swedish, French, Dutch, Polish, Scottish, Norwegian. Households (1980): 70% family, 39% with children, 59% married couples; 35.5% housing units rented; median monthly rent: $225; median house value: $64,600. Voting age pop. (1980): 2,081,151; 10% Spanish origin, 3% Black, 1% Asian origin, 1% American Indian. Registered voters (1988): 1,772,446; 552,164 D (31%), 592,677 R (33%), 627,605 unaffiliated and minor parties (35%).

1988 Share of Federal Tax Burden: $11,564,000,000; 1.31% of U.S. total, 22d largest.

1988 Share of Federal Expenditures

	Total		Non-Defense		Defense	
Total Expend	$12,973m	(1.47%)	$8,347m	(1.27%)	$5,575m	(2.44%)
St/Lcl Grants	1,241m	(1.08%)	1,241m	(1.08%)	0m	(0.01%)
Salary/Wages	2,522m	(1.88%)	1,277m	(1.91%)	1,246m	(1.91%)
Pymnts to Indiv	4,681m	(1.14%)	4,192m	(1.07%)	489m	(2.62%)
Procurement	3,831m	(2.03%)	949m	(2.04%)	3,831m	(2.03%)
Research/Other	698m	(1.87%)	688m	(1.86%)	10m	(1.86%)

Political Lineup: Governor, Roy R. Romer (D); Lt. Gov., Mike Callihan (D); Secy. of State, Natalie Meyer (R); Atty. Gen., Duane Woodard (R); Treasurer, Gail Schoettler (D). State Senate, 35 (24 R and 11 D); State House of Representatives, 65 (39 R and 26 D). Senators, William L. Armstrong (R) and Timothy E. Wirth (D). Representatives, 6 (3 R and 3 D).

1988 Presidential Vote

Bush (R)	728,155	(53%)
Dukakis (D)	621,453	(45%)

1984 Presidential Vote

Reagan (R)	821,817	(63%)
Mondale (D)	454,975	(35%)

GOVERNOR

Gov. Roy R. Romer (D)

Elected 1986, term expires Jan. 1991; b. Oct. 31, 1928, Garden City, KS; home, Denver; CO St. U, B.S. 1950, U. of CO, LL.B. 1952; Presbyterian; married (Bea).

Career: CO House of Reps., 1958–62; CO Senate, 1962–1966, Asst. Minor. Ldr., 1964–66; CO Ag. Commissioner, 1975; Chief of Staff, Gov. Richard D. Lamm, 1975–1977, 1982–1983; CO Treasurer, 1977–1986.

Offices: 136 State Capitol, Denver 80203, 303-866-2471.

Election Results

1986 gen.	Roy R. Romer (D)	616,325	(58%)
	Ted Strickland (R)	434,420	(41%)
1986 prim.	Roy R. Romer (D)	101,992	(100%)
1982 gen.	Richard D. Lamm (D)	627,960	(66%)
	John Fuhr (R)	302,740	(32%)

SENATORS

Sen. William L. Armstrong (R)

Elected 1978, seat up 1990; b. Mar. 16, 1937, Fremont, NE; home, Englewood; Tulane U., U. of MN; Episcopalian; married (Ellen).

Career: Pres., KEZW-Radio, KPVI-TV; CO House of Reps., 1963–64; CO Senate, 1965–72, Major. Ldr., 1969–72; U.S. House of Reps., 1973–78.

Offices: 528 HSOB 20510, 202-224-5941. Also 780 Dome Tower, 1625 Broadway, Denver 80202, 303-844-5980; 228 N. Cascade, Ste. 106, Colorado Springs 80903, 719-634-6071; 722 Thatcher Bldg., 5th and Main, Pueblo 81022, 719-545-9751; and 215 Fed. Bldg., 400 Rood Ave., Grand Junction 81501, 303-245-9553.

Committees: *Budget* (2d of 10 R). *Finance* (8th of 9 R). Subcommittees: Energy and Agricultural Taxation (Ranking Member); International Trade; International Debt.

Group Ratings

	ADA	ACLU	COPE	CFA	LCV	ACU	NTLC	NSI	COC	CEI
1988	5	8	2	8	20	96	90	100	93	81
1987	0	—	2	18	—	100	—	—	94	91

National Journal Ratings

	1988 LIB — 1988 CONS	1987 LIB — 1987 CONS
Economic	0% — 95%	0% — 94%
Social	18% — 81%	0% — 94%
Foreign	13% — 84%	0% — 76%

Key Votes

1) Cut Aged Housing $	AGN	5) Bork Nomination	FOR	9) SDI Funding	FOR
2) Override Hwy Veto	AGN	6) Ban Plastic Guns	FOR	10) Ban Chem Weaps	FOR
3) Kill Plnt Clsng Notice	FOR	7) Deny Abortions	FOR	11) Aid To Contras	FOR
4) Min Wage Increase	AGN	8) Japanese Reparations	FOR	12) Reagan Defense $	FOR

Election Results

1984 general	William L. Armstrong (R)	833,821	(64%)	($3,098,129)
	Nancy Dick (D)	449,327	(35%)	($840,595)
1984 primary	William L. Armstrong (R)	105,870	(100%)	
1978 general	William L. Armstrong (R)	480,596	(59%)	($1,081,944)
	Floyd K. Haskell (D)	330,247	(40%)	($664,249)

Sen. Timothy E. Wirth (D)

Elected 1986, seat up 1992; b. Sept. 22, 1939, Santa Fe, NM; home, Boulder; Harvard U., A.B. 1961, M. Ed. 1964, Stanford U., Ph.D. 1973; Episcopalian; married (Wren).

Career: White House Fellow, U.S. Dept. of HEW, Spec. Asst. to Secy., 1967–68; Dpty. Asst. Secy. of Educ., HEW 1969–70; Businessman, 1970–74; U.S. House of Reps., 1974–86.

Offices: 380 RSOB 20510, 202-224-5852. Also 1129 Pennsylvania St., Denver 80203, 303-866-1900.

Committees: *Armed Services* (9th of 11 D). Subcommittees: Conventional Forces and Alliance Defense; Defense Industry and Technology; Readiness, Sustainability and Support. *Banking, Housing and Urban Affairs* (10th of 12 D). Subcommittees: International Finance and Monetary Policy; Securities; *Budget* (9th of 13 D). *Energy and Natural Resources* (7th of 10 D). Subcommittees: Energy Regulation and Conservation; Energy Research and Development; Public Lands, National Parks and Forests.

Group Ratings

	ADA	ACLU	COPE	CFA	LCV	ACU	NTLC	NSI	COC	CEI
1988	95	78	83	92	70	0	24	0	36	27
1987	85	—	90	67	—	0	—	—	41	31

National Journal Ratings

	1988 LIB — 1988 CONS		1987 LIB — 1987 CONS	
Economic	74%	19%	44%	50%
Social	86%	0%	83%	16%
Foreign	77%	22%	81%	0%

Key Votes

1) Cut Aged Housing $	FOR	5) Bork Nomination	AGN	9) SDI Funding	AGN
2) Override Hwy Veto	FOR	6) Ban Plastic Guns	—	10) Ban Chem Weaps	AGN
3) Kill Plnt Clsng Notice	AGN	7) Deny Abortions	AGN	11) Aid To Contras	AGN
4) Min Wage Increase	FOR	8) Japanese Reparations	FOR	12) Reagan Defense $	AGN

Election Results

1986 general	Timothy E. Wirth (D)................	529,449	(50%)	($3,787,202)
	Ken Kramer (R).....................	512,994	(48%)	($3,785,577)
1986 primary	Timothy E. Wirth (D)................	97,044	(100%)	
1980 general	Gary W. Hart (D)....................	590,501	(50%)	($1,142,304)
	Mary Estill Buchanan (R)	571,295	(49%)	($1,099,945)

FIRST DISTRICT

"One mile above sea level," reads the plaque on the 14th step of the gold-domed Capitol in Denver, the mile-high city. For more than a century Denver, right where the High Plains yield to the sharp peaks of the Front Range of the Rockies, has been the metropolis of the vast region that Joel Garreau called "the Empty Quarter." For years Denver had steady, solid growth, reaching (with the suburbs) 400,000 in 1940, 900,000 in 1960, and 1.6 million in 1980. Now, with energy prices sharply down in the 1980s, Denver finds itself for the first time in serious trouble. Skyscrapers built in anticipation of $50 a barrel oil prices stand empty now, their vacant windows unlit at night; more people are moving out than moving in; big employers are moving more jobs out of town. Winter is the worst time: the city government has had trouble removing the snow, and the "brown cloud" of smog hangs over the city, so that not only the mountains but the high-rises are invisible. An inversion traps air over Denver, and in winter cold car engines take more gas to start and wood-burning fireplaces spew carbon particles that all contribute to the problem.

Denver remains the commercial and business center of the Rocky Mountains. Its mayor, Federico Peña, after barely avoiding a recall election in 1988, seems to be making some progress on his promises. Construction has begun on a new convention center near downtown, and in May 1989 voters approved a new airport 25 miles northeast of downtown to replace congested Stapleton.

The 1st Congressional District of Colorado is Denver—it is virtually coterminous with the incorporated city and county, which contains about 30% of the metropolitan area population. It is not a typical slice of the metropolitan area, though most of residential Denver looks like a comfortable, orderly suburb. It has most of the poor black and Hispanic neighborhoods, though there is less neighborhood segregation in Denver than in almost any major American city. More important, the district has a disproportionate share of the Denver area's singles and culturally liberal married people—the aging yuppies with all the right hiking and running shoes, the people who came to a prosperous Denver with its promise of easy access to outdoor recreation and its pleasant, natural lifestyle and now find themselves living in an economically besieged Denver with the nation's dirtiest air. Only one in four households here has children, and less than half include a married couple—one of the lowest figures in America. Denver increasingly is a city of the rich and poor, or at least the comfortable and the struggling; of large families of migrants and of young singles and older empty-nesters.

This has political consequences. In the 1950s and 1960s Denver was more Democratic than Colorado because it had more union members and low-income voters. Now it is more Democratic because it has more singles. Denver from 1950 to 1970 elected a Truman-ish Democrat to Congress. Since 1972, Denver has elected a prime representative of Colorado's baby boom generation liberal movement, and one of Congress's leading feminists, Representative Patricia Schroeder. She was an oddity when she was first elected in 1972: not only a woman and a feminist, but an opponent of the Vietnam war who got herself, over the objection of Chairman Edward Hébert, a seat on the House Armed Services Committee. Now she is one of the influential figures in the House of Representatives, a politician of enough stature to put herself forward, at least for a few months, as a candidate for President.

Schroeder's House career began in 1972, almost by accident, when the young activists who were campaigning against the Vietnam war and bringing the Winter Olympics to Colorado were casting about for a candidate for Congress: passing over Jim Schroeder, they lit on his wife Patricia. She had credentials in her own right. A lawyer with experience in government, she was also a licensed pilot: her father was an aviation insurance adjuster in the Midwest, and she earned her way through school with her own flying service. Used to being idiosyncratic, she was a baby boom liberal before the baby boom came along, and much to her surprise she was elected at 32 to Congress.

There she immediately became known as a tweaker of tigers' tails, seeking and with the help of Speaker Carl Albert getting a seat on the Armed Services Committee, challenging weapons systems and the Vietnam war, attacking the seniority system. To these fights she brought the gift for pithy phrase that led her to dub Ronald Reagan the "Teflon president" and the often flip demeanor that puts people off and distracts them from her usually serious substantive arguments. She also has a gift for taking on causes overlooked by others. On Armed Services she has interested herself in the situation of women in the military and in the wives of servicemen, and has done much useful work for them. On Post Office and Civil Service, she has been not only a champion of Denver's numerous federal workers, but a supporter of whistle-blowers and due process for civil servants accused of misdeeds and a backer of in-house grievance mechanisms even for those employees on Capitol Hill.

Schroeder decries the conservatives' appropriation of the label "family," and has her own raft of family programs: higher income tax exemptions, paid leave for new parents, a comprehensive child care program, universal health care coverage. She seems not much interested in the cost of such programs, or the effect such costs might have on economic growth; yet she takes these ideas to Armed Services and Post Office and Civil Service and puts them into practical form—and sometimes gets them passed. There is a certain Teflon-like aggressiveness to Schroeder's advocacy, but she is also a workmanlike legislator with a keen instinct for how public policies affect people's lives.

In early 1987 Schroeder was chairing Gary Hart's presidential campaign; when he left the race, many asked her to enter. Starting in June 1987 she gave it serious thought. Flying around the country, raising $787,000 (of a $2 million goal), relying on volunteers for advance work and fundraising, watching herself rise to third in the polls in a field of unknowns, she presented her record and her views. In Denver in September 1987 she faced a crowd of supporters and told them, choking as she did so with a few tears, that she wouldn't run. Attacked for the tears, she came back in feminist tones: "Tears signify compassion, not weakness." More seriously Schroeder suggested that her qualifications were as high as those of most of the male candidates—and so they were: the question was, were any of them ready to be President?

Schroeder has in any case shown she is capable of being a serious public official. On Armed Services, her position is still off-balance. She had enough credibility in the Democratic Caucus that her weighing in for Les Aspin in his chairmanship fight in 1987, despite their differences over the MX, made Aspin chairman again. But she had so few votes among the still mostly hawkish Armed Services Democrats that she made no attempt to claim the Personnel subcommittee she would be entitled to by seniority, but let hawkish Beverly Byron have it in 1987. She spends more of her efforts there on burden-sharing, arguing plausibly that the Europeans aren't doing enough, and on seeking a ban on testing of all but the smallest nuclear weapons if the Soviets reciprocate. On Post Office and Civil Service she has many causes, including advancing her family agenda; on Judiciary, on which she has also served, she is a solid vote against an anti-abortion Constitutional amendment and for the Equal Rights Amendment.

In Denver, where Michael Dukakis got more than 60% of the vote, Schroeder is reelected easily. And if she is not as plausible a Presidential candidate as she would like, she is a far more serious and effective national politician than her detractors would ever care to admit.

The People: Est. Pop. 1986: 493,200, up 2.4% 1980–86; Pop. 1980: 481,672, dn. 5.5% 1970–80. Households (1980): 55% family, 26% with children, 42% married couples; 50.7% housing units rented; median monthly rent: $214; median house value: $63,600. Voting age pop. (1980): 373,579; 15% Spanish origin, 11% Black, 1% Asian origin, 1% American Indian.

1988 Presidential Vote: Dukakis (D)...................124,474   (61%)
                                Bush (R) 73,759   (36%)

Rep. Patricia Schroeder (D)

Elected 1972; b. July 30, 1940, Portland, OR; home, Denver; U. of MN, B.A. 1961, Harvard U., J.D. 1964; United Church of Christ; married (James).

Career: Field Atty., Natl. Labor Relations Bd., 1964–66; Practicing atty.; Lecturer, Law instructor, Commun. Col. of Denver, 1969–70, U. of Denver, Denver Ctr., 1969, Regis Col., 1970–72; Hearing officer, CO Dept. of Personnel, 1971–72; Legal Counsel, CO Planned Parenthood.

Offices: 2410 RHOB 20515, 202-225-4431. Also 1600 Emerson St., Denver 80218, 303-866-1230.

Committees: *Armed Services* (5th of 31 D). Subcommittees: Military Installations and Facilities (Chairman); Military Personnel and Compensation; Research and Development. *Judiciary* (8th of 21 D). Subcommittees: Civil and Constitutional Rights; Courts, Civil Liberties, and the Administration of Justice; Economic and Commercial Law. *Post Office and Civil Service* (3d of 14 D). Subcommittee: Civil Service. *Select Committee on Children, Youth and Families* (3d of 18 D).

Group Ratings

	ADA	ACLU	COPE	CFA	LCV	ACU	NTLC	NSI	COC	CEI
1988	95	81	75	100	81	0	29	0	31	20
1987	72	—	74	71	—	9	—	—	27	18

National Journal Ratings

	1988 LIB — 1988 CONS	1987 LIB — 1987 CONS
Economic	87% — 8%	48% — 51%
Social	78% — 22%	78% — 0%
Foreign	79% — 16%	75% — 24%

Key Votes

1) Homeless $	AGN	5) Ban Drug Test	AGN	9) SDI Research	AGN
2) Gephardt Amdt	AGN	6) Drug Death Pen	AGN	10) Ban Chem Weaps	FOR
3) Deficit Reduc	FOR	7) Handgun Sales	AGN	11) Aid to Contras	AGN
4) Kill Plnt Clsng Notice	AGN	8) Ban D.C. Abort $	AGN	12) Nuclear Testing	FOR

Election Results

1988 general	Patricia Schroeder (D)	133,922	(70%)	($217,503)
	Joy Wood (R)	57,587	(30%)	($26,040)
1988 primary	Patricia Schroeder (D), unopposed			
1986 general	Patricia Schroeder (D)	106,113	(68%)	($156,237)
	Joy Wood (R)	49,095	(32%)	($13,251)

SECOND DISTRICT

Just north of Denver, across the arid flat plain just beneath the 12,000-plus foot, towering crags of the Rockies, in land that was mostly dry and vacant 50 years ago, is much of the high-tech heart of Colorado. This zone of free enterprise growth is anchored on two sides by government institutions: the University of Colorado in Boulder and the Rocky Mountain Flats nuclear plant northeast of Denver. The 2d Congressional District spans most of this area, from Boulder and the mountain counties just to the west, down across the plain almost all the way to the Rocky

Flats. Technically suburban, it is a mixture of communities. Most distinctive is Boulder, only 25 miles from downtown Denver, where the University is perched literally at the edge of the Front Range. College towns tend to go through short generational cycles, and Boulder has changed from the affluent Republican community of the 1960s to the almost radical Democratic stronghold of the early 1970s to a more mellow and ticket-splitting community in the 1980s. An important but changed political force are the grown-up Vietnam era generation, now young homeowners with backpacking gear spilling out of their closets; their concern for the environment is now tempered by economic concerns. No longer concerned with stopping the Vietnam war or prohibiting population growth, they are now into design, backing the city's plan to discourage stucco surfaces and Astroturf, drive-in windows, New Orleans railings, and Swiss chalets.

East of Boulder, down on the plains running north from Denver along Interstate 25 and the river, are working class suburbs like Westminster, Thornton, and Northglenn, with increasing numbers of Mexican-Americans, not isolated in small barrios but moving, mostly unnoticed, into middle-class neighborhoods in upwardly mobile fashion, like other immigrants before them. West, toward the mountains, is the higher income suburb of Arvada, and in the mountains themselves, near the remnants of what were once mining towns, are subdivisions of contemporary homes amid the rocks and first.

The 2d's diverse parts have one political thing in common: they are the least Republican of the Denver suburbs. Republican in 1970s and 1980s national politics, the 2d trended toward Michael Dukakis in 1988, as, for once, economics (the Colorado slump) and cultural issues worked in tandem. That movement reflected the 2d's long-term trend in congressional politics, for this district, and its somewhat differently-shaped predecessors, has elected Democratic congressmen since 1974. In six elections the winner, sometimes narrowly, was Timothy Wirth, who went on to win the Senate seat vacated by Gary Hart in 1986. In the last two elections the winner has been Wirth's first administrative assistant, David Skaggs.

Skaggs is part of the same generation of Democratic migrants who came to Colorado about 20 years ago and began dominating its politics in the 1970s. In the manner of the 19th century California Gold Rush—where the same generation of migrants held most major offices for 40 years, from 1850 when they were in their 30s to the 1890s when they were in their 70s—this pre-Baby Boom generation of politicians may monopolize at least the Democrats' share of offices for most of their adult lives. Unlike some of the earlier of these Democrats, Skaggs was a Marine and served in Vietnam; he is serious and seems to have little of the crackling wit of some of his Colorado contemporaries. He was elected to the Colorado House in 1980 and was one of the leaders of the Democratic minority there. In the 1986 primary he beat Democratic national vice-chair Polly Baca and then upset hard-campaigning Republican Mike Norton in the general. Skaggs emphasized the need for government support for education and scientific research—themes that resonated in Boulder and other Denver suburbs.

In the House he got seats on the Public Works and Science Committees, and spent time tending Rocky Flats and promoting the new Denver airport. He is as liberal on cultural and foreign issues as Schroeder and Wirth and even more liberal on economic issues. Two Republicans vied to oppose him in 1988: Mary Estill Buchanan, a moderate who nearly beat Gary Hart in 1980, and David Bath, a legislator who is a born-again Christian and fierce opponent of abortion. Bath won the primary but ran a hamhanded general election campaign, losing heavily in Boulder and the industrial suburbs and running behind even in Arvada. Skaggs's victory suggests that he is on the way to making this a safe Democratic seat—unless he chooses to run for Senator Bill Armstrong's seat in 1990, in which case the 2d should see another pitched battle.

The People: Est. Pop. 1986: 549,300, up 14.1% 1980–86; Pop. 1980: 481,617, up 50.4% 1970–80. Households (1980): 73% family, 44% with children, 62% married couples; 31.2% housing units rented; median monthly rent: $266; median house value: $70,500. Voting age pop. (1980): 339,617; 7% Spanish origin, 1% Asian origin, 1% Black.

1988 Presidential Vote:

Dukakis (D).	120,330	(50%)
Bush (R)	114,652	(48%)

Rep. David E. Skaggs (D)

Elected 1986; b. Feb. 22, 1943, Cincinnati, OH; home, Boulder; Wesleyan U., B.A. 1964, Yale U., L.L.B. 1967; Congregationalist; married (Laura).

Career: Marine Corps, 1968–71; CO House of Reps., 1980–86, Dem. Minor. Ldr. 1982–85; A.A. to Rep. Timothy E. Wirth, 1975–77, Campaign Dir., 1976; Practicing Attorney, 1977–86.

Offices: 1723 LHOB 20515, 202-225-2161. Also 9101 Harlan, Ste. 130, Westminster 80030, 303-650-7886.

Committees: *Public Works and Transportation* (20th of 31 D). Subcommittees: Aviation; Surface Transportation. *Science, Space and Technology* (26 of 30 D). Subcommittees: Natural Resources, Agricultural Research and Environment; Space Science and Applications; Science, Research and Technology. *Select Committee on Children, Youth and Families* (17th of 18 D).

Group Ratings

	ADA	ACLU	COPE	CFA	LCV	ACU	NTLC	NSI	COC	CEI
1988	95	83	83	82	75	16	28	0	57	27
1987	84	—	81	71	—	9	—	—	33	18

National Journal Ratings

	1988 LIB — 1988 CONS		1987 LIB — 1987 CONS	
Economic	50%	— 48%	68%	— 27%
Social	78%	— 20%	78%	— 0%
Foreign	79%	— 16%	81%	— 0%

Key Votes

1) Homeless $	AGN	5) Ban Drug Test	AGN	9) SDI Research	AGN
2) Gephardt Amdt	AGN	6) Drug Death Pen	AGN	10) Ban Chem Weaps	FOR
3) Deficit Reduc	FOR	7) Handgun Sales	AGN	11) Aid to Contras	AGN
4) Kill Plnt Clsng Notice	AGN	8) Ban D.C. Abort $	AGN	12) Nuclear Testing	FOR

Election Results

1988 general	David E. Skaggs (D).	147,437	(63%)	($721,647)
	David Bath (R).	87,578	(37%)	($85,095)
1988 primary	David E. Skaggs (D), unopposed			
1986 general	David E. Skaggs (D).	91,223	(51%)	($519,307)
	Michael J. (Mike) Norton (R)	86,032	(49%)	($491,329)

THIRD DISTRICT

Speckled across the steep mountainsides and deep-cut valleys of the Western Slope of Colorado are dozens of little towns, built in some boom—after the discovery of gold in the 1870s, in the uranium-exploring days of the 1950s, or during the oil shale boomlet of the 1970s. The Western Slope is everything west of the Front Range, and with dozens of peaks over 14,000 feet, it has always been a barrier to east-west transportation; but for the booms, almost no one would have settled here. But the miners who tracked gold and silver and lead ores also built Victorian towns with opera houses and gingerbread storefronts in valleys and defiles scarcely accessible to the outside world, which have been restored by ski resort operators and joined by dozens of new gleaming condominiums.

The political map of the Western Slope is as diverse as its history. Aspen and Telluride, with Victorian houses and counter-cultural substrata, are liberal and Democratic; Vail and Crested Butte, with contemporary condominiums and affluent empty-nesters like the Gerald Fords, are conservative and Republican. The rough-handed mining area around Grand Junction, where piles of tailings still crackle with radioactivity, is hostile to environmentalists, as is the once booming oil shale area up around the Utah and Wyoming borders. Cattle-raising counties are now switching to the care and feeding of tourists, with unclear partisan consequences. The small Hispanic and Indian communities in the south vote heavily for the Democrats.

The Western Slope forms more than half of Colorado's 3d Congressional District; the other part is around the small industrial city of Pueblo. There, on the banks of the Arkansas River, is one of the few major steel factories west of the Mississippi, built by the Rockefellers before World War I to make barbed wire and rails; it's still running and Pueblo has been weathering the decline of the industry better than steel towns back east. Pueblo is heavily Democratic, and so are the Hispanic counties just to the south. Hispanic, not Mexican-American: the Spanish-speaking people here, as in northern New Mexico, have been living here for 350 years.

The 3d District has one of the nation's most colorful congressmen. Ben Nighthorse Campbell is an Indian, only the eighth ever to serve in Congress, of the North Cheyenne tribe, and attends tribal ceremonies every year in Montana. He was an Olympic gold medalist in judo in 1964 and makes Indian-inspired silver and turquoise jewelry. As a state legislator he used to wear his hair in a pony tail and as a congressman got leave from Speaker Jim Wright to wear a scarf instead of a necktie on the House floor. On policy, however, he is more predictable. He defends the water rights of Western Slope ranchers and mining interests against the thirst of Denver. And his major goal in his first term, which he achieved, was approval of the Animas-La Plata dam and irrigation project.

That success helped Campbell convert what had been one of Colorado's most closely contested districts into a safe seat, for 1988 at least. Two years before he upset Republican Mike Strang, a freshman whose financial troubles as a rancher reflected Colorado's own economic problems; Campbell ran close to Strang in the Western Slope and won 63% in Pueblo County, enough to win. In 1988 his opponent, a staunch conservative, never got to the point of being taken seriously, and Campbell won with 78%. Well entrenched in the 3d, he seemed to be leaning toward running for the Senate seat Bill Armstrong was relinquishing, but decided not to in May 1989, citing the time involved in fund-raising as one reason.

The People: Est. Pop. 1986: 517,200, up 7.3% 1980–86; Pop. 1980: 481,854, up 29.5% 1970–80. Households (1980): 72% family, 40% with children, 62% married couples; 30.5% housing units rented; median monthly rent: $198; median house value: $48,900. Voting age pop. (1980): 345,175; 15% Spanish origin, 1% American Indian, 1% Black.

1988 Presidential Vote: Bush (R) 114,163   (52%)
                             Dukakis (D). 101,540   (46%)

Rep. Ben Nighthorse Campbell (D)

Elected 1986; b. April 13, 1933, Auburn, CA; home, Ignacio; B.A. 1957, Meiji U., Japan, 1960–64; no religious affil.; married (Linda).

Career: Air Force, 1951–54; CO House of Reps., 1982–86; Horse Breeder and Trainer, Jewelry Manufacturer.

Offices: 1724 LHOB 20515, 202-225-4761. Also P.O. Box 636, Pueblo 81002, 719-543-9621; 115 N. 5th St., Ste. 520, Grand Junction 81501, 303-242-2400; and 835 2d Ave., Ste. 105, Durango 81301, 303-247-9300.

Committees: *Agriculture* (22th of 26 D). Subcommittees: Forests, Family Farms and Energy; Livestock, Dairy and Poultry. *Interior and Insular Affairs* (22d of 26 D). Subcommittees: Mining and Natural Resources; Parks and Public Lands; Water and Power Resources.

Group Ratings

	ADA	ACLU	COPE	CFA	LCV	ACU	NTLC	NSI	COC	CEI
1988	65	65	90	64	69	21	29	40	43	20
1987	64	—	88	64	—	9	—	—	40	17

National Journal Ratings

	1988 LIB — 1988 CONS		1987 LIB — 1987 CONS	
Economic	48%	— 51%	48%	— 52%
Social	58%	— 40%	56%	— 43%
Foreign	64%	— 36%	56%	— 44%

Key Votes

1) Homeless $	FOR	5) Ban Drug Test	AGN	9) SDI Research	AGN
2) Gephardt Amdt	FOR	6) Drug Death Pen	FOR	10) Ban Chem Weaps	AGN
3) Deficit Reduc	FOR	7) Handgun Sales	FOR	11) Aid to Contras	AGN
4) Kill Plnt Clsng Notice	AGN	8) Ban D.C. Abort $	AGN	12) Nuclear Testing	FOR

Election Results

1988 general	Ben Nighthorse Campbell (D)	169,284	(78%)	($482,789)
	Jim Zartman (R).	47,625	(22%)	($17,936)
1988 primary	Ben Nighthorse Campbell (D), unopposed			
1986 general	Ben Nighthorse Campbell (D)	95,353	(52%)	($396,799)
	Michael L. Strang (R)	88,508	(48%)	($566,439)

FOURTH DISTRICT

Colorado is not all mountains: the eastern half of the state is part of the Great Plains, dusty brown gently rolling land that seems flat but slopes imperceptibly downward toward the Missouri River. The land is fertile but always needs more water: rainfall is scarce, the rivers most of the year are just a trickle, and in many places groundwater is equally scarce. With irrigation it is fine wheat country, and one of the foremost beef cattle regions. But wheat prices and exports have fallen in the 1980s and beef consumption is way down from the red-meat days of the middle

1970s. Often in its history, eastern Colorado has been a spawning ground of national farm rebellion and a politics of protest: its voting patterns are usually tilted toward the party out of power.

The 4th Congressional District of Colorado contains almost all of the state's eastern plains, plus the medium-sized towns of Greeley, Fort Collins, and Loveland—the northern end of the Front Range strip next to the mountains that contains 81% of Colorado's people. By heritage and usually by inclination, this is Republican territory. The major cities here, Greeley and Fort Collins, have universities, but not liberal student bodies; as Colorado trended Democratic in 1980, this area remained mildly Republican. The only Democratic part of the 4th is its small segment of the Denver metropolitan area, the working-class suburb of Commerce City and once completely agricultural Brighton, both with large Mexican-American populations.

Hank Brown, the congressman from the 4th, emerged as one of the most effective Republicans in the House in 1988. From a seat on the Ways and Means Committee, which he had been denied after the 1984 election and which he gained only in 1986, Brown became the most articulate and effective Republican critic of the House Ways and Means Democrats' welfare reform package—and the congressman who got the House to endorse instead a version which, in conference with the Senate, produced the workfare reform that was signed into law in 1988. Brown insisted that the Democrats erred in disallowing welfare recipients from taking low-paying jobs and he fought hard against their desire to insulate even two-parent families from a minimal work requirement. He sought tougher child support enforcement mechanisms, and he got the House to recede from its original $7 billion program to the Senate's $2.8 billion. Enough Democrats accepted his arguments that higher benefits and bans on low-paying jobs would just keep more people on welfare and get fewer into the work force, thus changing the House's position and producing a bill the Senate accepted and President Reagan signed.

Brown took on other interesting causes, urging that Congress be covered by civil rights laws and other regulations it imposes on others; and he served reluctantly on the ethics committee. A state legislator for four years before he was elected to the House in 1980, he also worked on local issues, getting EPA to allow Colorado farmers to use pesticides to control the Russian wheat aphid and urging that cities be allowed to turn their floodplains into parkland and receive rural federal land in return. His interest in agriculture is not theoretical: before 1980 he worked for Ken Monfort, the nation's biggest cattle feedlot operator and a maverick Democrat who nearly won the Democratic Senate nomination in 1968.

Brown's record in the House is partisan, but not lockstep. Conservative generally, he is more moderate on some cultural issues (abortion, wilderness), on foreign policy, and even on economics. He is respected enough at home that, when the Republican incumbent retired in 1980, he had no competition in the 4th District primary, and he has had no difficulty winning reelection. He considered running for governor in 1986, and when Bill Armstrong announced his retirement from the Senate in February 1989, Brown quickly made it known he would be a candidate for the seat. He has the potential of being a strong statewide candidate; in the meantime, the 4th seems likely to remain in Republican hands barring a severe recession or an especially strong Democratic candidate.

The People: Est. Pop. 1986: 527,000, up 9.5% 1980–86; Pop. 1980: 481,512, up 29.6% 1970–80. Households (1980): 73% family, 41% with children, 64% married couples; 32.9% housing units rented; median monthly rent: $191; median house value: $54,000. Voting age pop. (1980): 342,745; 11% Spanish origin, 1% Asian origin.

1988 Presidential Vote: Bush (R) 120,611   (55%)
Dukakis (D). 95,642   (44%)

Rep. Hank Brown (R)

Elected 1980; b. Feb. 12, 1940, Denver; home, Greeley; U. of CO, B.S. 1961, J.D. 1969; George Washington U., LL.M. 1986; United Church of Christ; married (Nan).

Career: Navy, Vietnam; Accountant, 1968–69; Vice Pres., Monfort of CO, Inc., 1969–80; CO Senate, 1972–76, Asst. Major. Ldr., 1974–76; Greeley City Planning Comm., 1979.

Offices: 1424 LHOB 20515, 202-225-4676. Also 1015 37th Ave. Ct., Ste. 101A, Greeley 80634, 303-352-4112; 301 S. Howes, Rm. 203, Ft. Collins 80521, 303-493-9132; 311 E. Platte Ave., Ft. Morgan 80701, 303-867-8909; and 243 P.O. Bldg., La Junta 81050, 303-384-7370; Adams and Arapahoe Counties, 303-466-3443.

Committees: *Ways and Means* (9th of 13 R). Subcommittees: Human Resources; Social Security (Ranking Member); Select Revenue Measures. *Standards of Official Conduct* (6th of 6 R).

Group Ratings

	ADA	ACLU	COPE	CFA	LCV	ACU	NTLC	NSI	COC	CEI
1988	30	39	10	18	31	72	89	80	100	79
1987	16	—	9	21	—	73	—	—	85	78

National Journal Ratings

	1988 LIB — 1988 CONS		1987 LIB — 1987 CONS	
Economic	0%	93%	28%	71%
Social	32%	68%	33%	66%
Foreign	36%	63%	33%	65%

Key Votes

1) Homeless $	FOR	5) Ban Drug Test	—	9) SDI Research	FOR
2) Gephardt Amdt	FOR	6) Drug Death Pen	FOR	10) Ban Chem Weaps	AGN
3) Deficit Reduc	AGN	7) Handgun Sales	FOR	11) Aid to Contras	FOR
4) Kill Plnt Clsng Notice	FOR	8) Ban D.C. Abort $	AGN	12) Nuclear Testing	FOR

Election Results

1988 general	Hank Brown (R).....................	156,202	(73%)	($109,146)
	Charles S. Vigil (D)	57,552	(27%)	($3,165)
1988 primary	Hank Brown (R), unopposed			
1986 general	Hank Brown (R).....................	117,089	(70%)	($212,172)
	David Sprague (D)	50,672	(30%)	($22,273)

FIFTH DISTRICT

Half a century ago Colorado Springs was a tourist attraction, known for the Broadmoor Hotel and Pike's Peak. In the years since it has become one of the military fortresses of the United States, safe in the fastness of the continent where the Rockies meet the High Plains, bristling with weapons and highly trained personnel. Here is the Army's Fort Carson; just to the north is the Air Force Academy, its striking modern buildings silhouetted against the mountains. Not far away is Falcon Air Force Base, the central planning site for Ronald Reagan's Strategic Defense Initiative, and Cheyenne Mountain, where NORAD in its underground headquarters patrols the skies for invading planes or missiles. In its surrealistic setting, with its lack of regional accent and identifiable ethnicity, with its service families living in neighborhoods filled with military personnel who have spent their lives moving from base to base and mixing always with similar and sometimes with the same people, Colorado Springs seems more American than most of America. Politically it tends to favor the party that has seemed for two decades more supportive of the military, the Republicans.

Colorado Springs is the heart and geographical center of Colorado's 5th Congressional District. It reaches north to the Denver metropolitan area and includes some of its suburbs: Golden, west of the city, an old mining town with a mining school and the Coors brewery, and some of the new suburbs at the southern edge of settlement, where the water lines have just been laid in and the pavement and sidewalks laid out off what was until recently an empty, dusty plain. The 5th District also proceeds east across the High Plains to the gas station junction of Limon and west into the Rockies to the old mining town of Leadville.

The 5th District is one of the most solidly Republican districts in the country; when Michael Dukakis was running even with George Bush in the Denver metropolitan area, he was running more than 2 to 1 behind here. The current incumbent, Joel Hefley, won the seat in the 1986 Republican primary, after his predecessor Ken Kramer decided to run for the Senate; Hefley held the seat in 1988 after Kramer said he'd run against him in the primary and was persuaded not to. His general election opponent was charged with distributing literature accusing Trans World Airlines of spreading AIDS; he was officially disavowed by the state Democratic party.

Hefley is a native of Oklahoma who made his way from the Panhandle of Texas to Colorado Springs in 1965; for 20 years he was a professional civic father, executive director of the Community Planning and Research Council in Colorado Springs. He served eight years in the legislature and rose to a leadership post in the state Senate. In Washington he was elected Republican freshman class president, and has concentrated on local issues, which in Colorado Springs includes SDI; he has also proposed a lunar outpost to spur the space program.

The People: Est. Pop. 1986: 596,900, up 23.9% 1980–86; Pop. 1980: 481,627, up 60.6% 1970–80. Households (1980): 76% family, 46% with children, 66% married couples; 32.2% housing units rented; median monthly rent: $209; median house value: $66,100. Voting age pop. (1980): 335,156; 6% Spanish origin, 4% Black, 1% Asian origin.

1988 Presidential Vote:

Bush (R)	169,819	(67%)
Dukakis (D)	79,437	(31%)

Rep. Joel Hefley (R)

Elected 1986; b. April 18, 1935, Ardmore, OK; home, Colorado Springs; OK Baptist U., B.A. 1957, OK St. U., M.S. 1962; Baptist; married (Lynn).

Career: CO House of Reps., 1977–78; CO Senate, 1979–86; Exec. Dir., Community Planning and Research Cncl., 1966–86.

Offices: 508 CHOB 20515, 202-225-4422. Also 2190A Vickers Ln., Colorado Springs 80918, 719-531-5555; 10394 W. Chattfield Ave., Ste. 104, Littleton 80127, 303-933-0044.

Committees: *Armed Services* (19th of 21 R). Subcommittees: Investigations; Military Personnel and Compensation; Readiness. *Small Business* (15th of 17 R). Subcommittees: Procurement, Tourism and Rural Development; Regulation, Business Opportunity and Energy.

Group Ratings

	ADA	ACLU	COPE	CFA	LCV	ACU	NTLC	NSI	COC	CEI
1988	5	13	7	36	31	100	81	100	100	69
1987	4	—	6	21	—	96	—	—	100	74

National Journal Ratings

	1988 LIB — 1988 CONS	1987 LIB — 1987 CONS
Economic	0% — 93%	0% — 89%
Social	24% — 75%	10% — 85%
Foreign	30% — 67%	0% — 80%

Key Votes

1) Homeless $	FOR	5) Ban Drug Test	FOR	9) SDI Research	FOR
2) Gephardt Amdt	AGN	6) Drug Death Pen	FOR	10) Ban Chem Weaps	AGN
3) Deficit Reduc	AGN	7) Handgun Sales	FOR	11) Aid to Contras	FOR
4) Kill Plnt Clsng Notice	FOR	8) Ban D.C. Abort $	FOR	12) Nuclear Testing	AGN

Election Results

1988 general	Joel Hefley (R)	181,612	(75%)	($183,229)
	John J. Mitchell (D)	60,116	(25%)	($930)
1988 primary	Joel Hefley (R), unopposed			
1986 general	Joel Hefley (R)	121,153	(70%)	($283,404)
	Bill Story (D)	52,488	(30%)	($51,253)

SIXTH DISTRICT

The affluent suburbs of Denver form a "U" around the city, occupying the high ground to the west and south, toward the Front Range and down the South Platte valley, and the flat land just east of the city out past Stapleton Airport and Lowry Air Force Base. The southern suburbs, Englewood and Littleton and Cherry Hills, pioneered in the 1940s and 1950s, are still the home of much of the city's elite. The western suburbs, Lakewood and Wheat Ridge, are creations of the 1960s and 1970s, affluent but not elite suburbs with winding streets and office complexes, notably Lakewood's gigantic Denver Federal Center. East of Denver is Aurora, a creation also of the 1960s and 1970s, comfortable but a little more tradition-minded and less environment-conscious.

In partisan politics these gradations and nuances make little difference: this is all Republican territory. The dominant tone is technical and managerial, and if more wives are working and more kids are taking drugs than anyone expected, people here are still yearning for the certainty of traditional limits. They do value their environment, but they also see the need for economic growth and scientific innovation—both of which they think liberals tend to undervalue. Ronald Reagan's Republicanism touched a chord here, and its appeal persisted even as the Colorado economy sagged, for it proclaimed the virtues of orderliness and predictability to people whose lives have been dominated by change and pulling up roots.

The 6th Congressional District of Colorado was created anew from the Denver suburbs after the 1980 Census, a political dividend of Colorado's rapid growth; it includes most of this "U" of suburbs and has proved solidly Republican. The congressman is Dan Schaefer, a public relations consultant who served six years in the legislature and was a Republican leader in the Senate. He was elected in March 1983, after astronaut Jack Swigert, elected in November 1982, died of cancer a month later before he could take office. Schaefer's record in the House is mostly conservative; the main event in his career came in 1985, when he got a seat on Energy and Commerce, one of the House's most important committees. Unfortunately for Schaefer, it has been pretty well dominated by Chairman John Dingell and his fellow Democrats, and Republicans are sometimes no more than spectators.

In 1988, Schaefer got what few members in such districts get: a well-known, well-financed Democratic opponent. She was Martha Ezzard, a former Republican state senator, who ran for the U.S. Senate nomination against Ken Kramer in 1986 but failed to get 20% at the party convention. Pro-choice on abortion, favoring more spending on some domestic programs, she changed parties, resigned her legislative seat, and ran. Articulate, hard-working, Ezzard charged that Schaefer was "the invisible congressman." But, warned by her effort, Schaefer campaigned hard, arguing that he was an effective behind-the-scenes operator, getting the C-470 Interstate built and supporting the Fitzsimmons Army Hospital. Despite initial polls to the contrary, the district's Republican strength held, and Schaefer won 63%–36%—a conclusive result that ends Ezzard's career and makes clear that Schaefer's seat is safe.

The People: Est. Pop. 1986: 583,200, up 21.1% 1980–86; Pop. 1980: 481,682, up 43.2% 1970–80. Households (1980): 73% family, 41% with children, 62% married couples; 32.3% housing units rented; median monthly rent: $261; median house value: $73,200. Voting age pop. (1980): 344,879; 4% Spanish origin, 2% Black, 1% Asian origin.

1988 Presidential Vote:

Bush (R)	135,173	(57%)
Dukakis (D)	100,030	(42%)

Rep. Dan L. Schaefer (R)

Elected 1983; b. Jan. 25, 1936, Guttenberg, IA; home, Lakewood; Niagara U., B.A. 1961, Potsdam U., 1963; Roman Catholic; married (Mary).

Career: USMC, 1955–57; Educator, 1961–67; Public Affairs Consultant, 1967–83; CO House of Reps., 1977–78; CO Senate, 1979–83.

Offices: 1317 LHOB 20515, 202-225-7882. Also 3615 S. Huron St., Ste. 101, Englewood 80110, 303-762-8890.

Committees: *Energy and Commerce* (14th of 17 R). Subcommittees: Transportation, Tourism and Hazardous Materials; Telecommunications and Finance.

Group Ratings

	ADA	ACLU	COPE	CFA	LCV	ACU	NTLC	NSI	COC	CEI
1988	15	22	19	55	19	83	80	100	71	65
1987	4	—	13	29	—	87	—	—	86	71

National Journal Ratings

	1988 LIB — 1988 CONS		1987 LIB — 1987 CONS	
Economic	30% —	69%	11% —	83%
Social	20% —	78%	19% —	78%
Foreign	16% —	78%	0% —	80%

Key Votes

1) Homeless $	FOR	5) Ban Drug Test	FOR	9) SDI Research	FOR
2) Gephardt Amdt	AGN	6) Drug Death Pen	FOR	10) Ban Chem Weaps	AGN
3) Deficit Reduc	AGN	7) Handgun Sales	FOR	11) Aid to Contras	FOR
4) Kill Plnt Clsng Notice	AGN	8) Ban D.C. Abort $	FOR	12) Nuclear Testing	AGN

Election Results

1988 general	Dan Schaefer (R)	136,487	(63%)	($636,204)
	Martha M. Ezzard (D)	77,158	(36%)	($489,303)
1988 primary	Dan Schaefer (R), unopposed			
1986 general	Dan Schaefer (R)	104,359	(65%)	($125,435)
	Chuck Norris (D)	53,834	(34%)	

CONNECTICUT

Through most of its history Connecticut—stony, chilly, out of the way, with no great city, no great natural resources—has been one of the richest of states. Half a century ago it had the nation's highest incomes behind bustling New York and tiny Delaware; in the late 1980s it was behind only Alaska. In 1831 Alexis de Tocqueville was struck by how this spot on the map gave America "the clock-peddler, the schoolmaster, and the senator. The first gives you time, the second tells you what to do with it, and the third makes your law and civilization." Connecticut was already almost 200 years old then, a crotchety, Federalist backwater; but it was also a cradle of civilization and hive of ingenuity that had placed its peculiar imprint on American civilization. The stony hills rising from the shores of Long Island Sound, the fast-flowing brooks and occasional meadows along the Connecticut River furnished only timber, water power, and rocky farmland—none of the advantages supposedly needed for economic growth.

But Connecticut had something else: this has always been a state of tinkerers and innovators, a place whose people—from the stern Congregational Yankees of the 17th century to the ethnic melange of today—have worked with vast ingenuity and unusual precision. Connecticut has produced Eli Whitney's rifle made of interchangeable components and his cotton gin; the brass fabrication business and hats made of felt; it invented vulcanized rubber; it has produced combs, cigars, clocks, silk thread, pins, matches, furniture; it has companies like Colt Industries and United Technologies, to the point that this small state has one of the largest shares of Pentagon spending; and it has Perkin Elmer, the high tech company that makes the machines that make semiconductor chips with lines no wider than a micron, one millionth of a meter. The industries here from time to time decline and are replaced by something else. And thanks to its ingenuity, Connecticut has always generated plenty of capital to export, in private placements and through the nation's largest insurance companies, long headquartered in Hartford, and it has enjoyed high incomes—with per capita incomes in 1988 the highest in the nation at $22,761, 33% above the average.

Connecticut's politics has been a struggle between the conservative tendencies fostered by its economic success and the more liberal proclivities which stem from its ethnic history. For most of the 20th century, politics has been an arena in which ethnic conflicts and rivalries were played out. Once the state was populated almost entirely by the kind of "Connecticut Yankees" celebrated by Mark Twain. If you drive around the state today, you still see towns with saltbox colonial houses, tourist attraction whaling ships, and low green mountains; and you can still talk to old Yankees with slightly dry New England accents (though not nearly as distinctive as in Massachusetts).

But Yankees are no longer the majority in Connecticut, and haven't been for years. In the 19th century, Connecticut's Yankees, more ornery and parochial than those in other parts of New England, were the last voters loyal to the Federalists and the Whigs; they were loyal enough to the Republicans who succeeded them to make Connecticut one of the few states to vote for Herbert Hoover in 1932. But in the years that followed, Connecticut became more Democratic—even as it grew more affluent. For in 1932, when a majority of the state's adults were Protestant, a majority of its children were Catholic. The Democrats' success was accelerated by the skill of John Bailey, Democratic State Chairman from 1946 to 1975. He was a master legislative strategist and ticket-balancer, and Connecticut's strong party and straight ticket voting traditions enabled him to exercise more clout than he could have in Massachusetts or New York. Bailey had a brilliant sense of timing: he endorsed, early, the state's first Jewish governor, Abraham Ribicoff, in 1954, and the nation's first Catholic president, John Kennedy. Bailey and his Democrats also gave the state honest and thrifty government: Connecticut does not have a state income tax nor a big bureaucracy like those of its neighbors.

Connecticut had, throughout the Democratic ascendancy, a vital Republican Party, a strong enough organization to have generated a couple of Republican national chairmen. It elected senators in the 1950s (including George Bush's father), and it swept the board when the Democrats were split on the Vietnam war and cultural issues in 1970. In the 1980s Connecticut has tipped first one way and then another. It has voted Republican in the last five Presidential elections, in all but 1988 by solid margins. It has tilted heavily to Republican congressmen in some years (1972, 1980, 1984) but toward Democrats in others (1982, 1986). It threw out a Democratic majority in the legislature in 1984 and then threw out the Republican majority in 1986.

Meanwhile Connecticut has had Democratic governors for all but four of the last 30 years, and has two Democratic senators now. But they came to office by different routes, and can expect serious Republican competition.

In the 1980s Connecticut's economy has been growing faster than the nation's, and one reason is the defense industry. Defense contractors have been prominent in Connecticut since World War II and now more so than ever. Connecticut's unemployment rates have been among the lowest in the country in the 1980s, and it would be hard for one living here to ignore the connection between defense work and economic recovery. Yet Connecticut's Democrats in Congress, and even more so former Republican Senator Lowell Weicker, have opposed major defense programs and Reagan foreign policy initiatives even as they continue to lobby, with some embarrassment, for local companies' defense contracts. It's a situation that refutes any Marxist notion of the economic determination of politics, and seems unsustainable over the long run.

Governor. Connecticut has a governor, William O'Neill, with a traditional Democratic background—and a longer time at the top than anyone expected. A bar owner in the town of East Hampton on the lower Connecticut River, he got active in local Democratic politics in the 1950s when he returned from the Air Force. In 1966 he was elected to the legislature—not a difficult feat since Connecticut's lower house has many seats, and a district is about the size of a neighborhood. He got his current job less for his leadership ability than for his loyalty. Governor Ella Grasso made him chairman of the state Democratic Party when John Bailey died, and when her lieutenant governor ran against her in the 1978 primary, she chose the faithful O'Neill as his successor. When Grasso resigned in late 1980 just before her death, O'Neill became Governor.

O'Neill has won the job in his own right now twice, and both times against opposition that initially looked formidable. In 1982 he withstood a primary challenge from state legislative leader Ernest Abate and then won with only 53% against Republican legislator Lewis Rome in

CONNECTICUT — Congressional Districts, Counties, County Subdivisions (Towns), and Places — (6 Districts)

Congressional districts established October 29, 1981; all other boundaries are as of January 1, 1980.

the general election. In 1986 at the state convention he did better, holding challenger Toby Moffett—a onetime Nader raider and four-term congressman—to less than the 20% he needed to get on the ballot (Moffett is now a local TV anchor); and then beating Republican Julie Belaga, a Weicker ally, in the general election by a 58%–41% margin. O'Neill has now served about as long as John Dempsey, who took Abraham Ribicoff's place when he became HEW secretary in 1961, and has done so without John Bailey at his side. It helped that for years the state's booming economy boosted revenues and painlessly produced surpluses; in 1988, he had a harder time balancing the budget, and by early 1989 the state was experiencing considerable budget shortfalls after double-digit state spending increases during the boom years of the mid-1980s. Will O'Neill run again? Many expect him to, although he says it will depend on his health. If he doesn't, Democratic House members Bruce Morrison and Barbara Kennelly are touted as likely possibilities, while their GOP colleague John Rowland may also run. Other Republican possibilities include state senate and house minority leaders Reginald Smith and Robert Jaekle, as well as businessman Joel Schiavone.

Senators. Connecticut now has two Democratic Senators who have crossed political paths during their careers. Christopher Dodd's father, Senator Thomas Dodd, was notably more conservative on cultural and foreign issues than other Connecticut Democrats; the current Senator Dodd has made his name as an opponent of efforts to oust Communist-backed forces in

Central America and as a backer of programs to accommodate Americans' changing family lifestyles. Joseph Lieberman started off as a liberal reformer, beating the incumbent state Senate majority leader in a primary in 1970; but he won his seat in 1988 by running slightly but noticeably to the right of Republican Lowell Weicker on cultural issues like school prayer and foreign policy.

Dodd has had an easier political rise and wields greater national power. He was a Watergate baby, first elected to Congress in 1974; in 1980, when Senator Abraham Ribicoff retired, he faced down Toby Moffett and got the Democratic nomination uncontested. He easily beat his Republican opponent, former New York Senator James Buckley. His name and family reputation helped (though his father was censured in 1967 for misuse of campaign funds); so did his pleasant demeanor and lack of overall enthusiasm for the Buckley brand of conservatism in the Buckleys' home state.

In the Senate Dodd immediately set to work on foreign policy. He had served in Latin America in the Peace Corps, and he seems to sympathize with the complaints of many Latin critics of U.S. policy. He has consistently worked against U.S. aid to and involvement with what he sees as repressive right-wing forces in the area. On El Salvador, he pushed the measure barring economic aid unless the President certified progress in human rights, and then opposed the certifications when Reagan made them. The decline of right-wing death squad activity and the election of President Jose Napoleon Duarte for a time seemed to prove Dodd's fears unfounded, but those things might not have happened without Dodd's pressure, and the death squads may be revived with the uncertainty which will follow Duarte's departure.

On Nicaragua Dodd is the lead spokesman in the Senate against aid to the contras, and has visited often with the Sandinista leaders. In 1987 he was part of a congressional delegation sent to observe the talks on the Arias plan, which he has strongly supported. He has been outspoken in his criticism of the contras, but has had little to say about human rights violations by the Sandinistas. On Central America generally, he seems more concerned about Vietnam-type involvement by the United States on the side of what he considers unprogressive forces than he does with human rights violations or aggression by Salvadoran guerrillas or the Sandinista government. On other Latin issues, he has demurred at using U.S. power heavyhandedly, arguing against decertifying Mexico for aid because of its lax drug enforcement and arguing that any action against Panama's Noriega should be multilateral.

Domestically, his first cause is his ABC child care bill. Supported by the AFL-CIO and Children's Defense Fund, the legislation would put $2.5 billion into child care, setting federal standards for child-staff ratios, classroom size, and caregiver training. It would make ineligible for federal grants and voucher assistance most of the churches that provide currently one-third of day care, and it wouldn't cover neighbors and relatives who take care of children. The aim is to institutionalize pre-kindergarten day care on a national basis, and to create a corps of caregivers in the image of the teaching profession, complete with postgraduate training and union representation. To do that for all children would of course cost much more than $2.5 billion; Dodd is interested now in making a start, and has modified his plan to meet various criticisms. Dodd's other great cause is parental leave; he has a bill which would require businesses to grant unpaid leave to new parents.

In March of 1989 Dodd was one of three Democratic Senators who voted for the nomination of John Tower as Secretary of Defense. Twenty-two years earlier, Tower was one of two Republicans dissenting on a 92–5 vote to censure Thomas Dodd.

Dodd has proved exceedingly popular in Connecticut in 1980 and 1986. He won his second term against a weak opponent with an impressive 65% of the vote. He has also taken a hand in presidential politics. He was the one senator supporting Gary Hart in 1984, giving him conspicuous support in the Connecticut primary which he carried handily and nominating him in San Francisco.

Joseph Lieberman came to the Senate in 1988 by beating one of the most original and most bumptious of American politicians, Lowell Weicker. A Republican who more or less stumbled into the Senate in 1970—as a young conservative he won a three-way race with only 42%— Weicker became a liberal force more from personality than ideas. Tall and imposing, aggressive and irritable, impassioned and self-righteous, he gloried in taking on forlorn causes and fighting them to the end. On the Senate Watergate Committee he was the one Republican aggressively going after Richard Nixon; on the Senate floor he relished fighting Jesse Helms on school prayer and abortion; in the Appropriations Committee he fought for money for the handicapped and AIDS victims. And with considerable success: he funneled lots of money into those programs and shot down lots of Helms's amendments. In the process he made political allies and enemies: allies like feminists and the state AFL-CIO, which endorsed him in 1988, and enemies like the Buckleys, a bunch of whom puckishly endorsed Lieberman that year. Liberal Republicans of Weicker's stripe used to be unbeatable, and many still are, winning many Democrats' and all Republicans' votes. But Weicker's self-righteousness irritated too many Republicans, while the fact that his fervor was directed mostly to cultural rather than economic issues left nonplussed many traditional Democrats who are themselves conservative on cultural issues.

Enter Joseph Lieberman, as well positioned as any Democrat these days to take advantage of Weicker's weaknesses. Lieberman started off the decade disastrously, losing a 3d District House race in 1980; two years later he was elected state attorney general. In that job he daringly sued the big insurance companies and issued a ruling forcing the resignation of a close friend of Governor O'Neill. He is a Democrat appreciative of the traditions of his party—he is the author of a 1966 biography of John Bailey which succeeds in being revealing and admiring at the same time—and of the tradition-minded views of many Democrats of ethnic stock. The son of a Stamford liquor store owner, he is an Orthodox Jew who observes the Sabbath so rigorously that he declined to appear at the convention that nominated him because it was held on Saturday. On some cultural and foreign issues he is more conservative than Weicker: he favors the death penalty and a moment of silence (but not prayer) in schools; he backed the invasion of Grenada and the bombing of Libya and strongly opposes Fidel Castro.

Weicker's slogan was "Nobody's man but yours," but Lieberman's ads showed a cartoon bear emitting *GRRRRRRs* and *ZZZZZZs* when irritated or sleeping. The bear ads seemed to click, not just because they were funny, but because they accurately described Weicker's strengths and weaknesses. Polls all along had shown about half the voters ready to vote against Weicker, by mid-October Lieberman was running even in the *Hartford Courant* poll, and on election day he won a dead heat. The contest cut across party lines, as many Democrats backed Weicker and many Republicans Lieberman. Lieberman ran especially strong, compared to the Democratic national ticket, in the industrialized area around Waterbury and the Naugatuck Valley and in the towns around his home in New Haven. Weicker ran ahead of his ticket in central city Hartford and heavily Jewish Bloomfield, in the college town of Storrs, and in the New York expatriate part of rural Litchfield County.

In the Senate Lieberman is likely to be more of a team player in his party than Weicker was in his—he could hardly be less so—and in his first moment in the spotlight joined most Democrats in opposing John Tower. With seats on the Environment and Public Works and the Governmental Affairs Committees, he is likely to focus on environmental issues. An interesting question: will his example as a Democrat winning in a Northeastern state with somewhat conservative cultural and foreign policy views move his colleagues to give such positions more serious consideration than they have during most of the 1980s?

Presidential politics. In the final days of the 1960 campaign, John Kennedy was scheduled to finish his day with a rally in Waterbury. He was far behind schedule (in those days when rallies weren't all staged before 6:30 so as to be on the TV news), but a crowd of 100,000 waited up past midnight to cheer him wildly. It was the clearest example of the enthusiasm Kennedy aroused in the Catholic voters of the Northeast, and of John Bailey's shrewdness in endorsing him early. In 1988 Waterbury voted against a son of immigrants and for George Herbert Walker Bush. While the Democrats have been carrying statewide elections in the 1980s, they seem to have lost the knack for carrying Connecticut in presidential races. The state went Democratic in the close elections of 1960 and 1968, but Republican in the close elections of 1976 and 1988. One reason is that the culturally liberal views of national Democrats have not kept in the party's ranks all the Catholics (or their descendants) who were so enthusiastically for the party of the Kennedys in the 1960s. Another is that the mistrust of technology national Democrats have portrayed—in their attacks on SDI and the space program—resonates negatively with many of Connecticut's technical and high-tech workers, the modern equivalents of the tinkerers of the 19th century.

The top of the ticket matters less to Connecticut politicians than it used to, because voters in 1986 by a 50.4%–49.6% margin outlawed the straight-party levers which for years dominated Connecticut politics. Straight-ticket voting was once required in Connecticut: until 1965 you had to pull one party's lever to activate the machine, and only then could fiddle with the levers down below to split your ticket. So the party with the winning presidential or gubernatorial candidate tended to sweep the state. Even in the early 1980s there wasn't much ticket-splitting here. But in 1988 there seemed to be lots of Bush-Lieberman and Dukakis-Weicker voters.

As for primaries, here you find a vestige of Connecticut's old machines: registration on both sides is low, because the machines used conventions rather than primaries for nominating statewide and congressional candidates, and didn't encourage uncontrollables to vote in what primaries there were. This has been changing only slowly: there have been statewide primaries, but not all that many, since 1970, and the 1986 Supreme Court case opened up the Republican primary to Independents. But only 241,000 Democrats and 103,000 Republicans voted in the 1988 Presidential primaries—turnout levels that approximate those of the Iowa caucuses, in a state that cast 1.4 million general election votes. The winners in the Connecticut primaries, incidentally, were Michael Dukakis and George Bush.

Congressional districting. The boundaries of Connecticut's six congressional districts received only marginal adjustments for the 1980s, and will probably not be much changed for the 1990s.

The People: Est. Pop. 1988: 3,241,000; Pop. 1980: 3,107,576, up 4.3% 1980–88 and 2.5% 1970–80; 1.32% of U.S. total, 28th largest. 16% with 1–3 yrs. col., 21% with 4+ yrs. col.; 8% below poverty level. Single ancestry: 11% Italian, 7% English, 6% Irish, 5% Polish, 3% French, German, 1% Russian, Portuguese, Swedish, Hungarian, Scottish, Greek. Households (1980): 74% family, 38% with children, 61% married couples; 36.1% housing units rented; median monthly rent: $203; median house value: $67,400. Voting age pop. (1980): 2,284,657; 6% Black, 3% Spanish origin, 1% Asian origin. Registered voters (1988): 1,612,971; 648,483 D (40%), 429,904 R (27%), 534,595 unaffiliated and minor parties (33%).

1988 Share of Federal Tax Burden: 17,979,000,000; 2.03% of U.S. total, 15th largest.

1988 Share of Federal Expenditures

	Total		Non-Defense		Defense	
Total Expend	$13,770m	(1.56%)	$8,272m	(1.26%)	$5,842m	(2.56%)
St/Lcl Grants	1,542m	(1.35%)	1,542m	(1.35%)	0m	(0.03%)
Salary/Wages	1,142m	(0.85%)	673m	(1.00%)	470m	(1.00%)
Pymnts to Indiv	5,215m	(1.27%)	5,094m	(1.30%)	121m	(0.65%)
Procurement	5,250m	(2.78%)	344m	(0.74%)	5,250m	(2.78%)
Research/Other	621m	(1.66%)	620m	(1.67%)	1m	(1.67%)

Political Lineup: Governor, William A. O'Neill (D); Lt. Gov., Joseph J. Fauliso (D); Secy. of State, Julia H. Tashjian (D); Atty. Gen., Clarine Riddle (D); Treasurer, Francisco L. Borges (D); Comptroller, J. Edward Caldwell (D). State Senate, 36 (23 D and 13 R); State House of Representatives, 151 (88 D and 63 R). Senators, Christopher J. Dodd (D) and Joseph I. Lieberman (D). Representatives, 6 (3 D and 3 R).

212 CONNECTICUT

1988 Presidential Vote

Bush (R)	750,241	(52%)
Dukakis (D)	676,584	(47%)

1988 Democratic Presidential Primary

Dukakis	140,291	(58%)
Jackson	68,372	(28%)
Gore	18,501	(8%)
Hart	5,761	(2%)
Simon	3,140	(1%)
Babbitt	2,370	(1%)

1984 Presidential Vote

Reagan (R)	890,877	(61%)
Mondale (D)	569,597	(39%)

1988 Republican Presidential Primary

Bush	73,501	(71%)
Dole	21,005	(20%)
Kemp	3,281	(3%)
Robertson	3,191	(3%)

GOVERNOR

Gov. William A. O'Neill (D)

Assumed office 1980, term expires Jan. 1991; b. Aug. 11, 1930, Hartford; home, East Hampton; New Britain Teacher's Col., U. of Hartford; Roman Catholic; married (Natalie).

Career: USAF, Korea; Dem. East Hampton Town Cmtee., 1954–80; CT House of Reps., 1966–78; Chmn., CT Dem. Central Cmtee., 1975–78; Lt. Gov. of CT, 1978–80.

Office: State Capitol, 210 Capitol Ave., Hartford 06106, 203-566-4840.

Election Results

1986 gen.	William A. O'Neill (D)	575,638	(58%)
	Julie D. Belaga (R)	408,489	(41%)
1986 prim.	William A. O'Neill (D), nominated by convention		
1982 gen.	William A. O'Neill (D)	578,264	(53%)
	Lewis B. Rome (R)	497,773	(46%)

SENATORS

Sen. Christopher J. Dodd (D)

Elected 1980, seat up 1992; b. May 27, 1944, Willimantic; home, East Haddam; Providence Col., B.A. 1966, U. of Louisville, J.D. 1972; Roman Catholic; divorced.

Career: Peace Corps, Dominican Republic, 1966–68; Army Reserve, 1969–75; Atty., 1972–74; U.S. House of Reps., 1974–80.

Offices: 444 RSOB 20510, 202-224-2823. Also 100 Great Meadow Rd., Wheathersfield 06109, 203-240-3470.

Committees: *Banking, Housing and Urban Affairs* (4th of 12 D). Subcommittees: Housing and Urban Affairs; Securities (Chairman). *Budget* (12th of 13 D). *Foreign Relations* (5th of 10 D). Subcommittees: East Asian and Pacific Affairs; International Economic Policy, Trade, Oceans and Environment; Western Hemisphere and Peace Corps Affairs (Chairman). *Labor and Human Resources* (5th of 9 D). Subcommittees: Aging; Children, Family, Drugs, and Alcoholism (Chairman); Education, Arts, and Humanities. *Rules and Administration* (8th of 9 D).

Group Ratings

	ADA	ACLU	COPE	CFA	LCV	ACU	NTLC	NSI	COC	CEI
1988	85	63	94	100	60	8	8	10	36	19
1987	65	—	95	75	—	0	—	—	13	27

National Journal Ratings

	1988 LIB — 1988 CONS		1987 LIB — 1987 CONS	
Economic	86% —	0%	58% —	41%
Social	71% —	27%	60% —	39%
Foreign	70% —	25%	81% —	0%

Key Votes

1) Cut Aged Housing $	AGN	5) Bork Nomination	AGN	9) SDI Funding	AGN
2) Override Hwy Veto	FOR	6) Ban Plastic Guns	—	10) Ban Chem Weaps	AGN
3) Kill Plnt Clsng Notice	AGN	7) Deny Abortions	FOR	11) Aid To Contras	AGN
4) Min Wage Increase	FOR	8) Japanese Reparations	FOR	12) Reagan Defense $	AGN

Election Results

1986 general	Christopher J. Dodd (D).............	632,695	(65%)	($2,276,764)
	Roger W. Eddy (R).................	340,438	(35%)	($183,632)
1986 primary	Christopher J. Dodd (D), nominated by convention			
1980 general	Christopher J. Dodd (D)..............	763,969	(56%)	($1,403,672)
	James L. Buckley (R)................	581,884	(43%)	($1,652,672)

Sen. Joseph I. Lieberman (D)

Elected 1988, seat up 1994; b. Feb. 24, 1942, Stamford; home, New Haven; Yale, B.A. 1964, LLB. 1967; Jewish; married (Hadassah).

Career: CT Senate, 1970–80, Major. Ldr., 1974-80; CT Atty. Gen., 1983–88.

Offices: 502 HSOB 20510, 202-224-4041. Also 1 Commercial Plaza, 21st fl., Hartford 06103, 203-240-3566.

Committees: *Environment and Public Works* (9th of 9 D). Subcommittees: Environmental Protection; Toxic Substances, Environmental Oversight, Research and Development; Water Resources, Transportation and Infrastructure. *Governmental Affairs* (8th of 8 D). Subcommittees: General Services, Federalism and the District of Columbia; Oversight of Government Management; Permanent Subcommittee on Investigations. *Small Business* (10th of 10 D). Subcommittees: Competition and Antitrust Enforcement; Export Expansion; Government Contracting and Paperwork Reduction.

Group Ratings and Key Votes: Newly Elected

Election Results

1988 general	Joseph I. Lieberman (D).............	688,499	(50%)	($2,570,779)
	Lowell P. Weicker, Jr. (R)............	678,454	(49%)	($2,609,902)
1988 primary	Joseph I. Lieberman (D), nominated by convention			
1982 general	Lowell P. Weicker, Jr. (R)............	545,987	(50%)	($2,306,615)
	Anthony Toby Moffett (D)	499,146	(46%)	($1,368,147)

FIRST DISTRICT

Before the War of 1812, Hartford was one of Connecticut's seaports; vessels could sail down the Connecticut River from its wharves straight to foreign ports. Jefferson's Embargo and the war stopped that trade, and the marine insurers who had gathered in the little Connecticut town turned to writing fire insurance policies: from this beginning sprung some of America's great insurance companies. As they were growing, Yankee tinkerers were producing new products—the Colt revolver in the 1850s, for example—and Hartford was on its way to being what it clearly became by 1940, Connecticut's first city, the center of its largest urban area, the state capital, and its economic capital as well. Since then, Hartford has continued to grow; it is the center of one of the nation's leading defense contractors, United Technologies, which produces a large percentage of the world's jet engines in the Pratt and Whitney plant in East Hartford. State government also provides Hartford with a stable employment base, though not a large one in thrifty Connecticut.

Politically metropolitan Hartford, which is, give or take a few suburbs, coterminous with Connecticut's 1st Congressional District, is the most Democratic part of Connecticut, not because of any industrial proletariat but because of its ethnic makeup. Hartford has proportionately one of the nation's largest Jewish communities; it also has many Irish, Italian, and French Canadian Catholics, and it has a fair number of blacks, including the city's present mayor Carrie Saxon Perry. Most of the original immigrants' grandchildren have moved moved out of the central city and into its hilly suburbs, but enough of them retain Democratic voting habits to make this white-collar, high-skill urban area one of the most Democratic in the country. Strengthening that allegiance was John Bailey, longtime state (1946–75) and national (1961–68) Democratic chairman, an old-fashioned political boss who had a career free of scandal and who promoted a raft of first-class candidates.

Fittingly, the House member from the 1st District today is Democrat Barbara Kennelly, who was known when she started off in politics as Bailey's daughter and former state Speaker James Kennelly's wife. But since she first won the seat in a 1982 special election, she has made a reputation of her own. First, she won a seat on the Ways and Means Committee in 1983, over the opposition of Chairman Dan Rostenkowski; Ways and Means's jurisdiction over taxes is vital to the insurance industry. Next, she was the chief House sponsor of the 1984 law to use the federal tax system to enforce child support payments. For years everyone was reluctant to use the IRS to enforce these state laws, and many legislators probably did not think non-paying ex-husbands were doing anything all that reprehensible. By focusing hard on the issue, and by coming up with a workable plan, Kennelly and the other members of the Women's Legislative Caucus who worked on this issue were able to turn around opinion on both counts. On the 1986 tax reform bill, Kennelly concentrated on getting a high deduction for single heads of household and saving the historic preservation and rehabilitation tax credit. She worked hard also on the 1988 welfare reform bill, first to protect or strengthen the child support provisions, but also to take off the cap on the dependent care tax credit.

And then there are the Hartford issues. Kennelly looked after the tax treatment of the ball bearing industry; she also looked after United Technologies; most important, she fought hard to save the single-premium insurance policies from what the insurance companies consider overtaxation. This was a tough fight, and she beat Rostenkowski in committee on it—which did not increase his warmth, but may have increased his respect, for her.

By inheritance and temperament, Kennelly is a team player Democrat. She was a booster of Geraldine Ferraro for Vice President in 1984 and nominated her in San Francisco; she was given a seat on the House Intelligence Committee in 1987. In the 1st District she has proved a strong vote-getter indeed, winning in 1986 and 1988 with more than 70%. She is mentioned as a possible candidate for governor in 1990, but only if William O'Neill retires: she is not the person to challenge an incumbent of her own party, but she has shown that she can both work with colleagues and take command, so it would not be a surprise to see her run—and win.

The People: Est. Pop. 1986: 523,900, up 1.5% 1980–86; Pop. 1980: 516,232, dn. 1.7% 1970–80. Households (1980): 71% family, 36% with children, 56% married couples; 42.2% housing units rented; median monthly rent: $205; median house value: $65,700. Voting age pop. (1980): 383,559; 10% Black, 5% Spanish origin, 1% Asian origin.

1988 Presidential Vote			
	Dukakis (D)	133,867	(55%)
	Bush (R)	106,890	(44%)

Rep. Barbara B. Kennelly (D)

Elected 1982; b. July 10, 1936, Hartford; home, Hartford; Trinity Col. (Washington, D.C.), B.A. 1958, Trinity Col. (Hartford, CT), M.A. 1971; Roman Catholic; married (James).

Career: Vice Chmn., Hartford Comm. on Aging, 1971–75; Hartford Crt. of Common Cncl., 1975–79; CT Secy. of State, 1979–82.

Offices: 204 CHOB 20515, 202-225-2265. Also One Corporate Center, Hartford 06103, 203-240-3120.

Committees: *Ways and Means* (18th of 23 D). Subcommittees: Human Resources; Select Revenue Measures. *Permanent Select Committee on Intelligence* (8th of 12 D). Subcommittees: Legislative; Oversight and Evaluation.

Group Ratings

	ADA	ACLU	COPE	CFA	LCV	ACU	NTLC	NSI	COC	CEI
1988	90	83	90	73	75	8	16	10	36	13
1987	84	—	89	86	—	0	—	—	21	7

National Journal Ratings

	1988 LIB — 1988 CONS			1987 LIB — 1987 CONS		
Economic	67%	—	30%	73%	—	0%
Social	83%	—	15%	78%	—	0%
Foreign	60%	—	37%	76%	—	19%

Key Votes

1) Homeless $	AGN	5) Ban Drug Test	AGN	9) SDI Research	AGN
2) Gephardt Amdt	FOR	6) Drug Death Pen	FOR	10) Ban Chem Weaps	FOR
3) Deficit Reduc	FOR	7) Handgun Sales	AGN	11) Aid to Contras	AGN
4) Kill Plnt Clsng Notice	AGN	8) Ban D.C. Abort $	AGN	12) Nuclear Testing	FOR

Election Results

1988 general	Barbara B. Kennelly (D)	176,463	(77%)	($471,530)
	Mario Robles, Jr. (R)	51,985	(23%)	($11,520)
1988 primary	Barbara B. Kennelly (D), nominated by convention			
1986 general	Barbara B. Kennelly (D)	128,930	(74%)	($388,045)
	Herschel A. Klein (R)	44,122	(25%)	($6,705)

SECOND DISTRICT

The hilly, wooded land of eastern Connecticut, with its Yankee villages and high-income havens like Old Saybrook and Old Lyme, doesn't look it, but it's one of the nation's high-tech industrial areas. New London and Norwich were among the 13 colonies' leading workshops and ports, and in the 19th century factories sprang up there and in the little villages on fast-flowing Quinebaug and Shetucket Rivers that provided waterpower. None of these became a metropolis—they have about the population New York did in 1790—and a sandbar across the mouth of the Connecticut River kept a big port from establishing itself there. But these towns kept their technical ingenuity and know-how and today, in a time when more Americans are moving out into the countryside, many are thriving. They also house big, high-risk, high-tech operations. The part of eastern Connecticut that makes up the state's 2d Congressional District has four nuclear power plants, the largest number in any area of similar population in the U.S. In Groton, across the Thames River from New London, is General Dynamics's Electric Boat Company, the major producer of the nuclear submarines which do so much to maintain nuclear stability—and which are also expensive and difficult to build.

The Nutmeg State landscape may look colonial or early industrial; the people are more often descended from the immigrants of 1840–1924 than from the Yankees who lived here during the Revolution. For many years, the balance of mostly Protestant Yankees and mostly Catholic immigrants produced a lively two-party politics here. Over the last 25 years the 2d District has been represented by both Republicans and Democrats, although none has actually lost an election: they usually have run for other offices. Most recently Christopher Dodd, after representing the 2d District for six years, became well enough known on Hartford and New Haven television to be elected senator in 1980.

The current congressman, Sam Gejdenson, says he wants to stay in the House. He worked hard to get there, beating the son of former Governor John Dempsey in his first primary and then beating Republican Tony Guglielmo in the Reagan year of 1980, though he started off little known and his name (*gay-den-son*) was often mispronounced. But he had other assets: an ability to organize a campaign, an instinctive feel for communicating issues to voters, a wry sense of humor, and the willingness to campaign hard personally. He has displayed all these in elections since, plus the ability to raise vast sums of money. Gejdenson won with only 56% in 1982 and sagged to 54% in 1984, when the straight-party lever hurt him. But in 1986 he won 67% against highly-touted but poorly-financed former FBI official Francis Mullen. For 1988, the straight-ticket lever was abolished, and Michael Dukakis almost carried the district anyway; Gejdenson won 63% against a spirited but underfinanced challenger.

Gejdenson has one of the more liberal records in the House, and his success at making this a safe district is a good illustration of how liberal Democrats stay in control. The son of survivors of the Holocaust, he is one of those talented Democratic politicos who came of age during the Vietnam war and whose attitudes were shaped then. He serves on the Foreign Affairs Committee, where he has been a leading opponent of aid to the Nicaraguan contras, taking on Administration spokesmen in televised debates. He is a critic as well of many weapons systems, opposing the MX, the B-1, and Trident II, though he adds that he supports Trident I, the Stealth bomber, and Minuteman. Furthermore, he stresses that he works hard to keep work coming into Electric Boat, and he talked with union and management officials there when workers went out on strike. He argued for stronger anti-drug laws (though he opposes the death penalty), and he is one of Congress's most vocal supporters of vast increases in the budget of the Coast Guard (whose academy is in New London). He serves also on the Interior Committee, where he has emerged as one of the leading critics of the nuclear power industry. He opposes, however, some measures to keep nuclear power plants out elsewhere: he wants other areas to share the problems he thinks eastern Connecticut's four nuclear plants pose. He works hard on local issues, returning to the district often and handling matters from loans to Connecticut flood victims to settling Indian land claims; he has proposed a Quinebaug River heritage corridor to urge landowners to limit development.

Gejdenson seems as happy where he is as most of his constituents seem happy to keep him there. He has declined to switch to Armed Services, and has not renewed his unsuccessful bid in 1984 to get on Appropriations; he now chairs a Foreign Affairs subcommittee. He promises never to run for Senator or governor. For all his strong views on issues, he seems to many constituents "just a farm boy who spends his week in Washington," and he made a point of announcing for reelection in 1988 on his parents' dairy farm.

The People: Est. Pop. 1986: 539,200, up 4.0% 1980–86; Pop. 1980: 518,244, up 6.4% 1970–80. Households (1980): 74% family, 40% with children, 63% married couples; 35.2% housing units rented; median monthly rent: $202; median house value: $56,800. Voting age pop. (1980): 378,132; 3% Black, 1% Spanish origin, 1% Asian origin.

1988 Presidential Vote:

Bush (R)	119,947	(50%)
Dukakis (D)	115,813	(49%)

Rep. Samuel Gejdenson (D)

Elected 1980; b. May 20, 1948, Eschwege, Germany; home, Bozrah; Mitchell Col., A.S. 1966, U. of CT, B.A. 1970; Jewish; married (Karen).

Career: CT House of Reps., 1974–78; Legis. Liaison to Gov. of CT, 1979–80.

Offices: 1410 LHOB 20515, 202-225-2076. Also P.O. Box 2000, Norwich 06360, 203-886-0139; and 94 Court St., Middletown 06457, 203-346-1123.

Committees: *Foreign Affairs* (9th of 28 D). Subcommittees: International Economic Policy and Trade (Chairman); Western Hemisphere Affairs. *House Administration* (10th of 13 D). Subcommittee: Accounts. *Interior and Insular Affairs* (11th of 26 D). Subcommittees: Energy and the Environment; Water, Power and Offshore Energy Resources; General Oversight and Investigations.

Group Ratings

	ADA	ACLU	COPE	CFA	LCV	ACU	NTLC	NSI	COC	CEI
1988	95	91	95	91	75	0	8	0	29	7
1987	92	—	96	93	—	0	—	—	20	5

National Journal Ratings

	1988 LIB — 1988 CONS		1987 LIB — 1987 CONS	
Economic	71% —	23%	73% —	0%
Social	86% —	0%	73% —	22%
Foreign	77% —	21%	81% —	0%

Key Votes

1) Homeless $	AGN	5) Ban Drug Test	AGN	9) SDI Research	AGN
2) Gephardt Amdt	FOR	6) Drug Death Pen	AGN	10) Ban Chem Weaps	FOR
3) Deficit Reduc	FOR	7) Handgun Sales	AGN	11) Aid to Contras	AGN
4) Kill Plnt Clsng Notice	AGN	8) Ban D.C. Abort $	AGN	12) Nuclear Testing	FOR

Election Results

1988 general	Samuel Gejdenson (D)	143,326	(64%)	($727,919)
	Glenn Carberry (R)	81,965	(36%)	($246,903)
1988 primary	Samuel Gejdenson (D), nominated by convention			
1986 general	Samuel Gejdenson (D)	109,229	(67%)	($987,167)
	Bud Mullen (R)......................	52,869	(33%)	($145,336)

THIRD DISTRICT

Once the capital and largest city of Connecticut, best known as the home of Yale, New Haven is really an industrial town, the place where Eli Whitney first mass-produced rifles—the forerunner of Connecticut's big defense industry. It is a town where tinkerers mass-produced clocks, locks, hardware, and toys in the 19th century and which still, despite the departure of the Winchester rifle company, shows signs of its factory town past. Politically, New Haven is the center of Connecticut's 3d Congressional District. You can still see the remains of New Haven's turn-of-the-century factories, but the children of the Irish, Italian, and Polish immigrants have long since spread out from their old neighborhoods of frame houses, huddled within walking distance of the factories, to the close-in suburbs and beyond.

For years New Haven politics centered on ethnic rivalries: the Irish became Democrats because the Yankee Republicans would have nothing to do with them; the Italians became Republicans because the Democratic Party was controlled by the Irish. (In all this Yale played little part: for all its national reputation, it has a small enrollment and, except for a few blocks near campus, New Haven is not really a college town.) But over time, as second- and third-generation Americans got educated, found good jobs, and raised their families in the suburbs, ethnic identity and ethnic jealousies came to matter less, and cultural attitudes more. New Haven's Yankees were staunch Republicans—cannons boomed out over the Green in 1860 when Lincoln was elected—and the Democratic loyalties of its Catholics were strongest when Kennedy was elected in 1960. In the years since, the conservative cultural attitudes that are strong in so many factory towns have become the determinant of political attitudes here. The city of New Haven, depopulated by urban renewal and the flight to the suburbs, is heavily Democratic, but the New Haven area and the 3d District have not voted for a Democrat for President since 1964.

The congressman from the 3d is a Democrat, however, and his success helps make clear why his party still controls the House. Bruce Morrison came to New Haven to go to law school and stayed to work in and run the legal services program. In 1982, fed up with the Reagan revolution, he decided to run for Congress; an outsider, with a WASP name in a district represented for 30 years by men named DeNardis, Giaimo, and Cretella, unconnected to the local pols, Morrison built an organization, raised $300,000, and ran some truly clever ads (the 3d, served primarily by two Connecticut TV stations, permits unusually spirited and specific campaigning, with plenty of charges and countercharges on TV). In the primary he beat the president of the board of aldermen and in the general incumbent Lawrence DeNardis, who had won the district in 1980 by beating Joseph Lieberman, now U.S. Senator. In the years since, in this Republican-leaning district, Morrison has simultaneously made a distinctive liberal record in the House and made the 3d District a safe seat.

In the House he has not been much of a gladhander and he is not afraid to make waves; he tried three times to get a seat on the Budget Committee, and lost each time, and in December 1988 lost a bid for a seat on Appropriations. But he has used his seat on Banking to advantage, voting against Fernand St Germain and in favor of keeping banks out of stock underwriting, and he has championed the interests of the insurance companies. He is interested in Third World debt, and has suggested an international agency to buy it up from the banks (presumably at some discount) and then repackage it and sell it elsewhere; he takes the common sense position that banks should lose something when they make bad loans. In the middle 1980s he led fights to freeze various parts of the budget. But he does seek more money to build public housing—one of the few members with real faith in that program—and he has resisted efforts to let tenants buy housing projects (lest they cut the wages of the projects' union-represented employees).

Morrison is not afraid of the L-word, arguing that "things that have been supported by liberal political leaders over the last half-century have built middle-class America." He casts lonely votes against measures like banning dial-a-porn calls on free speech grounds and opposes capital punishment. On foreign policy he is a vehement opponent of aid to the Nicaraguan contras, and in early 1987 he was arguing that Congress should think about whether Ronald Reagan should be impeached. In some quarters these views might get him in trouble, but among House Democrats they help. When Judiciary Committee Democrats voted Romano Mazzoli out of the chair of the immigration subcommittee by a 16-5 vote in 1989, they promptly installed Morrison.

How does he win at home? In 1982 Morrison won by stressing economic issues, by attacking trickle-down Reaganomics and charging DeNardis with voting to weaken Social Security. As the economy recovered, he has used the advantages of office to stay in office. He has raised vast sums from PACs and other contributors. He works the district hard, staying in touch with local businessmen even as he supports greater regulations on business, and helping out local defense contractors even as he supports cutbacks in the Pentagon budget. Against his political smarts and energy, the hapless Republicans who ran against him in 1986 and 1988 had no chance, and it hardly seems likely that this active and creative legislator will be seriously challenged in the future.

The People: Est. Pop. 1986: 527,900, up 1.8% 1980–86; Pop. 1980: 518,677, up 1.6% 1970–80. Households (1980): 73% family, 36% with children, 59% married couples; 37.0% housing units rented; median monthly rent: $212; median house value: $65,400. Voting age pop. (1980): 387,740; 9% Black, 2% Spanish origin, 1% Asian origin.

1988 Presidential Vote:

Bush (R)	....	119,329	(50%)
Dukakis (D)	....	117,432	(49%)

Rep. Bruce A. Morrison (D)

Elected 1982; b. Oct. 8, 1944, New York, NY; home, Hamden; MA Institute of Technology, S.B. 1965, U. of IL, M.S. 1970, Yale U., J.D. 1973; Lutheran; married (Jane).

Career: New Haven Legal Assistance Assn., Staff atty., 1973–74, Managing atty., 1974–76, Exec. Dir., 1976–81.

Offices: 330 CHOB 20515, 202-225-3661. Also 85 Church St., New Haven 06510, 203-773-2325.

Committees: *Banking, Finance and Urban Affairs* (14th of 31 D). Subcommittees: Housing and Community Development; Policy Research and Insurance; International Development, Finance, Trade and Monetary Policy. *District of Columbia* (7th of 8 D). *Judiciary* (13th of 21 D). Subcommittees: Administrative Law and Governmental Relations; Immigration, Refugees and International Law (Chairman). *Veteran's Affairs* (17th of 21). Subcommittee: Hospitals and Health Care. *Select Committee on Children, Youth and Families* (10th of 18 D).

Group Ratings

	ADA	ACLU	COPE	CFA	LCV	ACU	NTLC	NSI	COC	CEI
1988	100	91	94	82	100	4	16	0	43	17
1987	92	—	93	86	—	0	—	—	7	13

National Journal Ratings

	1988 LIB — 1988 CONS		1987 LIB — 1987 CONS	
Economic	67% —	30%	67% —	32%
Social	86% —	0%	72% —	27%
Foreign	79% —	16%	81% —	0%

Key Votes

1) Homeless $	AGN	5) Ban Drug Test	AGN	9) SDI Research	AGN
2) Gephardt Amdt	FOR	6) Drug Death Pen	AGN	10) Ban Chem Weaps	FOR
3) Deficit Reduc	FOR	7) Handgun Sales	AGN	11) Aid to Contras	AGN
4) Kill Plnt Clsng Notice	AGN	8) Ban D.C. Abort $	AGN	12) Nuclear Testing	FOR

Election Results

1988 general	Bruce A. Morrison (D)	147,394	(66%)	($506,799)
	Gerard B. Patton (R)	74,275	(34%)	($116,117)
1988 primary	Bruce A. Morrison (D), nominated by convention			
1986 general	Bruce A. Morrison (D)	114,276	(70%)	($567,868)
	Ernest J. Diette, Jr. (R)	49,806	(30%)	($14,307)

FOURTH DISTRICT

Each morning at the railroad station in Stamford the expensively dressed commuters getting on the train to New York are outnumbered by the more diverse lot getting off the trains and searching for a bus to take them to the corporate headquarters or the mirror-glassed office park where they work in Connecticut. What was 50 years ago a commuter suburb is now the center of one of the nation's hottest white collar job areas, as corporations flee the high taxes and costs of New York and relocate in airy settings in what once were almost exclusively residential suburbs but now make up one of the booming office centers in the United States.

This is Lower Fairfield County, a string of diverse towns along the New Haven Railroad line just above Long Island Sound. Politically, this was the Republican stronghold in Connecticut for years, one of the most affluent parts of the nation, a land of broad, well-manicured lawns sweeping down to Long Island Sound, of establishment Greenwich and woodsy New Canaan and artsy-craftsy Westport. Today real estate prices are higher—far higher—than ever, as New York's glitzy elite competes for prime property; most of the people who work in the new office buildings can't afford to live nearby. That means that, despite the commercial growth in Stamford and Greenwich and Fairfield, voters here are still oriented to New York, not Connecticut; they watch New York, not New Haven or Hartford, TV stations; they are Yankees, not Red Sox, fans; their political attitudes are shaped by what is happening in the City, not in Connecticut. Hartford is a lot farther away than Grand Central Station, and the major politicians produced by Greenwich—Senator Prescott Bush and his son George, Senator Lowell Weicker—lived very much in the New York orbit.

The 4th Congressional District of Connecticut is made up of the string of towns along the Sound plus the old industrial (but also park-laden) city of Bridgeport. Politics here was once a battle between factory workers and railroad commuters, back in the 1940s when Clare Boothe Luce won the seat and used her platform to denounce Franklin D. Roosevelt. Nowadays there are fewer factory workers and not so many commuters, and politics is more complicated. High-income voters in artsy-craftsy Westport are more liberal on cultural and foreign issues than blue-collar voters in Bridgeport; economic hard times may affect middle-income neighborhoods in Fairfield but not woodsy New Canaan; new rich are always replacing old rich in Greenwich, the Henry Luces and Prescott Bushes (new rich in their time) giving way to the Donald Trumps and the Ivan Lendls.

The political diversity of this district became apparent in the fight for the seat after the death in May 1987 of Stewart McKinney, the first member of Congress to die of AIDS, a liberal Republican who left his name on an act to help the homeless. The Democratic nominee, legislator Christine Niedermeier, grew up in working-class Bridgeport, and taking conservative stands on cultural issues won 46% against McKinney in 1986; she beat a black state Senator from Bridgeport in the July 1987 primary. The winner of the four-way Republican primary was legislator Christopher Shays, a former aide to Lowell Weicker and Congressman Paul Findley, a bitter critic of Israel. He was outspent by Niedermeier, but she managed to alienate liberals without gaining the trust of conservatives, and Shays won the August special 57%–42%.

Shays seems to be a Republican in the Weicker mode; quieter, perhaps, but still liable to make waves. He went to the length in 1985 of going to jail for three days to protest a corrupt judicial system; he is independent to the point of protest on occasion, and publicly criticized Republican leader Robert Michel when he didn't get the committee assignment he wanted. His record in his first year was arguably the most liberal of House Republicans. Shays won a full term in 1988 with 72%, even carrying Bridgeport, but he was saddened by Weicker's defeat—and Weicker's loss of many ordinarily Republican votes in the 4th suggests that sometimes a Republican can get too independent for his own good.

The People: Est. Pop. 1986: 511,300, dn. 1.4% 1980–86; Pop. 1980: 518,577, dn. 4.8% 1970–80. Households (1980): 74% family, 37% with children, 59% married couples; 38.8% housing units rented; median monthly rent: $230; median house value: $98,500. Voting age pop. (1980): 384,352; 9% Black, 6% Spanish origin, 1% Asian origin.

1988 Presidential Vote: Bush (R) 128,702   (57%)
Dukakis (D). 96,177   (42%)

Rep. Christopher Shays (R)

Elected Aug. 1987; b. Oct. 18, 1945, Stamford; home, Stamford; Principia Col., B.A. 1968, N.Y.U., M.B.A. 1974, M.P.A. 1978; Protestant; married (Betsi).

Career: Peace Corps 1968–70; Aide to Mayor of Trumbull, CT 1971–72; CT House of Reps., 1974-86.

Offices: 1531 LHOB 20515, 202-225-5541. Also 10 Middle St., Bridgeport 06604, 203-579-5870; 888 Washington Blvd., Stamford 06901, 203-357-8277; and 125 East Ave., Norwalk 06851, 203-866-6469.

Committees: *Government Operations* (9th of 15 R). Subcommittees: Employment and Housing; Legislation and National Security. *Science, Space and Technology* (16th of 19 R). Subcommittees: Natural Resources, Agriculture Research and Environment; Transportation, Aviation and Materials. *Select Committee on Narcotics Abuse and Control* (10th of 12 R).

Group Ratings

	ADA	ACLU	COPE	CFA	LCV	ACU	NTLC	NSI	COC	CEI
1988	90	78	70	82	89	24	58	40	57	39
1987	*	—	78	*	—	67	—	—	40	36

National Journal Ratings

	1988 LIB — 1988 CONS		1987 LIB — 1987 CONS	
Economic	35%	64%	*	*
Social	73%	25%	78%	0%
Foreign	49%	51%	*	*

Key Votes

1) Homeless $	—	5) Ban Drug Test	—	9) SDI Research	—
2) Gephardt Amdt	—	6) Drug Death Pen	AGN	10) Ban Chem Weaps	—
3) Deficit Reduc	AGN	7) Handgun Sales	AGN	11) Aid to Contras	AGN
4) Kill Plnt Clsng Notice	FOR	8) Ban D.C. Abort $	AGN	12) Nuclear Testing	AGN

Election Results

1988 general	Christopher Shays (R)	147,843	(72%)	($372,680)
	Roger Pearson (D)	55,751	(27%)	($44,410)
1988 primary	Christopher Shays (R), nominated by convention			
1987 special	Christopher Shays (R)	50,518	(57%)	
	Christine M. Niedermeier (D)	37,293	(42%)	
1986 general	Stewart B. McKinney (R)	77,212	(54%)	($534,663)
	Christine M. Niedermeier (D)	66,999	(46%)	($305,822)

FIFTH DISTRICT

Connecticut's 5th Congressional District is a slice of the stony hills where for 300 years its residents have been making comfortable livings in a cold land by tinkering, inventing, and precision fabricating. The talent seems to go with the soil: new ethnic groups now live in the place of the old Yankees, and old products that lose their markets are replaced by new. Danbury, at the western edge of the district, was once the nation's leading producer of hats; now it cuts almost no felt but is a major corporate headquarters city. The biggest of these cities, Waterbury, was until recently the nation's largest producer of brass products and one of its major clockmakers; the last of Waterbury's Big Three brass fabricators shut down in 1985, leaving less than 1,000 workers in a local industry that once employed 20,000 here; but the city is more prosperous than ever, with a low unemployment rate and a high level of satisfaction with the economic policies of the Republican Administration. The towns of the Naugatuck Valley used the river's fast-flowing waters to make things in the 19th century; now they are adapting to the high-tech world of the late 20th.

After the Revolution, this part of Connecticut was Yankee country. Its voters—first Federalists, later Whigs, then Republicans—were men who wanted to stop revolutionaries like Thomas Jefferson and Andrew Jackson from putting into effect their newfangled ideas, even as they themselves, in their factories, were making newfangled machines and products. By the 1940s Yankees were in a political minority, replaced by Democrats who went to Mass, lived in traditional ethnic neighborhoods, supported the New Deal, and revered John F. Kennedy. Now, as ethnic discrimination vanishes and market capitalism (and the Pentagon) produces new and unanticipated prosperity, this part of Connecticut has been moving perceptibly to the right. In the Kennedy and Johnson years the 5th was a solidly Democratic district. By the 1980s, with the Democratic factory towns balanced off by the smaller, still Yankee rural towns and by the wide Republican margins in the high-income woodsy suburbs of Weston, Wilton, and Ridgefield, it became Republican: in 1988 it gave George Bush a significantly higher percentage than the other Connecticut districts. The 5th District seat changed partisan hands in 1972, 1978, and 1984. But the Republican who holds it now seems likely to continue to do so.

He is John Rowland, still the youngest member of Congress as he was when he was first elected in 1984 at 27, who describes himself as a "Waterbury rat." He is from a political family: his grandfather, as Republican Controller of Waterbury, exposed the Democrats' shenanigans. One year out of college, while working in his father's insurance business, Rowland ran for the legislature and ousted a veteran Democrat; two years later he was a minority whip; two years after that he was in Congress. He speaks in the authentic language of the vast American middle class, eager to get ineligibles off the welfare rolls, determined not to deny college loans to students in families with incomes over $32,500. He is a strongly partisan politician who is also ready to break ranks with his party at almost any time.

That means he has caused trouble in the House for the leadership—of both parties. He was not shy about opposing the administration on Social Security or urging President Reagan to fire Edwin Meese; he signed up to support Claude Pepper's long-term health care bill. He has done some grandstanding on the POW issue, and he has urged more generous programs for Vietnam and other veterans. But he has mostly supported the Administration on defense votes—which probably helped him get on the House Armed Services Committee in 1987, the first Connecticut member there in 18 years. All of this means that Rowland is not a part of the New Right: "school prayer and those issues, I don't get excited about them," he says. He is against abortion and for the Equal Rights Amendment. And his opposition to drug use does not lead him to support absolute "user accountability"; he says he knows too many contemporaries who have used drugs and doesn't favor such a punitive approach.

But the leaders he really irked—and caught off guard—were the Democrats. In early September 1988, after George Bush had been attacking Michael Dukakis for vetoing a bill requiring teachers to lead students in the Pledge of Allegiance to the flag, Rowland rose in the House and proposed that the House say the Pledge every day. Kenneth Gray, in the chair, ruled this out of order, and his ruling was sustained on a party line vote; but Speaker Jim Wright, uneasy about leaving his Democrats vulnerable to the charge of voting against the Pledge, announced that the House would say it twice a week. This episode kept the Pledge issue on the TV newscasts for another day—which didn't hurt Bush.

Rowland won the seat in 1984, catching incumbent William Ratchford off guard, and benefiting from Connecticut's straight-party lever. He held it with 61% in 1986 and 74% against a former Meriden mayor in 1988—running far ahead of Bush. He has stayed in close touch with the district, and may consider running for governor in 1990, or even for senator in 1992 or 1994.

The People: Est. Pop. 1986: 546,400, up 5.3% 1980–86; Pop. 1980: 518,700, up 8.2% 1970–80. Households (1980): 78% family, 42% with children, 65% married couples; 32.2% housing units rented; median monthly rent: $179; median house value: $70,200. Voting age pop. (1980): 372,002; 4% Black, 3% Spanish origin.

1988 Presidential Vote:
Bush (R)	141,664	(58%)
Dukakis (D)	97,553	(40%)

Rep. John G. Rowland (R)

Elected 1984; b. May 24, 1957, Waterbury; home, Waterbury; Villanova U., B.S. 1979; Roman Catholic; married (Deborah).

Career: Insur. agent, 1979–84; CT House of Reps., 1980–84.

Offices: 329 CHOB 20515, 202-225-3822. Also 135 Grand St., Waterbury 06720, 203-573-1418.

Committees: *Armed Services* (14th of 21 R). Subcommittees: Procurement and Military Nuclear Systems; Seapower and Strategic and Critical Metals. *Veterans' Affairs* (9th of 13 R). Subcommittees: Hospitals and Health Care; Housing and Memorial Affairs. *Select Committee on Intelligence* (6th of 7 R). Subcommittee: Legislation.

Group Ratings

	ADA	ACLU	COPE	CFA	LCV	ACU	NTLC	NSI	COC	CEI
1988	45	61	51	82	63	60	71	100	54	39
1987	28	—	49	36	—	52	—	—	73	56

National Journal Ratings

	1988 LIB — 1988 CONS		1987 LIB — 1987 CONS	
Economic	34%	— 65%	36%	— 63%
Social	49%	— 51%	40%	— 59%
Foreign	16%	— 78%	36%	— 63%

Key Votes

1) Homeless $	FOR	5) Ban Drug Test	AGN	9) SDI Research	FOR
2) Gephardt Amdt	AGN	6) Drug Death Pen	FOR	10) Ban Chem Weaps	AGN
3) Deficit Reduc	AGN	7) Handgun Sales	AGN	11) Aid to Contras	FOR
4) Kill Plnt Clsng Notice	FOR	8) Ban D.C. Abort $	FOR	12) Nuclear Testing	AGN

Election Results

1988 general	John G. Rowland (R)	163,729	(74%)	($375,660)
	Joseph Marinan, Jr. (D)	58,612	(26%)	($54,524)
1988 primary	John G. Rowland, Jr. (D), nominated by convention			
1986 general	John G. Rowland (R)	98,664	(61%)	($425,746)
	Jim Cohen (D)	63,371	(39%)	($344,285)

SIXTH DISTRICT

From the urban corridor alongside the Connecticut River north of Hartford to the tiny Litchfield County towns just north and west of industrial Waterbury and Danbury and Bristol, extends the 6th Congressional District of Connecticut. This is an ethnic hodgepodge. Enfield and Windsor Locks, north of Hartford, are heavily Italian-American; New Britain, not far southwest of Hartford, is heavily Polish-American; the mill towns of Torrington and Winsted, in the clefts of river valleys amid mountains, are a mixture (Winsted is the hometown of Lebanese-American Ralph Nader). Interspersed are the Yankee Republican towns of Litchfield County, whose proud houses bear witness to its prosperity in the Revolutionary era, and whose communities and hidden estates are now sought out by elite New Yorkers. Also here are some high-income suburbs of Hartford like Farmington, home of the famous Miss Porter's School.

The 6th District has produced a series of interesting and successful congressmen, including two governors (Republican Thomas Meskill and Democrat Ella Grasso). The current incumbent, Republican Nancy Johnson, is in that tradition. She has also been an active and creative legislator. On roll calls she has compiled a record midway between standard Republicans and Democrats. But more important are the issues on which she has taken a lead.

The most prominent are child care and welfare reform. She is the lead House sponsor of the Republicans' major child care bill, which would give the states $250 million in block grants but which, unlike Christopher Dodd's ABC bill, would set up no federal standards. She also has a shorter-term reform, to change the day care tax credit by eliminating it for the highest income taxpayers and giving the $300 million saved as vouchers to mothers not on welfare but with incomes too low to take advantage of the credit. As part of welfare reform, she would require mothers to enter part-time training when their children are six months, but in return would pay for day care for a year while they are working at jobs that pay up to 150% of the poverty level. The principles behind these ideas are that those closest to the children, not federal authorities, can make the best decisions about child care, and that benefits should be targeted toward the needy and not lavished on the wealthy.

Johnson has also worked on budget issues, working with the 92 Group of liberal Republicans to produce their own budget. She is against further sharp cuts, but would like to hold down spending increases, and she would accept a small tax hike. On military issues, she tends to support the administration, though occasionally dissenting; her toughest vote, she says, was supporting aid to the contras. On cultural issues, she is more liberal, supporting the Equal Rights Amendment and abortion. One pet cause is the bearing industry, which has been losing jobs in Connecticut: with John Spratt of South Carolina she set up a Bearing Caucus. She charges that foreigners have been dumping bearings in the United States, and she persuaded the Pentagon to say it would buy only U.S.-made bearings for eight years. Johnson tried and failed earlier to get on the Armed Services Committee; but in December 1988 she got on the Ways and Means Committee, where she serves with her next-door neighbor (and possible future statewide rival), Democrat Barbara Kennelly.

Johnson, a doctor's wife and a teacher, raised three children and was active in charitable and community affairs before she was elected to the legislature in 1976 from heavily Democratic and industrial New Britain. Here being a woman may have helped, by suggesting that she would be somewhat more compassionate and generous than most Republicans. When 6th District Congressman Toby Moffett ran against Senator Lowell Weicker in 1982, Johnson beat a nuclear freeze organizer for the House seat. Since then she has won by wide margins, against a strong opponent in 1984 and weak ones in 1986 and 1988. She is mentioned as a candidate for governor in 1990, or perhaps as an opponent for one of Connecticut's two Democratic senators in 1992 or 1994. In the meantime she obviously has a safe seat and steady work.

The People: Est. Pop. 1986: 540,100, up 4.4% 1980–86; Pop. 1980: 517,146, up 6.4% 1970–80. Households (1980): 77% family, 39% with children, 65% married couples; 30.6% housing units rented; median monthly rent: $185; median house value: $63,300. Voting age pop. (1980): 378,872; 2% Black, 2% Spanish origin.

1988 Presidential Vote;	Bush (R)	133,709	(53%)
	Dukakis (D)	115,742	(46%)

Rep. Nancy L. Johnson (R)

Elected 1982; b. Jan. 5, 1935, Chicago, IL; home, New Britain; U. of Chicago, 1951–53, Radcliffe Col., B.A. 1957, U. of London, 1957–58; Unitarian; married (Theodore).

Career: Pres., Sheldon Commun. Guidance Clinic; Adjunct Prof., Central CT St. Col.; CT Senate, 1976–82.

Offices: 119 CHOB 20515, 202-225-4476. Also One Grove St., New Britain 06053, 203-223-8412; and 276 Hazard Ave., Enfield 06082, 203-745-5722.

Committees: *Ways and Means* (13th of 13 R). Subcommittees: Health; Human Resources.

Group Ratings

	ADA	ACLU	COPE	CFA	LCV	ACU	NTLC	NSI	COC	CEI
1988	50	74	54	64	56	56	63	90	69	31
1987	44	—	51	36	—	35	—	—	73	57

National Journal Ratings

	1988 LIB — 1988 CONS			1987 LIB — 1987 CONS	
Economic	37%	—	63%	38%	— 62%
Social	57%	—	42%	47%	— 52%
Foreign	37%	—	62%	44%	— 56%

Key Votes

1) Homeless $	FOR	5) Ban Drug Test	AGN	9) SDI Research	FOR
2) Gephardt Amdt	AGN	6) Drug Death Pen	FOR	10) Ban Chem Weaps	AGN
3) Deficit Reduc	AGN	7) Handgun Sales	FOR	11) Aid to Contras	FOR
4) Kill Plnt Clsng Notice	AGN	8) Ban D.C. Abort $	AGN	12) Imig Reform	AGN

Election Results

1988 general	Nancy L. Johnson (R)	157,020	(66%)	($399,370)
	James L. Griffin (D)	78,814	(33%)	($128,853)
1988 primary	Nancy L. Johnson (R), nominated by convention			
1986 general	Nancy L. Johnson (R)	111,304	(64%)	($425,553)
	Paul S. Amenta (D)	62,133	(36%)	($41,840)

DELAWARE

Deep in Delaware's chateau country, the rolling land where mansions sit behind acres of trees, above the cobblestone walls that line the narrow winding roads, is the place where Delaware's wealth creation got started, the site of the gunpowder mill that Eleuthere Irenee du Pont, the practical business-minded son of a dreamy, idealistic French immigrant, built on the banks of Brandywine Creek in 1802. This was the first of the enterprises of the family du Pont, which expanded to become one of America's great munitions and chemical companies, and which made the fortunes of the more than 2,000 of E. I. du Pont's descendants who are alive today.

A half century ago the Du Pont company also made Delaware America's richest state, with per capita income level 73% above the national average. Most heavy industry had bypassed Delaware in the early 20th century, moving inland to sites nearer coal and iron ore, and leaving the Du Pont company and the white-collar business of chartering most of the nation's leading corporations to a state that in 1940 had only 266,000 people, most of them clustered in or near Wilmington. In the postwar years, when more factories were built on low-lying coastlands, and as Du Pont prospered, pioneering new synthetics and plastics (rayon, nylon, cellophane, polyethylene, lucite, teflon: "better living through chemistry"), Delaware grew rapidly with new blue- and white-collar workers. Their comfortable but ordinary incomes diluted the impact of the du Ponts' wealth, and today the income levels of the 622,000 Delawareans are just above the national average—but still far ahead of where they were in 1940.

That this tiny territory—just three counties with a population the size of a congressional district—should be a separate state is one of those American anomalies that continually amaze foreigners. Delaware became a separate entity in the 17th century when three counties along the Delaware River split away from William Penn's Pennsylvania over some squabble. For 100 years it managed to stay separate by pitting Anglican London against Quaker Pennsylvania; it stood tough in the Constitutional Convention for equal representation by state; then it rushed and beat Pennsylvania and New Jersey by a few days to become the first state to ratify the Constitution.

Yet the politics of this small state is arguably a microcosm of the nation. Wilmington is an old-fashioned industrial city with distinct Polish, Italian, and black neighborhoods, heavily Democratic but casting only 10% of the state's votes. The two downstate counties, Kent and Sussex, have a southern air about them; they were once segregationist, have always been hawkish, and cast one-third of the state's votes. Most of the voters live in suburban New Castle County, in all manner of suburbs, from the working-class environs around a steel mill to the chateau country. But for all this diversity there is an intimacy to politics here. Most of Delaware is served by Philadelphia TV, so personal campaigning is still important. And the Thursday after the election is "Return Day," when winning and losing candidates—opponents ride in the same car—come back to the downstate town of Georgetown and receive the bipartisan cheers of the voters. Delaware chooses its small number of national convention delegates by caucus. Thinly attended, the caucuses were won by Jesse Jackson and George Bush in 1988.

Governor. Clearly the most influential governor of Delaware in the last generation has been Pete du Pont (officially Pierre S. du Pont IV). He is friendly and affable, crisply articulate, at ease with all sorts of people. He is also cerebral—arguably the brainiest candidate on the 1988 presidential campaign trail. He brings to politics the analytic skills and willingness to challenge with that received wisdom of a science major, which he was in college. When he was first elected to the House in 1970, he seemed a moderate Republican, opposing the Du Pont company on some environmental laws, for example. But he became convinced that government needed

DELAWARE - Congressional District, Counties, and Selected Places — *(1 At Large)*

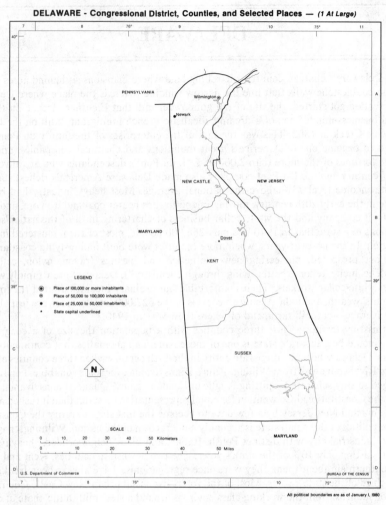

pruning and that the private economy needed to be liberated from overgovernance to be productive, and after he was elected governor in 1976 became an ardent conservative. Du Pont slashed tax rates and revised the state's banking laws to encourage out-of-state banks to move operations here; nationally, he would make Social Security voluntary and phase out farm subsidies.

His policies seemed to stimulate economic growth and were widely popular. Du Pont was reelected with 71% in 1980; his lieutenant governor, Mike Castle, was elected to succeed him with 56% in 1984, even as the Democrats were winning other statewide offices. Castle put through more tax cuts and claimed credit for more new jobs, but he also emphasized spending more on education and helping children in need. He was reelected with 71% in 1988 and brought in his choice as lieutenant governor, Dale E. Wolf.

Senators. William V. Roth is not a household name outside Delaware, nor is he particularly highly regarded in Washington. His career starts back in the 1960s, when some thought the Republican party was on the verge of extinction and almost no one thought it a party of ideas. But he has brought forward many original ideas and can lay claim to having been a successful and innovative senator. Roth's ideas tend to have this in common: their immediate benefit redounds to the suburban middle class which has always been his political base. His most famous initiative was what he calls the Roth-Kemp tax cut, the proposal to cut tax rates 10% every year for three years; he and Jack Kemp got almost every Republican candidate to back it as early as 1978, and Ronald Reagan got it (mostly) passed into law in 1981. Roth, who dislikes deficits, is quick to defend the tax cut as the generator of the 1980s economic growth, and notes that the rich are paying more, not less, in taxes now that rates are down.

Roth's other major stands include an antibusing initiative in the 1970s, co-sponsored by Joseph Biden when the Wilmington area was threatened with a busing order, and a tax credit for college tuitions. In the 1980s he was backing tax-free savings accounts of up to $6,000 a year, IRAs for housewives, and bigger business deductions for capital spending combined with what amounts to a value-added tax. Yet Roth is not always a party-line Republican. He supported the Democrats' factory closing notification provision in the 1988 trade bill, even over President Reagan's veto, and as ranking Republican on Governmental Affairs has attacked wasteful Pentagon spending. He called for delay in the reflagging of Kuwaiti tankers in the Persian Gulf. He co-sponsored the 1988 law prohibiting sludge dumping off the Atlantic coast and, further afield, was against oil drilling in the Coastal Plain of Alaska's Arctic National Wildlife Refuge. On the Finance Committee he ranks behind Bob Packwood and Bob Dole, and does not take a lead role on major legislation; but he was active in knitting together some of the provisions of the trade bill. On Government Operations he opposes repeal of the Hatch Act and supported the military base-closing bill that passed Congress in October 1988.

Delaware had a spirited, though ultimately not suspenseful, Senate race in 1988. Two Democrats vied to oppose Roth: Samuel Beard, a businessman with backing from Democratic pols, and Lieutenant Governor S. B. Woo, a Chinese-American scientist and political maverick. Initial returns in the September primary showed Beard ahead by some 2,700 votes. But it turned out that one precinct reported 2,828 votes for Beard when he only had 28, and after a recount Woo won by 71 votes. Woo argued that he had a special insight into science issues and American-Asian relations. But Roth, campaigning blandly as a backer of Social Security and purveyor of constituency services and charging that Woo favored a tax increase, won his fourth term at 67 with 62%, the highest percentage of his career.

About Delaware's junior Senator, Joseph Biden, it had long been the conventional wisdom in Washington that he was a gifted politician but not much of a policymaker and something of a phony as a human being. But the highs and lows, tragedies and triumphs that Biden suffered and won in 1987 and 1988 suggested that something more nearly the opposite is true: his political talents turned out to be more limited than either he or his detractors thought, his skills as a policymaker are notably greater, and his personal strengths, which perhaps have been the foundation of his political strength in Delaware all along, have turned out to be impressive.

Biden came into the national spotlight not so much when he announced for President in the spring of 1987 as when he was forced to leave the race in the fall. His strength as a candidate was his capacity to move an audience emotionally; he summoned up memories of the Kennedys, of the civil rights revolution and the opposition to the Vietnam war, and proclaimed that he was ready to take up where his generation's heroes left off. But this was hyperbole and overreaching: Biden, born in 1942, is a little too old to be a baby boomer; he supported integration in Wilmington but never went south; far from being an anti-war demonstrator, he was a desultory law student and a young suburban lawyer and family man in the late 1960s. Then in September 1987, a videotape circulated by Dukakis campaign manager John Sasso showed excerpts of Biden mouthing, almost word for word, a speech by British Labor party leader Neil Kinnock about how he was the first in his family to attend college—a refrain that resonates better in classbound Britain than in upwardly mobile America and which in any case didn't quite fit Biden, one of whose ancestors was a state senator in Pennsylvania. More videotape came out, showing Biden in New Hampshire claiming to have been a good student in law school. In a rush, he was forced to leave the presidential race.

But he did it with some grace and under the sternest of pressure. For he was in the middle of conducting, as chairman of the Senate Judiciary Committee, confirmation hearings on Judge Robert Bork's nomination to the Supreme Court. The hearings turned out to be as exhaustive an examination of constitutional law as the Senate has seen and Biden, never previously a constitutional scholar, mastered the issues and came up with his own view that the Constitution protects an undefined zone of personal privacy. Biden was careful, as some his colleagues and allies were not, to avoid the cheap shots and distortions when arguing against Bork. Yet at the same time he used his power to schedule and control the pace of the hearings shrewdly and to Bork's disadvantage. Without fraying the good working relations he enjoyed with ranking Republican Strom Thurmond, Biden helped move the critical votes on the committee—Democrats Howell Heflin and Dennis DeConcini, Republican Arlen Specter—away from Bork and dealt the Reagan Administration a serious defeat.

This was Biden's strongest performance since he was elected to the Senate at 29 in 1972 (he turned 30 by the time the term began). The popular incumbent, Caleb Boggs, seemed ready to retire, while the young challenger had energy, an attractive extended family, and an ability to connect with voters' emotions. A stutterer in school, he speaks now easily and fluently, and often with emotive force: in a political era dominated by the cool medium of television, he is a hot politician. But that was not a disadvantage in Delaware then, when no one bought Philadelphia TV time and most campaigning was in person. And Biden is not all mouth: he also has an acute political ear, a sure instinct for what is troubling voters, and a talent for articulating their complaints.

Biden has also had more than his share of tragedy. The month after he was first elected to the Senate his first wife and daughter died in an auto accident. And in February 1988, just days before the Iowa caucuses and New Hampshire primary in which he would have been competing had he not been forced to leave the race, he had to have emergency surgery to repair a life-threatening aneurysm in the brain. More surgery was needed later in the year, and he was not able to return to the Senate until the fall of 1988, with his health apparently fully restored.

In retrospect, Biden has said that he wasn't prepared to run for president, that he was not ready to run a national campaign and was not entirely prepared on the issues either. He was brought into the race more by the opportunity it presented to him than by the stature he brought to it. Now he says he will not run in 1992. He remains an important senator. As chairman of Judiciary, he has controlled the timing and pace—it has gotten very slow at times—of confirmation hearings for Republican-appointed judges. He has been against a constitutional amendment on abortion and for measures to limit court ordered busing; he was successful after at least six years getting his proposal for a drug enforcement director (or "drug czar") included in the 1988 antidrug law.

On Foreign Relations, his other plum committee assignment, Biden has concentrated on arms control. He was a staunch supporter of the SALT II treaty and in 1988 made a point of insisting on an amendment saying that the meanings of the INF treaty should be determined by administration statements—a slap at the Reagan theory that the ABM treaty means something different from what the Nixon Administration said at the time. On other foreign issues he has been less active, generally joining Democrats in their criticisms of the Republican administrations. On economic issues Biden has followed the mainstream of his party, voting for the more generous domestic spending alternatives but expressing some doubts about the effectiveness of government action. On cultural issues, he does not always support positions associated with liberal Democrats. On many issues Biden is torn between the advice of his political allies and advisers in Washington and by the impulses of the people he came from in Delaware.

Biden is up for reelection in 1990. Delaware Republicans had some hopes that the collapse of his presidential candidacy would hurt him at home. But by early 1989 they had not come up with a candidate, and his gallantry in defeat and illness probably strengthens his already strong position at home.

Congressman. Delaware's only congressman is Democrat Thomas Carper, who has been an active and sometimes effective legislator. He has used his seat on the Banking Committee to back bills letting banks into the securities business (much desired in Delaware) and to get rid of lead paint in public housing. On Merchant Marine he has pursued other environmental causes: preventing ocean sludge dumping (popular in Delaware's beach resorts), investigating the Atlantic dolphin epidemic, and questioning oil exploration in the Arctic National Wildlife Refuge. He has taken a lead as well on major issues outside his committees' venues. On foreign policy, he has opposed contra aid but has advanced ideas for some humanitarian aid. On welfare reform, he unveiled his own plan, much less costly than the Ways and Means version ($2.5 versus $6.2 billion) and with more work requirements, the basics of which eventually wound up in the bill. He decries the deficit and favors a balanced budget amendment and line-item veto.

Carper's stands have not always left him in the good graces of House Democratic leaders, but he has run well in Delaware. He won the seat in 1982 by beating Thomas Evans, who admitted an affair with Paula Parkinson, the lobbyist whose picture appeared in *Playboy*, and in the years since he has become unbeatable; he beat Elise du Pont, an AID administrator and Pete's wife, 58%–41% in 1984 and won 2 to 1 in 1986 and 1988. Many think he would be a strong Senate candidate, but he declined to run against William Roth in 1988. His next chance may not come until 1994, when he will have to weigh giving up a dozen years of House seniority to make the race.

Presidential politics. Back when Delaware was the nation's richest state, it was strongly Republican in national elections, voting for Hoover in 1932 and Dewey in 1948. But Delaware has been competitive in state elections since the Federalists were battling the Jeffersonians, and in Presidential elections over the last 30 years it has come close to matching the national result. Wilmington and the downstate counties, blacks (14% of the population) and southern-oriented whites, provide a divided base for the Democrats, counterbalanced by the Republicans' base in the affluent suburbs. Delaware voted for Kennedy in 1960, Nixon in 1968, Carter in 1976, and Bush in 1988—as good a barometer as any other state. So maybe it's not unfitting that Delaware produced two Presidential candidates, Republican Pete du Pont and Democrat Joseph Biden, in the 1988 cycle. Neither seems likely to run again in 1992, but both are young enough, and may be interested enough, to try in 1996.

The People: Est. Pop. 1988: 660,000; Pop. 1980: 594,338, up 11.1% 1980–88 and 8.4% 1970–80; 0.26% of U.S. total, 47th largest. 14% with 1–3 yrs. col., 16% with 4+ yrs. col.; 11.9% below poverty level. Single ancestry: 13% English, 6% Irish, German, 4% Italian, 2% Polish, 1% French, Scottish. Households (1980): 75% family, 41% with children, 61% married couples; 30.9% housing units rented; median monthly rent: $202; median house value: $44,600. Voting age pop. (1980): 427,743; 14% Black, 1% Spanish origin, 1% Asian origin. Registered voters (1988): 318,362; 138,878 D (44%), 114,833 R (36%); 64,651 unaffiliated and minor parties (20%).

1988 Share of Federal Tax Burden: $2,788,000,000; 0.32% of U.S. total, 43d largest.

1988 Share of Federal Expenditures

	Total		Non-Defense		Defense	
Total Expend	$2,088m	(0.24%)	$1,644m	(0.25%)	$528m	(0.23%)
St/Lcl Grants	319m	(0.28%)	318m	(0.28%)	1m	(0.46%)
Salary/Wages	336m	(0.25%)	182m	(0.27%)	154m	(0.27%)
Pymnts to Indiv	1,066m	(0.26%)	1,011m	(0.26%)	55m	(0.30%)
Procurement	318m	(0.17%)	85m	(0.18%)	318m	(0.17%)
Research/Other	49m	(0.13%)	49m	(0.13%)	1m	(0.13%)

Political Lineup: Governor, Michael N. Castle (R); Lt. Gov., Dale E. Wolf (R); Secy. of State, Michael E. Harkins (R); Atty. Gen., Charles M. Oberly, III (D); Treasurer, Janet C. Rzewnicki (R); Controller, R. Thomas Wagner, Jr. (R). State Senate, 21 (13 D and 8 R); State House of Representatives, 41 (23 R and 18 D). Senators, William V. Roth, Jr. (R) and Joseph R. Biden, Jr. (D). Representative, 1 D at large.

1988 Presidential Vote

Bush (R) 139,689 (56%)
Dukakis (D). 108,532 (43%)

1984 Presidential Vote

Reagan (R) 152,190 (60%)
Mondale (D) 101,656 (40%)

GOVERNOR

Gov. Michael N. Castle (R)

Elected 1984, term expires Jan. 1993; b. July 2, 1939, Wilmington; home, Dover; Hamilton Col., B.A. 1961, Georgetown U., J.D. 1964; Roman Catholic; single.

Career: DE Dpty. Atty. Gen., 1965–66; DE House of Reps., 1966–68; DE Senate, 1968–76, Minor. Ldr., 1975–76; DE Lt. Gov., 1980–84.

Offices: Legislative Hall, Dover 19901, 302-736-4101.

Election Results

1988 gen.	Michael N. Castle (R)	169,733	(71%)
	Jacob Kreshtool (D)	70,236	(29%)
1988 prim.	Michael N. Castle (R), nominated by convention		
1984 gen.	Michael N. Castle (R)	135,250	(56%)
	William T. Quillen (D)	108,315	(44%)

SENATORS

Sen. William V. Roth, Jr. (R)

Elected 1970, seat up 1994; b. July 22, 1921, Great Falls, MT; home, Wilmington; U. of OR, B.A. 1944, Harvard U., M.B.A., LL.B. 1947; Episcopalian; married (Jane).

Career: Army, WWII; Practicing atty.; Chmn., DE Repub. State Cmtee., 1961-64; U.S. House of Reps., 1967-70.

Offices: 104 HSOB 20510, 202-224-2441. Also 3021 Fed. Bldg., 844 King St., Wilmington 19801, 302-573-6291; 2215 Fed. Bldg., 300 S. New St., Dover 19901, 302-674-3308; and 2 S. Bedford St., Georgetown 19947, 302-856-7690.

Committees: *Banking, Housing and Urban Affairs* (7th of 9 R). Subcommittee: International Finance and Monetary Policy. *Finance* (3d of 9 R). Subcommittees: Health for Families and the Uninsured; International Trade; Taxation and Debt Management (Ranking Member). *Governmental Affairs* (Ranking Member of 6 R). Subcommittee: Investigations (Ranking Member). *Joint Economic Committee.* Subcommittees: International Economic Policy; Economic Growth, Trade and Taxes; Economic Goals and Intergovernmental Policy.

Group Ratings

	ADA	ACLU	COPE	CFA	LCV	ACU	NTLC	NSI	COC	CEI
1988	20	32	20	50	80	60	67	100	57	47
1987	20	—	19	50	—	80	—	—	94	68

National Journal Ratings

	1988 LIB — 1988 CONS		1987 LIB — 1987 CONS	
Economic	39%	— 59%	18%	— 81%
Social	22%	— 76%	41%	— 58%
Foreign	35%	— 64%	29%	— 68%

Key Votes

1) Cut Aged Housing $	AGN	5) Bork Nomination	FOR	9) SDI Funding	FOR
2) Override Hwy Veto	AGN	6) Ban Plastic Guns	FOR	10) Ban Chem Weaps	FOR
3) Kill Plnt Clsng Notice	FOR	7) Deny Abortions	FOR	11) Aid To Contras	FOR
4) Min Wage Increase	FOR	8) Japanese Reparations	AGN	12) Reagan Defense $	FOR

Election Results

1988 general	William V. Roth, Jr. (R)	151,115	(62%)	($1,942,119)
	S.B. Woo (D)	92,378	(38%)	($2,235,318)
1988 primary	William V. Roth, Jr. (R), nominated by convention			
1982 general	William V. Roth, Jr. (R)	105,472	(56%)	($797,516)
	David N. Levinson (D)	83,722	(44%)	($777,819)

Sen. Joseph R. Biden, Jr. (D)

Elected 1972, seat up 1990; b. Nov. 20, 1942, Scranton, PA; home, Wilmington; U. of DE, B.A. 1965, Syracuse U., J.D. 1968; Roman Catholic; married (Jill).

Career: Practicing atty., 1968–72; New Castle Cnty. Cncl., 1970–72.

Offices: 489 RSOB 20510, 202-224-5042. Also Fed. Bldg., 844 King St., Wilmington 19801, 302-573-6345; 1101 Fed. Bldg, 300 S. New St., Dover 17901, 302-678-9483; and Box 109, The Circle, Georgetown 19947, 302-856-9275.

Committees: *Foreign Relations* (2d of 10 D). Subcommittees: European Affairs (Chairman); East Asian and Pacific Affairs. *Judiciary* (Chairman of 8 D).

Group Ratings

	ADA	ACLU	COPE	CFA	LCV	ACU	NTLC	NSI	COC	CEI
1988	*	62	81	*	70	0	29	0	67	7
1987	70	—	81	75	—	0	—	—	17	20

National Journal Ratings

	1988 LIB — 1988 CONS			1987 LIB — 1987 CONS		
Economic	*	—	*	74%	—	0%
Social	*	—	*	87%	—	12%
Foreign	*	—	*	73%	—	26%

Key Votes

1) Cut Aged Housing $	—	5) Bork Nomination	AGN	9) SDI Funding	AGN
2) Override Hwy Veto	FOR	6) Ban Plastic Guns	AGN	10) Ban Chem Weaps	—
3) Kill Plnt Clsng Notice	AGN	7) Deny Abortions	—	11) Aid To Contras	—
4) Min Wage Increase	FOR	8) Japanese Reparations	—	12) Reagan Defense $	—

Election Results

1984 general	Joseph R. Biden, Jr. (D)	147,831	(60%)	($1,602,052)
	John M. Burris (R)	98,101	(40%)	($816,484)
1984 primary	Joseph R. Biden, Jr. (D), nominated by convention			
1978 general	Joseph R. Biden, Jr. (D)	93,930	(58%)	($494,718)
	James H. Baxter, Jr. (R)	66,479	(41%)	($206,250)

REPRESENTATIVE

Rep. Thomas R. Carper (D)

Elected 1982; b. Jan. 23, 1947, Beckley, WV; home, New Castle; OH State U., B.A. 1968, U. of DE, M.B.A. 1975; Presbyterian; married (Martha).

Career: Naval Flight Officer, 1968–73; Treas., James R. Soles for Congress Campaign, 1974; Industrial Devel. Specialist, DE Div. of Econ. Devel., 1975–76; DE Treas., 1976–82.

Offices: 131 CHOB 20515, 202-225-4165. Also 5021 Fed. Bldg., Wilmington 19801, 302-573-6181; and Fed. Bldg., 300 S. New St., Dover 19901, 302-736-1666.

Committees: *Banking, Finance and Urban Affairs* (17th of 31 D). Subcommittees: Financial Institutions Supervision, Regulation and Insurance; Housing and Community Development; International Finance, Trade and Monetary Policy. *Merchant Marine and Fisheries* (12th of 25 D). Subcommittees: Coast Guard and Navigation; Fisheries and Wildlife Conservation and the Environment.

Group Ratings

	ADA	ACLU	COPE	CFA	LCV	ACU	NTLC	NSI	COC	CEI
1988	75	74	71	82	88	24	38	30	64	29
1987	72	—	70	79	—	9	—	—	53	27

National Journal Ratings

	1988 LIB — 1988 CONS		1987 LIB — 1987 CONS	
Economic	40%	— 58%	45%	— 55%
Social	72%	— 27%	73%	— 22%
Foreign	79%	— 16%	59%	— 40%

Key Votes

1) Homeless $	AGN	5) Ban Drug Test	AGN	9) SDI Research	AGN
2) Gephardt Amdt	FOR	6) Drug Death Pen	FOR	10) Ban Chem Weaps	AGN
3) Deficit Reduc	AGN	7) Handgun Sales	AGN	11) Aid to Contras	AGN
4) Kill Plnt Clsng Notice	AGN	8) Ban D.C. Abort $	AGN	12) Nuclear Testing	FOR

Election Results

1988 general	Thomas R. Carper (D)	158,338	(68%)	($371,747)
	James P. Krapf (R)	76,179	(32%)	($184,712)
1988 primary	Thomas R. Carper (D), nominated by convention			
1986 general	Thomas R. Carper (D)	106,351	(66%)	($307,300)
	Thomas S. Neuberger (R)	53,767	(34%)	($270,563)

DISTRICT OF COLUMBIA

Fifty years ago Washington, D.C., was "a city conceived and built as a national government factory and nothing else—producing nothing but paper," writes David Brinkley in his insightful and delightful *Washington Goes to War.* "There was an army of politicians sent to decide what messages the paper would carry, assisted by their own army of couriers and clerks and along with them still another army of paper processors hired at low but steady wages to print, fold, type, bind, file and mail out the paper. This was an army that decamped at dusk and rode the Capital Transit trolleys to small houses bought with $5,000 mortgages at 3% interest and modestly embellished with hydrangeas and Atwater Kent radios. For their children, the Washington track was a segregated public school, Strayer Business College and then on into the government paper factory to work and wait for promotion, annual leave, retirement or pension."

This most political of American cities was then—and in a different way is now—the least political. Then it was apolitical because so many of its residents were civil servants, barred by the Hatch Act from partisan politics, and because the Founders, familiar with contemporary London and Paris mobs, had insisted on giving Congress control of the 10-mile-square enclave they called the District of Columbia. During most of the years since, Congress has kept close control over it, for its own advantage and out of distrust of the city's large black population. For blacks have made up as least one-quarter of metropolitan Washington's population since the 1790s (and today almost three-quarters), and the city was a center for free blacks before and after the Civil War and Emancipation. Radical Republicans gave the District self-government in the era of Reconstruction in 1871, but Governor Alexander ("Boss") Shepherd built great public works and spent the District into bankruptcy, and local self-government ended in 1874. Then during the civil rights revolution of the 1960s, it began to seem absurd to deny Washington, which officially became majority-black in 1960, the vote. So in 1964, Washingtonians began to cast three electoral votes for President and in 1968 they could vote for school board; in 1971 they finally got to elect a non-voting delegate to Congress; in 1974, after the defeat of longtime House District of Columbia Committee chairman John McMillan in his 1972 primary in South Carolina, they got home rule and could, like residents of every other American city, vote for mayor and council.

But Washington entered its second era of self-government with little in the way of local political institutions. It has no serious party organizations, being so overwhelmingly Democratic—not only more Democratic than any state, but more Democratic than any county—that neither party sees any advantage in centralized action. The District voted 83%–14% for Michael Dukakis over George Bush in 1988 while the rest of the country was voting 53%–46% the other way. Another reason for Washington's political underdevelopment is the sense that not much is at stake. Congress retains, under the Constitution, final authority over the District, and in 1988 it actually used it, forcing the District to repeal one law that required Georgetown University to sanction homosexual organizations and another that banned insurance companies from discriminating against AIDS virus carriers. Also, the District's prosecutor and judges are federal appointees, not responsible to the voters, and there are federal police forces that patrol buildings, embassies, parks and Capitol Hill.

But the most important cause for the District's political underdevelopment has been the failings of its leading politicians, most spectacularly that of Mayor Marion Barry. First elected in 1978, Barry came to office with credentials from the civil rights movement and from higher education. If he was known for wearing a dashiki and leading protests as head of an antipoverty

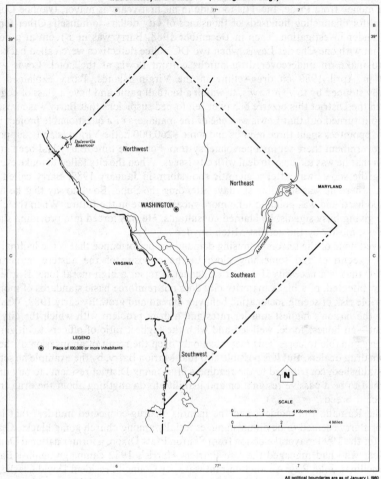

**DISTRICT OF COLUMBIA — Delegate District,
Quadrants, and Place — *(1 Delegate At Large)***

program called Pride, Inc., this son of a single mother who worked as a cleaning woman in Memphis had also completed all but the thesis requirements for a Ph.D. in chemistry at the University of Tennessee. In the three-way primary in which he won the mayoralty, Barry won similar percentages from the District's black majority and from the 30% of its voters, most of them in Ward 3 west of Rock Creek, who are white. Barry was not connected to the local black professional class, which for generations had led institutions like Howard University, Freedmen's Hospital and leading black churches. But he did have the makings of an exemplary role model for young people in the black underclass concentrated in Ward 8 east of the Anacostia River, while at the same time showing the administrative talents to rationalize the city's budget process and to help stimulate the city's extensive downtown development and build its Convention Center.

Yet by early 1989, Barry had gotten himself into political trouble and had seen his city get into terrible real life trouble in ways that overshadowed his earlier accomplishments and potential. Over the years, scandal did tend to accumulate around Barry. His first wife went to jail for skimming money from Pride, Inc. His top aide in his first years as mayor, Ivanhoe Donaldson, went to jail for channeling hundreds of thousands of city dollars to himself. Other former top aides are under investigation. Then in December 1988, Barry was in a room at a downtown Ramada Inn with one Charles Lewis, when two DC police detectives were called back from an attempt to make an undercover drug purchase from Lewis at the hotel. Lewis was later convicted in April 1989 on drug-selling in the Virgin Islands. Barry explained that he occasionally stopped by to visit Lewis, to watch a football game and have a glass of cognac, but for many in the District this bizarre behavior reinforced suspicions that Barry was himself using drugs. And it turned out that Lewis was one of the managers of a questionable project in which top Barry appointees spent three months and some $260,000 in the Virgin Islands, supposedly to help the government there set up a personnel system. For some time, Barry had been giving the impression that he was too busy to deal with city issues. When the city failed to make even a start at clearing the snow away after a gigantic snowstorm in January 1987, Barry called in from California, where he was spending six days attending the Super Bowl, to say that he had been working too hard and was going to take more vacation time in the future. When the city's 911 lines were giving busy signals, he blamed consultants. He was forced into providing shelter for the homeless, mostly by the activist Mitch Snyder.

He showed none of the uncompromising demand for performance that is the hallmark of any successful executive, and something close to the opposite of the austere intolerance for misbehavior that is a necessity if a political leader is to set a high moral tone. If a leader, no matter how talented, of a black majority city does not reinforce basic standards of morality, he runs a terrible risk of seeing sociopathic behavior spread and grow. By early 1989, Washington, D.C., had the nation's highest murder rates and a drug problem with which the city's police department—an honest force, well led and with the highest ratio of officers to citizens in the country—was unable to cope. This may have only been the result of an invasion of the city by out-of-town drug dealers. But it is possible also that Marion Barry, by the example he set and the tone he established, contributed to the readiness of so many District residents to buy drugs and what seemed to be a passive resignation and inability to do anything about the drug trade and the violence it breeds.

After the Ramada Inn incident and the months of drug-connected murders that followed, support for Barry seemed to be diminishing, especially among church-going blacks. Opposition appeared for the 1990 mayoral election from Sharon Pratt Dixon, a former national Democratic Party officer who had managed the late Patricia Harris's 1982 campaign against Barry, and from Councilman John Ray. Another entrant was City Council President David Clarke, a white with a long record of working with blacks going back to the civil rights era, who has genuine support from black voters. Barry's response seemed to be to portray himself as the champion of black voters against whites who want to take over city government—a phantom fear since city government and even the murder wave does not impinge much on the white minority in Washington, and the white voters tend to be liberal on most issues (most of them voted for Walter Mondale in 1984 and George McGovern in 1972). But Barry's strategy tends to pit whites, who regard the District government with a contempt that overlooks its genuine accomplishments, against blacks who regard the whites with apprehensions that have little basis in fact.

Then in April 1989, Jesse Jackson indicated he might be interested in moving to a house he has long owned in Washington and running for mayor, and though he said he would never run against Barry, who supported him vigorously in 1984 and 1988 for President, he also made it clear that he would see that Barry was well taken care of after he left office. Barry's rivals were miffed, but there seemed little doubt that Jackson could sweep the primary if he ran, and that

Washington's problems would give him an opportunity to prove that he could administer a government ably and set a higher moral tone, as he has tried to do with his imprecations on the campaign trail against drug use and "babies having babies," that will make a real change in people's lives.

The District has one non-voting Delegate in the House, Walter Fauntroy, who was first elected in a special 1971 election but who has not achieved influence in proportion to his seniority. Like other nonvoting members, he can vote in committee, and he is now the number three Democrat on the House Banking Committee and number two on the District of Columbia Committee behind Ron Dellums. Fauntroy has done some constructive work on Banking, where he could conceivably be chairman some day. And he affected the course of national policy on South Africa, moving even the Reagan Administration in his direction when he became the first congressman to be arrested demonstrating in front of the South African embassy in November 1984.

He has been less successful, ironically, on District matters. His crusade to give the District full voting representation in Congress came a cropper: he got Congress to approve a constitutional amendment doing so in 1978, but it died seven years later when far fewer than the required number of state legislatures voted to ratify it. And in 1988, he was ineffective in preventing the House from voting, in effect, to overturn two District laws—one which had been interpreted as requiring Georgetown University to extend official recognition to homosexual organizations, and another barring insurance companies from discriminating against AIDS virus carriers. On such issues Fauntroy's strength turns into a weakness—he tends to treat issues as simple moral questions of racial justice, without understanding that others may view them differently. On the two challenged pieces of District legislation, he neither warned District officials of the perilous unpopularity on Capitol Hill of the laws they were passing nor was he able to persuade his colleagues in the House to leave alone District laws which, while arguably wrongheaded, were nonetheless the product of a competent legislature. In the process the principle of home rule— for which Fauntroy and many others spent years fighting—took a terrible beating.

A minister with a proud past in the civil rights movement, Fauntroy is eager to defend his nearly two decades' record in the House. But in elections, even though he has not had serious opposition in years, he runs behind partisan levels; and with the discontent against Marion Barry, the District government, and Fauntroy's lack of success at defending home rule, it is just possible that he may have serious opposition in 1990.

The People: Est. Pop. 1988: 620,000; Pop. 1980: 638,333, dn. 2.8% 1980–88 and 15.6% 1970–80; 0.26% of U.S. total, 48th largest. 14% with 1–3 yrs. col., 28% with 4+ yrs. col.; 18.6% below poverty level. Households: 53% family, 29% with children, 30% married couples; 64.5% housing units rented; median monthly rent: $208; median house value: $70,700. Voting age pop. (1980): 494,842; 66% Black, 3% Spanish origin, 1% Asian origin. Registered voters (1988): 275,175; 217,142 D (78%); 24,928 R (9%); 31,272 unaffiliated and minor parties (11%).

1988 Share of Federal Tax Burden: $3,100,000,000; 0.36% of U.S. total.

1988 Share of Federal Expenditures

	Total		Non-Defense		Defense	
Total Expend	$15,257m	(1.73%)	$13,152m	(2.01%)	$3,805m	(1.67%)
St/Lcl Grants	1,615m	(1.41%)	1,615m	(1.41%)	0m	(0.09%)
Salary/Wages	8,223m	(6.12%)	7,227m	(10.78%)	996m	(10.78%)
Pymnts to Indiv	1,693m	(0.41%)	1,648m	(0.42%)	45m	(0.24%)
Procurement	2,759m	(1.46%)	1,700m	(3.66%)	2,759m	(1.46%)
Research/Other	967m	(2.59%)	962m	(2.60%)	5m	(2.60%)

Political Lineup: Representative, 1 D at large.

240 DISTRICT OF COLUMBIA

1988 Presidential Vote

Dukakis (D)...............	159,407	(83%)
Bush (R)..................	27,590	(14%)

1988 Democratic Presidential Primary

Jackson...................	68,480	(80%)
Dukakis..................	15,415	(18%)
Simon.....................	769	(1%)
Gore......................	648	(1%)

1984 Presidential Vote

Mondale (D)...............	180,408	(85%)
Reagan (R)................	29,009	(14%)

1988 Republican Presidential Primary

Bush	5,890	(88%)
Dole.......................	469	(7%)
Robertson..................	268	(4%)

REPRESENTATIVE

Rep. Walter E. Fauntroy (D)

Elected Mar. 23, 1971; b. Feb. 6, 1933, Washington, D.C.; home, Washington, D.C.; VA Union U., B.A. 1955, Yale U., B.D. 1958; Baptist; married (Dorothy).

Career: Pastor, New Bethel Baptist Church, 1958–present; Founder and former Dir., Model Inner City Commun. Org.; Dir., Washington Bureau, SCLC, 1960–71; Coordinator, Selma to Montgomery March, 1965; Vice Chmn., DC City Cncl., 1967–79; Natl. Coordinator, Poor Peoples Campaign, 1969; Chmn., Bd. of Dirs., Martin Luther King, Jr., Ctr. for Social Change, 1969–present.

Offices: 2135 RHOB 20515, 202-225-8050. Also 2041 Martin Luther King, Jr., Ave., S.E., Ste. 311, Washington, D.C. 20020, 202-426-2530.

Committees: *Banking, Finance and Urban Affairs* (3th of 31 D). Subcommittees: Domestic Monetary Policy; Housing and Community Development; International Development Institutions and Finance (Chairman); International Finance, Trade, and Monetary Policy. *District of Columbia* (2d of 8 D). Subcommittees: Fiscal Affairs and Health (Chairman); Government Operations and Metropolitan Affairs. *Select Committee on Narcotics Abuse and Control* (10th of 15 D).

Group Ratings and Key Votes: Does Not Vote

Election Results

1988 general	Walter E. Fauntroy (D)	121,817	(71%)	($68,523)
	W. Ronald Evans (R)	22,936	(13%)	
	Alvin C. Frost (SP)...................	13,802	(8%)	
	David H. Dabney (I)...................	10,449	(6%)	
1988 primary	Walter E. Fauntroy (D), unopposed			
1986 general	Walter E. Fauntroy (D)	101,604	(80%)	($74,681)
	Mary L. H. King (R)	17,643	(14%)	
	Julie McCall (SP)....................	6,122	(5%)	

FLORIDA

Who imagined a half century ago that Florida, swamp-ridden, geographically isolated, disease-ridden, bigoted, with no mineral resources but phosphate mines and not much agriculture outside its citrus groves, without major industries or universities, would become one of the most populous American states? Florida in 1940 was studded with a few fabulous resorts but more of its people lived in settlements like LaBelle where the *WPA Guide* found that "rough unpainted pine houses flank the many unpaved roads within the town; on the outskirts are primitive one-story cabins with palm thatched roofs; these cabins are perched high on stilts to provide dry quarters in the rainy season, and on hot days hogs, dogs, and children retire under them to keep cool. Kerosene lamps light the houses, and home-cured hides are sometimes used as bed 'kivers.'" Florida was the smallest state in the South, with 1.9 million people, its poverty only faintly relieved by winter visitors and northern migrants; it was anything but a model for the rest of the Union.

Now, 50 years later with 12 million people, Florida is the nation's second fastest growing and fourth largest state (it passed Ohio in 1984, Illinois in 1986, Pennsylvania in 1987), and an instructive though exaggerated model of the America that is to be. Florida's population is weighted toward the elderly, its migrants tend to be affluent, its economy is made up mostly of service industries, its voters are disconnected from state and national government—distrustful of neighbors and fellow citizens they scarcely know and alarmed about what they see as the proximate threats to their comfortable lives, crime and drugs. Florida offers the vision of a sunny, carefree, comfortable life in year-round warmth—and provides a glimpse at the dark problems that may lurk ahead.

What brought so many Americans there was warm weather. A climate that in all but the winter months was considered intolerable (and which was genuinely unhealthy) half a century ago is, now that air conditioning became commonplace, deemed desirable. As one cohort of older Americans after another has migrated from the cold industrial belt from Boston to St. Louis down to the funnel of the Florida peninsula, a new megastate was born. More than 90% of Florida's housing units have been built since 1945, hundreds of square miles of swampland have been drained, miles and miles of roads and parking lots have been laid down, shopping centers and restaurants and luxury resorts and trailer parks have been built. For millions of Americans, Florida has been a chance to start over, to create the kind of community they have always wanted to live in, to build if not a city on a hill then a suburb in what was until quite recently a swamp.

The result is a population and an electorate as diverse as any in America—but not in the same proportions. The old, pre-migration Florida, centered in the northern part of the state, was heavily Democratic, strongly segregationist, and interested in state politics because its shrewd legislators could bring money and jobs to impoverished local communities. To that Florida was added two distinct streams of migration. Starting in the late 1940s, affluent and mostly Protestant northerners, from pleasant suburbs and prosperous small towns, started moving to Florida to retire. They were joined, not too long after, by ethnic and blue-collar northerners—Jews moving to Miami were the most visible, but the new migrants included Catholics as well—who were mostly New Deal Democrats. Both streams continued in large volume, with many younger migrants as well; but Florida remains easily the most elderly of states, and the constant turnover in its elderly population has made for constant demographic and political change. Now Florida is becoming the home for much of what appears to be a third wave of migration to this

242   FLORIDA

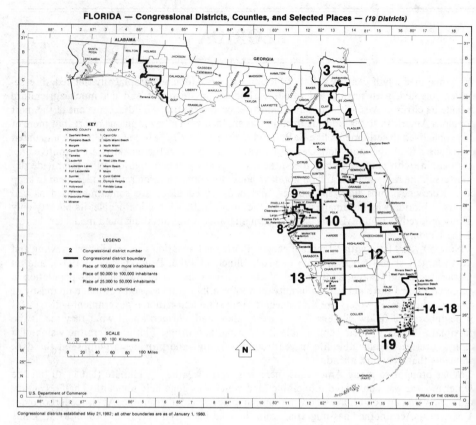

See pages 1443-1448 for additional metropolitan area maps.

country: not only the Cubans who came here first in the 1960s and then again in 1980 as refugees from Castro's dictatorship, but also immigrants legal and otherwise from Haiti and Nicaragua, Colombia and Jamaica.

This diversity has produced some cultural conflict and has had political repercussions. "Miami Vice" is not just a television program but living image to most Floridians, who see this commercial capital of Latin America and of the U.S. drug trade, with its flamboyantly untraditional Arquitectonica buildings lounging like lizards by the bayside, as beset by violence and dominated by criminals. Reaction to the Cubans is evident in the near-unanimity with which other Floridians voted in 1988 to declare English the official state language (it passed with 62% in Miami's Dade County and 88% in the rest of the state), and reaction to crime is apparent as Jews and other migrants from the East Coast have moved north into Broward and Palm Beach County; WASPs have settled in new condominium communities farther north or on the Gulf Coast. Similarly rapid though less turbulent migration has affected almost every part of the state.

The result is that few Florida voters have any permanent connection with the civic culture of the state; they know nothing of the antics of Governor Claude Kirk (1967–70), or how Reubin Askew came to office in 1970, or how the legislature was dominated for years by conservatives from north Florida called the Pork Chop Gang. Yet for all their diversity and newness Floridians have some things in common. They have an unfocused concern about Florida's physical environment, though the Florida they live in is anything but pristine. They are against any income tax and favor a high sales tax instead (because one-third of the revenue comes from tourists). They are cautious about proposals for casino gambling and wary of big-money crime.

Contributing also to Florida's political instability is its geographical size and the briefness of its political season. There are eight media markets here, none dominant; Miami's Dade County casts only 11% of the state's votes, and together with the other Gold Coast counties of Broward and Palm Beach only 29%. Another major metropolitan area has two contrasting central cities, bustling Tampa and the retiree-haven of St. Petersburg. Jacksonville is big enough to be significant in the state's economy and politics, and so is Orlando, the home of Disney World and its EPCOT Center as well as the center of the state's citrus industry. There are literally dozens of small cities, from Pensacola to Key West that, for most of their residents, are Florida, and most are growing more rapidly than the big centers. Then too, with no single dominant newspaper and a capital (tiny Tallahassee) tucked away in a corner of the state, state government and what sense of unity it may provide elsewhere is often invisible. Finally, to complete the sense of helter-skelter, Florida's political campaigns are decided in a rush: in 1988 the primary was September 6, the runoff was October 4, followed five weeks later by the general election.

All these factors make Florida elections subject to startling fluctuations. But as the 1980s have gone on, a trend is apparent—toward the Republican party of Ronald Reagan and (he is just about as strong here) George Bush. It is apparent first in presidential contests in which, since Jimmy Carter's razor-thin victory in 1976, Florida has voted Republican 56%–39% in 1980, 65%–35% in 1984, and 61%–39% in 1988. It is also apparent in party registration figures—numbers which in most states just measure historical preferences (because people tend to register in the party which historically has carried their locality) but which in Florida measure the allegiance of its constant streams of new migrants and their judgment about which party will govern in the future. The verdict is plain from the numbers. In the decade from 1978 to 1988 total registration in Florida rose from 4.2 million to 6 million. Democratic registration was up 452,000; Republican registration was up 1.2 million. In percentage terms the Democrats' registration edge dropped from 67% in 1978 to 54% in 1988. Since many southern-accented voters in the panhandle and elsewhere register Democratic and regularly vote Republican in top contests, it's clear that Florida is close to being a solid Republican state. The Democrats' comparative success in statewide races begins to look like evidence not of the strength of their party but of the strength of candidates. Bob Graham, after eight successful years as governor, was able to win only 55% of the vote for senator. Their 1988 Senate candidate, southern-accented moderate Buddy MacKay, managed a near-win by finishing second in the first primary, winning the runoff narrowly, and then rallying in the five weeks of the general election campaign. That used to be a recipe for decisive wins by Democrats like Graham in 1978 and Governor Reubin Askew and Senator Lawton Chiles in 1970. But this time the political balance was tipped enough to the Republicans to produce a narrow victory for Connie Mack.

At the same time, Republicans have been winning state offices. Not just the governorship, which their little-tested candidate Bob Martinez won over a liberal Democrat who in crime-crazed Florida opposed the death penalty. But also, for first time, down-the-line statewide offices in 1988: party-switcher Jim Smith was elected secretary of state with 63% and a Republican beat a perfectly acceptable Democrat for treasurer 53%–46%. A Republican victory put them behind the Democrats only 23–17 in the state Senate—a shift of three seats could put Republicans in control—of the state Senate at least—in time for post-1990 redistricting.

Demographics helped produce these results. Republicans are helped by increased registration among Miami-area Cuban-Americans, by rapid growth in the affluent Gulf coast south of St. Petersburg and Atlantic coast north of Palm Beach, by Republican trends in family-oriented central Florida around Orlando, and by the continuing Republican trend in the heavily military panhandle around Pensacola and Panama City. These shifts are only partially offset by Democratic trends in less affluent retirement areas on the Gulf coast north of St. Petersburg, the Atlantic coast between Cape Canaveral and Jacksonville, and in and around Tallahassee.

Issues also play a role. Drugs and crime are the front-burner issues working for Republicans. But they also stand to benefit on tax issues in a state whose elderly voters don't much want to pay to educate other people's kids. And they may be helped by resentment of immigration (although the Cubans in the legislature, all Republicans, split with party leaders over the English referendum).

The problem is that the solutions can make things worse. The legislature rewrote its gun laws in 1987 to allow any citizen without a criminal record to get a permit easily and cheaply to carry a concealed handgun—and, inadvertently, the law let anyone carry a handgun openly. As for holding down spending, Florida like most states needs more prisons and unlike all but the western states and Texas faces a significant increase in its school age population. Martinez and the Democratic legislature did in fact raise taxes (and about as clumsily as possible). But it's still not plain that Florida is providing the base for tomorrow's economic growth to match the pace of yesterday's and today's population growth.

Governor. The nation's fourth largest state has a governor who started off as a high school civics teacher, became an organizer for the teachers' union, and in 1979 became mayor of Tampa, just as this onetime port and cigar factory town was taking off into rapid Sun Belt growth. He is Florida's first Hispanic governor, but his style is not ethnic; he grew up in Tampa and speaks with a decidedly southern accent. A Democrat and supporter of Jimmy Carter in the 1970s, he switched to the Republican Party just in time to take advantage of Florida's Republican trend, the lack of seasoned state Republican politicians (in the 1986 primary he beat Louis Frey, a former congressman who spent most of his time in Washington after he lost the 1980 Senate primary), and the increasing prominence of liberals in the stagnant-sized pool of Democratic primary voters (his general election opponent Steve Pajcic took liberal stands on the death penalty, pornography, and taxes). Martinez campaigned as an experienced public official who would wipe out traffic jams, trim the state budget by $800 million, and not raise taxes, and won a not-so-narrow 55%–45% victory.

On taking office Martinez promptly changed course—and sailed right into a shoal. Instead of cutting taxes, he worked with Democratic leaders in the legislature to pass a tax on services, including lawyers and advertising. Newspapers claimed it infringed the First Amendment, national advertisers canceled their Florida ad buys, a TV campaign in August (when Floridians, unlike most Americans, tend to stay indoors) turned opinion sharply against the tax and Martinez, and in September 1987 he admitted, "I made a mistake. That mistake has cost me the confidence of the people of Florida." In December the legislature repealed the service tax and increased the sales tax to 6% instead, and his job rating was rock-bottom.

This was not the first such fiasco in Florida: Bob Graham in 1984 had to seek repeal of the unitary business tax he got in 1983—another attempt to make out-of-staters pay for Florida government. Martinez showed more deftness in 1988, hanging back for months and then pushing the legislature to enact solid waste management and transportation bond programs and pony up more money for education. And he was steadfast and early in his support of George Bush (whose son, Jeb Bush, was his commerce secretary from 1987–88), who carried Florida handily in March and November. But Martinez still had no base. His embrace of taxes and spending increases leaves Republicans with little enthusiasm for him; even Cubans were angry because he moved the State Hispanic Commission out of the governor's office. Several stronger candidates are on the scene. But the two who ran in 1986 and might have won if they had done just a little better in the Democratic and Republican primaries are now, after the 1988 elections, Republican statewide officials—Secretary of State (who as a Democrat used to be Attorney General) Jim Smith and Treasurer Tom Gallagher—and may not be well placed to challenge a governor of their own party. Congressman and onteme Space Shuttle crewmember Bill Nelson is mounting a strong Democratice challenge to Martinez though he has spent most of the 1980s in Washington. The stakes for both parties are high: Florida will gain House districts, and the Republicans would dearly like to control, or at least to prevent the Democrats from controlling, the redistricting process. Martinez's unsteady course is a problem for those wanting to make this a secure Republican state. But it may not be a disabling one.

Senators. Florida's unstable politics has produced flux in its Senate elections; only one senator, Lawton Chiles, has been reelected since 1964. But Chiles—a deeply religious man and a Democrat of southern origins and moderate to liberal views on policy, who won his first term in 1970 as an unknown 40-year-old state senator by inventing the tactic of walking across the state and became Chairman of the Senate Budget Committee—surprised almost everyone (including those who had raised $1.3 million in amounts no larger than $100 for his campaign) when he announced in December 1987 that he was retiring. So today, with Connie Mack III just elected and Bob Graham fresh from his victory in 1986, the fourth largest state has the least seniority in the Senate of any state in the union.

Bob Graham is careful, methodical, thorough, hard-working, steady: wearing his Florida ties (light outlines of the state on a field of blue), recording every meeting he attends and meal he eats (but not, it seems, his reactions to any of them) in the notebooks he carries everywhere, scheduling meetings with every member of the Florida House delegation and with lobbyists on both sides of environmental, banking, and crime issues. He comes from a prominent Florida family: his father started out with a Miami area dairy farm, which is now the planned mini-city of Miami Lakes; his half-brother Philip Graham was publisher of the *Washington Post* and proprietor of *Newsweek*. After 12 years in the legislature he ran for governor in 1978, finished second in the first primary, overtook Attorney General Robert Shevin in the runoff, then beat drugstore millionaire Jack Eckerd in the general. The attention-getting device in that campaign (it was invented by Senator Tom Harkin for his 1974 House race) was work days: Graham worked a day a week at some job, from bagging groceries to working construction; he keeps it up still, once a month.

He was a popular governor (one of 15 in the Senate now; 6 others lost governor races), backing some tax increases, setting up a water quality trust fund and passing a wetlands protection act, opposing any income tax and, as a capital punishment backer, signing death warrants. After the permitted two terms, he ran against Senator Paula Hawkins in 1986. She is an original, a spunky conservative who was the driving force behind the Missing Child Assistance Act and whose persistence drove many colleagues bonkers; "unique and irreplaceable" was her slogan. Against any other opponent she probably would have won; Graham beat her 55%–45%.

In the Senate Graham started out tight-lipped, careful not to commit himself until he had to, although his record has turned out to be that of a moderate Democrat, as expected. The issues he has concentrated on are as Florida-oriented as his ties: drug traffic, health care for elderly, campaign finance reform (Florida has a tradition of "sunshine laws," requiring full disclosure). His major legislative initiative was a banking bill, co-sponsored by Colorado's Tim Wirth, which would let banks into the securities business, but which would get non-financial companies like Sears out of banking, and would set up a commission to make sure banks don't endanger deposit in their securities operations—goals sought by Florida's aggressive statewide banks.

Graham holds a jinx seat: the last Senator reelected to it was George Smathers in 1962. He seems in strong shape for reelection in 1992, but must be careful of Florida's Republican trend. In national politics, Graham was a vehement Jimmy Carter backer in 1980 and a leader of the moderate Democratic Leadership Council later in the 1980s. He was mentioned as a possible vice presidential nominee in 1988, but had only spent 18 months on national issues at the time and didn't get the nod. But he could be a national candidate in the future. Florida's filing deadlines are late enough to let him run for President in 1992 and run for the Senate again if it doesn't work out. He is clearly able, well-positioned on issues, from a critical state, and perhaps not unwilling; his 1986 campaign manager has said, "I've always thought that doing work days in New Hampshire would look awfully good."

The election of Connie Mack III as only the third Florida Republican Senator in this century must be counted more as a triumph for his party and his positions than for him personally. A grandson and namesake of the longtime owner and manager of the Philadelphia Athletics (another grandfather was Morris Sheppard, Senator from Texas from 1913 to 1941), a banker in the comfortable Gulf Coast town of Cape Coral, Mack was a Democrat until 1979 and little involved in politics. When he ran for and won the heavily Republican newly created 13th District seat in 1982, he was attacked as insufficiently conservative, and led the first primary only 29%–22% and won the runoff by only 58%–42%. In 1987 he was still pro-choice on abortion and for the Equal Rights Amendment (though he switched positions on both issues the following year); he admitted in 1987 that he had smoked marijuana as a young adult. In the House he was part of Newt Gingrich's Conservative Opportunity Society, and by the mid-1980s was a fervent supply-sider. He delighted in hazing the Democrats and showcasing his ideas on C-SPAN; he was lead sponsor in the House of the Gramm-Rudman deficit-cutting measure that originated in the Senate.

Mack had good fortune along the way. He got out of the Senate race in April 1987, hesitating to take on Lawton Chiles; when Chiles got out in December, Mack got back in. For a time Mack was far overshadowed by former Governor Reubin Askew, a clear favorite for the nomination and election; but Askew, tired of the demands of fundraising, left the race abruptly in May 1988. Then Mack drew a primary opponent, former Tampa U.S. Attorney Robert "Mad Dog" Merkle, who carried a cutout of Mack around the state and called him "Cardboard Connie." But Merkle raised little money, and while carrying the Tampa-St. Petersburg media market 58%–42% lost statewide to Mack 62%–38%. Meanwhile the Democrats were having one of those multi-candidate primaries which in 1970 and 1978 produced their party's strongest candidates—and seemed about to do so again. Congressman Buddy MacKay, a southern-accented moderate who had worked hard on budget issues and for environmental causes, whose record as a legislator got him endorsements of 18 of the 20 papers who made a choice, finished ahead of Palm Beach County Congressman Dan Mica in the first primary by 26% to 18% and behind Insurance Commissioner Bill Gunter who had 38%. Gunter had been around the track many times: he was elected to Congress in 1972 and ran for the Senate in 1974 and 1980 (when he edged MacKay out of second place in the primary); as Insurance Commissioner he was collecting vast sums from insurance executives. MacKay scrambled to counter attacks in the heavily Jewish Gold Coast condo precincts for his support of a Saudi arms sale, and won 52%–48%.

MacKay's campaign emphasized his special talents; Mack's emphasized his stands on national issues. "Hey, Buddy, you're liberal," the chipped-tooth handsome Mack said in his ads, and called for "less taxing, less spending, less government, and more freedom." He attacked MacKay for opposing contra aid and the balanced budget amendment. He was the beneficiary of the undignified withdrawal of the Dukakis campaign from Florida and of $300,000 spent on ads by an import car dealer PAC. Worries about Social Security clearly helped MacKay, who carried St. Petersburg and ran far ahead of most Democrats in Mack's own retiree-heavy House district. But Mack ran far ahead of Paula Hawkins's losing showing in the heavily military Jacksonville area and in the family-oriented Orlando area. Mack was the subject of unfavorable newspaper stories and Bob Graham called him an "ideological wacko."

A majority of those who went to the polls and quite possibly a majority of all those voting were for MacKay. But Mack won the absentee vote heavily, and the ballot makeup in Palm Beach and Hillsborough (Tampa) Counties, where the Senate race appeared at the bottom of page 1 rather than at the top of page 2 as in most counties, apparently caused many voters to overlook the race. In Palm Beach the total voting in the Senate race was 16% lower than in the presidential race and in Hillsborough it was 24% lower—and much lower than the total voting for Insurance Commissioner and on the widowers' property tax exemption. Quite possibly this ballot design (which MacKay's campaign could have challenged, but didn't) cost MacKay the Senate seat. Mack went to bed thinking he had lost and was awakened Wednesday by a call from President Reagan saying he'd won. "I think we just won one more for the Gipper," Mack said, but the truth is that it was the other way around. Having arrived in the Senate much blessed by luck, Mack needs to prove he is the thoughtful innovator some of his House allies say he is rather than the lightweight who happens to take (after some false starts) the popular stands on issues, as his opponents and many Florida observers think.

Presidential politics. Florida now seems to be the safest Republican big state in presidential elections: Democratic presidential nominees throughout the 1980s won 39%, 35%, and 39% here. It still has a potentially pivotal primary, scheduled for years in early March, a date which other southern states adopted to make 1988's Super Tuesday. Florida's conservative southern Democrats, enough to give George Wallace a 42% victory here in 1972, are not so numerous now, and the last two Democratic primaries have been won by Michael Dukakis and Gary Hart. On the Republican side George Bush was a very big winner here in 1988, with percentages in some congressional districts—the hawkish Gulf Coast, Cuban Miami—as high as those he got anywhere while the contest was still on.

Congressional districting. Florida gained four House seats in the 1980 Census, more than any other state, and it stands to gain four to six more from the 1990 Census. The Democrats drew the lines last time, but it's not at all clear who will be in control in 1991, or if anyone will. There are two notable things about the House delegation now. One is that it continues to contain talented and powerful senior members, notably Dante Fascell, chairman of Foreign Affairs, and Sam Gibbons, number two on Ways and Means. The second thing is that the Democrats' edge was reduced to 10–9 by the Republicans' 1988 pickup of two seats. Florida's House delegation, once entirely Democratic, is now more heavily Republican than that of any megastate except Ohio.

The People: Est. Pop. 1988: 12,377,000; Pop. 1980: 9,746,324, up 27% 1980–88 and 43.5% 1970–80; 4.84% of U.S. total, 5th largest. 17% with 1–3 yrs. col., 15% with 4+ yrs. col.; 13.5% below poverty level. Single ancestry: 12% English, 6% German, 4% Irish, 3% Italian, 1% Polish, Russian, French, Scottish, Dutch. Households (1980): 72% family, 33% with children, 59% married couples; 31.7% housing units rented; median monthly rent: $209; median house value: $45,300. Voting age pop. (1980): 7,386,688; 11% Black, 9% Spanish origin, 1% Asian origin. Registered voters (1988): 6,047,347; 3,264,105 D (54%), 2,360,434 R (39%), 422,808 unaffiliated and minor parties (7%).

1988 Share of Federal Tax Burden: $45,687,000,000; 5.17% of U.S. total, 5th largest.

1988 Share of Federal Expenditures

	Total		Non-Defense		Defense	
Total Expend	$42,997m	(4.86%)	$32,679m	(4.98%)	$11,585m	(5.07%)
St/Lcl Grants	3,419m	(2.98%)	3,414m	(2.98%)	5m	(4.06%)
Salary/Wages	5,662m	(4.22%)	2,586m	(3.86%)	3,076m	(3.86%)
Pymnts to Indiv	26,800m	(6.55%)	24,891m	(6.37%)	1,909m	(10.24%)
Procurement	6,590m	(3.49%)	1,267m	(2.72%)	6,590m	(3.49%)
Research/Other	526m	(1.41%)	521m	(1.41%)	5m	(1.41%)

Political Lineup: Governor, Bob Martinez (R); Lt. Gov., Bobby Brantley (R); Secy. of State, Jim Smith (R); Atty. Gen., Robert A. Butterworth (D); Treasurer, Tom Gallagher (R); Comptroller, Gerald Lewis (D). State Senate, 40 (23 D and 17 R); State House of Representatives, 120 (73 D, 47 R). Senators, Robert Graham (D) and Connie Mack, III (R). Representatives, 19 (10 D, 9 R).

1988 Presidential Vote

Bush (R) 2,618,885 (61%)
Dukakis (D). 1,656,701 (39%)

1984 Presidential Vote

Reagan (R) 2,730,350 (65%)
Mondale (D) 1,448,816 (35%)

1988 Democratic Presidential Primary

Dukakis 520,868 (41%)
Jackson 254,825 (20%)
Gephardt 182,779 (14%)
Gore. 161,106 (13%)
Hart. 36,266 (3%)
Simon 27,592 (2%)
Babbitt 10,277 (1%)
Uncommitted 78,997 (6%)

1988 Republican Presidential Primary

Bush 559,359 (62%)
Dole. 190,934 (21%)
Robertson 95,721 (11%)
Kemp. 41,716 (4%)
Du Pont. 6,717 (1%)
Haig. 5,839 (1%)

GOVERNOR

Gov. Bob Martinez (R)

Elected 1986, term expires Jan. 1991; b. Dec. 25, 1934, Tampa; home, Tallahassee; U. of Tampa, B.A. 1957, U. of IL, M.A. 1964; Roman Catholic; married (Mary Jane).

Career: Teacher, 1952–62, 1963–66; Labor Relations Consult., 1963–67; Exec. Dir., Hillsboro Cnty. Classroom Teachers Assoc., 1966–75; Restaurant owner/mngr., 1975–83; Mayor of Tampa, 1979–86.

Office: The Capitol, Tallahassee 32301, 904-488-2272.

Election Results

1986 gen.	Bob Martinez (R)	1,847,525	(55%)
	Steve Pajcic (D)	1,538,620	(45%)
1986 runoff	Bob Martinez (R)	259,333	(66%)
	Lou Frey, Jr. (R)	131,652	(34%)
1986 prim.	Bob Martinez (R)	244,499	(44%)
	Lou Frey, Jr. (R)	138,017	(25%)
	Tom Gallagher (R)	127,709	(23%)
	Chester Clem (R)	44,438	(8%)
1982 gen.	Robert (Bob) Graham (D)	1,739,553	(65%)
	Lewis A. Bafalis (R)	949,023	(35%)

SENATORS

Sen. Robert (Bob) Graham (D)

Elected 1986, seat up 1992; b. Nov. 9, 1936, Coral Gables; home, Miami Lakes; U. of FL, B.A. 1959, Harvard U., J.D. 1962; United Church of Christ; married (Adele).

Career: Vice Pres., Chmn., Sengra Development Corp.; FL House of Reps., 1966–70; FL Senate, 1970–78; Gov. of FL, 1978–1986.

Offices: 241 DSOB 20510, 202-224-3041. Also 44 W. Flagler St., Miami 33130, 305-536-7293; and 325 John Knox Rd., Bldg. 600, Tallahassee 32308, 904-681-7726; and 101 E. Kennedy Blvd. Tampa 33602, 813-228-2476.

Committees: *Banking, Housing and Urban Affairs* (9th of 12 D). Subcommittees: Consumer and Regulatory Affairs; International Finance and Monetary Policy. *Environment and Public Works* (8th of 9 D) Subcommittees: Environmental Protection; Superfund, Ocean and Water Protection; Water Resources, Transportation and Infrastructure. *Veterans' Affairs* (6th of 6 D). *Special Committee on Aging* (9th of 10 D).

Group Ratings

	ADA	ACLU	COPE	CFA	LCV	ACU	NTLC	NSI	COC	CEI
1988	55	59	83	92	70	28	22	90	38	26
1987	60	—	100	83	—	23	—	—	28	28

National Journal Ratings

	1988 LIB — 1988 CONS		1987 LIB — 1987 CONS	
Economic	74%	— 19%	51%	— 45%
Social	56%	— 41%	90%	— 4%
Foreign	51%	— 48%	41%	— 57%

Key Votes

1) Cut Aged Housing $	AGN	5) Bork Nomination	AGN	9) SDI Funding	FOR
2) Override Hwy Veto	FOR	6) Ban Plastic Guns	AGN	10) Ban Chem Weaps	FOR
3) Kill Plnt Clsng Notice	AGN	7) Deny Abortions	FOR	11) Aid To Contras	FOR
4) Min Wage Increase	FOR	8) Japanese Reparations	FOR	12) Reagan Defense $	AGN

Election Results

1986 general	Robert (Bob) Graham (D)	1,877,231	(55%)	($6,173,663)
	Paula Hawkins (R)	1,551,888	(45%)	($6,723,729)
1986 primary	Robert (Bob) Graham (D)	851,586	(85%)	
	Robert P. (Bob) Kunst (D)	149,797	(15%)	
1980 general	Paula Hawkins (R)	1,822,460	(52%)	($696,969)
	Bill Gunter (D)	1,705,409	(48%)	($2,164,560)

250 FLORIDA

Sen. Connie Mack III (R)

Elected 1988, seat up 1994; b. Oct. 29, 1949, Philadelphia, PA home, Cape Coral; U. of FL, B.A. 1966; Roman Catholic; married (Priscilla).

Career: Banker, 1966–82; U.S. House of Reps., 1982–88.

Offices: 902 HSOB 20510, 202-224-5274. Also 1342 Colonia Blvd., Fort Myers 33907, 813-275-6252.

Committees: *Banking, Housing and Urban Affairs* (6th of 9 R) Subcommittees: Housing and Urban Affairs; International Finance and Monetary Policy. *Foreign Relations* (9th of 9 R). Subcommittees: African Affairs; Western Hemisphere and Peace Corps Affairs. *Joint Economic Committee.* Subcommittees: International Economic Policy; National Security Economics; Economic Growth, Trade and Taxes

Group Ratings (as Member of the U.S. House of Representatives)

	ADA	ACLU	COPE	CFA	LCV	ACU	NTLC	NSI	COC	CEI
1988	0	0	9	0	19	100	85	100	86	73
1987	0	—	10	0	—	95	—	—	93	88

National Journal Ratings (as Member of the U.S. House of Representatives)

	1988 LIB — 1988 CONS	1987 LIB — 1987 CONS
Economic	9% — 91%	0% — 89%
Social	0% — 95%	0% — 90%
Foreign	0% — 84%	0% — 80%

Key Votes (as Member of the U.S. House of Representatives)

1) Homeless $	FOR	5) Ban Drug Test	FOR	9) SDI Research	FOR
2) Gephardt Amdt	AGN	6) Drug Death Pen	FOR	10) Ban Chem Weaps	AGN
3) Deficit Reduc	AGN	7) Handgun Sales	—	11) Aid to Contras	FOR
4) Kill Plnt Clsng Notice	FOR	8) Ban D.C. Abort $	—	12) Nuclear Testing	AGN

Election Results

1988 general	Connie Mack, III (R)...............	2,049,329	(50%)	($5,181,639
	Kenneth H. (Buddy) MacKay (D)......	2,015,717	(50%)	($3,714,852
1988 primary	Connie Mack, III (R)	405,296	(62%)	
	Robert W. Merkle (R)................	250,730	(38%)	
1986 general	Lawton Chiles (D)	1,636,857	(62%)	($806,629
	Van B. Poole (R)...................	1,014,551	(38%)	($472,505

FIRST DISTRICT

The "Redneck Riviera" is the impolite name for the western end of Florida's northern panhandle, a part of the state that was always part of Dixie. Fifty years ago this was swamp and poor farmland; the beaches were little used—they were too chilly in the winter, too steamy in the summer, too far away from the ritzy resorts of the Gold and Gulf Coasts and not close to many people able to afford vacations. This land along the Gulf owes much of its current prosperity to the military. Since John Quincy Adams persuaded Spain to sell Florida to the United States in 1819 to get the port of Pensacola, the United States Navy had a base there (except for a spot of trouble in the 1860s); this was the birthplace of carrier aviation, a major base in World War II and a Navy homeport once again (though Pensacola had to threaten to join Alabama to get the state of Florida to pay for dredging the harbor). Inland to the east is Eglin Air Force Base, which spreads over the lion's share of three counties. In the 1940s and 1950s these facilities were the main engines of growth; since the 1960s, when the rural South started getting prosperous, this American riviera has become a major vacation and retirement spot for southerners.

Pensacola and the panhandle are 1,000 miles from Miami—and economically, culturally, and politically they have little to do with the rest of Florida. They are part of the Gulf Coast crescent that goes west through the southern tips of Alabama and Mississippi to the oil rigs of Louisiana and Texas and which in the 1980s has become arguably the most Republican part of the United States. Looking southward toward Castro's Cuba and the Sandinistas' Nicaragua, imbued with patriotic values and military experience, blessed with large families and religious faith, most voters here have difficulty understanding how any American could vote against Ronald Reagan and George Bush; Bush's highest winning percentage outside the state of Texas was in the Florida panhandle. Their Republicanism now goes far down the ballot: the panhandle is solidly Republican in statewide races now, even for the lower offices, and even elects Republicans as well as Democrats to the legislature.

The panhandle, which from Panama City west to Pensacola makes up Florida's 1st Congressional District, still elects a Democratic congressman—but one who comes about as close to a Republican voting record as any member of the majority caucus. He is Earl Hutto, who when he first ran in 1978 was probably more familiar in these small media markets for his work as a sportscaster than for his service in the state legislature. Hutto may have won because his politics was similar to that of his predecessor, Bob Sikes, first elected in 1940 and for years chairman of the Military Construction Appropriations Subcommittee, who pumped money into the 1st until he was reprimanded for unethical practices in 1976 and stripped of his chairmanship in 1977. Hutto does not have Sikes's forcefulness or seniority, but he does have seats on locally important committees—Armed Services and Merchant Marine—and he tends to the particular needs of the district: medicine for military retirees (this is one of the favorite spots for retired military personnel), the Pensacola homeport, funding for the Coast Guard. He's chaired a Coast Guard subcommittee, a hot spot with the drug issue, and he now chairs the Armed Services Readiness Subcommittee.

On other national issues, Hutto stays close to the district's views, a little mixed on economics, solidly conservative on foreign and cultural issues. That record, his practice of producing his own videotapes and popping them on the next airplane to local TV stations, and the benefits that accrue from his seniority have enabled him to withstand by comfortable margins challenges both from Democrats in the primary and Republicans in the general election.

The People: Est. Pop. 1986: 619,500, up 20.8% 1980–86; Pop. 1980: 512,821, up 22.6% 1970–80. Households (1980): 78% family, 44% with children, 64% married couples; 31.5% housing units rented; median monthly rent: $162; median house value: $35,500. Voting age pop. (1980): 362,491; 12% Black, 2% Spanish origin, 1% Asian origin, 1% American Indian.

1988 Presidential Vote:

Bush (R)	161,314	(73%)
Dukakis (D)	59,014	(27%)

252 FLORIDA

Rep. Earl Dewitt Hutto (D)

Elected 1978; b. May 12, 1926, Midland City, AL; home, Panama City; Troy St. U., B.S. 1949, Northwestern U., 1951; Baptist; married (Nancy).

Career: Navy, WWII; Pres., Earl Hutto Adv. Agency, 1974–78; Founder and Pres., WPEX Radio, 1960–65; TV Sports Dir., WEAR, WSFA, WJHG, 1954–72; FL House of Reps., 1972–78.

Offices: 2435 RHOB 20515, 202-225-4136. Also Fed. Bldg., Panama City 32401, 904-763-0709; and 4300 Bayou Blvd., Pensacola 32503, 904-478-1123.

Committees: *Armed Services* (8th of 31 D). Subcommittees: Military Installations and Facilities; Readiness (Chairman); Seapower and Strategic and Critical Materials. *Merchant Marine and Fisheries* (5th of 26 D). Subcommittees: Coast Guard and Navigation; Fisheries and Wildlife Conservation and the Environment.

Group Ratings

	ADA	ACLU	COPE	CFA	LCV	ACU	NTLC	NSI	COC	CEI
1988	20	38	36	73	44	76	40	100	69	36
1987	24	—	34	29	—	68	—	—	64	35

National Journal Ratings

	1988 LIB — 1988 CONS		1987 LIB — 1987 CONS	
Economic	44%	— 55%	41%	— 58%
Social	24%	— 75%	37%	— 63%
Foreign	0%	— 84%	0%	— 80%

Key Votes

1) Homeless $	FOR	5) Ban Drug Test	—	9) SDI Research	FOR
2) Gephardt Amdt	AGN	6) Drug Death Pen	FOR	10) Ban Chem Weaps	AGN
3) Deficit Reduc	FOR	7) Handgun Sales	FOR	11) Aid to Contras	FOR
4) Kill Plnt Clsng Notice	FOR	8) Ban D.C. Abort $	FOR	12) Nuclear Testing	AGN

Election Results

1988 general	Earl Dewitt Hutto (D)	142,449	(67%)	($210,940)
	E.D. Armbruster (R)	70,534	(33%)	($23,912)
1988 primary	Earl Dewitt Hutto (D)	72,508	(72%)	
	Durell Peaden, Jr. (D)...............	28,883	(28%)	
1986 general	Earl Dewitt Hutto (D)	97,465	(64%)	($134,745)
	Greg Neubeck (R)	55,415	(36%)	($54,046)

SECOND DISTRICT

Dixie, the still distinct culture of the rural South, dips south into the Florida counties just below the Georgia line. Here you find catfish farms, large families, small towns with big churches, black and white. But the new Florida full of migrants from the North is expanding into the rural counties between Jacksonville and the panhandle. The catalyst is Tallahassee, the state capital located here in the 19th century when it seemed unlikely that any non-Seminole would penetrate the swampy vastness south of Jacksonville. With a fast-growing state government, plus Florida State University, Tallahassee has boomed and with surrounding Leon County now is approaching 200,000 in population. Tallahassee has not attained the critical mass of the capitals of the three more populous states, Albany, Austin, and Sacramento. But it is growing and spreading into the surrounding counties which otherwise have been losing population for decades.

Tallahassee's growth has changed the political complexion of the 2d Congressional District of Florida, which extends westward almost to Panama City and eastward almost to Jacksonville. Historically, this was Democratic country, Jeffersonian and segregationist. In the 1980s, unlike so much of the South, it has remained Democratic, not voting for the national ticket to be sure (except for Carter in 1980), but supporting statewide Democrats by large margins. The district's blacks are joined by Tallahassee whites who believe in—sometimes have a vested interest in—an active and generous government, and together they support liberals in Democratic primaries and Democrats in November. The 2d District was solidly for Bob Graham in 1986 and Buddy MacKay in 1988, and nearly went for Steve Pajcic for governor in 1986.

The congressman from the 2d, Bill Grant, has seen in his adult lifespan this shift from old to new Democratic politics—and has decided to shift himself, to the Republican Party. Grant grew up poor in a rural county at a time when north Florida's Pork Chop Gang ran state government from the legislature. He made his way upward in life as the district itself was growing economically, graduating at 20 from Florida State and becoming one of the prominent citizens of Madison County as a local banker. In 1982, with a rural base, he was elected to the Florida Senate from the district that includes Tallahassee. In 1986, when Congressman Don Fuqua, chairman of the Science and Technology Committee, decided to retire after 24 years in the House, Grant ran for the seat and won the Democratic primary with 51%, avoiding a runoff in a district in which the Republicans didn't even bother to run a candidate.

In his first 25 months in the House, Grant made little splash, compiling a record rather middle of the road. But in February 1989 he suddenly switched parties and became a Republican. His motives were not entirely clear. Electorally, he would certainly have found it easier to win reelection in this Democratic district as a Democrat who could normally expect little (or, as in 1988, no) opposition than as a Republican who would virtually be guaranteed an opponent every time. As a Republican he would find it easier to win a spot on the statewide ticket in 1990—but for all the Republicans' recent gains in Florida, that would still be a chancy proposition at best. Being a member of the minority rather than the majority offers, certainly in the short run, no particular advantages. So perhaps the best explanation is that Grant acted out of conviction, and that his first term voting record was an attempt at accommodation with his then fellow Democrats of which he tired in early 1989. Should he run for reelection, he can certainly expect a seriously contested race: this will be one district both parties will be anxious to win.

The People: Est. Pop. 1986: 586,800, up 14.5% 1980–86; Pop. 1980: 513,127, up 33.5% 1970–80. Households (1980): 74% family, 42% with children, 60% married couples; 29.0% housing units rented; median monthly rent: $142; median house value: $30,700. Voting age pop. (1980): 363,447; 22% Black, 1% Spanish origin.

1988 Presidential Vote:

Bush (R)	123,524	(59%)
Dukakis (D)	83,458	(40%)

Rep. Bill Grant (R)

Elected 1986; b. Feb. 21, 1943, Lake City; home, Madison; FL St. U., B.A. 1963; Baptist; married (Janet).

Career: Bank pres., 1973–86; FL Senate, 1982–86.

Offices: 1330 LHOB 20515, 202-225-5235. 930 Thomasville Rd., Ste. 103, Tallahassee 32303, 904-681-7434; 1990-A S. 1st St., Lake City 32055, 904-755-5657; and P.O. Bldg., #109, Marianna 32446, 904-526-3525.

Committees: *Agriculture* (18th of 18 R). Subcommittees: Tobacco and Peanuts; Livestock, Dairy and Poultry. *Public Works and Transportation* (20th of 20 R). *Select Committee on Narcotics Abuse and Control* (12th of 12 R).

Group Ratings

	ADA	ACLU	COPE	CFA	LCV	ACU	NTLC	NSI	COC	CEI
1988	50	45	73	73	50	54	15	67	57	23
1987	52	—	69	50	—	25	—	—	47	17

National Journal Ratings

	1988 LIB — 1988 CONS		1987 LIB — 1987 CONS	
Economic	54% —	44%	68% —	27%
Social	42% —	57%	38% —	62%
Foreign	46% —	53%	46% —	54%

Key Votes

1) Homeless $	AGN	5) Ban Drug Test	AGN	9) SDI Research	AGN
2) Gephardt Amdt	FOR	6) Drug Death Pen	FOR	10) Ban Chem Weaps	AGN
3) Deficit Reduc	FOR	7) Handgun Sales	FOR	11) Aid to Contras	FOR
4) Kill Plnt Clsng Notice	AGN	8) Ban D.C. Abort $	FOR	12) Nuclear Testing	AGN

Election Results

1988 general	Bill Grant (D)	134,269	(100%)	($223,117)
1988 primary	Bill Grant (D), unopposed			
1986 general	Bill Grant (D)	110,120	(100%)	($266,070)

THIRD DISTRICT

In 1940 Jacksonville was Florida's largest metropolitan area, the biggest city on the whole southeastern coast from the Chesapeake Bay to the Florida Keys, a port surrounded by a swampy, sleepy rural South whose ways had changed little since Reconstruction. Today it is much larger and more prosperous, spreading over the lowlands on either side of the St. Johns River and along the Atlantic coast; if it has been overshadowed by larger Florida metro areas and by the big metro areas which dominate smaller southern states, it is still a big city itself: an important port, paper manufacturer, banking and insurance center, and site of military bases, with a metropolitan population approaching 1 million. More than other Florida cities, it is part of the South, with a large black population, plenty of blue-collar whites with southern accents, lots of children and relatively few retirees. Politically, its heritage is Democratic but it has been trending Republican in state as well as national elections.

Florida's 3d Congressional District, which includes almost all of Jacksonville and one county to the north, is represented by one of the senior members of the House, Charles Bennett, a Democrat first elected in 1948. A punctilious man and a stickler for propriety, he is one of the last World War II veterans in Congress; he enlisted after he was 30, performed heroically, and contracted polio in the service. Though he must use canes to walk, he answers every roll call. He was a pioneer supporter in the 1950s of ethical codes and disclosure of congressmen's finances; it was years before his code of ethics was applied to federal employees, and when the House finally did set up an Ethics Committee in 1967, he was pointedly kept off it for years. House leaders feared, justifiably, that he would not be understanding of members' difficulties. Finally, in 1978, with the Koreagate scandal looming and Bennett the committee's senior member, when he could no longer be denied the chair, he oversaw the Abscam investigation and recommended and secured the expulsion of Representative Ozzie Myers from the House.

Bennett's delay in receiving the ethics chair was not his only disappointment. He was deeply shaken by the death of his 22-year-old son from a drug overdose in 1977. "It was the greatest wound in my life," he said, and in the 1980s championed a measure to require the military to interdict drug traffickers outside U.S. borders. Opposed by the Defense Department, contrary to the principle of separation of the military from civilian life, it was passed by an overwhelming vote in the House in 1985. His major committee is Armed Services, and here too he has suffered disappointments. After the 1984 election, he supported aging Chairman Mel Price, and after Price was voted out by the Democratic Caucus sought the chair himself. But he was beaten by Les Aspin, whose seniority dates only to 1970. After the 1986 election, he opposed Aspin again, and was again painfully rejected, as the main opposition to the chairman came from the much less senior Marvin Leath.

Yet, at an age when most people are slowing down, and when many bowed down with disappointment simply withdraw, Bennett has returned to the fray in the late 1980s with apparently renewed zest. In May 1987 he led a successful floor fight to cut $500 million from the Administration's $3.1 billion Strategic Defense Initiative; Bennett questions whether it will be destabilizing or vulnerable to Soviet anti-satellite weapons or low-flying missiles. A vigorous supporter of the 600-ship Navy as chairman of the Seapower Subcommittee, he felt that the U.S. reflagging operation in the Persian Gulf did not have clear goals.

Back home in Jacksonville, support of the military leads to other local causes. Near Mayport Bennett has coerced Congress to establish the 35,000-acre Timucuan Historic Preserve. He sponsored the Abandoned Shipwreck Act and the Bennett-Moss Act allotting federal money to archaeology. He shepherded through the House money for a light rail system in Jacksonville and the Acosta Bridge Replacement project in Jacksonville. On issues like the MX and SDI, Bennett has become more of a national Democrat than ever, and he made a point of appearing with Michael Dukakis in Jacksonville in 1988. That has not made any difference in his local standing, which remains high: after 40 years he was reelected without opposition.

The People: Est. Pop. 1986: 575,500, up 12.2% 1980–86; Pop. 1980: 512,692, up 4.7% 1970–80. Households (1980): 73% family, 42% with children, 55% married couples; 36.6% housing units rented; median monthly rent: $165; median house value: $29,900. Voting age pop. (1980): 362,272; 25% Black, 2% Spanish origin, 1% Asian origin.

1988 Presidential Vote: Bush (R)   97,659   (60%)
                              Dukakis (D).   65,215   (40%)

Rep. Charles E. Bennett (D)

Elected 1948; b. Dec. 2, 1910, Canton, NY; home, Jacksonville; U. of FL, B.A., J.D. 1934; Disciples of Christ; married (Jean).

Career: Practicing atty., 1934–42, 1947–48; FL House of Reps., 1941–42; Army, WWII.

Offices: 2107 RHOB 20515, 202-225-2501. Also 314 Palmetto St., Jacksonville 32202, 904-791-2587.

Committees: *Armed Services* (2d of 31 D). Subcommittees: Seapower and Strategic and Critical Materials (Chairman); Research and Development. *Merchant Marine and Fisheries* (16th of 26 D). Subcommittees: Coast Guard and Navigation; Merchant Marine; Oceanography.

Group Ratings

	ADA	ACLU	COPE	CFA	LCV	ACU	NTLC	NSI	COC	CEI
1988	65	43	48	82	75	28	34	60	43	25
1987	48	—	47	79	—	22	—	—	60	18

National Journal Ratings

	1988 LIB — 1988 CONS	1987 LIB — 1987 CONS
Economic	54% — 44%	46% — 52%
Social	47% — 52%	45% — 54%
Foreign	55% — 45%	52% — 47%

Key Votes

1) Homeless $	FOR	5) Ban Drug Test	FOR	9) SDI Research	AGN
2) Gephardt Amdt	AGN	6) Drug Death Pen	FOR	10) Ban Chem Weaps	AGN
3) Deficit Reduc	FOR	7) Handgun Sales	AGN	11) Aid to Contras	FOR
4) Kill Plnt Clsng Notice	AGN	8) Ban D.C. Abort $	FOR	12) Nuclear Testing	FOR

Election Results

1988 general	Charles E. Bennett (D), unopposed	($19,500)
1988 primary	Charles E. Bennett (D), unopposed	
1986 general	Charles E. Bennett (D), unopposed	($19,564)

FOURTH DISTRICT

Between the broad St. Johns River, flowing northward from the swamps of central Florida toward Jacksonville and the ocean, and the hard sand beaches that stretch south from Jacksonville to Daytona Beach toward Cape Canaveral is the 4th Congressional District of Florida. Two generations ago the land was mostly swamps and orange groves: tourists on U.S. 1 heading south stopped to poke around the narrow streets of St. Augustine, the oldest city in the United States, settled by the Spanish in the 16th century. In the years since World War II, the beaches attracted migrants from North and South, while the little orange grove towns inland burgeoned; more recently the overspill of Jacksonville and its large military population spread south inland from the beaches and along the St. Johns River. Politically, this became border country, between northern migrants who tended to be Republicans or southerners who were often Democrats. For the moment none of these groups—white Southern Baptists or northern Episcopalians, southern country clubbers or factory-town ethnics—dominates.

In 1988 the 4th District was the scene of the biggest upset in any of the nation's 435 House districts. Congressman Bill Chappell had much going for him. He had deep roots in north Florida: he was elected to the legislature in 1956; he was part of the legendary Pork Chop Gang and served as speaker. He had 20 years of seniority in the House. He was chairman of the Defense Appropriations Subcommittee, responsible for the lion's share of the Pentagon spending—one of the weightiest responsibilities in Congress and one of the best perches from which to raise campaign money. Yet after the counting was over, Chappell had lost to Craig James, a 47-year-old lawyer who had never run for office before, had decided to run only 9 days before the July 1988 filing date, and then had to change his registration from Democratic to Republican.

"What happened was [that] he beat himself," James said after the election. Chappell was an old-style pol who smoked cigars and hated to issue press releases; he hid out from reporters and said little on the campaign trail. He made little of his record as a Navy pilot in World War II and the expertise he brought to his defense work—he liked to fly a lot of the planes he funded. What did get publicized were his ethical problems. Press reports said he was a target of the 1987 Pentagon procurement scandal, though that was never officially confirmed. Closer to home, from his 1983 income tax he deducted $30,000 for rent to a company he owned, which then promptly loaned him back the money; and he sold a failed health club in Palatka to a subsidiary of Martin Marietta for $195,000 in 1986. On top of that, his campaign raked in huge amounts—over $250,000—of contributions from defense-related PACs and individuals.

Chappell had little trouble beating a retired military officer in the primary 70%–30%. But James was made of tougher stuff. In his primary James showed that opponent Tom Visconti, a boyhood friend and recent legal client, had 42 bad check convictions in 1965–67; James won the three-man race with 50.3%—exactly 100 more votes than he needed to avoid a runoff. In the general he called Chappell "the embodiment of everything that is wrong with Congress," and marched into Chappell's Jacksonville headquarters and challenged him to a debate. The Republican campaign committee ran $55,000 worth of TV ads calling Chappell—whom national Republicans had not vigorously opposed in years because of his defense record—"an embarrassment." James, financed partly with his own money, started heavy advertising two weeks out; he called for abolishing PACs and limiting congressional terms. The result was exceedingly close. Chappell hoped the result would be overturned by military absentees, but absentee votes as usual went heavily Republican. Then Chappell argued that Flagler County's votes shouldn't be counted because they had not been handed in by the clerk by the legal deadline; this was brushed aside. James won by a 50.1%–49.9% margin. In March 1989 Chappell died of cancer.

James comes to Washington as a Mr. Smith decrying the way things are done. He wants to abolish PACs, long favored by House Republicans (though not any more by many), and when he was asked if losing Chappell's clout would hurt Florida, he said, "That's the kind of clout they need to lose. If he used that clout to bring companies to Florida, that was an abuse of power." He took on controversial causes as a lawyer, he says, including defending a local private school against sex abuse charges in the 1970s and stopping Volusia County from building a jail outside De Land in 1982. It will be interesting to see how he—and Washington—get along. His chances for reelection should be good. The 4th is used to Republicans; it elects as many Republicans as Democrats to the legislature; if he makes a credible record and takes the trouble to use the electoral advantages of incumbency as Chappell did not, he may be in solid shape.

The People: Est. Pop. 1986: 652,200, up 27.2% 1980–86; Pop. 1980: 512,672, up 56.8% 1970–80. Households (1980): 72% family, 33% with children, 61% married couples; 28.7% housing units rented;

median monthly rent: $196; median house value: $41,800. Voting age pop. (1980): 385,967; 9% Black, 2% Spanish origin.

1988 Presidential Vote: Bush (R) 169,949   (64%)
                              Dukakis (D). 95,362   (36%)

Rep. Craig T. James (R)

Elected 1988; b. May 5, 1941 Augusta, Georgia; home, Deland; Stetson U., B.S. 1963, J.D. 1967; Baptist; married (Katherine).

Career: Practicing Atty. 1967–88.

Offices: 1408 LHOB, 20515, 202-225-4035. Also 101 N. Woodland Blvd. Ste. 201, Deland 32720, 904-734-5523; 116 Seabreeze Blvd., St. 126, Daytona Beach 32018, 904-239-9823; and One San Jose Pl., Ste. 28, Jacksonville, 32207, 904-268-2038.

Committees: *Judiciary* (14th of 14 R). Subcommittees: Administrative Law and Governmental Relations; Civil and Constitutional Rights. *Veterans' Affairs* (11th of 12 R). Subcommittee: Oversight and Investigations. *Select Committee on Aging* (27 of 27 R).

Group Ratings and Key Votes: Newly Elected
Election Results

1988 general	Craig T. James (R)	125,608	(50%)	($313,415)
	Bill Chappell, Jr. (D)	124,817	(50%)	($1,069,699)
1988 primary	Craig T. James (R)	19,275	(50%)	
	Tom Visconti (R).	10,380	(27%)	
	Ken C. McCarthy (R)	8,694	(23%)	
1986 general	Bill Chappell, Jr. (D) unopposed			($139,758)

FIFTH DISTRICT

Orlando 50 years ago was a town of 40,000 amid acres of citrus grove; today it is the number one tourist destination in the world. It is also the center of a metropolitan area of about 1 million which has been growing more rapidly than just about any other in the country, with a diversified high-tech economy and a population weighted toward young families with children rather than retirees. Much of this change can be traced to the decision and vision of one man. Walt Disney invented the theme park in the flatlands of Orange County, California, but he perfected it in the 17,000 acres of swamp and lakes in Florida's Orange County. Disney not only invented the theme park, but he also pioneered in sophisticated communications, utility, and waste disposal methods—all out of sight and underground. Yet Disney World does not work mechanically; it requires some 17,000 people, with know-how and unfailing cheerfulness. Disney's vision of a future that was labor-intensive as well as high-tech, in which the critical variable is not industrial production but the provision of services, was a forecast of the service-driven economy that has grown so lustily—and despite adverse predictions—in the 1980s.

Disney World, on acreage bigger than a city itself, is 15 miles southwest of Orlando; but the city's growth is elsewhere—high income areas like Maitland and Altamonte Springs to the north, more modest places like Winter Garden and Apopka to the west and northwest. This means that the 5th Congressional District of Florida, which includes most of the Orlando metropolitan area, actually doesn't contain Disney World, though it is home to most of its work force. Once Democratic, Orlando is now Republican, and the 5th District is one of the most Republican in Florida, and in state and congressional as well as national elections.

Bill McCollum, the 5th District's congressman, was first elected in 1980, when the district ousted Richard Kelly, a dimwitted Republican caught stuffing bribe money in his pockets by Abscam cameramen. McCollum is not blow-dry handsome nor is he a speculative thinker, but he has become one of his party's most active and accomplished legislators. On Judiciary he was the lead spokesman in the debate on the immigration bill against an amnesty for illegal aliens, though he supported the bill when amnesty won. He supports a cutback in class-action work by the Legal Services Corporation. When a seven-day waiting period was proposed for gun purchases, McCollum substituted an amendment commanding the government to produce a nationwide list of convicted felons to which all gun dealers would have access; gun control advocates charged this would gut their bill, but McCollum called it a better way to see that the wrong people can't buy guns. On drugs he wrote a money laundering provision into the 1987 drug law, and sponsored the death penalty in drug-related matters and the "user accountability" provisions that went into the 1988 act—depriving convicted drug users of federal mortgage aid and student loans, for example. On AIDS he tried unsuccessfully to get the federal government to require marriage license testing in states with high AIDS incidences and notification of the spouses of HIV-positive patients.

Despite the lack of a relevant committee assignment, McCollum has also ventured into foreign policy. He organized a volunteer airlift of medical supplies to El Salvador in 1983 and he sponsored the law to airlift "non-lethal" supplies to the Afghan rebels, whose cause he strongly supported. He was one of the vocal Republican critics of the critics of the Reagan Administration on the Iran-contra committee. His proficiency at detail work and popularity among younger and older Republicans help explain why Minority Leader Robert Michel chose him as one of the Republicans on the Iran-contra investigating committee.

McCollum had his last serious challenge at home in 1982 and won 59%–41%; he had no opposition in 1988.

The People: Est. Pop. 1986: 644,200, up 25.6% 1980–86; Pop. 1980: 513,005, up 47.0% 1970–80. Households (1980): 73% family, 38% with children, 59% married couples; 33.9% housing units rented; median monthly rent: $200; median house value: $45,400. Voting age pop. (1980): 373,987; 14% Black, 3% Spanish origin, 1% Asian origin.

1988 Presidential Vote:

Bush (R)	131,585	(68%)
Dukakis (D)	59,038	(31%)

Rep. Bill McCollum (R)

Elected 1980; b. July 12, 1944, Brooksville; home, Altamonte Springs; U. of FL, B.A. 1965, J.D. 1968; Episcopalian; married (Ingrid).

Career: Navy, 1969–72; Practicing atty., 1973–81; Chmn., Seminole Cnty. Repub. Exec. Cmttees., 1976.

Offices: 1507 LHOB 20515, 202-225-2176. Also 1801 Lee Rd., Ste. 301, Winter Park 32789, 305-645-3100.

Committees: *Banking, Finance and Urban Affairs* (5th of 20 R). Subcommittees: Domestic Monetary Policy (Ranking Member); Financial Institutions Supervision, Regulation and Insurance; Housing and Community Development. *Judiciary* (5th of 14 R). Subcommittees: Crime (Ranking Member); Immigration, Refugees and International Law.

Group Ratings

	ADA	ACLU	COPE	CFA	LCV	ACU	NTLC	NSI	COC	CEI
1988	0	14	7	36	25	100	85	100	75	66
1987	0	—	6	29	—	87	—	—	100	73

National Journal Ratings

	1988 LIB — 1988 CONS	1987 LIB — 1987 CONS
Economic	21% — 77%	19% — 78%
Social	13% — 84%	10% — 85%
Foreign	0% — 84%	0% — 80%

Key Votes

1) Homeless $	FOR	5) Ban Drug Test	FOR	9) SDI Research	FOR
2) Gephardt Amdt	AGN	6) Drug Death Pen	FOR	10) Ban Chem Weaps	AGN
3) Deficit Reduc	AGN	7) Handgun Sales	FOR	11) Aid to Contras	FOR
4) Kill Plnt Clsng Notice	FOR	8) Ban D.C. Abort $	FOR	12) Nuclear Testing	AGN

Election Results

1988 general	Bill McCollum (R), unopposed	($304,853)
1988 primary	Bill McCollum (R), unopposed	
1986 general	Bill McCollum (R), unopposed	($121,052)

SIXTH DISTRICT

The growth that has transformed Florida's coasts for the last 50 years has now moved inland as well, to the lush grasslands of northern Florida. This is the site of some of the earliest development of the state. Here in Gainesville the state placed the University of Florida, where a large share of Florida's political elite share fond memories of the Gator Bowl. Here also is the bluegrass horse farm country around Ocala, where many of the nation's top thoroughbreds are raised and trained. Up Florida's turnpike and Interstate 75 the developers come with blueprints for new condominium villages and shopping centers and office blocks and trailer parks. This is the land that makes up the 6th Congressional District of Florida, from Gainesville and Ocala in the north to Lake County outside of Orlando and fast-growing, modest-income Hernando and Citrus Counties on the Gulf Coast.

Development has changed the politics of this area, which 25 years ago was simply southern Democratic. Now you can see the origins of the newcomers in the voting totals. Marion County around Ocala, like the bluegrass land around Lexington, Kentucky, is trending Republican, while Gainesville, like Ann Arbor, Michigan, is liberal and Democratic. The Gulf Coast counties, with many blue- as well as white-collar retirees, are mixed.

Change is also apparent in the election results, for the 6th District produced the nation's biggest upset in an open-seat race in 1988. This was created to be a Democratic district, and was won easily in 1982 by Buddy MacKay, a 12-year legislator who had come within 5% of making the runoff in the 1980 primary for U.S. Senator. He had no primary opposition for this House seat and won 61% in the general. In 1988 MacKay ran for Senate again, winning the Democratic nomination but losing to Connie Mack III by less than 1% and carrying the 6th with 56%. Jon Mills, the Speaker of the Florida House, who was unopposed for the 6th District seat in the Democratic primary and expected to win the general as MacKay had, instead lost 53%–47% to Republican Cliff Stearns.

It was a race of somebody versus nobody. Mills, born in Miami, went to college in Gainesville and stayed; he was in the legislature 10 years, was Speaker for four, was head of a university Center for Governmental Responsibility he set up. In presidential politics he supported Gary Hart in 1984 and Albert Gore in 1988. He was endorsed by every newspaper in the district. Stearns moved from Massachusetts to Ocala and started a business that owns five motels and three restaurants. He campaigned as "someone who works in the community, goes to church with his neighbors, and doesn't live in Tallahassee." He attacked Mills for his support of the sales tax on services, which had to be repealed because of public outcry. He campaigned less on George Bush's national issues than against the incumbent Congress, calling for limiting PACs and protecting congressional employees. Mills, expecting to win, took moderate lines on national issues and criticized Stearns for switching on long-term health care. The interesting question now is whether Stearns can sustain his citizen-in-politics appeal as an incumbent congressman— and whether this approach can work for Republican candidates elsewhere.

The People: Est. Pop. 1986: 679,800, up 32.5% 1980–86; Pop. 1980: 512,950, up 70.9% 1970–80. Households (1980): 73% family, 31% with children, 62% married couples; 27.0% housing units rented; median monthly rent: $174; median house value: $37,500. Voting age pop. (1980): 394,134; 12% Black, 2% Spanish origin.

1988 Presidential Vote:			
	Bush (R)	159,938	(61%)
	Dukakis (D)	101,833	(39%)

Rep. Clifford B. Stearns (R)

Elected 1988; b. April 16, 1941, Washington, DC; home, Ocala; Geo. Wash. U., B.S. 1963; Presbyterian; married (Joan).

Career: Air Force, 1963-67; Data Control Systems, Inc; Negotiator, CBS, 1969-70; Pres., Stearns House Inc., 1972-present.

Offices: 1630 LHOB 20515, 202-225-5744. Also 501 S.E. 26th Ct., #125, Ocala 32671, 904-351-8777; and 401 S.E. First Ave., #316, Gainesville 32601, 904-372-0382.

Committees: *Banking, Finance and Urban Affairs* (18th of 20 R). Subcommittees: Housing and Community Development; Financial Institutions Supervision, Regulation and Insurance. *Veterans' Affairs* (12th of 12 R). Subcommittee: Oversight and Investigations.

Group Ratings and Key Votes: Newly Elected

Election Results

1988 general	Clifford B. Stearns (R)	136,415	(54%)	($408,292)
	Jon Mills (D)	118,756	(46%)	($503,654)
1988 runoff	Clifford B. Stearns (R)	15,205	(54%)	
	Jim Cherry (R)	12,882	(46%)	
1988 primary	Jim Cherry (R)	13,355	(32%)	
	Clifford B. Stearns (R)	10,875	(26%)	
	Roy Abshier (R)	6,459	(16%)	
	Larry Gallagher (R)	5,984	(15%)	
	Others	4,532	(11%)	
1986 general	Kenneth H. (Buddy) MacKay (D)	143,583	(70%)	($462,732)
	Larry Gallagher (R)	61,053	(30%)	($14,522)

SEVENTH DISTRICT

Tampa, much to the surprise of many, has turned out to be one of Florida's boom communities in the 1980s. This is not what one would have predicted; 50 years ago Tampa was Florida's one industrial city, with a port and cigar factories—just the kind of place that had been stagnating for 20 years. But in the 1980s Tampa has a growing, gleaming skyline, a first-class airport, room for its subdivisions and condominiums to spread inland across swamps and lowlands, and the world's longest sidewalk (6.5 miles along Bayshore Boulevard). It is a city of families and younger people, a place with a blue-collar past which is fast moving upscale as it expands.

Tampa and most of surrounding Hillsborough County form the 7th Congressional District of Florida. This district has had the same congressman since it was created in 1962, Democrat Sam Gibbons. Historically Tampa has been as Democratic as St. Petersburg has been Republican, and the cities' legislative delegations still reflect this. But in seriously contested statewide races they have tended to converge and sometimes, as in the 1988 presidential election, Tampa is more Republican than St. Petersburg. It was Tampa, not some long-Republican-held constituency, that produced Republican Governor Bob Martinez in 1986.

Sam Gibbons has deep roots in Tampa and in the Democratic Party. He has the look of an old-fashioned southern congressman, and the philosophy of one: specifically, of Cordell Hull, who in decades in Congress and as Secretary of State singlemindedly championed the cause of free trade. From his study of the years before and after World War II Gibbons carries the conviction that free trade expands every economy and that the ties made by healthy trade relations help to prevent the outbreak of war. Gibbons has moved around a lot, at least when measured against his fellow Democrats, on other issues: he was one of the few southern Democrats to support the Kennedy and Johnson Administrations faithfully, but balked at some civil rights bills; he championed reforms to open up House procedures, and he ran a quixotic and aborted race for majority leader against Tip O'Neill in 1972; a foreign policy hawk, he wasn't in tandem opposing the Vietnam war, nor was he a champion of liberated cultural values.

But beyond all that he kept his interest in trade. He had a seat on Ways and Means and on its Trade Subcommittee, and by 1981, when he was number two in seniority on the full committee, he succeeded to the subcommittee chair. There he has been unable in the 1980s to do exactly as he wanted. He has recognized that the demand of House Democrats for restrictive trade legislation cannot be resisted without damaging his chances at succeeding to Rostenkowski's full committee chair some day. He allowed some restrictive trade bills—the textile bill, for example—to reach the floor despite his own opposition, and he voted for bills with provisions he found obnoxious—like the Gephardt trade retaliation measure—on the floor. He has reason to believe that Rostenkowski and Senate Finance Chairman Lloyd Bentsen are free traders too, but he is close to neither man and seems to have a grating relationship with Rostenkowski. Gibbons had hoped Rostenkowski would become party whip in 1981 and leave the chairmanship to him; Rostenkowski, who supports his other subcommittee chairmen, seems cool to Gibbons. Gibbons played virtually no part in the 1985 and 1986 tax reform bill, and Rostenkowski pointedly left him off the conference committee on the bill.

Events work against him too: it is hard to argue that the United States is not the target of some unfair trade practices in East Asia. And Gibbons has supported trade sanctions against South Africa and its apartheid policies. But he has also had his satisfactions, the success of the free trade treaty with Canada being the most notable.

Gibbons was challenged once at home in the 1980s, when Tampa Judge Michael Kavouklis held him to 59%—far below his earlier showings. Gibbons vowed to spend more time in the district and to raise more money for his campaigns. So he has become what anyone in his seat in Ways and Means can easily become, one of the leading PAC and individual fundraisers on Capitol Hill, with a pile of cash half a million or so high to spend if someone runs against him. In 1986 and 1988 no one has.

The People: Est. Pop. 1986: 600,500, up 17.1% 1980–86; Pop. 1980: 512,905, up 25.3% 1970–80. Households (1980): 71% family, 37% with children, 56% married couples; 35.1% housing units rented; median monthly rent: $188; median house value: $35,800. Voting age pop. (1980): 376,478; 13% Black, 11% Spanish origin, 1% Asian origin.

1988 Presidential Vote:

Bush (R)	107,474	(58%)
Dukakis (D)	76,831	(41%)

Rep. Sam M. Gibbons (D)

Elected 1962; b. Jan. 20, 1920, Tampa; home, Tampa; U. of FL; J.D. 1947; Presbyterian; married (Martha).

Career: Army, WWII; Practicing atty., 1947–62; FL House of Reps., 1952–58; FL Senate, 1958–62.

Offices: 2204 RHOB 20515, 202-225-3376. Also 101 E. Kennedy Blvd., Tampa 33602, 813-228-2101; and 201 S. Kings Ave., #6, Brandon 33511, 813-689-2847.

Committees: *Ways and Means* (2d of 23 D). Subcommittees: Social Security; Trade (Chairman). *Joint Committee on Taxation.*

Group Ratings

	ADA	ACLU	COPE	CFA	LCV	ACU	NTLC	NSI	COC	CEI
1988	60	65	55	73	63	35	20	40	64	31
1987	52	—	54	64	—	32	—	—	33	22

National Journal Ratings

	1988 LIB — 1988 CONS		1987 LIB — 1987 CONS	
Economic	40%	— 58%	60%	— 40%
Social	52%	— 48%	59%	— 40%
Foreign	54%	— 46%	57%	— 43%

Key Votes

1) Homeless $	AGN	5) Ban Drug Test	AGN	9) SDI Research	AGN
2) Gephardt Amdt	AGN	6) Drug Death Pen	FOR	10) Ban Chem Weaps	AGN
3) Deficit Reduc	FOR	7) Handgun Sales	AGN	11) Aid to Contras	FOR
4) Kill Plnt Clsng Notice	AGN	8) Ban D.C. Abort $	FOR	12) Nuclear Testing	FOR

Election Results

1988 general	Sam M. Gibbons (D), unopposed	($382,889)
1988 primary	Sam M. Gibbons (D), unopposed	
1986 general	Sam M. Gibbons (D), unopposed	($563,509)

EIGHTH DISTRICT

St. Petersburg has long been America's premier retiree city, a stereotype of old folks on a park bench, a butt of jokes, a bit of shorthand. Even before World War II a few retirees had come here; in the years afterward the Pinellas Peninsula on which St. Petersburg sits seemed to fill up with them. Others came too: St. Petersburg does have its young families and light manufacturing. But in the 8th Congressional District, which includes St. Petersburg and Pinellas County suburbs as far north as Clearwater, only 23% of households contain children, and 34% of adults are 65 or older—the highest percentage in any congressional district in the country. There are more than 40,000 people over 65 living alone in the constituency, accounting for one out of every six households.

Over four decades the politics of St. Petersburg has shifted at least twice, thanks to new migrants. In the 1940s and 1950s Yankee migrants of at least modest affluence—blue-collar workers at the time didn't get much in the way of pensions—voted as they had back home and made St. Petersburg Republican. It voted Republican for President in 1948 and elected a Republican congressman in 1954. Then in the 1970s St. Petersburg started trending Democratic. In 1976, Pinellas County almost went for Carter and in the 1980s it voted for Bob Graham and Buddy MacKay for senator. The inevitable turnover in elderly population was replacing affluent Republicans with retired blue-collar Democrats who increasingly could afford to retire to Florida. They settled in St. Petersburg, while their more affluent counterparts went to the newer, more glittery retirement towns.

This elderly district is represented by a man named Young, a Republican elected by white-collar retirees who comes from blue-collar Pennsylvania and started off in politics at an early age. In the 1950s, while he was in his 20s, Bill Young worked for Congressman William Cramer; in the 1960s, he served in the Florida Senate; in 1970, he was elected to the House from the St. Petersburg district to replace Cramer when he ran unsuccessfully for the Senate. Through careful attention to the district and devotion to Social Security, Young has gained a reputation for political strength, and has encountered no serious challenges. Against a respectable opponent in 1988 he won by nearly 3 to 1.

Young spends most of his time in Washington on his Appropriations subcommittees, Defense and Labor-HHS-Education. On the latter he is able to protect Social Security, but he devotes more attention to Defense, where he ranks just behind Republican Joseph McDade. Young is a strong supporter of Republican Administration military programs and is often the point man against Democrats.

The People: Est. Pop. 1986: 559,200, up 9.0% 1980–86; Pop. 1980: 512,909, up 30.3% 1970–80. Households (1980): 65% family, 23% with children, 54% married couples; 28.7% housing units rented; median monthly rent: $201; median house value: $39,600. Voting age pop. (1980): 413,853; 7% Black, 1% Spanish origin.

1988 Presidential Vote:

Bush (R)	131,100	(56%)
Dukakis (D)	103,040	(44%)

Rep. C. W. (Bill) Young (R)

Elected 1970; b. Dec. 16, 1930, Harmarville, PA; home, Largo; United Methodist; married (Beverly).

Career: Aide to U.S. Rep. William C. Cramer, 1957–60; FL Senate, 1960–70, Minority Leader, 1966–70.

Offices: 2407 RHOB 20515, 202-225-5961. Also 627 Fed. Bldg., St. Petersburg 33701, 813-893-3191.

Committees: *Appropriations* (6th of 22 R). Subcommittees: Defense; Labor, Health and Human Services, and Education.

Group Ratings

	ADA	ACLU	COPE	CFA	LCV	ACU	NTLC	NSI	COC	CEI
1988	10	18	15	36	31	88	61	100	79	60
1987	8	—	14	43	—	87	—	—	93	62

National Journal Ratings

	1988 LIB — 1988 CONS			1987 LIB — 1987 CONS		
Economic	30%	—	69%	24%	—	74%
Social	12%	—	87%	19%	—	78%
Foreign	16%	—	78%	25%	—	74%

Key Votes

1) Homeless $	FOR	5) Ban Drug Test	FOR	9) SDI Research	FOR
2) Gephardt Amdt	AGN	6) Drug Death Pen	FOR	10) Ban Chem Weaps	AGN
3) Deficit Reduc	AGN	7) Handgun Sales	AGN	11) Aid to Contras	FOR
4) Kill Plnt Clsng Notice	FOR	8) Ban D.C. Abort $	FOR	12) Nuclear Testing	AGN

Election Results

1988 general	C. W. (Bill) Young (R)	169,165	(73%)	($208,320)
	C. Bette Wimbish (D).................	62,539	(27%)	($37,947)
1988 primary	C. W. (Bill) Young (R), unopposed			
1986 general	C. W. (Bill) Young (R), unopposed			($96,142)

NINTH DISTRICT

In 1940—even in the late 1950s—you could have driven U.S. 19 north from St. Petersburg's Pinellas County and never noticed anything but the swamp. The road passed through intersections marked by gas stations, and every so often there was a sleepy little town, with low brick buildings constructed in some northern style, baking in the Florida sun. There weren't many people here. The coastline that looks so tempting on the map was then under the kind of water that fills a swamp. Any large development would have required investment in an infrastructure—water and sewer lines, underground electricity—that would have seemed hopelessly uneconomical.

Today all that investment has been made, and the Gulf Coast for 50 miles north of St. Petersburg is home now to half a million people (and that doesn't include the 350,000 right around St. Petersburg). This is not the Florida where the rich of Greenwich and Winnetka retire; it is the final home of more modest people, many of them blue-collar, most of them probably with Democratic rather than Republican heritages. Most of this area is in the 9th Congressional District, one of the four new districts created by the Florida legislature after the 1980 Census. The district begins in Largo and Clearwater, some eight miles from St. Petersburg, and continues up past the old resort of Tarpon Springs to the new condominium communities of Holiday, Elfers, New Port Richey, Bayonet Point, and Hudson in Pasco County. It also sweeps inland, circling Tampa and including the agricultural center of Plant City inland; but more than two-thirds of its population is along the coast.

The legislature intended this to be a Democratic district; it elects many Democrats to the legislature and voted in 1988 for Senate candidate Buddy MacKay; it can be mobilized for the Democrats if anyone suggests a Republican will cut Social Security. But it was won by Republican Michael Bilirakis in 1982 and he has made it a safe seat. Bilirakis is a lawyer and restaurant owner from the large Greek-American community in Tarpon Springs; he grew up in Pittsburgh and worked his way through college toiling in a steel mill; he served in the Air Force during the Korean War; he is pleasant and has been active in civic affairs. In 1982 he ran as a citizen-politician and beat experienced state legislators in the primary and general; he has won overwhelmingly since. He is a foe in general of government spending and profligacy, but is all for generous Social Security benefits and government-funded research on Alzheimer's disease. In Washington he has a plum committee assignment, Energy and Commerce, where he works amicably with Health Subcommittee Chairman Henry Waxman on issues important in Florida retirement spots, like health care for the elderly and clean air. But he is not a forceful or front rank legislator.

The People: Est. Pop. 1986: 636,900, up 24.1% 1980–86; Pop. 1980: 513,191, up 91.6% 1970–80. Households (1980): 74% family, 27% with children, 65% married couples; 22.2% housing units rented; median monthly rent: $208; median house value: $44,600. Voting age pop. (1980): 404,361; 3% Black, 2% Spanish origin.

1988 Presidential Vote:

Bush (R)	178,253	(60%)
Dukakis (D)	116,408	(39%)

Rep. Michael Bilirakis (R)

Elected 1982; b. July 16, 1930, Tarpon Springs; home, Palm Harbor; U. of Pittsburgh, B.S. 1959, U. of FL, J.D. 1963; Greek Orthodox; married (Evelyn).

Career: Air Force, Korea; Steelworker, 1955–59; Govt. contract negotiator, 1959–60; Petroleum engineer, 1960–63; Practicing atty., 1969–83.

Offices: 1130 LHOB 20515, 202-225-5755. Also 1100 Cleveland St., Ste. 1600, Clearwater 33515, 813-441-3721.

Committees: *Energy and Commerce* (14th of 17 R). Subcommittees: Energy and Power; Oversight and Investigations; Health and the Environment. *Veterans' Affairs* (7th of 21 R). Subcommittees: Compensation, Pensions and Insurance; Hospitals and Health Care.

Group Ratings

	ADA	ACLU	COPE	CFA	LCV	ACU	NTLC	NSI	COC	CEI
1988	10	39	22	45	44	96	86	100	93	72
1987	16	—	23	29	—	78	—	—	87	74

National Journal Ratings

	1988 LIB — 1988 CONS	1987 LIB — 1987 CONS
Economic	21% — 77%	24% — 74%
Social	13% — 87%	25% — 73%
Foreign	0% — 84%	0% — 80%

Key Votes

1) Homeless $	FOR	5) Ban Drug Test	FOR	9) SDI Research	FOR
2) Gephardt Amdt	AGN	6) Drug Death Pen	FOR	10) Ban Chem Weaps	AGN
3) Deficit Reduc	AGN	7) Handgun Sales	AGN	11) Aid to Contras	FOR
4) Kill Plnt Clsng Notice	FOR	8) Ban D.C. Abort $	FOR	12) Nuclear Testing	AGN

Election Results

1988 general	Michael Bilirakis (R)	223,925	(100%)	($193,901)
1988 primary	Michael Bilirakis, unopposed			
1986 general	Michael Bilirakis (R)	166,504	(71%)	($509,321)
	Gabe Cazares (D)	68,574	(29%)	($83,619)

TENTH DISTRICT

If you want to see what Florida looked like before the huge growth of the last 50 years, the best way is to drive inland from the coast and look at the parts of the state that have changed least. One such area is the citrus country of central Florida, south of Orlando. Of course there has been growth here: the population figures have grown by percentages unheard of in the Northeast; new shopping malls have sprung up on four-lane highways leading out of the old downtowns, and most people live in small, air-conditioned stucco houses or apartments built since 1950.

Yet a visitor from that year would not find utterly unrecognizable Lakeland or Winter Haven or Lake Wales or the citrus fields lying between these towns and the dozens of lakes of central Florida. None of these towns has grown to metropolitan size. None has reclaimed and developed hundreds of acres of swamp, as in so many other places in Florida. Nor would attitudes here be totally unrecognizable to our hypothetical visitor. Racial segregation, once firmly embedded in central Florida, is of course gone. But political attitudes associated with rural southern Democrats are not. People here tend to be southern in origin, faithful churchgoers, believers in traditional values, sympathetic to the idea of government intervention in the economy to help the ordinary person (though not always the poor). They still register Democratic and vote for local Democrats.

But in national and often in state elections they vote Republican. This is the country that forms most of Florida's 10th Congressional District, and its representation has reflected local changes in political attitudes. Most of the 10th District's people live in Polk County; it also extends to the Gulf Coast, taking in Bradenton, one of the more modest and less Yankeefied towns on the Gulf Coast. For years the 10th was represented by conservative southern Democrats. Then suddenly, in March 1984, it found itself represented by a Republican—not because of some election result, but because of the decision of Congressman Andy Ireland to switch parties. Ireland has always looked Republican anyway: he is from Republican Cincinnati, he went to prep school and the Ivy League, and he is a banker by trade. From his base in Winter Haven he ran for Congress as a Democrat in 1976 when the incumbent retired; he won the primary without a runoff and won the general decisively. In seven years he had made the seat utterly safe, and he had seniority on committees he liked—Foreign Relations, Small Business. Unlike some others, Ireland seems to have switched not out of opportunism, but because of his convictions, and somewhat against his political interest.

But only somewhat. He did lose his seat on Foreign Affairs, but moved to Armed Services and kept his committee assignment on Small Business. Ireland is all for spending more on defense, but he is a stickler for propriety and seems genuinely appalled by waste, fraud, and abuse. He sponsored a 1986 law to protect and compensate whistleblowers. In 1988 he served on a special panel on burden-sharing, which looked ahead toward significant reduction in American ground forces in Europe, but he spoke against Tommy Robinson's amendment to automatically cut troops in certain countries. He has looked after home causes, criticizing the 1986 treaty with the European Community for being too restrictive on citrus products and hailing the 1988 citrus accord with Japan, which is expected to increase Florida's citrus exports there manyfold. On the environment this booster of small businesses pushed through a one-year moratorium on offshore oil drilling in Florida's Gulf Coast.

Back home, the new party label was no handicap either in 1984, a very good year for Republicans, nor in 1986 or 1988, when Democrats Bob Graham and Buddy MacKay ran well in the district. Ireland won with more than 70% each time. In an age when voters split tickets and switch party preferences freely, party-switching is looked down on only when it seems opportunistic, and Ireland, in his quiet, thoughtful way, seems to have made his once safe Democratic seat safely Republican.

The People: Est. Pop. 1986: 605,700, up 18.1% 1980–86; Pop. 1980: 512,890, up 44.3% 1970–80. Households (1980): 75% family, 35% with children, 63% married couples; 27.9% housing units rented; median monthly rent: $170; median house value: $38,100. Voting age pop. (1980): 381,628; 11% Black, 3% Spanish origin.

1988 Presidential Vote:

Bush (R)	138,108	(66%)
Dukakis (D)	69,786	(33%)

Rep. Andy Ireland (R)

Elected 1976; b. Aug. 23, 1930, Cincinnati, OH; home, Winter Haven; Yale U., B.S. 1952, Columbia Univ., 1953–54, LA St. U., 1959; Episcopalian; married (Nancy).

Career: City Commissioner, Winter Haven, 1966–68; Dir., Federal Reserve Bank, Jacksonville; Chmn., Barnett Bank of Cypress Gardens, Winter Haven, Cloverdale, 1970–76.

Offices: 2416 RHOB 20515, 202-225-5015. Also 120 W. Central Ave., Winter Haven 33883, 813-299-4041; 1101 6th Ave., W., Bradenton 34206, 813-746-0766; and 1805 Bartow Hwy., P.O. Box 8758, Lakeland 33803, 813-687-8015.

Committees: *Armed Services* (12th of 21 R). Subcommittees: Investigations; Military Installations and Facilities; Procurement and Military Nuclear Systems. *Small Business* (4th of 17 R). Subcommittee: Exports, Tax Policy, and Special Problems (Ranking Member).

Group Ratings

	ADA	ACLU	COPE	CFA	LCV	ACU	NTLC	NSI	COC	CEI
1988	5	13	14	18	38	100	81	100	100	69
1987	4	—	14	21	—	96	—	—	100	73

National Journal Ratings

	1988 LIB — 1988 CONS		1987 LIB — 1987 CONS	
Economic	10%	— 88%	0%	— 89%
Social	9%	— 89%	0%	— 90%
Foreign	16%	— 78%	0%	— 80%

Key Votes

1) Homeless $	FOR	5) Ban Drug Test	FOR	9) SDI Research	FOR
2) Gephardt Amdt	AGN	6) Drug Death Pen	FOR	10) Ban Chem Weaps	AGN
3) Deficit Reduc	AGN	7) Handgun Sales	FOR	11) Aid to Contras	FOR
4) Kill Plnt Clsng Notice	FOR	8) Ban D.C. Abort $	FOR	12) Nuclear Testing	AGN

Election Results

1988 general	Andy Ireland (R)	156,563	(74%)	($460,468)
	David B. Higginbottom (D)	56,536	(26%)	($33,823)
1988 primary	Andy Ireland (R), unopposed			
1986 general	Andy Ireland (R)	122,368	(71%)	($402,873)
	David Higginbottom (D)	49,559	(29%)	($12,903)

ELEVENTH DISTRICT

In the 1940s, when Cape Canaveral was chosen as the nation's rocket testing site, there were only 20,000 people then in all of Brevard County, which stretches along 60 miles of the coast and includes the cape. It was a backward place, with no industry, picked because it was sunny and on the Atlantic coast: rockets have to be launched eastward and spent parts should fall into the ocean. Today Brevard County north and south of the cape, with more than 300,000 people, is a prototype of a future America, with no city center but plenty of shopping centers along strip highways, with a white collar and service economy, knit together by an interest in the space program.

The 11th Congressional District of Florida includes all of Brevard County and extends westward into booming metropolitan Orlando to include Walt Disney World—which brings in lots of tourists and almost no voters. To the south, the 11th extends as far as Vero Beach, once an old Dixie town with a large black community and now bristling with condominiums full of retirees from the affluent suburbs of the North. This has been Republican territory for three decades and elected a Republican congressman as long ago as 1962. Gratitude to the Kennedy Administration for its commitment to space is scanty, and locals spurred their politicians to get the cape's name changed back to Canaveral (though it's still the John F. Kennedy Space Center). Engineers and high-tech workers typically like the order and certitude of traditional Republican fiscal policy and traditional religious mores.

In congressional elections, however, it elects Democrat Bill Nelson. He is part of the generation of Democrats that came to the House in the 1970s: handsome, well educated, ambitious, and able to finance much of his own campaign. He was elected at 30 to the Florida legislature and at 36 to the House. In his first term, he was politically shrewd enough to get a seat on the Budget Committee, but once there, with a conservative district and moderate to conservative instincts himself, he wobbled under pressure, voting both for and against Reagan Administration tax and budget cuts—votes he came to regret later. After the 1984 election, the Democratic Caucus declined to change the rule limiting Budget Committee service to three terms, and Nelson rotated off.

At which point he put aside any statewide ambitions he had for 1986, stopped concentrating on broad national issues, and concentrated on an issue that in this district is local: space. Scrambling for committee assignments after rotating off Budget, he got on Banking, of major importance in booming Florida, and on Science and Technology he got his fellow Democrats to vote him rather than California's George Brown (a longtime dove and skeptic about space flight programs) as head of the Space Science Subcommittee. Nelson not only boosted the space program in every possible way, he also rode the space shuttle himself, in early January, 1986, and landed safely. Then, weeks later, the next shuttle, *Challenger*, blew up.

Nelson has not wavered in his support of the shuttle program, and he has used his chair and spent his time promoting the manned space station. In 1988 after shepherding the authorization bill through the Science Committee, he lobbied the Appropriations subcommittee. He ended up with $900 million in the bill, on top of the $800 million already spent; these funds institutionalize the program, Nelson says, just about assuring construction. He was pleased too when Lloyd Bentsen and other Texans twisted Michael Dukakis's arm and got him to join George Bush in promising to build the space station. Nelson can draw on his own experience in space and argue that manned programs like the shuttle and the space station capture people's imagination and promote scientific discovery. But he prefers to step lightly around the arguments that neither program stands to be routinized or commercially viable as originally promised, and that much more is to be learned from unmanned probes farther out in the solar system. Nelson's political career, for the moment, depends on building the space station.

Nelson is considered highly popular in the 11th District; an old saying there is that "running against Bill Nelson in this district is like practicing bleeding." In 1988, against a retired lobbyist, Nelson won with 61%—not overwhelming, but about 30% better than Michael Dukakis was running in the district. His longtime statewide ambitions were put aside when he took over the Space subcommittee in 1985, and he passed up chances to run for governor or senator in 1986. But Governor Bob Martinez's unpopularity has Nelson traveling around the state and thinking about running for governor in 1990.

The People: Est. Pop. 1986: 683,900, up 33.4% 1980–86; Pop. 1980: 512,691, up 39.8% 1970–80. Households (1980): 76% family, 37% with children, 64% married couples; 30.8% housing units rented; median monthly rent: $219; median house value: $47,400. Voting age pop. (1980): 380,011; 6% Black, 3% Spanish origin, 1% Asian origin.

1988 Presidential Vote:

Bush (R)	191,722	(70%)
Dukakis (D).	78,493	(29%)

Rep. Bill Nelson (D)

Elected 1978; b. Sept. 29, 1942, Miami; home, Melbourne; Yale U., B.A. 1965, U. of VA, J.D. 1968; Episcopalian; married (Grace).

Career: Army, 1968–70; Practicing atty., 1970–72; FL House of Reps., 1972–78.

Offices: 2404 RHOB 20515, 202-225-3671. Also Fed. Bldg., Ste. 300, Orlando 32801 407-841-1776; and 780 S. Apollo Blvd., Ste. 12, Melbourne 32901, 407-676-1776.

Committees: *Banking, Finance and Urban Affairs* (20th of 31 D). Subcommittees: Financial Institutions Supervision, Regulation and Insurance. *Science, Space and Technology* (9th of 30 D). Subcommittees: Space Science and Applications (Chairman); Transportation, Aviation and Materials.

Group Ratings

	ADA	ACLU	COPE	CFA	LCV	ACU	NTLC	NSI	COC	CEI
1988	45	35	43	73	75	56	20	100	43	26
1987	52	—	40	64	—	35	—	—	53	18

National Journal Ratings

	1988 LIB — 1988 CONS			1987 LIB — 1987 CONS		
Economic	57%	—	41%	57%	—	43%
Social	45%	—	54%	41%	—	59%
Foreign	33%	—	67%	42%	—	58%

Key Votes

1) Homeless $	AGN	5) Ban Drug Test	FOR	9) SDI Research	FOR
2) Gephardt Amdt	FOR	6) Drug Death Pen	FOR	10) Ban Chem Weaps	AGN
3) Deficit Reduc	FOR	7) Handgun Sales	AGN	11) Aid to Contras	FOR
4) Kill Plnt Clsng Notice	AGN	8) Ban D.C. Abort $	FOR	12) Nuclear Testing	AGN

Election Results

1988 general	Bill Nelson (D) 168,390	(61%)	($565,632)
	Bill Tolley (R) 108,373	(39%)	($158,208)
1988 primary	Bill Nelson (D), unopposed		
1986 general	Bill Nelson (D) 149,036	(73%)	($304,914)
	Scott Ellis (R) 55,904	(27%)	($11,896)

TWELFTH DISTRICT

The 12th Congressional District crosses the Florida peninsula, spanning the citrus groves and swamplands around Lake Okeechobee and the Everglades (which is actually a giant river with millions of islands draining Okeechobee out into the Gulf of Mexico). This was almost entirely uninhabited land before World War II, with perhaps 50,000 people scattered in little towns in territory that held 500,000 in 1980 and many more today. (The number of postal patrons in the district rose from 292,000 in 1982 to 430,000 in 1988—a rise of 47%). Inland the district extends all the way to super-rich Naples on the Gulf Coast. It takes in Sebring, in whimsically named Highlands County, where a Grand Prix auto race is held yearly, and the citrus and other farmlands around Lake Okeechobee. In cleared and drained swampland, acres of crops are planted, raised, sprayed, and finally harvested, mostly by blacks and Mexican-Americans whose wages and working conditions have long been among America's worst.

But most of the 12th's people and growth are on the Atlantic coast. The drowsy southern towns north of Palm Beach, where on steaming hot nights blacks and whites would fish off the causeways that connected the beach strips with the main town, were in the path of the northward movement of affluent development. Hobe Sound and Jupiter, longtime resorts of the wealthy, were joined by huge new developments around Stuart and Fort Pierce. Like Fort Lauderdale and West Palm Beach in earlier decades, so these towns in the 1980s became the centers of Yankee metropolises. But the 12th is not just a series of retirement villages. Palm Beach County has had lots of job growth too, over a wide range of wages. So the 12th also includes some modest suburbs and much of the area's black population on the north side of West Palm and in neighboring Riviera Beach.

Before the 1980 Census, most of what are now the 12th and 13th Districts was in a single district; so great has population growth been that both may split again into two districts after the 1990 Census. The boundaries of this district were designed to give Democrats a chance to pick up the seat in 1982, but the 1980s Republican trend and a strong Republican candidate prevailed instead. The candidate was Tom Lewis, who served 11 years in the Air Force and worked 17 years for Pratt & Whitney in West Palm Beach. He spent seven years on his town council and 10 years in the legislature. Lewis is anything but flashy in style, but in substance he has had impressive accomplishments in the House. He sponsored a program for a computerized study on how to manage Lake Okeechobee. With Senator Lawton Chiles he got through in 1988 expansion of the Big Cypress wilderness area in the Everglades; he signed onto the bill to trade Everglades land owned by the Barron Collier company for the government's Indian School on Central Avenue in Phoenix, Arizona. He sponsored a bill to set up outreach centers for Vietnam veterans' counseling and to reimburse veterans for expenses if they have to travel far to veterans' hospitals. With Democrat Dan Glickman of Kansas, he got $800 million for NASA for a study of metal fatigue and corrosion on aircraft. A pilot for 40 years, he sponsored a bill to make airplane interiors more survivable in case of a crash. He worked to open up Japan to U.S. (and Florida) citrus and beef imports; he characterized the 1988 citrus and beef accord (mixing up his Asian cuisines) as "sweet and sour."

On the voting charts Lewis stacks up as a pretty reliable conservative. But his more important role in Congress is to come up with creative solutions to questions that few other legislators have thought much about. His constituents seem to have concluded he has done a fine job. He was first elected in 1982 with large majorities in the Naples area and in the counties north of Palm Beach—a victory for Yankee Republicans. He has not had any opposition since.

The People: Est. Pop. 1986: 678,700, up 32.3% 1980–86; Pop. 1980: 513,121, up 67.0% 1970–80. Households (1980): 73% family, 32% with children, 61% married couples; 30.3% housing units rented; median monthly rent: $190; median house value: $47,700. Voting age pop. (1980): 384,221; 16% Black, 4% Spanish origin.

1988 Presidential Vote:

Bush (R) 168,433	(64%)
Dukakis (D). 92,448	(35%)

Rep. Tom Lewis (R)

Elected 1982; b. Oct. 26, 1924, Philadelphia, PA; home, North Palm Beach; Palm Beach Jr. Col., 1956–57, U. of FL, 1958–59; United Methodist; married (Marian).

Career: Air Force, WWII and Korea; Corp. Exec., Pratt & Whitney Aircraft, 1957–73; Mayor, Councilman, North Palm Beach, 1964–71; FL House of Reps., 1972–80; FL Senate 1980–82.

Offices: 1216 LHOB 20515, 202-225-5792. Also 2700 PGA Blvd. Ste. 1, Palm Beach Gardens 33410, 407-627-6192; and 2500 Midport Rd., Ste. 120, Port St. Lucie 33452, 407-283-7989.

Committees: *Agriculture* (10th of 18 R). Subcommittees: Cotton, Rice and Sugar; Domestic Marketing, Consumer Relations, and Nutrition; Livestock Dairy, and Poultry. *Science, Space and Technology* (5th of 19 R). Subcommittee: Space Science and Applications; Transportation, Aviation and Materials (Ranking Member). *Select Committee on Narcotics Abuse and Control* (7th of 12 R).

Group Ratings

	ADA	ACLU	COPE	CFA	LCV	ACU	NTLC	NSI	COC	CEI
1988	5	17	14	27	31	100	80	100	93	67
1987	4	—	14	29	—	83	—	—	93	64

National Journal Ratings

	1988 LIB — 1988 CONS		1987 LIB — 1987 CONS	
Economic	16%	— 83%	24%	— 74%
Social	16%	— 83%	10%	— 85%
Foreign	16%	— 78%	0%	— 80%

Key Votes

1) Homeless $	FOR	5) Ban Drug Test	FOR	9) SDI Research	FOR
2) Gephardt Amdt	AGN	6) Drug Death Pen	FOR	10) Ban Chem Weaps	AGN
3) Deficit Reduc	AGN	7) Handgun Sales	FOR	11) Aid to Contras	FOR
4) Kill Plnt Clsng Notice	FOR	8) Ban D.C. Abort $	AGN	12) Nuclear Testing	AGN

Election Results

1988 general	Tom Lewis (R), unopposed	($256,081)
1988 primary	Tom Lewis (R), unopposed	
1986 general	Tom Lewis (R), unopposed	($285,685)

THIRTEENTH DISTRICT

It was where Thomas Edison had his winter home, where Henry Ford used to visit, where even Walter Reuther took time off in the modest house he built with his own hands: Fort Myers, back in the days of World War II, when the Gulf Coast, with a permanent population from Sarasota all the way south to Naples of only 42,000, was the closest thing in the continental United States to a tropical paradise. The coastland is more varied than on the Atlantic side, the breakers gentler, the weather seems a bit milder, the geography of the coastline is more various: there are barrier islands on the Gulf, but they are not monotonous like those on the ocean; there are big gaps between them, wide estuaries, and places where the swampy lowlands seem to step right into the ocean. This environment (and Florida's lack of an income tax) has brought affluent people, retirees and professionals, mostly from the Midwest down to the lower Gulf Coast, to the point that there are close to 700,000 people living today where there were 42,000 half a century ago. And living comfortably. The sea is not blocked by miles of high-rise apartments; there are relatively few of the high rises that line the Atlantic, and the favored community is not the high-rise, but the sprawling, city-sized development like Cape Coral or Port Charlotte.

The Gulf Coast, Sarasota south to Naples, is Florida's 13th Congressional District. The population of the district is heavily tilted toward retirees: only 24% of households include children, and 33% of the adults are over 65—one of the highest percentages in the country. The population is also almost entirely white and usually affluent, and not surprisingly, this is one of the most Republican districts in Florida, and perhaps in the nation. From 1982 to 1988 it was represented by Connie Mack III, now U.S. senator. The real contest here in 1988 was in the Republican primary. Retired General Jim Dozier, who was held hostage by Italy's Red Brigades and then rescued in 1981, got just 19% here. Congressman Skip Bafalis, who gave up a seat containing most of this territory to run for governor in 1982, returned, but after a long absence got only 29%. The leader was Lee County Commissioner Porter Goss, who worked 10 years for the CIA, then moved to Sanibel Island, founded a prize-winning local newspaper, served on the city council and passed growth management laws, and was appointed originally to the Lee County Commission by Democratic Governor Bob Graham. He raised plenty of money, got 38% of the vote in the first primary and against Bafalis in the runoff won 72%–28%.

The Democratic nominee was high quality: Jack Conway, a top aide to Reuther in the UAW in the 1950s, one of the founding fathers of the anti-poverty program, and the first president of Common Cause. Conway got some 93,000 votes—more than several Democrats who won—but in this fast-growing district that was only 29% of the vote. Goss won 231,000 votes, more than any other House candidate in the country.

The People: Est. Pop. 1986: 674,300, up 31.4% 1980–86; Pop. 1980: 513,048, up 86.5% 1970–80. Households (1980): 73% family, 24% with children, 65% married couples; 23.3% housing units rented; median monthly rent: $238; median house value: $53,700. Voting age pop. (1980): 413,477; 4% Black, 2% Spanish origin.

1988 Presidential Vote: Bush (R) 225,798   (68%)
                          Dukakis (D). 106,428   (32%)

Rep. Porter J. Goss (R)

Elected 1988; b. Nov. 26, 1938, Waterbury, CT; home, Sanibel; Yale U., B.A., 1960; Presbyterian; married (Mariel).

Career: CIA Clandestine Svcs. 1962–72; City Council Mbr., Mayor of Sanibel 1974–82; Lee Cnty. Commissioner 1982–88.

Offices: 509 CHOB, 20515, 202-225-2536. Also 2000 Main St., Ste. 407, Fort Myers 33901, 813-332-4677; and 2002 Ringling Blvd., Ste. 152, Sarasota 34237, 813-951-7878.

Committees: *Foreign Affairs* (18th of 18 R). Subcommittees: Arms Control, International Security and Science; Western Hemisphere Affairs. *Merchant Marine and Fisheries* (17th of 17 R). Subcommittees: Coast Guard and Navigation; Oceanography.

Group Ratings and Key Votes: Newly Elected
Election Results

1988 general	Porter J. Goss (R)	231,170	(71%)	($836,224)
	Jack Conway (D)	93,700	(29%)	($210,296)
1988 runoff	Porter J. Goss (R)	49,272	(72%)	
	Skip Bafalis (R)	19,413	(28%)	
1988 primary	Porter J. Goss (R)	36,875	(38%)	
	Skip Bafalis (R)	27,958	(29%)	
	Jim Dozier (R)	18,048	(19%)	
	Others	13,222	(14%)	
1986 general	Connie Mack III (R)	187,794	(75%)	($313,639)
	Addison S. Gilbert III (D)	62,694	(25%)	($42,898)

FOURTEENTH DISTRICT

Palm Beach, on a barrier island created by nature, is a town that sprang entirely from the imagination of man. When Henry Flagler built his railroad this far south in 1894, he had the vision of a subtropical resort easily reachable from America's snowbound industrial cities in wintertime; the architect Addison Mizner, who came in 1918, had the vision of a pseudo-Spanish, pseudo-Mediterranean style that he used to build huge mansions and posh clubs and modest-sized storefront blocks. By the 1920s Palm Beach had become the premier winter resort for America's very rich, and to a considerable extent it still is: workers and help have since Flagler's time been sent to live in West Palm Beach, across Lake Worth, and resorts that cater to other tastes and pocketbooks have proliferated on both of Florida's coasts.

What Flagler, Mizner, and other Palm Beach pioneers didn't foresee is that the area around Palm Beach would become in time a workaday, commercial, even industrial metropolis on its own. In the 1970s and 1980s Palm Beach County has been one of the fastest-growing parts of the United States, spawning subdivisions and condominiums and even whole suburbs faster than the mapmakers can draw. In effect two paths of migration have converged here. One is the southward movement of retirees and of young working families as well to Florida's warm climate and suddenly growing, high-tech and service economy (Palm Beach County is where IBM developed its PC). The other is the northward movement along Florida's Gulf Coast of older and middle-aged residents looking for the quiet ambiance and crime-free atmosphere they can no longer find in Miami's Dade County or even Fort Lauderdale's Broward.

These two migrations have produced countervailing political trends in Florida's 14th Congressional District, which extends along the coast from Palm Beach to ultra-expensive Boca Raton (where Corky's delicatessen now serves "Flatbush special" and "Far Rockaway" sandwiches) and goes 12 miles inland, taking in fast-growing Florida Gardens, Country Club Acres, and, to the south along Broward County's Sawgrass Expressway, Margate and Tamarac. The Sun Belt family migration made the Palm Beach area, already heavily Republican in national elections, Republican in state and local elections as well. The condominium retiree migration, particularly by Jews heading north from Miami and Broward County, moves Palm Beach County toward the Democrats at all levels. For many years, while Miami was the most Democratic part of Florida, Palm Beach County was several points more Republican than the state as a whole. But starting in 1984, even as Miami's Cubans have been putting Dade County into the Republican column, Palm Beach County has been a few points more Democratic than Florida. In 1988 Florida voted for Republican Connie Mack III for the Senate, but Palm Beach County voted for Democrat Buddy MacKay.

This was all the more striking because MacKay won his nomination by edging 14th District Congressman Dan Mica out of second place in the first primary. Mica had held the district for the Democrats for 10 sometimes difficult years, despite his disappointment at being denied, because of his strong anti-Communist positions, the Latin America subcommittee chair he wanted on Foreign Affairs. The vacancy in the 14th attracted a large field, and both parties' nominations were won by men active in local government. Republican Ken Adams, who built a chain of hardware stores in New York, campaigned as a conservative on national issues, but stressed his work as a county commissioner aiding the poor and setting up an AIDS hospice. Harry Johnston, from a civically prominent West Palm Beach family, said he knew how to cut spending from his experience as state Senate president. Johnston served 12 years in the legislature. He was a candidate for governor in 1986, running third behind Steve Pajcic and Jim Smith in the primary; if he had run a few percentage points better, he might well have beaten either man in a runoff and could quite possibly have beaten Bob Martinez in the general and be governor of the nation's fourth largest state today.

Instead Johnston spent the fall of 1988 campaigning in condominiums and classrooms, sometimes caustically, sometimes in the more conciliatory manner of a man whose lifespan and career connects the older, southern-and-small-town-oriented Florida with the gleaming new, economically booming, environment-conscious metropolitan Florida of today. While citizen-politician Republicans were beating experienced Democratic legislators in the 4th and 6th Districts, the changing population of Palm Beach and Broward Counties was enough to enable Johnston to beat a candidate with a somewhat similar appeal. His 55%–45% victory gives him the chance to bring his considerable legislative talents to Washington and to make the 14th once again a safe Democratic district.

The People: Est. Pop. 1986: 674,200, up 31.5% 1980–86; Pop. 1980: 512,803, up 126.3% 1970–80. Households (1980): 74% family, 27% with children, 65% married couples; 22.0% housing units rented; median monthly rent: $278; median house value: $62,200. Voting age pop. (1980): 406,873; 4% Spanish origin, 3% Black.

1988 Presidential Vote: Bush (R) 167,352   (53%)
Dukakis (D). 147,665   (47%)

Rep. Harry A. Johnston (D)

Elected 1988; b. Dec. 2, 1931, West Palm Beach; home, West Palm Beach; VA Military Inst., B.A. 1953; U. of FL, J.D. 1958; Presbyterian, married (Mary).

Career: Practicing atty, 1958–88; FL Senate, 1974–86, Pres., 1985–86.

Offices: 1517 LHOB 20515, 202-225-3001. Also Pylon Park, 1501 Corporate Dr., Boynton Beach 33435, 407-732-4000.

Committees: *Foreign Affairs* (23d of 28 D). Subcommittees: Western Hemisphere Affairs; International Economic Policy and Trade. *Science, Space and Technology* (28th of 30 D). Subcommittees: Science, Research and Technology; Space Science and Applications; Oversight and Investigations.

Group Ratings and Key Votes: Newly Elected

Election Results

1988 general	Harry A. Johnston (D)	173,292	(55%)	($971,883)
	Ken Adams (R)	142,635	(45%)	($777,988)
1988 primary	Harry A. Johnston (D)	36,874	(59%)	
	Dorothy H. Wilken (D)	26,116	(41%)	
1986 general	Daniel (Dan) Mica (D)	171,961	(74%)	($386,905)
	Rick Martin (R)	61,185	(26%)	($11,072)

FIFTEENTH DISTRICT

Half a century ago it was a town of 17,000, with a long, mostly empty beach and a set of canal-surrounded streets just inland, before the gas station-lined strip of U.S. 1. Today Fort Lauderdale is the center of a county of nearly one million people, the centerpoint of the 10-to-20-mile strip of Gold Coast running from south of Miami to north of Palm Beach which is now home to four million people. Behind the lines of condominiums stalking along the Atlantic Coast, somewhere between the commercial strip boulevards, is the kernel of this development. But it is of little moment today, for Fort Lauderdale and surrounding Broward County have been changed beyond recognition, not once but several times, since the days before World War II.

Those changes can be charted, among other places, in the election returns. In the 1950s and 1960s, when it was famous for college students' spring vacation sand-and-beer brawls, Fort Lauderdale was growing as a retirement and vacation spot for WASPs from the high-income suburbs of the East and Midwest, the Locust Valleys and Winnetkas of America. Through the middle 1960s, Fort Lauderdale tended to exclude Jews: this was the WASPy part of south Florida. Its politics was straight out of the old *Chicago Tribune*: solidly Republican and conservative, even when that went against national trends. Broward County switched from the Democrats to Thomas E. Dewey and the Republicans in 1948 and stuck with the Republicans through 1964 when it voted for Barry Goldwater. Then in the late 1960s restrictions against Jews eased in Broward County. Hollywood, just south of Fort Lauderdale, became a mostly Jewish city; in Fort Lauderdale and towns inland rose huge condominium complexes most of whose residents were Jews. In 1976 Broward County went for Jimmy Carter, and by 1978 it started to vote more Democratic than the state as a whole. By 1984 it was consistently more Democratic than Miami's Dade County, as the Cuban voting population there increased and Jews moved

278   FLORIDA

north into Broward from Dade or moved directly there from their homes in the North. Entirely within Broward County is the 15th Congressional District of Florida, centered on Fort Lauderdale. On the coast it goes past Pompano Beach and Deerfield Beach up to the Palm Beach County line; inland it includes golf-course-laden suburbs like Plantation, Lauderhill, and Lauderdale Lakes past and just beyond the Sawgrass Expressway. As recently as 10 years ago this was solidly Republican country; Hollywood, to the south, was much more Jewish and much more Democratic. But today party registration is as Democratic as in the 16th, 18th, and 19th Districts, and more Democratic than in the 14th which the Democrats held in Republican 1988. Republican Congressman Clay Shaw owes his hold on the seat more to his own record in Fort Lauderdale politics and in the House than to his party's appeal.

Shaw first won the seat in 1980, after serving as mayor of Fort Lauderdale for five years; he was helped by a Democratic primary fight in which a conservative incumbent was dumped and the nomination went to a legislator who had represented Dade rather than Broward. Shaw won with 55% that time and with 57% against his predecessor who was attempting a comeback in 1982. Since then he has had no serious opposition.

Shaw has spent much of his House career visibly fighting crime and drugs. With a seat on the Judiciary Committee, he came forward with amendments to the drug laws that have become almost a part of the annual routine. Three of them were the death penalty for major drug dealers, a federal drug czar, and the use of the military to interdict drug smuggling: all were deleted from the drug bill in 1986, but were voted into the 1988 law. Three more would require drug testing as a condition of parole for drug-related offenders, property seizures for those in possession of illegal drugs, and higher penalties for crack use. He has also pushed for more drug testing of airline and railroad personnel. Presumably he will remain interested in these matters, though he had to give up his seats on Judiciary and Public Works when he won a place on Ways and Means in July 1988.

The People: Est. Pop. 1986: 552,200, up 7.7% 1980–86; Pop. 1980: 512,950, up 34.0% 1970–80. Households (1980): 65% family, 24% with children, 53% married couples; 33.2% housing units rented; median monthly rent: $261; median house value: $59,900. Voting age pop. (1980): 411,582; 13% Black, 3% Spanish origin.

1988 Presidential Vote: Bush (R) 102,768   (53%)
Dukakis (D) 90,113   (46%)

Rep. E. Clay Shaw, Jr. (R)

Elected 1980; b. Apr. 19, 1939, Miami; home, Ft. Lauderdale; Stetson U., B.A. 1961, U. of AL, M.B.A. 1963, Stetson U., J.D. 1966; Roman Catholic; married (Emilie).

Career: Practicing atty., 1966–68; Chf. City Prosecutor, 1968–69; Assoc. Municipal Judge, 1969–71, City Commissioner, 1971–73, Vice Mayor of Ft. Lauderdale, 1973–75, Mayor, 1975–80.

Offices: 440 CHOB 20515, 202-225-3026. Also 299 E. Broward Blvd., Ste. 100, Ft. Lauderdale 33301, 305-522-1800.

Committees: *Ways and Means* (11th of 13 R). Subcommittees: Oversight; Human Resources (Ranking Member).

Group Ratings

	ADA	ACLU	COPE	CFA	LCV	ACU	NTLC	NSI	COC	CEI
1988	5	9	10	36	31	96	80	100	92	59
1987	4	—	9	14	—	78	—	—	93	68

National Journal Ratings

	1988 LIB — 1988 CONS		1987 LIB — 1987 CONS	
Economic	21%	— 77%	19%	— 78%
Social	5%	— 91%	10%	— 85%
Foreign	0%	— 84%	0%	— 80%

Key Votes

1) Homeless $	FOR	5) Ban Drug Test	FOR	9) SDI Research	FOR
2) Gephardt Amdt	AGN	6) Drug Death Pen	FOR	10) Ban Chem Weaps	AGN
3) Deficit Reduc	AGN	7) Handgun Sales	FOR	11) Aid to Contras	FOR
4) Kill Plnt Clsng Notice	FOR	8) Ban D.C. Abort $	FOR	12) Nuclear Testing	AGN

Election Results

1988 general	E. Clay Shaw, Jr. (R)	132,090	(66%)	($455,578)
	Michael A. (Mike) Kuhle (D)	67,746	(34%)	($36,084)
1988 primary	E. Clay Shaw, Jr. (R), unopposed			
1986 general	E. Clay Shaw, Jr. (R), unopposed			($102,671)

SIXTEENTH DISTRICT

Fifty years ago the Florida land that is now its 16th Congressional District was almost entirely uninhabited: some empty coastal land between Miami and the small town of Fort Lauderdale and thousands of acres of unreclaimed Everglades that started just west of Miami and continued for miles inland. Today more than half a million people live here, in closely packed subdivisions, around new golf courses, or in high-rise condominiums. And some of the most explosive growth in south Florida is taking place here, on either side of the newly completed Sawgrass Expressway in Broward County, 12 to 15 miles west of the ocean, built in record time to meet the demand for development, and in the former swamplands west of the Palmetto Expressway that used to mark the edge of urban settlement in Miami's Dade County.

The 16th was the new district south Florida's Gold Coast got after the 1980 Census (the 17th, 18th, and 19th are descendants of the new districts the area got after the 1970, 1960, and 1950 Censuses respectively). In effect the 16th includes the products of two migrations. The first, and larger, is the migration of Jews and others who originally came from New York and the Northeast out from Dade County and into Broward. The most populous city here now is Hollywood, whose high-rise condominiums facing the ocean are full of former New Yorkers and Miamians; and similar populations live in Pembroke Pines to the west, Hallandale to the south, and Miramar to the southwest. Condominium activists are the big political force here. Large high-rise condominiums bring into one handy location, to which access can be controlled, hundreds and sometimes even thousands of voters. In many cases, they are articulate people with organizational literacy, an interest in issues, a knack for politics, and plenty of time on their hands. Properly organized, a condominium can give an endorsed candidate a margin of hundreds of votes—a huge advantage in a closely contested primary where most ordinary precincts are carried by 10 or 20 votes. In partisan politics this part of Broward County is heavily Democratic, with a 61%–32% Democratic registration edge.

The second part of the 16th District is in Miami's Dade County, not directly south of the Broward County portion of the 16th, but to the west. There it stretches south past the Tamiami

Trail, also known as Southwest 8th Street or, to Cuban-Americans, Calle Ocho. Between 60% and 80% of the residents here are of Spanish origin, living around and behind Miami International Airport in upwardly mobile communities like Westchester and Westwood Lakes. The Dade portion of the district is Republican in registrations (58%–34%) and usually in elections. Cuban-Americans know the evils of Communism, appreciate the virtues of free enterprise, cherish traditional moral values, and prefer Republicans to Democrats on all these counts. But Broward, though it has about 40% of the district's residents, casts only 25% of its votes, because many Cubans are still not citizens or are not registered.

The congressman from the 16th is Larry Smith, brought up in Brooklyn and Long Island, and possessed of a zest for argument and a brash New York style. He is voluble and argumentative, but seems to have no nasty or cynical edge; and his motives—to stop the drug trade, to aid Israel—are transparently sincere. Smith sits on Foreign Affairs, and in this district filled with residents who themselves or whose parents or grandparents fled tyranny, and who now live on a peninsula thrust downward toward Latin America, foreign issues arouse more passion than domestic. Smith is one of the House's leading and most aggressive backers of aid to Israel, and in the late 1980s was one of the first to oppose arms sales to Saudi Arabia and Kuwait; occasionally he has been successful in stopping them and on other occasions has seen the list of weapons cut. He was on both sides of the contra aid issue, depending on the circumstances, but has never been a romantic admirer of the Sandinistas like some of his Democratic colleagues.

Much of his effort in the late 1980s was directed against the drug trade, and he has been fairly bubbling over with proposals. He originated the law outlawing Quaaludes. From his seat on Foreign Affairs, he favored decertification of the Bahamas, Mexico, Peru, and Paraguay—a declaration that they were not enforcing drug laws, which would then require a cutoff of some U.S. aid. He wants assets of accused and convicted drug violators forfeited. He wants to revoke the passports of drug violators. He wants to sell more weapons and ammunition to drug enforcement officers in Latin countries. As chairman of the Task Force on International Economics Control, he wants to cut off drug traffickers like Manuel Noriega and give special aid to Colombia for its anti-drug efforts.

It would be easy to dismiss Smith's record as catering to the prejudices of his constituents, concerned about Israel, worried about Central America, cautious about leaving their condominium compounds for fear of drug-driven crime. But Smith seems to share their passions and fears, and seems determined to do something about them.

Smith first won this newly created seat in 1982, with a 55%–45% victory in a Democratic party battle of the condominiums. In general elections, he has not run strong in the Dade County portion of the district, leading Republicans to think about targeting him, as they did in 1984 when they held him to 56%. In 1988, his opponent, a young chiropractor who has become a perennial candidate, charged him with causing the October 1987 stock market crash. Smith was worried because this man's name is Joseph Smith, and so the Democrat ran ads saying "send the real Mr. Smith to Washington." They worked: Smith won with 69%. But he got only 55% in Dade County; when redistricting comes around, he might like to shed some of that territory, and probably will be able to, because the 16th's population has been rapidly increasing.

The People: Est. Pop. 1986: 578,200, up 12.6% 1980–86; Pop. 1980: 513,365, up 74.6% 1970–80. Households (1980): 74% family, 33% with children, 63% married couples; 25.8% housing units rented; median monthly rent: $278; median house value: $62,500. Voting age pop. (1980): 396,409; 20% Spanish origin, 4% Black, 1% Asian origin.

1988 Presidential Vote: Bush (R) 121,521   (55%)
                           Dukakis (D) 97,110   (44%)

Rep. Lawrence J. (Larry) **Smith (D)**

Elected 1982; b. Apr. 25, 1941, Brooklyn, NY; home, Hollywood; NYU, Brooklyn Law Sch., LL.B. 1964, J.D. 1976; Jewish; married (Sheila).

Career: Practicing atty., 1964–82; Hollywood Planning and Zoning Bd., 1974–78, Chmn., 1975–78; Broward Cnty. Advisory Bd., 1978; FL House of Reps., 1978–82.

Offices: 113 CHOB 20515, 202-225-7931. Also 4747 Hollywood Blvd., Hollywood 33021, 305-987-6484.

Committees: *Foreign Affairs* (13th of 28 D). Subcommittees: Europe and the Middle East; International Operations. *Judiciary* (15th of 21 D). Subcommittees: Crime; Economic and Commercial Law; Criminal Justice. *Select Committee on Narcotics Abuse and Control* (13th of 18 D).

Group Ratings

	ADA	ACLU	COPE	CFA	LCV	ACU	NTLC	NSI	COC	CEI
1988	85	70	96	64	75	17	6	30	23	14
1987	80	—	95	79	—	9	—	—	20	3

National Journal Ratings

	1988 LIB — 1988 CONS		1987 LIB — 1987 CONS	
Economic	79%	— 17%	73%	— 0%
Social	68%	— 31%	78%	— 0%
Foreign	58%	— 41%	68%	— 32%

Key Votes

1) Homeless $	AGN	5) Ban Drug Test	AGN	9) SDI Research	AGN
2) Gephardt Amdt	FOR	6) Drug Death Pen	FOR	10) Ban Chem Weaps	FOR
3) Deficit Reduc	FOR	7) Handgun Sales	AGN	11) Aid to Contras	FOR
4) Kill Plnt Clsng Notice	AGN	8) Ban D.C. Abort $	AGN	12) Nuclear Testing	FOR

Election Results

1988 general	Lawrence J. (Larry) Smith (D)	153,032	(69%)	($555,473)
	Joseph Smith (R)	67,461	(31%)	($15,325)
1988 primary	Lawrence J. (Larry) Smith (D), unopposed			
1986 general	Lawrence J. (Larry) Smith (D)	121,213	(70%)	($878,922)
	Mary Collins (R)	52,807	(30%)	($60,337)

SEVENTEENTH DISTRICT

The northern corner of Miami's Dade County, from the beach above Bal Harbour to the new town suburb of Miami Lakes developed by Senator Bob Graham in the west, makes up Florida's 17th Congressional District. It includes only a small part of Miami itself, but more than any other district votes like an old-style northern urban district: this is the only Florida district that regularly votes for national Democratic candidates. That is true even though about one-quarter of its residents, many in the once white working-class suburb of Hialeah, around the race track, are Cuban: they are heavily Republican, but don't all vote yet. The 17th is also about one-quarter black: just as Cubans move out from Miami along Southwest 8th Street, blacks tend to move north in a corridor between Northwest 7th and 27th Avenues. Yet the dominant political tone in the 17th is set by a group less numerous than either: the Jews, who tend to live in the communities along Biscayne Bay, especially North Miami and North Miami Beach. They turn out in Democratic primaries, which are tantamount to election here; they organize in condominium and neighborhood associations, which can deliver large margins to candidates.

William Lehman, the congressman from the 17th, was first elected in 1972, when the district was newly created; he had been active on the school board. Before that he had a long and successful career selling used cars under the name "Alabama Bill." Lehman entered Congress when he was almost 60, and is now one of the House's oldest members. He serves rather quietly on the Appropriations Committee, and since 1982 has been chairman of the Transportation Subcommittee. This is a position of potentially vast influence, but Lehman, a pleasant man, does not seem to have the aggressiveness and ambition to make high policy, although he has been successful in advancing Miami's Metrorail mass transit system and downtown Metromover. On other issues he votes with liberal Democrats more often than any other Florida congressman; he is one of only two Florida members to oppose contra aid regularly. At home, he has not had serious competition since his first and second campaigns; his major electoral effort is to scotch rumors that he is going to retire.

The People: Est. Pop. 1986: 560,100, up 9.2% 1980–86; Pop. 1980: 513,048, up 25.6% 1970–80. Households (1980): 72% family, 35% with children, 55% married couples; 38.3% housing units rented; median monthly rent: $237; median house value: $46,700. Voting age pop. (1980): 385,199; 24% Spanish origin, 22% Black, 1% Asian origin.

1988 Presidential Vote:

Dukakis (D)	84,029	(59%)
Bush (R)	58,053	(41%)

Rep. William Lehman (D)

Elected 1972; b. Oct. 5, 1913, Selma, AL; home, Biscayne Park; U. of AL, B.S. 1934; Jewish; married (Joan).

Career: Auto dealer, 1936–42, 1946–72; Teacher, airplane mechanics, Brazil, 1942–45; Teacher, Dade Cnty. Pub. Schools, 1963, Miami-Dade Jr. Col., 1964–66; Dade Cnty. Sch. Bd., 1966–72, Chmn., 1971–72.

Offices: 2347 RHOB 20515, 202-225-4211. Also 2020 N.E. 163rd St., N. Miami Beach 33162, 305-945-7518.

Committees: *Appropriations* (17th of 35 D). Subcommittees: Foreign Operations; Transportation (Chairman). *Select Committee on Children, Youth, and Families* (2d of 18 D).

Group Ratings

	ADA	ACLU	COPE	CFA	LCV	ACU	NTLC	NSI	COC	CEI
1988	100	96	88	82	81	8	8	0	36	17
1987	92	—	87	79	—	9	—	—	21	5

National Journal Ratings

	1988 LIB — 1988 CONS		1987 LIB — 1987 CONS	
Economic	54% —	44%	68% —	27%
Social	86% —	0%	78% —	0%
Foreign	79% —	16%	81% —	0%

Key Votes

1) Homeless $	AGN	5) Ban Drug Test	AGN	9) SDI Research	AGN
2) Gephardt Amdt	AGN	6) Drug Death Pen	AGN	10) Ban Chem Weaps	FOR
3) Deficit Reduc	FOR	7) Handgun Sales	AGN	11) Aid to Contras	AGN
4) Kill Plnt Clsng Notice	AGN	8) Ban D.C. Abort $	AGN	12) Nuclear Testing	FOR

Election Results

1988 general	William Lehman (D), unopposed	($257,487)
1988 primary	William Lehman (D), unopposed	
1986 general	William Lehman (D), unopposed	($172,800)

EIGHTEENTH DISTRICT

The hot night air, the moonlight reflecting off the bay onto the surrealistic high rises, the pastel, random-shaped, sharp-angled style of clothes and furniture and typography—a style that comes from Italian designers—the air of menace in streets where many are armed and vast quantities of drugs and cash are regularly changing hands: this is Miami as the 1990s begin. A resort city known for its pseudo-Spanish mansions and Art Deco beach hotels two generations ago, a city on its way to becoming a fairly typical American metropolitan area one generation ago, Miami today cannot be mistaken for any other American—or Latin American—city; its faults and its flair are all its own. It lives on the cusp of two civilizations: one English-speaking, confident that its liberty and property are secure, tolerant of diversity, and little interested in politics; the other Spanish-speaking, its liberty and property always under threat, ready to use violence to destroy contrary opinion, preoccupied with a politics of revenge. Miami's Dade County by the late 1980s was about 42% Hispanic (almost entirely Cuban), 40% white Anglo, and 18% black, and the Cuban community was growing. Miami is the one city in the country where you can rise to the top of your profession or business, patronize the best stores and restaurants, live in the best residential areas—and still speak nothing but Spanish. Miami is the economic capital of Latin America and the place of exile for many a loser in Latin American political wars; it is also the number one center of the U.S. drug trade. Young Cuban-Americans all know English, but the fact is that Cuban Miami has remained separate, is growing larger, and remains estranged from Anglo society—culturally and especially politically.

Miami is no longer the murder capital of the nation, as it was in the early 1980s; the drug trade has dispersed to other cities and west along the Gulf Coast; the kind of clothes Don Johnson wore in *Miami Vice* can now be seen in Wal-Marts in Arkansas and in Holidomes in South Dakota. Still, Miami is different. Concealed weapons and barely concealed bribery, vast sums of cash (most of the $100 bills in the country are in the Miami Federal Reserve district) and a constant commerce in illegal drugs, rampant police corruption (59 officers were suspended in the Miami River scandal): these are all part of Miami's daily life. Relations between Cubans and others are not growing more mellow. To goodhearted Anglo liberals, like those who run the *Miami Herald*, the Cubans' fanatic hatred of Fidel Castro's regime, their frequent disregard for the rules of political behavior here (remember that it was Cuban-Americans who burglarized the Watergate—not the first such operation by Cuban exiles), and their unwillingness to compromise or smooth over their differences on Cuban and other Latin American issues make them a dangerous force in American politics. To the Cubans, the Anglos' lack of sympathy for the tragedy that has befallen Cuba and their benign neutrality (or worse) toward Communist dictators who seize property and imprison their opponents make them an enemy force who must be opposed at all costs. From the 1940s to the 1970s, Miami was a Democratic town, dominated by a liberal establishment and a large Jewish community that stayed with the Democrats even during the civil rights revolution. But the Cubans—not just the initial exiles, but the younger generation, brought up and often born in the United States—are overwhelmingly Republican, even more enthusiastic in their support of George Bush (whose son Jeb and daughter-in-law Columba live in Miami) than they were of Ronald Reagan. So Miami and Dade County are now Republican—and likely to become more so.

Florida's 18th Congressional District covers most of the city of Miami and all of Miami Beach and Coral Gables. Its center is Southwest 8th Street—Calle Ocho—the main street of the Cuban community. Miami Beach is still mostly Jewish, and there are blacks in the corridor running north from the gleaming downtown. But in 1980, 50% of the district's residents were Cuban, and today the percentage is surely much higher.

Claude Pepper, who died of cancer May 30, 1989, represented the 18th District of Florida since 1962. He had been a pivotal figure in American politics and government over a longer span of time than anyone else in American history. Born in 1900 in Alabama, Pepper moved to Florida after Harvard Law School, was elected to the legislature in 1928, ran for the Senate and lost in 1934, and was appointed to the Senate to fill a vacancy in 1936. In 1938 Pepper was a vocal supporter of Franklin Roosevelt's minimum wage bill, which was thought unpopular in the South and which seemed to threaten his chances to win a full term. But he campaigned hard for the seat, and won 58% of the vote against an incumbent congressman and a former governor— and Congress passed the stalled bill within weeks. Pepper quickly became known as a brilliant orator, in the grandiloquent southern tradition but also of a high enough intellectual order that Robert Taft, no admirer of his New Deal politics, said he always made it a point to be on the floor when Pepper spoke because the man had a first-class mind. When Lyndon Johnson set about to provide speakers for Democratic House candidates in 1940, one of those most in demand was Senator Claude Pepper.

Pepper was also a force on foreign affairs, an opponent of isolationism before World War II and a skeptic about the cold war afterwards. That, plus his continuing support for unfashionable New Deal measures and his support of civil rights (he supported an anti-lynching bill in the 1930s), made him vulnerable to challenge, and he was beaten 55%–45% by George Smathers in a bitter primary in 1950. When Miami got a second House seat after the 1960 Census, Pepper was the obvious man to fill it and he won easily, as he did from that time on—even as the district changed from heavily Jewish to mostly Cuban. No member of the House spoke more passionately against Fidel Castro and for supporting the resistance to Communists in Latin America.

Pepper made an impact in the House early on, chairing a special crime committee from 1969 to 1974 and chairing the Select Committee on Aging; he pushed to passage the 1978 law raising the minimum mandatory retirement age from 65 to 70 and the 1986 law banning any compulsory retirement age. Always a New Dealer, he was not much concerned about costs; he denounced bitterly colleagues who did not share his generosity and perhaps his own experiences, from growing up poor in backward rural Alabama to living in rich urban Miami, that contribute to a belief that the United States will always prove rich enough to deliver on the promises he would have it make. In the 1980s he played a major role in resisting any Reagan cuts in social security, and in 1982 was the Democrats' most active and effective national campaigner, flying around to 70 districts denouncing Republicans and boosting Democrats. But he also suffered disappointments. When the Social Security Commission in 1983 came in with a bipartisan compromise, he tried to stop the proposal to gradually raise the retirement age. His colleagues gave him a standing ovation but most voted against him. The same thing happened in 1988 on his proposal for long-term health care. Ways and Means came forward with a catastrophic health care plan that would be paid for by a tax on the elderly's earnings; Pepper wanted instead a more generous program to be paid for by lifting the top limit on income subject to workers' payroll tax. Opposed by Dan Rostenkowski and John Dingell, Pepper spoke movingly, segueing gracefully from vivid descriptions of the plight of the infirm to an eloquent plea for generosity. But in a deficit-conscious House he didn't have the votes.

Pepper became chairman of the Rules Committee after Richard Bolling retired in 1982, and while he generally worked in tandem with the House leadership he used the committee's power to allow or prohibit votes on amendments to advance his pet causes. He was hard of hearing, but he could explain the complexities of legislation and procedure and stir the emotions of any listener much as he did 50 years ago. The Republicans once targeted him, but did not do better than 40% in 1980. Most politically active Cubans, it seems, thought it was more useful to have a sympathetic chairman of the Rules Committee than a freshman Cuban Republican representing them, though for the first time since the district was carved out for Pepper in 1962, it is possible for an Hispanic Republican to win the seat.

The People: Est. Pop. 1986: 542,600, up 5.7% 1980–86; Pop. 1980: 513,250, up 6.4% 1970–80. Households (1980): 62% family, 25% with children, 46% married couples; 64.7% housing units rented; median monthly rent: $210; median house value: $53,500. Voting age pop. (1980): 416,969; 50% Spanish origin, 13% Black, 1% Asian origin.

1988 Presidential Vote:

Bush (R)	72,421	(58%)
Dukakis (D)	52,368	(42%)

Rep. Claude Pepper (D)

Elected 1962; b. Sept. 8, 1900, Dudleyville, AL, d. May 30, 1989; home, Miami; U. of AL, A.B. 1921, Harvard U., LL.B. 1924; Baptist; widowed.

Career: Instructor in Law, U. of AR, 1924–25; Practicing atty., 1925–36, 1951–62; FL House of Reps., 1929–30; FL Bd. of Pub. Welfare, 1931–32; FL Bd. of Law Examiners, 1933–34; U.S. Senate, 1937–51.

Offices: 2239 RHOB 20515, 202-225-3931. Also 300 Courthouse Tower, 44 W. Flagler St., Miami 33130, 305-536-5565.

Group Ratings

	ADA	ACLU	COPE	CFA	LCV	ACU	NTLC	NSI	COC	CEI
1988	65	69	94	73	25	18	1	50	17	8
1987	68	—	94	93	—	14	—	—	9	3

National Journal Ratings

	1988 LIB — 1988 CONS		1987 LIB — 1987 CONS	
Economic	87% —	8%	73% —	0%
Social	58% —	42%	62% —	38%
Foreign	51% —	48%	56% —	44%

Key Votes

1) Homeless $	AGN	5) Ban Drug Test	—	9) SDI Research	AGN
2) Gephardt Amdt	FOR	6) Drug Death Pen	FOR	10) Ban Chem Weaps	FOR
3) Deficit Reduc	FOR	7) Handgun Sales	—	11) Aid to Contras	FOR
4) Kill Plnt Clsng Notice	AGN	8) Ban D.C. Abort $	AGN	12) Nuclear Testing	FOR

Election Results

1988 general	Claude Pepper (D), unopposed		($405,551)
1988 primary	Claude Pepper (D), unopposed		
1986 general	Claude Pepper (D) 80,047	(74%)	($1,395,549)
	Tom Brodie (R)....................... 28,803	(26%)	($15,888)

NINETEENTH DISTRICT

Fifty years ago, U.S. 1 heading southwest from Miami toward the 113-mile Florida Keys Highway was a narrow ribbon of highway next to Henry Flagler's Florida East Coast Railroad passing between acres of Everglades swamp, marked with an occasional tourist attraction and gas stations with red machines full of five cent Cokes. In the years since, the land three to 10 miles on each side of U.S. 1 has been reclaimed and subdivided into middle-class neighborhoods and has become as a result the southernmost inhabited part of the continental United States and the closest thing in the Miami area to the typical middle-class American ideal. This is Florida's 19th Congressional District, which starts in Miami's Coconut Grove area and passes through Coral Gables, planned as a ritzy suburb in the 1920s, to newer offspring of Miami like Kendall, Olympia Heights, Richmond Heights, and Perrine. In one way this constituency is not typical: 22% of its population is of Spanish origin. But if the Cubans still speak Spanish at home and at work, they also are upwardly striving, young, and family-oriented (40% of the households here contain children, one of the highest figures in Florida). More than many Americans whose immigrant ancestors are more remote, they are believers in the American dream.

The political tone here is still set mainly by Anglos, but Cubans have entered the electorate in significant numbers. For 40 years south Dade County has generally been Democratic. But some of the white residents have been moving to the Republicans, and Cuban-Americans tend to vote heavily Republican in serious contests. In congressional elections, however, the south Dade County district (numbered 4th in the 1950s, 12th in the 1960s, and 15th in the 1970s) has since 1954 regularly elected Dante Fascell. He is now Chairman of the House Foreign Affairs Committee and was a member as well of the special committee investigating the Iran-contra affair. These are strategic posts for a man who has been a force in foreign policy since the years of the bipartisan foreign policy of the 1950s and who, unlike most members of the House, has a district with two constituency groups strongly interested in foreign policy matters. Fascell has always been in sympathy with their views: he is pro-Israel and anti-Castro.

Institutionally, Fascell's chairmanship does not confer great power. The House is usually overshadowed in foreign policy by the Senate, with its power to approve treaties and nominations, and its chairman before Fascell had allowed Foreign Affairs subcommittee chairmen, most of them young liberals, to pretty much have their way. Fascell agrees with them on many issues, but not on Latin America, where he has strongly opposed Fidel Castro and strongly favored contra aid, nor does he share the mistrust many of the politicians who came of age during the Vietnam era seem to have in any assertion of American power in the Third World. On the contrary, Fascell has shown a desire to propagate the ideas of democracy, and a faith that the values America stands for are better than those espoused by Marxist-leaning Third World politicos. He has been part of the offensive for freedom as the main patron of the National Endowment for Democracy, which has helped advance democratic politics in Latin America and East Asia. He is also the prime sponsor of Radio Martí, which infuriates Castro by sending messages to Cubans he cannot control, and Fascell has proposed that it be joined by a Television Martí. Increasingly, he seems to be operating in bipartisan fashion with ranking Republican William Broomfield, backing the INF treaty, backing measures to combat the international drug trade, seeking investigations of Cuban human rights violations, launching a major review of foreign aid. But, fierce and ready to bellow with outrage, he is a force to be reckoned with on the House floor, determined and aggressive and well-informed.

He also tends to district matters, like keeping oil drillers out of the Gulf of Mexico and away from the Florida Keys and setting up nature sanctuaries there. In the 19th District he has been reelected by wide margins, despite Republican inroads in other contests in south Dade. His last serious opponent was TV newscaster Glenn Rinker in 1982, who held him to 59%, and it's possible he'll get another serious challenger again. But Cuban-Americans, who provide the vote base for any Republican challenge here, may very well conclude they're better off with a sympathetic and powerful Foreign Affairs chairman as their congressman.

The People: Est. Pop. 1986: 569,500, up 11.0% 1980–86; Pop. 1980: 512,886, up 45.0% 1970–80. Households (1980): 73% family, 40% with children, 60% married couples; 33.3% housing units rented; median monthly rent: $263; median house value: $69,900. Voting age pop. (1980): 373,329; 21% Spanish origin, 10% Black, 1% Asian origin.

1988 Presidential Vote:

Bush (R) 111,913	(59%)
Dukakis (D). 78,062	(41%)

Rep. Dante B. Fascell (D)

Elected 1954; b. Mar. 9, 1917, Bridgehampton, L.I., NY; home, Miami; U. of Miami, J.D. 1938; Protestant; married (Jeanne-Marie).

Career: Practicing atty., 1938–42, 1946–54; Army, WWII; Legal Attaché, Dade Cnty. St. Legis. Delegation, 1947–50; FL House of Reps., 1950–54; U.S. Delegation to U.N., 1969.

Offices: 2354 RHOB 20515, 202-225-4506. Also 7855 S.W. 104 St., Ste. 220, Miami 33156, 305-536-5301.

Committees: *Foreign Affairs* (Chairman of 28 D). Subcommittee: Arms Control, International Security and Science (Chairman). *Select Committee on Narcotics Abuse and Control* (8th of 18 D).

Group Ratings

	ADA	ACLU	COPE	CFA	LCV	ACU	NTLC	NSI	COC	CEI
1988	75	74	84	73	75	17	2	30	36	15
1987	80	—	84	86	—	9	—	—	20	4

National Journal Ratings

	1988 LIB — 1988 CONS		1987 LIB — 1987 CONS	
Economic	71% —	23%	73% —	0%
Social	68% —	31%	78% —	0%
Foreign	53% —	47%	64% —	35%

Key Votes

1) Homeless $	AGN	5) Ban Drug Test	AGN	9) SDI Research	AGN
2) Gephardt Amdt	FOR	6) Drug Death Pen	FOR	10) Ban Chem Weaps	FOR
3) Deficit Reduc	FOR	7) Handgun Sales	AGN	11) Aid to Contras	FOR
4) Kill Plnt Clsng Notice	AGN	8) Ban D.C. Abort $	AGN	12) Nuclear Testing	FOR

Election Results

1988 general	Dante B. Fascell (D).................	135,355	(72%)	($337,596)
	Ralph Carlos Rocheteau (R)	51,628	(28%)	($4,907)
1988 primary	Dante B. Fascell (D)..................	35,630	(85%)	
	Wesley F. (Wes) White (D)...............	6,416	(15%)	
1986 general	Dante B. Fascell (D)..................	99,203	(69%)	($293,227)
	Bill Flanagan (R)	44,455	(31%)	($359,382)

GEORGIA

A New South is rising in the red clay hills around Atlanta. You can see it in the clusters of high-rises towering above the thick trees near interchanges several miles apart, in the subdivisions leapfrogging miles out into the countryside, in the heaviest concentration of office complexes and shopping centers in the South in "the donut," as it is called, extending up to 60 miles around Atlanta. This is not the first time proclamations of a New South have rung out in Atlanta, and in the past the prophecies have often turned out false. In 1877, Atlanta editor Henry Grady predicted that an industrialized, progressive "New South" (he coined the term) would rise from the ashes of the Civil War. But, except for a few enterprises like Coca-Cola and many low-wage textile mills, the South had very little industrial development until after World War II. In the 1940s, Georgia Governor Ellis Arnall, in *The Shore Dimly Seen* envisioned a South that would embrace New Deal economic programs and labor unions, and where the race problem would be solved without struggle by greater education and higher incomes. Incomes *did* rise and legal segregation *was* ended—but not through unionization or economic redistribution, and not without a searing and sometimes violent struggle. In the 1980s, surging economic growth around Atlanta has made Georgia one of the nation's fastest growing states. But it's still not clear whether this version of the New South will produce enough well-educated young people to sustain the boom, and whether there will be room in the mostly white donut around Atlanta for many blacks, as well as whites, to get ahead.

The boom has strengthened Atlanta's and Georgia's claims to being the heart of the South. This is where the coastal South and the inland South meet, where the Appalachian chain ends and the Black Belt moves from the Carolina lowlands toward the Mississippi Delta. Georgia had inauspicious beginnings—philanthropist James Oglethorpe settling and trying to rehabilitate convicts around Savannah misfired, Andrew Jackson's troops driving the Civilized Tribes west over the Trail of Tears, slave proprietors extending their Cotton Kingdom across the hot flatlands. But Georgia did not lead the South in secession; it became the key to the outcome of the war because its geography made it the site of Sherman's march to the sea. The Union army cut a 60-mile swath through Georgia, burning towns and houses, destroying crops and the food they couldn't eat, not just to split the Confederacy but to humble a culture by teaching the Rebels that they were utterly beaten. Georgia and the South remained deeply moved by the memory of this terrible defeat, and *Gone With the Wind* sent chills up spines when it premiered in Atlanta in 1939, and still does 50 years later. Politically, Sherman made Georgia the most Democratic state, the number two state for John Kennedy in 1960 as well as the number one for Jimmy Carter in 1980, and the best Deep South state for Walter Mondale in 1984 (though it had switched to Barry Goldwater, George Wallace, and Richard Nixon in the civil rights years in between).

For Atlanta, defeat proved invigorating: Scarlett O'Hara's Atlanta was just a tiny railroad junction, but the Atlanta that grew after the Civil War became clearly the chief city of the South. Atlanta was the hub first of railroads and then airlines, the home of Joel Chandler Harris and Coca-Cola, of the South's biggest white establishment and of the black colleges and black middle class that were the backbone of the civil rights movement. And Georgia was the home of the first President produced from a southern statehouse in American history, Jimmy Carter, who was elected from a rural base and as governor placed a picture of Martin Luther King Jr. in the Capitol. Carter's 1970 victory was a turning point for Georgia and the South: it was the first time a candidate conspicuously supported by blacks still got enough white votes to win (Atlanta blacks used to send out endorsements in letters to arrive on election day, so that white voters wouldn't know whom black voters were backing). Similarly, Carter's nomination and election in 1976 marked a political union of black and white southerners—symbolized by Carter's endorsement by civil rights movement veteran Andrew Young.

Georgia politics before Carter's success was often a struggle between prosperous, relatively tolerant metropolitan Atlanta—"the city too busy to hate," as it liked to call itself—and rural Georgia. The rural counties, which cast 60% of the votes in general elections and 75% in Democratic primaries, usually won; the system was tilted even more toward these counties before a 1964 Supreme Court decision by Georgia's unit rule system, which gave each of the state's 159 counties 2, 4, or 6 votes in the decisive Democratic primary. Up through Carter's term as governor, Atlanta tended to favor candidates who favored civil rights, who were close to their national parties, whose accents were broadcaster-neutral, and whose clothes and bearing reflected the sophistication Atlanta is proud of. Rural Georgia went just the other way. Carter in 1970, Senator Sam Nunn in 1972, and Governor Joe Frank Harris in 1982 were all elected initially with majorities in the rural counties but, unlike the buffoonish Lester Maddox, they proved acceptable to Atlanta.

Over time the differences between the two areas diminished. The outlying parts of the Atlanta donut filled up with affluent young whites, mostly from the South, upbeat in mood and increasingly Republican in their politics; while in the rural counties, desegregation has long since been accepted and whites no longer see themselves as inevitably in conflict with blacks.

The two regions have not quite converged: metro Atlanta tends to be less tradition-minded on cultural issues and more market-oriented on economics. And there are interesting movements within the regions. In close-in Atlanta, notably DeKalb County just east of the city, where young people are moving close to universities and cultural institutions, high-toned shopping centers and black neighbors, the movement is toward the Democrats. Republicans are making their biggest gains in once entirely rural counties which are now filling up with blue- and white-collar breadwinners willing to commute 20 or 50 miles so they can raise their children in a country atmosphere.

But these trends tend to balance out, and on the bottom line, metropolitan and rural Georgia tend to end up same. In the 1982 Democratic primary for governor, there were no sharp differences between metro Atlanta and the rural counties. In the close 1986 election for Senate, Democrat Wyche Fowler, a congressman from Atlanta, got 51% of the vote in metropolitan Atlanta and 51% in the other 144 counties. And in 1988, George Bush, the son of a Connecticut Yankee, carried metropolitan Atlanta with 59% and rural Georgia with 61%, for a total of 60% statewide—exactly Ronald Reagan's percentage in 1984. In only six of the 159 counties were Bush's and Reagan's share of the vote more than 5% apart.

Today's Georgia seems fairly solidly Republican in presidential elections and fairly solidly Democratic in state and congressional elections. Yet the New South around Atlanta is strongly Republican and may provide a base for the party to be at last competitive in state contests. Symbolic of that trend was the defeat in 1988 in fast-growing Cobb County of 28-year legislator Joe Mack Wilson, attacked by Republicans for late tax filings, abuses of his expense account, and racial slurs. But there is a countervailing Democratic trend in some rural areas, which may

GEORGIA — Congressional Districts, Counties, and Selected Places — *(10 Districts)*

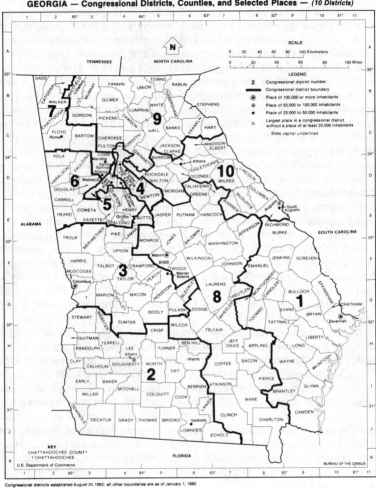

Congressional districts established August 24, 1982; all other boundaries are as of January 1, 1980.

reflect the influence of Sam Nunn, who in 1986 and 1988 campaigned heavily for his party's ticket. Symbolic of that trend was Michael Dukakis's running even in Macon, the south Georgia city which used to have a mayor nicknamed "Machine Gun" Thompson.

The demographic trends, however, favor the Republicans. Metro Atlanta cast only 34% of Georgia's votes in 1968, about 40% from 1972 to 1982, 42% in 1984, and 45% in 1986 and 1988: the growth is in Republican areas. Georgia's values too are those associated in national politics with Republicans. Support for the military is one: vanquished in one war, Georgia has been ready to fight ever since, and has produced some of the leading supporters of military preparedness in Congress—Armed Services chairmen Richard Russell, Carl Vinson, and Sam Nunn.

Another is religious faith. The state's most visible political executives, Governor Joe Frank Harris, Mayor Andrew Young, and Jimmy Carter, are all conspicuously religious, in different ways: Harris is abstemious and tradition-minded, Young worked in a civil rights movement whose tenets came from church and Gospel, while Carter stressed his faith as a born-again Christian. The Republicans, if they are to become a majority in Georgia and the South, must build on more than just the sparkling success evident in the interchange shopping centers, and the Democrats, if they are to extend their local success further up the ticket, need to show greater respect for the traditions which are so important in the lives of many loyal partisan voters as well as many who are movable.

Georgia has had a presidential primary since 1976 and has voted in early March, on what became 1988's Super Tuesday, since 1980. Since there is no party registration, turnout gives some suggestion of each party's strength. The Democrats' 1988 total of 622,000 votes was between the 502,000 they had in 1976 and the 684,000 of 1984; the Republicans' 1988 total of 400,000 was double their 200,000 in 1980 and 188,000 in 1976. The Democrats polled far fewer than the 900,000 who voted in their last seriously contested gubernatorial primary, in 1982; the Republicans polled far more than they have in any state primary. Among the Republicans, the clear favorite was Bush, with 54%; Pat Robertson, however, did have some support at conventions that elected delegates and sponsored a credentials challenge that was resolved just before the Republican Convention. Among the Democrats, Jesse Jackson led with 40%, a vast improvement over his 21% in 1984, when some blacks voted for Mondale; Albert Gore, with Nunn's and Murphy's support and his own ads, was second with 32%.

Governor. Georgia has one of the nation's more successful—and least known—governors. Joe Frank Harris is quiet to the point of reticence; he is steady rather than glib; even at the Democrats' Atlanta convention he did not make a strong impression. But in prosperous Georgia he has had significant contributions, especially his 1985 education package which raised spending on education to $200 million and required teachers to take competency tests; in three years teacher salaries increased 43%, per pupil expenditures were up 49%, and average SAT scores rose 15 points. By late 1988 the focus was turning to the 1990 governor's race (Harris is ineligible to run), and to the man who was in large part responsible for Harris's nomination in 1982, Speaker Thomas Murphy. A small town legislator for years, conservative on national issues and determined not to allow a gas tax increase and to keep road-building decisions in the legislature's hands, Murphy is also assertive and something of a kingmaker: in the 1988 presidential race, he supported Albert Gore early, got other states' speakers to do so, and saw Gore carry or finish second to Jesse Jackson in 10 states on Super Tuesday.

In early 1989, many candidates seemed to have a chance. One who is a Murphy favorite is Lauren "Bubba" McDonald, chairman of the same committee Harris headed before 1982. A frequent Murphy antagonist is Zell Miller, who says he will run after 16 years as lieutenant governor. Senator Roy Barnes may also run and Atlanta Mayor Andrew Young is almost certainly running. So the prospect is for a full Democratic primary and perhaps a spirited runoff. But the Republicans may compete seriously for the first time since 1970. They picked up seven state House seats in 1988, their largest gain in any state but New Hampshire, and they have at least two active candidates, House Republican Leader Johnny Isakson from Cobb County, former Macon Mayor George Israel and 1986 GOP nominee Guy Davis.

Senators. Senator Sam Nunn, chairman of the Senate Armed Services Committee, is one of the most powerful figures in American government—and one of the key players in American politics. He negotiates with Presidents, sets the course of military policy, and even plays presidential politics. His political position in Georgia is impervious to challenge, his position in the Democratic Party is strong, and if he is not well known to most voters nationally, he is familiar at least in the South. His ascent to the chair of Armed Services at age 48 was a prime example of the confluence of seniority and expertise. His leadership in the rejection of John Tower's nomination to be Secretary of Defense in March 1989 proved that he is one of a very few senators who can move a majority singlehandedly—even when it means overturning the ancient tradition that senators will never deny confirmation to a former colleague.

Nunn follows in the footsteps of his great-uncle, Carl Vinson, who was first elected to the House in 1914, served 50 years, and chaired the Naval Affairs and then the Armed Services Committee. When asked whether he would like to be Defense Secretary, Vinson is supposed to have replied, "I'd rather run the Pentagon from up here." Nunn, grumbled his critics, was motivated by similar feelings when he torpedoed the Tower nomination; but even they have to concede that Nunn has the in-depth knowledge and intellectual rigor that made him a powerful force in defense policy long before he became chairman. This combination of expertise and political position came about as a result of foresight, discipline, and luck. Like Vinson, Nunn grew up in a small south Georgia town, served in the legislature, was elected to Congress at a young age, got a seat on Armed Services and devoted most of his attention to military affairs, and rose in seniority and in skill. Like most southern Democrats of Vinson's era, the early Nunn was careful to separate himself from his national party. In 1972, when southern politics was still roiled by reverberations from the civil rights revolution, the 34-year-old Nunn, won a place in the runoff against a Jimmy Carter appointee by edging a former governor 23%–21% in the primary—an 18,000-vote margin; he won the runoff and general election by unspectacular 54%–46% margins. Each time he was the candidate of rural Georgia running against Atlanta, shunning George McGovern (who got 25% in Georgia) and courting George Wallace.

Nunn's Senate career has had two phases. In his first phase he got a seat on Armed Services, immersed himself in hard work, and essentially ignored the national party on most issues. He brought to his labors a disposition, not widely shared in the Senate then, to support military projects and spending; on domestic issues, he generally voted against most Democrats. He distinguished himself mainly by his hard work and curiosity about how the Pentagon's weapons and personnel policies and procedures really worked. He was never close to Jimmy Carter, but was circumspect about airing his disagreements with his Administration; in the Reagan years, as he rose in seniority, his hand became more evident. He was one of the architects, with Les Aspin of the House Armed Services Committee (who comes from the anti-Vietnam war branch of the Democratic Party), of the MX missile compromise that passed both houses of Congress, continuing development of the MX but also advancing as an alternative the Midgetman; he was one of the sponsors, with Barry Goldwater, of the 1986 military reform centralizing theater commands and the power of the chairman of the Joint Chiefs of Staff.

The second phase of Nunn's career began during the 1986 campaign. Before then Nunn almost never campaigned for or even endorsed other Democrats, and in 1985 he let it be known that he would do nothing to help beat his Republican colleague Mack Mattingly. But it was also apparent that, for all his bipartisan cooperation with Republicans, the only way Nunn would become chairman of Armed Services, then or ever, is if the Democrats gained a majority in the Senate. So he started stumping hard for Democratic Senate candidates in the South and North, vouching for the toughness on defense of the likes of Alan Cranston, and working vigorously for Mattingly's opponent, Atlanta liberal Wyche Fowler. At the same time his own ratings with some liberals were going up.

He also moved to assert mastery of arms policy. Right after the election, Nunn was quick to point out that President Reagan's proposals at the Reykjavik summit for getting rid of nuclear weapons would have left Europe undefended. Although he supported research on Reagan's Strategic Defense Initiative, he was quick to point out that it could never be an effective shield for the whole population. And in 1987 he redefined the whole SDI debate by challenging the Administration's reinterpretation of the ABM treaty which would have allowed testing of ABMs in space. Nunn, going back over the treaty text and record himself, delivered about as conclusive a refutation as is seen in politics. Afterwards, Nunn successfully insisted on writing his interpretation into law, holding up the defense bill for months to do so. When the INF treaty came up later, he insisted on an amendment stating that ratification was based on the public record of the treaty. In all these matters Nunn took positions that are intellectually respectable, even irrefutable. But they have had the additional advantages for him by making him a leading Democratic partisan in the Senate and out.

At the same time Nunn was one of the founders of the moderate Democratic Leadership Council, and was the lead proponent of its proposal for national service. He publicly teetered on the edge of running for president in early 1987, and may have been deterred largely by the almost unanimously dovish Democratic constituency in the first contest in Iowa. In the Senate he backed the INF treaty and passed his defense authorization bill, and was furious when it was vetoed at Bush's urging during the campaign season. He served on the Iran-contra committee, grilling former National Security Adviser John Poindexter. With Daniel Patrick Moynihan, he was the Senate Democrats' point man on the 1988 drug bill, both on the floor and in conference. He helped pass the ingenious base-closing bill. He turned aside talk that he could be Michael Dukakis's running mate. But in October 1988 he hosted Dukakis in Hawkinsville, just down U.S. 341 from his own home in Perry, and gave a riproaring speech on his behalf that overlooked their differences on defense policy and stressed their areas of agreement.

So even before Nunn took on John Tower, evidence was accumulating that he had ceased being the nonpartisan figure he was up through the early 1980s and had already become a capital *D* Democrat, albeit a very moderate one. Was this an opportunistic transformation? Nunn can claim, with some basis, that the national party was coming toward him, and was no longer reflexively supporting big spending domestic programs or opposing defense spending. He can claim as well that his views reflect a steady view of the world. He favors a flat defense budget with no increases except for inflation, is skeptical that SDI can do as much as its enthusiasts claim, wants to choose between Midgetman and the MX, and wants to strengthen U.S. conventional forces. He appears ready to take advantage of changes Mikhail Gorbachev may make in Soviet policies, but he is no starry-eyed admirer of the Soviet leader. Domestically, Nunn bemoans the large budget deficits, decries the lack of excellence in American schools, calls for national service; but he remains rather conservative on cultural issues, not at all convinced that traditional morals are outmoded. And he does not toady to the liberals. "We are losing the working and middle-class Americans who used to be the mainstay of our party's coalition," he told a Democratic Leadership Conference audience in 1989 that included Jesse Jackson.

All of which is intellectually consistent with the position he took that John Tower was unfit because of his personal behavior and his money dealings with defense contractors to be Defense Secretary. But it is also consistent with the fact that the only way Nunn can become president is to be nominated by Democrats who have historically differed from him on issues, just as the only way he could become and can remain Armed Services chairman is for these Democrats to retain their majority in the Senate. And if Nunn is torn on some of these issues, once he makes up his mind he acts decisively. He did not just cast his vote on Tower, but carried an almost entirely united Democratic majority with him, just as he carried the day on the ABM treaty interpretation. He may or may not be running for president—most likely he regards a run as an unlikely possibility, but one he'd like to leave open—but he is determined to exert control over the Pentagon and over public policy as his grand-uncle did a quarter and a half century ago. And if he has abandoned the above-partisan-politics posture he took in his first years in the Senate, there is an equally lively tradition of taking responsibility and exerting power as a partisan leader which he seems to be living up to.

Georgia's other senator is a Democrat who owes his seat to his own well-honed political talents—and to vigorous help from Sam Nunn. He is Wyche Fowler, who is politically adept enough to have been elected for nine years to represent the black-majority 5th Congressional District in Atlanta, and then to have beaten better known candidates in the primary and general elections statewide. In the primary Fowler beat Hamilton Jordan, one of America's premier political strategists, whose candidacy was strengthened by his gallant recovery from cancer and an absence of the arrogance that so many detected in him when he was Jimmy Carter's campaign manager and chief of staff. But Jordan relied too much on a stale anti-Atlanta theme, and in the last weeks Fowler, with more money by then, was able to campaign as the only candidate with experience in the Army and Congress and to tell voters to pronounce his name "Wyche—*ch* as in church." Fowler got 50.2%, avoiding a runoff.

In the general Fowler faced incumbent Senator Mack Mattingly, a former IBM salesman from Indiana who had upset scandal-tarred Herman Talmadge in 1980. Mattingly had made a respectable record in the Senate, managing Ted Stevens's nearly successful campaign for majority leader and championing the President's proposal for a line-item veto, but he made his major theme against Fowler absenteeism—a successful tactic against a little-known incumbent in Kentucky in 1984, but used by Republican strategists in 1986 in too many races like this one where it didn't apply (Mattingly was not hard-working, Fowler not unknown). Mattingly missed his chance to attack Fowler as a liberal, while Fowler stressed his rural roots, his guitar-strumming style, and Sam Nunn's wholehearted endorsement, and won with 51%.

In the Senate Fowler was one of the first southern Democrats to oppose Robert Bork's nomination and help defeat it. He was an environmentalist on the Energy Committee, trying to stop oil drilling in the Alaska National Wildlife Reserve and increase money for protection of wetlands; most of this was unsuccessful, and he gave up his Energy seat for the plum of a seat on Appropriations in 1989. He remains on Budget and Agriculture—one giving him leeway to indulge his interest in issues of national scope, the other enabling him to help particular interests in Georgia. On state projects he has established the sensible procedure in working in tandem with Nunn. Fowler was mentioned briefly as a possibility for the VP nomination in Atlanta, but wasn't in the running. In the fight for Senate majority leader in late 1988, Fowler went public several weeks before the vote in support of George Mitchell, the most liberal and the eventual winner, and against Daniel Inouye and fellow southerner (and Energy chairman) Bennett Johnston.

Presidential politics. Georgia goes Democratic when the Democrats nominate a Georgian for President—it did twice for Jimmy Carter, and by wide margins, and would surely do so if Sam Nunn were the nominee—and it goes Republican otherwise. Such is the lesson of the 1970s and 1980s. Despite the stumping of Georgia Democrats like Sam Nunn and (for a while) Speaker Tom Murphy, and despite the presence of Lloyd Bentsen on the ticket, the 1988 Democratic percentage was nearly the same as in 1984, an out-of-contention 39%. Since blacks cast about 22% of Georgia's votes, that means that the white vote went nearly 3 to 1 for Bush.

Congressional districting. Georgia will likely gain one seat after the 1990 Census, thanks to the rapid growth of metro Atlanta—the first gain for Georgia since 1910. The big controversy after the 1980 Census was over how black Atlanta's 5th District would be; so many blacks were put in by a court plan that the next-door 4th went Republican in 1984 and 1986. For 1992, debate will center on the boundaries of the new district. It will probably be in the fast-growing North Side suburbs from Gwinnett to Cobb Counties, in territory that almost surely would produce a Republican congressman. Why would Democratic legislators draw such a district? First, because the one-person-one-vote rule gives them little choice. Second, because it would relieve three Democratic incumbents of territory that could provide the basis for a successful Republican challenge.

The People: Est. Pop. 1988: 6,401,000; Pop. 1980: 5,463,105, up 17.1% 1980–88 and 19.1% 1970–80; 2.53% of U.S. total, 11th largest. 13% with 1–3 yrs. col., 15% with 4+ yrs. col.; 16.6% below poverty level. Single ancestry: 21% English, 5% Irish, 3% German, 1% French. Households (1980): 76% family, 44% with children, 61% married couples; 35.0% housing units rented; median monthly rent: $153; median house value: $36,900. Voting age pop. (1980): 3,816,975; 24% Black, 1% Spanish origin. Registered voters (1988): 2,941,339; no party registration.

1988 Share of Federal Tax Burden: $20,286,000,000; 2.29% of U.S. total, 12th largest.

1988 Share of Federal Expenditures

	Total		Non-Defense		Defense	
Total Expend	$18,451m	(2.09%)	$13,709m	(2.09%)	$5,084m	(2.23%)
St/Lcl Grants	2,964m	(2.59%)	2,963m	(2.59%)	1m	(0.85%)
Salary/Wages	4,175m	(3.11%)	1,688m	(2.52%)	2,488m	(2.52%)
Pymnts to Indiv	8,866m	(2.17%)	8,218m	(2.10%)	648m	(3.48%)
Procurement	1,944m	(1.03%)	342m	(0.74%)	1,944m	(1.03%)
Research/Other	502m	(1.34%)	498m	(1.34%)	4m	(1.34%)

Political Lineup: Governor, Joe Frank Harris (D); Lt. Gov., Zell Miller (D); Secy. of State, Max Cleland (D); Atty. Gen., Michael J. Bowers (D). State Senate, 56 (45 D and 11 R); State House of Representatives, 180 (144 D and 36 R). Senators, Sam Nunn (D) and Wyche Fowler (D). Representatives, 10 (9 D and 1 R).

1988 Presidential Vote

Bush (R)	1,081,331	(60%)
Dukakis (D)	714,792	(39%)

1984 Presidential Vote

Reagan (R)	1,068,722	(60%)
Mondale (D)	706,628	(40%)

1988 Democratic Presidential Primary

Jackson	247,831	(40%)
Gore	201,490	(32%)
Dukakis	97,179	(16%)
Gephardt	41,489	(7%)
Hart	15,852	(3%)
Simon	8,388	(1%)

1988 Republican Presidential Primary

Bush	215,516	(54%)
Dole	94,749	(24%)
Robertson	65,163	(16%)
Kemp	23,409	(6%)

GOVERNOR

Gov. Joe Frank Harris (D)

Elected 1982, term expires Jan. 1991; b. Feb. 16, 1936, Bartow Cnty.; home, Atlanta; U. of GA, B.B.A. 1958; United Methodist; married (Elizabeth).

Career: Army, 1958–64; Pres., Harris Georgia Corp., 1964–82; GA House of Reps., 1965–82.

Offices: 203 State Capitol, Atlanta 30334, 404-656-1776.

Election Results

1986 gen.	Joe Frank Harris (D)	828,461	(71%)
	Guy Davis (R)	346,508	(29%)
1986 prim.	Joe Frank Harris (D)	521,704	(85%)
	Kenneth B. Quarterman (D)	89,759	(15%)
1982 gen.	Joe Frank Harris (D)	732,686	(63%)
	Robert H. Bell (R)	434,204	(37%)

SENATORS

Sen. Sam Nunn (D)

Elected 1972, seat up 1990; b. Sept. 8, 1938, Perry; home, Perry; Emory U., A.B. 1960, LL.B. 1962; United Methodist; married (Colleen).

Career: Coast Guard, 1959–60; Legal Cnsl. to U.S. House Armed Svcs. Cmttee., 1962–63; Farmer, Practicing atty., 1963–72; GA House of Reps., 1968–72.

Offices: 303 DSOB 20510, 202-224-3521. Also Ste. 1700, 75 Spring Street, S.W., Atlanta 30303, 404-331-4811; 915 Main St., Perry 31069, 912-987-1458; 130 Fed. Bldg., Gainesville 30501, 404-532-9976; 600 E. 1st St., Rome 30161, 404-291-5696; and 120 Barnard St., Savannah 31069, 912-944-4300.

Committees: *Armed Services* (Chairman of 11 D). *Governmental Affairs* (2d of 8 D). Subcommittees: Government Information and Regulation; Investigations (Chairman). *Small Business* (2d of 10 D). Subcommittees: Rural Economy and Family Farming; Urban and Minority-Owned Business Development. *Select Committee on Intelligence* (2d of 9 D).

Group Ratings

	ADA	ACLU	COPE	CFA	LCV	ACU	NTLC	NSI	COC	CEI
1988	40	44	41	83	20	42	22	100	50	29
1987	55	—	40	67	—	23	—	—	28	30

National Journal Ratings

	1988 LIB — 1988 CONS	1987 LIB — 1987 CONS
Economic	41% — 58%	50% — 49%
Social	52% — 47%	53% — 42%
Foreign	46% — 53%	41% — 57%

Key Votes

1) Cut Aged Housing $	AGN	5) Bork Nomination	AGN	9) SDI Funding	FOR
2) Override Hwy Veto	FOR	6) Ban Plastic Guns	AGN	10) Ban Chem Weaps	FOR
3) Kill Plnt Clsng Notice	AGN	7) Deny Abortions	FOR	11) Aid To Contras	FOR
4) Min Wage Increase	FOR	8) Japanese Reparations	AGN	12) Reagan Defense $	AGN

Election Results

1984 general	Sam Nunn (D) 1,344,104	(80%)	($843,891)
	Mike Hicks (R) 337,196	(20%)	
1984 primary	Sam Nunn (D) 801,412	(90%)	
	Jim Boyd (D) 86,973	(10%)	
1978 general	Sam Nunn (D) 536,320	(83%)	($548,814)
	John W. Stokes (R) 108,808	(17%)	

Sen. Wyche Fowler (D)

Elected 1986, seat up 1992; b. Oct 6, 1940, Atlanta; home, Atlanta; Davidson Col., A.B. 1962, Emory U., J.D. 1969; Presbyterian; divorced.

Career: Army, 1962–64; Chief Asst. to U.S. Rep. Charles Weltner, 1965–66; Night Mayor for the City of Atlanta, 1968–69; Atlanta Bd. of Aldermen, 1970–74; Pres., Atlanta City Cncl., 1974–77; Practicing atty., 1970–77; U.S. House of Reps., 1977–87.

Offices: 204 RSOB 20510, 202-224-3643. Also 10 Park Place S., Ste. 210, Atlanta 30303, 404-331-0697.

Committees: *Agriculture, Nutrition and Forestry* (7th of 10 D). Subcommittees: Conservation and Forestry (Chairman); Nutrition and Investigations; Domestic and Foreign Marketing and Product Promotion. *Appropriations* (15th of 16 D). Subcommittees: Agriculture, Rural Development and Related Agencies; District of Columbia; VA-HUD-Independent Agencies; Military Construction. *Budget* (10th of 13 D).

Group Ratings

	ADA	ACLU	COPE	CFA	LCV	ACU	NTLC	NSI	COC	CEI
1988	75	56	88	92	60	8	4	10	43	24
1987	90	—	100	83	—	8	—	—	22	21

National Journal Ratings

	1988 LIB — 1988 CONS		1987 LIB — 1987 CONS	
Economic	47%	48%	65%	26%
Social	55%	44%	71%	26%
Foreign	69%	30%	59%	39%

Key Votes

1) Cut Aged Housing $	FOR	5) Bork Nomination	AGN	9) SDI Funding	AGN
2) Override Hwy Veto	FOR	6) Ban Plastic Guns	AGN	10) Ban Chem Weaps	AGN
3) Kill Plnt Clsng Notice	AGN	7) Deny Abortions	AGN	11) Aid To Contras	AGN
4) Min Wage Increase	FOR	8) Japanese Reparations	AGN	12) Reagan Defense $	AGN

Election Results

1986 general	Wyche Fowler (D)	623,705	(51%)	($2,779,297)
	Mack Mattingly (R)	601,235	(49%)	($5,119,249)
1986 primary	Wyche Fowler (D)	314,787	(50%)	
	Hamilton Jordan (D)	196,307	(32%)	
	John D. Russell (D)	100,307	(16%)	
1980 general	Mack Mattingly (R)	803,677	(51%)	($504,016)
	Herman E. Talmadge (D)	776,025	(49%)	($2,213,289)

FIRST DISTRICT

On the Atlantic coast of Georgia half a century ago you could find traces of history, where blacks on the Sea Islands still spoke in the African-linked dialect they called Geechee, where outsiders were called Gullah and where cotton was still traded on the Cotton Exchange on Savannah's waterfront. Savannah was built on a river just off the ocean at the center of the 13th British colony in North America; the proprietor, James Oglethorpe, tried to settle it with convicts and tried to regulate their conduct closely in hopes of rehabilitation. His hopes were frustrated, but Oglethorpe's rectangular street plan, with its straight streets and 19 parks remains amid the marshes of south Georgia. For 100 years Savannah was Georgia's only major city, its waterfront the emporium for the cotton and rice crops of the coastal plantations. After the Civil War, its port was eclipsed by Atlanta's railroads. Savannah industrialized slowly, with paper mills and chemical plants along the river; on farms, cotton was replaced by peanuts and tobacco and wood pulp.

In the last 50 years, Savannah's economy has grown, and if most of its residents have incomes as low as anywhere in the United States they are at least shopping in supermarkets rather than living off their little plots of land. Much of the growth can be ascribed to the federal government—nearby Fort Stewart is the Army's largest base east of the Mississippi—and to tourism. Visitors are attracted to resorts on the islands and to Savannah itself, where people have restored their old houses and whose squares are kept more tidily than they probably were in their antebellum heyday. With its variety of architectural styles, its occasional pastel buildings, its trees hanging with Spanish moss, Savannah suggests the tropics; the style is a cross between the stately harmony of Charleston and the funky eclecticism of New Orleans.

The 1st Congressional District of Georgia is centered on Savannah, and runs down the coast to the Florida line and inland through farming counties—tobacco and peanut country, plus Toombs County, the only place allowed to produce Vidalia onions—almost halfway to Atlanta. Savannah is not big enough to dominate the district, and whenever there is a contest the rural counties seem to gang up on the city. It is as if the small farmers, black and white, of the rural counties suppose that everyone in Savannah lives in a grand mansion, enjoying the profits made from the sweat of farmers' brows. The real division in elections here then is between town and country, not—as seemed likely 15 years ago—between black and white.

The incumbent congressman, Lindsay Thomas, spans that division, which helped him win when incumbent Bo Ginn ran for governor in 1982. Thomas was born in the rural areas, spent seven years in Savannah both in banking and civic affairs, then ran a family farm operation for nine years. He had held no political office, but he had good connections throughout the district and enough money to get his campaign started. That enabled him to build up big margins in the rural counties and a respectable vote in Savannah—enough to get him by a Savannah aristocrat in the primary and a Republican in the general election.

In the House, Thomas has concentrated on issues of local significance. On the Agriculture Committee he worked hard to protect peanut and tobacco subsidies, helped craft a dairy bill, and worked on the drought assistance bill. A tree farmer himself, he chairs a Forestry 2000 Task Force formed to improve and expand American forestry. He won a seat on the Appropriations Committee in 1987, but was already busy on projects like replacing the Talmadge Bridge in Savannah, building up Tybee Island beach, getting the Savannah airport named a foreign trade zone, and increasing funding for Fort Stewart. He takes some interest in environment issues, like the impact of the Kings Bay submarine base on Cumberland Island; with the growth of tourism the environment has become an economic asset. Those looking for process-minded reforms of the way in which the House does business will have to look elsewhere: Thomas is busy using the system to help his home folks.

Thomas made no moves to run for the Senate in 1986 and is not mentioned much as a candidate for governor in 1990; he seems strongly entrenched in the 1st District. In 1988 Republican Chris Meredith ran an aggressive and scurrilous campaign against Thomas; many of his charges were simply wrong—like calling Thomas a liberal when in fact Thomas, though he often votes with the Democratic leadership, did not have a liberal record on foreign and cultural issues. Thomas again won easily.

The People: Est. Pop. 1986: 588,900, up 8.8% 1980–86; Pop. 1980: 541,180, up 15.9% 1970–80. Households (1980): 77% family, 45% with children, 61% married couples; 36.0% housing units rented; median monthly rent: $125; median house value: $32,900. Voting age pop. (1980): 375,257; 30% Black, 1% Spanish origin, 1% Asian origin.

1988 Presidential Vote:

Bush (R)	94,646	(60%)
Dukakis (D)	62,529	(39%)

Rep. R. Lindsay Thomas (D)

Elected 1982; b. Nov. 20, 1943, Patterson; home, Statesboro; U. of GA, B.A. 1966; United Methodist; married (Melinda).

Career: Investment banker, 1966–73; Farmer, 1973–82.

Offices: 431 CHOB 20515, 202-225-5831. Also P.O. Box 10074, Savannah 31412, 912-944-4074; P.O. Box 333, Statesboro 30458, 912-489-8797; 304 Fed. Bldg., Brunswick 31520, 912-264-4040; and P.O.Box 767, Jesup 31545, 912-427-9231.

Committees: *Appropriations* (33d of 35 D). Subcommittees: Energy and Water Development; Military Construction.

Group Ratings

	ADA	ACLU	COPE	CFA	LCV	ACU	NTLC	NSI	COC	CEI
1988	50	41	48	55	50	48	30	90	64	28
1987	40	—	45	43	—	36	—	—	60	19

National Journal Ratings

	1988 LIB — 1988 CONS		1987 LIB — 1987 CONS	
Economic	40% —	58%	54% —	45%
Social	42% —	57%	33% —	67%
Foreign	46% —	54%	47% —	52%

Key Votes

1) Homeless $	AGN	5) Ban Drug Test	FOR	9) SDI Research	AGN
2) Gephardt Amdt	AGN	6) Drug Death Pen	FOR	10) Ban Chem Weaps	AGN
3) Deficit Reduc	FOR	7) Handgun Sales	FOR	11) Aid to Contras	FOR
4) Kill Plnt Clsng Notice	FOR	8) Ban D.C. Abort $	AGN	12) Nuclear Testing	FOR

Election Results

1988 general	R. Lindsay Thomas (D)	94,531	(67%)	($337,048)
	John Christian Meridith (R)	46,552	(33%)	($40,461)
1988 primary	R. Lindsay Thomas (D)	79,645	(100%)	
1986 general	R. Lindsay Thomas (D)	69,440	(100%)	($201,603)

SECOND DISTRICT

South Georgia has long been one of the lowest income parts of the United States, and statistically one of the most rural and backward. In the days before World War II, this was a land with little more than a subsistence farming economy; diseases like pellagra and rickets were rife; children were malnourished enough that their growth was stunted and they received little or no schooling; indoor plumbing and electricity even for well-off farmers were the exception rather than the rule. Today south Georgia continues to rank low on national statistics, but everyday life has changed radically. Endemic diseases have been wiped out, and infant mortality reduced to near-national levels. Electricity and indoor plumbing, washing machines, refrigerators and television are universal. Given the low cost of living, average incomes here are now in real dollars similar to what the very few local rich people made before the war. In one other important respect life has changed. Legal segregation has disappeared, despite predictions that whites would never tolerate integration; schools, restaurants, and shops are integrated; old forms of address are no longer required, though the sometimes elaborate politeness of the Deep South has not altogether vanished.

Accompanying this socio-economic change, but not precisely in tandem, has been political change. In Franklin Roosevelt's day, south Georgia was one of the most Democratic parts of the United States: blacks didn't vote, and whites still hated the party of Sherman and liked New Deal welfare, rural electrification, and farm programs, which pumped money into these otherwise moribund areas. Whites' preference for national Democrats vanished in the early 1960s, as they became associated with civil rights; blacks, when they could vote, went Democratic, but after years of outmigration were a minority. Economic growth followed the civil rights revolution, but much of it depended on federal spending and heavy industry. In the 1980s, as Atlanta boomed, south Georgia mostly sagged: the closing of the Firestone plant cost Albany 2,000 jobs; drought cut farm income to nearly zero; towns hustled to attract Japanese facilities. Whites' anger at the civil rights revolution wore off, and there was a perceptible trend toward the Democrats—enough for Michael Dukakis and Walter Mondale to win respectable totals in territory that was once death to liberal Democrats.

The southwest corner of Georgia, from the I-75 corridor and the piney woods around Valdosta west to the Alabama line, forms the state's 2d Congressional District. Since 1980 it has been represented by Charles Hatcher, a Democrat with a record somewhat less conservative than members from such districts had 20 years ago; most of the time he supports spending programs in close votes and quietly goes along with the majority of House Democrats—more often than any other rural Georgia congressman. On the Agriculture Committee, he is a nuts-and-bolts man, protecting the peanut subsidy (the 2d produces half of the nation's crop) and being careful about the details of the diesel tax repeal and pesticide regulations. Like many southern Democrats he is a supporter of the food stamp program, which, because need is determined on a national basis, is particularly generous to the South. His support of government programs, though it goes against current regional rhetoric, has roots in the region's history: for government—REA, the military, civil rights laws—has done so much here to improve people's everyday lives.

But Hatcher has had more than the usual competition for this seat, probably because he makes less than the usual noise of a district-minded congressman. Hatcher first won in 1980, when 2d District incumbent Dawson Mathis ran for the Senate; he was a protege in the legislature of his south Georgia neighbor, Governor George Busbee, and beat Mathis aide Julian Holland by only 53%–47% in the runoff. In 1982 Mathis ran for his old seat, and Hatcher won by only 52%–48%. In 1988 Holland ran, evidently convinced that Hatcher had not made much of an impact, but Hatcher won the primary with 67%. But he also had a Republican opponent, Ralph Hudgens, who accused him of being a liberal and attacked him for riding in a red Mercedes in Albany's Pecan Festival parade; Hatcher won that contest with 62%. The national and local Democratic percentages seem to be converging; two decades ago corresponding figures were 92% and 22%. That convergence may some day be good news for national Democrats, but it also gives a glimmer of hope for Republicans in historically Democratic south Georgia.

The People: Est. Pop. 1986: 566,500, up 3.0% 1980–86; Pop. 1980: 549,977, up 13.7% 1970–80. Households (1980): 78% family, 46% with children, 61% married couples; 35.1% housing units rented; median monthly rent: $100; median house value: $30,200. Voting age pop. (1980): 369,606; 32% Black, 1% Spanish origin.

1988 Presidential Vote:

Bush (R)	83,163	(58%)
Dukakis (D)	57,423	(40%)

Rep. Charles F. Hatcher (D)

Elected 1980; b. July 1, 1939, Doerun; home, Newton; GA Southern Col., Statesboro, B.S. 1965, U. of GA, J.D. 1969; Episcopalian; married (Ellen).

Career: Air Force, 1958–62; Practicing atty.; GA House of Reps., 1972–80.

Offices: 405 CHOB 20515, 202-225-3631. Also P.O. Box 1932, Albany 31702, 912-439-8067; and P.O. Box 1626, Valdosta 31603, 912-247-9705.

Committees: *Agriculture* (11th of 26 D). Subcommittees: Cotton, Rice and Sugar; Department Operations, Research and Foreign Agriculture. *Small Business* (7th of 27 D). Subcommittee: Procurement, Tourism and Rural Development.

Group Ratings

	ADA	ACLU	COPE	CFA	LCV	ACU	NTLC	NSI	COC	CEI
1988	50	50	56	55	31	43	22	80	64	20
1987	48	—	55	21	—	27	—	—	54	21

National Journal Ratings

	1988 LIB — 1988 CONS		1987 LIB — 1987 CONS	
Economic	43% —	57%	48% —	52%
Social	50% —	48%	39% —	61%
Foreign	46% —	54%	47% —	52%

Key Votes

1) Homeless $	AGN	5) Ban Drug Test	—	9) SDI Research	AGN
2) Gephardt Amdt	AGN	6) Drug Death Pen	FOR	10) Ban Chem Weaps	AGN
3) Deficit Reduc	FOR	7) Handgun Sales	FOR	11) Aid to Contras	FOR
4) Kill Plnt Clsng Notice	FOR	8) Ban D.C. Abort $	AGN	12) Nuclear Testing	FOR

Election Results

1988 general	Charles F. Hatcher (D)	85,029	(62%)	($368,470)
	Ralph T. Hudgens (R)	52,807	(38%)	($129,741)
1988 primary	Charles F. Hatcher (D)	77,789	(67%)	
	Julian Holland (D)	38,726	(33%)	
1986 general	Charles F. Hatcher (D)	72,482	(100%)	($140,185)

THIRD DISTRICT

The 3d Congressional District of Georgia is the birthplace of one Democratic President and the place where another died. Franklin Roosevelt first came to the bedraggled resort in Warm Springs, 75 miles south of Atlanta, in October 1924, the same month that Jimmy Carter was born in Plains, 75 miles farther south. The Georgia that Roosevelt looked out on from the hilltop of Warm Springs was ragged land, where most people lived in little cabins without electricity or plumbing and scratched out a bare living from overtilled soil. Yet history was made here too, at Fort Benning, where General George Marshall held manuevers that helped him choose most of the Army's generals in World War II; Benning still remains a giant Army training base, taking up most of a county. In the years since Carter went off to Annapolis in 1942 and Roosevelt died in Warm Springs in 1945 economic growth plus the works of government—electrification, the minimum wage, the military presence, interstate highways, better schools, the elimination of racial barriers—made life better here in the part of south Georgia between Atlanta and Albany, west of Macon and centered on Columbus, that currently makes up the 3d District.

It is the home also of Senator Sam Nunn, who hails from Perry, the county seat just down the road from Warner Robins Air Force Base. This was once cotton land, with some big plantations and plenty of smaller farmers; now it is devoted to soybeans, peanuts, and the softwood pine trees which grow almost as fast as cotton bolls in the warm, humid South. The economy of the rural counties, while far above the subsistence levels of the 1930s, has been sagging in the 1980s, and the political trend locally, after the severe reaction 20 years ago to the civil rights revolution, is toward the Democrats. There's a parallel here with Nunn, who has been more active as a national Democrat since 1984 than he ever was before, even bringing Michael Dukakis to Hawkinsville in Pulaski County—one of seven counties in the 3d District that Dukakis carried.

The congressman from the 3d is a Democrat whose career has been linked to Nunn's. Richard Ray, a pesticide business owner who was mayor of Perry when Nunn was city attorney, served as Nunn's administrative assistant for his first 10 years in the Senate. When Congressman Jack Brinkley retired in 1982, Ray got into the race and won the decisive primary with little difficulty. He has won reelection easily since. He serves on Armed Services and of course has views similar to Nunn's, and also works smoothly with Chairman Les Aspin. His instincts on economic issues are conservative, which is to say in today's environment advocating spending cuts on most domestic programs. His instincts on defense policy are to support generous defense spending but to be a stickler for details; he has balked at supporting the Administration's full requests for the Strategic Defense Initiative because of budgetary concerns, and he opposed some contra aid requests because he did not believe the contras were viable. On these and other issues he can be a pivotal vote in committee and on the floor—and a vote which can be won only on the merits.

The People: Est. Pop. 1986: 569,600, up 5.3% 1980–86; Pop. 1980: 540,865, up 8.9% 1970–80. Households (1980): 78% family, 46% with children, 61% married couples; 35.6% housing units rented; median monthly rent: $117; median house value: $30,200. Voting age pop. (1980): 376,128; 31% Black, 2% Spanish origin, 1% Asian origin.

1988 Presidential Vote:

Bush (R)	84,006	(57%)
Dukakis (D)	62,028	(42%)

Rep. Richard B. Ray (D)

Elected 1982; b. Feb. 2, 1927, Fort Valley; home, Perry; United Methodist; married (Barbara).

Career: Navy, WWII; Farmer, 1946–50; Owner, Ray Services Inc., 1950–62; S.E. Mngr., Getz Inc., 1962–72; Councilman, Perry, 1962–64; Mayor of Perry, 1964–70; Pres., GA Municipal Assoc., 1969; A.A. to Sen. Sam Nunn, 1973–82.

Offices: 425 CHOB 20515, 202-225-5901. Also 301 15th St., Columbus 31901, 404-324-0292; 200 Carl Vinson Pkwy., Warner Robins 31056, 912-929-2764; and 200 Ridley Ave., LaGrange 30240, 404-883-2195.

Committees: *Armed Services* (17th of 31 D). Subcommittees: Procurement and Military Nuclear Systems; Readiness. *Small Business* (15th of 27 D). Subcommittee: Exports, Tax Policy and Special Problems.

Group Ratings

	ADA	ACLU	COPE	CFA	LCV	ACU	NTLC	NSI	COC	CEI
1988	20	26	28	36	44	53	47	100	56	43
1987	32	—	25	25	—	63	—	—	73	38

National Journal Ratings

	1988 LIB — 1988 CONS	1987 LIB — 1987 CONS
Economic	38% — 62%	37% — 62%
Social	32% — 67%	27% — 72%
Foreign	* — *	* — *

Key Votes

1) Homeless $	FOR	5) Ban Drug Test	FOR	9) SDI Research	—
2) Gephardt Amdt	AGN	6) Drug Death Pen	FOR	10) Ban Chem Weaps	—
3) Deficit Reduc	AGN	7) Handgun Sales	FOR	11) Aid to Contras	FOR
4) Kill Plnt Clsng Notice	—	8) Ban D.C. Abort $	FOR	12) Nuclear Testing	—

Election Results

1988 general	Richard B. Ray (D)	97,663	(100%)	($256,751)
1988 primary	Richard B. Ray (D)	76,490	(100%)	
1986 general	Richard B. Ray (D)	75,850	(100%)	($150,796)

FOURTH DISTRICT

The 4th Congressional District of Georgia contains many of the leading institutions of the South. Here is Emory University, generously endowed with Coca-Cola money; across the street is the Center for Disease Control, one of those superbly competent government agencies that has saved thousands of lives; there, on the other side of Interstate 85, is Lenox Square, with not only the usual top-of-the-line luxury stores but probably the only antique book store in a mall in America. The 4th District was Atlanta's sprawl in the 1950s and 1960s, when whites were moving out of the central city; now the sprawl has moved into counties farther out than DeKalb, straight east of Atlanta. But much of the economic and cultural elite of the city remains here, in the hills around Buckhead in north Atlanta or north of Emory, and most of the neighborhoods have a comfortable, lived-in feel. This is the most highly educated, culturally sophisticated, and intellectually distinguished congressional district in Georgia and probably in the South.

It is also a district that had an election in 1988 as elevated in tone and rich in substance as a mud wrestling match. The genesis of this contest, oddly enough, goes back to the Voting Rights Act, under the current interpretation of which the next-door 5th District was redrawn by a federal court so that it would be 65% black. The removal of blacks and substitution of high-income whites in the 4th produced the surprise defeat of Democratic Congressman Elliott Levitas in 1984 by Republican Pat Swindall. Swindall was an odd duck for this district: an evangelical Republican who toted a "biblical scorecard" and campaigned as a Christian fundamentalist.

Swindall's legislative record was minimal; one achievement was getting a roll call on whether or not to fire the House's 14 elevator operators. In 1986 he was challenged by Democrat Ben Jones, the actor who plays the mechanic, Cooter (turtle, in southern dialect), on *The Dukes of Hazzard*. Jones was not considered a strong candidate and raised and spent only $118,000. But as more conservative young families move farther out and culturally liberal people stay close to the city and the university, the district has been trending Democratic, and Jones held Swindall, who raised $753,000 and spent $627,000, to 51% in DeKalb County and 53% districtwide.

1988 saw a Swindall-Cooter—Dickensian names!—rematch. Swindall was building a $1 million mansion near Stone Mountain and was strapped for cash; he met with an Atlanta businessman and an undercover agent who offered him an $850,000 loan and said it was "probably drug money." Swindall accepted—on videotape. When this was reported in June 1988 by the *Atlanta Constitution*, Swindall tearfully apologized and said that he had returned the money, and his ads promptly started attacking Jones as an alcoholic (he was, he admitted, and had stopped drinking several years before) and a wife-beater (he was charged with battery in a dispute with a former wife). In October, 22 days before the election, Swindall was indicted; he sought an immediate trial, but it was postponed after prospective jurors reported receiving his campaign literature. Jones in the meantime raised plenty of money and was attacking Swindall as an extremist and one who would impose religious tests on others. Swindall, standing revealed as a fraud, won 40% of the votes; Jones, who admitted to a turbulent past, won 60%. He is likely, given the changing composition of the district, to be able to win again.

The People: Est. Pop. 1986: 611,000, up 12.7% 1980–86; Pop. 1980: 542,368, up 24.1% 1970–80. Households (1980): 71% family, 38% with children, 58% married couples; 39.2% housing units rented; median monthly rent: $253; median house value: $57,100. Voting age pop. (1980): 399,703; 11% Black, 2% Spanish origin, 1% Asian origin.

1988 Presidential Vote: Bush (R) 142,998   (59%)
Dukakis (D). 99,212   (41%)

Rep. Ben Jones (D)

Elected 1988; b. Aug. 30, 1941, Tarboro; home, Covington; U. of NC, 1961–65; Southern Baptist; married (Vivian).

Career: Actor, 1966–86; TV producer, 1983-88.

Offices: 514 CHOB 20515, 202-225-4272; 150 E. Ponce de Leon Ave., Ste. 250, Decatur 30030, 404-371-9910

Committees: *Public Works and Transportation* (28th of 31 D). Subcommittees: Aviation; Surface Transportation; Water Resouces. *Veterans' Affairs* (20th of 21 D). Subcommittees: Compensation, Pension and Insurance; Housing and Memorial Affairs.

Group Ratings and Key Votes: Newly Elected

Election Results

1988 general	Ben Lewis Jones (D)...............	148,394	(60%)	($516,737)
	Patrick L. Swindall (R)	97,745	(40%)	($696,301)
1988 primary	Ben Lewis Jones (D)..................	32,982	(62%)	
	Nick Moraitakis (D).................	10,933	(21%)	
	John Stember, Jr. (D)................	8,944	(17%)	
1986 general	Patrick L. Swindall (R)	86,366	(53%)	($627,655)
	Ben Lewis Jones (D).................	75,892	(47%)	($118,085)

FIFTH DISTRICT

Venture out of the quiet of the Ebenezer Baptist Church or the shade of Martin Luther King Jr.'s boyhood home two blocks away and into the steam-heat blast of the sun on Auburn Avenue—Sweet Auburn—and you can see, a mile away, downtown Atlanta's atrium-skyscrapers towering in their glory. They are evidence of the wealth and vibrant growth of "the city," as it used to boast, "too busy to hate," the commercial capital of the South, the chic and sassy world city that has grown up where there was little more than a railroad junction at the time of the War Between the States. But the awesome achievement that is downtown Atlanta is overshadowed by the revolution in men's minds made in very large part by the man who grew up on Auburn Avenue, where people who never felt air conditioning moved slowly in the sweltering heat, where proud professionals worked hard and raised their families and yet never saw more than a few dollars cash at a time. Atlanta's white establishment, led by Mayors William Hartsfield and Ivan Allen and Coca-Cola's Robert Woodruff, deserve credit for abandoning segregation. But it was King and other civil rights leaders who took the risks that led them to do so. Atlanta's city fathers acted out of good will, but also with an eye for the economic growth of their city, which they knew would be hurt by violent resistance. King and his followers were motivated by their lonely vision of what American society could be. White Atlanta's decision to desegregate has helped Atlanta prosper. But King's movement to change the way Americans behave has made it possible for the whole nation to live up to its ideals.

But all is not entirely well in Atlanta. As metro Atlanta booms in the end of the 1980s and spreads over the hills of north Georgia and as affluent blacks move out to $250,000 houses in black subdivisions in DeKalb County, the poor blacks are left behind in the central city.

Atlanta's black institutions have long been the nation's leaders, and Atlanta's black politicians are of a high caliber; Mayor Andrew Young has an international reputation from his years as ambassador to the United Nations and his job-hunting trips for Atlanta, and the two men running in 1989 to succeed him—former Mayor Maynard Jackson and Fulton County Commission chairman Michael Lomax—are able as well. But Young's career was spotted in 1987 when prosecutors considered, but decided not to, charge him with obstruction of justice for allegedly trying to stymie the testimony of the estranged wife of Julian Bond after she claimed Bond and other politicians used cocaine; and the rise of Jesse Jackson has reduced Young's national influence to a point far below what it was when his endorsement helped nominate Jimmy Carter in 1976.

Georgia's 5th Congressional District includes most of Atlanta and a few suburbs, from posh white Sandy Spring in the north to middle-class and increasingly black East Point in the south, plus the rural precincts of southwest Fulton and mostly black southwest DeKalb counties. Its current boundaries were set by a federal court, which decided that the Georgia legislature's district did not count as black majority because it was less than 65% black. The effect on 5th District politics was minimal—the district elected Andrew Young in 1972, 1974, and 1976 when it had a white majority and Wyche Fowler in 1982 and 1984, even after the court's plan was adopted.

The current congressman from the 5th District, elected in 1986 when Fowler ran for the Senate, is John Lewis. He came to Congress already as an important figure in American history. In 1959 and 1960 Lewis, then 19, helped organize the first lunch counter sit-ins. In 1961, he was one of the leaders of the Freedom Rides, and was viciously beaten in Rock Hill, South Carolina, and Montgomery, Alabama. He spoke at the 1963 Washington march. In 1964, he helped coordinate the Mississippi Freedom Project. In 1965, he led the Selma-to-Montgomery march to petition for voting rights and was beaten by policemen using clubs, whips, and tear gas. Modestly, quietly, maintaining his poise and good judgment under harsh circumstances, Lewis was one of the people with roots in places like Auburn Avenue who made the civil rights revolution happen.

Lewis has also had his disappointments. His decade as head of the Voter Education Project in Atlanta and his stint at ACTION in the Carter Administration did not give him the publicity and fame that made a national celebrity of Jesse Jackson, whose movement credentials are much thinner. When Young left the House, Lewis ran for his seat and was soundly beaten by Fowler. After winning a seat on the Atlanta Council in 1981, he ran for Congress in 1986, and trailed Julian Bond 47%–35% in the first primary. Bond had his own illustrious record: he was denied his seat in the Georgia legislature in 1967 because of his opposition to the Vietnam war; he was nominated, at 28, for Vice President at the 1968 convention; he served for nearly 20 years in the legislature, and with a smooth and articulate style was a star of the national speaker circuit and his own syndicated TV show. Yet it was Lewis and not Bond who won in the runoff, and in a curious way: Bond won over 60% of the black votes, but Lewis, thanks to his hard work on local issues like zoning and city ethics, won nearly 90% of the whites.

Lewis was reelected without difficulty in 1988. In the House he has compiled a liberal voting record, pushing such causes as requiring 10% of all airport construction work be done by minority and women contractors; President Reagan singled him out for praise when he signed the 1988 fair housing law. And he was instrumental in getting the first federal building in the United States, in Atlanta, named after Martin Luther King Jr. Lewis's priority project is to set up a revolving fund for low-interest loans to stimulate commercial development in Sweet Auburn, back where his Atlanta started.

The People: Est. Pop. 1986: 570,700, up 3.7% 1980–86; Pop. 1980: 550,070, dn. 6.4% 1970–80. Households (1980): 66% family, 40% with children, 41% married couples; 53.5% housing units rented; median monthly rent: $154; median house value: $34,500. Voting age pop. (1980): 390,138; 60% Black, 1% Spanish origin.

1988 Presidential Vote:

Dukakis (D).	113,308	(68%)
Bush (R)	52,118	(31%)

Rep. John R. Lewis (D)

Elected 1986; b. Feb. 21, 1940, Troy, AL; home, Atlanta; Amer. Baptist Seminary, B.A. 1961, Fisk U, B.A. 1963; Baptist; married (Lillian).

Career: Chmn., Student Nonviolent Coordinating Cmtee., 1963–66; Staff Mbr., Field Foundation, 1966–67; Dir. of Community Organization, Southern Regional Cncl., 1967–70; Exec. Dir., Voter Education Project, 1970–76; Assoc. Dir., ACTION, 1977–80; Dir. of Community Affairs, Natl. Cooperative Bank, 1980–82; Atlanta City Cncl., 1982–86.

Offices: 501 CHOB 20515, 202-225-3801. Also Equitable Bldg. Ste. 750, 100 Peachtree St., N.W., Atlanta 30303, 404-659-0116.

Committees: *Interior and Insular Affairs* (21st of 26 D). Sub-committees: National Parks and Public Lands; Insular and International Affairs. *Public Works and Transportation* (19th of 31 D). Subcommittees: Surface Transportation; Public Buildings and Grounds; Aviation.

Group Ratings

	ADA	ACLU	COPE	CFA	LCV	ACU	NTLC	NSI	COC	CEI
1988	100	96	100	100	75	0	7	0	17	7
1987	96	—	100	79	—	0	—	—	20	8

National Journal Ratings

	1988 LIB — 1988 CONS			1987 LIB — 1987 CONS		
Economic	92%	—	0%	73%	—	0%
Social	86%	—	0%	73%	—	22%
Foreign	84%	—	0%	81%	—	0%

Key Votes

1) Homeless $	AGN	5) Ban Drug Test	AGN	9) SDI Research	AGN
2) Gephardt Amdt	FOR	6) Drug Death Pen	AGN	10) Ban Chem Weaps	FOR
3) Deficit Reduc	FOR	7) Handgun Sales	AGN	11) Aid to Contras	AGN
4) Kill Plnt Clsng Notice	AGN	8) Ban D.C. Abort $	AGN	12) Nuclear Testing	FOR

Election Results

1988 general	John R. Lewis (D).	135,194	(78%)	($101,540)
	J. W. Tibbs, Jr. (R)	37,693	(22%)	($6,047)
1988 primary	John R. Lewis (D).	38,507	(100%)	
1986 general	John Lewis (D)	93,229	(75%)	($380,314)
	Portia A. Scott (R)	30,562	(25%)	($75,862)

SIXTH DISTRICT

Metropolitan Atlanta is marching as relentlessly as General Sherman—but less destructively—into the countryside of Georgia. In the North Side suburbs of Atlanta the source of job creation is the office blocks going up at every interchange; in the South Side suburbs the biggest generator of growth is Hartsfield International Airport, in 1987 and 1988 the busiest airport in the world. Development on the South Side is not uniformly white-collar and the shopping malls are not all upscale: there is a mixture of subdivisions going up on the red clay hills, with various churches from mainline to fundamentalist. Suburbs merge into the always thickly-settled rural countryside of Georgia almost seamlessly. These new communities are affluent but not dominated by any establishment, liberation-minded in much of their lifestyle but tradition-minded often in their yearnings, places full of opportunity yet determined to be conservative. Politically this is conservative country, full of young families, almost all white, who have moved up economically and who like the homier cultural atmosphere of the smaller counties, where most people still attend church and the high school kids don't use drugs.

The 6th Congressional District of Georgia includes most of the South Side suburbs, starting off inside I-285 with College Park and Hapeville, both increasingly black, and moving out into almost entirely white rural counties. The political tradition here is Democratic, but increasingly this is Republican territory: in most counties Michael Dukakis got less than one-third of the vote, and Senator Wyche Fowler, though a familiar figure from Atlanta TV, lost the 6th District outside Fulton County to Senator Mack Mattingly 55%–45% in 1986. And the congressman here is a Republican, for several years one of his party's leading thinkers and in-the-front-of-the-scenes strategists, and since March 1989 the House Republican Whip, the number two position in the leadership. He is Newt Gingrich, history professor, transplanted Yankee, conservative intellectual, temperamentally a gadfly in a state which traditionally valued in its congressmen a kind of dull faithfulness to duty. His first election way back in 1978 was a better forecast of what the political direction of greater Atlanta, and it came in large part, as did his elevation to the leadership, because he had been campaigning against Democratic scandal. For he had nearly won the 6th District seat twice before, against scandal-plagued Democrat John Flynt in 1974 and 1976; congressional ethics—and the Democrats' lack thereof—is something he has been talking about for 13 years before he urged that the House Ethics Committee investigate Jim Wright.

Gingrich also owes his elevation to the kind of Republican he is—a very different kind of Republican than most of those who have made up the minority in the House for 36 years. Gingrich is a politician of ideas: he spews forth theories and political analogies and phrases like "visions, strategies, projects, tactics" like a broken water main spews out water; and at least some of his ideas have had serious consequences. In the late 1970s, he was one of those young Republicans who, with David Stockman and Jack Kemp, championed the Kemp-Roth tax cut, decontrol of oil prices, and higher defense spending—ideas that seemed quixotic when Gingrich was first elected and were law a few years later. Before then, House Republican ranks were no place for the intellectually adventurous; they were filled with middle-aged products of college fraternities and small town Rotary *bonhomie*. Congeniality was highly valued, and getting along with your colleagues (including the Democrats who ran your committees); your positions on issues were predictable, taken for granted, not the subject of much interest; your expectations were that sooner or later the other side would prevail, that the tide of history was in favor of the welfare state at home and socialism and neutralism abroad, and that the best you could hope for was to slow it down a bit.

Gingrich reads history another way. He lived as an Army brat in France and likes to tell how he visited the ossuary in Verdun; he is kind of an American Gaullist. He is a nationalist who believes that military force counts and that America needs an assertive foreign policy and an expensive, high-tech defense to combat Communists. He is sympathetic both to technical innovations and to the need for shrewd strategy and venturesome tactics. He sees no reason to accommodate the ideas of the leaders of the Third World, but believes that the American ideas of political freedom and market economics are sweeping the world from Britain to East Asia to the Soviet Union. He believes that a country must believe in something—some combination of values or religion—and that it must believe in itself; for him, the value-free skepticism of American liberals is a latter-day version of the anticlerical skepticism of Third Republic leaders who lost France to the Nazis in six weeks in 1940. He believes, in a Gingrichian phrase, in high tech and traditional values: a combination that seems oxymoronic to liberals but which is in fact building the New South Gingrich represents in the 6th District of Georgia.

His race against Edward Madigan for whip in March 1989 was a contrast of opposites. Madigan is a skilled legislator, working cooperatively with and aggressively opposing the Democratic chairmen of the two bodies on which he has been ranking Republican—the Agriculture Committee and the Health Subcommittee of Energy and Commerce. He has never been one to join Gingrich and his mostly younger friends waging guerrilla warfare against the Democrats over C-SPAN, nor would he have taken Tip O'Neill on on the floor of the House as Gingrich did—though on that occasion it was O'Neill who was ruled out of order. Gingrich, in contrast, can claim only minimal legislative achievements: in 1987 and 1988 he was starting to do something with his ranking position on Public Works, and in 1989 as ranking Republican on House Operations he got an agreement from the Democrats guaranteeing Republicans 20% of the staff on all committees.

But it is a mistake to say that the contrast was between a Madigan who wants to participate in governing and a Gingrich who wants to electioneer and campaign—both approaches are aimed at governing. Madigan operates as if he expects the Republicans never will have a majority; the best thing to do is to make the deals you can. Gingrich operates as if the Republicans can win a majority in the House, as they have at all other levels of government. He believes that to concentrate on short-term legislating is to accept the other side's premises and to produce policies which are not midway between extremes but going in the wrong direction.

He contrasts his "Conservative Opportunity Society" (he often adds 'Honest' before that) to what he calls the "corrupt liberal welfare state." He seeks not less government, but a "governing conservatism"—an active government that solves problems not just by eliminating barriers to market behavior but also by reinforcing traditional moral standards and creating a sense of common enterprise. He favors liberating markets from government regulation, but he also believes in major state enterprises, like a manned space program, which he hopes will stimulate technological innovation and, capture the national imagination and inspire national pride. He is untethered by the need that traditional and especially southern conservatives felt to justify racial segregation, and made a point of—and got some conservative flak for—opposing apartheid, just as he unhesitatingly supported Japanese American redress. He points out that he got support from 92 Group moderate Republicans like Olympia Snowe and Claudine Schneider who are interested in an active, innovative government—but also want Republicans to be a policy-forming majority rather than an occasionally policy-affecting minority.

Gingrich got to the point where he could win his 87–85 victory over Madigan by acting when no one else would and acting faster than anyone else did. In December 1987 he called on the Ethics Committee to investigate Jim Wright on a variety of charges, ranging from serious-sounding lapses to items in a newspaper clipping; Wright dismissed him as an "annoying gnat." But in May 1988 Common Cause called for an investigation of Wright, and in June the committee began one. Then in March 1989, when Republican Whip Richard Cheney's appointment as Secretary of Defense was announced on a Friday afternoon, Gingrich got on the phone immediately, nailing down commitments and making his candidacy an accomplished fact. That determination, plus Madigan's refusal to withdraw, kept out of the race others—Jerry Lewis, Henry Hyde—who might have won as consensus candidates, and forced Republicans to pick between two different approaches.

For such an aggressive politician, Gingrich has had his vulnerabilities. He was attacked in March 1989 when it was revealed that Republican activists and others raised $105,000 to promote his book *Window of Opportunity* in 1984, as he was attacked earlier for a $13,000 advance from a partnership to write a novel in 1977, before he was elected. Back home in the 6th District, the local tradition is Democratic, the black population is growing, and the House Democratic campaign committee has enjoyed pouring in money against Gingrich. In 1982 he was held to 56%, and in 1988 David Worley, a 30-year-old lawyer whose father was a security guard and who went to Harvard on scholarship, ran against him. Worley said Gingrich would do nothing about day care (although Gingrich backed George Bush's $1,000 day care tax credit), making college affordable, or giving notice of plant closings. He especially attacked his Social Security plan and charged it would cut benefits for the elderly; Gingrich, who had tried to design a plan that would not do that and who conceded that the plan had other political vulnerabilities, was enraged, called Worley's campaign "the most despicable I have ever seen," and refused to shake hands after a joint appearance. In the end Gingrich won with 59%—evidence that he has a safe seat.

The People: Est. Pop. 1986: 648,900, up 18.2% 1980–86; Pop. 1980: 548,959, up 41.4% 1970–80. Households (1980): 80% family, 49% with children, 67% married couples; 29.9% housing units rented; median monthly rent: $177; median house value: $38,200. Voting age pop. (1980): 375,209; 14% Black, 1% Spanish origin.

1988 Presidential Vote:

Bush (R) 121,128	(67%)
Dukakis (D). 59,118	(33%)

Rep. Newt Gingrich (R)

Elected 1978; b. June 17, 1943, Harrisburg, PA; home, Jonesboro; Emory U., B.A. 1965, Tulane U., M.A. 1968, Ph.D. 1971; Baptist; married (Marianne).

Career: Asst. Prof., W. GA Col., 1970–78; Repub. Nominee for U.S. House of Reps., 1974, 1976.

Offices: 2438 RHOB 20515, 202-225-4501. Also 6351 Jonesboro Rd., Ste. E, Morrow 30260, 404-968-3219; Carroll Cnty. Crthse., Carrollton 30117, 404-834-6398; P.O. Box 848, Griffin Fed. Bldg., Griffin 30224, 404-228-0389; and Cnty. Office Bldg., 19 E. Washington St., Newnan 30263, 404-253-8355.

Committees: *Minority Whip. House Administration* (3d of 8 R). Subcommittees: Accounts; Procurement and Printing. *Joint Committee on Printing.*

Group Ratings

	ADA	ACLU	COPE	CFA	LCV	ACU	NTLC	NSI	COC	CEI
1988	5	18	9	45	50	100	81	100	100	61
1987	4	—	8	14	—	96	—	—	93	77

National Journal Ratings

	1988 LIB — 1988 CONS			1987 LIB — 1987 CONS		
Economic	7%	—	91%	0%	—	89%
Social	20%	—	78%	16%	—	83%
Foreign	0%	—	84%	0%	—	80%

Key Votes

1) Homeless $	FOR	5) Ban Drug Test	FOR	9) SDI Research	FOR
2) Gephardt Amdt	AGN	6) Drug Death Pen	FOR	10) Ban Chem Weaps	AGN
3) Deficit Reduc	AGN	7) Handgun Sales	FOR	11) Aid to Contras	FOR
4) Kill Plnt Clsng Notice	FOR	8) Ban D.C. Abort $	FOR	12) Nuclear Testing	AGN

Election Results

1988 general	Newt Gingrich (R)	110,169	(59%)	($838,708)
	David Worley (D)	76,824	(41%)	($358,354)
1988 primary	Newt Gingrich (R)	19,615	(100%)	
1986 general	Newt Gingrich (R)	75,583	(60%)	($736,607)
	Crandle Bray (D)	51,352	(40%)	($251,751)

SEVENTH DISTRICT

One of the little-noted growth stories of the 1980s is Cobb County, Georgia. Just northwest of Atlanta, across the crease of the Chattahoochee River, Cobb County was known two decades ago as the site of the huge Lockheed Marietta plant and as a part of an otherwise sophisticated metropolitan area that has voted for the likes of George Wallace and Lester Maddox. Not far away on either side of four-laned U.S. 41 the developments thinned out, and you were looking at rural north Georgia, spread out over red clay hills. This was poor white country; it never had plantations or many blacks; it was one of the first industrialized parts of Georgia, with textile mills and carpet factories springing up here starting in the 1920s. The surging growth of metro Atlanta in the 1980s has transformed Cobb County. Shopping malls and huge office complexes have risen along the interstates, and subdivisions have been filling up the land in between. It is an upscale place now, sophisticated in its tastes, enchanted with its free enterprise success, hoping often to implant traditional values in a new land.

Politically, that means heavily Republican. Cobb County now produces some of the highest Republican percentages of any suburban county in the nation, and it has made the 7th Congressional District, which stretches northwest to the Georgia suburbs of Chattanooga, heavily Republican too; Cobb County cast 58% of the district's votes in 1980 and, after heavy growth, 67% in 1988. But in one respect—representation in the House—the 7th remains Democratic. This is the district that elected Larry McDonald, the urologist who was the Member of Congress on Korean Airlines flight 007 shot down by the Soviets—the first American congressman ever murdered by a foreign power. The current congressman is George (Buddy) Darden, one of those adept political operators whose success in districts as Republican as this is the main reason Democrats remain in control of the House. Darden was elected county prosecutor in 1972, at age 28, and beaten four years later; he was elected to the legislature in 1980 and 1982; when McDonald died, he was able to build on his local base and beat McDonald's widow by a solid 59%–41% margin.

In the House, Darden has one of those middle-of-the-road to conservative voting records which are common in southern delegations. You wouldn't mistake him for a northern big-city Democrat, but you wouldn't mistake him for a Republican either. He sits on the Armed Services Committee, where he supports big defense budgets and an assertive foreign policy; of course, he looks closely after the interests of Lockheed and was pleased to report in fall 1988 that the Pentagon was buying 32 more C-130 transports. He also sits on the Interior Committee.

At home Darden was held to 55% in 1984, but in 1986 and 1988 had weak opposition (the 1986 Republican was a Bircher who believed in "Theonomy") and won 74% each time outside Cobb County and 62% and 59% in Cobb. Obviously the growth in Cobb County is the main threat to Darden's tenure: new people for whom his long political record means nothing and who are strongly Republican. So far he has been able to win enough of them to win handily. But he should not be considered—and is not acting like—a congressman who has his seat locked up. He shares with two or three other north Georgia Democrats a common interest in the creation of a new Republican seat in the 1992 redistricting, so each of them can shed some of their most Republican territory and breathe a little easier during the next decade.

The People: Est. Pop. 1986: 648,100, up 18.7% 1980–86; Pop. 1980: 545,913, up 32.2% 1970–80. Households (1980): 78% family, 45% with children, 67% married couples; 30.2% housing units rented; median monthly rent: $207; median house value: $41,200. Voting age pop. (1980): 385,552; 5% Black, 1% Spanish origin.

1988 Presidential Vote:

Bush (R) 155,367	(70%)
Dukakis (D). 64,396	(29%)

Rep. George (Buddy) Darden (D)

Elected Nov. 8, 1983; b. Nov. 22, 1943, Hancock Cnty.; home, Marietta; N. GA Col., Geo. Wash. U., U. of GA, B.A. 1965, J.D. 1967; United Methodist; married (Lillian).

Career: Asst. Dist. Atty., Cobb Cnty., 1967–72; Dist. Atty., 1973–77; Practicing atty., 1977–83; GA House of Reps., 1980–83.

Offices: 228 CHOB 20515, 202-225-2931. Also 376 Powder Springs St., Marietta 30064, 404-422-4480; 301 Fed. Bldg., Rome 30161, 404-291-7777; and 125 S. Main St., Lafayette 30728, 404-638-7042.

Committees: *Armed Services* (21st of 31 D). Subcommittees: Research and Development; Investigations. *Interior and Insular Affairs* (15th of 26 D). Subcommittees: Energy and the Environment; Insular and International Affairs; National Parks and Public Lands.

Group Ratings

	ADA	ACLU	COPE	CFA	LCV	ACU	NTLC	NSI	COC	CEI
1988	45	30	47	45	50	50	32	100	64	36
1987	48	—	44	36	—	39	—	—	53	28

National Journal Ratings

	1988 LIB — 1988 CONS		1987 LIB — 1987 CONS	
Economic	37% —	63%	54% —	45%
Social	36% —	63%	36% —	64%
Foreign	41% —	58%	43% —	56%

Key Votes

1) Homeless $	FOR	5) Ban Drug Test	FOR	9) SDI Research	AGN
2) Gephardt Amdt	FOR	6) Drug Death Pen	FOR	10) Ban Chem Weaps	AGN
3) Deficit Reduc	FOR	7) Handgun Sales	FOR	11) Aid to Contras	FOR
4) Kill Plnt Clsng Notice	FOR	8) Ban D.C. Abort $	FOR	12) Nuclear Testing	AGN

Election Results

1988 general	George (Buddy) Darden (D).............	135,056	(65%)	($382,281)
	Robert Lamutt (R)....................	73,425	(35%)	($60,694)
1988 primary	George (Buddy) Darden (D).............	46,135	(100%)	
1986 general	George (Buddy) Darden (D).............	88,636	(66%)	($534,239)
	Joe Morecraft (R)...................	44,891	(34%)	($246,506)

EIGHTH DISTRICT

From Atlanta, General William Tecumseh Sherman's troops set out, without supplies or lines of communication, to march through Georgia to the sea. The path they cut through south Georgia has been mostly poor country ever since, its antebellum mansions mostly burned down, the memory of its crops destroyed and slaves freed handed down as family lore and still alive a century later. The 8th Congressional District of Georgia runs down the center of the state from a point not far south of Atlanta through the counties where 60% of the world's kaolin, used for china and ceramics, is mined and all the way to the Okeefenokee Swamp and the Florida line. Many blacks live here and many poor white farmers; new factories are being built around some of the towns, but there is nothing like the Atlanta boom here. The largest city is Macon, the home of music greats Otis Redding, Little Richard, and the Allman brothers, a city proud of its restored houses and Japanese cherry trees (it has 20 times as many as Washington). It can also be proud of changes in its civic tone: a city that used to elect a mayor nicknamed "Machine Gun" Thompson now has a county commission concerned about paying the expenses of Bibb County's four AIDS patients.

The 8th District has voted Democratic since Sherman came through, but has gone through some political transformations. Its whites soured on the national Democrats during the civil rights revolution, and a majority vote Republican in national elections today. But blacks vote heavily Democratic, and Senator Wyche Fowler, though cast as an Atlanta liberal, won 57% here in 1986, including 40% among whites. At the top of the ticket, Ronald Reagan and George Bush won, but with only 52% and 53% in 1984 and 1988. Here is one place in the South where Democrats have come up with a winning formula.

Congressman Roy Rowland, first elected in 1982, is a Democrat who has often but by no means always voted with his national party in the House. He is, as he likes to point out, one of two M.D.'s in Congress (freshman Jim McDermott of Washington is a psychiatrist). He spends most of his time on health issues. He sponsored a bill, adopted with changes, to outlaw the drug Quaalude. Serving on a veterans' subcommittee, he sponsored a law to pay for cancer treatment for veterans exposed to radiation during and after World War II. He also saw passed his bill to create a new national AIDS commission in 1988, to help take out of partisan politics difficult issues like testing and discrimination, he said; and he pushed to passage the 1988 bill continuing to pay for AZT for AIDS patients. He has served as vice-chairman of Lawton Chiles's National Commission to Prevent Infant Mortality, which pointed out that the United States ranks number 19 in the world on infant mortality and called for spending more to help poor mothers learn to take care of themselves and their babies. He also played a role on contra aid, fashioning the Democrats' alternative for humanitarian aid in early 1988.

Dr. Rowland won the seat in 1982 by beating incumbent Billy Lee Evans, who had been fined for accepting illegal campaign contributions and loans during his 1980 campaign. Rowland led in the primary 48%–42% and won the runoff 58%–42%. He has held the seat since without difficulty. For three terms he was disappointed in his attempts to get on the Energy and Commerce Committee and on its Health Subcommittee which handles so much health legislation; one reason may have been his successful opposition to Health Chairman Henry

Waxman's proposal to give heroin to terminal cancer patients. But he finally won seats on both after the 1988 election, and is likely to have some influence on a wide variety of health policies.

The People: Est. Pop. 1986: 566,100, up 4.5% 1980–86; Pop. 1980: 541,723, up 10.6% 1970–80. Households (1980): 78% family, 45% with children, 61% married couples; 31.9% housing units rented; median monthly rent: $94; median house value: $27,300. Voting age pop. (1980): 372,727; 32% Black, 1% Spanish origin.

1988 Presidential Vote:

Bush (R)	85,540	(54%)
Dukakis (D)	73,518	(46%)

Rep. J. Roy Rowland (D)

Elected 1982; b. Feb. 3, 1926, Wrightsville; home, Dublin; Emory U., S. GA Col., U. of GA, Medical Col. of GA, M.D. 1952; United Methodist; married (Luella).

Career: Army, WWII; Practicing physician 1954–82; GA House of Reps. 1976–82.

Offices: 423 CHOB 20515, 202-225-6531. Also P.O. Box 2047, Dublin 31040, 912-275-0024; P.O. Box 6258, Macon 31208, 912-743-0150; and Fed. Bldg., Rm. 16, Waycross 31501, 912-285-8420.

Committees: *Energy and Commerce* (25th of 26 D). Subcommittees: Health and the Environment; Commerce, Consumer Protection and Competitiveness. *Veterans' Affairs* (7th of 21 D). Subcommittees: Hospitals and Health Care; Housing and Memorial Affairs. *Select Committee on Children, Youth, and Families* (11th of 18 D).

Group Ratings

	ADA	ACLU	COPE	CFA	LCV	ACU	NTLC	NSI	COC	CEI
1988	55	48	47	73	44	46	32	80	69	26
1987	44	—	45	36	—	30	—	—	67	26

National Journal Ratings

	1988 LIB — 1988 CONS		1987 LIB — 1987 CONS	
Economic	39% —	61%	45% —	54%
Social	45% —	54%	41% —	59%
Foreign	48% —	52%	46% —	54%

Key Votes

1) Homeless $	FOR	5) Ban Drug Test	AGN	9) SDI Research	AGN
2) Gephardt Amdt	AGN	6) Drug Death Pen	FOR	10) Ban Chem Weaps	AGN
3) Deficit Reduc	FOR	7) Handgun Sales	FOR	11) Aid to Contras	AGN
4) Kill Plnt Clsng Notice	FOR	8) Ban D.C. Abort $	AGN	12) Nuclear Testing	FOR

Election Results

1988 general	J. Roy Rowland (D)	102,696	(100%)	($195,895)
1988 primary	J. Roy Rowland (D)	101,845	(86%)	
	R. Bayne Stone (D)	16,161	(14%)	
1986 general	J. Roy Rowland (D)	82,254	(86%)	($150,139)
	Eddie McDowell (R)	12,952	(14%)	

NINTH DISTRICT

The growth of metropolitan Atlanta, surging outward in all directions, is transforming the hills and mountains of north Georgia. Fifty years ago these were backward places, newly introduced to electricity, with textile mills in some of the railroad junctions and a way of life in the mountains that seemed little different from the 19th century. Electricity and the interstate highway transformed life here in the intervening years, and now as Atlantans move farther and farther out it is being transformed even more. This land, where the rolling hills of the Piedmont meet the southernmost Appalachians, is cooler in the summer than the rest of Georgia; its mountains are covered with fast-growing pines; the lakes created by dams which flooded old farmhouses are now prime recreational facilities. Racially and politically, it is a little apart from the rest of Georgia: there never were many plantations or slaves here, some of the mountain counties opposed secession in 1861 and supported the Union and voted Republican for decades afterwards. But this was not a sign of toleration: in Forsyth and Dawson Counties, blacks were driven out in 1912 after a white woman was raped and a black accused of the crime was lynched, and as late as 1981 a black Atlanta fireman was shot while picnicking in Forsyth County, now part of the Atlanta metro area; in 1987 and 1988, two thousand people came to Forsyth to march in protest of the heritage of a county that has more than doubled in population since 1970, but still has no blacks.

The 9th Congressional District of Georgia includes most of the hill counties, the textile mill country around Gainesville and along Interstate 85, and Forsyth and half of Gwinnett County in metro Atlanta. Gwinnett brings a new element to the political equation: young, affluent newcomers, living with the tension of being economically and geographically mobile and culturally traditional, and voting very heavily Republican. These voters far outbalance any Democrats among the urban retirees headed to the hill counties, and make the 9th District in national elections very Republican. And not just national: Gwinnett voters ousted the Democrats from the county courthouse in 1984, and in 1986 the district voted for Republican Senator Mack Mattingly over Atlanta Democrat Wyche Fowler.

The congressman from this district is one of the smartest operators on Capitol Hill, Democrat Ed Jenkins. He was first elected in 1976, and was a former aide to his predecessor, Phil Landrum, whose name remains attached to the Landrum-Griffin Act of 1959, the last major piece of labor law Congress passed, and who for many years was the textile industry's man on the House Ways and Means Committee. So is Jenkins, but he is a more important legislator than that, and his concerns are not just parochial, and if he has the appearance of a simple country lawyer he has, like so many other country lawyers, talents and shrewdness enough to do quite well, thank you, among the city slickers. His dispassionate questioning of Oliver North was one of the Democrats' better performances on the Iran-contra committee; he was the only Democrat whose selection for the committee did not result from a committee chair or some special expertise.

Still, his most visible legislative effort was the textile bill passed in 1986 and, as expected, vetoed by President Reagan as protectionist. The bill was attacked as a cynical effort by Democrats to raise an issue, but it was also an attempt to show low-wage, textile-producing countries the American determination to assert its interests. Jenkins is not in any way a naive man, and knows that on trade issues he is fighting a long-range, many-fronted battle, and he probably understands that protectionist measures, while they may protect jobs and investment in the short run, give a long-run incentive to economic inefficiency. It may have cost him some points with Chairman Dan Rostenkowski, who tends to be a free trader—Rostenkowski left Jenkins off the tax bill conference committee in 1986—but they continued to work and socialize together afterwards. But he can still oppose him: Jenkins was for capital gains reduction in 1988 and he sees long-term health care—Claude Pepper's cause, not Rostenkowski's—as a major issue for the 101st Congress.

Jenkins has made it a point to maintain cordial relationships with many northern Democratic colleagues, whatever their disagreements on issues, and to work with them to achieve compromise—making him one of the chief links between northern and southern Democrats—and on occasion he has voted with the northerners on issues not popular in his or other southern constituencies. He is affable, reliable, and endowed with sensitive political antennae. His seat on the Budget Committee, which he obtained in 1985, is less an avenue to power for him than a recognition that he is one of the critical members of the House.

Jenkins had to fight hard to win the district in 1976, and he even had a significant primary in 1978. He has won easily since. But his concentration on the problems of textiles—the industry which produced the district's growth in the past—has not helped him in Gwinnett where a quite different and more advanced economy of the future is coming rapidly into existence. In 1984, against a weak Republican opponent, he carried most parts of the district easily and won with 67% of the vote, but lost the 9th District's portion of Gwinnett County; in 1988 he again got more than 70% outside of Gwinnett, but lost it to Joe Hoffman, a Republican whose curriculum vitae—Michigan-born, Florida-raised, architect-entrepreneur, Jack Kemp supporter—was very Gwinnettish and not at all traditional north Georgia. Despite Hoffman's misstatements about his record, Jenkins's overall total slumped to 63%—a sign of Gwinnett's rising strength. It may be in Jenkins's interest for redistricting after 1990 to create a new district out of Gwinnett (big enough for half a district by itself now) and other fast-growing North Side areas which would be heavily Republican—and which would make the 9th more comfortably Democratic again.

The People: Est. Pop. 1986: 674,000, up 22.2% 1980–86; Pop. 1980: 551,782, up 35.1% 1970–80. Households (1980): 82% family, 47% with children, 71% married couples; 23.2% housing units rented; median monthly rent: $122; median house value: $36,400. Voting age pop. (1980): 384,588; 5% Black, 1% Spanish origin.

1988 Presidential Vote:

Bush (R)	139,037	(71%)
Dukakis (D)	56,681	(29%)

Rep. Ed Jenkins (D)

Elected 1976; b. Jan. 4, 1933, Young Harris; home, Jasper; Young Harris Col., A.A. 1951; U. of GA, LL.B. 1959; Baptist; married (Jo).

Career: Coast Guard, 1952–55; A.A. to U.S. Rep. Phil Landrum, 1959–62; Asst. U.S. Atty., N. Dist. of GA., 1962–64; Practicing atty., 1965–76.

Offices: 2427 RHOB 20515, 202-225-5211. Also P.O. Box 70, Jasper 30143, 404-692-2022; P.O. Box 1015, Gainesville 30503, 404-536-2531; and 307 Selvidge St., Dalton 30720, 404-226-5320.

Committees: *Budget* (4th of 21 D). Task Forces: Community Development and Natural Resources (Chairman); Economic Policy, Projections and Revenues. *Ways and Means* (8th of 23 D). Subcommittee: Trade.

Group Ratings

	ADA	ACLU	COPE	CFA	LCV	ACU	NTLC	NSI	COC	CEI
1988	45	41	40	55	50	54	27	90	71	37
1987	44	—	38	43	—	20	—	—	62	24

National Journal Ratings

	1988 LIB — 1988 CONS		1987 LIB — 1987 CONS	
Economic	33% —	67%	52% —	48%
Social	35% —	64%	36% —	63%
Foreign	48% —	52%	45% —	55%

Key Votes

1) Homeless $	FOR	5) Ban Drug Test	FOR	9) SDI Research	AGN
2) Gephardt Amdt	FOR	6) Drug Death Pen	FOR	10) Ban Chem Weaps	AGN
3) Deficit Reduc	FOR	7) Handgun Sales	FOR	11) Aid to Contras	FOR
4) Kill Plnt Clsng Notice	FOR	8) Ban D.C. Abort $	FOR	12) Nuclear Testing	FOR

Election Results

1988 general	Ed Jenkins (D)	121,800	(63%)	($405,040)
	Joe Hoffman (R).....................	71,905	(37%)	($64,400)
1988 primary	Ed Jenkins (D)	82,075	(100%)	
1986 general	Ed Jenkins (D)	84,303	(100%)	($144,641)

TENTH DISTRICT

Rural Georgia has its spots of urban economic growth, echoes of booming Atlanta: two of them, Augusta and Athens, are the main centers of population in the state's 10th Congressional District. Augusta's economy is based on the paper industry, stoked by the pines that grow in profusion on the flat Piedmont land; on the South Carolina border, only two hours' drive from Savannah, Augusta is part of the booming seaboard South, not the ailing inland South. A city with some urbanity spreading rapidly into the countryside, Augusta is best known nationally as the site of the Masters Golf Tournament, which finally in the 1980s allowed non-white players to compete. Athens is the home of the University of Georgia, famous for its football team and also as the retirement home of one-time Secretary of State and Georgia native Dean Rusk; it was not one of the South's leading state universities for years, but it is now stimulating some smart local growth. The 10th District also extends westward into metro Atlanta, taking in part of fast-growing, traffic-choked Gwinnett County. In the 1960s and 1970s, Augusta and Athens, with their black and university populations, were the liberal anchor of this area, with segregationist voting patterns in the smaller counties. Now the balance is different. The New South of Gwinnett and the Columbia County suburbs of Augusta make up some of the strongest Republican territory in the country, while blacks remain almost unanimously Democratic. Athens's Clarke County was almost precisely even: Michael Dukakis carried it by 4 votes out of 22,000 cast.

The congressman from the 10th, Doug Barnard Jr., was first elected in 1976 and, like his predecessor in the House, is a banker by trade. In the politics of the early 1970s Barnard was counted a moderate, a one-time aide to Governor Carl Sanders, Jimmy Carter's opponent in the 1970 gubernatorial runoff, and victor himself in 1976 over a former aide to Governor Lester Maddox. In the House, however, he is known primarily as a banker. He is a member of the House Banking Committee, and usually, though not quite always (he is a stickler about money laundering and cheating on appraisals), the point man for the banks. In the late 1980s, his chief cause has been deregulation, which means allowing banks into the securities business—to what exact extent, and whether to do it at all, are of course matters intensely debated and fought over. Former Chairman Fernand St Germain mostly wanted to keep the banks out of these businesses and, on another hot issue, maintain the current regulations for savings and loans. Barnard had bills to let bank affiliates underwrite mutual funds and otherwise get into securities operations.

318   GEORGIA

And, chairing the subcommittee with jurisdiction over all the bank regulatory agencies, he was an advocate of tighter regulation of the savings and loans even before the bankruptcy of the S&L's insurance agency, FSLIC, became obvious. Under Chairman Henry Gonzalez he may become more influential than under St Germain, who tended to keep issues to himself; but Barnard is only ninth in committee seniority and so unlikely ever to be chairman himself.

On other national issues Barnard tends to be conservative, the most market-oriented member of the Georgia Democrats, and by no means is he liberal on cultural or foreign issues. He has been renominated and reelected since 1976 without serious opposition.

The People: Est. Pop. 1986: 660,000, up 19.9% 1980–86; Pop. 1980: 550,268, up 32.1% 1970–80. Households (1980): 76% family, 45% with children, 62% married couples; 34.1% housing units rented; median monthly rent: $153; median house value: $39,200. Voting age pop. (1980): 388,067; 23% Black, 1% Spanish origin, 1% Asian origin.

1988 Presidential Vote: Bush (R) 123,328   (65%)
Dukakis (D). 66,579   (35%)

Rep. Doug Barnard, Jr. (D)

Elected 1976; b. Mar. 20, 1922, Augusta; home, Augusta; Augusta Col., Mercer U., B.A. 1942, LL.B. 1948; Baptist; married (Naomi).

Career: Army, WWII; Banker, GA Railroad Bank and Trust, 1948–49, 1950–76; Fed. Reserve Bank of Atlanta, 1949–50; Exec. Secy. to the Gov. of GA, 1963–66.

Offices: 2227 RHOB, 202-225-4101. Also Stephens Fed. Bldg. Rm. 128, Athens 30601, 404-546-2194; and 407 Telfair St., Augusta 30903, 404-724-0739.

Committees: *Banking, Finance and Urban Affairs* (9th of 31 D). Subcommittees: Domestic Monetary Policy; Economic Stabilization; Financial Institutions Supervision, Regulation and Insurance; General Oversight and Investigations; Consumer Affairs and Coinage. *Government Operations* (8th of 24 D). Subcommittee: Commerce, Consumer, and Monetary Affairs (Chairman).

Group Ratings

	ADA	ACLU	COPE	CFA	LCV	ACU	NTLC	NSI	COC	CEI
1988	25	17	26	27	50	64	48	100	67	46
1987	24	—	23	36	—	61	—	—	79	42

National Journal Ratings

	1988 LIB — 1988 CONS	1987 LIB — 1987 CONS
Economic	28% — 72%	37% — 63%
Social	20% — 80%	37% — 63%
Foreign	44% — 56%	37% — 62%

Key Votes

1) Homeless $	FOR	5) Ban Drug Test	AGN	9) SDI Research	AGN
2) Gephardt Amdt	AGN	6) Drug Death Pen	FOR	10) Ban Chem Weaps	AGN
3) Deficit Reduc	AGN	7) Handgun Sales	—	11) Aid to Contras	FOR
4) Kill Plnt Clsng Notice	—	8) Ban D.C. Abort $	FOR	12) Nuclear Testing	AGN

Election Results

1988 general	Doug Barnard, Jr. (D)................	118,156	(64%)	($193,123)
	Mark Myers (R).....................	66,521	(36%)	($6,760)
1988 primary	Doug Barnard, Jr. (D)................	59,863	(100%)	
1986 general	Doug Barnard, Jr. (D)................	79,548	(67%)	($210,274)
	Jim Hill (R)	38,714	(33%)	($117,315)

HAWAII

When Pearl Harbor was attacked almost 50 years ago, the universal reaction in the United States was the same as if the mainland had been bombed: we were under attack, and Hawaii, a territory 2,400 miles from California, most of its citizens of Asian or Polynesian origin, was an integral part of the United States. Fifty years before, when the last Hawaiian monarch, Queen Liliuokalani, was ousted from power and the Islands were annexed by the United States, that development could hardly have been predicted. In fact, of all the tropical islands acquired by western powers in the late 19th century, Hawaii is the only one which has become part of the acquiring nation.

One reason is that Hawaii's ties with the United States date back to the 1820s, when New England missionary families landed in the islands to proselytize. These New Englanders also engaged in trade—they came to do good and stayed to do well—and the Big Five companies and the charities they set up remain important in Hawaiian life. Another reason is that Hawaii quickly became a key American military outpost. In possession of the Philippines and Guam, with a sentimental interest always in China and an anxiety about Japan, early 20th century America felt Hawaii was the key to maintaining our presence in the Pacific; on that day of infamy in December 1941 almost all of the U.S. Pacific Fleet was gathered in Pearl Harbor. Today Hawaii is home to more than 100,000 military personnel and dependents.

The most important reason: Hawaiians wanted to be Americans. Half a million Americans lived in Hawaii on Pearl Harbor day, half the number of today; whites were just one-third of the total, then and now. The others' grandparents were Japanese, native Hawaiian, Portuguese, mainland whites, Chinese, Filipinos—most brought here as contract labor to work the rich and surprisingly extensive volcanic-soil farmlands. But their identity as Americans, their loyalties in war, and their tolerance of diversity—a sometimes weak tradition on the Mainland—were never in doubt.

The aloha spirit remains a real part of life in Hawaii. Like other Pacific islands, it developed a pidgin, called *da kine*, based on English, with Japanese, Chinese, Portuguese, and Filipino influences; so strong was its tolerance that it inspired segregationist southern Democrats to block Hawaii's admission to the Union for years, which moved many Hawaiians to vote Republican. Yet despite intermarriage, each group's traditions remain distinctive. The Japanese, the largest single migrant group after whites (who are sometimes called *haoles*), are by most measures the most successful, doing well in the professions and in organizations such as unions, government, and the Democratic Party, though they produce fewer entrepreneurs than the Chinese community. Whites still tend to have the highest incomes, many having come to Hawaii after they have been successful on the Mainland. Filipinos are more likely to be manual laborers. Native Hawaiians, from a culture that lived easily and well off a bounteous physical environment, also tend toward the lower end of the income scale. Outnumbered as early as the turn of the century, their share of the population is now rising because of high birth rates, and in 1986 the state elected its first native governor, John Waihee.

Hawaii's native and royal past have given it some unusual traditions, including large landholdings; homeowners typically hold their land on long-term (100 years or so) leases, though a state law, upheld by the U.S. Supreme Court in 1984, allows some to buy it outright. Much land is still held by estates, most notably the Bishop Estate (Mrs. Bishop was the last surviving member of the Hawaiian royal family) which owns about 10% of the state's land. Its five trustees, appointed by the state Supreme Court for life at $250,000 a year, are supposed to spend all the Estate's huge income on educating native Hawaiians; control of the Bishop Estate was finally cinched, after many years of waiting, by Governor George Ariyoshi's allies in the 1980s. Meanwhile, land development generally is closely controlled by the state—wisely to protect the environment, say some; foolishly to choke off economic growth with red tape, say others.

Hawaii has a standard of living today that matches the Mainland states. But there are reasons to worry about its economy. Even after three decades of explosive growth, Hawaii still has only 1.1 million people, not a big enough market for a self-sustaining economy, and none of its major industries is on solid footing. Tourism is Hawaii's biggest business, with 6 million visitors in 1988—with increasing numbers, almost one-third of the total, from Japan and East Asia. But if the hotels are increasingly expensive—like the new fantasy villages—too many of the jobs are low-wage and menial. And the tourism business is cyclical, slumping in the early 1980s due to recession and booming in the late 1980s thanks to the weak dollar and strong yen. Tourism has helped to produce a real estate boom, as Japanese buy up property, sometimes knocking on doors and offering a million dollars for a house; but this puts housing prices out of reach of the ordinary Hawaiian. Meanwhile, the military has been important since the Navy built fortifications and a huge drydock at Pearl Harbor in 1919, but the big military buildup of the 1980s is over. Sugar was once the mainstay of the Hawaiian economy, but slumped when quotas on sugar imports were removed between 1974 and 1981. Sugar employed 56,000 Hawaiians in the 1920s and less than 5,000 in 1988; and the industry would collapse if taxpayers get tired of paying 20 cents a pound for sugar which trades for a dime on the world market. The docks, for years big employers, have been mostly containerized. The International Longshoremen's and Warehouse-man's Union (ILWU) has long represented the sugar and dock workers and negotiated high wages for them, but its membership is down and its political clout vastly reduced.

One plausible future for Hawaii is as a center of Pacific trade, a meeting place between Occident and Orient: it has American political stability and is sensitive to East Asian ways, and it has a highly skilled labor force and first-rate transportation facilities. It is a place where you can get Korean kal bi ribs on the same menu as hamburgers, where sushi and ramen noodles, Filipino lumpia, Portuguese bread, and poi are staples. But Hawaii may not have the right habits of mind. It is used to being a producer of raw agricultural commodities and a site for tourism and military facilities, while its well-developed political machine has concentrated on propping up wages and modulating economic growth. But in the late 1980s wages are sagging and new sources of growth are needed. Governor John Waihee, elected in 1986, called the politicians who ran Hawaii since statehood "the first wave," and said, "Now it is time to take the gift they have given us and catch the second wave. Let us turn to the future." Yet Waihee is in effect the heir of the longest-entrenched and one of the toughest political machines in the United States.

Hawaii's Democratic machine had its beginning in the territorial politics of the 1950s, when returning World War II veterans like Daniel Inouye, Spark Matsunaga, and George Ariyoshi joined forces with former Mainlanders like Oren Long and John Burns, allied themselves with the then powerful ILWU, and cemented the allegiance of Japanese American voters. For a few years after statehood, in 1959, Hawaii tended to vote Republican. Burns was elected governor in 1962 and retired because of illness in 1974; Ariyoshi won in 1974, 1978, and 1982, and retired when he was ineligible for a fourth term. In time, Inouye split with Ariyoshi, and the ILWU's

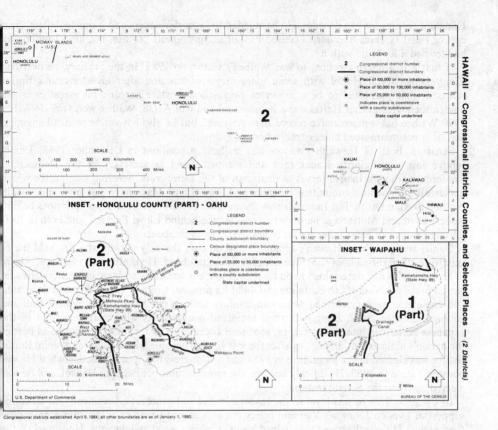

HAWAII — Congressional Districts, Counties, and Selected Places — (2 Districts)

power waned; the machine became centered on the governor's office and the patronage it controlled, from every state judgeship to the trustees of the Bishop Estate. But Waihee was Ariyoshi's man in 1986, and won after a rough campaign; there are echoes here of a Pacific Rim political style—cool, competent, tough, unsentimental.

Governor. For much of the 1970s and 1980s, Hawaii's politicians clamored to limit development. Now the Islands' two leading executives, Governor John Waihee and Honolulu Mayor Frank Fasi, are trying in different ways to encourage it. Waihee made a splash by trying, unsuccessfully, to get the America's Cup race run in Hawaii rather than San Diego. He supports the H-3 freeway (Hawaii has interstates though you can't get to another state on them) and has promoted a Big Island spaceport as a launching area for private spacecraft. At the same time, in the tradition of Hawaii politics, he is willing to use government to control business. He signed bills for special benefits for displaced workers and to raise the minimum wage, despite claims they would discourage business. And he told the directors of Amfac—one of Hawaii's Big Five companies—that he'd use the powers of the Land Commission to keep them from selling off their farmland for development if they sold to outsiders who would spin off units; they didn't.

Waihee's major failure was the inability of Honolulu council member Marilyn Bornhorst, for whom he campaigned personally, to beat Fasi in 1988. A Democrat when he was first elected in 1968, a tough challenger against Ariyoshi in 1974 and 1978, accused of bribery and defeated in a primary in 1980 and then winning his office back as a Republican in 1984, Fasi has dominated

Honolulu politics for two decades. He has tended to favor developers and wants to deflect them east of Pearl Harbor. Bornhorst accused Fasi of using "rumors" to win, but his $2 million ad budget had a lot to do with it.

If that was a rough election, so was Waihee's victory in 1986. In the primary, he overtook Congressman Cecil Heftel with some tough negative ads and after an anonymous tipster released what purported to be a report of suggestions to state narcotic investigators by an unidentified witness that Heftel was a homosexual and had AIDS. Waihee won 46%–36%. For 1990 Waihee has a more active record than Ariyoshi, but he also has active political enemies, and he is not guaranteed an easy reelection.

Senators. Both of Hawaii's senators lost leadership positions in December 1988: Daniel Inouye lost the majority leader race and stepped down as secretary of the Democratic Conference (though Inouye serves as chairman of the Democratic Steering Committee which makes all Democratic committee assignments), and Spark Matsunaga lost his deputy whip position to Alan Dixon. But Inouye is now the number two Democrat on Appropriations behind Robert Byrd and Matsunaga number two on Finance behind Lloyd Bentsen, and both in their different ways can exert influence on issues that they care about.

Daniel Inouye is now Hawaii's senior elected official, the only person who has held major statewide office throughout the three decades since statehood. He is above all else loyal—loyal to his principles and determined to do his duty. Inouye is one of those Japanese Americans who served in the all-Nisei 100th Battalion and 442d Regimental Combat Team, the most decorated and one of the most celebrated American military units in our history. The fighting skill and courage of these Nisei, along with their mainland counterparts who volunteered out of the Japanese American internment camps, produced acceptance of Japanese Americans as part of the nation's mainstream. In politics after the war Inouye became a loyal follower of John Burns; Inouye was elected to the legislature in 1954 and to Congress in a special election when Hawaii became a state in 1959. He quickly became the most popular politician in Hawaii, and he was elected easily to the Senate in 1962.

In Congress Inouye was loyal to the leadership and to Democratic Presidents; his steadfast support of Lyndon Johnson's Vietnam policy got him named keynoter at the 1968 Democratic Convention. His steadfastness also helped him get other special assignments. He served on the Watergate committee in 1973–74 with low-keyed dignity and clear skepticism about the stories of Nixon aides. He was the first chairman of the Senate Intelligence Committee in 1976–77. Yet for all his concern about propriety, he was unwilling to jump on the bandwagon and condemn a colleague: he was the chief defender in 1981–82 of Senator Harrison Williams, charged with bribery in the Abscam scandal. Since then, his loyalties have taken him in somewhat different directions. For years he championed traditional Democratic policies of generous spending at home and a strong defense abroad. Yet, beginning in 1983, he has opposed Reagan Administration policy in Central America, including military aid to El Salvador and help for the Nicaraguan contras; he opposed stationing the Marines in Lebanon and sending American forces to Grenada. And as chairman of the Iran-contra committee in 1987–88 he was sharply critical of Oliver North and others in the Reagan Administration for violating the law and covertly carrying on what he considered a provocative foreign policy.

Inouye is not one of those legislators who churns out bills with his name on them; he tends conscientiously to his committee business, and quietly takes up pet causes on which he can make a difference. His key committee is Appropriations, on which he ranks just behind Robert Byrd and chairs the Defense Subcommittee. He has handled other subcommittees before, notably the one with the headache of shepherding through the foreign aid appropriation while avoiding controversial amendments. Inouye is known as a friend of Israel (a Methodist, he says he once considered converting to Judaism), but not necessarily an enemy of Arab states; his penchant for detail got him in trouble in 1987 when it was revealed he had inserted in an appropriations bill a small sum to construct schools in France for North African Jewish refugees. Inouye admitted an error of judgment and said—strong criticism coming from him—"I fear that I have embarrassed my colleagues." Other assignments have evoked strong loyalties in him. He chaired the Commerce maritime subcommittee and is a strong supporter of federal maritime subsidies and restrictions.

In 1987–88 he chaired a special Indian Affairs committee and showed immense sympathy for Native Americans—very much including Native Hawaiians. He pushed hard to get the American Indian museum collection, now at three separate sites in New York City, transferred to a new building on the Smithsonian's Mall, and clashed with Daniel Patrick Moynihan, who wanted to keep it in New York. He worked to settle the Puyallup tribal claims issue in Washington and to get an Indian fishing rights activist released from jail.

For 10 years Inouye held a leadership position below Robert Byrd, and in 1986 there was talk that he had backed away from opposing Byrd in return for Byrd's promise to leave the majority leadership in two years. Whether that's true or not, Inouye refrained from rounding up votes till April 1988, and got started later than George Mitchell and Bennett Johnston. The apparent failure of the Iran-contra scandal to become a Democratic issue may have hurt him with colleagues who hoped he could help make it another Watergate, and his tendency to work in bipartisan harmony when possible—as he did with Warren Rudman on Iran-contra—may have disturbed some Democrats. Others were grateful for the help Mitchell gave them as campaign committee chairman in 1986, or thought he would be a better spokesman on television. For whatever reasons—leadership elections are by secret ballot, and not even senators know who votes for whom or why—Inouye had only 14 votes, the same as Johnston, while Mitchell had 27, at which point everyone agreed to dispense with a second ballot.

Inouye has many consolation prizes. He chairs the Steering Committee that makes committee assignments—a less important matter in the Senate than the House, since senators serve on more committees than House members do. He is the fourth most senior senator now, after Byrd, Republican Strom Thurmond, and ailing Democrat Quentin Burdick. His popularity in Hawaii remains exceedingly high. It is only partly transferable, however: he strongly supported John Waihee in 1986, but Inouye campaigned strenuously for Marilyn Bornhorst and Mary Bitterman who lost to Republicans Frank Fasi and Patricia Saiki in 1988, even though Michael Dukakis was carrying the state.

Senator Spark Matsunaga, also a 442d veteran, is a persistent man who has made his imprint on public policy by championing his own special ideas and getting them passed into law. He has a gentle Nisei manner and writes haiku when inspiration strikes. His leading issues are peace and space. After 22 years of lobbying he got Congress to set up a U.S. Peace Institute in 1984. He has pushed a joint U.S.-Soviet exploration of Mars and sponsored a proposal for an International Space Year in 1992. He has worked to make Hawaii a center for space exploration. Matsunaga has also looked closely after Hawaii's economic interests, such as sugar, pineapple, and macadamia nuts; he generally supports free trade, but naturally backs sugar price supports.

Matsunaga, first elected to the House in 1962 and the Senate in 1976, is now the second ranking Democrat on the Senate Finance Committee. He has not been a major force on the committee's big bills; despite his trade subcommittee chairmanship, it was Chairman Lloyd Bentsen, not Matsunaga, who managed the trade bill in 1987 and 1988, and he was not a leader on tax reform in 1986. But Matsunaga was the key leader who almost single-handedly got through the law to provide redress for the West Coast Japanese Americans interned during World War II. The law provides $1.25 billion in compensation, with $20,000 going to each internment survivor, and makes a formal apology for what was clearly an unjustified violation of constitutional rights and of simple decency. This was not an easy bill—it was unpopular with some vociferous World War II veterans and it was costly—and it could have been easily derailed. Matsunaga's success required genuine legislative skill and great persistence. Accordingly, Matsunaga has become an authentic hero among appreciative mainland Japanese Americans who strongly feel that after 46 years of waiting justice and vindication have arrived, with an indispensable and dogged role played by the senator from Hawaii.

Matsunaga's only problem in the 1988 election was that some had doubts about his health: he had a heart attack in 1984, and a stomach ulcer in 1987, and he lost 15 pounds in 1988 from a case of Shanghai flu; he skipped the 1988 Democratic National Convention and had to be helped out of his Senate chair because of a wrenched back. His Republican opponent, 70-year-old Molokai rancher Maria Hustace, made some tasteless jokes, but the 72-year-old Matsunaga returned from Washington and was able to allay any doubts. He was helped perhaps by his assiduous courting of voters, whom he rightly asserts should feel fully American and proudly Hawaiian. He won with an overwhelming 77%.

Congressmen. Hawaii has two congressional districts: the 1st includes Honolulu within its old city limits (city elections now cover all of Oahu) and extends westward to Pearl Harbor; the 2d includes the rest of Oahu and the Neighbor Islands.

Of Honolulu, the tourist usually only sees the airport and adjacent Hickam Air Force Base, the Arizona monument in the harbor, and Waikiki, with its 40-story hotels rising within a few feet of one another, its restaurants and souvenir shops. But few voters live in any of these places. The neighborhoods around Honolulu's downtown and the university campus are lower income, ethnically diverse, and usually Democratic. To the west, around the harbor, there are many military families; these modest neighborhoods may vote for Democrats but are sometimes attracted to Republicans. To the east, past Waikiki, around Diamond Head and out to the Kahala and Koko Head beach areas, is higher income territory; these places delivered the state's largest Reagan majorities in 1980 and 1984, and make the 1st the slightly more Republican of Hawaii's two districts.

Congresswoman Patricia Saiki of the 1st District is the only Republican ever elected to the House from Hawaii. She won the seat in a riproaring contest in 1986, when incumbent Cecil Heftel ran for governor. Bitterness erupted in the special primary election between Democratic candidates Neil Abercrombie, a pony-tail-wearing legislator who was hurt by flimsy charges that he used marijuana, and Mufi Hannemann, a Mormon native of Samoa and onetime White House Fellow. Abercrombie won the special election and served a few weeks in the House, while Hannemann eventually won the Democratic nomination for the full term but lost to Republican Saiki in the general. Saiki, a former teacher and teachers' union leader, an experienced legislator and of Asian descent, was well positioned to take advantage of this discord and won 60%–37%. In her first term she made a popular record against the textile bill and for catastrophic health insurance, and she argued that Hawaii needs at least one Republican to speak for it. She was also an early supporter of Bob Dole for President. Democrat Mary Bitterman, supported strongly by Daniel Inouye, argued that Saiki's record on senior citizens issues was conservative and that she was too pro-military. Saiki won 55%–43%, running well ahead of George Bush.

The 2d District includes not only the Neighbor Islands but most of the acreage of Oahu. It has the middle-class area around Pearl Harbor, with many military families, and the farmlands further out the island, between the two jagged chains of mountains that lift it out of the sea. Over the mountains to the west is the Leeward Coast, calm, sultry, and lightly populated; over the mountains to the northeast is the Windward Coast, windy as its name implies, with many prosperous and Republican subdivisions. The Neighbor Islands have distinct personalities. Hawaii, the Big Island, is large enough to boast huge cattle ranches, the active volcano of Kilauea, and Mauna Kea, the highest mountain in the world if you count from its base far under the ocean to the peak, rising in a slow, endless slant from Hilo or the Kona (western) Coast. On the north shore, with heavy rainfall and tropical foliage, are the old port of Hilo and Hawaii's macadamia nut industry; this is a blue-collar Democratic area. On the Kona Coast, where there is little rainfall and the landscape is dominated by lava flows, there are retirement condominiums and a higher-income, more Republican population. Maui in the 1980s has been the fastest-developing island, with dozens of luxury condominiums and rapidly rising real estate prices. Kauai, west of Oahu, is the least-developed and most agricultural of the main islands; parts of it have the nation's highest rainfall, while others seldom get wet. Its large farm work force makes it the most Democratic of the islands.

The congressman here, since he won a 1976 primary, is Democrat Daniel Akaka. A one-time Ariyoshi aide, Akaka serves quietly on Appropriations and its Agriculture Subcommittee—bodies with practical concerns that are especially important to Hawaii. His voting record on economic and cultural issues is generally liberal, but less so on foreign policy and defense. He sponsored a 1988 law regulating duty-free stores and an amendment allowing the government to buy electricity only from state-franchised utilities.

Presidential politics. Hawaii is one of the most Democratic of states, one of the six carried by Jimmy Carter in 1980 and one of the ten carried by Michael Dukakis in 1988. But in 1984 it did vote for President Reagan. Two sometimes countervailing forces seem to combine to produce these results: a strong Democratic partisan preference, plus an inclination to support incumbents. These two factors explain Hawaii's vote in every presidential election, its close elections when Republicans were in power (1960, 1976, 1984, and even 1988 since Dukakis did not carry the state overwhelmingly), its landslide margins for incumbents of different parties (1964, 1972), and its far higher than average percentages for Democrats when they were in power (1968, 1980). Hawaii is Democratic because it favors big government on economic issues and tolerance of diversity on cultural issues. It is pro-incumbent because it takes its patriotism very seriously, in part because the patriotism of so many of its citizens was once unjustly questioned, and in part because, out here in these heavily fortified islands in the Pacific, foreign threats seem more menacing. In the only state whose population center has come under direct foreign attack since the War of 1812, America can seem dangerously vulnerable.

Hawaii had presidential caucuses in 1988, which verged on farce; fewer than 30,000 people took part in a state of 1.1 million. The Democrats' choice was Jesse Jackson; the Republican state party establishment found its membership ranks swelled by Pat Robertson supporters, canceled a scheduled straw poll for a week, and then let Robertson win.

The People: Est. Pop. 1988: 1,093,000; Pop. 1980: 964,691, up 13.3% 1980–88 and 25.3% 1970–80; 0.44% of U.S. total, 39th largest. 18% with 1–3 yrs. col., 20% with 4+ yrs. col.; 9.9% below poverty level. Single ancestry: 3% Portuguese, English, 2% German, 1% Irish, Italian. Households (1980): 77% family, 45% with children, 63% married couples; 48.3% housing units rented; median monthly rent: $273; median house value: $119,400. Voting age pop. (1980): 689,108; 60% Asian origin, 6% Spanish origin, 2% Black. Registered voters (1988): 443,742; no party registration.

1988 Share of Federal Tax Burden: $3,755,000,000; 0.42% of U.S. total, 41st largest.

1988 Share of Federal Expenditures

	Total		Non-Defense		Defense	
Total Expend	$4,957m	(0.56%)	$2,392m	(0.36%)	$2,616m	(1.14%)
St/Lcl Grants	477m	(0.42%)	477m	(0.42%)	0m	(0.06%)
Salary/Wages	2,078m	(1.55%)	219m	(0.33%)	1,859m	(0.33%)
Pymnts to Indiv	1,715m	(0.42%)	1,553m	(0.40%)	162m	(0.87%)
Procurement	591m	(0.31%)	51m	(0.11%)	591m	(0.31%)
Research/Other	96m	(0.26%)	92m	(0.25%)	3m	(0.25%)

Political Lineup: Governor, John D. Waihee III (D); Lt. Gov., Benjamin Cayetano (D); Atty. Gen., Warren Price (D); Comptroller, Russell Nagata (D). State Senate, 25 (22 D and 3 R); State House of Representatives, 51 (45 D and 6 R). Senators, Daniel K. Inouye (D) and Spark M. Matsunaga (D). Representatives, 2 (1 D and 1 R).

1988 Presidential Vote

Dukakis (D)...............	192,364	(54%)	
Bush (R).................	158,625	(45%)	

1984 Presidential Vote

Reagan (R)...............	185,050	(55%)	
Mondale (D)..............	147,154	(44%)	

GOVERNOR

Gov. John D. Waihee III (D)

Elected 1986, term expires Dec. 1990; b. May 19, 1946, Honokaa; home, Honolulu; Andrews U., B.A. 1968; U. of HI, J.D. 1976; Christian; married (Lynne).

Career: Community Ed. Coord., Benton Harbor, MI, 1968–71; Program Planner, Honolulu Model Cities, 1971–73; Program Mgr., Honolulu Human Resources Office, 1973–74; Practicing atty., 1975–82; HI House of Reps. 1980–82; Lt. Gov. of HI, 1982–86.

Office: State Capitol, Executive Chambers, Honolulu 96813, 808-548-5420.

Election Results

1986 gen.	John D. Waihee (D)	173,655	(52%)
	D.G. Anderson (R)...........	160,460	(48%)
1986 prim.	John D. Waihee (D)	105,579	(46%)
	Cecil (Cec) Heftel (D).......	83,939	(36%)
	Patsy T. Mink (D)	37,998	(16%)
1982 gen.	George R. Ariyoshi (D)	141,043	(45%)
	D.G. Anderson (R)...........	81,507	(26%)
	Frank F. Fasi (I).............	89,303	(29%)

SENATORS

Sen. Daniel K. Inouye (D)

Elected 1962, seat up 1992; b. Sept. 7, 1924, Honolulu; home, Honolulu; U. of HI, B.A. 1950, Geo. Wash. U., J.D. 1952; United Methodist; married (Margaret).

Career: Army, WWII; Honolulu Asst. Prosecuting Atty., 1953–54; HI Territorial House of Reps., 1954–59; HI Territorial Senate, 1958–60; U.S. House of Reps., 1959–62.

Offices: 722 HSOB 20510, 202-224-3934. Also Prince Kuhio Fed. Bldg., 300 Ala Moana Blvd., Rm.7325, Honolulu 96850, 808-541-2542.

Committees: *Appropriations* (2d of 16 D). Subcommittees: Commerce, Justice, State, the Judiciary and Related Agencies; Defense (Chairman); Foreign Operations; Labor, Health and Human Services, Education and Related Agencies; Military Construction. *Commerce, Science, and Transportation* (2d of 11 D). Subcommittees: Aviation; Communications (Chairman); Merchant Marine; Surface Transportation; National Ocean Policy Study. *Rules and Administration* (4th of 9 D). *Select Committee on Indian Affairs* (Chairman of 5 D).

Group Ratings

	ADA	ACLU	COPE	CFA	LCV	ACU	NTLC	NSI	COC	CEI
1988	85	85	89	92	50	4	9	10	38	11
1987	95	—	89	83	—	0	—	—	29	18

National Journal Ratings

	1988 LIB — 1988 CONS		1987 LIB — 1987 CONS	
Economic	86%	— 0%	74%	— 0%
Social	79%	— 17%	84%	— 13%
Foreign	70%	— 25%	68%	— 31%

Key Votes

1) Cut Aged Housing $	FOR	5) Bork Nomination	AGN	9) SDI Funding	AGN
2) Override Hwy Veto	FOR	6) Ban Plastic Guns	AGN	10) Ban Chem Weaps	AGN
3) Kill Plnt Clsng Notice	AGN	7) Deny Abortions	AGN	11) Aid To Contras	AGN
4) Min Wage Increase	FOR	8) Japanese Reparations	FOR	12) Reagan Defense $	AGN

Election Results

1986 general	Daniel K. Inouye (D)	241,887	(74%)	($1,039,418)
	Frank Hutchinson (R)	86,910	(26%)	($31,843)
1986 primary	Daniel K. Inouye (D)	191,676	(100%)	
1980 general	Daniel K. Inouye (D)	224,485	(78%)	($480,113)
	Cooper Brown (R)	53,068	(18%)	($14,382)

Sen. Spark M. Matsunaga (D)

Elected 1976, seat up 1994; b. Oct. 8, 1916, Kukuiula, Kauai; home, Kailua; U. of HI, Ed.B. 1941, Harvard U., J.D. 1951; Episcopalian; married (Helene).

Career: Pub. sch. teacher, 1940–41; Army, WWII; Vet. Counselor, U.S. Dept. of Interior, 1945–47; War Assets Admin., 1947–48; Asst. Pub. Prosecutor, City and Cnty. of Honolulu, 1952–54; Practicing atty., 1954–63; HI Territorial House of Reps., 1954–59, Major. Ldr., 1959; U.S. House of Reps., 1962–76.

Offices: 109 HSOB 20510, 202-224-6361. Also 3104 Prince Kuhio Bldg., Honolulu 96813, 808-541-2534; and 101 Aupuni St., Ste. 214, Hilo 96720, 808-935-1114.

Committees: *Finance* (2nd of 11 D). Subcommittees: Energy and Agricultural Taxation; International Trade; Taxation and Debt Management (Chairman). *Labor and Human Resources* (4th of 9 D). Subcommittees: Aging (Chairman); Education, Arts, and Humanities; Labor. *Veterans' Affairs* (2d of 6 D). *Joint Committee on Taxation.*

Group Ratings

	ADA	ACLU	COPE	CFA	LCV	ACU	NTLC	NSI	COC	CEI
1988	90	88	85	92	80	0	9	0	36	13
1987	90	—	84	75	—	0	—	—	35	21

National Journal Ratings

	1988 LIB — 1988 CONS			1987 LIB — 1987 CONS	
Economic	72%	—	27%	74%	—	0%
Social	86%	—	0%	96%	—	0%
Foreign	86%	—	0%	81%	—	0%

Key Votes

1) Cut Aged Housing $	FOR	5) Bork Nomination	AGN	9) SDI Funding	AGN
2) Override Hwy Veto	FOR	6) Ban Plastic Guns	AGN	10) Ban Chem Weaps	AGN
3) Kill Plnt Clsng Notice	AGN	7) Deny Abortions	AGN	11) Aid To Contras	AGN
4) Min Wage Increase	FOR	8) Japanese Reparations	FOR	12) Reagan Defense $	AGN

Election Results

1988 general	Spark M. Matsunaga (D)	247,941	(77%)	($494,580)
	Maria M. Hustace (R)	66,987	(21%)	($33,325)
1988 primary	Spark M. Matsunaga (D)	180,853	(87%)	
	Bob Zimmerman (D)	27,360	(13%)	
1982 general	Spark M. Matsunaga (D)	245,386	(80%)	($655,713)
	Clarence J. Brown (R)	52,071	(17%)	
	E. Bernier-Nachtwey (I)	8,953	(3%)	

FIRST DISTRICT

The People: Est. Pop. 1986: 501,200, up 3.9% 1980–86; Pop. 1980: 482,321, up 16.0% 1970–80. Households (1980): 72% family, 39% with children, 59% married couples; 52.1% housing units rented; median monthly rent: $277; median house value: $139,800. Voting age pop. (1980): 362,478; 64% Asian origin, 5% Spanish origin, 1% Black.

1988 Presidential Vote:

	Dukakis (D)	95,347	(54%)
	Bush (R)	79,323	(45%)

Rep. Patricia Saiki (R)

Elected 1986; b. May 28, 1930, Hilo; home, Honolulu; U. of HI, B.S. 1952; Episcopalian; married (Stanley).

Career: School teacher, 1952–64; HI House of Reps., 1968–74; HI Senate, 1974–82; Chmn., HI Repub. Party, 1983–85.

Offices: 1609 LHOB 20515, 202-225-2726. Also 300 Ala Moana Blvd., Rm. 4104, Honolulu 96850, 808-541-2570.

Committees: *Banking, Finance and Urban Affairs* (15th of 20 R). Subcommittees: Housing and Community Development; Financial Institutions Supervision, Regulation and Insurance; Economic Stabilization; Internation Development, Finance, Trade and Monetary Policy. *Merchant Marine* (13th of 17 R). Subcommittees: Oceanography; Fisheries and Wildlife Conservation and the Environment. *Select Committee on Aging* (23d of 26 R). Subcommittees: Housing and Consumer Interest; Human Services.

Group Ratings

	ADA	ACLU	COPE	CFA	LCV	ACU	NTLC	NSI	COC	CEI
1988	50	50	48	82	56	39	60	100	50	22
1987	28	—	25	21	—	57	—	—	73	52

National Journal Ratings

	1988 LIB — 1988 CONS		1987 LIB — 1987 CONS	
Economic	48% —	52%	36% —	63%
Social	64% —	36%	37% —	63%
Foreign	41% —	58%	38% —	62%

Key Votes

1) Homeless $	FOR	5) Ban Drug Test	FOR	9) SDI Research	FOR
2) Gephardt Amdt	AGN	6) Drug Death Pen	FOR	10) Ban Chem Weaps	AGN
3) Deficit Reduc	AGN	7) Handgun Sales	AGN	11) Aid to Contras	FOR
4) Kill Plnt Clsng Notice	FOR	8) Ban D.C. Abort $	FOR	12) Nuclear Testing	AGN

Election Results

1988 general	Patricia Saiki (R)	96,848	(55%)	($686,165)
	Mary Bitterman (D)	76,394	(43%)	($638,351)
1988 primary	Patricia Saiki (R), unopposed			
1986 general	Patricia Saiki (R)	99,683	(60%)	($536,551)
	Mufi Hannemann (D)	63,061	(37%)	($500,716)

SECOND DISTRICT

The People: Est. Pop. 1986: 561,200, up 16.3% 1980–86; Pop. 1980: 482,370, up 36.2% 1970–80. Households (1980): 82% family, 53% with children, 68% married couples; 44.0% housing units rented; median monthly rent: $267; median house value: $102,300. Voting age pop. (1980): 326,630; 55% Asian origin, 7% Spanish origin, 2% Black.

1988 Presidential Vote:

	Dukakis (D)	97,017	(54%)
	Bush (R)	79,302	(44%)

Rep. Daniel K. Akaka (D)

Elected 1976; b. Sept. 11, 1924, Honolulu; home, Honolulu; U. of HI, B.A. 1953, M.A. 1966; Congregationalist; married (Mary Mildred).

Career: U.S. Army Corps of Engineers, WWII; Pub. sch. teacher and principal, 1953–71; Dir., HI Ofc. of Econ. Opp., 1971–74; Spec. Asst. to the Gov. of HI in Human Resources, 1975–76; Dir., Progressive Neighborhoods Program, 1975–76.

Offices: 2301 RHOB 20515, 202-225-4906. Also P.O. Box 50144, Honolulu 96850, 808-541-1993.

Committees: *Appropriations* (23d of 35 D). Subcommittees; Treasury, Postal Service and General Government; Rural Development, Agriculture and Related Agencies. *Select Committee on Narcotics Abuse and Control* (6th of 15 D).

Group Ratings

	ADA	ACLU	COPE	CFA	LCV	ACU	NTLC	NSI	COC	CEI
1988	85	90	86	82	56	0	5	20	23	7
1987	64	—	85	79	—	0	—	—	0	7

National Journal Ratings

	1988 LIB — 1988 CONS		1987 LIB — 1987 CONS	
Economic	79% —	17%	73% —	0%
Social	86% —	0%	78% —	0%
Foreign	57% —	43%	63% —	37%

Key Votes

1) Homeless $	AGN	5) Ban Drug Test	AGN	9) SDI Research	AGN
2) Gephardt Amdt	FOR	6) Drug Death Pen	AGN	10) Ban Chem Weaps	FOR
3) Deficit Reduc	FOR	7) Handgun Sales	AGN	11) Aid to Contras	AGN
4) Kill Plnt Clsng Notice	AGN	8) Ban D.C. Abort $	AGN	12) Nuclear Testing	FOR

Election Results

1988 general	Daniel K. Akaka (D)	144,802	(89%)	($153,163)
	Lloyd J. Mallan (L)	18,006	(11%)	
1988 primary	Daniel K. Akaka (D), unopposed			
1986 general	Daniel K. Akaka (D)	123,830	(76%)	($110,490)
	Maria M. Hustace (R)	35,371	(21%)	($32,339)

IDAHO

Idaho celebrates its centennial in 1990, but even before its first 50 years the character of the state was pretty well set. For as Randy Stapilus, author of the definitive *Paradox Politics*, puts it, "Idaho, they say, is what was left after they made Montana, Washington, Utah, Oregon, Wyoming, and Nevada." It was the last state Europeans set eyes on—fur traders who wandered here from their yearly rendezvous—and the first farmers here were New England Yankees, led by ministers, wending west on the Oregon Trail, in the broad Snake River valley. The northern panhandle, an extension of the Columbia valley of Washington, was first settled by miners seeking gold and silver; loggers followed. Mormons then moved north from Utah to settle in the east. But what brought the most settlers were federal water reclamation projects, first authorized in 1894, which transformed the barren Snake River valley into some of the nation's best volcanic soil-enriched farmlands. Idaho's economy is still based largely on agriculture, especially potatoes, and the state today, with only one city over 100,000 and much of its population still on the farm, uses more water per capita than any other state.

But the connection between Boise, with its gleaming towers and corporate headquarters (Boise Cascade, Morrison-Knudsen), tree-shaded streets and Spanish-style railroad station standing out against arid mountains, and the rest of the state is often tenuous. This is the only state with three separate state fairs; it lies in two separate time zones; the panhandle is connected to the rest of the state by a single two-lane road with tortuous switchbacks which is often closed in the winter. As Stapilus tells it, the state's politics was manipulated for decades by two bosses whose regional political origins barred them from thinking about high office themselves, but who could patch together statewide alliances—Democrat Tom Boise from the panhandle and Republican Lloyd Adams from the Mormon east. Today the regional divisions are plain in the 1988 presidential returns. Overall Idaho is a heavily Republican state, and the Boise area and the Magic Valley east along the Snake to Pocatello voted 62%–36% for George Bush over Michael Dukakis. But the panhandle favored Bush by only 51%–47%, looking much like Washington State which went for Dukakis. The mostly Mormon counties in the east, in contrast, voted 74%–25% for Bush, much like Utah.

Idaho's population has nearly doubled since 1940, with the rate picking up in the 1970s as its physical attractions and country lifestyle attracted some environmentalists and, even more, family people interested in a less hurried but still comfortable way of life in a small-town atmosphere where traditional values are given more respect than they are in big metropolitan areas. There are few trendy singles here; among all states, Idaho has the second highest percentage of households occupied by married people. Idaho also has attracted sophisticated outsiders for years: Averell Harriman developed Sun Valley as the nation's first ski resort in the 1930s; Ernest Hemingway's last home was nearby in Ketchum. Still, for every hip entertainer who comes here to groove on the environment, there are a dozen newcomers who left California because they thought Orange County was not conservative enough.

Over the years, Idaho has teetered and tottered from one party to another. Idaho's first settlers had a Republican heritage, but Idaho was for Bryan and free silver in 1896, and it was part of Woodrow Wilson's and Franklin Roosevelt's alliance of the colonial South and West against the rich East. Harry Truman carried it handily in 1948 and as late as 1960 John Kennedy (helped by sympathy from Mormons, as fellow sufferers from religious discrimination) was able to win 46% of the vote here. Then in the 1960s, ahead of the national trend, Idaho turned right. Idahoans began to think of themselves less as downtrodden employees of absentee corporations needing a protective federal government and more as pioneering entrepreneurs who need to get a bloated, bossy federal government off their backs. The federal government is a real presence here: it owns most of Idaho's land and when it blocks exploitation of local resources to protect the environment—by vetoing a logging operation or preventing sheep-ranchers from destroying coyotes—Washington arouses strong resentment. But in 1980, just as Ronald Reagan and the "Sagebrush Rebellion" seemed to be carrying all before it, Idahoans had second thoughts. They knew that Idaho has benefited over the years from railroad subsidies, government silver purchases, water reclamation projects, and federal maintenance of scenic lands and, as Stapilus says, they "don't want federal controls but neither do they want their land subdivided and turned into miracle miles."

That is one reason this nationally Republican state has elected nothing but Democratic governors since 1970. Another is the tendency of Democrats, who after all are fond of government and politics, to field some of the ablest men in the state as their candidates, while most able men and women who are Republicans dislike government so much they shun politics and stick with entrepreneurship and making money. Idaho has produced a few politicians of national distinction, notably William Borah, the silver-maned foreign policy expert, and Frank Church, who served 24 years until his defeat in 1980, both of whom chaired the Senate Foreign Relations Committee; and it had a bipartisan dynasty in the Clark family, whose current scions are lobbyist and Reagan family friend Nancy Reynolds and Bethine Church who was an active political partner of her late husband. Its leading politicians today, Governor Cecil Andrus and Senator James McClure, have made a national mark, but nothing yet like the impact Borah and Church had.

Governor. Cecil Andrus won his third gubernatorial term in 1986 by a narrow margin and after a long interval. He was first elected in 1970, an accidental candidate chosen after the Democratic nominee died in a plane crash, and the victor because voters bridled at plans to mine molybdenum in the "White Clouds" mountains east of Boise. Andrus won great popularity as governor and then lost it as Interior Secretary for Jimmy Carter, against whom three out of four Idahoans voted in 1980. Andrus's successor, John Evans, proved stronger than expected, winning in 1978 against a Mormon from the east who wanted to limit liquor sales, and in 1982 against a lieutenant governor who campaigned against farm workers' unions and for a right-to-work law. But in 1986 Andrus only narrowly defeated Lieutenant Governor David Leroy.

Andrus immediately began cooperating more closely with the Republican legislature than

IDAHO — Congressional Districts, Counties, and Selected Places — *(2 Districts)*

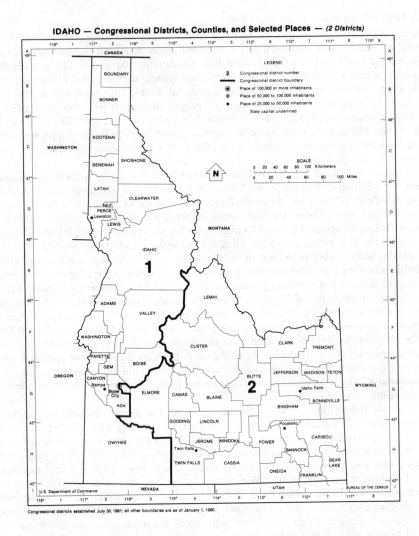

Congressional districts established July 30, 1981; all other boundaries are as of January 1, 1980.

Evans did on issues from taxes to wilderness areas, and his popularity ratings zoomed up toward the levels he enjoyed in the 1970s. He brings to politics some liberal impulses, but also the earthiness of a politician who got his start in the mining country and still likes nothing better than to go hunting: he got away with calling the National Rifle Association "the gun nuts of the world," for opposing bans on armor-piercing bullets, by noting that he had never seen an animal in a bullet-proof vest. Possible GOP opponents in 1990 are state Senators Roger Fairchild and Rachel Gilbert.

Senators. The most powerful member of Idaho's congressional delegation and the most enduring politician in Idaho is James McClure. He was elected to the legislature in 1960, the House in 1966, and the Senate in 1972—the most successful Idaho politician of his generation. He has held important posts in the Senate—he was Energy Committee chairman for six years and until 1984 was chairman of the Senate Republican Conference—but his biggest achievements have come through other avenues. As Energy chairman he was unable to push through complete deregulation of natural gas and did not try to cede federal lands to the states as Sagebrush Rebellion organizers demanded. When he ran for Senate majority leader after the 1984 election, he was the first of the five candidates to be eliminated from the race—even though he was the most conservative candidate. McClure was hurt at that time by charges that he pushed through a significant change in nuclear power law after telling senators it was uncontroversial; he maintains that he kept his colleagues fully informed and that some Democrat was asleep at the switch.

McClure's problem may be that he is betwixt and between. Starting off as a lawyer in a conservative Idaho farm county, rising in a decade when right-wing resentment at Washington was raging, he was drawn into a politics of protest. Yet he has the calm, judicious temperament of one accustomed to running things: he does not seem a natural rebel. He was quite ready to abandon the Sagebrush Rebellion when Ronald Reagan took office, to negotiate details of new wilderness areas with the likes of Cecil Andrus and, in 1988, to push bills through banning new dams on the Snake River and establishing the City of Rocks National Monument. On Energy and on the Interior Appropriations subcommittee he used to chair, he continues to do hard slogging detail work on important but unglamorous issues like liability for nuclear accidents and hydropower. In 1986 he won an important victory—and one likely to be appreciated by Idaho voters—when his McClure-Volkmer bill to relax federal gun control laws was passed into law. But in 1988 he compromised a bit: after sponsoring the NRA measure to set manufacturing standards for plastic guns, he finally agreed with Howard Metzenbaum on terms of the bill outlawing plastic guns altogether.

McClure is interested in foreign affairs, on which he is a hardliner. He was an early supporter of George Bush for President, and is a friend of Bush's from the time they were both House freshmen elected in 1966; some even speculated that McClure would end up with an appointment in the Administration. It is unlikely, however, that he would resign (and give Andrus a Senate appointment) before his term is up in 1990; and if he does run for reelection, he should win easily as he did in 1978 and 1984. His only tough elections have been in 1966, when he beat an incumbent Democratic congressman, and 1972, when he accused his opponent, a backer of Cesar Chavez's lettuce boycott, of contemplating a boycott of potatoes.

Idaho's junior Senator, Steven Symms, is as controversial and flamboyant as McClure is reserved and taciturn, although the two have similar voting records. Symms likes to portray himself as a simple apple-grower (which is what he was when he first ran for Congress in 1972), determined to get big government out of everybody's hair. But he is also a man who was investing heavily in the silver futures market and at the same time sponsoring legislation that would have helped him and his friend and supporter Nelson Bunker Hunt. And Symms, representing heavily Mormon and tradition-minded Idaho, has been dogged by rumors that he was a womanizer and showed up drunk on the floor of the Senate. There is something slapdash, almost whimsical, to Symms and his politics, a lack of gravity. In August 1988, for instance, he told national television cameras that he'd heard a rumor that Kitty Dukakis had burned an American flag at an anti-Vietnam war demonstration—although he admitted he had no proof and the charge was baseless. This was quite possibly the lowest point of the 1988 campaign.

Symms has good committee assignments: Budget, Environment, Finance and Joint Economic committees. But he is usually not a leader on issues and, when he is, his reputation for careless work and oddball ideas makes it difficult for him to win much support. For example, he led the fight on the Environment Committee to relax the terms of the Clean Air Act; but the result was near-unanimous passage of a bill backed by Chairman Robert Stafford that not only reaffirmed the terms of the original law but strengthened them. He was one of five senators voting to reject the INF treaty. He opposed the Idaho wilderness bill sought by James McClure and Cecil Andrus. But Symms has had some legislative successes; he was one of those western state senators backing the 65 mile per hour speed limit.

Although Symms is a staunch conservative in a staunch conservative state, he has been elected twice by only narrow margins—admittedly against tough opponents both times. In 1980 he beat Frank Church, then Foreign Relations chairman and in his 24th year in the Senate; in 1986 he beat John Evans, a popular governor for 10 years and as steady and solid in his personal character as Symms sometimes seems flaky and half-cocked. Despite this Symms carried the Mormon east by nearly 2 to 1 and carried Boise as well. The right-to-work referendum may have helped him by emphasizing to voters their disagreement with Democrats on national issues, even with a moderate and cautious Democrat like Evans. And Symms's hard work, intensive and good-natured personal campaigning, and nitty-gritty Republican organizing (in contrast to the computerized phone messages Republicans used in other states) all made a difference, boosting Republican turnout and enthusiasm and enhancing Symms's attractive personal qualities while deemphasizing his negatives. In 1992 he may have tough competition again: there will be strong pressure on 2d District Democrat Richard Stallings to take advantage of his proven electoral strength in the Mormon east and take on Symms.

Congressmen. Idaho's 1st District stretches from the Nevada border to Canada, taking in all the Democratic-leaning panhandle and including most of Boise. In statewide elections it is the less Republican of the districts, but has elected nothing but Republican congressmen since 1966. Two of them are now senators; the third is Larry Craig, elected in 1980, and reelected easily since 1984. Craig's number one cause is the balanced budget constitutional amendment, and he seems unfazed by its lack of progress. He is also a fervent opponent of gun control and, on the Interior Committee, of environmentalists' attempts to lock up resources. He supports IRAs for health care and home buying. He also pays close attention to district matters, monitoring local hazardous waste dumps and decrying Canadian restrictions on U.S. timber. He is a plausible Senate candidate should McClure or Symms retire.

The 2d District, from central Boise east to the Utah border, is one of America's most Republican districts in presidential elections, but it has elected a Democratic congressman now three times running. He is Richard Stallings, who in 1984 beat incumbent George Hansen by 170 votes after Hansen was convicted and sentenced to 5 to 15 months for filing false personal disclosure forms, omitting loans purportedly made to his wife from billionaire Nelson Bunker Hunt and a Virginia swindler. But if Hansen had weaknesses, Stallings had strengths. He was a professor from Ricks College in Rexburg, where the county gave Michael Dukakis 14% of the vote, a big jump over Walter Mondale's 7%; he is a practicing Mormon who describes himself as "very, very conservative."

In two terms Stallings has turned a political windfall into a safe seat. He has taken conservative stands on many issues, including the balanced budget amendment, abortion (pro-lifers cast three votes for him for President at the Democratic convention in Atlanta), and gun control. He has used his committee seat on Agriculture to sponsor bills on secondary markets, drought relief, rural health care, and more. He has worked to bring federal projects to eastern Idaho. Thomas Foley, from nearby Washington, has been a kind of mentor to him and Tony Coelho and Beryl Anthony of the Democrats' campaign committee helped him to outraise Republican opponents. By 1986 Stallings was carrying not only Pocatello, long the sole Democratic town in eastern Idaho, but also the Magic Valley; by 1988 he carried 22 of the 26 counties in the district and won 63%–34%.

Presidential politics. Idaho is not likely to vote Democratic for President again soon; the last time it did, in 1964, it gave Lyndon Johnson only 51%. For 1988 Idaho switched from a binding to a non-binding primary, with delegates chosen through caucuses; that made little difference, as in late contests Michael Dukakis and George Bush both won easily.

The People: Est. Pop. 1988: 999,000; Pop. 1980: 943,935, up 5.3% 1980–88 and 32.4% 1970–1980; 0.42% of U.S. total, 41st largest. 21% with 1–3 yrs. col., 16% with 4+ yrs. col.; 12.6% below poverty level. Single ancestry: 18% English, 10% German, 4% Irish, 2% Swedish, 1% French, Norwegian, Scottish, Dutch, Italian. Households (1980): 76% family, 44% with children, 67% married couples; 28.0% housing units rented; median monthly rent: $172; median house value: $45,900. Voting age pop. (1980): 637,270; 3% Spanish origin, 1% American Indian, 1% Asian origin. Registered voters (1988): 572,430; no party registration.

1988 Share of Federal Tax Burden: $2,521,000,000; 0.29% of U.S. total, 44th largest.

1988 Share of Federal Expenditures

	Total		Non-Defense		Defense	
Total Expend	$3,407m	(0.39%)	$3,097m	(0.47%)	$919m	(0.40%)
St/Lcl Grants	477m	(0.42%)	474m	(0.41%)	3m	(2.81%)
Salary/Wages	440m	(0.33%)	279m	(0.42%)	161m	(0.42%)
Pymnts to Indiv	1,495m	(0.37%)	1,410m	(0.36%)	85m	(0.45%)
Procurement	669m	(0.35%)	609m	(1.31%)	669m	(0.35%)
Research/Other	326m	(0.87%)	325m	(0.88%)	1m	(0.88%)

Political Lineup: Governor, Cecil D. Andrus (D); Lt. Gov., C. L. (Butch) Otter (R); Secy. of State, Pete T. Cenarrusa (R); Atty. Gen., Jim Jones (R); Treasurer, Lydia Justice Edwards (R); Auditor, J. D. Williams (D). State Senate, 42 (23 R and 19 D); State House of Representatives, 84 (64 R and 20 D). Senators, James A. McClure (R) and Steven D. Symms (R). Representatives, 2 (1 D and 1 R).

1988 Presidential Vote

Bush (R) 253,881 (62%)
Dukakis (D). 147,272 (36%)

1988 Republican Presidential Primary

Bush 55,464 (81%)
Robertson 5,876 (9%)
Others 6,935 (10%)

1984 Presidential Vote

Reagan (R) 297,523 (72%)
Mondale (D) 108,510 (26%)

GOVERNOR
Gov. Cecil D. Andrus (D)

Elected 1986, term expires Jan. 1991; b. Aug. 25, 1931, Hood River, OR; home, Boise; OR St. U., 1947–49; Lutheran; married (Carol).

Career: ID State Senate, 1960–66, 1969–70; Govenor of ID, 1971–77; U.S. Secy. of Interior, 1977–81; Pres., Cecil D. Andrus, Inc., 1981–87.

Office: State House, Boise 83720, 208-334-2100.

Election Results

1986 gen.	Cecil D. Andrus (D).	193,429	(50%)
	David Leroy (R).	189,794	(49%)
1986 prim.	Cecil D. Andrus (D).	49,663	(100%)
1982 gen.	John V. Evans (D)	165,365	(51%)
	Phil Batt (R)	161,157	(49%)

SENATORS

Sen. James A. McClure (R)

Elected 1972, seat up 1990; b. Dec. 27, 1924, Payette; home, McCall; U. of ID, J.D. 1950; United Methodist; married (Louise).

Career: Navy, WWII; Practicing atty., 1950–66; Payette Cnty. Prosecuting Atty., 1951–57; Payette City Atty., 1953–59, 1962–66; ID Senate, 1960–66; U.S. House of Reps., 1966–72.

Offices: 309 HSOB 20510, 202-224-2752. Also 304 N. 8th St., Rm. 149, Boise 83702, 208-334-1560; 305 Fed. Bldg., Coeur d'Alene 83814, 208-664-3086; 482 Constitution Way, Rm. 304, Idaho Falls 83401, 208-523-5541; FBUSCH, Rm. 210, 250 S. 4th Ave., Pocatello 83201, 208-236-6817; 401 2d St. N., Ste. 106, Twin Falls 83301, 208-734-6780; and 301 D St., Ste. 103, Lewiston 83501, 208-743-3579.

Committees: *Appropriations* (3d of 13 R). Subcommittees: Agriculture and Related Agencies; Defense; Energy and Water Development; Interior (Ranking Member); Labor, Health and Human Services, Education. *Energy and Natural Resources* (Ranking Member of 9 R). *Rules and Administration* (3d of 7 R).

Group Ratings

	ADA	ACLU	COPE	CFA	LCV	ACU	NTLC	NSI	COC	CEI
1988	5	4	8	8	0	91	79	90	83	73
1987	0	—	8	0	—	96	—	—	83	71

National Journal Ratings

	1988 LIB — 1988 CONS	1987 LIB — 1987 CONS
Economic	0% — 95%	0% — 94%
Social	0% — 89%	0% — 94%
Foreign	12% — 87%	0% — 76%

Key Votes

1) Cut Aged Housing $	AGN	5) Bork Nomination	FOR	9) SDI Funding	FOR
2) Override Hwy Veto	AGN	6) Ban Plastic Guns	FOR	10) Ban Chem Weaps	FOR
3) Kill Plnt Clsng Notice	FOR	7) Deny Abortions	FOR	11) Aid To Contras	FOR
4) Min Wage Increase	—	8) Japanese Reparations	AGN	12) Reagan Defense $	FOR

Election Results

1984 general	James A. McClure (R)	293,193	(72%)	($1,016,944)
	Peter Martin Busch (D)	105,591	(26%)	($31,001)
1984 primary	James A. McClure (R)	102,125	(100%)	
1978 general	James A. McClure (R)	194,412	(68%)	($434,871)
	Dwight Jensen (D)	89,635	(32%)	($55,163)

Sen. Steven D. Symms (R)

Elected 1980, seat up 1992; b. Apr. 23, 1938, Nampa; home, Caldwell; U. of ID, B.S. 1960; Free Methodist; separated.

Career: USMC, 1960–63; Personnel and Production Mngr., Vice Pres., Symms Fruit Ranch, Inc., 1963–72; U.S. House of Reps., 1972–80.

Offices: 509 HSOB 20510, 202-224-6142. Also P.O. Box 1190, Boise 83701, 208-334-1776; 207 Fed. Bldg., Pocatello 83201, 208-236-6775; 305 Fed. Bldg., Coeur d'Alene 83814, 208-664-5490; 105 Fed. Bldg., Moscow 83843, 208-882-5560; 301 D St., Ste. 103, Lewiston 83501, 208-743-1492; and 401 2d St., No. 106, Twin Falls 83301, 208-734-2515.

Committees: *Budget* (4th of 10 R). *Finance* (9th of 9 R). Subcommittees: Taxation and Debt Management; International Trade; Energy and Agricultural Taxation. *Environment and Public Works* (3d of 7 R). Subcommittees: Water Resources, Transportation and Infrastructure (Ranking Member); Superfund, Ocean and Water Protection; Nuclear Regulation. *Joint Economic Committee.* Subcommittees: Economic Resources and Competitiveness; Fiscal and Monetary Policy; Investment, Jobs and Prices.

Group Ratings

	ADA	ACLU	COPE	CFA	LCV	ACU	NTLC	NSI	COC	CEI
1988	0	0	2	8	0	100	81	100	86	87
1987	0	—	3	0	—	88	—	—	94	82

National Journal Ratings

	1988 LIB — 1988 CONS	1987 LIB — 1987 CONS
Economic	0% — 95%	14% — 85%
Social	0% — 89%	0% — 94%
Foreign	0% — 92%	0% — 76%

Key Votes

1) Cut Aged Housing $	AGN	5) Bork Nomination	FOR	9) SDI Funding	FOR
2) Override Hwy Veto	FOR	6) Ban Plastic Guns	FOR	10) Ban Chem Weaps	FOR
3) Kill Plnt Clsng Notice	FOR	7) Deny Abortions	FOR	11) Aid To Contras	FOR
4) Min Wage Increase	AGN	8) Japanese Reparations	AGN	12) Reagan Defense $	FOR

Election Results

1986 general	Steven D. Symms (R)...............	196,958	(52%)	($3,229,939)
	John V. Evans (D)..................	185,066	(48%)	($2,135,537)
1986 primary	Steven D. Symms (R)................	90,508	(100%)	
1980 general	Steven D. Symms (R)...............	218,701	(50%)	($1,780,777)
	Frank Church (D)..................	214,439	(49%)	($1,931,487)

FIRST DISTRICT

The People: Est. Pop. 1986: 504,600, up 6.8% 1980–86; Pop. 1980: 472,412, up 40.5% 1970–80. Households (1980): 77% family, 43% with children, 67% married couples; 26.7% housing units rented; median monthly rent: $173; median house value: $47,400. Voting age pop. (1980): 324,509; 3% Spanish origin, 1% American Indian, 1% Asian origin.

338 IDAHO

1988 Presidential Vote: Bush (R) 121,392   (59%)
                              Dukakis (D). 80,381   (39%)

Rep. Larry E. Craig (R)

Elected 1980; b. July 20, 1945, Council; home, Boise; U. of ID, B.A. 1969; United Methodist; married (Suzanne).

Career: Rancher, farmer; ID Senate, 1974–80.

Offices: 1034 LHOB 20515, 202-225-6611. Also 304 N. 8th St., Rm. 136, Boise 83702, 208-342-7985; 301 D St. Ste. 103, Lewiston, 83501 208-743-0792; and 103 N. 4th, Coeur d'Alene 83814, 208-667-6130.

Committees: *Interior and Insular Affairs* (4th of 15 R). Subcommittee: Mining and Natural Resources (Ranking Member); Water, Power and Offshore Energy Resources; National Parks and Public Lands. *Public Works and Transportation* (16th of 20 R). Subcommittees: Economic Development; Surface Transportation; Water Resources. *Standards of Official Conduct* (5th of 6 R).

Group Ratings

	ADA	ACLU	COPE	CFA	LCV	ACU	NTLC	NSI	COC	CEI
1988	5	22	9	18	6	100	90	100	92	75
1987	4	—	9	14	—	86	—	—	93	76

National Journal Ratings

	1988 LIB — 1988 CONS		1987 LIB — 1987 CONS	
Economic	0%	93%	11%	83%
Social	13%	84%	22%	78%
Foreign	30%	67%	27%	73%

Key Votes

1) Homeless $	FOR	5) Ban Drug Test	FOR	9) SDI Research	FOR
2) Gephardt Amdt	AGN	6) Drug Death Pen	FOR	10) Ban Chem Weaps	AGN
3) Deficit Reduc	AGN	7) Handgun Sales	FOR	11) Aid to Contras	FOR
4) Kill Plnt Clsng Notice	FOR	8) Ban D.C. Abort $	FOR	12) Nuclear Testing	—

Election Results

1988 general	Larry E. Craig (R)	135,221	(66%)	($361,113)
	Jeanne Givens (D).	70,328	(34%)	($116,109)
1988 primary	Larry E. Craig (R)	29,289	(100%)	
1986 general	Larry E. Craig (R)	120,553	(65%)	($310,471)
	William Currie (D).	59,723	(32%)	($12,507)
	David Shepherd (I).	4,848	(3%)	

SECOND DISTRICT

The People: Est. Pop. 1986: 498,000, up 5.6% 1980–86; Pop. 1980: 471,523, up 25.1% 1970–80. Households (1980): 76% family, 44% with children, 67% married couples; 29.3% housing units rented; median monthly rent: $170; median house value: $44,300. Voting age pop. (1980): 312,761; 4% Spanish origin, 1% American Indian, 1% Asian origin.

1988 Presidential Vote: Bush (R) 132,489   (65%)
Dukakis (D). 66,891   (33%)

Rep. Richard H. Stallings (D)

Elected 1984; b. Oct. 7, 1940, Ogden, UT; home, Rexburg; Weber St. Col., B.S. 1965, UT St. U., M.S. 1968; Mormon; married (Ranae).

Career: High sch. teacher, 1964–69; Chmn., History Dept., Ricks Col., Rexburg, ID, 1969–84.

Offices: 1233 LHOB 20515, 202-225-5531. Also 304 N. 8th, Rm. 434, Boise 83702, 208-334-1953; 250 S. 4th, Rm. 225, Pocatello 83201, 208-236-6734; 634 Falls Ave., Rm. 1180, Twin Falls 83301, 208-734-6329; and 482 Constitution Ave., Rm. 105, Idaho Falls, 208-523-5601.

Committees: *Agriculture* (16th of 27 D). Subcommittees: Conservation, Credit, and Rural Development; Cotton, Rice and Sugar; Forests, Family Farms, and Energy. *Science, Space and Technology* (17th of 30 D). Subcommittees: Energy Research and Development; Space Science and Applications. *Select Committee on Aging* (29th of 39 D). Subcommittees: Retirement Income and Employment.

Group Ratings

	ADA	ACLU	COPE	CFA	LCV	ACU	NTLC	NSI	COC	CEI
1988	55	55	57	64	38	48	43	50	71	28
1987	52	—	52	43	—	27	—	—	67	31

National Journal Ratings

	1988 LIB — 1988 CONS		1987 LIB — 1987 CONS	
Economic	43%	56%	35%	64%
Social	43%	55%	51%	48%
Foreign	56%	44%	53%	46%

Key Votes

1) Homeless $	FOR	5) Ban Drug Test	AGN	9) SDI Research	AGN
2) Gephardt Amdt	AGN	6) Drug Death Pen	FOR	10) Ban Chem Weaps	AGN
3) Deficit Reduc	AGN	7) Handgun Sales	FOR	11) Aid to Contras	AGN
4) Kill Plnt Clsng Notice	AGN	8) Ban D.C. Abort $	FOR	12) Nuclear Testing	—

Election Results

1988 general	Richard Stallings (D)	127,956	(63%)	($502,083)
	Dane Watkins (R).....................	68,223	(34%)	($206,960)
1988 primary	Richard Stallings (D), unopposed			
1986 general	Richard H. Stallings (D)	103,035	(54%)	($470,363)
	Mel Richardson (R)	86,528	(46%)	($325,004)

ILLINOIS

In 1940, as Hitler was sweeping through France and his ally Stalin was tightening his control of Eastern Europe, as the Japanese were advancing in China and eyeing the Pacific, the Democratic National Convention met in Chicago, the nation's second city in population, the center of its railroad network, the heart of America's vast interior. Just as President Franklin Roosevelt's letter disclaiming interest in the nomination was being read aloud to the hushed, surly delegates in Chicago Stadium on West Madison Street, a cry rang out over loudspeakers, "We want Roosevelt!" This was the famous "voice from the sewers," Chicago Sewer Commissioner Thomas McGarry shouting into a hidden microphone in a room beneath the hall. The demonstration this shouting inspired gave Roosevelt what he wanted—a draft nominating him for a third term as President. Roosevelt felt that only he could lead America against the forces of totalitarianism, and he knew that only Chicago's Mayor Ed Kelly, a beefy machine politician who worked his way up through the Sanitary Commission, was indebted and loyal to him and could control the convention hall.

Glaring across town at the convention hall from the Gothic Tribune Tower was Col. Robert Rutherford McCormick, publisher of the *Chicago Tribune*, "the World's Greatest Newspaper." With the second largest circulation in America, the *Tribune* was the voice of Midwest Republican isolationism and conservatism. "Only 100 days left to save your country," the *Tribune*'s countdown read in 1936, ticking off the days until its readers would vote out Franklin Roosevelt, and in the 1940s McCormick's front page editorials and partisan reportage blasted Roosevelt and the Democrats at every turn. Yet in Chicago McCormick was a friend and ally of Roosevelt's man Kelly. The Protestant Yankees who produced and controlled great wealth in this center of unbridled capitalism—where the agricultural abundance of the prairies came together with the iron ore from Great Lakes freighters and coal from inland hills—saw a need to cooperate with the Irish Catholics who controlled the votes of the millions of working men and women living in little villages of bungalows and low-rise apartments implanted in the inexorable grids radiating outward from Chicago's Loop.

Chicago was indisputably a world city in the days of Kelly and McCormick; a century before it barely existed. A traveler in 1836 reported that "four years ago it did not contain more than a hundred inhabitants, and now it boasts of nearly five thousand." Settled from New England and Kentucky, by Irishmen who dug the first canal connecting Lake Michigan and the Illinois River, by railroad promoters who saw its potential as the great connecting point between East and West and the Great Lakes and the Mississippi Valley, Chicago had 112,000 people as the Civil War began and 1.2 million when it hosted the world's fair of 1893. Chicago today is the nation's third largest city—not second as it was in 1940, but still a world city. Chicago may no longer be the hog butcher of the world (big meatpacking operations are now located near feedlots), and the Chicago of Saul Bellow does not command the awe of the Chicago of Theodore Dreiser. But Chicago has become the center of the world's futures markets and Illinois is the nation's center for producing and processing soybeans. Manufacturing is declining in Illinois, as in other Great Lakes states, and the farm sector is ailing. But the white-collar economy is of greater mass here than anywhere else between the coasts, and incomes remain well above the national average.

This Illinois is not conducive to philosophical speculation or airy dreams; it is a land of concrete and topsoil, of steel and water, of railroads and grain elevators and factories: people are here to make and grow things and earn a living. The state's economic growth and prosperity are the result, not of political theory or bureaucratic agency, but almost entirely of the strength and

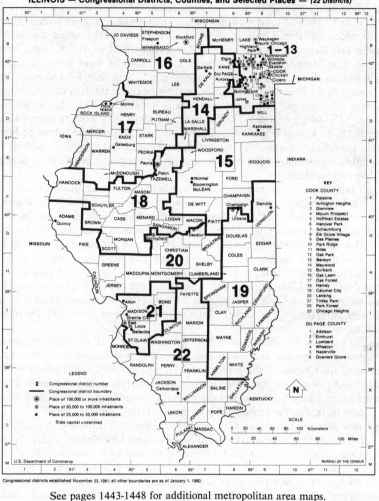

ILLINOIS — Congressional Districts, Counties, and Selected Places — (22 Districts)

KEY

COOK COUNTY

1 Palatine
2 Arlington Heights
3 Glenview
4 Mount Prospect
5 Hanover Park
6 Schaumburg
7 Schaumburg
8 Elk Grove Village
9 Des Plaines
10 Park Ridge
11 Niles
12 Oak Park
13 Berwyn
14 Maywood
15 Burbank
16 Oak Lawn
17 Oak Forest
18 Harvey
19 Calumet City
20 Lansing
21 Tinley Park
22 Park Forest
23 Chicago Heights

DU PAGE COUNTY

1 Addison
2 Elmhurst
3 Lombard
4 Wheaton
5 Naperville
6 Downers Grove

LEGEND

2 Congressional district number
─ Congressional district boundary
◉ Place of 100,000 or more inhabitants
◎ Place of 50,000 to 100,000 inhabitants
• Place of 25,000 to 50,000 inhabitants
   State capital underlined

SCALE
0   20   40   60   80   100 Kilometers
0   20   40   60   80   100 Miles

U.S. Department of Commerce   BUREAU OF THE CENSUS

Congressional districts established November 23, 1981; all other boundaries are as of January 1, 1980.

See pages 1443-1448 for additional metropolitan area maps.

growth of its private economy. Illinois likes to boast of Abraham Lincoln, the most important politician Illinois has produced; but Lincoln's greatest contribution to Illinois (dwarfed, to be sure, by his contributions to the nation), was his first-rate legal work for the east-west railroads. In this bustling and muscular Illinois, politicians have had the unglamorous job of managing the everyday government and keeping it from fouling up commerce and industry.

Thus it was before the days of Ed Kelly, when a Republican Mayor, Big Bill Thompson, threatened to "smash King George on the snoot" if he came to Chicago and opened up the city to Al Capone, and so it was after, when Richard J. Daley became mayor and county Democratic chairman in 1955. By keeping careful track of who got every public job and by building great public works—O'Hare Airport, McCormick Place convention hall—that helped business, Daley managed to keep both the voting masses and the downtown powers pleased with a machine politics that had vanished almost everywhere else in America long before his death in 1976.

Machine politics had its feudal aspects. It was sometimes violent: an upstart who dared challenge Thompson's ally, 20th ward committeeman and city collector Morris Eller, was murdered in the 1920s, and someone—no one was saying who—pumped bullets into 24th ward Democratic alderman Ben Lewis in 1964. And it made public office almost hereditary: Congressman Dan Rostenkowski, three-term Sheriff Richard Elrod, and of course former state's attorney and new Mayor Richard M. Daley are all sons of ward committeemen. Daley's admirers hailed his ability to make the city work—and to help elect John Kennedy in 1960 (he carried the state by 8,858 votes of 4.7 million cast, with dubious totals in some Chicago machine wards), just as Ed Kelly had helped reelect Franklin Roosevelt in 1940 (he carried Illinois by a 102,000-vote, 51%–49% landslide). The downside of Daley's work became more visible when he was succeeded by lackluster heir Michael Bilandic in 1977 and onetime appointee Jane Byrne in 1979: public payrolls laced with loyal but incompetent hacks, and a political machine—now that a growing public sector has opened up opportunities for competent people of all backgrounds—grown flabby and feckless.

Chicago's and Illinois's current chief executives both came up as squeaky-clean prosecutors, and are both from backgrounds typical of their party—though both have learned to play something more than their party's traditional politics. They made their way in an era when Illinois politics has become a kind of spectator sport—raucous, sometimes bawdy, full of play-acting, on a level somewhere between the Chicago Cubs and professional wrestling. It is fought out in ultra-competitive media, television newscasts and newspaper stories which focus so parochially on local politics that the most covered race in the March 1988 primaries in which a future President of the United States was running was the one for the Democratic nomination for Cook County Clerk of Circuit Court. It is a rough, inelegant game. "Ours is a one-syllable town," says its chronicler Studs Terkel. "Its character has been molded by the muscle rather than the word."

The first to rise was Governor James Thompson, who as U.S. attorney in the early 1970s brought indictments against major machine politicians, and helped the Better Government Association and the *Chicago Tribune* pretty well stamp out vote fraud. Thompson literally rose to the governorship over the ruins of the Daley machine. In November 1976 he won by beating a machine politician Daley had used to beat maverick incumbent (and in 1988 convicted tax evader) Daniel Walker in the primary. A month later Daley suddenly died.

Another new-style executive was Chicago Mayor Harold Washington. A longtime machine politician of great ability (he graduated from Northwestern Law School, as did Thompson) and a patchy record (he served time in jail for filing his income tax returns late), Washington was a South Side congressman and won 11% in the 1979 mayoral primary. But in 1983 he beat Jane Byrne and Richie Daley in a three-way race, sparking enormous enthusiasm among Chicago blacks and apprehension among neighborhood whites—and inspiring Chicago resident Jesse Jackson's presidential candidacy as well. Washington narrowly beat a Republican in 1983. In April 1987, he won a second term, beating Jane Byrne 54%–46% in the primary and his bitter council opponent Edward Vrdolyak 53%–42% in the general, amid byzantine maneuvering in which Vrdolyak left the Democratic party (whose Cook County chairman he was), and by 1988 became a Republican. Washington's forces also got a solid margin on the council, at which point former opponents came over to his side with Chicagoesque shamelessness and *sang-froid*. Washington's major achievements were to clean out many low-quality patronage appointees and make some good appointments himself; he made some progress assuring whites that his success would not destroy their neighborhoods, though few whites actually voted for him outside the liberal lakefront wards.

How he was replaced by the son of the man whose legacy he rejected—the current Mayor, Richard M. Daley—is a complex story. After Washington died suddenly in November 1987, most white aldermen joined several blacks in an all-night council session to elect Eugene Sawyer as mayor over Timothy Evans, who was the choice of most Washington supporters. Both Sawyer and Evans were interested in running and seemed likely to split the black vote, as Daley and Byrne had split the white vote in 1983; eventually, Evans was elbowed out of the primary and agreed to run as a third party candidate in the general. But more important, Daley had affirmative popularity, based on his record as state's attorney and bolstered by Washington's support when he ran for reelection in 1987. Washington's victories obscured the fact that blacks made up only about 40% of the total electorate, and Illinois's open primary allows even white Republicans to vote in city Democratic primaries; blacks moreover are moving to southern suburbs more than to the North Side, so that Hispanics, not necessarily loyal to black politicians, are the growing demographic force.

Daley, ironically considering his lineage, proved attractive to lakefront whites who had provided essential votes for the intelligent and articulate Washington but found Sawyer and Evans both unattractive: Sawyer attracted attention in 1988 when he refused for days to fire an aide who accused Jewish doctors of injecting black babies with AIDS virus, and then failed to rebuke black allies and appointees who said they didn't know whether there might not be something to this preposterous charge; Evans has said nothing either. Intensity of racial feelings were down, however, as indicated by the turnout, which was down 30% from 1987 in black wards and about 10% in the white bungalow wards at the edge of the city. Daley won with large margins the Hispanic and lakefront wards Washington had carried and beat Sawyer 56%–44%; his margin against the underfinanced Evans, was even greater. Daley's victories over Sawyer and Evans suddenly gave a city that seemed likely to have black mayors forever a white mayor with a solid white voting base of about 40%, with proven appeal to the lakefront liberals and Hispanics who hold the balance of votes, and with the desire and incentive to dull the sharp edge of hostility of many blacks. But his chances of proving as enduring as his father depend not just on mollifying voting blocs but on transmitting to forgotten parts of the city—the left-behind white ethnic neighborhoods, the bullet-pocked public housing projects—the dynamism and growth so apparent in the Loop and along North Michigan Avenue, in lakefront high-rises and in the zones of restoration that are spreading inland.

City elections remain the focus of Illinois politics; although Chicago casts only 23% of the state's votes, some 65% are cast in the Chicago media market, and the TV stations would rather be accused of anything but undercovering City Hall. City politics also helps to generate the animosities and anger that give Illinois the steadiest—or stubbornest—political alignments of any major state. Blacks vote for Jackson or blacks in primaries and for Democrats in the generals virtually unanimously, but their turnout in the 1988 general election, with no major black on the ballot, plummeted. Bungalow ward and inner suburban whites vote against Jackson and blacks nearly unanimously in primaries and increasingly for Republicans in generals; Illinois had the lowest white percentage for Jackson in 1988 of any state. High income whites in suburban Cook and the collar counties, making plenty of money in the private sector symbolized by Chicago's thriving but scandal-tarred commodity markets, are overwhelmingly and unguiltily Republican—if the *Tribune* is now more liberal or evenhanded, the spirit of the Colonel lives in suburban election returns. Downstaters, in communities hurt by the low farm prices and factory layoffs of the 1980s, have been trending Democratic.

While polls in the nation and other big states shifted sharply in the 1988 general election, they shifted hardly at all in Illinois; people knew who they were for—or, more important, who they were against—and were not about to change sides. George Bush's 51% in Illinois in 1988 was in between the Republican percentages in the two other recent close elections since 1984, the 1986 governor's race (53% for Thompson) and the 1984 Senate race (48% for loser Charles Percy); Ronald Reagan's 56% in 1984 was only a bit better. In those three close races the Republican vote in Chicago ranged from 30% to 32%, in the suburbs from 59% to 65%, and in Downstate from 50% to 55%.

It's beginning to look like a pattern, with a slight edge to the Republicans: the difference between Michael Dukakis's 49% and Franklin Roosevelt's 51% comes from the Republican trend among bungalow whites. But the Republican advantage is as tenuous as was Roosevelt's Democratic edge (the Democrats lost the governorship in 1940 and 1944 and Senate races in 1940 and 1942, as Roosevelt was winning statewide). Today Democrats hold both Senate seats, by virtue of Paul Simon's narrow win in 1984 and Alan Dixon's bipartisan popularity, most of the House seats, and majorities in both houses of the legislature. And for all the hoopla and controversy, turnout in Illinois has been in decline, from 3.7 to 3.1 million in the 1982–86 offyear cycle and 4.8 to 4.5 million—the lowest in 40 years—in the 1984–88 presidential cycle.

Governor. James Thompson, elected in 1976, is the nation's longest-serving governor, but far from the most popular; he is undeniably competent but leaves a record not full of accomplishments. He has consolidated his hold on office by accommodating the state's major economic interests, Democratic as well as Republican, winning the backing not only of business but in 1986 of the state AFL-CIO. This is a backward-looking strategy, more reminiscent of Nelson Rockefeller or Richard J. Daley than of recent big state governors like Richard Thornburgh or James Blanchard; it assumes that growth results from the nurturing of big economic units rather than the creation of a climate in which small units can flourish. He has encouraged foreign firms to locate in Illinois and he put together a package to keep the White Sox in Chicago; he has been less successful in getting money for education in a state where Education Secretary William Bennett called the Chicago public schools "the worst in the nation."

Thompson has been more successful as a political operator. He backed George Bush early and conspicuously in 1988, helping him to win what turned out to be the last seriously contested Republican primary, and he played a role too in helping him to carry Illinois's 24 electoral votes in November. But he did not win a place in Bush's Cabinet, nor was he seriously considered to be Bush's running mate. The speculation, often heard in the 1970s, that Thompson might become a presidential candidate has pretty much disappeared, replaced by stories about his taste for high living—like how he antiques set aside on particular shelves in stores where friends can buy them as presents for him.

Thompson's popularity in Illinois has declined since he won with 65% in 1976 and 59% in 1978. He squeaked through only 5,000 votes ahead of former Senator Adlai Stevenson III in 1982 and seemed in danger of losing to him in 1986. Stevenson was preparing to argue that Thompson's formula buttresses dying industries rather than nurtures growth. Thompson was prepared to counter by discussing how he brought business and labor together to agree on tax reform, how he got striking Chicago teachers and the board of education together to reach a contract, how he froze spending and built new prisons and set up an in-home care program for the elderly. Then Stevenson was struck by bad luck: his running mate George Sangmeister was beaten by a follower of Lyndon LaRouche in the Democratic primary (so much for the effectiveness of the Democratic machine) and Stevenson resigned from the Democratic ticket and formed a Solidarity party to run in the general. Stevenson got only 40% of the vote, but Thompson won with only 53%—an indication that under other circumstances he might have lost.

Will Thompson run again in 1990? Others are already lining up, especially holders of the statewide offices that have little power but build up name recognition. Attorney General Neil Hartigan, a statewide winner in 1972, 1982, and 1986, might finally run for governor; so might Treasurer Jerry Cosentino, who backed Jesse Jackson, and Controller Roland Burris, who is black. These are all Democrats. Republicans will wait on Thompson, but their likeliest candidates are Secretary of State Jim Edgar and Lieutenant Governor George Ryan. Big things will be at stake in this uncertain race, including redistricting the 20 House seats Illinois is expected to have in the 1990s. If he does run and wins, Thompson will break the 20th century record for tenure as governor—the 16 years in office of James Rhodes of Ohio.

Senators. Alan Dixon is Illinois's senior senator, one of its all-time leading vote-getters, and, since 1988, Democratic chief deputy whip. So why isn't he better known? One reason is that he doesn't take on many high-visibility issues: one of his pet causes was to get federal projects like the super collider for Illinois (it gets little defense money and pays high taxes); another was to stop the Army's Sergeant York gun (one jammed in his hands). Another reason is that he doesn't fit into the usual ideological niche. He backs the line-item veto; he is not a stringent opponent of weapons systems; he is conservative on many foreign and cultural issues. On Armed Services he got to procurement reform a little before other senators; he wants to let public housing residents manage their projects; he has proposed a five-regional-primary system for presidential campaigns.

Dixon won his first office, police magistrate in Belleville near St. Louis, in 1949, and has continued to win every race since. He served 20 years in the legislature, compiled an honest and efficient record, and got rid of patronage jobs as treasurer and secretary of state in the 1970s. He was elected to the Senate by a solid margin in 1980 and reelected by an overwhelming margin in 1986 against weak opposition; his good name helps deter Republicans from raising the vast sums needed to run statewide TV ads in Illinois. Curiously, he is a longtime friend of his colleague, Paul Simon, and was once Simon's business partner when he owned a small chain of Downstate papers.

Paul Simon's horn-rimmed glasses and bow tie, his extra-flat midwestern accent and his habit of writing his own newsletters and books (he has published 12), have long been well-known in Illinois; now, after his 1988 presidential candidacy, they are well-known nationally too. Simon ran as a liberal, a full-throated backer of big government at home and an opponent of an assertive policy abroad. He finished second in the Iowa caucuses, third in New Hampshire, and out of the running in the South on Super Tuesday; but at the importuning of Illinois politicos who were on his delegate slates he stayed in the race through the Illinois primary a week later, and won it. That was testimony to his popularity—and to the propensity of Illinois media to concentrate coverage on their home state candidates, Simon and Jesse Jackson, and to provide voters with little information about their unfamiliar opponents. Simon held onto his delegates a bit clumsily—Jackson claimed he was trying to keep them away from him—but his campaign seems not to have hurt and perhaps to have helped him at home.

It has changed his image at least a bit, however; for in Illinois Simon has been as much a reformer as a liberal. Simon got his start in public life when he bought the *Troy Tribune,* a paper published 15 miles from Dixon's Belleville, at age 19, and crusaded against local gangsters and machine politicians; he was elected to the legislature in 1954 and married a colleague in 1960; eventually, he owned 14 newspapers and sold the chain in 1966. In 1968 he was elected lieutenant governor, and was prepared to take on politically ailing Republican Governor Richard Ogilvie when he lost the Democratic primary to anti-Daley, anti-spending Daniel Walker. In 1974, when Ken Gray retired from the state's southernmost Downstate district, Simon ran and won; and in 1984, he won a heavily contested Democratic primary and then went on to beat Senate Foreign Relations Chairman Charles Percy 50%–48%. The key to both victories was Downstate, which Simon carried heavily in the primary and lost to the Chicago-based Percy by only 50%–49% in November.

Simon's reformism comes out in original proposals: an open meeting law in cynical Illinois, a pay-as-you-go constitutional amendment in free-spending Washington. He has sponsored legislation on missing children, rewritten his state adoption law, taken up the cause of spouses divided by the Iron Curtain and tried to direct foreign aid to poor countries' poorest inhabitants. He promotes water desalination projects and wants to do something to stop greenmail and golden parachutes. About his major projects he writes books. *The Tongue-Tied American* bemoaned our ignorance of foreign languages, and he got the State Department to require that every employee at several U.S. embassies speak the local language. His latest book, *Winners and*

Losers, gives his perspective on the 1988 presidential campaigns.

Before his presidential run, Simon got loaded with committee assignments. He has served on Judiciary, a non-lawyer scrutinizing Reagan judicial nominees; he is on Labor and on Foreign Relations. He seems unlikely to run for president again and does seem eager to gear up for the 1990 Senate race. Congresswoman Lynn Martin, a moderate Republican from Rockford with Irish Catholic roots in Chicago, would be a strong opponent.

Presidential politics. Illinois is a presidential bellwether; it has voted for every presidential winner for 100 years except for southerners Jimmy Carter in 1976 and Woodrow Wilson in 1916. It is arguably a microcosm of the nation: Cairo, at its southern tip, is closer to Mississippi than to Chicago; and Chicago itself has hundreds of thousands of black residents with roots in the South as well as the descendants of immigrants with roots in every part of Europe and now an increasing number from Latin America. A line across central Illinois marks the division between Democratic and Republican counties in Lincoln's day and almost exactly separates counties carried by Jimmy Carter and by Gerald Ford in the 1976 presidential election. Its close and stubborn divisions and its large electoral count make it a key state in any close election.

Illinois's March primary, one week after Super Tuesday, has been critical and arguably determinative in some nomination races. It provided key wins for Gerald Ford in 1976, Ronald Reagan and Jimmy Carter in 1980, Walter Mondale in 1984, and George Bush in 1988. The heavy focus on local politics makes Illinois unrepresentative when an Illinois candidate is in the race, as the Democrats in 1988 showed. But it could be critical in 1992. Jesse Jackson has one-third of the primary vote locked up, but can't seem to get more; Illinois could determine who emerges as the chief alternative to him, and hence the nominee.

Congressional districting. Illinois, for all its rough politics, has one of the most competent and distinguished House delegations—perhaps the most. It elects Republican House leader Robert Michel and Ways and Means Chairman Dan Rostenkowski as well as legislative leaders like Sidney Yates and Frank Annunzio, Edward Madigan and Lynn Martin. Current district lines were drawn by the Democrats (but adopted by a court that was 2 to 1 Republican!) and extend Chicago districts out into the suburbs; at least one Chicago district and probably one Downstate district will vanish after the 1990 Census.

The People: Est. Pop. 1988: 11,544,000; Pop. 1980: 11,426,518, up 1.0% 1980–88 and 2.8% 1970–80; 4.79% of U.S. total, 6th largest. 15% with 1–3 yrs. col., 15% with 4+ yrs. col.; 11.0% below poverty level. Single ancestry: 10% German, 6% English, 4% Irish, Polish, 3% Italian, 1% Swedish, Russian, Dutch, French, Greek. Households (1980): 73% family, 39% with children, 59% married couples; 37.4% housing units rented; median monthly rent: $201; median house value: $53,900. Voting age pop. (1980): 8,183,481; 13% Black, 5% Spanish origin, 1% Asian origin. Registered voters (1988): 6,356,940; no party registration.

1988 Share of Federal Tax Burden: $46,237,000,000; 5.23% of U.S. total, 4th largest.

1988 Share of Federal Expenditures

	Total		Non-Defense		Defense	
Total Expend	$31,962m	(3.62%)	$28,711m	(4.38%)	$4,362m	(1.91%)
St/Lcl Grants	4,670m	(4.07%)	4,668m	(4.08%)	2m	(2.01%)
Salary/Wages	4,271m	(3.18%)	2,810m	(4.19%)	1,461m	(4.19%)
Pymt to Indiv	18,181m	(4.44%)	17,898m	(4.58%)	284m	(1.52%)
Procurement	2,606m	(1.38%)	1,112m	(2.39%)	2,606m	(1.38%)
Research/Other	2,233m	(5.98%)	2,224m	(6.00%)	8m	(6.00%)

Political Lineup: Governor, James R. Thompson, Jr. (R); Lt. Gov., George H. Ryan (R); Secy. of State, James Edgar (R); Atty. Gen., Neil F. Hartigan (D); Treasurer, Jerry Cosentino (D); Comptroller, Roland W. Burris (D). State Senate, 59 (31 D and 28 R); State House of Representatives, 118 (67 D and 51 R). Senators, Alan J. Dixon (D) and Paul Simon (D). Representatives, 22 (14 D and 8 R).

1988 Presidential Vote

Bush (R) 2,310,939 (51%)
Dukakis (D) 2,215,940 (49%)

1984 Presidential Vote

Reagan (R) 2,707,103 (56%)
Mondale (D) 2,086,499 (43%)

1988 Democratic Presidential Primary

Simon 635,219 (42%)
Jackson 484,233 (32%)
Dukakis 245,289 (16%)
Gore 77,265 (5%)
Gephardt 35,108 (2%)
Hart 12,769 (1%)

1988 Republican Presidential Primary

Bush 469,151 (55%)
Dole 309,253 (36%)
Robertson 59,087 (7%)
Kemp 12,687 (2%)

GOVERNOR

Gov. James R. Thompson (R)

Elected 1976, term expires Jan. 1991; b. May 8, 1936, Chicago; home, Chicago; U. of IL, Chicago, B.A. 1956; Northwestern U., J.D. 1959; Presbyterian; married (Jayne).

Career: Prosecutor for Cook Cnty. States Atty., 1959–64; Assoc. Prof., Northwestern Law Sch., 1964–69; Chief, Dept. of Law Enforcement and Pub. Protection, IL Atty. Gen.'s Ofc., 1969–71; 1st Asst. U.S. Atty., N. Dist. of IL, 1970; U.S. Atty., 1971–75.

Office: State Capitol Bldg., Rm. 207, Springfield 62706, 217-782-6830.

Election Results

1986 gen.	James R. Thompson (R)	1,655,945	(53%)
	Adlai E. Stevenson III (SOL) . .	1,296,725	(40%)
	No candidate (D)	208,841	(7%)
1986 prim.	James R. Thompson (R)	452,685	(91%)
	Peter Bowen (R)	45,236	(9%)
1982 gen.	James R. Thompson (R)	1,816,101	(49%)
	Adlai E. Stevenson III (D)	1,811,027	(49%)

SENATORS

Sen. Alan J. Dixon (D)

Elected 1980, seat up 1992; b. July 7, 1927, Belleville; home, Belleville; U. of IL, B.S. 1949, Washington U., St. Louis, LL.B. 1949; Presbyterian; married (Joan).

Career: Navy, 1945–46; Belleville Police Magistrate, 1949; IL House of Reps., 1951–63; IL Senate, 1963–71; Treas. of IL, 1971–77; IL Secy. of State, 1977–81.

Offices: 331 HSOB 20510, 202-224-2854. Also 230 S. Dearborn St., Chicago 60604, 312-353-5420; 600 E. Monroe St., Springfield 62701, 217-492-4126; 8787 State St. E. St. Louis 62203 618-398-7920; and 105 S. 6th St., Mt. Vernon 62864, 618-244-6703.

Committees: *Armed Services* (6th of 11 D). Subcommittees: Conventional Forces and Alliance Defense; Projection Forces and Regional Defense; Readiness, Sustainability and Support (Chairman). *Banking, Housing, and Urban Affairs* (5th of 12 D). Subcommittees: International Finance and Monetary Policy; Consumer and Regulatory Affairs (Chairman). *Small Business* (5th of 10 D). Subcommittees: Government Contracting and Paperwork Reduction (Chairman); Rural Economy and Family Farming.

Group Ratings

	ADA	ACLU	COPE	CFA	LCV	ACU	NTLC	NSI	COC	CEI
1988	45	41	77	83	20	44	20	70	57	22
1987	60	—	78	67	—	20	—	—	41	29

National Journal Ratings

	1988 LIB — 1988 CONS		1987 LIB — 1987 CONS	
Economic	39%	59%	65%	26%
Social	43%	56%	51%	48%
Foreign	47%	52%	51%	45%

Key Votes

1) Cut Aged Housing $	AGN	5) Bork Nomination	AGN	9) SDI Funding	AGN
2) Override Hwy Veto	FOR	6) Ban Plastic Guns	FOR	10) Ban Chem Weaps	FOR
3) Kill Plnt Clsng Notice	AGN	7) Deny Abortions	FOR	11) Aid To Contras	AGN
4) Min Wage Increase	FOR	8) Japanese Reparations	FOR	12) Reagan Defense $	—

Election Results

1986 general	Alan J. Dixon (D)	2,033,926	(65%)	($1,928,750)
	Judy Koehler (R)	1,053,793	(34%)	($851,305)
1986 primary	Alan J. Dixon (D)	750,571	(85%)	
	Sheila Jones (D)	129,474	(15%)	
1980 general	Alan J. Dixon (D)	2,565,302	(56%)	($2,346,897)
	David C. O'Neal (R)	1,946,296	(42%)	($1,293,991)

Sen. Paul Simon (D)

Elected 1984, seat up 1990; b. Nov. 29, 1928, Eugene, OR; home, Makanda; attended U. of OR and Dana Col.; Lutheran; married (Jeanne).

Career: Editor-Publisher, *Troy Tribune*, and weekly newspaper chain owner 1948–66; Army, 1951–53; IL General Assembly, 1954–62; IL Senate, 1962–69; Lt. Gov. of IL, 1969–73; U.S. House of Reps., 1975–85.

Offices: 462 DSOB 20510, 202-224-2152. Also 230 S. Dearborn, Rm. 3892, Chicago 60604, 312-353-4952; 3 W. Old Capital Plaza, Ste. l, Springfield 62701, 217-492-4960; 250 W. Cherry, Rm 115B, Carbondale 62910, 618-457-3653; and 8787 State St., Ste. 212, E. St. Louis 62201, 618-398-7707.

Committees: *Budget* (7th of 13 D). *Judiciary* (7th of 8 D). Subcommittees: Antitrust, Monopolies and Business Rights; Constitution (Chairman); Immigration and Refugee Affairs. *Foreign Relations* (7th of 10 D). Subcommittee: African Affairs (Chairman); European Affairs. *Labor and Human Services* (6th of 9 D). Subcommittees: Education, Arts and Humanities; Employment and Productivity (Chairman); Handicapped.

Group Ratings

	ADA	ACLU	COPE	CFA	LCV	ACU	NTLC	NSI	COC	CEI
1988	85	88	90	50	40	0	8	0	42	2
1987	35	—	90	75	—	0	—	—	13	16

National Journal Ratings

	1988 LIB — 1988 CONS			1987 LIB — 1987 CONS		
Economic	86%	—	0%	74%	—	0%
Social	86%	—	0%	*	—	*
Foreign	86%	—	0%	*	—	*

Key Votes

1) Cut Aged Housing $	FOR	5) Bork Nomination	AGN	9) SDI Funding	AGN
2) Override Hwy Veto	FOR	6) Ban Plastic Guns	—	10) Ban Chem Weaps	—
3) Kill Plnt Clsng Notice	AGN	7) Deny Abortions	AGN	11) Aid To Contras	AGN
4) Min Wage Increase	FOR	8) Japanese Reparations	FOR	12) Reagan Defense $	—

Election Results

1984 general	Paul Simon (D)	2,397,165	(50%)	($4,545,786)
	Charles H. Percy (R)	2,308,039	(48%)	($5,391,567)
1984 primary	Paul Simon (D)	556,757	(36%)	
	Roland W. Burris (D)	360,182	(23%)	
	Alex R. Seith (D)	327,125	(21%)	
	Philip J. Rock (D)	303,397	(19%)	
1978 general	Charles H. Percy (R)	1,698,711	(53%)	($2,417,155)
	Alex R. Seith (D)	1,448,187	(46%)	($1,371,478)

FIRST DISTRICT

"A corner alive with people most of the time," was how the *WPA Guide* described 47th Street and South Park Way 50 years ago, when it was the heart of Bronzeville, the South Side Chicago black ghetto. "On adjoining side streets are small shops selling mystic charms and potions; curbstone stands with smoke rising from wood fires over which chicken and spareribs are being barbecued; lunchrooms serving hot fish, sweet potato pie, gumbo, and other southern dishes, markets bulging with turnip tops, mustard greens, and chitterlings; taverns and night clubs that resound with blues-singing and hot-foot music." But the South Side was home not just to recent migrants from the South, but to America's first black bourgeoisie, a center of black culture and distinguished black institutions since before the jazz age.

Illinois's 1st Congressional District, more than 90% black today, includes most of the South Side black community, from the mansions of Kenwood, once the home of the city's Jewish aristocracy and more recently the headquarters of the Black Muslims (where the Doric temple on East 50th Street that once belonged to the first Jewish congregation in Chicago is now the headquarters of Jesse Jackson's Operation Push), to the grim, crime-infested high-rise housing projects that line the Dan Ryan Expressway for what seems like miles. The 1st also includes the University of Chicago and the intellectual Hyde Park neighborhood around it, but the typical neighborhood here is one where the straight streets are lined with modest well-kept houses built around the turn of the century, in neighborhoods which have been entirely black for decades.

The 1st District has the longest continuous tradition of black representation in the nation. It elected its first black congressman, Republican Oscar DePriest in 1928; blacks then were still faithful to the party of Lincoln, and voted for Herbert Hoover even in the depression year of 1932. But the New Deal and the racial liberalism of Eleanor Roosevelt attracted blacks to the Democratic Party in the 1930s. DePriest was beaten by a black Democrat, Arthur Mitchell, in 1934; Mitchell was succeeded in 1942 by another black Democrat, William Dawson, the first black political boss of the 20th century, a mostly inert congressman and a stalwart of the Democratic machine until his death in 1970. Dawson's successor in Congress, Ralph Metcalfe, broke with Mayor Daley in 1972 when the Mayor refused to come to Metcalfe's office to discuss the beating of two black dentists by a policeman. Later that year, half the South Side's votes went to Republicans, Senator Charles Percy and Cook County State's Attorney Bernard Carey; the South Side never reliably supported the machine again. It elected Harold Washington to Congress in 1980, when he was a little-known state senator who received 11% of the vote in the 1979 mayoral primary; he spent most of his time running for mayor again and became the city's leading political figure from his election in April 1983 until his death in November 1988. In his final election he received 99% of the vote in most 1st District wards.

The 1st District is the home of many powerful black politicians, including Washington's successor, Eugene Sawyer, and his rival, Aldermen Timothy Evans, but the winner of the 1983 special election to succeed Washington in the House was Charles Hayes. He comes out of the labor movement, and from a part of it that has a heritage of old-time indigenous radicalism. He was a vice president of the United Food and Commercial Workers Union, and was an official in the Amalgamated Meatcutters and Packinghouse Workers before they merged; he has been a union official since the 1940s and has been lobbying Congress for more than 20 years. In campaigns he supported insurgents like Metcalfe and Washington over the Democratic machine. In the House he serves on the Education and Labor Committee, where he is an automatic vote for more generous federal programs and against efforts to cut racial quotas. He is a pro-union stalwart, favoring a higher minimum wage and seeking restrictions on textile and apparel imports. He has bills to provide job training for poor young people and to discourage school dropouts—genuine problems on the South Side. He has a Quality of Life Action bill to guarantee a job at a decent standard-of-living wage to every American and an Economic Bill of Rights. Hayes has been fighting for what he regards as social justice for nearly 50 years, and if his views are unfashionable now he has seen them go out of fashion before and then return. In this, the most Democratic of congressional districts in national elections, he can be reelected with ease.

The People: Est. Pop. 1986: 503,700, dn. 3.0% 1980–86; Pop. 1980: 519,045, dn. 18.9% 1970–80. Households (1980): 63% family, 39% with children, 32% married couples; 72.1% housing units rented; median monthly rent: $183; median house value: $37,300. Voting age pop. (1980): 358,925; 90% Black, 1% Spanish origin, 1% Asian origin.

1988 Presidential Vote:

Dukakis (D)	174,793	(95%)
Bush (R)	7,168	(4%)

Rep. Charles A. Hayes (D)

Elected 1983; b. Feb. 17, 1918, Cairo; home, Chicago; Baptist; married (Edna).

Career: Trade unionist; Intl. Vice Pres., Region 12, United Food and Commercial Workers Union, 1979–83.

Offices: 1028 LHOB 20515, 202-225-4372. Also 7801 S. Cottage Grove Ave., Chicago 60619, 312-783-6800.

Committees: *Education and Labor* (11th of 22 D). Subcommittees: Elementary, Secondary and Vocational Education; Labor-Management Relations; Labor Standards; Postsecondary Education. *Small Business* (16th of 27 D). Subcommittee: SBA, the General Economy and Minority Enterprise Development.

Group Ratings

	ADA	ACLU	COPE	CFA	LCV	ACU	NTLC	NSI	COC	CEI
1988	95	95	100	82	88	0	4	0	14	10
1987	100	—	100	93	—	0	—	—	7	4

National Journal Ratings

	1988 LIB — 1988 CONS		1987 LIB — 1987 CONS	
Economic	92%	— 0%	73%	— 0%
Social	86%	— 0%	78%	— 0%
Foreign	84%	— 0%	81%	— 0%

Key Votes

1) Homeless $	AGN	5) Ban Drug Test	AGN	9) SDI Research	AGN
2) Gephardt Amdt	FOR	6) Drug Death Pen	AGN	10) Ban Chem Weaps	FOR
3) Deficit Reduc	FOR	7) Handgun Sales	AGN	11) Aid to Contras	AGN
4) Kill Plnt Clsng Notice	AGN	8) Ban D.C. Abort $	AGN	12) Nuclear Testing	FOR

Election Results

1988 general	Charles A. Hayes (D)	164,125	(96%)	($145,905)
	Stephen J. Evans (R)	6,753	(4%)	($0)
1988 primary	Charles A. Hayes (D)	97,168	(87%)	
	Inez M. Garder (D)	13,930	(13%)	
1986 general	Charles A. Hayes (D)	122,376	(96%)	($136,347)
	Joseph C. Faulkner (R)	4,572	(3%)	

SECOND DISTRICT

The 2d Congressional District of Illinois forms a kind of *U* around the 1st District. In the days before World War II, this was a kind of white noose around the narrowly confined South Side black ghetto. Poles, Bohemians, and Lithuanians lived in neighborhoods like Slag Valley and the Island that sprouted up in grid streets amid the giant steel mills and the old Pullman factory around the city's artificial port in Lake Calumet. West of the Black Belt were Irish neighborhoods stretching parish to parish from south of the Back of the Yards area behind the Stockyards just up to the affluent Irish enclave of Morgan Park. Today Irish have long since left the western arm of the 2d District and the Jews have long since left the South Shore neighborhoods; blacks are moving southward into suburbs like Blue Island and Harvey which are now part of the district. Whites remain a majority only in the 10th ward, whose longtime Democratic ward leader and alderman, Edward Vrdolyak, was Mayor Harold Washington's most visible adversary in City Hall. Vrydolyak became a Republican and in 1988 supported George Bush—though the 10th ward still went for Michael Dukakis.

The 2d District now has a large black majority and since 1980 has had a black congressman, Gus Savage. He is temperamentally a rebel and has made a career running against Chicago's Democratic machine and against white politicians. For 25 years he ran a community newspaper and attacked the powers that be. He ran against Congressman Morgan Murphy in 1970, in a district whose white majority was just then vanishing; when Murphy retired in 1980, Savage ran again and won. He was an early backer of Harold Washington for mayor. His record in the House has been distinctive—and not usually positively so. In his first few years he was absent for many votes. He filed blatantly incomplete disclosure statements with the Federal Election Commission, and then said it was the fault of his campaign treasurer whom he couldn't find—although the treasurer was his son. Another son, though he seemed to be holding down a full-time job in Chicago, found his way onto the payroll of District Delegate Walter Fauntroy. In 1987, by the inexorable workings of the seniority system, Savage became chairman of a subcommittee handling economic development and public works programs, and he cites his sponsorship of laws reauthorizing the Economic Development Act (EDA) and the Appalachian Redevelopment Act, renaming a Chicago federal building for Harold Washington, and setting up a minority set-aside program for defense contracts as evidence that he has become an active legislator. But just as often he distinguishes himself by casting lone votes: he was one of five congressmen who voted against banning oil imports from Iran in 1987, one of three who voted against the resolution sponsored by Detroit's John Conyers impeaching Judge Alcee Hastings, a black District Court Judge from Florida charged with bribery.

If Savage were simply a scamp or a lone dissenter, he would not merit much attention. But he has a nasty habit of associating with bigots. Black Muslim leader Louis Farrakhan has extolled him as "our fighter in Congress." In 1988 Savage went to the trouble of inviting to the Democratic National Convention as his "honored guest" Steve Cokely, the tardily fired former aide of Mayor Eugene Sawyer, who charged that Jewish doctors have been intentionally injecting black babies with the AIDS virus. Few other Members of Congress have had such close association with such vicious bigotry.

For all his claims of representing Chicago blacks, Savage's performances in primaries have been consistently unimpressive. In 1982 he won only 39%, against 35% and 20% for two rivals; in 1984 he had 45% to 22% for the strongest of four weak opponents; in 1986 he got 51% to 21% and 12% for the strongest contenders; in 1988 he managed 52% against 25% and 14%. It has been charged that once he gets one opponent he puts another into the race to dilute opposition, an old tactic used by politicians of all stripes; whether or not that's true, he has never much exceeded the magic 50% and, given the volatility of voter preferences in primaries, must be considered vulnerable to challenge in 1990 or after redistricting in 1992.

The People: Est. Pop. 1986: 530,600, up 2.2% 1980–86; Pop. 1980: 518,931, dn. 1.9% 1970–80. Households (1980): 78% family, 50% with children, 50% married couples; 44.0% housing units rented; median monthly rent: $190; median house value: $37,700. Voting age pop. (1980): 340,827; 66% Black, 7% Spanish origin.

1988 Presidential Vote:

Dukakis (D)	150,387	(84%)
Bush (R)	25,896	(15%)

Rep. Gus Savage (D)

Elected 1980; b. Oct. 30, 1925, Detroit, MI; home, Chicago; Roosevelt U., B.A. 1951; Kent Col. of Law, 1952–53; Baptist; widowed.

Career: Army, WWII; Journalist, 1954–79; Editor-Publisher, Citizen Commun. Newspapers, 1965–79.

Offices: 1121 LHOB 20515, 202-225-0773. Also 11434 S. Halsted St., Chicago 60628, 312-660-2000.

Committees: *Public Works and Transportation* (9th of 31 D). Subcommittees: Economic Development (Chairman); Public Buildings and Grounds; Water Resources; Surface Transportation. *Small Business* (10th of 27 D). Subcommittee: SBA, the General Economy, Minority Enterprise Development.

Group Ratings

	ADA	ACLU	COPE	CFA	LCV	ACU	NTLC	NSI	COC	CEI
1988	100	95	98	100	88	0	7	10	23	9
1987	100	—	98	86	—	0	—	—	0	4

National Journal Ratings

	1988 LIB — 1988 CONS		1987 LIB — 1987 CONS	
Economic	92%	0%	73%	0%
Social	86%	0%	78%	0%
Foreign	58%	41%	81%	0%

Key Votes

1) Homeless $	AGN	5) Ban Drug Test	—	9) SDI Research	AGN
2) Gephardt Amdt	FOR	6) Drug Death Pen	AGN	10) Ban Chem Weaps	FOR
3) Deficit Reduc	FOR	7) Handgun Sales	AGN	11) Aid to Contras	AGN
4) Kill Plnt Clsng Notice	AGN	8) Ban D.C. Abort $	AGN	12) Nuclear Testing	FOR

Election Results

1988 general	Gus Savage (D).....................	138,256	(83%)	($242,487)
	William T. Hespel (R)	28,831	(17%)	($6,392)
1988 primary	Gus Savage (D).....................	56,405	(52%)	
	Emil Jones, Jr. (D)	26,767	(25%)	
	Melvin J. (Mel) Reynolds (D)	14,641	(14%)	
	Others	9,730	(9%)	
1986 general	Gus Savage (D).....................	99,268	(84%)	($150,979)
	Ron Taylor (R)	19,146	(16%)	

THIRD DISTRICT

Southward and southwest, following the Rock Island and Illinois Central rail lines and the Dan Ryan Expressway, to outer city neighborhoods and past the Chicago city limits into suburbs that were started as little ethnic enclaves on the prairie—out that path have moved thousands of South Side Chicago white ethnics, and following them, its lines moving farther out each decade, is the 3d Congressional District of Illinois. The 3d District includes the heavily Irish and virtually all white neighborhoods from the gritty area around Marquette Park and Midway Airport to the mansions and Prairie architecture homes of Beverly Hills and Morgan Park, where affluent Irish-Americans live atop some of Chicago's few perceptible hills. In the suburbs the district runs west along 95th Street to white-collar communities like Oak Lawn, a comfortable but not lavish product of the 1950s. In the south, from Blue Island to Markham, are suburbs with a little more of a working-class cast to them, and with significant black populations in some cases. The 3d also swings east to take in parts of the comfortable white-collar suburbs of Homewood and South Holland.

Politically this is marginal territory. Ancestral political preferences are mostly Democratic, but this is culturally conservative territory, hostile to black politicians like Jesse Jackson and the late Mayor Harold Washington. But even as Democratic percentages have been declining in city and national contests, they have been rising in state and legislative elections, as middle-aged descendants of Irish Democrats take the place in suburb after suburb of elderly descendants of Protestant Republicans.

The 3d District is represented by Marty Russo, a Democrat who manages not only to embody the values and speak in the tones of his constituency but also to be an energetic and productive legislator in Washington. He was one of the many Democratic winners in the Watergate year of 1974, but he came to Congress not with Ivy League credentials or Washington experience, but with a degree from DePaul, the alma mater of many local pols, and after a brief career of scrambling upward in the political world of Chicago. He showed a knack for getting onto key committees—first Energy and Commerce, then Ways and Means and Budget. In his early terms in the House he became known for being responsive to lobbies from funeral directors eager to avoid federal regulation, to Chicago-based businesses in need of special tax treatment and to hospitals opposed to cost-containment proposals. But he has also been an active and sometimes aggressive deputy whip.

Russo has the Chicagoesque instinct that politics is a matter of personal connections. He was shrewd enough to attach himself to his fellow Chicagoan, Ways and Means Chairman Dan Rostenkowski, who likes to team up in best-ball matches with Russo, a scratch golfer. But he is also close to several young liberal sparkplugs, like his Capitol Hill roommates George Miller, Leon Panetta, and Charles Schumer, and he tends to vote with them on foreign as well as economic issues, though less often on cultural ones.

Russo does not have the demeanor of one over-encumbered with abstract convictions. But he played a significant role on the tax reform bill of 1985 and 1986, pushing through a minimum tax clause which he claims has netted $9 billion from corporations and otherwise acting as a capable lieutenant for Rostenkowski, who named him over 10 more senior members to that conference committee. He is an opponent of plastic guns and an advocate of forcing states to have a death penalty for copkillers—positions which may hurt with both conservative and liberal activists, but which help with his constituents. On Budget he is now the third ranking Democrat not far below his old friend, Chairman Leon Panetta.

It is not totally unrewarding work. Russo is a close friend of Rostenkowski and a link between the Ways and Means chairman and many of the active younger members. Both have kept their roots in Chicago and maintain rather modest standards of living there, but even in comparatively humble surroundings they are treated in restaurants or convention halls or on the street with the deference and respect that dukes and earls received on campaign with medieval armies. As a political warrior, Russo has been impressively successful as to deter conflict: he has not had a serious opponent since 1976. Redistricting may be a little dicey; this is a district that could be sliced up but, given Russo's clout, probably won't be. Barring that, Russo seems likely to continue to be an important—for many, a strategic—congressman for many years to come.

The People: Est. Pop. 1986: 517,200, dn. 0.4% 1980–86; Pop. 1980: 519,040, dn. 2.0% 1970–80. Households (1980): 78% family, 39% with children, 65% married couples; 25.2% housing units rented; median monthly rent: $238; median house value: $55,600. Voting age pop. (1980): 379,396; 5% Black, 3% Spanish origin, 1% Asian origin.

1988 Presidential Vote: Bush (R) 130,606   (58%)
Dukakis (D). 92,108   (41%)

Rep. Martin A. (Marty) Russo (D)

Elected 1974; b. Jan. 23, 1944, Chicago; home, S. Holland; De Paul U., B.A. 1965, J.D. 1967; Roman Catholic; married (Karen).

Career: Law Clerk for IL Appellate Ct. Judge John V. McCormack, 1967–68; Cook Cnty. Asst. State's Atty., 1971–73.

Offices: 2233 RHOB 20515, 202-225-5736. Also 10634 S. Cicero, Oak Lawn 60453, 312-353-8093.

Committees: *Budget* (3d of 21 D). Task Forces: Budget Process, Reconciliation and Enforcement (Chairman); Defense, Foreign Policy and Space. *Ways and Means* (12th of 23 D). Subcommittee: Trade.

Group Ratings

	ADA	ACLU	COPE	CFA	LCV	ACU	NTLC	NSI	COC	CEI
1988	80	62	80	82	63	28	31	0	46	24
1987	84	—	79	64	—	17	—	—	33	16

National Journal Ratings

	1988 LIB — 1988 CONS		1987 LIB — 1987 CONS	
Economic	67%	30%	62%	35%
Social	43%	55%	60%	39%
Foreign	79%	16%	81%	0%

Key Votes

1) Homeless $	AGN	5) Ban Drug Test	AGN	9) SDI Research	AGN
2) Gephardt Amdt	FOR	6) Drug Death Pen	FOR	10) Ban Chem Weaps	FOR
3) Deficit Reduc	AGN	7) Handgun Sales	AGN	11) Aid to Contras	AGN
4) Kill Plnt Clsng Notice	AGN	8) Ban D.C. Abort $	FOR	12) Nuclear Testing	FOR

Election Results

1988 general	Martin A. (Marty) Russo (D)...........	132,111	(62%)	($558,273)
	Joseph J. McCarthy (R)................	80,181	(38%)	($81,325)
1988 primary	Martin A. (Marty) Russo (D)...........	76,930	(91%)	
	Maurice E. Johnson (D)................	7,793	(9%)	
1986 general	Martin A. (Marty) Russo (D)..........	102,949	(66%)	($483,102)
	James M. Tierney (R).................	52,618	(34%)	($42,977)

FOURTH DISTRICT

The southern fringe of metropolitan Chicago—where the suburbs generated by the growth of the great city start to thin out and the vast prairies, punctuated by neat rectangular-block towns, begin—makes up the 4th Congressional District of Illinois. Its eastern end is anchored in suburbs directly south of Chicago's Lake Calumet industrial district: Calumet City, Lansing, Chicago Heights. In the center, west and south of the Cook County line, is Joliet; in the northwest, Aurora. These are little cities with histories of their own: Downstate cities, really, factory towns and marketplaces for the surrounding rich farmland. Settled by Yankees and Germans, they are hard working and prosperous, orderly and pious. Historically they saw Chicago—with its rapid, disorderly growth, its tolerance of graft and vice, its vast peasant immigrant populations—as a cultural enemy; as solid Republicans, they have seen Democratic Chicago since the 1930s as a political enemy as well. Yet as white ethnics from the South Side of Chicago move farther out each generation, these communities are changing. Demographically they are becoming part of the Chicago metropolitan area, as the land between the old towns fills up with subdivisions, and politically they are becoming, if not reliably, Democratic.

This 4th District is one of a handful that the Democrats captured from the Republicans in 1988, and their victory owes something to special circumstances. The first is that the Republican that was beaten, Jack Davis, did not have the normal strength of incumbency. Davis was chosen in 1986 not in a primary but afterwards, in a party convention held after Congressman George O'Brien, fatally ill with cancer, resigned. An active Democrat, 28-year-old Shawn Collins, was already in the field, and although he was asked to step aside for his former boss, legislator George Sangmeister, he declined. Sangmeister at that point was known nationally for having lost the nomination for lieutenant governor in March 1986 to a follower of Lyndon LaRouche—a loss that may have cost the Democrats the governorship that fall—but he had long been well-known and remained popular in the Joliet area. Collins drew 48% of the vote against Davis; and Sangmeister lined up to run against Davis in 1988.

And so he did, running a well enough organized and active campaign to expunge the embarrassment of 1986. Davis could point to some accomplishments: he was one of the few Armed Services Committee members who favored using the military to enforce drug laws (most, from their years of experience, felt the military was inappropriate for this duty), he supported the new cabinet-level Veterans Affairs Department (ultimately to be headed by Edward Derwinski, who once represented the Cook County portion of the district, and after redistricting lost the 1982 primary to O'Brien), and championed a third Chicago airport near Joliet. But Sangmeister tied Davis to charges made by Republicans against local officeholders in Will County and accused Davis of illegal campaign spending in 1986. This turned out to be a bitter and negative battle between two men who had been top-rated legislators. Sangmeister was able to take advantage of his Joliet area base and to hold down Davis's vote in the Cook County portion of the district enough to win by about 1,000 votes. Given this performance against an incumbent and the probable Democratic trend in this outer edge of the metropolitan area, Sangmeister ought to be favored in 1990, but he could face a serious contest.

The People: Est. Pop. 1986: 528,700, up 1.9% 1980–86; Pop. 1980: 519,049, up 13.9% 1970–80. Households (1980): 79% family, 46% with children, 66% married couples; 28.6% housing units rented; median monthly rent: $221; median house value: $54,400. Voting age pop. (1980): 356,524; 10% Black, 5% Spanish origin, 1% Asian origin.

1988 Presidential Vote:

Bush (R)	103,720	(55%)
Dukakis (D)	82,662	(44%)

Rep. George E. Sangmeister (D)

Elected 1988; b. Feb. 16, 1931, Frankfort; home, Mokena; Elmhurst Col., B.A. 1957, John Marshall Law Sch., J.D. 1960; Lutheran; married (Doris).

Career: Army 1951–53; Practicing atty., 1960–87; State's Att., 1964–68; IL House of Reps., 1972–76; IL Senate, 1976–87.

Offices: 1607 LHOB 20515, 202-225-3635. Also 101 N. Joliet St., Joliet 60431, 815-740-2040; 274 Centre, Park Forest 60406; and 64 A Eastdowner Pl., Aurora 60505, 312-854-3554.

Committees: *Judiciary* (21st of 21 D). Subcommittees: Courts, Intelligence Property, and the Administration of Justice; Criminal Justice. *Veterans' Affairs* (18th of 21 D). Subcommittees: Compensation, Pension and Insurance; Education, Training and Employment.

Group Ratings and Key Votes: Newly Elected

Election Results

1988 general	George E. Sangmeister (D)	91,282	(50%)	($359,942)
	Jack Davis (R)	90,243	(50%)	($348,339)
1988 primary	George E. Sangmeister (D)	27,064	(78%)	
	George M. Laurence (D)	7,537	(22%)	
1986 general	Jack Davis (R)	61,633	(52%)	($272,420)
	Shawn Collins (D)	57,925	(48%)	($203,760)

FIFTH DISTRICT

If the Loop is the heart of Chicago and the University of Chicago its brains, the South Branch of the Chicago River is its guts. This is the site of one of western civilization's astonishing engineering feats: here in 1900 the course of the river was turned backward, so that sewage flowed downstate through a canal rather than out into Lake Michigan. The river wards—the old name for the neighborhoods along the river—performed an historic function, as important for Chicago as the Sanitary and Ship Canal: they provided a home for successive waves of immigrants from almost every quarter of Europe, the Mediterranean, and, more recently, Latin America. Work could be found nearby on the docks, in warehouses and factories, on the railroads, or on the canal itself. So the Jews came to Maxwell Street, the Czechs to Pilsen, the Irish to Bridgeport, the Italians near Halsted Street, where Jane Addams built Hull House.

358   ILLINOIS

These neighborhoods that were the guts of the city were essential to the success of the city's Democratic machine. Their residents needed the patronage jobs and the buckets of coal and turkeys the precinct committeeman or ward leader would supply at Christmas; and in return they were happy to give the Democratic ticket their votes. And more, so some people charged, since the river wards tended to report their vote totals late, and had a habit of supplying the Democratic ticket with almost exactly the margin it needed to prevail. Now that has changed. North of the river most residents are Mexican-Americans, and voter turnout is low. South of the river neighborhoods retain their Irish flavor; Archer Avenue, the diagonal that heads out toward Midway Airport, remains the path of outward migration of the South Side Irish. Even close-in Bridgeport and the Back of the Yards (the stockyards) area remain mostly white and Irish; Richard M. Daley still lives three blocks from where he grew up as the son of the mayor. But most families are older now and there are fewer freckle-faced kids.

The 5th Congressional District includes wards on both sides of the river and extends into suburban communities on both sides of the canal out to the Cook County line. Demographically, it is increasingly Mexican—21% of its adults and 40% of its children in 1980 were Hispanic. But politically, the older ethnic neighborhoods in the city and the close-in suburbs cast almost all the votes. This is not exactly a machine area any more—there hasn't been a single, coherent Democratic machine since Richard J. Daley died in 1976—and its city voters are not much more enthused about the national Democratic party than are voters in the gritty ancestrally Republican suburbs of Cicero and Berwyn. What they have in common is a sense of patriotism, a fear of blacks that can produce acts of bigotry when they move into the neighborhood or (as happened recently) join the Cicero police force, and a dislike of cultural liberalism.

The 5th District's Congressman, William Lipinski, is in line with most district attitudes. He started off as a parks patronage employee, was elected alderman, was slated for Congress against an aging incumbent and beat him 61%–36% in the 1982 primary. He serves on nuts-and-bolts committees (Public Works, Merchant Marine) and has spent much effort getting a southwest Chicago rail transit line built to Midway Airport—he even lobbied President Reagan on the subject. He is proud of his position as co-chairman of the national Democrats' Council on Ethnic Americans, and makes speeches lauding family values, opposing Libyan terrorism, and noting the advance of democracy around the world. His record on foreign and cultural issues is rather conservative; on economics he is more inclined to go along with liberal Democrats, but not always. He has been reelected by comfortable majorities, although his percentage fell somewhat abruptly in 1988 while George Bush was carrying the district.

The People: Est. Pop. 1986: 527,500, up 1.6% 1980–86; Pop. 1980: 518,971, dn. 2.7% 1970–80. Households (1980): 73% family, 37% with children, 56% married couples; 47.9% housing units rented; median monthly rent: $161; median house value: $52,600. Voting age pop. (1980): 377,195; 21% Spanish origin, 3% Black, 2% Asian origin.

1988 Presidential Vote: Bush (R) 83,892   (51%)
Dukakis (D) 77,783   (48%)

Rep. William O. Lipinski (D)

Elected 1982; b. Dec. 22, 1937, Chicago; home, Chicago; Loras Col., 1956–57; Roman Catholic; married (Rose Marie).

Career: Army Reserves, 1961–67; Chicago Parks and Recreation Dept., 1958–75; Chicago City Alderman, 1975–83.

Offices: 1032 LHOB 20515, 202-225-5701. Also 5832 S. Archer Ave., Chicago 60638, 312-886-0481.

Committees: *Merchant Marine and Fisheries* (10th of 26 D). Subcommittees: Panama Canal/Outer Continental Shelf; Merchant Marine. *Public Works and Transportation* (15th of 31 D). Subcommittees: Aviation; Investigations and Oversight; Surface Transportation.

Group Ratings

	ADA	ACLU	COPE	CFA	LCV	ACU	NTLC	NSI	COC	CEI
1988	55	58	92	64	75	35	22	78	45	15
1987	56	—	91	86	—	16	—	—	46	10

National Journal Ratings

	1988 LIB — 1988 CONS	1987 LIB — 1987 CONS
Economic	79% — 17%	61% — 39%
Social	53% — 47%	64% — 35%
Foreign	40% — 60%	43% — 57%

Key Votes

1) Homeless $	AGN	5) Ban Drug Test	AGN	9) SDI Research	FOR
2) Gephardt Amdt	FOR	6) Drug Death Pen	FOR	10) Ban Chem Weaps	AGN
3) Deficit Reduc	—	7) Handgun Sales	AGN	11) Aid to Contras	FOR
4) Kill Plnt Clsng Notice	AGN	8) Ban D.C. Abort $	FOR	12) Nuclear Testing	AGN

Election Results

1988 general	William O. Lipinski (D)	93,567	(61%)	($165,144)
	John J. Halowinski (R)	59,128	(39%)	($48,940)
1988 primary	William O. Lipinski, unopposed			
1986 general	William O. Lipinski (D)	82,466	(70%)	($152,573)
	Daniel John Sobieski (R)	34,738	(30%)	($11,303)

SIXTH DISTRICT

Half a century ago the land that is now Chicago's O'Hare Airport was an airstrip in an apple orchard (hence its current three-letter code: ORD) and the towns beyond were little suburban villages strung along rail lines, separated by cornfields. But in the 1950s, Mayor Richard J. Daley decided that Chicago needed a new airport, annexed the orchard, and named it after a World War II hero from a good Chicago Irish Catholic Democratic family. Today O'Hare is surrounded on all sides by suburbs as densely settled as the bungalow wards of the city, with hotels and office buildings clustered near the interchanges in Rosemont and other tiny suburbs with as much square footage as many American downtowns. The 6th Congressional District of Illinois, looking from the Loop, starts at O'Hare and spreads north to Park Ridge, Des Plaines, and Mount Prospect on the Chicago and Northwestern line and west through Elmhurst, Villa Park, Lombard, and Glen Ellyn on the Chicago & North Western lines running directly west. This is high income, almost all white, mostly but by no means exclusively WASP suburbia. Economically, it is market-oriented; politically, hostile to the Chicago Democratic machine; culturally, tradition-minded but with some ambivalence: this district has one of the highest percentages of working women in the nation. In partisan terms, it is one of the most heavily Republican districts in the nation.

This is the district that elects Henry Hyde, one of the Republicans' most competent and motivated legislators. He comes from hard-bitten Illinois, but he acts from deep belief more than political calculation. In time that often proves to be good politics. In the 1970s, for example, when abortion was hailed as a form of personal liberation and as science's answer to overpopulation, Hyde began proposing his amendments prohibiting the use of federal funds to pay for abortions in various circumstances. Most congressmen regarded this as a time-wasting diversion; Hyde, who regards abortion as murder, thought the issue was central. He brought not only dedication to his task, but ingenuity, attaching his amendments to all manner of bills. By the early 1980s, the House was routinely passing Hyde Amendments; and the number of federally-funded abortions was close to zero.

Since then, Hyde has made a difference on a variety of issues, and increasingly on foreign policy from his seat on the Foreign Affairs Committee and on the Intelligence Committee, on which he is now the ranking Republican (and which he would like to see folded into a joint House-Senate committee). He brings to his work intellectual honesty: he changed his position on the Voting Rights Act in 1982 because hearings convinced him it needed reauthorization. He brings a gift for invective: he called the SALT II treaty a "paper pussycat," and to the opponents of aid to the Nicaraguan contras—one of his favorite causes—he said that history "is going to assign to you Democrats the role of pallbearers at the funeral of democracy in Central America." He is politically fearless: he took on the nuclear freeze advocates in 1983, and by forcing them to defend in detail their attractive-sounding proposal, derailed it. He gives his adversaries the compliment of taking them seriously, by going to the trouble of finding out what they've said on issues in the past and quoting it back to them: he cited Stephen Solarz's prediction 10 years before that the Soviets would leave Angola if we didn't support their opponents, and quoted John Kennedy and Hubert Humphrey to Democrats arguing for a comprehensive test ban treaty. He has an aversion to the political cheap shot: he stands up and supports foreign aid, including money for international agencies, when members of right and left vote against it or encumber it with restrictions. He studies his facts and lets the chips fall where they may: on the Iran-contra committee he declined to draw the same self-righteous conclusions the Democrats did, but readily admitted that in trying to make a deal with the Iranians the Administration had gone awry.

Hyde's actions seem to stem from deep religious beliefs combined with a trial lawyer's combative instincts, a respect for rules combined with a certain compassion. Touched, apparently, by Barney Frank's jab that right-to-lifers cared about a child's quality of life from conception to birth, Hyde has gone out of his way to support programs to improve children's nutrition and to make sure that fathers support their children. He took the lead in pushing through a bill providing Medicaid for prenatal medical care and food stamps for pregnant women, and is co-sponsor with Henry Waxman of measures to reduce infant mortality. Congressmen who oppose abortion, Hyde says, should "consider whether we do not also have a positive obligation to protect a baby's life and health beyond the action of simply prohibiting abortion." He is sensitive to the burdens of obligation and responsibility: in 1984 he took the lead when Mario Cuomo argued at Notre Dame that in a pluralistic society Catholics should not seek to put their views on abortion into law. Hyde went to Notre Dame and argued that they have the obligation to do as much as they can within the limits of representative government. Citing a commitment to basic American principles, Hyde also strongly supporting the bill compensating Japanese Americans interned during World War II, legislation floor-managed by Barney Frank.

Hyde's zeal is sometimes impolitic, and he has lost out on leadership positions in the past. But Republican Leader Robert Michel did not hesitate to put him on the special panel investigating the Iran-contra scandal. Hyde started out in the House as a kind of gadfly but is now one of its most responsible Republican members, grappling honestly with major issues of policy, aggressively and yet at the same time with good humor. Like Ronald Reagan, Hyde grew up an Illinois Democrat and he retains many of the cultural attitudes of New Deal era Democrats while espousing the views of a Reagan era Republican. He first ran for Congress as long ago as 1962, losing in Chicago to Roman Pucinski; he served six years in the legislature and ran for the House in 1974, beating Black Panther prosecutor Edward Hanrahan. Hyde has been reelected since without difficulty as his district has moved farther out into the suburbs.

The People: Est. Pop. 1986: 541,700, up 4.4% 1980–86; Pop. 1980: 519,015, up 19.4% 1970–80. Households (1980): 79% family, 44% with children, 70% married couples; 24.4% housing units rented; median monthly rent: $293; median house value: $76,000. Voting age pop. (1980): 367,916; 3% Spanish origin, 2% Asian origin, 1% Black.

1988 Presidential Vote:

Bush (R)	147,384	(68%)
Dukakis (D).	67,355	(31%)

Rep. Henry J. Hyde (R)

Elected 1974; b. Apr. 18, 1924, Chicago; home, Bensenville; Georgetown U., B.S. 1947, Loyola U., J.D. 1949; Roman Catholic; married (Jeanne).

Career: Navy, WWII; Practicing atty., 1950–75; IL House of Reps., 1967–74, Major. Ldr., 1971–72.

Offices: 2104 RHOB 20515, 202-225-4561. Also 50 East Oak St., Addison 60101, 312-832-5950.

Committees: *Foreign Affairs* (7th of 18 R). Subcommittees: Arms Control, International Security and Science; Western Hemisphere Affairs. *Judiciary* (3d of 14 R). Subcommittees: Courts, Civil Liberties, and the Administration of Justice; Economic and Commercial Law. *Permanent Select Committee on Intelligence* (Ranking Member of 6 R). Subcommittee: Program and Budget Authorization.

Group Ratings

	ADA	ACLU	COPE	CFA	LCV	ACU	NTLC	NSI	COC	CEI
1988	15	23	15	27	19	92	66	100	100	59
1987	8	—	16	29	—	96	—	—	100	73

National Journal Ratings

	1988 LIB — 1988 CONS			1987 LIB — 1987 CONS		
Economic	19%	—	80%	0%	—	89%
Social	19%	—	81%	22%	—	78%
Foreign	0%	—	84%	0%	—	80%

Key Votes

1) Homeless $	FOR	5) Ban Drug Test	FOR	9) SDI Research	FOR
2) Gephardt Amdt	AGN	6) Drug Death Pen	FOR	10) Ban Chem Weaps	AGN
3) Deficit Reduc	AGN	7) Handgun Sales	AGN	11) Aid to Contras	FOR
4) Kill Plnt Clsng Notice	FOR	8) Ban D.C. Abort $	FOR	12) Nuclear Testing	AGN

Election Results

1988 general	Henry J. Hyde (R)	153,425	(74%)	($281,229)
	William J. Andrle (D)................	54,804	(26%)	($26,555)
1988 primary	Henry J. Hyde (R), unopposed			
1986 general	Henry J. Hyde (R)	98,196	(75%)	($229,898)
	Robert H. Renshaw (D)	32,064	(25%)	($6,378)

SEVENTH DISTRICT

In Chicago's Loop 100 years ago architects like Louis Sullivan and Daniel Burnham designed high-rise buildings and invented the American downtown. By the 1940s, the Loop—named in 1897 for the circle the El forms around the city's center—had as dazzling a set of skyscrapers as any city but New York, and by the 1970s, the John Hancock and Sears Towers enabled Chicago to claim once again the world's highest building. Running north from the Loop are the luxury shopping and office districts along North Michigan Avenue and the vast parks (including the railroad lines they all but conceal) along Lake Michigan. This is the face Chicago likes to present to the world: the giant buildings rising where the prairies meet the inland sea, a vast concentration of brains and muscle, the nerve center of the nation.

Behind the lakefront, Chicago has not always been so dazzling: the nation's largest skid row developed on West Madison, only blocks west of State, and a few blocks inland from North Michigan is the Cabrini-Green housing project where Mayor Jane Byrne once made news by spending the night. In the 1980s, many blocks on all sides of the Loop have been gentrified, but renovation has not reached the bedraggled West Side black ghetto. Blacks who do well may stay on the South Side, but West Side blacks who do well tend to get out as fast as they can. Farther west, there are more contrasts: cross Austin Boulevard and you come to the suburb of Oak Park, middle-class since Ernest Hemingway grew up there 80 years ago, and now integrated. Just beyond is River Forest, with grander streets and bigger lots; both Oak Park and River Forest contain a number of Frank Lloyd Wright houses. Still further out are Maywood, a black-majority suburb, and the modest working-class suburb of Bellwood.

Taken together, these disparate areas make up Illinois's 7th Congressional District. It has a solid black majority and is represented in the House by Democrat Cardiss Collins. She cuts a different figure than she did when she was first elected in 1973, to fill the seat vacated when her husband died in a plane crash; he had been a routine machine backer and she was expected to be the same. But Cardiss Collins was a voluble and independent chairman of the Black Caucus in 1979 and 1980; she serves on Energy and Commerce, the most sought after assignment for House Democrats; she has been an active Government Operations subcommittee chairman. Collins has concentrated on issues that affect her constituents: establishing health clinics in high schools and getting Medicare coverage for cancer tests, providing day care in government buildings and establishing GSA set-asides for minority contractors and businessmen.

Collins had some political problems, in the 1980s, dating back to her endorsement of Jane Byrne over her then-House colleague Harold Washington in the 1983 mayoral primary. It was a plausible thing to do: Washington started off a weak candidate (he received only 11% of the vote four years before) and Byrne had genuine black support (she ended up with 20% of the black vote). But the enthusiasm almost all Chicago blacks felt after Washington's victory spelled trouble for Collins. In the next two elections she had primary opposition from Alderman Danny Davis, a Washington supporter. In 1984, she beat him 48%–39%; in 1986, 60%–40%—not impressive scores for an incumbent. In 1987 she backed Washington and later that year he died; she had only weak opposition in 1988 and seems to have a much stronger hold on the district now.

The People: Est. Pop. 1986: 508,200, dn. 2.1% 1980–86; Pop. 1980: 519,034, dn. 15.8% 1970–80. Households (1980): 65% family, 42% with children, 36% married couples; 67.0% housing units rented; median monthly rent: $184; median house value: $54,500. Voting age pop. (1980): 343,964; 60% Black, 4% Spanish origin, 2% Asian origin.

1988 Presidential Vote:

Dukakis (D)	132,656	(77%)
Bush (R)	38,432	(22%)

Rep. Cardiss Collins (D)

Elected 1973; b. Sept. 24, 1931, St. Louis, MO; home, Chicago; Northwestern U.; Baptist; widowed.

Career: Stenographer, IL Dept. of Labor; Secy., Accountant, and Revenue Auditor, IL Dept. of Revenue.

Offices: 2264 RHOB 20515, 202-225-5006. Also 230 S. Dearborn St., Ste. 3880, Chicago 60604, 312-353-5754; and 328 West Lake, Oak Park 60302, 312-383-1400.

Committees: *Energy and Commerce* (11th of 26 D). Subcommittees: Oversight and Investigations; Health and the Environment; Telecommunications and Finance. *Government Operations* (2d of 24 D). Subcommittee: Government Activities and Transportation (Chairman). *Select Committee on Narcotics Abuse and Control* (5th of 15 D).

Group Ratings

	ADA	ACLU	COPE	CFA	LCV	ACU	NTLC	NSI	COC	CEI
1988	90	100	95	82	81	0	5	0	21	9
1987	92	—	95	86	—	0	—	—	0	4

National Journal Ratings

	1988 LIB — 1988 CONS			1987 LIB — 1987 CONS		
Economic	92%	—	0%	73%	—	0%
Social	86%	—	0%	69%	—	30%
Foreign	84%	—	0%	81%	—	0%

Key Votes

1) Homeless $	AGN	5) Ban Drug Test	—	9) SDI Research	AGN
2) Gephardt Amdt	FOR	6) Drug Death Pen	AGN	10) Ban Chem Weaps	FOR
3) Deficit Reduc	FOR	7) Handgun Sales	—	11) Aid to Contras	AGN
4) Kill Plnt Clsng Notice	AGN	8) Ban D.C. Abort $	AGN	12) Nuclear Testing	FOR

Election Results

1988 general	Cardiss Collins (D), unopposed			($127,487)
1988 primary	Cardiss Collins (D)	69,624	(89%)	
	Keith A. Klopfenstein (R)	8,408	(11%)	
1986 general	Cardiss Collins (D)	90,761	(80%)	($233,583)
	Caroline K. Kallas (R)	21,055	(19%)	($9,302)

EIGHTH DISTRICT

As polyglot a district as you can find in the nation is the 8th Congressional District of Illinois. This is a large chunk of the North Side of Chicago, with a couple of square miles of suburbs added on in 1982. For more than 100 years it has been home to immigrants and refugees from around the world. It is in particular a Polish-American district. As long ago as 1876, you could hear Polish spoken more often than English in the neighborhoods near Holy Trinity and St. Stanislaus Kostka—there are always two main Polish churches, it seems—and today you still can. In Chicago, ethnic groups tend to move out radial avenues, and the Polish have moved out along Milwaukee Avenue, which parallels the Kennedy Expressway and the North Branch of the Chicago River; Italians tended to move out along Grand Avenue, to the point that there are now more Italians in the suburbs than in the city; Ukrainians have their main churches and community in between. Following roughly in the same footsteps have been Mexican-Americans and Puerto Ricans. The 8th District's adult population in 1980 was 25% of Spanish origin; its under 18 population was 48% of Spanish origin. There are, by the way, virtually no blacks here. The boundary between the 7th and 8th Districts pretty closely tracks neighborhood racial barriers, and Mexican-Americans, here as elsewhere, seem to seek out white working-class rather than black neighborhoods.

In a comfortable but modest house looking across Pulaski park and at St. Stanislaus Kostka lives longtime 32d ward committeeman (he gave up the post in 1987) Dan Rostenkowski, who has also served as the 8th District's congressman for three decades and who, as Chairman of the House Ways and Means Committee since 1981, is one of the nation's most powerful and also one of its most productive legislators. Not many would have predicted that when he started off, the son of a ward committeeman who was elected to the state legislature when he was 24. But in a city where aldermen are considered the real power and where going to Washington is seen as a demotion or as an award to an elderly placeholder, Rostenkowski early on wanted to go to Congress, accumulate seniority, and become a national power; and when the local congressman retired in 1958, Rostenkowski at age 30 sold Mayor Daley on the idea. Rostenkowski rose over the years in the House, getting the Chicago seat on Ways and Means because at that time its Democratic members made their parties' committee assignments, winning and then in 1971 losing the post of Democratic Caucus chairman, becoming chief deputy whip after endorsing long-shot Jim Wright (he won by 1 vote) for majority leader in 1976. Much of his attention was directed at Chicago politics; he used to boast that he had spent fewer than a dozen weekends in Washington, and for years it was rumored that he might run for mayor.

Then in 1980 Al Ullman was defeated for reelection, and Rostenkowski had his choice of becoming Ways and Means chairman or majority whip. After some hesitation, he took Ways and Means. He started off badly. In 1981, his first year in the post, he seemed determined above all else to have his name on the tax bill that passed the House, and so he bid for the support of all manner of lobbies by letting them tack their favorite provisions on his bill—and lost anyway. For much of 1982 he lay low. Despite the constitutional requirement that revenue measures originate in the House—a provision that has been the source of much of Ways and Means's traditional power—he let the Senate pass the 1982 tax bill and then mostly went along with it.

Then he emerged as an active leader. He managed the 1983 Social Security rescue measure and supported a bill to cap the third year of the Reagan tax cut for high-income taxpayers. He helped lead the House to its prompt passage of budget and tax bills in 1984. What tied together most of his stands was his institutional interest, as chairman, in supporting his subcommittee chairmen. This rough-hewn politico proved in markups and in conference committees that he could master the technical details of legislation, line up solid majorities on his side, and out-negotiate just about anyone. He got comfortable with his post, and with taking risks.

He also developed what few people expected in a Chicago pol—some philosophical positions and what must be called a patriotic desire to make good public policy. Little else can explain why Rostenkowski embraced the tax reform proposal advanced by Bill Bradley and sponsored originally in the House by Richard Gephardt (Rostenkowski quickly saw to it that Gephardt, a Ways and Means member then running for President, got a low profile on the issue). For by cutting rates and eliminating preferences, this reform promised to destory much of the institutional power of his committee. And it was a bill that almost no one thought could pass. But Rostenkowski decided that the country was ripe for tax reform, that the Democratic Congress should get or share the credit, and—something entirely new for him—he went on TV in the spring of 1985 and asked voters to "write Rosty." Not a lawyer, not even a college graduate, and not generally considered a tax expert, he nonetheless brilliantly brokered the bill through his committee, recovered when the Republicans voted down the rule needed to get it on the floor, and got it passed by the House in December 1985. He made it a chairman's issue, on which he expected support from his subcommittee chairmen in return for the support he had given them (when Gibbons, number two on the committee, didn't back him up reliably, Rostenkowski coolly kept him off the conference committee). He stayed in touch with Bradley as the bill moved, stalled, then rushed through the Senate, and then in the conference committee had the upper hand. The House conferees were picked carefully so that Rostenkowski always could rely on every House Democrat; senior Ways and Means Republicans, none of them strong, he treated with contempt, and the word is that they learned what the conference decided by reading the papers the next morning. Senate Finance Chairman Bob Packwood lacked similar assurance about his conferees, and so Rostenkowski carried most of the points.

Rostenkowski has not topped this performance in the years since, but neither has anyone else. He has remained a busy chairman and a principled one. He resisted Ed Jenkins's textile restriction bill, and he fought for freer trade provisions in the trade bill passed in 1988; thanks largely to Rostenkowski and Senate Finance Chairman Lloyd Bentsen, the Democratic Congress was not swept along to pass the demagogic trade restriction bill many of the party's political consultants were urging. Rostenkowski also stood with John Dingell—another committee chairman, another Polish-American, another son of a successful politician (and of course with all this in common they don't usually get along)—and opposed Claude Pepper's long-term health care bill, backing Ways and Means's Pete Stark's catastrophic bill instead. Stark's bill had a payment mechanism, while Pepper was airily unconcerned about cost; Rostenkowski and Dingell got enough Democrats to go along with them—many of them members of their committees—to prevail.

What will Rostenkowski do next? He has ruled out running for Speaker or mayor for the time being, and probably forever. He has more than $1 million in his campaign treasury, and has shown restraint in not adding, as he easily could, millions more, which he can under law convert to personal funds when he leaves office; but, in his early 60s, he shows no sign of retiring. He likes a comfortable lifestyle—steak dinners at Morton's of Chicago, golf in Palm Springs and Boca Raton—and he has urged a sliding scale of pay for congressmen, saying he'd take the top dollar. He does not seem to care, though, about getting really rich. So the likelihood is that he will stay in the House and remain Chairman of Ways and Means. The 8th District as currently constituted will reelect him easily, and even if more of its Hispanics vote it seems inconceivable that they would want to pitch Rostenkowski out. Redistricting could conceivably be a problem, for one of the North Side districts in Chicago could easily be extinguished. But it is unlikely to be Rostenkowski's; the more likely chance is that Sidney Yates of the 9th District or Frank Annunzio of the 11th, both considerably older than Rostenkowski, would take the occasion to retire.

The People: Est. Pop. 1986: 521,200, up 0.4% 1980–86; Pop. 1980: 519,034, dn. 9.3% 1970–80. Households (1980): 68% family, 36% with children, 49% married couples; 61.3% housing units rented; median monthly rent: $174; median house value: $51,500. Voting age pop. (1980): 375,186; 25% Spanish origin, 3% Black, 2% Asian origin.

1988 Presidential Vote: Dukakis (D)...................... 92,135   (59%)
Bush (R) 63,885   (41%)

Rep. Dan Rostenkowski (D)

Elected 1958; b. Jan. 2, 1928, Chicago; home, Chicago; Loyola U., 1948–51; Roman Catholic; married (LaVerne).

Career: Army, Korea; IL House of Reps., 1953–55; IL Senate, 1955–59.

Offices: 2111 RHOB 20515, 202-225-4061. Also 2148 N. Damen Ave., Chicago 60647, 312-431-1111.

Committees: *Ways and Means* (Chairman of 23 D). Subcommittee: Trade. *Joint Committee on Taxation* (Chairman).

Group Ratings

	ADA	ACLU	COPE	CFA	LCV	ACU	NTLC	NSI	COC	CEI
1988	65	61	87	73	38	19	13	22	50	13
1987	72	—	87	64	—	18	—	—	22	12

National Journal Ratings

	1988 LIB — 1988 CONS	1987 LIB — 1987 CONS
Economic	60% — 37%	65% — 34%
Social	56% — 43%	55% — 45%
Foreign	55% — 45%	70% — 30%

Key Votes

1) Homeless $	AGN	5) Ban Drug Test	—	9) SDI Research	—
2) Gephardt Amdt	AGN	6) Drug Death Pen	FOR	10) Ban Chem Weaps	AGN
3) Deficit Reduc	FOR	7) Handgun Sales	—	11) Aid to Contras	AGN
4) Kill Plnt Clsng Notice	AGN	8) Ban D.C. Abort $	FOR	12) Nuclear Testing	—

Election Results

1988 general	Dan Rostenkowski (D)	107,726	(75%)	($428,607)
	V. Stephen Vetter (R)	34,659	(25%)	($0)
1988 primary	Dan Rostenkowski (D), unopposed			
1986 general	Dan Rostenkowski (D)	82,873	(79%)	($240,208)
	Thomas J. DeFazio (R)................	22,383	(21%)	

NINTH DISTRICT

There are few more dramatic panoramas of the works of man and nature than where Lake Michigan meets Chicago. Along the lakefront, behind the glorious parks that Daniel Burnham built early in this century, is one of the world's great collection of high-rise buildings. North of the skyscrapers of the Loop and the Near North Side are a row of apartment buildings, some the austere works of the masters of the International style, some in traditional styles evocative of some other place and time, some sleek works of the 1920s and 1930s. Lapping up against these buildings for some months in 1987 was the water—or the ice—of the Lake. Great Lakes levels reached a record high, beaches were eroded to nothing, sidewalks were flooded or covered with ice floes, and people wondered whether some high-rises would be undermined. Then in 1988 the lake levels fell again—no one knows just why.

Behind the apartment towers, however, is another Chicago—yeastier, grimier, more diverse. This is the Chicago of Studs Terkel's *Division Street*, a city full of life's losers and winners; of Saul Bellow, a city of successful small businessmen and irrationally vengeful hoodlums; of Nelson Algren, a city of drug addicts and drifters. Young professionals and gays are renovating old houses, Mexican-Americans and Asians are filling old apartment flats, blacks are moving here and there while white ethnics remain ensconced in some neighborhoods where they've lived for generations. This is the Chicago of Illinois's 9th Congressional District that begins at the Near North Side and follows the lakefront, and the varied neighborhoods just to the west, to Chicago's northern city limits and beyond into Evanston, the home of Northwestern University, and heavily Jewish Skokie, where the ACLU once defended Nazis' right to march. This district has far more singles and far more Jews than any other Chicago district; if the lakefront is not as liberal as cliche has it, it is far more so than any other part of the city. In mayoral elections, the lakefront wards have held the balance of power, giving Harold Washington enough votes to win in 1983 and 1987 and voting overwhelmingly for Richard M. Daley in 1989.

The 9th District's congressman, Sidney Yates, started representing Chicago lakefront wards 40 years ago; only Claude Pepper and Jamie Whitten in the current Congress were serving when he was first elected in 1948. But he lost seniority because he ran against Senator Everett Dirksen in 1962, and nearly beat him; he was returned to the House in 1964. Even if he had stayed, he would not yet chair Appropriations (Whitten does), and he has not gravitated to the big money issues. Instead he chairs the Appropriations Interior Subcommittee and concentrates on environmental issues and on federal support of the arts and humanities. He is a kind of federal Maecenas, and has nurtured the national endowments for arts, humanities, and historic preservation, not just by giving them money, but by breathing into them something more than bureaucratic life. He also takes care of local matters, working to get federal dollars to rehabilitate Chicago's Navy Pier, trying to do something to save the lakefront from the Lake. Only an appropriations subcommittee chairman would consider it part of his duty as well as clearly within his power to hold back the rising floods of one-quarter of the fresh water in the world.

Yates's political base has always been in Chicago's Jewish community, and he has been a spokesman for national Jewish causes; he is proud that he was one of the Members of Congress (Henry Jackson was another) who took on the cause of promoting Hyman Rickover to Admiral, and won over those in the Navy who feared his unorthodox ideas and perhaps disliked his ethnic background. At home he always had an accommodation with the Democratic machine; as the district gentrifies it becomes more suited to him politically. He was supposed to have had a hard race in 1982, when the district was extended into the suburbs and targeted by Republicans, but he was reelected with 67% then and has won easily since. But redistricting may eliminate the seat in 1992 when Yates turns 83.

The People: Est. Pop. 1986: 516,700, dn. 0.5% 1980–86; Pop. 1980: 519,120, dn. 8.9% 1970–80. Households (1980): 48% family, 22% with children, 37% married couples; 65.3% housing units rented; median monthly rent: $251; median house value: $88,100. Voting age pop. (1980): 422,900; 9% Black, 8% Spanish origin, 5% Asian origin.

1988 Presidential Vote:

Dukakis (D)	137,259	(61%)
Bush (R)	85,855	(38%)

Rep. Sidney R. Yates (D)

Elected 1964; b. Aug. 27, 1909, Chicago; home, Chicago; U. of Chicago, Ph.D. 1931, J.D. 1933; Jewish; married (Adeline).

Career: Practicing atty.; Asst. Atty. for IL St. Bank Receiver, 1935–37; Asst. Atty. Gen. attached to IL Commerce Comm., 1937–40; Navy, WWII; U.S. House of Reps., 1949–63; Dem. Nominee for U.S. Senate, 1962; U.N. Rep., Trusteeship Council, 1963–64.

Offices: 2234 RHOB 20515, 202-225-2111. Also 230 S. Dearborn St., Rm. 3920, Chicago 60604, 312-353-4596; and 2100 Ridge Ave., Rm. 2700, Evanston, 60204, 312-328-2610.

Committees: *Appropriations* (4th of 35 D). Subcommittees: Foreign Operations; Legislative; Interior and Related Agencies (Chairman); Treasury, Postal Service and General Government.

Group Ratings

	ADA	ACLU	COPE	CFA	LCV	ACU	NTLC	NSI	COC	CEI
1988	80	100	92	91	88	5	15	0	36	15
1987	96	—	92	100	—	9	—	—	7	9

National Journal Ratings

	1988 LIB — 1988 CONS		1987 LIB — 1987 CONS	
Economic	60% —	37%	66% —	33%
Social	86% —	0%	78% —	0%
Foreign	84% —	0%	81% —	0%

Key Votes

1) Homeless $	AGN	5) Ban Drug Test	AGN	9) SDI Research	AGN
2) Gephardt Amdt	AGN	6) Drug Death Pen	AGN	10) Ban Chem Weaps	FOR
3) Deficit Reduc	FOR	7) Handgun Sales	AGN	11) Aid to Contras	AGN
4) Kill Plnt Clsng Notice	AGN	8) Ban D.C. Abort $	AGN	12) Nuclear Testing	—

Election Results

1988 general	Sidney R. Yates (D)	135,583	(66%)	($122,900)
	Herbert Sohn (R)	67,604	(33%)	($28,324)
1988 primary	Sidney R. Yates (D), unopposed			
1986 general	Sidney R. Yates (D)	94,738	(72%)	($97,479)
	Herbert Sohn (R)	36,715	(28%)	($38,385)

TENTH DISTRICT

In 1855 the first railroad line from Chicago north along the shore of Lake Michigan opened, and almost from that time to the present the North Shore suburbs have been where most members of the metropolitan area's elite live. Running north from Evanston, founded by Methodists to promote temperance (a cause that has never prospered in Chicago), are a series of towns along Lake Michigan—Wilmette, Winnetka, Glencoe, Highland Park, Lake Forest—each with a slightly different personality and character, each long established and with a patina of age 50 years ago, and all similar economically: rich. Here you will find New Trier Township High School, which has long prided itself as the academically most distinguished public school in the nation; the Onwentsia Club, where patricians like Adlai Stevenson liked to dine; the winding lanes of Lake Forest with their college; the heavily treed lanes of Highland Park. Not far from the gritty, monosyllabic city, these are communities of pleasant, affluent, well-educated people living in an environment whose beautiful natural endowments are kept carefully disciplined.

The 10th Congressional District of Illinois is the North Shore district, starting at the Bahai Temple on the Wilmette lakefront, just north of Evanston, reaching up past Fort Sheridan (one of the military bases recommended for closure) to the industrial city of Waukegan (once famous as the home of Jack Benny) and the Wisconsin border beyond. The district also goes inland, where as you move away from the Lake, housing prices fall, slowly. Northbrook and Deerfield, just west of Glencoe and Highland Park, are still among the most affluent Chicago suburbs. Politically they are if anything more Republican than the lakefront towns; there is less tinge here of fashionable liberalism or radical chic, and more unalloyed devotion to the free-market system and opposition to the party of the Chicago machine. Farther inland you pass over land that was cornfields not long ago (some still are) to suburbs like Arlington Heights, developed in the 1950s and 1960s on the Northwestern railroad line, and Wheeling, developed in the 1960s and 1970s near Interstate 294 and now the home of one of the nation's most famed French restaurants.

The congressman from the 10th District is John Porter, a Republican who seems to fit the district exactly. He is a North Shore native, a graduate of Northwestern, a Republican who is against tax increases and looks with favor on free markets, but who takes liberal stands on some foreign and cultural issues. Porter serves on the Appropriations Committee, and on the subcommittees handling labor, health, and foreign aid issues. He is for population control abroad and for limiting tort liability for people who volunteer to help others. He is purist enough to vote against setting up a cabinet-level Veterans department and to phase out sugar price supports. He worries about the Social Security reserve getting too big, about the fate of refuseniks in the Soviet Union and about the greenhouse effect of deforestation in Brazil. Cynics might say that Porter's views correlate closely with his constituents' economic interests: they can afford some altruism abroad and don't need military bases near home, so long as they're allowed to keep the huge earnings they make out of unregulated and mostly untaxed free enterprise. But Porter does seem to be acting out of convictions and ideals, and even if he weren't, his particular combination of views is so unusual in Congress that it is good to have it so ably represented.

Actually, Porter had some difficulty winning his seat. He lost his first race, in 1978, to liberal Democrat Abner Mikva, by 650 votes, when the district included Evanston and Skokie; Mikva, one of the shrewdest and best-humored of House liberals, was appointed to a federal judgeship, and Porter won the ensuing special election. Reelected easily in 1980, he had a problem with redistricting; but as he moved north, fellow incumbent Robert McClory retired, and Porter has had no problem since. He has now the luxury and privilege of representing for many years a district that seems in line with his philosophic views and ready and able—redistricting should be no problem next time—to support them indefinitely.

370   ILLINOIS

The People: Est. Pop. 1986: 553,600, up 6.5% 1980–86; Pop. 1980: 519,660, up 5.7% 1970–80. Households (1980): 79% family, 45% with children, 69% married couples; 26.6% housing units rented; median monthly rent: $275; median house value: $92,100. Voting age pop. (1980): 368,611; 5% Black, 4% Spanish origin, 2% Asian origin.

1988 Presidential Vote: Bush (R) 143,022   (62%)
Dukakis (D). 86,280   (37%)

Rep. John E. Porter (R)

Elected 1980; b. June 1, 1935, Evanston; home, Winnetta; MIT, Northwestern U., B.A., B.S. 1957, U. of MI, J.D. 1961; Presbyterian; married (Kathryn).

Career: Atty., U.S. Dept. of Justice, 1961–63; Practicing atty., 1963–80; IL House of Reps., 1973–79.

Offices: 1501 LHOB 20515, 202-225-4835. Also 104 Wilmot Rd., Ste. 410, Deerfield 60015, 312-940-0202; 1650 Arlington Hgts. Rd., Ste. 104, Arlington Hgts. 60004, 312-392-0303; and 18 N. County St., County Bldg., No. 601A Waukegan 60085, 312-662-0101.

Committees: *Appropriations* (14th of 22 R). Subcommittee: Foreign Operations and Export Financing; Labor, Health and Human Services and Education; Legislative. *Select Committee on Aging* (24th of 27 R).

Group Ratings

	ADA	ACLU	COPE	CFA	LCV	ACU	NTLC	NSI	COC	CEI
1988	30	24	13	45	44	68	77	56	100	59
1987	20	—	13	14	—	62	—	—	100	72

National Journal Ratings

	1988 LIB — 1988 CONS		1987 LIB — 1987 CONS	
Economic	0%	93%	11%	83%
Social	30%	70%	25%	73%
Foreign	44%	55%	42%	58%

Key Votes

1) Homeless $	FOR	5) Ban Drug Test	FOR	9) SDI Research	FOR
2) Gephardt Amdt	AGN	6) Drug Death Pen	FOR	10) Ban Chem Weaps	FOR
3) Deficit Reduc	AGN	7) Handgun Sales	AGN	11) Aid to Contras	FOR
4) Kill Plnt Clsng Notice	FOR	8) Ban D.C. Abort $	FOR	12) Nuclear Testing	FOR

Election Results

1988 general	John E. Porter (R)	158,519	(73%)	($212,630)
	Eugene F. Friedman (D).	60,187	(28%)	($61,446)
1988 primary	John E. Porter (R), unopposed			
1986 general	John E. Porter (R)	87,530	(75%)	($176,228)
	Robert A. Cleland (D)	28,990	(25%)	($103,817)

ELEVENTH DISTRICT

Northwest of Chicago's Loop, out the Kennedy Expressway past the industrial zones along the North Chicago River and the rail lines, are the single-family-home, low-rise, bungalow neighborhoods where two and three generations of mostly ethnic Chicagoans have raised their families and worked their way up in the world. Fifty years ago, the city wards were just about as far out as anyone here expected to move; after World War II, suburbs burgeoned on arterial roads and rail lines, and the bungalow wards became a way station. They are, perhaps, again: young refugees from Communist Europe and immigrants from the Mediterranean and Mexico are moving into neighborhoods built by Greeks, Ukranians, Poles, Jews and others.

This is Illinois's 11th Congressional District, which includes most of the city's far northwest wards, from Greek Town to mostly Jewish Rogers Park, plus northern suburbs like Lincolnwood and part of mostly Jewish Skokie, and Niles and the western suburbs, with regular rectangular-blocked old neighborhoods interspersed with factories and warehouses, just south of O'Hare Airport, where Mexicans are now following in the footsteps of Italians. The Chicago wards all elect Democratic aldermen, but most vote Republican in contested statewide elections; the suburbs, historically Republican, have been trending Democratic.

Frank Annunzio, the Democratic congressman from the 11th District, is a veteran of Chicago politics who has made his way to the top of the House. He has the look of an old-time machine politico and the record of an independent-minded detail man. The political machine to which he had such loyalty has crumbled, and the labor movement which he worked for in the 1940s is in trouble. He charges on. Annunzio in all his years on the Banking Committee has never been cozy with the banking lobby, although he has always been a strong savings and loan man (old Chicago neighborhoods are strewn with ethnic-based S&Ls and small banks). He has been aggressive in regulating debt-collection agencies, which are sometimes guilty of incredible abuses, and in making a federal crime of serious credit card fraud; he pushed the bill to prohibit surcharges for credit card customers. His Banking subcommittee chairmanship has made him the czar of the nation's coinage, and he has taken his duties seriously. Annunzio thwarted a measure that would have allowed Armand Hammer's Occidental Petroleum to make money minting Olympic commemorative coins, and, by instituting his own government-managed coin program, raised $70 million for the 1984 Olympics—more than the Hammer program even promised. The Statue of Liberty commemorative he pushed raised $74 million in only 14 months. And as chairman of the House Administration Committee he has given congressional offices a desktop publishing ability by spending just $200,000 on computers.

In the 101st Congress Annunzio will be in hotter seats than ever before. The House Administration Committee, which he has chaired since 1984, has jurisdiction over campaign finance reform, which may be a hot issue indeed. Annunzio is a product of an old politics, but he has adapted to the new; he has not favored public financing or more severe limitations on PACs in the past, but he may work with Whip (and committee member) Tony Coelho on a Democratic bill even as Republicans try to pass one of their own. On Banking he will also be a high-ranking voice on tough issues. The 1988 defeat of Chairman Fernand St Germain—a longtime adversary of Annunzio's—leaves the mercurial Henry Gonzalez in the chair as the committee tries to figure out how to bail out the savings and loans. Annunzio ranks just behind Gonzalez and could provide some ballast in rough seas.

Annunzio started off in politics as a union staffer and an appointee of Governor Adlai Stevenson in 1949; he was first elected to Congress in 1964 as a machine loyalist from a district centered in the Loop, when the incumbent was dumped for alleged ties with organized crime. After the 1972 redistricting eliminated the seat, Annunzio leapfrogged to the 11th, whose congressman, Roman Pucinski, was running for the U.S. Senate and now holds the more

372　ILLINOIS

powerful office, for Chicagoans, of alderman. Annunzio adapted comfortably after the district moved out partially into the suburbs in 1982. But it's possible that the 11th will be squeezed out of existence in 1992, when he turns 77.

The People: Est. Pop. 1986: 523,500, up 0.9% 1980–86; Pop. 1980: 518,995, dn. 7.8% 1970–80. Households (1980): 72% family, 29% with children, 59% married couples; 40.6% housing units rented; median monthly rent: $239; median house value: $69,400. Voting age pop. (1980): 409,539; 5% Spanish origin, 4% Asian origin.

1988 Presidential Vote:　Bush (R) . . . . 117,883　(53%)
　　　　　　　　　　　　　Dukakis (D). 101,346　(46%)

Rep. Frank Annunzio (D)

Elected 1964; b. Jan. 12, 1915, Chicago; home, Chicago; De Paul U., B.S. 1940, M.A. 1942; Roman Catholic; married (Angeline).

Career: Pub. sch. teacher, 1935–43; Legis. and Ed. Dir., United Steel Workers of Amer., Chicago, Calumet Region Dist. 31, 1943–49; Dir., IL Dept. of Labor, 1949–52; Business, 1952–64.

Offices: 2303 RHOB 20515, 202-225-6661. Also 4747 W. Peterson Ave., Ste. 201, Chicago 60646, 312-736-0700; and Kluczynski Bldg., Ste. 3816, 230 S. Dearborn St., Chicago 60604, 312-353-2525.

Committees: *Banking, Finance and Urban Affairs* (2d of 31 D). Subcommittees: Financial Institutions Supervision, Regulation and Insurance (Chairman), General Oversight and Investigations. *House Administration* (Chairman of 13 D). *Joint Committee on the Library* (Chairman). *Joint Committee on Printing* (Vice Chairman).

Group Ratings

	ADA	ACLU	COPE	CFA	LCV	ACU	NTLC	NSI	COC	CEI
1986	75	67	92	73	44	17	8	0	25	7
1987	48	—	92	73	—	9	—	—	20	4

National Journal Ratings

	1988 LIB — 1988 CONS		1987 LIB — 1987 CONS	
Economic	86%	13%	73%	0%
Social	56%	43%	57%	42%
Foreign	56%	43%	*	*

Key Votes

1) Homeless $	—	5) Ban Drug Test	—	9) SDI Research	—
2) Gephardt Amdt	—	6) Drug Death Pen	FOR	10) Ban Chem Weaps	—
3) Deficit Reduc	FOR	7) Handgun Sales	AGN	11) Aid to Contras	AGN
4) Kill Plnt Clsng Notice	AGN	8) Ban D.C. Abort $	FOR	12) Nuclear Testing	FOR

Election Results

1988 general	Frank Annunzio (D)	131,753	(65%)	($239,158)
	George S. Gottlieb (R)	72,489	(36%)	($41,259)
1988 primary	Frank Annunzio (D), unopposed			
1986 general	Frank Annunzio (D)	106,970	(71%)	($171,298)
	George S. Gottlieb (R)	44,341	(29%)	($29,870)

TWELFTH DISTRICT

Somewhere in the Chicago metropolitan area there is an invisible line between the two different Chicagos. One is the Chicago dominated by blacks and the products of the vast immigration of 1840–1924, a Chicago where loyalties are taken for granted: loyalty to ethnic group, to church (usually the Catholic Church, but often with an ethnic prefix), and to party (almost always the Democratic Party, but occasionally, as in Cicero, the Republican). This Chicago is a gritty city, where occasional acts of cheerfulness and courtesy lighten up days otherwise as cold and as impersonal as the Chicago sky is gray during most of the winter. This part of Chicago sees the city not only as the center of life, but as the whole of it; people for whom there is not much life outside of Chicago, except perhaps a little beach house on the Indiana shore of Lake Michigan.

The other Chicago is the beginning of the Great Plains, a white Anglo-Saxon Protestant Chicago, a place whose residents are products of the first great wave of immigration to America. The tone of this Chicago is cheerier, its streets and highways cleaner and neater, its daily life somehow free from evidence of unpleasantness and deprivation. This is the Chicago of dozens of suburban and Downstate towns, all laid out on neat geometric grids on the flatness of the prairie, the Chicago which extends hundreds of miles out from the city and which seems separate from it. People in this Chicago think of themselves as the typical Americans, and their geographical vision takes in the vast plains. This is the Chicago of Colonel McCormick's *Chicago Tribune* and Don McNeill's *Breakfast Club*, of Paul Harvey and Sears catalogues. It is an optimistic world which knows personal, but not social or political, tragedy; a world in which all things are possible and most things are for the best. Ronald Reagan grew up in Downstate Illinois within the orbit of this kind of Chicago, and its spirit helped to characterize his presidency. His migration to southern California, incidentally, is not atypical: you can see in the geometric grids and Republican voting patterns of Orange County or Phoenix almost precise replicas of the grids and patterns in Chicago's suburban "collar counties," transported out on the Atchison, Topeka & Santa Fe or U.S. 66 from their beginnings in Chicago's Loop to the vast and once empty Southwest.

The line between these two Chicagos passes somewhere near the southern end of the 12th Congressional District of Illinois. This is part of metropolitan Chicago, beginning at the northwest corner of Cook County, taking in the western half of Lake County and most of McHenry County just to the west. And it contains many descendants of the second wave of immigrants who moved out from Chicago one or two generations ago. But the cultural style of this area is very much that of the second Great Plains Chicago.

That is apparent from the 12th District's voting habits, which are very much Republican. This is not just a function of income, though this area does have one of the highest income levels of any district in the Midwest or the nation; the 10th District, along Lake Michigan, is more wealthy and less Republican. The difference is cultural. The North Shore suburbanites are part of an urbane tradition, lineal descendants of the merchant princes who amassed great fortunes and patronized advanced arts and letters. The suburbanites inland are descendants of small town burghers, who uphold the traditions and observe the courtesies that are the fabric of life in cozy, affluent communities.

The 12th District is represented in Congress by a man who personifies many of the qualities of the kind of Chicago he represents. Philip Crane is the son of Dr. George Crane, who broadcast a medical advice radio program on Chicago's WGN for years and was a pillar of conservative thought; two of his sons have served as congressmen from Illinois and a third was a nearly successful candidate in Indiana. Phil Crane is handsome, congenial, loyal to his beliefs but full of good-hearted camaraderie.

He was one of the first announced presidential candidates for 1980, and one of the least

374   ILLINOIS

successful; his strategy depended on picking up support when the Reagan candidacy faded, but even when it looked, after the Iowa caucuses, like that might happen, Crane made no headway. Today no one thinks of him as a presidential candidate. Nor do many colleagues think of him as an original thinker or as an active legislator. He is a member of the Ways and Means Committee, but when he has shown up at meetings, it has been a source for comment; he had no role in passing the 1981 tax cuts; as ranking Republican on the trade subcommittee, he has stood valiantly for free trade principles. He has moved successfully to stop cost-of-living pay increases for the House but he has also moved to keep Supreme Court justices and diplomats out of the special parking lots congressmen use at Washington airports. His presence on the tax reform conference committee was an occasion for laughter and he skipped the final conference. He casts single votes against uncontroversial legislation and otherwise does little. In the 12th District, he is reelected by huge margins in what are for all practical purposes uncontested elections.

The People: Est. Pop. 1986: 565,400, up 8.9% 1980–86; Pop. 1980: 519,181, up 39.0% 1970–80. Households (1980): 79% family, 47% with children, 69% married couples; 25.7% housing units rented; median monthly rent: $300; median house value: $71,900. Voting age pop. (1980): 356,939; 3% Spanish origin, 1% Asian origin, 1% Black.

1988 Presidential Vote:

Bush (R)	161,488	(70%)
Dukakis (D)	66,474	(29%)

Rep. Philip M. Crane (R)

Elected 1969; b. Nov. 3, 1930, Chicago; home, Mt. Prospect; DePauw U., Hillsdale Col., B.A. 1952, IN U., M.A. 1961, Ph.D. 1963; Protestant; married (Arlene).

Career: Instructor, IN U., 1960–63; Asst. Prof., Bradley U., 1963–67; Dir. of Schools, Westminster Acad., 1967–68.

Offices: 1035 LHOB 20515, 202-225-3711. Also 1450 S. New Wilke Rd., Arlington Heights 60005, 312-394-0790; and 100 N. Walkup, Crystal Lake 60014, 815-459-3399.

Committees: *Ways and Means* (3d of 13 R). Subcommittees: Health; Trade (Ranking Member).

Group Ratings

	ADA	ACLU	COPE	CFA	LCV	ACU	NTLC	NSI	COC	CEI
1988	0	6	6	18	13	100	100	100	93	93
1987	4	—	6	14	—	100	—	—	92	94

National Journal Ratings

	1988 LIB — 1988 CONS			1987 LIB — 1987 CONS	
Economic	0%	—	93%	0%	— 89%
Social	0%	—	95%	18%	— 82%
Foreign	0%	—	84%	0%	— 80%

Key Votes

1) Homeless $	FOR	5) Ban Drug Test	—	9) SDI Research	FOR
2) Gephardt Amdt	AGN	6) Drug Death Pen	FOR	10) Ban Chem Weaps	AGN
3) Deficit Reduc	AGN	7) Handgun Sales	FOR	11) Aid to Contras	FOR
4) Kill Plnt Clsng Notice	FOR	8) Ban D.C. Abort $	FOR	12) Nuclear Testing	AGN

Election Results

1988 general	Philip M. Crane (R) 165,913	(75%)	($480,460)
	John A. Leonardi (D) 54,769	(25%)	($11,955)
1988 primary	Philip M. Crane (R), unopposed		
1986 general	Philip M. Crane (R) 89,044	(78%)	($365,932)
	John A. Leonardi (D) 25,536	(22%)	($7,879)

THIRTEENTH DISTRICT

The radial avenues that fan out from Chicago's Loop are the routes taken by the city's various ethnic groups—immigrants who came to Chicago and their descendants who have moved up and out as they prospered over the years. One of these routes runs almost straight west from the Loop, and the group that has trod it includes many of the Chicago area's white Anglo-Saxon Protestants. From anonymous clerks in Loop offices to the aristocratic Colonel Robert Rutherford McCormick, proprietor of the *Chicago Tribune,* they have made their way westward, past the Chicago city limits and the Bohemian suburbs of Cicero and Berwyn, to the westernmost suburbs of Cook County and beyond to affluent Du Page County.

This is the land of Illinois's 13th Congressional District. It begins, if you start nearest to Chicago, in the turn-of-the-century suburb of Riverside; with its curved streets and Frank Lloyd Wright houses, it was an elite place in the days of *art nouveau* and still is today. Farther west are affluent railroad commuter suburbs: the string of La Grange, Western Springs, and Hinsdale, more middle-income Downers Grove, and the newer suburb of Oak Brook which is the headquarters of McDonald's, among other enterprises. The boundaries of the 13th District were carefully crafted to exclude Democratic suburbs (the Democrats who drew the plan wanted them to pad the Chicago-based Democratic districts); the district has a salient into southwest Cook County, in somewhat different socioeconomic country (affluent Irish), to meet the population standard. People from elsewhere may think of Chicago as Democratic, but this part of Chicagoland is almost unanimously hostile to the city's Democratic machine, both for its reputed corruption and for its support of big government programs over the years. The 13th is, election after election, one of the most Republican districts in the nation.

The congressman from the 13th, Harris Fawell, has deep roots in Du Page County. He was first elected to the Illinois Senate in 1962, after losing a race for state Supreme Court. He practiced law in the county, and was a key supporter of Congressman John Erlenborn. When Erlenborn decided to retire in 1984, after some years of frustration as the ranking Republican on the liberal-dominated Education and Labor Committee, Fawell jumped into the race and got the local party endorsement. But he was attacked by his opponents as too liberal and won a four-way race 30%–23%–22%–12%.

So this pillar of the suburban establishment became a congressman at 53. He opposes federal spending, is against raising the minimum wage, doesn't want to require advance notice of plant closings and is unusually blunt about opposing protectionism. But Fawell supports ample funding for Argonne National Laboratory, which is in the district, and his voting record on cultural issues is rather liberal. He serves on the Science and Education and Labor Committees—forums where he might find in practical instances more need for federal spending than he is inclined generally to support. No doubt this leaves movement conservatives furious, but Fawell probably represents the balance of opinion in the upscale 13th better than they do, and he has won easily since 1984.

The People: Est. Pop. 1986: 568,100, up 9.4% 1980–86; Pop. 1980: 519,441, up 33.5% 1970–80. Households (1980): 79% family, 42% with children, 71% married couples; 24.0% housing units rented; median monthly rent: $291; median house value: $78,500. Voting age pop. (1980): 370,153; 2% Asian origin, 2% Spanish origin, 1% Black.

1988 Presidential Vote:

Bush (R)	179,219	(68%)
Dukakis (D)	81,899	(31%)

Rep. Harris W. Fawell (R)

Elected 1984; b. Mar. 25, 1929, West Chicago; home, Naperville; attended North Central Col., Chicago-Kent Col. of Law, J.D. 1953; United Methodist; married (Ruth).

Career: Practicing atty., 1953–84; IL Senate, 1963–77.

Offices: 318 CHOB 20515, 202-225-3515. Also 115 West 55th St., Ste. 100. Clarendon Hills 60514, 312-655-2052.

Committees: *Education and Labor* (9th of 13 R). Subcommittees: Elementary, Secondary, and Vocational Education; Labor-Management Relations; Labor Standards. *Science, Space and Technology* (11th of 19 R). Subcommittees: Energy Research and Development; International Scientific Cooperation. *Select Committee on Aging* (15th of 27 R). Subcommittees: Health and Long Term Care; Housing and Consumer Interests.

Group Ratings

	ADA	ACLU	COPE	CFA	LCV	ACU	NTLC	NSI	COC	CEI
1988	40	36	8	45	50	64	84	90	92	75
1987	24	—	6	36	—	70	—	—	100	75

National Journal Ratings

	1988 LIB — 1988 CONS		1987 LIB — 1987 CONS	
Economic	0%	— 93%	0%	— 89%
Social	26%	— 73%	10%	— 85%
Foreign	37%	— 63%	41%	— 58%

Key Votes

1) Homeless $	FOR	5) Ban Drug Test	FOR	9) SDI Research	FOR
2) Gephardt Amdt	AGN	6) Drug Death Pen	FOR	10) Ban Chem Weaps	AGN
3) Deficit Reduc	AGN	7) Handgun Sales	AGN	11) Aid to Contras	FOR
4) Kill Plnt Clsng Notice	FOR	8) Ban D.C. Abort $	AGN	12) Nuclear Testing	FOR

Election Results

1988 general	Harris W. Fawell (R)	174,992	(70%)	($289,190)
	Evelyn E. Craig (D)	74,424	(30%)	($45,760)
1988 primary	Harris W. Fawell (R)	36,233	(77%)	
	George T. Hamilton (R)	10,806	(23%)	
1986 general	Harris W. Fawell (R)	107,227	(73%)	($193,882)
	Dominick J. Jeffrey (D)	38,874	(27%)	

FOURTEENTH DISTRICT

In the "Collar Counties" around Chicago there is a subtle division between metropolitan Chicago and Downstate Illinois, between the zone where people feel they are part of a giant city anchored by those skyscrapers in the Loop and where people see the city as something alien, a foreign and even hostile force in their clean—physically clean, politically clean—and neat communities. The 14th Congressional district of Illinois straddles this invisible line. It gets as close as 30 miles to Chicago's Loop, in western Du Page County, where the subdivisions now are almost as built-up and densely populated as they are in Cook County. It contains the industrial city of Elgin and part of Aurora, both on the Fox River that runs parallel to Lake Michigan, 35 miles away. Past the Fox River, the subdivisions start thinning out and you see more cornfields; soon the fields devoted to producing fresh sweet corn for suburbanites in the summer give way to serious commercial farming operations. By the time you get as far west as De Kalb, site of Northern Illinois University, or as far southwest as the industrial towns of Ottawa, La Salle, and Peru on the Illinois River, you are unmistakably Downstate, in the midst of some of the richest and most productively cultivated agricultural land in the world.

This is also one of the most heavily Republican belts of territory in the country. Northern Illinois was settled, when Chicago was just one of thousands of frontier villages, by Yankees from Ohio, Indiana, Upstate New York, and New England, people who formed the heart of the Republican Party from the year it was founded, in 1854, just as they would form the core of the Grand Army of the Republic a few years later. Their descendants remain mostly loyal to the Republican Party today. There are parts of Northern Illinois, either first settled by southerners or by immigrants from Europe, which are Democratic; the major example is of course Chicago, and there are much smaller examples, like the ailing industrial towns of La Salle and Ottawa, which went for Michael Dukakis in 1988. But on the whole this is Republican territory that very seldom elects anyone but Republican congressmen.

The current congressman, Dennis Hastert, came to office in unusual circumstances. In the spring of 1986, freshman Congressman John Grotberg was struck down by a long dormant cancer. That was after the March primary, and the Republican Party chose as its new nominee Hastert, a high school teacher and coach who had served six years in the legislature. Some other Republicans who wanted the nomination themselves or thought Hastert insufficiently conservative objected and Hastert had strong opposition from Democrat Mary Lou Kearns, the Kane County coroner. He won the election with big margins in the areas closest to Chicago, and with just 52% of the total vote—low for a Republican in this district. In the House he seems to have concentrated on district matters: trying to do something about the high radium content of local groundwater, blocking a local landfill project, and trying—unsuccessfully—to get the Supercollider for this part of Illinois, to join the Fermi National Accelerator Laboratory in the eastern part of the district and the Argonne National Laboratory which is a few miles farther east. In 1988, Hastert won the sort of overwhelming percentage you would expect of a Republican incumbent here, and he seems now to have a safe seat.

The People: Est. Pop. 1986: 563,700, up 8.0% 1980–86; Pop. 1980: 521,909, up 17.7% 1970–80. Households (1980): 77% family, 44% with children, 67% married couples; 28.9% housing units rented; median monthly rent: $220; median house value: $63,200; Voting age pop. (1980): 367,441; 3% Spanish origin, 2% Black, 1% Asian origin.

1988 Presidential Vote:

Bush (R)	144,972	(64%)
Dukakis (D)	81,320	(36%)

378   ILLINOIS

Rep. Dennis Hastert (R)

Elected 1986; b. Jan. 2, 1942, Aurora, IL; home, Yorkville; Wheaton Col., B.A. 1964, Northern IL U., M.S. 1967; Protestant; married (Jean).

Career: Teacher and coach, Yorkville H.S., 1964–80; IL General Assembly 1980–86.

Offices: 515 CHOB 20515, 202-225-2976. Also 100 W. Lafayette, Ottawa 61350, 815-434-5666; 27 N. River, Batavia 60510, 312-406-1114; and 14 E. Chicago St. Elgin 60120, 312-697-6622.

Committees: *Government Operations* (7th of 15 R). Subcommittee: Commerce, Consumer and Monetary Affairs (Ranking Member). *Public Works and Transportation* (11th of 20 R). Subcommittees: Economic Development; Investigations and Oversight; Surface Transportation; Water Resources. *Select Committee on Children, Youth and Families* (5th of 12R).

Group Ratings

	ADA	ACLU	COPE	CFA	LCV	ACU	NTLC	NSI	COC	CEI
1988	10	22	17	36	19	92	78	100	86	65
1987	8	—	13	14	—	87	—	—	87	76

National Journal Ratings

	1988 LIB — 1988 CONS		1987 LIB — 1987 CONS	
Economic	21%	— 77%	11%	— 83%
Social	5%	— 91%	19%	— 78%
Foreign	0%	— 84%	0%	— 80%

Key Votes

1) Homeless $	FOR	5) Ban Drug Test	FOR	9) SDI Research	FOR
2) Gephardt Amdt	AGN	6) Drug Death Pen	FOR	10) Ban Chem Weaps	AGN
3) Deficit Reduc	AGN	7) Handgun Sales	FOR	11) Aid to Contras	FOR
4) Kill Plnt Clsng Notice	FOR	8) Ban D.C. Abort $	FOR	12) Nuclear Testing	AGN

Election Results

1988 general	Dennis Hastert (R)	161,146	(74%)	($346,785)
	Stephen Youhanaie (D)	57,482	(26%)	($0)
1988 primary	Dennis Hastert (R)	42,897	(100%)	
1986 general	Dennis Hastert (R)	77,288	(52%)	($327,219)
	Mary Lou Kearns (D)	70,293	(48%)	($322,625)

FIFTEENTH DISTRICT

South toward New Orleans the Illinois Central heads from Chicago on a railbed elevated slightly above some of the nation's richest farmland. The first settlers to reach the Illinois prairie found topsoil not just inches but feet deep; they turned it into some of the nation's most prosperous family farms—no populism in these parts—and today this is prime commercial agriculture country. Cultivating this soil is a big business, and often a risky one: choosing the right crops (soybeans and corn are the current favorites), maximizing yields, selecting proper pesticides, making marketing decisions, taking maximum advantage of any government programs, keeping watch on farm export prospects. Farmers here, like former Agriculture

Secretary John Block, typically own thousands of acres, though they may lease some out; even with lower land prices this soil is a serious financial asset that must be worked to yield the largest possible return. There is no room here for a little family vegetable garden or a horse corral: this is business.

The 15th Congressional District of Illinois occupies much of the prairie, beginning not quite 40 miles from Chicago, where the Illinois Central heads toward Kankakee, and moving over 150 miles of prairie to the courthouse towns of Lincoln and Monticello. Its largest city is Bloomington, whose best-known citizen was the first Adlai Stevenson, grandfather of the presidential candidate and one-term Vice President of the United States; he was only mildly sympathetic to populists like William Jennings Bryan and served under Grover Cleveland who was as doctrinaire a *laissez faire* Democrat as has ever been seen in American politics.

The congressman from the 15th is Edward Madigan, one of the Republican Party's leaders in the House and one of its best instinctive politicians, a successful businessman in Lincoln and one-time Republican state legislator—and the man who came 2 votes short of being elected House Republican Whip in March 1989. Madigan's father was an alderman in the small city of Lincoln, and Madigan, owner of a taxi company, was elected to the state legislature in 1966 and, after chairing the redistricting committee, to the U.S. House in 1972. Coming quietly into the then quiet ranks of House Republicans, he seemed indistinguishable from a dozen or so dull legislators. But he has made a vast difference.

He has done so by legislating from good committee positions. He got a seat on the Energy and Commerce Committee which by the middle 1970s became the cockpit for one important economic issue after another. Madigan specialized in transportation issues first and then, after becoming ranking Republican on Henry Waxman's subcommittee on Health and the Environment. (Like Madigan, Waxman also chaired his state house's redistricting committee.) Madigan's impulse usually is to reduce government regulation, but he is also interested in solving practical problems; and those two impulses put him at the fulcrum point in one policy-making decision after another. He backed the sale of Conrail, for example, and opposes acid rain bills that would put burdens on coal-burning midwestern utilities; but he also has originated successful organ transplant legislation, a nursing research center, a bill to encourage generic drugs, a compromise natural gas deregulation measure, and a new version of the Safe Drinking Water Act. He was the lead sponsor of the Administration version of catastrophic health care, and he worked closely with Waxman and against California Republican William Dannemeyer on AIDS legislation.

Madigan's second important position is as ranking Republican on the Agriculture Committee. He was off the committee altogether in 1981 and 1982, while serving as chairman of the Republican Research Committee; but he reclaimed his seat on Agriculture in 1983, in part to prevent Vermont's liberal James Jeffords (now in the Senate) from getting the ranking position. Representing a relatively prosperous farm area, Madigan has been a staunch opponent of what he considers overgenerous farm bill provisions. He led the fight against the Democrats' proposal for farmers' referenda to limit grain production. He has worked hard on refinancing the farm credit system and, after the droughts of the late 1980s, he pushed through a requirement that farmers take out crop insurance, to forestall putting the whole risk on the government.

On both Agriculture and Energy and Commerce, Madigan has shown himself to be a cool operator, maintaining orderly working relationships with Democrats and keeping his lines clearly open with his fellow Republicans; he works hard, knows his details, and obviously is genuinely interested in the issues. After the 1986 election he was chosen Chief Deputy Whip. When Whip Richard Cheney was nominated to be Defense Secretary in March 1989, Madigan jumped immediately into the race to succeed him, and soon had the wholehearted support of Minority Leader Robert Michel. It soon became a polarized race, between Madigan and Newt Gingrich, with Madigan's refusal to pull out squeezing out others—Jerry Lewis, Henry Hyde—

who might have been compromise choices. Madigan campaigned as a man who knows how to count votes, how to influence colleagues, and how to work with Democrats, a leader who would work with members inside the House, not one who would be talking constantly to the TV cameras and outsiders. He argued that if Republicans want to make a difference on policy, they have to work with Democrats and inside a framework Democrats control—premises which Gingrich directly challenged. In different circumstances, Madigan might have been elected easily. But House Republicans—and not just the conservatives among them—were frustrated with what they considered the highhanded leadership of Speaker Jim Wright, they felt that if their ideas could somehow get exposure they might sweep elections for the House as they had elections for other offices, and they were enraged by Madigan's references to working with Democrats. So on a secret ballot he lost 87–85.

That defeat probably ends any chance that Madigan will be Republican Leader some day, and will mean that he will probably remain busy at work on legislation in the 1990s. He is reelected easily every two years.

The People: Est. Pop. 1986: 517,100, dn. 0.4% 1980–86; Pop. 1980: 518,995, up 8.4% 1970–80. Households (1980): 75% family, 42% with children, 65% married couples; 31.6% housing units rented; median monthly rent: $182; median house value: $44,900. Voting age pop. (1980): 370,509; 5% Black, 1% Spanish origin.

1988 Presidential Vote: Bush (R) 124,915   (62%)
                              Dukakis (D). 74,312   (37%)

Rep. Edward R. Madigan (R)

Elected 1972; b. Jan. 13, 1936, Lincoln; home, Lincoln; Lincoln Col., B.A. 1956; Roman Catholic; married (Evelyn).

Career: Owner, Yellow-Lincoln Taxi Co., 1955–73; IL House of Reps., 1966–72.

Offices: 2109 RHOB 20515, 202-225-2371. Also 2401 E. Washington, Bloomington 61701, 309-662-9371; 70 Meadowview Ctr., Kankakee 60901, 815-937-0875; and 219 S. Kickapoo, Lincoln 62656, 217-735-3521.

Committees: *Agriculture* (Ranking Member of 17 R). *Energy and Commerce* (2d of 17 R). Subcommittee: Health and the Environment (Ranking Member); Telecommunications and Finance.

Group Ratings

	ADA	ACLU	COPE	CFA	LCV	ACU	NTLC	NSI	COC	CEI
1988	15	20	29	55	31	77	62	100	85	53
1987	8	—	29	7	—	76	—	—	92	64

National Journal Ratings

	1988 LIB — 1988 CONS		1987 LIB — 1987 CONS	
Economic	27%	73%	26%	73%
Social	23%	77%	22%	77%
Foreign	24%	74%	0%	80%

Key Votes

1) Homeless $	FOR	5) Ban Drug Test	—	9) SDI Research	FOR
2) Gephardt Amdt	AGN	6) Drug Death Pen	FOR	10) Ban Chem Weaps	AGN
3) Deficit Reduc	—	7) Handgun Sales	FOR	11) Aid to Contras	FOR
4) Kill Plnt Clsng Notice	FOR	8) Ban D.C. Abort $	—	12) Nuclear Testing	AGN

Election Results

1988 general	Edward R. Madigan (R)...............	140,171	(72%)	($374,760)
	Thomas J. (Tom) Curl (D)	55,260	(28%)	($37,785)
1988 primary	Edward R. Madigan (R), unopposed			
1986 general	Edward R. Madigan (R)..............	115,284	(100%)	($209,409)

SIXTEENTH DISTRICT

The 16th Congressional District of Illinois is one of the heartlands of the Republican Party. It was here in Freeport that Abraham Lincoln forced Stephen Douglas into the most damaging admission of their 1858 debates, and this was one part of Illinois that was overwhelmingly for Lincoln then and when he ran for President. During the 1930s, when most of America voted for Franklin Roosevelt, the 16th District voted for Hoover and Landon and was one of less than 100 congressional districts that always elected Republican congressmen. It did vote against Barry Goldwater in 1964, but only by the narrowest of margins. It was the home of one two-term Republican President, Ulysses S. Grant, who made a poor living in the old Mississippi River town of Galena, and the birthplace of another, Ronald Reagan. Yet—a nice ironic twist— Reagan was raised a Democrat in rented apartments in Tampico and Dixon; he has none of the smugness and suspicion that outsiders have of the Yankee small-town bank president who was the archetypical Republican here, but rather the expansiveness and inclusionary impulse of the President he continues to admire greatly though his home area never voted for him, Franklin Roosevelt. The ancestral Republican from the 16th District in the 1980 race—another nice twist—was John Anderson, who ran as a liberal Republican and then as a third-party candidate against Reagan and Jimmy Carter.

Despite the Democratic trend in Downstate Illinois, the 16th District has remained Republican. High unemployment in and around Rockford, its largest city, hurt Republicans here in the 1980s, and so did the woes of workers who used to make agricultural implements across the line in Rock Island and Moline. But the ancestral allegiance remained strong in small towns and farmlands, and the district went 63% for Ronald Reagan in 1984 and 57% for George Bush in 1988.

Lynn Martin, congresswoman from the 16th since Anderson retired in 1980, is one of the national leaders of her party. In the 1960s, she was a wife and teacher; in the 1970s, she was elected to the county board and to the Illinois House and Senate from Rockford; in the 1980s she has been a member of the Budget and Rules Committee and vice-chairman of the House Republican Conference. At each step she has shown political acumen combined with a sharp sense of humor. She is a moderate on cultural issues (she supported the Equal Rights Amendment, for example, and sometimes on foreign policy, and solidly conservative and market-oriented on economics). Martin is also a sharp and aggressive partisan, always ready to point out weaknesses in the Democrats' arguments and always ready to raise a standard to which all Republicans can repair. She was sharp enough, in several senses of the word, to be George Bush's sparring partner for his 1984 debate with Geraldine Ferraro. She combined her partisan and reformist impulses in her crusade in the 100th Congress to protect congressional employees from discrimination and poor working conditions, and to twit the Democrats for not subjecting themselves to the same laws they write for others. She had at least minor success in 1988 when the House established a committee to rule on discrimination against its employees.

Martin's strengths have not always translated into popularity with her fellow Republicans. After the 1986, election she tried for a seat on Appropriations and, despite the support of Republican Leader Robert Michel, lost it due to the opposition of Trent Lott and the small state coalition that dominated the Republican Committee on Committees. After the 1988 election, Martin ran for chairman of the Republican Conference, and was defeated by three votes by Jerry Lewis of California. As a kind of consolation prize she was given a seat on Rules and, as one of three new Republicans in four seats, has some chance to change how that committee operates; though partisan, she is also intellectually frank and personally congenial with Democrats—quite a contrast with Delbert Latta, whom she replaced during illness on Budget and now replaces on Rules—and so may have more impact on House proceedings than Republicans are used to.

Martin has a tough decision to make in 1989: whether to take on the risks of running against Senator Paul Simon in 1990. To do so, she would have to give up 10 years of seniority and an important place—though not as important as she wanted—in the House. She would have to give up as well a safe seat in the House; although Democrat Skip Schwerdtfeger held her under 60% in 1982 and 1984, she seems well established now. An Illinois Senate race is always iffy. Yet if she won—and that seems by no means impossible—she would put her party significantly closer to a Senate majority and make herself a visible and important national figure.

The People: Est. Pop. 1986: 512,300, dn.1.3% 1980–86; Pop. 1980: 519,035, up 2.8% 1970–80. Households (1980): 76% family, 42% with children, 65% married couples; 29.8% housing units rented; median monthly rent: $175; median house value: $42,300. Voting age pop. (1980): 364,824; 4% Black, 2% Spanish origin.

1988 Presidential Vote: Bush (R) 116,627   (57%)
                                Dukakis (D) 85,552   (42%)

Rep. Lynn M. Martin (R)

Elected 1980; b. Dec. 26, 1939, Chicago; home, Loves Park; U. of IL, B.A. 1960; Roman Catholic; married (Harry Leinenweber).

Career: High sch. teacher, 1960–69; Winnebago Cnty. Bd., 1972–76; IL House of Reps., 1977–79; IL Senate, 1979–81.

Offices: 1214 LHOB 20515, 202-225-5676. Also 308 W. State St., Ste. 175, Rockford 61101, 815-987-4326; and 420 Ave. A, Sterling 61081, 815-626-1616.

Committees: *Rules* (3d of 4 R). Subcommittee: Legislative Process (Ranking Member).

Group Ratings

	ADA	ACLU	COPE	CFA	LCV	ACU	NTLC	NSI	COC	CEI
1988	30	92	30	36	38	76	85	90	69	60
1987	20	—	28	21	—	74	—	—	73	73

National Journal Ratings

	1988 LIB — 1988 CONS		1987 LIB — 1987 CONS	
Economic	26% —	73%	19% —	78%
Social	34% —	65%	27% —	72%
Foreign	16% —	78%	28% —	70%

Key Votes

1) Homeless $	FOR	5) Ban Drug Test	FOR	9) SDI Research	FOR
2) Gephardt Amdt	AGN	6) Drug Death Pen	—	10) Ban Chem Weaps	FOR
3) Deficit Reduc	AGN	7) Handgun Sales	FOR	11) Aid to Contras	FOR
4) Kill Plnt Clsng Notice	AGN	8) Ban D.C. Abort $	AGN	12) Nuclear Testing	AGN

Election Results

1988 general	Lynn M. Martin (R)	128,365	(64%)	($329,598)
	Steven E. Mahan (D)	72,431	(36%)	($25,424)
1988 primary	Lynn M. Martin (R), unopposed			
1986 general	Lynn M. Martin (R)	92,982	(67%)	($239,059)
	Kenneth F. Bohnsack (D)	46,087	(33%)	($44,369)

SEVENTEENTH DISTRICT

Where the Illinois prairie rolls toward the Mississippi River are some of the most fertile farmlands of America—and, as land values and commodity prices have fallen spasmodically over the years, many of its citizens are troubled and disgruntled. In this quintessentially Middle American territory is the 17th Congressional District of Illinois. It has one major industrial center, around the cities of Rock Island and Moline on the Mississippi River. It has other, smaller industrial centers on the Illinois River, including some suburbs of Peoria, and the small city of Galesburg, the birthplace of Carl Sandburg. It has hundreds of square miles of prairie. This is an agricultural district; although only a handful of its residents are actually farmers, the economy of this part of Illinois depends almost entirely on agriculture. The main product of the industrial center is agricultural equipment: tractors and backhoes and plows and harrows; the main business of the white-collar sector is financing the production, storing, and transportation of agricultural commodities.

This land was first settled by Yankees coming overland from northern Indiana and Ohio and Upstate New York, and, after 1848, by Germans who left their homeland in search of better opportunities in a land that in so many ways resembles the flat, orderly plains of northern Germany. Their politics has been Republican since the 1850s. For many years the only sources of Democratic strength were the unionized factory workers, members of the United Auto Workers employed by John Deere plants, in Rock Island and Moline. But the 17th District, in much the same manner as neighboring Iowa, has trended sharply Democratic in the 1980s. It sees itself as a victim of Reaganomics: lower farm prices have resulted in closed ag-implement factories, big unionized paychecks have been replaced by lower, irregular earnings. But, as in Iowa—and most of this district is part of the Quad Cities media market, centered across the river from Rock Island and Moline in Davenport, Iowa—there is also an emotional aspect: people here feel left behind, ignored, not honored as they feel they ought to be, by a president who actually came from this area—for the road from Ronald Reagan's home town of Dixon to Eureka College passes through the 17th district. The Democratic trend is plain from the election figures. Walter Mondale almost carried this district in 1984, Republican Jim Thompson failed to win a majority here in 1986, and Michael Dukakis carried this very un-Brookline-like territory, as he carried Iowa, in 1988.

One beneficiary of this trend—or is he one of the reasons for it?—is 17th district Congressman Lane Evans. He started off as a political accident, a local legal services attorney angry at the Reagan recession who in 1982 ran in the district long represented by moderate Republican Tom Railsback. But Railsback had been mentioned in the Paula Parkinson affair and was beaten by a conservative legislator, Kenneth McMillan, in the primary; Evans beat McMillan with 65%. By historical standards, Evans should have been a one-term congressman. But instead he has thrived. He compiled one of the most anti-Reagan voting records in the House, but that didn't hurt in one of the few districts that trended away from Reagan in 1980–84 and which went solidly Democratic in 1988. It didn't hurt also that Evans served in the Marine Corps from 1969 to 1971 (when Dan Quayle was in the National Guard); that he has a pleasant, boyish demeanor and hair parted in the center which will never be mistaken for East Coast fashionable; that he returns constantly to the district and appears even more often on television.

Evans professes to believe in a populism which "is rooted in the realization that too few people control too much money and wealth, and this balance must be redressed." But he does not carry this to the logical end, as the 1890s Populists did, of urging steeply progressive income and estate taxes to redistribute income and wealth; and he has had only limited success with his proposals to let grain farmers vote to limit production, reregulate railroads, subsidize loans to farmers, and encourage employee stock ownership plans. He has done better on veterans issues, chairing a subcommittee and trying to get compensation for veterans allegedly harmed by their exposure to Agent Orange. But more important than his specific proposals is his earnestness: this is a young man with deep roots in this area who is comfortable with ordinary people and wants to help them.

In this light, the only political risk Evans takes is in becoming too comfortably esconced in Washington. He took some of that risk in May 1988 by giving up his seat on Agriculture in return for the seat he won, against some tough competition, on Armed Services formerly held by Mel Price. He promised to use it, among other things, to look after the Rock Island Arsenal, and can be counted on as a dovish vote on most issues. But that is not unpopular here in a district which has become as dovish as Iowa.

Electorally, Evans by his example may have moved the district to the left; certainly his Republican opponents have had no success in moving it to the right. He has used the advantages of incumbency to gain visibility for his ideas and to raise very unpopulistic sums—in the magnitude of half a million dollars every two years—to run for reelection. Some might think that Dukakis's showing here (53%) helped him in 1988; more likely, his own example helped Dukakis to carry the district.

The People: Est. Pop. 1986: 489,200, dn. 5.8% 1980–86; Pop. 1980: 519,333, up 4.0% 1970–80. Households (1980): 75% family, 40% with children, 65% married couples; 27.3% housing units rented; median monthly rent: $172; median house value: $42,500. Voting age pop. (1980): 372,502; 2% Black, 2% Spanish origin.

1988 Presidential Vote: Dukakis (D). 107,639   (53%)
                                 Bush (R) 95,672   (47%)

Rep. Lane Evans (D)

Elected 1982; b. Aug. 4, 1951, Rock Island; home, Rock Island; Augustana Col., B.A. 1974, Georgetown U. Law Sch., J.D. 1978; Roman Catholic; single.

Career: USMC, 1969–71; Practicing atty., 1978–82.

Offices: 328 CHOB 20515, 202-225-5905. Also 1535 47th Ave., Moline 61265, 309-793-5760; and 125 E. Main St., Galesburg 61401, 309-342-4411.

Committees: *Armed Services* (28th of 31 D). Subcommittees: Investigations; Procurement and Military Nuclear Systems. *Veterans' Affairs* (4th of 21 D). Subcommittees: Compensation, Pension, and Insurance; Education, Training, and Employment; Oversight and Investigation (Chairman). *Select Committee on Children, Youth and Families* (15th of 18 D).

Group Ratings

	ADA	ACLU	COPE	CFA	LCV	ACU	NTLC	NSI	COC	CEI
1988	100	91	95	100	100	0	5	0	14	7
1987	100	—	94	93	—	0	—	—	0	4

National Journal Ratings

	1988 LIB — 1988 CONS		1987 LIB — 1987 CONS	
Economic	92%	— 0%	73%	— 0%
Social	86%	— 0%	78%	— 0%
Foreign	84%	— 0%	81%	— 0%

Key Votes

1) Homeless $	AGN	5) Ban Drug Test	AGN	9) SDI Research	AGN
2) Gephardt Amdt	FOR	6) Drug Death Pen	AGN	10) Ban Chem Weaps	FOR
3) Deficit Reduc	FOR	7) Handgun Sales	AGN	11) Aid to Contras	AGN
4) Kill Plnt Clsng Notice	AGN	8) Ban D.C. Abort $	AGN	12) Nuclear Testing	FOR

Election Results

1988 general	Lane Evans (D).....................	132,130	(65%)	($471,233)
	William E. Steward (R)	71,560	(35%)	($124,133)
1988 primary	Lane Evans (D), unopposed			
1986 general	Lane Evans (D)....................	85,442	(56%)	($620,183)
	Sam McHard (R)...................	68,101	(44%)	($312,698)

EIGHTEENTH DISTRICT

Peoria, Illinois, is one of those small midwestern cities known better from its alleged typicalness than for its actual peculiarities. If it has been a useful test market for consumer products over the years, it is not necessarily a good barometer of political attitudes. "How will it play in Peoria?" turns out to be a question that produces misleading answers. Peoria and the 18th Congressional District which it dominates remained, for example, solidly Republican through the 1930s as America went Democratic, electing none other as its congressman than Everett McKinley Dirksen, later Senator (1951–69) and Senate Minority Leader (1959–69). Dirksen's current successor in the House, Robert Michel, first elected in 1956, has been the Republican Leader in the House since the 1980 election. This is Ronald Reagan country as well: he went to

Eureka College just across the Illinois River.

But Peoria and the 18th District in the Reagan years were hit hard by economic recession and layoffs and have trended sharply away from the President's party and their own ancestral allegiance. The collapse of farm prices and the strong dollar hurt Peoria's farm machinery manufacturers—especially Caterpillar, long the world's leading producer of earth-moving and construction equipment. The Democratic trend enabled Paul Simon to carry the 18th District in 1984; James Thompson failed to win a majority here in 1986; and Michael Dukakis made a respectable showing the 18th in 1988.

The trend has even put in jeopardy the incumbency of Bob Michel and made even more difficult the already frustrating job he has of marshalling a Republican minority when Republicans have been in the majority in just about every other part of Washington. In the 1982 general election, Peoria lawyer G. Douglas Stephens gave Michel a scare and eventually held him to 52%; in 1988 Stephens ran again and held Michel to 55%. Yet having survived 1982, when the Democrats' campaign committee was pouring money in, Michel seems not to have let his possible peril at home affect his performance as Leader in Washington—though he does take care to tend to things Peorian.

As House Republican Leader Michel has performed ably, under often trying circumstances, throughout the 1980s. In 1981 and 1982, when Republicans had enough votes to have a working majority in the House, he nurtured unprecedented party unanimity: there were virtually no dissenters from the Reagan budget or tax cuts of 1981. After the 1982 elections, he came under attack from the younger conservatives around Newt Gingrich for being insufficiently confrontational. Michel has served three decades in a Democratic-majority House, and he is a man of old-fashioned personal decency and good fellowship. But he is also capable of being a tough partisan on occasion. In 1985 and 1986 he helped lead the Republicans' hopeless fight on the Indiana 8th challenge, helped put together a House Republican alternative budget that united much of the party, and argued strongly and finally effectively for aid to the Nicaraguan contras. But in 1987 he was antagonizing Republicans by his (accurate) prediction that they would lose a vote on the contras and by his vote to override the President's veto of the highway bill because it included a project in the 18th District ("The President doesn't see Route 121 as I do," Michel said). But he still managed to carry some contra aid votes in the House, till the Iran-contra scandal destroyed its chances, and he has maintained Republican Party unity at something near the historic high, a considerable achievement considering the wide breadth of views.

Despite the warm feelings most House Republicans have for Michel, they administered him something of a rebuke in March 1989 when they elected as Whip, the number two position in the leadership, his sometime antagonist Newt Gingrich over his endorsed favorite and Downstate Illinois neighbor Edward Madigan. The contest arose suddenly, when Richard Cheney was nominated to be Secretary of Defense, and Gingrich and Madigan—representing opposite views on party posture—jumped into the race so quickly as to squeeze out possible consensus candidates like Jerry Lewis and Henry Hyde. The race was portrayed by some as liberal versus conservative, but the difference was more over basic strategy: whether to try to accommodate to Democratic control and make the best legislatively of it, as Madigan argued, or whether to challenge the premises of the Democrats' policies, in the House and out, in the hope of producing a Republican majority, as Gingrich argued. To Gingrich's side went not just 1980s conservatives but also 92 Group moderates who are attracted to new ideas and want a Republican majority and they turned out to be enough to produce an 87–85 Gingrich victory. Gingrich was careful to say this was no repudiation of Michel, but the glum expression of Michel as he stood by his side was eloquent: he looked like a man less comfortable with what the House and his party were becoming than with what they had been over the 40 years since he had come to Washington as a staffer in 1949.

Michel's father came to isolationist Peoria from Alsace-Lorraine (an area long fought over in

European wars), and Michel himself was wounded in the Battle of the Bulge, not far away. His predecessor, Richard Velde, was chairman of the House Un-American Activities Committee; Michel himself, on the floor and in the Appropriations Committee, was a steady and unflagging but often unsuccessful opponent of federal spending. He chaired the Republicans' campaign committee in its tough years in the middle 1970s and was party whip in the late 1970s. After the 1980 election, he beat Guy VanderJagt, then and now chairman of the Republican campaign committee, for the party leadership. Although he must have at one time expected that the Republicans would regain their majority, at some point he evidently gave up hope that they would, and decided to shoulder on, to uphold the party's cause and to act in what he considered the country's interest; through it all he has almost always remained of good cheer. In early 1989 there was once again talk that Michel will retire from the House, weary of being in the minority and of having to campaign hard in Peoria; if he does he will have to tip his hand early, for Illinois has a December filing deadline, the first in the nation. That announcement will probably produce a battle royal for the leadership, occupying most of 1990, with candidates calling for this and that change; they might do well to remember and build on the strengths of the leader they have, which may look greater after he retires than they have to some in the 1980s.

The People: Est. Pop. 1986: 490,700, dn. 5.4% 1980–86; Pop. 1980: 519,026, up 8.3% 1970–80. Households (1980): 75% family, 41% with children, 65% married couples; 28.3% housing units rented; median monthly rent: $185; median house value: $44,400. Voting age pop. (1980): 368,659; 4% Black, 1% Spanish origin.

1988 Presidential Vote:

Bush (R)	114,566	(55%)
Dukakis (D)	94,582	(45%)

Rep. Robert H. Michel (R)

Elected 1956; b. Mar. 2, 1923, Peoria; home, Peoria; Bradley U., B.S. 1948; Apostolic Christian; married (Corinne).

Career: Army, WWII; A.A., U.S. Rep. Harold Velde, 1949–56.

Offices: 2112 RHOB 20515, 202-225-6201. Also 100 N.E. Monroe, Rm. 107, Peoria 61602, 309-671-7027; and 236 W. State St., Jacksonville 62650, 217-245-1431.

Committees: *Minority Leader.*

Group Ratings

	ADA	ACLU	COPE	CFA	LCV	ACU	NTLC	NSI	COC	CEI
1988	10	10	12	36	6	92	76	100	85	60
1987	0	—	11	14	—	86	—	—	86	86

National Journal Ratings

	1988 LIB — 1988 CONS			1987 LIB — 1987 CONS		
Economic	21%	—	77%	11%	—	83%
Social	9%	—	89%	0%	—	90%
Foreign	0%	—	84%	0%	—	80%

Key Votes

1) Homeless $	FOR	5) Ban Drug Test	FOR	9) SDI Research	FOR
2) Gephardt Amdt	AGN	6) Drug Death Pen	FOR	10) Ban Chem Weaps	AGN
3) Deficit Reduc	AGN	7) Handgun Sales	FOR	11) Aid to Contras	FOR
4) Kill Plnt Clsng Notice	FOR	8) Ban D.C. Abort $	FOR	12) Nuclear Testing	AGN

Election Results

1988 general	Rober H. Michel (R) 114,458	(55%)	($861,969)
	G. Douglas Stevens (D) 94,763	(45%)	($231,511)
1988 primary	Robert H. Michel (R)................. 33,395	(88%)	
	Justin Zachary West (R)................ 4,553	(12%)	
1986 general	Robert H. Michel (R)................. 94,308	(63%)	($639,765)
	Jim Dawson (D) 56,331	(37%)	($11,949)

NINETEENTH DISTRICT

The first white settlers who moved west of the Wabash River encountered suddenly the great American prairie; a vast sea of flat, unforested land that stretched much farther than the eye could see, all the way to the Mississippi River and beyond. For 200 years settlers had to chop down trees and clear the stumps—backbreaking work that kept the frontier from marching forward very fast. The prairie soil was difficult to plough, but the settlers could begin farming in Illinois much faster than they had in Ohio or Indiana, and the soil proved wondrously rich. The prairie lands of Illinois even today are among the richest croplands in the nation.

Settlers came to the prairie of Illinois from two directions. The northern half of the state was settled originally by Yankees coming overland from Ohio, Upstate New York, and New England, people who soon formed the bedrock of the new Republican Party. The southern part was settled by people we would now call southerners, people born in Kentucky (like Abraham Lincoln) or Virginia or Tennessee. The rough boundary between these two migrations runs through the middle of the 19th Congressional District, along the old National Road—now U.S. 40, paralleled by Interstate 70. North of this the accents are hard and the politics traditionally Republican; Danville, in the northern end of the district, used to elect Joseph Cannon, the Speaker of the House against whom the progressives rebelled in 1910. South of the National Road, the accents are softer and more drawling and the politics traditionally Democratic. Voters here have had little use for national Democrats, but as late as 1976 they regularly reelected a Democratic congressman.

Now it elects a Democrat again, Terry Bruce, one of those natural politicians with which his party seems so much better endowed than the opposition. He spent two years on the staff of the Illinois Senate president, then was elected senator himself in 1970 at age 26. He showed himself able to pass bills on everything from education to grain elevators and was reelected regularly. He ran in 1978 for the House but lost to Republican Dan Crane; in 1984, after Crane had been censured by the House for having sex with a female page, and despite Crane's repentance and a tearful appearance with his family back home, Bruce defeated him 52%–48%. The composition of the 19th District in 1984 was a little more favorable for him than it was in 1978: it stretched along the eastern Illinois prairie, extending south almost to the Ohio River, and going north far enough to take in not only the old manufacturing town of Danville but Champaign-Urbana, home of the University of Illinois.

In the House Bruce got seats on the Agriculture, Education and Labor, and Science Committees, and got busy getting scientific grants for the University of Illinois, working on student loan programs, and encouraging ethanol production. He proclaimed himself a fiscal conservative, supporting Gramm-Rudman and insisting on work requirements in welfare reform

After two years, and with some adroit lobbying, he got a seat on the Energy and Commerce Committee, helped partly by the understanding that, with coal mines in the southern part of his district, he would be less stringent than many on clean air. He used his committee post to advantage by pushing to passage a law requiring federal utility rate decreases to go into effect as rapidly as increases, and he pushed to limit advertising on children's TV programs and decried the tendency of cartoon programs to be nothing more than advertising displays of commercial products.

In this district that sits on a political borderland, tottering between two regions and two parties, Bruce has shown his mastery of the political game by winning reelection twice by overwhelming margins.

The People: Est. Pop. 1986: 513,000, dn. 1.0% 1980–86; Pop. 1980: 518,350, up 4.9% 1970–80. Households (1980): 70% family, 36% with children, 61% married couples; 30.3% housing units rented; median monthly rent: $161; median house value: $35,100. Voting age pop. (1980): 386,732; 3% Black, 1% Asian origin, 1% Spanish origin.

1988 Presidential Vote:

Bush (R)	114,219	(54%)
Dukakis (D)	95,602	(45%)

Rep. Terry L. Bruce (D)

Elected 1984; b. Mar. 25, 1944, Olney; home, Olney; U. of IL, B.S. 1966, J.D. 1969; United Methodist; married (Charlotte).

Career: U.S. Dept. of Labor, 1965; Staff asst., IL Senate Pres., 1969–70; Practicing atty., 1970–84; IL Senate, 1970–84.

Offices: 419 CHOB 20515, 202-225-5001. Also 202 E. Main St., P.O. Box 206, Olney 62450, 618-395-8585; 106 N. Vermillion St., Danville 61832, 217-446-7445; and 102 E. University Ave., Champaign 61820, 217-398-0020.

Committees: *Energy and Commerce* (24th of 26 D). Subcommittees: Health and the Environment; Energy and Power. *Science, Space and Technology* (16th of 30 D). Subcommittees: Energy Research and Development; Science, Research and Technology.

Group Ratings

	ADA	ACLU	COPE	CFA	LCV	ACU	NTLC	NSI	COC	CEI
1988	75	61	92	73	69	24	7	0	36	18
1987	80	—	89	86	—	9	—	—	13	7

National Journal Ratings

	1988 LIB — 1988 CONS			1987 LIB — 1987 CONS	
Economic	60%	—	37%	73% — 0%	
Social	54%	—	45%	66% — 32%	
Foreign	84%	—	0%	81% — 0%	

Key Votes

1) Homeless $	AGN	5) Ban Drug Test	AGN	9) SDI Research	AGN
2) Gephardt Amdt	FOR	6) Drug Death Pen	FOR	10) Ban Chem Weaps	—
3) Deficit Reduc	FOR	7) Handgun Sales	FOR	11) Aid to Contras	AGN
4) Kill Plnt Clsng Notice	AGN	8) Ban D.C. Abort $	FOR	12) Nuclear Testing	FOR

Election Results

1988 general	Terry L. Bruce (D)	132,889	(64%)	($193,205)
	Robert F. Kerans (R)	73,981	(36%)	($16,241)
1988 primary	Terry L. Bruce (D)	38,221	(100%)	
1986 general	Terry L. Bruce (D)	111,105	(66%)	($278,421)
	Al Salvi (R)	56,186	(34%)	($37,570)

TWENTIETH DISTRICT

The 20th District of Illinois is a descendant of the district that elected a 37-year-old railroad lawyer and Whig opponent of the Mexican War named Abraham Lincoln to the House of Representatives in 1846. The western part of the district, to outward appearances, hasn't changed much since the 19th century. It remains a land of fertile prairies, the bottomlands of the Mississippi and Illinois Rivers, farm marketing towns and courthouse villages. The river port of Quincy on the Mississippi River looks pretty much the way it did at the turn of the century. Some of these counties are historically Democratic (one produced Henry Rainey, Speaker of the House during Franklin Roosevelt's first 100 days); others historically Republican.

The largest city in the district is Springfield, with 99,000 people. It must have been a bustling, perhaps even a gracious town in Abe Lincoln's and Mary Todd's time. Today it is a middle-sized state capital with an old capitol building, several not-so-elegant hotels, a small black ghetto, a little industry and a few shopping centers, but little of the gentrification and glitter that has made Albany and Sacramento and Austin into considerable cities in the last 10 years. The other major city here is Decatur, an old factory town important now as the headquarters of Dwayne Andreas's Archer-Daniels-Midland soybean and corn combine.

The 20th District is now a solid political base for Democratic Representative Richard Durbin. He is another one of those workhorse younger members who, as the local Republican paper that carries Lincoln's picture on the masthead noted while endorsing him, has a 98% attendance record and yet came home 48 weekends a year. In Springfield he worked for Democrats in the state Senate and for Senator Paul Simon when he was lieutenant governor (1969–73); he lost two races for office in the 1970s, but developed an in-depth knowledge of parliamentary procedure and an instinctive understanding of the legislative process. In 1982 he was able to win the nomination to oppose a clearly vulnerable congressman and to raise and spend a large campaign budget intelligently. He won a seat on the Agriculture Committee and on Science and Technology as well; after the 1984 election he had the political savvy to win a seat on Appropriations over tough competition. He serves on the Agriculture and Transportation subcommittees, and is proud of his work funneling money to Springfield and Illinois. A reflector of contemporary opinion, he was proud of measures aimed at drug-exporting nations and to get states to raise the drinking age to 21. He wants to require that half of all gasoline be blended with ethanol and he opposes ethanol imports—positions that help Andreas and ADM. He is the author of the ban on smoking on airline flights of less than two hours which, to his surprise, was passed on the floor of the House 198–193 in July 1987.

Durbin won the district in 1982 by beating Republican Paul Findley, a 22-year House veteran. Findley won easily when he concentrated on farm issues, but as a senior Foreign Affairs Committee member in the late 1970s he met with Yasir Arafat and was happy to characterize himself as Arafat's best friend in Congress—thus generating plenty of campaign money to any serious opponent. Since his first victory Durbin has won by very large margins and has made Lincoln's old district a safe Democratic seat.

The People: Est. Pop. 1986: 507,600, dn. 2.2% 1980–86; Pop. 1980: 519,015, up 3.2% 1970–80. Households (1980): 72% family, 38% with children, 61% married couples; 28.0% housing units rented.

median monthly rent: $162; median house value: $37,200. Voting age pop. (1980): 375,764, 4% Black.

1988 Presidential Vote:

Bush (R)	113,676	(51%)
Dukakis (D)	110,072	(49%)

Rep. Richard J. Durbin (D)

Elected 1982; b. Nov. 21, 1944; East St. Louis; home, Springfield; Georgetown U., B.S. 1966, J.D. 1969; Roman Catholic; married (Loretta).

Career: Staff of Lt. Gov. Paul Simon, 1969–72; Legal cns. to IL Sen. Judiciary Cmtee., 1972–82; Professor, Southern IL Sch. of Medicine, 1978–82.

Offices: 129 CHOB 20515, 202-225-5271. Also 1307 S. 7th St., Springfield 62703, 217-492-4062; 363 S. Main St., Rm. 110, Decatur 62523, 217-428-4745; and 531 Hampshire, Rm. 305, Quincy 62301, 217-228-1042.

Committees: *Appropriations* (30th of 35 D). Subcommittees: Rural Development, Agriculture and Related Agencies; Transportation. *Budget* (11th of 21 D). Task Forces: Economic Policy, Projections and Revenues; Human Resources. *Select Committee on Children, Youth and Families* (16th of 18 D).

Group Ratings

	ADA	ACLU	COPE	CFA	LCV	ACU	NTLC	NSI	COC	CEI
1988	90	65	88	82	75	16	7	0	36	14
1987	92	—	86	93	—	4	—	—	0	7

National Journal Ratings

	1988 LIB — 1988 CONS			1987 LIB — 1987 CONS		
Economic	60%	—	37%	73%	—	0%
Social	61%	—	38%	66%	—	32%
Foreign	84%	—	0%	81%	—	0%

Key Votes

1) Homeless $	AGN	5) Ban Drug Test	AGN	9) SDI Research	AGN
2) Gephardt Amdt	FOR	6) Drug Death Pen	FOR	10) Ban Chem Weaps	FOR
3) Deficit Reduc	FOR	7) Handgun Sales	AGN	11) Aid to Contras	AGN
4) Kill Plnt Clsng Notice	AGN	8) Ban D.C. Abort $	FOR	12) Nuclear Testing	FOR

Election Results

1988 general	Richard J. Durbin (D)	153,341	(69%)	($251,634)
	Paul E. Jurgens (R)	69,303	(31%)	($57,708)
1988 primary	Richard J. Durbin (D), unopposed			
1986 general	Richard J. Durbin (D)	126,556	(68%)	($289,085)
	Kevin B. McCarthy (R)	59,291	(32%)	($108,129)

TWENTY-FIRST DISTRICT

Through the Gateway Arch you can see, across the Mississippi River, the tangle of rail lines and old factories that are the major sights of East St. Louis, Illinois, where the major railroads and Interstate highways from Chicago, the East, and the South funnel into the bridges over the Mississippi. This is one of America's poorest and most troubled cities, an industrial slum with a

high crime rate, declining population and job base, with a stormy history (in 1896 angr
aldermen drew their pistols and killed the mayor at a council meeting); and the towns just behin
and north, Belleville and Granite City, while in better shape, are scarcely garden spots. Th
Illinois side of the St. Louis metropolitan area has a disproportionate share of its poor and low
income working-class residents; the rich stay on the Missouri side of the river.

The 21st proceeds north and inland from the river enough to take in territory more typical c
Downstate Illinois. There is Alton, home of the antislavery martyr Elijah Lovejoy and, later, c
Robert Wadlow, at 8'11" the world's tallest man, and Phyllis Schlafly. And there are the fla
farmlands of southern Illinois, alive with the latest miracle plant, soybeans, a crop exported i
great quantities to Japan. Politically this has been a solidly Democratic district since the 1940s
In the close presidential elections of the 1940s, 1960, 1968, and 1976, well as the not-so-clos
contests of 1952 and 1956, it delivered Democratic majorities; it has not elected a Republica
congressman since 1942. Yet it may be moving away from the Democratic column. The vote i
down in East St. Louis (some of which has been moved from the 21st district which contain
most of the St. Louis suburbs to the southern 22d). Voting is up in two rural counties added afte
the 1980 Census, which have attracted young, tradition-minded families from the St. Louis orb
and are heavily Republican. So the area fell out of the Democratic column in 1972, 1980, an
1984. It delivered modest majorities to Senator Paul Simon, a native son, in 1984, and t
Michael Dukakis in 1988. But as much of Downstate Illinois trends toward the Democrats, the
can no longer rely on this industrial district.

That was demonstrated also in the House race in 1988. Congressman Mel Price, first electe
in 1944, died in May 1988 after serving for years on the old Joint Atomic Energy Committee an
on Armed Services, which he chaired from 1975 to 1985. By 1984 Price was inactive: he bea
Republican Robert Gaffner by only 60%–40% that year, then was voted out of the chairmanshi
by the Democratic caucus; in 1986, he was opposed by 40-year-old Madison County Auditc
Pete Fields in the primary and won by only 52%–40%, and then beat Gaffner by only 943 vote
50.4%–49.6%, in the general.

It was no surprise when Price announced his retirement; what was a surprise was how difficu
it was for Jerry Costello, St. Clair County board chairman, son of a former St. Clair Count
treasurer and sheriff, supported by organized labor, to hold the seat for the Democrats. Field
ran against him in the regular primary, charging that he accepted contributions from tri
lawyers and exerted undue influence on the choice of judges (though an inquiry board cleare
Costello of wrongdoing); also running was former Price aide Mike Mansfield. Costello, even wit
the endorsement of Belleville native Senator Alan Dixon, won with only 46% to 27% for Field
and 25% for Mansfield; Costello won the July special primary scheduled after Price's deat
without serious opposition. In the general, Gaffner ran again, charging that in St. Clair Count
"politics are administered Chicago-style"; Costello claimed a record of streamlining gover
ment, beefing up law enforcement, and cleaning out corruption in the local poverty progran
Though known to be Price's heir apparent for years, Costello won by just a 53%–47% margir

The likelihood is that he will use the powers of incumbency and his seat on Public Works—a
appropriate spot for a nuts and bolts politician—to make this a safe seat. But the local politic
trends and recent political turbulence may mean there's another rough contest coming up on th
other side of the river from the Arch.

The People: Est. Pop. 1986: 526,400, up 1.0% 1980–86; Pop. 1980: 521,036, dn. 2.0% 1970–8
Households (1980): 76% family, 42% with children, 62% married couples; 29.1% housing units rente
median monthly rent: $155; median house value: $36,700. Voting age pop. (1980): 367,291; 12% Blac
1% Spanish origin.

1988 Presidential Vote: Dukakis (D). 110,653   (54%)
Bush (R) 92,957   (45%)

Rep. Jerry F. Costello (D)

Elected August 1988; b. Sept. 25, 1949, East St. Louis; home, Belleville; Belleville Area Col. A.A. 1970, Maryville Col. B.A. 1972; Roman Catholic; married (Georgia).

Career: Dir., Crt. Services, Probation; Chrmn., Region's Council of Governments; Chrmn., St. Clair Cnty. Bd, 1980-88.

Offices: 1529 LHOB 20515, 202-225-5661. Also 1316 Niedringhaus Ave., Granite City, 618-451-2122; 8787 State St. E. St. Louis 618-397-8833.

Committees: *Public Works and Transportation* (26th of 31 D). Subcommittees: Aviation; Surface Transportation; Water Resources. *Science, Space and Technology* (27th of 30 D). Subcommittees: Energy Research and Development; Science, Research and Technology. *Select Committee on Aging* (35th of 39 D).

Group Ratings and Key Votes: Newly Elected

Election Results

1988 general	Jerry F. Costello (D)	105,836	(53%)	($394,412)
	Robert H. (Bob) Gaffner (R)	95,385	(47%)	($69,486)
1988 special	Jerry F. Costello (D)	33,144	(51%)	($239,564)
	Robert H. (Bob) Gaffner (R)	31,257	(49%)	($155,362)
1986 general	Melvin Price (D)......................	65,722	(50%)	($143,009)
	Robert H. Gaffner (R)	64,779	(50%)	($137,353)

TWENTY-SECOND DISTRICT

The southern end of Illinois is not one of the gentler parts of rural America. The Egypt region down where the Ohio River meets the Mississippi is flat, fertile farmland, protected by giant levees because it is susceptible to yearly floods; there is more than a touch of Dixie here, and the unofficial capital of Egypt, Cairo (pronounced *KAYroh*), is a declining town closer to Mississippi than Chicago which has seen outbreaks of violence between the races. North of Egypt are the coal mining counties, where coal used to be brought to the surface through shafts and is now mostly strip-mined; John L. Lewis started his path upward in the United Mine Workers in an Illinois coal town called Panama. Southern Illinois also has its amenities— Southern Illinois University in Carbondale primary among them—and its pleasant scenery. But for most of its citizens this is unsentimental, workaday country.

The 22d Congressional District of Illinois includes most of the southern end of the state, from Cairo in Egypt north almost to Panama in the coal country, taking in Carbondale and proceeding north along the Mississippi River in a salient that goes far enough to take in some precincts of the slum-city of East St. Louis. Nearly all this territory is Democratic in most elections, because of ancestral southern preference (this is southern drawl, not midwestern hard R territory) or because of the Democratic leanings of coal miners and industrial workers. But it has not been reliably Democratic in national elections. The 21st went against the Catholic John Kennedy in 1960 and the Great Society's Hubert Humphrey in 1968; it gave southerner Jimmy Carter a majority in 1976 but turned sharply against him, as did many border areas, in 1980. It went for Michael Dukakis in 1988, but only by a narrow margin.

Southern Illinois's Democratic preference was very apparent in the 1988 House race, when it chose as its new congressman Democrat Glenn Poshard. That election keeps alive a string the

394   ILLINOIS

party has going back to 1954, when Kenneth Gray—auctioneer, magician, pork barrel politician—first won the district. It continues through 1974, when Gray retired for health reasons and newspaper editor and reform legislator Paul Simon, now U.S. Senator, won it, and through 1984, when Simon ran for the Senate and Gray returned to win. It finishes off (for now) with Gray's second retirement for health reasons and Poshard's win. When Gray announced in November 1987 that he wasn't running, Poshard was so strong that he drew no Democratic primary opponents; Republican Randy Patchett, who had given Gray a couple of good fights, did not run, and Poshard won the general election by nearly 2 to 1.

Like a number of his contemporaries who have won House seats in their 40s (Jerry Costello of the 21st district is another), and unlike many born in the same years who won them in their 20s and 30s in the 1970s, Poshard does not have an elite background: he went into military service after high school, graduated from college a little late, does not share the liberal views on cultural and foreign issues that were obligatory on Ivy League campuses half a generation ago. But Poshard is not a rube either: he has a Ph.D., he won an Illinois Senate seat over serious competition, he rose to chair a committee, he worked to cut down pollution from coal use. He seems to have no bias against government spending, especially when it is directed at southern Illinois; he can be expected to be a bread-and-butter Democrat, devoted to helping his district. There is no reason to expect that he will not make this a safe Democratic seat.

The People: Est. Pop. 1986: 523,600, up 0.4% 1980–86; Pop. 1980: 521,303, up 9.3% 1970–80. Households (1980): 73% family, 37% with children, 62% married couples; 25.6% housing units rented; median monthly rent: $131; median house value: $29,500. Voting age pop. (1980): 381,684; 6% Black, 1% Spanish origin.

1988 Presidential Vote:

Dukakis (D)	113,071	(52%)
Bush (R)	104,885	(48%)

Rep. Glenn W. Poshard (D)

Elected 1988; b. Oct. 30, 1945, White Cnty.; home, Carterville; S IL U., B.A. 1970, M.S. 1974, Ph.D. 1984; Baptist; married (Jo).

Career: Army, Korea 1962–65; State Senator 1984; Dir., Area Service Center for Educators of Gifted, 1974–84.

Offices: 1229 LHOB 20515, 202-225-5201. Also 234 W. Main, West Frankfort 62896, 618-937-6402; 110 N. Division, Carterville 62918, 618-985-6300; 4831 Bond Ave., Alorton 62207, 618-271-7500.

Committees: *Education and Labor* (16th of 22 D). Subcommittees: Elementary, Secondary and Vocational Education; Human Resources; Postsecondary Education. *Small Business* (26th of 27 D). Subcommittees: Procurement, Tourism and Rural Development; Environment and Labor.

Group Ratings and Key Votes: Newly Elected

Election Results

1988 general	Glenn Poshard (D)	139,392	(65%)	($392,791)
	Patrick J. Kelly (R)	75,462	(35%)	($80,675)
1988 primary	Glenn Poshard (D), unopposed			
1986 general	Kenneth J. Gray (D)	97,585	(53%)	($304,950)
	Randy Patchett (R)	85,733	(47%)	($220,564)

INDIANA

In August 1940, Wendell Willkie, the Republican nominee for President, returned home to Indiana. At his mother-in-law's in Rushville, as his biographer Steve Neal tells the story, he ate his favorite meal of fried chicken and hot cherry pie; on that hot evening they may have sat on the darkened porch, listening to the soft thud of moths hitting screens while heading for light. The next day Willkie went to his boyhood home town of Elwood, to formally accept the Republican nomination for President before a crowd of 150,000 in 103 degree heat. As 60,000 cars came into this town of 10,000, 55 miles north of Indianapolis, the streets were designated one-way, food prices were jacked up 20%, Willkie hats and tie clips and tumblers were sold everywhere, and Homer Capehart, later a U.S. Senator, boasted to H. L. Mencken that each of the latrines he had set up in Callaway Park where the nominee would speak was "a 32-holer!" Willkie was not the hayseed he liked to appear; "the barefoot boy from Wall Street," as Harold Ickes called him, lived in a Fifth Avenue apartment across from the Metropolitan Museum, was knowledgeable enough to appear on "Information Please," and was given to naive-sounding political statements that were actually very popular.

But the backdrop was authentic. Indiana in 1940 was the center of population in the United States; it was where sociologists Robert and Helen Lynd conducted their study of "Middletown" (actually Muncie); in partisan politics, it was a fulcrum point, a crucial state since the Civil War in the struggles between Republicans and Democrats. Willkie was a politician who held himself above party, but Indiana—then and now—had some of the toughest and most professional political machines in the United States. Party identification was handed down with religious affiliation—the Lynds noted that the Presbyterians had little to do with Methodists, but that was nothing next to Republicans and Democrats—in a state that had relatively few immigrants since it was first settled by Yankees from Ohio and the Northeast and "Butternuts" (as they were called in the Civil War years) from Kentucky and the South.

But if Indiana was classically Middle American long before that term was coined, it has always celebrated its distinctiveness. It is the Hoosier state—a unique word, about whose origins and meanings you can get plenty of argument—with its own poet in James Whitcomb Riley, its own novelist in Booth Tarkington, and its own politics in its two still surprisingly hardy political party machines. While other states have long since moved away from their political heritage, splitting over the economic issues of the 1930s or the cultural conflicts that started in the 1960s, Indiana has stuck to its Civil War alignments: a map of the results of the 1980 Senate campaign show liberal Democratic Senator Birch Bayh carrying half the counties south of the old National Road (later U.S. 40) that bisects the state, while conservative Republican Dan Quayle carried all but four of the counties to the north—a result eerily similar to that of 1868. Indiana's machines have lost some of their control: the mandatory 2% contributions by state employees to the state party were banned in the 1980s by the Republicans (in anticipation of a 1988 defeat, the Democrats said). The Republican machine which had controlled the state government for 20 years, since Dan Quayle was looking for a state job to work his way through law school, finally lost the governorship and control of one house of the legislature to the son of the Senator that Quayle beat, Evan Bayh, in the year in which Quayle was elected Vice President of the United States.

Indiana politics has changed less because life here has changed less than in other states. The cultural and ethnic patterns in Indiana today are not much different from what the Lynds found in the 1920s and 1930s. Ethnically, except for the steel area around Gary—really an extension of

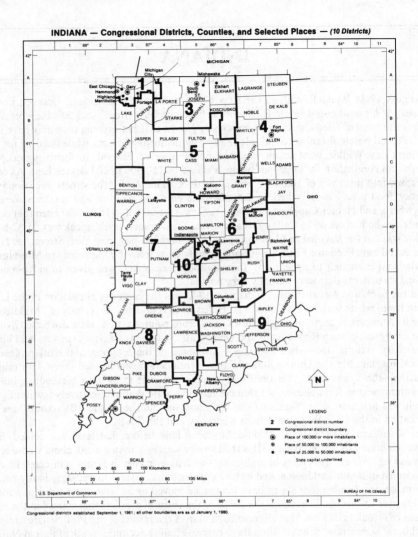

INDIANA — Congressional Districts, Counties, and Selected Places — *(10 Districts)*

the Chicago metropolitan area—Indiana has relatively few ethnics from the 1840–1924 wave of immigration. It has no great metropolitan areas: greater Indianapolis now has more than one million people, but nothing like the singles and gay cultures of other metropolises. The divorce rate here is lower than the American average, and the percentage of households occupied by families and married people higher. The percentage of households with children is also high and, if the population weren't a little older than the national average, would be among the highest in the United States. Even the singles ads in *Indianapolis Monthly* emphasize physical fitness and Christian values. This is a state not far from the more innocent America of barbershop quartets and ice cream socials.

These patterns have important political consequences in a time when the old economic antagonisms between union members and management supporters seem to have dissipated. Indianapolis, by far the largest metropolitan area, is consistently more Republican than the rest of the state, if you leave the northwest industrial zone from Gary to South Bend aside; it went nearly 2 to 1 for Reagan in 1984 and Bush in 1988. And while the northwest's share of the statewide vote is falling, the share of booming and growing metro Indianapolis, which extends into eight counties, is growing. The auto factory towns of Kokomo and Anderson, Muncie and Fort Wayne, though once Democratic and suffering from some of the nation's highest unemployment in the early 1980s, nevertheless voted for Reagan-Bush in 1984 and Bush-Quayle in 1988. In the 1920s the Lynds, liberal academics influenced by Marx's idea that political acts were determined by economic interests, were puzzled as to why the factory workers didn't vote against the bosses; in the 1930s, they were cheered by signs that they were. Why don't they now? The answer is that cultural identity and personal values have usually been more important determinants of political allegiance in an America where economic status is so often readily changeable.

This does not mean that the Republicans always win—although they have held national Democratic tickets to no more than 40% of the vote in all but three elections since 1952. Evan Bayh's capture of the governorship in 1988 was presaged by his defeat of former Governor and Health and Human Services Secretary Otis Bowen's son for secretary of state in 1976, and despite a fiercely partisan Republican redistricting plan, the Democrats have held half or more of the state's U.S. House delegation throughout the 1980s. In 1988, they won an even split in the state House—each party will have a "speaker du jour," alternating in the chair—and cut the Republican margin in the state Senate to 26–24. Over the long run the large number of Hoosiers with ancestral ties to each party has given both a base and the ability of the out-party to adapt to local circumstances and attack the ins' shortcomings has assured a pretty regular rotation in office. The national Republicans' occasional emphasis on free market economics has not played very well in this factory state, which lost jobs during much of the decade; and the national emphasis on conservative cultural values does not help Republicans against local Democrats because they represent no challenge to them. So after a long and mostly successful 20 years in office, the Republicans fell victim in 1988 to the forces which for 150 years have produced closely contested two-party politics in Indiana.

Governor. In 1988 Indiana exchanged the nation's oldest governor, Robert Orr (born in 1917), for the youngest, Evan Bayh (born in 1955). Orr, barred from a third term, vigorously supported Lieutenant Governor John Mutz, and Indianapolis Mayor William Hudnut did not run. (Indiana parties for years nominated statewide candidates in conventions dominated by party officials; now there can be primaries, but usually they don't amount to much.) Mutz had run Orr's campaign to encourage and attract businesses and new jobs; he had an encyclopedic knowledge of Hoosier businesses and could claim considerable success. But the Republicans wasted much time charging that Bayh didn't meet the state residency requirement, and Bayh put them on the defensive on abolishing the 2% fee, even though a Republican law did end it in July 1988. Bayh in the meantime charged that the Republicans had made too many concessions to attract a Subaru-Isuzu plant and campaigned for spending and tax controls and, though the issue was largely moot, against overpoliticization. In effect he got on the opposite side of two issues on which national Democrats are usually poorly positioned.

The result was a comfortable, though not huge, Bayh victory, accompanied by Democratic gains in the legislature. An interesting question is whether Bayh will stick with the traditionally low levels of state taxes and services. The likelihood is that he, like earlier Democratic governors, will.

Senators. If you had told almost anyone in Washington in early 1988 that an Indiana Senator would have been George Bush's choice for Vice President, the immediate assumption would have been that you were talking about Richard Lugar. As chairman of the Senate Foreign Relations Committee in 1985 and 1986, after the defeat of Charles Percy and before Republicans lost their Senate majority, Lugar was a national and international figure of great stature. He did as much as anyone in Congress, perhaps as much as anyone in government, to get Ferdinand Marcos out of the Malacanang Palace in Manila and a democratic government, headed by Corazon Aquino, in. He fought the Democrats on contra aid and the Reagan Administration on South African sanctions, yet he seems better positioned to—and more interested in—establishing a genuinely bipartisan foreign policy. He has long taken time out each day to read and write, and his 1988 book, *Letters to the Next President*, is thoughtful and definitely not ghost-written.

On one issue after another his philosophy and his analysis have led him into positions that are politically risky. He led the 1978 filibuster against the AFL-CIO's labor law reform bill; like most Indiana Republicans, he has always been an adversary of organized labor, but he went out of his way to antagonize a group that then had a large constituency in the state. He provided key support in 1978 for the loan guarantees to Chrysler, a big employer in Indiana, but he also insisted on requiring bigger wage and benefit concessions than the UAW wanted. He voted against several versions of the Civil Rights Restoration Act because he believed it impinged on the free exercise of religious beliefs. He voted against the 1988 trade bill in a midwestern state where workers have been trained to think that foreigners are taking their jobs—though, as he pointed out, Indiana exports plenty of agricultural products, pharamaceuticals, steel, and auto parts.

He has also taken some leadership positions in the Senate. He chaired the Republican Senate campaign committee in the 1983–84 cycle, and held control for the Republicans. He became an admirer and close lieutenant of Majority Leader Howard Baker, and ran for majority leader himself after the 1984 election, running behind Bob Dole and Ted Stevens but ahead of James McClure. Then he became the chairman of the Senate Foreign Relations Committee, and became a major and positive force in American foreign policy. Lugar quickly took command over a committee sharply divided between Jesse Helms, who tends to conduct his own foreign policy, and liberal Democrats. Lugar supported the Reagan foreign policy generally and is a vigorous advocate of aid to the Nicaraguan contras. But on the Philippines he was ahead of the Administration: keeping in touch with Corazon Aquino as well as Ferdinand Marcos, and observing the elections. Lugar quickly concluded that Marcos's "victory" was fraudulent and, at a decisive point, called on him to leave office; the Administration followed. On South Africa Lugar backed the Senate bill that Reagan vetoed and then led the fight to override the veto. For all this he received some criticism from the right. But he had done much to forge a bipartisan consensus to advance democracy abroad and to oppose dictatorship, and Lugar is the first Foreign Relations chairman since William Fulbright to genuinely move the mind of the nation. He also seems to have moved Senate Republicans.

After the 1986 elections, Republicans lost control of the Senate, and Helms invoked his seniority to take the ranking minority position on Foreign Relations rather than Agriculture. Helms claimed he was released from a 1984 campaign promise because he was seeking not the chair but the ranking position. In early January 1987 committee Republicans voted 7–0 for Lugar, but that victory was overturned by the whole body of Republican Senators, 24–17. Helms quickly threw out Lugar's staff and installed his own; Lugar, who got the ranking position on Agriculture Helms had vacated, did likewise. This diminishes Lugar's central position on foreign policy in the short run and makes it harder for him to establish himself as the spokesman for his party. But the committee vote, and the narrowness of the wider vote despite the seniority principle, shows that Lugar in the long run is in the stronger and more respected position. In the meantime he has the ranking position on Agriculture which Helms abandoned—which means that he will have a major role in the difficult business of fashioning a 1989 farm bill, just as he did in the farm credit law of 1987.

Lugar is not the sort of man you would expect to rise out of a machine politics. He is bookish rather than gregarious, more unimposing than charismatic, his voice has a nasal undertone rather than a deep resonance. That he has brains and works hard are quickly apparent, but his strength of character and quiet persistence show up only over time. Yet perhaps it is only a machine that would advance a man of this demeanor, in the confidence that his competence would sustain his career. It has, and over a few bumps. Republican Party leaders slated him for mayor of Indianapolis in 1967, when he was 35; he consolidated the city and county into Unigov, which added tax resources to the city and also had the happy effect of adding more Republican votes to city elections. In the late 1960s, Lugar bucked fashion among big-city mayors and called for fewer rather than more federal programs, and nonetheless upset the much-ballyhooed John Lindsay for the presidency of the National League of Cities in 1970. He became known as Richard Nixon's favorite mayor—not a political asset in 1974, when he ran against and lost 51%–46% to Senator Birch Bayh. But in the more favorable climate of 1976 and against a weaker Democratic incumbent, Vance Hartke, he won 59%–40%.

In 1988 Lugar's reelection campaign set records. Against an underfinanced Democrat who never got any ads on the air, Lugar won 68% of the vote—well above the record for Indiana, Dan Quayle's 61% in 1986. This was far better than Lugar's 54% against incumbent Congressman Floyd Fithian in the recession year of 1982; this time, Lugar lost Lake County (Gary and the adjacent steel towns) and carried the other 91 counties in the state, all but 8 of them with more than 60% of the vote. No Indiana senator has ever been elected to a fourth term. Lugar will surely break that jinx if he runs again in 1994.

For eight years Lugar's Hoosier colleague in the Senate was Dan Quayle, now Vice President. Now the junior Senator is Dan Coats, Quayle's aide when he was a congressman and his successor in the House, appointed in his stead by outgoing Governor Robert Orr. But Coats is not Quayle's creature or anyone else's. When Quayle won his House seat in 1976, he hired Coats as his district representative, and it was Coats, an insurance man with a strongly traditional religious background, who put Quayle in touch with conservative Christians and others concerned about moral issues at a time when most Indiana Republicans' personal contacts were with economic, not cultural, conservatives. When Quayle ran for the Senate in 1980, Coats ran for the House and after beating Paul Helmke, now the mayor of Fort Wayne, in the primary, won the general election easily: the once marginal district around Fort Wayne had become by then heavily Republican.

In the House Coats sat on the hyperactive Energy and Commerce Committee, where he opposed total natural gas decontrol and zeroing out Amtrak. But he spent much of his time as the ranking Republican on the Select Committee on Children. There he shared the desire of Democrats like George Miller to do something to help children, but opposed what he considered the Democrats' overbureaucratic schemes and favored Republican plans to raise the income tax exemption and provide tax credits for child care. He and other committee Republicans split sharply from Miller and the Democrats over the issue of teenage pregnancy; Coats believes that sex counseling in schools that includes dispensing of contraceptives encourages premarital sex, and believes the emphasis should be put on encouraging abstinence until marriage. He has sponsored an amendment to cut off federal education funds to states banning voluntary school prayer.

In the Senate, Coats inherited Quayle's committee assignments, Labor and Armed Services and can be expected to have a similar voting record. Under Indiana law, although Quayle was elected in 1986, Coats must face the voters again in 1990 for the remaining two years of the term. A few years older than Quayle, not as telegenic or effervescent, he has not been tested in a statewide forum, and the Democrats are upbeat after their recent victories; so the 1990 contest could turn out to be the kind of spirited contest Indiana was used to up to 1980, rather than the much tamer and more one-sided campaigns it has had since. Marion County Prosecutor Stephen Goldsmith, widely known after 10 years on Indianapolis TV, wants to run for the Republican nomination; but present law, according to state chairman Gordon Durnil, says the state committee chooses the nominee. Possible Democratic nominees include Congressman Frank McCloskey and former Secretary of State Larry Conrad.

Presidential politics. Indiana remains one of the most Republican of states in presidential elections. Did Dan Quayle's popularity make it more Republican in 1988? Maybe in his old congressional district, the 4th, where the Bush-Quayle ticket ran even with Reagan-Bush '84; but not in the rest of the state. Indiana has a presidential primary that was once one of the earlier contests: in May 1968, for example, it was the scene of an epic battle between Robert Kennedy, Eugene McCarthy and Roger Branigin, the hapless governor who was a stand-in for President Johnson. In 1984 Indiana's primary was overshadowed by Ohio's the same day; curiously enough, Gary Hart won both by similar margins. In 1988 Indiana voted after both parties' nominees had been determined.

Congressional districting. Indiana's 1981 redistricting went up to the Supreme Court in 1986. It's decision was a classic muddle: it ruled that state legislatures can draw lines for partisan advantage but that courts can overturn them if they're egregious; then it went on to uphold Indiana's lines, although it's not likely that anyone could come up with a clearer case of partisan motivation. The better course would have been to uphold these lines and any that meet the equal-population standard, because the advantage any party can get from district-drawing is limited severely by the one-person-one-vote rule. Indiana is a fine example of this. In 1982 Republicans won 51% of House votes and 5 of the 10 seats. In 1984 they won 53% of the House votes and 5 seats, counting the bitterly contested 8th District the way the House did, for Democrat Frank McCloskey. In 1986, they won 49% of House votes and in 1988, 48%, and each time took 4 of the 10 seats. Altogether under their own plan Republicans have won 51% of the votes but only 17 of 40 seats. And by trying to maximize the number of seats they can carry, they also maximized their vulnerability by spreading their strength too thin: Governor Evan Bayh carried 9 of the 10 districts while winning statewide with just 53% in 1988.

The prospects for 1990, with a Democratic governor and a legislature that the Democrats do not yet control, are for a compromise plan, protecting most incumbents, with little change in district lines.

The People: Est. Pop. 1988: 5,575,000; Pop. 1980: 5,490,224, up 1.5% 1980–88 and 5.7% 1970–80; 2.28% of U.S. total, 14th largest. 12% with 1–3 yrs. col., 12% with 4+ yrs. col.; 9.7% below poverty level. Single ancestry: 13% German, 12% English, 4% Irish, 1% Polish, French, Dutch, Italian. Households (1980): 76% family, 42% with children, 64% married couples; 28.3% housing units rented; median monthly rent: $166; median house value: $37,200. Voting age pop. (1980): 3,871,906; 7% Black, 1% Spanish origin. Registered voters (1988): 2,865,870; no party registration.

1988 Share of Federal Tax Burden: $17,634,000,000; 1.99% of U.S. total, 16th largest.

1988 Share of Federal Expenditures

	Total		Non-Defense		Defense	
Total Expend	$14,807m	(1.67%)	$11,661m	(1.78%)	$2,559m	(1.12%)
St/Lcl Grants	1,960m	(1.71%)	1,199m	(1.05%)	0m	(0.43%)
Salary/Wages	1,606m	(1.20%)	901m	(1.34%)	706m	(1.34%)
Pymnts to Indiv	8,583m	(2.10%)	8,414m	(2.15%)	168m	(0.90%)
Procurement	1,681m	(0.89%)	173m	(0.37%)	1,681m	(0.89%)
Research/Other	977m	(2.62%)	974m	(2.63%)	3m	(2.63%)

Political Lineup: Governor, Evan Bayh (D); Lt. Gov., Frank O'Bannon (D); Secy. of State, Joseph Hogsett (D); Atty. Gen., Linley E. Pearson (R); Treasurer, Marjorie H. O'Laughlin (R); Auditor, Ann DeVore (R). State Senate, 50 (26 R and 24 D); State House of Representatives, 100 (50 R and 50 D). Senators, Richard G. Lugar (R) and Daniel R. Coats (R). Representatives, 10 (6 D and 4 R).

1988 Presidential Vote

Bush (R) 1,297,763 (60%)
Dukakis (D)............... 860,643 (39%)

1984 Presidential Vote

Reagan (R) 1,377,230 (62%)
Mondale (D)............... 841,481 (38%)

1988 Democratic Presidential Primary

Dukakis.................. 449,495 (69%)
Jackson 145,021 (22%)
Gore...................... 21,865 (3%)
Gephardt.................. 16,777 (3%)
Simon 12,555 (2%)

1988 Republican Presidential Primary

Bush 350,632 (83%)
Dole..................... 42,650 (10%)
Robertson 28,967 (7%)

GOVERNOR

Gov. Evan Bayh (D)

Elected 1988, term expires Jan. 1993; b. Dec. 26, 1955, Terre Haute; home, Indianapolis; IN U., B.A. 1978, U. of VA, J.D. 1981; Episcopalian; married (Susan).

Career: Practicing atty., 1985–86; IN Secy. of State, 1986–89.

Office: 206 State House, Indianapolis 46204, 317-232-4567.

Election Results

1988 gen.	Evan Bayh (D)	1,138,574	(53%)
	John Mutz (R)	1,002,207	(47%)
1988 prim.	Evan Bayh (D)	493,198	(83%)
	Stephen J. Daily (D)	66,242	(11%)
	Frank O'Bannon (D).........	34,360	(6%)
1984 gen.	Robert D. Orr (R)	1,146,497	(52%)
	W. Wayne Townsend (D)	1,036,832	(47%)

SENATORS

Sen. Richard G. Lugar (R)

Elected 1976, seat up 1994; b. Apr. 4, 1932, Indianapolis; home, Indianapolis; Denison U., B.A. 1954; Rhodes Scholar, Oxford U., M.A. 1956; Methodist; married (Charlene).

Career: Navy, 1957–60; V.P. and Treas., Thomas L. Green & Co., 1960–67; Indianapolis Bd. of Sch. Commissioners, 1964–67; Mayor of Indianapolis, 1968–75; Repub. Nominee for U.S. Senate, 1974; Visiting prof., U. of Indianapolis, 1976.

Offices: 306 HSOB 20510, 202-224-4814. Also 46 E. Ohio, Rm. 447, Indianapolis 46204, 317-269-5555; Fed. Bldg., 1300 S. Harrison St., Rm. 340, Fort Wayne 46802, 219-422-1505; Fed. Bldg., 101 N.W. 7th St., Rm. 103, Evansville 47708, 812-465-6313; Fed. Ctr., Rm. 103, 1201 E. 10th St., Jeffersonville 47132, 812-288-3377; and Fed. Bldg., 5500 Sohl Ave., Hammond 46320, 219-937-5380.

Committees: *Agriculture, Nutrition, and Forestry* (Ranking Member of 9 R). *Foreign Relations* (2nd of 9 R). Subcommittees: International Economic Policy, Trade, Oceans and Environment; East Asian and Pacific Affairs; Western Hemisphere and Peace Corps Affairs (Ranking Member).

Group Ratings

	ADA	ACLU	COPE	CFA	LCV	ACU	NTLC	NSI	COC	CEI
1988	10	30	11	50	40	88	71	90	92	56
1987	5	—	10	33	—	72	—	—	88	64

National Journal Ratings

	1988 LIB — 1988 CONS	1987 LIB — 1987 CONS
Economic	9% — 81%	6% — 87%
Social	28% — 70%	26% — 73%
Foreign	31% — 66%	27% — 71%

Key Votes

1) Cut Aged Housing $	AGN	5) Bork Nomination	FOR	9) SDI Funding	FOR
2) Override Hwy Veto	AGN	6) Ban Plastic Guns	FOR	10) Ban Chem Weaps	FOR
3) Kill Plnt Clsng Notice	FOR	7) Deny Abortions	FOR	11) Aid To Contras	FOR
4) Min Wage Increase	AGN	8) Japanese Reparations	FOR	12) Reagan Defense $	FOR

Election Results

1988 general	Richard G. Lugar (R)	1,430,525	(68%)	($3,244,601)
	Jack Wickes (D)	668,778	(32%)	($314,233)
1988 primary	Richard G. Lugar (R), unopposed			
1982 general	Richard G. Lugar (R)	978,301	(54%)	($2,987,573)
	Floyd Fithian (D)	828,400	(46%)	($870,023)

Sen. Daniel R. Coats (R)

Appointed Jan. 1989 to fill term of Vice President J. Danforth Quayle, term up 1990; b. May 16, 1943, Jackson, MI; home, Fort Wayne; Wheaton Col., B.A. 1965, IN U., J.D. 1971; Baptist; married (Marcia).

Career: Army Corps of Engineers, 1966–68; Asst. V.P. and Counsel, Mutual Security Life Ins. Co., 1972–76; Dist. Rep. for U.S. Rep. J. Danforth Quayle, 1976–80; U.S. House of Reps., 1980–88.

Offices: 411 RSOB 20515, 202-224-5623. Also 46 E. Ohio St., Rm. 247, Indianapolis 46204, 317-226-5555; Fed. Bldg., 1300 S. Harrison St., Rm. 340, Fort Wayne 46802, 219-422-1505; 1201 E. 10th St., Bldg. 66, Rm. 103, Jeffersonville 47132, 812-288-3377; 127 N.W. 7th St., Evansville 47708, 812-465-6313; and 5500 Sohl Ave., Hammond 46320, 219-937-5380.

Committees: *Armed Services* (9th of 9 R). Subcommittees: Conventional Forces and Alliance Defense; Defense Industry and Technology; Readiness, Sustainability and Support. *Labor and Human Resources* (4th of 7 R). Subcommittees: Aging; Children, Family, Drugs and Alcoholism.

Group Ratings (as Member of the U.S. House of Representatives)

	ADA	ACLU	COPE	CFA	LCV	ACU	NTLC	NSI	COC	CEI
1988	10	13	13	64	38	92	75	80	93	60
1987	8	—	11	7	—	91	—	—	100	74

National Journal Ratings (as Member of the U.S. House of Representatives)

	1988 LIB — 1988 CONS		1987 LIB — 1987 CONS	
Economic	27% —	72%	0% —	89%
Social	20% —	78%	0% —	90%
Foreign	27% —	71%	20% —	76%

Key Votes (as Member of the U.S. House of Representatives)

1) Homeless $	FOR	5) Ban Drug Test	FOR	9) SDI Research	FOR
2) Gephardt Amdt	AGN	6) Drug Death Pen	FOR	10) Ban Chem Weaps	FOR
3) Deficit Reduc	AGN	7) Handgun Sales	FOR	11) Aid to Contras	FOR
4) Kill Plnt Clsng Notice	AGN	8) Ban D.C. Abort $	FOR	12) Nuclear Testing	AGN

Election Results

1986 general	J. Danforth (Dan) Quayle (R)	936,143	(61%)	($1,979,561)
	Jill Long (D)	595,192	(38%)	($127,187)
1986 primary	J. Danforth (Dan) Quayle (R)	357,612	(100%)	
1980 general	J. Danforth (Dan) Quayle (R)	1,182,414	(54%)	($2,289,838)
	Birch E. Bayh, Jr. (D)	1,015,922	(46%)	($2,773,254)

FIRST DISTRICT

"Striking by day and beautiful by night," the writer of the *WPA Guide* half a century ago called "the 16-mile crescent of the lake shore, from the Illinois line on the west to the eastern edge of Gary." It was and is "broken only by three small parks, a continuous array of manufacturing plants. Over the entire district are the smoke of the steel mill, the smell of the oil refinery, and the glow of the blast furnace. Column after column of stacks pour forth steamy white or heavy black smoke. Giant steel towers supporting high-tension cables stride over the region. Great gas reservoirs move imperceptibly up and down in huge steel frameworks. Cranes, oil distilleries, collieries, and giant factories stand silhouetted against the sky. Freight engines weave in and out with long strings of cars. Great banks of coal lie waiting for blast furnaces. Bridges lift over the ship canal so that steamers and ore boats may pass. Everywhere in the composite of movement and noise thousands of workers hurry in and out. At night, myriads of light outline shafts, tanks, and framework. Flames from open hearth furnaces light the sky for miles." This is the heart of the 1st Congressional District of Indiana, the northwest corner of Hoosier America.

Steel created this part of the Midwest in the first half of this century. The largest city, Gary, was founded in 1906 on the sand dunes by the shores of Lake Michigan by J. P. Morgan's colossal United States Steel Corporation and named for one of Morgan's partners, Chicago Judge Elbert Gary. The site chosen seemed ideal. Iron ore from the Lake Superior ranges could be carried on Great Lakes freighters to the huge man-made port at the southern tip of Lake Michigan. Coal from West Virginia and Pennsylvania could be shipped in by rail on the great east-west rail lines that pass through Gary, Hammond and East Chicago on their way to Chicago. The local political environment was favorable: Indiana has always been a low-tax state, and for years the Lake County assessor let the steel companies' own auditors set their assessments. For nearly 70 years the steel mills attracted a diverse work force, much like that in Chicago and quite unlike the rest of Indiana—Irish, Poles, Czechs, Ukrainians and blacks from the American South. These groups live today in uneasy proximity, and much of the politics in the area has reflected ethnic and racial rivalries.

Today the steel country of the Indiana dunes is in trouble. Some mills stand cold and silent; storefronts are empty block after block; unemployment is high and population declining. Yet there has been some recovery and adaptation. As total U.S. steel production sinks to the amount produced as the nation was mobilizing for war nearly 50 years ago, northern Indiana has become the number one steel-producing area in the country.

Politically, this part of Indiana is overwhelmingly Democratic, but not out of any Civil War heritage, for this was heavily Republican territory when the steel mills and oil refineries were being built: it became Democratic after the great and sometimes violent CIO organizing drives in the late 1930s. By the late 1960s, this Democratic coalition of workers was being fractured by racial tensions. Blacks became the majority in Gary in the middle 1960s, and in 1967 elected Richard Hatcher, a newcomer from the factory town of Michigan City 25 miles east, as mayor. That infuriated other local politicians who missed the patronage and boodle they had been used to in Gary's fortress-like City Hall; and local whites, afraid their neighborhoods would be ruined by blacks, reacted with unremitting hostility that made Gary and the surrounding mostly all-white towns the most racially polarized constituency in America. That may have abated in the middle 1980s. Hatcher, nationally visible as a leading Jesse Jackson backer in 1984, got in trouble at home as city government was unable to improve life in an economically-troubled and crime-beset environment. He was defeated in his 1987 primary.

The racial divisions here have occasionally played a role in the politics of the 1st District, which includes all the steel and refineries cities, their suburbs to the south, and stretches east along the dunes, where affluent ethnic Chicagoans vacation, to Michigan City. The current congressman, Pete Visclosky, was a staff member for six years of Representative Adam Benjamin, a savvy politico and hard-working legislator first elected in 1976, who collapsed and died while working late in 1982. That left the Democratic nomination vacant and it was filled by the district party chairman, none other than Richard Hatcher. He chose Katie Hall, a black state senator who was undergoing personal misfortunes of her own. She served one term and was the name sponsor of the Martin Luther King holiday, but in this racially polarized environment predictably lost two-thirds of the votes in the next primary in 1984; she had 33% to Visclosky's 34% and another white candidate's 31%.

Visclosky's secret in the 1st District was assiduous door-to-door campaigning; his secret in Washington is, unsurprisingly, heavy attention to the politics of steel. Visclosky will concede that the area needs to diversify and that steel might not need protection forever, but he is a vigilant enforcer of the misnamed Voluntary Restraint Agreement barring many steel imports. He uses seats on the Public Works and Interior Committees to lobby for a Little Calumet River flood control project, to add acreage to the Indiana Dunes National Lakeshore (done in 1986) as part of a so-called Marquette Project, and to make Gary's airport the third Chicago area regional facility. A solid union supporter on Education and Labor, he has worked to protect benefits for employees and retirees of bankrupt steel companies, and he is opposed to drug-testing by the government without a warrant. In a rematch, Visclosky beat Hall 57%–35% in the 1986 primary; having pretty well sewed up the votes of whites, he has spent time with blacks, and he seems to have a safe seat.

The People: Est. Pop. 1986: 515,600, dn. 5.8% 1980–86; Pop. 1980: 547,100, dn. 5.9% 1970–80 Households (1980): 77% family, 45% with children, 60% married couples; 32.7% housing units rented median monthly rent: $170; median house value: $40,100. Voting age pop. (1980): 375,863; 22% Black 7% Spanish origin.

1988 Presidential Vote:

Dukakis (D)	112,270	(59%)
Bush (R)	78,515	(41%)

Rep. Peter J. Visclosky (D)

Elected 1984; b. Aug. 13, 1949, Gary; home, Merrillville; IN U., B.S. 1970, U. of Notre Dame, J.D. 1973, Georgetown U., LL.M. 1982; Roman Catholic; married (Anne).

Career: Practicing atty., 1973–76, 1983–84; Aide to U.S. Rep. Adam Benjamin Jr., 1976–82.

Offices: 420 CHOB 20515, 202-225-2461. Also 215 W. 35th St., Gary 46408, 219-884-1177.

Committees: *Education and Labor* (20th of 22 D). Subcommittee: Labor-Management Relations. *Interior and Insular Affairs* (16th of 26 D). Subcommittee: National Parks and Public Lands. *Public Works and Transportation* (16th of 31 D). Subcommittees: Aviation; Investigations and Oversight; Surface Transportation.

Group Ratings

	ADA	ACLU	COPE	CFA	LCV	ACU	NTLC	NSI	COC	CEI
1988	100	91	89	91	63	0	11	0	36	18
1987	92	—	85	79	—	0	—	—	13	8

National Journal Ratings

	1988 LIB — 1988 CONS		1987 LIB — 1987 CONS	
Economic	65%	— 34%	68%	— 27%
Social	78%	— 20%	78%	— 0%
Foreign	79%	— 16%	71%	— 27%

Key Votes

1) Homeless $	AGN	5) Ban Drug Test	AGN	9) SDI Research	AGN
2) Gephardt Amdt	FOR	6) Drug Death Pen	AGN	10) Ban Chem Weaps	FOR
3) Deficit Reduc	FOR	7) Handgun Sales	AGN	11) Aid to Contras	AGN
4) Kill Plnt Clsng Notice	AGN	8) Ban D.C. Abort $	AGN	12) Nuclear Testing	FOR

Election Results

1988 general	Peter J. Visclosky (D)	138,251	(77%)	($141,855)
	Owen W. Crumpacker (R)	41,076	(23%)	
1988 primary	Peter J. Visclosky (D)	75,785	(84%)	
	Sandra K. Smith (D)	14,527	(16%)	
1986 general	Peter J. Visclosky (D)	86,983	(73%)	($163,283)
	William Costas (R)	30,395	(26%)	($63,460)

SECOND DISTRICT

"As one prowls Middletown"—actually Muncie, Indiana—"about six o'clock of a winter morning one notes two kinds of homes: the dark ones where people still sleep, and the ones with a light in the kitchen where the adults of the household may be seen moving about, starting the business of the day. For the seven out of ten of those gainfully employed who constitute the working class, getting a living means being at work in the morning anywhere between 6:15 and 7:30, chiefly 7:00." Nearly three-fourths of working-class wives were up by 5:30, while business-class wives, whose husbands don't have to get to work till 8:00 or 8:30, mostly sleep past 7:00. With such detail, Robert and Helen Lynd reported in *Middletown* on their visit to Muncie in

1924 and 1925, showing a culturally homogeneous but economically riven factory town. But those divisions, the radical Lynds were disappointed to find, did not show up in politics; people still voted their Civil War loyalties, choosing between parties which both favored limited government and traditional cultural values. *Middletown Revisited* showed a political upheaval in the Muncie of 1935, with the business elite—local bankers, merchants, executives at the Ball family's glass company and at the General Motors plants—who saw themselves as typical Muncie citizens and ran community affairs in what they believed was the common interest, fiercely opposed by the working class, which was voting Democratic and joining unions. Muncie, like most of the industrial Midwest, was unionized in what amounted sometimes to a violent uprising; partisan politics took on the sharp, bitter tone of a struggle for shares of the wealth between two rival classes whose claims seemed irreconcilable. The New Deal majority, which some Democrats are always trying to revive, was forged in an atmosphere of class hatred and mistrust.

Now the picture seems to have changed once more. A team of sociologists following the Lynds' footsteps in 1976–78 found both economic life and cultural values changed. As incomes tripled over 40 years, class antagonisms cooled; it turned out there was plenty for everyone. At the same time, increasing affluence and the waning of some traditions allowed for more variety in personal life. As cultural issues came to the fore, the cultural and family values shared by the majority of Middletowners of various income levels tended to bring them together. Politically, party labels are not now so firmly fixed as they were in the 1930s. The Republicans' sleek party machine tends to carry most elections here as Republicans did in the 1920s. But they have been conspicuously unsuccessful in attempts to unseat Democratic Representative Philip Sharp, who has represented Muncie and the surrounding area in the 2d Congressional District of Indiana since 1974.

Sharp's career illustrates the movement in Middle America from a class-conscious politics to something rather different. When Sharp first ran for Congress here, in 1970, it was assumed that, if elected, he would vote a straight liberal-labor line on economic issues, like almost every non-southern Democrat in the House. But Sharp, who lost that year and in 1972, ultimately won the seat on non-economic as much as economic issues. Republican economic policies were unpopular in 1974, when he beat Republican David Dennis, but as important a factor was Dennis's opposition, on the House Judiciary Committee, to the impeachment of Richard Nixon. Once in the House, Sharp opposed the Democratic orthodoxy of oil and gas price controls and, as chairman of a special task force appointed by Speaker O'Neill, helped fashion a compromise energy program which phased out the price controls over several years. By 1981 he was well-placed on the Interior Committee and was one of the high-ranking members on the sought-after Energy and Commerce Committee and chairman of the subcommittee on Fossil and Synthetic Fuels, which after the 100th Congress expanded its jurisdiction and became the Energy and Power Subcommittee.

This is not quite as hot a seat as it once was, now that the price controls issue has been mostly settled, but plenty of detail work and ancillary issues remain, on which Sharp is constantly making policy. Temperamentally, he tends to seek compromise and consensus, which also helps him bridge the gap between his environmentalist supporters and a constituency which produces automobiles and emits lots of sulfur dioxide. He got the amount of insurance for nuclear accidents in the Price-Anderson Act increased to $7 billion. He opposed the oil import fee and suggested a broader energy tax instead. In 1987 and 1988 he promoted ethanol, minimum appliance standards and a stop to a $1.75 billion uranium bailout. He got gas companies to pass through $400 million in savings to Indiana consumers. This is not earthshaking work, but with some evidence of global warming the subcommittee may become more critical, and Sharp is a chairman who can carry a bill in full committee and on the floor. On other issues he is often but not always liberal, not always voting the AFL-CIO line; on day care, for example, he wants to draw on both the Democrats' (Act for Better Child Care) and Republicans' tax credit bills. At home, Sharp has been a target of the Republicans for years; he has risen to 60% only in 1976 and 1986. The 1980s redistricting gave him a tough district, but his appeal went across old party lines and, spread by television, across county and old district boundaries. With more than 2 to 1 margins in Muncie's Delaware County and more than 60% in Wayne County, which centers on the heavily Republican old Quaker center of Richmond, he won with 56% in 1982. In the presidential years of 1984 and 1988, he was held to 53%; in the latter year Republican Mike Pence attacked him for accepting over the years more than $1 million in PAC contributions. The movement of affluent young families southeast from Indianapolis into the 2d District hasn't helped him.

1990 will be the 20th anniversary of Sharp's first campaign; he still looks young and seems serene, while his wife has written bestselling mysteries set in Washington. Most political systems would not retire such an experienced and competent legislator; but his Indiana seat, even with favorable redistricting for 1990, can never be regarded as completely safe.

The People: Est. Pop. 1986: 545,300, dn. 1.5% 1980–86; Pop. 1980: 553,510, up 7.8% 1970–80. Households (1980): 77% family, 43% with children, 66% married couples; 28.0% housing units rented; median monthly rent: $165; median house value: $38,200. Voting age pop. (1980): 390,981; 2% Black, 1% Spanish origin.

1988 Presidential Vote:

Bush (R)	144,206	(65%)
Dukakis (D)	76,764	(35%)

Rep. Philip R. Sharp (D)

Elected 1974; b. July 15, 1942, Baltimore, MD; home, Muncie; Georgetown U., B.S. 1964, Oxford U., 1966, Georgetown U., Ph.D. 1974; United Methodist; married (Marilyn).

Career: Legis. Aide to U.S. Sen. Vance Hartke, 1964–69; Asst. and Assoc. Prof., Ball St. U., 1969–74.

Offices: 2217 RHOB 20515, 202-225-3021. Also 2900 W. Jackson, Ste. 101, Muncie 47304, 317-747-5566.

Committees: *Energy and Commerce* (4th of 26 D). Subcommittees: Commerce, Consumer Protection and Competitiveness; Energy and Power (Chairman). *Interior and Insular Affairs* (3d of 26 D). Subcommittees: Energy and the Environment; Water, Power and Offshore Resources.

Group Ratings

	ADA	ACLU	COPE	CFA	LCV	ACU	NTLC	NSI	COC	CEI
1988	75	76	75	73	75	20	35	10	50	25
1987	76	—	73	71	—	4	—	—	38	30

National Journal Ratings

	1988 LIB — 1988 CONS		1987 LIB — 1987 CONS	
Economic	53%	— 46%	53%	— 46%
Social	64%	— 34%	64%	— 36%
Foreign	60%	— 37%	74%	— 25%

Key Votes

1) Homeless $	FOR	5) Ban Drug Test	AGN	9) SDI Research	AGN
2) Gephardt Amdt	FOR	6) Drug Death Pen	AGN	10) Ban Chem Weaps	FOR
3) Deficit Reduc	FOR	7) Handgun Sales	FOR	11) Aid to Contras	AGN
4) Kill Plnt Clsng Notice	AGN	8) Ban D.C. Abort $	AGN	12) Nuclear Testing	FOR

Election Results

1988 general	Philip R. Sharp (D).................	116,915	(53%)	($444,422)
	Mike Pence (R).....................	102,846	(47%)	($332,880)
1988 primary	Philip R. Sharp (D), unopposed			
1986 general	Philip R. Sharp (D).................	102,456	(62%)	($384,009)
	Don Lynch (R)	62,013	(37%)	($117,598)

THIRD DISTRICT

"Win one for the Gipper" is a phrase that first became familiar in 1940, when a 29-year-old Ronald Reagan starred in *Knute Rockne—All-American*. Rockne, the football coach who died in a 1931 plane crash, was almost universally known then, and so was Notre Dame. Founded in 1842, Norte Dame became famous in the 20th century for its football teams, the Fighting Irish, the favorites of many Catholics in New York, Chicago, and all across the country. Under Rockne and ever after, Notre Dame has been known also for its academic rigor, with no special admissions or lowered academic standards for football (or basketball) players—a rigor that seems appropriate in these stony buildings on the flat, usually frigid north Indiana campus.

Notre Dame is certainly better known than South Bend, one of those industrial cities set incongruously on the limestone-bottomed plains of the Midwest. Surrounded by farm counties whose origins—and Republican allegiance—go back to the days when they served as northern terminals on the Underground Railroad, South Bend is mostly the creation of the early 20th century, when its factories attracted an ethnic population, which has always voted Democratic. Sixty years ago South Bend was a boom town, like Silicon Valley in the late 1970s, but since World War II the place has frequently been in trouble. South Bend saw the collapse of a portion of the auto industry long before Detroit or Flint: in the 1960s, Studebaker went out of business, and South Bend lost its largest employer. More recently its economy has suffered from other, less dramatic shutdowns and layoffs, even though the surrounding agricultural countryside—economically stagnant earlier in the century—is now sprouting factories and jobs; the district may be the nation's largest maker of "manufactured housing" (trailers).

The 3d Congressional District of Indiana has centered for years on South Bend; but it has mattered a great deal what other territory is included. Democrats have joined South Bend with the similar industrial city of Michigan City, to the west; Republicans have joined it with Elkhart, a higher income and heavily Republican city to the east, and with the rural counties directly south (one of which, however, Starke, often votes Democratic). The current Republican redistricting plan follows these lines, and resulted in the election of a Republican congressman by narrow margins throughout the 1980s.

He is John Hiler, one of the prototypes of the "Reagan robots" in the early 1980s, the subject of Fred Barnes's "The Unbearable Lightness of Being a Congressman" in *The New Republic*. But Hiler does not seem mindless and has been at least a little politically adept. Elected at age 27, when he beat House Democratic Whip John Brademas, Hiler came to Washington with an elite education and experience in his family's foundry business, plus a conviction that government must be cut back. He made a point of not seeking federal money for the district—though by 1986 he was bragging about landing an Army contract to build the Hummer vehicle for AM General in South Bend. He prided himself in the early 1980s on his lockstep support of Reagan Administration programs, though by 1986 dissented occasionally, on Superfund and South Africa sanctions.

Hiler had five tough races in the 1980s and won them all. In 1986 and 1988 he faced rural county prosecutor Tom Ward, who attacked him as a "PAC puppet" and benefactor of "the wealthy and the powerful" and called for "fair trade" and keeping jobs in the district. He came within 47 votes of Hiler in 1986; Hiler was not sworn in until January 23, 1987. In 1988 this was one of the nation's most expensive House races. The candidates fought it out over South Bend television (which covers the district at reasonable cost) and in constant personal campaigning. Hiler won 54%–46%, running just 5% behind of George Bush. In the House Hiler is not a major power, nor likely to become one soon; but for all his concentration on local issues, he does seem dedicated enough to continue running—while the Democrats seem determined, and with their South Bend base able, to give him a serious contest once again.

The People: Est. Pop. 1986: 571,300, up 2.4% 1980–86; Pop. 1980: 558,100, up 5.5% 1970–80. Households (1980): 76% family, 41% with children, 65% married couples; 24.9% housing units rented; median monthly rent: $168; median house value: $35,600. Voting age pop. (1980): 395,121; 4% Black, 1% Spanish origin.

1988 Presidential Vote: Bush (R) 128,039   (59%)
Dukakis (D). 87,080   (40%)

Rep. John P. Hiler (R)

Elected 1980; b. Apr. 24, 1953, Chicago, IL; home, LaPorte; Williams Col., B.A. 1975, U. of Chicago, M.B.A. 1977; Roman Catholic; married (Catherine).

Career: Mktg. Dir., Charles O. Hiler and Sons, Accurate Castings, Inc., 1977–80; Delegate, White House Conf. on Small Businesses, 1980.

Offices: 407 CHOB 20515, 202-225-3915. Also 120 River Glenn Ofc. Plaza, 501 E. Monroe, South Bend 46601, 219-236-8282.

Committees: *Banking, Finance, and Urban Affairs* (9th of 20 R). Subcommittees: Consumer Affairs and Coinage; Financial Institution Supervision, Regulation and Insurance; Housing and Community Development. *Small Business* (5th of 16 R). Subcommittee: Environment and Labor (Ranking Member). *House Administration* (7th of 8 R). Subcommittees: Accounts; Elections.

Group Ratings

	ADA	ACLU	COPE	CFA	LCV	ACU	NTLC	NSI	COC	CEI
1988	5	9	6	36	38	100	78	100	100	67
1987	0	—	5	14	—	87	—	—	93	82

National Journal Ratings

	1988 LIB — 1988 CONS		1987 LIB — 1987 CONS	
Economic	15%	— 85%	11%	— 83%
Social	5%	— 91%	0%	— 90%
Foreign	0%	— 84%	0%	— 80%

Key Votes

1) Homeless $	FOR	5) Ban Drug Test	FOR	9) SDI Research	FOR
2) Gephardt Amdt	AGN	6) Drug Death Pen	FOR	10) Ban Chem Weaps	AGN
3) Deficit Reduc	AGN	7) Handgun Sales	FOR	11) Aid to Contras	FOR
4) Kill Plnt Clsng Notice	FOR	8) Ban D.C. Abort $	FOR	12) Nuclear Testing	AGN

Election Results

1988 general	John Hiler (R)	116,309	(54%)	($1,085,140)
	Thomas W. Ward (D)	97,934	(46%)	($584,006)
1988 primary	John Hiler (R), unopposed			
1986 general	John P. Hiler (R)	75,979	(50%)	($336,768)
	Thomas W. Ward (D)	75,932	(50%)	($189,509)

FOURTH DISTRICT

Will Indiana's 4th Congressional District end up in the ranks of districts (the Ohio 16th, Massachusetts 8th, Texas 10th, California 33d, Michigan 5th, to use their current numbers) that in this century have produced a President of the United States? It's not something anyone would have bet on in the summer of 1976, when 29-year-old Dan Quayle was challenging eight-term incumbent Ed Roush, or even in July 1988. But Dan Quayle, elected Senator in 1980, is now Vice President of the United States, and stands as good a chance as any American of being President some day.

The House district that elected Quayle in 1976 and 1978, and then elected his former aide Dan Coats in 1980—and then in 1989, just after Quayle took national office and Coats went to the Senate, elected Democrat Jill Long in their place—is the 4th Congressional District of Indiana, the northeast corner of the state. It centers on Fort Wayne, Indiana's second largest city (though not its second largest metropolitan area), a medium-sized midwestern manufacturing community, with a small black ghetto and nondescript frame houses that belong to factory workers and a cluster of larger houses on the same side of town as the country club. Like many other such cities, Fort Wayne faced rough times in the early 1980s: an International Harvester plant closed down, wiping 4,500 jobs in one fell swoop, and unemployment went into double digits. But the town got together, Mayor Winfield Moses and Lieutenant Governor John Mutz worked to bring in a new General Motors factory with 3,000 jobs and, probably more important, small businesses began expanding until by 1988 employers were having a hard time finding workers for even entry-level jobs. The city under Mayor Paul Helmke found itself having to raise taxes to pay for increased services. Fort Wayne and similar parts of Indiana and Ohio have had an unnoticed mini-boom, or at least a smart economic rebound in the late 1980s.

The mini-boom had the political effect of strengthening in national elections Fort Wayne's and the 4th District's already strong Republican allegiance, which goes back to the days when their ancestors fought for the Union in the Civil War. The Bush-ticket carried the 4th with 67% in 1988, the same percentage by which Ronald Reagan carried it in 1984; Quayle's home town appeal probably added 2% or 3% to the district total. Coats won reelection to the House with 70%. Yet in the March 1989 special election to replace Coats, Jill Long—the unsuccessful candidate against Quayle in 1986 and Coats in 1988—won. What accounted for the difference? One issue was taxes. Dan Heath, chosen the Republican candidate in a contested district convention, had been Helmke's public safety director in Fort Wayne, and the Democrats pounced on Helmke's support of an income tax and attempt to annex a Republican township; Long campaigned on a read-my-lips platform of no new taxes. In addition, the dignified and positive campaigns she had run in 1986 and 1988 plus the experience she built up served her well. As a harbinger of national trends, this 4th district special election result will probably not amount to much; it is hard to think of anything short of a Bush-sponsored tax increase that will make the Democrats nationally the party with greater credibility on the issue of not raising taxes. But it did represent a shot in the arm for House Democrats as Jim Wright was under attack and a setback for House Republicans like Newt Gingrich who had just won the whip position while calling for a Republican House majority. Long certainly should go into the 1990 election with the advantages of an incumbent, but given the strong Republican leanings of the 4th in national contests she is likely to have serious competition for this seat.

The People: Est. Pop. 1986: 559,700, up 1.1% 1980–86; Pop. 1980: 553,698, up 7.2% 1970–80. Households (1980): 76% family, 43% with children, 66% married couples; 24.4% housing units rented; median monthly rent: $168; median house value: $38,100. Voting age pop. (1980): 382,150; 4% Black, 1% Spanish origin.

1988 Presidential Vote:

Bush (R)	143,461	(66%)
Dukakis (D)	71,156	(33%)

Rep. Jill Long (D)

Elected March 28, 1989; b. July 15, 1952, Warsaw, IN; home, Larwill; Valparaiso U., B.S. 1974, IN U., M.B.A. 1978, Ph.D. 1984; Methodist; single.

Career: Asst. Prof., Valparaiso U. 1981–85, 1987–88; Adjunct Prof., IN U., 1987–89.

Offices: 1632 LHOB, 20515, 202-225-4436. Also 1300 S. Harrison, Ste. 3105, Fort Wayne 46802, 219-424-3041.

Committees: *Agriculture* (24th of 27 D). Wheat, Soybeans and Feedgrains; Livestock, Dairy and Poultry; Conservation, Credit and Rural Development. *Veterans' Affairs* (21st of 21 D). Oversight and Investigations; Educations, Training and Employment.

Group Ratings and Key Votes: Newly Elected
Election Results

1989 special	Jill Long (D)	65,272	(51%)	($313,724)
	Dan Heath (R)	63,494	(49%)	($378,441)
1988 general	Daniel R. Coats (R)	132,843	(62%)	($266,016)
	Jill Long (D)	80,915	(38%)	($114,454)
1986 general	Daniel R. Coats (R)	99,865	(70%)	($225,157)
	Greg Scher (D)	43,105	(30%)	($20,082)

FIFTH DISTRICT

In the 1930s and 1940s, Cole Porter, the songwriter who was the epitome of Manhattan sophistication, returned with an assemblage of luggage to spend Christmas in his family home in Peru, Indiana. It was then and is now a place entitled to consider itself the heartland of America. In north central Indiana it is near the divide between the Great Lakes and Mississippi River systems, on the major east-west railroads and highways that connect the nation's largest cities and industrial areas. The small cities and large towns display a geometric regularity and neatness that bespeak the virtues we think of as peculiarly American; and if they have a few criminals or suffer from layoffs and unemployment, people there remain confident that most Americans are competent, decent, sensible people who will do the right thing in time of crisis. It is a part of America with little immigrant heritage, with relatively few blacks, with only a handful of the Latin and Asian immigrants who are so prominent in other parts of the country.

This is the land of the 5th Congressional District of Indiana, which extends most of the way across northern Indiana from the suburbs of Gary to the factory town of Marion and the much smaller town of North Manchester, home of Thomas R. Marshall, Woodrow Wilson's Vice President. There are notes of discord here and there: echoes in the northwest corner of the racial animosities that dominate Gary politics, very high unemployment rates in Kokomo, where the Chrysler plant nearly closed down. But basic values have not been shaken so much here as in many other parts of the nation: in 1980, fully 79% of the households here contain families and 69% married couples—among the highest figures in the Midwest—and 45% have children, a high percentage given the rather old age structure.

The 5th District also tells why the Democrats control the House of Representatives in this era of Republican Presidents: this quintessentially Middle American district elects a Democratic congressman with a pretty straightforward Democratic record. He is Jim Jontz, an incredibly hardworking and gifted natural politician. A year out of school, at age 22, Jontz was elected to the Indiana House by beating its majority leader by two votes (and may have won because he insisted on campaigning after 10 p.m. the night before the election when two laundromats were still open); this was in Democratic 1974 but in a very Republican part of rural northwestern Indiana. Single, interested almost exclusively in politics, he has been politically successful ever since. He has a flair for trademarks, riding his sister's rusty blue Schwinn with mismatched tires in parades and handing out potholders to voters. He has rotated the same four pairs of shoes in and out of a local shoe repair shop every week for five years. He took one afternoon off in six months and missed only five roll call votes—three when his grandfather died and two when he was in the district.

Jontz has a flair as well for issues. Running in 1986 in a district where General Motors moved Delco operations from Kokomo to Matamoros, Mexico, Jontz ran ads denouncing the "theft" of U.S. jobs through unfair foreign trade. In the House he introduced a bill to let rural cities and towns buy back their Farmers Home Administration loans to get better interest rates; 12 towns in the district saved $5 million. He gave his last pay increase to college scholarships for local kids.

He also proved a conqueror in the campaign finance wars. A narrow winner in 1986 over an evangelical Christian in a district held easily by a Republican for 16 years, Jontz was an obvious target; Republican Patricia Williams, an active realtor who had served as administrative assistant to former Congressman Elwood (Bud) Hillis, was a respectable candidate. The huge Realtors PAC gave Williams $1,000 and Jontz $10,000; Jontz who had raised $305,000 in PAC money for 1986 raised $471,725 by for 1988—the seventh highest figure of all House incumbents. And so the Democrat outspent the Republican in a Republican district in a Republican-controlled state by better than 3 to 1, and won the election 56%–44%.

It's plain from those results that a less talented and hardworking incumbent might not have prevailed; it's also plain that Jontz will be hard to beat next time. In April 1989, Jontz took himself out of the running for the 1990 Senate race, though he did not rule out a challenge in 1992.

The People: Est. Pop. 1986: 537,800, dn. 1.9% 1980–86; Pop. 1980: 548,257, up 13.2% 1970–80. Households (1980): 79% family, 45% with children, 69% married couples; 24.4% housing units rented; median monthly rent: $166; median house value: $40,300. Voting age pop. (1980): 380,248; 2% Black, 1% Spanish origin.

1988 Presidential Vote:
    Bush (R) 136,223   (65%)
    Dukakis (D). 73,065   (35%)

Rep. James Jontz (D)

Elected 1986; b. Dec. 18, 1951, Indianapolis; home, Monticello; IN U., B.A. 1973; United Methodist; single.

Career: IN House of Reps., 1974–84; IN Senate, 1984–86.

Offices: 1039 LHOB 20515, 202-225-5037. Also 104 W. Walnut, Kokomo 46901, 317-459-4375; 302 E. Lincolnway, Valparaiso 46383, 219-462-6499.

Committees: *Agriculture* (18th of 27 D). Subcommittees: Department Operations, Research and Foreign Agriculture; Forests, Family Farms and Energy; Wheat, Soybeans and Feed Grains. *Education and Labor* (21st of 22 D). Subcommittee: Select Education. *Veterans' Affairs* (15th of 21 D). Subcommittee: Hospital and Health Care. *Select Committee on Aging* (34th of 39 D). Subcommittee: Retirement, Income and Employment.

Group Ratings

	ADA	ACLU	COPE	CFA	LCV	ACU	NTLC	NSI	COC	CEI
1988	95	87	97	100	100	4	13	0	21	10
1987	100	—	94	86	—	0	—	—	20	9

National Journal Ratings

	1988 LIB — 1988 CONS			1987 LIB — 1987 CONS		
Economic	92%	—	0%	73%	—	0%
Social	76%	—	23%	78%	—	0%
Foreign	84%	—	0%	81%	—	0%

Key Votes

1) Homeless $	AGN	5) Ban Drug Test	AGN	9) SDI Research	AGN
2) Gephardt Amdt	FOR	6) Drug Death Pen	AGN	10) Ban Chem Weaps	FOR
3) Deficit Reduc	FOR	7) Handgun Sales	FOR	11) Aid to Contras	AGN
4) Kill Plnt Clsng Notice	AGN	8) Ban D.C. Abort $	AGN	12) Nuclear Testing	FOR

Election Results

1988 general	James Jontz (D)	116,240	(56%)	($689,086)
	Patricia L. Williams (R)	90,163	(44%)	($244,985)
1988 primary	James Jontz (D)	44,788	(92%)	
	F. Gopal Raju (D)	3,752	(8%)	
1986 general	James Jontz (D)	80,772	(52%)	($462,970)
	James R. Butcher (R)	75,507	(48%)	($424,538)

SIXTH DISTRICT

In a circle, or rather in a mosaic of seven counties, around Indianapolis are some of the most heavily Republican suburbs in the United States. Indianapolis was a compact city 50 years ago, radiating outward four or five miles from the Soldiers' and Sailors' Monument downtown. The few rich neighborhoods were on the streets directly north of the city's core, beyond the home of Benjamin Harrison, Indiana's one President. But most of Indianapolis consisted of modest neighborhoods of frame houses with clapboard shutters where most people voted Republican in most elections. In the years since, real incomes have risen here as elsewhere, and people have moved farther and farther outward. The old central neighborhoods have populations more Democratic and sometimes more black. And the once vacant flat fields and low hills 10 to 20 miles from downtown have become filled with people seemingly self-selected as strong Republicans. Affluent young families and older couples have moved out past the extended Indianapolis city limits, which are coextensive with Marion County, and into the once rural and now increasingly suburban counties that surround it.

Most residents of these suburbs are confident upholders of the local order of things and believers that the American system sees that merit and hard work are rewarded. To them it seems natural that those who have not done so well—people with low incomes, union members, and the like—will be Democrats, and that intelligent people will usually be Republicans. Almost all articulate opinion in Indianapolis—the Pulliam newspapers, most leading public officials (though not the governor since Evan Bayh won in 1988), leading businessmen and civic leaders—are Republicans, and they are boosters of free enterprise and traditional values, of the flag and motherhood and the other institutions that bind the less successful to the more successful here. The 6th Congressional District of Indiana covers most of the Indianapolis suburbs, including some 120,000 people on the affluent north side of Indianapolis, counties that gave Ronald Reagan as much as 82% of the vote in 1984. It also takes in the gritty industrial city of Anderson.

The congressman from the 6th District is Dan Burton, an active and enthusiastic Republican who has been running for office since he was in his 20s. He had a rough childhood, with an abusive father, a divorced mother, and a stint in the county guardian's home; he enlisted in the Army at 18, but never finished college. A hearty, bluff backslapper, he made his way up selling insurance. He was elected to the Indiana House in 1966, 1976, and 1978, and to the Indiana Senate in 1968 and 1980; he lost elections for the U.S. House in 1970 (to Democrat Andrew Jacobs) and 1972 (in the primary to William Hudnut, who beat Jacobs that year, lost in 1974, and is now Indianapolis's Mayor). In 1982, when the legislature created a new and much more heavily Republican 6th District, he took on the Republican state chairman in the party and beat him 28%–22% (there were four other candidates).

Burton is nothing if not voluble. "Generally speaking," Andy Jacobs says, "Dan Burton is generally speaking." He is a true believer in an assertive and aggressive anti-Communist foreign policy, and is willing to take on what others regard as lost or unpopular causes. He championed the Nicaraguan contras as enthusiastically, if not as effectively, as anyone in the House; he opposes sanctions on South Africa, charging they'd be harmful to blacks and helpful to Communists. On other issues as well he takes a position that few others do: he has favored mandatory AIDS testing for all Americans. It's likely that Burton's enthusiasm and sometimes less than complete command of the facts make his arguments unpersuasive to many wavering in the middle. But it should be said in his behalf that it is useful to have a House member standing up for what he plausibly believes is human freedom abroad when others are eager to conciliate and compromise with totalitarians.

Loud and controversial, Burton does not seem to be disliked by most colleagues; it may help that he has been known as the Republicans' best golfer. At home, for all his lack of polish, he seems firmly entrenched in one of the nation's safest Republican districts.

The People: Est. Pop. 1986: 554,700, up 2.5% 1980–86; Pop. 1980: 540,939, up 16.1% 1970–80. Households (1980): 77% family, 42% with children, 67% married couples; 27.6% housing units rented; median monthly rent: $200; median house value: $45,600. Voting age pop. (1980): 381,833; 3% Black, 1% Spanish origin.

1988 Presidential Vote: Bush (R) 188,615   (69%)
Dukakis (D). 82,201   (30%)

Rep. Dan Burton (R)

Elected 1982; b. June 21, 1938, Indianapolis; home, Indianapolis; IN U., 1956–57, Cincinnati Bible Seminary, 1958–60; Protestant; married (Barbara).

Career: Army, 1956–57; Founder, Dan Burton Insur. Agency; IN House of Reps., 1967–68, 1977–78; IN Senate, 1969–70, 1981–82.

Offices: 120 CHOB 20515, 202-225-2276. Also 8900 Keystone-at-the-Crossing, Ste. 1050, Indianapolis 46240, 317-848-0201; and 922 Meridian Plaza, Anderson 46016, 317-649-6887.

Committees: *Foreign Affairs* (11th of 18 R). Subcommittees: Africa (Ranking Member); Western Hemisphere Affairs. *Post Office and Civil Service* (5th of 9 R). Subcommittee: Human Resources (Ranking Member). *Veterans' Affairs* (6th of 13 R). Subcommittees: Hospitals and Health Care; Housing and Memorial Affairs (Ranking Member).

Group Ratings

	ADA	ACLU	COPE	CFA	LCV	ACU	NTLC	NSI	COC	CEI
1988	0	5	9	27	13	100	91	100	93	83
1987	4	—	11	7	—	100	—	—	93	83

National Journal Ratings

	1988 LIB — 1988 CONS			1987 LIB — 1987 CONS		
Economic	0%	—	93%	0%	—	89%
Social	5%	—	91%	10%	—	85%
Foreign	27%	—	71%	0%	—	80%

Key Votes

1) Homeless $	FOR	5) Ban Drug Test	FOR	9) SDI Research	FOR
2) Gephardt Amdt	AGN	6) Drug Death Pen	FOR	10) Ban Chem Weaps	AGN
3) Deficit Reduc	AGN	7) Handgun Sales	FOR	11) Aid to Contras	FOR
4) Kill Plnt Clsng Notice	FOR	8) Ban D.C. Abort $	FOR	12) Nuclear Testing	AGN

Election Results

1988 general	Dan Burton (R).....................	192,064	(73%)	($333,723)
	George T. Holland (D)	71,447	(27%)	($11,743)
1988 primary	Dan Burton (R), unopposed			
1986 general	Dan Burton (R).....................	118,363	(68%)	($216,290)
	Tom McKenna (D)	53,431	(31%)	($48,045)

SEVENTH DISTRICT

In the 1940s, the old Wabash Cannonball ran along the Wabash River across the rolling farmland of northern Indiana on its way from Detroit to St. Louis. The railroad heads west and the river heads south, crossing the old National Road, now U.S. 40, which runs in a nearly straight line from Indianapolis to St. Louis. This part of central Indiana, with its neat farms and its frame-bungalowed towns, looks much as it did in the 1940s. But life has changed, with new levels of affluence, new levels of household comfort, and new transportation arteries. The

Cannonball no longer runs; people bounce around the Midwest on commuter airlines or fly from one hub city to another. And the National Road and U.S. 40 have been replaced for through traffic by Interstate 70. This is the land of the 7th Congressional District of Indiana, the central part of the state west of, and including the western suburbs of, Indianapolis.

Terre Haute, its largest city—and despite its elegant French name—was once known for its gambling and vice. Today it is known as the home of Indiana State University (training ground for Boston Celtic great, Larry Bird) and as the home of Sony Records compact disc plant. Politically Terre Haute has long had a strong Democratic machine (although it was the home town of the great Socialist leader Eugene Debs), which more often than not has controlled the Vigo County Courthouse; it nearly carried the county for Michael Dukakis. To get people's political leanings, listen to the way they talk. North of Terre Haute and the National Road people tend to speak with the hard-edged accent of the Midwest; to the south they drawl in a manner reminiscent of Dixie. The counties to the north are traditionally Republican, those to the south traditionally Democratic. You can see the demarcation in maps of voting behavior in the 1860s, and more than a century later, it surfaced again when Jimmy Carter, of Plains, Georgia, ran against Gerald Ford, of Grand Rapids, Michigan, in 1976. Carter carried the southern part of the district in 1976 and even in 1980.

The 7th District was created in something like its present form by a Democratic legislature in 1966 with the intention of electing a Democratic congressman. Instead it has elected Republican John Myers ever since. He has benefited from weak opposition and from the 1982 redistricting, which added two suburban Indianapolis counties, and substituted for Bloomington and liberal arts Indiana University, engineering-oriented Purdue and the city of Lafayette, which is eagerly welcoming an Isuzu assembly plant. Myers has not been seriously opposed and has won easily.

That makes Myers one of the more senior House Republicans. He is not one of the raucous young conservative partisans, nor the small town conservative he looks. His record on economic issues has been rather liberal, and in his important committee positions he has sought consensus rather than conflict with his Democratic counterparts. On Appropriations he is the third-ranking Republican, and he is ranking Republican on the Energy and Water Development Subcommittee, which parcels out money for rivers and harbor projects. He and chairman Tom Bevill typically report out a bipartisan bill with projects for many districts, and resent sharply what they consider cheap shot votes against their bills by environmentalists or economizers. Myers also plays a role on farm issues.

Myers has also been ranking Republican on the Ethics Committee since May 1988—a hot seat if ever there was one. He was in on the beginning of the investigation of Jim Wright. Myers does not show strong partisanship and has exhibited a get-along-go-along approach to public works projects, but he is also a stickler for what he thinks is proper. He had a successful bill to prohibit commercial or political fundraising exploitation of names of government programs like social security, and he was one of the few who spoke up against Republican Robert Walker's unworkable "drug-free workplace" amendment in 1988. This approach was reflected in Myers's decision to take a tough stand against Wright on the committee.

The People: Est. Pop. 1986: 559,200, up 0.7% 1980–86; Pop. 1980: 555,192, up 9.2% 1970–80. Households (1980): 75% family, 40% with children, 66% married couples; 26.2% housing units rented; median monthly rent: $159; median house value: $36,400. Voting age pop. (1980): 403,139; 2% Black, 1% Spanish origin, 1% Asian origin.

1988 Presidential Vote: Bush (R) 136,233   (63%)
                                 Dukakis (D) 79,244   (37%)

Rep. John T. Myers (R)

Elected 1966; b. Feb. 8, 1927, Covington; home, Covington; IN St. U., B.S. 1951; Episcopalian; married (Carol).

Career: Army, WWII; Cashier and Trust Officer, Foundation Trust Co., 1954–66.

Offices: 2372 RHOB 20515, 202-225-5805. Also 107 Fed. Bldg., Terre Haute 47808, 812-238-1619; and 107 Halleck Fed. Bldg., Lafayette 47901, 317-423-1661.

Committees: *Appropriations* (3d of 22 R). Subcommittees: Energy and Water Development (Ranking Member); Legislative; Rural Development, Agriculture and Related Agencies. *Post Office and Civil Service* (3d of 9 R). Subcommittees: Compensation and Employee Benefits (Ranking Member); Postal Personnel and Modernization. *Standards of Official Conduct* (Ranking Member of 6 R).

Group Ratings

	ADA	ACLU	COPE	CFA	LCV	ACU	NTLC	NSI	COC	CEI
1988	15	27	16	36	31	83	52	100	92	54
1987	12	—	16	14	—	87	—	—	60	54

National Journal Ratings

	1988 LIB — 1988 CONS		1987 LIB — 1987 CONS	
Economic	18%	— 81%	19%	— 78%
Social	26%	— 74%	10%	— 85%
Foreign	24%	— 74%	0%	— 80%

Key Votes

1) Homeless $	FOR	5) Ban Drug Test	FOR	9) SDI Research	FOR
2) Gephardt Amdt	AGN	6) Drug Death Pen	FOR	10) Ban Chem Weaps	AGN
3) Deficit Reduc	AGN	7) Handgun Sales	FOR	11) Aid to Contras	FOR
4) Kill Plnt Clsng Notice	FOR	8) Ban D.C. Abort $	FOR	12) Nuclear Testing	AGN

Election Results

1988 general	John T. Myers (R)	130,578	(62%)	($157,671)
	Mark Waterfill (D)	80,741	(38%)	($55,524)
1988 primary	John T. Myers (R), unopposed			
1986 general	John T. Myers (R)	104,965	(67%)	($163,877)
	L. Eugene Smith (D)	49,675	(32%)	($27,139)

EIGHTH DISTRICT

In a state with hard-bitten politics, the 8th Congressional District of Indiana covers the southwest portion of the state. Its boundaries are as irregular as pieces of a jigsaw puzzle, because the legislature wanted to maximize the number of Republicans and minimize the Democrats. So Indiana University's Bloomington is split while the district bulges in and out to take in Republican courthouse towns and spew out Democratic hills. It has bipartisan traditions: it was Democratic enough since its Doughface days in the Civil War period to vote for Jimmy Carter in 1976, Birch Bayh in 1980, and Evan Bayh in 1988; its largest city, Evansville, produced three-term Democratic Senator Vance Hartke. But it also has a Republican tradition, as the boyhood home of Senator William Jenner, a McCarthy ally who once said General

George Marshall would sell out his grandmother to the Communists, and Admiral and Iran-contra defendant John Poindexter who grew up in Odum. This partisan history goes back nearly 200 years, when this southwest corner of Indiana was, oddly, the first part of the state settled by whites. Vincennes, now a small town on the banks of the Wabash River, was once the metropolis of Indiana, and Robert Owen, the Scottish philanthropist and visionary, established the town of New Harmony downstream. Owen's son was the first congressman from the area, elected in 1842 and 1844.

In House elections, the 8th has been one of the nation's most furiously contested districts. It elected four different congressmen in four election years in the 1970s—the only district in the nation to do so. It ousted incumbents of varying parties in 1958, 1966, 1974, 1978, and 1982. In 1984, incumbent Democrat Frank McCloskey, Mayor of Bloomington for 11 years, led 27-year-old Republican Richard McIntyre in the first count by 72 votes out of 233,000 cast; then some double-counting in a Democratic county was corrected, giving McIntyre a 34-vote lead which Republican state officials quickly certified; then a recanvass in another county put McCloskey ahead by 72 votes, and the House declined to seat either man. This became the nasty partisan dispute of 1985, with a special task force set up to decide it, and McCloskey ultimately was seated by a partisan vote with the Republicans yelling foul. In 1986, there was a rematch, in which McIntyre charged that McCloskey, who had admitted trying marijuana briefly, had used opium; there was no evidence for this, and it hurt McIntyre and McCloskey won 53%–47%.

Since then, McCloskey in his plodding way has concentrated mainly on constituency service and local issues. He uses his seat on Armed Services to keep the Crane Naval Ammunition Depot humming; on larger issues he tends to go along with other Democrats. He chairs a Post Office subcommittee and has pushed bills to stop the government from mailing biological materials and to stop others from sending out mailings that look like they are official Social Security or other government documents. He works to get strip-mined land reclaimed after bonding companies have defaulted; he gets funds for a study of a direct Indianapolis-Evansville highway. In 1988 he was a bit nervous when his Republican opponent turned out to be one John Myers, namesake of the popular 7th District congressman. But this Myers, despite campaign help from his old classmate John Poindexter, raised little money and won a lower percentage of votes than anyone has received in this district since 1972. But it's still possible that McCloskey will get tougher opposition in this tough partisan territory.

The People: Est. Pop. 1986: 554,900, up 1.5% 1980–86; Pop. 1980: 546,744, up 9.3% 1970–80. Households (1980): 74% family, 39% with children, 64% married couples; 26.1% housing units rented; median monthly rent: $154; median house value: $34,700. Voting age pop. (1980): 395,151; 2% Black.

1988 Presidential Vote: Bush (R) 133,017   (57%)
Dukakis (D). 97,530   (42%)

Rep. Francis X. (Frank) **McCloskey (D)**

Elected 1982; b. June 12, 1939, Philadelphia, PA; home, Smithville; IN U., B.A. 1968, J.D. 1971; Roman Catholic; married (Roberta).

Career: USAF, 1957–61; Journalist; Mayor of Bloomington, 1971–82.

Offices: 127 CHOB 20515, 202-225-4636. Also 501 S. Madison, Bloomington 47401, 812-334-1111; 10 N.E. 4th St., Washington 47501, 812-254-6646; and Fed. Bldg., Rm. 124, 101 N.W. 7th St., Evansville 47708, 812-465-6484.

Committees: *Armed Services* (19th of 31 D). Subcommittees: Procurement and Military Nuclear Systems; Investigations. *Foreign Affairs* (27th of 28 D). Subcommittee: Africa. *Post Office and Civil Service* (9th of 15 D). Subcommittees: Civil Service; Postal Personnel and Modernization (Chairman).

Group Ratings

	ADA	ACLU	COPE	CFA	LCV	ACU	NTLC	NSI	COC	CEI
1988	75	77	89	91	69	16	9	0	21	10
1987	80	—	87	71	—	4	—	—	14	10

National Journal Ratings

	1988 LIB — 1988 CONS	1987 LIB — 1987 CONS
Economic	87% — 8%	55% — 43%
Social	76% — 23%	66% — 32%
Foreign	74% — 23%	75% — 24%

Key Votes

1) Homeless $	FOR	5) Ban Drug Test	AGN	9) SDI Research	AGN
2) Gephardt Amdt	FOR	6) Drug Death Pen	FOR	10) Ban Chem Weaps	FOR
3) Deficit Reduc	FOR	7) Handgun Sales	FOR	11) Aid to Contras	AGN
4) Kill Plnt Clsng Notice	AGN	8) Ban D.C. Abort $	FOR	12) Nuclear Testing	FOR

Election Results

1988 general	Francis X. (Frank) McCloskey (D)	141,355	(62%)	($551,484)
	John L. Myers (R)	87,321	(38%)	($130,243)
1988 primary	Francis X. (Frank) McCloskey (D)	62,944	(89%)	
	John W. Taylor (D)	8,101	(11%)	
1986 general	Francis X. (Frank) McCloskey (D)	106,662	(53%)	($625,188)
	Richard D. McIntyre (R)	93,586	(47%)	($581,786)

NINTH DISTRICT

Down the Ohio River in the early 19th centurry came the first white settlers of Indiana. Most of them were southerners, from across the river in Kentucky or over the mountains in Virginia. The old city of Madison, on the Ohio, still has many of its marvelous old buildings from the days when it was one of the busiest ports on the Ohio River; but it has been a backwater since the middle of the 19th cetury. Farther down the river is Corydon, from 1816 to 1825 the state capital. Many other towns have 19th century buildings, well preserved because they were bypassed by railroads. The river is still an artery of commerce, but utilitarian barges have replaced the steamers, and even the barges have been overbuilt; the last Ohio River shipyard in

Jeffersonville, across from Louisville, closed in 1986.

The settlers in this part of Indiana retained their affection for things southern into the Civil War and beyond; one of their number, Jesse Bright, was expelled from the Senate in 1862 because of his Confederate sympathies. The hills along the Ohio typically deliver Democratic majorities, as they did in the close gubernatorial elections of 1984 and 1988; Democratic as well are the Indiana suburbs of Louisville.

Most of Indiana's Ohio River counties, and an oddly shaped collection of lightly populated counties inland form Indiana's 9th Congressional District. The boundaries are irregular because Republican legislators wanted to pack as much Democratic territory as possible into the 9th. In effect, they were conceding it to Democratic Representative Lee Hamilton, as well they might.

First elected in the 1964 landslide, Hamilton has become one of the most respected members of the House. Second ranking Democrat on the Foreign Affairs Committee, he was chosen by Speaker Tip O'Neill to chair the House Intelligence Committee after the 1984 election, and after the 1986 election he was chosen by Jim Wright to chair the special committee investigating the Iran-contra scandal. When those choices were made, Hamilton was still little known outside the House. He seldom appeared on national news shows; he was not a regular at tweedy foreign affairs seminars; his name did not often get in the paper. But for years he has commanded vast respect in the House. Other members rise and talk and sway one or two votes. When Hamilton comes down on one side, he often persuades dozens of different members, of widely varying views, to support that position. Such influence is acquired painstakingly and slowly. Hamilton instinctively approaches difficult issues cautiously, hears out all sides, researches the facts personally, reaches decisions or makes recommendations judiciously and on the merits. He seems impervious to personal influence and the blandishments of friendship and camaraderie. His reluctance to take stands makes him all the more influential when he does so. As a result, on an area as controversial as the Middle East, he is one of the few Members of Congress who is genuinely respected—and spoken of in hushed tones—on all sides. Even the most aggressive and contemptuous of the young House Republicans speak his name only in tones of respect.

The Middle East, where he is one Foreign Affairs member the Israel lobby cannot count on but can sometimes persuade, is not the only touchy issue Hamilton has played a major role on. He staunchly supported the Pershing II missile deployment in Europe. He works against trade barriers. He is one of the House's leading experts on international lending institutions. On all these matters he has helped to lead a Democratic House in the same direction as the Republican Administration. But he is only a cautious supporter of covert activity, as the Iran-contra hearings showed. And he has consistently opposed aid to the Nicaraguan contras; while sometimes seeking compromise, he is probably as responsible as any member for the end of contra aid. On intelligence, on contra aid, on Angola and other trouble spots, he believes in close congressional oversight of intelligence activities and is cautious about U.S. government involvement in hostilities abroad. Operators like Oliver North may be all sail; Hamilton seeks to provide anchor.

To his task of co-chairing the Iran-contra hearings, Hamilton brought the convictions and demeanor that have made this minister's son a successful small town lawyer and rural politician. He is always ready to concede others' good faith and is open to their arguments; he likes to avoid positions at the extremes, and he tends to advise caution at home as well as abroad. As chairman of the Democratic freshmen elected in 1964, he sent Lyndon Johnson a letter in September 1965 calling for "a time to pause" in Great Society legislation. He is unconcerned about fashion: he has kept his crew cut till it is almost back in style again. He is concerned about morality and regularity, and tellingly lectured the Administration on the deception and irregularity that were at the heart of Iran-contra.

Hamilton will probably be in the national spotlight again. He favorably impressed Michael Dukakis and was on his short list of vice presidential candidates. He is almost sure to be chairman some day of Foreign Affairs, and his work and that of chairman Dante Fascell have made this committee more influential and listened to than it has been in years. He can also have, if he chooses, influence on other issues in the House. He served on the ethics committee during the Koreagate and Abscam scandals and takes a stern tone and insists on harsh penalties for what he considers transgressions.

Hamilton has had no difficulty winning reelection in the 9th District for many years, and although the Republican redistricters took his home town of Columbus out of the 9th, they otherwise gave him a seat as favorable as he has ever had. He seems certain to win reelection indefinitely here.

The People: Est. Pop. 1986: 554,500, up 1.8% 1980–86; Pop. 1980: 544,873, up 14.2% 1970–80. Households (1980): 77% family, 44% with children, 67% married couples; 25.2% housing units rented; median monthly rent: $158; median house value: $36,500. Voting age pop. (1980): 383,018; 2% Black, 1% Spanish origin.

1988 Presidential Vote:

Bush (R)	123,198	(58%)
Dukakis (D)	89,744	(42%)

Rep. Lee H. Hamilton (D)

Elected 1964; b. Apr. 20, 1931, Daytona Beach, FL; home, Nashville; DePauw U., B.A. 1952, Goethe U., Frankfurt, Germany, 1952–53, IN U., J.D. 1956; United Methodist; married (Nancy).

Career: Practicing atty., 1956–64; Instructor, American Banking Inst. 1960–61.

Offices: 2187 RHOB 20515, 202-225-5315. Also 107 Fed. Ctr., Bldg. 66, 1201 E. 10th St., Jeffersonville 47130, 812-288-3999.

Committees: *Foreign Affairs* (2d of 28 D). Subcommittee: Europe and the Middle East (Chairman). *Science, Space and Technology* (19th of 30 D). Subcommittees: Science Research and Technology; International Scientific Cooperation. *Joint Economic Committee* (Chairman). Task Forces: International Economic Policy; Economic Growth, Trade and Taxes; Economic Goals and Intergovernmental Policy (Chairman).

Group Ratings

	ADA	ACLU	COPE	CFA	LCV	ACU	NTLC	NSI	COC	CEI
1988	85	74	68	82	69	8	34	10	36	24
1987	72	—	67	57	—	9	—	—	47	27

National Journal Ratings

	1988 LIB — 1988 CONS		1987 LIB — 1987 CONS	
Economic	60%	— 37%	42%	— 56%
Social	58%	— 40%	68%	— 31%
Foreign	60%	— 37%	61%	— 38%

Key Votes

1) Homeless $	FOR	5) Ban Drug Test	AGN	9) SDI Research	AGN
2) Gephardt Amdt	FOR	6) Drug Death Pen	AGN	10) Ban Chem Weaps	AGN
3) Deficit Reduc	AGN	7) Handgun Sales	FOR	11) Aid to Contras	AGN
4) Kill Plnt Clsng Notice	AGN	8) Ban D.C. Abort $	FOR	12) Nuclear Testing	FOR

Election Results

1988 general	Lee H. Hamilton (D)	147,193	(71%)	($333,957)
	Floyd E. Coates (R)	60,946	(29%)	($0)
1988 primary	Lee H. Hamilton (D), unopposed			
1986 general	Lee H. Hamilton (D)	120,586	(69%)	($306,485)
	Robert Kilroy (R)	46,398	(31%)	($16,610)

TENTH DISTRICT

Indianapolis, long the home of some of America's strongest political machines, is a state capital of perfect dimensions. Situated precisely in the center of the state, with avenues radiating out from Monument Circle in eight directions to all its ends and corners, Indianapolis is both Indiana's largest city and its capital. Right on the Circle are headquartered the state's two biggest banks, one historically Republican and one Democratic; a few blocks away on North Meridian are the World War Memorial and the headquarters of the American Legion. Fifty years ago this Indianapolis was the headquarters of presidential hopeful Paul McNutt, a former American Legion national commander and Democratic governor who systematized Indiana's political patronage and schemed to push aside Franklin Roosevelt.

He failed, but Indianapolis remained the cockpit of partisan conflict, the center of the state's media—notably of the Indianapolis newspapers owned by Eugene Pulliam, Dan Quayle's grandfather—and the headquarters of its big insurance and pharmaceutical companies. Indianpolis today remains the engine of Indiana's economic growth, with a white-collar economy resembling that of a Sun Belt city and suburbs spreading well beyond the Marion County line. Indianapolis is proud that it spirited away the Colts from Baltimore and the Hudson Institute from Westchester County; it is proud of its huge Medical Center; it is proud that it was the host of the 1987 Pan American Games as well as the annual Indianapolis 500. With more than one million people, Indianapolis is now a city worthy of its monumental core.

Politically, Indianapolis has always had two-party competition, yet in national contests has been distinctly Republican; it was nearly 2 to 1 for the Bush-Quayle ticket. It lacks the groups that have moved other cities leftward. It does not have the yeasty ethnic mix of most midwestern cities—there are some blacks here and some identifiable ethnics, but the dominant tone is very much white Protestant—it has never had really big CIO unions nor large singles or gay communities. It has grown pretty steadily and sees little reason to be dissatisfied with the free enterprise system or any need to redistribute income.

Yet the larger part of Indianapolis has been represented in the House for all but two years since 1964 by Andrew Jacobs, Jr., a Democrat of idiosyncratic views and puckish demeanor. He has some reason to take pride in his quirkiness: a cheapskate, he refused in 1975 to board a plane because only first class seats were available; it crashed, killing all aboard. He flouted tradition later that year when he married Representative Martha Keys of Kansas (who is also the sister of Lee Hart, Gary Hart's wife); they met in the House Ways and Means Committee. On weekends Jacobs flew to Indianapolis and Keys took the same plane on to Kansas City, until she was defeated for reelection in 1978. (They have since divorced; his first wife was the daughter of an Indiana governor; his third wife is an anchor on Indianapolis's Channel 13.)

Jacobs owed his initial election to the Democratic sweep in 1964 and his first reelections to Democratic redistricting in 1966 and 1968. Because 1970 was a recession year, it was a good Democratic year in Indiana; in 1972, he was defeated by William Hudnut, now Indianapolis's mayor. Returned to office in the Watergate year of 1974, Jacobs has developed a record that has made him close to unbeatable. He has grown less enthusiastic and more skeptical about federal spending programs over the years; he has been backing a constitutional amendment to require a balanced budget since 1979. Jacobs is chairman of the Social Security Subcommittee of Ways and Means and has played—and may play again—a key role in holding down medicare spending. He is one congressman who will stand up and say that the government doesn't owe "Notch Babies" (those born between 1917 and 1921) any extra Social Security benefits. He does serve local interests, helping Eli Lilly get a tax exemption and the Marion County Sheriff department an airplane and Pan Am game athletes get refunds for duties they paid on sports equipement when coming into the U.S. He is active on other measures, allowing blood donors to give their Social Security numbers so their blood could be traced back and allowing federal courts to enforce child support laws. He has also proposed reprinting political cartoons in the *Congressional Record* and wrote one complainant who penned a roman numeral a "IV" after his name that he might be in violation of a state statute upheld because, in the words of Justice Holmes, "three generations of imbeciles are enough."

He opposed sending the Marines to Lebanon and, as a Marine veteran who sustained a disability in combat in Korea, he twitted young Republican hawks like Newt Gingrich and Vin Weber by calling them "war wimps." For months many of them were unaccustomedly silent on the issue. Then Jacobs asked former California Republican Representative Pete McCloskey about his recollections of presidential candidate Pat Robertson's service in the Marines during the Korean war; McCloskey replied that he had heard that Robertson was kept out of combat by his father, who was a Senator from Virginia at the time. Jacobs gave McCloskey's letter wide circulation, and Robertson, who admits that he was not under fire but claims that he served in a rear echelon in what was technically a combat zone, sued them both for libel, then withdrew the suit after it came up for trial in March 1988 at a key point in the campaign. McCloskey's story may be particularly interesting to Jacobs because like Robertson he had a father in Congress when the Korean war broke out, but served in combat anyway and now is eligible for disability pay but doesn't take it.

Jacobs's self-denial extends to campaigning. He accepts no PAC contributions, raises and spends little money even when seriously opposed, and wins anyway. In 1982 his Democratic colleague David Evans, redistricted into a heavily Republican seat, raised plenty of money and opposed Jacobs in the primary; he outspent Jacobs, but Jacobs won 60%–35%. In 1984 and 1988 he won about 60% against black Republicans. In 1986 the American Medical Association was miffed when Jacobs moved successfully to limit doctors' fees ("Vote for the canes, not for the stethoscopes," he said) and went into Indianapolis and spent $300,000 on an independent expenditure campaign against him. His Republican opponent outspent him by more than 10–1, and his percentage fell to 58%. Many incumbents would feel uncomfortable with this, even though the 10th District, which includes almost all of Indianapolis inside the Interstate 465 loop, except for the rich precincts directly north of downtown, has many black and white working-class precincts, and had enough Democrats to go for Michael Dukakis in 1988. But Jacobs, going his own way as always, seems entirely comfortable in this political situation, and seems likely to continue being himself in the House for some time to come.

The People: Est. Pop. 1986: 550,600, up 1.6% 1980–86; Pop. 1980: 541,811, dn. 12.4% 1970–80. Households (1980): 68% family, 39% with children, 51% married couples; 43.0% housing units rented; median monthly rent: $164; median house value: $28,400. Voting age pop. (1980): 384,402; 25% Black, 1% Spanish origin.

1988 Presidential Vote:

Dukakis (D)	91,726	(51%)
Bush (R)	86,331	(48%)

Rep. Andrew Jacobs, Jr. (D)

Elected 1974; b. Feb. 24, 1932, Indianapolis; home, Indianapolis; IN U., B.S. 1955, LL.B. 1958; Roman Catholic; married (Kim).

Career: USMC, Korea; Practicing atty., 1958–65, 1973–74; IN House of Reps., 1959–60; U.S. House of Reps., 1965–73.

Offices: 2313 RHOB 20515, 202-225-4011. Also 441-A Fed. Bldg., 46 E. Ohio St., Indianapolis 46204, 317-226-7331.

Committees: *Ways and Means* (6th of 23 D). Subcommittees: Oversight; Social Security (Chairman).

Group Ratings

	ADA	ACLU	COPE	CFA	LCV	ACU	NTLC	NSI	COC	CEI
1988	95	87	74	82	94	12	47	0	42	33
1987	96	—	72	71	—	4	—	—	33	30

National Journal Ratings

	1988 LIB — 1988 CONS		1987 LIB — 1987 CONS	
Economic	57%	— 41%	53%	— 46%
Social	78%	— 20%	73%	— 22%
Foreign	84%	— 0%	73%	— 26%

Key Votes

1) Homeless $	FOR	5) Ban Drug Test	AGN	9) SDI Research	AGN
2) Gephardt Amdt	FOR	6) Drug Death Pen	AGN	10) Ban Chem Weaps	FOR
3) Deficit Reduc	FOR	7) Handgun Sales	AGN	11) Aid to Contras	AGN
4) Kill Plnt Clsng Notice	AGN	8) Ban D.C. Abort $	AGN	12) Nuclear Testing	FOR

Election Results

1988 general	Andrew Jacobs, Jr. (D)	105,846	(61%)	($35,786)
	James C. Cummings (R)	68,978	(39%)	($24,919)
1988 primary	Andrew Jacobs, Jr. (D)	40,116	(92%)	
	Joe Turner (D)	3,393	(8%)	
1986 general	Andrew Jacobs, Jr. (D)	68,817	(58%)	($40,577)
	Jim Eynon (R)	49,064	(41%)	($531,148)

IOWA

"The panorama," read the *WPA Guide* 50 years ago, "is of corn, growing in great square and rectangular fields, of grain ripening in the prairie winds; of grazing cattle, red barns, tall silos, white farmhouses; and of towns bordering the highway at regular intervals and dominated by grain elevators and church spires. The bird's-eye view shows a land of independent farmers of rich soil, and prosperity." But that was not the whole picture, not after the falling farm prices of the 1920s and depression of the 1930s. Farmers lost their land and became tenants; when they moved off one piece of rented land to another in February for spring planting in March, "trucks and wagons crowded with furniture rumble[d] over the frozen roads and tired herds of cattle and sheep trudge[d] in their wake. Load after load jolt past the farm houses, stretching out like a gypsy caravan going on to camp elsewhere for a brief time, hoping that the next farm will be a little better than the last one."

Today Iowa is much more prosperous than it was 50 years ago; its agriculture, enhanced by scientific research, is far more productive; its small cities comfortable and progressive. Since its first settlement, Iowa has prided itself on education: it was dotted with colleges and had the nation's highest literacy rates. Yet Iowa remains afflicted with many of the same problems it had 50 years ago, and none more agonizing than "the phenomenal emigration of its people." Farm prices fell sharply in the early 1980s, many farmers lost their land and tenancy became more common, and outmigration from the state was even higher than historic levels so that Iowa lost more people in the last decade than any other state. From 1940 to 1980, the population of 10 of Iowa's city and university counties increased 62%, while the other 89 saw their population fall 6%; people have been leaving farms and small towns for jobs in tractor and farm machinery factories and offices in Waterloo, Des Moines, Cedar Rapids and Sioux City. But in the 1980s, as the demand for new farm machinery sunk toward zero, the cities were hit as well as the countryside; only Des Moines and the college towns of Iowa City and Ames had some growth. As the 1980s were ending, the state's population started growing again, and Governor Terry Branstad was proclaiming that computers and fiber optics would enable Iowa's highly literate and skilled work force to make growing contributions to the world's economy. If that does happen, it will be the first time that Iowa has managed to generate an economy capable of absorbing all its children.

Iowa responded to the downturns of the 1930s and the 1980s as it has to almost every development—contrary to the national trend. For a state which looks like classical Middle America—the natural home, it would seem, of Norman Rockwell's freckle-faced boys and turkey-serving grandmothers, with most of its housing stock dating from before 1950—Iowa economically, culturally, and politically is atypical almost to the point of being quirky and eccentric. Economically, it remains dependent on the farm economy and has a vested interest in inflation, which increases farm and land prices. Culturally, it was settled in a rush in the generation following the Mexican War of 1846–48 by yeomen of Yankee and German stock. With outmigration since 1900 it is almost entirely white and northern European today. These first Iowans stressed hard work and learning, and today Iowa has the cultural conservatism that comes from steady habits: Iowa boasts that it has the nation's highest literacy rate and one of the lowest divorce rates.

Politically, Iowa has been almost perfectly countercyclical. Discontent with the farm economy is one reason, since farm prices tend to fall in times of general prosperity. Farm incomes are profits rather than salaries or wages, and so are particularly volatile; a small shift in

IOWA — Congressional Districts, Counties, and Selected Places — (6 Districts)

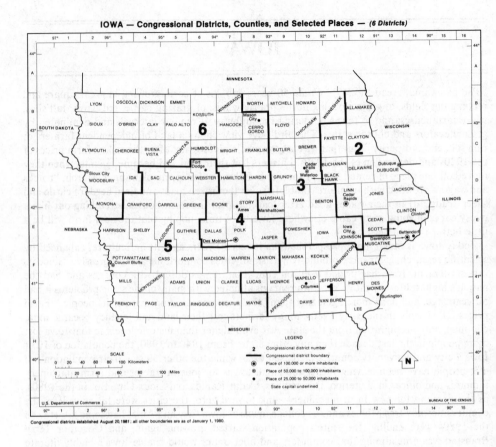

crop prices or interest rates or the cost of fertilizer or pesticide requirements or simply a break in the weather can have huge effects on a farmer's income. That volatility generates near-constant dissatisfaction and continual demands for government action. When prices fall, Iowa demands that the government prop them up in various complicated ways; when interest rates rise, Iowa demands that they be forced back down; when presidential candidates come to Iowa's precinct caucuses in January, as they did in droves in the 1980s, Iowa forces most of them to pledge that they will not embargo grain sales or interrupt the flow of grain to the Soviet Union whatever the foreign policy consequences. The high grain prices of the late 1970s generated complaints that land was becoming too expensive and that government must act to keep small farmers from being squeezed out. The lower grain prices of the 1980s generated demands for subsidizing farm credit and maintaining federal price support payments, in some cases at more than 100% of the world market price. The result is that Iowa tends to swing against the party in power, even when it is gaining nationally, as in 1956, 1972, and 1984, and it swings harder against a party in power than most other states, as in 1968 and 1980.

On foreign policy issues, Iowa has consistently been one of the most dovish states. In 1940, Franklin Roosevelt was moving from the New Deal to preparedness for war—even though his running mate, Henry Wallace, was an Iowan; Iowa was the number six Republican state then, trailing only the Dakotas, Nebraska, Kansas, and Vermont. In 1988, after eight years of Ronald

Reagan's defense buildup and assertive foreign policy. Iowa was the number two Democratic state, favoring Michael Dukakis over George Bush by a percentage exceeded only in the District of Columbia and Rhode Island. One reason is its German heritage. German-Americans were pilloried for their opposition to American entry into World War I, and their skepticism about American involvement in a foreign war made Iowa an isolationist state in the 1930s until Pearl Harbor Day and may have contributed to its dovishness in the Vietnam period. Another contributing factor is the dovish tone of articulate opinion, led by the *Des Moines Register & Tribune* (one of the few American papers with statewide circulation), accompanied by the mainline Protestant denominations (which seem to have more vitality here than elsewhere in the nation), and completed by the lack of any significant military bases or major defense contractors in the state.

Iowa's counter-cyclical politics are the result of its combined proclivities on issues. First, this farm state is usually conservative on economic questions but used to relying on government assistance in agriculture. But, second, Iowa is otherwise stingy about other forms of spending, particularly if it spots waste. Some of the all-time congressional pinch-pennies come from Iowa. Third, it abhors corruption. Iowa gave Richard Nixon in 1972 a lower percentage than in 1968; Watergate was then only a minor issue elsewhere, but it cut in Iowa. Fourth, Iowa is tolerant generally but not particularly pleased with new cultural styles. This is family country. Finally, Iowa has been dovish at least since the First World War. It is wary of military involvements abroad now, and hostile to large defense budgets.

This is an unusual mix. You find something like it in adjacent parts of Wisconsin and Minnesota, and nowhere else—a product of Yankee settlement and Scandinavian leavening, moral uprightness and a penchant for reform. It resulted in the landslide 1986 reelection of Republican Senator Charles Grassley, who shrewdly combines a reputation as a tightwad on domestic spending and at the Pentagon with a willingness to use government to help farmers, and in the 1988 near-landslide for Michael Dukakis. An added element is the affirmative unpopularity in Iowa of Ronald Reagan, the only President who has lived as an adult in Iowa (Herbert Hoover left when he was 9). His cheeriness and ingratiating quips seemed only to grate on voters here; the very familiarity of his Middle American idiom seemed to enrage these Middle Americans; perhaps his own Iowa connections made them even more resentful of the policies which they feel have wreaked havoc on Iowa's economy, ripping apart its small towns and depopulating its rural counties, and threatening its way of life. Iowans seem to feel left behind in the economic recovery of the 1980s and left out of the surge of patriotism and nationalistic feeling. Their consistently negative job ratings of Reagan and their scathingly low votes for George Bush—44% in the general election and a pathetic 19% in the Republican precinct caucuses—show that Iowa as it approaches the 1990s is more countercyclical than ever.

Presidential politics. Every four years, on a frigid Monday night in January or February, Iowa Democrats and Republicans gather in some 4,000 designated schools, public buildings and private houses, and begin America's presidential delegate selection process. These are the Iowa precinct caucuses, technically gatherings to select delegates to each party's 99 county conventions; but in fact Iowa has become so important that candidates spend literally months here, wooing political activists, speaking to every gathering they can find. Presidents and Vice Presidents phone and send out hand-written notes to gas station owners and bank tellers; Bruce Babbitt pedaled across the state in RAGBRAI (the *Register*'s Annual Great Bicycle Race Across Iowa) and Michael Dukakis, as incumbent governor of Massachusetts, spent 82 days here in 1987–88.

That such an idiosyncratic state begins the presidential selection process is one of the anomalies of American politics. It evidently started accidentally: caucus scholar Hugh Winebrenner says Iowa Democrats chose a date that made them the earliest contest in the nation in 1972 solely because it was the required number of days before the available date of a hall suitable for their state convention. The 1972 caucuses, in which George McGovern ran close behind Edmund Muskie, were little noted outside the state, and not many were paying attention in 1975 as former Georgia Governor Jimmy Carter spent nights in Iowans' homes and made the beds; his victory in an October 1975 Jefferson-Jackson dinner straw poll gave his campaign credibility for the first time. Carter's 27% of "state delegate equivalents," though it was behind the 37% who were uncommitted, made him the frontrunner for the Democratic nomination. Gerald Ford led Ronald Reagan 45%–43% in a straw poll of 600 Republican caucus-goers—a ludicrously small sample, but about the margin by which Ford won the nomination.

By 1980 the caucuses were a full-fledged contest: Ronald Reagan passed up an Iowa debate and promptly lost to George Bush; Jimmy Carter walloped Edward Kennedy. In 1984 the Democrats had the only contest: Walter Mondale from neighboring Minnesota won half the state delegate equivalents in an eight-candidate field, but Gary Hart's 16% second place finish made him a national contender. By 1988 the caucuses were bringing $25 million to Iowa's economy, the bar at the Savery Hotel (owned by the husband of the Democratic state chairwoman) was jammed with the nation's premier political reporters night after night, and on caucus night half the satellite transmitters in North America were in Des Moines to beam the results of the caucuses to the world.

The results showed Iowa at its most parochial. The Democratic winner, with 31%, was Richard Gephardt, co-author of the Harkin-Gephardt mandatory farm production control bill and the Gephardt trade bill, with heavy support from union and elderly caucus-goers; second with 27% was Paul Simon, from neighboring Downstate Illinois, endorsed by the *Register* (on the curious ground, for an independent newspaper, that he was the most traditional Democrat); in third, with 22% thanks to a crackerjack organizational and turnout effort, was Michael Dukakis. Jesse Jackson surprised some by winning 9%; Bruce Babbitt, had he been endorsed by the *Register* as expected, would have done much better than his poor fifth and might have become a genuine contender; Albert Gore, charging that Iowa Democrats' almost unanimous dovishness made it impossible for a candidate with his defense views to win, withdrew. Among the Republicans the easy winner was Bob Dole, with his record on farm issues and endorsement from Charles Grassley, with 37%. Pat Robertson rallied some 26,000 Iowans, enough for a 25% second-place finish. George Bush's 19% third-place finish led to speculation that he was finished.

The justification for the Iowa caucuses is that they require candidates to get in touch with actual voters, give little-known outsiders a chance to compete, and provide some forecast of later contests. On all three counts the 1988 Iowa caucuses failed. Thanks to the parties' computer technology, candidates can target and thus spend vast amounts of time with party activists, who are chipper and articulate and pleasant but not necessarily representative even of Iowa voters: just 126,000 Democrats and 108,000 Republicans participate in a state of nearly 3 million. As for giving little-known candidates a break, the caucuses arguably helped drive all but little-known candidates out of the Democratic race, and some would argue that giving an edge to a minister who has never held public office is not a good idea. As for Iowa's general election forecasting ability, it has deteriorated since 1976 when Iowa in November was within 1% of the national result. In 1988 Iowa was the most anti-Reagan state in poll after poll, and the caucus results came close to being replicated only in next-door South Dakota. On Super Tuesday, five weeks later, the top two Iowa finishers in both parties were effectively eliminated: Gephardt stopped campaigning and Simon ran seriously only in his home state of Illinois a week later; Dole withdrew before Illinois and Robertson retired in confusion.

Will Iowa be the first in the nation again in 1992? And should it be? Many Democrats, at least, have doubts, and in early 1989 were thinking about jimmying their party rules once again. The unanimous dovishness of Iowa's Democratic caucus-goers means that any candidate without a purely dovish record not only can't win here, but can't win any appreciable number of votes at all; if Iowa has a veto, that means the Democrats can never nominate a candidate with a foreign and defense policy acceptable to the 151 electoral votes in the South. As for the Republicans, in 1988 at least Iowa was the most unfavorable ground in the entire country for George Bush. It is impossible to find a state that is perfectly representative of the country. But it is hard to see why the process should start in a state which has become so completely unrepresentative.

Governor. Governor Terry Branstad, a conservative Republican governing a state profoundly disillusioned with the national conservative Republican Administration, has nonetheless had his successes and maintained his popularity in office in the 1980s. He has reason to hope that the 1990s will be better for Iowa and reason as well to hope that the 1990 election will be as favorable for him as 1982 and 1986 were when he won as much because of his Democratic opponents' problems as his own strength. The first time, he was age 35 and owed more money on his farm than its market value. But he criticized the Reagan Administration and pushed for a moratorium on farm foreclosures, and was helped because opponent Roxanne Conlin had legally avoided paying state taxes. In 1986, another Republican year in Iowa, opponent Lowell Junkins offered a plan to issue $400 million in bonds to stimulate new business and trade, to be paid back out of proceeds from the lottery; parsimonious and abstemious Iowans seemed uncertain that government could allocate money intelligently and worried that lottery proceeds would, as they have in other states, drop after the novelty wore off. Branstad, a 53% winner in 1982, won with 52% in 1986.

Branstad cut business taxes in his first term, proposed spending increases for teachers, highways and prisons plus some tax changes—an activist agenda—in his second. He hailed the recovery of the state's economy following a rise in farm and farm land prices in 1987, and a net rise in jobs during his two terms. For 1990 he is still likely to have a tough race. Democrats have controlled the legislature throughout his term, and possible opponents include Attorney General Tom Miller, Speaker Don Avenson, banker John Chrystal, and Lieutenant Governor Jo Ann Zimmerman.

Senators. Charles Grassley has been underestimated throughout his political career. He likes to point out that he is a simple farmer, that he worked as a machinist while serving in the legislature; he talks and looks like an archetypical hayseed. But he is also a shrewd and successful politician, winning a seat in the Iowa legislature in the Democratic year of 1958, a House seat in the Democratic year of 1974, and a Senate seat by beating a strong incumbent, John Culver, in 1980. He began by sponsoring a budget freeze proposal, emphasizing the frugality and fairness Iowans have always believed in; he went on to attack the Pentagon for wasting money, and made headlines when he asked Pentagon analyst Chuck Spinney to testify before Congress, which he did only after making the cover of *Time*—a perfect episode for Iowa's dovish, pinch-penny voters. In 1985 someone in the White House said publicly that if Grassley did not vote for the MX missile, the President was not going to come in and campaign for him. Grassley, no doubt aware that Reagan had won only 53% in 1984 in Iowa, said that was just fine with him.

From that point on, other incumbent Republicans eagerly recorded their dissents from this or that item on the Administration's agenda and tailored their reelection campaigns closely to the views and priorities of their home states. Pretty much lost was the kind of national theme that accounted for so many Republican gains in 1980 and 1984 and minimized the number of Republican losses in 1982. Not all his colleagues were as successful as Grassley; but then he has been winning with this kind of formula for three decades. In 1986 Grassley became the first Iowa Senator to win reelection in 20 years. No serious candidate filed to run against him, and he was reelected with 66% of the vote—more than any other Iowa Senator has ever received. In 1988 Grassley supported Bob Dole for President and helped him to his solid win in Iowa.

Legislatively, Grassley has not had much impact in a Democratic Senate. Yet he has shown the capacity to change the terms of debate, and future historians may date the end of the Reagan

Administration's huge increases in defense spending to Grassley's initiatives. He charges there is a black market in military secrets and also calls on Pentagon employees to violate a secrecy pledge. He still has his seats on the Budget and Judiciary committees and moved, unwillingly, from Finance to Appropriations.

Iowa's other Senator, Tom Harkin, has a different formula that has also played quite well with Iowa politics for nearly two decades now. He is one of the Democrats' Watergate babies, but he has a craggy and almost worn look; he grew up poor in a tiny rural town, worked his way through college and law school, spent five years in the 1960s in the Navy. He has a brother who became deaf at age 9 whose experiences made a deep impression on him. He worked on Representative Neal Smith's staff. He was the man who exposed the South Vietnamese "tiger cage" prison. He then ran for Congress in a Republican district in the Republican year of 1972 and nearly won: the incumbent wasn't working hard, and Iowa's countercyclical voting habits were working for Harkin. In 1974 he ran again and invented "work days," a campaign technique widely imitated since: he spent a day working at each of a dozen or two jobs. He won solidly and held the seat with good percentages. Well before the 1984 election, he cornered the Democratic nomination to run against Senator Roger Jepsen, who was gravely weakened by, among other things, insisting he was entitled to commute to work alone in the highway lane reserved for cars with four passengers, and having visited years ago a massage parlor despite his campaigning for family values and against abortion. 1984 was a tough year for Democrats elsewhere, but a marvelous year for Harkin; he was elected to the Senate with 56% of the vote and carried all six congressional districts.

Harkin regards himself as a populist, he has set up a New Populist Forum, and he argues that "too few people have too much money and too much power," summoning up memories of the Populist party of the 1890s. He talks generally of redistributing wealth and power, but his specific proposals tend to hone in on redistributing certain kinds of wealth to certain kinds of people. He was tied with five other senators with the most liberal ratings from *National Journal* for the 100th Congress. He was the lead sponsor of the Harkin-Gephardt bill to let farmers vote on whether to have mandatory production controls—a proposal to take money from food consumers and give it to farmers with six-figure net worths; even in farm districts it elicited only a mixed response in 1986 and was little heard of in 1988. He is an outspoken opponent of American military involvement in Central America and has opposed contra aid. He has also called for linking human rights progress to aid for the Duarte government. He has worked for grants for "assistive technology" for the handicapped and a new NIH Institute on Deafness and Other Communications Disorders. He serves on the Appropriations, Agriculture, and Labor committees—nice posts for an Iowa Democrat—and chairs the Labor-HHS subcommittee, a post where his generous impulses can make a big difference.

Unless opinion in Iowa takes a sharp turn from 1988, Harkin's formula seems well adapted to win him a second term in 1990; if so, it will be the first time the holder of this seat has been reelected since 1966 and the first time Iowa voters have elected a Democrat to two consecutive six-year terms. On military and farm issues Harkin's convictions leave him well-positioned, and issues on which he is not in tune with the Iowa electorate—abortion and spending generally—don't seem likely to be as important. After Michael Dukakis swept five of Iowa's six districts (losing the 6th by 98 votes), the race against Harkin looked unattractive to some Iowa Republicans. But 2d district Congressman Tom Tauke in early 1989 started fundraising and speaking around the state, and there was some speculation that if he didn't run 6th district Congressman Fred Grandy would. Either one would provide serious competition, even if opinion remains favorable to the Democrats—and Iowa's history shows that it can sometimes shift as quickly as the weather coming in across the plains.

Congressional districting. In 1981 a state redistricting commission presented plans for the legislature to vote up or down; the then Republican legislature voted a plan that endangered one

Republican incumbent. The 1990 Census is likely to cost Iowa a seat, and the Democrats, if they control the legislature, will probably try to unseat one of the state's four Republicans, probably by combining the two western districts.

The People: Est. Pop. 1988: 2,834,000; Pop. 1980: 2,913,808, dn. 2.7% 1980–88 and up 3.1% 1970–80; 1.18% of U.S. total, 29th largest. 15% with 1–3 yrs. col., 14% with 4+ yrs. col.; 10.1% below poverty level. Single ancestry: 21% German, 7% English, 4% Irish, 2% Dutch, Norwegian, 1% Swedish, French. Households (1980): 73% family, 39% with children, 64% married couples; 26% housing units rented; median monthly rent: $176; median house value: $40,600. Voting age pop. (1980): 2,087,935; 1% Black, 1% Spanish origin. Registered voters (1988): 1,690,093; 610,537 D (36%), 524,934 R (31%), 554,622 unaffiliated and minor parties (33%).

1988 Share of Federal Tax Burden: $8,613,000,000; 0.97% of U.S. total, 30th largest.

1988 Share of Federal Expenditures

	Total		Non-Defense		Defense	
Total Expend	$9,697m	(1.10%)	$8,633m	(1.32%)	$883m	(0.39%)
St/Lcl Grants	1,199m	(1.05%)	880m	(0.77%)	1m	(0.74%)
Salary/Wages	666m	(0.50%)	561m	(0.84%)	105m	(0.84%)
Pymnts to Indiv	4,827m	(1.18%)	4,752m	(1.22%)	75m	(0.40%)
Procurement	699m	(0.37%)	139m	(0.30%)	699m	(0.37%)
Research/Other	2,305m	(6.17%)	2,302m	(6.21%)	3m	(6.21%)

Political Lineup: Governor, Terry E. Branstad (R); Lt. Gov., Jo Ann Zimmerman (D); Secy. of State, Elaine Baxter (D); Atty. Gen., Tom Miller (D); Treasurer, Michael L. Fitzgerald (D); Auditor, Richard D. Johnson (R). State Senate, 50 (30 D and 20 R); State House of Representatives, 100 (61 D and 39 R). Senators, Charles E. Grassley (R) and Tom Harkin (D). Representatives, 6 (4 R and 2 D).

1988 Presidential Vote

Dukakis (D). 670,557 (55%)
Bush (R) 545,355 (44%)

1984 Presidential Vote

Reagan (R) 703,088 (53%)
Mondale (D) 605,620 (46%)

GOVERNOR

Gov. Terry E. Branstad (R)

Elected 1982, term expires Jan. 1991; b. Nov. 17, 1946, Leland; home, Des Moines; U. of IA, B.A. 1969, Drake U. Law Sch., J.D. 1974; Roman Catholic; married (Christine).

Career: Army, 1969–71; IA House of Reps., 1973–79; Practicing atty., Farmer, 1974–1982; Lt. Gov., 1979–83.

Office: State Capitol, Des Moines 50319, 515-281-5211.

Election Results

1986 gen.	Terry E. Branstad (R)	472,712	(52%)
	Lowell L. Junkins (D)	436,924	(48%)
1986 prim.	Terry E. Branstad (R)	104,482	(100%)
1982 gen.	Terry E. Branstad (R)	548,313	(53%)
	Roxanne Conlin (D)	483,291	(47%)

432   IOWA

SENATORS

Sen. Charles E. Grassley (R)

Elected 1980, seat up 1992; b. Sept. 17, 1933, New Hartford; home, New Hartford; U. of N. IA, B.A. 1955, M.A. 1956, U. of IA, 1957–58; Baptist; married (Barbara).

Career: Farmer, 1960–74; IA House of Reps., 1958–74; U.S. House of Reps., 1974–80.

Offices: 135 HSOB 20510, 202-224-3744. Also 721 Fed. Bldg., 210 Walnut St., Des Moines 50309, 515-284-4890; 210 Waterloo Bldg., 531 Commercial St., Waterloo 50701, 319-232-6657; 116 Fed. Bldg., 131 E. 4th St., Davenport 52801, 319-322-4331; 103 Fed. Bldg., 320 6th St., Sioux City 51101, 712-233-3331; and 206 Fed. Bldg., 101 1st St., S.E., Cedar Rapids 52401, 319-399-2555.

Committees: *Appropriations* (11th of 13 R). Subcommittees: Agriculture, Rural Development and Related Agencies; HUD-Independent Agencies; Military Construction (Ranking Member); Transportation and Related Agencies. *Budget* (5th of 10 R). *Judiciary* (4th of 6 R). Subcommittees: Courts and Administrative Practice (Ranking Member); Patents, Copyrights and Trademarks. *Small Business* (6th of 9 R). Subcommittees: Government Contracting and Paperwork Reduction (Ranking Member); Rural Economy and Family Farming. *Special Committee on Aging* (4th of 9 R).

Group Ratings

	ADA	ACLU	COPE	CFA	LCV	ACU	NTLC	NSI	COC	ACA
1988	5	22	19	42	30	88	53	70	93	59
1987	25	—	19	50	—	81	—	—	83	49

National Journal Ratings

	1988 LIB — 1988 CONS	1987 LIB — 1987 CONS
Economic	9% — 81%	30% — 68%
Social	15% — 83%	13% — 85%
Foreign	26% — 72%	37% — 61%

Key Votes

1) Cut Aged Housing $	AGN	5) Bork Nomination	FOR	9) SDI Funding	AGN
2) Override Hwy Veto	AGN	6) Ban Plastic Guns	FOR	10) Ban Chem Weaps	AGN
3) Kill Plnt Clsng Notice	FOR	7) Deny Abortions	FOR	11) Aid To Contras	FOR
4) Min Wage Increase	AGN	8) Japanese Reparations	AGN	12) Reagan Defense $	FOR

Election Results

1986 general	Charles E. Grassley (R)	588,880	(66%)	($2,513,319)
	John P. Roehrick (D).................	299,406	(34%)	($255,673)
1986 primary	Charles E. Grassley (R)	108,370	(100%)	
1980 general	Charles E. Grassley (R)	683,014	(53%)	($2,183,028)
	John C. Culver (D).................	581,545	(46%)	($1,750,680)

Sen. Tom Harkin (D)

Elected 1984, seat up 1990; b. Nov. 19, 1939, Cumming; home, Cumming; IA St. U., B.S. 1962, Catholic U., J.D. 1972; Roman Catholic; married (Ruth).

Career: Navy, 1962–67; Practicing atty., 1972–74; U.S. House of Reps., 1974–84.

Offices: 316 HSOB 20510, 202-224-3254. Also 733 Fed. Bldg., 210 Walnut St., Des Moines 50309, 515-284-4574; Box H, Fed. Bldg., Council Bluffs 51501, 712-325-5533; Lindale Mall, Ste. 101, 4444 1st Ave. N.E., Cedar Rapids 52407, 319-393-6374; 131 E. 4th St., 314B Fed. Bldg., Davenport, 52801, 319-322-1338; 880 Locust, Ste. 125, Dubuque 52001, 319-588-2130; and 4th and Jackson Sts. 901 Badgerow Bldg., Sioux City 51101, 712-252-1550.

Committees: *Agriculture, Nutrition, and Forestry* (5th of 10 D). Subcommittees: Agricultural Production and Stabilization of Prices; Domestic and Foreign Marketing and Product Promotion; Nutrition and Investigations (Chairman). *Appropriations* (11th of 16 D). Subcommittees: Agriculture, Rural Development and Related Agencies; Defense; Foreign Operations; Labor, Health and Human Services, Education (Chairman); Transportation and Related Agencies. *Labor and Human Services* (6th of 9 D). Subcommittees: Children, Family, Drugs and Alcoholism; Employment and Productivity; Labor; Handicapped (Chairman). *Small Business* (7th of 10 D). Subcommittees: Competition and Antitrust Enforcement (Chairman); Export and Expansion.

Group Ratings

	ADA	ACLU	COPE	CFA	LCV	ACU	NTLC	NSI	COC	ACA
1988	95	81	92	100	70	0	9	0	36	15
1987	95	—	91	83	—	4	—	—	44	21

National Journal Ratings

	1988 LIB — 1988 CONS		1987 LIB — 1987 CONS	
Economic	86%	— 0%	65%	— 26%
Social	86%	— 0%	90%	— 4%
Foreign	86%	— 0%	81%	— 0%

Key Votes

1) Cut Aged Housing $	FOR	5) Bork Nomination	AGN	9) SDI Funding	AGN
2) Override Hwy Veto	FOR	6) Ban Plastic Guns	AGN	10) Ban Chem Weaps	AGN
3) Kill Plnt Clsng Notice	AGN	7) Deny Abortions	AGN	11) Aid To Contras	AGN
4) Min Wage Increase	FOR	8) Japanese Reparations	FOR	12) Reagan Defense $	AGN

Election Results

1984 general	Tom Harkin (D)	716,883	(55%)	($2,838,277)
	Roger W. Jepsen (R).................	564,381	(44%)	($3,420,153)
1984 primary	Tom Harkin (D)	106,005	(100%)	
1978 general	Roger W. Jepsen (R).................	421,598	(51%)	($728,268)
	Dick Clark (D)	395,066	(48%)	($860,774)

FIRST DISTRICT

In Burlington, Iowa, half a century ago, Front Street along the Mississippi was described by the *WPA Guide* as "noisy with the rattle and clatter of trucks and the air is redolent with the odor of fruits in season, for the wholesale dealers whose buildings dominate the south end of the street are always loading and unloading—perhaps cantaloupe today, apples tomorrow. Barges tie up at the municipal dock, motor boats race by, or an occasional excursion boat pulls out with its paddle wheels splashing. Bridges bound the street at either end. Autos stream over the MacArthur Bridge, and frequently the draw of the railroad bridge swings open to allow a large steamboat to pass. In the bottoms north along the river lies a commercial district that surrounds the Willow Patch, a settlement started previous to the Civil War, known for the fine woven nets and seines that the people make. Life here is simple and somewhat primitive. In West Burlington are the shops of the Chicago, Burlington and Quincy Railroad where more than 500 men are employed." In its century of existence, Burlington had been traversed by Indian-hunters, railroad workers, and searchers for fugitive slaves; it was settled mostly by Germans, for whom the bluffs above the Mississippi recalled their native river towns, and who set about recreating Mitteleuropa in Middle America, complete with pork sausage factories and musical societies.

In the half century since that description, Burlington and other Iowa towns up and down the river have outwardly changed little: they are more affluent, but have grown less than the nation; their ethnic distinctiveness has grown muted; the old river craft have been replaced by giant barges and the rail lines employ fewer men. The largest town is Davenport which, with Rock Island, Moline and East Moline, Illinois, across the river, make up the Quad Cities; Davenport was where Ronald Reagan got his first job, at radio station WOC, owned by the Palmer School of Chiropractic. The river towns along the Mississippi from Davenport south to the Missouri border, and westward through rolling farm country, make up the 1st Congressional District of Iowa.

Politically, the 1st District is typical of the state: historically Republican, in the 1960s and 1970s oscillating between the parties, in 1988 fairly solidly Democratic. But it has a Republican congressman, Jim Leach, whose often liberal positions on many issues have helped to give him a lengthy and seemingly secure tenure. On economic issues, he is rather frugal with the taxpayers' money. But on cultural issues he is one of the chamber's more liberal members, and on foreign policy he votes more often on seriously contested issues with the Democrats than with his fellow Republicans. He has supported and occasionally has been one of the leaders of the fight against U.S. involvement in El Salvador and Nicaragua; in 1985, he co-sponsored legislation that would even prohibit private citizens from sending money to the contras. He was one of four Foreign Affairs Committee Republicans to vote to cut off U.S. trade with South Africa. His vote is not often crucial on the committee, but he often gives a bipartisan appearance to policies which are supported by a large majority of Democrats and only a few Republicans.

Leach would argue that he is more in line with Republican tradition, and historically in the Iowa 1st he may well be. But he has edged back from moves that once provoked his fellow Republicans to fury. He has abandoned the "Mainstream Committee" he set up in 1984, whose name echoes a 1964 Nelson Rockefeller slogan, and which scarcely rang true in a year in which a very un-Leach-like Republican won 61% of the votes for President. And in 1988, he stepped down after seven years as chairman of the Ripon Society, a small group of liberal Republican intellectuals founded in the 1960s when the words conservative and intellectual were considered oxymorons. Instead, he has found places to cooperate with his fellow partisans—or they with him. He was an early backer of George Bush, an old friend, and chaired his Iowa campaigns in 1980 and 1988; in 1988 he pointedly refrained from challenging the Bush-approved platform at the convention. And in the House, the Common Cause campaign finance reform bill he co-sponsored with many Democrats now looks much more attractive to Republicans, from Robert Michel to Newt Gingrich, as they contemplate how the Democrats have gotten the lion's share of PAC money and seem to have permanent control of the House. On the Banking Committee, Leach is a stickler for strict regulation of insolvent savings and loans—a subject that embarrassed Jim Wright, who had pushed through legislation that allowed sharp operators to stuff their own pockets and let the taxpayers foot the bill.

Before Leach first won this seat in 1976, it had been one of the nation's prime marginal seats for a dozen years. Since then he has won easily, though his percentage was a bit reduced in the 1988 Dukakis sweep.

The People: Est. Pop. 1986: 473,400, dn. 2.6% 1980–86; Pop. 1980: 485,961, up 5.0% 1970–80. Households (1980): 74% family, 40% with children, 64% married couples; 25% housing units rented; median monthly rent: $178; median house value: $39,600. Voting age pop. (1980): 345,540; 2% Black, 1% Spanish origin.

1988 Presidential Vote:

Dukakis (D)	106,756	(55%)
Bush (R)	86,724	(44%)

Rep. James A. S. (Jim) Leach (R)

Elected 1976; b. Oct. 15, 1942, Davenport; home, Davenport; Princeton U., B.A. 1964, Johns Hopkins U., M.A. 1966, London Sch. of Econ., 1966–68; Episcopalian; married (Elisabeth).

Career: Staff Asst., U.S. Rep. Donald Rumsfeld, 1965–66; U.S. Foreign Svc., 1968–69, 1971–72; A.A. to Dir. of U.S. Ofc. of Equal Opp., 1969–70; Pres., Flamegas Co., Inc., 1973–75; Dir., Fed. Home Loan Bank Bd., Midwest Region, 1975–76.

Offices: 1514 LHOB 20515, 202-225-6576. Also 322 W. 3d St., Davenport 52801, 319-326-1841; 306 F&M Bank Bldg., 3rd & Jefferson Sts., Burlington 52601, 319-752-4584; and Park View Plaza, Rm. 204, 107 E. 2nd St., Ottumwa 52501, 515-682-8549.

Committees: *Banking, Finance and Urban Affairs* (2d of 20 R). Subcommittees: Financial Institutions Supervision, Regulation and Insurance; Domestic Monetary Policy; International Development; Finance, Trade and Monetary Policy. *Foreign Affairs* (4th of 18 R). Subcommittees: Asian and Pacific Affairs (Ranking Member); Europe and the Middle East.

Group Ratings

	ADA	ACLU	COPE	CFA	LCV	ACU	NTLC	NSI	COC	ACA
1988	75	68	34	64	69	32	78	0	64	39
1987	48	—	31	64	—	38	—	—	79	56

National Journal Ratings

	1988 LIB — 1988 CONS		1987 LIB — 1987 CONS	
Economic	31%	— 67%	34%	— 65%
Social	58%	— 40%	53%	— 46%
Foreign	84%	— 0%	68%	— 30%

Key Votes

1) Homeless $	—	5) Ban Drug Test	—	9) SDI Research	AGN
2) Gephardt Amdt	AGN	6) Drug Death Pen	AGN	10) Ban Chem Weaps	FOR
3) Deficit Reduc	AGN	7) Handgun Sales	FOR	11) Aid to Contras	AGN
4) Kill Plnt Clsng Notice	AGN	8) Ban D.C. Abort $	FOR	12) Nuclear Testing	FOR

Election Results

1988 general	James A. S. (Jim) Leach (R)	112,746	(61%)	($218,707)
	Bill Gluba (D)	71,280	(38%)	($59,204)
1988 primary	James A. S. (Jim) Leach (R), unopposed			
1986 general	James A. S. (Jim) Leach (R)	86,834	(66%)	($231,937)
	John R. Whitaker (D)	43,985	(34%)	($23,526)

SECOND DISTRICT

"Wide bottomlands, often flooded over, spread out to the north and south," announces the *American Guide*. "High bluffs, some of them rocky precipices, all but jut out over the business center where tall buildings reach to their height." This is Dubuque, in supposedly monotonously flat Iowa, a hilly town settled mostly by German immigrants which was once the largest city in Iowa and still sometimes casts (because of German Catholics' ancestral preferences) the largest Democratic margins in the state. Harold Ross remarked that his *New Yorker* was not edited for "the little old lady in Dubuque," but Dubuque County voted as heavily for liberal presidential candidates Dukakis and McGovern as Ross's precincts in trendy Manhattan. The 2d Congressional District of Iowa, geographically the northeast corner of the state, is a combination of Dubuque, several hilly rural counties on the river and farming counties with smoother rolling Grant Wood-like hills just inland, plus the rather different city of Cedar Rapids, now Iowa's second largest urban center. If its biggest industry 50 years ago was Quaker Oats, its biggest employer more recently has been Collins Radio, a high-tech firm with big (and Iowa's only significant) defense contracts. Cedar Rapids now prides itself as a high-tech manufacturing center: it has attracted a big new Kodak biotech research facility, which will draw on the corn and soybean crops of the area; more important, it will utilize Iowa's highly-educated, highly-skilled work force.

Politically, Dubuque is very Democratic (except when its heavily Catholic population was voting against the Democrats on the abortion issue a decade ago), Cedar Rapids is marginally Democratic, and the rural counties vary. This gives the 2d District about the same leanings as Iowa generally. In House elections this district has been contested seriously in almost half the elections of the last 20 years. It was held by Democrats from 1964 to 1978 and has been held by a Republican, Tom Tauke, since then.

Tauke was only 28 when he came to the House, but he was already a veteran of four years in the Iowa legislature, a Republican from Democratic Dubuque, and one of those instinctive politicians who are found more often among the Democrats than the Republicans. Tauke spent some $250,000 in that election—a lot for the time—and has been a first-class fundraiser since; his money-raisers work the political action committees so aggressively that he puts ceilings on how much they may raise. Tauke has also proved himself an active and thoughtful if not, in this Democratic House, always an effective politician. His forum is the Energy and Commerce Committee, which handles most federal regulatory, health, and environmental issues. He serves also on Education and Labor.

In those positions Tauke is by no means a foe of all government action, but he usually backs—and sometimes is one of the lone supporters of—Republican initiatives that entail less spending and less bureaucratic supervision than the Democrats' bills. He would prefer to let broadcasters rather than the government work out guidelines for children's advertising. He is dubious about the worth of federal aid to education. He opposes the ABC child care plan, pushing instead for a tax credit, arguing that parents can be trusted to get better child care than federal regulators. He thinks government should play a role curbing infant mortality, and looks to patching up holes in the Medicaid fabric. He has also worked on the drug patent extension bill and to get demonstration rural mental health programs. His 1988 coalition with Democrat Tim Penny and Republican Dick Armey for across-the-board budget cuts mostly failed. But the moderate Republican 92 Group budget he helped draft in 1985 was closely followed by Budget Chairman William Gray.

Tauke does have his cheap shot issues. He makes a point of turning down the congressional pay increase and champions the cause of the Social Security "Notch Babies" (numerous in Iowa). From 1980 to 1984, Tauke won by wide margins. As Iowa has become more Democratic, he has been pressed by Democrat Eric Tabor; if Tauke is Iowa's biggest House fundraiser, Tabor is the best-financed challenger. Tauke's percentage declined from 64% in 1984 to 61% in 1986 and 57% in 1988. That was the lowest reelection margin of all six Iowa congressmen, and while it may not be danger territory, it evidently got Tauke thinking that the 1990 Senate race against Tom Harkin, while certainly not a risk-free proposition, might be worth making. In early 1989 Tauke was raising money and speaking around the state, and while he insisted "I have never been into political suicide," he looked as if he hoped to run.

The People: Est. Pop. 1986: 474,400, dn. 2.3% 1980–86; Pop. 1980: 485,708, up 2.9% 1970–80. Households (1980): 74% family, 41% with children, 65% married couples; 25% housing units rented; median monthly rent: $180; median house value: $43,200. Voting age pop. (1980): 338,272; 1% Black.

| **1988 Presidential Vote:** | Dukakis (D)................113,993 | (56%) |
| | Bush (R).................86,874 | (43%) |

Rep. Thomas J. Tauke (R)

Elected 1978; b. Oct. 11, 1950, Dubuque; home, Dubuque; Loras Col., B.A. 1972, U. of IA, J.D. 1974; Roman Catholic; married (Beverly).

Career: Newspaper reporter, 1969–71; Editor, *The Daily Iowan*, 1973; Practicing atty., 1977–79; IA House of Reps., 1975–79.

Offices: 2244 RHOB 20515, 202-225-2911. Also 698 Central Ave., Dubuque 52001, 319-557-7740; 176 1st Ave., N.E., Cedar Rapids 52402, 319-366-8709; and 116 S. 2d St., Clinton 52732, 319-242-6180.

Committees: *Education and Labor* (7th of 13 R). Subcommittees: Human Resources (Ranking Member); Postsecondary Education. *Energy and Commerce* (7th of 17 R). Subcommittees: Health and the Environment; Telecommunications and Finance; Transportation and Hazardous Materials. *Select Committee on Aging* (6th of 26 R). Subcommittee: Retirement Income and Employment (Ranking Member).

Group Ratings

	ADA	ACLU	COPE	CFA	LCV	ACU	NTLC	NSI	COC	ACA
1988	45	61	19	55	50	67	87	50	85	69
1987	36	—	19	29	—	50	—	—	80	75

National Journal Ratings

	1988 LIB — 1988 CONS		1987 LIB — 1987 CONS	
Economic	0% —	93%	11% —	83%
Social	31% —	69%	35% —	64%
Foreign	48% —	51%	48% —	51%

438   IOWA

Election Results

1988 general	Thomas J. Tauke (R)	113,543	(57%)	($581,514)
	Eric Tabor (D)	86,438	(43%)	($258,106)
1988 primary	Thomas J. Tauke (R), unopposed			
1986 general	Thomas J. Tauke (R)	88,708	(61%)	($387,840)
	Eric Tabor (D)	55,903	(39%)	($170,816)

THIRD DISTRICT

To look at "the wild plum trees—a white mist of blossoms in the spring on the hills and by the roadside," as the *American Guide* did five decades ago, or at the wild crab apple blossoms that "fill the air with fragrance," you would not have guessed that Floyd County, in north central Iowa, was one of the nation's most productive farm counties—and had been buzzing with innovation. In 1896 two local college graduates hooked up a gasoline engine to a farm machine and called it a "tractor"; in town lived the suffragist Carrie Catt; down the road were nurseries whose owners developed new breeds of apples and evergreens even before Iowa State got into that work. Two counties south on the Cedar River is Waterloo, which grew rapidly after 1900 as the John Deere tractor and Rath meatpacking factories expanded.

Waterloo and Floyd County are at the geographical and political heart of Iowa's 3d Congressional District. It extends southward to Iowa City, home of the University of Iowa, and the Amana colonies nearby. Historically, this is Republican country. But in the early 1970s Iowa City became a liberal bastion, and in the 1980s, as the Rath plant was taken over by workers and then shut down, and as John Deere had big layoffs, Waterloo moved to the Democrats. So did Floyd County: it voted 59%–41% against John Kennedy in 1960, 57%–43% (about the same as the 3d District) for Michael Dukakis in 1988.

The switchover in House elections was in 1986, when Democrat Dave Nagle was elected. For 26 years the 3d was represented by conservative curmudgeon H. R. Gross, then by Charles Grassley; after 1980 it was held by Cooper Evans, a Republican expert on farm programs until his retirement in 1986. Democrat Dave Nagle, the party's state chairman during the 1984 Iowa presidential caucuses, won the seat in part by ridiculing his opponents' proposal that farmers tackle their storage problem by leaving crops in the fields over the winter and has held it in part by working on the Agriculture Committee on farm credit bills. The brashness and salty tongue that made him a favorite of the national press in 1984 were turned to inside-the-House work, mostly on farm issues, but also on one of Jim Wright's contra aid compromises. He is willing to take stands—voting for a tax increase to cut the deficit and backing flagging tankers in the Persian Gulf—unpopular in thrifty, dovish Iowa. He opposed Republican Robert Walker's bill to cut off all funds to any non-drug-free workplace. And he joined Republican Robert Dornan to ban testing depressed trajectory missiles, which they say are a first-strike weapon. Nagle's record, plus the Democratic trend here enabled him to make big gains in rural counties and win reelection in 1988 with a whopping 63%; the 3d now seems a safe Democratic seat.

The People: Est. Pop. 1986: 468,900, dn. 3.4% 1980–86; Pop. 1980: 485,529, up 3.9% 1970–80. Households (1980): 72% family, 38% with children, 64% married couples; 28% housing units rented; median monthly rent: $185; median house value: $43,500. Voting age pop. (1980): 352,455; 2% Black.

1988 Presidential Vote:

Dukakis (D).....................	118,602	(57%)
Bush (R)	89,365	(43%)

Rep. David R. Nagle (D)

Elected 1986; b. Apr. 15, 1943, Grinnell; home, Cedar Falls; U. of N. IA, 1961–65, U. of IA, LL.B. 1968; Roman Catholic; married (Diane).

Career: Asst. Black Hawk Cnty. Atty., 1969–70; Evansdale City Atty., 1971–74; Chmn., IA Dem. Party, 1982–85.

Offices: 214 CHOB 20515, 202-225-3301. Also 524 Washington St., Waterloo 50701, 319-234-3623; and 102 S. Clinton, Rm. 505, Iowa City 52240, 319-351-0789.

Committees: *Agriculture* (17th of 27 D). Subcommittees: Conservation, Credit, and Rural Development; Livestock, Dairy and Poultry; Wheat, Soybeans and Feed Grains. *Science, Space and Technology* (24th of 30 D). Subcommittees: Investigations and Oversight; Science, Research and Technology.

Group Ratings

	ADA	ACLU	COPE	CFA	LCV	ACU	NTLC	NSI	COC	CEI
1988	80	86	97	73	75	8	7	10	36	17
1987	88	—	94	71	—	0	—	—	7	13

National Journal Ratings

	1988 LIB — 1988 CONS		1987 LIB — 1987 CONS	
Economic	67% —	30%	73% —	0%
Social	85% —	15%	66% —	32%
Foreign	68% —	28%	68% —	30%

Key Votes

1) Homeless $	AGN	5) Ban Drug Test	AGN	9) SDI Research	AGN
2) Gephardt Amdt	FOR	6) Drug Death Pen	AGN	10) Ban Chem Weaps	FOR
3) Deficit Reduc	FOR	7) Handgun Sales	FOR	11) Aid to Contras	AGN
4) Kill Plnt Clsng Notice	AGN	8) Ban D.C. Abort $	AGN	12) Nuclear Testing	FOR

Election Results

1988 general	David R. Nagle (D)	129,204	(63%)	($595,911)
	Donald B. Redfern (R)................	74,682	(37%)	($261,911)
1988 primary	David R. Nagle (D)	15,803	(92%)	
	James R. Cox (D).....................	1,396	(8%)	
1986 general	David R. Nagle (D)	83,504	(55%)	($294,811)
	John McIntee (R).....................	69,386	(45%)	($418,486)

FOURTH DISTRICT

Over 50 years ago, when Ronald Reagan started work as an announcer at WHO, he had no more reason to believe that Walnut Street and Locust, a block away in downtown Des Moines, would become the political capital of the United States than he had to expect that he would become President of the United States. Des Moines was the state capital then, an insurance and printing center, the home of the statewide-circulation *Register & Tribune*; but as you looked up Locust

440   IOWA

Street at the five-gold-domed state Capitol across the Des Moines River, you would never have imagined that this small city would be the political center of anything bigger than Iowa. But in the same years when dissatisfaction with inflation and the welfare state would make Dutch Reagan president, the Democrats' reform rules and the scheduling of the Iowa precinct caucuses made Des Moines in the winters of 1980, 1984, and 1988 the political focus of the world.

Des Moines is the center and casts most of the votes in Iowa's 4th Congressional District, which also includes Ames, the home of Iowa State University, and the small manufacturing towns of Webster City, Boone and Newton. With its white-collar base, Des Moines has grown moderately in the 1980s, strengthening its position as the state's dominant city, though it still is no metropolis; get on the interstate, and you are out of town in six minutes. Even as Des Moines has grown more prosperous, it has become more Democratic, and the 4th District's congressman, Neal Smith, is now one of the senior Democrats in the House. Smith is an old-fashioned farm belt Democrat, one whose liberalism is tempered by a moderate personal temperament and by a constituency which seems reluctant to go overboard in any direction. In his early years in the House he embarked on what seemed quixotic crusades, and had notable successes: passing a tougher meat inspection law and imposing an anti-nepotism rule on congressmen. He was the sponsor of the rule requiring committee chairmen to be chosen by votes in the Democratic caucus, rather than by automatic operation of seniority. But he was not so adept at the buttonholing required by the new system: in 1975 he ran to be the first chairman of the Budget Committee and lost to Brock Adams.

Now Smith is the number three Democrat on Appropriations and, approaching 70, just behind two men a decade older. But he didn't get a subcommittee chairmanship until 1980, and the body he chairs—Commerce, Justice, State and Judiciary—was much more powerful in the hands of a ruthless chairman like John Rooney than it is in the hands of a man as scrupulous and fair-minded as Smith. The budgets it handles are not large, and a chairman not determined to interfere in operations will have relatively little influence in policymaking. Smith tends to be a force for institutional continuity. He was a champion on the Legal Services program, resisting efforts to zero it out; he questioned the need to tear down the heavily bugged U.S. embassy in Moscow and build a new one; he has worked on farm programs and feels that "in the long run, things will work out pretty good." Much of his energy is directed at squeezing a few dollars out of this and that budget.

Smith has a fair chance of becoming chairman of the full Appropriations Committee some day, and his Democratic colleagues would probably be happy to see him in that position: he is hard-working and capable but not overbearing or dictatorial. He has had only one serious challenge in recent years, in 1980, when he won with 54%; he has been reelected easily since then in a district not at all enamored of its only resident (Ronald Reagan) who has gone on to the White House.

The People: Est. Pop. 1986: 496,600, up 2.3% 1980–86; Pop. 1980: 485,480, up 6.6% 1970–80. Households (1980): 70% family, 37% with children, 60% married couples; 30% housing units rented; median monthly rent: $214; median house value: $46,900. Voting age pop. (1980): 356,227; 3% Black, 1% Spanish origin, 1% Asian origin.

1988 Presidential Vote: Dukakis (D).......................131,356   (59%)
                              Bush (R) 90,855   (41%)

Rep. Neal Smith (D)

Elected 1958; b. Mar. 23, 1920, Hedrick; home, Altoona; MO U. Col., B.A. 1946, Syracuse U., 1946–48, Drake U., LL.B. 1950; United Methodist; married (Beatrix).

Career: Farmer; Army Air Corps, WWII; Asst. Polk Cnty. Atty., 1950–52; Practicing atty., 1952–58; Chmn., Polk Cnty. Bd. of Social Welfare, 1956.

Offices: 2373 RHOB 20515, 202-225-4426. Also 544 Insurance Exchange Bldg., Des Moines 50309, 515-284-4634; and 215 P.O. Bldg., Ames 50010, 515-232-5221.

Committees: *Appropriations* (3d of 35 D). Subcommittees: Commerce, Justice, State, the Judiciary and Related Agencies (Chairman); Labor, Health and Human Services, Education and Related Agencies; Rural Development, Agriculture and Related Agencies. *Small Business* (2d of 27 D). Subcommittee: SBA, the General Economy and Minority Enterprise Development.

Group Ratings

	ADA	ACLU	COPE	CFA	LCV	ACU	NTLC	NSI	COC	ACA
1988	80	95	79	73	50	16	17	30	46	21
1987	76	—	79	79	—	9	—	—	14	12

National Journal Ratings

	1988 LIB — 1988 CONS	1987 LIB — 1987 CONS
Economic	49% — 50%	68% — 27%
Social	75% — 25%	66% — 32%
Foreign	60% — 37%	59% — 41%

Key Votes

1) Homeless $	AGN	5) Ban Drug Test	AGN	9) SDI Research	AGN
2) Gephardt Amdt	AGN	6) Drug Death Pen	AGN	10) Ban Chem Weaps	AGN
3) Deficit Reduc	FOR	7) Handgun Sales	FOR	11) Aid to Contras	AGN
4) Kill Plnt Clsng Notice	AGN	8) Ban D.C. Abort $	AGN	12) Nuclear Testing	FOR

Election Results

1988 general	Neal Smith (D)	157,065	(72%)	($83,474)
	Paul Lunde (R)	62,056	(28%)	
1988 primary	Neal Smith (D)	12,101	(90%)	
	Maurice W. Stoutenberg (D)	1,293	(10%)	
1986 general	Neal Smith (D)	107,271	(68%)	($100,675)
	Robert R. Lockard (R)	49,641	(32%)	($65,866)

FIFTH DISTRICT

There are many lines between East and West, dotted state boundaries on the map, the 100th parallel that runs straight down the Great Plains, the more jagged and irregular lines that separate well-watered green croplands from arid brownish lands. You'll have a hard time finding such lines on the ground, since most Plains farmers fatten hogs with their corn and most who raise cattle grow some of their own feed. But as you drive west from the Mississippi to the Missouri River, the croplands grow sparser and the horizons open wider. And just before you get to the Missouri itself, you come to another boundary marker between the regions, the city of

Council Bluffs across the river from Omaha. There in 1859 General Grenville Dodge lobbied Illinois lawyer Abraham Lincoln on the need for a transcontinental railroad; Lincoln got it through Congress in 1863, Dodge became its chief engineer, and Council Bluffs became its eastern terminus when it was completed in 1869. Fast progress, and with a war in between—and Dodge lived on in Council Bluffs until 1916!

These lines between East and West pass through the southwestern part of Iowa that makes up the state's 5th Congressional District. The eastern counties near Des Moines are classic corn and hog country, with a little metropolitan development; ancestrally Republican, they were hurt by falling prices (their commodities were not supported as much by government as wheat prices) and became Democratic in the 1980s. The northwest counties, around the small farm machine manufacturing city of Fort Dodge, are getting close to wheat country, though crop patterns are mixed; Fort Dodge is usually Democratic, and so are some rural Catholic counties. The southeast counties around Council Bluffs raise more beef and fewer hogs, they are more western in aspect, and they are much more heavily Republican. Well beyond the range of Des Moines television stations and the liberal *Des Moines Register & Tribune*, they are in the Omaha TV market and get the conservative *Omaha World-Herald*.

Democrat Tom Harkin won this district by solid margins for 10 years starting in 1974; he was helped by the presence of the university town of Ames, removed in the post-1980 redistricting. In 1984 Harkin ran for the Senate, and Jim Ross Lightfoot recaptured the seat for the Republicans. He was a folksy-mannered farm broadcaster well known (as Jim Ross) in the counties around Omaha, which cast 40% of the district's votes, and there he got 63% of the vote. That was enough for a 51% district-wide victory over Jerry Fitzgerald, a former legislator and unsuccessful candidate for governor.

Lightfoot has turned out to be not only a folksy campaigner but a supple politician. He managed to put a relief provision for farmers forced out of business into the tax reform bill. He organized a plan to help drought-stricken southern farmers ship their cattle to winter in Iowa, which is cheaper than shipping hay south. He hustled to get more federal loan money for small businesses, to support the Job Corps because of local successes. On cultural issues he is the most conservative member of the Iowa delegation. But he was one of the few Republicans to oppose aid to the Nicaraguan contras. He has proved strong in the district, winning in 1986 with 59% and 1988 with 64%. That was particularly impressive, since Michael Dukakis was carrying the district at the same time, and was competitive even in the Omaha area counties. If the 5th district is carved up in redistricting, however, he may be in for a tough race.

The People: Est. Pop. 1986: 469,800, dn. 3.3% 1980–86; Pop. 1980: 485,639, up 1.5% 1970–80. Households (1980): 75% family, 39% with children, 67% married couples; 24% housing units rented; median monthly rent: $144; median house value: $33,400. Voting age pop. (1980): 346,800; 1% Spanish origin.

1988 Presidential Vote: Dukakis (D)...................... 100,734   (52%)
                               Bush (R) 92,323   (47%)

Rep. Jim Ross Lightfoot (R)

Elected 1984; b. Sept. 27, 1938, Sioux City; home, Shenandoah; Roman Catholic; married (Nancy).

Career: Army, 1955–56; Mgr., farm equip. manufacturing facility 1970–76; Corsicana City Comm., 1974–76; Farm editor, KMA Radio, 1976–84.

Offices: 1222 LHOB 20515, 202-225-3806. Also 501 W. Lowell, Shenandoah 51601, 712-246-1984; 105 Pearl, Council Bluffs 51503, 712-325-5572; 220 W. Salem, Indianola 50125, 515-961-0591; Warden Plaza, Ste. 7, Ft. Dodge 50501, 515-955-5319.

Committees: *Interior and Insular Affairs* (14th of 15 R). Subcommittes: Energy and the Environment; National Parks and Public Lands. *Public Works and Transportation* (10th of 20 R). Subcommittees: Aviation; Public Buildings and Grounds; Water Resources. *Select Committee on Aging* (14th of 26 R). Subcommittee: Health and Long-Term Care.

Group Ratings

	ADA	ACLU	COPE	CFA	LCV	ACU	NTLC	NSI	COC	ACA
1988	10	14	15	27	31	90	89	78	85	68
1987	8	—	15	21	—	74	—	—	87	67

National Journal Ratings

	1988 LIB — 1988 CONS		1987 LIB — 1987 CONS	
Economic	12%	— 88%	19%	— 78%
Social	12%	— 88%	0%	— 90%
Foreign	37%	— 63%	33%	— 65%

Key Votes

1) Homeless $	FOR	5) Ban Drug Test	FOR	9) SDI Research	FOR
2) Gephardt Amdt	AGN	6) Drug Death Pen	FOR	10) Ban Chem Weaps	AGN
3) Deficit Reduc	AGN	7) Handgun Sales	FOR	11) Aid to Contras	—
4) Kill Plnt Clsng Notice	FOR	8) Ban D.C. Abort $	FOR	12) Nuclear Testing	AGN

Election Results

1988 general	Jim Ross Lightfoot (R)...............	117,761	(64%)	($420,730)
	Gene Freund (D).....................	66,599	(36%)	($115,701)
1988 primary	Jim Ross Lightfoot (R), unopposed			
1986 general	Jim Ross Lightfoot (R)...............	85,025	(59%)	($474,179)
	Scott Hughes (D)	58,552	(41%)	($250,384)

SIXTH DISTRICT

Sioux City, nestled below and running up the bluffs above the Missouri River, is the largest town on the Plains west of Des Moines and north of Omaha. "Late on Sunday nights and early on Monday mornings," the *WPA Guide* reported 50 years ago, "the highways leading into the city are filled with trucks of livestock for the week's opening market. The trade territory reaches as far as Montana and includes portions of Wyoming, Colorado, North Dakota, South Dakota, Nebraska, and Minnesota. Hundreds of trucks rumble along the streets of Sioux City at all hours of the day. Truck drivers loiter about the taverns and dance halls during the evenings. Like the boat hands of the old days, they add color to night life." The trucks don't rumble in like that any more; the Sioux City stockyards have now been replaced by Armand Hammer's IBP factory across the river in Nebraska as a major meat-producer; and Sioux City has had no significant growth in the past five decades. But it is still the main commercial center of the fertile plains of northwestern Iowa, and the leading city of Iowa's 6th Congressional District. The counties on the gently rolling landscape are an ethnic melange: Irish Catholics in Palo Alto (one of the nation's bellwether counties until it voted for Walter Mondale in 1984), Dutch in Sioux (the most heavily Republican county in Iowa), and the descendants of the English lords who built huge cattle ranches around Le Mars in Plymouth County.

The 6th District was the unlikely setting in 1986 for the election of a television actor to Congress. Fred Grandy is known to millions of Americans after 10 years of prime time (and will be known to millions more thanks to reruns) as Gopher, the purser on *The Love Boat*. Now he is a Republican congressman. He has genuine roots in the district, but he left to attend prep school, where he roomed with David Eisenhower, and then went on to Harvard. His Republican allegiance must have been cemented in fire then: those were years of students riots, but after college Grandy went to work for the 6th District's Republican congressman, Wiley Mayne. Mayne, hard pressed in the 1972 election, in an act of political courage which has not been appreciated, cast a damaging vote against the impeachment of Richard Nixon, and was beaten in 1974 by Democrat Berkley Bedell; it was Bedell's retirement, because of a chronic illness he got from a tick bite, that set off the 1986 race Grandy won.

The Democrats licked their chops at the prospect of campaigning against a Hollywood actor; but Grandy has had the last laugh. He had two secret weapons: brains and hard work. Beginning in the campaign, and continuing in the House Agriculture Committee, Grandy has studied the minutiae of farm programs, and can discuss at length farm credit, PIK, set-asides, target prices, price supports, groundwater contamination—you name it. He also worked the district hard and obviously impressed people who may have come out to see Gopher that he was interested in what they thought and cared about. He won 68% in the 1986 Republican primary and beat Clayton Hodgson, Bedell's former top aide, by a 51%–49% margin. In office Grandy worked hard on farm credit legislation, but probably got more publicity off a couple of casework items: he helped farmer Arlo Van Veldhuizen save his favorite cow, Old Mama, from slaughter under the whole herd buyout program, and he got an extension of a deadline for a widow to redeem expired PIK certificates she found in her husband's drawer. Grandy also serves on Education and Labor where, among other things, he sponsored an amendment to allow vouchers under the Democrats' ABC child care plan to be used for religious schools. He took a major political risk by becoming the only House member in dovish Iowa to vote for contra aid. And he conducted 93 town meetings across the district.

In 1988 Grandy was opposed by Dave O'Brien, member of a long-prominent Sioux City Democratic family. But Grandy, who bought a house in Sioux City, seems to have convinced 6th District voters that he is really committed to Iowa, and he won by a whopping 64%–36% margin in a district that came within 98 votes of going for Michael Dukakis. The day afterward, he responded to a mysterious letter circulating in the district which said that his second wife Catherine Mann-Grandy condoned some of the practices described in her two steamy novels. There is some talk that Grandy may run for the Senate against Tom Harkin in 1990, but he has said he would not run against Tom Tauke or Jim Leach in any primary, and he may conclude that it is just too soon after his return from California to make that jump, or that Harkin is too popular.

The People: Est. Pop. 1986: 467,700, dn. 3.7% 1980–86; Pop. 1980: 485,491, dn. 0.8% 1970–80. Households (1980): 74% family, 38% with children, 66% married couples; 25% housing units rented; median monthly rent: $152; median house value: $36,600. Voting age pop. (1980): 348,641; 1% Spanish origin.

1988 Presidential Vote: Bush (R) 99,214 (50%)
Dukakis (D). 99,116 (50%)

Rep. Fred Grandy (R)

Elected 1986; b. June 29, 1948, Sioux City; home, Sioux City; Harvard U., B.A. 1970; Episcopalian; married (Catherine).

Career: Asst. to U.S. Rep. Wiley Mayne, 1970–71; Entertainer, 1971–85.

Offices: 418 CHOB 20515, 202-225-5476. Also 508 Pierce St., Sioux City 51101, 712-252-3733; 211 N. Delaware, Rm. 307, Mason City 50401, 515-424-0233; and 14 W. 5th St., Spencer 51301, 712-262-6480.

Committees: *Agriculture* (14th of 17 R). Subcommittees: Wheat, Soybeans and Feed Grains; Conservation, Credit and Rural Development; Department Operations, Research and Foreign Agriculture. *Education and Labor* (11th of 13 R). Subcommittees: Elementary, Secondary and Vocational Education; Labor-Management Relations; Human Resources. *Select Committee on Children, Youth and Families* (7th of 12 R).

Group Ratings

	ADA	ACLU	COPE	CFA	LCV	ACU	NTLC	NSI	COC	CEI
1988	40	30	37	55	38	64	82	80	86	46
1987	20	—	19	21	—	57	—	—	80	67

National Journal Ratings

	1988 LIB — 1988 CONS		1987 LIB — 1987 CONS	
Economic	31%	— 67%	27%	— 73%
Social	26%	— 73%	30%	— 69%
Foreign	41%	— 58%	38%	— 62%

Key Votes

1) Homeless $	FOR	5) Ban Drug Test	FOR	9) SDI Research	FOR
2) Gephardt Amdt	AGN	6) Drug Death Pen	FOR	10) Ban Chem Weaps	AGN
3) Deficit Reduc	AGN	7) Handgun Sales	FOR	11) Aid to Contras	FOR
4) Kill Plnt Clsng Notice	AGN	8) Ban D.C. Abort $	FOR	12) Nuclear Testing	FOR

Election Results

1988 general	Fred Grandy (R).	125,859	(64%)	($523,108)
	Dave O'Brien (D)	69,614	(36%)	($175,951)
1988 primary	Fred Grandy (R), unopposed			
1986 general	Fred Grandy (R).	81,861	(51%)	($677,082)
	Clayton Hodgson (D)	78,807	(49%)	($407,916)

KANSAS

Even half a century ago, Kansas was the image of dull, prim, old-fashioned Middle America. Gazing at the bold colors of the land of Oz, Dorothy said to Toto, "I have a feeling we're not in Kansas any more,"and clearly she wasn't: for in the 1939 movie *The Wizard of Oz* the scenes of Kansas were shot in dreary black and white. An unpainted wood house, flimsy enough to be swept up into the sky by a cyclone, meddling neighbors and cold surrogate parents. This was MGM's view of Kansas, and the wonder of the movie is that Dorothy wanted to get back home. Smack in the center of the 48 contiguous states, about as far as you can get from either ocean, and hundreds of miles from the Rockies, which start rivers moving down over the slightly rolling plains that tilt imperceptibly toward the east, Kansas seemed geographically normal; settled almost entirely by white Anglo-Saxon Protestants, full of small towns and farms and entirely lacking a big city, Kansas was and mostly still is the demographic picture of ordinary small town America.

Even Kansas's politicians 50 years ago seemed the picture of ordinariness. Alf Landon, oil promoter, depression era governor who pushed relief programs similar to the New Deal, smiling jauntily in his wire-rimmed glasses and three-piece midwestern suit, became the 1936 Republican nominee and the candidate of those who opposed Roosevelt jot and tittle—and won just 37% of the vote. Supporting Landon, was William Allen White, the editor of the *Emporia Gazette*, nationally famous for his editorials, his Calvin Coolidge biography and his celebration of corny Republican virtues at a time when the Republican Party was at its nadir. Both were men of good humor; both, uncharacteristically for Republicans and for Kansans, supported Roosevelt's preparedness measures for World War II; both lived, as disproportionately large numbers of Kansans do, to ripe old ages, White succumbing finally in 1944 at age 76, Landon living on to see his daughter (only 4 when he ran for President) elected U.S. Senator in 1978 and to welcome President and Mrs. Reagan to a visit in his home in September 1987 to celebrate his 100th birthday.

Landon and White were typical of how Kansas's seeming ordinariness makes it atypical. A state that seemed half a century ago and seems today the essence of ordinary Americanness has in fact had a history as turbulent as one of its sudden cyclones. Its beginnings were anything but placid. Most of this vast geographic expanse was still regarded as "the Great American Desert" when the Kansas-Nebraska Act of 1854 left the question of whether Kansas would be free or slave territory to its voters. Almost immediately pro-slavery southerners and abolitionist New Englanders were financing like-minded settlers and moving them to Kansas. Armed fighting broke out between Democratic "bushwhackers" and free soil "jayhawkers." Pro-slavery raiders from Missouri rode into the territory, and John Brown massacred anti-abolitionists at Pottawatomie Creek. This was "Bleeding Kansas"—one of the proximate causes of the Civil War. When the South seceded in 1861, Kansas was admitted to the Union as a free state, with a solid Republican majority, and it has been—mostly—a Republican state ever since.

It was never an easy land. Sod houses, historian Everett Dick wrote in 1937, were so cold in winter that "housewives froze their feet on the cold floor." The capital of Topeka had not sidewalks but mud "slippery as lard, adhesive as tar." But there were few towns: Kansas was a farm state, its livelihood always at risk—a hailstorm, a grasshopper invasion, a dry season, or a drop in world farm prices could mean disaster for thousands of Kansans. The 1880s were years of high rainfall on the plains, when Kansas attracted hundreds of thousands of new settlers. In 1890, rainfall and wheat prices plummeted all at once, the boom went bust; some Kansas

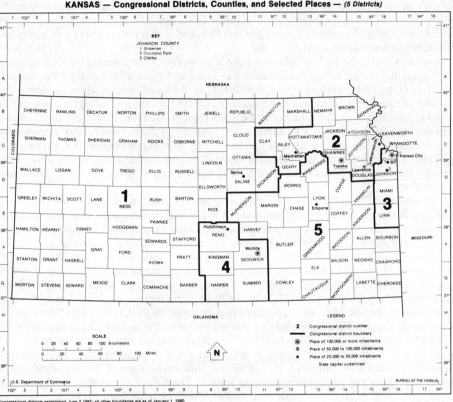

KANSAS — Congressional Districts, Counties, and Selected Places — (5 Districts)

counties never again reached the population levels recorded in the 1890 Census. Suddenly Populists were winning Kansas elections, politicians like "Sockless Jerry" Simpson and Mary Ellen Lease ("What you farmers should do is to raise less corn and more hell"). Populists advocated arcane doctrines like free silver and commodity credit programs. William Jennings Bryan, the lion of the prairies, was their man, and he swept Kansas in 1896. But soon afterwards the nation began to enjoy an extended period of agricultural prosperity so great that parity prices are still based on those years, and small town Republicans were back in the majority. Echoes of the Populist revolt have reverberated in Kansas every few years, with farm revolts against the Republicans in the early 1930s, the late 1950s, and the early 1970s, and farm revolts against the Democrats in the late 1960s and again in the late 1970s. Fewer Kansans than ever are farmers; the state's 96 rural counties' population fell 25% from 1940 to 1980 while the nine metropolitan counties more than doubled. But the state's economy still depends heavily on agriculture; and however much they may favor free enterprise in the abstract, Kansans believe that government is responsible for the condition of the farm economy.

Yet no really serious farm rebellion materialized in the 1980s. One reason may be that the leading maker of farm policy in Congress has been Kansas's own Senator Bob Dole, whom most voters trust to do the right thing. Another is that the metropolitan areas, not entirely dependent on agriculture, continued to grow, and increasingly set the tone of life in the state. County seat storefronts are boarded up as farmers and townspeople drive 100 miles to the mall; Carrie Nation's home state finally legalized liquor by the drink in 1987, and 36 counties, mostly metropolitan and along the interstates, voted themselves wet. Life is less precarious in Kansas now and less old-fashioned than it was when Bob Dole and so many other young men nearly half a century ago left Kansas to go off to war.

Senators. Clearly the leading politician from Kansas, one of the towering political figures in Washington despite his switch from Majority to Minority Leader after the 1986 elections and his defeat in the 1988 presidential race, is Robert Dole of Russell, Kansas. He is also now one of the most experienced politicians in Washington: he was first elected to Congress in 1960, and has served longer there than all but four other Senators (Inouye, Burdick, Thurmond, Byrd) and has been serving as a Republican in Congress longer than any of them. He is an active, aggressive, often successful Minority Leader; although technically he ranks just behind Bob Packwood on the Finance Committee and just behind Richard Lugar on Agriculture, he has not only more seniority but on many issues more expertise and casts a long shadow over those committees' deliberations.

Dole is an old-fashioned Kansas kind of Republican: old-fashioned in what he believes in, old-fashioned in how he operates, old-fashioned in the grit and determination that have taken the grievously wounded son of a cream-and-egg station operator in small town Kansas to the summit of politics and government in the most powerful nation in the world. Yet he remains a bitter man, his bitterness barely camouflaged by Washington's most caustic wit. Ask Bob Dole about his boyhood and he segues forward to his wound in the war; ask him about his early career, and he refers back to the war; then take a moment to remember the date on which Dole, fighting on a static front in Italy, attempting to help a buddy, had his arm shattered and upper body wounded by shrapnel—April 14, 1945, two days after Franklin Roosevelt died, three weeks before the end of the war in Europe. Then remember that this strong-bodied high school athlete lost nearly half his weight, that he nearly died, that he spent four years in hospital wards, regarded by some as a hopeless case. With help from people in his hometown of Russell, he went through largely successful rehabilitation programs, though he still does not have use of his right hand, suffers considerable pain, and has difficulty dressing himself. The note of bitterness in his reference to "Democrat wars" in his 1976 debate with Walter Mondale comes from the same experiences that have made him one of the leading congressional advocates of the handicapped.

But if Dole was bitter, he was also determined and ambitious. He went to college and law school, came home and hung out his shingle, served a term in the legislature and eight years as county attorney. His own experience and knowledge of the community where most people at all levels—not just the banker and the country club member, but the mechanic at the garage and the clerk at the feed store—are Republicans helped make him a Republican who has always felt the party should do something for "people in this country with real problems and no place to go. And they're not cheats and they're not lazy." With George McGovern, he was the architect of the food stamp program—the one form of aid to the really poor that grew in the 1970s and which, thanks to Dole and the perception that it is a voucher system, was cut back little in the 1980s. And he shares the traditional Republican belief in civil rights. Operating from a seat on the Judiciary Committee, he rescued the Voting Rights Act from deadlock in 1982 and got it renewed. His support was critical in passing the Martin Luther King holiday.

To these views Dole appends an old-fashioned Republican partisanness. In his first Senate term, he was chosen in 1971 by the Nixon White House to be Republican National Chairman because of his vehement and usually volunteered defenses of Administration policy. Relieved of that job in early 1973, he made some acerbic comments about Watergate, but was a faithful enough party man to be considered a conservative ticket-balancer when he was chosen as Gerald Ford's vice presidential candidate in 1976. In the first Reagan term, as chairman of the Senate Finance Committee, he aroused the ire of Administration supply-siders by his lack of enthusiasm for their doctrine and his constant pushing, dazzlingly successful in 1982, for tax increases. But Dole was moved by nothing more than the long-time Republican belief in balanced budgets; as a young congressman in the 1960s, he voted against the Kennedy tax cuts and deficits; on the 1988 campaign trail, he talked of the necessity to make painful choices—the traditional Republican language of austerity.

Dole has had surprise victories and defeats in the 1980s. One victory was in the race for Majority Leader after the 1984 elections, when with support from Jesse Helms and others on the right, Dole beat Ted Stevens, Richard Lugar, and James McClure. He was pleased to see his wife Elizabeth appointed Secretary of Transportation by President Reagan in 1983 and Secretary of Labor by President Bush in 1989. He stood up in 1985 against what he considered overgenerous farm bills, even though he was up for reelection in Kansas in 1986. He supported vigorously aid to the Nicaraguan contras and to Angola rebel Jonas Savimbi. He held back from sanctions on South Africa. He jumped ahead of the Administration in denouncing SALT II. Even more than Howard Baker, and more like Tip O'Neill in the House, Dole relied almost entirely on his own party to get his majorities, and didn't dicker with the opposition. Before 1986 he won some stunning victories with his Republican majority; after 1986, he was more often frustrated in the minority.

At the beginning of 1988, Dole seemed to many in Washington and elsewhere as the likeliest next President. Ten weeks later his candidacy was in ruins. What happened? One problem was that Dole operates as almost all politicians did 50 years ago, as a one-man band rather than as an executive with a large bureaucratic staff. He never clearly delegated control of his campaign to any one manager; he involved himself unpredictably in minute decisions and antagonized his staff. "He's one of us" was his theme in Iowa, where it usefully emphasized his Farm Belt roots; but he also showed a fierce and counterproductive antagonism for George Bush as the son of a rich man. He flared up in anger in February 1988, confronting Bush on the Senate floor, when Bush's Iowa chairman charged him with "meanspiritedness" and noted that aspects of Elizabeth Dole's blind trust were being examined by government agencies. In the Iowa caucuses that month, he won a handsome victory and thoughts of "President Dole" were going through many people's heads. But eight days later he lost to George Bush in New Hampshire. On NBC News that night, Dole was asked what he would say to Bush; he gave not the expected sportsmanlike answer, but snarled, "Stop lying about my record"—a reference to Bush campaign suggestions that Dole might raise taxes and Bush wouldn't. Dole won again a week later in the Minnesota caucuses and South Dakota primary. A couple of days later Dole's manager Bill Brock fired two other top aides within camera range—newscast footage showing a campaign in disarray. On Super Tuesday, March 8, Bush swept the South—always his strongest region. In Illinois a week later, Dole canceled some TV ads and seemed to be giving up, and before the primary he as much as said he was quitting, thus missing a last chance to beat Bush on Farm Belt turf. If campaigns are a test of how a politician can run an organization and get his ideas across over the media, George Bush passed and Bob Dole failed. The very qualities which make Dole a successful Senate leader—hands-on attention to detail, an emotional engagement on issues, strong personal involvement—worked against him in the presidential campaign.

That was not the end of Dole's 1988 disappointments. He obviously wanted to be named Bush's Vice President, and it was out of concern for Dole's discomfiture that Bush jumped his own deadline and, on his own, named Dan Quayle on the Tuesday of the Republican Convention. During the campaign, Dole made less than enthusiastic comments about Quayle— just the sort of behavior that was probably the reason Bush didn't pick him. Dole's professional strengths as a legislator, however, and their similar views on almost all for ign and most domestic policies suggest that Dole will do constructive work with the Executive Branch—as he did the first month of the new Bush Administration by working diligently on the Tower nomination.

In Kansas Dole's popularity has had its ups and downs. Elected to the House from western Kansas as a farm revolt was receding, he had a fairly safe seat, and moved to the Senate without much problem in politically divisive 1968. But he was nearly beaten in 1974 by Representative Bill Roy, and had to resort to the abortion issue in the last weeks. He did not attract serious opposition in 1980 or 1986, and was reelected with large margins both times, and probably can be again in 1992.

Nancy Landon Kassebaum, after a decade in the Senate, has emerged as a thoughtful politician others listen to—and one of steely enough will to be paid some respect. Her impulses are moderate: she worked for bipartisan budgets on the Budget Committee, backed limited economic sanctions against South Africa, and tried to put together a bipartisan humanitarian aid package for the Nicaraguan contras. She has become one of the critics of the Senate's incredibly inefficient ways of doing business. She works to help refugees in Mozambique, but claims credit also for getting the Pentagon to buy as training planes more business jets (most of which are built in Wichita). Her vote cannot be taken for granted by other Republicans, even Bob Dole, but she does not try to hurt her fellow Republicans either: she was the only Republican to vote against the confirmation of John Tower in 1989, but reportedly said she would have voted for him if her vote had made the difference.

In 1989, Kassebaum quit Budget and Commerce and went on the Labor and Banking Committees, and in May 1989 announced she would run for a third term in the Senate— contrary to her earlier promise that she would only serve two terms. If Kassebaum had retired, Congressman Dan Glickman, popular in the Wichita media market that serves half the state, would have been a strong contender for the seat. He may still challenge her; however, Kassebaum is a strong favorite for reelection, and Glickman could decide to wait until 1992 to see if Bob Dole retires. Kansas incidentally, has not elected a Democratic Senator since 1932— the longest such interval in the country.

Governor. Governor Mike Hayden, first elected in 1986, had a busy first two years, pushing a $1.7 billion highway construction plan to supplement the rather thin network of interstates, responding with a tort reform limiting damage awards after insurance companies stopped writing malpractice policies in Kansas, getting the legislature to repeal the prevailing wage law and cut meatpacking disability payments (thus enraging unions). In late 1988 he was proposing refunds to taxpayers from the state's income tax windfall from federal tax reform. So Hayden, Vietnam veteran, rough-hewn rancher, environmentalist, may be making Kansas a laboratory of conservative reform. A tough opponent in 1990 would be Congressman Jim Slattery, highly popular in the Topeka media market, who served six years in the legislature.

Presidential politics. Kansas is so heavily Republican in presidential elections that it's not closely watched: everyone knows where it will go. Actually Michael Dukakis drew almost the same percentage here that Jimmy Carter got in his winning race in 1976. That may reflect some farm belt dissatisfaction with the Republicans, or disappointment with the failure of the Republicans to nominate Bob Dole. You can see a similar disappointment factor in especially poor showings by George McGovern in Edmund Muskie's Maine in 1972, Richard Nixon in George Romney's Michigan in 1968, Jimmy Carter in Edward Kennedy's Massachusetts in 1980, and Walter Mondale in Gary Hart's Colorado in 1984. Kansas's not very large delegations to national conventions are chosen by caucuses which attract little attention.

Congressional districting. Kansas may lose one of its five seats in the 1990 Census. If so, geography suggests the Wichita, Kansas City, and the huge western districts will survive pretty much as is, putting the 2d District, now represented by Democrat Jim Slattery and the 5th, now represented by Republican Bob Whittaker together. Both congressmen are therefore thinking about running statewide in 1990 or 1992.

KANSAS 451

The People: Est. Pop. 1988: 2,487,000; Pop. 1980: 2,363,679, up 5.2% 1980–88 and 5.1% 1970–80; 1.02% of U.S. total, 32d largest. 17% with 1–3 yrs. col., 16% with 4+ yrs. col.; 10.1% below poverty level. Single ancestry: 15% German, 11% English, 4% Irish, 1% Swedish, French, Dutch. Households (1980): 73% family, 38% with children, 63% married couples; 29.8% housing units rented; median monthly rent: $168; median house value: $37,800. Voting age pop. (1980): 1,714,644; 5% Black, 2% Spanish origin, 1% Asian origin, 1% American Indian. Registered voters (1988): 1,265,958; 361,045 D (29%), 522,519 R (41%); 382,394 unaffiliated and minor parties (30%).

1988 Share of Federal Tax Burden: $8,424,000,000; 0.95% of U.S. total, 31st largest.

1988 Share of Federal Expenditures

	Total		Non-Defense		Defense	
Total Expend	$8,995m	(1.02%)	$7,827m	(1.19%)	$2,252m	(0.99%)
St/Lcl Grants	880m	(0.77%)	1,765m	(1.54%)	1m	(1.25%)
Salary/Wages	1,553m	(1.16%)	589m	(0.88%)	965m	(0.88%)
Pymnts to Indiv	4,251m	(1.04%)	4,077m	(1.04%)	173m	(0.93%)
Procurement	1,111m	(0.59%)	198m	(0.43%)	1,111m	(0.59%)
Research/Other	1,199m	(3.21%)	1,198m	(3.23%)	1m	(3.23%)

Political Lineup: Governor, Mike Hayden (R); Lt. Gov., Jack Walker (R); Secy. of State, Bill Graves (R); Atty. Gen., Robert T. Stephan (R); Treasurer, Joan Finney (D); Commissioner of Insurance, Fletcher Bell (R). State Senate, 40 (22 R and 18 D); State House of Representatives, 125 (67 R and 50 D). Senators, Robert Dole (R) and Nancy Landon Kassebaum (R). Representatives, 5 (3 R and 2 D).

1988 Presidential Vote

Bush (R) 549,049 (56%)
Dukakis (D). 422,636 (43%)

1984 Presidential Vote

Reagan (R) 677,296 (66%)
Mondale (D) 333,149 (33%)

GOVERNOR

Gov. Mike Hayden (R)

Elected 1986, term expires Jan. 1991; b. Mar. 16, 1944, Atwood; home, Topeka; KS St. U., B.S. 1966; Ft. Hayes U., M.S. 1974; United Methodist; married (Patti).

Career: Army, 1967–70; Executive Manager, Rawlins Co. 1973–76; insurance agt., 1976–86; KS House of Reps., 1972–86, Speaker, 1983–86.

Office: State Capitol, 2d Flr., Topeka 66612, 913-296-3232.

Election Results

1986 gen.	Mike Hayden (R).	436,267	(52%)
	Tom Docking (D)	404,338	(48%)
1986 prim.	Mike Hayden (R).	99,669	(37%)
	Larry Jones (R)	85,989	(32%)
	Jack Brier (R).	37,410	(14%)
	Gene Bicknell (R).	25,733	(10%)
	Richard Peckham (R)	18,876	(7%)
1982 gen.	John W. Carlin (D).	405,309	(53%)
	Sam Hardage (R).	339,700	(44%)

SENATORS
Sen. Robert Dole (R)

Elected 1968, seat up 1992; b. July 22, 1923, Russell; home, Russell; U. of KS, A.B., Washburn U., LL.B. 1952; United Methodist; married (Elizabeth).

Career: Army, WWII; KS House of Reps., 1951–53; Russell Cnty. Atty., 1953–61; U.S. House of Reps., 1960–68; Chmn., Repub. Natl. Cmtee., 1971–73; Repub. Nominee for Vice Pres., 1976; U.S. Senate Maj. Ldr., 1984–86; Min. Ldr., 1986–present.

Offices: 141 HSOB 20510, 202-224-6521. Also 636 Minnesota Ave., Kansas City 66101, 913-371-6108; 444 S.E. Quincy, Ste. 392, Topeka 66603, 913-295-2745; 100 N. Broadway, Wichita 67202, 316-263-4956; and 76 Parsons Plaza, Ste. 102, Parsons 67357, 316-421-5380.

Committees: *Agriculture, Nutrition, and Forestry* (2d of 9 R). Subcommittees: Agricultural Production and Stabilization of Prices; Nutrition and Investigations. *Finance* (2d of 9 R). Subcommittees: Medicare and Long-Term Care; International Debt (Ranking Member); Social Security and Family Policy (Ranking Member). *Rules and Administration* (5th of 7 R). *Joint Committee on Taxation.*

Group Ratings

	ADA	ACLU	COPE	CFA	LCV	ACU	NTLC	NSI	COC	CEI
1988	15	25	17	33	20	91	77	100	91	51
1987	5	—	16	17	—	77	—	—	83	67

National Journal Ratings

	1988 LIB — 1988 CONS		1987 LIB — 1987 CONS	
Economic	22%	75%	0%	94%
Social	26%	72%	22%	77%
Foreign	28%	70%	27%	71%

Key Votes

1) Cut Aged Housing $	AGN	5) Bork Nomination	FOR	9) SDI Funding	FOR
2) Override Hwy Veto	AGN	6) Ban Plastic Guns	FOR	10) Ban Chem Weaps	FOR
3) Kill Plnt Clsng Notice	FOR	7) Deny Abortions	FOR	11) Aid To Contras	FOR
4) Min Wage Increase	AGN	8) Japanese Reparations	FOR	12) Reagan Defense $	FOR

Election Results

1986 general	Robert Dole (R)	576,902	(70%)	($1,517,585)
	Guy MacDonald (D)	246,664	(30%)	
1986 primary	Robert Dole (R)	228,301	(84%)	
	Shirley J. Ashley Landis (R)	42,237	(16%)	
1980 general	Robert Dole (R)	598,686	(64%)	($1,224,494)
	John Simpson (D)	340,271	(36%)	($323,792)

Sen. Nancy Landon Kassebaum (R)

Elected 1978, seat up 1990; b. July 29, 1932, Topeka; home, Burdick; U. of KS, B.A. 1954, U. of MI, M.A. 1956; Episcopalian; divorced.

Career: Member, Maize Sch. Bd., 1972–75; Staff of U.S. Sen. James B. Pearson, 1975.

Offices: 302 RSOB 20510, 202-224-4774. Also 444 S.E. Quincy St., Topeka 66683, 913-295-2888; 8th and Grant, Garden City 67846, 316-276-3423; 4200 Somerset, Ste. 152, Prairie Village 66208, 913-648-3103; and 111 N. Market, Wichita 67202, 316-269-6251.

Committees: *Banking, Housing and Urban Affairs* (8th of 9 R). Subcommittees: Housing and Urban Affairs; Securities. *Foreign Relations* (3rd of 9 R). Subcommittees: African Affairs (Ranking Member); Western Hemisphere and Peace Corps Affairs; Near Eastern and South Asian Affairs. *Labor and Human Resources* (2d of 7 R). Subcommittees: Education, Arts and Humanities (Ranking Member); Children, Family, Drugs and Alcoholism; Employment and Productivity. *Special Committee on Aging* (9th of 9 R).

Group Ratings

	ADA	ACLU	COPE	CFA	LCV	ACU	NTLC	NSI	COC	CEI
1988	30	39	21	42	40	61	63	80	71	52
1987	30	—	21	17	—	60	—	—	71	61

National Journal Ratings

	1988 LIB — 1988 CONS		1987 LIB — 1987 CONS	
Economic	27%	— 70%	6%	— 87%
Social	39%	— 60%	38%	— 61%
Foreign	39%	— 59%	39%	— 60%

Key Votes

1) Cut Aged Housing $	AGN	5) Bork Nomination	FOR	9) SDI Funding	FOR
2) Override Hwy Veto	AGN	6) Ban Plastic Guns	—	10) Ban Chem Weaps	AGN
3) Kill Plnt Clsng Notice	FOR	7) Deny Abortions	—	11) Aid To Contras	FOR
4) Min Wage Increase	AGN	8) Japanese Reparations	FOR	12) Reagan Defense $	FOR

Election Results

1984 general	Nancy Landon Kassebaum (R)	757,402	(76%)	($355,077)
	James R. Maher (D)	211,664	(21%)	($30,444)
1984 primary	Nancy Landon Kassebaum (R)	214,664	(100%)	
1978 general	Nancy Landon Kassebaum (R)	403,354	(54%)	($856,644)
	Bill Roy (D)	317,602	(42%)	($813,754)

FIRST DISTRICT

When Kansas 1st District Congressman Pat Roberts annually sets out at 6:30 a.m. in Dodge City to meet constituents at each of the district's county seats, he has a big job ahead: it takes two weeks and puts 3,000 miles on his van. For there are 58 counties in the "Big First," more than in any other congressional district except three directly to the north, the 3d of Nebraska and the at-large districts of North and South Dakota. That's more than just a bit of trivia; it shows the expectations of the first settlers, mostly from Illinois, Iowa, and Missouri, who came here in the

1870s and 1880s. As this area's population was rising from 56,000 to 428,000, they organized counties 30 or 36 miles square, just like those in their old states, assuming that this new land would soon be as thickly populated as the places they came from. But out here past 98° longitude, rainfall is usually half what it is in Illinois, and since those dry years of the 1890s, people have been moving out of western Kansas: from 428,000 in the 1880s, the population rose only to 505,000 in 1940, and dropped to 477,000 in 1986.

That is not to say that life is dismal in the "Big First" or its economy moribund, only that it hasn't generated enough jobs for its natural population increase. There are prosperous towns out here on the plains, and some growth in the southwest cattle and oil country; since electrification in the 1930s and the post-1945 economic boom life on the farm has been much easier than it once was. But even here in this very unmetropolitan area, most of the growth is absorbed into a few towns, like Salina, the largest with 41,000, Dodge City, terminus of the old cattle drives and once the home of Wyatt Earp, with 18,000 residents, and Holcomb, made famous by Truman Capote's *In Cold Blood*, with exactly 816.

This is livestock and wheat country, one of the most agricultural districts in the nation. For miles on end you can see nothing but rolling brown fields, sectioned off here and there by barbed wire fence, and in the distance a grain elevator towering over a tiny town and its miniature railroad depot. The winds and rain and tornadoes that come suddenly out of the sky remind you that the original settlers likened this part of Kansas to an ocean and thought themselves in their wooden wagons almost as helpless as passengers at sea in a wooden rowboat. The political culture is Republican, though there are ancestral Democratic spots, like Ellis County, with its German Catholics and their Cathedral of the Plains. But the real substance of politics here is farm policy, and no one understands that better than Congressman Pat Roberts. He admits "spending most of this session of the 100th Congress stamping out brushfire issues and problems important to the state and the Western Kansas 'Big First' District."

In 1987 and 1988 that meant working to repeal the diesel fuel tax and the heifer tax which were part of the 1986 tax reform act, lobbying the Transportation Department against designating, as a United Nations treaty was said to require, the fertilizer anhydrous ammonia as a poison gas, and persuading the IRS to give more favorable treatment to the Conservation Reserve Program. He got provisions favorable to U.S. agriculture in the 1988 trade bill. He seems to see himself as protecting Great Plains farmers from outsiders—tax reformers, UN apparatchiks, tax collectors—who ignorantly and carelessly cause them problems while engaged in some work of their own. Of course, he serves on Agriculture and will try to influence the 1989 farm bill.

On national issues Roberts tends to be conservative, though not always on foreign policy. He has a Republican pedigree—his father served briefly as national party chairman in the Eisenhower years—but more important to winning this seat were his 12 years as chief aide to Congressman Keith Sebelius. When Sebelius retired in 1980, Roberts moved from Topeka to Dodge City, ran and won the 1980 Republican primary (56%–36% over his nearest rival), and won the general election easily. If Bob Dole had been elected President, Governor Mike Hayden would probably have appointed him Senator; and he may run for the Senate if Dole retires in 1992. In the meantime, he continues to campaign, in formal meetings and over cups of coffee in small-town cafes or at barbecues and chili suppers, in all 58 county seats of the 1st District.

The People: Est. Pop. 1986: 477,400, up 1.1% 1980–86; Pop. 1980: 472,139, up 0.2% 1970–80. Households (1980): 73% family, 36% with children, 66% married couples; 25.3% housing units rented; median monthly rent: $133; median house value: $31,300. Voting age pop. (1980): 342,439; 2% Spanish origin, 1% Black.

1988 Presidential Vote:

Bush (R)	120,325	(60%)
Dukakis (D)	74,716	(38%)

Rep. Pat Roberts (R)

Elected 1980; b. Apr. 20, 1936, Topeka; home, Dodge City; KS St. U., B.A. 1958; United Methodist; married (Franki).

Career: USMC, 1958–62; Co-owner, editor, *The Westsider* (AZ Newspaper) 1962–67; A.A. to U.S. Sen. Frank Carlson, 1967–68; A.A. to U.S. Rep. Keith G. Sebelius, 1968–80.

Offices: 1323 LHOB 20515, 202-225-2715. Also P.O. Box 550, Dodge City 67801, 316-227-2244; P.O. Box 128, Norton 67654, 913-877-2454; and P.O. Box 1334, Salina 67402, 913-825-5409.

Committees: *Agriculture* (6th of 18 R). Subcommittees: Department Operations, Research and Foreign Agriculture (Ranking Member); Wheat, Soybeans, and Feed Grains. *House Administration* (5th of 8 R). Subcommittees: Elections; Personnel and Police (Ranking Member); Procurement and Printing. *Joint Committee on Printing.*

Group Ratings

	ADA	ACLU	COPE	CFA	LCV	ACU	NTLC	NSI	COC	CEI
1988	10	14	7	18	31	79	85	90	100	70
1987	4	—	5	14	—	86	—	—	100	65

National Journal Ratings

	1988 LIB — 1988 CONS		1987 LIB — 1987 CONS	
Economic	12%	— 87%	0%	— 89%
Social	16%	— 83%	10%	— 85%
Foreign	30%	— 67%	33%	— 67%

Key Votes

1) Homeless $	FOR	5) Ban Drug Test	FOR	9) SDI Research	FOR
2) Gephardt Amdt	AGN	6) Drug Death Pen	FOR	10) Ban Chem Weaps	AGN
3) Deficit Reduc	AGN	7) Handgun Sales	FOR	11) Aid to Contras	FOR
4) Kill Plnt Clsng Notice	FOR	8) Ban D.C. Abort $	FOR	12) Nuclear Testing	AGN

Election Results

1988 general	Pat Roberts (R), unopposed			($81,140)
1988 primary	Pat Roberts (R), unopposed			
1986 general	Pat Roberts (R)...................	141,297	(75%)	($87,221)
	Dale Lyon (D)......................	43,359	(25%)	($8,637)

SECOND DISTRICT

A surprising amount of history has taken place in the valley of the Kansas River, in the 60 miles west of where it flows into the Missouri in Kansas City. This was the heart of "Bleeding Kansas" before the Civil War, where the pro-slavery bushwhackers set up a state capital in tiny Lecompton and anti-slavery New Englanders set up their stronghold down the river at Lawrence. Farther up the river was Fort Riley, once an outpost against the Indians, now still a major Army base. Topeka, the state capital, sits here on low bluff above the river: 50 years ago it was a focus of national attention as the home of presidential candidate Alf Landon; 35 years ago it was known both as the home of the Menninger Psychiatric Clinic and as the city whose system of legal segregation was overturned in the 1954 landmark case of *Brown v. Board of Education.* Topeka, together with the university towns of Lawrence (KU) and Manhattan (Kansas State), plus surrounding rural counties which have been slowly drained of population, some small Indian reservations and the Army prison at Fort Leavenworth on the heights overlooking the Missouri River, make up the 2d Congressional District of Kansas. It has a Republican heritage and a Democratic congressman. The Republicans of Lawrence far outnumbered the Democrats of Lecompton when the votes were counted honestly, and Topeka produced in Landon the only major party nominee in our history who lived to be 100. But Democrats—Dr. Bill Roy and Martha Keys—won the House seat in the 1970s, and after an interval of a notably untalented Republican, Democrat Jim Slattery won in 1982 and has held the seat since. Born and raised in Atchison County farmland, he won a state legislative seat in 1972 while still in law school in Topeka. He is one of those young Democrats who seems to have a knack for politics. He was speaker pro tem of the state House at age 28, after the Democrats won control (for the only time in 80 years) in 1976. His timing has been good: he retired from the legislature, to make money in the real estate business, when the Democrats lost control in 1978; he passed up a chance to run for Congress in the Republican year of 1980 and chose 1982 instead. He won his first election in 1982 rather easily, with no primary opposition and 57% of the vote in the general election; in 1984 he had 60% and in 1986 and 1988 more than 70%. He carried every precinct in the district in the last election.

Slattery's political acumen is also apparent from his work in the House. In his first term he won a seat on the Energy and Commerce Committee—the most coveted committee in the House. In his second term he won a seat on Budget too. Slattery insists that he is a fiscal conservative, bringing "Kansas values" to the budget process; he is a real bug on the deficit and wants to use any tax increase to reduce it. He is often anxious, as he demonstrated on natural gas decontrol, to carve out on issues a position that distinguishes him from either side. As a result, his is usually one of the last votes to be counted and gets ratings near 50% from almost every rating group. Yet he falls in line with the Democratic leadership on most Energy and Commerce and national issues. He works energetically as well on the little issues that still make a difference, like promoting rural health care and getting federal retirement credit to cadet nurses from World War II.

Slattery has been speaking around Kansas outside the 2d District since 1988, and in light of his fellow Democrat Dan Glickman's interest in the Senate, it's widely assumed that Slattery will run for governor in 1990. He has another incentive: redistricting will quite likely put most of the 2d and 5th Districts together, which would force Slattery, if still in the House, to run against Republican incumbent Bob Whittaker in territory which would be unfamiliar. The Democrats have made inroads in the legislature and are within range of control of both Senate and House, and Republican Governor Mike Hayden has taken some political risks; so Slattery's chances look pretty good and the omens for success in office are better than one might expect for a Democrat in Kansas.

The People: Est. Pop. 1986: 490,500, up 3.7% 1980–86; Pop. 1980: 472,988, up 5.8% 1970–80. Households (1980): 71% family, 38% with children, 61% married couples; 35.9% housing units rented; median monthly rent: $176; median house value: $40,600. Voting age pop. (1980): 348,994; 7% Black, 3% Spanish origin, 1% Asian origin, 1% American Indian.

1988 Presidential Vote: Bush (R) 99,411   (53%)

Dukakis (D) 85,689   (46%)

Rep. Jim Slattery (D)

Elected 1982; b. Aug. 4, 1948, Atchison; home, Topeka; Washburn U., B.S. 1970, J.D. 1974, Netherlands Sch. of Intl. Bus. and Econ., 1969–70; Roman Catholic; married (Linda).

Career: Natl. Guard, 1970–75; KS House of Reps., 1972–78; Brosius, Slattery and Meyer, Inc., real estate, 1974–82;

Offices: 1440 LHOB 20515, 202-225-6601. Also 400 N. 8th St., Topeka 66602, 913-295-2811.

Committees: *Budget* (8th of 21 D). Task Forces: Urgent Fiscal Issues; Economic Policy, Projections and Revenues (Chairman). *Energy and Commerce* (18th of 26 D). Subcommittees: Commerce, Consumer Protection and Competitiveness; Telecommunications and Finance; Transportation and Hazardous Materials.

Group Ratings

	ADA	ACLU	COPE	CFA	LCV	ACU	NTLC	NSI	COC	CEI
1988	55	70	62	55	75	33	47	60	38	27
1987	68	—	58	57	—	4	—	—	47	36

National Journal Ratings

	1988 LIB — 1988 CONS		1987 LIB — 1987 CONS	
Economic	42%	— 57%	50%	— 49%
Social	54%	— 45%	51%	— 48%
Foreign	53%	— 46%	53%	— 47%

Key Votes

1) Homeless $	AGN	5) Ban Drug Test	AGN	9) SDI Research	AGN
2) Gephardt Amdt	FOR	6) Drug Death Pen	FOR	10) Ban Chem Weaps	AGN
3) Deficit Reduc	FOR	7) Handgun Sales	FOR	11) Aid to Contras	AGN
4) Kill Plnt Clsng Notice	AGN	8) Ban D.C. Abort $	FOR	12) Nuclear Testing	AGN

Election Results

1988 general	Jim Slattery (D)	135,694	(73%)	($388,866)
	Phil Meinhardt (R)....................	49,498	(27%)	($110,263)
1988 primary	Jim Slattery (D), unopposed			
1986 general	Jim Slattery (D)	110,737	(71%)	($377,067)
	Phillip Kline (R).....................	46,029	(29%)	($20,414)

THIRD DISTRICT

Kansas is not all farmlands and plains: one-fifth of the people in the state live in greater Kansas City, one of the nation's 30-odd metropolitan areas with more than one million people. The big Kansas City, the one with the big office buildings, is in Missouri, separated from Kansas by the Missouri River and, as you go south, by only a rather minor residential street. Directly west of downtown Kansas City is Kansas City, Kansas, an industrial, meatpacking town. On the low-lying land near the river used to be one of the nation's largest stockyards, and Kansas City, Kansas is still a working-class town, with a few slummy looking streets, the largest black neighborhood in the state, and lots of modest frame houses; it is heavily ethnic and Catholic, and supports a machine Democratic politics which you won't find anywhere west of here until you

458   KANSAS

get to San Francisco.

To the south is Johnson County, adjoining high-income neighborhoods in Missouri. Johnson County is white-collar, middle- to high-income; it contains some of metro Kansas City's newest and fastest-growing suburbs, with gleaming office parks and cul-de-sac streets; it is easily the highest-income county in Kansas. It is also one of the most Republican parts of a Republican state, and when rural Kansas is upset with farm prices or programs and starts leaning Democratic, Johnson County provides a strong Republican anchor and keeps Kansas one of the nation's most Republican states. Yet when an issue pits metropolitan areas against rural Kansas—as liquor by the drink did in 1970 or 1987 or the oil severance tax did in 1982—Johnson County votes metropolitan, for bars and for taxing oilmen.

Growth patterns here are a paradigm of those throughout the country: over the last 50 years working class Kansas City has hardly grown at all (and casts fewer votes in 1988 than in 1940), while Johnson County has grown, at first steadily and then in the 1970s and 1980s explosively. In 1940, Kansas City's Wyandotte County cast 66,000 votes to Johnson's 16,000; in 1960, Wyandotte cast 76,000 to Johnson's 65,000; in 1988 Wyandotte's 57,000 was overwhelmed by Johnson's 150,000. Democratic presidential candidates carried the four counties of the current 3d District in close elections in 1940 and 1948, but John Kennedy lost it in 1960, and it hasn't come close to voting for a national Democrat since LBJ in 1964.

The congresswoman from the 3d District is Jan Meyers, a five-year Overland Park council member and 12-year veteran of the legislature who ran and lost in the 1978 Senate primary and who was first elected to the House in 1984. Her real contest was in the Republican primary. Meyers supports the Supreme Court decision legalizing abortion, and has taken other positions considered relatively liberal by Republican activists. Although she began the race as by far the best known of five Republicans, she ended up winning with just 35% of the vote. In the general election she faced Kansas City Mayor Jack Reardon (who died young in 1988), who would have won when Wyandotte County cast most of the votes, but lost as Meyers carried Johnson 63%–32%.

In office, Meyers has had a middle-of-the-road record on most issues, which seems to suit her constituents just fine. Her predecessor, Larry Winn, was never nationally prominent nor especially active as a constituency service representative, and Meyers seems not to have exceeded his standard yet, though she may in time.

The People: Est. Pop. 1986: 523,200, up 10.7% 1980–86; Pop. 1980: 472,456, up 8.9% 1970–80. Households (1980): 76% family, 42% with children, 64% married couples; 29.0% housing units rented; median monthly rent: $216; median house value: $52,000. Voting age pop. (1980): 334,153; 8% Black, 2% Spanish origin, 1% Asian origin.

1988 Presidential Vote: Bush (R) 121,658   (54%)
Dukakis (D). 99,785   (45%)

Rep. Jan Meyers (R)

Elected 1984; b. July 20, 1928, Lincoln, NE; home, Overland Park; Williams Wood Col., A.A. 1948, U. of NE, B.A. 1951; United Methodist; married (Louis).

Career: Member, Overland Park City Cncl., 1967–72; KS Senate, 1972–84.

Offices: 315 CHOB 20515, 202-225-2865. Also 204 Fed. Bldg., Kansas City 66101, 913-621-0832; and 7133 W. 95th St., Ste. 217, Overland Park 66212, 913-383-2013.

Committees: *Foreign Affairs* (12th of 18 R). Subcommittees: Europe and the Middle East; Human Rights and International Organizations. *Small Business* (8th of 17 R). Subcommittees: Exports, Tax Policy and Special Problems; SBA, the General Economy and Minority Enterprise Development. *Select Committee on Aging* (16th of 27 R). Subcommittees: Health and Long-Term Care; Human Services.

Group Ratings

	ADA	ACLU	COPE	CFA	LCV	ACU	NTLC	NSI	COC	CEI
1988	35	26	15	36	56	58	76	80	85	54
1987	12	—	13	29	—	61	—	—	93	66

National Journal Ratings

	1988 LIB — 1988 CONS		1987 LIB — 1987 CONS	
Economic	13%	— 85%	28%	— 71%
Social	38%	— 61%	30%	— 69%
Foreign	42%	— 58%	40%	— 59%

Key Votes

1) Homeless $	FOR	5) Ban Drug Test	FOR	9) SDI Research	AGN
2) Gephardt Amdt	AGN	6) Drug Death Pen	FOR	10) Ban Chem Weaps	AGN
3) Deficit Reduc	AGN	7) Handgun Sales	AGN	11) Aid to Contras	FOR
4) Kill Plnt Clsng Notice	FOR	8) Ban D.C. Abort $	AGN	12) Nuclear Testing	FOR

Election Results

1988 general	Jan Meyers (R)	150,223	(74%)	($234,583)
	Lionel Kunst (D)	53,959	(26%)	($13,483)
1988 primary	Jan Meyers (R)	25,993	(85%)	
	Charles B. Masterson (R)	4,570	(15%)	
1986 general	Jan Meyers (R)	109,266	(100%)	($139,791)

FOURTH DISTRICT

In the years before World War II, Wichita was a small city of 114,000, a trading center for farm commodities, living off the agricultural yield of the surrounding counties. Today Wichita is a substantial medium-sized city, with a metropolitan population of 470,000, at the northern limit of the Sun Belt. Wichita owes most of its growth to the general aviation industry. During World War II and the years immediately after, aircraft factories sprouted up here on the Kansas plains. Today Boeing has a major plant here, its only one outside Washington state; so do Cessna, Beechcraft, and Gates Learjet. Wichita is far and away the nation's leading center for producing small airplanes—everything short of jetliners. At times this has been a boom business, and at times a bust: the market for small planes depends on business profits, and when they are squeezed, sales plummet. During most of the 1970s, Wichita did very well: the market for small planes was robust, and the rise in oil prices made the stripper wells around Wichita economically attractive once again. In the middle 1980s, general aviation was once again on hard times, as bankruptcy trustees sold off planes once owned by oil drillers and corporations pared down their fleets. Low wheat and oil prices completed the picture, and left Wichita eager for some revival in general aviation.

Wichita's politics is the product of two conflicting tendencies. Its belief in free enterprise tilts it toward the Republicans in most elections. But the need for federal help and subsidy for wheat, oil, and general aviation, plus the southern origin of many residents, sometimes incline it to the Democrats.

The 4th Congressional District of Kansas includes all of Wichita and Sedgwick County; the much smaller city of Hutchinson to the northwest; and rural areas like Sumner County, often the number one wheat-producing county in Kansas. Its congressman is Dan Glickman, a Democrat first elected in 1976, who combines political acumen with energy and an interest in a wide variety of policy areas. From the beginning, he was more skeptical about government programs than most Democrats and more inclined to hold down spending. Since the Carter years, when many of the creative ideas in politics came from Republicans, Glickman has been coming forth with many ideas on how government can be made to work better—or can be done without.

He has had useful committee assignments for the district: a seat on Agriculture, chairmanship (for over four years) of the aviation subcommittee of Science, Space and Technology, plus seats on Judiciary and Intelligence. On Agriculture, he has not only worked on the wheat program but has been attentive to and an expert on regulation of the futures markets and pushed to passage a bill tightening up their regulation. In early 1987, he became chairman of the Wheat Subcommittee, and is likely to play a major role shaping the wheat portions of the 1989 farm bill. In the meantime he has been pushing a clean grain bill, to raise standards for stored grain. He worries about a trade war with Europe, and warns U.S. negotiators that Europeans won't give up their farm subsidies. He provokes a flurry of activity on aviation: he wants changes in Mode C requirements, he opposes higher general aviation fees in Boston's Logan Airport, he got more funds and development on structural fatigue in older aircraft, and he wants to study pilot fatigue.

Glickman ranges far afield from his committee assignments, which would ordinarily be resented; but usually he is so well-prepared on the facts that he prevails. He has been a stickler on government ethics, calling for repeal of the loophole that lets members elected before 1980 convert their campaign funds upon retirement to personal use. But he is also popular with his colleagues and in 1987 got a seat on the Steering and Policy Committee that makes Democratic committee assignments. He was the original House sponsor of the U.S. Institute of Peace and wants to replace the Nuclear Regulatory Commission with a single administrator.

Glickman first won this seat in 1976 against a quiet, older incumbent named Garner Shriver. His flurry of activity in Washington and in the district have given him high ratings. Against the most serious opponent he's faced in 10 years, he won 65% in 1986; in presidential 1988 he won with 64%. Glickman has thought about running statewide before, but decided not to challenge Bob Dole or Nancy Kassebaum. Although Kassebaum decided to run for a third term, it is unclear whether Glickman will risk a safe seat to challenge her; he was saying he'd never intended to spend a lifetime in the House. He probably could; even if redistricting splits up the 4th, he should be strong enough to win (which is why it isn't likely to be split).

The People: Est. Pop. 1986: 498,400, up 5.3% 1980–86; Pop. 1980: 473,180, up 4.7% 1970–80. Households (1980): 72% family, 38% with children, 61% married couples; 33.9% housing units rented; median monthly rent: $192; median house value: $40,100. Voting age pop. (1980): 341,718; 6% Black, 2% Spanish origin, 1% Asian origin, 1% American Indian.

1988 Presidential Vote: Bush (R) 108,417 (55%)
Dukakis (D). 84,235 (43%)

Rep. Dan Glickman (D)

Elected 1976; b. Nov. 24, 1944, Wichita; home, Wichita; U. of MI, B.A. 1966; Geo. Wash. U., J.D. 1969; Jewish; married (Rhoda).

Career: Trial atty., SEC, Washington, D.C., 1969–70; Practicing atty., 1971–76; President, Wichita Bd. of Ed., 1973–76.

Offices: 1212 LHOB 20515, 202-225-6216. Also 401 N. Market, Rm. 134, Wichita 67202, 316-262-8396; and 115 W. 2d St., Hutchinson 67501, 316-669-9011.

Committees: *Agriculture* (8th of 27 D). Subcommittees: Department Operations, Research and Foreign Agriculture; Domestic Marketing, Consumer Relations, and Nutrition; Wheat, Soybeans, and Feed Grains (Chairman). *Judiciary* (9th of 21 D). Subcommittees: Administrative Law and Governmental Relations; Economic and Commercial Law. *Science, Space and Technology* (6th of 30 D). Subcommittee: Transportation, Aviation and Materials. *Permanent Select Committee on Intelligence* (9th of 12 D). Subcommittees: Program and Budget Authorization; Legislation.

Group Ratings

	ADA	ACLU	COPE	CFA	LCV	ACU	NTLC	NSI	COC	CEI
1988	80	74	64	73	94	16	33	30	43	30
1987	80	—	62	71	—	9	—	—	47	24

National Journal Ratings

	1988 LIB — 1988 CONS		1987 LIB — 1987 CONS	
Economic	50% —	48%	54% —	45%
Social	61% —	38%	62% —	36%
Foreign	74% —	23%	62% —	37%

Key Votes

1) Homeless $	AGN	5) Ban Drug Test	AGN	9) SDI Research	AGN
2) Gephardt Amdt	AGN	6) Drug Death Pen	FOR	10) Ban Chem Weaps	AGN
3) Deficit Reduc	FOR	7) Handgun Sales	AGN	11) Aid to Contras	AGN
4) Kill Plnt Clsng Notice	AGN	8) Ban D.C. Abort $	AGN	12) Nuclear Testing	FOR

Election Results

1988 general	Dan Glickman (D)	122,777	(64%)	($545,755)
	Lee Thompson (R)	69,165	(36%)	($149,035)
1988 primary	Dan Glickman (D), unopposed			
1986 general	Dan Glickman (D)	111,164	(65%)	($523,533)
	Bob Knight (R).....................	61,178	(35%)	($227,587)

FIFTH DISTRICT

Even if it looks that way on the interstate, Kansas is not a monotonous state, and to find out why you need only go down to the 5th Congressional District in southeast Kansas, where there are no interstates and only a 15-mile stretch of four-lane highway. Right up against the Missouri line is "the Balkans"—a reference to the Eastern European origin of some of the residents and to its low hill country, the outer fringe of the Ozarks. The hills here contain some coal, and the main town was named Pittsburg—another example of the unrealistic optimism of the people who first settled Kansas. This was a gritty industrial center, and in 1908 the little town of Girard was a Socialist center where Clarence Darrow and Upton Sinclair made pilgrimages, and its paper, *Appeal to Reason*, had a nationwide 750,000 circulation. Today Girard and the Balkans are not at all Socialist, but as an industrial and agricultural area that has for years been in unmistakable decline, they are seething with resentment of Wall Street and commodities speculators. Girard voted for Michael Dukakis in 1988, and he came close to carrying the whole Balkans region.

West of the Balkans, about 100 miles west of the Missouri line, are Kansas's sand hills—a formidable barrier to the pioneers, not agriculturally productive and therefore lightly populated today. Then you come to the Kansas prairie: rich farmland planted mostly with winter wheat. One famous town here is Emporia, home of William Allen White, editor of the *Emporia Gazette*—a more conventional paper than *Appeal to Reason*. White was horrified by the Populists in the 1890s, but was enchanted by Theodore Roosevelt and became a progressive Republican; from isolationist Kansas, he chaired a committee to aid Britain in the years before Pearl Harbor.

The Balkans may swing left occasionally, but the sand hills and the prairie are pretty solid Republican territory, and the 5th District has been a safe Republican seat. The current incumbent, Bob Whittaker, is a generally conservative Republican first elected in 1978. A friendly man who served two terms in the legislature, Whittaker went door to door talking with voters and worked at various jobs around the district for a day at a time. He won a six-candidate primary and then got 57% in the general, and has not been seriously challenged since.

Generally conservative on economic issues, moderate on cultural issues, usually hawkish on foreign policy, Whittaker has a record in step with his constituency. He devotes much of his energy to getting the four-lane road to Wichita built. He has become one of the senior Republicans on the Energy and Commerce Committee. When Energy and Commerce ranking Republican James Broyhill moved to the Senate in July 1986, Whittaker became ranking Republican on the Transportation and Hazardous Materials Subcommittee that handles such issues as the Superfund, hazardous waste and railroads. In the past, the panel was dominated by its chairman, James Florio of New Jersey, but Whittaker is in a position to weld alliances with some subcommittee Democrats. He sponsored the law requiring drug testing of railroad employees. Another bill he got through the House requires that telephones be compatible with hearing aids. And he got the House to pass his bill against telemarketing fraud. This may be a conservative record, but it is also an active one.

Whittaker does have one political problem: redistricting after the 1990 Census may combine most of the 5th District with much of the 2d now represented by popular Democrat Jim Slattery. Slattery may run for governor in 1990, and a redistricted seat would at least require him to get known in a lot of new territory.

The People: Est. Pop. 1986: 471,300, dn. 0.3% 1980–86; Pop. 1980: 472,916, up 6.2% 1970–80. Households (1980): 73% family, 36% with children, 65% married couples; 25.2% housing units rented; median monthly rent: $128; median house value: $28,600. Voting age pop. (1980): 347,340; 2% Black, 1% Spanish origin, 1% American Indian.

1988 Presidential Vote: Bush (R) 104,238   (56%)

Dukakis (D) 78,211   (42%)

Rep. Robert (Bob) Whittaker (R)

Elected 1978; b. Sept. 18, 1939, Eureka; home, Augusta; IL Col. of Optometry, Doctor of Optometry 1962; Christian Church; married (Marlene).

Career: Optometrist, 1962–78; KS House of Reps., 1974–77.

Offices: 2436 RHOB 20515, 202-225-3911. Also P.O. Box 280, Augusta 67010, 316-775-1127; P.O. Box 1102, Emporia 66801, 316-342-6464; P.O. Box 1003, McPherson 67460, 316-241-5797; and P.O. Box 1111, Pittsburg 66762, 316-232-2320.

Committees: *Energy and Commerce* (6th of 17 R). Subcommittees: Health and the Environment; Transportation and Hazardous Materials (Ranking Member).

Group Ratings

	ADA	ACLU	COPE	CFA	LCV	ACU	NTLC	NSI	COC	CEI
1988	10	17	10	9	38	88	74	100	100	68
1987	8	—	9	31	—	73	—	—	87	58

National Journal Ratings

	1988 LIB — 1988 CONS		1987 LIB — 1987 CONS	
Economic	16%	83%	19%	78%
Social	24%	75%	19%	78%
Foreign	16%	78%	31%	69%

Key Votes

1) Homeless $	FOR	5) Ban Drug Test	FOR	9) SDI Research	FOR
2) Gephardt Amdt	AGN	6) Drug Death Pen	FOR	10) Ban Chem Weaps	—
3) Deficit Reduc	AGN	7) Handgun Sales	FOR	11) Aid to Contras	FOR
4) Kill Plnt Clsng Notice	FOR	8) Ban D.C. Abort $	AGN	12) Nuclear Testing	AGN

Election Results

1988 general	Robert (Bob) Whittaker (R)	127,722	(70%)	($117,312)
	John Barnes (D)	54,327	(30%)	
1988 primary	Robert (Bob) Whittaker (R), unopposed			
1986 general	Robert (Bob) Whittaker (R)	116,800	(71%)	($97,850)
	Kym E. Myers (D)	47,540	(29%)	

KENTUCKY

In July 1938 Franklin Roosevelt came to Kentucky to campaign for Senate Majority Leader Alben Barkley against the primary challenge of Governor Happy Chandler. As the President's car was leaving the train station for the parade, Chandler stepped over Roosevelt's crippled legs and took the seat beside him before Barkley could get around and into the car. At Latonia Race Track near Covington Roosevelt praised Barkley mightily and slighted Chandler, and had the satisfaction later of seeing Barkley beat a challenger who had all the strengths of an incumbent governor.

Since that contest more than 50 years ago, Kentucky politics has changed remarkably little— just as life in Kentucky has changed less than in most states. Its population has risen just 30% in five decades—a low figure that indicates considerable outmigration and very few outsiders moving in. Kentuckians today are still largely the descendants of the settlers who poured over the mountains in the 40 years after Daniel Boone made his way through the Cumberland Gap in 1775, raising Kentucky's population from 73,000 in the first census in 1790 to 564,000 in 1820. Only 21% of Kentuckians today live in metropolitan Louisville and only 7% in the Kentucky suburbs of Cincinnati, its largest metro areas. Living conditions have improved since 1938, when central heating, indoor plumbing and electricity were rare outside the cities; cable TV and satellite dishes, four-lane highways and RVs are more common than electricity and running water were decades ago; people no longer feel isolated by the mountains from the rest of the world. But among Kentuckians who have stayed and the thousands who have gone to northern industrial cities or Sun Belt metroplexes to make their livings there is an attachment to roots, to place and family.

The traveler from Roosevelt's time, once off the interstates and parkways, would not be much surprised at the Kentucky landscape today. The tobacco fields, the thoroughbred horse country of the Bluegrass region and the flat fields of western Kentucky look the same as they have for years, though they are more likely to be planted in soybeans than cotton now. The small towns, with their 19th century courthouses, look mostly the same except for the fast food operations and small shopping centers that have grown up on the roads leading out. The coal industry, important 50 years ago, grew again in the 1970s after two rough decades; with fewer underground mines, the work is less hazardous, but the new strip mines leave scars all over the landscape.

Kentucky's political structure seems little changed from the days of Henry Clay, who came to Lexington from Virginia as a penniless youth and did well enough in law and land speculation to build a mansion with silver doorknobs and become a United States Senator by age 30. Political manners have improved—Clay fought in duels, and Kentucky governors now must swear they won't; gubernatorial claimant William Goebel was murdered in 1900 in a dispute over who was entitled to the office—but Kentuckians still fight bitterly, sometimes over economic issues, but more often over long-maintained political rivalries, some of them still based on the splits caused by the Civil War. Kentucky was a slave state, but it voted to stay with the Union, and there were strong feelings on both sides. Most of the hill country was pro-Union and remains Republican today, except for counties where coal miners joined the United Mine Workers in the 1930s and became Democrats. The Blue Grass region and the western Jackson Purchase and Pennyrile areas were more likely to be slaveholding territory and today remain mostly Democratic, but with a Republican trend around growing Lexington. Louisville, with many German immigrants, was an anti-slavery town, and for years supported a strong Republican organization. These

KENTUCKY — Congressional Districts, Counties, and Selected Places — *(7 Districts)*

Congressional districts established March 10, 1982; all other boundaries are as of January 1, 1980.

patterns, which have prevailed now for more than 100 years, were glaringly apparent in the 1976 and 1980 presidential races, when the Democrats nominated a southerner who lost Louisville's Jefferson County and carried the mining counties in the east, the Blue Grass country around Lexington, and Jackson Purchase and the Pennyrile—patterns similar to those of 1940, 1920 or 1880. In 1984 and 1988, the Democrats ran slightly stronger in Louisville and weaker in the urban areas, but the differences were not striking.

The other enduring feature of Kentucky politics is faction—and notably the factions represented in 1938 by Barkley and Chandler and in the 1987 gubernatorial primary by Steve Beshear (endorsed by Bert Combs, the leader of Barkley's faction after his death in 1956) and Wallace Wilkinson (endorsed by the 90-year-old Chandler). The old leaders were more prominent nationally: Barkley was Senate Majority Leader from 1937 to 1947 and Vice President under Harry Truman; he died, again a Senator, in mid-oration. Chandler became senator, baseball commissioner, and governor again in 1947 and 1955, and was active in the late 1980s. There is a direct line from the Barkley faction to the group around Governor Bert Combs, a mountain liberal elected in 1959, whose choices, Edward Breathitt and Julian Carroll, won in 1963 and 1975. Descending from the Chandler faction is the group around Combs's one-time top assistant, Wendell Ford, who beat Combs for the gubernatorial nomination in 1971 and whose candidate, Martha Layne Collins, won the office in 1983 over Combs's candidate, Harvey

Sloane. The last two governors, Collins and Wilkinson, are both from Versailles (pronounced vur-sayles), which is also Chandler's home town. Ford himself went to the Senate in 1974, not sure that giving up the governorship to Carroll for a year was worth what seems to have turned out to be a lifetime Senate seat. John Gunther quotes a story told by Fred Vinson (longtime congressman, Chief Justice of the Supreme Court 1946–53, and member of the Barkley faction) about a Kentucky politician who had not decided whom to support in a primary a few weeks away: "I don't know yet. I'm waiting to see what the opposition does, so I can take the other side."

Not all elections are won by Democrats. In the 1950s and 1960s, Kentucky slowly became more Republican, until during one four-year period (1967–71) Republicans held the governorship and both Senate seats. The first Republican victories were won by moderates from the Louisville area and the Cumberland Plateau, men like John Sherman Cooper and Thurston Morton, Republicans who supported civil rights. The Democrats they beat were southern in style and usually well to the right of the party on national issues. Then, in the 1960s, Kentucky began to fit more into the national pattern. The Republicans, under Governor Louie Nunn, were conservative on economics and civil rights (not a burning issue in Kentucky, where blacks are only 7% of the population). The Democrats had a resurgence beginning with the 1971 gubernatorial election, and have won statewide races by large margins except for Senator Dee Huddleston who was upset by Republican Mitch McConnell in 1984. But Republicans lost the 1986 race to Ford by a record margin, their 1983 governor candidate, Jim Bunning, settled for a suburban House seat which is safe Republican in 1986, and just as the party seemed about to field an active candidate for governor in 1987, he announced (weeks before the filing date) that he would not run.

Governor. There is no question who stands at the apex of Kentucky politics: the governor. The governor's appointment powers are wide; this is not a state with a vibrant civil service tradition. The legislature can meet only 60 days every two years; then the governor can shift around line items in the budget as he likes. The governor is also the undisputed leader of his state party. To prevent governors from becoming too powerful, Kentucky is one of two states (Virginia is the other) to bar them from a second consecutive term.

Wallace Wilkinson came to office after a 35%–25% upset victory in the primary (Kentucky has no runoff) and a general election margin that was not quite as large as expected. He made his fortune by starting with a used book store, making money off textbooks and then branching into real estate, hotels and a charter airline service. In between there were some odd incidents, including one when Wilkinson claims he was kidnapped by and paid $500,000 ransom to a former business associate. Wilkinson did not have the support of outgoing Governor Martha Layne Collins, whom he criticized for making too many concessions to attract a giant Toyota plant to the Blue Grass town of Georgetown. Wilkinson called for a lottery, opposed new taxes, promised that he could find jobs for Kentuckians and combined denunciations of the state's current conditions and standard politicos with home-state boosterism. The best-known candidate was former Governor John Y. Brown Jr., the Kentucky Fried Chicken millionaire; Lieutenant Governor Steve Beshear attacked Brown for high living and high-stakes gambling. But the beneficiary was not Beshear but Wilkinson, who led Brown in the May 26 primary by 35%–25%, with Beshear lagging far behind. Wilkinson won the general election over an underfinanced Republican who called him a "weasel" by 65%–35%. He got the venture capital bill he sought in the legislature, but lost on the issue of second terms; in November 1988 voters approved his lottery proposal 61%–39%.

Senators. Wendell Ford, who looks like a weatherbeaten old pro, has risen from humble beginnings to positions of considerable power in his 15 years in the Senate. He is now third ranking Democrat on the Commerce Committee, third on Energy and Natural Resources, and chairman of Rules. Ford's fierce determination to champion Kentuckians' interests seems rooted in a sense that they are little guys who are victims or targets of big selfish guys elsewhere—that they are as humble as Ford's own economic background. He not only beat John Chafee's amendment to stop export subsidies for tobacco, but he threatened to retaliate against Rhode Island for it. To advocates of a coal slurry pipeline, which would compete with Kentucky coal, he promised "blood on the carpet of the Senate." He is a fierce champion of clean-coal technology. He stands firmly against a warning on bottles of Kentucky bourbon or other liquor. He also champions strongly the institutional interests of agencies he superintends, calling for an FAA separate from the Transportation Department, and he would prohibit anyone from using videotapes of televised Senate proceedings except Senators. He has taken up other causes too: he wants to stop the purchase of dogs and cats at auctions (to protect pets); he favors a rescue of the uranium industry.

On Rules, Ford has been a champion of changing the way the Senate does business, while he seems less enthusiastic about changing the way Senate candidates raise money. He would like the Senate to work more efficiently and with a more predictable schedule. He made those points also when he ran against Alan Cranston for whip after the 1988 elections, but lost. He supported, but was not a leader of, David Boren and Robert Byrd's effort to limit the role of PACs and introduce some public financing into Senate elections. His instincts on campaign money seem traditional: when he chaired the Democrats' Senate campaign committee (1977–82), he specialized in raising big contributions from business sources, and didn't build up a big base of direct mail contributors. Finally, he proposes a five-regional-primary system of nominating presidential candidates, with the first state selected at random.

Ford won his seat in 1974 by beating incumbent Republican Marlow Cook in a close and bitter race. Since then he has had only the weakest of opposition. In 1980 Kentucky still seemed heavily Democratic, nearly voting for Jimmy Carter; Ford got 65%, a record for a Kentucky Senate candidate. After Huddleston's defeat in 1984, Democrats looked more vulnerable. But Ford preempted all serious opposition and in 1986 was reelected with 75%, breaking his own record. Amazingly, in a state where partisan tradition is so strong that George McGovern carried 8 counties and Barry Goldwater 21, Ford carried all of Kentucky's 120 counties, the first opposed candidate ever to do so. He has made it known he intends to run for reelection in 1992.

Kentucky's junior Senator, Mitch McConnell, is the only Republican to win a statewide race here since 1968. He won in 1984 thanks to his own unstinting ambition and to incumbent Dee Huddleston's low profile. McConnell had been aiming for the Senate over a long career. He served on the staff of Senator Marlow Cook during his single and often stormy term in office (1968–74), then moved back to Louisville and won, in an upset, the office that had been Cook's political stepping stone: Jefferson County judge. This is the executive position in the county that includes Louisville and most of its suburbs; it is the largest constituency in the state in which Republicans are competitive. It also, unlike the governorship or the mayoralty of Louisville, allows incumbents to run for a second consecutive term; McConnell won reelection in 1982, though by a lackluster margin. In 1984 he pounced on Huddleston's weakness with ads that showed bloodhounds sniffing for Huddleston in vacation locales where he had collected fees for speeches while the Senate was in session. Huddleston had striven more to avoid controversy than to advertise his record, and the bloodhound ads, by suggesting he'd been doing little but feathering his nest, cost him just enough votes to keep him from getting the 11% he needed to run ahead of Walter Mondale. McConnell ran unimpressively in Jefferson County, but ran strongly enough in rural counties to win.

In the Senate McConnell has moved aggressively to protect interests he cares about: Kentucky tobacco farmers and the Republican Party. He pushed through a sodbuster clarification act for the tobacco farmers, and ceaselessly promotes tobacco exports. He upholds other Kentucky interests as well, cutting red tape for the pari-mutuel tracks and making sure that state parkways (of which there are 669 miles) could raise their speed limits to 65 as soon as interstates could. For his party, he supplied most of the energy that killed the Boren-Byrd campaign finance bill. McConnell's substitute would outlaw PAC contributions but would not try to prevent them from "bundling" members' individual contributions (handing them over to a candidate in a lump sum, thus avoiding the legal limit), and it would not limit overall campaign spending. There are serious arguments for these positions, but the upshot was a standoff. He has another interesting reform, to prevent incumbents from raising money after the election to pay off personal loans they took out in their campaigns.

On Foreign Relations since 1987, McConnell became active on John Kerry's subcommittee investigating Caribbean drug dealing. He co-sponsored with Kerry a money laundering provision of the 1988 drug bill. But he also charged in 1988 that Kerry's investigation of alleged contra or U.S. involvement in the drug trade was politically motivated—a charge given credence by the fact that the minimal results never matched the initial headlines. He did break with the Reagan Administration on South African sanctions. McConnell was also one of the first Senators to support George Bush for President.

McConnell may face a tough challenge in 1990 from Harvey Sloane, the doctor who has been mayor of Louisville and won McConnell's old job of Jefferson County judge; but McConnell is not likely to be unprepared. Sloane would have the state's Democratic leanings and his own record working for him, but McConnell has been preparing both a record and a campaign treasury that will make him a strong candidate.

Presidential politics. Kentucky had a presidential primary, abolished it, then joined southern Super Tuesday for 1988. That produced solid wins for Albert Gore and George Bush. Kentucky is a closely contested state if the Democratic nominee has appeal to the South, as in 1976 and 1980; Michael Dukakis was able to make a respectable but not truly competitive showing here in November 1988.

Congressional districting. Kentucky's Democrats typically redraw its congressional district lines without major change and without much controversy.

The People: Est. Pop. 1988: 3,721,000; Pop. 1980: 3,660,777, up 1.6% 1980–88 and 13.7% 1970–80; 1.55% of U.S. total, 23d largest. 11% with 1–3 yrs. col., 11% with 4+ yrs. col.; 17.6% below poverty level. Single ancestry: 25% English, 7% German, 6% Irish, 1% French. Households (1980): 78% family, 44% with children, 65% married couples; 30.0% housing units rented; median monthly rent: $151; median house value: $34,200. Voting age pop. (1980): 2,578,047; 7% Black, 1% Spanish origin. Registered voters (1988): 2,026,307; 1,361,631 D (67%), 596,443 R (29%), 58,233 unaffiliated and minor parties (3%).

1988 Share of Federal Tax Burden: $9,755,000,000; 1.10% of U.S. total, 26th largest.

1988 Share of Federal Expenditures

	Total		Non-Defense		Defense	
Total Expend	$10,686m	(1.21%)	$9,378m	(1.43%)	$1,934m	(0.85%)
St/Lcl Grants	1,766m	(1.54%)	2,135m	(1.86%)	0m	(0.24%)
Salary/Wages	1,861m	(1.39%)	743m	(1.11%)	1,118m	(1.11%)
Pymnts to Indiv	6,142m	(1.50%)	5,955m	(1.52%)	187m	(1.00%)
Procurement	629m	(0.33%)	257m	(0.55%)	629m	(0.33%)
Research/Other	288m	(0.77%)	288m	(0.78%)	0m	(0.78%)

Political Lineup: Governor, Wallace G. Wilkinson (D); Lt. Gov., Brereton C. Jones (D); Secy. of State, Bremer Erhler (D); Atty. Gen., Fred Cowan (D); Treasurer, Robert Mead (D); Auditor, Robert Babbage (D). State Senate, 38 (30 D and 8 R); State House of Representatives, 100 (72 D and 28 R). Senators, Wendell H. Ford (D) and Mitch McConnell (R). Representatives, 7 (4 D and 3 R).

1988 Presidential Vote

Bush (R) 734,281 (56%)
Dukakis (D). 580,368 (44%)

1984 Presidential Vote

Reagan (R) 821,702 (60%)
Mondale (D) 539,539 (39%)

1988 Democratic Presidential Primary

Gore. 145,988 (46%)
Dukakis. 59,433 (19%)
Jackson 49,667 (16%)
Gephardt. 28,982 (9%)
Hart. 11,798 (4%)
Simon 9,393 (3%)
Others 13,460 (4%)

1988 Republican Presidential Primary

Bush 72,020 (59%)
Dole. 27,868 (23%)
Robertson 13,526 (11%)
Kemp. 4,020 (3%)
Others 3,768 (3%)

GOVERNOR

Gov. Wallace G. Wilkinson (D)

Elected 1987; term expires Jan. 1992; b. Dec. 12, 1941, Liberty; home, Frankfort; U. of KY; married (Martha).

Career: Businessman; Founder, Wallace's College Book Company, Wilkinson Enterprises.

Office: Office of the Governor, State Capitol, Frankfort 40601, 502-564-2611.

Election Results

1987 gen.	Wallace G. Wilkinson (D)	504,674	(65%)
	John Harper (R).	273,141	(35%)
1987 prim.	Wallace G. Wilkinson (D)	221,138	(35%)
	John Y. Brown (D)	163,204	(25%)
	Steve Beshear (D)	114,439	(18%)
	Grady Stumbo (D).	84,613	(13%)
	Julian Carroll (D).	42,137	(7%)
1983 gen.	Martha Layne Collins (D)	561,674	(54%)
	Jim Bunning (R).	454,650	(44%)

470 KENTUCKY

SENATORS

Sen. Wendell H. Ford (D)

Elected 1974, seat up 1992; b. Sept. 8, 1924, Daviess Cnty.; home, Owensboro; U. of KY, MD School of Insurance; Baptist; married (Jean).

Career: Army, WWII; Family insur. bus.; Chf. A.A. to Gov. Bert Combs; KY Senate, 1965–67; Lt. Gov. 1967–71; Governor, 1971–74.

Offices: 173A RSOB 20510, 202-224-4343. Also 172-C New Fed. Bldg., 600 Fed. Pl., Louisville 40202, 502-582-6251; 305 Fed. Bldg., Frederica St., Owensboro 42301, 502-685-5158; 343 Waller Ave., Ste. 204, Lexington 40504, 606-233-2484; 19 U.S. P.O. and Crthse., Covington 41011, 606-491-7929.

Committees: *Commerce, Science, and Transportation* (3rd of 11 D). Subcommittees: Aviation (Chairman); Communications; Consumer; National Ocean Policy Study. *Energy and Natural Resources* (3rd of 10 D). Subcommittees: Energy, Research and Development (Chairman); Mineral Resources Development and Production; Water and Power. *Rules and Administration* (Chairman of 9 D). *Joint Committee on Printing* (Chairman).

Group Ratings

	ADA	ACLU	COPE	CFA	LCV	ACU	NTLC	NSI	COC	CEI
1988	65	23	76	92	30	24	7	20	21	11
1987	75	—	75	75	—	19	—	—	22	17

National Journal Ratings

	1988 LIB — 1988 CONS	1987 LIB — 1987 CONS
Economic	65% — 30%	74% — 0%
Social	19% — 78%	35% — 62%
Foreign	59% — 39%	69% — 27%

Key Votes

1) Cut Aged Housing $	FOR	5) Bork Nomination	AGN	9) SDI Funding	AGN
2) Override Hwy Veto	FOR	6) Ban Plastic Guns	FOR	10) Ban Chem Weaps	AGN
3) Kill Plnt Clsng Notice	AGN	7) Deny Abortions	FOR	11) Aid To Contras	AGN
4) Min Wage Increase	FOR	8) Japanese Reparations	AGN	12) Reagan Defense $	AGN

Election Results

1986 general	Wendell H. Ford (D).................	503,755	(75%)	($1,201,624)
	Jackson M. Andrews (R)	173,330	(25%)	($58,572)
1986 primary	Wendell H. Ford (D), unopposed			
1980 general	Wendell H. Ford (D).................	720,891	(65%)	($491,522)
	Mary Louise Foust (R)...............	386,029	(35%)	($7,406)

Sen. Mitch McConnell (R)

Elected 1984, seat up 1990; b. Feb. 20, 1942, Sheffield, AL; home, Louisville; U. of Louisville, B.A. 1964, U. of KY, J.D. 1967; Baptist; divorced.

Career: Chief Legis. Asst. to U.S. Sen. Marlow Cook, 1968–70; Dpty. Asst. Atty. Gen., 1974–75; Judge, Jefferson Cnty., 1977–1984.

Offices: 120 RSOB 20510, 202-224-2541. Also 600 Federal Pl., Rm. 136-C, Louisville 40202, 502-582-6304; Fed. Bldg., Rm 307, Covington 41011, 606-261-6304; Irvin Cobb Bldg., 602 Broadway, Paducah 42001, 502-442-4554; 1501 S. Main St., Ste. N, London 40741, 606-864-2026; Fed. Bldg., 241 Main St., Rm. 305, Bowling Green 42101; and 155 E. Main St., Ste. 210, Lexington 40508, 606-252-1781.

Committees: *Agriculture, Nutrition, and Forestry* (6th of 9 R). Subcommittees: Agricultural Production and Stabilization of Prices; Rural Development and Rural Electrification (Ranking Member); Domestic and Foreign Marketing and Product Promotion. *Energy and Natural Resources* (9th of 9 R). Subcommittees: Energy Research and Development; Mineral Resources Development and Production. *Foreign Relations* (7th of 9 R). Subcommittees: East Asian and Pacific Affairs; Terrorism, Narcotics and International Operations (Ranking Member); Western Hemisphere and Peace Corps Affairs.

Group Ratings

	ADA	ACLU	COPE	CFA	LCV	ACU	NTLC	NSI	COC	CEI
1988	5	15	17	33	30	92	71	100	93	47
1987	10	—	13	25	—	80	—	—	89	57

National Journal Ratings

	1988 LIB — 1988 CONS		1987 LIB — 1987 CONS	
Economic	9%	81%	27%	72%
Social	11%	88%	30%	68%
Foreign	25%	74%	0%	76%

Key Votes

1) Cut Aged Housing $	AGN	5) Bork Nomination	FOR	9) SDI Funding	FOR
2) Override Hwy Veto	FOR	6) Ban Plastic Guns	FOR	10) Ban Chem Weaps	FOR
3) Kill Plnt Clsng Notice	FOR	7) Deny Abortions	FOR	11) Aid To Contras	FOR
4) Min Wage Increase	AGN	8) Japanese Reparations	AGN	12) Reagan Defense $	FOR

Election Results

1984 general	Mitch McConnell (R)	644,990	(50%)	($1,767,114)
	Walter D. (Dee) Huddleston (D)	639,721	(49%)	($2,444,091)
1984 primary	Mitch McConnell (R)	39,465	(79%)	
	Three others (R)	10,352	(21%)	
1978 general	Walter D. (Dee) Huddleston (D)	290,730	(61%)	($461,808)
	Louie Guenthner, Jr. (R)	175,766	(37%)	($76,445)

FIRST DISTRICT

The western end of Kentucky has a Democratic tradition that goes back to 1818, when General Andrew Jackson and Kentucky Governor Isaac Shelby agreed that the United States would pay the Chickasaw Indians $300,000 for more than 8,000 square miles of land between the Tennessee and Mississippi rivers. This Jackson Purchase, now the western end of Kentucky and part of Tennessee, in many ways seems part of the Deep South. This is low-lying land, like the cotton and soybean fields of west Tennessee or the bootheel of Missouri or Illinois's Little Egypt, protected from the great muddy Mississippi by levees and cut off from the rest of Kentucky by the dammed-up Tennessee and Cumberland rivers. The first settlers came to the Jackson Purchase not long after 1818, and most people here now are their descendants. They retain a living memory of the generations that came before, in family lore and in the annual Big Singing in the courthouse in Benton, on the fourth Sunday in May, in which perhaps 50 Jackson Purchase residents sing hymns in an old style called Southern Harmony.

Just to the east of the Tennessee and the Cumberland rivers is a region called the Pennyrile (after pennyroyal, a common variety of local wild mint). Here you find a land of low hills and small farms. It is also where you find the west Kentucky coal fields, the site of much strip mining in recent years. The Jackson Purchase and the Pennyrile have a southern atmosphere: they grow southern crops, they speak in what sound to northerners like deep southern accents, they have a significant black population (whereas otherwise in Kentucky there are few blacks outside Louisville), and in most elections they vote Democratic.

This forms the 1st Congressional District of Kentucky, which is made up of the Jackson Purchase and much of the Pennyrile, one of the most Democratic parts of the state. Paducah, the largest city here, produced one of the most enduring Democratic politicians of this century, Alben Barkley, who served 14 years in the House, 24 in the Senate, four as Vice President, and keynoted four Democratic National Conventions. Since Barkley's time, the 1st District House seat has passed to winners of successive Democratic primaries.

The current incumbent, Carroll Hubbard, was first elected in 1974 after he had the foresight to challenge a weak incumbent in the primary. On arrival in Washington, he was chosen chairman of the Freshman Caucus, though he was very far from typical of the Democrats first elected that year. Not only did he have more conservative views on most issues, but he had a different political style. Most freshman Democrats were independent and even critical of the Democratic leadership; Hubbard has cooperated closely with Jim Wright. They used subcommittee seats or personal expertise to sponsor legislation that got voters' and other legislators' eyes; Hubbard, challenged in the 1988 primary, could name no significant piece of legislation he had introduced. They have been outspoken voices on major national issues; Hubbard has not.

He is a congressman who works hard at keeping in touch with his constituents, sending them letters and memorializing their contributions to society in the *Congressional Record*. He was also interested, for a while, in state politics, and ran for governor in 1979; against millionaire John Y. Brown Jr., he received only 12% of the vote, though he carried the 1st District with 33%. Back home in 1988 Hubbard got his first serious opposition when Lacey Smith, a former Louisville legislator and aide to Louisville Mayor Harvey Sloane, moved from Florida back to his family's ancestral western Kentucky home and ran for office. This prompted one of the nastier primary campaigns of 1988. Smith charged that Hubbard accomplished little and missed chances to switch from the Banking Committee to Agriculture because he could collect so much PAC money on Banking. Hubbard got his subcommittee to request a GAO investigation of a bank loan to Smith. Hubbard also got involved in a local drug traffic investigation, charging that drug smugglers were using airstrips in western Kentucky and that federal officials asked him not to speak out on the subject until after the sentencing of a Florida man, to whom

Smith had past ties, who was convicted of providing a gun used to kill a prosecutor. Old charges were aired, notably that Smith had solicited a bribe from an insurance agency while on Sloane's staff—a charge on which Smith had been acquitted in 1974.

The bottom line was a big 73%–27% victory for Hubbard. Unless this was solely a negative response to Smith, it indicates that Hubbard has a pretty safe seat.

The People: Est. Pop. 1986: 517,100, dn. 1.7% 1980–86; Pop. 1980: 525,844, up 12.3% 1970–80. Households (1980): 78% family, 42% with children, 68% married couples; 25.8% housing units rented; median monthly rent: $128; median house value: $29,900. Voting age pop. (1980): 379,011; 8% Black, 1% Spanish origin.

1988 Presidential Vote:

Bush (R)	96,150	(51%)
Dukakis (D)	92,391	(49%)

Rep. Carroll Hubbard, Jr. (D)

Elected 1974; b. July 7, 1937, Murray; home, Mayfield; Georgetown Col., B.A. 1959, U. of Louisville, J.D. 1962; Baptist; married (Carol).

Career: Practicing atty., 1962–74; KY Senate, 1967–75.

Offices: 2182 RHOB 20515, 202-225-3115. Also 145 E. Center St., Madisonville 42431, 502-825-1371; Fed. Bldg.,501 Broadway, Rm. 100, Paducah 42002, 502-442-9804; Municipal Bldg., Henderson 42420, 502-826-5776; 109 Hammond Plaza, Hopkinsville 42240, 502-885-2625; and Hall Hotel, Mayfield, 502-247-7128.

Committees: *Banking, Finance and Urban Affairs* (5th of 31 D). Subcommittees: Financial Institutions Supervision, Regulation and Insurance; Housing and Community Development; Consumer Affairs and Coinage. *Merchant Marine and Fisheries* (3d of 26 D). Subcommittees: Merchant Marine; General Oversight and Investigations (Chairman).

Group Ratings

	ADA	ACLU	COPE	CFA	LCV	ACU	NTLC	NSI	COC	CEI
1988	50	59	65	82	38	54	39	80	50	24
1987	56	—	64	50	—	19	—	—	53	37

National Journal Ratings

	1988 LIB — 1988 CONS		1987 LIB — 1987 CONS	
Economic	53%	— 46%	49%	— 51%
Social	42%	— 57%	52%	— 48%
Foreign	43%	— 56%	42%	— 58%

Key Votes

1) Homeless $	—	5) Ban Drug Test	AGN	9) SDI Research	FOR
2) Gephardt Amdt	FOR	6) Drug Death Pen	FOR	10) Ban Chem Weaps	AGN
3) Deficit Reduc	AGN	7) Handgun Sales	FOR	11) Aid to Contras	FOR
4) Kill Plnt Clsng Notice	AGN	8) Ban D.C. Abort $	FOR	12) Nuclear Testing	AGN

Election Results

1988 general	Carroll Hubbard, Jr. (D)	117,288	(95%)	($546,908)
	Charles K. Hatchett (I)	6,106	(5%)	
1988 primary	Carroll Hubbard, Jr. (D)	63,136	(73%)	
	Lacey T. Smith (D)	23,153	(27%)	
1986 general	Carroll Hubbard, Jr. (D)	64,315	(100%)	($237,748)

SECOND DISTRICT

Even before the Revolutionary War was won, Kentucky pioneers were laying out Bardstown. It was incorporated in 1778; an academy was started in 1788; in 1797, Louis Philippe, the exiled Duke of Orleans and later King of France, spent the night at Bean's Tavern. Bardstown has had a rich history since: it is the site of Stephen Collins Foster's "My Old Kentucky Home," it contributed dozens of soldiers to both Union and Confederacy in the Civil War, and it suffered disproportionate losses in Vietnam. Midway between Fort Knox, where the nation's gold bullion is kept, and Abraham Lincoln's birthplace, Bardstown has just 6,000 people today—probably the size the Founders expected most American communities would be.

The 2d Congressional District of Kentucky, in hilly land south of Louisville, has a lot of communities like Bardstown. Its largest cities are Owensboro, a factory town on the Ohio River, and Bowling Green, in the cave country near Tennessee, each with about 50,000 people. This is rural and small town country, where in the last 50 years people have gained almost all the modern conveniences and luxuries that only the rich in the cities used to have. But they also have family roots that go back generations and a connection with the past that isn't often found in big metropolitan areas. Much of that past goes back to the Civil War. Kentucky was sharply divided when the South seceded; families were split. It finally stayed in the Union, but most Kentuckians were unenthusiastic for the cause of Mr. Lincoln, who won 1% here in 1860. The current 2d District was divided: the map shows splotches of counties pro-South and splotches pro-Union, but the bits of color only hint at the deep and often bitter feelings caused by the splits over the war and the losses people suffered. Of those splits and feelings current partisan preferences are a dim but persistent reflection.

William Natcher, one of the House's most hard-working and conscientious members, has represented this district since he won a special election in 1953. He is one of a kind—one of the men and women who makes the House work, and work much better than its detractors think. He is above all meticulous and attentive to detail; he abhors waste and disorder; he is appalled by anything that smacks of corruption. He insists on doing what he regards as his duty, even when it means staying in the chair for long, wearying days during the debate on immigration reform, or when it means responding to harassing quorum calls.

Natcher is often called on to take the chair when the House meets under the Committee of the Whole procedure. He is the ideal presiding officer: courteous, scrupulously fair, but determined to keep the proceedings moving along. He is an active committee member as well. He is the number two Democrat on the House Appropriations Committee, and chairs the Labor-HHS-Education Subcommittee. His appropriations bill is the target for a wide variety of amendments, particularly those to limit abortions; it takes a long time to consider, and often Natcher has been frustrated after doing his duty to see it stalled in the Senate and his appropriations folded into the continuing resolution. In conference committees, he is adroit enough to strike many a compromise, but he is also willing to stick stubbornly to the House point of view, rather than accede to the Senate. His record, perhaps surprisingly for one of his temperament and district, is similar on many though by no means all issues to those of most House Democrats.

Natcher prides himself on never having missed a roll call vote or quorum call since he was elected in 1953. By the end of the 1988 session he had responded to roll and quorum calls 15,902 times—the all-time record. Natcher also, in the old-fashioned manner, resists relying on staff; he does his own reading and research and prides himself on being well prepared. But a lot of the roll call votes on the House floor are on trivial matters or are delaying tactics. Natcher's presence on the floor cuts into his study time; and he has a jurisdiction which cannot be mastered by any single person anyway. Still, there is something awesome about his stubborn devotion to duty.

Natcher brings the same old-fashioned attitudes to elections in the 2d District. He usually spends under $10,000—all of it his own personal money—on a campaign and, in an age when voters will not pay attention to politicians unless they slip their messages into the middle of television shows, he communicates with them by making his rounds of courthouse towns on days when Congress is not in session. The press is not welcome at these gatherings, however; a Kentucky reporter who got to Natcher's house at 5:30 a.m. to follow him on his rounds found that he was already on his way.

For 35 years this has been a winning formula. Four primary opponents in 1982 held him to 60% of the vote, but Kentucky does not have runoffs and so this seems like a comfortable showing. Since then he has been returned to office with overwhelming support and shows no sign of slowing down as he reaches his 80th birthday in 1989.

The People: Est. Pop. 1986: 546,800, up 5.0% 1980–86; Pop. 1980: 520,634, up 17.5% 1970–80. Households (1980): 80% family, 47% with children, 69% married couples; 28.0% housing units rented; median monthly rent: $150; median house value: $34,500. Voting age pop. (1980): 361,229; 6% Black, 1% Spanish origin.

1988 Presidential Vote:

Bush (R)	102,721	(58%)
Dukakis (D)	72,768	(41%)

Rep. William H. Natcher (D)

Elected Aug. 1, 1953; b. Sept. 11, 1909, Bowling Green; home, Bowling Green; W. KY U., A.B. 1930, OH St. U., LL.B. 1933; Baptist; married (Virginia).

Career: Practicing atty., 1934–54; Fed. Conciliation Commissioner, W. Dist. of KY, 1936–37; Warren Cnty. Atty., 1937–49; Navy, WWII; Commonwealth Atty., 8th Judicial Dist. of KY, 1951–53.

Offices: 2333 RHOB, 202-225-3501. Also 414 E. 10th St., Bowling Green 42101, 502-842-7376; and #11, The Mall, 50 Public Square, Elizabethtown 42701, 502-765-4360.

Committees: *Appropriations* (2d of 35 D). Subcommittees: District of Columbia; Labor, Health and Human Services, Education and Related Agencies (Chairman); Rural Development, Agriculture and Related Agencies.

Group Ratings

	ADA	ACLU	COPE	CFA	LCV	ACU	NTLC	NSI	COC	CEI
1988	75	78	74	82	38	16	5	50	21	7
1987	76	—	73	71	—	13	—	—	13	9

National Journal Ratings

	1988 LIB — 1988 CONS		1987 LIB — 1987 CONS	
Economic	87% —	8%	73% —	0%
Social	70% —	28%	56% —	43%
Foreign	58% —	41%	50% —	48%

Key Votes

1) Homeless $	AGN	5) Ban Drug Test	AGN	9) SDI Research	FOR
2) Gephardt Amdt	FOR	6) Drug Death Pen	FOR	10) Ban Chem Weaps	FOR
3) Deficit Reduc	FOR	7) Handgun Sales	FOR	11) Aid to Contras	AGN
4) Kill Plnt Clsng Notice	AGN	8) Ban D.C. Abort $	AGN	12) Nuclear Testing	FOR

Election Results

1988 general	William H. Natcher (D)	92,184	(61%)	($8,397)
	Martin A. Tori (R)	59,907	(39%)	($84,102)
1988 primary	William H. Natcher (D)	26,918	(76%)	
	Bob Evans (D)	8,324	(24%)	
1986 general	William H. Natcher (D)	57,644	(100%)	($5,717)

THIRD DISTRICT

Half a century ago Louisville (pronounced *LOOuhv'l*) was very much in the running to be the major city of the South. It had as many people as Atlanta or Birmingham, and a stronger economy; it was not so fixated on a peculiar history as were New Orleans and Richmond. And if its location seemed at the outer periphery of the South, in a state that after all had not seceded, Louisville and Kentucky in those days were, as Alistair Cooke wrote, the most self-consciously southern places in the country. Steamboats still tied up in front of Louisville's downtown, following the channel around the Falls of the Ohio which prompted George Rogers Clark to found the town in 1778; mint juleps were served on the verandas of country mansions; horse racing was a preoccupation not just during Derby Week in May, but year-round, with the *Racing Form* sold in downtown Louisville like a newspaper.

The Louisville of today still has its southern and Kentucky customs, but is not an especially southern city, and is certainly not the first city of the South. Atlanta has quadrupled in population in 50 years, while Louisville has not even doubled; its manufacturing economy—appliances, car assembly, whiskey, cigarettes—has not boomed, and even close by it is overshadowed by Cincinnati, St. Louis, even Indianapolis. Louisville's biggest business now is health: Humana, the nation's second-largest operator of for-profit hospitals, has its headquarters here a few blocks from the riverfront, in a Michael Graves building which is one of the monuments of postmodern architecture.

Politically, Louisville has always had an un-southern aspect, and has often voted against the rest of Kentucky; this comes from its past as a heavily German river town, a Republican and anti-slavery island in a secessionist and pro-slavery sea. Ever since, it has been usually more liberal and more Republican than Kentucky as a whole—and usually badly outnumbered in state politics. Locally, Louisville and Jefferson County have long had a robust two-party politics. Jefferson County judges (county executives) have become U.S. Senators: Republicans Marlow Cook and his one-time aide Mitch McConnell made that move in 1968 and 1984, and current Judge and former Louisville Mayor Harvey Sloane may try to do so in 1990.

The 3d Congressional District includes all of Louisville and some of its less affluent suburbs. Its congressman is Democrat Romano Mazzoli, who won the seat in 1970 by all of 211 votes, beating a Republican incumbent who had been mayor of Louisville. At a time when most congressmen choose committee seats and issues to maximize their reelection chances, Mazzoli has stayed from the beginning on Judiciary, a committee increasingly shunned by Democrats with anything close to marginal seats, because of the difficult issues it handles. And on Judiciary he concentrated on an issue with zero political payoff for him, immigration reform. In 1981 he became chairman of the Immigration Subcommittee of Judiciary, and worked with Senator Alan Simpson to produce a reform bill that responded to the sharp increases in illegal immigration in the 1970s by promising both an amnesty for illegal migrants who had been in the country for several years and employer sanctions to discourage future illegal immigration. The Simpson-Mazzoli bill passed the Senate in 1982 and 1983 and the House in 1984, but stalled in conference in 1984. In 1985, after Mazzoli had voted with the Republicans rather than the Democrats on the Indiana 8th challenge, he ceded his lead role on immigration to Judiciary

Chairman Peter Rodino. After many perils of Pauline, immigration reform finally became law at the end of the 1986 session—for which Mazzoli deserves much and got a little of the credit. In fact, he has gotten the opposite. At the beginning of the 101st Congress, Judiciary Committee Democrats voted Mazzoli out of the chairmanship altogether and installed Bruce Morrison in his place. They seem to have been acting out of a not unjustified feeling that Mazzoli has not been a loyal party man lately. He voted against the party on the Indiana 8th challenge; he not only opposes abortion, but voted against at least one version of the Civil Rights Restoration Act; his record on economic and foreign policy issues over the years has become less and less liberal. House Democrats were evidently unwilling to tolerate such a record in a colleague from an urban Democratic district, even though Mazzoli could argue that he has done constructive work on immigration and on issues like crime and drugs and gun control as well.

This change in Mazzoli's stance has been reflected in the opposition he has received in his district. In 1988 Mazzoli's challenge came in the primary, from Jeffrey Hutter, a Humana executive, former TV reporter, and former aide to Harvey Sloane. Hutter won the endorsement of the AFL-CIO and the support of many liberals unhappy with Mazzoli's record. Mazzoli won renomination by only 61%–39%—not an impressive margin for an incumbent. Although he says he wants to stay in Congress for some time, it's entirely possible his House career will end in 1990.

The People: Est. Pop. 1986: 512,100, dn. 1.9% 1980–86; Pop. 1980: 522,252, dn. 9.3% 1970–80. Households (1980): 70% family, 37% with children, 53% married couples; 38.1% housing units rented; median monthly rent: $162; median house value: $33,100. Voting age pop. (1980): 381,792; 18% Black, 1% Spanish origin.

1988 Presidential Vote:

Dukakis (D)	101,458	(53%)
Bush (R)	88,129	(46%)

Rep. Romano L. Mazzoli (D)

Elected 1970; b. Nov. 2, 1932, Louisville; home, Louisville; U. of Notre Dame, B.S. 1954, U. of Louisville, J.D. 1960; Roman Catholic; married (Helen).

Career: Army, 1954–56; Law Dept., L & N Railroad Co., 1960–62; Practicing atty., 1962–70; Lecturer, Bellarmine Col., 1964–68; KY Senate, 1968–70.

Offices: 2246 RHOB 20515, 202-225-5401. Also Fed. Bldg., 600 M.L.King Jr. Place, Louisville 40202, 502-582-5129.

Committees: *Judiciary* (5th of 21 D). Subcommittees: Crime; Immigration, Refugees and International Law; Economic and Commercial Law. *Small Business* (5th of 27 D). Subcommittees: Exports, Tax Policy and Special Problems; SBA, the General Economy and Minority Enterprise Development.

Group Ratings

	ADA	ACLU	COPE	CFA	LCV	ACU	NTLC	NSI	COC	CEI
1988	75	52	66	82	56	21	15	40	54	20
1987	56	—	65	86	—	30	—	—	33	13

National Journal Ratings

	1988 LIB — 1988 CONS			1987 LIB — 1987 CONS	
Economic	50%	—	48%	50%	—	49%
Social	61%	—	38%	44%	—	56%
Foreign	73%	—	26%	52%	—	48%

Key Votes

1) Homeless $	AGN	5) Ban Drug Test	FOR	9) SDI Research	AGN
2) Gephardt Amdt	AGN	6) Drug Death Pen	FOR	10) Ban Chem Weaps	FOR
3) Deficit Reduc	AGN	7) Handgun Sales	AGN	11) Aid to Contras	AGN
4) Kill Plnt Clsng Notice	AGN	8) Ban D.C. Abort $	FOR	12) Nuclear Testing	FOR

Election Results

1988 general	Romano L. Mazzoli (D)	131,981	(70%)	($371,431)
	Philip Dunnagan (R).	57,387	(30%)	($4,931)
1988 primary	Romano L. Mazzoli (D)	31,288	(61%)	
	Jeffrey Hutter (D).	20,207	(39%)	
1986 general	Romano L. Mazzoli (D)	81,943	(73%)	($125,577)
	Lee Holmes (R)	29,348	(26%)	($169)

FOURTH DISTRICT

On hills above the Ohio River, east of Louisville and south of Cincinnati, are the two major concentrations of suburbs in Kentucky. Together, connected by a strip of rural Kentucky extending 120 miles along the Ohio River, they make up the state's 4th Congressional District. On the riverfront across from Cincinnati are the two old, gritty cities of Covington and Newport on the lowlands by the river, as well as old affluent suburbs like Fort Thomas and new middle-income suburbs like Florence and Erlanger on the heights which overlook Cincinnati. Historically these counties, like Cincinnati, have leaned Republican; and so they go in most Kentucky elections. But, with media oriented more to Ohio than Kentucky, people here seem to have political attitudes less anchored to a traditional party preference, and so they are often swing areas. The Louisville suburbs, on the other hand, which include about 40% of the 4th District's voters, are Republican both by heritage and current inclination. The 4th goes right up to the city limits on Louisville's more affluent east side; it includes the farther out, more Republican suburbs on the less affluent south and west sides.

The central, connecting corridor of the district is quite different. Here you find tobacco fields along the Ohio River bottomlands, small farms with wooden fences in the knobby hills a few miles inland, and the old river town of Carrollton near where the Kentucky River that winds through the Bluegrass country flows into the Ohio. This part of Kentucky was settled nearly 200 years ago, and it has been heavily—often almost unanimously—Democratic since the Civil War. It casts only 10% of the 4th District's votes, but those are heavily Democratic.

The 4th District has a freshman congressman who made headlines 30 years before he was elected, Republican Jim Bunning. Bunning was a major league baseball pitcher and a good one; he threw a no-hitter for the Detroit Tigers in 1958 and pitched a perfect game for the Philadelphia Phillies in 1964; he also played for the Pittsburgh Pirates, the Los Angeles Dodgers and the Phillies again and retired in 1971 with a 224–184 record. He also had one of the highest totals in baseball history for hitting batters, 160, as compared to 18 for his contemporary Sandy Koufax and 40 for Juan Marichal. He just missed getting into the Hall of Fame in 1987 and 1988.

Though he never played for the Cincinnati Reds, Bunning got involved in Kentucky politics, was elected to the state Senate in 1979, and won a respectable 44% as the Republican nominee against Governor Martha Layne Collins in 1983. Gene Snyder, 4th District incumbent from the Louisville suburbs and ranking Republican on the Public Works Committee called it quits early in 1986. Bunning quickly sewed up the Republican nomination and, as it turned out, the election. Democratic legislator Terry Mann from the Cincinnati suburbs had run a strong race against Snyder in 1982. But Mann's tenure was hurt when it was revealed that he had jimmied his automatic voting device with a rubber band in Frankfort so that he would be recorded as present when he was not. Mann still carried the river counties. But Bunning, with 52% in the Cincinnati suburbs and 63% around Louisville, won with 55% of the vote.

In his first term, Bunning showed himself an aggressive conservative. He spent some time on the Banking Committee attacking the policies of the World Bank—a favorite target of supply-siders. He votes against any spending increase over 2% but was proud of getting $27 million for an IRS center in Covington. Reelected easily in 1988, he seems to have a long House career ahead of him—if not statewide office.

The People: Est. Pop. 1986: 539,000, up 3.0% 1980–86; Pop. 1980: 523,090, up 18.6% 1970–80. Households (1980): 79% family, 46% with children, 68% married couples; 26.6% housing units rented; median monthly rent: $175; median house value: $43,400. Voting age pop. (1980): 363,075; 2% Black.

1988 Presidential Vote:

Bush (R)	135,832	(65%)
Dukakis (D)	72,430	(35%)

Rep. Jim Bunning (R)

Elected 1986; b. Oct 23, 1931, Campbell County; home, Southgate; Xavier U., B.S. 1953; Roman Catholic; married (Mary).

Career: Professional baseball player, 1950–71; investment broker and agent, 1960–86; Ft. Thomas City Cncl., 1977–79; KY Senate, 1979–83.

Offices: 116 CHOB 20515, 202-225-3465. Also 1717 Dixie Hwy., Ste. 160, Fort Wright 41011, 606-341-2602; and 10301 Linn Station Rd., Ste. 105, Louisville 40223, 502-429-5588.

Committees: *Banking, Finance and Urban Affairs* (16th of 20 R). Subcommittees: Housing and Community Development; Financial Institutions Supervision, Regulation and Insurance; Domestic Monetary Policy. *Merchant Marine and Fisheries* (15th of 17 R). Subcommittees: Merchant Marine; Coast Guard and Navigation.

Group Ratings

	ADA	ACLU	COPE	CFA	LCV	ACU	NTLC	NSI	COC	CEI
1988	0	17	7	45	19	100	87	100	100	74
1987	4	—	6	14	—	87	—	—	93	79

National Journal Ratings

	1988 LIB — 1988 CONS		1987 LIB — 1987 CONS	
Economic	9% —	91%	11% —	83%
Social	20% —	78%	0% —	90%
Foreign	0% —	84%	0% —	80%

Key Votes

1) Homeless $	FOR	5) Ban Drug Test	FOR	9) SDI Research	FOR
2) Gephardt Amdt	AGN	6) Drug Death Pen	FOR	10) Ban Chem Weaps	AGN
3) Deficit Reduc	AGN	7) Handgun Sales	FOR	11) Aid to Contras	FOR
4) Kill Plnt Clsng Notice	FOR	8) Ban D.C. Abort $	FOR	12) Nuclear Testing	AGN

Election Results

1988 general	Jim Bunning (R).....................	145,609	(74%)	($468,870)
	Richard V. Beliles (D).................	50,575	(26%)	($23,636)
1988 primary	Jim Bunning (R), unopposed			
1986 general	Jim Bunning (R).....................	67,626	(55%)	($895,709)
	Terry L. Mann (D)..................	53,906	(44%)	($332,845)

FIFTH DISTRICT

If you wanted to find the congressional district most consistently and solidly Republican over the course of the 20th century, you would do well to look not in high-income suburbs or Rocky Mountain redoubts. You would be well advised to avoid the Sun Belt and high-income areas altogether, and go to the Cumberland Plateau in the south central part of Kentucky. There, in an area with some of the lowest income levels in the United States, is the 5th Congressional District of Kentucky, one of the most Republican parts of the nation.

Roots run deep here. Most people in these hills are the descendants of people whose families had already been there two or three generations by the time of the Civil War; and over the years, cousins have married so that it seems that practically everyone in a community is related to everyone else. Handed down are living memories of the old ways of doing things, when the only contact with the outside world was a steamboat coming up a narrow river, as one did as late as the 1930s, or a coal company owner's agent suddenly ordering the digging up of farmers' land. Harriet Arnow's *Seedtime in the Cumberland* relays the memories of her parents, that go back to the time when thousands of settlers were following Daniel Boone through the Cumberland Gap into Kentucky; and John Egerton's *Generations* tells the story of Burnam and Addie Ledford, born in 1876 and 1885, who remembered a great-grandparent who had come to Kentucky in the 1790s and who were the proofreaders of Egerton's book in 1982. In this perspective, the 1931 feud that divides the numerous Sizemores of Clay County is only yesterday, and the Civil War, which threatened people's lives and everything they had, is recent history. Here in the mountains of Kentucky, people are still living in the same communities, attending the same churches, farming the same land, and voting the same party as their grandparents and great-great-grandparents did, and in most cases, in this pro-Union, anti-slaveholding area, it is the Republican Party. The major exception is Harlan County, known as Bloody Harlan during the union organizing days of the 1930s, where the influence of the United Mine Workers is evident in its Democratic voting habits.

The 5th District always goes Republican in presidential and congressional elections, and its congressman is an aggressive Republican, Hal Rogers. Rogers won the seat in the 1980 primary, an 11-candidate contest in which he played up his association with his predecessor, Dr. Tim Lee Carter. In the House, Rogers served first on Energy and Commerce and then on the Appropriations Committee—plum assignments for this (or any) district. Rogers is a conservative on most issues, but not always on economics; politically, he was for Gerald Ford over Ronald Reagan in 1976. But clearly what is most important to him is serving the interests of his district. He is a tiger on coal and tobacco issues. He gets interested in broader issues when they affect folks back home: pipeline safety after several natural gas explosions in Kentucky, restricting textile imports because there are 13,000 textile workers in the district. He is a vociferous critic of any form of smoking ban and a supporter of tobacco programs; they ban cigarette advertising in Poland, he says, and yet have the world's highest smoking rate. He aggressively pushes forward the Cumberland Gap Tunnel, the Big South Fork flood control, clean coal technology and fish farming.

With his record and the 5th District's strong Republican leanings, Rogers has a safe seat.

The People: Est. Pop. 1986: 543,700, up 3.8% 1980–86; Pop. 1980: 523,664, up 22.4% 1970–80. Households (1980): 82% family, 47% with children, 70% married couples; 26.2% housing units rented; median monthly rent: $100; median house value: $25,000. Voting age pop. (1980): 359,513; 2% Black, 1% Spanish origin.

1988 Presidential Vote:

Bush (R)	120,671	(66%)
Dukakis (D)	59,945	(33%)

Rep. Harold (Hal) Rogers (R)

Elected 1980; b. Dec. 31, 1937, Barrier; home, Somerset; U. of KY, B.A. 1962, J.D. 1964; Baptist; married (Shirley).

Career: Practicing atty., 1964–69; Pulaski-Rockcastle Commonwealth Atty., 1969–81; Repub. Nominee for Lt. Gov. of KY, 1979.

Offices: 206 CHOB 20515, 202-225-4601. Also 203 E. Mount Vernon St., Somerset 42501, 606-679-8346.

Committees: *Appropriations* (15th of 22 R). Subcommittee: Commerce, Justice, State, the Judiciary and Related Agencies (Ranking Member). *Budget* (6th of 14 R). Task Forces: Community Development and Natural Resources; Economic Policy, Projections and Revenues.

Group Ratings

	ADA	ACLU	COPE	CFA	LCV	ACU	NTLC	NSI	COC	CEI
1988	5	13	26	45	19	96	67	100	100	56
1987	4	—	27	14	—	78	—	—	80	52

National Journal Ratings

	1988 LIB — 1988 CONS		1987 LIB — 1987 CONS	
Economic	17% —	82%	31% —	68%
Social	20% —	78%	0% —	90%
Foreign	16% —	78%	0% —	80%

Key Votes

1) Homeless $	FOR	5) Ban Drug Test	FOR	9) SDI Research	FOR
2) Gephardt Amdt	AGN	6) Drug Death Pen	FOR	10) Ban Chem Weaps	AGN
3) Deficit Reduc	AGN	7) Handgun Sales	FOR	11) Aid to Contras	FOR
4) Kill Plnt Clsng Notice	FOR	8) Ban D.C. Abort $	FOR	12) Nuclear Testing	AGN

Election Results

1988 general	Harold (Hal) Rogers (R), unopposed		($119,720)
1988 primary	Harold (Hal) Rogers (R), unopposed		
1986 general	Harold (Hal) Rogers (R)	56,760 (100%)	($253,110)

SIXTH DISTRICT

When Queen Elizabeth II came to America in 1984 on an unofficial tour to inspect horseflesh, it was almost inevitable that she would come to a farm (owned by George Bush's frequent host, Will Farish) outside Lexington in the Bluegrass country of Kentucky. Lexington was founded in 1779, just a few years after Daniel Boone led the first settlers through the Cumberland Gap; horse racing started here in 1787, and the jockey club was founded in 1797. The Bluegrass has been horse country ever since. Lexington has the fastest-growing economies of Kentucky, with an IBM plant and the headquarters of Island Creek Coal and dozens of smaller operations, but when you get past the built-up areas, you find the rolling green meadows where thoroughbreds graze behind white wooden fences; stately mansions on hillocks overlooking the fields; you might almost imagine for a minute the colonel sitting on the porch, dressed in a white suit and sipping a mint julep. The Bluegrass country around Lexington is one of those places where a cliche comes (almost) true; and despite the growth of new horse-breeding areas, a huge percentage of North America's fastest horses are bred and nurtured here in this land of mineral-rich grass.

The Bluegrass area has history too. These fertile valleys and hills, where the grass seems to shine blue in the spring, were the promised land that Daniel Boone and the thousands who came over the Cumberland Gap were seeking in the late 1700s and early 1800s—the first American West. Coming around a corner from a horse farm you may run into small towns with houses built as long ago as the 1810s—like Georgetown; although the next sight there is the Toyota plant that Kentucky coaxed and cajoled to locate here. Lexington's growth has spread into adjacent counties, leapfrogging the horse farms and jumping into places like Frankfort, the small town where the state Capitol sits between the Kentucky River and hills and trees. At the same time, Lexington has been sprucing up its downtown with a Festival Market and a Victorian Square, trolley cars and new museums.

The Bluegrass has countervailing historic tendencies. Lexington's Henry Clay was a Whig, and surely would have opposed secession (though one of his sons backed it); but Lexington's John Breckinridge, elected Vice President in 1856 at 35 (the youngest ever), fought on the Confederate side; Mary Todd Lincoln was a Lexington girl, and all her relatives were Rebels. For most of the 20th century, the political tendency in these parts has been Democratic, enough so that Jimmy Carter carried the 6th Congressional District that includes most of the Bluegrass country in both 1976 and 1980. But even then there was an obvious Republican trend in Lexington, as its population grew increasingly faster; and by the late 1980s, that trend seemed to have spread to the adjacent Bluegrass counties. Michael Dukakis, despite a respectable 44% statewide showing in Kentucky, carried only one tiny county in the 6th District in 1988.

The congressman from the 6th District is a Republican, Larry Hopkins, who was first elected in 1978 in something of a fluke, and who is now rising to the top of the House Armed Services Committee. Hopkins was not even the Republican nominee in 1978 when the incumbent, Democrat John C. Breckinridge (a descendant of the original), was beaten by a liberal in the primary; the Republicans dumped their 68-year-old nominee, Mary Louise Foust, and named Hopkins, then a state senator, instead. They gave him a $300,000 campaign budget and helped him campaign against the Democrat by calling him a backer of big government, big labor and big spending. That was enough to give him a 2 to 1 margin in Lexington and a 51%–46% districtwide victory. In 1980 and 1982, he won by solid margins; since then he has won overwhelmingly.

On Armed Services Hopkins's major accomplishment was to sponsor, with the late Bill Nichols of Alabama, the Pentagon reorganization bill. This was one of the major legislative products of 1986, and had its genesis in trips Nichols and Hopkins took to Beirut when American Marines were stationed there: both warned that the Marines were in danger and were appalled when 249 Marines were killed by an explosion. They were appalled also that the command structure of the military is so convoluted as to make it very difficult to take sensible precautions. Nichols, who was gravely wounded in World War II, and Hopkins, who served in the Marines in Korea, took the lead in fashioning a positive response, and pushed it through despite the opposition of Caspar Weinberger's Pentagon.

Otherwise, Hopkins tends to local matters. He is interested in nerve gas, especially since the Army has agreed to study how to destroy old nerve gas in the Blue Grass Army Depot just south of Lexington. On the Agriculture Committee—in contrast to many Republicans who have seats on no important committees, Hopkins has seats on two—Hopkins naturally looks after the interests of burley tobacco growers. (Kentucky is the number two tobacco state, and essentially the only producer of burley.) He is ranking Republican on the Tobacco and Peanuts Subcommittee, and of course he opposes any changes in the small tobacco subsidy or cozy tobacco allotment programs. But on both military and farm issues he has shown some originality and thoughtfulness which, together with the general Republican shift in the Bluegrass country, help to explain his very strong electoral showings in the 6th District.

The People: Est. Pop. 1986: 537,600, up 3.6% 1980–86; Pop. 1980: 519,009, up 18.5% 1970–80. Households (1980): 74% family, 41% with children, 61% married couples; 38.7% housing units rented; median monthly rent: $174; median house value: $43,800. Voting age pop. (1980): 377,249; 9% Black, 1% Spanish origin.

1988 Presidential Vote:

Bush (R)	112,162	(57%)
Dukakis (D)	82,755	(42%)

Rep. Larry J. Hopkins (R)

Elected 1978; b. Oct. 25, 1933, Detroit, MI; home, Lexington; Murray St. U.; United Methodist; married (Carolyn).

Career: USMC, 1954–56; stockbroker; Fayette Cnty. Clerk, 1969–72; KY House of Reps., 1972–78; KY Senate, 1978.

Offices: 2437 RHOB, 202-225-4706. Also Vine Ctr., 333 W. Vine St., Rm. 207, Lexington 40507, 606-233-2848.

Committees: *Agriculture* (4th of 17 R). Subcommittees: Livestock, Dairy and Poultry; Tobacco and Peanuts (Ranking Member). *Armed Services* (5th of 21 R). Subcommittees: Procurement and Military Nuclear Systems; Investigations (Ranking Member).

Group Ratings

	ADA	ACLU	COPE	CFA	LCV	ACU	NTLC	NSI	COC	CEI
1988	20	26	26	27	19	76	84	90	93	57
1987	0	—	25	14	—	77	—	—	93	76

National Journal Ratings

	1988 LIB — 1988 CONS		1987 LIB — 1987 CONS	
Economic	13% —	85%	22% —	78%
Social	26% —	73%	0% —	90%
Foreign	27% —	71%	20% —	76%

Key Votes

1) Homeless $	FOR	5) Ban Drug Test	FOR	9) SDI Research	FOR
2) Gephardt Amdt	AGN	6) Drug Death Pen	FOR	10) Ban Chem Weaps	AGN
3) Deficit Reduc	AGN	7) Handgun Sales	FOR	11) Aid to Contras	FOR
4) Kill Plnt Clsng Notice	FOR	8) Ban D.C. Abort $	FOR	12) Nuclear Testing	AGN

Election Results

1988 general	Larry J. Hopkins (R)	128,898	(74%)	($295,333)
	Milton Patton (D).....................	45,339	(26%)	($46,610)
1988 primary	Larry J. Hopkins (R), unopposed			
1986 general	Larry J. Hopkins (R)	75,906	(74%)	($160,669)
	Jerry W. Hammond (D)	26,315	(26%)	($10,141)

SEVENTH DISTRICT

Fifty years ago, in the counties of eastern Kentucky that now make up the 7th Congressional District, there were 579,000 people; by 1970 there were only 459,000. You can liven up those statistics by recalling the ballads that record the loneliness of the hillbilly in Detroit City, or by noting the number of cars heading south on I-75 on any three-day weekend, hill people heading home. The Appalachian region of Kentucky has been one of the poorest parts of the nation since it was first settled; there is hardly a flat acre of ground anywhere, and almost no good farmland; the roads even today are twisting, up and down hills and through hollows, and there is an air of isolation, of being out of touch with anywhere else, even today. And yet these mountains are still home to hundreds of thousands of hill people, almost all of them descendants of the original settlers, who came here with or not long after Daniel Boone, right after the Revolutionary War. When the economy turns up, as when coal prices rose in the 1970s, people come back: the population rose from 459,000 in 1970 to 526,000 in 1980; since then prices have sagged, and some residents have moved out, and in 1986 the population was just barely up to 532,000.

In the 19th century people found that these mountain ridges were undergirded with thick veins of coal. That meant prosperity, and suffering: coal is a difficult mistress. Conditions in underground mines were usually dreadful; the old songs probably understate the miners' misery and dependence and isolation. Then, in the 1930s, the United Mine Workers moved in and organized most of eastern Kentucky's mines, but this was no easy task; there was violence, bloodshed, something approaching civil war. Mostly the union won, and in the short run raised wages and built hospitals for the miners and their families; in the longer run, the UMW planned to and did phase out jobs in the mines, in return for job security and health benefits, as coal was replaced by oil as our major fuel.

Economic change was accompanied by political change. The hills had been solidly Republican since they supported the Union during the Civil War. But the UMW organizing drives and the New Deal converted many miners and their families to the Democratic Party, raising Democratic percentages as much as 40%—a vast change in Kentucky, where political allegiances otherwise have mostly stayed the same for a century. The 7th District has voted Democratic in every election since the New Deal except 1972.

The plight of the 7th District, and other parts of Appalachia like it, inspired in the 1960s many of the nation's antipoverty programs. One of the architects of those programs was Carl Perkins, the district's congressman from 1948 until his death in 1984. During the days when the Great Society laws were enacted, Perkins was the number two Democrat on the House Education and Labor Committee, which had jurisdiction over many of the bills; when Adam Clayton Powell was thrown out of the House in 1967, Perkins became chairman. He held that position for 17 years, tenaciously guarding his programs, fighting first to expand them and later against cuts. He was one of the last really strong committee chairmen, making sure that only sympathetic Democrats got on his committee, negotiating like a master poker player, and fighting for what he believed in. The Appalachia program, the various aid to education programs, the more generous welfare programs of the 1960s, have improved life in the 7th District and made it more prosperous and more comfortable. He died suddenly, after pushing through the equal access (for extracurricular religious groups) bill in 1984.

The current congressman is his son, Carl C. Perkins, generally known as Chris, born six years after his father was first elected. A Kentucky legislator for four years, the younger Perkins was given the Democratic nomination, the seat and spots on the Education and Labor and Science committees. Perkins has stoutly supported higher minimum wages, more generous education programs, black lung benefits, highways; in his first term, he passed vocational education and Kentucky wilderness bills. In 1988, after a hasty divorce and remarriage, he was challenged by Republican Will Scott, a former Pike County Judge, who charged that Perkins, brought up in northern Virginia, educated in North Carolina and Louisville, was an outsider and had a lifestyle that required $23,000 a month. Scott made inroads into the base Democratic vote in Pike and Floyd Counties, but still Perkins won 59% overall—something of a rebuke, but not a real threat to his seat. He reportedly says he wants to be a congressman "for the rest of my life," and he may very well be.

The People: Est. Pop. 1986: 532,000, up 1.1% 1980–86; Pop. 1980: 526,284, up 23.4% 1970–80. Households (1980): 83% family, 49% with children, 71% married couples; 25.1% housing units rented; median monthly rent: $113; median house value: $27,900. Voting age pop. (1980): 356,178; 1% Black, 1% Spanish origin.

1988 Presidential Vote:

Dukakis (D)	98,621	(55%)
Bush (R)	78,616	(44%)

Rep. Carl C. (Chris) Perkins (D)

Elected 1984; b. Aug. 6, 1954, Washington, D.C.; home, Leburn; Davidson Col., B.S. 1976, U. of Louisville, J.D. 1978; Baptist; married (Jan).

Career: Practicing atty., 1979–84; law clerk and Asst. Commonwealth Atty.; Jefferson Cnty., 1977–78; TV talk show host; KY House of Reps., 1981–84.

Offices: 1004 LHOB 20515, 202-225-4935. Also Fed. Bldg., Pikeville 41501, 606-432-4191; P.O. Box 127, Ashland 41101, 606-325-8530; and P.O. Box 486, Morehead 40351, 606-784-1000.

Committees: *Education and Labor* (12th of 22 D). Subcommittees: Elementary, Secondary, and Vocational Education; Labor Standards; Postsecondary Education. *Science, Space and Technology* (21st of 29 D). Subcommittees: Science, Research and Technology; Space Science and Applications.

Group Ratings

	ADA	ACLU	COPE	CFA	LCV	ACU	NTLC	NSI	COC	CEI
1988	85	78	95	82	44	12	5	0	14	6
1987	84	—	94	86	—	4	—	—	7	6

National Journal Ratings

	1988 LIB — 1988 CONS	1987 LIB — 1987 CONS
Economic	87% — 8%	73% — 0%
Social	64% — 34%	56% — 43%
Foreign	79% — 16%	76% — 19%

Key Votes

1) Homeless $	AGN	5) Ban Drug Test	AGN	9) SDI Research	AGN
2) Gephardt Amdt	FOR	6) Drug Death Pen	FOR	10) Ban Chem Weaps	FOR
3) Deficit Reduc	FOR	7) Handgun Sales	FOR	11) Aid to Contras	AGN
4) Kill Plnt Clsng Notice	AGN	8) Ban D.C. Abort $	FOR	12) Nuclear Testing	FOR

Election Results

1988 general	Carl C. (Chris) Perkins (D)	96,946	(59%)	($411,699)
	William T. Scott (R)	68,165	(41%)	($432,403)
1988 primary	Carl C. (Chris) Perkins (D), unopposed			
1986 general	Carl C. (Chris) Perkins (D)	90,619	(80%)	($240,757)
	James T. (Jim) Polley (R)	23,209	(20%)	($57,712)

LOUISIANA

More than 50 years ago, on September 8, 1935, in the halls of the 34-story state Capitol he built in Baton Rouge, Huey P. Long was shot down; two days later, after malpractice by his doctors, he died. No other American politician has cast a longer shadow over his state's politics after such a short career. Long had been elected governor only in 1928, he had been nearly impeached early in his term, he recovered and was elected Senator in 1932, but remained in Baton Rouge, in iron control by then of the legislature, wandering to the podium with drafts of bills he insisted be passed without changing a comma. By 1935, he had a following all over the country and was considering running for President. Long came from no political background, he had no money or connections, yet he moved up so quickly that he was only 42 when he died; nor was his platform—"Share the wealth, Every man a king"—so very unusual in an American politics that saw periodically local demagogues demand a redistribution of wealth.

What was extraordinary about Long was that he was so talented and competent that he actually did what he promised. He took over a Louisiana that had the economy and labor force and public services of an underdeveloped country—a thin layer of rich people and some big oil company operations layered over a mass of barely literate poor people of both races, Baptist and Cajun—and within a few years he built the Capitol and Louisiana State University and the biggest bridge over the Mississippi River and the second-highest number of paved roads in the entire country. He also built a political machine so effective it reminded many Americans of contemporary dictatorships in Europe. What scared people about Huey Long was not what he promised but what they feared he could deliver.

For America, as it turned out, what he delivered was little more than entertainment; for Louisiana, he delivered a political structure that revolved around him long after he was dead—and a class of political leaders who, lacking his talents, treated the state as his doctors treated his wound, leaving Louisiana without either a fully developed economy or a fully competent public sector. For the next half-century, until Senator Russell Long's retirement in 1986, protégés of Huey and members of the Long family held high political office in Louisiana; elections up through the 1956 gubernatorial primary won by Earl Long split on pro- and anti-Long lines. Huey Long built a coalition of the poor, including some blacks, against the rich and better off; he never did well in New Orleans, where even the poor had paved streets, electricity, and public schools—unlike the rural parishes when the Kingfish came along.

But in time other divisions in Louisiana reasserted themselves. A state that in many ways seemed nonchalant about race got caught up in the 1950s with violent opposition to school desegregation, and in the 1960, 1964 and 1968 state campaigns voted for the candidates who seemed most anti-desegregation and anti-New Orleans. Then, around 1970, as racial animosity cooled and as the price of oil—Louisiana was then the nation's number two producer, and a big refiner—shot up, state politics seemed redolent of Louisiana's peculiar historic and cultural heritage. For Louisiana, as A. J. Liebling described it 25 years ago, is an outpost of the Levant along the Gulf of Mexico. While most of the United States faces east toward the Atlantic Ocean or west toward the Pacific, Louisiana faces resolutely south, to the Gulf of Mexico and the steamy heat and volatile societies of Latin America beyond; New Orleans is our one major city that preserves the look and feel it had as a French and Spanish outpost in the New World; Louisiana is the only state whose legal system comes not from British common law but from the Napoleonic Code of continental Europe.

Traditions of centralized control and lazy corruption are part of this heritage. Control was necessary, because the delta land that makes up half of the state—soggy, swampy, below sea level, laced with tributaries and offshoots of the Mississippi, bayous and major rivers like the Atchafalaya—can only be cultivated with vast capital expenditures for levees and drainage. Even today, houses here don't have basements, people are buried in above-ground cemeteries (with grandiose headstones), and at the outskirts of metro New Orleans, the swamp abruptly begins at the edges of subdivisions and people find alligators in their back yards. New Orleans, the nation's fifth largest city when the Civil War broke out, and the grand plantations along the Mississippi housed some of the nation's richest plutocrats and vast numbers of its poorest people; in the years after, some of the rich held onto their wealth (and are notoriously unventuresome and tight-knit) and New Orleans remained a great port—its position at the mouth of the Mississippi and as the terminus of the Illinois Central Railroad guaranteed that.

But Louisiana became one of the poorest of states, its large black population still working on what had been sugar, rice, and cotton plantations, its large Cajun population—descended from French settlers forced out of Nova Scotia by the British in 1755—spread out among the bayous in the swampy southern part of the state. But that is also where most of Louisiana's oil is, and the towns that service its offshore rigs; and in the 1960s, as the rural South sent migrants northward, the Cajun country was generating more than enough jobs for its numerous sons and daughters. Coinciding with this development was the emergence in 1972 of Edwin Edwards—very much a Cajun, despite the name—a young congressman running for governor. Although one-third of Louisianans are Catholic—not just Cajuns, but most New Orleans area whites as well—no Catholic had been elected governor for years; but Edwards joyously proclaimed his heritage. He won only narrowly that year, beating Bennett Johnston in the runoff 50.2%–49.8% and David Treen in the general election 57%–43%.

For the next dozen years Edwards set the tone of government and public life in Louisiana. *"Laissez les bons temps rouler!"* Edwards proclaimed, savoring life with the zest of spicy, crawfish-laden, heavy-on-the-roux Cajun cuisine. As oil prices soared, Louisiana enjoyed a prosperity it had never dreamed of. This was one state which did not see itself as a victim of economic trends and in which big economic institutions were regarded with respect rather than mistrust. In Latin fashion politicians and businessmen were judged by results, not procedure. Under Edwards, Louisiana politics combined a Levantine tolerance of the means by which the world's business must be done with a Latin American gaudiness and fondness for display.

But the times that rolled ahead were not good. Edwards could easily have won a third term in

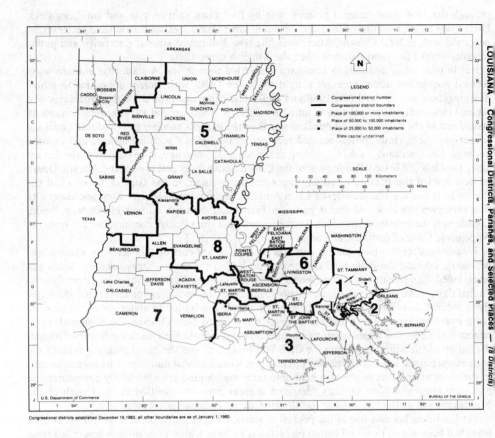

LEGEND

2 Congressional district number
   Congressional district boundary
⊙ Place of 100,000 or more inhabitants
◉ Place of 50,000 to 100,000 inhabitants
• Place of 25,000 to 50,000 inhabitants
   State capital underlined

SCALE
0 20 40 60 80 100 Kilometers
0 20 40 60 80 100 Miles

U.S. Department of Commerce   BUREAU OF THE CENSUS

Congressional districts established December 19, 1983; all other boundaries are as of January 1, 1980.

1979 had he been eligible. Instead, Republican David Treen won after a multi-candidate campaign of expenditures so lavish as to rival those in the contemporaneous contest in that other oil republic of Venezuela on the other side of the Caribbean. (The campaign was run under a system Edwards invented, after having to contest three elections in 1972 when Treen had to fight only one. All candidates run in a first primary, and anyone who wins 50% is elected; if no one does, the top two finishers, regardless of party, run off several weeks later.) Edwards came back and beat Treen handily in 1983, but the *bons temps* were not *roulezing* any more: oil prices had collapsed, and so had Louisiana's economy.

Forty years ago, the state's income level was about 60% of the national average, and in 1970 it had reached only about 75%; by 1982 it reached 90%, within striking distance, given the local low cost of living. But in 1985 it was back down to 81% and falling, and in 1986 Louisiana lost population for the first time in history, and by March 1989 the state's unemployment rate was estimated and 9.6%, down from 13% in 1986, but still the highest in the nation. The state government that had a $700 million surplus in 1982 faced a $400 million deficit in 1986, and was forced to sell its own bonds to recoup its losses. Even as the 1984 Summer Olympics in Los Angeles were a symbol of the nation's mood of optimism and pride, the financial fiasco of New Orleans's 1984 World's Fair became a metaphor for Louisiana's troubles.

Louisiana was further humiliated by the trials of Edwin Edwards, in 1985 on bribery charges, and in 1986 on federal charges of steering to his brother profits that he and others made by obtaining approval certificates for hospitals from state government officials, who in exchange were promised promotions when Edwards returned to office. Edwards admitted—bragged—that he made $2 million on the deal, but argued the deal was made when he was a private citizen and was perfectly legal. One jury hung 11 to 1 for acquittal and another let him off: the prosecution seemed as competent as Huey Long's doctors. But politically Edwards's ratings plummeted while he went off during recesses in the trial to pay telephones to confer with appointees and legislators about the state's burgeoning deficits. Within two years of returning to office as the most popular and commanding politician Louisiana had seen since Huey Long, Edwards had rock-bottom ratings in polls, and his proposals for populist solutions—a state lottery, licensing 13 casinos in New Orleans, letting the governor rearrange the state budget single-handedly—were rejected by the legislature.

With the collapse of oil prices, Louisiana in the middle 1980s developed something closer to a classic economics-based politics than could be found anywhere else in the United States. Just as the economic politics following the Second New Deal of 1935, and the accompanying CIO industrial union movement, took deepest root in the part of the country that had grown most rapidly in the previous decade (the coal-steel-auto industrial country from Pittsburgh through Ohio and Michigan to Chicago), so this economic politics has become rooted in the part of the country—Louisiana and the southeast corner of Texas—where giddily rapid growth was followed suddenly by sickeningly rapid collapse. Louisiana's affection for free enterprise and opposition to government regulation, always based on self-interest rather than principle, vanished in a trice, to be replaced among the less well-off by a fervent desire to use government to redistribute income and among the more affluent by a rigid desire to prevent such redistribution at almost all costs.

The two sides turn out to be pretty well balanced in Louisiana. The quarter of the electorate that is black is joined by enough less well-off whites to make Louisiana's last three big elections close—and to guarantee victory to neither side. In 1986, when Senator Russell Long retired, Republican Henson Moore proclaimed, "the party's over, it's morning in Louisiana"—an obvious attack on Edwards. But he was beaten by Democrat John Breaux who had solid support in Cajun areas and was the beneficiary of a big black vote after a hamhanded Republican attempt to dampen black turnout by a "ballot security" program was publicized.

In the 1987 governor's race, Edwards was the populist candidate, backing more spending on education and welfare, his roguishness and irregularities tolerated by voters who idolized Huey Long and have few scruples about the political process. Edwards won near-unanimous support from blacks and ran well among some low-income whites. But his Cajun base was badly eroded: he lost votes there not only to Congressman Billy Tauzin, a fellow Cajun and former ally who entered the race before Edwards announced and ultimately won 10%, but also to Shreveport area Congressman Buddy Roemer. Republican Congressman Bob Livingston hoped to make a strong race, but a moment of weakness when his mind wandered in debate undermined his candidacy, and he carried only his affluent base in metro New Orleans, enough for 19% statewide. Roemer started with his base in northern Louisiana, but also ran well among affluent whites in Baton Rouge, Lake Charles and Lafayette, all of which he carried, and got one out of five votes in metro New Orleans as well. That gave him a statewide total of 33%, putting him ahead of Edwards, who had 28%. Edwards, saying that if he couldn't finish first he shouldn't be running, and probably calculating that he couldn't expand much on his base, conceded without a runoff, and suddenly Buddy Roemer was the new governor of Louisiana.

Breaux's sensational victory in 1986 was hailed as evidence that Louisiana was now a populist state, but Roemer's gubernatorial victory in 1987 is evidence that the anti-populist side can also win. The 1988 presidential election, in which Michael Dukakis held George Bush to a 54%–44% win in this culturally not very liberal state, is evidence of the same. In recent decades most

American states have been moving away from an economics-based politics toward one in which voters are divided more along cultural lines. Louisiana provides another model, and a picture—not an altogether pretty one—of where American politics, if the whole country goes through the boom-bust cycle that Louisiana did, might go.

Governor. Buddy Roemer came to office proclaiming a "Roemer revolution" and portraying himself as an anti-political reformer—an interesting feat since his father, Charles Roemer, was one of Edwards's top staffers and went to jail on bribery charges. Impatient, impulsive, given to inspiring oratory, he rubs many politicians the wrong way. But he should not be mistaken for an Edwards or Long style populist. In Congress, he voted more often with Republicans on economic issues than just about any other Democrat, and his fiscal reform plan—to shift taxes from businesses to the property tax which is often a dead letter now because of a generous homestead exemption—was largely drawn up by Jim Bob Moffett, head of New Orleans's biggest company, Freeport-McMoRan. What he is selling is uplift and reform, not spending and sharing the wealth.

When he came to office, Louisiana had the nation's highest unemployment, illiteracy, and school dropout rate. It was facing a $750 million deficit on a $5 billion budget and had $1.37 billion in outstanding debt. Roemer got emergency budget powers, cut payrolls and $500 million in spending (mostly on social services), and maintained a $700 million "temporary" sales tax. He raised teachers' salaries but took away tenure. He pushed through a campaign finance bill limiting contributions, raised fines for industrial pollution, and cut unemployment benefits and workmen's compensation. He even modified Louisiana's Napoleonic Code to get it in line with the English common law tradition. How this agenda of conservative reform works will be tested when Roemer comes up for reelection in fall 1991.

Presidential politics. With its economics-based politics, Louisiana has the potential to become a competitive state in presidential elections; it certainly was when southerner Jimmy Carter was running, and it almost was in 1988. There is a large black vote here, and the Cajun vote has gone Democratic in national contests.

Senators. Bennett Johnston, Louisiana's senior Senator, is one of Capitol Hill's smarter political operators—but also one of its more disappointed ones. At home he seems strong, and he chairs one of the Senate's major committees. But he failed in late 1988 to achieve his ambition of becoming Senate Majority Leader. He remains an important Senator as chairman of the Energy and Natural Resources Committee. In the 1970s, this committee was drafting complex energy price legislation, and Johnston was in the thick of the details. In the late 1980s, as energy prices were decontrolled, difficulties with nuclear weapons facilities and possible shortfalls in electricity production emerged as problems; but oil and natural gas still present plenty of issues. Naturally, Johnston is sympathetic to producers' interests, but he emphasizes that he is not a creature of Big Oil; he is much more responsive to the more numerous small producers (who tend to be very rich individuals and able political fundraisers). On the Appropriations Committee, Johnston is chairman of the Energy and Water Development Subcommittee, which together with the Energy chair gives him as much to say on a wide range of environmental issues as any Senator. Like most Louisianans, he is alert to the need for economic growth and not interested in curtailing development, but is also aware that some development really can ruin things worth keeping.

Johnston spent much of the second Reagan term running for Majority Leader. Discontented with Robert Byrd, he backed Lawton Chiles against Byrd in 1984, and in 1986 was himself a declared candidate for the Democratic leadership; he took himself out of the race before the election, when it became clear that Byrd had the votes. For 1988, he ran early and hard against Daniel Inouye and George Mitchell. In 1987, with superb timing, he became the first conservative southern Democrat to announce he would vote against the confirmation of Robert Bork—a move that made the Bork nomination a partisan issue and, in a Democratic Senate, defeated it. Yet, in the contest for Majority Leader, Johnston was unable to win many northerners' votes and did not hold the South. In the end, when Mitchell led 27–14–14, Johnston and Inouye sensibly decided to dispense with a second ballot. Will Johnston rebound from this setback? He has high committee positions on Budget as well as Energy and Appropriations (though not a warm relationship with the new Appropriations chairman, Robert Byrd), he has a natural dealmaking ability and he is capable of mastering details well enough to make him one of the Senate's toughest negotiators in conference. He can also be a key fundraiser for other Senate Democrats.

At least once earlier in his career, Johnston ended up winning big by losing. In 1972, he lost the gubernatorial primary to Edwin Edwards by 4,488 votes out of 1.1 million cast. Months later, he was the only major politician to file against Senator Allen Ellender, a Huey Long protege who had held the seat since 1936; Ellender died between the filing date and the primary, and Johnston won the seat easily. In 1978, he was held to 59% by conservative legislator Woody Jenkins, who was not taken too seriously; in 1984, he drew only nuisance opposition (one candidate appeared on the ballot as Larry Napoleon "Boo-Ga-Loo" Cooper) and won the seat with 86% in the September primary. For 1990, Johnston seems well positioned in Louisiana's increasingly economic-based politics. No serious Democrat is likely to challenge such a senior Senator, and Johnston has some claim on the same geographic and economic base—northern Louisiana and affluent voters—that elected Buddy Roemer governor.

John Breaux has emerged in his first term as an active and effective Senator: after only two years in the Senate he was named to head the Democratic Senatorial Campaign Committee during the 1989-90 election cycle. This is quite a turnaround considering he entered the 1986 Senate race under a cloud named Edwin Edwards. Breaux is from the same small Cajun town as Edwards, served four years on his staff, and won Edwards's House seat when Edwards became governor in 1972. He was known for an Edwards-like response he gave when asked after voting for the 1981 Reagan budget cuts after getting an agreement to reinstate sugar price supports, "Does that mean your vote is for sale?" "No," he replied, "but it is available for rent." Actually, Breaux had shown some creativity in the House as a legislator, using his seat on the Public Works and Commerce committees not only to get projects for his coastal district but also for such larger causes as torpedoing the Law of the Sea treaty and getting the state a $605 million windfall in offshore oil payments.

Breaux's 1986 Senate Republican opponent, Baton Rouge Congressman Henson Moore, who had an overwhelming money advantage and was attacking the unpopular Edwards, made some bad mistakes—notably letting national Republicans stage a "ballot security" drive aimed supposedly at stopping vote fraud but in fact at intimidating blacks. This succeeded in infuriating blacks and increasing their turnout while—no one would have believed this two decades ago—doing nothing for Moore among whites. Moore failed to get 50% in the first primary and Breaux, emphasizing economic issues, overtook him by November. Black voters gave Breaux margins as large as anyone has ever won in Louisiana; the Cajun parishes came in for him at better than 2 to 1; he carried or ran about even in white Baptist parishes and blue-collar neighborhoods. Moore carried all affluent suburbs, the growing cities of Baton Rouge, Shreveport, Monroe and Alexandria, his own congressional district (though only barely) and not much else.

In the Senate, Breaux got seats on the Environment and Public Works and the Commerce Committees—expanded versions of his House assignments—and showed the sureness of foot he had at his best in the House. With Johnston, he plays a key role on nuclear issues. Politically, his 1986 experience persuaded him to be "a Democrat trying to be a power in the party." As Republicans become more competitive in state races, Democrats increasingly find themselves identified with the national party they used to pretty much ignore; Breaux's conclusion is that they—he—had better determine what that national party stands for. Hence his active work for

Michael Dukakis in 1988; hence his successful campaign to head the Senate campaign committee and his less successful efforts to get former Congressman Jim Jones elected Democratic national chairman.

Congressional districting. Louisiana's congressional redistricting eventually went to court in the 1980s, where the New Orleans 2d District was redrawn to produce a black majority. It continued to reelect Lindy Boggs. Redistricting is not likely to make major changes in the delegation for 1992, except to expand the population-losing 2d's boundaries outward. Louisiana's unique all-party primary means that the critical congressional election here for incumbents is in September, for if they win 50% then they are reelected; in the 1980s, only one incumbent has failed to win in September—Republican Clyde Holloway in the Democratic 8th in 1988—and he won in November.

The People: Est. Pop. 1988: 4,420,000; Pop. 1980: 4,205,900, up 5.1% 1980–88 and 15.4% 1970–80; 1.87% of U.S. total, 18th largest. 13% with 1–3 yrs. col., 13% with 4+ yrs. col.; 18.6% below poverty level. Single ancestry: 11% French, 10% English, 3% Irish, German, 2% Italian. Households (1980): 76% family, 45% with children, 60% married couples; 34.5% housing units rented; median monthly rent: $156; median house value: $43,000. Voting age pop. (1980): 2,875,432; 27% Black, 2% Spanish origin, 1% Asian origin. Registered voters (1988): 2,161,395; 1,628,405 D (75%); 355,964 R (16%); 177,026 unaffiliated and minor parties (8%).

1988 Share of Federal Tax Burden: $11,240,000,000; 1.27% of U.S. total, 23d largest.

1988 Share of Federal Expenditures

	Total		Non-Defense		Defense	
Total Expend	$12,682m	(1.43%)	$8,713m	(1.33%)	$3,098m	(1.36%)
St/Lcl Grants	2,135m	(1.86%)	663m	(0.58%)	2m	(1.51%)
Salary/Wages	1,585m	(1.18%)	809m	(1.21%)	776m	(1.21%)
Pymnts to Indiv	6,479m	(1.58%)	6,196m	(1.59%)	283m	(1.52%)
Procurement	2,036m	(1.08%)	599m	(1.29%)	2,036m	(1.08%)
Research/Other	448m	(1.20%)	446m	(1.20%)	1m	(1.20%)

Political Lineup: Governor, Buddy Roemer (D); Lt. Gov., Paul Hardy (R); Secy. of State, Wallace Fox McKeithen (D); Atty. Gen., William J. Guste, Jr. (D); Treasurer, Mary Landrieu (D). State Senate, 39 (34 D and 5 R); State House of Representatives, 105 (87 D and 18 R). Senators, J. Bennett Johnston, Jr. (D) and John B. Breaux (D). Representatives, 8 (4 D and 4 R).

1988 Presidential Vote

Bush (R)	883,702	(54%)
Dukakis (D)	717,460	(44%)

1984 Presidential Vote

Reagan (R)	1,037,299	(61%)
Mondale (D)	651,586	(38%)

1988 Democratic Presidential Primary

Jackson	221,532	(35%)
Gore	174,976	(28%)
Dukakis	95,667	(15%)
Gephardt	66,434	(11%)
Hart	26,442	(4%)
Duke	23,390	(4%)
Simon	5,155	(1%)

1988 Republican Presidential Primary

Bush	83,687	(58%)
Robertson	26,295	(18%)
Dole	25,626	(18%)
Kemp	7,722	(5%)

GOVERNOR

Gov. Buddy Roemer (D)

Elected 1987, term expires Mar. 1992; b. Oct. 4, 1943, Shreveport; home, Bossier City; Harvard U., B.A. 1964, M.B.A. 1967; United Methodist; married (Patti).

Career: Businessman, farmer, banker, 1967–80; Delegate, LA Constitutional Convention, 1972; U.S. House of Reps., 1980–88.

Offices: State Capitol, Baton Rouge 70804, 504-342-7015.

Election Results

1987 gen.	Buddy Roemer (D), unopposed		
1987 prim.	Buddy Roemer (D)...........	516,078	(33%)
	Edwin Edwards (D)	437,801	(28%)
	Bob Livingston (R)...........	287,780	(18%)
	Billy Tauzin (D)	154,079	(10%)
	Four others	162,992	(10%)
1983 prim.	Edwin W. Edwards (D)	1,006,561	(62%)
	David C. Treen (R)	588,508	(36%)

SENATORS

Sen. J. Bennett Johnston, Jr. (D)

Elected 1972, seat up 1990; b. June 10, 1932, Shreveport; home, Shreveport; Wash. & Lee U., 1950–51, 1952–53, U.S. Military Academy, 1951–52, LA St. U., LL.B. 1956; Baptist; married (Mary).

Career: Army, 1956–59; Practicing atty., 1959–72; LA House of Reps., 1964–68; LA Senate, 1968–72.

Offices: 136 HSOB 20510, 202-224-5824. Also Hale Boggs Fed. Bldg., 500 Camp St., Rm. 1010, New Orleans 70130, 504-589-2427; Joe D. Waggoner Jr. Fed. Bldg., 500 Fannin St., Ste. 7A12, Shreveport 71161, 318-226-5085; and 1 American Pl., Ste. 1510, Baton Rouge 70825, 504-389-0395.

Committees: *Appropriations* (4th of 16 D). Subcommittees: Defense; Energy and Water Development (Chairman); Foreign Operations; HUD-Independent Agencies; Interior. *Budget* (3d of 13 D). *Energy and Natural Resources* (Chairman of 10 D). *Special Committee on Aging* (5th of 10 D).

Group Ratings

	ADA	ACLU	COPE	CFA	LCV	ACU	NTLC	NSI	COC	CEI
1988	55	38	51	92	20	36	11	60	50	13
1987	70	—	49	67	—	20	—	—	33	19

National Journal Ratings

	1988 LIB — 1988 CONS	1987 LIB — 1987 CONS
Economic	57% — 40%	74% — 0%
Social	36% — 63%	45% — 52%
Foreign	62% — 37%	51% — 45%

Key Votes

1) Cut Aged Housing $	FOR	5) Bork Nomination	AGN	9) SDI Funding	AGN
2) Override Hwy Veto	FOR	6) Ban Plastic Guns	FOR	10) Ban Chem Weaps	FOR
3) Kill Plnt Clsng Notice	AGN	7) Deny Abortions	FOR	11) Aid To Contras	FOR
4) Min Wage Increase	FOR	8) Japanese Reparations	FOR	12) Reagan Defense $	AGN

Election Results

1984 primary	J. Bennett Johnston, Jr. (D)	838,181	(86%)	($1,046,293)
	Robert M. Ross (R)	86,546	(9%)	
	Larry Napoleon Cooper (R)	52,746	(5%)	
1978 primary	J. Bennett Johnston, Jr. (D)	498,773	(59%)	($857,860)
	Louis (Woody) Jenkins (D)	340,896	(41%)	($327,340)

Sen. John B. Breaux (D)

Elected 1986, seat up 1992; b. Mar. 1, 1944, Crowley; home, Lafayette; U. of S.W. LA, B.A. 1964, LA St. U., J.D. 1967; Roman Catholic; married (Lois).

Career: Practicing atty., 1967–68; Legis. Asst., Dist. Mgr. to U.S. Rep. Edwin W. Edwards, 1968–72; U.S. House of Reps., 1972–87.

Offices: 516 HSOB 20510, 202-224-4623. Also 705 Jefferson, Rm. 13, Lafayette 70501, 318-264-6871; 500 Camp St., Ste. 1005, New Orleans 70130, 504-589-2531; 534 Murray St., Alexandria 71301, 318-473-7370; and 211 N. 3d St., Monroe 71201, 318-325-3320.

Committees: *Commerce, Science and Transportation* (9th of 11 D). Subcommittees: Communications; Merchant Marine (Chairman); Surface Transportation; National Ocean Policy Study. *Environment and Public Works* (6th of 9 D). Subcommittees: Environmental Protection; Nuclear Regulation (Chairman); Water Resources, Transportation and Infrastructure. *Special Committee on Aging* (6th of 10 D).

Group Ratings

	ADA	ACLU	COPE	CFA	LCV	ACU	NTLC	NSI	COC	CEI
1988	50	35	87	92	30	44	11	60	43	15
1987	70	—	90	67	—	19	—	—	28	21

National Journal Ratings

	1988 LIB — 1988 CONS	1987 LIB — 1987 CONS
Economic	52% — 45%	65% — 26%
Social	35% — 64%	66% — 31%
Foreign	52% — 45%	51% — 45%

Key Votes

1) Cut Aged Housing $	AGN	5) Bork Nomination	AGN	9) SDI Funding	AGN
2) Override Hwy Veto	FOR	6) Ban Plastic Guns	AGN	10) Ban Chem Weaps	FOR
3) Kill Plnt Clsng Notice	AGN	7) Deny Abortions	FOR	11) Aid To Contras	FOR
4) Min Wage Increase	FOR	8) Japanese Reparations	FOR	12) Reagan Defense $	AGN

Election Results

1986 general	John B. Breaux (D)...................	723,586	(53%)	($2,958,313)
	W. Henson Moore (R).................	646,311	(47%)	($5,986,460)
1986 primary	John B. Breaux (D)...................	447,328	(37%)	
	W. Henson Moore (R).................	529,433	(44%)	
	Samuel B. Nunez (D).................	73,505	(6%)	
	J.E. Jumonville (D)..................	53,394	(5%)	
	Sherman A. Bernard (D)	52,479	(5%)	
1980 primary	Russell B. Long (D)	484,770	(58%)	($2,166,838)
	Louis (Woody) Jenkins (D)............	325,922	(39%)	($237,242)
	Three others (D, R, No party)	30,321	(4%)	

FIRST DISTRICT

Surrounding the historic center of New Orleans, like a doughnut around the Crescent City, are the affluent and not-so-affluent residential neighborhoods that have grown up on the spongy soil of this Mississippi delta land over the last 30 or 40 years. Without topographic interest—the only rises are the bridges over the canals or the freeway overpasses—and almost always without architectural distinction, lacking the funkiness of the French Quarter or the gracious patina of the Garden District, radiating outward in remorseless grids to Lake Pontchartrain or the river or a swamp, these are the streets where you'll find New Orleans's middle class, comfortable and not so comfortable, white and in some places black. They are places most tourists never see—but where they would feel most at home if they had to live here.

The 1st Congressional District of Louisiana includes most of these areas. In the city it includes the neat, all-white, 1950s neighborhoods on straight streets headed out to Lake Pontchartrain west of City Park. Just to the west is Metairie, the suburb that is home to more of the city's middle- and upper-income whites than is New Orleans itself, and which made itself nationally infamous when one of its districts in early 1989 elected unrepentant former Ku Klux Klansman David Duke to the legislature. Stretching farther out, along canals and just south of Lake Pontchartrain, is the more modest suburb of Kenner; and below the railroad lines, beneath the levees on the west and east banks of the Mississippi River, lined with docks and grain elevators and the Avondale Shipyard, are working-class suburbs. All this land is Jefferson Parish, which still has the politics of a rural satrapy, with a fine cast of Louisiana characters, like assessor Lawrence Chehardy, who despite his Democratic label appeared at a Republican rally in 1986 and opposed Governor Buddy Roemer's tax reform program in 1988. From Jefferson Parish over the 26-mile Lake Pontchartrain Causeway, is St. Tammany Parish, the fastest-growing part of the metropolitan area in the 1980s.

Demographically, this district is almost all-white; blacks were put into the 2d in a Voting Rights Act case. Politically, this is Republican territory in national and sometimes—though not always—in local contests. Louisiana has a politics almost of economic class warfare these days, and those who are well off—not just the inbred elite with their preoccupation over blood lines and Mardi Gras krewes, but the slightly-pinched middle class masses—are solidly conservative. Like the comfortable classes in an underdeveloped country, where it seems inconceivable that most people could make decent livings or find anything more than menial jobs, people here are quite unsentimental about maintaining their privilege and position, and completely unapologetic about what the guiltily affluent of the Northeast would call their selfishness. Why give away what you have? And what would others do with it anyway? That kind of thinking, which you would encounter inside the houses in Caracas, Venezuela, where the tops of the surrounding walls are studded with broken glass, you will find in the neater and more gracious looking homes of lakefront New Orleans, Metairie or St. Tammany Parish.

The congressman from this district represents the views and also some of the virtues of this constituency. Bob Livingston is from an aristocratic family and bears the name of the New York chancellor who administered the oath of office to George Washington 200 years ago. Chancellor Livingston helped negotiate the Louisiana Purchase, and some of his Hudson Valley relatives settled in the state and helped run it. But this Livingston grew up in modest circumstances, enlisting in the Navy after high school, working his way through school at the Avondale Shipyard. He was once a federal prosecutor and approaches politics with a prosecutorial frame of mind; he won the seat in a 1977 special, after the Democrat who won it in 1976 was forced to resign due to fraud and eventually a jail sentence, and he was a tough judge of his colleagues while on the House Ethics Committee.

On foreign policy, Livingston takes stern views too. He strongly backed contra aid, he moved to beat the Democrats' bill requiring congressional notification of covert actions within 48 hours, and he had a bill of his own to make it a felony for any Member of Congress or other congressional employee to disclose classified information. On the Appropriations Committee he has worked to fund Louisiana projects, from I-49 to coastal hurricane and flood protection; he wants to stop coastal erosion (a major cause in a state that is losing territory to the Gulf of Mexico); he helped set aside the Bogue Chitto National Wildlife Reserve. He looks out for shrimp fisherman who don't want to be required to use Turtle Excluding Devices.

Livingston did not fare well in his gubernatorial campaign in 1987. As the sole Republican, he hoped to survive into a runoff with the unpopular Edwin Edwards. But he faltered after losing his train of thought in a debate, and ended up carrying only his base in the New Orleans suburbs; Buddy Roemer got the affluent vote he sought in Baton Rouge, the Cajun country, and the Baptist north. Still, Livingston seems popular in the 1st District and busy and productive in the House.

The People: Est. Pop. 1986: 584,000, up 11.1% 1980–86; Pop. 1980: 525,883, up 35.2% 1970–80 Households (1980): 76% family, 44% with children, 64% married couples; 33.2% housing units rented median monthly rent: $243; median house value: $59,100. Voting age pop. (1980): 367,724; 9% Black 4% Spanish origin, 1% Asian origin.

1988 Presidential Vote: Bush (R) 149,519   (70%)
Dukakis (D). 61,214   (29%)

Rep. Robert L. (Bob) Livingston (R)

Elected Aug. 27, 1977; b. Apr. 30, 1943, Colorado Springs, CO; home, Metairie; Tulane U., B.A. 1967, J.D. 1968; Episcopalian; married (Bonnie).

Career: Navy, 1961–63; Asst. U.S. Atty., 1970–73; Chf. Spec. Prosecutor, Orleans Parish Dist. Atty.'s Ofc., 1974–75; Chf. Prosecutor, LA Atty. Gen.'s Ofc., Organized Crime Unit, 1975–76.

Offices: 2412 RHOB 20515, 202-225-3015. Also 111 Veterans Blvd., Ste. 700, Metairie 70005, 504-589-2753.

Committees: *Appropriations* (11th of 22 R). Subcommittee: Defense. *Permanent Select Committee on Intelligence* (2d of 7 R). Subcommittees: Legislation (Ranking Member); Program and Budget Authorization.

Group Ratings

	ADA	ACLU	COPE	CFA	LCV	ACU	NTLC	NSI	COC	CEI
1988	5	0	11	9	25	100	66	100	100	66
1987	0	—	11	14	—	73	—	—	78	60

National Journal Ratings

	1988 LIB — 1988 CONS		1987 LIB — 1987 CONS	
Economic	12%	88%	31%	69%
Social	0%	95%	0%	90%
Foreign	0%	84%	28%	72%

Key Votes

1) Homeless $	—	5) Retain Gun	—	9) SDI Research	—
2) Gephardt Amdt	AGN	6) Drug Death Pen	FOR	10) Ban Chem Weaps	AGN
3) Deficit Reduc	AGN	7) Handgun Sales	FOR	11) Aid to Contras	FOR
4) Kill Plnt Clsng Notice	FOR	8) Ban D.C. Abort $	FOR	12) Nuclear Testing	AGN

Election Results

1988 primary	Robert L. (Bob) Livingston (R)	69,679	(79%)	($555,058)
	George Mustakas (D)	13,091	(15%)	($99,065)
	Eric Honig (D)	5,457	(6%)	($26,106)
1986 primary	Robert L. (Bob) Livingston (R), unopposed			($201,033)

SECOND DISTRICT

The stucco sidings were chipped off the brick walls, the stone pavements in the courtyards were uneven, the shutters were askew and the grillwork needed paint—the old sections of New Orleans, the French Quarter and the commercial district upriver from Canal Street, were looking run down in the *WPA Guide* of five decades ago. Founded by the French in 1718, New Orleans was an alien Creole city—part French, a bit Spanish—when the Americans flag was raised over what is now Jackson Square in 1803. It was the fourth largest American city from 1840 until the Civil War, the only sizeable city in the South; yet even as it was sending southern cotton out to the mills of Lancashire, it was an alien cultural force in the South. Urbanized and developed, yet poor and in many ways primitive, New Orleans had yellow fever epidemics late in the 19th century, even as it was installing electric lights; it had a riot in which Italian immigrants were massacred, even as it was laying its streetcar tracks and telephone lines. New Orleans was one of the most corrupt of American cities in the years of Reconstruction and after, when its votes were regularly bid for and bought; and like other southern cities, it became rigidly segregated after 1890. Today, New Orleans remains a major port, but ships out mostly oil products; its place as the chief entrepot of Latin American trade has been ceded to Miami.

The 2d Congressional District of Louisiana includes almost all the city of New Orleans, as well as all its older, more distinctive neighborhoods. Here is the French Quarter, its 19th century homes still intact because the Americans who moved here after 1803 wanted to stay away from the snobbish Creoles and built a new downtown west of Canal Street. Just above the Quarter is the site of Storyville, where prostitution was legal before 1918 and where jazz was probably first played; the old frame houses have long since been torn down and replaced by housing projects. But many similar neighborhoods remain, where blacks and some working-class whites live in rickety frame houses, not always strong enough to keep the rain out and never tight enough to keep out the summer humidity or the damp winter chill, along the vividly named streets that go north from the river wharves east of the Quarter. In the other direction, you go through the downtown flecked with skyscrapers, past the old slum known as the Irish Channel—a reminder that New Orleans had more foreign immigrants than any other part of the South—to the Garden District. This was the home of the rich, early American settlers, and its antebellum homes are still covered with vines and Spanish moss. Quaintly named trolley cars still roll out St. Charles Avenue, passing out of the 2d District in the affluent Uptown area and back into it when they reach a poor black neighborhood beyond.

Going out east and north from the French Quarter, you find another New Orleans. Past the old frame houses, off Interstate 10, are garden apartment complexes and shopping centers, built on recently reclaimed swampland; just beyond it is still more swamp, and you find yourself on a causeway, heading to the Mississippi border. This current 2d District was drawn after the 1982 election and was intended to meet the requirements of the Voting Rights Act by maximizing the number of blacks within its borders (thereby minimizing the number of blacks, and the influence of black voters, in the neighboring 1st and 3d Districts). It has created a black-majority district whose voters seem pleased to continue electing their now long-time representative, congresswoman Lindy Boggs.

When Members of Congress assembled in Philadelphia in 1987 to reenact the Constitutional Convention, the member selected to take the role of George Washington was Lindy Boggs. It was an apt choice in many ways. Boggs may or may not be the descendant of any of the delegates, but one forebear was the first territorial governor of Louisiana, and she has distinguished roots that go back well before the Revolution. She also is a link with our own recent past: she first came to Washington in 1940, when her husband Hale Boggs was elected congressman as an anti-Huey Long reformer; only a few other Members of Congress (notably Claude Pepper, John Dingell) go back farther on Capitol Hill. Hale Boggs became one of the leaders of the House, but not without taking risks; he courageously supported the civil rights laws of 1965 and 1968 (and was nearly beaten in 1968), and he was campaigning with a colleague in Alaska when their plane was lost in 1972. Had he lived, Boggs would have been Speaker of the House.

Lindy Boggs was the obvious choice to succeed him and is now a senior member on her own. For years she was considered one of the most knowledgeable of congressional wives and she managed her husband's campaigns in New Orleans—not a job for a political innocent. She has the manners of a girl raised on a plantation (which she was), the panache of someone with an elegant old house in the French Quarter (which she has), and the political savvy of one who has managed tough campaigns and moved in the highest circles of Washington for years (which she also has). She was mentioned occasionally as a possible vice presidential candidate in 1984, although she was not given the consideration younger women like Dianne Feinstein and

Geraldine Ferraro received.

In the House, she serves on the Appropriations Committee and on the HUD-Independent Agencies and Energy and Water Development Subcommittees. On major issues she is inclined to support the House Democratic leadership: she tends to be somewhat generous on economic issues, cautious on cultural issues, and supportive of defense spending (though not the MX). She spends great effort building levees in Algiers and Jefferson Parish, getting Navy contracts for the Avondale Shipyard, getting the Mississippi River dredged 45 feet up to Mile 181, getting $33 million for restoring New Orleans's streetcars—local projects on which she is increasingly well-positioned to help.

No one doubts that Boggs played an important role in persuading her husband to vote for civil rights legislation, and that—plus her current voting record and constituency services—enabled her to overcome a challenge from a serious black candidate, Judge Israel Augustine in 1984; in a district where 55% of the voters are black, she got 60% of the votes. There was talk that former Mayor Dutch Morial might run against her. But the current mayor, Sidney Barthelemy, is less given to racial confrontation, and Boggs had no serious opposition in 1986 or 1988. Redistricting will mean adding territory—and therefore whites—to the district, which may strengthen Boggs. But she has shown the capacity to deliver for her constituents and to win their votes regardless of race and can probably hold this seat as long as she wants.

The People: Est. Pop. 1986: 522,500, dn. 0.5% 1980–86; Pop. 1980: 525,331, dn. 5.3% 1970–80. Households (1980): 64% family, 37% with children, 41% married couples; 62.0% housing units rented; median monthly rent: $151; median house value: $48,500. Voting age pop. (1980): 370,324; 52% Black, 3% Spanish origin, 1% Asian origin.

1988 Presidential Vote:

Dukakis (D)	112,977	(68%)
Bush (R)	51,739	(31%)

Rep. Corinne C. (Lindy) Boggs (D)

Elected 1973; b. Mar. 13, 1916, Brunswick Plantation; home, New Orleans; Newcomb Col. of Tulane U., B.A. 1935; Roman Catholic; widowed.

Career: Pub. sch. teacher, 1936–37; Gen. Mgr., campaigns of U.S. Rep. Hale Boggs; Co-chwmn., Presidential Inaugural Balls, 1961, 1965; Chwmn., 1976 Dem. Natl. Convention.

Offices: 2353 RHOB 20515, 202-225-6636. Also Hale Boggs Fed. Bldg., Ste. 1012, 500 Camp St., New Orleans 70130, 504-589-2274.

Committees: *Appropriations* (14th of 35 D). Subcommittees: Energy and Water Development; VA, HUD and Independent Agencies; Legislative. *Select Committee on Children, Youth, and Families* (4th of 18 D).

Group Ratings

	ADA	ACLU	COPE	CFA	LCV	ACU	NTLC	NSI	COC	CEI
1988	80	81	77	73	38	5	3	22	18	12
1987	72	—	76	79	—	5	—	—	13	9

National Journal Ratings

	1988 LIB — 1988 CONS			1987 LIB — 1987 CONS	
Economic	57%	—	43%	73%	—	0%
Social	60%	—	39%	57%	—	43%
Foreign	59%	—	40%	63%	—	36%

Key Votes

1) Homeless $	AGN	5) Ban Drug Test	AGN	9) SDI Research	AGN
2) Gephardt Amdt	FOR	6) Drug Death Pen	AGN	10) Ban Chem Weaps	FOR
3) Deficit Reduc	FOR	7) Handgun Sales	AGN	11) Aid to Contras	AGN
4) Kill Plnt Clsng Notice	AGN	8) Ban D.C. Abort $	FOR	12) Nuclear Testing	FOR

Election Results

1988 primary	Corinne C. (Lindy) Boggs (D)	63,762	(89%)	($252,835)
	Roger C. Johnson (R)...................	7,505	(11%)	
1986 primary	Corinne C. (Lindy) Boggs (D)	105,661	(91%)	($261,984)
	Roger C. Johnson (R).................	8,474	(7%)	

THIRD DISTRICT

From the air, it is an expanse of green, unrelieved except for the occasional trickle of a bayou and an even more rare ribbon of highway: the great wetlands of southern Louisiana. Actually, this is part of a broad river mouth with unnumerable islands, through which the waters of the Mississippi and its tributaries drain out into the Gulf. It is rich with animal life, with birds and shellfish and small game, and supports a larger population than one in the air might think. There are cabins along the bayous and crossroads towns where Cajun French remains the first language and roadside diners feature crawfish étouffé. But Cajun country looks not just to tradition. Near the Gulf of Mexico there are rough oil-rig towns where men come ashore after two-week stints to raise hell or, more often today, linger in hopes of a job. In the 1960s and 1970s, the oil industry helped preserve Cajun culture here, by providing jobs at home for residents' children as they grew up; now, with oil payrolls down and the wetlands themselves threatened by coastal erosion, the Cajun country feels its way of life is threatened—which is probably why politically so many of these southern whites have switched to the national Democrats.

The 3d Congressional District of Louisiana includes the Cajun country from the swamplands south of New Orleans west almost to Lafayette. In greater New Orleans, it includes parts of the working-class towns of Jefferson Parish along the Mississippi River, hemmed in by swamps and the river (elevated behind levees above street level) and the grain elevators that flank it: here you find the garish strip of motels on Airline Highway where televangelist Jimmy Swaggart was revealed in 1988 to have engaged in bizarre sex sessions with prostitutes. Then, on the other side of industrial New Orleans, the 3d crosses over swampland to include St. Bernard and Plaquemines Parishes. St. Bernard was once a tightly controlled fiefdom but is now white working-class suburbia. Closer in, as you get near the Gulf, is Plaquemines Parish, where the Perez family held sway for decades. The late Leander Perez Sr., once a Huey Long lieutenant, was excommunicated from the Catholic Church for opposing desegregation, but was still able to deliver a virtually unanimous vote for any candidate he chose. He also managed to make vast sums—no one knows how much—off the oil and sulfur deposits here; no one else seemed interested in extracting them so long as his family controlled local government.

The 3d District's congressman is a politically canny Cajun who has become a talented operator in the House but who has failed to realize (yet anyway) all his ambitions in Louisiana. He is Billy Tauzin, a Democrat from Thibodaux in Lafourche Parish, who was first elected in a

1980 special election when the district included some high-income Republican suburbs. He has been routinely reelected since, usually without opposition.

Tauzin serves on the Merchant Marine and Fisheries Committee, where he can work for wildlife preservation and against coastal erosion, and also help the local oil industry. He also has a much-sought-after seat on Energy and Commerce. That is the body with jurisdiction over oil and gas price controls, and Tauzin has of course opposed them; but more than that, he has been an active, competent and aggressive advocate of what he considers to be Louisiana's interest on oil and gas issues. Sometimes combative, Tauzin is not afraid to oppose Energy and Commerce's imposing chairman John Dingell, but he also specializes in biding his time on many issues, establishing himself as a key deciding vote, and then dickering with both sides for an agreement that is most favorable to his position.

Tauzin spent much of 1987, however, running for governor of Louisiana. As a former legislator and legislative staffer, he knew Baton Rouge, and he argued that he could solve the problems left by Governor Edwin Edwards. But Tauzin was an Edwards floor leader in the legislature and had been supported by Edwards in 1980; he drew from the same Cajun core constituency; he entered the race when it was not clear whether Edwards was running. But when Edwards announced, Tauzin was probably doomed. He stayed in anyway and won 10% of the vote, carrying four parishes in the 3d District. But unless the winner, Governor Buddy Roemer, proves a bust, Tauzin will probably have to delay any statewide ambitions until 1995. And by that time he could be one of the higher-ranked members of Energy and Commerce, and may be reluctant to leave.

The People: Est. Pop. 1986: 560,400, up 6.3% 1980–86; Pop. 1980: 527,280, up 19.5% 1970–80. Households (1980): 82% family, 52% with children, 69% married couples; 28.9% housing units rented; median monthly rent: $168; median house value: $46,100. Voting age pop. (1980): 346,013; 18% Black, 3% Spanish origin, 1% American Indian, 1% Asian origin.

1988 Presidential Vote:

Bush (R)	114,277	(54%)
Dukakis (D)	90,809	(43%)

Rep. W. J. (Billy) Tauzin (D)

Elected 1980; b. June 14, 1943, Chackbay; home, Thibodaux; Nicholls St. U., B.A. 1964, LA St. U., J.D. 1967; Roman Catholic; married (Gayle).

Career: Legis. Aide, LA Senate, 1964–68; Practicing atty., 1968–80; LA House of Reps., 1971–79.

Offices: 2342 RHOB 20515, 202-225-4031. Also 2439 Manhattan Blvd., Ste. 304, Harvey 70058, 504-361-1892; 107 Fed. Bldg., Houma 700360, 504-876-3033; and 210 E. Main St., New Iberia 70560, 318-367-8231.

Committees: *Energy and Commerce* (13th of 26 D). Subcommittees: Energy and Power; Telecommunications and Finance; Transportation and Hazardous Materials. *Merchant Marine and Fisheries* (6th of 26 D). Subcommittees: Fisheries and Wildlife Conservation and the Environment; Coast Guard and Navigation (Chairman).

Group Ratings

	ADA	ACLU	COPE	CFA	LCV	ACU	NTLC	NSI	COC	CEI
1988	45	39	45	64	25	64	31	100	62	32
1987	24	—	40	36	—	53	—	—	56	33

National Journal Ratings

	1988 LIB — 1988 CONS	1987 LIB — 1987 CONS
Economic	40% — 58%	52% — 48%
Social	33% — 66%	* — *
Foreign	30% — 67%	35% — 65%

Key Votes

1) Homeless $	—	5) Ban Drug Test	FOR	9) SDI Research	—
2) Gephardt Amdt	FOR	6) Drug Death Pen	FOR	10) Ban Chem Weaps	AGN
3) Deficit Reduc	AGN	7) Handgun Sales	FOR	11) Aid to Contras	FOR
4) Kill Plnt Clsng Notice	AGN	8) Ban D.C. Abort $	FOR	12) Nuclear Testing	AGN

Election Results

1988 primary	W. J. (Billy) Tauzin (D)	72,110	(89%)	($707,085)
	Millard Clement (D)	8,602	(11%)	
1986 primary	W. J. (Billy) Tauzin (D), unopposed			($329,823)

FOURTH DISTRICT

Out the still uncompleted Interstate 49, far from New Orleans, you reach northern Louisiana's largest city, Shreveport. This is an oil town with none of the Creole ambience of New Orleans or the French accents of the Cajun country; in most ways it is similar to neighboring east Texas or southern Arkansas. Baptist farmers have been working this land for 150 years, voting against cosmopolitan New Orleans, whether for conservative anti-government Republicans or riproaring populists. The 4th Congressional District of Louisiana occupies this northwest corner of the state, with Shreveport and adjacent suburban areas in Caddo and Bossier (pronounced bohzh-yer) Parishes forming about half the district. The rural parishes to the west and south usually vote for Democrats, sometimes even national ones; Caddo and Bossier, which are oil communities, have become Republican strongholds like the oil-rich Tyler and Longview, Texas. But in local contests they have backed Shreveport natives like Senator Bennett Johnston and Governor Buddy Roemer, who of course have voted for many Republican programs at different stages in their careers.

Perhaps it is this split heritage, perhaps it is what W. J. Cash in *The Mind of the South* called the "hell of a fellow" spirit, perhaps simply because this has been an open seat. For whatever reason, the 4th District has had some of the most turbulent politics and flamboyantly contested elections of any congressional district in the nation. And expensive: $2.6 million was spent in the 1978 and 1980 contests. Buddy Roemer, now Governor, won the seat here in 1980 by beating Claude (Buddy) Leach, who was under indictment on vote fraud charges; Roemer, intense, inspirational, grandstanding was unopposed in the next three elections until he won the governorship in October 1987.

The special election to fill his place resulted in the victory of a former Roemer staffer, Jim McCrery—except that he, unlike them, ran as a Republican and not a Democrat. By many standards McCrery did not have much going for him: his name was little known, he was a bachelor who had been working as a lobbyist in Baton Rouge. But the Republican label helped him to make it into the April 1988 runoff, and he was probably helped when his Democratic opponent, state Senator Foster Campbell was badly injured (he lost an eye) in March while driving illegally on an unopened section of Interstate 49. Campbell's populist style evidently went over badly in Caddo and Bossier Parishes, and calls for a more assertive trade policy did not produce enough votes to compensate.

McCrery had Roemer's vote in that contest. But in the October 1988 primary for the full term his opponent, after several Democratic politicians bowed out, was none other than Adeline Roemer, the Governor's mother. But her candidacy did not catch on and McCrery won 68%–27%. In the House McCrery got two good committee assignments, Budget and Armed Services (Fort Polk is in the southern end of the district)—perhaps because Republicans hope this former Democrat will make this formerly Democratic seat safe for them, and serve as an example to others. McCrery seems on his way to achieving at least part of this goal.

The People: Est. Pop. 1986: 573,700, up 9.2% 1980–86; Pop. 1980: 525,194, up 11.3% 1970–80. Households (1980): 76% family, 44% with children, 60% married couples; 31.6% housing units rented; median monthly rent: $139; median house value: $34,900. Voting age pop. (1980): 363,684; 29% Black, 2% Spanish origin.

1988 Presidential Vote:

Bush (R) 112,042	(59%)
Dukakis (D) 77,197	(40%)

Rep. Jim McCrery (R)

Elected April 1988; b. Sept. 18, 1949, Shreveport; home, Shreveport; LA Tech U., B.A. 1971, LA St. U., J.D. 1975; Methodist; single.

Career: Practicing atty. 1975–78; Asst. City Atty., Shreveport, 1979–80; Legis. Dir. for Rep. Buddy Roemer, 1981–84; Regional Manager, Georgia-Pacific Corp., 1984–88.

Offices: 1721 LHOB 20515, 202-225-2777. Also 621 Edwards St., Shreveport 71101, 318-226-5080; and 110 E. Lula St., Leesville 71446, 318-238-4550.

Committees: *Armed Services* (20th of 21 R). Subcommittees: Military Personnel and Compensation; Investigations. *Budget* (10th of 14 R). Subcommittees: Defense, Foreign Policy and Space; Urgent Fiscal Issues.

Group Ratings

	ADA	ACLU	COPE	CFA	LCV	ACU	NTLC	NSI	COC	CEI
1988	12	22	20	27	25	94	68	100	100	57
1987	*	—	*	*	—	*	—	—	*	*

National Journal Ratings

	1988 LIB — 1988 CONS		1987 LIB — 1987 CONS	
Economic	9% —	91%	* —	*
Social	19% —	81%	* —	*
Foreign	0% —	84%	* —	*

Key Votes

1) Homeless $	—	5) Ban Drug Test	—	9) SDI Research	—
2) Gephardt Amdt	—	6) Drug Death Pen	FOR	10) Ban Chem Weaps	—
3) Deficit Reduc	—	7) Handgun Sales	FOR	11) Aid to Contras	—
4) Kill Plnt Clsng Notice	—	8) Ban D.C. Abort $	FOR	12) Nuclear Testing	AGN

Election Results

1988 primary	Jim McCrery (R)	72,228	(68%)	($286,813)
	Adeline Roemer (D)	28,027	(27%)	($175,450)
	Robert Briggs (D)	5,103	(5%)	($127)
1988 special	Jim McCrery (R)	63,590	(51%)	($455,345)
	Foster Campbell (D)	62,214	(49%)	($447,139)
1986 primary	Buddy Roemer (D), unopposed			($197,235)

FIFTH DISTRICT

From the low-lying delta lands along the Mississippi River, west toward the Red River and Texas, northern Louisiana is part of the Deep South. People here are Protestant, not Catholic; they live in small towns or in the countryside or maybe in the small city of Monroe, not in a large metropolitan area; the whites don't believe any longer in racial segregation but they dislike the cultural views of the liberal elite. The agricultural establishments in this cotton and piney woods country range from large plantations along the Mississippi River to small, poor hill farms in places like Winn Parish, the boyhood home of Huey P. Long. This is the 5th Congressional District of Louisiana. In contrast to a quarter century ago, politics is biracial today, and 28% of the district's registered voters are black—the same as the 28% black voting age population for the state. At the same time, fully 38% of the district's children are black. With black outmigration from the South long since ended, that statistic matters for the future: black voters will almost certainly be more numerous and more powerful in districts like this 20 years from now than they are today.

The congressman from the 5th District is Jerry Huckaby, a dairy farmer and former Western Electric management employee, who had the shrewdness to challenge 30-year incumbent Otto Passman in 1976 and the attractiveness to beat him. Huckaby has held the district ever since, and had serious competition only in 1978; in the September 1988 primary, he won 71% of the vote and under Louisiana's unique all-party-primary law, was declared elected. Huckaby has good prospects for holding the seat as long as Passman did.

The reason: In 1983 he succeeded to the chairmanship of the Agriculture Committee's Subcommittee on Cotton, Rice, and Sugar. Those are Louisiana's three main crops, and historically producers of all three have depended on heavy subsidies, support programs or import restrictions. The care and maintenance of such programs has been Huckaby's main work, and he can be counted on to further the interests of Louisiana farmers and middlemen—against foes as dreaded as Republicans, bankers, or Energy and Commerce Chairman John Dingell. On other issues he will take a quieter role. His instincts are to the political right; he was one of the Boll Weevil Democrats who supported the Reagan budget and tax cut bills in 1981, and he seems to feel no particular obligation to go along with the Democratic leadership. But as the 1980s have gone on, he has begun to go along with other Democrats more often. That may reflect changing issues, a desire to stay in favor with the Democratic caucus, and also the potential rise in the black voting percentage back home, which mean that Huckaby has a long-term incentive to keep his record not too far out of line with those of most of his fellow Democrats.

The People: Est. Pop. 1986: 546,700, up 3.7% 1980–86; Pop. 1980: 527,220, up 12.6% 1970–80. Households (1980): 76% family, 44% with children, 61% married couples; 26.7% housing units rented; median monthly rent: $96; median house value: $29,400. Voting age pop. (1980): 360,687; 28% Black, 1% Spanish origin.

1988 Presidential Vote:

	Bush (R)	122,014	(62%)
	Dukakis (D)	70,397	(36%)

Rep. Jerry Huckaby (D)

Elected 1976; b. July 19, 1941, Hodge; home, Ringgold; LA St. U., B.S. 1963, GA St. U., M.B.A. 1968; United Methodist; married (Sue).

Career: Mgmt. position, Western Electric, 1963–73; farmer, businessman, 1973–76.

Offices: 2182 RHOB 20515, 202-225-2376. Also 211 N. 3d St., Monroe 71201, 318-387-2244; and P.O. Box 34, Old Court House Bldg., Natchitoches 71458, 318-352-9000.

Committees: *Agriculture* (7th of 27 D). Subcommittees: Cotton, Rice, and Sugar (Chairman); Forests, Family Farms and Energy. *Budget* (15th of 21 D). Subcommittees: Budget Process, Reconciliation and Enforcement; Community Development and Natural Resources.

Group Ratings

	ADA	ACLU	COPE	CFA	LCV	ACU	NTLC	NSI	COC	CEI
1988	40	24	32	55	31	65	42	100	77	42
1987	40	—	30	50	—	35	—	—	64	30

National Journal Ratings

	1988 LIB — 1988 CONS		1987 LIB — 1987 CONS	
Economic	38%	62%	46%	52%
Social	30%	70%	32%	67%
Foreign	39%	60%	44%	55%

Key Votes

1) Homeless $	FOR	5) Ban Drug Test	FOR	9) SDI Research	FOR
2) Gephardt Amdt	FOR	6) Drug Death Pen	FOR	10) Ban Chem Weaps	AGN
3) Deficit Reduc	AGN	7) Handgun Sales	FOR	11) Aid to Contras	FOR
4) Kill Plnt Clsng Notice	AGN	8) Ban D.C. Abort $	FOR	12) Nuclear Testing	—

Election Results

1988 primary	Jerry Huckaby (D)	51,113	(71%)	($194,021)
	Jack Wright (D)	14,343	(20%)	($9,007)
	Bradley T. Roark (R)	6,403	(9%)	
1986 primary	Jerry Huckaby (D)	96,200	(68%)	($326,332)
	Thomas (Bud) Brady (D)	32,284	(23%)	($41,293)
	Fred Huenefeld (D)	11,966	(9%)	($25,634)

SIXTH DISTRICT

When Huey P. Long came to Baton Rouge as governor-elect in 1928, Louisiana's capital was a small, sleepy southern town of 30,000 people. Today Baton Rouge is a bustling city of 241,000, with a population up nearly 50% since 1970. The change has been brought about by both the Kingfish and his bitterest political enemies. Long built a major university in Baton Rouge (Louisiana State) and vastly increased the size and scope of state government. Others have contributed as well. Exxon, a Long adversary when it was still Standard Oil of New Jersey, has its biggest refinery in Baton Rouge. And Baton Rouge is also the home base of a man who has something of Long's eloquence and even greater weaknesses, the television preacher Jimmy

Swaggart.

Baton Rouge (except for a few black precincts) and its suburban fringe make up about two-thirds of Louisiana's 6th Congressional District. The remainder of the district is to the east, in farming and piney woods country, stretching northeast to the Mississippi border. This area is known as the Florida Parishes, because it was acquired by the United States when West Florida was annexed in 1810. Ancestral politics here is Democratic, but both Baton Rouge and the Florida parishes have been supporting many Republicans for 20 years. In congressional politics, the 6th District has been a Republican district since 1975 and perhaps 1974: the 1974 election had to be rerun, because the machines in one heavily Democratic precinct did not work; the winner of the runoff was Republican Henson Moore, congressman for 11 years, member of the House Ways and Means Committee, and nearly successful candidate for the U.S. Senate in 1986.

The 6th District congressman now is Republican Richard Baker. Politics in Louisiana sometimes sounds mixed-up, and nowhere more than in the 1986 House race here. Baker was a Democratic legislator first elected in 1972 at age 24, and chairman of the roads committee for years; he represented a blue-collar Baton Rouge district; but he became a Republican in 1985. His opponent, state Senator Tommy Hudson, once served on Senator Bennett Johnston's staff; he represented a Baton Rouge country club district; but he stayed a Democrat. In the September primary, Baker managed to make more inroads into Hudson's territory than Hudson did into Baker's; high income voters showed more party loyalty than low. The district's overall vote for Senate candidate Henson Moore the same day was reflected in the result here: 51% for Baker, 45% for Hudson, which under Louisiana's all-party primary law meant Baker was elected. This was good news for Republicans—they held an endangered House seat—and bad—they ended up losing the Senate seat when Moore had no local race to boost turnout while there was a runoff between two Democrats in John Breaux's 7th District.

In Washington, Baker got assigned to the Interior Committee in his first term and switched to Banking in his second. He worked to get funding to open the Pennington Center for nutrition research at LSU, the old West Pearl Canal in the Florida parishes, and to make Baton Rouge a Foreign Trade Zone. With this record and the usual assiduous constituency service operation (helping 2,000 constituents, answering 185,000 letters), Baker faced no opposition in October.

The People: Est. Pop. 1986: 578,900, up 10.3% 1980–86; Pop. 1980: 524,770, up 29.5% 1970–80. Households (1980): 75% family, 45% with children, 61% married couples; 32.6% housing units rented; median monthly rent: $194; median house value: $50,800. Voting age pop. (1980): 362,252; 23% Black, 1% Spanish origin.

1988 Presidential Vote:

Bush (R)	128,304	(60%)
Dukakis (D)	83,704	(39%)

Rep. Richard H. Baker (R)

Elected 1986; b. May 22, 1948, New Orleans; home, Baton Rouge; LA St. U., B.A. 1971; United Methodist; married (Kay).

Career: Real estate developer, 1972–86; LA House of Reps., 1972–86.

Offices: 404 CHOB 20515, 202-225-3901. Also 5757 Corporate Blvd., Ste. 104, Baton Rouge 70808, 504-929-7711; and 105 S. Cherry, Hammond 70403, 504-345-4845.

Committees: *Banking, Finance and Urban Affairs* (17th of 20 R). Subcommittees: Financial Institutions Supervision, Regulation and Insurance; International Development, Finance, Trade and Monetary Policy; Housing and Community Development. *Small Business* (10th of 17 R). Subcommittees: Procurement, Tourism and Rural Development; SBA, the General Economy and Minority Enterprise Development.

Group Ratings

	ADA	ACLU	COPE	CFA	LCV	ACU	NTLC	NSI	COC	CEI
1988	5	10	10	18	19	100	81	100	100	61
1987	4	—	6	29	—	81	—	—	100	73

National Journal Ratings

	1988 LIB — 1988 CONS		1987 LIB — 1987 CONS	
Economic	10% —	88%	0% —	89%
Social	17% —	83%	0% —	90%
Foreign	30% —	67%	30% —	69%

Key Votes

1) Homeless $	—	5) Ban Drug Test	FOR	9) SDI Research	FOR
2) Gephardt Amdt	AGN	6) Drug Death Pen	FOR	10) Ban Chem Weaps	AGN
3) Deficit Reduc	—	7) Handgun Sales	FOR	11) Aid to Contras	FOR
4) Kill Plnt Clsng Notice	FOR	8) Ban D.C. Abort $	FOR	12) Nuclear Testing	AGN

Election Results

1988 primary	Richard Baker (R), unopposed			($270,899)
1986 primary	Richard Baker (R)	76,833	(51%)	($433,281)
	Thomas H. Hudson (D)	67,774	(45%)	($712,083)
	Willis E. Blackwell (D).	6,120	(4%)	

SEVENTH DISTRICT

In the low-lying land north of the swamps along the Gulf of Mexico and west of the almost impenetrable Atchafalaya, along the route of Interstate 10, is the heart of Cajun Louisiana, one of the few parts of the nation where almost half the people grew up speaking a language other than English—Cajun French. The 7th Congressional District of Louisiana covers most of this territory, hugging the Gulf Coast and taking in the oil refinery city of Lake Charles and the oil exploration center of Lafayette, which for a short time a decade ago was producing more millionaires than any other small city in the country.

Many rural backwaters like this have died in the years since World War II; the Cajun country has mostly thrived, because of petroleum. It lies in plentiful quantities under the swampy soil and in even greater amounts below the Gulf of Mexico a few miles out to sea. Oil and attendant industries have generated money to keep Cajuns who wish to stay in their homeland and to attract others as well. Cajun culture—language, music, cuisine—remains healthy as well. For years the use of French was discouraged, and seemed to be dying out; but in the 1970s, people here worked to keep the language alive—even while making sure, sensibly, that their children learned to become completely proficient in English.

But in the middle 1980s, the Cajun country was caught in a crisis of rising expectations. Rising, because the giddy growth of the oil industry in the late 1970s seemed to promise ever-rising prosperity here—and then, in the early 1980s, it fell. That left borrowers overextended, plungers ruined and ordinary homeowners unable to maintain a standard of living they expected to achieve. The Cajun country has always been less unfavorable to the national Democratic Party than other parts of the South. In 1984, Walter Mondale got his national percentage in the 7th District. In 1986, 7th District Congressman John Breaux won more than 60% here in his successful race for the Senate. In 1988, Michael Dukakis ran ahead of his national average here, carrying everything but Lafayette and one other small parish, and coming within a thousand votes of carrying the district. And in 1984, it gave the Mondale-Ferraro ticket a respectable percentage. There seems to be a liberal trend in this region which a decade ago had total confidence in free enterprise. That helps to explain why the Republican Party, on the rise elsewhere in Louisiana, did not even field a serious candidate here to fill the House seat Breaux left open.

The new congressman is Jimmy Hayes, a successful real estate developer who was a contributor to and appointee of Governor (and former 7th District congressman) Edwin Edwards. Hayes threaded his way adroitly through Louisiana's unique process, winning 30% in the first primary, in which a more liberal candidate was eliminated, and then running in tandem with Breaux and beating a pro-business, anti-union state Senator in the general. The AMA and Realtors' PACs made independent expenditures against Hayes, but he was able to outspend them and his opponent out of his own pocket. He serves on the Public Works and Science Committees, and like Breaux and Edwards seems to be concentrating on aiding the district, with highways, antipollution efforts, and aid to the shellfish industry.

The People: Est. Pop. 1986: 570,700, up 8.6% 1980–86; Pop. 1980: 525,361, up 19.6% 1970–80. Households (1980): 78% family, 47% with children, 66% married couples; 28.5% housing units rented; median monthly rent: $154; median house value: $41,500. Voting age pop. (1980): 355,571; 18% Black; 2% Spanish origin.

1988 Presidential Vote:

Bush (R)	106,573	(49%)
Dukakis (D)	105,908	(49%)

Rep. Jimmy Hayes (D)

Elected 1986; b. Dec. 21, 1946, Lafayette; home, Lafayette; U. of S.W. LA, B.A. 1967, Tulane U., J.D. 1970; United Methodist; married (Leslie).

Career: Asst. City Atty., Lafayette, 1971–72; Asst. Dist. Atty., Lafayette Parish, 1974–83; Real estate developer, 1978–86; LA Commissioner of Fin. Institutions, 1983–85.

Offices: 503 CHOB, 202-225-2031. Also 109 E. Vermillion, Lafayette 70501, 318-233-4773; and 901 Lake Shore Dr., Ste. 402, Lake Charles 70601, 318-433-1613.

Committees: *Public Works and Transportation* (23d of 31 D). Subcommittees: Aviation; Water Resources. *Science, Space and Technology* (25th of 30 D). Subcommittees: Investigations and Oversight; Science, Research and Technology; Space Science and Applications.

Group Ratings

	ADA	ACLU	COPE	CFA	LCV	ACU	NTLC	NSI	COC	CEI
1988	55	43	79	55	38	52	22	50	62	28
1987	52	—	69	57	—	22	—	—	53	21

National Journal Ratings

	1988 LIB — 1988 CONS		1987 LIB — 1987 CONS	
Economic	42%	— 57%	49%	— 50%
Social	40%	— 58%	39%	— 60%
Foreign	49%	— 50%	47%	— 52%

Key Votes

1) Homeless $	AGN	5) Ban Drug Test	AGN	9) SDI Research	FOR
2) Gephardt Amdt	FOR	6) Drug Death Pen	FOR	10) Ban Chem Weaps	AGN
3) Deficit Reduc	AGN	7) Handgun Sales	FOR	11) Aid to Contras	FOR
4) Kill Plnt Clsng Notice	AGN	8) Ban D.C. Abort $	FOR	12) Nuclear Testing	FOR

Election Results

1988 primary	Jimmy Hayes (D), unopposed			($268,116)
1986 general	Jimmy Hayes (D)	109,205	(57%)	($846,953)
	Margaret Lowenthal (D)	82,293	(43%)	($350,505)
1986 primary	Jimmy Hayes (D)	51,136	(30%)	
	Margaret Lowenthal (D)	41,938	(25%)	
	James David Cain (D)	40,407	(24%)	
	David Thibodaux (R)	21,082	(13%)	
	Phil Bell (D)	7,479	(4%)	

EIGHTH DISTRICT

Along the Mississippi River, as it makes snakelike loops through Louisiana, during Louisiana's antebellum days were some of the state's biggest plantations: beneath the levees, behind aisles overcrowned with flowering trees, stood some of the nation's grandest plantation houses. The crops then were sugar, rice and cotton, and most of the people were black slaves. Today, some of the plantation houses still stand, but the Mississippi, enclosed by levees and due (thanks to the clout of the Louisiana delegation) to be deepened to 45 feet, is now petroleum alley, with one of

510   LOUISIANA

the nation's biggest concentrations of oil refineries and petrochemical plants. These have provided jobs and some prosperity to what otherwise might be bedraggled areas; but they may also be responsible for some of the nation's highest disease rates.

The 8th Congressional District of Louisiana follows the river, from just above the New Orleans airport to the Mississippi line; it doesn't include Baton Rouge, however, except for a few all-black precincts. It also includes, across the Atchafalaya swamp, a couple of Cajun precincts and the small city of Alexandria, the point where Louisiana changes from Catholic to Baptist. In political terms, the river counties, with their large black populations and their white workers sometimes unionized and often angry with their employers, are national Democratic territory; the Cajun country has been trending Democratic; only Alexandria is Republican in national or seriously contested state elections. This is one of two Louisiana districts which Michael Dukakis carried over George Bush in 1988; it even came within 5,000 votes of going for Walter Mondale in 1984.

Yet the 8th District elects a Republican congressman, Clyde Holloway. The seat was long held by Gillis Long, chairman of the House Democratic Caucus when he died in January 1985; it was held the rest of 1985 and 1986 by his widow Cathy Long. But she decided not to run in 1986, at which point a gaggle of Democrats and one Republican, Holloway, made the race. The leader in Louisiana's all-party primary, with 26%, was Faye Williams, a black former NEA and Democratic Party staffer in Michigan, California, and Capitol Hill, who returned home to make the race; number two was Holloway, with 23%; following them were three white Democrats with 20%, 19% and 12%. Holloway, who raised a family and built a successful nursery business in the district, had run before and won just 25% of the vote against Gillis Long in September 1980, and 16% against Cathy Long in March 1985. But this time, national Republicans channeled money his way, and he was helped when it was revealed that in 1971 Williams's estranged husband broke into her house, beat her and shot to death the college professor—a Communist, Holloway said—she had been dating. Williams, as she pointed out, was the victim, but this lurid stuff surely must have dominated conversations over coffee or backyard fences more than the candidates' opposite positions on aid to the contras, gay rights, abortion, and gun control. Holloway won 51%–49%.

In the House Holloway's first term was far from routine. He had a seat on the Agriculture Committee, but he spent more effort on the Select Committee on Children, Youth, and Family. He became lead sponsor of the Republicans' bill to provide a tax credit to parents for child care, with a refund to those with incomes too low to qualify for the credit; this proposal killed any momentum for the ABC plan to subsidize group day care facilities in 1988. In 1988 there was a rematch. Again other candidates were eliminated in the primary, and again Williams faced Holloway in November. This time Holloway won 57%–43%, running ahead of George Bush; he won 80% of the white vote while Williams won 95% of the black vote, even though both Holloway and Williams made genuine efforts to win votes of the other race. Can Holloway keep this seat? It's beginning to look like he can. "I think I will have a tough race in 1990," he said after the election. "But I believe if I can get through 1990, then Katy can bar the door." It may depend on his opposition—or on the course of the child care issue.

The People: Est. Pop. 1986: 564,500, up 7.6% 1980–86; Pop. 1980: 524,861, up 10.4% 1970–80. Households (1980): 80% family, 49% with children, 63% married couples; 29.0% housing units rented; median monthly rent: $93; median house value: $32,600. Voting age pop. (1980): 349,177; 36% Black, 1% Spanish origin.

1988 Presidential Vote:

Dukakis (D)	115,224	(53%)
Bush (R)	99,234	(45%)

Rep. Clyde Holloway (R)

Elected 1986; b. Nov. 28, 1943, Lecompte, LA; home, Forest Hill; Natl. Sch. of Aeronautics; Baptist; married (Cathy).

Career: Founder and owner, Holloway's Nursery, 1969–86; Pan Amer. Airways 1965–1980.

Offices: 1206 LHOB 20515, 202-225-4926. Also 515 Murray St., P.O. Box 410, Alexandria 71309, 318-473-7430; City Hall Bldg., 120 S. Erma Blvd., Gonzales 70737, 504-647-2000; and P.O. Box 907, Opelousas 70570, 318-942-1115.

Committees: *Agriculture* (16th of 18 R). Subcommittees: Cotton, Rice and Sugar; Conservation, Credit and Rural Development. *Small Business* (14th of 17 R). Subcommittees: SBA, the General Economy and Minority Enterprise Development; Procurement, Tourism and Rural Development. *Select Committee on Children, Youth and Families* (6th of 12 R).

Group Ratings

	ADA	ACLU	COPE	CFA	LCV	ACU	NTLC	NSI	COC	CEI
1988	0	5	28	36	19	96	76	100	92	58
1987	0	—	20	21	—	82	—	—	93	73

National Journal Ratings

	1988 LIB	—	1988 CONS	1987 LIB	—	1987 CONS
Economic	19%	—	80%	19%	—	78%
Social	0%	—	95%	0%	—	90%
Foreign	16%	—	78%	0%	—	80%

Key Votes

1) Homeless $	FOR	5) Ban Drug Test	FOR	9) SDI Research	FOR
2) Gephardt Amdt	AGN	6) Drug Death Pen	FOR	10) Ban Chem Weaps	AGN
3) Deficit Reduc	AGN	7) Handgun Sales	FOR	11) Aid to Contras	FOR
4) Kill Plnt Clsng Notice	FOR	8) Ban D.C. Abort $	FOR	12) Nuclear Testing	AGN

Election Results

1988 general	Clyde Holloway (R)	116,241	(57%)	($629,950)
	Faye Williams (D)	88,564	(43%)	($434,854)
1988 primary	Clyde Holloway (R)	58,831	(44%)	
	Faye Williams (D)	46,088	(34%)	
	Robert L. Freeman (D)	14,814	(11%)	
	J.E. Jonesville, Jr. (D)	14,009	(10%)	
1986 general	Clyde Holloway (R)	102,276	(51%)	($454,661)
	Faye Williams (D)	96,864	(49%)	($403,804)

MAINE

The stereotypical state-of-Mainer is a figure still known to all: a flinty Yankee farmer, dressed in plain clothes and living in a plain clapboard house, speaking in dry and deeply accented monosyllables and occasionally with mordant wit. John Gunther in the 1940s described Maine's character: "One element is intrepidity. The state is largely marked by fingers of land poking out into the sea; in the most literal sense its lobstermen and other fishermen make their living by combat with the elements. Another factor is the complete simplicity and financial integrity of almost all old Maine citizens; money doesn't count for everything in their scale of values; people will spend their last cent on a coat of pale yellow paint for their houses; drop a pocketbook in the streets of Augusta, and a dozen passers-by will return it. Another element is humor. This is not as wry and bitter as is humor in Vermont, say; it has a glow; it has been softened by Atlantic fogs. Still, it can be sharp." An old lobsterman was called as a witness in a lawsuit. "You live in Bayley Island?" he was asked. "Yes." "Lived there all your life?" "Not yet."

Fifty years ago the stereotype hit the mark. Next to Vermont, Maine was the most Yankee state in the nation, stable and conservative but not especially prosperous, a believer in Prohibition and ancestrally Republican since before the Civil War. Maine held its state elections in September up through 1958, a date originally chosen because it followed the state's early harvest; in the days before polls, the results here were taken as a gauge of national partisan movement—hence the saying, "As Maine goes, so goes the nation." Actually, Maine with Yankee stubbornness has been politically contrarian. In 1936, the only state to go with Maine and vote for Alf Landon was Vermont. In 1940, when war was breaking out in Europe and Franklin Roosevelt was trailing far behind his 1936 showings in the heartland and big industrial states, he polled 7% more in Maine as a supporter of aid to the Yankees' British cousins than he had as a New Dealer. Since then, Maine has voted for the loser in the close elections of 1948, 1960, 1968 and 1976, and nearly did so again in 1980—a record equalled by no other state.

But as that contrariness suggests, Maine has not remained solidly Yankee or solidly Republican. Higher birth rates and migration patterns mean that the immigrants who were a minority two generations ago have produced offspring who are very nearly the majority in Maine now: a near-majority that in many ways shares traditional Yankee traits and values, but that is also more Democratic than Republican. Maine was represented in Congress for years by Republican Yankees only: today its delegation is bipartisan. Its Senators over the last decade have been the sons of Polish, Jewish and Lebanese immigrants, and its two House members are of Greek and Irish descent.

But even as Maine's politics have changed to reflect the migration patterns of 50 and 60 years ago, its migration patterns are changing again—and affecting politics—in the 1980s. Maine was frontier when the rest of the East was settled, but it filled up quickly after becoming a state in 1820, and like the Great Plains states some decades later, basically quit growing. Maine had 600,000 people by 1860, 700,000 in about 1905, 800,000 in the 1930s, and over one million in 1971—extraordinarily low population growth that reflects steady outmigration, a not very buoyant economy and an aging population. But now the New England boom has touched at least southern Maine, and the population is rising and will likely top 1.2 million in 1990, indicating as much growth in the last 19 years as in the 40 before that (or the 70 before that). The rocky coast of Maine, always a favored vacation spot—and now the vacation home of President George Bush—has been attracting young migrants, professionals and craftsmen seeking a simpler life than in the great metropolitan areas; at the same time, the antique dockside buildings of

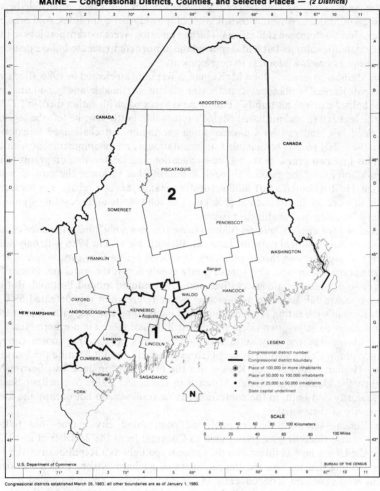

MAINE — Congressional Districts, Counties, and Selected Places — *(2 Districts)*

Portland's Commercial Street have been renovated and the Portland area has had some of the fastest-rising real estate prices in the country.

Yet not all of Maine is as buzzing with unpretentious prosperity as Freeport's L. L. Bean store, open 24 hours a day. Not far inland up some narrow two-lane highway is the home of Carolyn Chute's *The Beans of Egypt, Maine*, a region of poor, ignorant, ill-clothed swamp Yankees in a backwater from which they have not a clue how to extricate themselves. Many of Maine's paper and textile mill towns have the air of neglect and abandonment that comes to places that have been losing jobs and young people for a generation, and it seems to get harder every year to scratch a living out of the cold earth of the Aroostook County potato country. The mostly coastal counties that make up Maine's 1st Congressional District grew 7% in the first six years of the 1980s, while the mostly inland counties of the 2d District grew only 1%. But by the late 1980s, the inland counties and mill towns were growing too. That leaves Maine voters concerned about the environment that brought or kept so many of them here. In 1987, they approved a law directing the state to buy up land before it's developed, but that's only a part of the solution, since almost all of Maine is privately owned, most of it by lumber companies. And even effective regulation can have unforeseen side effects. The ban on using rivers to transport logs in the 1970s has saved the Atlantic salmon, but it also spurred the lumber companies to build a dense network of roads that opens much wilderness to development.

Governor. Maine's governor is John McKernan, a Republican elected in 1986 after two terms in Congress. McKernan is photogenic and a star athlete, personable and good-humored. As a teenager, he helped manage his family's Bangor newspaper when his father died; in 1972, he was elected to the legislature and authored Maine's returnable bottle law; he left the legislature in 1976, practiced law, and ran for Congress when the incumbent challenged Senator George Mitchell in 1982. His record has justified his reputation as an environmentalist with business support. In his first two years, he started new education and job training programs to upgrade Maine's work force, and he pushed through a reform plan to lower the cost of workmen's compensation. He distributed a $61 million surplus to taxpayers as a rebate. For his second two, he promised to work on environmental problems like solid waste and recycling styrofoam, and also affordable housing and health care issues.

How secure is McKernan's hold on Blaine House (the governor's mansion once occupied by Maine's 19th century political paladin, James G. Blaine)? He won in 1986 with only 40% of the vote. The rest was split among three candidates: Democrat James Tierney won just 30%, nuclear power critic Sherry Huber won 15% spread pretty evenly across the state, and former Portland city manager John Menario, a conservative, won 15% centered around Portland. But the anti-nuclear cause took a fall when an anti-nuclear power referendum was defeated 59%–41% in 1988. If McKernan's job rating remains high, he is likely to be a strong candidate in 1990, and the contest is likely to be just two-sided, which is still the norm even in northern New England.

Senators. Maine was the only state with two Senators on the Iran-contra committee—Republican William Cohen and Democrat George Mitchell—and it became the fourth state in this century (Indiana, Illinois, and Kansas are the others) to produce two Senate Majority Leaders when the Democrats selected Mitchell in December 1988. Yet neither Senator has enormous seniority and both, in the contrarian Maine tradition, do not occupy the ideological center of gravity of their parties.

William Cohen—son of a baker, published poet, small city mayor—has followed an independent course since he was first elected to Congress from the 2d District in 1972. In his first term in the House he was thrust into the national spotlight as a Republican on the Judiciary Committee holding hearings on the impeachment of Richard Nixon. Cohen was one of the Republicans who caucused independently of his party leaders and who ended up voting to impeach. On some, though not all, other issues he took liberal stances as well. Yet when he ran against Senator William Hathaway in 1978, his platform was military preparedness; and after beating Hathaway by a wide margin, Cohen immediately got a seat on the Armed Services Committee, opposed the SALT II treaty, and supported a big defense buildup—though he was not a lockstep supporter of Reagan programs. In the early Reagan years, he opposed the nuclear freeze and was one of the originators of the build-down proposal, working to get the Administration to agree to a build-down in return for congressional support of the MX missile. He chaired the Seapower Subcommittee and, with Gary Hart of Colorado (his co-author on a spy novel published in 1985), argued for building more small ships rather than fewer big ones (and inevitably for a Maine Senator, for building them at the Bath Iron Works rather than in Pascagoula, Mississippi).

By the late Reagan years, he was taking another turn. In 1987 he became vice chairman of the Intelligence Committee, and turned out to be much less leak-prone than his Republican predecessor David Durenberger. On the Iran-contra committee, this sometime opponent of contra aid tended to support the chairmen and bipartisan majority. Afterwards he wrote a book with George Mitchell, decrying Oliver North and his colleagues as "men of zeal" who undermined the Constitution and the legal process, and conceding that the committee did not succeed in making its case persuasively to the public. But in 1989 on Armed Services he was one of the Republicans most strongly critical of the Democrats for their attacks on John Tower.

On other issues, Cohen has usually not taken a leading role. On economic issues, he shares with most Republicans a faith in the free-market mechanism, but his experience growing up in a family that owned a bakery and then serving as mayor in Bangor inclines him to believe that government should help people out. But rather than get into arguments about economic redistribution, he prefers to find ways to make government work better. He also works to stop federal computer matching of benefits recipients, to ban chemical exports to Iran and Iraq, and to stop WIC overcharges. On cultural issues, he is one of those East Coast Republicans who take positions which are generally considered liberal.

One common thread in Cohen's record is that he has often (though not always) been ahead of the curve. Another is that he generally favors strengthening Congress against the executive branch. In 1987 and 1988, for example, he was pushing bills to further insulate independent counsels from the Justice Department and to require more notice to Congress of covert action. But he does not always oppose Republican administrations on the merits, as so many Democrats do, and he recognizes that Congress has responsibilities which it may fail to fulfill—as he charged that former Speaker Jim Wright did when he attacked the CIA for provoking the Sandinistas.

Cohen has proved to be a strong vote-getter in Maine, winning a formerly Democratic House seat in 1972, beating an incumbent senator 57%–37% in 1978, and winning 73% in 1984 against a Democratic legislator who stressed the already withering issue of the nuclear freeze. He did nothing to help the right-wing Republican who ran against George Mitchell in 1988. His prospects for 1990 are excellent, and probably enhanced rather than diminished by the fact that his sometimes liberal, not always predictable Republican from this contrarian corner of the country has not been considered a likely candidate for national office.

After a decade in Washington, and a political career that has had its downs as well as ups, George Mitchell is now the Senate Majority Leader—one of the major power wielders in Washington. He brings to the job a genial temperament, a gift for argumentation, and a strong belief in the principles of old-fashioned liberalism. He is courteous, but he is also a strong partisan, and if he recognizes the strength in national elections of the tenets of Reagan-Bush conservatism, he waits patiently for a chance to oppose them successfully with the confidence of a man who has taken some hard defeats and then has seen things turn his way again.

Mitchell got his political start as a protégé of Senator Edmund Muskie; as a young lawyer he became Democratic state chairman in 1966, the beginning of a series of dreadful years for Democrats in most places, but in contrarian Maine the year their party captured both the state's House seats. In 1974 he was the Democratic nominee for governor, and was humiliated when he lost 40%–37% to Independent James Longley. When he got an appointment as a federal judge during the Carter Administration—a nice plum, since dour state of Mainers are notoriously unlitigious and the state's federal judges typically are assigned duty in mostly pleasant spots all around the country—it seemed that his political career was over. Unpredictable events in spring 1980 changed that: the failed rescue mission in Iran, the resignation of Secretary of State Cyrus Vance, the selection of Edmund Muskie to succeed him, the decision by Governor Joseph Brennan (now an obscure congressman, while Mitchell leads the Senate) to appoint Judge Mitchell in May 1980.

It was expected that Mitchell would be slaughtered by 1st District Congressman David Emery in 1982; instead, it was the other way around. Emery made some big mistakes, while Mitchell stayed cool, delivered his basic message, and in a recession year won with 61%.

Mitchell was underestimated again when he got himself selected chairman of the Democratic Senatorial Campaign Committee after the 1984 election. For most of the biennium it seemed possible the Republicans would hold the Senate, but Mitchell plugged on, raising money, monitoring the races closely, encouraging strong candidates to run. Democrats ended up with 55 seats, more than anyone thought possible; especially critical were several victories in the South, which won control of the Senate for the Democrats and ended up winning the majority leadership for Mitchell.

Mitchell was not legislatively idle during this time. On Environment, where Muskie had made his original mark, Mitchell became a well-informed and active critic of Reagan environmental policies and pushed a clean air (and anti-acid rain) bill excruciatingly close to passage in the Senate. On Senate Finance, he advanced the key alternative to the 1986 tax reform bill, calling for higher rates on high-income taxpayers; but this classic progressive policy, despite Mitchell's skilled advocacy, failed to pass, as most Senators concluded that high rates either impeded growth or inevitably promoted tax avoidance schemes and hence inequity. Nor was he successful in getting continuation of tax exemptions for investments in low-income housing. On the Iran-contra committee, Mitchell was as skilled an interrogator of Oliver North and other witnesses as any member, bringing to his work both a knowledge of the facts and a conviction that both the illegal acts of Administration officials and the substantive policies of the Administration were in important ways wrong. But he did not neglect local issues, claiming that the Canadian free trade treaty improperly treated lobsters and potatoes. His reelection in 1988 was taken for granted, and against a religious conservative activist he won 81% of the vote—the all-time record for a Maine Senator.

How did Mitchell get to be Majority Leader? By campaigning softspokenly, out of the way of the press; by cornering the votes of most northern liberals; by making inroads in the South and among the class of 1986 he helped elect; by being considered a more polished and appropriate (i.e., not a southern conservative) spokesman for the Democratic Party. On the first ballot Mitchell had 27 votes; Daniel Inouye and Bennett Johnston, with 14 each, sensibly decided to forego a second ballot. What does Mitchell intend to do with the majority leadership? In early 1989 he issued a Democratic program which was more specific in its contents and more liberal in its thrust than many political consultants would have advised. Mitchell's key lieutenant, Tom Daschle of South Dakota, is one of several young senators who call themselves populists and who believe that there is a market among voters for policies that aggressively use government to protect individuals and workers. There are only about 25 solid liberal Democrats in the Senate, far fewer than in the 1960s and 1970s though more than in in the 1940s and 1950s; but the Democrats have shown unexpected solidarity in opposing the Bork and Tower appointments, and Mitchell undoubtedly hopes they will on positive initiatives as well. Mitchell does not seem to be looking for confrontation on all issues; in April 1989 he reached a budget agreement with the Bush administration. But he does seem to be trying to use the Senate Democrats power aggressively and skillfully to advance views that many think a majority have repudiated but which he believes can win wide support.

Presidential politics. Maine is now the home of President George Bush—or at least the site of the only home he owns. Bush has spent every summer of his life in Kennebunkport (except when on wartime duty), and he bought the family house there from a relative's estate while he was Vice President. He has claimed Maine as one of his many home states ever since he first ran for President in 1980, and the claim was strong enough to give him what amounted to an uncontested victory in Maine's 1988 caucuses, February 28. It also helped him, but only marginally, in November: only in the towns around Kennebunkport did Bush, by running ahead of Ronald Reagan's 1984 showings, demonstrate a strong personal appeal. Otherwise Bush carried Maine by a comfortable but not overwhelming margin on national issues.

The Maine caucuses, coming so early, have been looked to by many candidates as the site of a possible breakthrough. But none has materialized. Ernest Hollings, despite much personal campaigning, did poorly here in 1984, and George Bush's and Michael Dukakis's wins were discounted well in advance. Anyway, only 18,744 voters took part in a state of 1.2 million. The only omen was Jesse Jackson's surprisingly strong second place in a state with virtually no blacks—an accurate omen that Jackson's appeal to leftish Democratic activists would make him a stronger candidate in caucuses in 1988 than in primaries.

Congressional districting. Maine's redistricting plan has been only slightly modified since the state lost its 3d District in the 1960 Census. A Republican plan, it was intended to split areas of Democratic strength; but Maine is politically homogeneous enough that the lines make less difference than the strength of the incumbents and their challengers. Slight modifications were made in 1983 and probably will be again in 1991 to adjust for the greater population growth in the 1st District.

1st Congressional District. This district stretches from southernmost Kittery and nearby Kennebunkport and the booming Portland area to the craggy-shored ancestrally Republican counties farther east. The congressman is Joseph Brennan, a liberal Democrat who was the only incumbent governor backing Edward Kennedy in 1980 and who later barred Maine National Guard troops from training in Honduras; barred from a third term, he in effect changed places with 1st District Republican Jock McKernan who won his place in Blaine House. But Brennan won by an unimpressive 53%–44% margin over a little-known candidate, and in 1988 attracted two serious Republican challengers. Linda Bean-Jones, well-known and well-financed L. L. Bean heiress, was a hardshell conservative; she spent pots of money on media but lost the primary 52%–48% to Ted O'Meara, who ran only a few ads, featuring his former boss, William Cohen, and relied on support from organization Republicans.

After all this hubbub, Brennan beat O'Meara 63%–37% in the general election—a comfortable margin typical of an established incumbent. Liberal in his impulses on most issues, but not quite always (he made a name in Maine opposing Indian claims), a pugnacious professional politician, Brennan can have a long career in the House. He serves on the Armed Services and Merchant Marine Committees.

2nd Congressional District. Republican Olympia Snowe, elected in 1978 to replace Bill Cohen in the 2d District, is now one of the more senior Republicans in the House, and one of the more aggressive and conspicuous. She is one of the founders of the 92 Group, the cluster of somewhat more liberal but still usually partisan Republicans who are working for their party to become the majority by 1992. That desire led her to be one of the most active supporters of Newt Gingrich's candidacy for minority whip, much to the surprise of some. She is also one of two deputy minority whips in the House, and is mostly conservative and market-oriented on economic issues; on cultural and foreign issues, her record is somewhat more liberal. It is in the last that her committee work, as a member of the Foreign Affairs Committee and ranking Republican on the International Operations Subcommittee, is concentrated. She is a key vote on many issues, giving Republican support to the committee Democrats' approach on South Africa, for instance, or representing a swing vote on contra aid. But she also wants the administration to abrogate the treaty that gave the Soviets one of Washington's highest points for their embassy while the U.S. got swampy land and a heavily bugged building, which she wants torn down. With the rest of the Maine delegation, she opposed the Canadian free trade bill, arguing that the Canadians were unfairly subsidizing sawmills and potato growers in competition with Mainers. She is of Greek descent, and has been one of the Congress's leading advocates of cutting military aid to Turkey; but she is also a vigorous critic of the anti-American and intellectually dishonest government of Andreas Papandreou (a reminder that the Greeks gave us the word not only for democracy but for demagogue). She is also, since her early 1989 marriage to John McKernan, the only member of Congress married to an incumbent governor.

Geographically, the 2d District covers the northern three-quarters of the state; in the more thickly populated part of Maine, however, the boundary line is actually rather jagged, and it takes in the traditionally Democratic mill town of Lewiston as well as the traditionally Republican coastal area down east. In contrast to the coastal south, where the labor market is so tight some jobs go begging, there is still some slack in the economy up north; people in the potato country hope their low wage rates will attract employers and some were in terror that the automatic base-closing bill would spell the end for Loring Air Force Base.

In 1988, Snowe faced the strongest competition she has seen recently and won 66% of the vote—lower than in 1986 or 1984 but still solid.

The People: Est. Pop. 1988: 1,206,000; Pop. 1980: 1,124,660, up 7.2% 1980–88 and 13.2% 1970–80; 0.49% of U.S. total, 37th largest. 15% with 1–3 yrs. col., 14% with 4+ yrs. col.; 13.0% below poverty level. Single ancestry: 23% English, 13% French, 5% Irish, 2% German, Scottish, 1% Italian, Polish, Swedish. Households (1980): 74% family, 41% with children, 63% married couples; 29.1% housing units rented; median monthly rent: $173; median house value: $37,900. Voting age pop. (1980): 803,273. Registered voters (1988): 854,764; 264,375 D (31%), 237,883 R (28%), 284,414 unaffiliated and minor parties (33%).

1988 Share of Federal Tax Burden: $3,702,000,000; 0.42% of U.S. total, 42d largest.

1988 Share of Federal Expenditures

	Total		Non-Defense		Defense	
Total Expend	$4,024m	(0.46%)	$4,492m	(0.69%)	$1,044m	(0.46%)
St/Lcl Grants	665m	(0.58%)	2,004m	(1.75%)	0m	(0.09%)
Salary/Wages	496m	(0.37%)	249m	(0.37%)	246m	(0.37%)
Pymnts to Indiv	2,114m	(0.52%)	2,008m	(0.51%)	107m	(0.57%)
Procurement	690m	(0.37%)	173m	(0.37%)	690m	(0.37%)
Research/Other	59m	(0.16%)	58m	(0.16%)	0m	(0.16%)

Political Lineup: Governor, John R. McKernan, Jr. (R); Sec. of State, G. William Diamond (D); Atty. Gen., James Tierney (D); Treasurer, Samuel Shapiro (D); Controller, David Bourne (D). State Senate, 35 (20 D and 15 R); State House of Representatives, 151 (97 D and 54 R). Senators, William S. Cohen (R) and George J. Mitchell (D). Representatives, 2 (1 D and 1 R).

1988 Presidential Vote			**1984 Presidential Vote**		
Bush (R)	307,131	(55%)	Reagan (R)	336,500	(61%)
Dukakis (D)	243,569	(44%)	Mondale (D)	214,515	(39%)

GOVERNOR

Gov. John R. McKernan, Jr. (R)

Elected 1986, term expires Jan. 1991; b. May 2, 1948, Bangor; home, Cumberland; Dartmouth Col., A.B. 1970, U. of ME, J.D. 1974; Protestant; married (U.S. Rep. Olympia J. Snowe).

Career: Practicing atty.; ME House of Reps., 1973–77; Asst. House Minor. Ldr., 1975–76; U.S. House of Reps., 1982–86.

Office: State House, Station 1, Augusta 04333, 207-289-3531.

Election Results

1986 gen.	John R. McKernan, Jr. (R)	170,312	(40%)
	James Tierney (D)	128,744	(30%)
	Sherry F. Huber (I)	64,317	(15%)
	John E. Menario (I)	63,474	(15%)
1986 prim.	John R. McKernan, Jr. (R)	79,393	(68%)
	Porter D. Leighton (R)........	36,705	(32%)
1982 gen.	Joseph E. Brennan (D)........	281,066	(61%)
	Charles L. Cragin (R)	172,949	(38%)

SENATORS

Sen. William S. Cohen (R)

Elected 1978, seat up 1990; b. Aug. 28, 1940, Bangor; home, Bangor; Bowdoin Col., B.A. 1962, Boston U., LL.B. 1965; Unitarian Universalist; divorced.

Career: Practicing atty., 1965–72; Asst. Penobscot Cnty. Atty., 1968; Instructor, Husson Col., 1968, U. of ME, 1968–72; Bangor City Cncl., 1969–72, Mayor of Bangor, 1971–72; U.S. House of Reps., 1973–79.

Offices: 322 HSOB 20510, 202-224-2523. Also 154 State St., Augusta 04330, 207-622-8414; Fed. Bldg., Rm. 204, 202 Harlow St., Bangor 04401, 207-945-0417; 2 Adams St., Biddeford 04005, 207-283-1101; 11 Lisbon St., Lewiston 04240, 207-784-6969; 15 Monument Sq., Portland 04104, 207-780-3575; and 523 Main St., Presque Isle 04769, 207-764-3266.

Committees: *Armed Services* (4th of 9 R). Subcommittees: Conventional Forces and Alliance Defense; Strategic Forces and Nuclear Deterrence; Projection Forces and Regional Defense (Ranking Member). *Governmental Affairs* (3d of 6 R). Subcommittees: Government Information and Regulation; Investigations; Oversight of Government Management (Ranking Member). *Select Committee on Intelligence* (Ranking Member of 7 R). *Special Committee on Aging* (2d of 9 R).

Group Ratings

	ADA	ACLU	COPE	CFA	LCV	ACU	NTLC	NSI	COC	CEI
1988	35	58	39	75	80	46	42	100	57	19
1987	55	—	37	83	—	58	—	—	67	36

National Journal Ratings

	1988 LIB — 1988 CONS	1987 LIB — 1987 CONS
Economic	43% — 55%	40% — 59%
Social	61% — 38%	39% — 59%
Foreign	41% — 58%	43% — 56%

Key Votes

1) Cut Aged Housing $	FOR	5) Bork Nomination	FOR	9) SDI Funding	FOR
2) Override Hwy Veto	AGN	6) Ban Plastic Guns	FOR	10) Ban Chem Weaps	FOR
3) Kill Plnt Clsng Notice	AGN	7) Deny Abortions	AGN	11) Aid To Contras	FOR
4) Min Wage Increase	AGN	8) Japanese Reparations	FOR	12) Reagan Defense $	AGN

Election Results

1984 general	William S. Cohen (R)................	404,414	(73%)	($1,063,188)
	Elizabeth H. Mitchell (D)	142,626	(26%)	($410,611)
1984 primary	William S. Cohen (R)................	36,606	(100%)	
1978 general	William S. Cohen (R)................	212,294	(57%)	($648,739)
	William D. Hathaway (D)	127,327	(37%)	($423,027)
	Hayes Gahagan (I)..................	27,824	(7%)	($115,901)

Sen. George J. Mitchell (D)

Appointed May 17, 1980, elected 1982, seat up 1994; b. Aug. 20, 1933, Waterville; home, South Portland; Bowdoin Col., B.A. 1954, Georgetown U., J.D. 1960; Roman Catholic; divorced.

Career: Army counter-intelligence, 1954–56; U.S. Dept. of Justice, 1960–62; Exec. Asst. to U.S. Senator Edmund S. Muskie, 1962–65; Practicing atty., 1965–77; Asst. Atty., Cumberland Cnty., 1971; U.S. Atty. for ME, 1977–79; U.S. Dist. Judge for ME, 1979–80; U.S. Sen. Major. Ldr., 1989–present.

Offices: 176 RSOB 20510, 202-224-5344. Also 537 Congress St., P.O. Box 8300, Portland 04104, 207-874-0883; Fed. Bldg., 40 Western Ave., Rm. 101C, Augusta 04330, 207-622-8292; 231 Main St., Biddeford 04005, 207-282-4144; Maine and Winter Sts., Rockland 04841, 207-596-0311; Fed. Bldg., 202 Harlow St., P.O. Box 1237, Bangor 04401, 207-945-0451; 11 Lisbon St., Lewiston 04240, 207-784-0163; 33 College Ave., P.O. Box 786, Waterville 04901, 207-873-3361; and 6 Church St., Presque Isle 04769, 207-764-5601.

Committees: *Environment and Public Works* (3d of 9 D). Subcommittees: Environmental Protection; Superfund, Ocean and Water Protection; Water Resources, Transportation and Infrastructure. *Finance* (7th of 11 D). Subcommittees: International Trade; Health for Families and the Uninsured; Medicare and Long-Term Care. *Veterans' Affairs* (4th of 6 D).

Group Ratings

	ADA	ACLU	COPE	CFA	LCV	ACU	NTLC	NSI	COC	CEI
1988	95	70	87	92	80	0	7	10	21	11
1987	95	—	86	100	—	8	—	—	28	21

National Journal Ratings

	1988 LIB — 1988 CONS		1987 LIB — 1987 CONS	
Economic	86% —	0%	74% —	0%
Social	79% —	17%	78% —	17%
Foreign	79% —	16%	81% —	0%

Key Votes

1) Cut Aged Housing $	FOR	5) Bork Nomination	AGN	9) SDI Funding	AGN
2) Override Hwy Veto	FOR	6) Ban Plastic Guns	AGN	10) Ban Chem Weaps	AGN
3) Kill Plnt Clsng Notice	AGN	7) Deny Abortions	AGN	11) Aid To Contras	AGN
4) Min Wage Increase	FOR	8) Japanese Reparations	FOR	12) Reagan Defense $	AGN

Election Results

1988 general	George J. Mitchell (D)	452,590	(81%)	($1,471,426)
	Jasper S. Wyman (R)	104,758	(19%)	($147,760)
1988 primary	George J. Mitchell (D), unopposed			
1982 general	George J. Mitchell (D)	279,819	(61%)	($1,209,599)
	David F. Emery (R)	179,882	(39%)	($1,081,122)

FIRST DISTRICT

The People: Est. Pop. 1986: 605,100, up 7.5% 1980–86; Pop. 1980: 563,073, up 17.2% 1970–80. Households (1980): 73% family, 39% with children, 62% married couples; 30.4% housing units rented; median monthly rent: $186; median house value: $42,000. Voting age pop. (1980): 405,831.

1988 Presidential Vote:	Bush (R)	169,292	(56%)
	Dukakis (D)	131,078	(43%)

Rep. Joseph E. Brennan (D)

Elected 1986; b. Nov. 2, 1934, Portland; home, Portland; Boston Col., B.S. 1958, U. of ME, J.D. 1963; Roman Catholic; divorced.

Career: Practicing atty.; ME House of Reps., 1965–71; Cumberland Cnty. Atty., 1971–73; ME Senate, 1973–75, Dem. Flr. Ldr.; Atty. Gen. of ME, 1975–79; Governor of ME 1979–87.

Offices: 1428 LHOB 20515, 202-225-6116. Also 177 Commercial St., Portland 04101; 207-772-8240, 107-780-3382; and 128 State St., Ste. 102, Augusta 04330, 207-623-2883.

Committees: *Armed Services* (25th of 31 D). Subcommittees: Investigations; Seapower and Strategic and Critical Materials. *Merchant Marine and Fisheries* (19th of 26 D). Subcommittees: Coast Guard and Navigation; Oceanography; Merchant Marine.

Group Ratings

	ADA	ACLU	COPE	CFA	LCV	ACU	NTLC	NSI	COC	CEI
1988	90	87	97	100	88	12	18	0	29	17
1987	100	—	94	85	—	0	—	—	7	8

National Journal Ratings

	1988 LIB — 1988 CONS		1987 LIB — 1987 CONS	
Economic	60% —	37%	73% —	0%
Social	76% —	23%	78% —	0%
Foreign	68% —	28%	73% —	26%

Key Votes

1) Homeless $	AGN	5) Ban Drug Test	AGN
2) Gephardt Amdt	FOR	6) Drug Death Pen	AGN
3) Deficit Reduc	FOR	7) Handgun Sales	FOR
4) Kill Plnt Clsng Notice	AGN	8) Ban D.C. Abort $	AGN

9) SDI Research	AGN
10) Ban Chem Weaps	FOR
11) Aid to Contras	AGN
12) Nuclear Testing	FOR

Election Results

1988 general	Joseph E. Brennan (D)	190,989	(63%)	($464,541)
	Edward S. O'Meara, Jr. (R)	111,125	(37%)	($286,699)
1988 primary	Joseph E. Brennan (D), unopposed			
1986 general	Joseph E. Brennan (D)	121,848	(53%)	($287,695)
	H. Rollin Ives (R)	100,260	(44%)	($261,403)

SECOND DISTRICT

The People: Est. Pop. 1986: 568,700, up 1.3% 1980–86; Pop. 1980: 561,587, up 9.4% 1970–80. Households (1980): 76% family, 42% with children, 64% married couples; 27.7% housing units rented; median monthly rent: $161; median house value: $33,600. Voting age pop. (1980): 397,442.

1988 Presidential Vote:

Bush (R) 137,839	(55%)
Mondale (D) 112,491	(45%)

Rep. Olympia J. Snowe (R)

Elected 1978; b. Feb. 21, 1947, Augusta; home, Auburn; U. of ME, B.A. 1969; Greek Orthodox; married (Gov. John R. McKernan).

Career: Dir., Superior Concrete Co.; Member, Bd. of Voter Regis., Auburn, 1971–73; ME House of Reps., 1973–76; ME Senate, 1976–78.

Offices: 2464 RHOB 20515, 202-225-6306. Also 1 Cumberland Place, Ste. 306, Bangor 04401, 207-945-0432; 197 State St., P.O. Box 722, Presque Isle 04769, 207-764-5124; and 2 Great Falls Plaza, Ste. 7B, Auburn 04210, 207-786-2451.

Committees: *Foreign Affairs* (6th of 18 R). Subcommittees: Arms Control, International Security and Science; International Operations (Ranking Member). *Select Committee on Aging* (5th of 26 R). Subcommittee: Human Services (Ranking Member). *Joint Economic Committee.* Task Forces: Education and Health; Economic Goals and Intergovernmental Policy; International Economic Policy.

Group Ratings

	ADA	ACLU	COPE	CFA	LCV	ACU	NTLC	NSI	COC	CEI
1988	60	57	48	82	75	40	56	60	50	22
1987	56	—	44	50	—	22	—	—	73	40

National Journal Ratings

	1988 LIB — 1988 CONS	1987 LIB — 1987 CONS
Economic	49% — 50%	40% — 59%
Social	49% — 51%	48% — 50%
Foreign	51% — 48%	50% — 48%

Key Votes

1) Homeless $	FOR	5) Ban Drug Test	AGN	9) SDI Research	AGN
2) Gephardt Amdt	FOR	6) Drug Death Pen	FOR	10) Ban Chem Weaps	FOR
3) Deficit Reduc	AGN	7) Handgun Sales	FOR	11) Aid to Contras	FOR
4) Kill Plnt Clsng Notice	AGN	8) Ban D.C. Abort $	AGN	12) Nuclear Testing	FOR

Election Results

1988 general	Olympia J. Snowe (R)	167,229	(66%)	($202,317)
	Kenneth P. Hayes (D)	85,346	(34%)	($68,390)
1988 primary	Olympia J. Snowe (R), unopposed			
1986 general	Olympia J. Snowe (R)	148,770	(77%)	($215,659)
	Richard R. Charette (D)	43,614	(23%)	($23,779)

MARYLAND

Fifty years ago, when H. L. Mencken—chronicler of the American language, explicator of political buncombe, and excoriator of Prohibition—was still writing for the *Baltimore Sun*, Maryland was a kind of city-state, occupying both shores of the Chesapeake Bay and centered on Baltimore. Almost precisely half of all Marylanders lived within the city limits of Baltimore, "charmingly picturesque," the *WPA Guide* said then, "in its ugliness. Red brick houses, row on row, with scrubbed white steps, line the narrow streets of the old town; yellow brick houses, miles of them, run uphill and down through the purgatories of the 20th century realtors; crooked alleys with odd names meander behind the old red brick fronts; lordly mansions of the rich preen themselves in groves and parks in the smart suburbs to the north." Other Marylanders then were spread in distinct hinterlands: the southern-oriented counties of both shores of the Chesapeake, the northern-accented wheat-growing country around the antique small cities of Frederick and Hagerstown, where railroad tracks ran on the street right in front of lace-curtained houses, and the mountain-bound industrial city of Cumberland.

The puritan impulse was never lively in Maryland; it has been tolerant and even proud of its foibles and eccentricities since its founders, the Lords Baltimore, allowed religious freedom for the sensible reason that they were a Catholic family in a Protestant country. Prohibition was enforced only laxly in Baltimore; slot machines were legal in the rural counties of the Western Shore; the state's old law guaranteeing blacks equal access to public accommodations specifically excluded the Eastern Shore. Baltimore, the *Guide* notes, was "rough and boisterous" and, "like ancient European metropolises, had its 'mob,' which the gentlemen of the town were sometimes hard put to quell"; "Maryland, My Maryland," sung (or hummed: almost no one knows the words) proudly on state occasions, commemorates an attack by a racist mob on Union troops. Parts of Maryland's political history read like a chronicle of rogues, from Luther Martin, the drunken haranguer at the Constitutional Convention, to Spiro Agnew, who took cash bribes as governor and Vice President.

Maryland's genial tolerance may have given it a history a little too savory, but it has also held together this diverse—northerners and southerners, blacks and ethnics, civil servants and Chesapeake Bay watermen—and oddly-shaped commonwealth. It has helped to create a pride and a local patriotism as vibrant as that of any state, even after two generations of rapid growth in which an almost entirely new Maryland has grown up as large as the old around the Beltways that circle Baltimore and Washington. While 16% of Marylanders live in Baltimore City now, and 14% in the Eastern Shore and western counties (though most have grown), they have a much smaller share of the state's population than they did 50 years ago. Most Marylanders now live in the suburbs, 34% in suburban counties around Baltimore and 36% in the five suburban counties around Washington, D.C.

But the tone of public life in the Free State is still set in Baltimore. The Washington suburbs may be more upscale (and also more black), but they remain a bit disconnected; while in the suburbs of "Bawlmer" (as it's called in the distinctive local accent) pride in Harborplace and the Orioles and Johns Hopkins and Pulitzer Prize winning novelist Anne Tyler are as strong as in the city. William Donald Schaefer, in 15 years as mayor—from 1971 to 1986—transformed Baltimore's image from that of a dowdy, inbred industrial city to a city where people vacation, where movies are made, where people are happy that the local economy—changing steadily from blue-collar to white-collar—is providing enough good jobs to enable them to stay. Baltimore's and Maryland's surge of local pride was never more apparent than in 1986, when Schaefer was elected governor by an overwhelming margin and Baltimore Congresswoman Barbara Mikulski was elected to the Senate as colleague to Baltimore's Paul Sarbanes. These are politicians with backgrounds in modest Maryland neighborhoods, with ties in Schaefer's case to old-fashioned politicos and in its Senators' to political reformers—politicians who, in a city and a state known for corruption, worked their way up without a hint of scandal.

This same pride may have played a role in the most surprising result of the 1988 campaign, the passage of a referendum endorsing the state's new gun control law. Schaefer led this fight, making it a battle of his state's law versus the NRA outsiders who were spending millions. With unremitting support from the *Washington Post* and *Baltimore Sun* editorial pages, Schaefer and his allies carried not only Montgomery County and Baltimore City but Prince George's and the Baltimore suburbs as well; they held down negative margins in the rural counties—where turnout swollen by gun control opponents nevertheless may have helped George Bush edge Michael Dukakis statewide—and even carried one county on the Eastern Shore. Maryland has been a landmark state on gun control, ever since attacks on his pro-gun control position helped cause the upset of Senator Joseph Tydings in 1970. This time, the result went the other way, as the referendum passed 58%–42%.

Governor. William Donald Schaefer is rumpled, unphotogenic, squirms when interviewed and feuds with the press; his tastes and style are that of the meatloaf middle class of the 1950s; he summers in a vacation trailer in Ocean City. He is anything but smooth; he pouts at the slightest criticism; he is often nervous before any group that he suspects is not uncritically admiring; he balks at even mentioning the names of some political adversaries like former Attorney General Stephen Sachs and current Baltimore Mayor Kurt Schmoke, though they would not be averse to having pleasant relations with him. Schaefer looks the opposite of today's media politician, and yet he is the most popular politician in Maryland and quite possibly the politically strongest governor in the nation. He won the governorship in 1986 by soundly beating a strong candidate, Stephen Sachs, in the primary, and by winning the general election with 1986's highest percentage in a contested gubernatorial or senate race.

Schaefer's secret is that he is utterly dedicated to serving his constituents. "That's my whole motivation: people," he says, in words that from a less corny politician would sound insincere; but few in Maryland doubt that it is true. Schaefer is famous for his personal inspections, sending city and state appointees memos demanding that this alley be cleaned by 10 a.m. tomorrow and that that bit of red tape be cut by Wednesday afternoon. His theoretical policy

MARYLAND — Congressional Districts, Counties, Independent City, and Other Selected Places — *(8 Districts)*

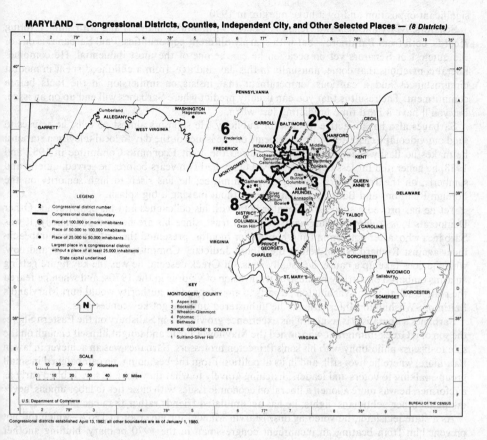

MARYLAND — Congressional Districts, Counties, Independent City, and Other Selected Places — *(8 Districts)*

LEGEND

2 Congressional district number

— Congressional district boundary

◉ Place of 100,000 or more inhabitants

◎ Place of 50,000 to 100,000 inhabitants

● Place of 25,000 to 50,000 inhabitants

○ Largest place in a congressional district without a place of at least 25,000 inhabitants

State capital underlined

KEY

MONTGOMERY COUNTY
1 Aspen Hill
2 Rockville
3 Wheaton-Glenmont
4 Potomac
5 Bethesda

PRINCE GEORGE'S COUNTY
1 Suitland-Silver Hill

SCALE

0 10 20 30 40 50 Kilometers

0 10 20 30 40 50 Miles

U.S. Department of Commerce

BUREAU OF THE CENSUS

Congressional districts established April 13, 1982; all other boundaries are as of January 1, 1980.

instincts tend to be conservative; on cultural issues he is traditional, not liberation-minded; on economics he talks about the need to encourage business. In a state that is 21% and a city that is more than 50% black, his core political base has always been among whites (though he won a majority of black votes against a black in 1983 and again in 1986). But confront him with a specific problem, and his instinct is to insist that it be solved—whether the problem is lack of job skills or traffic jams on the Chesapeake Bay Bridge.

With the legislature, his relations are often stormy and adversarial; yet he has been mostly successful. In his first years, he got an increased gas tax, changes in workmen's compensation and medical malpractice and legislation authorizing construction of two new stadiums—one for football, one for baseball—in the Camden Yards near Harborplace. These are typical Schaefer projects, which probably are not at all cost-effective, but which he hopes will boost morale and community pride. He froze spending for Medicaid abortions and increased spending on local schools. He has traveled to every county and has long since disarmed those who were wary of a Baltimore politician in Annapolis. It can safely be predicted that Schaefer will be criticized further by the press, will storm at and be stormed at by leading legislators, that he will be attacked for his friendliness to disgraced former Governor Marvin Mandel and other machine politicians. But this is a man who didn't hesitate to take on the National Rifle Association in 1988—and who won. There is every reason to believe that Schaefer will be reelected, without significant opposition and by a huge margin, in 1990.

Senators. Maryland has two Senators elected with similar margins and with similar voting records, both from Baltimore—but with sharply different personalities. Paul Sarbanes is one of the quietest of Senators yet on occasion he can be one of the most influential. He combines liberal convictions that come, unusually in this day and age, from a childhood spent in modest circumstances and a cautious temperament that insists on immersion in the facts before commitment. The result is that you can usually predict where Sarbanes will end up on an issue, but you'll have a hard time predicting just when.

Sarbanes also has an active disdain for publicity. He sponsors almost no bills; he refuses to send out videotape cassettes of his comments on the issues of the day to local television stations; he makes no flashy speeches. When he chaired the Joint Economic Committee in 1987 and 1988, he generated far less news than David Obey had two years before; he served, quietly and somberly, on the Iran-contra investigating committee; he has risen to high seniority on the Foreign Relations and Banking Committees without making a big splash.

Yet he has proved a successful Senator both with his colleagues and his constituents. Other Democrats look to him for judgments they can trust, since his are never made hastily: it was Sarbanes who, after not committing himself for months, presented the first counts of impeachment against Richard Nixon before the House Judiciary Committee in 1974. Then and now, when he does take up a cause, he usually wins. Of Greek descent, he was the key figure getting an arms embargo on Turkey because of its invasion of Cyprus in the 1970s; and when he feared the plan to sell the two Washington airports to an independent authority would hurt Maryland's Baltimore-Washington International, he filibustered until he got key concessions.

Sarbanes's liberalism is rooted in his experience growing up in Salisbury on the Eastern Shore, the son of a Greek immigrant who owned the Mayflower Grill, and taught himself enough on the side to discuss philosophy with his son's Princeton professors. Sarbanes was an achiever in law in Baltimore, where he lives still, and in local politics. From the beginning, he campaigned in small groups, talking to voters and leaders, listening gravely to what they have to say. Tabbed early as a reformer, he was more a loner, a liberal on economic issues with close ties to labor unions, never taking on other politicians' fights; he has accumulated friends rather than enemies.

As a state legislator, he voted against Marvin Mandel for governor in 1969—which did not prevent him from beating an incumbent congressman in the 1970 primary, bluffing another incumbent out of the race after they were redistricted together in 1972, and winning the admiration of Mandel admirer and ally William Donald Schaefer. In 1976, he beat former Senator Joseph Tydings in the primary and Republican Senator Glenn Beall in the general, by 55%–35% and 59%–41% margins. Sarbanes won reelection in 1982 and 1988 by almost precisely similar margins, distributed almost precisely the same way across the state. In 1988, the original Republican nominee dropped out, and the party picked Alan Keyes, a black former State Department appointee. He got some visible support from Ronald Reagan, but made no perceptible impact: the results were almost the same as six years before.

A footnote on Sarbanes: he was a classmate of two other Greek-Americans at Harvard Law, Michael Dukakis and Paul Brountas, and supported Dukakis back in 1958 when he was running for town office in Brookline. He endorsed him again for the 1988 race, but characteristically waited 10 months after his announcement and came out for him publicly just before the Iowa caucuses.

Senator Barbara Mikulski came to the Senate with a distinctive personal style and with deep roots in east Baltimore and a rapport with Baltimoreans that is unshakeable. She got her start in politics as a social worker organizing Highlandtown (where her parents ran a bakery) to stop a highway from going through; she won, and in the process was elected to the Baltimore Council in 1971, in time to serve (and spar) with the then new mayor, Donald Schaefer. As a local official with genuine ethnic roots and a woman with genuine liberal impulses, she was chosen head of the national Democratic Party's commission on delegate selection in 1973, and avoided the pitfalls on either side. She ran for the Senate in 1974, and got a respectable percentage (43%) against Charles Mathias; when Paul Sarbanes ran for the other Senate seat in 1976, Mikulski ran for his 3d District seat and won. Ten years later she gave up that seat for what seemed like a chancy Senate race, and won handily.

Mikulski is loud and brash, humorous and warm, brusque and aggressive when she feels she should be, curious and thoughtful when she encounters another new part of the world. She knows Baltimore warp and woof—its neighborhoods and government agencies, charitable institutions and ethnic politicians—and she still lives there, in the Fells Point neighborhood being restored on the waterfront: Fells Point and Don Schaefer's Harborplace, she points out, stand where the highway she opposed was supposed to go through.

She has also proven to be an effective political operator in the Senate. With help from Paul Sarbanes, she got a seat on Appropriations her first year. In her second year she got her spousal impoverishment amendment to the catastrophic health care bill passed, to keep one spouse from losing everything because the other spouse needs expensive care. Never a subcommittee chair in her 10 years in the House, she took over the HUD-Independent Agencies Appropriations Subcommittee in 1989—a good spot from which to help Maryland's Goddard Space Flight Center and EPA Chesapeake Bay cleanups. She works on local projects—the FAA weather station in Salisbury, oyster bed research—but she also takes on longer-range issues. In 1988, she came forward with a proposal for national service, in which any adult could perform public services on a National Guard-like schedule and get credits convertible to student loans or partial down payments on a house. Mikulski is regarded by some as an unthinking reflexive liberal. But on national service and other issues she draws on her own experiences in Baltimore and her knowledge of how people can suffer—and how they can help each other—in the real world.

In 1986, Mikulski had tough competition in the primary from Montgomery County Congressman Michael Barnes and Governor Harry Hughes. But Hughes was weakened by the Maryland state S&L failures and Barnes could not loosen Mikulski's hold on Baltimore voters. Nearly 60% of the votes were cast in the Baltimore metropolitan area, and Mikulski got 63% there to 19% for Barnes and 13% for Hughes. Barnes's 62% in the Washington suburbs was not nearly enough to prevent her from winning 50%–31%–14%. In the general, Mikulski's opponent, former White House aide Linda Chavez, was well-informed on issues. But she had the handicap of having only recently moved over the D.C. line into the Maryland suburbs in a year in which local pride was sweeping the state; and Chavez, with her cool demeanor, seemed the type who had never had Maryland crab seasonings caked under her fingernails. Chavez tried to attack Mikulski by innuendo, citing her hiring in 1981 of an Australian feminist whose works Mikulski required other staffers to read. But, as Schaefer pointed out to Mikulski, most Maryland voters knew her and liked her the way she was. One Mikulski ad showed a shopper in Baltimore's Lexington Market compliment her on losing weight, to which Mikulski replied, spontaneously, "I'm counting my calories, I'm counting my votes, and I'm counting my blessings." This 4'11" Polish-American woman from Highlandtown has a lot of blessings to count—and probably will have some more when her seat comes up again in 1992.

Presidential politics. For 1988, Maryland switched its presidential primary from May to Super Tuesday in March. It used to attract attention—in 1972, when George Wallace was shot while campaigning in Prince George's County the day before voting, and in 1976, when Jerry Brown, with the help of some old-fashioned pols, beat Jimmy Carter. In the 1980s, it has been more conventional, with wins for Carter, Walter Mondale, and Michael Dukakis. The Republican primary electorate is still rather small and mostly conservative; George Bush won in 1988.

In the general election Maryland, in the 1960s one of the nation's better bellwethers, has now become one of its most Democratic states. In 1980, it was one of only six states for Jimmy Carter, and in 1984 and 1988, it just narrowly missed voting for Walter Mondale and Michael

Dukakis. The reason: Maryland's black population is increasing rapidly (it was 23% in 1980), as many Washington area blacks move out from the District to Prince George's County which, in the middle 1980s, had the nation's highest concentration of affluent suburban blacks. The black percentage will likely increase, even if that migration slows down, because 27% of Maryland's under-18 population in 1980 was black.

Congressional districting. For the 1980s, Maryland's Democratic legislature extended the two Baltimore districts, which had lost population, out into the suburbs, leaving them with convoluted but sharply defined boundaries. The one incumbent really hurt was Democrat Clarence Long of Baltimore County, who was beaten in 1984 by Helen Bentley. Incidentally, in 1978 and 1984 four of Maryland's eight districts elected women to the House; in 1986 and 1988 three did, with Mikulski beating Linda Chavez in the Senate race.

The People: Est. Pop. 1988: 4,644,000; Pop. 1980: 4,216,975, up 10.1% 1980–88 and 7.5% 1970–80; 1.85% of U.S. total, 19th largest. 15% with 1–3 yrs. col., 20% with 4+ yrs. col.; 9.8% below poverty level. Single ancestry: 10% English, 9% German, 4% Irish, 2% Italian, Polish, 1% Russian, French. Households (1980): 75% family, 42% with children, 59% married couples; 38% housing units rented; median monthly rent: $222; median house value: $59,200. Voting age pop. (1980): 3,049,445; 21% Black, 1% Asian origin, 1% Spanish origin. Registered voters (1988): 2,305,422; 1,478,680 D (64%); 638,020 R (28%); 188,722 unaffiliated and minor parties (8%).

1988 Share of Federal Tax Burden: $19,810,000,000; 2.24% of U.S. total; 13th largest.

1988 Share of Federal Expenditures

	Total		Non-Defense		Defense	
Total Expend	$4,024m	(0.46%)	$4,492m	(0.69%)	$1,044m	(0.46%)
St/Lcl Grants	665m	(0.58%)	2,004m	(1.75%)	0m	(0.09%)
Salary/Wages	496m	(0.37%)	249m	(0.37%)	246m	(0.37%)
Pymnts to Indiv	2,114m	(0.52%)	2,008m	(0.51%)	107m	(0.57%)
Procurement	690m	(0.37%)	173m	(0.37%)	690m	(0.37%)
Research/Other	59m	(0.16%)	58m	(0.16%)	0m	(0.16%)

Political Lineup: Governor, William Donald Schaefer (D); Lt. Gov., Melvin A. Steinberg (D); Secy. of State, Winfield M. Kelly, Jr. (D); Atty. Gen., J. Joseph Curran, Jr. (D); Treasurer, Lucille Maurer (D); Comptroller, Louis L. Goldstein (D). State Senate, 47 (40 D and 7 R); State House of Delegates, 141 (125 D and 16 R). Senators, Paul S. Sarbanes (D) and Barbara A. Mikulski (D). Representatives, 8 (6 D and 2 R).

1988 Presidential Vote

Bush (R)	876,167	(51%)
Dukakis (D).	826,304	(48%)

1988 Democratic Presidential Primary

Dukakis	242,479	(46%)
Jackson	152,642	(29%)
Gore.	46,063	(9%)
Gephardt	42,059	(8%)
Simon	16,513	(4%)
Hart	9,732	(2%)
Babbitt	4,750	(1%)

1984 Presidential Vote

Reagan (R)	879,918	(53%)
Mondale (D)	787,935	(47%)

1988 Republican Presidential Primary

Bush	107,021	(53%)
Dole	64,987	(32%)
Robertson	12,860	(7%)
Kemp	11,909	(6%)
Du Pont	2,551	(1%)
Haig	1,421	(1%)

GOVERNOR

Gov. William Donald Schaefer (D)

Elected 1986, term expires Jan. 1991; b. Nov. 2, 1921, Baltimore; home, Annapolis; Baltimore City Col., B.A. 1939, U. Baltimore, LL.B. 1942, LL.M. 1951; Episcopalian; single.

Career: Army, WWII; Practicing atty., 1955–67; Baltimore City Cncl., 1955–71, Pres., 1967–71; Mayor of Baltimore, 1971–87.

Offices: State House, Annapolis 21404, 301-974-3901.

Election Results

1986 gen.	William Donald Schaefer (D) ..	907,291	(82%)
	Thomas J. Mooney (R)........	194,185	(18%)
1986 prim.	William Donald Schaefer (D) ..	395,170	(62%)
	Stephen H. Sachs (D)	224,755	(35%)
1982 gen.	Harry R. Hughes (D).........	705,910	(62%)
	Robert A. Pascal (R)	432,826	(38%)

SENATORS

Sen. Paul S. Sarbanes (D)

Elected 1976, seat up 1994; b. Feb. 3, 1933, Salisbury; home, Baltimore; Princeton U., A.B. 1954, Rhodes Scholar, Oxford U., B.A. 1957, Harvard U., LL.B. 1960; Greek Orthodox; married (Christine).

Career: Law Clerk to Judge Morris A. Soper, U.S. 4th Circuit Crt. of Appeals, 1960–61; Practicing atty., 1961–62, 1965–70; A.A. to Chmn. Walter W. Heller of the Pres. Cncl. of Econ. Advisers, 1962–63; Exec. Dir., Baltimore Charter Revision Comm., 1963–64; MD House of Delegates, 1969–70; U.S. House of Reps., 1971–77.

Offices: 332 DSOB 20510, 202-224-4524. Also 1518 Fed. Ofc. Bldg., 31 Hopkins Plaza, Baltimore 21201, 301-962-4436; 11160 Viers Mill Rd., 503 Wheaton Plaza So., Wheaton 20902, 301-946-1252; 111 Baptist St., Ste. 115, Salisbury 21801, 301-546-4998; and 141 Baltimore St., Ste. 206, Cumberland 21502, 301-722-5369.

Committees: *Banking, Housing and Urban Affairs* (3d of 12 D). Subcommittees: Housing and Urban Affairs; International Finance and Monetary Policy (Chairman). *Foreign Relations* (3d of 10 D). Subcommittees: European Affairs; International Economic Policy, Trade, Oceans and Environment (Chairman); Near Eastern and South Asian Affairs. *Joint Economic Committee* (Vice Chairman). Subcommittees: International Economic Policy (Chairman); Technology and National Security Economics; Economic Resources and Competitiveness.

Group Ratings

	ADA	ACLU	COPE	CFA	LCV	ACU	NTLC	NSI	COC	CEI
1988	90	70	98	100	80	4	9	0	29	11
1987	100	—	97	100	—	0	—	—	28	10

National Journal Ratings

	1988 LIB — 1988 CONS	1987 LIB — 1987 CONS
Economic	86% — 0%	74% — 0%
Social	74% — 24%	78% — 17%
Foreign	86% — 0%	81% — 0%

Key Votes

1) Cut Aged Housing $	FOR	5) Bork Nomination	AGN	9) SDI Funding	AGN
2) Override Hwy Veto	FOR	6) Ban Plastic Guns	AGN	10) Ban Chem Weaps	AGN
3) Kill Plnt Clsng Notice	AGN	7) Deny Abortions	AGN	11) Aid To Contras	AGN
4) Min Wage Increase	FOR	8) Japanese Reparations	FOR	12) Reagan Defense $	AGN

Election Results

1988 general	Paul S. Sarbanes (D)	999,166	(62%)	($1,466,477)
	Alan L. Keyes (R)...................	617,537	(38%)	($662,651)
1988 primary	Paul S. Sarbanes (D)	309,923	(86%)	
	B. Emerson Sweatt (D)...............	25,932	(7%)	
	A. Robert Kaufman (D)...............	25,450	(7%)	
1982 general	Paul S. Sarbanes (D)	707,356	(63%)	($1,623,533)
	Lawrence J. Hogan (R)	407,334	(37%)	($90,976)

Sen. Barbara A. Mikulski (D)

Elected 1986, seat up 1992; b. July 20, 1936, Baltimore; home, Baltimore; Mt. St. Agnes Col., B.A. 1958, U. of MD, M.S.W., 1965; Roman Catholic; single.

Career: Social worker, Admin., Baltimore Dept. of Soc. Services.; Baltimore City Cncl., 1971–76; Adjunct prof., Loyola Col., 1972–76; Chwmn., Natl. Dem. Comm. on Delegate Selection, 1972; Dem. nominee for U.S. Senate, 1974; U.S. House of Reps., 1976–86.

Offices: 320 HSOB 20510, 202-224-4654. Also World Trade Center, Ste. 253, Baltimore 21202-3041, 301-962-4510; 419 S. Highland Ave., Baltimore 21224, 301-563-4000; 3 Church Cir., Annapolis 21401, 301-263-1805; City Ctr. on the Plaza, 213-219 W. Main St., Salisbury 21801, 301-546-7711; 9658 Baltimore Ave., Ste. 103, College Park 20740, 301-345-5517; and 82 W. Washington St., Ste. 402, Hagerstown 21740, 301-797-2826.

Committees: *Appropriations* (12th of 16 D). Subcommittees: Foreign Operations; HUD-Independent Agencies (Chairman); Legislative Branch; Transportation and Related Agencies; Treasury, Postal Service, and General Government. *Labor and Human Resources* (9th of 9 D). Subcommittees: Education, Arts and Humanities; Employment and Productivity; Labor. *Small Business* (9th of 10 D). Subcommittees: Export Expansion (Chairman); Urban and Minority-owned Business Development.

Group Ratings

	ADA	ACLU	COPE	CFA	LCV	ACU	NTLC	NSI	COC	CEI
1988	95	77	100	100	70	0	4	0	29	10
1987	100	—	100	100	—	4	—	—	28	13

National Journal Ratings

	1988 LIB — 1988 CONS			1987 LIB — 1987 CONS		
Economic	86%	—	0%	74%	—	0%
Social	86%	—	0%	74%	—	24%
Foreign	86%	—	0%	81%	—	0%

Key Votes

1) Cut Aged Housing $	FOR	5) Bork Nomination	AGN	9) SDI Funding	AGN
2) Override Hwy Veto	FOR	6) Ban Plastic Guns	AGN	10) Ban Chem Weaps	AGN
3) Kill Plnt Clsng Notice	AGN	7) Deny Abortions	AGN	11) Aid To Contras	AGN
4) Min Wage Increase	FOR	8) Japanese Reparations	FOR	12) Reagan Defense $	AGN

Election Results

1986 general	Barbara A. Mikulski (D)	675,225	(61%)	($2,097,216)
	Linda Chavez (R)....................	437,411	(39%)	($1,699,175)
1986 primary	Barbara A. Mikulski (D)	307,876	(50%)	
	Michael D. Barnes (D)................	195,086	(31%)	
	Harry Hughes (D).....................	88,908	(14%)	
1980 general	Charles McC. Mathias, Jr. (R).........	850,970	(66%)	($841,446)
	Edward T. Conroy (D)	435,118	(34%)	($46,456)

FIRST DISTRICT

Fifty years ago "the 20th century has made little impression on Leonardtown," the *WPA Guide* says, "where oxen trundle tobacco along the tree-lined lanes to the warehouses and boat landings, and the warm hospitality of the people has not yet been commercialized." Leonardtown is in St. Mary's County, on the Western Shore of Chesapeake Bay, where the colony of Maryland was first settled in 1634. For the next 150 years, ocean-going ships sailed up the bay, which is really the flooded river valley of the Susquehanna, and built tobacco farms on its wide estuaries. This was the most thickly settled part of the American colonies in the 17th century; the bay was the avenue by which the rich tobacco crops of Maryland and Virginia reached the world.

On the Western Shore of the Chesapeake and its branch river the Potomac have grown two of America's metropolises, Baltimore and Washington. But in St. Mary's County and on the whole Eastern Shore, things did not change much until the last several decades. There are a surprisingly small number of family names here, and population growth was low, scarcely more than doubling on the Eastern Shore between 1790 and 1970. The Western Shore, first settled by the Catholics for whom Maryland was founded as a religious haven, was famous for the slot machines legal there in the 1940s; the Eastern Shore, southern segregationist country for years, now has, on land jutting out toward the Bay, big estates of some of the nation's richest families and, inland, some of the nation's largest chicken producing operations.

The 1st Congressional District of Maryland includes the whole Eastern Shore, the Western Shore counties below Annapolis and the Washington suburbs, and part of suburban Baltimore's Harford County. Republican in national elections, conservative on cultural issues like gun control, the 1st has had some of the nation's most outlandish congressional politics of recent years. One congressman killed himself amid charges of financial improprieties. Another, caustic conservative Robert Bauman, lost his seat in 1980 after he was charged with soliciting sex from a 16-year-old boy in circumstances suggesting he was courting discovery. The winner of that race was Roy Dyson, a Democratic legislator from a St. Mary's family active in politics for nine generations. In 1988 Dyson was nearly defeated following some unusual charges.

Their target was Dyson's top aide, Tom Pappas who, the *Washington Post* reported in May 1988, hired only men for staff jobs, required them to refrain from dating and to socialize with him, and even asked one to perform a strip tease at a staff retreat. He advertised for staffers in small town newspapers and hired inexperienced young men at high salaries. The day the article appeared, Pappas, in New York with Dyson on a trip financed by a defense contractor, killed himself. Dyson was already under investigation for having reported that campaign checks were issued to two aides when the money went to Pappas's own companies. Dyson said he didn't know about the personnel practices and denied that he was a homosexual.

In the House, the revelations sparked demands for protecting congressional employees from abuses of power. In the 1st District they vastly increased the previously nil political prospects of the Republican nominee, community college guidance counselor and summer-season house painter Wayne Gilchrest. The Republicans had never had much critical to say about Dyson's generally conservative but occasionally inconsistent voting record, and there wasn't much political mileage in the accurate charge that he had little impact of national and international issues because he devoted himself to local projects. On the Armed Services Committee, for example, he makes little intellectual contribution to the debate. He is "quite proud" of the 1980s military buildup, he says, but "more importantly" he's proud of his efforts to steer it to Maryland. He uses his seat on Merchant Marine for similar purposes in this two-sides-of-the-Bay district. As for his vote on the floor, he told President Reagan to his face that he wouldn't support one contra aid measure until the Pentagon agreed to keep a squadron at Patuxent Naval Air Station.

With all his woes and his unspectacular record, Dyson barely survived in 1988. The Republicans couldn't get Gilchrest to drop out or to campaign with maximum effectiveness. He did carry the Upper Eastern Shore, but Dyson carried his home area heavily and the Lower Eastern Shore by enough for a 1,540-vote victory. It will be interesting to see whether Dyson attracts stronger opposition in 1990.

The People: Est. Pop. 1986: 586,400, up 11.4% 1980–86; Pop. 1980: 526,206, up 21.7% 1970–80. Households (1980): 78% family, 45% with children, 65% married couples; 28.1% housing units rented; median monthly rent: $159; median house value: $49,500. Voting age pop. (1980): 369,721; 17% Black; 1% Spanish origin, 1% Asian origin.

1988 Presidential Vote: Bush (R) 131,161   (63%)
Dukakis (D) 75,575   (36%)

Rep. Roy Dyson (D)

Elected 1980; b. Nov. 15, 1948, Great Mills; home, Great Mills; U. of Baltimore, 1970, U. of MD, 1971; Roman Catholic; single.

Career: Legis. Asst., Ed. and Labor Cmtee., U.S. House of Reps., 1973–74; MD House of Del., 1974–80.

Offices: 326 CHOB 20515, 202-225-5311. Also 1 Plaza E., Salisbury 21801, 301-742-9070; P.O. Box 742, Waldorf 20601, 301-645-4844; and 20 W. Bel Air Ave., Aberdeen 21001, 301-272-7070.

Committees: *Agriculture* (25th of 27 D). Subcommittee: Wheat, Soybeans and Feed Grains. *Armed Services* (13th of 31 D). Subcommittees: Readiness; Procurement and Military Nuclear Systems. *Merchant Marine and Fisheries* (9th of 26 D). Subcommittees: Fisheries and Wildlife Conservation and the Environment; Panama Canal/Outer Continental Shelf (Chairman).

Group Ratings

	ADA	ACLU	COPE	CFA	LCV	ACU	NTLC	NSI	COC	CEI
1988	55	61	75	82	44	50	29	88	36	16
1987	44	—	73	57	—	32	—	—	27	20

National Journal Ratings

	1988 LIB — 1988 CONS		1987 LIB — 1987 CONS	
Economic	77%	— 23%	55%	— 45%
Social	46%	— 53%	47%	— 52%
Foreign	47%	— 53%	39%	— 60%

Key Votes

1) Homeless $	FOR	5) Ban Drug Test	AGN	9) SDI Research	FOR
2) Gephardt Amdt	FOR	6) Drug Death Pen	FOR	10) Ban Chem Weaps	AGN
3) Deficit Reduc	FOR	7) Handgun Sales	FOR	11) Aid to Contras	AGN
4) Kill Plnt Clsng Notice	AGN	8) Ban D.C. Abort $	FOR	12) Nuclear Testing	AGN

Election Results

1988 general	Roy Dyson (D)	96,128	(50%)	($684,204)
	Wayne T. Gilchrest (R)	94,588	(50%)	($118,568)
1988 primary	Roy Dyson (D)	39,207	(86%)	
	Morris C. Durham (D)	6,379	(14%)	
1986 general	Roy Dyson (D)	88,113	(67%)	($354,240)
	Harlan C. Williams (R)	43,764	(33%)	($171,876)

SECOND DISTRICT

For more than 50 years, Baltimore has been moving outward from the square boundaries, over rolling hills into suburban Baltimore County and beyond. City and County are separate governmental units, but they share the "Bawlmer" accent and the city's infectious local pride. Most people here grew up in Baltimore; they may remember when the St. Louis Browns moved to Baltimore in 1954 and the glory days of Johnny Unitas's Baltimore Colts; they may recall when a Towson lawyer named Spiro Agnew won an upset victory in the race for county executive in 1962. County residents today may work in nearby low-rise office buildings and seldom get down to Harborplace or Memorial Stadium, but their picture of local government is more likely to be Baltimore's ornate jewel of a city hall than the old-fashioned county courthouse building in a park a few blocks off the six-lane highways in Towson.

The 2d Congressional District of Maryland includes almost three-quarters of Baltimore County, plus some of Harford County just beyond. On the soggy low-lying peninsulas jutting into the Chesapeake Bay are the Democratic working-class communities of Dundalk and Essex, extensions of east Baltimore where many residents worked for years at Bethlehem Steel's Sparrows Point mill. Directly north of Baltimore are Towson, Lutherville, Timonium—relatively high-income suburbs situated, geographically and sociologically, between the more modest suburbs to the east and the green horse country to the west. This is solid Republican territory. In the western part of the district Baltimoreans are moving out from older Jewish neighborhoods and in the eastern part they are moving out from older Catholic neighborhoods to the countryside.

The congresswoman from the 2d District is Helen Delich Bentley, a Republican who is as tough as nails, as sentimental as Ronald Reagan, and as dedicated to "Bawlmer" as any politician in the state. The daughter of an immigrant from Yugoslavia to Nevada, Bentley was for 24 years a reporter for the *Baltimore Sun*, specializing in maritime news; for six years she was chair of the Federal Maritime Commission. Her major issue, when she first challenged Representative Clarence (Doc) Long in 1980, was dredging the harbor of Baltimore, which Long opposed on environmental grounds; in 1982, her main issue was dredging the harbor; in 1984, her main issue again was dredging the harbor, which by this time Long favored. But Long was 75, had concentrated for years on his work as chairman of the appropriations subcommittee handling the foreign aid bill, and did not seem likely to pursue the dredging issue vigorously. Bentley, a tough-talking and (at least in the past) profane woman, did.

She won with 51% of the vote and, in her first term, she delivered. She got federal money for the dredging. She got funding for the Brewerton Channel extension and Chesapeake and Delaware Canal improvements. She got Baltimore declared an extension of the Norfolk Navy home port, bringing Baltimore shipyards big repair contracts. She got an aircraft carrier superstructure ship contract shifted from Canada to Sparrows Point. This record enabled her to beat no less attractive a candidate than Kathleen Kennedy Townsend, who is not only a daughter of the late Robert Kennedy, but is also a thoughtful and original thinker in her own right, with experience in the Maryland attorney general's office. But in a year when Baltimore was bursting with local pride, Townsend still looked like a carpetbagger to many. Both candidates spent over $1 million—this was the only district in 1986 where both did—but Bentley got the votes, carrying not only the Republican areas but Dundalk and Essex and winning with 59%.

In the House, Bentley is generally a conservative Republican. But she is a strong believer in trade restrictions and retaliation, and was one of the House members photographed bashing in a Toshiba product. And she sharply criticized the state party chairman, a religious conservative, and beat his candidate for national committeewoman. She continues to back the shipping industry on Merchant Marine and Baltimore projects on Public Works. Against a hapless Harford area legislator, she was reelected overwhelmingly in 1988.

The People: Est. Pop. 1986: 544,400, up 3.4% 1980–86; Pop. 1980: 526,354, up 13.6% 1970–80. Households (1980): 78% family, 41% with children, 66% married couples; 34.7% housing units rented; median monthly rent: $227; median house value: $57,100. Voting age pop. (1980): 388,788; 5% Black, 1% Asian origin, 1% Spanish origin.

1988 Presidential Vote:	Bush (R)	141,948	(62%)
	Dukakis (D)	85,451	(37%)

Rep. Helen Delich Bentley (R)

Elected 1984; b. Nov. 28, 1923, Ely, NV; home, Lutherville; U. of MO, B.A. 1944, U. of NV, Geo. Wash. U.; Greek Orthodox; married (William).

Career: Reporter and Maritime Ed., *The Sun*, Baltimore, 1945–69; Chmn., Fed. Maritime Comm., 1969–75; Businesswoman, 1975–85; Columnist and Ed., *World Ports Magazine*, 1981–85.

Offices: 1610 LHOB 20515, 202-225-3061. Also 200 E. Joppa Rd., Shell Bldg., Ste. 400, Towson 21204, 301-337-7222; 6 N. Main St., Bel Air 21014, 301-879-2517; and 7458 German Hill Rd., Dundalk 21222, 301-285-2747.

Committees: *Budget* (14th of 14 R). Subcommittees: Defense, Foreign Policy and Space; Human Resources. *Merchant Marine and Fisheries* (13th of 17 R). Subcommittees: Coast Guard and Navigation; Merchant Marine; Panama Canal and Outer Continental Shelf. *Select Committee on Aging* (15th of 26 R). Subcommittee: Health and Long-Term Care.

Group Ratings

	ADA	ACLU	COPE	CFA	LCV	ACU	NTLC	NSI	COC	CEI
1988	10	43	53	55	31	86	58	100	79	33
1987	28	—	49	43	—	57	—	—	73	39

National Journal Ratings

	1988 LIB — 1988 CONS		1987 LIB — 1987 CONS	
Economic	36%	— 63%	41%	— 58%
Social	17%	— 82%	27%	— 72%
Foreign	24%	— 74%	20%	— 76%

Key Votes

1) Homeless $	FOR	5) Ban Drug Test	AGN	9) SDI Research	FOR
2) Gephardt Amdt	FOR	6) Drug Death Pen	FOR	10) Ban Chem Weaps	AGN
3) Deficit Reduc	AGN	7) Handgun Sales	FOR	11) Aid to Contras	FOR
4) Kill Plnt Clsng Notice	FOR	8) Ban D.C. Abort $	FOR	12) Nuclear Testing	AGN

Election Results

1988 general	Helen Delich Bentley (R)	157,956	(71%)	($779,318)
	Joseph Bartenfelder (D)	63,114	(29%)	($64,263)
1988 primary	Helen Delich Bentley (R), unopposed			
1986 general	Helen Delich Bentley (R)	96,745	(59%)	($1,070,161)
	Kathleen Kennedy Townsend (D)	68,200	(41%)	($1,071,713)

THIRD DISTRICT

Baltimore is a city with a savor all its own. Two generations ago, it was inward-looking: "there are no songs entitled 'Way Down upon the Patapsco,' nor 'The Baltimore Blues'; the city has inspired no outstanding novels," wrote the *WPA Guide* 50 years ago, "it is not planning a world's fair; it does not boast of the biggest, the newest, or the fastest anything. This does not indicate lack of city pride; it merely means that Baltimoreans are too sure of themselves and their city to feel the need of advertising their virtues." Sometime between 1940 and 1970 that sureness evaporated. With the usual problems of central cities—declining population, aging housing, slow job growth, racial tensions—Baltimore and its image needed sprucing up. Under Mayor William Donald Schafer, from 1971 to 1986, they got it. The economy has charged ahead, the city's downtown and some of its neighborhoods have been revitalized with new building that is also respectful of the old, and Schaefer has captured the imaginations of Baltimoreans, suburbanites, and ultimately the whole nation with projects like Harborplace and the Aquarium. In the process, Baltimore has avoided the racial divisiveness of many cities. With a black majority it reelected Schaefer three times, and in 1987 had a non-divisive mayoral contest between two blacks, Schaefer's chosen successor Clarence (Du) Burns and the winner by a narrow margin, State's Attorney Kurt Schmoke.

The 3d Congressional District of Maryland is centered on Baltimore. Its convoluted boundaries take in most of the white-majority precincts in the city, plus adjacent parts of Baltimore County, plus—added on to meet the population standard—most of the planned town of Columbia, 15 miles from downtown Baltimore. The central focus is Harborplace, overlooking the city's busy harbor; across the bay, not far away, is Fort McHenry, where Francis Scott Key saw the star-spangled banner yet wave. Going counterclockwise from downtown, the district moves east to include the mostly Polish Highlandtown neighborhood, the political base of Senator Barbara Mikulski; the middle-class northeastern corner of the city; upper-income WASPy neighborhoods north of Johns Hopkins University and in the Baltimore County suburb of Towson; and the mostly Jewish area around the Pimlico Race Track and the suburb of Pikesville. West of downtown, this time clockwise, the 3d takes in the old ethnic neighborhoods overlooking the harbor, the modest suburbs of Arbutus and Catonsville, and goes out to Howard County and Columbia. Now 15 years old, Columbia was a much heralded "new town" whose architecture is less distinctive than one might think, but which has attracted a population of nearly 40,000 which is, by suburban standards, unusually well integrated (20% black) and politically liberal.

One of the reasons Baltimore has been so visibly bursting with pride is that this city, once depicted as the home of political hacks and crooks, has been producing outstanding politicians. They include Schaefer, now governor, and Senators Sarbanes and Mikulski, who both represented the 3d District in the House; and they include the 3d District's new congressman, Ben Cardin. Though just 43 when he ran, he had a political career running back 20 years and impressive political strength. He was elected to the Maryland House of Delegates from a Jewish district in northwest Baltimore, an area full of political talent, as long ago as 1966; he chaired the Ways and Means Committee by 1975; he served as Speaker from 1979 to 1986. The Maryland legislature is a fast track with a dizzying pace, where Cardin demonstrated great finesse and skill as well as complete honesty. It was logical that he was thinking about running for governor in 1986, and logical that he was deterred by Donald Schaefer's strength; logical as well that when Mikulski ran for the Senate, he ran for her seat and won the Democratic primary—tantamount to election—with 82% of the vote.

Cardin's first months in the House must have been disappointing. He sought seats on the Ways and Means and Budget Committees, which freshmen usually don't get, and settled for Public Works and Judiciary instead, on which he remains. Cardin, accustomed to being a central figure in Annapolis, became a peripheral figure in Washington. But he seemed pleased with the change of pace, pushing local projects and stepping forward to oppose such popular measures as the "user accountability" parts of the drug law. He wins by huge margins at home and has a safe seat.

The People: Est. Pop. 1986: 533,100, up 1.0% 1980–86; Pop. 1980: 527,699, dn. 3.3% 1970–80. Households (1980): 71% family, 35% with children, 54% married couples; 38.9% housing units rented; median monthly rent: $197; median house value: $43,500. Voting age pop. (1980): 399,019; 14% Black, 1% Spanish origin, 1% Asian origin.

1988 Presidential Vote: Dukakis (D)................113,869 (54%)
Bush (R).................95,071 (45%)

Rep. Benjamin L. Cardin (D)

Elected 1986; b. Oct. 5, 1943, Baltimore; home, Baltimore; U. of Pittsburgh, B.A. 1964, U. of MD, LL.B., J.D. 1967; Jewish; married (Myrna).

Career: MD House of Delegates, 1966–86, Speaker, 1979–86; Practicing atty., 1967–86.

Offices: 507 CHOB 20515, 202-225-4016. Also 540 E. Belvedere Rd., Ste. 201, Baltimore 21212, 301-433-8886; 754 Frederick Rd., Catonsville 21228, 301-788-2041; 412 S. Highland Ave., Baltimore 21224 301-563-9177.

Committees: *Judiciary* (20th of 21 D). Subcommittees: Administrative Law and Governmental Relations; Courts, Intellectual Property and the Administration of Justice. *Public Works and Transportation* (21st of 31 D). Subcommittees: Surface Transportation; Public Buildings and Grounds; Water Resources.

Group Ratings

	ADA	ACLU	COPE	CFA	LCV	ACU	NTLC	NSI	COC	CEI
1988	90	83	93	82	81	4	7	0	36	11
1987	88	—	94	79	—	0	—	—	13	8

National Journal Ratings

	1988 LIB — 1988 CONS	1987 LIB — 1987 CONS
Economic	67% — 30%	73% — 0%
Social	86% — 0%	62% — 36%
Foreign	68% — 28%	81% — 0%

Key Votes

1) Homeless $	AGN	5) Ban Drug Test	AGN	9) SDI Research	AGN
2) Gephardt Amdt	FOR	6) Drug Death Pen	AGN	10) Ban Chem Weaps	FOR
3) Deficit Reduc	FOR	7) Handgun Sales	AGN	11) Aid to Contras	AGN
4) Kill Plnt Clsng Notice	AGN	8) Ban D.C. Abort $	AGN	12) Nuclear Testing	FOR

Election Results

1988 general	Benjamin L. Cardin (D)................	133,779	(73%)	($354,701)
	Ross Z. Pierpont (R)................	49,733	(27%)	($18,893)
1988 primary	Benjamin L. Cardin (D)................	52,850	(86%)	
	Charles Walker (D)................	8,451	(14%)	
1986 general	Benjamin L. Cardin (D)................	100,161	(79%)	($487,797)
	Ross Z. Pierpont (R)................	26,452	(21%)	($46,542)

FOURTH DISTRICT

Annapolis, said one *WPA Guide* writer 50 years ago, "has that air of age and gracious dignity found only where old centers of wealth and culture have kept their importance but have not been overwhelmed by industry and commerce." Even in the 1980s, as Eugene Meyer points out in *Maryland Lost and Found*, downtown Annapolis still resembles the 1856 overlook on display in the Georgian William Paca house. Annapolis has been Maryland's capital since 1694 and the

State House, still in the circle where it was built in 1772, is America's oldest capitol still in use. In these blocks, down to the waterfront and the United States Naval Academy, Annapolis is an 18th century town—not preserved under glass, but a working city not entirely gentrified, a waterman's as well as a yachtist's port, a market town as much as a lobbying emporium, a little bit gritty under the fingernails even as another coat of white enamel is applied to its Georgian woodwork.

Annapolis is the center and focal point of Maryland's 4th Congressional District, most of which is thoroughly unquaint, unhistorical suburban territory, stretching from the Baltimore city limits to the District of Columbia line. It includes all of Anne Arundel County and part of Prince George's County. Between Annapolis and Baltimore are the Anne Arundel suburbs where about half the 4th District's residents live: Linthicum, Glen Burnie, Severna Park. West of Annapolis and along the bay are new subdivisions; the Prince George's County part, near Washington, has a black majority.

Representing the 4th is one of Congress' scholar-athletes, Tom McMillen. He was a basketball star at the University of Maryland, a Rhodes Scholar, a pro with the Atlanta Hawks and Capital Bullets; he settled in Maryland, started a business, and set about running for the House. He passed up the race against Republican incumbent Marjorie Holt in 1984: the district is fairly heavily Republican in presidential years. But when Holt retired in 1986 he was off and running, the heavy favorite. Yet by November he had flagged and Republican Robert Neall, an experienced Anne Arundel legislator, nearly overtook him. McMillen ended up winning by only 428 votes—the closest margin in the country.

In his first term, McMillen worked hard to learn the legislative ropes in Congress and win support in the district. He spent much of his time on local issues, trying to save the Curtis Bay Coast Guard Yard, repave the Baltimore-Washington Parkway, and spur the cleanup of the bay. On the Banking Committee, he took something of a lead role on some savings and loan issues; he was on the board of a (solvent) Maryland S&L when the state had its S&L crisis earlier in the 1980s. He drew as a Republican opponent a man who exaggerated his combat service in Vietnam and charged there was a plot by Rhodes Scholars to win public office; McMillen won easily. He seems a long way toward making this a safe seat. Incidentally, at 6'11", he is exactly two feet taller than Maryland's Senator Barbara Mikulski, giving Maryland the biggest height differential of any state's delegation now and maybe ever.

The People: Est. Pop. 1986: 571,200, up 8.7% 1980–86; Pop. 1980: 525,453, up 17.7% 1970–80. Households (1980): 78% family, 47% with children, 64% married couples; 35.3% housing units rented; median monthly rent: $261; median house value: $66,200. Voting age pop. (1980): 372,900; 19% Black, 1% Asian origin, 1% Spanish origin.

1988 Presidential Vote: Bush (R) 120,027   (57%)
Dukakis (D) 87,650   (42%)

Rep. Thomas McMillen (D)

Elected 1986; b. May 26, 1952, Elmira, NY; home, Crofton; U. of MD, B.S., 1974; Rhodes Scholar, Oxford U., M.A., 1978; Roman Catholic; single.

Career: Prof. basketball player, 1974–86; founder, McMillen Communications, 1983–present.

Offices: 327 CHOB 20515, 202-225-8090. Also Arundel Center N., 101 Crain Hwy. N., Ste. 509, Glen Burnie 21061, 301-768-8050; 132 Holiday Ct., Ste. 207, Annapolis 21403, 301-261-8401; and 6196 Oxon Hill Rd., Ste. 370, Oxon Hill 20745, 301-567-9212.

Committees: *Banking, Finance and Urban Affairs* (23d of 31 D). Subcommittees: Financial Institution Supervision, Regulation and Insurance; International Development, Finance, Trade and Monetary Policy. *Science, Space and Technology* (22d of 30 D). Subcommittees: Natural Resources, Agriculture Research and Environment; Space Science and Applications; Transportation, Aviation and Materials.

Group Ratings

	ADA	ACLU	COPE	CFA	LCV	ACU	NTLC	NSI	COC	CEI
1988	75	87	100	73	69	12	13	50	36	15
1987	80	—	100	79	—	4	—	—	27	8

National Journal Ratings

	1988 LIB — 1988 CONS	1987 LIB — 1987 CONS
Economic	67% — 30%	62% — 35%
Social	83% — 15%	78% — 0%
Foreign	56% — 43%	53% — 46%

Key Votes

1) Homeless $	AGN	5) Ban Drug Test	AGN	9) SDI Research	FOR
2) Gephardt Amdt	FOR	6) Drug Death Pen	FOR	10) Ban Chem Weaps	AGN
3) Deficit Reduc	AGN	7) Handgun Sales	AGN	11) Aid to Contras	AGN
4) Kill Plnt Clsng Notice	AGN	8) Ban D.C. Abort $	AGN	12) Nuclear Testing	FOR

Election Results

1988 general	Thomas McMillen (D)	128,624	(68%)	($599,881)
	Bradlyn McClanahan (R)	59,688	(32%)	
1988 primary	Thomas McMillen (D)	39,661	(87%)	
	Edward B. Quirk, Jr. (D)	3,941	(9%)	
	John Rea (D)	1,877	(4%)	
1986 general	Thomas McMillen (D)	65,071	(50%)	($796,344)
	Robert R. Neall (R)	64,643	(50%)	($640,939)

FIFTH DISTRICT

Two generations ago, Prince George's County, Maryland, just north and east of Washington, D.C., was mostly low-lying farmland, with a few suburbs strung out along U.S. 1 from Washington toward Baltimore. Today Prince George's is home to nearly 700,000 people, and is one of the nation's most important counties— and a place that gives us a hopeful glimpse of a possible future. This is not conventional wisdom in official Washington, where Prince George's is seen as a working class haven, overshadowed by faster-growing and higher-income Montgomery to the west and Fairfax in Virginia. But Prince George's is by national standards affluent, and it has its own impressive and accelerating growth. All this is especially interesting because Prince George's is the nation's biggest black suburban community.

The black percentage here increased from 14% in 1970 to 37% in 1980; by 1990 it will probably be about 45%. Through all that change, levels of achievement have remained high. Prince George's 5th Congressional District ranked 36th out of 435 in 1979 median family income; in black family income it ranked 13th, behind 12 suburban districts with far smaller black populations. For some years, Prince George's was buoyed upward by the high level of federal wages. In 1970, when federal salaries were at their most generous, 38% of the 5th District's work force here was employed by Uncle Sam—the highest figure in the nation. But by 1980, when federal pay was starting to fall behind the private sector, the federal share was down to 25%; more Prince George's residents were moving into the private sector. And make no mistake about it, this is a hard-working community. Fully 65% of women age 16 and over in the 5th District were in the work force in 1980—the highest figure for any congressional district in the nation.

The racial change in Prince George's has occasioned some strain—but less than might be thought. The county was riven by a school busing case in the 1970s and early 1980s. But in the middle 1980s, school superintendent John Murphy instituted a set of magnet schools and promised to raise black students' test scores to the level of whites—and quickly made impressive progress. Local politics in the 1970s and early 1980s was filled with bickering, and blacks complained about police misconduct. But under County Executive Parris Glendenning, product of a competent and biracial Democratic organization, such complaints appear to have tapered off. Prince George's seems to be giving the nation lesson after lesson in how successful, hard-working blacks can work with whites to build a productive, tolerant, attractive community.

Maryland's 5th Congressional District includes most of Prince George's County, all but the close-in suburb of Oxon Hill and a strip of land to the south. Its congressman is Steny Hoyer, one of those instinctive politicians who seem to rise out of the Maryland soil and flourish in Annapolis and Washington. He was elected to the Maryland Senate at age 27 and was Senate president from 1975 to 1978; he made a misstep running for lieutenant governor on a losing ticket in 1978. But when the 5th District was declared vacant in 1981, after Representative Gladys Spellman went into an irreversible coma, Hoyer edged out Spellman's husband and several other Democrats in the primary and beat a well-financed, competent Republican candidate in the general.

In office, Hoyer has followed the usual Washington suburban pattern of providing extensive constituency services, especially to federal employees, and he is a key man on Appropriations not only for all of Prince George's but for Maryland and the D.C. metropolitan area. He is universally regarded as hard-working, straight-shooting, easy to deal with, but tenacious in pursuit of his own goals, from getting Metro's Green Line subway out into Prince George's to consolidating the National Archives at the University of Maryland. In addition, as federal payrolls have become less important locally, he has moved into national politics too, and for 1989 was elected chairman of the Democratic Caucus. He co-chairs the Helsinki Commission and is well-versed in Eastern European and Soviet affairs.

Hoyer's record on issues generally is liberal, except sometimes on foreign and defense issues. Given the demographic nature of the 5th District, he would appear vulnerable to a black primary challenger, like State's Attorney Alex Williams who beat a long-entrenched white in 1986. But Hoyer has been campaigning among Prince George's blacks since 1966, and for them as well (he supported Williams). He prudently declined to endorse in the 1988 presidential race as Jesse Jackson was carrying the district. The political clout he has accumulated and the political skills he has shown seem likely to keep him very strong in a constituency which, as much as any in America, has developed a genuinely biracial politics.

The People: Est. Pop. 1986: 538,000, up 2.0% 1980–86; Pop. 1980: 527,469, up 0.5% 1970–80. Households (1980): 74% family, 45% with children, 56% married couples; 44.1% housing units rented; median monthly rent: $282; median house value: $64,100. Voting age pop. (1980): 374,737; 31% Black, 2% Asian origin, 2% Spanish origin.

1988 Presidential Vote:

Dukakis (D).	107,195	(59%)
Bush (R)	72,873	(40%)

Rep. Steny H. Hoyer (D)

Elected 1981; b. June 14, 1939, New York City; home, Forestville; U. of MD, B.S. 1963, Georgetown U., J.D. 1966; Baptist; married (Judith).

Career: Practicing atty., 1966–80; MD Senate, 1966–78, Pres., 1975–78; Mbr., MD Bd. of Higher Education, 1978–81.

Offices: 1513 LHOB 20515, 202-225-4131. Also 4351 Garden City Dr., Ste. 625, Landover 20785, 301-436-5510.

Committees: *Appropriations* (27th of 35 D). Subcommittees: District of Columbia; Labor, Health and Human Services and Education; Treasury, Postal Service and General Government.

Group Ratings

	ADA	ACLU	COPE	CFA	LCV	ACU	NTLC	NSI	COC	CEI
1988	95	96	94	91	63	0	2	10	21	6
1987	84	—	94	93	—	0	—	—	7	3

National Journal Ratings

	1988 LIB — 1988 CONS		1987 LIB — 1987 CONS	
Economic	92% —	0%	73% —	0%
Social	86% —	0%	78% —	0%
Foreign	60% —	37%	66% —	32%

Key Votes

1) Homeless $	AGN	5) Ban Drug Test	AGN	9) SDI Research	AGN
2) Gephardt Amdt	FOR	6) Drug Death Pen	AGN	10) Ban Chem Weaps	AGN
3) Deficit Reduc	FOR	7) Handgun Sales	AGN	11) Aid to Contras	AGN
4) Kill Plnt Clsng Notice	AGN	8) Ban D.C. Abort $	AGN	12) Nuclear Testing	FOR

Election Results

1988 general	Steny H. Hoyer (D)	128,437	(79%)	($416,187)
	John E. Sellner (R).	34,909	(21%)	($0)
1988 primary	Steny H. Hoyer (D), unopposed			
1986 general	Steny H. Hoyer (D)	82,098	(82%)	($368,388)
	John Eugene Sellner (R).	18,102	(18%)	

SIXTH DISTRICT

Long vistas of cornfields, pasturelands, mountains of ancient stone rising above the plains; then narrow streets, lined with rowhouses with Baltimore steps and overhung with telephone and streetcar wires: this is what George R. Stewart found in the 1940s as he followed U.S. 40, the old National Road, west from Baltimore through the Maryland countryside. The old road quickly escaped the metropolis and passes into rich farmlands and the Catoctins and the Appalachian ridges, past Frederick, where Barbara Fritchie supposedly reared her old gray head, and Hagerstown, where Oliver Wendell Holmes found refuge after being wounded in the Civil War. This is a part of Maryland settled less by Chesapeake Bay southerners than by Pennsylvania Dutch and Scots-Irish hill people. Politically, it was pro-Union in the Civil War and, more than the rest of Maryland, pro-Republican ever since (though sometimes Democratic in the factory town of Cumberland in the mountains). Even as strong a Democrat as Paul Sarbanes, running for reelection against an unknown black Republican, did no better than break even here in 1988.

The 6th Congressional District of Maryland takes in all of western Maryland and touches on Washington and Baltimore suburbs besides. It includes the very high-income suburb of Potomac all the way to the Capital Beltway; in the Baltimore area it reaches the edge of the planned town of Columbia. For the most part, however, this is a rural and not a cosmopolitan district, a place where family patterns are traditional and patriotism is never scoffed at.

Beverly Byron, the representative from the 6th District, is the fourth Byron elected to Congress in western Maryland. Her husband's father and mother served in the 1940s, and her husband, Goodloe Byron, was elected in 1970 and served until he died while jogging in October 1978. Mrs. Byron got the nomination then and was easily elected. She seemed a political neophyte, but she had some background: she had worked (unpaid) for her husband, and her father was one of Dwight D. Eisenhower's top wartime aides. She continues her husband's general voting pattern, conservative on most issues, but not all: you might call her the northernmost southern Democrat.

From a military family, Byron has devoted much of her legislative career to military issues. On the Armed Services Committee, she is part of the solid committee majority sympathetic to requests for military spending; she enjoys examining military equipment first hand on inspection trips. Byron does not like being counted as an automatic pro-Pentagon vote; she has occasionally dissented from Pentagon positions, but has not been shy about championing the interests of western Maryland defense contractors and has helped local companies like London Fog bid on military contracts. She chairs a personnel subcommittee and spends considerable time and effort on the problems and situations—ignored by most other politicians—of Americans serving their country around the world.

Byron also serves on Interior and, while not satisfying some environmentalists, has been sympathetic enough to avoid the primary opposition which gave her husband close races in the 1976 and 1978 primaries. She has passed some bills there too, preserving Civil War landmarks by expanding the Antietam Battlefield park and promoting conversion of old rail lines, like those paralleling the National Road, to hiking trails. Byron is now the dean of the Maryland House delegation and, with more of a record than many expected, the holder of a safe seat.

The People: Est. Pop. 1986: 575,600, up 9.0% 1980–86; Pop. 1980: 528,168, up 24.3% 1970–80. Households (1980): 80% family, 45% with children, 70% married couples; 27.4% housing units rented; median monthly rent: $167; median house value: $58,100. Voting age pop. (1980): 376,405; 4% Black, 1% Spanish origin, 1% Asian origin.

Rep. Beverly B. Byron (D)

Elected 1978; b. July 27, 1932, Baltimore; home, Frederick; Hood Col., 1963–64; Episcopalian; married (Kirk Walsh).

Career: Campaign Asst., U.S. Rep. Goodloe E. Byron.

Offices: 2430 LHOB 20515, 202-225-2721. Also 10 E. Church St., Frederick 21701, 301-662-8622; 100 W. Franklin St., #110, Hagerstown 21700, 301-797-6043; P.O. Box 3275, Cumberland 21504, 301-729-0300; and 6 N. Court St., Westminster 21157, 301-848-5366.

Committees: *Armed Services* (6th of 31 D). Subcommittees: Research and Development; Military Personnel and Compensation (Chairman). *Interior and Insular Affairs* (9th of 26 D). Subcommittees: National Parks and Public Lands; Water, Power and Offshore Energy Resources. *Select Committee on Aging* (9th of 39 D). Subcommittee: Housing and Consumer Interests.

Group Ratings

	ADA	ACLU	COPE	CFA	LCV	ACU	NTLC	NSI	COC	CEI
1988	30	48	50	64	44	68	41	89	69	37
1987	52	—	48	71	—	35	—	—	60	31

National Journal Ratings

	1988 LIB — 1988 CONS		1987 LIB — 1987 CONS	
Economic	42% —	58%	42% —	56%
Social	31% —	68%	40% —	59%
Foreign	39% —	61%	39% —	60%

Key Votes

1) Homeless $	FOR	5) Ban Drug Test	AGN	9) SDI Research	FOR
2) Gephardt Amdt	FOR	6) Drug Death Pen	FOR	10) Ban Chem Weaps	AGN
3) Deficit Reduc	AGN	7) Handgun Sales	FOR	11) Aid to Contras	FOR
4) Kill Plnt Clsng Notice	AGN	8) Ban D.C. Abort $	FOR	12) Nuclear Testing	—

Election Results

1988 general	Beverly B. Byron (D)	166,753	(75%)	($213,554)
	Kenneth W. Halsey (R)................	54,528	(25%)	
1988 primary	Beverly B. Byron (D)	38,123	(81%)	
	Anthony P. Puca (D)...................	9,101	(19%)	
1986 general	Beverly B. Byron (D)	102,975	(72%)	($206,120)
	John Vandenberge (R)	39,600	(28%)	($137,069)

SEVENTH DISTRICT

Since the city was founded, Baltimore has had a large black community; by 1940 there were 142,000 blacks, 18% of the population, enough to support the *Afro-American* newspaper and a symphony orchestra. In addition, blacks had their own shopping street where, the *WPA Guide* reports, "are all the usual stores, five-and-dime, small groceries where two cigarettes can be had for a cent, expensive restaurants with the best of everything, and little eating places where hot dogs cost a nickel or free soup is given with all meals costing more than ten cents. It is still possible to purchase 'charms' here, but the old folkways are rapidly disappearing." Baltimore's main black neighborhood then was on the west side of downtown, with a smaller one on the east side; the latter has been hemmed in by ethnic white neighborhoods for most of the last 50 years, while the west side black population—their numbers increased by migrants from the South in the postwar years—has grown to include almost all the western half of the city.

This has changed Baltimore politics, though less than one might suppose. Blacks always voted here, and were courted by pro-civil rights Republicans like Theodore McKeldin, once Mayor and Governor, as well as by urban Democrats. "Walking around money" was always floating around in black precincts on election day, but Baltimore's black community also produced strong institutions and political leaders, the most brilliant of whom was Clarence Mitchell, for many years the NAACP's lobbyist in Washington. The emergence of a black mayor was delayed by the talents of Mayor William Donald Schaefer, who won majorities from black as well as white voters in 1971, 1975, 1979 and 1983, and by the legal problems of Mitchell's sons who served in the state legislature. Schaefer's successor as mayor, after Schaefer was elected governor in 1986, was Clarence (Du) Burns, who worked himself up from locker room attendant to city council president; he did a competent job and was edged out only narrowly in the Democratic primary by State's Attorney Kurt Schmoke. Young, a Yale graduate and Rhodes Scholar from a modest home in west Baltimore, Schmoke has little connection with traditional politics in Baltimore and is willing to make some waves: he was widely spotlighted and attacked in 1988 when he proposed decriminalizing drugs.

Schmoke represents one new face of Baltimore politics; another is the congressman from the 7th District. The 7th includes almost all of the mostly black neighborhoods and, aside from most of Johns Hopkins University and the old patrician neighborhood of Bolton Hill, very few white areas, and extends out directly west into the Baltimore County suburbs of Lochearn and Milford Mill, both of which have black majorities. The congressman is Kweisi Mfume, former councilman and radio talk show host, whose name echoes the rebellious Black Power movement of the 1960s, whose personal history is caught up in the social pathology that is at the root of the problems of the black underclass—and who himself has moved on from and above these aspects of the past. Mfume's original name was Frizzell Gray; he was 16 when his mother died, at which point he dropped out of school, held only low-paying jobs, and fathered five children out of wedlock. Then he took control of his life and moved it in another direction. He adopted his current Swahili name, studied radio broadcasting and eventually graduated from Morgan State, and got elected to the Baltimore City Council at 31. There he was a political critic of Mayor Schaefer. But he was also a stern critic of drug use and immoral conduct. Mfume seems to be a classic example of a black politician who has moved from demanding black power to emphasizing the need for self-discipline.

When 7th District Congressman Parren Mitchell retired in 1986, Mfume ran for the seat. Against Clarence Mitchell III, a veteran state senator with many legal problems, and minister and legislator Wendell Phillips, Mfume won 44% of the vote to their 23% and 17%. Only then was it revealed he had fathered five sons; he replied that he supported them and met his responsibilities. He won the general election with 87%. In Congress, he has worked quietly in the Banking and Small Business Committees, particularly on housing programs, and compiled a solid liberal voting record. Politically, he has gotten along well with Schaefer and the rest of the Maryland delegation. With a serious demeanor, a safe seat, and a politics in touch with the realities of life in black Baltimore today, he seems one of the more interesting politicians in the House.

The People: Est. Pop. 1986: 508,300, dn. 3.6% 1980–86; Pop. 1980: 527,590, dn. 11.2% 1970–80. Households (1980): 67% family, 40% with children, 37% married couples; 58.1% housing units rented; median monthly rent: $158; median house value: $28,300. Voting age pop. (1980): 376,566; 70% Black, 1% Spanish origin, 1% Asian origin.

1988 Presidential Vote:

Dukakis (D)	123,261	(81%)
Bush (R)	26,360	(17%)

Rep. Kweisi Mfume (D)

Elected 1986; b. Oct. 24, 1948, Baltimore; home, Baltimore; Morgan St. U., B.S. 1976, Johns Hopkins U., M.A. 1984; Baptist; divorced.

Career: Baltimore City Cncl., 1979–87.

Offices: 128 CHOB 20515, 202-225-4741. Also 3000 Druid Park Dr., Baltimore 21205, 301-367-1900; 223 N. Charles St., Baltimore 21218, 301-235-2700; 6326 Security Blvd., Baltimore 21207, 301-298-5997.

Committees: *Banking, Finance and Urban Affairs* (26th of 31 D). Subcommittees: Housing and Community Development; Financial Institutions Supervision, Regulation and Insurance. *Education and Labor* (22d of 22D). Subcommittee: Employment Opportunities. *Small Business* (19th of 27 D). Subcommittees: SBA, the General Economy and Minority Enterprise Development; Procurement, Tourism and Rural Development. *Select Committee on Narcotics Abuse and Control* (16th of 18 D).

Group Ratings

	ADA	ACLU	COPE	CFA	LCV	ACU	NTLC	NSI	COC	CEI
1988	95	87	100	100	100	4	10	0	21	10
1987	100	—	100	93	—	0	—	—	7	5

National Journal Ratings

	1988 LIB — 1988 CONS		1987 LIB — 1987 CONS	
Economic	87% —	8%	73% —	0%
Social	83% —	15%	78% —	0%
Foreign	74% —	23%	81% —	0%

Key Votes

1) Homeless $	AGN	5) Ban Drug Test	AGN	9) SDI Research	AGN
2) Gephardt Amdt	FOR	6) Drug Death Pen	FOR	10) Ban Chem Weaps	FOR
3) Deficit Reduc	FOR	7) Handgun Sales	AGN	11) Aid to Contras	AGN
4) Kill Plnt Clsng Notice	AGN	8) Ban D.C. Abort $	AGN	12) Nuclear Testing	FOR

Election Results

1988 general	Kweisi Mfume (D), unopposed			($110,565)
1988 primary	Kweisi Mfume (D), unopposed			
1986 general	Kweisi Mfume (D)	79,226	(87%)	($104,550)
	St. George I.B. Crosse, III (R)	12,170	(11%)	($52,593)

EIGHTH DISTRICT

Out the old roads down which colonial farmers rolled their barrels of tobacco, now called Wisconsin and Georgia Avenues, past the straight lines that mark the edges of the District of Columbia, marched the growth of the most affluent part of the Washington metropolitan area. In 1940, Montgomery County, Maryland, directly north and northwest of the White House, had just 83,000 people, dwarfed by the District's 663,000; its public services were still rudimentary and some parents paid tuition to send their kids to D.C. public schools. But growth, driven first by the expansion of the District and then by the federal facilities—Bethesda Naval Hospital, the National Institutes of Health, the Food and Drug Administration—that have made Montgomery County the center of America's health industry, has made Montgomery boom. By 1990 there will be about 700,000 people there, well ahead of the 620,000 in the District. And they will be, as they have been since the 1940s, on average the most affluent and best-educated people in America, living in a community with first-rate public services and the *élan* of successful, committed professionals who have done well while doing good.

Montgomery County, and the 8th Congressional District which includes most of its land area and 90% of its people, has always been a bit apart from the rest of Maryland. The typical voter here is a high-ranking civil servant, a lawyer in private practice, or, increasingly, a professional employee of a firm that does consulting for the government. He (or she) is as likely as not to have a graduate degree and to belong to a liberal-oriented Protestant church or a Reform Jewish temple. He is sympathetic to the striving nations of the Third World, to efforts to clean up political campaigns and to environmentalists. He professes a vaguely liberal sort of politics. Montgomery County voters are usually willing to support Democrats, and the 8th District, in a nice refutation of the theory that Americans always vote their pocketbooks, favored Michael Dukakis and Walter Mondale over George Bush and Ronald Reagan. For years their favorite candidates have been liberal Republicans who care deeply about civil rights and process issues, like former Senator (and Congressman) Charles Mathias and former Congressman Gilbert Gude, and liberal Democrats who are brainy and hard-working and take the lead on national issues, like former Congressman Michael Barnes. It may be though that Montgomery demands too much of its congressmen: it is just too exhausting being a national leader and tending to the local (and civil service) problems of half a million constituents who are only a local phone call away. Mathias, Gude and Barnes, all still in the prime of life, relinquished their seats voluntarily.

Today the 8th District is represented by a Republican in the Mathias-Gude tradition, Connie Morella. She also brings credentials of her own: an ethnic background that not many old-line Republicans, but an increasing number of Montgomery voters, share; a personal history of raising nine children, six of them her late sister's; eight years experience in the legislature. In 1986, when Barnes ran for the Senate, she beat, 53%–47%, legislator Stewart Bainum, a liberal with accomplishments of his own and a nursing home business owner who spent $1.5 million on the campaign, the third highest in the country. In 1988, legislator Peter Franchot, a knowledgeable former House staffer, ran an aggressive campaign lampooning Morella's co-sponsorship (as a ranking subcommittee member) of commemorative resolutions. But she responded with endorsements from everyone from the Fraternal Order of Police to PeacePAC to the Sierra Club, based on a voting record liberal on cultural issues, somewhat less so on foreign policy, and rather market-oriented on economics, while her seats on the Post Office and Civil Service and Science Committees were obviously useful for Montgomery. Morella won with 63%, running 16% ahead of George Bush.

The People: Est. Pop. 1986: 606,300, up 14.8% 1980–86; Pop. 1980: 528,036, up 7.3% 1970–80. Households (1980): 72% family, 38% with children, 60% married couples; 37.1% housing units rented; median monthly rent: $332; median house value: $96,900. Voting age pop. (1980): 391,309; 8% Black, 4% Spanish origin, 4% Asian origin.

1988 Presidential Vote:

Dukakis (D)	150,522	(53%)
Bush (R)	129,919	(46%)

Rep. Constance A. Morella (R)

Elected 1986; b. Feb. 12, 1931, Somerville, MA; home, Bethesda; Boston U., A.B. 1954; American U., M.A. 1967; Roman Catholic; married (Anthony).

Career: Teacher, Montgomery Cnty. Pub. Schls., 1956-60; Instructor, American U., 1968-70; Prof., Montgomery Col., 1970-86; MD House of Delegates, 1979–86.

Offices: 1024 LHOB 20515, 202-225-5341. Also 11141 Georgia Ave., Ste. 302, Wheaton 20902, 301-946-6801.

Committees: *Science, Space and Technology* (15th of 19 R). Subcommittees: Science, Research and Technology; Space Science and Applications. *Post Office and Civil Service* (6th of 9 R). Subcommittees: Civil Service (Ranking Member); Compensation and Employee Benefits. *Select Committee on Aging* (22th of 27 R). Subcommittee: Human Services.

Group Ratings

	ADA	ACLU	COPE	CFA	LCV	ACU	NTLC	NSI	COC	CEI
1988	90	91	63	100	88	8	32	22	46	21
1987	60	—	50	71	—	22	—	—	40	33

National Journal Ratings

	1988 LIB — 1988 CONS		1987 LIB — 1987 CONS	
Economic	48% —	52%	34% —	66%
Social	83% —	15%	62% —	36%
Foreign	68% —	28%	66% —	34%

Key Votes

1) Homeless $	FOR	5) Ban Drug Test	AGN	9) SDI Research	AGN
2) Gephardt Amdt	AGN	6) Drug Death Pen	AGN	10) Ban Chem Weaps	AGN
3) Deficit Reduc	AGN	7) Handgun Sales	AGN	11) Aid to Contras	AGN
4) Kill Plnt Clsng Notice	AGN	8) Ban D.C. Abort $	AGN	12) Nuclear Testing	FOR

Election Results

1988 general	Constance A. Morella (R)	172,619	(63%)	($821,574)
	Peter Franchot (D)	102,478	(37%)	($460,847)
1988 primary	Constance A. Morella (R), unopposed			
1986 general	Constance A. Morella (R)	92,917	(53%)	($640,270)
	Stewart Bainum, Jr. (D)	82,825	(47%)	($1,500,531)

MASSACHUSETTS

Half a century ago, when President Franklin Roosevelt came to Boston in his last week of campaigning for a third term, he was arriving not in safe Democratic territory but in a state that was politically marginal and even treacherous. The Bay State's Yankees, descended from the first Puritan settlers, had been loyal to the Republican Party since it was founded in 1854; they were hostile to the New Deal and all its works. The Democratic vote in Massachusetts came almost entirely from Catholics, and mainly from descendants of the Irish immigrants who arrived on the frigid shores of New England after fleeing the Irish potato famine of the 1840s; loyal followers of an insular, bitter Church, they were hostile to Roosevelt's cultural liberalism and unsympathetic to his obvious desire to aid their ancient enemies the British in their desperate fight against Hitler.

After saluting "my ambassador" to Britain, Joseph P. Kennedy, whom he had just relieved of office, Roosevelt gave an assurance "to you mothers and fathers" that would be quoted back at him by his enemies, "I have said this before, but I shall say it again and again and again: Your boys are not going to be sent into any foreign wars." Roosevelt carried Massachusetts that year, gaining just enough pro-British votes from Yankees to offset his large losses among Irish Catholics. But Massachusetts was one of the most evenly—and bitterly—divided states in the nation 50 years ago. How had it gotten that way? And how did it become by 1968 one of the most liberal and Democratic states?

The story goes back to the settlement of this stony and infertile land during an age of religious controversy in the 17th century by Calvinist Puritans convinced they had a special mission on earth. Their austere creed told them that only the elect would be saved and that they must extirpate the forces of Satan—Indians, Papists, tolerationists—in their way. For about 150 years, New England was insular, hostile to outsiders, economically stagnant. Then, for a moment after the American Revolution, the Napoleonic wars in Europe let New England shipowners become the leading merchants of the world; they soon lost that advantage but with shrewdness and ingenuity they plowed their profits into textile mills, the great growth industry of the day, then into railroads, then into coal-mining and steel-making. New Englanders surged through Upstate New York, the Midwest, and across the continent; they built new cities and new colleges in the wilderness; they helped to start the Republican Party and did much to start—and win— the Civil War. They planted their economic system and their values—articulated in the McGuffey readers—across the continent: by the 1820s they were as far west as Syracuse, by the 1850s in Iowa and bleeding Kansas and Oregon's Willamette Valley, by the 1880s in Los Angeles.

But as each year brought more Catholics from Ireland, these descendants of Yankee Protestants believed those values were under attack at home in Massachusetts. As for the Irish, 100 years later they remembered "No Irish need apply" signs, and as successful an Irish Catholic as Joseph Kennedy felt obliged to move to New York in 1927 because he would never be treated as an equal by the Brahmins. By the Yankees' standards many of the Irish immigrants were undesirable. But the reception the Irish got from them was as hostile as any group of immigrants have received in this country.

With a bitterness not found in other big states, with grievances and suspicions rooted in the experiences of the 17th century when the Puritans set up their "city on a hill," a model they expected would be imitated in Cromwell's England, and the Irish were conquered by Protestants, Massachusetts's political struggles for years were a kind of cultural war between Yankee

MASSACHUSETTS — Congressional Districts, Counties, County Subdivisions (Towns), and Places — *(11 Districts)*

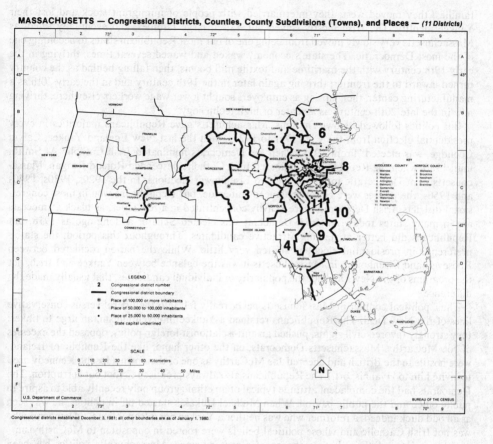

Congressional districts established December 3, 1981; all other boundaries are as of January 1, 1980.

Republicans and Irish Democrats, with arguments not so much over the distribution of income or the provision of services, as over whose vision of Massachusetts should be honored, whose mores regarded as the norm.

Sometimes the stakes were concrete—control of patronage jobs, command of the Boston Police Department—more often they were symbolic. Yankee Republicans tended to back programs of an activist government: public works and protective tariffs to help business, war and Reconstruction to help suitably distant oppressed people like the blacks of the South, uplifting (and productivity-enhancing) social movements like temperance. The Irish found 19th century Democrats, a party promoting not government action but laissez-faire, more congenial. They came from a place where the government was the enemy; they didn't want government spending money to help the rich or to stimulate commerce (with which they had little acquaintance in agricultural Ireland); they didn't want government to restrict immigration; they didn't want it to advance the blacks who might compete with them in the labor market; and they didn't want it to prohibit the consumption of liquor. They were people familiar with competing hierarchies—the hierarchy of the hated English lords and the hierarchy of their own, often suppressed, Roman Catholic Church. The Democratic Party, with its ward organization and rituals, seemed like a sympathetic hierarchy. So the Irish went into politics, determined to beat the Protestants.

Over the years the percentage of Irish and Catholics slowly rose. Yankees had smaller families, they moved west, they intermarried with people of immigrant stock and lost their Yankee identity. The Irish mostly stayed put, raised large families, and eventually ruled, as Massachusetts very slowly moved from being one of our most Republican states to becoming one of the most Democratic. The state's economy waxed and waned several times, thriving in the early 19th century with the maritime and textile mill booms, then falling behind as the country turned inward to the frontier; thriving again later in the 19th century and in the early 20th as a manufacturing center, then lapsing as employers sought lower wage workers elsewhere; thriving now in the late 20th century as a center of high technology.

But politics followed its own rhythms. Massachusetts gave Republicans majorities in every presidential election from the Civil War to 1924, when the last New England Yankee, Calvin Coolidge, was elected. From 1928, when the Democrats nominated Irish Catholic Al Smith, until 1980, when the Republicans nominated Irish Catholic-descended Ronald Reagan, Massachusetts went Democratic in all but the two Eisenhower elections. In the 1920s, 1930s, 1940s and 1950s, the parties were closely balanced statewide, but Republicans won in most congressional districts; Irish Democrats were heavily concentrated in a few cities, as black Democrats are in many states today. An Irish Democrat was elected Senator as long ago as 1918, but Republicans did better at fielding attractive candidates. Throughout this period, the state's preference in presidential elections shifted very little. While the nation oscillated between Roosevelt and Eisenhower, in Massachusetts it was the balance between Yankee and Irish, not the programs of the New Deal nor the popularity of individual candidates, that usually made the difference.

Thus, political conflict in Massachusetts never really fell into the liberal-versus-conservative lines of the New Deal. The Republicans retained a Yankee interventionism, an urge to tinker: they strongly favored civil rights, pushed an anti-isolationist foreign policy, opposed the excesses of Joe McCarthy. Massachusetts Democrats, on the other hand, like the Republic of Ireland, were hostile to the British and cheered Joe McCarthy as one of their own. (Joseph Kennedy used to invite him to Hyannisport.) The Republicans also always promised to root out corruption. The Democrats had the complacent attitude typical of an ethnic group only recently able to aspire to public office and the public payroll. When Michael Dukakis started off in politics, he was seen as an odd duck indeed: a reformer who was neither a Yankee nor a Republican, a Democrat who was not Irish Catholic and whose political beliefs were rooted in opposition to McCarthyism.

What is interesting is that, in the quarter century since, Massachusetts politics has been transformed: the Democrats have become reformist, liberal to varying extents on economics, liberal (to the point of ludicrousness in the views of voters elsewhere) on almost every conceivable cultural issue; the Republicans have become enthusiasts for free economic markets and vitriolic opponents of all taxes, and increasingly conservative on cultural issues. The catalysts were two young men first elected to public office in 1962: 30-year-old U.S. Senator Edward Kennedy and 29-year-old state Representative Michael Dukakis. For a time in the 1960s and 1970s, under Kennedy's influence, Irish Democrats and Yankee Republicans were moving in the same direction. Kennedy's support of civil rights even during the 1970s Boston busing controversy, his opposition to the war in Vietnam, his stand against corruption during Watergate—all appealed to Yankee sensibilities, while his appeal to the Irish changed their attitudes. By 1968, Massachusetts was 20% more Democratic than the nation; in 1972—when it was the only state to vote for George McGovern—it was 17% more Democratic than the nation. This was a consensus response: upper-crust Yankee Lincoln as well as lower-income Irish Somerville both voted for McGovern in the election that allowed Bay Staters to display during Watergate bumper stickers that said "Don't blame me, I'm from Massachusetts."

That new consensus politics also made Michael Dukakis's election as governor possible. In 1974, he beat an Irish Catholic in the primary and a Yankee liberal in the general—a triumph over both of the state's previously dominant strains. But in his first term he ran up against the limits of government, and foundered. Dukakis raised taxes after he promised not to, and Massachusetts's tax burdens—the highest or second highest in the nation—choked off economic growth. Dukakis lost the 1978 primary to Ed King, a conservative on cultural issues and an opponent of taxes; King's tax cuts and Proposition 2½, plus the cut in federal capital gains, got the state's high-tech economy humming in the 1980s. Dukakis, returned to office, helped it along with state projects helping old mill towns revitalize and welfare mothers get job training, and for a time Massachusetts's economy seemed to be leading the national recovery. But, like New Hampshire's very different tax haven strategy, this was not a model the nation could follow. Massachusetts for decades has been exporting low-skill people (textile workers, high school grads) and importing high-skill people (Harvard and MIT grads, computer whizzes); once taxes were lowered even mildly, the high-skill people produced an economy that zoomed—and were able to keep their cultural liberalism in the bargain. But the United States as a whole can't export anybody (nobody, demographically speaking, leaves this country) and can't replenish its work force with super-educated people as fast as Massachusetts can.

And by the late 1980s, Massachusetts's high-tech growth seemed to be turning many voters toward free market economics, even as some Catholics were following the national trend to cultural conservatism. Massachusetts was only 8% more Democratic than the national average in 1984 and 7% more so in 1988; Michael Dukakis, a native son, got just 53% of the vote here, lower than George McGovern's 54% in 1972. The upshot is that the Republicans may be on the verge of being competitive in statewide races once again. The national Republican vote base, under 40% two decades ago, is now around the 45% Raymond Shamie got against John Kerry in 1984, or the 46% George Bush got against Dukakis in 1988, within shooting distance of the 51% Ronald Reagan got in 1984.

Governor. Michael Dukakis announced in January 1989 that he wouldn't run for reelection in 1990; the nearly two decades in which he has been the major figure in state politics are coming to an end. The verdict is not clear. His greatest political asset going into the 1988 presidential race was the perception, in Massachusetts and out, that he had not merely done a good job as governor, but that he had set the state on a course that offered great promise for the nation. In the few months after he lost the 1988 race, as he faced a burgeoning state deficit and prepared to boost taxes, the verdict looked different. "Competence, not ideology" was Dukakis's cry in Atlanta, and on the trail he emphasized how he balanced nine state budgets.

The tenth budget seemed to undercut his entire argument. Even with Massachusetts's huge 1980s growth in revenues, Dukakis had allowed the public sector to balloon in size until it required $700 million in new taxes that, to judge from voters' opinions as rendered in referenda, threaten to throttle the private economy. And much of that private sector growth, it might be added, depends on the big defense budgets which Dukakis almost reflexively opposes—more certainly than the growth that has been produced by Dukakis's creative encouragement of local enterprises and limited workfare plan. It would be going too far to claim, as Republicans might, that Dukakis has done more to curb economic growth than promote it. The cultural liberalism he champions, after all, has helped to attract many productive newcomers to the state who are, inconveniently for the conservatives' arguments, prominent among the entrepreneurs and innovators who make the high-tech economy grow.

But it is not apparent that the Dukakis approach which has governed state affairs during most of the last 20 years will govern during much of the next 20. The state's youngest voters, as well as most of its high-tech communities, tended to vote against him. The generation that came of age during Vietnam and Watergate, the core of his support, has reached its maximum as a share of the electorate. For them Dukakis's extreme liberalism on issues like crime may not be a drawback: Massachusetts remained, until Dukakis grudgingly signed the repeal after 12 years of opposition, the only state to give weekend furloughs to prisoners sentenced to life-without-parole; it is the only state to permit prisoners to vote and to send state officials in to sign the convicts up.

But it is not clear that a majority of Massachusetts voters want a governor whose appointees and staffers will come up with policies as liberal as these.

Lieutenant Governor Evelyn Murphy led in polls after Dukakis announced his retirement, but she must obviously build something more on top of name identity. Former Attorney General Frank Bellotti has an honorable career in statewide politics that goes back to 1962 and could be a serious competitor. Boston Mayor Raymond Flynn, popular with blacks though not in his Irish South Boston base, quickly took himself out of the race, but reconsidered running after Congressman Joseph Kennedy, also popular with older Catholic voters, took himself out of the race in March 1989. Another possible candidate with Kennedy out is former national party chairman (and longtime Edward Kennedy aide) Paul Kirk, who moved back to Boston to practice law. There were reports that Edward Kennedy, Jr., would run for lieutenant governor, a nomination he could probably have for the asking.

The Republican Party as recently as 1986 was a joke in the gubernatorial race; one candidate after another was forced to leave the race after embarrassing revelations. But for 1990 the Republicans have a bevy of respectable or semi-respectable candidates. One is William Weld, former U.S. assistant attorney general who resigned out of disagreement with Edwin Meese. Others are White House deputy chief of staff Andy Card, who helped George Bush carry the Boston media market in 1988; State House Minority Leader Steven Pierce, who attacked Dukakis all fall; former Congressman Paul Cronin, who beat Senator John Kerry in the 5th district in 1972; and former Boston EPA office head Michael Deland, a moderate who is distinctive because he is ambulatory in a wheelchair. In a state that has gone far beyond the days when the Kennedys—John Kennedy in 1952, Edward Kennedy in 1962—promised to "do more for Massachusetts,"(that is, to pump more government money into a stagnant private economy), and now seems past the Dukakis era when the argument was that government was playing a key role stimulating the private sector, Massachusetts appears ready to recognize the primacy of the market-oriented businesses which are mostly responsible for its bounteous growth—and may even vote accordingly.

Senators. Edward Kennedy—graying, full-framed, not only older than his brothers ever lived to be but past the age of his father when he became a national political figure—is Massachusetts's most enduring politician. Senator Kennedy may not occupy as big a place on the national scene as he once did: 30 years after his brother's victory in 1960, it is clear that this Kennedy will never be President, and the rumor mills that once buzzed with speculation over when he would be in the White House are now twittering about whether this or that next-generation Kennedy is about to win a congressional or legislative seat somewhere. In retrospect, it is plain that Edward Kennedy's presidential chances were ended in July 1969, with the accident at Chappaquiddick; in 1980, when he finally ran, he was unable to beat an incumbent the public, it became apparent from the November results, was eager to get rid of. When he announced he wouldn't run in 1984 and 1988, there was no draft movement to change his mind, no sense that the Democrats were doomed without a candidate from this one family. Most voters can't remember, or never knew, what made the Kennedys so exciting.

All of which has enabled Kennedy to do what he evidently wants, to work conscientiously for what he considers the interests of the poorest and most helpless in our society. For this he had little preparation and no firsthand knowledge: he spent his first three decades as a rich playboy and his next three as a celebrity who could not walk down a street without being mobbed. He came from a political family whose concern for the poor was limited, until about 1963, to how many votes the poor would cast for them and, in some places, how much those votes would cost In his early years in the Senate Edward Kennedy was quiet, listened respectfully to his elders learned the rules, written and unwritten, and prepared himself to be the legislator his brothers never were. After the deaths of his brothers John and Robert, after the awful year of urban riots and anti-war demonstrations and the murder of Martin Luther King, Edward Kennedy evidently decided he had a mission to help the helpless; and ever since, he has been America's most conspicuous supporter of greater government spending on programs aimed at helping the poor.

In the process, he assembled a crackerjack staff (many members of which had daydreams about their White House offices) that became a model for other Democrats, generating one big-government bill after another, working as part of iron triangles with agency bureaucrats and think tank professionals to create and nurture new government programs, under the sometimes loose supervision of the Senator. Kennedy himself worked hard to master details and shepherded to passage such diverse measures as immigration reform (the 1965 bill; he opposed the thrust of the 1986 reform), criminal code revision, and airline deregulation. He became chairman of the Judiciary Committee in 1979, on the retirement of James Eastland, and undertook the burden of upholding liberal positions on issues like abortion, capital punishment, busing, and the balanced budget constitutional amendment; when the Republicans took the majority, he relinquished his rank on Judiciary for Labor and Human Resouces, and has chaired that committee since 1987.

That post has given him scope to push legislation he cares about. He has been successful on a $1 billion bill for AIDS education and treatment, the "Star Schools" bill for stronger math, science, and foreign languages, a lie detector ban law, the Civil Rights Restoration Act, and fair housing. He has been less successful on long-term health care, and employer-paid health insurance (like the bill Dukakis pushed through in Boston in 1988). He is not, however, resurrecting his proposals of the 1970s, of which little has been heard since his 1980 campaign: national health insurance, labor law reform, a guaranteed annual income. Increasingly, he seeks to put costs on the private sector rather than in the federal budget, though of course costs still must be paid out of what the private economy generates.

The Democrats' capture of the Senate in 1986 did not make Kennedy "King of the Congress," as some have said; but he clearly sets the tone and much of the agenda for the two dozen or so Senators who can be counted on as solid liberals. And if he increasingly seems mellow and at ease with his place in life, Kennedy is also capable of throwing some pretty sharp elbows: he does not like to be pushed around. He helped launch the successful campaign against Judge Robert Bork by issuing a strong statement that was less than completely factual. And he got his friend Fritz Hollings to insert a provision in a communications bill that forced publisher Rupert Murdoch to sell the *Boston Herald*, an aggressively conservative paper that counters the preachily liberal *Boston Globe* and which attacks and ridicules Kennedy constantly.

Kennedy's strength in Massachusetts is different from what it was 15 or 20 years ago. Then he was revered by Irish voters who remembered discrimination and loved him as a member of the family that had brought them all into the American mainstream; now he is more likely to be respected as a hardworking, competent, earnest public official. His conduct at Chappaquiddick in 1969 still causes some voters problems, as it did when he ran for President in 1980, and probably always will; and he stirs Republican as well as Democratic partisan juices, both among Massachusetts voters and among recipients of Republican and New Right direct mail. Since 1970, his reelection percentage has oscillated in the 60% range: high-tech entrepreneur Raymond Shamie held him to 61% in 1982; in 1988 against 33-year-old Republican staffer Joe Malone, who ran a high-road campaign, Kennedy won 65%–34%, cutting at least 10 points into the core Republican vote.

Massachusetts's junior Senator, John Kerry, is in his first term but has been in the national spotlight for some time. He first won fame as one of the organizers of Vietnam Veterans Against the War in 1971, when he tossed a set of medals (someone else's, he later explained) over a fence in a rally; Kerry's leadership attracted attention because of his background, unusual for a Vietnam veteran (he went to Yale and his mother is from the Brahmin Forbes family), and because of his genuine record of heroism in combat. He also was plainly politically ambitious, buying a house in Worcester as preparation to challenge one congressman in 1972, then moving to Lowell when another retired. There he had vitriolic opposition from the *Lowell Sun* and, even while George McGovern was carrying the district, lost to a Republican. There had been talk of Kerry as a presidential candidate some day; chastened by his loss, he went to law school, worked for a prosecutor, was elected lieutenant governor on the Dukakis ticket in 1982, and squeaked to a narrow victory in the 1984 Senate primary over then congressman (and since 1986, attorney general) James Shannon, who made the mistake of attacking him for serving in the military.

In the meantime, Republican primary voters were surprising observers across the nation by rejecting the candidacy of Elliot Richardson—former holder of several Cabinet offices, as well as lieutenant governor and attorney general of Massachusetts—and selecting instead Raymond Shamie. The once Yankee and socially interventionist ranks of the Republican Party have been so thinned that the children of immigrants who believe in Ronald Reagan's politics now are a majority in primaries here as elsewhere, and naturally they preferred Shamie to Richardson. But newly rising groups make mistakes in politics: Shamie, it seems, used to be involved with the John Birch Society and kept Birch literature around his office; this is pretty weird stuff, and the leftish *Boston Globe* had a lot of fun with it. Kerry won with 55%—a good share for a freshman Senator, but also a sign that Massachusetts is not so one-sidedly Democratic on national issues as it once was.

Kerry is one of those Democrats for whom Vietnam seems to be the paradigmatic event in American history. He sits on the Foreign Relations Committee and chairs a subcommittee which has been investigating drug dealing and dictators in Central America; Kerry has focused not on the Sandinistas but on trying to link the contras to the drug trade. He has also accused Fidel Castro of drug trafficking; he made similar charges against Panama's Noriega regime, but failed to deliver on hinted-at revelations that George Bush somehow knew or was chargeable with knowing about Noriega's operations. Kerry was eventually criticized by ranking Republican Mitch McConnell for relying excessively on testimony of a drug trafficker (sentenced to 43 years), and for refusing to let a Bush ally testify to clear himself of the man's charges.

At the same time Kerry was chairing the Democrats' Senate campaign committee. He had the satisfaction of seeing his party gain one seat on balance, a gain that was pretty well cinched in 1987 when many strong Republicans decided not to run. Kerry ran an efficient and aggressive operation, and only a few bad breaks in ultra-close races prevented him from picking up two or three more seats himself.

How will Kerry himself fare in 1990? As a Democrat whose views seem unexceptional in Massachusetts, if not elsewhere, he will surely not face a serious primary challenge, and the odds are he will not face a serious challenger in November either. But the Republicans have a bigger vote-base in Massachusetts than is generally acknowledged, and the possibility of a serious gubernatorial candidacy in 1990; if they can avoid stumbling and settle on a strong ticket, they may be able to exploit the weaknesses in the Democrats' programs suggested by the Dukakis budget deficit and make a head-on assault on liberalism in what has come to be seen as its home fortress. In that case, Kerry might have a more difficult race than most pros expect.

Presidential politics. Massachusetts, 20% more Democratic than the national average in 1968 and 17% more so in 1972, was only 8% more Democratic than average in 1984 and, even with "the governor of Massachusetts," as Republicans liked to call him, running for President, just 7% more Democratic than the nation in 1988. That still leaves Massachusetts as one of the most Democratic states, but its belief in welfare state liberalism has been sapped. The recent spectacular private-sector driven local growth has undermined the view that voters need politicians who can do more for Massachusetts, and has strengthened the idea that big government will kill the high-tech goose that lays the golden eggs. If you take the whole Boston media market, including southern New Hampshire where so many tax-hating Bay Staters have moved, Dukakis ran almost precisely even with Bush—not much of a home base. Between 1972 and 1988, the corridors along the old-fashioned four-lane Route 2 west from Cambridge and Route 9 west from Boston have become more Democratic, as has the college-strewn Pioneer

Valley in the west: they have attracted the culturally liberal and what might be called the graduate student proletariat to their comfortable old houses. At the same time, the corridors along newer limited-access highways—Interstate 93 north toward New Hampshire, Interstate 95 north to Maine, Route 24 south to Taunton, Route 3 south toward Plymouth, and the Interstate 495 circumferential, 20 miles out past 128—have become more Republican as their newer, less tree-shaded subdivisions fill up with high-tech employees and entrepreneurs who regard Dukakis, despite his national reputation, as someone who is savaging growth rather than helping it. The Republican Party is almost pathetically weak in the trenches in Massachusetts. But if high-tech expands faster than the radical graduate student communities, there is a potential majority for it.

Massachusetts's presidential primary has long been in early March; it was one of the Super Tuesday contests in 1988. It was won by Dukakis and Bush, both of whom were born in Norfolk County, Massachusetts—the only time in American history both major party candidates were born in the same county, and one which already had produced three presidents before (the Adamses and Kennedy).

Congressional districting. Massachusetts will probably lose another congressional district after the 1990 Census as it did after 1980. This means a game of musical chairs in the Great and General Court (the official name for the legislature). The losers last time were Barney Frank and Republican Margaret Heckler, who were thrown in together; Frank won. This time possible victims include Joe Kennedy and Edward Markey, both of whose districts could easily be sliced up among their neighbors and neither of whom has many friends in the legislature. Another possibility is joining much of the 1st District to Springfield if the 1st's Silvio Conte retires.

The People: Est. Pop 1988: 5,871,000; Pop. 1980: 5,737,037, up 2.3% 1980–88 and 0.8% 1970–80; 2.42% of U.S. total, 12th largest. 16% with 1–3 yrs. col., 20% with 4+ yrs. col.; 9.8% below poverty level. Single ancestry: 12% Irish, 8% English, Italian, 5% French, 3% Portuguese, Polish, 2% German, 1% Russian, Swedish, Greek, Scottish. Households (1980): 71% family, 36% with children, 57% married couples; 42.5% housing units rented; median monthly rent: $197; median house value: $48,500. Voting age pop. (1980): 4,246,648; 3% Black, 2% Spanish origin, 1% Asian origin. Registered voters (1988): 2,969,506; 1,378,262 D (46%); 400,544 R (13%); 1,190,700 unaffiliated and minor parties (40%).

1988 Share of Federal Tax Burden $27,402,000,000; 3.10% of U.S. total, 10th largest.

1988 Share of Federal Expenditures

	Total		Non-Defense		Defense	
Total Expend	$25,079m	(2.84%)	$16,936m	(2.58%)	$8,806m	(3.85%)
St/Lcl Grants	3,328m	(2.90%)	3,327m	(2.91%)	0m	(0.39%)
Salary/Wages	2,383m	(1.77%)	1,682m	(2.51%)	701m	(2.51%)
Pymnts to Indiv	10,456m	(2.56%)	10,234m	(2.62%)	223m	(1.19%)
Procurement	7,862m	(4.17%)	663m	(1.43%)	7,862m	(4.17%)
Research/Other	1,049m	(2.81%)	1,029m	(2.78%)	20m	(2.78%)

Political Lineup: Governor, Michael S. Dukakis (D); Lt. Gov., Evelyn F. Murphy (D); Secy. of Commonwealth, Michael Joseph Connolly (D); Atty. Gen., James Shannon (D); Treasurer, Robert Q. Crane (D); Auditor, Joseph DeNucci (D). State Senate, 40 (32 D and 8 R); State House of Representatives, 160 (128 D and 32 R). Senators, Edward M. Kennedy (D) and John F. Kerry (D). Representatives, 11 (10 D and 1 R).

1988 Presidential Vote

Dukakis (D).	1,401,415	(53%)
Bush (R)	1,195,635	(45%)

1988 Democratic Presidential Primary

Dukakis	418,256	(59%)
Jackson	133,141	(19%)
Gephardt	72,944	(10%)
Gore	31,631	(4%)
Simon	26,176	(4%)
Hart	10,837	(2%)

1984 Presidential Vote

Reagan (R)	1,310,936	(51%)
Mondale (D)	1,239,606	(48%)

1988 Republican Presidential Primary

Bush	141,113	(59%)
Dole	63,392	(26%)
Kemp	16,791	(7%)
Robertson	10,891	(5%)
Du Pont	3,522	(2%)
Haig	1,705	(1%)

GOVERNOR

Gov. Michael S. Dukakis (D)

Elected 1982, term expires Jan. 1991; b. Nov. 3, 1933, Brookline home, Brookline; Swarthmore Col., B.A. 1955, Harvard U., LL.B. 1960; Greek Orthodox; married (Kitty).

Career: Army, Korea; Practicing atty., 1960–74; MA House of Reps., 1963–70; Dem. Nominee for Lt. Gov., 1970; Moderator of public TV show "The Advocates," 1971–73; Gov. of MA, 1975–79; Lecturer, Dir., Intergovernmental Studies, JFK Sch. of Govt. Harvard U., 1979–82. Dem. Nominee for Pres., 1988.

Office: State House, Rm. 360, Boston 02133, 617-727-3600.

Election Results

1986 gen.	Michael S. Dukakis (D)	1,157,786	(69%)
	George S. Kariotis (R)	525,364	(31%)
1986 prim.	Michael S. Dukakis (D)	499,572	(100%)
1982 gen.	Michael S. Dukakis (D)	1,219,109	(59%)
	John W. Sears (R)	749,679	(37%)

SENATORS

Sen. Edward M. Kennedy (D)

Elected 1962, seat up 1994; b. Feb. 22, 1932, Boston; home, Boston; Harvard U., B.A. 1956, The Hague, 1958, U. of VA, LL.B. 1959; Roman Catholic; divorced.

Career: Army, 1951–53; Asst. Dist. Atty., Suffolk Cnty., 1961-62.

Offices: 315 RSOB 20510, 202-224-4543. Also JFK Fed. Bldg. Rm. 2400A, Boston 02203, 617-565-3170.

Committees: *Armed Services* (4th of 11 D). Subcommittees: Manpower and Personnel; Strategic Forces and Nuclear Deterrence; Projection Forces and Regional Defense (Chairman). *Judiciary* (2d of 8 D). Subcommittees: Constitution; Immigration and Refugee Affairs (Chairman); Patents, Copyrights and Trademarks; *Labor and Human Resources* (Chairman of 9 D). *Joint Economic Committee.* Subcommittees: International Economic Policy; Fiscal and Monetary Policy (Chairman); Economic Goals and Intergovernmental Policy.

Group Ratings

	ADA	ACLU	COPE	CFA	LCV	ACU	NTLC	NSI	COC	CEI
1988	95	88	93	100	70	0	5	0	27	14
1987	90	—	93	92	—	0	—	—	24	22

National Journal Ratings

	1988 LIB — 1988 CONS		1987 LIB — 1987 CONS	
Economic	86%	— 0%	74%	— 0%
Social	86%	— 0%	96%	— 0%
Foreign	86%	— 0%	74%	— 0%

Key Votes

1) Cut Aged Housing $	FOR	5) Bork Nomination	AGN	9) SDI Funding	AGN
2) Override Hwy Veto	FOR	6) Ban Plastic Guns	AGN	10) Ban Chem Weaps	AGN
3) Kill Plnt Clsng Notice	AGN	7) Deny Abortions	AGN	11) Aid To Contras	AGN
4) Min Wage Increase	FOR	8) Japanese Reparations	—	12) Reagan Defense $	AGN

Election Results

1988 general	Edward M. Kennedy (D)	1,693,344	(65%)	($2,702,865)
	Joseph D. Malone (R)	884,267	(34%)	($587,323)
1988 primary	Edward M. Kennedy (D), unopposed			
1982 general	Edward M. Kennedy (D)	1,247,084	(61%)	($2,470,473)
	Raymond Shamie (R)	784,602	(38%)	($2,305,996)

Sen. John F. Kerry (D)

Elected 1984, seat up 1990; b. Dec. 11, 1943, Denver, CO; home, Boston; Yale U., A.B. 1966, Boston Col., LL.B. 1976; Roman Catholic; divorced.

Career: Navy, Vietnam; Organizer, Vietnam Veterans Against the War; Asst. Dist. Atty., Middlesex Cnty., 1976–81; Practicing atty., 1981–82; Lt. Gov. of MA, 1982–84.

Offices: 421 RSOB 20510, 202-224-2742. Also Transportation Bldg., 10 Park Plaza, Rm. 3220, Boston 02216, 617-565-8519.

Committees: *Banking, Housing and Urban Affairs* (11th of 12 D). Subcommittees: Housing and Urban Affairs; Consumer and Regulatory Affairs. *Commerce, Science and Transportation* (8th of 11 D). Subcommittees: Aviation; Communications; Science, Technology and Space. *Foreign Relations* (6th of 10 D). Subcommittees: International Economic Policy, Trade, Oceans and Environment; Western Hemisphere and Peace Corps Affairs; Terrorism, Narcotics and International Operations (Chairman). *Small Business* (8th of 10 D). Subcommittee: Rural Economy and Family Farming; Innovation, Technology and Productivity; Urban and Minority-Owned Business Development (Chairman).

Group Ratings

	ADA	ACLU	COPE	CFA	LCV	ACU	NTLC	NSI	COC	CEI
1988	90	85	95	92	100	0	7	0	36	12
1987	85	—	96	92	—	4	—	—	25	27

National Journal Ratings

	1988 LIB — 1988 CONS		1987 LIB — 1987 CONS	
Economic	86% —	0%	65% —	26%
Social	86% —	0%	96% —	0%
Foreign	86% —	0%	74% —	19%

Key Votes

1) Cut Aged Housing $	FOR	5) Bork Nomination	AGN	9) SDI Funding	AGN
2) Override Hwy Veto	FOR	6) Ban Plastic Guns	AGN	10) Ban Chem Weaps	AGN
3) Kill Plnt Clsng Notice	AGN	7) Deny Abortions	AGN	11) Aid To Contras	AGN
4) Min Wage Increase	FOR	8) Japanese Reparations	FOR	12) Reagan Defense $	AGN

Election Results

1984 general	John F. Kerry (D)	1,393,150	(55%)	($2,070,004)
	Raymond Shamie (R)	1,139,913	(45%)	($4,180,961)
1984 primary	John F. Kerry (D)	322,470	(41%)	
	James M. Shannon (D)	297,941	(38%)	
	David M. Bartley (D)	85,910	(11%)	
	Michael Joseph Connolly (D)	82,999	(11%)	
1978 general	Paul E. Tsongas (D)	1,093,283	(55%)	($768,383)
	Edward W. Brooke (R)	890,584	(45%)	($1,284,855)

FIRST DISTRICT

The valleys of western Massachusetts, settled by Yankees coming up the Connecticut River in the years before and after the Indian uprising known as King Philip's War of 1676, were for many years the essence of flinty, thrifty, chilly Yankeedom. Fifty years ago they were symbolized by their best known recent resident, Calvin Coolidge, who left the White House after choosing not to run in 1928 and settled back into the comfortable college town of Northampton where he had started out practicing law. Even after Coolidge died in 1933, at the depth of the Depression, much of western Massachusetts remained loyal to Yankee Republicanism. By the 1940s, the Irish and other mill workers of Springfield and other industrial cities along the Connecticut River and Pittsfield and the smaller mill towns in the Berkshires were producing Democratic majorities big enough to carry the area; but the hillsides, where you could stumble on old farmers' stone walls in now dense woods, and college towns, where the sons and daughters of America's elite matriculated, stayed Yankee.

Today western Massachusetts is very different political territory. In the 1988 presidential election, it was one of the most Democratic parts of the United States. Partly, this reflects Michael Dukakis's popularity in places like the old mill town of North Adams where he has used state government to revive local economies. But more important is that much of western Massachusetts has become an extended college town. The influence of the University of Massachusetts and Amherst College spreads out from Amherst; the radical tone of today's Smith College spreads out from Northampton; free-wheeling Hampshire College is nearby in Hadley and Mount Holyoke is in South Hadley. Over the mountains, beneath the Berkshires, are Williams College in Williamstown; and just south of Pittsfield are the communities of Lenox and Stockbridge, home of the Tanglewood Music Festival, celebrated in *Alice's Restaurant*. All these schools tended to attract liberal to leftish students, but the important voting bloc is made up of older baby boomers, attracted to this area by its physical beauty and cultural tone, some carrying around slightly sanitized memories of the great days of rebellion and drugtaking in the late 1960s and early 1970s, when it seemed their movement would sweep the whole world. This graduate student proletariat is the cutting edge of politics in western Massachusetts now, and Dukakis's strongest cities here in 1988 were not industrial Springfield or Holyoke but Amherst and Calvin Coolidge's Northampton, where he got 76% and 70% of the votes.

All of western Massachusetts, except Springfield and the towns just around on the east bank of the Connecticut River, make up the state's 1st Congressional District. By 1988, its younger voters made it one of the state's most Democratic districts, but its congressman is a Republican with roots deep in the area's old politics. Silvio Conte comes from industrial Pittsfield, was elected to the legislature in 1950, when Michael Dukakis was still in Brookline High, and won the 1st District seat in 1958, when the Yankee Republican retired, against none other than Williams Professor James MacGregor Burns, the Roosevelt and Kennedy biographer. Conte's politics are mostly those of old-fashioned liberal Republicans: fairly liberal on economics, quite liberal on cultural and foreign policy. To these he added a flair for the business that few WASPy liberal Republicans had. On many substantive issues he votes with the Democrats, which is a bit embarrassing to Republicans since he is now their ranking member on the Appropriations Committee (though he did support the 1981 Reagan budget cuts). On procedural issues like committee ratios, he is as partisan a Republican as can be. He flares up at programs that he thinks waste the taxpayers' money on the well-positioned: for years he has crusaded against subsidies to big farmers, against politically targeted water projects—the glue that Democrats use to hold their rural and urban members together. And for years he was one of the leaders on the Republicans' great softball team.

Conte was out sick during part of the 100th Congress. But his usual disposition is to be roaring with indignation. He bellows against cuts in programs that help feed the poor and elderly and finance student loans and medical research; he bellows at the Budget Committee for its transgressions against Appropriations; he bellows against subsidies to boat-users and the depredations of acid rain; he denounces his colleagues for not having the courage to vote for pay raises. He is self-righteous, but in the hearty, competitive way of most politicians he can roar in indignation with the best of them but is not offended when his opponents do the same. He is shrewd enough to advance his views and his district's interests with considerable success, but he is not at all devious or underhanded. He is on excellent terms with Minority Leader Robert Michel as he was with Tip O'Neill.

In fact Michel, who served with him on the Appropriations Committee for years, supported him in 1979 when some conservatives wanted to deny him the position, to which the seniority principle entitled him, of ranking Republican on the committee. Seniority was not the only reason; Michel seems to feel that Conte does real service to his party, and probably most House Republicans agree.

His constituents recognize it also. In 1986 against an active Democrat he was reelected with 78%; in 1988, he won with 83%, running more than 40% ahead of George Bush. He can hold onto his seat as long as he wants, though if he retires by 1992 it might be merged with Springfield to accommodate Massachusetts's expected loss of a House seat.

The People: Est. Pop. 1986: 524,300, up 0.3% 1980–86; Pop. 1980: 522,540, up 4.1% 1970–80. Households (1980): 71% family, 36% with children, 58% married couples; 37.5% housing units rented; median monthly rent: $176; median house value: $38,600. Voting age pop. (1980): 391,008; 1% Spanish origin, 1% Black.

1988 Presidential Vote: Dukakis (D) 134,252   (58%)

Bush (R) 96,012   (41%)

Rep. Silvio O. Conte (R)

Elected 1958; b. Nov. 9, 1921, Pittsfield; home, Pittsfield; Boston Col., Boston Col., LL.B. 1949; Roman Catholic; married (Corinne)

Career: Seabees, SW Pacific, WWII; Practicing atty., 1949–58 MA Senate, 1951–59.

Offices: 2300 RHOB 20515, 202-225-5335. Also 78 Center Arterial, Pittsfield 01201, 413-442-0946; and 187 High St., #202 Holyoke 01040, 413-532-7010.

Committees: *Appropriations* (Ranking Member of 22 R). Sub committees: Labor, Health and Human Services and Education (Ranking Member); Legislative; Transportation and Related Agencies. *Small Business* (2d of 16 R). Subcommittee: Procurement Tourism and Rural Development (Ranking Member).

Group Ratings

	ADA	ACLU	COPE	CFA	LCV	ACU	NTLC	NSI	COC	CEI
1988	90	78	66	91	75	8	26	10	46	24
1987	80	—	65	57	—	9	—	—	29	20

National Journal Ratings

	1988 LIB — 1988 CONS		1987 LIB — 1987 CONS	
Economic	54%	— 44%	48%	— 52%
Social	68%	— 31%	47%	— 53%
Foreign	64%	— 34%	76%	— 19%

Key Votes

1) Homeless $	AGN	5) Ban Drug Test	AGN	9) SDI Research	AGN
2) Gephardt Amdt	FOR	6) Drug Death Pen	AGN	10) Ban Chem Weaps	FOR
3) Deficit Reduc	AGN	7) Handgun Sales	AGN	11) Aid to Contras	AGN
4) Kill Plnt Clsng Notice	AGN	8) Ban D.C. Abort $	FOR	12) Nuclear Testing	FOR

Election Results

1988 general	Silvio O. Conte (R)..................	186,356	(83%)	($131,566
	John R. Arden (D)	38,907	(17%)	($472
1988 primary	Silvio O. Conte (R), unopposed			
1986 general	Silvio O. Conte (R)..................	113,653	(78%)	($204,921
	Robert S. Weiner (D)	32,396	(22%)	($123,426

SECOND DISTRICT

Overshadowed by Boston in Massachusetts, by Hartford on the Connecticut River, by the influence of the college towns of the Pioneer Valley just to the north in cultural matters Springfield, Massachusetts, is nonetheless a town of considerable significance. It is the center c a metropolitan area of half a million, the city that produced the nation's unabridged dictionarie (2d and 3d editions) and the game of basketball (invented at a YMCA here in 1891), and constituency that has produced more than its share of canny politicians. With its surroundin towns it has produced over the years Lawrence O'Brien, the Kennedy campaign manager an Democratic national chairman; Joseph Napolitan, long one of the leading national an international political consultants; James B. King, the first chief of personnel in the Carte

White House and known by insiders for years as the best advance man in the business.

Springfield is the largest city in Massachusetts's 2d Congressional District, which includes its suburbs on the east (but not the west) bank of the Connecticut River and then stretches inward to the stony hills and small towns of Worcester County. There are a few old mill towns here, notably Fitchburg, but this area is by no means all Yankee and Protestant anymore, and not necessarily very picturesque: fewer clapboard villages than gritty towns with store signs bearing names of Italian or Polish proprietors. This has become Republican territory lately, and is only narrowly balanced off by Democratic Springfield. The 2d District was competitive for 30 years in House races until 1952, when it was captured by one canny Irish Democrat who held it for 36 years; now it is held by a man who appears to be another. The veteran was Edward Boland, elected at age 41, a bachelor who roomed with Tip O'Neill; he married the president of the Springfield council at age 61 and they had four children. Boland, tight-lipped and austere, a reliable ally and well-prepared foe, rose to be number two on Appropriations, chairman of the Intelligence Committee, and sponsor of the various Boland amendments to prevent U.S. aid to the Nicaraguan contras.

When Boland decided to retire in 1988, he was succeeded by a politician who seems very much in the same mold. Richard Neal was elected to the Springfield Council in 1977; he became mayor in 1984; when he ran for Boland's seat in 1988 at age 39, he had no opposition in the primary, a show of astonishing strength in a safe Democratic seat. He could boast of a record of urban revival in Springfield; he seemed to combine circumspect liberalism on economics with some cultural conservatism; he had shown himself adept at political maneuver and compromise. One major difference from Boland: he was already married and had four children before he was elected.

By all odds Neal, who is on the Banking and Small Business Committees, should hold one of the safest of congressional seats. Redistricting is his only conceivable problem, but it is unlikely that legislators would slice up the 2d unless one of his two House neighbors, Silvio Conte or Joseph Early, should choose to retire.

The People: Est. Pop. 1986: 533,200, up 2.2% 1980–86; Pop. 1980: 521,949, dn. 2.2% 1970–80. Households (1980): 74% family, 39% with children, 60% married couples; 38.5% housing units rented; median monthly rent: $158; median house value: $37,100. Voting age pop. (1980): 377,798; 4% Black; 3% Spanish origin.

1988 Presidential Vote:

Dukakis (D)	113,877	(52%)
Bush (R)	102,349	(47%)

Rep. Richard E. Neal (D)

Elected 1988; b. Feb. 14, 1949, Worcester; home, Springfield; Am. Intl. Col., B.A. 1972, U. Hartford, M.A. 1976; Catholic; married (Maureen).

Career: Asst. to Mayor of Springfield, 1973–78; Springfield City Cncl., 1978–83; Mayor of Springfield, 1984–89.

Offices: 437 CHOB 20515, 202-225-5601. Also Fed. Office Bldg., Rm. 309, 1550 Main St., Springfield 01103, 413-785-0325; and 881 Main St., Philbin Bldg., Fitchburg 01420, 617-342-8722.

Committees: *Banking, Finance and Urban Affairs* (27th of 27 D). Subcommittees: Housing and Community Development; Economic Stabilization; General Oversight and Investigations. *Small Business* (25th of 27 D). Subcommittees: Antitrust, Impact of Deregulation and Privatization; Procurement, Tourism and Rural Development.

Group Ratings and Key Votes: Newly Elected
Election Results

1988 general	Richard E. Neal (D)...............	156,262	(80%)	($268,094
	Louis R. Godena (PJ&J).............	38,446	(20%)	
1988 primary	Richard E. Neal (D)................	24,523	(100%)	
1986 general	Edward P. Boland (D)...............	91,033	(66%)	($281,963
	Brian P. Lees (R)..................	47,022	(34%)	($100,628

THIRD DISTRICT

One of the unheralded success stories of America in the 1980s is Worcester, Massachusetts. Known hitherto as a small manufacturing city, with sluggish growth for more than half a century, its name pronounced with a particularly pungent Massachusetts accent that makes it sound as if it had no Rs, Worcester has for years been the second largest city in Massachusetts. but has never bulked much larger in the consciousness of greater Boston than Framingham or Natick. It was long a small manufacturing city with a high-skill, high-wage labor market: its four big industries 50 years ago were making wire, textiles, grinding wheels, and envelopes. None has been a major growth industry since then, at least not in Worcester. But in the 1980s a major growth industry has made its way here, as the computer and electronics industries were built up along Interstate 495, the circumferential highway just 20 miles east of Worcester, just as they did around circumferential Route 128 closer to Boston many years ago. The biggest such company is Digital, the sometimes surging, sometimes troubled giant of the mini-computer industry. The movement of high-tech industry into the district has brought with it prosperity, new residents, a labor shortage, and higher housing prices to the towns and suburbs along I-495 and in Worcester—always a pleasant, hilly, park-filled city—itself.

The 3d Congressional District of Massachusetts is roughly coincident with the Worcester metropolitan area, stretching south to the old textile towns in the Blackstone Valley on the Rhode Island line and north through Yankee towns almost all the way to New Hampshire. I-495 cuts through its eastern half. The historical voting preference here is Democratic, but as the area has grown in the 1980s Republicans have made gains. Massachusetts's liberalism is mostly the product of humanities graduates; the high-tech industries are staffed much more than lawyers' or government planners' offices with Republicans. Worcester itself and the Blackstone Valley voted for Michael Dukakis in 1988. But the ring of towns around Worcester and the computer towns along I-495 voted for George Bush, as did the 3d District as a whole.

Joseph Early, congressman from the 3d District, is a man with roots deep in Worcester: he grew up there, went to Holy Cross there, raised eight children there, taught school there, and represented the city in the Great and General Court (i.e., the legislature) for 12 years. In 1974 he was strong enough to win the 3d District seat in a seriously contested primary and against a serious Republican in a general election complicated by an independent candidate. Early's voting record is generally liberal, though a little less so on cultural issues. But he spends most of his time and effort as an insider on the Appropriations Committee—an old-fashioned legislator who doesn't get much publicity but who can steer hundreds of millions of dollars to the National Institutes of Health and biotechnical research. His interests, it should be added, are broad-gauged and generous, not small-minded and petty; and he seems to appreciate the new growth and trends in his home town and district even as he represents much that is best about its traditions. The 3d District voted for Ronald Reagan in 1984 and George Bush in 1988, but the last time Early had Republican opposition, in 1984, he won with 67%.

The People: Est. Pop. 1986: 533,700, up 2.4% 1980–86; Pop. 1980: 521,354, up 2.2% 1970–80. Households (1980): 75% family, 40% with children, 62% married couples; 38.5% housing units rented.

median monthly rent: $175; median house value: $46,800. Voting age pop. (1980): 376,641; 2% Spanish origin, 1% Black.

1988 Presidential Vote: Bush (R) 123,471   (50%)
                                 Dukakis (D). 120,907   (49%)

Rep. Joseph D. Early (D)

Elected 1974; b. Jan. 31, 1933, Worcester; home, Worcester; Col. of the Holy Cross, B.S. 1955; Roman Catholic; married (Marilyn).

Career: Navy, 1955–57; High sch. teacher and coach, 1957–63; MA House of Reps., 1963–75.

Offices: 2349 RHOB, 202-225-6101. Also 34 Mechanic St., Rm. 203, Worcester 01608, 508-752-6718.

Committees: *Appropriations* (12th of 35 D). Subcommittees: Commerce, Justice, State, the Judiciary and Related Agencies; Labor, Health and Human Services and Education and Related Agencies; Treasury, Postal Service and General Government.

Group Ratings

	ADA	ACLU	COPE	CFA	LCV	ACU	NTLC	NSI	COC	CEI
1988	85	86	86	73	69	8	11	0	36	11
1987	92	—	86	86	—	0	—	—	8	14

National Journal Ratings

	1988 LIB — 1988 CONS		1987 LIB — 1987 CONS	
Economic	79%	— 17%	53%	— 47%
Social	72%	— 27%	78%	— 0%
Foreign	84%	— 0%	81%	— 0%

Key Votes

1) Homeless $	FOR	5) Ban Drug Test	—	9) SDI Research	AGN
2) Gephardt Amdt	FOR	6) Drug Death Pen	FOR	10) Ban Chem Weaps	FOR
3) Deficit Reduc	FOR	7) Handgun Sales	AGN	11) Aid to Contras	AGN
4) Kill Plnt Clsng Notice	AGN	8) Ban D.C. Abort $	AGN	12) Nuclear Testing	FOR

Election Results

1988 general	Joseph D. Early (D)	191,005	(100%)	($205,989)
1988 primary	Joseph D. Early (D)	23,729	(100%)	
1986 general	Joseph D. Early (D)	120,222	(100%)	($186,651)

FOURTH DISTRICT

As convoluted and irregularly shaped a congressional district as any in the country is the 4th District of Massachusetts. Configured to throw two unfortunate incumbents together after Massachusetts lost a seat in the 1980 Census, the 4th extends through territory so diverse that to drive its length you would start near busy Kenmore Square in Boston, surge through expressways and thread your way over country lanes, and end up on the beach on Rhode Island Sound. Politically, it is diverse country too. Just next to Boston are Brookline, the lifelong home of

Michael Dukakis, and Newton just to the west, the home of columnist Ellen Goodman, both long-settled suburbs with comfortable houses and capacious trees; Yankee and Republican 50 years ago, they are now filled with culturally liberal professionals who are happy to use government to change society as they contemplate the astronomically rising local housing values. Aside from black ghettos, Brookline and Newton were among the most Democratic places in the country in 1988: 70% for Dukakis.

Far to the south, on the Rhode Island line, is Fall River, an old textile mill town which seems on the verge of finally reviving its economy 60 years after the mills started moving south. Culturally conservative but liberal on economics, heavily ethnic, with many French Canadians, Fall River and surrounding towns voted 66% for Dukakis. But the 4th District is not all liberal. Brookline and Newton cast just 30% of its votes, the Fall River area about 20%; half come from the towns in the middle, which include high-income suburbs like leafy Wellesley and countrified Dover, and more modest Yankee towns like North Attleboro, home of onetime (1947–49, 1953–55) Republican House Speaker Joseph Martin. They also include working-class Natick, newly built and upper middle-income Medfield, Sharon with its large Jewish population, Foxboro, home of the New England Patriots—places within range of Boston TV but outside its trendy cultural orbit. Taken together, the middle area voted 53%–47% for George Bush; overall the district was 57% for Dukakis, solid but not overwhelming.

This unlikely district elects one of the truly gifted legislators of our time, Barney Frank. He is a liberal Democrat in conservative times; he engages in genuine intellectual interchange in a chamber where many members rely on canned speeches produced by staffers and letterhead interest groups; he has a mind so fast that he sometimes can change the outcome of a vote in a single extemporized one-minute speech. He understands politics and cares about policy, and if he can be called a steadfast liberal he is also intellectually original enough that you cannot be sure just where he'll come out on many issues and which issues he'll work hard on, unless you listen to the torrent of words coming out in his New Jersey accent. After compiling and defending one of the most liberal records in Congress, he chided liberals after the 1988 election as "scolds" for opposing the 65-mile-per-hour speed limit and for pursuing an impossible goal like federal gun control. Liberals are on the popular side of many issues, he says, but are hurt because they feel they are not supposed to say that Communism is terrible, that free enterprise has worked better than any other economic system, and that most people in prison are bad people.

Frank's list of accomplishments as he rounds out his first decade in Congress is long. He was one of the major reasons the Immigration Reform Act of 1986 was passed. He took over the subcommittee sitting on the bill for compensating Japanese Americans interned in World War II and got it through the House and signed into law. He is now a hero among an Asian ethnic group on the West Coast. His subcommittee also passed renewal of the independent counsel law which was strong enough to avoid a Reagan veto and an ethics in government act that he did veto. Frank got passed a housing bill requiring adequate new housing for poor people displaced by urban renewal. He has pushed through two year-by-year repealers of the McCarran-Walter Act which barred from the United States foreigners deemed subversive, and is working on making them permanent and on repealing the bans on gays and low-level criminals. He pushed successfully for amendments to the fair housing bill for AIDS victims and those with the HIV virus. He shepherded a bill through the House allowing servicemen to sue the military for negligence, fought unsuccessfully to avoid cuts in public housing, and got the House to vote momentarily to build only 40 rather than 50 MX missiles.

Sometimes he wins arguments with his wit. Of abortion opponents who oppose child nutrition programs, he said, "Sure, they're pro-life. They believe that life begins at conception and ends at birth." On congressmen taking honoraria he opined, "Elected officials are the only human beings in the world who are supposed to take large sums of money on a regular basis from absolute strangers without it having any effect on their behavior." Frank's power goes beyond his subcommittee chair; it comes not from specialization and seniority, but from his knowledge of a wide range of issues and skill at argumentation.

In an earlier generation, Barney Frank, overweight (until he lost 70 pounds after the 1982 election), Jewish, speaking with a slight lisp, and (as he admitted in response to a reporter's question in 1987) gay, would probably have been a staffer rather than an elected official. In fact, he did move from graduate school to work for Boston Mayor Kevin White and Congressman Michael Harrington before winning election to the Massachusetts legislature in 1972. In 1980, after orders from Rome caused Father Robert Drinan to retire from Congress, Frank was elected in a differently configured 4th District that veered west from Brookline and Newton, but with only 52% in primary and general. In 1982, he ran against 16-year Republican incumbent Margaret Heckler in territory most of which was hers. But he raised $1 million and capitalized on her mistakes to win with 60%. Now he has a safe seat and with his base in Brookline and Newton is well-positioned for redistricting. He says he intends to run again in 2014 when he will be 74, but will see how he's feeling before he decides whether to run in 2016.

The People: Est. Pop. 1986: 528,600, up 1.3% 1980–86; Pop. 1980: 521,995, up 1.8% 1970–80. Households (1980): 74% family, 38% with children, 61% married couples; 39.2% housing units rented; median monthly rent: $202; median house value: $58,900. Voting age pop. (1980): 386,245; 1% Spanish origin, 1% Asian origin, 1% Black.

1988 Presidential Vote:

Dukakis (D)	141,008	(57%)
Bush (R)	104,853	(42%)

Rep. Barney Frank (D)

Elected 1980; b. Mar. 31, 1940, Bayonne, NJ; home, Newton; Harvard Col., B.A. 1962, J.D. 1977; Jewish; single.

Career: Chf. of Staff to Boston Mayor Kevin White, 1967–71; A. A. to U.S. Rep. Michael Harrington, 1971–72; MA House of Reps., 1973–80; Lecturer on Pub. Policy, JFK Sch. of Govt., Harvard U., 1979–80.

Offices: 1030 LHOB 20515, 202-225-5931. Also 437 Cherry St., West Newton 02165, 617-332-3920; 10 Purchase St., Fall River 02722, 508-674-3551; and 140 Park St., Attleboro 02703, 508-226-4723.

Committees: *Banking, Finance and Urban Affairs* (12th of 31 D). Subcommittees: Financial Institutions Supervision, Regulation and Insurance; Housing and Community Development. *Government Operations* (9th of 24 D). Subcommittee: Employment and Housing. *Judiciary* (10th of 21 D). Subcommittees: Administrative Law and Governmental Relations (Chairman); Immigration, Refugees and International Law. *Select Committee on Aging* (15th of 39 D). Subcommittees: Health and Long-Term Care.

Group Ratings

	ADA	ACLU	COPE	CFA	LCV	ACU	NTLC	NSI	COC	CEI
1988	100	100	91	91	94	0	14	0	21	18
1987	100	—	91	86	—	0	—	—	7	11

National Journal Ratings

	1988 LIB — 1988 CONS			1987 LIB — 1987 CONS		
Economic	71%	—	23%	73%	—	0%
Social	86%	—	0%	78%	—	0%
Foreign	84%	—	0%	81%	—	0%

Key Votes

1) Homeless $	AGN	5) Ban Drug Test	AGN	9) SDI Research	AGN
2) Gephardt Amdt	FOR	6) Drug Death Pen	AGN	10) Ban Chem Weaps	FOR
3) Deficit Reduc	FOR	7) Handgun Sales	AGN	11) Aid to Contras	AGN
4) Kill Plnt Clsng Notice	AGN	8) Ban D.C. Abort $	—	12) Nuclear Testing	FOR

Election Results

1988 general	Barney Frank (D)	169,729	(70%)	($343,097)
	Debra R. Tucker (R)	71,661	(30%)	($34,368)
1988 primary	Barney Frank (D)	22,990	(100%)	
1986 general	Barney Frank (D)	134,387	(89%)	($213,909)
	Thomas D. DeVisscher (R)	16,857	(11%)	($1,017)

FIFTH DISTRICT

The banks of the fast-flowing Merrimack River have been, not once but twice in the last two centuries, the site of some of America's greatest technological innovation and economic growth. In the early 19th century, when Massachusetts was a kind of maritime republic, with a few farmers struggling to scratch a living from the stony soil, a few ingenious Yankees flush with profits from the sea trade decided to tame the rapidly flowing Merrimack River and build cotton spinning mills. They created the cities of Lowell and Lawrence, built model housing for the local farm girls and, later, the Irish and French Canadian immigrants they used as their work force. For when the maritime trading business faded, Massachusetts continued to grow because of the textile industry; it lasted here for nearly 100 years. Then, in the 1920s, the price of labor rose in New England and newly built mills in the Carolinas, nearer the cotton supply, essentially ended the businesses Lawrence and Lowell built. Yet many in the work force, by then rather elderly, waited forlornly for some upturn in the local economy.

It came from an unexpected source. Starting in the 1960s in Cambridge, around MIT, moving out to the old Route 128 circumferential highway, and more recently locating also along Interstate 495, which passes through Lowell and Lawrence, high-tech has powered growth for Massachusetts. Wang, headquartered in Lowell, grew prodigiously; and the city was upgraded by the national historical restoration of its old mill area sparked by former Senator and Congressman Paul Tsongas and supported by Governor Michael Dukakis. The computer, software, and defense industries here have had their ups and downs; but in the early 1980s, when the rest of the country was in recession, Massachusetts had one of the nation's lowest unemployment rates. As the 1980s went on, as one computer company foundered, dozens of others seemed to sprout up, and the high-tech area around interstates 128 and 495 was one of the most prosperous parts of the country.

The 5th Congressional District of Massachusetts takes in much of this country, including Lawrence and Lowell, which with surrounding suburbs around I-495 account for about half its population. The other half is mostly to the south, high-income country between 128 and 495, with elite suburbs like Lincoln and Concord, plus more modest-income Framingham. The district also extends west of 495, to Fort Devens and the almost mountainous towns along the New Hampshire line. Most of this area (Lowell and Lawrence are exceptions) is ancestrally

Yankee Republican; culturally liberal, it trended toward the Democrats in the early 1970s; booming with high-tech, market-driven growth, it has trended toward Republicans in national and even statewide contests in the 1980s. Some of it is perversely countercyclical: Lincoln (home of presidential sister Nancy Bush Ellis) voted for McGovern in 1972, Ford in 1976, 28% for John Anderson in 1980, and for Mondale in 1984 and Dukakis in 1988, switching parties but sticking with losers in every case. Lowell and Lawrence, in the meantime, have been trending toward the Republicans and almost voted for George Bush in 1988. An additional local factor was at work in Lawrence: this was where Willie Horton brutally stabbed a 17-year-old gas station attendant to death in 1977, for which he was sentenced to life-without-parole; and it was the *Lawrence Eagle-Tribune*, in a Pulitzer Prize winning series, which exposed how the Dukakis administration gave him weekend furloughs, and how Dukakis tried to cover up the furlough program for lifers even as he resisted for 12 years demands that it be changed.

Overall the 5th District is a kind of Baja New Hampshire: it is one of the few districts in the country that voted for George McGovern in 1972 and for George Bush in 1988. In congressional elections, however, it has stayed Democratic largely because of the political skill—one might almost say the political genius—of Congressman Chester Atkins. Large almost to the point of being rotund, soft-spoken almost to the point of being shy, a Yankee in a state where any other ethnic origin is more advantageous but with a thick townie accent that will strike no one as distinguished, Atkins has rung up one political triumph after another. He was elected to the state House at 22, in 1970. In 1972, in hitherto Republican territory, he was elected to the state Senate. In 1977 he became chairman of the Massachusetts Democratic Party, perhaps the most fractious in the country; after five years in Washington he still holds that job. In 1979, at 30, Senate President Billy Bulger, a brilliant old-fashioned South Boston pro, made Atkins of the Yankee suburbs chairman of the Massachusetts Senate Ways and Means Committee. There he brokered the state budget and, on the side, cut a housing judge's salary when the latter wouldn't give local legend Sonny McDonough's son a job Bulger had made a deathbed promise to Sonny to deliver.

But Atkins was not just a hack: he really did know the budget and did a brilliant job of adapting to the Proposition 2½ property tax cut. When 5th District Congressman James Shannon ran for Senator in 1984, Atkins ran for the House, and beat a Lawrence legislator in the primary and a Proposition 2½ leader in the general. As a freshman, he got a seat on Budget from Tip O'Neill; in 1986, he moved from Public Works to Foreign Affairs; in 1988, against competition from Joe Kennedy and Connecticut's Bruce Morrison, he won Eddie Boland's seat on Appropriations. This wasn't a razzle-dazzle victory; the voting was among New England (and Puerto Rico and the Virgin Islands) House Democrats, by secret ballot. Atkins's victory is a sign he is held in high regard by his ultra-critical peers—and that he was willing, as Kennedy was not at the time, to pledge he wouldn't run for governor in 1990.

Atkins's secret is that he is good on policy as well as politics. He works hard, learns the details, and knows how to make a deal and stick to it. He works to get grants for bilingual education for Cambodians in Lowell, was the sparkplug in getting Emerson College to move from Boston's Beacon Hill to Lawrence, and helped to get Fort Devens expanded rather than shut down. He also takes on bigger issues—crusading against smoking (he would require cigarettes to be sold as liquor is, only over-the-counter to adults), working to help Southeast Asian refugees and condemning the Khmer Rouge, and he has worked on child nutrition programs.

His record and his willingness to stay in a district seat which two young members (Tsongas in 1978, Shannon in 1984) have left have helped Atkins win reelection unopposed in 1986 and with 84% of the vote in 1988. Just 40 that year, he has the potential of a long House career.

The People: Est. Pop. 1986: 535,700, up 3.4% 1980–86; Pop. 1980: 518,313, up 3.3% 1970–80. Households (1980): 75% family, 42% with children, 62% married couples; 40.0% housing units rented;

median monthly rent: $207; median house value: $61,100. Voting age pop. (1980): 368,925; 3% Spanish origin, 1% Black, 1% Asian origin.

1988 Presidential Vote: Bush (R) 120,945   (51%)
                            Dukakis (D). 112,301   (47%)

Rep. Chester G. Atkins (D)

Elected 1984; b. Apr. 14, 1948, Geneva, Switzerland; home, Concord; Antioch Col., B.A. 1970; Unitarian; married (Corinne).

Career: MA House of Reps., 1971–73; MA Senate, 1973–85; Chmn., MA State Dem. Cmtee., 1977–present.

Offices: 504 CHOB 20515, 202-225-3411. Also 134 Middle St., Ste. 301, Lowell 01852, 508-459-0101, 800-831-3125.

Committees: *Appropriations* (34th of 35 D). Subcommittees: Interior; VA, HUD and Independent Agencies. *Standards of Official Conduct* (6th of 6 D).

Group Ratings

	ADA	ACLU	COPE	CFA	LCV	ACU	NTLC	NSI	COC	CEI
1988	100	91	92	100	88	0	5	0	23	9
1987	96	—	89	86	—	0	—	—	7	8

National Journal Ratings

	1988 LIB — 1988 CONS			1987 LIB — 1987 CONS		
Economic	92%	—	0%	73%	—	0%
Social	86%	—	0%	78%	—	0%
Foreign	84%	—	0%	81%	—	0%

Key Votes

1) Homeless $	AGN	5) Ban Drug Test	AGN	9) SDI Research	AGN
2) Gephardt Amdt	FOR	6) Drug Death Pen	AGN	10) Ban Chem Weaps	FOR
3) Deficit Reduc	FOR	7) Handgun Sales	AGN	11) Aid to Contras	AGN
4) Kill Plnt Clsng Notice	AGN	8) Ban D.C. Abort $	AGN	12) Nuclear Testing	FOR

Election Results

1988 general	Chester G. Atkins (D).................	181,860	(84%)	($344,930)
	T. David Hudson (LIB)................	34,399	(16%)	($15,396)
1988 primary	Chester G. Atkins (D).................	15,567	(100%)	
1986 general	Chester G. Atkins (D)................	113,690	(100%)	($563,019)

SIXTH DISTRICT

In the Salem around Nathaniel Hawthorne's *House of the Seven Gables*, an observer 50 years ago saw "the eerie atmosphere that still lingers in the narrow streets which the master of delicate impressions frequented. Here are the more robust memories of docks and wharves from which poured crude wealth in fish and ships' supplies, and into which, after many turnovers of cargo, flowed all the exotic treasure of the Indies and China. Here stored in old landmarks is the romance of swift clipper ships, of bellying sails, of masts stripped for the gale, of sailors' oaths and sailors' roaring chanteys, of ambition and avarice, of mansions built by merchant princes and delicate women nurtured in them." From this small port for only a few years, from 1785 to 1812, America's China trade was carried on leaving wealth and artifacts that changed the country ever after: Massachusetts capital has financed everything from 1820s textile mills to 1980s computer companies, and the china of the federal period has been imitated to this day.

Today Salem's historic sites are protected by national legislation, but otherwise it is one of several ethnic factory towns—from Lynn on up through next-door Peabody to Newburyport—which alternate with the high-income enclaves from Marblehead up through Beverly, Rockport and Ipswich on Boston's North Shore. The North Shore also includes the old fishing village of Gloucester, whose atmosphere is probably closer to the Salem of the clipper ships than are the manicured estates of today. Nearby are the boating suburbs of Marblehead and Swampscott, and Lynn, whose troubled shoe industry pressed for years for protection against imports and whose biggest factory today is a General Electric jet engine plant. The Merrimack River flows through the northern edge of the district, just below New Hampshire, past the old mill towns of Haverhill, John Greenleaf Whittier's town, and Newburyport.

The North Shore from Lynn onward, plus towns and cities several miles inland, form Massachusetts's 6th Congressional District. This is a varied area demographically and politically. High-income Yankees tend to be Republicans, but liberal ones; Lynn, Salem, and Peabody are basically Irish working-class Democratic, as are the Merrimack mill towns. On balance it is a Democratic district, but Republicans have a base here; they represented the district in Congress until 1969 and made serious attempts to win it that year and in 1976, 1978, 1980 and 1982. This is, by the way, the site of the original gerrymander, named because its architect, Elbridge Gerry, a Jeffersonian, wanted to corral all the area's Federalist towns into one grotesquely shaped district. Ironically, the current 6th District's boundaries are about as regular and politically unobjectionable as those of any district in the country.

The district's current congressman, Nicholas Mavroules, has deep roots in local politics, and was mayor of Peabody for 11 years; he planned in 1978 to challenge liberal incumbent Michael Harrington in the Democratic primary and then got the nomination when Harrington retired. Ironically, Mavroules, who came to office as a critic of Harrington's preoccupation with the Vietnam war and the ouster of Salvador Allende in Chile, has been distinguished in the House primarily by his liberal positions on foreign and defense policy. Mavroules inherited Harrington's seat on the Armed Services Committee, probably intending to concentrate on keeping defense business in the GE plant in Lynn. But in 1981 he became the chief advocate for the nuclear freeze resolution, and in 1983 he became the House's primary spokesman in the fight against the MX missile. He has led this fight, with varying levels of success, sometimes pitted against Armed Services chairman Les Aspin. In early 1987, Mavroules became one of several challengers for Aspin's chair; but he got just 35 votes and was eliminated on the first ballot, and Aspin ultimately won. Some might take that as a humiliating defeat. But for a member whose credentials on major national issues had not been taken seriously a few years before it can also be seen as something of an achievement. In 1988, after the death of Dan Daniel, he became Chairman of the Subcommittee on Readiness and in the 101st Congress he chairs the Investigations Subcommittee.

Mavroules's prominence on the nuclear freeze and the MX have vastly strengthened him in the 6th District, although it doesn't hurt that he is prepared to argue in the same breath for GE jet engines and other local defense contractors. He also tends to local issues like the Salem historic district and protecting the North Shore from Boston's raw sewage and New Hampshire's Seabrook nuclear plant. He overcame his last tough challenge, in 1982, with 58% of the vote; he won with 70% in 1988.

570 MASSACHUSETTS

The People: Est. Pop. 1986: 531,100, up 2.4% 1980–86; Pop. 1980: 518,841, dn. 0.8% 1970–80 Households (1980): 72% family, 37% with children, 59% married couples; 38.5% housing units rented median monthly rent: $216; median house value: $55,000. Voting age pop. (1980): 383,191; 1% Spanish origin, 1% Black.

1988 Presidential Vote:

Dukakis (D)	131,246	(50%)
Bush (R)	125,871	(48%)

Rep. Nicholas Mavroules (D)

Elected 1978; b. Nov. 1, 1929, Peabody; home, Peabody; Greek Orthodox; married (Mary).

Career: Sprvsr. of Personnel, Sylvania Electronics Corp., 1949–67; Peabody Ward Councillor, 1958–61, Councillor-at-Large 1964–65; Mayor of Peabody, 1967–78.

Offices: 2432 RHOB, 202-225-8020. Also 70 Washington St. Salem 01970, 508-745-5800; 140 Union St., Lynn 01902, 617-599-7105; and 10 Welcome St., Haverhill, 01830, 508-372-3461.

Committees: *Armed Services* (7th of 31 D). Subcommittees Military Installations and Facilities; Investigations (Chairman) *Small Business* (6th of 27 D). Subcommittee: SBA, the General Economy and Minority Enterprise Development. *Select Committee on Intelligence* (10th of 12 D). Subcommittee: Oversight and Evaluation.

Group Ratings

	ADA	ACLU	COPE	CFA	LCV	ACU	NTLC	NSI	COC	CEI
1988	90	81	94	91	88	8	6	10	23	8
1987	76	—	93	93	—	0	—	—	7	3

National Journal Ratings

	1988 LIB —	1988 CONS	1987 LIB —	1987 CONS
Economic	92% —	0%	73% —	0%
Social	66% —	32%	78% —	0%
Foreign	79% —	16%	70% —	29%

Key Votes

1) Homeless $	AGN	5) Ban Drug Test	AGN	9) SDI Research	AGN
2) Gephardt Amdt	FOR	6) Drug Death Pen	FOR	10) Ban Chem Weaps	FOR
3) Deficit Reduc	FOR	7) Handgun Sales	AGN	11) Aid to Contras	AGN
4) Kill Plnt Clsng Notice	AGN	8) Ban D.C. Abort $	FOR	12) Nuclear Testing	FOR

Election Results

1988 general	Nicholas Mavroules (D)	177,643	(70%)	($337,199
	Paul McCarthy (R)	77,186	(30%)	($63,013
1988 primary	Nicholas Mavroules (D)	13,783	(100%)	
1986 general	Nicholas Mavroules (D)	131,051	(100%)	($184,485

SEVENTH DISTRICT

Two generations ago through the suburbs north of Boston ran the battle lines of a conflict that went back to the 17th century, between Puritan Yankee Protestants and Papist Irish Catholics. Both sides had memories of how they arrived in boats, the Yankees to a cold stony land with a few Indians, the Irish to a crowded city with Yankees who were even less welcoming. By 1940, they had built their own communities. The Yankee suburban towns were filled with solid brick and white frame houses, furnished in Early American furniture, with a view out the paned windows of a large tree in the back yard; the local public school was a bit empty as young people with children had moved out, and attendance at the Protestant churches was down. The Irish, heavily concentrated in the crowded wards of Boston, were moving out into the Yankee suburbs, filling their houses with large families and the local Catholic schools with nuns and kids. There were other ethnic groups here and there—Jews in the only entry port of Chelsea, Italians in Revere and elsewhere; but the major conflict—fought out in neighborhood playgrounds, in school committee meetings, and not least in political campaigns—was between Protestant Yankee Republicans and Catholic Irish Democrats.

That conflict is pretty well over today, and both sides have won. The election of President Kennedy in 1960 symbolized for Catholics that they were accepted as full Americans at about the same time as Vatican II reforms made it far less distinctive to be a Catholic. For a time Massachusetts politics reached a consensus, with the Irish accepting the cultural liberalism of Yankee Republicans and the Yankees accepting the economic liberalism of Irish Democrats. Members of both groups scrambled to take part in Massachusetts's high-tech, white-collar economic growth of the 1980s. In the process the northern suburbs that make up Massachusetts's 7th Congressional District, from the edge of Logan Airport northwest out past Route 128 to Interstate 495, became a very heavily Democratic, then a mildly Democratic constituency. The oldest towns like Chelsea, whose schools are being taken over by Boston University, continue to be immigrant entry ports, but their votes are down; onetime Yankee Protestant towns like Malden and Melrose are now Democratic; but the high-tech towns near and beyond 128, once Democratic, are now trending Republican, even working-class Woburn (pronounced as if with two Os). The 7th was Republican until 1954; in 1976, when the incumbent died, 12 Democrats filed to run in the primary—and no Republican. Now it is trending the other way: it voted twice for Ronald Reagan and gave Michael Dukakis an uninspiring margin over George Bush.

The congressman from the 7th District is Edward Markey, a Democrat who is a product of Malden Catholic High, Boston College and the Massachusetts legislature. He was elected to the House in 1976, at age 30—like Jimmy Stewart in *Mr. Smith Goes to Washington* he had never been in Washington before—and now he chairs one of the most important subcommittees (telecommunications) in Congress. Markey's early years in the House were marked by a certainty amounting almost to zealotry. He had been a rebel on Beacon Hill, and it helped him politically when he got publicity for losing his state seat; Washington was full of Watergate era Democrats eager to put what they considered the lessons of civil rights, Vietnam and Watergate to work. On the Interior Committee Markey was one of the most resolute opponents of nuclear power, and from the Oversight Committee chair he reached in only four years he pummeled the power companies. On Energy and Commerce he was a vehement backer of energy price controls. On foreign policy he drew the lesson from Vietnam that almost any exertion of American military power was wrong, and was one of the leading political organizers and House cheerleaders for the nuclear freeze in 1983, as well as a backer of the comprehensive test ban treaty in 1986. On economic issues he almost invariably supported greater government spending. Such enthusiasm and certainty, coming from a young man with limited experience in the world (he was single and had spent all his life in school or in public office) infuriated many of his opponents; and they thought they detected in him both irritating self-righteousness and over ambition.

Events of the 1980s have convinced many that the 1974 Democrats' assumptions were wrong, although Markey has not changed his views much. But his committee responsibilities and electoral vicissitudes have changed the way he has used the power the seniority system has given him. When he came to the House he inherited, with a boost from fellow Boston College alumnus Tip O'Neill, his predecessor's seat on Energy and Commerce, which soon became one of the most sought-after committees in the House; he is now 6th ranking Democrat on Energy and Commerce and 4th on Interior. He got on what was then called the Communications Subcommittee early because, he says now, he was convinced by the high-tech boom out on I-128 that the post would handle key issues. He rose rapidly: two subcommittee members ahead of him were beaten in 1980 (one later went to jail) and another in 1978 (after acquiring 60,000 surplus books from the Library of Congress); Marty Russo switched to Ways and Means when Dan Rostenkowski became chairman and Tim Wirth, after six hectic years as chairman and holder of a marginal seat, opted for the comparative leisure of running for the Senate. And Markey was subjected to the discipline of Energy and Commerce Chairman John Dingell, who likes aggressive young colleagues, but demands full preparation and mastery of arguments. The voters of the 7th District also exerted some discipline. Markey started running for the Senate in 1984, when Paul Tsongas retired at 42; then he jumped back into the House race when he failed to raise enough money. But several local politicians were running in the 7th, and one of them, Winchester legislator Sam Rotondi, stayed in and held Markey to an embarrassing 54%–41% margin in the primary. Markey's hot-button approach to nuclear power and the freeze proved bad politics at home and was not Dingell's style—important, since Dingell probably could have denied Markey the subcommittee chairmanship that was opening up.

That was the Energy Conservation and Power Subcommittee, and Markey did workmanlike jobs on extending daylight savings time, relicensing hydroelectric power plants, and trying to keep the Chinese from nuclear proliferation. In 1987, after Tim Wirth moved to the Senate, he became chairman of the Telecommunications and Finance Subcommittee, with jurisdiction over the communications industry and the securities business. This is a juicy position, with fabulous possibilities for campaign fundraising (but Markey doesn't take PAC money or accept honoraria) and with subject matter that is intellectually more demanding and in lobbying terms more fiercely contested than just about anything else in Congress.

On communications issues Markey like Dingell is a regulator, backing the fairness doctrine and supporting regulation of children's advertising. But he is also striving for consensus, as on his appliance energy-efficiency bill which passed with support from the industry. On securities, he is proud of his insider trading bill that received unanimous support in 1988, of the praise he got from various quarters for the reforms he proposed (similar to the Brady Commission's) after the October 1987 stock market crash. He promises to prepare bills on corporate takeovers (Markey is skeptical about leveraged buyouts), high definition television (he would like to see American firms do the manufacturing) and computer viruses. Still a critic of the workings of various markets, Markey is also aware that any proposal he makes can move billions of dollars on markets, and in contrast to his pre-1984 legislating he is looking for bipartisan solutions and consensus proposals, in one of the most challenging positions in the 101st Congress.

The People: Est. Pop. 1986: 523,800, no % chg. 1980–86; Pop. 1980: 523,982, dn. 3.7% 1970–80. Households (1980): 75% family, 38% with children, 61% married couples; 38.9% housing units rented; median monthly rent: $220; median house value: $58,100. Voting age pop. (1980): 387,217; 1% Spanish origin, 1% Black, 1% Asian origin.

1988 Presidential Vote: Dukakis (D). 133,241   (53%)
                             Bush (R) 114,124   (45%)

Rep. Edward J. Markey (D)

Elected 1976; b. July 11, 1946, Malden; home, Malden; Boston Col., B.A. 1968, J.D. 1972; Roman Catholic; married (Susan).

Career: Practicing atty.; MA House of Reps., 1973–76.

Offices: 2133 RHOB 20515, 202-225-2836. Also JFK Fed. Bldg., Rm. 2100A, Boston 02203, 617-565-2900.

Committees: *Energy and Commerce* (6th of 26 D). Subcommittees: Energy and Power; Telecommunications and Finance (Chairman). *Interior and Insular Affairs* (4th of 26 D). Subcommittees: Energy and the Environment; Water, Power and Offshore Energy Resources.

Group Ratings

	ADA	ACLU	COPE	CFA	LCV	ACU	NTLC	NSI	COC	CEI
1988	90	100	90	100	88	0	8	0	23	10
1987	96	—	90	93	—	0	—	—	0	3

National Journal Ratings

	1988 LIB — 1988 CONS		1987 LIB — 1987 CONS	
Economic	87%	— 8%	73%	— 0%
Social	86%	— 0%	78%	— 0%
Foreign	84%	— 0%	81%	— 0%

Key Votes

1) Homeless $	AGN	5) Ban Drug Test	AGN	9) SDI Research	AGN
2) Gephardt Amdt	FOR	6) Drug Death Pen	AGN	10) Ban Chem Weaps	FOR
3) Deficit Reduc	FOR	7) Handgun Sales	AGN	11) Aid to Contras	AGN
4) Kill Plnt Clsng Notice	AGN	8) Ban D.C. Abort $	AGN	12) Nuclear Testing	FOR

Election Results

1988 general	Edward J. Markey (D)	188,647	(100%)	($134,388)
1988 primary	Edward J. Markey (D), unopposed			
1986 general	Edward J. Markey (D)	124,183	(100%)	($314,410)

EIGHTH DISTRICT

Fifty years ago, when Tip O'Neill was a young state representative from North Cambridge, Harvard and MIT, the city's two great universities, were closely hemmed in by a not very friendly town, full of Irish Catholics like O'Neill whose only contact with the universities was mowing the lawn in Harvard Yard and who knew that they would never be welcome in Yankee institutions. Today, there is still a town-gown divide in Cambridge and surrounding communities, but the proportions have changed. The old ethnic neighborhoods of Cambridge and Somerville and of the Allston, Brighton and Charlestown sections of Boston across the Charles have shrunk, encroached on first by impecunious graduate students and more recently by young

574   MASSACHUSETTS

professionals willing to pay enormous sums for a bedraggled three-decker. The elite neighbor
hoods, out Brattle Street in Cambridge and on Beacon Hill and Back Bay in Boston have
expanded and spawned glitzy shopping strips.

This is the land of the 8th Congressional District of Massachusetts, where 15% of the adult
are students and where many more are part of the one consistently leftish segment of the
American electorate, the graduate student proletariat; a district with great historic sites from
the gold dome of the State House on Beacon Hill to the frigate *Constitution* in the Charlestown
docks; a district which, with MIT and the software concentration in Cambridge's once
downscale Lechmere Square, is one of the high-tech capitals of America. For all its high-tech
and glitz, it still has funky ethnic areas, like Portuguese East Cambridge and Armenian
Watertown. Politically, except for black ghetto congressional districts, this is one of the most
Democratic House seats in the nation, and one with the further distinction of having elected a
its two previous representatives President John F. Kennedy and Speaker Thomas P. O'Neill.

The current congressman is Joseph P. Kennedy II, elected when O'Neill retired in 1986. He i
the oldest son of the late Robert Kennedy, and obviously won because of his family background
Before 1986, he didn't live anywhere near the district and maintained that he was only interested
in running an energy corporation he set up with family money and which purported to buy oil in
bulk and distribute it to low-income citizens. He spoke disdainfully of politics, telling the *Boston
Globe*, "It's just not in me to do it. It's such a crummy system. It's just a bog. I really wonder
whether it's better to go out and do something than fight this ball of molasses. Every time I get
near government, it strikes me that it just doesn't work. I hate things that don't work."

But when O'Neill announced his retirement, and half a dozen leftish candidates with various
local bases filed, Kennedy overcame his distaste. Other candidates began to withdraw
photographers from *People* began thronging in, and what had been a battle of lefties ended up a
battle between a Kennedy capitalizing on the sentimental attachments of older, culturally
conservative voters, versus a left-leaning, neighborhood-based Cambridge state senator, George
Bachrach, who made the mistake of charging Kennedy with having ties with Qaddafi's Libya
Kennedy said it was "totally off base" to suggest that he was tied to a country that offered
asylum to his father's assassin. At the same time, O'Neill endorsed Kennedy. Before that he'd
been running only even in the polls; after, he beat Bachrach 52%–30%.

Kennedy has a boyish, boisterous charm, with the physical impulsiveness and verbal
clumsiness of a teenager. He talks hesitatingly and makes arguments only with some effort
grinning when he gets it right; he has leaped from one philosophy to another—from the strident
leftism of his speech at the Kennedy Library dedication in 1979 to his emphasis on capital
punishment in 1986—with all the appearance of a young man looking for something plausible to
say. But he's not a kid. He turns 38 in 1990—older than many young congressmen are when first
elected, and older than his father was when he played a critical role in the Cuban missile crisis
No one can imagine Joseph Kennedy doing anything like that any time soon. He has not been
especially successful in the House, where he failed to get a seat on the Energy and Commerce
Committee in 1987 and lost to Chester Atkins a race among New England Democrats for a seat
on Appropriations in 1988. It was widely expected that he would run for governor in 1990 but
facing a divorce, he took himself out of the race in March 1989; he had been the early leader in
the polls, but it was not clear that he had the gravity and intellect needed to maintain that
support, much less build on it.

The People: Est. Pop. 1986: 513,300, dn. 1.6% 1980–86; Pop. 1980: 521,548, dn. 7.1% 1970–80
Households (1980): 50% family, 22% with children, 37% married couples; 69.1% housing units rented
median monthly rent: $236; median house value: $60,600. Voting age pop. (1980): 434,109; 4% Black
3% Asian origin, 3% Spanish origin.

1988 Presidential Vote: Dukakis (D)....................... 141,366 (66%)
   Bush (R) 70,811 (33%)

Rep. Joseph P. Kennedy II (D)

Elected 1986; b. Sept. 24, 1952, Brighton; home, Brighton; U. of MA, B.A. 1976; Roman Catholic; separated.

Career: Community Services Admin., 1977–79; Founder and Pres., Citizens Energy Corp., 1979–86; Founder, Citizens Conservation Corp., 1981.

Offices: 1208 LHOB 20515, 202-225-5111. Also 1111 Thomas P. O'Neill, Jr. Fed. Bldg., 10 Causeway St., Boston 02222, 617-565-8686.

Committees: *Banking, Finance and Urban Affairs* (24th of 31 D). Subcommittees: Financial Institutions Supervision, Regulation and Insurance; Housing and Community Development; International Development, Finance, Trade and Monetary Policy. *Veterans' Affairs* (12th of 21 D). Subcommittees: Hospitals and Health Care; Oversight and Investigations. *Select Committee on Aging* (32th of 39 D). Subcommittee: Human Services.

Group Ratings

	ADA	ACLU	COPE	CFA	LCV	ACU	NTLC	NSI	COC	CEI
1988	95	91	93	100	88	4	11	0	21	8
1987	96	—	88	86	—	0	—	—	13	10

National Journal Ratings

	1988 LIB — 1988 CONS		1987 LIB — 1987 CONS	
Economic	92% —	0%	57% —	40%
Social	81% —	18%	78% —	0%
Foreign	84% —	0%	81% —	0%

Key Votes

1) Homeless $	AGN	5) Ban Drug Test	AGN	9) SDI Research	AGN
2) Gephardt Amdt	AGN	6) Drug Death Pen	FOR	10) Ban Chem Weaps	FOR
3) Deficit Reduc	FOR	7) Handgun Sales	AGN	11) Aid to Contras	AGN
4) Kill Plnt Clsng Notice	AGN	8) Ban D.C. Abort $	AGN	12) Nuclear Testing	FOR

Election Results

1988 general	Joseph P. Kennedy II (D)	165,745	(80%)	($1,186,852)
	Glenn W. Fiscus (R)	40,316	(20%)	($17,288)
1988 primary	Joseph P. Kennedy II (D)	37,390	(99%)	
1986 general	Joseph P. Kennedy II (D)	104,651	(72%)	($1,800,781)
	Clark C. Abt (R)	40,259	(28%)	($591,652)

NINTH DISTRICT

The "Hub of the Universe," the elder Oliver Wendell Holmes called it in the 19th century, and for a time in the 1988 campaign it was the hub of American politics, as the Dukakis campaign at 105 Chauncy Street sent out organizers with George V. Higgins character accents to win one primary state after another for the candidate George Bush referred to as the Governor of Massachusetts. The Boston from which they were dispatched is very different from the Boston to which Joseph P. Kennedy, long a resident of New York, sent his sons to run for office in the 1940s. Boston then was a grey city with no new buildings and dust on every windowsill; the sky was dark with pollution and the air was thick with the ancient animosity of Yankee and Irish. The big office buildings were full of Yankees, seeking safe investments for their old family fortunes; the State House and City Hall were full of Irishmen, scampering after good patronage jobs and regaling each other with political battle stories and pure blarney with a fluency found nowhere else in the land. Today that old Boston is mostly gone. The new skyscrapers are full of venture capitalists and lawyers of every ethnic description; the stores are stocked with the latest glitzy merchandise; the advertising slogans crackle with a sauciness and double entendre you can find only here and maybe in New York and Los Angeles.

The changes have not come to all of Boston neighborhoods. South Boston, the Irish peninsula into the harbor that resisted the 1970s school busing orders, today is angry with its native son, Mayor Raymond Flynn, for supporting measures wanted by blacks, and it looks out over the Boston Harbor that, as the Bush campaign informed America in 1988, has become one of the nation's dirtiest bodies of water. If Roxbury and north Dorchester have deteriorated as they have become majority-black, South Boston still has a 1940s look, and Jamaica Plain and West Roxbury, comfortable neighborhoods to the southwest, have not yet acquired a trendy look. But most of Boston is beyond the city limits now; its population is down from nearly 800,000 to under 600,000 after 50 years as the suburbs have expanded. Irish Catholics, who were still heavily clustered in Boston in 1940, have long since moved out into the suburbs, though the Irish resentment of the Yankees, while muted, lingers on. You can still find little ladies in Boston who will tell you that they don't know much about the candidates but "I always vote for all the good Irish names"; and you will find people who, when asked about discrimination, say, "Oh, yes. You mean 'No Irish need apply.'" Even in the majority, in a city governed by a series of Irish mayors since 1906, the Irish still feel beleaguered and put down, resentful of the privileges and connections Boston's Brahmins seem to enjoy, disdainful of what they consider the disrespectful behavior of many blacks, confused by the denunciations of their neighborhoods during the busing crisis by intellectuals from Boston's universities and writers for the *Boston Globe*.

As the Boston Irish and other city residents have moved out, so has the 9th Congressional District, which includes the central core of Boston but which, to keep up with the equal population standard, has expanded some 40 miles south from the city. It includes the well-to-do suburbs of Needham and Westwood, more modest towns like Stoughton, the small industrial city of Taunton far south of Boston, and several small rural towns roundabout. Less than half the district's population is now in Boston.

The congressman from the 9th, Joe Moakley, has the appearance and demeanor of an old Boston Irish pol, and the pedigree as well: he holds the 9th District seat represented from 1925 to 1970 by Speaker John McCormack and the Rules Committee seat held from 1954 to 1972 by Speaker Tip O'Neill of the 8th District. Moakley is a solid party man, a deputy majority whip who was always responsive on Rules to O'Neill (although, sitting in the chair, he was forced to rule O'Neill in violation of House rules when the Speaker attacked Newt Gingrich in the spring of 1984); he is less well connected with, but not unresponsive to, the leadership under Jim Wright. In June of 1989 Moakley became chairman of the Rules Committee upon the death of Claude Pepper. Moakley is solidly liberal on economic and foreign issues, but not on cultural ones—an attractive combination in Boston and many of the 9th District suburbs. As Rules chairman, he is well-positioned to get things done as an insider, and doesn't speak out often on substantive issues. His major personal battle has been a fight to allow Central Americans in this country to qualify to remain as refugees; he was an early and has been a consistent critic of anti satellite weapons tests and the Reagan Administration's Strategic Defense Initiative.

Oddly, given his party regularity, Moakley was first elected, in 1972, as an Independent; he was running against Louise Day Hicks, the busing opponent who had won the Democratic nomination over Moakley and the seat in 1970 by pluralities in multi-candidate fields. Moakley was an experienced legislator (he served in both houses in Massachusetts and on the Boston Council) and competent parliamentarian who was not going to give up his political career, so he used his Independent candidacy to beat Hicks in 1972 and got the Rules Committee seat shortly hereafter. Moakley has not had serious competition for years, even though in national contests the addition of the suburbs has left the 9th barely Democratic. Given his powerful position in the House and rapport with State House pols, he is likely to get a favorable seat out of redistricting.

The People: Est. Pop. 1986: 525,100, up 1.1% 1980–86; Pop. 1980: 519,226, dn. 5.2% 1970–80. Households (1980): 68% family, 36% with children, 49% married couples; 51.5% housing units rented; median monthly rent: $172; median house value: $49,400. Voting age pop. (1980): 380,987; 14% Black, 4% Spanish origin, 1% Asian origin.

1988 Presidential Vote:

Dukakis (D)	115,814	(54%)
Bush (R)	96,849	(45%)

Rep. John Joseph (Joe) Moakley (D)

Elected 1972; b. Apr. 27, 1927, Boston; home, Boston; U. of Miami, Suffolk U., LL.B. 1956; Roman Catholic; married (Evelyn).

Career: Navy, WWII; MA House of Reps., 1953–65, Major. Whip, 1957; Practicing atty., 1957–72; MA Senate, 1965–69; Boston City Cncl., 1971.

Offices: 221 CHOB 20515, 202-225-8273. Also 4 Court St., Taunton 02780, 617-824-6676; and World Trade Ctr., Ste. 220, Boston 02210, 617-565-2920.

Committees: *Rules* (Chairman of 9 D).

Group Ratings

	ADA	ACLU	COPE	CFA	LCV	ACU	NTLC	NSI	COC	CEI
1988	90	73	93	91	94	8	5	0	21	7
1987	84	—	93	100	—	5	—	—	7	4

National Journal Ratings

	1988 LIB — 1988 CONS		1987 LIB — 1987 CONS	
Economic	92% —	0%	73% —	0%
Social	73% —	25%	72% —	27%
Foreign	84% —	0%	81% —	0%

Key Votes

1) Homeless $	—	5) Ban Drug Test	AGN	9) SDI Research	AGN
2) Gephardt Amdt	FOR	6) Drug Death Pen	FOR	10) Ban Chem Weaps	FOR
3) Deficit Reduc	FOR	7) Handgun Sales	AGN	11) Aid to Contras	AGN
4) Kill Plnt Clsng Notice	AGN	8) Ban D.C. Abort $	FOR	12) Nuclear Testing	FOR

Election Results

1988 general	John Joseph (Joe) Moakley (D)	160,799	(100%)	($273,488
1988 primary	John Joseph (Joe) Moakley (D)	36,424	(100%)	
1986 general	John Joseph (Joe) Moakley (D)	110,026	(84%)	($314,452
	Robert W. Horan (I)	21,292	(16%)	

TENTH DISTRICT

If you had gone to Cape Cod half a century ago, when it was a not-too-thickly settled summe vacationland, you would have had little idea that this outstretched arm into the Atlantic, where the Pilgrims first put ashore before scuttling across Cape Cod Bay and settling in Plymouth, had a bustling industrial past. The picturesque towns here and on the islands of Nantucket and Martha's Vineyard were once whaling and China trade ports; a railroad steamed up the spine of the Cape; lumber was harvested here as in northern Maine or the Pacific Northwest. The bigges city in these parts was New Bedford, also once a whaling port. Then, around the beginning of the 20th century, quiet set into this southeastern corner of Massachusetts. New Bedford continue as a port and factory town; its population stabilized at about 100,000 for seven decades, but there was considerable turnover, as the Yankees died out, moved west, or intermarried, and wer replaced by the nation's largest Portuguese-American (actually, mostly Azorean-American community.

As for the Cape and the area around Plymouth, its industry withered away, it became vacation and poor farming country. Fifty years ago this was almost vacant territory, one of the more sparsely settled parts of the Northeast. But as metropolitan Boston spread down the South Shore, and as rising affluence enabled more and more people to buy second homes or to retire i comfortable circumstances, the Plymouth area and the Cape have been growing at rates tha seem to be accelerating each decade and which are now the fastest in Massachusetts. Too fas perhaps: strong support sprang up in 1988 for the call by former Senator Paul Tsongas for temporary moratorium on new construction.

This is the land of the 10th Congressional District of Massachusetts, starting at the beac suburb of Hull on Boston's South Shore and proceeding down through Plymouth and the town on Buzzards Bay to the Cape and New Bedford. Historically, this whole area, except for Ne Bedford and a few smaller mill towns, was heavily Republican. In the Vietnam years it trende liberal in cultural issues: the 10th went for Richard Nixon over George McGovern, but onl narrowly—a striking result in an area always heavily against Franklin D. Roosevelt. Wit Massachusetts's economic boom of the 1980s, the Plymouth area has become more Republica attracting some free marketeers who on the North Shore might head on to low-tax Ne Hampshire. But the Cape and the Islands, their retirees joined by the affluent trendy, ar trending ever more left, and New Bedford remains Democratic: the 10th as a whole voted fo Michael Dukakis in 1988.

The congressman here is Gerry (pronounced "Gary") Studds, a Democrat who is distinctiv in several respects. He got his start in politics as a New Hampshire prep school teacher who wa a top Eugene McCarthy volunteer; he remains one of the House's and the Foreign Affair Committee's most liberal voices on foreign policy, convinced that almost any America intervention abroad is dangerous for us and harmful for others. He ran for the 10th District sea in 1970 and nearly won; for 1972, he learned Portuguese, and won an ancestrally Republica seat in a national Republican year. In his first term he took a seat on the Merchant Marine an Fisheries Committee, a body shunned by most members, and made political capital—an important public policy—on it. His third asset is his support of the fishing industry. The 10t District may be the single House district most dependent on commercial fishing, and Studds ha shown great energy and skill advancing that industry's interests. In his first term, he succeeded in pushing through to passage a bill extending the territorial waters of the United States to 200 miles off the shoreline; since then he has been looking out for the interests of small fishermen, trying to keep their waters free from foreign trawlers and oil spills, trying to stop Canadian patrol boats from firing on them. This may seem humdrum work, but surely it has some fascination, and it helped Studds politically when he really needed it.

That time came in 1983, when it was revealed that Studds had had sex with a 17-year-old male page 10 years before. The House quite properly censured Studds and also Daniel Crane of Illinois, who had sex with a female page; under House rules Studds lost his Merchant Marines subcommittee chairmanship. With the same kind of stubbornness he brings to issues from El Salvador to fishing rights to "Notch Babies" (he is one of the few congressmen with the courage to say out loud they don't have a case), he maintained that he had done nothing wrong, rejecting the argument that members of Congress had a responsibility not to engage in such intimacy with young people in their charge. He proceeded to run for reelection as he had before. He had serious opposition in both primary and general, but he drew on the support he had won on foreign policy and fishing and from his indefatigable constituency service efforts and weekly reports (which seem clearly not staff-written). He marched in the annual New Bedford parade and was greeted with dozens of cheers and only a few catcalls; he got two-thirds of the votes in the New Bedford area in both the primary and general elections in 1984. The traditionally Republican Cape he carried with more than 80% of the vote in the primary and by a solid margin in the general. He beat Plymouth Sheriff Peter Flynn 61%–34% in the primary and a strong Republican, Lewis Crampton, 56%–44% in the general.

In the House in 1984, he attended briskly and effectively to his legislative duties, faithfully supporting the Coast Guard, winning passage of the Striped Bass Conservation bill, working on a variety of maritime, environmental and foreign policy bills; in 1985, he got his subcommittee chair back. In 1987, on Foreign Affairs, he declined to seek the chair of the Western Hemisphere subcommittee to which his seniority entitled him. Instead Studds took over the Fisheries, Wildlife Conservation and Environment Subcommittee on Merchant Marine, where he has continued to churn out legislation to protect marine mammals, keep fishing boats safe, restrict use of driftnets, and expand the National Wildlife Refuge System. Studds is now heir to the chair of the full name committee, where he ranks just behind the much older and ailing Walter Jones of North Carolina. Would House Democrats elect Studds chairman of the full committee? If competence and hard work and a determination to stick to principles right or wrong are the criteria, they will respond as Studds's 10th District constituents have.

The People: Est. Pop. 1986: 563,800, up 8.0% 1980–86; Pop. 1980: 522,200, up 26.6% 1970–80. Households (1980): 75% family, 38% with children, 62% married couples; 29.5% housing units rented; median monthly rent: $161; median house value: $48,800. Voting age pop. (1980): 377,639; 1% Black, 1% Spanish origin.

1988 Presidential Vote:

Dukakis (D).	. . . .	143,938	(51%)
Bush (R)	. . . .	136,345	(48%)

Rep. Gerry E. Studds (D)

Elected 1972; b. May 12, 1937, Mineola, NY; home, Cohasset Yale U., B.A. 1959, M.A.T. 1961; Episcopalian; single.

Career: U.S. Foreign Svc., 1961–63; Exec. Asst. to William R Anderson, Pres. Consultant for a Domestic Peace Corps, 1963 Legis. Asst. to U.S. Sen. Harrison J. Williams, 1964; Prep. sch teacher, 1965–69.

Offices: 1501 LHOB 20515, 202-225-3111. Also P.O. Bldg., Nev Bedford 02740, 508-999-1251; Barston's Landing, Ste. 6, 2 Colum bia Rd., Pembroke 02359, 617-826-3866; and 146 Main St. Hyannis 02601, 508-771-0666.

Committees: *Foreign Affairs* (5th of 28 D). Subcommittees Arms Control, International Security and Science; Western Hemi sphere Affairs. *Merchant Marine and Fisheries* (2d of 26 D) Subcommittees: Coast Guard and Navigation; Fisheries and Wild life Conservation and the Environment (Chmn.); Oceanography.

Group Ratings

	ADA	ACLU	COPE	CFA	LCV	ACU	NTLC	NSI	COC	CEI
1988	100	96	91	100	94	0	11	0	21	13
1987	100	—	90	93	—	0	—	—	0	4

National Journal Ratings

	1988 LIB — 1988 CONS		1987 LIB — 1987 CONS	
Economic	67%	— 30%	73%	— 0%
Social	86%	— 0%	78%	— 0%
Foreign	84%	— 0%	81%	— 0%

Key Votes

1) Homeless $	AGN	5) Ban Drug Test	AGN	9) SDI Research	AGN
2) Gephardt Amdt	FOR	6) Drug Death Pen	AGN	10) Ban Chem Weaps	FOR
3) Deficit Reduc	FOR	7) Handgun Sales	AGN	11) Aid to Contras	AGN
4) Kill Plnt Clsng Notice	AGN	8) Ban D.C. Abort $	AGN	12) Nuclear Testing	FOR

Election Results

1988 general	Gerry E. Studds (D)	187,178	(67%)	($235,946
	Jon L. Bryan (R)	93,564	(33%)	($121,056
1988 primary	Gerry E. Studds (D)	31,200	(100%)	
1986 general	Gerry E. Studds (D)	121,578	(65%)	($396,216
	Ricardo M. Barros (R)	49,451	(26%)	($97,191
	Alexander Byron (I)	15,687	(8%)	

ELEVENTH DISTRICT

Out the chronically clogged Southeast Expressway, over randomly curving streets and aroun hills, the descendants of Irish and other immigrants have for several generations been slowl making their way to the South Shore suburbs of Boston. This was Yankee territory originall the birthplace of John and John Quincy Adams; it is also the 11th Congressional District o Massachusetts, which includes the southern third of Boston, most of the city's South Shor suburbs, and more suburban territory stretching to the shoe manufacturing city of Brockton an the towns just beyond, and which was represented in the last years of his life by John Quinc

Adams. It includes Milton, the site of a famous prep school and the birthplace of President George Bush; it includes some Italian and Jewish neighborhoods; its Boston wards now have a large black population. The 11th District was represented by a Republican with the grand Yankee name of Richard Wigglesworth as late as 1958; it is only a generation since Catholics and Democrats have become numerous enough to dominate elections here.

The congressman from the 11th is Brian Donnelly, a man whose political roots are in Dorchester. He was a teacher and coach, a state legislator for six years, a politician who showed deference to his elders; he won the seat in 1978, when James Burke retired, partly because Burke and other local pols backed him over an upstart who had challenged Burke two years before. Donnelly, pretty liberal on economic and foreign issues, is the member of the Massachusetts delegation most conservative (but not very) on cultural issues. With Tip O'Neill's help he got a seat on Budget in 1981 (he has rotated off now) and on Ways and Means in 1985. He works hard on local issues like pollution in Quincy Bay and he has bills for tax incentives for investment in Northern Ireland and an excise tax on smokeless tobacco. But he has not made many waves on national issues. He has been reelected easily since he first won, and he can hold this seat for years, as Burke did; it seems unlikely he'll run for other office.

The People: Est. Pop. 1986: 519,100, dn. 1.1% 1980–86; Pop. 1980: 525,089, dn. 2.8% 1970–80. Households (1980): 73% family, 38% with children, 56% married couples; 42.2% housing units rented; median monthly rent: $211; median house value: $42,600. Voting age pop. (1980): 382,888; 7% Black, 1% Spanish origin, 1% Asian origin.

1988 Presidential Vote:

Dukakis (D)	113,465	(51%)
Bush (R)	104,005	(47%)

Rep. Brian J. Donnelly (D)

Elected 1978; b. Mar. 2, 1946, Dorchester; home, Dorchester; Boston U., B.S. 1970; Roman Catholic; married (Virginia).

Career: Dir. of Youth Activities, Dorchester YMCA, 1968–70; High sch. and trade sch. teacher and coach, 1969–72; MA House of Reps., 1973–78.

Offices: 2229 RHOB, 202-225-3215. Also 47 Washington St., Quincy 02169, 617-472-1800; JFK Fed. Bldg., Rm. 2307, Boston 02203, 617-565-2910; and 61 Main St., Brockton 02401, 617-583-6300.

Committees: *Ways and Means* (19th of 23 D). Subcommittees: Select Revenue Measures; Health.

Group Ratings

	ADA	ACLU	COPE	CFA	LCV	ACU	NTLC	NSI	COC	CEI
1988	80	73	89	64	75	8	9	0	23	13
1987	76	—	89	100	—	5	—	—	21	8

National Journal Ratings

	1988 LIB — 1988 CONS		1987 LIB — 1987 CONS	
Economic	78%	— 21%	66%	— 33%
Social	61%	— 38%	78%	— 0%
Foreign	73%	— 27%	62%	— 38%

Key Votes

1) Homeless $	AGN	5) Ban Drug Test	AGN	9) SDI Research	FOR
2) Gephardt Amdt	FOR	6) Drug Death Pen	FOR	10) Ban Chem Weaps	FOR
3) Deficit Reduc	FOR	7) Handgun Sales	AGN	11) Aid to Contras	AGN
4) Kill Plnt Clsng Notice	AGN	8) Ban D.C. Abort $	FOR	12) Nuclear Testing	FOR

Election Results

1988 general	Brian J. Donnelly (D)	169,692	(81%)	($167,960)
	Michael C. Gilleran (R)	40,277	(19%)	($18,090)
1988 primary	Brian J. Donnelly (D)	40,122	(86%)	
	David J. Peterson (D)	6,709	(14%)	
1986 general	Brian J. Donnelly (D)	114,926	(100%)	($46,171)

MICHIGAN

It was empty, swampy land 50 years ago, the square mile next to a little-used airfield along a little creek named Willow Run. But by the time America got into the war in December 1941, the corrugated steel walls and roofs were being hammered into place to create the huge building, a mile long and a quarter-mile wide, in which the Ford Motor Company would ultimately assemble 8,600 bombers. Thus did big government and big business, with cooperation from what was rapidly becoming big labor, create out of scratch the biggest bomber factory in the world. Ford hired 42,000 workers, many brought in by the government from the South and from local farmlands, and they were represented by the United Auto Workers which Henry Ford, stubborn and nearly 80, agreed to recognize as his employees' bargaining agent only in 1941. A 30-mile expressway was built to get workers in from Detroit (they were given extra gasoline rations); and the government built temporary housing—a 5,000-unit dormitory in early 1943, and, then, a few months later, dingy gray prefabricated units with coal stoves and iceboxes for 14,000 people were completed.

Willow Run was not fully used after the war, but it foreshadowed the growth of Michigan. This was growth directed and managed by big units—big government, big business, big labor. Big government by deliberate decision made the industrial arc of Michigan around Detroit the biggest center of war production in the interior of the country—"the arsenal of democracy," to use a phrase familiar to one growing up in Michigan in the 1950s. The government contracted directly with the big auto companies which had grown up serendipitously (Chicago and Cleveland bankers were less venturesome in staking auto pioneers) in this stove-making, crop-growing and lumber-harvesting state. After the war it was the auto companies—which soon became the Big Three of General Motors, Ford and Chrysler—who directed growth into Michigan, setting up new auto assembly and parts plants, and subcontracting work to local job shops. Michigan also became a key state for Big Labor, and housed the headquarters of the UAW whose president from 1947 to 1970, Walter Reuther, was a social democratic visionary. From his office in Solidarity House on the Detroit River, Reuther sought to use union power and union members' votes to move America toward a redistribution of income and wealth to workers and to build a Scandinavian-style welfare state in the richest nation in the world.

For more than a generation the big units were successful. Michigan was the fastest growing state in the Midwest from 1940 to 1965 (it gained congressional seats in the 1930, 1940, 1950 and 1960 Censuses); its residents' incomes were growing even faster; it became committed, after resistance from outstate Republicans accustomed to running things their way from their county seat main streets, to generous public expenditures and liberal social policies. Its politics was conducted as if it were class warfare, with a bitterness that recalled the violent days of the sit-down strikes and the Battle of the Overpass in 1937; but as the postwar period went on, growth continued, and it seemed there was plenty for everyone. The bitterness subsided and something like a consensus evolved, symbolized by Henry Ford II joining Walter Reuther in backing Lyndon Johnson in the election of 1964.

In the quarter-century since then, Michigan at first boomed, as one-car families became two-car families, and as UAW wages rose faster than the economy; recessions hit the state hard, dependent as it was on the biggest of big-ticket consumer items, but it always seemed to rebound. Until, that is, the recessions following the oil shock of 1979. Suddenly it became clear that Americans did not *have* to buy a new full-sized American-made car every two or three years, that clever ad campaigns couldn't force them to, and that foreign competitors were producing better and cheaper cars than those made by the Big Three managers and UAW workers, and more responsive to changes in consumer preferences. The big units, so well-adapted for growth in the quarter century after war production started in 1940, proved to be poorly-adapted for the quarter century that followed, when most growth came from small units. So Michigan has spent most of the 1980s adapting to the new small unit economy—eventually with considerable success.

This is not the first time in Michigan's history this geographically separate and distinct state—two peninsulas jutting out into the Great Lakes—has suffered from overreliance on a single industry. It boomed first with furs, as French *courreurs du bois* sailed up the Great Lakes and icy rivers of Ontario in the 17th century and sprinkled the land with French and French-Indian names (Mackinac, Sault Ste. Marie, Detroit, Michigan). But when the fashion for beaver hats passed, Michigan was left to the Indians. It boomed in the late 19th century when Michigan was the nation's leading lumber state, until the forests were clear-cut or swept by blazes like the 1881 fire that burned out half the Thumb. In the early 20th century, the rich iron and copper veins created miners' cities in the frigid Upper Peninsula, but the area has been losing population since the mines started petering out around 1920.

Politics in Michigan had its beginning in the 1830s and 1840s, when settlers poured into its empty forests from Upstate New York. This was part of the vast westward migration of New England Yankees, believers in learning and founders of colleges, reformers who hated slavery, manned the underground railroad, and promoted temperance, civilizing influences who in the 1850s made Michigan the first state to ban capital punishment and promoted temperance. Michigan was one of the birthplaces of the Republican Party, which was founded in Jackson in 1854 and swept the state in the elections later that year.

Republican Michigan was a bustling, well-educated, orderly commonwealth—but, until the auto industry grew up here in the 30 years after 1900, something of a backwater. Then, during those 30 years Detroit was a boom town—the nation's fastest growing big city after Los Angeles (the three-county metro area grew from 426,000 to 2.2 million)—and one of the world's leading immigrant destinations. The auto industry drew labor from outstate Michigan and southern Ontario and from the farms of Ohio and Indiana; it brought whites from the mountains of Kentucky and Tennessee and (mostly after 1940) blacks from Alabama and Mississippi. Michigan was mostly a native stock state before 1900, leavened by a Dutch colony (the nation's largest) around Grand Rapids and Holland, and Finns in the mining towns of the Upper Peninsula. But Detroit attracted Poles and Italians, Hungarians and Belgians, Greeks and Jews.

This sudden influx of a polyglot proletariat also changed Michigan's politics. The catalyst was the Great Depression of the 1930s, and the impetus came not so much from actual privation, for the auto companies paid good wages, as from the fact that the companies' managers and time-study engineers, in their desire to use machines efficiently, treated employees mechanically and

MICHIGAN — Congressional Districts, Counties, and Selected Places — (18 Districts)

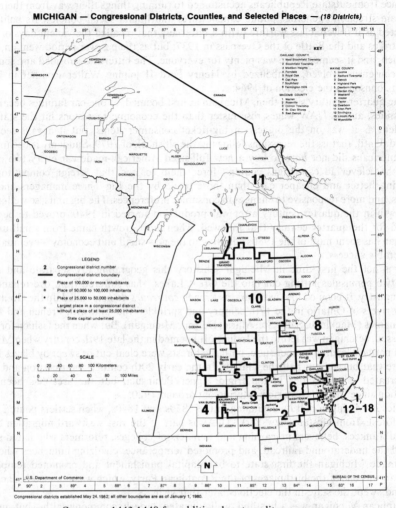

Congressional districts established May 24, 1982; all other boundaries are as of January 1, 1980.

See pages 1443-1448 for additional metropolitan area maps.

with great distrust. The result was the sit-down strikes of 1937 organized by the new United Auto Workers; management and labor were fighting, sometimes literally, for shares of what both sides thought was a static-sized pie. The UAW won and organized most of the companies, after Democratic Governor Frank Murphy refused to send in troops to break the strikes, even though they were clearly illegal.

The success of the union organizing drives set the tone of Michigan politics for at least 25 years. The union won, but many others resented its tactics and success: Murphy's Democrats lost the 1938 elections, not only statewide but in factory towns like Flint, and Republicans won most contests for nearly 20 years after. Their demographics finally worked for the Democrats: the auto workers and post-1900 immigrants were producing more children than outstate Yankees or management. Following Walter Reuther's election as UAW president in 1947, they elected G. Mennen Williams, then a young liberal, governor in 1948, and by 1954 the Democrats, closely allied to and heavily supported by the UAW, seemed to have become the natural majority in the state. The class-warfare atmosphere of Michigan politics ended after 1962, when Republican George Romney was narrowly elected governor: Romney and his successor William Milliken accepted the welfare state policies which were the goal of the UAW leadership and the Democrats. In the 1970s, as auto wages rose to levels unsurpassed by those in any other industry but steel, and as Michigan's standard of living surged ahead of those of other states, this seemed to be a state that had built an exemplary standard of living and had reached a solid political consensus. Michigan had income levels at least 10% above the national average, it had the nation's highest blue-collar wages, its residents had one of the highest rates of ownership of second homes and pleasure boats. The state government was one of the nation's most generous, to the poor and the unemployed and to others as well; it supported one of the nation's most distinguished and extensive systems of higher education; it had a fine system of state parks and recreation areas; it had been a pioneer in many efforts to end racial discrimination.

The collapse of the auto industry in 1979–82 changed all that. A state which seemed admirably governed by talented and enlightened moderates found itself suddenly faced with a crisis it seemed unable to handle. Chrysler nearly went bankrupt, Ford was in financial difficulty, and even General Motors had its first losses in years. The auto industry, which had grown faster than the economy for most of the 20th century, now seemed doomed to grow more slowly; no one expected auto employment in Michigan ever again to reach the level of 1978. Workers came to the end of their 65 weeks of unemployment benefits; housing prices in factory areas plummeted toward zero; hundreds of thousands left, many for oil-rich Texas. After several years, this shock convinced Michiganians that the old days of seemingly automatic growth would never return, and that the focus of Michigan politics should not be on dividing up an ever-growing pie but on how to bake a new pie from scratch. For years, people in Michigan had put their trust in big units, counting on the Big Three, the Union and big government to make it possible for them to earn more while working less. Now it was becoming clear that in an economy where all the growth was coming in small units, Michigan had to learn how to nurture that growth and that workers, instead of seeking more vacations and earlier retirements, would have to hustle and work harder than they used to.

In partisan terms this meant that Michigan was no longer, as it was in the 1960s and 1970s, a Democratic state on national economic issues. In the era of class-conscious politics, the UAW and its Democratic allies registered tens of thousands of working-class voters in the Detroit area and carried what was otherwise a Republican state: Franklin Roosevelt won Michigan with 50% in 1944 by carrying 61% of the votes in the three-county Detroit area while losing 60%–40% outstate, and John Kennedy won 51% in 1960 by carrying 62% in metro Detroit while losing 60%–40% outstate. That sharp regional division and the Democratic margin continued through the 1968 election, and in 1972, had it not been for controversy over a metropolitan busing order in the Detroit area, Michigan would have been among George McGovern's top three or four states. In the 1960s and 1970s, Michigan was voting 4% to 6% more Democratic than the nation (except when Michigan's Gerald Ford ran). In the 1980s, Michigan voted zero percent more Democratic than the nation. Since 1968 Democrat tickets have been running around 40% outstate, which used to be enough for a statewide victory. But since 1968 the Democrats have carried metro Detroit only in 1976, and then just 53%–46%. In the 1950s and 1960s, unemployment figures like those of 1979–83 would have boosted the Democrats' totals. But the national Democrats have not carried metro Detroit, much less Michigan, since the auto industry collapse. And metro Detroit has been losing population: it cast 49% of the state's votes in 1964 and 41% in 1988.

Governor. Even as the national Democrats lose their appeal, Michigan's state government has been led by a popular Democrat who has done much of the work of changing the state's basic attitudes. This is especially surprising since James Blanchard's major credential when he first ran in 1982 was his congressional floor management of the Chrysler loan guarantee—a classic partnership of big government, big labor and one of the Big Three. But circumstances suggested that Republican anti-tax and low-government ideas were in the ascendancy: Blanchard won by only 51%–45% against a mistake-prone Republican, and when he got the legislature to raise taxes in 1983, the Democrats lost control of the state Senate when two of their incumbents were recalled and replaced by Republicans.

But the new governor did not stick with old solutions. Instead of seeking federal aid or new Big Three installations, Blanchard and his crackerjack top appointees concentrated on seeking smaller, more diverse new businesses. Shrewdly, he refused to pursue fashionable high-tech industries, as so many states did, and instead concentrated on using Michigan's existing manufacturing expertise to specialize in high-skill, capital-intensive, flexible manufacturing State government, drawing on $750 million of its pension funds, has provided venture capital for small companies manufacturing everything from tape drives for microcomputers to fiberglass coffins.

The results, in an era of small units, included few big, highly visible successes (and to get one of those, the Mazda plant in Flat Rock, the local government had given up so much revenue it had to come begging the state for help). But they show up in the numbers, demographically and politically. Michigan's population loss of 2.3% in 1980–83 was the sharpest drop of any state But in 1983–86, Michigan grew 1%, more than any other Great Lakes industrial state, while unemployment fell from 15% at its recession peak down to under 9% in 1986, dropping by 1.9% in the single month of August 1986 alone. Unemployment was estimated in May of 1989 to be a 6.7%. Manufacturing jobs in 1986 were still down more than 200,000 from 1979's 1.2 million but the decline had levelled off and the total number was estimated in April 1989 to be 953,000.

As the state's economy picked up, Blanchard was able to get rid of the temporary tax hike thus depriving Republicans of their major issue, and to identify himself with the pride that was bursting out in almost every quarter of Michigan. One example: Blanchard's plan to let families pay into a tax-free trust fund to guarantee tuition for their children in Michigan's excellent state college and university system attracted 82,000 families—16 times as many as anticipated. "Say Yes! to Michigan" read bumper stickers all over the state, and the voters in 1986 said Yes! to Blanchard and their incumbent legislators—to the frustration of Republicans who believed with some justice, that Blanchard had borrowed many of their own policies. The Republican made a big to-do of persuading black Wayne County Executive William Lucas to switch partie and run for governor; a former FBI agent and Wayne County Sheriff with a stern attitude toward crime and government spending, he provided a vivid contrast with Detroit Mayo Coleman Young, who is highly unpopular in the suburbs and outstate. Pundits speculate whether primary opposition from car customizer Dick Chrysler would hurt Lucas (probably not no one was paying attention) and whether his race would hurt him (unlikely: Secretary of Stat Richard Austin, who is black, was reelected with 70%). More likely, voters were simply not i the market for a new governor; they wanted to reelect Blanchard and didn't care who else was or the ballot. Blanchard won 68%–31%, the highest percentage since Fred Green in 1928 and the best Democratic percentage since Stevens T. Mason in 1835. Lucas, nominated in 1989 to be assistant attorney general for civil rights in the Bush Administration, was initially opposed by the civil rights lobby for what they considered his lack of experience in civil rights affairs, as well a his questionable judgement on a few sensitive rulings.

Looking ahead to 1990, Blanchard is the commanding figure of Michigan politics and governor who, if the economic revival of the state continues, could remain in office as long as hi predecessor William Milliken, who lasted 14 years—or more. The state's economy continued to grow after 1986, and the results of the 1988 elections—Republican at the presidential level, big margin for Democratic Senator Donald Riegle statewide, solid reelection for the overwhelm ing majority of congressmen and legislators locally—suggested a satisfaction with the change direction of the state and a confidence about Michigan's apparently bright economic future. Blanchard himself gained some national prominence, chairing the Democrats' platform committee in 1988, conspicuously holding the key drafting session on Mackinac Island. As for potential challengers, the Republicans have some possibilities who, if they could get some attention, might be attractive candidates—state Senators John Engler or Dick Posthumus or former Legal Services Corporation chairman Clark Durant. They argue strenuously that Blanchard really backs higher taxes and more government than he lets on. But there is little evidence that voters are interested in a change.

Senators. Senator Donald Riegle, after spending most of the last two decades in the minority (as a Republican congressman from 1966 to 1973 and as a Democratic Senator from 1980 to 1986), now occupies one of the critical committee chairmanships in the 101st Congress. With the retirement of William Proxmire and Alan Cranston retaining the post of whip, Riegle became Chairman of the Banking, Housing and Urban Affairs Committee, and therefore the Senate's chief designated handler of the hot potato of the savings and loan crisis. Thus, a man who has been a critical outsider—he supported Pete McCloskey against Richard Nixon in 1972 and switched to the Democratic Party in 1973—has now become a consummate political insider, supported by the UAW and Big Three auto company executives in Michigan, cadres of lobbyists in Washington and the panjandrums of the securities industry in New York.

Riegle has made these transformations more easily and with less break from his principles than might be thought. He came to Congress as part of the large Republican class of 1966, from a small business family in the factory town of Flint and after a stint at Harvard Business School; but this was just as class warfare politics was dying out in Michigan, when it seemed natural for big business and big labor to work together—as they did, with some prodding from and compromises engineered by Riegle a dozen years later when he managed the Chrysler bailout bill in the Senate. And beginning as a member of the out party during an increasingly intractable and unpopular war, it was not unnatural for him to become a Vietnam dove and to turn against Richard Nixon because he did not end U.S. involvement there quickly enough.

Where Riegle has changed is in the scope of his ambition. When he first came to Congress, and in his book *O Congress*, based on his diary in 1971 and 1972, he was not shy about confessing his ambitions, and a city full of politicians who want to be President twitted him because he admittedly openly that what most of the others keep quiet about. Ironically, the course of the race that typically is the first step to a presidential run probably foreclosed him from making one. When Riegle was running for the Senate in 1976, in a close race against Congressman Marvin Esch, a class-of-1966 Republican who had stayed in the party, the *Detroit News* ran a particularly nasty story featuring extracts from tapes of Riegle and a woman he had an affair with; a backlash against the often harshly partisan *News* probably helped elect Riegle Senator at age 38. Since then Riegle has shown no interest in running for President. Instead he has worked hard as a Senator and has become a solid family man (his 1988 campaign ads featured shots of his 4-year-old daughter).

Riegle now serves on three money committees: not only Banking but also Budget, and Finance. Although he supported the Reagan tax cut in 1981, he has an almost entirely liberal voting record on economic (and other) issues. He has not always been successful: he was unable to save the UDAG (Urban Development Action Grants) program, which made many grants in Michigan, from extinction. But he has had his successes, like the Riegle trade amendment of 1988, which aimed at increasing American exports to cut our trade deficit. This was a compromise, worked out with Chrysler and the UAW among others, and passed by an 87–7 margin; it was endorsed, rather hastily, by Michael Dukakis in his desperate attempt to summon up enthusiasm in the Michigan presidential "firehouse primary." Riegle also has worked to limit corporate takeovers and has pushed for tougher rules on insider trading. He opposes repeal of the Glass-Steagall Act which separates commercial banking from the securities business; this enabled him to raise record sums from the securities business for his reelection campaign in 1988.

That was a typical Riegle effort, with an early start, smart strategy, and all-out effort by the candidate. Riegle had won with 53% against Esch in 1976 and 58% against Philip Ruppe, another Republican class-of-1966 veteran, in 1982; but that was a recession year, and few Senate seats in big states can be counted as safe. Riegle made the most of his fundraising advantages and was blessed with weak opposition. Riegle's 1988 Republican opponent, Jim Dunn, a businessman from the Lansing area, had won a House seat in 1980 which he then lost in 1982, and had lost a Senate nomination in 1984. He has a taste for the acerbic quip without the instinct of making it politically telling. By the fall of 1988, Dunn was suing the Republicans' Senate campaign committee for refusing to give him as much money as promised—a sure sign of political bankruptcy. Riegle won 60%–39%, carrying not only metro Detroit (65%) but outstate as well (57%).

Michigan's junior Senator, Carl Levin, is an example of a politician who has taken a set of principles seemingly in political eclipse and has managed to apply them with some success, passing some important legislation and getting himself elected twice now to the Senate in years unfavorable to his party and his ideas. He began his public career as head of Detroit's public defender office, and in 1969 was elected to the Detroit Council, where he won support equally from blacks and whites. In 1978, he was elected to the Senate 52%–48% after incumbent Robert Griffin, defeated for Republican Party Leader the year before, first announced his retirement and then got back into the race; Levin was reelected 52%–47% in 1984 when he enjoyed a 2 to 1 fundraising edge over former astronaut Jack Lousma, after showing tapes of Lousma praising his Toyota to an audience of Japanese executives.

In the Senate, Levin became one of the first Vietnam doves on the Armed Services Committee, on which he now ranks third, behind Chairman Sam Nunn and James Exon. There he has led opposition to SDI and tried to channel money away from it toward conventional weapons; he opposed the MX missile and the Reagan Administration's interpretation of the ABM treaty; he has urged that defense contractors' employees be required to file disclosure forms and be subject to conflict-of-interest rules.

On domestic issues, he is a stickler at advancing his principles. He has even gone so far as to insist with Texas Republican Senator Phil Gramm that committees specify cutbacks in spending to match their unwillingness to raise taxes. In line with a Michigan tradition that goes back to 1855, he is the Senate's leading opponent of the death penalty, fighting to keep it out of drug bills. He led the successful fight in the Senate to renew the independent counsel bill. He was one of only three Senators to vote against the 1986 tax reform bill. Most rating groups count him as having a liberal record, but there are exceptions to that rule, and he has shown a stubborn independence that seems innocent of political calculation through not closed to intellectual argument.

Levin seems likely to be one of the national Republicans' major targets in 1990—partly because there aren't any really weak Democrats running, partly because Levin's 52% wins don't look too strong, partly because any big state Senator has a hard time establishing a linkage with his voters. What was not clear in early 1989 was who his opponent would be. One possibility is Congressman Bill Schuette of Midland who has a proven record as a fundraiser and may argue that Levin is captive to the old economic interests of southeast Michigan, not to the vibrantly growing economy outstate. Richard DeVos Jr., son of the co-founder of Amway, also may run and make similar arguments. A map of the results of the 1984 election in fact shows that Levin does well north and east of Interstate 75, once a route out which Detroiters went to vacation and increasingly the path by which they have moved out of the metropolitan area altogether. These former Detroiters and ancestral Democrats seem to have a happier view of liberal politicians than do those who have remained closer to Detroit, in the suburbs (Levin lost both Oakland and

Macomb Counties). In contrast, Levin ran quite weakly south and west in the historically Republican heart of the state, which has been the center of recent economic growth. Outstate, in any case, is where the lion's share of movable votes are, and this may be a hotly contested race.

Presidential politics. Michigan had the nation's wildest and wooliest presidential politics of 1988—not in the fall, but early in the year and going back in to 1987 and 1986. The reason is that since 1968 Michigan has been unable to settle on a presidential delegate selection system that seems even mildly satisfactory. After George Wallace won the 1972 primary, the Democratic legislature abolished the primary, leaving both parties to improvise their own systems or use the pre-1972 system, in which precinct delegates elected two years before the presidential year select state convention delegates who select national convention delegates in the presidential year. For 1988, Michigan Republicans, hopeful of attracting national attention, went back to this old system, which made the precinct delegate contests in the August 1986 primary the first event of the 1988 campaign. Pat Robertson, using his non-profit Freedom Council, and George Bush, using his supposedly non-presidential PAC, both bent if not broke the rules to pour millions into the state in 1986, and got about 45% and 40% of the precinct delegates (there is no official designation or count). Jack Kemp won most of the balance and formed an alliance with Robertson that lasted into 1987. But Bush operatives managed to split the coalition apart in what one of them called "the Beirut of American politics," and the January 1988 state convention was a solid Bush victory, with Robertson followers holding a rump convention downstairs in the hall. In New Orleans these wounds were healed. But Michigan Republicans were left with a large and not entirely digestible body of dissidents, as Democrats had been after 1968: will the Robertson evangelicals move the Republican Party toward them as the McCarthy followers moved the Democrats?

Michigan Democrats, prevented by party rules from using a system that starts before calendar year 1988, in 1984 and 1988 used a "firehouse primary," in which anyone could show up at one of several hundred designated sites around the state and vote. But they used far fewer and different sites than in ordinary primaries, and so organization is of paramount importance: the key is getting out your vote. In 1988 that worked to the advantage of Jesse Jackson. His Michigan manager Joel Ferguson, an experienced Democrat, had organized outstate blacks for Blanchard when he was opposed by Bill Lucas in 1986. Ferguson's contacts and talents enabled him to produce wins for Jackson not only in the two black-majority Detroit districts, but in outstate districts as well. In a state with 6.8 million voters, only 213,000 turned out; 44% of those were in the two black Detroit congressional districts, where Jackson won over 90%; outstate, Ferguson organized black activists in every small city, carrying six of the 10 outstate districts and losing two others by 1%. This was not as hard as it sounds: a few busloads of church congregations can notch up many percentage points in a congressional district where the turnout is 6,000 to 10,000.

Much of the national press, eager to find the populist unity of white and black blue-collar workers which Jackson was constantly saying he could produce, found it in the Michigan results—it turned out that this was the one state where none of the networks conducted exit polls. Suddenly a wave of fear went through Democrats all over the country as many began to think Jackson might have a chance to actually win the nomination, and some expected him to win in the next state, Wisconsin. Actually in Michigan as elsewhere, white blue collar workers were the Democrats least likely to vote for Jackson after Orthodox Jews. Michigan stands not as the harbinger of a new populist coalition but as an example of how a talented organizer can take advantage of a caucus system when his candidate has enthusiastic supporters and his opponents are, for practical purposes, unknown.

Congressional districting. Michigan, which gained seats in the 1930, 1940, 1950 and 1960 Censuses, lost one each in 1970 and 1980, and may well lose two House seats in 1990. The 1980 situation was eased when James Blanchard ran for governor; 1990 will be bad news for at least

590   MICHIGAN

one white incumbent in the Detroit metropolitan area—although probably not senior committee chairmen John Dingell or William Ford. The exact lines will be part of a political compromise, unless the Democrats end the Republicans' 20–18 edge in the state Senate in 1990.

The People: Est. Pop. 1988: 9,300,000; Pop. 1980: 9,262,078, up 0.4% 1980–88 and up 4.3% 1970–80; 3.79% of U.S. total, 8th largest. 16% with 1–3 yrs. col., 15% with 4+ yrs. col.; 10.4% below poverty level. Single ancestry: 8% German, English, 4% Polish, 3% Irish, 2% Dutch, Italian, French, 1% Scottish, Swedish, Hungarian. Households (1980): 75% family, 42% with children, 61% married couples; 27.3% housing units rented; median monthly rent: $197; median house value: $39,000. Voting age pop. (1980): 6,510,092; 12% Black, 1% Spanish origin, 1% Asian origin. Registered voters (1988): 5,952,513; no party registration.

1988 Share of Federal Tax Burden: $34,147,000,000; 3.86% of U.S. total, 9th largest.

1988 Share of Federal Expenditures

	Total		Non-Defense		Defense	
Total Expend	$23,651m	(2.68%)	$21,539m	(3.29%)	$2,450m	(1.07%)
St/Lcl Grants	4,243m	(3.70%)	4,241m	(3.70%)	2m	(1.71%)
Salary/Wages	2,167m	(1.61%)	1,519m	(2.27%)	648m	(2.27%)
Pymnts to Indiv	14,835m	(3.63%)	14,640m	(3.75%)	195m	(1.05%)
Procurement	1,598m	(0.85%)	337m	(0.73%)	1,598m	(0.85%)
Research/Other	808m	(2.16%)	801m	(2.16%)	7m	(2.16%)

Political Lineup: Governor, James J. (Jim) Blanchard (D); Lt. Gov., Martha W. Griffiths (D); Secy. of State, Richard H. Austin (D); Atty. Gen., Frank J. Kelley (D); Treasurer, Robert Bowman (D). State Senate, 38 (20 R and 18 D); State House of Representatives, 110 (61 D and 49 R). Senators, Donald W. Riegle, Jr. (D) and Carl Levin (D). Representatives, 18 (11 D and 7 R).

1988 Presidential Vote			**1984 Presidential Vote**		
Bush (R)	1,965,485	(54%)	Reagan (R)	2,251,571	(59%)
Dukakis (D)	1,675,783	(46%)	Mondale (D)	1,529,638	(40%)

GOVERNOR
Gov. James J. (Jim) Blanchard (D)

Elected 1982, term expires Jan. 1991; b. Aug. 8, 1942, Detroit; home, Ferndale; MI St. U., B.A. 1964, M.B.A. 1965, U. of MN, J.D. 1968; Unitarian; divorced.

Career: Legal Aide, MI Secy. of State, 1968; Asst. Atty. Gen. of MI, 1969–73; U.S. House of Reps., 1974–1982.

Office: Capitol Bldg., Lansing 48909, 517-373-3400.

Election Results

1986 gen.	James J. (Jim) Blanchard (D)	1,632,138	(68%)
	William Lucas (R)	753,647	(31%)
1986 prim.	James J. (Jim) Blanchard (D)	428,125	(93%)
	Henry Wilson (D)	28,940	(3%)
1982 gen.	James J. (Jim) Blanchard (D)	1,561,291	(51%)
	Richard H. Headlee (R)	1,369,582	(45%)

SENATORS

Sen. Donald W. Riegle, Jr. (D)

Elected 1976, seat up 1994; b. Feb. 4, 1938, Flint; home, Flint; Flint Jr. Col., W. MI U., U. of MI, B.A. 1960, MI St. U., M.B.A. 1961, Harvard Bus. Sch., 1964-66; United Methodist; married (Lori).

Career: Consultant, IBM Corp., 1961-64; Faculty Mbr., MI St. U., Boston U., Harvard U., U. of Southern CA; U.S. House of Reps., 1967-77.

Offices: 105 DSOB 20510, 202-224-4822. Also 1850 McNamara Bldg., Detroit 48226, 313-226-3188; 30800 Van Dyke, 3d fl., Warren 48093, 313-573-9017; Sabuco Bldg., Ste. 910, 352 Saginaw St., Flint 48502, 313-234-5621; Washington Sq. Bldg., Ste. 705, 109 W. Michigan Ave., Lansing 48933, 517-377-1713; Fed. Bldg., Rm. 716, Grand Rapids 49503, 616-456-2592; 309 E. Front St., Traverse City 49685, 616-946-1300; and 200 W. Washington, Ste. 31, Marquette 49855, 906-228-7457.

Committees: *Banking, Housing and Urban Affairs* (Chairman of 12 D). *Budget* (4th of 13 D). *Finance* (9th of 11 D). Subcommittees: Health for Families and the Uninsured (Chairman); International Debt; International Trade.

Group Ratings

	ADA	ACLU	COPE	CFA	LCV	ACU	NTLC	NSI	COC	CEI
1988	90	67	94	100	80	4	4	10	36	11
1987	100	—	94	83	—	4	—	—	17	15

National Journal Ratings

	1988 LIB — 1988 CONS		1987 LIB — 1987 CONS	
Economic	83% —	14%	74% —	0%
Social	85% —	14%	90% —	4%
Foreign	86% —	0%	81% —	0%

Key Votes

1) Cut Aged Housing	FOR	5) Bork Nomination	AGN	9) SDI Funding	AGN
2) Override Hwy Veto	FOR	6) Ban Plastic Guns	AGN	10) Ban Chem Weaps	AGN
3) Kill Plnt Clsng Notice	AGN	7) Deny Abortions	AGN	11) Aid To Contras	AGN
4) Min Wage Increase	FOR	8) Japanese Reparations	FOR	12) Reagan Defense $	AGN

Election Results

1988 general	Donald W. Riegle, Jr. (D)	2,116,865	(60%)	($3,383,849)
	Jim Dunn (R)	1,348,216	(39%)	($442,693)
1988 primary	Donald W. Riegle, Jr. (D), unopposed			
1982 general	Donald W. Riegle, Jr. (D)	1,728,793	(58%)	($1,583,439)
	Philip E. Ruppe (R)	1,223,286	(41%)	($1,045,545)

Sen. Carl Levin (D)

Elected 1978, seat up 1990; b. June 28, 1934, Detroit; home, Detroit; Swarthmore Col., B.A. 1956, Harvard U., LL.B. 1959; Jewish; married (Barbara).

Career: Practicing atty., 1959–64, 1978–79; Asst. Atty. Gen. of MI and Gen. Counsel for MI Civil Rights Comm., 1964–67; Chief Appellate Defender for the City of Detroit, 1967–69; Detroit City Cncl., 1969–77, Pres., 1973–77.

Offices: 459 RSOB 20510, 202-224-6221. Also 1860 McNamara Bldg., 477 Michigan Ave., Detroit 48226, 313-226-6020; Fed. Bldg., 145 Water St., Rm. 102, Alpena 49707, 517-354-5520; 2409 1st Ave., Escanaba 49829, 517-789-0052; Gerald R. Ford Fed. Bldg., 110 Michigan Ave. N.W., Rm. 134, Grand Rapids 49503, 616-456-2531; 124 W. Michigan Ave., Rm. G30, Lansing 48933, 517-377-1508; P.O. Box 817, Saginaw 48606, 517-754-4562; and 24580 Cunningham, Rm. 110, Warren 48091, 313-759-0477.

Committees: *Armed Services* (3d of 11 D). Subcommittees: Strategic Forces and Nuclear Deterrence; Conventional Forces and Alliance Defense (Chairman); Readiness, Sustainability and Support. *Governmental Affairs* (3d of 8 D). Subcommittees: Investigations; Oversight of Government Management (Chairman); Government Information and Regulation. *Small Business* (5th of 10 D). Subcommittees: Rural Economy and Family Farming; Innovation, Technology and Productivity (Chairman).

Group Ratings

	ADA	ACLU	COPE	CFA	LCV	ACU	NTLC	NSI	COC	CEI
1988	80	70	93	100 ·	50	0	14	10	21	13
1987	90	—	94	100	—	4	—	—	17	18

National Journal Ratings

	1988 LIB — 1988 CONS		1987 LIB — 1987 CONS	
Economic	82%	— 17%	74%	— 0%
Social	78%	— 21%	71%	— 26%
Foreign	86%	— 0%	81%	— 0%

Key Votes

1) Cut Aged Housing $	FOR	5) Bork Nomination	AGN	9) SDI Funding	AGN
2) Override Hwy Veto	FOR	6) Ban Plastic Guns	AGN	10) Ban Chem Weaps	AGN
3) Kill Plnt Clsng Notice	AGN	7) Deny Abortions	FOR	11) Aid To Contras	AGN
4) Min Wage Increase	FOR	8) Japanese Reparations	FOR	12) Reagan Defense $	AGN

Election Results

1984 general	Carl Levin (D)	1,915,831	(52%)	($3,569,330)
	Jack Lousma (R)...................	1,745,302	(47%)	($1,765,786)
1984 primary	Carl Levin (D) unopposed			
1978 general	Carl Levin (D)	1,484,193	(52%)	($971,775)
	Robert P. Griffin (R)...............	1,362,165	(48%)	($1,681,550)

FIRST DISTRICT

From 1900 to 1930, the great auto factories had been built in a semicircular ring about five miles from downtown Detroit on swampy, flat land that was then at the edge of urban settlement. In the flat farmlands beyond, on the remorseless grid street pattern enforced by conscientious city planners, grew up mile after mile of residential neighborhoods, with commercial streets exactly one mile apart and, as late as the 1940s, a few farms still surviving inside the city limits. This was one of the first American cities built to automobile scale, and in the years after 1940 one group after another moved out the broad avenues and, in time, the giant freeways that headed outward from downtown. The biggest movement was by blacks, very few of whom lived in any part of pre-war Detroit and, except for a couple of small ghetto pockets, none of whom lived out past the auto factories. But both during the war (and after thousands of southern blacks streamed in to work in Detroit's factories), and after the war, they left the small ghettos where they had been confined, as whites fled to outer FHA-financed suburbs. Whole square miles of Detroit changed racial composition—just as rapidly as they had been built—in the 1950s and 1960s, and even faster after the riot of 1967, when most of the area's Jews left northwest Detroit for the suburbs. Some of the city's most affluent areas were opened up to blacks, even as some of the old factories—most of the Highland Park plant, where Henry Ford wowed the world in 1914 by announcing he'd pay $5 a day, and the old DeSoto and Cadillac factories—were abandoned.

Much of this Detroit just beyond the factories makes up Michigan's 1st Congressional District. About three out of four of its residents are black, as compared to fewer than one in 20 a half century ago. In income terms the 1st District, with much of Detroit's professional black elite, is not badly off. But the quality of life is bad: crime is high, shootings common, elaborate alarm systems and thick plexiglass enclosures around cashiers commonplace. Politically, this is one of the three or four most heavily Democratic districts in the country, with support for Republicans well-nigh nonexistent. Yet it is not apparent that the solutions of local Democrats—guaranteed annual incomes, more racial set-asides, more government jobs—would solve the problems that people here encounter daily on the streets.

The congressman from the 1st district is one of the senior black members of the House and, beginning in 1989, a full committee chairman, John Conyers. Conyers's father was an activist in the United Auto Workers, allied with the group ousted by Walter Reuther in 1947 and attacked by some Reuther supporters as allies of the Communists. When Conyers was first elected in 1964, he was only the fifth black in the House, and he was the first who took a militant liberal posture, distancing himself from the Johnson Administration, criticizing from the beginning the Vietnam war, charging that liberals were not doing enough for the poor. He was instrumental in setting up the Congressional Black Caucus, in part to get around the mellow ways of the older black members; now it is some of the younger blacks who are more inclined to work quietly within the system while Conyers seems more interested in denouncing and expressing his disgust. For a while, in the 1960s, he seemed to be an operator within the system; but, jeered by Detroit blacks when he tried to calm the 1967 riot, rebuffed totally when he tried to get a high guaranteed annual income for the poor, and disgusted when white Democratic colleagues opposed busing in 1972 (although they would have been defeated if they had not), he seems to have soured on everything but his own principles; for most of the 1970s and 1980s he was more a disgruntled observer than an involved participant in the House.

At the same time, he has developed his own specialties—one is as the House's leading aficionado, legislatively and otherwise, of jazz musicians—and has taken a workmanlike approach to his committee responsibilities on Judiciary and, now as chairman, on Government Operations. As chairman of the Judiciary subcommittees first on Crime and then on Criminal Justice, he opposed the death penalty in drug bills, the abolition of the insanity defense after the Reagan assassination attempt in 1981 and the revised criminal code—all futilely. In 1988, after intensive hearings, he recommended the impeachment of Alcee Hastings, a black federal judge from Florida acquitted of criminal bribery but accused by his fellow judges of lying. After the 1988 elections, he inherited the Government Operations chairmanship from Jack Brooks, who is now chairman of the Judiciary Committee, and promised to continue Brooks's involvement in procurement reform and to pursue his own interest in whether government purchasing policies can't do more for minority businessmen and aging industrial areas.

594   MICHIGAN

Over the years, Conyers has grown disengaged from local politics. His own position in the 1st District is impregnable; his only tough race was his first primary, in 1964, when he beat Richard Austin, now Michigan's secretary of state, by 108 votes out of 60,000 cast. In 1988, he spent much time across the country campaigning with and for Jesse Jackson.

The People: Est. Pop. 1986: 482,000, dn. 6.3% 1980–86; Pop. 1980: 514,560, dn. 10.0% 1970–80. Households (1980): 73% family, 44% with children, 44% married couples; 33.0% housing units rented; median monthly rent: $166; median house value: $21,400. Voting age pop. (1980): 349,182; 66% Black, 2% Spanish origin.

1988 Presidential Vote:

Dukakis (D)	126,551	(89%)
Bush (R)	15,099	(11%)

Rep. John Conyers, Jr. (D)

Elected 1964; b. May 16, 1929, Detroit; home, Detroit; Wayne St. U., B.A. 1957, LL.B. 1958; Baptist; single.

Career: Army, Korea; Legis. Asst. to U.S. Rep. John D. Dingell, 1958–61; Practicing atty., 1959–61; Referee, MI Workmen's Compensation Dept., 1961–63.

Offices: 2426 RHOB 20515, 202-225-5126. Also 669 Fed. Bldg., 231 W. Lafayette St., Detroit 48226, 313-961-5670.

Committees: *Government Operations* (Chairman of 24 D). Subcommittee: Legislation and National Security (Chairman). *Judiciary* (4th of 21 D). Subcommittees: Civil and Constitutional Rights; Criminal Justice; Crime. *Small Business* (17th of 27 D). Subcommittee: SBA, the General Economy and Minority Enterprise Development.

Group Ratings

	ADA	ACLU	COPE	CFA	LCV	ACU	NTLC	NSI	COC	CEI
1988	90	100	94	100	88	0	8	0	21	7
1987	92	—	92	79	—	0	—	—	0	1

National Journal Ratings

	1988 LIB — 1988 CONS		1987 LIB — 1987 CONS	
Economic	92% —	0%	73% —	0%
Social	86% —	0%	73% —	22%
Foreign	77% —	21%	81% —	0%

Key Votes

1) Homeless $	AGN	5) Ban Drug Test	AGN	9) SDI Research	AGN
2) Gephardt Amdt	FOR	6) Drug Death Pen	AGN	10) Ban Chem Weaps	FOR
3) Deficit Reduc	FOR	7) Handgun Sales	AGN	11) Aid to Contras	AGN
4) Kill Plnt Clsng Notice	AGN	8) Ban D.C. Abort $	AGN	12) Nuclear Testing	FOR

Election Results

1988 general	John Conyers, Jr. (D)	127,800	(91%)	($124,823)
	Bill Ashe (R)	10,979	(8%)	
1988 primary	John Conyers, Jr., unopposed			
1986 general	John Conyers, Jr. (D)	94,307	(89%)	($163,360)
	Bill Ashe (R)	10,407	(10%)	

SECOND DISTRICT

In the years before World War II, the comfortable towns and small cities of southern Michigan were celebrating their centennials. A hundred years before, Yankees from New England and Upstate New York, fresh from steamer rides across Lake Erie, trudged over the hills of southern Michigan, still wet with thawing snows, and founded new towns, bringing their habits of literacy, community self-improvement and strict morality. They led the nation on issues like women's rights, temperance, opposition to capital punishment, resistance to the extension of slavery, and support of the new Republican Party. Joined by German refugees from the failed revolutions of 1848, they formed prosperous farming and industrial communities, governed for years by folksy members of the local elite—the kind of men who, in Congress and the state legislature, formed the core of opposition to New Deal measures as their home towns marked their first 100 years.

The 2d Congressional District of Michigan includes much of this historic territory: Ann Arbor, where the University of Michigan was established in 1817; Jackson, where the Republican Party was founded in 1854; and Hillsdale, a picturebook old town and home of Hillsdale College, founded in the 1850s, which has always admitted women and blacks but has refused federal money because it doesn't want equal opportunity investigators around. The 2d District's eastern extremity also verges on the Detroit metropolitan area. It includes half of Livonia, which was farmland in 1940 and filled up with more than 100,000 people 25 years later, and the affluent suburban territory around the old town, redolent of its New England namesake, of Plymouth.

On balance, this is a Republican district, though parts of it have gone Democratic: Livonia, when economic issues recall residents' working-class origins and loyalties; Ann Arbor, when cultural or war issues turn out a leftish student vote. This made it a seriously contested seat in the 1970s, though no Democrat has been able to combine the trends and win. Since the 1970s Ann Arbor was almost perfectly countercyclical, an indicator of the way the nation is not going: it went for George McGovern in 1972, U of M alumnus Gerald Ford in 1976, gave John Anderson a big vote in 1980, and voted twice against Ronald Reagan and once against George Bush.

This rather disparate district was assembled to suit the political needs of Representative Carl Pursell and has done so. Pursell is a Republican, a rumpled and often tieless man who has been a professional legislator for almost 20 years. Elected to the House in 1976, he got a seat on the Appropriations Committee in his second term, and there has been a quiet but often effective legislator. He is one of those Republicans known briefly in the early 1980s as Gypsy Moths, who were uncomfortable with many of the Reagan budget cuts, and a leader of the '92 Group— moderate Republicans whose goal is to make their party a majority in the House by 1992. Pursell is not flashy or voluble on the floor, but works on the Labor-HHS-Education Subcommittee for programs to help nursing, graduate students and workers needing re-training. He organized a group of Northeast and Midwest Republicans to protect their regional interests, for much of the detail work on Capitol Hill comes in writing the formulas for federal disbursements that can make vast differences for local communities. He has tried to forge compromises on Central America and the Caribbean Basin.

But Pursell's overall record on economic issues is more Republican than Democratic, and his liberalism on cultural and foreign issues is not so strong as to protect him from challenges from Ann Arbor liberals; he is a George Bush supporter, after all, and they are not. In 1986, graduate student Dean Baker, without much of a campaign, carried Ann Arbor and held Pursell to 59% districtwide. In 1988, Ann Arbor state Senator Lana Pollack raised much more money, and so did Pursell; the issue was joined in TV ads; they held a nasty-tempered debate. But the result was not much different from 1986. Pollack carried Ann Arbor, but Pursell got more than 60% in the rest of the district and won with 54%. Such a figure ordinarily indicates a marginal seat. But Ann

Arbor, which has the votes in the primary, is not likely to nominate a Democrat acceptable to the rest of the district. The major threat to Pursell is redistricting, for Michigan will lose at least a seat, and it would be possible to divide the 2d among its Detroit area and outstate neighbors.

The People: Est. Pop. 1986: 509,400, dn. 1.0% 1980–86; Pop. 1980: 514,560, up 10.1% 1970–80. Households (1980): 73% family, 40% with children, 62% married couples; 30.7% housing units rented; median monthly rent: $251; median house value: $52,200. Voting age pop. (1980): 375,911; 5% Black, 1% Asian origin, 1% Spanish origin.

1988 Presidential Vote:

Bush (R)	130,585	(58%)
Dukakis (D)	94,358	(42%)

Rep. Carl D. Pursell (R)

Elected 1976; b. Dec. 19, 1932, Imlay City; home, Plymouth; E. MI U., B.A. 1957, M.A. 1962; Protestant; married (Peggy).

Career: Army, 1957–59; Educator; Businessman; Mbr., Wayne Cnty. Bd. of Commissioners, 1969–70; MI Senate, 1971–76.

Offices: 1414 LHOB 20515, 202-225-4401. Also 361 W. Eisenhower Pkwy., Ann Arbor 48104, 313-761-7727; 134 N. Main, Plymouth 48170, 313-455-8830; and 111 N. West Ave., Jackson 49201, 517-787-0552.

Committees: *Appropriations* (9th of 22 R). Subcommittees: Energy and Water Development; Labor, Health and Human Services, Education and Related Agencies.

Group Ratings

	ADA	ACLU	COPE	CFA	LCV	ACU	NTLC	NSI	COC	CEI
1988	45	59	44	73	38	46	54	60	79	40
1987	24	—	43	36	—	55	—	—	71	52

National Journal Ratings

	1988 LIB — 1988 CONS		1987 LIB — 1987 CONS	
Economic	39%	— 61%	27%	— 72%
Social	49%	— 50%	35%	— 65%
Foreign	44%	— 56%	41%	— 58%

Key Votes

1) Homeless $	FOR	5) Ban Drug Test	FOR	9) SDI Research	AGN
2) Gephardt Amdt	AGN	6) Drug Death Pen	FOR	10) Ban Chem Weaps	FOR
3) Deficit Reduc	AGN	7) Handgun Sales	AGN	11) Aid to Contras	FOR
4) Kill Plnt Clsng Notice	AGN	8) Ban D.C. Abort $	AGN	12) Nuclear Testing	FOR

Election Results

1988 general	Carl D. Pursell (R)	120,070	(54%)	($876,779)
	Lana Pollack (D)	98,290	(45%)	($750,493)
1988 primary	Carl D. Pursell, unopposed			
1986 general	Carl D. Pursell (R)	79,567	(59%)	($140,396)
	Dean Baker (D)	55,204	(41%)	($32,181)

THIRD DISTRICT

From their settlement by Yankees from New England and Upstate New York 150 years ago until today, the small cities and towns that spot the farmland of southern Michigan have been incubators of innovation. The state's public school system was established by two politicians from Marshall, whose dashed hopes to become the state capital have resulted in the preservation of many 19th century houses whose counterparts in Lansing, which won the contest instead, have long since been demolished. A few miles away, in Battle Creek, sanitarium operator W.K. Kellogg invented corn flakes as a health food; he and his onetime client C.W. Post both established factories in the late 19th century and created the American breakfast cereal industry. Kalamazoo, another little ways to the west, has been a pharmaceutical center for more than 100 years.

This diversified and innovation-minded tradition provided a better economic base for the part of outstate Michigan contained in the state's 3d Congressional District than existed in much of the rest of the state. The auto industry is an important presence here too, especially in Lansing (the western portion of which is in the district), but it's not so dominant as in Detroit or Flint or Saginaw. Historically, this is all Republican territory, and has been since the party was founded nearby in Jackson in 1854—but, at the same time, interested in fostering activist institutions and promoting reformist moral agendas. It rejected with some indignation New Deal tinkering and was mostly hostile to the United Auto Workers: people were proud of taking care of each other and didn't want distant big city intellectuals telling them how to live their lives. But they also were receptive to moral claims being made by the reformers of the 1960s, challenging racial segregation, the Vietnam war and the Watergate coverup: this is one part of the country where their cultural liberalism helped the Democrats. On economic issues, the makeshift American welfare state came to be taken for granted, and even welcomed. State government and education were big employers in this part of Michigan, and people who believed in them found the Democrats more generous and more likeminded.

These changes help to (but don't fully) explain the successful political career of 3d District Democratic Congressman Howard Wolpe. He came to the district from the West Coast and Washington to be a teacher at Western Michigan University in Kalamazoo; he was elected to the city council and the state legislature; he ran for Congress in 1976, barely lost, and worked the next two years as a staffer for Senator Donald Riegle in Lansing. Then he ran again and won in 1978. In his first term, he got a seat on the Foreign Affairs Committee. In his second term, he became chairman of the Africa Subcommittee—an appropriate assignment: he had lived for two years in Nigeria and later taught African political systems at Western Michigan University. In his third term, he got a seat on the Budget Committee.

He has been active as a legislator and as a district representative. On African issues, he has generally been a leader, though he deferred somewhat to Congressional Black Caucus members in the successful drive for sanctions legislation against South Africa; he was bitterly critical of the Reagan Administration's "constructive engagement" policy toward the South African regime. He argues that we need to get on good terms with the blacks who will ultimately run South Africa. He has always been sympathetic to African leaders who wish to remain unaligned, away from the two superpowers, and has called on Americans to look at issues there more from these Africans' point of view. He has urged the United States to spend more on famine relief and seems to see more aid, rather than a turn to free enterprise, as providing the best chance for economic growth. He has opposed aid to the Savimbi group in Angola and has called for South Africa to withdraw from Namibia, rejecting arguments that support for Savimbi would help get Cuban troops out of Angola and help persuade the South Africans to leave Namibia.

Wolpe has been a legislative powerhouse not just on Africa. His bill for foreign lobbyist

598   MICHIGAN

registration, barring officials from lobbying for foreigners for a year after they leave government, was enacted; his Hazardous Waste Reduction Act, to encourage cleanups during manufacturing, passed the House. He believes strongly in government acting to boost economic development, and strongly supported programs like UDAG (Urban Development Action) and EDA (Economic Development Action) grants which are supposed to give seed money to development. He has worked hard to get such money into the 3d District, and maintains excellent relations with officials of both parties; in Michigan, during its economic downturn and in revival as well, such federal programs have become part of the fabric of local life and Wolpe, in working on them, is a frantically busy Burkean conservative, busy with the practical business of everyday life. Yet he has been willing to antagonize local interests: Kellogg, with facilities in South Africa, opposed sanctions, but Wolpe would support no exemption; Kellogg's PAC supported the Republican in 1988.

Wolpe has been blessed with opponents who, in contrast, sound themes that are abstract and theoretical and verge on the shrilly intolerant. Jackie McGregor, the Republican who ran against him in 1984 and 1986, called him "the liberal, far left radical puppet of the anti-American Third World," and was the intended beneficiary of a 1984 letter from then 4th District Republican Mark Siljander—a student to whom Wolpe gave a C at Western Michigan—urging ministers to "send another Christian to Congress"; to that Wolpe, who is Jewish, and quite a lot of other 3d District voters, took umbrage. In 1988, his Republican opponent Cal Allgaier's attacks were blunted when it was revealed that his chain of groceries was writing bad checks to the state liquor and lottery bureaus. Motivated, knowledgeable, and well-connected in Washington, Wolpe has vastly outraised the Republicans and outhustled and outsmarted them too. The major threat to his tenure seems not so much the opposition but the possibility of fatigue: Wolpe has been carrying a heavy load legislatively and on district projects, and in fact may be a little relieved that he rotated off the Budget Committee in 1989.

The People: Est. Pop. 1986: 515,900, up 0.3% 1980–86; Pop. 1980: 514,560, up 3.7% 1970–80. Households (1980): 71% family, 40% with children, 58% married couples; 32.0% housing units rented; median monthly rent: $199; median house value: $35,800. Voting age pop. (1980): 367,512; 8% Black, 2% Spanish origin.

1988 Presidential Vote:

Bush (R)	108,143	(54%)
Dukakis (D)	91,318	(45%)

Rep. Howard E. Wolpe (D)

Elected 1978; b. Nov. 2, 1939, Los Angeles, CA; home, Lansing; Reed Col., B.A. 1960, M.I.T., Ph.D., 1967; Jewish; divorced.

Career: Prof., W. MI U., 1967–72; Kalamazoo City Cncl., 1969–72; MI House of Reps., 1972–76; Regional Rep. to U.S. Sen. Donald W. Riegle, Jr., 1976–78.

Offices: 1535 LHOB 20515, 202-225-5011. Also P.O. Box 1202, Battle Creek 49015, 616-963-0133; 707 Academy St., Kalamazoo 49007, 616-385-0039; and 316 N. Capitol, Lansing 48933, 517-482-9386.

Committees: *Foreign Affairs* (6th of 28 D). Subcommittees: Africa (Chairman); International Economic Policy and Trade. *Science, Space and Technology* (8th of 30 D). Subcommittees: Natural Resources, Agriculture Research and Environment; Energy Research and Development; Science, Research and Technology.

Group Ratings

	ADA	ACLU	COPE	CFA	LCV	ACU	NTLC	NSI	COC	CEI
1988	100	95	91	91	88	0	10	0	36	16
1987	92	—	91	86	—	0	—	—	7	8

National Journal Ratings

	1988 LIB — 1988 CONS	1987 LIB — 1987 CONS
Economic	85% — 15%	73% — 0%
Social	86% — 0%	78% — 0%
Foreign	79% — 16%	81% — 0%

Key Votes

1) Homeless $	AGN	5) Ban Drug Test	AGN	9) SDI Research	AGN
2) Gephardt Amdt	FOR	6) Drug Death Pen	AGN	10) Ban Chem Weaps	FOR
3) Deficit Reduc	FOR	7) Handgun Sales	AGN	11) Aid to Contras	AGN
4) Kill Plnt Clsng Notice	AGN	8) Ban D.C. Abort $	AGN	12) Nuclear Testing	FOR

Election Results

1988 general	Howard E. Wolpe (D)................	112,605	(57%)	($600,940)
	Cal Allgaier (R)	83,769	(43%)	($164,856)
1988 primary	Howard E. Wolpe (D), unopposed			
1986 general	Howard E. Wolpe (D)................	78,720	(60%)	($852,746)
	Jackie McGregor (R)	51,678	(40%)	($223,082)

FOURTH DISTRICT

The southwest corner of Michigan, where people tune in Chicago rather than Michigan television stations and root for the Cubs or the White Sox rather than the Tigers, makes up the 4th Congressional District of Michigan. Settled partly by the Yankee rush westward in the mid-19th century that populated most of outstate Michigan, and partly by Germans and Dutch who came up later, it is a collection of small manufacturing cities, like the Benton Harbor-St. Joseph area, towns proud of their Underground Railroad pasts like Calvin Center, tiny Vicksburg (where townspeople swear they saw Elvis Presley in 1987) and the nation's premier Dutch-American community, centered around the town of Holland. The Dutch brought with them tulip bulbs, wooden shoes, native costumes and a determination to preserve their rigorous Christian Reformed religion; they have built small businesses and prospered, but have kept their mores very much the same, and their politics, in this already very conservative and Republican corner of Michigan. Holland is in the only county of Michigan's 83 that voted against Governor James Blanchard in 1986; 6 of the 14 counties that voted against Democratic Senator Donald Riegle in 1988 are wholly or partially in the 4th.

For more than 50 years, the 4th District has been represented by Republicans who are vitriolic critics of the welfare state. They include the crusty anti-New Dealer Clare Hoffman (1935–63); Edward Hutchinson (1963–77), the ranking Republican on the Judiciary Committee who defended Richard Nixon in the impeachment hearings; and David Stockman (1977–81), who as a provocative backbencher in the House spent the Carter years learning the details of the federal budget that would serve him so well as President Reagan's OMB Director. Stockman has been followed, after a five-year interval, by a protege of similar but less vehement views. He is Fred Upton, an aide to Stockman at OMB and grandson of the founder of Whirlpool, a big employer in St. Joseph. Upton has a conservative voting record, especially on economics, has pushed spending cut amendments (with varying success) and supports the balanced budget amendment and the line-item veto. He wants to use market mechanisms to produce better public policies,

600   MICHIGAN

and was proud that his first amendment to be passed into law—a measure changing federal flood insurance to allow demolition of threatened buildings before they are inundated—creates incentives that tend to reduce government expenditures.

Upton won the seat in rather unusual fashion, upsetting incumbent Republican Mark Siljander 55%–45% in the 1986 primary. Siljander, an evangelical Christian, was bizarre enough to put the seat in jeopardy in the general election by sending a tape to ministers during the 1986 campaign in which he said, "We need to break the back of Satan and the lies that are coming our way." Upton, in contrast, seems to stir no controversy at all and has every prospect of representing this district for years if he likes.

The People: Est. Pop. 1986: 518,700, up 0.8% 1980–86; Pop. 1980: 514,560, up 12.8% 1970–80. Households (1980): 77% family, 43% with children, 66% married couples; 24.4% housing units rented; median monthly rent: $178; median house value: $35,600. Voting age pop. (1980): 355,746; 6% Black, 1% Spanish origin.

1988 Presidential Vote:

Bush (R)	124,506	(63%)
Dukakis (D)	71,397	(36%)

Rep. Frederick S. Upton (R)

Elected 1986; b. Apr. 23, 1953, St. Joseph; home, St. Joseph; U. of MI, B.A. 1975; Protestant; married (Amey).

Career: U.S. Office of Mgt. and Budget, Staff Asst, 1975–81, Asst. Dir. for Legis. Affairs, 1984–85.

Offices: 1607 LHOB 20515, 202-225-3761. Also 421 Main St., St. Joseph 49085, 616-982-1986; 225 W. 30th St., Holland 49423, 616-394-4900; and P.O. Box 425, 108 Portage Ave., Three Rivers 49093, 616-273-9122.

Committees: *Public Works and Transportation* (15th of 20 R). Subcommittees: Investigations and Oversight; Surface Transportation; Water Resources. *Small Business* (13th of 16 R). Subcommittees: Procurement, Tourism and Rural Development; Environment and Labor. *Select Committee on Hunger* (7th of 11 R).

Group Ratings

	ADA	ACLU	COPE	CFA	LCV	ACU	NTLC	NSI	COC	CEI
1988	30	52	30	64	38	64	82	100	100	54
1987	16	—	13	21	—	70	—	—	87	77

National Journal Ratings

	1988 LIB — 1988 CONS			1987 LIB — 1987 CONS		
Economic	26%	—	73%	23%	—	76%
Social	36%	—	63%	30%	—	69%
Foreign	16%	—	78%	28%	—	72%

Key Votes

1) Homeless $	FOR	5) Ban Drug Test	FOR	9) SDI Research	FOR
2) Gephardt Amdt	AGN	6) Drug Death Pen	FOR	10) Ban Chem Weaps	AGN
3) Deficit Reduc	AGN	7) Handgun Sales	FOR	11) Aid to Contras	FOR
4) Kill Plnt Clsng Notice	FOR	8) Ban D.C. Abort $	AGN	12) Nuclear Testing	AGN

Election Results

1988 general	Frederick S. Upton (R)................	132,270	(71%)	($323,829)
	Norman Rivers (D)....................	54,428	(29%)	($8,577)
1988 primary	Frederick S. Upton (R), unopposed			
1986 general	Frederick S. Upton (R)................	70,331	(62%)	($382,663)
	Daniel Roche (D)	41,624	(37%)	($15,314)

FIFTH DISTRICT

Grand Rapids half a century ago was the home base of one of the most powerful politicians of the 1940s, Arthur Vandenberg. A former editorial writer of grandiloquent and rather gassy prose, he had allied himself with the state's Republican boss, Frank McKay, whose office was in another of Grand Rapids's little skyscrapers, and had gotten himself appointed to a vacancy that occurred when a Senator died in 1928. A shrewd taker of the public pulse, Vandenberg sponsored federal deposit insurance after Michigan's February 1933 bank holiday and was the only industrial state Republican Senator reelected in the New Deal year of 1934. Grand Rapids, settled not just by New England Yankees but prominently by Calvinist Dutch, its economy undergirded by the usually solid furniture business, was not a typical American city, but it was typical enough to follow Vandenberg from his foreign policy isolationism, as senior Republican on Foreign Relations in 1940, to his support for the United Nations in 1945 and the Truman Doctrine, as chairman in 1947. Grand Rapids showed its confidence not only by reelecting Vandenberg in 1940 and 1946, but also by ousting incumbent 5th District Congressman Bartel Jonkman in 1948 and electing in his place a 35-year-old Republican lawyer named Gerald Ford.

Congenial, hard-working, faithful to party and principle, Ford became House Minority Leader after the Republicans' 1964 debacle and Vice President in 1973, when Richard Nixon needed someone the Democratic Congress would confirm after Spiro Agnew's resignation. The 5th District in turn helped to make Ford President, by electing (much to his surprise and shock) a Democrat as his successor in the House. That was one of the four Democratic victories in Republican districts, two of them in Michigan, that convinced many Republicans in 1974 that Nixon had to go. In fact, there had been a minor Democratic trend in Grand Rapids for several years, and for the next 10 years the 5th District seat was seriously contested more often than not.

Since 1984, the congressman from the 5th has been Paul Henry, who seems in line with most of its current political leanings. Henry served in the state Senate, he worked (as David Stockman did, later) for Congressman John Anderson, he was a professor at Calvin College singled out for praise by no less than David Broder of the *Washington Post*. Henry won his primary easily against his predecessor, Harold Sawyer's son, then got the best percentage in the general election since Ford. In 1986 and 1988, he was reelected with 71% and 73%—better than Ford ever got.

Henry is counted as a liberal in some quarters and is a member of the moderate Republican '92 Group, and opposed the Reagan Administration on some key votes. But he is also a solid opponent of abortion and is not especially liberal on other cultural issues, has a mixed record on foreign policy, and sticks pretty close to Republican and free market principles on economics, apart from trade. One of his chief initiatives has been what he calls his college savings bond proposal, which amounts to an IRA for parents to save for their children's college education; it was endorsed by George Bush in 1988, and Henry launched an attack on Michael Dukakis's different plan. Henry has been mentioned as a possible candidate for the Senate in 1990, a race that might require different skills and would certainly require more money than he has had to spend in the convenient-sized (roughly coincident with the Grand Rapids TV market) 5th.

The People: Est. Pop. 1986: 552,000, up 7.3% 1980–86; Pop. 1980: 514,560, up 9.5% 1970–80. Households (1980): 75% family, 43% with children, 63% married couples; 26.8% housing units rented; median monthly rent: $188; median house value: $38,400. Voting age pop. (1980): 359,611; 5% Black, 2% Spanish origin.

1988 Presidential Vote:

Bush (R)	151,994	(64%)
Dukakis (D)	83,993	(35%)

Rep. Paul B. Henry (R)

Elected 1984; b. July, 9, 1942, Chicago, IL; home, Grand Rapids; Wheaton Col., B.A. 1963, Duke U., M.A. 1968, Ph.D. 1970; Christian Reformed; married (Karen).

Career: Peace Corps, 1963–65; Legis. Asst. to U.S. Rep. John B. Anderson, 1968–69; Instructor, Duke U., 1969–70; Prof., Calvin Col., 1970–78; Mbr., MI Bd. of Ed., 1975–78; MI House of Reps., 1979–82; MI Sen., 1983–84.

Offices: 215 CHOB 20515, 202-225-3831. Also 166 Federal Bldg., Grand Rapids 49503, 616-451-8383.

Committees: *Education and Labor* (10th of 13 R). Subcommittees: Employment Opportunities; Postsecondary Education; Employment Opportunities; Health and Safety. *Science, Space and Technology* (10th of 19 R). Subcommittees: Natural Resources, Agriculture Research and Environment; Energy Research and Development; Science, Research and Technology. *Select Committee on Aging* (18th of 26 R). Subcommittee: Retirement Income and Employment.

Group Ratings

	ADA	ACLU	COPE	CFA	LCV	ACU	NTLC	NSI	COC	CEI
1988	50	48	40	73	63	52	67	60	93	58
1987	36	—	35	43	—	45	—	—	87	59

National Journal Ratings

	1988 LIB — 1988 CONS		1987 LIB — 1987 CONS	
Economic	30% —	69%	35% —	64%
Social	32% —	67%	31% —	68%
Foreign	45% —	55%	48% —	52%

Key Votes

1) Homeless $	FOR	5) Ban Drug Test	FOR	9) SDI Research	AGN
2) Gephardt Amdt	FOR	6) Drug Death Pen	FOR	10) Ban Chem Weaps	FOR
3) Deficit Reduc	AGN	7) Handgun Sales	AGN	11) Aid to Contras	AGN
4) Kill Plnt Clsng Notice	FOR	8) Ban D.C. Abort $	FOR	12) Nuclear Testing	AGN

Election Results

1988 general	Paul B. Henry (R)	166,569	(73%)	($309,436)
	James Catchick (D)	62,868	(27%)	($50,977)
1988 primary	Paul B. Henry (R), unopposed			
1986 general	Paul B. Henry (R)	100,577	(71%)	($304,765)
	Teresa Decker (D)	40,608	(29%)	($17,074)

SIXTH DISTRICT

Long before district caucuses and PAC contributions, Ice Age glaciers scooped out tons of earth from the path before them and deposited them where they stopped, along a diagonal line in what now is the Lower Peninsula of Michigan. They left behind a row of lakes and hills through the monotonously flat landscape. Through one of these belts of hills, and over rolling land to the north and west, lies the state's 6th Congressional District. It is anchored, on either end, by the giant auto factories that produce Oldsmobiles (in Lansing) and Pontiacs (in Pontiac). In between is Livingston County, sparsely settled for years; in the last two decades, it has sprouted subdivisions, trailer parks and rows of lakeside cottages for new residents who have left metro Detroit. These are people who left the city to seek a more rural, culturally traditional environment in which to live and raise their children. Even Pontiac, though part of affluent suburban Oakland County, is outside the Detroit orbit, with its own newspaper and radio station, and its own population mix of blacks from the Black Belt of Alabama and whites from Appalachian Kentucky and Tennessee. It was the site of one of the nation's most bitter busing disputes in the early 1970s, with many of the whites leaving for its lake-studded suburb of Waterford Township.

The congressman from the 6th District is Bob Carr, a battle-scarred but still thriving member of the Democrats' class of 1974. He first ran for Congress in 1972, and with the help of new 18-year-old voters, nearly beat a 16-year Republican incumbent. Two years later the incumbent retired, and Carr won and became one of the most outspoken of Watergate babies; it was he who in March 1975 got the Democratic Caucus to vote against military aid to Cambodia as the Khmer Rouge were closing in on Phnom Penh; he served on the Armed Services Committee and opposed its hawkish majority often. On economics, he was a conventional pro-labor Democrat for years, but since the late 1970s, when he supported the Kemp-Roth tax cut, has been more cautious on economic issues. His foreign policy stands helped him in the 1970s, and like almost all of the Watergate class, he was reelected in 1976 and 1978. But in 1980, after Iran and Afghanistan, his dovish stands were a liability and he lost to Republican Jim Dunn. State Democrats pretty much gave up on him and took away some of his most Democratic precincts to help Howard Wolpe in the 3d District.

But Carr ran against Dunn in 1982 and, in the trough of the recession, won 51%–48%. He then got a seat on the Appropriations Committee, steered clear of most defense issues (though he calls on his expertise as a pilot sometimes and champions fliers of small planes), and concentrated on arranging federal aid programs for local areas, boosting Pontiacs and Oldses, and raising plenty of campaign dollars. He has been an adroit campaigner blessed with less than adroit opponents. In 1984, Carr was able to run ads attacking his "family values" Republican opponent for being late in child support payments. In 1986 he faced Dunn (who lost a Senate primary in 1984), charging him with supporting the (bipartisan) 1982 tax increase and turning aside Dunn's criticism of his early 1970s support of liberalization of marijuana laws by saying that he (like many voters) had changed his mind. In 1988, Carr vastly outraised his opponent, winning 65% in Oakland and even carrying Livingston, for a 59% win—his best ever in a career that is now 9–2, and an indication that the more practical, politics Carr has practiced in the 1980s has more staying power than the idealistic, venturesome politics he championed in the 1970s.

The People: Est. Pop. 1986: 518,800, up 0.8% 1980–86; Pop. 1980: 514,559, up 19.0% 1970–80. Households (1980): 74% family, 45% with children, 62% married couples; 30.0% housing units rented; median monthly rent: $234; median house value: $46,700. Voting age pop. (1980): 360,961; 6% Black, 2% Spanish origin, 1% Asian origin.

1988 Presidential Vote: Bush (R) 120,819 (57%)
Dukakis (D). 89,071 (42%)

Rep. Robert (Bob) Carr (D)

Elected 1982; b. Mar. 27, 1943, Janesville, WI; home, Okemos; U. of WI, B.S. 1965, J.D. 1968, MI State U., 1968–69; Baptist; divorced.

Career: Staff Mbr., MI Senate Minor. Ldr.'s Ofc., 1968–69; A. A. to Atty. Gen. of MI, 1969–70; Asst. Atty. Gen. of MI, 1970–72; Counsel to MI Legislature Special Comm. on Legal Educ., 1972; Dem. Nominee for U.S. House of Reps., 1972, 1980; U.S. House of Reps., 1975–81.

Offices: 2439 RHOB 20515, 202-225-4872. Also 2848 E. Grand River, Ste. 1, E. Lansing 48823, 517-351-7203; and 91 N. Saginaw, Pontiac 48058, 313-332-2510.

Committees: *Appropriations* (28th of 35 D). Subcommittees: Commerce, Justice, State, and the Judiciary; District of Columbia; Transportation. *Select Committee on Hunger* (9th of 16 D).

Group Ratings

	ADA	ACLU	COPE	CFA	LCV	ACU	NTLC	NSI	COC	CEI
1988	80	65	84	82	50	21	18	0	46	26
1987	92	—	84	71	—	9	—	—	31	15

National Journal Ratings

	1988 LIB — 1988 CONS		1987 LIB — 1987 CONS	
Economic	53% —	46%	55% —	43%
Social	57% —	42%	70% —	28%
Foreign	63% —	37%	68% —	30%

Key Votes

1) Homeless $	AGN	5) Ban Drug Test	AGN	9) SDI Research	FOR
2) Gephardt Amdt	FOR	6) Drug Death Pen	FOR	10) Ban Chem Weaps	FOR
3) Deficit Reduc	AGN	7) Handgun Sales	FOR	11) Aid to Contras	AGN
4) Kill Plnt Clsng Notice	AGN	8) Ban D.C. Abort $	AGN	12) Nuclear Testing	FOR

Election Results

1988 general	Robert (Bob) Carr (D)	120,581	(59%)	($504,217)
	Scott Schultz (R)	81,079	(40%)	($81,586)
1988 primary	Robert (Bob) Carr (D), unopposed			
1986 general	Robert (Bob) Carr (D)	74,927	(57%)	($692,787)
	Jim Dunn (R)	57,283	(43%)	($244,913)

SEVENTH DISTRICT

Half a century ago Flint, Michigan may very well have been the most class-conscious city in America. It was then, and is now, a company town, a city of 150,000 with five major General Motors plants and over half its wage-earners on the GM payroll. Flint was the scene in the early months of 1937 of the first sit-down strikes started by United Auto Workers organizers; GM was forced to recognize the UAW as bargaining agent when Governor Frank Murphy refused to use troops to clear the plants. Until the depression set in, Flint was a boom town, with migrants from local rural areas, the American South, and Eastern Europe. Local businessmen feared and tried to smooth over evidence of class conflict; Charles Stewart Mott, GM's biggest individual stockholder and for 60 years a member of its board, established a foundation that built civic institutions and improved life in Flint in dozens of ways. So when Flint was split by the sit-downs, it may not be surprising that many, perhaps most, voters supported the companies: if the Democrats carried Flint in the next several presidential elections, the Republicans held the House seat (which included a couple of smaller counties) until 1954.

The 1979–82 collapse of the auto industry hit Flint hard. Unemployment rose to 20%, and thousands ran through their 65 weeks of 95% unemployment benefits and suddenly found themselves with no job and owning a house with no market value. Flint has come back a ways now; the factories are now running, and there is a traffic jam again at 3:30 when the shifts break. But there are fewer jobs at Buick, Chevrolet and Fisher Body, and more of the GM payroll is working for the EDS computer processing subsidiary GM bought from H. Ross Perot. Flint's downtown is spruced up with new (federally aided) projects, its shopping malls are humming and real estate is worth something again. Politically, the conventional wisdom always has been that recession turns Flint to the Democrats, inflation or racial problems to the Republicans. But in the middle 1980s Flint, while more Democratic than most of Michigan, still voted for Ronald Reagan in 1984, though it went for Michael Dukakis and overwhelmingly for native son Donald Riegle in 1988.

Michigan's 7th Congressional District includes most of Flint—all of the city, and most of Genesee County and the Flint TV market. Since 1976, when Riegle first ran for the Senate, it has been represented in the House by Democrat Dale Kildee. Kildee studied for the priesthood, and he brings to his politics a certain intensity of conviction, derived from the liberal tradition that has been lively in the American Catholic Church since the early 1900s—a tradition that has little regard for market economics and feels a strong obligation to care for the needy. His door-to-door campaigning got him elected to a new state legislative seat created by redistricting in 1964 and enabled him to beat a 26-year veteran of the state Senate 10 years later. His popularity was such that he was elected to this safe Democratic seat in the House in 1976 by 3 to 1 margins in both the primary and general election. He has been reelected easily ever since, even though he spends relatively little; this is one of those districts which coincides closely with a TV market, and so Kildee can get free air time easily.

Kildee was assigned to the Education and Labor and Interior Committees at a time when the former's programs were about to be squeezed while environmentalists held sway on the latter; this must have been frustrating, since his interests lie in what is now called human services. (Now he is chairman of the Human Resources Subcommittee of Education and Labor.) He tried to switch to Ways and Means after the 1982 election and failed, evidently because with characteristic austerity he had opposed the pay raise shortly before. In 1988, he did win a seat on Budget, for which he took temporary leave from Interior.

Kildee's most important role in Congress has been as chief House sponsor of the ABC child care bill also spearheaded by Chris Dodd in the Senate. This measure, developed by the Alliance for Better Childcare and other lobbying groups, seeks to encourage expanded day care options by providing subsidies and requiring federal regulation of them. Some proponents argue that current day care is inadequate and that group day care can provide services that many neighborhood providers and relatives can't. Kildee also argues that not all parents are able to insist on needed health or safety standards any more than airline passengers can be counted on to demand safety of airliners. The bill has passed through Education and Labor and has many votes on the floor, but it has also run into some knotty problems, most notably the question of whether and under what terms church-run day care programs should be eligible. Some liberals bridle at any church involvement, while conservatives point out that a large share of existing programs are run by churches and are no different than church-run colleges, for example, that receive various kinds of subsidy. Kildee, eager not to hurt church schools and not to overstep constitutional limits, has tried to forge compromises. ABC is likely to get a thorough airing in the 101st Congress, in which Kildee should play a major role.

The People: Est. Pop. 1986: 499,800, dn. 2.9% 1980–86; Pop. 1980: 514,560, up 5.0% 1970–80. Households (1980): 77% family, 47% with children, 61% married couples; 24.4% housing units rented; median monthly rent: $209; median house value: $36,800. Voting age pop. (1980): 346,868; 14% Black, 1% Spanish origin.

1988 Presidential Vote:
Dukakis (D)..................... 112,101	(55%)
Bush (R)......................... 89,235	(44%)

Rep. Dale E. Kildee (D)

Elected 1976; b. Sept. 16, 1929, Flint; home, Flint; Sacred Heart Seminary, Detroit, B.A. 1952, U. of MI, M.A. 1961, Rotary Fellow, U. of Peshawar, Pakistan; Roman Catholic; married (Gayle).

Career: High sch. teacher, 1954–64; MI House of Reps., 1965–75; MI Senate, 1975–77.

Offices: 2262 RHOB 20515, 202-225-3611. Also 303 W. Water St., Flint 48503, 313-239-1437.

Committees: *Budget* (13th of 21 D). Task Forces: Community Development and Natural Resources; Human Resources. *Education and Labor* (7th of 22 D). Subcommittees: Elementary, Secondary, and Vocational Education; Human Resources (Chairman); Labor-Management Relations.

Group Ratings

	ADA	ACLU	COPE	CFA	LCV	ACU	NTLC	NSI	COC	CEI
1988	95	87	95	100	88	4	7	0	14	7
1987	96	—	94	100	—	4	—	—	7	5

National Journal Ratings

	1988 LIB — 1988 CONS		1987 LIB — 1987 CONS	
Economic	87% —	8%	73% —	0%
Social	78% —	20%	73% —	22%
Foreign	84% —	0%	81% —	0%

Key Votes

1) Homeless $	AGN	5) Ban Drug Test	AGN	9) SDI Research	AGN
2) Gephardt Amdt	FOR	6) Drug Death Pen	AGN	10) Ban Chem Weaps	FOR
3) Deficit Reduc	FOR	7) Handgun Sales	AGN	11) Aid to Contras	AGN
4) Kill Plnt Clsng Notice	AGN	8) Ban D.C. Abort $	FOR	12) Nuclear Testing	FOR

Election Results

1988 general	Dale E. Kildee (D) 150,832	(76%)	($150,594)
	Jeff Coad (R) 47,071	(24%)	($1,310)
1988 primary	Dale E. Kildee (D), unopposed		
1986 general	Dale E. Kildee (D) 101,225	(80%)	($101,545)
	Trudie Callihan (R)................. 24,848	(19%)	

EIGHTH DISTRICT

A century ago the Thumb of Michigan (to see why it's called that, look at the map) was new cropland, much of it burned over from the great fire of 1881, tended by farmers of Yankee and German descent raising potatoes and navy beans (used in the Senate's bean soup) and sugar beets—crops that can thrive in places with short growing seasons. Today the Thumb is still mostly farmland, tilled by those pioneers' descendants. Saginaw and Bay City to the west were lumber mill towns a century ago, to where logs were floated down the rivers and sawed into finished lumber; today they are factory towns, with Saginaw known as the place where General Motors makes its power steering. Politically, the Thumb counties are among the most Republican in Michigan; Bay City though, with its Polish population, is Democratic; Saginaw leans slightly Republican.

Michigan's 8th Congressional District, made up today of these distinct areas, has had mostly a somnolent but occasionally an explosive political history. Mostly it has elected Republican congressmen, but when the 8th has a special election anything can happen. In November 1931, after the death of Republican Bird Vincent, Democrat Michael Hart won the special election, an astonishing upset that not only helped deliver control of the House to the Democrats, but was the first indicator of the political revolution that produced the Roosevelt Democratic landslide of 1932. In April 1974, when Republican James Harvey was appointed a federal judge, the 8th District elected Democrat Bob Traxler, in an upset that was one of several signalling popular discontent with Richard Nixon over the Watergate scandal. Ludicrously, Nixon campaigned in the Thumb, thus increasing his downside risk—but then he never need have given Harvey the judgeship anyway.

Traxler has held the seat ever since, mostly without difficulty and against desultory competition. Bay City and Saginaw are now solidly Democratic (both went for Dukakis in 1988) while the Thumb is marginally less Republican and has been courted by Traxler on agricultural issues steadily. His 72% reelection in 1988 was a typical result.

In the House, Traxler became in 1989 a member of the "college of cardinals," the old name for the chairmen of House Appropriations subcommittees—not an unfitting accomplishment for a man who has been a professional legislator for most of three decades. The occasion for his elevation was the retirement of Edward Boland, and the chair he takes over is that of VA, HUD and Independent Agencies. It is something of a hot seat: Traxler will be besieged on one side by those who want to put more money into the space program (none more so than Bill Nelson, who is using his chairmanship of the authorizing space subcommittee as a launching pad for his race for governor of Florida) and on the other by Democrats who are trying to figure some way to put more money into housing programs; institutionally, he will be pressed to hold his subcommittee's total within the limits authorized by the budget process. But this, and his service on the Agriculture subcommittee chaired by Jamie Whitten, is not wholly unhappy work. There are opportunities always for deflecting more money to the needy and to 8th District residents—all the better if they fall into both categories. HUD projects for Saginaw and Bay City and for subsidies maintaining U.S. sugar prices at well above world levels may be two such worthy causes. With his political acumen, subcommittee chairmanship and safe seat, Traxler seems in the prime of a long political career.

The People: Est. Pop. 1986: 497,500, dn. 3.3% 1980–86; Pop. 1980: 514,560, up 8.3% 1970–80. Households (1980): 78% family, 45% with children, 65% married couples; 22.0% housing units rented; median monthly rent: $189; median house value: $35,600. Voting age pop. (1980): 350,577; 6% Black, 3% Spanish origin.

1988 Presidential Vote: Bush (R) 101,657   (50%)

                             Dukakis (D). 101,061   (50%)

Rep. Bob Traxler (D)

Elected Apr. 16, 1974; b. July 21, 1931, Kawkawlin; home, Bay City; MI St. U., B.A. 1952, Detroit Col. of Law, LL.B. 1959; Episcopalian; divorced.

Career: Army, 1953–55; Asst. Bay Cnty. Prosecutor, 1960–62; MI House of Reps., 1962–74, Major. Flr. Ldr., 1965–66.

Offices: 2366 RHOB 20515, 202-225-2806. Also New Fed. Bldg., Rm. 1052, 100 S. Warren St., Saginaw 48606, 517-754-4226; and Fed. Bldg., Rm. 323, 1000 Washington Ave., Bay City 48708, 517-894-2906.

Committees: *Appropriations* (11th of 35 D). Subcommittees: VA, HUD and Independent Agencies (Chairman); Legislative; Rural Development, Agriculture and Related Agencies.

Group Ratings

	ADA	ACLU	COPE	CFA	LCV	ACU	NTLC	NSI	COC	CEI
1988	80	74	87	73	63	14	9	0	21	12
1987	80	—	87	71	—	4	—	—	14	8

National Journal Ratings

	1988 LIB — 1988 CONS		1987 LIB — 1987 CONS	
Economic	65%	— 34%	73%	— 0%
Social	64%	— 34%	57%	— 42%
Foreign	84%	— 0%	73%	— 27%

Key Votes

1) Homeless $	AGN	5) Ban Drug Test	AGN	9) SDI Research	FOR
2) Gephardt Amdt	FOR	6) Drug Death Pen	AGN	10) Ban Chem Weaps	FOR
3) Deficit Reduc	FOR	7) Handgun Sales	FOR	11) Aid to Contras	AGN
4) Kill Plnt Clsng Notice	AGN	8) Ban D.C. Abort $	FOR	12) Nuclear Testing	FOR

Election Results

1988 general	Bob Traxler (D)......................	139,904	(72%)	($128,400)
	Lloyd Buhl (R)	54,195	(28%)	($2,188)
1988 primary	Bob Traxler (R), unopposed			
1986 general	Bob Traxler (D)......................	97,406	(73%)	($98,670)
	John Levi (R)	36,695	(27%)	($31,955)

NINTH DISTRICT

The 19th century lumbering country on the eastern shore of Lake Michigan, the fruit orchards behind the giant sand dunes that line the Lake's shores, the pleasant resort country and occasional polluted industrial harbors, from Holland in the south to Traverse City in the north—the little finger of the hand that, on the map, forms Michigan's Lower Peninsula—make up the 9th Congressional District of Michigan. Fifty years ago, this was aging industrial country or cut-over forest; today some of the industrial towns are aging and some of the forest is virgin, but much of western Michigan is growing smartly. The frugal, heavily Dutch area around Holland is prosperous without being glitzy; the resort area around Traverse City and the Sleeping Bear Dunes National Lakeshore is one of the fastest-growing and most prosperous parts of Michigan. This is one of the nation's most solidly Republican districts, despite some Democratic precincts in Muskegon and a couple of the lumber towns, and it elects one of the nation's most prominent Republican congressmen, Guy Vander Jagt. His background is diverse: he was a television newscaster and a state senator, he is an attorney and an ordained minister. He prides himself on his speaking ability, and he is not one of those new-fashioned orators who speaks conversationally to the television camera. Vander Jagt thunders out his speeches, which he likes to practice while walking through the woods, and which he insists on delivering extemporaneously. He is cited by speech professors as an exemplary orator, though his style seems suited less to the television age than to some earlier America, where eloquent phrases, heart-warming stories, and homey similes had the capacity to send chills up rapt listeners' spines.

Vander Jagt occupies two important positions but exerts little power in the House. First, he is chairman of the House Republican campaign committee, and has been since 1975. As chairman he has had some considerable accomplishments. He helped Republicans make gains in 1978 and 1980 from their Watergate nadir. In those same years he far outdistanced the Democrats in direct mail fundraising and sophisticated media operations. The 1980 election results gave Vander Jagt a plausible basis for running for House Republican Leader and gave the Republicans some reasonable hope of capturing control of the House in the 1980s. Neither anticipation materialized. Despite considerable support from the class of 1980, Vander Jagt lost the leadership to Robert Michel, who was much more experienced inside the House. And in 1982 Republicans, instead of making gains, lost 26 seats.

One reason was the sharp recession. But another was that Vander Jagt was outperformed by the Democrats' Tony Coelho. Coelho personally lobbied PACs and business contributors to give money to Democrats as well as Republicans, and fed them reliable information about strong Democrats and weak Republicans. Vander Jagt tended to concentrate on speechmaking, take for granted that business money would go Republican, and puff the chances of many of his candidates. Vander Jagt never recovered: despite a favorable economy, the Republicans did not recoup their 1982 losses in 1984 or 1986 or 1988. In early 1989 the Campaign Committee hired as its head Ed Rollins, manager of Ronald Reagan's 1984 campaign and an aggressive strategist who seemed determined to make Republican gains.

Vander Jagt's other major position in the House is as second ranking Republican on the Ways and Means Committee. He has used this to pass minor measures which help his district, to which he has remained for all his national politicking closely attentive. But for many years he spent little time in committee and has been ignored by Chairman Dan Rostenkowski. He continues to push for an income tax write-off to support the U.S. Olympic team and for repeal of the 22d Amendment, lifting the two-term presidential limit. But these are not exactly pressing matters (Ronald Reagan wasn't going to run in 1988 at age 77 and George Bush is not going to run in 1996 at 72). On legislation as in politics, Vander Jagt has tended, perhaps because of his initial successes as an orator and campaign chairman, to lose sight of the ball, to use his not inconsiderable political talents to focus on peripheral matters even when he has achieved institutional positions that give their holders the opportunity to affect the outcome of central issues.

The People: Est. Pop. 1986: 534,700, up 3.9% 1980–86; Pop. 1980: 514,560, up 13.9% 1970–80. Households (1980): 77% family, 43% with children, 67% married couples; 20.9% housing units rented; median monthly rent: $163; median house value: $33,500. Voting age pop. (1980): 356,896; 4% Black, 1% Spanish origin.

1988 Presidential Vote: Bush (R) 143,764   (62%)
Dukakis (D) 85,457   (37%)

Rep. Guy Vander Jagt (R)

Elected 1966; b. Aug. 26, 1931, Cadillac; home, Luther; Hope Col., B.A. 1953, Yale U., B.D. 1955, Rotary Fellow, Bonn U., Germany, 1956, U. of MI, LL.B. 1960; Presbyterian; married (Carol).

Career: Practicing atty., 1960–64; MI Senate, 1965–66.

Offices: 2409 RHOB 20515, 202-225-3511. Also Roosevelt Park, 950 W. Norton Ave., Muskegon 49441, 616-733-3131; 124 N. Division St., Traverse City 49684, 616-946-3832.

Committees: *Ways and Means* (2d of 13 R). Subcommittees: Select Revenue Measures (Ranking Member); Trade.

Group Ratings

	ADA	ACLU	COPE	CFA	LCV	ACU	NTLC	NSI	COC	CEI
1988	15	24	16	36	13	91	76	100	100	61
1987	0	—	16	14	—	90	—	—	93	60

National Journal Ratings

	1988 LIB — 1988 CONS	1987 LIB — 1987 CONS
Economic	10% — 88%	28% — 72%
Social	5% — 91%	0% — 90%
Foreign	0% — 84%	0% — 80%

Key Votes

1) Homeless $	FOR	5) Ban Drug Test	—	9) SDI Research	FOR
2) Gephardt Amdt	AGN	6) Drug Death Pen	FOR	10) Ban Chem Weaps	AGN
3) Deficit Reduc	AGN	7) Handgun Sales	FOR	11) Aid to Contras	FOR
4) Kill Plnt Clsng Notice	FOR	8) Ban D.C. Abort $	FOR	12) Nuclear Testing	AGN

Election Results

1988 general	Guy Vander Jagt (R)	149,748	(70%)	($450,801)
	David Gawron (D)	64,843	(30%)	($14,866)
1988 primary	Guy Vander Jagt (R), unopposed			
1986 general	Guy Vander Jagt (R)	89,991	(64%)	($398,996)
	Richard Anderson (D)	49,702	(36%)	($18,006)

TENTH DISTRICT

Even half a century ago, the northern part of Michigan's Lower Peninsula, north of Grand Rapids and Saginaw, was already losing population. This area was passed over by the Yankee farmers who were Michigan's first settlers: the land thawed too late in the spring to plow and the frost came too soon in the fall to harvest crops. So the forests of the northern half of the Lower Peninsula were left to the lumber barons to clear-cut late in the 19th century, leaving behind sawdust and stumps that caused huge forest fires. To this day, the timber growth along the inland lakes of the northern Lower Peninsula is new forest, only barely regenerated since that terrific pillage.

On both sides of the boundary of these forest lands and the farmland just to the south is the 10th Congressional District of Michigan, for many years one of the forgotten parts of America. It contains no great cities, although it has some small towns like Owosso (the boyhood home of Thomas E. Dewey), which once had reason to think it might turn into a Lansing or a Grand Rapids; it has college towns like Alma and Mount Pleasant and Big Rapids, where parka-clad students stomp to class through snow and under winter grey skies; it has Midland, home of Dow Chemical, a company that inspires almost unanimous loyalty here and bitter ostracism of any critic; it also has many of Michigan's ski resorts and some of its inland lakes. Here thousands of midwesterners spend summers, sleeping four to a room in log cabins or knotty pine cottages tightly spaced around the lakes, getting up at dawn to fish or, after sleeping late, watching the children swim in the icy green waters. In the fall there are traffic jams as thousands of men drive up north to hunt; in the winter thousands of young people come north to ski. Rapidly rising incomes in auto-affluent Michigan made this resort country accessible not just to white-collar and professional families, but increasingly to blue-collar families as well. And, as everyone got even more affluent and economically secure in the 1970s, they began moving their homes here: retirees, planning to spend the worst of the winter in Florida; young parents willing to give up larger paychecks to raise their families in a natural environment free from the social problems (drugs, crime, racial tensions) they felt existed in Detroit. Since 1970, this part of Michigan has had the state's most rapid population growth.

That growth has made for political change. Ancestrally, these were all Republican counties, suspicious of big cities and labor unions; many of their new residents come from Democratic families. As a result, what was a safe Republican district for decades was the scene of close House elections in 1978, 1980, 1984 and 1986. The winner of the first two was Donald Albosta, a farmer and a Democrat who made a name protesting the state's handling of PBB contamination; he was beaten in a bitter 1984 contest by a new-style Republican, the current congressman, Bill Schuette.

Old-style Republicans here were middle-aged, overweight businessmen from small towns; Schuette (pronounced *Shootie*) is young and looks younger, the stepson of the chairman of Dow Chemical, who has spent over $2 million in his three carefully computerized campaigns. In 1984, the rough-hewn Albosta was attacked by the sleek Schuette for not serving on the Agriculture Committee; Schuette has served there getting aid for farmers who suffered first from flood and then from drought. He got the USDA to buy surplus Michigan cherries and sought government aid for local bean farmers. On most though not all other issues his record has been conservative. He faced bitter opposition from Albosta in 1986, and only barely beat him; in 1988, he won with the second best percentage of any Michigan Republican. In 1989, he got a seat on the Budget Committee, and co-sponsored Senator Pete Domenici's budget-cutting initiative, and in some quarters it was rumored that he would run against Senator Carl Levin in 1990. His youthful good looks might cause him to be underestimated in some quarters. But he showed staying power and good political instincts in his races against Albosta, and a George Bush-like ability to make himself a spokesmen for ordinary voters of varied origins despite what some Democrats (many of them products of an elite class themselves) would call a privileged background.

The People: Est. Pop. 1986: 525,000, up 2.0% 1980–86; Pop. 1980: 514,560, up 23.5% 1970–80. Households (1980): 78% family, 44% with children, 68% married couples; 20.1% housing units rented; median monthly rent: $170; median house value: $34,400. Voting age pop. (1980): 357,369; 1% Spanish origin, 1% Black.

1988 Presidential Vote:

Bush (R)	126,899	(58%)
Dukakis (D)	90,335	(41%)

Rep. Bill Schuette (R)

Elected 1984; b. Oct. 13, 1953, Midland; home, Sanford; Georgetown U., B.S. 1976, U. of San Francisco, J.D. 1979; Episcopalian; single.

Career: Practicing atty., 1979–84.

Offices: 415 CHOB 20515, 202-225-3561. Also 304 E. Main St., P.O. Box 631, Midland 48640, 517-631-2552; 300 W. Main St., Owosso 48867, 517-723-6759; and 120 W. Harris St., Parkview Plaza N., Cadillac 49601, 616-775-2722.

Committees: *Agriculture* (13th of 17 R). Subcommittees: Forests, Family Farms and Energy; Wheat, Soybeans and Feed Grains. *Budget* (13th of 14 R). Subcommittees: Budget Process, Reconciliation and Enforcement; Urgent Fiscal Issues. *Select Committee on Aging* (19th of 26 R). Subcommittees: Housing and Consumer Interests; Retirement Income and Employment.

Group Ratings

	ADA	ACLU	COPE	CFA	LCV	ACU	NTLC	NSI	COC	CEI
1988	40	43	25	64	44	63	74	100	93	41
1987	12	—	17	21	—	65	—	—	80	56

National Journal Ratings

	1988 LIB — 1988 CONS			1987 LIB — 1987 CONS		
Economic	24%	—	74%	34%	—	65%
Social	35%	—	64%	25%	—	73%
Foreign	22%	—	76%	20%	—	76%

Key Votes

1) Homeless $	FOR	5) Ban Drug Test	FOR	9) SDI Research	FOR
2) Gephardt Amdt	AGN	6) Drug Death Pen	FOR	10) Ban Chem Weaps	AGN
3) Deficit Reduc	AGN	7) Handgun Sales	FOR	11) Aid to Contras	FOR
4) Kill Plnt Clsng Notice	FOR	8) Ban D.C. Abort $	FOR	12) Nuclear Testing	AGN

Election Results

1988 general	Bill Schuette (R)....................	152,646	(73%)	($728,533)
	Mathias Forbes (D)...................	55,398	(26%)	($7,809)
1988 primary	Bill Schuette (R)....................	37,969	(100%)	
1986 general	Bill Schuette (R)....................	78,475	(51%)	($897,825)
	Donald Joseph (Don) Albosta (D)	74,941	(49%)	($405,971)

ELEVENTH DISTRICT

"In October, usually, the first snow falls steady on the northland," writes Dixie Lee Franklin in *A Most Superior Land*, "whispering teasing promises of more to come. White fluffy flakes drift lazily from the skies, then turn to whirl off through the trees or to flatten themselves in wet globby flakes against Upper Peninsula windowpanes." The snow continues through May or even June: in the winter of 1978–79 the Keweenaw Peninsula in the northernmost UP (as it is called here) got 390 inches of snow. Far away from any major city, with ground too frozen and a growing season too short for most crops, nearly surrounded by frigid Lake Superior and Lake Michigan, the Upper Peninsula wouldn't have been settled at all but for the ores that prospectors found here—through 1987 the Keweenaw Peninsula copper veins and immediate surrounding areas produced 13.5 billion pounds of copper, the Marquette, Menominee and Gogebic iron ranges more than one billion tons of iron ore. Starting in the 1880s, immigrants came flocking here to work the mines—Irish, Italians, Swedes, Norwegians, miners' sons from Wales and Cornwall and most prominently Finns, who must have found this cold land with its lakes and hills much like their home. By 1900, the UP was a northern industrial belt, with a few bosses and some absentee overlords, and a work force disposed to radical ideas and union movements.

A major strike in 1913–14, falling ore prices after World War I—events that would be long forgotten elsewhere—are remembered in the UP as the beginning of its decline: the UP's population peaked at 332,000 in 1920. The copper veins were mostly worked out by then, mining iron ore became less labor-intensive, and lumber and farming provided only a few thousand jobs. In the last half-century there has been constant outmigration, for Detroit, Chicago, the West Coast; the UP's population has hovered around 300,000, rising to 318,000 in 1980. The Upper Peninsula forms about 60% of Michigan's 11th Congressional District, which has 40% of Michigan's land but only 6% of its people and extends 477 miles from end to end. Its Lower Peninsula portions are fast-growing, especially the affluent resort towns of Petoskey and Charlevoix on the Lake Michigan side, the ski areas around Boyne City and Gaylord, and the less flashy Tawas-Oscoda area on Lake Huron.

Politically, most of the UP is Democratic while the Lower Peninsula is Republican; but recent population movements have both regions trending in the other direction. In House elections the UP has, except for 1964, elected Republicans since the 1940s. This has reflected the strength of successive incumbents, most recently of Robert Davis, a mortician and former state legislator who has concentrated mostly on bringing federal dollars to the UP and northern Michigan. Davis serves on the Armed Services Committee (there are a couple of Air Force bases in the 11th protecting our northern borders) and is also ranking Republican on Merchant Marine and Fisheries and on the Coast Guard Subcommittee (working to clean up the St. Mary's River). He works to bring community health centers to and keep airports in the 11th District, and he has sponsored a National Historic Park in the Calumet copper mining district. His voting record is rather liberal economically, and mixed otherwise—again responsive to the district.

For Davis, this seems to be a winning formula. The Democrats, for some reason, run their best-financed challengers in presidential years; state Senator Mitch Irwin, their 1988 nominee, carried his own Republican-leaning base around Sault Ste. Marie but lost the Democratic-leaning western and central UP to Davis, who as usual won about 60% of the vote.

The People: Est. Pop. 1986: 514,000, dn. 0.1% 1980–86; Pop. 1980: 514,560, up 10.9% 1970–80. Households (1980): 75% family, 40% with children, 65% married couples; 22.8% housing units rented; median monthly rent: $160; median house value: $30,800. Voting age pop. (1980): 367,779; 1% American Indian, 1% Black.

1988 Presidential Vote:

Bush (R)	117,173	(52%)
Dukakis (D)	105,030	(47%)

Rep. Robert W. (Bob) Davis (R)

Elected 1978; b. July 31, 1932, Marquette; home, Gaylord; N. MI U., 1950, 1952, Hillsdale Col., 1951–52, Wayne St. U., B.S. 1954; Episcopalian; separated.

Career: Mortician, 1954–66; St. Ignace City Cncl., 1964–66; MI House of Reps., 1966–70; MI Senate, 1970–78, Major. Whip, 1970–74, Minor. Ldr., 1974–78.

Offices: 2417 RHOB 20515, 202-225-4735. Also 2400 U.S. 41 W, Marquette 49855, 906-228-3700; 145 Main St., Ste. 103B, Gaylord, 49735, 517-732-3151; City-County Bldg., Sault Ste. Marie 49783, 906-635-5261; 144 S. 2d St., Alpena 49707, 517-356-2028; 18 N. 22d St., Escanaba 49829, 906-786-4504; 100 Portage, Haughton 49931, 906-482-2464; 200 E. 410 N. Main St., Cheboygan 49721, 616-627-4603; and 207 E. Mitchell St., Petoskey 49770, 616-347-4960.

Committees: *Armed Services* (6th of 21 R). Subcommittees: Procurement and Military Nuclear Systems; Research and Development. *Merchant Marine and Fisheries* (Ranking Member of 17 R). Subcommittees: Coast Guard and Navigation (Ranking Member).

Group Ratings

	ADA	ACLU	COPE	CFA	LCV	ACU	NTLC	NSI	COC	CEI
1988	60	68	64	82	31	42	30	100	29	19
1987	44	—	61	43	—	33	—	—	40	20

National Journal Ratings

	1988 LIB — 1988 CONS	1987 LIB — 1987 CONS
Economic	71% — 23%	42% — 56%
Social	48% — 51%	47% — 53%
Foreign	35% — 64%	32% — 67%

Key Votes

1) Homeless $	FOR	5) Ban Drug Test	AGN	9) SDI Research	FOR
2) Gephardt Amdt	FOR	6) Drug Death Pen	FOR	10) Ban Chem Weaps	AGN
3) Deficit Reduc	AGN	7) Handgun Sales	FOR	11) Aid to Contras	FOR
4) Kill Plnt Clsng Notice	AGN	8) Ban D.C. Abort $	FOR	12) Nuclear Testing	AGN

Election Results

1988 general	Robert W. (Bob) Davis (R)	129,085	(60%)	($680,819)
	Mitch Irwin (D)	86,526	(40%)	($415,660)
1988 primary	Robert W. (Bob) Davis (R), unopposed			
1986 general	Robert W. (Bob) Davis (R)	91,575	(63%)	($207,080)
	Robert Anderson (D)	53,180	(37%)	($58,826)

TWELFTH DISTRICT

One of the most pivotal political constituencies in the United States—visited by hordes of journalists, traversed by presidential candidates and attendant camera crews, the place where Michael Dukakis took his ride in the tank—is Macomb County, Michigan, just northeast of Detroit. These billiard-table flat lands 50 years ago were mostly empty, with farms and occasional gas stations and mom-and-pop stores at crosslights or summer cottages along the shores of Lake St. Clair. There were 107,000 people in Macomb County in 1940, many of them in the old sulphur-water spa town of Mount Clemens; in 1980, Macomb's population was 694,000. Almost all of that difference represents a pouring out of excess people from Detroit: Polish-Americans marching out Van Dyke from Detroit and Hamtramck to Warren, Italian-American heading out Gratiot from the east side of Detroit to Roseville and Clinton township, Belgian-Americans from the Mack Avenue corridor moving out farther to St. Clair Shores.

These new suburbanites were heavily Catholic, often blue collar, at least modestly affluent and ancestrally Democratic. They accepted the New Deal as part of their natural heritage, but also resented the efforts of Detroit politicians to tax them to pay for welfare and were fearful of the high crime rates they had left behind in Detroit's black neighborhoods. As more Detroiters moved north of the Eight Mile Road line, Macomb became more Democratic, and in 1960, the county voted 63% for America's first Catholic President, John F. Kennedy: it was the most Democratic major suburban county in the United States. Since then, Macomb has been moving away from the Democrats. It deserted Governor John Swainson in 1962 for supporting Detroit's right to tax suburbanites. It voted for a Republican governor in 1970 when he supported state aid to parochial schools. It voted against Democrats up and down the line in 1972 in protest against a federal judge's plan (never put into effect) requiring busing of suburban public schoolers to Detroit. Northern Macomb County voters in 1983 recalled a Democratic state senator who backed a tax increase and replaced him with a Republican. Macomb voted twice for Ronald Reagan for President in the 1980s, and in 1988 for the very unethnic George Bush. This represents a sharp shift: in 1960, Macomb was 17% more Democratic than next-door, more upscale Oakland County; in 1984 and 1988, it voted only 1% more Democratic than Oakland.

But perhaps the interesting question is why it's still considered noteworthy when Macomb votes Republican. True, it does elect nominal Democrats to local office and mostly Democrats to the state legislature, but it has not given a Democratic presidential candidate a majority since 1968. Why should it, when its list of grievances and differences with national Democrats has grown with every quadrennium, while its memories of Franklin Roosevelt and John Kennedy grow dimmer? Macomb's voters are affluent and able to advance themselves, not huddled masses in need of economic redistribution, and in the 1970s and 1980s, these suburbs have grown perceptibly more white-collar and less blue-collar, more market-oriented and less unionized. At the same time, they are mostly hostile to the culturally liberal themes which so many national Democrats like to sound. It remains true that it's hard for a Democrat to carry Michigan without carrying Macomb (though Senator Carl Levin did in 1984). But that may be more a symptom than a cause of the fact that Michigan in the 1980s has become as Republican in national contests as the nation generally.

Michigan's 12th Congressional District, which includes most of Macomb plus most of St. Clair County and the old industrial city of Port Huron to the north, still elects a Democratic congressman though, indeed one of the leaders of the Democratic Party in the House; but in 1988, after his first term in the leadership, he won with a less than impressive margin, which may augur serious contests here in the future. David Bonior has deep roots in Macomb, he was a Vietnam-era veteran (serving stateside), he has campaigned hard on environmental issues, he wears a gray-sprinkled beard and, usually, a serious or even sad expression. Conscientious, intense, concerned about the environment and determined to keep the United States out of any Vietnam-type war, he is a fine representative of the generation of Democrats whose attitudes were stamped by the years of Vietnam and Watergate.

Bonior has also shown the talent and ambition that are characteristic of this group. He was elected to the state legislature in 1972 and, after a tough primary and general election, to the House in 1976; running after an ice storm had killed many Macomb County trees, he gave out thousands of pine seedlings as a campaign gimmick. He formed the Vietnam Veterans caucus in the House and wrote a book on the subject of the neglect of Vietnam veterans. As an environmentalist, he opposed not only water projects in other states, but also the Army Corps of

616   MICHIGAN

Engineers' proposal for year-round navigation on the Great Lakes, which he knew would be expensive and believed would damage fish and lakefront property. Early on, Bonior became known as a close student of House procedures, and he won a seat—a sure sign of leadership favor—on the House Rules Committee. One of the best House athletes, he became known as a team player and a leader: he played a lead role from 1983 to 1988 as one of the Democrats' chief opponents of aid to the Nicaraguan contras. From his days in Catholic school and college, Bonior had heard of the evils of the Somoza regime; he traveled to Nicaragua in 1985 and talked with President Daniel Ortega; he argued his case passionately, suggesting Nicaragua could be another Vietnam, and had the satisfaction of seeing military aid to the contras shut off.

One of Bonior's chief allies in that fight was then Majority Leader Jim Wright, and when Wright became Speaker he surprised many by naming Bonior as chief deputy Democratic whip, the number four position in the leadership. That has required Bonior to temper his own views on occasion, as in some of the compromise contra packages, but Wright was evidently impressed by Bonior's unassuming temperament and capacity for hard work, and he could not have failed to understand how his selection of Bonior would impress others in the Vietnam generation, who opposed contra aid with religious fervor, that the new Speaker was really on their side. Bonior has continued also on the Rules Committee, using his power there to advance his views on national issues and on local matters as well; he serves too on the board of Gallaudet University for the deaf, and played a role in acceding to student protests and selecting a deaf president in 1988.

Bonior is by no means inattentive to the 12th District, and can cite local projects from obtaining a UDAG (urban development grant) for St. Clair to keeping open the Can-Am shop on the Blue Water Bridge from Port Huron to Canada to working to maintain water quality in the Great Lakes and maintaining Selfridge Air Force Base near Mount Clemens. He still distributes seedlings—"Bonior pines"—to local students by the thousands and is the chief congressional promoter of Arbor Day. But his increasing prominence as a national Democratic leader may not have helped him with Macomb County voters and may have stimulated the serious challenge in 1988 from Doug Carl, the state senator elected in 1983 in northern Macomb. In the manner of House Democrats these days, Bonior vastly outraised Carl and with the advantages of incumbency outcampaigned him. Yet his percentage declined from 66% in 1986 to 54% in 1988—not entirely illogical when you remember that Michael Dukakis, whose issue stands are similar to Bonior's, was winning 39% in Macomb. This was easily the closest contest for any member of the Democratic leadership, and it will be interesting to see whether the national Republicans will target this district again, and whether Carl, whose legislative seat was not up in 1988 but will be in 1990, will run again.

The People: Est. Pop. 1986: 520,600, up 1.2% 1980–86; Pop. 1980: 514,560, up 9.4% 1970–80. Households (1980): 78% family, 44% with children, 66% married couples; 22.1% housing units rented; median monthly rent: $243; median house value: $47,200. Voting age pop. (1980): 362,035; 2% Black, 1% Spanish origin.

1988 Presidential Vote:

Bush (R)	126,846	(60%)
Dukakis (D)	82,413	(39%)

Rep. David E. Bonior (D)

Elected 1976; b. June 6, 1945, Detroit; home, Mt. Clemens; U. of IA, B.A. 1967, Chapman Col., M.A. 1972; Roman Catholic; divorced.

Career: Probation officer and adoption caseworker, 1967–68; USAF, 1968–72; MI House of Reps., 1973–77.

Offices: 2242 RHOB 20515, 202-225-2106. Also 82 Macomb Pl., Mt. Clemens 48043, 313-469-3232; and 526 Water St., Port Huron 48060, 313-987-8889.

Committees: *Rules* (5th of 9 D). Subcommittee: Rules of the House.

Group Ratings

	ADA	ACLU	COPE	CFA	LCV	ACU	NTLC	NSI	COC	CEI
1988	95	95	94	82	69	4	5	0	21	7
1987	88	—	93	83	—	0	—	—	8	8

National Journal Ratings

	1988 LIB — 1988 CONS		1987 LIB — 1987 CONS	
Economic	92%	— 0%	73%	— 0%
Social	82%	— 17%	69%	— 30%
Foreign	84%	— 0%	81%	— 0%

Key Votes

1) Homeless $	AGN	5) Ban Drug Test	AGN	9) SDI Research	AGN
2) Gephardt Amdt	FOR	6) Drug Death Pen	AGN	10) Ban Chem Weaps	FOR
3) Deficit Reduc	FOR	7) Handgun Sales	AGN	11) Aid to Contras	AGN
4) Kill Plnt Clsng Notice	AGN	8) Ban D.C. Abort $	—	12) Nuclear Testing	FOR

Election Results

1988 general	David E. Bonior (D)	108,158	(54%)	($434,200)
	Douglas Carl (R).....................	91,780	(45%)	($143,886)
1988 primary	David E. Bonior (D), unopposed			
1986 general	David E. Bonior (D)	87,643	(66%)	($283,904)
	Candice Miller (R)	44,442	(34%)	($62,244)

THIRTEENTH DISTRICT

Detroit is America's first automobile city, not just the city that manufactured most of the nation's cars but the first big city built to automobile scale. When Henry Ford drove his first car out of his garage in 1903, Detroit was a second-rank industrial city, no bigger than Milwaukee, with less than half a million people and extending no further than four or five miles out from the site where the French built Fort Pontchartrain on the Detroit River in 1701. As the Motor City boomed, it grew outward along nine-lane-wide avenues and six-lane freeways; the auto companies themselves put their factories and headquarters out near the edge of urban settlement; as early as 1954, the nation's first big suburban shopping center, with parking for 10,000 cars, drew the retail trade from downtown. As Detroit expanded to 4 million, each generation seemed to move out the roadways rapidly and in all directions, leaving behind the previous generation's neighborhoods and civic institutions.

Today, all of turn-of-the-century Detroit could be fitted into the inner city 13th Congressional District. Here is downtown, where the giant Hudson's department store is closed and the 70-story Renaissance Center with one empty tower is inaccessible from the sidewalk (you can only get there by car); here are radial avenues with boarded-up stores and hulks of movie palaces; here are side streets with abandoned houses, many of them burned by arsonists, often on Halloween, some occupied by squatters. The 13th District still has some viable middle-class neighborhoods and even includes two of the exclusive Grosse Pointe suburbs. But overall its population has declined from about 800,000 in 1960 to 688,000 in 1970 to 444,000 in 1986—the biggest decline in the United States. Put another way: inner city Detroit has lost about 40% of its population since the riot of 1967. No wonder the Catholic Church closed more than one-third of its Detroit churches in 1988.

The chief reason for the population loss is crime. Readers of Elmore Leonard will know that Detroit has never been a gentle city, but first in the middle 1970s and then again in the late 1980s Detroit has had murder rates far higher than those in any other major American city, until Washington, D.C., surpassed it in 1988. Robbery and drug traffic rates are harder to measure, but it's likely that Detroit is also at the top—or bottom—of the list on these as well. With the proliferation of guns, criminal or personal altercations quickly become homicide; neighbors, frustrated by the police's inability to act, set fire to the crack house next door. This social disorganization cannot be blamed necessarily on lack of government action: for 25 years Detroit has had mayors, civic activists, and union leaders who have supported anti-poverty and anti-discrimination programs. But liberal spending programs and black hiring initiatives can't make up for the loss of neighborhoods' natural leaders, who have long since fled as crime grew, and the deterioration of civic institutions. Nor can the local government cure the habits of non-cooperation with the police and passive acquiescence in the face of drug-dealing and stolen goods sales. Those who argue that liberal teachings, which stress society's injustices and deny the individual's responsibility for his acts have, by undermining confidence in the legitimacy of existing institutions, helped to create the moral climate in which violent crime can flourish.

In early 1989, there were even signs that in this overwhelmingly liberal and Democratic city, the liberal Democratic mayor, Coleman Young, might be in trouble seeking a fifth term in November 1989. Young has emphasized for years his ability to bring federal money into the city, as for his downtown Peoplemover project, and he has done an effective job reviving the warehouse district on the river east of the Renaissance Center; he tried in 1976, 1981, and 1988 to get voters to legalize casino gambling. But he angrily rejected demands for gun control and even more angrily has denied that there is anything unusual or especially alarming about Detroit's crime rate. When Young was first elected in 1973, it was enough that he was a talented black politician running against a somewhat less talented white. But despite his accomplishments, Detroit voters may now be holding Young responsible for the desperate and scarcely civilized quality of life they see every day around them; and if they do, his political career may be over.

The congressman from the 13th District is George Crockett, a longtime political ally of Young and a major figure in Detroit's public life for decades himself. Crockett was general counsel of the United Auto Workers in 1946 and 1947, part of the left-wing group sometimes allied with Communists which was thrown out by Walter Reuther's liberal anti-Communist group in 1947. In those days, when most conventional politicians resisted even the mildest civil rights measures (the Fair Employment Practices bureaucracy Crockett worked on in the war was created only after A. Philip Randolph threatened to disrupt the war effort if it was not), the Communists seemed the surest friends of civil rights—long before the execrable record of the Soviet dictatorship and the great success of American democracy on civil rights had become apparent. As a judge on Detroit's criminal court in the 1960s, Crockett aroused great controversy when, prompted only by his own ideas of justice, he went down to the courthouse in the middle of the night, held hearings, and released on bail men arrested for killing a policeman. Whites launched a movement to recall him; but he had solid black support and was never defeated. Forced to retire as a judge after age 70, he ran for the 13th District seat from which Charles Diggs, convicted of payroll-padding, was forced to retire, and was easily elected in 1980 at age 71. Routinely reelected, he does not seem to address the appalling reign of crime in his district; implicit in his voting record is a conviction that it should be addressed by more government aid to the poor.

In 1987, Crockett became chairman of the Foreign Affairs subcommittee handling Latin America, a potentially visible post, to which he brings the suspicions of one who sees the United States as too often the supporter of right-wing dictatorships and racist regimes, and which sees Soviet-allied states like Nicaragua and Cuba as progressive to the extent they redistribute income, provide welfare state services, and stamp out racism. Some conservatives attacked him as "a threat to national security," but they dwelled on his actions as counsel for Communists in the 1940s and his being jailed while serving as a counsel to a witness before the old House Un-American Activities Committee. In the process, they largely missed the point that the views of this congressman, who abstained on the resolution passed 416–0 criticizing the Soviet Union for the shooting down of Korean Air Lines 007, had views not much different on Latin policy from those of most Democrats. The fact that many were unjustly accused of being Communists in the past does not obscure the fact that Crockett's views seem consistently over the years to have followed something like a pro-Soviet line, one that few Democratic congressmen share and most would be uncomfortable defending to their constituents. But of course Crockett kept his chair (the Democrats were not about to vote out a black) and he in turn kept quiet and not very visible, performing his duties with the courtesy and serenity that have marked his public career for nearly 50 years, and in times of controversy much more bitter than these. He is certain to be reelected in the 13th District, which despite its depopulation is likely to survive as a black-majority constituency for the 1990s, since no Michigan politician wants to be seen as depriving blacks of a seat.

The People: Est. Pop. 1986: 444,600, dn. 13.6% 1980–86; Pop. 1980: 514,560, dn. 30.8% 1970–80. Households (1980): 60% family, 36% with children, 31% married couples; 59.1% housing units rented; median monthly rent: $143; median house value: $17,900. Voting age pop. (1980): 360,241; 67% Black, 3% Spanish origin, 1% Asian origin.

1988 Presidential Vote:

Dukakis (D)		100,969	(86%)
Bush (R)		16,127	(14%)

Rep. George W. Crockett, Jr. (D)

Elected 1980; b. Aug. 10, 1909, Jacksonville, FL; home, Detroit; Morehouse Col., A.B. 1931, U. of MI, J.D. 1934; Baptist; married (Harriette).

Career: Practicing atty., 1934–39, 1946–66; Sr. Atty., U.S. Dept. of Labor, 1939–43; Founder-Dir., UAW Fair Practices Dept., 1944–46; Judge, Recorder's Crt., 1966–78; Visiting Judge, MI Crt. of Appeals, 1979; Acting Corp. Cnsl., Detroit, 1980.

Offices: 2235 RHOB 20515, 202-225-2261. Also 8401 Woodward Ave., Detroit 48202, 313-874-4900.

Committees: *Foreign Affairs* (7th of 28 D). Subcommittees: Africa; Western Hemisphere Affairs (Chairman). *Judiciary* (11th of 21 D). Subcommittees: Civil and Constitutional Rights; Courts, Intellectual Property and the Administration of Justice. *Select Committee on Aging* (17th of 39 D). Subcommittee: Retirement Income and Employment.

Group Ratings

	ADA	ACLU	COPE	CFA	LCV	ACU	NTLC	NSI	COC	CEI
1988	85	95	94	100	75	0	9	0	33	12
1987	84	—	93	79	—	0	—	—	0	7

National Journal Ratings

	1988 LIB — 1988 CONS		1987 LIB — 1987 CONS	
Economic	92%	— 0%	73%	— 0%
Social	82%	— 17%	78%	— 0%
Foreign	84%	— 0%	81%	— 0%

Key Votes

1) Homeless $	AGN	5) Ban Drug Test	—	9) SDI Research	—
2) Gephardt Amdt	FOR	6) Drug Death Pen	AGN	10) Ban Chem Weaps	FOR
3) Deficit Reduc	FOR	7) Handgun Sales	AGN	11) Aid to Contras	AGN
4) Kill Plnt Clsng Notice	AGN	8) Ban D.C. Abort $	AGN	12) Nuclear Testing	FOR

Election Results

1988 general	George Crockett, Jr. (D)	99,751	(87%)	($84,024)
	John Savage II (R)	13,196	(12%)	
1988 primary	George Crockett, Jr. (D)	18,250	(51%)	
	Barbara-Rose Collins (D)	15,438	(43%)	
	Others	21,045	(6%)	
1986 general	George W. Crockett, Jr. (D)	76,435	(85%)	($56,271)
	Mary Griffin (R)	12,395	(14%)	($13,663)

FOURTEENTH DISTRICT

Hamtramck may be surrounded by Detroit but half a century ago you could tell where you were by the signs: "a chain drug store is advertised by a huge *apteka* sign, and on the second floor windows are *adwokayt* and *dentysta*. There are many 'bazaars,' their windows a melange of dream books, pictures of saints, razor strops, chewing tobacco, and first communion dresses. The windows of the white and gleaming *sklad wedlin* are neatly packed with Polish foods and display an amazing variety of sausages—big, small, round, loaf-shaped, red, brown, black, ringed, and curled." This was America's premier Polish-American city, and today it remains the spiritual heart of Detroit's Polish-Americans (Pope John Paul II visited here in 1987), though most have long since dispersed to the suburbs. Michigan's 14th Congressional District includes many of these areas—Hamtramck, much of Detroit's east side, and the suburbs of Warren and Sterling Heights; it also spreads to the east where the ethnic flavor is more Flemish, to affluent Grosse Pointe Shores on Lake St. Clair and Rochester far to the north, and to Hazel Park and Madison Heights where most people speak in the accents of the Kentucky and Tennessee hills.

The congressman from the 14th is Democrat Dennis Hertel. Hertel serves on the Armed Services Committee, where he is one of the members more skeptical about military projects; he has led moves against the rail-based MX missile and against SDI deployment unless approved by Congress; he has proposed a new civilian procurement agency which would keep operational officers away from purchasing decisions. Hertel wants to target defense spending in high-unemployment states; Michigan, the arsenal of democracy in World War II, has little defense spending these days, though what there is tends to be in this district, including the Sterling Heights tank plant where Michael Dukakis took his famous ride. He also chairs the Oceanography Subcommittee of Merchant Marine.

Hertel is from a political family; his two brothers also hold elective office on the east side. His own critical election was in 1980, when his popularity as a state legislator enabled him to win an eight-candidate primary with 62% of the vote and his hard work enabled him to beat a Republican and former TV anchor. His next hurdle, the 1982 redistricting, turned out to be easy when James Blanchard gave up his House seat to run for governor; Hertel got some of Blanchard's old territory in Oakland County. Now he looks ahead to 1992 and the squeeze in Detroit area districts; Republicans in the meantime give him no problem.

The People: Est. Pop. 1986: 487,200, dn. 5.3% 1980–86; Pop. 1980: 514,559, dn. 1.2% 1970–80. Households (1980): 76% family, 39% with children, 62% married couples; 20.8% housing units rented; median monthly rent: $223; median house value: $39,000. Voting age pop. (1980): 372,422; 4% Black, 1% Asian origin, 1% Spanish origin.

1988 Presidential Vote:

Bush (R)	107,535	(55%)
Dukakis (D)	84,746	(44%)

Rep. Dennis M. Hertel (D)

Elected 1980; b. Dec. 7, 1948, Detroit; home, Harper Woods; E. MI U., B.S. 1971, Wayne St. U., J.D. 1974; Roman Catholic; married (Cynthia).

Career: Practicing atty.; MI House of Reps., 1974–80.

Offices: 2442 RHOB 20515, 202-225-6276. Also 28221 Mound Rd., Warren 48092, 313-574-9420; and 18927 Kelly Rd., Detroit 48224, 313-526-5900.

Committees: *Armed Services* (14th of 31 D). Subcommittees: Military Personnel and Compensation; Investigations; Research and Development. *Merchant Marine and Fisheries* (8th of 26 D). Subcommittees: Oceanography (Chairman); Merchant Marine. *Select Committee on Aging* (19th of 39 D). Subcommittee: Health and Long-Term Care.

Group Ratings

	ADA	ACLU	COPE	CFA	LCV	ACU	NTLC	NSI	COC	CEI
1988	95	91	94	100	81	4	16	0	21	10
1987	88	—	94	100	—	0	—	—	13	8

National Journal Ratings

	1988 LIB — 1988 CONS		1987 LIB — 1987 CONS	
Economic	92%	0%	73%	0%
Social	83%	15%	78%	0%
Foreign	79%	16%	76%	19%

Key Votes

1) Homeless $	AGN	5) Ban Drug Test	AGN	9) SDI Research	AGN
2) Gephardt Amdt	FOR	6) Drug Death Pen	AGN	10) Ban Chem Weaps	FOR
3) Deficit Reduc	FOR	7) Handgun Sales	AGN	11) Aid to Contras	AGN
4) Kill Plnt Clsng Notice	AGN	8) Ban D.C. Abort $	AGN	12) Nuclear Testing	FOR

Election Results

1988 general	Dennis M. Hertel (D)	111,612	(63%)	($137,560)
	Kenneth McNealy (R)	64,750	(36%)	($3,537)
1988 primary	Dennis M. Hertel (D), unopposed			
1986 general	Dennis M. Hertel (D)	92,328	(73%)	($172,835)
	Stanley Grot (R).......................	33,831	(27%)	($73,988)

FIFTEENTH DISTRICT

It is, literally, the Detroit Industrial Expressway, built in 1942 so workers from Detroit could get to the Willow Run bomber plant 30 miles away; for years it was known by travelers for its pothole-pocked pavement and the giant Goodyear tire over the billboard with the digital counter showing this year's (American) car production. Nowadays this stretch of Interstate 94 just west of the city limits of Detroit has been repaved and renamed. Governor James Blanchard has taken to calling it Automation Alley and touting it as the world center of robotic manufacturing. In fact this longtime industrial corridor is sprouting new factories and new businesses, built not by Ford or one of the other automotive Big Three but by smaller entrepreneurs, seeking out market niches and responding to market cues around the world, using the fabricating expertise and skilled labor force that has been built up over generations in the Detroit area.

Michigan's 15th Congressional District follows I-94 and Automation Alley from the city limits of the Ford headquarters city of Dearborn, west past Willow Run and Ypsilanti almost to Ann Arbor. In the half century since the Willow Run expressway was built, the area around it has filled up with working-class suburbs and some that are more upscale. Some are gleaming and carefully trimmed, like Westland (named after a shopping center) and Canton Township (one of the few parts of the district with recent population growth). Others, like Romulus, have the look of places where people with not much money worked a little at a time to build their own houses, on land so flat that the ground oozes with water after it rains. Historically, this has been Democratic country since the UAW forced an unwilling Henry Ford to sign a collective bargaining contract in 1941. But as working-class wages went up and working-class conscious-ness went down, and grievances with liberal Democrats over busing and other issues have arisen, the Democratic margins here have diminished, and the 15th District voted twice for Ronald Reagan and voted pretty close to the national average for George Bush in 1989.

The congressman from the 15th District is William Ford, a Democrat first elected in 1964 and a big enough man in the House now that it need hardly be noted that he is no relation to Henry or

Gerald. Ford is chairman of the Post Office and Civil Service Committee and the heir apparent, second behind octogenarian Chairman Augustus Hawkins, on Education and Labor. Ford has a political faith considered a little old-fashioned in some quarters: he is a believer in labor unions, and in strengthening them; he believes in the Great Society programs he voted for as a freshman; he believes in a generous, active federal government, helping people who cannot help themselves. Since 1974, he has been the major sponsor of the plant closing notice bill that was attached to the 1988 trade bill and, after its veto, passed separately. On cultural and foreign issues, he also has a liberal voting record. But his real fervor and energy seems concentrated on economic issues, in the broad sense of the term.

The Post Office chair is an often thankless job. Ford is a strong supporter of unions for government workers, and wants to repeal the Hatch Act and let them engage fully in politics. But he doesn't want them to have the right to strike. He pushed through a new federal retirement system and wants to put the Postal Service off budget to protect postal wages from cuts. He stakes out liberal positions but is willing sometimes to compromise, as he did on the Carter civil service reform. Education and Labor, in contrast, was the glamour committee of the House when Ford came to Washington, with jurisdiction over the new and exciting anti-poverty programs. Now it is a very practical body, on which organized labor and education lobbies are counting to protect the gains they have won in the past. Ford and some other canny politicians have managed to save programs and preserve benefits more than almost anyone thought possible. On the committee, Ford has specialized in the big money education bills (such as ESEA—the Elementary and Secondary Education Act).

Ford wins reelection without serious competition in the 15th District. But in the last two presidential elections, his percentages were 60% and 64%, the lowest of his House career. But these are more a sign of national Democratic weakness in Automation Alley than of any serious threat to Ford's tenure.

The People: Est. Pop. 1986: 509,600, dn. 1.0% 1980–86; Pop. 1980: 514,560, up 11.1% 1970–80. Households (1980): 78% family, 48% with children, 65% married couples; 28.6% housing units rented; median monthly rent: $258; median house value: $46,400. Voting age pop. (1980): 356,253; 5% Black, 1% Spanish origin, 1% Asian origin.

1988 Presidential Vote:

	Bush (R)	95,010	(54%)
	Dukakis (D)	79,994	(45%)

Rep. William D. Ford (D)

Elected 1964; b. Aug. 6, 1927, Detroit; home, Taylor; Wayne St. U., 1947–48, U. of Denver, B.S. 1949, J.D. 1951; United Church of Christ; divorced.

Career: Navy, 1944–46; Practicing atty., 1951–60; Taylor Township Justice of the Peace, 1955–57; Melvindale City Atty., 1957–59; MI Senate, 1962–64.

Offices: 239 CHOB 20515, 202-225-6261. Also Federal Bldg., Wayne 48184, 313-722-1411; and 31 S. Huron St., Ypsilanti 48197, 313-482-6636.

Committees: *Education and Labor* (2d of 22 D). Subcommittees: Elementary, Secondary and Vocational Education; Health and Safety; Labor-Management Relations; Postsecondary Education. *Post Office and Civil Service* (Chairman of 15 D). Subcommittee: Investigations (Chairman).

Group Ratings

	ADA	ACLU	COPE	CFA	LCV	ACU	NTLC	NSI	COC	CEI
1988	100	95	97	82	69	0	6	0	23	10
1987	92	—	97	64	—	0	—	—	0	7

National Journal Ratings

	1988 LIB — 1988 CONS	1987 LIB — 1987 CONS
Economic	87% — 8%	73% — 0%
Social	86% — 0%	70% — 28%
Foreign	84% — 0%	81% — 0%

Key Votes

1) Homeless $	AGN	5) Ban Drug Test	AGN	9) SDI Research	AGN
2) Gephardt Amdt	FOR	6) Drug Death Pen	AGN	10) Ban Chem Weaps	FOR
3) Deficit Reduc	FOR	7) Handgun Sales	AGN	11) Aid to Contras	AGN
4) Kill Plnt Clsng Notice	AGN	8) Ban D.C. Abort $	AGN	12) Nuclear Testing	FOR

Election Results

1988 general	William D. Ford (D)................	104,596	(64%)	($234,435)
	Burl Adkins (R)	56,963	(35%)	($7,993)
1988 primary	William D. Ford (D).................	20,062	(100%)	
1986 general	William D. Ford (D).................	77,950	(75%)	($306,543)
	Glenn Kassel (R).....................	25,078	(24%)	($5,600)

SIXTEENTH DISTRICT

Along the Detroit River, the chokepoint of the Great Lakes, is one of America's great industrial corridors: steel and chemical plants line the water, their dark and rusted hulks glaring across at Canada. Up the sluggish Rouge River lies the giant Rouge complex, built by Henry Ford in the 1910s for $1 billion so that he could convert Great Lake freighter and railroad car loads of iron ore, coal, limestone and sand into automobiles in 48 hours. This swampy, low-lying land, along the nation's most heavily trafficked waterway and within easy reach of the great east-west rail lines, was a natural place for industry in the early 20th century, and the residential neighborhoods around the older factories and well within range of their sulfurous odors, with their neat, tightly packed houses, were the natural homes of the migrants—Polish, Hungarian, black, Italian, more recently Mexican and Arab (the area has America's largest concentration of Arab-Americans)—who came to work there. This industrial area has seen better times: some of the factories give out no sulfurous flares night or day, and the nearby neighborhoods have been abandoned as the original migrants' children have moved outward in the Detroit area or beyond. The 16th Congressional District, which in the 1960s consisted of Dearborn and the downriver communities, has now had to spread south into Monroe County along Lake Erie and inland to the old Yankee town of Adrian to meet the equal-population standard. The political tradition here, heavily Democratic from the New Deal until the late 1960s, has become more inconstant today in national and even state elections. But it remains solidly supportive of its congressman, John Dingell.

And for good reason. Dingell is one of the three or four most powerful Members of the House, the chairman since 1981 of the House Energy and Commerce Committee, and simply "the best congressman" according to *Washington Monthly* magazine. A *National Journal* poll of lobbyists voted him "the most effective House Member." These are judgments few would quibble with. Under Dingell, Energy and Commerce "claims jurisdiction over anything that moves, burns or is sold," according to *National Journal's* Richard E. Cohen and Burt Solomon:

over health, securities markets, telecommunications, energy, railroads, consumer protection, clean air. In the 1980s, it has been the most sought-after committee assignment for Democrats; it handles up to 40% of all House bills and has the largest budget and staff of any House committee. But John Dingell's power comes not just from that. It comes from his aggressiveness, his ability, his hard work and his determination to do his duty, and to see that others do theirs. He has assembled a top-notch staff that is solidly loyal to him—and never condescends to him or smirks about him behind his back, as so many staffers do. He insists that facts be solidly documented. He gives leeway—and often valuable publicity—to subcommittee chairmen and to junior members, particularly on the Oversight and Investigations Subcommittee he chairs. But only those he respects and believes have played fair with him; others get nothing—like James Scheuer, number two Democrat on the committee but chairman of none of its subcommittees. Dingell knows the rules, and is willing to use them to the utmost in his own interest; he swings a very fast gavel indeed when he wants to; his temper will flare up and he doesn't mind being called "Big John" or "the Truck." But it's hard to find anyone who will say he is unfair.

Dingell's committee and subcommittee made news and law again and again in the Reagan years. It was a Dingell request for information from the General Accounting Office that triggered the investigation of Michael Deaver for lobbying the White House before he'd been out of office for the requisite time; Dingell's curiosity was piqued when he read that Deaver, ordinarily uninterested in policy, worked to shape an agreement with Canadians on acid rain which Dingell, who thinks the acid rain problem is overstated and many proposed remedies unwarranted, opposed. It was Dingell's demands for subpoenas that drove Anne Burford out as head of the Environmental Protection Agency and led to the conviction of EPA official Rita Lavelle. It was Dingell's subcommittee that found out that the Pentagon had paid $640 for a toilet seat and that General Dynamics had billed the Pentagon for country club dues and dog kennel boarding. It was Dingell's committee that held up the sale of Conrail to the Norfolk Southern, which resulted in its sale by public offering instead. It is Dingell's committee which superintends the communications industry, handling issues like the AT&T breakup and its consequences. It is Dingell's committee that passes bills on insider trading, leveraged buyouts, greenmail and hostile takeovers. It has jurisdiction over health (Dingell wants to stop drug companies from giving doctors free samples of prescription medicines), energy (Dingell has resisted proposals to complete the deregulation of natural gas), and the environment.

Dingell has not been successful on every issue. He has clashed with subcommittee chairmen Henry Waxman on the Clean Air Act and James Florio on the Superfund. In general, Dingell supports government regulation, but he is open to the argument, and not only when the auto and steel industries are involved, that regulation is strangling an enterprise. On trade, he strongly favors retaliating against Japan and other countries whose practices he considers unfair; and though Ways and Means tends to have jurisdiction here, he is a force to be reckoned with on the issue. He has a reputation, earned over many years, as a conservationist; he is an enthusiastic hunter (and opponent of gun controls) and an avid outdoorsman, and he fought to maintain natural habitats and environments long before it was fashionable. For years he stayed on the Merchant Marine and Fisheries Committee not, as most Members do, to funnel subsidies to the maritime industry, but to advance conservation.

Dingell has been around Capitol Hill longer than just about anyone. His father was elected to Congress in 1932, one of the first Polish-Americans in the House and a sponsor of the Social Security Act and the Truman-supported national health insurance. John Dingell Jr., was a House page from 1938 to 1943, when Claude Pepper was a Senator, Jamie Whitten won a special election (in 1941), and no other current Member of Congress was around. After his father's death in 1955, the 29-year-old son was elected from a district with large Polish, black and Jewish minorities. He had one serious fight, because of redistricting, in 1964, beating a fellow Democrat who opposed the Civil Rights Act, even though most of the district was new to

Dingell; he has been reelected easily since. He has had an interesting personal life, raising his children after his divorce (his son Christopher was elected to the Michigan Senate in 1986) and marrying in 1981 a granddaughter of one of General Motors's Fisher brothers; professionally he worked as a law clerk to the uncle of Michigan delegation members Sander and Carl Levin and employed as his own staffer his current colleague John Conyers. He is the most powerful and formidable member of the Michigan delegation, and the heavily industrial 16th District surely would not want to be represented by anyone else.

The People: Est. Pop. 1986: 491,100, dn. 4.6% 1980–86; Pop. 1980: 514,560, dn. 0.7% 1970–80. Households (1980): 77% family, 41% with children, 65% married couples; 24.0% housing units rented; median monthly rent: $208; median house value: $44,000. Voting age pop. (1980): 367,589; 3% Black, 2% Spanish origin.

1988 Presidential Vote:

Bush (R)	106,007	(53%)
Dukakis (D)	91,270	(46%)

Rep. John D. Dingell (D)

Elected Dec. 13, 1955; b. July 8, 1926, Colorado Springs, CO; home, Trenton; Georgetown U., B.S. 1949, J.D. 1952; Roman Catholic; married (Deborah).

Career: Army, WWII; Practicing atty., 1952–55; Wayne Cnty. Asst. Prosecuting Atty., 1953–55.

Offices: 2221 RHOB 20515, 202-225-4071. Also 5461 Schaefer Rd., Dearborn 48126, 313-846-1276; and 241 E. Elm, Ste. 105, Monroe 48161, 313-243-1849.

Committees: *Energy and Commerce* (Chairman of 26 D). Subcommittee: Oversight and Investigations (Chairman).

Group Ratings

	ADA	ACLU	COPE	CFA	LCV	ACU	NTLC	NSI	COC	CEI
1988	80	86	93	64	69	13	2	11	29	10
1987	92	—	93	71	—	0	—	—	7	7

National Journal Ratings

	1988 LIB — 1988 CONS		1987 LIB — 1987 CONS	
Economic	79% —	17%	73% —	0%
Social	76% —	23%	78% —	0%
Foreign	66% —	33%	71% —	27%

Key Votes

1) Homeless $	AGN	5) Ban Drug Test	AGN	9) SDI Research	AGN
2) Gephardt Amdt	FOR	6) Drug Death Pen	FOR	10) Ban Chem Weaps	AGN
3) Deficit Reduc	FOR	7) Handgun Sales	FOR	11) Aid to Contras	AGN
4) Kill Plnt Clsng Notice	AGN	8) Ban D.C. Abort $	AGN	12) Nuclear Testing	FOR

Election Results

1988 general	John D. Dingell (D)	132,775	(97%)	($462,180)
	Russell Leone (WAC)	3,561	(3%)	
1988 primary	John D. Dingell (D), unopposed			
1986 general	John D. Dingell (D)	101,659	(78%)	($510,044)
	Frank W. Grzywacki (R)	28,971	(22%)	

SEVENTEENTH DISTRICT

The 17th Congressional District of Michigan forms almost a semicircle around the city of Detroit—at a point just beyond, in most cases, where significant numbers of blacks live. Most of Detroit's blacks are in the 1st and 13th Districts, whose boundaries were drawn to make safe black constituencies; what is left over, on the far northwest side of Detroit, and in its near western and northwestern suburbs, is the 17th. That means that the 17th has plenty of variety. Some of its suburbs, like Ferndale and Royal Oak, along Woodward Avenue in Oakland County, or Redford Township just west of Detroit, are aging now: originally mixed Protestant and Catholic, and leaning Republican, Royal Oak has become more Democratic and older, as young families move farther out. Southfield, once empty swampland, has now become the high-rise office center of Michigan, with more square footage than downtown Detroit. The 17th's portion of Detroit includes what was once one of the metropolitan area's high-income neighborhoods, Rosedale Park, as well as miles of straight streets lined by frame and white aluminum siding workingmen's houses from the 1940s. Blacks have been moving westward in Detroit, and the 17th's portion of the city is already one-third black; there are also a significant number of blacks in the mostly Jewish suburbs of Oak Park and Southfield. To the south, the 17th takes in white working-class Dearborn Heights and, just next door, the mostly black suburb of Inkster.

The 17th District's congressman, Sander Levin, has a wealth of political experience. Twice he came within a hairsbreadth of beating William Milliken and becoming Michigan's governor, in 1970 and 1974; before that he was an important state legislator and Michigan's Democratic chairman in the turbulent year of 1968. In the Carter Administration, he was in charge of population control programs in AID—not a noncontroversial job. He is the older brother of Senator Carl Levin, and came to Congress later; but he was the first in his family to run for office, and the two brothers seem to have an entirely comfortable relationship. Sander Levin had not been expecting to run for Congress at all in 1982, but 18th District incumbent James Blanchard (who worked in Levin's gubernatorial campaigns) ran for governor, and 17th District incumbent William Brodhead retired at age 40; their districts were collapsed and included Levin's home base, so he ran and after a spirited primary won.

Sandy Levin is a natural legislator: a hard worker, a detail man, a strong partisan who is less interested in trumpeting his own opinions than he is in working out compromise and agreement among everyone involved in an issue, and who is willing to spend endless hours doing so. He is also willing to tell colleagues things they don't want to hear and to stand behind legislation he has backed when it's attacked. In his first term, he was a member of the Freshman Budget Group which pushed both the Democratic leadership and the Reagan Administration to do more to close the budget deficit. In his second term, he chaired the House Democrats' task force which helped lay the groundwork for the 1988 workfare law. Levin's task force recommended increased help for the working poor, but shifted the historical focus of many Democrats on benefit levels by urging better education, training and child care to enable welfare recipients to get into the work force.

In 1987, Levin got a seat on the Ways and Means Committee, in time to work on such laws as workfare, the 1988 trade and factory closing bill, catastrophic health care and the U.S.-Canada

Free Trade Treaty. He was also busy in national politics, going into Iowa to campaign for House and Ways and Means colleague Dick Gephardt in 1987 and early 1988, backing Michael Dukakis in May 1988, and working on the Democratic platform committee chaired by Blanchard. For 1992, he has proposed a new system in which primaries would be held on six dates, on each one of which one state in each of six regions would vote.

At home, since his first election, Levin was unopposed in 1984 and ran well ahead of party lines, with 76% and 70%, in 1986 and 1988.

The People: Est. Pop. 1986: 484,400, dn. 5.9% 1980–86; Pop. 1980: 514,560, dn. 11.7% 1970–80. Households (1980): 73% family, 36% with children, 60% married couples; 25.4% housing units rented; median monthly rent: $268; median house value: $41,200. Voting age pop. (1980): 382,414; 10% Black, 1% Spanish origin, 1% Asian origin.

1988 Presidential Vote:

Dukakis (D).	105,431	(53%)
Bush (R)	92,015	(46%)

Rep. Sander M. Levin (D)

Elected 1982; b. Sept. 6, 1931, Detroit; home, Southfield; U. of Chicago, B.A. 1952, Columbia U., M.A. 1954, Harvard U., LL.B. 1957; Jewish; married (Victoria).

Career: Practicing atty.; Oakland Bd. of Sprvrs., 1961–64; MI Senate, 1965–70; Fellow, Kennedy Sch. of Govt., Harvard U., 1975; Asst. Admin., Agency for Intl. Develop., 1977–81.

Offices: 323 CHOB 20515, 202-225-4961. Also 17117 W. Nine Mile Rd., Ste. 1120, Southfield 48075, 313-559-4444.

Committees: *Ways and Means* (22d of 23 D). Subcommittees: Health; Social Security. *Select Committee on Children, Youth, and Families* (9th of 18 D).

Group Ratings

	ADA	ACLU	COPE	CFA	LCV	ACU	NTLC	NSI	COC	CEI
1988	100	90	95	82	75	0	9	10	31	13
1987	84	—	94	93	—	0	—	—	13	6

National Journal Ratings

	1988 LIB — 1988 CONS		1987 LIB — 1987 CONS	
Economic	78% —	22%	73% —	0%
Social	86% —	0%	78% —	0%
Foreign	79% —	16%	76% —	19%

Key Votes

1) Homeless $	AGN	5) Ban Drug Test	AGN	9) SDI Research	AGN
2) Gephardt Amdt	FOR	6) Drug Death Pen	AGN	10) Ban Chem Weaps	FOR
3) Deficit Reduc	FOR	7) Handgun Sales	AGN	11) Aid to Contras	AGN
4) Kill Plnt Clsng Notice	AGN	8) Ban D.C. Abort $	AGN	12) Nuclear Testing	FOR

Election Results

1988 general	Sander M. Levin (D) 135,493	(70%)	($233,421)
	Dennis Flessland (R)................. 55,197	(29%)	
1988 primary	Sander M. Levin (D), unopposed		
1986 general	Sander M. Levin (D) 105,031	(76%)	($134,327)
	Calvin Williams (R) 30,897	(22%)	

EIGHTEENTH DISTRICT

It is only a few miles—just minutes on the freeway—from the black ghettos of inner city Detroit, where abandoned houses and gunshot wounds are commonplace, to the affluent suburbs north and west of the city. This is the growing part of the Detroit area, with increasing population even in the troubled 1980s, where the inner city was being depopulated; the suburbs are white-collar and professional, entrepreneurial and executive, while the inner city looks to government and factory payrolls if not to welfare and crime. Even physically there is a distinction. Detroit is on some of the flattest land in the country, while the northwest suburbs of Oakland County run along a line of hills and lakes that marks the southernmost advance of an Ice Age glacier. Politically, there is a distinction as well. The affluent Oakland County suburbs are not as unanimously Republican as the inner city precincts of Detroit are Democratic; there are enough descendants of Jewish and Catholic immigrants and cultural liberals to leaven up the local political scene considerably. But the definite climate of opinion, once you get beyond mostly Jewish Southfield and Oak Park, is Republican: people here who vehemently took the side of management in the days when Michigan's politics represented a kind of company-versus-union class war now speak respectfully of market economics and entrepreneurs and are dead earnest in their opposition to higher taxes.

This is the 18th Congressional District of Michigan, which includes most of Oakland County, following on the map the lines that show both the glacial hills and the zones of greatest affluence. In the center are Birmingham and Bloomfield Hills, the former once a small outstate Michigan town and now a major shopping and office center, the latter the highest-income suburb in the Detroit area. To the northeast are the affluent parts of Troy, Rochester and, across the Macomb County line, Shelby Township. Southwest of Birmingham are Farmington Hills and the suburb of Novi; the 18th proceeds west, across hilly country almost all the way to Ann Arbor. This is not only the most affluent, but also the most heavily Republican district in Michigan; it was designed to take in the most heavily Republican parts of the metropolitan area, leaving safe Democratic constituencies for its other congressmen.

The congressman here is William Broomfield, one of the two senior Republicans in the House. First elected in 1956, he is not a man who seeks the spotlight or looks particularly comfortable in it. Nonetheless, he is a professional politician, first elected to the Michigan legislature in 1948, and a solid party man, who wants never to embarrass his party or its administration. He is the ranking Republican on the Foreign Affairs Committee, and in that capacity was the Reagan Administration's spokesman on contra aid and arms control. Broomfield is old enough to remember when the phrase "bipartisan foreign policy" was more than a cliche, and his instinct is to cooperate with administrations of either party, to present a united front abroad. Often quiet and pro forma in his support of measures his committee position gives him the lead on, he was a vigorous, sincere, and effective—in 1986 anyway—supporter of the Reagan Administration policy of aid to the Nicaraguan Contras; he surprised some of the younger Republicans who did not suspect him of such fervor. And he has occasionally shown some of the same fervor when breaking ranks, as he did on South African sanctions (though he opposed the Democrats' bills), and he had the same visceral negative reaction most voters did when it appeared the

Administration was going to make a deal dropping the drug indictment of Manuel Noriega.

Broomfield has hit the spotlight a few times, on the Iran-contra committee, for example, and when he met with Mikhail Gorbachev to present a list of Jewish refuseniks to him. Broomfield has always been a strong supporter of aid to Israel and the rights of Soviet Jews, and arms sales to Arab states is one issue on which he has opposed the Reagan Administration. He fought successfully to get Macomb County resident Peter Ivezaj released from a Yugoslav prison and, with Democrats Sander Levin and Bob Carr, welcomed the Soviet wife of Keith Braun when she arrived in Oakland County.

From 1956 to 1962, Broomfield had to fight hotly contested general elections when his district included the tough working-class town of Pontiac and the affluent suburbs were not so populous. He survived the Democratic year of 1958 nimbly and beat another Republican incumbent in the 1972 primary when they were redistricted together. Now he has a safe seat for as long as he wants: he is regularly reelected with more than 70% of the vote.

The People: Est. Pop. 1986: 549,700, up 6.8% 1980–86; Pop. 1980: 514,560, up 31.4% 1970–80. Households (1980): 79% family, 45% with children, 70% married couples; 22.0% housing units rented; median monthly rent: $314; median house value: $80,500. Voting age pop. (1980): 360,726; 1% Asian origin, 1% Spanish origin, 1% Black.

1988 Presidential Vote:

Bush (R)	192,072	(70%)
Dukakis (D)	80,288	(29%)

Rep. William S. Broomfield (R)

Elected 1956; b. Apr. 28, 1922, Royal Oak; home, Birmingham; MI St. U.; Presbyterian; married (Jane).

Career: MI House of Reps., 1949–55, Spkr. Pro Tem, 1953; MI Senate, 1955–57; Amb. to Gen. Assembly of U.N., 1967.

Offices: 2306 RHOB 20515, 202-225-6135. Also 430 N. Woodward, Birmingham 48011, 313-642-3800; and 371 N. Main, Milford 48042, 313-685-2640.

Committees: *Foreign Affairs* (Ranking Member of 18 R). Subcommittee: Arms Control, International Security and Science (Ranking Member). *Small Business* (3d of 16 R). Subcommittee: Regulation, Business Opportunity and Energy (Ranking Member).

Group Ratings

	ADA	ACLU	COPE	CFA	LCV	ACU	NTLC	NSI	COC	CEI
1988	30	35	19	55	31	84	77	100	92	50
1987	0	—	18	29	—	96	—	—	93	70

National Journal Ratings

	1988 LIB — 1988 CONS		1987 LIB — 1987 CONS	
Economic	24% —	74%	11% —	83%
Social	29% —	70%	0% —	90%
Foreign	16% —	78%	0% —	80%

Key Votes

1) Homeless $	FOR	5) Ban Drug Test	FOR	9) SDI Research	FOR
2) Gephardt Amdt	AGN	6) Drug Death Pen	FOR	10) Ban Chem Weaps	AGN
3) Deficit Reduc	AGN	7) Handgun Sales	AGN	11) Aid to Contras	FOR
4) Kill Plnt Clsng Notice	FOR	8) Ban D.C. Abort $	FOR	12) Nuclear Testing	AGN

Election Results

1988 general	William S. Broomfield (R)	195,579	(77%)	($77,103)
	Gary Kohut (D)	54,643	(21%)	($9,459)
1988 primary	William S. Broomfield (R), unopposed			
1986 general	William S. Broomfield (R)	110,099	(74%)	($68,497)
	Gary Kohut (D)	39,144	(26%)	($5,929)

MINNESOTA

Harold Stassen was governor; the Farmer-Labor party, with a frankly socialist platform, had controlled state government for most of the last decade; Charles Lindbergh's America First crusade against American involvement in the European war was widely popular in a state where his father had voted in Congress against the declaration of war in 1917; Trotskyites controlled the local Teamsters union, while Communists held leadership roles in the CIO; Hubert Humphrey was a graduate student at the state university, taking classes from Evron Kirkpatrick and debating with Orville Freeman and Richard Scammon. This was Minnesota half a century ago.

If Minnesota is distinctive today as the most consistently Democratic state—Democratic for President since 1960 except for 1972, when it was number three for George McGovern behind Massachusetts and Rhode Island—it was far more distinctive in 1940 for its three-party politics, its economic radicalism, its resemblance to the politics of Scandinavia. For our American regions seem to reflect eerily the geography of Europe, with the East Coast resembling the British Isles and France, the industrial Midwest reminiscent of Germany and Poland, the poor and always hawkish South a Baptist Mediterranean, and the Upper Midwest of Minnesota, Wisconsin and North Dakota reflections of Scandinavia. Like Scandinavia, which pioneered the European welfare state, these three have had an effect on continental politics out of proportion to their numbers. Minnesota's Democratic-Farmer-Labor party, through its leaders (especially Hubert Humphrey) and by its example, has shaped the post-1945 Democrats and done more to reshape the nation than any other state political party.

This is no accident, as the Marxists would say; but the explanation, as Marxists would not say, is not economic but ethnic. For Minnesota, far north of the nation's great paths of east-west migration, was bypassed by most of the Yankee immigrants moving west on the great east-west railroads into Iowa, Nebraska and Kansas. In its icy lakes and ferocious winters, others saw their opportunities. James J. Hill, the builder of the Great Northern Railroad ("You can't interest me in any proposition in any place where it doesn't snow"), and others operating out of Minneapolis and St. Paul—already twin cities by 1860—worked to attract Norwegian, Swedish and German migrants who would find the terrain and climate congenial. Within two decades the Twin Cities were the nerve center of a sprawling and rich agricultural empire stretching west from Minnesota through the Dakotas and eventually into Montana and beyond; Minneapolis and St. Paul became the termini of its rail lines and the site of its grain-milling companies.

Thus was a wilderness converted quickly into one of the most productive parts of the world. But the Scandinavians and Germans were alarmed by the unprecedented concentration of economic power and wealth into the hands of just a few identifiable millionaires on Minneapolis's and St. Paul's Summit Avenue. The immigrants had brought to Minnesota traditions of cooperative activity and bureaucratic socialism, and their rebellion against market capitalism and the magnates' dominance gave the politics of Minnesota from the turn of the 20th century a Scandinavian flavor. As in Wisconsin and North Dakota, a strong third party developed here in the years after the Populist era; and this Farmer-Labor Party elected Senators in the 1920s and dominated state politics in the 1930s. The Farmer-Laborites, hurt by their ties to Communists, were beaten by Harold Stassen's Republicans in 1938, but this was still a New Deal state; by 1944, the bedraggled local Democrats were merged with anti-Communist Farmer-Laborites to form the Democratic-Farmer-Labor party. A key role was played by Humphrey—graduate student in 1940, mayor of Minneapolis in 1945, the dazzling advocate of the civil rights plank at the 1948 national convention. Humphrey's DFL—clean, idealistic, closely tied to labor, backed by many farmers—attracted dozens of talented politicians, including Eugene McCarthy, Orville Freeman, Walter Mondale and Minneapolis's current mayor, Donald Fraser. In 1948, Humphrey's speech helped put the Democrats on record for civil rights, and he was elected to the Senate at 37.

For years after, the DFL dominated Minnesota politics, winning most elections and setting the agenda for policy even when, usually because of internal feuds, it lost an election. It stood for a generous, compassionate federal government, for strong labor unions and high wages, for an expansionist fiscal policy to encourage consumer-led economic growth, for civil rights, for an anti-Communist but not bombastic foreign policy. Its base was among blue-collar workers in the Twin Cities and in Duluth and the Iron Range and among farmers of Scandinavian origin. The party succeeded in getting most of its policies adopted in St. Paul and Washington, and helped its constituents achieve affluence. But at some time in the 1970s, the party lost much of its appeal and saw its base splinter on cultural issues like abortion and wilderness preservation in the same year (1978) when it was hurt by Humphrey's death and by Governor Wendell Anderson's appointing himself to the Senate.

By the late 1980s, the DFL was winning most elections again (though the Independent-Republicans, as they renamed themselves, held both Senate seats), but the policies the DFL was advocating were different. Since 1978, Minnesota has been pruning back its government, aggressively recruiting new business, abandoning the assumption that the big milling companies and the rich will generate enough revenue to fulfill every campaign promise. Noting that most of Minnesota's growth in the last 50 years has come in the Twin Cities metro area as it spreads farther into the countryside, DFL Governor Rudy Perpich has concentrated not on increasing farm or blue-collar jobs, but on trying to make Minnesota "the Brainpower state," criticizing the University president publicly for not pushing hard enough on the President's Commitment to Focus program, and signing an education bill (he chairs the U.S. Education Commission) that gives every parent in the state the choice of which public school his child will attend. State social services continue to be generous, but are supplemented by the commitment of 78 of Minnesota's biggest companies to donate 5% of their earnings for charity—which should count as a dozen or so of George Bush's thousand points of light.

And for all of Minnesota's tolerance of diversity, culturally conservative points of view have been advanced in politics with some success. If Minnesota has the nation's strictest anti-smoking-in-public law, it also has one of the most active right-to-life movements, which in 1984 supplied the impetus for the Republicans' only capture of the state House in the 1980s. As Norway, Sweden and Denmark debate cutting back on welfare state measures and even question aspects of cultural liberalism, so does Minnesota.

That may be happening not because Minnesota's welfare state failed but because it has

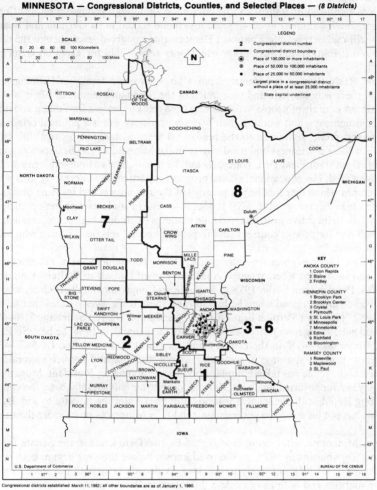

MINNESOTA — Congressional Districts, Counties, and Selected Places — (8 Districts)

succeeded—and because the economy has changed in the process. Thanks to economic growth, which high tax levels did not choke off and which public spending helped to produce, fewer voters are demanding services or income redistribution from the state, and more are seeing themselves as the ones who have to pay for these things. Higher education levels have helped the Twin Cities develop a diversified economy. Big companies like General Mills and troubled Pillsbury still play a major role here, but even big Twin Cities firms—3M, Control Data, Dayton Hudson, Northwest Airlines— have prospered by being responsive to rapidly changing markets. And as in the country at large more jobs have been generated here by small businesses, by entrepreneurial startups and spinoffs, than by big firms. Workers and even (the much less numerous) farmers no longer feel at the mercy of a few big milling firms and railroads, young people starting out have many more career choices, and consumers have a much wider range of brand and product choices than they did 50 years ago: the need for New Deal-style intervention and regulation is less.

Minnesota's cultural liberalism and its dovishness on foreign policy—it retains tinges of the isolationism which Samuel Lubell 40 years ago found rooted in its German and Scandinavian heritage—still makes this state a national Democratic stronghold, even though the demand for economic redistribution and regulation which was responsible for early DFL successes has tapered off.

Governor. Rudy Perpich is a dentist from a large Croatian family in Hibbing in the Iron Range, and there is in his style and tone much of the rough-and-tumble of life in a community made up almost entirely of people with working class roots living in a forbidding and unforgiving physical environment—and working their way up in society. He is a political original, without close allies and prone sometimes to the feuds that seem a staple of political life on the Iron Range. His wooing of business and his desire to make Minnesota "the Brainpower state" are at least a shift from traditional DFL policy, though he also defends Minnesota against the charge that it is overtaxed. His educational choice program is particularly interesting. It is attacked by teachers' unions which fear for the job security of their members and by some blacks who fear blacks won't take advantage of it; what it does is to reward students with get-up-and-go, to give school districts an incentive to attract and hold students (including high school seniors, for whom the state will pay for college courses), and to provide special schools for those who seek special help or discipline.

Perpich first became governor without the DFL endorsement, as a maverick lieutenant governor who succeeded when Wendell Anderson named himself to Walter Mondale's Senate seat in 1976. Perpich then lost in 1978 to Republican Congressman Albert Quie, who cut taxes and then was so embarrassed when he had to raise them back several times that he didn't run again in 1982. That year Perpich beat DFL party-endorsed Warren Spannaus 51%–46% in the primary and got 59% against Wheelock Whitney in the general; in 1986, he beat St. Paul Mayor George Latimer 57%–41% in the primary and then beat a conservative IR 56%–43% in the general. These primary showings in particular are not stunning, and Perpich's job rating has not always been high, yet he has talked, implausibly, about running for President. More plausibly he hints he may run for governor again in 1990 and, despite his still not solid base, the apparent lack of any strong Republican challengers will probably make him the favorite to win. By this time certainly he has put his stamp on government and life in Minnesota much more than anyone had expected.

Senators. Minnesota, after being represented by two Democrats in the Senate for 20 years, elected two Republicans in 1978, neither well known before the year began, both regarded as beneficiaries of good luck not likely to last long. A decade later both have been reelected by impressive margins and both have made a difference in Washington.

David Durenberger has made the biggest splash and won against the toughest electoral competition. His most visible post was as chairman of the Senate Intelligence Committee in 1985 and 1986. Suddenly he took vehement exception to contra aid, attacked CIA director William Casey and began leaking intelligence matters to the press, which brought him not only off-the-record criticism from the administration but an unmistakable public rebuke from House Intelligence Committee chairman Edward Boland. Eventually, he was rebuked by the Senate for telling a Jewish group in Florida that the CIA was recruiting spies in Israel. Durenberger's leaks and outbursts may have been related to turbulence in his personal life: he separated from his wife in 1985, moved to a nondenominational Christian retreat house amid rumors that he had had an affair with a staffer and was drinking too much, and got into an altercation with an airport policeman in Boston where he was traveling to see a counselor. It turned out he was giving speeches there so he could collect fees and have his travel paid for; also, he arranged to receive some $100,000 in "promotional fees" for giving speeches supposedly to boost sales on a book he published.

Against this erratic behavior Durenberger had a record of hard work and some independence on issues. On the Finance Committee he specialized in health care, promoting choice, peer review and cost control in Medicare; he backed some increases in domestic spending but favored Gramm-Rudman and opposes tax increases. He has a generally liberal attitude on cultural issues, but as a Catholic raised at St. John's in Collegeville opposes both abortion and capital punishment on pro-life grounds.

This seems to have been a winning combination in Minnesota. In 1978, he resoundingly beat Bob Short, who antagonized many liberals by the way he beat Donald Fraser in the DFL primary; in 1982, Durenberger edged Mark Dayton, the department store heir who spent $7 million, 53%–47% in a recession year. In 1988, his opponent was Hubert H. Humphrey III, generally known as Skip, a champion vote-winner as state attorney general. Though competitive in early polls, Humphrey was unable to stir grievances against the Republican. In a series of harsh ads he charged that Durenberger was cutting social security and medicare to pay for defense, that he was AWOL in the war against drugs, and even suggested (based on an incautious statement by Durenberger) that he favored "pulling the plug" on old people. Humphrey's big-spending programs—supply management for farmers, long-term health care for the elderly, the ABC child care bill—didn't generate much support. Many Minnesotans complained about the negative tone of the ad campaigns, but the more important fact was that Humphrey's approach to issues, which carried the day in Minnesota in his father's time, failed to do so in 1988. He narrowed the gap in September, fell farther behind in October, then in the last few weeks ran out of money (as his father did in 1968) and went off the air. Durenberger won 56%–41%, a solid and impressive win, and an indication that his politics can consistently command majority support in what is still in presidential elections America's premier Democratic state.

Another test of this proposition will come in 1990, when Senator Rudy Boschwitz comes up for reelection. Much of his record can be traced to his personal history. He came to the United States at age five, as a refugee from Nazi Germany; raised and educated in the East, he came to Minnesota, established a discount chain of Plywood Minnesota stores, was active in Jewish charities and went into politics. He has specialized first of all in refugee issues, traveling to Thailand to learn about Cambodian and Hmong refugees, and helping those in the United States stay here. Minnesota, with its tolerance and strong economy, has attracted many, and so the issue has resonance at home. On foreign policy he has been a strong, though not entirely uncritical, supporter of Israel; he drafted and signed a 1988 letter from U. S. Senators to Prime Minister Shamir criticizing some of his policies. Although a city boy, he has a seat on the Agriculture Committee and has worked hard on farm problems. He put his impress on the 1987 Farm Credit Act and he would like to see in the 1989 farm bill his approach decoupling payments from production of particular crops . He champions the dairy industry and argues that its problem is not overproduction but underconsumption (Americans do consume less milk than 30 years ago); which he attacks by, inter alia, serving cherry, banana and root beer flavored milk at Rudy's Super Duper Milk House at the Minnesota State Fair every year.

More than most Minnesota politicians, Boschwitz trusts economic markets, which after all have worked very well in his experience; aware from his personal history of the impact of totalitarianism, he takes a more hawkish line on foreign policy than most politicians from what was half a century ago (and arguably still is) America's isolationist belt. On cultural issues, his record is more mixed. On campaign finance, he is influenced by his role as a big fundraiser for himself and other Republicans and his service as chairman of the Republicans' Senate campaign committee in 1987 and 1988. He did not have the satisfaction of seeing the Republicans gain control or even gain seats; but seeing as they had considerably more vulnerable seats up, he may be pleased that they had a net loss of only one seat.

One seat Boschwitz does not want to lose in 1990 is his own. He won it in 1978 against

Wendell Anderson, who had, in effect, appointed himself to fill Walter Mondale's seat. (This is always an unpopular tactic—only one such governor-turned-senator has won in 50 years—and Boschwitz, drawing on his TV exposure in ads for his plywood business, won 57%–40%.) In 1984, after several potentially strong opponents dropped out, Boschwitz beat Secretary of State Joan Anderson Growe 56%–43%, in the one state Ronald Reagan was (though only narrowly) losing. There was talk that Walter Mondale would run for the seat he formerly held, but in May of 1989 he decided not to make the race, as did Congressman Gerry Sikorski. Two who may run are Mark Dayton, the department store heir who ran well in 1982 and can finance any level of campaign, and Minneapolis lawyerTom Berg. Others may jump in: Hennepin County Commissioner, John Derus and Paul Wellstone, a Carlton College professor who has already announced he is running.

Presidential politics. Since 1968, Minnesota has voted 5% to 11% more Democratic than the national average in presidential elections, reflecting its special traditions and the strength of Hubert Humphrey and Walter Mondale, who were either on, or were top competitors for, a place on every Democratic ticket for 20 years.

Minnesota hasn't had a presidential primary since 1956 and never had old-fashioned political machines; both its parties pride themselves on their strong volunteer-based organizations, which endorse state candidates and select presidential delegates in caucuses and conventions, not primaries. Unlike other states where caucuses are easily dominated by small gaggles of enthusiasts, Minnesota's parties have enough people involved so that the results bear some sensible relation to public preference. In 1988, the February 23 caucuses were won by Michael Dukakis, with 33% of the DFL votes, and Robert Dole, with 42% of the IR votes—which is quite possibly how ordinary people would have voted if they'd had the information caucus-goers did (although it should be added that the two ministers, Jesse Jackson and Pat Robertson, finished second). In 1989, however, the state legislature voted to hold presidential primaries in 1992, the first in 26 years.

Congressional districting. For the 1980s, a federal court adopted a DFL plan for Minnesota's House districts. All signs are that it need be changed only slightly for 1990, with the outstate and central city districts nibbling little bits off the fast-growing suburban 3d and 6th Districts.

The People: Est. Pop. 1988: 4,306,000; Pop. 1980: 4,075,970, up 5.6% 1980–88 and 7.1% 1970–80; 1.75% of U.S. total, 21st largest. 17% with 1–3 yrs. col., 17% with 4+ yrs. col.; 9.5% below poverty level. Single ancestry: 17% German, 7% Norwegian, 4% Swedish, 3% English, 2% Irish, Polish, 1% French, Dutch, Italian. Households (1980): 72% family, 40% with children, 62% married couples; 28.3% housing units rented; median monthly rent: $212; median house value: $54,300. Voting age pop. (1980): 2,904,162; 1% Black, 1% American Indian, 1% Spanish origin, 1% Asian origin. Registered voters (1988): 2,916,957; no party registration.

1988 Share of Federal Tax Burden: $15,751,000,000; 1.78% of U.S. total, 20th largest.

1988 Share of Federal Expenditures

	Total		Non-Defense		Defense	
Total Expend	$13,840m	(1.57%)	$11,445m	(1.75%)	$2,624m	(1.15%)
St/Lcl Grants	2,120m	(1.85%)	2,114m	(1.85%)	5m	(4.65%)
Salary/Wages	1,163m	(0.87%)	967m	(1.44%)	195m	(1.44%)
Pymnts to Indiv	6,168m	(1.51%)	6,052m	(1.55%)	116m	(0.62%)
Procurement	2,306m	(1.22%)	228m	(0.49%)	2,306m	(1.22%)
Research/Other	2,084m	(5.58%)	2,083m	(5.62%)	2m	(5.62%)

Political Lineup: Governor, Rudy Perpich (DFL); Lt. Gov., Marlene Johnson (DFL); Secy. of State, Joan Anderson Growe (DFL); Atty. Gen., Hubert H. Humphrey III (DFL); Treasurer, Michael McGrath (DFL); Auditor, Arne Carlson (IR). State Senate, 67 (44 DFL and 23 IR); State House of Representatives, 134 (80 DFL and 54 IR). Senators, David Durenberger (IR) and Rudy Boschwitz (IR). Representatives, 8 (5 DFL and 3 IR).

1988 Presidential Vote

Dukakis (D)............... 1,109,471 (53%)
Bush (R).................. 962,337 (46%)

1984 Presidential Vote

Mondale (D).............. 1,036,364 (50%)
Reagan (R).............. 1,032,603 (50%)

GOVERNOR

Gov. Rudy Perpich (DFL)

Elected 1982, term expires Jan. 1991; b. June 27, 1928, Carson Lake; home, Gilbert; Hibbing Jr. Col., A.A. 1950, Marquette U., D.D.S. 1954; Roman Catholic; married (Lola).

Career: Army, 1946–48; Dentist; Hibbings Bd. of Ed., 1952–62; MN Senate, 1963–71; Lt. Gov., 1971–76; Gov., 1976–79; Vice Pres., World Tech, Inc., 1979–82.

Office: 130 State Capitol Bldg., Aurora Ave., St. Paul 55155, 612-296-3391.

Election Results

1986 gen.	Rudy Perpich (DFL)	790,138	(56%)
	Cal R. Ludeman (IR)........	606,755	(43%)
1986 prim.	Rudy Perpich (DFL)	293,426	(57%)
	George Latimer (DFL).......	207,198	(41%)
1982 gen.	Rudy Perpich (DFL)	1,049,104	(59%)
	Wheelock Whitney (IR).......	711,796	(40%)

SENATORS

Sen. David Durenberger (IR)

Elected 1978, seat up 1994; b. Aug. 19, 1934, St. Cloud; home, Minneapolis; St. John's U., B.A. 1955, U. of MN, J.D. 1959; Roman Catholic; married (Penny).

Career: Army, 1955–57; Practicing atty., 1959–66; Exec. Secy. to Gov. Harold LeVander, 1967–71; Counsel for Legal & Commun. Affairs, Corporate Secy., Mgr., Intl. Licensing Div., H.B. Fuller Co., 1971–78.

Offices: 154 RSOB 20510, 202-224-3244. Also 1020 Plymouth Bldg., 12 S. 6th St., Minneapolis 55402, 612-349-5111.

Committees: *Environment and Public Works* (4th of 7 R). Subcommittees: Water Resources, Transportation and Infrastructure; Environmental Protection; Superfund, Ocean and Water Protection (Ranking Member). *Finance* (7th of 9 R). Subcommittees: Health for Families and the Uninsured; Social Security and Family Policy; Medicare and Long-Term Care (Ranking Member). *Labor and Human Resources* (6th of 7 R). Subcommittees: Employment and Productivity; Handicapped (Ranking Member); Aging.

Group Ratings

	ADA	ACLU	COPE	CFA	LCV	ACU	NTLC	NSI	COC	CEI
1988	60	54	47	58	80	26	35	30	43	34
1987	55	—	44	75	—	28	—	—	56	37

638   MINNESOTA

National Journal Ratings

	1988 LIB — 1988 CONS	1987 LIB — 1987 CONS
Economic	56% — 43%	43% — 56%
Social	48% — 49%	30% — 68%
Foreign	56% — 43%	57% — 42%

Key Votes

1) Cut Aged Housing $	FOR	5) Bork Nomination	FOR	9) SDI Funding	AGN
2) Override Hwy Veto	FOR	6) Ban Plastic Guns	FOR	10) Ban Chem Weaps	AGN
3) Kill Plnt Clsng Notice	AGN	7) Deny Abortions	FOR	11) Aid To Contras	AGN
4) Min Wage Increase	AGN	8) Japanese Reparations	FOR	12) Reagan Defense $	AGN

Election Results

1988 general	David Durenberger (IR)	1,176,210	(56%)	($5,410,783)
	Hubert H. Humphrey III (DFL)	856,694	(41%)	($2,477,068)
1988 primary	David Durenberger (IR)	112,413	(93%)	
	Sharon Anderson (IR)	5,464	(5%)	
1982 general	David Durenberger (IR)	949,207	(53%)	($4,189,619)
	Mark Dayton (DFL)	840,401	(47%)	($7,172,312)

Sen. Rudy Boschwitz (IR)

Elected 1978, seat up 1990; b. Nov. 7, 1930, Berlin, Germany; home, Plymouth; Johns Hopkins U., B.S., 1950; N.Y.U., LL.B. 1953; Jewish; married (Ellen).

Career: Army, 1953–55; Founder and Pres., Plywood Minnesota, Inc., 1963–78.

Offices: 506 HSOB 20510, 202-224-5641. Also 215 Kellogg Square Bldg., 111 E. Kellogg Blvd., St. Paul 55101, 612-221-0904.

Committees: *Agriculture, Nutrition, and Forestry* (5th of 9 R). Subcommittees: Agricultural Production and Stabilization of Prices; Agricultural Credit; Nutrition and Investigations (Ranking Member). *Budget* (3d of 10 R). *Foreign Relations* (4th of 9 R). Subcommittees: European Affairs; International Economic Policy, Trade, Oceans and Environment; Near Eastern and South Asian Affairs (Ranking Member). *Small Business* (Ranking Member of 9 R).

Group Ratings

	ADA	ACLU	COPE	CFA	LCV	ACU	NTLC	NSI	COC	CEI
1988	20	38	18	58	50	70	69	90	69	56
1987	25	—	17	33	—	76	—	—	94	59

National Journal Ratings

	1988 LIB — 1988 CONS	1987 LIB — 1987 CONS
Economic	33% — 65%	15% — 82%
Social	44% — 55%	42% — 56%
Foreign	17% — 81%	34% — 64%

Key Votes

1) Cut Aged Housing $	AGN	5) Bork Nomination	FOR	9) SDI Funding	FOR
2) Override Hwy Veto	AGN	6) Ban Plastic Guns	AGN	10) Ban Chem Weaps	FOR
3) Kill Plnt Clsng Notice	FOR	7) Deny Abortions	FOR	11) Aid To Contras	FOR
4) Min Wage Increase	AGN	8) Japanese Reparations	FOR	12) Reagan Defense $	FOR

Election Results

1984 general	Rudy Boschwitz (IR)	1,119,926	(56%)	($6,657,484)
	Joan Anderson Growe (DFL)	852,844	(43%)	($1,592,885)
1984 primary	Rudy Boschwitz (IR)	162,555	(97%)	
	Two others (IR).	5,739	(3%)	
1978 general	Rudy Boschwitz (IR)	894,092	(57%)	($1,872,443)
	Wendell Anderson (DFL)	638,375	(40%)	($1,154,351)

FIRST DISTRICT

South of Minneapolis-St. Paul the Mississippi River flows through narrow passages and broad calm lakes, with shoulders of rolling hills on each side—one of the finest river landscapes of North America. This far north the westward tide of Yankee migrants thinned out, and in the years after the Civil War most of the settlers following the railroads on the floodplains and over the Minnesota farmlands west of the river were Germans and Scandinavians, bringing their families to this terrain that reminded some of the Rhine. Southeastern Minnesota is a borderland between Yankee and Germanic settlement—politically, between Civil War Republicans and Farmer-Laborites favoring interventionist economic and isolationist foreign policies.

The southeastern corner of Minnesota today is the state's 1st Congressional District. Within its compact bounds is considerable diversity. Rochester, home of the Mayo Clinic, with its large professional population, is prosperous and one of the most heavily Republican parts of Minnesota; Austin, a county away, headquarters of the Hormel meatpacking firm that beat a bitter strike in 1986, is one of the most Democratic places south of the Iron Range. The 1st District extends north to new subdivisions spreading out from the Twin Cities and to Northfield, the home of Carleton College; it also includes the river towns of Red Wing and Wabasha and Winona, with their 19th century stone storefronts and mountain-like rock outcroppings that overlook the river. There are farms here, but not the big—and troubled—commercial farms you find as the land smooths out farther west.

The 1st District, narrowly Republican in 1980s presidential elections, elects a Democratic congressman, Tim Penny. Not yet 40, and looking considerably younger, Penny is one of those young Democrats who startles everyone with his instinctive feel for politics and his energy—and who is an example of why the Democrats have a majority in the House. Penny was elected to the state Senate in 1976 at age 24, after visiting every home in the Republican district. In 1982, he used the same door-to-door, personal campaigning tactics, plus $182,000, to win in a congressional seat into which two Republicans had been redistricted.

He also proceeded immediately to follow a political course that has proved exceedingly popular. Penny became chairman of the Freshman Budget Group in 1983 and called himself a "compassionate conservative," and he compiled a more conservative record on economic issues than any DFL congressman has for years; ever since, he has been struggling to come up with proposals to cut the deficit. He got a seat on the Agriculture Committee, where he worked on drought legislation and to increase payments for dairy farmers. A family man with four children, he kept a middle-of-the-road profile on cultural issues. On foreign affairs he is more liberal, like most Upper Midwest Democrats.

Penny's politics has proved very successful. In 1984 he was reelected with 57%; in 1986 and

1988 he won 72% and 70%. By every indication Penny has made southeast Minnesota into a safe Democratic district.

The People: Est. Pop. 1986: 513,400, up 0.8% 1980–86; Pop. 1980: 509,460, up 5.2% 1970–80. Households (1980): 74% family, 40% with children, 66% married couples; 24.7% housing units rented; median monthly rent: $180; median house value: $45,800. Voting age pop. (1980): 362,626; 1% Spanish origin.

1988 Presidential Vote:

Bush (R)	122,629	(51%)
Dukakis (D)	116,414	(48%)

Rep. Timothy J. Penny (DFL)

Elected 1982; b. Nov. 19, 1951, Freeborn Cnty.; home, New Richland; Winona St. U., B.A. 1974; U. of MN; Lutheran; married (Barbara).

Career: MN Senate, 1976–82.

Offices: 436 CHOB 20515, 202-225-2472. Also Park Towers, 22 N. Broadway, Rochester 55904, 507-281-6053; and Blue Earth Cnty. Gov. Ctr., P.O. Box 3148, Mankato 56001, 507-625-6921.

Committees: *Agriculture* (15th of 27 D). Subcommittees: Livestock, Dairy and Poultry; Conservation, Credit and Rural Development; Wheat, Soybeans, and Feed Grains. *Veterans' Affairs* (5th of 21 D). Subcommittees: Compensation, Pension and Insurance; Education, Training and Employment (Chairman). *Select Committee on Hunger* (8th of 19 D).

Group Ratings

	ADA	ACLU	COPE	CFA	LCV	ACU	NTLC	NSI	COC	CEI
1988	60	55	58	64	75	36	56	30	64	36
1987	68	—	56	64	—	30	—	—	53	49

National Journal Ratings

	1988 LIB — 1988 CONS		1987 LIB — 1987 CONS	
Economic	46% —	52%	39% —	61%
Social	46% —	53%	60% —	39%
Foreign	58% —	41%	64% —	35%

Key Votes

1) Homeless $	FOR	5) Ban Drug Test	AGN	9) SDI Research	AGN
2) Gephardt Amdt	AGN	6) Drug Death Pen	AGN	10) Ban Chem Weaps	FOR
3) Deficit Reduc	AGN	7) Handgun Sales	FOR	11) Aid to Contras	AGN
4) Kill Plnt Clsng Notice	AGN	8) Ban D.C. Abort $	FOR	12) Nuclear Testing	FOR

Election Results

1988 general	Timothy J. Penny (DFL)	161,118	(70%)	($165,016)
	Curt Schrimpf (IR)	67,709	(30%)	($85,532)
1988 primary	Timothy J. Penny (DFL), unopposed			
1986 general	Timothy J. Penny (DFL)	125,115	(72%)	($334,484)
	Paul H. Grawe (IR)	47,750	(27%)	($44,112)

SECOND DISTRICT

"The creek bank, shaded by plum trees and thick with bushes, is a cozy place, and the dugout house (you can see only the outlines of it now) was protected from the elements, but just above, the land levels out and treeless croplands are open to the sky, unsheltered from the sun and locusts in summer and from the wind and snow in winter." This is the home Laura Ingalls Wilder describes in *By the Shores of Plum Creek*, near Walnut Grove, Minnesota. The plains of southwestern Minnesota, spotted with occasional hills and cut by dozens of creeks, were settled 100 years ago by Yankee, German and Scandinavian farmers, and like the Great Plains from the Dakotas to Oklahoma they have been hard places to make a living; Laura's family, after all their struggles, left the farm for town as soon as they could.

Plum Creek is in the 2d Congressional District of Minnesota, which covers most of the southwest quadrant of the state. In 1940, there were 515,000 people here; by the middle 1980s, there were 500,000, with more movement than the figures suggest. The small towns on the Minnesota River and the courthouse towns which have been graced with state colleges have grown, absorbing people from the farms; with far higher farm productivity, far fewer people live on the land, and even in town people here have had a hard time developing an economy that can provide jobs for all their children, much less attract newcomers.

That has caused a certain volatility to politics here. Ancestrally, this is mostly Republican territory. But there is also a Democratic base and it is prone to countercyclical farm revolts. The current congressman is Vin Weber, one of the Republican Party's best instinctive politicians and most resourceful strategists. But he was caught off guard and nearly beaten, mainly on farm issues, in 1986, and he has proved to be a rather different congressman in the late 1980s than he was in the early Reagan years. Weber, fresh from managing Senator Rudy Boschwitz's 1978 campaign, won a seat abandoned by a Watergate era Democrat in 1980, and came to Washington with a conservative tilt, a respect for free markets, a belief in conservative cultural values, and an opposition to the dovish foreign policy views that became orthodox in the Upper Midwest in the 1970s. He enthusiastically supported the Reagan programs and, with Newt Gingrich, was one of the leaders of the Conservative Opportunity Society that used the House's special orders procedure to appeal to a C-SPAN audience. He needled the Democrats for the intellectual weakness of some of their positions and demagogued them on others.

At the same time, Weber was not a robot, opposing the administration on South African sanctions, the MX missile, chemical warfare and the AWACs sales to Saudi Arabia. He was the leader on the Science, Space and Technology Committee of the ultimately successful fight to stop the Clinch River Breeder Reactor, which he opposed as a waste of money and as a threat to the environment. In 1988, he was a strong supporter of Jack Kemp for President.

He was also successful back home, persuading another Republican incumbent from the 2d to run in the 1st District instead in 1982 (the man lost), and winning in 1984 by nearly 2 to 1. Then in 1986, with farm prices low and land prices a fraction of their 1970s highs, Weber got strong opposition from Dave Johnson, a successful farmer and a Reagan delegate to the 1984 Dallas convention where Weber was busy working on platform planks; Johnson ran against the trends that "threaten to change what I grew up in. Our small towns are being turned into old age homes." Weber spent $909,000 and was confident enough to leave $165,000 in the bank afterwards—perhaps a little too confident, since his margin was only 52%–48%.

Back in the House, Weber changed his tack, switching to Appropriations and its Agriculture Subcommittee, scrounging for those local aid and job creation projects he used to have little time for, holding dozens of town meetings, working on drought relief, and staying away from the Republican national convention. All this paid off in 1988, when Weber was reelected with 58% of the vote. He has not totally given up national politics. He was a Jack Kemp backer in 1988, he was elected after 1988 to be secretary of the House Republican Conference (the number eight position in the leadership), and he played a role in getting Louis Sullivan, President Bush's choice to be HHS Secretary, to agree to hire right-to-lifers to top posts. He forswears interest in the 1990 governor's race and so seems likely to remain in the House.

The People: Est. Pop. 1986: 500,900, dn. 1.7% 1980–86; Pop. 1980: 509,500, up 2.1% 1970–80. Households (1980): 74% family, 38% with children, 67% married couples; 23.4% housing units rented; median monthly rent: $142; median house value: $37,300. Voting age pop. (1980): 363,087.

1988 Presidential Vote:
Bush (R)	118,769	(51%)
Dukakis (D)	112,838	(48%)

Rep. Vin Weber (IR)

Elected 1980; b. July 24, 1952, Slayton; home, N. Mankato; U. of MN, 1970–74; Roman Catholic; married (Cheryl).

Career: Press Secy., researcher for U.S. Rep. Tom Hagedorn, 1974–76; Co-publisher, *The Murray County Herald*, 1976–78; Campaign Mgr., Chief MN Aide, Sen. Rudy Boschwitz, 1978–80.

Offices: 106 CHOB 20515, 202-225-2331. Also P.O. Box 279, New Ulm 56073, 507-354-6400; 919 S. 1st St., Willmar 56201, 612-235-6820; and P.O. Box 1214, Marshall 56258, 507-532-9611.

Committees: *Appropriations* (19th of 22 R). Subcommittees: Labor, Health and Human Services and Education; Rural Development, Agriculture and Related Agencies.

Group Ratings

	ADA	ACLU	COPE	CFA	LCV	ACU	NTLC	NSI	COC	CEI
1988	15	39	12	36	69	96	74	90	93	55
1987	20	—	12	29	—	87	—	—	80	62

National Journal Ratings

	1988 LIB — 1988 CONS		1987 LIB — 1987 CONS	
Economic	7% —	91%	19% —	78%
Social	27% —	72%	32% —	67%
Foreign	0% —	84%	20% —	76%

Key Votes

1) Homeless $	FOR	5) Ban Drug Test	FOR	9) SDI Research	FOR
2) Gephardt Amdt	AGN	6) Drug Death Pen	AGN	10) Ban Chem Weaps	FOR
3) Deficit Reduc	AGN	7) Handgun Sales	FOR	11) Aid to Contras	FOR
4) Kill Plnt Clsng Notice	FOR	8) Ban D.C. Abort $	FOR	12) Nuclear Testing	AGN

Election Results

1988 general	Vin Weber (IR)	131,639	(58%)	($623,776)
	Doug Peterson (DFL)	96,016	(42%)	($152,295)
1988 primary	Vin Weber (IR), unopposed			
1986 general	Vin Weber (IR)	100,249	(52%)	($909,607)
	Dave Johnson (DFL)	94,048	(48%)	($296,080)

THIRD DISTRICT

The suburbs of the Twin Cities are the fastest growing part of Minnesota and the most prosperous. If Minneapolis and St. Paul have the big buildings and cultural landmarks, the suburbs have most of the people. Some are modest blue-collar towns, extensions of older central city neighborhoods. But even an affluent suburb like Edina, with the highest incomes in the area, is modest and comfortable, not at all showy or extravagant. They are places where people can enjoy their success without bragging about it, where they can savor the pleasure (and endure the pain) of Minnesota's environment without ostentation.

Since the 1980 Census, two of Minnesota's eight congressional districts are made up entirely of Twin Cities suburbs (there are also suburbs in the 4th and 5th Districts, and newer suburbs reach into each of the other four). The southern of the two is the 3d Congressional District of Minnesota. The 3d includes high-income Protestant suburbs like Edina, predominantly Jewish St. Louis Park, and the younger suburbs of Burnsville, Eagan and Inver Grove Heights. To the south and west the suburbs thin out, and you come to farmlands; the district extends as far as 30 miles outward from the Twin Cities. This is the most affluent, most highly educated, most Republican district in Minnesota.

The 3d District's congressman, Bill Frenzel, is now the senior member of the Minnesota delegation and one of the hardest working and most influential Republicans in the House. First elected by a narrow margin in 1970, Frenzel has won big ever since. Loud and brainy, partisan and thoughtful, he puts his stamp on every debate in which he participates. With long experience in a family-owned business, he is a strong supporter of free enterprise, and looks with suspicion on government interference in the marketplace. On the Ways and Means Committee, he was one of the leaders in efforts to cut taxes. He is perhaps the premier free trade advocate on both sides of the aisle in the House: knowledgeable about the arcana of trade law, ready to pounce upon any hint of protectionism in any bill. His importance comes not from his committee position, but from a combination of conviction and expertise. On other Ways and Means matters he is also important, although on tax reform his partisan instincts seem to have outweighed his desire for lower rates. He was one of the Republicans who nearly derailed the tax reform bill in December 1985; he said he wanted more incentives for business, but it's hard to escape the conclusion that he was bridling at supporting a measure concocted by the other side.

Frenzel was the ranking Republican on House Administration (until he took a leave of absence to serve on Budget), where he was a vigorous, even vitriolic, opponent of public financing of campaigns—to the point of cheering proposals to abolish the presidential fund check-off on tax returns—and of limitations on political action committees. He is, in effect, the Republican Party's lead player on these issues, which are of such great personal importance to so many of his colleagues.

Over the years Frenzel has become more partisan and increasingly hostile to government interference in business. He retains, however, a reputation as a moderate Republican, justified because of some of his stands on many cultural and foreign policy issues— a political asset in a district of this nature, where even strong Republican voters like to think of themselves as moderate and thoughtful. But he seems more frustrated than fulfilled. His ideas have made great progress since he came to Congress, but his party has not, and he is not the player on Ways and Means his talents would entitle him to be. He wants to cut the deficit and served on the National Economic Commission, but the deficit remains and President Bush promised to ignore the commission. He performs ably, but his judgment is sometimes tilted askew by anger and partisanship; he is a talented man who has not quite found an institutional fit. He is now ranking Republican on the Budget Committee, and it will be interesting to see if he finds one there.

The People: Est. Pop. 1986: 585,600, up 14.9% 1980–86; Pop. 1980: 509,499, up 25.3% 1970–80. Households (1980): 77% family, 46% with children, 67% married couples; 24.9% housing units rented; median monthly rent: $289; median house value: $73,900. Voting age pop. (1980): 352,682; 1% Asian origin, 1% Black.

1988 Presidential Vote: Bush (R) 182,877   (54%)
                                 Dukakis (D). 150,082   (45%)

Rep. Bill Frenzel (IR)

Elected 1970; b. July 31, 1928, St. Paul; home, Golden Valley; Dartmouth Col., B.A. 1950, M.B.A. 1951; no religious affil.; married (Ruth).

Career: Navy, Korea; Pres., MN Terminal Warehouse Co., 1960–71; MN House of Reps., 1962–70.

Offices: 1026 LHOB 20515, 202-225-2871. Also 8120 Penn Ave. S., Bloomington 55431, 612-881-4600.

Committees: *Budget* (Ranking Member of 14 R). *Ways and Means* (4th of 13 R). Subcommittees: Trade.

Group Ratings

	ADA	ACLU	COPE	CFA	LCV	ACU	NTLC	NSI	COC	CEI
1988	35	36	15	36	50	57	83	100	92	74
1987	16	—	14	29	—	40	—	—	87	80

National Journal Ratings

	1988 LIB — 1988 CONS		1987 LIB — 1987 CONS	
Economic	0%	— 93%	18%	— 82%
Social	50%	— 50%	27%	— 72%
Foreign	29%	— 71%	45%	— 54%

Key Votes

1) Homeless $	FOR	5) Ban Drug Test	AGN	9) SDI Research	AGN
2) Gephardt Amdt	AGN	6) Drug Death Pen	FOR	10) Ban Chem Weaps	AGN
3) Deficit Reduc	AGN	7) Handgun Sales	AGN	11) Aid to Contras	FOR
4) Kill Plnt Clsng Notice	FOR	8) Ban D.C. Abort $	AGN	12) Nuclear Testing	AGN

Election Results

1988 general	Bill Frenzel (IR) 215,322	(68%)	($381,646)
	Dave Carlson (DFL)................. 99,770	(32%)	($20,733)
1988 primary	Bill Frenzel (IR), unopposed		
1986 general	Bill Frenzel (IR) 127,434	(70%)	($323,232)
	Ray Stock (DFL) 54,261	(30%)	($52,716)

FOURTH DISTRICT

Above the Mississippi River bluffs, forested when the first settlers arrived in the 1850s and one of America's great urban vistas today, stand the two edifices which stamp the character of St. Paul: the Minnesota Capitol and Archbishop Ireland's Cathedral. St. Paul is the older and smaller of the Twin Cities, a river town that soon became the state capital. It was settled mainly by Catholic Irish and German immigrants, while Minneapolis was attracting Protestant Swedes and Yankees; it became a major transportation hub, a railroad center and river port, while Minneapolis, farther upriver at the Falls of St. Anthony, became the nation's largest grain milling center. Though second in size, St. Paul has its share of civic amenities: beneath the Capitol and the cathedral, its skywalk-linked downtown is home to the Ordway Music Theater, the headquarters of Minnesota Public Radio and a burgeoning pop music industry.

Politically, St. Paul was one of the few Democratic parts of Minnesota even before the Democratic-Farmer-Labor Party was formed in 1944; ever since, St. Paul and Ramsey County have remained staunchly Democratic. The neighborhoods of St. Paul, soberly lined up on grid streets in solidly built houses, and the close-in suburbs, with their more irregular street patterns and shopping nodes, remained determinedly Democratic in the 1980s, voting solidly in 1984 for Walter Mondale—who announced his candidacy in the Capitol and lived during the campaign in his house in the woodsy suburb of North Oaks just north of St. Paul—and in 1988 for Michael Dukakis.

St. Paul and its close-in suburbs make up Minnesota's 4th Congressional District. It includes the working-class, DFL suburbs south, east and northeast of the city, as well as the wealthier suburbs to the north and the old-fashioned rich neighborhood along Summit Avenue, where F. Scott Fitzgerald grew up amid sturdy mansions west of where the cathedral overlooks the Capitol, the river and downtown. The 4th District has been held by the DFL since 1948, when Eugene McCarthy—a hardworking politician then—won it. The current congressman, Bruce Vento, was first elected in 1976; coming from a blue-collar background and a career as a science teacher, elected to the state House and to a leadership post, he won the party endorsement at the district DFL convention and then won the primary easily.

Vento is one of those fairly senior House Members who sometimes make policy but seldom break into the national consciousness. He is counted as a supporter of the environmental movement, though not always a successful one; he promoted state cost-sharing of federal water projects in the early 1980s, but pork-minded colleagues balked at this obviously sensible idea. He has been busy in other areas as well, pushing for a stronger Clean Air Act and trying to get more funding to help the homeless.

Vento became chairman of the Interior subcommittee handling national parks and recreation after the 1984 election; after 1986, his subcommittee added public lands to its jurisdiction. That gives it one of the busiest schedules in Congress, for national parks seem to have replaced dams and post offices as plums sought by almost every congressmen, and Vento's subcommittee must sort through the applications for wilderness areas and national parks, national seashores and lakeshores and historic sites, and decide which will be sent to the floor, and in what form.

Vento ordinarily has uninteresting IR opposition, but in 1986 he faced Harold Stassen, wildly popular as Minnesota's governor in 1939–1943, who returned to the state after years of presidential campaigns and Pennsylvania residency at age 79. Vento won with 73%, similar to his showings in 1982, 1984 and 1988.

The People: Est. Pop. 1986: 524,600, up 3.0% 1980–86; Pop. 1980: 509,532, dn. 3.4% 1970–80. Households (1980): 67% family, 36% with children, 55% married couples; 37.5% housing units rented; median monthly rent: $226; median house value: $60,700. Voting age pop. (1980): 375,922; 2% Black, 2% Spanish origin, 1% Asian origin.

1988 Presidential Vote: Dukakis (D)...................... 160,154   (61%)
Bush (R) 99,961   (38%)

Rep. Bruce F. Vento (DFL)

Elected 1976; b. Oct. 7, 1940, St. Paul; home, St. Paul; U. of MN, A.A. 1961; WI St. U., B.S. 1965; Roman Catholic; married (Mary Jean).

Career: Teacher, 1965–76; MN House of Reps., 1971–77, Asst. Major. Ldr., 1974–76.

Offices: 2304 RHOB 20515, 202-225-6631. Also 5th & Minnesota Ave., Ste. 905, St. Paul 55101, 612-224-4503.

Committees: *Banking, Finance and Urban Affairs* (8th of 31 D). Subcommittees: Financial Institutions Supervision, Regulation and Insurance; Housing and Community Development; Economic Stabilization. *Interior and Insular Affairs* (7th of 26 D). Subcommittees: Energy and the Environment; National Parks and Public Lands (Chairman). *Select Committee on Aging* (13th of 39 D). Subcommittee: Health and Long-Term Care.

Group Ratings

	ADA	ACLU	COPE	CFA	LCV	ACU	NTLC	NSI	COC	CEI
1988	90	96	93	100	88	4	9	0	36	11
1987	100	—	92	71	—	0	—	—	8	7

National Journal Ratings

	1988 LIB — 1988 CONS		1987 LIB — 1987 CONS	
Economic	71%	— 23%	73%	— 0%
Social	81%	— 18%	78%	— 0%
Foreign	74%	— 23%	81%	— 0%

Key Votes

1) Homeless $	AGN	5) Ban Drug Test	AGN	9) SDI Research	AGN
2) Gephardt Amdt	FOR	6) Drug Death Pen	AGN	10) Ban Chem Weaps	FOR
3) Deficit Reduc	FOR	7) Handgun Sales	AGN	11) Aid to Contras	AGN
4) Kill Plnt Clsng Notice	AGN	8) Ban D.C. Abort $	AGN	12) Nuclear Testing	FOR

Election Results

1988 general	Bruce F. Vento (DFL).................	181,227	(72%)	($216,172)
	Ian Maitland (IR).....................	67,073	(27%)	($35,789)
1988 primary	Bruce F. Vento (DFL).................	15,117	(93%)	
	Harold Dorland (DFL).................	1,168	(7%)	
1986 general	Bruce F. Vento (DFL).................	112,662	(73%)	($197,906)
	Harold Stassen (IR)	41,926	(27%)	($76,954)

FIFTH DISTRICT

From most of downtown Minneapolis they are hardly visible, sealed off below bridges and far from the skywalks where people can walk for blocks without their winter coats: the Falls of St. Anthony which are the reason the city grew up here. This is the head of navigation of the Mississippi River, and the greatest source of waterpower in the area, and it was here that early pioneers built the grist mills which were the beginning of the biggest grain mills in the United

States. By 1890, Minneapolis together with St. Paul was the center of one of America's largest urban areas, living mainly off grain. Today Minneapolis is a center of high-tech industry and of banking and finance; it is a regional railroad center, and the headquarters of one of the nation's largest airlines, Northwest (the nation's first non-smoking airline, as well); it is also the nerve center of an economic area that extends almost 1,000 miles west to the Rocky Mountains in Montana.

The city of Minneapolis itself, together with some working-class suburbs just to the northwest and some middle-income suburbs directly to the south, make up Minnesota's 5th Congressional District. The central city has been declining in population—521,000 in 1950, 370,000 in 1980—but increasing in vigor. Small frame houses on grid streets in the old working-class neighborhoods which once held large families now typically hold an elderly widow or couple; the children are in bigger houses out in the suburbs. The large old houses along the chain of lakes in western and southern Minneapolis, which once held the families of some of the city's richest citizens, now hold young double-income couples with few or no children who like being close to downtown and the arts center. In northeastern Minneapolis, behind the railroad and warehouse district along the Mississippi, is an old working-class neighborhood which has become the new home of many Hmongs from the mountains of Laos.

Minneapolis has a political liberalism drawn from its Scandinavian and Yankee heritage, given to extremes in clean government, original reforms (like its no-smoking laws) and cultural tolerance. Its mayor, Donald Fraser, was the DFL congressman from the 5th District from 1962 until he ran unsuccessfully for the Senate in 1978; quiet, seemingly dull, he is one of the most dedicated and intellectually honest liberal politicians in America.

The congressman from the 5th District since 1978 is another talented DFL politician, Martin Olav Sabo. On the surface he is anything but flashy: he has a Lake Wobegonish taciturnity, which comes perhaps from his Scandinavian heritage; he is not gladhanding or ebullient. But he is experienced and competent at what he does. In 1960, he was elected to the Minnesota House of Representatives at age 22; at 30, he was the minority leader (members were elected without party labels then, putting the DFL at a disadvantage); at 34, speaker. Sabo won the Congressional seat easily in 1978, though it was a Republican year in Minnesota, and got a seat on the Appropriations Committee; Tip O'Neill, who was speaker of the Massachusetts House before he came to Congress, had a soft spot in his heart for former speakers.

Sabo became, in 1988, chairman of the Democratic Study Group, and appropriately his record on all issues is one of the most liberal in the House. He now serves on both Budget and Appropriations—a powerful combination. He is willing to be an insurgent on occasion, supporting Les Aspin for the Armed Services Committee chairmanship in the Democratic Caucus after the 1984 election; he was less successful in his own race for party whip, leaving the race in May 1986 well before the election. "I think I know how to count," Sabo said, and he knew that campaign chairman Tony Coelho had too many votes to be stopped. As a sort of consolation prize he got the seat on the Defense Appropriations Subcommittee vacated when Chairman Joseph Addabbo died in 1986, leaving this crucial subcommittee with only one liberal; he advanced further up the ladder when the new chairman, Bill Chappell, was defeated in the 1988 election.

Sabo does much of his work in subcommittee and has taken on only a few visible causes. One was to restore federal funding for the University of Minnesota's supercomputer, which was cut off by the National Science Foundation; in this he succeeded. Another is to funnel money into buses for urban mass transit systems, especially in Minneapolis. A third is to get health insurance for the uninsured, along the lines, he says, of a program he pushed through the Minnesota legislature in 1975. He would require employers to offer group policies and the government to set up a pool for non-employees who aren't covered; this one still seems a long way from passage. At home Sabo is reelected regularly, without difficulty.

The People: Est. Pop. 1986: 494,200, dn. 3.0% 1980–86; Pop. 1980: 509,506, dn. 15.3% 1970–80. Households (1980): 56% family, 27% with children, 44% married couples; 45.8% housing units rented; median monthly rent: $220; median house value: $57,800. Voting age pop. (1980): 401,381; 5% Black, 1% American Indian, 1% Asian origin, 1% Spanish origin.

1988 Presidential Vote:			
	Dukakis (D).	166,580	(65%)
	Bush (R)	85,100	(33%)

Rep. Martin Olav Sabo (DFL)

Elected 1978; b. Feb. 28, 1938, Crosby, ND; home, Minneapolis; Augsburg Col., B.A. 1959, U. of MN; Lutheran; married (Sylvia).

Career: MN House of Reps., 1961–78, Minor. Ldr., 1969–73, Spkr., 1973–78.

Offices: 2201 RHOB 20515, 202-225-4755. Also 462 Fed. Courts Bldg., 110 S. 4th St., Minneapolis 55401, 612-348-1649.

Committees: *Appropriations* (18th of 35 D). Subcommittees: Defense; Transportation; Treasury, Postal Service and General Government. *Budget* (16th of 21). Task Forces: Budget Process, Reconciliation and Enforcement; Human Resources.

Group Ratings

	ADA	ACLU	COPE	CFA	LCV	ACU	NTLC	NSI	COC	CEI
1988	100	100	92	82	81	0	8	10	21	11
1987	100	—	91	79	—	0	—	—	7	9

National Journal Ratings

	1988 LIB — 1988 CONS		1987 LIB — 1987 CONS	
Economic	79% —	17%	73% —	0%
Social	86% —	0%	78% —	0%
Foreign	79% —	16%	76% —	19%

Key Votes

1) Homeless $	AGN	5) Ban Drug Test	AGN	9) SDI Research	AGN
2) Gephardt Amdt	FOR	6) Drug Death Pen	AGN	10) Ban Chem Weaps	FOR
3) Deficit Reduc	FOR	7) Handgun Sales	AGN	11) Aid to Contras	AGN
4) Kill Plnt Clsng Notice	AGN	8) Ban D.C. Abort $	AGN	12) Nuclear Testing	FOR

Election Results

1988 general	Martin Olav Sabo (DFL)	174,416	(72%)	($281,455)
	Raymond C. Gilbertson (IR)	60,646	(25%)	($16,915)
1988 primary	Martin Olav Sabo (DFL)	15,240	(92%)	
	Ole Savior (DFL)	1,370	(8%)	
1986 general	Martin Olav Sabo (DFL)	105,410	(73%)	($208,403)
	Rick Serra (IR)	37,583	(26%)	($22,088)

SIXTH DISTRICT

The northern suburbs of Minneapolis and St. Paul make up the 6th Congressional District of Minnesota. This is the less upscale of the two suburban Twin Cities districts. Its oldest part is the town of Stillwater, facing Wisconsin on hills above the St. Croix River, which nearly became Minnesota's capital and is full of Midwest Victoriana from its days as a lumber port. The 6th District has Minnesota's—and one of the nation's—highest percentages of households with families, married couples, children and working women. To the west, the 6th extends almost all the way to St. Cloud and to Hubert Humphrey's lakeside home in Waverly. Closer to Minneapolis, it includes the very high-income Minneapolis suburbs around Lake Minnetonka.

The congressman here is one of the DFL's aggressive, ambitious young politicos, Gerry Sikorski. When current 6th District lines were drawn in 1982, Sikorski had already served in the legislature for six years and run for Congress once; this time he got into a rematch with Republican incumbent Arlen Erdahl. But aside from Stillwater's Washington County, the district was new to Erdahl and well-suited to Sikorski, and he won 51%–49%.

In the House, Sikorski got a seat on the much coveted Energy and Commerce Committee; he has worked hard on acid rain legislation (which can do no political harm in a state with 10,000 lakes); he sponsored gas pipeline safety legislation after a fatal pipeline explosion in Mounds View; he serves on John Dingell's Oversight and Investigations Subcommittee and took part in the investigations of General Dynamics (which billed the Pentagon for kennel fees). He sponsored a bill to help sufferers of multiple sclerosis and ended up with a law making it easier for all disabled people to get medicare benefits. He got a law passed to stop lead poisoning of drinking water. He attacked the secrecy forms Pentagon workers and many other civil servants were asked to sign. Sikorski did get some bad publicity when it was reported that he had staffers run personal errands for him and his wife—though why voters should have a stake in having their congressman stand in line in the cleaners or the bank is not clear.

Since 1982, Sikorski has won by impressive margins, and against opponents with some credentials. He is interested in going statewide though he decided in June 1989 not to challenge Senator Boschwitz in 1990. Given Walter Mondale's earlier departure, some had seen Sikorski as the favorite for that race.

The People: Est. Pop. 1986: 586,200, up 15.1% 1980–86; Pop. 1980: 509,446, up 38.8% 1970–80. Households (1980): 81% family, 54% with children, 72% married couples; 20.6% housing units rented; median monthly rent: $249; median house value: $65,000. Voting age pop. (1980): 332,303; 1% Asian origin, 1% Spanish origin.

1988 Presidential Vote:

Dukakis (D)	148,030	(51%)
Bush (R)	140,362	(48%)

Rep. Gerry Sikorski (DFL)

Elected 1982; b. Apr. 26, 1948, Breckenridge; home, Stillwater; U. of MN, B.A. 1970, J.D. 1973; Roman Catholic; married (Susan).

Career: Practicing atty.; MN Senate, 1976–82, Major. Whip, 1980–82.

Offices: 414 CHOB 20515, 202-225-2271. Also 277 Coon Rapids Blvd. N.W., Ste. 414, Coon Rapids 55433, 612-780-5801.

Committees: *Energy and Commerce* (19th of 26 D). Subcommittees: Health and the Environment; Oversight and Investigations; Transportation and Hazardous Materials. *Post Office and Civil Service* (8th of 15 D). Subcommittees: Civil Service (Chairman); Human Resources. *Select Committee on Children, Youth, and Families* (12th of 18 D).

Group Ratings

	ADA	ACLU	COPE	CFA	LCV	ACU	NTLC	NSI	COC	CEI
1988	90	83	96	100	94	12	14	0	36	11
1987	92	—	95	79	—	9	—	—	13	9

National Journal Ratings

	1988 LIB — 1988 CONS		1987 LIB — 1987 CONS	
Economic	71%	23%	73%	0%
Social	76%	23%	73%	22%
Foreign	84%	0%	81%	0%

Key Votes

1) Homeless $	AGN	5) Ban Drug Test	AGN	9) SDI Research	AGN
2) Gephardt Amdt	FOR	6) Drug Death Pen	AGN	10) Ban Chem Weaps	FOR
3) Deficit Reduc	FOR	7) Handgun Sales	FOR	11) Aid to Contras	AGN
4) Kill Plnt Clsng Notice	AGN	8) Ban D.C. Abort $	FOR	12) Nuclear Testing	FOR

Election Results

1988 general	Gerry Sikorski (DFL)	169,486	(65%)	($320,437)
	Ray Ploetz (IR)	89,209	(34%)	($100,941)
1988 primary	Gerry Sikorski (DFL), unopposed			
1986 general	Gerry Sikorski (DFL)	110,598	(66%)	($492,385)
	Barbara Zwach Sykora (IR)	57,460	(34%)	($154,337)

SEVENTH DISTRICT

"It has been a quiet week in Lake Wobegon." Garrison Keillor's town, founded by New England Yankees as New Albion in 1852, renamed when Norwegians got a majority on the council in 1880, is in Mist County, which, due to some long-ago error, has disappeared from Minnesota's maps, but appears to lie somewhere west of Little Falls and east of Moorhead and north of Interstate 94 that connects the Twin Cities with Fargo, North Dakota. Keillor does not get much into partisan politics, except to note that in this area, peopled mainly with Norwegians and German Catholics, the Norwegian flag flies on holidays but no one has seen a German flag since 1917. This is a Wobegonishly quiet reminder of the persecution of all things German in World War I, when most residents of this area (and their congressman, Charles Lindbergh's father) did not want their country to go to war against Germany, and of how resentments began and continued to smolder politically as isolationist sentiment in the 1930s and 1940s, and as McCarthyism in the early 1950s.

If Mist County were on the political map, it would be about in the middle of the 7th Congressional District of Minnesota. This is farming country running along the rail lines stretching northwest from the Twin Cities to North Dakota and Puget Sound. Nearer the Twin Cities is the German Catholic country around St. Cloud, dotted with farm villages with saints' names; the boyhood home of Sinclair Lewis, Sauk Centre, is here, thinly disguised in his *Main Street*, and Collegeville, where Benedictine monks taught Senators Eugene McCarthy and David Durenberger. This area is volatile politically, Democratic but isolationist and anti-abortion. On the other side of Lake Wobegon are the wheat and sugar beet lands along the Red River of the North. Otter Tail County, heavily Norwegian, leans Republican; farther north the counties are more DFL; not far away is the lake and resort country around Bemidji, where you can find the statues of Paul Bunyan and his blue ox, Babe.

The 7th District is closely divided politically, with a history of close elections. It made national headlines in 1958, when Coya Knutson was congresswoman here; her husband Andy issued a plaintive statement urging her to come home and make his breakfast again. Knutson was the only Democratic incumbent to lose in the heavily Democratic year of 1958. The seat was held by Republican Odin Langen until 1970, by DFL-er Bob Bergland until he became Secretary of Agriculture in 1977, and since then by Republican Arlan Stangeland. His electoral career is like the Perils of Pauline: he is a farmer of Norwegian descent, which helps, and favors some government aid to farmers, which helps too, but he is also conservative on most other issues and a Republican in a district whose historical attraction to the DFL has enough vitality that Michael Dukakis nearly carried the district. On the Agriculture Committee, he boasts of getting sugar price supports up, and in 1985 just barely failed in getting the committee to adopt a new system of supports through a marketing loan aimed at cutting costs and moving U.S. grain into world markets while holding up farm income. Presumably, he will be pushing the same approach in 1989. On Public Works, he tends to go along with the committee's pro-pork majority and to be dubious about spending too much to clean up rivers and lakes.

Stangeland beat DFL state Senator Collin Peterson with 57% in 1984 but by only 121 votes in 1986; Peterson tried again in 1988, but spent little money and lost the primary to former state Senator Marvin Hanson. But Hanson had little money, and Stangeland accused Dukakis of wanting to use rejected sites in northwest Minnesota for dumping nuclear waste; Dukakis replied that he wanted it put in Nevada, which did the Democratic Senate candidate there little good. Hanson ran ahead of Dukakis in his home area up near the Canadian border, but overall Stangeland led his national ticket, in contrast to 1984, and won with 55%. Unlike most congressmen, he seems unworried about his electoral prospects and unfazed at the possibility of defeat.

The People: Est. Pop. 1986: 514,500, up 1.0% 1980–86; Pop. 1980: 509,521, up 10.8% 1970–80. Households (1980): 75% family, 42% with children, 66% married couples; 22.7% housing units rented; median monthly rent: $168; median house value: $39,300. Voting age pop. (1980): 355,632; 1% American Indian.

1988 Presidential Vote: Bush (R) 119,691 (51%)
Dukakis (D). 110,605 (47%)

Rep. Arlan Stangeland (IR)

Elected 1977; b. Feb. 8, 1930, Fargo, ND; home, Barnesville; Lutheran; married (Virginia).

Career: Farmer; MN House of Reps., 1966–74; Mbr., Barnesville Bd. of Ed., 1976–77.

Offices: 2245 RHOB 20515, 202-225-2165. Also M-F Bldg., 403 Center Ave., Moorhead 56560, 218-233-8631; and Fed. Bldg., 720 Mall Germain, St. Cloud 56301, 612-251-0740.

Committees: *Agriculture* (5th of 18 R). Subcommittees: Cotton, Rice and Sugar (Ranking Member); Livestock, Dairy and Poultry; Wheat, Soybeans and Feed Grains. *Public Works and Transportation* (3d of 20 R). Subcommittees: Aviation; Surface Transportation; Water Resources (Ranking Member).

Group Ratings

	ADA	ACLU	COPE	CFA	LCV	ACU	NTLC	NSI	COC	CEI
1988	5	13	13	27	25	92	64	100	93	54
1987	8	—	11	36	—	83	—	—	93	56

National Journal Ratings

	1988 LIB — 1988 CONS		1987 LIB — 1987 CONS	
Economic	21%	77%	11%	83%
Social	13%	84%	0%	90%
Foreign	26%	73%	0%	80%

Key Votes

1) Homeless $	FOR	5) Ban Drug Test	FOR	9) SDI Research	FOR
2) Gephardt Amdt	AGN	6) Drug Death Pen	FOR	10) Ban Chem Weaps	AGN
3) Deficit Reduc	AGN	7) Handgun Sales	FOR	11) Aid to Contras	FOR
4) Kill Plnt Clsng Notice	FOR	8) Ban D.C. Abort $	FOR	12) Nuclear Testing	AGN

Election Results

1988 general	Arlan Stangeland (IR)	121,396	(55%)	($288,782)
	Marvin Hanson (DFL)	101,011	(45%)	($320,437)
1988 primary	Arland Stangeland (IR), unopposed			
1986 general	Arlan Stangeland (IR)	94,024	(50%)	($547,810)
	Collin C. Peterson (DFL)	93,903	(50%)	($465,898)

EIGHTH DISTRICT

The Iron Range of northern Minnesota, where the Arctic winds that blow down over the Canadian Shield's thousands of inland lakes often make nearby International Falls the nation's coldest town, is also the northern end of the lifeline of America's heavy industry. It runs south along rail lines to the port of Duluth, nestled beneath bluffs near the always cold and every winter frozen waters of Lake Superior. Since before the turn of the century, millions of tons of ore have been dug out of the Range, shipped into rail cars for the ride down to Duluth, and loaded into Great Lakes freighters for shipment to Cleveland, Gary, Detroit, Chicago, Pittsburgh and Buffalo. Over all that time about 100,000 people have lived on the Iron Range and another 100,000 in Duluth, most of them the products of America's 1880–1924 wave of immigration—Italians, Poles, Serbs and Croats, Jews, Swedes and Finns. In this punishing environment, they worked to the point of exhaustion, built solid houses with staunch central heating, and bought layers of warm clothing to survive the winter.

These were rough-and-ready communities, with little local elite: the men who owned the mines and the freighters were having lunch in their clubs in Chicago or Detroit while the miners stopped briefly for a bite out of their lunchpails. Life was rough: the work was hard, the hours long, pay low. There was little time and few facilities for recreation back in those days when working people couldn't afford special winter sports clothes or summer gear; the churches, a separate one for each ethnic group, were the main community institution. Living conditions improved vastly in the decades of great economic growth after World War II, but there remains a rough-hewn tone to life here today. And there has also been economic distress. As the iron and steel industry got more efficient, they needed fewer workers; as the American steel industry collapsed after 1979, they needed even fewer, or none at all. Unemployment topped 20% in the early 1980s, and young people have been moving out for years. Now the Iron Range and Duluth seem to be diversifying, hoping that tourism, UDAG grants and an enterprise zone will provide growth and jobs. They are proud of the new chopsticks factory in Hibbing that hopes to produce a billion units for export to Japan.

The Iron Range and Duluth have been voting for the Democratic-Farmer-Labor party since it was created in 1944. The current congressman, James Oberstar, is the product of a Catholic education, and his views seem to reflect the social gospel side of Catholicism. He believes government has an obligation to help the poor and disadvantaged and to stimulate economic growth; he is dubious about American military involvement abroad, especially in Central America; he is also culturally traditional and an opponent of abortion. With high seniority on the Public Works Committee, he has hopped from one subcommittee chairmanship to another. On Economic Development in the early 1980s he defended EDA and other local aid programs from Reagan Administration attacks. In 1985, he switched to Oversight and Investigations and in 1989 to Aviation.

Oberstar's father was a miner and local union official on the Iron Range; the son studied French and other languages abroad and then landed a job with Congressman John Blatnik in Washington. When Blatnik, then chairman of Public Works, retired in 1974, Oberstar ran and won a primary victory over Governor Rudy Perpich's brother Tony; Republicans are not a problem here. Oberstar has had serious primary opposition from Duluth council member Thomas Dougherty in 1980 and 1984; the second race came after Oberstar returned to the House contest after failing to win endorsement for the Senate race at the DFL state convention. But now he looks safely ensconced.

The People: Est. Pop. 1986: 494,600, dn. 2.9% 1980–86; Pop. 1980: 509,506, up 10.7% 1970–80. Households (1980): 74% family, 40% with children, 65% married couples; 22.0% housing units rented; median monthly rent: $166; median house value: $38,100. Voting age pop. (1980): 360,529; 1% American Indian.

1988 Presidential Vote:

Dukakis (D)	144,768	(60%)
Bush (R)	92,948	(39%)

Rep. James L. Oberstar (DFL)

Elected 1974; b. Sept. 10, 1934, Chisholm; home, Chisholm; St. Thomas Col., B.A. 1956, Col. of Europe, Bruges, Belgium, M.A. 1957; Roman Catholic; married (Jo).

Career: Civilian language teacher, U.S. Navy, Haiti, 1959–63; A. A. to U.S. Rep. John A. Blatnik, 1963–74; Administrator, U.S. House of Reps. Cmtee. on Pub. Works, 1971–74.

Offices: 2209 RHOB 20515, 202-225-6211. Also 231 Fed. Bldg., Duluth 55802, 218-727-7474; Chisolm City Hall, Chisholm 55719, 218-254-5761; and Brainerd City Hall, 501 Laurel St., Brainerd 56401, 218-828-4400.

Committees: *Budget* (9th of 21 D). Task Forces: Budget Process, Reconciliation and Enforcement; Defense, Foreign Policy and Space. *Public Works and Transportation* (4th of 31 D). Subcommittees: Aviation (Chairman); Investigations and Oversight; Water Resources.

Group Ratings

	ADA	ACLU	COPE	CFA	LCV	ACU	NTLC	NSI	COC	CEI
1988	90	86	93	73	88	12	8	0	21	14
1987	96	—	93	86	—	4	—	—	7	6

National Journal Ratings

	1988 LIB — 1988 CONS		1987 LIB — 1987 CONS	
Economic	67%	— 30%	73%	— 0%
Social	75%	— 24%	73%	— 22%
Foreign	84%	— 0%	81%	— 0%

Key Votes

1) Homeless $	AGN	5) Ban Drug Test	AGN	9) SDI Research	AGN
2) Gephardt Amdt	FOR	6) Drug Death Pen	AGN	10) Ban Chem Weaps	FOR
3) Deficit Reduc	FOR	7) Handgun Sales	FOR	11) Aid to Contras	AGN
4) Kill Plnt Clsng Notice	AGN	8) Ban D.C. Abort $	FOR	12) Nuclear Testing	FOR

Election Results

1988 general	James L. Oberstar (DFL)..............	165,656	(75%)	($157,802)
	Jerry Shuster (IR)....................	56,630	(25%)	($7,743)
1988 primary	James L. Oberstar (DFL), unopposed			
1986 general	James L. Oberstar (DFL).............	135,718	(73%)	($163,619)
	Dave Rued (IR)	51,315	(27%)	($68,931)

MISSISSIPPI

Magnolia trees on the lawn of the antebellum mansion, golden-haired young women in white dresses on the veranda, faithful black servants and retainers: this was the stereotype of Mississippi 50 years ago. But behind that image was the reality of the tarpaper shack of the black sharecropper and the hardbitten lot of the small white farmer. Black Mississippians were a separate caste, with their own folkways and customs. And most white Mississippians were, as the *WPA Guide* put it, "A farmer people with a mental background of furrowed hot fields and a hope for rain, we are both dependent on and modified by the sporadic blessings of forces that we cannot control. We are tolerant but not susceptible, easy to amuse but hard to convince. Our faith is in God, next year's crop, and the Democratic Party."

This 1940s Mississippi—superstitious, improvident, and most of all poor—was another country to most Americans. Along its dusty roads leading from market towns were loose-jointed frame farmhouses, where people lived without automobiles and farmed without machines; they had no electricity and no leisure time to speak of; their isolation was more like the life of farmers in the age of Andrew Jackson than that of Americans about to enter the freeway age. Many Mississippians were still sharecroppers, living outside the money economy; and many others considered themselves lucky to make $100 a month. In 1940 Mississippi's per capita income was just 36% of the national average. There were successful businesses and plantations in Mississippi, but somehow the wealth here never seemed to trickle down. The families who had money had mostly had it for generations; they considered it inconceivable that most other Mississippians could make much money or, if they did, would know how to spend it. Mississippi was more like what we now call an underdeveloped country than it was like most of the United States.

In that era, Mississippi politics had no match in the nation for crudity and, on occasion, savagery. There was always an economic division, between the rich white planters of the Delta and the river valley and the poor white farmers of the hillier north and east. Even more important was the division between the races. In 1940, 49% of Mississippians were black—and their high numbers made whites even more determined to maintain a system of segregation as rigid and severe as South Africa's is today. Blacks were not allowed to vote; they could not mingle with whites in schools or public accommodations; they had to address whites with particular phrases. Infractions were sometimes punished with death; lynchings were not uncommon in the 1940s and occurred up through the murder of Emmet Till in 1955 and the murders of three civil rights workers in Neshoba County in the summer of 1964. In politics, blacks were relevant only as objects of vituperation; they were denounced by all politicians and described as monkeys by Theodore Bilbo, elected governor in 1915 and 1927 and senator in 1934, 1940 and 1946.

Few states have made as much progress in the 25 years since the civil rights revolution, and few states feel they still have so far to go, as Mississippi. In 1964, civil rights workers were murdered for encouraging blacks to register and vote; in 1986, Mississippi had a black congressman and black Supreme Court justice, and its secretary of state, in a glossy brochure, recalled the "oppression of the black population of the state," and said, "a change from the old racial status quo was necessary and morally correct." Yet black voter turnout has lagged in many rural counties, and voting has often been polarized: in 1988, more than 80% of Mississippi blacks voted for Michael Dukakis and more than 70% of Mississippi whites voted for George Bush. In other elections, for governor in 1983 and Senator in 1984, there has been less polarization, but few Republicans aside from Senator Thad Cochran have won many black

MISSISSIPPI — Congressional Districts, Counties, and Selected Places — (5 Districts)

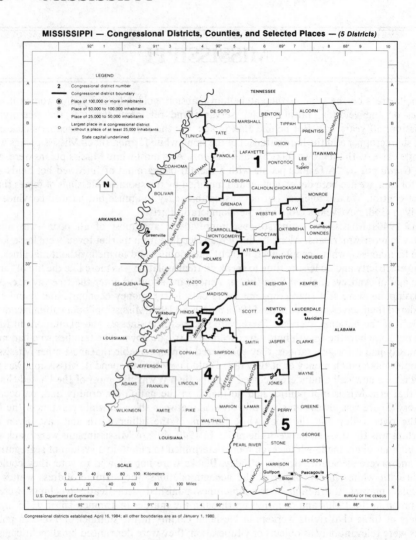

Congressional districts established April 16, 1984; all other boundaries are as of January 1, 1980.

votes. Economically, Mississippi has grown along with the rest of the nation, and faster—
Mississippi incomes were 70% of the national average in 1984, up from 65% in 1970. But even
accounting for Mississippi's lower cost of living, which is still perceptibly lower than the norm, as
on so many other indexes, Mississippi is uncomfortably aware that for all its progress it remains
number 50 among the states in many respects.

As the state changed its way of life, Mississippi went through some uncomfortable political
contortions. For a time it voted almost as another country, as the only state backing an
independent slate of electors in 1960, voting 87% for Barry Goldwater as he was losing nationally
by a landslide, casting 63% of its votes for George Wallace in his obviously futile 1968
campaign. But in the 1970s, as desegregation was accepted so much more readily than almost
anyone imagined, Mississippi's politics moved back into the national mainstream. In national
elections it voted much like the rest of the country: for Richard Nixon in 1972, though by an

unusually big majority, narrowly for Jimmy Carter in 1976, against him in 1980. In county seats and in the state capital, blacks were gaining political influence. Black support was no longer the kiss of death for a white politician; it was for William Winter, for example, in the gubernatorial races of 1967 and 1975, but not in 1979. In these circumstances, Mississippi blacks have become adroit at exerting political pressure and have, quietly and out of the national spotlight, been getting more of what they want out of government. A politician who runs in a constituency that is 10% or 30% black is going to try to give those voters what they want, once it's clear that doing so isn't going to mean certain defeat at the hands of the other 70% or 90%.

There was another reason for the change: the state's economy, long 50th in the nation, took off. State per capita income, 36% of the national average in 1940 and 54% in 1960, was 65% in 1970 and 70% in 1984. This growth may be one result of integration: the economy got a boost just as Mississippi was forced to get rid of segregation. That makes sense. Investors are more willing to put up money in a state with no racial strife; integration helped improve Mississippians' education and skills, even while wages and tax levels in many northern states were soaring to uncompetitive levels. Another reason—not mentioned by those who focus only on the motives of white businessmen and the performance of politicians—is that Mississippi's blacks themselves, finally free to express themselves and to make their livings as they wish, have been more likely, if they are skilled, to stay in Mississippi, and more likely, whether skilled or not, to work harder and put out more effort than they were in the days when it seemed that anything they might gain could be taken away by whites. Lots of small changes can add up: Governor Ray Mabus claims that Mississippi has surpassed North Carolina in furniture production by producing low-priced chairs and tables for discounters in hundreds of little shops.

Politicians have made some contributions to this progress. One is increasing support for public education in order to provide a better work force; yeoman work was done by former Governor William Winter and is being done by Mabus. The other is in developing political appeals that cross racial lines. In the 1970s, Mississippi elections featured fights between black Independents and Democrats versus Republicans who focused almost entirely on whites. But Republican Thad Cochran and Democrat Winter both won elections while appealing to both races, and so paved the way for others. National politics, particularly with Jesse Jackson prominently on the scene, may polarize the races, but the state that was once the symbol of resistance to civil rights shows other possibilities. Mississippi still has a ways to go. But this is progress.

Governor. Mississippi's Governor Raymond Mabus is a symbol of how far the state has come. Mabus was starting high school when James Meredith integrated the University of Mississippi in 1962; he was still in high school when Goodman, Cheney and Schwerner were murdered in 1964; he went off to Ole Miss just as the Voting Rights Act for the first time was putting blacks on the voting rolls in Mississippi. He is part of the first generation of white Mississippians who never took part in the old system of segregation. Mabus went to Harvard Law and was practicing in Washington when he decided to come back in 1979 to work for newly-elected Governor William Winter. He was a supporter of William Winter when he was running for governor, and of Winter's education package, which for the first time committed Mississippi to state-supported kindergartens, raised the school leaving age to 14, and raised taxes specifically for education. When Mississippi's (later abolished) one-term limitation forced Winter out, Mabus ran for state auditor in 1983, and used the powers of office to make a name as a reformer, attacking county auditors and hacking away at the power bases of seemingly permanent state legislative leaders.

In 1987, he ran for governor, promising to revise the 1890 Constitution, reorganize state government, and raise Mississippi teacher salaries to the southeastern average: "Mississippi," he proclaimed, echoing an old segregationist slogan, "will never be last again!" It was a popular program: Mabus won the Democratic runoff against businessman Mike Sturdivant 65%–35%, and he beat Republican Jack Reed—interestingly, a Tupelo businessman who eased adjustment to integration—in the general election, handily. Mabus's platform is a continuation of Winter's:

to provide Mississippi with an education system that will upgrade its work force to the level of others. Even more than Winter, he takes on locally-based politicians and the businessmen who, doing well in the state's current low-wage economy, don't want it changed. His allies include other young politicians of his generation—Secretary of State Dick Molpus, Attorney General Mike Moore and Speaker Tim Ford. In 1988, Mabus got his teacher pay raise and county government reorganization—major achievements—through the legislature. In early 1989, he was pushing for state government reorganization—a tougher goal in a state where the legislature has kept tight rein on the executive for years. But he's still popular and eligible now for a second term.

Senators. For three decades Mississippi was represented by two Democratic Senators who were both powers on Capitol Hill, James Eastland and John Stennis. Now that Stennis has retired after 41 years, Mississippi is represented by two Republicans, both politically skilled, but with different attitudes, and neither as powerful as his predecessor.

Thad Cochran has risen and thrived in Mississippi politics almost without controversy or acrimony. He was elected to the House in 1972 against a white Democrat and a black Independent from the district that included Jackson; he was elected to the Senate in 1978 in a similar three-way contest. In both cases, he won with less than an absolute majority, and then won by impressive margins in his next contests. Cochran's pleasant personal demeanor, his refusal to engage in any kind of racial politics, his conservative stands on almost all issues, and his Republican Party label in a state where most whites have been voting Republican for President for two decades, have made him acceptable to most Mississippi voters and unacceptable to very few. Cochran looks and sounds like the successful young professionals you'll find in the Jackson area, along the Gulf Coast, and in some smaller towns which increasingly are setting the tone in state politics in both parties.

In Washington, Cochran is far less doctrinaire than many conservatives. As secretary of the Senate Republican Conference, he is a member of the party leadership, and he supported Bob Dole for President in 1988. As a member of the Appropriations Committee, he is tending to the practical business of governing, concentrating not just on old-fashioned pork barrel projects (like the Tennessee-Tombigbee Waterway Stennis nursed along for so many years) but also holding down spending on domestic programs generally. On the Agriculture Committee, he has been a player in shaping the 1985 farm bill and the 1987 farm credit system fix. On economics Cochran is a solid conservative, but not always so on cultural or foreign issues.

Cochran proved his strength at home in the 1984 election. He faced the strongest possible opponent, William Winter, just a year after Winter retired as governor. But Winter dithered over whether to run, announcing he would become chancellor of Ole Miss and then weeks later declining the post to make the Senate race. Cochran won that race by 58%–42%, winning white votes by a large margin and making inroads, despite Winter's own pro-civil rights record, among blacks. This race could turn out to be a preview of what Republican National Chairman Lee Atwater, seeking black votes, hopes to make more common in the South: if Republicans can add some black votes to a solid white vote base, they will become unbeatable. It is perhaps too soon to say that about Cochran for 1990. But he has an attractive record and voters have few grievances against him; it will be hard for the Democrats to find a strong candidate.

Mississippi's junior Senator, Trent Lott, enters the Senate a political veteran though still in his forties. But he won the seat after a tougher contest than he might have expected. Starting from a modest background, Lott has risen fast, showing an eye for opportunity but also a steadiness and strength of conviction that have led him to take what seemed at the time political risks but which have turned out, in an increasingly Republican country and state, to have been political masterstrokes. Lott worked his way through law school by running the Ole Miss alumni affairs office there, and has accumulated a stateful of good contacts; he got a job on the staff of Democrat William Colmer, the aged Gulf Coast congressman who chaired the House Rules

Committee. When Colmer retired in 1972, Lott ran for the seat with Colmer's encouragement and endorsement—as a Republican. He was elected with 55% in what turned out to be Nixon's best congressional district in the country. In 1974, Lott was the youngest member of the Judiciary Committee, defending Richard Nixon as long as anyone in the impeachment hearings. In 1975, he got a seat on Rules. In 1980, he was elected Republican whip, the number two position in the leadership. In 1980 and 1984, he ran the Republican National Convention's platform committees. He supported Jack Kemp for President in 1987 and 1988, even as he was running for the Senate himself.

Lott was working his way through college and law school during the civil rights revolution, but it seems not to have affected him one way or the other; he shows no sign of racial prejudice but has trouble understanding how others will perceive racial issues: he was the man who kept urging the Reagan Administration to grant a tax exemption to Bob Jones University. Like many self-made men, he has a visceral dislike for taxes and big government, developed in his case to an articulate belief in supply-side economics and deregulation, though not always free trade. Culturally, he wants to strengthen belief in traditional moral values and in the rightness of the existing order: he wants people to believe that America is good to the core, not riddled with rottenness. He believes in an assertive foreign policy and plenty of defense spending, and on SDI in particular. Gregarious and personable, he is on good terms with otherwise feuding conservatives, and he has long cultivated his contemporaries among southern Democrats, looking for a vote here and a vote there. But he can be sharp in debate, aggressively partisan and exceedingly combative.

Lott gave up not only a safe seat in the House but the number two spot in the Republican leadership to make the Senate race, and it seemed for a while to be dicier than he might have thought. In the Democratic primary, 4th District Congressman Wayne Dowdy ran a populist campaign against reformer and Mabus ally Dick Molpus; with heavy support from his home base, Dowdy won 54%–42%. Then Dowdy attacked Lott for backing economic policies that help the rich and ran an ad criticizing him for having a chauffeur. Lott responded by showing the employee in question, a law enforcement professional named George Awkward, who explained he was guarding Lott as a member of the leadership: "I'm nobody's chauffeur, Mr. Dowdy." Lott ran a smooth, well-financed campaign; Dowdy didn't raise enough money and couldn't make strategic decisions. The results show the potential—and the limit—for Dowdy's populist appeal. He carried the black-majority Delta and the northeastern hills, and also most of his old district. But, in the Jackson area, the Gulf Coast, and other counties where turnout increased 10% since 1980, Lott beat Dowdy 61%–39%; in the rest of the state, Dowdy prevailed 51%–49%. It's an interesting illustration of which kind of politics represents the future of Mississippi and which the past.

In the Senate Lott serves on Armed Services and Commerce, where his votes are predictable. But his political skills and continuing enthusiasm for the game suggest he'll soon make a difference there, just as he did in the House.

Presidential politics. Jesse Jackson won Mississippi's Democratic primary, though not by a wide margin, over Albert Gore; George Bush was an easy winner in the Republican primary and in the general election. Mississippi's performance in presidential elections is easily predictable. Jimmy Carter's success here in 1976 and near-success in 1980 shows that a Democrat with appeal to white southerners can carry Mississippi; Walter Mondale and Michael Dukakis showed that liberal northerners are no longer ignored by white voters as Hubert Humphrey or George McGovern were, but they don't win enough votes to make it close either. There is an eerie similarity between Ronald Reagan's 62–37% margin in 1984 and George Bush's 60%–39% in 1988.

Congressional districting. Mississippi's congressional districting plans have been changed twice to comply with the Voting Rights Act, in each case increasing the black percentage in the

2d Congressional District. In 1986, that helped elect Mike Espy, the first black to represent Mississippi in Congress since Reconstruction. By 1988, he was popular enough to win easily, whatever the boundaries.

The People: Est. Pop. 1988: 2,627,000; Pop. 1980: 2,520,638, up 4.2% 1980–88 and 13.7% 1970–80; 1.09% of U.S. total, 31st largest. 14% with 1–3 yrs. col., 13% with 4+ yrs. col.; 23.9% below poverty level. Single ancestry: 20% English, 6% Irish, 2% German, 1% French. Households (1980): 78% family, 46% with children, 62% married couples; 29.0% housing units rented; median monthly rent: $113; median house value: $31,400. Voting age pop. (1980): 1,706,441; 31% Black, 1% Spanish origin. Registered voters (1988): 1,595,826; no party registration.

1988 Share of Federal Tax Burden $5,531,000,000; 0.63% of U.S. total, 33d largest.

1988 Share of Federal Expenditures

	Total		Non-Defense		Defense	
Total Expend	$9,895m	(1.12%)	$6,445m	(0.98%)	$3,583m	(1.57%)
St/Lcl Grants	1,324m	(1.16%)	1,311m	(1.14%)	14m	(11.93%)
Salary/Wages	1,208m	(0.90%)	442m	(0.66%)	766m	(0.66%)
Pymnts to Indiv	4,465m	(1.09%)	4,250m	(1.09%)	215m	(1.16%)
Procurement	2,586m	(1.37%)	134m	(0.29%)	2,586m	(1.37%)
Research/Other	311m	(0.83%)	309m	(0.83%)	2m	(0.83%)

Political Lineup: Governor, Ray Mabus (D); Lt. Gov., Brad Dye (D); Secy. of State, Dick Molpus (D); Atty. Gen., Mike Moore (D); Treasurer, Marshall Bennett (D); Auditor, Pete Johnson (R). State Senate, 52 (44 D and 8 R); State House of Representatives, 122 (113 D and 9 R). Senators, Thad Cochran (R) and Trent Lott (R). Representatives, 5 (4 D and 1 R).

1988 Presidential Vote

Bush (R)	557,921	(60%)
Dukakis (D)	363,921	(39%)

1984 Presidential Vote

Reagan (R)	582,377	(62%)
Mondale (D)	352,192	(37%)

1988 Democratic Presidential Primary

Jackson	160,651	(44%)
Gore	120,304	(33%)
Dukakis	29,947	(8%)
Gephardt	19,693	(5%)
Hart	13,304	(4%)
Simon	2,090	(1%)
Babbitt	2,053	(1%)
Others	12,491	(4%)

1988 Republican Presidential Primary

Bush	104,814	(66%)
Dole	26,855	(17%)
Robertson	21,378	(13%)
Kemp	5,479	(4%)

GOVERNOR

Gov. Ray Mabus (D)

Elected 1987, term expires Jan. 1992; b. Oct. 11, 1948, Ackerman; home, Jackson; U. of MS, B.A. 1969, Johns Hopkins U., M.A. 1970, Harvard U., J.D. 1976; Methodist; married (Julie).

Career: Practicing atty., 1976–80; Aide, Gov. William Winter, 1980–83; State Auditor, 1984–88

Office: P.O. Box 139, Jackson 39205, 601-359-3100.

Election Results

1987 gen.	Ray Mabus (D)	385,689	(61%)
	Jack Reed (R)	336,006	(39%)
1987 runoff	Ray Mabus (D)	428,883	(52%)
	Mike Sturdivant (D).	238,039	(48%)
1987 prim.	Ray Mabus (D)	304,559	(37%)
	Mike Sturdivant (D).	131,180	(16%)
	William (Bill) Waller (D)	105,056	(13%)
	John A. Eaves (D)	98,517	(12%)
	Maurice Dantin (D)	83,603	(10%)
	Ed Pittman (D).	73,667	(9%)
1983 gen.	William A. (Bill) Allain (D).	409,209	(55%)
	Leon Bramlett (R)	288,764	(39%)

SENATORS

Sen. Thad Cochran (R)

Elected 1978, seat up 1990; b. Dec. 7, 1937, Pontotoc; home, Byram; U. of MS, B.A. 1959, J.D. 1965, Rotary Fellow, Trinity Col., Ireland, 1963–64; Baptist; married (Rose).

Career: Navy, 1959–61; Practicing atty., 1965–72; U.S. House of Reps., 1973–78.

Offices: 326 RSOB 20510, 202-224-5054. Also 226 Eastland Fed. Court Bldg. 245 E. Capitol St., Jackson 39201, 601-965-4459.

Committees: *Agriculture, Nutrition, and Forestry* (4th of 9 R). Subcommittees: Agricultural Production and Stabilization of Prices; Domestic and Foreign Marketing and Product Promotion (Ranking Member); Rural Development and Rural Electrification. *Appropriations* (5th of 13 R). Subcommittees: Agriculture, Rural Development and Related Agencies (Ranking Member); Defense; Energy and Water Development; Interior; Labor, Health and Human Services, Education, and Related Agencies. *Labor and Human Resources* (7th of 7 R). Subcommittees: Aging (Ranking Member); Labor; Education, Arts and Humanities. *Select Committee on Indian Affairs* (3d of 3 R).

Group Ratings

	ADA	ACLU	COPE	CFA	LCV	ACU	NTLC	NSI	COC	CEI
1988	5	27	15	33	10	96	69	100	100	50
1987	20	—	15	17	—	68	—	—	78	51

National Journal Ratings

	1988 LIB — 1988 CONS			1987 LIB — 1987 CONS		
Economic	9%	—	81%	19%	—	79%
Social	28%	—	70%	27%	—	71%
Foreign	28%	—	70%	0%	—	76%

Key Votes

1) Cut Aged Housing $	AGN	5) Bork Nomination	FOR	9) SDI Funding	FOR
2) Override Hwy Veto	FOR	6) Ban Plastic Guns	FOR	10) Ban Chem Weaps	FOR
3) Kill Plnt Clsng Notice	FOR	7) Deny Abortions	FOR	11) Aid To Contras	FOR
4) Min Wage Increase	AGN	8) Japanese Reparations	FOR	12) Reagan Defense $	FOR

Election Results

1984 general	Thad Cochran (R).....................	508,314	(58%)	($2,870,894
	William Winter (D)	371,926	(42%)	($738,739
1984 primary	Thad Cochran (R) unopposed			
1978 general	Thad Cochran (R).....................	263,089	(45%)	($1,052,303
	Maurice Danton (D)...................	185,454	(32%)	($873,518
	Charles Evers (I).....................	133,646	(23%)	($135,119

Sen. Trent Lott (R)

Elected 1988, seat up 1994; b. Oct. 9, 1941, Grenada; home Pascagoula; U. of MS, B.A. 1963, J.D. 1967; Baptist; married (Tricia).

Career: Practicing atty., 1967–68; A. A. to U.S. Rep. William M Colmer, 1968–72; U.S. House of Reps., 1973–1988.

Offices: 487 RSOB 20510, 202-224-6253. Also 1 Gov. Plaza, Ste 428, Gulfport 39501, 601-863-1988; 245 E. Capitol St., Ste. 309 Jackson 39201, 601-965-4644; 3100 S. Pascagoula St., Pascagoula 39567, 601-762-5400; Golden Triangle Regional Airport, Rte. 3 P.O. Box 282, Columbus 39701, 601-329-3897; 911 Jackson Ave. Fed. Bldg., Ste. 127, Oxford 38655, 601-234-3774; and 200 E Washington St., Ste. 145, Greenwood 38930, 601-453-5681.

Committees: *Armed Services Committee* (8th of 9 R). Sub committees: Projection Forces and Regional Defense; Defense Industry and Technology; Manpower and Personnel. *Commerce Science and Transportation* (9th of 9 R). Subcommittees: Merchant Marine (Ranking Member) Science, Technology and Space; Surface Transportation; National Ocean Policy Study. *Small Busines* (7th of 9 R). Subcommittees: Innovation, Technology and Productivity (Ranking Member); Urban and Minority-Owned Business Development. *Select Committee on Ethics* (3d of 3 R).

Group Ratings (as Member of the U.S. House of Representatives)

	ADA	ACLU	COPE	CFA	LCV	ACU	NTLC	NSI	COC	CEI
1988	5	18	15	18	6	95	74	100	82	53
1987	4	—	15	14	—	91	—	—	77	71

National Journal Ratings (as Member of the U.S. House of Representatives)

	1988 LIB — 1988 CONS			1987 LIB — 1987 CONS		
Economic	28%	—	72%	11%	—	83%
Social	0%	—	95%	17%	—	82%
Foreign	0%	—	84%	0%	—	80%

Key Votes (as Member of the U.S. House of Representatives)

1) Homeless $	FOR	5) Ban Drug Test	FOR	9) SDI Research	FOR
2) Gephardt Amdt	AGN	6) Drug Death Pen	FOR	10) Ban Chem Weaps	AGN
3) Deficit Reduc	AGN	7) Handgun Sales	FOR	11) Aid to Contras	FOR
4) Kill Plnt Clsng Notice	FOR	8) Ban D.C. Abort $	FOR	12) Nuclear Testing	AGN

Election Results

1988 general	Trent Lott (R)	510,380	(54%)	($3,405,242)
	Wayne Dowdy (D)	436,339	(46%)	($2,355,957)
1988 primary	Trent Lott (R), unopposed			
1982 general	John C. Stennis (D)	414,099	(64%)	($944,054)
	Haley Barbour (R)	230,927	(36%)	($1,133,384)

FIRST DISTRICT

The keystone of William Faulkner's fictional universe, the university town of Oxford in northern Mississippi, sits on a divide between two parts of the state. To the east are the mostly white hill counties, going all the way up to the northeast corner where Mississippi's Tishomingo County meets the Tennessee River. The Tennessee Valley Authority brought electricity here, and the Tennessee-Tombigbee Waterway provided construction jobs for years and a new shipping canal when it was completed in 1985: this is one part of Mississippi where the federal government is regarded as a helper and not a meddling intruder by articulate white opinion. To the west is Mississippi's Delta, the swampy land pioneered by large planters around the turn of the century, with large black work forces little removed—in the conditions of their daily lives or long-term economic chances—from slavery. In the center is Oxford, the home of Ole Miss and the town that was the inspiration for Faulkner's mythical and often savage Jefferson. "His spirit is still here, of course," Willie Morris wrote in *National Geographic* of Faulkner's home territory: "in the woodsmoke of November from forlorn country shacks, in the fireflies in driftless random in the town in June, in the summer wisteria on the greenswards and the odor of verbena, in the ruined old mansions in the Yocona bottoms, in the echoes of an ax on wood and of dogs barking far away, in the languid human commerce on the courthouse square, in the aged whites and blacks bantering on the brick wall beside the jail."

All this land is part of Mississippi's 1st Congressional District, which also includes the Mississippi suburbs of Memphis, Tennessee, touches on the river itself, and goes as far west as Tallahatchie County, the home of Representative Jamie Whitten. Whitten is the dean of the House and chairman of the Appropriations Committee. He was first elected in 1941, a month before Pearl Harbor. Since 1949 (except for 1953–55, when Republicans had control) he has chaired the Agriculture Subcommittee of Appropriations—the longest service of any House subcommittee chairman in history. This has enabled him to become a kind of permanent "secretary of agriculture"; the top bureaucrats in the department believe that Whitten will be around a lot longer than the official Secretary; so far they have been right. Whitten is not afraid to use his influence. He was a strong force for large subsidy payments to cotton farmers; for years the cotton program was the most costly of the Agriculture Department's crop subsidy operations. He has strongly backed attempts to kill vermin with pesticides, and is unsympathetic to critics who claim the chemicals are harmful or in the long run self-defeating: he wants to protect farmers from sudden and potentially catastrophic crop failures and drops in prices. Whitten has developed a network of friends in state agriculture departments and among county agricultural agents all over the country. A Secretary of Agriculture who ignores him is a fool.

But Whitten's mastery of politics goes beyond farm issues. He is one of the few southern politicians from the pre-civil rights days who has made the transition to today's House, and made it skillfully, gracefully, and with powers enhanced. Though he is from a Delta county, almost all of his constituency from 1941 to 1962 was in hill counties, and like many hill county southerners, he supported some New Deal economic programs, including generous spending for farmers, and of course absolutely opposed any change in the system of racial segregation. In 1962, he was placed in the same district with a colleague reputed to be a moderate and given many Delta counties, where of course no blacks were then voting; Whitten ran as the more conservative candidate and won. For a dozen years, as issues changed and Mississippi whites seethed with anger at Washington liberals, Whitten concentrated on agriculture and compiled a conservative voting record on other issues.

Then in 1974, the Democratic Caucus began to elect all committee chairmen by secret ballot, and Whitten, by this time the second ranking member of Appropriations behind 74-year-old George Mahon, took note. On the Agriculture Subcommittee he fought attempts to kill the food stamp program—not a Whitten favorite before 1975, but well-loved by most House Democrats and by the increasing number of black voters in his district. On other issues, his rating from organized labor jumped from the 10% level to about 40%. In effect, he rejoined the national Democratic Party, compiling a liberal voting record on economic issues and sometimes agreeing with most other Democrats on cultural and foreign issues. When Mahon retired in 1978 and it came time to elect a new Appropriations chairman, Edward Boland, popular, respected, liberal and one notch below Whitten, decided not to run, and Whitten won the secret ballot 157–88. Whitten is pleased to point out that after six years as chairman the secret ballot vote was 212–5. "Being a lawyer, you look at the jury and you look at the situation," he has said. "A lawyer who doesn't realize when you've changed the judge and jury is not much for you. I have adjusted to changing conditions."

Whitten has not only adjusted his voting record; he has become one of the leaders of his party, helping younger members with their projects, carrying the party flag on major issues, accumulating favors. He opposes Republican economic programs, fights Republican cuts on the Appropriations Committee, and uses his parliamentary skills (despite an accent unintelligible to many Members) to good advantage. For a time it seemed his power as Appropriations chairman was diminished by the congressional budget process, which sets limits on spending which are supposed to and often do bind the Appropriations subcommittees. But there remains plenty of room for subcommittee chairmen—known collectively as the College of Cardinals—to steer federal programs in the direction they want. For several years, Whitten's power was augmented as most subcommittees missed their deadlines and saw their appropriations jammed into a single continuing resolution in the fall; as the floor manager and conference committee head handling the continuing resolution, Whitten held life and death power over most of government. But as Whitten points out, he hasn't sought this power: he generally has steered House appropriations bills through on schedule, and in 1988 he seemed pleased that a Reagan veto threat meant there was no need for a continuing resolution.

Whitten has never been inattentive to things in Mississippi. He got the Tennessee-Tombigbee waterway built by arranging to have work started at both ends and then in the middle; so when the crunch came, he could argue that it made no sense not to connect the parts already completed. The waterway cost $2 billion and was projected to carry 27 to 40 million tons of cargo a year; in its first 20 months it carried 5 million, plus a lot of pleasure craft. But Whitten is still enthusiastic about its prospects, and proud as well of the $11 million acoustics lab the Congress told the Agriculture Department to build at Ole Miss, or the watershed protection and flood control project for the foothills of the Delta, or money to build Route 302 to connect I-55 and U.S. 72. Whitten is also working to build the space shuttle's rocket boosters in Yellow Creek at an abandoned TVA nuclear plant. "My district is a part of the nation," he has said, "and if you handle a national program and leave out your district, you would not want to go home."

Whitten is not afraid to go home, and the same geniality and marbles-in-the-mouth diction that works for him in Washington works in Mississippi. Redistricting in the 1980s has pared away the Delta counties and black Democratic voters, leaving him with a whiter and more Republican district, but he wins by wide margins, 78% in 1988. Whitten has seen every President since Franklin Roosevelt come and go, most of them (including Ronald Reagan) younger than he is. He seems as politically wily as ever and has plenty of energy, and he is closing in on Carl Vinson's record of 50 years and two months service in the House. Expect to see him in his chair in January 1992 when he will break Vinson's record.

The People: Est. Pop. 1986: 525,500, up 4.2% 1980–86; Pop. 1980: 504,136, up 18.2% 1970–80. Households (1980): 80% family, 46% with children, 67% married couples; 24.2% housing units rented; median monthly rent: $98; median house value: $30,000. Voting age pop. (1980): 345,943; 21% Black, 1% Spanish origin.

1988 Presidential Vote:

Bush (R)	109,304	(59%)
Dukakis (D)	73,839	(40%)

Rep. Jamie L. Whitten (D)

Elected 1941; b. Apr. 18, 1910, Cascilla; home, Charleston; U. of MS, 1927–1931; Presbyterian; married (Rebecca).

Career: Practicing atty.; sch. principal; MS House of Reps., 1932–33; Dist. Atty., 1933–41.

Offices: 2314 RHOB 20515, 202-225-4306. Also P.O. Bldg., Charleston 38921, 601-647-2413; P.O. Box 667, Oxford 38655, 601-234-9064; and P.O. Box 1482, Tupelo 38801, 601-844-5437.

Committees: *Appropriations* (Chairman of 35 D). Subcommittee: Rural Development, Agriculture and Related Agencies (Chairman).

Group Ratings

	ADA	ACLU	COPE	CFA	LCV	ACU	NTLC	NSI	COC	CEI
1988	65	77	44	73	38	20	5	40	15	10
1987	72	—	42	79	—	13	—	—	13	10

National Journal Ratings

	1988 LIB — 1988 CONS		1987 LIB — 1987 CONS	
Economic	71% —	23%	68% —	27%
Social	70% —	30%	53% —	47%
Foreign	56% —	43%	50% —	48%

Key Votes

1) Homeless $	AGN	5) Ban Drug Test	AGN	9) SDI Research	AGN
2) Gephardt Amdt	FOR	6) Drug Death Pen	FOR	10) Ban Chem Weaps	FOR
3) Deficit Reduc	FOR	7) Handgun Sales	FOR	11) Aid to Contras	AGN
4) Kill Plnt Clsng Notice	AGN	8) Ban D.C. Abort $	AGN	12) Nuclear Testing	FOR

Election Results

1988 general	Jamie L. Whitten (D)................	137,445	(78%)	($58,370)
	Jim Bush (R).......................	38,381	(22%)	
1988 primary	Jamie L. Whitten (D)................	56,222	(85%)	
	John Hargett (D)	9,594	(15%)	
1986 general	Jamie L. Whitten (D)................	59,870	(66%)	($170,878)
	Larry Cobb (R).....................	30,267	(34%)	($112,195)

SECOND DISTRICT

The Mississippi Delta, the flat, incredibly fertile land between the Mississippi and the Yazoo, criss-crossed and refertilized by tributaries, is a fabled land, a source of great wealth and a scene of great misery. It was swampy land, often flooded, until well after the Civil War; but wanderers through the Delta wilderness discovered that the topsoil here, accumulated over centuries of Mississippi spring floods, reached depths of 25 feet. To nature, late 19th century entrepreneurs applied technology: the Delta was drained by great machines, the river was lined with levees, and the Illinois Central tracks were laid down on elevated tracks from Memphis to New Orleans. Labor was attracted from the older black belts of the Deep South, and the Delta became, in the words of the *WPA Guide*, "a land of cotton and cotton planters. In the fall, or cotton-picking time, it is a sea of white, broken at intervals by dark lines of trees that grow along the bayous. The plantation big houses are substantial but not pretentious; the tenant cabins are all alike. Smaller towns, hardly more than plantation centers, are of a single pattern; each is centered about a gin, a filling station, a loading platform, and a short line of low-roofed, brick stores."

There was a kind of industrial revolution in agriculture, and the workers were treated with the same indifference and callousness that northern factory owners treated the immigrants and farmboys who worked their machines. The patina of graciousness which often covered the brutality of slavery was not often seen in the Delta. Most new planters were capitalists, not cavaliers, and when they replaced labor with capital by bringing in cotton-picking machines in the 1940s, in later decades switching to crops like soybeans and catfish, they did everything they could (perhaps in anticipation of the day when blacks would get the vote) to encourage local blacks to move north to Chicago or Memphis. Welfare payments and aid to the poor are as stingy—or nonexistent—in the Delta as anywhere in the United States.

This was the land that produced some of the most obdurate segregationists in American politics, like Delta planter James Eastland, U.S. Senator from 1941 to 1979, chairman of the Judiciary Committee from 1955 to 1979, and unrelenting foe of civil rights laws. But it is also the land that has produced, for the first time since Reconstruction, and 20 years after the Voting Rights Act first gave black Mississippians the vote, a black congressman, Mike Espy. Born the year before *Brown v. Board of Education* and 11 years old when the Voting Rights Act was passed, he was elected in 1986 in the 2d Congressional District, which includes all of the Delta plus a few of the foothills to the east, a small part of the city of Jackson, and the Mississippi Valley just below Vicksburg.

Espy succeeded in 1986 where another black candidate had failed in 1982 and 1984 partly because the district lines were changed in Voting Rights Act cases, and partly because of his background: his grandfather decided to build a hospital and asked every black in audiences around the state to contribute $1 for a brick. He also built 28 funeral homes and became one of the biggest landowners in the state. A third advantage was eloquence: Espy, a lawyer, educated in northern schools, experienced after several years in state government enforcing land laws over recalcitrant locals, was at ease on the stump attacking Republican Webb Franklin's record. And there was sheer luck: in the low-turnout primary, Espy beat a nephew of former Governor Paul

Johnson and a cousin of James Eastland with 50.1% of the vote—just 79 more votes than he needed to avoid a runoff. Finally, Espy ran a superior campaign, with a targeted voter registration and turnout drive as sophisticated as any Mississippi had seen; he raised plenty of money and got support from leading Democrats; he attacked the Republican incumbent for his votes on farm programs and carried around in his pocket a promise from then Speaker-to-be Jim Wright that if Espy was elected, he would get a seat on the Agriculture Committee. This combination was enough for Espy to carry the Delta with enough extra votes to overcome Franklin's edge in Vicksburg and one mostly-white rural county.

Once in office, Espy has used the standard formulas to consolidate his hold on the district, and they have worked. He got a seat not only on Agriculture but on Budget. He has deluged constituents with mail, run a good constituency service operation, and highlighted his success in passing the Lower Mississippi River Valley Development Act setting up a multistate Delta Commission, in getting the Army to increase its purchases of catfish (a big Delta product these days) by 65%, and in steering federal money to the 2d district. He was endorsed by the National Rifle Association and, after the election, appeared in one of their "I'm the NRA" print ads. Shrewdly, he worked with Jamie Whitten on the Delta bill and other matters. In 1988, he outraised and outcampaigned his Republican opponent, and won by a 65%–34% margin. In the process, he ran well ahead of Michael Dukakis and Senate candidate Wayne Dowdy and won more than one in three white votes. This was a stunning performance: Espy broke the back of the old segregationist politics, and proved that it is possible for a black candidate to win anywhere in the country.

The People: Est. Pop. 1986: 499,600, dn. 0.9% 1980–86; Pop. 1980: 503,935, up 0.4% 1970–80. Households (1980): 76% family, 47% with children, 56% married couples; 37.3% housing units rented; median monthly rent: $78; median house value: $26,800. Voting age pop. (1980): 323,647; 53% Black, 1% Spanish origin.

1988 Presidential Vote: Dukakis (D)...................... 87,386   (51%)
                             Bush (R) 82,403   (48%)

Rep. Mike Espy (D)

Elected 1986; b. Nov. 30, 1953, Yazoo City; home, Madison; Howard U., B.A. 1975, U. of Santa Clara, J.D. 1978; Baptist; married (Sheila).

Career: Managing atty., Central MS Legal Services, 1978–80; Asst. Secy. of State, MS, 1980–84; Asst. Atty. Gen., Dir. of MS Consumer Protection, 1984–85.

Offices: 216 CHOB 20515, 202-225-5876. Also 300 S. Main St., Yazoo City 39194, 1-800-746-247-9395, 601-746-1400; Vicksburg City Hall, 1401 Walnut St., Rm. 302, Vicksburg 39180, 601-638-3779; Clarksdale City Hall, 416 3d St., 1st flr., Clarksdale 38614, 601-624-9929; and Greenville City Hall, City Hall Annex, 340 Main St., Greenville 38701, 601-334-3779.

Committees: *Agriculture* (22d of 27 D). Subcommittees: Conservation, Credit, and Rural Development; Domestic Marketing, Consumer Relations and Nutrition; Cotton, Rice and Sugar. *Budget* (12th of 21 D). Task Forces: Community and Natural Resources; Human Resources. *Select Committee on Hunger* (12th of 16 D).

Group Ratings

	ADA	ACLU	COPE	CFA	LCV	ACU	NTLC	NSI	COC	CEI
1988	85	77	90	73	50	12	5	10	25	7
1987	84	—	88	50	—	0	—	—	7	9

National Journal Ratings

	1988 LIB — 1988 CONS		1987 LIB — 1987 CONS	
Economic	71% —	29%	73% —	0%
Social	63% —	37%	65% —	34%
Foreign	84% —	0%	74% —	25%

Key Votes

1) Homeless $	AGN	5) Ban Drug Test	AGN	9) SDI Research	AGN
2) Gephardt Amdt	FOR	6) Drug Death Pen	FOR	10) Ban Chem Weaps	FOR
3) Deficit Reduc	FOR	7) Handgun Sales	FOR	11) Aid to Contras	AGN
4) Kill Plnt Clsng Notice	AGN	8) Ban D.C. Abort $	AGN	12) Nuclear Testing	FOR

Election Results

1988 general	Mike Espy (D)	112,401	(65%)	($886,540)
	Jack Coleman (R)....................	59,827	(34%)	($225,873)
1988 primary	Mike Espy (D)	59,801	(88%)	
	J. F. (Boja) Clarke (D)	8,250	(12%)	
1986 general	Mike Espy (D)	73,119	(52%)	($591,002)
	Webb Franklin (D)..................	68,292	(48%)	($574,120)

THIRD DISTRICT

The Neshoba County fair, held every August in Philadelphia, Mississippi since 1892, is traditionally the place where Mississippi politicians announce their candidacies, with the crowds watching their performance to take their measure. It is a mostly white crowd (though Philadelphia is the center of Mississippi's Choctaw Indians), and when Ronald Reagan came here in 1980 and Michael Dukakis in 1988, neither mentioned what Philadelphia and Neshoba County are best known for in history : it was here in "Freedom Summer" of 1964 that three civil rights workers, two white and one black, were murdered for the crime of urging American citizens to register and vote. Philadelphia geographically is near the center of Mississippi and of its 3d Congressional District, a mostly rural area that stretches from Columbus and Starkville, home of Mississippi State University, in the north, to Laurel in the south, and touches on the Jackson suburbs of Rankin County in the west. Most whites probably don't want to be reminded of the brutal way in which Mississippi's old segregationist order was maintained and, considering how amiably blacks and whites get along in public accommodations, at workplaces and in politics, it is hard to imagine how such hate could have existed.

The 3d District's congressman, Sonny Montgomery, is an old-fashioned southern Democrat: devoted to his work, a delightful companion, dedicated to his principles, possessed of a fine sense of humor. A veteran of both World War II and Korea, Montgomery serves on the Armed Services and Veterans' Affairs Committee. In 1981 he became chairman of Veterans' Affairs, a body led for years by conservative southerners. Veterans' Affairs bills are traditionally considered on the floor of the House under a closed rule, which means that no amendments are allowed; which means in turn that the bill Montgomery and his allies on the committee report out is the one that passes.

On some issues Montgomery has represented the traditional views of older veterans' organizations against those of younger veterans. He has tended to be skeptical about the claims that Agent Orange caused injuries for which victims should be compensated, and he resisted a proposal by California Democrat Don Edwards to allow veterans to hire lawyers to make claims on the Veterans' Administration rather than rely on traditional veterans' organizations to pursue them. But his biggest achievement as chairman is the new G.I. education bill, passed in 1985 with improvements in 1988. This allows servicemen to put aside $100 a month of their first 12 months pay and receive $300 a month for 36 months in education aid. He argues that this will help recruitment in the all-volunteer military and provide thousands of servicemen and women with a chance to improve their skills and earnings. In 1988, he was pleased to support the upgrading of the VA to a Cabinet department, and backed adding a statue in honor of the women who served to the Vietnam war memorial.

On the Armed Services Committee, Montgomery is Capitol Hill's strongest champion of the Reserves and National Guard, which do not boast as many Members of Congress in their ranks as they used to; he sponsored the successful amendment to take away governors' powers to veto assignment of their states' guards to overseas training exercises (some have been held in Honduras). He has not been successful in his effort to require doctors and nurses to register for a possible draft. On military issues Montgomery is invariably hawkish, on cultural matters traditional, on economic issues sometimes willing to spend money domestically. Over the years he has usually voted with Republican administrations. But he remains on friendly terms with the Democratic leadership, seldom opposes them volubly, and is sometimes available to help—a party loyalist, in his own way. Back home, his 89% in 1988 was his *lowest* percentage in 20 years; the dropoff is due to the increasing vote in Jackson suburbs, where he won with 79% as compared to 91% in the rest of the district.

The People: Est. Pop. 1986: 526,600, up 4.3% 1980–86; Pop. 1980: 505,169, up 16.5% 1970–80. Households (1980): 78% family, 45% with children, 64% married couples; 26.1% housing units rented; median monthly rent: $114; median house value: $31,800. Voting age pop. (1980): 348,335; 28% Black, 1% Spanish origin, 1% American Indian.

1988 Presidential Vote:

Bush (R)	124,841	(66%)
Dukakis (D)	64,007	(34%)

Rep. G. V. (Sonny) Montgomery (D)

Elected 1966; b. Aug. 5, 1920, Meridian; home, Meridian; MS St. U., B.S. 1943; Episcopalian; single.

Career: Army, WWII and Korea; Owner, Montgomery Insur. Agcy.; MS Senate, 1956–66.

Offices: 2184 RHOB 20515, 202-225-5031. Also P.O. Box 5618, Meridian 39301, 601-693-6681; Fed. Bldg., Laurel 39440, 601-649-1231; Golden Triangle Airport, Columbus 39701, 601-327-2766; and 110-D Airport Rd., Pearl 39208, 601-932-2410.

Committees: *Armed Services* (3d of 31 D). Subcommittees: Military Installations and Facilities; Military Personnel and Compensation. *Veterans' Affairs* (Chairman of 21 D). Subcommittees: Hospitals and Health Care (Chairman).

Group Ratings

	ADA	ACLU	COPE	CFA	LCV	ACU	NTLC	NSI	COC	CEI
1988	25	39	15	64	25	71	42	100	71	35
1987	20	—	13	21	—	65	—	—	71	37

National Journal Ratings

	1988 LIB — 1988 CONS	1987 LIB — 1987 CONS
Economic	43% — 56%	42% — 58%
Social	29% — 70%	28% — 71%
Foreign	30% — 67%	32% — 67%

Key Votes

1) Homeless $	AGN	5) Ban Drug Test	FOR	9) SDI Research	FOR
2) Gephardt Amdt	AGN	6) Drug Death Pen	FOR	10) Ban Chem Weaps	AGN
3) Deficit Reduc	FOR	7) Handgun Sales	FOR	11) Aid to Contras	FOR
4) Kill Plnt Clsng Notice	FOR	8) Ban D.C. Abort $	FOR	12) Nuclear Testing	AGN

Election Results

1988 general	G. V. (Sonny) Montgomery (D)	164,651	(89%)	($116,761)
	Jimmie Ray Boukland (R)	20,729	(11%)	($671)
1988 primary	G. V. (Sonny) Montgomery (D), unopposed			
1986 general	G. V. (Sonny) Montgomery (D)	80,575	(100%)	($70,580)

FOURTH DISTRICT

Two generations ago, Jackson, Mississippi was a sleepy small city of 48,000, proud of its state capital, but defensive about its state's national reputation as a stronghold of bigotry and poverty. As life in Mississippi has changed, a new spirit and new vibrancy have become apparent in Jackson. On the north side of town, in new subdivisions of pleasant, large colonial houses under huge, overhanging trees, you can get a sense of what growth has meant to Jackson—especially when you consider that at least some of the people in these neighborhoods came from humble houses in rural Mississippi. Even the less well-to-do people who grew up poor and now make $40,000 a year—more than they ever dreamed of—tend to think of themselves as the new rich, and in fact money goes a good deal further in Jackson than in a large metropolitan area.

This kind of economic growth has made white Jackson one of the Republican strongholds of Mississippi. Evidently, these white voters have not paused to ask whether the civil rights revolution, which coincides with the beginnings of boom times for Jackson and the Sun Belt, had anything to do with the economic explosion from which they have benefited. Yet surely it has, if only to make places like Jackson more attractive to investors and to the talented blacks who used to migrate en masse to northern cities. The other side of this paradox is that black Jackson, almost unanimously Democratic, does not have much appreciation for what free markets and gutsy entrepreneurs have done to raise living standards for everyone in Jackson. Central to their political experience has been the fact that civil rights were won only by an activist, even meddlesome federal government, and reflexively they see big government as their ally and even savior generally. Between these points of view there is little room for accommodation. Politicians like William Winter and Thad Cochran have made biracial political themes acceptable across Mississippi, but in Jackson most of the votes tend to be cast along racial lines.

Jackson and some of its affluent suburban fringe form almost half of Mississippi's 4th Congressional District. The rest consists of the rural areas and small towns of south central and southwestern Mississippi, from the antebellum mansions of Natchez to small cities like Brookhaven, McComb and Columbia. These are mini-Jacksons: they have growing white affluent populations plus black near-majorities. Nationally, they have been trending Republican, but there are still many rural white Democratic voters in congressional elections. They tend to balance off Jackson, and to make this one of the more spiritedly contested congressional districts in the South.

It certainly was in 1988, when Congressman Wayne Dowdy, a rich businessman with populist instincts, was running for the Senate. Both Democrats and Republicans had runoff primaries; both produced candidates who sounded general themes but did not get much into specifics. The Republican nominee was Jackson-based Tom Collins, a prisoner of war during the Vietnam war; the Democrat was Mike Parker, a funeral home owner from Brookhaven. Indignantly, Collins accused Parker of being a Dukakis Democrat; as if injured, Parker replied that he was not endorsing Dukakis and added a criticism of Dukakis' mandatory health insurance proposal in the bargain. Parker mellifluously and in an expensive ad campaign presented himself as backer of family values and believer in things American. The *Jackson Clarion-Ledger* found the candidates so vapid it refused to endorse either one.

That left the race a battle of the smaller counties versus Jackson. Collins squeezed out only a narrow 50%–48% margin in the Jackson area, while in the smaller counties Parker led smartly, 61%–39%, for an overall win of 55%–44%—in yet another seriously contested election in which the Democrat vastly outspent the Republican. In the House, Parker sits on the Public Works and Veterans' Affairs Committees, not his first choice, which was Energy and Commerce.

The People: Est. Pop. 1986: 521,700, up 3.7% 1980–86; Pop. 1980: 503,297, up 12.5% 1970–80. Households (1980): 76% family, 44% with children, 59% married couples; 29.4% housing units rented; median monthly rent: $129; median house value: $34,200. Voting age pop. (1980): 345,335; 37% Black, 1% Spanish origin.

1988 Presidential Vote: Bush (R) 114,110   (57%)
Dukakis (D). 85,094   (42%)

Rep. Mike Parker (D)

Elected 1988; b. Oct. 31, 1949, Laurel; home, Brookhaven; William Carey Col., B.A. 1970; Presbyterian; married, (Rosemary).

Career: Small businessman, funeral homes, 1971–88.

Offices: 1725 LHOB 20515, 202-225-5865. Also 245 E. Capitol St., Ste. 222, Jackson 39201, 601-965-4086.

Committees: *Public Works and Transportation* (29th of 31 D). Subcommittees: Public Buildings and Grounds; Surface Transportation; Water Resources. *Veterans' Affairs* (19th of 21 D). Subcommittees: Compensaton, Pension and Insurance; Housing and Memorial Affairs.

Group Ratings and Key Votes: Newly Elected

Election Results

1988 general	Mike Parker (D)	110,184	(55%)	($843,142)
	Thomas Collins (R)	88,433	(44%)	($394,250)
1988 run off	Mike Parker (D)	34,507	(61%)	
	Brad Pigott (D)	22,122	(39%)	
1988 primary	Brad Pigott (D)	23,489	(25%)	
	Mike Parker (D)	17,303	(19%)	
	Steve Patterson (D)	16,695	(18%)	
	Bobby Moak (D)	12,037	(13%)	
	Clint Watkins (D)	9,127	(10%)	
	Terrell Stubbs (D)	8,425	(9%)	
	Others	5,481	(6%)	
1986 general	Wayne Dowdy (D)	85,819	(72%)	($325,665)
	Gail Healy (R)	34,190	(28%)	($62,347)

FIFTH DISTRICT

The Gulf Coast of Mississippi is the part of the state that was the first to be settled and that most recently has grown the fastest. Biloxi was founded by the French in 1699, before New Orleans or St. Louis, and was capital of an empire extending to Yellowstone Park; it was on this strand that Jefferson Davis built his mansion, Beauvoir. But for years its growth was limited by yellow fever and lack of farmland. Now, with heavy 1970s and 1980s growth in vacation areas, the Gulf Coast is booming. Here are the cities of Biloxi and Gulfport, greatly enlarged in recent years after a nasty hurricane. To the east are Pascagoula and Moss Point, beneficiaries of the giant Litton shipyard often favored with military contracts; to the west are smaller resort towns frequented by the rich and not-so-rich of nearby New Orleans. The Gulf Coast includes about 60% of the people of the 5th Congressional District of Mississippi. The remainder live inland, in farm counties or in the medium-sized cities of Hattiesburg and Laurel. Much of this land is piney woods and paper mill country—scrubby land that was not good enough for antebellum plantations. As a result, there are relatively few blacks here: only one in six of the district's adults are black, the lowest percentage in Mississippi. With its low black percentage and booming economy, the 5th District, like most of the Gulf Coast, has become prime Republican territory. It went Republican twice against fellow southerner Jimmy Carter, and in 1972 it gave Richard Nixon his highest percentage in any of the 435 congressional districts, a whopping 87%. It was represented for 16 years in the House by Trent Lott, who rose to become Republican whip before he was elected to the Senate in 1988.

Lott's successor is a Republican too, but his victory was not automatic. Larkin Smith was elected sheriff of Harrison County (Biloxi, Gulfport) in 1983, after 17 years in law enforcement; he ran well ahead of George Robert Hall, a former Vietnam prisoner of war. But Democrats still hold many local offices in southern Mississippi, and they fielded candidates with local followings; Bay St. Louis state Senator Gene Taylor beat Forrest and Perry Counties (Hattiesburg) District Attorney Glenn White in the runoff. Smith emphasized law enforcement issues. Taylor did not differ much from him on these or other matters. Taylor ended up running better on the coast, holding Smith to a 51%–49% edge there. But in the counties inland, Smith led 60%–40%, and won districtwide 55%–45%. In the House, Smith is a member of the Government Operations and Judiciary Committees; on the latter he ranks just behind Lamar Smith of Texas.

The People: Est. Pop. 1986: 550,800, up 9.3% 1980–86; Pop. 1980: 504,101, up 23.7% 1970–80. Households (1980): 78% family, 47% with children, 65% married couples; 28.3% housing units rented; median monthly rent: $156; median house value: $33,500. Voting age pop. (1980): 343,181; 17% Black, 1% Spanish origin, 1% Asian origin.

1988 Presidential Vote: Bush (R) 126,860   (69%)
Dukakis (D). 53,595   (29%)

Rep. Larkin Smith (R)

Elected 1988; b. June 26, 1944, Poplarville; home, Long Beach; LA State U. Law Enforcement Inst. 1969, William Carey Col., B.A. 1979; Roman Catholic; married (Sheila).

Career: Chief Depty. Sheriff, Pearl River Cnty., 1966–72; Chief Investigator, Harrison Cnty., 1972–77; Chief of Police, Gulfport, 1977–83; Sheriff, Harrison Cnty., 1984–89.

Offices: 516 CHOB 20515, 202-225-5772. Also 1 Govt. Plaza, P.O. Box 1557, Gulfport 39501, 601-864-7670; and 215 Fed. Bldg., Hattiesburg 39401, 601-582-3246.

Committees: *Government Operations* (13th of 15 R). Subcommittee: Human Resources and Intergovernmental Relations (Ranking Member). *Judiciary* (12th of 14 R). Subcommittees: Crime; Administrative Law and Governmental Relations; Criminal Justice.

Group Ratings and Key Votes: Newly Elected
Election Results

1988 general	Larkin Smith (R)	100,185	(55%)	($569,830)
	Gene Taylor (D)	82,034	(45%)	($165,041)
1988 run off	Larkin Smith (R)	25,470	(67%)	
	George R. Hall (R).	12,553	(33%)	
1988 primary	Larkin Smith (R)	26,294	(48%)	
	George R. Hall (R).	17,855	(32%)	
	Glenn Mitchell (R).	6,870	(12%)	
	Christopher Roosa (R)	3,606	(7%)	
1986 general	Trent Lott (R).	75,288	(82%)	($264,822)
	Larry L. Albritton (D)	16,143	(18%)	($531)

MISSOURI

The second most important American election 50 years ago, after the presidential contest, was the Democratic primary for Senator in the state of Missouri. It was a close contest between crime-busting Governor Lloyd Stark and one-term incumbent Harry Truman, who had close ties to Kansas City boss Tom Pendergast, convicted and sent to jail the year before. But Truman's New Deal voting record helped him win the support of union members and blacks, St. Louis boss Bob Hannegan switched to him at the last minute, Truman's residual sympathies for the Confederacy helped him in rural areas. He beat Stark by 8,300 votes out of 665,000, cast going on to win by a party-line vote in November. This primary wasn't much watched at the time, but if the result had been different, Truman never would have been President, and the way he won the contest—through appeals to unions and blacks, neither of whom had Truman's personal sympathy—foreshadowed the way he would win the 1948 election and the coalition that Democrats would attempt to assemble, with varying success, over the next half-century.

Truman was running in a state that was as good a political laboratory for national politics as any. In the middle of Middle America, at once southern and northern, eastern and western, at the confluence of the continent's two greatest rivers, with the geographical center of the nation's population in 1980 and not far from the geographic midpoint of the 48 continental states, Missouri is *the* central American state. Fifty years ago, more than today, it bulked large in the national consciousness. Kansas City was an "up-to-date" major metropolitan area, and St. Louis, with 816,000 people living in street grids bending back from the Mississippi levees, was one of the few cities with two major league baseball teams. Missouri was one of the hubs of the nation's railroad network, one of its major farm as well as manufacturing states, and for years had been America's leading producer of mules (Truman's father was a mule trader). In 1940, there were 6 million farms, 1.5 million tractors and 4 million mules; the mule was most farmers' most efficient source of agricultural power, and Missouri mules were still bred in large numbers and sent out over the rail lines to states from Mississippi to Nebraska, Ohio to Texas.

Missouri had been, a century before, the frontier—the first state created entirely out of territory west of the Mississippi River, jutting far out past white settlement. St. Louis had been just a trading post when Lewis and Clark passed through, and the site of Kansas City was just another point on the bluffs that overlooked the Missouri River as it rushed down from Montana and the Dakotas. The northernmost slave state, Missouri sent pro-slavery raiders over the border into the Kansas Territory in the 1850s to fight settlers sent in by abolitionists, and in the 1860s it had its own civil war in the hilly counties along the Missouri River. But Missouri's most important historical role was that of a gateway to the West, an avenue for the great Yankee migrations west from Ohio, Indiana and Illinois and the southern migration west from Kentucky (Missouri is where Daniel Boone finally stopped looking for elbow room), the eastern terminus of the Pony Express and the Transcontinental Railroad.

Missouri has had below-average population growth since 1900, as its rural residents leave for big cities and suburbs and its cities grow at no more than ordinary rates; Missouri had 13 congressmen when Truman was renominated and has 9 today. Since 1940, population growth has been mostly at the periphery of the nation, and inland states like Missouri have become demographically old. But having continuity, Missouri retains a civic life and politics akin to what it had when mules were an industry here. As in other border states, political divisions split along Civil War lines, but the geographical pattern is not what you might expect. Little Dixie, first settled by Virginians, lies in the northeast part of the state; the southwest, in the Ozarks, was Union and is Republican country today. Meanwhile, St. Louis, once a Republican island in a southern Democratic sea, became heavily Democratic in the 1930s, though now metropolitan St. Louis seems to be trending Republican (partly because some of its most Democratic areas are across the river in Illinois). The Kansas City area, less anchored to the state, is more volatile and usually more Democratic (partly because most of its richest suburbs are across State Line Road in Kansas). So political preference is still a matter of economic status and cultural attitudes only lightly superimposed on Civil War regional allegiances. On cultural and foreign controversies as defined nationally, Missouri is closer than the coasts to the consensus that the nation had 30 years ago.

In state elections, Missouri has followed (or led) national trends, voting mostly Democratic from the 1930s through the 1960s and mostly Republican at the top of the ticket (Democrats still win most legislative and local offices) since 1968. In those last two decades it has elected a Democratic governor only once, a Democratic Senator (Tom Eagleton) twice; not only are its current governor and Senators all Republicans, but so are all statewide officials except the lieutenant governor. For years it favored rough-hewn politicos, but Governor John Ashcroft and Senators John Danforth and Christopher Bond are all Ivy League graduates and reformers who have made their political careers exposing scandal and running against old boy networks.

Rural Missouri still casts nearly half the votes and sets much of the tone. These voters' traditional attitudes on cultural issues were never undermined by the kind of explosive economic

MISSOURI — Congressional Districts, Counties, Independent City, and Other Selected Places — *(9 Districts)*

LEGEND

2 Congressional district number
Congressional district boundary
◉ Place of 100,000 or more inhabitants
◎ Place of 50,000 to 100,000 inhabitants
• Place of 25,000 to 50,000 inhabitants
State capital underlined

U.S. Department of Commerce
BUREAU OF THE CENSUS

Congressional districts established January 7, 1982; all other boundaries are as of January 1, 1980.

growth that took wives out of kitchens and put them into offices; they have gone Democratic only in the recessions of the mid-1970s and 1982. Also, the Democrats have often nominated St. Louis-based candidates who call the state Missour*ee*—a distinct handicap against outstate candidates who say, as Truman did and most Missourians do, Missour*ah*. Whichever way you say it, Missouri may be the number one success story for the Republican Party in the nation, a state where they have run better candidates and run government better than the Democrats, and have outpoliticked them at every turn.

Presidential politics. Near the center of the nation geographically, Missouri is also near the center in presidential elections: it is a pretty good bellwether, voting for only one presidential loser in the 20th century—Adlai Stevenson in 1956. Stevenson was an urban sophisticate who had Farm Belt discontent going for him; so did Michael Dukakis, but not enough for him to win: he got 44% in the rural areas, compared to Jimmy Carter's 51% in 1976, which made the difference between Carter's 51%–47% statewide victory and Dukakis's 48%–52% statewide loss. Dukakis's campaign in Missouri was marked by one memorable goof: he went to the Moog automotive plant in St. Louis County to praise union-management cooperation in American-owned plants—only to have television viewers learn that night that Moog is owned by an Italian company.

Missouri joined the Super Tuesday primary in 1988, discarding its old-fashioned caucuses.

Democratic legislators wanted to help Richard Gephardt, who won a smart and uncontested victory in his home state. On the Republican side, Bob Dole of next-door Kansas missed a chance to win a much-needed primary state on Super Tuesday; he was so close that just a little more effort—a few more ads, another touchdown at an airport—might have made the difference and made him a credible candidate in Illinois the week after.

Governor. Missouri's Governor John Ashcroft is one of the state's most popular politicians. The son of a fundamentalist minister, a gospel singer and songwriter from the southwest part of the state, he combines rural style and culturally conservative views with the articulateness and argumentativeness you might expect from a graduate of Yale and the University of Chicago Law School and a man who with his wife, also a lawyer, has co-authored two legal textbooks. He is against taxes almost always, although he favored a bipartisan effort to adopt a four cent gas tax hike in his first term to pay for building roads. He is against abortion, though he does not make that a high-priority issue. He is against the St. Louis and Kansas City school busing programs which courts have ordered, saying that these orders would "bleed" more than $210 million from the state budget. As governor, he stresses education, putting 70% of revenue growth into education programs, to bring Missouri up from its rather middling performance. He claims credit for improved test scores during his first term and wants to persuade more students to stay in school until graduation in his second. He wants to attract new business, and during the 1988 campaign claimed credit for 179,000 (or 204,000: he used different figures and these things aren't precise anyway) new jobs.

To this, his Democratic opponent Betty Hearnes, a veteran legislator and wife of former Governor (1964–72) Warren Hearnes, argued that Ashcroft was claiming credit for what the legislature did—or alternatively that the new jobs were low-paying service jobs. Some also attacked Ashcroft for opposing the 1988 MedAssist ballot measure calling for a .6% earnings tax to provide universal health insurance. But his record and stands proved popular with the voters. Hearnes campaigned gamely, but never had a chance; approval of Ashcroft was high throughout. In 1984, he won two tough races, against the St. Louis county executive in the primary and against the Democratic lieutenant governor, a veteran legislator from the St. Louis area, in the general; he barely carried the metro areas but got 63% in the rest of the state, for a 57% victory. In 1988, he won 112 of 114 counties, carrying both metropolitan areas handily and winning 64% of the vote statewide—the best percentage for a governor in Missouri since the Civil War.

Senators. Missouri's two Senators are political allies whose careers have run in tandem. Both are Republicans who first ran for office in 1968, both have suffered defeats and won big victories, both have similar philosophies, and together they have made the Republicans the majority party in Missouri.

John Danforth, now in his third term and third decade in public office, comes from the rich (and philanthropic) family that started Ralston Purina. He is also the only ordained minister in the Senate: he attended Yale Law and Divinity Schools at the same time. Danforth brings a certain moral intensity but not starchiness to politics: he is rumpled, informal and candid, with a taste for country music and baseball, but not a natural horse-trader or storyteller. He tends to arrive at positions after a moral inventory rather than a political calculus; he is unusual in the Senate because he opposes both abortion and capital punishment. Danforth was elected attorney general of Missouri at age 32 in 1968—the breakthrough victory for Republicans in Missouri— but he lost narrowly to Senator Stuart Symington in 1970 and was not the favorite six years later when Symington retired. But the Democratic nominee, Congressman Jerry Litton, died in a plane crash on primary night, and in November Danforth easily beat the substitute candidate, former Governor Warren Hearnes.

Danforth sits on the Finance Committee and is ranking member on the subcommittee on trade; he has been throughout the 1980s a major player on trade issues. Working with Finance Chairman Lloyd Bentsen, he sponsored the 1988 trade bill that passed, seeking reciprocity of market access and more predictable U.S. behavior. The legislation is hardly a hymn to free trade, but Danforth, like Bentsen, seems aware of the pitfalls of protectionism and determined, despite sometimes responding to pleas from Missouri shoe and auto interests, not to fall into them. Danforth has had other legislative successes: a $1.85 billion high school basic skills program, a law to promote methanol as a motor fuel and was a co-sponsor on the airport improvement bill of 1987. He sponsored the critical amendment to the civil rights bill of 1988, preventing it from requiring Catholic hospitals' insurance policies to cover abortions; without this, the law would not have passed. He also pushed for random testing of railroad and other transportation workers after the crash of a Maryland train that one of his daughters had almost boarded. In 1989 Danforth moved from Budget to Intelligence in 1989, where he hopes to promote bipartisan foreign policy.

Occasionally Danforth has flinched or switched on major issues. After opposing the plant closing notice amendment to the 1988 trade bill, he switched and supported it. And in 1986, after initially supporting the concept of the tax reform bill, he decided that the final version raised taxes on corporations and hurt defense contractors (McDonnell-Douglas and General Dynamics are both headquartered in Missouri) too much and voted against it. No one doubts that Danforth's objections were on the merits, but such switches tend to undermine his effectiveness as a legislator.

Danforth has other interests. He made a trip to a number of Sub-Saharan countries in 1984 well before their starving children began appearing on television screens and newsmagazine covers, and in 1985 he led the Senate to pass a major relief bill for famine victims throughout Africa. But he draws the lesson that encouraging market economics, not subsidies for state socialism, will serve Africans' best interests in the long run. At home he is one of those Republicans, like his former Finance Chairman Bob Dole, willing to raise taxes to cut the deficit, to the point of favoring a higher tax on tobacco and keeping intact the later repealed withholding requirement for interest on dividend income. So for a man of rather unconventional temperament, Danforth ends up with a fairly conventional, oldfashioned Republican voting record. If he is not exactly a team player and certainly not a vote-trader, he is not a boat-rocker either.

Danforth has had an off-again, on-again record as a vote-getter in Missouri: winning for attorney general in 1968 and 1972, losing for Senator narrowly in 1970, winning in odd circumstances in 1976, then only narrowly beating Democrat Harriett Woods in 1982. In that recession year Woods, of suburban St. Louis, ran a populist campaign emphasizing the woes of farmers, while attacking mounting surpluses, the huge cost of subsidies, and rising food prices for consumers: all problem and no solution. She criticized Danforth for supporting Reaganomics and for being rich, and in mid-October was running even; then she ran out of money and went off the air, while Danforth went negative, accusing her of demagoguery and distortion. Danforth won by only 51%–49%. In 1988 he redeemed himself. Democrat Jay Nixon, a brash 32-year-old state senator, used Woods's themes. But he raised little money, had turmoil in his campaign organization and failed to show the stature for the job. Danforth, emphasizing some of his positive stands, won easily, carrying all 114 counties and losing only St. Louis City, and winning 68% of the vote—the all-time record for a Senate candidate in Missouri.

Missouri's junior Senator, Christopher Bond, is also rounding out two decades in public life: a narrowly unsuccessful run for the House in 1968, election as governor in 1972 at age 33, unexpected defeat for reelection in 1976, a comeback victory after Democrat Joseph Teasdale compiled a weak record in 1980 and then, after two years out of office, a close Senate race in 1986. His opponent was the same Harriett Woods, by then lieutenant governor, who had nearly beaten Danforth in 1982. She created a furor by running a three-part ad showing a farmer breaking into tears as he and his wife told Woods about their foreclosure and then named Bond as a member of the board of the insurance company that foreclosed. This struck most voters as going too far, whether in invading the farmer's privacy or making too long a stretch to indict Bond; Woods dropped the ad as she dropped in the polls, especially in urban areas; she ended up running weaker in rural areas than four years before. Bond started with the asset of a popular, no-tax-rise record as governor and had the advantage of being, as governor for most of the preceding 14 years, the best-known public figure in Missouri. He played smartly on the home state pride that was as evident in Missouri as it was in so many other states in 1986. Bond carried rural Missouri handily and the St. Louis area as well and won 53%–47%.

Bond comes from a comfortable background (though he is nowhere near as rich as Danforth); he is a strong partisan Republican, a conservative who believes in holding down taxes, is willing to entertain innovative solutions for new problems, and tends to be culturally conservative and to support an assertive foreign policy, but not invariably. In the Senate, he is a lead backer of such partisan initiatives as the Republican campaign finance reform and the modified line-item veto; in the pinch, he switched from support of the plant closing notice measure in 1988 to opposition. With seats on the Agriculture (for industrial uses of existing crops) and Banking Committees, he has worked on some minor bills affecting Missouri farmers and savings and loans, but in 1989 and 1990 will have to handle some of the hottest potatoes on Capitol Hill, the 1989 farm bill and the savings and loan bailout. In 1989 he also got a seat on Budget. He was the only Republican freshman in a Senate just turned Democratic in 1987; now he is likely to be busier and his next election is coming up in 1992.

Congressional districting. Missouri now has nine congressional districts, one less than in the 1970s. Missouri lost a House seat in the 1980 Census, forcing out Republican Wendell Bailey, now state treasurer. It seems unlikely to lose one in 1990, and incumbents are likely to be safe.

The People: Est. Pop. 1988: 5,139,000; Pop. 1980: 4,916,686, up 4.5% 1980–88 and 5.1% 1970–80; 2.1% of U.S. total, 15th largest. 14% with 1-3 yrs. col., 14% with 4+ yrs. col.; 12.2% below poverty level. Single ancestry: 13% German, 11% English, 5% Irish, 1% Italian, French, Polish, Dutch. Households (1980): 73% family, 39% with children, 62% married couples; 30.4% housing units rented; median monthly rent: $153; median house value: $36,700. Voting age pop. (1980): 3,554,203; 9% Black, 1% Spanish origin. Registered voters (1988): 2,943,025; no party registration.

1988 Share of Federal Tax Burden $17,333,000,000; 1.96% of U.S. total, 17th largest.

1988 Share of Federal Expenditures

	Total		Non-Defense		Defense	
Total Expend	$21,559m	(2.44%)	$14,666m	(2.24%)	$7,948m	(3.48%)
St/Lcl Grants	1,942m	(1.69%)	1,939m	(1.69%)	3m	(2.57%)
Salary/Wages	2,622m	(1.95%)	1,520m	(2.27%)	1,102m	(2.27%)
Pymnts to Indiv	9,015m	(2.20%)	8,728m	(2.23%)	287m	(1.54%)
Procurement	6,553m	(3.47%)	1,056m	(2.27%)	6,553m	(3.47%)
Research/Other	1,427m	(3.82%)	1,425m	(3.84%)	3m	(3.84%)

Political Lineup: Governor, John Ashcroft (R); Lt. Gov., Mel Carnahan (D); Secy. of State, Roy D. Blunt (R); Atty. Gen., William Webster (R); Treasurer, Wendell Bailey (R); Auditor, Margaret Kelly (R). State Senate, 34 (22 D and 12 R); State House of Representatives, 163 (105 D and 58 R). Senators, John C. Danforth (R) and Christopher S. (Kit) Bond (R). Representatives, 9 (5 D and 4 R).

1988 Presidential Vote

Bush (R) 1,084,953 (52%)
Dukakis (D) 1,001,619 (48%)

1988 Democratic Presidential Primary

Gephardt 305,287 (59%)
Jackson 106,386 (20%)
Dukakis 61,303 (12%)
Simon 21,433 (4%)
Gore 14,549 (3%)
Hart 7,607 (1%)

1984 Presidential Vote

Reagan (R) 1,274,188 (60%)
Mondale (D) 848,583 (40%)

1988 Republican Presidential Primary

Bush 168,812 (42%)
Dole 164,394 (41%)
Robertson 44,705 (11%)
Kemp 14,180 (4%)

GOVERNOR

Gov. John Ashcroft (R)

Elected 1984, term expires Jan. 1993; b. May 9, 1942, Chicago, IL; home, Jefferson City; Yale U., B.A. 1964, U. of Chicago, J.D. 1967; Assembly of God; married (Janet).

Career: Practicing atty.; Professor, 1968–1973; MO Auditor, 1973–75; Asst. Atty. Gen. of MO, 1975–76; Atty. Gen. of MO, 1976–84.

Office: P.O. Box 720, Jefferson City 65102, 314-751-3222.

Election Results

1988 gen.	John Ashcroft (R)	1,339,531	(64%)
	Betty Hearnes (D)	724,919	(35%)
1988 prim.	John Ashcroft (R), unopposed		
1984 gen.	John Ashcroft (R)	1,194,506	(57%)
	Kenneth J. Rothman (D)	913,700	(43%)

SENATORS

Sen. John C. Danforth (R)

Elected 1976, seat up 1994; b. Sept. 5, 1936, St. Louis; home, Newburg; Princeton U., A.B. 1958, Yale U., B.D., LL.B. 1963; Episcopalian; married (Sally).

Career: Practicing atty., 1963–69; Ordained Clergyman; Atty. Gen. of MO, 1969–77.

Offices: 249 RSOB 20510, 202-224-6154. Also 1795 E. Sunshine, Plaza Towers, Ste. 705, Springfield 65804, 417-881-7068; 1815 Olive St., St. Louis 63101, 314-425-6381; 1233 Jefferson St., Jefferson City 65101, 314-635-7292; and 811 Grand Ave., 943 U.S. Crthse., Kansas City 64106, 816-374-6101.

Committees: *Commerce, Science, and Transportation* (Ranking Member of 9 R). *Finance* (4th of 9 R). Subcommittees: International Trade (Ranking Member); Taxation and Debt Management; Medicare and Long-Term Care. *Select Committee on Intelligence* (6th of 7 R).

Group Ratings

	ADA	ACLU	COPE	CFA	LCV	ACU	NTLC	NSI	COC	CEI
1988	20	31	31	50	50	72	40	80	71	45
1987	35	—	31	42	—	54	—	—	61	44

National Journal Ratings

	1988 LIB — 1988 CONS			1987 LIB — 1987 CONS		
Economic	35%	—	63%	37%	—	62%
Social	31%	—	68%	32%	—	65%
Foreign	30%	—	69%	36%	—	63%

Key Votes

1) Cut Aged Housing $	AGN	5) Bork Nomination	FOR	9) SDI Funding	FOR
2) Override Hwy Veto	FOR	6) Drug Death Pen	FOR	10) Ban Chem Weaps	AGN
3) Kill Plnt Clsng Notice	FOR	7) Deny Abortions	FOR	11) Aid To Contras	FOR
4) Min Wage Increase	AGN	8) Japanese Reparations	AGN	12) Reagan Defense $	FOR

Election Results

1988 general	John C. Danforth (R)	1,407,416	(68%)	($4,060,441)
	Jeremiah W. Nixon (D)	660,045	(32%)	($880,160)
1988 primary	John C. Danforth, unopposed			
1982 general	John C. Danforth (R)	784,876	(51%)	($1,849,025)
	Harriett Woods (D)	758,629	(49%)	($1,193,966)

Sen. Christopher S. (Kit) Bond (R)

Elected 1986, seat up 1992; b. Mar. 6, 1939, St. Louis; home, Mexico; Princeton U., B.A. 1960, U. of VA, LL.B. 1963; Presbyterian; married (Carolyn).

Career: Practicing atty., 1964–69; MO Asst. Atty. Gen., 1969–70; MO State Auditor, 1971–72; Gov. of MO, 19723–76, 1980–84.

Offices: 293 RSOB 20510, 202-224-5721. Also 811 Grand Ave., Rm. 911, Kansas City 64106, 816-374-2748; 320 Jackson St., Jefferson City 65101, 314-634-2488; and Old P.O. Bldg., 815 Olive St., Rm. 224, St. Louis 63101, 314-425-5067.

Committees: *Agriculture, Nutrition and Forestry* (7th of 9 R). Subcommittees: Agricultural Research and General Legislation; Conservation and Forestry (Ranking Member); Domestic and Foreign Marketing and Product Promotion. *Banking, Housing and Urban Affairs* (5th of 9 R). Subcommittees: International Finance and Monetary Policy; Consumer and Regulatory Affairs (Ranking Member). *Budget* (10th of 10 R). *Small Business* (5th of 9 R). Subcommittees: Export Expansion; Rural Economy and Family Farming.

Group Ratings

	ADA	ACLU	COPE	CFA	LCV	ACU	NTLC	NSI	COC	CEI
1988	0	20	24	33	10	88	53	100	86	46
1987	10	—	25	17	—	81	—	—	82	69

National Journal Ratings

	1988 LIB — 1988 CONS			1987 LIB — 1987 CONS		
Economic	32%	—	67%	32%	—	66%
Social	22%	—	76%	15%	—	84%
Foreign	21%	—	77%	0%	—	76%

Key Votes

1) Cut Aged Housing $	AGN	5) Bork Nomination	FOR	9) SDI Funding	FOR
2) Override Hwy Veto	FOR	6) Drug Death Pen	FOR	10) Ban Chem Weaps	FOR
3) Kill Plnt Clsng Notice	FOR	7) Deny Abortions	FOR	11) Aid To Contras	FOR
4) Min Wage Increase	AGN	8) Japanese Reparations	AGN	12) Reagan Defense $	FOR

Election Results

1986 general	Christopher S. (Kit) Bond (R)	777,612	(53%)	($5,376,255)
	Harriet Woods (D)	699,624	(47%)	($4,397,780)
1986 primary	Christopher S. (Kit) Bond (R)	239,961	(89%)	
	Richard J. Gimpelson (R).............	10,471	(4%)	
	David A. Brown (R)	10,407	(4%)	
	Joyce Padgett Lea (R)	9,407	(3%)	
1980 general	Thomas F. Eagleton (D)	1,074,859	(52%)	($1,272,272)
	Gene McNary (R)	985,399	(48%)	($1,173,161)

FIRST DISTRICT

St. Louis—the starting and stopping point for Lewis and Clark's expedition in 1804 and 1806, the site of the World's Fair of 1904 that produced the hot dog, the ice cream cone, and, eventually, *Meet Me in St. Louis*—was the first major American city west of the Mississippi River. Just below the point where the waters of the Missouri plunge into the flow of the Mississippi, about halfway between New Orleans and Lake Superior, the Atlantic and the Pacific, the terminus of the National Road and the last resting place for Daniel Boone, St. Louis was a natural gateway to the West. At the turn of the century it was the nation's fourth largest city, still rivaling Chicago as the transportation hub of America.

But Chicago streaked ahead, and St. Louis has been one of the nation's second-line metro areas, with a central city that has become depopulated. St. Louis's old street grids radiating from downtown were filled with densely-packed brick houses in the pre-auto days when people lived within walking distance of streetcar lines; but they had little appeal to later Americans who wanted large lots and two-car garages. In 1930, 821,000 people lived within the city limits; in 1950, 856,000; in 1980, 453,000—about the same as in 1890. Whole neighborhoods, and the Pruitt-Igoe housing project, have been bulldozed; others have been thinned out. The north side of the city, north of the expressways that feed into downtown, has essentially become all black; the south side has remained all white. Blacks live in suburbs north and west of the city; virtually none have chosen to live on the south side.

Missouri's 1st Congressional District includes the north side of St. Louis and adjacent parts of St. Louis County. Once entirely within the city limits, the district now has 59% of its voters in the suburbs. They include the mostly black towns along St. Charles Rock and Natural Bridge Roads northwest of the city; high-income Clayton, with its office high-rises, and white-collar University City (once mostly Jewish, by 1980 43% black), Richmond Heights and Maplewood, directly west; and virtually all-white Bellefontaine Neighbors, Spanish Lake and Black Jack, directly north. This is the most Democratic seat in Missouri by a good margin.

Since 1968, this district has been represented by Bill Clay, who got his political start as a union staffer and civil rights activist. Only five years before he was first elected, he served 105 days in jail for participating in a civil rights demonstration; in the middle 1980s, he was arrested again, as one of several congressmen demonstrating before the South African embassy. In between, his career has had its ups and downs. For a time it appeared he might be brought down by charges of scandal. In 1976, it was revealed that he had been billing the government for numerous auto trips home, although he was actually buying less expensive airline tickets and, presumably, pocketing the difference. The next year he was under investigation for tax fraud. His administrative assistant was sent to jail for falsification of payroll records. In four consecutive primaries, from 1976 to 1982, he won by rather small margins, losing or just barely carrying the suburbs. He was not doing well in Washington either. His efforts to repeal the Hatch Act's limitations on the political activities of federal employees were unsuccessful. His effort to help public employee unions defeat the Carter civil service reforms also lost. Despite his pro-labor record, he was passed over for a labor subcommittee chairmanship.

Lately Clay has done better. He has his labor-management relations subcommittee chair, and has even done some things with it: he got a bill through the House in 1986 to stop construction firms from setting up non-union subsidiaries, though it died in the Senate. In October 1987, he got unanimous committee approval for a Hatch Act revision although it, too, died in the Senate. He got an amendment through banning U.S. airlines from hiring foreigners as strikebreakers. He worked on the plant closing legislation passed in 1988, on trade adjustment assistance, and on a bill to prohibit lie detector tests for most workers. He is poised to take a more visible role: he is fourth ranking Democrat on Education and Labor and second on Post Office and Civil Service; should William Ford succeed Augustus Hawkins, who turns 85 in 1990, as chairman of the former, Clay will become chairman of the latter.

At home, Clay has consolidated his position in the 1st District. He won his 1982 primary with just 61%, with voters divided on racial lines; but in 1984 and 1988 he had no primary opposition and in 1986 he won 80% against nuisance candidates. The 1st District has lost only a little population this decade, and minor adjustments to its boundaries should keep Clay's district safe—a contrast from a decade ago, when Missouri lost a seat and the legislature was on the verge of abolishing this district.

The People: Est. Pop. 1986: 530,700, dn. 2.8% 1980–86; Pop. 1980: 546,208, dn. 20.7% 1970–80. Households (1980): 66% family, 36% with children, 45% married couples; 45.6% housing units rented; median monthly rent: $145; median house value: $31,800. Voting age pop. (1980): 393,146; 46% Black, 1% Spanish origin, 1% Asian origin.

1988 Presidential Vote:	Dukakis (D)	143,802	(72%)
	Bush (R)	54,578	(27%)

Rep. William (Bill) Clay (D)

Elected 1968; b. Apr. 30, 1931, St. Louis; home, St. Louis; St. Louis U., B.S. 1953; Roman Catholic; married (Carol).

Career: Real estate broker; Life insur. bus., 1959–61; St. Louis City Alderman, 1959–64.

Offices: 2470 RHOB 20515, 202-225-2406. Also 6197 Delmar Blvd., St. Louis 63112, 314-725-5770; and 12263 Bellefontaine Rd., St. Louis 63138, 314-355-6811.

Committees: *Education and Labor* (4th of 22 D). Subcommittees: Labor-Management Relations (Chairman); Labor Standards. *House Administration* (8th of 13 D). Subcommittees: Elections; Libraries and Memorials (Chairman). *Post Office and Civil Service* (2d of 15 D). Subcommittees: Postal Operations and Services; Investigations. *Joint Committee on the Library*.

Group Ratings

	ADA	ACLU	COPE	CFA	LCV	ACU	NTLC	NSI	COC	CEI
1988	90	100	96	82	81	0	6	0	18	6
1987	92	—	95	57	—	0	—	—	0	4

National Journal Ratings

	1988 LIB — 1988 CONS		1987 LIB — 1987 CONS	
Economic	92%	— 0%	73%	— 0%
Social	86%	— 0%	78%	— 0%
Foreign	84%	— 0%	81%	— 0%

Key Votes

1) Homeless $	AGN	5) Ban Drug Test	AGN	9) SDI Research	AGN
2) Gephardt Amdt	FOR	6) Drug Death Pen	AGN	10) Ban Chem Weaps	FOR
3) Deficit Reduc	FOR	7) Handgun Sales	AGN	11) Aid to Contras	AGN
4) Kill Plnt Clsng Notice	—	8) Ban D.C. Abort $	AGN	12) Nuclear Testing	FOR

Election Results

1988 general	William (Bill) Clay (D)	140,751	(72%)	($134,200)
	Jerry Inman (R)	53,109	(27%)	
1988 primary	William (Bill) Clay, unopposed			
1986 general	William (Bill) Clay (D)	91,044	(66%)	($217,113)
	Robert J. Wittman (R)	46,599	(34%)	($28,414)

SECOND DISTRICT

The city of St. Louis, tired of paying for dusty back roads, separated itself from St. Louis County in 1876, when there were about 350,000 people in the city and 31,000 in the rest of the county. As late as 1940 the city was still far larger, 816,000 to 274,000; but by 1980 Census the city was down to 453,000 and the county up to 973,000, as the St. Louis metropolitan area moves farther and farther away from the Mississippi River that gave it birth. About half of St. Louis County, mostly beyond the Inner Belt Expressway, plus a small part of fast-growing St. Charles County across the Missouri River, make up Missouri's 2d Congressional District. North of Interstate 70 it includes the blue-collar suburbs of Hazelwood, Berkley, St. John, St. Ann and Overland, centered on the big McDonnell-Douglas aircraft plants near the airport; these are filled mostly with whites who grew up on the north side of St. Louis, though most towns have blacks; no one is quite sure whether this represents stable integration or rapid neighborhood change. To the south are comfortable white-collar suburbs like Kirkwood, pleasant but not rich places filled with older whites. In the center of the county are high-income Ladue, the home of most of St. Louis's elite, Creve Coeur and the more Jewish suburb of Olivette. Farther west, you come to new subdivisions, with few trees and large, air-conditioned houses which keep their storm doors up all year; they are interspersed among a few crumbling remains of rural houses built higgledy-piggledy by their owners years ago and grimy enclaves like Times Beach, site of a toxic waste dump which was a center of national attention in 1983.

Politically, the 2d is a mixed bag. The working-class suburbs are traditionally Democratic, mainly on economic issues, but often leave the party on cultural issues; the southern suburbs and most of the new subdivisions are pretty solidly Republican, though with a variety of perspectives. In the 1970s the demographic balance favored the northern, working class suburbs and the Democrats. But by the 1980s the working class areas had grown little or saw their residents move to semi-rural surroundings far beyond the county line, while the affluent suburbs in the west were growing fast.

This helps to account for, but does not entirely explain, the victories of Republican Jack Buechner (pronounced *beekner*) in 1986 and 1988 after his loss in 1984. Buechner is a Republican with a sense of humor and an irreverent approach, who became known as a moderate in the legislature because he backed the Equal Rights Amendment. On economic issues he is a strong free market man, and a decrier of government waste—even when it helps the folks back home. In 1984, he took on Bob Young, a pipefitter who represented St. Ann for 20 years in the legislature and the 2d for 8 years after that, a genial political pro who prided himself on a perfect AFL-CIO voting record. Buechner lost that time, but returned in 1986 and criticized Young, a member of the Public Works Committee, as a "back-scratching, back room deal maker" for pushing for pork barrel projects for the district. Young's solid support of labor didn't help in the southern end of the district. Buechner's campaign was outspent and Young raised much more PAC money. But Buechner's message, delivered via an exceedingly effective TV ad, was enough to make him the one Republican who beat an incumbent Democratic congressman in 1986.

In Washington Buechner got seats on the Budget Committee and Science Committees, the latter of importance to McDonnell-Douglas. In the House, he took some unusual stands, calling for free mailing privileges for challengers in House campaigns, for example, and paring down the NASA authorization to what it is likely to get in the appropriations process. He allowed during the 1988 campaign as how he didn't think the death penalty was a relevant issue. But he was also ready to take up the cudgels for a 2d District low-bidder that didn't get a defense contract and for a refusenik who eventually got out of the Soviet Union. In 1988, Democratic legislator Bob Feigenbaum, one of the exposers of dioxin pollution in Times Beach, ran, emphasizing hazardous waste disposal. But his campaign was not well-financed, some of his arguments were far-fetched, and in a year when George Bush was carrying St. Louis County comfortably, Buechner won by a 2 to 1 margin. With his personal appeal and his party's strength, he seems to have a safe seat.

The People: Est. Pop. 1986: 573,700, up 5.1% 1980–86; Pop. 1980: 546,039, up 11.4% 1970–80. Households (1980): 79% family, 44% with children, 68% married couples; 24.3% housing units rented; median monthly rent: $232; median house value: $53,700. Voting age pop. (1980): 386,511; 5% Black, 1% Asian origin, 1% Spanish origin.

1988 Presidential Vote: Bush (R) 173,205   (61%)
                               Dukakis (D). 111,172   (39%)

Rep. Jack Buechner (R)

Elected 1986; b. June 4, 1940, St. Louis; home, Kirkwood; Benedictine Col., B.A. 1962, St. Louis U., J.D. 1965; Roman Catholic; married (Marietta).

Career: Practicing atty.; MO House of Reps., 1972–82.

Offices: 502 CHOB 20515, 202-225-2561. Also 13545 Barrett Pkwy. Dr., Ste. 150, Ballwin 63021, 314-965-1101; and St. Charles City Hall, 200 N. 2d St., St. Charles 63361, 314-946-9377.

Committees: *Budget* (8th of 14 R). Task Forces: Budget Process, Reconciliation and Enforcement; Human Resources. *Science, Space and Technology* (14th of 19 R). Subcommittees: Science, Research and Technology; Space Science and Applications.

Group Ratings

	ADA	ACLU	COPE	CFA	LCV	ACU	NTLC	NSI	COC	CEI
1988	15	35	17	55	50	88	82	100	79	60
1987	12	—	6	21	—	86	—	—	100	75

National Journal Ratings

	1988 LIB — 1988 CONS		1987 LIB — 1987 CONS	
Economic	16%	— 83%	0%	— 89%
Social	26%	— 74%	15%	— 84%
Foreign	0%	— 84%	31%	— 68%

Key Votes

1) Homeless $	FOR	5) Ban Drug Test	FOR	9) SDI Research	FOR
2) Gephardt Amdt	AGN	6) Drug Death Pen	FOR	10) Ban Chem Weaps	AGN
3) Deficit Reduc	AGN	7) Handgun Sales	FOR	11) Aid to Contras	FOR
4) Kill Plnt Clsng Notice	FOR	8) Ban D.C. Abort $	FOR	12) Nuclear Testing	AGN

Election Results

1988 general	Jack Buechner (R)	186,450	(66%)	($693,066)
	Robert H. Feigenbaum (D)	91,645	(33%)	($254,492)
1988 primary	Jack Buechner (R), unopposed			
1986 general	Jack Buechner (R)	101,010	(52%)	($326,375)
	Robert A. Young (D)	93,538	(48%)	($528,101)

THIRD DISTRICT

The center of the United States, or at least the geographical center of its population in 1980, is in the 3d Congressional District of Missouri. This is the southern part of the St. Louis metropolitan area—a slice of pie with its apex near the Gateway Arch, extending outward and widening in suburban St. Louis County and finally ending in Jefferson County, once a rural area and now part of suburban St. Louis. The city's south side is almost entirely white, with signs still there of the German immigrants who made St. Louis one of the nation's most bustling and progressive cities in the late 1800s; the most famous St. Louis German was Carl Schurz, friend of Lincoln, Union Army officer in the Civil War, Secretary of the Interior and Senator from Missouri. St. Louis's south side, like the north, has lost about half its population in the last 40 years, much of it moving directly out to St. Louis County, where the solid middle class of St. Louis lives, people who keep its offices humming, its stores and warehouses bustling, its schoolchildren instructed and disciplined. Others have moved out to Jefferson County, where old towns sitting near the banks of the fast-flowing Mississippi are now receiving an infusion of shopping centers, new subdivisions, and apartment complexes. Republican during most of the post-Civil War period, middle-class St. Louis became Democratic in the New Deal years; it still is in local elections but has trended Republican in national and state contests.

One product of south side St. Louis is Missouri's most recent candidate for President, 3d District Congressman Richard Gephardt. He has accomplished in a dozen years the considerable feat of making himself both a respected leader inside the House and a serious, if so far not successful, candidate for President in the great world beyond the Washington Beltway. He has the ambitious politician's knack of seeing his openings, widening them and making his way through to still more. The knock on him is that he has gone through a few too many changes, and that it's not clear what he stands for. To that, his reply is to painstakingly set out his positions, how he came to them, and how he hopes to reach his goals.

Gephardt's origins are not quite so humble as he likes to suggest; his father was a milkman but also a real estate salesman, the family lived in one of the more comfortable wards in south St. Louis, and both sons were sent to prestige colleges. Gephardt returned after law school, clearly seeking a political career; he joined a big downtown law firm, but unlike most associates moved not to an affluent suburb but to the south side. There he ran for alderman in 1971, and was one of a band of south side reformers on the council. He was thinking about running for mayor when 3d District Congresswoman Leonor Sullivan announced her retirement, and he jumped into the race running as an anti-establishment candidate. He beat a labor union official in the 1976 primary and a former board of aldermen president in the general, outspending and outcampaigning both of them.

Unlike most Democrats of the time, Gephardt came to the House not with the blessings of organized labor, but over its opposition; he was one of the newer breed of Democrats who did not automatically favor big-government and high-tax solutions. Yet he was also adroit enough to get a seat on the Ways and Means Committee in his first term, when there were more than 100 freshman and sophomore Democrats and only a half dozen seats available. He helped to scuttle a Carter proposal for hospital cost controls and came up with a competition-based alternative (co-sponsored by David Stockman) offering employees choices between different health insurance plans. On taxes he, unlike most Democrats, was open to arguments that they should be lowered to encourage investment and recognized that nominal high rates were actually unsustainable and could be sacrificed to get rid of loopholes for the wealthy. In the early 1980s, he supported the Reagan tax cut and was the House co-sponsor with Bill Bradley of rate-cutting, preference-eliminating tax reform. He was one of the founders of the moderate Democratic Leadership Council, and he also got himself elected chairman of the House Democratic Caucus in 1984.

Gephardt is a good listener, a hard-working detail man, and a natural molder of political compromise—qualities that make him popular with his colleagues. They helped him wrap up the caucus chairman race early, when David Obey dropped out, acknowledging he didn't have the votes. Gephardt had the support—often active, enthusiastic support—of dozens of his colleagues in his 1988 presidential race. But as he started running seriously for President in 1985 and moved from seeking the support of mixed liberal-and-moderate constituencies in the 3d District and the House to seeking votes in the lopsidedly liberal constituencies of Democratic endorsing groups and Iowa caucusgoers, his approach to issues seemed to change. He played little part on tax reform (Dan Rostenkowski didn't want him to). In 1986, he abandoned his long-time support of anti-abortion measures in a bow to the power of feminists in the Democratic nominating process. In 1987, he was advocating a referendum to let farmers authorize the government to impose mandatory production controls, a step that would probably be impracticable and certainly would be costly to consumers. This Harkin-Gephardt amendment never came close to passing either house, but he talked about it a lot in Iowa. Even more prominently, he went on the offensive on the trade issue. Repelled, he says, by the spectacle of industries coming into Congress looking for special relief—he cites the auto industry and UAW's domestic content bill, which he voted against—he came up with the Gephardt amendment requiring countermeasures against countries running large trade surpluses with the United States. It passed the House in late 1987 by a 218–214 margin—a gift to Gephardt's presidential campaign, for it clearly was going nowhere in the Senate or in conference committee.

Meanwhile, Gephardt was spending more time in Iowa than any other candidate; his entire family moved there. He built an organization and with his emphasis on trade and production controls he attracted support from union organizers, older voters and those who want the government to revive Iowa's ailing farm economy. He sloughed over the tension in his record between his earlier moves toward market-oriented solutions attractive to young upscale voters and his campaign year support of control-oriented solutions attractive to older downscale voters. He won the Iowa caucuses with 31% of the vote, to 27% for Paul Simon and 22% for Michael Dukakis. But, like every other early primary winner, he failed to get any momentum in 1988's cluttered media, and instead in New Hampshire found himself under attack for changing his positions in a super-prosperous state that hates taxes and government regulation; he finished second with 20% to Dukakis's 36%. Gephardt won the South Dakota primary February 23 with 44% by running an ad attacking Dukakis for urging Iowa farmers to grow Belgian endive. But that released Dukakis from any scruples on negative campaigning, and his well-financed campaign ran a devastating flip-flop ad against Gephardt before Super Tuesday on March 8. Gephardt's campaign, by previous years' standards well-financed, could not match Dukakis's, and made some bad decisions (spending heavily in hopeless Florida, as Dukakis would in the general). On Super Tuesday, Gephardt won only Missouri and was effectively out of the race. He kept his campaign theoretically alive until the Michigan caucus March 26, but, despite vigorous support from Congressman John Dingell and several UAW leaders, won only 13% there. That left him with time to meet Missouri's filing deadline of March 29 and to win reelection (although with a slightly lower than usual 63%) in November.

Gephardt had to give up the caucus chairmanship, a temporary position; he remains an important House Member nonetheless. He traveled to Japan and China, continues to study the trade issue, as he writes a book and learns Japanese. He remains interested also, it appears, in the presidency. Many Gephardt backers argue that he had the message—an I'm on your side populistic appeal—that would have prevailed if he had only had enough money. But on Super Tuesday Gephardt failed to beat either Dukakis or Albert Gore in media markets where he was matching their spending.

There was not much doubt that Gephardt was interested in running again for President in 1992, and before the Democratic Leadership Council in March 1989, he laid out his basic approach. His presidential aspirations were sidelined however when, with the resignations of Jim Wright and Tony Coelho, he jumped in to fill the vacuum. He won a decisive victory in the Democratic Caucus for majority leader over Georgia's Ed Jenkins, 181–76, in June of 1989. After the scrutiny of the 1988 presidential campaign, Gephardt's ethics seemed beyond reproach, a factor which, along with his reputation as a pragmatic consensus builder, made him a highly attractive candidate to replace now Speaker Tom Foley.

But many will watch closely to see how Gephardt performs. Will he assume the role of Coehlo, the aggressive partisan, or will he extend his ample ability to compromise to the other side of the aisle? Whatever the case, he now has the chance to prove his political skills and ability—to a degree that even he might not have imagined so soon after his decisive Super Tuesday losses—in a forum not too far from 1600 Pennsylvania Avenue.

688 MISSOURI

The People: Est. Pop. 1986: 558,700, up 2.3% 1980–86; Pop. 1980: 546,102, up 0.3% 1970–80. Households (1980): 72% family, 36% with children, 61% married couples; 31.2% housing units rented; median monthly rent: $151; median house value: $43,900. Voting age pop. (1980): 403,646; 1% Black, 1% Spanish origin.

1988 Presidential Vote:

Bush (R)	126,310	(53%)
Dukakis (D)	111,956	(47%)

Rep. Richard A. Gephardt (D)

Elected 1976; b. Jan. 31, 1941, St. Louis; home, St. Louis; Northwestern U., B.S. 1962, U. of MI, J.D., 1965; Baptist; married (Jane).

Career: Practicing atty., 1965–71; St. Louis City Alderman, 1971–76.

Offices: 1432 LHOB 20515, 202-225-2671. Also 9959 Gravois, St. Louis 63123, 314-631-9959.

Committees: *Majority Leader.*

Group Ratings

	ADA	ACLU	COPE	CFA	LCV	ACU	NTLC	NSI	COC	CEI
1988	75	73	82	73	19	10	15	0	20	9
1987	20	—	81	21	—	0	—	—	0	8

National Journal Ratings

	1988 LIB — 1988 CONS		1987 LIB — 1987 CONS	
Economic	92% —	0%	73% —	0%
Social	72% —	28%	* —	*
Foreign	64% —	34%	* —	*

Key Votes

1) Homeless $	—	5) Ban Drug Test	AGN	9) SDI Research	AGN
2) Gephardt Amdt	FOR	6) Drug Death Pen	FOR	10) Ban Chem Weaps	—
3) Deficit Reduc	—	7) Handgun Sales	AGN	11) Aid to Contras	AGN
4) Kill Plnt Clsng Notice	AGN	8) Ban D.C. Abort $	FOR	12) Nuclear Testing	FOR

Election Results

1988 general	Richard A. Gephardt (D)	150,205	(63%)	($512,206)
	Mark F. Hearne (R)	86,763	(36%)	($202,524)
1988 primary	Richard A. Gephardt (D)	45,784	(82%)	
	James Vires (D)	4,073	(7%)	
	James W. Whitt (D)	3,442	(6%)	
	Ed Roche (D)	2,747	(5%)	
1986 general	Richard A. Gephardt (D)	116,403	(69%)	($881,325)
	Roy Amelung (R)	52,382	(31%)	

FOURTH DISTRICT

In Warrensburg, on the western prairie of Missouri, was delivered the classic "Eulogy to a Dog" in 1870, in a lawsuit brought by a hunter against a sheep farmer who shot his black and tan hound, Old Drum, who "never lies. I can always tell the kind of game he is chasing by his bark." The defendant's lawyer Francis Cockrell—formerly a Confederate general, later U.S. Senator for 30 years, appointed to settle a boundary dispute with Mexico in 1910—won the case on appeal, but on retrial plaintiff's lawyer George G. Vest—later Senator for 24 years himself—quoting the story of Lazarus and a poem by Byron, eulogized the dog as ready to stand by his master's grave, "watchful, faithful, and true," and won damages of $25. This story, recounted in the *WPA Guide*, gives a picture of early life in a Missouri teeming with westward settlers and fought over in the Civil War.

The 4th Congressional District of Missouri includes Warrensburg and much of the prairie of western Missouri, from Jefferson City, the state capital at the center of the state, through the old prairie counties and the new developments, filled with retirees from cities and from ranks of the career military, around Lake of the Ozarks, all the way to Independence (though not including Harry Truman's home). Political attitudes are still shaped by the Civil War: Truman, who set up his 1940 campaign headquarters in Sedalia, a county over from Warrensburg, was born in Lamar in the southern end of the district and lived in Independence, next door to (and now a suburb of) Kansas City; the Trumans were strong Democrats and his mother could remember when her house was attacked by Yankee soldiers. Jefferson City has been heavily Republican since then; but ancestrally the 4th is mostly Democratic.

Ike Skelton, congressman from the 4th District, looks the part of an old-fashioned rural Missouri Democrat. His record on economics tends often to put him in line with his party; he is more tradition-minded on cultural matters and foreign policy. His main work comes on the Armed Services Committee and its issues. While he tends to support higher defense spending, he also demands to know what it's being spent on—and is willing to speak out when he thinks mistakes are being made. After the 1984 election he played a major role in elevating Les Aspin as chairman over the elderly and out-of-touch Mel Price. In 1986 he was a strong proponent of reorganizing the Pentagon command structure, unifying the service commands and strengthening the power of the chairman of the Joint Chiefs of Staff, and played a key role in passing the reorganization law. He is also able to look after the interests of Whiteman Air Force Base near Warrensburg, the site for deployment of the B-2 Stealth bomber. Also in 1986 he was also a lead sponsor of the successful move to fund the Nicaraguan contras; in 1988 he was trying to forge yet another compromise on contra aid. In 1987, he was calling for better strategic thinking in the services and in their war colleges.

Skelton has been given leave to do this work by his constituency. The current 4th District lines put Skelton in with another incumbent, Republican Wendell Bailey, in 1982, but Skelton had represented 64% of the new district and won with 55%; Bailey was elected state treasurer in 1984. Since then, Skelton's reelection has been routine and in 1986 unanimous. He was mentioned as a Senate candidate in 1988, but didn't run.

The People: Est. Pop. 1986: 587,300, up 7.4% 1980–86; Pop. 1980: 546,637, up 19.7% 1970–80. Households (1980): 77% family, 42% with children, 69% married couples; 25.5% housing units rented; median monthly rent: $141; median house value: $35,600. Voting age pop. (1980): 390,415; 3% Black, 1% Spanish origin.

1988 Presidential Vote:

Bush (R)	139,370	(59%)
Dukakis (D)	95,117	(40%)

Rep. Ike Skelton (D)

Elected 1976; b. Dec. 20, 1931, Lexington; home, Lexington Wentworth Military Acad., U. of MO, B.A. 1953, LL.B. 1956 Disciples of Christ; married (Susan).

Career: Lafayette Cnty. Prosecuting Atty., 1957–60; Spec. Asst Atty. Gen. of MO, 1961–63; Practicing atty., 1957–76; MO Senate, 1971–76.

Offices: 2134 RHOB 20515, 202-225-2876. Also 1616 Industrial Dr., Jefferson City 65109, 314-635-3499; 1700 W. 40 Hwy., Blue Springs 64015, 816-228-4242; and 319 S. Lamine, Sedalia 65301 816-826-2675.

Committees: *Armed Services* (9th of 31 D). Subcommittees Military Installations and Facilities; Military Personnel and Compensation; Procurement and Military Nuclear Systems. *Small Business* (4th of 27 D). Subcommittee: Procurement, Tourism and Rural Developments (Chairman). *Select Committee on Aging* (18th of 39 D). Subcommittee: Health and Long-Term Care.

Group Ratings

	ADA	ACLU	COPE	CFA	LCV	ACU	NTLC	NSI	COC	CEI
1988	40	62	69	73	44	58	24	100	62	25
1987	48	—	68	36	—	38	—	—	40	25

National Journal Ratings

	1988 LIB — 1988 CONS		1987 LIB — 1987 CONS	
Economic	49%	— 50%	57%	— 43%
Social	37%	— 62%	50%	— 50%
Foreign	39%	— 61%	39%	— 60%

Key Votes

1) Homeless $	—	5) Ban Drug Test	AGN	9) SDI Research	FOR
2) Gephardt Amdt	FOR	6) Drug Death Pen	FOR	10) Ban Chem Weaps	AGN
3) Deficit Reduc	AGN	7) Handgun Sales	FOR	11) Aid to Contras	FOR
4) Kill Plnt Clsng Notice	AGN	8) Ban D.C. Abort $	FOR	12) Nuclear Testing	AGN

Election Results

1988 general	Ike Skelton (D)	166,480	(72%)	($273,316
	David Eyerly (R)	65,393	(28%)	
1988 primary	Ike Skelton (D), unopposed			
1986 general	Ike Skelton (D)	129,471	(100%)	($183,973

FIFTH DISTRICT

Is everything up to date in Kansas City? The singers in *Oklahoma!*, written in the 1940s but se in 1907, apparently thought so; and so do most people who visit here today. The 5th Congressional District of Missouri includes the heart of Kansas City—the confident Art Deco skyscrapers of the old downtown, over which stands Hallmark's Crown Center; Country Club Plaza, one of the first shopping centers in America, built in the 1920s, and the adjacent high income neighborhood; the city's black neighborhood to the northeast, famous for its barbecue places; the industrial areas below the bluffs down by the river and the Kansas City stockyards The district goes out past the new Harry Truman Sports Complex and the old Chevrolet and

Ford assembly plants, east to Independence, which includes the old white Truman home—actually it belonged to Mrs. Truman's family, the Wallaces, and she didn't let him forget it—on Truman Road.

As befits a district that was home to a Democratic President, and was represented by one of the party's most thoughtful and effective House leaders, Richard Bolling, for 34 years, this is a Democratic district, and seems to be getting more so, as middle-class Republicans move further out into the suburbs, often out of Missouri altogether and into Kansas. The 5th elects a Democratic congressman, and by wide margins, which would not be notable except that the congressman, Alan Wheat, is black, and he has made his political fortune in a district that is and is likely to remain for many years mostly white.

Wheat is not even from Kansas City (but then neither was Bolling): he is the son of an Air Force colonel, and grew up all over the world. That makes him one of the few Members of Congress from a career military family, and the only black congressman who grew up in what has been for 40 years the most thoroughly integrated sector of American life. He was a state legislator from a mostly black district when he ran for the House in 1982, and his base helped him win the Democratic primary with 32% of the vote. It's possible that he would not have won if Missouri, like most southern states, had a runoff law. But Wheat understood that he could not win any further elections in an 80% non-black district with only black votes, and he made sure to appeal to whites. With solid support from Bolling, he won the 1982 general election with 58% of the vote—below the normal Democratic share, but still comfortable. Then he used his two years of incumbency shrewdly. Against two opponents he won 82% in the 1984 Democratic primary, and won with 66% in the general election. In 1986 and 1988, he had no primary opposition and won with over 70%.

Wheat has done this by using traditional political tactics. In his first term he won Bolling's seat on the Rules Committee—an unusual achievement for a freshman—and he has used it to pass measures important to his district or key constituents. He is proud of having secured flood control projects for the Blue River and Brush Creek and funds for the Bruce Watkins Memorial Drive. He tacked a measure banning foreign servicing of U.S. planes—of interest to employees at Kansas City's big Eastern and TWA facilities—to the rule allowing consideration of the continuing resolution. His major substantive legislative effort in 1987 and 1988 was to get EPA regulation of firms transporting toxic PCBs, on which he worked with no less than Energy and Commerce Chairman John Dingell and moved the bill through the House though it didn't move in the Senate. Two further causes are getting a cleanup study of nuclear weapons production plants (including at Kansas City's old Bendix plant) and protecting the Truman historic site.

Wheat has taken some political risks, and in 1988 his Republican opponent attacked him for opposing the death penalty for drug dealers and for opposing dial-a-porn bans. But he has refused to get involved in the controversial Kansas City school desegregation case. In an era when Jesse Jackson seems the only black candidate on national television, Wheat points to a different strategy by which blacks can advance politically, and he does it as someone who has been winning elections since 1976: by working to represent mostly non-black constituencies. This does not necessarily mean ignoring black issues or avoiding all unpopular stands. But it does mean avoiding inflammatory rhetoric and blatant appeals to racial solidarity. The fact is that the Voting Rights Act has long since maximized the number of black-majority constituencies in the country. Further gains by black politicians are going to be made in districts that are majority non-black, like the 5th of Missouri.

The People: Est. Pop. 1986: 542,400, dn. 0.8% 1980–86; Pop. 1980: 546,882, dn. 10.3% 1970–80. Households (1980): 65% family, 34% with children, 51% married couples; 40.2% housing units rented; median monthly rent: $167; median house value: $35,100. Voting age pop. (1980): 405,263; 20% Black, 2% Spanish origin, 1% Asian origin.

692 MISSOURI

1988 Presidential Vote: Dukakis (D)...................... 129,433 (60%)
Bush (R)........................ 83,926 (39%)

Rep. Alan Wheat (D)

Elected 1982; b. Oct. 16, 1951, San Antonio, TX; home, Kansa» City; Grinnell Col., B.A. 1972; Church of Christ; single.

Career: Economist, U.S. Dept. of HUD, Kansas City and Mid« America Regional Cncl., 1972–74; Aide to Jackson Cnty. Exec. Mike White, 1974–75; MO House of Reps., 1977–82.

Offices: 1204 LHOB 20515, 202-225-4535. Also 811 Grand Ave. Rm. 935, Kansas City 64106, 816-842-4545; and 301 W. Lexing ton, Rm. 221, Independence 64050, 816-833-4545.

Committees: *Rules* (7th of 9 D). Subcommittee: The Legislativ« Process. *District of Columbia* (6th of 8 D). Subcommittees: Gov ernment Operations and Metropolitan Affairs (Chairman); Judi« ciary and Education. *Select Committee on Children, Youth an«*
Families (13th of 18 D).

Group Ratings

	ADA	ACLU	COPE	CFA	LCV	ACU	NTLC	NSI	COC	CEI
1988	100	95	96	91	81	0	3	0	21	11
1987	100	—	96	86	—	0	—	—	0	2

National Journal Ratings

	1988 LIB — 1988 CONS		1987 LIB — 1987 CONS	
Economic	79%	— 17%	73%	— 0%
Social	86%	— 0%	78%	— 0%
Foreign	84%	— 0%	81%	— 0%

Key Votes

1) Homeless $	AGN	5) Ban Drug Test	AGN	9) SDI Research	AGN
2) Gephardt Amdt	FOR	6) Drug Death Pen	AGN	10) Ban Chem Weaps	FOR
3) Deficit Reduc	FOR	7) Handgun Sales	AGN	11) Aid to Contras	AGN
4) Kill Plnt Clsng Notice	AGN	8) Ban D.C. Abort $	AGN	12) Nuclear Testing	FOR

Election Results

1988 general	Alan Wheat (D)......................	149,166	(70%)	($240,623
	Mary Ellen Lobb (R)..................	60,453	(29%)	($14,636
1988 primary	Alan Wheat (D), unopposed			
1986 general	Alan Wheat (D)......................	101,030	(71%)	($192,612
	Greg Fisher (R)......................	39,340	(28%)	

SIXTH DISTRICT

The farmland along and behind the bluffs that line the Missouri and other rivers of northwes Missouri: these are the originals of Thomas Hart Benton's rolling, surging fields. This is a part o America that was quickly settled in the late 19th century and has been losing people ever since Fewer men are now needed on farms than half a century ago, far fewer than at the turn of th« century; and the biggest town in northwest Missouri, St. Joseph, has declined as well. In 1940, i» had "the fifth largest meat-packing industry in the world, out of which has risen a modern city o skyscrapers and chromium-plated facades. But even in the maturity of its development, St. Joseph keeps its sidewalk lounging chairs, and clings to the river and to memories of the wagon trails and the Pony Express of its early days." Alas, the meat-packing business has generated no more new jobs than farming, and St. Joseph has no more people than 50 years ago and fewer than in 1900. All the counties of northwest Missouri, aside from those in the Kansas City metro area, had 508,000 people in 1900, 452,000 in 1940 and 301,000 in 1980.

These counties, plus Clay and Platte Counties, which include the parts of Kansas City north of the Missouri River, make up the 6th Congressional District; the two metro counties have increased in numbers almost precisely as the rural counties have declined. The Kansas City area has almost half the population but—newly developed, decentralized, without strong political organizations—it cast only 36% of the district's votes. The historic political tradition in these parts is mostly Democratic, tempered by dislike for national Democrats' cultural liberalism, but strengthened by anger at what people regard as neglect of this salt-of-the-earth farming area—an attitude similar to what you find across the border in left-leaning Iowa. Michael Dukakis carried the rural counties of the 6th District and lost the Kansas City portions only barely, for a district-wide dead heat.

The House seat here, however, remains in the hands of Republican Thomas Coleman, who won it in 1976 (when the Republican National Convention was, coincidentally, in Kansas City) and has held onto it through hard work and attention to farm issues. His election was serendipitous—the *Kansas City Star* revealed that Democratic nominee Morgan Maxfield was an utter fraud, lying about his education, his business, and his family.

Coleman is now one of the more senior Republicans in the House, and the second ranking minority member on both Agriculture and Education and Labor. On Agriculture, he worked in the 1980s to shore up the farm credit system and develop the sodbuster soil conservation programs. But he does not favor the Democrats' wheat and corn price support programs. On Education and Labor, he has worked to cut defaults in student loans, particularly to for-profit trade schools where a lot of federal money is being siphoned to sharp operators. For college students, he tends to oppose Pell Grants and to favor loans, from which after all the government gets back most of its money. But when toting up students' eligibility for loans, he would exclude the value of homes—a big help to many middle-class families.

In some years Coleman has been reelected easily. But in 1986 and 1988 he got vocal opposition from Livingston County farmer Doug Hughes. In 1986, he won with 57%, getting just 53% in the rural counties and 62% in the urban areas. In 1988, he did a bit better, with 59% district-wide, raising his percentage to 58% in the rural counties and holding on with 61% in the urban areas. These are good showings, given the continuing distress and the high Dukakis vote in a district which is a long cultural distance from Brookline; but for all Coleman's seniority, he may not have an utterly safe seat.

The People: Est. Pop. 1986: 549,800, up 0.6% 1980–86; Pop. 1980: 546,614, up 7.2% 1970–80. Households (1980): 74% family, 38% with children, 65% married couples; 27.2% housing units rented; median monthly rent: $151; median house value: $34,800. Voting age pop. (1980): 396,507; 2% Black, 1% Spanish origin.

1988 Presidential Vote: Bush (R) 115,674   (50%)
Dukakis (D) 115,469   (50%)

Rep. E. Thomas (Tom) Coleman (R)

Elected 1976; b. May 29, 1943, Gladstone; home, Gladstone; William Jewell Col., B.A. 1965, N.Y.U., M.P.A. 1969, Washington U., J.D. 1969; Protestant; married (Marilyn).

Career: Asst. Atty. Gen. of MO, 1969–72; MO House of Reps., 1973–76.

Offices: 2468 RHOB 20515, 202-225-7041. Also 851 N.W. 45th St., Kansas City 64116, 816-454-7117; and 8th and Edmond, St. Joseph 64501, 816-364-3900.

Committees: *Agriculture* (2d of 18 R). Subcommittees: Conservation, Credit and Rural Development (Ranking Member); Department Operations, Research and Foreign Agriculture. *Education and Labor* (2d of 13 R). Subcommittees: Elementary, Secondary and Vocational Education; Human Resources; Postsecondary Education (Ranking Member).

Group Ratings

	ADA	ACLU	COPE	CFA	LCV	ACU	NTLC	NSI	COC	CEI
1988	25	41	21	55	31	76	61	100	93	42
1987	0	—	18	21	—	62	—	—	87	55

National Journal Ratings

	1988 LIB — 1988 CONS		1987 LIB — 1987 CONS	
Economic	34%	65%	22%	78%
Social	29%	70%	25%	75%
Foreign	16%	78%	20%	76%

Key Votes

1) Homeless $	FOR	5) Ban Drug Test	AGN	9) SDI Research	FOR
2) Gephardt Amdt	AGN	6) Drug Death Pen	FOR	10) Ban Chem Weaps	AGN
3) Deficit Reduc	AGN	7) Handgun Sales	AGN	11) Aid to Contras	FOR
4) Kill Plnt Clsng Notice	FOR	8) Ban D.C. Abort $	FOR	12) Nuclear Testing	AGN

Election Results

1988 general	E. Thomas (Tom) Coleman (R)	135,883	(59%)	($341,344)
	Doug Hughes (D)	93,128	(41%)	($198,617)
1988 primary	E. Thomas (Tom) Coleman (R)	28,762	(90%)	
	Robert L. Buck (R)....................	3,278	(10%)	
1986 general	E. Thomas (Tom) Coleman (R)	95,865	(57%)	($250,606)
	Doug R. Hughes (D)...................	73,155	(43%)	($134,325)

SEVENTH DISTRICT

Most Americans' image of the Ozarks of Missouri is precisely wrong. They think of mountains, but most of the residents of the Ozark area live in and around Springfield, on a plateau of rolling high land between two river systems. They think of tarpaper shacks, but while Springfield and Joplin have their share of fine antique homes this is one part of Missouri that has had recent steady growth: new subdivisions pop up around Springfield and retirement developments and condominiums in the mountains to the south around the tourist center of Branson. Incomes in this area are below the national average, but so is the cost of living, and crime, as many recent migrants from St. Louis and Chicago will tell you, is very low. The climate here is relatively temperate, and the cultural tone is distinctly traditional. Springfield is home to the Assemblies of God, one of the fastest growing American churches, and traditional and fundamentalist Protestantism are strong here, although it is also home to America's most generous (per capita) Catholic diocese.

Politically, southwestern Missouri is historically Republican. It was not slaveholding or secession territory in 1861, and though Springfield changed hands several times in Missouri's Civil War, its sympathies were Union. Its conservative responses to the big-spending government of the 1960s and cultural liberalism of the 1970s reinforced its Republicanism, but Farm Belt discontent has moved it toward the Democrats. The 7th Congressional District of Missouri, which covers the southwest corner of the state, generally goes Republican and elects Republican congressmen who are faithful followers of the party leadership in the House. But in 1988, when incumbent Gene Taylor retired, it had a real race, and a rather different result.

There were serious contests in both primaries. On the Republican side, Taylor supported his district aide Gary Nodler, as his predecessor, Durward Hall, had supported him in 1972. But Mel Hancock, promoter of a successful anti-tax referendum in 1980 and an unsuccessful candidate for Senate in 1982 and for lieutenant governor in 1984, edged him 39%–36%. On the Democratic side, businessman Keith Jaspers, a newcomer to the area, ran a strong race, but was beaten 51%–37% by Max Bacon, a former judge famed for his tough sentences and with deep roots in the district (he grew up friends with Governor John Ashcroft). In the general, Bacon ran about even with Hancock in the Springfield area. But Hancock carried the western part around Joplin and the mountain counties by enough for a narrow 53%–46% victory. This was not an impressive victory for the booming-voiced, anti-tax Hancock in a district where George Bush won with more than 60%. Hancock, the oldest House freshman at age 59, will have the advantages of incumbency and a seat on Public Works to make this a safe seat.

The People: Est. Pop. 1986: 586,700, up 7.5% 1980–86; Pop. 1980: 545,921, up 22.2% 1970–80. Households (1980): 75% family, 37% with children, 66% married couples; 25.7% housing units rented; median monthly rent: $135; median house value: $31,100. Voting age pop. (1980): 399,610; 1% Black, 1% American Indian, 1% Spanish origin.

1988 Presidential Vote:
Bush (R)	148,460	(61%)
Dukakis (D).	92,866	(38%)

Rep. Mel Hancock (R)

Elected 1988; b. Sept. 14, 1929, Cape Fair; home, Springfield; Southwestern MO St. Col., B.S. 1951; Church of Christ; married, ("Sug").

Career: Intl. Harvester Co., 1953–59, Sentry Insurance, 1959–69, Pres. and owner, Federal Protection Inc., 1969–89.

Offices: 511 CHOB 20515, 202-225-6536. Also 322-B E. Pershing, Springfield 65806, 417-862-4317; and 302 Fed. Bldg., Joplin 64801, 417-781-1041.

Committees: *Public Works and Transportation* (18th of 20 R). Subcommittees: Aviation; Surface Transportation; Water Resources. *Small Business* (15th of 17 R). Subcommittees: SBA, the General Economy and Minority Enterprise Development; Regulation, Business Opportunities and Energy.

Group Ratings and Key Votes: Newly Elected

Election Results

1988 general	Melton D. Hancock (R)	127,939	(53%)	($338,125)
	Max Bacon (D)	111,244	(46%)	($215,064)
1988 primary	Melton D. Hancock (R)	37,067	(39%)	
	Gary Nodler (R)	33,940	(36%)	
	Dennis Smith (R)	20,354	(21%)	
	Cecil W. Huff (R)	4,176	(4%)	
1986 general	Gene Taylor (R)	114,210	(67%)	($143,284)
	Ken Young (D)	56,291	(33%)	

EIGHTH DISTRICT

Rows of barges tethered together, full of coal or soybeans, not steamboats sending puffs of steam high above the water, account nowadays for most of the traffic on the Mississippi, the life along which Mark Twain chronicled more than a century ago. Outwardly, the communities along the river from the old French settlement town of Ste. Genevieve down to the Bootheel that dips south of the rest of the state toward the Mississippi Delta, have not changed much in the last 50 years; neither have the lowland rural counties to the west and the less populous communities in the hills that begin a few dozen miles west of the river. The only big growth here in that time has been around the manufacturing town of Cape Girardeau on the Mississippi and along the route of Interstate 44 (which follows the route of the late lamented U.S. 66); there has been a big population outflow from the Bootheel, as machines replace low-wage farm workers, and from some mining communities, as ores give out or become too expensive to extract.

Politically, there is much variation. The Bootheel is Dixiecratic, Cape Girardeau heavily Republican, Ste. Genevieve and St. Francois just inland heavily Democratic; the overall result is a district that was about 1% more for George Bush than the national average in 1988. Most of this area has been represented by Democrats in the House since the Civil War. But since 1980 it has been represented by Republican Bill Emerson, who has held on despite some serious challenges.

It has helped that he seems to have the natural political instincts not always evident in the Republicans who captured Democratic districts in 1980. Before that, he was a Washington lobbyist with roots in the district, and he spotted the vulnerability, on personal grounds, of Democratic Representative Bill Burlison and went back to run in 1980 and won with 55%. He got a seat on the Agriculture Committee (he's now on Public Works as well) that enabled him to make a popular record in this agricultural district. Chubby, irrepressible, he works for higher soybean supports and for holding down the cost of the food stamp program (though he supported it against Reagan cuts), and supported Claude Pepper's long-term health care program: certainly he is more of an operator than an ideologue. He has worked the district hard, sending his mobile office around to 40 stops each month. And he championed the cause of embattled farmers, notably that of Puxico farmer Wayne Cryts, who removed from a bankrupt grain elevator 30,000 bushels of soybeans he had pledged on a loan he had never repaid; Cryts became a national folk hero, evidently on the theory that the whole economy could be revived if folks could sell their collateral and pocket the proceeds without paying off their loans.

But Emerson may rue his support of Cryts. If it helped him fend off a Democratic challenge in 1982, it also propelled Cryts to challenge him in 1986 and 1988. In 1986, Cryts held Emerson to a 53%–47% margin. After 1986, Cryts faced some hearings on whether he could pay back his loan; Emerson checked into the Betty Ford clinic for a month to solve an alcohol problem. Despite campaigning from Richard Gephardt, Cryts ran weaker in 1988, carrying only 4 of the district's 26 counties; Emerson won 58%–42%. Whether that will insulate him from further tough competition is unclear.

The People: Est. Pop. 1986: 552,300, up 1.1% 1980–86; Pop. 1980: 546,112, up 14.3% 1970–80. Households (1980): 76% family, 41% with children, 66% married couples; 26.3% housing units rented; median monthly rent: $105; median house value: $26,500. Voting age pop. (1980): 387,786; 3% Black.

1988 Presidential Vote:

Bush (R)	111,605	(55%)
Dukakis (D)	91,370	(45%)

Rep. Bill Emerson (R)

Elected 1980; b. Jan. 1, 1938, St. Louis; home, Cape Girardeau; Westminster Col., B.A. 1959, U. of Baltimore, LL.B. 1964; Presbyterian; married (Jo Ann).

Career: Spec. Asst. to U.S. Rep. Bob Ellsworth, 1961–65; A. A. to U.S. Rep. Charles Mathias, 1965–70; Dir. of Govt. Rel., Fairchild Indus., 1970–73; Dir. of Public Affairs, Interstate Natural Gas Assn., 1974–75; Exec. Asst. to Chmn., Fed. Elec. Comm., 1975; Dir., Fed. Rel., TRW, Inc., 1975–79; Govt. rel. consultant, 1979–80.

Offices: 438 CHOB, 202-225-4404. Also Fed. Bldg., 339 Broadway, Cape Girardeau 63701, 314-335-0101; and 4612 Pine St., Ste. 101, Rolla 65401, 314-364-2455.

Committees: *Agriculture* (7th of 18 R). Subcommittees: Cotton, Rice, and Sugar; Domestic Marketing, Consumer Relations, and Nutrition (Ranking Member); Wheat, Soybeans and Feed Grains. *Public Works and Transportation* (15th of 20 R). Economic Development; Surface Transportation; Water Resources. *Select Committee on Hunger* (Vice Chairman).

Group Ratings

	ADA	ACLU	COPE	CFA	LCV	ACU	NTLC	NSI	COC	CEI
1988	10	39	24	73	19	90	69	100	83	47
1987	4	—	22	21	—	78	—	—	87	55

National Journal Ratings

	1988 LIB — 1988 CONS		1987 LIB — 1987 CONS	
Economic	37% —	62%	29% —	69%
Social	5% —	91%	10% —	85%
Foreign	26% —	74%	0% —	80%

Key Votes

1) Homeless $	FOR	5) Ban Drug Test	FOR	9) SDI Research	FOR
2) Gephardt Amdt	AGN	6) Drug Death Pen	FOR	10) Ban Chem Weaps	AGN
3) Deficit Reduc	AGN	7) Handgun Sales	FOR	11) Aid to Contras	FOR
4) Kill Plnt Clsng Notice	—	8) Ban D.C. Abort $	FOR	12) Nuclear Testing	—

Election Results

1988 general	Bill Emerson (R)	117,601	(58%)	($768,792)
	Wayne Cryts (D)	84,801	(42%)	($516,239)
1988 primary	Bill Emerson (R), unopposed			
1986 general	Bill Emerson (R)	79,142	(53%)	($598,090)
	Wayne Cryts (D)	71,532	(47%)	($309,504)

NINTH DISTRICT

Mark Twain's home country, in the Mississippi River town of Hannibal in northern Missouri, is smack in the middle of Little Dixie. Settled by southerners, it was pro-slavery and Democratic, though Twain himself had scorn for slavery and was a Civil War Republican. The area around Hannibal, however, has remained Democratic, and the 9th Congressional District, which historically has included most of Little Dixie, has elected such notable Democratic congressmen as Champ Clark, Speaker of the House from 1911 to 1919 and presidential candidate in 1912, and Clarence Cannon, author of the definitive text on the House's parliamentary procedure and curmudgeonly chairman of the House Appropriations Committee until his death in 1963.

Little Dixie remains heavily Democratic: Hannibal and 10 counties voted for Michael Dukakis over George Bush in 1988. But the 9th Congressional District as a whole has been trending Republican. This is partly a matter of changing opinions, but even more a matter of changing demographics. Little Dixie has been losing population: the 9th District Little Dixie counties had more people in 1940 than in 1980. Columbia, home of the University of Missouri, trended left as students got the vote in the early 1970s, but now its is voting more white-collar—a bit liberal on cultural issues and conservative on economics, the opposite of Little Dixie. The fastest-growing areas are in St. Charles and Franklin Counties, the outlying parts of the St. Louis metropolitan area, with spanking new suburbs full of young Upbeats (the Times Mirror-Gallup survey term) who have little use for preachy, gloomy Democrats like Jimmy Carter or Michael Dukakis and like the cheery optimism of Ronald Reagan and George Bush. As St. Charles and Franklin grow, the 9th moves more into the Republican column; and they even erode slightly the percentages for 9th District Democratic Congressman Harold Volkmer.

Volkmer has been around since 1976 and has cinched his hold on the district while making an impact in Congress. By far his biggest achievement there was passage of the McClure-Volkmer amendments, weakening federal gun control laws, in 1986. Volkmer was a tireless proponent, getting the signatures of a majority of members to pry this measure out of the Judiciary Committee, pressing the issue when many others would rather leave it to campaign rhetoric. Not surprisingly, it is highly popular in Little Dixie and in the St. Louis suburbs as well. Volkmer himself is less popular in the House, where his nettlesome personality and sometimes tactless persistence work against him. At home he stresses his seniority, his work on the Agriculture Committee for farmers (he chairs the Forest, Family Farms and Energy Subcommittee), his insistence that foreigners open their markets to American farm products, his support of the U.S. 36 widening, rural hospitals and Hannibal flood control.

Little Dixie has elected nothing but Democratic congressmen since the irascible Cannon was elected in 1922, but Volkmer had serious opposition in his first election in 1976, as well as in 1980, 1984 and 1986. He got only 53% against former John Danforth staffer Carrie Francke in 1984, and lost Columbia; against abortion opponent state Senator John Uthlaut he won 57% in 1986. Volkmer won easily in 1988 and remains popular in Little Dixie, but he is potentially vulnerable in the St. Louis suburbs, which casts 30% of the district's votes, and the Columbia area, which casts 19%.

The People: Est. Pop. 1986: 584,700, up 7.0% 1980–86; Pop. 1980: 546,171, up 20.6% 1970–80. Households (1980): 75% family, 41% with children, 66% married couples; 25.8% housing units rented; median monthly rent: $143; median house value: $35,700. Voting age pop. (1980): 391,319; 3% Black, 1% Spanish origin.

1988 Presidential Vote:

Bush (R)		131,825	(54%)
Dukakis (D)		110,434	(45%)

Rep. Harold L. Volkmer (D)

Elected 1976; b. Apr. 4, 1931, Jefferson City; home, Hannibal; Jefferson City Jr. Col., St. Louis U., U. of MO, LL.B. 1955; Roman Catholic; married (Shirley).

Career: Army, 1955–57; Practicing atty.; Marion Cnty. Prosecuting Atty., 1960–66; MO House of Reps., 1967–77.

Offices: 2411 RHOB 20515, 202-225-2956. Also 370 Fed. Bldg., Hannibal 63401, 314-221-1200.

Committees: *Agriculture* (10th of 27 D). Subcommittees: Livestock, Dairy and Poultry; Wheat, Soybeans, and Feed Grains; Department Operations, Research and Foreign Agriculture; Forests, Family Farms and Energy (Chairman). *Science, Space and Technology* (7th of 30 D). Subcommittee: Space Science and Applications. *Select Committee on Aging* (25th of 39 D). Subcommittees: Housing and Consumer Interests; Retirement Income and Employment.

Group Ratings

	ADA	ACLU	COPE	CFA	LCV	ACU	NTLC	NSI	COC	CEI
1988	60	61	71	73	56	35	18	56	50	18
1987	68	—	69	64	—	9	—	—	27	13

National Journal Ratings

	1988 LIB — 1988 CONS		1987 LIB — 1987 CONS	
Economic	57%	— 41%	62%	— 35%
Social	43%	— 55%	53%	— 47%
Foreign	51%	— 48%	55%	— 44%

Key Votes

1) Homeless $	AGN	5) Ban Drug Test	AGN	9) SDI Research	AGN
2) Gephardt Amdt	FOR	6) Drug Death Pen	FOR	10) Ban Chem Weaps	AGN
3) Deficit Reduc	FOR	7) Handgun Sales	FOR	11) Aid to Contras	AGN
4) Kill Plnt Clsng Notice	AGN	8) Ban D.C. Abort $	FOR	12) Nuclear Testing	—

Election Results

1988 general	Harold L. Volkmer (D)...............	160,872	(68%)	($210,841)
	Ken Dudley (R)	76,008	(32%)	($9,565)
1988 primary	Harold L. Volkmer, unopposed			
1986 general	Harold L. Volkmer (D)................	95,939	(57%)	($383,791)
	Ralph Uthlaut, Jr. (R)	70,972	(43%)	($147,986)

MONTANA

Helena, Montana's capital, in the 1940s was a "mountain village 4,124 feet high," wrote John Gunther in *Inside U.S.A.* "Nowhere have I come across more bizarre or more typical American contradictions. The civic center is in the form of a Mohammedan shrine, complete with tall minaret; the main street winds through the town like a shallow letter S, because it follows the route of Last Chance Gulch, where gold was found in 1864; Helena, a backwater, contains one of the most brilliantly satisfying restaurants in the whole country; the building of the leading hotel was partially financed by gold found in digging its own foundations." In the 1980s Dayton Duncan, between stints as a Democratic nominee's press secretary, found Helena "small but cosmopolitan, active but with a laid-back sophistication." Many of the people, he writes in *Out West*, "have come from somewhere else—often to escape the big cities that Great Falls is trying so hard to emulate. They like being close to the mountains, the forests, the rivers, close to the plains and the big sky." Duncan saw the same Moorish civic center but not the restaurant, but he did go into Hap's where, amid businessmen stopping in after work and yuppies starting a night on the town, he found "an old man with bib overalls with a chain looping to his watch pocket, a bushy white goatee, a crumpled hat, and thick work boots. He takes the spot next to me at the bar and orders a beer. Guessing him to be a rail worker getting off a shift, I ask if he just got in from a train, and he nods. 'Work for the Burlington Northern, do you?' I ask. He takes a deep pull at his beer and looks at me. 'I'm Fry Pan Jack,' he says. 'King of the Hoboes. On my way to the Hobo Convention in Britt, Iowa.'"

Montana has changed and Montana has stayed the same. The Big Sky is still everywhere: Montana remains a land of great empty vistas, with mountains in the west but hundreds of miles of plateaus and plains in the east—the 4th largest state in area and 44th in population, with 800,000 people in an area larger than Michigan and Indiana and Illinois. This is still small-town America—the largest metropolitan area, Billings, has about 100,000 people—but with an industrial as well as rural accent. Even in towns, you're only a few miles from hunting, fishing, camping and boating in unspoiled surroundings and wide open spaces. In the last four or five decades, Montana's mining towns and ranching counties have lost population, and people have converged on small cities—Billings, Missoula, Kalispell, Helena—with growing economies. But the muscular tone of a land settled by ranch hands and miners and railroad workers, of cowboy hats and boots and blue jeans, of men who do hard physical work and relax hard afterwards, remains a common thread in Gunther's and Duncan's Montanas—and attracts tourism, which is now the state's third industry. Montanans see a need to change their economy but also to keep their culture much the same.

The first white Americans here were Lewis and Clark in 1805; after them came the mountain men, fur traders who rendezvoused every year at a prearranged location; then came miners, seeking gold, silver, copper—sudden riches that would make them kings not of this barren land but of the metropole back East. Raucous mining towns sprang up, complete with outlaws and vigilantes. Butte, sitting on "the richest hill on earth," was for many years the state's largest city—and, aside from Denver and Salt Lake City, the only real city in the Rockies, known all over the country as a wild place, full of company goons and IWW organizers, with a Socialist mayor and millionaires who bought seats in the U.S. Senate. The heir to their financial power was the Anaconda Mining company, which from about 1900 to the 1940s bought up almost all of Montana's newspapers and many of its politicians. But Anaconda also had strong opponents like Senators Thomas Walsh, who exposed the Teapot Dome scandal, and Burton Wheeler, a

MONTANA — Congressional Districts, Counties, National Park, and Selected Places — *(2 Districts)*

Congressional districts established March 4, 1983; all other boundaries are as of January 1, 1980.

progressive who broke with Roosevelt over court packing and isolationism.

For years Montana's politics were a matter of economics, with Anaconda, Montana power, the Stockmen's Association (the cattle drive that started in Texas in *Lonesome Dove* ended in Montana), and the Farm Bureau on the Republican side and the old progressives, the labor unions (Montana has no right-to-work law and is the most pro-union state in the Rockies), small farmers' groups and pork barrel beneficiaries (for a while in the 1930s Montana received more federal money per capita than almost any other state) for the Democrats. The echoes of class warfare have grown dimmer over the years. Anaconda sold its newspapers in 1959, and closed its big Montana smelter in the 1970s; government is now the biggest employer in the state. The mines are still worked, though they're now run by a Japanese concern that pellitizes low-grade ore and hauls it off to the Far East. Only a few extremes of partisan division remain, with depopulated Butte and the Indian reservations Democratic, fast-growing Kalispell and some farm counties Republican.

Senators. Except for the 1964 Johnson-Goldwater race, Montana has had a 40-year habit of voting Republican for President and Democratic for Senator. In 1988, it almost did the opposite, coming within a few points of voting for Michael Dukakis and electing for only the second time in history a Republican Senator, Conrad Burns. That leaves Montana with a bipartisan Senate delegation for the first time since the election in 1952 of Mike Mansfield, Senate majority leader from 1961–77 and Ambassador to Japan from 1977–89.

Max Baucus, little known to the national public, still in his forties, sits in one of the potentially most powerful seats in the Senate: on the Finance Committee he ranks just behind Chairman Lloyd Bentsen, who turns 69 in 1990, Spark Matsunaga, who turns 74, and Daniel Patrick Moynihan, who turns 63. That means that Baucus, who turns 49 in 1990, has a good chance to chair Finance in the first part of the 21st century.

Baucus comes from a ranching family near Helena; he went to Stanford, worked a bit in Washington, ran for the legislature in 1972. His big race was for the western 1st District House seat in 1974: in the primary he led current Congressman Pat Williams 44%–32%, with 25% for former Congressman Arnold Olsen. Then he beat Republican incumbent Richard Shoup, who had won against Olsen in 1972 more because of Olsen's problems than his own strength. Two years later Mansfield retired, and 2d District Democrat John Melcher ran for the seat. In 1978, Senator Lee Metcalf was expected to retire, and Baucus was running for the seat. Then Metcalf died in January and Governor Thomas Judge appointed state Chief Justice Paul Hatfield to take his place. Baucus stayed in the race, however, and, much better known and not saddled with a vote for the Panama Canal treaties, beat Hatfield 65%–19% in the primary. In the general, he beat a conservative Republican investment adviser 56%–44%, after pictures of Baucus on a bucking bronco and his opponent in love beads were circulated. His 1984 opponent called Baucus a "wimp" who "talks out of both sides of his mouth and lives in fear that we'll get wise to his games." That wasn't credible in a state where voters are used to chatting with their Senators over coffee in the local cafe, and Baucus won 57%–41%.

Baucus spent much of his first years in the Senate on Montana issues, tending to local projects and making sure that big bills don't hurt Montana's volatile farm or fragile mining economy. On national issues he tended to be cautious, usually but not always in line with other Democrats. Occasionally, as when he was a leader in the move to prevent federal courts from being stripped of jurisdiction over controversial constitutional issues, did he take a visible role on a hot issue. On the Finance Committee, he specialized in health care issues, trying to expand coverage under medicare, leaving taxes and trade mostly to others.

But since around 1985, Baucus has been staking out a lead role on trade. He now chairs the trade subcommittee of Finance. Naturally, he tends to the interests of Montana lamb, beef and wheat, notably on the U.S.-Canada Free Trade Agreement. He authored a Section 301 revision to define currency manipulations, as in South Korea and Taiwan, as unfair trade practices. In fall 1988, he came out for a bilateral treaty with Japan, based on the Canadian model, though not in this case for full free trade, but covering macroeconomic policy and military burden-sharing as well; he sees only limited progress possible under the GATT Uruguay Round talks. Baucus's general disposition is toward free trade; like other Finance leaders, he is wary of another Smoot-Hawley and does not like protectionism. Yet he is frustrated that East Asian countries won't open their markets, and he is not going to be inattentive to the needs of his home state. From the other side of the Pacific Rim, Montana looks like an almost empty treasure trove, with minerals and timber so needed in East Asia, and with only a small but skilled labor force and a minuscule number of consumers. That this sparsely populated, remote part of America should elect a Senator who may have major say over our trade policy with Asia and Europe is one of the things that makes American politics a source of fascination.

On other issues, Baucus chairs a Small Business subcommittee on Rural Economy and Family Farms, has passed the Rural Health Care Viability Act of 1987, promotes gasohol, crusades for air service to Montana (deregulation hurt here). He used his seat on Finance to put in the 1987 deficit reduction bill a provision allowing small businesses, partnerships and personal service corporations to determine their own fiscal years. He also supported an across-the-board budget freeze and voted for Gramm-Rudman. Without having to give up any other committee assignments, Baucus was able to pick up Melcher's seat on Agriculture—a bonus for Montana's farmers and ranchers. Baucus comes up for reelection in 1990, with a good job rating in a state with a large Democratic base. But for all his vote-getting prowess and committee positions, he still has to hustle to win convincingly in 1990.

For this is a state that surprised many by defeating its other Democratic Senator, John Melcher, in 1988, and electing in his place Conrad Burns, Billings farm news broadcaster, livestock auctioneer, livestock fieldman, tobacco chewer and for two years Yellowstone County Commissioner. Burns started off an underdog: Melcher had been representing Montana since he won a 1969 House special election; he won his two Senate races 64%–36% and 54%–42%. Melcher had seats on the Agriculture and Energy Committees, a middle-of-the-road voting record, and a deserved reputation as a maverick who often balked at following party leaders, holding up farm bills to get higher support levels and voting against the Panama Canal Treaties. Burns attacked Melcher as "a liberal who is soft on drugs, soft on defense, and very high on social programs," and as a supporter of ousted Philippine President Ferdinand Marcos. He may have been helped, too, when President Reagan vetoed a wilderness bill Melcher supported and Burns opposed, and by opposition to the "let-it-burn" policy that resulted in the huge Yellowstone fires of summer 1988.

Melcher responded with a reprise of the talking cows ads that worked for him when NCPAC ran ads against him in 1982. But this time the target was different. Burns, who ended every speech with a Western "You bet!" was plainly not an outsider (being a "greenhorn" in politics is not a disadvantage here). Melcher's aim was less than true. Melcher ran ahead of Dukakis in every county but one in his old congressional district and behind Dukakis in all but four counties in the other district: testimony, even 12 years later, to the strength a hard-working incumbent House member can build. But Burns won statewide with 52%.

Burns is not likely to be an influential Senator immediately: he is 100th in seniority, a member of the minority party, from a small state. His wry country sense of humor will serve him well, but whether his conservative policies will is less clear. He sits on the Energy Committee, a good assignment for Montana, and on Commerce, Science and Transportation. The only other Republican elected Senator from Montana, Zales Ecton, lost for reelection to Mike Mansfield in 1952. Burns might well do better.

Governor. Governor Ted Schwinden, smart and unassuming, could have been reelected easily in 1988, but chose to retire. This triggered contests in both parties, resulting in the first Republican gubernatorial victory since 1964. The Democratic contest was won by former Governor Thomas Judge, elected in 1972 and 1976 and beaten in 1980 by Schwinden, who charged campaign finance irregularities. Judge had a JOBS economic program featuring public-private partnerships to promote Montana products at home and abroad. Republican Stan Stephens, a longtime state senator and broadcaster, opposed state government involvement; he appears to be as pristine a conservative as you can find in the ranks of Rocky Mountain governors. Montana's problem is that its economy depends heavily on basic commodities—minerals, coal, wheat—whose prices (the platinum of Stillwater County is an exception) tend to fall as the economy grows. The state has done well with tourism, but needs to develop new industries to generate enough jobs for its young people.

Presidential politics. Montana is clearly the most marginal of the Rocky Mountain states, and in 1988 George Bush carried it by only 52%–46%—the only Rockies state where he ran behind his national average. Yet it never sees much campaigning: even on jets it takes a long time to fly up here, and it still has only four electoral votes. Nor does the primary, held in June, attract many candidates: California votes the same day.

Congressional districting. Montana waited for the 1984 election to redistrict, switching just a couple of counties from the 1st to the 2d District. Latest estimates show them with virtually identical populations. There has been speculation, taken seriously by some, that Montana might lose one of its two House seates after the 1990 Census and might become the seventh state in the nation to be represented by a Congressman-At-Large.

1st Congressional District. The mountainous western 1st District has had a turbulent political history: half a century ago it elected Communist party-liner Jerry O'Connell, vicious anti-Semite Jacob Thorkelson, Jeanette Rankin who voted against the declaration of war in 1941 as she had in 1917, and Mike Mansfield. Since then it has been mostly Democratic. The current congressman is Pat Williams, a former teacher, state legislator and Melcher aide. He is an old-fashioned liberal Democrat, close enough to organized labor that the state AFL-CIO director is godfather to one of his children. In 1985, Williams became one of seven deputy majority whips. He also serves on Education and Labor—a solid pro-labor, pro-teacher vote—and in 1987 became chairman of the Postsecondary Education Subcommittee. This gives him jurisdiction over such issues as college loans and grants, libraries and brittle books (books disintegrating in libraries). He is probably Education and Labor's strongest opponent of aid to church schools and voted against the ABC child care bill for that reason. He sponsored a successful bill to ban (the notoriously unreliable) employer-administered lie detector tests.

The bulk of voters in the 1st has long since shifted from heavily Democratic Butte to Missoula, Kalispell, Helena and Bozeman. Williams, who first won the seat, runs enough ahead of his party to carry the district with over 60%. He considered running for governor but bowed out of the race in September 1987.

2d Congressional District. The eastern 2d District lies mostly east of the mountains: a vast expanse of plains—the fourth largest district in the nation in area—where cattle ranches stretch as far as the eye can see and towering buttes rise over the magnificently eroded High Plains. It has most of Montana's farms and coal strip mines, but about half the population is in and around Billings and Great Falls.

Congressman Ron Marlenee, first elected in 1976, is now one of the senior Republicans on the House Agriculture Committee. He has had a say in fashioning the 1985 farm bill, the 1987 farm credit bill and the 1988 drought relief bill, and undoubtedly will play a part on the 1989 farm bill. Generally conservative, he is no doctrinaire free marketer, and supports generous farm programs, though he made a point of opposing the sodbuster section of the 1985 bill. He also sits on Interior and as ranking Republican on the Public Lands Subcommittee—a key assignment since much congressional politicking revolves around wilderness areas, national trails and the like; in 1988, a Montana wilderness bill was passed over Marlenee's objections, but President Reagan vetoed it. The fact that Marlenee was beaten on a home state matter is not surprising: he is a man of some temper and his usual (though not invariable) style is one of vehement denunciations, not bipartisan compromising.

Marlenee has not always had an easy time getting reelected. In 1988, Democrat Buck O'Brien ran even with him in Billings and Great Falls and held him to 55% district-wide; in 1986 O'Brien held Marlenee to 53%. He barely ran ahead of George Bush in an agricultural district—a sign that this seat could be seriously contested in the future.

The People: Est. Pop. 1988: 804,000; Pop. 1980: 786,690, up 2.2% 1980–88 and 13.3% 1970–80; 0.34% of U.S. total, 44th largest. 20% with 1–3 yrs. col., 17% with 4+ yrs. col.; 12.3% below poverty level. Single ancestry: 14% German, 7% English, 5% Irish, Norwegian, 2% Swedish, 1% French, Scottish, Dutch, Italian, Polish. Households (1980): 72% family, 40% with children, 63% married couples; 31.4% housing units rented; median monthly rent: $165; median house value: $46,400. Voting age pop. (1980): 554,795; 4% American Indian, 1% Spanish origin. Registered voters (1988): 505,541; no party registration.

1988 Share of Federal Tax Burden: $2,139,000,000; 0.24% of U.S. total, 46th largest.

1988 Share of Federal Expenditures

	Total		Non-Defense		Defense	
Total Expend	$2,929m	(0.33%)	$2,664m	(0.41%)	$334m	(0.15%)
St/Lcl Grants	546m	(0.48%)	545m	(0.48%)	1m	(0.91%)
Salary/Wages	445m	(0.33%)	315m	(0.47%)	130m	(0.47%)
Pymnts to Indiv	1,368m	(0.33%)	1,314m	(0.34%)	54m	(0.29%)
Procurement	149m	(0.08%)	69m	(0.15%)	149m	(0.08%)
Research/Other	421m	(1.13%)	421m	(1.14%)	0m	(1.14%)

Political Lineup: Governor, Stan Stephens (R); Lt. Gov., Allen Kolstad (R); Secy. of State, Mike Cooney (D); Atty. Gen., Marc Racicot (R); Auditor, Andrea (Andy) Bennett (R). State Senate, 50 (27 R and 23 D); State House of Representatives, 100 (52 D and 48 R). Senators, Max Baucus (D) and Conrad Burns (R). Representatives, 2 (1 D and 1 R).

1988 Presidential Vote
Bush (R)	190,412	(52%)
Dukakis (D)	168,956	(46%)

1988 Democratic Presidential Primary
Dukakis	83,684	(69%)
Jackson	26,908	(22%)
Gephardt	3,369	(3%)
Gore	2,261	(2%)
Simon	1,566	(1%)

1984 Presidential Vote
Reagan (R)	232,450	(60%)
Mondale (D)	146,742	(38%)

1988 Republican Presidential Primary
Bush	63,098	(73%)
Dole	16,762	(19%)
Others	6,520	(8%)

GOVERNOR

Gov. Stan Stephens (R)

Elected 1988, term expires Jan. 1993; b. Sept. 16, 1929, Calgary, Alberta, Canada; home, Helena; Lutheran; married (Ann).

Career: Korean War; Radio announcer, newswriter, correspondent, 1947–1953; Cable TV executive, 1968–85; MT Senate, 1968–86.

Office: Office of the Governor, Helena 59620, 406-444-3111.

Election Results

1988 gen.	Stan Stephens (R)	190,604	(53%)
	Tom Judge (D)	169,313	(47%)
1988 prim.	Stan Stephens (R)	44,022	(50%)
	Cal Winslow (R)	37,875	(43%)
	Jim Waltermire (R)	6,024	(7%)
1984 gen.	Ted Schwinden (D)	266,578	(70%)
	Pat M. Goodover (R)	100,070	(26%)

SENATORS

Sen. Max Baucus (D)

Elected 1978, seat up 1990; b. Dec. 11, 1941, Helena; home Missoula; Stanford U., B.A. 1964, LL.B. 1967; Protestant; married (Wanda).

Career: Staff Atty., Civil Aeronautics Bd., 1967–69; Legal Asst. Securities and Exch. Comm., 1969–71; Practicing atty., 1971–75; MT House of Reps., 1973–75; U.S. House of Reps., 1975–78.

Offices: 706 HSOB 20510, 202-224-2651. Also Granite Bldg., 3. N. Last Chance Gulch, Helena 59601, 406-449-5480; 202 Frat Bldg., 2817 2d Ave. N., Billings 59101, 406-657-6970; Fed. Bldg. 32 E. Babcock, Rm. 114, P.O. Box 1689, Bozeman 59715, 406-586 6104; Silver Bow Ctr., 125 W. Granite, Butte 59701, 406-782-8700 107 5th St. N., Great Falls 59401, 406-761-1574; and 211 N Higgins, Ste. 102, Missoula 59802, 406-329-3123.

Committees: *Agriculture, Nutrition and Forestry* (9th of 10 D) Subcommittees: Agricultural Production and Stabilization of Prices; Domestic and Foreign Marketing and Product Promotion; Conservation and Forestry. *Environ ment and Public Works* (4th of 9 D). Subcommittees: Environmental Protection (Chairman); Toxic Substances, Environmental Oversight, Research and Development; Superfund Ocean and Wate Protection. *Finance* (4th of 11 D). Subcommittees: International Trade (Chairman); Taxation and Deb Management; Medicare and Long-Term Care. *Small Business* (3d of 10 D). Subcommittees: Innova tion, Technology and Productivity; Rural Economy and Family Farming (Chairman).

Group Ratings

	ADA	ACLU	COPE	CFA	LCV	ACU	NTLC	NSI	COC	CEI
1988	80	63	75	100	60	8	24	0	29	19
1987	75	—	74	67	—	8	—	—	28	29

National Journal Ratings

	1988 LIB — 1988 CONS		1987 LIB — 1987 CONS	
Economic	73% —	26%	65% —	26%
Social	67% —	31%	52% —	47%
Foreign	79% —	16%	81% —	0%

Key Votes

1) Cut Aged Housing $	AGN	5) Bork Nomination	AGN	9) SDI Funding	AGN
2) Override Hwy Veto	FOR	6) Ban Plastic Guns	—	10) Ban Chem Weaps	AGN
3) Kill Plnt Clsng Notice	AGN	7) Deny Abortions	AGN	11) Aid To Contras	AGN
4) Min Wage Increase	FOR	8) Japanese Reparations	FOR	12) Reagan Defense $	AGN

Election Results

1984 general	Max Baucus (D)	215,704	(57%)	($1,386,561
	Chuck Cozzens (R)	154,308	(41%)	($492,391
1984 primary	Max Baucus (D)	80,726	(79%)	
	Bob Ripley (D)	20,979	(21%)	($233,018
1978 general	Max Baucus (D)	160,353	(56%)	($653,756
	Larry Williams (R)	127,589	(44%)	($346,72

Sen. Conrad Burns (R)

Elected 1988, seat up 1994; b. Jan. 25, 1935, Gallatin, MO; home, Billings; U. of MO; Lutheran; married (Phyllis).

Career: USMC, 1955; TWA and Ozark Airlines, 1958–61; Field Rep., *Polled Hereford World Mag.*, 1962; Mgr., Billings Livestock Show, 1968; Radio, TV broadcaster, 1968–86; Commissioner, Yellowstone Cnty., 1986–88.

Offices: 183 DSOB 20510, 202-224-2644. Also 2708 First Ave. N., Billings 59101, 406-252-0550; 208 N. Montana Ave., Rm 202-A, Helena 59601, 406-449-5401; 415 N. Higgins, Missoula 59802, 406-329-3528; and 104 4th St. N., Great Falls 59401, 406-252-9585.

Committees: *Commerce, Science and Transportation* (7th of 9 R). Subcommittees: Communications; Foreign Commerce and Tourism; Surface Transportation. *Energy and Natural Resources* (7th of 9 R). Subcommittees: Energy Research and Development; Public Lands, National Parks and Forests; Water and Power. *Small Business* (8th of 9 R). Subcommittees: Rural Economy and Family Farming; Urban and Minority-Owned Business Development (Ranking Member).

Group Ratings and Key Votes: Newly Elected

Election Results

1988 general	Conrad Burns (R)	189,445	(52%)	($1,076,010)
	John Melcher (D)	175,809	(48%)	($1,338,622)
1988 primary	Conrad Burns (R)	63,330	(85%)	
	Tom Faranda (R)	11,427	(15%)	
1982 general	John Melcher (D)	174,861	(54%)	($830,892)
	Larry Williams (R)	133,789	(42%)	($708,286)

FIRST DISTRICT

The People: Est. Pop. 1986: 410,900, up 4.5% 1980–86; Pop. 1980: 393,298, up 19.0% 1970–80. Households (1980): 71% family, 40% with children, 62% married couples; 31.3% housing units rented; median monthly rent: $163; median house value: $46,900. Voting age pop. (1980): 280,180; 3% American Indian, 1% Spanish origin.

1988 Presidential Vote:

	Bush (R)	95,054	(50%)
	Dukakis (D)	91,519	(48%)

Rep. Pat Williams (D)

Elected 1978; b. Oct. 30, 1937, Helena; home, Helena; U. of MT; U. of Denver, B.A. 1961; Roman Catholic; married (Carol).

Career: Pub. sch. teacher; MT House of Reps., 1967, 1969; Reg Dir., Humphrey Pres. Camp., 1968; Exec. Asst. to U.S. Rep. Johr Melcher, 1969–71; MT State Coord., Family Ed. Prog., 1971–78.

Offices: 2457 RHOB 20515, 202-225-3211. Also 32 N. Las Chance Gulch, Helena 59601, 406-443-7878; Finlen Complex Butte 59701, 406-723-4404; and 302 W. Broadway, Missoula 59802, 406-549-5550.

Committees: *Education and Labor* (8th of 22 D). Subcommittees Elementary, Secondary and Vocational Education; Labor Standards; Postsecondary Education (Chairman). *Interior and Insular Affairs* (8th of 26 D). Subcommittee: National Parks and Public Lands.

Group Ratings

	ADA	ACLU	COPE	CFA	LCV	ACU	NTLC	NSI	COC	CEI
1988	85	91	89	73	75	0	10	0	15	3
1987	100	—	88	64	—	0	—	—	7	10

National Journal Ratings

	1988 LIB — 1988 CONS		1987 LIB — 1987 CONS	
Economic	92%	0%	73%	0%
Social	85%	15%	78%	0%
Foreign	84%	0%	81%	0%

Key Votes

1) Homeless $	AGN	5) Ban Drug Test	AGN	9) SDI Research	AGN
2) Gephardt Amdt	FOR	6) Drug Death Pen	AGN	10) Ban Chem Weaps	FOR
3) Deficit Reduc	FOR	7) Handgun Sales	—	11) Aid to Contras	AGN
4) Kill Plnt Clsng Notice	AGN	8) Ban D.C. Abort $	AGN	12) Nuclear Testing	FOR

Election Results

1988 general	Pat Williams (D)..................... 115,278	(61%)	($250,276)
	Jim Fenlason (R)..................... 74,405	(39%)	($58,204)
1988 primary	Pat Williams (D), unopposed		
1986 general	Pat Williams (D)..................... 98,501	(62%)	($252,708)
	Don Allen (R)..................... 61,230	(38%)	($154,551)

SECOND DISTRICT

The People: Est. Pop. 1986: 408,000, up 3.7% 1980–86; Pop. 1980: 393,392, up 8.1% 1970–80 Households (1980): 73% family, 41% with children, 64% married couples; 31.6% housing units rented median monthly rent: $167; median house value: $46,100. Voting age pop. (1980): 274,615; 5% American Indian, 1% Spanish origin.

1988 Presidential Vote:

Bush (R) 95,358	(54%)
Dukakis (D)...................... 77,437	(44%)

Rep. Ron Marlenee (R)

Elected 1976; b. Aug. 8, 1935, Scobey; home, Scobey; MT St. U., U. of MT, Reisch Sch. of Auctioneering; Lutheran; married (Cynthia).

Career: Farmer, rancher, and businessman, 1953–76.

Offices: 2465 RHOB, 202-225-1555. Also 103 N. Broadway St., Billings 59401, 406-657-6753; and 111 5th St., N., Great Falls 59401, 406-453-3264.

Committees: *Agriculture* (3d of 18 R). Subcommittees: Forests, Family Farms and Energy; Wheat, Soybeans, and Feed Grains (Ranking Member). *Interior and Insular Affairs* (3d of 15 R). Water, Power and Offshore Energy Resources; Mining and Natural Resources; National Parks and Public Lands (Ranking Member).

Group Ratings

	ADA	ACLU	COPE	CFA	LCV	ACU	NTLC	NSI	COC	CEI
1988	0	17	19	18	19	96	54	100	86	75
1987	8	—	20	36	—	83	—	—	93	69

National Journal Ratings

	1988 LIB — 1988 CONS		1987 LIB — 1987 CONS	
Economic	0%	— 93%	11%	— 83%
Social	5%	— 91%	0%	— 90%
Foreign	27%	— 71%	20%	— 76%

Key Votes

1) Homeless $	FOR	5) Ban Drug Test	FOR	9) SDI Research	FOR
2) Gephardt Amdt	AGN	6) Drug Death Pen	FOR	10) Ban Chem Weaps	AGN
3) Deficit Reduc	AGN	7) Handgun Sales	FOR	11) Aid to Contras	FOR
4) Kill Plnt Clsng Notice	FOR	8) Ban D.C. Abort $	FOR	12) Nuclear Testing	AGN

Election Results

1988 general	Ron Marlenee (R).....................	97,465	(55%)	($380,928)
	Buck O'Brien (D)	78,069	(45%)	($394,102)
1988 primary	Ron Marlenee (R), unopposed			
1986 general	Ron Marlenee (R).....................	84,548	(53%)	($251,163)
	Buck O'Brien (D)	73,583	(47%)	($223,231)

NEBRASKA

"The traveler crossing Nebraska," wrote the *WPA Guide* in the late 1930s, "gets an impression of broad fields, deep skies, wind, and sunlight; clouds racing over prairie swells; herds of cattle grazing on the sandhills; red barns and white farmhouses surrounded by fields of tasseling corn and ripening wheat; windmills and wire fences; and men and women who take their living from the soil." That was two generations after Nebraska was settled, in one giant rush, in the 1880s, when its population increased from 452,000 to 1,062,000 in a single decade, more than it has increased ever since (it is now 1.6 million). Within that same decade Nebraska became a major regional center and Lincoln a state capital. Today Nebraska remains heavily dependent on farming and related industries, and Omaha and Lincoln are still its only significant cities. This is a state that sprang suddenly into existence and has changed strikingly little in the years since.

That is not what its founders intended: they hoped Nebraska would develop into diversified farming, industrial and commercial centers like Ohio or Illinois or Missouri or Minnesota. But while the 1880s were a time of plentiful rain here, the 1890s were a decade of drought, and Nebraska stopped growing. Many rural counties and even Omaha lost population, and have been exporting people ever since; and the creative energies in the economy seem to have skipped over the Great Plains and moved far to the West. Most of Nebraska's settlers, like most migrants, were young people, optimistic and motivated, in search of opportunity, with families full of children. Fully 48% of the one million Nebraskans of 1890 were children, and a very large percentage of them moved elsewhere when they grew up. Since 1890, Nebraska has exported people to the West, the great metropolitan areas of the Midwest, and to Texas and the Southwest; since 1940, it has grown in percentage terms less than all but seven other states (Pennsylvania, West Virginia, Mississippi, Arkansas, Iowa, and the Dakotas). Only 28% of Nebraska's 1.6 million residents today are children, meaning that there are actually 60,000 fewer children then there were 90 years ago.

The sudden boom of the 1880s and the bust of the 1890s produced the most colorful—and atypical—politics of Nebraska's history: namely the populist movement and William Jennnings Bryan, the "silver tounged orator of the Platte." Bryan was only 36 when he delivered the famous Cross of Gold speech at the 1896 Democratic National Convention and was swept to the Democratic nomination; he was thought so radical that Democratic President Grover Cleveland wouldn't support him, but Bryan still won 47% of the vote. Nebraskans supported Bryan, whose program may have been forward-looking, but whose purpose was retrograde: to restore Nebraska to the prosperity and prospects it enjoyed a few years before. Bryan won the Democratic nomination again in 1900 and 1908 but never came as close to winning as he did the first time. By then Nebraska had already gone to the Republicans, and Bryan himself eventually moved to Florida. Since Bryan's time, Nebraska's most notable politician has been George Norris, representative (1909–13) and Senator (1913–43). During the progressive era, Norris led the House rebellion against Speaker Joseph Cannon; during the 1930s, he pushed through the Norris-LaGuardia Anti-Injunction Act, the first national pro-union legislation, and the Tennessee Valley Authority.

Governor. Heavily Republican, Nebraska has had Democratic governors for most of the last 20 years, thanks largely to the personal popularity of Jim Exon and Bob Kerrey, both of whom have gone on to become Senators. The state's current governor, Kay Orr, is a Republican, an aggressive conservative who started off as a staffer to Governor Charles Thone, became state treasurer in 1981, and won the nation's first two-woman governor's race against Democrat Helen

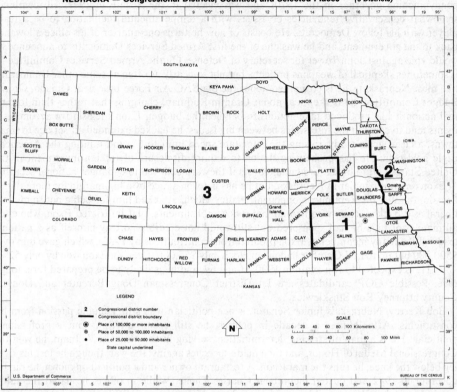

NEBRASKA — Congressional Districts, Counties, and Selected Places — *(3 Districts)*

Boosalis, the mayor of Lincoln, in 1986. (This easy acceptance of women as leaders is not so surprising when you remember pioneer women built sod houses, raised children, and taught them the classics of Western culture.) In her first term, spurred by the chief executive of giant ConAgra, Orr and the legislature in 1987 pushed through a tax package lowering the top rates of the state income tax and cutting some business taxes; in return, ConAgra expanded operations rather than make good on its threat to move its headquarters from Omaha. Orr argues that this program will produce much needed economic growth; some opponents say that it is an undeserved break for the rich and well-placed. This may turn out to be a central issue in the 1990 election.

Orr's other major initiative did not turn out quite as she hoped. In March 1987, when Senator Edward Zorinsky suddenly died, she spurned the pleas of Congressman Hal Daub and former state chairman Kermit Brashear, who had their eyes on the seat, and appointed agribusiness executive David Karnes, whose main political experience was in serving on the Omaha board of education and backing Orr's candidacy in 1986. In 1988, Karnes beat Daub after a bitter primary, but ran far behind Bob Kerrey in the general; probably no Republican had a chance against Kerrey, but the intra-party fight did not help. If Orr decides to seek reelection in 1990 (she says she'll announce in January of that year), she might face Lincoln mayor Bill Harris, whom some speculate may seek the Democratic nomination.

Senators. Nebraska's senior Senator is James Exon, who served eight years as a popular pennypinching governor in the 1970s and was elected to the Senate in 1978. He combines somewhat conservative tendencies on issues with a temperamental inclination to be a team player with his fellow Democrats. He boasts of how he turns one-quarter of his office allowance back to the government, and he was one of the first Armed Services Democrats to announce he would vote against John Tower for secretary of Defense. On the Armed Services Committee he is sometimes skeptical of weapons projects, but not so nearly as often as some other Democrats; like most Nebraskans he is concerned about the big SAC Air Force base near Omaha. On the Budget Committee, he is skeptical about Gramm-Rudman, charging that rather than forcing real action it has produced fake actions to balance the budget. Exon's legislative accomplishments tend to come in the interstices between big issues: he backed extended air service to small towns, a clean grain study, raising the interstate speed limit to 65, and minting the American eagle gold coin. He has pushed legislation to require disclosure of foreign investment in the United States and to block foreign takeovers if they are believed to endanger national security.

Exon remains popular in Nebraska, but he has not won a race by a big margin for more than a decade. In 1984 his Republican opponent, Nancy Hoch, attacked him for being not so much a liberal as a backbencher, who had no major accomplishments; that infuriated Exon, who cited all manner of bills he had sponsored but still could not credibly portray himself as a national leader. Like many incumbents, Exon profited from contributions by PACs, which gave him over $500,000 but up to mid-October had given Hoch only $57,000. Even so, Exon won by only 52%–48%. He is expected to run again in 1990, at age 69, and he is likely to be prepared for a tough race. Possible GOP candidates are 1st District Congressman Doug Bereuter and Douglas County attorney Ron Staskiewicz.

Bob Kerrey, Nebraska's junior Senator, is one politician who stirs genuine passion from his constituents. After almost a decade in politics, he still seems anything but a professional politician. He is a man of striking determination: serving in the Navy in Vietnam, he won the Congressional Medal of Honor, and then made speeches against the war; though he lost his right leg below the knee, he runs the marathon. A restaurant owner and a political unknown, he ran for governor in 1982 and ousted incumbent Charles Thone. While in office, he dated the sultry movie star Debra Winger, which seemed to charm Nebraskans. In 1986, Kerrey shocked most politicians by deciding at 43 not to seek reelection, despite 70%-plus job approval ratings (and even though voters repealed his seat belt law and sales tax for education); in 1988, he surprised very few by winning the Senate seat held by appointee David Karnes after the death of Edward Zorinsky.

The most bitter part of that Senate race came not in the general, but in the Republican primary between Karnes and Omaha Congressman Hal Daub. After Daub spoke favorably of an across-the-board spending freeze, a Karnes ad charged he'd cut Social Security, and Karnes noted that Daub lived in a $400,000 Washington area house. Daub said Karnes's policy of not finishing old water projects before starting new ones would make Nebraska a desert, and noted that Karnes supported a May 1987 vote that would have cut social security COLAs. There was an edge of personal nastiness to the contest, which Karnes finally won by piling up a 2 to 1 margin in the west compared to Daub's 3 to 2 margin in the Omaha area. But Karnes made a couple of classic gaffes, agreeing in a pre-primary debate that he would accept tax increases to cut deficits, and saying after the primary, "We need fewer farmers at this point in time." This effectively prevented him from making any headway against Kerrey's lead, and he fell off Republican moneygivers' priority lists, and ended up losing by a 57%–42% margin.

In the Senate, Kerrey got some plum committee assignments—Agriculture, a plus for any Nebraska Senator, and Appropriations, not usually given to freshmen. His personal magnetism leads many who know him to wonder whether he might be a presidential candidate some day; he starts out well known in the western part of the first caucus state, Iowa. In the meantime he is just getting his introduction to national and international issues, with which he doesn't claim to be deeply conversant.

Presidential politics. Nebraska is one of the most Republican of states in presidential elections. But Farm Belt discontent sometimes tips it a little toward the Democrats: in 1980 it was the second most Republican state, in 1984 the fourth, in 1988 the eighth. There is a bit of an urban-rural split, with greater Omaha and Lincoln, which now cast almost half the state's votes, running less Republican than the western counties, which vote like adjacent Wyoming.

Nebraska has a presidential primary in May which once attracted attention; the whole national press followed Robert Kennedy and Eugene McCarthy out here in 1968 and took note when Frank Church won in 1976. No more. The big event in the 1988 primary was the Republican Senate race; the presidential nominations were already sewed up.

Congressional districting. Nebraska hasn't lost a House seat since the Census of 1960, and it changes its House district lines just a little every 10 years. It's likely to do so again after the 1990 Census.

The People: Est. Pop. 1988: 1,601,000; Pop. 1980 1,569,825, up 2.0% 1980-88 and 5.7% 1970-80; 0.66% of U.S. total, 36th largest. 17% with 1-3 yrs. col., 16% with 4+ yrs. col.; 10.7% below poverty level. Single ancestry: 22% German, 6% English, 4% Irish, 2% Swedish, Polish, 1% French, Italian, Dutch, Norwegian. Households (1980): 72% family, 38% with children, 63% married couples; 31.6% housing units rented; median monthly rent: $170; median house value: $38,000. Voting age pop. (1980): 1,122,655; 3% Black, 1% Spanish origin. Registered voters (1988): 898,959; 378,360 D (42%), 455,472 R (51%), 65,127 unaffiliated and minor parties (7%).

1988 Share of Federal Tax Burden: $4,972,000,000; 0.56% of U.S. total, 34th largest.

1988 Share of Federal Expenditures

	Total		Non-Defense		Defense	
Total Expend	$5,935m	(0.67%)	$5,112m	(0.78%)	$958m	(0.42%)
St/Lcl Grants	712m	(0.62%)	711m	(0.62%)	1m	(0.82%)
Salary/Wages	832m	(0.62%)	383m	(0.57%)	449m	(0.57%)
Pymnts to Indiv	2,679m	(0.65%)	2,564m	(0.66%)	115m	(0.62%)
Procurement	392m	(0.21%)	135m	(0.29%)	392m	(0.21%)
Research/Other	1,319m	(3.53%)	1,318m	(3.56%)	1m	(3.56%)

Political Lineup: Governor, Kay A. Orr (R); Lt. Gov., Bill Nichol (R); Secy. of State, Allen J. Beermann (R); Atty. Gen., Robert Spire (R); Treasurer, Frank Marsh (R); Comptroller, Ray A. C. Johnson (R). Unicameral legislature, 49 (no party affiliation). Senators, J. James Exon (D) and Robert Kerrey (D). Representatives, 3 (2 R and 1 D).

1988 Presidential Vote

Bush (R)	397,956	(60%)
Dukakis (D).	259,235	(39%)

1984 Presidential Vote

Reagan (R)	460,054	(71%)
Mondale (D)	187,866	(29%)

1988 Democratic Presidential Primary

Dukakis...................	106,334	(63%)
Jackson	43,380	(26%)
Gephardt..................	4,948	(5%)
Hart......................	4,220	(2%)
Gore......................	2,519	(1%)
Simon	2,104	(1%)
Uncommitted	4,763	(3%)

1988 Republican Presidential Primary

Bush	138,784	(68%)
Dole......................	45,572	(22%)
Robertson	10,334	(5%)
Kemp......................	8,423	(4%)

GOVERNOR

Gov. Kay A. Orr (R)

Elected 1986, term expires Jan. 1991; b. Jan. 2, 1939, Burlington, IA; home, Lincoln; U. of IA; Protestant; married (William).

Career: Executive Asst. to NE Gov. Charles Thone, 1979–81; NE Treasurer, 1981–86; Chwmn., Repub. Natl. Platform Cmtee., 1988.

Office: State Capitol Bldg., Rm. 2316, Lincoln 68509, 402-471-2244.

Election Results

1986 gen.	Kay A. Orr (R).............	298,325	(53%)
	Helen Boosalis (D)...........	265,156	(47%)
1986 prim.	Kay A. Orr (R).............	75,914	(39%)
	Kermit Brashear (R).........	60,308	(31%)
	Nancy Hoch (R).............	42,649	(22%)
1982 gen.	Robert Kerrey (D)...........	277,436	(51%)
	Charles Thone (R)...........	270,203	(49%)

SENATORS

Sen. J. James Exon (D)

Elected 1978, seat up 1990; b. Aug. 9, 1921, Geddes, SD; home, Lincoln; U. of Omaha; Episcopalian; married (Patricia).

Career: Army, WWII; Branch Mgr., Universal Finance Co., 1946–54; Pres., Exon's Inc., office equip. business, 1954–70; Gov. of NE, 1970–78.

Offices: 330 HSOB 20510, 202-224-4224. Also 8305 New Fed. Bldg., 215 N. 17th St., Omaha 68102, 402-221-4665; 287 Fed. Bldg., 100 Centennial Mall N., Lincoln 68508, 402-471-5591; and 275 Fed. Bldg., North Platte 69101, 308-534-2006.

Committees: *Armed Services* (2d of 11 D). Subcommittees: Manpower and Personnel; Strategic Forces and Nuclear Deterrence (Chairman); Projection Forces and Regional Defense. *Budget* (5th of 13 D). *Commerce, Science, and Transportation* (4th of 11 D). Subcommittees: Aviation; Communications; Surface Transportation (Chairman).

Group Ratings

	ADA	ACLU	COPE	CFA	LCV	ACU	NTLC	NSI	COC	CEI
1988	35	33	46	75	10	48	31	90	50	22
1987	65	—	43	58	—	38	—	—	50	37

National Journal Ratings

	1988 LIB — 1988 CONS			1987 LIB — 1987 CONS		
Economic	37%	—	61%	39%	—	60%
Social	38%	—	61%	45%	—	52%
Foreign	52%	—	45%	46%	—	49%

Key Votes

1) Cut Aged Housing $	AGN	5) Bork Nomination	AGN	9) SDI Funding	FOR
2) Override Hwy Veto	FOR	6) Ban Plastic Guns	AGN	10) Ban Chem Weaps	FOR
3) Kill Plnt Clsng Notice	AGN	7) Deny Abortions	FOR	11) Aid To Contras	FOR
4) Min Wage Increase	AGN	8) Japanese Reparations	FOR	12) Reagan Defense $	AGN

Election Results

1984 general	J. James Exon (D)..................	332,217	(52%)	($886,760)
	Nancy Hoch (R).....................	307,147	(48%)	($583,632)
1984 primary	J. James Exon (D) unopposed			
1978 primary	J. James Exon (D)..................	334,096	(68%)	($234,862)
	Don Shasteen (R)	159,706	(32%)	($218,148)

Sen. Robert Kerrey (D)

Elected 1988, seat up 1994; b. Aug. 27, 1943, Lincoln; home, Omaha; U of NE, M.S. 1966; Congregationalist; divorced.

Career: US Navy, 1966–69; Restauranteur; Gov., NE, 1983–87.

Offices: 302 HSOB 20510, 202-224-6551. Also 7602 Pacific St. Omaha 68114, 402-391-3411; and 100 Centennial Mall N., Rm. 294, Fed. Bldg, Lincoln 68508, 402-437-5246.

Committees: *Agriculture, Nutrition and Forestry* (10th of 10 D). Subcommittees: Agricultural Production and Stabilization of Prices; Nutrition and Investigations; Agricultural Research and General Legislation. *Appropriations* (16th of 16 D). Subcommittees: Agriculture, Rural Development and Related Agencies; District of Columbia; VA, HUD and Independent Agencies; Treasury, Postal Service, and General Government.

Group Ratings and Key Votes: Newly Elected

Election Results

1988 general	Robert Kerrey (D)	378,717	(57%)	($3,461,148)
	David Karnes (R)	278,250	(42%)	($3,411,361)
1988 primary	Robert Kerrey (D)	156,498	(91%)	
	Ken L. Michaelis (D)	14,248	(8%)	
1982 general	Edward Zorinsky (D)	363,350	(67%)	($523,141)
	Jim Keck (R)	155,760	(29%)	($489,186)

FIRST DISTRICT

The plains sweep west from the bluffs of the Missouri River, along the always wide and shallow Platte River and a dozen less daunting and dustier tributaries. Eastern Nebraska for just a century, has been an area of well-ordered farmlands and square-gridded small towns, with land that is just irregular enough in its contours and weather that is just unreliable enough in its heat and rainfall to make it difficult though still possible to make a decent living here. The 1st Congressional District of Nebraska is a band of 26 counties covering most of eastern Nebraska, except for a few counties around and including Omaha. The largest city, Lincoln, state capital and home of the University of Nebraska Cornhuskers, is the only fast-growing part of the district and now casts nearly 40% of its votes. The political inclination of the region is Republican, but

Lincoln has become almost Democratic, voting heavily against Governor Kay Orr in 1986 and nearly favoring Michael Dukakis over George Bush in 1988.

The 1st District's congressman, Douglas Bereuter, is a Republican with experience in and positive feelings about government; he was a city planner and a top aide to Governor Norbert Tiemann, who was beaten by Jim Exon in 1970 after raising taxes. He spends much time on trade issues. According to *National Journal*, he "understands the connection between agricultural policy and international trade," and he boosted in the 1988 trade bill provisions to open foreign markets to American farm products. His style on farm and other issues tends to be bipartisan: with Florida Democrat Richard Lehman he wrote the Farmer Mac provision in the 1987 farm credit bill, and with California Democrat Mel Levine he became head of the House Export Task Force in 1988. He tends to other farming matters—grain quality, the diesel tax, groundwater recharge—as well. He joined Intelligence in 1989.

Bereuter has been reelected regularly by handsome margins and could indefinitely hold this district which was fiercely contested from 1964 to 1976 and probably will be again if he doesn't run. He is thinking about running for Jim Exon's seat in 1990, and if he does, that should be a tough race between two politicians both classed as moderates but with contrasting approaches to issues.

The People: Est. Pop. 1986: 530,300, up 1.4% 1980–86; Pop. 1980: 523,079, up 6.6% 1970–80. Households (1980): 71% family, 36% with children, 63% married couples; 31.1% housing units rented; median monthly rent: $167; median house value: $38,300. Voting age pop. (1980): 383,987; 1% Spanish origin, 1% Black, 1% American Indian.

1988 Presidential Vote:

Bush (R)	123,674	(56%)
Dukakis (D)	96,134	(43%)

Rep. Douglas K. (Doug) Bereuter (R)

Elected 1978; b. Oct. 6, 1939, York; home, Utica; U of NE, B.A. 1961, Harvard U., M.C.P. 1966, M.P.A. 1973; Lutheran; married (Louise).

Career: Army, 1963–65; Urban Planner, U.S. Dept. of HUD., 1965–66; Div. Dir., NE Econ. Devel. Dept., 1967–68; Dir., NE Office of Planning, 1969–71; NE Senate, 1974–78.

Offices: 2446 RHOB 20515, 202-225-4806. Also 1045 K St., Lincoln 68508, 402-471-5400.

Committees: *Banking, Finance and Urban Affairs* (7th of 20 R). Subcommittees: Financial Institutions Supervision, Regulation and Insurance; Housing and Community Development; International Development, Finance, Trade and Monetary Policy; Policy Research and Insurance (Ranking Member). *Foreign Affairs* (8th of 18 R). Subcommittees: Human Rights and International Organizations (Ranking Member); International Economic Policy and Trade. *Select Committee on Hunger* (6th of 10 R). *Permanent Select Committee on Intelligence* (5th of 7 R). Subcommittee: Oversight and Evaluation.

Group Ratings

	ADA	ACLU	COPE	CFA	LCV	ACU	NTLC	NSI	COC	CEI
1988	20	39	21	55	44	76	71	90	93	47
1987	20	—	18	36	—	57	—	—	80	51

National Journal Ratings

	1988 LIB — 1988 CONS			1987 LIB — 1987 CONS		
Economic	29%	—	70%	28%	—	71%
Social	33%	—	66%	25%	—	73%
Foreign	38%	—	61%	41%	—	58%

Key Votes

1) Homeless $	FOR	5) Ban Drug Test	FOR	9) SDI Research	FOR
2) Gephardt Amdt	AGN	6) Drug Death Pen	FOR	10) Ban Chem Weaps	AGN
3) Deficit Reduc	AGN	7) Handgun Sales	FOR	11) Aid to Contras	FOR
4) Kill Plnt Clsng Notice	FOR	8) Ban D.C. Abort $	FOR	12) Nuclear Testing	AGN

Election Results

1988 general	Douglas K. (Doug) Bereuter (R)	146,231	(67%)	($221,530)
	Corky Jones (D)	72,167	(33%)	($96,278)
1988 primary	Doug K. (Doug) Bereuter (R), unopposed			
1986 general	Douglas K. (Doug) Bereuter (R)	121,772	(64%)	($227,910)
	Steve Burns (D)	67,137	(36%)	($92,746)

SECOND DISTRICT

Omaha is a city with a 19th century economic base that has grown gracefully into the late 20th century, the site selected by Abraham Lincoln as the eastern terminus of the transcontinental railroad, the home of the stockyards and livestock exchange that made it the nation's third largest livestock town. Over the years Omaha filled up with cattle hands from the West and immigrants from Europe (especially Germans and Czechs); it developed fine civic institutions from the Joslyn Art Museum to the Ak-Sar-Ben (spell it backwards) Exhibition to its refurbished old theaters; it developed a competitive politics, with Democrats strong on the south side around the stockyards and Republicans in the higher-income neighborhoods west of 72d Street. Already a major city by the 1880s, Omaha is still a small enough city—famous on Wall Street as the place where Warren Buffett lives and works—to be readily comprehensible; you don't feel distant, physically or psychologically, from neighborhoods on the other side of town, and you usually know people from a broader range of backgrounds than you would in a large homogeneous neighborhood within a big metropolitan area.

Omaha, which together with a few counties 80 miles up and down the Missouri River forms Nebraska's 2d Congressional District, was the site of one of America's most strenuously contested House races in 1988—and one which in a mostly apathetic year inspired some genuine enthusiasm and a large turnout. Congressman Hal Daub was running for the Senate seat traditionally allotted to Omaha, though he had to run in the primary against appointed incumbent David Karnes and, if he had won that, face popular former Governor Bob Kerrey in the general. The favorite to replace Daub was Democrat Cece Zorinsky, widow of former Omaha Mayor and Senator Edward Zorinsky, who died in March 1987; another strong candidate was Republican Jerry Schenken, a doctor active in AMA affairs. But the winner, by a narrow margin in both primary and general, was Democrat Peter Hoagland, a former state senator and lawyer from an old-line Omaha Republican family. Hoagland challenged Zorinsky to debate seven months before the primary; she, unsteady on the facts of national policy, refused, and he kept renewing his challenge and running ads stressing how tough the times were. Hoagland edged her 51%–44%.

Schenken, meanwhile, beat a state senator 38%–30% in his primary and, fortified by contributions from doctors across the country, was spending freely. He attacked Hoagland for backing tax increases in the legislature and also for votes on crime and drugs, and ran an ad showing him next to Michael Dukakis. But Dukakis ended up losing the 2d District by 58%–42%, not an insurmountable problem for a ticketmate. Hoagland hit Schenken on his medicare reform plans, backed plant closing laws, a higher minimum wage and a waiting period for handguns, and built an organization that fielded 1,200 volunteers in Omaha, bringing out his vote in both the south and west sides. The two campaigns together spent about $2 million by the end of the race, the fourth highest of any district race in the country. Ultimately, Hoagland won by a 51%–49% margin.

In the House, Hoagland got the seat on the Banking Committee he sought, and will be concentrating on the savings and loan problem, among others. He will have the advantages of incumbency for two years, but given the narrow margin, this could be a seriously contested seat in 1990.

The People: Est. Pop. 1986: 551,400, up 5.5% 1980–86; Pop. 1980: 522,919, up 6.2% 1970–80. Households (1980): 72% family, 42% with children, 60% married couples; 35.7% housing units rented; median monthly rent: $190; median house value: $40,500. Voting age pop. (1980): 364,998; 7% Black, 2% Spanish origin, 1% Asian origin.

1988 Presidential Vote:

Bush (R)	130,193	(58%)
Dukakis (D).......................	94,071	(42%)

Rep. Peter Hoagland (D)

Elected 1988; b. Nov. 17, 1941, Omaha; home, Omaha; Stanford U., A.B. 1963, Yale U., J.D. 1968; Espiscopalian; married (Barbara).

Career: Practicing atty, 1968–88; NE House of Reps., 1979–87.

Offices: 1415 LHOB, 20515, 202-225-4155. Also 8424 Zorinsky Fed. Bld., 215 N. 17th St., Omaha 68102, 402-221-4216.

Committees: *Banking, Finance and Urban Affairs* (30th of 31 D). Subcommittees: Domestic Monetary Policy; General Oversight and Investigations; Housing and Community Development; Financial Institutions Supervision, Regulation and Insurance; International Development, Finance, Trade and Monetary Policy. *Small Business* (24th of 27 D). Subcommittee: Exports, Tax Policy and Special Problems.

Group Ratings and Key Votes: Newly Elected

Election Results

1988 general	Peter Hoagland (D)...................	112,174	(51%)	($858,762)
	Jerry Schenken (R)....................	109,193	(49%)	($1,158,294)
1988 primary	Peter Hoagland (D)....................	33,394	(51%)	
	Cece Zorinsky (D)	28,635	(44%)	
	David A. Wilken (D)	2,922	(4%)	
1986 general	Harold J. (Hal) Daub (R)..............	99,569	(59%)	($509,019)
	Walter M. Calinger (D)	70,372	(41%)	($57,627)

THIRD DISTRICT

"The Middle West merges with the West" in central Nebraska, where "fields give way to the great cattle ranches of the sand hill area, life is more leisurely and manners more relaxed. Something of the old West still survives," wrote the *WPA Guide* 50 years ago, "a cowboy riding hard against the sky, a herd of white faces coming down from the hills to water, bawling calves at branding time. Here neighbors think nothing of strolling a mile or two of prairie to pay an evening call, and one can travel for hours without finding a sign of human habitation. On the high plateaus of the Panhandle, where the wind cuts along the broad valley of the Platte, rocks and buttes rise. Occasionally a coyote may be seen crossing a 'blowout' hollowed by the wind among the dunes." This is now Nebraska's 3d Congressional District, with one-third of the state's people spread over three-quarters of its acreage; except for the towns along the interstate, the 3d has been losing population for decades; in 1988, it cast 214,000 votes, down from 253,000 in 1940.

Politically, the 3d District merges Midwest and West as well. It has the Farm Belt's demand for farm subsidy and aid programs and the West's angry opposition to federal interference on all other fronts. Presidentially, it is as heavily Republican as the Rockies: 74% and 81% for Ronald Reagan, 67% for George Bush. In congressional elections, it is ultra-safe territory for Virginia Smith, a chipper and enthusiastic Republican first elected, narrowly, in Democratic 1974. She is now the dean of Republican women in the House. For 20 years, Smith chaired the American Farm Bureau Women, once one of the free enterprise pillars of Republican strength in the Farm Belt; she was an active Republican as well. Now she has a seat on the Appropriations Committee and is a vote for frugality, sometimes even on defense issues. But on farm programs, she is a quick and persistent voice against cuts and looks out closely, as the ranking Republican on Jamie Whitten's Agriculture Subcommittee, for the interests of wheat growers. She fights congressional pay raises and boosts rural health care programs, backs senior citizen aid and subsidies for local bus lines. She tends carefully to even the minutest water projects in often arid western Nebraska; her late-in-the-primary support for Senator David Karnes's water policy (though technically she kept her pledge to be neutral) helped Karnes beat Smith's Omaha colleague Hal Daub 2 to 1 in the west and win the 1988 primary.

In June 1989, Smith announced she would retire, saying, "there is a time in life for everything." With the overwhelming Republican voter registration in this district, it seems likely that her successor will retain her party label.

The People: Est. Pop. 1986: 516,000, dn. 1.5% 1980–86; Pop. 1980: 523,827, up 4.2% 1970–80. Households (1980): 73% family, 38% with children, 66% married couples; 28.1% housing units rented; median monthly rent: $142; median house value: $34,700. Voting age pop. (1980): 373,670; 2% Spanish origin.

1988 Presidential Vote:
Bush (R)	144,089	(67%)
Dukakis (D)	69,030	(32%)

Rep. Virginia Smith (R)

Elected 1974; b. June 30, 1911, Randolph, IA; home, Chappell; U. of NE, B.A. 1936; United Methodist; married (Haven).

Career: Owner, wheat ranch, 1931–74; Mbr., NE Bd. of Ed. for St. Colleges, 1950–60; Natl. Chwmn., Amer. Farm Bureau Women, 1955–74; Mbr., Amer. Farm Bur. Fed., 1955–74; Chwmn. and Pres., Task Force on Rural Devel., 1971–72.

Offices: 2202 RHOB 20515, 202-225-6435. Also 312 W. 3d St., P.O. Box 2146, Grand Island 68802, 308-381-5555; and 1502 2d Ave., Scotts Bluff 69361, 307-622-3333.

Committees: *Appropriations* (8th of 22 R). Subcommittees: Rural Development, Agriculture and Related Agencies (Ranking Member); Energy and Water Development.

Group Ratings

	ADA	ACLU	COPE	CFA	LCV	ACU	NTLC	NSI	COC	CEI
1988	25	27	12	64	19	80	66	80	93	54
1987	4	—	10	29	—	78	—	—	93	59

National Journal Ratings

	1988 LIB — 1988 CONS	1987 LIB — 1987 CONS
Economic	29% — 70%	24% — 74%
Social	29% — 70%	0% — 90%
Foreign	30% — 67%	28% — 70%

Key Votes

1) Homeless $	FOR	5) Ban Drug Test	FOR
2) Gephardt Amdt	AGN	6) Drug Death Pen	FOR
3) Deficit Reduc	AGN	7) Handgun Sales	FOR
4) Kill Plnt Clsng Notice	FOR	8) Ban D.C. Abort $	FOR

9) SDI Research	FOR
10) Ban Chem Weaps	AGN
11) Aid to Contras	FOR
12) Nuclear Testing	AGN

Election Results

1988 general	Virginia Smith (R)	107,302	(79%)	($229,109)
	John D. Racek (D)	45,183	(21%)	($13,451)
1988 primary	Virginia Smith (R), unopposed			
1986 general	Virginia Smith (R)	136,985	(70%)	($253,292)
	Scott E. Sidwell (D)	59,182	(30%)	($74,227)

NEVADA

"As it was in the days of the Old West," wrote Richard Lillard in *Desert Challenge* half a century ago, "Nevada is a civilization of gay town-cities, lonely ranches, and mines. The talk is still on shafts and ore samples, range stock, hay, and horseflesh. The townspeople are as tolerant of personal morals and as likely to ask a man to have a drink as were the Comstockers of John Mackay's time. Reno and Las Vegas are amazingly near in spirit to the Virginia City and the Tonopah of the past. Money comes easy, goes easy. Every night is a Saturday night, every Sunday an open house. Out in the long grassy valleys—the Monitor, Paradise, Pahranagat—cowboys still roll their own, brand calves, court the new schoolma'am, and bulldog steers at rodeos." There were only 110,000 Nevadans then, gambling had just been legalized (to raise money in a mining state whose economy ground to a halt during the depression), and Reno divorces were only starting to become a national tradition.

Today's Nevada has almost one million people, about 570,000 of them in and around Las Vegas (where Clark County gains some 4,000 people a month) and another 250,000 in and around Reno; beneath the bare mountains, surrealistically rising from desert in the distance, has arisen a prospering, urban civilization. Yet outside the gleaming new cities, in the vast expanse of the Cow Counties, Nevada remains as empty as it always has been, or in ghost towns even emptier. But almost everywhere you can still find an anything-goes atmosphere. For this is a state largely built by legalized gambling; even with competition from Atlantic City, Nevada is still a booming tourist and convention mecca and a place where a large part of America likes to gaudily kick up its heels. Gaming—the Nevada word—is not a gentle business. Bugsy Siegel, who built the Flamingo, the first big hotel on the Las Vegas Strip in 1947, was gunned down in his Beverly Hills home, and it is well known now that most of the casinos were mob-owned until Howard Hughes bought them up in the mid-1960s. Today, casinos are owned by publicly traded companies, and Nevada has used its low taxes to build another economy as a distribution center for the western (especially California) market. With the Hoover Dam, military bases, the nation's nuclear weapons testing facilities, and 87% of its land owned by Uncle Sam, Nevada remains dependent on federal government much more than its rugged individualists would like to recognize.

Politically, Nevada has always been in danger of domination by outside forces. It was admitted to the Union in 1864 to provide three quick electoral votes for Abraham Lincoln's reelection. The Comstock Lode and other mines had absentee owners, like California's Big Four, but up through the 1930s, silver called the shots politically in the state; Senator Key Pittman, Chairman of Foreign Relations, backed FDR's foreign policy only after Roosevelt agreed to buy absurdly large amounts of silver. Senator Pat McCarran, a pennypincher and author of the repressive McCarran Act, shamelessly pushed aid for Reno and Las Vegas (the airport there is named for him) and became suddenly solicitous of civil liberties when mobsters and casino owners were called to testify before the Kefauver committee investigating crime and racketeering. For years, Nevada delegations wanted to keep the nuclear test facilities here; now they fight to keep nuclear waste out.

In the last half-century, as Nevada has boomed and filled with people, it has changed from Democratic to Republican. This comes not out of devotion to family values, for Nevada is the least family-oriented state: 32% of its households do not contain families (number one in the nation), while 64% don't have children (only Florida has a higher percentage) and 44% aren't occupied by married couples (exceeded only by California and New York). It allows not only

NEVADA — Congressional Districts, Counties, Independent City, and Other Selected Places — *(2 Districts)*

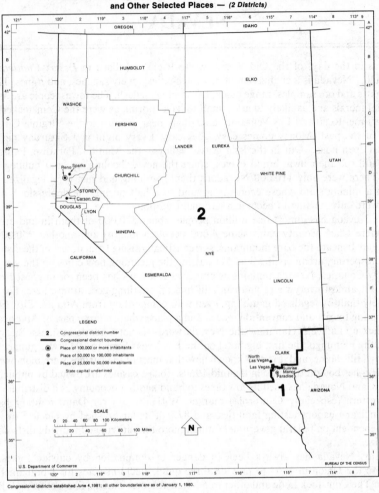

Congressional districts established June 4, 1981; all other boundaries are as of January 1, 1980.

gambling but lets the Cow Counties legalize prostitution. Nevada's conservatism comes more from economic issues, from the new migrants who come here thinking they are sharper than others, that they have a special angle, that they are a step ahead of the market, that they can and will beat the odds. It makes for lively and sometimes cynical politics.

Governor. Nevada's governor, elevated to office from lieutenant governor when Richard Bryan was elected to the Senate in 1988, is Democrat Bob Miller. (The full term election is in 1990.) His own biography contains much of the state's recent history. His father, Ross Miller, was a bookmaker in Chicago and owner of the Slots-A-Fun casino in Las Vegas; he was indicted in 1967, but the charges were dismissed. Bob Miller was elected district attorney in Las Vegas— a sensitive position indeed—in 1978 and reelected in 1982; some charges have been made against him but nothing has come close to sticking, and he was elected lieutenant governor in 1986. If he represents a second generation in Nevada public life—knowledgeable about the gaming industry, but utterly clean—he seems also interested in a second generation of issues: improving public education, diversifying the state's economy, reducing child abuse and teenage suicide. He supported a successful May 1989 referendum to increase the amount of taxes the mining industry must pay and supports further increases to see that the mining industry pays what he feels should be a greater share of the tax burden.

Miller is considered a strong candidate for a full term in 1990. His best-known possible competitor is Attorney General Brian McKay, a former Democrat and New Yorker who is quick to attack politicians of both parties, who could have the Republican nomination for the asking but may want to wait and run against Senator Harry Reid in 1992.

Senators. As recently as 1986, Nevada was represented by two Republicans in the Senate. But Paul Laxalt retired while his friend and fellow former governor was in the White House, and was replaced by Democrat Harry Reid that year; while Republican Chic Hecht, never a strong figure, was beaten two years later by Governor Richard Bryan. So now Republican Nevada is represented by two Democrats.

The senior Senator, and a veteran officeholder as he approached 50, is Harry Reid. He was elected to the legislature back in 1968 and was elected lieutenant governor in 1970; from there he challenged and nearly beat Paul Laxalt in the 1974 Senate race. He lost a race for mayor of Las Vegas in 1976, and then became head of the Gaming Commission from 1977 to 1981—a position more sensitive than any other in Nevada. When Jim Santini, then a Democrat, ran for the Senate in 1982, Reid ran for the new 1st District seat that covers most of Las Vegas and suburbs—the 1980 Census had given Nevada a second House member for the first time—and won. Reelected in 1984, he had no serious competition for the Democratic nomination when Laxalt announced his retirement from the Senate in 1986.

Reid combines a rather conservative temperament with Democratic alliances. Like many of his fellow Mormons in sinful Nevada, he is culturally conservative, pushing for tough standards against drunk drivers, for example. Yet he has also been an ally of organized labor, which has always been strong in Las Vegas, and spoke out against IRS seizure of money obtained from blackjack dealers' "tokes" to prevent tax avoidance on these tips. He was unable to prevent the designation of Yucca Mountain as the nation's sole high-level nuclear waste depository in 1987 or to increase funding for safety and accountability checks, but he moved successfully in 1988 to put limits on underground nuclear testing. He is also pushing for a comprehensive water plan for his part of the West, including some disposition of Indian water rights. He is not afraid to voice lonely complaints against the uranium bailout bill or against the confirmation of Treasury Secretary Nicholas Brady.

Reid won his seat 50%–45% after one of the wildest and wooliest contests of 1986. His Republican opponent was former Democrat Jim Santini, who preceded Reid in the House and nearly beat Senator Howard Cannon in the 1982 primary; hours before the 1986 deadline, Santini changed parties and filed for Laxalt's seat. This switch seemed motivated less by Santini's views on issues, which had changed little if at all, than by sheer opportunism. Nevadans might have supported a clone of Laxalt or supporter of Ronald Reagan, but for those roles Santini was poorly cast; instead he appeared in Reid's ads as Goliath to Reid's David—ads that captured not only Santini's weaknesses but the quiet, straight-arrow, persistent Reid's strengths. And just as Reid has overcome political reversals to win, he may overcome some of his policy reversals in the Senate as well. His seats on the Appropriations and Environment Committees certainly will help him do so.

Senator Richard Bryan won by a similar, 50%–46%, margin—but that race was not expected to be so close, even though Bryan beat the incumbent Republican Chic Hecht. Hecht, a Las Vegas clothing store owner and former legislator, won 50%–48% in 1982 largely because of Howard Cannon's weaknesses (he was named in the indictment of Teamsters president Roy Lee Williams and mob figure Allen Dorfman and testified extensively in their trial a month before the election). Hecht is short, speaks with a squeaky voice and a lisp, and spews forth malapropisms. He failed in his major quest—to stop the Yucca Mountain nuclear depository (he called it a "nuclear suppository" at one point). But Hecht's very weakness as a candidate may have helped him. He was undeniably sincere. He was not out of line with the state on most issues. He had built a successful business in Nevada. He had been one of the most persistent backers of the 65-mile-per-hour speed limit—popular in Nevada, which had no speed limit at all before 1974.

Bryan began the campaign with high job ratings as governor and great popularity. But his attacks on Hecht on the nuclear depository issue lost a little of their force because of controversy over Bryan's signing of a bill creating a new, zero-population Bullfrog County on the site. The idea was to funnel any federal property tax payments to the state rather than to Nye County if the depository was built, but some critics charged that the bill paved the way for the facility, and in any case the new county was declared illegal by the state Supreme Court. Bryan was not helped when Michael Dukakis, under attack in Minnesota for considering a nuclear waste site there, said no, he was in favor of putting it all in Nevada. Hecht's ads also attacked Bryan for leasing a state airplane. Hecht forces brought up Bob Miller's father's indictment and pointed out that Miller would become governor if Bryan was elected. Independent expenditure groups—foreign car dealers, doctors, right-to-lifers—spent liberally against Bryan and for Hecht. Ultimately, Bryan won rather narrowly, carrying the Las Vegas area by only 54%–43%, but running strong for a Democrat in carrying the Reno area 50%–46%. Hecht has gone on to be nominated to be Ambassador to the Bahamas—actually, a sensitive post given the alleged drug connections of some in that country's government and its proximity to Florida.

In the Senate Bryan is on the Commerce Committee, where he chaired the Consumer Subcommittee right from the start, and on Banking, where he presumably will be involved in the savings and loan bill, as well as the Joint Economic Committee. He claims to be somewhat more conservative than other Democrats, favoring some forms of contra aid and a balanced budget amendment. But given the increasing partisan tilt of the Senate, he is likely to be a fairly solid Democrat.

Presidential politics. In the 1940s, Nevada was a Democratic state; in the 1960s, it was divided much as the nation was, voting narrowly for John Kennedy in 1960 and Richard Nixon in 1968. Today it is heavily Republican. Ronald Reagan carried the state 63%–27% over Jimmy Carter and 66%–32% over Walter Mondale; there is simply not much backing for national Democrats here any more, despite the fact that Michael Dukakis' 38% to George Bush's 59% in 1988 was something of an improvement. New residents, attracted by Nevada's glitz and sure they're smarter than the rubes, have been heavily Republican. Nevada at one time had a presidential primary, predictably ignored by the candidates.

1st Congressional District. Nevada's congressional districts are of vastly different physical size; the 1st consists roughly of the southern half of Clark County, and the 2d is the whole rest of the state. The 1st includes almost all of Las Vegas, the Strip (actually in a suburban area called Paradise Valley), North Las Vegas with its large black population, and the Hoover Dam area. It is a solidly Democratic constituency in local elections, but seriously contested in statewide contests; after all, Nevada has few voters who like the Democrats' national politics. Bush carried this district with 59% to Dukakis' 38%. When Reid ran for the Senate in 1986, the district was hotly contested—and one of many districts in which the Democrat greatly outspent the Republican.

The winner was Democrat James Bilbray, from a well-connected Las Vegas family (his father was Clark County assessor), conqueror at 34 of longtime conservative Democratic Congressman-at-Large Walter Baring in the 1972 primary (but loser of the general election). Bilbray was a state legislator for six years before running for the House in 1986 and beating Bob Ryan, a blind state senator, 54%–44%. Bilbray quickly established a reputation for plugging away at district issues. After the May 1988 chemical plant explosion in Henderson south of Las Vegas, he worked on victims relief and got Kerr-McGee to guarantee loans for them. He was active in getting the first veterans' cemetery in Nevada. Using his seat on Armed Services and with the support of Chairman Les Aspin, he delayed deactivation of the 474th fighter wing at Nellis Air Force Base. He supported the administration on nuclear weapons testing and the B-1 and was a swing vote on contra aid. He favors a 700,000-acre Nevada wilderness package.

His 1988 opponent Lucille Lusk ran, according to the *Las Vegas Review Journal*, "a campaign that borders on the absurd, enlisting partisan flunkies to don prison garb and march in front of Bilbray's Las Vegas headquarters to rail against the congressman's vote to 'let rapists and child molesters out of jail in Washington, D.C.,' or some such nonsense." In response, Bilbray ran "I Love Lucy"-type ads and won 2 to 1. Without any higher office to run for, he seems well ensconced in the House, with his only potential problem being to stay in touch with a rapidly growing district.

2d Congressional District. This is the more Republican district. The 2d's portion of Clark County—about one-sixth of the whole district—is heavily Democratic; most of the Cow Counties and Reno's Washoe County are heavily Republican. Congresswoman Barbara Vucanovich, elected in 1982 with Senator Paul Laxalt's support, is now one of the state's leading Republican officeholders in her own right. Widowed in her 40s, she started a speed reading school, a travel agency and raised five children. The daughter of a Catholic Democrat whose father was New York state's chief engineer under Al Smith and FDR, she scorns welfare and believes firmly in self-reliance. She does favor some additional spending—on breast cancer research, on fighting AIDS, on helping the homeless—and though she decries federal bossiness, she boasts of sponsoring the Great Basin National Park. She was one of the first (though not quite the first, as she claimed for a time) to move to repeal the 55-mile-per-hour speed limit. Her biggest political mistake was that she wasn't initially against the nuclear waste dump in Yucca Mountain; by 1988, after the bill had passed, she had switched to solid opposition. Vucanovich sits on the Interior and House Administration Committees. She left her seat on the National Parks and Public Lands Subcommittee to serve as ranking Republican on General Oversight and Investigations. Despite her disagreements with the Democrats, she gets on with them without too much abrasion; she is a staunch fan of her former committee colleague, Interior Secretary Manuel Lujan.

Except in 1984, when she won overwhelmingly, Vucanovich has held the seat with solid but not huge margins. Against the mayor of Reno she won 58%–42% in 1986. Her 1988 opponent, Jim Spoo, mayor of the Reno suburb of Sparks, raised much more money; a Seventh Day Adventist, family man and active objector who served as a medic during the Vietnam years, he was an attractive candidate and it was a relatively civil campaign. The result was about the same: Vucanovich won 57%–41%. This is creditable, but may not be enough to forestall serious opposition in the future.

The People: Est. Pop. 1988: 1,060,000; Pop. 1980: 800,493, up 32.5% 1980–88 and 63.8% 1970–80; 0.40% of U.S. total, 43d largest. 20% with 1–3 yrs. col., 15% with 4+ yrs. col.; 8.7% below poverty level. Single ancestry: 10% English, 7% German, 4% Irish, Italian, 1% French, Polish, Swedish, Scottish, Norwegian, Dutch, Russian. Households (1980): 68% family, 36% with children, 56% married couples; 40.4% housing units rented; median monthly rent: $268; median house value: $69,200. Voting age pop. (1980): 584,694; 6% Spanish origin, 5% Black, 2% Asian origin, 1% American Indian. Registered voters (1988): 444,930; 209,048 D (47%), 188,571 R (42%), 47,312 unaffiliated and minor parties (11%).

1988 Share of Federal Tax Burden: $3,988,000,000; 0.45% of U.S. total, 38th largest.

1988 Share of Federal Expenditures

	Total		Non-Defense		Defense	
Total Expend	$3,429m	(0.39%)	$2,793m	(0.43%)	$1,310m	(0.57%)
St/Lcl Grants	336m	(0.29%)	336m	(0.29%)	0m	(0.00%)
Salary/Wages	517m	(0.39%)	274m	(0.41%)	243m	(0.41%)
Pymnts to Indiv	1,658m	(0.41%)	1,471m	(0.38%)	187m	(1.00%)
Procurement	880m	(0.47%)	674m	(1.45%)	880m	(0.47%)
Research/Other	39m	(0.10%)	39m	(0.10%)	0m	(0.10%)

Political Lineup: Governor, Bob Miller (D); Secy. of State, Frankie Sue Del Papa (D); Atty. Gen., Brian McKay (R); Treasurer, Ken Santor (R); Controller, Darrel R. Daines (R). State Senate, 21 (13 R and 8 D); State Assembly, 42 (27 D and 15 R). Senators, Harry Reid (D) and Richard H. Bryan (D). Representatives, 2 (1 D and 1 R).

1988 Presidential Vote

Bush (R)	206,040	(59%)
Dukakis (D)	132,738	(38%)

1984 Presidential Vote

Reagan (R)	188,770	(66%)
Mondale (D)	91,655	(32%)

GOVERNOR

Gov. Bob Miller (D)

Assumed office Jan. 1989, term expires Jan. 1991; b. March 30, 1945, Chicago, IL; home, Carson City; U. of Santa Clara, B.A. 1967, Loyola U., J.D. 1971; Roman Catholic; married (Sandra).

Career: Practicing atty., 1971–87; Clark Cnty. Dpty. Dist. Atty., 1971–73; Legal Advisor, Las Vegas Metro. Police Dept., 1973–75; Justice of the Peace, Las Vegas Tnshp., 1975–78; Lt. Gov. NV 1987–88.

Office: Executive Chambers, Capitol Bldg., Carson City 89710, 702-885-5670.

Election Results

1986 gen.	Richard H. Bryan (D)		187,268	(72%)
	Patty Cafferata (R)		65,081	(25%)
1986 prim.	Richard H. Bryan (D)		71,920	(80%)
	Herb Tobman (D)		13,776	(15%)
1982 gen.	Richard H. Bryan (D)		128,132	(53%)
	Robert F. List (R)		100,104	(42%)

SENATORS

Sen. Harry Reid (D)

Elected 1986, seat up 1992; b. Dec. 2, 1939, Searchlight; home, Searchlight; UT St. U., B.S. 1961, Geo. Wash. U., J.D. 1964; Mormon; married (Landra).

Career: Practicing atty.; City Atty., Henderson, 1964–66; NV Assembly, 1968–70; Lt. Gov. of NV, 1970–74; Chmn., NV Gaming Comm., 1977–81; U.S. House of Reps., 1982–86.

Offices: 324 HSOB 20510, 202-224-3542. Also 300 Booth St., Reno 89509, 702-784-5568; 500 S. Rancho Rd., Ste. 7, Las Vegas 89106, 702-388-6547; and 600 E. Williams St., Ste. 302, Carson City 89701, 702-882-7343.

Committees: *Appropriations* (13th of 16 D). Subcommittees: Energy and Water Development; Interior and Related Agencies; Labor, Health and Human Services, Education and Related Agencies; Legislative Branch (Chairman); Military Construction. *Environment and Public Works* (7th of 9 D). Subcommittees: Toxic Substances, Environmental Oversight, Research and Development (Chairman); Water Resources, Transportation and Infrastructure; Nuclear Regulation. *Select Committee on Aging* (8th of 10 D).

Group Ratings

	ADA	ACLU	COPE	CFA	LCV	ACU	NTLC	NSI	COC	CEI
1988	55	36	91	92	50	28	18	50	29	16
1987	80	—	90	83	—	19	—	—	22	22

National Journal Ratings

	1988 LIB — 1988 CONS	1987 LIB — 1987 CONS
Economic	65% — 30%	65% — 26%
Social	37% — 62%	53% — 42%
Foreign	61% — 38%	59% — 39%

Key Votes

1) Cut Aged Housing $	FOR	5) Bork Nomination	AGN	9) SDI Funding	FOR
2) Override Hwy Veto	FOR	6) Ban Plastic Guns	AGN	10) Ban Chem Weaps	AGN
3) Kill Plnt Clsng Notice	AGN	7) Deny Abortions	FOR	11) Aid To Contras	AGN
4) Min Wage Increase	FOR	8) Japanese Reparations	FOR	12) Reagan Defense $	—

Election Results

1986 general	Harry Reid (D)	130,955	(50%)	($2,055,756)
	Jim Santini (R)	116,606	(45%)	($2,656,747)
	Others	14,271	(5%)	
1986 primary	Harry Reid (D)	74,275	(83%)	
	Manny Beals (D)	7,039	(8%)	
	Others	8,486	(9%)	
1980 general	Paul Laxalt (R)	144,224	(59%)	($1,126,826)
	Mary Gojack (D)	92,129	(37%)	($285,619)
	Others	3,163	(4%)	

Sen. Richard H. Bryan (D)

Elected 1988, seat up 1994; b. July 16, 1937, Washington, D.C.; home, Carson City; U.of NV, B.A. 1959, U. of CA, Hastings Col. of Law., LL.B. 1963; Episcopalian; married (Bonnie).

Career: Dpty. Dist. Atty., Clark Cnty., 1964–66; Clark Cnty. Public Defender, 1966–68; Counsel to Clark Cnty. Juv. Crt., 1968–69; NV Asembly, 1969–73; NV Senate, 1973–79: Atty. Gen. of NV, 1978–83; Gov. of NV, 1982–1988.

Offices: 364 RSOB 20510, 202-224-6244. Also 300 Las Vegas Blvd. S., Ste. 420, Las Vegas 89101, 702-388-6605; 300 Booth St., Ste. 2014, Reno 89509, 702-784-5007; and 308 N. Curry St., Ste. 201, Carson City 89701, 702-885-9111.

Committees: *Banking, Housing and Urban Affairs* (12th of 12 D). Subcommittees: Housing and Urban Affairs; Consumer and Regulatory Affairs. *Commerce, Science and Transportation* (10th of 11 D). Subcommittees: Consumer (Chairman); Foreign Commerce and Tourism; Science, Technology and Space. *Joint Economic Committee* Subcommittees: National Security Economics; Economic Resources and Competitiveness; Investment, Jobs, and Prices.

Group Ratings and Key Votes: Newly Elected

Election Results

1988 general	Richard H. Bryan (D).................	175,548	(50%)	($2,957,789)
	Jacob (Chic) Hecht (R)	161,336	(46%)	($3,007,864)
	Others	12,765	(4%)	
1988 primary	Richard H. Bryan (D).................	62,278	(79%)	
	Patrick Fitzpatrick (D).................	4,721	(6%)	
	Others	11,346	(14%)	
1982 general	Jacob (Chic) Hecht (R)	120,377	(50%)	($1,657,070)
	Howard W. Cannon (D)	114,720	(48%)	($1,592,094)

FIRST DISTRICT

The People: Est. Pop. 1986: 494,800, up 23.5% 1980–86; Pop. 1980: 400,636, up 69.5% 1970–80. Households (1980): 67% family, 36% with children, 54% married couples; 42.3% housing units rented; median monthly rent: $267; median house value: $68,400. Voting age pop. (1980): 292,870; 8% Black, 7% Spanish origin, 2% Asian origin, 1% American Indian.

1988 Presidential Vote:	Bush (R)	90,541	(56%)
	Dukakis (D).......................	67,519	(42%)

Rep. James Bilbray (D)

Elected 1986; b. May 19, 1938, Las Vegas; home, Las Vegas; U. of NV, American U., B.A. 1962, J.D. 1964; Roman Catholic; married (Michaelene).

Career: U. Regent, U. of NV, 1968–72; Dpty. Dist. Atty., Clark Cnty., 1964–68; Alt. Mun. Judge, Las Vegas 1978–80; NV Senate, 1980–86.

Offices: 319 CHOB 20515, 202-225-5965. Also 1701 W. Charleston, Ste. 300, Las Vegas 89101, 702-477-7000; and 201 Lead St., Rm. 26, Henderson 89015, 702-565-4788.

Committees: *Armed Services* (29th of 31 D). Subcommittees: Military Installations and Facilities; Readiness. *Small Business* (18th of 27 D). Subcommittees: Procurement, Tourism and Rural Development; Antitrust, Impact of Deregulation and Privatization; Exports, Tax Policy and Special Problems. *Select Committeee on Hunger* (14th of 16 D).

Group Ratings

	ADA	ACLU	COPE	CFA	LCV	ACU	NTLC	NSI	COC	CEI
1988	60	61	93	82	69	44	27	44	43	21
1987	68	—	94	64	—	26	—	—	33	15

National Journal Ratings

	1988 LIB — 1988 CONS		1987 LIB — 1987 CONS	
Economic	53%	— 46%	62%	— 35%
Social	50%	— 48%	58%	— 42%
Foreign	50%	— 49%	48%	— 52%

Key Votes

1) Homeless $	AGN	5) Ban Drug Test	FOR	9) SDI Research	AGN
2) Gephardt Amdt	FOR	6) Drug Death Pen	FOR	10) Ban Chem Weaps	FOR
3) Deficit Reduc	AGN	7) Handgun Sales	FOR	11) Aid to Contras	AGN
4) Kill Plnt Clsng Notice	AGN	8) Ban D.C. Abort $	FOR	12) Nuclear Testing	AGN

Election Results

1988 general	James Bilbray (D).....................	101,764	(64%)	($652,199)
	Lucille Lusk (R)......................	53,588	(34%)	($147,891)
1988 primary	James Bilbray (D), unopposed			
1986 general	James Bilbray (D).....................	61,830	(54%)	($387,717)
	Bob Ryan (R)........................	50,342	(44%)	($276,138)

SECOND DISTRICT

The People: Est. Pop. 1986: 469,600, up 17.4% 1980–86; Pop. 1980: 399,857, up 58.5% 1970–80. Households (1980): 69% family, 37% with children, 58% married couples; 38.5% housing units rented; median monthly rent: $269; median house value: $70,200. Voting age pop. (1980): 291,824; 5% Spanish origin, 2% Black, 2% American Indian, 2% Asian origin.

1988 Presidential Vote:	Bush (R)	115,499	(62%)
	Dukakis (D)......................	65,219	(35%)
	Others...........................	6,798	(4%)

Rep. Barbara F. Vucanovich (R)

Elected 1982; b. June 22, 1921, Camp Dix, NJ; home, Reno; Manhattanville Col., 1938–39; Roman Catholic; married (George).

Career: Owner, NV franchise of Evelyn Wood Speed Reading Co., 1964–68; Owner, travel agcy., 1968–74; Campaign staffer for U.S. Sen. Paul Laxalt, 1974, 1980; Dist. Rep. for U.S. Sen. Paul Laxalt, 1974–81.

Offices: 206 CHOB 20515, 202-225-6155. Also 300 Booth St., Reno 89509, 702-784-5003; and P.O. Box A, 2200 Civic Ctr. Dr., N. Las Vegas 89030, 702-399-3555.

Committees: *House Administration* (4th of 8 R). Subcommittee: Accounts (Ranking Member). *Interior and Insular Affairs* (Ranking Member of 15 R). Subcommittees: Energy and the Environment; Mining and Natural Resources; General Oversight and Investigations (Ranking Member). *Select Committee on Children, Youth and Families* (3d of 12 R).

Group Ratings

	ADA	ACLU	COPE	CFA	LCV	ACU	NTLC	NSI	COC	CEI
1988	10	26	10	36	13	92	77	100	77	66
1987	16	—	9	29	—	74	—	—	86	74

National Journal Ratings

	1988 LIB — 1988 CONS		1987 LIB — 1987 CONS	
Economic	19%	80%	22%	78%
Social	5%	91%	30%	69%
Foreign	27%	71%	0%	80%

Key Votes

1) Homeless $	FOR	5) Ban Drug Test	FOR	9) SDI Research	FOR
2) Gephardt Amdt	AGN	6) Drug Death Pen	FOR	10) Ban Chem Weaps	AGN
3) Deficit Reduc	AGN	7) Handgun Sales	FOR	11) Aid to Contras	FOR
4) Kill Plnt Clsng Notice	FOR	8) Ban D.C. Abort $	FOR	12) Nuclear Testing	AGN

Election Results

1988 general	Barbara F. Vucanovich (R)	105,981	(57%)	($614,853)
	Jim Spoo (D)	75,163	(41%)	($430,155)
1988 primary	Barbara F. Vucanovich (R), unopposed			
1986 general	Barbara F. Vucanovich (R)	83,479	(58%)	($367,044)
	Pete Sferrazza (D)	59,433	(42%)	($69,777)

NEW HAMPSHIRE

Just a little more than half a century ago, the six-story red brick Amoskeag Mills that line the banks of the Merrimack River in Manchester, New Hampshire—the largest cotton mills in the world, once employing 17,000 workers in 30 major mills covering 8 million square feet and producing enough cloth every two months to put a band around the world—were lying cold and idle: in 1935 the Amoskeag company went into bankruptcy. They were a casualty of competition from low-wage southern mills, of a divisive strike in 1922, of a management out of touch with technological innovation. Amoskeag was the central focus of New Hampshire's economy half a century ago: by far the largest employer in the only true city, with one-fifth of the state's population—a city of red brick mill dormitories and frame three-family houses filled with immigrants from Quebec, Ireland, Poland and Greece, amid the mountains and villages still inhabited by flinty Yankee farmers and mechanics. New Hampshire was then part of the backwoods of New England, an odd corner off to one side of the country; if anyone had suggested that New Hampshire represented any wave of the future, he would have been looked at askance, if not locked up for his own good.

Yet as the 1980s move into the 1990s, New Hampshire can make a strong claim to be the state that has, more than any other, set the course of public policy and the tone of public debate. The bedraggled New Hampshire of 50 years ago, where small operators were setting up little low-wage, low-skill operations in the deserted Amoskeag buildings, where Frank Knox had left behind his *Manchester Union Leader* to be run by the son of a one-time Teddy Roosevelt staffer named William Loeb—that New Hampshire has largely disappeared, and in its place has arisen one of the nation's fastest-growing, most prosperous economic communities. This "Nouvelle Hampshire," to use the *Washington Post*'s Henry Allen's term, has none of the architectural purity of Amoskeag: its shopping centers, which you have to wait through five cycles of red lights to get into, look half finished; its new subdivisions and condominium developments have the look of plaster no thicker than the nail it takes to hang a picture and fiberboard not capable of taking a second coat of paint; its new company headquarters and bank branches, located off dirty-snow-lined arterial highways, seem built of one of the shinier but not necessarily more durable forms of plastic. Yet, for all that, there can be no question but that New Hampshire is prospering. The economy, which fared so badly for the immigrants who lost their jobs when the Amoskeag Mills folded, now seems to be doing very well indeed for their grandchildren, and for the tens of thousands who have flocked here from the nearby high-tax states of the Northeast.

The public policy that has been the key to New Hampshire's success has been low taxes, and the political instrumentality that has helped this small state, with one-tenth of 1% of the nation's population, to convert the rest of the United States to its gospel has been New Hampshire's first-in-the-nation primary. Neither the policy nor the politics proceeded out of any deliberate plan, but together they produced results around 1980 that have had reverberations around the world.

New Hampshire's first first-in-the-nation primary was held in 1920, but for three decades only slates of unpledged delegates were fielded; only in 1952, when Estes Kefauver beat Harry Truman and Dwight Eisenhower beat Robert Taft, did New Hampshire see how it could exert vast leverage by choosing first. Since 1952, no one has won a presidential election without winning the New Hampshire primary first; Eisenhower, Kennedy, Johnson, Nixon, Carter, Reagan and Bush all won. New Hampshire has not done as well picking the losing party's nominee, choosing Kefauver in 1952 and 1956, Henry Cabot Lodge in 1964, Lyndon Johnson in 1968, Edmund Muskie in 1972 and Gary Hart in 1984, but it has voted for three of the last four:

NEW HAMPSHIRE — Congressional Districts, Counties,
County Subdivisions, and Places — *(2 Districts)*

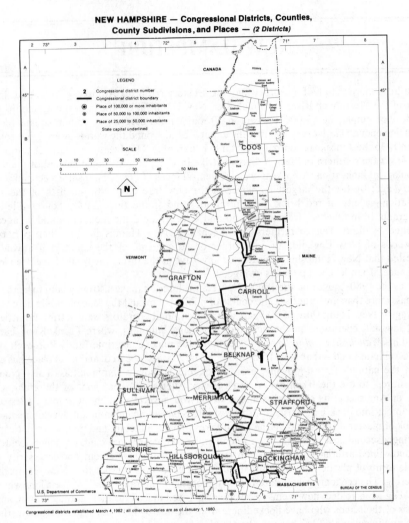

Congressional districts established March 4, 1982 ; all other boundaries are as of January 1, 1980.

Gerald Ford in 1976, Jimmy Carter in 1980 and Michael Dukakis in 1988. It has played two other roles, hurting front-runners by giving them fewer votes than expected (Goldwater in 1964, Johnson in 1968, Muskie in 1972, Mondale in 1984), and propelling little-known or little-considered candidates into the national spotlight (Lodge in 1964, Eugene McCarthy in 1968, George McGovern in 1972, Gary Hart in 1984).

New Hampshire's status as the nation's most visible tax haven is relatively new. Back when the Amoskeag Mills closed, New Hampshire had no sales or income tax, but neither did most other states; as late as the middle 1960s, many states had no income tax and sales taxes were not universal. The difference is that New Hampshire, under the far from gentle prodding of William Loeb and the *Union Leader,* resisted the temptation to which all the other 49 states succumbed (Alaska later repealed its income tax) to pass a broad-based tax. They did so primarily to pay for education, while New Hampshire insisted on keeping schools a local expense, giving local property taxpayers an incentive to keep teachers' salaries down; the states did so also to provide welfare payments for the unfortunate, which New Hampshire decided it could do without. The closest New Hampshire came to a broad-based tax was under Governor Walter Peterson, a Republican defeated by Loeb's man, Meldrim Thomson, in the primary in 1972 (a big year for Loeb: the suspect forged "Cannocks" letter he printed helped sink the candidacy of Edmund Muskie). Since then, New Hampshire candidates have been asked to "take the pledge" to oppose any broad-based tax; no candidate who refused has been elected governor.

In the 1960s and 1970s, New Hampshire's low tax policy resulted in above-average population growth; by the 1980s, it resulted in an astonishing boom. As Massachusetts crackled with high-tech growth, it occurred to many that just on the other side of the state's northern border, less than an hour's drive from Faneuil Hall, was a place where you could live comfortably, make an excellent living, watch Boston TV, and not only not pay Massachusetts's still high taxes, but in fact pay no income or sales tax at all.

Since 1970, New Hampshire's population has grown more than 40%, to more than one million, as compared to 3% growth in Massachusetts. New Hampshire has also moved from the middle of the pack in per capita income to near the top, and it often has the nation's lowest unemployment rates. The old Amoskeag Mills are now filled with high-tech offices and warehouses, and once grimy Manchester is now one of the centers of America's high-tech economy.

This growth has made an imprint on politics. New Hampshire Republicans and Democrats used to vote about the same as Republicans and Democrats across the country; as late as 1976, the New Hampshire primary results foreshadowed the candidates' national showings. But in the 1980s, both parties' constituencies showed an anti-tax bias. New Hampshire's not terribly numerous Democrats chose Jimmy Carter over Edward Kennedy of neighboring "Taxachusetts" in 1980, and preferred Gary Hart's new ideas to Walter Mondale's New Dealism in 1984. In 1988, Michael Dukakis won out of gratitude for blocking the Seabrook nuclear plant—not just an environmental issue, but a fiscal one—running well ahead of more traditional Democrats like Richard Gephardt and Paul Simon.

As for New Hampshire Republicans, there is no more fervent anti-tax constituency in the western world. In 1980, they gave half their votes to a 69-year-old former movie actor who promised to cut federal tax rates 30%, despite the momentum from Iowa working for George Bush. Nor did Iowa momentum help Bob Dole in 1988: as he was talking about the need for painful solutions, George Bush was travelling from truck stop to Catholic college with three-term Governor John Sununu, an enthusiastic pledge-taker, promising that he would back "no new taxes" and challenging Dole to do the same. The result was Bush's come-from-behind 38%–28% victory over Dole, and the nomination of a Republican candidate whose New Hampshire-like views on taxes contrasted most vividly with those of his later opponent he took to referring to as "the governor of Massachusetts."

In early 1989 George Bush was President of the United States, John Sununu was White House chief of staff, and tax rates in all the major western countries seemed to be following the same downward course they took in the United States in the 1980s. Those who are pleased with this trend, and those who are not, have good reason to say, as George Bush did on primary night and later, "Thank you, New Hampshire."

Governor. In late February, within 24 hours after the primary returns are in, the politicians and the press clear out of the Sheraton Wayfarer parking lot and are not seen again for another three years. New Hampshire has its politics to itself. Its key issues have been "the (anti-tax) pledge" and the Seabrook nuclear plant. The former is now deeply ingrained, and not even Democrats challenge it. And controversy over the latter has cooled down since the departure of John Sununu for Washington. Sununu came to politics as an engineer; besides believing strongly in free markets, he believes strongly that New England needs more electric power and that

Seabrook would provide it safely and economically; he scorns Michael Dukakis's claims that it is unsafe. His problem was that, even unbuilt, Seabrook was costing New Hampshire voters money, and in 1986 he beat Democrat Paul McEachern, a one-issue, anti-Seabrook candidate, by only 54%–46%.

The current governor, Republican Judd Gregg, is more conciliatory; calling for a "more constructive dialogue" on Seabrook, he beat McEachern by a comfortable 61%–39% margin. In 1988, Gregg's father Hugh served as governor from 1953–55 and was a major player in presidential politics later. Judd Gregg was elected to Congress in 1980, where he was not entirely conciliatory, but was rather vocal in his criticisms of the majority Democrats. He had no trouble taking the pledge, though he does favor more spending on education and environment, but with local towns making most of the decisions. New Hampshire, by the way, has antique political institutions: its governors are elected every two years, it has an executive council to advise the governor and rule on appointments, and it has a House with 400 members, the nation's largest, most of whom are retirees, students, housewives and others who can use the tiny salary.

Senators. New Hampshire has two Republican Senators, of different styles and views.

Gordon Humphrey, the senior Senator, is the kind of conservative who likes to take on lost causes and complain about being sold out—but in this conservative era he has also gotten some results. He cast lonely votes against the Civil Rights Restoration Act and its handicapped provisions, against World Bank policies, against a separate Veterans Affairs Department, against the welfare reform and catastrophic health care bills and against the INF Treaty, all without perceptible effect.

But he has made a difference on other things. In 1984 and 1985, he criticized the Reagan Administration for not helping the Afghan rebels, and set up a Senate Afghan Task Force; he is one of those who changed U.S. policy and provided the weapons—notably the Stinger hand-held missile launcher—that helped force the Soviets out. Never a George Bush loyalist (he was for Jack Kemp), he let it be known at the 1988 Republican National Convention that he'd lead a revolt if an abortion proponent like Thomas Kean or Alan Simpson was chosen Vice President; he purred with satisfaction when a name on his list, Dan Quayle, was chosen. When HHS nominee Louis Sullivan waffled on abortion, he announced that although he wouldn't vote against Bush's only black cabinet member, he would demand right-to-life appointees under him—and mostly got them. He was one of those who led the successful (95–5) fight against the pay raise in the Senate in 1989.

Humphrey has other interests. He is something of an environmentalist, a backer of the balanced budget amendment, a founder of the bipartisan Congressional Coalition on Adoption. He was a fervent and frustrated backer of Judge Robert Bork on Judiciary; in 1989, he switched from Armed Services to Foreign Relations and from Labor and Human Resources to Public Works. A former airline pilot (many of whom live in New Hampshire to avoid taxes), he has an electronic console in his Capitol hideaway office where he keeps in touch with his staff via computer screens. The Democrats have long thought he is a little offbeat, but on at least some things he has been more in touch with the future than they have. One of those is New Hampshire electoral politics. In 1978, Humphrey took on Senator Thomas McIntyre, a Democrat twice reelected against right-wing Republicans. Humphrey raised money, ran TV ads, and empha-sized the Panama Canal Treaties as well as his opposition to abortion. McIntyre's defeat was the biggest upset of the year. In 1984, Humphrey took a different tack, emphasizing his work against acid rain when opposed by Congressman Norman D'Amours. Humphrey was reelected 59%–41%, the sort of numbers that have come to seem normal for New Hampshire Republicans. In early 1989 he announced his retirement, saying "Two terms is enough" and that he took "a lot of satisfaction" in his accomplishments.

The leading Republican candidate who emerged in the ensuing weeks was 1st District Congressman Bob Smith, who officially announced his candidacy on March 20, 1989. Possible primary opponents include lawyer Tom Christo, state Senator Susan McLean, freshman Chuck Douglas of the 2nd District and John Sununu. Democratic state chairman Joseph Grandmaison and former Congressman Norm D'Amours (who lost to Humphrey in 1984) seem interested in running, as do Nashua Mayor Jim Donchess, who lost to Douglas in 1988, and attorney John Rauh. But any of them would be laboring under the handicap of the unpopularity of national Democratic stands in a state where the Republican approach seems to have had so much success.

Senator Warren Rudman has made a national name for himself twice, in his first term as co-sponsor of the Gramm-Rudman deficit reduction law, in his second as vice chairman of the Senate Iran-contra committee. In both cases he has gone against form, taken an innovative approach, mastered the facts, and come out politically ahead. Rudman instinctively is a centrist, a compromiser among Republicans, not necessarily a strong partisan; his Senate mentor was Majority Leader Howard Baker. Yet he gets aggressive once he gets into a fight and plays to win. Back in 1982, for example, he took on and licked the AMA while defending the Federal Trade Commission's regulation of doctors' fees. In 1985, dismayed by the deficit, he joined forces with Texas's Phil Gramm in support of what purported to be a mechanism to automatically reduce it to zero by 1990; he had to work to readjust it after the Supreme Court ruled it partly unconstitutional. If Gramm-Rudman has not had all the good results its backers hoped, it has not been the disaster its critics feared.

In early 1987, Rudman became vice chairman of the Senate Iran-contra committee, where he cooperated closely with Democrat Daniel Inouye and signed the majority report. Rudman especially questioned the Justice Department's work and Admiral Poindexter's concealment of the diversion of money to the contras from President Reagan; he did not flinch when Oliver North briefly enjoyed a flurry of popularity. Rudman kept busy at other things as well. He worked on the ethics and lobbying bill, which Reagan ultimately vetoed, applying it to Members of Congress. He was the chief Senate drafter of the 1988 omnibus drug bill, which he insisted was more than just a campaign year measure. He pushed through a bill to preserve 45,000 acres in northern New Hampshire threatened by development. He challenged Logan Airport's higher fees for commuter airlines, and got them cut back. He is something of a workhorse, and not a Washington partygoer—he has turned down four White House invitations and refuses to wear a black tie.

Rudman won the seat in 1980 by beating former Governor Wesley Powell and future Governor John Sununu in the Republican primary and then longtime adversary Senator John Durkin in the general 52%–48%. He said he considered retiring in 1986, but ran after Gramm-Rudman passed and beat former Massachusetts Governor Endicott Peabody 63%–32%. In 1988 he backed Bob Dole, and gulped as he watched him decline to sign New Hampshire's anti-tax pledge; he says he's undecided about running for reelection in 1992. Certainly he could win.

Presidential politics. You can sum up the politics of the 1980s by saying that the Democrats have been dominated by dovish, generous-spending Iowa and the Republicans by low-tax, hawkish New Hampshire, and that the Republicans have won. New Hampshire's first-in-the-nation status doesn't seem threatened by Republicans, and certainly would not be challenged by George Bush; and in early 1989, at least, the Democrats seemed to have no stomach for their usual quadrennial debate over the rules. This means that the New Hampshire law setting its primary a week before anyone else's will probably govern the whole nation's primary schedule. (But what would happen if another state passed a law setting its primary for the same day as New Hampshire's, or a week before?)

The argument for the New Hampshire primary is that it provides one arena for what columnist Mark Shields calls "retail politics": the state is small enough for candidates to talk to voters personally. But as New Hampshire continues to grow, retail campaigning is less important, and television ads on the Boston stations more so. (*The Union Leader* can swing few votes: publisher Nackey Loeb, much wooed, backed Pete du Pont who got all of 10% of the vote.) The argument against New Hampshire is that it is atypical: it voted 63%–36% for George Bush in 1988, a showing he exceeded in just a few small western states. Bush carried all the major towns except Portsmouth, with its restored 18th century houses and trendy shopping, and the college towns of Hanover and Durham.

Congressional districting. With only slight changes, New Hampshire's two congressional districts have had the same boundaries since 1881, neatly separating the Merrimack River mill towns of Manchester and Nashua, the state's largest cities. That was done to split the Catholic Democratic vote; but both cities are now high-tech Republican towns.

1st Congressional District. This district includes Manchester, its suburbs, and most of the state's southeast corner—booming, fast-growing, anti-tax New Hampshire. The *Manchester Union-Leader* used to set the tone here, but the district's conservatism has outgrown it. For 10 years it was held by Manchester-based Democrat Norman D'Amours, but he ran for the Senate in 1984, and the district's new personality asserted itself. The new congressman is Bob Smith, a real estate agent who grew up in New Jersey, a firm opponent of taxes, and a cultural conservative. He won a four-way primary with 42% of the vote, carrying most of the small towns, and won 59%–40% over liberal Executive Councillor Dudley Dudley. He beat another council member in the 1986 primary 77%–23% and won the general 56%–44%; in 1988 he was reelected 60%–40%. This is beginning to look like a pattern.

Smith is one of the House's staunchest conservatives, though he has pushed bills on acid rain, and was an early and strong backer of Jack Kemp in 1988. In the House, Smith's committee positions give him little clout. But he was one of the three major opponents of the 1989 congressional pay raise, prevailing on the floor but antagonizing the leadership and losing a seat on Armed Services. The district may not care: local businessmen were glad Portsmouth's Pease Air Force Base was on the base-closing list; now they can make it a private airport. And Smith probably does not either. When Senator Gordon Humphrey announced his retirement, Smith jumped into the race and became the early favorite for the Republican nomination and the seat.

2d Congressional District. The 2d District includes Nashua (the state's booming second city on the Massachusetts border), the capital of Concord, and the somewhat liberal towns along the Connecticut River. When the 2d's Judd Gregg ran for governor in 1988, the Republicans had a tough primary and the Democrats put up a tough candidate, but a strong conservative Republican, Chuck Douglas, won anyway. His Republican primary opponent, Betty Tamposi, the daughter of a big developer, was attacked by Senator Gordon Humphrey for putting "political ambition ahead of the welfare of an infant" because she had two children, ages four and one. After some uproar, Humphrey apologized. Douglas said the Reagan Administration was "a disappointment" because of the appointment of "a bunch of squishes." A protégé of former Governor Meldrim Thomson, Douglas emerged as the strongest anti-tax candidate and won 47%–41%. In the general he faced Democrat Jim Donchess, fresh from reelection as Mayor of Nashua with over 80%, who ran ads attacking Douglas's decisions while on the state Supreme Court. But in this race Donchess carried Nashua by just 52%–47% and lost just about everything else but Dartmouth College's Hanover. Douglas won 57%–43% and seems to have a safe seat— unless he chooses to run for the Senate seat Gordon Humphrey is leaving in 1990.

In Washington Douglas kicked up a fuss when before an insurance industry audience he illustrated the Judiciary Committee's liberalness by mentioning that committee member Barney Frank's homosexuality. Frank called that "the kind of mean-spirited performance that degrades the level of public debate," and Douglas, after refusing for several days, finally apologized.

The People: Est. Pop. 1988: 1,097,000; Pop. 1980: 920,610, up 19.1% 1980–88 and 24.8% 1970–80; 0.43% of U.S. total, 40th largest. 17% with 1–3 yrs. col., 18% with 4+ yrs. col.; 8.5% below poverty level. Single ancestry: 14% English, 12% French, 6% Irish, 2% German, Italian, Polish, 1% Scottish, Greek, Swedish. Households (1980): 74% family, 40% with children, 63% married couples; 32.4% housing units rented; median monthly rent: $206; median house value: $48,000. Voting age pop. (1980): 662,528; 1% Spanish origin. Registered voters (1988): 649,924; 197,409 D (30%), 252,720 R (39%), 199,795 unaffiliated and minor parties (31%).

1988 Share of Federal Tax Burden: $4,691,000,000; 0.53% of U.S. total, 35th largest.

1988 Share of Federal Expenditures

	Total		Non-Defense		Defense	
Total Expend	$3,198m	(0.36%)	$2,229m	(0.34%)	$1,006m	(0.44%)
St/Lcl Grants	398m	(0.35%)	398m	(0.35%)	0m	(0.01%)
Salary/Wages	612m	(0.46%)	228m	(0.34%)	384m	(0.34%)
Pymnts to Indiv	1,601m	(0.39%)	1,499m	(0.38%)	103m	(0.55%)
Procurement	516m	(0.27%)	37m	(0.08%)	516m	(0.27%)
Research/Other	71m	(0.19%)	68m	(0.18%)	3m	(0.18%)

Political Lineup: Governor, Judd Gregg (R); Secy. of State, William Gardner (D); Atty. Gen., John Arnold (R); Treasurer, Georgie A. Thomas (R); State Senate, 24 (16 R and 8 D); State House of Representatives, 400 (278 R and 118 D). Senators, Gordon J. Humphrey (R) and Warren B. Rudman (R). Representatives, 2 R.

1988 Presidential Vote:

Bush (R)	281,537	(63%)
Dukakis (D)	163,696	(36%)

1984 Presidential Vote:

Reagan (R)	267,051	(69%)
Mondale (D)	120,377	(31%)

1988 Democratic Presidential Primary

Dukakis	44,112	(36%)
Gephardt	24,513	(20%)
Simon	21,094	(17%)
Jackson	9,615	(8%)
Gore	8,400	(7%)
Babbitt	5,644	(5%)
Hart	4,888	(4%)
Uncommitted	5,246	(4%)

1988 Republican Presidential Primary

Bush	59,290	(38%)
Dole	44,797	(28%)
Kemp	20,114	(13%)
DuPont	15,885	(10%)
Robertson	14,775	(9%)

GOVERNOR

Gov. Judd Gregg (R)

Elected 1988, term expires Jan. 1991; b. Feb. 14, 1947, Nashua; home, Greenfield; Columbia U., A.B. 1969, Boston U., J.D. 1972; Congregationalist; married (Kathleen).

Career: Practicing atty., 1976–80; NH St. Exec. Cncl. 1979–80. U.S. House of Reps. 1980–88.

Office: State House, Concord 03301, 603-271-2121.

Election Results

1988 gen.	Judd Gregg (R)	267,064	(61%)
	Paul McEachern (D)	172,543	(39%)
1988 prim.	Judd Gregg (R)	65,957	(79%)
	Bob Shaw (R).	15,133	(18%)
1986 gen.	John H. Sununu (R).	134,824	(54%)
	Paul McEachern (D)	116,142	(46%)

SENATORS

Sen. Gordon J. Humphrey (R)

Elected 1978, seat up 1990; b. Oct. 9, 1940, Bristol, CT; home, Chichester; Geo. Wash. U., U. of MD, Burnside-Ott Aviation Inst.; Baptist; married (Patricia).

Career: Air Force, 1958–62; Pilot, 1965–78.

Offices: 531 HSOB 20510, 202-224-2841. Also One Eagle Sq., Concord 03301, 603-228-0453; and 157 Main St., Berlin 03570, 603-752-2600.

Committees: *Environmental and Public Works* (7th of 7 R). Water Resources, Transportation and Infrastructure; Environmental Protection. *Foreign Relations* (8th of 9 R). Subcommittees: International Economic Policy, Trade, Oceans and Environment (Ranking Member); Terrorism, Narcotics and International Operations. *Judiciary* (6th of 6 R). Subcommittees: Antitrust, Monopolies and Business Rights; Technology and the Law (Ranking Member).

Group Ratings

	ADA	ACLU	COPE	CFA	LCV	ACU	NTLC	NSI	COC	CEI
1988	5	4	6	33	80	100	87	100	79	81
1987	5	—	6	33	—	96	—	—	94	89

National Journal Ratings

	1988 LIB — 1988 CONS			1987 LIB — 1987 CONS		
Economic	9%	—	81%	6%	—	87%
Social	13%	—	86%	11%	—	87%
Foreign	0%	—	92%	0%	—	76%

Key Votes

1) Cut Aged Housing $	AGN	5) Bork Nomination	FOR	9) SDI Funding	FOR
2) Override Hwy Veto	AGN	6) Ban Plastic Guns	FOR	10) Ban Chem Weaps	FOR
3) Kill Plnt Clsng Notice	FOR	7) Deny Abortions	FOR	11) Aid To Contras	FOR
4) Min Wage Increase	AGN	8) Japanese Reparations	AGN	12) Reagan Defense $	FOR

Election Results

1984 general	Gordon J. Humphrey (R).............	225,828	(59%)	($1,806,653)
	Norman E. D'Amours (D)............	157,447	(41%)	($1,066,485)
1984 primary	Gordon J. Humphrey (R).............	57,763	(100%)	
1978 general	Gordon J. Humphrey (R).............	133,745	(51%)	($357,107)
	Thomas J. McIntyre (D)..............	127,945	(49%)	($289,628)

Sen. Warren B. Rudman (R)

Elected 1980, seat up 1992; b. May 18, 1930, Boston, MA; home, Hollis; Syracuse U., B.S. 1952, Boston Col., LL.B. 1960; Jewish; married (Shirley).

Career: Army, Korea; Practicing atty. 1960–70, 1976–80; Atty. Gen. of NH, 1970–76; Pres., Natl. Assn. of Attys. Gen., 1975.

Offices: 530 HSOB 20510, 202-224-3324. Also Thomas J. McIntyre Fed. Bldg., 80 Daniel St., Portsmouth 03801, 603-431-5900; 125 N. Main St., Concord 03301, 603-225-7115; Norris Cotton Fed. Bldg., 275 Chestnut St., Manchester 03103, 603-666-7591; and 157 Main St., Berlin 03570, 603-752-2604.

Committees: *Appropriations* (8th of 13 R). Subcommittees: Commerce, Justice, State and Judiciary (Ranking Member); Defense; Foreign Operations; Interior; Labor, Health and Human Services, Education. *Budget* (8th of 10 R). *Governmental Affairs* (4th of 6 R). Subcommittees: Government Information and Regulation (Ranking Member); Oversight of Government Management; Investigations. *Select Committee on Ethics* (Vice Chairman of 3 R).

Group Ratings

	ADA	ACLU	COPE	CFA	LCV	ACU	NTLC	NSI	COC	CEI
1988	15	38	19	50	50	68	68	100	93	44
1987	25	—	18	42	—	80	—	—	75	71

National Journal Ratings

	1988 LIB — 1988 CONS		1987 LIB — 1987 CONS	
Economic	22% —	75%	26% —	73%
Social	51% —	48%	42% —	56%
Foreign	24% —	75%	0% —	76%

Key Votes

1) Cut Aged Housing $	AGN	5) Bork Nomination	FOR	9) SDI Funding	FOR
2) Override Hwy Veto	AGN	6) Ban Plastic Guns	AGN	10) Ban Chem Weaps	FOR
3) Kill Plnt Clsng Notice	FOR	7) Deny Abortions	FOR	11) Aid To Contras	FOR
4) Min Wage Increase	AGN	8) Japanese Reparations	FOR	12) Reagan Defense $	FOR

740 NEW HAMPSHIRE

Election Results

1986 general	Warren Rudman (R).................	154,090	(63%)	($831,098)
	Endicott Peabody (D).................	79,222	(32%)	($307,760)
1986 primary	Warren Rudman (R)..................	52,003	(98%)	
1980 general	Warren Rudman (R).................	195,559	(52%)	($634,264)
	John A. Durkin (D).................	179,455	(48%)	($676,150)

FIRST DISTRICT

The People: Est. Pop. 1986: 523,800, up 13.7% 1980–86; Pop. 1980: 460,863, up 27.4% 1970–80. Households (1980): 73% family, 40% with children, 62% married couples; 33.8% housing units rented; median monthly rent: $205; median house value: $49,000. Voting age pop. (1980): 332,498; 1% Spanish origin.

1988 Presidential Vote: Bush (R) 145,996   (64%)
Dukakis (D)...................... 80,604   (35%)

Rep. Robert C. Smith (R)

Elected 1984; b. Mar. 30, 1941, Allentown, NJ; home, Tuftonboro; Lafayette Col., B.A. 1965; Roman Catholic; married (Mary Jo).

Career: Navy, Vietnam; Teacher, 1975–85; Businessman (real estate); Chmn., Gov. Wentworth Reg. Sch. Bd., 1978–83.

Offices: 115 CHOB 20515, 202-225-5456. Also Technology Ctr., 340 Commercial St., 2d Fl., Manchester 03101, 603-644-3387; 90 Washington St., Ste. 303, Dover 03820, 603-742-0404; and P.O. Box 737, Wolfeboro 03894, 603-569-4993.

Committees: *Science, Space and Technology* (9th of 19 R). Subcommittees: Natural Resources, Agriculture Research and Environment; Space Science and Applications. *Veterans' Affairs* (10th of 13 R). Subcommittees: Oversight and Investigations; Housing and Memorial Affairs.

Group Ratings

	ADA	ACLU	COPE	CFA	LCV	ACU	NTLC	NSI	COC	CEI
1988	5	13	15	27	63	100	93	100	93	88
1987	4	—	15	29	—	96	—	—	100	85

National Journal Ratings

	1988 LIB — 1988 CONS		1987 LIB — 1987 CONS	
Economic	7% —	91%	0% —	89%
Social	5% —	91%	19% —	78%
Foreign	27% —	71%	0% —	80%

Key Votes

1) Homeless $	FOR	5) Ban Drug Test	FOR	9) SDI Research	FOR
2) Gephardt Amdt	AGN	6) Drug Death Pen	FOR	10) Ban Chem Weaps	AGN
3) Deficit Reduc	AGN	7) Handgun Sales	FOR	11) Aid to Contras	FOR
4) Kill Plnt Clsng Notice	FOR	8) Ban D.C. Abort $	FOR	12) Nuclear Testing	AGN

Election Results

1988 general	Robert C. Smith (R)	131,520	(60%)	($333,695)
	Joseph F. Keefe (D)	86,546	(40%)	($262,895)
1988 primary	Robert C. Smith (R), unopposed			
1986 general	Robert C. Smith (R)	70,739	(56%)	($409,068)
	James Demers (D)	54,787	(44%)	($242,845)

SECOND DISTRICT

The People: Est. Pop. 1986: 503,100, up 9.4% 1980–86; Pop. 1980: 459,747, up 22.3% 1970–80. Households (1980): 74% family, 41% with children, 64% married couples; 30.9% housing units rented; median monthly rent: $208; median house value: $46,900. Voting age pop. (1980): 330,030.

1988 Presidential Vote:

Bush (R)	135,541	(61%)	
Dukakis (D)	83,092	(38%)	

Rep. Charles G. (Chuck) Douglas III (R)

Elected 1988; b. Dec. 2, 1942 Abington, PA; home, Concord; U. N.H., B.A. 1965, Boston U., J.D. 1968; Episcopalian; divorced.

Career: A. A. to Majority Leader, NH House of Reps., 1965; Legal and Legis. Cnsl. to Gov.of NH, 1973–74; Assoc. Justice, NH Superior Crt., 1974–76; Assoc. Justice, NH Supreme Crt. 1977–85.

Offices: 1338 LHOB 20515, 202-225-5206. Also 197 Loudon Rd., Concord 03301, 603-228-0315; 40 E. Pearl St., Ste. 202, Nashua 03060, 603-883-0800; and 157 Main St., Berlin 03570, 603-752-5358.

Committees: *Judiciary* (13th of 14 R). Subcommittees: Economic and Commercial Law; Administrative Law and Governmental Relations. *Government Operations* (12th of 15 R). Subcommittees: Environment, Energy and Natural Resources; Commerce, Consumer and Monetary Affairs.

Group Ratings and Key Votes: Newly Elected

Election Results

1988 general	Charles G. (Chuck) Douglas III (R)	119,742	(57%)	($730,803)
	James W. Donchess (D)	89,677	(43%)	($519,336)
1988 primary	Charles G. (Chuck) Douglas III (R)	22,774	(47%)	
	Betty Tamposi (R)	19,827	(41%)	
	Steven Gregg (R)	2,546	(5%)	
	Three others	2,581	(5%)	
1986 general	Judd Gregg (R)	85,479	(74%)	($138,713)
	Laurence Craig-Green (D)	29,688	(26%)	($5,309)

NEW JERSEY

When Orson Welles was rewriting the old H. G. Wells *War of the Worlds*, to broadcast it live on his *Mercury Theater on the Air* the night before Halloween 1938, where better to have the Martians land than in a small town in New Jersey? In those days a short drive out from Manhattan took you past oil tank farms and swamplands to the heart of Middle America, to small industrial towns thick with overhead wires and fraternal lodges, to vacant flat vegetable fields dotted by gas station junctions. New Jersey in 1938 was a state of 4.1 people million sandwiched between the metropolises of New York City (8.6 million with the suburbs of Long Island and Westchester) and Philadelphia (2.7 million with its four densely settled Pennsylvania suburbs). Both New York and Philadelphia were heavily Democratic in those New Deal days; New Jersey, except for the ridge of Hudson County across the river from Manhattan, which was ruled absolutely by boss Frank Hague, was Republican. In those days when the bridges and tunnels across the Hudson and Delaware were still new (or not yet built), when big city radio stations were only beginning to create a metropolitan tone to life, New Jersey was still a place apart: you might as well be in the middle of Ohio or Indiana as in New Jersey, 40-odd miles from Times Square.

In those days New Jersey's insularity protected it from domination by the metropolises across the rivers. Now it has its own sources of pride. The demographic balance has changed, for one thing: if metro New York City is up to 10.5 million and Philadelphia to 3.5 million, New Jersey has almost doubled in 50 years to 7.6 million, and in the late 1980s it was generating more jobs and growing more rapidly than all of New York state. More than that, it is no longer, as someone said in colonial times, "a valley of humility between two mountains of conceit," but a state with a new-found identity: "New Jersey and you," as Governor Thomas Kean's tourist slogan has it, "perfect together." It is the home of Bruce Springsteen and of big league football, basketball, and hockey franchises; it has spawned at least two politicians of national stature, Kean and Senator Bill Bradley. Its Atlantic City has America's only gambling casinos outside Nevada. It is seeing its manufacturing base being overshadowed by high-tech growth that builds on a large existing base, such as Bell Labs. Meanwhile, Americans are becoming aware that there is more to New Jersey than the swamps of the Meadowlands and the grimy New Jersey Turnpike corridor. To the west are rolling countryside and mountains of surprising height; to the east are the mysterious Pine Barrens, still as virgin as they were in colonial times, and the kaleidoscopic variety of the resort towns of the Jersey Shore.

New Jersey's new prominence and pride have resulted partly from the fact that American urban centers increasingly are centered not in a single downtown, but in "urban villages" scattered throughout metropolitan areas—which means that New Jersey is suddenly on the right side of the rivers. But the buoyant growth that produced subdivisions and factories and shopping centers in the 1950s and 1960s, suddenly in the 1980s was producing office and high-tech and even entertainment centers. Freeway interchanges in northern New Jersey and in the corridor around Princeton are sprouting office buildings, corporate headquarters and luxury hotels. State government has also played an important role here. The Meadowlands complex, first developed during Brendan Byrne's terms as governor in the 1970s, has taken land once used only for truck terminals and oil tank farms and turned it into the prime real estate its proximity to Manhattan suggests it should have been all along. In the process, New Jersey has gotten its own sports teams. The legalization of casino gambling in Atlantic City, also during the Byrne years, has not only spruced up that bedraggled resort, but has made New Jersey a national

NEW JERSEY — Congressional Districts, Counties, and Selected Places — *(14 Districts)*

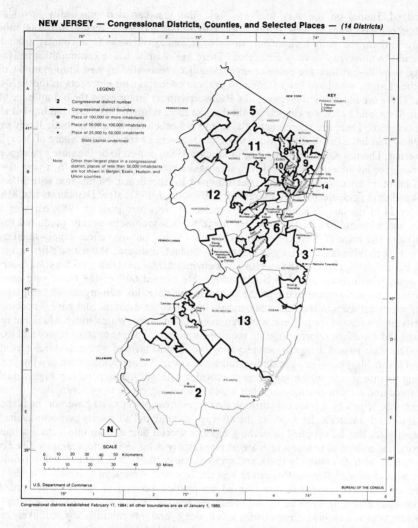

LEGEND

2 Congressional district number

Congressional district boundary

● Place of 100,000 or more inhabitants

● Place of 50,000 to 100,000 inhabitants

• Place of 25,000 to 50,000 inhabitants

State capital underlined

Note: Other than largest place in a congressional district, places of less than 50,000 inhabitants are not shown in Bergen, Essex, Hudson, and Union counties.

KEY
PASSAIC COUNTY
1 Paterson
2 Clifton
3 Passaic

U.S. Department of Commerce   BUREAU OF THE CENSUS

Congressional districts established February 17, 1984; all other boundaries are as of January 1, 1980.

entertainment center. New Jersey now has its own VHF television station, but the big network affiliates in New York and Philadelphia still give it less attention than their home states receive.

Even politics has helped New Jersey establish its identity. Public financing of gubernatorial campaigns has, at last, made New Jersey politicians personally known statewide through their TV ads, and a succession of strong governors, first Democrat Byrne and then Republican Kean, has made a genuine impact on people's lives. In the years when New Jersey was overshadowed by the big cities, politics was left to the county political bosses, a few of them outstanding leaders but most low- and middle-grade hacks: the result was corruption, a state government that didn't live up to its potential, and a mostly ineffective congressional delegation. Now all that is no more.

All of which makes certain sense: for New Jersey has had all along most of the ingredients of a separate American commonwealth. The outsider's image of New Jersey is of the industrial turnpike corridor and the soot-blackened row houses that you can see before entering the Lincoln or Holland Tunnel on the way to New York. But you can find practically any kind of neighborhood you want in New Jersey. Especially in northern New Jersey, within 60 miles of New York, there are many high-income suburbs, as well as the horse farm country around Far Hills and the university town of Princeton. There are old row house communities in Hudson County as well—but they are being changed and often renovated by new immigrants, Cubans and other Latins, who have been thronging to these once stagnant entrepots in the 1970s and 1980s. There are old industrial towns, like Paterson with its factories on the old millrace of the Passaic River, and 1950s working-class suburbs, like those south of Elizabeth that line both sides of the turnpike. There are retirement villages and old beach resorts and in south Jersey even a few towns that have the southern atmosphere of Delaware or the Eastern Shore of Maryland.

Governor. Thomas Kean, leaving office in January 1990, proved to be the state's most popular governor since his ancestor William Livingston was elected to the office in 1776, a year in which two of his other ancestors signed the Declaration of Independence. Nominated with 31% in an eight-candidate field, elected by a margin of 1,797 votes in 1981, after Democrats had held the office for 24 of the last 28 years, Kean was reelected overwhelmingly in 1985, carrying every county and winning 70% of the vote. He made his Massachusetts accent (acquired in prep school) into the voice of New Jersey on the state's TV ads, put into effect supply-side tax cuts after having to raise taxes initially to balance his budget, instituted the nation's first enterprise zones, built highways and started a clean water environmental trust fund, taking state money out of companies with investments in South Africa. He carried 60% of the black vote against a Democrat who had represented half the blacks in the state; his well-organized campaign also captured critical seats in the Assembly, mostly in blue-collar districts, and gave Republicans a majority. In his second term, Kean was even more venturesome, with a tough education reform package and a welfare reform program requiring welfare recipients to go to school and look for work. The state passed a mandatory recycling law, took control of wetlands development and banned ocean dumping of sewage sludge. But Kean's overall vision remains one of a buoyant and growing private sector, which government provides with an infrastructure, a highly qualified work force and a clean environment, but which it must not overtax or overregulate.

Kean was helped by a state constitution that gives great power to its governor: he is the only official elected statewide, he appoints the attorney general and all county prosecutors, he has a line-item veto. But he supplied something more: a special flair and an intellectual originality, integrity, and a sense of humor which are on nice display in his 1988 autobiography *The Politics of Inclusion*, with its unusually frank and sympathetic portraits of still active fellow politicians. Kean, who convinced Ronald Reagan to sign the Japanese American redress bill in 1988, was passed over for the 1988 vice presidential nomination because of his reluctant pro-choice position on abortion. In 1989 he agreed to become head of Drew University after leaving office. But Kean, who as a child stuttered badly, was dyslexic, and was painfully shy, will likely remain on the short list of prime potential appointees in the Bush Administration.

The 1989 gubernatorial election will be a match between two Members of Congress from opposite ends of the state: Democrat James Florio of Camden, across the river from Philadelphia, and Republican Jim Courter of Hackettstown in northern New Jersey. Florio, who ran just 1,797 votes behind Kean in 1981, defeated Princeton mayor Barbara Boggs Sigmund and assemblyman Alan Karcher in the June Democratic primary, while Courter won a close eight-way primary, defeating former New Jersey attorney general Cary Edwards and state Assembly Speaker Charles Hardwick. Among the tough issues a new governor will have to face are garbage disposal (local dumps have been closed) and auto insurance.

Senators. If Democratic nominees for President were chosen by secret ballot of their peers, the winner would almost certainly be Senator Bill Bradley of New Jersey. A Senator for just a decade, Bradley has already produced a major reform of our tax system and attracts respectful attention whenever he weighs in on a major issue. He has demonstrated a special strength of character and self-discipline not often seen in politicians and a piercing insight into issues that goes quickly beyond the conventional wisdom and to the heart of the matter. Not only many Democrats but many Republicans as well think the country would be lucky if in eight years of the next three decades its government were headed by a President Bill Bradley.

This admiration is all the more striking because Bradley comes to politics by a route that more often inspires both jealousy and derision: he ran for and won a Senate seat in 1978 after 15 years as a celebrity athlete. But as a basketball player at Princeton and then for the New York Knicks, Bradley showed an unusual mental discipline that complemented his physical skills. He gave up two years in the pros to take a Rhodes Scholarship at Oxford; he turned down commercial endorsements that could have made him millions; he wrote a thoughtful book, *Life on the Run*. He established residency in New Jersey and became quietly involved in politics years before he ran. His first race in 1978 showed his strengths: his aggressiveness in taking on a Senate race at age 35, for a seat held by four-term Republican Clifford Case; his shrewd judgment that Case might be vulnerable because of his age and liberal views; his openness to genuine intellectual engagement—both when he accepted the challenge of Jeffrey Bell, the supply-sider who beat Case in the primary, to debate him 21 times, and when he took seriously Bell's backing of Kemp-Roth in a year of tax revolts then underway from Jerry Brown's California to Michael Dukakis's Massachusetts.

Bradley rejected the supply-side answers and voted against the 1981 Reagan tax cuts; with Dale Bumpers and Ernest Hollings, he was one of three Democrats who voted for the Reagan budget and against tax cuts, votes which would have eliminated most of the 1980s deficits. But he wasn't satisfied either with traditional Democratic economics. Government spending was growing more rapidly than the private economy, revenues were ballooning because of inflation, and the Democratic Congress was adjusting tax rates to help the well-placed while the economy as a whole was winding down. In 1982, Bradley came up with his "fair tax" proposal to cut tax rates sharply and eliminate most preferences and tax shelters. Characteristically, he took a broad concept and then filled in the details with great care.

Bradley's "fair tax" led directly to the 1986 tax reform—a stunning achievement for a politician with little seniority on the minority side of the aisle and freighted with the kind of celebrity that other politicians usually resent. Ronald Reagan called for (post-election) tax reform in his 1984 State of the Union; Donald Regan's and then James Baker's Treasury advanced proposals; Ways and Means chairman Dan Rostenkowski took up the cause enthusiastically; Senate Finance chairman Bob Packwood, on the verge of being rolled in his own committee and rejected by primary voters in Oregon, embraced the idea and got a bill through the Senate. At each stage Bradley was there, quietly encouraging others, avoiding the spotlight but offering advice and lobbying key Members; he even played basketball (which he has otherwise given up) with House Members. Despite his unobtrusive approach, all the other principals agree that Bradley was the indispensable man.

On taxes, as on other issues, Bradley has been careful to concentrate on a few key issues where he can master the facts and the arguments and make an original and telling contribution. He doesn't seem to care whom he takes on in the process. His first cause was to build up the Strategic Petroleum Reserve, and he beat then chairman Russell Long in Finance. On tax reform, he in effect took on the entire Washington lobbying community, and won. He has urged debt relief for underdeveloped countries, with lower interest rates and partial debt cancellation for countries serious about growth, making him the major critic of James Baker's debt plan and at least the partial inspirer of Nicholas Brady's. He voted for contra aid in 1986 and for at least some consideration of SDI research, opposing sacred causes of many liberal Democrats. He has more respect for economic markets than most Democrats, spurning plans to discourage leveraged buyouts for example, but also urges more spending on health care for low-income pregnant women. Looking at the Soviet Union he notes that, as in the United States, "decentralized economic power erodes centralized political power." But he has argued strongly that Americans should not finance perestroika unless it makes sense in market terms. Two other pet causes: he worked with Frank Lautenberg on the ocean dumping bill, and he wants children to learn more geography.

Bradley comes up for reelection in 1990, and no one doubts he will win; he had 64% of the vote in 1984. Will he run for President in 1992? No one is sure, except that he is one politician (Mario Cuomo is another) who kept his word in 1988 when he said he wasn't running. How will he decide? As he told the *New York Times*, "The point is you develop a sense. I will run when I have that explicit sense of where I'd take the country. People ask me, when will that be? October? Next year? Year after? The answer is, I'll know it when I'm there."

Senator Frank Lautenberg is neither as famous nor as politically secure as Bradley. As the 1980s began, his only involvement in politics was as a Democratic moneygiver; now he has shown he knows how to play the game. It helps to start with a large pile of chips. Lautenberg grew up poor, the son of an immigrant silk worker in Paterson who died young, a World War II veteran who would never have gone to college without the G.I. Bill of Rights. In 1952, he started a company called Automatic Data Processing, which by 1982 employed 16,000 people and processed the payroll for 1 of every 14 non-government workers in the entire country. That year, Lautenberg ran in a crowded field for the Senate, spending $5 million of his own money in this second most expensive media state in the country (expensive because you have to buy New York and Philadelphia TV). Spotlighting his high-tech experience, he beat several professional politicians in the primary and upset Congresswoman Millicent Fenwick 51%–48% in the general.

In the Senate, Lautenberg concentrated on issues of special interest in New Jersey: the Superfund; ocean dumping, on which he pushed a new law in 1988 after hospital waste was dumped off the Jersey Shore; a national 21-year drinking age (it was 18 for years in New York). Even so, his low name identification and liberal record drew a seemingly strong opponent in Pete Dawkins, former Heisman Trophy winner and Rhodes Scholar, Pentagon general and Wall Street celebrity exec, who started running after he moved to New Jersey in 1987. But Dawkins was hurt by his own statements (that he'd "blow his brains out" if he had to live in a small town) and a *Manhattan, inc.* article calling him essentially a phony. A spring flight of ads didn't help much either. Dawkins raised $8 million, but Lautenberg always had reserves. In a brilliant strategic campaign, Lautenberg started advertising late, with an ad showing Dawkins's announcement and an announcer saying, "Be real, Pete." Then he pummeled it out as Dawkins responded with negatives and called him a "swamp dog." Dawkins tried to switch tactics late in the campaign, but Lautenberg had more money for positive ads, and won 54%–46%.

Presidential politics. New Jersey has been mostly a Republican state presidentially for 50 years; with its large Catholic population, it still went only narrowly to John Kennedy in 1960. In the close elections of 1968 and 1976 it went Republican; in 1988 Michael Dukakis came in gamely to compete, and then slunk out by mid-October. George Bush meanwhile blanketed the state and won 56%–42%.

New Jersey has a presidential primary late in the season which has been overshadowed publicly by California, though because it chose delegate slates by congressional districts it produced almost unanimous delegations for winning Democrats like Walter Mondale and Michael Dukakis. That feature was threatened by the rules concessions the Dukakis campaign made to Jackson in 1988, and so New Jersey may be less important in 1992.

Congressional districting. New Jersey redistricted a couple of times in the 1980s; the courts threw out a Democratic plan after 1982, and the Democrats lost a seat in 1984. Unless New Jersey loses a seat, its districts will not have to be changed much for the 1990s. With a Democratic State Senate, a Republican assembly and a 1989 governor's race that will probably be closely contested, it seems unlikely that one party will have control.

The People: Est. Pop. 1988: 7,720,000; Pop. 1980: 7,364,823, up 4.9% 1980–88 and 2.7% 1970–80; 3.16% of U.S. total, 9th largest. 13% with 1–3 yrs. col., 19% with 4+ yrs. col.; 9.5% below poverty level. Single ancestry: 11% Italian, 6% Irish, German, 4% English, Polish, 1% Russian, Hungarian, Dutch, Ukrainian, Scottish, Portuguese, Greek. Households (1980): 76% family, 39% with children, 61% married couples; 38.0% housing units rented; median monthly rent: $228; median house value: $61,400. Voting age pop. (1980): 5,373,962; 11% Black, 6% Spanish origin, 1% Asian origin. Registered voters (1988): 3,699,057; 1,168,608 D (32%), 741,913 R (20%), 1,788,536 unaffiliated and minor parties (48%).

1988 Share of Federal Tax Burden: $40,506,000,000; 4.58% of U.S. total, 7th largest.

1988 Share of Federal Expenditures

	Total		Non-Defense		Defense	
Total Expend	$23,984m	(2.71%)	$18,997m	(2.90%)	$5,605m	(2.45%)
St/Lcl Grants	3,328m	(2.90%)	3,325m	(2.90%)	2m	(1.84%)
Salary/Wages	3,148m	(2.34%)	1,776m	(2.65%)	1,371m	(2.65%)
Pymnts to Indiv	13,174m	(3.22%)	12,919m	(3.31%)	256m	(1.37%)
Procurement	3,972m	(2.11%)	618m	(1.33%)	3,972m	(2.11%)
Research/Other	362m	(0.97%)	359m	(0.97%)	3m	(0.97%)

Political Lineup: Governor, Thomas H. Kean (R); Secy. of State, Jane Burgio (R); Atty. Gen., Peter Perretti (R); Treasurer, Feather O'Connor (R). State Senate, 40 (24 D and 16 R); State Assembly, 80 (41 R and 39 D). Senators, Bill Bradley (D) and Frank R. Lautenberg (D). Representatives, 14 (8 D and 6 R).

1988 Presidential Vote			1984 Presidential Vote		
Bush (R)	1,743,192	(56%)	Reagan (R)	1,933,630	(60%)
Dukakis (D)	1,320,352	(42%)	Mondale (D)	1,261,323	(39%)

1988 Democratic Presidential Primary			1988 Republican Presidential Primary		
Dukakis	414,289	(63%)	Bush	241,033	(100%)
Jackson	213,705	(33%)			
Gore	18,062	(3%)			

GOVERNOR

Gov. Thomas H. Kean (R)

Elected 1981, term expires Jan. 1990; b. Apr. 21, 1935, New York City; home, Livingston; Princeton U., B.A. 1958, Columbia U., M.A. 1964; Episcopalian; married (Deborah).

Career: Educator; TV news commentator; NJ Assembly, 1967–74, Speaker, 1972–73; Chmn. and Pres., Realty Transfer Co., 1967–81.

Office: State House, 125 W. State St., CN–001, Trenton 08625, 609-292-6000.

Election Results

1985 gen.	Thomas H. Kean (R)	1,372,631	(70%)
	Peter Shapiro (D)	578,402	(30%)
1985 prim.	Thomas H. Kean (R)	151,259	(100%)
1981 gen.	Thomas H. Kean (R)	1,145,999	(45%)
	James J. Florio (D)	1,144,202	(45%)
	Eleven others	269,380	(11%)

SENATORS

Sen. Bill Bradley (D)

Elected 1978, seat up 1990; b. July 28, 1943, Crystal City, MO; home, Denville; Princeton U., B.A. 1965, Rhodes Scholar, Oxford U., M.A. 1968; Presbyterian; married (Ernestine).

Career: U.S. Olympic Team, 1964; Pro basketball player, New York Knicks, 1967–77.

Offices: 731 HSOB, 202-224-3224. Also P.O. Box 1720, 1609 Vauxhall Rd., Union 07083, 201-688-0960; and 1 Greentree Ctr., Ste. 303, Rte. 73, Marlton 08053, 609-983-4143.

Committee: *Energy and Natural Resources* (5th of 10 D). Subcommittees: Energy Regulation and Conservation; Public Lands, National Parks and Forests; Water and Power (Chairman). *Finance* (6th of 11 D). Subcommittees: International Debt (Chairman); International Trade; Health for Families and the Uninsured. *Select Committee on Intelligence* (4th of 8 D). *Special Committee on Aging* (3d of 10 D).

Group Ratings

	ADA	ACLU	COPE	CFA	LCV	ACU	NTLC	NSI	COC	CEI
1988	75	67	86	75	70	9	11	20	25	26
1987	80	—	87	92	—	21	—	—	28	28

National Journal Ratings

	1988 LIB — 1988 CONS		1987 LIB — 1987 CONS	
Economic	81%	— 18%	59%	— 37%
Social	84%	— 15%	70%	— 29%
Foreign	68%	— 31%	61%	— 36%

Key Votes

1) Cut Aged Housing $	AGN	5) Bork Nomination	AGN	9) SDI Funding	AGN
2) Override Hwy Veto	FOR	6) Ban Plastic Guns	—	10) Ban Chem Weaps	AGN
3) Kill Plnt Clsng Notice	AGN	7) Deny Abortions	AGN	11) Aid To Contras	AGN
4) Min Wage Increase	—	8) Japanese Reparations	FOR	12) Reagan Defense $	AGN

Election Results

1984 general	Bill Bradley (D) 1,986,644	(64%)	($5,142,316)
	Mary V. Mochary (R)............... 1,080,100	(35%)	($956,398)
1984 primary	Bill Bradley (D) 404,301	(93%)	
	Elliot Greenspan (D)................. 30,680	(7%)	
1978 general	Bill Bradley (D) 1,082,960	(56%)	($1,688,499)
	Jeffrey Bell (R)..................... 844,200	(43%)	($1,418,931)

Sen. Frank R. Lautenberg (D)

Elected 1982, seat up 1994; b. Jan. 23, 1924, Paterson; home, Montclair; Columbia U., B.S. 1949; Jewish; married (Lois).

Career: Army, WWII; Cofounder, Automatic Data Processing, 1952–82; Commissioner, Port Authority of NY and NJ, 1978–82.

Offices: 717 HSOB 20510, 202-224-4744. Also Gateway 1, Gateway Ctr., Newark 07102, 201-645-3030; Court Plaza N., 25 Main St., Hackensack 07601, 201-342-0610, 201-342-0610; and 3 Cooper Plaza, Ste 408, S. Camden 08103, 609-757-5353.

Committees: *Appropriations* (10th of 16 D). Subcommittees: Commerce, Justice, State, and Judiciary; Defense; Foreign Operations; HUD-Independent Agencies; Transportation (Chairman). *Budget* (6th of 13 D). *Environment and Public Works* (5th of 9 D). Subcommittees: Water Resources, Transportation and Infrastructure; Environmental Protection; Superfund, Ocean and Water Protection (Chairman).

Group Ratings

	ADA	ACLU	COPE	CFA	LCV	ACU	NTLC	NSI	COC	CEI
1988	90	73	95	100	90	0	11	0	17	12
1987	85	—	94	92	—	8	—	—	33	22

National Journal Ratings

	1988 LIB — 1988 CONS		1987 LIB — 1987 CONS	
Economic	86%	0%	64%	35%
Social	86%	0%	76%	22%
Foreign	79%	16%	81%	0%

Key Votes

1) Cut Aged Housing $	AGN	5) Bork Nomination	AGN	9) SDI Funding	AGN
2) Override Hwy Veto	FOR	6) Ban Plastic Guns	AGN	10) Ban Chem Weaps	AGN
3) Kill Plnt Clsng Notice	AGN	7) Deny Abortions	AGN	11) Aid To Contras	AGN
4) Min Wage Increase	FOR	8) Japanese Reparations	FOR	12) Reagan Defense $	AGN

Election Results

1988 general	Frank R. Lautenberg (D)	1,599,905	(54%)	($7,298,663)
	Peter M. Dawkins (R)	1,349,937	(46%)	($7,616,249)
1988 primary	Frank R. Lautenberg (D)	326,072	(78%)	
	Elnardo Webster (D)	51,938	(12%)	
	Harold Young (D)	41,303	(10%)	
1982 general	Frank R. Lautenberg (D)	1,117,549	(51%)	($6,435,743)
	Millicent Fenwick (R)	1,047,626	(48%)	($2,606,633)

FIRST DISTRICT

It is not the broadest and it certainly is not the most picturesque of the estuaries along the Atlantic Coast; it doesn't have the tributaries or the scenery of the Hudson or the broadness and fishing riches of the Chesapeake, but the Delaware River is probably the premier industrial inlet on the East Coast, with a concentration of steel factories, chemical plants and oil tank farms equal to any in the country. To the west, the land rises above Wilmington and Philadelphia harbors; to the east, on the New Jersey side, it is almost perfectly flat, occasionally marshy, punctuated every few miles by a slow-moving stream snaking quietly and sluggishly through the cattails on its way from New Jersey's mysterious Pine Barrens. Philadelphia was built on the other bank of the river, and farmers seeking fertile land moved west toward the Pennsylvania Dutch country. As late as 1900, southern New Jersey was a backwater: the small industrial city of Camden, across the river from Philadelphia, once the home of Walt Whitman and later of Campbell soups and RCA records; miles of vegetable fields, producing for the huge canneries then coming on line; quiet, small towns which seem even today far from any metropolis.

By the beginning of World War II, however, the second industrial revolution, featuring especially petrochemicals, was well established here, and still is today. With easy access to cheap water transport and plenty of skilled labor from the Philadelphia area, this was one of the fast-growing industrial areas of the country in the quarter-century starting around 1940. Today, it is known for, literally, the residue of that growth: nowhere will you find such a high concentration of toxic waste, such malodorous smells, such high cancer rates as in southern New Jersey opposite Philadelphia, much of which forms the 1st Congressional District.

The 1st District is concentrated on the urbanized industrial riverfront, from Riverton and Palmyra, connected by bridge with northeast Philadelphia, through Camden and down to a point opposite Delaware. It proceeds inland as well, out the Lindenwold commuter line to thinly settled barren land halfway to Atlantic City. Settled first by Swedes and Dutch, it was one of the polyglot middle colonies; its 20th century industrialization brought in Irish and Italians from across the river and elsewhere. Petrochemicals provided these people with well-paying jobs, houses in the suburbs in stable communities and a level of affluence of which most of their parents never dreamed. But levels of pollution and threats to health once considered tolerable or just ignored are today a major political issue. This is an area with a Democratic heritage, and a tendency to vote for the candidate who promises to do the most to clean up toxic wastes.

Congressman James Florio of the 1st District is a Democrat who has built his political career—one which includes serious races for governor in 1981 and 1989—on these issues. Florio came to Camden from Brooklyn, won a seat in the assembly in 1969, then with the help of Camden Mayor Angelo Errichetti won the 1st District House seat in 1974 from a Republican who was a strong defender of Richard Nixon. Florio got a seat on Interstate and Foreign Commerce (as it then was called), not nearly so sought after as a seat on Energy and Commerce (its current name) is now. The key year in his career was 1978. At home he broke with Errichetti (who was later implicated in the Abscam scandal) and took over control of the local party. In Washington, he succeeded to the chairmanship of the subcommittee that handled railroad bills, which at the time didn't seem a terribly important post; one of the two previous chairmen switched to become a Republican, and the other was defeated in a traditionally Democratic district.

However, the subcommittee also had jurisdiction over what became the Superfund. The idea was to accumulate money for cleaning up toxic wastes by assessing major chemical companies and other polluters; naturally, great sums of money were at stake in the details, and the bills were heavily lobbied. The Superfund was aimed at just the kind of pollution that was becoming obvious in places like the 1st District of New Jersey in the 1970s, where chemical waste dumps turned out, against everyone's expectations, to be poisoning the soil and groundwater. Florio became one of the fathers of the Superfund, and a candidate for governor of New Jersey. With a good Italian name, and as the only candidate from South Jersey, he won the 1981 Democratic gubernatorial primary; leading most of the way in the general, he ended up losing to Thomas Kean by 1,797 votes in the nation's ninth largest state.

Florio was hurt both in that campaign and also later in the House by his operating style: he was something of a loner, studious about details, but long on self-righteousness and short on schmoozing with fellow politicians. That, and his stands on environmental issues, won him the opposition of Energy and Commerce chairman John Dingell during one of the fights over

Superfund revision; Dingell won that one and, as is his wont, trimmed back the jurisdiction of Florio's subcommittee. But in the late 1980s, Florio seems to have become more expansive and easier to deal with. At the same time, he has used his position to become visibly involved in dozens of issues. He moved successfully to outlaw three-wheeled, all-terrain vehicles and less successfully to remove Reagan's chairman of the Consumer Product Safety Commission. He investigated the agency that disposes of bankrupt savings and loans' property, and he kicked up a ruckus about a contract that the Pentagon awarded to Unisys and took away from an RCA plant in South Jersey. He called for tougher asbestos removal in schools and for federal regulation of auto insurance—a very hot topic in New Jersey, where premiums have skyrocketed.

For Florio, 1989 looks like the high point of his political career. He easily won the Democratic nomination for governor in June, and he has a good possiblity to win. Certainly he seems more prepared for what is inevitably a collegial job than he was in 1981. If he wins, the 1st District seat will be vacant and will probably be won by some ambitious local Democratic politico; if he loses, he can remain an active and influential Member of the House for many years to come.

The People: Est. Pop. 1986: 544,400, up 3.5% 1980–86; Pop. 1980: 526,069, up 6.0% 1970–80. Households (1980): 75% family, 42% with children, 59% married couples; 31.7% housing units rented; median monthly rent: $211; median house value: $39,600. Voting age pop. (1980): 370,997; 13% Black, 3% Spanish origin, 1% Asian origin.

1988 Presidential Vote:

Bush (R)	107,784	(52%)
Dukakis (D)	97,658	(47%)

Rep. James J. Florio (D)

Elected 1974; b. Aug. 29, 1937, Brooklyn, NY; home, Gloucester; Trenton St. Col., B.A. 1962, Columbia U., 1962–63, Rutgers U., J.D. 1967; Roman Catholic; married, (Lucinda).

Career: Navy, 1955–58; Practicing atty., 1967–74; NJ Gen. Assembly, 1970–74.

Offices: 2162 RHOB 20515, 202-225-6501. Also 208 White Horse Pike, Ste. 5, Barrington 08007, 609-546-0888.

Committees: *Energy and Commerce* (5th of 26 D). Subcommittees: Commerce, Consumer Protection and Competitiveness (Chairman); Transportation and Hazardous Materials. *Veterans' Affairs* (8th of 21 D). Subcommittees: Hospitals and Health Care; Housing and Memorial Affairs; Oversight and Investigations. *Select Committee on Aging* (3d of 39 D). Subcommittees: Health and Long-Term Care; Housing and Consumer Interests (Chairman).

Group Ratings

	ADA	ACLU	COPE	CFA	LCV	ACU	NTLC	NSI	COC	CEI
1988	80	83	93	82	100	9	12	0	21	16
1987	92	—	92	93	—	4	—	—	0	3

National Journal Ratings

	1988 LIB — 1988 CONS		1987 LIB — 1987 CONS	
Economic	85% —	14%	62% —	35%
Social	70% —	28%	78% —	0%
Foreign	57% —	42%	76% —	19%

Key Votes

1) Homeless $	FOR	5) Ban Drug Test	AGN	9) SDI Research	AGN
2) Gephardt Amdt	FOR	6) Drug Death Pen	FOR	10) Ban Chem Weaps	FOR
3) Deficit Reduc	FOR	7) Handgun Sales	AGN	11) Aid to Contras	AGN
4) Kill Plnt Clsng Notice	AGN	8) Ban D.C. Abort $	AGN	12) Nuclear Testing	FOR

Election Results

1988 general	James J. Florio (D)...................	141,988	(70%)	($924,427)
	Frank A. Cristaudo (R)	60,037	(30%)	($55,301)
1988 primary	James J. Florio (D), unopposed			
1986 general	James J. Florio (D)....................	93,497	(76%)	($322,534)
	Frederick A. Busch, Jr. (R)	29,173	(24%)	($9,719)

SECOND DISTRICT

Did the builders of the Camden & Atlantic Railroad know in 1852, when they began their line to the little inlet town of Absecon, that they were starting America's biggest beach resort, Atlantic City? Like all resorts, it was a product of developments elsewhere: of industrialization and widespread affluence, of railroad technology and the conquest of diseases which used to make summer a time of terror for parents and doctors. In the years after the Civil War, first Altantic City and then the whole oceanfront strand from Brigantine to Cape May became America's first seaside resort, and Atlantic City developed its characteristic features: the Boardwalk in 1870, the amusement pier in 1882, the rolling chair in 1884, salt water taffy in the 1890s, Miss America in 1921. By 1940, when 16 million Americans visited every summer, Atlantic City was a common man's resort of ancient traditions, and it declined in the years after World War II as people could afford nicer vacations. By the early 1970s, it was grim and bedraggled. When New Jersey voters legalized casino gambling for Atlantic City in 1977, gleaming new hotels sprang up, big name entertainers came in and Atlantic City became more glamorous than it had been in 90 years—though there are still slums a few blocks from the Boardwalk.

Behind the beach is swamp and flatland, the Pine Barrens and vegetable fields that gave New Jersey the name of Garden State. Here and there amidst this flatness are small towns and gas station intersections, communities in whose eerie calmness in the summer you can hear the mosquitoes whining. In the flatness you can also find factory towns, clustered around low-wage apparel factories or petrochemical plants on the Delaware estuary: the high-tech service economy of the northeast has not reached this far in south Jersey yet. This is the land that makes up New Jersey's 2d Congressional District.

Democrat William Hughes has been congressman from the 2d since he was first elected in 1974, beating Charles Sandman, the most vitriolic defender of Richard Nixon in the House Judiciary Committee impeachment hearings. In the House, Hughes is self-effacing, hardworking and moderate on the issues. As chairman of the Judiciary Subcommittee on Crime (an interesting post for one of the three House Members who represents a district with legalized gambling) he has been responsible for drafting and floor managing a series of politically sensitive bills, including the 1988 anti-drug act, the child pornography law, the plastic gun bill vehemently opposed by the National Rifle Association and a contract fraud law. He was the major House sponsor of the 1988 law to ban ocean dumping and to stop the disposal of plastics and medical waste in the ocean which had closed many Jersey beaches in 1987 and 1988. He also put together the 1984 anti-crime and 1986 anti-drug bills, and conducted an investigation of alleged drug smuggling by the Nicaraguan contras. He was one of the prime backers of a law to keep government appointees from moving directly into jobs in industries they used to oversee and a law banning unauthorized use of a computer, public or private. He also has worked to ban cop-killer bullets, product tampering and money laundering.

Hughes's 1988 drug bill has provisions against large-scale distributors of pornography and against distributing certain chemicals used in making drugs. It also prohibits dispensing steroids without prescription and imposes a 20-year mandatory sentence for child pornography. Hughes's bills tend to be responsive to the headlines, but he usually stays on the right side of the line between responsiveness to public concern and cheap-shot grandstanding. He also spends time on New Jersey matters, including the Pinelands bill and the coastal trail. He has remained highly popular in the 2d District, winning reelection usually by wide margins.

The People: Est. Pop. 1986: 552,600, up 5.0% 1980–86; Pop. 1980: 526,070, up 13.5% 1970–80. Households (1980): 73% family, 38% with children, 57% married couples; 31.8% housing units rented; median monthly rent: $201; median house value: $42,300. Voting age pop. (1980): 381,227; 12% Black, 3% Spanish origin.

1988 Presidential Vote:

Bush (R)	127,331	(58%)
Dukakis (D)	89,369	(41%)

Rep. William J. Hughes (D)

Elected 1974; b. Oct. 17, 1932, Salem; home, Ocean City; Rutgers U., A.B. 1955, J.D. 1958; Episcopalian; married (Nancy).

Career: Practicing atty., 1959–78; Cape May Cnty. Asst. Prosecutor, 1960–70.

Offices: 341 CHOB 20515, 202-225-6572. Also Central Park E., Ste. 405, 222 New Rd., Linwood, 08221, 609-927-9063; and P.O. Box 248, Pennsville 08070, 609-678-3333.

Committees: *Judiciary* (6th of 21 D). Subcommittees: Courts, Intellectual Property and the Administration of Justice; Crime (Chairman). *Merchant Marine and Fisheries* (4th of 26 D). Subcommittees: Fisheries and Wildlife Conservation and the Environment; Oceanography; Coast Guard and Navigation. *Select Committee on Aging* (5th of 39 D). Subcommittee: Human Services. *Select Committee on Narcotics Abuse and Control* (10th of 18 D).

Group Ratings

	ADA	ACLU	COPE	CFA	LCV	ACU	NTLC	NSI	COC	CEI
1988	70	70	75	82	81	16	35	30	43	24
1987	80	—	74	86	—	9	—	—	27	16

National Journal Ratings

	1988 LIB — 1988 CONS		1987 LIB — 1987 CONS	
Economic	50%	— 48%	46%	— 52%
Social	54%	— 45%	62%	— 36%
Foreign	68%	— 28%	66%	— 32%

Key Votes

1) Homeless $	FOR	5) Ban Drug Test	AGN	9) SDI Research	AGN
2) Gephardt Amdt	AGN	6) Drug Death Pen	FOR	10) Ban Chem Weaps	FOR
3) Deficit Reduc	FOR	7) Handgun Sales	AGN	11) Aid to Contras	AGN
4) Kill Plnt Clsng Notice	AGN	8) Ban D.C. Abort $	AGN	12) Nuclear Testing	FOR

Election Results

1988 general	William J. Hughes (D)	134,505	(66%)	($235,629)
	Kirk W. Conover (R).	67,759	(34%)	($47,159)
1988 primary	William J. Hughes (D), unopposed			
1986 general	William J. Hughes (D)	83,821	(68%)	($241,948)
	Alfred J. Bennington (R)	35,167	(29%)	($138,115)

THIRD DISTRICT

For more than 100 years the Jersey Shore had been one of the nation's foremost resort areas. Connected to New York City by train in 1874, Long Branch for a time became the summer home of Presidents from Grant to Wilson (Garfield, convalescing after he was shot, died there in 1881) and of New York race horse owners and socialites, including Diamond Jim Brady and Lillian Russell. When the racetrack closed, high society moved to Saratoga, and the Shore north and south of Long Branch was settled by all kinds of people, reflected in the diversity of the beach towns: grand and rather forbidding houses in Deal, clapboard Victorians in Allenhurst, slummy neighborhoods in parts of Long Branch, and stucco contemporary condominiums, freshly built to attract retiring New Yorkers afraid to remain in the city, farther south in Ocean County or a few miles back of the beach. A permanent population, many of them offspring of Italian immigrants, built up modest subdivisions in the townships behind the beaches; it is their progeny, growing up in the fast lanes of the highways leading from one Shore adventure to another, who are the inspiration for the music of Shore native (and current resident) Bruce Springsteen.

For all its continuing celebrity, however, it was apparent in the late 1980s that the Shore had seen better days. The ferris wheels and carnival rides had chipped paint and gnashing gears, the old brick hotels lording over the boardwalks may have no lights in their windows after the sun sets over the lagoons behind the beach; worst of all, in the summers of 1987 and 1988 untreated sludge, plastic containers and medical waste washed up on the beaches in large quantities. Vacationers canceled their reservations; hotel rooms and summer rentals went empty; Shore stores and restaurants languished; a depression economy seized the area.

This event transformed the politics of the 3d Congressional District of New Jersey, which covers the Shore and proceeds a few miles inland from Sandy Hook and the Jersey Highlands area on the south side of Lower New York Bay south through Long Branch, Asbury Park and other Monmouth County Shore towns to Seaside Heights and Toms River in Ocean County. This district, its lines drawn variously by Democrats, Republicans and courts, had been represented since the 1964 election by Democrat James Howard, a former teacher who became chairman of the House Public Works Committee and the House's impresario of highway construction and water projects, and the father of the 55-mile-per-hour speed limit as well; reelected by varying margins, he was in strong political shape when he died of a heart attack in March 1988. For Republicans, this was an opportunity that seldom occurs: an open seat race in a district which, while it connects most of the more Democratic territory in the area, is still on balance Republican (it voted for Bush over Dukakis 62%–37% in November). Joseph Azzolina, a local supermarket chain owner and former state senator in his sixties, was already running when Howard died; some Republicans wanted to push him aside, but he got the nomination without strong opposition.

The Democrats' candidate was Frank Pallone, a state senator in his thirties, the son of a disabled Long Branch policeman, and a professional politician who has run for office since law school. Pallone entered Middlebury College in Vermont in 1969, just as the environmental movement was beginning. He was one of those working for Vermont's first-in-the-nation bottle deposit law, and he brought to the politics of the Jersey Shore a focus on environmental issues and rather conservative attitudes on issues such as crime and foreign policy. Pallone was already legislating against ocean dumping before the summer of 1987; where other candidates' signs featured their party, his said "Stop Ocean Dumping"; he had the support as well of Howard's family. With all these advantages, Pallone ended up carrying all but the more high-income towns in the district and won 52%–48%. His victory is a paradigmatic example of how Democrats, using superior political talents and emphasizing local issues, continue to win House seats that are Republican on major national issues in numbers large enough to make the difference in control of the House.

In Washington, Pallone was given seats on the Public Works and Merchant Marine Committees—perfect assignments for his district. Given his already demonstrated political skills, he appears in strong shape. Howard, first elected at 37, held the seat for 23 years, and Pallone, first elected at 37, could hold it at least as long: so it's possible that an essentially Republican district could be held by two Democrats, one the political heir of the other, for half a century or more.

The People: Est. Pop. 1986: 552,400, up 5.0% 1980–86; Pop. 1980: 526,074, up 15.4% 1970–80. Households (1980): 74% family, 38% with children, 61% married couples; 30.8% housing units rented; median monthly rent: $243; median house value: $57,700. Voting age pop. (1980): 382,244; 7% Black, 2% Spanish origin, 1% Asian origin.

1988 Presidential Vote:

Bush (R)	151,582	(62%)
Dukakis (D)	91,100	(37%)

Rep. Frank Pallone, Jr. (D)

Elected 1988; b. Oct. 30, 1951, Long Branch; home, Long Branch; Middlebury Col., B.A. 1973, Fletcher Sch. of Law and Diplomacy, M.A. 1974, Rutger U., J.D. 1978; Roman Catholic, single.

Career: Asst. Prof., Rutgers U., 1979–80; Practicing atty., 1981–83; NJ Senate, 1983–88; Instructor, Monmouth Col., 1984–86.

Offices: 1207 LHOB 20515, 202-225-4671. Also 808 Belmar Plaza, Belmar 07719, 201-681-3321; and 1174 Fischer Blvd., Toms River 08753, 201-929-1400; 540 Broadway Ave., Ste. 119, Long Branch 07740, 201-571-1140.

Committees: *Merchant Marine and Fisheries* (23d of 26 D). Subcommittees: Fisheries and Wildlife Conservation and the Environment; Merchant Marine; Oversight and Investigations. *Public Works and Transportation* (27th of 31 D). Subcommittees: Investigations and Oversight; Surface Transportation; Water Resources. *Select Committee on Aging* (37th of 39 D). Subcommittees: Housing and Consumer Interests; Human Services.

Group Ratings and Key Votes: Newly Elected

Election Results

1988 general	Frank Pallone, Jr. (D)	117,024	(52%)	($678,647)
	Joseph Azzolina (R)	107,479	(48%)	($981,865)
1988 primary	Frank Pallone, Jr. (D), unopposed			
1986 general	James J. Howard (D)	73,743	(59%)	($540,240)
	Brian T. Kennedy (R)	51,882	(41%)	($202,242)

FOURTH DISTRICT

"Trenton makes, the world takes," the large neon sign proclaims over the old manufacturing city where New Jersey's State House perches overlooking the Delaware River. This is the largest city in and was historically the center of New Jersey's 4th Congressional District which now, as the central cities have thinned out and its countryside filled in, sprawls across the middle of the state, straddling the New York and Philadelphia TV markets, stretching to within 5 miles of the Philadelphia city limits and within 10 miles across Raritan Bay to New York's Staten Island. The district includes the rolling hill country, suburban and rural, north of Trenton, and the old industrial towns south along the Delaware. It also stretches far inland, through the northern part of the Pine Barrens, and gets within a mile of the Jersey Shore.

You can read some of the political history of this part of New Jersey in the 1988 election returns. Senator Frank Lautenberg, son of an immigrant mill worker with a record tailored to local concerns, carried the 4th District by a comfortable 56%–44%: an echo of its Democratic past. Michael Dukakis, with his cultural liberalism and support of furloughs for life-without-parole prisoners, carried Trenton by a wide margin but lost the district by the same margin. And Republican Congressman Christopher Smith, a seeming political fluke when he first won the district by beating Abscam defendant Frank Thompson in 1980, proved once again that he is solidly rooted in this territory, beating the wife of the 26-year mayor of Trenton by a 2 to 1 margin.

When Smith came to the House, he was identified as a single-issue right-to-lifer, and his opposition to abortion does help to stitch together his record. Like many of his constituents, he is Catholic. He has seen his efforts to sever any connection between federal spending and abortions largely succeed and his efforts to outlaw abortions generally fail. But these are not his only concerns: Smith also is in line with the Catholic tradition of providing care for individuals who are in need but do not worship too much the values of the economic marketplace. He is proud of getting authorization for a Child Survival Fund to spend $170 million in immunizing Third World children against diseases, and he fought against Administration cuts in the Peace Corps. He sponsored a bill to provide $5 million to buy orthopedic shoes for American diabetics. He has worked to admit Amerasian children to the United States and to help handicapped children. Like most congressmen, he hustles to provide federal money and aid for his local communities, and he got some publicity as well by accompanying a "pro-active" Trenton police squad on all-night drug raids.

The election returns suggest that Smith's views come closer to paralleling those of 4th District voters than do those of the liberal candidates who share most voters' historic Democratic identification. He beat a longtime Trenton state senator in 1982, the head of New Jersey's AFSCME in 1984, an experienced young liberal in 1986 and Trenton mayor Arthur Holland's wife Betty in 1988. He seems to have a safe seat and redistricting in any direction (except liberal Princeton just to the north) is likely to help rather than hurt him.

The People: Est. Pop. 1986: 580,400, up 10.3% 1980–86; Pop. 1980: 526,080, up 10.6% 1970–80. Households (1980): 77% family, 42% with children, 63% married couples; 29.3% housing units rented; median monthly rent: $234; median house value: $54,700. Voting age pop. (1980): 379,038; 12% Black, 2% Spanish origin, 1% Asian origin.

1988 Presidential Vote: Bush (R) 139,824   (55%)
Dukakis (D). 110,623   (44%)

Rep. Christopher H. Smith (R)

Elected 1980; b. Mar. 4, 1953, Rahway; home, Hamilton Township; Worcester Col., England, 1974, Trenton St. Col., B.S. 1975; Roman Catholic; married (Marie).

Career: Sales exec., family-owned sporting goods business, 1975–80; Exec. Dir., NJ Right to Life, 1976–78; Legis. Agent, NJ Senate and Assembly, 1979.

Offices: 2440 RHOB 20515, 202-225-3765. Also 1720 Greenwood, Trenton 08609, 609-890-2800; 427 High St., Rm. 1, Burlington City 08016, 609-386-5534; and 655 Park Ave., Rte. 33, Freehold 07728, 201-780-0707.

Committees: *Foreign Affairs* (9th of 18 R). Subcommittees: Europe and the Middle East; Human Rights and International Organizations. *Veterans' Affairs* (5th of 13 R). Subcommittees: Education, Training and Employment (Ranking Member); Hospitals and Health Care. *Select Committee on Aging* (10th of 27 R). Subcommittee: Health and Long-Term Care. *Select Committee on Hunger* (5th of 12 R).

Group Ratings

	ADA	ACLU	COPE	CFA	LCV	ACU	NTLC	NSI	COC	CEI
1988	60	57	75	91	56	48	39	60	43	24
1987	52	—	71	64	—	39	—	—	53	23

National Journal Ratings

	1988 LIB — 1988 CONS		1987 LIB — 1987 CONS	
Economic	54%	44%	42%	56%
Social	45%	54%	42%	57%
Foreign	38%	61%	38%	62%

Key Votes

1) Homeless $	AGN	5) Ban Drug Test	AGN	9) SDI Research	FOR
2) Gephardt Amdt	FOR	6) Drug Death Pen	AGN	10) Ban Chem Weaps	FOR
3) Deficit Reduc	AGN	7) Handgun Sales	AGN	11) Aid to Contras	FOR
4) Kill Plnt Clsng Notice	AGN	8) Ban D.C. Abort $	FOR	12) Nuclear Testing	FOR

Election Results

1988 general	Christopher H. Smith (R)	115,283	(66%)	($252,823)
	Betty Holland (D)	79,006	(34%)	($53,964)
1988 primary	Christopher H. Smith (R), unopposed			
1986 general	Christopher H. Smith (R)	78,699	(61%)	($338,244)
	Jeffrey Laurenti (D)	49,290	(38%)	($304,077)

FIFTH DISTRICT

At the northern edge of New Jersey, just south of a dotted line stretching from the Palisades of the Hudson River to the hill-enclosed upper reaches of the Delaware, crossing one ridge of mountains after another, runs the 5th Congressional District. Two-thirds of the population is clustered in the eastern end, in Bergen County. Just west of the Palisades are affluent suburbs built along the old Dutch farm communities, in the valley of the Hackensack River and in the hills beyond. Half a century ago this land was only starting to be filled in, between the nuclei of old villages. Paramus, said the *WPA Guide*, was "an old Dutch farming community still growing vegetables for the city market. A wide area on both sides of State 2 is covered with a black muck, especially suited to celery growing, giving Paramus the name of Celery Town. Dutch colonists first settled here in 1666." Celery Town, indeed: Paramus today is criss-crossed by Routes 4 and 17 and the Garden State Parkway and is the site of several giant shopping centers. Not far away is Saddle River, with million-dollar houses on multi-acre lots, the latest home of that most migratory of Presidents, Richard Nixon. To the west, beyond the Ramapo Mountains, are little subdivisions filling up with young families set amid the lakes of western Passaic County; farther west is once rural, now fast-growing Sussex County.

This is an affluent district, historically heavily Protestant though quite varied ethnically now, and heavily Republican—often the most Republican in New Jersey. The congresswoman since 1980 has been Marge Roukema, who has always been well-positioned on issues for this affluent constituency. A teacher who gave up working to raise her children, she became involved in community activities before she became a political candidate—founding a senior citizens' housing corporation and serving on a local school board. Like some of the other Republican congresswomen, she brings to politics maturity and wide experience in the actual workings of civic institutions. She ran for the House in 1980 as an opponent of incumbent liberal Democrat Andrew Maguire's liberal economic and foreign policies, and she remains distinctly market-oriented on economics. But she also feels strongly that government should do more in some areas. She is co-sponsor, along with Bill Clay, of a bill to require large employers to grant family and medical leaves to employees, and criticized the national Republican Party for its opposition. She supported the 1988 welfare reform, tough penalties for failure to pay child support and sterner drug laws in the Education and Labor Committee and on the floor. She wants to get the government to do more to help the hungry; she opposes further cuts in federal housing spending. On child care, she favors incentive grants to the states and a tax credit for parents of small children. On education, she thinks better results will come not so much from spending more money as from making the system more accountable.

Both the problems Roukema identifies and the kinds of solutions she backs seem in line not just with voter sentiment, but with the fabric of life in the 5th District, and in many less affluent parts of America as well. Certainly she seems to win the approval of her constituents. Her first two elections were struggles: she challenged an incumbent in 1980, and she had to survive a musical chairs struggle after New Jersey lost a seat in redistricting. But she has been reelected without difficulty ever since, and seems to have a safe seat.

The People: Est. Pop. 1986: 536,800, up 2.0% 1980–86; Pop. 1980: 526,075, up 3.8% 1970–80. Households (1980): 84% family, 46% with children, 72% married couples; 17.3% housing units rented; median monthly rent: $306; median house value: $78,600. Voting age pop. (1980): 377,765; 2% Spanish origin, 1% Asian origin, 1% Black.

1988 Presidential Vote: Bush (R) 164,951   (66%)
                              Dukakis (D) 82,324   (33%)

Rep. Margaret S. (Marge) Roukema (R)

Elected 1980; b. Sept. 19, 1929, Newark; home, Ridgewood; Montclair St. Col., B.A. 1951, Rutgers U.; Protestant; married (Richard).

Career: High sch. teacher, 1951–55; Ridgewood Bd. of Educ., 1970–73; Cofounder, Ridgewood Sr. Citizens Housing Corp., 1973; Repub. Nominee for U.S. House of Reps., 1978.

Offices: 303 CHOB 20515, 202-225-4465. Also 58 Trinity St., Newton 07860, 201-579-3039; and 555 Rte. 17 S., Ridgewood 07450, 201-447-3900.

Committees: *Banking, Finance and Urban Affairs* (6th of 20 R). Subcommittees: Economic Stabilization; Financial Institutions Supervision, Regulation and Insurance; Housing and Community Development (Ranking Member). *Education and Labor* (4th of 13 R). Subcommittees: Elementary, Secondary and Vocational Education; Labor-Management Relations (Ranking Member); Postsecondary Education. *Select Committee on Hunger* (2d of 12 R).

Group Ratings

	ADA	ACLU	COPE	CFA	LCV	ACU	NTLC	NSI	COC	CEI
1988	40	28	34	73	81	50	62	80	69	30
1987	32	—	29	64	—	52	—	—	87	43

National Journal Ratings

	1988 LIB — 1988 CONS		1987 LIB — 1987 CONS	
Economic	35%	64%	35%	64%
Social	48%	51%	38%	61%
Foreign	45%	54%	46%	54%

Key Votes

1) Homeless $	FOR	5) Ban Drug Test	FOR	9) SDI Research	AGN
2) Gephardt Amdt	AGN	6) Drug Death Pen	FOR	10) Ban Chem Weaps	FOR
3) Deficit Reduc	AGN	7) Handgun Sales	AGN	11) Aid to Contras	FOR
4) Kill Plnt Clsng Notice	FOR	8) Ban D.C. Abort $	AGN	12) Nuclear Testing	AGN

Election Results

1988 general	Margaret S. (Marge) Roukema (R)	175,562	(76%)	($400,555)
	Lee Monaco (D)	54,828	(24%)	($14,083)
1988 primary	Margaret S. (Marge) Roukema (R), unopposed			
1986 general	Margaret S. (Marge) Roukema (R)	94,253	(75%)	($304,786)
	H. Vernon Jolley (D)	32,145	(25%)	($23,139)

SIXTH DISTRICT

It has been imitated thousands of times since, and has been altered beyond recognition today: the nation's first cloverleaf intersection, at the junction of U.S. 1 and U.S. 9 in Woodbridge, New Jersey. This is a crowded, industrial corner of the Garden State, just west of Staten Island and Arthur Kill, whose sluggish oily waters drain into Raritan Bay, Kill Van Kull and New York Bay. On the water inch giant tankers filled with crude oil and feedstock for the refineries and chemical plants of New Jersey; just inland, locomotives on the Conrail main line and trucks roaring along the 12-lane-wide New Jersey Turnpike that now dwarfs U.S. 1 are ready to ship refined oil and chemicals to the rest of the country. This heavily industrialized stretch of New Jersey, from Linden in Union County to south of Perth Amboy in Middlesex, and going inland to New Brunswick, forms the 6th Congressional District.

This is high-tech country too. Thomas Edison came here and set up his laboratory in Menlo Park, when it was still surrounded by fields but accessible to New York; and today it has some of the nation's biggest and most successful high-tech research operations that have been fueling New Jersey's vibrant growth in the 1980s. As a result, the descendants of the immigrants who came here two or three generations ago have been able to move up economically and intellectually and still live not far from their roots. The 6th District has the largest concentration of Hungarian-Americans in the nation, in and around New Brunswick; it also has sizeable neighborhoods of Italian-Americans in Woodbridge and Polish-Americans in Perth Amboy. You can still see little ethnic towns like Polish-American South River, while in the heavily cloverleafed surrounding area people are mixed.

The political tradition here is Democratic and machine-dominated, and the Middlesex County machine (headed for almost 50 years by the late David Wilentz who first gained fame in the 1930s as the prosecutor of accused Lindbergh kidnapper Bruno Hauptmann and whose Perth Amboy law office in later years somehow seemed to attract some of the nation's largest corporations as clients) has selected honest and competent, if rather lackluster, officeholders who have continued to win local elections. What they have not been able to do is to recapture the enthusiasm that made heavily Catholic Middlesex County vote 58% for John Kennedy in 1960; this generation's Massachusetts liberal, Michael Dukakis, won only 45% in Middlesex and 46% in the 6th District in 1988. As life here has become less distinctive and less visibly different from the experiences of other Americans, its political behavior has been, in the language of political scientists, regressing toward the mean.

The congressman from the 6th District is Bernard Dwyer, a Democrat chosen by the Wilentz machine in 1980 when he was a 59-year-old state senator and veteran Edison Township mayor and councilman. His voting record is on the liberal side of the spectrum, and not only on economic issues. He was always assumed to be a solid leadership man, and won important committee assignments as a result. He got a seat on Appropriations in his first term, and works hard and concentrates on details. He is busy getting more research funds for Princeton, Rutgers and New Jersey private companies, beginning the New York Bight Restoration Plan and getting outpatient veterans centers in New Jersey. He was tapped by Speaker O'Neill for a seat on the Intelligence Committee, where he still sits and has been a cautious opponent of contra aid, and by Speaker Wright for a seat on Budget, where he helps to determine general spending levels. But his most prominent assignment turned out to be the Ethics Committee, where he cast several crucial votes, along with Chet Atkins, against Wright in early 1989—an example of an organization Democrat voting his conscience on the basis of his own detailed study of the issues.

Dwyer depends on the Democratic organization to deliver votes for him, although that is a bit risky these days: in 1980 and 1984 he won only 53% and 56% of the vote. He did better in 1988, with 62%, and does not seem disposed to retire.

The People: Est. Pop. 1986: 548,900, up 4.3% 1980–86; Pop. 1980: 526,075, dn. 3.1% 1970–80. Households (1980): 77% family, 39% with children, 63% married couples; 36.9% housing units rented; median monthly rent: $259; median house value: $59,600. Voting age pop. (1980): 394,413; 8% Black, 5% Spanish origin, 1% Asian origin.

1988 Presidential Vote:　　Bush (R) . . . . 115,133　　(53%)
　　　　　　　　　　　　　　　Dukakis (D). . . . . 101,046　　(46%)

Rep. Bernard J. Dwyer (D)

Elected 1980; b. Jan. 24, 1921, Perth Amboy; home, Edison; Roman Catholic; married (Lilyan).

Career: Navy, WWII; Insur. exec., 1945–80; Edison Township Cncl., 1958–70; Mayor of Edison Township, 1970–74; NJ Senate, 1974–80.

Offices: 2428 RHOB 20515, 202-225-6301. Also 214 Smith St., Perth Amboy 08861, 201-826-4610; 86 Bayard St., New Brunswick 08901, 201-545-5655; and 628 Wood Ave. N., Linden 07036, 201-486-4600.

Committees: *Appropriations* (26th of 35 D). Subcommittees: Commerce, Justice, State, and Judiciary; Labor, Health and Human Services and Education. *Budget* (17th of 21 D). Task Forces: Budget Process, Reconciliation and Enforcement; Community Development and Natural Resources. *Standards of Official Conduct* (3d of 6 D). *Permanent Select Committee on Intelligence* (6th of 12 D). Subcommittees: Program and Budget Authorization; Oversight and Evaluation.

Group Ratings

	ADA	ACLU	COPE	CFA	LCV	ACU	NTLC	NSI	COC	CEI
1988	85	83	97	82	75	4	8	0	31	12
1987	84	—	96	64	—	0	—	—	7	8

National Journal Ratings

	1988 LIB — 1988 CONS		1987 LIB — 1987 CONS	
Economic	84%	— 15%	62%	— 35%
Social	83%	— 15%	73%	— 22%
Foreign	60%	— 37%	81%	— 0%

Key Votes

1) Homeless $	FOR	5) Ban Drug Test	AGN	9) SDI Research	AGN
2) Gephardt Amdt	FOR	6) Drug Death Pen	AGN	10) Ban Chem Weaps	FOR
3) Deficit Reduc	FOR	7) Handgun Sales	AGN	11) Aid to Contras	AGN
4) Kill Plnt Clsng Notice	AGN	8) Ban D.C. Abort $	AGN	12) Nuclear Testing	FOR

Election Results

1988 general	Bernard J. Dwyer (D)	120,125	(62%)	($123,632)
	Peter J. Sica (R)	74,827	(38%)	($38,919)
1988 primary	Bernard J. Dwyer (D), unopposed			
1986 general	Bernard J. Dwyer (D)	67,460	(69%)	($115,192)
	John D. Scalamonti (R)	28,286	(29%)	($18,461)

SEVENTH DISTRICT

"The colors of the town," wrote the *WPA Guide* of Elizabeth, New Jersey, 50 years ago, "with the exception of its greenery, are those of a manufacturing place; faded and stained reds, grays, yellows, and browns. Houses range from the yellow brick flats and nondescript frame structures of the poorer sections to the commuters' and businessmen's compact, modern homes in the early American or English cottage style." Even then, the radial highways running west from Elizabeth and Newark were already thickly settled. In the intervening five decades people have moved slowly out from the industrial city, with its oil tank farms and its main street running under both the Amtrak and Jersey Central tracks at "the Arch" through Union and Roselle, to Westfield and Scotch Plains and Somerville beneath the ridge of the First Watchung Mountain. As a political unit, this is the 7th Congressional District of New Jersey. The district offers a nice picture of American upward mobility. Elizabeth, its biggest city, now has a large Cuban and Puerto Rican population, poised it seems to move upward and out as generations of ethnics did before them. Out U.S. 22, once the main highway into New York, you pass through suburbs which once considered themselves WASPy, and are now a little more ethnic in flavor, with Italian and Spanish names and a black presence quite common (a solid majority in Plainfield) where they were seldom seen a generation ago. Up around the mountain are high-income enclaves like Summit, with successful local businessmen and professionals and some commuters who get the morning train to New York.

Historically, this territory is closely divided between the parties, although in national elections Elizabeth now is only slightly Democratic while most of the suburbs are more than 60% Republican. In congressional elections its tradition is to elect liberal Republicans, with voting records acceptable to organized labor, once important here, and to Jewish voters. The current congressman, Matthew Rinaldo, a Republican first elected in 1972, plays variations on this theme. Institutionally, there is no equivalent of the role labor once played in forestalling opposition for such incumbents; so Rinaldo has done it himself, by taking the popular position on just about every hot button issue and by using his now high-seniority seat on the Energy and Commerce Committee to raise huge amounts of campaign money. He is one of those congressmen ready to promise more aid regardless of how much it costs: with the social security system rescued again in the 1980s from financial ruin, Rinaldo sponsors more generous COLAs and increased survivor benefits, and votes for Claude Pepper's long-term health care plan. Without regard to revenue loss, he backs IRAs for homebuyers' down payments. He is a fearless crusader against dial-a-porn and ads on children's TV programs. He charges into the fray against acid rain, ocean dumping and local aircraft noise (though taking the lead only on the last). As ranking Republican on the Energy and Commerce Subcommittee on Telecommunications and Finance, with jurisdiction over the securities markets, he is eager to do something about insider trading and leveraged buyouts, though except for some minor changes in the law it is not clear what he has in mind.

What is clear is that Rinaldo has a marvelous instinct for the popular side of any issue. It helps, of course, to serve on Energy and Commerce, which under Chairman John Dingell has jurisdiction over just about every business in the country. The committee decides issues on which literally billions of dollars hang, and perhaps the fate of the economy: so Rinaldo in his quiet way has the potential of great influence indeed. On many issues the decision is between deregulation to spur competition and regulation to provide stability. Rinaldo is found with regulators on some issues (oil prices, trucking) and deregulators on others (telephones), in patterns that seem to be explained less by consistent convictions than by the politics of the interests involved. Rinaldo's view is that he decides issues on their merits on a case-by-case basis, and that his judgment is vindicated since he is reelected overwhelmingly every two years.

His popularity was tested in 1982, the most Democratic year in the last decade, when shopping center heir Adam Levin spent $2.3 million against him; Rinaldo, who spent $719,000 himself, won 56%–43%. He has had no serious competition since, and is not likely to.

The People: Est. Pop. 1986: 524,100, dn. 0.4% 1980–86; Pop. 1980: 526,076, dn. 6.8% 1970–80. Households (1980): 78% family, 38% with children, 64% married couples; 35.1% housing units rented; median monthly rent: $248; median house value: $73,300. Voting age pop. (1980): 393,910; 10% Black, 7% Spanish origin, 1% Asian origin.

1988 Presidential Vote: Bush (R) 132,400   (59%)
                              Dukakis (D). 90,800   (40%)

Rep. Matthew J. Rinaldo (R)

Elected 1972; b. Sept. 1, 1931, Elizabeth; home, Union; Rutgers U., B.S. 1953, Seton Hall U., M.B.A. 1959, NYU, D.P.A. 1979; Roman Catholic; single.

Career: Pres., Union Township, Zoning Bd. of Adjustment, 1962–63; Union Cnty. Bd. of Freeholders, 1963–64; NJ Senate, 1967–72.

Offices: 2469 RHOB 20515, 202-225-5361. Also 1961 Morris Ave., Union 07083, 201-687-4235; and 290 Rte. 22, Green Brook 08812, 201-981-9090.

Committees: *Energy and Commerce* (4th of 17 R). Subcommittees: Telecommunications and Finance (Ranking Member); Transportation and Hazardous Materials. *Select Committee on Aging* (Ranking Member of 26 R). Subcommittee: Health and Long-Term Care.

Group Ratings

	ADA	ACLU	COPE	CFA	LCV	ACU	NTLC	NSI	COC	CEI
1988	45	59	83	91	75	54	38	90	36	21
1987	56	—	82	71	—	39	—	—	47	29

National Journal Ratings

	1988 LIB — 1988 CONS	1987 LIB — 1987 CONS
Economic	54% — 44%	42% — 56%
Social	47% — 53%	51% — 48%
Foreign	30% — 67%	36% — 63%

Key Votes

1) Homeless $	AGN	5) Ban Drug Test	AGN	9) SDI Research	FOR
2) Gephardt Amdt	FOR	6) Drug Death Pen	FOR	10) Ban Chem Weaps	FOR
3) Deficit Reduc	AGN	7) Handgun Sales	AGN	11) Aid to Contras	FOR
4) Kill Plnt Clsng Notice	AGN	8) Ban D.C. Abort $	FOR	12) Nuclear Testing	AGN

Election Results

1988 general	Matthew J. Rinaldo (R)	153,350	(75%)	($370,387)
	James Hely (D)......................	52,189	(25%)	
1988 primary	Matthew J. Rinaldo (R), unopposed			
1986 general	Matthew J. Rinaldo (R)	92,254	(79%)	($387,616)
	June S. Fischer (D)...................	24,462	(21%)	($7,644)

EIGHTH DISTRICT

Paterson, New Jersey, wrote the *WPA Guide* 50 years ago, "is one of the few American cities that have turned out exactly as they were planned." The planner was none less than Alexander Hamilton, who in the 1790s journeyed 20 miles from Manhattan into the interior of New Jersey to the Great Falls of the Passaic River. Watching the water surge down 72 feet—the highest falls along the East Coast—he predicted that an industrial city would rise at this place. It did. Paterson became America's "Silk City," employing 25,000 silk mill workers before the great strike of 1913 led by the radical Industrial Workers of the World, at a time when the city fathers were erecting imposing public buildings and the narrow streets were buzzing with rumors of anarchist plots. Paterson also had big locomotive factories, and after the silk mills started closing down following another unsuccessful strike in 1924, it became a center of the cloth-dying industry. Throughout, it attracted immigrants from England, Ireland and, after the turn of the century, Italy and Poland.

Today Paterson is a kind of misfit in its time and place: still a manufacturing center at a time when manufacturing is no longer considered the nation's prime work, still an old fashioned central city, though it is surrounded by suburbs of New York and Newark and is an easy freeway ride away from the George Washington Bridge. Paterson is the center of New Jersey's 8th Congressional District, which includes most of the surrounding Passaic County communities and, to the south, Essex County's working-class Nutley and Belleville, white-collar Bloomfield and, up on the ridge with views of New York City, the mixed rich and black Montclair. To the north and west are the higher-income suburbs of Passaic County, notably Wayne Township. The political heritage of the 8th District is Democratic, less because of its radical past than because of the allegiances of its immigrant groups. But in recent political behavior, while Paterson, Passaic and Montclair remain Democratic, almost all the suburbs are heavily Republican. Only blacks remain a reliably Democratic group; the immigrants' blue-collar descendants are conservative on cultural issues, while the white-collar vote, as in many factory towns, is heavily Republican. The 8th District voted not only for Ronald Reagan in 1980 and 1984, but for George Bush in 1988.

The 8th District's congressman, Robert Roe, is now the dean of the New Jersey delegation; he first won in a special election in 1969. Appropriately for a congressman from a district whose economy was first built on water power, much of his congressional career has centered on water. He is second on the Public Works Committee, and it was the Water Resources Subcommittee which he chaired that fashioned the water projects bill of which Congress overrode President Reagan's veto in early 1987, making it the first major water projects bill to pass in 10 years. The bill had near-unanimous support on Capitol Hill—testimony to Roe's hard work and knowledge of detail, and to his willingness to lace the bill with projects for almost every Member's district, take your pick. Roe is an engineer, experienced in local government, a workaholic who is familiar with every detail in his bill. Not afraid of the charge of pork barrel politics, he has been willing to take on Presidents and beat them—as he took on Jimmy Carter in 1977 and Reagan 10 years later.

Roe is now chairman of the Science, Space and Technology Committee, on which he was less active until 1986. But after the space shuttle *Challenger* blew up, and with the retirement of the previous chairman, Roe became instantly more active and brought his habit of insisting on details into play. He supports the new shuttle program and the manned space station, but also wants to advance the less expensive and more far-ranging unmanned space exploration. But the Science Committee handles more than just the space program, and Roe has an exceptional opportunity here. He has conducted wide-ranging hearings on the super collider, biomedical products and the Anarctic ozone hole; he has passed bills encouraging commercial space vehicles, ending ocean sludge dumping, getting the government involved in nutrition monitoring and improving steel technology. He may have had something to do with EPA's decision to put their National Toxic Waste Center in the New Jersey Institute of Technology in Newark. These are not partisan issues, and Roe, knowledgeable, respected on both sides of Capitol Hill, has been effective in his position.

He was less effective when he ran for governor, finishing second in the 1977 primary to Brendan Byrne and second again, after he declined New Jersey's public financing, to James Florio in 1981. He got 86% and 71% in those races in Passaic County—strong showings which, together with his solid reelection percentages, suggest that he has a safe seat.

The People: Est. Pop. 1986: 536,300, up 2.0% 1980–86; Pop. 1980: 526,087, dn. 6.4% 1970–80. Households (1980): 74% family, 37% with children, 57% married couples; 48.8% housing units rented;

median monthly rent: $219; median house value: $66,900. Voting age pop. (1980): 390,558; 12% Black, 10% Spanish origin, 1% Asian origin.

1988 Presidential Vote:

Bush (R)	102,412	(53%)
Dukakis (D)	85,605	(45%)

Rep. Robert A. Roe (D)

Elected 1969; b. Feb. 28, 1924, Wayne; home, Wayne; OR St. U., WA St. U.; Roman Catholic; single.

Career: Army, WWII; Mbr., Wayne Township Cmtee., 1955–56; Mayor of Wayne Township, 1956–61; Mbr., Passaic Cnty. Bd. of Freeholders, 1959–63, Dir., 1962–63; Commissioner, NJ Dept. of Conserv. and Econ. Devel., 1963–69.

Offices: 2243 RHOB 20515, 202-225-5751. Also 158 Boonton Rd., Wayne 07470, 201-696-2077; 102 Law Bldg., 66 Hamilton St., Paterson 07505, 201-523-5152; and U.S. P.O. Bldg., Bloomfield Ave., Bloomfield 07003, 201-645-6299.

Committees: *Public Works and Transportation* (2d of 31 D). Subcommittees: Investigations and Oversight; Surface Transportation; Water Resources. *Science, Space and Technology* (Chairman of 30 D). Subcommittee: Investigations and Oversight (Chairman). *Permanent Select Committee on Intelligence* (4th of 12 D). Subcommittee: Oversight and Evaluation.

Group Ratings

	ADA	ACLU	COPE	CFA	LCV	ACU	NTLC	NSI	COC	CEI
1988	70	68	91	82	56	13	8	10	21	11
1987	80	—	91	64	—	9	—	—	23	0

National Journal Ratings

	1988 LIB — 1988 CONS		1987 LIB — 1987 CONS	
Economic	87% —	8%	73% —	0%
Social	66% —	34%	53% —	46%
Foreign	60% —	37%	71% —	27%

Key Votes

1) Homeless $	AGN	5) Ban Drug Test	AGN	9) SDI Research	AGN
2) Gephardt Amdt	FOR	6) Drug Death Pen	FOR	10) Ban Chem Weaps	FOR
3) Deficit Reduc	FOR	7) Handgun Sales	AGN	11) Aid to Contras	AGN
4) Kill Plnt Clsng Notice	AGN	8) Ban D.C. Abort $	FOR	12) Nuclear Testing	FOR

Election Results

1988 general	Robert A. Roe (D), unopposed			($267,609)
1988 primary	Robert A. Roe (D), unopposed			
1986 general	Robert A. Roe (D)	57,820	(63%)	($298,400)
	Thomas P. Zampino (R)	14,699	(37%)	($14,848)

NINTH DISTRICT

One of the great American success stories of the 1980s is the development of the Jersey Meadowlands. Until the middle 1970s this was a giant swamp on both sides of the Hackensack River before it emptied into Newark Bay, known for its landscape of gas stations and their giant signs, oil tank farms, truck terminals and 12 lanes of New Jersey Turnpike. The Meadowlands symbolized the old New Jersey—a smelly, ugly place that meant that you were still not where you wanted to go. But in the 1970s, during Brendan Byrne's term as governor, the state built the Meadowlands Sports Complex—including Giants Stadium (Giants and Jets), the Meadowlands Racetrack and the Meadowlands (formerly Brendan Byrne) Arena (Nets and Devils)—at the intersection of the Turnpike and Route 3, and set the stage for private development. At first mostly warehouses were built. But developers noted a demand for offices and hotels, and now the biggest of them—Hartz Mountain—is building what amount to cities; about 100,000 people now work in what was once a swamp.

The Meadowlands are the focus of New Jersey's 9th Congressional District, made up of cities, towns and boroughs around and north of the Meadows complexes. Huddled to the west on high land overlooking the Passaic River are the old towns like Rutherford and Carlstadt, peopled with Polish, German and Italian-Americans; with Secaucus, in Hudson County, they have most of the Meadowlands within their limits. Another major part of the 9th District, with almost half its population, is a series of towns running along the spine of land which forms the Palisades along the Hudson River. This area, psychologically and almost physically, is part of New York City. The giant apartment complexes in Fort Lee and Cliffside Park advertise the good view they have of New York they have and how easy it is to get into the city on an express bus; these are renter and condominium towns where people have only the vaguest sense that they are in New Jersey. Farther north and west are suburbs on the roads that lead into the George Washington Bridge: the leafy and pleasantly aged Englewood; Alpine; Teaneck, a predominantly Jewish suburb of somewhat more recent vintage; Hackensack, an old industrial town that is the Bergen County seat; and Fair Lawn, a planned town with a large Jewish population. Demographically, this area was growing in the 1950s and 1960s, as New Yorkers moved out of the City; it lost population in the 1970s, as young people moved out and left empty nesters; parts of it, the Meadowlands and the apartment towns, have been gaining in the 1980s.

Politically, these southern Bergen County towns mostly have a Republican heritage: they voted against Franklin Roosevelt and his Democrats throughout the depression, little white-collar enclaves where people struggled to get by on their paychecks and resented the idea of their taxes going to the political machines of Hudson County and New York City. In the years since, Englewood, Teaneck and other towns near the Bridge have become more Democratic as they have become extensions of the Upper West Side, while the old ethnic towns in the Meadowlands have trended Republican. The balance today is pretty close: George Bush carried the 9th District 53%–46%—his national average.

The congressman from the 9th is Robert Torricelli, who started off as an aide to Brendan Byrne and Walter Mondale in the 1970s and was politically able enough to have been the resident director of the Carter-Mondale campaign in Illinois six months before the 1980 primary—Carter's crucial victory over Edward Kennedy—and to have been Carter's leading spokesman on the rules at the 1980 Democratic National Convention. In 1982 he returned home to New Jersey, amassed a substantial campaign treasury and took on Republican Representative Harold Hollenbeck, who had a generally liberal record but had voted for the Reagan economic program and against gun control. Torricelli won 53%–46% and has been reelected without trouble since.

He has shown his political acumen by taking committee assignments seemingly removed from local affairs and making them political assets. On the Foreign Affairs Committee, he is not surprisingly a strong supporter of Israel, but has also paid close attention to Greece, Korea and the Philippines—countries of great interest to some in the 9th. On Central America, he went down to El Salvador and personally recovered the body of a Bergen County journalist killed there; he has opposed contra aid, though he insists that he will demand that the Sandinistas stop violating human rights in return for the cutoff. As for the Science and Technology Committee, North Jersey, though not so glamorous perhaps as Massachusetts or California, is one of the most important research and development centers for the rest of the country; it is the home, most notably, of Bell Labs, perhaps the single most consistently productive research facility in history. Torricelli is a supporter of manned (and therefore expensive) space flight, urging a new space shuttle after the *Challenger* blew up, backing a joint American-Soviet manned flight to Mars. Torricelli has also used his Science seat to push a Superfund amendment for better toxic waste technology and to clean up toxic thorium in Maywood. On other issues, he is a strong supporter of gun control and has a bill to require universal national service. Torricelli also served as a member of Jim Wright's legal defense team during Wright's final weeks as Speaker.

But Torricelli's interests don't seem limited to Congress—or maybe to politics. He has been eyeing the governorship of New Jersey for some time, and staked out positions—for mass transit and gun control, for state land-use control—on state issues. He was harshly critical of 1985 gubernatorial candidate Peter Shapiro after he lost (as he was of his former boss Walter Mondale in 1984 and the candidate he endorsed in 1988, Richard Gephardt). But in the summer of 1988 he endorsed South Jersey Congressman James Florio, the 1981 Democratic gubernatorial nominee, in part to beat Senate president John Russo. In January 1989 Russo left the race, but that leaves Torricelli out of the governor's race in that year and probably until 1997—rather long for this hard-charging young man to wait. Torricelli has hinted that he may go on to something else: "I consider public life to be a stage of life." In the meantime, unless he shows uncharacteristic lassitude on the job, he seems sure to be reelected comfortably in the 9th district and to continue as an active Member of the House, if he wants.

The People: Est. Pop. 1986: 517,900, dn. 1.5% 1980–86; Pop. 1980: 526,066, dn. 6.0% 1970–80. Households (1980): 72% family, 31% with children, 60% married couples; 45.9% housing units rented; median monthly rent: $270; median house value: $67,800. Voting age pop. (1980): 415,175; 5% Black, 4% Spanish origin, 2% Asian origin.

1988 Presidential Vote:

Bush (R)	122,284	(53%)
Dukakis (D)	105,839	(46%)

Rep. Robert G. Torricelli (D)

Elected 1982; b. Aug. 26, 1951, Paterson; home, Englewood; Rutgers U., B.A. 1974, J.D., 1977, JFK Sch. of Govt., Harvard U., M.P.A. 1980; United Methodist; married (Susan).

Career: Asst. to NJ Gov. Brendan Byrne, 1975–77; Cnsl. to Vice Pres. Walter Mondale, 1978–81; Practicing atty., 1981–82.

Offices: 317 CHOB 20515, 202-225-5061. Also 25 Main St., Court Plaza, Hackensack 07601, 201-646-1111.

Committees: *Foreign Affairs* (12th of 28 D). Subcommittees: Asian and Pacific Affairs; Europe and the Middle East. *Science, Space and Technology* (14th of 30 D). Subcommittees: Space Science and Applications; International Scientific Cooperation.

Group Ratings

	ADA	ACLU	COPE	CFA	LCV	ACU	NTLC	NSI	COC	CEI
1988	85	73	94	82	69	4	9	10	25	13
1987	84	—	93	86	—	5	—	—	15	3

National Journal Ratings

	1988 LIB — 1988 CONS			1987 LIB — 1987 CONS		
Economic	79%	—	17%	73%	—	0%
Social	73%	—	25%	68%	—	31%
Foreign	68%	—	28%	76%	—	19%

Key Votes

1) Homeless $	AGN	5) Ban Drug Test	—	9) SDI Research	AGN
2) Gephardt Amdt	FOR	6) Drug Death Pen	FOR	10) Ban Chem Weaps	FOR
3) Deficit Reduc	FOR	7) Handgun Sales	AGN	11) Aid to Contras	AGN
4) Kill Plnt Clsng Notice	AGN	8) Ban D.C. Abort $	AGN	12) Nuclear Testing	FOR

Election Results

1988 general	Robert G. Torricelli (D)	142,012	(68%)	($403,059)
	Roger J. Lane (R).	68,363	(32%)	($57,260)
1988 primary	Robert G. Torricelli (D), unopposed			
1986 general	Robert G. Torricelli (D)	89,634	(69%)	($408,779)
	Arthur F. Jones (R).	40,226	(31%)	($64,091)

TENTH DISTRICT

"The metropolis of New Jersey," the *WPA Guide* called it as America was about to go to war, was "the focus of the vast complex of industrial and suburban cities that modern machinery and transport has made of the northeastern corner of the state." By 1940, "this two-century-old city presents the picture of a huge industrial beehive built over the staid old seaport and local market center that was once Newark." Its skyscrapers looked across the Jersey Meadows to Manhattan, its "Four Corners" at Broad and Market was called the third busiest intersection in the United States, its three big businesses—Bamberger's, the Prudential and Public Service Corporation—employed 22,000 people downtown. "It has been said that every kind of product sold in the United States is manufactured in Newark," the *Guide* continued, and the city was known for its fine parks and its "uniformly excellent school system."

Today no one would describe Newark in such terms. The city still has many big factories, and Prudential and Public Service have kept their headquarters downtown. But their new employment has all been in the suburbs, and in the rapidly growing New Jersey of the 1980s, Newark has been not a vibrant center but something more like an empty core. With a falling population and a high crime rate, neighborhoods that are emptying out and public facilities that have become empty husks, Newark today is one of America's sadder cities.

What happened in between is a story of political corruption, racial change and increasing violence that made many of Newark's old neighborhoods unlivable, as the city's population declined from 438,000 in 1950 to 329,000 in 1988. The key event was the major riot of 1967; after that not only many of the city's whites but most of its middle-class blacks fled to the suburbs, leaving behind a population with high unemployment and serious problems. The Jews who once lived in Philip Roth's Weequahic Park have long since moved to places like Maplewood and Short Hills; the Irish have vanished far beyond the city limits into Livingston or West Orange; the Yankees are now even farther away in Morris or Somerset Counties. But many Italians stayed behind in the North Ward in close-knit neighborhoods where everyone knows everyone else, there is little crime or violence, and people still speak Italian in the streets and shops. Blacks have been moving west and south instead of north: to East Orange (83% black in 1980), Orange (57%), Irvington (38%), Hillside (30%) and high-income South Orange (10%).

All these suburbs except the last, plus Newark and a few precincts in Belleville just above the North Ward, make up the 10th Congressional District of New Jersey. For 40 years the 10th and its predecessor districts were represented by Congressman Peter Rodino. First elected in 1948, replacing the Republican co-author of the Taft-Hartley Act, Rodino was a young Roosevelt Democrat, who for years labored quietly in Washington and at home; where others sought publicity and some sought money, he just wanted to do his duty. Suddenly in 1973 he was thrust into the national spotlight as the chairman of the Judiciary Committee considering the impeachment of Richard Nixon, and he performed superbly: at a careful pace, with fairness to those on all sides of the issue, insisting on a thorough sifting of the facts and consideration of legal precedent, and then shepherding the committee through its vote soberly and with dignity. Rodino remained an active chairman afterwards, bottling up bills and amendments he considered unconstitutional or unwise, while pushing through measures like the Immigration Reform Act of 1986. At home he suddenly found himself with a black-majority district beginning in 1972. But Rodino had always worked closely with black constituents and fought for civil rights bills; his standing with black voters was strong enough that he beat several strong black challengers in primaries and was elected eight times from a black-majority district before he decided to retire at 79 in 1988—typically spending his last session in a whirlwind of legislative activity.

The new congressman, Donald Payne, ran against Rodino in 1986 (though he praised him often and said nothing negative about him) and had the support of Newark Mayor Sharpe James (who had just beaten Kenneth Gibson, a Rodino backer) and Jesse Jackson. But he won just 36% then; with Rodino out of the race, he got 73% against another black in 1988. The general election was not seriously contested, and Payne became the first black Member of Congress from New Jersey. He got good committee assignments—Education and Labor, Foreign Affairs and the Africa Subcommittee, plus Government Operations—which take advantage of his experience both in civic affairs in Newark and in foreign aid and development. He recognized in his campaign that drugs was the major issue in the district, and called for more community involvement as well as government action. But he is upbeat about Newark's prospects, citing new housing starts and a new industrial park; it has one of Governor Thomas Kean's enterprise zones. Certainly his own prospects for continued reelection appear good.

The People: Est. Pop. 1986: 513,900, dn. 2.3% 1980–86; Pop. 1980: 525,886, dn. 8.8% 1970–80. Households (1980): 69% family, 42% with children, 39% married couples; 74.6% housing units rented; median monthly rent: $197; median house value: $37,000. Voting age pop. (1980): 360,309; 54% Black, 12% Spanish origin, 1% Asian origin.

1988 Presidential Vote:

Dukakis (D)	90,963	(74%)
Bush (R)	24,123	(20%)
Others	7,362	(6%)

Rep. Donald M. Payne (D)

Elected 1988; b. July 16, 1934, Newark; home, Newark; Seton Hall U., B.A. 1957; Baptist; widowed.

Career: Exec., Prudential Ins. Co.; Vice Pres., Urban Data Systems, Inc.; Pres., YMCAs of USA; Essex Cnty. Bd. of Chosen Freeholders, 1972–78, Dir. 1977–78; Newark Mun. Cncl., 1982–89.

Offices: 417 CHOB 20515, 202-225-3436. Also Fed. Bldg., 970 Broad St., Ste. 1435-B, Newark 07102, 201-645-3213.

Committees: *Foreign Affairs* (28th of 28 D). Subcommittee: Africa. *Education and Labor* (14th of 22 D). Subcommittees: Elementary, Secondary and Vocational Education; Labor Standards; Select Education. *Government Operations* (23d of 24 D). Subcommittee: Human Resources and Intergovernmental Relations.

Group Ratings and Key Votes: Newly Elected

Election Results

1988 general	Donald M. Payne (D)	84,681	(86%)	($413,338)
	Michael Webb (R)	13,848	(14%)	
1988 primary	Donald M. Payne (D)	40,608	(73%)	
	Ralph T. Grant, Jr. (D)	14,908	(27%)	
1986 general	Peter W. Rodino, Jr. (D)	46,666	(96%)	($407,220)
	Chris Brandlon (R)	1,977	(4%)	

ELEVENTH DISTRICT

Fifty years ago, if you traveled west of the First and Second Watchung Mountains—the ridges that overlook Newark and the valley of the Passaic River—you were out in the country. This part of New Jersey, western Essex County and Morris County farther west—were, to be sure, fairly densely settled, with many little towns that could trace their histories back to colonial times and farmlands with mostly small plots. And you could find some suburban subdivisions, starting with West Orange's Llewellyn Park, developed in the 19th century and the home of Thomas Edison and his bride, and nearby South Orange, a small high-income suburb of Newark. In the half century since, the land west from West Orange going far out into Morris County, following Interstate 280 and then 80 west—land that today makes up the 11th Congressional District of New Jersey—has become suburbanized, as Newark and the New York metropolitan area generally have spread westward over hills, swamps and mountain ridges. The magnitude of the movement is graspable if you remember that there were 400,000 whites living within the Newark city limits in 1940 and about 75,000 today.

It took some time for the congressional district boundary lines to catch up with this movement. Newark for years was split among three House districts, all of them Republican through most of the 1940s; one was represented by Governor Thomas Kean's father until 1958, but the other two were captured by Democrats—Peter Rodino and Hugh Addonizio—in 1948. Newark lost one of these seats in the 1966 redistricting, and all of the city was concentrated in Rodino's district in 1972. Finally, the redistricting for 1984 produced the current 11th, which is as heavily Republican as Newark was 50 years ago—and partly for the good reason that the voters here include the grandchildren of many of the voters there. The largest town in the 11th is not even in Essex County, but is a Morris County township with the ungainly name of Parsippany-Troy Hills. It is overall a very Republican district, with only speckles of Democratic territory here and there. Outsiders may assume that people here feel they are part of metropolitan New York. But they tend to identify more with Newark or with New Jersey generally. Most people here work in New Jersey rather than commute to the city; they enjoy entertainment and cultural events more often at home than in New York; they share much more of the traditional cultural outlook you would find in a suburb of Chicago or even Indianapolis rather than the one that might embrace the latest fashion or intellectual trend found in Manhattan.

The congressman from the 11th is Dean Gallo, a Republican who grew up in the mill town of Boonton, where iron ore once came down from the Delaware River in canals, and who served on the Parsippany-Troy Hills Council, on the Morris County Board of Freeholders, and in the New Jersey Assembly. There he was a Republican leader working closely with Kean, and he shares Kean's liking for positive governmental action and low tax rates. In the House, Gallo has worked closely with Democrats, including Robert Roe from the next-door 8th District, on such Public Works issues as ocean dumping, toxic waste cleanup and hazardous waste transportation procedures. Gallo backs the Clean Air Act to get rid of acid rain. He also backs catastrophic health insurance and takes an interest in home health care; in 1989, he unsnarled a local medicare funding problem that was about to force patients to pay hospitals in cash.

In 1989, Gallo moved from Public Works to Appropriations and Budget. He promises to work on the deficit, and backs the line-item veto and the balanced budget constitutional amendment. But most likely he will continue to emphasize local and New Jersey issues and to approach them in a problem-solving mode. Also, he is the chairman of his 12th District colleague Jim Courter's campaign for governor.

Gallo first won the seat by taking 56% of the vote against incumbent Democrat Joseph Minish, a low-key Democrat with few achievements who had always relied on old organization retainers and the Democratic label to reelect him. Since then, Gallo has won easily and has a safe seat.

The People: Est. Pop. 1986: 535,900, up 1.9% 1980–86; Pop. 1980: 526,078, up 2.6% 1970–80. Households (1980): 82% family, 44% with children, 71% married couples; 24.5% housing units rented; median monthly rent: $299; median house value: $78,300. Voting age pop. (1980): 381,844; 2% Spanish origin, 2% Black, 2% Asian origin.

1988 Presidential Vote: Bush (R) 156,769   (64%)
                             Dukakis (D). 85,011   (35%)

Rep. Dean A. Gallo (R)

Elected 1984; b. Nov. 23, 1935, Hackensack; home, Parsippany; United Methodist; divorced.

Career: Parsippany-Troy Hills Cncl., 1968–71, Pres., 1970–71; Morris Cnty. Bd. of Freeholders, 1971–1975, Dir., 1973–75; NJ House of Reps., 1975–84.

Offices: 1318 LHOB 20515, 202-225-5035. Also 22 N. Sussex St., Dover 07801, 201-328-7413; 101 Gilbraltar Dr., Ste. 2D, Morris Plains 07950, 201-984-0711; and 3 Fairfield Ave., W. Caldwell 07006, 201-228-9262.

Committees: *Appropriations* (22d of 22 R). Subcommittees: District of Columbia (Ranking Member); Foreign Operations, Export Financing and Related Programs. *Budget* (12th of 14 R). Subcommittee: Budget Process, Reconciliation and Enforcement.

Group Ratings

	ADA	ACLU	COPE	CFA	LCV	ACU	NTLC	NSI	COC	CEI
1988	30	52	40	64	63	72	70	100	79	47
1987	32	—	43	50	—	57	—	—	67	51

National Journal Ratings

	1988 LIB — 1988 CONS		1987 LIB — 1987 CONS	
Economic	18%	— 82%	33%	— 66%
Social	36%	— 64%	41%	— 59%
Foreign	16%	— 78%	0%	— 80%

Key Votes

1) Homeless $	FOR	5) Ban Drug Test	FOR	9) SDI Research	FOR
2) Gephardt Amdt	AGN	6) Drug Death Pen	FOR	10) Ban Chem Weaps	AGN
3) Deficit Reduc	AGN	7) Handgun Sales	AGN	11) Aid to Contras	FOR
4) Kill Plnt Clsng Notice	FOR	8) Ban D.C. Abort $	AGN	12) Nuclear Testing	AGN

Election Results

1988 general	Dean A. Gallo (R)	154,654	(70%)	($490,751)
	John C. Shaw (D)	64,773	(30%)	
1988 primary	Dean A. Gallo (R), unopposed			
1986 general	Dean A. Gallo (R)	75,037	(68%)	($660,059)
	Frank Askin (D)	35,280	(32%)	($167,857)

TWELFTH DISTRICT

In January 1935, Flemington, New Jersey, was the news center of the world, during the trial of Bruno Hauptmann for the kidnapping of Charles Lindbergh Jr. Only 50 miles west of New York, Flemington was for the *WPA Guide* the essence of small town America: "Here in a setting of white, green-shuttered houses, business makes haste slowly. There is still a general store where the latest sheet music dangles invitingly over silk hose, and penny candy fills a counter carrying a copy of Pearson and Allen's *Nine Old Men*, a testament to the existence of open minds in this conservative stronghold. The cars parked near the County Courthouse seldom bestir themselves the day long, and the side streets are all but deserted. Just opposite, the four-story Union Hotel—a lumbering, Hudson-River-bracketed structure of nondescript date, sparrow-grass architecture, tall double-decker porches, and the genial vapidity of the nineties—serves the barristers who amble back and forth across the street to the courthouse."

Today Flemington is not yet home to a high-rise cluster of office parks, but it is just nine miles off Interstate 78, and the tide of metropolitan growth is reaching out to embrace it. Flemington, geographically and perhaps otherwise, is the center of New Jersey's 12th Congressional District, which starts off in some of the state's metropolitan corridors and proceeds west to the Delaware River. Its jagged, irregular boundaries take in the campus of Princeton University and the horse farm country around Far Hills and Bernardsville, the Delaware Water Gap and the Great Swamp National Wildlife Refuge near Morristown. It includes most of the Princeton corridor, the area along U.S. 1 that is becoming the state's biggest office center (and producing some of its worst traffic jams) in what used to be boring countryside. Most of the 12th District is white-collar, high-tech, affluent and solidly Republican, though it does include a few Democratic mill towns, and Princeton, once a Republican bastion, is now culturally liberal and safely Democratic. Fifty years ago there were only about one-third as many people within the current 12th District's limits as were needed for a congressional district, and old-time politicos looking at its boundaries may scratch their heads and wonder where the city is with enough people to entitle this countryside to its own representative. But there are plenty of people and plenty of Republican voters.

The 12th District's congressman, Jim Courter, is a Republican with an unusual background whose original ideas and strength of conviction have made him an important Member of the House and an important figure in New Jersey state politics. Courter started out as a Peace Corps volunteer and a legal services lawyer—the sort of background that has produced many liberal Democrats—but he emerged a strong conservative. Settling in Hackettstown, a town much like Flemington, he ran for Congress in 1978, won his Republican primary by 134 votes, and beat incumbent Democrat Helen Meyner 52%–48%. Courter was a leading supporter of Ronald Reagan's 1980 campaign when you didn't find many in New Jersey, and an early backer of Governor Thomas Kean in 1981.

Some of Courter's critics argue that he's not a consistent conservative; he has in fact been one of the Republicans who have been redefining its terms. He strongly favored the Kemp-Roth tax cut and the Reagan military buildup; he has backed civil rights measures, enterprise zones and the Martin Luther King holiday; he voted for the plant closing notification law and pushed a ban on offshore oil and gas drilling off New Jersey. To some, this combination of views may seem anomalous. But Courter is intellectually consistent by his own rights, and his combinations of positions are similar to those of Jack Kemp and Thomas Kean.

In the House, Courter's greatest influence has been on things military. He serves on the Armed Services Committee, where he is one of the most intellectually active members. He is an enthusiastic backer of the Strategic Defense Initiative, an advocate of abrogating the ABM treaty, a supporter of the reform strengthening the chairman of the Joint Chiefs of Staff, a strong advocate of building the MX missile and giving military aid to the Nicaraguan contras. On SDI he has been particularly effective, prodding even President Reagan to move ahead more aggressively on the program. He is also well thought of by the Republican leadership and was appointed to the committee investigating the Iran-contra scandal.

Courter has a safe seat in the House (he avoided a musical chairs primary in 1982 when Millicent Fenwick ran for the Senate), but some of his allies—Kemp, Trent Lott—are gone and for several years he has been aiming at running for governor. He even missed the crucial vote for Republican whip in March 1989 because he was in New Jersey campaigning and declined the offer of a plane to fly him back to Washington, though as it turned out his rather uncharacteristic support of Edward Madigan over Newt Gingrich would have made Gingrich's margin one vote rather than two. Although by early 1989 Kean had not endorsed anyone, Courter's instincts on policies are similar: he believes in lower taxes, in encouraging the vibrant private sector growth that has been booming in New Jersey, in improving education not just by spending more money but by helping people learn, in making sure that blacks and other minorities have real opportunities. Against desultory opposition in his 1988 campaign, he waged one of the nation's most expensive House races and bought New York TV; that probably helped him win the governor's race in early 1989 against primary opponents Chuck Hardwick and Cary Edwards. Courter's greater strength will be the intellectual originality and the strong motivation he has brought to his career in the House; and if can beat the Democratic candidate, 1st District Congressman James Florio, he may well become as important a national political figure as Kean has been.

The People: Est. Pop. 1986: 571,600, up 8.7% 1980–86; Pop. 1980: 526,063, up 11.8% 1970–80. Households (1980): 80% family, 43% with children, 69% married couples; 26.5% housing units rented; median monthly rent: $275; median house value: $74,000. Voting age pop. (1980): 380,628; 5% Black, 2% Asian origin, 2% Spanish origin.

1988 Presidential Vote Bush (R) 162,819   (62%)
Dukakis (D). 98,355   (37%)

Rep. James A. (Jim) Courter (R)

Elected 1978; b. Oct. 14, 1941, Montclair; home, Hackettstown; Colgate U., B.A. 1963, Duke U., J.D. 1966; United Methodist; married (Carmen).

Career: Peace Corps, Venezuela, 1967–69; Practicing atty., 1969–70; Atty., Union Cnty. Legal Svcs., 1970–71; 1st Asst. Warren Cnty. Prosecutor, 1973–77.

Offices: 2422 RHOB, 202-225-5801. Also P.O. Bldg., 1 Morris St., Morristown 07960, 201-538-7267; and 3084 Rte. 27, Ste. 12, Kendall Park 08824, 201-297-1550.

Committees: *Armed Services* (4th of 21 R). Subcommittees: Procurement and Military Nuclear Systems (Ranking Member); Military Installations and Facilities. *Select Committee on Aging* (7th of 26 R). Subcommittee: Health and Long-Term Care.

Group Ratings

	ADA	ACLU	COPE	CFA	LCV	ACU	NTLC	NSI	COC	CEI
1988	25	32	31	55	56	74	63	100	62	41
1987	24	—	27	64	—	57	—	—	62	53

National Journal Ratings

	1988 LIB — 1988 CONS		1987 LIB — 1987 CONS	
Economic	34%	— 65%	33%	— 66%
Social	33%	— 67%	41%	— 58%
Foreign	22%	— 76%	0%	— 80%

Key Votes

1) Homeless $	FOR	5) Ban Drug Test	—	9) SDI Research	FOR
2) Gephardt Amdt	AGN	6) Drug Death Pen	FOR	10) Ban Chem Weaps	AGN
3) Deficit Reduc	—	7) Handgun Sales	AGN	11) Aid to Contras	FOR
4) Kill Plnt Clsng Notice	AGN	8) Ban D.C. Abort $	FOR	12) Nuclear Testing	AGN

Election Results

1988 general	James A. (Jim) Courter (R)	165,918	(70%)	($1,333,882)
	Norman J. Weinstein (D)	71,559	(30%)	($13,556)
1988 primary	James A. (Jim) Courter (R)	25,816	(89%)	
	Thomas Young (R)	3,177	(11%)	
1986 general	James A. (Jim) Courter (R)	72,966	(63%)	($779,078)
	David B. Crabiel (D)	41,967	(37%)	($318,869)

THIRTEENTH DISTRICT

The Pine Barrens of New Jersey as late as 1940 were a backward land, described by the *WPA Guide* as,"a deep scrub forest threaded by occasional trails and a few wretched roads, unmarked and not safe for automobile travel except in dry weather. The inhabitants are called the Pineys, and gain some income by cutting timber, and by gathering sphagnum moss, cranberries, and huckleberries." Not many years before, a researcher had found the Pineys inbred, with no formal marriage; "no one knows how many tiny hovels of cast-off cranberry boxes and miscellaneous lumber still remain the recesses of the pine forest." The Barrens are no longer terra incognita, but they are still not thickly populated; encroached by the Philadelphia suburbs of South Jersey on the west and the burgeoning retirement developments of the Jersey Shore on the east, they are crossed even today mostly by narrow two-lane roads and are the site of the Army's Fort Dix and the Great Adventure theme park. For years, the Barrens were seen as a barrier to civilization; only recently have environmentally-minded Jerseyites decided that their natural ecology should be preserved.

New Jersey's 13th Congressional District spans the Pine Barrens. Two-thirds of its residents are in the Philadelphia orbit, in the more affluent of the south Jersey suburbs of Philadelphia, close-in enclaves like Collingswood and the newer, more spread out Cherry Hill. One-third are on the other side of the Barrens in Ocean County, including the barrier islands from Seaside Park south to Little Egg Inlet and the inland townships with their new apartment complexes and the beachfront communities on the Long Beach sand spit facing the ocean. As you get further away from the Delaware River with its oil tank farms and factories, the suburbs get more Republican. Ocean County politically is much like Florida, with a large and relatively affluent elderly population, conservative on cultural issues and on taxes, but determined to extract the largest possible social security benefits and concerned about the local environment.

Congressman James Saxton was a real estate broker who served nine years in the legislature, the kind of locally connected politician who is cautiously conservative about most national issues but cares about the home district first. He was one of the original sponsors of the 1988 ocean dumping law, which bans plastics dumping and requires tracing of medical waste—this was the hottest issue on the Shore that year. He wants to do something about the acid rain that hurts the Pinelands and he voted for Claude Pepper's long-term health care bill. He uses his seat on Merchant Marine and Fisheries to do something about red tides on the Shore and is working on the plutonium cleanup at a district missile site. He serves on the Banking Committee and wistfully strives to do something to make local housing in booming South Jersey more affordable.

Saxton's key election was the 1984 Republican primary. It was a regional contest in which Saxton carried his home county of Burlington with 85% and lost Camden only narrowly to a Cherry Hill candidate, while his main opponent won 84% in Ocean County; overall that gave him a 45%–41%–14% victory. Saxton's heavy concentration on Shore issues since then can be seen as a so far successful attempt to forestall any Ocean County primary challenge, so far. The Democrats have not seriously contested this seat, though Senator Frank Lautenberg came close to carrying the district in his 1988 Senate race.

The People: Est. Pop. 1986: 584,200, up 11.1% 1980–86; Pop. 1980: 526,062, up 29.0% 1970–80. Households (1980): 81% family, 42% with children, 70% married couples; 18.8% housing units rented; median monthly rent: $244; median house value: $50,100. Voting age pop. (1980): 377,446; 7% Black, 2% Spanish origin, 1% Asian origin.

1988 Presidential Vote:

Bush (R)	159,742	(61%)
Dukakis (D)	98,736	(38%)

Rep. H. James Saxton (R)

Elected 1984; b. Jan. 22, 1943, Scranton, PA; home, Vincentown; East Stroudsburg St. Col., B.A. 1965, Temple U., 1967–68; United Methodist; married (Helen).

Career: Teacher, 1965–68; Real estate broker, 1968–84; NJ House of Reps., 1975–81; NJ Senate, 1981–84.

Offices: 324 CHOB 20515, 202-225-4765. Also P.O. Box 38., Mt. Holly 08060, 609-261-5800; 1 Maine Ave., Cherry Hill 08002, 609-428-0520; and 23 Crestwood Village Shopping Ctr., Schoolhouse Rd., Whiting 08759, 201-350-3535.

Committees: *Banking, Finance and Urban Affairs* (14th of 20 R). Subcommittees: Consumer Affairs and Coinage; Financial Institutions Supervision, Regulation and Insurance; Housing and Community Development; International Development, Finance, Trade and Monetary Policy. *Merchant Marine and Fisheries* (8th of 17 R). Subcommittees: Fisheries and Wildlife Conservation and the Environment; Merchant Marine; Oceanography; Oversight and Investigations. *Select Committee on Aging* (12th of 26 R). Subcommittee: Health and Long-Term Care.

Group Ratings

	ADA	ACLU	COPE	CFA	LCV	ACU	NTLC	NSI	COC	CEI
1988	30	48	38	73	56	72	70	100	79	44
1987	24	—	34	50	—	52	—	—	73	54

National Journal Ratings

	1988 LIB — 1988 CONS		1987 LIB — 1987 CONS	
Economic	31% —	67%	29% —	69%
Social	35% —	64%	42% —	57%
Foreign	16% —	78%	20% —	76%

Key Votes

1) Homeless $	FOR	5) Ban Drug Test	AGN	9) SDI Research	FOR
2) Gephardt Amdt	AGN	6) Drug Death Pen	FOR	10) Ban Chem Weaps	AGN
3) Deficit Reduc	AGN	7) Handgun Sales	AGN	11) Aid to Contras	FOR
4) Kill Plnt Clsng Notice	FOR	8) Ban D.C. Abort $	FOR	12) Nuclear Testing	AGN

Election Results

1988 general	H. James Saxton (R)	167,470	(69%)	($411,620)
	James B. Smith (D)	73,561	(31%)	
1988 primary	H. James Saxton (R), unopposed			
1986 general	H. James Saxton (R)	82,866	(65%)	($331,286)
	John Wydra (D)	43,920	(35%)	($60,843)

FOURTEENTH DISTRICT

"Thoroughfares leading to the waterfront" of Jersey City 50 years ago, described the *WPA Guide*, "meet with a chaos of side streets that cross and interlace, forming odd-shaped islands upon which squat equally odd-shaped structures. Skeletons of abandoned buildings stand crumbling in the shadow of newer factories, humming with the roar of machinery. The residential streets are lined with tightly packed rows of two- and three-story brownstone or brick houses. Some are old and unoccupied, seemingly held erect only by the support of neighboring structures." Such was the face Jersey City presented, already old and a bit crumbling, sitting as the largest of the Hudson County cities atop the granite and gneiss ridge that rises between the Meadowlands and the Hudson. Each has its own aspect: the five-story Victorian apartment buildings of Hoboken, unshaded by trees, sparkle in light that takes on tone from the river; the substantial 1920s houses in Weehawken stare across from the skyscrapers of Manhattan, guarding middle-class values against the sophistication of the city. But Hudson County is a unit, economically, ethnically and geographically, cut off from New York by the Hudson, from the rest of New Jersey by the Meadowlands, from the rest of America by an insular local culture.

Yet its geographical position, on the west side of New York Harbor, gives it economic connections to every corner of the country. Into Hudson County came the railroads and highways from the interior of America heading to its largest metropolitan area; into its docks steamed cargo ships and liners; out of its factories poured soap, pencils, cans, mouthwash, cigarettes, pasta, steel. Here, within easy sight of the Statue of Liberty, generation after generation of immigrants gathered in ethnic neighborhoods reminiscent of home, building churches and civic institutions in the few hours left over after their usually backbreaking work: Hudson County's function throughout its history was to house some of America's millions of immigrants, to provide them with jobs, on the waterfront or in the great factories or on the railroads or in Jersey City's huge City Hall.

In this industrial landscape, people's primary interest was, according to the *WPA Guide*, "politics. In city and county employees and in their families has been instilled a political awareness that transcends interest in other civic and cultural problems. An elaborate framework of political clubs provides a social outlet for voters of all leading nationalities. Nonpolitical recreation is found in motion pictures and sports, since dance halls and night clubs are prohibited." Mayor Frank Hague, boss from 1917 to 1949, said, "I am the law," and mostly he was: his machine chose governors and U.S. Senators, prosecutors and judges, and had influence in the White House of Franklin D. Roosevelt. He collected high taxes from the industries clustered here—who then passed them on to consumers all over the country—and in return gave them an orderly city, free of most crime and vice, and a work force insulated against racketeers and militant unions. (He drove the CIO out of town in what became a major Supreme Court case.) Hague's votes came from an organization manned by employees on swollen public payrolls and financed by a 3% assessment on their salaries; scattered through every neighborhood, with connections to relatives and friends and fellow parishioners, in a place so insular that many Hudson Countians have never been to Manhattan, those connections produced heavy majorities for Hague's candidates even before the New Deal. Statewide Democratic candidates could expect a 100,000-vote margin in Hudson County, and since they often lost the rest of the state by less than that, they were indebted indeed.

Perhaps one reason the machine lasted so long—Hague was in power from 1917 to 1949 and his successor John V. Kenny held sway from 1949 to 1971—was that Hudson County was insulated against change for years by the closing off of immigration in 1924, and the lack of industrial and commercial growth for four decades after the Depression of the 1930s. Young people moved out and these insular Catholic, blue-collar, mostly Irish and Italian neighborhoods became uninviting physically and psychologically; few new people moved in, and the county's population fell from 690,000 in 1930 to 555,000 in 1980. But in the 1980s, Hudson County has begun to change again, as rapidly and yeastily as it did 100 years before.

One change has been the resumption of immigration, particularly from Latin America. Union City has become predominantly Cuban (64% Spanish origin in 1980, according to the Census Bureau), while there are mixed Latin-American communities in West New York (63%), Hoboken (40%) and Jersey City itself (19%). These new migrants, like those earlier in the century, tend to be young people with many children, who will some day pay the taxes to finance the social security of today's baby boomers who have not had large enough families to support themselves. Another change has been the development of some high-rise condominiums on the northern part of the ridge for Manhattanites. Also, young people have been rehabbing row houses in Hoboken, near the PATH tubes that take you straight to Manhattan. These changes, by the way, have countervailing political effects: the Cubans vote heavily Republican, the ex-Manhattanites are liberal Democrats.

Even more important is the commercial development of the Meadowlands, most of it just outside Hudson's borders, and of the waterfront facing New York: what used to be physical barriers have become Hudson County's economic assets. On the Jersey City waterfront, developer Samuel LeFrak is building Newport, with thousands of housing units and hundreds of thousands of square feet of office space; not far away, the old Colgate-Palmolive factory is being redeveloped as Liberty Place; opposite the Statue of Liberty is Port Liberté; up in Weehawken, Lincoln Harbor is filled with New York bank employees overlooking the traffic waiting to go through the Lincoln Tunnel; then there is Liberty Harbor North, Evertrust, Exchange Place Centre, Harborside Financial Center, Roc Harbour, Grand Cove. It has taken some time, but it has occurred to people that Hudson County is a sensible location for lots of the back office work of New York's financial services industry; and now that Hudson County no longer exacts an inordinate tribute from its taxpayers, it is far cheaper to build here than across the river. If public services still lag behind—the Jersey City school system was taken over by the state for failing to meet minimum standards—and if local politics in places like Hoboken still seems insular to newcomers, these are not huge barriers. After all, the employees are being drawn from all over New Jersey, and local politics doesn't intrude on most residents' lives as it once did.

Politically, Hudson County has become less Democratic since the 1960s, as the cultural conservatism of its longtime residents became more important than their historic party allegiance and the machine became less important in their lives. Tussles between local politicos continued, and were written up by outsiders as titanic battles for control of an all-powerful machine. But if the machine could still pick judges and state legislators, and if it still had influence in Democratic gubernatorial primaries, its power to affect votes in general elections became very limited. The 100,000-plus Democratic margins in Hudson County have vanished. Ronald Reagan started his fall 1980 campaign here, overlooking the Statue of Liberty; he lost the county by 4,000 votes in 1980 and carried it in 1984. That son of immigrants Michael Dukakis carried it over Greenwich WASP George Bush by only 17,000 votes. Hudson County has even voted for Republicans for the state legislature at the prodding of Governor Thomas Kean.

New Jersey's 14th Congressional District includes almost all of Hudson County—a change from Hague's day when there were two Hudson seats. The congressman is Frank Guarini, a sure-footed lawyer who served in the state Senate and was county Democratic chairman before he won the crucial 1978 primary. Guarini has moved up smartly in the House, while tending to the changing needs of Hudson County. He is a member of the Ways and Means Committee, taking more of a role on trade than on tax issues. In many areas he supports free trade: he co-chairs a congressional Friends of the Caribbean Basin and he supported the U.S.-Canada Free Trade Agreement. But he also backed Ed Jenkins's protectionist textile bill: Hudson County, he pointed out, has 700 textile and apparel plants with 16,000 workers. He did wage one tax fight in 1988, to save the tax credit for employee educational assistance, rounding up 302 co-sponsors at one stage. Guarini has naturally represented New Jersey in its battles with New York, but has moved to set up a bi-state Hudson River coalition for cooperation.

Guarini is not a particular gladhander, but he seems to have good political moves. In the House he got a seat on the Budget Committee; in national politics he was early and prominently on board supporting Walter Mondale in 1984 and Michael Dukakis in 1988. He retains support from the vestiges of the Hudson County machine, but has the polish to appeal to Hudson County's new upscale voters and the adaptability to win votes among its latest immigrants; he is routinely reelected by 2 to 1 margins and without serious primary challenges.

The People: Est. Pop. 1986: 520,000, dn. 1.2% 1980–86; Pop. 1980: 526,062, dn. 8.7% 1970–80. Households (1980): 69% family, 35% with children, 48% married couples; 71.8% housing units rented; median monthly rent: $186; median house value: $40,100. Voting age pop. (1980): 388,408; 24% Spanish origin, 11% Black, 3% Asian origin.

1988 Presidential Vote:

Dukakis (D)	93,287	(55%)
Bush (R)	76,021	(44%)

Rep. Frank J. Guarini (D)

Elected 1978; b. Aug. 20, 1924, Jersey City; home, Jersey City; Dartmouth Col., B.A. 1947, NYU, J.D. 1950, LL.M. 1955, Acad. of Intl. Law, The Hague, Holland; Roman Catholic; single.

Career: Navy, WWII; Practicing atty.; NJ Senate, 1965–72.

Offices: 2458 RHOB 20515, 202-225-2765. Also 15 Path Plaza, Jersey City 07306, 201-659-7700; and 654 Ave. C, Bayonne 07002, 201-823-2900.

Committees: *Budget* (10th of 21 D). Task Forces: Defense, Foreign Policy and Space; Economic Policy, Projections and Revenues. *Ways and Means* (11th of 23 D). Subcommittee: Trade. *Select Committee on Narcotics Abuse and Control* (7th of 15 D).

Group Ratings

	ADA	ACLU	COPE	CFA	LCV	ACU	NTLC	NSI	COC	CEI
1988	70	70	92	82	81	14	8	20	46	16
1987	88	—	91	93	—	0	—	—	20	4

National Journal Ratings

	1988 LIB — 1988 CONS		1987 LIB — 1987 CONS	
Economic	71% —	23%	73% —	0%
Social	61% —	38%	73% —	22%
Foreign	77% —	23%	71% —	27%

Key Votes

1) Homeless $	AGN	5) Ban Drug Test	AGN	9) SDI Research	AGN
2) Gephardt Amdt	FOR	6) Drug Death Pen	FOR	10) Ban Chem Weaps	FOR
3) Deficit Reduc	FOR	7) Handgun Sales	AGN	11) Aid to Contras	AGN
4) Kill Plnt Clsng Notice	AGN	8) Ban D.C. Abort $	AGN	12) Nuclear Testing	—

Election Results

1988 general	Frank J. Guarini (D)................ 104,001	(69%)	($369,578)
	Fred J. Theemling, Jr. (R) 47,293	(31%)	
1988 primary	Frank J. Guarini (D)................. 35,964	(67%)	
	Robert P. Haney, Jr. (D).............. 10,680	(20%)	
	Edward A. Allen (D) 7,027	(13%)	
1986 general	Frank J. Guarini (D)................. 63,057	(71%)	($407,120)
	Albio Sires (R) 23,822	(27%)	($62,073)

NEW MEXICO

"For greatness of beauty," wrote British writer D. H. Lawrence in the 1920s, after traveling from Sardinia to Australia, "I have never experienced anything like New Mexico. All those mornings when I went with a hoe along the ditch to the *Canon*, at the ranch, and stood in the fierce proud silence of the Rockies, on their foothills, to look far over the desert to the blue mountains away in Arizona, blue as Chalcedony, with the sage-brush desert sweeping grey-blue in between, dotted with tiny cube crystals of houses, the vast amphitheater of lofty, indomitable desert, sweeping round to the ponderous Sangre de Cristo Mountains on the east, and coming up flush at the pine-dotted foothills of the Rockies! What splendour!" Lawrence was part of a group of artists and writers who came to New Mexico, as early as the 1890s, and were enchanted by its vast vistas and unique life, and by the special civilization developed here long before the Pilgrims landed at Plymouth Rock and quite unlike anything else in the United States.

For much of what makes New Mexico distinctive is the product of the Pueblo peoples the Spanish conquistadors found here—something that is true of no other state but Hawaii. When the Pilgrims were building flimsy wood houses, the Indians in New Mexico were living in dwellings hundreds of years old, holding thousands of people, made with the adobe that is New Mexico's characteristic building material and which lasts so long that you can't tell a 1680 building from its 1980 neighbor. Every other state's culture is based on what its early white settlers brought to the land; natives, except in Hawaii, have mostly disappeared. Not so in much of New Mexico. The English-speaking culture here is superimposed, rather lightly it sometimes seems, on a society whose written history dates back to 1609, when the Spaniards first established a settlement in Santa Fe, and to centuries long past when the Pueblo Indians set up stable agricultural societies on the sandy, rocky lands of northern New Mexico. A very substantial minority of New Mexicans are descendants of these Indians or the Spanish, or both. Nearly one-third of the people in this state speak Spanish in ordinary everyday life, and only a few of them are recent migrants from Mexico. This is the northernmost salient of the great Indian civilizations of the Cordillera, which extend along the mountain chain through Mexico and Central America to South America, as far away as Chile and Argentina.

The Hispanic-Indian culture dominates most of northern and western New Mexico, except for enclaves—usually related to mining or, in the case of Los Alamos, nuclear research—where Anglos have settled in the last 50 years. In vivid contrast to the Hispanic part of New Mexico is the area called Little Texas. With small cities, plenty of oil wells, vast cattle ranches and desolate military bases, this region resembles, economically and culturally, the adjacent High Plains of west Texas. Oil is important here, but not as vital as the military presence: a couple of Air Force bases and the Army's White Sands Missile Range, near Alamogordo, where the first atomic bomb was detonated.

In the middle of the state is Albuquerque which, with the arrival of the air conditioner, grew from a small desert town of 35,000 in 1940 into the Sun Belt city of almost 500,000 today. Albuquerque has a large Hispanic minority, as many of our fastest-growing cities do; its economy is based heavily on high technology, particularly the nuclear variety. Metropolitan Albuquerque now has almost precisely one-third of the state's population—about the same percentage as the Hispanic areas and Little Texas. By happy coincidence, the three regions also coincide quite closely with the state's three congressional districts.

For many years New Mexico politics was a somnolent business. Local bosses—first Republican, later Democratic—controlled the large Hispanic vote. Elections in many counties featured irregularities that would have made a Chicago ward committeeman blush. New Mexico also had for years another evidence of boss-controlled politics, the balanced ticket: one Spanish and one Anglo Senator, with the offices of governor and lieutenant governor split between the groups. But for all its distinctiveness, in national politics New Mexico was a bellwether, never voting for a losing presidential candidate from 1912 when it became a state until 1976 when it backed Gerald Ford; in 1988 it voted 52%–47% for George Bush, one point less Republican than the national average. In congressional and state elections, there was a conservative tilt in the 1980s, but they remain competitive between the parties. There is some ethnic voting, and the Democrats usually have a solid base in the Hispanic areas, but no great polarization. New Mexico tends to attract the least affluent of the migrants, low-skill laborers and retirees who can afford a trailer but not a Scottsdale condominium. But any desire for a more active government or for boosting local wages or redistributing income may be diminished by the unseen but always remembered proximity of Mexico. New Mexico has not seen all that much migration from Mexico; its Hispanic population is growing rapidly because of high birth and low death rates. But Mexicans could start coming here, and that possibility must exert some discipline over wage levels.

Governor. In the 1980s, New Mexico, governed for years by conservative, politically well-connected Democrats, elected ideological governors, a liberal Democrat and a conservative Republican. The former, Toney Anaya, won narrowly in 1982 and became highly unpopular. But he didn't change his views: in his last weeks in office he commuted the sentences of New Mexico's five men on death row, and in 1988, he went around the country stumping for Jesse Jackson.

The current governor, Republican Garrey Carruthers, seems to have done better. In his campaign he made much of the fact that he was not a legislator; he won with 53% over a Democrat who was assistant head of the Sandia Laboratories. Carruthers was something of an intellectual too, an assistant secretary of the Interior under James Watt and then a professor of agricultural economics at New Mexico State in Las Cruces. He came into office promising to streamline government and attract economic development; he delved into the minutiae of governance in a government small enough probably to be comprehensible to one person. He recommended a tax increase in 1987 and has avoided antagonizing the legislature. New Mexico has repealed its law barring incumbent governors from seeking reelection; only two states still have such a prohibition, Kentucky and Virginia. But the repeal doesn't apply to Carruthers, so there will be a free-for-all again in 1990; one possible candidate is 1st District Democratic Congressman Bill Richardson. Former Democratic governor Bruce King has already announced his bid for governor, and former attorney general Paul Bardacke has also expressed an interest, among others.

Senators. New Mexico's most prominent politician is Senator Pete Domenici, chairman of the Senate Budget Committee for the first six Reagan years, now ranking minority member of Budget, mentioned as a possible vice presidential nominee in 1988. He was largely unknown when the Republicans' capture of the Senate in 1980 put him in the Budget chair, and not long removed from the time when his major governmental responsibility was superintending the

NEW MEXICO — Congressional Districts, Counties, and Selected Places — *(3 Districts)*

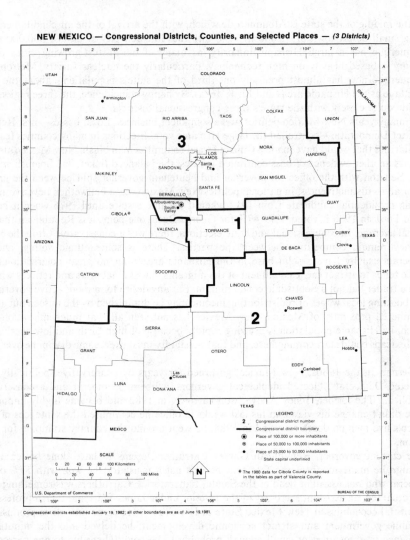

Congressional districts established January 19, 1982; all other boundaries are as of June 19, 1981.

budget of the city of Albuquerque. Only one of the other Republicans on Budget had any experience on the committee, and none had both the knowledge and the tenacity to compete with Domenici as the Republicans' driving force. For his first months as Budget chairman, Domenici worked closely with OMB Director David Stockman and the Reagan Administration, cutting domestic programs and boosting defense. But by the beginning of 1982, he had embarked on the constantly frustrating course he followed for five long years: trying to squeeze the deficit down while Reagan resisted tax increases, the Administration urged large defense increases, and everyone recognized that almost all the politically palatable domestic cuts had already been made. Hard-working, intense, frank often to the point of belligerence, genuinely worried about the deficit, but reluctant to set an entirely separate course from the Republican Administration, Domenici found himself again and again in the midst of grinding negotiations unable to accomplish what he wanted. He was beset by supply-siders who attacked him as a green-eyeshaded inflicter of austerity and by Democrats who saw him as being too faithful to the Reagan Administration. Support has come from Senate Republican Leaders Howard Baker and Bob Dole—and from the voters of New Mexico.

He seemed a bit more comfortable after 1986, with his friend Lawton Chiles taking over the chairmanship of the Budget Committee, the Gramm-Rudman law setting targets and limits that helped to force others in the direction that Domenici had been wanting to go all along, and a deal for 1988 having been made after everyone got good and scared by the October 1987 stock market crash. It seems unlikely that he will get on as well with the new chairman, Jim Sasser, to whom he is not as close personally and who is more of a national Democrat. In any case, Domenici has other things to attend to as well. He is a member of Appropriations and of Energy and Natural Resources, the latter being the old Interior Committee which is so important in western states; through these he can do things like push a uranium bailout law and get money to restore the irrigation canals—acequias—built by the Spanish in New Mexico.

Domenici's political position in New Mexico is very strong. He lost when he ran for governor in 1970 and only narrowly defeated a Democrat named Jack Daniels in his first Senate race in 1972; he was reelected in 1978 by an unimpressive margin over the then much less well-known Toney Anaya. But in 1984, he got 72% of the vote—the highest percentage any New Mexico Senator has ever won—and his job rating has continued to be very high, discouraging any serious opposition in 1990. This is one case where a Senator's national stature has been a political asset, and not just because federal spending is important to New Mexico. New Mexico voters saw Domenici being subjected to some very demanding circumstances, and he was not found wanting.

New Mexico's junior Senator, Jeff Bingaman, was labelled "the invisible senator" by an Albuquerque magazine and is little known in Washington; he has not held high committee positions, he is not particularly voluble or distinctive, and in a business full of people who hog the spotlight, he seems to avoid it. Yet his political career has prospered. He started off well-connected in New Mexico; his father was a professor at Western New Mexico in Silver City, and his uncle was campaign manager for Senator Clinton Anderson, one of the savviest politicians of his generation. A year out of law school, he was counsel to the state constitutional convention; a few years later, he went into law practice in Santa Fe with former Governor Jack Campbell; Bingaman's wife started a highly successful law practice of her own that helped finance his first campaigns. But Bingaman's rise was not mindless nepotism: in a small state important people are on the lookout for bright young individuals who are not nearly as numerous as they are in New York or Washington or Los Angeles. Bingaman ran for attorney general in 1978 and won; in 1982, he ran against Senator Harrison Schmitt, the former astronaut, also from Silver City. Bingaman won with 54%, partly because it was a recession year, but also because of Schmitt's own negative TV spots, which made damaging and, it quickly became apparent, misleading charges against Bingaman.

In the Senate he worked quietly on Armed Services, where he took much guidance from Sam Nunn, and compiled a record that became more conservative just as Governor Toney Anaya's liberal politics was growing more unpopular at home. On Armed Services, he is a promoter of SDI research (much of which is done in New Mexico) without being a zealot for the program; he was an opponent of Navy Secretary John Lehman's homeporting (a position that may come naturally to a Senator from a state whose largest body of water is the Rio Grande). He also got seats on the Energy and Natural Resources Committee and on Governmental Affairs; he worked on Indian affairs, competitiveness, child care; with Domenici he created the San Juan Basin Wilderness Protection Act, the Santa Fe Trail and the El Malpais National Monument. There is an earnestness to Bingaman—taking lessons to learn Spanish, trying to stop cut-rate cigarette sales to soldiers, fighting bubonic and pneumonic plague (most U.S. cases are in New Mexico), promoting physical fitness through his HealthNet program which encourages 90% of the state's population to refrain from smoking, exercise regularly, and keep their weight within 10% of the ideal. In the winter of 1986–87, his program got 7,000 New Mexicans, including the two Senators, to sign up to abide by an "Eat Right New Mexico" regimen, and they lost a total of 34,000 pounds.

Bingaman's opponent in 1988 was Bill Valentine, an Albuquerque dentist who was the Republican leader in the state Senate. Valentine flailed out in all directions, accusing Bingaman of having liberal ratings, taking contributions from defense PACs and cancelling out Domenici's vote. But Valentine was vastly outspent by Bingaman, who had developed a big network of contributors in New Mexico as well as in Washington. "Serious about New Mexico" was his slogan and a good description of his approach. Bingaman won 63%–37%, and while that may not discourage some serious Republican from challenging him in 1994, it is an impressive performance—the best by a Democratic Senate candidate in New Mexico since Clinton Anderson won his third term in 1960.

Presidential politics. New Mexico, heavily Republican in presidential elections from 1968 to 1984, was suddenly closer in 1988, and an object of attention of both the Bush and Dukakis campaigns. Michael Dukakis's fluent Spanish may have helped him appeal to Hispanic voters, and he made his biggest gains over the Democrats' 1984 showings in Hispanic counties including Santa Fe. Dukakis's widely advertised distaste for nuclear power and his desire to unilaterally give up nuclear weapons may have hurt him in the state where nuclear energy was first developed and the first atomic bomb detonated: George Bush held the Reagan vote best in Albuquerque, Los Alamos, and Alamogordo, homes respectively of the Sandia Labs, the original nuclear research center, and the White Sands firing range where the first A-bomb was set off in 1945.

Congressional districting. New Mexico got a third congressional district out of the 1980 Census and created a new, heavily Hispanic and Democratic district in the northern part of the state. The other two are competitive, at least when an incumbent isn't running, as in the 1st in 1988 and the 2d in 1980. Only minor adjustments to boundaries are likely to be needed in the 1990s.

The People: Est. Pop. 1988: 1,510,000; Pop. 1980: 1,302,894, up 15.9% 1980–88 and 28.1% 1970–80; 0.61% of U.S. total, 37th largest. 17% with 1–3 yrs. col., 17% with 4+ yrs. col.; 17.6% below poverty level. Single ancestry: 9% English, 5% German, 3% Irish, 1% Italian, French, Scottish. Households (1980): 75% family, 45% with children, 62% married couples; 31.9% housing units rented; median monthly rent: $178; median house value: $45,400. Voting age pop. (1980): 884,987; 33% Spanish origin, 7% American Indian, 2% Black, 1% Asian origin. Registered voters (1988): 674,766; 395,010 D (59%), 238,676 R (35%), 41,080 unaffiliated and minor parties (6%).

1988 Share of Federal Tax Burden: $3,904,000,000; 0.44% of U.S. total, 39th largest.

1988 Share of Federal Expenditures

	Total		Non-Defense		Defense	
Total Expend	$8,685m	(0.98%)	$7,152m	(1.09%)	$4,997m	(2.19%)
St/Lcl Grants	831m	(0.72%)	829m	(0.72%)	2m	(2.12%)
Salary/Wages	1,202m	(0.89%)	542m	(0.81%)	660m	(0.81%)
Pymnts to Indiv	2,369m	(0.58%)	2,159m	(0.55%)	209m	(1.12%)
Procurement	4,124m	(2.19%)	3,464m	(7.45%)	4,124m	(2.19%)
Research/Other	160m	(0.43%)	158m	(0.43%)	2m	(0.43%)

Political Lineup: Governor, Garrey E. Carruthers (R); Lt. Gov., Jack L. Stahl (R); Secy. of State, Rebecca Vigil Giron (D); Atty. Gen., Hal Stratton (R); Treasurer, James B. Lewis (D); Auditor, Harroll H. Adams (D). State Senate, 42 (26 D and 16 R); State House of Representatives, 70 (45 D and 25 R). Senators, Peter V. (Pete) Domenici (R) and Jeff Bingaman (D). Representatives, 3 (2 R and 1 D).

1988 Presidential Vote

Bush (R) 270,341 (52%)
Dukakis (D). 244,497 (47%)

1984 Presidential Vote

Reagan (R) 307,101 (60%)
Mondale (D) 201,769 (39%)

1988 Democratic Presidential Primary

Dukakis 114,968 (61%)
Jackson 52,988 (28%)
Hart...................... 6,898 (4%)
Gore...................... 4,747 (3%)
Babbitt 2,913 (2%)
Simon 2,821 (2%)

1988 Republican Presidential Primary

Bush 69,359 (78%)
Dole...................... 9,305 (11%)
Robertson 5,350 (6%)
Haig...................... 2,161 (2%)

GOVERNOR

Gov. Garrey E. Carruthers (R)

Elected 1986, term expires Jan. 1991; b. Aug. 29, 1939, Alamosa, CO; home, Las Cruces; NM State U., B.S. 1964, M.S. 1965, IA St. U., Ph.D. 1968; United Methodist; married (Katherine).

Career: Asst. Secy., U.S. Dept. of Int., 1981–84; Dir., NM Water Resources Research Inst., 1976–78; Prof., NM State U., 1968–85.

Office: State Capitol, Rm. 417, Santa Fe 87503, 505-827-3000.

Election Results

1986 gen.	Garrey E. Carruthers (R)......	209,455	(53%)
	Ray B. Powell (D)	185,378	(47%)
1986 prim.	Garrey E. Carruthers (R)......	27,671	(31%)
	Joseph H. Mercer (R)	23,560	(26%)
	Colin R. McMillan (R)	19,807	(22%)
	Frank M. Bond (R)	10,619	(12%)
	Paul F. Becht (R)	6,566	(7%)
1982 gen.	Toney Anaya (D)	215,840	(53%)
	John Irick (R).	190,626	(47%)

SENATORS

Sen. Peter V. (Pete) Domenici (R)

Elected 1972, seat up 1990; b. May 7, 1932, Albuquerque; home, Albuquerque; U. NM, B.S. 1954, Denver U., LL.B. 1958; Roman Catholic; married (Nancy).

Career: Practicing atty., 1958–72; Albuquerque City Comm., 1966–70, Mayor Ex-Officio, 1967–70.

Offices: 434 DSOB 20510, 202-224-6621. Also Fed. Bldg. and U.S. Crthse., Rm. 10013, Albuquerque 87102, 505-766-3481; New Postal Bldg., Rm. 3004, Santa Fe 87501, 505-988-6511; 202 E. New Fed. Bldg., Las Cruces 88001, 505-523-8150; and Fed. Bldg. and U.S. Crthse., Rm. 140, Roswell 88201, 505-623-6130.

Committees: *Appropriations* (10th of 13 R). Subcommittees: District of Columbia; Energy and Water Development; Interior; Treasury, Postal Service, General Government (Ranking Member). *Budget* (Ranking Member of 10 R). *Energy and Natural Resources* (3d of 9 R). Subcommittees: Energy Regulation and Conservation; Energy Research and Development (Ranking Member); Public Lands, National Parks and Forests. *Special Committee on Aging* (6th of 9 R).

Group Ratings

	ADA	ACLU	COPE	CFA	LCV	ACU	NTLC	NSI	COC	CEI
1988	15	31	23	50	30	72	62	100	79	40
1987	20	—	22	25	—	65	—	—	78	53

National Journal Ratings

	1988 LIB — 1988 CONS		1987 LIB — 1987 CONS	
Economic	9%	— 81%	21%	— 74%
Social	24%	— 75%	16%	— 78%
Foreign	31%	— 66%	34%	— 64%

Key Votes

1) Cut Aged Housing $	AGN	5) Bork Nomination	FOR	9) SDI Funding	FOR
2) Override Hwy Veto	AGN	6) Ban Plastic Guns	FOR	10) Ban Chem Weaps	FOR
3) Kill Plnt Clsng Notice	FOR	7) Deny Abortions	FOR	11) Aid To Contras	FOR
4) Min Wage Increase	AGN	8) Japanese Reparations	FOR	12) Reagan Defense $	FOR

Election Results

1984 general	Peter V. (Pete) Domenici (R)	361,371	(72%)	($2,658,008)
	Judith A. Pratt (D)	141,253	(28%)	($301,661)
1984 primary	Peter V. (Pete) Domenici (R)	42,760	(100%)	
1978 general	Peter V. (Pete) Domenici (R)	183,442	(53%)	($914,634)
	Toney Anaya (D)	160,045	(47%)	($175,633)

Sen. Jeff Bingaman (D)

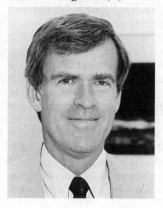

Elected 1982, seat up 1994; b. Oct. 3, 1943, El Paso, TX; home, Santa Fe; Harvard Col., B.A. 1965, Stanford U., LL.B. 1968; United Methodist; married (Anne).

Career: NM Asst. Atty. Gen., 1969; Practicing atty., 1970–78; NM Atty. Gen., 1979–82.

Offices: 502 HSOB 20510, 202-224-5521. Also 123 E. Marcy, Ste. 207, Santa Fe 87501, 505-988-6647; Dennis Chavez Fed. Bldg., Rm. 9017, 500 Gold Ave. S.W., Albuquerque 87102, 505-766-3636; Runnels Fed. Bldg., Ste. 201-B, Las Cruces 88001, 505-523-8237; and Fed. Bldg., Ste. 175, Roswell 88201, 505-622-7113.

Committees: *Armed Services* (5th of 11 D). Subcommittees: Defense Industry and Technology (Chairman); Readiness, Sustainability and Support; Strategic Forces and Nuclear Deterrence. *Energy and Natural Resources* (6th of 10 D). Subcommittees: Energy, Regulation, and Conservation; Mineral Resources Development and Production (Chairman); Public Lands, National Parks and Forests. *Governmental Affairs* (6th of 8 D). Subcommittees: General Services, Federalism and the District of Columbia; Government Information and Regulation (Chairman); Oversight of Government Management. *Joint Economic Committee*. Subcommittees: Economic Resources and Competitiveness; Education and Health; National Security Economics.

Group Ratings

	ADA	ACLU	COPE	CFA	LCV	ACU	NTLC	NSI	COC	CEI
1988	70	56	84	83	50	20	20	50	43	21
1987	65	—	85	67	—	13	—	—	40	32

National Journal Ratings

	1988 LIB	—	1988 CONS	1987 LIB	—	1987 CONS
Economic	52%	—	45%	44%	—	50%
Social	67%	—	31%	58%	—	40%
Foreign	59%	—	39%	55%	—	44%

Key Votes

1) Cut Aged Housing $	AGN	5) Bork Nomination	AGN	9) SDI Funding	FOR
2) Override Hwy Veto	FOR	6) Ban Plastic Guns	—	10) Ban Chem Weaps	FOR
3) Kill Plnt Clsng Notice	AGN	7) Deny Abortions	AGN	11) Aid To Contras	AGN
4) Min Wage Increase	FOR	8) Japanese Reparations	FOR	12) Reagan Defense $	AGN

Election Results

1988 general	Jeff Bingaman (D)	321,983	(63%)	($2,808,659)
	Bill Valentine (R)	186,579	(37%)	($659,624)
1988 primary	Jeff Bingaman (D), unopposed			
1982 general	Jeff Bingaman (D)	217,682	(54%)	($1,586,245)
	Harrison H. (Jack) Schmitt (R)	187,682	(46%)	($1,692,204)

FIRST DISTRICT

Fifty years ago Albuquerque, named for a 16th century Spanish grandee, was the largest of several small cities in New Mexico, with just 35,000 people. Built at the junction of a river that is just a trickle most of the year and a road which was nothing more than a line on a surveyor's map when the Santa Fe Railroad was constructed, Albuquerque was huddled in the blocks around the Old Town and the Indian School, just above the Rio Grande, a place you could pass through quickly on the Santa Fe or U.S. 66. Since then it has grown more than any place in New Mexico and, with a metropolitan population approaching 500,000, has as many people as the whole state did 50 years ago. Albuquerque's prosperous neighborhoods have climbed the gently rising heights to the east, and its poorer people spread north and south of downtown in the Rio Grande valley. Albuquerque is counted as part of the Sun Belt, but its climate is closer to that of the High Plains of west Texas: hot in the summer, sometimes very cold in the winter, with high winds most of the time. Unlike most other Sun Belt cities, it owes its growth more to the public than the private sector: its biggest employers include the Sandia Labs, military bases and defense contractors.

The 1st Congressional District of New Mexico is, for all practical purposes, the city of Albuquerque and its suburbs. Albuquerque itself accounts for 76% of the district's population, with 21% more in the suburban fringe; that leaves just 3% in the three desert counties which have most of the district's land area. In the 1960s it trended Republican but is now among the least Republican of Sun Belt cities. In 1988 it voted for George Bush, but by only a 54%–45% margin—far lower than his 3 to 1 margins in greater Phoenix.

Albuquerque and the 1st District, so closely divided, were the site of one of the nation's more fiercely contested House races in 1988. It was occasioned by the retirement after 20 years of Manuel Lujan Jr., first elected in a local Republican upsurge in 1968, a member of a family with a local insurance business long prominent in the Republican Party. With his seniority, Lujan was ranking Republican on the Interior and Science Committees, both important locally, in the 1980s; but he also had some close calls back home and a heart attack in 1986. As it turned out, he ended up as Secretary of the Interior in the Bush Administration.

Both parties had seriously contested primaries. The Democrats had no less than 10 candidates. Tom Udall, son of former Interior Secretary Stewart Udall, nephew of House Interior Committee chairman Morris Udall and loser to Bill Richardson in the 1982 primary in the 3d District, won with 25% of the vote, ahead of former Judge Patricia Madrid and former state Land Commissioner Jim Baca, who both had 21%. In the Republicans' three-candidate race, Albuquerque District Attorney Steven Schiff edged out Lujan's brother Edward, who runs the family insurance business, by a 41%–37% margin. Udall campaigned against transporting nuclear waste through Albuquerque and stressed his own experience as a federal prosecutor in drug cases and his pro-environment stance. Schiff, a Chicago native who came to New Mexico to go to law school, is acerbic and aggressive, proud of the death penalty convictions he has obtained, and his service as a lieutenant colonel in the New Mexico Air National Guard. With high visibility from eight years as DA, he stressed that and his strong support of SDI, and after a rather contentious race he won 51%–47%.

In the House, Schiff has seats on the Government Operations and Science and Technology Committees. The latter is important to Albuquerque, and if Schiff continues to show the political skills that enabled him to win two tough races in 1988, he has a good chance to make this a safe seat.

The People: Est. Pop. 1986: 490,200, up 12.9% 1980–86; Pop. 1980: 434,141, up 32.1% 1970–80. Households (1980): 72% family, 41% with children, 58% married couples; 36.3% housing units rented; median monthly rent: $202; median house value: $55,000. Voting age pop. (1980): 307,647; 33% Spanish origin, 2% American Indian, 2% Black, 1% Asian origin.

1988 Presidential Vote: Bush (R) 96,586   (54%)
　　　　　　　　　　　　　　Dukakis (D). 81,687   (45%)

Rep. Steve Schiff (R)

Elected 1988; b. March 18, 1947, Chicago, IL; home, Albuquerque; U. of IL, B.A. 1968, U. of NM, J.D. 1972; Jewish; married (Marcia).

Career: Asst. Dist. Atty., Bernalillo Cnty., 1972–77; Practicing atty. 1977–79; Asst. City Atty. and Cnsl., Albuquerque Police Dept., 1979–81; Dist. Atty., Bernalillo Cnty., 1981–89.

Offices: 1520 LHOB, 202-225-6316. Also 500 Gold Ave. S.W., Ste. 10001, Albuquerque 87102, 505-766-2538.

Committees: *Government Operations* (11th of 15 R). Subcommittees: Commerce, Consumer and Monetary Affairs; Government Information, Justice and Agriculture. *Science, Space and Technology* (18th of 19 R). Subcommittees: Energy Research and Development; Space Science and Applications.

Group Ratings and Key Votes: Newly Elected

Election Results

1988 general	Steve Schiff (R)	89,985	(51%)	($559,134)
	Tom Udall (D)	84,138	(47%)	($576,677)
1988 primary	Steve Schiff (R)	14,028	(41%)	
	Edward L. Lujan (R)	12,801	(37%)	
	John A. Budagner (R)	7,393	(22%)	
1986 general	Manuel Lujan, Jr. (R)	90,476	(71%)	($243,795)
	Manny Garcia (D)	37,138	(29%)	($71,407)

SECOND DISTRICT

The plains of southern and eastern New Mexico are about as vacant a landscape as you can imagine: miles of sagebrush-strewn acreage, and then suddenly 9,000-foot mountain peaks rising in the distance. This is New Mexico's 2d Congressional District, which can be divided into two roughly equally populated parts. In the east is Little Texas—an extension of the High Plains of west Texas over the invisible New Mexico state border. Oil is the mainstay of the economy here; cattle ranching is common; cotton is grown on irrigated land. There is a considerable Hispanic population—at least 19% in each county—and yet the regional accent is the twang of west Texas, not the lilt of northern New Mexico. As you move west from the towns near the Texas border—Clovis, Portales, Lovington, Hobbs—the towns become fewer and agricultural settlement sparser. Politically, the partisan tradition is Democratic and the politics culturally conservative and concerned about oil; in national politics that makes this the most consistently Republican part of New Mexico.

The other part of the 2d District is centered on Las Cruces, the fast-growing second largest city in the state, only 45 miles north of El Paso, Texas, on the Rio Grande. Las Cruces has New Mexico State University, a big military presence, and a rising Mexican-American population; it is the home base of Republican Governor Garrey Carruthers, but nearly voted for Dukakis in 1988. More Democratic is the old mining country to the west around Silver City and the tiny border town of Columbus, which was raided by Pancho Villa's revolutionary army in 1916.

The 2d District is represented by a Little Texas Republican, Joe Skeen. He is a sheep rancher who chaired the state Republican Party in the 1960s and nearly was elected governor twice, in 1974 and 1978. His record in the House is solidly conservative, in a rough-and-ready rather than intellectual way. Generally opposed to high government spending, he is happy to make exceptions for defense, science and agriculture. After the 1984 election, he switched off two good committees for a congressman from his district, Agriculture and Science and Technology, for an even better one, Appropriations; he serves on Jamie Whitten's Agriculture Subcommittee and is ranking Republican on the panel that handles funding for the Treasury Department and Postal Service, among other agencies.

Skeen won the seat the hard way, by a write-in in 1980, when Democratic incumbent Harold "Mud" Runnels died and the Democrats put Governor Bruce King's nephew on the ballot. But Skeen got 38% of the vote to 34% for King and 28% for Runnels's widow, also a write-in. In 1986, Skeen beat Runnels's son Mike 63%–37% and in 1988 was unopposed; this is a safe seat. He declined to run against Senator Jeff Bingaman in 1988. In the spring of 1989 he announced he would not run for governor, and since whoever is elected in 1990 will be able to run for a second term and Skeen will be 67 in 1994, that surely will be his last chance.

The People: Est. Pop. 1986: 498,200, up 14.2% 1980–86; Pop. 1980: 436,261, up 17.9% 1970–80. Households (1980): 77% family, 45% with children, 66% married couples; 31.7% housing units rented; median monthly rent: $154; median house value: $33,400. Voting age pop. (1980): 297,158; 29% Spanish origin, 3% Black, 1% American Indian, 1% Asian origin.

1988 Presidential Vote:

Bush (R)	96,142	(58%)
Dukakis (D)	67,307	(41%)

Rep. Joseph R. (Joe) **Skeen (R)**

Elected 1980; b. June 30, 1927, Roswell; home, Picacho; TX A&M U., B.S. 1950; Roman Catholic; married (Mary).

Career: Navy, WWII; Engineer, Navajo Reservation, 1950–51; Sheep rancher, 1951–89; NM Senate, 1960–70, Minor. Ldr., 1965–70; Repub. Nominee for Gov. of NM, 1974, 1978.

Offices: 1007 LHOB 20515, 202-225-2365. Also Fed. Bldg., A-206, Las Cruces 88001, 505-523-8245; and Fed. Bldg., Rm. 127, Roswell 88201, 505-622-0055.

Committees: *Appropriations* (16th of 22 R). Subcommittees: Rural Development, Agriculture and Related Agencies; Treasury, Postal Service and General Government (Ranking Member).

Group Ratings

	ADA	ACLU	COPE	CFA	LCV	ACU	NTLC	NSI	COC	CEI
1988	5	22	13	36	19	100	47	100	93	43
1987	16	—	11	21	—	83	—	—	80	52

National Journal Ratings

	1988 LIB — 1988 CONS			1987 LIB — 1987 CONS		
Economic	19%	—	80%	24%	—	74%
Social	20%	—	78%	10%	—	85%
Foreign	27%	—	71%	20%	—	76%

Key Votes

1) Homeless $	FOR	5) Ban Drug Test	FOR	9) SDI Research	FOR
2) Gephardt Amdt	AGN	6) Drug Death Pen	FOR	10) Ban Chem Weaps	AGN
3) Deficit Reduc	AGN	7) Handgun Sales	FOR	11) Aid to Contras	FOR
4) Kill Plnt Clsng Notice	FOR	8) Ban D.C. Abort $	FOR	12) Nuclear Testing	AGN

Election Results

1988 general	Joseph R. (Joe) Skeen (R), unopposed			($67,727)
1988 primary	Joseph R. (Joe) Skeen (R), unopposed			
1986 general	Joseph R. (Joe) Skeen (R)	77,787	(63%)	($293,428)
	Mike Runnels (D).....................	45,924	(37%)	($48,409)

THIRD DISTRICT

Since the 1890s artists have been coming to northern New Mexico around Santa Fe, "the dancing ground of the sun," as the Pueblo Indians called it. They were attracted first by the clear air, the massive mountains, the long, cold empty vistas in which physical detail stands out with pinpoint clarity; but they were enchanted even more by the unique civilization here—part Indian, part Spanish, only a little Mexican (for northern New Mexico was Mexican only briefly, from 1821 to 1846), part Anglo-American. The Spanish language, Indian pottery and dances, the adobe pueblos and most of all a sense that here was a civilization rooted in the unlikeliest of desert soil and rock outcroppings, a place not settled a few decades or generations ago like most of the United States, but where life had gone on for centuries under these same skies in much the same way.

Actually, life here has not been so stable: the pueblos were built in sudden spurts; the Spanish conquistadors and priests brought the Catholic religion, the baroque accents of the adobe buildings and the Spanish language in a rush; successive waves of American settlement have changed New Mexico, including the flocking of unprecedented numbers of affluent and bohemian migrants of the 1980s. The Indian crafts which are thriving today nearly died out in the 1880s, and the Palace of the Governors, built in 1610, had its Victorian balustrade torn off and its original appearance restored in 1913. The unchanged look must be carefully maintained. Yet up the back roads in Rio Arriba or Taos Counties, one can find a religion that is a mixture of Catholicism with adaptations of Indian festivals, and buildings not that much different from the old pueblos. Politics here, too, is a unique blend. Debate is conducted and votes are bartered often in Spanish, but the Republican and Democratic Parties have been firmly established here for a century, and there has been nothing smacking of cultural revolution or massive income redistribution coming from any politician. Quite the contrary: politics tends to be a cynical, sometimes corrupt, business; loyalties run to families and communities more than to principles or parties. In the back country, you can still find more than vestiges of the old communities and the old politics—though no one is going to let you in on them much, even if you speak good Spanish.

The 3d Congressional District of New Mexico contains most of the Spanish-speaking and Indian parts of the state. Its largest and dominant city is Santa Fe, which grew lustily in the 1980s, but the district covers most of the northern part of the state, from the High Plains as they rise to the haunting Sangre de Cristo Mountains in the east, through the vast ridges and isolated buttes in the center (on one such isolated butte the government built Los Alamos in World War II, to create the atomic bomb), to the windy and dusty desert-like plains, dotted occasionally by mountains, with their Indian reservations in the west. The population is 39% Spanish origin and 21% Indian (there is some overlap between the categories). In national as well as state contests, this is Democratic territory. Although Los Alamos and the uranium country around Farmington are heavily Republican, the 3d voted 54%–44% for Michael Dukakis in 1988.

The congressman from the 3d District is something of a political anomaly as well as a political dynamo: a Hispanic with an Anglo name, a newcomer to New Mexico who carries towns where families go back 300 years, a patently ambitious politician who has also taken some impolitic stands for no apparent reason except that the conviction that they were right on the merits. Bill Richardson was born in California; his mother is Mexican and he was raised in Mexico City; he has always been bilingual. He came to New Mexico in 1978 after holding staff jobs on Capitol Hill (the importance of which was exaggerated in 1980 campaign brochures), worked as executive director of the state Democratic Party for a month, and started running against Republican Congressman Manuel Lujan in a district that then included Albuquerque and most of northern New Mexico. He raised $200,000 ($100,000 of it in a loan ultimately declared legal by the Federal Election Commission) and won 49% in the Republican year of 1980. He carried the area within the bounds of the new 3d district which was created after the 1980 Census, and in 1982 he beat former Lieutenant Governor Roberto Mondragon 36%–31% in the primary and clobbered a Republican with 64% to become, four years after he moved to the state, New Mexico's only Democratic congressman.

Richardson has worked hard to hold the seat, spending three out of four weekends in the district and holding constant town meetings, as well as winning impressive committee assignments in the House. He is a member of the Energy and Commerce Committee, where he has generally voted with the Democrats. But he backed the bill for national product liability, which got him denounced by Ralph Nader, and he has tended to favor market pricing of oil and gas (of which New Mexico, but not the 3d District, produces a lot). He voted for immigration reform in 1984, when the other Hispanic Members were against it; eventually some joined him. And he has voted for humanitarian, though not military, contra aid. He presses for enterprise zones (a cause most advanced by Republicans) as well as for tax breaks to new businesses in depressed areas.

Richardson also won a seat on the Interior Committee, always important in a western state, and is proud of establishing the El Malpais National Monument in his district and blocking the Waste Isolation Pilot Plant supported by the rest of the delegation in Joe Skeen's 2d District. (He and Skeen don't seem to have much use for each other.) He occasionally goes far afield, as on a bipartisan panel seeking readjustments of the American role in NATO. But he also uses his skills in political organizing. He campaigned in 13 states and ran Michael Dukakis's Hispanic vote program, spending a $1 million media budget and organizing to bring Hispanic turnout up from 60% to 70% and the Democratic percentage from 66% to 70%. These efforts seem to have been successful on both counts and are of prime importance to national Democrats, since Hispanics will cast an increasing share of the vote, especially in California and Texas.

Richardson does not deny that he is interested in statewide office some day; his problem is to figure out which office, and when. Governor Garrey Carruthers can't run in 1990 and the new governor could serve for eight years; but Richardson has not been much interested in the office. As for the Senate, he decided not to take Pete Domenici on in 1984, and might conceivably do so in 1990; but Domenici's job ratings are very high, and that race would be risky at best. Obviously, he is not going to run against Senator Jeff Bingaman. He may well decide to stay in the House, where he has fine committee assignments and the prospect, as a Hispanic with campaign organizing skills, of playing a part in the next Democratic presidential campaign as he did in the last. There is no reason to believe he would ever have trouble winning reelection in the 3d District.

The People: Est. Pop. 1986: 491,100, up 13.6% 1980–86; Pop. 1980: 432,492, up 35.8% 1970–80. Households (1980): 77% family, 50% with children, 63% married couples; 27.2% housing units rented; median monthly rent: $166; median house value: $47,900. Voting age pop. (1980): 280,182; 37% Spanish origin, 17% American Indian, 1% Black.

1988 Presidential Vote:

Dukakis (D)	95,503	(54%)
Bush (R)	77,613	(44%)

Rep. Bill Richardson (D)

Elected 1982; b. Nov. 15, 1947, Pasadena, CA; home, Tesuque; Tufts U., B.A. 1970, Fletcher Sch. of Law and Diplomacy, M.A. 1971; Roman Catholic; married (Barbara).

Career: Congressional Rel., U.S. Dept. of State, 1973–75; Staff, Sen. Subcmtee. on Foreign Relations Assistance, 1975–78; Businessman, 1978–82.

Offices: 332 CHOB 20515, 202-225-6190. Also 548 Agua Fria, Santa Fe 87501, 505-988-6177; Gallup City Hall, 2d and Aztec, Gallup 87301, 505-722-6522; San Miguel Cnty. Cthse., P.O. Box 1805, Las Vegas 87701, 505-425-7270; and The Harvey House, 104 N. 1st St., Belen 87003, 505-864-1419.

Committees: *Energy and Commerce* (17th of 26 D). Subcommittees: Health and the Environment; Energy and Power; Telecommunications and Finance. *Interior and Insular Affairs* (14th of 26 D). Subcommittees: Energy and the Environment; National Parks and Public Lands. *Select Committee on Aging* (24th of 39 D). Subcommittees: Housing and Consumer Interests; Human Services. *Select Committee on Intelligence* (10th of 12 D).

Group Ratings

	ADA	ACLU	COPE	CFA	LCV	ACU	NTLC	NSI	COC	CEI
1988	75	70	90	82	50	21	13	30	42	18
1987	80	—	90	64	—	9	—	—	29	8

National Journal Ratings

	1988 LIB — 1988 CONS		1987 LIB — 1987 CONS	
Economic	59% —	41%	62% —	35%
Social	58% —	40%	58% —	42%
Foreign	57% —	43%	54% —	45%

Key Votes

1) Homeless $	AGN	5) Ban Drug Test	AGN	9) SDI Research	FOR
2) Gephardt Amdt	FOR	6) Drug Death Pen	FOR	10) Ban Chem Weaps	FOR
3) Deficit Reduc	AGN	7) Handgun Sales	FOR	11) Aid to Contras	AGN
4) Kill Plnt Clsng Notice	AGN	8) Ban D.C. Abort $	AGN	12) Nuclear Testing	FOR

Election Results

1988 general	Bill Richardson (D)	124,938	(73%)	($267,633)
	Cecilia Salazar (R)	45,954	(27%)	($41,669)
1988 primary	Bill Richardson (D), unopposed			
1986 general	Bill Richardson (D)	95,760	(71%)	($354,849)
	David F. Cargo (R)	38,552	(29%)	($86,865)

NEW YORK

On October 21, 1944, Franklin D. Roosevelt, campaigning for a fourth term as President of the United States, rode 50 miles in an open car in the rain through the four large boroughs of New York City. At Ebbets Field on Bedford Avenue in Brooklyn, where the Dodgers had yet to win their first World Series, he was helped out of his car and spoke on behalf of Senator Robert Wagner, author of the Wagner Labor Relations Act that had made possible the surging CIO industrial union movement and the sponsor as well of Social Security and public housing, and a colleague of Roosevelt's in the state legislature in 1911 and 1912. Passing crowds all along the route, the limousine drove through Queens, past the site of the 1939–40 World's Fair which Mayor Fiorello LaGuardia, on the jump seat beside Roosevelt, had put together to celebrate the city's achievements even as the world was headed to war. On the Grand Concourse on the spine of the Bronx, lined with sturdy Art Deco apartments, Roosevelt appeared in the borough—part Jewish, Irish and Italian—where the sons and daughters of immigrants had moved out along the subway lines from the tenements of the Lower East Side and now, under the leadership of Bronx boss and former Democratic National Chairman Ed Flynn, also delivered 3 to 1 Democratic margins.

The cold rain continued to pour down on the frail and sickly President as he rolled through Harlem and past the Upper East Side of Manhattan, where his mother kept a house on East 65th Street, down Broadway to vast cheers in the garment district, and finally to the apartment Eleanor Roosevelt maintained on Washington Square in Greenwich Village. That night he spoke before the Foreign Policy Association, flanked by his appointees Henry Stimson, the embodiment of the Protestant public service elite, James Forrestal, an Irish Catholic who climbed fast on Wall Street, and Herbert Lehman, scion of one of the German Jewish families who had long been part of New York's financial and cultural aristocracy.

New York that day was the most powerful city in the world. Two million people saw Roosevelt drive through the rain, and on election day two weeks later New York City cast 3.3 million votes—7% of the nation's total, one out of 14 in the entire country, the highest proportion in history—61% of them for Roosevelt. And although this was a campaign trip, it was also a triumphal parade. Four months before, American troops had landed in Normandy, and now they were sweeping across France into Hitler's Germany; just two days before, American troops landed again in the Philippines, even as they were island-hopping within secure airfield range of Japan. Washington was the capital of the nation, where the commands were given, but New York, far more than any other city, supplied the capital and brains and infantrymen who won the war. Included among them was a commander-in-chief who came from one of those Dutch families who had first settled the city and who like most American immigrants were not counted as particularly distinguished people by the country they left behind. London was in ruins, Berlin and Tokyo were being bombed, Moscow was starving, Paris and Rome were shamed. The people cheering Roosevelt in Brooklyn, Queens, the Bronx, and Manhattan were immigrants and the children of immigrants; they spoke with the greasy and coarse accents whose rasps echoed the shrieks of brakes on the pavements and horns echoing through the high-rise streets; their fingers were dirty with the ink from the *Daily News* and the other tabloids they picked up on their way into the subways and their fingernails were caked with the remnants of grease and mustard from the hot dogs and soft pretzels they chomped on. In other great cities not so long before vast crowds had cheered grandiose leaders who in pomp and ceremony hailed their followers' racial purity and called on them to slaughter their inferiors. In this great city vast crowds cheered a

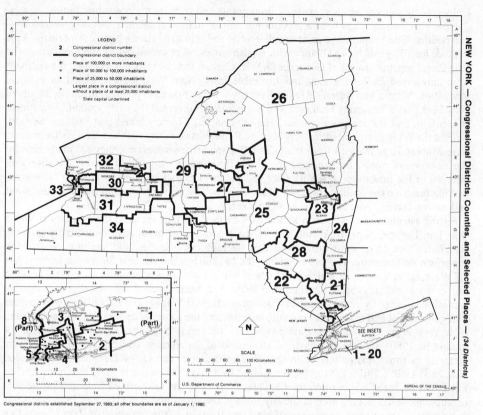

Congressional districts established September 27, 1983; all other boundaries are as of January 1, 1980.

See pages 1443-1448 for additional metropolitan area maps.

leader who eschewed pomp and was, in this moment of his greatest triumph, content to parade as a coarse politician seeking the votes of his equals, from a mass who reveled in the humbleness of their beginnings and the diversity of their origins. The great immigrant metropolis of New York, with its skyscrapers and public housing projects, its unequalled infrastructure of subways and bridges and parks, and its concentration of America's and the world's intellectuals and writers and artists, was at the beginning of the American half century, the city that was conquering the world.

New York was not always such a leader. Nature gave New York an excellent harbor, but during the Revolution it was only America's third city. Not until the 19th century did the descendants of Dutch patroons, Huguenot refugees, English West Indies traders, and Yankee farmers become the nation's most successful merchants and capitalists, forging the first routes to the great American interior through the valleys of the Hudson and the Mohawk, over the Finger Lakes and the Great Lakes, and building grand brownstone mansions on broad avenues in midtown Manhattan. That early diversity provides one clue to New York's success: if it has been a cynical town, ready to cooperate with Loyalists and Revolutionaries depending on which was ahead, it has also been tolerant, and ready to accept anyone smart or rich enough to be counted a success. It has been propelled upward at each stage—forging ahead of London as a financial and manufacturing center by the First World War, and staying ahead of surging

Chicago—by welcoming every wave of immigrants and consistently rewarding brains.

New York's success has been a product not only of market economics, but of government—and politics. The Iroquois, the most deeply-rooted and militarily strong Native Americans, kept in place for 100 years by an alliance with British troops, were driven out by the Revolution; the Erie Canal was the project of Governor DeWitt Clinton and the state government; the railroads were subsidized by land grants and favorable laws. New York led the nation in political innovation: Martin Van Buren's Albany Regency was the first state political machine, an ally of New York City's Tammany Hall, and Van Buren himself invented the party system, the national convention, and the inaugural parade. His adversaries, Thurlow Weed and William Seward, formed the Whig party and ultimately became Republicans; noting that Van Buren's Democrats were winning large margins from Irish Catholics and other immigrants, they too made bids for the newcomers' votes. Both parties serve the function of mediating between the divergent interests of the masses in New York City and the farmers and burghers of Upstate New York, making bearable the conflict you can still see in New York between city and country, immigrant and native, the Big Apple and the appleknockers.

Sitting astride a cultural chasm almost as wide as those that spawned the trenches of World War I in Europe, New York built one of the world's most productive and rapidly growing economies, one of its most progressive and tolerant communities, and the prototype of the American welfare state. The key event was the 1911 fire in the Triangle Shirtwaist factory, just off Washington Square, in which hundreds of women died, many jumping 11 stories, because fire escapes had not been installed and exits had been blocked off. To the investigative committee headed by young Tammany Democrats Robert Wagner and Al Smith, it was obvious that government had to step in to regulate business and use some of the great wealth produced in New York to protect the 2.3 million people then packed into Manhattan (as compared to 1.4 million in 1980) and the hundreds of thousands of immigrants and others working in tiny factories in thousands of loft buildings all over the city. The canny Democrat who headed Tammany Hall, Charles F. Murphy, recognized that there were votes in these measures, and he knew that he faced competition for the votes of Jews in the Lower East Side and in the new neighborhoods developing around subway stops in the Bronx and Brooklyn both from Socialists (who were winning some congressional elections then) and from progressive Republicans like Fiorello LaGuaradia. Tammany Democrats, disciplined by Murphy and led by Smith and Wagner (Roosevelt was an Upstate party rebel and a Wilson administration official then), wrote wage and working condition laws, passed a minimum wage, got New York state into the electric power business and built the nation's best system of roads.

So New York was a forerunner of the New Deal, and New York politics in the 1920s was a harbinger of American politics in the 1930s and 1940s. In the four decades after World War I, New York produced fully half the nation's prominent politicians: Smith, Roosevelt, Wagner and Averell Harriman among the Democrats, Thomas E. Dewey, Wendell Willkie, Dwight Eisenhower (a New York resident as president of Columbia in 1952) and Nelson Rockefeller among the Republicans. New York pioneered public housing and fair housing laws, industry-wide unions (in the garment trades), high minimum wages, rent control and dairy price fixing (to help New York City tenants and Upstate farmers). It took largely for granted the productivity of Wall Street and New York's thousands of small entrepreneurs, the factories of the Upstate industrial corridor and the affluence of its growing suburbs. Just as it led the nation in the canal and railroad eras, so in the 20th century New York spawned high-tech headquarters in the suburbs and Upstate: General Electric and IBM, Eastman Kodak and Xerox.

The Democrats carried New York by amassing big enough margins in New York City (771,000 in 1944, for example) to overcome the Republican margins Upstate (265,000 that year)—enough to carry the state by small percentages (52%–47% in 1944). The key swing voters were the Jews, then, as now, about one-quarter of New York City's population. Their aversion for Tammany and their affection for vaguely socialist ideas were reflected in the creation of separate American Labor and Liberal parties, so that Jewish immigrants who didn't read much English could vote for Roosevelt and LaGuardia's candidates by pulling the same party lever. The Democrats' welfare state policies held the governorship for 22 of the 24 years from 1918 to 1942; the liberal Republican policies—acceptance and enlargement of the welfare state—represented by Thomas Dewey and Nelson Rockefeller, enabled Republicans to hold the governorship for 28 of the 32 years from 1942 to 1974. National strategists took the peculiarities of New York—particularly the presence of a large leftish voting bloc—as a model for the nation, and built political strategies on the theory that Republicans couldn't win without backing liberal policies.

But what served as a good model up through the middle 1960s has been a poor one since—and one that hasn't worked very well even at home. New York state's population rose 32% from 1940 to 1965, and although New York City lost many people to the suburbs after World War II, the metropolitan area still easily led the nation in population and wealth. After the middle 1960s, the costs of New York's welfare state started to increase vastly and the benefits tended to dwindle in value, and between 1965 and 1987 the state's population grew just 1%. By the middle 1970s, New Yorkers were fleeing by hundreds of thousands to low-tax New Jersey, Connecticut and Florida (or New Hampshire: former Governor John Sununu made his way from Brooklyn to the White House via New Hampshire's low-tax politics), and New York's welfare state politics collapsed. Overgenerous spenders—ironically, they were mostly Republicans, Rockefeller and Mayor John Lindsay—spent the city almost to bankruptcy in 1975; the state government nearly went belly up shortly after. Retrenchment followed, supervised not by Governor Hugh Carey but by private leaders heading ad hoc public organizations, like Felix Rohatyn (who in the 1980s became a prophet of doom and gloom). Public employees unions had to accept cutbacks in jobs and salaries; citizens had to endure loss of services and deterioration of streets, bridges, subways; even renters lost some of their advantages after rent control helped devastate vast city neighborhoods by forcing landlords to abandon buildings, leaving them open to arsonists and looters. In the 1970s, the population of New York, city and state, dropped by 1 million—an unprecedented hemorrhage of the talented and the productive, a flight of the middle class away from a polity that seemed to be dying.

New York by the end of the 1980s was once again brimming with confidence, and the buzzing of economic growth and cultural innovation could again be heard over the never-ending blaring of its car horns. Its economy was growing, its population was rising, it was attracting immigrants once again. Manhattan was booming as an office center and remained the center of America's financial, clothing, entertainment, media and publishing industries. The outer boroughs were attracting migrants from Latin America, the eastern Mediterranean, Asia, even Russia—Colombians and Salvadorans, Greeks and Russian Jews, Haitians and Koreans—injecting vitality and a younger generation into what were aging, listless communities. With two genuinely bright leaders, Governor Mario Cuomo and Mayor Edward Koch, New York has balanced its budgets and paid off its debts, cut its taxes and seen enough revenue come in to permit at least some experiments and exercises of compassion. The clash between trendy Manhattan and the tradition-minded outer boroughs, so violent in John Lindsay's day, has now been muted as the outer boroughs grow and change (see the 1987 movie *Moonstruck*) and Manhattan rediscovers the virtues of homeownership and monogamy.

The divide in New York City politics in the late 1980s is between blacks, whose votes provided a strong showing in 1984 and a plurality victory in 1988 for Jesse Jackson in the presidential primary, and white homeowners in the outer boroughs. This divide has been widened by tragic incidents: the Howard Beach killings in late 1986 and the Tawana Brawley hoax. (Both are foreshadowed dimly in Tom Wolfe's savage *The Bonfire of the Vanities*: a case of life outdoing satiric art.) In fact, what the two sides want is not very different. New York's black voters, as

Jackson's rhetoric recognizes, are desperate to do something about the drug epidemic that threatens to turn their often middle-class neighborhoods into burned out shells, as large parts of the South Bronx and Brownsville were in John Lindsay's 1970s. (Koch has been talking about drugs too since 1983: these two savvy pols, who can't stand each other, both have good ears.) The outer boroughs' white voters, with investments in their houses now in the hundreds of thousands, living in neighborhoods of increasing vitality, are terrified themselves by the specter of the South Bronx and Brownsville. Rhetoric from Jackson and Koch which, taken literally, is not racial at all, seems incendiary in this atmosphere, and in early 1989 seemed likely to be replicated at least mildly in the year's mayoral race, with Koch being strongly challenged by black Manhattan Borough president David Dinkins. The winner of that contest will probably face Republican former federal prosecutor Rudolph Giuliani in the general who is likely to have the Liberal line on the ballot as well.

Whatever the outcome of that race, Koch in the city government and Cuomo in the state—even as they remain political rivals and, as in 1977 and 1982, opponents—have set a tone for New York politics and a course for New York government that is likely to prevail after they are gone. The tone is acerbic, insulting and smart, in many senses of the word: these may be nasty guys, but they are as brainy as any two politicians in the United States. Products of the outer boroughs who made their way upward in Manhattan without much help from anyone else, they speak in the natural idiom of the street in New York, both wise guy and wise: Al Smith would understand them in a minute. He might not be quite as pleased with the course they have set for government. Liberals of the Smith-Roosevelt-Wagner generation wanted to expand government almost indefinitely; they thought the opposition to such expansion was so strong that it was not incumbent on them to worry about the limits. Cuomo and Koch, chastened by the bankruptcy of the middle 1970s, worry a lot about the limits and, despite their rhetoric and tradition, don't propose much in the way of expansion. Cuomo has been determined to stick with his tax-cutting plans, whatever the effect on public programs—almost as if his 1982 opponent, supply-sider Lewis Lehrman, had won (as he nearly did). Koch has worked hard to encourage new development and has resisted urgings to pour new billions into programs for the poor. Up through the 1960s, New York politicians promised their constituents that they could solve all their problems. Now the best of them are promising that solving even minor problems is going to take a while longer.

And neither Koch nor Cuomo, for all their talents, have come up with solutions to two problems which, when analyzed, start to melt into one. The first is corruption, symbolized by the 1986 suicide of Queens Borough president Donald Manes when stories of payoffs to him began to appear. Bronx Democratic boss Stanley Friedman, Brooklyn Democratic boss Meade Esposito and others went to jail; some city officials were implicated. Not all were Koch appointees and no one believed Koch was involved; but damage was done at least to his reputation for competence.

The other issue is the ineffectiveness, even clumsiness, of the public sector. The government that was once supposed to solve everyone's problems now seems incapable of getting anything done: it can't finish a Sixty-third Street subway tunnel, although New Yorkers generations ago built dozens of subways; it can't find parents and homes for the boarder babies, who live in nurseries for years because of social workers' arguments; it couldn't resurface the Wollman Rink in Central Park for years, when Donald Trump could do it at his own expense in weeks.

Why these failures? Because government is so hedged in by requirements to make it responsive to this deserving constituency and impervious to that malign influence and invulnerable to graft and corruption, that a public sector designed to be fail-safe ends up simply failing. Koch's critics write as if the only mistake in New York was Koch's decision to yield a few small departments to favorites the likes of Esposito, Manes, and Friedman. The bigger mistake is that New York has over the years developed a public sector densely interwoven into daily life which is so good at stopping needed action and so poor at expediting it that those who want to do things that move society ahead—to run a vegetable stand or maintain an apartment house or drive a taxi—feel that they must give bribes just to keep government from getting in their way.

The decline of faith in the efficacy of the public sector has infected even the effete precincts of liberalism in Manhattan. Even as the liberal population grows somewhat in Manhattan—as the numbers of young singles, young married professionals and highly cultured mature New Yorkers increase, spreading from Central Park West and Riverside Drive to cover the entire West Side (as a generation ago they spread from Park Avenue and Carl Schurz Park to cover the East Side) and as SoHo and TriBeCa join Greenwich Village as trendy places to live—it is becoming somewhat less liberal in sentiment. Given the chance to repudiate the *Village Voice's* *bête blanche*, Edward Koch, in 1985, liberals backed him instead, and could conceivably do so again in 1989.

But not all of New York is New York City or in the orbit of its suburbs; nearly 40% of New York lives north of the Westchester and Rockland County lines, in Upstate. It no longer has the central transportation arteries it did in the days of the New York Central's water level route, and is instead off the beaten path: passenger trains no longer run, its freight lines were long bankrupt and poorly run and its airports are not very busy. Its population has not risen much since the 1950s. Its largest city, Buffalo, is one of those Great Lakes factory cities where old steel mills are closed and the economy sagged for a dozen years after the recession of 1973–74. But Upstate has great assets. It has a fine physical environment—green hills, majestic mountains, glistening lakes, a plentiful water supply—and its winters are no colder than those in booming Minnesota or New Hampshire. It has a high-skills labor force and high-tech employment base (Rochester's Kodak, Xerox and IBM) all over the place.

Meanwhile, the U.S.-Canada Free Trade Agreement (FTA) puts Upstate New York on the doorstep of the biggest and most prosperous parts of Canada: it is only a few minutes drive from Buffalo's Niagara Frontier to the Golden Horseshoe of Ontario that extends from St. Catharines to Hamilton and Toronto, and Interstate 87 leads straight from Montreal to Albany. The FTA may finally help Upstate solve its greatest problem, that it gets so little attention. For years it has been overshadowed by New York City, overlooked by those who concentrate on the East Coast or the Great Lakes, ignored by those who do not know that it was one of America's first frontiers, that it has fine colleges and cultural institutions that go back to the wave of Yankee settlements in the early 1800s, that it set the dominant cultural tone of the Yankee America that won the Civil War, settled the West and built an America that stretched all the way to the Pacific Ocean.

New York's major politicians do not neglect Upstate: Mario Cuomo has been through every county many times; Daniel Patrick Moynihan repairs to his farm in Pindar's Corners to write his annual book, and can tell you the history of every one of Upstate's 53 courthouses; even Edward Koch combed Upstate when he ran for governor in 1982. The Manhattan mega-rich—the Donald Trumps and Henry Kravises and Saul Steinbergs and Tom Wolfe's Bavardages—have become a source of fascination to millions, though they never seem to step out of a few luxury-lined buildings and blocks, in a time when speculator Ivan Boesky (temporarily not hobnobbing with the above) proclaimed that greed was good. Yet New York's leading politicians have set a different example. They come from backgrounds that were humble but proud, they won their initial elections by hairsbreadth margins—Moynihan beat Bella Abzug in the 1976 primary by 9,992 votes out of 916,000 cast; Koch beat Cuomo in the 1977 mayoral runoff; and Cuomo beat Koch by 60,000 in the 1982 gubernatorial primary and Lew Lehrman in the general with just 51% of the vote—and they are all original thinkers who usually say what they think. In office, they have helped to make the city and state once again a lesson to all Americans in how things can work and how government can make a better life for people. That may not be as great an achievement as the creation of New York's productive economy and the building of its generous welfare state, but it is no small achievement in a time when many had given up on government and politics, and in a state where any voice has a hard time being heard over the noise and clangor that are part—perhaps the heart—of everyday life.

Presidential politics. Fifty years ago New York was the key state in assembling Franklin Roosevelt's New Deal coalition, not because it was safely Democratic, but because it was so large (it had 47 electoral votes in the 1930s and 1940s, as many as California in the 1980s) and so closely divided. A huge vote in New York City (2,042,000 votes in 1944) enabled Roosevelt to carry the state narrowly (52%–47%). By the late 1980s, New York's place in presidential general elections had become less pivotal: it has 36 electoral votes, and is the most reliably Democratic of the 10 largest states. In 1988, it was the only one of the 10 to vote for Michael Dukakis, by a 51%–48% margin reminiscent of the margins by which Jimmy Carter and John Kennedy carried it in 1976 and 1960 (52%–47% and 53%–47% respectively). All three, and Roosevelt in 1944, got between 56% and 58% in the New York City metropolitan area and between 44% and 46% Upstate. The difference now is that the metropolitan area vote has changed. The huge margins Roosevelt and Kennedy won from Jews and Catholics in the Bronx, Brooklyn and parts of Queens have disappeared; there are now pockets of Jewish neighborhoods in each borough (along Ocean Parkway in Brooklyn, Rego Park and Flushing in Queens, Co-op City in the Bronx) which Democrats carry by wide margins, but white Catholics and Protestants in the city were as likely to vote for George Bush as Michael Dukakis and in the suburbs gave Bush significant margins.

It is now blacks who give the Democratic nominees their biggest margins, but they add up to only about 25% of the city and 12% of the state electorate; Puerto Ricans are also heavily Democratic, but their numbers have not increased much since Leonard Bernstein wrote *West Side Story* in the 1950s. The other Democratic base is concentrated in, but not limited to, Manhattan: young singles, affluent childless couples, feminists, gays and lesbians, the often underpaid highly educated people who flock to this center of arts and letters and long to be worthy of a scathing reference in *Spy* magazine. This segment of the electorate is not as leftish as it was in the 1970s, but they are still a good deal more liberal in the voting booth—more likely to vote for Dukakis, more likely to consider voting for Jesse Jackson—than any other white voters.

The big fireworks in New York's presidential politics are now shot off not in October or November but in its presidential primary in late March or early April. For years New York elected only delegates, with candidate preference not indicated: an attempt to preserve machine control which failed as early as 1968, when Eugene McCarthy candidates won most of the slots. With a tradition of statewide primaries that goes back only 20 years, New York has had low turnout: in a state where six million people vote in November, only 989,000 cast votes in the 1980 Carter-Kennedy contest. Jewish voters formed perhaps one-third of that electorate, and the 1980 and 1984 New York Democratic primaries were the one point in the presidential process that Jewish voters could exert maximum political leverage. Hence, Kennedy walloped Carter just after U.N. Ambassador Andrew Young made what was construed as an anti-Israel vote in the United Nations, and Walter Mondale and Gary Hart in 1984 argued about who would be more likely to move the U.S. Embassy from Tel Aviv to Jerusalem. But that year, Jesse Jackson's appeal to black voters started to stir the electorate, and the acrimonious 1988 contest increased turnout, black and white, even more. In 1984, Jackson won 355,000 out of 1.4 million votes cast; in 1988, 585,000 out of 1.6 million.

But Jackson also inspired great fear among many voters. In 1984, his "Hymietown" statement and his featuring of the anti-Jewish bigot Louis Farrakhan as warmup speaker at his rallies, alienated many, not all of them Jews, and these offenses were not entirely forgotten in 1988. On the other side, Mayor Edward Koch aroused a storm of protest in 1988 when he said that "Jews and others who care about Israel would be crazy" to vote for Jackson—a statement which, if he had simply omitted the first two words, would have been nothing more than a pungent argument based on genuine differences on a legitimate issue. But it was taken by many liberals as an incitement to racism or at least an appeal to ethnic solidarity, and Koch's endorsement of Albert Gore in the last days of the primary, far from helping him, destroyed whatever small chance Gore had of attracting attention to himself and away from the question, which seemed to dominate the primary, of whether you were for or against Jesse Jackson.

New York in 1984 had been a genuine three-way contest, with Mondale beating Hart 45%–27%, with 26% for Jackson. In 1988, it boiled down to a two-way race, in which Dukakis beat Jackson 51%–37%. Jackson did carry New York City, 46%–45%, which some took as an indication that a more conciliatory black like David Dinkins would be able to beat Ed Koch; but it is probably a mistake to assume that there is a straight carryover of preferences in contests involving such distinctive candidates. Interestingly, at this stage of the race, Dukakis's immigrant background seems to have helped him with Ellis Islanders generally: he not only beat Jackson among Jews 77%–7%, but won among white Catholics 70%–13%, a much better showing than his 57%–25% lead among white Protestants.

Republican primaries are as heavily tilted toward Upstate as Democratic contests are toward New York City. They are dominated not by laconic Yankees or upscale WASPs, but by Italian-Americans, who indeed form practically the entire Republican primary electorate in New York City and much of it in the suburbs and Upstate. They are not averse to a little government interference in the economy, but on cultural issues their approach is traditional, and even on economic issues like rent control they see themselves as adversaries of the great Democratic majority in New York City. In presidential contests, the Republicans elect delegates whose presidential preference is not identified on the ballot; there is no direct vote on the candidates themselves.

Any observer of New York politics should resist the temptation to focus on the machinations of New York City's Democratic bosses, the county chairmen in each of the four biggest boroughs—just as Edward Koch should have resisted the temptation to heed their recommendations for appointments. It should be apparent to anyone by now that they have little to do with the outcome of statewide or national elections. They are in a different business, the brokering of patronage; for higher office, a county chairman's endorsement is more often a liability than an asset. Probably the most powerful boss today is Joseph Mondello, who is not a Democrat and not from New York City, but is the Republican leader in suburban Nassau County. As for the state's minor parties, they have some potential influence because they can threaten to run separate candidates, but they no longer seem to move state politics in the direction they want, as the Liberals did in the 1950s and early 1960s and the Conservatives did in the late 1960s and 1970s. Both of these minor parties have never recovered from supporting mayoral candidates their constituents came to consider unsatisfactory: the Liberals for backing John Lindsay in 1965 and 1969, the Conservatives for backing Mario Biaggi in 1973.

Governor. Mario Cuomo, the governor of New York, is one of the nation's most interesting politicians and, to the press, often one of the most maddening. Reporters assume that he is always running for President, and try to see in every statement and act some hint of presidential campaign maneuvering. But in presidential politics Cuomo has done just exactly what he said he would—not run. What is more interesting about him is what he believes and the way he governs, and the tension between them. For he is his generation's most eloquent defender of the American welfare state and, at least inferentially, an advocate of its extension. Yet in practice, as the governor of the state that initiated so many welfare state mechanisms, he has cut taxes, held the line on much, though not all, spending and struggled to repair patches in the existing fabric of the welfare state rather than begin weaving anew.

Cuomo's roots are deep in New York. He grew up in South Jamaica, a rough neighborhood even then in Queens, the son of an immigrant grocer, speaking only Italian until he entered school, watching his parents work incredibly hard. The competitiveness Cuomo shows today must have been ingrained in him then: he got top grades at St. John's University and law school, clerked for a top judge, had a tryout in baseball's minor leagues. He had established a successful law practice in Brooklyn, one of thousands of outer borough lawyers, when he was appointed by Mayor John Lindsay in 1972 as a mediator between advocates and opponents of a low-income housing project in middle-income Forest Hills. His political rise was choppy: he lost a lieutenant governorship primary in 1974 (to Mary Ann Krupsak), was appointed secretary of state by Hugh Carey afterwards, ran for mayor and lost to Ed Koch in 1977, was elected lieutenant governor in 1978, and ran as an underfinanced underdog for governor in 1982. But he conquered Koch 52%–48% in the primary and Rite-Aid drug entrepreneur Lew Lehrman 51%–47% in the general—and promptly became one of the most popular New York politicians of all time.

As governor, Cuomo has increased education spending sharply and cut New York state's top state income tax rates from 10% to 7% in 1990. He vetoed capital punishment and has built many new prison cells. He pushed to raise New York's drinking age to 21 (it had been 18 since the repeal of prohibition). He opposed the Shoreham nuclear plant on Long Island and eventually succeeded in preventing it from opening. He got bills passed on enterprise zones and $400 million for low and moderate income housing. With billion dollar bond issues, he pushed programs to rebuild roads and clean up the environment, and he worked to help rebuild New York City's transportation system.

This record has disappointed those who hoped he would push for a more active government to help the poor, and some charge that he is responding to the political initiatives of conservatives (on taxes and prisons, for example) rather than taking the initiative himself. Certainly, there is a tension here with the vision he presented in his 1984 Democratic National Convention keynote speech in which he depicted two Americas, one rich and cynical and glutted with gain, the other hungry and impoverished and in need of a helping hand. But with the logic and reasoning he learned from the Vincentians, and from a long Catholic tradition that understands the need to reconcile lofty ideals with the demands of the world, Cuomo seems to be saying that, as governor of New York, and as one part of a much larger political process, he is constrained from raising taxes too high and has a responsibility to foster economic growth, even at the cost of not doing some things he would like to do. "We stand on the shoulders of giants," Cuomo said in San Francisco, talking of the achievements of immigrants like his father; and as governor he is standing on the shoulders of the giants who built New York's generous—overgenerous—welfare state, trying to maintain as much of their work as he can, and extending it a little if he is able.

Consider, in this connection, Cuomo's metaphor of the family. It has been taken as suggesting that government has an all-encompassing responsibility to take care of each member of society, and to ignore costs in doing so (and Cuomo generally, in line with Catholic tradition, has negative attitudes toward free economic markets). But if Cuomo uses the idea of family to preach toleration (his argument on AIDS starts: how would you feel if your child were gay?), he also sees the state as paternalistic (hence the 21-year-old drinking age). A parent does not just give a child everything he wants, and—especially for a man whose parents struggled in South Jamaica—a parent cannot always afford to give his children everything he would like. For Cuomo, family means not just compassion and interrelatedness; it also implies traditional standards of personal morality and a sense of limits. Cuomo's is the kind of politics that naturally comes from the product of a hard-working family in a tight-knit neighborhood in Queens.

The federal government, as Cuomo suggested in 1984 and since, can and should do more. In 1988, he formed his own Cuomo Commission, which came up with recommendations, some familiar and some not. It would cut the deficit with higher taxes, reduced defense and farm programs, and social security cutbacks for high-income recipients: all except the first have been tried, at least to some extent. One that hasn't been tried much is his recommendation for an industrial policy—business-labor-government task forces to restructure vital industries; but appeals by Gary Hart and others for industrial policy in 1982 and 1983 could not be sustained in the face of skepticism (voiced by some prominent Democrats as well as Republicans) that government can pick winners and make intelligent plans for future growth. The commission would also attack the trade deficit by rescheduling Third World debt (as Bill Bradley has proposed) and putting pressure on Japan and Europe to import more and export less.

That sounds something like a platform for a presidential campaign. But Cuomo has tantalized and teased and toyed with a New York and national press that seem obsessed with the idea that he is running for President. At each stage, he has done just exactly what he said he would do, which of course goes against every insider's expectation. In 1982, he said he wouldn't run for President if he were elected governor, and he didn't; he said he would endorse a candidate after a series of New York forums, and he held the forums and endorsed Walter Mondale. His 1984 keynote stimulated speculation again, but in 1986 he repeated that he wasn't planning to run for President and he was easily reelected governor in New York, beating whimsical Westchester County Executive Andrew O'Rourke 65%–32%, a state record, in a race chiefly characterized by Cuomo's acerbic exchanges with the press. Then, in February 1987, on a radio call-in show after newspaper reporters' deadlines, he took himself out of the presidential race (one side effect: another northeastern governor, Michael Dukakis, started thinking seriously about running). Then began speculation that Cuomo was waiting for a draft (which ignored utterly the arithmetic of delegate gathering, making that scenario exceedingly unlikely) and endless questions about when Cuomo was going to endorse (as if New York and other voters were waiting around, unable to decide between Dukakis and Jesse Jackson, until Cuomo gave them the word).

This game is likely to be played out again in 1989 and 1990, even—or especially—if Cuomo surprises everyone by not running for reelection as governor. Analysts will examine every statement for the slightest nuance and ambiguity. They will speculate that he is worried about anti-Italian prejudice, about attacks on his son Andrew who has been his chief adviser or on other relatives, or about his relations with the press. They will ignore the fact that he has been entirely frank so far about what he would do. It is possible, after all, that he doesn't particularly want to either run for or be President, that the job is not that attractive for a man who, even as governor of a large state, tends to keep counsel with only a few close advisers and who cherishes his privacy and his chances for quiet intellectual introspection. His mother, he likes to say, asks him when he will get a secure job and become a judge. When you think about where Cuomo has come from, and how narrow the margins were by which he got where he is, that becomes less funny and more poignant, and suggests that Mario Cuomo regards the challenges of the governorship of the nation's second largest state as quite enough for him, thank you.

Senators. Every year a tall, gray-haired former Harvard professor spends several weeks in an old one-room schoolhouse in Pindar's Corners, deep in the hills of Upstate New York, writing in distinctive prose another book filled with original thought about—oh, almost anything: arms control or the Constitution and deficits, the tendency of opposing organizations to resemble each other or the rising proportion of children raised in single-parent homes. He is Senator Daniel Patrick Moynihan, the kind of philosopher-politician who would fill the ranks of the Senate in many people's ideal republic. Yet for all his academic credentials, Moynihan has had a range of experience in American government as broad as any Member of Congress. He worked for Governor Averell Harriman in the 1950s, served as Assistant Secretary of Labor in the Kennedy and Johnson Administrations, was chief domestic adviser to President Nixon and his ambassador to India, and was ambassador to the United Nations under President Ford—the only person in American history, he likes to note, who has served in the cabinet or subcabinet of four successive Presidents.

In all these jobs he displayed his penchant for original thinking and his taste for controversy. For years he was regarded with hostility by black political activists because of his warning about the breakup of black families in the middle 1960s (though they are now concerned about the same trend, much worsened) and by foreign policy doves for his assertive beliefs in American principles (though they now realize that those principles provide the strongest basis for their own beliefs). He crafted the Nixon Administration's family assistance program and saw it savaged by the left and scuttled by the right in the Senate Finance Committee, where he now sits and on which he sponsored the successful welfare reform package of 1988. At the United Nations, he spoke out against Russia and for Israel and ignored the conventional wisdom that policymakers should accept the premises of Third World and Soviet demands and negotiate quietly for small concessions; his policy is now approaching consensus status, as leaders of the Third World and even of the Soviet Union have been forced by events and stands like Moynihan's to admit that market economics and political democracy provide better guides than anything they have come up with. Moynihan's prescience, his ability to spot rising issues, is almost eerie. In the early 1960s, to cite just one example, before Ralph Nader, he was writing about auto safety. In 1969, to cite another, he was negotiating an agreement with the French and Turkish governments to end the drug traffic known as "the French connection."

Moynihan showed the same uncanny instinct for spotting issues throughout the 1980s. In the spring of 1981, when he pounced on Reagan Administration proposals to cut scheduled future social security benefits, striding forward with a resolution denouncing any benefit cuts, which was beaten only by a 49–48 vote; promptly, the Senate adopted a resolution by Bob Dole, that said much the same thing, by 96–0. In his 1985 Godkin Lectures at Harvard, published as *Family and Nation*, Moynihan returned 20 years after his family report on the Negro (the term then in use) family to the subject of society's treatment of children, and found it wanting. "We have eliminated poverty for the elderly," he said in essence, "only to see it burgeon for children." Quickly, he translated this insight into legislation that became the 1988 welfare reform act. It starts out by recognizing for the first time the responsibilities of fathers to provide for their children, then it puts single mothers under an obligation to obtain work, and only then does it provide some benefits—education and training programs, residual aid and medicaid—to help them do so. It has been dismissed by some as just tinkering with the problem, and it does not throw large sums of money at it. But if one of the evils of the existing system has been to create a mentality sanctioning dependency by mothers and irresponsibility by fathers, then Moynihan's law makes a move toward withdrawing that sanction and insisting that those who receive benefits must meet responsibilities, as well. If fortified on other fronts, these ideas may do as much to break down the underclass as proposals that rest solely on providing (or withdrawing) specific amounts of aid.

Moynihan was busy on other legislative duties as well. In 1985 and 1986, he was vice-chairman of the Intelligence Committee, resigning momentarily after CIA Director William Casey withheld required information, and returning again to cooperate with chairman Barry Goldwater. On the Finance Committee, he worked on the tax reform bill, insisting early on maintaining deductions for state and local taxes (worth more in New York than anywhere else) and supporting steadfastly thereafter the bill that passed. He worked closely with Sam Nunn in fashioning the Senate version of the 1988 drug bill. He had one significant defeat, yielding to Frank Lautenberg of New Jersey on ocean sludge dumping (New York City wanted to keep dumping; New Jersey wanted it to stop). He started a long-term fight to keep the current surpluses in the social security system from being used for other purposes or counted against other deficits under Gramm-Rudman. He has attacked the Reagan deficits as having been purposefully created to block increases in domestic spending, citing his onetime in-house babysitter in Cambridge, former OMB Director David Stockman; but he does not want to imperil social security in order to have a few more dollars, even for domestic programs. In an odd moment, he pushed through the repeal of the McCarran Act provision requiring the State Department to deny foreign writers and artists entry to the United States if they are deemed somehow subversive. And he is Congress's only promoter of "maglev," trains that are run above special tracks by magnetic levitation at speeds much greater than can be achieved on rails. He is alarmed that West Germany and Japan are ahead of us in this technology (Germans want to build a track between Los Angeles and Las Vegas), and wants the federal government to fund research for this mode of transportation as it did for canals, railroads, and airplanes in the past.

To many, Moynihan seemed an unlikely politician; he lost a race for New York City council president in 1965 and only narrowly beat Bella Abzug in the 1976 Democratic senatorial primary. But electoral politics has proved surprisingly congenial to him, and holding electoral office seems to have made him intellectually even more original and daring. In the 1976 general election he won routinely over incumbent James Buckley, who improved on the percentage with which he had won the three-way race of 1970 but not enough to win a two-way battle. For 1982, Moynihan avoided primary opposition from the left by emphasizing his disagreement with Reagan on social security, the Equal Rights Amendment and aid to cities, and he eliminated Republican Congressman Bruce Caputo when it became known that Caputo had a falsified military record. That fall, he won 65%–34%—a record for a New York Senate race. In 1988, there was not even a hint of opposition from Democrats, and potentially serious Republicans— notably U.S. Attorney Rudolph Giuliani—took a look at the race and backed away. His opponent, Garden City attorney Robert McMillan, Dan Rather of CBS said, "had as much business in this race as a moose in a phone booth," and Moynihan won 67%–31%, breaking his own record, carrying all but one county (Hamilton), and winning more votes than any other Senator in American history except for the two current incumbents from California. Another (apparent) record: he carried the Hasidic Orthodox village of New Square in Rockland County 756–21, while George Bush was carrying it 773–9, indicating that more than 95% of the voters split their tickets. His wife Elizabeth, otherwise a scholar of Mogul gardens, serves as his campaign manager; they met while campaigning for Harriman. Perhaps they will set more records in 1994; Moynihan has refrained from indicating whether he will run for another term then.

Alfonse D'Amato, in the middle of his second term, is to many "Senator Pothole," concentrating almost entirely on local matters, not taken seriously as a thinker (though sometimes respected as an operator) on national issues. He comes from Nassau County, the suburban tract just east of Queens which filled up in the two decades after World War II. He is a product of its Republican machine politics and was one of its biggest operatives, as presiding supervisor of the town of Hempstead (a big town, with 800,000 people, but a post of limited powers) in a county where employees had to give 1% of their salaries to the Republican Party and where D'Amato regularly used insurance brokers recommended by county boss Joseph Margiotta, who went to jail for taking kickbacks from them. D'Amato's great political insight was that he could win the 1980 Republican primary against Senator Jacob Javits, who was, as D'Amato's ads bluntly pointed out, 76, ailing and liberal. He won that fall with 45% of the vote, as Javits stayed in the race as the Liberal nominee; after six years of practical-minded service, he was reelected over former Ralph Nader associate Mark Green, who renounced all PAC money and would have been vastly outspent anyway. By that time, most voters seemed satisfied with D'Amato's responsiveness and uninterested in charges that his 1980 campaign had received loans below prime from a bank into which he'd put public monies, or the fact that he testified for a night club owner accused of conspiring with organized crime figures—D'Amato brushed all such charges aside as unimportant.

As a Senator, D'Amato has also been shrewd to the point of shamelessness in taking practically any position, espousing any cause, and lobbying for any project or program that could be popular with even the smallest segment of the New York electorate, while turning his back without a moment's hesitation on those who helped him get where he is (Margiotta, for example). All the while he remains jovial and good-humored—as if he were elbowing erstwhile opponents in the ribs and saying, it's only a game, right? "O.K., I love ya, babes," he signs off his phone conversations. Shamelessly, he fastens on the momentary popularity of a figure like subway shooter Bernhard Goetz or a tragedy like the terrorist murder of Leon Klinghoffer. D'Amato's major legislative achievements are of the same ilk, though policy arguments can be made for them. He champions the death penalty for drug dealers at every opportunity, and works to put it in must-pass defense bills. He originated a residential drug-free program. He pounced hard on the Reagan Administration for not being tougher in going after Panama's Manuel Noriega. On the Banking Committee, he seeks to do something to get builders to put up more affordable housing and proposes higher limits on FHA mortgage guarantees, without much regard to risk for the government.

He is anything but shy about using his seats on committees—Appropriations and Banking—to pump money into New York, and perhaps into his own campaign. When it looked like Geraldine Ferraro might run against him in 1986, he was busy raising $5 million, including some $500,000 in contributions from New York's financial district; on Banking, he invariably backs Wall Street firms in their fights against big banks. The massive power he has over New York patronage has gotten him into some embroilments; some of his appointments have been attacked, and he blocked Rudolph Giuliani's choice as successor in the key U.S. attorney job in Manhattan. D'Amato continues to have a good job rating and is probably in strong shape for reelection in 1992. But if Mario Cuomo decides not to run for reelection as governor, D'Amato has said he would be interested in that office; and it would be interesting to see whether New York would be ready to put the former presiding supervisor of the town of Hempstead and the current "Senator Pothole" in charge of the state government, its huge budget, and all its appointments.

Mayor. For many years the budget of New York City was bigger than the budget of New York state, and in many ways the mayor of New York sets the tone for public life in the city. Edward Koch, elected in 1977, 1981 and 1985, was highly popular with most voters in the outer boroughs—whose views he tends to express volubly and often at length and whose gritty style he personifies—until the breaking of the Queens and Bronx scandals in 1986. He can still claim to have made a success of city government in New York, restoring its finances, raising slowly the quality of public services, forestalling the excesses of racial quotas while appointing the city's first black police commissioner. And he might add that even if one concedes, as Jack Newfield and Wayne Barrett have charged, that he gave up a couple of commissionerships to hacks named by the party bosses who turned out to be crooks, the damage to New York's governance has been limited. (Who cares if someone might made some extra dough off parking meters?)

The more difficult question Koch might address as he seeks to become New York's first four-term mayor, and which David Dinkins, Rudolph Giuliani, and others might address as they seek the office, is the balance between corruption and regulation in this money-making and money-mad commercial metropolis. On the one hand, the pressure for corruption is great. Yet the complex rules and administration set up to prevent corruption tend to increase that pressure: the only way to get around the red tape and actually get something done is to grease someone's palm. In commerce, New Yorkers are used to getting things done and paying for them, quite legitimately. In government, when they do that they're corrupting the system. One solution to this might be less regulation and more reliance on market mechanisms, with more political accountability for elected officials than has seemed sensible in a city where voters throw up their hands and say everyone does it.

The city in any case must change its government structure because of a March 1989 court decision ruling that the borough presidents cannot have equal votes on the Board of Estimate. The borough presidents' major power came from those votes, since the Board had to approve the city budget and major expenditures, and the charter commission set up to write new rules had to decide whether to increase the borough presidents' power or allow the office to become relatively unimportant. All this came when the outlook for the mayoral election was anything but clear. In early polls Koch trailed Dinkins, but he has not been tested in the superacerbic environment of a New York campaign. Neither for that matter has Giuliani, a onetime Democrat who won the Liberal party nomination and spurned the Conservatives, and who led both Koch and Dinkins in early polls. If Giuliani wins he will be the first Republican mayor of New York since John Lindsay left office in 1972.

Congressional districting. Every 10 years since 1950 the New York legislature has been faced with the unhappy task of reducing the number of New York's congressional districts—in 1982, it went from 39 to 34; in 1992, it will go from 34 to 31 or 32. This sets up a game of musical chairs with the losers usually being the political mavericks with little clout. The New York delegation, while not cohesive, is not as fractious as it was, for example, in the early 1970s. It has good clout on Ways and Means, which helped preserve the deduction for state and local taxes in the 1986 tax reform; it is weaker now in Appropriations and Armed Services, which worries the big defense contractors on Long Island.

The People: Est. Pop. 1988: 17,898,000; Pop. 1980: 17,558,072, up 1.9% 1980–88 and dn. 3.7% 1970–80; 7.37% of U.S. total, 2d largest. 14% with 1–3 yrs. col., 19% with 4+ yrs. col.; 13.4% below poverty level. Single ancestry: 11% Italian, 6% Irish, 5% German, English, 3% Polish, 2% Russian, 1% French, Greek, Hungarian. Households (1980): 70% family, 37% with children, 54% married couples; 51.4% housing units rented; median monthly rent: $211; median house value: $45,900. Voting age pop. (1980): 12,870,209; 12% Black, 8% Spanish origin, 2% Asian origin. Registered voters (1988): 8,581,276; 3,494,050 D (41%); 2,472,438 R (29%); 1,692,919 unaffiliated and minor parties (20%).

1988 Share of Federal Tax Burden: $77,852,000,000; 8.80% of U.S. total, 2d largest.

1988 Share of Federal Expenditures

	Total		Non-Defense		Defense	
Total Expend	$60,677m	(6.86%)	$51,331m	(7.83%)	$10,899m	(4.77%)
St/Lcl Grants	12,494m	(10.90%)	12,493m	(10.91%)	1m	(1.31%)
Salary/Wages	5,952m	(4.43%)	4,618m	(6.89%)	1,334m	(6.89%)
Pymnts to Indiv	31,110m	(7.60%)	30,804m	(7.89%)	306m	(1.64%)
Procurement	9,243m	(4.90%)	1,552m	(3.34%)	9,243m	(4.90%)
Research/Other	1,878m	(5.03%)	1,864m	(5.03%)	14m	(5.03%)

Political Lineup: Governor, Mario M. Cuomo (D); Lt. Gov., Stanley N. Lundine (D); Secy. of State, Gail Shaffer (D); Atty. Gen., Robert Abrams (D); Comptroller, Edward V. Regan (R). State Senate, 61 (34 R and 27 D); State Assembly, 150 (92 D and 58 R). Senators, Daniel Patrick Moynihan (D) and Alfonse M. D'Amato (R). Representatives, 34 (21 D and 13 R).

1988 Presidential Vote

Dukakis (D)	3,347,882	(51%)
Bush (R)	3,081,871	(48%)

1984 Presidential Vote

Reagan (R)	3,664,763	(54%)
Mondale (D)	3,119,609	(46%)

1988 Democratic Presidential Primary

Dukakis	801,457	(51%)
Jackson	585,076	(37%)
Gore	157,559	(10%)
Simon	17,011	(1%)

GOVERNOR

Gov. Mario M. Cuomo (D)

Elected 1982, term expires Jan. 1991; b. June 15, 1932, Queens; home, Queens; St. John's U., B.A. 1953, LL.B. 1956; Roman Catholic; married (Matilda).

Career: Confidential Legal Asst. to Judge Adrian T. Burke, NY State Crt. of Appeals, 1956–58; Practicing atty., 1958–74; Prof., St. John's U. Sch. of Law, 1958–74; Secy. of State of NY, 1975–78; Lt. Gov., 1978–82.

Office: Executive Chamber, State Capitol, Albany 12224, 518-474-8390.

Election Results

1986 gen.	Mario M. Cuomo (D)	2,775,229	(65%)
	Andrew J. O'Rourke (R)	1,363,810	(32%)
	Dillon Droseskey (RTL)	130,802	(3%)
1986 prim.	Mario M. Cuomo (D) unopposed		
1982 gen.	Mario M. Cuomo (D-L)	2,675,213	(51%)
	Lewis E. Lehrman (R-C-SI)	2,494,827	(47%)

SENATORS

Sen. Daniel Patrick Moynihan (D)

Elected 1976, seat up 1994; b. Mar. 16, 1927, Tulsa, OK; home, Pindars Corners; CCNY, 1943, Tufts U., B.A. 1948, M.A. 1949, Ph.D. 1961, LL.D. 1968; Roman Catholic; married (Elizabeth).

Career: Navy, 1944–47; University professor; Aide to Gov. Averell Harriman, 1955–58; U.S. Asst. Secy. of Labor, 1963–65; Dir., Joint Ctr. for Urban Studies, MIT and Harvard, 1966–69; Asst. to the Pres. for Urban Affairs, 1969–70; Ambassador to India, 1973–75; Ambassador to the U.N., 1975–76.

Offices: 464 RSOB 20510, 202-224-4451. Also 733 3d Ave., New York 10017, 212-661-5150; Guaranty Bldg., 28 Church St., Buffalo 14202, 716-846-4097; and 214 Main St., Oneonta 13820, 607-433-2310.

Committees: *Environment and Public Works* (2d of 9 D). Subcommittees: Environmental Protection; Nuclear Regulation; Water Resources, Transportation and Infrastructure (Chairman). *Finance* (3d of 11 D). Subcommittees: International Trade; Social Security and Family Policy (Chairman); Private Retirement Plans and Oversight of the Internal Revenue Service. *Foreign Relations* (9th of 10 D). Subcommittees: African Affairs; Near Eastern and South Asian Affairs (Chairman); Terrorism, Narcotics and International Operations. *Rules and Administration* (7th of 9 D). *Joint Committee on the Library. Joint Committee on Taxation.*

Group Ratings

	ADA	ACLU	COPE	CFA	LCV	ACU	NTLC	NSI	COC	CEI
1988	90	74	92	92	90	8	9	20	31	13
1987	95	—	92	100	—	0	—	—	31	19

National Journal Ratings

	1988 LIB — 1988 CONS		1987 LIB — 1987 CONS	
Economic	74% —	19%	74% —	0%
Social	74% —	24%	90% —	4%
Foreign	70% —	25%	81% —	0%

Key Votes

1) Cut Aged Housing $	FOR	5) Bork Nomination	AGN	9) SDI Funding	AGN
2) Override Hwy Veto	FOR	6) Ban Plastic Guns	AGN	10) Ban Chem Weaps	AGN
3) Kill Plnt Clsng Notice	AGN	7) Deny Abortions	FOR	11) Aid To Contras	AGN
4) Min Wage Increase	FOR	8) Japanese Reparations	FOR	12) Reagan Defense $	AGN

Election Results

1988 general	Daniel Patrick Moynihan (D-L) 4,048,649	(67%)	($4,809,810)
	Robert R. McMillan (R-C). 1,875,784	(31%)	($528,989)
1988 primary	Daniel Patrick Moynihan (D), unopposed		
1982 general	Daniel Patrick Moynihan (D-L) 3,232,146	(65%)	($2,708,660)
	Florence Sullivan (R-C-RTL) 1,696,766	(34%)	($117,875)

Sen. Alfonse M. D'Amato (R)

Elected 1980, seat up 1992; b. Aug. 1, 1937, Brooklyn; home, Island Park; Syracuse U., B.S. 1959, J.D. 1961; Roman Catholic; separated.

Career: Nassau Cnty. Public Admin., 1965–68; Hempstead Town Receiver of Taxes, 1969, Sprvsr., 1971–77; Presiding Sprvsr., Vice Chmn., Nassau Cnty. Bd. of Sprvsrs., 1977–80.

Offices: 520 HSOB 20510, 202-224-6542. Also 420 Leo O'Brien Fed. Bldg., Albany 12207, 518-463-2244; Fed. Bldg., 111 W. Huron, Rm. 620, Buffalo 14202, 716-846-4111; 7 Penn Plaza, 7th Ave., Ste. 600, New York 10001, 212-947-7390; 1259 Fed. Bldg., 100 S. Clinton St., Syracuse 13260, 315-423-5471; and 100 State St., 304 Fed. Bldg., Rochester 14614, 716-263-5866.

Committees: *Appropriations* (7th of 13 R). Subcommittees: Defense; Foreign Operations; VA, HUD and Independent Agencies; Treasury, Postal Service and General Government; Transportation (Ranking Member). *Banking, Housing, and Urban Affairs* (3d of 9 R). Subcommittees: Housing and Urban Affairs (Ranking Member); Securities; Consumer and Regulatory Affairs. *Select Committee on Intelligence* (7th of 7 R).

Group Ratings

	ADA	ACLU	COPE	CFA	LCV	ACU	NTLC	NSI	COC	CEI
1988	15	28	46	50	40	80	40	100	64	31
1987	30	—	45	58	—	56	—	—	44	30

National Journal Ratings

	1988 LIB — 1988 CONS		1987 LIB — 1987 CONS	
Economic	33% —	65%	44% —	50%
Social	25% —	74%	16% —	78%
Foreign	9% —	89%	0% —	76%

Key Votes

1) Cut Aged Housing $	AGN	5) Bork Nomination	FOR	9) SDI Funding	FOR
2) Override Hwy Veto	FOR	6) Ban Plastic Guns	AGN	10) Ban Chem Weaps	FOR
3) Kill Plnt Clsng Notice	AGN	7) Deny Abortions	FOR	11) Aid To Contras	FOR
4) Min Wage Increase	AGN	8) Japanese Reparations	FOR	12) Reagan Defense $	FOR

Election Results

1986 general	Alfonse M. D'Amato (R-C-RTL)	2,378,197	(57%)	($12,914,822)
	Mark Green (D)	1,723,216	(41%)	($1,635,676)
1986 primary	Alfonse M. D'Amato (R), unopposed			
1980 general	Alfonse M. D'Amato (R-C-RTL)	2,699,965	(45%)	($1,699,709)
	Elizabeth Holtzman (D)	2,618,661	(44%)	($2,173,056)
	Jacob K. Javits (L)	664,544	(11%)	($1,846,313)

FIRST DISTRICT

Fifty years ago, the eastern half of Long Island—America's largest island—was a backwater. Its landmarks—the Montauk Lighthouse, the old fishing ports of Sag Harbor and Shelter Island, the mansions behind the dunes at Southampton—were just recovering from the 1938 hurricane which leveled everything in its path; the fields inland were sown with potatoes, and shoreline inlets were used to raise thousands of Long Island ducklings. Rich people from New York came out here in the summer, but almost no one dreamed that the New York metropolitan area would march out into eastern Suffolk County.

But by the middle 1960s it had. As Nassau County filled up in the 15 years after World War II, developers looked eastward to cheaper land amid the potato fields and the aircraft factories, and the suburbs moved out past the docks of the Fire Island ferries almost to the Hamptons. The people here tended to be less upscale and less liberal than the suburbanites of Nassau; there were more young families and fewer aficionados of Manhattan culture, more Catholics and Protestants and fewer Jews. The result is that Suffolk County is one of the most conservative parts of New York state in national politics; Suffolk was the only county to give an absolute majority to Conservative Senator James Buckley when he won the three-way race of 1970. Yet in congressional politics, all three of Suffolk's districts are represented by Democrats, and have been through most of the 1980s.

The reason, in the case of the 1st District, which covers the North Shore eastward from Nissequogue and the South Shore east from Patchogue, can be summed up in a single word: Shoreham. This is an old town on the North Shore, where the local utility Lilco had been trying to build a nuclear power plant since the 1970s. In a familiar pattern, costs have skyrocketed while safety concerns have grown; a federal regulatory official was fired because he would not say Lilco's evacuation procedures were satisfactory; residents were threatened with higher electricity rates. Governor Mario Cuomo strongly opposed Shoreham and in 1987 finally engineered a bailout, leaving the plant permanently unopened and putting much of the cost on local rate-payers. In the meantime, the issue came up in House politics. Congressman Robert Carney, a registered Conservative when he was first elected in 1978, stoutly defended Lilco and Shoreham. The issue nearly cost him reelection in 1984: he got only 52% in the primary and 53% in the general, and in 1986, a month after the Chernobyl nuclear accident in the Soviet Union, Carney decided to retire from the House at age 44.

That left the field open for George Hochbrueckner, the Democrat who nearly beat Carney in 1984. An engineer who worked his way up in the aerospace industry despite the lack of a college degree, a member of the New York Assembly for eight years starting in 1975, Hochbrueckner was an outspoken opponent of Shoreham. Meanwhile, local Republicans, forever feuding among themselves and with Conservatives over local politics and patronage, gave less than whole-hearted backing to Hochbrueckner's opponent, and the Democrat won 51%–42%. Hochbrueckner had a busy and eventful two years. He at first backed, then backed away from the Cuomo Shoreham solution, because of the rise in local rates; he got a seat on the Armed Services Committee, of vital importance to Long Island's defense plants; at first, he stuck with New York City's insistence on dumping sludge in the ocean 106 miles off New Jersey, then, after beaches were littered with plastic and medical waste, switched and, along with New Jersey's Members, pushed the bill that outlawed the dumping.

The 1988 Republican candidate, Suffolk County legislator Edward Romaine, attacked Hochbrueckner for switching on Shoreham and ocean dumping and for opposing the death penalty for drug dealers. Hochbrueckner defended himself, telling *Newsday*, "I used Shoreham [as an issue] to get me here because it is clearly what people care about. As part of my getting here, I had to tackle that issue and do something about it." Like most incumbents, Hochbrueckner worked hard on constituency service and returned often to the district. But Romaine's attacks must have hit home since, though outspent, he made this one of the closest races in the nation and lost by just 51%–49%.

Hochbrueckner is not without resources for 1990. With the retirement of Sam Stratton, he is New York state's senior Democrat on Armed Services and, with the death of Joseph Addabbo, the member best positioned to defend Long Island's defense contractors. He is the sponsor of the Lyme Disease Act of 1989. (Suffolk is America's number one Lyme disease county.) But sentiment on national issues remains Republican and the Shoreham issue may be fading. So the prospects are that this will be a seriously contested race once more.

The People: Est. Pop. 1986: 545,300, up 5.6% 1980–86; Pop. 1980: 516,407, up 36.7% 1970–80. Households (1980): 81% family, 49% with children, 69% married couples; 21.5% housing units rented; median monthly rent: $281; median house value: $43,700. Voting age pop. (1980): 350,987; 4% Black, 3% Spanish origin, 1% Asian origin.

1988 Presidential Vote:

Bush (R)	131,180	(60%)
Dukakis (D)	85,652	(39%)

Rep. George Hochbrueckner (D)

Elected 1986; b. Sept. 20, 1938, Jamaica, Queens; home, Coram; St. U. of NY, Stonybrook, Hofstra U.; Roman Catholic; married (Carol Ann).

Career: Navy, 1956–59; Engineer, 1961–75; NY Assembly, 1975–84.

Offices: 124 CHOB 20515, 202-225-3826. Also 3771 Nesconset Hwy., Ste. 213, Centereach 11720, 516-689-6767.

Committees: *Armed Services* (24th of 31 D). Subcommittees: Research and Development; Seapower and Strategic and Critical Materials; Military Personnel and Compensation. *Merchant Marine and Fisheries* (20th of 26 D). Subcommittees: Fisheries and Wildlife Conservation and the Environment; Coast Guard and Navigation.

Group Ratings

	ADA	ACLU	COPE	CFA	LCV	ACU	NTLC	NSI	COC	CEI
1988	80	74	93	100	88	12	12	20	36	13
1987	92	—	93	93	—	4	—	—	27	4

National Journal Ratings

	1988 LIB — 1988 CONS			1987 LIB — 1987 CONS		
Economic	79%	—	17%	73%	—	0%
Social	56%	—	43%	62%	—	36%
Foreign	74%	—	23%	76%	—	19%

Key Votes

1) Homeless $	AGN	5) Ban Drug Test	AGN	9) SDI Research	AGN
2) Gephardt Amdt	FOR	6) Drug Death Pen	AGN	10) Ban Chem Weaps	FOR
3) Deficit Reduc	FOR	7) Handgun Sales	AGN	11) Aid to Contras	AGN
4) Kill Plnt Clsng Notice	AGN	8) Ban D.C. Abort $	FOR	12) Nuclear Testing	FOR

Election Results

1988 general	George J. Hochbrueckner (D-ARE)......	105,624	(51%)	($732,956)
	Edward P. Romaine (R-C-RTL).........	102,327	(49%)	($217,971)
1988 primary	George J. Hochbrueckner (D-ARE), unopposed			
1986 general	George J. Hochbrueckner (D)	67,139	(51%)	($416,332)
	Gregory J. Blass (R-CAL)	55,413	(42%)	($277,947)
	Dominic J. Santoro (C).................	4,345	(3%)	
	William J. Doyle (RTL)	4,134	(3%)	

SECOND DISTRICT

Into the potato fields of central Long Island, in the 20 booming years after World War II, poured hundreds of thousands of New Yorkers—mostly people who thought they would always live within the boundaries of the city and never imagined that they would find their way—except for Sunday outings—this far out on the Island. The highways that Robert Moses built to connect Jones Beach with the masses of Queens and Brooklyn suddenly became routes of migration, commuter paths, as young veterans and their families found they could afford to leave the row-house neighborhoods where they had grown up for the comparatively spacious lots and single-family houses of Levittown and other Long Island subdivisions. The first wave of postwar migration moved into Nassau County, and it was a pretty accurate cross-section of all but the poorest New Yorkers: almost half Catholic, about one-fourth Jewish and one-fourth Protestant. Then, as Long Island developed an employment base of its own, the next wave of migration started, this time far out into Suffolk County. This second wave was more Catholic and less Jewish, more blue collar (aircraft manufacturers are Suffolk County's biggest employers) and less white-collar, more Democratic perhaps in ancestral politics but culturally more firmly traditional and conservative in their approach to life.

The 2d Congressional District of New York covers a large part of Suffolk County—essentially the South Shore towns of Babylon and Islip, which within them contain dozens of suburbs with different names—one community after another strung out along the Sunrise Highway. With a few exceptions (notably Dix Hills in the north) this is the lowest-income part of Long Island, situated out past the fashionable and expensive suburbs with their minimum acreage zoning, far from the picturesque North Shore and separated by the Great South Bay from the beaches of Fire Island. The area filled up with people in the 1950s and 1960s and has grown little since, but with some of the lowest-priced housing on the Island, it has continued to attract young families. It also has minorities: black neighborhoods in North Amityville and Wyandanch and enough blacks and Hispanics scattered elsewhere to make the district 9% black and 7% Spanish origin.

The 2d District leans Republican in national elections, but it has a Democratic Congressman,

Thomas Downey, who, while still in his thirties, has been one of the most active and productive members of the House in the late 1980s. He has sometimes also been the brashest: he was the youngest member of the Watergate class of 1974, elected when he was just 25 and the veteran of a few years in the Suffolk County legislature; he spotted the weakness of an overconfident Republican and has been working the district hard, and winning, ever since. In his first two terms, he was a member of the Armed Services Committee, dovish on policy generally, but eager to promote the programs of Long Island's aircraft manufacturers. In 1979, he switched to Ways and Means, and from 1981 to 1987 he had a seat on Budget. He was one of the House's voluble and sarcastic critics of the Reagan Administration, regularly denouncing it for stinginess on domestic programs and profligacy on defense. He attacked, in particular, the MX missile, criticized the Strategic Defense Initiative, and called for a nuclear test moratorium. And although he is often sarcastic in tone, he also knows enough facts and figures to keep up with his arguments.

The late 1980s were a busy time for Downey, on Ways and Means and off. Once Chairman Dan Rostenkowski agreed to deductibility of state and local taxes, Downey became a solid backer of the 1986 tax reform bill. After Harold Ford temporarily stepped aside as chairman of the Human Resources Subcommittee, Downey took over the chair and became the leading House legislator on welfare reform. When it was clear that the House version, with its generous increases in payments and lack of insistence on the responsibilities of recipients, would not fly in conference, Downey showed impressive knowledge of details and considerable negotiating skills in patching together a compromise that mostly followed Daniel Patrick Moynihan's bill in the Senate, including a work requirement, as well, and managed to sell it in the House despite the opposition of Education and Labor Chairman Augustus Hawkins. Downey was also active in the presidential campaign as an enthusiastic backer and adviser of Albert Gore, a close friend despite their differences on issues like the MX missile and Grenada.

Downey may continue to talk like an unreconstructed liberal when he is scalding the Republicans. But when he gets down to work as a legislator or politician, he has fought for positions and candidates who seem in line with the less-government, somewhat more nationalistic America of the 1980s rather than maintaining a nostalgia for the apparently lost days of the early 1970s. He has worked to preserve Section 8 housing in Babylon and Islip and to maintain funding for T-46 trainer jets built by Fairchild in Farmingdale, just over the Nassau County line, and for the F-14, built by Grumman in Suffolk County.

Downey had serious opposition in 1984 and won with 55%; the next two elections he won impressively, with 64% and 62%. Uninterested in statewide office, Downey has remained in close touch with his district, and not just with politicians but with those "little platoons" (in Charles Murray's and Edmund Burke's phrase) of people who create high school antidrug curricula and start job centers and set up Foster Grandparents programs. He has strong local popularity and the only threat to his tenure is the possibility that strains on the local economy, caused by Lilco's record high utility rates and possible losses of defense contracts, may create enough discontent to fuel a serious challenge. But so far no serious challenger has appeared.

The People: Est. Pop. 1986: 520,000, up 0.9% 1980–86; Pop. 1980: 515,595, up 5.1% 1970–80. Households (1980): 85% family, 53% with children, 71% married couples; 21.4% housing units rented; median monthly rent: $314; median house value: $41,700. Voting age pop. (1980): 351,055; 8% Black, 6% Spanish origin, 1% Asian origin.

1988 Presidential Vote: Bush (R) 112,570   (61%)
Dukakis (D) 70,748   (38%)

Rep. Thomas J. Downey (D)

Elected 1974; b. Jan. 28, 1949, Ozone Park; home, Amityville; Cornell U., B.S. 1970, St. John's U. Sch. of Law, 1972–74, American U., J.D. 1978; United Methodist; married (Chris).

Career: Personnel mgt. and labor rel., Macy's Dept. Store, 1970; Suffolk Cnty. Legislature, 1971–74.

Offices: 2232 RHOB 20515, 202-225-3335. Also 4 Udall Rd., West Islip 11795, 516-661-8777.

Committees: *Ways and Means* (10th of 23 D). Subcommittees: Trade; Human Resources (Acting Chairman). *Select Committee on Aging* (2d of 39 D). Subcommittees: Human Services (Chairman); Retirement Income and Employment.

Group Ratings

	ADA	ACLU	COPE	CFA	LCV	ACU	NTLC	NSI	COC	CEI
1988	100	91	87	91	81	0	14	10	36	14
1987	92	—	87	93	—	9	—	—	20	10

National Journal Ratings

	1988 LIB — 1988 CONS		1987 LIB — 1987 CONS	
Economic	65%	— 34%	68%	— 27%
Social	86%	— 0%	78%	— 0%
Foreign	84%	— 0%	76%	— 19%

Key Votes

1) Homeless $	AGN	5) Ban Drug Test	AGN	9) SDI Research	AGN
2) Gephardt Amdt	AGN	6) Drug Death Pen	AGN	10) Ban Chem Weaps	FOR
3) Deficit Reduc	FOR	7) Handgun Sales	AGN	11) Aid to Contras	AGN
4) Kill Plnt Clsng Notice	AGN	8) Ban D.C. Abort $	AGN	12) Nuclear Testing	FOR

Election Results

1988 general	Thomas J. Downey (D-VCH)	107,646	(62%)	($627,584)
	Joseph Cardino (R-C-RTL).	66,972	(38%)	($35,057)
1988 primary	Thomas J. Downey (D-VCH), unopposed			
1986 general	Thomas J. Downey (D-RAL)	69,771	(64%)	($739,062)
	Jeffrey A. Butzke (R-CAL-RTL)	35,132	(33%)	($30,153)
	Veronica Windishman (RTL)	3,651	(3%)	

THIRD DISTRICT

The North Shore of Long Island, where peninsulas jutting out into the Sound are covered with vast green lawns leading to the mansions of America's greatest capitalists: this was the original Gatsby country, where the richest people in business and show business took their leisure and watched as their servants unloaded the bootleggers' boats at their docks. Inland, behind the bright green lawns, Long Island was still mostly farm country as late as 1940, with little villages clustered at railroad stations, occasional colonial era houses, and acres of billboard-strewn wasteland on the main highways to New York City. Then, in the years after World War II, settlers streamed in from the city. The North Shore suburbs, hilly and green, attracted many of the better educated and higher income migrants in the 1940s and 1950s; by the 1960s, they were pretty well built up through Syosset in Nassau County and into Huntington in Suffolk County. Since then, their population has not grown much. Households have lost people as children have grown up and moved away; new housing units, mostly apartments and condominiums, have been added.

New York's 3d Congressional District consists of the North Shore suburbs from Manhasset, Port Washington, and the New York City line in the west, all the way through Nassau and into Suffolk County to Smithtown in the east. The southern boundary throughout runs near the Long Island Expressway. This is almost entirely affluent country, with the second highest housing prices of any New York suburban district, just behind the 20th District in Westchester County. It tends to vote Republican in national and state elections, although its Jewish voters provide a solid liberal base for a Democratic candidate.

Robert Mrazek, the Democratic congressman from the 3d, has built a solid House career on an initial break. He won the seat as a Suffolk County legislator in 1982 by beating Republican John LeBoutillier, the brash freshman descendant of Vanderbilts and Whitneys who called Speaker Tip O'Neill "fat, bloated, and out of control—just like the federal budget." O'Neill made sure Mrazek's campaign was well funded, and Mrazek used the money ably, charging that LeBoutillier was ineffective and uninterested in the practical problems of Long Island. In the House he became, with O'Neill's help, the only freshman on the House Appropriations Committee.

Mrazek takes up causes which catch his fancy and often succeeds on them. He introduced a law banning the use of pound animals for scientific research. Spurred by efforts of Huntington High School students to help a handicapped Amerasian boy in Vietnam, Mrazek amended a big appropriations bill to let more Amerasian children into the United States and brought the boy back to the U.S. himself. He was the House's lead proponent of a bill to save part of the Manassas Civil War battlefield in Virginia from becoming a shopping center. He authored a National Film Preservation Act to discourage colorization and a bill regulating timbering practices in Alaska's Tongass National Forest. He introduced legislation outlawing plastic guns that can't be detected in airport security machines.

In 1984 and 1988, Mrazek was opposed by businessmen who made a lot of money in Manhattan and promised to spend some in the 3d District, and in 1986, he was opposed by a local Nassau County official. But only in 1984 did his opponent spend serious amounts of money, and Mrazek's mixture of local and national issues seems to have struck a chord on the North Shore.

The People: Est. Pop. 1986: 510,300, dn. 1.2% 1980–86; Pop. 1980: 516,610, dn. 3.3% 1970–80. Households (1980): 83% family, 44% with children, 73% married couples; 20.1% housing units rented; median monthly rent: $325; median house value: $70,500. Voting age pop. (1980): 378,027; 3% Black, 2% Spanish origin, 1% Asian origin.

1988 Presidential Vote:

Bush (R)	141,465	(59%)
Dukakis (D)	94,781	(40%)

Rep. Robert J. Mrazek (D)

Elected 1982; b. Nov. 6, 1945, Newport, RI; home, Centerport; Cornell U., B.A. 1967; United Methodist; married (Catherine).

Career: Navy, 1967–68; Staff Asst., U.S. Sen. Vance Hartke, 1969–71; Small business owner, 1971–75; Suffolk Cnty. Legislature, 1975–82, Minor. Ldr., 1979–82.

Offices: 306 CHOB 20515, 202-225-5956. Also 143 Main St., Huntington 11743, 516-673-6500.

Committees: *Appropriations* (29th of 35 D). Subcommittees: Foreign Operations, Export Financing and Related Programs; Transportation.

Group Ratings

	ADA	ACLU	COPE	CFA	LCV	ACU	NTLC	NSI	COC	CEI
1988	95	91	85	73	75	4	12	0	31	13
1987	96	—	87	86	—	9	—	—	13	12

National Journal Ratings

	1988 LIB — 1988 CONS		1987 LIB — 1987 CONS	
Economic	57%	— 43%	53%	— 46%
Social	86%	— 0%	78%	— 0%
Foreign	84%	— 0%	81%	— 0%

Key Votes

1) Homeless $	AGN	5) Ban Drug Test	AGN	9) SDI Research	AGN
2) Gephardt Amdt	AGN	6) Drug Death Pen	AGN	10) Ban Chem Weaps	FOR
3) Deficit Reduc	FOR	7) Handgun Sales	AGN	11) Aid to Contras	AGN
4) Kill Plnt Clsng Notice	AGN	8) Ban D.C. Abort $	AGN	12) Nuclear Testing	FOR

Election Results

1988 general	Robert J. Mrazek (D)................	128,336	(57%)	($364,087)
	Robert Previdi (R-C)	91,122	(40%)	($90,892)
1988 primary	Robert J. Mrazek (D), unopposed			
1986 general	Robert J. Mrazek (D)................	83,985	(56%)	($646,610)
	Joseph A. Guarino (R-C)	60,367	(41%)	($200,651)
	Charles W. Welch (RTL)	4,440	(3%)	

FOURTH DISTRICT

In September 1947, 300 families moved into 750 square foot houses, put up in record time with mass production methods, and selling for $6,990, with no down payment for veterans. This was Levittown, and by the time the last new house was sold in November 1951, for $9,500, the name had become a metaphor for rapid suburban development. Developer William Levitt had the insight that lots of young veterans and their families were eager to move out of crowded New York City neighborhoods and bought a potato field in Nassau County, east of Queens, planted trees on the lots, designed the floor plans to allow easy additions—he didn't want them to become slums a few decades later—and built a community of 65,000 people. Four decades later,

Levittown houses, with much added on, trade at well into six figures, and they are attracting young families once again. That may be happening in Nassau County generally, where the population rose from 450,000 in 1940 to 1.3 million in 1960, 1.4 million in 1970, then back to 1.3 million in 1980 as youngsters moved out and empty nesters remained.

Would the new suburbanites take Democratic voting habits out to the Island or blend in with the Republican landscape? people asked in the early postwar years. The answer is that they have mostly voted Republican—and that their parents made up the much larger Republican vote that existed in New York City in the 1940s than does today. It helps that Nassau County is the home of what may be the nation's premier county Republican machine. It was the creation of Nassau Republican Chairman J. Russel Sprague, who managed to carry the county for Alf Landon in 1936 and that same year persuade the voters to adopt a county executive form of government, in which control of political patronage would center in one man responsible to the Nassau County Republican chairman; it is headed these days by Joseph Mondello. Nassau's Republican machine is attacked by many. But it has this to say for itself: it has provided competent local government and candidates who are returned to office by an intelligent and well-informed electorate. The county's Republican margins remain large in national as well as most local elections.

The 4th Congressional District of New York, wholly within Nassau County and including most of Levittown, is one of the political units within the realm of the Nassau machine. It includes much of central Nassau around Levittown, plus a string of suburbs along the South Shore of Long Island (actually along the shore of the bay that separates the sand spits of Long Beach and Jones Beach from the main part of the Island). These suburbs were tiny separate towns in 1945 but have long since grown together, from East Rockaway to Massapequa—places where you find Nassau County zoning lawyers and New York City policemen, owners of small businesses and stores, and engineers at Long Island's big aircraft factories. When it came time for the county Republican organization to find a candidate to run against anti-Vietnam war activist Allard Lowenstein, who had won a 1968 race in a House district then mostly on the South Shore, it picked a lawyer still in his thirties, who had served in the state Senate for eight years, who had made a name as an opponent of a local busing plan, and whose father was a Nassau County judge—Norman Lent.

Lent won and has been the congressman from this district ever since. Now he is one of the most senior Republicans in the House and ranking minority member on the House Energy and Commerce Committee—one of the busiest and most powerful committees in Congress, which handles a host of regulatory and environmental matters. For years Lent was not particularly voluble or visible, but he did make significant contributions—to the original Superfund law, as well as the update he co-sponsored with Ohio's Dennis Eckart (which prevailed over James Florio's version), to an insurance liability risk retention act he co-sponsored with Oregon's Ron Wyden and to a bill allowing Conrail to be sold on the open market. Lent generally respects market principles, but he also is a practical politician. His instinct often is to come up with a bipartisan compromise, whether on clean air, on insider trading or on product liability reform; he has been successful on the latter two. He can be a blunt negotiator, but of course he has fewer chits—votes, clout or staff—than Chairman John Dingell. Interestingly, on clean air, Lent, with his white-collar district, favors tougher regulation than Dingell, who represents the smokestacks of Dearborn and Downriver Detroit; Lent also claims credit for Congress's 1988 limits on ocean dumping—important in a district increasingly concerned about its environment and its garbage—and he worked with George Hochbrueckner to put Peconic Bay and its threatened shellfish waters into the National Estuary Program.

Democrats have long since given up serious attempts to defeat Lent in the heartland of the Nassau Republican machine, and he is reelected every two years, routinely.

The People: Est. Pop. 1986: 520,100, up 0.7% 1980–86; Pop. 1980: 516,641, dn. 8.9% 1970–80. Households (1980): 88% family, 46% with children, 77% married couples; 14.3% housing units rented; median monthly rent: $321; median house value: $55,800. Voting age pop. (1980): 376,675; 3% Black, 3% Spanish origin, 1% Asian origin.

1988 Presidential Vote: Bush (R) 134,515   (58%)
Dukakis (D). 94,111   (41%)

Rep. Norman F. Lent (R)

Elected 1970; b. Mar. 23, 1931, Oceanside; home, E. Rockaway; Hofstra U., B.A. 1952, Cornell U., LL.B. 1957; United Methodist; married (Barbara).

Career: Navy, Korea; Practicing atty., 1957–70; Asst. E. Rockaway Police Justice, 1960–62; NY Senate, 1962–70.

Offices: 2408 RHOB 20515, 202-225-7896. Also 2280 Grand Ave., Ste. 300, Baldwin 11510, 516-223-1616.

Committees: *Energy and Commerce* (Ranking Member of 17 R). Subcommittee: Oversight and Investigations. *Merchant Marine and Fisheries* (3d of 17 R). Subcommittee: Merchant Marine (Ranking Member).

Group Ratings

	ADA	ACLU	COPE	CFA	LCV	ACU	NTLC	NSI	COC	CEI
1988	25	38	32	45	44	68	55	100	69	40
1987	8	—	31	43	—	59	—	—	79	46

National Journal Ratings

	1988 LIB — 1988 CONS	1987 LIB — 1987 CONS
Economic	31% — 67%	24% — 74%
Social	34% — 66%	31% — 69%
Foreign	22% — 76%	20% — 76%

Key Votes

1) Homeless $	FOR	5) Ban Drug Test	AGN	9) SDI Research	FOR
2) Gephardt Amdt	AGN	6) Drug Death Pen	FOR	10) Ban Chem Weaps	AGN
3) Deficit Reduc	AGN	7) Handgun Sales	AGN	11) Aid to Contras	FOR
4) Kill Plnt Clsng Notice	FOR	8) Ban D.C. Abort $	FOR	12) Nuclear Testing	AGN

Election Results

1988 general	Norman F. Lent (R-C)	151,038	(70%)	($436,310)
	Francis T. Goban (D-L)	59,479	(28%)	($4,452)
1988 primary	Norman F. Lent (R-C), unopposed			
1986 general	Norman F. Lent (R-C)	92,214	(65%)	($337,118)
	Patricia Sullivan (D-L)	43,581	(31%)	($11,829)
	George F. Patterson (RTL)	6,493	(4%)	

FIFTH DISTRICT

Fifty years ago Nassau County, just beyond the New York City line, was a mishmash of small suburban villages clustered around railroad stations, occasional precincts of country estates, the remaining potato fields whose owners were waiting for a good offer, and commercial buildings and gas stations strung along the arteries leading east out Long Island. In the two decades following World War II, the Nassau suburbs pretty well filled up: one town ran into another (though most did not lose their separate identities), freeways replaced the strip highways as the movers of traffic, shopping centers sprang up at intersections and schools and places of worship dotted the landscape. Politically, most of this territory, including most of the part of central and southwestern Nassau that make up New York's 5th Congressional District, has remained as heavily Republican as it was when it was lightly populated. Garden City, a model suburb laid out in the 1870s, is heavily Protestant and Republican; places like Valley Stream, East Meadow and Uniondale are more Catholic but still pretty solidly Republican. Only the Five Towns of Lawrence, Inwood, Cedarhurst, Hewlett and Woodmere between Kennedy Airport and the ocean, which are heavily Jewish, and the black pockets of Hampstead and Roosevelt, are heavily Democratic.

The 5th District, marginal political territory in the early 1970s, has become solidly Republican in the 1980s. Its congressman, Raymond McGrath, has thinner credentials than any other Long Island member and no particular reputation for hard work, but he seems to have made the seat entirely safe. A former teacher, deputy parks commissioner, and state legislator, an "ordinary guy" in his own words, McGrath was tapped for the seat by Nassau County Republican boss Joseph Margiotta in 1980, and beat tough Democrats that year and in 1982. He tended to mix well with most Republicans, though his stands on various issues—Superfund and foreign policy—were sometimes more liberal.

McGrath's great moment in the House so far, and it may turn out to be his moment in history, came in 1985, when as a first-year member of the House Ways and Means Committee, he announced that the only issue in the tax reform debate he cared about was the deductibility of state and local taxes, and that he would vote for any bill that made them deductible and against any that wouldn't. Like a good Nassau Republican politician, he kept his word. When Chairman Dan Rostenkowski accepted state and local deductibility, McGrath became a solid supporter of the bill, always accepting the chairman's mark, to the point where other Republicans were miffed when he caucused with them. McGrath ended up standing behind the President when he signed the bill and his district was the recipient of special benefits—tax breaks for the towns of Hempstead and Oyster Bay, for a Garden City firm, for Merrill Lynch, and 19 of the 21 transition rules he sought—from Chairman Rostenkowski.

McGrath has been quieter since, compiling a moderate-to-conservative voting record on major issues, working on Ways and Means against taxing public employee's fringe benefits and changing a law to save Long Island Rail Road workers' pension benefits. To those who attack him as a hack, McGrath can reply that the voters of this affluent, well-educated and well-informed district have in the last two elections returned him to office by nearly 2 to 1 margins. That seems likely to continue for some time.

The People: Est. Pop. 1986: 515,500, dn. 0.2% 1980–86; Pop. 1980: 516,712, dn. 7.6% 1970–80. Households (1980): 81% family, 39% with children, 68% married couples; 25.5% housing units rented; median monthly rent: $300; median house value: $56,900. Voting age pop. (1980): 386,288; 10% Black, 3% Spanish origin, 1% Asian origin.

1988 Presidential Vote:

Bush (R)	124,622	(56%)
Dukakis (D)	97,312	(43%)

Rep. Raymond J. McGrath (R)

Elected 1980; b. Mar. 27, 1942, Queens; home, Valley Stream; St. U. of NY, Brockport, B.A. 1963, N.Y.U., M.A. 1968; Roman Catholic; married (Sheryl).

Career: Teacher, 1963–64; Hempstead Dpty. Commissioner of Parks and Recreation, 1964–75; NY Assembly, 1976–80.

Offices: 205 CHOB 20515, 202-225-5516. Also 203 Rockaway Ave., Valley Stream 11580, 516-872-9550.

Committees: *Ways and Means* (8th of 13 R). Subcommittees: Oversight; Select Revenue Measures.

Group Ratings

	ADA	ACLU	COPE	CFA	LCV	ACU	NTU	NSI	COC	CEI
1988	25	43	39	64	75	55	48	80	82	37
1987	24	—	34	36	—	59	—	—	64	47

National Journal Ratings

	1988 LIB — 1988 CONS		1987 LIB — 1987 CONS	
Economic	37%	— 63%	27%	— 73%
Social	39%	— 61%	31%	— 68%
Foreign	24%	— 74%	36%	— 63%

Key Votes

1) Homeless $	—	5) Ban Drug Test	FOR	9) SDI Research	FOR
2) Gephardt Amdt	AGN	6) Drug Death Pen	FOR	10) Ban Chem Weaps	FOR
3) Deficit Reduc	AGN	7) Handgun Sales	AGN	11) Aid to Contras	FOR
4) Kill Plnt Clsng Notice	FOR	8) Ban D.C. Abort $	FOR	12) Nuclear Testing	AGN

Election Results

1988 general	Raymond J. McGrath (R-C)	134,881	(65%)	($337,792)
	William G. Kelly (D)	68,930	(33%)	($35,627)
1988 primary	Raymond J. McGrath (R-C), unopposed			
1986 general	Raymond J. McGrath (R-C)	93,473	(65%)	($294,365)
	Michael T. Sullivan (D-L-RTL)	49,728	(35%)	($66,389)

SIXTH DISTRICT

Fifty years ago, when the land that is now Kennedy Airport was part of the tidal marsh of Jamaica Bay, the neighborhoods of southern Queens were already built. The writers of the *WPA Guide* sniffed at "the architectural monotony of block upon block of boxlike frame and brick houses," noting that "swimming is prohibited in the polluted waters," while Springfield, Laurelton and Rosedale, near the Nassau County line, were "undistinguished products of the Queens building boom of the 1920s." The Rockaway peninsula, across the Bay, was "a resort for lower-middle class families," and "south of the railroad embankment in South Jamaica," where an immigrant from Salerno named Andrea Cuomo had a grocery store, "about 15,000 Negroes dwell in miserable shacks." They were about the only blacks in Queens in those days, when it was still a haven—the Manhattan-loving *Guide* writers notwithstanding—for New Yorkers eager for a little space around their homes and a little light in their windows, even if it meant moving out a bus line past the last subway stop in a borough which until a few years before had been mostly empty.

These mostly middle-class white areas of the 1940s have become the mostly middle-class black areas that make up New York's 6th Congressional District. It was one of the still white areas, Howard Beach, that made headlines in late 1986 when three blacks were beaten by a gang of teenagers and one, fleeing, was run over by a car on Belt Parkway. Ironically, this happened in a constituency which has had successful multi-racial politics. In 1982 and 1984, the black-majority 6th continued to renominate and reelect Joseph Addabbo, congressman from the area since 1960, a lead opponent of the Cambodia bombing in 1973 and of weapons systems like the MX, and a booster of Long Island aerospace firms as a member and, since 1979, chairman of the Defense Appropriations Subcommittee.

When Addabbo died of cancer in April 1986, however, it was clear that a black congressman would be elected. The primary election winner for the remainder of his term was Alton Waldon, supported by the remnants of the Queens machine disgraced after the suicide of county leader Donald Manes in March 1986. But something was fishy: the name of one of his opponents, Floyd Flake, was kept off the absentee ballots by one of New York election law's endless number of technicalities. Flake, noting that he won by 167 votes at the polls but was declared defeated by 276 votes when the absentees were counted, understandably felt cheated. He campaigned hard in the fall, and with the endorsement of Mayor Edward Koch as well as of many local blacks, defeated Waldon in the primary in the next full term and was elected without difficulty in this overwhelmingly Democratic district in November.

Flake is minister of a 4,000-member church that built a big senior citizens' home and runs small businesses. Flake himself has diverse experience in the private sector and academics; he has a big following in the middle class communities along the Nassau County line. With a seat on the Banking Committee, he wants to do something to increase the amount of public housing. Wisely, he is concentrating less on the non-starter of building more new units and more on the notion of conserving existing units: he has sponsored, and urged the administration to implement, a bill allowing public housing authorities to use renovation funds for what is now classified as routine maintenance.

The People: Est. Pop. 1986: 523,400, up 1.4% 1980–86; Pop. 1980: 516,312, dn. 5.7% 1970–80. Households (1980): 77% family, 43% with children, 55% married couples; 44.7% housing units rented; median monthly rent: $222; median house value: $42,800. Voting age pop. (1980): 368,500; 47% Black, 8% Spanish origin, 1% Asian origin.

1988 Presidential Vote:

Dukakis (D)	103,007	(71%)
Bush (R)	39,327	(27%)

Rep. Floyd H. Flake (D)

Elected 1986; b. Jan. 30, 1945, Los Angeles, CA; home, Queens; Wilberforce U., B.A., 1967; African Methodist Episcopal; married (Elaine).

Career: Mktg. Analyst, Xerox Corp., 1969–70; Assoc. Dean, of Students, Lincoln U. 1970–73; Dean of Students, U. Chaplin, Boston U. 1973–76; Founder of Allen Christian School, Allen Home Care Agency.

Offices: 1427 LHOB, 202-225-3461. Also 114-60 Merrick Blvd., Jamaica 11434, 718-657-2968; and 20-80 Seagirt Blvd., Far Rockaway 11691, 718-327-9791.

Committees: *Banking, Finance and Urban Affairs* (25th of 31 D). Subcommittees: Financial Institutions Supervision, Regulation and Insurance; Housing and Community Development; International Development, Finance, Trade and Monetary Policy; General Oversight and Investigations. *Small Business* (20th of 27 D). Subcommittee: SBA, the General Economy and Minority Enterprise Development. *Select Committee on Hunger* (11th of 19 D).

Group Ratings

	ADA	ACLU	COPE	CFA	LCV	ACU	NTU	NSI	COC	CEI
1988	95	86	100	100	88	0	8	0	30	9
1987	92	—	100	64	—	0	—	—	0	5

National Journal Ratings

	1988 LIB — 1988 CONS		1987 LIB — 1987 CONS	
Economic	92%	0%	73%	0%
Social	78%	20%	73%	22%
Foreign	84%	0%	75%	24%

Key Votes

1) Homeless $	AGN	5) Ban Drug Test	AGN	9) SDI Research	AGN
2) Gephardt Amdt	FOR	6) Drug Death Pen	AGN	10) Ban Chem Weaps	FOR
3) Deficit Reduc	FOR	7) Handgun Sales	AGN	11) Aid to Contras	AGN
4) Kill Plnt Clsng Notice	AGN	8) Ban D.C. Abort $	FOR	12) Nuclear Testing	FOR

Election Results

1988 general	Floyd H. Flake (D-L)	94,506	(86%)	($370,236)
	Robert L. Brandofino (C-FGY)	15,547	(14%)	($3,071)
1988 primary	Floyd H. Flake (D-L), unopposed			
1986 general	Floyd H. Flake (D)	58,317	(68%)	($359,382)
	Richard Dietl (R-C)	27,773	(32%)	($55,318)

SEVENTH DISTRICT

Along most of Queens Boulevard, on both sides of the Grand Central Parkway at it goes from LaGuardia Airport to the Nassau County line at Lake Success, runs the 7th Congressional District of New York, entirely within the borough of Queens. The epicenter of the district is somewhere between the unimpressive brick Borough Hall on Queens Boulevard—just after it passes over the Parkway, across from the Pastrami King and Crossroads Drugs, the site of the worst recent scandal in New York politics—and St. John's University a mile to the east, off the

Grand Central on Utopia Parkway where a grocer's son named Mario Cuomo went to college and law school. Fifty years ago there were plenty of gas stations and vacant lots in what was only a partly built-up area; now it has dozens of high-rise apartments in that light gray brick which was evidently the cheapest building material in New York in the 1950s and 1960s. Queens, with nearly two million people, the home base of such national politicians as Cuomo and Geraldine Ferraro, is more sophisticated than Manhattanites would have you believe, more affluent and more tolerant.

Yet this is still a borough without an image and one that doesn't get much attention. Part of the problem is history: Queens doesn't have much of it. It was nondescript farmland for most of the 19th century, and as recently as 50 years ago was known mainly for the West Side Tennis Club in Forest Hills. Its communities had no focus, and when residents talked of going into "the city" they meant Manhattan. In those days the built-up parts of Queens consisted mostly of modest one- and two-family houses, inhabited by Irish, Italian and German immigrants, as well as a considerable number of people of Yankee stock. It was a Republican stronghold that happened, technically, to be part of a much larger Democratic city. Since World War II, most of the new housing units in Queens have been in apartment buildings, many of them giant, like the units in Lefrak City. Added to its older residents have been a large number of Jews, mostly from Manhattan and Brooklyn. It is an airier place to live and raise a family than Manhattan; there are good public schools; rents are lower and, via the subway, Manhattan offices are not so far away. It was here, on 64th Road in Rego Park, a couple of blocks off Queens Boulevard, that the first condominium conversion in New York took place in 1966: an opportunity for the owners to get out from under rent control and the tenants to convert their low rental into a capital asset.

The 7th district is mostly white, heavily Jewish, with large numbers of many other minorities, from Haitians to Koreans. It has a significant Caribbean community in Corona and Latins in Elmhurst; in the southwest it includes some black neighborhoods. Politically, it is heavily Democratic. Its congressman is Gary Ackerman, a Democrat elected in March 1983 to replace Benjamin Rosenthal who died after 20 years in office. Ackerman, a former teacher and community newspaper owner, had served four years in the state Senate.

In the House he is distinctive in a number of ways, first physically: he lost over 100 pounds in 1987 and shaved off his goatee in 1988, but he still lives in a houseboat in Washington and wears a carnation in his lapel every day. He serves on Foreign Affairs, where he is a strong supporter of Israel and worked to help Ethiopian Jews; he has aggressively criticized the Ethiopian and Sudanese governments for blocking distribution of food to their starving peoples for political reasons. On Post Office and Civil Service, this representative of many public employees has always taken positions backed by unions—opposing compulsory drug tests (asking a Reagan Administration witness to produce a urine sample himself), opposing privatization of government jobs, sponsoring a bill for leave-sharing, opposing any relaxation of the rules against homeworking. He is in a good position to help, as chairman of the Compensation and Employee Benefits Subcommittee. He wrote the youth suicide prevention act of 1986. At home Ackerman seems to be in strong shape; as an old adversary of the late Queens boss Donald Manes, he was not adversely affected when Manes got into trouble and killed himself. Barring a redistricting mishap, he has a safe seat for another 12 years.

The People: Est. Pop. 1986: 529,200, up 2.5% 1980–86; Pop. 1980: 516,544, dn. 2.5% 1970–80. Households (1980): 67% family, 29% with children, 52% married couples; 70.4% housing units rented; median monthly rent: $266; median house value: $56,300. Voting age pop. (1980): 407,309; 17% Spanish origin, 11% Black, 6% Asian origin.

1988 Presidential Vote:
Dukakis (D)	87,214	(60%)
Bush (R)	57,353	(39%)

Rep. Gary L. Ackerman (D)

Elected Mar. 1, 1983; b. Nov. 19, 1942, Brooklyn; home, Jamaica; Queens Col., B.A. 1965; Jewish; married (Rita).

Career: Pub. sch. teacher, 1966–72; Newspaper ed. and publisher; Owner, adv. agcy.; NY Senate, 1979–83.

Offices: 238 CHOB, 202-225-2601. Also 118–35 Queens Blvd., Forest Hills 11375, 718-263-1525.

Committees: *Foreign Affairs* (18th of 28 D). Subcommittees: Asian and Pacific Affairs; Europe and the Middle East; Human Rights and International Organizations. *Post Office and Civil Service* (10th of 15 D). Subcommittees: Compensation and Employee Benefits (Chairman); Postal Operations and Services. *Select Committee on Hunger* (9th of 19 D).

Group Ratings

	ADA	ACLU	COPE	CFA	LCV	ACU	NTU	NSI	COC	CEI
1988	95	95	99	82	94	0	3	0	23	6
1987	96	—	99	71	—	0	—	—	14	7

National Journal Ratings

	1988 LIB — 1988 CONS		1987 LIB — 1987 CONS	
Economic	92% —	0%	73% —	0%
Social	86% —	0%	78% —	0%
Foreign	84% —	0%	81% —	0%

Key Votes

1) Homeless $	AGN	5) Ban Drug Test	AGN	9) SDI Research	AGN
2) Gephardt Amdt	FOR	6) Drug Death Pen	AGN	10) Ban Chem Weaps	FOR
3) Deficit Reduc	FOR	7) Handgun Sales	AGN	11) Aid to Contras	AGN
4) Kill Plnt Clsng Notice	AGN	8) Ban D.C. Abort $	AGN	12) Nuclear Testing	FOR

Election Results

1988 general	Gary L. Ackerman (D-L), unopposed			($142,041)
1988 primary	Gary L. Ackerman (D-L), unopposed			
1986 general	Gary L. Ackerman (D)	62,836	(77%)	($116,950)
	Edward Nelson Rodriguez (R-C)	18,384	(23%)	($8,456)

EIGHTH DISTRICT

The Trylon and Perisphere, rising over what had been "a thousand acres of malodorous eyesore," is the still-remembered symbol of the New York World's Fair of 1939–40, an exposition intended to be "the Fair of the Future" at a time when in the immediate future loomed a world war. The symbols of the Fair linger on in memory, as do those of the 1964–65 World's Fair held here. Today, on the same site is Flushing Meadow Park, with its own zoo and the National Tennis Center, and Shea Stadium, across Roosevelt Avenue where the Fair's parking lot used to be. The Fair was in a part of Queens already built up in 1939, with a grid of streets and the Queens numbering system superimposed awkwardly over the trails that once led to the 17th century Dutch village of Flushing.

Flushing is the heart of the 8th Congressional District of New York, which includes most of northern Queens plus small parts of the Bronx and suburban Nassau County. The Queens portion includes the working-class neighborhoods of Whitestone and College Point, the more affluent double-house neighborhood of Bayside, and higher-income Douglaston, right next to the rich, mostly Jewish suburb of Great Neck in Nassau County, most of which is also in the 8th. In Queens the district goes south, below the Long Island Expressway, to pleasant home-owner neighborhoods with names like Utopia, Fresh Meadows and Oakland Gardens. But even here, far from Manhattan and in relatively affluent areas, there are plenty of high-rises, with a population density not approached, except for a few odd neighborhoods, in other metropolitan areas.

The population in this part of the district includes few blacks or Hispanics; there are more in the Bronx portion of the 8th. This area is a little misleading: it looks like a sliver on the map, but it has 29% of the district's population; its statistics make it sound mostly black (24%) and Spanish origin (30%), but most of the voters here are Jewish. The district's rather jagged boundaries take in several of the Bronx's longstanding Jewish neighborhoods and shopping districts, including the Parkchester apartment project, which houses some 40,000 people.

For Congressman James Scheuer, representing this district means he has come full circle: he was first elected to the House in 1964, when he lived in Manhattan, from a Bronx district that included some of his present territory; he was beaten for reelection as a result of redistricting in 1972; he was elected again in 1974 from a district that included southern portions of Queens and Brooklyn, around Jamaica Bay, and even bought a house there; he lost that district in 1982, but with the help of Queens Borough President Donald Manes cinched the nomination in the new incumbentless 8th. He is thus the Flying Dutchman of New York congressmen: he has represented parts of four different counties (while coming originally from another) and has run against two other Democratic incumbents (beating Jacob Gilbert in 1964, losing to Jonathan Bingham in 1972). This is a heavily Democratic district and will likely keep Scheuer in Congress up until 1992, when New York will lose at least two districts, and many are eyeing the two-borough 8th as one to be divided among its neighbors. So the Flying Dutchman may have to set sail again.

Scheuer's good fortune is all the more remarkable because he is not particularly popular with his fellow politicians or congressmen. He suffered the indignity of seeing Energy and Commerce Committee chairman John Dingell abolish his subcommittee out from under him in 1981, even though he is the second-ranking Democrat on the full committee; he has not been active there since and he seems likely to be passed over for the chair in favor of third-ranking Henry Waxman—though it should be added that Dingell is not likely to step down. Scheuer now chairs a Science, Space and Technology subcommittee of considerably less legislative importance, although it did give him a piece of the action in investigating former EPA Administrator Anne Burford and her subordinates in 1982 and 1983, and he has been looking into biotech issues—which could be as important for the future as was the work he was doing in the 1970s on Energy and Commerce.

But Scheuer's problems should not be overstated. He is an active, aggressive legislator who works hard at his job, takes it seriously, and does his homework. He was one of the Science Committee members who sternly admonished NASA and its officials after the *Challenger* accident. He tends to local problems, trying to keep the noisy Concorde out of Kennedy Airport in the 1970s and trying to get better wind shear radar for Kennedy and LaGuardia in the 1980s. Once he had other ambitions: he ran for mayor in 1969 and finished fifth among five candidates, behind Mario Procaccino, Robert Wagner, Herman Badillo and novelist Norman Mailer; perhaps he even dreamed of statewide office as well. Now he has to work hard and fight as contentiously as ever to remain an important congressman after more than 20 years in the House. But he hasn't quit fighting.

The People: Est. Pop. 1986: 530,600, up 2.8% 1980–86; Pop. 1980: 516,165, dn. 6.5% 1970–80. Households (1980): 73% family, 32% with children, 57% married couples; 62.5% housing units rented; median monthly rent: $246; median house value: $68,400. Voting age pop. (1980): 402,776; 12% Spanish origin, 9% Black, 4% Asian origin.

1988 Presidential Vote:

Dukakis (D)......................	101,681	(59%)
Bush (R)	69,870	(40%)

Rep. James H. Scheuer (D)

Elected 1974; b. Feb. 6, 1920, New York City; home, Douglaston; Swarthmore Col., A.B. 1945, Harvard Business Sch., 1946 Columbia U., LL.B. 1948; Jewish; married (Emily).

Career: Army Air Corps, WWII; Economist, U.S. Foreign Econ. Admin., 1945–46; Legal Staff, U.S. Ofc. of Price Stabilization, 1951–52; U.S. House of Reps., 1964–72; Pres., NYC Citizens Housing and Planning Cncl., 1972–74; Pres., Natl. Housing Conf., 1972–74.

Offices: 2466 RHOB 20515, 202-225-5471. Also 137-08 Northern Blvd., Flushing 11354, 718-445-8770; 708 Lydig Ave, Ste. 203, Bronx, 10462 212-823-6512; and Nassau, 516-466-3939.

Committees: *Energy and Commerce* (2d of 26 D). Subcommittees: Commerce, Consumer Protection, and Competitiveness; Health and the Environment. *Science, Space and Technology* (3d of 30 D). Subcommittees: International Scientific Cooperation; Natural Resources, Agriculture Research and Environment (Chairman); Space Science and Applications. *Select Committee on Narcotics Abuse and Control* (4th of 18 D). *Joint Economic Committee.*

Group Ratings

	ADA	ACLU	COPE	CFA	LCV	ACU	NTU	NSI	COC	CEI
1988	85	95	91	82	75	5	14	0	46	19
1987	84	—	92	93	—	5	—	—	9	10

National Journal Ratings

	1988 LIB — 1988 CONS		1987 LIB — 1987 CONS	
Economic	59% —	41%	73% —	0%
Social	80% —	19%	61% —	38%
Foreign	74% —	23%	81% —	0%

Key Votes

1) Homeless $	AGN	5) Ban Drug Test	—	9) SDI Research	AGN
2) Gephardt Amdt	FOR	6) Drug Death Pen	AGN	10) Ban Chem Weaps	FOR
3) Deficit Reduc	FOR	7) Handgun Sales	—	11) Aid to Contras	AGN
4) Kill Plnt Clsng Notice	AGN	8) Ban D.C. Abort $	AGN	12) Nuclear Testing	FOR

Election Results

1988 general	James H. Scheuer (D-L), unopposed			($98,919)
1988 primary	James H. Scheuer (D-L), unopposed			
1986 general	James H. Scheuer (D-L)...............	70,605	(90%)	($65,543)
	Gustave Reifenkugel (C-RTL)	7,679	(10%)	

NINTH DISTRICT

It was the week before the 1988 New York presidential primary, a clammy late winter night, but spirits were high and the dancing energetic in Astoria, Queens, one of America's premier Greek immigrant neighborhoods, where the residents were celebrating the visit and impending victory of the first Greek-American presidential candidate, Michael Dukakis. Astoria was celebrating itself as well. Known to national reporters for the grimy storefronts they see on the cab ride in from LaGuardia to Manhattan, Astoria has an entirely different aspect when you get off the Long Island Expressway. The stores and restaurants on Broadway are sparkling and affluent; the houses on the side streets have the crisp look that says they are not only maintained spotlessly outside, they have been renovated inside; the people coming in off the El from Manhattan are well dressed and not intimidated by what people in Queens still call "the City."

Astoria is just one of the neighborhoods in the outer boroughs of New York which, fortified with new immigrants and maintained by determined homeowners, is doing much better than almost anyone predicted 20 years ago. They are holding the successful people who grew up here, raising a new generation of children, building net worths in their real estate in the hundreds of thousands. They are proof that the answer to city housing problems is not for government to build more public housing, but for homeowners to maintain the solid and sturdy units they already have.

Astoria is part of the 9th Congressional District of Queens, a jagged-boundaried part of the borough of Queens that contains all manner of ethnic neighborhoods, from Greek Astoria to Colombian Jackson Heights, German Ridgewood, Irish Middle Village and affluent Jewish and mixed Forest Hills. Long Island City, long the site of factories opposite Manhattan across the East River, is now sporting an office high-rise where Citicorp employees do back office work; more development is sure to follow.

In the early 1970s, the 9th District's attitudes were symbolized by the Archie Bunker character on Norman Lear's *All in the Family*. In the late 1980s, they might better be represented by the character played by Cher in John Patrick Shanley's *Moonstruck*. The Bunker mentality was one of fear and hatred of the cultural liberals across the river in Manhattan, and of the blacks not too many blocks away in Brooklyn. The current attitude is more hopeful: some traditional values have been quietly jettisoned, but others seem secure; and as the neighborhoods visibly improve, the specter of becoming another Brownsville seems to recede. The change can be tracked from the 9th District's representatives, all Democrats with ethnic roots in the district. James Delaney, congressman from 1942 to 1978, became a sour opponent of Great Society legislation, an adversary of the Democratic leadership as chairman of the Rules Committee. Geraldine Ferraro, first elected in 1978, adapted easily to the liberal and feminist ways of her peers on Capitol Hill and was a good enough team player to become, when they were looking for a woman, the Democrats' vice presidential nominee in 1984. Thomas Manton, the former councilman who replaced Ferraro, is quieter and looks more traditional, but his voting record and general attitude are much closer to Ferraro's than to Delaney's.

Manton is a former policeman who served on the City Council from 1969 to 1984; he ran against Delaney in 1972 as the tribune of anti-Vietnam war liberals and as the organization choice against Ferraro in 1978, losing both times. He is the son of Irish immigrants—a personal link between the older stock second- and third-generation residents of the district and the newer residents who are immigrants themselves. His critical race was the 1984 primary, which he won 30%–27%–22%–21%. Serphin Maltese, the longtime Conservative party leader who was the Republican nominee in the general, simply did not have the political moves to take advantage of the issues and the year, and Manton won 53%–47%. Now he seems firmly ensconced; he was reelected in 1986 easily and in 1988 was unopposed.

In 1989, Manton became one of two new members on the Energy and Commerce Committee, with support from Chairman John Dingell and Jim Wright. He also serves on Merchant Marine and Fisheries, which handles some environmental measures and where he often involves himself with legislation which has a local angle. He is eager to increase the FHA mortgage ceiling, to cover those appreciating prices in places like Astoria, and he modified the Alaska National Wildlife Reserve oil drilling proposal to require that all work be done at wages negotiated by the building trades, which are of course strong in New York.

The People: Est. Pop. 1986: 525,500, up 1.8% 1980–86; Pop. 1980: 516,143, dn. 4.5% 1970–80. Households (1980): 66% family, 29% with children, 50% married couples; 72.0% housing units rented; median monthly rent: $206; median house value: $57,600. Voting age pop. (1980): 407,420; 15% Spanish origin, 5% Asian origin, 3% Black.

1988 Presidential Vote:

Dukakis (D)	70,331	(51%)
Bush (R)	66,627	(48%)

Rep. Thomas J. Manton (D)

Elected 1984; b. Nov. 3, 1932, New York City; home, Sunnyside; St. John's U., B.B.A. 1958, LL.B. 1962; Roman Catholic; married (Diane).

Career: USMC, 1951–53; NYC Police Officer, 1955–60; IBM Salesman, 1960–64; Practicing atty., 1964–84; NYC Cncl., 1969–84.

Offices: 331 CHOB 20515, 202-225-3965. Also 46–12 Queens Blvd., Sunnyside 11104, 718-706-1400.

Committees: *Energy and Commerce* (26th of 26 D). Subcommittees: Telecommunications and Finance; Transportation and Hazardous Materials. *Merchant Marine and Fisheries* (17th of 26 D). Subcommittees: Coast Guard and Navigation; Fisheries and Wildlife Conservation and the Environment; Oceanography. *Select Committee on Aging* (27th of 39 D). Subcommittees: Housing and Consumer Interests; Retirement Income and Employment.

Group Ratings

	ADA	ACLU	COPE	CFA	LCV	ACU	NTU	NSI	COC	CEI
1988	60	74	95	82	56	18	0	25	23	7
1987	80	—	93	71	—	4	—	—	7	6

National Journal Ratings

	1988 LIB — 1988 CONS		1987 LIB — 1987 CONS	
Economic	92% —	0%	73% —	0%
Social	61% —	38%	73% —	22%
Foreign	72% —	27%	71% —	27%

Key Votes

1) Homeless $	AGN	5) Ban Drug Test	AGN	9) SDI Research	AGN
2) Gephardt Amdt	FOR	6) Drug Death Pen	FOR	10) Ban Chem Weaps	AGN
3) Deficit Reduc	FOR	7) Handgun Sales	AGN	11) Aid to Contras	AGN
4) Kill Plnt Clsng Notice	AGN	8) Ban D.C. Abort $	FOR	12) Nuclear Testing	—

Election Results

1988 general	Thomas J. Manton (D), unopposed		($256,832)
1988 primary	Thomas J. Manton (D), unopposed		
1986 general	Thomas J. Manton (D) 50,738	(69%)	($416,151)
	Salvatore J. Calise (R) 18,040	(25%)	
	Thomas V. Ognibene (C) 4,348	(6%)	

TENTH DISTRICT

Most of the heart of Brooklyn, from the green rises of Prospect Park to the marshy flats of Canarsie, from the Lefferts homestead built by 17th century Dutch settlers to the new shopping center and high-rises along Sheepshead Bay, is contained within the 10th Congressional District of New York, which starts in the borough's old downtown and goes out to the Atlantic Ocean. Here are mile after mile of grid streets, built up with solid brick houses and three- and four-story apartment buildings: the Brooklyn that grew up along the subway lines in the 1910s and 1920s. Its population is mostly Jewish: this and the next-door 13th District may be the only majority-Jewish congressional districts in the whole United States. In the 1970s, blacks began moving in large numbers into Flatbush, formerly a mostly Jewish neighborhood, but most of the Flatbush blacks are in the neighboring 12th District. And the Jewish neighborhoods along Ocean Parkway and Coney Island Avenue seem likely to remain mostly Jewish in the future.

There is a renaissance of Orthodox Judaism here, and to some extent a turning away from the goals of secular education and advancement; the Jews here are not, in many cases, tremendously affluent, and they seem more interested in celebrating their traditions than in trying to emulate the dazzling successes of Jews who have long since moved on to Great Neck or Beverly Hills. Similar attitudes, on the part of both Jews and Gentiles, seem to prevail in the two-family house neighborhoods farther out, from Sheepshead Bay near Coney Island to Flatlands and Canarsie.

The 10th District is heavily Democratic country in partisan terms; but not in quite the way it used to be. In the 1930s, it was enthusiastically for liberal Democrats at the top of the ticket like Franklin D. Roosevelt but suspicious of the Irish politicians and, sometimes, the Italian gangsters who ran the local Democratic machine. Now, increasingly conservative on many cultural issues, hostile to racial quotas and suspicious that dovish politicians may abandon Israel, it votes overwhelmingly for local Democratic candidates but does not always give national Democrats huge margins. Jimmy Carter actually lost many Jewish neighborhoods here to Ronald Reagan in 1980, and neither Walter Mondale in 1984 nor Michael Dukakis in 1988 reached historic levels of support from Jewish voters.

The congressman from the 10th District is Charles Schumer, a Democrat first elected in 1980 who, in a decade when Republicans made most of the public policy in Washington, has become one of the legislative powerhouses in the House. He has done so through energy, imagination and a certain amount of chutzpah. He comes forward with interesting and imaginative ideas and works and lobbies and nags until they are adopted. In his second term, operating from the Banking Committee, he enacted the Nehemiah program, an idea advanced by black churches in Brooklyn, to set up a revolving fund to subsidize mortgages for self-help home buying and renovation, often with whole blocks of homes being bought rather than rented by residents. This is the major innovation in housing programs in the 1980s, and one with the additional advantage for Schumer of making it possible to rehabilitate the vast acres of abandoned housing in Brownsville and East New York just at the edge of his district. But he also ranges far afield, coming up with a key compromise on the farm labor provisions of the long-deadlocked immigration reform bill which was directly responsible for its enactment in 1986.

On the Banking Committee, he is almost always a critic of the big banks and often an advocate of things sought by the securities business; he is stoutly against the repeal of Glass-Steagall, which would let the banks into securities underwriting. It was at his insistence that a provision was inserted into the trade bill forcing the Japanese to open their securities markets to American firms (otherwise we would bar them from underwriting American securities). But he has not been a patsy for the banks' longtime adversaries, the savings and loans; in 1988, when regulator Danny Wall was pooh-poohing the problem, Schumer insisted that the S&L crisis could cost $70 billion to fix—one of the higher estimates at the time. And he played a key role in fashioning the committee's relatively tough response to the S&L crisis in early 1989.

How does Schumer do it? For one thing, he is not shy. He is constantly advancing his own proposals, and keeping his lines out to others, while remaining unburdened by many special interests in his district and schmoozing on the floor of the House and in the cloakroom. "I have never seen anyone like that guy," Senator Alan Simpson, a collaborator on immigration reform, said. "I don't know whether he ever slows down; there is an audible hum about him."

Schumer is helped by his friendship with three other Members with whom he shares a Capitol Hill townhouse, Californians George Miller and Leon Panetta and Illinois' Marty Russo. This gives him lines to the big California delegation and to Ways and Means Chairman Dan Rostenkowski, and helped him easily win a seat on the Budget Committee in 1985. But not all the ideas he bubbles over with are passed into law. He has been frustrated in trying to reduce the cost of farm programs and their benefits for the rich; his proposal for a national presidential primary doesn't seem to be going anywhere; he was campaign manager for Charles Rangel's unsuccessful bid for House majority whip. He was the Dukakis co-chair of the testy New York delegation in Atlanta and was booed when he spoke out against the Jesse Jackson-sponsored Palestinian resolution—which couldn't have hurt him too much in his district.

Schumer is safe back home. This natural legislator had found his metier early: he was elected to the New York Assembly at 23, just after finishing law school, and is now a prominent congressman though he turns 40 in 1990. He won the 1980 primary with 59% of the vote; his biggest problem then was the charge that he violated election laws by using his employees in that campaign, but nothing came of it. Redistricting worried him for a while in 1981, and both he and Stephen Solarz, anticipating a primary fight, amassed huge campaign war chests for 1982. But both, partly for that reason, got safe districts; in 1988 Schumer had over $700,000 sitting in his treasury. Brooklyn has not lost much population, so both men should have no trouble getting safe seats for the 1990s. The only threat to Schumer's tenure then is the suggestion, advanced by Clay Felker of *Manhattan, inc.*, that he run for mayor of New York.

The People: Est. Pop. 1986: 544,000, up 5.3% 1980–86; Pop. 1980: 516,471, dn. 6.9% 1970–80. Households (1980): 71% family, 30% with children, 56% married couples; 66.2% housing units rented; median monthly rent: $228; median house value: $53,600. Voting age pop. (1980): 401,703; 7% Spanish origin, 4% Black, 2% Asian origin.

1988 Presidential Vote:　Dukakis (D)..................... 89,508　(56%)
　　　　　　　　　　　　　　Bush (R) .... 68,898　(43%)

Rep. Charles E. Schumer (D)

Elected 1980; b. Nov. 23, 1950, Brooklyn; home, Brooklyn; Harvard Col., B.A. 1971, J.D. 1974; Jewish; married (Iris).

Career: Practicing atty.; NY Assembly, 1974–80.

Offices: 126 CHOB 20515, 202-225-6616. Also 1628 Kings Hwy., Brooklyn 11229, 718-965-5400.

Committees: *Banking, Finance and Urban Affairs* (11th of 31 D). Subcommittees: Consumer Affairs and Coinage; Financial Institutions Supervision, Regulation and Insurance; Housing and Community Development; International Finance, Trade, and Monetary Policy. *Budget* (6th of 21 D). Task Forces: Budget Process, Reconciliation and Enforcement; Urgent Fiscal Issues (Chairman). *Judiciary* (12th of 21 D). Subcommittees: Criminal Justice (Chairman); Immigration, Refugees, and International Law.

Group Ratings

	ADA	ACLU	COPE	CFA	LCV	ACU	NTLC	NSI	COC	CEI
1988	100	90	91	82	88	4	15	0	36	17
1987	88	—	92	86	—	9	—	—	21	14

National Journal Ratings

	1988 LIB — 1988 CONS		1987 LIB — 1987 CONS	
Economic	60%	37%	57%	40%
Social	82%	17%	78%	0%
Foreign	84%	0%	81%	0%

Key Votes

1) Homeless $	AGN	5) Ban Drug Test	AGN	9) SDI Research	AGN
2) Gephardt Amdt	AGN	6) Drug Death Pen	AGN	10) Ban Chem Weaps	FOR
3) Deficit Reduc	FOR	7) Handgun Sales	AGN	11) Aid to Contras	AGN
4) Kill Plnt Clsng Notice	AGN	8) Ban D.C. Abort $	AGN	12) Nuclear Testing	FOR

Election Results

1988 general	Charles E. Schumer (D-L)	107,056	(78%)	($87,129)
	George S. Popielarski (R)	24,313	(18%)	
	Alice E. Gaffney (C)	5,119	(4%)	
1988 primary	Charles E. Schumer (D-L), unopposed			
1986 general	Charles E. Schumer (D-L)	76,318	(93%)	($65,543)
	Alice E. Gaffney (C)	5,472	(7%)	

ELEVENTH DISTRICT

"Bedford, in the mauve decade, was one of Brooklyn's most fashionable neighborhoods," wrote the *WPA Guide* years later. "Except for one or two quiet, less crowded streets, few traces of its past elegance survive. The brownstones of its heyday, faded and neglected for the most part, are now crowded by frame houses, small industrial establishments and warehouses." So the faded elegance of Bedford-Stuyvesant's massive brownstones is nothing new; it dates back to the years when most of the area's residents were white, living near downtown Brooklyn and its retail center on Fulton Street. Bedford-Stuyvesant is the heart of New York's 11th Congressional District, which includes several of Brooklyn's older neighborhoods. It includes the downtown area, less congested than it once was, and Williamsburg, which was much more densely populated in the years right after the Williamsburg Bridge from the Lower East Side of Manhattan opened in 1903. This was a polyglot area 50 years ago, and is again today, but with different groups: there are still some Hasidic Jews in Williamsburg, and there are Italians left in Carroll Gardens amid the young professionals spreading out from Brooklyn Heights and renovating brownstones. But there are not many Germans left in Bushwick, near the Queens border, or Italians farther out in East New York. Bedford-Stuyvesant itself is heavily black, with many immigrants from the West Indies and their descendants, as well as blacks whose family origins are in the American South.

In 1980, 47% of the 11th's residents were black and 34% Hispanic; there is, it should be noted, some overlap between these categories. It was created to be a minority district, but it does not form a unit with much of a civic culture. Part of the reason may be that the civic loyalties of many residents remain elsewhere. Blacks and the Hispanics from the Caribbean often move to Brooklyn intending to stay only a while, to make enough money to set themselves up back home. They continue to read newspapers from San Juan or Kingston or Barbados; they may pay U.S. taxes and become U.S. citizens (if they are not already), but their hearts are elsewhere.

The congressman from the 11th District is Ed Towns, a black Democrat from East New York more experienced in government than politics and used to serving members of all races. Towns has been a teacher, social worker and hospital administrator and active in the civic affairs of a racially changing community. He served as Brooklyn's deputy borough president for six years. That is an office with duties more mundane than it sounds, but nonetheless one which keeps a conscientious incumbent in close touch with organized communities across Brooklyn. Towns evidently succeeded in making himself both popular and non-controversial, and keeping himself from becoming involved in the political feuds that have captivated Bedford-Stuyvesant. In Washington, Towns is a member of the Government Operations and Public Works and Transportation Committees and maintains a solidly liberal voting record on most issues. A student-athlete himself at North Carolina A&T, he is a co-sponsor of the "Student Athlete Right-to-Know Act" and has criticized colleges for failing to see that student athletes receive an education and graduate with a degree.

Throughout his career, Towns has been the opposite of controversial. When the 11th District was drawn in 1982 to satisfy the Voting Rights Act, it seemed at first as if white incumbent Frederick Richmond would win. But Richmond, a rich businessman who had been pouring political and charitable money into Brooklyn for years, was forced to retire after it was revealed, four years after his arrest on homosexual charges, that he had gotten an ex-convict a job in the House under a false name. Towns won easily and now seems to have a safe seat, the only possible (but unlikely) threat to which is redistricting in 1992.

The People: Est. Pop. 1986: 503,200, dn. 2.6% 1980–86; Pop. 1980: 516,554, dn. 26.6% 1970–80. Households (1980): 70% family, 47% with children, 35% married couples; 83.4% housing units rented; median monthly rent: $174; median house value: $33,700. Voting age pop. (1980): 331,181; 47% Black, 34% Spanish origin, 1% Asian origin.

1988 Presidential Vote:

Dukakis (D)	80,095	(83%)
Bush (R)	15,298	(16%)

Rep. Edolphus Towns (D)

Elected 1982; b. July 21, 1934, Chadbourn, NC; home, Brooklyn; NC A&T U., B.S. 1956, Adelphi U., M.S.W. 1973; Presbyterian; married (Gwendolyn).

Career: Army, 1956–58; Prof., Medgar Evers Col.; Dpty. hospital admin., 1965–71; Dpty. Borough Pres. of Brooklyn, 1976–82.

Offices: 1726 LHOB 20515, 202-225-5936. Also 93 Prospect Pl., Brooklyn 11217, 718-622-5700; and 276 Stuyvesant Ave., Brooklyn 11221, 718-965-5124.

Committees: *Government Operations.* (14th of 24 D). Subcommittees: Environment, Energy, and Natural Resources; Government Information, Justice, and Agriculture. *Public Works and Transportation* (14th of 31 D). Subcommittees: Aviation; Surface Transportation; Economic Development. *Select Committee on Narcotics Abuse and Control* (14th of 18 D).

Group Ratings

	ADA	ACLU	COPE	CFA	LCV	ACU	NTLC	NSI	COC	CEI
1988	90	94	99	82	63	0	1	0	33	8
1987	92	—	99	79	—	0	—	—	0	4

National Journal Ratings

	1988 LIB	—	1988 CONS	1987 LIB	—	1987 CONS
Economic	85%	—	14%	73%	—	0%
Social	86%	—	0%	78%	—	0%
Foreign	84%	—	0%	81%	—	0%

Key Votes

1) Homeless $	AGN	5) Ban Drug Test	—	9) SDI Research	AGN
2) Gephardt Amdt	FOR	6) Drug Death Pen	—	10) Ban Chem Weaps	FOR
3) Deficit Reduc	FOR	7) Handgun Sales	—	11) Aid to Contras	AGN
4) Kill Plnt Clsng Notice	AGN	8) Ban D.C. Abort $	AGN	12) Nuclear Testing	FOR

Election Results

1988 general	Edolphus Towns (D-L)	73,755	(87%)	($278,709)
	Riaz B. Hussain (R)	7,418	(9%)	($226,722)
	Two others	1,985	(4%)	
1988 primary	Edolphus Towns (D-L)	13,998	(76%)	
	Riaz B. Hussain (D)	4,468	(24%)	
1986 general	Edolphus Towns (D-L)	41,689	(89%)	($185,565)
	Nathaniel Hendricks (R)	4,053	(9%)	($543)

TWELFTH DISTRICT

In the 1947, when Jackie Robinson suited up for the Brooklyn Dodgers and became the first black major league baseball player, there weren't that many blacks in Brooklyn. New York's large black ghetto was Manhattan's Harlem, with only a scattering of blacks at the southern edge of Brooklyn's Bedford-Stuyvesant, where landlords would rent cheap apartments to blacks "in the least desirable part of the neighborhood," Brooklyn historian Elliott Willensky explains, in the two blocks between "the unsightly old Fulton Street elevated and the Long Island Rail Road's equally unkempt Atlantic Avenue route." An IND subway built to replace the El connected these Bedford-Stuyvesant blacks with the center of black life and entertainment in Harlem, and in 1941, as the El was being demolished, inspired Duke Ellington's "Take the A Train."

In the 50 years since, Harlem has been depopulated, and large parts of the South Bronx have become vacant as landlords abandon rent controlled apartments and young thugs burn them up. But Bedford-Stuyvesant has grown and, to some extent, prospered. By 1980, Harlem had withered so much that there were more blacks in Queens and in the Bronx than in Manhattan. Nearly twice as many, 722,000, lived in Brooklyn, most in the few square miles of Bedford-Stuyvesant and in adjoining Crown Heights, Brownsville and East Flatbush.

Together these areas form New York's 12th Congressional District, a more varied area than it appears on the surface to many outsiders. The solid stone row houses of Bedford-Stuyvesant, many of them renovated or sparkling with new paint, house many upwardly mobile families, some of them straight from the West Indies; the blacks who have moved recently into once all-white East Flatbush are by no means impoverished. Brownsville, on the other hand, is about as wretched and disorganized a place as there is in America. Fifty years ago it had "large shops, a movie palace, and restaurants; great crowds of shoppers and strollers," says the *WPA Guide*. "The open-air pushcart market on Belmont Avenue, where Yiddish is the shopkeepers' tongue, and all the varieties of kosher foods, as well as delicacies particularly favored by Jews, are the leading articles of sale." Brownsville gave birth to Socialist politicians and Communist and bitterly anti-Communist writers, to novelists and wardheeling politicians. But today it looks bombed-out, with vacant lots giving hints of the outlines of the houses that once stood there and streets controlled by youth gangs, drug dealers and arsonists.

The 12th District is 80% black, heavily Democratic and possessed of a political culture which, though lively, seems to directly touch very few of its citizens. Voter turnout for years was about as low here as any place in the United States; elections were decided by small groups of hardy civic activists. Turnout rose suddenly in the 1984 presidential primary, thanks almost entirely to Jesse Jackson; while Manhattan's leading black politician, Congressman Charles Rangel, was uncomfortably keeping his word and supporting Walter Mondale, Bedford-Stuyvesant Assemblyman Albert Vann, with more than an eye on the next year's mayor race, was chairing Jackson's campaign. Jackson did indeed sweep the district, and won 38% of the vote in Brooklyn, an impressive showing; but Vann and other anti-Koch politicians were unable to agree on a single opponent for the mayor in 1985 and were routed.

The congressman from the 12th District, Major Owens, has had a long career in New York politics and government. He started out as a librarian, worked in the Brownsville Community Council, was commissioner of New York City's Community Development Agency under Mayor John Lindsay from 1968 to 1973, and was called by critic Charles Morris "the most capable and canny" of New York's anti-poverty program directors. That was a high-pressure job, with few guidelines to draw on; Owens may have been relieved when he was elected to serve in the antique chamber of the New York Senate in 1974. In 1982, when Congresswoman Shirley Chisholm, immigrant from Barbados and presidential candidate in 1972, announced her retirement, Owens got into the primary to succeed her. Chisholm backed another state Senator, Vander Beatty, who also had support from the Brooklyn organization; but Owens won.

He sits on two committees—Education and Labor and Government Operations—that have obvious relevance to this district and on which Owens can use his experience. He can be counted to look after the interests of libraries; as he likes to point out, he is the only librarian in the House. On national issues, Owens can be counted on as a solid liberal Democratic vote. General elections are, of course, no problem for him, but he must always be wary of the primary: even Chisholm, after years of incumbency and national fame, had to worry about primary opposition. One of Owens's sons, incidentally, plays Elvin on the "Bill Cosby Show."

The People: Est. Pop. 1986: 534,800, up 3.4% 1980–86; Pop. 1980: 516,983, dn. 12.5% 1970–80. Households (1980): 70% family, 46% with children, 37% married couples; 83.2% housing units rented; median monthly rent: $203; median house value: $46,200. Voting age pop. (1980): 348,549; 78% Black, 9% Spanish origin, 2% Asian origin.

1988 Presidential Vote:

Dukakis (D)	101,326	(88%)
Bush (R)	10,748	(9%)

Rep. Major R. Owens (D)

Elected 1982; b. June 28, 1936, Memphis, TN; home, Brooklyn; Morehouse Col., B.A. 1956, Atlanta U., M.S. 1957; Baptist; divorced.

Career: V.P., Metropolitan Cncl. of Housing, 1964; Commun. Coord., Brooklyn Pub. Library, 1964–65; Exec. Dir., Brownsville Commun. Cncl., 1966–68; Commissioner, NYC Commun. Devel., 1968–73; Dir., Commun. Media Library Prog., Columbia U., 1973–74; NY Senate, 1974–82.

Offices: 114 CHOB 20515, 202-225-6231. Also 289 Utica Ave., Brooklyn 11213, 718-773-3100.

Committees: *Education and Labor* (10th of 22 D). Subcommittees: Elementary, Secondary, and Vocational Education; Labor–Management Relations; Postsecondary Education; Select Education (Chairman). *Government Operations* (13th of 24 D). Subcommittee: Government Activities and Transportation.

Group Ratings

	ADA	ACLU	COPE	CFA	LCV	ACU	NTLC	NSI	COC	CEI
1988	95	100	99	100	81	0	6	0	15	10
1987	88	—	99	71	—	0	—	—	0	5

National Journal Ratings

	1988 LIB — 1988 CONS			1987 LIB — 1987 CONS		
Economic	92%	—	0%	73%	—	0%
Social	81%	—	18%	78%	—	0%
Foreign	84%	—	0%	81%	—	0%

Key Votes

1) Homeless $	AGN	5) Ban Drug Test	AGN	9) SDI Research	AGN
2) Gephardt Amdt	FOR	6) Drug Death Pen	AGN	10) Ban Chem Weaps	FOR
3) Deficit Reduc	FOR	7) Handgun Sales	AGN	11) Aid to Contras	AGN
4) Kill Plnt Clsng Notice	AGN	8) Ban D.C. Abort $	AGN	12) Nuclear Testing	FOR

Election Results

1988 general	Major R. Owens (D-L)	74,304	(93%)	($189,684)
	Owen Augustin (R-C)	5,582	(7%)	($7,099)
1988 primary	Major R. Owens (D-L), unopposed			
1986 general	Major R. Owens (D-L)	42,138	(91%)	($167,617)
	Owen Augustin (R)	2,752	(6%)	($24,506)
	Joseph N.O. Caesar (C)	1,168	(3%)	($1,895)

THIRTEENTH DISTRICT

Past the Navy Yard that once employed 30,000 men in the war and is now silent, past the empty piers near the huge Bush Terminal buildings, from Williamsburg with its Hasidic Jewish community and its single skyscraper, past downtown Brooklyn and the old Brooklyn Heights neighborhood overlooking downtown Manhattan and Wall Street from Columbia Heights, past the old and often abandoned docks of South Brooklyn, Red Hook and the Bush Terminal, dodging inland to avoid middle-class Bay Ridge and then facing the ocean, and going almost all the way the Brooklyn waterfront, stretches the 13th Congressional District of New York. Seldom more than a mile wide, the district is extensive enough to take most of a working day to drive through. It has high-income pockets, like trendy Brooklyn Heights, and some poverty-stricken slums here and there; it has Hasidic neighborhoods in the north, burgeoning Orthodox communities in Borough Park and along Ocean Parkway, and neighborhoods brimming with new Jewish emigrants from Soviet Russia in Brighton Beach and Coney Island on the ocean. The 13th is basically the poor Jewish district, one of the few majority-Jewish districts in the nation and the home of many of the nation's least affluent Jewish communities.

It is a district with mixed political leanings. On economic issues the tradition here is liberal, even socialistic: government should act to help the ordinary person. On civil liberties, of course the tradition is for tolerance—though some of the Orthodox would rather not tolerate practices other than their own. On cultural issues, there is fear of crime and dislike of racial quotas. On foreign policy, the trend has been conservative. Brooklyn was ready early on to support candidates who didn't favor the Vietnam war. But this part of Brooklyn is always worried about the survival of Israel and is as hostile as any part of the country today toward the Soviet Union; it is suspicious of Gorbachev's sincerity or skeptical about his chances and has little use for Third World dictators of any sort.

The congressman from the 13th District is Stephen Solarz, an able, ambitious and powerful member of the large Democratic class of 1974. Solarz is a Brooklyn politician and a foreign policy scholar, an elected official who has been supple in adapting to the changing views and priorities of his constituency, a leader on foreign policy who has had a major effect on American actions, and a player in NATO meetings and Philippine showdowns. Solarz has roots in Brooklyn, but he was also a graduate student studying under Zbigniew Brzezinski at Columbia in the 1960s; he was opposed to the Vietnam war, but he also believes that the United States must assert leadership and not simply accept whatever Soviet and Third World leaders decide to do. He has been a political insurgent, beating the rotted old Brooklyn machine in a race for the New York Assembly in 1968 and beating a scandal-tarred incumbent congressman in the Democratic primary in 1974. But he is by now a member of the establishment, fourth ranking Democrat on the Foreign Affairs Committee, chairman of a major subcommittee, a widely respected participant in foreign policy debate.

The critical period in his career came after the 1980 election, following the Republicans' surprising victory. For two years, Solarz had been chairman of the subcommittee covering Africa, an area on which there was predictably going to be a clash between Democratic liberals and Reagan Republicans. But there was an opening on the Asian and Pacific Affairs Subcommittee, where the issues were not so polarized, and on which, given the fate of Cambodia and Vietnam, it was hard for Democratic liberals to wax as self-righteous as they could on South Africa. Solarz chose the Asia chair. It has given him an opportunity to be a leader and to have a considerable effect on the course of events. He started off as a critic of countries like South Korea and the Philippines for their lack of democracy, but he did not believe we should withdraw our military presence in response; instead he backed and exerted his own pressures on them to change. He was one of the four or five key figures developing American policy to the

Philippines in 1985 and 1986. Travelling often to Manila, keeping up a barrage of criticism of Ferdinand Marcos since before Benigno Aquino was murdered in 1983, and he was harshly critical of the elections Marcos held in 1986; joined by Republicans like Senate Foreign Relations chairman Richard Lugar, he helped create a climate in which the Administration tilted sharply toward Corazon Aquino and signalled Marcos into exile without bloodshed. He deserves much of the credit for the revolution that put Aquino into office, and he was even with her in the Malacanang Palace when they discovered the closet with Imelda Marcos's 3,000 pairs of shoes.

On South Korea, as well, he backed that country's leaders strongly when they moved in the direction of democracy and opposed them subtly when they moved away from it. On Afghanistan he was one of the early backers of aid to the Afghan rebels, which helped them stymie the Soviets and perhaps made the difference in forcing them out of a country they once thought was theirs.

Solarz has been able to help forge a bipartisan foreign policy in Asia partly because the limits of both liberal and conservative policies are apparent there. It is clear that Vietnam and Cambodia are worse off than they would have been if U.S.-backed forces had won (though it is not clear whether or not they could have won), but clear also that Communist victories in those countries have not proved an attractive example for the rest of East Asia, as many conservatives feared they would. It is apparent that authoritarian East Asia countries like South Korea have produced much greater economic growth and more tolerable living conditions than Communist alternatives, but clear also that human rights there could be improved.

But Solarz is involved in issues outside Asia too, and in 1989 added a seat on the Intelligence Committee (thanks to Jim Wright) to his Foreign Affairs slot. He helps to shepherd foreign aid bills through, making sure they contain plenty for Israel. He backed the U.S. reflagging of Kuwaiti tankers in the Persian Gulf, but believed the War Powers Act should have been invoked. He keeps a hand in arms control, calling for a willingness to trade the Strategic Defense Initiative for Soviet concessions, and he criticized unilateral disarmers like the British Labor party. He also criticized Colombia and Peru for not doing enough to stop the illegal drugs. He issued his own conclusions on the Iran-contra scandal. He came out for the U.S.-Japan nuclear agreement.

Solarz sometimes talks as if he were bucking constituency pressures, but his views fit his district closely, and he has essentially a safe seat. During the redistricting process after the 1980 Census it looked as though Solarz and the 10th District's Charles Schumer would be put in the same seat, and both accumulated huge campaign treasuries in anticipation of that. But they both got safe, separate districts and have good prospects of doing so again for 1992. Even so, Solarz still raises enough money that he had over $1 million in his campaign treasury after the 1988 election. But not all his ambitions are electoral. Many think he would like to be secretary of state in a Democratic administration, and it's just possible that he could.

The People: Est. Pop. 1986: 539,000, up 4.4% 1980–86; Pop. 1980: 516,512, dn. 9.8% 1970–80. Households (1980): 67% family, 31% with children, 51% married couples; 77.5% housing units rented; median monthly rent: $195; median house value: $53,600. Voting age pop. (1980): 387,947; 13% Spanish origin, 6% Black, 2% Asian origin.

1988 Presidential Vote:

Dukakis (D)............................	73,438	(56%)
Bush (R)...............................	56,129	(43%)

Rep. Stephen J. Solarz (D)

Elected 1974; b. Sept. 12, 1940, New York City; home, Brooklyn; Brandeis U., A.B. 1962, Columbia U., M.A. 1967; Jewish; married (Nina).

Career: NY Assembly, 1968–74.

Offices: 1536 LHOB 20515, 202-225-2361. Also 532 Neptune Ave., Brooklyn, 11224, 718-372-8600.

Committees: *Foreign Affairs* (4th of 28 D). Subcommittees: Arms Control, International Security and Science; Asian and Pacific Affairs (Chairman); Western Hemisphere Affairs. *Merchant Marine and Fisheries* (22d out of 26 D). Subcommittees: Fisheries and Wildlife Conservation and the Environment; Merchant Marine. *Joint Economic Committee.* Task Forces: Fiscal and Monetary Policy; International Economic Policy; Investment, Jobs and Prices. *Permanent Select Committee on Intelligence* (12th of 12 D). Subcommittees: Legislation; Program and Budget Authorization.

Group Ratings

	ADA	ACLU	COPE	CFA	LCV	ACU	NTLC	NSI	COC	CEI
1988	95	91	89	91	81	4	10	10	33	16
1987	92	—	89	93	—	0	—	—	8	7

National Journal Ratings

	1988 LIB — 1988 CONS	1987 LIB — 1987 CONS
Economic	71% — 23%	73% — 0%
Social	86% — 0%	78% — 0%
Foreign	79% — 16%	76% — 19%

Key Votes

1) Homeless $	AGN	5) Ban Drug Test	AGN	9) SDI Research	AGN
2) Gephardt Amdt	FOR	6) Drug Death Pen	AGN	10) Ban Chem Weaps	FOR
3) Deficit Reduc	FOR	7) Handgun Sales	AGN	11) Aid to Contras	AGN
4) Kill Plnt Clsng Notice	AGN	8) Ban D.C. Abort $	AGN	12) Nuclear Testing	FOR

Election Results

1988 general	Stephen J. Solarz (D-L)	81,305	(75%)	($553,532)
	Anthony M. Curci (R-C)	27,536	(25%)	
1988 primary	Stephen J. Solarz (D-L), unoppposed			
1986 general	Stephen J. Solarz (D-L)	61,089	(82%)	($417,975)
	Leon Nadrowski (R)	10,941	(15%)	($294,811)
	Samuel Roth (C).	2,106	(3%)	

FOURTEENTH DISTRICT

As you approached New York by ferry (5 cents) 50 years ago, you saw "factories topped by high smoking chimneys along the north and northeast shore. Farther inland, one could find modest middle-class communities, many of them independent towns and villages at the time of the consolidation of Greater New York in 1898. Large estates and pretentious mansions extend along the central ridge," which included Todt Hill, the highest point on the eastern seacoast from Maine to Florida. Staten Island then had only 175,000 people and was connected with the

7.3 million other residents of New York only by ferry. Today there are 380,000 Staten Islanders, connected not only by ferry (25 cents) but by the Verrazano Narrows Bridge. A sense of remoteness from the city still remains, however. Geographically, Staten Island is way off to one side of New York, and looks from the air to be part of New Jersey. Some of it is still rural: cows still graze in the nation's largest city.

Culturally, the attitudes of Staten Islanders are traditional and conservative—more so than in many, perhaps most, of New York's suburbs—quite a contrast from the island at the other end of the ferry. This is a place of Italian and Irish Catholic homeowners, registered Democrats perhaps but behavioral Republicans; families, not singles; religious people, not skeptics.

Staten Island forms two-thirds of New York's 14th Congressional District. The other one-third is the part of New York City that may be closest to Staten Island in attitudes, as well as in proximity: the Bay Ridge section of Brooklyn. At the eastern terminus of the Verrazano Narrows Bridge, Bay Ridge is mostly Catholic, mostly middle-class; there are some large apartment buildings and even high-rises, but 30% of the housing units are owner-occupied, and there are even some large single-family homes overlooking New York Harbor. In heavily Democratic Brooklyn, Bay Ridge consistently votes Republican.

The congressman from the 14th District is Staten Islander Guy Molinari, a Republican first elected in 1980. He owed his victory less to the Reagan landslide than to local circumstances: other Republicans had been beaten by Democratic Representative John Murphy in Republican presidential years, but in 1980 Murphy ran after having been convicted in the Abscam scandal, and lost. Since then, Molinari has remained in office more by tending local interests than by following national conservative agendas. He has championed the Navy's homeporting plan, dispersing ships from Norfolk and San Diego; one result is that Staten Island will become a Navy port. Like many northeastern Republicans, he is as eager as his Democratic neighbors to be seen cleaning up the environment, but rather than get involved in the New York City-New Jersey dispute on ocean dumping, he just inserted his own amendment banning sludge disposal in Staten Island's Fresh Kills, for which he is also busy getting a sea wall and new docks.

Molinari has had his reverses, and was disappointed when Newt Gingrich took away (as he was entitled to by seniority) his ranking position on a Public Works subcommittee in 1985—although he is now ranking member on the Investigations and Oversight Subcommittee. But by concentrating his efforts on a small number of issues, most of which have clear local impact, he has made a difference on policy and helped establish himself in a strong political position. In 1982, redistricting put him in a race against Bay Ridge Democratic incumbent Leo Zeferetti, but Molinari won with a big margin in Staten Island. He was the leader of nine New York Republican congressmen who made a show in 1986 of endorsing George Bush over their New York colleague, Jack Kemp. He has been reelected easily ever since, even against a Democrat in 1988 who raised and spent more money. Recruited by Republican mayoral candidate Rudolph Giuliani, Molinari is running for Staten Island borough president in November 1989. A Republican has not held that seat since 1973, and if Molinari does win and resign his House seat, a possible successor might be his daughter, Susan Molinari, a city councilwoman.

The People: Est. Pop. 1986: 546,800, up 5.9% 1980–86; Pop. 1980: 516,537, up 8.7% 1970–80. Households (1980): 75% family, 38% with children, 60% married couples; 50.5% housing units rented; median monthly rent: $217; median house value: $62,000. Voting age pop. (1980): 379,638; 6% Spanish origin, 4% Black, 2% Asian origin.

1988 Presidential Vote:

Bush (R)	105,315	(61%)
Dukakis (D)	67,361	(39%)

Rep. Guy V. Molinari (R)

Elected 1980; b. Nov. 23, 1928, New York City; home, Staten Island; Wagner Col., B.A. 1949, NY Law Sch., LL.B. 1951; Roman Catholic; married (Marguerite).

Career: USMC, Korea; Practicing atty., 1953–74; NY Assembly, 1974–80.

Offices: 2453 RHOB 20515, 202-225-3371. Also Naval Station, Bldg. 203, Staten Island 10305, 718-981-9800; and 1305 73d St., Brooklyn 11228, 718-236-9292.

Committees: *Public Works and Transportation* (5th of 20 R). Subcommittees: Aviation; Investigations and Oversight (Ranking Member); Water Resources.

Group Ratings

	ADA	ACLU	COPE	CFA	LCV	ACU	NTLC	NSI	COC	CEI
1988	30	30	31	55	56	63	64	90	91	42
1987	28	—	27	43	—	74	—	—	71	55

National Journal Ratings

	1988 LIB — 1988 CONS		1987 LIB — 1987 CONS	
Economic	30%	— 70%	19%	— 78%
Social	28%	— 71%	35%	— 65%
Foreign	24%	— 74%	32%	— 68%

Key Votes

1) Homeless $	FOR	5) Ban Drug Test	FOR	9) SDI Research	FOR
2) Gephardt Amdt	AGN	6) Drug Death Pen	FOR	10) Ban Chem Weaps	FOR
3) Deficit Reduc	AGN	7) Handgun Sales	AGN	11) Aid to Contras	FOR
4) Kill Plnt Clsng Notice	—	8) Ban D.C. Abort $	FOR	12) Nuclear Testing	AGN

Election Results

1988 general	Guy V. Molinari (R-C-RTL)	99,179	(63%)	($206,796)
	Jerome X. O'Donovan (D-IVP)	57,503	(37%)	($218,849)
1988 primary	Guy V. Molinari (R-C-RTL), unopposed			
1986 general	Guy V. Molinari (R-C-RTL)	64,647	(69%)	($152,312)
	Barbara Walla (D)	27,950	(30%)	($41,310)

FIFTEENTH DISTRICT

"Rockefeller Center," writes Jan Morris, remembering what it looked like in *Manhattan '45*, "stood in the heart of midtown, the area of the smartest shops, the grandest hotels, the plush offices, the theaters, the expensive apartment houses, which set the civic reputation. Manhattan's midtown occupied 20 or 30 blocks, perhaps a mile square, around the focus of, say, Fifth Avenue and 59th Street. Beyond it there stretched away wide areas of slum and dullness." "The perfumed stockade," Theodore White called it when the cities seemed beset by riots, the rather few blocks around his own house on East 64th Street where the richest people of the richest city in the world lived, uncomfortably aware that they were only a few blocks away from rather tawdry apartment buildings and not that far away from the violent slums of Harlem. And, as

Morris points out, "provincial America never felt far distant—just over the Hudson River, only a few hundred yards away, all the rest began"—as you could see when you looked far enough west on almost any Manhattan cross street.

This upper class enclave in Manhattan was set apart in a separate congressional district as early as 1918, called as early as the 1930s, the Silk Stocking District. What has happened through the five decades since is that elite, affluent Manhattan has spread from this narrow enclave and taken over the greater part of the island, at least when you are counting residents who take the trouble to vote. In the process, the political attitudes of this much-broadened upper class—defined partly by income, but also by association with elite tastes in the arts, fashion, letters, all the things in which New York remains clearly the nation's capital—have changed, and changed again, in a progress that needs some charting.

Fifty years ago the Silk Stocking District went no farther east of Central Park than Third Avenue, where the El separated the rich area from the rest of the East Side and its factories, breweries, and the German immigrant community of Yorkville. Today's Silk Stocking District, the 15th Congressional District of New York, extends as far south as City Hall, just a few blocks north of the financial district (which could easily have been included: there aren't many residents or voters in those blocks), covers the Lower East Side, all of Midtown north of 14th Street, and even the Times Square area. It bypasses Greenwich Village and SoHo, but only by a few blocks, and many of the denizens of their nightlife actually live and vote (if they bother) within the bounds of the 15th District.

Most of the voters in this district live on the Upper East Side, from the East 50s to the East 90s, between Central Park and the East River. This is the largest concentration of singles in America. These are the people who make Manhattan the center of the nation's securities, publishing, advertising, entertainment, broadcasting and communications industries.

The Silk Stocking District has always been culturally more liberal and tolerant than the rest of the nation that it sees glowering over the Hudson. In partisan terms it was, from its creation in 1918 until the 1960s, more Republican than the nation—more than that, the heartland of the robust, confident, ruling Republican Party of the era of Theodore Roosevelt and William Howard Taft. In the 1950s, when it was one of six Manhattan districts, it was the embodiment of liberal Republicanism—a philosophy articulated in the old *New York Herald-Tribune* and Henry Luce's *Time* magazine that accepted the New Deal and embraced America's commitments abroad, but that felt that the natural executors of those policies were the well-educated Protestant gentlemen one saw strolling down Madison Avenue to their clubs, not the creatures of political bosses who made deals with labor union leaders and racketeers. Successful in 1952, hopeful that Nelson Rockefeller would capture the presidency in 1960, these establishment Republicans had their last success in the election of John Lindsay, then Silk Stocking District congressman, as mayor of New York in 1965, just a couple of years before the *Herald Tribune* merged and folded.

Lindsay proved a disaster as mayor, running up huge debts that nearly bankrupted the city in 1975 and allowing neighborhoods to deteriorate so badly that the city lost one million people in the 1970s, but he personified nicely the change in Silk Stocking politics. Starting off as a member of an establishment, he became scathingly critical of almost all existing institutions except those whose heads parroted his line, carrying the tone of black power advocates and student rioters to middle-class life in the outer boroughs (which never voted for him). It is a measure of the power of New York-based media that with this record he was considered by some a plausible candidate for President in 1972. In the process, he switched to the Democratic Party—a switch most Silk Stocking district voters made by 1968 when they elected a Greenwich Village reformer named Edward Koch as their congressman.

Koch went on to be elected mayor in 1977 as the candidate of the outer boroughs, using his Manhattan liberal critics as foils. The Silk Stocking District, with its constant population

842   NEW YORK

turnover, turned inward—away from poverty programs and toward exercise programs. The surge in New York's financial industry in the 1980s made the rich much richer, and much less ashamed of their wealth; a raft of publications—*Vanity Fair, Manhattan, inc., Avenue, Conde Nast Traveler, Connoisseur,* and of course *New York Magazine*—flaunt it and have made Donald Trump the Silk Stocking District's dominant intellectual presence in a way that even Tom Wolfe and *Spy* can only begin to satirize. The more attractive side of the change is that the Silk Stocking District seems less disdainfully critical of those who don't share its values, less certain that it has the answer to how all those people in those icky middle class places should live. It will go its way and others can go theirs.

In politics, the Silk Stocking District went back to electing a Republican to Congress when Koch moved to Gracie Mansion. Bill Green was elected at first because of the weaknesses of his Democratic opponents, but now is reelected because of his own strengths. Green is smart and rich, and was the last Republican elected (in 1965) to the New York Assembly from Manhattan. He won the House seat in the 1978 special election by beating Bella Abzug, then in the 1978 general, he beat Carter Burden; he has won usually by wide margins, but after some expensive campaigns, in the 1980s. On cultural issues, Green is more liberal than most Democrats; he is an ardent backer of gay rights measures and of having all federal medical programs cover abortions. On foreign policy, he is a bit more cautious, and on economics in this district which lives off markets, he is quite market-oriented. He moves quickly to help local constituencies, as when he got the IRS's absurd capitalization rules for writers repealed. He has a seat on the Appropriations Committee and is ranking Republican on the HUD Subcommittee; he is hard-working and knowledgeable, and manages to channel a lot of money to New York housing programs. The Republican leadership probably does not much mind: they understand that this is the only kind of Republican who could hold this district. Careful, diffident, almost shy, possessed of a quiet sense of humor, Green is not a natural gladhander or spellbinder and does not seem fascinated by the glitz that has mesmerized too many others in the district.

The 15th was a Mondale and Dukakis district, and Green is one Republican who had to run ahead of Reagan and Bush to win. He did so, and in 1988 got 61% of the vote, some 28 points more than Bush.

The People: Est. Pop. 1986: 541,300, up 4.8% 1980–86; Pop. 1980: 516,409, dn. 3.2% 1970–80. Households (1980): 37% family, 14% with children, 28% married couples; 89.3% housing units rented; median monthly rent: $317; median house value: $185,800. Voting age pop. (1980): 444,395; 12% Spanish origin, 9% Asian origin, 5% Black.

1988 Presidential Vote: Dukakis (D)...................... 131,052   (66%)
                              Bush (R) 65,134   (33%)

Rep. Bill Green (R)

Elected Feb. 14, 1978; b. Oct. 16, 1929, New York City; home, New York City; Harvard U., B.A. 1950, J.D. 1953; Jewish; married (Patricia).

Career: Army, 1953–55; Law Secy., U.S. Court of Appeals for DC Circuit, 1955–56; Practicing atty., 1956–70; NY Assembly, 1965–68; NY Reg. Admin., U.S. Dept. of HUD, 1970–77.

Offices: 1110 LHOB 20515, 202-225-2436. Also 60 E. 42d St., Rm. 2308, New York 10165, 212-826-4466.

Committees: *Appropriations* (12th of 22 R). Subcommittees: District of Columbia; VA, HUD and Independent Agencies (Ranking Member).

Group Ratings

	ADA	ACLU	COPE	CFA	LCV	ACU	NTLC	NSI	COC	CEI
1988	75	64	55	64	81	25	38	20	64	44
1987	60	—	55	57	—	13	—	—	47	32

National Journal Ratings

	1988 LIB — 1988 CONS			1987 LIB — 1987 CONS		
Economic	30%	—	69%	39%	—	60%
Social	72%	—	27%	48%	—	50%
Foreign	60%	—	37%	56%	—	43%

Key Votes

1) Homeless $	AGN	5) Ban Drug Test	AGN	9) SDI Research	AGN
2) Gephardt Amdt	AGN	6) Drug Death Pen	FOR	10) Ban Chem Weaps	FOR
3) Deficit Reduc	AGN	7) Handgun Sales	AGN	11) Aid to Contras	AGN
4) Kill Plnt Clsng Notice	FOR	8) Ban D.C. Abort $	AGN	12) Nuclear Testing	FOR

Election Results

1988 general	Bill Green (R-IN)	107,599	(61%)	($602,942)
	Peter G. Doukas (D)	64,425	(37%)	($162,157)
1988 primary	Bill Green (R-IN), unopposed			
1986 general	Bill Green (R-IN)	58,214	(58%)	($709,384)
	George A. Hirsch (D-L)	42,147	(42%)	($395,185)

SIXTEENTH DISTRICT

Harlem in 1940, said the *WPA Guide,* was an area "into which are crowded more than a quarter of a million Negroes from the southern states, the West Indies, and Africa, [and it] has many different aspects. To whites seeking amusement, it is an exuberant, original, and unconventional entertainment center; to Negro college graduates, it is an opportunity to practice a profession among their own people; to those aspiring to racial leadership, it is a domain where they may advocate their theories unmolested; to artists, writers, and sociologists, it is a mine of rich material; to the mass of Negro people, it is the spiritual capital of Black America." Blacks started moving into this street-grid filled with five-story tenements in 1901. Central Harlem was mostly black by 1920, a place where blacks built "a cosmopolitan Negro capital which exerts an influence over Negroes everywhere."

In the years since, blacks spread north along the Harlem River and south into part of what was "Spanish Harlem," but the larger movement has been away from Harlem altogether. Some 70% of Harlem's dwellings have been abandoned by owners and now belong to the city; hoped-for rehabilitation and rise in property values have not yet happened. A few middle-class pockets are left, but crime and drugs have driven most people out who can get out. Harlem, if you include the area east of Morningside Heights and north of West 110th and East 96th Streets, is home to 250,000 fewer people than in the 1940s. There are now more blacks in southeast Queens than there are in Harlem, and many more in Brooklyn's black neighborhoods; nor have Harlem's cultural institutions or places of entertainment retained their central role in black life. Harlem is a place American blacks have outgrown, without entirely replacing.

Harlem has had its own congressional district since 1944—a district whose size has had to expand every 10 years because it has been losing population. The present 16th District, centered on Harlem, includes, on the east, the Hispanic (once Italian) neighborhood of East Harlem and, on the west, dips down into the Upper West Side almost as far south as Zabar's delicatessen at 80th Street and includes Columbia University, most of Morningside Heights (an academic neighborhood), virtually all of Washington Heights (once Jewish, now mostly hispanic), and the Inwood neighborhood at the northern tip of Manhattan (still mostly Irish). Less than a majority, 49%, of its residents are black; some 38% are of Spanish origin (there is an overlap here); given turnout rates, probably a significant majority of voters here are white, though like the blacks, they are heavily Democratic.

In the 40 years during which it has formed the nucleus of a congressional district, Harlem has had only two congressmen: Adam Clayton Powell and Charles Rangel. Powell was an accomplished legislator, an able chairman of the Education and Labor Committee during the years the Great Society and antipoverty laws were passed through it; he was one of the most eloquent, gifted—and most flawed—black leaders of his generation. He was ousted from the House in 1967—the Supreme Court later ruled the procedure illegal—because of outrage over payroll-padding charges. Powell believed, with some justice, that voters were far more outraged when he did such things than when white congressman did them; still, why did he have to? Powell won two elections afterwards, but never really returned to Congress. He lost the 1970 primary to 40-year-old Charles Rangel, a four-year verteran of the New York Assembly

Rangel is now one of the most senior and arguably the most powerful member of New York delegation. He was spotlighted early in his House career as a member of the Judiciary Committee in the Nixon impeachment hearings. In 1975, he won a seat on Ways and Means and he is now the fourth ranking Democrat on the committee. There he is an advocate for New York's interests and an ally usually of chairman Dan Rostenkowski. In the tax reform fight, once Rostenkowski accepted state and local tax deductibility, Rangel supported him strongly; Rangel chairs the Select Revenues Subcommittee, and while Rostenkowski keeps control over special tax breaks and transition rules, Rangel has some say too. Rangel, representing a district ravaged by drugs, is chairman of the Select Committee on Narcotics Abuse and Control, and a hardline believer in suppressing drug use by almost any means—by taking action against Latin drug-producing countries, for example, or by refusing to let doctors prescribe heroin for terminal cancer patients. Rangel says that drugs are the number one national security problem, and that "Communists aren't killing kids—drugs are."

Rangel has not always been successful in his political maneuvering. He supported Walter Mondale early in 1984 and had the courage to stick with him, but he saw Harlem vote heavily for Jesse Jackson. He ran for majority whip, the number three position in the leadership, after the 1986 election, but ended up far behind (167–78) the harder-charging Tony Coelho. In New York City politics Rangel has often been a critic and adversary of his onetime Manhattan House colleague Edward Koch, came out early for Jackson in the 1988 presidential primary and was one of the fiercest critics of what he considered Koch's incendiary statements. Rangel himself has a good record of avoiding demagoguery: when whites were accused in the beatings and death of blacks in Howard Beach, Rangel urged the black witnesses to testify when their lawyers, later visible in the Tawana Brawley hoax, said they would not.

One of Rangel's chief assets, through all these vicissitudes and under the spotlight, has been the good humor and ebullience which have served him well in his political career. He is a firm believer in enough causes which seem to give him varying groups of allies—in promoting civil rights, but also in sternly suppressing the drug trade, for example—that he seems to have a wide range of sympathies and a broad-gauged view of society. He is regularly reelected without serious opposition or difficulty.

The People: Est. Pop. 1986: 515,200, dn. 0.2% 1980–86; Pop. 1980: 516,405, dn. 16.7% 1970–80. Households (1980): 58% family, 34% with children, 29% married couples; 96.0% housing units rented; median monthly rent: $169; median house value: $37,800. Voting age pop. (1980): 381,724; 49% Black, 35% Spanish origin, 1% Asian origin.

1988 Presidential Vote:

Dukakis (D)	114,237	(87%)
Bush (R)	14,960	(11%)

Rep. Charles B. Rangel (D)

Elected 1970; b. June 11, 1930, New York City; home, New York City; N.Y.U., B.S. 1957, St. John's U., LL.B. 1960; Roman Catholic; married (Alma).

Career: Army, Korea; Asst. U.S. Atty., S. Dist. of NY, 1961; Legal Cnsl., NYC Housing and Redevel. Bd., Neighborhood Conservation Bur.; Gen. Cnsl., Natl. Advisory Comm. on Selective Svc., 1966; NY Assembly, 1966–70.

Offices: 2252 RHOB 20515, 202-225-4365. Also 163 W. 125 St., Rm. 730, New York 10027, 212-663-3900; 601 W. 181st St., New York 10033, 212-927-5333; and 2110 1st Ave., New York 10029, 212-348-9630.

Committees: *Ways and Means* (4th of 23 D). Subcommittees: Oversight; Select Revenue Measures (Chairman). *Select Committee on Narcotics Abuse and Control* (Chairman of 18 D).

Group Ratings

	ADA	ACLU	COPE	CFA	LCV	ACU	NTLC	NSI	COC	CEI
1988	85	90	94	73	94	0	3	0	31	8
1987	88	—	94	93	—	0	—	—	0	5

National Journal Ratings

	1988 LIB — 1988 CONS			1987 LIB — 1987 CONS		
Economic	85%	—	14%	73%	—	0%
Social	86%	—	0%	78%	—	0%
Foreign	84%	—	0%	81%	—	0%

Key Votes

1) Homeless $	AGN	5) Ban Drug Test	AGN	9) SDI Research	AGN
2) Gephardt Amdt	FOR	6) Drug Death Pen	AGN	10) Ban Chem Weaps	FOR
3) Deficit Reduc	FOR	7) Handgun Sales	AGN	11) Aid to Contras	AGN
4) Kill Plnt Clsng Notice	AGN	8) Ban D.C. Abort $	AGN	12) Nuclear Testing	FOR

Election Results

1988 general	Charles B. Rangel (D-R-L).............	107,620	(97%)	($479,427)
1988 primary	Charles B. Rangel (D-R-L), unopposed			
1986 general	Charles B. Rangel (D-R-L).............	61,262	(96%)	($375,344)

SEVENTEENTH DISTRICT

The West Side of Manhattan, facing the Hudson River docks and New Jersey across the river, has always been the more raffish side of the island. As Fifth Avenue channeled New York's carriage trade northward to the precincts east of Central Park, Broadway—the slanted avenue running past the mass department stores and the marquees and billboards of Times Square—was the route northward for those with slightly less aristocratic and more theatrical tastes. The West Side 50 years ago was a melange of neighborhoods from the Italian and Bohemian blocks in the irregular grids of Greenwich Village; the dockside slums of Chelsea and Hell's Kitchen; Central Park West, with its almost solid blocks of apartment buildings with grand towers confidently overlooking the Park and the skyscrapers of midtown—"New York's finest street at large scale" in the view of Paul Goldberger, architectural critic for the *New York Times*—and finally to the mansions of Riverside Drive, with blocks of brownstones and West End Avenue apartment houses in between. Up on Morningside Heights was Columbia University and farther north City College and a collection of museums on the bluff around 155th Street, looking north to the majesty of what was, from 1931 to 1937, the world's longest span, the George Washington Bridge.

Politically, the West Side was not a particularly left-wing place: New York's Socialist and pro-Communist politicians came from Italian East Harlem (Congressman Vito Marcantonio) and Jewish Brownsville. In the early 1940s, many West Side brownstone blocks were included in the Silk Stocking District that elected a Republican congressman. But by the middle 1960s, the two heavy voting concentrations here—Greenwich Village and the Upper West Side from 61st Street to the 90s—were full of Adlai Stevenson liberal reform Democrats, determined to wrest control of the party from the local bosses and the scattered ethnics and rooming house residents who supplied their votes. In battles whose epic character derives almost solely from the fact that so many of the participants were writers, the reformers won total victory as their constituency—young singles, gays, liberals from the sticks come to the big city, the young professionals making their way in Manhattan's word businesses—grew, while the bosses' constituencies dwindled.

This is the land of New York's 17th Congressional District, which covers the West Side from the tip of Manhattan (in a nice touch, it includes the financial district and the offices of *The Wall Street Journal*'s editorial writers) up through Battery Park City and TriBeCa and SoHo, Greenwich Village and Chelsea, and the Upper West Side up to 90th Street. From there it covers only a block or two along the Hudson and then, to meet the population standard, includes two neighborhoods in the Bronx: high-income Riverdale, with its estates, apartments and big houses and, across two golf courses and a cemetery, middle-income and mostly black Williamsbridge.

This is now one of the most leftish congressional districts in the country, where majority opinion has been inclined to see America working for evil dictators abroad and to compel cultural uniformity and enforce middle class values at home. In the early 1970s, when the United States was sending troops to help the Thieu government in South Vietnam and National Guard troops were shooting peaceful student demonstrators in Ohio, this seemed a supportable view. It seemed to make less sense in the late 1980s, when the Soviet Union's leader was proclaiming the viability of market economics, and those who once extolled personal liberation from all restraint and who lived comfortably in a city where nothing seems forbidden were urging moderation in food and drink, abstinence from drugs, and monogamy or safe sex. On stylishly affluent Columbus Avenue or in the glittering Village, it is hard now to see oneself as part of an oppressed proletariat, exploited by greedy corporations, mad generals, rapacious landlords, vicious speculators, or hypocritical fundamentalist preachers. As restaurant-goers become couch potatoes and liberated young people start to contemplate the implications of mortality, it becomes apparent that their most dangerous enemies are not others with different lifestyles but, like Pogo's, themselves.

Politically, that leaves the West Side a slightly demoralized constituency, no longer quite so sure it has all the answers for everyone else. Once solid for John Lindsay and George McGovern, the West Side is now often fragmented, voting for Edward Koch in 1985 despite the attacks of the *Village Voice*, for example, and admitting that it finds resistible the blandishments of the most leftish presidential candidate in 1984 and 1988, Jesse Jackson.

The congressman from the 17th District is Ted Weiss, a veteran of the reform movement who has applied its liberal philosophy relentlessly and cheerfully in the House. He was elected to the City Council back in 1961, before Ed Koch was known outside of Greenwich Village, and ran for Congress as long ago as 1966 and 1968. When Bella Abzug left the House to run for the Senate in 1976, Weiss was strong enough on the West Side that he was elected without opposition in the primary. Weiss has a solidly liberal record and has been chairman of Americans for Democratic Action. On foreign policy, his sympathies are often with those most congressmen regard as the adversaries of America. Like some other Democrats, he calls for normalization of relations with Cuba, and he criticized the invasion of Grenada harshly as being unjustified by its stated reasons and illegal under international law; like many liberals he shows more outrage over the evildoings of right-wing regimes than those of the murderous Grenada Communists or the Sandinistas in Nicaragua. It should be added that Weiss, who came to America as a refugee one step ahead of the Nazis in 1938, is a strong supporter of civil liberties in this country; he reacted sharply when an Education Department bureaucrat objected to a course on the Holocaust on the grounds it did not explain the views of the Nazis.

Much of Weiss's legislative work has come on the Government Operations subcommittee he chairs which, despite a general name (Human Resources and Intergovernmental Relations), has for years devoted most of its oversight to the Food and Drug Administration. He has insisted on tougher testing of food additives and has tracked down charges of conflict of interest. An advocate of aggressive research to find a cure for AIDS, he has faced squarely the dilemma caused by the fact that drugs that seem to do some good have not gone through the full FDA process, required by previous law, of being found both safe and efficacious. Weiss insists that FDA procedures be respected, and that the flexibility regarding the use of these drugs must derive from the FDA. His other causes include bills for conversion of defense industries to peacetime work and to enable disabled veterans to get funds so they can father children through artificial insemination.

Weiss seems to have a safe seat. Challenged for renomination in 1986 by a Democrat whose views are well to his right, especially on foreign policy, he won an overwhelming 83% victory. Redistricting will be a problem only if the legislature decides to collapse the 15th and 17th districts, and even then Weiss's West Side margins have been larger than those of East Side Republican Bill Green.

The People: Est. Pop. 1986: 550,600, up 6.7% 1980–86; Pop. 1980: 516,239, up 0.3% 1970–80. Households (1980): 39% family, 16% with children, 28% married couples; 89.8% housing units rented; median monthly rent: $271; median house value: $51,800. Voting age pop. (1980): 442,060; 14% Black, 13% Spanish origin, 3% Asian origin.

1988 Presidential Vote:

Dukakis (D)	169,463	(78%)
Bush (R)	44,801	(21%)

Rep. Theodore S. (Ted) **Weiss** (D)

Elected 1976; b. Sept. 17, 1927, Gava, Hungary; home, New York City; Syracuse U., B.A. 1951, LL.B. 1952; Jewish; married (Sonya).

Career: Army, 1946–47; Practicing atty., 1953–76; Asst. Dist. Atty., NY Cnty., 1955–59; NYC Cncl., 1961–77.

Offices: 2467 RHOB 20515, 202-225-5635. Also 252 7th Ave., New York 10001, 212-620-3970; 4060 Broadway, New York 10032, 212-620-3970; 131 Waverly Pl., New York 10011, 212-420-9393; 490 W. 238th St., Bronx 10463, 212-884-0441; and 655 E. 233d St., Bronx 10466, 212-652-0400.

Committees: *Foreign Affairs* (17th of 28 D). Subcommittees: Human Rights and International Organizations; International Operations; Western Hemisphere Affairs. *Government Operations* (5th of 24 D). Subcommittees: Human Resources and Intergovernmental Relations (Chairman); Employment and Housing. *Select Committee on Children, Youth, and Families* (6th of 18 D).

Group Ratings

	ADA	ACLU	COPE	CFA	LCV	ACU	NTLC	NSI	COC	CEI
1988	75	100	92	100	88	0	14	0	21	11
1987	92	—	92	100	—	0	—	—	14	8

National Journal Ratings

	1988 LIB — 1988 CONS		1987 LIB — 1987 CONS	
Economic	83%	— 16%	73%	— 0%
Social	86%	— 0%	78%	— 0%
Foreign	77%	— 21%	81%	— 0%

Key Votes

1) Homeless $	AGN	5) Ban Drug Test	AGN	9) SDI Research	AGN
2) Gephardt Amdt	FOR	6) Drug Death Pen	AGN	10) Ban Chem Weaps	FOR
3) Deficit Reduc	FOR	7) Handgun Sales	AGN	11) Aid to Contras	AGN
4) Kill Plnt Clsng Notice	AGN	8) Ban D.C. Abort $	AGN	12) Nuclear Testing	FOR

Election Results

1988 general	Theodore S. (Ted) Weiss (D-L)	157,339	(84%)	($170,567)
	Myrna C. Albert (R-C)	29,156	(16%)	($2,851)
1988 primary	Theodore S. (Ted) Weiss (D)	28,185	(86%)	
	Harry Fotopoulos (D)	4,453	(14%)	
1986 general	Theodore S. (Ted) Weiss (D)	95,094	(85%)	($242,860)
	Thomas A. Chorba (R)	15,587	(14%)	($13,305)

EIGHTEENTH DISTRICT

"The beautiful Bronx," Lloyd Utlan, historian of the borough, calls it, remembering the 1930s and 1940s when Presidents Roosevelt and Truman rode down 138th Street, when Babe Ruth was hitting home runs out of Yankee Stadium, when one Art Deco apartment building after another went up along the Grand Concourse, when shoppers thronged Tremont Avenue stores and New Yorkers from all over came to the Bronx Zoo. The Bronx was built in a trice, starting in 1906 when the first subway came in, enabling the sons and daughters of immigrants who grew up in dimly lit tenements on the Lower East Side to move to comparatively spacious quarters on the crests and valleys of the ridges of granite and gneiss that run north and south in the borough. The population of the Bronx rose from 200,000 in 1900 to 430,000 in 1910, 732,000 in 1920, and 1.3 million in 1930—more than in the 1980s.

Most of that growth occurred within what is today the 18th Congressional District of New York, which is more or less coextensive with what is generally thought of as the South Bronx. In the late 1970s and early 1980s, the South Bronx was the nation's most famous slum, and for good reasons. Politicians came here—Jimmy Carter in 1976, Ronald Reagan in 1980—and said something must be done, though they were understandably vague about just what that was; local politicians—Mayor Koch, the South Bronx's representatives in Washington and Albany—didn't have many ideas either. One reason was that the depopulation of the South Bronx that occurred in the 1980s was without precedent in American experience. Within the limits of what was, in the 1970s, the 21st congressional district, there were 476,000 residents (mostly white) in 1960 and 460,000 (mostly Hispanic and black) in 1970. In 1980, there were just half as many, 233,000.

One reason was rent control, insisted on by New York tenants, which guarantees that owners of low-rent property who spend any decent amount on maintenance and repairs will be bankrupted. The result is that properties are abandoned and revert to the city for nonpayment of taxes. Then there is crime. With no community institutions and little parental supervision, the black and Hispanic teenagers here committed hundreds of crimes every day, with seeming impunity. Arson became an increasingly common crime, committed by kids for kicks or on behalf of landlords who want to get insurance money for their rent controlled buildings. The rise in crime helped drive away businesses that provided low-wage jobs—historically the mainstay of the local economy that helped so many immigrants move upward in the years from 1906 to the 1960s. Union demands, high minimum wages, the high cost of doing business generally in New York also persuaded low-wage employers to take their businesses to the places where their most recent workers had come from, the southeastern states and Puerto Rico. The migrants who had stayed in the South Bronx were left to welfare, which tends to split families. In no other part of America have so many low-wage jobs been lost so fast; and nowhere else has there been a community so large and so suddenly depopulated as the South Bronx was in the 1970s.

So elderly whites moved out, either farther into the Bronx, to the suburbs, or to Florida; middle class residents, including blacks and Hispanics who worked at steady jobs, moved out too, to the Bronx or other boroughs or even the suburbs. Programs for revitalizing the South Bronx didn't work because they ignored the fact that most of the people who could help with revitalization had already left the area for safer and more stable neighborhoods, and because they tended to anchor people to a place where there was little opportunity. The obvious solutions—roundups of those committing crime, an end to rent control, the encouragement of low-wage jobs—were politically or constitutionally unfeasible.

Now there are signs that things are getting better. The population of the current 18th District has stabilized, falling only from 517,000 to 485,000 between 1980 and 1986. Community institutions have taken hold in some parts of the South Bronx, more criminals are sent to jail for longer terms, and the freezing of welfare payments for a decade discouraged low-skill people from moving to New York. Finally, the city government in the 1980s found some programs that would work: a few isolated housing units in the midst of cleared land, and commercial property for light industry and warehousing. The South Bronx is actually well located: right on main trucking lines, with access to rail spurs, not far from airports and port facilities.

One program that helped for a while, but which has harmed the political system, is the minority set-aside law that created a niche for, among others, a South Bronx firm called Wedtech. Eligible for preference because it was founded by someone from Spain, Wedtech got Defense Department contracts and sought lobbying support from Edwin Meese and Members of

Congress. In return, it allegedly paid bribes to various officials including, according to a November 1988 indictment, 18th District Congressman Robert Garcia.

The word that Garcia would be indicted surprised many familiar with his career. First elected in a 1978 special election, Garcia is an articulate, fast-talking, enthusiastic legislator who has been active on a number of fronts. He was, with Jack Kemp, the House's lead sponsor of enterprise zones, a proposal which promises to do more for the South Bronx than earlier anti-poverty programs; it has been stifled by opposition from Ways and Means chairman Dan Rostenkowski and organized labor, though it has spawned a number of state enterprise zones programs, including one in New York. Garcia was an active opponent of immigration reform, arguing that employer sanctions would lead to discrimination against Hispanics. He has worked hard to maintain federal housing programs and even to encourage some innovations. He used his former chair of the Census and Population Subcommittee to push for adjustments to the census counts—a proposal of obvious appeal to a Member whose district lost half its people in one decade. Despite the rumors of indictment in an environment where other Bronx officials—borough president Stanley Simon, Democratic leader Stanley Friedman—were sentenced to jail, Garcia was reelected by a wide margin in 1988.

Now Garcia's future hinges on what happens in court. The accusation is that Wedtech paid money to a Puerto Rico lawyer who then passed it along to Garcia's wife disguised as consulting fees, though it was intended as a bribe; Garcia maintains that he is innocent. Should he be convicted, probably another Hispanic politician would be elected in his place, perhaps Assemblyman Jose Serrano, who was passed over in favor of Fernando Ferrer for the borough presidency.

The People: Est. Pop. 1986: 485,200, dn. 6.2% 1980–86; Pop. 1980: 517,278, dn. 37.0% 1970–80. Households (1980): 70% family, 50% with children, 31% married couples; 94.4% housing units rented; median monthly rent: $177; median house value: $35,200. Voting age pop. (1980): 327,637; 49% Spanish origin, 44% Black, 1% Asian origin.

1988 Presidential Vote:

Dukakis (D)	91,928	(86%)
Bush (R)	13,055	(12%)

Rep. Robert Garcia (D)

Elected 1978; b. Jan. 9, 1933, Bronx; home, New York City; Brooklyn Commun. Col., CCNY, R.C.A. Institute; Pentecostal; married (Jane).

Career: Army, Korea; Computer engineer, 1957–65; NY Assembly, 1965–67; NY Senate, 1966–78;

Offices: 2338 RHOB 20515, 202-225-4361. Also 890 Grand Concourse, Bronx 10451, 212-860-6200; and 1185 Boston Rd., Bronx 10456 212-542-4273.

Committees: *Banking, Finance and Urban Affairs* (10th of 31 D). Subcommittees: Economic Stabilization; Housing and Community Development; Policy Research and Insurance. *Post Office and Civil Service* (4th of 15 D). Subcommittees: Census and Population; Postal Operations and Services.

Group Ratings

	ADA	ACLU	COPE	CFA	LCV	ACU	NTLC	NSI	COC	CEI
1988	85	89	96	55	88	4	5	0	31	11
1987	100	—	96	86	—	0	—	—	8	4

National Journal Ratings

	1988 LIB — 1988 CONS			1987 LIB — 1987 CONS		
Economic	70%	—	29%	73%	—	0%
Social	86%	—	0%	78%	—	0%
Foreign	84%	—	0%	81%	—	0%

Key Votes

1) Homeless $	AGN	5) Ban Drug Test	—	9) SDI Research	AGN
2) Gephardt Amdt	FOR	6) Drug Death Pen	AGN	10) Ban Chem Weaps	FOR
3) Deficit Reduc	FOR	7) Handgun Sales	—	11) Aid to Contras	AGN
4) Kill Plnt Clsng Notice	AGN	8) Ban D.C. Abort $	AGN	12) Nuclear Testing	FOR

Election Results

1988 general	Robert Garcia (D-L)...................	75,459	(91%)	($448,391)
	Fred Brown (R)........................	5,764	(7%)	
1988 primary	Robert Garcia (D).....................	16,517	(60%)	
	Pedro Espada, Jr. (D)..................	7,515	(27%)	
	Ismael Betancourt, Jr. (D)	3,471	(13%)	
1986 general	Robert Garcia (D-L)..................	43,343	(94%)	($314,485)
	Melanie Chase (R)	2,479	(5%)	

NINETEENTH DISTRICT

The Bronx, it is sometimes forgotten, was originally a collection of middle-class neighborhoods, a borough where the upwardly mobile and striving children of immigrants left dark Manhattan tenements for the sunlight of the wide Bronx avenues and the vistas of a city where the street grid was adapted to nature's ridges and hills. Today's 19th Congressional District of New York, with its jagged boundaries, is a collection of such middle class Bronx neighborhoods, plus most of the middle-income suburb of Yonkers to the north. It includes Bedford Park, an Italian enclave sandwiched between parks and Fordham University, and the Irish precincts of Kingsbridge, in the valley between Riverdale and the Grand Concourse. It includes the heavily Italian East Bronx thrusting out into Long Island Sound and neighborhoods just south of the Westchester County line with middle class blacks. Its most prominent feature is Co-op City, the giant apartment complex (with thirty-five 35-story towers: only in New York) which was built in the 1960s on landfill surrounded by two limited access highways; it attracted many middle-class Jews fleeing the crime of the lower Concourse with its low rents (and naturally tenants staged a rent strike when asked to pay for the rise in maintenance costs).

Its most famous place is Yonkers, whose city government in 1988 refused to enforce a public housing integration order to which it had previously agreed. The racial separation in the units was not in dispute, but Yonkers could complain that richer Westchester towns (including the judge's home) were not required to do anything for blacks, while defenders of the government could say that the town council could easily have avoided its problem by sensible efforts to comply with what it had agreed to anyway: the case does not reflect well on anyone.

The 19th District was one of the few House seats in the nation that saw its congressman ousted in 1988. That congressman was Mario Biaggi, a Democrat first elected in 1968, who was once the most decorated member of the New York City police department, sponsor of the law to ban "copkiller" bullets and a serious candidate for mayor in 1977 until it became known that he had, contrary to his own statement, taken the Fifth Amendment before a grand jury. The charge that brought Biaggi down spoke more to personal than systemic corruption: he accepted expenses for a quick Florida vacation for himself, and someone who seems to have been a girlfriend, from

Brooklyn Democratic boss Meade Esposito, and did some favors for Esposito in return. Convicted in that case in September 1987, he was convicted in August 1988 of accepting a bribe from Wedtech, the South Bronx minority contractor; the day after, he resigned, though his name was still on the September primary ballot.

Biaggi comes from Bedford Park, one of the district's older neighborhoods. His successor, Eliot Engel, was a guidance counselor who was living in Co-op City when he was first elected to the New York Assembly in 1977—to replace an incumbent ousted on corruption charges. Engel filed to run against Biaggi in June, giving up his Assembly seat; he won 48% of the vote against Biaggi's 26% and Vincent Marchiselli's 26%; in November Biaggi was on the ballot as the Republican nominee and Engel beat him 56%–27%. He probably has a safe seat for 1990, but then he must deal with redistricting; the Bronx will probably not lose a seat, but he will need friends in the Assembly to make sure he continues to have a congenial seat. He would probably like some of the Bronx territory now in James Scheuer's 8th District. In the House he has seats on the Foreign Affairs and Small Business Committees.

The People: Est. Pop. 1986: 546,900, up 5.9% 1980–86; Pop. 1980: 516,498, up 1.2% 1970–80. Households (1980): 69% family, 32% with children, 51% married couples; 73.4% housing units rented; median monthly rent: $219; median house value: $58,000. Voting age pop. (1980): 398,578; 11% Black, 13% Spanish origin, 1% Asian origin.

1988 Presidential Vote:

Dukakis (D)	85,832	(54%)
Bush (R)	72,262	(45%)

Rep. Eliot L. Engel (D)

Elected 1988; b. February 18, 1947, Bronx; home, Bronx; Lehman Col., B.A. 1969, M.A. 1973; NY Law Schl., J.D. 1987; Jewish, married (Patricia).

Career: Teacher, guidance counselor, NYC Public Schls., 1969–77; NY Assembly, 1977–88.

Offices: 1407 LHOB, 20515, 202-225-2464. Also, 3250 Westchester Ave., Bronx 10461, 212-823-7200; 641 Yonkers Ave., Yonkers 10704, 914-376-1600; and Co-op City, 177 Dreiser Loop, Rm. 3, Bronx 10475, 212-320-2314.

Committees: *Foreign Affairs* (24th of 28 D). Subcommittees: Africa; Arms Control, International Security and Science; International Economic Policy and Trade. *Small Business* (27th of 27 D). Subcommittees: Environment and Labor; Regulation, Business Opportunities, and Energy. *Select Committee on Hunger* (17th of 17 D).

Group Ratings and Key Votes: Newly Elected

Election Results

1988 general	Eliot L. Engel (D-L)	77,158	(56%)	($183,145)
	Mario Biaggi (R)	37,454	(27%)	
	Martin J. O'Grady (RTL)	11,271	(8%)	
	Robert Blumetti (C)	11,182	(8%)	
1988 primary	Eliot L. Engel (D)	12,181	(48%)	
	Vincent A. Marchiselli (D)	6,700	(26%)	
	Mario Biaggi (D)	6,525	(26%)	
1986 general	Mario Biaggi (D-R-L)	87,774	(90%)	($252,790)
	Alice Farrell (C)	6,906	(7%)	
	John J. Barry (RTL)	2,669	(3%)	

TWENTIETH DISTRICT

It was the quintessential suburb 50 years ago. From White Plains and Larchmont, from Scarsdale and Mamaroneck and New Rochelle, half the breadwinners assembled every morning at the railroad stations, across from the faux Tudor drugstore and soda fountain and down the street from the cobblestone post office, and waited for the train to take them into Manhattan. On the way home at night, they would have a martini in the bar car, decompressing as they awaited the short drive over narrow asphalt roads to the driveway of their tree-shaded brick or white-frame colonial houses. This was Westchester County, though even then not everyone there lived that way. There were also Italian-Americans clustered in little industrial villages from Mount Vernon to Port Chester to Pleasantville, men who repaired shoes or worked in local machine shops; there were oldstock Yankees or New York Dutchmen whose descendants had worked modest jobs in this county for years. And there were signs of metropolitanization as well. Big New York stores already had branches on Mamaroneck Avenue in White Plains, and *Reader's Digest*, with its colonial campus-like buildings north of Pleasantville, was one of the first employers to leave Manhattan for a suburban site.

Today, Westchester retains much of the physical ambiance that made it attractive to the affluent 50 years ago. Large plots of land are set aside in greenery, some made into parks, some kept in private hands like the Rockefeller family estate at Pocantico Hills. Intensive development has not proceeded too far north of White Plains, for just to the north Westchester is crossed by the first of several mountain ridges—the closest, someone said, the Appalachians come to the ocean. Some of its most elite settlements—Bronxville, Scarsdale, Harrison—were already pretty well filled up then and have not grown much since. Big corporations have headquarters here and there, notably along the Cross-Westchester Expressway, and most Westchesterites drive to work in their cars rather than queue up for the train. But to a much greater extent than in almost any other suburban jurisdiction, you could imagine yourself in the 1940s here.

Politically there has been a change. Westchester used to be solidly Republican, with local government run by an efficient and honest Republican machine and big Republican margins in national elections: the county was 62% for Dewey in 1944, for example, when New York City was 61% for Roosevelt. Today, as the grandchildren of immigrants have grown up and moved out past the city line, as once Protestant Scarsdale has become mostly Jewish and as blacks have moved out in large numbers to Mount Vernon and here and there to the suburbs beyond, Westchester has become more Democratic, giving George Bush only 51% of the vote in 1988, and far less than he got in many historically Democratic sections of the outer boroughs of New York City. For all its comfortably aged suburban patina, Westchester votes like a central city neighborhood these days.

The 20th Congressional District of New York includes most of Westchester, all of the county facing Long Island Sound on the east—from the ethnic neighborhoods of Mount Vernon, through the rich, Catholic and conservative suburbs of Pelham, Eastchester, and Bronxville, up through more Jewish and liberal Scarsdale—and the Sound towns of New Rochelle, Larchmont, Mamaroneck and Rye. Just above them is White Plains, the county seat/corporate headquarters/shopping mall center; the 20th also includes part of the city of Yonkers, on the Hudson. North of White Plains are the tiny villages and the little cities on the Hudson, Washington Irving's Tarrytown and John Cheever's Ossining, and the woodsy surrounding suburbs like Briarcliff Manor and Chappaqua. Everywhere residential real estate values, fed by the local and Manhattan boom, skyrocketed, though after the Wall Street plunge in October 1987 prices stabilized. Nevertheless, the once small village of Mount Kisco in northern Westchester is plagued by traffic jams, as residents call for a lid on future development.

854   NEW YORK

In 1988, the 20th was the scene of one of the few seriously contested House races in the country, one in which a Democrat ousted a Republican—but that's not so unusual, since most of Westchester has been represented by Democrats in the House during most of the last 25 years. The Democrats were helped by the clumsiness of Republican incumbent Joseph DioGuardi, who never seemed comfortably adapted to the district or perhaps to the House. Nominated in 1984, when Democrat Richard Ottinger retired, DioGuardi beat Ottinger aide Orin Teicher by only 50%–48%, even though Teicher backed Walter Mondale's tax increase. In 1986 DioGuardi faced former Manhattan Congresswoman Bella Abzug (who had raised her family in Westchester years before) and beat her by only 54%–45%. DioGuardi was always talking about how he was a CPA and arguing that government should be run like a business—the kind of talk most Republican political consultants despair of hearing in their clients. For DioGuardi, nothing is so appealing as a column of figures; his answer to the Iran-contra scandal was for the government to be reimbursed for the arms sale proceeds that went to the contras—which misses every conceivable point.

This fascination with figures may have helped do him in and elect Democrat Nita Lowey in 1988. In the 1970s, she worked for Mario Cuomo when he was New York's secretary of state, and she was appointed assistant secretary of state by him in 1987; she won a close three-way primary against businessman Dennis Mehiel and the former *Nation* publisher Hamilton Fish III, son and grandson of Hudson River congressmen. Lowey criticized DioGuardi for overspending on defense and was helped late in the campaign by charges that a car dealer involved in DioGuardi's campaign had been promising to reimburse his employees for $1,000 contributions. This looked like an illegal funneling of money into a campaign with a candidate whose self-advertised fetish for figures made any protestations of ignorance seem unlikely. Lowey won 50%–47%. She has seats on the Education and Labor and Merchant Marine Committees, wants to work for better education and against drugs and to build bridges between suburban and black Members.

The People: Est. Pop. 1986: 511,200, dn. 1.0% 1980–86; Pop. 1980: 516,507, dn. 4.9% 1970–80. Households (1980): 73% family, 36% with children, 59% married couples; 49.5% housing units rented; median monthly rent: $272; median house value: $92,400. Voting age pop. (1980): 388,570; 14% Black, 5% Spanish origin, 2% Asian origin.

1988 Presidential Vote:

Bush (R)	112,224	(51%)
Dukakis (D)	104,728	(48%)

Rep. Nita M. Lowey (D)

Elected 1988; b. July 5, 1937, New York City; home, Harrison; Mt. Holyoke Col., B.A. 1959; Jewish, married (Stephen).

Career: Asst. to NY Secy. of State for Econ. Devel. and Neighborhood Pres., Deputy Dir., Div. of Econ. Opp., 1975–85; NY Asst. Secy. of State, 1985–87.

Offices: 1313 LHOB 20515, 202-225-6506. Also 235 Mamaroneck Ave., White Plains 10605, 914-428-1707.

Committees: *Education and Labor* (15th of 22 D). Subcommittees: Elementary, Secondary and Vocational Education; Human Resources; Postsecondary Education. *Merchant Marine and Fisheries* (25th of 26 D). Subcommittees: Coast Guard and Navigation; Oceanography. *Select Committee on Narcotics Abuse and Control* (18th of 18 D).

Group Ratings and Key Votes: Newly Elected

Election Results

1988 general	Nita M. Lowey (D)	102,235	(50%)	($1,309,873)
	Joseph J. DioGuardi (R-C)	96,465	(47%)	($1,567,129)
1988 primary	Nita M. Lowey (D)	10,533	(44%)	
	Hamilton Fish III (D)	8,578	(36%)	
	Dennis Mehiel (D)	4,849	(20%)	
1986 general	Joseph J. DioGuardi (R)	80,220	(54%)	($1,264,167)
	Bella A. Abzug (D)	66,359	(45%)	($902,535)

TWENTY-FIRST DISTRICT

It is the place where the Atlantic coast gives way to the interior of America: the Hudson Highlands, where the river carrying the waters from most of Upstate New York breaks through the first of the big Appalachian ridges and then flows south into the wide Tappan Zee down to New York Harbor. During the Revolutionary War, the colonials built a chain across the river to keep the British from sailing north; and it was over control of this part of the Hudson that Benedict Arnold betrayed the country which he had, at Saratoga, helped to create. From the Storm King Highway, carved from one of the cliffs along the Hudson, or from one of the terraces at West Point, you can look up the river to the interior or down toward the sea; in either direction is some of the most spectacular scenery on the continent. The Highlands may have inspired the builders of the Erie Canal and the water-level New York Central, the great projects that connected New York City with the interior and made it the nation's leading commercial city; it may have inspired Franklin Roosevelt as well, that son of coastal America whose winning margins came mostly from the interior, and who knew this stretch of river intimately from hundreds of trips up from the city or from Washington to his home overlooking the Hudson in Hyde Park.

The Roosevelts are not the only old family in this part of the Hudson. Another is the Fish's, one of whom currently represents New York's 21st Congressional District, a seat that covers most of the lower Hudson, starting in northern Westchester County, taking in both sides of the river through most of the Highlands, and proceeding as far north on the east bank as Poughkeepsie, just a few miles short of Hyde Park. This is an affluent area, historically Republican (Roosevelt never carried it for President), with old villages and small industrial cities, but now within the orbit of metropolitan New York, with some large estates of the very rich but (politically more important) modest subdivision homes for the teachers and civil servants and policemen who can't afford the higher prices in Westchester and are seeking a more tradition-minded, drug-free environment in which to raise their children. These new residents, far from bringing Democratic voting habits from the city, have made the Lower Hudson area one of the most Republican parts of New York state; Mario Cuomo, while winning the state 2 to 1 in 1986, ran no better than even here.

The current congressman, Hamilton Fish, is a descendant of another Hamilton Fish who was governor, Senator, and Ulysses S. Grant's Secretary of State; and he is the son of Hamilton Fish Sr., congressman from a Hudson district from 1920 to 1944 and a bitter critic and enemy of Roosevelt (who would not allow him in the White House and made him part of his "Martin, Barton and Fish" refrain). This Fish was defeated in 1944, much to Roosevelt's satisfaction, but he lived on, celebrating his 100th birthday in 1988 by marrying his live-in companion and denouncing, along with many old enemies, his grandson Hamilton Fish III who was running for Congress as a Democrat in the 20th District in Westchester.

To all this, the current Congressman Fish took a dignified and tolerant attitude. He is now one of the more senior Republicans in the House, having first been elected in 1968, when he beat none other than future Watergate burglar G. Gordon Liddy by 8,000 votes in the Republican primary and John Dyson, later originator of the "I Love New York" ads, 48%–46% in the general. (How history would have changed if either of those had come out differently!) Rather market-oriented on economics, more liberal on cultural matters, Fish's main role in the House is as ranking Republican on the House Judiciary Committee. This is not always a pleasant role. Judiciary handles (or bottles up) many controversial proposals and must deal with the unpleasant business of impeachment. Fish is much less conservative than most of the other Republicans on the committee, while remaining somewhat less liberal than most of its Democrats. He has been a staunch supporter of civil rights (as was his father, who led a black unit in battle in World War I), and he deserves credit for the passage of the Fair Housing Act of 1988. It was Fish who sat down with the realtors and the civil rights lobby in the spring of 1988 and got agreement on an enforcement mechanism which seemed stronger than anyone else had proposed and yet was acceptable to both sides—a sterling bit of creative legislation. Fish has also played constructive roles on immigration reform, on breaking down barriers to voting and on the law reversing the Grove City decision, reaffirming that institutions receiving federal funds cannot discriminate. Having worked for years with former Chairman Peter Rodino, who was steadfast but not overbearing, he must now work with new Chairman Jack Brooks, who is brainy but aggressive and occasionally partisan.

Fish wins reelection every two years by wide margins.

The People: Est. Pop. 1986: 547,200, up 5.9% 1980–86; Pop. 1980: 516,778, up 11.3% 1970–80. Households (1980): 78% family, 45% with children, 66% married couples; 31.4% housing units rented; median monthly rent: $234; median house value: $56,600. Voting age pop. (1980): 365,060; 6% Black, 3% Spanish origin, 1% Asian origin.

1988 Presidential Vote:

Bush (R)	135,851	(61%)
Dukakis (D)	83,633	(38%)

Rep. Hamilton Fish, Jr. (R)

Elected 1968; b. June 3, 1926, Washington, D.C.; home, Millbrook; Harvard Col., A.B. 1949, N.Y.U., LL.B. 1957; Episcopalian; married (Mary Ann).

Career: Navy, WWII; Vice Consul, U.S. Foreign Svc., Ireland, 1951–53; Practicing atty. 1957–68; Counsel, NY Assembly Judiciary Cmtee., 1961; Dutchess Cnty. Civil Def. Dir., 1967–68.

Offices: 2269 RHOB 20515, 202-225-5441. Also 82 Washington St., Poughkeepsie 12601, 914-452-4220; 36 Gleneida Ave., Carmel 10512, 914-225-5200; and Bldg. 710, Stewart Intl. Airport, Newburgh 12550, 914-564-4302.

Committees: *Judiciary* (Ranking Member of 14 R). Subcommittees: Courts, Intellectual Property, and the Administration of Justice; Economic and Commercial Law (Ranking Member); Immigration, Refugees and International Law. *Joint Economic Committee.* Task Forces: Education and Health; Investment, Jobs and Prices; National Security Economics.

Group Ratings

	ADA	ACLU	COPE	CFA	LCV	ACU	NTLC	NSI	COC	CEI
1988	60	52	48	73	81	32	49	60	71	28
1987	48	—	46	43	—	35	—	—	53	39

National Journal Ratings

	1988 LIB	—	1988 CONS	1987 LIB	—	1987 CONS
Economic	40%	—	58%	39%	—	60%
Social	55%	—	44%	42%	—	57%
Foreign	49%	—	51%	49%	—	50%

Key Votes

1) Homeless $	AGN	5) Ban Drug Test	AGN	9) SDI Research	AGN
2) Gephardt Amdt	AGN	6) Drug Death Pen	FOR	10) Ban Chem Weaps	FOR
3) Deficit Reduc	AGN	7) Handgun Sales	FOR	11) Aid to Contras	FOR
4) Kill Plnt Clsng Notice	FOR	8) Ban D.C. Abort $	FOR	12) Nuclear Testing	FOR

Election Results

1988 general	Hamilton Fish, Jr. (R-C)..............	150,443	(75%)	($277,680)
	Lawrence W. Grunberger (D)...........	47,294	(23%)	
1988 primary	Hamilton Fish, Jr. (R-C), unopposed			
1986 general	Hamilton Fish, Jr. (R-C)..............	102,070	(77%)	($217,637)
	Lawrence W. Grunberger (D)...........	28,339	(21%)	($6,340)

TWENTY-SECOND DISTRICT

From Sunnyside, the whimsical house Washington Irving built in Tarrytown, you can see across the waters of the Tappan Zee, the widest point of the Hudson, and get some sense of the land as it looked when it was settled by the Dutchmen who were ancient legends even when Irving was writing early in the 19th century. All around is Irving country—the old towns of Tarrytown, Irvington, Dobbs Ferry and Hastings-on-Hudson, now comfortable affluent suburbs. On the other side of the Tappan Zee, spanned by the Thruway bridge in the 1950s, is Rockland County, full of little towns with Dutch names long since surrounded by suburban developments. When James A. Farley grew up here nearly 100 years ago, this was Upstate, but now it is an extension of the New York metropolitan area. Politically, it is mildly Republican, as most affluent New York suburbs are, but its large number of Jewish residents help to make it a bit more liberal on cultural and economic issues than many other suburbs.

The 22d Congressional District of New York spans the Tappan Zee, connecting most of the Irving suburbs with Rockland County and proceeding over the Ramapos some 120 miles inland to where the state borders New Jersey and Pennsylvania. Past the Ramapos is Orange County— a part of Upstate whose population has been swelled for 20 years by people from New York City, many of them policemen, firemen, teachers and other civil servants. Farther out, past the Shawangunk Mountains, is Sullivan County, the heart of the Catskills Borscht Belt resort district, part of which is in the 22d District. This is one of the few predominantly Jewish non-metropolitan areas in the United States, and has been a Jewish resort area, with huge kosher hotels, since before the turn of the century. Politically, this is a district that usually goes Republican, but not always by huge margins. Westchester has been trending mildly toward the Democrats, but the outlying areas, with their many new residents fleeing the city, have tilted them farther toward the Republicans.

The 22d's congressman is Benjamin Gilman, a moderate Republican first elected in 1972. Gilman sometimes votes with the Democrats on economic issues and is quite liberal on cultural issues, but less so on foreign policy. This is important, since he is the second ranking Republican on the Foreign Affairs Committee. Like ranking member William Broomfield, he is a strong supporter of Israel, a co-sponsor of the bill to move the U.S. embassy in Israel from Tel Aviv to Jerusalem, and an opponent of Arab arms deals. He has other international concerns too: he

858   NEW YORK

wants Soviet refugees admitted more expeditiously to the United States, is concerned about human rights in Tibet, wants information on MIAs before any concessions are made to Vietnam, and has worked with Patricia Schroeder on the global warming issue. He has also crusaded against the international narcotics trade for some time, and has had a hand in all recent drug legislation, strongly supporting, for example, the concept of a drug czar. He is now the ranking Republican on Post Office and Civil Service.

Gilman first won the seat in 1972, beating ultra-liberal John Dow, who had won in unusual circumstances (the LBJ landslide of 1964, a scandal affecting the Republican incumbent in 1970), and his most difficult race came in 1982, when he was placed in the same district with Westchester Democrat Peter Peyser. A former Republican Member of the House, Peyser left to run a quixotic primary campaign against Senator James Buckley in 1976 and in 1978 was elected to the House as a Democrat, while Gilman remained quietly working within Republican ranks. In the face-off, Peyser won 65% in Westchester, but Gilman won 70% of the vote in Orange County and carried Sullivan and Rockland as well. He won handily in 1984 and 1986, though he does not seem to have sewed up the Westchester vote: in 1988 and 1986, against septuagenarian Eleanor Burlingham who wears a trademark shawl, he won only 54% and 52% in Westchester while winning districtwide with 71% and 69%, respectively.

The People: Est. Pop. 1986: 539,000, up 4.3% 1980–86; Pop. 1980: 516,625, up 14.4% 1970–80. Households (1980): 79% family, 45% with children, 68% married couples; 31.5% housing units rented; median monthly rent: $267; median house value: $63,000. Voting age pop. (1980): 363,184; 6% Black, 4% Spanish origin, 1% Asian origin.

1988 Presidential Vote:

Bush (R) 129,459	(57%)
Dukakis (D) 97,516	(43%)

Rep. Benjamin A. Gilman (R)

Elected 1972; b. Dec. 6, 1922, Poughkeepsie; home, Middletown; U. of PA, B.S. 1946, NY Law Sch., LL.B. 1950; Jewish; married (Rita).

Career: Army Air Corps, WWII; Asst. Atty. Gen. of NY, 1953–55; Practicing atty., 1955–72; Atty., NY Temp. Comm. on the Courts; NY Assembly, 1967–72.

Offices: 2185 RHOB 20515, 202-225-3776. Also 44 East Ave., P.O. Box 358, Middletown 10940, 914-343-6666; 223 Rte. 59, Monsey 10952, 914-357-9000; and 32 Main St., Hastings-on-Hudson 10706, 914-478-5550.

Committees: *Foreign Affairs* (2d of 18 R). Subcommittees: Europe and the Middle East (Ranking Member); International Operations. *Post Office and Civil Service* (Ranking Member of 9 R). Subcommittee: Investigations. *Select Committee on Hunger* (4th of 12 R). *Select Committee on Narcotics Abuse and Control* (2d of 12 R).

Group Ratings

	ADA	ACLU	COPE	CFA	LCV	ACU	NTLC	NSI	COC	CEI
1988	55	77	74	91	94	42	41	90	50	24
1987	68	—	73	79	—	26	—	—	21	23

National Journal Ratings

	1988 LIB — 1988 CONS			1987 LIB — 1987 CONS		
Economic	49%	—	50%	45%	—	54%
Social	63%	—	37%	66%	—	32%
Foreign	40%	—	59%	41%	—	58%

Key Votes

1) Homeless $	AGN	5) Ban Drug Test	AGN	9) SDI Research	FOR
2) Gephardt Amdt	FOR	6) Drug Death Pen	FOR	10) Ban Chem Weaps	AGN
3) Deficit Reduc	AGN	7) Handgun Sales	FOR	11) Aid to Contras	FOR
4) Kill Plnt Clsng Notice	AGN	8) Ban D.C. Abort $	AGN	12) Nuclear Testing	AGN

Election Results

1988 general	Benjamin A. Gilman (R)	144,227	(71%)	($411,056)
	Eleanor F. Burlingham (D)	54,312	(27%)	($10,427)
1988 primary	Benjamin A. Gilman (R), unopposed			
1986 general	Benjamin A. Gilman (R)	94,244	(69%)	($305,258)
	Eleanor F. Burlingham (D)	36,852	(27%)	($16,066)
	Richard Bruno (RTL)	4,560	(4%)	

TWENTY-THIRD DISTRICT

Fifty years ago, Albany was already a kind of antique: its solid rowhouses showed its 19th century prosperity, its once teeming lumberyards and railroad car shops, its old restaurants and hotels carried the patina of age and the accumulated soot and grime of decades of coal smoke rising in its six-month-long winters. It could trace its history back more than 300 years, to 1624 when the Dutch built Fort Orange on the banks of the Hudson where seagoing ships could dock, at the edge of the great gloomy forests teeming with beaver and Iroquois, near the confluence of the Hudson and the Mohawk—the natural crossroads of Upstate New York then and even more so after the building of the Erie Canal and the water-level New York Central Railroad. This was one of America's early industrial centers. Troy, up the river just a few miles, was a steel town rivaling Pittsburgh in the 1840s; Cohoes, at the junction of the Hudson and the Mohawk, became one of America's leading textile producers; Schenectady a few miles up the Mohawk was the site of Charles Steinmetz's fabled General Electric laboratories and has been a big GE town ever since. As for Albany, it was one of America's biggest lumber towns, as well as the state capital.

Albany had and still has one of the nation's most famed political machines, which dates back exactly to 1921, when Daniel O'Connell and his brothers and local aristocrat Edwin Corning took control of City Hall. They never really relinquished it: Daniel O'Connell died, still boss after 56 years, in 1977 at age 91, and his early partner's son, Erastus Corning 2d, was mayor from 1942 until his death in 1983. The machine was sustained by legions of city and county employees, by a certain creativity when it came to counting votes, by the raffish atmosphere that you found in the speakeasies of so many cities during Prohibition and which lingered in Albany for decades after.

Albany today has a shiny new face, as its bard William Kennedy makes clear in *O Albany!* Mayor Corning provided the creative financing for Governor Nelson Rockefeller's monumental South Mall, yuppies began buying up and renovating old townhouses, expressways were built, and even the old Union Station was spruced up. The capital area around Albany is now one of the faster-growing parts of Upstate New York, not quite a high tech boom area like Boston or New Hampshire, but doing much better than almost anyone expected. The Albany Democratic machine still seems to be in power in the H. H. Richardson City Hall that faces up to the gaudy State House, but slowly the bulk of voters in the capital region have moved to the suburbs and, while they tend to favor Democrats, they have to be persuaded just as voters anywhere else do to support them.

The 23d Congressional District of New York includes Albany, Troy, Schenectady, the old carpet manufacturing town of Amsterdam on the Mohawk, and the old industrial towns, suburban subdivisions and rural land in between. Oddly enough, it was not represented by a product of the Albany machine between 1966 and 1988. Samuel Stratton was a maverick Democrat from Schenectady, first elected in 1958, who ended up in Albany after two redistrictings when Republicans gave up trying to beat him and the machine embraced him to beat a Republican reformer. Stratton, a domestic policy liberal and foreign policy hawk, was a senior member of Armed Services who scathingly attacked Democratic doves. In July 1988, four days after the deadline for filing for reelection and on the last day for withdrawal, he announced his retirement for health reasons. This gave the Democratic machine a chance to name its replacement, which it promptly did by picking assemblyman Michael McNulty. His loyalty to the machine was assured not only by his own 13 years of service as a town supervisor and mayor in the Albany industrial suburb of Green Island and his six years in the Assembly, but also by the fact that his father and grandfather were Albany County sheriffs; they started off as opponents of the O'Connells, but the families evidently learned to live together.

Of course the candidate did have to win the general election, against a venture capital specialist with a state-funded foundation who attacked McNulty for avoiding the issues and for having been selected by party bosses rather than primary voters. But the Democrat won 62%–38%, carrying not only Albany County but the pieces of adjacent counties that are in the district. He surely now has one of the safest seats in the House. He got Stratton's spot, though not his seniority, on Armed Services, where he can look after the Watervliet Arsenal; he is likely to have a record, though not an acerbic temperament, similar to Stratton's.

The People: Est. Pop. 1986: 510,900, dn. 1.2% 1980–86; Pop. 1980: 516,943, dn. 4.0% 1970–80. Households (1980): 67% family, 33% with children, 54% married couples; 42.3% housing units rented; median monthly rent: $169; median house value: $38,900. Voting age pop. (1980): 389,983; 4% Black, 1% Spanish origin, 1% Asian origin.

1988 Presidential Vote: Dukakis (D). 140,440   (56%)
Bush (R) 106,755   (43%)

Rep. Michael R. McNulty (D)

Elected 1988; b. Sept. 16, 1947, Troy; home, Green Island; Holy Cross Col., A.B. 1969; Catholic; married (Nancy).

Career: Spvsr., Green Island, 1969–77; Mayor, Green Island, 1977–82; NY Assembly, 1982–88.

Offices: 1431 LHOB 20515, 202-225-5076. Also P.O. Bldg., Jay St., Schenectady 12305, 518-374-4547; O'Brien Fed. Bldg., Albany 12207, 518-465-0700; P.O. Bldg., Amsterdam 12010, 518-843-3400; and 33 2d St., Troy 12180, 518-271-0822.

Committees: *Armed Services* (31st of 31 D). Subcommittees: Readiness; Research and Development. *Small Business* (22d of 27 D). Subcommittees: Exports, Tax Policy and Special Problems; Regulation, Business Opportunities, and Energy; Procurement, Tourism and Rural Development. *Select Committee on Hunger* (15th of 19 D).

Group Ratings and Key Votes: Newly Elected

Election Results

1988 general	Michael R. McNulty (D)	145,040	(62%)	($273,505)
	Peter M. Bakal (R-C)	89,858	(38%)	($174,790)
1988 primary	Michael R. McNulty (D), unopposed			
1986 general	Samuel S. Stratton (D)	140,759	(96%)	($38,035)
	James Joseph Callahan (SW)	5,279	(4%)	

TWENTY-FOURTH DISTRICT

It is not one of America's great metropolitan centers now, and even 50 years ago it was not the subject of much notice. But in the 19th century the Hudson River Valley was one of the heartlands of American culture and politics. From the jagged hills that rise above the river, you can see even today the vistas that inspired the romantic Hudson River painters. An arm of the ocean and an artery of commerce for 300 years, the Hudson and the hills and mountains around it still look wild: nature writes in bigger letters than the canal and railroad giants of the 19th century.

The Hudson Valley was one of the nation's centers of political innovation as well. It was on a trip up the Hudson in the 1790s that James Madison and Aaron Burr welded the Virginia-New York alliance that made possible Jeffersonian Democracy. And two descendants of Dutch settlers on the Hudson helped create the Democratic Party as we know it. Martin Van Buren, an innkeeper's son from Kinderhook, created the first Democratic organizations—the Albany Regency in New York, Andrew Jackson's Democracy in Washington—and was nominated vice president at the first national convention in 1832. Franklin Roosevelt, an aristocrat's son from Hyde Park, forged the New Deal Democratic coalition which seems to have lasted longer and won more elections than Van Buren's and Jackson's.

Yet, ironically, the Hudson Valley is not at all Democratic these days, and hasn't been for about 100 years. New York's 24th Congressional District, which includes most of the river valley from Roosevelt's Hyde Park north through Van Buren's Kinderhook and, skipping the cities of Albany and Troy, goes up through the old battlefield, spa and racetrack town of Saratoga to the mountains around the headwaters of the Hudson, is one of the most Republican districts in New York; the town-by-town voting figures may show it to be the only district that went for Republican Andrew O'Rourke over Democrat Mario Cuomo in the 1986 gubernatorial race.

The 24th District has a congressman, Gerald Solomon, who is one of the staunchest and most forthright of Republicans, with probably the most conservative record of any New York Member. He also has his name on significant legislation: the Solomon Amendment, to bar young men who have not registered for the draft from receiving federal scholarship or college loan aid. This was initially a matter of some controversy, with Democrats professing to see it as a violation of freedom of expression and charging that it was punitive; but as time went on, and as it has been upheld by the courts, it has come to be seen as a rather unremarkable piece of legislation. Why should people who violate a federal law be entitled to collect federal money? If there is fault to be found, it is with the registration law, which has no real effect on our adversaries but which gives conscientious and other opponents of current American policies something to object to.

Up through 1988 Solomon was a member of the Foreign Affairs Committee, where he was a staunch, even fierce, backer of an assertive foreign policy. He was also ranking Republican on the Veterans' Affairs Committee. There he was a strong supporter of the successful 1984 G.I. Bill and of the 1988 measure giving the VA cabinet status; the first has had major positive effects on thousands of Americans' lives, while the second will get the Veterans head invited to more White House dinners. In 1989, Solomon shifted to the Rules Committee, where he immediately became the second ranking of four Republicans. Currently Rules Republicans, outnumbered 9–4, have little say over how issues are decided on the floor, but in a different political environment, and especially if Republicans should ever win a majority in the House, Solomon could become a major legislative force.

Solomon's positions seem to be popular in the 24th District. He first won the seat in 1978, defeating a Democrat elected in 1974 who held on, barely, in 1976 and then confessed he had once smoked marijuana. Solomon has been reelected easily since and seems likely to be for some time to come.

The People: Est. Pop. 1986: 535,900, up 3.9% 1980–86; Pop. 1980: 515,614, up 15.8% 1970–80. Households (1980): 76% family, 42% with children, 65% married couples; 26.9% housing units rented; median monthly rent: $174; median house value: $38,500. Voting age pop. (1980): 364,047; 1% Black, 1% Spanish origin.

1988 Presidential Vote:

Bush (R)	142,169	(58%)
Dukakis (D)	98,965	(41%)

Rep. Gerald B. H. Solomon (R)

Elected 1978; b. Aug. 15, 1930, Okeechobee, FL; home, Glens Falls; Siena Col., St. Lawrence Col.; Presbyterian; married (Freda).

Career: USMC, Korea; Founding partner, Associates of Glens Falls, Inc., 1964–78; Queensbury Town Sprvsr., Warren Cnty. Legis., 1968–72; NY Assembly, 1972–78.

Offices: 2265 RHOB 20515, 202-225-5614. Also Gaslight Square, Saratoga Springs 12866, 518-587-9800; 568 Columbia Turnpike, East Greenbush 12061, 518-477-2703; 419 Warren St., Hudson 12534, 518-828-0181; and 21 Bay St., Glens Falls 12801, 518-792-3013.

Committees: *Rules* (2d of 4 R).

Group Ratings

	ADA	ACLU	COPE	CFA	LCV	ACU	NTLC	NSI	COC	CEI
1988	15	18	23	64	31	88	86	100	86	64
1987	4	—	20	14	—	91	—	—	86	76

National Journal Ratings

	1988 LIB — 1988 CONS		1987 LIB — 1987 CONS	
Economic	35%	— 64%	11%	— 83%
Social	5%	— 91%	24%	— 75%
Foreign	0%	— 84%	0%	— 80%

Key Votes

1) Homeless $	FOR	5) Ban Drug Test	—	9) SDI Research	FOR
2) Gephardt Amdt	AGN	6) Drug Death Pen	FOR	10) Ban Chem Weaps	AGN
3) Deficit Reduc	AGN	7) Handgun Sales	FOR	11) Aid to Contras	FOR
4) Kill Plnt Clsng Notice	FOR	8) Ban D.C. Abort $	FOR	12) Nuclear Testing	AGN

Election Results

1988 general	Gerald B. H. Solomon (R-C-RTL)	162,962	(72%)	($151,276)
	Fred Baye (D)	62,177	(28%)	($15,936)
1988 primary	Gerald B. H. Solomon (R), unopposed			
1986 general	Gerald B. H. Solomon (R-C-RTL)	117,285	(70%)	($153,651)
	Edward James Bloch (D)	49,225	(30%)	($79,334)

TWENTY-FIFTH DISTRICT

The American frontier, when it got to the Mississippi moved rapidly west, but for 150 years, from the establishment of Fort Orange in what now is Albany until the Revolutionary War, the line of settlement was stuck in the Mohawk Valley of Upstate New York. The British used their allies, the fierce Iroquois, as a buffer against the French and in return kept New England Yankees from moving west of Albany. Only after the French were driven from North America in 1759 did the pressures for westward settlement prevail; the British tried to keep their word but the colonials started a revolution, one of the results of which was the end of Iroquois dominion.

This is the background of *Drums Along the Mohawk*, and there is little in these rolling hills today to give any hint of the shrieks of war whoops or the bloody violence whose conclusion made possible the digging of the Erie Canal, the building of the New York Central and the forging of the great path westward into the interior of America. This route accounted for much of the phenomenal growth in the 19th century of New York City and its port; Boston and Philadelphia, with no similar access inland, were left behind. As migration slowed and trade increased, the Mohawk Valley became one of the early industrial centers of the nation. The little Oneida County hamlets of Utica and Rome grew to become sizable factory towns. First settled by New England Yankees, these towns attracted a new wave of immigration from the Atlantic coast in the early 20th century. Today they are the most heavily Italian and Polish-American communities between Albany and Buffalo.

The 25th Congressional District of New York consists of most of the Mohawk Valley, from Amsterdam (but not including Herkimer) through Utica and Rome, where the canal builders had to dig through the route's highest ground. It also includes a row of counties to the south which are more sparsely settled. These hilly areas are not along any major east-west route; the population here remains more Yankee, the area less industrial. The most famous town here is Cooperstown, once a resort, with 19th century houses and commercial buildings maintained in better-than-pristine condition, thanks in large part to the money brought in by the Baseball Hall of Fame. Politically, these counties are heavily Republican under practically all circumstances; they gave Mario Cuomo only a bare margin when he was winning overwhelmingly in 1986. The Mohawk Valley, on the other hand, is more marginal: it almost went for Cuomo in 1982 when he barely won, and it was almost even in the Bush-Dukakis race; evidently, the key factor is the presence of a Democrat with appeal to ethnic voters.

Congressman Sherwood Boehlert is a Republican who worked for his two predecessors and won the seat in the 1982 Republican primary. After working for Alexander Pirnie, who retired in 1972, and Donald Mitchell, Boehlert returned to Utica, and in 1978 was elected Oneida County Executive. When Mitchell retired, he ran for Congress and won easily; he was strong enough to keep incumbent Gary Lee from running in the district, though it contained his legal residence, and Lee was beaten by another incumbent elsewhere.

Boehlert is one of the more liberal Republicans in the House. He has supported the government economic aid programs which free market ideologues like David Stockman scorn. He has formed a Northeast Agriculture Caucus, to help local farmers, and he is a big fan of student financial aid programs. When Robert Walker came forward with his "drug-free workplace" amendment, Boehlert pointed out that it would be "disastrous in terms of implications"—exposing it for the political ploy it is. He is chairman of the working group on Acid Rain, made up of Republicans who would like to see some toughening of clean air legislation. They have tried to put pressure on Energy and Commerce chairman John Dingell and his environmentalist adversaries to compromise, they got George Bush to speak on the issue in 1988, and they have advanced the compromise suggested by Cuomo and Ohio Governor Richard Celeste—but so far to little avail. As ranking Republican on the Science, Research and Technology Subcommittee, he has been pushing for more government aid in developing robotics. He is a co-founder of the House Fire Services Caucus. But he can be a partisan Republican too. He charged that a money-raising group headed by James Roosevelt was employing scare tactics in its direct mail to senior citizens, and initiated hearings that produced some changes. He is a co-chair of the 92 Group of moderate Republicans who nonetheless are working to make their party the majority in the House, and he provided key support for Newt Gingrich in his race against Edward Madigan for Republican whip.

At least through 1989 Boehlert's voting record kept him from choicer committee assignments. But he has managed to protect Rome's Griffiss Air Force Base anyway, and he is reelected regularly by wide margins.

The People: Est. Pop. 1986: 509,300, dn. 1.3% 1980–86; Pop. 1980: 516,201, dn. 0.4% 1970–80. Households (1980): 73% family, 39% with children, 61% married couples; 32.5% housing units rented; median monthly rent: $155; median house value: $32,400. Voting age pop. (1980): 374,606; 2% Black, 1% Spanish origin.

1988 Presidential Vote: Bush (R) 114,277   (54%)
Dukakis (D). 94,653   (45%)

Rep. Sherwood L. Boehlert (R)

Elected 1982; b. Sept. 28, 1936, Utica; home, New Hartford; Utica Col., B.A. 1961; Roman Catholic; married (Marianne).

Career: Army, 1956–58; Mgr., pub. relations, Wyandotte Chemicals Corp., 1961–64; A.A. to Rep. Alexander Pirnie, 1964–73; A.A. to Rep. Donald Mitchell, 1973–79; Oneida Cnty. Exec., 1979–82.

Offices: 1127 LHOB, 202-225-3665. Also 200 Fed. Bldg., 10 Broad St., Utica 13501, 315-793-8146; 41 S. Main St., Oneonta 13820, 607-432-5524; 17 Main St., Cortland 13045, 607-753-9324; and 42 S. Broad St., Norwich 13815 607-336-7160.

Committees: *Public Works and Transportation* (9th of 20 R). Subcommittees: Aviation; Investigations and Oversight; Surface Transportation. *Science, Space and Technology* (4th of 19 R). Subcommittees: Investigations and Oversight; Science, Research and Technology (Ranking Member). *Select Committee on Aging* (11th of 27 R). Subcommittees: Health and Long-Term Care; Housing and Consumer Interests.

Group Ratings

	ADA	ACLU	COPE	CFA	LCV	ACU	NTLC	NSI	COC	CEI
1988	65	78	69	73	81	24	40	70	64	28
1987	60	—	66	43	—	9	—	—	67	31

National Journal Ratings

	1988 LIB — 1988 CONS	1987 LIB — 1987 CONS
Economic	48% — 52%	42% — 58%
Social	72% — 27%	54% — 45%
Foreign	47% — 52%	55% — 44%

Key Votes

1) Homeless $	FOR	5) Ban Drug Test	AGN	9) SDI Research	FOR
2) Gephardt Amdt	FOR	6) Drug Death Pen	FOR	10) Ban Chem Weaps	AGN
3) Deficit Reduc	AGN	7) Handgun Sales	AGN	11) Aid to Contras	AGN
4) Kill Plnt Clsng Notice	AGN	8) Ban D.C. Abort $	AGN	12) Nuclear Testing	AGN

Election Results

1988 general	Sherwood L. Boehlert (R), unopposed			($145,883)
1988 primary	Sherwood L. Boehlert (R), unopposed			
1986 general	Sherwood L. Boehlert (R)	104,216	(69%)	($268,122)
	Kevin J. Conway (D)	33,864	(22%)	($2,660)
	Robert S. Barstow (C-RTL)	12,999	(9%)	($31,567)

TWENTY-SIXTH DISTRICT

Some of the northernmost farmland in the United States sits on the far north edge of Upstate New York, between the Adirondacks, "forever wild" in their state park, and the St. Lawrence River and Canadian border just below Montreal. This was land settled by hardy New Englanders in the early 1800s and bypassed in the westward migrations of the rest of the century. It was not without its cultural institutions—churches, colleges, early public schools—and not without its business innovations: it was in Watertown in 1878 that 26-year-old Frank Woolworth put a sign over a table of odds and ends reading "Any Article 5 cents," starting America's first retail chain and inventing the concept of discount stores. The 26th Congressional District of New York includes most of this far north country, the counties at the northern margin of the state and at the east end of Lake Ontario, dipping south as far as Herkimer on the Mohawk River.

In the late 20th century, the north country has been looking for government to stimulate its not terribly fast-growing economy. It had great hopes for the St. Lawrence Seaway, which is headquartered in Massena on the St. Lawrence River, but its yield has been disappointing. Its locks are too slow for most shippers and too small for the large container ships that have become the rule in most oceangoing trade. The seaway freezes over three months a year, and most people here don't want it kept open with icebreakers; that would harm the shore land. More enthusiasm is being shown for two state prisons set in Ogdensburg and Cape Vincent. The private sector has put up big malls in Watertown and Massena. But the biggest initiative has been the enlargement of Fort Drum, near Watertown. Largely at the behest of 26th District Congressman David Martin, the Army in 1985 stationed a new light infantry division of more than 10,000 men there, and began a $1.3 billion construction program at the base. This went against the longstanding Army preference for training in warm weather climates, but Martin and others pointed out that American infantry may be required to fight in cold weather; our chief adversary, after all, is not a tropical country.

The Fort Drum expansion has been the single biggest achievement of Congressman Martin, a Republican first elected in 1980. He is a solid, not at all flashy, native of the north country who served in the Marines, went to law school, and on returning home almost immediately ran for local office. In 1976, he was elected to the New York Assembly; in 1980, he won a two-man primary with 70% and beat former Lieutenant Governor Mary Ann Krupsak 64%–32% in the general. He serves on Armed Services, has a somewhat mixed voting record, and concentrates on district issues. He is reelected every two years without difficulty.

The People: Est. Pop. 1986: 516,600, up 0.1% 1980–86; Pop. 1980: 516,196, up 3.1% 1970–80. Households (1980): 74% family, 42% with children, 63% married couples; 29.5% housing units rented; median monthly rent: $144; median house value: $29,200. Voting age pop. (1980): 364,170; 1% Black, 1% Spanish origin, 1% American Indian.

1988 Presidential Vote:
Bush (R) 109,749	(55%)
Dukakis (D). 87,213	(44%)

Rep. David O'B. Martin (R)

Elected 1980; b. Apr. 26, 1944, St. Lawrence County; home, Canton; U. of Notre Dame, B.A. 1966, Albany Law Sch., J.D. 1973; Roman Catholic; married (DeeAnn).

Career: USMC, 1966–70; Practicing atty., 1973–80; St. Lawrence Cnty. Legis., 1973–77; NY Assembly, 1976–80.

Offices: 442 CHOB 20515, 202-225-4611. Also E.J. Noble Med. Ctr. Bldg., Main St., Canton 13617, 315-379-9611.

Committees: *Armed Services* (8th of 21 R). Subcommittees: Military Installations and Facilities (Ranking Member); Readiness.

Group Ratings

	ADA	ACLU	COPE	CFA	LCV	ACU	NTLC	NSI	COC	CEI
1988	25	36	33	82	50	68	49	100	79	32
1987	20	—	28	8	—	64	—	—	57	49

National Journal Ratings

	1988 LIB — 1988 CONS			1987 LIB — 1987 CONS		
Economic	44%	—	55%	33%	—	66%
Social	31%	—	69%	29%	—	70%
Foreign	26%	—	74%	0%	—	80%

Key Votes

1) Homeless $	FOR	5) Ban Drug Test	AGN	9) SDI Research	FOR
2) Gephardt Amdt	AGN	6) Drug Death Pen	FOR	10) Ban Chem Weaps	AGN
3) Deficit Reduc	AGN	7) Handgun Sales	FOR	11) Aid to Contras	FOR
4) Kill Plnt Clsng Notice	FOR	8) Ban D.C. Abort $	FOR	12) Nuclear Testing	AGN

Election Results

1988 general	David O'B. Martin (R-C) 131,043	(75%)	($120,423)
	Donald Ravenscroft (D) 43,585	(25%)	($10,635)
1988 primary	David O'B. Martin (R-C), unopposed		
1986 general	David O'B. Martin (R-C) 94,840	(100%)	($76,301)

TWENTY-SEVENTH DISTRICT

A middle American city in the middle of Upstate New York, halfway between Albany and Buffalo on the Erie Canal and the old New York Central Railroad (for years the nation's major east-west transportation routes) Syracuse is a manufacturing city with a growing economy that is sufficiently typical to have been for many years a favorite test marketing site. Syracuse, built on a swamp that was a salt spring, invented the dental chair, Stickley mission furniture, the drive-in bank teller, and the foot measuring devices used in shoe stores; it was one of the first big manufacturers of typewriters, and is the site of the New York State Fair. Its agricultural hinterland is rich with specialty crops like wine grapes, its industrial jobs mostly high skill. The weather may have helped to motivate its achievements. Syracuse gets as much snow as any city in the United States, and if you are going to live up here you are going to have to earn enough money to build a solid, well-insulated house to protect you through the winter.

In the late 1980s, Syracuse was trending Democratic. One reason is the presence of a popular Catholic Democrat at the center of state politics, Governor Mario Cuomo; the last time Syracuse trended Democratic, in the middle 1960s, was in the days of Senator Robert Kennedy. Another reason is the weakness of some local Republican nominees, notably former Congressman George Wortley, who came within 1% of losing in 1986 to Democrat Rosemary Pooler in the 27th Congressional District, which includes Syracuse, surrounding Onondaga County, and most of Madison County to the east. Wortley, a local businessman who was never much of a vote-getter, was hurt in 1986 after firing the director of his Syracuse office who then threatened to sue him, and after he asked former Banking Committee chairman Fernand St Germain, a Democrat, to attend one of his fundraisers while Wortley also served on the Ethics Committee that was then investigating St Germain. Pooler, a public service commissioner, was ahead in October polls when she was charged with accepting a campaign contribution from a director of New York Telephone as the PSC was considering a phone rate increase.

Pooler started running right away for 1988, and Wortley seemed in trouble when he dropped out of the race. The new Republican, James Walsh, the son of a former Syracuse mayor and congressman, served on the Syracuse Council and was the 49-vote loser in the 1987 Republican primary for county executive. In her campaign against Walsh, Pooler argued that the district's economy was in trouble and called for trade restrictions; Walsh said the economy was coming back and claimed credit for Syracuse's getting an AT&T tower and an enterprise zone designation. Michael Dukakis, an apostle of government aid to business, ran well here for a Democrat, losing the district by only 52%–47%. But despite Pooler's high-profile campaign, Walsh ran ahead of Bush and won 57%–42%. He seems in a strong position to hold the seat.

The People: Est. Pop. 1986: 517,300, up 0.2% 1980–86; Pop. 1980: 516,364, dn. 1.1% 1970–80. Households (1980): 71% family, 39% with children, 58% married couples; 36.8% housing units rented; median monthly rent: $186; median house value: $38,100. Voting age pop. (1980): 372,785; 5% Black, 1% Spanish origin, 1% American Indian, 1% Asian origin.

1988 Presidential Vote:

Bush (R)	116,123	(52%)
Dukakis (D)	103,274	(47%)

Rep. James T. Walsh (R)

Elected 1988; b. June 19, 1947, Syracuse; home, Syracuse; St. Bonaventure U., B.A. 1970; Catholic; married (Diane).

Career: Peace Corps, 1970–72; Marketing exec., NYNEX, 1974–88; Syracuse Common Cncl., 1977–88, Pres. 1985–88.

Offices: 229 CHOB 20515, 202-225-3701. Also 1269 Fed. Bldg., Clinton Sq., Syracuse 13260, 315-423-5657.

Committees: *Agriculture* (17th of 17 R). Subcommittees: Livestock, Dairy, and Poultry; Department Operations, Research and Foreign Agriculture. *House Administration* (8th of 8 R). Subcommittees: Elections; Libraries and Memorials. *Select Committee on Children, Youth and Families* (11th of 12 R). *Joint Committee on the Library.*

Group Ratings and Key Votes: Newly Elected

Election Results

1988 general	James T. Walsh (R-C)................. 124,928	(57%)	($594,965)
	Rosemary S. Pooler (D-JBS) 90,854	(42%)	($645,123)
1988 primary	James T. Walsh (R)....................... 439	(67%)	
	David Floss (R)......................... 212	(33%)	
1986 general	George C. Wortley (R-C) 83,430	(50%)	($697,045)
	Rosemary S. Pooler (D-ECP)........... 82,491	(49%)	($505,254)

TWENTY-EIGHTH DISTRICT

The southern tier of New York is the name for the counties running along the southern edge of western Upstate, just north of Pennsylvania (they are actually well to the north of New York City). Through the narrow crevices between the hills that cluster in this part of the state came the Erie Railroad as long ago as 1848, and later the Delaware Lackawanna and Delaware Hudson; these opened the fastnesses of these still little-known parts of the east to industry and commerce. On the banks of the Susquehanna River that flows through Pennsylvania and becomes Chesapeake Bay arose the city of Binghamton; to the north through the hills, at the southern end of the largest of the Finger Lakes, grew Ithaca, home of Cornell University.

New York's 28th Congressional District is a swath along the state's southern border, from the ancient Hudson River city of Kingston to Binghamton and Ithaca in the southern tier. Ulster County around Kingston was first settled by Dutch patroons and their retainers and includes much of the Catskill Mountains: Rip Van Winkle country. On the other side of the Catskills is the Borscht Belt resort district, part of which is in the 28th; here a predominantly Jewish clientele has been summering for nearly 100 years. Westward into the vastness of Upstate New York is the Delaware River, the source of much of New York City's excellent water supply.

This whole area has had little population growth in the past several decades, but it would be a mistake to see it as economically stagnant. Old industries have been replaced rather steadily by new ones, like the IBM plants near Binghamton; low-wage jobs have been replaced by high-wage jobs. Some children choose to leave, to seek opportunities elsewhere; but this part of Upstate New York continues to provide good livings for its citizens. Politically, their heritage is Republican; in the late 1980s they seemed to be trending Democratic: in 1988, Ithaca with its graduate school community, voted heavily for Michael Dukakis, while Binghamton's Broome

County was evenly split.

The congressman from the 28th is Matthew McHugh, a former Ithaca district attorney and a Democrat first elected in the Watergate year of 1974. Originally from Philadelphia, McHugh is earnest, careful, hard-working and slow (perhaps impossible) to anger. He has served quietly but effectively on the Appropriations Committee since 1978. Most of his time seems devoted to the Foreign Operations Subcommittee, to foreign aid programs and foreign policy generally. That subcommittee handles aid to Israel and Egypt; it handles money for international organizations; it can get involved with contra aid and other Central American issues—in other words, some of the most controversial issues in Congress. In most of these controversies McHugh is an emollient rather than an abrasive. He tends to support aid to Israel and Egypt more heartily than subcommittee chairman David Obey, but not uncritically; he tends to support economic aid more than the Republican administration, but not uncritically either. He was one of the few Democrats to support aid for the UNITA rebels in Angola in 1988; he had opposed it in 1985, but switched because he became convinced that the Reagan Administration was pushing for a negotiated settlement for the Angolan civil war. He is also a member of the Intelligence Committee, and there is trying to craft some formula that will make effective the recently ignored requirement that Congress be given timely notice of covert intelligence operations. He serves as well on the Agriculture Subcommittee chaired by Jamie Whitten, where he has fought cuts in rural housing programs. On broader issues he is inclined to oppose protectionist measures and would like to reduce Third World debt.

In this historically Republican territory, McHugh has sometimes drawn strong opponents, and has only topped 60% of the vote three times—the most recent in 1988, when his only opponent was the nominee of New York's Right-To-Life party. The strong Dukakis showing suggests the Democratic base here is bigger than when he started out, but this is not a district that the incumbent can take utterly for granted and is one in which redistricting could make a considerable difference.

The People: Est. Pop. 1986: 520,900, up 0.9% 1980–86; Pop. 1980: 516,402, up 4.1% 1970–80. Households (1980): 71% family, 37% with children, 59% married couples; 33.8% housing units rented; median monthly rent: $185; median house value: $39,400. Voting age pop. (1980): 382,338; 3% Black, 2% Spanish origin, 1% Asian origin.

1988 Presidential Vote:

Bush (R)	118,542	(52%)
Dukakis (D)	108,155	(47%)

Rep. Matthew F. (Matt) McHugh (D)

Elected 1974; b. Dec. 6, 1938, Philadelphia, PA; home, Ithaca; Mt. St. Mary's Col., B.S. 1960, Villanova U., J.D. 1963; Roman Catholic; married (Alanna).

Career: Practicing atty., 1964–68, 1972–74; Ithaca City Prosecutor, 1968; Tompkins Cnty. Dist. Atty., 1969–72.

Offices: 2335 RHOB 20515, 202-225-6335. Also 100A Fed. Bldg., Binghamton 13902, 607-773-2768; Terrace Hill-Carriage House, Ithaca 14850, 607-273-1388; and 291 Wall St., Kingston 12401, 914-331-4466.

Committees: *Appropriations* (16th of 35 D). Subcommittees: Foreign Operations, Export Financing and Related Programs; Rural Development, Agriculture and Related Agencies. *Select Committee on Children, Youth, and Families* (4th of 17 D). *Permanent Select Committee on Intelligence* (5th of 12 D). Subcommittees: Legislation (Chairman); Oversight and Evaluation.

Group Ratings

	ADA	ACLU	COPE	CFA	LCV	ACU	NTLC	NSI	COC	CEI
1988	95	87	82	73	81	4	17	0	46	22
1987	92	—	81	93	—	9	—	—	13	9

National Journal Ratings

	1988 LIB — 1988 CONS		1987 LIB — 1987 CONS	
Economic	52% —	47%	68% —	27%
Social	78% —	20%	78% —	0%
Foreign	68% —	28%	81% —	0%

Key Votes

1) Homeless $	AGN	5) Ban Drug Test	AGN	9) SDI Research	AGN
2) Gephardt Amdt	AGN	6) Drug Death Pen	AGN	10) Ban Chem Weaps	FOR
3) Deficit Reduc	FOR	7) Handgun Sales	AGN	11) Aid to Contras	AGN
4) Kill Plnt Clsng Notice	AGN	8) Ban D.C. Abort $	AGN	12) Nuclear Testing	FOR

Election Results

1988 general	Matthew F. (Matt) McHugh (D) 141,976	(93%)	($172,905)
	Mary C. Dixon (RTL)................. 10,395	(7%)	
1988 primary	Matthew F. (Matt) McHugh (D), unopposed		
1986 general	Matthew F. (Matt) McHugh (D) 103,908	(68%)	($287,642)
	Mark R. Masterson (R-C-RTL) 48,213	(32%)	($7,218)

TWENTY-NINTH DISTRICT

The Finger Lakes of Upstate New York, the long, thin, deep-blue lakes in folds between the rolling hillsides, many thick with grapevines, look rural and empty and little changed from the days when New England Yankees first settled here in the early 1800s. Yet they have been among America's most dynamic places. In the old town squares are monuments to the enthusiasms of the 1830s and 1840s, a time when these communities were almost brand new, full of young families on the move and on the rise. In this threshold of the American interior, the religious revivals were so fervent that the area was known as the Burnt-Over district. Here in the village of Palmyra, near the Erie Canal, Joseph Smith had his vision of the angel Moroni and saw the golden tablets which led him to found the Mormon Church. Preachers fanned the local enthusiasm for abolition of slavery, greater here than anywhere else in the country. This was the birthplace of the women's suffrage movement; the great 1848 women's convention was held in Seneca Falls, at the head of one of the Finger Lakes. It was the birthplace as well of the temperance movement—and, hard as it may be for today's liberated women to believe, the two causes were often linked in those days. Finally, this part of Upstate New York has always had a taste for learning. It is full of small colleges, and some anonymous scholar gave many of its towns classical names: Scipio, Marcellus, Cicero, Ovid, Romulus, Hannibal.

The Finger Lakes region forms about half of New York's 29th Congressional District; the other half is on the east side of Rochester and includes some of its eastern suburbs. Here are the mansions on East Avenue of Kodak's George Eastman and other inventors who made Rochester a high-tech city, and also some of its cultural institutions. Followers of the progressive historians might ask why, after all its initial cultural ferment, this part of Upstate New York has been so somnolently Republican ever since. But the reformers of the Burnt-Over District were Whigs and later Republicans interested in changing other Americans' conduct, not Jeffersonian Democrats who wanted to leave them alone; and their ardor cooled not because they failed, but because they mostly succeeded. Women were liberated, temperance did cut down drinking, slavery was abolished, new churches were built, and the personal and moral lives of these communities were put on a solid footing where they have remained ever since.

The Republican Party, which believed in restricting slavery in territories and building land-grant schools in colleges, was an activist party which helped to achieve these goals and then to consolidate them. Well into the 20th century, Upstate Republicans saw themselves as the upholders of standards and learning against the immigrant mobs of New York City, and as the conservers of an economic system, which proved vastly productive, against the importers of foreign socialism. And so it does today, as the welfare state has stopped short of socialism but embedded itself in the lives of local communities, and as traditional morality has again asserted its claims against those who denigrated it.

The congressman from this district is Frank Horton, one of the more senior Republicans in the House and one of the more liberal on most issues. Horton was first elected in 1962, one of a long line of liberal Republicans from the east side of Rochester, which included former Senator Kenneth Keating. He is now ranking Republican on Government Operations, a committee that produces little ongoing legislation and has a power to investigate that in practice, is difficult to focus. Horton was also a lead sponsor of revenue sharing, which has now been phased out, and a founder and co-chairman of the Northeast-Midwest Coalition, which focused attention on the distribution of federal funds throughout the nation and lobbied for the older industrial areas—the first time the regions, long the richest in the nation, saw themselves needing help. Horton was also a mover behind the establishment of inspectors general in federal departments.

Horton serves on Post Office and Civil Service, where he led the move to take the Postal Service off-budget. Horton is the New York representative on the Republican Committee on Committees, and it was he who got Raymond McGrath a Ways and Means seat in 1985—useful for New York, since McGrath was the most obdurate proponent of maintaining state and local tax deductibility in the tax reform bill—and James Walsh on Agriculture in 1989.

To many House Republicans Horton must seem an anachronism. His generally liberal voting record, his amiable bipartisanship (he was proud of his election as chairman of the majority-Democratic New York delegation), his amiable relations with longtime Government Operations Chairman Jack Brooks of Texas (from where Horton also hails: both sides of Rochester are represented now by native southerners), his support of the Education and Energy Departments and his quick repudiation of the catastrophic health bill once some squawks began—are all things which infuriate many young Republicans who think he is conceding intellectual premises and the moral high ground to liberal Democrats. Horton does, however, seem to remain popular in his district which in its current boundaries, would surely support a Republican congressman of whatever stripe.

The People: Est. Pop. 1986: 523,400, up 1.5% 1980–86; Pop. 1980: 515,404, up 2.1% 1970–80. Households (1980): 72% family, 40% with children, 60% married couples; 31.7% housing units rented; median monthly rent: $190; median house value: $36,600. Voting age pop. (1980): 365,972; 4% Black, 1% Spanish origin.

1988 Presidential Vote: Bush (R) 113,994   (53%)
Dukakis (D) 99,637   (46%)

Rep. Frank Horton (R)

Elected 1962; b. Dec. 12, 1919, Cuero, TX; home, Rochester; LA St. U., B.A. 1941, Cornell U., LL.B. 1947; Presbyterian; (Nancy).

Career: Army, WWII; Practicing atty., 1947–62; Rochester City Cncl., 1955–61.

Offices: 2108 RHOB 20515, 202-225-4916. Also 314 Kenneth B. Keating Bldg., 100 State St., Rochester 14614, 716-454-7490; 304 Metcalf Plaza, 144 Genesee St., Auburn 13021, 315-255-1125; and Riverfront Office Bldg., Oswego 13126, 315-342-4688.

Committees: *Government Operations* (Ranking Member of 15 R). Subcommittee: Legislation and National Security (Ranking Member). *Post Office and Civil Service* (2d of 9 R). Subcommittee: Postal Operations and Services (Ranking Member).

Group Ratings

	ADA	ACLU	COPE	CFA	LCV	ACU	NTLC	NSI	COC	CEI
1988	65	70	68	82	69	22	25	40	50	14
1987	56	—	67	29	—	10	—	—	43	25

National Journal Ratings

	1988 LIB — 1988 CONS		1987 LIB — 1987 CONS	
Economic	56%	— 43%	44%	— 56%
Social	62%	— 37%	38%	— 62%
Foreign	50%	— 50%	52%	— 47%

Key Votes

1) Homeless $	—	5) Ban Drug Test	AGN	9) SDI Research	FOR
2) Gephardt Amdt	FOR	6) Drug Death Pen	FOR	10) Ban Chem Weaps	FOR
3) Deficit Reduc	AGN	7) Handgun Sales	FOR	11) Aid to Contras	AGN
4) Kill Plnt Clsng Notice	AGN	8) Ban D.C. Abort $	AGN	12) Nuclear Testing	AGN

Election Results

1988 general	Frank J. Horton (R)	132,608	(69%)	($130,597)
	James R. Vogel (D)...................	51,243	(26%)	($4,514)
	Two others...........................	8,810	(5%)	
1988 primary	Frank J. Horton (R), unopposed			
1986 general	Frank J. Horton (R)	99,704	(71%)	($96,489)
	James R. Vogel (D)...................	34,194	(24%)	($20,893)
	Two others	7,110	(5%)	

THIRTIETH DISTRICT

The big cities of Upstate New York are strung out not along any natural feature, but along the route of the artery that made the region's fortune, the Erie Canal. One of them is Rochester, situated just beyond the point where the canal had to be curved sharply into a turning basin and then put across the Irondequoit River with a bridge as conduit. From this beginning, Rochester became one of America's early high-tech cities. Its great industries include Bausch and Lomb, the lensmakers; Eastman Kodak, a company that thrived for years thanks to technological breakthroughs and good management; and Xerox, which started here as Haloid though its headquarters is now in Stamford, Connecticut. Technical innovation, precision workmanship, high reliability, customer service—these have given Rochester an affluent and well-educated population which maintains fine civic institutions and provides a more elevated tone of life than found in many 20th century American cities.

The 30th Congressional District of New York includes most of the Rochester metropolitan area plus a swath of rural and small-town Upstate New York to the south along the New York Thruway. It is shaped oddly, with one wide end along Lake Ontario, a narrow pinched waist through downtown Rochester, and then a vast base running along the Thruway. It includes Rochester's highest-income suburb, Pittsford, site of the canal turnaround; and it also includes the lakefront suburbs, where working people move out when they move up: Irondequoit, Greece and Parma. Its southern portion contains the kind of small towns, originally settled by Yankees from New England, which, for so many years in Upstate New York and through the Midwest, produced the leaders of the Republican Party in the House.

But the 30th District is represented now not by a Republican man with roots deep in Upstate New York, but by a Democratic woman whose accent reflects her origins in eastern Kentucky. She is Louise Slaughter, who like many women first ran for office in her forties and became an experienced and popular Monroe County legislator and New York assemblywoman. Slaughter's predecessor-but-one was a prototypical Upstater, Barber Conable, a lover of ancient rolltop desks and Upstate history, thoughtful and moderate in temperament but capable of partisan crusading on occasion. Conable retired in 1984, and after a year was tapped to be president of the World Bank; his successor, for one term, was Republican Fred Eckert, whose abrasive and unpersonable conservatism simply didn't go over well.

Slaughter, in contrast, with her Harlan County, Kentucky accent, is ebullient, pleasant and active. In 1986, she attacked Eckert as "Congressman No" for his blunt opposition of revenue sharing to abortion and, before the Iran-contra revelations, ran TV ads showing a Rochester area woman accusing Eckert of refusing to do anything to help her brother, a hostage held in Lebanon. She raised piles of money, as much as Eckert—one of many examples of Democratic challengers matching Republican incumbents. In a city where local media cover the area's two House seats closely, this race received plenty of notice, and Slaughter won 51%–49%.

In the House, Slaughter showed the political skills Eckert lacked, using her seats on the Public Works and Government Operations Committees. She claimed credit for a new health and food benefit program for the elderly based, she said, on complaints she heard from 30th District senior citizens, and for a walkway for schoolchildren in the town of Pavilion. She also got money for repair of the Barge Canal in Fairport and for the Rochester airport. In 1988, her Republican opponent attacked her for voting for the protectionist textile bill. But the Rochester *Democrat and Chronicle* said, "it's hard to imagine a more effective freshman representative than Louise Slaughter." She was reelected by a 57%–39% margin, carrying every Rochester suburb in Monroe County and the other three counties as well. She is so strong that it's possible that the legislature, with control divided between the parties, will give her a safer seat, with more of Rochester and the Democratic suburbs, for 1990, particularly since she obtained a seat on the Rules Committee in June 1989.

The People: Est. Pop. 1986: 522,200, up 1.0% 1980–86; Pop. 1980: 516,819, up 3.5% 1970–80. Households (1980): 74% family, 41% with children, 62% married couples; 31.4% housing units rented; median monthly rent: $211; median house value: $44,100. Voting age pop. (1980): 371,098; 4% Black, 1% Spanish origin, 1% Asian origin.

1988 Presidential Vote:

Bush (R)	127,474	(54%)
Dukakis (D)	106,375	(45%)

Rep. Louise M. Slaughter (D)

Elected 1986; b. Aug. 14, 1929, Harlan Cnty., KY; home, Fairport; U. of KY, B.S. 1951, M.S. 1953; Episcopalian; married (Robert).

Career: Monroe Cnty. Legis., 1976–79; Regional Coord., Lt. Gov. Mario Cuomo, 1976–79; NY Assembly, 1983–86.

Offices: 1707 LHOB 20515, 202-225-3615. Also 311 Fed. Bldg., 100 State St., Rochester 14614, 716-232-4850; and 216 Main St., 3d floor, Batavia 14020, 716-343-2524.

Committees: *Rules* (9th of 9 D). *Select Committee on Aging* (32d of 38 D). Subcommittee: Human Services.

Group Ratings

	ADA	ACLU	COPE	CFA	LCV	ACU	NTLC	NSI	COC	CEI
1988	85	86	93	91	88	8	23	0	43	19
1987	76	—	87	86	—	10	—	—	29	13

National Journal Ratings

	1988 LIB — 1988 CONS	1987 LIB — 1987 CONS
Economic	50% — 48%	61% — 39%
Social	78% — 20%	68% — 32%
Foreign	74% — 23%	68% — 30%

Key Votes

1) Homeless $	—	5) Ban Drug Test	AGN	9) SDI Research	AGN
2) Gephardt Amdt	FOR	6) Drug Death Pen	AGN	10) Ban Chem Weaps	FOR
3) Deficit Reduc	AGN	7) Handgun Sales	AGN	11) Aid to Contras	AGN
4) Kill Plnt Clsng Notice	AGN	8) Ban D.C. Abort $	AGN	12) Nuclear Testing	FOR

Election Results

1988 general	Louise M. Slaughter (D)	128,364	(57%)	($802,886)
	John D. Bouchard (R)	89,126	(39%)	($310,704)
	Two others	8,222	(4%)	
1988 primary	Louise M. Slaughter (D), unopposed			
1986 general	Louise M. Slaughter (D)	86,777	(51%)	($558,744)
	Fred J. Eckert (R-C))	83,402	(49%)	($565,374)

THIRTY-FIRST DISTRICT

Across the gentle hills of Upstate New York, from the Finger Lakes to the Buffalo city limits, just south of the great historic east-west paths—the Erie Canal, the New York Central and the New York Thruway— stretches the 31st Congressional District of New York. Most of the land is rolling hill country, with deep crevices filled sometimes with finger-shaped lakes, that is part of the historic homeland of the Republican Party—dairy country settled mostly by New England Yankees more than 150 years ago and loyal to the Republicans since the party was founded in the days of ferment before the Civil War. Most of the people in this district, however, live well within the orbit of Buffalo, the easternmost of the Great Lakes industrial cities on the

U.S. side, which filled up in the late 19th and early 20th century with immigrants from industrial corners of Britain, Ireland, Germany, Poland and Italy. Some of the suburbs, like high-income Hamburg, are management-Republican, but most of Buffalo and Erie County have been Democratic territory since the New Deal, with a formidable Democratic organization, though sometimes there has been robust competition between the parties here.

For 18 years the congressman from this district (and its predecessors) was Jack Kemp, a Republican who came to the House thanks to a split among Democrats, who started off with a reputation as a football quarterback and left having transformed American public policy and American politics. Much like Hubert Humphrey, Kemp has been an entrepreneur of political ideas, many of which turned out, to many people's surprise, to be in tune with the times. Like Humphrey, and like Ronald Reagan, Kemp came to politics from an unusual profession, is an ebullient optimist, was associated with labor unions, won in a constituency conceded for years to the opposition, and learned, from his own experience and observations of the world around him, lessons that he then applied in politics. Kemp grew up in sunny, booming southern California, and what he noticed in snowy, declining Buffalo was that the New Deal policies of taxing and spending weren't building a stronger economy; unlike other conservatives, he didn't hate government spending programs, and he seemed genuinely to care about blue collar workers and blacks who were hurt by slow growth. But he understood early what it took more sophisticated observers years to catch on to: that Keynesian economics and wage-price controls weren't producing growth. People, he thought, could and would produce growth, if government would just cut their taxes and let them keep most of what they made. So by 1975, he was arguing that lower tax rates would produce greater economic growth and possibly even more revenue; by 1978, he got every Republican in Congress to back his 30%, three-year Kemp-Roth tax cut; in 1981, he had the satisfaction of seeing Ronald Reagan propose that cut and Congress pass most of it.

Kemp did not stop there, backing his own variant of the Bradley-Gephardt tax plan and thus foreshadowing the 1986 tax reform; boosting enterprise zones, adopted in 36 states though not in Congress; pushing to sell public housing to tenants, which he is now in a position to do as HUD Secretary. He boosted the gold standard and, more practically, was chairman of the House Republican Conference until 1987. About the only area in which Kemp was singularly unsuccessful was in his 1988 presidential candidacy. Votes that might have gone to him in early contests were splintered off by Pete du Pont and Pat Robertson, and in a year in which voters were not much interested in politics, he never got the attention which might have made him competitive with the better-known George Bush and Bob Dole.

Kemp's successor in the House is a politician with similar enthusiasm and similar ideas, but his own independent career which stretches back more than a decade though he was, at 34, the youngest freshman elected to the House in 1988. He is Bill Paxon, son of an Erie County family judge, who at age 15 worked in Kemp's first House campaign and at 23, in 1977, was elected to the Erie County legislature. In 1982, he was elected to the New York Assembly, where he championed enterprise zones and opposed most forms of business regulation; a fine natural campaigner, with much enthusiasm, he was reelected without serious opposition in 1984 and 1986. Paxon had Kemp's early endorsement in his congressional race and won the Republican nomination without opposition, but he did not have a free ride in the general. Two Democrats vied to run, noting that Buffalo councilman James Keane, in 1986, had held Kemp to 57% of the vote districtwide and 51% in Erie County—by far his worst showing since he was first elected. In their primary, George Hasiotis, member of a Buffalo restaurant-owning family, was beaten by Erie County Clerk David Swarts, who had the backing of longtime county Democratic chairman Joe Crangle. In the general Swarts charged Paxon with taking ideologically rigid positions. Paxon won with just 53% districtwide and 51% in Erie County.

Paxon promises to be more district-oriented than Kemp was when he was running for

President, and ordinarily a competent incumbent can be expected to improve his position. Paxon's greater problem is that he is beginning to look like the odd man out in redistricting. Upstate New York will lose at least one district and the elongated 31st, sandwiched between two parallel neighbors, looks easy to carve up (though 75% of its votes and population are in Erie County). Paxon's 1988 showing suggests he would have a hard time beating Henry Nowak with his Buffalo base or John LaFalce if he had his base in Niagara Falls; he would probably be an underdog against Rochester-based Louise Slaughter. Perhaps Amory Houghton, who will be 66 in 1992, might retire from his southern tier seat, but he first won it only in 1986, and so may not be inclined to leave unless he gets a top Bush appointment. In any case, as Paxon hustles to win reelection in 1990, the 1992 redistricting will not be far from his mind.

The People: Est. Pop. 1986: 518,600, up 0.5% 1980–86; Pop. 1980: 516,271, up 9.0% 1970–80. Households (1980): 78% family, 42% with children, 68% married couples; 25.3% housing units rented; median monthly rent: $201; median house value: $45,300. Voting age pop. (1980): 369,104; 1% Black, 1% Spanish origin, 1% Asian origin.

1988 Presidential Vote:			
	Bush (R)	130,130	(56%)
	Dukakis (D)	101,868	(44%)

Rep. L. William (Bill) Paxon (R)

Elected 1988; b. April 29, 1954, Buffalo; home, East Aurora; Canisius Col., B.A. 1977; Roman Catholic; single.

Career: Erie County Legis., 1978–82; NY Assembly, 1983–88.

Offices: 1711 LHOB 20515, 202-225-5265. Also 5500 Main St., Williamsville, 14221, 716-634-2324; 236 Buffalo St., Hamburg 14075, 716-648-7023; and Ontario Cnty. Crthse., N. Main St., Canandaigua 14424, 716-394-1423.

Committees: *Banking, Finance and Urban Affairs* (20th of 20 R). Subcommittees: Economic Stabilization; Housing and Community Development; International Development, Finance, Trade and Monetary Policy; Policy Research and Insurance. *Select Committee on Narcotics Abuse and Control* (11th of 12 R).

Group Ratings and Key Votes: Newly Elected

Election Results

1988 general	L. William Paxon (R-C-RTL)	117,710	(53%)	($688,382)
	David J. Swarts (D-L)	102,777	(47%)	($453,462)
1988 primary	L. William Paxon (R-C-RTL), unopposed			
1986 general	Jack F. Kemp (R-C-RTL)	92,508	(57%)	($2,613,605)
	James P. Keane (D-FTP)	67,574	(42%)	($234,487)

THIRTY-SECOND DISTRICT

Fifty years ago the honeymooners and other tourists coming to Niagara Falls stayed not in motels but in the few hotels downtown near the Falls or in rooms in people's houses; the Maid of the Mist was running in the churning waters below the Horseshoe and American Falls, but the Rainbow Bridge was not yet built, and you had to cross far downriver; the waters rushing down the Niagara River had been partly diverted to power stations, but Niagara was generating nothing like the power it does today. Niagara Falls was and is a tourist city, glamorous at least by middle-class tastes with a history of cross-border warfare almost unique in North America and an attraction that is truly worth seeing. Yet for the people who live here, it is more an industrial small city, with power lines strung out on giant pylons fanning out in every direction to provide cheap electric power to the industrial heartland, and industrial plants and dumps, some idle, like the Hooker Chemical facility that poisoned the Love Canal area: the gritty little frame houses, built where Hooker warned the city that no one should live, sitting abandoned near piles of dirt-covered hard late-season ice.

The 32d Congressional District of New York includes the heart of the Niagara Frontier: the Falls; the Buffalo suburbs of Tonawanda, Kenmore and Amherst, with its big new state university campus and more new office buildings than downtown Buffalo; the towns and farm country along the south shore of Lake Ontario to the Rochester suburbs; and a salient of low income black neighborhoods in Rochester itself. Like most of Upstate New York this was once Republican territory. But as its industrial base has declined, it has become less interested in the production of wealth and more in its distribution, and has trended Democratic. The area that from 1950 to 1962 elected William Miller, Republican national chairman in the early 1960s and Barry Goldwater's running mate in 1964, now routinely reelects a Democratic congressman.

He is John LaFalce, who as a young state legislator became part of the large Watergate congressional class of 1974. Politically, he has been eminently successful, following up his easy capture of a district that had been held by Republicans for years but which often voted for national Democrats with 2 to 1 or better margins ever since; the only threat to his tenure, and it is not a menacing one, is redistricting. On policy, he has worked to use government to stimulate economic growth in a variety of ways, but he does not seem to have any overarching vision of how this can be done, and some of his approaches have not been successful.

His forums have been the Banking and Small Business Committees. On Banking in the 1970s he helped establish the UDAG program, a favorite of mayors across the country because it provides government financing of private projects which might otherwise not be built and which become tangible evidence of accomplishment in reelection campaigns; but many argued that it just shifted projects around that would have been built anyway, and it was finally abolished in 1988. In 1983 and 1984, LaFalce used his Banking subcommittee chair to champion industrial policy—a hot subject of discussion among Democrats at the time. But it was shot down by the skepticism not only of Republicans but of Democratic economists like Charles Schultze. Next, LaFalce took up the banner of promoting competitiveness, and he got a competitiveness provision inserted in the 1988 trade bill. He came up with his own proposal for Third World debt in 1987, calling for an intermediary agency to buy up the debt with backing from the IMF's gold fund. He is not, it should be added, reflexively protectionist like some Democrats these days; to the contrary, he backed the U.S.-Canada Free Trade Agreement which promises to make the Niagara Frontier, with its low land costs and rents, an appendage of Canada's booming Toronto-based Golden Horseshoe, perhaps because he represents a border constituency. The FTA may very well bring a boom economy to an area that has long hoped for it.

In 1987, LaFalce moved from the Banking subcommittee chair to the chair of the Small Business Committee. This is a full committee that should not exist: it has jurisdiction over the Small Business Administration, a small agency which helps a few businesses which have learned its cumbersome procedures; but large numbers of congressmen like to say they've done something for small business, and a seat on the committee gives them an opportunity. LaFalce has shifted from the preoccupation with the SBA of previous chairmen to a broader focus, though he has tried to patch up the minority enterprise provisions which contributed to the Wedtech scandal. He has looked at parental leave, the minimum wage, mandated health benefits and liability insurance; he also took the trouble to move an SBA regional office from the New York City area to Niagara Falls.

LaFalce was mentioned, incidentally, as a possible successor when Banking Committee

Chairman Fernand St Germain was defeated in 1988. The committee could do worse: LaFalce is not closely tied to the S&L industry that is threatening now to cost the Treasury $100 billion; his general impulse seems to favor competition (which the big New York banks think they can do well in) without relaxing regulation altogether. But neither LaFalce nor anyone else challenged Henry Gonzalez, so he remains chairman of Small Business.

The People: Est. Pop. 1986: 495,100, dn. 4.1% 1980–86; Pop. 1980: 516,387, dn. 6.6% 1970–80. Households (1980): 74% family, 39% with children, 61% married couples; 32.5% housing units rented; median monthly rent: $174; median house value: $37,600. Voting age pop. (1980): 375,165; 7% Black, 1% Spanish origin, 1% American Indian.

1988 Presidential Vote: Dukakis (D). 104,508   (51%)
　　　　　　　　　　　　　　　Bush (R) 98,419   (48%)

Rep. John J. LaFalce (D)

Elected 1974; b. Oct. 6, 1939, Buffalo; home, Tonawanda; Canisius Col., B.S. 1961, Villanova U., J.D. 1964; Roman Catholic; married (Patricia).

Career: Law Clerk, Ofc. of Gen. Cnsl., U.S. Dept. of the Navy, 1963; Lecturer, Geo. Wash. U., 1965–66; Practicing atty.; Army, 1965–67; NY Senate, 1971–73; NY Assembly, 1973–74.

Offices: 2367 RHOB 20515, 202-225-3231. Also Fed. Bldg., 111 W. Huron St., Buffalo 14202, 716-846-4056; Main P.O. Bldg., 615 Main St., Niagara Falls 14302, 716-284-9976; and Fed. Bldg., 100 State St., Rochester 14614, 716-263-6424.

Committees: *Banking, Finance and Urban Affairs* (6th of 31 D). Subcommittees: Economic Stabilization; Financial Institutions Supervision, Regulation and Insurance; International Development, Finance, Trade and Monetary Policy. *Small Business* (Chairman of 27 D). Subcommittee: SBA, the General Economy and Minority Enterprise Development (Chairman).

Group Ratings

	ADA	ACLU	COPE	CFA	LCV	ACU	NTLC	NSI	COC	CEI
1988	80	84	84	64	81	8	16	10	38	14
1987	88	—	83	93	—	5	—	—	14	12

National Journal Ratings

	1988 LIB — 1988 CONS		1987 LIB — 1987 CONS	
Economic	60%	— 37%	55%	— 43%
Social	66%	— 32%	78%	— 0%
Foreign	68%	— 28%	66%	— 32%

Key Votes

1) Homeless $	AGN	5) Ban Drug Test	—	9) SDI Research	FOR
2) Gephardt Amdt	FOR	6) Drug Death Pen	AGN	10) Ban Chem Weaps	FOR
3) Deficit Reduc	AGN	7) Handgun Sales	AGN	11) Aid to Contras	AGN
4) Kill Plnt Clsng Notice	AGN	8) Ban D.C. Abort $	FOR	12) Nuclear Testing	FOR

Election Results

1988 general	John J. LaFalce (D-L)	133,917	(73%)	($133,738)
	Emil K. Everett (R-C-RTL)	50,229	(27%)	($13,702)
1988 primary	John J. LaFalce (D-L), unopposed			
1986 general	John J. LaFalce (D-L)	99,745	(91%)	($108,258)
	Dean L. Walker (C)	6,234	(6%)	
	Anthony M. Murty (RTL)	3,678	(3%)	

THIRTY-THIRD DISTRICT

It's possible that the success story city of the early 1990s will be Buffalo. Buffalo? The city famous for the snows piled up at the eastern end of Lake Erie which supposedly keep it immobilized half the year, for the cold steel furnaces of Lackawanna and the emptying working-class quarters south of the railroad tracks, for the empty grain elevators in what was once, before the St. Lawrence Seaway, America's number one grain milling city? A city that is eclipsed in state politics by New York City and economically by the bigger Great Lakes industrial cities of Cleveland and Detroit and Chicago, and whose architecturally bold City Hall and downtown skyscrapers are now far overshadowed by the high-rise horizon of Toronto, not so many miles away across Lake Ontario? *Buffalo?* Well, yes. You see, Buffalo has some considerable assets which no one noticed much in the 1980s. It has a high-skill labor force that works now at reasonably low wage rates; it has exceedingly cheap real estate; it has spruced up and gentrified its rather handsome waterfront on what is now a fairly clean Lake Erie; it even has an interesting history, as the western terminus of the Erie Canal and as home of two Presidents (Fillmore and Cleveland) and the place where another (McKinley) was fatally shot.

But the key to Buffalo's recent resurgence can be summed up in one word: Canada. Canada is literally right across the Peace Bridge, and Buffalo is the major metropolitan area right on the doorstep of the richest part of Canada, whose Free Trade Agreement with the United States was signed in late 1988. Toronto's wages and real estate prices and taxes, it seems, all tend to be higher than Buffalo's; its labor market is much tighter and its unions much more militant. Canadian investment is flowing into Buffalo, and investors from all over anticipate that its economy will be booming. The climate which seemed to be more forbidding now seems, economically and even meteorologically, to be healthier than that of, say, Houston, just as it did in the 19th century when Buffalo's better educated and motivated work force was protected from the diseases that debilitated the South by early frosts and mostly cool summers.

Virtually all of Buffalo, with the steel-mill town of Lackawanna just to the south, the white-collar suburb of Grand Island in the Niagara River to the north, and the blue-collar suburbs of Cheektowaga, Depew and Lancaster directly to the east, make up the 33d Congressional District of New York. This is a very heavily Democratic district—the most Democratic of any in Upstate New York. Republican voters have died or moved to the suburbs, and Buffalo's apparent upturn has not yet been matched by any Republican revival in the city limits.

Congressman Henry Nowak has represented the Buffalo district since 1974, when he was tapped by Erie County chairman Joseph Crangle's organization. Nowak was then county comptroller, an amiable organization Democrat. Nowak chairs the Water Resources sub-committee of Public Works, in which capacity he is one of the chief organizers and dispensers of federal water projects around the country; he passed a two-year water projects authorization in 1988, and superintended the ocean dumping law that was of so much concern in New Jersey. He is working on groundwater legislation. He has not neglected Buffalo and can claim credit for the creative adaptation of the waterfront; even while Great Lakes levels were high in 1987 he resisted calls that Chicago be allowed to divert more water down the Sanitary Canal.

If anyone in Congress has a safe seat, Henry Nowak does. He is a practical politician, one adept at persuading his colleagues to help him on a project, but quiet almost to the point of silence in debate. The only threat to him is redistricting, but unless his base of Buffalo is split between two districts, which is unlikely, he seems sure to carry any Buffalo district against anyone.

The People: Est. Pop. 1986: 477,300, dn. 7.6% 1980–86; Pop. 1980: 516,392, dn. 17.4% 1970–80. Households (1980): 67% family, 34% with children, 48% married couples; 47.5% housing units rented; median monthly rent: $138; median house value: $32,400. Voting age pop. (1980): 383,256; 17% Black, 2% Spanish origin.

1988 Presidential Vote:

Dukakis (D)	130,129	(66%)
Bush (R)	65,216	(33%)

Rep. Henry J. Nowak (D)

Elected 1974; b. Feb. 21, 1935, Buffalo; home, Buffalo; Canisius Col., B.A. 1957, U. of Buffalo, J.D. 1961; Roman Catholic; married (Rose).

Career: Army, 1957–58, 1961–62; Practicing atty.; Erie Cnty. Asst. Dist. Atty., 1964; Confidential Secy. to NY Supreme Ct. Justice Arthur J. Cosgrove, 1965; Erie Cnty. Comptroller, 1966–74.

Offices: 2240 RHOB 20515, 202-225-3306. Also U.S. Crthse., 68 Court St., Rm. 212, Buffalo 14212, 716-853-4131.

Committees: *Public Works and Transportation* (5th of 32 D). Subcommittees: Aviation; Public Buildings and Grounds; Surface Transportation; Water Resources (Chairman). *Science, Space and Technology* (20th of 30 D). Subcommittee: Natural Resources, Agriculture Research and Environment.

Group Ratings

	ADA	ACLU	COPE	CFA	LCV	ACU	NTLC	NSI	COC	CEI
1988	90	71	92	100	81	12	14	10	36	8
1987	76	—	92	93	—	4	—	—	7	5

National Journal Ratings

	1988 LIB — 1988 CONS		1987 LIB — 1987 CONS	
Economic	71% —	23%	73% —	0%
Social	72% —	27%	73% —	22%
Foreign	68% —	32%	71% —	27%

Key Votes

1) Homeless $	AGN	5) Ban Drug Test	AGN	9) SDI Research	AGN
2) Gephardt Amdt	FOR	6) Drug Death Pen	AGN	10) Ban Chem Weaps	AGN
3) Deficit Reduc	FOR	7) Handgun Sales	AGN	11) Aid to Contras	AGN
4) Kill Plnt Clsng Notice	AGN	8) Ban D.C. Abort $	FOR	12) Nuclear Testing	FOR

Election Results

1988 general	Henry J. Nowak (D-L), unopposed			($94,042)
1988 primary	Henry J. Nowak (D)	39,860	(91%)	
	Charles H. Carman (D)	3,706	(9%)	
1986 general	Henry J. Nowak (D-L)	109,256	(85%)	($76,902)
	Charles A. Walker (R-C)	19,147	(15%)	($8,432)

THIRTY-FOURTH DISTRICT

The western half of New York's southern tier—the local name for the counties on the northern side of the border between Upstate New York and Pennsylvania—makes up the 34th Congressional District of New York. Stretching from the small city of Elmira to Lake Erie, the district contains the Corning Glass Works in Steuben County, two small Indian reservations, miles and miles of dairy farms, and much of New York's wine country. Near the western end, not far from Lake Erie, is Lake Chautauqua, where the Chautauqua gatherings of the late 19th century were held: in the summer, down by the lake, on wide green lawns and on porches and in gazebos decorated with ornate white Victorian gingerbread, whole families came and listened to educational talks and inspirational lectures from the likes of William Jennings Bryan.

The small cities scattered among the district's valleys—Jamestown, Olean, Hornell, Corning—and on the shores of Lake Erie—Dunkirk, Fredonia—tend to be Democratic or politically marginal, reflecting the preference of the Irish and Italian Catholics who came to this part of Upstate New York after it had first been settled by New England Yankees. Outside the towns, the Yankee Republicans still predominate and overall this is usually a Republican district.

The current congressman won the seat almost by inheritance—yet he was also the beneficiary of political accidents. He is Amory Houghton Jr., known as Amo, scion of the exceedingly wealthy family that owns the Corning Glass Works, and a top executive at Corning for 25 years who had considered retiring and becoming a missionary in Africa as he approached age 60. The Houghtons, moreover, are not just rich folks in a small town, they are charter members of the American establishment: Houghton's father was ambassador to France, his grandfather, while congressman in the 1920s, built one of the biggest mansions on Washington's Embassy Row, his family endowed the rare books library at Harvard, and this latest Houghton sat on boards of companies like IBM, Citicorp and Procter and Gamble. But Amory Houghton's missionary plans were changed when Representative Stan Lundine, a Democrat who captured the district in a 1976 special election and held it ever since, was tapped by Mario Cuomo to be his lieutenant governor candidate. Suddenly Houghton decided to run for Congress, at which point the other Republicans in the race dropped out. He had a serious Democratic opponent, a young district attorney who carried the eastern part of the district. But Houghton got 77% in his home county of Steuben and won with a comfortable 60%. In the 1988 campaign, when he was opposed only by a Liberal who at 24 was too young to serve, he did "work days"as a disc jockey at Elmira's WENY, as a cook at the Texas Hots restaurant in Wellsville, and as a man-on-the-street reporter for the *Olean Times-Herald*.

Houghton was not the typical freshman congressman when first elected, but he may well be more what the Founding Fathers had in mind than the politically adept youngsters with few local ties who win in so many districts. He seems to have the cheerful unassuming nature of one to whom much is given, who has been busy most of his life living up to his responsibilities and has enjoyed himself in the process. He said during the campaign that he understood how to create jobs, though he may find it was easier to do that as CEO at Corning than in the Democratic House. His voting record was somewhat varied; he supported the plant closing law, for example, saying that big businesses do it anyway; he thought the trade bill a step in the right direction as someone with some experience in doing foreign business. Houghton surely will be able to serve the 34th District as long as he chooses; redistricting is unlikely to hurt an incumbent with his standing in a district that is in a corner of the state.

The People: Est. Pop. 1986: 500,600, dn. 3.0% 1980–86; Pop. 1980: 516,154, up 1.3% 1970–80. Households (1980): 74% family, 40% with children, 63% married couples; 27.3% housing units rented; median monthly rent: $152; median house value: $30,600. Voting age pop. (1980): 368,422; 1% Black, 1% Spanish origin.

1988 Presidential Vote:

Bush (R)	118,065	(59%)
Dukakis (D)	78,927	(40%)

Rep. Amory Houghton, Jr. (R)

Elected 1986; b. Aug. 7, 1926, Corning; home, Corning; Harvard, B.A. 1950, M.B.A. 1952; Episcopalian; separated.

Career: USMC, WWII; Corning Glass Works, 1951–86, Chmn. of the Bd., C.E.O., 1964–83.

Offices: 1217 LHOB 20515, 202-225-3161. Also 700 W. Gate Plaza, W. State St., Olean 14760, 716-372-2127; 203 Lake St., Hazlett Bldg., Ste. 411, Elmira 14902, 607-734-8580; 32 Denison Pkwy. W., Corning 14830, 607-937-3333; and Fed. Bldg., Rm. 122, Prendergast & 3d Sts., Jamestown 14701, 716-484-0252.

Committees: *Budget* (9th of 14 R). Task Forces: Budget Process, Reconciliation and Enforcement; Community Development and Natural Resources. *Foreign Affairs* (17th of 18 R). Subcommittees: Africa; International Economic Policy and Trade.

Group Ratings

	ADA	ACLU	COPE	CFA	LCV	ACU	NTLC	NSI	COC	CEI
1988	45	52	47	82	38	56	64	90	100	41
1987	24	—	38	21	—	39	—	—	80	67

National Journal Ratings

	1988 LIB — 1988 CONS		1987 LIB — 1987 CONS	
Economic	37% —	63%	33% —	66%
Social	33% —	67%	37% —	63%
Foreign	35% —	64%	35% —	65%

Key Votes

1) Homeless $	FOR	5) Ban Drug Test	AGN	9) SDI Research	FOR
2) Gephardt Amdt	AGN	6) Drug Death Pen	FOR	10) Ban Chem Weaps	AGN
3) Deficit Reduc	AGN	7) Handgun Sales	FOR	11) Aid to Contras	AGN
4) Kill Plnt Clsng Notice	FOR	8) Ban D.C. Abort $	AGN	12) Nuclear Testing	AGN

Election Results

1988 general	Amory Houghton, Jr. (R-C)	131,078	(96%)	($319,098)
	Ian Kelly Woodward (L)	4,797	(4%)	
1988 primary	Amory Houghton, Jr. (R-C), unopposed			
1986 general	Amory Houghton, Jr. (R-C)	85,856	(60%)	($465,710)
	Larry M. Himelein (D)	56,898	(40%)	($107,100)

NORTH CAROLINA

In North Carolina, wrote V.O. Key in the 1940s, "it has been the vogue to be progressive. Willingness to accept new ideas, sense of community responsibility toward the Negro, feeling of common purpose, and relative prosperity have given North Carolina a more sophisticated politics than exists in most southern states." This was the creation, wrote Jonathan Daniels, then publisher of the *Raleigh News and Observer*, of elite groups "which create a unity that—beyond the uniformity of taxes and laws—may very well be called North Carolina. Strongest of all, perhaps, is the alumni of the University of North Carolina. Sometimes regarded with suspicion, sometimes attacked with bitterness, the university nevertheless is more often held in almost pathetic affection by the state. North Carolina was so long in ignorance, so long in poverty!" Yet by most measures it still was as Daniels was writing; the state's much praised colleges and universities did train an admirable elite, but most North Carolinians 50 years ago did not graduate from high school, worked most of their lives on small farms or in textile mills, and lived out in the countryside in houses that had gotten electricity and indoor plumbing only recently, if at all.

Yet for all the gap between the small groups of elites and the rest of North Carolinians, there was an egalitarian tone you wouldn't find in aristocratic South Carolina—"any Sunday in the social columns of the state newspapers a picture of some mill-town bride may appear alongside that of the mill owner's daughter," writes the *WPA Guide*—and an "omnipresent southern hospitality [that] comes largely from a spirit of delightful informality, or from just plain 'southern don't care.'" And there was an unspoken connection with the past in a place where most people had roots going back 200 years. "Almost every county has its backwoods districts where old English ballads are still sung, where old women know how to dye and weave, and where pottery churns and jugs are made from the local clay." Churchgoing was deeply ingrained and revivals were common. "Sometimes a revivalist will sweep together all the elements of a section, rich and poor, town and country, into a fanatical band," and religiosity was reflected "in the strictness of Sunday blue laws, in the rules of certain sects that frown on card playing, in the prohibition of dancing at some of the largest colleges."

How did this North Carolina of 50 years ago become the North Carolina that emerged in the 1980s as the nation's tenth largest state, as "the prototype of America's future," as John Herbers calls it in *The New American Heartland*? The answer is that there is plenty of continuity, and that some of the things that made North Carolina seem, under its university-educated veneer, backward and unprogressive in the 1940s have helped to put it on the cutting edge of national growth in the 1980s. One is its lack of a metropolis. The idea of Chapel Hill (1940 population 3,654) as an intellectual center was preposterous to most Americans of the 1940s, accustomed to taking their cultural cues from New York and educating their elite in universities within the orbits of its great cities; but in the 1980s, Chapel Hill is one of the three centers of North Carolina's Research Triangle (the others are Durham, home of Duke University, and Raleigh, state capital and home of North Carolina State), and together they make up a metropolitan economy that *Inc.* magazine ranked fourth in the country for 1989. North Carolina still has no city larger than Charlotte, with just over 300,000 people. But at a time when interstate highways, airport hubs (the state has two big ones) and computers connect workers, North Carolina has, in Herbers's words, "pioneered scattered growth away from its cities and suburbs," and become, in one expert's words, a "countrified city"—one with new housing not in towns or on their edges, but built on land surrounded by forests and farms and at least several

NORTH CAROLINA — Congressional Districts, Counties, and Selected Places — *(11 Districts)*

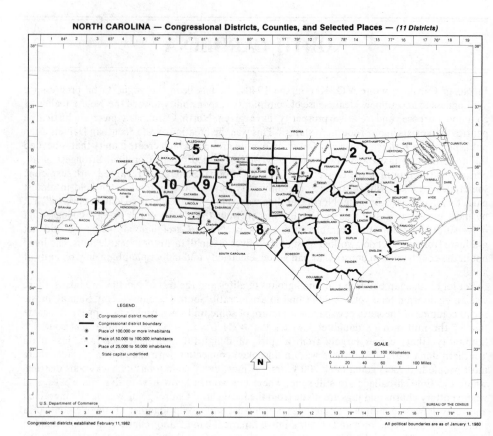

LEGEND

2　Congressional district number

────　Congressional district boundary

◉　Place of 100,000 or more inhabitants

⊛　Place of 50,000 to 100,000 inhabitants

•　Place of 25,000 to 50,000 inhabitants

　State capital underlined

SCALE

0　20　40　60　80　100 Kilometers

0　20　40　60　80　100 Miles

U.S. Department of Commerce　　　　BUREAU OF THE CENSUS

Congressional districts established February 11, 1982　　　All political boundaries are as of January 1, 1980

miles' drive away from shopping centers and workplaces. In the 1970s, jobs were coming in large numbers to rural North Carolina; in the 1980s the movement seems to be closer to the state's still mid-sized metropolitan clusters, and the jobs more upscale and higher-paying.

Another connecting thread between the North Carolina of 1940 and 1990 is its historic poverty and egalitarianism. Two generations ago North Carolina lived on textiles, tobacco, and furniture, none of them high-wage industries. North Carolina was settled mostly by poor colonists, many of whose offspring (including Presidents Jackson, Polk and Johnson) moved west; it contributed more troops to the Confederacy than any other state, but not many leaders. Throughout, North Carolina's leaders have not been transfixed by their aristocracy or obsessed, as some in other southern states are, with the notion that they are born to lead. And although the state's tradition of education has its underside (its great champion was Governor Charles Aycock, elected in 1900 on a platform of universal education and disenfranchisement of blacks), it has also produced a system where merit is rewarded and an able man with humble origins can get ahead.

The third connection between the old and new North Carolina is a sense of roots and tradition that has remained through successive stages of economic growth. Neither tobacco nor textiles took many Tarheels far from their native counties, tobacco kept them near home because it is cultivated intensively on small plots (a family can make a living off 15 acres, which is true of no other legal crop), textiles because the mills have been built in small cities, rural crossroads and interstate interchanges. Industrial unions did not emerge here, as they did in the northern cities with their southern migrants, as intermediaries between workers and management and between politicians and voters; North Carolina, for reasons made plain in *Norma Rae*, has long been the least unionized state in the country—which for a long time looked like a lagging, and now looks like a leading, indicator.

So too the continued strength of traditional and fundamentalist religion in a society of increasing cultural variety has turned out to be more of a harbinger of the future than many thought. Television preacher Jim Bakker, whose South Carolina base is in the Charlotte media market, may have been disgraced, but there remains a churchy tone to public life in the 10th megastate that folks there at least don't see as inconsistent with increasing cultural sophistication or economic complexity.

In politics, North Carolina has developed what seems to be a prototype for politics in the South and may prove in time a prototype for national politics—but which is also the product of some pungent and unique individuals. It is a polarized, increasingly party-line politics, but one which also seems adaptable to issues that are arising and not hung up on the issues of the past, a politics in which Democrats and Republicans are distinctive, non-overlapping in their ideas, and bitter in their rivalries. Its fiercest battle was the 1984 Senate race between Senator Jesse Helms and then Governor Jim Hunt, the most expensive Senate race in American history and one of the most vitriolically contested. That contest may or may not be repeated in 1990—by early 1989 Helms had not committed himself to run and Hunt, who passed up the 1986 Senate race, seemed reluctant—and its bitter intensity seems to have exhausted both sides. Yet ironically the winner, Helms, does not seem to have captured the future, as other Republicans, even in North Carolina, take a different path; while Hunt, the loser, has seen the policies he has backed and the stands he has taken vindicated in state and local elections even when his political allies have not won.

Hunt comes from the progressive Democratic strain that goes back to the Daniels family and Governors Luther Hodges, elected in 1956 and the founder of Research Triangle Park, and Terry Sanford, elected in 1960 and known as the man who accepted desegregation. Hunt is not a believer in economic redistribution, and on cultural issues tends to be tradition-minded: strongly in favor of capital punishment and teaching basics in the schools, very comfortable beginning a meeting with a prayer. He believes in an activist government working with local businessmen and lawyers to encourage economic growth. His 1976 campaign was one of the first in the nation to raise issues like competency tests for teachers and students, a prison-building program, and an active economic development program to bring in high-wage, high-skill jobs. He delivered on these promises at the same time that North Carolina's pleasant physical environment and high tech strength was attracting talented migrants and producing record economic growth. It had reason to believe it was a prototype for what the rest of the nation would—or might hope to—become. As David Broder has pointed out, if Hunt had been elected Senator in 1984, he could have become a presidential candidate by 1986—and might very well have ended up the Democratic nominee and perhaps have been elected President.

If Hunt is a doer, Helms is an attitudinizer. His philosophy by now is well known: fierce opposition to every form of cultural liberalism, dislike of most domestic government spending, an anti-Communism so strong that it produces a reflexive support of odious dictatorships from Chile to the Philippines to South Korea and of apartheid in South Africa, an opposition to civil rights measures that seems to go beyond differences of principle to genuine hostility. For example, when Spark Matsunaga was making the case for Japanese American redress, Helms and his staff countered with positions racially and factually preposterous. In general, Helms thrives in opposition and withers a bit when he must bear the responsibilities of governing.

Helms began his political career in the 1950 race against Senator Frank Graham, the longtime president of the University of North Carolina, and made his name with voters as a

Raleigh television and Tobacco Radio Network commentator denouncing Richard Nixon's recognition of Communist China and the latest civil rights legislation. He has never held or sought executive office: his only political office before he ran for the Senate was as a member of the Raleigh city council in the 1950s. As a manager of legislation Helms has been a flop, from his mismanagement of the farm bill in 1981 (which nearly cost the tobacco growers their subsidy) to his bungling of the abortion issue (in which he ended up himself voting against an embattled anti-abortion constitutional amendment) to his attempt to dominate the Foreign Relations Committee (he got Republicans to make him ranking minority member in 1987, but the year before the committee pointedly refused to confirm a Helms protégé as ambassador to Belize).

But in 1984, Helms made his clarity on issues an asset by contrasting it with Hunt's positions in between extremes; Helms the complainer was tellingly asking Hunt the doer in ad after ad, "Where do you stand, Jim?" He has raised money for himself and others primarily by direct mail, a medium in which the shrillest apocalyptic appeal usually does best; Helms's Congressional Club, based in Raleigh, has become one of the nation's largest direct mail fund raisers. The club not only gives contributions as a PAC but has provided at low cost (some argue, at illegally low cost) campaign services to Helms-backed candidates. Helms has always done best in presidential years when national issues are in the forefront: he first won his seat in 1972, his protégé John East won in 1980; in 1984, after registration drives which produced more new evangelicals for Helms than blacks for Hunt, Helms won 52% against Hunt. Democrats do better in off years: Helms won unimpressively in 1978, and East's seat was won by Democratic former Governor Terry Sanford in 1986.

The common way to analyze this is to speculate about presidential coattails. But in North Carolina it is the state races which dominate the airwaves. What is happening here, in a pattern being echoed in the rest of the South, is a convergence of national and state tickets. In 1968 and 1972, the Democratic national ticket got only 29% of North Carolina's votes, while the party's candidates for governor and Senator got 53% and 61% in 1968 and 48% and 46% in 1972, respectively. In 1984 and 1988, national Democratic tickets headed by northern liberals did better, with 38% and 42%, though they still were far from winning the state's 13 electoral votes. But the Democratic candidates for governor and senator got 45% and 48%, respectively, in 1984 and the gubernatorial candidate in 1988 got 44%. Put it another way: 20 years ago the gubernatorial candidate ran 24% ahead of the national ticket and House candidates ran 26% ahead; in 1988 the gubernatorial candidate ran 2% ahead of the national ticket and House candidates 14% ahead. North Carolina has in effect reinvented straight-ticket politics. Given the close balance here, that has produced unusual volatility: 8 of the 11 congressional districts have been seriously contested in the 1980s, more than in any other state, with three changing hands, one of them (the 11th) four times in four elections.

Meanwhile, the techniques used in the 1984 Helms-Hunt race have been a prototype for other political contests, including the 1988 presidential race. The huge sums of money raised enabled both candidates to poll constantly on the issues and to prepare instant rebuttals and response ads for broadcasting across the 100 counties of the state. Those who yearn for the revival of old-fashioned political debate have decried such back-and-forth ads, and yet they serve the same function as protracted debate did in the days of Lincoln and Douglas. Then the candidates would come to town and provide entertainment, speaking for hours amid crowds that included romping children and dogs, gossiping wives and spirited—sometimes drunken—hecklers. Now the candidates must bring their messages and make their debating points in the forum where voters seek entertainment, on television, and so make their cases amid episodes of "L.A. Law" and "Murphy Brown" to an audience many of whose members are also reading the paper or are out in the kitchen breaking open a bag of potato chips.

Governor. Jim Martin, elected governor in 1984 and reelected in 1988, has put his impress on state government more deeply than almost anyone expected and has provided an alternative to the Republicanism of Helms and the Democracy of Hunt. Starting off as a chemistry professor at Davidson College, elected congressman in 1972 and serving as a member of the Ways and Means Committee, he does not have a conventional politician's temperament; he is no backslapper or vote-trader. He won with 54% in 1984 largely because of splits among the Democrats, beating Rufus Edmisten, then attorney general and now secretary of state, but best known as Senator Sam Ervin's counsel in the Watergate hearings. North Carolina's system provides for a weak governor with no veto, and in his first term Martin did not get along with the legislature; he refused to buy votes with public works projects and did not advance as many programs as Hunt had. He defied the conventional wisdom that he had to wheel and deal with the Democrats, and mostly won. He deliberately concentrated on just a few issues and had some successes, reducing business taxes, starting a highway improvement program, following through on Hunt's education program with his "career ladders" $397 million merit pay program. He overpowered Helms's forces at the 1987 state convention and got his man in as party chairman. Opposed by Lieutenant Governor Robert Jordan in 1988, he bragged about the state's 300,000 new jobs, its tax cuts, its increases in education as a percentage of the state budget; when Jordan told a black group he couldn't back their demands because he needed the "redneck vote," Republicans handed out bumper stickers that said "another redneck for Martin."

Martin won a smashing success in 1988, not just beating Jordan 56%–44%, but electing a Republican lieutenant governor, James C. Gardner—important because Gardner names all committee chairmen in (and essentially runs) the state Senate—and picking up more legislative seats for Republicans than in any other state. In the state House a coalition of 20 Democrats and the 46 Republicans ousted liberal, pork-barreling Speaker Liston Ramsey in January 1989, and elected a pro-Martin Democrat. So Martin now has a friendly legislature. He can presumably win support for some of his activist programs—preschool for "at risk" children, for example—while holding down the tax rates, a move which he believes is important for continuing economic growth. With a high job rating and a strong economy, he looks well positioned to challenge Terry Sanford for the Senate in 1992, when he can't run for a third term as governor anyway. But then Jim Hunt was well positioned to run against Jesse Helms in 1984 too.

Senators. Jesse Helms, nearing 70, has seen some of his North Carolina base melt away. He saw his protege David Funderburk lose the 1986 Senate nomination to moderate James Broyhill by a 67%–30% margin. He saw his candidate for state chairman lose to Jim Martin's in 1987. The man who helped Ronald Reagan win the come-from-behind victory in the North Carolina presidential primary that kept him in the 1976 presidential race and in presidential politics took no public position in the 1988 Republican race: some of his allies perfunctorily endorsed Jack Kemp, but Helms seems to have covertly preferred Bob Dole, who has bailed him out many times in the Senate, and kept quiet about it lest he upset his conservative constituency. The Congressional Club no longer is a major force in the rest of the country and hasn't had many wins in North Carolina. Against Hunt in 1984, Helms felt compelled to pledge that he would remain chairman of Agriculture and not take the Foreign Relations chair, to which a loss by Chairman Charles Percy would have entitled him. Percy did lose and Helms kept his word, but when the Democrats took control in 1986, Helms considered himself released from his pledge, and got the ranking minority position on Foreign Relations, though not before committee Republicans voted for Richard Lugar over him 7–0. (Helms made an issue of his seniority—four years more than Lugar in the Senate—and swayed crucial votes from fellow Members who feared their own seniority might be endangered.) Helms' hard fought position enabled him to hold up ambassadorial appointments and put pressure on the State Department to select his appointees and adopt his views, and in doing so be a power in foreign policy. It leaves him less well positioned to come to the aid of North Carolina's beleaguered tobacco farmers, which might bother voters if he seeks reelection.

On other issues, Helms has done far better than a temperamental aginner probably ever expected and not nearly so well as an adept politician with his advantages might have done. On cultural issues he has been largely frustrated: abortion is still legal, state-written prayers are forbidden in public schools, practices Helms regards as immoral are condoned and sometimes even approved all across the country, the Martin Luther King holiday Helms inveighed against (and won some votes on in 1984) is established. The Senate passed an AIDS bill Helms had many objections to, though he did manage to amend it to bar funding for organizations that "promote or encourage" homosexuality. But many of Helms's issues remain alive, capable of generating embarrassing roll call votes which he can use in direct mail fundraising and direct mail campaigning against his colleagues.

On foreign policy, Helms has had more successes—though again he does not recognize them as such. The United States is stronger, the Soviet Union is weaker, the premises of conservative policy—that peace comes through strength, not conciliation; that the Soviet system and Third World theocracies are morally evil, not just friendly rivals—are more widely accepted. But Helms insists on looking at the down side, seeing in the accession of Corazon Aquino and the return of electoral democracy in Chile advances for Communism. Helms is a foe of most domestic spending, but he seems far less engaged on that subject than he does on non-economic issues.

In 1990, he can claim, if he chooses to run, to have salvaged most of the tobacco programs. But is his heart in that? It is said that Helms is waiting to see if Hunt runs, and will run again if he does, to keep Hunt out of the seat; it is said also that Hunt is waiting, to see if he can edge Helms out before he gets in. Who knows? What does seem true is that neither man looks forward to a campaign that raises as much money, spends so much time and energy on negative ads, and becomes as intense as their 1984 contest. That was perhaps, in a state more typical than it used to be, too much politics for a country that in this stage of its history doesn't have much taste for politics at all.

Certainly the 1986 Senate race was less intense, and for a while the Democrats, who ended up winning the seat, had a hard time finding a candidate when John East, a protégé of Helms's elected in 1980 by a 50%–49%, a professor confined to a wheelchair, announced he was retiring. Hunt, weary from 1984, passed; so did several other Democrats; Terry Sanford, elected governor in 1960, an unsuccessful presidential candidate in 1972 and 1976, president of Duke University from 1970 to 1985, decided to run. Then East committed suicide in June 1986; James Broyhill, long the ranking Republican on John Dingell's Energy and Commerce Committee, already the easy winner of the Republican primary, was appointed by Martin to take his place. In this Senate race only $9 million was spent, as opposed to $26 million in Helms-Hunt, and the arguments were rather tame: Sanford attacked Broyhill for failing to get Reagan to veto the protectionist textile bill, Broyhill attacked Sanford for the sales tax on food he passed as governor. Sanford racked up the big majorities in east Carolina that Hunt had been unable to amass against Helms, ran even in the urban counties and the west as Hunt did, and won 52%–48% despite Broyhill's home district strength.

Sanford started off on the wrong foot, dithering over whether to vote to override a Reagan veto of a highway bill, voting "present" and then switching two minutes later to sustain, then on reconsideration voting to override. He took some flak too from Helms in a dispute they had over a western Carolina wilderness area. But he also had some achievements. He won a seat on Foreign Relations and was one of the creators of an International Commission for Central American Recovery and Development, and got Costa Rica's President Oscar Arias to endorse it; he wants a sort of mini-Marshall plan in the area. Aroused by the leveraged buyouts of Burlington Industries and RJR Nabisco, two firms historically based in North Carolina, he has a bill to discourage them by denying some deals the interest deduction. He wants the surpluses Social Security is starting to generate not to be reflected in the budget. Burned a bit by the highway vote, he has come out early on other tough calls, against the Bork nomination, for Albert Gore's presidential candidacy and for George Mitchell for Majority Leader. Sanford insists he will run for reelection in 1992, when he will be 75. The likeliest opponent, and a tough one, will be Governor Jim Martin; another possibility might be drug czar, former Education Secretary, and onetime North Carolina professor William Bennett.

Presidential politics. North Carolina long had a May presidential primary. Ronald Reagan's victory here in 1976 kept him in the race and in presidential politics; without it the 1980s might have been much different. For 1988 the Democratic legislature put North Carolina's primary on Super Tuesday. Albert Gore, endorsed by Terry Sanford and Jim Hunt, won a narrow victory over Jesse Jackson; Michael Dukakis used his ample treasury to advertise and win 20% of the votes, enough to break the threshold and split the delegates with the two front-runners. On the Republican side, North Carolina is Elizabeth Dole's home state and was Bob Dole's strongest state in the South; he spent time and money here and had Jesse Helms's benign neutrality. But George Bush's strength among southern Republicans was just too much and he won 45%–39%.

In the general election, North Carolina has been winnable for the Democrats when they nominate a southerner for president and tantalizingly close, but still out of reach when they don't: Michael Dukakis's 42% here was a big improvement over George McGovern's 29%, but George Bush still won easily 58%–42%.

Congressional districting. North Carolina's congressional districts, with boundaries influenced by a long history and the Voting Rights Act, produced the most competitive House elections in any state in the 1980s. This, in turn, has had an effect in the House. North Carolina Democrats have become party loyalists, sticking together to get favors—like support of their tobacco positions and trade restrictions on textiles—from other Democrats, and to exert leverage to keep the caucus from getting too liberal. The Democratic leadership in turn has helped the North Carolinians all it can.

This may change in the 1990s if North Carolina gets a new seat from the 1990 Census. In that case everybody but Helms Republicans and those who savor competition stand to be the winners. The Republicans are likely to get the new seat: politically they are strong in the legislature and demographically the sensible place for a new district is in the textile and hill country between Winston-Salem and Charlotte, in counties now heavily Republican. But incumbent Democrats will be winners too: for to create such a seat, the legislature must remove heavily Republican counties from districts only narrowly carried by Steve Neal, Bill Hefner, and Jamie Clarke, who should be much safer in 1992 if they can manage to get through 1990.

The People: Est. Pop. 1988: 6,526,000; Pop. 1980: 5,881,766, up 10.9% 1980–88 and 15.7% 1970–80; 2.63% of U.S. total, 10th largest. 14% with 1–3 yrs. col., 13% with 4+ yrs. col.; 14.8% below poverty level. Single ancestry: 23% English, 5% German, 4% Irish, 1% Scottish, French. Households (1980): 77% family, 43% with children, 63% married couples; 31.6% housing units rented; median monthly rent: $135; median house value: $36,000. Voting age pop. (1980): 4,224,031; 20% Black, 1% American Indian, 1% Spanish origin. Registered voters (1988): 3,432,042; 2,247,759 D (65%), 1,016,546 R (30%), 167,737 unaffiliated and minor parties (5%).

1988 Share of Federal Tax Burden: $19,390,000,000; 2.19% of U.S. total, 14th largest.

1988 Share of Federal Expenditures

	Total		Non-Defense		Defense	
Total Expend	$17,743m	(2.01%)	$13,280m	(2.03%)	$4,914m	(2.15%)
St/Lcl Grants	2,299m	(2.01%)	2,290m	(2.00%)	9m	(7.68%)
Salary/Wages	3,691m	(2.75%)	1,075m	(1.60%)	2,616m	(1.60%)
Pymnts to Indiv	9,504m	(2.32%)	8,908m	(2.28%)	596m	(3.20%)
Procurement	1,690m	(0.90%)	451m	(0.97%)	1,690m	(0.90%)
Research/Other	560m	(1.50%)	556m	(1.50%)	4m	(1.50%)

Political Lineup: Governor, James G. (Jim) Martin (R); Lt. Gov., Jim Gardner (R); Secy. of State, Rufus Edmisten (D); Atty. Gen., Lacy H. Thornburg (D); Treasurer, Harlan Boyles (D); Auditor, Edward Renfrow (D). State Senate, 50 (37 D and 13 R); State House of Representatives, 120 (74 D and 46 R). Senators, Jesse A. Helms (R) and Terry Sanford (D). Representatives, 11 (8 D and 3 R).

1988 Presidential Vote			**1984 Presidential Vote**		
Bush (R)	1,237,258	(58%)	Reagan (R)	1,346,481	(62%)
Dukakis (D).	890,167	(42%)	Mondale (D)	824,287	(38%)

1988 Democratic Presidential Primary			**1988 Republican Presidential Primary**		
Gore.	235,669	(35%)	Bush	124,260	(45%)
Jackson	224,177	(33%)	Dole.	107,032	(39%)
Dukakis.	137,993	(20%)	Robertson	26,861	(10%)
Gephardt.	37,553	(6%)	Kemp.	11,361	(4%)
Hart.	16,381	(2%)			
Simon	8,032	(1%)			
Babbitt	3,816	(1%)			

GOVERNOR

Gov. James G. (Jim) Martin (R)

Elected 1984, term expires Jan. 1993; b. Dec. 11, 1935, Savannah, GA; home, Raleigh; Davidson Col., B.S. 1957, Princeton U., Ph.D. 1960; Presbyterian; married (Dorothy).

Career: Prof., Davidson Col., 1960–72; Mecklenburg Cnty. Bd. of Commissioners, 1966–72, Chmn., 1967–68, 1970–71; U.S. House of Reps., 1972–84.

Office: State Capitol, Raleigh 27611, 919-733-4240.

Election Results

1988 gen.	James G. (Jim) G. Martin (R).	1,222,338	(56%)
	Robert G. Jordan III (D)	957,687	(44%)
1988 prim.	James G. (Jim) Martin (R), unopposed		
1984 gen.	James G. (Jim) Martin (R)	1,208,167	(54%)
	Rufus Edmisten (D).	1,011,209	(45%)

SENATORS

Sen. Jesse A. Helms (R)

Elected 1972, seat up 1990; b. Oct. 18, 1921, Monroe; home, Raleigh; Wingate Col., Wake Forest U.; Baptist; married (Dorothy).

Career: Navy, WWII; City Ed., *Raleigh Times*; A. A. to U.S. Sens. Willis Smith, 1951–53 and Alton Lennon, 1953; Exec. Dir., NC Bankers Assn., 1953–60; Raleigh City Cncl., 1957–61; Exec. V.P., WRAL-TV and Tobacco Radio Network, 1960–72.

Office: 403 DSOB 20510, 202-224-6342. Also P.O. Box 2888, Raleigh 27602, 919-856-4630; and P.O. Box 2944, Hickory 28603, 704-322-5170.

Committees: *Agriculture, Nutrition, and Forestry* (3d of 9 R). Subcommittees: Agricultural Production and Stabilization of Prices (Ranking Member); Domestic and Foreign Marketing and Product Promotion; Nutrition and Investigation. *Foreign Relations* (Ranking Member of 9 R). *Rules and Administration* (4th of 7 R). *Select Committee on Ethics* (2d of 3 R).

Group Ratings

	ADA	ACLU	COPE	CFA	LCV	ACU	NTLC	NSI	COC	CEI
1988	5	4	8	10	0	100	93	100	75	75
1987	10	—	7	8	—	100	—	—	89	87

National Journal Ratings

	1988 LIB — 1988 CONS		1987 LIB — 1987 CONS	
Economic	7%	— 92%	6%	— 87%
Social	0%	— 89%	6%	— 89%
Foreign	19%	— 80%	0%	— 76%

Key Votes

1) Cut Aged Housing $	AGN	5) Bork Nomination	FOR	9) SDI Funding	FOR
2) Override Hwy Veto	AGN	6) Ban Plastic Guns	FOR	10) Ban Chem Weaps	FOR
3) Kill Plnt Clsng Notice	FOR	7) Deny Abortions	FOR	11) Aid To Contras	FOR
4) Min Wage Increase	AGN	8) Japanese Reparations	AGN	12) Reagan Defense $	—

Election Results

1984 general	Jesse A. Helms (R)	1,156,768	(52%)	($16,917,559)
	James B. (Jim) Hunt, Jr. (D)	1,070,488	(48%)	($9,461,924)
1984 primary	Jesse A. Helms (R)	134,675	(91%)	
	George Wimbish (R)	13,899	(9%)	
1978 general	Jesse A. Helms (R)	619,151	(55%)	($8,123,205)
	John R. Ingram (D)	516,663	(45%)	($264,088)

Sen. Terry Sanford (D)

Elected 1986, seat up 1992; b. Aug. 20, 1917, Laurinburg, IL; home, Durham; U. of NC, B.A. 1939, J.D. 1946; United Methodist; married (Margaret).

Career: FBI Agent, 1941–42; Army, WWII; Asst. Dir., U. of NC Inst. of Govt., 1946–48; Practicing atty., 1948–60, 1965–86; Gov. of NC, 1961–65; Pres., Duke U., 1969–85.

Offices: 716 HSOB 20510, 202-224-3154. Also P.O. Box 25009, Raleigh 27661, 919-856-4401; P.O. Box 2137, Asheville 28802, 704-254-3099; and 401 W. Trade St., Rm. 212, Charlotte 28202, 704-371-6800.

Committees: *Banking, Housing, and Urban Affairs* (7th of 12 D). Subcommittees: International Finance and Monetary Policy; Securities. *Budget* (8th of 13 D). *Foreign Relations* (8th of 10 D). Subcommittees: International Economic Policy, Trade, Oceans and Environment; Terrorism, Narcotics and International Operations; Western Hemisphere and Peace Corps Affairs. *Select Committee on Ethics* (3d of 3 D).

Group Ratings

	ADA	ACLU	COPE	CFA	LCV	ACU	NTLC	NSI	COC	CEI
1988	90	76	87	92	80	4	9	11	43	8
1987	85	—	90	75	—	8	—	—	28	25

National Journal Ratings

	1988 LIB — 1988 CONS		1987 LIB — 1987 CONS	
Economic	74%	— 19%	74%	— 0%
Social	70%	— 29%	58%	— 40%
Foreign	86%	— 0%	81%	— 0%

Key Votes

1) Cut Aged Housing $	FOR	5) Bork Nomination	AGN	9) SDI Funding	AGN
2) Override Hwy Veto	FOR	6) Ban Plastic Guns	—	10) Ban Chem Weaps	AGN
3) Kill Plnt Clsng Notice	AGN	7) Deny Abortions	AGN	11) Aid To Contras	AGN
4) Min Wage Increase	FOR	8) Japanese Reparations	FOR	12) Reagan Defense $	AGN

Election Results

1986 general	Terry Sanford (D)	823,662	(52%)	($4,168,509)
	James T. Broyhill (R)	767,668	(48%)	($5,188,244)
1986 primary	Terry Sanford (D)	409,394	(60%)	
	John Ingram (D)	111,557	(16%)	
	Fountain Odom (D)	49,689	(7%)	
	William Irwin Belk (D)	33,821	(5%)	
1980 general	John P. East (R)	898,064	(50%)	($1,175,875)
	Robert Morgan (D)	887,653	(49%)	($948,209)

FIRST DISTRICT

"Beaufort retains the charm and flavor of an 18th century seacoast town," wrote the *WPA Guide* 50 years ago. "Narrow streets curve between neatly whitewashed rows of spreading oaks and elms. Houses with narrow porches and no eaves front the sea and churches with low wooden steeples, surrounded by cemeteries filled with weather-stained monuments, appear much as they did a century ago." Morehead City, next door on Bogue Sound, was "the more modern town, a resort, fishing center, and ocean port. The Atlantic & North Carolina R.R., nicknamed the Old Mullet because of the quantities of mullet formerly shipped over it, bisects the broad main street. Summer cottages are scattered over treeless blocks to the west, separated from the business district by the Promised Land, shacks and small houses occupied by boatmen and commercial fishermen." This was coastal North Carolina 50 years ago—old, deeply rooted, but poor and not very picturesque. On the Outer Banks stood the monument to the Wright Brothers, where they made their first flight at Kitty Hawk; near Manteo was the site where the only record left of the first English settlement 400 years ago was the word "Croatoan" carved on a tree.

Today Morehead City and Manteo are the centers of thriving resort areas, where newcomers savor the bleakly beautiful beaches on either side of treacherous Cape Hatteras. Inland, in the counties where towns held celebrations for the ripening of each crop 50 years ago, there is also growth, not only small factories but also from military bases and East Carolina University in Greenville. The Outer Banks from Kitty Hawk to Morehead City and east Carolina inland to Greenville and Ahoskie, make up North Carolina's 1st Congressional District. This has always been Democratic country, and still is: Michael Dukakis carried 9 of its 21 counties and won 46% here, and statewide Democrats always carry it, though Jesse Helms tends to cut into their margins. National Democratic politicians now come from the required-to-be-smoke-free rooms of Minnesota, New York and San Francisco. But they cannot forget, if they count their votes, that it's hard for them to win 270 electoral votes without carrying a big margin in tobacco-growing east Carolina.

The congressman from the 1st District, Walter Jones, reelected in 1988 at 75, often wheelchair-bound, looks like an archetypal southern Democrat, and for years he looked after local crops from the chair of the Tobacco and Peanuts Subcommittee of Agriculture. But he handed it over to the 7th District's Charlie Rose in 1980 to take over the chairmanship of the Merchant Marine and Fisheries Committee. This aging and often ill congressman has taken an aging and often ailing committee and pumped life and verve into it. He is working to patch up the tattered system of maritime subsidies and exemptions, and has adeptly attached his cause to every topical issue that comes along. If you are concerned about oil shortages and the environment, his committee has passed his bill to allow oil exploration in the Arctic National Wildlife Refuge with a "protective management zone" to save animals. If you are worried about the drug traffic, he has a plan to expand the Coast Guard. Just when you're reading about the divers who found the wreck of the Titanic, here he is with a bill to prevent commercial exploitation of it. And if you're not worried now about the Navy's sealift capacity in time of war, here is Chairman Jones with facts and figures about why we must subsidize and protect high-wage U.S. flag ships in order to have the sealift capacity when we need it.

Of course there are local interests at stake. Jones is pushing a five-year Albemarle-Pamlico Estuary study and is urging stabilization of the oft-wandering Oregon Inlet between the barrier isles. He got passed a bill giving inshore shrimp fishermen a delay from the requirement to use Sea Turtle Excluder Devices on their trawlers, another bill requiring commercial fishing boats to carry safety equipment and a declaration that beaches affected by red tide were disaster areas. It begins to look as if Jones has been aiming through his long congressional career at holding this chairmanship, which was also held by his 1st District predecessor Herbert Bonner. One tipoff is this: he votes a solid national Democratic line on most issues. Committee chairmen are elected by the Democratic Caucus, and Jones has obviously been taking care for years, long before most members thought he wanted the post, to make sure that most northern liberal Democrats would have no reason to vote reflexively against him for this chairmanship he dearly wants. At the same time he has taken care to keep his standing high at home. In 1984 a high-spending primary opponent held him to 61% of the vote, but he has had no primary opponent since, and seems determined to convince voters that he is an active and useful representative.

The People: Est. Pop. 1986: 581,400, up 8.4% 1980–86; Pop. 1980: 536,219, up 13.2% 1970–80. Households (1980): 77% family, 43% with children, 61% married couples; 32.4% housing units rented; median monthly rent: $111; median house value: $33,600. Voting age pop. (1980): 382,422; 32% Black, 1% Spanish origin.

1988 Presidential Vote:

Bush (R)	97,424	(54%)
Dukakis (D).	83,301	(46%)

Rep. Walter B. Jones (D)

Elected 1966; b. Aug. 19, 1913, Fayetteville; home, Farmville; NC St. U., B.S. 1934; Baptist; married (Elizabeth).

Career: Office supply business, 1934–49; Mayor of Farmville, 1949–53; NC House of Reps., 1955–59; NC Senate, 1965–66.

Offices: 241 CHOB 20515, 202-225-3101. Also 108 E. Wilson St., P.O. Drawer 90, Farmville 27828, 919-753-3082.

Committees: *Agriculture* (2d of 27 D). Subcommittees: Cotton, Rice and Sugar; Tobacco and Peanuts. *Merchant Marine and Fisheries* (Chairman of 26 D). Subcommittee: Merchant Marine (Chairman).

Group Ratings

	ADA	ACLU	COPE	CFA	LCV	ACU	NTLC	NSI	COC	CEI
1988	80	72	50	64	50	13	6	0	46	12
1987	56	—	49	57	—	0	—	—	21	7

National Journal Ratings

	1988 LIB — 1988 CONS		1987 LIB — 1987 CONS	
Economic	57% —	41%	62% —	35%
Social	66% —	34%	55% —	45%
Foreign	64% —	36%	57% —	42%

Key Votes

1) Homeless $	AGN	5) Ban Drug Test	AGN
2) Gephardt Amdt	FOR	6) Drug Death Pen	—
3) Deficit Reduc	FOR	7) Handgun Sales	FOR
4) Kill Plnt Clsng Notice	AGN	8) Ban D.C. Abort $	AGN

9) SDI Research	—
10) Ban Chem Weaps	—
11) Aid to Contras	AGN
12) Nuclear Testing	FOR

Election Results

1988 general	Walter B. Jones (D)	118,027	(65%)	($82,147)
	Howard D. Moye (R)	63,013	(35%)	($16,758)
1988 primary	Walter B. Jones (D), unopposed			
1986 general	Walter B. Jones (D)	91,122	(70%)	($87,114)
	Howard Moye (R).	39,912	(30%)	($47,184)

SECOND DISTRICT

Half a century ago, one-quarter of American cigarettes including the leading brand of the time, Lucky Strikes, all came from the small city of Durham, North Carolina. It had been farmland 75 years before, when a young Confederate veteran returned home to his family's farm and began grinding tobacco and selling it to mustered-out soldiers. His son, James B. Duke, invented the cigarette in 1880 and created the American Tobacco Trust in 1890; he built Durham as the site for his cigarette factories and near the end of his life, from his mansion in New York City, he endowed Durham's Duke University, now one of the great institutions in the land. By 1940, the Trust had been broken up, but Lucky Strikes were just on the verge of going to war—a war in which smoking would become almost universal.

The coastal plain of North Carolina had been tobacco growing country since it was settled in the 18th century, and tobacco has remained central to its economy ever since. For tobacco is a labor-intensive crop, requiring lots of labor and capable of producing a living off a small plot of land—if, that is, it has one of the tobacco allotments the government handed out during the Depression. North Carolina's 2d Congressional District occupies a major portion of its tobacco lands north of Raleigh and south of the Virginia line. Durham is the district's largest city, with its boundary wiggling around and excluding Raleigh just to the east; on the other side of Raleigh it includes the town of Rocky Mount. You can still find tobacco marketed here in the old courthouse towns, and there are textiles produced in mills scattered here and there, usually near rivers or main highways; new subdivisions are being built on farm and forest land out in the country. Historically, textile mills didn't hire blacks, but Duke's and the other tobacco factories did, and many black farmers grow tobacco as well (and today a higher proportion of blacks than whites smoke cigarettes). The 2d District has more blacks than any other House seat in North Carolina, 36% of the population in 1980, 28% of the registered voters in 1981 and 37% in 1986.

The 2d District used to be represented by a black in Congress—but not since the last century. George White, a Republican and a contemporary of James B. Duke, won the seat in 1896 and 1898; the Democrats, running on a platform of education and segregation, won it in 1900 and have held it ever since. For 30 years it was held by a conservative, white-linen-suited Democrat, L. H. Fountain; when he retired in 1982, he was succeeded by a Democrat of similar ilk, Tim Valentine, who beat two strong black candidates from Durham. The first was H. M. (Mickey) Michaux, the local U.S. attorney in the Carter years, who sparked a large black turnout in the 1982 runoff—109,000 people voted, as opposed to 93,000 in the general election—and got 46% of the vote; he got 14% as a write-in in the general election that year, though he repudiated the effort. His defeat was cited constantly by Jesse Jackson in 1984 as one reason for abolishing runoff primaries. In 1984, the challenger was Ken Spaulding, a state legislator and member of the family that owns a big insurance company in Durham. In a turnout of 125,000, Spaulding won 48% of the vote.

Since then Valentine has not had primary opposition. One reason is that it is hard to paint him as a Reagan conservative. His voting record is smack at the midpoint of the House on most issues, and with other Democrats in the partisan North Carolina delegation he works with the party leadership on tough issues. A second is that he has an obvious political incentive to provide services to black constituents and vote their way on major issues; for a black-based candidacy is the only one to which he could lose. Finally, he has some locally useful committee assignments. He now serves on the Public Works and Transportation and Science, Space and Technology committees; he chairs the Transportation, Aviation and Materials Subcommittee which, along with his other seats, provides a politically useful post for a congressman whose district takes in part of the Research Triangle high-tech park between Raleigh, Durham and Chapel Hill. On that subcommittee, he distinguished himself in 1988 by ridiculing and helping to sidetrack

Pennsylvania Congressman Robert Walker's "drug-free workplace" amendment as a cheap shot.

The People: Est. Pop. 1986: 568,100, up 5.9% 1980–86; Pop. 1980: 536,210, up 10.4% 1970–80. Households (1980): 76% family, 43% with children, 59% married couples; 39.0% housing units rented; median monthly rent: $119; median house value: $34,700. Voting age pop. (1980): 382,220; 36% Black, 1% Spanish origin.

1988 Presidential Vote:
Dukakis (D)........................	93,736	(50%)
Bush (R)	92,768	(49%)

Rep. Tim Valentine (D)

Elected 1982; b. Mar. 15, 1926, Nash County; home, Nashville; The Citadel, A.B. 1948, U. of NC, LL.B., 1952; Baptist; married (Barbara).

Career: Air Force, WWII; NC House of Reps., 1955–60; Legal Advisor to the Gov., 1965, Cnsl. to the Gov., 1967; Chmn., NC Dem. Exec. Cmtee., 1966–68; Practicing atty., 1952–82.

Offices: 1510 LHOB 20515, 202-225-4531. Also 121 E. Parrish St., Durham 27701, 919-683-1495; and 124 Station Sq., Rocky Mount 27804, 919-446-1147.

Committees: *Public Works and Transportation* (13th of 31 D). Subcommittees: Aviation; Surface Transportation. *Science, Space and Technology* (13th of 30 D). Subcommittees: Energy Research and Development; Natural Resources, Agriculture Research and Environment; Transportation, Aviation and Materials (Chairman).

Group Ratings

	ADA	ACLU	COPE	CFA	LCV	ACU	NTLC	NSI	COC	CEI
1988	45	52	46	82	63	48	38	70	62	36
1987	44	—	42	43	—	29	—	—	60	27

National Journal Ratings

	1988 LIB — 1988 CONS		1987 LIB — 1987 CONS	
Economic	43% —	56%	49% —	50%
Social	50% —	48%	38% —	61%
Foreign	43% —	56%	40% —	59%

Key Votes

1) Homeless $	FOR	5) Ban Drug Test	FOR	9) SDI Research	AGN
2) Gephardt Amdt	FOR	6) Drug Death Pen	FOR	10) Ban Chem Weaps	AGN
3) Deficit Reduc	FOR	7) Handgun Sales	FOR	11) Aid to Contras	AGN
4) Kill Plnt Clsng Notice	FOR	8) Ban D.C. Abort $	AGN	12) Nuclear Testing	AGN

Election Results

1988 general	Tim Valentine (D).....................	128,832	(100%)	($84,671)
1988 primary	Tim Valentine (D), unopposed			
1986 general	Tim Valentine (D).....................	95,320	(75%)	($164,680)
	Bud McElhaney (R)..................	32,515	(25%)	($69,193)

THIRD DISTRICT

One of the economic growth success stories of the last 50 years in the United States is the flat coastal plain of eastern North Carolina. Today, it lacks metropolitan glitter and stands below the national average in income; but it has come far. Fifty years ago, its small farms and little cities were homes mainly to tenant farmers and mill hands, people raising families in thin-walled frame houses often with no electricity or running water, in an economy where most people didn't handle paper money every day and had no occasion to have bank accounts. Today, most of the farmers here mostly own their own land, the textile mill workers are better paid, and the variety of jobs from which people can choose is far greater—for the four-lane roads and interstates take you quickly from the coastal counties to the booming Raleigh-Durham metropolitan area and to dozens of new businesses that are sprouting up in the countryside. Yet it is not necessary to leave your roots or your family, and you can live in a community where traditional moral principles are valued and where traditional religion remains strong.

The 3d Congressional District of North Carolina covers much of this coastal plain. Most of its people are clustered within 50 miles of Raleigh; settlement is sparser in the sandy-soiled counties nearer the coast. Coastal North Carolina was settled by Englishmen who were Anglicans and became Methodists, they tended to have a few slaves and support the Confederacy, and they have tended to vote Democratic ever since. Farther west in the Piedmont the settlement was Scots-Irish, the church Presbyterian, the 1861 sentiment Union, and the politics ever since often Republican.

Tobacco remains the most important crop, especially politically, since its profitable cultivation depends heavily on government programs which are constantly under political attack. Another major buttress of the economy here is the military. The 3d District is the home of Seymour Johnson Air Force Base near Goldsboro and the Marine Corps's Camp Lejeune on the swampy coast; just over the district line is the Army's Fort Bragg near Fayetteville. The sight of servicemen with their short haircuts cruising on one of the garish strip highways outside the base is not an exotic one here.

With a lower black percentage and greater military concentrations, the 3d District ends up somewhat less Democratic than the other North Carolina coastal districts. In presidential elections, it voted twice for Jimmy Carter, but is otherwise Republican; it has voted three times for Senator Jesse Helms, but in House races has stayed Democratic.

The current congressman is Martin Lancaster, an experienced state legislator from Goldsboro who ran when incumbent Charles Whitley decided to retire in 1986. Lancaster grew up on a tobacco farm, served in the Navy in the Vietnam war, served since 1978 in the legislature and in his third session was voted the fifth most effective legislator of 120 by the state Center for Public Policy Research. He was an ally of Governor Jim Hunt and shepherded major bills, like a tough drunk driving measure, through the legislature. The primary contest turned out to be a classic friends-and-neighbors contest; Lancaster got 85% in a big turnout in his home county and only 13% in his major opponent's. But Lancaster did best where no other candidate was strong and led 44%–26% in the first primary, and the opponent declined to call for a runoff. He was not seriously challenged in the 1986 general and was unopposed in 1988.

Lancaster bills himself as a conservative; in the North Carolina context, however, he stood with progressive Democrats like Jim Hunt, and he has a voting record in the House similar to that of the other North Carolina Democrats, at the midpoint of the House between conservative and liberal on economic, cultural and foreign policy issues. He seems to spend lots of time on local issues and serves on Armed Services, of obvious importance to the district. He won a temporary seat on Agriculture, in time for the 1989 farm bill: since coastal North Carolina already has two of the four top-ranked Democrats on the committee (and the Democrat from the next-door South Carolina is on too), the tobacco and peanuts programs seem well protected. Lancaster protested when the Agriculture Department appointed a burley man as a local tobacco inspector (burley is the tobacco grown in Kentucky) and when the Small Business Administration wouldn't declare red tide a disaster. He got a bill through for disaster relief for the fishermen and has introduced a bill to require plastic containers to be biodegradable (the 3d District produces biodegradable plastic). Lancaster can obviously remain congressman here as long as he wants; the only question is whether he might want to run for governor or Senator some day.

The People: Est. Pop. 1986: 572,600, up 6.9% 1980–86; Pop. 1980: 535,906, up 13.2% 1970–80. Households (1980): 80% family, 47% with children, 65% married couples; 33.2% housing units rented; median monthly rent: $123; median house value: $31,500. Voting age pop. (1980): 379,853; 25% Black, 2% Spanish origin, 1% American Indian.

1988 Presidential Vote: Bush (R)   85,776   (58%)
Dukakis (D).   62,862   (42%)

Rep. H. Martin Lancaster (D)

Elected 1986; b. Mar. 24, 1943, Wayne Cnty.; home, Goldsboro; U. of NC, A.B. 1965, J.D. 1967; Presbyterian; married (Alice).

Career: Research Asst., U.S. Senate Sbcmtee. on Constitutional Rights, 1966; Navy, 1967–70; Practicing atty.; NC House of Reps., 1978–86.

Offices: 1417 LHOB 20515, 202-225-3415. Also Fed. Bldg., Goldsboro 27530, 919-736-1844.

Committees: *Agriculture* (26th of 27 D). Subcommittee: Tobacco and Peanuts. *Armed Services* (27th of 31 D). Subcommittees: Military Personnel and Compensation; Readiness. *Small Business* (21st of 27 D). Subcommittees: Procurement, Tourism and Rural Development; Exports, Tax Policy and Special Problems.

Group Ratings

	ADA	ACLU	COPE	CFA	LCV	ACU	NTLC	NSI	COC	CEI
1988	60	65	73	73	69	40	34	80	64	27
1987	60	—	75	57	—	17	—	—	40	22

National Journal Ratings

	1988 LIB — 1988 CONS		1987 LIB — 1987 CONS	
Economic	44%	— 55%	50%	— 49%
Social	50%	— 50%	51%	— 48%
Foreign	46%	— 53%	44%	— 55%

Key Votes

1) Homeless $	FOR	5) Ban Drug Test	AGN	9) SDI Research	AGN
2) Gephardt Amdt	FOR	6) Drug Death Pen	FOR	10) Ban Chem Weaps	AGN
3) Deficit Reduc	FOR	7) Handgun Sales	FOR	11) Aid to Contras	AGN
4) Kill Plnt Clsng Notice	FOR	8) Ban D.C. Abort $	AGN	12) Nuclear Testing	AGN

Election Results

1988 general	Martin Lancaster (D)	95,323	(100%)	($98,956)
1988 primary	Martin Lancaster (D), unopposed			
1986 general	H. Martin Lancaster (D)	71,460	(64%)	($439,725)
	Gerald B. Hurst (R)	39,408	(36%)	($61,265)

FOURTH DISTRICT

Half a century ago, almost no one would have thought Raleigh-Durham, North Carolina, would have one of the nation's fastest growing economies. But there it is, number four on *Inc.* magazine's list for 1989. In the 1940s, Raleigh was a sleepy state capital, with aging downtown buildings; Durham was a cigarette factory town, with a university off to the side; Chapel Hill was a tiny university town nearby. But in the middle 1950s, Governor Luther Hodges opened Research Triangle Park between the three towns, as an attempt to get high-tech business into North Carolina's low-wage environment before anyone heard the term high-tech. With continued boosts from government (there's a big EPA research center there), it has plainly succeeded. By the middle 1980s, the Raleigh-Durham area had one of the nation's lowest unemployment rates, and wage levels and economic growth which North Carolinians of Hodges's era would have found unbelievable. There are still some poor neighborhoods here, and the downtowns are not glittering; but evidence of the growth is apparent in the shopping centers and pine-shaded neighborhoods of colonial houses farther out.

The 4th Congressional District of North Carolina includes Raleigh, Chapel Hill and three rural counties, one north of Raleigh and two to the west (Durham is in the 2d District). The politics in the rural counties is typical of old North Carolina: two are conservative Democratic; the farthest west, which has a Quaker tradition, is solidly Republican. But Chapel Hill and surrounding Orange County vote like a liberal university town in California or the Midwest; Raleigh and Wake County, the home base of Jesse Helms and Jim Hunt, of Terry Sanford's law firm and Tom Ellis's Congressional Club, have been much fought over. For a time it seemed that Helms's side had the advantage, capturing the lion's share of votes of affluent technical-minded newcomers. But in the late 1980s Helms's vitriolic style and his allies' increasing religiosity has repelled new voters, while the Democrats have come up with candidates who have appealed to them.

The prime case in point is the 4th District's Congressman, David Price. A political science professor at Duke, he had practical political experience as the state Democratic Party chairman when Jim Hunt was governor; he also had national political experience as executive director of the Hunt commission that revised the Democrats' rules between the 1980 and 1984 elections, and for the first time brought party and elected officials into the process. In a state where traditional religion is strong, Price also had an authentic religious background; he graduated from divinity school at Yale and has been active as a lay Baptist preacher.

All this put Price in a strong position in 1986 when he challenged 4th District Republican Bill Cobey, former University of North Carolina athletic director and a strong Helms man. Cobey had beaten a weak Democrat hobbled by a drunk driving conviction and with only a rural base in 1984; Cobey sent out letters beginning "Dear Christian friend" that cost him support. Price had already won a 48%–32% victory over state Senator Wilma Woodard, and this was a district that had backed Hunt over Helms two years before; he won 56%–44%.

In the House, Price became one of the political entrepreneurs he has written about. Noting that his district was full of young, shallowly rooted, upwardly mobile independent voters, he homed in on issues that would affect their lives. He pushed to passage a law requiring greater disclosure of the terms of home equity loans, he pushed a bill for lower down payments on FHA-insured mortgages, he got a new veterans' counseling center in Raleigh and pushed for a new environmental lab at Research Triangle. He was just a bit more independent of the Democratic leadership than other North Carolina Democrats, voting against the 1987 budget bill that Jim Wright carried by just one vote, and voting for the House to say the Pledge of Allegiance each legislative day.

Price's theory was tested in the 1988 general election and it worked. He was opposed by Tom Fetzer, a protégé of Helms and the late Senator John East, who, as Price pointed out in an ad, had done little in his adult life except work for the Congressional Club and its allies. Fetzer's attacks, in contrast, didn't dent Price, and the incumbent won by a 58%–42% margin. This is not only the best margin anyone has won in this district since 1976, it is also the first time an incumbent (except for one election when he was unopposed) has improved his percentage since 1974. Price hesitates to say that he has made a safe seat out of what was once one of the most fiercely contested districts in the country. Price has been mentioned as a possible senatorial candidate against Jesse Helms in 1990.

The People: Est. Pop. 1986: 618,500, up 15.9% 1980–86; Pop. 1980: 533,580, up 27.3% 1970–80. Households (1980): 73% family, 40% with children, 60% married couples; 35.0% housing units rented; median monthly rent: $182; median house value: $47,000. Voting age pop. (1980): 395,635; 18% Black, 1% Spanish origin, 1% Asian origin.

1988 Presidential Vote:

Bush (R)	132,495	(55%)
Dukakis (D)	105,357	(44%)

Rep. David E. Price (D)

Elected 1986; b. Aug. 17, 1940, Johnson City, TN; home, Chapel Hill; U. of NC, Chapel Hill, B.A. 1961, Yale U., B.D. 1964, Ph.D. 1969; Baptist; married (Lisa).

Career: Legis. Aide to U.S. Sen. E.L. Bartlett, 1963–67; Duke U., Asst. Prof., 1967–73, Prof.,1973–86; NC Dem. Party, Exec. Dir., 1979–80, Chmn., 1983–84; Staff Dir., DNC Comm. on Pres. Nominations, 1981–82.

Offices: 1224 LHOB 20515, 202-225-1784. Also 225 Hillsborough St., Ste, 330 Raleigh 27603, 919-857-8611; 1777 Chapel Hill-Durham Blvd., Ste. 100, Chapel Hill 27514, 919-967-8500; and 101 Fed. Bldg., Sunset Ave., Asheboro 27203, 919-625-3060.

Committees: *Banking, Finance and Urban Affairs* (27th of 31 D). Subcommittees: Consumer Affairs and Coinage; Financial Institutions Supervision, Regulation and Insurance; Housing and Community Development. *Science, Space and Technology* (23d of 30 D). Subcommittees: Natural Resources, Agriculture Research and Environment; Science, Research and Technology.

Group Ratings

	ADA	ACLU	COPE	CFA	LCV	ACU	NTLC	NSI	COC	CEI
1988	75	70	87	73	69	24	30	20	62	25
1987	80	—	81	71	—	9	—	—	33	21

National Journal Ratings

	1988 LIB	—	1988 CONS	1987 LIB	—	1987 CONS
Economic	46%	—	52%	53%	—	46%
Social	58%	—	40%	62%	—	36%
Foreign	59%	—	40%	66%	—	32%

Key Votes

1) Homeless $	AGN	5) Ban Drug Test	AGN	9) SDI Research	AGN
2) Gephardt Amdt	FOR	6) Drug Death Pen	FOR	10) Ban Chem Weaps	FOR
3) Deficit Reduc	AGN	7) Handgun Sales	FOR	11) Aid to Contras	AGN
4) Kill Plnt Clsng Notice	AGN	8) Ban D.C. Abort $	AGN	12) Nuclear Testing	FOR

Election Results

1988 general	David E. Price (D)	131,896	(58%)	($1,006,641)
	Tom Fetzer (R)	95,482	(42%)	($745,726)
1988 primary	David E. Price (D), unopposed			
1986 general	David E. Price (D)	92,216	(56%)	($854,616)
	William W. Cobey (R)	73,469	(44%)	($792,031)

FIFTH DISTRICT

The Piedmont, wrote Jonathan Daniels 50 years ago, "has always been a more serious-minded land. In contrast to the east" of North Carolina, "it seems to have grown from the stern spirits of the Quakers of Guilford, the Moravians of Forsyth, the Calvinists of Mecklenburg, the ubiquitous Baptists, and that practical Methodism from which the Dukes emerged. The plantation disappeared at the fall line. Where there was little Negro labor, there was water falling in the streams. Hard-working, hard-headed men, with no foreknowledge of the inevitable change in relationship from money and land to money and machinery, attached themselves and their region to the change. Doing so long ago, they took the Piedmont into the direct stream of mechanical America. Its people are stirring or struggling. Wealth here has more sharply stratified society than in the older and more aristocratic east. But unlike some other industrial areas, its people are homogeneous. There are more foreign corporations than there are foreign workers. It is modern and American in almost every familiar connotation of these terms."

That description still suffices: the Piedmont's economy has diversified, but textiles and tobacco are still of exceeding importance; it has grown more prosperous; ethnically, it is still mostly Scots-Irish but differences in religious beliefs sometimes produce political conflicts over cultural issues. One of the largest cities in the Piedmont, within sight of the first Appalachian ridges, is Winston-Salem, the combination of the 18th century Mennonite Salem and 19th century Presbyterian Winston. For years this was the home of the R. J. Reynolds tobacco company, which became part of RJR Nabisco, was moved by one hotshot CEO to Atlanta, was the object in 1988 of the largest leveraged buy-out to date, and is now moving some of its operations to New York. In the meantime, many in Winston-Salem have become millionaires, including members of the Reynolds family who have endowed Wake Forest University here and other institutions.

Winston-Salem is the largest city in North Carolina's 5th Congressional District, which extends eastward to the industrial town of Eden and west to the mountains on both sides of the Blue Ridge in the west. The mountain Republican tradition lives on here, particularly in Wilkes County, home of the Holly Farms chicken operation which, only on the most unusual occasions, votes Democratic; the Piedmont has long tended to be Republican. Its differences from the east Carolina coastal plain seem to go back to the days of settlement: the English, Episcopal and Methodist, slaveholding east favored secession and has always been Democratic; the Scots-Irish, Presbyterian and sectarian, non-slaveholding Piedmont has leaned strongly to the Republicans, though never much to Jesse Helms, whose crypto-segregationist politics has appeal in the east but turns off traditional Republicans in the Piedmont and mountains.

The congressional politics of the 5th District has been dominated by types whom Daniels would recognize. The incumbent congressman, Steve Neal, is a quiet, unoratorical former mortgage banker who is, among other things, the grandnephew of R. J. Reynolds—part of the elite in this stratified society. He upset a Republican incumbent in the Watergate year of 1974 and has held the district ever since by narrow margins in every year but 1980, the best Republican year in the last 20, in which Republicans unaccountably didn't have a serious candidate. Like other North Carolina Democrats, he has a voting record in the middle of the road in the House. Early in his House career Neal won note for stopping a power plant and saving the New River, which flows into the Piedmont.

Neal has spent much time on the Banking Committee, on which he currently ranks fourth. He used to chair the subcommittee which handled the International Monetary Fund and the Export-Import Bank, and was attacked for helping countries that compete with North Carolina textiles. In 1987, he took over the subcommittee that handles monetary policy, on which he has backed Federal Reserve Chairman Alan Greenspan's early 1989 efforts to hold the economy down to stop inflation. On Banking, Neal has been a deregulator, voting to break down the barriers that have kept the banks out of the securities business since 1933 and to let the savings and loans into businesses other than housing. The latter helped produce the S&L crisis of the late 1980s, and Neal may be called on to explain why he blocked earlier efforts to have the S&Ls bail themselves out before the taxpayers had to be called in to do the job for tens of billions of dollars more.

In 1984 and 1986, Neal had close races against Stuart Epperson, a Republican of the religious right. In 1988, his opponent was Lyons Gray, son and grandson of presidents of R.J. Reynolds and first cousin of top George Bush aide C. Boyden Gray. Lyons Gray argued not that Neal is a liberal, which was not very credible, but that he was mediocre: "Not bad isn't good enough." But Gray made one terrible mistake when he allowed a questionnaire to be returned to the AFL-CIO indicating he opposed the protectionist textile bills which every other Carolina congressman supports. He also erred in calling for the closing down of 3,500 foreign bases (there aren't nearly that many), and Neal ran ads saying, "Lyons Gray? You can't believe him." After all this, Neal won 53%–47%, not a strong showing for a veteran, but a win after all in a district that was voting 60%–40% for Bush and which went Republican for governor, lieutenant governor and auditor general as well. It would be prudent to expect another serious contest in the 5th in 1990.

The People: Est. Pop. 1986: 563,800, up 5.3% 1980–86; Pop. 1980: 535,212, up 16.5% 1970–80 Households (1980): 77% family, 42% with children, 64% married couples; 27.8% housing units rented; median monthly rent: $136; median house value: $36,500. Voting age pop. (1980): 388,006; 15% Black 1% Spanish origin.

1988 Presidential Vote:

Bush (R)	123,725	(60%)
Dukakis (D)	81,340	(40%)

Rep. Stephen L. Neal (D)

Elected 1974; b. Nov. 7, 1934, Winston-Salem; home, Winston-Salem; U. of CA at Santa Barbara, U. of HI, A.B. 1959; Presbyterian; married (Landis).

Career: Bank executive, 1959–66; Newspaper business, 1966–74; Pres., Community Press, Inc., Suburban Newspapers, Inc., King Publishing Co., and Yadkin Printing Co., Inc.

Offices: 2463 RHOB 20515, 202-225-2071. Also 421 Fed. Bldg., Winston-Salem 27101, 919-761-3125.

Committees: *Banking, Finance and Urban Affairs* (4th of 31 D). Subcommittees: Domestic Monetary Policy (Chairman); Financial Institutions Supervision, Regulation and Insurance; Housing and Community Development; International Development, Finance, Trade and Monetary Policy. *Government Operations* (7th of 24 D). Subcommittee: Legislation and National Security.

Group Ratings

	ADA	ACLU	COPE	CFA	LCV	ACU	NTLC	NSI	COC	CEI
1988	70	76	54	82	75	21	39	33	50	28
1987	68	—	52	57	—	5	—	—	60	30

National Journal Ratings

	1988 LIB — 1988 CONS		1985 LIB — 1987 CONS	
Economic	48% —	52%	46% —	52%
Social	70% —	28%	61% —	39%
Foreign	66% —	33%	62% —	37%

Key Votes

1) Homeless $	AGN	5) Ban Drug Test	—	9) SDI Research	AGN
2) Gephardt Amdt	FOR	6) Drug Death Pen	FOR	10) Ban Chem Weaps	AGN
3) Deficit Reduc	FOR	7) Handgun Sales	FOR	11) Aid to Contras	AGN
4) Kill Plnt Clsng Notice	AGN	8) Ban D.C. Abort $	AGN	12) Nuclear Testing	FOR

Election Results

1988 general	Stephen L. Neal (D)..................	110,516	(53%)	($756,115)
	Lyons Gray (R).......................	99,540	(47%)	($718,015)
1988 primary	Stephen L. Neal (D), unopposed			
1986 general	Stephen L. Neal (D)..................	86,410	(54%)	($494,014)
	Stuart Epperson (R)	73,261	(46%)	($939,377)

SIXTH DISTRICT

For more than 50 years, furniture store managers and owners from all over the country have gathered in the huge furniture mart in High Point, the center of the U.S. furniture business, for a giant trade show put on by manufacturers. The business grew here early in the 20th century because of the proximity of hardwoods in the mountains not far west and the abundance of low-wage labor in the flatlands not far east. Half a century ago, there were already 30 furniture factories and 22 hosiery mills in High Point, where 12,000 people worked in factories in a town of 36,000; another 12,000 worked in factories in Greensboro (population 53,000), 15 miles away. Once this had been rolling farmland settled by Quakers, the site of the Battle of Guilford Courthouse in the Revolutionary War. But by 1940, smokestacks were puffing at all hours and the local saying in High Point was that "only a wise man knows his own factory whistle."

Today, there are about 330,000 people in Guilford County, which contains Greensboro and High Point, and their economies are somewhat more diversified. Greensboro had its moment in history in 1960, when black students at North Carolina A&T started the lunch counter sit-in at a local five-and-dime; later in the year, a transfer student named Jesse Jackson joined their cause. The 6th Congressional District of North Carolina includes Guilford County, furniture-manufacturing Davidson County to the west and textile-producing Alamance County just to the east. For all its growth, this area still feels dependent on textiles which, as the classic cheap-labor industry, is always vulnerable to competition from abroad. In the first half of the 1980s, the 6th District had a revolving door politics, ousting incumbents in 1980, 1982 and 1984. But now it seems to have found a congressman it likes, Republican Howard Coble, who has made textile protection his number one cause.

Coble first won in 1984 when he beat a Jesse Helms-backed candidate in the Republican primary, for although his voting record is heavily conservative by Washington standards, his roots in Republican politics are with the mountain moderates; in the general he beat Democrat Robin Britt by 2,662 votes in a race in which $753,000 was spent. In 1986, there was a rematch in which $1.1 million was spent, and Coble won by exactly 79 votes—one of the closest margins in the country. In 1988, Coble was opposed by Tom Gilmore, a businessman who was a college roommate of Jim Hunt and an active campaigner who raised enough to make this another $1 million race. But this time Coble won by the comfortable margin of 62%–38%—even though Cone Mills closed down a mill in Gibsonville in October.

Coble claims he went to Washington with a sharp pencil and with no intention of sponsoring many new bills; he was one of the most vociferous opponents of the proposed 1989 pay raise and will oppose any pay increase for federal judges. He is a strong backer of the protectionist textile bill Ronald Reagan vetoed. Why the big change in the 1988 election? Coble is a likeable man at a time when North Carolina politics seemed less polarized; the textile industry seemed perhaps less beleaguered; no one is sure—just as no one is quite sure yet that Coble has a safe seat.

The People: Est. Pop. 1986: 548,700, up 3.6% 1980–86; Pop. 1980: 529,635, up 10.2% 1970–80. Households (1980): 76% family, 41% with children, 62% married couples; 32.9% housing units rented; median monthly rent: $144; median house value: $38,900. Voting age pop. (1980): 386,301; 19% Black, 1% Spanish origin.

1988 Presidential Vote: Bush (R) 118,565   (61%)
Dukakis (D). 76,208   (39%)

Rep. Howard Coble (R)

Elected 1984; b. Mar. 18, 1931, Greensboro; home, Greensboro; Guilford Col., A.B. 1958, U. of NC, J.D. 1962; Presbyterian; single.

Career: Coast Guard, 1952–56, 1977–78; NC House of Reps., 1969, 1979–83; Asst. U.S. Atty., Middle Dist. of NC, 1969–73; Commissioner, NC Dept. of Revenue, 1973–77; Practicing atty., 1979–84.

Offices: 430 CHOB 20515, 202-225-3065. Also P.O. Box 299, 324 W. Market St., Greensboro 27402, 919-333-5005; P.O. Box 1813, 116A W. 2d St., Lexington 27293, 704-246-8230; P.O. Box 814, 124 W. Elm St., Graham 27253, 919-229-0159; and 510 Ferndale Blvd., High Point 27260, 919-886-5106.

Committees: *Judiciary* (9th of 14 R). Subcommittees: Courts, Intellectual Property, and the Administration of Justice; Criminal Justice. *Merchant Marine and Fisheries* (11th of 17 R). Subcommittees: Coast Guard and Navigation; Fisheries and Wildlife Conservation and the Environment.

Group Ratings

	ADA	ACLU	COPE	CFA	LCV	ACU	NTLC	NSI	COC	CEI
1988	10	13	18	64	31	92	75	80	93	56
1987	4	—	17	7	—	87	—	—	100	76

National Journal Ratings

	1988 LIB — 1988 CONS		1987 LIB — 1987 CONS	
Economic	21%	— 77%	23%	— 76%
Social	5%	— 91%	0%	— 90%
Foreign	27%	— 71%	20%	— 76%

Key Votes

1) Homeless $	FOR	5) Ban Drug Test	FOR	9) SDI Research	FOR
2) Gephardt Amdt	AGN	6) Drug Death Pen	FOR	10) Ban Chem Weaps	FOR
3) Deficit Reduc	AGN	7) Handgun Sales	FOR	11) Aid to Contras	FOR
4) Kill Plnt Clsng Notice	FOR	8) Ban D.C. Abort $	FOR	12) Nuclear Testing	AGN

Election Results

1988 general	Howard Coble (R)	116,534	(62%)	($738,088)
	Tom Gilmore (D)	70,008	(38%)	($583,013)
1988 primary	Howard Coble (R), unopposed			
1986 general	Howard Coble (R)	72,329	(50%)	($585,703)
	Charles Robin Britt (D)	72,250	(50%)	($562,711)

SEVENTH DISTRICT

The economy of coastal North Carolina, since it was settled by Englishmen in the early 18th century and even before, has been based primarily on a single crop, tobacco. This is a plant indigenous to North America that can be cultivated profitably only in a few places in the world; it is a labor-intensive crop, requiring close tending and serial picking (one leaf on a stalk matures before the one above it); and it is valuable. Colonial farmers could make a living off 10 or 15 acres of tobacco, and today North Carolina farmers, if they have one of the tobacco allotments handed out in the 1930s or have bought the rights to one, can too. Tobacco thus produces more voters per federally assisted acre than for any other crop.

Nowhere is this more apparent than in the 7th Congressional District of North Carolina, in the southern portion of the state's coastal plain. Between its two cities—Wilmington, an old port now in the center of growing beach communities, and Fayetteville, next door to the Army's Fort Bragg—are miles of flat land, much of it used for tobacco. Also there is Robeson County, with a population that is 40% white, 35% black and 25% Lumbees Indian; altogether the Lumbees, whose ethnic origin is shrouded in history, make up 8% of the district, making the 7th the most Indian district east of the Mississippi. In recent years, new textile and apparel mills have gone up here, as well as factories built by European and Japanese companies. But wages are still well below the national average, and tobacco retains its symbolic and economic importance.

This is one of the most Democratic parts of North Carolina, and elects a Democratic congressman, Charlie Rose. He first won the seat in 1972 and has built something of a power base in the House since then. He has a seat on the House Administration Committee, and is the resident expert on the House's computer systems; he helped computerize the House in the early 1970s and has continued to refine the systems which help congressmen and their staffs in many unanticipated ways. He also set up the system by which the House, with cameras controlled by the Speaker, has televised its sessions since 1979.

For most of the 1980s, Rose has concentrated on protecting tobacco and peanuts, something he is well-positioned to do as chairman of Agriculture's Tobacco and Peanuts Subcommittee, though he has a few other pet causes (stopping patents of animals, Tibetan human rights). Since 1981, when he took the chair, he has saved the tobacco and peanut allotment systems, invented in the 1930s and 1940s to control production, which give only allotment owners the right to produce those crops and be eligible for federal assistance. Rose is of course a strong backer of subsidies and price supports for tobacco and peanuts, and has used his standing and alliances within the Democratic Party to push his position. He naturally opposes tougher warnings on cigarette packages or any other measure that discourages or penalizes smoking.

To win these fights he has played politics within the House Democratic Caucus, making unlikely alliances with northerners and persuading the leadership that a defeat on tobacco would defeat every North Carolina Democrat. The North Carolina group has been careful to support the leadership often on roll calls, and especially on tough issues; Speakers Tip O'Neill and Jim Wright have attempted to return the favors. Rose doesn't always win in intra-caucus fights: he backed Phil Burton for Majority Leader in 1976 and Charles Rangel for whip in 1986, and both lost. But in general he has been successful: the North Carolina delegation is still mostly Democratic, and tobacco and peanuts still have most of their protections.

Rose's seat in the House seems to be safe. He was tested in 1986, when during the campaign it was announced that between 1978 and 1985 he had diverted $64,000 of campaign funds for personal use. This violates House rules, but Rose admitted the violations, amended his forms, and the House Ethics Committee, acting with typical speed and rigor, ruled in March 1988 that he had violated the law but recommended no disciplinary action because of mitigating circumstances. Rose's ethics problems resurfaced in May, 1989, when the Justice Department filed a civil lawsuit that charged him with failing to report over $138,000 in loans on his financial disclosure forms. Rose claimed the Justice Department was acting out of "simple political retaliation," accusing assistant attorney general John Bolton of punishing Rose for having filed a complaint with the FEC against Jesse Helms' National Congressional Club.

The 7th District is Democratic enough—Michael Dukakis came within 3% of carrying it— that the Republicans do not run serious candidates, and Rose was reelected without difficulty in 1988. His prospects are for a continued House career (but this latest spate of ethics problems must be watched), though not as prominent a one had some of his leadership choices won.

The People: Est. Pop. 1986: 578,500, up 7.3% 1980–86; Pop. 1980: 539,055, up 19.5% 1970–80. Households (1980): 79% family, 49% with children, 63% married couples; 35.4% housing units rented; median monthly rent: $148; median house value: $33,500. Voting age pop. (1980): 371,808; 25% Black, 7% American Indian, 2% Spanish origin, 1% Asian origin.

1988 Presidential Vote:

Bush (R)	....	77,438	(51%)
Dukakis (D)	....	73,231	(48%)

Rep. Charles G. (Charlie) Rose (D)

Elected 1972; b. Aug. 10, 1939, Fayetteville; home, Fayetteville; Davidson Col., A.B. 1961, U. of NC, LL.B. 1964; Presbyterian; married (Joan).

Career: Practicing atty., 1964–72; Chf. Dist. Crt. Prosecutor, 12th Judicial Dist., 1967–70.

Offices: 2230 RHOB 20515, 202-225-2731. Also P.O. Bldg., Rm. 208, Wilmington 28401, 919-343-4959; and 218 Fed. Bldg., Fayetteville 28301, 919-323-0260.

Committees: *Agriculture* (4th of 27 D). Subcommittees: Department Operations, Research and Foreign Agriculture; Livestock, Dairy and Poultry; Tobacco and Peanuts (Chairman). *House Administration* (3d of 13 D). Subcommittees: Elections; Office Systems (Chairman).

Group Ratings

	ADA	ACLU	COPE	CFA	LCV	ACU	NTLC	NSI	COC	CEI
1988	60	73	64	64	50	11	14	25	25	14
1987	76	—	63	36	—	5	—	—	43	15

National Journal Ratings

	1988 LIB — 1988 CONS			1987 LIB — 1987 CONS		
Economic	59%	—	40%	66%	—	33%
Social	63%	—	37%	50%	—	50%
Foreign	64%	—	36%	61%	—	38%

Key Votes

1) Homeless $	AGN	5) Ban Drug Test	AGN	9) SDI Research	FOR
2) Gephardt Amdt	FOR	6) Drug Death Pen	FOR	10) Ban Chem Weaps	FOR
3) Deficit Reduc	—	7) Handgun Sales	FOR	11) Aid to Contras	AGN
4) Kill Plnt Clsng Notice	AGN	8) Ban D.C. Abort $	AGN	12) Nuclear Testing	—

Election Results

1988 general	Charles G. (Charlie) Rose (D)	102,392	(67%)	($185,039)
	George G. Thompson (R)	49,855	(33%)	
1988 primary	Charles G. (Charlie) Rose (D), unopposed			
1986 general	Charles G. (Charlie) Rose (D)	70,471	(64%)	($302,654)
	Thomas J. Harrelson (R)	39,289	(36%)	($403,005)

EIGHTH DISTRICT

The thickest concentration of the nation's textile industry for more than half a century has been along the route of Interstate 85 in the Carolina Piedmont. From Atlanta to Durham, the mills are so thick you can almost see the lint. Within North Carolina, I-85 passes through the nation's leading textile-producing area, past Salisbury, Concord and Kannapolis, a company town for years owned by Cannon Mills. Eastern North Carolina was settled by English coming up the rivers or overland from the coast, and as far west as the Sand Hills counties, not far east of Interstate 85. But the Piedmont land along Interstate 85 was settled primarily by Scots, plus diverse groups like Quakers and Moravian sects, coming down along the valleys and hills just east of the Blue Ridge from Pennsylvania through Virginia to North Carolina. These migratory patterns were reflected in Civil War divisions and in current voting habits. The coastal counties all the way up through the Sand Hills (except for the rich golfing condominium country around Southern Pines) were Confederate and are now Democratic. The textile mill towns along 85 were anti-secession and are now Republican.

The 8th Congressional District of North Carolina combines many of the textile mill counties with several Sand Hill counties. The textile counties have more people, but even so the district has been electing a Democratic congressman since Bill Hefner first won in 1974. Hefner used to be a country music disc jockey and radio station owner in Kannapolis, and his campaigns typically have featured a little Democratic oratory and a lot of country music. His politics, however, have been an adroit mix of Democratic principle and southern sentiment—adroit, because he has used his support and that of his fellow North Carolina Democrats for many Democratic programs to win crucial victories for their causes, like textile restrictions and tobacco subsidies. Hefner and others from the state stuck with the Democrats on the tough Reagan budget votes in 1981, and have been reaping the benefits ever since.

Defense is Hefner's major preoccupation. He serves on the Defense Appropriations Subcommittee and, after only eight years in the House, became Chairman of the Military Construction Appropriations Subcommittee. This is a key pork barrel committee which determines, among other things, spending on military bases including the Army's Fort Bragg (partly in the 8th District) and other North Carolina bases. Hefner must balance his desire for frugality on the one hand with the institutional bias of his chairmanship toward heavy military construction spending on the other. Hefner has been less successful in his own leadership aspirations. In 1986, he ran for whip, the number three position in the leadership, but was unable to win much support beyond his North Carolina base. He wound up with only 15 votes in the Democratic Caucus, far behind winner Tony Coelho and runner-up Charles Rangel. He was appointed a deputy whip afterwards.

Against Republicans, Hefner won reelection easily in the 1970s, but has had tougher competition in the 1980s. Jesse Helms protege Harris Blake got 49% of the vote against Hefner in 1984, and Salisbury attorney and former Senate aide Ted Blanton got 49% against him in 1988; Union County, once heavily Democratic, but now filling with young families from Charlotte, went Republican. The key election for this district could turn out to be 1990. If Hefner, who had a heart attack in 1985, should hold on with his usual off year margin in 1990, he will be well positioned for redistricting, since the likelihood is that any new North Carolina district will be a Republican seat in the foothills of the Piedmont, taking away at least several counties from the current 8th and giving Hefner in return some more Democratic territory in the Sand Hills. But if Hefner is beaten, the legislature may choose to build the new district around the new Republican.

The People: Est. Pop. 1986: 576,100, up 7.6% 1980–86; Pop. 1980: 535,526, up 17.6% 1970–80. Households (1980): 79% family, 43% with children, 66% married couples; 24.9% housing units rented; median monthly rent: $106; median house value: $32,400. Voting age pop. (1980): 381,299; 18% Black, 1% American Indian, 1% Spanish origin.

1988 Presidential Vote:

Bush (R)	119,272	(62%)
Dukakis (D)	73,450	(38%)

Rep. W. G. (Bill) Hefner (D)

Elected 1974; b. Apr. 11, 1930, Elora, TN; home, Concord; Baptist; married (Nancy).

Career: Entertainment, radio business, 1954–74.

Offices: 2161 RHOB 20515, 202-225-3715. Also P.O. Box 385, 101 Union St. S., Concord 28025, 704-933-1615, 704-786-1612; P.O. Box 4220, 507 W. Innes St., Ste. 225, Salisbury 28144, 704-636-0635; and P.O. Box 1503, 202 E. Franklin St., Rockingham 28379, 919-997-2070.

Committees: *Appropriations* (21st of 35 D). Subcommittees: Defense; Military Construction (Chairman).

Group Ratings

	ADA	ACLU	COPE	CFA	LCV	ACU	NTLC	NSI	COC	CEI
1988	65	52	55	73	31	25	17	50	50	22
1987	64	—	53	57	—	4	—	—	40	14

National Journal Ratings

	1988 LIB — 1988 CONS		1987 LIB — 1987 CONS	
Economic	52% —	47%	57% —	40%
Social	48% —	51%	45% —	54%
Foreign	49% —	50%	54% —	45%

Key Votes

1) Homeless $	AGN	5) Ban Drug Test	AGN	9) SDI Research	AGN
2) Gephardt Amdt	FOR	6) Drug Death Pen	FOR	10) Ban Chem Weaps	AGN
3) Deficit Reduc	FOR	7) Handgun Sales	FOR	11) Aid to Contras	AGN
4) Kill Plnt Clsng Notice	AGN	8) Ban D.C. Abort $	FOR	12) Nuclear Testing	FOR

Election Results

1988 general	W. G. (Bill) Hefner (D)	99,214	(52%)	($581,888)
	Ted Blanton (R)	93,463	(49%)	($242,782)
1988 primary	W. G. (Bill) Hefner (D), unopposed			
1986 general	W. G. (Bill) Hefner (D)	80,959	(58%)	($157,576)
	William G. Hamby (R)	58,941	(42%)	($50,554)

NINTH DISTRICT

"Towering business buildings" the writers of the *WPA Guide* found 50 years ago in Charlotte, the biggest city in a big state that doesn't have big cities, "great warehouses, and numerous factories. Near the South Carolina border, a score of miles east of the Appalachian foothills, the city reaches into fertile, cultivated lands from which it draws much of its life and wealth." Charlotte had "fine old trees, landscaping, and gardening" in its residential sections, and large estates beyond; but "on the southeastern edge, the city is surrounded by textile-mill villages where long rows of square, identical four-room houses are occupied by hundreds of white operatives." Blacks, 30% of the population, "live in scattered, segregated districts."

Charlotte has continued to grow in the years since, a banking and distribution center for much of the Piedmont South, and it has grown much richer; but like all American cities, it has its variations in wealth, ethnicity and race. Charlotte has handled its racial divisions probably better than most southern cities. The site of a busing order that became a landmark Supreme Court case in 1971, Charlotte complied not only peacefully but creatively, managing to improve its public schools even as it bused kids back and forth across town to attend them. In 1983 and 1985, it elected a black mayor, Harvey Gantt, who in 1963 integrated Clemson University in South Carolina; Gantt was defeated in 1987, but the chief issue appears to have been traffic rather than race.

Politically, Charlotte has long been Republican, part of the belt in the western Piedmont settled overland by Scots and Quakers and German sects from Virginia and Pennsylvania; and on economic issues it is pretty devoted to market economics. Culturally, it is more split: Jesse Helms's cultural conservatism grates on some in a city that prides itself on its tolerance. The 9th Congressional District, which includes Charlotte and all of Mecklenburg County, plus the textile county of Iredell to the north and rural Lincoln County to the northwest, elected a Republican congressman as long ago as 1928, and has elected nothing else since 1952, including Jim Martin, who left the seat in 1984 and was elected governor in 1984 and 1988. And it has a Republican congressman now, Alex McMillan, although he had to work hard to win the seat.

The reason was not any weakness of McMillan, but the strength of his opponent, Democrat D. G. Martin, a civically active lawyer with a good speaking style who promised not to take any money from PACs. He lost by only 321 votes in 1984 and won 49% in 1986, carrying Charlotte but losing the smaller counties; his promise hurt, as McMillan outraised him with the help of $316,000 he got from PACs. But McMillan had assets of his own; he is from a Charlotte family prominent in local business, a longtime civic activist, a moderate in North Carolina Republican terms who beat a candidate supported by Helms's Congressional Club 58%–42% in the 1984 primary. In 1988, with Martin no longer in the picture, McMillan won 66%–34%.

After the 1986 race, Martin made it clear he would not run again, and McMillan had more time to concentrate on legislation. His major achievement was the Transitional Housing Program, allowing a limited number of public housing tenants to retain some welfare benefits if they are working to finish high school, get job training, undergo drug treatment, or improve themselves in other specified ways. A modest, experimental program, it advances two useful ideas, that aid recipients have some responsibilities in return and that government programs should encourage and reward upwardly mobile behavior. McMillan has also spoken out for greater burden sharing, i.e., for Western Europe and Japan to pay more of the cost of their defense. His record on issues generally, moderate in North Carolina Republican circles, is one of the more conservative in the House. In 1989, McMillan moved to the powerful Energy and Commerce Committee, where although in the minority to chairman John Dingell's Democrats, he can have at least some voice in the crafting of its far-reaching legislation.

The People: Est. Pop. 1986: 593,000, up 10.6% 1980–86; Pop. 1980: 536,325, up 15.3% 1970–80. Households (1980): 74% family, 42% with children, 60% married couples; 35.7% housing units rented; median monthly rent: $164; median house value: $44,800. Voting age pop. (1980): 385,849; 21% Black, 1% Spanish origin, 1% Asian origin.

1988 Presidential Vote:

Bush (R)	140,777	(61%)
Dukakis (D)	89,322	(39%)

Rep. J. Alex McMillan III (R)

Elected 1984; b. May 9, 1932, Charlotte; home, Charlotte; U. of NC, B.A. 1954, U. of VA, M.B.A. 1958; Presbyterian; married (Caroline).

Career: Army Intelligence, 1954–56; Salesman, Carolina Paper Board Corp., 1958–83; Secy., Vice Pres., R.S. Dickson & Co., 1963–70; Secy., Vice Pres., Ruddick Corp., 1968–83; Mecklenburg Cnty. Bd. of Commissioners, 1973; Pres., CEO, Harris-Teeter Super Markets, 1976–83.

Offices: 401 CHOB 20515, 202-225-1976. Also 401 W. Trade St., Charlotte 28202, 704-372-1976; 207 W. Broad St., Statesville 28677, 704-872-7331; Municipal Bldg., Mooresville 28115, 704-663-1976; and P.O. Bldg., Rm. B-01, Lincolnton 28092, 704-735-1976.

Committees: *Energy and Commerce* (17th of 17 R). Subcommittees: Oversight and Investigations; Transportation and Hazardous Materials.

Group Ratings

	ADA	ACLU	COPE	CFA	LCV	ACU	NTLC	NSI	COC	CEI
1988	15	22	16	45	38	88	76	100	100	57
1987	4	—	15	29	—	83	—	—	100	70

National Journal Ratings

	1988 LIB — 1988 CONS			1987 LIB — 1987 CONS		
Economic	16%	—	83%	28%	—	71%
Social	18%	—	81%	0%	—	90%
Foreign	16%	—	78%	0%	—	80%

Key Votes

1) Homeless $	FOR	5) Ban Drug Test	FOR	9) SDI Research	FOR
2) Gephardt Amdt	AGN	6) Drug Death Pen	FOR	10) Ban Chem Weaps	AGN
3) Deficit Reduc	AGN	7) Handgun Sales	AGN	11) Aid to Contras	FOR
4) Kill Plnt Clsng Notice	FOR	8) Ban D.C. Abort $	FOR	12) Nuclear Testing	AGN

Election Results

1988 general	J. Alex McMillan III (R)	139,014	(66%)	($440,082)
	Mark Sholander (D)	71,802	(34%)	($32,949)
1988 primary	J. Alex McMillan III (R), unopposed			
1986 general	J. Alex McMillan III (R)	80,352	(51%)	($884,385)
	D.G. Martin (D)	76,240	(49%)	($475,545)

TENTH DISTRICT

Wreathed in the haze that gave them the name Smokies, heavily wooded, the mountains of North Carolina seem placid and old. Geologically, they are some of the oldest ranges in the world; economically, however, they are churning with activity. The hilly North Carolina counties west of Charlotte are in fact the heaviest manufacturing area in the country, not with steel plants or petrochemical machinery, but with hundreds of textile mills and some of the biggest furniture factories in the world. The 10th Congressional District of North Carolina includes six counties, plus part of another, in the western Piedmont, just where the mountains begin. The southern part of the district, on the South Carolina border, is textile country; Gaston County here has more textile workers than any other single American county. North of Gastonia, the hills rise to mountains around such towns as Morganton, the home of former Senator Sam Ervin, who died in 1985 at age 88. The nearby hardwood forests provide some of the raw materials for the big furniture factories here, like the Broyhill establishment in the town of Lenoir. Farther north, you reach some of North Carolina's most pleasant vacation country, around Grandfather Mountain.

This district, running from Piedmont to mountains, also spans the gamut of political preferences which date back to the Civil War. Even though there were not many slaves this far west, the lowland areas were pro-Confederate then and are Democratic now, though with a distinct Dixie accent. Gaston County was once a George Wallace stronghold; Cleveland County next door years ago produced a string of Democratic governors. In the northern part of the district, you come to some of North Carolina's most heavily Republican counties; Democrats are as scarce here as big plantation owners were before the war. The counties in the middle are split between the parties; on balance, however, the district has been Republican.

The congressman from this district is Cass Ballenger, a Republican who, appropriately for this area, started his own business in 1957 making plastic wrappings for J.C. Penney underwear and other garments, which now has a payroll of 220 and annual sales of $20 million. Ballenger also served, as businessmen do in these parts, on the Catawba County board of commissioners for 8 years and in the legislature for 12. He ran for Congress in 1986 after James Broyhill, scion of the furniture family and ranking Republican on the House Energy and Commerce Committee for 6 years, decided to run for the Senate; when incumbent John East killed himself, Broyhill was appointed to fill the seat. In the House primary, Ballenger promised to be a "Broyhill Republican," and beat an opponent backed by Helms's Congressional Club by winning 80% of the vote in his home county and majorities in the southern part of the district. In the general election, against the former mayor of Shelby, he lost the Democrat's home county but won comfortably elsewhere.

Like most Republicans counted as moderates in North Carolina, Ballenger has one of the most conservative voting records in the House. He serves on the Education and Labor Committee and was proud of killing OSHA regulations which he thought would have destroyed the furniture industry; he fought the Democrats' plant closing legislation; he opposed a higher minimum wage and would raise the earned income tax credit instead. He raised money for paper for Nicaragua's *La Prensa*. Serving on Public Works, he also showed some concern about the environment, closing down a hazardous waste incinerator, looking into groundwater pollution, and trying to do something about the water supply in Shelby County. His approach seems to the liking of his constituents. Ballenger was reelected 61%–39%, despite attacks on the social security "Notch Baby" issue and should have no trouble holding the seat.

The People: Est. Pop. 1986: 563,000, up 5.6% 1980–86; Pop. 1980: 532,954, up 15.6% 1970–80. Households (1980): 80% family, 44% with children, 66% married couples; 27.6% housing units rented; median monthly rent: $125; median house value: $33,400. Voting age pop. (1980): 379,876; 9% Black, 1% Spanish origin.

1988 Presidential Vote:

Bush (R)	120,503	(65%)
Dukakis (D)	63,589	(34%)

Rep. Cass Ballenger (R)

Elected 1986; b. Dec. 6, 1926, Hickory; home, Hickory; U. of NC, Amherst Col., B.A. 1948; Episcopalian; married (Donna).

Career: Catawba Cnty. Bd. of Commissioners, 1966–74, Chmn. 1970–74; NC House of Reps., 1974–76; NC Senate, 1976–86.

Offices: 218 CHOB 20515, 202-225-2576. Also P.O. Box 1830, Hickory 28603, 704-327-6100; and 832 E. Garrison Blvd., Gastonia 28054, 704-864-9922.

Committees: *Education and Labor* (12th of 13 R). Subcommittee: Health and Safety; Labor–Management Relations; Select Education. *Public Works and Transportation* (13th of 20 R). Subcommittees: Aviation; Economic Development; Water Resources.

Group Ratings

	ADA	ACLU	COPE	CFA	LCV	ACU	NTLC	NSI	COC	CEI
1988	10	13	17	27	25	92	77	100	100	73
1987	8	—	19	14	—	82	—	—	93	71

National Journal Ratings

	1988 LIB — 1988 CONS		1987 LIB — 1987 CONS	
Economic	7% —	91%	29% —	71%
Social	0% —	95%	0% —	90%
Foreign	0% —	84%	0% —	80%

Key Votes

1) Homeless $	FOR	5) Ban Drug Test	FOR	9) SDI Research	FOR
2) Gephardt Amdt	FOR	6) Drug Death Pen	FOR	10) Ban Chem Weaps	AGN
3) Deficit Reduc	AGN	7) Handgun Sales	FOR	11) Aid to Contras	FOR
4) Kill Plnt Clsng Notice	FOR	8) Ban D.C. Abort $	FOR	12) Nuclear Testing	AGN

Election Results

1988 general	Cass Ballenger (R)	112,554	(61%)	($302,215)
	Jack L. Rhyne (D)	71,865	(39%)	($44,329)
1988 primary	Cass Ballenger (R), unopposed			
1986 general	Cass Ballenger (R)	83,902	(57%)	($463,830)
	Lester D. Roark (D)	62,035	(43%)	($196,438)

ELEVENTH DISTRICT

Western North Carolina, the protrusion of the Tarheel state deep into the fastness of the eastern United States' highest and oldest mountains, is a land of long and ornery traditions. First settled by whites not long after Independence, it still has its tiny Indian communities, and has also hollow towns where people are descended from the first white settlers. Its biggest city, Asheville, is memorialized in Thomas Wolfe's novels and was a retreat for lung patients in the early 20th century. It was also the home of the eccentric George Washington Vanderbilt who built the chateau-like Biltmore mansion, now a tourist attraction, and who started the scientific study of forestry by hiring Gifford Pinchot to oversee the forests on the property. Over a ridge is the Smoky Mountains National Park, the nation's most heavily visited, 20° cooler in the summer than the lowland towns not far away. The climate and the forested, green, fog-wisped mountains have attracted millions of tourists, thousands of retirees, and people who could live anywhere—like Carl Sandburg and Billy Graham—to this area.

The orneriness of the mountains has come out in its politics. During the Civil War, it was the part of the state most reluctant to secede. With few slaves (only 5% of the people here today are black), many of the small farmers in the hollows remained loyal to the Union, and those who took up the Confederate cause did so largely because of the efforts of Governor Zebulon Vance, an Asheville native and reluctant secessionist himself. Ancestral party loyalties are strong, and evenly balanced between the parties; the retirees who have come to Asheville and pleasant places like Hendersonville and Rutherford County haven't tipped things much. The western end of the state makes up the 11th Congressional District of North Carolina, which, over the past dozen decades has been the most closely contested district in the entire nation.

It is also the only district which in four consecutive elections threw out its incumbent congressman: first in 1980, when Lamar Gudger, a one-time beneficiary of Jimmy Carter's and Jim Hunt's Democratic coattails, lost in a Republican year to 36-year-old Republican Bill Hendon; then in 1982, when Hendon was upset by 65-year-old Democrat James Clarke; again in 1984, when Hendon came back and beat Clarke with 51%; and finally in 1986, when Clarke came back and beat Hendon with 51%. At that point Hendon quit. Charles Taylor, a rich tree farmer and former state legislator, ran an aggressive race in 1988, but Clarke broke the jinx and won 50.4%–49.6%. No one would bet the house that he'll repeat in 1990.

Clarke is an apple farmer, originally from Vermont, who lives in an 1834 stagecoach inn and has made many friends in western North Carolina granting scholarships endowed by his relative and namesake James McClure. He is a loyal North Carolina Democrat, with a typically middle-of-the-road voting record. On Foreign Affairs, he opposed contra aid and favored South African sanctions. He has a seat on the Interior Committee, and was proud in 1988 of having produced a new visitors' center for the National Park on the North Carolina side. He also got a veterans' cemetery in Black Mountain and an armory for Marion. His biggest asset may have been the money he got for apple farmers who were hurt in a deep freeze in 1987; this helped him cut the Republican edge in Henderson County. Taylor attacked Clarke for his liberal ratings and for supporting congressional pay raises, but it wasn't quite enough; he may run again in 1990. Clarke, though in his 70s, asserts that he will serve as long as his health remains good. Redistricting, by the way, is not likely to affect the 11th much, since it's at one end of the state.

The People: Est. Pop. 1986: 567,500, up 6.9% 1980–86; Pop. 1980: 531,144, up 15.6% 1970–80. Households (1980): 78% family, 39% with children, 66% married couples; 24.5% housing units rented; median monthly rent: $126; median house value: $34,300. Voting age pop. (1980): 390,762; 5% Black, 1% American Indian, 1% Spanish origin.

1988 Presidential Vote:

Bush (R)	128,515	(59%)
Dukakis (D).	87,771	(40%)

Rep. James McClure Clarke (D)

Elected 1986; b. June 12, 1917, Manchester, VT; home, Fairview; Princeton U., A.B., 1939; Presbyterian; married (Elspeth).

Career: USN, 1942–45; Farmers Fed. Coop., 1939–59; Assoc. Ed., *Asheville Citizen Times*, 1961–69; Chmn., Buncombe Cnty. Bd. of Educ., 1969–76; Asst. to Pres., Warren Wilson Col., 1970–82; NC House of Reps., 1977–80; NC Senate, 1981–82; U.S. House of Reps., 1983–85; Dairy Farmer and Orchard Operator.

Offices: 217 CHOB 20515, 202-225-6401. Also 1 N. Pack Sq., Ste. 434, Ashville 28801, 704-254-1747; 301 W. Main St., Spindale 28160, 704-286-4890; and 319 W. Main St., Sylva 28779, 704-586-6631.

Committees: *Interior and Insular Affairs* (19th of 26 D). Subcommittees: Energy and the Environment; Insular and International Affairs; National Parks and Public Lands. *Foreign Affairs* (20th of 28 D). Subcommittees: Arms Control, International Security and Science; Asian and Pacific Affairs. *Select Committee on Aging* (30th of 39 D). Subcommittee: Human Services.

Group Ratings

	ADA	ACLU	COPE	CFA	LCV	ACU	NTLC	NSI	COC	CEI
1988	60	55	76	91	75	29	25	20	57	30
1987	72	—	88	64	—	0	—	—	27	14

National Journal Ratings

	1988 LIB — 1988 CONS			1987 LIB — 1987 CONS		
Economic	43%	—	56%	73%	—	0%
Social	49%	—	51%	52%	—	47%
Foreign	63%	—	36%	62%	—	37%

Key Votes

1) Homeless $	AGN	5) Ban Drug Test	AGN	9) SDI Research	AGN
2) Gephardt Amdt	FOR	6) Drug Death Pen	FOR	10) Ban Chem Weaps	FOR
3) Deficit Reduc	FOR	7) Handgun Sales	FOR	11) Aid to Contras	AGN
4) Kill Plnt Clsng Notice	FOR	8) Ban D.C. Abort $	FOR	12) Nuclear Testing	FOR

Election Results

1988 general	James McClure Clarke (D)	108,436	(50%)	($494,092)
	Charles H. Taylor (R).	106,907	(50%)	($503,289)
1988 primary	James McClure Clarke (D), unopposed			
1986 general	James McClure Clarke (D)	91,575	(51%)	($435,435)
	William M. Hendon (R).	89,069	(49%)	($474,166)

NORTH DAKOTA

North Dakota, which turns 100 in 1989, seemed "a young state" to the *WPA Guide* half a century ago. "Ruts left by the wagon trains of early explorers, military expeditions, and home seekers have not yet been effaced from the prairies. Red men and white men, who hunted buffalo and fought at the Little Big Horn, who saw the railroads push their gleaming paths across the Plains, who recall a puny young man named Theodore Roosevelt hunting in the Badlands with his short-stocked rifle, still survive to tell their tales. In those fledgling days, the land was rich with promise. Bonanza farms"—giant industrial operations in the Red River Valley—"unfolded their ample acres of wheat, thousands of cattle roamed unchecked in the gullies and over the plains of the western counties. The word spread, and from Europe and the eastern states came men and women to break the new soil. Sod houses and barns and frame homes and windmills set their seal on the prairies"—a vast, treeless expanse of the North American steppe always at the mercy of the wind, freezing cold much of the year, but swept by tornadoes and blazing hot in July and August. But it was also, once the soil was broken, some of the best wheat land in the world, empty now of Indians and buffalo, connected to markets by the rails, ready to become a cog in the industrial world which was being created by entrepreneurs and raising living standards to unparalleled heights.

And so in a sudden rush of settlement during the 20 years before World War I, North Dakota filled up to pretty much its present population; there were 632,000 people here in 1920 and the number has fluctuated in the 600,000s ever since. Wheat is not the only crop; as the plains become more arid in the west, ranching and livestock grazing—along with strip mining and oil production—become more important than wheat, and other hardy root crops like potatoes and sugar beets are grown as well. But wheat is still number one. Typically the state produces about one-tenth of the nation's crop, and a fair percentage of the world's; its durum wheat is the main ingredient of pasta, a growing market of late.

Few other states have an economy that serves the same functions as it did 90 years ago; North Dakota does. It has the nation's largest share of population—almost 25%—still living on farms and ranches. Naturally this affects people's politics. In most states, prosperity depends on the level of wages; but in North Dakota, where farmers are really small businessmen, prosperity depends on the level of profits. This is inherently volatile and uncertain: the demand for food is always there, but commodity prices in any market system are unstable—they have to be, if the market is to keep suppliers informed about demand—just as the weather is undependable. So entrepreneurs, who must make their plans on worst-case analyses, try to minimize their risks by calling on government, and in a democracy, government usually complies. The resulting farm programs are so complicated, and the circumstances of the business so uncertain that there is almost always some sort of raging dissatisfaction with the federal government's farm programs. This has made North Dakota temperamentally inclined to vote against all incumbent adminis-trations, and was the driving force behind the radical strain in its politics.

That radical strain also owes much to the immigrant origins of so many of its early settlers: Norwegians in the eastern part of the state, Canadians along the northern border, Volga Germans in the west, colonies of Poles and Czechs and Icelanders, and native Germans throughout the state. (Volga Germans were people who had migrated to Russia from Germany in the early 19th century, but who retained their German language and character. They are recorded in census figures as Russian stock.) There is an orderliness to North Dakota's small cities, a tradition of cooperative action, a willingness to support government programs even by

NORTH DAKOTA — Congressssional District, Counties, and Selected Places — *(1 At Large)*

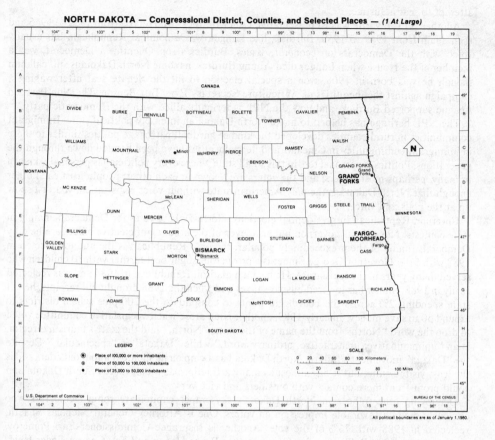

conservatives that is almost entirely absent in South Dakota and can be traced to North Dakota's German and Scandinavian heritage.

Another product, chronicled colorfully and with unusual frankness in the North Dakota Heritage Museum in Bismarck, was the Non-Partisan League (NPL) formed in 1915. Its constituency was the lonely marginal farmer, cut off in many cases from the wider American culture by the barrier of language, his fate at the mercy of the grain millers of Minneapolis, the railroads of St. Paul, the banks of New York, and the commodity traders of Chicago. The NPL's program was frankly socialistic—government ownership of the railroads and grain elevators—and, like many North Dakota ethnics, the League opposed going to war with Germany. The positions taken by the NPL won it many adherents in North Dakota, and the League spread to neighboring states. But North Dakota was its bastion. The NPL often determined the outcome of the usually decisive Republican primary and sometimes swung its support to the otherwise heavily outnumbered Democrats. It achieved some of its goals in North Dakota, such as establishing a state-owned bank. A particular favorite of the NPL was "Wild Bill" Langer, who served intermittently as governor during the 1930s. He was elected to the Senate in 1940 but was allowed to take his seat only after a lengthy investigation of campaign irregularities. His subsequent career was fully as controversial; one of his pet projects was to get a North Dakotan on the Supreme Court, and he filibustered every nomination from 1954 on in an unsuccessful attempt to seat a Justice.

Another NPL favorite was Representative Usher Burdick, who served from 1935 to 1945 and then again from 1949 to 1959. Burdick, like Langer, was a nominal Republican, but usually voted with the Democrats on economic issues. Burdick's son Quentin, a Democrat, was a member of the House when Langer died. Young Burdick, as some North Dakotans still call him though he was born in 1908, won a special election to fill the Senate seat after waging a campaign against the inequities of Agriculture Secretary Ezra Taft Benson. The Non-Partisan League supported Burdick, and now the NPL is formally allied with the Democratic party.

The NPL heritage has helped to make North Dakota an intensely political state. Immigrant communities in rural counties developed the kind of hardball patronage politics similar to those in immigrant communities in Chicago, and fierce loyalties have been handed down through the generations. Politics is personal too, in this small state where every politician is personally known to many, perhaps most, voters; and the voters are known to each other: people trust each other enough that North Dakota is the only American state without voter registration: you just show up at the polls and vote.

Governor. Republican in presidential elections, North Dakota votes for Democrats mainly in state contests. Not only its governor, but also seven of the other eight elective offices are held by Democrats, many of them exceedingly popular; the only Republican is the auditor, elected in 1988 with 51%. Governor George Sinner is a prosperous sugar beet farmer with 10 children who served many years in the legislature. He beat a maladroit Republican in 1984 and was reelected easily in 1988. Sinner has lowered business taxes and when the 1988 drought cut receipts, he cut state spending 2% across the board. He wants to consolidate the 200-plus school districts to around 50 to save money. In early 1989, another issue arose when a legislative committee voted to drop the word "North" from the name of the state; "North," said the state's tourism director, is an "unimaginative, unattractive, ordinary word," while "Dakota" is "spectacular." Despite the "Dakota" movement's failure, North Dakota has a chip on its shoulder about outsiders and is the least visited state, but it has almost as many attractions as much-visited South Dakota and could profit from more contact with outsiders and vice versa.

Occupying other offices in North Dakota's skyscraper capitol are some Democrats who obviously made a favorable impression on voters. One is Attorney General Nicholas Spaeth, reelected in 1988 with 73% of the vote. Another is Insurance Commissioner Earl Pomeroy, reelected with 68%. Public Service Commissioner Bruce Hagen and Tax Commissioner Heidi Heitkamp were not far behind with 66%. Any of them might reasonably hope to follow the path of Byron Dorgan, who won great popularity as tax commissioner and has been congressman since 1980.

Senators. North Dakota's strongest link with its Non-Partisan League past is Senator Quentin Burdick. It was rumored for some time that he would retire and many, notably Byron Dorgan, hoped he would in 1988, when he turned 80 and his health seemed precarious. For years Burdick with his rumpled clothes, 'aw shucks' manner, and habit of rotating off committees before he could become chairman, seemed anything but a formidable figure in Washington. He left Judiciary (which has had two Democratic chairmen with less seniority than he has) and saw Post Office and Civil Service abolished out from under him in 1977 just as he was about to take the chair. But one effect of the Democratic capture of the Senate in 1986 is that Burdick, the second ranking minority member on Environment and Public Works in 1986, suddenly became chairman in 1987. Burdick also became chairman of the Appropriations Committee's Agriculture Subcommittee. To help stave off a 1988 primary challenge from the popular Dorgan, Burdick, with help from an aggressive staff, pushed the clean water bill President Reagan vetoed through the Senate in early 1987 and spent a much-publicized night with the homeless in Fargo; he began running "public service announcements" (paid for out of campaign funds) on North Dakota TV showing him as chairman; he announced that his major legislative priority was getting a highway bill; he stepped up and challenged the congressional pay raise; he started billing himself as "one of the most powerful people in Washington." He was trying to elbow aside Dorgan, for whom he felt something of the distaste and jealousy that his longtime Republican colleague Milton Young ("Mr. Wheat") felt for Republican Congressman Mark Andrews; Young was reelected at 77 in 1974 after he ran an ad showing him take a karate chop through a block of wood. Burdick succeeded as Young had. Despite polls showing him far ahead of the incumbent, Dorgan decided not to challenge him.

That decision pretty well settled the contest. The Republican candidate was Earl Strinden, an acerbic and competent veteran of many years in the state Senate. But Strinden was unable to make the charge stick that Young Burdick was a dangerous liberal—and in fact his voting record has many deviations from the L-word. Burdick argued that his power in Washington brought two-thirds of a billion dollars into the state, and he seemed to be in good health even though he had intestinal surgery in a Fargo hospital in August 1987. He won by the comfortable margin of 59%–39%, and he swears he has not ruled out running again in 1994, although his health deserves watching. In the meantime he promises to work on a 1990 highway bill, on strengthening the Clean Air Act, on protecting groundwater, and on the 1989 farm bill.

North Dakota's junior Senator, Kent Conrad, was elected in what would have been one of the big upsets of 1986—except that political reporters and pollsters watch the races so closely now that every upset is anticipated months in advance. Conrad was running against Mark Andrews, who finally won Young's seat in 1980 and had in six years in the Senate and 17 in the House never hesitated to bellow out in support of wheat and against the farm policies of the President in power at the time. But Andrews had some personal weaknesses in a state where politicians are closely watched: some voters resented a medical malpractice suit he filed on behalf of his wife, others bridled when a close Andrews friend in Washington hired a private detective to monitor the personal life of Representative Byron Dorgan, who as state tax commissioner was Conrad's boss and then saw Conrad succeed him as tax commissioner when he was elected to the House in 1980. Andrews, with his penchant for loud denunciations, seemed something of a blowhard, while Conrad quietly and methodically talked about what could be done about low wheat prices and his own record of squeezing more money from out-of-state corporations. Drawing on North Dakota's longtime mistrust of outside corporations and market forces and its affection for those who would use government to help the small farmer-entrepreneur, he carried most of the rural counties while Andrews carried most of North Dakota's small cities. But nowhere was the vote lopsided, as Conrad won 50%–49%.

In the Senate Conrad has spent most of his efforts on farm issues, working on the 1987 farm credit and 1988 drought relief bills; he will be involved in the 1989 farm bill. Often he comes out against big bills: he criticized Andrews for backing the 1985 farm bill and he opposed the U.S.-Canada Free Trade Agreement. He put through a bill to block the sale of the Great Plains coal gasification plant in Morton County without congressional approval, but did ultimately approve its sale to a cooperative. From his days as tax commissioner, he favors tougher tax law enforcement. Farther afield, he started a Deficit Reduction Caucus and on the Budget Committee has championed an across-the-board (except Social Security) spending cut; he wants to force greater burden sharing with Western Europe and Japan.

Presidential politics. Like other farm states, North Dakota is countercyclical in presidential politics: lower farm prices are good news for most Americans and bad news for North Dakota. The historic tradition was progressive and Republican, in favor of an interventionist government in the domestic economy and a non-interventionist government abroad; since this comes closer to the national Democrats than Republicans these days, North Dakota is cross-pressured. A Republican President in power doesn't do well: Gerald Ford carried the state by only 52%–46% in 1976. But after four years of Democrats North Dakota favored Ronald Reagan over Jimmy Carter 64%–26%. Over the next four years Reagan's percentage rose 8% nationally but only 1%

in North Dakota; in 1988 George Bush carried the state 56%–43%. The 1980s have been tough years for many farmers, and over the decade North Dakota's rural counties seem to have been drained of population; but its small cities have gained, its unemployment rate is low, and Bush's success may be an indication that the state's economy has adapted better than most political rhetoric suggests.

Congressman-at-large. Byron Dorgan has missed two chances to run for the Senate, against Andrews in 1986 and Burdick in 1988, yet he seems likely to end up there anyway. He has been by most measures the most popular politician in North Dakota for a decade now, winning his House seat easily in the Republican year of 1980 and winning reelection four times with more than 70% of the vote. Dorgan's political career was hatched in the unlikely precincts of the office in Bismarck's 19-story Capitol of the state tax commissioner, an elective office to which he was appointed in 1969 and elected and reelected in the 1970s. He started by getting out-of-state corporations to pay more taxes in North Dakota—a technical, legalistic battle, the kind of battle prairie farmers are accustomed to losing to big-city lawyers, but Dorgan won and brought back memories of the old Non-Partisan League struggles.

Dorgan harks back to North Dakota's prairie populism, its distrust of big institutions (especially banks and grain companies) and its solicitude for the individual family farmer. An opponent of the Vietnam war when that was an issue, he is skeptical about much defense spending and foreign aid. (North Dakota, as it happens, is loaded with missile silos; if it seceded, it would be the world's third nuclear power.) He is an unyielding supporter of the state's wheat growing interests. He is a low-interest-rate man and a denouncer of big bankers and the Federal Reserve. But he was sophisticated enough in the ways of the House to win a seat on the Ways and Means Committee in his second term. He approaches issues with a zest and the kind of cornball good humor that New Deal enthusiasts liked to summon up when liberals thought they represented the ordinary, inarticulate little guy, and saw the conservatives as representing the stuck-up old stuffed shirts; and he continues to work hard at home in a state where people are used to meeting with their representatives.

Dorgan worked on the drought bill and will weigh in surely on the 1989 farm bill. On Ways and Means he backed the 1986 tax reform, then worked in 1987 to repeal the diesel fuel and heifer taxes for farmers. He was an early supporter of Richard Gephardt's presidential candidacy. Like an old-time populist, he is perturbed by the wave of mergers, acquisitions, and leveraged buyouts, and his impulse is to do something about them—perhaps limit the deductibility of interest on corporate takeover loans. He wants to get Social Security off-budget, so that its surpluses are not used to offset the deficits in the rest of the budget. Another Dorgan cause is providing prosthetic devices and other help to children who are victims of violence in Central America.

It is widely assumed that Dorgan will run for and be elected to the Senate in 1994 when Burdick's term ends, and that Governor Sinner will appoint him to any vacancy that may exist.

The People: Est. Pop. 1988: 663,000; Pop. 1980 652,717, up 1.5% 1980-88 and 5.7% 1970-80; 0.29% of U.S. total, 45th largest. 20% with 1-3 yrs. col., 15% with 4+ yrs. col.; 12.6% below poverty level. Single ancestry: 26% German, 15% Norwegian, 2% English, Irish, Swedish, 1% French, Polish. Households (1980): 73% family, 40% with children, 65% married couples; 31.3% housing units rented; median monthly rent: $175; median house value: $43,800. Voting age pop. (1980): 461,726; 2% American Indian. Enrolled Voters (1988): 474,000; no party registration.

1988 Share of Federal Tax Burden: $1,911,000,000; 0.22% of U.S. total, 47th largest.

1988 Share of Federal Expenditures

	Total		Non-Defense		Defense	
Total Expend	$2,881m	(0.33%)	$2,470m	(0.38%)	$459m	(0.20%)
St/Lcl Grants	462m	(0.40%)	459m	(0.40%)	3m	(2.44%)
Salary/Wages	464m	(0.35%)	198m	(0.30%)	267m	(0.30%)
Pymnts to Indiv	1,071m	(0.26%)	1,047m	(0.27%)	24m	(0.13%)
Procurement	166m	(0.09%)	49m	(0.10%)	166m	(0.09%)
Research/Other	717m	(1.92%)	717m	(1.94%)	0m	(1.94%)

Political Lineup: Governor, George A. Sinner (D); Lt. Gov., Lloyd Omdahl (D); Secy. of State, James Kusler (D); Atty. Gen., Nicholas Spaeth (D); Treasurer, Robert Hanson (D); Auditor, Robert W. Peterson (R). State Senate, 53 (32 D and 21 R); State House of Representatives, 106 (61 R and 45 D). Senators, Quentin N. Burdick (D) and Kent Conrad (D). Representatives, 1 D at large.

1988 Presidential Vote

Bush (R) 166,559 (56%)
Dukakis (D). 127,739 (43%)

1984 Presidential Vote

Reagan (R) 200,336 (65%)
Mondale (D) 104,429 (34%)

1988 Democratic Presidential Primary

Dukakis 2,890 (85%)
Jackson 515 (15%)

1988 Republican Presidential Primary

Bush 37,062 (94%)
Rachner................... 2,372 (6%)

GOVERNOR

Gov. George A. Sinner (D)

Elected 1984, term expires Jan. 1993; b. May 29, 1928, Fargo; home, Casselton; St. John's U., B.A. 1950; Roman Catholic; married (Jane).

Career: Partner, Sinner Bros. & Bresnahan (Farming partnership); ND Senate, 1962–66; Mbr., St. Bd. Higher Educ., 1967–74, Chrmn., 1970; ND House of Reps., 1982–84.

Office: State Capitol, Bismarck 58505, 701-224-2200.

Election Results

1988 gen.	George A. Sinner (D).........	179,094	(60%)
	Arthur A. Link (R)	119,986	(40%)
1988 prim.	George A. Sinner (D), unopposed		
1984 gen.	George A. Sinner (D).........	173,992	(55%)
	Allen I. Olson (R)...........	140,460	(45%)

SENATORS

Sen. Quentin N. Burdick (D)

Elected June, 1960, seat up 1994; b. June 19, 1908, Munich; home, Fargo; U. of MN, B.A. 1931, LL.B. 1932; Congregationalist; married (Jocelyn).

Career: Practicing atty., 1932–58; Dem. Nom. for Gov., 1946; U.S. House of Reps., 1958–60.

Offices: 511 HSOB, 202-224-2551. Also Fed. Bldg., Fargo 58102, 701-237-4000, Fed. Bldg., Bismarck 58501, 701-255-2553; and Fed. Bldg., Minot 58701, 701-852-4503; 108 Fed. Bldg., Grand Forks 58201, 701-746-1014.

Committees: *Appropriations* (5th of 16 D). Subcommittees: Agriculture, Rural Development and Related Agencies (Chairman); Energy and Water Development; Interior; Labor, Health and Human Services, Education. *Environment and Public Works* (Chairman of 9 D). *Select Committee on Indian Affairs* (3d of 5 D). *Special Committee on Aging* (4th of 10 D).

Group Ratings

	ADA	ACLU	COPE	CFA	LCV	ACU	NTU	NSI	COC	CEI
1988	85	70	86	100	60	16	9	20	29	10
1987	95	—	85	83	—	8	—	—	24	19

National Journal Ratings

	1988 LIB — 1988 CONS	1987 LIB — 1987 CONS
Economic	65% — 30%	74% — 0%
Social	77% — 22%	66% — 31%
Foreign	65% — 32%	81% — 0%

Key Votes

1) Cut Aged Housing $	FOR	5) Bork Nomination	AGN	9) SDI Funding	AGN
2) Override Hwy Veto	FOR	6) Ban Plastic Guns	FOR	10) Ban Chem Weaps	AGN
3) Kill Plnt Clsng Notice	AGN	7) Deny Abortions	AGN	11) Aid To Contras	AGN
4) Min Wage Increase	FOR	8) Japanese Reparations	FOR	12) Reagan Defense $	AGN

Election Results

1988 general	Quentin N. Burdick (D)	171,899	(59%)	($2,026,617)
	Earl Strinden (R)	112,937	(39%)	($906,807)
1988 primary	Quentin N. Burdick (D), unopposed			
1982 general	Quentin N. Burdick (D)	164,873	(62%)	($783,020)
	Gene Knorr (R)	89,304	(34%)	($406,601)

Sen. Kent Conrad (D)

Elected 1986, seat up 1992; b. March 12, 1948, Bismarck; home, Bismarck; Stanford U., B.A. 1971; Geo. Wash. U., M.B.A. 1975; Unitarian; married (Lucy).

Career: Asst. to ND Tax Commissioner, 1974–80; Dir., Mgt. Planning and Personnel, ND Tax Dept., 1980; ND Tax Commissioner, 1981–86.

Offices: 361 DSOB 20510, 202-224-2043. Also Fed. Bldg., Rm. 232, 3d and Roffer Ave., Bismarck 58501, 701-258-4648; 657 2d Ave. N., Fed. Bldg., Rm. 306, Fargo 58102, 701-232-8030; 100 1st St. S.W., Minot 58701, 701-852-0703; and 102 N. 4th St., Ste. 106, Grand Forks 58201, 701-775-9601.

Committees: *Agriculture, Nutrition and Forestry* (6th of 10 D). Subcommittees: Agricultural Credit (Chairman); Agricultural Production and Stabilization of Prices; Domestic and Foreign Marketing and Product Promotion. *Budget* (11th of 13 D). *Energy and Natural Resources* (8th of 10 D) Subcommittees: Mineral Resources Development and Production; Public Lands, National Parks and Forests; Water and Power. *Select Committee on Indian Affairs* (5th of 5 D).

Group Ratings

	ADA	ACLU	COPE	CFA	LCV	ACU	NTU	NSI	COC	CEI
1988	80	67	92	83	60	24	16	10	29	24
1987	85	—	90	67	—	8	—	—	39	29

National Journal Ratings

	1988 LIB — 1988 CONS		1987 LIB — 1987 CONS	
Economic	65%	30%	44%	50%
Social	53%	46%	53%	42%
Foreign	65%	32%	69%	27%

Key Votes

1) Cut Aged Housing $	FOR	5) Bork Nomination	AGN
2) Override Hwy Veto	FOR	6) Ban Plastic Guns	FOR
3) Kill Plnt Clsng Notice	AGN	7) Deny Abortions	FOR
4) Min Wage Increase	FOR	8) Japanese Reparations	FOR

9) SDI Funding	AGN
10) Ban Chem Weaps	AGN
11) Aid To Contras	AGN
12) Reagan Defense $	AGN

Election Results

1986 general	Kent Conrad (D)	143,932	(50%)	($908,374)
	Mark Andrews (R)	141,797	(49%)	($2,270,557)
1986 primary	Kent Conrad (D)	58,213	(100%)	
1980 general	Mark Andrews (R)	210,347	(70%)	($402,129)
	Kent Johanneson (D)	86,658	(29%)	($139,203)

REPRESENTATIVE

Rep. Byron L. Dorgan (D)

Elected 1980; b. May 14, 1942, Dickinson; home, Bismarck; U. of ND, B.S. 1965, U. of Denver, M.B.A. 1966; Lutheran; married (Kimberly).

Career: Martin-Marietta Exec. Develop. Prog., 1966–68; ND Dpty. Tax Commissioner, 1968–69, Tax Commissioner, 1969–80.

Offices: 109 CHOB 20515, 202-225-2611. Also 358 Fed. Bldg., Bismarck 58502, 701-255-4011; and 112 Robert St., Fargo 58107, 701-237-5771.

Committees: *Ways and Means* (17th of 23 D). Subcommittees: Oversight; Select Revenue Measures. *Select Committee on Hunger* (6th of 18 D).

Group Ratings

	ADA	ACLU	COPE	CFA	LCV	ACU	NTU	NSI	COC	CEI
1988	75	68	76	82	69	17	27	20	38	23
1987	92	—	74	86	—	0	—	—	14	15

National Journal Ratings

	1988 LIB — 1988 CONS		1987 LIB — 1987 CONS	
Economic	54%	— 44%	73%	— 0%
Social	50%	— 48%	70%	— 28%
Foreign	67%	— 32%	81%	— 0%

Key Votes

1) Homeless $	AGN	5) Ban Drug Test	—	9) SDI Research	AGN
2) Gephardt Amdt	FOR	6) Drug Death Pen	FOR	10) Ban Chem Weaps	FOR
3) Deficit Reduc	FOR	7) Handgun Sales	FOR	11) Aid to Contras	AGN
4) Kill Plnt Clsng Notice	AGN	8) Ban D.C. Abort $	FOR	12) Nuclear Testing	FOR

Election Results

1988 general	Byron L. Dorgan (D)	212,583	(71%)	($143,210)
	Steve Sydness (R)....................	84,475	(28%)	($1,154)
1988 primary	Byron L. Dorgan (D), unopposed			
1986 general	Byron L. Dorgan (D)	216,258	(76%)	($391,909)
	Syver Vinje (R)......................	66,989	(23%)	($73,278)

OHIO

Ohio half a century ago was "a nucleus to 70% of all industrial activity in the nation," wrote John Gunther. "It is first in an extraordinary variety of products and enterprises—machine tools, rubber, publishing of periodicals, ceramics, nuts and bolts, steel barrels, washers and rivets, oilcloth, sporting goods, cranes and derricks, playing cards, china and, among oddities, sewer pipe and false teeth. Ohio is the second state in motor vehicles, steel, and blast furnace products; third in paints and varnishes and job printing; fourth in chemicals, aviations, men's clothing, and bakery goods; fifth in footwear; sixth in paper."

It was also, in those years before Depression had turned into war, a cockpit of what seemed like class warfare. Early in 1937, General Motors workers in Toledo, Cleveland and Cincinnati staged sitdown strikes which were ruled illegal but resulted in GM recognizing the United Auto Workers; in May, 50,000 workers were out at "Little Steel" plants in Youngstown, Canton, Massillon, Warren and Niles; seven strikers were killed in riots when National Guard troops were called in as the companies tried to bring in replacement workers and the nascent United Steel Workers tried to maintain the strike.

In this atmosphere of violent crisis, politics came to be centered around issues of union organization and income redistribution. Workers and management alike assumed that the economy had stopped growing; they were fighting, sometimes physically, for bigger shares of the same pie. New Deal Democrats, who refused to send in troops to break the sitdown strikes, were seen as allies of the CIO unions; conservative Republicans like Robert Taft feared that unions would organize most of the work force and would, through their support of New Deal Democrats, control government and institute something like Marxist Socialism in the United States.

Ohio, with its big manufacturing cities and dozens of small towns, its ethnic factory neighborhoods and its productive farms, its southern-accented counties below the National Road and U.S. 40 which had been Copperhead in the Civil War and its New England Yankee-settled northeast which voted overwhelmingly for Abraham Lincoln, was closely divided in this new economic politics, as it had been in partisan politics for most of the years since it was admitted to the Union in 1803. In 1938, after the sitdown strikes, Ohioans ousted Democrats and elected Republicans Robert Taft, Senator, and John Bricker, Governor, by 54%–46% and 52%–48% margins; in 1940, Ohio went for Franklin Roosevelt over Wendell Willkie by a 52%–48% margin. It has remained closely divided in the 50 years since, voting for Harry Truman by 7,000 votes in 1948, for Richard Nixon by 90,000 in 1968, and for Jimmy Carter by 11,000 in 1976. It has voted within 2% of the national average in every presidential election since 1964.

But not every part of Ohio is closely divided; rather, the state typically seems split into two sharply different Ohios. Before the New Deal, the split was between the Copperhead or Butternut south and the Yankee north, and that division surfaces again from time to time: John Glenn, at the beginning of his career, was especially strong south of U.S. 40 and it was Jimmy Carter's extra strength in those rural counties, not his lackluster margins in the industrial cities, that enabled him to carry the state in 1976. But the more usual division in the past two decades is between the industrial north-and-east, where the CIO union organizing drives of the late 1930s were successful, and the rest of the state, much of which is industrial but has been much less heavily unionized. The industrial north-and-east includes the coal strip-mining counties on the Ohio River across from Wheeling, West Virginia, which were strong United Mine Workers country in their day; it includes the steel mill corridors of the Mahoning Valley in Youngstown

OHIO — Congressional Districts, Counties, and Selected Places — (21 Districts)

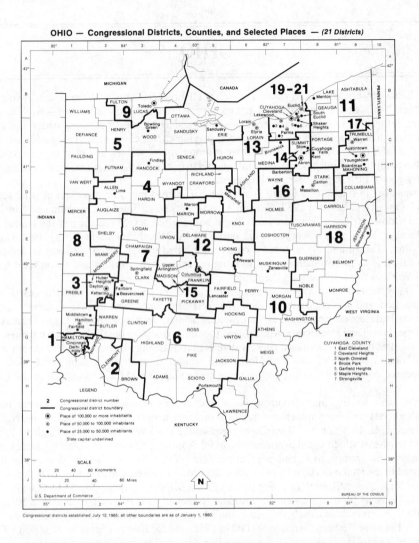

and Warren and the Cuyahoga River corridor in Cleveland, a center of the national strength of the United Steelworkers for years; it includes Akron which, in the days when all the big American rubber companies had factories operating there (none does today) was the center of the United Rubber Workers; it passes along the shore of Lake Erie (much less polluted now than 15 years ago, and even swimmable) to Toledo, with its glass and auto plants which, like those scattered throughout northern Ohio in Cleveland suburbs and Lordstown, halfway between Akron and Youngstown, were organized by the United Auto Workers. In contrast, the machine tool and soap factories of Cincinnati, the cash register and box factories of Dayton, and the various shops of Columbus were not, for the most part, organized by militant CIO unions.

North-and-east industrial Ohio, which casts about 45% of the votes in the state, has become one of the most Democratic parts of the nation. Walter Mondale ran about as well here as he did in Minnesota, and Michael Dukakis ran about as well here as he did in Massachusetts; Mondale barely lost it and Dukakis carried this half of Ohio 54%–46%. Governor Richard Celeste won 68% and 70% of its votes—the sort of near-unanimous response you usually don't get outside city-states like Massachusetts, Rhode Island and Maryland—and Senator Howard Metzenbaum, running against Cleveland Mayor George Voinovich in 1988, carried it 64%–36%.

The collapse of the auto, steel and rubber industries after the oil shock of 1979 caused a political earthquake here. The suddenness of the collapse meant that people who had counted on making well-above-average wages even for low-skill work, and who were looking forward to an early and comfortable retirement, suddenly found themselves facing the end of their unemployment benefits in communities where the traditional big employers had pretty much shut down and there seemed to be no visible job openings in new firms. Many people left the state and found work elsewhere. Among those who stayed, there was a political reaction approaching panic. In 1980, they turned sharply against Jimmy Carter, who won only 46% of the vote in north-and-east Ohio, slightly under Ronald Reagan's share. In 1982, after two more years of record unemployment, they turned back toward the Democrats, backing Celeste and Metzenbaum with overwhelming margins. Since then, north-and-east Ohio's economy has been slowly diversifying and growing. But the process is far less visible than the still cold steel plants and rubber factories. Politically, north-and-east Ohio has been voting about 8% or 9% more Democratic than the rest of the country. That's a sharp contrast with 50 years ago, when it was slightly more Republican than the nation. Then, its New England Yankee traditions were still strong; now, the sons and daughters of its immigrants and CIO members vastly outnumber those who trace their ancestry to Revolutionary war veterans.

The rest of Ohio has moved in quite different directions. It nearly voted for Roosevelt and Truman in the 1940s. But without either strong CIO unions or Democratic political machines, it drifted toward the Republicans as early as the 1950s. In the 1960s and 1970s, it found congenial the policies of James Rhodes, governor for 16 of the 20 years between 1962 and 1982: low taxes, limited public services, attempts to attract business and new jobs. This is the part of Ohio that has continued to grow during the recession years: it cast 52% of the state's votes in 1968 and 55% in 1988. And in the 1980s it has swung as solidly to the Republicans as next-door Indiana. In 1976, Jimmy Carter won 43% of the votes here and in 1980 slipped to 37%, a figure the Democrats have not exceeded since; Michael Dukakis had only 36% of the votes, losing by nearly a 2 to 1 margin. Cultural conservatism and patriotic nationalism, combined with faith in a growing economy, continue to produce very different results than in north-and-east Ohio.

The combination of these two quite different and nearly equal-sized Ohios produces some anomalous results. Until the 1980s, Jim Rhodes dominated state government for two decades and until the 1970s, the Republicans had a stranglehold on the state legislature and statewide offices; now Democrats, through a combination of smart political footwork and underlying political trends, hold the governorship, most of the statewide offices, and a big margin in the state House. It should be added, however, that these will all be up for grabs in 1990, with no sure winners in the offing. Democrats narrowly control Ohio's delegation to the U.S. House, and Democrats John Glenn and Howard Metzenbaum—with Glenn an increasingly partisan figure—have had a firm hold on the state's two Senate seats since the middle 1970s.

Even with a big election cycle coming up in 1990, the sense of urgency seems gone in Ohio politics. When the state seemed to be facing economic disaster in the early 1980s, turnout rose to historic highs, with off-year turnout up from 2.8 to 3.3 million between 1978 and 1982, and presidential turnout up from 4.3 to 4.6 million between 1980 and 1984. But as the economy improved and population started increasing again, turnout sank back to 3.1 million in 1986 and 4.3 million in 1988. Raging dissatisfaction in north-and-east Ohio has been replaced by something between resignation and calm acceptance of a less than exciting but still not scary economic fate.

Ohio's current leaders, in government, business and labor, have not managed to do what the inventors, business founders and Republican politicians of the turn of the century, or the industrial union leaders and Democratic politicians of the 1940s, did—to capture people's imagination, to attract them with a vision of a better tomorrow. The Ohio that produced Thomas Edison and the Wright brothers, the cash register and auto safety glass, showed its citizens that a more comfortable and more exciting future was possible through mechanical technology and business organization; the Ohio that produced the big CIO unions showed Americans that mass production and job security could win a war and create an affluent life for the masses who had previously been confined to misery.

Ohio today remains mostly a manufacturing state, but by no means a dull-witted one; many of its visible old industries have been shut down, but the number of jobs is on the rise again, increasing more rapidly in small businesses than they had been decreasing in the more visible big units. Unemployment is down, and Ohio's Thomas Edison state investment program is helping to stimulate innovation and to build on Ohio's industrial strengths. But Ohio has not thrown up leaders in the private sector who epitomize these developments, and its politicians have failed to do so, with Richard Celeste dogged at home by scandal and John Glenn and Howard Metzenbaum more preoccupied with national issues.

Governor. As the 1980s end, so does Richard Celeste's eight-year service as governor. He came to office in 1982 at 45, already a veteran of two statewide races (the saying in Ohio is you have to run once statewide and lose before you can win: it applies to Celeste, Rhodes, Glenn and Metzenbaum) and with a resume that included being head of the Peace Corps. His instincts were to spend and tax more than Rhodes had, and he took the heat for a tax increase and beat a 1983 referendum that would have overturned it. But he fell into the habit of hiring rouges with a glint in their eye and worse, elevating them to high offices, and was enmeshed in a number of scandals. The most visible was the collapse in 1985 of the state-insured Home State Savings and Loan; it was owned by Democratic campaign contributor and political operator Marvin Warner, who gave Celeste crucial financial support in the 1982 primary season, without which he would never have been elected. Other state-insured S&Ls folded, and the state had to meet depositors' guarantees, which was done before the 1986 campaign.

In that contest Celeste had the fortune to face James Rhodes, still a wily pro but by then too old (77) to be a credible candidate, even in the era of Ronald Reagan. And if Celeste's margin was increased by Rhodes's weakness, he could still argue that his 61% (70% in north-and-east industrial Ohio, 53% in the rest of the state) was matched by the 55% to 65% showings of Democrats for lower state offices and was almost exactly equal to Senator John Glenn's percentage. But when Celeste's name was mentioned as a possible presidential candidate in 1987, there was no significant support; instead, the Cleveland *Plain Dealer*, without naming any sources, charged that Celeste had been "romantically linked" with three women other than his wife, one as recently as 1985. One can't help imagining that Celeste was a bit wistful as the Democratic nomination went to another big state ethnic governor of his own generation; but Celeste himself was busy fending off charges that he steered state contracts to big contributors and calls by state Republicans for his impeachment. Celeste's Democrats were unable to recapture the state Senate in 1988, and his call in 1989 for higher taxes to pay for education was received negatively not only by Republicans but by longtime Democratic Speaker Vern Riffe.

But in Columbus in 1989, more eyes were on the 1990 governor's race than on Celeste, who is ineligible to run. Two prominent Democrats were thinking of running: attorney general Anthony Celebrezze Jr. and auditor Tom Ferguson. Among the Republicans interested were Cleveland Mayor George Voinovich, despite his loss to Metzenbaum in 1988 and Cincinnati county commissioner Robert Taft. One of these candidates will probably win, but it's not clear whether any of them can provide the inspiration that Ohio needs as it rebuilds its economy and strengthens its public services.

Senators. Ohio's best known politician in the 1980s has been Senator John Glenn. Since his moment in the spotlight when he became the first American to orbit the earth in 1962, Glenn has been a personification of the small town virtues of family, God-fearing religion, duty, patriotism and hard work. He actually is from the small town of New Concord, right on the National Road divide, and he really does believe in its values. Yet he is also aggressive enough to have become a brilliant fighter pilot in World War II and Korea, to have gotten himself into the astronaut program, to have been a successful businessman, to have succeeded in being elected, after a couple of missteps, to the Senate, and to have made himself, despite his failure as a presidential candidate, a useful and effective leader in national politics.

In retrospect, a case can be made that Glenn's failure in the Democratic presidential process reflects more negatively on the party than on him. It was presaged by the less than overwhelming reception to Glenn's keynote speech at the 1976 convention, in contrast to the tumultuous reception to Barbara Jordan's; Glenn's delivery was indeed wooden, but his speech had more content than hers, and Democratic activists' desire to spotlight blacks, women and members of other groups not considered for the highest offices in the past have left them arguably less advantageously represented on the national screen than they would be by supposedly dull, gray-haired, middle-aged white Protestant males like Glenn and Lloyd Bentsen.

The 1988 campaign tends to support that supposition. Bentsen performed ably and was clearly an asset, and Glenn—the apparent runner-up in the selection process—delivered a corker of a nominating speech for Bentsen which suggests he could have done just as well. And there are some who think that a Bentsen-Dukakis or a Glenn-Dukakis ticket might have beaten the Bush-Quayle ticket in 1988, just as Bentsen beat Bush in Texas in 1970 and Glenn has beaten every Republican candidate who has run against him in the pivotal state of Ohio, by overwhelming margins.

Glenn would have brought to either end of that ticket a record in the Senate that is a bit more moderate than those of most other Democrats, especially on foreign policy issues, and a mastery of several difficult issues on which a President, or a well-informed and aggressive Senator, can make a difference. A prime example is nuclear proliferation, on which he has been vigilant about transfers of nuclear technology and materials to countries like India and Pakistan. On this critical issue he knows the details, masters the arguments, and never quits fighting his good fight, towering over everyone else in American government. Naturally, Glenn is interested in military matters—so much so, in fact, that after the 1984 election he gave up a high-ranking seat on Foreign Relations to serve on Armed Services. On Foreign Relations, he followed the SALT talks very closely and, despite an obvious desire to support the treaty, hesitated because of concerns about verification (later resolved, he said, by technical innovations).

Glenn did not start off as an environmental activist and, as a Senator from Ohio, does not come out against all smokestacks. But he has been an aggressive proponent of cleaning up the government's nuclear materials plants—a visible issue in Ohio, where the Fernald plant is just outside Cincinnati, and one on which he, as chairman of the Governmental Affairs Committee, has played a lead role. On cultural issues, this son of middle America has always been willing to vote against abortion restrictions and school prayer amendments; who is going to say he is insufficiently patriotic or pious?

Glenn's senatorial career had two false starts: he began running in 1964, then left the race when he injured himself in a household accident; he ran again in 1970, but was upset in the primary by Howard Metzenbaum, who in turn lost the general election narrowly to Robert Taft Jr. In 1974 Glenn and Metzenbaum ran against each other again, in one of the most bitter primaries of recent times; this time Glenn won. He won the general election easily that year and has had no trouble holding the seat. (Metzenbaum won the other Ohio Senate seat in 1976 and he and Glenn are now on friendly terms.) Glenn won reelection with a record-breaking 69% of the vote in 1980, running 29% ahead of Jimmy Carter.

Yet Glenn's presidential candidacy in 1984 was not a success. In critical debates in the winter of 1983–84 he did not seem to have the suppleness of mind some of his competitors possessed and failed to give a sense of command over them. He was hurt as well, as he has been in Democratic primaries in Ohio, because the same wholesomeness which makes him so appealing to the general electorate tends to turn off the party activists and self-conscious minorities who are disproportionately influential in Democratic politics. Within this constituency, he was unable to frame the issues in ways favorable to his candidacy, and instead found himself trying to convince nuclear freeze activists that he would utter enough of their catechism to be acceptable. In any case, this competent and engaging Senator was not able to convince many party activists and voters that he had the stuff it takes to be President. Left over from the 1984 campaign was a $2 million-plus debt, most of it accumulated when Glenn struggled to win a primary in the South. Although other candidates, notably Alan Cranston, paid off their debts, Glenn still owed money in 1988, when he signed an agreement with the Federal Election Commission agreeing to pay a nominal fine and not to contest the FEC's contention that bank loans advanced after Glenn's campaign provided "letters of comfort" (not guarantees but pledges from rich Ohioans, including Marvin Warner, that they would try to raise money to repay the debt) were illegal. Glenn's 1986 opponent, Thomas Kindness, attacked this arrangement, with cause; it's a bit jarring to see a man whose integrity is unquestionable skate so close to, if not over, the edge of what campaign finance laws allow.

In the 1970s, Glenn was seen as a kind of nonpartisan figure, with broad enough appeal to carry just about every group and county in Ohio. In the more partisan climate of the 1980s, he has become a more partisan Democrat in his voting record and in voters' perceptions, although he remains a very popular one. His percentage declined just a bit, to 62% against Congressman Thomas Kindness in 1986; and he failed to win some traditionally Republican counties, carrying 71% in industrial north-and-east Ohio and 56% in the rest of the state.

Senator Howard Metzenbaum has a background almost entirely different from Glenn's. Metzenbaum is from Cleveland; spent most of his life in business, making his fortune in airport parking lots (not a business one enters for love). Politically active for years, he was campaign manager for Senator Stephen Young's two surprise victories: in 1958 against John Bricker at age 74, and in 1964 against Robert Taft Jr. Then Metzenbaum ran himself, beat Glenn and almost beat Taft in 1970; he then lost to Glenn in the 1974 primary after having been appointed to fill a vacancy by Governor John Gilligan; he finally won the seat in 1976, beating Cleveland Congressman James Stanton in the primary and Taft in the general. Winning reelection by handsome margins in 1982 and 1988, he has now had a hand in elections for this Ohio Senate seat for terms totalling 30 years.

Metzenbaum has fought his way up in business, in politics, and now in the Senate without much regard for traditional rules or the sensibilities of others. His record on issues is one of the most liberal in the Senate. But more distinctive and important has been his role as a watchdog for legislation that in his view benefits special interests. On the floor of the Senate, he is a kind of Horatius at the bridge, putting holds near the end of the session on dozens of pieces of what he considers to be special interest legislation and then filibustering them if they come up. In effect, Metzenbaum forces Senators backing these bills to negotiate with him, even if they have a large majority and he represents only himself. He first got interested in the possibilities for delay in the Senate rules when he and James Abourezk of South Dakota staged a two-man filibuster against deregulation of oil and gas prices; that failed, but Metzenbaum saw that the potential for such tactics was tremendous, and that at the end of the session delay means death for a bill. So he is ready with amendments (as many as 100 to a single bill) and with extended comment. Metzenbaum himself has proposed changing the rules that allow him to do this; but in the meantime, he proposes to take advantage of them. Colleagues get infuriated with Metzenbaum—they vow to deny him any special breaks he might seek—but they cannot get around him and so, grumbling, make their plans with him in mind. "He's like the security guard at the airport," Arkansas's David Pryor said. "You know he's going to X-ray your baggage, so you have to be clean."

Metzenbaum takes on big issues and small. He held up passage of a bill giving the Alaska Railroad to the state until an outraged Ted Stevens persuaded the state to pay something for it. He almost singlehandedly forced Judiciary Committee Chairman Strom Thurmond to put an indefinite hold on the nomination of presidential counselor Edwin Meese as Attorney General in 1984, while an independent counsel investigated charges that Meese had used his White House office for personal gain; when the nomination was resubmitted in 1985, Metzenbaum again led the campaign against it—even though the independent counsel had cleared Meese of criminal wrongdoing and the appointment was headed for confirmation. Nonetheless, Metzenbaum himself wasn't immune to charges of ethical improprieties: he was criticized in 1984 for accepting a $250,000 "finder's fee" for making a phone call putting a prospective buyer in touch with the owner of Washington's Hay-Adams hotel, and Metzenbaum returned the money when the transaction was revealed.

Metzenbaum has some positive accomplishments as well. He was one of the leaders in framing a tough savings and loan bill in early 1989, arguing for high capital requirements for S&Ls and insisting that accounting sheet "goodwill is not worth doodly-doo, and I want to eliminate it." He has backed banning plastic handguns that can't be caught by metal detectors. He supported Bill Armstrong's stockholders' bill of rights, to limit the powers of entrenched managements to fend off takeovers (Metzenbaum, who graduated from law school in 1941, when none of Cleveland's big companies or law firms would hire Jews, is not a big fan of established management.) He wants workers given notice of toxic chemicals on the job. The most important one, especially for the 1988 campaign, was the plant-closing notification legislation that became law after the fight over the 1988 trade bill. This was Metzenbaum's idea originally, and with Democrats casting about for a way to make their more liberal stance on economics attractive to voters it was taken up by his colleagues and pressed to passage. In Ohio, full of highly visible closed factories, it resonated more than in just about any other state in the union.

Metzenbaum also capitalized adroitly on the mistakes of his enemies. His opponent, George Voinovich, is widely regarded as a moderate and has a pleasant, non-abrasive personality. But in July 1987, a Senate Republican campaign committee memo was released recommending attacks on Metzenbaum as a "Communist sympathizer" for organizational ties in the 1940s; Republican Leader Bob Dole and campaign committee chairman Rudy Boschwitz promptly apologized. In September 1988, Voinovich ran an ad criticizing Metzenbaum for opposing "laws that will put child pornographers out of business." John Glenn—a good friend since Metzenbaum came to his side after his unsuccessful 1984 campaign—was outraged and quickly cut a spot attacking Voinovich's "gutter politics." That put the kibosh on any chances Voinovich's campaign had. In 1982, Metzenbaum won 57%–43%, carrying 68% in north-and-east Ohio and 52% in the rest of the state; in 1988, he won 57%–43%, carrying 64% in north-and-east Ohio (Voinovich's home base, after all) and 52% in the rest of the state. It is beginning to look like a familiar pattern. Metzenbaum has long since transcended the negatives of the liberal label by making political assets out of his own authentic virtues—working hard and fighting hard for what he believes is in the ordinary citizen's interest. Though he is past 70, he could be pardoned for wondering whether he might not, in the words of that fighter for rather different causes, Margaret Thatcher, "go on and on."

Presidential politics. Ohio is one of the linchpins of presidential politics. The old saw was that no Republican can win the presidency without Ohio, and given the Democrats' current weakness in the South—Michael Dukakis ran behind his national average in every southern state—it's probably true that no Democrat can win the presidency without Ohio either. In 1984, Reagan campaign manager Ed Rollins acted on that assumption, cutting special Ohio ads comparing

Mondale to Celeste and putting extra money into the state; in 1988, George Bush showed up in the state of his father's birthplace (his grandfather owned a small steel factory in Columbus) practically as often as Howard Metzenbaum. The Republican appeal, based on opposition to higher taxes and to cultural liberalism, seems strong here, and the wideness of Bush's margin— 55%–44%, more than his national average—suggests that even with John Glenn on the ticket Michael Dukakis might not have carried Ohio.

There was talk before 1988 that Ohio would switch its primary from May to March, but it didn't. Not since 1972 has a primary this late had significant impact on the outcome of the nomination, and 1988 was no exception. Michael Dukakis and George Bush won big victories here that were scarcely noticed anywhere else.

Congressional districting. Congressional redistricting was a bipartisan exercise in Ohio in 1982, not because its politicians are altruistic, but because the Democrats controlled the state House of Representatives, and Republicans the state Senate and governorship. The bipartisanship is apparent in the Cincinnati and Columbus areas, where partisans of either side would have drawn the lines differently. The outcome of the next redistricting thus will hinge heavily on the 1990 elections. Either party could conceivably win control of the process, though the Republicans will have an awfully uphill battle to win the state House; the most likely outcome, however, is another bipartisan plan. Because of slow population growth, Ohio is liable to lose two districts, one in Cleveland or the northeast, one in the rest of the state—which is exactly what happened in 1982.

The People: Est. Pop. 1988: 10,872,000; Pop. 1980: 10,797,630, dn. 0.7% 1980–88 and up 1.3% 1970–80; 4.46% of U.S. total, 7th largest. 13% with 1–3 yrs. col., 15% with 4+ yrs. col.; 10.3% below poverty level. Single ancestry: 13% German, 9% English, 4% Irish, 2% Italian, Polish, 1% Hungarian, French. Households (1980): 74% family, 41% with children, 62% married couples; 31.6% housing units rented; median monthly rent: $167; median house value: $45,100. Voting age pop. (1980): 7,703,310; 9% Black, 1% Spanish origin. Registered voters (1988): 6,323,352; 2,023,473 D (32%), 1,327,904 R (21%); 2,971,975 unaffiliated and minor parties (47%).

1988 Share of Federal Tax Burden: $37,174,000,000; 4.20% of U.S. total, 8th largest.

1988 Share of Federal Expenditures

	Total		Non-Defense		Defense	
Total Expend	$33,521m	(3.79%)	$26,634m	(4.06%)	$8,283m	(3.63%)
St/Lcl Grants	4,693m	(4.10%)	4,691m	(4.10%)	3m	(2.45%)
Salary/Wages	3,484m	(2.59%)	2,000m	(2.98%)	1,484m	(2.98%)
Pymnts to Indiv	17,968m	(4.39%)	17,630m	(4.51%)	337m	(1.81%)
Procurement	6,442m	(3.41%)	1,396m	(3.00%)	6,442m	(3.41%)
Research/Other	934m	(2.50%)	917m	(2.47%)	17m	(2.47%)

Political Lineup: Governor, Richard F. Celeste (D); Lt. Gov., Paul R. Leonard (D); Secy. of State, Sherrod Brown (D); Atty. Gen., Anthony J. Celebrezze, Jr. (D); Treasurer, Mary Ellen Withrow (D); Auditor, Thomas E. Ferguson (D). State Senate, 33 (19 R and 14 D); State House of Representatives, 99 (59 D and 40 R). Senators, John H. Glenn, Jr. (D) and Howard M. Metzenbaum (D). Representatives, 21 (11 D and 10 R).

1988 Presidential Vote

Bush (R) 2,416,549 (55%)
Dukakis (D). 1,939,629 (44%)

1988 Democratic Presidential Primary

Dukakis 862,201 (63%)
Jackson 378,766 (28%)
Gore. 29,889 (2%)
Hart. 28,415 (2%)
Simon 15,457 (1%)
Others 61,407 (4%)

1984 Presidential Vote

Reagan (R) 2,678,559 (59%)
Mondale (D) 1,825,440 (40%)

1988 Republican Presidential Primary

Bush 637,697 (81%)
Dole. 93,076 (12%)
Robertson 55,949 (7%)

GOVERNOR

Gov. Richard F. Celeste (D)

Elected 1982, term expires Jan. 1991; b. Nov. 11, 1937, Lakewood; home, Columbus; Yale U., B.A. 1959, Rhodes Scholar, Oxford U., 1960–62; United Methodist; married (Dagmar).

Career: Exec. Asst. to U.S. Ambassador to India, 1963–67; Real estate developer, Natl. Housing Corp., 1967–75; OH House of Reps., 1971–75; Lt. Gov. of OH, 1975–79; Dir., Peace Corps, 1979–81.

Office: State House, Columbus 43266-0601, 614-466-3555.

Election Results

1986 gen.	Richard F. Celeste (D)	1,858,372	(61%)
	James A. Rhodes (R)	1,207,264	(39%)
1986 prim.	Richard F. Celeste (D)	684,206	(100%)
1982 gen.	Richard F. Celeste (D)	1,981,882	(59%)
	Clarence J. Brown (R)	1,303,962	(39%)

SENATORS

Sen. John H. Glenn Jr. (D)

Elected 1974, seat up 1992; b. July 18, 1921, Cambridge; home, Columbus; Muskingum Col., B.S. 1943; Presbyterian; married (Annie).

Career: USMC, 1942–65; NASA Astronaut, 1959–65, First American to orbit the Earth, 1962; Vice Pres., Royal Crown Cola Co., 1966–68, Pres., Royal Crown Intl., 1967–69.

Offices: 503 HSOB 20510, 202-224-3353. Also 200 N. High St., Rm. 600, Columbus 43215, 614-469-6697; 201 Superior Ave., Cleveland 44114, 216-522-7095; and 550 Main St., Ste. 10407, Cincinnati 45202, 513-684-3265.

Committees: *Armed Services* (7th of 11 D). Subcommittees: Conventional Forces and Alliance Defense; Strategic Forces and Nuclear Deterrence; Manpower and Personnel (Chairman). *Governmental Affairs* (Chairman of 8 D). Subcommittee: Permanent Subcommittee on Investigations (Vice Chairman). *Special Committee on Aging* (2d of 10 D).

Group Ratings

	ADA	ACLU	COPE	CFA	LCV	ACU	NTLC	NSI	COC	CEI
1988	80	78	81	100	50	9	2	70	31	21
1987	80	—	81	92	—	12	—	—	18	13

National Journal Ratings

	1988 LIB — 1988 CONS	1987 LIB — 1987 CONS
Economic	74% — 19%	74% — 0%
Social	86% — 0%	84% — 13%
Foreign	58% — 41%	46% — 49%

Key Votes

1) Cut Aged Housing $	FOR	5) Bork Nomination	AGN	9) SDI Funding	FOR
2) Override Hwy Veto	FOR	6) Ban Plastic Guns	AGN	10) Ban Chem Weaps	FOR
3) Kill Plnt Clsng Notice	AGN	7) Deny Abortions	AGN	11) Aid To Contras	AGN
4) Min Wage Increase	FOR	8) Japanese Reparations	FOR	12) Reagan Defense $	AGN

Election Results

1986 general	John H. Glenn Jr. (D)...............	1,949,208	(62%)	($1,319,026)
	Thomas N. Kindness (R)	1,171,893	(38%)	($657,908)
1986 primary	John H. Glenn Jr. (D).................	678,171	(88%)	
	Don Scott (D)........................	96,309	(12%)	
1980 general	John H. Glenn Jr. (D)...............	2,770,786	(69%)	($1,157,965)
	James E. Betts (R)	1,137,695	(28%)	($423,060)

Sen. Howard M. Metzenbaum (D)

Elected 1976, seat up 1994; b. June 4, 1917, Cleveland; home, Lyndhurst Heights; OH State U., B.A. 1939, LL.D. 1941; Jewish; married (Shirley).

Career: Practicing atty.; Cofounder, Airport Parking Co. of America, ComCorp Communications Corp.; Chmn. of the Bd., ITT Consumer Services Corp., 1966–68; OH House of Reps., 1943–46; OH Senate, 1947–50; Campaign Mgr. for U.S. Senator Stephen M. Young, 1958, 1964.

Offices: 140 RSOB 20510, 202-224-2315. Also 200 N. High St., Rm. 405, Columbus 43215, 614-469-6774; 1240 E. 9th St., Rm. 2919, Cleveland 44114, 216-544-7272; City Ctr. One, Ltd., 100 Fed. Plaza E., Ste. 510, Youngstown 44503, 216-746-1132; 10411 Fed. Bldg., Cincinnati 45202, 513-684-3894; and 234 Summit St., Toledo 43603, 419-259-7536.

Committees: *Energy and Natural Resources* (4th of 10 D). Subcommittees: Energy Regulation and Conservation (Chairman); Energy Research and Development; Water and Power. *Judiciary* (3d of 8 D). Subcommittees: Antitrust, Monopolies and Business Rights (Chairman); Constitution; Courts and Administrative Practice. *Labor and Human Resources* (3d of 9 D). Subcommittees: Aging; Education, Arts and Humanities; Handicapped; Labor and Human Resources (Chairman).

Group Ratings

	ADA	ACLU	COPE	CFA	LCV	ACU	NTLC	NSI	COC	CEI
1988	80	70	94	100	70	4	9	0	15	14
1987	100	—	94	100	—	4	—	—	22	18

National Journal Ratings

	1988 LIB — 1988 CONS			1987 LIB — 1987 CONS		
Economic	86%	—	0%	74%	—	0%
Social	83%	—	16%	90%	—	4%
Foreign	86%	—	0%	81%	—	0%

Key Votes

1) Cut Aged Housing $	FOR	5) Bork Nomination	AGN	9) SDI Funding	AGN
2) Override Hwy Veto	FOR	6) Ban Plastic Guns	AGN	10) Ban Chem Weaps	AGN
3) Kill Plnt Clsng Notice	AGN	7) Deny Abortions	AGN	11) Aid To Contras	AGN
4) Min Wage Increase	FOR	8) Japanese Reparations	FOR	12) Reagan Defense $	AGN

Election Results

1988 general	Howard M. Metzenbaum (D)	2,480,038	(57%)	($8,547,545)
	George V. Voinovich (R)	1,872,716	(43%)	($8,233,859)
1988 primary	Howard M. Metzenbaum (D)	1,070,934	(83%)	
	Ralph A. Applegate (D)	210,508	(17%)	
1982 general	Howard M. Metzenbaum (D)	1,923,767	(57%)	($2,794,172)
	Paul E. Pfeifer (R)	1,396,790	(41%)	($1,025,595)

FIRST DISTRICT

Cincinnati "spreads back from the Ohio River over a disarray of rugged hills," wrote the *WPA Guide* 50 years ago. "The growth of the city from its nucleus has been much like the rise of the flood waters that periodically have swept into the lower sections. Homes and streets seeped into the adjoining valleys, curved around the hills, and then crept higher on the hillsides." This was America's first inland metropolis, the fourth largest city in the nation at the outbreak of the Civil War, a heavily German beehive of riverboats and sausage factories (the city was known as Porkopolis and celebrated its bicentennial in 1988 with a sculpture topped with four flying pigs). Over the past century Cincinnati has not had the growth spurts of cities like Cleveland or Houston, but it has not had the sharp contractions such cities have suffered from either; it has spawned not flashy but solid industries, like the Procter & Gamble soap business, now headquartered in a striking two-towered office complex at the edge of downtown, and America's biggest concentration of machine tool makers.

Most of Cincinnati and suburban Hamilton County, west of the central dividing line of Mill Creek, forms Ohio's 1st Congressional District. The 1st includes some of the oldest and poorest parts of the city, like the Over-the-Rhine area (once German and crowded, now black and mostly empty) and some of the city's black slums (though only 16% of its residents are black). More typical are the old neighborhoods, some dating back more than 100 years, of wooden houses tucked in the valleys or ravines between Cincinnati's many hills. Here immigrant Germans moved, commuting to work in the factories on foot or downtown by the horsecar; in such neighborhoods today you could easily imagine yourself in the America of 50 or even 80 years ago. The comfortable urbanity of Cincinnati at the turn of the century is still apparent in many of its streets and neighborhoods.

Cincinnati's main ethnic group is German, and its ancestral politics is Republican. As its more prosperous offspring have moved off to the suburbs, the city of Cincinnati itself has become more Democratic; the suburbs in most elections are overwhelmingly Republican. Nevertheless, this is a district which elects a Democratic congressman. He is Thomas Luken, by now a House veteran and chairman of the Transportation and Hazardous Materials Subcommittee of the powerful Energy and Commerce Committee. Yet in Cincinnati he is remembered by many from his days on the Cincinnati Council—a body with limited jurisdiction since the charter reform of 1925, but which gets enough publicity to make its members the strongest candidates for other offices in the whole metropolitan area, even though they represent only a fraction of it. In some ways Luken resembles his district: he is an old-fashioned, not especially articulate congressman, who reflects old values and plods on with considerable success.

Luken was elevated to a subcommittee chairmanship in 1987, to his own surprise. When Chairman John Dingell reshuffled the jurisdiction of Energy and Commerce subcommittees, everyone expected James Florio of New Jersey to take the panel handling transportation and the Superfund which is so popular in his New Jersey district. But Florio opted for the subcommittee with jurisdiction over trade and consumer affairs instead, which gave Luken transportation.

In that important post, Luken has responded to more than initiated legislation, and he has followed the lead in almost every case of lobbying groups with something specific to gain or lose. He has tended, for example, to back reregulation of railroad rates in response to complaints from shippers—in spite of the fact that deregulation has lowered rates generally and enabled the railroads to compete with other modes of transportation better than they have for years. On acid rain legislation, he has been an ally of Energy and Commerce Chairman John Dingell and of the coal-burning industries and their unions in Ohio, which favor less stringent restrictions than Health Subcommittee Chairman Henry Waxman of Los Angeles. Luken was the leader in the effort to overturn the Federal Trade Commission's regulations on funeral homes. And after a fatal 1987 rail crash in Maryland sparked demands for random testing of engineers and other transportation workers, Luken took no action for months, in apparent support of the transportation unions which opposed all testing. Only when parents of children killed in the crash spoke out in his district after he refused to meet with them, and after he was criticized by editorials in the Cincinnati papers did he support some limited testing.

Luken is also is known as one of the Energy and Commerce members most responsive to the appeals of PACs, and most assiduous in seeking political contributions from them. Luken may or may not be overly responsive to lobbyists' pressures, but he is certainly aware that well-positioned Energy and Commerce members can easily raise hundreds of thousands of dollars of campaign money, money that can be very useful for a congressman who started off without a firm hold on his seat. Against nuisance opposition he collected $225,000 from PACs in 1986 and against stronger competition collected $468,000 in 1988. His record is notably less liberal on economic issues than those of most northern Democrats, and his approach to cultural issues reflects traditional Catholic attitudes; he is a fervent opponent of abortion, for example, though an equally fervent backer of a national lottery.

Luken's 1988 Republican opponent, Councilman Steve Chabot, used the issue of drug testing of railroad employees against Luken, and apparently made some headway. The result was a 56%–44% race, the closest in Ohio in 1988, but not the first close one for Luken. He first won the east side district seat in a special election in the spring of 1974, in one of those contests that helped end Richard Nixon's career. But Willis Gradison, the loser in the spring, came back in the fall and beat Luken. Two years later Luken ran in the west Cincinnati district against an incumbent who spent most of his time in Florida. He won narrowly in 1978, and in 1984 won with just 56%. Those results, and the 1988 election, suggest that Luken, for all the power of his subcommittee chairmanship and his ability to raise PAC money, may remain vulnerable in the 1st District.

The People: Est. Pop. 1986: 511,000, dn. 0.6% 1980–86; Pop. 1980: 514,190, dn. 2.2% 1970–80. Households (1980): 72% family, 40% with children, 57% married couples; 40.2% housing units rented; median monthly rent: $171; median house value: $47,900. Voting age pop. (1980): 364,014; 14% Black, 1% Spanish origin.

1988 Presidential Vote: Bush (R) 131,747   (63%)
                                Dukakis (D)..................... 76,661   (36%)

Rep. Thomas A. Luken (D)

Elected 1976; b. July 9, 1925, Cincinnati; home, Cincinnati; Bowling Green U., 1943–44, Xavier U., A.B. 1947, Salmon P. Chase Law Sch., LL.B. 1950; Roman Catholic; married (Shirley).

Career: USMC, WWII; Practicing atty.; Deer Park City Solicitor, 1955–61; U.S. Dist. Atty. for S. Dist. of OH, 1961–64; Cincinnati City Cncl., 1964–67, 1969–71, 1973; Mayor of Cincinnati, 1972–73; U.S. House of Reps., 1973–74.

Offices: 2168 RHOB 20515, 202-225-2216. Also Gwynne Bldg., Ste. 712, 602 Main St., Cincinnati 45202, 513-684-2723.

Committees: *Energy and Commerce* (7th of 26 D). Subcommittees: Commerce, Consumer Protection, and Competitiveness; Transportation and Hazardous Materials (Chairman). *Small Business* (3d of 27 D). Subcommittee: Antitrust, Impact of Deregulation and Privatization. *Select Committee on Aging* (8th of 39 D). Subcommittee: Health and Long-Term Care.

Group Ratings

	ADA	ACLU	COPE	CFA	LCV	ACU	NTLC	NSI	COC	CEI
1988	70	71	78	82	56	14	23	30	46	27
1987	56	—	77	64	—	14	—	—	29	17

National Journal Ratings

	1988 LIB — 1988 CONS		1987 LIB — 1987 CONS	
Economic	63% —	36%	52% —	47%
Social	53% —	46%	55% —	44%
Foreign	60% —	37%	58% —	42%

Key Votes

1) Homeless $	AGN	5) Ban Drug Test	AGN	9) SDI Research	AGN
2) Gephardt Amdt	FOR	6) Drug Death Pen	—	10) Ban Chem Weaps	AGN
3) Deficit Reduc	AGN	7) Handgun Sales	AGN	11) Aid to Contras	AGN
4) Kill Plnt Clsng Notice	AGN	8) Ban D.C. Abort $	FOR	12) Nuclear Testing	FOR

Election Results

1988 general	Thomas A. Luken (D)................	117,682	(56%)	($908,765)
	Steve Chabot (R)	90,738	(44%)	($262,162)
1988 primary	Thomas A. Luken (D), unopposed			
1986 general	Thomas A. Luken (D)................	90,477	(62%)	($261,455)
	Fred E. Morr (R)	56,100	(38%)	($127,653)

SECOND DISTRICT

"With all its manufacturing," the *WPA Guide* wrote 50 years ago, Cincinnati "is essentially commercial." At first an Ohio River crossroads, then a rail center (though overshadowed by St. Louis and Chicago), always a trade center for the territory to the south and west, Cincinnati may have big factories but the dynamism of its economy comes more from trade. Those who have done well in Cincinnati's commerce have, since the city's early days, tended to live on its east side. Starting on Mount Adams overlooking downtown, moving out the spine of the ridges running northward from the Ohio River, in the pleasant rolling country of the northern suburbs and of the estate-filled Village of Indian Hill, are concentrated Cincinnati's higher income and more prestigious residents. Its Reform Jews—an important group since the German immigrations of the 1840s—are as much a part of this fabric as are the Tafts who still live in Cincinnati.

Since 1852, Cincinnati and Hamilton County have been divided by a vertical line into two congressional districts; after the 1980 Census, the redistricters, to meet the population standard, had to move out into Clermont County where many east side Cincinnatians had been moving anyway and even farther, to Brown County, up the Ohio River, where Liza crossed the ice in Cincinnati author Harriet Beecher Stowe's *Uncle Tom's Cabin*. The east side of Cincinnati and its eastern Hamilton County suburbs, plus most of Clermont and Brown Counties, now make up the 2d Congressional District of Ohio. This is not an entirely upscale constituency. There are blacks here and enclaves like Norwood, site of a big General Motors plant, settled mostly by people who still regard the hills of eastern Kentucky and Tennessee as home.

Politically, Cincinnati's historical tradition is Republican, from the time Stowe composed her novel here in an island of German, pro-Union, Republican sentiment in a southern, Democratic pro-slavery sea. In later years, Cincinnati did not attract as many southern and eastern European immigrants as did Great Lakes industrial cities like Cleveland, Detroit and Chicago; its ethnic character (like its physical appearance) and its political preference have remained pretty well fixed. Even many of the Appalachians here are Republicans, from Civil War Republican counties in the hills. Culturally, it is the home of one of the most successful anti-pornography drives of any city in the nation. In 1988, Cincinnati lived up to its history: its metropolitan area, which extends into Kentucky and Indiana, produced a higher percentage for George Bush than any other million-plus metro area except Phoenix, Arizona.

Out of Cincinnati have come several prominent Republicans, including Salmon P. Chase (Lincoln's Treasury Secretary and Chief Justice), President and Chief Justice William Howard Taft, Speaker of the House Nicholas Longworth (who married Teddy Roosevelt's daughter Alice), and the late Senator Robert Taft. All were men of urbanity and learning, conservatives who sought to maintain the values and the political system which had allowed the growth and prosperity of ordered communities like Cincinnati, articulate advocates of a system that worked. In the 1960s, this district has had a series of prominent congressmen: John Gilligan, later governor of Ohio, and Robert Taft Jr., later U.S. Senator.

The current congressman from the district, Willis Gradison, is in Cincinnati's tradition of urbane conservatives. He is a believer in free market economics and shares the traditional Republican belief that business should be taxed lightly if you want investment and economic growth. He was never enthusiastic about supply-side economic theories and places a greater value on balanced budgets than supply-siders do. His strength—and his problem with other Members of his own party, as well as the opposition—is that he tends to take his beliefs and arguments where they go intellectually, regardless of political consequences. He is a clear-sighted and fair-minded analyst of what is going on, the kind of man to which members of both parties go to find out what is happening and what is at stake.

These traits have helped him to play a major role in fashioning legislation in the middle 1980s. In 1985, he was one of the few Ways and Means Republicans who was a steady supporter of tax reform, not even flinching when other Republicans gleefully but temporarily derailed Dan Rostenkowski's bill in December 1985. As ranking Republican on the Ways and Means Health Subcommittee, he worked with Chairman Pete Stark to piece together what became the catastrophic health care act of 1988—a bill that extended new benefits and levied a new tax to pay for them, and that was one of the major legislative achievements of the 100th Congress. In the 101st Congress, he is second ranking Republican on the Budget Committee, as he has been before; but the difference is that the ranking member is Bill Frenzel of Minnesota, whose cast of mind is similar to Gradison's, though his temperament is more mercurial. If there is the possibility of reaching a bipartisan budget accord in the House, or if the Republicans have a chance of fashioning an alternative that can command a majority there, these are two members with the technical ability and the policy creativity to do it.

Gradison won this seat on his second try: he lost to Thomas Luken in a 1974 special election, in which the main issue was Richard Nixon and Watergate; then, with Nixon gone, he beat Luken in November. (Luken went on to win the west Cincinnati district in 1976.) Since 1974, Gradison has been reelected by very large margins and has not attracted serious opposition; the extension of the district out beyond Hamilton County has strengthened him.

The People: Est. Pop. 1986: 523,700, up 1.9% 1980–86; Pop. 1980: 514,168, dn. 0.8% 1970–80. Households (1980): 70% family, 39% with children, 57% married couples; 39.4% housing units rented; median monthly rent: $168; median house value: $49,500. Voting age pop. (1980): 370,100 16% Black, 1% Spanish origin; 1% Asian origin.

1988 Presidential Vote:

Bush (R) 138,698	(62%)
Dukakis (D). 83,366	(37%)

Rep. Willis D. (Bill) Gradison, Jr. (R)

Elected 1974; b. Dec. 28, 1928, Cincinnati; home, Cincinnati; Yale U., B.A. 1948, Harvard U., M.B.A. 1951, D.C.S. 1954; Jewish; married (Heather).

Career: Investment broker; Asst. to U.S. Undersecy. of the Treasury, 1953–55; Asst. to U.S. Secy. of HEW, 1955–57; Cincinnati City Cncl., 1961–74, Vice-Mayor, 1967–71, Mayor, 1971.

Offices: 2311 RHOB 20515, 202-225-3164. Also 8008 Fed. Bldg., 550 Main St., Cincinnati 45202, 513-684-2456.

Committees: *Budget* (2d of 14 R). *Ways and Means* (6th of 13 R). Subcommittees: Health (Ranking Member); Social Security.

Group Ratings

	ADA	ACLU	COPE	CFA	LCV	ACU	NTLC	NSI	COC	CEI
1988	35	39	14	73	44	62	75	100	83	62
1987	20	—	14	29	—	65	—	—	100	78

National Journal Ratings

	1988 LIB — 1988 CONS			1987 LIB — 1987 CONS		
Economic	26%	—	74%	11%	—	83%
Social	43%	—	55%	19%	—	78%
Foreign	34%	—	66%	38%	—	61%

Key Votes

1) Homeless $	FOR	5) Ban Drug Test	FOR	9) SDI Research	FOR
2) Gephardt Amdt	AGN	6) Drug Death Pen	FOR	10) Ban Chem Weaps	AGN
3) Deficit Reduc	AGN	7) Handgun Sales	AGN	11) Aid to Contras	FOR
4) Kill Plnt Clsng Notice	FOR	8) Ban D.C. Abort $	AGN	12) Nuclear Testing	—

Election Results

1988 general	Willis D. (Bill) Gradison, Jr. (R) 153,162	(72%)	($125,682)
	Chuck R. Stidham (D)................. 58,637	(28%)	($13,961)
1988 primary	Willis D. (Bill) Gradison, Jr. (R), unopposed		
1986 general	Willis D. (Bill) Gradison, Jr. (R) 105,061	(70%)	($68,473)
	William F. Stineman (D)................ 43,448	(30%)	($1,474)

THIRD DISTRICT

Dayton, Ohio, just below the old National Road that spans the Midwest, a synonym sometimes for the ordinary mid-sized middle American city, is also one of America's centers of historic technological innovation. Dayton was the home of James Ritty, who in 1879 invented the cash register—that indispensable instrument for mass retail trade—and of John Henry Patterson, who bought it from Ritty for $6,500 in 1884 and established the National Cash Register company. It was home for a while of a trusted Patterson subordinate who feuded with him, Tom Watson Sr., the founder of IBM. It was in Dayton in the 1890s, that Wilbur and Orville Wright, tinkering in their bicycle shop and observing the horseless carriages that were being driven through Dayton's streets, experimented with kites and gliders, and constructed the first wind tunnel in the world and the first heavier-than-air flying machine which they brought down to ever-windy Kitty Hawk, North Carolina, to fly in 1903. Dayton, at the turn of the century, was a town buzzing with mechanical innovations, and with inventors like Charles Kettering who invented the automatic starter for cars, practical enough to turn them into profitable businesses.

In the early 1980s, the atmosphere was different. Dayton's major businesses seemed beleaguered: NCR by the volatility of the office and personal computer markets; Mead Paper by a huge antitrust verdict; companies supplying the Big Three auto firms by the collapse of auto sales. Dayton's population started to decline as young people left to find jobs elsewhere. Had the spirit of tinkering and innovation, of practical organization and mechanical dreaming entirely vanished? The experience of the early 1980s showed Dayton it could no longer coast on the achievements of its old inventors. It got Piedmont Airlines and Emery Air Freight to make Dayton a major airline hub, built on the aerospace base it got from nearby Wright-Patterson Air Force Base—the largest Air Force base in the world, with 35,000 workers on 8,000 acres—and sought to build on its engineering and manufacturing expertise. The unemployment rate was down by 1987, but the verdict was still out on whether Dayton was going to create anew its old spirit.

Dayton's economic troubles were accompanied by political volatility in a city which has never had really strong political machines or politically domineering business establishments or unions. In the off year elections, Dayton voted heavily for Democrats, Governor Richard Celeste and Senators Howard Metzenbaum and John Glenn; in presidential years, it gave Ronald Reagan and George Bush large majorities (though it voted for Metzenbaum in the 1988 Senate race). The apparent conclusion is that the Dayton area and the 3d Congressional District of Ohio, which includes almost all of Montgomery County, was not sure whether the Democrats' active-government or the Republicans' less-government approach was the best for Dayton's ills—or maybe they just voted for whomever seemed best at the moment.

The congressman from Dayton's 3d District is a Democrat with a distinctive approach to issues, Tony Hall. In many of the causes he has undertaken he has seemed good-hearted and guileless to the point of naivete—and yet he has been as successful in public life as the craftiest politico. Hall comes by his interest in politics partly through family—his father was once mayor of Dayton—but his views also owe much, as do those of many elected officials of his generation, to his service in the Peace Corps. He was in the by no means primitive, but also rather cynical, country of Thailand in 1966 and 1967, when the Vietnam war was raging not far away. When he returned to Dayton, he was elected to the state House of Representatives, evidently without much struggle, in the otherwise hideously turbulent political year of 1968.

Hall seems to have the gift of maintaining a serenity and focus on issues of pure morality while toiling in the vicinity of the most worldly strife. He advanced to the Ohio Senate in 1972, and was routinely reelected; when Congressman Charles Whalen, a liberal Republican, retired in 1978, Hall ran to succeed him, and won rather easily, with 80% in the primary and, despite the Republican trend that year, 55% in the general. In the House, he acquired a seat on the Rules Committee in his second term, yet while his record on most issues is predictably Democratic, he has not proved utterly malleable to the Democratic leadership; he backed a Republican budget alternative in 1981, and in 1988 he blocked a major education bill, despite strong lobbying by Jim Wright, because it did not include a total ban on dial-a-porn that Hall wanted attached.

Hall has sometimes used his leverage on Rules for local causes, but more often, since he became a born-again Christian in the early 1980s, for issues whose moral content catches his attention—although the solutions he offers do not always seem to rise to the level of the problem they're intended to address. Moved by reports that millions of children throughout the world are forced to labor under terrible conditions, he has urged the State Department to provide more information on child labor in its annual human rights reports. Moved by indications that many Americans (including some in the Dayton area) live in hunger, he has been active on the Select Committee on Hunger. Moved by the spate of attacks on blacks and others because of their race, religion, or ethnic group, he has denounced hate groups and proposed a national Commission on Values Education. He does attend to Dayton area problems and to Wright-Patterson Air Force Base (actually, it's just outside the district); but he paid less official attention to the fate of his brother, Sam P. Hall, who was shot down as an apparent mercenary over Nicaragua in 1986, than did next-door Republican Congressman Michael DeWine on the Iran-contra committee.

It is perhaps too cheap a shot to contrast the gravity of the problems Hall attacks with the scope of the solutions he proposes; who has come up with better? In Dayton and Montgomery County, to feed the hungry and help the homeless, he has revived the age-old practice of gleaning, persuading farmers to let him and other volunteers come into their fields after harvest and pick the crops missed by mechanical reapers and pickers—something like the polar opposite of Dayton's technical ingenuity. Politically, his almost saintly guilelessness pays off much better than the machinations of many a wily politico.

The People: Est. Pop. 1986: 506,400, dn. 1.5% 1980–86; Pop. 1980: 514,173, dn. 7.6% 1970–80. Households (1980): 72% family, 39% with children, 57% married couples; 37.0% housing units rented; median monthly rent: $159; median house value: $39,500. Voting age pop. (1980): 370,952; 16% Black, 1% Spanish origin.

1988 Presidential Vote:

Bush (R)	106,157	(54%)
Dukakis (D)	87,465	(45%)

Rep. Tony P. Hall (D)

Elected 1978; b. Jan. 16, 1942, Dayton; home, Dayton; Denison U., A.B. 1964; Presbyterian; married (Janet).

Career: Peace Corps, Thailand, 1966–67; Real estate broker, 1968–78; OH House of Reps., 1969–73; OH Senate, 1973–79.

Offices: 2448 RHOB 20515, 202-225-6465. Also 501 Fed. Bldg., 200 W. 2d St., Dayton 45402, 513-225-2843.

Committees: *Rules* (6th of 9 D). Subcommittee: Rules of the House. *Select Committee on Hunger* (2d of 19 D).

Group Ratings

	ADA	ACLU	COPE	CFA	LCV	ACU	NTLC	NSI	COC	CEI
1988	75	55	80	73	50	17	17	10	23	16
1987	76	—	79	64	—	9	—	—	29	19

National Journal Ratings

	1988 LIB — 1988 CONS		1987 LIB — 1987 CONS	
Economic	87%	— 8%	65%	— 35%
Social	55%	— 45%	46%	— 53%
Foreign	77%	— 21%	74%	— 26%

Key Votes

1) Homeless $	AGN	5) Ban Drug Test	AGN	9) SDI Research	AGN
2) Gephardt Amdt	FOR	6) Drug Death Pen	FOR	10) Ban Chem Weaps	FOR
3) Deficit Reduc	FOR	7) Handgun Sales	AGN	11) Aid to Contras	AGN
4) Kill Plnt Clsng Notice	AGN	8) Ban D.C. Abort $	FOR	12) Nuclear Testing	FOR

Election Results

1988 general	Tony P. Hall (D)	141,953	(77%)	($182,889)
	Ron Crutcher (R)	42,664	(23%)	($46,403)
1988 primary	Tony P. Hall (D), unopposed			
1986 general	Tony P. Hall (D)	98,311	(74%)	($76,558)
	Ron Crutcher (R)	35,167	(26%)	($48,368)

FOURTH DISTRICT

"What impressed me most," John Gunther wrote in the 1940s, "was the feeling this part of Ohio gave of being a crossroads. Take Mansfield. This town of 37,154 people is on the main line of both the Pennsylvania and Erie railroads, with direct service to both New York and Chicago; it is on a branch line of the Baltimore & Ohio, and the New York Central is only 12 miles distant. A stone's throw away northward is Norwalk, a pure New England town; a stone's throw southward is Mount Vernon, a pure southern town. Consider, too, crossroads in another dimension. Mansfield has 60 industrial plants, but it is the center of one of the richest agricultural areas on earth."

Politically, this crossroads on the flat limestone plains of northern Ohio is one of the

Republican heartlands of the United States. On the B&O tracks from Dayton to Toledo that intersect the east-west rail lines that go through Mansfield, Richard Nixon in 1968 and Ronald Reagan in 1984 made whistle-stop campaign tours to summon up the memories of past campaign styles and past loyalties. The TV cameras showed Reagan in Wapakoneta, the typically modest home town of the first man on the moon, Neil Armstrong, and Lima, an old industrial city that is in the largest county east of Chicago and north of Richmond to have voted for Barry Goldwater in 1964.

Much of this territory is in the 4th Congressional District of Ohio. This is a shallow, upside-down U-shaped group of counties, rural in appearance but with most of its people in small cities and towns in western and central Ohio. It includes Wapakoneta, Lima, Findlay, the prosperous home of Marathon Oil (acquired by U.S. Steel after some brouhaha), Bucyrus, which gave its name to a company producing giant earth-moving equipment, and Mansfield, home of John Sherman, one of Ohio's great Republican statesmen of the 19th century. This has been a Republican stronghold since the Civil War, yet it was momentarily shaken by the woes of Ohio's manufacturing economy. For the chief economic activity here is not farming—most of its fields are pretty marginal operations—but manufacturing; this is one of the most gadget-prone, mechanically inclined parts of the country. In the late 1980s, it recovered its confidence and its Republicanism: this is one of the few Ohio districts that voted against Senator Howard Metzenbaum in 1988.

The congressman from the 4th is Michael Oxley, a Republican chosen by an uncharacteristically narrow margin of 378 votes in a special election in the recession year of 1981. The Ohio Republican delegation was long dominated by men of the World War II generation; now it is mostly made up of men like Oxley, 20 and even 30 years younger. Their politics is a bit less orthodox and more venturesome: they are less worried about balancing the budget and getting along with the Democratic majority, and more concerned with nurturing economic growth and creating a Republican majority. Oxley was called a moderate when he ran because he supported George Bush in 1980; but just as Bush has done, he has backed conservative positions with vigor and consistency.

Oxley has a seat on one of the key committees in Congress, Energy and Commerce, where he has consistently voted to reduce federal regulation; and of course he is sympathetic to the problems of midwestern industries. That leaves him mostly against, but occasionally allied with, the committee's aggressive chairman, John Dingell. He has worked to establish a foreign trade zone in Findlay, to allow an extension for schools to get rid of asbestos, and to allow sting-obtained evidence to be used against accused money launderers. Energy and Commerce is a marvelous base from which to raise campaign contributions, but ever since his narrow victory in the special election, Oxley does not seem to need much. He has won easily and by overwhelming margins.

The People: Est. Pop. 1986: 513,000, dn. 0.2% 1980–86; Pop. 1980: 514,172, up 5.1% 1970–80. Households (1980): 77% family, 42% with children, 67% married couples; 26.1% housing units rented; median monthly rent: $153; median house value: $39,600. Voting age pop. (1980): 360,450; 3% Black, 1% Spanish origin.

1988 Presidential Vote:

Bush (R)	....	140,598	(67%)
Dukakis (D)	....	65,901	(32%)

Rep. Michael G. Oxley (R)

Elected June 25, 1981; b. Feb. 11, 1944, Findlay; home, Findlay; Miami U. of OH, B.A. 1966, OH State U., J.D. 1969; Lutheran; married (Patricia).

Career: FBI Spec. Agent, 1969–72; OH House of Reps., 1972–81; Practicing atty., 1972–1981.

Offices: 1131 LHOB 20515, 202-225-2676. Also 3121 W. Elm Plaza, Lima 45805, 419-999-6455; 24 W. 3d St., Rm. 314, Mansfield 44902, 419-522-5757; and 110 W. Main Cross, Rm. 206, Findlay 45840, 419-423-3210.

Committees: *Energy and Commerce* (11th of 17 R). Subcommittees: Energy and Power; Oversight and Investigations; Telecommunications and Finance. *Select Committee on Narcotics Abuse and Control* (3d of 12 R).

Group Ratings

	ADA	ACLU	COPE	CFA	LCV	ACU	NTLC	NSI	COC	CEI
1988	20	25	7	18	13	88	84	100	100	61
1987	4	—	6	7	—	95	—	—	100	82

National Journal Ratings

	1988 LIB — 1988 CONS	1987 LIB — 1987 CONS
Economic	15% — 85%	0% — 89%
Social	22% — 77%	0% — 90%
Foreign	16% — 78%	25% — 74%

Key Votes

1) Homeless $	FOR	5) Ban Drug Test	FOR	9) SDI Research	FOR
2) Gephardt Amdt	AGN	6) Drug Death Pen	FOR	10) Ban Chem Weaps	AGN
3) Deficit Reduc	AGN	7) Handgun Sales	AGN	11) Aid to Contras	FOR
4) Kill Plnt Clsng Notice	FOR	8) Ban D.C. Abort $	FOR	12) Nuclear Testing	AGN

Election Results

1988 general	Michael G. Oxley (R)................	160,099	(100%)	($207,157)
1988 primary	Michael G. Oxley (R), unopposed			
1986 general	Michael G. Oxley (R)................	115,751	(75%)	($215,276)
	Clem T. Cratty (D)...................	26,320	(17%)	

FIFTH DISTRICT

Undergirded by limestone, as flat and fertile as any part of the country, astride the land routes from the parts of the country which were economically the most productive in the years just after they were settled, northern Ohio has been blessed with a favorable location since its New England Yankees were joined by German Protestants around the middle of the 19th century. Northwest Ohio is the beginning of the great corn and hog belt that stretches into Illinois and Iowa, and has been one of the heartlands of the Republican Party since it was founded in 1854. It is also prime industrial country: its limestone, its rail connections, its location near the Great Lakes have spurred the growth of a factory economy which in dollar terms is more important than agriculture. Since its first settlement, northern Ohio hasn't had spectacular growth. But it has grown steadily, gaining population in the 1950s and 1960s when most farm areas were losing, gaining jobs in the 1970s and 1980s when so many heavy industrial areas saw the collapse of their old economic bases. Northern Ohio facing the 1990s has a big edge over many larger metropolitan areas, with lower labor costs, less obdurate unions, lower taxes, and almost no racial tensions.

The 5th Congressional District covers most of northwestern Ohio, except for Toledo and most of its suburbs which make up the 9th District. The 5th has been one of the most solidly Republican districts in the nation over the years. Franklin Roosevelt lost nearly 2 to 1 here, and despite the Democratic trend in industrial north-and-east Ohio, Michael Dukakis did not do much better. The contest for congressman, if there is any, is determined in the Republican primary, and that is very much what happened in 1988 when Congressman Delbert Latta retired after 30 years of partisan and mostly frustrating service. Partisan, because Latta is one of the most bitter and unyielding of Republican partisans, as shown by his defense of Richard Nixon in the 1974 impeachment hearings and his refusal to cooperate with Democrats during almost all of his 14 years as ranking Republican on the House Budget Committee. Frustrating, because— with the exception of the 1981 Reagan budget cut packages, known as Gramm-Latta I and II— Latta has seldom prevailed. On the Rules Committee, where he was a senior Republican for many years, he was usually on the losing end of partisan 9–4 votes.

Partisan and frustrating must also describe Latta's political year in 1988, when he decided to retire. He wanted very much to hand this House seat down to his son, Robert Latta, a 32-year-old Toledo lawyer, and to block the ambitions of state Senate President Paul Gillmor, who had long been eyeing it. Gillmor and Latta quarreled over the 1982 redistricting and over a bill Gillmor slipped through in 1985 that blocked Latta from resigning his seat and having the local Republican committee give it to his son. In the campaign Gillmor argued that, as the leading Republican in Columbus and a 22-year legislator, he had much the greater experience; Latta cited his work in his father's behalf and said he would carry on in his tradition. The contest came down to a matter of friends-and-neighbors, with Gillmor carrying his home territory and the eastern half of the district by 8,540 votes, and Latta carrying the western half by 8,483 votes. When absentee ballots were counted, Gillmor won by exactly 27 votes out of 63,000 cast. The general election was much easier, with Gillmor winning with 61%; the Democrat, rich businessman Tom Murray, did carry one county on Lake Erie.

The People: Est. Pop. 1986: 511,900, dn. 0.4% 1980–86; Pop. 1980: 514,173, up 7.7% 1970–80. Households (1980): 77% family, 44% with children, 67% married couples; 24.4% housing units rented; median monthly rent: $165; median house value: $43,200. Voting age pop. (1980): 358,616; 2% Spanish origin, 2% Black.

1988 Presidential Vote: Bush (R) 128,479 (61%)
Dukakis (D). 79,946 (38%)

Rep. Paul E. Gillmor (R)

Elected 1988; b. Feb. 1, 1939, Tiffin; home, Port Clinton; OH Wesleyan, B.A. 1961, U. of MI, J.D. 1964; Protestant; married (Karen).

Career: Air Force, 1965–66; OH Senate, 1967–88.

Offices: 1008 LHOB 20515, 202-225-6405. Also 100 Fed. Bldg., 280 S. Main St., Bowling Green 43402, 419-353-8871; 120 Jefferson St., Port Clinton 43452, 800-541-6446; 608 N. Clinton St., Defiance 43512, 800-541-6446; and 165 E. Washington Row, Sandusky 44870, 800-541-6446.

Committees: *Banking, Finance and Urban Affairs* (19th of 20 R). Subcommittees: Economic Stabilization; Financial Institutions Supervision, Regulation and Insurance; General Oversight and Investigations; Housing and Community Development.

Group Ratings and Key Votes: Newly Elected

Election Results

1988 general	Paul E. Gillmor (R)	123,838	(61%)	($769,548)
	Tom Murray (D)	80,472	(39%)	($846,905)
1988 primary	Paul E. Gillmor (R)	28,694	(45%)	
	Robert E. Latta (R)	28,667	(45%)	
	Rex Damschroder (R)	5,769	(9%)	
1986 general	Delbert L. Latta (R)	102,016	(65%)	($268,667)
	Tom Murray (D)	54,864	(35%)	($146,492)

SIXTH DISTRICT

After the Revolutionary War, George Washington procured for his Virginia veterans bounty grants of land in what was then called the Virginia Military District of Ohio. The metropolis of this region, between the Scioto and Miami rivers, and briefly the capital of Ohio, was Chillicothe, where the young Virginians who were the new state's first leaders built houses of native sandstone designed by the architect Benjamin Latrobe. But in 1810, the capital was moved away, and while Columbus is now the center of a million-plus metro area, Chillicothe keeps its old buildings. The writers of the *WPA Guide* noted that 50 years ago you could still see "Mount Logan, familiar to all Ohioans because it is stamped on the Great Seal of the State, with the sun rising over its shoulder and looking down on a field of ripened wheat extending to Chillicothe's front and back door, as it was on that morning of 1803 when Thomas Worthington and his friends (after, some say, an all-night card game) looked upon it, thought it a fine view, and decided to adopt it as the State symbol." The traces of the Virginians still lie on this landscape, which is laid out in irregular-shaped parcels as in Virginia, not in the checkerboard grid of most of the Midwest; and there is a political effect as well, for until recent decades this part of southern Ohio usually voted Democratic. It still elects some notable Democrats, like Ohio House Speaker Vern Riffe, a power in Columbus and the senior House speaker in the nation, but it has been solidly Republican in congressional elections since 1960.

The lands of the Virginia Military District take up most of the expanse of Ohio's 6th Congressional District. It touches the metropolitan areas of Cincinnati, Dayton and Columbus, and includes the gritty industrial city of Portsmouth on the Ohio River; it also includes Kings Island, one of the biggest theme parks in the country, off I-71 northeast of Cincinnati. But little in this district partakes of metropolitan ambience; this is mostly small-town America.

The current congressman, Bob McEwen, came to office in 1980 after serving in the legislature and working for his predecessor, William Harsha, and at first he, like Harsha, seemed to concentrate on bringing public works projects to the district. But by the middle 1980s, McEwen, still in his mid-thirties, started thinking about running for statewide office. In 1985, he began to stake out some interesting positions on issues, becoming lead sponsor of measures to require the President to state a national strategy statement with each military budget, to target the about-to-be-phased-out revenue sharing funds to poorer cities and towns, and to put the highway trust funds off budget so no one can use their surpluses to balance the overall budget. He then announced he was thinking about running for the Senate in 1988 against Howard Metzenbaum. But when it became apparent in 1987 that this would mean a primary against Cleveland Mayor George Voinovich, McEwen withdrew from the race.

Could he have won? He started off in the primary behind in name identification, but Voinovich's reputation as a moderate and McEwen's record of down-the-line conservative and pro-Reagan voting might have given McEwen a chance to overtake him. The general election might have been more problematic. Metzenbaum's reputation as a fighter for the little guy helped him win 57% in both 1982 and 1988, and it's not obvious that McEwen's supply-side economics and cultural conservatism could put a dent in him, nor that the thirty-something and handsome McEwen would have equalled Metzenbaum in stature.

Returned to the House with a record vote in 1988, McEwen seems again fixated on issues with a local, 6th District angle: he wants to make sure the transportation trust funds are spent on roads, aviation, and inland waterways, and not squirreled away or used for general deficit reduction. He has been mentioned only fleetingly as a candidate for the governorship, which is open in 1990, perhaps because his involvement with state issues has been limited. But he reportedly has been offered the lieutenant governor's nomination by more than one gubernatorial candidate. What that is worth is another matter. It might put him in position to run for governor in 1994 or 1998. But it would also cost him control of his political fate—something few politicians with as safe a seat as McEwen has in the 6th District do.

The People: Est. Pop. 1986: 525,300, up 2.2% 1980–86; Pop. 1980: 514,173, up 13.0% 1970–80. Households (1980): 79% family, 45% with children, 69% married couples; 26.1% housing units rented; median monthly rent: $143; median house value: $39,800. Voting age pop. (1980): 359,077; 2% Black.

1988 Presidential Vote: Bush (R) 136,915   (64%)
Dukakis (D). 74,200   (35%)

Rep. Bob McEwen (R)

Elected 1980; b. Jan. 12, 1950, Hillsboro; home, Hillsboro; U. of Miami (FL), B.B.A. 1972; Protestant; married (Liz).

Career: Real estate developer; OH House of Reps., 1974–80.

Offices: 2431 RHOB 20515, 202-225-5705. Also P.O. Bldg., Portsmouth 45662, 614-353-5171; and P.O. Bldg., Rm. 202, Hillsboro 45133, 513-393-4223.

Committees: *Public Works and Transportation* (6th of 20 R). Subcommittees: Aviation; Economic Development (Ranking Member); Surface Transportation. *Veterans' Affairs* (4th of 13 R). Subcommittees: Compensation, Pension and Insurance (Ranking Member); Hospitals and Health Care.

Group Ratings

	ADA	ACLU	COPE	CFA	LCV	ACU	NTLC	NSI	COC	CEI
1988	5	14	17	36	19	96	88	100	100	65
1987	4	—	18	7	—	86	—	—	90	74

National Journal Ratings

	1988 LIB — 1988 CONS		1987 LIB — 1987 CONS	
Economic	10%	88%	24%	76%
Social	13%	84%	17%	82%
Foreign	0%	84%	0%	80%

Key Votes

1) Homeless $	—	5) Ban Drug Test	FOR	9) SDI Research	FOR
2) Gephardt Amdt	AGN	6) Drug Death Pen	FOR	10) Ban Chem Weaps	AGN
3) Deficit Reduc	AGN	7) Handgun Sales	FOR	11) Aid to Contras	FOR
4) Kill Plnt Clsng Notice	FOR	8) Ban D.C. Abort $	FOR	12) Nuclear Testing	AGN

Election Results

1988 general	Bob McEwen (R)	152,235	(74%)	($884,754)
	Gordon R. Roberts (D)................	52,635	(26%)	($43,485)
1988 primary	Bob McEwen (R), unopposed			
1986 general	Bob McEwen (R)	106,354	(70%)	($248,157)
	Gordon R. Roberts (D)................	42,155	(28%)	($21,324)

SEVENTH DISTRICT

"Although Springfield has become a big city of many manufacturers," wrote the *WPA Guide* 50 years ago, "it still has a rural atmosphere lingering from the days when farmers and their wives hitched their horses on the Esplanade and alighted to sell firewood and trade chickens, eggs and country butter for calico, buttons and lace. The farmer in overalls busy with his produce near the markethouse, or loafing at the corner of Limestone and Main, is today as much a part of Springfield as the shop worker from the International Harvester Plant and the girl and pressman from the Crowell-Collier Publishing Company. This is the center of one of the richest valleys in Ohio, where corn grows as long as a man's forearm, the loamy soil is black and deep, and the price of hogs is watched as closely as the weather forecast." International Harvester has now gone bankrupt and been renamed Navistar, and Crowell-Collier is not the giant it once was, but there remains a certain steadiness in Springfield and the central Ohio country around it. For just as the farm atmosphere remained long after agriculture was replaced by heavy manufacturing as the chief generator of economic activity here, so the atmosphere of heavy manufacturing remains even as the local economy adapts to different times with suppleness and skill. And just as people remembered the old days fondly 50 years ago, so do they reminisce about them today—forgetting the hard work and drudgery that were the lot of almost all men and women in those supposedly easier times.

Springfield is the largest town in the 7th Congressional District of Ohio, an odd-shaped unit which forms a sort of horseshoe some 20 to 50 miles around Columbus. It includes such notable places as Bellefontaine, site of the first concrete street in America; Marion, where young Socialist-to-be Norman Thomas delivered newspapers edited by President-to-be Warren Harding; and Marysville, site of Honda's first U.S. plant. Historically, this is Republican territory. The policies of the party of William McKinley—tariff protection, railroad regulation, antitrust suits against monopolies, discouragement of labor unions—seemed to work very well to produce economic growth in the years 1900–30; the low-tax Republican policies of the 1950s also seemed to work; this was the last decade in which Ohio had a significant increase in the number of manufacturing jobs. And in the 1980s, as Honda's decision to build another assembly plant in nearby Shelby County suggests, this part of Ohio has again built a growing economy and developed a new political consensus. In presidential contests it supports the low-tax, culturally conservative, nationalistically assertive politics of Ronald Reagan and George Bush. But to hedge its bets in statewide elections it has supported government intervention in the economy by giving small margins to Senator Howard Metzenbaum and Governor Richard Celeste.

In congressional elections, Springfield and the 7th follow their national political instincts and since 1982, when Clarence (Bud) Brown ran for governor, have elected Republican Michael DeWine. He spent four years as the elected prosecutor in Greene County, just south of Springfield, which covers Dayton suburbs, farming and covered-bridge countryside, and the small town of Xenia made famous by the octogenarian Helen Hooven Santmyer's ... And Ladies of the Club. For two years he was in the Ohio Senate. He brings to the House a prosecutorial air plus an enthusiasm for conservative causes which has made him one of the feistiest young Republicans—one who delights in harassing the Democrats, supporting aid to the Nicaraguan contras on the Foreign Affairs Committee and tussling with liberals on Judiciary. In 1986, DeWine was appointed to serve on the special committee investigating the Iran-contra scandal. There his staunch defenses of Ronald Reagan got him labelled "DeWhine" by some critics, and others noticed that he dozed off from time to time (he says he was working long hours, and anyway lack of energy is not one of his vices). He was a prosecutor in the impeachment trial of Judge Harry Claiborne, and sponsored a tough anti-drunk driving bill in the House, similar to one he got passed in the Ohio Senate in 1982.

DeWine's aggressiveness is carried over into electoral politics. He has won by wide margins when he is opposed in the 7th District, and in 1989 he was travelling across Ohio running for governor. He begins probably less well known than some other likely Republican contenders, but name recognition is only the initial hurdle and it's possible that if he can get past it, he can make a positive impression. He points out, for example, that Ohio's increased spending on education has produced fewer teachers and more administrators—a vivid way of making a criticism that is not confined to conservatives. By early 1990, he has said, he will know for sure if he's going to make the chancy race for governor or run for surefire reelection.

950   OHIO

The People: Est. Pop. 1986: 513,600, dn. 0.1% 1980–86; Pop. 1980: 514,170, up 3.7% 1970–80. Households (1980): 78% family, 44% with children, 67% married couples; 28.2% housing units rented; median monthly rent: $153; median house value: $41,500. Voting age pop. (1980): 362,126; 5% Black, 1% Spanish origin.

1988 Presidential Vote:

Bush (R)	126,434	(64%)
Dukakis (D)	69,649	(35%)

Rep. Michael DeWine (R)

Elected 1982; b. Jan. 5, 1947, Springfield; home, Cedarville; Miami U. of OH, B.S. 1969, OH Northern U., J.D. 1972; Roman Catholic; married (Frances).

Career: Practicing atty.; Asst. Prosecuting Atty., Greene Cnty., 1973–75, Prosecuting Atty., 1977–81; OH Senate, 1981–82.

Offices: 1705 LHOB 20515, 202-225-4324. Also 150 N. Limestone St., Rm. 220, Springfield 45501, 513-325-0474; and 399 E. Church St., Marion 43302, 614-387-5300.

Committees: *Foreign Affairs* (10th of 18 R). Subcommittees: International Economic Policy and Trade; Western Hemisphere Affairs. *Judiciary* (7th of 14 R). Subcommittees: Crime; Economic and Commercial Law.

Group Ratings

	ADA	ACLU	COPE	CFA	LCV	ACU	NTLC	NSI	COC	CEI
1988	5	22	13	55	50	100	80	100	93	64
1987	20	—	13	21	—	87	—	—	93	77

National Journal Ratings

	1988 LIB — 1988 CONS		1987 LIB — 1987 CONS	
Economic	21% —	79%	0% —	89%
Social	24% —	75%	25% —	73%
Foreign	0% —	84%	25% —	74%

Key Votes

1) Homeless $	FOR	5) Ban Drug Test	FOR	9) SDI Research	FOR
2) Gephardt Amdt	AGN	6) Drug Death Pen	FOR	10) Ban Chem Weaps	AGN
3) Deficit Reduc	AGN	7) Handgun Sales	FOR	11) Aid to Contras	FOR
4) Kill Plnt Clsng Notice	FOR	8) Ban D.C. Abort $	FOR	12) Nuclear Testing	AGN

Election Results

1988 general	Michael DeWine (R)	142,597	(74%)	($299,553)
	Jack Schira (D)	50,423	(26%)	($51,478)
1988 primary	Michael DeWine (R), unopposed			
1986 general	Michael DeWine (R)	119,238	(100%)	($142,205)

EIGHTH DISTRICT

In the middle of Middle America, the old National Road, now U.S. 40, heads straight as an arrow in its last miles across Ohio to Indiana. By the early 20th century, this had become industrial country: Dayton was already a major factory city; Middletown and Hamilton, downstream on the Great Miami River, were smaller versions; the little towns around were increasingly sustained by their factories rather than farm markets. Yet nature still exerted its force. U.S. 40 must jog southward twice to go over the dams on the Miami and the Stillwater built after the great flood of 1913 killed 361 people in Dayton and caused $1 billion in damage. And as George Stewart noted while driving through in the 1940s to prepare his book *U.S. 40*, the forest was still thick here.

The 8th Congressional District of Ohio occupies part of this territory on the western edge of Ohio. The southern end of the district, in Butler County around Hamilton and Middletown, had many settlers from around the Ohio River and farther south and still has a trace of southern accent and Dixiecrat politics; George Wallace got 18% of the vote here in the 1968 general election, his highest percentage in any district of a state that barred slavery at the time of the Civil War. The counties north of U.S. 40, more sparsely populated, were settled overland and have little southern accent or heritage. People here rooted for the Union in the Civil War, and most of their descendants have voted Republican ever since, except for some Catholic communities and in deep recession years.

The congressman from this district is Donald "Buz" Lukens, who has had a long career as a conservative *enfant terrible* but lately seems more terrible than enfant. With marvelous symmetry he has been elected to the House in 1966 and 1968 and 1986 and 1988; in 1970 gave up his House seat to run for statewide office, unsuccessfully, then served in the legislature in Columbus from 1971–86 during which time he suffered a bout with cancer and recovered. In 1986, he gained his House seat back after the incumbent, Thomas Kindness, ran unsuccessfully for statewide office. In early 1989, his tenure seemed threatened by personal scandal. Even apart from that, Lukens has not cut a commanding figure in the House. He seemed an oddity in the early 1960s, when most insiders assumed quite wrongly that the future of the Republican Party lay with its liberal wing; Lukens was an activist conservative who won attention as head of the Young Republicans in 1963 and then made it to the House from a district created by the one-person-one-vote decisions so many conservatives abhorred.

In the House once again he is an exhorter who is not very effective—his main causes have been stopping South African sanctions and backing contra aid—and a thinker who is simply not in the league with some of the younger conservatives. In January 1989 a Columbus TV station charged that he had had sex with a 13-year-old black girl; he said, "I didn't really know she was a teenager . . . I do now, of course." He was convicted of morals charges and asserted both his innocence and intention to run again. However, Kindness, out of public office, announced he'd run if there was a vacancy, and the odds are that the symmetry of Luken's congressional record will continue, and that in 1990, as in 1970, Lukens will not be reelected to the House.

The People: Est. Pop. 1986: 526,200, up 2.3% 1980–86; Pop. 1980: 514,171, up 11.3% 1970–80. Households (1980): 78% family, 44% with children, 68% married couples; 26.5% housing units rented; median monthly rent: $164; median house value: $44,800. Voting age pop. (1980): 361,343; 3% Black, 1% Spanish origin.

1988 Presidential Vote:
Bush (R)	147,196	(69%)
Dukakis (D)	65,826	(31%)

Rep. Donald E. (Buz) Lukens (R)

Elected 1986; b. Feb. 11, 1931, Harveysburg; home, Middletown; OH State U., B.A. 1951; Quaker; divorced.

Career: USAF, 1954–60; U.S. House of Reps., 1967–70; OH Senate, 1971–86.

Offices: 117 CHOB 20515, 202-225-6205. Also 646 High St., Hamilton 45011, 513-895-5656; 202 E. Main St., Greenville 45331, 513-548-8817; and 1345 Central Ave., Middletown 45044, 513-423-2100.

Committees: *Foreign Affairs* (14th of 18 R). Subcommittees: Africa; Europe and the Middle East. *Government Operations* (6th of 15 R). Subcommittee: Employment and Housing.

Group Ratings

	ADA	ACLU	COPE	CFA	LCV	ACU	NTLC	NSI	COC	CEI
1988	0	5	12	18	13	96	94	100	85	74
1987	4	—	0	14	—	100	—	—	100	78

National Journal Ratings

	1988 LIB — 1988 CONS		1987 LIB — 1987 CONS	
Economic	18%	— 81%	0%	— 89%
Social	0%	— 95%	24%	— 76%
Foreign	0%	— 84%	0%	— 80%

Key Votes

1) Homeless $	FOR	5) Ban Drug Test	—	9) SDI Research	FOR
2) Gephardt Amdt	AGN	6) Drug Death Pen	FOR	10) Ban Chem Weaps	AGN
3) Deficit Reduc	AGN	7) Handgun Sales	FOR	11) Aid to Contras	FOR
4) Kill Plnt Clsng Notice	FOR	8) Ban D.C. Abort $	FOR	12) Nuclear Testing	AGN

Election Results

1988 general	Donald E. (Buz) Lukens (R).	154,164	(76%)	($147,712)
	John W. Griffin (D)	49,084	(24%)	
1988 primary	Donald E. (Buz) Lukens (R), unopposed			
1986 general	Donald E. (Buz) Lukens (R).	98,475	(68%)	($218,387)
	John W. Griffin (D)	46,195	(32%)	($3,814)

NINTH DISTRICT

On Toledo's Maumee River, reported the *WPA Guide* 50 years ago, "from the breakup of the ice in spring until winter halts navigation, boats ranging in size from 700-foot ore freighters to saucy catboats go busily up and down the waterway. Its shores, once described as 'well-defined projecting headlands,' are now lined solidly with wharves, factories, warehouses and refineries where furnaces glow red and a forest of stacks rise against the sky. Twenty-four railroads converge on the city. Coal trains rumble in from Ohio, West Virginia, and Kentucky. At 40 wharves, huge machines pick up freight cars one by one and dump their contents into the holds of freighters with the ease of a farm girl emptying a pail of water. Equally Gargantuan are the scoops that unburden the incoming freighters of their red ore." Toledo was then "the world's greatest shipper of bituminous coal," one of those heavy industrial, heavily ethnic cities on the Great Lakes whose factories and muscles would build the machines—notably the Jeeps—that enabled America to win the war.

Toledo was largely built by the automobile business, its major products being Jeeps and auto glass; it more than doubled in size between 1900 and 1930, the boom auto years; and it suffered in the 1970s and 1980s from the collapse of the American manufacturers. Now Toledo is being reshaped by the economic changes of the 1970s and 1980s. In 1978, just before the second oil shock, there were 79,000 manufacturing and 185,000 non-manufacturing employees in the Toledo metropolitan area. By the 1982 trough, manufacturing employment was down to 60,000 while non-manufacturing held steady at 184,000. After four years of recovery, in 1989 manufacturing bounced back only to 61,700, but non-manufacturing was up to 224,000. Toledo's economy has been hurt or threatened by widely publicized events, like big companies' plant closings and the purchase of a major interest in Libbey-Owens-Ford glass by a Japanese firm. These hurt well-established local institutions, especially labor unions. Toledo has been helped visibly by new developments on the waterfront—office buildings, a fancy hotel, an apartment tower—and less visibly by small businesses hiring new workers and starting to make new products or provide new services.

Historically, Toledo and surrounding Lucas County, which together make up most of today's 9th Congressional District, have been heavily Democratic since the CIO unions organized the plants in the late 1930s; Toledo was the only Ohio city carried by George McGovern in 1972. But in 1980, a year after the auto industry collapsed, Toledo switched to the Republicans, voting for Ronald Reagan and ousting 26-year Democratic Congressman Thomas Ashley, an old college friend of George Bush, for Republican businessman Ed Weber. But after two more years of recession, Toledo was heavily Democratic again, ousting Weber and electing Democrat Marcy Kaptur, who remains 9th District congresswoman today.

Kaptur spent 15 years as an urban planner in a city famous half a century ago for its city planning; she had a job on the Carter White House staff and was shrewd enough to return home to Toledo in 1982 when no one else wanted to run. In that campaign and ever since she has been fixated on the trade issue and the Japanese. She calls for measures to get the Japanese to buy their fair share of American auto parts and co-chairs the Congressional Competitiveness Caucus, which released a study of foreign ownership of U.S. assets; Kaptur seems troubled even by the Japanese investment in Libbey-Owens-Ford, though it helps a home-town business keep going and penetrate the Japanese market. She is co-sponsor of a major provision of the ethics bill, vetoed by President Reagan in 1988, which would prohibit government officials from representing foreign interests for four years after they leave government.

Among House Democrats Kaptur has been a hard-working team player. After the 1986 election, she won a seat on the Steering and Policy Committee, which makes committee assignments; after the 1988 election, she won a seat on the Budget Committee. At home she won reelection against a former local newscaster by only a 55%–43% margin in 1984, but won by better than 3 to 1 in 1986 and 1988.

The People: Est. Pop. 1986: 506,200, dn. 1.5% 1980–86; Pop. 1980: 514,174, up 1.0% 1970–80. Households (1980): 71% family, 39% with children, 57% married couples; 32.4% housing units rented; median monthly rent: $179; median house value: $42,600. Voting age pop. (1980): 364,640; 11% Black, 2% Spanish origin.

1988 Presidential Vote: Dukakis (D) 107,960   (53%)
                               Bush (R) 92,563   (46%)

Rep. Marcy Kaptur (D)

Elected 1982; b. June 17, 1946, Toledo; home, Toledo; U. of WI, B.A. 1968, U. of MI, M.A. 1974; Roman Catholic; single.

Career: Urban planner, Toledo–Lucas Cnty. Planning Comm., 1969–75; Development and Urban Planning Consultant, 1975–77; Asst. Dir. for Urban Affairs, Domestic Policy Staff, White House, 1977–80; Dpty. Secy., Natl. Consumer Coop. Bank, 1980–81.

Offices: 1228 LHOB 20515, 202-225-4146. Also Fed. Bldg., 234 Summit St., Rm. 719, Toledo 43604, 419-259-7500.

Committees: *Banking, Finance and Urban Affairs* (15th of 31 D). Subcommittees: Consumer Affairs and Coinage; Economic Stabilization; Financial Institutions Supervision, Regulation and Insurance; Housing and Community Development. *Budget* (20th of 21 D). Task Forces: Defense, Foreign Policy and Space; Human Resources.

Group Ratings

	ADA	ACLU	COPE	CFA	LCV	ACU	NTLC	NSI	COC	CEI
1988	75	74	92	73	81	13	16	10	43	18
1987	84	—	91	86	—	0	—	—	21	8

National Journal Ratings

	1988 LIB — 1988 CONS		1987 LIB — 1987 CONS	
Economic	67%	— 30%	73%	— 0%
Social	56%	— 43%	72%	— 27%
Foreign	74%	— 23%	81%	— 0%

Key Votes

1) Homeless $	AGN	5) Ban Drug Test	AGN	9) SDI Research	AGN
2) Gephardt Amdt	FOR	6) Drug Death Pen	FOR	10) Ban Chem Weaps	FOR
3) Deficit Reduc	FOR	7) Handgun Sales	AGN	11) Aid to Contras	AGN
4) Kill Plnt Clsng Notice	AGN	8) Ban D.C. Abort $	FOR	12) Nuclear Testing	FOR

Election Results

1988 general	Marcy Kaptur (D)	157,557	(81%)	($244,030)
	Al Hawkins (R).....................	36,183	(19%)	($47,945)
1988 primary	Marcy Kaptur (D), unopposed			
1986 general	Marcy Kaptur (D)	105,646	(78%)	($317,798)
	Mike Shufeldt (R)	30,643	(22%)	($47,514)

TENTH DISTRICT

Fifty years ago a traveler on U.S. 40 still encountered, in central Ohio, some of the S-bridges built in the 1820s, when the federal government was laying the road west into Ohio and cared less about avoiding sharp curves than building the shortest possible bridge over a river. A major federal project then, the National Road and its successors, U.S. 40 and Interstate 70 remain a major landmark, culturally and politically, in Ohio today. South of these roads is southern-accented Ohio, the part of the state first settled by whites, historically Copperhead and Democratic; north was Yankee-settled, industrial, historically Republican.

The 10th Congressional District of Ohio is situated almost entirely south of the National Road. The 10th includes Marietta, on the Ohio River, the first permanent American settlement in 1788 in the old Northwest Territory, and the land north and west of the Ohio River ceded to the new nation by the British after the Revolutionary War; it includes the industrial city of Ironton on the Ohio River; and it takes in the small industrial cities of Lancaster and Newark not far from Columbus. The hills here have been for years the least thickly settled part of Ohio, a part of America seemingly left behind by progress, but in the 1970s and 1980s some of these small cities, including Athens, home of Ohio University, have been growing while Ohio's industrial cities have been losing people. Even so, about half the 10th's voters live within 50 miles of Columbus.

Politically the heritage here is mixed, between the Democratic tendencies of some of the areas settled by Virginians and the Republican leanings of parts like Marietta settled by Yankees. The national trend has been Republican now for a long time; in congressional elections this was prime marginal territory from 1958 to 1966, when party control changed hands four times. But the 10th District has stayed solidly Republican since then.

Representative Clarence Miller, elected that year, is an engineer and seems to approach politics seeking precision and orderliness. He established a record of never missing a House roll call vote since he was elected—an example of stern discipline, particularly since many roll calls are demanded for dilatory or mischievous reasons. As a member of the Appropriations Committee he has introduced numerous amendments to require across-the-board cuts of specific percentages in departmental spending. But like so many other critics of big government, he has been less successful than he would like at the hard work of actually paring down appropriations; it must have been frustrating for him to see huge deficits piled up under a Republican President who styled himself a conservative. But Miller perseveres. His old-fashioned brand of politics remains hugely popular in the 10th District, and he is routinely reelected by large margins.

The People: Est. Pop. 1986: 521,300, up 1.4% 1980–86; Pop. 1980: 514,173, up 12.7% 1970–80. Households (1980): 77% family, 43% with children, 67% married couples; 26.0% housing units rented; median monthly rent: $150; median house value: $37,700. Voting age pop. (1980): 362,509; 2% Black.

1988 Presidential Vote:

Bush (R)	125,699	(61%)
Dukakis (D)	79,608	(38%)

Rep. Clarence E. Miller (R)

Elected 1966; b. Nov. 1, 1917, Lancaster; home, Lancaster; United Methodist; widowed.

Career: Electrical engineer; Lancaster City Cncl., 1957–63; Mayor of Lancaster, 1963–65.

Offices: 2308 RHOB 20515, 202-225-5131. Also 212 S. Broad St., Lancaster 43130, 614-654-5149; and 27 S. Park Pl., Newark 43055, 614-349-8279.

Committees: *Appropriations* (4th of 22 R). Subcommittee: Defense.

Group Ratings

	ADA	ACLU	COPE	CFA	LCV	ACU	NTLC	NSI	COC	CEI
1988	15	18	13	45	31	92	64	100	93	57
1987	8	—	12	17	—	100	—	—	71	57

National Journal Ratings

	1988 LIB — 1988 CONS			1987 LIB — 1987 CONS	
Economic	29%	—	70%	24%	—	74%
Social	5%	—	91%	17%	—	82%
Foreign	16%	—	78%	0%	—	80%

Key Votes

1) Homeless $	FOR	5) Ban Drug Test	—	9) SDI Research	FOR
2) Gephardt Amdt	AGN	6) Drug Death Pen	FOR	10) Ban Chem Weaps	AGN
3) Deficit Reduc	AGN	7) Handgun Sales	FOR	11) Aid to Contras	FOR
4) Kill Plnt Clsng Notice	FOR	8) Ban D.C. Abort $	FOR	12) Nuclear Testing	AGN

Election Results

1988 general	Clarence E. Miller (R)	143,673	(72%)	($99,247)
	John M. Buchanan (D)	56,893	(28%)	($8,535)
1988 primary	Clarence E. Miller (R)	52,243	(84%)	
	Ronald E. Shoemaker (R)	9,782	(16%)	
1986 general	Clarence E. Miller (R)	106,870	(70%)	($67,073)
	John M. Buchanan (D)	44,847	(30%)	($1,023)

ELEVENTH DISTRICT

Ohio's Western Reserve—the northeast corner of the state that belonged to Connecticut until 1800—still has something of the Yankee imprint on it. Inland from Lake Erie, east of Cleveland or north of Youngstown and Warren, you can still see, as the *WPA Guide* described 50 years ago, landscapes of "white farmhouses lying next to boulder-strewn fields, orchards, groves of maples, and wooded ravines silvered with tiny streams." The Western Reserve was one of the nation's strongest anti-slavery constituencies before the Civil War and one of its most heavily Republican areas afterwards. Its thrifty, hard-working, well-educated citizens built communities with fine schools and, with their accumulated savings, invested in what became some of the nation's leading industries. That brought in great masses of immigrants to Cleveland and the other cities of northeast Ohio, who remained solidly Republican until the Great Depression and the bloody CIO organizing drives of the late 1930s; then, for 30 years, the Western Reserve was Democratic in Ohio's class warfare politics.

Now the Western Reserve may be moving toward a post-industrial economy similar to that of Connecticut or Massachusetts. Factory employment has been falling, but total jobs are rising again; small, adaptive business units and highly skilled work are the growth sectors. In politics, the Western Reserve now seems to prefer Democrats as it once did Republicans, with only a few Republicans with liberal reputations, like Cleveland Mayor George Voinovich, surviving. Yet the Democrats are careful to promise lower rather than higher taxes and to sketch out a future in which entrepreneurs play a bigger role than union leaders.

The 11th Congressional District of Ohio takes in most of the geographical expanse of the Western Reserve, the northeast corner of Ohio. But it skirts the central cities. Cleveland and Akron are just to the west, Canton and Youngstown to the south. The 11th does include the Cleveland suburbs strung out along Lake Erie, in Lake County; Ashtabula, also on the lake; and Kent, site of Kent State University, where students were shot and killed by National Guardsmen in 1970. It still includes some rural areas in between the industrial cities, like Hiram, the home of James Garfield, who once (1863–81) represented a very similarly shaped district (then numbered the 19th) when it was the most Republican part of Ohio, and who was the last President elected directly from the House, in 1880.

The current congressman from the Western Reserve district, Dennis Eckart, does not seem likely to be elected President from the House, but otherwise he has done pretty well. First elected in 1980, he has become one of the leaders of the younger Democrats and a crucial swing vote on some issues. He has achieved a certain national prominence, playing Dan Quayle in practice debates with Lloyd Bentsen. Eckart came to the House after six successful years in the Ohio legislature, with a reputation for competence as a legislator and the ability to express his own views yet go along generally with the leadership. In his second term he got the plum committee assignment of Energy and Commerce and he works closely with Chairman John Dingell on his Oversight and Investigations Subcommittee.

On Energy and Commerce Eckart finds himself continually torn between environment-minded Democrats who want to toughen anti-pollution laws and regulations on business and industry and (often more vocal) labor unions which want to relax them. There are usually strong arguments on either side, forcefully made, and both with political supporters in the 11th District. Eckart keeps in touch with both sides, and has been part of a group seeking compromise; but when he has been forced to choose on tough issues like clean air and acid rain, he has usually come out on the side of the more relaxed standards. He is proud of his work on reauthorizing the Superfund, opposing the stringent version backed by James Florio; on reauthorization of the Safe Drinking Water Act; on blocking the sale of Conrail to the Norfolk Southern; and on regulating the disposal of hazardous wastes.

These positions have hurt him with Health Subcommittee Chairman Henry Waxman, but helped him with full committee Chairman John Dingell, to whom Eckart has become very close. They have much in common: both are of Eastern European descent (though neither has a distinctively ethnic name), both had fathers in politics (Dingell's was congressman, Eckart's a Euclid city councilman), both were elected to Congress as young men (Dingell at 29, Eckart at 30), both represent suburban districts of industrial cities where most voters have working-class roots, and both have shown great skill at handling the details of complex legislation. They hunt and socialize together on off hours, and then legislate together at work—though occasionally Eckart will dissent from even a chairman as strong-minded as Dingell.

Eckart has shown skill on the campaign trail as well. He won a Democratic primary against a senior legislator in 1980 to represent the 22d District in the close-in Cleveland suburbs. Then, after redistricting carved up this seat, he moved outward to the 11th District being vacated by moderate Republican William Stanton and won there as well. He has been reelected by overwhelming margins since then. Redistricting will probably not be a problem this time, since the 11th, as a corner district, is hard to slice up among its neighbors.

The People: Est. Pop. 1986: 515,800, up 0.5% 1980–86; Pop. 1980: 514,173, up 10.1% 1970–80. Households (1980): 80% family, 46% with children, 70% married couples; 23.6% housing units rented; median monthly rent: $208; median house value: $55,700. Voting age pop. (1980): 355,787; 2% Black.

1988 Presidential Vote:

Bush (R)		116,101	(55%)
Dukakis (D)		93,849	(44%)

Rep. Dennis E. Eckart (D)

Elected 1980; b. Apr. 6, 1950, Euclid; home, Mentor; Xavier U.. B.A. 1971, Cleveland St. U., J.D. 1974; Roman Catholic; married (Sandra).

Career: Asst. Lake Cnty. Prosecutor, 1974; OH House of Reps., 1975–80.

Offices: 1210 LHOB, 202-225-6331. Also 5970 Heisley Rd., Mentor 44060, 216-522-2056.

Committees: *Energy and Commerce* (16th of 26 D). Subcommittees: Oversight and Investigations; Telecommunications and Finance; Transportation and Hazardous Materials. *Small Business* (9th of 27 D). Subcommittees: Antitrust, Impact of Deregulation and Privatization (Chairman).

Group Ratings

	ADA	ACLU	COPE	CFA	LCV	ACU	NTLC	NSI	COC	CEI
1988	90	78	89	100	88	8	24	10	29	15
1987	88	—	88	93	—	4	—	—	29	12

National Journal Ratings

	1988 LIB — 1988 CONS		1987 LIB — 1987 CONS	
Economic	71%	— 23%	62%	— 35%
Social	68%	— 31%	78%	— 0%
Foreign	74%	— 23%	76%	— 19%

Key Votes

1) Homeless $	AGN	5) Ban Drug Test	AGN	9) SDI Research	AGN
2) Gephardt Amdt	FOR	6) Drug Death Pen	FOR	10) Ban Chem Weaps	FOR
3) Deficit Reduc	AGN	7) Handgun Sales	AGN	11) Aid to Contras	AGN
4) Kill Plnt Clsng Notice	AGN	8) Ban D.C. Abort $	AGN	12) Nuclear Testing	FOR

Election Results

1988 general	Dennis E. Eckart (D)	124,600	(62%)	($561,070)
	Margaret R. Mueller (R)	78,028	(38%)	($860,766)
1988 primary	Dennis E. Eckart (D), unopposed			
1986 general	Dennis E. Eckart (D)	104,740	(70%)	($348,852)
	Margaret R. Mueller (R)	39,944	(29%)	($275,584)

TWELFTH DISTRICT

"Columbus, in terms of its people rather than its buildings, is three cities in one," the sprightly writer of the *WPA Guide* explained in 1940. "In the low, gray stone capitol in its 10-acre square. and in the mobile 'little capitol' that moves from one smoke-filled room to another in the hotels across High Street, the political city has its life. Politicians and legislators come and go, lobbyists throng the hotels and the corridors of the State office buildings and do their political trading.' The second city was up High Street, at the campus of Ohio State University, too far away to dominate downtown; the third "is one of commerce and industry. It is visibly symbolized in the lofty American Insurance Union Citadel, and in the smoking stacks of foundries and shops scattered about town, where several hundred plants make products ranging from violins to steel.

railroad cars." Today's Columbus is more than twice as populous, with glass high-rises across from the capitol, and pleasant neighborhoods fanning out on high ground in all directions. It is increasingly a white-collar town, proud of being the third largest repository of data in the world, after Washington and Moscow: between Ohio State, Bell Labs, Chemical Abstracts Service, On-Line Computer Library, and the Battelle Memorial Institute, Columbus is evidently just crammed with data. This makes sense: not built on a navigable river, Columbus has never had much heavy industry. Politically and culturally conservative, it prides itself on its economic innovativeness: Columbus had the first 24-hour automated bank teller in 1973; it had the first two-way cable TV system, QUBE, in 1977; it will build the C-17 plane. It also grew smartly in the 1970s and 1980s while much of Ohio has sent its young people elsewhere, and it is getting ready to celebrate the 500th anniversary of Columbus's voyage with an extravagant flower show called Ameriflora '92.

If its economy is up-to-date, sometimes its local politics seems old-fashioned, with a Republican organization that wins most local elections and politicians possessed of the common touch of longtime Governor James Rhodes, who was elected auditor of Columbus in 1939 and mayor in 1943. Yet the congressman from the 12th District of Ohio, which includes the east side of Columbus and its suburbs plus two adjacent rural counties, is a very up-to-date Republican who rose through his own efforts. This should be a heavily Republican district. Though it includes more than half of Columbus's blacks, most of its wards in Columbus and all of the affluent suburbs of Bexley and Gahanna are heavily Republican, and it includes none of the academic community around Ohio State University. Yet the last time an old-style Republican won the seat comfortably was in 1968.

In that year the current congressman, Republican John Kasich, was a 16-year-old high school student living with his parents in McKees Rocks, Pennsylvania. Kasich got to Columbus by attending Ohio State; in 1978, at age 26, he ran a strenuous door-to-door campaign and beat an incumbent Democratic state Senator. Four years later, in the second election in which he was constitutionally eligible, he ran for the House and won. With the help of favorable redistricting, he beat Bob Shamansky, a Democrat who had beaten veteran Republican Samuel Devine in 1980; Kasich was the only Republican to beat an incumbent Democrat in 1982, and the 12th was the only district to oust a Republican incumbent in the Republican year of 1980 and then oust a Democratic incumbent in the Democratic year of 1982.

Kasich is peppery, brash, spewing forth ideas, a fairly good percentage of which are good and some of which even get enacted into law. He serves on Armed Services (the only Ohioan there) and in 1989 went on Budget. He was one of the tigers who pushed through the military base closing bill (chief sponsor Dick Armey wasn't on Armed Services), he got the welfare reform bill to withhold tax refunds from those who have defaulted on government loans (he says this is worth $2 billion to Uncle Sam), he has got the government working harder collecting its debts, and he increased the awards for government employees who disclose instances of waste and fraud.

His approach seems popular, and the 12th District's years of countercyclical politics seem to be over: Kasich was reelected by huge margins in 1984, 1986 and 1988.

The People: Est. Pop. 1986: 537,200, up 4.5% 1980–86; Pop. 1980: 514,173, up 14.1% 1970–80. Households (1980): 72% family, 41% with children, 58% married couples; 37.7% housing units rented; median monthly rent: $179; median house value: $47,100. Voting age pop. (1980): 366,117; 14% Black, 1% Spanish origin.

1988 Presidential Vote: Bush (R) 138,992   (61%)
Dukakis (D) 86,297   (38%)

Rep. John R. Kasich (R)

Elected 1982; b. May 13, 1952, McKees Rocks, PA; home, Westerville; OH St. U., B.A. 1974; Roman Catholic; divorced.

Career: A.A. to OH St. Sen. Donald Lukens, 1975–77; OH Senate, 1979–82.

Offices: 1133 LHOB 20515, 202-225-5355. Also Fed. Bldg., 200 N. High St., Columbus 43215, 614-469-7318.

Committees: *Armed Services* (9th of 21 R). Subcommittees: Procurement and Military Nuclear Systems; Readiness (Ranking Member). *Budget* (11th of 14 R). Task Forces: Defense, Foreign Policy and Space; Human Resources.

Group Ratings

	ADA	ACLU	COPE	CFA	LCV	ACU	NTLC	NSI	COC	CEI
1988	15	30	15	55	25	92	77	100	93	58
1987	8	—	13	14	—	78	—	—	93	74

National Journal Ratings

	1988 LIB — 1988 CONS		1987 LIB — 1987 CONS	
Economic	19%	— 80%	31%	— 68%
Social	20%	— 78%	23%	— 76%
Foreign	16%	— 78%	24%	— 76%

Key Votes

1) Homeless $	FOR	5) Ban Drug Test	AGN	9) SDI Research	FOR
2) Gephardt Amdt	AGN	6) Drug Death Pen	FOR	10) Ban Chem Weaps	AGN
3) Deficit Reduc	AGN	7) Handgun Sales	FOR	11) Aid to Contras	FOR
4) Kill Plnt Clsng Notice	FOR	8) Ban D.C. Abort $	FOR	12) Nuclear Testing	AGN

Election Results

1988 general	John R. Kasich (R)	204,892	(80%)	($351,517)
	Mark P. Brown (D)	50,782	(20%)	
1988 primary	John R. Kasich (R), unopposed			
1986 general	John R. Kasich (R)	117,905	(73%)	($424,678)
	Timothy C. Jochim (D)	42,727	(27%)	($22,945)

THIRTEENTH DISTRICT

The westward track of New England Yankee migration, from Upstate New York west to Chicago, passes along the south shore of Lake Erie in Ohio. The Yankees, cooped up in New England for 200 years, shot across the country to the West Coast in just two or three generations, providing the inspiration and much of the manpower and technical might for the Union victory in the Civil War, and leaving a deep imprint in many places along the way. One of those places was the Western Reserve, the northeast corner of Ohio along Lake Erie, which was marked out early as a reserve for the excess population of Connecticut, and whose towns and colleges and cultural institutions were mostly set up by Yankees, in time for the great migration of eastern and southern Europeans to its industrial centers. Consider Oberlin College, founded in 1832 as the first co-educational college in the world, though no women dared apply till 1837; it accepted black students a few years later, and the town became a center of the Underground Railroad. In partisan terms, the area was naturally Republican territory. The Yankees, with their reformist ideas and dislike of slavery and the South, were the natural Republican base wherever they moved in the young nation, and this was a heavily Republican area for years.

But now northern Ohio, like most areas of early Yankee settlement, is inclined away from the Republicans and toward the Democrats. The industrial development which changed the face of Cleveland also affected the shoreline of Lake Erie to the west. Here are pleasant suburbs on the lake, but also electric generating plants and giant factories. This is the land of Ohio's 13th Congressional District, which contains the factory towns of Lorain and Elyria, which have become part of the Cleveland metropolitan area, and the shoreline west to the picturesque town of Vermillion, and goes inland to include Medina County, which filled up in the 1970s and 1980s with outmigrants from Cleveland, and the once rural area around Ashland and Mansfield.

Yet the switch from a Republican to a Democratic congressman did not come until 1976. You could say, however, that it happened in stages: Republican Charles Mosher, of Oberlin, first elected in 1960, had a voting record that increasingly resembled that of a Democrat, especially on cultural issues; it was a metamorphosis typical of what was going on at the same time among many New England Yankees. Mosher's successor in Congress is Donald Pease, also of Oberlin, who followed Mosher as editor of the *Oberlin News-Tribune,* in the Ohio Senate, and in basic political leanings—although Pease is a Democrat.

Pease is a member of the House Ways and Means Committee. On economic issues he, like other Ohio Democrats, is inclined toward generosity—an inclination that becomes focused when the issue is trade adjustment assistance or unemployment benefits—as it was in the high-unemployment atmosphere of the early 1980s. His instincts on foreign policy are for interna-tional amity and cooperation, and for arms control and multilateral development agencies. On taxes he supported the rate-lowering, preference-eliminating tax reform of 1986, and was one of the Democrats Dan Rostenkowski hand-picked to serve on the conference committee.

Increasingly, he has concentrated on trade issues. As one of the leading Ways and Means Democrats from a constituency that feels beleaguered by foreign imports, Pease supported the Democrats' 1986 initiative on trade and came forward with his own proposal, passed in modified form in the 1988 trade bill, to set up labor standards stipulating that any country that doesn't pay its workers enough and provide them with good enough working conditions has violated U.S. trade laws and can't get its products into the U.S. market—a sort of international minimum wage and working conditions law. He also got provisions through to prevent steel quotas from being evaded by shipments through third countries and the effects on trade to be noted as part of the budget process. Pease seems drawn toward something like the tariff policy followed by Republicans for 70 years after the Civil War (for they, like Pease's Democrats, represented most of the high-wage working-class areas) to protect high American wages by building barriers against low-wage imports from abroad. But Pease is aware, as these Republicans were not, that trade restrictions like the Smoot-Hawley tariff of 1930 can grind international trade to a virtual halt. Many of Pease's fellow Democrats have embraced the trade issue with little regard for the consequences, glad at last to have an economic issue on which they can take a macho posture. Pease, who comes out as they do on some points, takes a much more thoughtful and careful approach, one that arguably draws on the longer traditions of the Western Reserve which he represents.

The People: Est. Pop. 1986: 513,800, dn. 0.1% 1980–86; Pop. 1980: 514,176, up 11.9% 1970–80. Households (1980): 80% family, 47% with children, 69% married couples; 25.0% housing units rented; median monthly rent: $181; median house value: $50,600. Voting age pop. (1980): 350,858; 5% Black, 2% Spanish origin.

1988 Presidential Vote:

Bush (R)	109,471	(53%)
Dukakis (D).	93,497	(46%)

Rep. Donald J. (Don) **Pease (D)**

Elected 1976; b. Sept. 26, 1931, Toledo; home, Oberlin; OH U., B.S. 1953, M.A. 1955, Fulbright Scholar, U. of Durham, England, 1954–55, OH U., LL.D. 1987; United Methodist; married (Jeanne).

Career: Army, 1955–57; Co-editor and publisher, *Oberlin News-Tribune*, 1957–68, Ed., 1968–77; Oberlin City Cncl., 1961–64; OH Senate, 1965–67, 1975–77; OH House of Reps., 1969–75.

Offices: 2410 RHOB 20515, 202-225-3401. Also 1936 Cooper Foster Park Rd., Lorain 44053, 216-282-5003; 144 N. Broadway, Medina 22456, 216-725-6120; 180 Milan Ave., Norwalk 44857, 419-668-0206; 42 E. Main St., Ste. 101, Ashland 44805, 419-325-4148; and 200 N. Diamond St., Mansfield 44901.

Committees: *Ways and Means* (13th of 23 D). Subcommittees: Human Resources; Trade.

Group Ratings

	ADA	ACLU	COPE	CFA	LCV	ACU	NTLC	NSI	COC	CEI
1988	90	78	83	73	81	8	20	10	50	29
1987	88	—	82	93	—	0	—	—	7	13

National Journal Ratings

	1988 LIB — 1988 CONS		1987 LIB — 1987 CONS	
Economic	54% —	44%	68% —	27%
Social	73% —	25%	73% —	22%
Foreign	79% —	16%	68% —	30%

Key Votes

1) Homeless $	AGN	5) Ban Drug Test	AGN	9) SDI Research	FOR
2) Gephardt Amdt	FOR	6) Drug Death Pen	FOR	10) Ban Chem Weaps	FOR
3) Deficit Reduc	FOR	7) Handgun Sales	AGN	11) Aid to Contras	AGN
4) Kill Plnt Clsng Notice	AGN	8) Ban D.C. Abort $	AGN	12) Nuclear Testing	—

Election Results

1988 general	Donald J. (Don) Pease (D)	137,074	(70%)	($157,632)
	Dwight Brown (R).	59,287	(30%)	($16,682)
1988 primary	Donald J. (Don) Pease (D)	52,388	(83%)	
	John M. Ryan (D).	11,307	(17%)	
1986 general	Donald J. (Don) Pease (D)	88,612	(63%)	($415,486)
	William D. Nielsen, Jr. (R).	52,452	(37%)	($256,604)

FOURTEENTH DISTRICT

Akron is one of America's premier factory towns which in the 1980s is turning into something else. "Neither booster pamphlets nor fact books are needed," wrote the *WPA Guide* in 1940, "to inform the visitor that Akron is the rubber manufacturing center of the world; it is proclaimed by Akron's air, especially on hot summer days. It is written on the clothing and the hands and faces of the workers who, unless they have scrubbed and brushed vigorously, bear a thin coating of soapstone. And rubber dominates their talk: they discuss the big industry, expansion, the threat of decentralization, strikes, A.F. of L., C.I.O. and the future. The very composition of the people is a product of the rubber boom; 152,000 of its 243,000 are of southern origin, who flocked from their native hills into Akron in the war decade and the 1920s. The West Virginia Day picnic is one of the rubber town's bigger events."

"Rubber town" it is not any more. The companies started decentralizing their plants, looking for cheaper labor; the European competitors they scorned started making money on radials; the auto market sagged. The last auto tire plant was shut down in the 1970s, and the last truck and airplane tires were made in 1984 and 1985. Firestone even moved its headquarters to Chicago and was sold to a Japanese company. General Tire was bought by a German firm. Goodyear fought off a takeover attempt by Sir James Goldsmith. Akron has been busy diversifying too. It built new hotels and meeting centers downtown even as its tire factories were closing; its small businesses added white-collar jobs as its big businesses cut their blue-collar payrolls. It got out of tires and into polymers—plastics and other such materials that can be formed or shaped (like rubber!) into useful industrial products. "The Pontiac Fiero should be a symbol for Akron," Mayor Tom Sawyer said in 1986, because its outer skin is made of polymers; "our goal should be nothing less than making this region the polymer capital of the world." All this is part of the so-called materials revolution in high-tech.

The politics of Akron for years after the 1930s was a kind of class warfare, between rubber company management and the Republicans on one side and the United Rubber Workers and the Democrats on the other. Elections were closely contested, and a premium went to party leaders who could fashion appeals across class lines. Akron was the home of Ray Bliss, for years Ohio and once national Republican chairman; his candidate for Congress in the 14th District, which included Akron and its Summit County suburbs, was an affable plumber named William Ayres who won enough working class votes to stay in office from 1950 to 1970. To beat him, the Democrats came up with a liberal lawyer and environmentalist who was the grandson of one of the rubber company founders, the rather reserved John Seiberling, who represented the district from 1970 to 1986 and whose politics was validated by the increasing liberalism of the *Akron Beacon Journal*. His successor was Tom Sawyer, a man of similar political views, but his victory was anything but automatic. In the primary, he was opposed by Oliver Ocasek, an old-time state senator first elected in 1958; Sawyer won by only 50%–40%. In the general, Sawyer had serious opposition from Republican county prosecutor Lynn Slaby, who attacked Sawyer in ads on Cleveland TV for being too liberal. Sawyer campaigned on his record of solving the problems of the city's troubled Recycle Energy System and of being the only mayor in Ohio not to raise taxes—enough for him to win 54% in a district where Richard Celeste was winning over 70% of the vote.

Sawyer made a few missteps in office, telling a TV interviewer that Firestone wanted to expand its retail business and "Akron is not suited for that kind of operation," and failing to get the Navy to buy a blimp from an Akron company. But he helped Akron get the National Inventors Hall of Fame and, as an Education and Labor Committee member and former teacher, he sought to get the Defense Department to give enlistees full credit for evening high school diplomas. He serves as chairman of the Post Office and Civil Service Subcommittee on the Census and Population, and could figure significantly in the 1990 census. With no serious opposition in 1988, he won reelection with 75% of the vote.

The People: Est. Pop. 1986: 497,500, dn. 3.2% 1980–86; Pop. 1980: 514,172, dn. 5.6% 1970–80. Households (1980): 74% family, 38% with children, 60% married couples; 30.4% housing units rented; median monthly rent: $180; median house value: $44,700. Voting age pop. (1980): 373,433; 10% Black.

1988 Presidential Vote: Dukakis (D).....................110,222   (52%)
Bush (R) 98,111   (47%)

Rep. Thomas C. Sawyer (D)

Elected 1986; b. Aug. 15, 1945, Akron; home, Akron; U. of Akron, B.A. 1968, M.A. 1970; Presbyterian; married (Joyce).

Career: OH House of Reps., 1977–83; Mayor of Akron, 1984–86.

Offices: 1518 LHOB 20515, 202-225-5231. Also Fed. Bldg., 2 S. Main St., Akron 44308, 216-375-5710.

Committees: *Education and Labor* (13th of 22 D). Subcommittees: Elementary, Secondary and Vocational Education; Labor–Management Relations; Human Resources. *Post Office and Civil Service* (12th of 15 D). Subcommittees: Census and Population (Chairman); Postal Personnel and Modernization.

Group Ratings

	ADA	ACLU	COPE	CFA	LCV	ACU	NTLC	NSI	COC	CEI
1988	95	83	90	91	94	4	11	10	36	18
1987	88	—	88	86	—	0	—	—	20	6

National Journal Ratings

	1988 LIB — 1988 CONS		1987 LIB — 1987 CONS	
Economic	71% —	23%	73% —	0%
Social	73% —	25%	78% —	0%
Foreign	79% —	16%	76% —	19%

Key Votes

1) Homeless $	AGN	5) Ban Drug Test	AGN
2) Gephardt Amdt	FOR	6) Drug Death Pen	FOR
3) Deficit Reduc	FOR	7) Handgun Sales	AGN
4) Kill Plnt Clsng Notice	AGN	8) Ban D.C. Abort $	AGN

9) SDI Research	AGN
10) Ban Chem Weaps	FOR
11) Aid to Contras	AGN
12) Nuclear Testing	FOR

Election Results

1988 general	Thomas C. Sawyer (D)...............	148,951	(75%)	($419,005)
	Loretta Lang (R)	50,356	(25%)	($13,244)
1988 primary	Thomas C. Sawyer (D), unopposed			
1986 general	Thomas C. Sawyer (D)................	83,257	(54%)	($546,302)
	Lynn Slaby (R)......................	71,713	(46%)	($411,539)

FIFTEENTH DISTRICT

The idea of Columbus as a major American city takes a bit of getting used to. Yet there it is: the capitol of Ohio is now the center of a metropolitan area with more than one million people, the headquarters of major research centers, of financial powers like insurance companies and a major interstate bank, and the home of a major university. Fifty years ago it was a symbol of Middle America: the place where James Thurber grew up, the town *My Sister Eileen* left behind for New York, the college town to which Philip Roth's Newark-born hero was finally able to say goodbye. Then it seemed that most Americans were leaving places like Columbus behind. Now it seems that most Americans are moving to places like Columbus—and a fair number of them to Columbus itself.

The 15th Congressional District of Ohio is made up of the west and south sides of Columbus and suburban Franklin County, plus most of rural Madison County directly to the west. The 15th includes some (but not most) of Columbus's black population, some white working-class areas on the south side of the city, and the Ohio State University campus area. These are more than balanced by the heavily Republican suburb of Upper Arlington, across the Olentangy River from Ohio State, and by the Republican subdivisions that seem to be sprouting in the rural land and in between the old villages all around.

The congressman from the 15th is Chalmers Wylie, an old-school Columbus Republican, a 33d degree Mason and political veteran who served in city government in the 1940s and 1950s and in the legislature in the 1960s and then was elected to the House when redistricting produced a second Columbus district in 1966. Wylie has risen through seniority to become one of the House Republicans' leaders on economic policies. In 1989, he became ranking House Republican on the Joint Economic Committee, and as such the chief dissenter from the Democrats' doom-and-gloom view of six years of economic growth. Wylie is not, however, one of those conservatives with a fancy theory to spin nor is he given to speak in highfalutin' technical lingo. "Most Americans feel like they're better off than they were 10 years ago," he says simply but not unprofoundly, "and I agree with them."

The hottest seat Wylie occupies is as ranking Republican on the House Banking, Finance and Urban Affairs Committee. For six years Wylie, a pleasant and low-keyed man, had to work with hard-driving and abrasive Chairman Fernand St Germain. Wylie's impulses have been to minimize federal regulation and big government: he wouldn't go as far as the Democrats on interest rate disclosure or in expanding federal housing programs. But he has been readier to embrace some new ideas, like tenant management for public housing projects, and he has supported a number of federal housing programs. On a number of issues he worked with St Germain and others of both parties to push measures like check-hold legislation, interest rate disclosure, anti-money laundering bills, emergency grants for the homeless, and continuation of International Monetary Fund programs.

Where was Wylie on the savings and loan issue? Mostly outvoted by St Germain is the answer. St Germain played his own peculiar brand of politics with the S&Ls and didn't cut other Democrats in on the policymaking much, much less the Republicans. On banking deregulation, Wylie co-sponsored a St Germain bill in 1988 to give banks some limited entry into the securities business, but he withdrew his support later when the Democrats added some consumer provisions. The new chairman, Henry Gonzalez, is so very much his own man that it's not likely that Wylie will get heavily involved, but who knows? Though Gonzalez has a temper, he is not malicious as St Germain seems to have been and he is completely honest. In any case Wylie, a man used to representing a broad constituency made up of all levels of society—and one which had its own Ohio savings and loan scandal in 1985—must now play a major role on the savings and loan repair measure, and on pending housing measures as well.

In early 1989, there was talk that Dale Butland, a top aide to both Senators John Glenn and Howard Metzenbaum, would take on Wylie in 1990. But in 1986, the last off year contest, he beat a well-regarded opponent, Dr. David Jackson, former head of the state health department, with 64% of the vote, and the odds are that he has a safe seat.

The People: Est. Pop. 1986: 539,200, up 4.9% 1980–86; Pop. 1980: 514,176, up 0.8% 1970–80. Households (1980): 68% family, 37% with children, 54% married couples; 42.6% housing units rented; median monthly rent: $168; median house value: $47,500. Voting age pop. (1980): 377,458; 10% Black, 1% Asian origin, 1% Spanish origin.

1988 Presidential Vote:

Bush (R)	137,729	(62%)
Dukakis (D)	81,708	(37%)

Rep. Chalmers P. Wylie (R)

Elected 1966; b. Nov. 23, 1920, Norwich; home, Columbus; Otterbein Col., OH State U., Harvard U., J.D. 1948; United Methodist; married (Marjorie).

Career: Army, WWII; Asst. Atty. Gen. of OH, 1948, 1951–53; Asst. Columbus City Atty., 1949–50, City Atty., 1954–57; Admin., OH Bureau of Workmen's Comp., 1957; First Asst. to the Gov. of OH, 1957; OH House of Reps., 1961–66.

Offices: 2310 RHOB 20515, 202-225-2015. Also 200 N. High St., Rm. 500, Columbus 43215, 614-469-5614.

Committees: *Banking, Finance and Urban Affairs* (Ranking Member of 20 R). Subcommittees: Consumer Affairs and Coinage; Financial Institutions Supervision, Regulation and Insurance (Ranking Member); Housing and Community Development. *Veterans' Affairs* (3d of 13 R). Subcommittees: Compensation, Pension, and Insurance; Education, Training and Employment. *Joint Economic Committee.* Task Forces: Fiscal and Monetary Policy; International Economic Policy.

Group Ratings

	ADA	ACLU	COPE	CFA	LCV	ACU	NTLC	NSI	COC	CEI
1988	30	22	23	36	25	80	71	90	92	51
1987	4	—	22	21	—	73	—	—	100	68

National Journal Ratings

	1988 LIB — 1988 CONS		1987 LIB — 1987 CONS	
Economic	15% —	85%	18% —	81%
Social	27% —	73%	10% —	85%
Foreign	29% —	70%	24% —	75%

Key Votes

1) Homeless $	FOR	5) Ban Drug Test	FOR	9) SDI Research	FOR
2) Gephardt Amdt	AGN	6) Drug Death Pen	FOR	10) Ban Chem Weaps	AGN
3) Deficit Reduc	—	7) Handgun Sales	AGN	11) Aid to Contras	FOR
4) Kill Plnt Clsng Notice	FOR	8) Ban D.C. Abort $	FOR	12) Nuclear Testing	AGN

Election Results

1988 general	Chalmers P. Wylie (R)	154,694	(75%)	($211,963)
	Mark S. Froehlich (D)	51,172	(25%)	($6,682)
1988 primary	Chalmers P. Wylie (R), unopposed			
1986 general	Chalmers P. Wylie (R)	97,745	(64%)	($338,230)
	David L. Jackson (D)	55,750	(36%)	($319,640)

SIXTEENTH DISTRICT

Canton, Ohio is an industrial city, but different from huge factory towns like Youngstown and Akron. It has many employers, not just a few, and its work has typically been high-skill not low-skill; it was fashioning new kinds of plows and reapers and making watches in the 19th century, and has been making roller bearings since 1899. Canton did not attract masses of immigrants; its factories did not run on harsh stopwatch discipline. "There is no large class distinction in the city," wrote the *WPA Guide* 50 years ago; "even the most affluent residents do not make a special display of wealth." The class warfare politics created during the CIO union organizing drives and sitdown strikes of the late 1930s did not really take in Canton; its politics remains something closer to that of its (today mostly forgotten) President, William McKinley.

Fifty years ago, his name was synonymous with outmoded, standpat politics, but in fact McKinley was a very successful politician in his time, who won two elections by decisive margins and began a period of three decades in which the Republican Party, with scarcely a bit of support in the one-third of the nation that was the South, was nonetheless the clear majority party in the United States—the only time it has been so. His policies—the protective tariff, the gold standard, the enforcement of law and order in labor relations—were summed up in the phrase the "full dinner pail" and for many years produced economic growth and technological progress that improved the lives of people living in all quarters of cities like Canton.

Some of McKinley's politics remains alive in his home town of Canton, Ohio, and in the 16th Congressional District, of which it is the largest and dominant urban center. Here on North Market Avenue McKinley sat on his front porch and received delegations of thousands of voters, carefully selected by Republican organizations around the country, and heard that he had been elected President over William Jennings Bryan. Canton and the 16th District remain Republican territory, and elect a Republican congressman whose pragmatism and political instincts are reminiscent of McKinley, who was himself elected to the House six times from the Canton area and served as chairman of the Ways and Means Committee.

He is Ralph Regula, a graduate of the William McKinley School of Law, who in the 1970s worked to retain the name Mount McKinley for the highest mountain in North America (although Alaska natives did get the surrounding area named Denali National Park). Regula is considered a moderate, a man with an instinct to be a party regular but also one who works amicably and constructively with those across the aisle. He is an advocate of greater coal use and of research for cleaner coal, and a booster of steel import restrictions.

Regula is a member of the Appropriations Committee, and, since 1985, ranking Republican on the Interior Subcommittee. There he works with Chairman Sidney Yates on most, but not all issues; Regula is a bit more inclined to favor economic development over protecting the environment than Yates is. But their differences are limited and cooperation is usually the order of the day. Regula spent much time, for example, negotiating an agreement on offshore oil drilling in California. On the Commerce, State, Justice Subcommitteee he pushed for more foreign exchange programs. Once a teacher, Regula is often favorable to claims for more domestic spending. He has a moderate record on cultural and foreign policy issues. Regula has held the 16th District with ease.

The People: Est. Pop. 1986: 513,700, dn. 0.1% 1980–86; Pop. 1980: 514,171, up 5.2% 1970–80. Households (1980): 78% family, 42% with children, 67% married couples; 27.3% housing units rented; median monthly rent: $167; median house value: $45,600. Voting age pop. (1980): 363,139; 4% Black, 1% Spanish origin.

1988 Presidential Vote: Bush (R) 116,353   (57%)

Dukakis (D) 86,957   (42%)

Rep. Ralph S. Regula (R)

Elected 1972; b. Dec. 3, 1924, Beach City; home, Navarre; Mt. Union Col., B.A. 1948, Wm. McKinley Sch. of Law, LL.B. 1952; Episcopalian; married (Mary).

Career: Navy, WWII; Teacher and school principal, 1948–52; Practicing atty., 1952–73; OH Bd. of Educ., 1960–64; OH House of Reps., 1965–66; OH Senate, 1967–72.

Offices: 2207 RHOB 20515, 202-225-3876. Also 4150 Belden Village Ave., N.W., Canton 44718, 216-489-4414.

Committees: *Appropriations* (7th of 22 R). Subcommittees: Commerce, Justice, State, and Judiciary; District of Columbia; Interior (Ranking Member). *Select Committee on Aging* (3d of 27 R). Subcommittee: Health and Long-Term Care (Ranking Member).

Group Ratings

	ADA	ACLU	COPE	CFA	LCV	ACU	NTLC	NSI	COC	CEI
1988	30	48	36	64	44	76	52	90	93	40
1987	28	—	34	57	—	52	—	—	67	46

National Journal Ratings

	1988 LIB — 1988 CONS	1987 LIB — 1987 CONS
Economic	35% — 64%	40% — 60%
Social	24% — 76%	34% — 65%
Foreign	40% — 59%	42% — 57%

Key Votes

1) Homeless $	FOR	5) Ban Drug Test	AGN	9) SDI Research	AGN
2) Gephardt Amdt	FOR	6) Drug Death Pen	FOR	10) Ban Chem Weaps	FOR
3) Deficit Reduc	AGN	7) Handgun Sales	AGN	11) Aid to Contras	FOR
4) Kill Plnt Clsng Notice	FOR	8) Ban D.C. Abort $	FOR	12) Nuclear Testing	AGN

Election Results

1988 general	Ralph S. Regula (R).................	158,824	(79%)	($94,492)
	Melvin J. Gravely (D).................	43,356	(21%)	
1988 primary	Ralph S. Regula (R), unopposed			
1986 general	Ralph S. Regula (R).................	118,206	(76%)	($103,471)
	William J. Kennick (D)	36,639	(24%)	

SEVENTEENTH DISTRICT

"Steel makes Youngstown run," wrote the *WPA Guide* 50 years ago. "From the city square, on nights when production is up and the mills are roaring, the horizon is painted with an uncertain light where the stack-flung ceiling of smoke gives back the glare of the mill fires. And when production is down and only a few furnaces carry 'heats,' the forlornness of the squat and silent mills seeps out into the whole city." The Mahoning River, a small stream that flows down from Akron through the flat land of eastern Ohio into the hills of western Pennsylvania, was for a long time one of the leading steel-producing regions of the United States. The Valley seemed marked for steel: it is halfway between the Lake Erie docks that unload iron ore from Great Lakes freighters and the coalfields of western Pennsylvania and West Virginia. After the turn of the century, the capitalists from downtown Pittsburgh and Cleveland put immense amounts of money into building giant steel mills here, huge industrial hulks that must have taken people's breath away then—as do now, standing empty and smokeless and silent. The first steel-mill builders were ahead of the technological curve, anticipating correctly the gigantic demand for steel the 20th century would bring—for automobiles, skyscrapers, airplanes.

But American steel has been in trouble for at least 25 years. Foreign producers gained a technological edge on American companies in the 1950s and 1960s, and overcapacity was built into the industry when practically every nation decided that, to show it was an advanced industrial power, it must have its own steel mill. Foreign producers had cost advantages not only because of efficiency, but because of lower wage costs. The steel industry and the United Steel Workers, after the long strike which held the nation's attention through much of 1959, decided to avoid strikes and grant large wage and benefit increases which, they were confident, could be passed along to consumers who would always need a lot of steel; if there were problems with imports, they could be barred. This strategy worked in the short run but in the long run it helped to wreck the industry; foreign steel made its way in, and users found lower-priced substitutes. Recently American steel has snapped back strongly, but mostly in smaller, decentralized mills, not in Youngstown.

The result was economic disaster for the Mahoning Valley. Most of its steel mills have been shut down; some have even been dynamited. During the early 1980s, metropolitan Youngstown had one of the nation's highest unemployment rates—in some months the highest. The high-wage standard of living that was maintained through the late 1970s has vanished, and here, in contrast to other industrial areas in Ohio, it does not seem likely to return soon. Young people have been leaving since at least 1960, looking for new opportunities; those who have remained seem anchored here by community ties or by an inertia that seems to have been at least partly encouraged by safety nets like unemployment compensation and welfare.

These events have naturally had political reverberations. Republican in the 1920s, the Mahoning Valley was a solidly Democratic area for years after the United Steelworkers organized the plants following sometimes bloody skirmishes in the late 1930s, and usually votes even more Democratic in times of recession. But as the steel industry collapsed, it flirted for a while with the Republicans. In 1978, the voters of the congressional district that includes Youngstown, Warren and most of the Mahoning Valley, actually elected a Republican congressman, and reelected him in 1980 and 1982. They gave Jimmy Carter in 1980 no higher a percentage of their votes than they had given George McGovern eight years before. Then, as recession lingered they switched back to the Democrats, but not necessarily old-timers. In 1984, they voted for Walter Mondale in the fall, but not before backing Gary Hart, who said he had new solutions for the problems of old industries, in the May 1984 primary.

Among the political beneficiaries of this thrashing around is Congressman James Traficant, former Mahoning County sheriff, a politician who would not likely be elected in ordinary times and whose style is redolent of the high times when the steel mill smokestacks were pouring out soot, the bars across from the plant gates were thronged at shift break, and mobsters prowled the streets in shiny black Cadillacs. Much of the controversy over Traficant goes back to his campaign for Mahoning County sheriff in 1980. He admitted taking large bribes from mobsters to overlook gambling, loan-sharking, drug trafficking and prostitution in Mahoning County and argued, when presented with tapes of some of these transactions, that this was part of his own sting operation (the man he said he returned the money to had, however, disappeared). The charges did not come out during the 1980 campaign, which Traficant won, and when he was tried on criminal charges in 1983 he acted as his own lawyer and persuaded the jury to find him not guilty. Already he had become a kind of local hero for refusing to enforce foreclosures, and he ran for Congress in 1984. Politicians mostly hated him; in 1982, the Mahoning County Democratic chairman called him "a nitwit, a lunatic, a raving maniac." But in 1984, he won a seven-candidate Democratic congressional primary with 56% of the vote, an election in which the astonishing total of 120,000 votes were cast, and he beat the three-term Republican incumbent in a Republican year 53%–46%.

That contest and the general election proved Traficant a gifted demagogue, capable of articulating the discontents of people who feel suddenly cheated by history. In Congress, he scarcely calmed down. Wearing bell bottom pants and cowboy boots, using coarse language (he predicted President Reagan's Persian Gulf policy would "jump up and bite him right on the keister"), he pressed "buy American" amendments to any bill he could think of, proposed across-the-board cuts in foreign aid, jumped in with other steel district representatives to protect benefits of LTV workers and retirees when the company went bankrupt, introduced a bill to delay foreclosures six months, and pushed for the canal from Lake Erie to the Ohio sought by longtime Mahoning Valley Representative Michael Kirwan. Except for the LTV issues, none of these initiatives were successful. And while he was pursuing them, the Mahoning Valley was starting to grow again, gaining 19,000 new jobs—not in the big steel mills, but in minimills, small plastics factories, fancy window frame makers, and dozens of other small businesses that have grown up once people realized the big mills weren't going to reopen.

Meanwhile, Traficant's legal troubles continue. The government brought civil tax evasion charges for the bribe money he took in 1979 (he acted as his own lawyer again) and in September 1987 a federal judge held him liable and ordered him to pay back taxes and penalties of $180,000. Traficant, who had already announced he was thinking of running for President, responded, "I am no Gary Hart. I am going to kick the IRS's butt. The IRS can go to hell." He is currently awaiting appeal of the case. Traficant did in fact run for President, winning 18% of the votes in his home district, putting him just behind Jesse Jackson there, but no more than 3% anywhere else in Ohio. Traficant continues to provide good political theater. He can articulate some of the anger that lingers as coal dust once did in the Mahoning Valley, and he is reelected to the House by overwhelming majorities. But as the Mahoning Valley economy changes and revives, Traficant may find himself out of tune—and it's possible that his district could be carved up by redistricters.

The People: Est. Pop. 1986: 492,600, dn. 4.2% 1980–86; Pop. 1980: 514,172, dn. 1.6% 1970–80. Households (1980): 77% family, 40% with children, 64% married couples; 26.7% housing units rented; median monthly rent: $168; median house value: $39,300. Voting age pop. (1980): 372,108; 10% Black, 1% Spanish origin.

1988 Presidential Vote: Dukakis (D) 130,383   (62%)
Bush (R) 79,756   (38%)

Rep. James A. Traficant, Jr. (D)

Elected 1984; b. May 8, 1941, Youngstown; home, Poland; U. of Pittsburgh, B.S. 1963; Youngstown St. U., M.S. 1973, M.S. 1976; Roman Catholic; married (Patricia).

Career: Dir., Mahoning Cnty. Drug Program, 1971–81; Mahoning Cnty. Sheriff, 1981–85.

Offices: 312 CHOB 20515, 202-225-5261. Also 11 Overhill Rd., Boardman 44512, 216-788-2414; and City Hall, 391 Mahoning Ave., Warren 44483, 216-399-3513.

Committees: *Public Works and Transportation* (17th of 31 D). Subcommittees: Aviation; Surface Transportation; Water Resources. *Science, Space and Technology* (18th of 29 D). Subcommittees: Energy Research and Development; Space Science and Applications. *Select Committee on Narcotics Abuse and Control* (15th of 18 D).

Group Ratings

	ADA	ACLU	COPE	CFA	LCV	ACU	NTLC	NSI	COC	CEI
1988	95	70	100	91	69	8	12	10	21	10
1987	88	—	100	86	—	5	—	—	0	5

National Journal Ratings

	1988 LIB — 1988 CONS		1987 LIB — 1987 CONS	
Economic	92%	— 0%	73%	— 0%
Social	61%	— 38%	78%	— 0%
Foreign	68%	— 28%	64%	— 35%

Key Votes

1) Homeless $	AGN	5) Ban Drug Test	AGN	9) SDI Research	AGN
2) Gephardt Amdt	FOR	6) Drug Death Pen	FOR	10) Ban Chem Weaps	FOR
3) Deficit Reduc	—	7) Handgun Sales	AGN	11) Aid to Contras	AGN
4) Kill Plnt Clsng Notice	AGN	8) Ban D.C. Abort $	AGN	12) Nuclear Testing	FOR

Election Results

1988 general	James A. Traficant, Jr. (D)	162,526	(77%)	($96,003)
	Frederick W. Lenz (R)	47,929	(23%)	($2,391)
1988 primary	James A. Traficant, Jr. (D)	98,341	(86%)	
	Van Williams (D)	16,130	(14%)	
1986 general	James A. Traficant, Jr. (D)	112,855	(72%)	($91,338)
	James H. Fulks (R)	43,334	(28%)	($91,035)

EIGHTEENTH DISTRICT

From its earliest settlement in the 1790s, the hilly land of east central Ohio has been industrial country. The local clay was used to make pottery, the coal that lies just on the surface was dug up, a green vitriol works was built, and a nail factory went into operation, all before 1814. For more than 100 years this area has been part of the great coal and steel belt that centers on Pittsburgh and Cleveland and stretches from the coal mines of West Virginia to Lake Erie, the destination of the once common freighters filled with iron ore from Minnesota's Mesabi Range. This area is filled with small cities, each with its little steel mill or factory, most of them old towns whose storefronts and wooden, working-class houses, with hills rising behind them, bearing the unmistakable imprint of the early 20th century. There is nothing chic or fashionable here: these are gritty places where working people have toiled long hours at physically demanding work for whatever pay might be available. For a time the pay was good. But in the late 1970s, the coal and steel economy, long in trouble, seemed about to collapse; and while the impact here was cushioned by continuing demand for coal from electric utilities, wage levels have sagged and the hopes many had of getting ahead have been disappointed.

The 18th District lies along the Ohio River, a land of marginal farms and hills pockmarked by strip mines, beginning in the north just below Youngstown and proceeding almost all the way to Marietta, Ohio, and Parkersburg, West Virginia. Some of the people here are from the Scots-Irish stock, part of the first wave of migration over the Appalachians. But more are descended from later immigrants: Italians, Poles, Czechs, Germans. The 18th District, sociologically and politically, is a kind of ethnic working-class neighborhood. Politically, the district is heavily Democratic; it voted for Ronald Reagan in 1984, but only barely, and gave Michael Dukakis a comfortable margin in 1988. Economically, the area has prospered only occasionally in the last few decades, but its lack of really large factories has made it less vulnerable to the sudden economic dislocation caused by the unexpected closing of such factories, which has been so common in much of Ohio.

The congressman from this district is Democrat Douglas Applegate, a veteran state legislator who was elected in 1976 after Wayne Hays, chairman of the House Administration Committee and tyrant of the House, was forced to leave office because of the Elizabeth Ray scandal. Applegate is a member of the kind of practical committees—Public Works and Transportation and Veterans' Affairs—that help him do something concrete for his district. He chairs the Veterans' Affairs subcommittee that handles military pensions and he sits on the Surface Transportation Subcommittee of Public Works. He has a moderate voting record on most issues and makes few waves in the House, concentrating it seems on local issues. He is routinely reelected, but could face a tougher race if Republicans persuade state Senator Bob Ney, son of a Wheeling newscaster who beat Wayne Hays in a state House race in 1980, to run.

The People: Est. Pop. 1986: 496,700, dn. 3.4% 1980–86; Pop. 1980: 514,173, up 4.1% 1970–80. Households (1980): 77% family, 41% with children, 67% married couples; 24.0% housing units rented; median monthly rent: $132; median house value: $34,200. Voting age pop. (1980): 367,705; 2% Black.

1988 Presidential Vote: Dukakis (D)...................... 102,998   (52%)
Bush (R) 93,959   (47%)

Rep. Douglas Applegate (D)

Elected 1976; b. Mar. 27, 1928, Steubenville; home, Steubenville; Presbyterian; married (Betty).

Career: Real estate salesman, 1950–56, broker, 1956–76; OH House of Reps., 1961–69; OH Senate, 1969–77.

Offices: 2183 RHOB 20515, 202-225-6265. Also 46060 Nat'l Rd. W., St. Clairsville 43950, 614-695-4600; Ohio Valley Tower, Rm. 610, Steubenville 43952, 614-283-3716; 109 W. 3d St., E. Liverpool 43920, 216-385-5921; and 1330 4th St., N.W., New Philadelphia 44663, 216-343-9112.

Committees: *Public Works and Transportation* (7th of 31 D). Subcommittees: Economic Development; Investigations and Oversight; Surface Transportation. *Veterans' Affairs* (3d of 21 D). Subcommittees: Compensation, Pension and Insurance (Chairman); Oversight and Investigations.

Group Ratings

	ADA	ACLU	COPE	CFA	LCV	ACU	NTLC	NSI	COC	CEI
1988	70	52	75	82	44	24	31	50	29	24
1987	60	—	74	71	—	13	—	—	27	19

National Journal Ratings

	1988 LIB — 1988 CONS			1987 LIB — 1987 CONS		
Economic	57%	—	41%	44%	—	55%
Social	35%	—	65%	53%	—	47%
Foreign	52%	—	47%	49%	—	51%

Key Votes

1) Homeless $	FOR	5) Ban Drug Test	AGN	9) SDI Research	FOR
2) Gephardt Amdt	FOR	6) Drug Death Pen	FOR	10) Ban Chem Weaps	FOR
3) Deficit Reduc	AGN	7) Handgun Sales	FOR	11) Aid to Contras	AGN
4) Kill Plnt Clsng Notice	AGN	8) Ban D.C. Abort $	FOR	12) Nuclear Testing	FOR

Election Results

1988 general	Douglas Applegate (D)................	151,306	(78%)	($86,061)
	William C. Abraham (R)	43,628	(22%)	($7,095)
1988 primary	Douglas Applegate (D), unopposed			
1986 general	Douglas Applegate (D)................	126,526	(100%)	($83,591)

NINETEENTH DISTRICT

Far from the twisting Cuyahoga River, where giant Great Lakes freighters dodge daring pleasure boats, beyond sight or smell of the steel mills that line the Cuyahoga or the factories in the blocks on either side, the suburbs in the ring around Cleveland give little hint that they are part of a metropolis dependent on declining heavy industry. Fifty years ago, some of these suburbs were already well established: Lakewood and Rocky River, west of downtown, with their substantial houses within wind-gust distance of Lake Erie, separated by one of the Cleveland area's deep ravines; Euclid on the east side, just beyond the big General Electric plant, where working class families were moving out from Cleveland's east side cosmo wards. Other suburbs scarcely existed, except as farmland or empty fields. Parma, directly south of the west side of Cleveland, was a mostly uninhabited township. Today, many of the older suburbs have that patina of age and quaint commercial centers which many young upscale people find attractive, and are doing better than many critics 20 years ago expected; the newer suburbs, boom towns like Parma which shot up to 100,000 people in the postwar decades, are perhaps a little frazzled, as their populations age and find their cultural values under attack.

The Cleveland area now seems to be emerging from two decades of controversies and shocks. City politics was torn by racial division in the late 1960s and early 1970s, and echoed in charges in the 1980s that suburbs like Parma excluded blacks. The city's heavy industries suffered a severe and evidently permanent contraction beginning in the late 1970s, and thousands of Clevelanders left the area or found new ways to make their livings in a metropolis where health services and government payrolls now account for more jobs than steel mills and auto assembly plants. The change has been a wrenching process in many people's personal lives, but in the long run it may be seen as part of a natural economic evolution—painfully and perhaps unnecessarily concentrated in just a few years—a progression upward that began when poor immigrants from eastern and southern Europe arrived at Cleveland's railroad terminal and which has ended, for the moment anyway, somewhere in the comfortable ring of suburbs around the city.

Much of this suburban ring makes up Ohio's 19th Congressional District. It forms a kind of convoluted U around Cleveland and some of its close-in suburbs, encircling the 20th and 21st Districts. The 19th can be divided into three distinct sections. One is the southern blue-collar suburbs. Parma is the largest town here, and is reputed to have the nation's largest concentration of bowling alleys; accordingly, it has been subjected to more than its fair share of analysis from the nation's political reporters looking for trends in ethnic blue-collar America. The suburbs south of Parma enjoy higher real estate values, largely because their houses and condominiums are newer. This is the home of comfortable blue-collar families, those with skilled workers and two paychecks, prime beneficiaries of the rises in real income in metropolitan Cleveland over the past three decades.

Quite different are the white-collar suburbs running west from Cleveland along Lake Erie and south along the Rocky River, comfortable and long-settled communities whose people tend to be older, more Protestant, and more Republican. The eastern suburbs are in many cases even better off, but they are also more ethnic, with many Italians and Jews; the Jewish suburbs in particular vote Democratic. Throughout the district, however, there is a sort of warfare going on in voters' hearts, between the Democratic leanings of most of their forebears and the Republican preference they have had on many issues since the middle 1960s. This is the most affluent congressional district in Ohio, yet it tends to vote right along the statewide average, as it did for President in 1988 and governor in 1986. In theory, then, it should be seriously contested in House elections.

It was in the early 1980s, but seems not to be any more, thanks to the political skills and energy of Congressman Edward Feighan. A former state legislator, county commissioner and candidate for mayor of Cleveland in 1977, Feighan beat incumbent Ron Mottl in the 1982 primary by a 49%–47% margin. Mottl was a Parma Democrat who backed the Reagan budget and tax cuts in 1981—the only Boll Weevil this far north of the Mason-Dixon line. In 1984, Feighan beat back a well-financed challenge from Republican Matt Hatchadorian by a 55%–43% margin, and in 1986 he beat state Senator Gary Suhadolnik 55%–45%. These opponents were about as tough as could be found in two races where the candidates together spent over $1 million.

How has Feighan won? Not so much by emphasizing his fervent opposition to contra aid and his generally liberal record on the Foreign Affairs Committee, though that does not seem to be a handicap; nor through his support for Israel and advocacy of human rights, which may well have been an asset at home. (He had the distinction of being one of the Americans who received a cool welcome from South Korean police as they accompanied dissident Kim Dae Jung on his return to Seoul in early 1985.) More important is his hard work bringing federal money into the different municipalities in the district. Also important has been his record on gun control. Feighan was the lead House sponsor of what became known as the Brady bill, to force a seven-day waiting period for gun purchases; taking advantage of a favorable statement by President Reagan, he pushed it to passage in the House in 1988. He pushed another measure to ban the sale of plastic guns and is the lead sponsor of the 1989 measure to ban semiautomatic weapons like those used by drug dealers to execute rivals and by a maniac to murder schoolchildren in California. He also seems to be bubbling over with proposals to deal with other things that affect ordinary people's daily lives, like unwanted direct mail solicitations, lawsuits against charitable volunteers, financing 911 lines.

With that record, Feighan had no serious challenge in 1988 and seems unlikely to in 1990. His major political problem is redistricting. Ohio will probably lose two districts for 1992, as it did 10 years before, and geographically the elongated 19th would be very easy to divide among its neighbors. But Feighan may be politically adroit enough to overcome this obstacle too.

The People: Est. Pop. 1986: 509,900, dn. 0.8% 1980–86; Pop. 1980: 514,174, dn. 1.4% 1970–80. Households (1980): 76% family, 35% with children, 66% married couples; 25.7% housing units rented; median monthly rent: $257; median house value: $67,300. Voting age pop. (1980): 386,888; 1% Black, 1% Asian origin.

1988 Presidential Vote:

Bush (R)	140,174	(55%)
Dukakis (D)	115,180	(45%)

Rep. Edward F. Feighan (D)

Elected 1982; b. Oct. 22, 1947, Lakewood; home, Lakewood; Loyola U., B.A. 1969, Cleveland St. U., J.D. 1977; Roman Catholic; married (Nadine).

Career: High sch. teacher, 1969–72; OH House of Reps., 1973–79; Cuyahoga Cnty. Commissioner, 1979–82; Practicing atty., 1978–82.

Offices: 1124 LHOB 20515, 202-225-5731. Also 2951 Fed. Bldg., Cleveland 44199, 216-522-4382.

Committees: *Foreign Affairs* (16th of 28 D). Subcommittees: Europe and the Middle East; Human Rights and International Organizations; International Economic Policy and Trade. *Judiciary* (14th of 21 D). Subcommittees: Crime; Economic and Commercial Law.

Group Ratings

	ADA	ACLU	COPE	CFA	LCV	ACU	NTLC	NSI	COC	CEI
1988	95	83	92	82	94	0	15	10	38	13
1987	92	—	91	86	—	0	—	—	29	6

National Journal Ratings

	1988 LIB — 1988 CONS		1987 LIB — 1987 CONS	
Economic	71% —	23%	67% —	32%
Social	78% —	22%	78% —	0%
Foreign	84% —	0%	76% —	19%

Key Votes

1) Homeless $	AGN	5) Ban Drug Test	AGN	9) SDI Research	AGN
2) Gephardt Amdt	FOR	6) Drug Death Pen	AGN	10) Ban Chem Weaps	FOR
3) Deficit Reduc	FOR	7) Handgun Sales	AGN	11) Aid to Contras	AGN
4) Kill Plnt Clsng Notice	AGN	8) Ban D.C. Abort $	AGN	12) Nuclear Testing	FOR

Election Results

1988 general	Edward F. Feighan (D)	168,065	(70%)	($226,086)
	Noel F. Roberts (R)	70,359	(30%)	($522)
1988 primary	Edward F. Feighan (D), unopposed			
1986 general	Edward F. Feighan (D)	97,814	(55%)	($630,626)
	Gary Suhadolnik (R)	80,743	(45%)	($524,243)

TWENTIETH DISTRICT

"Once almost entirely Nordic and Celtic in makeup, Cleveland was transformed by the expanding steel industry into one of the most racially diversified communities in the United States," wrote the *WPA Guide* in 1940. "Forty-eight nationalities have representation here; more than 40 languages are spoken in the city. First in numbers are the Czechoslovaks, followed by the Poles, Italians, Germans, Yugoslavs, Irish, and Hungarians." Early in the 20th century, Cleveland's ethnicity was a jarring note in a section of Ohio settled almost exclusively by New England Yankees and in a state much of which remained vaguely southern in its origins and sympathies. To some, these masses seemed threatening: would they produce revolution or corruption or a multilingual society?

None of those apprehensions has been realized. In the early 20th century, Cleveland got honest, efficient, activist government under Mayors Tom Johnson and Newton Baker; the residents of its cosmo wards proved themselves patriots in two world wars and the decades after; the closest it has come to revolution was the CIO union organizing drives of the late 1930s, which produced constructive and stabilizing institutions that, together with a vigorous private economy and a helping-hand government, enabled hundreds of thousands of Clevelanders to move up from nonstop drudgery and subsistence living to pleasant working conditions and a standard of living their parents would have regarded as unthinkably affluent.

Cleveland had a bad decade in the 1970s, and became momentarily an object of ridicule by national sophisticates. Its heavy industries were in trouble, Lake Erie and the Cuyahoga River were badly polluted (yes, the river did catch fire once), city politics was racially polarized in the late 1960s and dominated in the late 1970s by Mayor Dennis Kucinich, a neighborhood-based demagogue who managed to bankrupt the city government. But the enduring strengths of Cleveland remained as solid as the Terminal Tower on the Public Square and the massive government buildings a few blocks away on the Mall. For Cleveland was always more than just a factory town. True, the Cuyahoga, winding beneath limestone walls toward Lake Erie, has been lined with factories for nearly 100 years; it's one of the few places on shallow Lake Erie where the giant Great Lakes freighters can unload their iron ore so it can be smelted by West Virginia coal. But as long as there have been steel mills along the Cuyahoga, there have been skyscrapers in downtown Cleveland, as well as a thriving business district; and if Cleveland is no longer America's fourth largest city, as it was in 1910, it has consistently been a national leader in surgery and symphony—a city whose spacious downtown parks are thronged on festival days. It went through a painful economic adjustment in the 1980s in which many individuals were been hurt; city government has been cleaned up and cut back by Republican Mayor George Voinovich.

The 20th Congressional District of Ohio includes the west side of Cleveland and adjacent suburbs. It spans both sides of the Cuyahoga to include the cosmo wards east of the river, along Broadway and in the suburb of Garfield Heights; and it includes most of downtown. Technically it is not a pure big city district: half its residents live in suburbs which are mostly modest and working-class. The 20th is almost entirely white, with lower incomes than the other white suburban district; one reason is high unemployment, another is that these are older neighborhoods.

This has been a heavily Democratic district since Franklin Roosevelt first fired the enthusiasm of the ethnic residents of industrial Cleveland in the 1930s. The current representative, Mary Rose Oakar, is an important Member of the House with deep roots in her district and a background that would have been unusual in politics not so long ago. She comes from a modest ethnic (Arab-American) family, and worked her way through college as a telephone operator. She was elected to the Cleveland City Council while the city was in the midst of racial and fiscal turmoil, and was one west side representative who maintained good relations with blacks. She was popular enough to have won a 12-candidate primary with 24% of the vote in 1976, and has not been seriously challenged since. She is an ardent Cleveland booster and Cleveland, or at least the 20th District, seems an ardent booster of Mary Rose Oakar.

Oakar has a solidly liberal record on economic issues but is somewhat more conservative on cultural issues. An active member of various women's movements, she is also an opponent of abortion. Preparing for the reauthorization of the Defense Production Act from the Banking subcommittee she chairs, she has a proposal emphasizing conversion of defense industries to civilian use and limiting use of foreign sources (reflecting the preoccupation with trade issues common in northern Ohio). She has also been an advocate of requiring banks to provide services like checking at less than exorbitant rates; on Post Office, she favors generous treatment of federal employees; everywhere, she argues for more equitable and favorable treatment for women.

Oakar has been frustrated in her pursuit of a House leadership position. After the 1984 election, she was chosen secretary of the House Democratic Caucus, the leadership position Geraldine Ferraro had held. But her attempt to become caucus chairman in 1988 was hurt by revelations in 1987 that she paid one staffer a high salary, though the staffer lived and worked in New York, and that she promoted another woman with whom she shares a house and mortgage payments. The House ethics committee found the first of these arrangements in violation of House rules but recommended no disciplinary action. Even so, she ran far behind William Gray in the race for caucus chairman. The charges also got wide circulation in Cleveland, and Dennis Kucinich ran against her in the 1988 primary. But Oakar won 77%–23%, a margin similar to those she wins by in general elections. The major threat to her seat seems to be redistricting, and even that is not too great; there will continue to be a west side of Cleveland district after the 1992 Census, and she seems likely to be strong there.

The People: Est. Pop. 1986: 489,500, dn. 4.8% 1980–86; Pop. 1980: 514,164, dn. 14.7% 1970–80. Households (1980): 70% family, 34% with children, 56% married couples; 36.6% housing units rented; median monthly rent: $167; median house value: $45,700. Voting age pop. (1980): 383,041; 2% Spanish origin, 2% Black, 1% Asian origin.

1988 Presidential Vote:

Dukakis (D)	. . . .	103,933	(57%)
Bush (R)	. . . .	77,551	(42%)

Rep. Mary Rose Oakar (D)

Elected 1976; b. Mar. 5, 1940, Cleveland; home, Cleveland; Ursuline Col., B.A. 1962, John Carroll U., M.A. 1966; Roman Catholic; single.

Career: Operator, OH Bell Telephone Co., 1957–62; Instructor, Lourdes Acad., 1963–70; Asst. Prof., Cuyahoga Commun. Col., 1968–75; Cleveland City Cncl., 1973–76.

Offices: 2231 RHOB, 202-225-5871. Also 523 Fed. Crt. Bldg., 215 Superior Ave., Cleveland 44114, 216-522-4927.

Committees: *Banking, Finance and Urban Affairs* (7th of 31 D). Subcommittees: Economic Stabilization (Chairman); Financial Institutions Supervision, Regulation and Insurance; Housing and Community Development. *House Administration* (6th of 13 D). Subcommittees: Accounts; Personnel and Police (Chairman). *Post Office and Civil Service* (7th of 15 D). Subcommittee: Compensation and Employee Benefits. *Select Committee on Aging* (7th of 39 D). Subcommittees: Health and Long-Term Care; Retirement Income and Employment. *Joint Committee on the Library.*

Group Ratings

	ADA	ACLU	COPE	CFA	LCV	ACU	NTLC	NSI	COC	CEI
1988	90	76	94	91	81	8	5	10	17	8
1987	96	—	93	79	—	5	—	—	0	2

National Journal Ratings

	1988 LIB — 1988 CONS	1987 LIB — 1987 CONS
Economic	84% — 15%	73% — 0%
Social	72% — 27%	70% — 28%
Foreign	67% — 33%	76% — 19%

Key Votes

1) Homeless $	AGN	5) Ban Drug Test	—	9) SDI Research	AGN
2) Gephardt Amdt	FOR	6) Drug Death Pen	FOR	10) Ban Chem Weaps	FOR
3) Deficit Reduc	FOR	7) Handgun Sales	AGN	11) Aid to Contras	AGN
4) Kill Plnt Clsng Notice	AGN	8) Ban D.C. Abort $	FOR	12) Nuclear Testing	FOR

Election Results

1988 general	Mary Rose Oakar (D).................	146,715	(83%)	($783,180)
	Michael Sajna (R)	30,944	(17%)	
1988 primary	Mary Rose Oakar (D).................	64,417	(77%)	
	Dennis J. Kucinich (D)...............	19,530	(23%)	
1986 general	Mary Rose Oakar (D).................	110,976	(85%)	($378,170)
	William Smith (R)	19,794	(15%)	

TWENTY-FIRST DISTRICT

Fifty years ago blacks were only one of many distinctive groups living in Cleveland, and by no means the most numerous. "Most of Cleveland's Negroes," the *WPA Guide* reported, "who came in during the labor famine of the World War and immediately after, live in the slum area extending from the fringes of the business section to East 105th Street and south of Carnegie Avenue. The few who become affluent move to other sections of the city, but the birth rate of those who remain has created a serious housing problem." A few years later, the wartime demand for labor brought many more thousands of blacks from the South to Cleveland, and their numbers continued to grow in the postwar years as steel mills and auto assembly plants hired new hands. By the middle 1960s, Cleveland east of the Cuyahoga River, once a checkerboard of Polish, Czech, Hungarian, Italian and Jewish neighborhoods, was mostly black; and in 1967, the city elected Carl Stokes as its first black mayor. In the years since, blacks continued to move east, not only into comfortable neighborhoods at the northeast and southeast extremes of the city, but into suburbs, from modest East Cleveland to luxurious Shaker Heights, laid out on broad boulevards by the streetcar magnates the Van Sweringen brothers in 1905. But these form only a part of Cleveland's black community.

The 21st Congressional District of Ohio includes most of the east side of Cleveland, plus many of the suburbs into which blacks have been moving. Its congressman, now in his third decade of service is Louis Stokes. He was first elected in 1968, when his younger brother was mayor; Carl Stokes left that office in 1971, abandoning politics for a job as a TV anchor in New York, and then returned to Cleveland and was elected judge; for all that time Louis Stokes remained in the House. The Stokes brothers have a rags-to-riches family history; able and successful, they changed the course of Cleveland politics. Before they became powerful, Cleveland's blacks felt excluded from high civic positions and were unhappy particularly with the city's police department. Now they are integrated into city politics. Blacks and whites combined to get rid of

Mayor Dennis Kucinich and blacks, as well as whites, have supported the Republican Mayor, George Voinovich; controversies over the school board or city council members have split the city not on racial lines but on other divides.

Louis Stokes is now a senior congressman of recognized abilities who has been called on for one difficult assignment after another. One was the chairmanship of the Select Committee on Presidential Assassinations, which he assumed after Henry Gonzalez resigned in 1977. Stokes supervised responsible hearings and the production of a report which has held up as the last word on the subject. In 1981, in the wake of the Abscam scandal, Stokes was called on to chair the Committee on Standards of Official Conduct—the official name of the House Ethics Committee—and handled that assignment until after the 1984 election. In 1987 and 1988, he was chairman of the House Intelligence Committee and a member of the special committee investigating the Iran-contra scandal. Stokes seems profoundly mistrustful of the CIA after the revelations of late 1986, and in early 1987 proposed legislation reducing to zero the Executive Branch's discretion about when to notify Congress of covert activities. Stokes is a high-ranking member of the Appropriations Committee, generally inclined to favor generous federal domestic spending. He has done yeoman work on producing the Congressional Black Caucus budget resolution alternatives which, while attracting relatively few votes, provide a useful perspective on what a more generous government would look like. He is routinely reelected every two years.

The People: Est. Pop. 1986: 487,000, dn. 5.3% 1980–86; Pop. 1980: 514,169, dn. 19.7% 1970–80. Households (1980): 66% family, 36% with children, 43% married couples; 52.1% housing units rented; median monthly rent: $143; median house value: $38,000. Voting age pop. (1980): 372,949; 58% Black, 1% Spanish origin, 1% Asian origin.

1988 Presidential Vote:

Dukakis (D).	144,023	(80%)
Bush (R)	33,866	(19%)

Rep. Louis Stokes (D)

Elected 1968; b. Feb. 23, 1925, Cleveland; home, Shaker Heights; Western Reserve U., 1946–48, Cleveland Marshall Law Sch., J.D. 1953; United Methodist; married (Jeanette).

Career: Army, 1943–46; Practicing atty., 1954–68.

Offices: 2365 RHOB 20515, 202-225-7032. Also New Fed. Ofc. Bldg., 1240 E. 9th St., Rm. 2947, Cleveland 44199, 216-522-4900; and 2140 Lee Rd., Cleveland Hgts. 44118, 216-522-4907.

Committees: *Appropriations* (7th of 35 D). Subcommittees: District of Columbia; VA–HUD–Independent Agencies; Labor–Health and Human Services–Education.

Group Ratings

	ADA	ACLU	COPE	CFA	LCV	ACU	NTLC	NSI	COC	CEI
1988	70	100	95	82	81	0	5	0	25	7
1987	88	—	95	71	—	0	—	—	7	5

National Journal Ratings

	1988 LIB — 1988 CONS			1987 LIB — 1987 CONS		
Economic	92%	—	0%	73%	—	0%
Social	86%	—	0%	78%	—	0%
Foreign	84%	—	0%	81%	—	0%

Key Votes

1) Homeless $	AGN	5) Ban Drug Test	AGN	9) SDI Research	AGN
2) Gephardt Amdt	FOR	6) Drug Death Pen	AGN	10) Ban Chem Weaps	FOR
3) Deficit Reduc	FOR	7) Handgun Sales	AGN	11) Aid to Contras	AGN
4) Kill Plnt Clsng Notice	AGN	8) Ban D.C. Abort $	AGN	12) Nuclear Testing	—

Election Results

1988 general	Louis Stokes (D).....................	148,388	(86%)	($173,534)
	Franklin H. Roski (R).................	24,804	(14%)	
1988 primary	Louis Stokes (D), unopposed			
1986 general	Louis Stokes (D).....................	99,878	(82%)	($164,171)
	Franklin H. Roski (R).................	22,594	(18%)	

OKLAHOMA

No other state was hit as hard by the Depression of the 1930s as Oklahoma. A state which had grown from 1.5 million at statehood in 1907—well within the living memory of most adult Oklahomans then—to 2.4 million in 1930 suddenly found its way of life destroyed as farm prices plummeted and the farmland itself vanished in dust storms. "On a single day, I heard, 50 million tons of soil were blown away," John Gunther reported later. "People sat in Oklahoma City, with the sky invisible for three days in a row, holding dust masks over their faces and wet towels to protect their mouths at night, while the farms blew by." The famed Okies headed westward on U.S. 66 to the green land of California—the biggest internal migration of the 1930s—and Oklahoma's population sank to 2.3 million in 1940 and 2.2 million in 1950; it did not rise above the 1930 level again until the census of 1970.

The episode was not atypical. Boom and bust has been the history of Oklahoma, over and over again. This is a state with a history as short as any, and as tragic. It was home first to the Cherokee and other Civilized Tribes driven here by Andrew Jackson's troops over the Trail of Tears. Not until 1889 was even part of Oklahoma opened up to white settlement; then, on the morning of the great land rush memorialized in the Rodgers and Hammerstein musical, an Edna Ferber novel, and half a dozen Hollywood movies, thousands of would-be homesteaders drove their wagons across the territorial line, the most adventurous or unscrupulous of them jumping the gun—the Sooners. Of course, it wasn't such attractive land in the first place, or Jackson wouldn't have given it to the Indians. Interestingly, there are many Indians left: Oklahoma has the second largest Indian population of any state, not on reservations, but assimilated into the rest of the population.

Oklahoma boomed once again in the 1970s, as the oil shocks of 1973 and 1979 sent oil prices up; the population rose from 2.5 million in 1970 to 3 million in 1980 and 3.3 million in 1983. Then, with the collapse of oil prices and the collapse of Oklahoma's farm economy as well, it was bust again. Just as the dust cloud was the symbol of Oklahoma's 1930s bust, so the auction of oil drilling equipment might be the symbol of the 1980s calamity. Alongside Oklahoma highways in the middle 1980s you could see rows of drill rigs and tractors, their still bright paint flecked with rust; in muddy lots, you could see bidders watch as yet another oil man's derrick trailers, rig-up trucks, cranes, compressors and Mercedes were auctioned off.

To understand how sickening Oklahoma's fall has been, you need to understand how giddy was its rise. In January 1982, the rig count was 882; in February 1983, 232, and by 1986, 128. In parallel fashion, between 1980 and 1983, 186,000 people moved into the state; between 1983 and 1986, more than that moved out. In the early 1980s, it was the scene of feverish oil drilling in established fields and of deep-well gas exploration in the Anadarko Basin which promised to take care of America's energy needs for years. In the midst of national recession in 1982, Oklahoma had the nation's lowest unemployment rate, below 4%; by 1986, it was above 8%, after the state lost 59,000 oil and gas jobs. By April of 1989, the unemployment rate had fallen back to 5.7%—though this increase in jobs was due to improvements in the service and transportation economies. Oil and gas have continued to wither; by May 1989, the rig count was 93—the lowest level since 1973. Historians may record that Oklahoma ended up after the oil bust pretty much where it was headed before the oil boom, but that ignores the human cost. Thousands of Oklahomans, many from dirt-poor backgrounds, for a fleeting moment struck it rich—and then found themselves shorn of their money and their dreams.

Governor. Governor Henry Bellmon is Oklahoma's most durable politician: he was elected governor in 1962, Senator in 1968 and 1974, and governor again as the state's economy languished in 1986. Bellmon is a taciturn wheat farmer who disliked Washington life and refuses to serve liquor in the governor's mansion, and an old-fashioned Republican who dislikes deficits and cultural conservatives. His policy has been austerity. Oil and gas revenues used to provide one-third of Oklahoma's budget, but these revenues are off by two-thirds; as a result, the sales and gas taxes have been doubled and the income tax left unadjusted after federal tax reform, but local property taxes are low (and county governments often overstaffed and corrupt) so the demand for state education spending is high. Bellmon wants to spend more for education, to insist on tobacco-free schools, to bar dropouts from getting driver's licenses, and to institute a no-pass-no-play rule for high school athletes.

In April 1989 Bellmon unexpectedly announced he would retire in 1990, stimulating long lists of candidates for the office. Republicans include current or former legislators Mike Fair, Tim Leonard and Tom Cole; Transportation department head Neal McCaleb; former Human Services chairman V. Burns Hargis and U.S. attorney Bill Price. Democrats include Congressman Wes Watkins, former Governor George Nigh, 1986 nominee and narrow loser (47%–45%) David Walters, Lieutenant Governor Robert Kerr II, Treasurer Ellis Edwards, and state Speaker Steve Lewis.

Senators. Oklahoma's Senator David Boren has become, in his second term, an important national figure. When he entered the Senate he seemed to be one of its most conservative young Democrats, a supporter of the Kemp-Roth tax cut before 1980 and a resolute backer of decontrol of oil and gas prices. He snagged a seat on the Finance Committee, where Oklahoma's Robert Kerr once reigned, and he has had considerable success in his original objectives: taxes have been cut and energy prices mostly decontrolled. But in the process of achieving these objectives, Boren has become popular with his fellow Democrats, partly because he has voted with them more often than they anticipated, partly because he is pleasant and competent. He is capable of sharp partisan maneuver: he led a filibuster of Edwin Meese's nomination for Attorney General in early 1985 until Republican leaders agreed to consideration of his farm credit proposals. He played a more nonpartisan role shaping the 1987 farm credit bill.

In the late 1980s, he has concentrated on two new issues. One was campaign finance reform. He has never accepted PAC contributions himself, and the Boren bill which he introduced with Barry Goldwater in 1985 would have limited the total amount of PAC money candidates could receive and provide the option of federal financing which would be conditioned on accepting

OKLAHOMA — Congressional Districts, Counties, and Selected Places — *(6 Districts)*

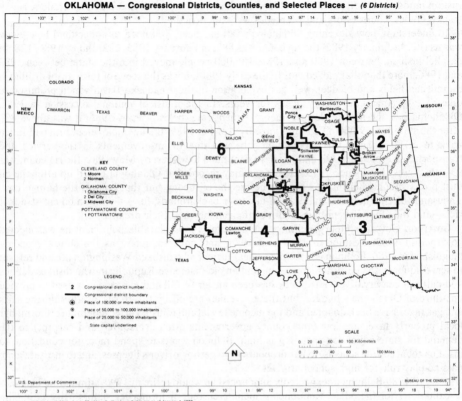

limits on campaign and personal spending. Boren had to struggle to get a vote on it, but finally succeeded and saw 69 Senators agree—although the number might have been inflated because it was clear it would not pass the House.

The other major area for Boren's attention is foreign policy, now that he is chairman of the Senate Intelligence Committee. Boren seems likely to be a quieter chairman than David Durenberger was, less prone to go to the press with complaints and disclosures, more willing to work with the CIA which has itself seemed more willing to work with Congress. He played a part in strengthening the verification provisions of the INF Treaty but has otherwise been quiet— perhaps a sign of success in that job.

Boren has been the most popular politician in recent Oklahoma history. He has long experience in politics: his father was a congressman, and after Yale and a Rhodes scholarship he returned to Oklahoma for law school, was elected to the legislature, and was elected governor in 1974. In the Democratic primary he beat an incumbent who later went to jail; Boren's symbol was a broom. Boren was an early Carter supporter, but was disappointed when Carter didn't back total decontrol of energy prices. He ran for the Senate when Republican Dewey Bartlett retired in 1978 and won reelection easily in 1984. He has been mentioned locally as a possible favorite son candidate for President; when Oklahoma's Robert Kerr ran as a favorite son at the 1952 national convention, Boren, then 11, was a page for him. He is up for reelection in 1990, and by early 1989 no credible opponent had surfaced.

Oklahoma's other Senator, Don Nickles, turns out to have a safer seat than many Washington observers thought. Nickles was one of the real surprise winners in 1980, a 31-year-old state senator with little command of national issues and a Catholic whose strongest support came from Protestant fundamentalists. But that is an asset here: if polls could measure intensity of religious feeling, Oklahoma would probably rank near the top of the nation. This is Southern Baptist and evangelical country: Oklahoma only recently has allowed liquor by the drink, and Tulsa is the headquarters of evangelist and Pentecostal faith healer Oral Roberts. With that support, Nickles won typically light-turnout Republican primary and runoff contests and prevailed over a not very well-known Democrat in the general. In Washington, Nickles was one of the least visible of the Republican freshmen, not coming forward with venturesome legislation or constitutional amendments, not denouncing colleagues for backing conventional policy.

This may have been shrewder than it looked. Certainly the Democrats seemed to underestimate Nickles going into 1986. His opponent was Tulsa Congressman Jim Jones, chairman of the House Budget Committee for the first four Reagan years, 14-year House incumbent from a basically Republican district, an aide when a very young man to President Lyndon Johnson. By any measure of legislative competence or raw ability, Jones was the superior candidate, but he had some liabilities which Nickles shrewdly exploited. To Oklahomans, Nickles seemed the patently sincere and plausible candidate.

Nickles has been more active legislatively than expected in the Democratic Senate, and had the satisfaction of finally seeing the 55-mile-per-hour speed limit and the windfall profits tax repealed in 1988. He serves on the Appropriations and Budget Committees—assignments that could give him real leverage in a Republican Senate—and he was chosen to chair the Republican Senate campaign committee in 1989 and 1990.

This is a tough assignment: Republicans go into the cycle behind 55–45; the Democrats probably have more obvious targets; and the early retirements of Bill Armstrong and Gordon Humphrey make holding their two seats considerably iffier. Nevertheless, Democrats who scoff at Nickles's skills should recall how he did against Jim Jones. The Republicans have long had a fine fundraising operation, and they have often done brilliantly at sending the money in the right directions. The harder part is to frame the issues in a way that works for their candidates. Nickles seems to have done that in Oklahoma better than anyone expected, or at least better than most of the Republican Senators of the class of 1980, and it will be interesting to see if he surprises the pundits once again in 1990.

Presidential politics. Curiously, neither the dust bowl nor the oil bust vastly changed Oklahoma's party politics. Historically, party preference was determined by where you came from: southern Oklahoma's Little Dixie was Democratic; the wheat country in the northwest, settled from Kansas, was Republican. Southerners and Democrats were more numerous, and Oklahoma was mostly Democratic, and became a bit more so in the bust of the 1930s. The same split remains today, in different proportions. In the close presidential race of 1976, Gerald Ford carried almost every county north of Interstate 40 and west of Tulsa and lost almost every one on the other side of that line; Republican Henry Bellmon did the same in the close gubernatorial contest of 1986. The balance favors the Republicans, however, because of their strength in the two big cities, Oklahoma City and Tulsa, which have long been Republican, and among people in the oil business, who believe they prosper from free markets and were hurt by regulation—except for regulations and tax preferences that helped them, of course.

That Republican trend in the two metropolitan areas, which between them cast 47% of the state's votes, kept Oklahoma solidly Republican despite the oil bust of the 1980s. It favored Ronald Reagan over Walter Mondale 69%–31%, and in 1986, when most of the country trended mildly Democratic, Oklahoma reelected a Republican Senator who had a strong opponent and, like its Oil Patch neighbor Texas (known here sometimes as Baja Oklahoma), replaced a

Democratic governor with a Republican. In 1988, however, it moved toward the Democrats; Oklahoma, outside the two metropolitan areas, (though nothing like Brookline, Massachusetts in its cultural attitudes) gave George Bush no better than his national margin of 53%–46%. He still carried the state smartly by winning 64% and 63% in greater Oklahoma City and Tulsa.

Congressional districting. Oklahoma's congressional districting plan is, to put it bluntly, a Democratic gerrymander. It was designed to safeguard the seats of the state's five Democratic congressmen and to place the maximum number of Republican voters in the seat of its one Republican House Member. It succeeded through 1986, when Jim Jones's decision to run for the Senate enabled the Republicans to take the Tulsa-based 1st District that always seemed likely to be theirs if Jones were not a candidate—though they didn't win it by a large margin in 1988 and it may be seriously contested in 1990.

The People: Est. Pop. 1988: 3,263,000; Pop. 1980: 3,025,290, up 7.9% 1980–88 and 18.2% 1970–80; 1.37% of U.S. total, 26th largest. 16% with 1–3 yrs. col., 16% with 4+ yrs. col.; 13.4% below poverty level. Single ancestry: 13% English, 6% German, 5% Irish, 1% French, Dutch. Households (1980): 74% family, 40% with children, 63% married couples; 29.3% housing units rented; median monthly rent: $164; median house value: $35,600. Voting age pop. (1980): 2,170,406; 6% Black, 5% American Indian, 2% Spanish origin, 1% Asian origin. Registered voters (1988): 2,199,014; 1,436,147 D (65%), 704,901 R (32%), 57,966 unaffiliated and minor parties (3%).

1988 Share of Federal Tax Burden: $9,219,000,000; 1.04% of U.S. total, 27th largest.

1988 Share of Federal Expenditures

	Total		Non-Defense		Defense	
Total Expend	$10,762m	(1.22%)	$8,434m	(1.29%)	$2,665m	(1.17%)
St/Lcl Grants	1,406m	(1.23%)	1,405m	(1.23%)	1m	(0.97%)
Salary/Wages	2,232m	(1.66%)	747m	(1.11%)	1,485m	(1.11%)
Pymnts to Indiv	5,640m	(1.38%)	5,332m	(1.37%)	308m	(1.65%)
Procurement	870m	(0.46%)	336m	(0.72%)	870m	(0.46%)
Research/Other	614m	(1.65%)	614m	(1.66%)	1m	(1.66%)

Political Lineup: Governor, Henry Bellmon (R); Lt. Gov., Robert S. Kerr, II (D); Secy. of State, Hannah Atkins (D); Atty. Gen., Robert Henry (D); Treasurer, Ellis Edwards; Controller, Clifton H. Scott (D). State Senate, 48 (33 D and 15 R); State House of Representatives, 101 (69 D and 32 R). Senators, David Lyle Boren (D) and Don Nickles (R). Representatives, 6 (4 D and 2 R).

1988 Presidential Vote

Bush (R)	678,367	(58%)
Dukakis (D)	483,423	(41%)

1984 Presidential Vote

Reagan (R)	861,530	(69%)
Mondale (D)	385,080	(31%)

1988 Democratic Presidential Primary

Gore	162,584	(41%)
Gephardt	82,596	(21%)
Dukakis	66,278	(17%)
Jackson	52,417	(13%)
Hart	14,336	(4%)
Simon	6,901	(2%)

1988 Republican Presidential Primary

Bush	78,224	(38%)
Dole	73,016	(35%)
Robertson	44,067	(21%)
Kemp	11,439	(6%)

GOVERNOR

Gov. Henry Bellmon (R)

Elected 1986, term expires Jan. 1991; b. Sept. 3, 1921, Tonkawa; home, Red Rock; OK St. U., B.S. 1942; Presbyterian; married (Shirley).

Career: USMC, WWII; Farmer; OK House of Reps., 1946–48 ; Gov. of OK, 1962–66; U.S. Senate, 1968–80.

Office: State Capitol Bldg., Rm. 212, Oklahoma City 73105, 405-521-2342.

Election Results

1986 gen.	Henry Bellmon (R)...........	431,762	(47%)
	David Walters (D)...........	405,295	(45%)
	Jerry Brown (I)..............	60,115	(7%)
1986 prim.	Henry Bellmon (R)...........	111,665	(70%)
	Mike Fair (R)................	33,266	(21%)
	Three others (R).............	13,968	(7%)
1982 gen.	George P. Nigh (D)	548,159	(62%)
	Tom Daxon (R)...............	332,207	(38%)

SENATORS

Sen. David Lyle Boren (D)

Elected 1978, seat up 1990; b. Apr. 21, 1941, Washington, D.C.; home, Seminole; Yale U., B.A. 1963, Rhodes Scholar, Oxford U., 1965, U. of OK, J.D. 1968; United Methodist; married (Molly).

Career: OK House of Reps., 1968–74; Prof. and Chmn., Dept. of Govt., OK Baptist U., 1968–74; Practicing atty.; Gov. of OK, 1975–79.

Offices: 453 RSOB 20510, 202-224-4721. Also 621 N. Robinson, Rm. 350, Oklahoma City 73102, 405-231-4381; 440 S. Houston, Tulsa 74127, 918-581-7785; and Municipal Bldg., Seminole 74868, 405-382-6480.

Committees: *Agriculture, Nutrition, and Forestry* (3d of 10 D). Subcommittees: Agricultural Credit; Agricultural Production and Stabilization of Prices; Domestic and Foreign Marketing and Product Promotion (Chairman). *Finance* (5th of 11 D). Subcommittees: Energy and Agricultural Taxation (Chairman); International Trade; Taxation and Debt Management. *Small Business* (6th of 10 D). Subcommittees: Government Contracting and Paperwork Reduction; Rural Economy and Family Farming. *Select Committee on Intelligence* (Chairman of 8 D).

Group Ratings

	ADA	ACLU	COPE	CFA	LCV	ACU	NTLC	NSI	COC	CEI
1988	25	41	41	58	20	48	33	90	58	17
1987	35	—	39	42	—	63	—	—	50	33

National Journal Ratings

	1988 LIB — 1988 CONS			1987 LIB — 1987 CONS		
Economic	35%	—	63%	41%	—	58%
Social	40%	—	59%	29%	—	70%
Foreign	48%	—	51%	40%	—	59%

Key Votes

1) Cut Aged Housing $	AGN	5) Bork Nomination	FOR	9) SDI Funding	FOR
2) Override Hwy Veto	FOR	6) Ban Plastic Guns	AGN	10) Ban Chem Weaps	FOR
3) Kill Plnt Clsng Notice	FOR	7) Deny Abortions	FOR	11) Aid To Contras	FOR
4) Min Wage Increase	AGN	8) Japanese Reparations	FOR	12) Reagan Defense $	AGN

Election Results

1984 general	David Lyle Boren (D)	906,131	(76%)	($1,192,026)
	William E. (Bill) Crozier (R)	280,638	(23%)	($6,925)
1984 primary	David Lyle Boren (D)	432,534	(90%)	
	Marshall Luse (D)	48,761	(10%)	
1978 general	David Lyle Boren (D)	493,953	(65%)	($751,286)
	Robert B. Kamm (R)	247,857	(33%)	($443,712)

Sen. Don Nickles (R)

Elected 1980, seat up 1992; b. Dec. 6, 1948, Ponca City; home, Ponca City; OK St. U., B.A. 1971; Roman Catholic; married (Linda).

Career: Natl. Guard, 1970–76; Vice Pres. and Gen. Mgr., Nickles Machine Co., 1976–80; OK Senate, 1979–80.

Offices: 713 HSOB, 202-224-5754. Also 215 Dean McGee Ave., Rm. 820, Oklahoma City 73102, 405-231-4941; 3310 Mid-Continent Tower, 401 S. Boston, Tulsa 74103, 918-581-7651; 1916 Lake Rd., Ponca City 74601, 405-767-1270; and 106 Fed. Bldg., 5th and E Ave., Rm. 115, Lawton 73501, 405-357-9878.

Committees: *Appropriations* (12th of 13 R). Subcommittees: Foreign Operations; Interior; Legislative Branch (Ranking Member); VA, HUD, and Independent Agencies. *Budget* (7th of 10 R). *Energy and Natural Resources* (6th of 9 R). Subcommittees: Energy Regulation and Conservation (Ranking Member); Energy Research and Development; Mineral Resources Development and Production.

Group Ratings

	ADA	ACLU	COPE	CFA	LCV	ACU	NTLC	NSI	COC	CEI
1988	0	4	3	17	0	92	73	100	86	71
1987	5	—	3	8	—	100	—	—	94	87

National Journal Ratings

	1988 LIB — 1988 CONS			1987 LIB — 1987 CONS		
Economic	25%	—	73%	6%	—	87%
Social	0%	—	89%	6%	—	89%
Foreign	0%	—	92%	0%	—	76%

Key Votes

1) Cut Aged Housing $	AGN	5) Bork Nomination	FOR	9) SDI Funding	FOR
2) Override Hwy Veto	AGN	6) Ban Plastic Guns	FOR	10) Ban Chem Weaps	FOR
3) Kill Plnt Clsng Notice	FOR	7) Deny Abortions	FOR	11) Aid To Contras	FOR
4) Min Wage Increase	AGN	8) Japanese Reparations	AGN	12) Reagan Defense $	FOR

Election Results

1986 general	Don Nickles (R)	493,436	(55%)	($3,252,965)
	James R. Jones (D)..................	400,230	(45%)	($2,564,982)
1986 primary	Don Nickles (R), unopposed			
1980 general	Don Nickles (R)	587,252	(53%)	($828,346)
	Andy Coats (D).....................	478,283	(44%)	($996,447)

FIRST DISTRICT

"A dramatic view of Tulsa from the southwest," wrote the *WPA Guide* 50 years ago, "across the vast refinery dominated by West Tulsa and the wide sand-carpeted bed of the river, shows tall, smoke-stained stacks giving way, on the skyline, to the taller modern-city group of skyscrapers that serve the office and hotel needs of its hundreds of oil companies. It is a visual summary of the city's description of itself as the oil capital of the world." The label was grandiose, but Tulsa, almost spanking new in the 1920s and 1930s (it was Indian country not long before that, within living memory) already had the character it still shows today. Its buildings may not have been air-conditioned, but its economy was based on oil; Oral Roberts had not yet built his church headquarters, his university, or his 60-story City of Faith hospital, but Tulsa was already a city inspired by the tradition of enthusiastic religion; its leading citizens did not shop then in galleries, but they already had pretentions for culture and looked down on the mud-on-their-boots sorts in Oklahoma City.

Politically, Tulsa was then and is now one of America's most conservative cities—which means, paradoxically, that it wants to change the way a lot of things are going. Despite the collapse of oil prices in the 1980s, Tulsa is still full of a contagious enthusiasm for new business enterprises and innovations. Ordinary people here do not resent or attack the oil companies or the new rich; they identify with them. They see not class conflict, but a coincidence of economic interests. They see government as interfering with efforts to produce goods and services people want and are ready to pay for—although Tulsans are pleased that the federal government built the McClellan-Kerr Waterway that has made the Tulsa suburb of Catoosa a seaport. They are only mildly embarrassed by Oral Roberts's declaration that "God would call him home" unless he raised $4.5 million by April 1, 1987 for his plans for medical programs. (He was saved at the last minute when a Florida dog track owner gave him $1.3 million.)

Oklahoma's 1st Congressional District consists of most of Tulsa County, plus parts of several of the surrounding counties, into which Tulsa's suburban growth has just been starting to pour in the 1970s and 1980s. By all odds it should be a solidly Republican district. It has voted for nothing but Republican presidential candidates over the last 50 years. Yet the 1st was represented by a Democrat, Jim Jones, for most of the 1970s and 1980s, and its current Republican congressman, Jim Inhofe, seems in weak political shape. This can be explained partly by political skills. Jones, a onetime aide to President Lyndon Johnson, has a subtle political mind and had a successful House career, serving on the Ways and Means Committee (important always to oil interests) and serving for four years as chairman of the Budget Committee. Inhofe, in contrast, has had a rocky political (and business) career; an insurance company of which he was president left debts of $2 million, and he was hurt during the 1988

988   OKLAHOMA

campaign by reports that in 1986 he took out a $20,000 personal loan and immediately donated it to the campaign—an end run, it seemed, around campaign finance law restrictions. He was beaten for reelection to the Oklahoma Senate in 1978 and as mayor of Tulsa in 1983; he lost the governor's race to David Boren in 1974 and the 1st District race to Jim Jones in 1976.

But Inhofe came back and won the House seat in 1986 against weak opposition in the primary and general, when Jones ran unsuccessfully for the Senate. Inhofe takes pride in being outspoken and a staunch conservative, criticizing colleagues George Crockett for supporting the Communist party line and Barney Frank for being homosexual. In 1988, he had tougher opposition from 33-year-old Kurt Glassco, who had been an aide to former Governor George Nigh. Glassco was for contra aid, against gun control, for silent school prayer and the death penalty; he said he knew people's problems from being a prosecutor while Inhofe had been on the public payroll too long. If he seemed to be singing a Republican tune, he may have been doing it more harmoniously than the incumbent Republican, who was dogged by a lawsuit brought by his brother over a family estate, which generated unfavorable publicity about the congressman's business practices, and by charges that in 1987 his campaign borrowed $20,000 from the same supporter who had illegally contributed to his 1986 campaign. Inhofe won reelection by the weak margin of 52%–48%. This may stimulate serious competition from Glassco or someone else in 1990, or after redistricting in 1992.

The People: Est. Pop. 1986: 552,400, up 9.7% 1980–86; Pop. 1980: 503,739, up 14.1% 1970–80. Households (1980): 71% family, 38% with children, 59% married couples; 34.3% housing units rented; median monthly rent: $204; median house value: $42,500. Voting age pop. (1980): 365,006; 8% Black, 4% American Indian, 1% Spanish origin, 1% Asian origin.

1988 Presidential Vote: Bush (R) 120,873   (61%)
Dukakis (D).   76,349   (38%)

Rep. James M. Inhofe (R)

Elected 1986; b. Nov. 17, 1934, Des Moines, IA; home, Tulsa; U. of Tulsa, B.A. 1961; Presbyterian; married (Kay).

Career: OK House of Reps., 1968–69; OK Senate, 1969–77, Repub. Ldr., 1975–77; Mayor of Tulsa, 1978–84.

Offices: 408 CHOB 20515, 202-225-2211. Also 201 W. 5th St., Tulsa 74103, 918-581-7111.

Committees: *Merchant Marine and Fisheries* (16th of 17 R). Subcommittees: Coast Guard and Navigation; Merchant Marine. *Public Works and Transportation* (12th of 20 R). Subcommittees: Aviation; Investigations and Oversight; Water Resources. *Select Committee on Narcotics Abuse and Control* (8th of 12 R).

Group Ratings

	ADA	ACLU	COPE	CFA	LCV	ACU	NTLC	NSI	COC	CEI
1988	10	13	17	27	19	92	87	100	92	68
1987	4	—	0	7	—	100	—	—	100	83

National Journal Ratings

	1988 LIB —	1988 CONS	1987 LIB —	1987 CONS
Economic	21% —	77%	0 —	89%
Social	0% —	95%	0 —	90%
Foreign	0% —	84%	0 —	80%

Key Votes

1) Homeless $	—	5) Ban Drug Test	FOR	9) SDI Research	FOR
2) Gephardt Amdt	AGN	6) Drug Death Pen	FOR	10) Ban Chem Weaps	AGN
3) Deficit Reduc	AGN	7) Handgun Sales	FOR	11) Aid to Contras	FOR
4) Kill Plnt Clsng Notice	FOR	8) Ban D.C. Abort $	FOR	12) Nuclear Testing	AGN

Election Results

1988 general	James M. Inhofe (R).................	103,458	(52%)	($484,585)
	Kurt Glassco (D).....................	93,101	(48%)	($253,585)
1988 primary	James M. Inhofe (R), unopposed			
1986 general	James M. Inhofe (R)..................	78,919	(55%)	($410,286)
	Gary D. Allison (D)	61,663	(43%)	($119,550)

SECOND DISTRICT

Indian Territory—that was, literally, what northeast Oklahoma was, from the time in the 1830s the Five Civilized Tribes were driven here from Georgia and Alabama over the Trail of Tears. Oklahoma was not open to white settlement until 1889, and today 12% of the people in this part of Oklahoma report their race as American Indian; many more claim some percentage of Indian blood. The Indian percentage is highest in the hilly counties just west of the Ozarks of Arkansas, where the county names—Cherokee, Delaware, Sequoyah—recall what were called the Civilized Tribes. "Steadily there is being woven into the fabric of Oklahoma's citizenship this red thread of Indian," wrote the *WPA Guide* 50 years ago. "Through intermarriage, Indian blood in Oklahoma is becoming more widely diffused. The time may come when an Indian recognizable as such will be hard to find within the state, but perhaps through wider dissemination the influences of Indian blood may be greater in the future than they have ever been in the past." Much attention nationally is focused on the problems of Indians in states where there are large reservations. But no one seems to be asking whether the experience of the Indians in Oklahoma—where they are now relatively prosperous, assimilated and living comfortably with the white population—has any useful lessons for Indians and whites in other parts of the country.

Most of northeastern Oklahoma, minus most of Tulsa and its immediate surroundings, makes up the 2d Congressional District of Oklahoma. It is represented by a man from Muskogee, Mike Synar, who is not an ordinary Oklahoma politician. Synar is aggressive, pushy, independent to the point of cussedness, yet possessed of a self-effacing sense of humor. His record on the issues is about as liberal as that of any Oklahoma congressman, and his energy is not concentrated on parochial issues. He made headlines in 1985 when he brought a lawsuit challenging the constitutionality of Gramm-Rudman—after several colleagues who said they'd join him ducked out—and more headlines in 1986 when the Supreme Court ruled that Gramm-Rudman's trigger mechanism was indeed unconstitutional. He has fought for years to ban all forms of tobacco advertising. With David Obey of Wisconsin, he is the lead House sponsor of the campaign finance reform to limit PAC contributions, and he takes no PAC money himself. Synar sometimes seems to be a fly in every well-entrenched group's ointment—which occasionally costs him. He ran for Democratic caucus chairman in 1988, and was unwilling to make campaign contributions to colleagues, as William Gray did, or to politick much for support; he ran far behind Gray and Mary Rose Oakar.

But he is not a down-the-line liberal either. He worked hard on the bankruptcy law in 1986 and on some issues supported the views advanced by big creditors. He has worked out compromises on such sticky issues as who should pay for state and local costs imposed by the immigration reform bill and family farm bankruptcy procedures. He was a vitriolic opponent of the Synthetic Fuels Corporation, despite its strong support from Jim Wright. On the Energy and Commerce Committee, he pushed for natural gas deregulation against the never-to-be-underestimated opposition of Chairman John Dingell. He supports the seven-day waiting period for gun purchases opposed by the National Rifle Association. In his first term, as a young member of the Judiciary Committee, he sponsored a key amendment strengthening the fair housing law the House passed in 1980, which passed by a 205–204 vote. More recently, he has been pushing for a mandatory parental leave law.

Synar has managed to combine this record of positions which are not always popular, and priorities which are not always shared in his district, with impressive popularity among the voters. He first won the seat in a fluke, beating in the 1978 Democratic primary an incumbent who had recently been divorced and was rumored to have a heart-shaped waterbed, and winning reelection by a lesser margin in 1980. After winning more than 70% against weak opponents in suceeding elections, he got stronger primary opposition in 1988. Frank Shurden, a state senator whose seat was not up, challenged him in the primary, swearing that he would vote for contra aid and against all tax increases and deficits, and boasting of his bill requiring castration of convicted sex offenders. But Synar, who returned most weekends to the district and took care to have a strong constituency service operation, won 70%–30%. In the general, Republican businessman Ira Phillips, though not very articulate, made the standard Republican case against liberalism. Synar replied, "If fighting for senior citizens, veterans, farmers and ranchers, families and the future of children is liberal, I claim proudly to be one." In a year when Michael Dukakis ran even with George Bush in most of the district, Synar carried every county in the district but Tulsa and won 65%–35%. These victories pretty well dispose of the notion that Synar is vulnerable, and as he enters his forties he has the prospect of a long House career ahead of him.

The People: Est. Pop. 1986: 559,400, up 10.7% 1980–86; Pop. 1980: 505,149, up 33.6% 1970–80. Households (1980): 78% family, 42% with children, 68% married couples; 23.0% housing units rented; median monthly rent: $118; median house value: $31,500. Voting age pop. (1980): 353,938; 10% American Indian, 4% Black, 1% Spanish origin.

1988 Presidential Vote: Bush (R) 110,246   (53%)
Dukakis (D). 97,194   (47%)

Rep. Michael L. (Mike) Synar (D)

Elected 1978; b. Oct. 17, 1950, Vinita; home, Muskogee; U. of OK, B.A. 1972, J.D. 1977, Northwestern U., M.S. 1973, U. of Edinburgh, Rotary Intl. Scholar, 1974; Episcopalian; single.

Career: Rancher, practicing atty., real estate broker.

Offices: 2441 RHOB 20515, 202-225-2701. Also Fed. Bldg., 125 S. Main, Rm. 2B22, Muskogee 74401, 918-687-2533.

Committees: *Energy and Commerce* (12th of 26 D). Subcommittees: Energy and Power; Health and the Environment; Telecommunications and Finance. *Government Operations* (6th of 24 D). Subcommittee: Environment, Energy, and Natural Resources (Chairman). *Judiciary* (7th of 21 D). Subcommittees: Courts, Intellectual Property, and the Administration of Justice; Economic and Commercial Law. *Select Committee on Aging* (11th of 39 D). Subcommittees: Health and Long-Term Care; Retirement Income and Employment.

Group Ratings

	ADA	ACLU	COPE	CFA	LCV	ACU	NTLC	NSI	COC	CEI
1988	100	91	62	91	69	0	17	10	38	20
1987	84	—	60	86	—	13	—	—	13	13

National Journal Ratings

	1988 LIB — 1988 CONS	1987 LIB — 1987 CONS
Economic	65% — 34%	55% — 43%
Social	86% — 0%	78% — 0%
Foreign	68% — 28%	71% — 27%

Key Votes

1) Homeless $	AGN	5) Ban Drug Test	AGN	9) SDI Research	AGN
2) Gephardt Amdt	AGN	6) Drug Death Pen	AGN	10) Ban Chem Weaps	FOR
3) Deficit Reduc	FOR	7) Handgun Sales	AGN	11) Aid to Contras	AGN
4) Kill Plnt Clsng Notice	AGN	8) Ban D.C. Abort $	AGN	12) Nuclear Testing	FOR

Election Results

1988 general	Michael L. (Mike) Synar (D)	136,009	(65%)	($358,705)
	Ira Phillips (R)	73,659	(35%)	($81,634)
1988 primary	Michael L. (Mike) Synar (D)	62,936	(70%)	
	Frank Shurden (D)	27,604	(30%)	
1986 general	Michael L. (Mike) Synar (D)	114,543	(73%)	($268,187)
	Gary K. Rice (R)	41,795	(27%)	($11,276)

THIRD DISTRICT

Fifty years ago, Little Dixie was the most backward part of Oklahoma. This southeast part of the state was settled between 1889 and 1907 by white southerners, most of them dirt poor; some county names here (Leflore, Pontotoc) were taken directly from Mississippi. The politics, too, was from the old one-party South: Little Dixie remains the most Democratic part of Oklahoma, giving even Michael Dukakis a near victory in 1988. The 3d Congressional District of Oklahoma includes most of the Little Dixie counties, and juts up into the center of the state, into the old university town of Stillwater, which is Republican territory, to include enough people to meet the population standard.

This is the district that for 30 years elected Carl Albert to the House of Representatives. Albert was chosen by Speaker Sam Rayburn early in his career, in 1955, to be majority whip, but he did not get to be Speaker until 1971, when he seemed tired; he deferred to committee chairmen and had trouble relating to the younger Members who were potential allies for a strong Speaker. Nonetheless, as a national leader of the area's historic party, he was widely popular in Little Dixie.

The current congressman from Little Dixie succeeded Carl Albert and has a different approach. Rather than seek a national leadership post, Congressman Wes Watkins has concentrated on getting projects for the district. He is a member of the Appropriations Committee, and of two subcommittees which can do his district a lot of good: Agriculture and Energy and Water Development. He devotes much time, energy and ingenuity in snaring more water projects for Little Dixie; and he has been active as a promoter of rural areas generally, and was for three terms chairman of a Rural Caucus. He has taken a role on national issues with implications for rural America, like the farm credit bill of 1987. But he seems to devote most of his attention to local projects. He was proud to have helped create the Winding Stair Mountain National Recreation and Wilderness Area and the Robert S. Kerr Memorial Arboretum, named after the Senator who, in the 1950s and early 1960s, brought plenty of pork to Oklahoma. These projects may have done some good, too. At least the economy of Little Dixie has been growing more robustly than that of the rest of the state in the 1980s; it is less dependent on oil and more on leisure time activities, and in 1986 and 1987 it generated more than one-third of the state's new jobs.

On other issues, Watkins voted a very conservative line in his first four years in the House and since Ronald Reagan came in has been much closer to other Democrats. This probably reflects a shrewd appreciation of how the increasingly partisan House does business. Committee and subcommittee chairmen are elected by secret ballot by their fellow Democrats, and conservatives who buck the party too often lose these contests. Watkins has not caused party leaders any trouble, and in return they are happy to help him with what he cares about the most. This has proved a winning formula in 3d District elections, which have not been seriously contested since 1976, when Watkins beat Albert's longtime administrative assistant, Charles Ward, in the primary.

But Watkins may leave the 3d to run for governor. In April 1989 when Governor Henry Bellmon announced his retirement, Watkins emerged as one of the leading Democratic contenders for the office, and seemed poised to run. If he does the favorite in this district that almost voted for Michael Dukakis will be the next Democratic nominee. The most prominent early possibility was state Attorney General Robert Henry.

The People: Est. Pop. 1986: 536,800, up 6.5% 1980–86; Pop. 1980: 504,268, up 20.1% 1970–80. Households (1980): 74% family, 39% with children, 64% married couples; 27.6% housing units rented; median monthly rent: $113; median house value: $25,100. Voting age pop. (1980): 365,865; 6% American Indian, 4% Black, 1% Spanish origin.

1988 Presidential Vote:

Bush (R)	95,225	(50%)
Dukakis (D)	94,615	(49%)

Rep. Wes Watkins (D)

Elected 1976; b. Dec. 15, 1938, DeQueen, AR; home, Ada; OK St. U., B.S. 1960, U. of MD, M.S. 1961 ; Presbyterian; married (Lou).

Career: USDA, 1963; Asst. Dir. of Admissions, OK St. U., 1963–66; Exec. Dir., Kiamichi Econ. Develop. Dist. of OK, 1966–68; Realtor and homebuilder, 1968–76; OK Senate, 1975–76.

Offices: 2348 RHOB 20515, 202-225-4565. Also 232 P. O. Bldg., Ada 74820, 405-436-1980; 118 Fed. Bldg., McAlester 74501, 918-423-5951; and 720 S. Husband, Stillwater 74074, 405-743-1400.

Committees: *Appropriations* (24th of 35 D). Subcommittees: Energy and Water Development; Rural Development, Agriculture and Related Agencies.

Group Ratings

	ADA	ACLU	COPE	CFA	LCV	ACU	NTLC	NSI	COC	CEI
1988	50	64	46	73	38	46	19	60	57	25
1987	64	—	44	43	—	17	—	—	21	22

National Journal Ratings

	1988 LIB — 1988 CONS		1987 LIB — 1987 CONS	
Economic	45%	54%	57%	40%
Social	40%	58%	58%	41%
Foreign	50%	49%	49%	51%

Key Votes

1) Homeless $	FOR	5) Ban Drug Test	AGN	9) SDI Research	AGN
2) Gephardt Amdt	FOR	6) Drug Death Pen	FOR	10) Ban Chem Weaps	AGN
3) Deficit Reduc	FOR	7) Handgun Sales	FOR	11) Aid to Contras	FOR
4) Kill Plnt Clsng Notice	FOR	8) Ban D.C. Abort $	AGN	12) Nuclear Testing	AGN

Election Results

1988 general	Wes Watkins (D), unopposed			($174,437)
1988 primary	Wes Watkins (D), unopposed			
1986 general	Wes Watkins (D)	114,008	(78%)	($210,936)
	Patrick K. Miller (R)	31,913	(22%)	

FOURTH DISTRICT

The 4th Congressional District of Oklahoma starts out within a few miles of the oil-derrick-surrounded state Capitol in Oklahoma City, smack dab in the middle of the state, and proceeds south and west to cover half of Oklahoma's Red River Valley. It includes Lawton, a small city whose major industries are Goodyear and the Army's Fort Sill; Norman, home of the University of Oklahoma; and some mostly blue-collar parts of Oklahoma City itself and its suburbs of Midwest City and Moore. But the predominant tone, demographically and politically, is rural. Even in the cities and towns, the red or brown dust gets tracked indoors by your boots, and the entree of choice is still chicken-fried steak. Politically, this country is ancestrally Democratic, although Republicans, helped by Republican trends in the parts of the district with population growth like Norman, Lawton and the Oklahoma City suburbs, have carried it in recent national elections.

The congressman from the 4th District, Dave McCurdy, has emerged as one of the national leaders of his party on several defense and foreign policy issues, even though he was first elected only in 1980, and then by a narrow margin. He occupies that position partly because of his expertise and committee assignments, but even more because he is poised at the fulcrum of opinion in the House: with a few other like-minded members, he can determine the outcome of votes on bitterly contested issues like contra aid and the MX missile. This he has gone out and done, with an adroitness hailed by his admirers or (take your choice) an opportunism denounced by his detractors.

He embarked on this course by getting a seat in his first term on Armed Services, a natural assignment for a Member from a hawkish district laden with military bases (Fort Sill, Oklahoma City's Tinker Air Force Base, Altus Air Force Base). While generally supporting increased military spending, he sparked the movement to oust the elderly Mel Price as Armed Services chairman and install Les Aspin in his place, a move that succeeded in 1984 despite the opposition of Speaker Tip O'Neill. He worked with Aspin in 1985 to fashion a compromise on the MX missile which was opposed by most House Democrats but accepted by the Administration and adopted by Congress. He also became a player on contra aid in 1985, as the lead sponsor of the proposal to give the contras $27 million in "humanitarian" aid, but no military aid. All this was premised on progress in negotiations and continuing review by Congress—and also, in practical terms, on acts of the Sandinistas; McCurdy switched to a tougher position at one point when Daniel Ortega flew off to Moscow after the House voted down military aid. McCurdy supported the Arias plan and Speaker Jim Wright's policy on the contras, and seemed pleased when the contra movement seemed to surrender in early 1988. He insists he doesn't like the Sandinistas, but clearly the Republicans are correct when they say that his first priority was blocking American military aid and they are probably right in saying that the various amendments and changes in policy he has helped to produce have weakened pressure on the Sandinistas to honor human rights.

McCurdy wanted to become chairman of the Intelligence Committee in 1989, and in December 1987 resigned from it for a year so that he would not be subject to the six-year limit on consecutive service. Jim Wright appointed him to another six-year term, but named Anthony Beilenson of California, a liberal but not a political deal-maker, to be chairman. Beilenson, however, must rotate off the committee when he reaches the six-year limit in 1990, and McCurdy, as the second ranking Democrat, is in line to become chairman. He could keep that potentially powerful position for five years, provided that he has the favor of Speaker Tom Foley and that (as everyone expects) the Democrats retain control of the House. He was also prominent in 1989 as the lead House sponsor of the Democratic Leadership Council's national service plan. Volunteers could serve in the military or in civilian service jobs and earn vouchers that could be used for college expenses or down payments on a house. McCurdy does more mundane things as well. He got himself a seat in 1987 on an Armed Services subcommittee handling military bases—obviously of importance in the 4th District.

In the midst of all this involvement in foreign and defense policy, McCurdy has transformed the 4th District from the most marginal of districts to a safe seat. In 1988, he won 83% in the primary and was unopposed in the general. He has made no move to run for the Senate and is one congressman who would have greater power if he stayed in the House.

The People: Est. Pop. 1986: 563,200, up 11.3% 1980–86; Pop. 1980: 505,869, up 24.3% 1970–80. Households (1980): 77% family, 44% with children, 67% married couples; 30.6% housing units rented; median monthly rent: $181; median house value: $37,200. Voting age pop. (1980): 356,658; 6% Black, 3% Spanish origin, 3% American Indian, 1% Asian origin.

1988 Presidential Vote: Bush (R) 105,170   (58%)
Dukakis (D). 74,429   (41%)

Rep. Dave McCurdy (D)

Elected 1980; b. Mar. 30, 1950, Canadian, TX; home, Norman; U. of OK, B.A. 1972, J.D. 1975, U. of Edinburgh, Scotland, Rotary Fellow, 1977–78; Lutheran; married (Pam).

Career: OK Asst. Atty. Gen., 1975–77; Practicing atty., 1978–80.

Offices: 2344 RHOB 20515, 202-225-6165. Also P.O. Box 1265, Norman 73070, 405-329-6500; 103 Fed. Bldg., Lawton 73501, 405-357-2131; and P.O. Box 1051, Duncan 73534, 405-252-1434.

Committees: *Armed Services* (11th of 31 D). Subcommittees: Military Installations and Facilities; Research and Development. *Science, Space and Technology* (11th of 30 D). Subcommittees: Natural Resources, Agriculture Research and Environment; Transportation, Aviation and Materials. *Permanent Select Committee on Intelligence* (2d of 12 D). Subcommittees: Oversight and Evaluation (Chairman); Program and Budget Authorization.

Group Ratings

	ADA	ACLU	COPE	CFA	LCV	ACU	NTLC	NSI	COC	CEI
1988	60	78	44	82	56	30	31	70	64	31
1987	44	—	41	50	—	27	—	—	40	25

National Journal Ratings

	1988 LIB — 1988 CONS		1987 LIB — 1987 CONS	
Economic	46%	— 52%	45%	— 54%
Social	55%	— 45%	57%	— 43%
Foreign	50%	— 50%	48%	— 52%

Key Votes

1) Homeless $	AGN	5) Ban Drug Test	AGN	9) SDI Research	FOR
2) Gephardt Amdt	AGN	6) Drug Death Pen	—	10) Ban Chem Weaps	AGN
3) Deficit Reduc	FOR	7) Handgun Sales	FOR	11) Aid to Contras	AGN
4) Kill Plnt Clsng Notice	FOR	8) Ban D.C. Abort $	AGN	12) Nuclear Testing	AGN

Election Results

1988 general	Dave McCurdy (D), unopposed			($251,956)
1988 primary	Dave McCurdy (D).	52,366	(83%)	
	Howard Bell (D)	10,728	(17%)	
1986 general	Dave McCurdy (D).	94,984	(76%)	($176,096)
	Larry Humphreys (R).	29,697	(24%)	

FIFTH DISTRICT

Oklahoma City, created within the memory of many then living, had an unfinished, hastily assembled look to the *WPA Guide* 50 years ago. "Downtown, on the streets, in the stores, and in lodging places that range from 25 cents a night to the luxury of fine hotel suites, fur coats and overalls, oil-field workers and clerks, farmers and their families, and sophisticates who know Europe and South America as well as they know the playgrounds of the United States—all these mingle and make Oklahoma City a truly American metropolis." Truly Oklahoman, certainly:

situated almost precisely in the middle of the state and the middle of the continent, with the oil derrick outside the state Capitol still pumping some oil, Oklahoma City is the metropolis of Oklahoma. Like many state capitals, it was not the spontaneous creation of commerce but the deliberate creation of government, built on land that is browner and more eroded by creeks than the greener, rolling Oklahoma farther east. During the 1960s, the city fathers decided that they would not let the old city limits fence them in, so Oklahoma City, unlike most American central cities, started annexing land, so that it now spills over into five counties and four congressional districts, and includes hundreds of acres which even today are farms or grazing land.

The 5th Congressional District of Oklahoma includes most of Oklahoma City, but it is a carefully chosen part: the most Democratic sections of the city, including its black areas, are chopped off and included in Democratic districts. The 5th is intended to be Republican. Besides the prosperous parts of Oklahoma City, which are heavily Republican as only prosperous parts of oil cities are, it includes wheat-growing counties to the north, and the market town of Ponca City, which is as Republican as any similar-sized town in nearby Kansas. Connected by a strip of mostly uninhabited Osage County is the well-to-do oil town of Bartlesville, headquarters of Phillips Petroleum, whose management, allied with the equally worried townspeople-employees, succeeded in warding off T. Boone Pickens, but only after saddling the firm with huge debt. The 5th District is a collection of urban Republican voting precincts stitched together by swaths of thinly populated rural territory.

The congressman from the 5th District is Mickey Edwards, a Republican regarded as far outside the national consensus when he was first elected in 1976 but today one of the leaders of his party in the House—and one of the more originally thoughtful members of either party. Edwards believes in market economics and has long believed in deregulating energy markets; he also, as one expects in the Oil Patch, favors a higher oil depletion allowance and other incentives for production, plus an oil import fee. On foreign policy, he was one of the leading and most vehement backers of military aid to the Nicaraguan contras; he is proud that he helped push through contra aid in June 1986, and he seems disgusted with the group of swing votes, evidently including his Oklahoma neighbor Dave McCurdy, who withdrew their support of military aid and, as he sees it, insured the contras' defeat in return for promises the Sandinistas are certain not to keep. The ranking Republican on the Appropriations subcommittee on Foreign Operations, he opposes giving assistance to countries like Mozambique and Peru. But he seems open to evidence of possible change in the Soviet Union, though skeptical. Will Gorbachev and perestroika produce real progress in human rights and market economics? "They're trying, but they still don't quite get it," he says.

After the 1988 election, Edwards was elected chairman of the House Republican Policy Committee, the number four position in the leadership. It was an impressive victory, all the more so because Edwards is not associated with either of the two groups symbolized by the two contenders in the 1989 contest for whip. He has little affection for the guerrilla tactics of the young Members around Newt Gingrich, and he has criticized both parties in the House for not doing more constructive legislating. His senior position on Appropriations clearly has influenced him here. Yet at the same time he is not one of the "old bulls" like Edward Madigan, devoted to getting along with the Democrats in fashioning legislation and temperamentally averse to publicizing new ideas. Edwards was chairman of the American Conservative Union for five years, and he has advanced some unorthodoxies of his own. He opposed the line-item veto, for example, after it had become a campaign staple of Republicans, because it would increase the power of the Executive Branch and diminish that of Congress; he asked his fellow conservatives how they would like it if a Democratic President could zero out weapons systems if he had the support of the one-third-plus-one of one house needed to prevent an overriding of his veto.

Edwards is now the oldest member of the youngish Oklahoma delegation and one of the most senior; he is also one of the politically most secure. He passed up his chance to run for the Senate and seems committed to a career in the House, just as his constituents seem committed to keeping him there.

The People: Est. Pop. 1986: 560,700, up 11.5% 1980–86; Pop. 1980: 502,974, up 17.1% 1970–80. Households (1980): 71% family, 37% with children, 61% married couples; 30.8% housing units rented; median monthly rent: $199; median house value: $43,600. Voting age pop. (1980): 367,630; 5% Black, 3% American Indian, 2% Spanish origin, 1% Asian origin.

1988 Presidential Vote:

Bush (R)	145,247	(67%)
Dukakis (D)	68,735	(32%)

Rep. Mickey Edwards (R)

Elected 1976; b. July 12, 1937, Cleveland, OH; home, Oklahoma City; U. of OK, B.A. 1958, OK City U., J.D. 1969; Presbyterian; married (Lisa).

Career: Practicing atty.; Editor, *Private Practice* magazine; Asst. City Editor, *Oklahoma City Times*; Instr., OK City U.

Offices: 2330 RHOB 20515, 202-225-2132. Also 900 N.W. 63d St., Ste. 105, Oklahoma City 73116, 405-231-4541; 1200 S.E. Frank Phillips Blvd., Ste. 102, Bartlesville 74003, 918-336-5436; and 102 S. 5th, Ponca City 74601, 405-762-8121.

Committees: *Appropriations* (10th of 22 R). Subcommittees: Foreign Operations, Export Financing and Related Programs (Ranking Member); Military Construction.

Group Ratings

	ADA	ACLU	COPE	CFA	LCV	ACU	NTLC	NSI	COC	CEI
1988	10	26	10	45	25	92	72	100	93	61
1987	12	—	8	14	—	90	—	—	100	77

National Journal Ratings

	1988 LIB — 1988 CONS			1987 LIB — 1987 CONS		
Economic	24%	—	74%	0%	—	89%
Social	13%	—	84%	27%	—	73%
Foreign	16%	—	78%	0%	—	80%

Key Votes

1) Homeless $	FOR	5) Ban Drug Test	FOR	9) SDI Research	FOR
2) Gephardt Amdt	AGN	6) Drug Death Pen	FOR	10) Ban Chem Weaps	AGN
3) Deficit Reduc	AGN	7) Handgun Sales	FOR	11) Aid to Contras	FOR
4) Kill Plnt Clsng Notice	FOR	8) Ban D.C. Abort $	FOR	12) Nuclear Testing	AGN

Election Results

1988 general	Mickey Edwards (R)	139,182	(72%)	($318,822)
	Terry J. Montgomery (D)	53,668	(28%)	($302)
1988 primary	Mickey Edwards (R)	25,311	(83%)	
	Bill Maguire (R)	5,142	(17%)	
1986 general	Mickey Edwards (R)	108,774	(71%)	($289,552)
	Donna Compton (D)	45,256	(29%)	($16,217)

SIXTH DISTRICT

Western Oklahoma 50 years ago was "fertile, but the crops are at the mercy of the elements. Wheat, broomcorn, and forage yields are large when drought and wind temper their fury. Many of the acres, particularly the broad plateaus with their terraced canyons, are used as grazing land for cattle. The flat, even terrain creates mirages on a wavering horizon. Inhabitants tell of standing in the open and being able to see towns many miles away. Tumbleweeds, which grow profusely here, are blown about by the wind and pile against houses and outbuildings. On especially windy days,"—and this is one of the windiest parts of America—"sand swirls over the fields, burying seeds and young plants deeply, and justifying the term 'dust bowl'." The western plains of Oklahoma are a demanding land, scorching hot under the summer sun, snow-blown in winter. The rural counties today have far fewer people than before the dust bowl of the 1930s (in the counties wholly within the 6th District, the population dropped from 423,000 to 282,000), and the once booming oil and natural gas exploration here in the Anadarko Basin and other fields has not done much for the region now that it has gone bust.

The western plains of Oklahoma, plus the blue-collar and black neighborhoods in Oklahoma City form Oklahoma's 6th Congressional District. Most of its acreage has long been Republican: it was settled by farmers moving south from Kansas, starting when (or a little before) the gun went off the morning of the great land rush in 1889. A few of its counties in the south are heavily Democratic, and always have been; most of the rest are heavily Republican, and always have been: these divisions are as permanent as if Oklahoma had been split down the middle during the Civil War, except that of course there were no white people settled in the state at all at that time.

Yet the 6th District elects and reelects a Democratic congressman, Glenn English. He was helped in the 1980s by redistricting, which carefully included a part of Oklahoma City which is 25% black and contains most of the city's white working-class areas; but he is by no means dependent on these votes. English was once an aide to liberal Democrats in the California Assembly, but you wouldn't know it from his voting record, which tends toward the conservative. His Oklahoma credentials are in order: he grew up here and served as executive director of the state Democratic Party before he ran for Congress in 1974. Perhaps his greatest political achievement so far was to seize a propitious moment—just four days before the showdown on the 1981 Reagan tax cut—and extract from Ronald Reagan, in a letter in his own handwriting, a commitment to veto "with pleasure" any windfall profits tax on natural gas. That promise effectively protected that otherwise vulnerable revenue source in 1982, when Republicans were scrambling around looking for politically painless ways to, in the phrase of the day, enhance revenues.

English serves on the Agriculture Committee, which of course is of great interest to this wheat-growing district, and chairs the Subcommittee on Conservation, Credit and Rural Development. In this capacity he has oversight over the commodities markets, and in early 1989 was planning an in-depth investigation in the wake of revelations of fraud. A fiscal conservative on most issues, he makes exceptions for local pork barrel projects and especially for wheat programs; a free trader generally, he is a hawk when it comes to restricting meat imports. He wants to stimulate U.S. farm exports and advocates an oil import fee. He also serves on Government Operations, which he has used to concentrate on the difficult and important, but not at all parochial, problems of government computers, individual privacy, and the Freedom of Information Act. He has also been, to the surprise and delight of many of his fellow Democrats, a tiger in preventing relaxation of the FOIA. He is one of several congressmen who have tried to reduce the federal expenditure on presidential libraries, and has authored legislation that would require private endowments to pay for their upkeep. (In early 1985, he discovered that the Administration supported his initiative, but only if it exempted the Reagan library.) National

Republicans, apparently respectful of English's strength, have never targeted him, and he has won reelection by huge margins most years; in 1988 he beat a hapless Republican 73%–27%.

The People: Est. Pop. 1986: 532,900, up 5.9% 1980–86; Pop. 1980: 503,291, up 4.1% 1970–80. Households (1980): 73% family, 38% with children, 62% married couples; 29.1% housing units rented; median monthly rent: $152; median house value: $32,500. Voting age pop. (1980): 361,309; 9% Black, 3% American Indian, 2% Spanish origin.

1988 Presidential Vote:

Bush (R)	101,606	(58%)
Dukakis (D)	72,101	(41%)

Rep. Glenn English (D)

Elected 1974; b. Nov. 30, 1940, Cordell; home, Cordell; Southwestern St. Col., B.A. 1964; United Methodist; married (Jan).

Career: Chf. Asst., Major. Caucus, CA Assembly; Exec. Dir., OK Dem. Party, 1969–73; Petroleum leasing business.

Offices: 2206 RHOB 20515, 202-225-5565. Also 264 Old P.O. Bldg., 215 Dean A. McGee Ave., Oklahoma City 73102, 405-231-5511; Fed. Bldg., P.O. Box 3612, Enid 73702, 405-233-9224; and 1120 9th St., Woodward 73801, 405-256-5752.

Committees: *Agriculture* (5th of 27 D). Subcommittees: Conservation, Credit and Rural Development (Chairman); Tobacco and Peanuts; Wheat, Soybeans, and Feed Grains. *Government Operations* (3d of 24 D). Subcommittees: Government Information, Justice, and Agriculture; Legislation and National Security.

Group Ratings

	ADA	ACLU	COPE	CFA	LCV	ACU	NTLC	NSI	COC	CEI
1988	40	52	32	73	44	60	40	90	71	35
1987	44	—	30	50	—	39	—	—	73	39

National Journal Ratings

	1988 LIB — 1988 CONS			1987 LIB — 1987 CONS		
Economic	39%	—	60%	40%	—	60%
Social	26%	—	73%	47%	—	53%
Foreign	43%	—	56%	43%	—	57%

Key Votes

1) Homeless $	FOR	5) Ban Drug Test	AGN	9) SDI Research	AGN
2) Gephardt Amdt	AGN	6) Drug Death Pen	FOR	10) Ban Chem Weaps	AGN
3) Deficit Reduc	AGN	7) Handgun Sales	FOR	11) Aid to Contras	FOR
4) Kill Plnt Clsng Notice	FOR	8) Ban D.C. Abort $	FOR	12) Nuclear Testing	AGN

Election Results

1988 general	Glenn English (D)	122,887	(73%)	($306,600)
	Mike Brown (R)	45,239	(27%)	($85,059)
1988 primary	Glenn English (D)	51,733	(84%)	
	Batch Batchelder (D)	9,490	(16%)	
1986 general	Glenn English (D) unopposed			($149,998)

OREGON

"Pictorially, Oregon is this," the *WPA Guide* explained 50 years ago, "tidy white houses and church spires of the Willamette Valley settlements, like transplanted New England towns, among pastoral scenery warm and graceful as the landscapes of Innes; the Alice-through-the-looking-glass effect of a swift incredible geographic change that lifts motorists out of lush green forests and over the wind-scoured ridgepole of the Cascades, and plummets them into a grim never-never land of broken rim-rock and bare-boned plains beyond the range; the lamplit frontier towns of eastern Oregon, the rolling, golden wheatlands, great ranches where booted and spurred men still ride. Or if the bird's eye view is toward the west coast, a humid, forested, mountainous region, fronting the Pacific, to which it presents, abruptly, a precipitous escarpment, relieved here and there by long stretches of sand beaches, an occasional lumber port or fishing village, or a river mouth." This Oregon was known to Americans since Lewis and Clark spent the winter of 1805–06 at the mouth of the Columbia. John Jacob Astor's fur traders set up Astoria in 1811, and settlers came up the Oregon Trail, through the rapids of the Columbia Gorge to the fertile, well-watered Willamette Valley. Oregon was a hot political issue then: James K. Polk won the 1844 election on the cry of "54°40′ or Fight!" although in 1846 he settled with the British for the 49th parallel instead.

In this remote land, nearly 2,000 miles and weeks of travel away from the Mississippi River frontier and at least 700 miles from the equally small settlements in California, was established the orderly, productive society of Oregon. It grew steadily over the years, with only a few booms—in 1900–10 as the timber industry was growing, and in the 1940s when war workers raised the state's population by 40%. Culturally, it is quintessentially American, but geographically it is remote from most of the United States and looks out across the Pacific Rim to the Orient: most of the Japanese cars sold in the United States are unloaded in Portland, and this is one state which resolutely backs free trade. Its major product for many years was—and in good years, still is—lumber, but there is less of the raucousness of the lumber camp to its history and more of the decorum of the New England Yankee small town with its library and literary society. When the West was the stronghold of populism, Oregon was different; and it was the most Republican of the western states as late as 1948, when it favored Thomas E. Dewey over Harry Truman.

This well-ordered little commonwealth had another boom in the 1970s. As Americans became aware of pollution and to appreciate their natural environment, they began to seek out places like Oregon, with its small cities (even metropolitan Portland is only about 1.3 million) and nearby wilderness, its pristine mountains, seacoast and desert. Oregonians, however, did not want to see their state follow the same path as the big metro areas in California. Its attitude was summed up by Governor Tom McCall (1966–74), who urged people to visit Oregon, "but for heaven's sake don't come to live here." That attitude changed by the late 1970s, when recession and an ailing lumber industry made environment-conscious Oregon yearn for a little more of the economic growth it had been taking for granted. For a time, migration into the state—long heavy, despite McCall's admonition—stopped, and unemployment rates zoomed up to some of the nation's highest levels. The problem was the vulnerability of the lumber industry: demand for lumber depends on the level of new construction, which in turn depends on interest rates; the combination of high interest rates and recession during the first Reagan term hit Oregon especially hard.

In the late 1980s, growth returned and concern for the environment was again high; Oregon

OREGON — Congressional Districts, Counties, and Selected Places — *(5 Districts)*

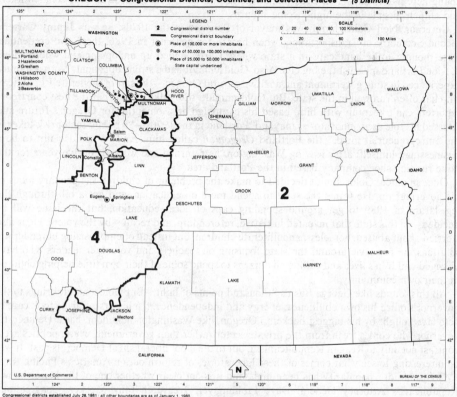

Congressional districts established July 28, 1981 ; all other boundaries are as of January 1, 1980.

which elected a conservative, belt-tightening Republican governor in 1978 and 1982, was ready to elect an expansive liberal Democrat, Neil Goldschmidt, in 1986. A similar trend was apparent in the 1988 presidential election when Oregon, after voting Republican in all but one of the last nine elections, cast its electoral votes for Michael Dukakis. His emphasis on economic growth and on the liberal cultural values important to so many highly educated professionals struck a chord in Oregon; this is a culturally liberal state on many issues, with many young and single voters, and one that is proud of being the first state to ban throwaway bottles and among the first to allow abortions (though it may be a little sheepish about having decriminalized marijuana in the early 1970s). On economics, Oregon is less liberal, cautious in its enthusiasm for big government (even though public works like the Columbia River dams are so visible here) and turned off by the Democrats' increasing emphasis on restrictive trade policies.

Oregon seems to have reached these conclusions not after dialectical struggle, but through the emergence of a consensus. Unlike most states, it does not have long-standing political differences between different regions. The coastal areas and the lower Columbia River valley are marginally more Democratic than the rest of the state; Salem, the state capital, is usually more Republican than Eugene, the site of the University of Oregon; the low-lying, less affluent sections of Portland east of the Willamette River are usually Democratic, while the more affluent city neighborhoods and suburbs in the hills in the west tend to be Republican. But the differences are small, and there is not the vast gap between lifestyles you find in California. The longhaired young here like to backpack and think of themselves as middle-class; so do blue-collar workers and affluent people in the high-income suburbs.

Governor. Neil Goldschmidt was mayor of Portland in the 1970s; he was Jimmy Carter's second Secretary of Transportation; when he ran for governor in 1986, these two credentials were thought to be handicaps in a state where Carter ended up unpopular and where voters outside Portland mistrust the big city. Also, Goldschmidt had a strong opponent, Norma Paulus, experienced in state government and a native of rural Oregon—the sort of moderate Republican who has often run well in the state. But Goldschmidt, who talks so fast that the best courtroom reporters can't keep up with him, based his campaign on a blueprint for Oregon's future and stressed his role as an innovator as mayor of Portland in the 1970s—"a public-sector risk-taker in the entrepreneurial mold," the Portland *Oregonian* called him. And he could claim to be a businessman himself; after leaving Washington, he returned and worked for five years for the Nike running shoe company based in the Portland area.

Once in office, Goldschmidt decided to make the problems of children the primary focus of his governorship. He wants the state to spend more on education, and got a bill through the legislature in 1989 to get around spending caps on local education; but the issue will be decided—in this state that invented initiative, referendum, and recall—by the voters. He is also worried about abused, homeless, and illiterate children, but instead of emphasizing bureaucratic solutions, he has gone around the state focusing on teachers and volunteer leaders who have changed children's lives and calling on citizens to spend some of their own time helping children in their own community.

All this sounds like George Bush's "thousand points of light." But Goldschmidt brings to the governor's office his own ebullience, energy and independence. (In his first year he took care to veto laws sought by his biggest backers.) Oregon, like Washington next door, has a Democratic governor who comes fresh from the private sector rather than government, whose politics are a contrast not only to Reagan Republicanism, but to the labor liberalism of Democrats past. It will be interesting to see what comes of these laboratories of reform out on America's Pacific Rim.

Goldschmidt's popularity has been high, and it is not clear whether one of the better known Republicans—Attorney General Dave Frohnmayer, Treasurer Tony Meeker, Congressman Denny Smith—will choose to run against him in 1990. If not, he may be opposed by a member of Oregon's religious right, like Joe Lutz the activist minister who challenged Bob Packwood in the 1986 primary.

Senators. Oregon has two of the senior Republicans in the Senate, the chairmen of the Appropriations and Finance Committees when their party was in control, and important legislators now that it is in the minority. Both are men of considerable intellect, character and distinctive views. And, as so often is the case when a state is represented by two Senators of the same party, considered to be in the same place on the ideological scale, and roughly the same age, their relations have been sometimes friendly, sometimes edgy.

The senior Senator is Mark Hatfield, ranking member of the Senate Appropriations Committee and holder of statewide office in Oregon since 1956, when he was elected secretary of state at 34. In 1958, he was elected governor and served for eight years; in 1966, he was elected to the Senate and has been there ever since. The issue about which Hatfield has always cared most is peace. He is a deeply religious man, and as a young serviceman was one of the first Americans to see Hiroshima after it was bombed. That experience—and deep convictions—have left him a strong proponent of disarmament and of understanding our adversaries. He was the cosponsor of the McGovern-Hatfield amendment to end the Vietnam war in the early 1970s; he was an enthusiastic backer of the nuclear freeze in the 1980s; he has never voted for a defense authorization bill. But as Appropriations chairman, he presided over the huge defense spending increases in the early 1980s; Hatfield is a man who will always vote his convictions, but will not bend the rules or use underhanded means to achieve them. On other foreign issues, he has been a staunch opponent of contra aid, he believes American Middle East policy is too pro-Israel, and he strongly opposes the death penalty and tried to get it dropped from the 1988 drug bill. With Edward Kennedy, he is sponsoring a two-year U.S.-Soviet moratorium on underground nuclear testing of over one kilton. He has worked for years to give aid to Vietnamese refugees.

On other issues, Hatfield is not so unconventional a politician. He is not an unqualified believer in free-market economics, but he has favored—long before the current slump in the lumber industry—measures to give the lumber companies more access to Oregon's forests than many environmentalists would like. He is not an enthusiast for most domestic spending programs. On cultural issues, his strong religious beliefs usually do not make him join forces usually with the New Right, but he does oppose abortion, in vivid contrast to fellow Oregon Senator Bob Packwood. He has used his Appropriations seat to funnel money to Oregon and he worked hard to prevent restarting of a shut-down nuclear plant across the river in the Hanford Reservation in Washington. Hatfield also welded together the usually fractious Oregon delegation to push through a Wild and Scenic Rivers bill in 1988, protecting 40 rivers; all but eastern Oregon's Bob Smith supported the bill.

Hatfield chaired the Appropriations Committee for six years—an often frustrating assignment, since it is constantly being muscled by the Budget Committee and by Gramm-Rudman, its bills must be defended against dozens of controversial amendments, and it had to do much of its work in one end-of-session continuing resolution. Hatfield is not a cynical horse-trader at such times, but he is willing to take on some fights and is able to win some. In 1987 Hatfield turned his gavel over to the Democrats, but since his power was not based on either partisan staffing or aggressive use of the chair, much of it remains.

Hatfield's seat is up in 1990, when he will have held public office for 40 years. He is considered popular, but it is hard for any Oregon politician to stay in close touch with constituents so many miles away, so there is speculation that he may retire or encounter serious opposition. In 1984, he ran very well despite some charges that would have hurt a Senator whose integrity is not so universally taken for granted. Before the election, it was revealed that Mrs. Hatfield, a real estate broker, had received a $40,000 fee in return for little or no services from one Basil Tsakos, and that Hatfield had been soliciting support on official stationary for Tsakos's proposal to build a $15 billion oil pipeline across Africa. The Hatfields changed their story several times, then appeared together in Portland, confessed an error in judgment, promised to donate the money to charity, and asked the voters' forgiveness. Another odd episode came in 1989 when Hatfield, stopped at a red light in Washington with his wife and son in the car, saw one man on foot shoot at another. When bullets passed close to his car, he floored it—a natural and prudent reaction—but he did not report the incident to the police.

After the Tsakos affair, Hatfield won reelection in 1984 with 67% of the vote—his best showing ever. He has said he will announce in fall 1989 whether he will run again, and has been raising money. Two of the state's Democratic congressmen clearly have senatorial ambitions, but one of them, Les AuCoin, has worked closely with Hatfield on Appropriations matters and says he will not run against him. The other, Ron Wyden, has not ruled it out; either or both might run if Hatfield retires, and so might Republican Congressman Denny Smith.

Oregon's junior Senator, Bob Packwood, made history in 1986 as the Chairman of the Senate Finance Committee who played a major role in producing America's most sweeping tax reform act in 45 years. His role was all the more surprising, since it was such a departure from his previous posture. Packwood spent most of his years on the Finance Committee when Russell Long was chairman, and for years he shared Long's view that government should use the tax code—granting tax credits and accelerated depreciation, allowing deductions and tax shelters—to achieve policy goals; and he also seemed to share Long's unspoken view that a Finance chairman maximizes his power by keeping tax rates high and then doling out exemptions and favors and lower rates to his colleagues and constituents. Far from sharing Jimmy Carter's view that the tax code was a disgrace to the human race, he stated openly that it was pretty good as it was. In the first months of 1986, after Dan Rostenkowski's Ways and Means Committee passed its tax reform bill lowering rates and eliminating preferences, Packwood followed his old approach. He announced early on that he would insist on favorable treatment for the timber industry—a maladroit move that gave others leverage over him—and watched as fellow Finance members piled preference after preference into the bill.

By mid-April 1986, enough preferences had been voted to boost the deficit by $100 billion—and kill the bill. Packwood was being lampooned in the Portland *Oregonian* as "H & R Packwood with another of my 17 versions of tax reform," and he was facing opposition in the May 20 primary from a charismatic young conservative named Joe Lutz. Packwood had amassed some $4 million in campaign contributions (not difficult when you're Finance chairman doling out tax preferences), but Lutz was attacking him with style and humor, and was drawing on the anti-Packwood base among registered Republicans that had held him to 62% against weak opposition in the 1980 primary. A fiasco on tax reform would undercut Packwood's greatest strength with Republican primary voters, namely his reputation for competence and his ability as a committee chairman to get things done.

So in late April, Packwood repaired to a Capitol Hill bar with an aide and over a pitcher of beer started pencilling out some figures—and came up with a bill that stripped away far more preferences than the House or Reagan version and which would lower rates far more, to a high of 27%. "I came around full circle to think [Bill] Bradley was right," Packwood said. "We ought to get the rates as low as we can, [and] let economic efficiency guide decisions." Packwood's turnaround stunned Washington, which had been writing off tax reform for 18 months, and carried the day in early May on the Finance Committee and in the Senate. There was almost an audible sigh of relief from the politicians at the prospect of getting out of the business of doling out preferences to favored causes and lobbyists.

Packwood was banged around somewhat later by Dan Rostenkowski in the conference committee, where Rostenkowski controlled his House conferees while Packwood didn't control his Senate counterparts. But the bill finally passed into law. In the meantime, Packwood won renomination over Joe Lutz May 20 by the none too huge margin, for a primary, of 58%–42%. That was the contest for him: the Democratic nominee, Representative James Weaver, withdrew from the race in August while he was being investigated by the House Ethics Committee, and the Democrats nominated a young man who had won 14% in their primary. Packwood, with millions left in campaign funds and his reputation for competence and clout restored, won easily.

The loss of the Finance chair left Packwood less powerful but still busy. He is one of the Senate's stronger free traders, backing the U.S.-Canada Free Trade Agreement (but getting changes to help Oregon's plywood industry) and opposing the protectionist textile bill in 1988; the former was passed and Packwood organized enough senators to prevent an override of the veto of the latter. On the Commerce Committee, which he chaired from 1981 to 1985, he is a force for deregulation. He supported the catastrophic health care bill and the Civil Rights Restoration Act and was the first Senate Republican to oppose the nomination of Robert Bork. He is co-sponsoring with Daniel Patrick Moynihan a bill to change the child care tax credit. He worked on the Oregon Wild and Scenic Rivers bill. On campaign finance reform he has partisan expertise from his days as chairman of the National Republican Senatorial Committee (he lost the post in 1982 after he was critical of Reagan), and he upheld the Republican filibuster against the Democrats' bill; late at night in February 1988, Majority Leader Robert Byrd, frustrated by the lack of a quorum, ordered the sergeant-at-arms to arrest Packwood making him the first Senator ever to be carried into the chamber under arrest.

Packwood has causes as well as committees. In the early 1970s, he was the Senate's leading advocate of zero population growth, and in the late 1970s, he became its leading opponent of bans on abortion. The Senate, despite New Right gains, is still the branch of government least inclined to restrict abortions; Packwood has proven skillful at using parliamentary devices to rally the majority he has on this issue in the face of attacks from Jesse Helms and others. The issue has also been a major electoral asset to Packwood. Women's rights advocates made his reelection their number one priority in 1980 and they, in turn, were the single biggest bloc of contributors to his campaign that year, even providing a substantial share of his funds in 1986, though most, of course, could be attributed to his Finance chair. Yet he is also a strong party man, one who put together the fundraising capability and technical services which were crucial in keeping Republican control of the Senate in the 1980s. He was also the originator of the yearly Tidewater talks, when Republican officeholders from around the country, wearing sweaters and using first names, meet on Maryland's Eastern Shore and try to share the new ideas they have had about policy.

Packwood, like many prominent Senators, first won office in an upset: he was a surprise winner when he ran, at age 36, against four-term incumbent Wayne Morse in 1968. He won reelection in 1974 and 1980 by margins that have to be considered unimpressive, especially considering the fact that he heavily outspent his opponents both times. In 1986, his real challenge was in the primary, and it now looks as if the religious right will always oppose him (but not Hatfield, because of his well-known deep religious beliefs). The distance factor may be playing a part here. Much of Oregon is nine flying hours from Washington, D.C., and it's harder for Oregon's Members of Congress to keep in close touch with their constituents.

Packwood is a man of calculation more than passion, an experienced observer of the game and one who still plays it to win. Those who see him as a cynical man who believes in nothing have got it wrong; he does have strong beliefs—encouraging free enterprise, women's rights, the Republican Party to name three—but he is also interested in surviving, and other issues—tax preferences, for example—may become negotiable. His strategy for 1992, as it has been for previous races, is to raise plenty of money and try to avoid serious competition; and the surprise of previous elections is not that he has won, but that some of his margins have been so close.

Presidential politics. Oregon, with seven electoral votes, and geographically closer to Vancouver, British Columbia than it is to any population concentration in any state but neighboring Washington, does not see much of presidential candidates, even in primaries, and even when, as in 1988, the contest in the general election here is close. Since environmental issues started becoming important, Oregon has tended to vote more Democratic than the nation when the Democrats run a culturally liberal candidate and less Democratic than the nation when they do not. Oregon was one of the few states to cast almost as high a percentage of its votes for George McGovern as for Hubert Humphrey, yet in 1976 it went narrowly for Gerald Ford over Jimmy Carter. Walter Mondale did not sell particularly well here; Michael Dukakis did. The difference in response is even more striking when you consider that these Democratic nominees got 30% of their votes from blacks in some industrial states, while there are almost no blacks in Oregon, nor is there a large low-income population. Oregon is part of America's Northern Tier—so is Washington, Minnesota, Wisconsin, Massachusetts—the only place in the country where the Democrats' cultural liberalism is affirmatively popular.

The halcyon days of Oregon's presidential primary are probably over. This late May contest ended Harold Stassen's career as a serious presidential candidate in 1948, when he lost 52%–48% to Thomas Dewey, and it gave Robert Kennedy his only defeat in 1968. Oregon in those days was part of a West Coast swing, since it came just before the California primary; at a time when campaigners were not yet used to flying all over the country they, like National Football League teams in the 1950s, scheduled West Coast contests together, to minimize travel time. By the 1980s, Oregon seemed to come too late in the season and to have too few delegates at stake to earn much attention.

1006   OREGON

Congressional districting. Oregon House races have a certain volatility: the distance factor makes it hard for even the most conscientious and attractive congressman to keep winning by the kinds of percentages that members whose districts are within two hours of Washington's National Airport can count on. Oregon is not likely to gain a seat in 1992, as it did in 1982, nor will its district lines have to be changed much because of population growth. The Democrats who control the redistricting process may, however, adjust the lines in the Portland area to make the 1st and 5th Districts more favorable to their candidates.

The People: Est. Pop. 1988: 2,741,000; Pop. 1980: 2,633,105, up 4.1% 1980–88 and 25.9% 1970–80; 1.12% of U.S. total, 30th largest. 20% with 1–3 yrs. col., 17% with 4+ yrs. col.; 10.7% below poverty level. Single ancestry: 10% English, 9% German, 4% Irish, 2% Norwegian, 1% Swedish, French, Scottish, Italian, Dutch. Households (1980): 70% family, 37% with children, 60% married couples; 34.9% housing units rented; median monthly rent: $212; median house value: $59,000. Voting age pop. (1980): 1,910,048; 2% Spanish origin, 1% Asian origin, 1% Black, 1% American Indian. Registered voters (1988): 1,528,478; 737,489 D (48%); 590,648 R (39%); 200,341 unaffiliated and minor parties (13%).

1988 Share of Federal Tax Burden: $8,659,000,000; 0.98% of U.S. total, 29th largest.

1988 Share of Federal Expenditures

	Total		Non-Defense		Defense	
Total Expend	$8,237m	(0.93%)	$7,420m	(1.13%)	$1,115m	(0.49%)
St/Lcl Grants	1,322m	(1.15%)	1,320m	(1.15%)	2m	(1.95%)
Salary/Wages	1,001m	(0.75%)	831m	(1.24%)	170m	(1.24%)
Pymnts to Indiv	4,878m	(1.19%)	4,685m	(1.20%)	193m	(1.03%)
Procurement	749m	(0.40%)	298m	(0.64%)	749m	(0.40%)
Research/Other	287m	(0.77%)	286m	(0.77%)	1m	(0.77%)

Political Lineup: Governor, Neil Goldschmidt (D); Secy. of State, Barbara Roberts (D); Atty. Gen., Dave Frohnmayer (R); Treasurer, Tony Meeker (R). State Senate, 30 (19 D and 11 R). State House of Representatives, 60 (32 D and 28 R). Senators, Mark O. Hatfield (R) and Robert W. Packwood (R). Representatives, 5 (3 D and 2 R).

1988 Presidential Vote

Dukakis (D)	616,206	(51%)
Bush (R)	560,126	(47%)

1988 Democratic Presidential Primary

Dukakis	221,048	(57%)
Jackson	148,207	(38%)
Gephardt	6,772	(2%)
Gore	5,445	(1%)
Simon	4,757	(1%)

1984 Presidential Vote

Reagan (R)	685,700	(56%)
Mondale (D)	536,479	(44%)

1988 Republican Presidential Primary

Bush	199,938	(73%)
Dole	49,128	(18%)
Robertson	21,212	(8%)

GOVERNOR

Gov. Neil Goldschmidt (D)

Elected 1986, term expires Jan. 1991; b. June 16, 1940, Eugene; home, Salem; U. of OR, B.A. 1963, U. of CA at Berkeley, J.D. 1967; Jewish; married (Margie).

Career: Practicing atty., 1967–70; Legal Aide, Portland City Comm., 1971–73; Mayor of Portland, 1973–79; U.S. Secy. of Transportation, 1979–81; Vice Pres., Nike, Inc., 1981–85.

Office: State Capitol, Rm. 254, Salem 97310, 503-378-3111.

Election Results

1986 gen.	Neil Goldschmidt (D)	549,456	(52%)
	Norma Paulus (R)	506,989	(48%)
1986 prim.	Neil Goldschmidt (D)	214,148	(68%)
	Edward N. Fadeley (D)	81,300	(26%)
1982 gen.	Victor G. Atiyeh (R)	639,841	(61%)
	Ted Kulongoski (D)	374,316	(36%)

SENATORS

Sen. Mark O. Hatfield (R)

Elected 1966, seat up 1990; b. July 12, 1922, Dallas; home, Tigard; Willamette U., B.A. 1943, Stanford U., M.A. 1948; Baptist; married (Antoinette).

Career: Navy, WWII; Assoc. Prof. of Pol. Sci., Dean of Students, Willamette U., 1949–57; OR House of Reps., 1951–55; OR Senate, 1955–57; OR Secy. of State, 1957–59; Gov. of OR, 1959–67.

Offices: 711 HSOB 20510, 202-224-3753. Also 475 Cottage St. N.E., Salem 97301, 503-363-1629; and 114 Pioneer Crthse., 555 S.W. Yamhill, Portland 97204, 503-221-3380.

Committees: *Appropriations* (Ranking Member of 13 R). Subcommittees: Commerce, Justice, State, the Judiciary and Related Agencies; Energy and Water Development (Ranking Member); Foreign Operations; Labor, Health and Human Services, Education; Legislative Branch. *Energy and Natural Resources* (2d of 9 R). Subcommittees: Public Lands, National Parks and Forests; Water and Power. *Rules and Administration* (2d of 7 R). *Joint Committee on the Library. Joint Committee on Printing.*

Group Ratings

	ADA	ACLU	COPE	CFA	LCV	ACU	NTLC	NSI	COC	CEI
1988	70	56	51	75	70	30	40	0	57	37
1987	65	—	50	58	—	28	—	—	61	41

National Journal Ratings

	1988 LIB — 1988 CONS			1987 LIB — 1987 CONS		
Economic	43%	—	55%	28%	—	71%
Social	45%	—	54%	35%	—	62%
Foreign	75%	—	24%	64%	—	35%

Key Votes

1) Cut Aged Housing $	AGN	5) Bork Nomination	FOR	9) SDI Funding	AGN
2) Override Hwy Veto	AGN	6) Ban Plastic Guns	FOR	10) Ban Chem Weaps	AGN
3) Kill Plnt Clsng Notice	AGN	7) Deny Abortions	FOR	11) Aid To Contras	AGN
4) Min Wage Increase	FOR	8) Japanese Reparations	FOR	12) Reagan Defense $	AGN

Election Results

1984 general	Mark O. Hatfield (R)	808,152	(67%)	($671,167)
	Margie Hendriksen (D).	406,122	(33%)	($257,512)
1984 primary	Mark O. Hatfield (R)	214,114	(79%)	
	John T. Scheiss (R).	26,848	(10%)	
	Sherry Reynolds (R).	18,590	(7%)	
	Ralph H. Preston (R)	12,662	(5%)	
1978 general	Mark O. Hatfield (R)	550,165	(62%)	($223,874)
	Vernon Cook (D).	341,616	(38%)	($38,976)

Sen. Robert W. (Bob) Packwood (R)

Elected 1968, seat up 1992; b. Sept. 11, 1932, Portland; home, Portland; Willamette U., B.A. 1954, N.Y.U., LL.B. 1957; Protestant; married (Georgie).

Career: Law clerk, OR Supreme Crt., 1957–58; Practicing atty., 1959–69; OR House of Reps., 1963–69.

Offices: 259 RSOB 20510, 202-224-5244. Also 101 S.W. Main St., Ste. 240, Portland 97204-3210, 503-294-3448.

Committees: *Commerce, Science, and Transportation* (2d of 9 R). Subcommittees: Communications (Ranking Member); Foreign Commerce and Tourism; Surface Transportation. *Finance* (Ranking Member of 9 R). Subcommittees: International Trade; Medicare and Long Term Care. *Joint Committee on Taxation.*

Group Ratings

	ADA	ACLU	COPE	CFA	LCV	ACU	NTLC	NSI	COC	CEI
1988	55	63	46	75	60	40	44	67	57	37
1987	60	—	45	58	—	31	—	—	61	49

National Journal Ratings

	1988 LIB — 1988 CONS			1987 LIB — 1987 CONS		
Economic	47%	—	48%	35%	—	64%
Social	65%	—	34%	84%	—	13%
Foreign	43%	—	56%	46%	—	49%

Key Votes

1) Cut Aged Housing $	AGN	5) Bork Nomination	AGN	9) SDI Funding	FOR
2) Override Hwy Veto	AGN	6) Ban Plastic Guns	AGN	10) Ban Chem Weaps	AGN
3) Kill Plnt Clsng Notice	AGN	7) Deny Abortions	AGN	11) Aid To Contras	AGN
4) Min Wage Increase	FOR	8) Japanese Reparations	FOR	12) Reagan Defense $	AGN

Election Results

1986 general	Robert W. (Bob) Packwood (R)	656,317	(63%)	($6,523,492)
	Rick Bauman (D)	375,735	(36%)	($64,139)
1986 primary	Robert W. (Bob) Packwood (R)	171,985	(58%)	
	Joe P. Lutz, Sr. (R)	126,315	(42%)	
1980 general	Robert W. (Bob) Packwood (R)	594,290	(52%)	($1,534,607)
	Ted Kulongoski (D).	501,963	(44%)	($190,047)

FIRST DISTRICT

In the northwest corner of Oregon, near the antique town of Astoria, where John Jacob Astor's fur traders were the state's first white settlers, around the mouth of the Columbia River, and in the coastal counties of Clatsop, Tillamook and Lincoln, the countryside still has a frontier ambience to it: rain falls constantly on the weathered frame houses, and men in plaid flannel jackets work in lumber mills and on docks. The towns have an unfinished look to them, as if they were villages in the late 19th century, waiting for a railroad hookup or a new factory to make one of them into one of Oregon's major cities. This land is part of the 1st Congressional District of Oregon. The 1st also includes part of the Willamette Valley south of Portland, which has long been farmland—the most fertile land in the state, settled by Yankees in the middle 19th century. But in recent years, areas close to Portland have had an influx of settlers from the metropolitan area—people looking for wider spaces, closer access to the countryside, and a more traditional atmosphere in which to raise their families.

That is the historical 1st District, the descendant of a congressional district first established in 1892, that stretches along the lower Columbia River and almost half of Oregon's Pacific shore. The newer 1st District is part of the Portland metropolitan area. It starts with the sparkling new downtown, with its handsome postmodern high-rises—the pyramid-crested brick KOIN Tower, the wedge-shaped Justice Center—and Victorian storefronts and transit mall with trolleys and the river walk where a freeway was torn down, on the west bank of the Willamette River. It continues up through the hills that jut up just west of downtown, through Portland's most affluent neighborhoods, with old lumber barons' mansions overlooking downtown, the river and Mount Hood. Over those hills are the new suburbs of Washington County. Fifty years ago this was a farm county, with 39,000 people; now Portland has spread out over the lowlands, and the population is about 265,000. This is an affluent area with a high-tech aura; computer and high tech companies have been flocking here, attracted by an environment—at the foot of mountains, woodsy and even rustic, but outfitted with all the comforts and services of modern civilization— that appeals to a high-skill work force. People have started to call the area Silicon Forest.

Historically, this was mostly Republican country, and the 1st elected only Republicans to the House from 1892 to 1972. Then in the Watergate year of 1974 it elected Les AuCoin, a Democrat who is one of the leaders of, and perhaps the archetypical member of, the Watergate generation. His approach to issues is as different from that of typical labor-liberal Democrats as the 1st District is different from typical big city Democratic districts, and he has shown the capacity to win elections in difficult territory and bad years for his party. He typifies the Watergate class also in legislative skill; after one term in the Oregon state legislature he became House Majority Leader. His base was not on the Democratic coast, but in high-income Washington County; his primary emphasis was not on economic issues but on non-economic matters like Vietnam, Watergate and the environment.

In the 1980s, he emerged from his seat on the Appropriations Committee as one of the most visible and fervent opponents of the Reagan Administration's foreign and defense policy. He is one of only two doves on the Defense Appropriations Subcommittee, and took the lead role opposing the MX missile, for example; he is strongly opposed to aiding the Nicaraguan contras; he has argued against the loose interpretation of the 1972 ABM treaty and opposes the Strategic Defense Initiative as "a first-strike capable offensive technology"; he criticized the Reagan Administration bitterly for doing nothing on arms control; he infuriated Republicans by urging that funds be cut from SDI and used instead for Coast Guard drug enforcement. On all these issues, he shows genuine passion plus considerable political skill. He has also taken a lead role on some environmental issues: working with Senator Mark Hatfield to pass the Columbia River Gorge bill in 1986; helping to put together the 1984 Oregon Wilderness bill and getting it passed over the objections of the two Oregon House Republicans; and working with Hatfield to get all but one member of the delegation to support the 1988 Scenic and Wild Rivers bill. He is one of the most passionate opponents of restrictions on abortion—a losing position in the House.

On economic issues, in contrast, AuCoin's views are not reflexively pro-spending. Representing a port that unloads a lot of cars from Japan and ships a lot of lumber to the Far East, he is inclined to be a free trader. He is ready to hear arguments why business needs incentives, and has cultivated many of the business interests in his district.

For all this, AuCoin has some rough political sledding. In the late 1970s and early 1980s Washington County and the Silicon Forest were trending Republican. That, plus the native Republican strength and simple distance from Washington, D.C. stimulated several serious Republican candidacies; moreover, AuCoin with his cheeriness and his burning opposition to many of their favorite causes is just the kind of Democrat that enrages many conservative Republicans. He was held under the 60% mark, which most incumbents easily exceed, in 1974, 1976, 1982, and 1984.

But in the late 1980s Oregon west of the Cascades, like coastal California and the burgeoning suburbs around Seattle, trended Democratic. The historically Republican 1st district gave Michael Dukakis 51% of its votes—5% above his national average. AuCoin continued to raise and spend very substantial amounts of money every electoral cycle, but he had only weak opposition in 1986 and 1988 and won easily. With his free and paid exposure on the Portland television stations that cover three-quarters of the state, AuCoin is a natural to run for the Senate. But he isn't the only Oregon Democrat who has been thinking about that; so has Ron Wyden of the 3d District across the Willamette. But AuCoin, who has been working closely with Hatfield on Appropriations matters and shares many of his strong feelings on foreign policy, has said he will not run against Hatfield in 1990. He may run for the seat if Hatfield retires, or he may seek Bob Packwood's seat in 1992.

The People: Est. Pop. 1986: 562,300, up 6.7% 1980–86; Pop. 1980: 526,840, up 32.4% 1970–80. Households (1980): 67% family, 35% with children, 58% married couples; 38.1% housing units rented; median monthly rent: $226; median house value: $68,100. Voting age pop. (1980): 387,395; 2% Spanish origin, 2% Asian origin, 1% American Indian, 1% Black.

1988 Presidential vote: Dukakis (D)...................... 137,972   (51%)

Bush (R) 126,763   (47%)

Rep. Les AuCoin (D)

Elected 1974; b. Oct. 21, 1942, Redmond; home, Portland; Pacific U., B.A. 1969; Protestant; married (Susan).

Career: Army, 1961–64; Reporter, *Portland Oregonian*, 1965–66; Dir. of Public Info., Pacific U., 1966–73; OR House of Reps., 1971–75, Major. Ldr., 1973–75; Admin., Skidmore, Owings, and Merrill, architectural firm, 1973–74.

Offices: 2159 RHOB 20515, 202-225-0855. Also 860 Montgomery Park, 2710 N.W. Vaughn St., Portland 97210, 503-326-2901.

Committees: *Appropriations* (22d of 35 D). Subcommittees: Defense; District of Columbia; Interior.

Group Ratings

	ADA	ACLU	COPE	CFA	LCV	ACU	NTLC	NSI	COC	CEI
1986	95	86	73	73	100	8	21	0	43	22
1987	88	—	71	86	—	14	—	—	20	18

National Journal Ratings

	1988 LIB	—	1988 CONS	1987 LIB	—	1987 CONS
Economic	57%	—	41%	49%	—	50%
Social	86%	—	14%	73%	—	22%
Foreign	64%	—	34%	81%	—	0%

Key Votes

1) Homeless $	AGN	5) Ban Drug Test	AGN	9) SDI Research	AGN
2) Gephardt Amdt	AGN	6) Drug Death Pen	AGN	10) Ban Chem Weaps	FOR
3) Deficit Reduc	FOR	7) Handgun Sales	FOR	11) Aid to Contras	AGN
4) Kill Plnt Clsng Notice	AGN	8) Ban D.C. Abort $	AGN	12) Nuclear Testing	FOR

Election Results

1988 general	Les AuCoin (D)	179,915	(70%)	($542,224)
	Earl Molander (R)	78,626	(30%)	($11,741)
1988 primary	Les AuCoin (D), unopposed			
1986 general	Les AuCoin (D)	141,585	(62%)	($946,767)
	Anthony Meeker (R).	87,874	(38%)	($492,655)

SECOND DISTRICT

The Cascades, the string of volcanic-origin mountains that run north and south through Oregon, in the words of the *WPA Guide*, "walled eastern Oregon away from the humid winds, the warm rains of the coast, and turned most of the land, through countless eons of slow dehydration, into a country of drought and distances, of grim and tortured mountains and high desert grown sparsely with stunted juniper and windblown sage." The mountains made the first settlers "out of sheer necessity, into cattlemen and sheepmen and 'dry' farmers, just as more benign circumstances made western Oregon residents into lumbermen, dairymen, fishermen, and farmers, and—in the more populous centers—into artisans and politicians and financiers." Thus it was 50 years ago and mostly is still today. Eastern Oregon, with 70% of the state's land, has less than 15% of its people; and if the rest of the state is perched on the Pacific Rim, eastern Oregon is part of the vast, mostly empty intermountain basin.

All of which produces a chip-on-the-shoulder attitude, as when Neil Goldschmidt, then running for governor, declined to debate in Bend, the biggest city east of the Cascades, because it is "the middle of nowhere." He apologized and should have, for Bend had in 1988 the nation's largest percentage of VCRs (74% of households had one), and it is right next door (by western standards) to Crook County, the one county out of more than 3,100 in the United States that has voted for the popular vote winner in every presidential election since its creation. Crook County is lumbering country, almost entirely white Protestants, "a red-neck, white-sock county," Jay Mathews of *The Washington Post* quotes a school librarian as saying. National reporters flocked to the county seat of Prineville in 1988 to see where the country was going. Crook County lived up to its reputation by voting 52%–46% for George Bush, almost precisely the national percentages.

The 2d Congressional District of Oregon covers all of the state east of the Cascades and the southernmost valley between the Cascades and the Coast Range. This is the barren land that some of the first settlers of the Willamette Valley came from—and many died on the way. To the south, the terrain is desertlike, and mostly uninhabited. To the east, along the Idaho border, are the irrigated farmlands along the Snake River as it flows northwest to the Columbia. The northern part of eastern Oregon is forested land, with occasional lumber mill towns; settlements are sparse and separated by many miles. There are a few larger towns here—Pendleton in the northeastern wheat fields, La Grande in the rich Grande Ronde Valley, The Dalles where the Columbia River Gorge begins, and Bend. Much of the district's population is clustered in the southwestern corner, in an area separated from the rest by the Cascades and the once huge volcano whose blown-off cone is now 2,000-foot deep Crater Lake. This is lumbering and pear orchard country. Medford, Ashland, Klamath Falls and Grants Pass are pleasant towns whose ornate Victorian houses remind you of the past.

The 2d District, like most of the intermountain west, is mostly Republican, and it is represented in the House by Bob Smith, a cattle rancher and 22-year veteran of the Oregon legislature who led the Republicans in both houses. He looks rough-hewn in his cowboy boots and western shirts, but he is also a skilled legislator. His proudest accomplishment was an amendment to the 1988 drought relief act, limiting feed grain aid to only those farmers who grow their own feed grain; why should the government, Smith reasoned, pay $2 billion to subsidize feed prices to those who don't grow any? Although not high in seniority, Smith may play an important role in the Agriculture Committee on the 1989 farm bill; he claims also to have opened markets for Oregon products—pears in Taiwan, beef in Japan, potatoes in South Korea. On environmental issues, Smith has consistently been rolled by western Oregon members; he opposed the 1984 Oregon Wilderness law and the 1988 Wild and Scenic Rivers Act, but both passed anyway, and his opposition actually seems to have helped in the 1988 campaign. In 1989 he finally got a seat on Interior where he can fight further battles.

Smith may not have been planning to go to Congress, but when Denny Smith chose to run in the new Willamette Valley district in 1982, the 2d was an open seat, and Bob Smith won 63% in the Republican primary. Against two spirited Democrats he has won four comfortable victories and seems to have a safe seat. Incidentally, there is another Congressman Bob Smith, from New Hampshire, with a similar voting record but an entirely different background and constituency.

The People: Est. Pop. 1986: 548,800, up 4.1% 1980–86; Pop. 1980: 526,968, up 34.2% 1970–80. Households (1980): 75% family, 39% with children, 65% married couples; 30.5% housing units rented; median monthly rent: $186; median house value: $49,900. Voting age pop. (1980): 374,066; 3% Spanish origin, 1% American Indian, 1% Asian origin.

1988 Presidential vote:
Bush (R) 122,981 (54%)
Dukakis (D). 98,308 (43%)

Rep. Robert F. (Bob) Smith (R)

Elected 1982; b. June 16, 1931, Portland; home, Burns; Willamette U., B.A. 1953; Presbyterian; married (Kaye).

Career: Cattle rancher; OR House of Reps., 1960–72, Spkr. 1968–72; OR Senate, 1972–82.

Offices: 118 CHOB 20515, 202-225-6730. Also 1150 Crater Lake Ave., Ste. K, Medford 97504, 503-776-4646.

Committees: *Agriculture* (11th of 17 R). Subcommittees: Forests, Family Farms, and Energy; Livestock, Dairy, and Poultry; Wheat, Soybeans, and Feed Grains. *Interior and Insular Affairs* (12th of 15 R). Subcommittees: National Parks and Public Lands; Water, Power and Offshore Energy Resources. *Select Committee On Hunger* (5th of 12 R).

Group Ratings

	ADA	ACLU	COPE	CFA	LCV	ACU	NTLC	NSI	COC	CEI
1988	5	22	14	45	19	92	81	80	86	65
1987	24	—	13	21	—	64	—	—	86	64

National Journal Ratings

	1988 LIB — 1988 CONS		1987 LIB — 1987 CONS	
Economic	19%	— 80%	22%	— 77%
Social	13%	— 84%	25%	— 73%
Foreign	16%	— 78%	32%	— 68%

Key Votes

1) Homeless $	FOR	5) Ban Drug Test	FOR	9) SDI Research	FOR
2) Gephardt Amdt	AGN	6) Drug Death Pen	FOR	10) Ban Chem Weaps	FOR
3) Deficit Reduc	—	7) Handgun Sales	FOR	11) Aid to Contras	FOR
4) Kill Plnt Clsng Notice	FOR	8) Ban D.C. Abort $	FOR	12) Nuclear Testing	AGN

Election Results

1988 general	Robert F. (Bob) Smith (R)	125,366	(63%)	($340,643)
	Larry Tuttle (D)	74,700	(37%)	($208,513)
1988 primary	Robert F. (Bob) Smith (R), unopposed			
1986 general	Robert F. (Bob) Smith (R)	113,566	(60%)	($323,210)
	Larry Tuttle (D)	75,124	(40%)	($104,266)

THIRD DISTRICT

Fifty years ago, it was known as the Rose City for its beautiful flowers on hillsides overlooking the Willamette River and, looming in the distance on clear days, the snowy peak of Mount Hood. Portland, then as now, was Oregon's metropolis, with about 45% of Oregonians living in its metropolitan area. Portland was founded by New England Yankees (had a coin toss come up heads, it would be called Boston) and started off as a muscular blue-collar town—the place where Oregon unloaded its supplies from the east, on the docks or in the railroad yards, and where it shipped out Oregon's products, mainly lumber and fruit. And it still has a large blue collar population.

But since the late 1960s, the tone of the city has been set by younger people with white-collar jobs and liberal cultural attitudes. It is a city where the former mayor (and now governor, Neil Goldschmidt) worked for an athletic shoe company; where he tore down a riverfront freeway to make a park with summer festivals; where a transit mall runs through the downtown core and you can ride the mass transit line for free; and where the current mayor, Bud Clark, a bearded tavern owner and bicyclist, fired three police chiefs in two years. Portland is tolerant in its cultural attitudes, innovative in its public policies and almost religiously devoted to its environment. These attitudes may be more pronounced in the affluent hills that rise just west of the Willamette River and in some of the more expensive suburbs; but they are also present on the flat plains east of the Willamette, which slope exceedingly gradually toward Mount Hood, where most Portlanders are just plain folks. These attitudes are reinforced by the changing focus of the economy here. Portland is very much aware that it is on the Pacific Rim; it lives in very large part on foreign trade, and sees East Asians as potential customers rather than competitors. This is the one American million-plus metro area from which you cannot fly nonstop to Washington or New York—but from which you can fly nonstop to Tokyo.

The 3d Congressional District of Oregon takes in all of Portland and Multnomah County east of the Willamette River, plus a couple of suburbs along the Willamette just to the south. These are mostly modest-looking areas, with small houses and rows of commercial buildings on the main streets built in the 1950s. The population begins to thin out as you go east toward Mount Hood; there is even a little agricultural land there. The congressman from the 3d District is Ron Wyden, who in his twenties started off in the 1970s as director of the Oregon Gray Panthers, a militant organization for the elderly; he was, among other things, the spark behind the successful statewide referendum to reduce the price of dentures. In 1980, he ran against the incumbent congressman, Bob Duncan, who evidently had not kept in touch with Portland, and won with a solid 60%.

Wyden has a pleasant personality and a low-key style which contrasts with his aggressiveness and creativity as a legislator. He was a freshman Democrat in a Republican year, but won easily; he got a seat on the Energy and Commerce Committee, which has jurisdiction over almost everything that moves, just when the aggressive and competent John Dingell became chairman; he serves on Henry Waxman's Health Subcommittee and Dingell's Investigations panel and has remained on excellent terms with both even when they were fighting fiercely over the Clean Air Act. Wyden has used his committee slots shrewdly, including his chairmanship of a Small Business subcommittee which technically has little legislative power. Among his achievements are a bill delaying access charges on single business phones, a bill imposing severe penalties for computer crime, a $350 million Nurse Education Act, a national data bank for disciplinary records of doctors, nurses and other health practitioners, making nationwide the restrictions on dumping of medical wastes, a reservation to the U.S.-Canada Free Trade Agreement to open up their plywood market to U.S. (especially Oregon) producers. Wyden has conducted investigations of medical labs that did a slipshod job of assessing tests for AIDS and other diseases. He has pushed the Patent Office to speed up the processing of biotechnical patent applications; he wants an antitrust exemption to allow small companies to join in "flexible manufacturing networks" to get new business; he wants to experiment with letting workers take unemployment benefits in a lump sum to use as seed capital for small businesses.

For the 101st Congress, Wyden wants to keep tabs on private long-term health care insurance policies and to see if more Medicaid dollars can be used for home care. He has a bill, supported by the industry and environmentalists, for better tax treatment of small woodlot owners. He wants to encourage rehabilitation and sweat equity, recognizing that the biggest source of low income housing is conservation of existing units rather than building new ones. A law he sponsored set up college scholarships for students who want to go into teaching. Usually Wyden is always looking for issues on which he can make common cause with conservatives and Republicans as well as younger and older Democrats. He approaches issues with almost a childlike wonder but works out solutions that are politically shrewd and make sense as policy.

Wyden's performance at the polls has been superlative. The 3d is a Democratic district; it has voted Democratic for President three times in the 1980s. But Wyden surpassed all records when he received 86% of the vote here in 1986—the highest percentage ever won by a congressional candidate with major party opposition in Oregon's history; in 1988, he had opposition only in the primary and won 95%–5%. Well-positioned in the House, he decided after some thought not to run for the Senate in 1986. But he is thought to be considering running for Mark Hatfield's seat in 1990 or perhaps Bob Packwood's in 1992; there is some rivalry here with Les AuCoin of the 1st District (though AuCoin says he won't run against Hatfield), but those two Democrats could conceivably end up as Oregon's Senators for a couple of decades as those two Republicans have.

The People: Est. Pop. 1986: 529,300, up 0.5% 1980–86; Pop. 1980: 526,715, up 2.6% 1970–80. Households (1980): 65% family, 33% with children, 51% married couples; 39.8% housing units rented; median monthly rent: $220; median house value: $56,400. Voting age pop. (1980): 394,345; 5% Black, 2% Asian origin, 2% Spanish origin, 1% American Indian.

1988 Presidential vote:

Dukakis (D)	143,542	(61%)
Bush (R)	89,744	(38%)

Rep. Ron Wyden (D)

Elected 1980; b. May 3, 1949, Wichita, KS; home, Portland; Stanford U., B.A. 1971, U. of OR, J.D. 1974; Jewish; married (Laurie).

Career: Campaign aide to Sen. Wayne Morse, 1972, 1974; Codir. and Cofounder, OR Gray Panthers, 1974–80; Dir., OR Legal Svcs. for the Elderly, 1977–79; Prof. of Gerontology, U. of OR, 1976, Portland St. U., 1979, U. of Portland, 1980.

Offices: 2452 RHOB 20515, 202-225-4811. Also 500 N.E. Multnomah, Ste. 250, Portland 97232, 503-231-2300.

Committees: *Energy and Commerce* (14th of 26 D). Subcommittees: Health and the Environment; Oversight and Investigations; Telecommunications and Finance. *Small Business* (8th of 27 D). Subcommittee: Regulation, Business Opportunities, and Energy (Chairman). *Select Committee on Aging* (16th of 39 D). Subcommittee: Health and Long-Term Care.

Group Ratings

	ADA	ACLU	COPE	CFA	LCV	ACU	NTLC	NSI	COC	CEI
1988	90	73	81	100	81	16	26	0	43	21
1987	84	—	80	79	—	9	—	—	14	12

National Journal Ratings

	1988 LIB — 1988 CONS			1987 LIB — 1987 CONS		
Economic	60%	—	37%	57%	—	40%
Social	64%	—	34%	78%	—	0%
Foreign	64%	—	34%	76%	—	19%

Key Votes

1) Homeless $	AGN	5) Ban Drug Test	AGN	9) SDI Research	AGN
2) Gephardt Amdt	AGN	6) Drug Death Pen	FOR	10) Ban Chem Weaps	FOR
3) Deficit Reduc	FOR	7) Handgun Sales	FOR	11) Aid to Contras	AGN
4) Kill Plnt Clsng Notice	AGN	8) Ban D.C. Abort $	AGN	12) Nuclear Testing	FOR

Election Results

1988 general	Ron Wyden (D).....................	190,684	(99%)	($287,996)
1988 primary	Ron Wyden (D).....................	84,978	(95%)	
	Sam Kahl, Jr. (D).....................	4,790	(5%)	
1986 general	Ron Wyden (D).....................	180,067	(86%)	($242,600)
	Thomas Phelan (R)...................	29,321	(14%)	

FOURTH DISTRICT

At the southern end of Oregon's Willamette Valley, set between two buttes, is Eugene, the state's second largest city. White settlers first arrived in 1846, farming in the valley and cutting timber in the hills, and in 1876, the University of Oregon was set up here—a symbol of Oregon's Yankee cultural ethic and of how sparsely inhabited Oregon was: there were just five students in the first graduating class. Thousands of miles from most Americans, this has never been a thickly populated place, though it has grown steadily: Eugene and the next-door lumber mill town of Springfield had 25,000 people between them in 1940 and 150,000 in 1980. Lumber and the University give this part of Oregon its special tone. Eugene has bicycle paths along the river banks and on main streets and likes to bill itself as the Running Capital of the Universe; the annual Bach Festival includes a Bach Run, a one-to-five kilometer dash through downtown. It is a place where graduate students stay on forever and where people have an almost religious enthusiasm for the environment.

Springfield and the lumber towns to the south and over on the coast have a different preoccupation. Oregon's 4th Congressional District that includes Eugene and Springfield, the valley around and to the south, and the southern half of the Oregon coast, produces more lumber than any other district in the nation. That means that the local economy is exceedingly sensitive to interest rates and economic conditions which affect construction in the United States and—this is the increasing market here—East Asia; the early 1980s were rough times here, the late 1980s much easier. It also means that there are arguments over how much and how timber should be harvested and processed. Small mill workers and owners, for example, want heavy harvesting and a ban on export of unprocessed logs. The big lumber companies want to manage the harvest and to export unprocessed logs if there is a market for them (as there is). Environmentalists want to limit harvest, and especially to keep timber men from building roads.

Resolving these conflicting demands is one of the things electoral politics in the 4th District is all about. The current congressman, Peter DeFazio, a Democrat first elected in 1986, seems to have done more to resolve them than anyone thought possible. His predecessor and onetime employer, James Weaver, a Democrat first elected in 1974 who was proud of being the grandson of the 1892 Populist party candidate for President, took the environmentalists' side totally, which was not unimportant because, thanks to the vagaries of seniority, he quickly became a high-ranking member of the Interior Committee. Weaver in turn was bitterly opposed by local lumbermen, the big companies and conservative Republicans. Still, he won routinely, and was planning a Senate race against Bob Packwood in 1986 when he was tripped up by reports that he had lost $80,000 in campaign funds in commodities speculation; he left the Senate race and retired from politics.

DeFazio, who moved from Washington to Springfield and won a seat on the county commission, made a name for himself suing the Washington Public Power Supply System; with what one reporter called his "sharp views and sardonic wit" he seemed similar to Weaver. But he navigated carefully to a 34%–33%–31% primary victory over a state senator from the Coast and the Eugene liberal who had lost to Senator Mark Hatfield in 1984, and in the general against Weaver's 1984 opponent, Bruce Long, he trumpeted his opposition to unprocessed log exports. Each carried his home areas again, which was enough to produce a 54% win for DeFazio.

In the House, he quickly emerged as a more accomplished legislator than anyone expected. He was the first freshman to pass a law settling a problem involving the Cow Creek Band of Umpqua Indians. He got consumer protection provisions into the Airline Passenger Protection Act which passed the House and Senate, and was named to the conference committee reconciling the details of the issue. He moved to make permanent the income tax exemption granted to graduate students for tuition waivers. Unlike Weaver, he put most of his staff into district offices and held dozens of town meetings; he also got environmentalists and timber people talking to each other. One issue was whether to allow salvage of usable timber from the 100,000-acre Silver fire; DeFazio arranged a compromise that allowed lots of salvage but few new roads. With a seat on the Interior Committee, he helped to put together the Oregon Wild and Scenic Rivers Act. Like other Oregon Democrats, he wasn't far to the left on economic policy, opposing some spending programs as well as congressional pay increases above the social security COLA. There is a certain feistiness about DeFazio: he was the only Pacific Northwest Member to vote for Richard Gephardt's trade amendment, and he came out against the Reagan policy in the Persian Gulf. But he has also shown a gift for creative compromise.

All this was nicely rewarded when he was reelected in 1988 with 72% of the vote; Weaver, in contrast, never exceeded 60%. His only problem is the "redeye." This is probably the district farthest from Washington in the continental U.S. in flying time: to get back to the nation's capital without losing a day, you have to drive two hours from Eugene to Portland, take a plane that leaves around midnight, stops at O'Hare or somewhere else in the middle of the country and then gets into Washington at something like 8:37 a.m. Taking this redeye every other weekend all year can exhaust even the healthiest and most motivated young politician, and DeFazio may be pardoned for wondering whether he hasn't spoiled his constituents by his frequent trips back home and whether he can sustain this pace over what otherwise has every prospect of being a long congressional career.

The People: Est. Pop. 1986: 509,400, dn. 3.2% 1980–86; Pop. 1980: 526,462, up 26.9% 1970–80. Households (1980): 73% family, 39% with children, 63% married couples; 33.0% housing units rented; median monthly rent: $208; median house value: $57,100. Voting age pop. (1980): 378,675; 2% Spanish origin, 1% American Indian, 1% Asian origin.

1988 Presidential vote:

Dukakis (D)	120,036	(54%)
Bush (R)	99,085	(44%)

Rep. Peter A. DeFazio (D)

Elected 1986; b. May 27, 1947, Needham, MA; home, Springfield; Tufts U., B.A. 1969, U. of OR, M.S. 1977; Roman Catholic; married (Myrnie).

Career: District Ofc. Dir., Rep. James Weaver, 1977–82; Lane Cnty. Bd. of Commissioners, 1982–86, Chmn., 1984–86.

Offices: 1729 LHOB 20515, 202-225-6416. Also 215 S. 2d, Coos Bay 97420, 503-269-2609; P.O. Box 123, Fed. Bldg., 211 E. 7th Ave., Eugene 97401, 503-687-6732; and 621 W. Madrone, Rm. 406, P.O. Box 126, Roseburg 97470.

Committees: *Interior* (23d of 26 D). Subcommittees: Mining and Natural Resources; National Parks and Public Lands; Water, Power and Offshore Energy Resources. *Public Works and Transportation* (20th of 31 D). Subcommittees: Aviation; Water Resources.

Group Ratings

	ADA	ACLU	COPE	CFA	LCV	ACU	NTLC	NSI	COC	CEI
1988	80	83	90	100	94	13	20	0	25	19
1987	100	—	93	71	—	4	—	—	20	14

National Journal Ratings

	1988 LIB — 1988 CONS		1987 LIB — 1987 CONS	
Economic	63%	37%	61%	38%
Social	81%	19%	78%	0%
Foreign	68%	28%	81%	0%

Key Votes

1) Homeless $	AGN	5) Ban Drug Test	AGN	9) SDI Research	AGN
2) Gephardt Amdt	FOR	6) Drug Death Pen	FOR	10) Ban Chem Weaps	FOR
3) Deficit Reduc	AGN	7) Handgun Sales	FOR	11) Aid to Contras	AGN
4) Kill Plnt Clsng Notice	AGN	8) Ban D.C. Abort $	AGN	12) Nuclear Testing	FOR

Election Results

1988 general	Peter A. DeFazio (D)	108,483	(72%)	($279,809)
	Jim Howard (R)	42,220	(28%)	($58,563)
1988 primary	Peter A. DeFazio (D), unopposed			
1986 general	Peter A. DeFazio (D)	105,697	(54%)	($295,654)
	Bruce Long (R)	89,795	(46%)	($333,647)

FIFTH DISTRICT

Fifty years ago Oregon's capital, Salem, had only 30,000 people; with its domeless capitol it was one of several small cities in the Willamette Valley, established by the first wave of New England Yankees who came here on the Oregon Trail. This was one of the few valleys which settlers to the West found that nature had already made suitable for agriculture. California's great valleys depend on irrigation; so does the cultivation of wheat in eastern Washington. But things grow in the Willamette Valley without much man-made help. The soil is fertile, the plain created by the waters of the Willamette sweeping down from the Cascades and the Coast Range are broad, and the rains everyone hears about in Oregon are dependable most of the year. These assets made this good farming country for years; more recently it has attracted young people looking for a clean and pleasant environment and an air of tolerance. In the process Salem grew to 89,000 in 1980, in a county of 204,000.

The 5th Congressional District of Oregon includes much of the northern Williamette Valley. Near Portland it has the old pioneer town of Oregon City, and part of the high-income suburb of Lake Oswego. In the south it includes Corvallis, home of Oregon State University. In the center is Salem. Historically this was Republican country—typical of New England Yankee settlements. But like most of Oregon it has trended Democratic in recent years, irregularly. The legislature created this district after the 1980 Census and gave Oregon a new seat expecting that it would lean Republican. It has, but it has produced three close elections out of four.

The congressman from this district, Denny Smith, has a political pedigree but sees himself, mostly accurately, as a political amateur. His father, Elmo Smith, was governor in 1956 and 1957. Denny Smith was an Air Force and commercial pilot and Vietnam veteran who headed his family's newspaper chain and then ran against and upset House Ways and Means Committee Chairman Al Ullman in 1980. Smith's platform then and voting record since is fairly simple. He believes in cutting, if not eliminating, every domestic government program. And he believes in spending a lot more on defense. In addition, he attacked Ullman for not owning a home in the district and for backing a value-added tax when Oregon has always refused to have a sales tax (as it did again by a 4 to 1 margin in a 1985 referendum; the smart thing to do in these parts is live and work in Washington state, which has no income tax, and shop in Oregon). Smith's 49%–47% victory was one of the big upsets of 1980 and also changed the House—and maybe the country. If Smith had lost, Dan Rostenkowski would not have become chairman of Ways and Means, in which case he, and not Thomas Foley, would have probably become Democratic Whip and then, as Majority Leader, would have become Speaker after Jim Wright resigned in 1989.

Smith has devoted much of his attention to military issues, though he doesn't serve on the Armed Services Committee. But when he sets his pilot's eye on some projects, he doesn't like what he sees. Armed with test results and testimony from military men, he launched a non-stop attack on the Army's Sergeant York antiaircraft gun, and in August 1985 Defense Secretary Caspar Weinberger scrapped it after the Pentagon spent $1.8 billion—the first time a weapons system in production had been scrapped in 20 years. Smith drew a bead as well at the Navy's Aegis antiaircraft missile in 1984—several years before an Aegis on the USS Vincennes shot down an Iranian 747. Smith's work on weapons and testing was cited approvingly as an exercise of power in Hedrick Smith's *The Power Game*.

But Smith has not been converted to liberalism. On the Budget Committee, where he is now the fourth-ranking Republican, he favors across-the-board freezes on domestic spending and suggested saving money on social security COLAs. There he has sacrificed effectiveness for purity. On Oregon issues, Smith opposed the 1984 Oregon Wilderness and 1986 Columbia River Gorge bills, only to see them passed over his opposition. In 1988, he supported the Wild and Scenic Rivers Act, after gaining some concessions. He also got heavily involved in state politics in 1988 by backing an anti-crime initiative, banning parole, probation and early release of repeat violent offenders; Governor Neil Goldschmidt complained it would require expensive new prison places, but it passed 79%–21%.

But while Smith was winning on that issue, he almost got blindsided in the 5th District. State legislator Mike Kopetski, a former congressional staffer, was running an active organizational campaign, and Michael Dukakis was running about even in the district. The graduate student proletariat around Corvallis disliked Smith for his unapologetic conservatism. And during October, Marilyn Wilson, wife of the owner of the Soloflex exercise equipment company, ran a $150,000 independent expenditure campaign of ads against Smith showing, for example, a schoolchild getting a small slice of pie and a cigar-smoking, sunglass-wearing general getting a huge piece. Smith called the ads vicious and claimed the Wilsons were leading activists for liberalized drug laws. Kopetski carried Corvallis with nearly 60% and ran just ahead of Dukakis; Smith ended up, after a recount, winning by 707 votes.

But Smith seemed unfazed. The job does not seem to have a psychological hold on him; back in 1982, when Oregon got its fifth House seat, he could have chosen to run in the much more Republican 2d District and won handily. He chose the 5th because he lives in Salem, though he could have easily moved. He has been mentioned as a candidate for statewide office, though he has said he won't run for governor in 1990 and won't run against one of the state's two Republican Senators. If Mark Hatfield should retire in 1990 or Bob Packwood in 1992, however, Smith might very well go for it.

The People: Est. Pop. 1986: 547,900, up 4.1% 1980–86; Pop. 1980: 526,120, up 41.1% 1970–80. Households (1980): 74% family, 40% with children, 63% married couples; 32.4% housing units rented; median monthly rent: $207; median house value: $62,100. Voting age pop. (1980): 375,567; 2% Spanish origin, 1% Asian origin, 1% American Indian.

1988 Presidential vote:

Bush (R)	121,553	(50%)
Dukakis (D)	116,348	(48%)

Rep. Denny Smith (R)

Elected 1980; b. Jan. 19, 1938, Ontario; home, Salem; Willamette U., B.A. 1961; Baptist; divorced.

Career: Air Force, 1958–67; Pilot/Flight Engineer, Pan-Am Airways, 1967–76; Chmn., family newspaper chain, 1976–present.

Offices: 1213 LHOB 20515, 202-225-5711. Also P.O. Box 13089, 4035 12th St. S.E., Ste. 40, Salem 97309, 503-399-5756.

Committees: *Budget* (4th of 14 R). Task Forces: Community Development and Natural Resources; Defense, Foreign Policy and Space; Economic Policy, Projections and Revenues. *Interior and Insular Affairs* (5th of 15 R). Subcommittees: Energy and the Environment; Water, Power and Offshore Energy Resources (Ranking Member).

Group Ratings

	ADA	ACLU	COPE	CFA	LCV	ACU	NTLC	NSI	COC	CEI
1988	5	5	8	9	25	96	93	100	92	83
1987	4	—	7	14	—	95	—	—	100	89

National Journal Ratings

	1988 LIB — 1988 CONS			1987 LIB — 1987 CONS		
Economic	7%	—	91%	0%	—	89%
Social	0%	—	95%	10%	—	85%
Foreign	0%	—	84%	27%	—	73%

Key Votes

1) Homeless $	FOR	5) Ban Drug Test	FOR	9) SDI Research	AGN
2) Gephardt Amdt	AGN	6) Drug Death Pen	FOR	10) Ban Chem Weaps	AGN
3) Deficit Reduc	AGN	7) Handgun Sales	FOR	11) Aid to Contras	FOR
4) Kill Plnt Clsng Notice	FOR	8) Ban D.C. Abort $	FOR	12) Nuclear Testing	AGN

Election Results

1988 general	Denny Smith (R)	111,489	(50%)	($559,616)
	Mike Kopetski (D)	110,782	(50%)	($351,806)
1988 primary	Denny Smith (R), unopposed			
1986 general	Denny Smith (R)	125,906	(60%)	($312,236)
	Barbara Ross (D)	82,290	(40%)	($87,129)

PENNSYLVANIA

Fifty years ago Pennsylvania was, as its nickname noted, the Keystone State. It was the nation's major producer of energy at a time when almost all industry was fueled and most homes were heated with coal. It was also the nation's most important heavy manufacturing state, with its huge steel plants and small foundries, and one of its chief transportation hubs: the home of the Pennsylvania Railroad (the nation's largest) and the pathway through which passed most of the freight traveling between the interior of the country and the Atlantic. "Today, the mention of Pennsylvania probably calls up, first of all," wrote the *WPA Guide* 50 years ago, "a picture of an industrial commonwealth, with belching blast furnaces, labor problems, and all the spectacular features of an industrial civilization." The Guide points out that Pennsylvania still had many fertile farming regions and quaint Pennsylvania Dutch and Quaker remnants, but it concedes that more typical were regions "where the plow no longer turns the furrow but has been permanently laid aside for the hydraulic drill. Fields no longer tilled have been gutted by quarry or mine shaft, and mountains have surrendered their wealth of coal and iron."

This was not the future that seemed likely to the men who voted the Declaration of Independence and drafted the Constitution in 1776 and 1787 in Philadelphia, a city which, with 43,000 people, was America's first city, and a state which had a fair claim to being its first state. Pennsylvania was one of the newer colonies, founded 50 years after the Puritans established New England and 70 years after the settlement of the first of the Chesapeake tobacco colonies, Virginia. Under the benevolent rule of the Penns and with its Quaker traditions, Pennsylvania soon became the major settlement in the Middle Colonies: its tolerance attracted Englishmen of all sects and Germans as well. Its vast and available farmlands west to the first Appalachian ridge attracted thousands of yeoman farmers, and poor Scots-Irish farmers were crossing the corduroy-like ridges and settling the mountainous interior where Braddock had been beaten by the French and Indians not long before and where George Washington would lead troops again when the Whiskey Rebellion flared up a decade later. On the banks of a wide estuary, with its thriving commerce and rich hinterland, Philadelphia seemed destined to be the London of America, the capital and metropolis and academy all rolled into one.

But history took a few unexpected turns. Philadelphia and Pennsylvania have remained among the most important American cities and states, but they have not occupied the central position the Founding Fathers expected. The nation's capital went to the Potomac, as part of a political deal, rather than to the Delaware. The Appalachian chains stalled the early development of transportation arteries west from Philadelphia, while New Yorkers were building the Erie Canal and the water-level railroad line which became the New York Central. By 1830, Philadelphia was eclipsed by Washington in government and New York in commerce, and rivaled by Boston in culture.

Pennsylvania in the 19th century became instead the energy and heavy industry capital of America. The key was coal: northeast Pennsylvania was the nation's primary source of anthracite, the hard coal used for home heating; western Pennsylvania was the major source of bituminous coal, the soft coal used in producing steel and other industrial products. As a result, the area around Pittsburgh, where the Allegheny and Monongahela rivers join to become the Ohio, was the center of the nation's steel industry by 1890. Immigrants poured in from Europe and from the surrounding hills to work in the mines and the factories; and Pittsburgh became synonymous with industrial prosperity, the inspiration behind the civic pride that celebrated chuffing smokestacks. In 1900, Pennsylvania was the nation's second largest state and growing rapidly.

The boom ended conclusively with the Depression of the 1930s, and in parts of Pennsylvania good times have never really returned. The coal industry collapsed after World War II, as both home heating and industry switched out of coal; John L. Lewis's United Mine Workers decided to seek higher pay and benefits for fewer workers, and cooperated in sharply cutting the coal work force. Even when coal use rose sharply in the 1970s, the emphasis was on capital-intensive means of extraction, such as strip mines, and there are still far fewer jobs than in the 1940s; the anthracite country now lives on the apparel industry, and has had almost constant outmigration over the past 40 years. Most important, Pennsylvania steel has long since ceased to be a growth industry. American steel companies dispersed their operations, made bad guesses about new technology, and suffered from low-wage competition in a world in which almost every nation thinks it must have the prestige of having its own steel industry. By 1969, the steel manufacturers and the United Steelworkers—after a series of amicable agreements for ever higher wages—persuaded the federal government to limit steel imports. Predictably, that stimulated rather than assuaged demands for protection, which in the late 1980s became fiercer than ever. A century ago the steel producers made Pennsylvania the classic high-tariff state, when they sought protection for what they called infant industries. Now, in the late 20th century, Pennsylvania seems to be seeking protection for industries which have grown senile.

These economic developments left Pennsylvania in sorry shape for a long time. People growing up here were as likely to leave the state as stay, and out-of-staters showed no interest in moving in. Compared to the growth areas of the Sun Belt, with their garden condominiums and shopping malls, the cities and small towns of Pennsylvania give the traveler a sense of being 40 or 50 years back in time; you can see, little changed, the suburb where John Updike lived as a boy and the gritty coal town where John O'Hara grew up. Sometimes the trip is pleasant, as in the spanking clean 1920s downtown of Lancaster, surrounded by early 19th century row houses. Sometimes it is grim, as in the coal towns where houses stand unoccupied and the woods and brush creep up to the edge of neighborhoods built 60 years ago. In 1930, after its last decade of above-national-average economic growth, Pennsylvania had 9.5 million people. In 1986, the number stood at 11.9 million—by far the smallest long-term growth among the nation's biggest states. Pennsylvania, easily the second largest state in 1940, by the late 1980s had been passed long since not only by California and then the new energy capital of Texas, but more recently by Florida. This sluggish growth has had political consequences. As recently as 1950, Pennsylvania had 32 seats in the House of Representatives. Now it has 23, and after the 1990 Census it is expected to have 21.

As the 1980s end, increasingly there seem to be two Pennsylvanias, separated by the same first Appalachian ridge that marked the edge of well-ordered English and German settlement in Franklin's time and the ragged and lawless Scots-Irish settlements in the mountains. Today the same ridge separates the state's population into two equal halves. Southeast of the ridge is Philadelphia and its suburban fringe reaching almost to Reading and Lancaster County, as well as the Pennsylvania Dutch country and the industrial Lehigh Valley. Here in what might be called Cismontane Pennsylvania the economy is shifting away from heavy manufacturing and toward services, an economic gentrification lagging perhaps a decade behind what you see around New York and New England to the north and around Washington and Baltimore to the

PENNSYLVANIA — Congressional Districts, Counties, and Selected Places — *(23 Districts)*

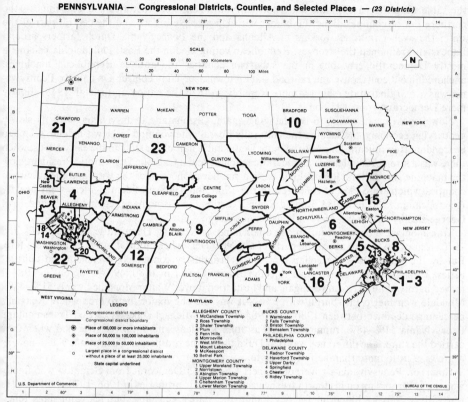

south. In the land beyond that first ridge, which might be called Transmontane Pennsylvania, the economy has always been more dependent on coal and steel, and the pains of contraction are still apparent. Population continues to decline, wage levels are depressed, traditional cultural patterns remain unchallenged in places where there is not enough work for men, much less women. Yet there are signs of a turnaround here. Pittsburgh, the center of Transmontane Pennsylvania, seems to be expanding its high-tech, white-collar economy even as the steel furnaces go cold.

Traditionally Pennsylvania was heavily Republican, the most Republican of all the big states. It was for Lincoln and the Union, for the steel industry and the high tariff; its malodorous Republican machines built parties which were not, like Tammany or the New York Republicans, just the representatives of one ethnic segment but rather an organization with a place for just about everybody. In 1932, Pennsylvania was the only big state that stuck with Herbert Hoover and voted against Franklin Roosevelt. But the New Deal changed the politics of Pennsylvania more than any other state. The immediate reactions to Roosevelt's New Deal, the thundering endorsement of Roosevelt by the United Mine Workers' John L. Lewis in 1936, the founding by Lewis of the CIO industrial union movement and the success of the United Steelworkers, after a series of bloody strikes, in organizing the big steel companies—all these occurrences made most of the industrial parts of Pennsylvania almost as Democratic in the

1930s and after as they had been Republican in the 1920s going back to the Civil War. Yet at the same time the parts of the state not heavy with big steel factories and coal mines—the northern tier of counties along the border with Upstate New York and the central part of the state, the Welsh railroad workers in Altoona and the Pennsylvania Dutch farmers around Lancaster—remained the strongest Republican voting bloc in the East. Philadelphia became a mostly Democratic city, but in the suburban counties the antique Republican machines, anchored in old courthouse and railroad station towns, stayed in control. On balance Pennsylvania was a marginal state, slightly more Republican than the nation up through 1948, slightly more Democratic from 1952 on.

Now Pennsylvania seems to be changing again. Cismontane Pennsylvania, with its slowly gentrifying economy and lacking the culturally liberal elite you find in New England, seems to be trending Republican. This was the more Democratic half of the state in the early 1960s, when there was a strong Philadelphia Democratic machine and a Catholic Democratic President; now the machine is in tatters, Philadelphia casts a smaller proportion of the vote, and the suburban counties which were closely contested in the 1960 and 1968 presidential races went heavily Republican in 1980 and 1984. Ronald Reagan carried the Cismontane region by 10% and 11%; George Bush won it 53%–46%—the national average.

Transmontane Pennsylvania, on the other hand, is trending Democratic. In the 1960s and 1970s it grew lukewarm about the party of the New Deal when cultural issues came to the fore. But by the early 1980s the collapse of the steel industry completely overshadowed cultural issues. Transmontane Pennsylvania rejected Jimmy Carter in 1980, 49%–45%, but in 1984 it moved hardly at all to Ronald Reagan, and he carried it over Walter Mondale by only 51%–48%. Mondale won metro Pittsburgh with 55%—it was the one major metro area where Reagan's percentage declined between 1980 and 1984. In 1988 Michael Dukakis carried Transmontane Pennsylvania 51%–48%, running as well as John Kennedy and Jimmy Carter had when they carried the state. The difference was that Dukakis lost the prosperous Cismontane side—now, as it grows, a little more than half of the state.

Governor. Pennsylvania's governor, Robert Casey, is a Democrat from Scranton who finally won the governorship on his fourth try; he lost Democratic primaries in 1966, 1970 and 1978. He ran with a 76-page blueprint for developing the state's economy, but his campaigns relied heavily on precisely targeted negative ads in the hardball accents of Transmontane Pennsylvania. He lanced primary opponent Edward Rendell, the Philadelphia D.A., for accumulating 96 parking tickets. He attacked Republican William Scranton, son of the governor elected in 1962, for neglecting meetings of boards he belonged to as lieutenant governor: "They gave him the job because of his father's name. The least he could do is show up to work." In late October Scranton pulled his negative ads, but Casey declined to do so, running the last week an ad featuring sitar music, a picture of the Maharishi Mahesh Yogi, and a picture of Scranton 15 years ago with long hair and a beard. Scranton, who admitted using marijuana recreationally as "my generation" did, was cast as the candidate of cultural liberalism, while in the older Casey the Democrats had for once a convincing representative of traditional values. Scranton got 54% of the vote in Cismontane Pennsylvania. But Casey got 56% in Transmontane Pennsylvania, enough for a 51%–48% victory.

As governor, Casey is scrapping the approach used by his Republican predecessor and now U.S. Attorney General Richard Thornburgh, who relied on stimulating small business and financing their technical innovations, and is setting up a partnership of government, business and labor, concentrating on the big companies whose numbers of jobs have been declining sharply for more than a decade. He is also stressing cleaning up the environment, but has disappointed some of his backers by not increasing welfare programs much after eight years of sharp contraction under Thornburgh. Under pressure from the Republicans, he backed a tax cut in 1987 but not in 1988; in early 1989, neither side was calling for one.

Casey looks to be a strong candidate for reelection in 1990, but not one assured of victory. He had heart bypass surgery in September 1987, but his health afterwards seemed good. Thornburgh has been mentioned as a possible opponent, but he's unlikely to leave his position as Attorney General to make the race. A flock of other people have been suggested: 21st District Congressman Thomas Ridge, Pennsylvania GOP chair and state Senator Earl Baker, Senate president Robert Jubelirer and state Senator D. Michael Fisher, and Delaware County lawyer and former Reagan White House aide Faith Whittlesey. Demography, it should be added, mildly favors the Republicans. In minor statewide contests in 1988, their attorney general candidate, Ernie Preate, beat former Iowa Congressman and Pennsylvania party chairman Edward Mezvinsky 51%–48%, and Republican Barbara Hafer beat incumbent Auditor General Don Bailey, another former congressman, 49%–48%.

Senators. Both of Pennsylvania's Senators are Republicans, both with unusual backgrounds: one is the scion of one of Pittsburgh's great industrial empires, the other a former Democrat scarred in the political battles of Philadelphia. In this state, which has few residents who grew up elsewhere, one of these Senators lived as a boy in San Francisco and the other grew up in Kansas. Both have shown the political skill that has enabled Republicans to monopolize U.S. Senate seats in this Democratic state; Democrats have not won one since Joseph Clark squeaked through to a second term in 1962.

John Heinz, now past 50, is Pennsylvania's longest surviving top officeholder. Heir to the H. J. Heinz food fortune, he is one of the two richest members of the Senate, with wealth of the same magnitude as Jay Rockefeller. (The Rockefeller family fortune is bigger, but he has many cousins; Heinz is the only child of an only child.) He was elected to the House in a special election from the Pittsburgh suburbs in 1971 and became very popular in western Pennsylvania. His 1976 Senate race against William Green, then congressman and later mayor of Philadelphia, was a kind of Pirates versus Phillies contest, between two young politicians very popular in the two major parts of the state. The difference was money: Heinz spent $2.9 million of his own money, and won. Now he seems to hold one of the few safe seats that either party can count on in a major state.

For that, credit must go not only to his money, which does tend to intimidate opponents, but also to his political skill. Even when he was in the House, Heinz had already identified trade as an issue that resonated in western Pennsylvania, and he has been one of Congress's most assiduous practitioners of what he might call a retaliatory (and others would call a protectionist) trade policy ever since. On the Senate Finance Committee, he has pushed for aggressive enforcement of antidumping laws and has worked to deny administrations discretion in granting relief from injury due to imports; he is almost always ready with a "Buy America" provision for government procurement contracts. He was not a major player on the tax bill early on, but supported Finance Chairman Bob Packwood's stringent low-rate, preference-cutting approach at a critical point in late spring 1986, and apparently in return was able to get provisions helping the steel companies, notably a carryback procedure that let money-losing and even bankrupt companies get refunds on taxes they paid on profits as long as 15 years ago. Now, while many politicians talking about trade focus on East Asia, Heinz is looking at Europe: he wants to make sure that the 1992 Common Market initiative will not shut American manufacturers out of European markets.

Heinz has a couple of other important committee niches. He is ranking Republican and formerly was chairman of the Special Committee on Aging; he used that platform to help put together the 1983 social security rescue bill and to prevent medicare cost-cutting reforms from hurting the quality of medical care for the elderly; he pushed for eliminating mandatory retirement ages. None of this hurts in Pennsylvania, which has one of the oldest populations of the states and hundreds of thousands of voters heavily dependent on social security and medicare. On the environment, he has teamed with Tim Wirth of Colorado (a prep-school roommate) to sponsor Project 88, in which a Kennedy School expert recommended market-based strategies in tandem with command-control regulations to handle environmental problems.

For all this there is something disappointing in his career. He is not a popular member of the Senate and is never mentioned in speculation for national office. In the Senate he seems to be intense and aloof; he got less credit for his work as National Republican Senatorial Committee chairman in the 1979–80 cycle and more blame for his work as chairman in the 1985–86 cycle than he deserved; in fact he helped produce the Republican Senate in 1980 and nearly saved it, despite the weak political instincts of many of the incumbents who were up for reelection in 1986. But in 1980, he lost the chairmanship of the Senate Republican Conference to James McClure of Idaho, and in 1984, he won the campaign chairmanship by only one vote over Malcolm Wallop of Wyoming.

As for national ambitions, it would have been unnatural if this rich, handsome, well-connected young man did not think about being President at the start of his career. But in 1971, when he first won office, it was widely assumed that a Republican could be elected President only by supporting a bigger welfare state and currying credit with organized labor; Barry Goldwater had only recently lost overwhelmingly, Richard Nixon had just barely beaten Hubert Humphrey, and political insiders scoffed at Kevin Phillips's *The Emerging Republican Majority*. Heinz followed the traditional liberal Republican strategy and adapted it, as on the trade issue, to Pennsylvania, with fine results: he beat Bill Green for Senator in the Democratic year of 1976 and was easily reelected over underfinanced opposition in 1982 and 1988. Heinz conspicuously avoided spending his own money in those races, but it nevertheless deters competition, as does his genuine popularity in the Pittsburgh metropolitan area which is otherwise the Democratic bulwark of the state. But it is apparent that a candidate with Heinz's voting record could not have been nominated Vice President, much less President, by any of the last four Republican national conventions. In early 1989, it was bruited about that he was considering running for governor, (though Heinz later seemed to quash this speculation) presumably to somehow make himself a national candidate. But that motive seldom enchants voters, Heinz has had little involvement in state government, Governor Robert Casey led him in early polls, and even if he should win, the national press spends very little time in Harrisburg.

Pennsylvania's other Senator is Arlen Specter. A one-time Democrat and a top staffer for the Warren Commission, Specter was a kind of boy wonder when, as a Republican, he was elected district attorney in Philadelphia in 1965. He won again in 1969, but didn't win another election for 11 years. He lost reelection in an increasingly Democratic city in 1973, lost the 1976 Senate primary to Heinz and lost the 1978 gubernatorial nomination to Richard Thornburgh. Finally, he beat former Republican state chairman Bud Haabestad 36%–33% in the 1980 Senate primary and then beat former Pittsburgh Mayor Peter Flaherty, who refused to spend much money, 50%–48% in the general. Not an awe-inspiring record. Yet in 1986, when the Democrats were recapturing the Senate, Specter won reelection in Pennsylvania by a 56%–43% margin.

His secrets are brains and hard work—and not much else. Specter is respected by other Senators (perhaps because he is a Kansas native, he gets on well with Bob Dole), but not well-liked; he is seen as calculating and self-serving. "They can't say I'm dumb or crooked," he once said, "so what do they say? That I'm calculating or ambitious? I have always thought those were good qualities, to think about what you want to do and to seek achievement." He managed not to dissent heavily from Reagan economic policies early in his first term, but has compiled a record that seems to reflect the views of a state that sees itself in need of federal help. He has taken his prosecutorial background to the Judiciary Committee, where he sponsored the 1984 law to give career criminals 15-year-to-life sentences; but he also cast critical votes against Robert Bork and William Bradford Reynolds. He will continue to be a crucial vote on Judiciary. He supported an inspector general entirely independent of the CIA director, but he also voted to uphold the administration view of the ABM treaty ratification process—both losing causes. He flip-flops on issues like South Africa sanctions. Active, energetic, sometimes frenetic, Specter leaves no locally crucial issue unmined for publicity or votes.

While Washington rests, however, Specter criss-crosses Pennsylvania, from Philadelphia (where his wife Joan is a city councilwoman) to Pittsburgh and in little planes touching down on small airstrips sandwiched in between two mountain ridges. Specter also worked hard, with help from his onetime opponent Heinz, to raise a large campaign treasury. These proved to be unbeatable assets in 1986. The Democrats had a riproaring primary between two candidates who represented, in exaggerated form, their party's activists in the two major regions of the state. Auditor general and former Representative Don Bailey, a Vietnam veteran from a county outside Pittsburgh, was pugnacious, traditional on cultural issues like abortion, still bitter against opponents of the Vietnam war; but he relied on support from Democratic organizations that were paper tigers and raised relatively little money. Representative Bob Edgar, a Methodist minister from suburban Philadelphia was a longtime opponent of the war, a congressional critic of pork barrel politics, an unbending liberal with enough political savvy to put together a large volunteer organization, win the endorsement of the state AFL-CIO, and raise far more money than Bailey (though far less than Specter). Edgar won 47%–45% in a fascinating regional battle: he rolled up a 68%–25% edge in Cismontane Pennsylvania, while losing to Bailey 58%–33% in Transmontane Pennsylvania.

But Edgar, who had won six House elections by narrow margins, did not pull off another miracle in the general election. He tried to argue that Specter was not for social security or unemployment benefits and was overly political, with ads showing a bust of Specter crumbling as his contradictory votes are ticked off: "Arlen Specter is just not what he is cracked up to be." Edgar attracted enthusiastic activists from Citizens Action and other groups determined to show that a leftish candidate can win in an industrial state. This is one race where money made a difference: if Edgar had had as much as Specter, he might have made the race closer and could conceivably have won. Yet the results must be disappointing for those who think the American working class is ready to vote for a principled backer of bigger government and liberal cultural values. Edgar ran no better than even in the Pittsburgh metro area and won only 44% of the vote in Transmontane Pennsylvania—12% behind Bob Casey. He ran close to even in his old congressional district, but otherwise in Cismontane Pennsylvania took only about one-third of the vote except among Philadelphia blacks. Specter's ultra-adaptable politics and frenetic activity seem to be more what the voters want.

Presidential politics. One of these days Pennsylvania may vote Democratic for President again, as it did in 1960, 1968 and 1976; it came the closest of the biggest eight states to doing so in 1984 and was second to New York, the only one which voted for Dukakis, in 1988. But there is a problem for the Democrats here. They like to campaign as the party of change. But their support comes from Transmontane Pennsylvania from people who want to keep things as they are—or, rather, restore them as they think they used to be. If the state as a whole does succeed in turning its economy around, as most of Cismontane Pennsylvania has, then credit will go to any party associated with that effort; but it will not necessarily rub off on national Democrats who argue that they can move things back to what they used to be.

Pennsylvania's presidential primary, scheduled for years in late April, has not been crucial since the 1976 Democratic race, when Jimmy Carter cinched the Democratic nomination by beating Henry Jackson and Morris Udall here. In 1984, Transmontane Pennsylvania backed the candidate of big government, Walter Mondale, while Gary Hart carried Cismontane Pennsylvania. In 1988, Michael Dukakis carried everything but Philadelphia where black votes gave a narrow edge to Jesse Jackson. The Democratic primary remains heavily blue-collar, with few voters in the Philadelphia suburbs where registration remains, anachronistically, overwhelmingly Republican; the Republican primary is fairly representative of the state, except for the big cities and some industrial areas.

Congressional districting. Pennsylvania lost three congressional districts in the 1950 Census, two in 1960, two more in 1970 and two in 1980, reducing its delegation from 32 to 23; it is expected to lose two more in 1990. With the legislature divided between the parties, and the Democrats controlling the House for several years now by the narrowest of margins, it is quite possible that redistricting will be a compromise, dictated as much by the demographics of population loss as anything else. Pennsylvania's House delegation, not to put too fine a point on it, has long been considered a collection of political hacks, with not much talent for self-advancement. But John Murtha, an youngish old-time politician who likes to operate out of the limelight, helped put together the big cities and Black Caucus coalition that elected Philadelphia's William Gray chairman of the House Budget Committee in 1984, and Gray followed that up by being elected Democratic caucus chairman in 1988 and majority whip in 1989. So Pennsylvania has emerged as one of the power blocs among House Democrats.

The People: Est. Pop. 1988: 12,027,000; Pop. 1980: 11,863,895, up 1.4% 1980–88 and 0.5% 1970–80; 5.93% of U.S. total, 4th largest. 11% with 1–3 yrs. col., 14% with 4+ yrs. col.; 10.5% below poverty level. Single ancestry: 15% German, 6% English, Italian, 5% Irish, 3% Polish, 1% Russian, Dutch, Hungarian, Ukrainian. Households (1980): 74% family, 38% with children, 61% married couples; 30.1% housing units rented; median monthly rent: $174; median house value: $39,100. Voting age pop. (1980): 8,740,599; 8% Black, 1% Spanish origin. Registered voters (1988): 5,875,943; 3,069,234 D (58%), 2,518,282 R (43%), 288,427 unaffiliated and minor parties (5%).

1988 Share of Federal Tax Burden: $42,896,000,000; 4.85% of U.S. total, 6th largest.
1988 Share of Federal Expenditures

	Total		Non-Defense		Defense	
Total Expend	$39,569m	(4.48%)	$33,719m	(5.14%)	$7,038m	(3.08%)
St/Lcl Grants	5,793m	(5.05%)	5,791m	(5.06%)	2m	(1.85%)
Salary/Wages	4,752m	(3.54%)	2,666m	(3.98%)	2,085m	(3.98%)
Pymnts to Indiv	23,469m	(5.73%)	23,055m	(5.90%)	415m	(2.22%)
Procurement	4,526m	(2.40%)	1,188m	(2.55%)	4,526m	(2.40%)
Research/Other	1,029m	(2.75%)	1,019m	(2.75%)	9m	(2.75%)

Political Lineup: Governor, Robert P. Casey (D); Lt. Gov., Mark Singel (D); Secy. of Commonwealth, James Haggerty (D); Atty. Gen., Ernest Preate, Jr. (R); Treasurer, Catherine Baker Knoll (D). State Senate, 50 (27 R and 23 D); State House of Representatives, 203 (104 D and 99 R). Senators, H. John Heinz, III (R) and Arlen Specter (R). Representatives, 23 (12 D and 11 R).

1988 Presidential Vote

Bush (R)	2,300,087	(51%)
Dukakis (D)	2,194,944	(48%)

1984 Presidential Vote

Reagan (R)	2,584,323	(53%)
Mondale (D)	2,228,131	(46%)

1988 Democratic Presidential Primary

Dukakis	1,002,480	(67%)
Jackson	411,260	(27%)
Gore	44,542	(3%)
Hart	20,473	(1%)
Simon	9,692	(1%)
Gephardt	7,254	(1%)

1988 Republican Presidential Primary

Bush	687,323	(79%)
Dole	103,763	(12%)
Robertson	79,463	(9%)

GOVERNOR

Gov. Robert P. Casey (D)

Elected 1986, term expires Jan. 1991; b. Jan. 9, 1932, Jackson Heights, NY; home, Scranton; Holy Cross Col., A.B. 1953 ; Geo. Wash. U., J.D. 1956; Roman Catholic; married (Ellen).

Career: Practicing atty., 1956–86; PA Senate, 1963–67; PA Auditor Gen., 1969–77.

Office: 225 Main Capitol Bldg., Harrisburg 17120, 717-787-2500.

Election Results

1986 gen.	Robert Casey (D)	1,717,484	(51%)
	William W. Scranton (R)	1,638,268	(48%)
1986 prim.	Robert Casey (D)	549,376	(51%)
	Edward G. Rendell (D)	385,539	(40%)
	Steve Douglas (D)	38,295	(4%)
1982 gen.	Richard L. Thornburgh (R)	1,872,784	(51%)
	Allen E. Ertel (D)	1,772,353	(48%)

SENATORS

Sen. H. John Heinz III (R)

Elected 1976, seat up 1994; b. Oct. 23, 1938, Pittsburgh; home, Pittsburgh; Yale U., B.A. 1960, Harvard U., M.B.A. 1963; Episcopalian; married (Teresa).

Career: Special Asst. to U.S. Sen. Hugh Scott, 1964; Fin. and Mktg. Div., H. J. Heinz Co., 1965–70; U.S. House of Reps., 1971–76.

Offices: 277 RSOB 20510, 202-224-6324. Also 6th and Arch Sts., Philadelphia 19106, 215-925-8750; 2031 Fed. Bldg., Pittsburgh 15222, 412-562-0533; P.O. Box 55, Harrisburg 17108, 717-233-5849; 130 Fed. Sq. Bldg., Erie 16501, 814-454-7114; and Scranton Electric Bldg., 507 Linden St., Scranton 18503, 717-347-2341.

Committees: *Banking, Housing, and Urban Affairs* (2d of 9 R). Subcommittees: International Finance and Monetary Policy; Securities (Ranking Member). *Finance* (6th of 9 R). Subcommittees: International Trade; Medicare and Long-Term Care; Private Retirement and Oversight of IRS (Ranking Member). *Governmental Affairs* (5th of 6 R). Subcommittees: General Services, Federalism, and the District of Columbia (Ranking Member); Government Information and Regulation; Oversight of Government Management. *Special Committee on Aging* (Ranking Member of 9 R).

Group Ratings

	ADA	ACLU	COPE	CFA	LCV	ACU	NTLC	NSI	COC	CEI
1988	55	60	66	75	50	41	26	60	46	18
1987	70	—	65	67	—	35	—	—	50	28

National Journal Ratings

	1988 LIB — 1988 CONS			1987 LIB — 1987 CONS		
Economic	47%	—	48%	55%	—	43%
Social	59%	—	40%	49%	—	50%
Foreign	42%	—	57%	61%	—	36%

Key Votes

1) Cut Aged Housing $	AGN	5) Bork Nomination	FOR	9) SDI Funding	AGN
2) Override Hwy Veto	FOR	6) Drug Death Pen	FOR	10) Ban Chem Weaps	AGN
3) Kill Plnt Clsng Notice	AGN	7) Deny Abortions	FOR	11) Aid To Contras	FOR
4) Min Wage Increase	FOR	8) Japanese Reparations	FOR	12) Reagan Defense $	AGN

Election Results

1988 general	H. John Heinz III (R) 2,901,715	(67%)	($5,151,512)
	Joe Vignola (D)................... 1,416,764	(32%)	($544,137)
1988 primary	H. John Heinz III (R), unopposed		
1982 general	H. John Heinz III (R) 2,136,418	(59%)	($2,952,829)
	Cyril H. Wecht (D)................ 1,412,965	(39%)	($424,507)

Sen. Arlen Specter (R)

Elected 1980, seat up 1992; b. Feb. 12, 1930, Wichita, KS; home, Philadelphia; U. of PA, B.A. 1951, Yale U., LL.B. 1956; Jewish; married (Joan).

Career: Air Force, 1951–53; Practicing atty.; Asst. Cnsl., Warren Comm., 1964; PA Asst. Atty. Gen., 1964–65; Philadelphia Dist. Atty., 1966–74.

Offices: 331 HSOB, 202-224-4254. Also Fed. Bldg., 600 Arch Street, Ste. 9400, Philadelphia 19106, 215-597-7200; 2017 Fed. Bldg., Pittsburgh 15222, 412-644-3400; 118 Fed. Bldg., Erie 16501, 814-453-3010; Fed. Bldg, 228 Walnut St., Rm. 1159, Harrisburg 17101, 717-782-3951; P.O. Bldg., 5th and Hamilton Sts., Rm. 201, Allentown 18101, 215-434-1444; Park Plaza, 225 N. Washington Ave., Ste. 501, Scranton 18503, 717-346-2006; and 116 S. Main St., Main Towers, Wilkes-Barre 18701, 717-826-6265.

Committees: *Appropriations* (9th of 13 R). Subcommittees: Agriculture, Rural Development and Related Agencies; Defense; Energy and Water Development; Foreign Operations; Labor–Health and Human Services–Education (Ranking Member). *Judiciary* (5th of 6 R). Subcommittees: Antitrust, Monopolies and Business Rights; Constitution (Ranking Member). *Veterans Affairs* (4th of 5 R). *Select Committee on Intelligence* (4th of 7 R).

Group Ratings

	ADA	ACLU	COPE	CFA	LCV	ACU	NTLC	NSI	COC	CEI
1988	60	67	70	58	30	33	30	30	62	19
1987	80	—	69	83	—	15	—	—	47	27

National Journal Ratings

	1988 LIB — 1988 CONS			1987 LIB — 1987 CONS		
Economic	60%	—	39%	55%	—	43%
Social	66%	—	33%	61%	—	36%
Foreign	36%	—	61%	65%	—	32%

Key Votes

1) Cut Aged Housing $ AGN	5) Bork Nomination AGN	9) SDI Funding AGN
2) Override Hwy Veto FOR	6) Drug Death Pen FOR	10) Ban Chem Weaps AGN
3) Kill Plnt Clsng Notice AGN	7) Deny Abortions AGN	11) Aid To Contras AGN
4) Min Wage Increase FOR	8) Japanese Reparations FOR	12) Reagan Defense $ FOR

Election Results

1986 general	Arlen Specter (R)	1,906,537	(56%)	($5,993,230)
	Robert W. Edgar (D)	1,448,219	(43%)	($3,968,994)
1986 primary	Arlen Specter (R)	434,623	(76%)	
	Richard A. Stokes (R)	135,673	(24%)	
1980 general	Arlen Specter (R)	2,230,404	(50%)	($1,488,588)
	Peter Flaherty (D)	2,122,391	(48%)	($633,861)

FIRST DISTRICT

William Penn, 37 feet high, stands atop the 548-foot tower of City Hall at Market and Broad, surveying Philadelphia, the city he founded—and looking up at the new One Liberty Place tower, with its "romantic modernist" spire, the first building to break the tradition that no building here should be taller than City Hall. The first American colonies were settled by practical men, out to make money or replicate a farm settlement back home; Penn was a Quaker, a member of one of those rationalizing sects of the 17th century, who intended to impose a greater regularity on his new environment, and did. Hence Philadelphia was designed not with a cowpath street pattern like Boston or Charleston, but with a grid of numbered and named streets, with occasional open squares, which was replicated in dozens of American cities for more than 200 years afterwards.

Penn would never, as the writers of the *WPA Guide* 50 years ago put it, recognize "in what today is a sprawling industrial giant" what had been "his 'greene countrie towne'." But Philadelphia, unlike New York or Chicago, has grown slowly and deliberately enough that there are places on which William Penn looks down today in which you can see the distant past: in the restored townhouses of Society Hill and the tree-shaded public buildings around Independence Hall, and, on the way to the ornate City Hall, the Federal and Greek Revival buildings, little temples of commerce, built when Philadelphia was the nation's largest city, and left standing as bigger buildings—1920s masonry-faced skyscrapers and 1970s glass-and-steel towers—were built around City Hall and in Center City farther west.

Most of Penn's original city and most of Philadelphia's Delaware River waterfront, plus a wide swath of territory to the north and south, form the 1st Congressional District of Pennsylvania. It includes all of South Philadelphia, where Italian families, groceries and restaurants have been pressed tightly into narrow streets with English and Indian names under a tangle of overhead wires, as well as the neighborhood around the University of Pennsylvania. North of Center City, it mostly stays east of Broad Street, taking in some black wards but, as you get closer to the river, you suddenly find that the closely packed 19th century houses are inhabited not by blacks but whites. Here is the old Kensington neighborhood, a place along the Delaware River where people of Irish and Italian descent live in rude frame houses, and income levels are lower than in most black neighborhoods. As you walk around this neighborhood, you could easily imagine yourself (if you could blot out the cars) back in the 1930s. Overall, the 1st is about one-third black; blacks are just one more minority in the ethnic mix here.

The 1st District is a heavily Democratic district in national elections, although South Philly and Kensington voted for George Bush. The Democratic congressman from the 1st, Thomas Foglietta, is an Italian-American who represented South Philadelphia on the City Council for 20

1032   PENNSYLVANIA

years as a Republican; but he now has one of the more liberal records in a Democratic Congress. He is a man with deep roots in his district but who concentrates heavily on national issues. He first won the seat in 1980 as an Independent, running against convicted Abscam defendant Ozzie Myers (one of former Mayor Frank Rizzo's gifts to Congress), 38%–34%; he held it in 1982 against another incumbent, Joseph Smith, when they were thrown together by redistricting, by 52%–48%. In 1982 and 1984 he was challenged in the Democratic primary by South Philadelphia politico James Tayoun, who criticized Foglietta for not coming back to the district every night and listening to constituents' problems as longtime congressman (1945–47, 1949–76) William Barrett did; Tayoun held Foglietta to 52%–45% and 62%–38%, respectively.

These close victories don't seem to phase Foglietta. His record on issues remains staunchly liberal with a few exceptions such as his opposition to abortion. He is a member of the Armed Services Committee and a staunch supporter of chairman Les Aspin; and the committee does help him to channel business to the Philadelphia Navy Yard, which he successfully fought to protect from closure. He is concerned about commercial jobs on the waterfront too: with Senator John Heinz he sprung into action in early 1989 as the Chilean grape scare threatened the Chilean fruit trade which gives the Philly docks most of their work in the winter.

Having increased his margin in 1986, Foglietta had no serious opposition in 1988. But that's no guarantee he won't in 1990: Philadelphia politics continues to be as spicy as the peppers on a cheese steak or the mustard on a hot pretzel. Redistricting could conceivably threaten Foglietta. Philadelphia will have almost enough population to sustain the three districts it has now, but William Gray might want some of the black wards now in the 1st District in his 2d District instead, and there is an outside chance that the 1st could be chosen as the eastern Pennsylvania district to be sliced up among its neighbors.

The People: Est. Pop. 1986: 495,400, dn. 3.8% 1980–86; Pop. 1980: 515,145, dn. 16.6% 1970–80. Households (1980): 65% family, 35% with children, 40% married couples; 43.4% housing units rented; median monthly rent: $148; median house value: $26,000. Voting age pop. (1980): 374,046; 29% Black, 7% Spanish origin, 2% Asian origin.

1988 Presidential Vote:

Dukakis (D)	121,095	(66%)
Bush (R)	60,033	(33%)

Rep. Thomas M. Foglietta (D)

Elected 1980; b. Dec. 3, 1928, Philadelphia; home, Philadelphia; St. Joseph's Col., B.A. 1949, Temple U., J.D. 1952; Roman Catholic; single.

Career: Practicing atty., 1952–80; Philadelphia City Cncl., 1955–75; Reg. Dir., U.S. Dept. of Labor, 1976.

Offices: 231 CHOB 20515, 202-225-4731. Also Wm. J. Green Fed. Bldg., 600 Arch St., Rm. 10402, Philadelphia 19106, 215-925-6840; 1806 S. Broad St. 19125, 215-463-8702; and 2630 Memphis St., Philadelphia 19125, 215-426-4616.

Committees: *Armed Services* (12th of 31 D). Subcommittees: Military Installations and Facilities; Research and Development; Seapower and Strategic and Critical Materials. *Merchant Marine and Fisheries* (7th of 26 D). Subcommittees: Merchant Marine Oversight and Investigations (Chairman). *Select Committee on Hunger* (13th of 19 D).

Group Ratings

	ADA	ACLU	COPE	CFA	LCV	ACU	NTLC	NSI	COC	CEI
1988	90	82	96	73	69	4	3	0	42	11
1987	84	—	96	57	—	0	—	—	8	5

National Journal Ratings

	1988 LIB — 1988 CONS	1987 LIB — 1987 CONS
Economic	71% — 29%	73% — 0%
Social	81% — 18%	68% — 32%
Foreign	79% — 16%	74% — 26%

Key Votes

1) Homeless $	AGN	5) Ban Drug Test	—	9) SDI Research	AGN
2) Gephardt Amdt	FOR	6) Drug Death Pen	AGN	10) Ban Chem Weaps	—
3) Deficit Reduc	FOR	7) Handgun Sales	AGN	11) Aid to Contras	AGN
4) Kill Plnt Clsng Notice	AGN	8) Ban D.C. Abort $	AGN	12) Nuclear Testing	FOR

Election Results

1988 general	Thomas M. Foglietta (D)	128,076	(76%)	($234,957)
	William J. O'Brien (R)	39,749	(24%)	($1,643)
1988 primary	Thomas M. Foglietta (D), unopposed			
1986 general	Thomas M. Foglietta (D)	88,224	(75%)	($399,872)
	Anthony J. Mucciolo (R)	29,811	(25%)	($1,991)

SECOND DISTRICT

From Center City up the oaring-club-lined Schuylkill, up Fairmount Park and Wissahickon Creek, runs the 2d Congressional District of Pennsylvania, through some of the most pleasant and some of the most dangerous neighborhoods of Philadelphia. It contains most of the Center City high-rises and office centers on City Line Avenue, where the Main Line suburbs begin, but has few factories and is primarily residential. The 2d District includes North Philadelphia and West Philadelphia, where the MOVE rowhouse was firebombed by the city in May 1985; it also includes the 18th century stone houses and 19th century rowhouses of Germantown farther out from Center City, and beyond that are the post-war Jewish subdivisions just below the city line. All these are black neighborhoods now, and more than 80% of the 2d District's residents are black: this is Philadelphia's black district.

Pennsylvania never had slavery—part of William Penn's Quaker legacy—and Philadelphia has a long-established black community, going back well before the Civil War. For years it was Republican, and many blacks have voted Republican recently, against Mayor Frank Rizzo in 1971 and 1975, for example, for District Attorney and Senator Arlen Specter in 1965, 1969 and 1980, and for Governor Richard Thornburgh in 1978. Blacks are still not quite a majority of the city's electorate, but their solid support made possible the election of a black mayor, Wilson Goode, in 1983 and his reelection in 1987 despite the MOVE bombing. Goode, like many mayors and governors of different backgrounds, campaigned on the theme of local pride, and Philadelphia—long an object of derision in sophisticated precincts of New York and Washington—was justifiably proud of its new buildings, its commercial, rather than industrial driven prosperity. But Wilson Goode is barred from seeking a third term in 1991; the most powerful black politician in Philadelphia, and probably in Washington, is the 2d District's congressman, William Gray.

Gray has been in Congress just over 10 years, and is now the third highest ranking Democrat, getting the posts on his own initiative and his own terms. He has a solid base back home in

Philadelphia—he preaches every Sunday at the Bright Hope Baptist Church, at 12th Street and Columbia Avenue, as his father did before him—and he does not have any serious political challengers at home. He won the House seat from an aged, underperforming incumbent in the 1978 primary, after nearly winning in 1976, and in 1982 beat state Senator Milton Street—a militant who switched to the Republican Party to give it control of the state Senate, and then ran for the House seat as an Independent. Gray won by a convincing 76%–22% margin. He stays mostly aloof from city politics—though he endorsed a white candidate for district attorney in 1989 and helped him carry black wards—while he has worked in the House to build a constituency that covers all parts of the Democratic party.

Gray has produced steady results. He was named head of the Democrats' 1978 freshman class. Two years later he won a seat on the Appropriations Committee. After the 1982 election he won a seat on the Budget Committee, and soon was running for chairman. He worked with fellow Pennsylvanian John Murtha to round up votes from old-line Democrats, even as he got the support of younger members, and with adroit politicking, won the chairmanship. He got Tip O'Neill to oppose any waiver of the three-term limit on Budget membership, which eliminated outgoing chairman, James Jones and heir apparent Leon Panetta, both of whom O'Neill mistrusted. Gray's election was an even more considerable achievement than first appears. The Pennsylvania delegation hasn't shown such clout in recent years; quite the contrary. And House Democrats were in no mood to elect a black as chairman at a time when most voters associated blacks with unpopular big-spending programs.

As Budget Chairman, Gray saw his role as creating a consensus of Democrats around budget resolutions—a sensible procedure, since ranking Republican Delbert Latta was totally uncooperative—and he succeeded: over four years there were 919 Democratic votes for his resolutions and 77 against. He has delighted in working with Marvin Leath and Charles Stenholm of Texas, who were Boll Weevils in 1981 but are also cooperation-minded Democrats; in the process he heard some grumbling from northern liberals who felt he was not cutting defense enough and was not spending enough domestically. Gray's response is that he was not constructing a budget resolution that would be his own personal first choice, but one that could win 218 Democratic votes in the House. Gray was also assisted by circumstance. The budget process, for all the criticism of it, does tend to narrow down choices: you can't credibly propose vast new domestic spending unless you're prepared to support some hefty new taxes which Gray, like most other Democrats, was not ready to do. You can get Members from hawkish districts to agree to some defense cuts, but not huge ones.

None of this means that Gray has entirely abandoned his convictions or shunned issues of special interest to many black voters. He provided some impassioned leadership, together with tactical surefootedness, on South African sanctions, helping to frame the House's and ultimately the nation's position on that difficult issue. He has also shown a self-confidence and, for all his talkativeness, a self-discipline when it comes to other black politicians' ambitions. He defers to Mayor Goode in city politics, though rather gingerly, and did not endorse him for reelection in 1987 with much enthusiasm; he did nothing to take the spotlight away from Charles Rangel's unsuccessful bid to become majority whip in 1986. He played no particular role in Jesse Jackson's campaign. Rather, and characteristically, he chaired the drafting committee for the Democratic platform in Mackinac Island, producing a document that was easily adopted in Atlanta and caused the party's nominees none of the trouble past Democratic platforms have.

Gray was also running for another leadership post, the Democratic Caucus chairmanship being vacated by Richard Gephardt. Again he put together an interesting coalition of support, taking care to contribute to many colleagues' campaigns and won easily on the first ballot. When Jim Wright got into trouble in early 1989 and Tony Coelho resigned his seat, Gray became House majority whip, winning with 134 votes to 97 for David Bonior of Michigan and 30 for Beryl Anthony of Arkansas. The first black to hold a position in the House leadership, Gray is in line with the old and noble American tradition of the politician with a solid base in his own ethnic group who reaches out to make coalitions, sometimes unlikely ones, with others. He is a politician who, without betraying his own views or those of his constituents, is able to fashion a consensus in a Congress representing a diverse nation. Articulate and well-informed, inspirational when he wants to be yet also conciliatory, armed with formidable political intuition, liked and respected by his colleagues, deeply rooted in his own constituency yet able to understand and empathize with others, he has the potential to be a national leader, and not just in the House. He has made no move yet to run statewide, and perhaps does not have to: it has occurred to more than one national strategist that it might be advantageous to have Gray on a national ticket, in either spot.

The People: Est. Pop. 1986: 495,700, dn. 4.2% 1980–86; Pop. 1980: 517,215, dn. 17.5% 1970–80. Households (1980): 61% family, 35% with children, 32% married couples; 48.4% housing units rented; median monthly rent: $157; median house value: $25,700. Voting age pop. (1980): 378,182; 76% Black, 1% Spanish origin, 1% Asian origin.

1988 Presidential Vote:

Dukakis (D)	187,254	(91%)
Bush (R)	17,151	(8%)

Rep. William H. Gray III (D)

Elected 1978; b. Aug. 20, 1941, Baton Rouge, LA; home, Philadelphia; Franklin and Marshall Col., B.A. 1963, Drew Theological Seminary, M. Div. 1966, Princeton Theological Sch., Th.M. 1970; Baptist; married (Andrea).

Career: Minister; Prof., Jersey City St. Col., Montclair St. Col., Rutgers U., 1968–74.

Offices: 2454 RHOB 20515, 202-225-4001. Also 6753 Germantown Ave., Philadelphia 19119, 215-951-5388; 2316 W. Columbia Ave., Philadelphia 19121, 215-232-2770; and 22 N. 52d St., Philadelphia 19139, 215-476-8725.

Committees: *Majority Whip. Appropriations* (25th of 35 D). Subcommittees: Foreign Operations, Export Financing and Related Programs; Transportation. *District of Columbia* (4th of 8 D). Subcommittees: Fiscal Affairs and Health; Government Operations and Metropolitan Affairs.

Group Ratings

	ADA	ACLU	COPE	CFA	LCV	ACU	NTLC	NSI	COC	CEI
1988	95	90	97	64	69	0	5	0	31	8
1987	88	—	97	86	—	0	—	—	0	3

National Journal Ratings

	1988 LIB —	1988 CONS	1987 LIB —	1987 CONS
Economic	87% —	8%	73% —	0%
Social	86% —	0%	78% —	0%
Foreign	84% —	0%	81% —	0%

Key Votes

1) Homeless $	AGN	5) Ban Drug Test	—	9) SDI Research	AGN
2) Gephardt Amdt	FOR	6) Drug Death Pen	AGN	10) Ban Chem Weaps	FOR
3) Deficit Reduc	FOR	7) Handgun Sales	AGN	11) Aid to Contras	AGN
4) Kill Plnt Clsng Notice	AGN	8) Ban D.C. Abort $	AGN	12) Nuclear Testing	FOR

Election Results

1988 general	William H. Gray III (D)	184,322	(94%)	($660,456)
	Richard L. Harsh (R)	12,365	(6%)	
1988 primary	William H. Gray III (D), unopposed			
1986 general	William H. Gray III (D)	128,399	(98%)	($551,836)

THIRD DISTRICT

In northeast Philadelphia, out Roosevelt Boulevard, you could still see farms and empty fields 50 years ago; the alley-wide streets of North and South Philadelphia and the river wards were already tightly packed with houses and people, and the Main Line suburbs might already be well-settled near the stations, but the transit lines and the workers of Philadelphia's docks and factories and Center City offices had not yet moved out in any great numbers to the northeast. But today, northeast Philadelphia includes almost one-third of the city's population and its population is still growing. Along the Delaware River, with its blocks of closely packed brick row houses and neighborhood bars with neon lights, with mostly Irish and Italian residents and their pungent accents, you expect to see a Democratic ward leader (except in Philadelphia it would usually have been a Republican) knocking on the doors and distributing coal for the winter. Away from these old neighborhoods, 10 to 20 miles from Independence Hall, middle-income tract housing was still going up in the 1960s; more than half the housing units here, in fact, were built after 1950 (as compared to 20% in the rest of the city).

A sizable percentage of northeast Philadelphia's population is Jewish, in neighborhoods that are like neither Brooklyn nor Scarsdale. The houses are pleasant, but modest; the politics Democratic, but not always liberal and many are part of the hard-pressed lower-middle class. Quite a few voted for Frank Rizzo for mayor, some joined him when he reregistered in the Republican party and many live in fear that blacks will move into their neighborhoods. Northeast Philadelphia also has a sizable Catholic population, which is still pretty conservative on cultural issues. In many ways, this is a district out of the 1950s.

The congressman from the 3d District is Robert Borski, a young former stockbroker and state legislator from the older part of the district who got the 1982 nomination when other Democrats failed to see how Democratic a year it would be. To everyone's surprise, Borski beat Republican Charles Dougherty, who had been elected in 1978 when Democrat Joshua Eilberg was indicted for accepting $100,000 to help a Philadelphia hospital get a federal grant. Borski has won reelection easily since; the one highlight came in 1986 when Dougherty, who had become a Democrat, switched back to run as a Republican the day of the filing deadline. But Dougherty lost that primary 2 to 1 to a more constant Republican who in turn lost to Borski by almost as great a margin. Borski makes few waves in the House, where he generally votes a liberal line except on cultural issues like abortion; he is a member of the Public Works Committee and is one of two Philadelphia Democrats on Merchant Marine and Fisheries. He is friendly to groups which support the Irish Republican Army. He stays close to local issues and, like most of his constituents, backed Ed Rendell against Mayor Wilson Goode in the May 1987 mayoral primary.

The People: Est. Pop. 1986: 513,800, dn. 0.5% 1980–86; Pop. 1980: 516,154, dn. 6.6% 1970–80. Households (1980): 74% family, 34% with children, 59% married couples; 26.6% housing units rented; median monthly rent: $201; median house value: $32,700. Voting age pop. (1980): 391,605; 7% Black, 1% Spanish origin, 1% Asian origin.

1988 Presidential Vote:

	Bush (R)	115,312	(51%)
	Dukakis (D)	110,228	(48%)

Rep. Robert A. Borski (D)

Elected 1982; b. Oct. 20, 1948, Philadelphia; home, Philadelphia; U. of Baltimore, B.A. 1972; Roman Catholic; divorced.

Career: Stockbroker, Raymond James, Assoc., Inc., 1972–76; PA House of Reps., 1976–82.

Offices: 314 CHOB 20515, 202-225-8251. Also 7137 Frankford Ave., Philadelphia 19135, 215-335-3355.

Committees: *Merchant Marine and Fisheries* (11th of 26 D). Subcommittees: Merchant Marine; Oceanography. *Public Works and Transportation* (11th of 31 D). Subcommittees: Economic Development; Investigations and Oversight; Water Resources. *Select Committee on Aging* (20st of 39 D). Subcommittee: Health and Long-Term Care.

Group Ratings

	ADA	ACLU	COPE	CFA	LCV	ACU	NTLC	NSI	COC	CEI
1988	80	6	98	91	75	12	5	10	23	8
1987	80	—	97	79	—	5	—	—	13	7

National Journal Ratings

	1988 LIB — 1988 CONS		1987 LIB — 1987 CONS	
Economic	92%	— 0%	73%	— 0%
Social	56%	— 43%	72%	— 27%
Foreign	64%	— 34%	74%	— 25%

Key Votes

1) Homeless $	AGN	5) Ban Drug Test	AGN	9) SDI Research	—
2) Gephardt Amdt	FOR	6) Drug Death Pen	FOR	10) Ban Chem Weaps	FOR
3) Deficit Reduc	FOR	7) Handgun Sales	AGN	11) Aid to Contras	AGN
4) Kill Plnt Clsng Notice	AGN	8) Ban D.C. Abort $	FOR	12) Nuclear Testing	FOR

Election Results

1988 general	Robert A. Borski (D)	135,590	(63%)	($250,480)
	Mark Matthews (R)	78,909	(37%)	($23,101)
1988 primary	Robert A. Borski (D)	61,440	(91%)	
	John J. Hughes (D)	5,801	(9%)	
1986 general	Robert A. Borski (D)	107,804	(62%)	($391,980)
	Robert A. Rovner (R)	66,693	(38%)	($446,282)

FOURTH DISTRICT

Fifty years ago, the Jones & Laughlin steel mill, which employed 9,000 men in Aliquippa, Pennsylvania in Beaver County northwest of Pittsburgh, was "surrounded by a high wire fence. Workers' houses squat on the flats or cling to the grassless slopes. When the mills are running full blast, the town is bustling and houses receive a new coat of paint. The shores of the Ohio are lined with piles of iron ore, limestone and coal, and with cranes, stocks and furnaces." Aliquippa wasn't picturesque, but it was one of the sinews of America, where immigrants and their sons worked their way up by pouring the steel that built the country and won the war. Now the mills are cold and silent; LTV, the supposedly synergistic conglomerate that bought Jones &

Laughlin, has gone into bankruptcy; the population is declining as workers who have long since exhausted their unemployment benefits finally give in and move somewhere else to find work. The western Pennsylvania steel country has seven congressional districts today; 35 years ago, before the decline of the steel industry and the outmigration that has accompanied it, the same area had 11 districts. Most of Beaver County forms about half of the 4th Congressional District of Pennsylvania, which travels east across the hills north of Pittsburgh to take in the mountainous country around the towns of Indiana and Ligonier. The irregular boundaries were drawn by a Republican legislature in 1982 in a vain attempt to preserve the seat of one of the Reagan Administration's prized Democrats-turned-Republicans; the attempt failed, but the lines remain. The 4th and its predecessor districts, which have produced football players of the caliber of Joe Namath and Tony Dorsett, have also produced a melancholy string of incompetent congressmen. For 20 years, Beaver County and the surrounding area were represented by Frank Clark, a Democrat who managed to lose his seat in the ultra-Democratic Watergate year of 1974 (he was held in such low regard by his colleagues that after losing he was able to win only 34 of 244 votes for the post of Clerk of the House). His conqueror was Gary Myers, a Republican who decided after two terms to return to his post as a foreman in a steel mill. The next congressman, Democrat Eugene Atkinson, who had lost to Myers in 1976, won unimpressively in 1978, backed Edward Kennedy in the 1980 primary in which he lost western Pennsylvania, and then switched to the Republican Party just as the steel industry was going into its worst tailspin and the steel country was about to be the one part of the country trending Democratic: bad political moves every step of the way.

The craziest district lines in the world couldn't save a politician like this, and didn't. The new congressman, Joe Kolter, is a step above—when he sticks to what he knows best, the woes of the steel country—and he beat Atkinson (who nearly lost his Republican primary!) by a 60%–39% margin. Kolter was a 13-year veteran of the legislature, with solid labor support. He now serves on the Government Operations, Public Works and House Administration Committees. He has a record that is generally liberal on economics and foreign policy and traditional on cultural issues. In the fall of 1988, he introduced a bill to provide financial assistance to individuals unable to afford the high cost of organ and tissue transplants. As lead sponsor of a measure to cut contra aid, he embarrassed himself on C-SPAN when he said the contras were Communist, Daniel Ortega was freely elected, and most Latin countries had been communist at one time. He is reelected easily every two years, and the only threat to his tenure is the possibility—not an entirely unlikely one—that his district will collapse in redistricting.

The People: Est. Pop. 1986: 507,000, dn. 1.7% 1980–86; Pop. 1980: 515,572, up 6.1% 1970–80. Households (1980): 78% family, 40% with children, 68% married couples; 24.1% housing units rented; median monthly rent: $155; median house value: $39,400. Voting age pop. (1980): 375,245; 2% Black.

1988 Presidential Vote:

Dukakis (D)	97,784	(54%)
Bush (R)	81,028	(45%)

Rep. Joe P. Kolter (D)

Elected 1982; b. Sept. 3, 1926, McDonald; home, New Brighton; Geneva Col., B.S. 1950, Duquesne U., U. of Pittsburgh; Roman Catholic; married (Dorothy).

Career: Army, 1944–47; Accountant, 1950–67; High sch. teacher, 1950, 1965–67; New Brighton Borough Cncl., 1961–65; PA House of Reps., 1969–82.

Offices: 212 CHOB 20515, 202-225-2565. Also 1322 7th Ave., Beaver Falls 15010, 412-846-3600; 20 S. Mercer St., New Castle 16101, 412-658-4525; 104 P.O. Bldg., Butler 16001, 412-282-8081; and 21 S. 7th St., Indiana 15701, 412-349-3755.

Committees: *Government Operations* (16th of 24 D). Subcommittees: Commerce, Consumer, and Monetary Affairs; Environment, Energy, and Natural Resources. *House Administration* (10th of 13 D). Subcommittees: Accounts; Office Systems. *Public Works and Transportation* (12th of 31 D). Subcommittees: Aviation; Economic Development; Water Resources.

Group Ratings

	ADA	ACLU	COPE	CFA	LCV	ACU	NTLC	NSI	COC	CEI
1988	60	57	93	73	50	22	6	60	17	10
1987	64	—	92	71	—	5	—	—	36	11

National Journal Ratings

	1988 LIB — 1988 CONS		1987 LIB — 1987 CONS	
Economic	92%	0%	61%	38%
Social	49%	50%	59%	40%
Foreign	55%	45%	54%	46%

Key Votes

1) Homeless $	AGN	5) Ban Drug Test	AGN	9) SDI Research	FOR
2) Gephardt Amdt	FOR	6) Drug Death Pen	FOR	10) Ban Chem Weaps	AGN
3) Deficit Reduc	—	7) Handgun Sales	FOR	11) Aid to Contras	AGN
4) Kill Plnt Clsng Notice	AGN	8) Ban D.C. Abort $	FOR	12) Nuclear Testing	FOR

Election Results

1988 general	Joseph P. Kolter (D)	124,041	(70%)	($90,710)
	Gordon R. Johnston (R)	52,402	(29%)	
1988 primary	Joseph P. Kolter (D), unopposed			
1986 general	Joseph P. Kolter (D)	86,133	(60%)	($249,885)
	Al Lindsay (R)	55,165	(39%)	($9,029)

FIFTH DISTRICT

The countryside outside Philadelphia is studded with separate settlements that have histories and personalities which date back to the times when Philadelphia was a day or so's horse ride away. Chester, a small industrial town on the Delaware River, is really an old city which for years had its own Republican machine; most of its residents are black now. The Chadds Ford area, where the Wyeth family lives and paints, is peaceful countryside far from the brawling tone of Philadelphia public life. Kennett Square nearby is the center of the nation's mushroom industry. Coatesville, at the western edge of the district, is really part of the Pennsylvania Dutch

1040　PENNSYLVANIA

country, although no one is sure just where the boundary is. Not far away is Oxford, home of Lincoln University, one of the nation's oldest black colleges—a symbol of the area's Lincoln Republican heritage and a reminder that there are many blacks scattered over this area; on the next field, from a country mansion, you may see an A.M.E. church surrounded by what look like 19th century cabins.

These outer edges of the Philadelphia metropolitan area—technically in western Montgomery and Delaware counties, plus most of Chester County farther out—make up the 5th Congressional District of Pennsylvania. The 5th is one of the premier Republican congressional districts in the nation. Its Main Line commuters at the Paoli station, its Pennsylvania Dutch country, even the area around Chester—are all heavily Republican. This is one of those heartland Republican districts which for decades has supplied the House Republican Conference with its backbenchers and its most reliable supporters.

The current congressman, Richard Schulze, is a Republican Party loyalist with roots in the richest part of the district. He has taken jobs of sufficient modesty—Chester County register of wills, state representative—to suggest that he was seen as the kind of faithful local functionary who is allowed, by men of great power who commute to offices in the big city, to handle affairs in their small local community.

Schulze easily won the Republican primary for this seat in 1974 and has been reelected without perceptible difficulty since. His record on major issues is solidly Republican. He serves on the Ways and Means Committee and is now ranking minority member on its Oversight Subcommittee. Schulze also has a seat on the Trade Subcommittee, and has concentrated on those issues. Here he is true to Pennsylvania's century-old protectionist tradition, introducing bills calling for reciprocity and fairness and mandating vigorous retaliation against countries that do not comply. In 1986, he was an early sponsor of the steel-textiles-apparel-telecommunications trade bill that passed the House in May. By early 1987, he appeared with "trade competitiveness" bills giving small businesses tax breaks and reinstating the investment tax credit for "productive equipment and machinery." In 1988, he insisted that the U.S-Canada Free Trade Agreement be monitored to prevent dumping of steel. He is particularly vigilant against imports of cheap Chinese mushrooms, and has put through technical amendments to protect the religious rights of the apolitical Amish.

Schulze, who tends so carefully the traditional economic interests of this district, is reelected easily every two years.

The People: Est. Pop. 1986: 549,700, up 6.6% 1980–86; Pop. 1980: 515,528, up 9.8% 1970–80. Households (1980): 77% family, 42% with children, 64% married couples; 31.1% housing units rented; median monthly rent: $225; median house value: $57,300. Voting age pop. (1980): 370,556; 10% Black, 1% Spanish origin, 1% Asian origin.

1988 Presidential Vote:　Bush (R) . . . . 133,148　　(65%)
　　　　　　　　　　　　　Dukakis (D). . . . . 70,808　　(34%)

Rep. Richard T. Schulze (R)

Elected 1974; b. Aug. 7, 1929, Philadelphia; home, Berwyn; U. of Houston, 1949, Villanova U., 1952, Temple U., 1968; Presbyterian; married (Nancy).

Career: Army, 1951–53; Businessman, appliances; Committeeman, Tredyffrin Township, 1960–67; Chester Cnty. Regis. of Wills and Clerk of Orphans Crt., 1967–69; PA House of Reps., 1969–74.

Offices: 2369 RHOB 20515, 202-225-5761. Also 10 S. Leopard St., Ste. 204, Paoli 19301, 215-648-0555.

Committees: *Ways and Means* (5th of 13 R). Subcommittees: Oversight (Ranking Member); Trade; Social Security.

Group Ratings

	ADA	ACLU	COPE	CFA	LCV	ACU	NTLC	NSI	COC	CEI
1988	30	24	22	55	56	76	69	100	92	52
1987	8	—	21	29	—	77	—	—	85	62

National Journal Ratings

	1988 LIB — 1988 CONS		1987 LIB — 1987 CONS	
Economic	15%	— 84%	36%	— 63%
Social	31%	— 69%	10%	— 85%
Foreign	30%	— 67%	27%	— 72%

Key Votes

1) Homeless $	FOR	5) Ban Drug Test	FOR	9) SDI Research	FOR
2) Gephardt Amdt	AGN	6) Drug Death Pen	FOR	10) Ban Chem Weaps	AGN
3) Deficit Reduc	—	7) Handgun Sales	FOR	11) Aid to Contras	FOR
4) Kill Plnt Clsng Notice	FOR	8) Ban D.C. Abort $	FOR	12) Nuclear Testing	AGN

Election Results

1988 general	Richard T. Schulze (R)...............	153,453	(78%)	($444,205)
	Donald A. Hadley (D)	42,758	(22%)	
1988 primary	Richard T. Schulze (R), unopposed			
1986 general	Richard T. Schulze (R)...............	87,593	(66%)	($320,232)
	Tim Ringgold (D)....................	45,648	(34%)	($115,056)

SIXTH DISTRICT

The 6th Congressional District of Pennsylvania is betwixt and between—a part of eastern Pennsylvania beyond the Philadelphia orbit, south of the center of the anthracite area of northeastern Pennsylvania, and northeast of the Pennsylvania Dutch country. Fifty years ago the *WPA Guide* found in Reading the greatest concentration of Pennsylvania Germans, who make "a fetish of orderliness and thriftiness, and these traits are reflected in the city's appearance. The central section is laid out with gridiron simplicity; urban residential areas are made up of row upon row of red brick houses. Despite the encroachment of railroad and industrial activity there is little grime or dirt." The Reading Railroad and textile mills were the big employers then in this orderly community, in one of whose suburbs where John Updike grew up. But go over Blue

Mountain, and you are in anthracite country, where the *Guide* found little towns abandoned because their streets had sunk, settled because of the mines underneath, boarded-up textile mills, and Pottsville—John O'Hara's "Gibbsville"—whose anthracite industry was already in decline after strikes in 1922 and 1925 prompted many consumers to switch to oil for home heating. These were not well-ordered German cities, but hard-bitten towns where the rich people schemed with bootleggers to get a supply of the best smuggled liquor, where people of more modest background tried and usually failed to imitate upper-class manners, and where tough-talking miners and factory workers stayed menacingly in the background unless a character stumbled into the wrong roadhouse at night or diner at dawn.

In the 1930s, there were more people in Schuylkill County around Pottsville than in Berks County around Reading; now the reverse is true, and about 60% of the 6th District's people live south of Blue Mountain. The anthracite country has continued its decline (Schuylkill County had a population of 228,000 in 1940 and 160,000 in 1980), while Reading, once a high-wage manufacturing center, has been doing fairly well on lower-wage work and by converting its old brick factories to factory outlet stores that attract bargain hunters from all over the East. The Dutch country is not far away, and the 6th District now includes a small sliver of heavily Dutch Lancaster County.

The 6th District, in national elections, is not as Democratic as you might expect. A lot of the working-class people who would have been good Democratic voters have long since moved away in search of jobs. And in Berks County the Pennsylvania Dutch (i.e., German) tradition has been heavily Republican since the region split in 1858 over the slavery issue, as did two prominent local Democrats, James Buchanan of Lancaster and his lieutenant, J. Glancy Jones of Reading, then chairman of the House Ways and Means Committee.

Nevertheless, the congressional representation here has been Democratic since 1948. The current incumbent, Gus Yatron, was first elected in 1968, and continues to win by overwhelming margins. His general voting record in the House is liberal on economic issues, conservative on cultural matters—which seems in line with his district. His chief focus, however, has been on foreign policy, and he is now, starting his third decade in Congress, the third ranking Democrat on the House Foreign Affairs Committee.

After the 1982 election, he took over the chair of the Human Rights and International Organizations Subcommittee from Don Bonker of Washington, who relinquished it for another chair. There he has attended to his duties in a more than perfunctory way. He has risen with other committee Democrats to oppose aid to the Nicaraguan contras, but he has also pointed out, as some of them have been reluctant to do, that the Sandinistas in charge in Managua have been some pretty nasty human rights violators themselves. He criticized both Pinochet of Chile and Marcos of the Philippines when they were still in power, and has criticized China's human rights record in Tibet. He is working to support the United Nations, was early in criticizing deforestation in Brazil and is increasingly vocal about the threat of global warming. Yatron is of Greek descent, and remains interested in and sympathetic to Greek interests, but has sharply criticized the demagogic Papandreou government for its policies in dealing with terrorists.

So generally Yatron has been in line with his fellow Democrats. It is not likely he will be voted out of a chairmanship again, (as he was in 1981 on the Inter-American Affairs Subcommittee, in favor of Michael Barnes of Maryland). Perhaps he hopes to succeed to the full committee chairmanship some day. That's unlikely, but it is possible; Yatron has proved to be a more enduring Member in the House than many expected a few years ago.

The People: Est. Pop. 1986: 522,900, up 1.3% 1980–86; Pop. 1980: 515,952, up 3.9% 1970–80. Households (1980): 75% family, 36% with children, 63% married couples; 25.5% housing units rented; median monthly rent: $154; median house value: $32,400. Voting age pop. (1980): 384,537; 1% Black, 1% Spanish origin.

1988 Presidential Vote: Bush (R) 112,048 (61%)

Dukakis (D). 70,915 (38%)

Rep. Gus Yatron (D)

Elected 1968; b. Oct. 6, 1927, Reading; home, Reading; Kutztown St. Teachers Col., 1950; Greek Orthodox; married (Millie).

Career: Pro heavyweight boxer, 1947–50; Proprietor, Yatron's Ice Cream, 1950–69; Mbr., Reading Sch. Bd., 1955–60; PA House of Reps., 1957–60; PA Senate, 1961–68.

Offices: 2205 RHOB 20515, 202-225-5546. Also 1940 N. 13th St., Reading 19604, 215-929-9233; and American Bank Bldg., Pottsville 17901, 717-622-4212.

Committees: *Foreign Affairs* (3d of 28 D). Subcommittees: Human Rights and International Organizations (Chairman); International Operations. *Post Office and Civil Service* (6th of 15 D). Subcommittees: Human Resources; Investigations.

Group Ratings

	ADA	ACLU	COPE	CFA	LCV	ACU	NTLC	NSI	COC	CEI
1988	65	57	84	73	50	24	18	33	36	18
1987	84	—	83	79	—	13	—	—	33	10

National Journal Ratings

	1988 LIB — 1988 CONS		1987 LIB — 1987 CONS	
Economic	67%	— 30%	62%	— 35%
Social	36%	— 63%	60%	— 39%
Foreign	54%	— 46%	64%	— 36%

Key Votes

1) Homeless $	AGN	5) Ban Drug Test	AGN	9) SDI Research	AGN
2) Gephardt Amdt	FOR	6) Drug Death Pen	FOR	10) Ban Chem Weaps	FOR
3) Deficit Reduc	AGN	7) Handgun Sales	FOR	11) Aid to Contras	AGN
4) Kill Plnt Clsng Notice	AGN	8) Ban D.C. Abort $	FOR	12) Nuclear Testing	FOR

Election Results

1988 general	Gus Yatron (D).....................	114,119	(63%)	($121,435)
	James R. Erwin (R)	65,278	(36%)	($12,002)
1988 primary	Gus Yatron (D), unopposed			
1986 general	Gus Yatron (D).....................	98,142	(69%)	($97,114)
	Norm Bertasavage (R)	43,858	(31%)	($18,211)

SEVENTH DISTRICT

One of America's distinctive political constituencies is Delaware County, Pennsylvania, just outside Philadelphia, long the home of the old Delaware War Board, one of the premier Republican political machines in the country. The War Board harks back to the days when Republicans carried everything in Pennsylvania, and when working-class neighborhoods were serviced and rallied by Republican ward heelers. For although Delaware County has its rich neighborhoods, much of it is modest. You might not notice the difference if you drove over

Cobbs or Darby Creeks, which separate the county from Philadelphia: the mostly white working-class neighborhood in Philadelphia looks a lot like the modest, long-settled close-in suburbs nearby, in Upper Darby Township and a dozen or so small incorporated boroughs. These are increasingly the homes of older people whose families are grown, who still treasure traditional cultural values but also felt pinched during the recession and worry about how they will fare in retirement. Farther along, the houses spread out, and real estate values rise in leafy suburbs like Swarthmore; these are also old areas, but the people are more secure and less anxious. (Swarthmore College, alma mater of Michael Dukakis, is liberal; the town is not.) To the north are some of the suburbs of the Main Line—the highest income and highest status communities in the Philadelphia area.

Politically, the War Board is one of the last of the Republican machines which dominated so much of the middle-class American North in the 1920s, when Republicanism was the norm from which few decent-minded Protestant voters in such neighborhoods deviated, and political machines were as much a part of the urban landscape as trolley lines or overhead electrical wires. Philadelphia, after all, kept electing machine Republican mayors until 1951 and the War Board provided stable and reliable, if undistinguished and dull, local government and representation in Washington and Harrisburg. And if that era seems long gone, it may have returned: the entire Philadelphia metropolitan area, its economy reviving, gave majorities to Ronald Reagan in 1980 and 1984, and Delaware County Republicans have elected a congressman with genuine roots in a working class community and wide popularity and appeal.

He is Curt Weldon, and he first came to attention as mayor of Marcus Hook, Pennsylvania's southernmost town on the Delaware River, the home of oil tank farms and a rusty-looking old steel mill. Weldon was an active and popular mayor, went on the county council, and then ran in 1984 in the 7th Congressional District, which includes most of Delaware County and one ward of Philadelphia, against incumbent Bob Edgar. Edgar was an archetypical member of the class of 1974, a Methodist minister from a working-class background and an opponent of the Vietnam war and Richard Nixon, who entered politics suddenly in 1974, profited from an internal Republican split and a national trend of opinion, established a liberal and anti-pork-barrel record and surprised everyone (probably including himself) by winning reelection five times. Against Weldon, Edgar won by 412 votes out of 248,000 cast. In 1986, Edgar ran for the Senate, won the Democratic primary narrowly, but lost the general election by a large margin to Arlen Specter. Weldon was elected to the House fairly easily, with no primary opposition and 61% in the general.

Weldon made a distinctive record in the House, not just protecting the Philadelphia Navy Yard on the Armed Services Committee, but also establishing a Congressional Fire Services Caucus, which has 286 members and sponsored measures calling for new alarm systems in congressional offices and a new Fire Training Center in Illinois. Weldon personally helped to put out a fire in Speaker Jim Wright's office. He also came forward with the distinctive proposal to identify the sponsors, beneficiaries and costs of targeted tax measures—something sure not to ingratiate him with Ways and Means Chairman Dan Rostenkowski, but obviously justified. He got the period in which convicted individuals cannot lobby the Defense Department extended from one to five years. He helped set up an EPA recycling clearinghouse.

With a voting record that made occasional bows to liberals on economic and cultural issues, Weldon was in fine shape for the 1988 general in which he beat former Gary Hart delegate counter David Landau 68%–32%.

The People: Est. Pop. 1986: 519,500, up 0.7% 1980–86; Pop. 1980: 515,766, dn. 8.3% 1970–80. Households (1980): 75% family, 36% with children, 62% married couples; 26.3% housing units rented; median monthly rent: $233; median house value: $45,600. Voting age pop. (1980): 387,309; 5% Black, 1% Asian origin, 1% Spanish origin.

1988 Presidential Vote: Bush (R) 140,716   (60%)
Dukakis (D). 93,286   (39%)

Rep. Curt Weldon (R)

Elected 1986; b. July 22, 1947, Marcus Hook; home, Aston; West Chester State Col., B.A. 1969; Protestant; married (Mary).

Career: Teacher, Vice Principal, 1969–76; Dir., Training and Manpower Devel., INA Corp., 1976–81; Mayor, Marcus Hook, 1977–82; Delaware Cnty. Cncl., 1984–86, Chmn. 1985–86.

Offices: 1233 LHOB 20515, 202-225-2011. Also 1554 Garrett Rd., Upper Darby 19082, 215-259-0700; and 2501 S. 71st St., Philadelphia 19145, 215-365-7755.

Committees: *Armed Services* (15th of 21 R). Subcommittees: Research and Development; Seapower and Strategic and Critical Materials. *Merchant Marine and Fisheries* (12th of 17 R). Subcommittees: Fisheries, Wildlife Conservation and the Environment; Oceanography. *Select Committee on Children, Youth, and Families* (8th of 12 R).

Group Ratings

	ADA	ACLU	COPE	CFA	LCV	ACU	NTLC	NSI	COC	CEI
1988	30	47	57	82	56	59	71	90	71	42
1987	36	—	40	29	—	55	—	—	73	54

National Journal Ratings

	1988 LIB — 1988 CONS		1987 LIB — 1987 CONS	
Economic	40%	— 58%	39%	— 60%
Social	37%	— 62%	40%	— 60%
Foreign	16%	— 78%	31%	— 69%

Key Votes

1) Homeless $	FOR	5) Ban Drug Test	FOR	9) SDI Research	FOR
2) Gephardt Amdt	AGN	6) Drug Death Pen	FOR	10) Ban Chem Weaps	FOR
3) Deficit Reduc	AGN	7) Handgun Sales	AGN	11) Aid to Contras	FOR
4) Kill Plnt Clsng Notice	AGN	8) Ban D.C. Abort $	FOR	12) Nuclear Testing	—

Election Results

1988 general	Curt Weldon (R).	155,387	(68%)	($507,360)
	David Edward Landau (D).	73,745	(32%)	($203,582)
1988 primary	Curt Weldon (R), unopposed			
1986 general	Curt Weldon (R).	110,118	(61%)	($617,063)
	Bill Spingler (D)	69,557	(39%)	($166,612)

EIGHTH DISTRICT

One of the original three counties of William Penn's colony, Bucks County had its dual nature from the beginning: it was a paradise of bucolic hills and creeks running into the Delaware, and in 1727 James Logan, Penn's secretary, established the Durham Furnace iron works there. Fifty years ago, it was still the bucolic Bucks that captured the imagination, the by that time mellow and well-settled farmland, with old stone houses and covered bridges, easily reached by train from New York as well as Philadelphia, and long the residence of well-known writers and artists, including the late yippie Abbie Hoffman, who committed suicide in New Hope in 1989. In the years after World War II, the location of Lower Bucks County—directly between Philadelphia and industrial Trenton, New Jersey, along the ocean-navigable Delaware River and several rail lines—led to huge new developments here. U.S. Steel built its Fairless Works, one of the few big postwar steel plants, down by the river. And the Levitt organization created one of its Levittowns in what had been farmland and swamp between U.S. 13 and U.S. 1, which the *WPA Guide* described in 1940 as "flat country inappropriately known as Penn Valley. Gasoline stations, refreshment stands, and farm produce stands clutter the roadside; billboards also intrude."

Politically, Bucks County, like all of Pennsylvania, was solidly Republican: it was the home of Senator Joseph Grundy, longtime head of the Pennsylvania Manufacturers Association, who opposed the Smoot-Hawley tariff of 1930 on the grounds that it was not protectionist enough. But in contrast to the other suburban Philadelphia counties, where most of the blue-collar immigration took place a long time ago, when Philadelphia itself was solidly Republican and the suburban county machines ready to enroll new residents in their party, development came after the New Deal in Bucks. So Lower Bucks, around the Fairless Works and Levittown, has been fairly solidly Democratic, while Upper Bucks is Republican but sometimes liberal on issues like the environment and foreign policy. The 8th Congressional District of Pennsylvania includes all of Bucks County plus a small slice of Montgomery County directly north of Philadelphia's Center City. And although it leans Republican, it has elected Democratic Congressman Peter Kostmayer for all but two years since 1976.

Kostmayer's political formula has been to emphasize his liberal stands on environmental and foreign issues, to vote somewhat more conservatively on economic issues, and to work hard on constituency services. He was a product of the Democratic politics of the middle 1970s: a McGovern coordinator and press aide to Governor Milton Shapp who got it into his head to run for Congress at age 30 and was shrewd enough to figure out how to win. Vigorous opposition to corruption (he urged early investigations of Koreagate and of his fellow Pennsylvania Democrats Daniel Flood and Joshua Eilberg) and emphasis on environmental issues (he helped kill the Tocks Island Dam on the Delaware) enabled Kostmayer to solidify support in Upper Bucks; he easily won reelection in 1978. But in 1980, the district went Republican, in a year in which economic issues were the center of attention, and elected James Coyne. Coyne in turn stumbled when he showed a lack of feel for the political process, attacking Kostmayer for continuing to help 8th District residents with problems and flip-flopping in public view on the nuclear freeze. Kostmayer regained the seat with a 50%–49% victory in 1982.

In this second stint in Congress, he has gotten along better with his colleagues and slowly increased his percentages with the voters. He sits on the Interior Committee and now chairs the Oversight and Investigations Subcommittee and cites as proud achievements a Pennsylvania Wilderness Act and making the Delaware & Lehigh Canal a National Heritage Corridor. On economic issues, he supports Gramm-Rudman and the line-item veto. Kostmayer has worked hard to defeat the MX missile, and as a member of the Foreign Affairs Committee has taken a front-row position opposing aid to the Nicaraguan contras. But he has been flexible enough to invite House Armed Services Chairman Les Aspin, who took the opposite view on both issues, into the 8th District to persuade him to save the Naval Air Defense Command in Warminster, the second biggest employer in the district.

In the 8th District, Kostmayer has tried to keep his opponents from launching attacks on his record by preemptive strikes at them—and has succeeded. In 1988, Kostmayer launched an attack on the supposed absenteeism of former state Senator Ed Howard by emphasizing the 1,234 roll calls he missed; Howard claimed he was present at 92%. Oddly, Howard attacked Kostmayer as a tool of developers; the Upper County is worried about overdevelopment, but as Kostmayer said the charge had the credibility of accusing Colonel Sanders of being a friend of chickens.

Howard might have aimed more fire at what Kostmayer said while at the Democratic National Convention. "We are not going to blow it this time," he told a liberal gathering. "Just shut up, gays, women and environmentalists. Just shut up. You'll get everything you want after the election. But just, for the meantime, shut up so that we can win. There's a real strong feeling that we don't want to start trouble. Nobody wants to take the rap for messing this up." As a confession of disingenuousness in politics, this can hardly be beaten. But Kostmayer had a huge money advantage—in mid-October he was the number 10 fundraiser in House races, with more than $1.1 million raised—and pressed it home for his biggest victory since 1978. It's hard to say he has a safe seat, but hard to say what he could do to make it safer.

The People: Est. Pop. 1986: 559,900, up 1.0% 1980–86; Pop. 1980: 516,902, up 14.1% 1970–80. Households (1980): 80% family, 45% with children, 70% married couples; 25.9% housing units rented; median monthly rent: $255; median house value: $57,100. Voting age pop. (1980): 364,239; 2% Black, 1% Spanish origin, 1% Asian origin.

1988 Presidential Vote:

Bush (R)	138,869	(60%)
Dukakis (D)	88,081	(38%)

Rep. Peter H. Kostmayer (D)

Elected 1982; b. Sept. 27, 1946, New York, NY; home, Solebury; Columbia U., B.A. 1971; Episcopalian; separated.

Career: Reporter, *The Trentonian*, 1971–72; Press Secy. to Atty. Gen. of PA, 1972–73; Dpty. Press Secy. to PA Gov. Milton Shapp, 1973–76; U.S. House of Reps., 1977–81; Pub. rel. consultant, 1981–82.

Offices: 123 CHOB 20515, 202-225-4276. Also 100 S. Main St., Doylestown 18901, 215-345-8543; 1 Oxford Valley, Ste. 700, Langhorne 19047, 215-757-8181; and 515 S. West End Blvd., Quakertown 18951, 215-538-2222.

Committees: *Foreign Affairs* (11th of 28 D). Subcommittees: International Economic Policy and Trade; Western Hemisphere Affairs. *Interior and Insular Affairs* (12th of 26 D). Subcommittees: General Oversight and Investigations (Chairman); National Parks and Public Lands; Water, Power and Offshore Energy Resources. *Select Committee on Hunger* (5th of 19 D).

Group Ratings

	ADA	ACLU	COPE	CFA	LCV	ACU	NTLC	NSI	COC	CEI
1988	85	91	89	91	88	4	11	10	31	13
1987	96	—	88	79	—	0	—	—	7	6

National Journal Ratings

	1988 LIB — 1988 CONS		1987 LIB — 1987 CONS	
Economic	71% —	23%	73% —	0%
Social	82% —	17%	78% —	0%
Foreign	74% —	23%	81% —	0%

Key Votes

1) Homeless $	AGN	5) Ban Drug Test	AGN	9) SDI Research	AGN
2) Gephardt Amdt	FOR	6) Drug Death Pen	AGN	10) Ban Chem Weaps	FOR
3) Deficit Reduc	FOR	7) Handgun Sales	AGN	11) Aid to Contras	AGN
4) Kill Plnt Clsng Notice	AGN	8) Ban D.C. Abort $	AGN	12) Nuclear Testing	FOR

Election Results

1988 general	Peter H. Kostmayer (D)	128,153	(57%)	($1,089,612)
	Ed Howard (R)	93,648	(42%)	($507,682)
1988 primary	Peter H. Kostmayer (D)	34,298	(90%)	
	Edward T. Czyzyk (D)	3,947	(10%)	
1986 general	Peter H. Kostmayer (D)	85,731	(55%)	($682,526)
	David A. Christian (R)	70,047	(45%)	($353,180)

NINTH DISTRICT

Like a series of vertebrae through central Pennsylvania, the Appalachian mountain chain has been a formidable barrier through most of Pennsylvania's history. Up close the mountains look tantalizingly low: you imagine that you could hike over them in an hour or so. But they are much more formidable than they seem. The colonials and British regulars led by General Braddock to his defeat near Pittsburgh in 1754 found it hard going, despite their guidance from George Washington; Scots-Irish settlers and 19th century pioneers in Conestoga wagons found it not much easier, for there are few gaps in the ridges and unless you can build a tunnel you have to climb over the top.

During the 18th century, the mountains provided Quaker Pennsylvania with a rampart against Indian attacks, and allowed the commonwealth to become the richest and most populous of the colonies. But in the 19th century, when people wanted to open up and trade with the vast interior, the mountains stopped them, and they went over New York's Erie Canal and New York Central Railroad instead. It took the aggressive capitalists who built the Pennsylvania Railroad to get trains over these ridges, and a nation at war in the 1940s to build the first highway, the Pennsylvania Turnpike, that could dependably get trucks over them. Today, the old towns look much as they did 60 years ago, and the farmhouses and red barns still sit on rolling hills in the shadow of one or another of the ridges, isolated and out of touch with the pulsing rhythms of the America of the 1980s.

The 9th is the only one of Pennsylvania's congressional districts to lie wholly within these mountains. This part of the Alleghenies (the term is often used interchangeably with Appalachians in Pennsylvania) was first settled by poor Scottish and Ulster Irish farmers just after the Revolutionary War. They were a people of fierce independence and pride, as the Whiskey Rebellion demonstrated—corn was not an article of commerce out here unless distilled into easily portable alcohol. The settlers worked their hardscrabble farms and built their little towns. Sometimes coal was found nearby, and their communities changed. But for the most part the 9th is not really coal country, and the area was denied—or spared—the boom-bust cycles of northeastern Pennsylvania and West Virginia. This was an important area for the Pennsylvania Railroad, however. Near Altoona was the Pennsylvania Railroad's famous Horseshoe Curve, and in Altoona itself the railroad built the nation's largest car yards. As rail transportation became less important, and the Pennsylvania Railroad moved from prosperity to merger to bankruptcy, Altoona's population declined from 82,000 at the end of the 1920s to 58,000 in 1989.

This part of Pennsylvania has been solidly Republican since the election of 1860, and it has not come close to electing a Democrat to Congress for years. The current incumbent, E. G. (Bud) Shuster, is an entrepreneur who made a fortune building up a computer business. He decided to settle in the southern Pennsylvania mountains, became interested in local affairs, decided to run for Congress, and beat the favorite, a local state senator, in the 1972 Republican primary. Shuster has won easily since.

He has had essentially two careers in the House. In the 1970s he was a hard-driving partisan, the House's most vociferous opponent of the air bag, and chairman of the Republican Policy Committee until the 1980 election. Then he ran for minority whip against Trent Lott and lost. Since then he has concentrated his efforts on the Public Works Committee, working with Democrats, including the late Chairman James Howard, to raise the gasoline tax and build more highways. One of the most vocal sounders of conservative themes in the late 1970s, by the late 1980s his main work was getting the water and highway bills passed over President Reagan's veto. Shuster had a hand in writing the Clean Water Act Amendments and the Surface Transportation Uniform Relocation Assistance Act of 1987. The largest single "demonstration project" by far was the $9 million project to close a gap in the U.S. 220 freeway between Altoona and the borough of Tyrone "for the purpose of demonstrating state-of-the-art delineation technology." All of which is ironic in terms of 1980s politics, but makes more sense when you think in terms of the 1780s or 1880s: for the conquest of these Appalachian ridges by western civilization, now as then, depends critically on support and subsidy from government, and a congressman from these parts, unless perhaps he has a national leadership role, is not in any position to forget that.

The People: Est. Pop. 1986: 521,200, up 1.1% 1980–86; Pop. 1980: 515,430, up 8.5% 1970–80. Households (1980): 78% family, 41% with children, 67% married couples; 24.6% housing units rented; median monthly rent: $137; median house value: $32,600. Voting age pop. (1980): 368,331; 1% Black.

1988 Presidential Vote:

Bush (R)	106,383	(63%)
Dukakis (D)	61,408	(36%)

Rep. E. G. (Bud) Shuster (R)

Elected 1972; b. Jan. 23, 1932, Glassport; home, Everett; U. of Pittsburgh, B.S. 1954, Duquesne U., M.B.A. 1960, American U., Ph.D. 1967; United Church of Christ; married (Patricia).

Career: Army, 1954–56; Vice Pres., Electronic Computer Div., RCA; Founder and Chmn., computer software companies.

Offices: 2268 RHOB 20515, 202-225-2431. Also RD 2, Box 711, Altoona 16601, 814-946-1653; and 179 E. Queen St., Chambersburg 17201, 717-264-8308.

Committees: *Public Works and Transportation* (2d of 20 R). Subcommittees: Aviation; Investigations and Oversight; Surface Transportation (Ranking Member). *Select Committee on Intelligence* (3d of 7 R). Subcommittees: Oversight and Evaluation; Program and Authorization.

Group Ratings

	ADA	ACLU	COPE	CFA	LCV	ACU	NTLC	NSI	COC	CEI
1988	5	13	18	27	19	100	75	100	100	77
1987	20	—	18	29	—	70	—	—	80	63

National Journal Ratings

	1988 LIB — 1988 CONS		1987 LIB — 1987 CONS	
Economic	13% —	85%	32% —	67%
Social	5% —	91%	27% —	72%
Foreign	16% —	78%	0% —	80%

1050　　PENNSYLVANIA

Key Votes

1) Homeless $	FOR	5) Ban Drug Test	AGN	9) SDI Research	FOR
2) Gephardt Amdt	FOR	6) Drug Death Pen	FOR	10) Ban Chem Weaps	AGN
3) Deficit Reduc	AGN	7) Handgun Sales	FOR	11) Aid to Contras	FOR
4) Kill Plnt Clsng Notice	FOR	8) Ban D.C. Abort $	FOR	12) Nuclear Testing	AGN

Election Results

1988 general	E. G. (Bud) Shuster (R), unopposed			($332,647)
1988 primary	E. G. (Bud) Shuster (R), unopposed			
1986 general	E. G. (Bud) Shuster (R)	120,890	(100%)	($276,463)

TENTH DISTRICT

"Coal is the theme song of this city in the hills," wrote the *WPA Guide* of Scranton 50 years ago. "Coal brought prosperity and also despair. Coal built its mansions, stores, banks, hotels, and hovels; it blackened the beautiful Lackawanna, scarred the mountain sides, made artificial hills of unsightly coal refuse, and undermined the city itself—but it created an anthracite kingdom, the importance of which merits a considerable place in American history. It exalted the hardiness of the Pennsylvania miner and brought into existence one of the most powerful labor unions in the country—the United Mine Workers of America. It did more than any other factor to diversify Pennsylvania's population," bringing 30 nationalities to Scranton, where each "clings to a particular area: the Welsh concentrate in Hyde Park on the west; Germans and Irish in South Scranton; Poles, Russians, Lithuanians, and Italians in separate outlying sections." But as those words were written, the anthracite kingdom was dying, or dead. Demand for hard coal as a home heating fuel started to decline in the 1920s and plummeted in the 1940s; the three major anthracite counties fell in population from 991,000 in 1930 to 731,000 in 1980. Lackawanna County fell from 310,000 to 227,000, and Scranton from 143,000 to 87,000.

In the process, many of the characteristic features of the anthracite kingdom vanished. One was coal dust and air pollution; another was the hills of refuse; the ethnic groups became less distinctive as the generations went on and what had been communities of young families became communities of old people. In the 1960s and 1970s, there was an influx of textile and apparel mills, bringing low-wage, non-union jobs to what had once been a high-wage, unionized area.

Scranton and Lackawanna County make up almost half of Pennsylvania's 10th Congressional District. The rest of it is made up of the kind of territory Scranton was before the anthracite boom: Scots-Irish mountain counties in the Poconos (a favorite resort of many middle-class New Yorkers) and the northern tier of counties just below Upstate New York. The railroads on which Scranton was a major switching point and roundhouse stop plow through here, often on high viaducts, occasionally through tunnels. But they have few reasons to stop in these small towns and quiet hills.

The politics of the 10th District for many years could be easily summarized: Scranton was Democratic, the rest of the district Republican. But by 1988, a combination of cultural conservatism and skepticism that government would bring back the old days, made Lackawanna County only 51% for Michael Dukakis, while the mountain counties, some of them filling with New York expatriates, were as Republican as ever. The result is that what had been basically a Democratic district when Scranton Republican Joseph McDade won it in 1962 has become basically a Republican district.

This may prove fortunate for McDade, whose career has taken a couple of not terribly good turns in the late 1980s. For years, he had been ranking Republican on the Interior Appropriations Subcommittee, where he was able to cooperate with an often like-minded chairman Sidney

Yates on programs that could produce visible good effects—national parks, aid to the arts, historic preservation, energy research—and mostly didn't cost very much. In 1985, after the retirement of Jack Edwards, he switched to the Defense Subcommittee where he is ranking Republican. There some expected—or feared—that he would oppose Reagan Administration policies, and others felt he simply wasn't as familiar with them as would be desirable. In fact, he seems to have made a conscientious effort to support them, and certainly did not embarrass himself. But at the same time, he does not conceal his lack of enthusiasm for many Pentagon spending increases and some weapons systems. In 1985 and early 1986, when New York's Joseph Addabbo was chairman, he sometimes worked with hawkish and nuts-and-bolts minded Bill Chappell of Florida; then Chappell succeeded to the chair after Addabbo's death; now, with Chappell defeated, the new chairman is another Pennsylvanian, John Murtha. This surely means that the Pentagon will be forced to keep buying 300,000 tons of anthracite—one-tenth the national production—it doesn't need.

But in December 1988, *The Wall Street Journal* charged that McDade had received $45,000 in campaign contributions and speaking fees from officials and others involved in a company with a plant in his district for which he arranged a Defense Department minority set-aside contract, and that some of the employees were reimbursed by the company for their contributions—which would make them illegal. In January 1989, McDade refused to provide some records subpoenaed by a federal grand jury investigating this United Chem-Con case. How this case will turn out no one can say. But it threatens to give McDade at least a bit of a black eye. A week after the *Journal* story broke, McDade was defeated for secretary of the Republican Conference by Vin Weber. The questions now, pending legal action or an ethics committee investigation, are whether McDade can retain his effectiveness on the Defense Appropriations Subcommittee and whether he will remain popular in his increasingly Republican district. It's quite possible he will survive. But he may be threatened in 1990, either by serious opposition or by unfavorable redistricting (it's unlikely, but the redistricters could put Scranton and nearby Wilkes-Barre in the same district). Either of those threats could prove politically fatal or could persuade McDade to retire.

The People: Est. Pop. 1986: 528,700, up 2.6% 1980–86; Pop. 1980: 515,442, up 7.1% 1970–80. Households (1980): 76% family, 38% with children, 64% married couples; 28.4% housing units rented; median monthly rent: $140; median house value: $34,400. Voting age pop. (1980): 376,348.

1988 Presidential Vote:

Bush (R)	112,038	(58%)
Dukakis (D)	80,528	(41%)

Rep. Joseph M. McDade (R)

Elected 1962; b. Sept. 29, 1931, Scranton; home, Clarks Summit; U. of Notre Dame, B.A. 1953, U. of PA, LL.B. 1956; Roman Catholic; married (Sarah).

Career: Clerk to Chf. Fed. Judge John W. Murphy, 1956–57; Practicing atty., 1957–62; Scranton City Solicitor, 1962.

Offices: 2370 RHOB 20515, 202-225-3731. Also 514 Scranton Life Bldg., Scranton 18503, 717-346-3834.

Committees: *Appropriations* (2d of 22 R). Subcommittees: Defense (Ranking Member); Interior. *Small Business* (Ranking Member of 17 R). Subcommittee: SBA, the General Economy and Minority Enterprise Development (Ranking Member).

Group Ratings

	ADA	ACLU	COPE	CFA	LCV	ACU	NTLC	NSI	COC	CEI
1988	40	55	69	91	38	54	44	100	50	23
1987	40	—	68	50	—	37	—	—	36	29

National Journal Ratings

	1988 LIB — 1988 CONS			1987 LIB — 1987 CONS		
Economic	50%	—	48%	41%	—	58%
Social	38%	—	61%	43%	—	56%
Foreign	24%	—	76%	33%	—	67%

Key Votes

1) Homeless $	FOR	5) Ban Drug Test	—	9) SDI Research	FOR
2) Gephardt Amdt	FOR	6) Drug Death Pen	FOR	10) Ban Chem Weaps	AGN
3) Deficit Reduc	AGN	7) Handgun Sales	FOR	11) Aid to Contras	FOR
4) Kill Plnt Clsng Notice	AGN	8) Ban D.C. Abort $	FOR	12) Nuclear Testing	AGN

Election Results

1988 general	Joseph M. McDade (R)	140,096	(73%)	($430,322)
	Robert C. Cordaro (D)	51,179	(27%)	($66,299)
1988 primary	Joseph M. McDade (R), unopposed			
1986 general	Joseph M. McDade (R)	118,603	(75%)	($291,757)
	Robert C. Bolus (D)	40,248	(25%)	($10,195)

ELEVENTH DISTRICT

Three miles east of the town square of Wilkes-Barre, the *WPA Guide* pointed out 50 years ago, you could see over the mountainside "a pall of steam in rainy weather. Below the surface here rages a mine fire started in 1917"—the peak year of local anthracite production—"after a forgetful mule driver had left his lamp hanging on a mine prop. Millions of tons of coal have already been consumed, and millions more will be destroyed before the fire encounters underground barriers set up to save adjoining mining properties. But many more millions will remain, for the coal veins of Luzerne County, of which Wilkes-Barre is the seat, are almost inexhaustible and produce 40% of the world's hard coal." To this town, named by Revolutionary-era pioneers after two Englishmen who supported their cause, thousands of immigrants came in the late 19th and early 20th centuries, attracted by the high wages they were paid to scrape out the coal needed to heat the houses and smudge the skies of New York and Boston and Philadelphia. But the endless supplies were never to be exhausted, for anthracite was replaced by oil and gas heat, and by the 1930s, this region was in decline; Luzerne County's population, 445,000 in 1930, was 343,000 in 1980.

This is the land of Pennsylvania's 11th Congressional District, which includes all of Luzerne County and similar territory to the east and west. The miners have been a Democratic voting bloc since the 1930s, but there were also a lot of Republicans here, people in white-collar occupations and ancestral Pennsylvania Republicans of all walks of life. For more than 30 years, the district was represented by Daniel Flood, a mustachioed Democrat who, from his perch on the Appropriations Committee, brought millions in federal dollars to the anthracite country. But in 1978, he was charged with wrongly accepting money, was stripped of his subcommittee chairmanship, and resigned. In the next six years, the 11th District had a series of bizarre elections and no less than four different congressmen.

The first was Democratic legislator Ray Musto, who won the April 1980 special election to fill the rest of Flood's term and probably expected to stay in Congress the rest of his life. But he lost in the November 1980 landslide to Republican James Nelligan. Nelligan, in turn, lost the 1982 election to Democrat Frank Harrison. Harrison was subsequently beaten 47%–43% in the 1984 primary by Paul Kanjorski after Harrison was caught travelling in Central America while Wilkes-Barre area residents had to boil their tap water because it was contaminated. This succession, curiously, exactly matches the order of finish in the 1980 special election: Musto (with 27%), Nelligan (23%), Harrison (17%), Kanjorski (16%). The jinx finally ended in 1986— or fell on the challenger, 25-year-old Marc Holtzman, son of a Wilkes-Barre jewelry manufacturer who flew 1980 presidential candidate Ronald Reagan around in the company plane and let Marc tag along. Holtzman raised $1.3 million from Reagan connections, but evidently convinced voters in the 11th District, who had given Reagan only a narrow margin anyway, that he was nothing more than a kind of mascot. Kanjorski just plodded on, returning to the district, serving constituents and, for all of Holtzman's hoopla, raising enough money to spend an entirely respectable $713,000 himself; the Democrat won with 71% of the vote.

This was the first time an incumbent had won since Flood's last victory in 1978; the 1988 election, when Kanjorski was unopposed, was the second. In 1989, he took a seat on the Post Office and Civil Service Committee and immediately became chairman of the Human Resources Subcommittee. He continues to work on local issues, to change the formula to make sure Luzerne County gets homeless assistance and to keep the Pentagon buying lots of anthracite.

The People: Est. Pop. 1986: 505,300, dn. 2.0% 1980–86; Pop. 1980: 515,729, up 2.7% 1970–80. Households (1980): 74% family, 34% with children, 61% married couples; 29.0% housing units rented; median monthly rent: $136; median house value: $30,100. Voting age pop. (1980): 388,822; 1% Black.

1988 Presidential Vote:

Bush (R)	94,061	(52%)
Dukakis (D)	84,893	(47%)

Rep. Paul E. Kanjorski (D)

Elected 1984; b. April 2, 1937, Nanticoke; home, Nanticoke; Temple U., Dickinson U.; Roman Catholic; married (Nancy).

Career: Practicing atty., 1966–85; Nanticoke City Solicitor, 1969–81; Admin. Law Judge, 1971–80.

Offices: 424 CHOB 20515, 202-225-6511. Also 10 E. South St., Wilkes-Barre 18701, 717-825-2200.

Committees: *Banking, Finance and Urban Affairs* (21st of 31 D). Subcommittees: Economic Stabilization; Financial Institutions Supervision, Regulation and Insurance; Housing and Community Development; Policy Research and Insurance. *Post Office and Civil Service* (13th of 15 D). Subcommittee: Human Resources (Chairman).

Group Ratings

	ADA	ACLU	COPE	CFA	LCV	ACU	NTLC	NSI	COC	CEI
1988	70	52	90	82	63	20	13	40	36	18
1987	80	—	87	64	—	4	—	—	13	6

National Journal Ratings

	1988 LIB — 1988 CONS		1987 LIB — 1987 CONS	
Economic	79%	— 17%	73%	— 0%
Social	43%	— 55%	54%	— 45%
Foreign	60%	— 37%	60%	— 40%

Key Votes

1) Homeless $	AGN	5) Ban Drug Test	AGN	9) SDI Research	FOR
2) Gephardt Amdt	FOR	6) Drug Death Pen	FOR	10) Ban Chem Weaps	FOR
3) Deficit Reduc	FOR	7) Handgun Sales	FOR	11) Aid to Contras	AGN
4) Kill Plnt Clsng Notice	AGN	8) Ban D.C. Abort $	FOR	12) Nuclear Testing	FOR

Election Results

1988 general	Paul E. Kanjorski (D), unopposed		($310,305)
1988 primary	Paul E. Kanjorski (D), unopposed		
1986 general	Paul E. Kanjorski (D)................ 112,405	(71%)	($713,740)
	Marc Holtzman (R) 46,785	(29%)	($1,353,170)

TWELFTH DISTRICT

The mountains and hills of western Pennsylvania, eastern Ohio and northern West Virginia, which encircle the Pittsburgh metropolitan area, form the largest industrial section of the country without a major city. The urban focus here is Pittsburgh, though it may be 100 miles away; the economy throughout has been based for years on steel and coal. Once upon a time, up through the 1920s, this was one of the most Republican parts of America, and Republican policies—the high tariff, discouragement of labor unions—were thought to have contributed greatly to steel's growth. Now people in these parts seem to see the Democrats—with their support for unions, for trade restrictions, perhaps for industrial policy—as the only possible savior of steel; and the steel country has been one of the few parts of America where Republican policies have grown more unpopular during the 1980s.

Much of the easternmost part of Pennsylvania's steel country, north of West Virginia and east of Pittsburgh, forms Pennsylvania's 12th Congressional District. It consists of two distinct areas. The largest city in the first is Johnstown, a steel town known best for the disastrous flood which occurred on May 31, 1889, when a dam broke and a 75-foot wall of water half a mile wide swept through the town killing more than 2200 people. The city had 67,000 people in 1920, 35,000 in 1980. This area was first settled by Scots-Irish farmers when it was still the frontier in the 1790s; in the 19th century bituminous coal was discovered here, and immigrants from other parts of Europe were attracted to work the mines and the blast furnaces. The other part of the district, containing about half its population, is almost all of Westmoreland County, just east of Pittsburgh's Allegheny County. Technically, this is a suburban county, which means that many people commute to jobs in Allegheny. Nevertheless, Westmoreland is large—40 miles east to west—and full of separate little industrial communities established on their own long before Pittsburgh's influence reached out this far. Both parts of the district are Democratic in local and congressional elections, and somewhat less reliably so in presidential contests. In the politics of the 1980s, both are liberal on economic and conservative on cultural and foreign issues.

This 12th District is represented by John Murtha, the undisputed power broker of the Pennsylvania and steel country delegations, the chairman of the Defense Appropriations Subcommittee, and the leading example, in a House full of Members air-expressing videotapes and faxing press releases to their districts, of a silent, behind-the-scenes power. Murtha is an old-fashioned Democrat, with no prejudice against supporting big-government programs, but no abstract yearning to do so either; his decisions tend to depend on how it will help areas like the 12th District or on whether it is a *quid* that he can trade for someone else's *quo*. On foreign policy he is strongly hawkish, a supporter of major defense systems and of U.S. aid to the Nicaraguan contras. His rare floor speeches are mostly on foreign policy and sometimes fervent: he was a Marine veteran of the Korean era who reenlisted in his middle thirties to serve in Vietnam, and was the first Vietnam veteran to be elected to the House.

Murtha shuns publicity as almost no 1980s politician does, to the point of refusing to be interviewed by reporters writing a story on him; you will not find him at a fashionable gathering of any kind. He depends on fellow Members, not just national reporters, to transmit his messages; his audience is the House Democratic Caucus, nothing wider, though he will work with Administration lobbyists from time to time; evidently he has enough pride in his own work not to need the praise of others.

In 1989 this anonymity-prizing member ascended to one of the most powerful, and ordinarily one of the most obscure, power positions in the House the chair of the Defense Appropriations Subcommittee. Murtha is not as liberal as Joseph Adabbo, Chairman until his death in April 1986, nor as enamored with high-powered weapons systems as pilot Bill Chappell, Chairman until his defeat in November 1988. As a combat-minded Marine, Murtha focuses especially on the condition of the enlisted man, insisting on maintaining benefits and pay for the rank and file in the military. Pennsylvania has few big military installations or prominent defense contractors for Murtha to protect, as Addabbo looked after aircraft plants in Long Island and Chappell contractors in Florida and others to whom he was linked; and the subcommittee has just a couple of defense policy doves. So Murtha will have considerable leeway, within the limits of the military budget, to advance the causes he believes in.

He seems confident he can win reelection in the 12th District. He first won the district in a 1974 special election to replace a Republican who had died, and he has not had serious Republican competition since; this has become a safe district as the steel country has trended Democratic. His one problem came in 1982, when he was placed in the same district with likeminded Democrat Don Bailey, also a Vietnam veteran; Murtha won 52%–38%, mostly because he had already represented most of the new district. Redistricting could conceivably be a problem for the 1990s, except that it seems unlikely the Pennsylvania legislature would want to jeopardize Murtha's seat. His prospects are for continued reelection and continued power in the House.

The People: Est. Pop. 1986: 499,300, dn. 3.2% 1980–86; Pop. 1980: 515,915, up 4.7% 1970–80. Households (1980): 78% family, 40% with children, 68% married couples; 24.9% housing units rented; median monthly rent: $153; median house value: $38,400. Voting age pop. (1980): 374,878; 1% Black.

1988 Presidential Vote:

Dukakis (D)	96,166	(52%)
Bush (R)	86,183	(47%)

Rep. John P. Murtha (D)

Elected Feb. 5, 1974; b. June 17, 1932, New Martinsville, WV; home, Johnstown; U. of Pittsburgh, B.A. 1962, Indiana U. of PA; Roman Catholic; married (Joyce).

Career: USMC, Vietnam; Owner, Johnstown Minute Car Wash; PA House of Reps., 1969–74.

Offices: 2423 RHOB 20515, 202-225-2065. Also Vine and Walnut Sts., 2d Fl., Center Town Mall, Johnstown 15907, 814-535-2642; P.O. Bldg., 201 N. Center St., Somerset 15501, 814-445-6041; and 206 N. Main St., Greensburg 15601, 412-832-3088.

Committees: *Appropriations* (12th of 35 D). Subcommittees: Defense (Chairman); Interior; Legislative.

Group Ratings

	ADA	ACLU	COPE	CFA	LCV	ACU	NTLC	NSI	COC	CEI
1988	55	70	86	64	38	46	2	100	29	11
1987	60	—	85	71	—	26	—	—	13	9

National Journal Ratings

	1988 LIB — 1988 CONS		1987 LIB — 1987 CONS	
Economic	79% —	17%	73% —	0%
Social	52% —	47%	60% —	39%
Foreign	44% —	56%	44% —	56%

Key Votes

1) Homeless $	AGN	5) Ban Drug Test	AGN	9) SDI Research	AGN
2) Gephardt Amdt	FOR	6) Drug Death Pen	FOR	10) Ban Chem Weaps	AGN
3) Deficit Reduc	FOR	7) Handgun Sales	FOR	11) Aid to Contras	FOR
4) Kill Plnt Clsng Notice	AGN	8) Ban D.C. Abort $	FOR	12) Nuclear Testing	AGN

Election Results

1988 general	John P. Murtha (D), unopposed			($401,945)
1988 primary	John P. Murtha (D), unopposed			
1986 general	John P. Murtha (D)	97,135	(67%)	($272,436)
	Kathy Holtzman (R)	46,937	(33%)	

THIRTEENTH DISTRICT

For most of the 20th century, the Main Line has been a synonym for lush, rich, snobby suburbia. The towns strung out along the Main Line of the old Pennsylvania Railroad today look better than ever, their vast comfortable houses are now coming back into fashion, and their huge overhanging trees are as verdant as ever. On the Main Line and behind it, in suburbs like Gladwyne back toward the Schuylkill River, live most of greater Philadelphia's richest and most influential people. The Main Line forms part, but only part, of the 13th Congressional District of Pennsylvania; in fact, the Main Line past Bryn Mawr is outside the district, in the 7th and 5th, and the greatest growth is in outer Montgomery County. This is nonetheless the highest income district in Pennsylvania and one of the most affluent in the nation. But it has its patches of variety, reflecting an old and varied history.

Out past the Main Line, for example, you come to the old Schuylkill factory towns of Conshohocken and Norristown and then to the shopping mall and high-rise office center at King of Prussia, just short of Valley Forge. On the eastern side of the 13th District are some of Philadelphia's more Jewish suburbs, just north of the city. Farther out in Montgomery County are small towns surrounded now by subdivisions where some of the residents are still members of the old German sects which settled these rolling hills in the 18th century; among their members are Richard Schweiker who was the 13th's congressman for eight years before he was elected to the Senate in 1968 and then served as Secretary of Health and Human Services in the first Reagan term. The 13th also includes two wards in Philadelphia: the old Chestnut Hill neighborhood, a posh area with grass tennis courts, and funkier, more working-class Manayunk, perched on the hills above the Schuylkill River.

The congressman from this district is Lawrence Coughlin, a Republican first elected in 1968, a Yale contemporary of George Bush and graduate of Harvard Business School who, with his ever-present bowtie, looks the picture of comfortable Main Line chic. Coughlin is the fifth-ranking Republican on the Appropriations Committee, a supporter of mass transit spending generally and particularly in Philadelphia. Coughlin has also been a lead sponsor of amendments to prohibit testing the antisatellite weapons connected with the Reagan Administration's Strategic Defense Initiative so long as the Russians don't test theirs. Coughlin is ranking minority member of the Select Committee on Narcotics and oversaw the Drug Abuse Act of 1986. Overall, Coughlin's voting record can be described as conservative on economic issues and mildly liberal on cultural and foreign issues—which probably matches opinion in the district pretty well.

Coughlin had a couple of tough challenges in the 1980s from state legislator Joseph Hoeffel. In 1984, he caught Coughlin unaware and held him to 56% of the vote; in 1986, he ran again, in a somewhat less Republican year, but Coughlin was better prepared and won with 59%. Against weak competition in 1988, Coughlin won 67%—probably more typical of what he can expect in the future.

The People: Est. Pop. 1986: 526,200, up 2.3% 1980–86; Pop. 1980: 514,346, dn. 2.9% 1970–80. Households (1980): 74% family, 34% with children, 62% married couples; 30.9% housing units rented; median monthly rent: $269; median house value: $58,000. Voting age pop. (1980): 392,167; 6% Black, 1% Asian origin, 1% Spanish origin.

1988 Presidential Vote:

Bush (R)	....	135,283	(56%)
Dukakis (D)	....	104,266	(43%)

Rep. Lawrence Coughlin (R)

Elected 1968; b. Apr. 11, 1929, Wilkes-Barre; home, Plymouth Meeting; Yale U., A.B. 1950, Harvard U., M.B.A. 1954, Temple U., LL.B. 1958; Episcopalian; married (Susan).

Career: USMC, Korea; Practicing atty., 1958–69; PA House of Reps., 1965–67; PA Senate, 1967–69.

Offices: 2309 RHOB 20515, 202-225-6111. Also 2 Stony Creek Ofc. Ctr., 151 W. Marshall St., Norristown 19401, 215-277-4040; and 4390 Main St., Philadelphia 19127, 215-482-3672.

Committees: *Appropriations* (5th of 22 R). Subcommittees: Transportation (Ranking Member); VA, HUD and Independent Agencies. *Select Committee on Narcotics Abuse and Control* (Ranking Member of 12 R).

Group Ratings

	ADA	ACLU	COPE	CFA	LCV	ACU	NTLC	NSI	COC	CEI
1988	50	59	37	64	69	48	52	60	79	43
1987	36	—	36	50	—	52	—	—	60	47

National Journal Ratings

	1988 LIB — 1988 CONS		1987 LIB — 1987 CONS	
Economic	30%	— 69%	31%	— 68%
Social	46%	— 54%	45%	— 54%
Foreign	46%	— 53%	45%	— 55%

Key Votes

1) Homeless $	FOR	5) Ban Drug Test	FOR	9) SDI Research	FOR
2) Gephardt Amdt	AGN	6) Drug Death Pen	FOR	10) Ban Chem Weaps	FOR
3) Deficit Reduc	AGN	7) Handgun Sales	AGN	11) Aid to Contras	FOR
4) Kill Plnt Clsng Notice	AGN	8) Ban D.C. Abort $	AGN	12) Nuclear Testing	FOR

Election Results

1988 general	Lawrence Coughlin (R)	152,191	(67%)	($225,412)
	Bernard Tomkin (D)	76,424	(33%)	($60,672)
1988 primary	Lawrence Coughlin (R), unopposed			
1986 general	Lawrence Coughlin (R)	100,701	(59%)	($702,834)
	Joseph M. Hoeffel (D)	71,381	(41%)	($455,101)

FOURTEENTH DISTRICT

Pittsburgh, the center of America's steel industry for more than 100 years, was a strategic site long before that: it was toward Fort Duquesne, where the Allegheny and Monongahela rivers join to form the Ohio, that Braddock's army was headed (with George Washington helping to lead the way) when it was ambushed and defeated in 1754. Not so many years later, trees were felled and a city was carved out of the wilderness here and named after the English statesman Pitt—the first urban center in the American interior. Pittsburgh grew rapidly in those days when most of the nation's commerce moved over water; when traffic switched to railroads, Pittsburgh also did nicely, since they had to run at riverside rather than scale the mountains. Soon Pittsburgh became the leading producer of one commodity the railroads needed, steel. With large deposits of coal nearby and ready access to iron ore from across the Great Lakes, Pittsburgh firmly established itself by 1890 as the nation's leading steel producer.

Fifty years ago Pittsburgh was known for its steel—and its smoke. "The triangle formed by the rivers is packed with smoke-grimed buildings," wrote the *WPA Guide.* "From the manufacturing establishments come clouds of devastating smoke that unite with the river fog to form Pittsburgh's traditional nuisance, 'smog.' Except for the Golden Triangle and a few outlying sections, the city stretches its length and breadth over hills. Dwellings on the South Side and East End heights look down upon mill stacks and skyscrapers. Streams of traffic pour through tunnels, over numerous bridges and along highways skirting cliffs." Today Pittsburgh's air is clear, long since cleaned up by a city government-business-labor partnership. And increasingly, it wants to be known not as the steel city, but as a major white-collar center, a city most of whose jobs are in services, government, research and development; a city whose future is pegged not to a declining industry, but to rising businesses, and as a center for research on robotics, for health care and for computer programming. It has good air service, now that it has become the main hub for USAir. It is even, people are discovering, a pleasant place to live: in 1985, Rand McNally even named it the best place to live in the country.

The 14th Congressional District of Pennsylvania includes all of the city of Pittsburgh plus a few adjacent suburbs. It takes in most of the Pittsburgh area's landmarks: the Golden Triangle; the University of Pittsburgh and its skyscraper campus; Carnegie-Mellon University, a center of artificial intelligence research. Not that many of the Pittsburgh area's steel mills lay in the 14th, but some present and former steelworkers do live here, mostly in ethnic neighborhoods nestled in the Pittsburgh hills. But the 14th also includes some of the metropolitan area's higher income neighborhoods, at a time when they seem to have new vitality: Shadyside, with newly renovated shops near some of Pittsburgh's old mansions, and the predominantly Jewish Squirrel Hill. About 24% of Pittsburgh's residents are black, a smaller figure than in most industrial cities because employment opportunities here peaked before the big wave of black migration from the South. Before the 1930s, in the heyday of Henry Clay Frick and Andrew Mellon, Pittsburgh was a solidly Republican town. Since the New Deal, the 14th District has been solidly Democratic, in every election—and even more strongly in the 1980s.

The congressman from the 14th District, first elected in 1980, is William Coyne. He was an ally of the late Pittsburgh Mayor Richard Caliguiri on the city council, and demonstrated a strong base by beating the son of his predecessor, William Moorhead, in the 1980 Democratic primary by a 65%–35% margin. After the 1984 election, in a campaign managed by the 12th District's Jack Murtha, he won a seat on the Ways and Means Committee, just in time to look after the needs of the steel industry. Legislatively, Coyne has come up with bills to target revenue sharing and low-interest loans for infrastructure to places with high unemployment or business failure rates, and he would require a community impact statement for mergers and would have the FTC deny interest deductibility for those which cost too many jobs in its judgment. He is reelected without difficulty, beating by wide margins in both 1986 and 1988, Richard Caligiuri, a distant cousin of the late mayor.

The People: Est. Pop. 1986: 474,700, dn. 8.1% 1980–86; Pop. 1980: 516,629, dn. 17.6% 1970–80. Households (1980): 63% family, 28% with children, 45% married couples; 47.7% housing units rented; median monthly rent: $174; median house value: $32,500. Voting age pop. (1980): 405,532; 19% Black, 1% Spanish origin, 1% Asian origin.

1988 Presidential Vote:

Dukakis (D)	140,594	(72%)
Bush (R)	51,387	(26%)

Rep. William J. Coyne (D)

Elected 1980; b. Aug. 24, 1936, Pittsburgh; home, Pittsburgh; Robert Morris Col., B.S. 1965; Roman Catholic; single.

Career: Army, Korea; Corporate accountant; PA House of Reps., 1971–72; Pittsburgh City Cncl., 1974–80.

Offices: 2455 RHOB 20515, 202-225-2301. Also 2009 Fed. Bldg., 1000 Liberty Ave., Pittsburgh 15222, 412-644-2870.

Committees: *Ways and Means* (20th of 23 D). Subcommittees: Health; Human Resources.

Group Ratings

	ADA	ACLU	COPE	CFA	LCV	ACU	NTLC	NSI	COC	CEI
1988	95	91	96	73	88	0	5	0	31	9
1987	96	—	96	86	—	0	—	—	7	8

National Journal Ratings

	1988 LIB — 1988 CONS		1987 LIB — 1987 CONS	
Economic	87%	— 8%	73%	— 0%
Social	86%	— 0%	78%	— 0%
Foreign	79%	— 21%	81%	— 0%

Key Votes

1) Homeless $	AGN	5) Ban Drug Test	AGN	9) SDI Research	AGN
2) Gephardt Amdt	FOR	6) Drug Death Pen	AGN	10) Ban Chem Weaps	FOR
3) Deficit Reduc	FOR	7) Handgun Sales	AGN	11) Aid to Contras	AGN
4) Kill Plnt Clsng Notice	AGN	8) Ban D.C. Abort $	AGN	12) Nuclear Testing	FOR

Election Results

1988 general	William J. Coyne (D)	135,181	(79%)	($80,730)
	Richard E. Caligiuri (R)	36,719	(21%)	
1988 primary	William J. Coyne (D), unopposed			
1986 general	William J. Coyne (D)	104,726	(90%)	($60,903)
	Richard E. Caligiuri (LIB)	6,058	(5%)	
	Mark Weddleton (SW)	3,120	(3%)	

FIFTEENTH DISTRICT

Tucked in among the rolling hills of eastern Pennsylvania, little known to the rest of America, is the Lehigh Valley, long one of America's original heavy industrial areas, now apparently on its way to becoming something else. Much of the Valley was settled by Pennsylvania Dutch, notably the Moravian sect who founded Bethlehem in 1741 (they are the same people who started the Salem of Winston-Salem, North Carolina); a farm area in the early 1800s, its dependable labor force and its location on a river emptying into the Delaware made it a natural location for early industries. As recently as the early 1980s, the Lehigh Valley was the source of some of America's best-known products: Easton produced Crayola crayons and Dixie cups,

Allentown was the home of the Mack Truck factory, and Bethlehem was the home base of the number two steelmaker, Bethlehem Steel. By early 1987, the Valley was still producing crayons and cups, but Mack Truck had moved one plant to Winnsboro, South Carolina. Meanwhile, Bethlehem's furnaces were mostly cold and the company for several years tottered on the brink of bankruptcy.

Yet the Lehigh Valley does not seem to be sinking into permanent decrepitude. It retains important appliance factories, cement operations and a big AT&T facility in Allentown. The completion of Interstate 78 across New Jersey means that the Lehigh Valley is just one and a half hours straight west from New York City. Its lower cost of living is attracting new residents, and its low wage costs have inspired insurance companies to move some of their office jobs here. New office buildings and shopping centers are springing up. Together with a small portion of an adjacent rural county, the Lehigh Valley forms Pennsylvania's 15th Congressional District. Once solidly Democratic, it has elected a Republican congressman for a decade and voted in 1988 for George Bush over Michael Dukakis.

That political change and the evident economic growth here are both vindications of the political views of the 15th District's unusual congressman, Republican Don Ritter. He is unusual in Congress because he is an engineer, and because he spent a year in the Soviet Union and speaks Russian. He is unusual for Pennsylvania industrial districts because he is a devotee of free-market economics, with little interest in wooing union leaders or suburban liberals. He is unusual among market-oriented conservative Republicans, because he seems to have a flair for politics which has translated consistently into winning margins in this district. Ritter does fall away from the free-market crowd on trade issues. But otherwise he has preached the gospel that free enterprise will provide jobs and economic growth better than government can, and he and his constituents have seen it happen, evidently, in the Lehigh Valley.

Ritter serves on the Energy and Commerce Committee, perhaps the single most important committee when it comes to government regulation of business. In general, he supports deregulation and relaxation of rigid government regulations, as on clean air. He is on the Science, Space and Technology Committee and is ranking Republican on the Investigations and Oversight Subcommittee. His record on cultural and foreign issues, as well as economics, is solidly conservative. He is an especially strong—and well-informed—critic of Soviet internal repression. He is proud of having gotten the Lehigh & Delaware Canals declared a National Heritage Corridor, and he is co-chair of the High Definition Television Task Force. He is interested in helping the families of victims who died in the December 1988 bombing of Pan Am flight 103, and would like to see a joint congressional investigation.

Ritter has perhaps been fortunate in his opposition. He won the seat in 1978 by upsetting Democrat Fred Rooney, who had not been spending much time in the district; Ritter's family still lives there, and he returns every weekend. In 1980 Ritter beat 65-year-old state Senator Jeanette Reibman; in 1988 he defeated Reibman's son by the same 57%–43% margin by which he won in 1986. Some incumbents would regard that as uncomfortably close; Ritter, with his sense of where the economy is going nationally and in the Lehigh Valley, probably regards it as satisfactory.

The People: Est. Pop. 1986: 537,900, up 4.4% 1980–86; Pop. 1980: 515,259, up 7.7% 1970–80. Households (1980): 75% family, 37% with children, 64% married couples; 28.8% housing units rented; median monthly rent: $189; median house value: $44,600. Voting age pop. (1980): 385,814; 2% Spanish origin, 1% Black.

1988 Presidential Vote:

Bush (R)	103,803	(55%)
Dukakis (D)	84,625	(44%)

Rep. Donald L. (Don) Ritter (R)

Elected 1978; b. Oct. 21, 1940, New York, NY; home, Coopersburg; Lehigh U., B.S. 1961, M.I.T., M.S. 1963, Sc.D. 1966; Unitarian; married (Edith).

Career: Scientific Exchange Fellow, Moscow, USSR, 1967–68; Asst. Prof., CA St. Poly. U., 1968–69; Prof., Asst. to Vice Pres. for Research, Lehigh U., 1969–76; Mgr., Res. Devel. Prog., Lehigh U., 1976–79.

Offices: 2447 RHOB 20515, 202-225-6411. Also 2 Bethlehem Plaza, Ste. 300, Bethlehem 18018, 215-866-0916; 1444 Hamilton St., Hotel Traylor, Ste. 206, Allentown 18102, 215-439-8861; and Alpha Bldg., Rm. 705, Easton 18042, 215-258-8383.

Committees: *Energy and Commerce* (8th of 17 R). Subcommittees: Commerce, Consumer Protection and Competitiveness (Ranking Member); Telecommunications and Finance. *Science, Space and Technology* (6th of 19 R). Subcommittees: Investigations and Oversight (Ranking Member); Science, Research and Technology.

Group Ratings

	ADA	ACLU	COPE	CFA	LCV	ACU	NTLC	NSI	COC	CEI
1988	10	27	37	55	31	84	66	100	77	54
1987	20	—	34	29	—	64	—	—	73	62

National Journal Ratings

	1988 LIB — 1988 CONS	1987 LIB — 1987 CONS
Economic	35% — 64%	31% — 68%
Social	17% — 83%	27% — 72%
Foreign	16% — 78%	0% — 80%

Key Votes

1) Homeless $	FOR	5) Ban Drug Test	FOR	9) SDI Research	FOR
2) Gephardt Amdt	FOR	6) Drug Death Pen	FOR	10) Ban Chem Weaps	AGN
3) Deficit Reduc	AGN	7) Handgun Sales	FOR	11) Aid to Contras	FOR
4) Kill Plnt Clsng Notice	AGN	8) Ban D.C. Abort $	FOR	12) Nuclear Testing	AGN

Election Results

1988 general	Donald L. (Don) Ritter (R)	106,951	(57%)	($752,332)
	Ed Reibman (D)	79,127	(43%)	($355,016)
1988 primary	Donald L. (Don) Ritter (R), unopposed			
1986 general	Donald L. (Don) Ritter (R)	74,829	(57%)	($440,370)
	Joe Simonetta (D)	56,972	(43%)	($51,639)

SIXTEENTH DISTRICT

One part of America that has not changed much in half a century is where the Plain People live in Pennsylvania Dutch country. Tourists—more of them these days—can still see Amish families clad in black, clattering over the back roads in horse-drawn carriages, scrupulously tended farms set amid rolling hills, barns decorated with hex signs. The Pennsylvania Dutch are actually German in origin ("Dutch" comes from Deutsch), descended from members of Amish, Mennonite and other pietistic sects who left the principalities of 18th-century Germany for the religious freedom of the Quaker-dominated colony of Pennsylvania. The Quakers were happy to welcome the Germans, but not so eager to have them in Philadelphia. So they were sent to Germantown, a few miles away, until they could move out to what was then the frontier, where they could protect the pacifist Quakers against the Indians. Thus the Dutch came to the rolling green hills of the part of Pennsylvania centered on Lancaster County. The land was naturally fertile, and careful cultivation by the Dutch increased its productivity. Today the small farms in Lancaster County continue to produce some of the highest per-acre yields on earth.

There is no sign in the Pennsylvania Dutch country of the farm crises you hear about on the Great Plains. Farms here are small, equipment simple, chemical fertilizer use very limited, cultivation intensive, with all the children in the usually large Amish families pitching in. The commercial ethos of farming on the prairies and Great Plains has always been tempered here by communal values and family responsibility. In the Sun Belt and on the Great Plains, Americans seek the reassurance of cultural continuity in the midst of the economic change inevitably produced by market capitalism. In the Pennsylvania Dutch country, cultural continuity is a fact and helps to sustain what other Americans might regard as an unduly modest standard of living. Most of the Pennsylvania Dutch, it should be added, are not plain people. But the heritage is important: most people here are of German descent and have a strong work ethic. Small industries have settled in the Lancaster area because of the skills and work habits of the labor force, and agriculture continues to be important economically. The brick townhouses of Lancaster, like the frame farmhouses of the Amish, are sparklingly well kept and seem little different from what they must have looked like 50 years ago.

The 16th Congressional District of Pennsylvania includes almost all of Lancaster County, mostly Dutch Lebanon County to the north and part of Chester County to the east. Of all eastern congressional districts, it consistently casts the highest Republican percentages in presidential elections. For years the Pennsylvania Dutch area was represented by Republican congressmen who were as languid in their demeanor as they were conservative on substantive issues.

The current incumbent, Robert Walker, is different. He is fully as conservative as any Republican—and eager to proclaim himself so. He is one of the leaders of the group of young Republicans who took advantage of the "special orders" procedure, which allows speechmaking after the legislative business of the day is completed, to present on the C-SPAN cable network—which broadcasts congressional proceedings—extensive denunciations of all things Democratic—and he was the one caught at the podium, gesturing and asking rhetorical questions, when Speaker Tip O'Neill ordered the C-SPAN cameras to show that the Republicans were speaking to an empty House. But Walker and his allies have surely had the last laugh. They have found a forum in which to attract attention for their cases, substantive and procedural, against the Democrats, and they have goaded the majority into acting in an overbearing manner that suggests they are abridging the minority's rights. And they have moved their Republican colleagues to challenge the Democratic majority more aggressively, on issues and procedure in the House and in elections back home—as symbolized by the election of Walker's ally Newt Gingrich as House Republican whip, and his own appointment as chief deputy whip, in March 1989.

Walker has another forum these days: he is ranking Republican on the Science, Space and Technology Committee. Under Chairman Robert Roe this is not a terribly partisan body, and Walker has distinguished himself by pushing for an expanded space program and, with Bill Nelson who represents Cape Canaveral, he resuscitated the National Space Council over Administration opposition headed by the Vice President. Walker also prides himself as the House Member who has offered the most successful floor amendments in the 99th and 100th Congress; 38 of the 63 he proposed were adopted. The most famous—or notorious—of these is his "Drug-free Workplace" amendment, offered when Members were desperate to be seen doing something to fight drugs. Opponents ridiculed Walker's proposal, arguing that it is impossible for the government to police the workplaces of every contractor and that it would be onerous and often harmful to the government to cancel the contract of an employer one of whose employees, despite its precautions and against its wishes, used drugs on the job. This led to all sorts of amendments to the amendment. But even if most Members thought Walker's amendment was a cheap shot, they voted for it.

Few people would have predicted such an influential career for Walker, who is gifted neither with the intellectual adventurousness of Gingrich or the oratorical virtuosity of Michel. He is, however, a hard worker, a plugger, a believer and one whose views are thought through rather than reflexive: he was one of those conservatives who, for example, rather than defending South Africa in late 1984 and early 1985, organized a letter of protest to its government. Many of Walker's Republican allies represent marginal or iffy districts, or have run for statewide office. Walker's seat is safe as safe can be, and no one has noted yet the glint of senatorial or gubernatorial ambition in his eye.

The People: Est. Pop. 1986: 550,700, up 7.0% 1980–86; Pop. 1980: 514,585, up 12.9% 1970–80. Households (1980): 77% family, 41% with children, 67% married couples; 30.4% housing units rented; median monthly rent: $179; median house value: $46,400. Voting age pop. (1980): 369,823; 2% Black, 2% Spanish origin.

1988 Presidential Vote:

Bush (R)	132,402	(69%)
Dukakis (D)	57,214	(30%)

Rep. Robert S. Walker (R)

Elected 1976; b. Dec. 23, 1942, Bradford; home, East Petersburg; Millersville U., B.S. 1964, U. of DE, M.A. 1968; Presbyterian; married (Sue).

Career: Teacher, 1964–67; A. A. to U.S. Rep. Edwin D. Eshleman, 1967–77.

Offices: 2445 RHOB 20515, 202-225-2411. Also Lancaster Cnty. Crthse., 50 N. Duke St., Lancaster 17603, 717-393-0666; 307 Municipal Bldg., 400 S. 8th St., Lebanon 17402, 717-274-1641; and P.O. Box 69, Cochranville 19330, 215-593-2155.

Committees: *Science, Space and Technology* (Ranking Member of 19 R).

Group Ratings

	ADA	ACLU	COPE	CFA	LCV	ACU	NTLC	NSI	COC	CEI
1988	5	13	14	27	50	100	89	100	93	86
1987	4	—	15	7	—	96	—	—	87	88

National Journal Ratings

	1988 LIB — 1988 CONS		1987 LIB — 1987 CONS	
Economic	0% —	93%	0% —	89%
Social	13% —	84%	10% —	85%
Foreign	0% —	84%	0% —	80%

Key Votes

1) Homeless $	FOR	5) Ban Drug Test	FOR	9) SDI Research	FOR
2) Gephardt Amdt	AGN	6) Drug Death Pen	FOR	10) Ban Chem Weaps	AGN
3) Deficit Reduc	AGN	7) Handgun Sales	FOR	11) Aid to Contras	FOR
4) Kill Plnt Clsng Notice	FOR	8) Ban D.C. Abort $	FOR	12) Nuclear Testing	AGN

Election Results

1988 general	Robert S. Walker (R)	136,944	(74%)	($91,950)
	Ernest E. Guyll (D)	48,169	(26%)	
1988 primary	Robert S. Walker (R), unopposed			
1986 general	Robert S. Walker (R)	100,784	(75%)	($75,730)
	James D. Hagelgans (D)	34,399	(25%)	

SEVENTEENTH DISTRICT

The Susquehanna is one of America's largest, and yet most obscure rivers—the longest river in the East, if you include the Chesapeake Bay, which is really the flooded lower Susquehanna valley. The Susquehanna is the one river strong enough to break through the mountain chains that run, like rugged corduroy, through central Pennsylvania. But few songs are written to celebrate the Susquehanna, it occupies nothing like the place of the Hudson or even the Schuylkill in our art, it has not given a name to a fever (Potomac), a school of painting (Hudson) or economics (Charles), or to a state (Ohio, Mississippi, Alabama, Missouri, Colorado).

The 17th Congressional District of Pennsylvania is a string of counties along the Susquehanna River, from Harrisburg in the south to Williamsport, up almost to the New York state border in the north. Cut diagonally by dozens of mountain ridges, the 17th includes several very different areas. About half its population is in and around the state capital of Harrisburg, an old city with a declining population and a large black community, not far upstream from the Three Mile Island nuclear plant. Several hours' drive north is Williamsport, a small manufacturing town that hosts the Little League World Series and has been the home for years of *Grit*, the world's largest family weekly newspaper. In the middle of the district, on the east shore of the Susquehanna, is Northumberland County, a onetime anthracite mining area. On the west shore are three counties reaching inland between the mountain chains, containing small manufacturing firms and such diverse institutions as Bucknell University and the cushiest of federal penitentiaries, Allenwood.

In most elections, this is a solidly Republican district. Harrisburg seems to retain, from the 1860–1930 era of Republican dominance in Pennsylvania, a Republican preference that survives all ethnic and racial change; Williamsport is quintessential Republican country. Northumberland is sometimes Democratic, but the west shore counties are among the most Republican in the nation; two of the three went for Barry Goldwater in 1964. The district did elect a Democratic congressman, Allan Ertel, in 1976, 1978 and 1980; he went on to close defeats in the 1982 race for governor and 1984 race for attorney general.

The congressman now is Republican George Gekas, former state senator from Harrisburg who helped to design the district boundaries and, when Ertel ran for governor, won the primary with 60% and the general election with 58%. Gekas specialized in crime legislation as a member of the Pennsylvania legislature, and is proud of sponsoring the state's mandatory sentencing and child abuse laws. In the House he is ranking Republican on the Judiciary Subcommittee on Criminal Justice, where he has led the governments impeachment proceedings against U.S. District Judge Alcee L. Hastings. Since his second term, Gekas has been heavily involved in the antidrug package, and he called for the death penalty against those who commit murder in the course of a drug felony. His brand of politics seems very popular along the Susquehanna, and he has been reelected twice by overwhelming margins.

The People: Est. Pop. 1986: 525,700, up 1.9% 1980–86; Pop. 1980: 515,900, up 7.2% 1970–80. Households (1980): 74% family, 38% with children, 62% married couples; 31.4% housing units rented; median monthly rent: $164; median house value: $37,800. Voting age pop. (1980): 376,440; 6% Black, 1% Spanish origin.

1988 Presidential Vote: Bush (R) 112,911   (63%)
Dukakis (D) 64,505   (36%)

Rep. George W. Gekas (R)

Elected 1982; b. April 14, 1930, Harrisburg; home, Harrisburg; Dickinson Col., B.A. 1952, Dickinson Law Sch., J.D. 1958; Greek Orthodox; married (Evangeline).

Career: Asst. Dist. Atty., Dauphin Cnty., 1960–66; PA House of Reps., 1967–75; PA Senate, 1977–83.

Offices: 1519 LHOB 20515, 202-225-4315. Also 1 Riverside Ofc. Ctr., Ste. 301, 2101 N. Front St., Harrisburg 17110, 717-232-5123; Herman Schneebeli Fed. Bldg., P.O. Box 606, Williamsport 17703, 717-327-8161; and R.D. 5, Box 198, Ste. L, Selinsgrove 17870, 717-743-1575.

Committees: *Judiciary* (6th of 14 R). Subcommittees: Crime; Criminal Justice (Ranking Member).

Group Ratings

	ADA	ACLU	COPE	CFA	LCV	ACU	NTLC	NSI	COC	CEI
1988	10	26	20	27	50	92	76	100	93	76
1987	8	—	19	36	—	83	—	—	87	66

National Journal Ratings

	1988 LIB — 1988 CONS		1987 LIB — 1987 CONS	
Economic	0%	— 93%	0%	— 89%
Social	13%	— 84%	30%	— 69%
Foreign	16%	— 78%	0%	— 80%

Key Votes

1) Homeless $	FOR	5) Ban Drug Test	FOR	9) SDI Research	FOR
2) Gephardt Amdt	AGN	6) Drug Death Pen	FOR	10) Ban Chem Weaps	AGN
3) Deficit Reduc	AGN	7) Handgun Sales	FOR	11) Aid to Contras	FOR
4) Kill Plnt Clsng Notice	FOR	8) Ban D.C. Abort $	AGN	12) Nuclear Testing	AGN

Election Results

1988 general	George W. Gekas (R)	166,289	(100%)	($97,611)
1988 primary	George W. Gekas (R), unopposed			
1986 general	George W. Gekas (R)	101,027	(74%)	($90,963)
	Michael S. Ogden (D)	36,157	(26%)	($3,335)

EIGHTEENTH DISTRICT

Surrounding Pittsburgh like a thick but irregularly shaped doughnut with one bite taken out of it is the 18th Congressional District of Pennsylvania. The Republican legislature packed into this single seat just about all the strong Republican suburbs it could find, and connected them using as few Democratic areas as possible. So within the 18th you will find the residences of most of Pittsburgh's elite, in leafy, secluded suburbs like Fox Chapel and Sewickley. The district also includes solid high income, but not elite, suburbs like Mount Lebanon and Upper St. Clair Township, south of the Golden Triangle. But when you go down to the flood plain or over the next hill from these places, you run into much more modest suburban territory, from pleasant 1950s tract housing to gritty little factory towns built in a hurry 80 or 100 years ago.

This makes the 18th District a mixed bag politically—the most Republican constituency possible in metropolitan Pittsburgh, but still not Republican by any margin in most races. It elected John Heinz to Congress in 1972 and 1974, but when he ran for the Senate in 1976, the 18th elected Democrat Doug Walgren and has reelected him ever since. Walgren has had some luck: he had weak opponents in his first election and in the 1980 and 1984 presidential years.

Walgren is blessed with committee assignments which did not look interesting when he got them, but do now. He has a seat on the Science, Space and Technology Committee and chairs a subcommittee on Science, Research and Technology at just the time when voters want more and better research—and nowhere more so than in the Pittsburgh area, where Walgren can argue that he has bills to spur steel technology, make Pittsburgh the nation's supercomputer center, invest in clean coal technology, and promote cogeneration from coal. He has increased funding of the National Science Foundation and sponsored a Computer Security Act to protect information in civilian computer databases. He has pushed to give inventors more patent rights and to have Japanese technical literature translated. He also sits on the Energy and Commerce Committee—the most sought-after committee assignment in the 1980s, because it covers so much federal regulatory law. On this body he has been less active. Walgren is a bit out of place in the Pennsylvania delegation, a bit less liberal on economics and more so on non-economic issues than most of his colleagues; he voted for Gramm-Rudman, supported John Glenn for President in 1984 and was the only Pennsylvanian not to back the measure that allowed William Gray to win the Budget chairmanship.

Walgren's visibility on the technology issues increased greatly in the middle 1980's, just in time for the 1986 election, in which he faced a well-financed challenge from businessman Ernie Buckman. With this new record he could point to, and a voting record well-tailored to the most affluent part of the steel belt, Walgren won reelection with 63% of the vote. He got the same 63% in 1988, as he once again drew weak opposition in the presidential year.

The People: Est. Pop. 1986: 503,100, dn. 2.5% 1980–86; Pop. 1980: 516,050, dn. 0.8% 1970–80. Households (1980): 78% family, 38% with children, 68% married couples; 24.2% housing units rented; median monthly rent: $237; median house value: $57,300. Voting age pop. (1980): 382,408; 2% Black, 1% Asian origin.

1988 Presidential Vote:

Bush (R)	....	123,583	(53%)
Dukakis (D)	....	106,535	(46%)

Rep. Douglas (Doug) Walgren (D)

Elected 1976; b. Dec. 28, 1940, Rochester, NY; home, Mt. Lebanon; Dartmouth Col., B.A. 1963, Stanford U., LL.B. 1966; Roman Catholic; married (Carmala).

Career: Staff atty., Neighborhood Legal Svcs., 1967–68; Asst. Solicitor, Allegheny Cnty., 1967–69; Practicing atty., 1969–72; Corp. Cnsl., Behavioral Research Lab., 1973–75.

Offices: 2441 RHOB 20515, 202-225-2135. Also 2117 Fed. Bldg., 1000 Liberty Ave., Pittsburgh 15222, 412-391-4016.

Committees: *Energy and Commerce* (8th of 26 D). Subcommittees: Energy and Power; Health and the Environment; Oversight and Investigations. *Science, Space and Technology* (5th of 30 D). Subcommittees: Energy Research and Development; Science, Research and Technology (Chairman).

Group Ratings

	ADA	ACLU	COPE	CFA	LCV	ACU	NTLC	NSI	COC	CEI
1988	90	77	85	91	81	4	15	0	25	17
1987	92	—	84	86	—	0	—	—	13	6

National Journal Ratings

	1988 LIB — 1988 CONS		1987 LIB — 1987 CONS	
Economic	79%	— 17%	73%	— 0%
Social	68%	— 31%	72%	— 27%
Foreign	84%	— 0%	81%	— 0%

Key Votes

1) Homeless $	AGN	5) Ban Drug Test	AGN	9) SDI Research	AGN
2) Gephardt Amdt	FOR	6) Drug Death Pen	FOR	10) Ban Chem Weaps	FOR
3) Deficit Reduc	FOR	7) Handgun Sales	AGN	11) Aid to Contras	AGN
4) Kill Plnt Clsng Notice	AGN	8) Ban D.C. Abort $	AGN	12) Nuclear Testing	FOR

Election Results

1988 general	Douglas (Doug) Walgren (D)	136,924	(63%)	($321,074)
	John A. Newman (R)	80,975	(37%)	($16,349)
1988 primary	Douglas (Doug) Walgren (D), unopposed			
1986 general	Douglas (Doug) Walgren (D)	104,164	(63%)	($557,031)
	Ernie Buckman (R).	61,164	(37%)	($983,798)

NINETEENTH DISTRICT

The rolling green farmland of southern Pennsylvania, just west of the Pennsylvania Dutch country and southwest of the state capital of Harrisburg and running up to the base of the first Appalachian chains, makes up the 19th Congressional District of Pennsylvania. The most famous part of this district, Gettysburg—the tourist-thronged site of the Civil War's northernmost battle—is also the most sparsely populated, at least by permanent residents. Outside the town is the retirement home of President Eisenhower, who was of Pennsylvania Dutch stock himself; his father migrated in the late 19th century with a group of Mennonite brethren out into Kansas and Texas.

The largest city here is York, which from September 1777 to June 1778 was the capital of the young nation. When the Continental Congress met at York, it passed the Articles of Confederation, received word from Benjamin Franklin in Paris that the French would help with money and ships, and issued the first proclamation calling for a national day of thanksgiving. The other large population center of the 19th District encompasses the west shore suburbs of Harrisburg, opposite the state capital on the other side of the Susquehanna River. During the past two decades, the west shore has absorbed a considerable white flight away from Harrisburg and has been growing more Republican. Farther west is the town of Carlisle, home of Dickinson College, one of the nation's oldest, and the Army's Carlisle Barracks.

York, for some years, was more Democratic than other Pennsylvania Dutch areas, and this district was hotly contested by the two major parties; Democrats actually won it in 1954, 1958 and 1964. Except for two years, it has been held by members of the Goodling family since 1961. The current congressman, William Goodling, started off as one of the most conservative members of the Pennsylvania delegation after he was first elected in 1974. But in the ensuing years, Goodling, who was a teacher and principal, has risen to be ranking Republican on the Education and Labor Committee and has supported, sometimes vehemently, education and school lunch programs slated for extinction or cuts by the Reagan Administration. He worked closely with the late Chairman Carl Perkins to save Chapters 1 and 2 of the Education and Consolidation Improvement Act from inclusion in block grants to the states; he worked with current Chairman Augustus Hawkins on a bipartisan reauthorization of the act, with a new Even Start plan to attack illiteracy among adults as well as children. He has gotten through initiatives on technical assistance centers for teachers, vocational education and the Talented Teacher Act; with the practical sense of a teacher, he pushed a policy that children be offered different foods but not served what they won't eat. For the 101st Congress he sponsored the Bush Administration bill on the minimum wage, and he wants to look at vocational education, child nutrition and the Job Training Partnership Act.

He serves also on the Budget Committee, where he watches education spending; this is one Republican who believes in concentrating on his committee agendas and working with colleagues of both parties to shape legislation. He rotated off Intelligence after one term, dissatisfied with the CIA's mining of the Nicaraguan harbors. He does have one other cause, which now seems lost: he wants the Census Bureau not to count illegal aliens, so that states like Pennsylvania which have very few will do better when House districts are reapportioned among the states. Goodling himself is likely to face no problems from redistricting or from the voters.

The People Est. Pop. 1986: 541,800, up 4.9% 1980–86; Pop. 1980: 516,605, up 14.4% 1970–80. Households (1980): 77% family, 40% with children, 67% married couples; 26.9% housing units rented; median monthly rent: $180; median house value: $46,500. Voting age pop. (1980): 376,801; 2% Black, 1% Spanish origin.

1988 Presidential Vote:

Bush (R)	125,523	(65%)
Dukakis (D)	65,656	(34%)

Rep. William F. (Bill) Goodling (R)

Elected 1974; b. Dec. 5, 1927, Loganville; home, Jacobus; U. of MD, B.S. 1953, Western MD Col., M.Ed. 1957; United Methodist; married (Hilda).

Career: Army, 1946–48; Pub. sch. teacher and admin., 1952–74; Pres., Dallastown Sch. Bd., 1966–67.

Offices: 2263 RHOB 20515, 202-225-5836. Also Fed. Bldg., 200 S. George St., York 17405, 717-843-8887; 212 N. Hanover St., Carlisle 17013, 717-243-5432; 140 Baltimore St., Gettysburg 17325, 717-334-3430; 2020 Yale Ave., Camp Hill 17011, 717-763-1988; and 44 Frederick St., Hanover 17331, 717-632-7855, 800-631-1811.

Committees: *Budget* (3d of 14 R). Task Forces: Community Development and Natural Resources; Human Resources (Ranking Member). *Education and Labor* (Ranking Member of 13 R). Subcommittees: Elementary, Secondary, and Vocational Education (Ranking Member); Health and Safety; Postsecondary Education.

Group Ratings

	ADA	ACLU	COPE	CFA	LCV	ACU	NTLC	NSI	COC	CEI
1988	30	35	27	55	44	63	64	80	93	38
1987	24	—	26	43	—	48	—	—	80	60

National Journal Ratings

	1988 LIB — 1988 CONS	1987 LIB — 1987 CONS
Economic	27% — 72%	29% — 69%
Social	35% — 65%	25% — 73%
Foreign	30% — 67%	44% — 56%

Key Votes

1) Homeless $	FOR	5) Ban Drug Test	FOR	9) SDI Research	FOR
2) Gephardt Amdt	AGN	6) Drug Death Pen	AGN	10) Ban Chem Weaps	FOR
3) Deficit Reduc	AGN	7) Handgun Sales	FOR	11) Aid to Contras	FOR
4) Kill Plnt Clsng Notice	FOR	8) Ban D.C. Abort $	FOR	12) Nuclear Testing	AGN

Election Results

1988 general	William F. (Bill) Goodling (R)	145,381	(77%)	($57,091)
	Paul E. Ritchey (D)	42,819	(23%)	($2,358)
1988 primary	William F. (Bill) Goodling (R), unopposed			
1986 general	William F. (Bill) Goodling (R)	100,055	(73%)	($49,648)
	Richard F. Thornton (D)...............	37,223	(27%)	($19,535)

TWENTIETH DISTRICT

The Mon Valley today is a monument to the headiest days of American heavy manufacturing—and a clear indication that they are over. Fifty years ago the *WPA Guide* noted that "the river banks bristle with factories, principally steel and glass, and workers' villages huddle around the gigantic plants." The Monongahela—the shortened version is increasingly in formal use—winds through steep Pennsylvania hills north from West Virginia, and on the flat lands along its sweeping curves are built the steel mills, coke furnaces, and glass factories almost all the way to Pittsburgh. The working-class towns or neighborhoods were built on higher land nearby, where frame houses were crowded into narrow streets and almost piled one on top of another. Then, over the next hill, an entirely different, white-collar community might develop, connected to the city by entirely different streets. The working class towns started losing population 50 years ago, as sons and daughters in these numerous families were able to move to more pleasant suburbs; Braddock, on the site where the British general fought and died in 1754, had 21,000 people in 1920 and 11,000 in 1980. Then, as the steel industry collapsed and mills were shut down, the number of steel jobs in the Mon Valley dropped by 58,000 from 1979 to 1985. In these tiny towns, where row houses cling to the hillside, places once prosperous due to high steel wages are now seeing most of their residents on unemployment or moving out. Ministers have barricaded themselves in their churches, preaching against the executives of the big companies—actually against the economies that no longer need the high-price steel produced by the high-wage, high-skill workers that used to man these steel mills, that now sit cold and black, brooding and unavoidable presences beside the rivers on which all the houses look down.

This is the land of the 20th Congressional District of Pennsylvania, most of whose residents are strung out in the towns along the Monongahela. There is a similar population concentration to the north, on the Allegheny. Connecting them are modest working-class suburbs, interspersed with a few of higher status, just outside of Pittsburgh itself. Almost all of this district is heavily Democratic. It is populated by people of almost every ethnic background; the politics of Franklin D. Roosevelt not only gave them hope of economic recovery, but assured them that they were included and valued in America. They turned from their longtime Republican voting habits to support FDR, and their Democratic allegiance was cemented in the struggle over unionization that made the United Steelworkers the major economic force here for years. That Democratic allegiance is sometimes strained by the party's cultural liberalism; this is a place where the population is old and the old patterns remain very much the rule. But in the 1980s, this has been one of the most solidly Democratic parts of the country in presidential as well as House elections.

The 20th District's congressman is Joseph Gaydos, a former state senator and attorney for United Mine Workers District 5. He had Democratic organization and union backing when he first won the seat in 1968; in Washington, he has been a reliable vote for organized labor and, usually, the Democratic leadership. There is no doubt where his loyalties lie as a member of the Education and Labor Committee. He has chaired the Subcommittee on Health and Safety, which has had jurisdiction over the Occupational Safety and Health Administration, since 1977. During that time, there have been all manner of controversies over OSHA; the burden of regulations was reduced by Jimmy Carter's commissioner as well as Ronald Reagan's. Gaydos has seen his job as defending the agency from attack and preventing any relaxation of enforcement. Cost-cutting here, as he argues, can cost lives. Gaydos introduced a bill to establish safeguards for workers exposed to toxic substances in high-risk jobs. He also wants to resurrect the Civilian Conservation Corps of the 1930s to provide a workforce for improvement projects on public lands.

By all odds Gaydos should have a safe seat. But politics along the Monongahela can be turbulent; he won primaries in 1982 and 1984 with 67% and 73%—not quite the unanimous support some congressmen get. In general elections he is reelected overwhelmingly. The serious threat to him is the redistricting that will follow the 1990 Census. The steel towns have been losing population rapidly, and the 20th District, elongated in shape and sandwiched between other Democratic districts, could easily be sliced up, putting him in a primary battle with another incumbent.

The People: Est. Pop. 1986: 490,900, dn. 4.9% 1980–86; Pop. 1980: 516,028, dn. 8.0% 1970–80. Households (1980): 76% family, 35% with children, 62% married couples; 28.9% housing units rented; median monthly rent: $157; median house value: $37,800. Voting age pop. (1980): 390,171; 5% Black.

1988 Presidential Vote:

Dukakis (D)......................	125,909	(65%)
Bush (R)	67,172	(34%)

Rep. Joseph M. Gaydos (D)

Elected 1968; b. July 3, 1926, Braddock; home, McKeesport; Duquesne U., U. of Notre Dame, LL.B. 1951; Roman Catholic; married (Alice).

Career: Navy, WWII; Dpty. Atty. Gen. of PA; Asst. Allegheny Cnty. Solicitor; Gen. Cnsl., United Mine Workers of Amer., Dist. 5; PA Senate, 1967–68.

Offices: 2186 RHOB 20515, 202-225-4631. Also 318 5th Ave., McKeesport 15132, 412-673-7756; and Crown Bldg., 979 4th Ave., Rm. 217, New Kensington 15068, 412-339-7070.

Committees: *Education and Labor* (3d of 22 D). Subcommittees: Health and Safety (Chairman); Postsecondary Education. *House Administration* (2d of 13 D). Subcommittees: Accounts (Chairman); Personnel and Police. *Standards of Official Conduct* (5th of 6 D). *Joint Committee on Printing.*

Group Ratings

	ADA	ACLU	COPE	CFA	LCV	ACU	NTLC	NSI	COC	CEI
1988	65	57	91	73	44	24	6	60	25	10
1987	64	—	90	64	—	9	—	—	27	8

National Journal Ratings

	1988 LIB — 1988 CONS		1987 LIB — 1987 CONS	
Economic	78% —	21%	73% —	0%
Social	46% —	53%	56% —	43%
Foreign	54% —	45%	50% —	50%

Key Votes

1) Homeless $	AGN	5) Ban Drug Test	AGN	9) SDI Research	FOR
2) Gephardt Amdt	FOR	6) Drug Death Pen	FOR	10) Ban Chem Weaps	AGN
3) Deficit Reduc	FOR	7) Handgun Sales	FOR	11) Aid to Contras	AGN
4) Kill Plnt Clsng Notice	AGN	8) Ban D.C. Abort $	FOR	12) Nuclear Testing	FOR

Election Results

1988 general	Joseph M. Gaydos (D)	137,472	(98%)	($137,023)
1988 primary	Joseph M. Gaydos (D), unopposed			
1986 general	Joseph M. Gaydos (D)	136,638	(98%)	($119,321)

TWENTY-FIRST DISTRICT

Erie "has the restful quiet of a resort center," wrote the *WPA Guide* 50 years ago,"but the waterfront presents a scene of activity when the lake, ice-locked several months of the year, is open to navigation. Here the 44,000 vessels annually warp into and away from the piers, carrying heavy cargoes of lumber, coal, petroleum, grain, iron ore and fish; until 1925, more fresh-water fish were shipped from Erie than from any other port in the world." Erie is the one part of Pennsylvania that looks to the Great Lakes, not to the Atlantic or to Pittsburgh; it's 428 miles from here to Center City Philadelphia.

Erie is the largest city in Pennsylvania's 21st Congressional District, about half of which is in

Erie County. The other half is part of western Pennsylvania's steel country: Sharon, right on the Ohio border and part of the Youngstown-Warren area, was long a major steel-producing town, and so was New Castle, whose suburbs are also part of the district. But there are rural areas, too. Crawford County, between Sharon and Erie, is mostly farming country. This combination produces a pretty even political balance, with the Democratic majorities of Erie and the steel towns balanced off by the Republican majorities of Crawford County and other rural areas; Michael Dukakis narrowly carried this district in 1988. In congressional elections, this was for years one of the classic marginal districts in the nation, but now seems very happy with its Republican congressman, Tom Ridge.

Ridge has the perfect background for such a seat. He is from a Catholic Slovak-and-Irish working-class family in Erie who once lived in a housing project; he went to Harvard and—an unusual combination—served in Vietnam. On the Banking Committee he has worked with Democrats on some issues and has worked to further local projects. He has paid particular attention to local issues and local angles. He spent much effort trying to help constituents after tornados swept the area in May 1985, and he developed what became the Disaster Relief and Emergency Assistance Amendments of 1988, although he is not on the relevant committee. He has worked to let banks into the securities business. He worked on the McKinney Homeless Act and on protecting veterans programs from budget cuts. He has worked with Bob Mrazek to let Amerasian children into the United States. He wants to prevent the Census Bureau from counting illegal aliens and to have it count servicemen abroad in the 1990 Census. He is inclined toward trade restrictions; he was one of the few Republicans to speak out for the Gephardt amendment.

Ridge won the seat in the recession year of 1982 by only 729 votes against an abrasive and overconfident Democrat, state Senator Anthony "Buzz" Andrezeski. Ridge, a Bush supporter in 1980, stressed his independence and his background. In a district where Democrats usually vote in lockstep with union leaders, and where Republicans are usually lackluster choices of local country club denizens or eccentric loners, Ridge seemed earnest, hardworking and thoughtful. His personal touch has helped him to reelection with 65% in 1984, 81% in 1986 and 79% in 1988. He has been mentioned as a possible candidate for governor in 1990. If he does run, there will probably be a hotly contested race in this closely divided district.

The People: Est. Pop. 1986: 509,500, dn. 1.4% 1980–86; Pop. 1980: 516,645, up 5.5% 1970–80. Households (1980): 76% family, 40% with children, 64% married couples; 27.1% housing units rented; median monthly rent: $156; median house value: $37,600. Voting age pop. (1980): 370,614; 3% Black.

1988 Presidential Vote:

Dukakis (D)	94,351	(50%)
Bush (R)	91,555	(49%)

Rep. Thomas J. Ridge (R)

Elected 1982; b. Aug. 26, 1945, Munhall; home, Erie; Harvard Col., B.A. 1967, Dickinson Sch. of Law, J.D. 1972; Roman Catholic; married (Michele).

Career: Army, Vietnam; Practicing atty., 1972–82.

Offices: 1714 LHOB 20515, 202-225-5406. Also 108 Fed. Bldg., Erie 16501, 814-456-2038; 305 Chestnut St., Meadville 16335, 814-724-8414; and 91 E. State St., Sharon 16146, 412-981-8440.

Committees: *Banking, Finance and Urban Affairs* (10th of 20 R). Subcommittees: Consumer Affairs and Coinage; Financial Institutions Supervision, Regulation and Insurance; Housing and Community Development. *Post Office and Civil Service* (7th of 9 R). Subcommittees: Civil Service; Census and Population (Ranking Member). *Veterans' Affairs* (8th of 13 R). Subcommittees: Education, Training and Employment; Hospitals and Health Care. *Select Committee on Aging* (9th of 27 R). Subcommittees: Health and Long-Term Care; Housing and Consumer Interests.

Group Ratings

	ADA	ACLU	COPE	CFA	LCV	ACU	NTLC	NSI	COC	CEI
1988	50	61	57	73	75	36	56	50	71	32
1987	44	—	51	50	—	19	—	—	64	43

National Journal Ratings

	1988 LIB — 1988 CONS		1987 LIB — 1987 CONS	
Economic	49%	— 50%	38%	— 61%
Social	33%	— 66%	50%	— 49%
Foreign	46%	— 54%	50%	— 48%

Key Votes

1) Homeless $	FOR	5) Ban Drug Test	AGN	9) SDI Research	AGN
2) Gephardt Amdt	FOR	6) Drug Death Pen	FOR	10) Ban Chem Weaps	AGN
3) Deficit Reduc	AGN	7) Handgun Sales	FOR	11) Aid to Contras	FOR
4) Kill Plnt Clsng Notice	AGN	8) Ban D.C. Abort $	AGN	12) Nuclear Testing	AGN

Election Results

1988 general	Thomas J. Ridge (R)	141,832	(79%)	($370,619)
	George R. H. Elden (D)	38,288	(21%)	
1988 primary	Thomas J. Ridge (R), unopposed			
1986 general	Thomas J. Ridge (R)	111,148	(81%)	($267,525)
	Joylyn Blackwell (D)	26,324	(19%)	

TWENTY-SECOND DISTRICT

Fifty years ago, according to the *WPA Guide,* Uniontown, "in a wild setting at the foot of the Alleghenies, [was] one of the bituminous coal centers in Pennsylvania. The rambling city of narrow streets has an appearance of prosperity. Coal, iron, lumber, natural gas, and glass, radiator, and textile manufacture contribute to its income." Prosperity is not a word most people would use to describe the southwest corner of Pennsylvania these days—although in fact incomes, even for unemployed workers, are much higher and living standards much more comfortable than they were for all but a few 50 years ago. In the small towns and little cities wedged in the interstices between hills and rivers, where frame houses were built 70 years ago to house the immigrants from Italy, Poland, Scotland and later Czechoslovakia, factories have closed, old jobs have disappeared, and young people have long since moved away.

This is the land of the 22d Congressional District of Pennsylvania—a region of rugged hills and polluted rivers, lined with steel mills and smaller factories. The 22d is one of Pennsylvania's—and the nation's—most blue-collar and most Democratic districts. The long slide of the steel industry has made this a depressed area for going on two decades now. Its ethnic composition, its high union membership, its depressed economy, its appetite for federal help—all these make this a heavily Democratic district. It voted 57% for Walter Mondale in 1984 and 65% for Michael Dukakis in 1988.

The 22d District's congressman, Austin Murphy, is a native of the Mon Valley, a veteran of the Marine Corps, a supporter of organized labor and a Democrat. Murphy's voting record is solidly Democratic and pro-labor; on cultural issues and foreign policy, his record is mixed. Murphy sits on the Interior Committee, where he naturally supports the interests of coal and pushed for the Southwestern Pennsylvania Industrial Heritage Commission, and on Education and Labor, where he spends most of his time. Beginning in 1985, he has chaired the Labor Standards Subcommittee, where he supports a higher minimum wage, a stronger Davis-Bacon Act (requiring high construction wages on government projects), and tougher occupational disease legislation. In March 1989, he was the lead sponsor of the Murphy-Ridge-Robinson minimum wage—well above the Bush Administration's—that passed the House. Yet when it comes to protecting local governments, he may be willing to subordinate the interests of their employees; in the 99th Congress, he moved successfully to allow cities to set retirement ages for police and fire officers and to give employees compensatory time rather than overtime pay. He has fought to protect the black lung compensation program against cuts and to make it more generous. Like all western Pennsylvanians, he clamors for a tougher trade policy.

Murphy's record was besmirched in 1987 when he was charged with letting another person cast his vote on the floor, diverting supplies to his former law firm, and paying a staffer for work not done. The ethics committee found him in violation of the rules, and in December 1987 the House voted 324–68 to formally reprimand him. This did not cause him much problem back home in the 22d District. Murphy first won the 22d District seat when he drew 29% of the vote in a 12-candidate primary in 1976 and 55% in the general, after 32-year incumbent Thomas Morgan, chairman of the House Foreign Affairs Committee, retired. In 1988, Murphy beat a turnpike equipment manager by a 73%–27% margin in the primary and won the general election with 72%.

The People: Est. Pop. 1986: 502,500, dn. 2.5% 1980–86; Pop. 1980: 515,122, up 2.4% 1970–80. Households (1980): 78% family, 38% with children, 65% married couples; 26.0% housing units rented; median monthly rent: $136; median house value: $35,500. Voting age pop. (1980): 378,475; 3% Black.

1988 Presidential Vote:

Dukakis (D)	115,106	(65%)
Bush (R)	61,947	(35%)

Rep. Austin J. Murphy (D)

Elected 1976; b. June 17, 1927, North Charleroi; home, Mononga-hela; Duquesne U., B.A. 1949, U. of Pittsburgh, LL.B. 1952; Roman Catholic; married (Ramona).

Career: USMC, WWII; Practicing atty.; Washington Cnty. Asst. Dist. Atty., 1956–57; PA House of Reps., 1959–71; PA Senate, 1971–77.

Offices: 2210 RHOB 20515, 202-225-4665. Also 306 Fallowfield Ave., Charleroi 15022, 412-489-4217; 96 N. Main St., Washington 15301, 412-228-2777; 45-51 E. Penn St., Uniontown 15401, 412-438-1490; 1801 C. Broadhead Rd., Aliquippa 15001, 412-375-1199; and 93 High St., Waynesburg 15370, 412-627-7611.

Committees: *Education and Labor* (6th of 22 D). Subcommittees: Labor–Management Relations; Labor Standards (Chairman). *Interior and Insular Affairs* (5th of 26 D). Subcommittees: Energy and the Environment; Mining and Natural Resources; National Parks and Public Lands.

Group Ratings

	ADA	ACLU	COPE	CFA	LCV	ACU	NTLC	NSI	COC	CEI
1988	60	60	82	82	31	24	24	50	33	23
1987	60	—	80	57	—	5	—	—	15	11

National Journal Ratings

	1988 LIB — 1988 CONS	1987 LIB — 1987 CONS
Economic	63% — 36%	51% — 48%
Social	52% — 47%	44% — 55%
Foreign	53% — 47%	54% — 46%

Key Votes

1) Homeless $	AGN	5) Ban Drug Test	—	9) SDI Research	FOR
2) Gephardt Amdt	FOR	6) Drug Death Pen	FOR	10) Ban Chem Weaps	AGN
3) Deficit Reduc	—	7) Handgun Sales	FOR	11) Aid to Contras	AGN
4) Kill Plnt Clsng Notice	AGN	8) Ban D.C. Abort $	FOR	12) Nuclear Testing	AGN

Election Results

1988 general	Austin J. Murphy (D)	123,428	(72%)	($183,335)
	William Hodgkiss (R)	47,039	(28%)	
1988 primary	Austin J. Murphy (D)	64,187	(73%)	
	Thomas J. Fullard (D)	23,193	(27%)	
1986 general	Austin J. Murphy (D)	131,650	(100%)	($118,557)

TWENTY-THIRD DISTRICT

The 23d Congressional District of Pennsylvania is the rural north central part of the state. The region is the most sparsely populated area in all the eastern states. The district's terrain is mountainous, and its valleys have only a few towns here and there; this was a route ignored in the great migrations west, and it contains none of the great historical east-west transportation routes. The only significant concentrations of people are found in the Nittany Valley in the southern part of the district and around Oil City in the extreme west. The Nittany Valley is the home of Pennsylvania State University, commonly called Penn State, long known for the powerful football teams coached by Joe Paterno (who gave the seconding speech for George Bush at the Republican Convention and is mentioned as a possible gubernatorial candidate in 1990). Oil City is near the site of the nation's first oil well, sunk in 1859. Today Pennsylvania crude—a relatively scarce oil but of higher quality than that found in the Southwest—continues to occupy an important place in the area's economy.

North central Pennsylvania now has easy connections with the rest of the country through Interstate 80, the shortest main road from New York to Chicago, and through commuter airlines; yet the air of isolation persists. The solidly built courthouses and banks in the center of each county seat testify to the long prosperity of this part of the country; yet unemployment rates have been high in most counties. The 23d remains a rural and small-town district, populated mainly by descendants of the English stock farmers who moved here in the early 19th century; it is one part of America that no further wave of immigration has reached.

Pennsylvania has a long Republican tradition going back to the years just before the Civil War, and no part of Pennsylvania more so than this. Yet the 23d District's Republican congressman, Bill Clinger, had to fight hard to win the district in 1978 over a one-term Democratic incumbent, and he had to fight hard to hold it through the 1980s. This is all the more striking because Clinger is the kind of moderate Republican who presumably appeals across party lines. He chaired the House Wednesday Group, made up mostly of moderate and liberal Republicans, which, under his leadership, generated some actual legislation. He moved to repeal the requirement that EPA must indemnify pesticide makers when it bans their products; he lost on a procedural vote 209–206, but is likely to return to the issue. He also sponsored with three Democrats a bill to close loopholes in the regulation of toxic PCBs. He pushed to adjust the 1986 tax reform to allow municipalities to invest funds they received from selling bonds pending completion of the projects they were intended to pay for. He is one of the congressional promoters of a federal capital budget, to set capital spending apart from current operations, and presumably to generate more of it. He helped to originate the individual training account idea popularized in the 1984 presidential campaign by Gary Hart.

But none of this prevented Democratic legislator Bill Wachob from running strong races in 1984 and 1986. A liberal from College Station, Wachob caught Clinger by surprise in 1984; Wachob won 48% that year and started running for 1986. But Clinger started running hard too. For a moment in 1986, the race in the remote 23d looked like Star Wars: Ed Asner came in to campaign for Wachob and his rival in the Screen Actors Guild, Charlton Heston, came in to campaign for Clinger. It's not clear how much either knew about the candidates; Heston took potshots at Asner for working with Communist-connected supporters of the Sandinista regime. In the end, with both candidates campaigning hard, the district's native Republicanism asserted itself, and Clinger won with 55%, running slightly ahead of losing gubernatorial candidate William Scranton and well behind winning Senator Arlen Specter. In 1988, he had a much weaker opponent and won with 62%. His major problem now seems to be redistricting. It would be hard but not impossible to carve this geographically large district among its neighbors, and that might well be done if Clinger signals he wishes to retire in 1992.

The People: Est. Pop. 1986: 507,800, dn. 1.6% 1980–86; Pop. 1980: 515,976, up 6.1% 1970–80. Households (1980): 74% family, 39% with children, 64% married couples; 27.3% housing units rented; median monthly rent: $154; median house value: $34,100. Voting age pop. (1980): 378,256; 1% Black.

1988 Presidential Vote:

Bush (R)	97,551	(56%)
Dukakis (D)	73,737	(43%)

Rep. William F. (Bill) Clinger, Jr. (R)

Elected 1978; b. Apr. 4, 1929, Warren; home, Warren; Johns Hopkins U., B.A. 1951, U. of VA, LL.B. 1965; Presbyterian; married (Julia).

Career: Navy, 1951–55; Adv. Dept., New Process Co., 1955–62; Practicing atty., 1965–75, 1977–78; Chf. Cnsl., Econ. Devel. Admin., U.S. Dept. of Commerce, 1975–77.

Offices: 2160 RHOB 20515, 202-225-5121. Also 315 S. Allen St., Ste. 219, State College 16801, 814-238-1776; and 805 Pennbank Bldg., Warren 16365, 814-726-3910.

Committees: *Government Operations* (3d of 15 R). Subcommittee: Environment, Energy, and Natural Resources (Ranking Member). *Public Works and Transportation* (4th of 20 R). Subcommittees: Aviation (Ranking Member); Investigations and Oversight; Surface Transportation. *Select Committee on Aging* (21st of 27 R). Subcommittees: Health and Long-Term Care; Human Services.

Group Ratings

	ADA	ACLU	COPE	CFA	LCV	ACU	NTLC	NSI	COC	CEI
1988	25	59	43	64	38	63	53	100	86	38
1987	24	—	41	36	—	43	—	—	73	48

National Journal Ratings

	1988 LIB — 1988 CONS		1987 LIB — 1987 CONS	
Economic	34%	65%	33%	66%
Social	39%	60%	44%	56%
Foreign	34%	65%	37%	63%

Key Votes

1) Homeless $	FOR	5) Ban Drug Test	AGN	9) SDI Research	FOR
2) Gephardt Amdt	AGN	6) Drug Death Pen	FOR	10) Ban Chem Weaps	AGN
3) Deficit Reduc	AGN	7) Handgun Sales	FOR	11) Aid to Contras	FOR
4) Kill Plnt Clsng Notice	FOR	8) Ban D.C. Abort $	FOR	12) Nuclear Testing	AGN

Election Results

1988 general	William F. (Bill) Clinger, Jr. (R).........	105,575	(62%)	($336,675)
	Howard Shakespeare (D)..............	63,476	(37%)	($106,463)
1988 primary	William F. (Bill) Clinger, Jr. (R), unopposed			
1986 general	William F. (Bill) Clinger, Jr. (R).........	79,595	(55%)	($695,266)
	Bill Wachob (D)....................	63,875	(45%)	($577,853)

RHODE ISLAND

As turbulent a political history as any in the country can be found in the tidy little city-state of Rhode Island. A successful trading community since the 1600s, a leader in manufacturing since Samuel Slater replicated from memory an English water-powered cotton textile mill in Pawtucket in 1791, Rhode Island also had its beginning as an upstart community, a refuge for religious dissenters, "the sewer of New England," as the orthodox Cotton Mather put it. Rhode Island profited from slavery (two-thirds of America's slaves arrived on ships owned by Rhode Islanders) and war (the state boomed during the Civil War), while it carried its dissenting tradition into politics. Rhode Island refused to pay for the Revolutionary war, declined to send delegates to the 1787 Constitutional Convention, and delayed joining the Union till the other 12 states had, prompting George Washington to say, "Rhode Island still perseveres in that impolitic, unjust—and one might add without much impropriety—scandalous conduct, which seems to have marked all her public counsels of late." In the 1840s, conflict between hard money merchants and soft money farmers resulted in two state governments and what is known now as Dorr's War.

And just over 50 years ago, Rhode Island had the closest thing America has had to a political revolution. The textile industry and later manufacturing, notably costume jewelry, attracted thousands of immigrants to Rhode Island, from French Canada, Ireland and Italy, and by the early 1900s, this erstwhile colony of dissident Protestants had become the most heavily Catholic state in the nation. The Yankee Republicans had some success in appealing to Catholics, running French Canadians for high office for example; but national events—Al Smith's candidacy in 1928, when he carried Rhode Island, and the New Deal of Franklin Roosevelt—moved the Catholics toward the Democrats. Then came the revolution: in 1935, the Democrats under Governor Theodore Green, although they had won only 20 of the 42 state Senate seats, refused to seat two Republicans. With the lieutenant governor's tie-breaker they voted Democrats into the seats and proceeded, within 14 minutes, to declare the state Supreme Court seats vacant, abolish state boards that controlled Democratic cities, strengthen the power of the governor and reorganize state government so as to get rid of Republicans.

This was a body blow to Rhode Island's "Five Families"—the Browns, Metcalfs, Goddards, Lippitts and Chafees—who owned or ran many of the textile mills, the Rhode Island Hospital Trust (one of the state's largest banks), the *Providence Journal*, the Rhode Island School of Design and the state Republican Party. Rhode Island politics has operated ever since in the backwash of the Green revolution of 1935. The Democrats, winning the lion's share of votes from Rhode Island's 64% Catholic majority, have won most elections, starting with Theodore Green who in 1936, at age 69, was elected to the first of his four terms as U.S. Senator. From 1940 to 1980, Democrats won every election for the U.S. House. And in 1988, this was Michael Dukakis's best state in the union. But Republicans have been able to capitalize on scandal and on the power of the Five Families to win some elections at the top of the ticket, the most notable example being John Chafee, elected governor and Senator three times each.

Rhode Island's competitive and, if not violent, then sometimes scandalous politics has continued to operate in pretty much the same way even as the state's economy has vastly changed. For years the unions remained politically powerful, but they represent fewer and fewer workers; the state's economy was quietly upgraded from blue-collar to white-collar, from textiles to high-tech; the electorate, instead of being a mass of Catholic factory workers pressed into neighborhoods of three-story three-family houses, has become comfortably affluent and subur-

**RHODE ISLAND — Congressional Districts, Counties,
County Subdivisions (Towns), and Places — *(2 Districts)***

Congressional districts established April 9, 1982 ; all other boundaries are as of January 1, 1980.

ban. There was a pause in growth when the Newport Navy base closed in 1973, and for a while that attracted everyone's attention. But by the early 1980s, both parties were ready with ways to adapt to change and build for the future.

The voters responded unfavorably to the Democrats' ideas and favorably, at least so far, to those of the Republicans. Both parties, including Democratic Governor (1976–84) Garrahy agreed that Rhode Island's high taxes and pro-labor laws (since the 1930s union members could collect unemployment benefits while on strike) were stifling the state's economy. Garrahy's response was a commission of business and civic leaders which under the guidance of business consultant Ira Magaziner (who as an undergraduate had helped restructure Brown University in the 1970s) produced the Greenhouse Compact, a kind of state industrial policy that would use government to encourage and incubate industry. But the voters, perhaps concerned that the $250 million package would lead to higher taxes, perhaps skeptical of government's ability to produce economic growth, rejected the Greenhouse Compact by almost an 80%–20% margin in a 1984 referendum. Instead, the state took another turn in policy by electing Republican Governor Edward DiPrete, who despite some perils of Pauline political adventures has stayed in office and helped to set the state's course ever since.

Governor. DiPrete has had some considerable achievements. He got the Democratic legislature to pass a 16% cut in the state income tax, got the strikers' unemployment benefits abolished, repealed the state gift and estate tax and restructured the state unemployment compensation system. He also established a state Partnership for Science and Technology and increased funding for education, Head Start and other children's programs and he ran ads in national newspapers saying "If you want to talk business in Rhode Island, talk to a businessman: The Governor."

DiPrete's problem in 1988 was not his policies but scandal. In July 1988, it was revealed that DiPrete, three of his family members and a close adviser had made $2 million in a land deal; also there was a messy Department of Environmental Management incident that smacked of favoritism and impropriety. DiPrete's image as a modest family man and honest businessman was cast into doubt, and Democrat Bruce Sundlun, a rich entrepreneur who had lost badly in 1986, attacked fiercely. But DiPrete recovered, and enough doubts were raised about Sundlun's abilities and past that DiPrete was able to eke out a modest victory. In 1989, with Rhode Island's economy growing and an unemployment rate well under the national average, DiPrete and the heavily Democratic legislature faced issues like crime, drugs, medicare fees and the right-to-die dilemma. The basic course of state policy seemed set. DiPrete seems likely to run again in 1990. Possible opponents include Providence Mayor Joe Paolino, Warwick Mayor Francis X. Flaherty, former Lieutenant Governor Richard Licht (who lost to John Chafee in 1988) and his 1988 opponent, Bruce Sundlun.

Senators. It must strike anyone as odd that heavily Catholic and ethnic Rhode Island has two blue-blooded Protestant Senators. Both of them, Democrat Claiborne Pell and Republican John Chafee, have had unusual careers. Pell, first elected to the Senate in 1960, is now the state's senior politician. His father was congressman from New York for a term, a friend of Franklin Roosevelt, and minister to Portugal and Hungary—important listening posts—in the early years of World War II. Pell himself served as a foreign service officer for several years, then settled on Bellevue Avenue in Newport, where you find the Vanderbilt and Auchincloss "cottages." (Rhode Island's Five Families tend to live on Providence's College Hill, with comfy summer places on Rhode Island Sound; the oceanfront palaces of Newport were built mostly by New Yorkers.) He is now what he always wanted to be, chairman of the Senate Foreign Relations Committee.

It is obligatory in Washington to deprecate Pell's political skills. He has an old-fashioned aristocratic accent, seems remote and diffident, uses corny old phrases and seems unable to rally his colleagues around his standard. Yet there is evidence that if he wears a velvet glove, there is an iron fist inside. He has gotten everything he wanted in politics, and by whipping the toughest competition this tough little state could offer. In the 1960 Democratic primary, he beat former Governor Dennis Roberts and former Governor, Senator and U.S. Attorney General J. Howard McGrath; this was the first time since Green's governorship that a candidate endorsed by the Democratic organization was beaten. One opponent in that race called Pell a "cream puff"; he promptly went out and got the endorsement of the bakers' union. In 1972, when Rhode Island was going Republican for President, Pell faced John Chafee, then a popular former governor and Secretary of the Navy. Although Chafee began ahead, Pell turned the campaign around and won again. It is worth noting that Pell holds the seat won by Theodore Green in 1936 when he was 69, a seat that a generation of Rhode Island politicians assumed would soon become open; Green, who chaired Foreign Relations himself, retired in 1960 at age 93. Pell has now been elected to serve a total of 30 years in that seat, longer than Green, and he will be 71 when it comes up again in 1990.

As Chairman of Foreign Relations, Pell has not been a powerhouse. He has done nothing comparable to William Fulbright's hearings on Vietnam or Richard Lugar's work on the Philippines. Pell's instincts are dovish—toward the Democrats' disarmament position, normalization of diplomatic relations with Cuba, banning nuclear weapons on the ocean floor, and banning environmental alteration as a weapon of war—at a time when the more confrontational policies of the Reagan Administration produced the INF Treaty, which Pell supported and which the Senate ultimately ratified 93–5 but with some reservations. The ranking Republican on the committee is Jesse Helms, with his own right-wing agenda, his willingness to obstruct nominations and his lack of interest in bipartisan cooperation; and Pell does not have a reliable majority on the committee. But Pell has had his successes. His opposition to contra aid succeeded, though he was not a lead player on the issue; the opponents had a majority in the House, not the Senate. He saw the Senate vote South African sanctions.

Pell's other major legislative interest is education. He is the second ranking Democrat on Labor and Human Resources and for years has chaired the subcommittee in charge of education programs. He made a particular mark in setting up a grant program for needy college and university students; these Pell grants, as they are now officially called, were attacked unsuccessfully by the Reagan Administration. Those who disdain Pell's political talents should ask how many other Senators have their name on a program that sends money to tens of thousands of families in their states every year. He has also been one of the main promoters of federal aid to the arts and of ocean research (Rhode Island's license plates call it the "Ocean State").

After Chafee's challenge, Pell was reelected with 75% and 73% in 1978 and 1984, respectively. Although Congresswoman Claudine Schneider declined to take him on in 1984, she was reported in early 1989 to be seriously considering the race. But Pell shows no signs of quitting, and he continues to make the rounds of Rhode Island political meetings and christenings and backyard gatherings, quietly and politely keeping in touch with the mostly ethnic and Catholic voters whom polls indicate have warm feelings toward him. Schneider would be a strong candidate, but it's not clear that she or any other Republican will find Pell a "cream puff" when the 1990 results are in.

Senator John Chafee is Rhode Island's most successful Republican politician in the last 50 years. Even so, he has had his setbacks: he was defeated when he sought a fourth term as governor in 1968, and he lost to Pell in 1972. He came back, however, in 1976 when Senator John Pastore retired, profiting from then-Governor Philip Noel's defeat in the Democratic Senate primary by a Cadillac dealer who ran a self-financed campaign but exhausted most of his resources.

Chafee's popularity comes from a solid, pleasant personality and from his liberal stands on many issues. On economics, while he is not always a solid conservative, he cannot be mistaken for a Democrat either. On the Finance Committee he is a critic of greenmail, hostile takeovers, and "golden parachutes"—all populist stands, though somewhat vulnerable to the charge that they entrench incompetent managements or oldtimers like the Five Families. On trade issues, he has been inclined toward free trade positions and supported the 1988 trade law.

Chafee is most active on environmental issues. He was the chief packager in the Senate of the water projects bill that President Reagan vetoed in 1986, and cooperated with the Democrats in bringing it forward and getting it passed over Reagan's veto in early 1987. On Environment and Public Works, where he is ranking minority member, Chafee worked with his fellow New England Republican Robert Stafford, now retired, to get a stronger Superfund and to reauthorize the Clean Air Act. He works hard on clean water as well, making sure that Rhode Island gets its share of funds. He worked on the 1988 ocean dumping law and produced a commercial fishing vessel safety act. In return, environmentalists provided critical support, both in money and volunteers, for Chafee in his tough reelection fights of 1982 and 1988.

Chafee tends to be rather liberal on cultural and foreign policy issues and is anything but a favorite of the New Right; he supports the ABC child care bill and the 1988 plant closing notification law. Yet, easy-going and popular, he won a leadership post after the 1984 elections—chairman of the Republican Conference—over the sometimes intense and abrasive Jake Garn of Utah, 28–25. He continues to hold that post.

For all his popularity in Rhode Island, where he won his first statewide election in 1962, Chafee was nearly defeated for reelection in the recession year of 1982 and faced a vigorous challenge in 1988. In 1982, former attorney general and state AFL-CIO counsel Julius Michaelson denounced Reaganomics and drew 49% against Chafee. In 1988, Lieutenant Governor Richard Licht, nephew of the Democrat who beat Chafee for governor in 1968, attacked Chafee for his social security and medicare votes, and charged that he used influence to have his beachfront house included in a federally protected area, and that he used his Finance Committee seat to give tax breaks to rich friends. Licht showed great energy and matched Chafee in fundraising—a formidable task. But he was unable to besmirch the Republican's reputation, and Chafee's support from environmentalists and his liberal positions on some economic issues sustained him with many swing voters. In the end, Chafee won with 55% of the vote—an impressive score in the number one Dukakis state.

Presidential politics. Rhode Island in 1988 was the number one Dukakis state in the nation. It gave him 56% of its votes in the general election, more than Massachusetts; the Boston media market may have gone for Bush, but the Providence media market (which includes Fall River and New Bedford, Massachusetts) voted for Dukakis. The ancestral Democratic preference of the nearly two-thirds of Rhode Islanders who are Catholics played some role here; so did Dukakis's record of encouraging economic development of smaller New England mill towns, of which Rhode Island has some. Dukakis's liberal stands on cultural issues were not much of a liability. Some might suppose that Catholics here would dislike Dukakis's positions on abortion and other family issues. In states where Catholics are a beleaguered minority, they do often cling to church positions. But in Rhode Island, where they are a big majority, they don't feel under siege; and the mostly Irish clergy has never had a commanding power over the state's mostly Italian and French Canadian Catholics whose family traditions are often anticlerical rather than pious.

Rhode Island's presidential primary, held the same day as Massachusetts's, has some of the lowest turnout in the nation, a vestige of the days when Democratic party bosses had sway. Now they don't (Gary Hart won here in 1984), but few Rhode Islanders bother to vote anyway.

The People: Est. Pop. 1988: 995,000; Pop. 1980: 947,154, up 5.1% 1980–88 and dn. 0.3% 1970–80; 0.40% of U.S. total, 42d largest. 13% with 1–3 yrs. col., 15% with 4+ yrs. col.; 10.3% below poverty level. Single ancestry: 13% Italian, 8% French, English, Irish, 7% Portuguese, 2% Polish, 1% German, Scottish, Swedish, Russian. Households (1980): 72% family, 37% with children, 59% married couples; 41.2% housing units rented; median monthly rent: $158; median house value: $47,000. Voting age pop. (1980): 704,303; 2% Black, 2% Spanish origin, 1% Asian origin. Registered voters (1988): 548,758; no party registration.

1988 Share of Federal Tax Burden: $3,818,000,000; 0.43% of U.S. total, 40th largest.

1988 Share of Federal Expenditures

	Total		Non-Defense		Defense	
Total Expend	$3,567m	(0.40%)	$2,768m	(0.42%)	$860m	(0.38%)
St/Lcl Grants	644m	(0.56%)	641m	(0.56%)	2m	(1.98%)
Salary/Wages	503m	(0.37%)	205m	(0.31%)	298m	(0.31%)
Pymnts to Indiv	1,848m	(0.45%)	1,779m	(0.46%)	69m	(0.37%)
Procurement	489m	(0.26%)	61m	(0.13%)	489m	(0.26%)
Research/Other	84m	(0.22%)	82m	(0.22%)	2m	(0.22%)

Political Lineup: Governor, Edward D. DiPrete (R); Lt. Gov., Roger Begin (D); Secy. of State, Kathleen S. Connell (D); Atty. Gen., James E. O'Neil (D); Treasurer, Anthony Solomon (D). State Senate, 50 (41 D and 9 R); State House of Representatives, 100 (83 D and 17 R). Senators, Claiborne Pell (D) and John H. Chafee (R). Representatives, 2 (2 R).

1988 Presidential Vote

Dukakis (D).	225,123	(56%)
Bush (R)	177,761	(44%)

1984 Presidential Vote

Reagan (R)	208,513	(52%)
Mondale (D)	194,292	(48%)

1988 Democratic Presidential Primary

Dukakis	34,211	(70%)
Jackson	7,445	(15%)
Gephardt	2,028	(5%)
Gore.	1,939	(4%)
Simon	1,395	(3%)
Hart.	733	(2%)
Babbitt	399	(1%)

1988 Republican Presidential Primary

Reagan	10,403	(65%)
Dole.	3,637	(23%)
Robertson	921	(6%)
Kemp.	783	(5%)

GOVERNOR

Gov. Edward D. DiPrete (R)

Elected 1984, term expires Jan. 1991; b. July 8, 1934, Cranston; home, Cranston; Col. of the Holy Cross, B.S. 1955; Roman Catholic; married (Patricia)

Career: Cranston School Comm., 1970–74, Chmn., 1972–74; Cranston City Cncl., 1974–78; Mayor of Cranston, 1978–84; Pres., DiPrete Realty Co.

Office: 222 State House, Providence 02903, 401-277-2080.

Election Results

1988 gen.	Edward D. DiPrete (R)	203,550	(51%)
	Bruce G. Sundlun (D)	196,936	(49%)
1988 prim.	Edward D. DiPrete (R), unopposed		
1986 gen.	Edward D. DiPrete (R)	203,203	(65%)
	Bruce G. Sundlun (D)	101,437	(32%)

SENATORS

Sen. Claiborne Pell (D)

Elected 1960, seat up 1990; b. Nov. 22, 1918, New York, NY; home, Newport; Princeton U., A.B. 1940, Columbia U., A.M. 1946; Episcopalian; married (Nuala).

Career: Coast Guard, WWII; U.S. Foreign Svc. and State Dept., Czechoslovakia and Italy, 1945–52; Exec. Asst. to RI Dem. St. Chmn., 1952, 1954; Consultant, Dem. Natl. Cmtee., 1953–60.

Offices: 335 RSOB 20510, 202-224-4642. Also 418 Fed. Bldg., Providence 02903, 401-528-5456.

Committees: *Foreign Relations* (Chairman of 10 D) Subcommittees: East Asian and Pacific Affairs; International Economic Policy, Trade, Oceans and Environment; Near Eastern and South Asian Affairs. *Labor and Human Resources* (2d of 9 D). Subcommittees: Aging; Children, Family, Drugs and Alcoholism; Education, Arts, and Humanities (Chairman). *Rules and Administration* (2d of 9 D). *Joint Committee on the Library* (Vice Chairman).

Group Ratings

	ADA	ACLU	COPE	CFA	LCV	ACU	NTLC	NSI	COC	CEI
1988	100	85	92	100	80	0	4	0	36	15
1987	90	—	92	100	—	0	—	—	28	17

National Journal Ratings

	1988 LIB — 1988 CONS		1987 LIB — 1987 CONS	
Economic	74%	— 19%	74%	— 0%
Social	86%	— 0%	90%	— 4%
Foreign	78%	— 21%	81%	— 0%

Key Votes

1) Cut Aged Housing $	FOR	5) Bork Nomination	AGN	9) SDI Funding	AGN
2) Override Hwy Veto	FOR	6) Drug Death Pen	AGN	10) Ban Chem Weaps	AGN
3) Kill Plnt Clsng Notice	AGN	7) Deny Abortions	AGN	11) Aid To Contras	AGN
4) Min Wage Increase	FOR	8) Japanese Reparations	FOR	12) Reagan Defense $	AGN

Election Results

1984 general	Claiborne Pell (D)	286,780	(73%)	($430,739)
	Barbara M. Leonard (R)	108,492	(27%)	($143,842)
1984 primary	Claiborne Pell (D), unopposed			
1978 general	Claiborne Pell (D)	229,557	(75%)	($373,077)
	James G. Reynolds (R)	76,061	(25%)	($85,614)

Sen. John H. Chafee (R)

Elected 1976, seat up 1994; b. Oct. 22, 1922, Providence; home, Warwick; Yale U., B.A. 1947, Harvard U., LL.B. 1950; Episcopalian; married (Virginia).

Career: USMC, WWII, Korea; Practicing atty., 1952–63; RI House of Reps., 1957–63, Minor. Ldr., 1959–63; Gov. of RI, 1963–69; Secy. of the Navy, 1969–72.

Offices: 567 DSOB 20510, 202-224-2921. Also 301 John O. Pastore Fed. Bldg., Kennedy Plaza, Providence 02903, 401-528-5294.

Committees: *Environment and Public Works* (Ranking Member of 7 R). Subcommittees: Environmental Protection (Ranking Member); Water Resources, Transportation, and Infrastructure. *Finance* (5th of 9 R). Subcommittees: Health for Families and the Uninsured (Ranking Member); Medicare and Long-Term Care; International Trade.

Group Ratings

	ADA	ACLU	COPE	CFA	LCV	ACU	NTLC	NSI	COC	CEI
1988	90	81	49	83	100	4	31	10	36	30
1987	80	—	46	92	—	16	—	—	56	40

National Journal Ratings

	1988 LIB — 1988 CONS		1987 LIB — 1987 CONS	
Economic	83%	— 14%	38%	— 61%
Social	79%	— 17%	78%	— 17%
Foreign	64%	— 35%	65%	— 32%

Key Votes

1) Cut Aged Housing $	FOR	5) Bork Nomination	AGN	9) SDI Funding	AGN
2) Override Hwy Veto	AGN	6) Drug Death Pen	AGN	10) Ban Chem Weaps	AGN
3) Kill Plnt Clsng Notice	FOR	7) Deny Abortions	AGN	11) Aid To Contras	AGN
4) Min Wage Increase	FOR	8) Japanese Reparations	AGN	12) Reagan Defense $	AGN

Election Results

1988 general	John H. Chafee (R)	217,273	(55%)	($2,841,985)
	Richard A. Licht (D)	180,717	(45%)	($2,735,917)
1988 primary	John H. Chafee (R), unopposed			
1982 general	John H. Chafee (R)	175,248	(51%)	($1,065,627)
	Julius C. Michaelson (D)	167,283	(49%)	($438,630)

FIRST DISTRICT

The 1st Congressional District is the eastern half of Rhode Island, east of Narragansett Bay, a line that cuts through Providence and then proceeds west and north to the Massachusetts border. There are several Democratic strongholds here: Providence (although this includes elite College Hill around Brown University) and next-door Pawtucket; the onetime textile mill towns of the Blackstone Valley, Woonsocket and Central Falls; and, south on the ocean, the old city of Newport, with its restored 18th-century houses and its so-called cottages that are really palaces. Most of the rest of the district is Democratic by national standards, except for the high-income suburb of Barrington and the old Yankee beach town of Little Compton. Ethnically, this is the more French Canadian and less Italian of the two Rhode Island districts.

In 1988, the 1st District was the scene of the defeat of one of the few incumbents to lose—and of the most important: Fernand St Germain, Chairman of the House Banking, Finance and Urban Affairs Committee, one of the politically sharpest but ethically most dubious members of the House of Representatives. St Germain had genuine abilities, riding herd over a usually fractious committee charged with handling tough and complicated issues, holding back on bank deregulation, keeping the international banking agencies open, using an administration gaffe to get a new housing program through in 1983. He also managed to see that a large share of the nation's senior citizen housing was built in eastern Rhode Island.

But St Germain's ethical standards weren't as high as his skills. In 1985, *The Wall Street Journal* charged that a top St Germain aide called regulators about a savings and loan in which St Germain had a potential interest, that St Germain obtained better than 100% financing from a bank to purchase International House of Pancakes restaurants and that he had accumulated $2 million in assets while on the public payroll for 25 years. While the ethics committee was investigating, St Germain took a pounding in the 1986 election on ethical issues from Republican John Holmes, but in this heavily Democratic district St Germain won 58%–42%. In April 1987, the ethics committee finally reported, finding that St Germain had made minor errors in filing disclosure forms and accepting one too many rides on an S&L plane, but declining to draw the obvious inferences about the aide's phone calls, and recommending no disciplinary action. A move by Newt Gingrich to take up the case on the floor failed by a 291–111 vote, with only one Democrat (Romano Mazzoli of Kentucky) voting to investigate. In July 1987, *The Wall Street Journal* reported that the Justice Department was conducting a criminal investigation of St Germain, partly for receiving dozens of free meals at Washington's Prime Rib restaurant from S&L lobbyist James "Snake" Freeman.

The Justice Department announced in May 1988 that it was closing the investigation and would issue no indictments, but the unrefuted *Journal* stories raised at the least the likelihood that undue influence had been exerted on St Germain on the biggest issue of his chairmanship, the S&L crisis. The S&Ls had been deregulated by a bill he co-sponsored, and when they started running up losses that would have to be met by FSLIC, St Germain blocked the tougher of two bills. As a result, the government will have to make up losses estimated in 1988 at $50 billion and in 1989 at $100 billion: money that could buy a lot of rare roast beef at the Prime Rib.

For the first time in years, St Germain had strong opposition in both primary and general election. In the primary, Providence political consultant Scott Wolf said that St Germain had shown "insensitivity to the maintenance of a high standard of ethical conduct" and was "part of the old-style politics." He called on St Germain to debate and labeled him arrogant and out of touch. Wolf raised large amounts for a challenger and mounted a professional-quality campaign for the September primary. He won 45% of the vote—a very strong showing for a challenger, even though his chances had been heavily discounted by Washington campaign and PAC operatives. The result might have been different if a Public Citizen lawsuit in Washington had produced a couple of months earlier the disclosure it reported in the last week of October from records of the Justice Department investigation—when it forwarded documents to the ethics committee, the Department had said that it found "substantial evidence of serious and sustained misconduct." This was a total refutation of St Germain's argument that he had been cleared by the decision not to indict.

The beneficiary was Republican Ronald Machtley, who had been running a game campaign all year, raising good money against St Germain, and parading a 250-pound hog named Lester H. Pork ("Les Pork") to symbolize his opposition to St Germain's big spending policies. Machtley was a latecomer to Rhode Island: he grew up in Pennsylvania, graduated from the Naval Academy, and was homeported in Rhode Island; he returned after he left the Navy and became a fishing and admiralty lawyer in Newport County—not exactly a member of the establishment. But he was at the right place at the right time, and in November 1988 beat St Germain and became the first Republican elected to Congress in the 1st District in 50 years.

Can he stay there? He got a seat on the Armed Services Committee, which has some local importance, and he says he wants to emphasize issues like acid rain, global warming, and ocean dumping—popular here and not exactly a New Right agenda. But he's certain to have serious opposition. Wolf has said he will run again and seems to have the capacity to be a serious candidate, and some of the Democrats who supported St Germain or were simply too cowardly to oppose him may run too. Certainly this is a seat that both parties expect to be seriously contested.

The People: Est. Pop. 1986: 480,700, up 1.3% 1980–86; Pop. 1980: 474,429, dn. 2.8% 1970–80. Households (1980): 71% family, 35% with children, 58% married couples; 45.3% housing units rented; median monthly rent: $157; median house value: $48,600. Voting age pop. (1980): 357,096; 2% Black, 2% Spanish origin, 1% Asian origin.

1988 Presidential Vote:	Dukakis (R)................	112,949	(57%)
	Bush (D)................	83,140	(42%)

Rep. Ronald Keith Machtley (R)

Elected 1988; b. July 8, 1934, Johnstown, PA; home, Portsmouth; U.S. Naval Academy, B.S. 1970, Suffolk U. J.D., 1978; Protestant; married (Kati).

Career: U.S. Navy, 1970–75; Practicing atty. 1978–88.

Offices: 1123 LHOB 20515, 202-225-4911. Also 200 Main St., Pawtucket 02860, 401-725-9400.

Committees: *Armed Services* (21st of 21 R). Subcommittees: Military Personnel and Compensation; Readiness. *Small Business* (18th of 18 R). *Select Committee on Children, Youth and Families* (12th of 12 R).

Group Ratings and Key Votes: Newly Elected

Election Results

1988 general	Ronald K. Machtley (R)...............	105,506	(56%)	($385,402)
	Fernand J. St Germain (D).............	84,141	(44%)	($801,289)
1988 primary	Ronald K. Machtley (R), unopposed			
1986 general	Fernand J. St Germain (D).............	85,077	(58%)	($848,082)
	John A. Holmes Jr. (R)...............	62,397	(42%)	($340,458)

SECOND DISTRICT

The 2d Congressional District is the western half of Rhode Island. While the 1st includes many mill towns, the 2d has most of its population in working and middle-class suburbs like Cranston and Warwick, which despite their Anglo-Saxon names are inhabited mostly by people with Irish, Italian, French and Portuguese surnames. Some of Providence's rich suburbs are also here, and to a very marginal degree this is Rhode Island's more Republican district.

Its Congresswoman since 1980 has been Republican Claudine Schneider. She got her start in politics by opposing a nuclear plant and running a losing race in 1978 against Edward Beard, house-painter-turned-congressman; she came back and won in 1980. That victory she may owe to Beard's weaknesses; her four reelection wins, by increasing margins, she owes to her own strengths. In her first term, she voted against Reagan budget cuts and sponsored a law to prohibit construction of Navy ships abroad. She was one of the leaders in the fight, finally successful in 1983, to kill the Clinch River breeder reactor. She has specialized in environmental issues—popular in this ocean-conscious district—and claims some of the credit for the 1988 laws limiting ocean dumping and promoting the protection of endangered species. She has worked as well on hazardous waste and the Civil Rights Restoration Act.

Schneider is generally given the label of liberal Republican, but on economic issues she often votes with market-oriented Republicans, and her interest in new approaches and ideas prompted her to vote for Newt Gingrich, a conservative similarly interested in new ideas, in the March 1989 race for whip. Schneider considered running against Senator Claiborne Pell in 1984, and in early 1989 the talk was that she was likely to do so in 1990. Her own popularity statewide is high, as witnessed by her rousing reelection victory; but Pell is also exceedingly popular and has beaten a highly popular Republican, his current colleague John Chafee, before. Pell will turn be 71 in November 1990, but he seems in good health, and Schneider needs to come up with a rationale for replacing a Senator with whom most Rhode Islanders have no quarrel. If he retires, however, she will almost certainly run and might very well be the favorite to win. Already, Democratic attorney general James E. O'Neal is rumored to be interested in this seat if Schneider does decide to challenge Pell.

The People: Est. Pop. 1986: 494,200, up 4.5% 1980–86; Pop. 1980: 472,725, up 2.4% 1970–80. Households (1980): 74% family, 38% with children, 60% married couples; 37.0% housing units rented; median monthly rent: $159; median house value: $45,700. Voting age pop. (1980): 347,207; 3% Black, 2% Spanish origin, 1% Asian origin.

1988 Presidential Vote:

Dukakis (D)	112,174	(54%)
Bush (R)	94,621	(46%)

Rep. Claudine Schneider (R)

Elected 1980; b. Mar. 25, 1947, Clairton, PA; home, Narragansett; Rosemont Col., U. of Barcelona, Spain, Windham Col., B.A. 1969; Roman Catholic; divorced.

Career: Founder, RI Cmtee. on Energy, 1973; Exec. Dir., Conservation Law Foundation, 1973–78; Producer, pub. affairs prog. on Providence TV, 1979–80.

Offices: 1512 LHOB 20515, 202-225-2735. Also 30 Rolfe Sq., Cranston 02910, 401-528-5020.

Committees: *Merchant Marine and Fisheries* (6th of 17 R). Subcommittees: Fisheries and Wildlife Conservation and the Environment; Oversight and Investigations (Ranking Member). *Science, Space and Technology* (3d of 19 R). Subcommittees: Natural Resources, Agriculture Research and Environment (Ranking Member); Science, Research and Technology. *Select Committee on Aging* (8th of 27 R). Subcommittee: Health and Long-Term Care.

Group Ratings

	ADA	ACLU	COPE	CFA	LCV	ACU	NTLC	NSI	COC	CEI
1988	80	71	73	91	81	17	53	10	38	26
1987	72	—	69	57	—	26	—	—	60	34

National Journal Ratings

	1988 LIB — 1988 CONS	1987 LIB — 1987 CONS
Economic	46% — 52%	38% — 62%
Social	66% — 32%	62% — 36%
Foreign	68% — 32%	66% — 32%

Key Votes

1) Homeless $	FOR	5) Ban Drug Test	AGN	9) SDI Research	AGN
2) Gephardt Amdt	AGN	6) Drug Death Pen	FOR	10) Ban Chem Weaps	FOR
3) Deficit Reduc	AGN	7) Handgun Sales	AGN	11) Aid to Contras	AGN
4) Kill Plnt Clsng Notice	AGN	8) Ban D.C. Abort $	AGN	12) Nuclear Testing	FOR

Election Results

1988 general	Claudine Schneider (R)	145,218	(72%)	($443,267)
	Ruth S. Morgenthau (D)	56,129	(28%)	($328,335)
1988 primary	Claudine Schneider (R), unopposed			
1986 general	Claudine Schneider (R)	110,524	(72%)	($325,052)
	Donald J. Ferry (D)	43,149	(28%)	($67,685)

SOUTH CAROLINA

Fifty years ago South Carolina was more like what is now called an underdeveloped country than part of an advanced country like the United States. Beneath its very thin veneer of rich people, it was the poorest state in the union, with income levels less than half the national average; its levels of illiteracy and of disease were among the nation's highest. "In this country where natural growth borders on the semitropical," wrote the *WPA Guide*, "and midday heat in the summer is prostrating except where sea breezes creep in under the thick foliage of live oak and myrtle or between the tall trunks of longleaf pine, there seems to be no hard grinding necessity for thinking too much about money in the bank, fine clothes, and weather-tight houses. The outdoors is too free, fishing is too good, and crops grow with only part of a year's work."

Some 43% of South Carolinians were black, almost all of them living in the Low Country—the swampy territory within 50 miles of the coast, where the great planters of the 18th and 19th century built rice paddies and cultivated exotic crops like indigo in the days before, as one South Carolina politician put it in the 1850s, "Cotton is King." The great wealth of the Low Country planters was destroyed by the war they did more than any other southerners to provoke, but their pride and their way of life continued. "The Low Countryman himself will not change. He will still have his afternoon nap, eat his rice, revere his ancestors, go hunting and fishing in season, and take time out from his labors to entertain his friends and guests with courtesy, ease, and graceful hospitality." Up-country South Carolina, settled by Scots-Irish and even Germans, with few slaves before the Civil War, had begun 50 years ago to develop the lowest-wage of industries, textiles. "Enterprising businessmen came in and established cotton mills, built towns around them, with schools, churches, banks, stores, and hospitals. Into the mills came the up-country farmer who was barely making a living, and out of the mountains came the barefoot man and sunbonneted woman, to take charge of spindles and looms." The mills in those days never hired blacks; even before World War II fair numbers of South Carolina blacks took the bus north to New York or Philadelphia to make a living.

Politics in this underdeveloped South Carolina was a rough business, with harsh appeals to racial fears and economic envies. And not many people participated. Only 99,000 South Carolinians voted for President in 1940, and 96% of them voted Democratic—the highest percentage in the nation. And in the Democratic primary in the year Strom Thurmond ran for governor, 1946, only 271,000 voted in a state of more than two million.

In the decades since, life in South Carolina has changed as much as in any state: the underdeveloped country has joined the First World. Today the state's incomes, discounted for its somewhat lower cost of living, are close to national levels; health standards are similar to the rest of the nation; education levels, though low, are now not far from the national average. South Carolina was helped upward for some years by the military bases clustered around Charleston (helped along by Mendel Rivers, chairman of the House Armed Services Committee), by the textile mills that dotted the hilly up-country landscape around Greenville and Spartanburg, and by the outmigration of Low Country blacks to the big cities of the Northeast. But that was only the beginning. By the 1970s South Carolina became the most aggressive state in the South in attracting new industry. It went over to Europe and enticed French and German firms to set up major operations in the Piedmont and the Lowlands. It advertised its business climate (translation: one of the lowest rates of unionization), its taxes (low), and its willingness to meet local employers' needs (very high). Gradually, its standard of living moved up toward the national average, even as that average was itself rising rapidly. And it has used some of that increase in affluence to upgrade the quality of its local work force, through public expenditures on schools as well as highways, teachers as well as policemen.

Much of this was made possible because South Carolina was relieved, quite against the will of its white majority, of the burdens and stigma of racial segregation. Beginning in the 1950s, fewer people were kept from the polls by the poll tax, and turnouts surged as South Carolina became competitive in the presidential elections of 1952, 1956 and 1960. Then the Civil Rights Act of 1964 and the Voting Rights Act of 1965 ended segregation of public accommodations and in the workplace and brought blacks suddenly into the electorate. Politically, the reaction was a sharp rightward trend toward Republicans led by Strom Thurmond, who had turned Republican in September 1964 and had indicated his disapproval of this process. But even while candidates were denouncing school busing after a bus in one rural district had been burned, South Carolina was learning to live with integration and getting on with the work of economic development.

Politically South Carolina reached a not entirely uncomfortable equilibrium by the early 1970s. Almost 30% of its voters were black, almost all of them solid national Democrats. But while the white majority was polarized against them in the 1968 and 1972 presidential elections, there were enough movable white votes to elect a Democratic governor in 1970 and to cast South Carolina's electoral votes for Jimmy Carter in 1976. Affluent whites vote heavily Republican. But less affluent whites have become a swing vote, loyal to Strom Thurmond but favorable to Ernest Hollings, making most of South Carolina's gubernatorial elections over the last 20 years very close indeed. They yearn on the one hand for an end to old-style politics, to control of the legislature by an oligarchy of rural-based bosses: Edgar Brown, elected to the legislature in 1920, chaired the Senate Finance Committee from 1942 to 1972, when he retired at 84; Sol Blatt, elected in 1932, was Speaker of the House for all but four years from 1937 to 1972 and served in the House until he died in 1986; but on the other hand, they are afraid that higher taxes will choke off growth. They are people at one and the same time exhilarated and terrified by the changes they have seen in South Carolina in the last generation—both around them and in their own lives. They live in affluence beyond their dreams, and if their pleasant subdivisions and small houses amid strip-development highways look quite ordinary to visiting intellectuals and journalists, they represent an undreamed-of comfort for many South Carolinians who grew up without indoor plumbing or electricity or, often enough that they can remember it, enough to eat. They are leery of policies—and institutions, like labor unions—that seem to threaten the economic order which has proved so bountiful. Yet there is an underlying appreciation that

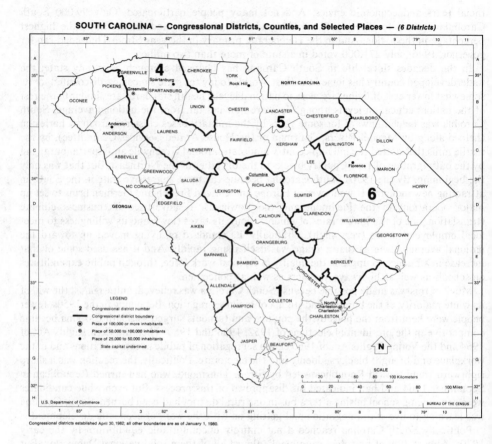

SOUTH CAROLINA — Congressional Districts, Counties, and Selected Places — (6 Districts)

Congressional districts established April 30, 1982; all other boundaries are as of January 1, 1980.

government—building highways, running schools, maintaining social security—has made some contribution to this bounty and to their affluence.

Many surely have an uneasy sense that old rules, however unjust some of them were, are no longer in force, that the affluent South Carolina they inhabit, so different from the underdeveloped country they grew up in, also is a land of divorce and abortion, of places where traditional moral values are flouted and even patriotism seems to be mocked. This is a state where traditional religion has strong roots, and where cultural conservatism thrives, despite—or because—most people live in an environment where traditional rules do not always apply. South Carolina, hotblooded enough to have started our only civil war, is perhaps the most bellicose of states, the least inclined to support a conciliatory foreign policy. Most South Carolina voters find it simply implausible that large numbers of their fellow Americans would mock traditional values or cast aspersions on patriotism, and they find it hard to vote for a candidate who seems sympathetic to those views.

The legacy of these voters is Democratic, and for a while in the 1970s, when Jimmy Carter appeared at the Firecracker 400 stock car race in 1976, the Democrats seemed to be speaking their language. But in the 1980s, as South Carolina has been growing more affluent and the Democrats seemed to be increasingly liberal on cultural and foreign policy issues, the South Carolina swing voters have been moving Republican. The voters who were entirely happy with

Democratic Governor Richard Riley, elected in 1978 and 1982 by large margins, were also happy to elect Republican Governor Carroll Campbell in 1986, albeit by a much narrower margin, and it is surely not without significance that these two governors—political rivals and not especially friendly ones—should choose to emphasize the same issue: education. And it may turn out that this not-so-long-ago underdeveloped country is leading the nation on this important part of national life.

Governor. Richard Riley's 1984 education reform package has been called "in many respects . . . the most comprehensive, sophisticated, thoughtful approach to reform in the country." It contained merit pay and pay raises for teachers and a tough new testing program including a high school graduation test, a building program, remedial classes and gifted-children programs, cash bonuses to schools that improve and penalties for those who do poorly. It was passed after Riley convinced businessmen and voters that the state needed a better educated work force to enjoy further economic growth, and that the extra taxes he was seeking would be worth it. In four years South Carolina chalked up some of the highest increases in test scores in the country, attendance is up, the high school graduation rate is up, and more teachers report morale gains that in any other state. Building on that record, Campbell got teachers' salaries up to the regional average and committed the biggest share of five years of budget increases to education. He set up a statewide Governor's School for Mathematics and Science, and stepped up spending on colleges and technical schools, and created a higher education program with student scholarships, endowed professorships and accountability and assessment measurements.

This is all the more interesting, because on the national political spectrum Campbell is counted as a conservative. His political career—from his days in the legislature to a controversial race for Congress in 1978 (Democrats claimed and Campbell denied that he encouraged a minor candidate to attack the Democrat on the grounds that as a Jew he did not believe in Jesus) to his election for the governorship and strong support of George Bush in 1987 and 1988—has been closely associated with Lee Atwater, the South Carolinian who is now chairman of the Republican National Committee. Campbell is adamant about lowering taxes, but his approach to government is anything but *laissez faire*. Campbell wants to lower auto insurance rates and reorganize state government, and his work on education, like Riley's, shows an appreciation that South Carolina needs to improve the skills of its work force if its economy is to continue to grow, and that market forces by themselves are not going to do that. Those who want to see an example of what Newt Gingrich calls "governing conservatism" would do well to go down to South Carolina.

Campbell won his 1986 race against Lieutenant Governor Mike Daniel by only 51%–49%, and only after labelling him as one of the insider politicians. His margins came in urban and suburban areas, especially in his home base of Greenville, and he may have been helped by increased turnout up-country; most rural counties went for Daniel. Tom Hartnett, his colleague in Congress, agreed to run for lieutenant governor rather than give Campbell a primary fight; but he was beaten 50%–49% by Democrat Nick Theodore—one reason why Campbell had none of the rumored interest in an appointment by George Bush. Since his election Campbell's ratings have been high and he has gone some distance toward building a stronger Republican Party; his candidates have captured several Democratic districts in state legislative elections. Campbell also had success in his backing of Bush. The South Carolina Republican primary was scheduled on the Saturday before Super Tuesday, presumably at Atwater's instigation, to give Bush an opportunity to start out with a big win before the rest of the South voted; Campbell campaigned actively with him, helped build his organization, and had the satisfaction of seeing him win a strong victory. For 1990, Campbell himself starts out a strong favorite. Riley, reported to be considering the race, announced late in 1988 that he would not run; possible Democrats include 1986 contenders Mike Daniel, Phil Lader and Hugh Leatherman amd Theo Mitchell, a black state Senator from Greenville.

Senators. For a long time South Carolina's Senate seats have in effect been the political reward of the most politically formidable of its governors: Burnet Maybank (first elected governor in 1938 and Senator in 1940), Olin Johnston (1934, 1944), Thurmond (1946, 1954), and Hollings (1958, 1966). The current Senators are commanding men who rose from humble beginnings, made their careers in the courtrooms, and ran unsuccessfully for President of the United States. They have proved to be two of the most durable and forceful members of the Senate today—or maybe ever. Strom Thurmond's career goes back nearly 60 years now: he was first elected to the legislature at 29, in 1932, and is plotting his reelection campaign for 1990. Hollings won his first election at 26, in 1948, and says those who think he may retire in 1992 are "non-thinkers."

Thurmond has combined a reputation for firmness and steadfastness with a flexibility and adroitness that has enabled this onetime symbol of racial segregation to prosper politically in an era of integration. He was elected governor in 1946 and won 39 electoral votes as the States' Rights—i.e., anti-civil rights—Democratic candidate for President in 1948. In 1954 he was elected to the Senate, stunningly, as a write-in candidate; he promised the voters that if he won he would resign and seek election in the ordinary manner, and in 1956 he did. During the 1964 campaign he switched to the Republican Party and supported Barry Goldwater for President; in 1968 he was the key power broker at the Republican National Convention, when he held the South for Richard Nixon.

This was his peak of national influence, but it was also a moment of peril: South Carolina's blacks were getting the vote, and for a moment Thurmond seemed to be in trouble. But he reacted to the enfranchisement of South Carolina's blacks by working as doggedly for them as he had for others: he hired black staffers in the early 1970s, pushed through the appointment of black federal judges, helped black local officials and citizens' groups with federal projects. He has ended up voting for renewal of the Voting Rights Act and the Martin Luther King Holiday. He probably gets few black votes, but he has softened black voters' hostility; they don't turn out in large numbers to vote against him or form a strong political base for a possible opponent. His switch was an example of his mind at work. There are no baroque embellishments to his thoughts; he is not interested in nuance or qualification. His intellect is simple but strong: he decides where he wants to go, figures out how to get there, and then does it.

Thurmond, as the senior Republican Senator, was president pro tempore of the Senate from 1980 to 1986, a ceremonial post he enjoyed, and which put him in the theoretical line of succession to the Presidency. He also served as chairman of the Judiciary Committee, having taken care in the 1970s to use his seniority to outrank the liberal Charles Mathias. As chairman Thurmond was courteous, cooperative, conciliatory, but ready to move fast when he had the votes. He seems to have a pleasant working relationship with the current chairman, Joseph Biden. In his middle 80s, he remains in excellent health, and if he doesn't seem attentive to detail to some observers, those who think he might overlook some legislative point or particle of procedure may find him alert and ready if the matter is something he cares about.

Thurmond is a WWII veteran and an unabashed enthusiast for things military, and a supporter of an aggressive and assertive foreign policy. But in 1987 he did not exercise his option of becoming ranking Republican on the Armed Services Committee, declining to elbow aside Virginia's John Warner as he had Mathias. He is also a member of Veterans' Affairs and, as of 1985, Labor and Human Resources Committees. Thurmond has surprised some observers by not aggressively pursuing conservative causes. Instead he has worked on consensus measures like stopping cop-killer bullets, outlawing plastic guns, reforming the antitrust laws, outlawing designer drugs, and keeping South Carolina from getting more nuclear waste. He wants to bar former federal officials from lobbying for foreign countries. A proud teetotaler—he pushes lemonade in the summertime—he wants large warning labels on liquor bottles. He did push the death penalty when he could and stoutly backed all Reagan judicial nominations. But one gets the impression that some time around 1970 Thurmond got tired of being a controversial figure who was widely hated, and decided to seek maximum acceptance and to make himself a consensus national leader instead. Not many then would have guessed he could do it, but he has.

Thurmond's seat came up in 1984, and he was reelected with scarcely any fuss. He has a solid bedrock of support in South Carolina that is well over 50%; he showed that in 1978 when he beat back a strong challenge by Democrat Charles Ravenel. There's been speculation about a possible Thurmond successor for 20 years now. But Thurmond shows no sign of tiring or retiring. With the same directness and steadiness of purpose he brings to all political enterprises, he has set out since early 1985 to put himself in a strong position to win reelection in 1990, and he seems to have succeeded. Some Republicans grumble that he supported Bob Dole rather than George Bush in 1988; some Democrats argue that he's not quite as strong as he seems. But the professional politicians seem convinced he still has his 50%-plus base and more, and in early 1989 he seemed likely to be a vigorous candidate—and a winner. The span of his career is awesome: Thurmond knew Pitchfork Ben Tillman, the South Carolina governor and Senator who was born in 1847, and his children have a good chance of living into the 2050s; this is a man in touch with two centuries of American politics.

South Carolina's other Senator, Ernest Hollings, ran for President in 1984 and made less impact than he wished—and less than his talents and program might seem to have warranted. Then in 1985 on the same issue he had emphasized in his campaign for the presidency with such dismal results he made a great impact indeed. The issue was the federal deficit, and while he won few votes with the budget freeze he proposed on the stump and on the Senate Budget Committee, he was successful in proposing the Gramm-Rudman-Hollings deficit-cutting bill. Hollings has been tussling with budgets for a long time, as chairman of the Senate Budget Committee in 1980 after Edmund Muskie resigned to become Secretary of State, and as ranking Democrat on the committee in 1981 and 1982, when the groundwork for the deficits was laid by the Reagan budget and tax cuts. He continues to be the second ranking Democrat on the Budget Committee, and his proposal for 1989 is a budget freeze combined with a 5% value-added tax on everything but food, housing and health care. This is typical Hollings: he believes in an activist federal government, but he also believes in subjecting it to strict discipline.

Now, however, Hollings is devoting much attention to his duties as chairman of the Senate Commerce Committee. He was careful to relinquish the ranking seat on Budget and take it on Commerce in 1983; for Commerce, which has jurisdiction over most federal regulation, is much the better place from which to raise funds for campaigns, presidential or otherwise. As chairman, Hollings is well-informed and aggressive. He is the major opponent of deregulating broadcasting, and has been trying to reinstate the Fairness Doctrine and to start regulation of advertising on children's programs. As a young lawyer he made his living as a plaintiffs' lawyer in negligence cases (he looks like a Charleston aristocrat, but has a modest background) and is opposed to laws limiting tort claims. He has worked on various ocean issues on the committee, including the 1988 ocean dumping law; he has championed a National Global Climate Change Research Act; he worked on reviving the National Space Council to be chaired by the Vice President. He is pushing a constitutional amendment to allow Congress to limit campaign spending. On trade issues he proudly proclaims himself a "hawk," supporting vigorously the textile bill that was widely criticized as protectionist.

Why did Hollings fall flat as a presidential candidate? One reason is the times: appeals for shared sacrifice fall flat in a peaceful, prosperous America. Another reason is the constituency. The Democrats' selection process is geared to mostly liberal party activists, and Hollings failed some of their litmus tests. He may have been the Senate's leading opponent of the MX missile in 1983, for example, but the party activists recognized, accurately, that on most military and foreign issues he is an unreconstructed hawk. He may have been the Senate's most effective fighter against hunger in the 1960s and 1970s, when he was spurred to action by discovering how poorly many people were eating in South Carolina, but he expressed a not-at-all-veiled scorn for schemes of income redistribution and job guarantee programs.

Confident and impressive in person even more than on television, Hollings has worked hard in Washington and campaigned hard in South Carolina. He seems well-positioned to run for reelection in 1992.

Presidential politics. South Carolina has become one of the most Republican of the southern states in presidential elections; in November 1988 it was, no doubt to Lee Atwater's great satisfaction, one of George Bush's strongest states in the country. He got 62% of the vote here, down only slightly from Ronald Reagan's 64% in 1984. One thing that is helping the Republicans is demographic change. The proliferation of Hilton Head Island-style condominium communities on the coast made two Low Country counties become more Republican between 1984 and 1988; the other big population gaining areas are counties just outside cities like Charleston, Columbia, and Greenville. With relatively few blacks and many upwardly mobile and/or deeply religious whites, they are heavily Republican. The election results tell the story. In counties where voter turnout rose more than 10% from 1980 to 1988, Bush beat Michael Dukakis 65%–34%; in counties where turnout rose less than 10% in the 1980s, Bush led Dukakis by the lesser margin of 59%–40%; in counties where turnout fell during the 1980s— many of them rural black-majority counties with little economic growth—Bush only barely beat Dukakis, 53%–46%.

South Carolina's Republican primary played a significant role in the 1988 contest; it was scheduled to help George Bush, and did. Carroll Campbell was one of three governors—John Sununu of New Hampshire and James Thompson of Illinois were the others—who were credited by Lee Atwater with major responsibility for Bush's three early crucial victories in their states. Bush's victory was especially sweet since it effectively extinguished the chances of Pat Robertson showing any significant primary strength to go with the support he had been able to win in packable caucuses.

As for the Democrats, they scheduled their caucus the weekend after Super Tuesday, presumably to deflect attention from it. Predictably, it was won by South Carolina-born Jesse Jackson, with blacks apparently accounting for more than half the turnout.

Congressional districting. South Carolina's congressional districts were changed only slightly in 1980s redistricting, and probably will not be changed significantly for the 1990s.

The People: Est. Pop. 1988: 3,493,000; Pop. 1980: 3,121,820, up 11.9% 1980–88 and 20.5% 1970–80; 1.40% of U.S. total, 24th largest. 13% with 1–3 yrs. col., 14% with 4+ yrs. col.; 16.6% below poverty level. Single ancestry: 19% English, 5% Irish, 4% German, 1% French, Scottish. Households (1980): 78% family, 46% with children, 63% married couples; 29.8% housing units rented; median monthly rent: $133; median house value: $35,100. Voting age pop. (1980): 2,179,854; 27% Black, 1% Spanish origin. Registered voters (1988): 1,437,628; no party registration.

1988 Share of Federal Tax Burden:　$9,141,000,000; 1.03% of U.S. total, 28th largest.

1988 Share of Federal Expenditures

	Total		Non-Defense		Defense	
Total Expend	$10,934m	(1.24%)	$8,023m	(1.22%)	$4,279m	(1.87%)
St/Lcl Grants	1,354m	(1.18%)	1,353m	(1.18%)	1m	(0.97%)
Salary/Wages	2,322m	(1.73%)	450m	(0.67%)	1,872m	(0.67%)
Pymnts to Indiv	5,139m	(1.26%)	4,666m	(1.19%)	473m	(2.54%)
Procurement	1,932m	(1.02%)	1,368m	(2.94%)	1,932m	(1.02%)
Research/Other	187m	(0.50%)	186m	(0.50%)	0m	(0.50%)

Political Lineup: Governor, Carroll A. Campbell, Jr. (R); Lt. Gov., Nick A. Theodore (D); Secy. of State, John T. Campbell (D); Atty. Gen., Travis Medlock (D); Treasurer, Grady L. Patterson, Jr. (D); Comptroller General, Earle E. Morris, Jr. (D). State Senate, 46 (35 D and 11 R); State House of Representatives, 124 (87 D and 37 R). Senators, Strom Thurmond (R) and Ernest F. Hollings (D). Representatives, 6 (4 D and 2 R).

1988 Presidential Vote

Bush (R) 606,443 (62%)
Dukakis (D). 370,554 (38%)

1984 Presidential Vote

Reagan (R) 615,539 (64%)
Mondale (D) 344,459 (36%)

1988 Republican Presidential Primary

Bush 94,738 (49%)
Dole. 40,265 (21%)
Robertson 37,261 (19%)
Kemp. 22,431 (11%)

GOVERNOR

Gov. Carroll A. Campbell, Jr. (R)

Elected 1986, term expires Jan. 1991; b. July 24, 1940, Greenville; home, Greenville; U. of SC, American U., M.A. 1985; Episcopalian; married (Iris).

Career: Real estate and farming; SC House of Reps., 1970–74; Exec. Asst. to Gov. James B. Edwards, 1975–76; SC Senate, 1976–78; U.S. House of Reps., 1978–86.

Office: P.O. Box 11369, The State House, Columbia 29211, 803-734-9818.

Election Results

1986 gen.	Carroll A. Campbell, Jr. (R) . . .	384,565	(51%)
	Mike Daniel (D).	361,325	(49%)
1986 prim.	Carroll A. Campbell, Jr. (R), unopposed		
1982 gen.	Richard W. Riley (D).	468,819	(70%)
	William D. Workman, Jr. (R) . .	202,806	(30%)

SENATORS
Sen. Strom Thurmond (R)

Elected 1954 seat up 1990; b. Dec. 5, 1902, Edgefield; home, Aiken; Clemson U., B.S. 1923; Baptist; married (Nancy).

Career: Teacher and coach, 1923–29; Edgefield Cnty. Super. of Educ., 1929–33; Practicing atty., 1930–38, 1951–55; SC Senate, 1933–38; Circuit Judge, 1938–42; Army, WWII; Gov. of SC, 1947–51; States Rights cand. for U.S. Pres., 1948; Pres. Pro Tempore, U.S. Senate, 1981–87.

Offices: 217 RSOB 20510, 202-224-5972. Also 1835 Assembly St., Ste. 1558, Columbia 29201, 803-765-5496; 334 Meeting St., Rm. 600, Charleston 29493, 803-724-4282; 211 York St. N.E., Ste. 29, Aiken 29801, 803-649-2591; and 401 W. Evans St., Florence 29501, 803-662-8873.

Committees: *Armed Services* (2d of 9 R). Subcommittees: Conventional Forces and Alliance Defense; Readiness, Sustainability and Support; Strategic Forces and Nuclear Deterrence (Ranking Member). *Judiciary* (Ranking Member of 6 R). Subcommittees: Antitrust, Monopolies and Business Rights (Ranking Member); Courts and Administrative Practice. *Labor and Human Resources* (5th of 7 R). Subcommittees: Employment and Productivity (Ranking Member); Education, Arts, and Humanities; Labor. *Veterans' Affairs* (3d of 5 R).

Group Ratings

	ADA	ACLU	COPE	CFA	LCV	ACU	NTLC	NSI	COC	CEI
1988	0	11	11	42	20	92	71	100	93	56
1987	15	—	11	17	—	96	—	—	71	62

National Journal Ratings

	1988 LIB — 1988 CONS	1987 LIB — 1987 CONS
Economic	22% — 75%	15% — 82%
Social	0% — 89%	16% — 78%
Foreign	8% — 91%	0% — 76%

Key Votes

1) Cut Aged Housing $	AGN	5) Bork Nomination	FOR	9) SDI Funding	FOR
2) Override Hwy Veto	AGN	6) Ban Plastic Guns	AGN	10) Ban Chem Weaps	FOR
3) Kill Plnt Clsng Notice	FOR	7) Deny Abortions	FOR	11) Aid To Contras	FOR
4) Min Wage Increase	AGN	8) Japanese Reparations	AGN	12) Reagan Defense $	FOR

Election Results

1984 general	Strom Thurmond (R)	644,815	(67%)	($1,682,962)
	Melvin Purvis (D)	306,982	(32%)	($9,023)
1984 primary	Strom Thurmond (R)	44,662	(94%)	
	Robert H. Cunningham (R)	2,693	(6%)	
1978 general	Strom Thurmond (R)	351,733	(56%)	($2,013,431)
	Charles D. Ravenel (D)	281,119	(44%)	($1,134,168)

Sen. Ernest F. (Fritz) Hollings (D)

Elected 1966, seat up 1992; b. Jan. 1, 1922, Charleston; home, Charleston; The Citadel, B.A. 1942, U. of SC, LL.B. 1947; Lutheran; married (Peatsy).

Career: Army, WWII; Practicing atty.; SC House of Reps., 1949–54, Speaker Pro Tempore, 1951–54; Lt. Gov. of SC, 1955–59; Gov. of SC, 1959–63.

Offices: 125 RSOB 20510, 202-224-6121. Also 1835 Assembly St., Columbia 29201, 803-765-5731; 112 Custom House, 200 E. Bay St., Charleston 29401, 803-724-4525; and 126 Fed. Bldg., Greenville 29304, 803-585-3702; 103 Fed. Bldg., Spartanburg 29301, 803-585-3702.

Committees: *Appropriations* (3d of 16 D). Subcommittees: Commerce, Justice, State, and Judiciary (Chairman); Defense; Energy and Water Development; Interior; Labor, Health and Human Services, Education. *Budget* (2d of 13 D). *Commerce, Science, and Transportation* (Chairman of 11 D). Subcommittees: Communications; Foreign Commerce and Tourism; Surface Transportation. *Select Committee on Intelligence* (3d of 8 D).

Group Ratings

	ADA	ACLU	COPE	CFA	LCV	ACU	NTLC	NSI	COC	CEI
1988	55	41	58	83	50	48	27	100	29	22
1987	40	—	57	50	—	62	—	—	17	27

National Journal Ratings

	1988 LIB — 1988 CONS		1987 LIB — 1987 CONS	
Economic	52%	— 45%	63%	— 36%
Social	60%	— 39%	35%	— 62%
Foreign	39%	— 59%	24%	— 75%

Key Votes

1) Cut Aged Housing $	FOR	5) Bork Nomination	FOR	9) SDI Funding	FOR
2) Override Hwy Veto	FOR	6) Ban Plastic Guns	AGN	10) Ban Chem Weaps	FOR
3) Kill Plnt Clsng Notice	FOR	7) Deny Abortions	AGN	11) Aid To Contras	FOR
4) Min Wage Increase	FOR	8) Japanese Reparations	AGN	12) Reagan Defense $	AGN

Election Results

1986 general	Ernest F. (Fritz) Hollings (D)	456,500	(63%)	($2,233,843)
	Henry D. McMaster (R)	262,886	(36%)	($584,288)
1986 primary	Ernest F. (Fritz) Hollings (D), unopposed			
1980 general	Ernest F. (Fritz) Hollings (D)	612,554	(70%)	($723,427)
	Marshall Mays (R)	257,946	(30%)	($62,472)

FIRST DISTRICT

There are few, if any, more beautiful urban scenes in America than the pastel "single houses" of Charleston, built flush with the sidewalk, turning their shoulders to the streets, with open "piazzas" inside their gateways facing south to catch the breeze, wreathed with the springtime flowers of blossoming trees. Charleston, founded in 1670 and blessed with one of the finest harbors on the Atlantic, was one of the South's two leading cities up to the Civil War. Across its docks went cargoes of rice, indigo, cotton—all cultivated by black slaves and enriching the white planters and merchants who dominated the state's economic and political life. Many of the old houses south of Broad were kept in families and preserved, but in the rest of the city, wrote the *WPA Guide* 50 years ago, "along streets no longer fashionable, clothes lines flap above abandoned gardens, and several Negro families are crowded out into some tumble-down big houses, spilling their progeny out on the sidewalk." In the years that followed the Civil War, Charleston became an economic backwater. Today prosperity has come back to Charleston, restoration has crept far north of the Battery, and the old part of the city, where the Ashley and Cooper Rivers meet to form the Atlantic Ocean, is still beautifully preserved and still the home of the city's elite, housing fewer people than it did when it rained out shots on Fort Sumter in 1861.

This is an old society. The old South Carolina aristocracy, very private today, was once a leading force in American political life. The Democrats held their national convention in Charleston in 1860, and the hotheaded dandies in the galleries hooted down the northerners and so disrupted the proceedings that the northerners adjourned and reconvened in Baltimore while the southerners nominated a separate ticket that enabled Lincoln to be elected with 38% of the popular vote. South Carolina's blacks also have a colorful history. There were free blacks here before the Civil War (some even owned slaves themselves), and Charleston's black culture was memorialized in *Porgy and Bess*. The local accent, which seems to outsiders to have a touch of New Jersey and which, rapidly spoken, can be incomprehensible, is best appreciated in the speech of Charleston native (but not aristocrat) Ernest Hollings.

Since World War II, Charleston has been growing again. At first the impetus was the military, with the big Navy and Air Force bases here nurtured by Mendel Rivers, chairman of the House Armed Services Committee from 1965 until his death in 1971; at one point they accounted for one-third of the payrolls in the Charleston area. The white working-class area around the port and the bases in North Charleston remembers: its main street is Rivers Avenue. The military continues to be important, but the economy has diversified since Rivers's death and has prospered by the influx of Yankees and southerners to the condominium communities on the barrier islands. The first of these, Hilton Head, was started by Charles Fraser in 1957; it was an untested, risky concept at the time. Nearby were some of the poorest areas in the United States, where lowland blacks lived in poverty and malnutrition; many spoke a distinct dialect called Gullah. Now the blacks are much better off, and practically the entire coast is covered with developments inspired, in varying degrees, by the original.

The 1st Congressional District of South Carolina includes Charleston and its suburbs, the Low Country south and west of Charleston, and a couple of black-majority counties inland. Historically this was one of the most Democratic of constituencies in Franklin Roosevelt's time; now it leans Republican. High-income whites in these new areas, and in the affluent areas of Charleston, both in the old downtown and in new neighborhoods east of the Ashley River and out in the suburbs, have proved to be heavily Republican; blacks, who did not vote in most of this area until after 1965, are even more heavily Democratic.

The congressman from this district is Republican Arthur Ravenel, an experienced Charleston politician with a fine old South Carolina Huguenot name. He is a cousin of Charles Ravenel, the young Democrat who was about to be elected governor in 1974 until his name was yanked off the ballot for failure to meet a residency requirement; he ran against Strom Thurmond in 1978 and in the 1st District in 1980, and lost both times. The Republican Ravenel is folksy ("Hi, I'm your cousin Arthur," he greets passers-by), worked hard on constituency service as a state legislator, and has, unusually for a Republican, significant support from black voters. The seat was up in 1986 because Republican Tom Hartnett, who showed a flip contempt for the business of legislating, left the House to run for lieutenant governor (an office he narrowly lost); Arthur Ravenel beat Democrat Jimmy Stuckey 52%–48%.

In his first term Ravenel compiled a somewhat mixed record ideologically and got a seat on

Armed Services—more or less a political necessity for this district—and worked to channel dollars into the Charleston Shipyard and military health care. He was concerned about acid rain because of damage to the Medway Plantation. His most vivid moment may have come when he told Defense Secretary Carlucci of the need for military involvement in fighting drugs, saying, by his own account, "What we need to do, upon positive identification, which is very important, is begin shooting down the drug-carrying planes and machine-gunning any survivors. I believe that very quickly these tough measures will put an end to drug smuggling. I further told the Secretary to think of all the money that will be saved by not having to have lengthy trials or having to maintain the drug traffickers in jail." He did not record Carlucci's reaction, but the voters in the 1st District responded favorably and reelected him by a 64%–36% margin.

The People: Est. Pop. 1986: 584,200, up 12.3% 1980–86; Pop. 1980: 520,338, up 25.3% 1970–80. Households (1980): 77% family, 47% with children, 61% married couples; 36.1% housing units rented; median monthly rent: $174; median house value: $41,400. Voting age pop. (1980): 362,866; 29% Black, 2% Spanish origin, 1% Asian origin.

1988 Presidential Vote:

Bush (R)	100,179	(61%)
Dukakis (D)	62,594	(38%)

Rep. Arthur Ravenel, Jr. (R)

Elected 1986; b. Mar. 29, 1927, St. Andrews Parish; home, Mount Pleasant; Col. of Charleston, B.A. 1950; French Huguenot; married (Jean).

Career: USMC, 1945–46; Realtor, gen. contractor, cattleman; SC House of Reps., 1952–58; SC Senate, 1980–86.

Offices: 508 CHOB 20515, 202-225-3176. Also 640 Fed. Bldg., Rm. 640, Charleston 29403, 803-724-4175; 263 Hampton St., Walterboro 29488, 803-549-5395; P.O. Box 550, Estill 29918, 803-625-3177; and P.O. Box 1538, Beaufort 29902, 803-524-2166.

Committees: *Armed Services* (17th of 21 R). Subcommittees: Military Installations and Facilities; Military Personnel and Compensation.

Group Ratings

	ADA	ACLU	COPE	CFA	LCV	ACU	NTLC	NSI	COC	CEI
1988	25	41	47	64	56	76	57	100	86	35
1987	24	—	31	29	—	61	—	—	87	51

National Journal Ratings

	1988 LIB — 1988 CONS		1987 LIB — 1987 CONS	
Economic	34% —	65%	29% —	69%
Social	40% —	58%	32% —	67%
Foreign	30% —	67%	28% —	70%

Key Votes

1) Homeless $	FOR	5) Ban Drug Test	AGN	9) SDI Research	FOR
2) Gephardt Amdt	AGN	6) Drug Death Pen	FOR	10) Ban Chem Weaps	AGN
3) Deficit Reduc	AGN	7) Handgun Sales	FOR	11) Aid to Contras	FOR
4) Kill Plnt Clsng Notice	FOR	8) Ban D.C. Abort $	FOR	12) Nuclear Testing	AGN

Election Results

1988 general	Arthur Ravenel, Jr. (R)................	101,572	(64%)	($118,702)
	Wheeler Tillman (D)...................	57,691	(36%)	($82,035)
1988 primary	Arthur Ravenel, Jr. (R), unopposed			
1986 general	Arthur Ravenel, Jr. (R)................	59,969	(52%)	($265,574)
	Jimmy Stuckey (D)...................	55,262	(48%)	($457,810)

SECOND DISTRICT

In 1786, just after the Revolution, the South Carolina legislature decided to move the state's capital away from the aristocrats of Charleston and into the up-country interior, away from a city named after a king to a new city they created smack dab in the middle of the state and named after a discoverer of America. So began Columbia. The State House was built on high ground above the Congaree River, amid a town of Columbia cottages—1½ story houses with first floor porticoes, dormers and raised brick basements. The big event in Columbia's later history was the arrival of Sherman's Army: "Except for the State House," the *WPA Guide* noted in 1940, "no structure on Main Street antedates 'The Burning' by Sherman, in 1865. His name is still anathema to Columbians." In the post-Sherman years Columbia grew slowly, with state government and the university, the Army's Fort Jackson and local insurance companies proving steady employers. More recently it has started to boom, attracting plants from Michelin and Allied Chemical, United Technologies and FN of Belgium, Du Pont and Square D. The Columbia metropolitan area on both sides of the Congaree is the largest and most prosperous in South Carolina, and some are projecting it as one of the fastest-growing U.S. metro areas of the 1990s.

Columbia is one of those southern metropolitan areas that has been trending Republican for at least 30 years. The Columbia where Sherman was remembered in the 1940s and where Jimmy Byrnes, after years in top posts in Democratic Washington, returned as governor to lament the *Brown v. Board of Education* decision in 1954, has trended Republican in the years since. Upwardly mobile South Carolinians, transplanted from rural areas with no electricity to comfortable subdivisions with two-car garages, preferred Republicans first in national and then in state and local elections. The Columbia area went for Eisenhower in the 1950s; even when blacks got the vote in 1965, they were outnumbered usually by the increasingly Republican whites—particularly if you count not just Columbia's Richland County, but also the once rural and now suburban Lexington County across the river. South Carolina's 2d Congressional District is made up of those two counties, plus part of the South Carolina lowland country around Orangeburg. This was plantation country before 1865, most of the people who live here now are black, and politics follows racial lines.

The congressman from the 2d District is Republican Floyd Spence, who has been running for office in the Columbia area since 1956. Spence became a Republican in 1962, two years before Strom Thurmond, narrowly lost a House race that year to Albert Watson (a Democrat who supported Barry Goldwater in 1964, and was kicked out of the Democratic Caucus for it), and became a Republican in 1965. When Watson ran for governor in 1970, Spence ran for the House seat and won it.

Spence won a close reelection in 1988 after a difficult year: in May he underwent a double-lung transplant. His illness had forced him to relinquish the increasingly hot seat of ranking Republican on the House Ethics Committee, and he was necessarily less active on the Armed Services Committee. But he insisted that he came out of surgery with "the lungs of an 18-year-old." Spence has often had serious opponents, tempted by the rather close balance of racial and political forces in the district, including Matthew Perry, a black later appointed a federal judge by Strom Thurmond, and Jack Bass, a top newspaper reporter and the writer of the definitive work on the Orangeburg massacre when highway patrolmen shot black students in 1968. In 1988 his opponent was Jim Leventis, a Columbia county councilman and prominent attorney and banker, considered to be at least as strong as the opponents who had held Spence (with one exception) to the 54% to 59% range from 1974 to 1986. Spence recovered physically and started generating news about military contracts, a computer virus bill, and expanding the Congaree Swamp National Monument. Leventis actually raised more money and campaigned hard.

But in this polarized constituency the results were almost the same as in the close 1986 race. Spence won 53%–46%, carrying 68% in Lexington County and winning the Columbia area 54%–45%. After the election, Spence was still generating news, announcing a partnership between Hughes Aircraft and South Carolina State in Orangeburg. But the same factors which produced a serious challenge and a close race may well be operating in 1990.

The People: Est. Pop. 1986: 562,400, up 7.6% 1980–86; Pop. 1980: 522,688, up 24.6% 1970–80. Households (1980): 76% family, 45% with children, 60% married couples; 32.7% housing units rented; median monthly rent: $160; median house value: $40,800. Voting age pop. (1980): 372,290; 32% Black, 1% Spanish origin, 1% Asian origin.

1988 Presidential Vote:

Bush (R)	103,577	(59%)
Dukakis (D).	67,446	(39%)

Rep. Floyd D. Spence (R)

Elected 1970; b. Apr. 9, 1928, Columbia; home, Lexington; U. of SC, A.B. 1952, LL.B. 1956; Lutheran; married (Deborah).

Career: Navy, 1952–54; Practicing atty.; SC House of Reps., 1956–62; SC Senate, 1966–70, Minor. Ldr., 1966–70.

Offices: 2405 RHOB 20515, 202-225-2452. Also 140 Stone Ridge Dr., Ste. 104, Columbia 29201, 803-254-5120; and 1681 Chestnut St. N.E., P.O. Box 1609, Orangeburg 29116-1609, 803-536-4641.

Committees: *Armed Services* (2d of 21 R). Subcommittees: Military Installations and Facilities; Seapower and Strategic and Critical Materials (Ranking Member). *Select Committee on Aging* (20th of 27 R). Subcommittees: Human Services; Retirement Income and Employment.

Group Ratings

	ADA	ACLU	COPE	CFA	LCV	ACU	NTLC	NSI	COC	CEI
1988	10	18	16	18	44	85	73	100	71	38
1987	4	—	15	14	—	73	—	—	93	56

National Journal Ratings

	1988 LIB — 1988 CONS			1987 LIB — 1987 CONS		
Economic	*	—	*	29%	—	69%
Social	13%	—	84%	15%	—	84%
Foreign	0%	—	84%	0%	—	80%

Key Votes

1) Homeless $	FOR	5) Ban Drug Test	FOR	9) SDI Research	FOR
2) Gephardt Amdt	AGN	6) Drug Death Pen	—	10) Ban Chem Weaps	AGN
3) Deficit Reduc	—	7) Handgun Sales	FOR	11) Aid to Contras	FOR
4) Kill Plnt Clsng Notice	FOR	8) Ban D.C. Abort $	FOR	12) Nuclear Testing	AGN

Election Results

1988 general	Floyd D. Spence (R)...................	94,960	(53%)	($369,698)
	Jim Leventis (D).....................	83,978	(46%)	($376,727)
1988 primary	Floyd D. Spence (R), unopposed			
1986 general	Floyd D. Spence (R)...................	73,455	(54%)	($294,665)
	Fred Zeigler (D).....................	63,592	(46%)	($179,860)

THIRD DISTRICT

The South Carolina up-country, many days' travel by wagon from the Low Country plantations owned by Charleston aristocrats, was first settled by Scots-Irish farmers, like the family of John C. Calhoun in the years just before and after the Revolutionary War. The pioneers wanted to make big plantations of these forests, but the land did not always cooperate: it was too hilly for the labor-intensive rice crop grown in the lowlands and sometimes too cold for cotton. So while the coastal plantations were tended by thousands of slaves, relatively few were brought here, and the land went mostly to smaller white farmers. That history has consequences today. The 3d Congressional District of South Carolina, which follows the Savannah River border with Georgia for most of its length, starts in the lowlands in Allendale County, which is 62% black, and proceeds north to 3,500-foot Sassafras Mountain, in Pickens County, which is 7% black.

The southern part of this district is Strom Thurmond country. He grew up in Edgefield and as county judge there in the 1930s maintained stern white control of the black majority. He maintains his residence now in Aiken, a prosperous town which was long a winter haven for New York huntsmen, and which now is the chief commercial center for the huge (15,000 employees) and troubled Savanah River Plant, which produces nuclear weapons material. The northern part of the district, where Calhoun had his mansion and his son-in-law created Clemson College nearby, is Piedmont and textile country, with mountains in the north. Here the Savannah River intersects with Interstate 85, the main street of America's textile belt, near Anderson, the largest city in the district.

The politics of this area, ancestrally Democratic, has been trending Republican for some time now. Aiken started voting Republican for Dwight Eisenhower in the 1950s, well before Thurmond switched parties in 1964; it has been steadily Republican ever since. Anderson, in contrast, has jumped around. It voted for George Wallace in 1968, Richard Nixon in 1972, Jimmy Carter in 1976 and 1980, Ronald Reagan in 1984, and by almost as large a margin, more than 2 to 1, for George Bush in 1988. Some of the river counties with their large black populations remain Democratic. But the textile mill counties from Clemson to the mountains are heavily Republican. The result is that what was a Carter district in 1976 and 1980 had become a Bush district by 1988.

This poses some problems for Butler Derrick, the Democratic congressman from the 3d District since 1974. The national Democratic strength here early in his career gave him leeway to fashion a distinctive record. He got a seat on the Rules Committee in 1979, where he was free to concentrate on whatever issues he liked with the understanding that he'd be helpful to the Democratic leadership. He also served two rotations on the Budget Committee, from 1975–79 and 1983–89.

But as the 1980s have gone on, he has gravitated more to district causes. He served as the chairman of the Congressional Textile Caucus, sponsoring a ban on Soviet textile imports and the requirement that the country of origin be named on garment labels. He was a lead sponsor of the 1987 textile protection bill vetoed by President Reagan. He argues that he vetoed in a conference committee session proposals to put Monitored Receivable Storage of nuclear waste in the Savannah River Plant area, by tying that measure to the selection of a permanent nuclear waste repository, which is expected to be in Nevada. On the other hand, he has been a staunch advocate of the Energy Department's selection of Savannah River for a new nuclear production facility; the area was badly hurt by the closedown of facilities due to charges of unsafety or obsolescence in 1988.

All of this must have helped Derrick in his 1988 reelection fight, his first rough contest in years. His opponent was Henry Jordan, an Anderson surgeon who lost the nomination to face Ernest Hollings in 1986; this time he had good financing, though much less than Derrick. Jordan accused Derrick of being a johnny-come-lately on the textile bill, though Jordan himself seemed to talk quite fondly of free trade; he also accused the Democrat of voting to release non-violent federal prisoners 90 days early to ease overcrowding—a way of linking him with one of Michael Dukakis's vulnerabilities. He got Oliver North to come to Clemson to campaign. Derrick was a familiar figure in his horn-rimmed glasses and trademark suspenders, and his work on textiles and the Savannah River plant must surely have worked in his favor. Yet he won with just 54% of the vote—one of two Democrats on Rules (David Bonior of Michigan was the other) with this not very impressive showing. Derrick carried Anderson with 54%, but only barely won the textile counties to the north; for all his work on Savannah River, he lost Aiken County, with its increasing numbers of affluent suburbanites. Derrick gave up any plans he had for statewide office in 1984, and he has a fine future ahead in the House: on Rules he ranks just behind the new chairman, Joe Moakley; he could easily be chairman some day and in the meantime is in fine position to exert leverage on all manner of things. But the 1988 result indicates that he may get more serious competition and may be hard pressed to hold this Republican-trending district.

The People: Est. Pop. 1986: 554,600, up 6.8% 1980–86; Pop. 1980: 519,280, up 20.2% 1970–80. Households (1980): 79% family, 44% with children, 65% married couples; 25.3% housing units rented; median monthly rent: $104; median house value: $32,000. Voting age pop. (1980): 366,318; 20% Black, 1% Spanish origin.

1988 Presidential Vote:

Bush (R)	108,043	(66%)
Dukakis (D)	54,507	(33%)

Rep. Butler Derrick (D)

Elected 1974; b. Sept. 30, 1936, Springfield, MA; home, Edgefield; U. of SC, U. of GA, LL.B. 1965; Episcopalian; married (Beverly).

Career: Practicing atty., 1965–74; SC House of Reps., 1969–74.

Offices: 201 CHOB 20515, 202-225-5301. Also 315 S. McDuffie St., Anderson 29622, 803-224-7401; 211 York St. N.E., Rm. 5, Aiken 29801, 803-649-5571; and 129 Fed. Bldg., Greenwood 29622, 803-223-8251.

Committees: *Rules* (2d of 9 D). Subcommittee: Legislative Process (Chairman). *Select Committee on Aging* (12th of 39 D). Subcommittee: Health and Long-Term Care.

Group Ratings

	ADA	ACLU	COPE	CFA	LCV	ACU	NTLC	NSI	COC	CEI
1988	70	59	57	82	69	36	23	30	54	23
1987	72	—	56	43	—	17	—	—	40	23

National Journal Ratings

	1988 LIB — 1988 CONS	1987 LIB — 1987 CONS
Economic	45% — 54%	60% — 39%
Social	42% — 57%	44% — 56%
Foreign	51% — 48%	58% — 41%

Key Votes

1) Homeless $	AGN	5) Ban Drug Test	FOR	9) SDI Research	AGN
2) Gephardt Amdt	FOR	6) Drug Death Pen	FOR	10) Ban Chem Weaps	FOR
3) Deficit Reduc	FOR	7) Handgun Sales	FOR	11) Aid to Contras	AGN
4) Kill Plnt Clsng Notice	AGN	8) Ban D.C. Abort $	AGN	12) Nuclear Testing	FOR

Election Results

1988 general	Butler Derrick (D)	89,071	(54%)	($641,429)
	Henry Jordan (R)	75,571	(45%)	($354,575)
1988 primary	Butler Derrick (D), unopposed			
1986 general	Butler Derrick (D)	79,109	(68%)	($177,714)
	Richard Dickison (R)	36,495	(32%)	($4,261)

FOURTH DISTRICT

When northern investors were looking for sites for textile mills as long ago as the 1880s, they looked to the up-country of South Carolina, to which they "were attracted by the mild climate, abundant water power, proximity to the cotton fields, and plenty of native [and white] labor already accustomed to a low standard of living." And so the textile industry of the South became centered by 1900 along the Southern Railway tracks between Charlotte and Atlanta, mainly in the Piedmont of North and South Carolina; and as the mills fled New England and the Northeast in the 1920s, the concentration here became even more thick. The textile country could look bucolic, as it did 50 years ago to a WPA writer in Greenville, where "winding streets, following old paths and roads, cross and recross the Reedy River," but Spartanburg, like Greenville, was "not so much a city as it is the civic center of a county highly developed agriculturally and industrially. The business district, where tall buildings, handsome stores, and modern hotels hobnob with shabby little old structures, occupies several blocks on narrow streets converging at Morgan Square. In the entire city, blocks are of irregular length and, without civic plan, streets have evolved from twisting woodland paths and lanes."

Today, this same stretch of land along South Carolina's Interstate 85, which parallels the Southern, remains the number one textile-producing area in the United States. But it is more than that. Greenville and Spartanburg Counties have attracted new businesses producing Michelin tires and Stouffer's Lean Cuisine and Digital Computer, most of them requiring higher skills and paying higher wages than the mills. This has long been one of the most industrialized and blue-collar parts of the nation, because of textiles; now with diversification it is becoming one of the economic growth centers of the South or, for that matter, the western world. It also stages the largest balloon race east of the Mississippi, with some 200 balloons competing each year.

Northern observers have always thought that textiles and the textile belt would go the way of big northern industries like steel and autos: that the manufacturers would be concentrated into a few big companies, operating huge factories, and that the workers would join unions which would bargain for high wages and fringe benefits. But history has taken a different course. There are big textile companies, like Roger Milliken's operation which is headquartered in Greenville. But there are lots of small producers as well, and the concentration of textile companies has not squeezed other businesses out as autos squeezed others out of Michigan. The plants have become not more concentrated, but more scattered—in some large mills and small, not usually in cities (which aren't very large here anyway) but at the edge of small towns or in the middle of heavily settled rural landscapes, near an interchange or on a side highway. Wages have not risen, and workers who want more go to the newer industries; and unions, despite a few publicized exceptions, have made almost no headway at all. Yet the textile country is thriving and diversification is more than compensating for jobs lost because of cheap foreign competition. And the industrial North which set itself up as a model is now—with smaller companies growing and unions' power eroding—coming to resemble the textile country rather than vice versa.

The textile mill country has its own sets of civic institutions: business leaders and their allies in press and politics and religious fundamentalists and evangelicals like the proprietors of Greenville's Bob Jones University. The two biggest towns here have divergent political traditions. Spartanburg has been more Democratic and was the home base of politicians like James Byrnes when he was Senator (he was also congressman, Supreme Court Justice, Secretary of State, and finally governor in the early 1950s) and Olin Johnston (governor 1935–39 and 1943–45 and Senator 1945–65), who tended to support their party on economic issues. Greenville's products have included moderate Democrats and Republicans, like Judge and defeated Supreme Court nominee Clement Haynsworth, Democratic Governor (1979–87) Richard Riley, and his Republican successor Carroll Campbell.

The 4th Congressional District of South Carolina, which includes Greenville and Spartanburg and one small county, has had seriously contested races when it has been open, as in 1978 and 1986. The most recent winner was Liz Patterson, a state Senator and former council member from Spartanburg and daughter of Olin Johnston. The primary action, interestingly, was on the Republican side—a struggle between William Workman III, a newspaper editor with many business and Republican ties, and two candidates with strong religious backing; Workman won, but got just 49% in the first primary and was hurt in the strife. Patterson has a history of government service in the Peace Corps and Vista, civic involvement on college and agency boards, Sunday school teaching; she was attacked as a liberal but campaigned convincingly as a fiscal conservative concerned about human needs. Workman won 56% in Greenville County, but she won 60% in Spartanburg and 63% in Union, for a 52% victory.

In the House Patterson was proud of her work setting up child care centers in Veterans' Administration medical centers and of her fiscal voting record; like other South Carolina Democrats she is about in the middle of the House on economic, cultural and foreign issues. In 1988 there was again a Republican primary, with former Campbell aide Knox White beating a fundamentalist airline pilot 56%–45%. The general election was almost a carbon copy of 1986. White won 54% in Greenville County, but Patterson won 60% in Spartanburg and 67% in Union, for a 52% victory. This was 20% ahead of Michael Dukakis's showing here, but suggests another close race in 1990 if Knox White should challenge Patterson again.

The People: Est. Pop. 1986: 549,200, up 5.5% 1980–86; Pop. 1980: 520,525, up 17.3% 1970–80. Households (1980): 78% family, 43% with children, 63% married couples; 30.4% housing units rented; median monthly rent: $132; median house value: $34,300. Voting age pop. (1980): 373,015; 17% Black, 1% Spanish origin.

1988 Presidential Vote:

Bush (R)	....	114,191	(67%)
Dukakis (D)	....	54,572	(32%)

Rep. Elizabeth J. (Liz) **Patterson (D)**

Elected 1986; b. Nov. 18, 1939, Columbia; home, Spartanburg; Columbia Col., B.A. 1961; United Methodist; married (Dwight).

Career: Recruiting office, Peace Corps, 1962–64, VISTA, 1965–66; VISTA SC Coordinator, 1966–67; Head Start Coordinator, SC Ofc. of Econ. Opp., 1967–68; Aide to Rep. James R. Mann, 1969–70; Mbr., Spartanburg Cnty. Cncl., 1975–76; SC Senate, 1979–86.

Offices: 1641 LHOB 20515, 202-225-6030. Also P.O. Box 10408, Fed. Station, Greenville 29603, 803-232-1141; P.O. Box 1330, Spartanburg 29304, 803-582-6422; and P.O. Box 904, Union 29379, 803-427-2205.

Committees: *Banking, Finance and Urban Affairs* (22d of 31 D). Subcommittees: Economic Stabilization; Financial Institutions Supervision, Regulation and Insurance; Housing and Community Development. *Veterans' Affairs* (13th of 21 D). Subcommittees: Education, Training and Employment; Hospitals and Health Care. *Select Committee on Hunger* (12th of 19 D).

Group Ratings

	ADA	ACLU	COPE	CFA	LCV	ACU	NTLC	NSI	COC	CEI
1988	45	52	67	100	50	48	39	60	57	32
1987	72	—	63	43	—	26	—	—	60	32

National Journal Ratings

	1988 LIB — 1988 CONS		1987 LIB — 1987 CONS	
Economic	40%	— 58%	41%	— 58%
Social	40%	— 58%	48%	— 50%
Foreign	44%	— 55%	50%	— 48%

Key Votes

1) Homeless $	FOR	5) Ban Drug Test	FOR	9) SDI Research	AGN
2) Gephardt Amdt	FOR	6) Drug Death Pen	FOR	10) Ban Chem Weaps	FOR
3) Deficit Reduc	AGN	7) Handgun Sales	FOR	11) Aid to Contras	FOR
4) Kill Plnt Clsng Notice	FOR	8) Ban D.C. Abort $	FOR	12) Nuclear Testing	AGN

Election Results

1988 general	Elizabeth J. Patterson (D)	90,234	(52%)	($1,143,351)
	Knox White (R)	82,793	(48%)	($630,913)
1988 primary	Elizabeth J. Patterson (D), unopposed			
1986 general	Elizabeth J. Patterson (D)	67,012	(52%)	($594,026)
	Bill Workman (R)	61,648	(47%)	($639,859)

FIFTH DISTRICT

In the late 18th century Scots-Irish farmers moved from the sluggish rivers of Low Country Carolina to the up-country and Piedmont, where were fought some of the fiercest battles of the Revolutionary War. Kings Mountain and the brilliantly executed Cowpens were fought here, and Andrew Jackson as a boy was scarred when he defied a British soldier; and the fighting spirit has never really subsided. Nor has the strong Calvinist religion which the earliest settlers brought with them; it lives on in various forms of Protestantism today—including the preaching of Jim Bakker and his wife Tammy Faye, who built their headquarters and their Heritage USA

Christian theme park and vacation retreat here in Fort Mill, South Carolina. What has changed, however, is that what looks like farming country—and still has many farms on it—has economically long since been a part of industrial America. Textile mills have been the biggest employers in up-country South Carolina, and the picture the *WPA Guide* gives of the city of Rock Hill 50 years ago is scarcely bucolic: "Railroad tracks run through the middle of the town, and the Memorial Bridge viaduct, honoring the military dead, connects the business district with the north residential section. While the houses are not outstanding architecturally, many along the wide, tree-bordered thoroughfares are distinguished for their lawns and gardens. Homes of the better educated and more prosperous Negroes are on the southern outskirts, with the usual fringe of cabins and 'shotgun' houses where the poorer classes of both races live."

In the 1970s metropolitan growth is moving out into these textile and tobacco farm counties, from Charlotte, North Carolina, just to the north, from the Greenville-Spartanburg strip along Interstate 85 which now specializes in more than textiles, from the state capital of Columbia. Eleven such counties in north and central South Carolina make up the state's 5th Congressional District.

The congressman from the 5th District is John Spratt. He comes from a politically active family in Rock Hill and has degrees from Davidson, Yale Law and Oxford; he was one of the young Democrats involved in Charles Ravenel's unsuccessful 1974 campaign for governor and have stayed in South Carolina politics since. Spratt was first elected in 1982, when incumbent Ken Holland announced his retirement a week before the filing deadline; he was able to put a campaign together readily and won 38% in the primary, 55% in the runoff against a candidate who spent $929,000, and 68% in the general election. He has been reelected easily, winning 70% in 1988.

Spratt has made a name for himself in the House as a smart and hard-working Member whose knowledge and judgments can be relied on. As a freshman he failed to get a seat on Energy and Commerce and went to Armed Services instead. There he has become, according to *National Journal*, "one of the House's more influential members on matters military." His secret has been to study hard and master the details personally. Early on he became an expert on the issue of procurement, mastering the details while others were making headlines, with an understanding of the hard choices and tradeoffs that must be made in any procurement reform. He has been one of the Democrats most immersed in the details of the Strategic Defense Initiative, about which he has neither the unalloyed enthusiasm of a Jack Kemp nor the not very well informed opposition of some northern liberal Democrats; he favored only restricted funds for the Phase One SDI deployment. He worked on the difficult and for a South Carolinian sensitive issue of the safety of the Savannah River Plant nuclear reactors. He conducted breakfast seminars on chemical warfare and came up with a compromise that allowed carefully limited research to continue.

He has spent some time on domestic issues as well, sponsoring a bill requiring recycling for most consumer product packaging, supporting the "Buy American Bearings" cause, and transferring title to the Sandhills Forest to the state of South Carolina. On economic, cultural and foreign issues generally he has taken positions that put him at about midpoint in the House. Some have pushed Spratt to run for statewide office, but he says he has no interest in becoming governor, and seems uninterested in running against either incumbent Senator or against Richard Riley if he runs for Senate. So the likelihood is that he will continue what has been a productive career in the House.

The People: Est. Pop. 1986: 549,300, up 5.7% 1980–86; Pop. 1980: 519,716, up 12.9% 1970–80. Households (1980): 80% family, 47% with children, 64% married couples; 26.5% housing units rented; median monthly rent: $104; median house value: $31,000. Voting age pop. (1980): 357,907, 29% Black, 1% Spanish origin.

1988 Presidential Vote: Bush (R) 91,385   (60%)

Dukakis (D). 61,398   (40%)

Rep. John M. Spratt, Jr. (D)

Elected 1982; b. Nov. 1, 1942, Charlotte, NC; home, York; Davidson Col., A.B. 1964, Oxford U., M.A. 1966, Yale U., LL.B. 1969; Presbyterian; married (Jane).

Career: Operations Ofc. of Asst. Secy. of Defense, 1969–71; Practicing atty., 1971–82; Pres., Bank of Ft. Mill, 1973–82; Pres., Spratt Insur. Agcy., 1973–82.

Offices: 1533 LHOB 20515, 202-225-5501. Also Box 350, Rock Hill 29731, 803-327-1114; 39 E. Calhoun St., Sumter 29150, 803-773-3362; and Box 964, Laurens 29360, 803-984-5323.

Committees: *Armed Services* (18th of 31 D). Subcommittees: Investigations; Procurement and Military Nuclear Systems. *Government Operations* (15th of 24 D). Subcommittees: Commerce, Consumer, and Monetary Affairs; Government Information, Justice, and Agriculture.

Group Ratings

	ADA	ACLU	COPE	CFA	LCV	ACU	NTLC	NSI	COC	CEI
1988	55	57	61	64	75	29	30	33	57	29
1987	72	—	57	50	—	9	—	—	47	21

National Journal Ratings

	1988 LIB — 1988 CONS	1987 LIB — 1987 CONS
Economic	40% — 58%	53% — 46%
Social	50% — 50%	48% — 50%
Foreign	56% — 43%	56% — 44%

Key Votes

1) Homeless $	AGN	5) Ban Drug Test	FOR	9) SDI Research	FOR
2) Gephardt Amdt	FOR	6) Drug Death Pen	FOR	10) Ban Chem Weaps	AGN
3) Deficit Reduc	FOR	7) Handgun Sales	FOR	11) Aid to Contras	AGN
4) Kill Plnt Clsng Notice	FOR	8) Ban D.C. Abort $	FOR	12) Nuclear Testing	AGN

Election Results

1988 general	John M. Spratt, Jr. (D).	107,959	(70%)	($105,620)
	Robert Carley (R).	46,622	(30%)	($8,449)
1988 primary	John M. Spratt, Jr. (D), unopposed			
1986 general	John M. Spratt, Jr. (D), unopposed			($66,944)

SIXTH DISTRICT

The 6th Congressional District of South Carolina is part of the state's Low Country, north and east of Charleston, up to the North Carolina border. Here the rivers wind lazily toward the shoreline, where they come upon the barrier islands now developed as South Carolina's Grand Strand. Inland you find tobacco fields; 15 acres can support a family, though not very well, which helps to explain why tobacco area politicians defend its interests so assiduously. This was once plantation country, and a large percentage of the people here are black; three of the counties have black majorities, and overall the district is 37% black. This is the highest percentage in a South Carolina district, and the percentage of blacks is no longer declining as it was before 1970. For years blacks from this area lined up after high school graduation and got on the bus to New York (called the "chicken bone special," because they packed chicken dinners) to make their livings. Now they remain in South Carolina, and over the long run the black percentage here may rise. Still, the places here with the most rapid recent growth are along the coast, especially the Grand Strand on either side of Myrtle Beach in Horry County. This is attracting migrants from other parts of the South, many of them affluent retirees, and almost all of them white.

Nonetheless this is a district where black voters have had the satisfaction of influencing congressional politics greatly since the Voting Rights Act of 1965. In 1972 they ousted the chairman of the House District of Columbia Committee, John McMillan, who was often accused of being a racist. In 1974 and 1982 they ousted Republican congressmen who had gotten in under special circumstances. The current congressman, Robin Tallon, is a Democrat who had the happy assignment of facing in 1982 the Republican who had beaten convicted Abscam defendant John Jenrette in 1980. Tallon, a Democratic legislator and clothing chain store owner, had strong support from blacks as Jenrette did, and concentrated his campaign efforts on turning out the black vote. He ran close to racial percentages in most counties, but won enough white votes in Horry County to win districtwide with 52%. Since then it has been no contest. Tallon was reelected with 76% in 1986 and 1988. Even the national ticket doesn't hurt much. Michael Dukakis lost the district, but only by a 56%–44% margin. Any incumbent with the franking privilege who can't run 7% ahead of the head of his ticket doesn't deserve to be in Congress.

No one has ever accused Tallon of being an intellectual. He has a good old boy style, as you might expect of a small city clothing store owner, that goes over well at Rotary Club meetings and in black churches. His record is fairly liberal on economic and foreign policy, solidly conservative on cultural issues. In the House he is a member of the Agriculture Committee and of Charlie Rose's Tobacco and Peanuts Subcommittee. He has worked for South Carolina research projects, to beef up the Grand Strand beaches, to fund a hybrid striped bass project, and to maintain tobacco export credits despite reports of corruption by leaf dealers. His approach is not subtle. "South Carolina has the potential to become the Holly Farms of striped bass," he said on one issue. "The tobacco farmer in my district and elsewhere should be the point of reference for any government program, domestic or export," he said on another.

The People: Est. Pop. 1986: 575,900, up 10.9% 1980–86; Pop. 1980: 519,273, up 23.6% 1970–80. Households (1980): 80% family, 49% with children, 63% married couples; 28.4% housing units rented; median monthly rent: $104; median house value: $33,100. Voting age pop. (1980): 347,458; 37% Black, 1% Spanish origin.

1988 Presidential Vote:

Bush (R)	89,068	(56%)
Dukakis (D)	70,037	(44%)

Rep. Robin M. Tallon, Jr. (D)

Elected 1982; b. Aug. 8, 1946, Hemingway; home, Florence; U. of SC, 1964–65; United Methodist; married (Amy).

Career: Retail clothing store owner, 1965–present; Real estate broker and developer, 1982–present; SC House of Reps., 1980–82.

Offices: 432 CHOB 20515, 202-225-3315. Also P.O. Box 6286, Florence 29502, 803-669-9084; and Horry Cnty. Cthse., Conway 29526, 803-248-6256.

Committees: *Agriculture* (12th of 27 D). Subcommittees: Conservation, Credit, and Rural Development; Cotton, Rice, and Sugar; Tobacco and Peanuts. *Merchant Marine and Fisheries* (14th of 25 D). Subcommittees: Fisheries and Wildlife Conservation and the Environment; Merchant Marine.

Group Ratings

	ADA	ACLU	COPE	CFA	LCV	ACU	NTLC	NSI	COC	CEI
1988	40	52	69	73	69	60	33	90	62	28
1987	44	—	67	50	—	39	—	—	60	25

National Journal Ratings

	1988 LIB — 1988 CONS		1987 LIB — 1987 CONS	
Economic	46% —	52%	49% —	50%
Social	40% —	58%	48% —	50%
Foreign	44% —	55%	28% —	70%

Key Votes

1) Homeless $	FOR	5) Ban Drug Test	AGN	9) SDI Research	FOR
2) Gephardt Amdt	FOR	6) Drug Death Pen	FOR	10) Ban Chem Weaps	AGN
3) Deficit Reduc	AGN	7) Handgun Sales	FOR	11) Aid to Contras	FOR
4) Kill Plnt Clsng Notice	AGN	8) Ban D.C. Abort $	FOR	12) Nuclear Testing	AGN

Election Results

1988 general	Robin M. Tallon, Jr. (D).	120,719	(76%)	($243,559)
	Bob Cunningham (R)	37,958	(24%)	($10,604)
1988 primary	Robin M. Tallon, Jr. (D).	65,608	(89%)	
	Luther Lightly, Jr. (D)	8,448	(11%)	
1986 general	Robin M. Tallon, Jr. (D).	92,398	(76%)	($269,708)
	Bob Cunningham (R)	29,922	(24%)	($61,949)

SOUTH DAKOTA

Half a century ago, work was stopped on Mount Rushmore. Sculptor Gutzon Borglum's design had not been fully chiseled out of the granite-crested mountain; Lincoln's beard was not finished, and Washington had been carved only to the lapels. But the looming war cut off federal subsidy of the project, and the four likenesses were recognizable—a national monument, the American political tradition embodied in a physically remote, forbidding environment. By this time Mount Rushmore had already become a symbol not just of patriotism but of the American can-do spirit; the seemingly wacky idea of carving statues out of a faraway mountaintop had been sanctioned when it was dedicated by President Calvin Coolidge in 1927, on the same summer vacation when he handed out slips of paper to reporters that read, "I do not choose to run for president in 1928."

And it was built in the Black Hills where the state that became South Dakota got its start, all of a sudden, a half century before in 1876. That year, as General George Custer suited up in the Dakota Territory on his way to be slaughtered by Crazy Horse's Sioux at Little Big Horn, prospectors discovered gold in the Black Hills—a discovery that marked the end for the Indians and their buffalo, as prospectors swarmed into land that treaties had reserved for the Indians. It was the year Calamity Jane ruled in the saloons of Deadwood, and Wild Bill Hickock was shot in the back there while holding up two pair, aces and eights. It was a year when hunters started slaughtering the buffalo, who could not be contained by barbed wire fences so thoroughly that by the time Teddy Roosevelt got to the Dakota Territory in 1885 he had a hard time finding one to shoot.

The mining towns flared brightly and then went dim or flickered out, though they're still taking gold out of one mine in Lead. But their fame attracted settlers, already headed west, to the plains of the Dakota Territory. It was not long before the railroad came through, before the Indians were massacred in 1890 at Wounded Knee, before enough settlers, many of them German and Scandinavian immigrants recruited by the railroads and land speculators, had built sodhouses and broken the land and set down roots to justify admitting both Dakotas to the Union in 1889.

That was just the moment that the Census Bureau and historian Frederick Jackson Turner proclaimed the closing of the American frontier. But bits and pieces of frontier, of marchland between the English-speaking American civilization and the civilizations that preceded it, remained then and remain now around the country. You can still see them in South Dakota. In the 25 years between statehood and World War I, the eastern third of the state, sectioned off Midwestern style into 640 acre square miles, filled up with farmers. But before you get to the Missouri River in the middle of the state, green turns to brown, cultivation grows sparser and then stops, the land is punctuated not by roads meeting every mile at precise angles but by buttes and gullies and grasslands sweeping all the way to the horizon with no sign of human habitation. These are the plains where the Sioux once built a civilization based on hunting the buffalo, and where the Sioux live today, on or just off reservations; currently, 7% of South Dakotans are Indians. This is not an entirely peaceful frontier even yet: in 1973 Wounded Knee was occupied by Indian militants, and not until 1984 did Indian leader Dennis Banks return to serve his sentence for riot and assault.

By 1910 South Dakota's settlement patterns were established—with patches of frontier left here and there—and the state's political character had been pretty well set. During the 1890s voters here flirted briefly with the Populists and William Jennings Bryan; but by the 1920s, South Dakota had become almost as monolithically Republican as Nebraska. Voters in South

SOUTH DAKOTA — Congresssional District, Counties, and Selected Places — (1 At Large)

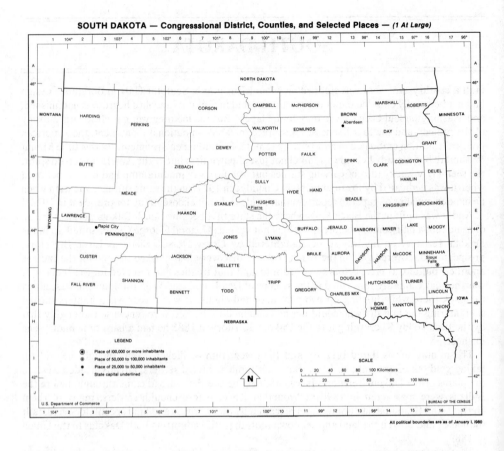

Dakota never had much use for the Non-Partisan League, which caught on in the more Scandinavian soil of North Dakota (though they embodied some of its socialistic ideas in their constitution), and there was never anything here comparable to the Farmer-Labor Party of Minnesota. As in most other Great Plains states, there have been periodic farm revolts against incumbent administrations. Nearly one-fourth of the state's residents live on farms, and its day-to-day economy depends on farmers' profits, not revenues, and hence is subject to wide fluctuations. But South Dakota began with a large enough Republican base that, despite such revolts, the state between 1936 and 1970 had a Democratic governor for only two years and elected only one Democrat to the Senate, George McGovern.

The last two decades, in contrast, have seen sharp political fluctuations in South Dakota. For a while McGovern's Democrats were on the rise, capturing at various times the governorship, the legislature, both Senate seats, both House seats, and nearly carrying the state for McGovern's presidential campaign in 1972. This trend owed something to McGovern's personal popularity and something to South Dakotans' revulsion at Vietnam and Watergate. Like other Upper Midwest states, South Dakota tends to be dovish on foreign policy (as it was isolationist before Pearl Harbor) and sternly intolerant of corruption. Then, around the time of the American Indian Movement's occupation of Wounded Knee, South Dakota shifted sharply to the right. Republicans picked up one House seat in 1972 and the other (when the state had a 2d) in 1974;

they won one Senate seat in 1978 and soundly beat McGovern, the symbol of the state's Democratic Party, in 1980. In the early 1970s one house of the legislature went Democratic; since 1976 Republicans have had big majorities in both houses.

Then in the middle 1980s another shift, to the Democrats, evidently on the farm issue. Democrat Thomas Daschle was elected to the Senate and Democrat Tim Johnson to the House in 1986, and a Democrat was nearly elected governor to follow Janklow. Yet it's not clear that the farm issue has swept all before it. Farm prices and farm land values did fall abruptly, local banks were endangered, and local businessmen were squeezed. But thanks to recent strength in commodity prices, the agricultural economy hereabouts has improved. South Dakota has also attracted, partly by changing its banking laws, new white-collar jobs in numbers which wouldn't make a ripple in other states but which, in a state of only 700,000 whose economy hasn't generated enough jobs to employ all its young people since 1914, make a major difference. The state's unemployment rate is well under the national average; its income levels are pulled down by the Indians, but are otherwise well above the poverty range. It may be that South Dakota is approaching a time, 100 years after the farmers started coming in, when farming won't be the be-all and end-all of the economy here.

Governor. Governor George Mickelson is a pleasant, consensus-minded Republican, a vivid contrast to his feisty, aggressive Republican predecessor Bill Janklow. Janklow made his name by a stand-tough stance against Indians and by enticing Citicorp and other big banks to set up their credit card and other operations in Sioux Falls and Rapid City. He got the state to buy 936 miles of Milwaukee Road railroad tracks and then to lease them to the Burlington Northern, to hold down farmers' freight rates; he launched a state hail insurance program, coal operation, gas station chain and cement plant. Mickelson has concentrated on economic development, raising the sales tax one cent to amass a $40 million fund for loans to local communities, and making grants for research. He has defended some new developments against environmental attacks. But he was under attack in early 1989 for conditions in the Sioux Falls state prison, after the acting warden was accused of swapping marijuana for hacksaw blades with an inmate some years ago. Lurking in the background of state politics is the threat raised by a Sioux lawsuit seeking lands confiscated after—that crucial year 1876 again—Custer's defeat, and a bill sponsored by Senator Bill Bradley of New Jersey that would return 1.3 million acres of the Black Hills to the Sioux.

Mickelson won the governorship in 1986, with 52% of the vote; both he and his opponent, Lars Herseth, are the sons of governors. Mickelson's crucial margins came in Sioux Falls and Rapid City, the state's two largest cities and the two places that were growing in the 1980s. Among the Democrats who may run against him in 1990 are Herseth; behind-the-scenes operator, Bob Samuelson; and state Senator Leonard Andera.

Senators. South Dakota's senior Senator is Republican Larry Pressler. He has demonstrated his vote-getting prowess over and over again: he beat an incumbent Democratic congressman in the Democratic year of 1974; he beat a respectable opponent 2 to 1 in the 1978 Senate race; and he won the largest vote total, largest percentage, and by the largest margin in South Dakota history when he won his second term in 1984. He is one of those politicians who came of age in the early 1970s who seems to have an instinct for capitalizing on the latest turn in public opinion. What is not evident in Pressler's record is whether he has any internal compass, any central core of beliefs at all. Early in his career he had a reputation as a liberal Republican; in 1987 and 1988, according to *National Journal*, he had as conservative a voting record as any member of the Senate. Yet it is hard to find either a connecting thread or a moment of conversion to explain the difference.

With a seat on the Foreign Relations Committee and the chairmanship for a time of a subcommittee on arms control, he might have become a respected expert there. But his record shows wobbles and ineffectiveness. In the early 1980s, when Ronald Reagan was under attack from the nuclear freeze movement which had some reverberations in dovish South Dakota, Pressler opposed the MX missile, opposed the Strategic Defense Initiative, and was the only Republican to oppose the arms control nomination of Kenneth Adelman—all to no effect. Yet when the INF Treaty came up for consideration in 1988, when the rumors in South Dakota were that conservative former Governor Bill Janklow might oppose him in the primary, Pressler moved first to block the INF Treaty until NATO and Warsaw Pact forces were in parity and then to block it unless the Soviets were declared in accord with the Helsinki accords; the amendments were beaten 15–2 in committee and 86–10 on the floor. Yet for all his hawkishness, his name was advanced as the first Republican thinking of voting against the John Tower nomination in early 1989, though he did not.

On domestic matters Pressler is eminently switchable, switching from support of the Civil Rights Restoration Act, for example, to upholding President Reagan's veto of it. He seems to specialize in a potpourri of issues, many of which have a local South Dakota angle. Some are useful, if arguably minor: he sponsored a successful measure to encourage shelter belts, the rows of trees which helped stop erosion on the Great Plains in the 1930s and could be useful again. He wants to make telephones compatible with hearing aids. Others are just demagoguery: he got an amendment recommending the appointment of a small business owner or farmer to the Federal Reserve Board through the Senate. He has worked to stop railroads from abandoning track on the Great Plains and to get funds for the Mount Rushmore Highway and a prison in Yankton.

Pressler's political modus operandi has been to take any position with strong short-term appeal to South Dakota voters; the question is whether he can make a viable long-term career of it. Before Bush was nominated he was saying, "If Bush were President when I run for reelection in 1990, I think I would have a tough time. I am not sure I could be reelected." Few prominent Democrats in early 1989 seemed interested in the race (although political operative Ted Muenster has indicated an interest), so Pressler may win a third term by another overwhelming margin. If so, the question will remain when South Dakota voters are going to understand that Pressler's ability to articulate their moment-to-moment reactions to issues is not matched by an ability to support long-term public policies in directions they would end up approving.

South Dakota's other Senator, Tom Daschle, has followed a different course and in a much shorter time has emerged as one of the genuine leaders in the Senate. As recently as 1978 he won a seat in the House by 139 votes, and in 1986 he was elected to the Senate by just 52%–48%; but in January 1989, as co-chairman of the Senate Democratic Policy Committee, he was effectively the number two man in the Senate leadership, just behind Majority Leader George Mitchell. Daschle came to these positions not by playing the odds or by catering to voters' momentary prejudices, but by standing for a set of positions on issues and by effectively campaigning for them in good political times and bad.

Daschle has spent his adult life in politics: when he returned from service in the Air Force in 1972, at the high point of South Dakota Democrats' fortunes, he became a staffer to Senator James Abourezk; in 1978, as Abourezk was about to retire, he returned to South Dakota, ran for the eastern House district Larry Pressler was leaving, and won by a hairsbreadth margin over the former prisoner of war who had come close to beating George McGovern in 1974. In the House he was the chief promoter of compensation to Vietnam veterans who believe they have been hurt by Agent Orange, and in the farm credit crisis of 1985 he got his bill for restructuring farm debt and advancing loans through the House. He also became a prime political organizer, employing in his 1986 Senate campaign many of the same populist-minded operatives who had helped elect Tom Harkin Senator in Iowa in 1984; and if his voting record was liberal, especially on economic issues, that was not out of line with opinion in a hard-stricken farm state, while Daschle's seriousness and dogged hard work personified qualities South Dakota values.

The Senate seat Daschle was running for was held by James Abdnor, a not very articulate but pleasant man with a conservative record who had overwhelmed McGovern in 1980. But Abdnor had primary opposition from outgoing Governor Bill Janklow, and won by only 55%–45% after trailing much of the time. In the general Abdnor ran an ad attacking Daschle for, among other things, inviting Jane Fonda to testify before a congressional hearing, even though "Jane Fonda has been identified with more radical causes than practically anyone in America, including warning people against eating red meat." But Daschle doggedly stressed farm woes, attacked the 1985 farm bill, and argued for continued high crop subsidies, production controls, and export subsidies. In the end this was enough for a 52%–48% victory, with Daschle carrying most of his old congressional district (the two were collapsed into one after the 1980 Census) and Abdnor most of the western district he had once represented.

Daschle and some of his allies saw his victory as the blueprint for a national Democratic populism, and worked with Democrats in other states in 1988. Daschle was less successful in his support of Richard Gephardt, whose restrictive trade amendment and production controls plan enabled him to win Farm Belt contests like the Iowa caucus and South Dakota primary but not to carry anything else but his home state of Missouri. In the Senate Daschle had more success. With a seat on the Agriculture Committee, he played a major role in fashioning the 1987 farm credit act. He continues to work on Agent Orange compensation. And as an early supporter of and organizer for George Mitchell's campaign for the majority leadership, he reaped a bounteous prize as co-chairman of the Policy Committee—a committee previously chaired by the majority leader alone. Under Mitchell and Daschle, the liberal-dominated Senate Democrats prepared an ambitious agenda for the 101st Congress, which—in line with Daschle's modus operandi—left themselves open for criticism but also put them in a position to claim credit if events and opinions move their way. With that venturesome approach this still young man from one of the nation's smallest states has taken some very narrow political victories and made himself a major force in national politics.

Congressman. The House Member who represents the most populous district in the nation according to the 1980 Census (and the second most populous, after the Texas 26th, according to 1986 estimates) is South Dakota's Congressman-at-Large Tim Johnson. Until the 1980 Census results came in, South Dakota elected two congressmen; now it has one. He is Tim Johnson, a Democrat who, beneath the noise and furor of a multi-million dollar Senate contest, won two seriously contested elections in 1986. He beat fellow state Senator Jim Burg in the Democratic primary 48%–45%; Burg carried most of the counties in the state, but Johnson piled up big majorities in his home area in the southeast and in Sioux Falls and Rapid City. In the general election his opponent was Dale Bell, a Republican much touted by conservative strategists who had run against Daschle in 1984. But Bell proved to be a weak candidate, carrying only a scattering of counties, and Johnson won with a thumping 59%.

In the House, the Democrats gave Johnson a seat on the Agriculture Committee. He claimed credit for passing eight different pieces of legislation, including authorization of three South Dakota water projects, several agricultural measures, and a Drunk Driving Prevention Act. With an attractive family and with frequent visits back to the state, he built up high popularity, and against longtime state Treasurer Dale Volk won reelection with 72% in 1988—close to a state record. Johnson thus already is a proven statewide winner.

Presidential politics. With only three electoral votes, South Dakota is not a great prize in presidential contests. Nevertheless it has been close in three of the last five elections. With typical Farm Belt contrariness, it came close to going Democratic in 1972 (when George McGovern was the nominee), 1976 and 1988; in 1980, with a Democrat in the White House, it was heavily Republican and in 1984 it stuck with Ronald Reagan. In 1988 George Bush won by a far from comfortable 53%–47%; the race was essentially even in the eastern counties of the state (with Michael Dukakis carrying booming Sioux Falls), with the west giving Bush the decisive margin.

For years South Dakota's presidential primary was overshadowed by California's, held on the same day; for 1988 it was moved up to February 23, one week after New Hampshire—in violation of the Democrats' rules. That didn't matter much—but then neither did the primary results, which turned out to be a replication of the results of the Iowa caucuses, and which were paid little heed by the national press. Bob Dole, who started off his campaign here by saying he was going to Mount Rushmore "for a fitting," easily won the Republican primary, while Richard Gephardt beat Michael Dukakis among the Democrats. Incidentally, conservative Republicans around the country have begun a movement to add Ronald Reagan's likeness to Mount Rushmore.

The People: Est. Pop. 1988: 715,000; Pop. 1980: 690,768, up 3.4% 1980–88 and 3.7% 1970–80; 0.29% of U.S. total, 45th largest. 18% with 1–3 yrs. col., 14% with 4+ yrs. col.; 16.9% below poverty level. Single ancestry: 26% German, 7% Norwegian, 4% English, 3% Irish, 2% Dutch, Swedish, 1% French. Households (1980): 73% family, 40% with children, 64% married couples; 30.7% housing units rented; median monthly rent: $148; median house value: $36,600. Voting age pop. (1980): 485,162; 5% American Indian. Registered voters (1988): 440,301; 188,552 D (43%); 216,510 R (49%); 35,239 unaffiliated and minor parties (8%).

1988 Share of Federal Tax Burden: $1,837,000,000; 0.21% of U.S. total, 48th largest.

1988 Share of Federal Expenditures

	Total		Non-Defense		Defense	
Total Expend	$2,691m	(0.30%)	$2,416m	(0.37%)	$350m	(0.15%)
St/Lcl Grants	443m	(0.39%)	443m	(0.39%)	1m	(0.49%)
Salary/Wages	428m	(0.32%)	244m	(0.36%)	184m	(0.36%)
Pymnts to Indiv	1,195m	(0.29%)	1,158m	(0.30%)	37m	(0.20%)
Procurement	128m	(0.07%)	75m	(0.16%)	128m	(0.07%)
Research/Other	497m	(1.33%)	497m	(1.34%)	0m	(1.34%)

Political Lineup: Governor, George S. Mickelson (R); Lt. Gov., Walter D. Miller (R); Secy. of State, Joyce Hazeltine (R); Atty. Gen., Roger Tellinghuisen (R); Treasurer, David L. Volk (R); Auditor, Vernon L. Larson (R). State Senate, 35 (20 R and 15 D); State House of Representatives, 70 (46 R and 24 D). Senators, Larry Pressler (R) and Thomas A. Daschle (D). Representative, 1 D at-large.

1988 Presidential Vote

Bush (R)	165,415	(53%)
Dukakis (D)	145,560	(47%)

1988 Democratic Presidential Primary

Gephardt	31,184	(44%)
Dukakis	22,349	(31%)
Gore	5,993	(8%)
Simon	3,992	(6%)
Hart	3,875	(5%)
Jackson	3,867	(5%)
Babbitt	346	(1%)

1984 Presidential Vote

Reagan (R)	200,267	(63%)
Mondale (D)	116,113	(37%)

1988 Republican Presidential Primary

Dole	51,599	(55%)
Robertson	18,310	(20%)
Bush	17,404	(19%)
Kemp	4,290	(5%)
Du Pont	576	(1%)

GOVERNOR
Gov. George S. Mickelson (R)

Elected 1986, term expires Jan. 1991; b. Jan. 31, 1941, Mobridge; home, Brookings; U. of SD, B.S. 1963, J.D. 1965; United Methodist; married (Linda).

Career: Army, 1965–67; Brookings Cnty. States Atty., 1970–74; SD House of Reps., 1975–80, Speaker, 1978–79.

Office: State Capitol Bldg., Pierre 57501, 605-773-3212.

Election Results

1986 gen.	George S. Mickelson (R)	152,543	(52%)
	R. Lars Herseth (D)	141,898	(48%)
1986 prim.	George S. Mickelson (R)	40,979	(35%)
	Clint Roberts (R)	37,250	(32%)
	Lowell Hanson (R)	21,884	(19%)
	Alice Kundert (R)	15,985	(14%)
1982 gen.	William J. Janklow (R)	197,426	(71%)
	Michael O'Connor (D)	81,136	(29%)

SENATORS
Sen. Larry Pressler (R)

Elected 1978, seat up 1990; b. Mar. 29, 1942, Humboldt; home, Humboldt; U. of SD, B.A. 1964, Rhodes Scholar, Oxford U., 1966, Harvard U., M.A., J.D. 1971; Roman Catholic; married (Harriet).

Career: Army, Vietnam; U.S. House of Reps., 1974–78.

Offices: 133 HSOB 20510, 202-224-5842. Also 520 S. Main, Aberdeen 57402, 605-226-7471; Rushmore Mall, Rm. 105, Rapid City 57701, 605-341-1185, 1-800-952-3591; Empire Mall, 4001 W. 41st St., Sioux Falls 57106, 605-336-2980; and 224 E. Capitol, Pierre 57501, 605-224-9552.

Committees: *Banking, Housing, and Urban Affairs* (9th of 9 R). Subcommittees: Housing and Urban Affairs; Securities. *Commerce, Science, and Transportation* (3d of 9 R). Subcommittees: Communications; Science, Technology and Space (Ranking Member); Surface Transportation. *Foreign Relations* (5th of 9 R). Subcommittees: European Affairs (Ranking Member); Near Eastern and South Asian Affairs. *Small Business* (3d of 9 R). Subcommittees: Export Expansion (Ranking Member); Rural Economy and Family Farming. *Special Committee on Aging* (3d of 9 R).

Group Ratings

	ADA	ACLU	COPE	CFA	LCV	ACU	NTLC	NSI	COC	CEI
1988	0	15	35	42	30	96	62	100	79	58
1987	25	—	35	50	—	81	—	—	82	46

National Journal Ratings

	1988 LIB — 1988 CONS			1987 LIB — 1987 CONS		
Economic	5%	—	93%	36%	—	63%
Social	0%	—	89%	23%	—	74%
Foreign	0%	—	92%	0%	—	76%

Key Votes

1) Cut Aged Housing $	FOR	5) Bork Nomination	FOR	9) SDI Funding	FOR
2) Override Hwy Veto	FOR	6) Ban Plastic Guns	FOR	10) Ban Chem Weaps	FOR
3) Kill Plnt Clsng Notice	FOR	7) Deny Abortions	FOR	11) Aid To Contras	FOR
4) Min Wage Increase	AGN	8) Japanese Reparations	AGN	12) Reagan Defense $	FOR

Election Results

1984 general	Larry Pressler (R)...................	235,176	(74%)	($1,155,683)
	George V. Cunningham (D).............	80,537	(26%)	($166,426)
1984 primary	Larry Pressler (R), unopposed			
1978 general	Larry Pressler (R)...................	170,832	(67%)	($449,541)
	Don Barnett (D).....................	84,767	(33%)	($152,006)

Sen. Thomas A. Daschle (D)

Elected 1986, seat up 1992; b. Dec. 9, 1947, Aberdeen; home, Aberdeen; SD St. U., B.A. 1969; Roman Catholic; married (Linda).

Career: Air Force, 1969–72; Legis. Asst. to U.S. Sen. James Abourezk, 1972–77; U.S. House of Reps., 1978–86.

Offices: 317 HSOB 20510, 202-224-2321. P.O. Box 1274, Sioux Falls 57101, 605-334-9596; P.O. Box 1536, Aberdeen 57401, 605-225-8823; and P.O. Box 8168, Rapid City 57709, 605-348-3551.

Committees: *Agriculture, Nutrition and Forestry* (8th of 10 D). Subcommittees: Agricultural Credit; Agricultural Research and General Legislation (Chairman); Rural Development and Rural Electrification. *Finance* (11th of 11 D). Subcommittees: International Trade; Social Security and Family Policy; Medicare and Long-Term Care. *Select Committee on Indian Affairs* (4th of 5 D).

Group Ratings

	ADA	ACLU	COPE	CFA	LCV	ACU	NTLC	NSI	COC	CEI
1988	85	67	91	92	50	13	13	0	36	5
1987	85	—	89	67	—	8	—	—	33	24

National Journal Ratings

	1988 LIB — 1988 CONS			1987 LIB — 1987 CONS		
Economic	86%	—	0%	74%	—	0%
Social	63%	—	36%	71%	—	26%
Foreign	79%	—	16%	74%	—	19%

Key Votes

1) Cut Aged Housing $	FOR	5) Bork Nomination	AGN	9) SDI Funding	AGN
2) Override Hwy Veto	FOR	6) Ban Plastic Guns	AGN	10) Ban Chem Weaps	AGN
3) Kill Plnt Clsng Notice	AGN	7) Deny Abortions	AGN	11) Aid To Contras	AGN
4) Min Wage Increase	FOR	8) Japanese Reparations	FOR	12) Reagan Defense $	AGN

Election Results

1986 general	Thomas A. Daschle (D)	152,657	(52%)	($3,485,870)
	James Abnor (R)	143,173	(48%)	($3,410,387)
1986 primary	Thomas A. Daschle (D), unopposed			
1980 general	James Abdnor (R)	190,594	(58%)	($1,801,653)
	George McGovern (D)	129,018	(39%)	($3,237,669)

REPRESENTATIVE

Rep. Tim Johnson (D)

Elected 1986; b. Dec. 28, 1946, Canton; home, Vermillion; U. of SD, B.A. 1969, M.A. 1970, J.D. 1975; Lutheran; married (Barbara).

Career: Practicing atty.; Clay Cnty. Dpty. State's Atty., 1985; SD House of Reps., 1978–82; SD Senate, 1982–86.

Offices: 513 CHOB 20515, 202-225-2801. Also 1610 S. Minnesota Ave., P.O. Box 57101, Sioux Falls, 605-332-8896; 429 Kansas City St., P.O. Box 1098, Rapid City 57709, 605-341-3990; and 615 S. Main, P.O. Box 1554, Aberdeen 57401, 605-226-3440.

Committees: *Agriculture* (19th of 27 D). Subcommittees: Forests, Family Farms and Energy; Livestock, Dairy, and Poultry; Wheat, Soybeans, and Feed Grains. *Veterans' Affairs* (14th of 21 D). Subcommittee: Hospitals and Health Care.

Group Ratings

	ADA	ACLU	COPE	CFA	LCV	ACU	NTLC	NSI	COC	CEI
1988	70	—	87	82	75	28	24	10	36	19
1987	80	—	81	64	—	13	—	—	27	24

National Journal Ratings

	1988 LIB — 1988 CONS			1987 LIB — 1987 CONS		
Economic	49%	—	50%	55%	—	43%
Social	40%	—	58%	62%	—	36%
Foreign	74%	—	23%	58%	—	41%

Key Votes

1) Homeless $	AGN	5) Ban Drug Test	AGN	9) SDI Research	FOR
2) Gephardt Amdt	FOR	6) Drug Death Pen	FOR	10) Ban Chem Weaps	FOR
3) Deficit Reduc	AGN	7) Handgun Sales	FOR	11) Aid to Contras	AGN
4) Kill Plnt Clsng Notice	AGN	8) Ban D.C. Abort $	FOR	12) Nuclear Testing	FOR

Election Results

1988 general	Tim Johnson (D)	223,759	(72%)	($632,105)
	David Volk (R)	88,157	(28%)	($199,420)
1988 primary	Tim Johnson (D), unopposed			
1986 general	Tim Johnson (D)	171,462	(59%)	($430,806)
	Dale Bell (R)	118,261	(41%)	($483,394)

TENNESSEE

In few states 50 years ago was the imprint of the past more plain than in Tennessee. The state had four medium-sized cities, but two-thirds of its people were scattered in its 95 rural counties stretching 500 miles from Bristol to Memphis—most of them in the same county where their ancestors had settled in the years from 1796, when it was admitted to the Union, until 1829, when its first President, Andrew Jackson, left the Hermitage to go to the White House. The state these small farmers built was as feisty and quick to take umbrage as Jackson; it peopled the armies of our early wars so eagerly it became known as the Volunteer state; and it took sides so strongly in the Civil War that almost all of its counties in 1940 and most of them in the 1980s voted the way they fought in the 1860s: the Union counties of the east and scattered in the west solidly Republican, the Confederate counties in middle and west Tennessee heavily Democratic.

The enduring nature of these political divisions is one of the uncanny features of the American political system. Fifty years ago they enabled a crafty political boss, Edward Crump, longtime mayor of Memphis, to manipulate state politics to his liking: with near-unanimous margins from both blacks and whites in Memphis, the state's largest city; and with a series of entangling alliances, particularly with patronage-hungry Democrats in the Republican east, Crump was able to produce pluralities in the Democratic primary—Tennessee is the one formerly Confederate state without a runoff—for his candidates. Through Kenneth McKellar, a viciously unpleasant man with a monstrous appetite for patronage, he controlled federal jobs, and grasped for others in the then new Tennessee Valley Authority; through governors in Nashville he controlled state policy and patronage. But Crump's power was based on little more than manipulativeness. As Tennessee's economy slowly grew, partly because of the cheap electric power generated by TVA, which brought aluminum plants to the Knoxville area, atomic energy to Oak Ridge, and less heralded factories to smaller places, the old courthouse politicians were undermined; and others were welded into a reform coalition by sharp and ambitious politicians.

Two of them beat Crump's Senators and set the course for a liberal Democratic Party in Tennessee—Estes Kefauver in 1948 and Albert Gore Sr. in 1952, even as Dwight Eisenhower was carrying the state and setting a tone which has prevailed among its Republicans in the years since. Kefauver and Gore refused to sign the Southern Manifesto against integration in 1957, and survived politically; Republican Howard Baker, running for the Senate in 1966, refused to oppose civil rights, and ended up thriving politically. Much of Tennessee, with its 16% black population (small for a southern state), half of which is concentrated in Memphis, was almost untouched by the racial divisions and hatreds that seared so much of the South in the 1950s and 1960s, thanks in very large part to the actions of its leading politicians—and in part also to the continuing hold that ancestral partisan preferences had on most voters.

Tennessee's basic divisions are still in place. East Tennessee still remains a distinctive region politically, as do middle Tennessee and west Tennessee. Their political personalities—the east has been feisty and Republican, middle Tennessee has been devoutly Democratic since the days of Nashville's Andrew Jackson, the west has long been racially polarized—are well known even to ordinary Tennesseans. Their persistence is matched, and their particular personalities analogous, to the musical traditions which have made Tennessee for many Americans the music capital of the nation. Tennessee is associated with country music, but there are several strains of it. That of east Tennessee has been influenced by the bluegrass music and fiddling tradition of the mountains. The country music of Nashville, in contrast, seems to have roots in the gospel music which is also centered in that city—which, as it happens, is also the nation's leading center

TENNESSEE — Congressional Districts, Counties, and Selected Places — *(9 Districts)*

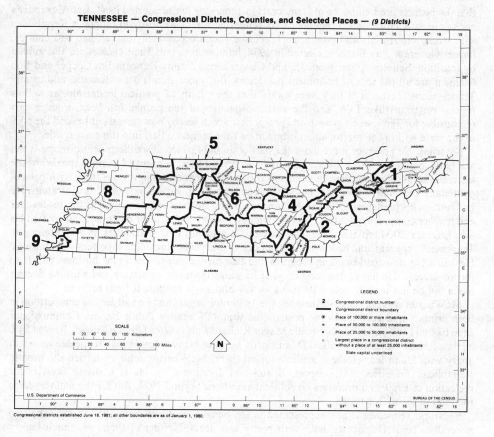

Congressional districts established June 18, 1981; all other boundaries are as of January 1, 1980.

of religious publishing. Nashville's Grand Ole Opry, broadcast since 1925, and Knoxville's Tennessee Barn Dance, broadcast since 1942, have names that suggest the differences between them. West Tennessee, the Mississippi lowlands around Memphis, is a northern extension of the Mississippi Delta and the part of America that gave birth to blues music in the 1890–1920 period. Memphis produced many blues musicians, and others who drew on their tradition, from the jazz musicians of Beale Street in the 1920s to Elvis Presley of Graceland mansion in the 1950s and 1960s.

Those traditions have remained in place as Tennessee has grown and prospered. The 1980s have not been boom economic times in most of the Mississippi Valley core of the United States, but they have been in Tennessee. The state has attracted more Japanese investment than any other state but California—not just the big Nissan plant in Smyrna in middle Tennessee, but dozens of plants in all parts of the state. And they in turn helped to attract General Motors' Saturn project to Spring Hill, also near Nashville. For these developments much of the credit should go to Republican Governor Lamar Alexander, elected in 1978 and 1982, who also sponsored one of the most thorough of the education reform programs in the South. Both the attraction of industry and education reform have been continued by Democratic Governor Ned McWherter, elected in 1986.

McWherter's victory and those of Senators Jim Sasser and Albert Gore Jr., make it appear that the historic predominance of Democrats in Tennessee has reasserted itself. But Alexander's not so distant victories are a reminder that Tennessee voters are ready to support a Republican with strong credentials and programs. Tennessee voters occasionally make some bad choices; former Governor Ray Blanton, elected in 1974, later went to jail. Their choices are also guided by tradition: Senator Albert Gore Jr., and Congressmen Jimmy Duncan, Jim Cooper and Bob Clement are all the sons of prominent politicians. But succession is not automatic, and mostly Tennesseeans choose as if they were aware that the quality of political leadership, as well as federal programs like TVA, and the native capacities of the people, has been in large part responsible for Tennessee's growth and prosperity, which has by now spread out beyond the 55% of the state within the metropolitan orbits of its four biggest cities, into the countryside.

Governor. No governor more looks the part of an old-fashioned southern politician: he is tall and hefty, he speaks with a thick accent and tells droll stories, he spent 14 years as speaker of the state House and became known as one of the craftiest operators in a state thick with natural politicians. But Ned McWherter has shown a capacity for policy as well as political strategy. He has built on his predecessor Lamar Alexander's Better Schools program, with its master teacher and teacher competency features, put through his own $1,575 teacher pay raise, and created his own Literacy 2000 initiative. He took his cabinet around to all 95 counties on a "Listening to Tennessee" program, and he keeps his door open to everyone—including reporters—at all times. He has a big new road-building program and has carried Alexander's new business efforts to record success. He has gotten most of what he wants from the legislature and when he doesn't like a bill he has usually gotten its sponsors to withdraw it to spare it from his veto.

McWherter was not the favorite when the 1986 race began, and he had serious competition in both primary and general. In the primary, he won 42% against Public Service Commissioner Jane Eskind (30%) and then Nashville Mayor Richard Fulton (26%). In the general, he won 54% against former Governor Winfield Dunn, partly because many voters in east Tennessee were still angry with Dunn for vetoing a medical school there; McWherter actually carried the usually Republican Tri-Cities of Kingsport, Bristol and Johnson City. He is a strong favorite for reelection in 1990, and professes no political ambitions beyond 1994. But for the moment he is the man to see in Tennessee.

Senators. Tennessee is now represented in the Senate, as it was from 1952 to 1963, by two generally liberal Democrats, both with pretty safe seats. Neither of them was much known outside Tennessee in 1987, but in 1988 and 1989 they have become national figures.

Tennessee's senior Senator, James Sasser, after two mostly behind-the-scenes terms, emerged as chairman of the Senate Budget Committee in 1989. For some years, he has been known as a senator interested in the details of federal programs; now, while he must continue to master details, he will become known for how they all add up together. To these assignments, he brings some of the impulses native to Tennessee's Democratic tradition. His father was an agriculture official who moved all over rural Tennessee, one of those men who make government programs work to help people; and Sasser tends to favor increased spending on domestic programs that help people, though he is not wholly uncritical of them. On balance, he sees government as a friend, not an enemy. In another era, he would be proposing new government programs; in the 1980s, his major initiative of that kind has been a home ownership proposal that would enable the FHA to insure mortgages on homes with down payments as low as 3%.

But much of Sasser's substantive work has concentrated on details. He has a seat on Appropriations and is close to Robert Byrd, who often sent him on inspection trips—to Thailand, to see how Cambodian refugees were being treated; to Pakistan, to get a better view of the Afghan *mujaheddin*; to Central America, to find out exactly how much U.S. military construction has taken place; to the Persian Gulf, to see the U.S.S. Stark after it was hit by Iraqi missiles. On Central America, he ended up as an opponent of contra aid; on the Persian Gulf, he was critical of the U.S. reflagging operation and wondered why the Europeans and Japanese weren't paying for it. On trade, his impulse was at once populistic and vague: he wants to limit imports and subsidize exports without being protectionist. And he will get right down to the picayune, as he did when he got former Attorney General William French Smith to reimburse the government $11,207 for his wife's trips via his government car to the grocery.

Sasser keeps in touch with Tennessee, making a point of visiting each of the state's 95 counties once a year, hiking through the Cherokee National Forest in Tennessee to see how much timber is harvested, boating over Kentucky Lake to see how the fish are affected by water pollution. He keeps money flowing to TVA and the Appalachian Regional Commission, protects Millington Naval Air Station, and opposes monitored retrievable storage of nuclear materials in east Tennessee.

On the Budget Committee, he was not a major player before 1989. He is frustrated that the current fiscal condition leaves little money for new domestic programs, and would like to cut defense below administration requests. Yet he favors Gramm-Rudman-Hollings, which squeezes legislators into making unpleasant choices, and he has said that he won't consider new taxes unless they are proposed by the Bush administration. When Bush OMB Director Richard Darman came forward with a budget with blank spaces left for tough choices, Sasser insisted that the Administration present its own proposals. At some point someone is going to blink—and Sasser's mettle is going to be tested in the process.

The tests Sasser has met at the ballot box he has passed nicely. In 1976, he beat well-known entrepreneur and trial lawyer John J. Hooker Jr. in the primary, and then beat Senator Bill Brock in the general—both upset wins. In 1982, he overwhelmed Congressman Robin Beard, who ran an ad with a Castro look-alike taking a puff on a cigar and saying, "Muchas gracias, Señor Sasser," with 62% of the vote. In 1988, Republicans tried to get former Governor Lamar Alexander to run, but he declined, and the nomination eventually went to Bill Andersen, a lawyer from east Tennessee who had been thinking about running against Congressman Jimmy Quillen in the primary; Andersen campaigned by doing work days, but had little money and got little attention, and Quillen publicly praised Sasser. Sasser's strength was so great that he carried 94 of Tennessee's 95 counties (losing only in Sevier County in eastern Tennessee)—an unheard of feat in a state where partisan loyalties run so deep—and won with 65% of the vote.

Tennessee's junior Senator has a name long familiar in Tennessee politics and now familiar in national politics as well, Albert Gore Jr. A dozen years after he ran for Congress at age 28, Gore was running for President—and was one of the top three candidates for the Democratic nomination. If one or another factors had been slightly altered, he might even have been the party's nominee.

Even so, Gore owes his initial election to the House to his father. Albert Gore Sr., 40 years before, served as Smith County superintendent of schools by day and put himself through law school at night; in 1938, he ran for Congress and, winning the Democratic primary, was elected in the heavily Democratic hill country of middle Tennessee. This was the start of what became the family business: every two years he was reelected, until 1952 when he was elected to the Senate; reelected in 1958 and 1964, he lost to Bill Brock in one of the hardest-fought campaigns of 1970 after opposing the Vietnam war and voting against Richard Nixon's two southern Supreme Court nominees. At that time Albert Gore Jr., was just about to serve in the Army in Vietnam and, after he returned to Nashville, became a reporter for *The Tennesseean*, went to divinity school at night and sprung at the chance to run for Congress when his father's successor, Joe Evins, announced his retirement in 1976.

In the House, Gore quickly made an impressive name for himself. He became one of the most thoughtful members of the Science Committee, and conducted useful hearings on difficult issues like organ transplants. He was a member of the Select Committee on Intelligence. He was a leading member of the increasingly important Energy and Commerce Committee. And in areas not covered by his committees he also made a contribution. He studied arms control issues intensively for months, and came forward with a proposal—to de-MIRV missiles, that is, remove their multiple warheads—which was echoed by no less than Henry Kissinger (who had backed MIRVing in the first place) and which soon became the conventional wisdom on arms control of both left and right. Gore also played a key role in fashioning a compromise that saved the MX missile in 1983 and 1984. When Howard Baker retired from the Senate in 1984, Gore ran and won easily; he had no primary opposition and won the general election against Victor Ashe (now mayor of Knoxville) 61%–34%.

In the Senate, Gore was equally active. After the *Challenger* disaster, he ferreted out proof that NASA had cut back on quality monitoring. He continued to work on defense issues on the Armed Services Committee. More than any other Senator, he has been àlert to the potentialities—and dangers—of new technologies: fiber optics, biotechnology, superconductivity, the dangers to the ozone layer. And more than most Senators, he seems to do his own research and thinking, hone in on the details and not just repeat the conventional wisdom that reverberates so loudly in Washington meeting rooms. He is not the only member of the family that makes headlines, by the way: his wife Tipper, together with James Baker's wife Susan, lobbied the record industry to voluntarily rate and label obscene and violent lyrics.

Gore's presidential candidacy began when an opening appeared in the field and ended when it appeared boxed in. The opening occurred when Sam Nunn and Dale Bumpers declined to run in early 1987, leaving the field without a southerner, even though southern legislators had set up the "Super Tuesday" contests for March 8, 1988, with the intention of giving a boost to a southerner or a candidate whose policies would be attractive to southern primary voters. Gore won the support of leading fundraisers like Nathan Landow, and in April 1987 entered the race. Reporters later complained that Gore changed tacks on issues, but they lacked a simple one-word label for the positions he had long taken and which he emphasized in the campaign. On domestic issues, Gore was closer to traditional Democratic big government views than other Democrats, notably Michael Dukakis; he vigorously defended the traditional rationale for non-means-tested social security against Bruce Babbitt's argument that benefits should be given only to the needy. On foreign policy issues, he was a little tougher—not a full-fledged hawk, to be sure, but he was the only Democrat to resist Iowa STARPAC's demand that candidates oppose missile flight-testing (which was almost universally supported in Congress), he supported the reflagging operation in the Persian Gulf while the other Democrats opposed or ridiculed it, and he emphasized that he supported humanitarian (not military) aid to the Nicaraguan contras while the other candidates competed to denounce them.

Thus on both domestic and foreign policy issues, this youngest of the Democratic candidates could plausibly claim to be closer to the post-World War II Democratic tradition that runs from Harry Truman through John Kennedy and Lyndon Johnson to Henry Jackson—and Albert Gore Sr., as well—the Cold War liberals who built a strong America abroad and an affluent America at home. To that he added, a bit hesitantly, his future-oriented views on technology.

Why didn't Gore's views find him a large constituency? The answer is that they did, but that the Super Tuesday super-primary which had been created to put the national spotlight on candidates like him had the opposite effect. He was obviously going nowhere in Iowa, where caucus-goers are almost unanimously dovish. He made a feint at New Hampshire, but had no hope of cracking Dukakis's lead. He did win early March caucuses in Wyoming and Nevada—not insignificant victories. Then on Super Tuesday, he won more votes in southern states than any other candidate, 30% to Jesse Jackson's 28% and Michael Dukakis' 23%. He finished first in five states (North Carolina, Kentucky, Tennessee, Arkansas, Oklahoma) and second to Jesse Jackson in five states (Virginia, Georgia, Alabama, Mississippi, Louisiana). But Gore had not telegraphed his punch. He campaigned quietly, relying mainly on a $3 million television blitz to show southerners he was a candidate with views and a background they would find congenial. In television debates, he showed command of himself and the issues and an almost pit-bull aggressiveness at times; but the national press was discounting his chances heavily, and then when he did win, they were preoccupied with the other legitimately major stories coming out of Super Tuesday—George Bush's sweep on the Republican side, Jesse Jackson's carrying five once Confederate states, Michael Dukakis's four-cornered (Massachusetts, Florida, Texas and Washington state) national victories. In a campaign when most of the candidates started out unknown or little known, exposure on national newscasts and election specials was critical to later success. But Gore was a victim of clutter. He ran ahead of every other Democrat with a conceivable chance to be nominated or elected in 10 states, one-fifth of the nation. But that gave him only third or fourth spot on one day's newscast—with the inevitable compensating negative stories to follow.

After his success in winning votes and his failure to win attention, Gore struggled to get voters' support—and failed. In Illinois, local news coverage focused on home town candidates Paul Simon and Jesse Jackson, who got 75% of the votes there. In Connecticut, Wisconsin and most notably New York, Michael Dukakis, with his lead in the polls and his ethnic roots, became clearly the strongest opponent to Jesse Jackson, whom most voters wanted to see defeated; and as the national press exaggerated Jackson's chances after his victory in the Michigan caucus, Gore's chances plummeted to zero. They got even lower in New York as Mayor Edward Koch, while endorsing Gore, seized the spotlight the weekend before the election with his statement that "Jews and others who care about Israel would be crazy to vote for Jackson."

The morning after conclusion was that Gore never had a chance and that there was no market for his kind of politics outside the South. It's true that all of the candidates tended to win votes from those who shared their ethnic roots, with Dukakis winning because more ethnics than blacks or white southerners vote in Democratic primaries. But imagine a Democratic field without Jesse Jackson: it is quite possible that Gore with his southern roots and his more traditional Democratic economic policies would have won the lion's share of black votes (as Jimmy Carter did in 1976), which would have enabled him to sweep over half the southern vote on Super Tuesday and would have made him competitive with Dukakis in the big states of the North. Of course Jackson may continue to run and preempt the black vote. But the outlook for a future Gore candidacy need not be as bleak as the post mortems on his 1988 campaign suggest.

Gore is expected to win reelection to the Senate in Tennessee in 1990 with an overwhelming percentage and probably without serious opposition. That would leave him in a position to run for President if he likes in 1992, and as for the future, Tennessee's state primaries are held in August, long after the presidential contest is over, so Gore need not give up his Senate seat to run in 1996.

Presidential politics. The eerie continuity in Tennessee politics comes out in presidential elections: Tennessee gave George Bush in 1988 the same 58% it gave Ronald Reagan in 1984; it went for Ronald Reagan over Jimmy Carter in 1980 by almost exactly the same small margin— not just statewide, but in almost every county—that it gave Dwight Eisenhower over Adlai Stevenson in 1952 and 1956. That means that Tennessee remains one of the Democrats' targets in the South—though, without a southerner or someone with a hawkish foreign policy, an elusive one. Tennessee's presidential primary was switched to the southern Super Tuesday date for 1988, and Albert Gore and George Bush won expected victories.

Congressional districting. Tennessee gained one House seat from the 1980 Census, the same one it lost in 1970. The Democratic legislature tried to gain two seats, and got one. No major changes seem needed for 1992.

The People: Est. Pop. 1988: 4,919,000; Pop. 1980: 4,591,120, up 7.1% 1980–88 and 16.9% 1970–80; 1.99% of U.S. total, 16th largest. 12% with 1–3 yrs. col., 12% with 4+ yrs. col.; 16.5% below poverty level. Single ancestry: 23% English, 5% Irish, 4% German, 1% French, Scottish. Households (1980): 77% family, 42% with children, 63% married couples; 31.4% housing units rented; median monthly rent: $148; median house value: $35,600. Voting age pop. (1980): 3,292,560; 14% Black, 1% Spanish origin. Registered voters (1988): 2,590,923; no party registration.

1988 Share of Federal Tax Burden: $14,475,000,000; 1.64% of U.S. total, 21st largest.

1988 Share of Federal Expenditures

	Total		Non-Defense		Defense	
Total Expend	$15,705m	(1.78%)	$13,735m	(2.09%)	$3,772m	(1.65%)
St/Lcl Grants	2,225m	(1.94%)	2,220m	(1.94%)	6m	(5.02%)
Salary/Wages	2,356m	(1.75%)	1,877m	(2.80%)	479m	(2.80%)
Pymnts to Indiv	7,855m	(1.92%)	7,496m	(1.92%)	359m	(1.92%)
Procurement	2,927m	(1.55%)	1,802m	(3.88%)	2,927m	(1.55%)
Research/Other	342m	(0.92%)	340m	(0.92%)	2m	(0.92%)

Political Lineup: Governor, Ned McWherter (D); Lt. Gov., John Wilder (D); Secy. of State, Gentry Crowell (D); Atty. Gen., Charles Burson (D); Treasurer, Steve Adams (D); Controller, William Snodgrass (D). State Senate, 33 (22 D and 11 R); State House of Representatives, 99 (59 D and 40 R). Senators, James R. Sasser (D) and Albert Gore, Jr. (D). Representatives, 9 (6 D and 3 R).

1988 Presidential Vote

Bush (R)	947,233	(58%)
Dukakis (D)	679,794	(42%)

1984 Presidential Vote

Reagan (R)	990,212	(58%)
Mondale (D)	711,714	(42%)

1988 Democratic Presidential Primary

Gore	416,861	(72%)
Jackson	119,248	(21%)
Dukakis	19,348	(3%)
Gephardt	8,470	(2%)
Hart	4,706	(1%)
Simon	2,647	(1%)

1988 Republican Presidential Primary

Bush	152,515	(60%)
Dole	55,027	(22%)
Robertson	32,015	(13%)
Kemp	10,911	(4%)

GOVERNOR

Gov. Ned McWherter (D)

Elected 1986, term expires Jan. 1991; b. Oct. 15, 1930, Palmersville; home, Dresden; United Methodist; widowed.

Career: Farmer, businessman; TN House of Reps., 1969–86, Speaker, 1973–86.

Office: State Capitol, Nashville 37219, 615-741-2001.

Election Results

1986 gen.	Ned McWherter (D)	656,602	(54%)
	Winfield Dunn (R)	553,449	(46%)
1986 prim.	Ned McWherter (D)	314,449	(42%)
	Jane Eskind (D)	225,551	(30%)
	Richard H. Fulton (D)	190,016	(26%)
1982 gen.	Lamar Alexander (R)	737,963	(60%)
	Randall Tyree (D)	500,937	(40%)

SENATORS

Sen. James R. (Jim) **Sasser (D)**

Elected 1976, seat up 1994; b. Sept. 30, 1936, Memphis; home, Nashville; Vanderbilt U., B.A. 1958, J.D. 1961; United Methodist; married (Mary).

Career: Practicing atty., 1961–76; Chmn., TN St. Dem. Cmtee., 1973–76.

Offices: 363 RSOB 20510, 202-224-3344. Also 569 U.S. Crthse., Nashville 37203, 615-736-7353; 239 Fed. Bldg., Chattanooga 37402, 615-756-8836; 320 P.O. Bldg., Knoxville 37902, 615-673-4204; 390 Fed. Bldg., 167 N. Main, Memphis 38103, 901-521-4187; B-8 U.S.P.O. Bldg., Jackson 38301, 901-424-6600; and Tri-City Airport, Blountville 37617, 615-323-6207.

Committees: *Appropriations* (7th of 16 D). Subcommittees: Commerce, Justice, State, and Judiciary; Defense; Energy and Water Development; Military Construction (Chairman); Transportation. *Banking, Housing, and Urban Affairs* (6th of 12 D). Subcommittees: Housing and Urban Affairs; Securities. *Budget* (Chairman of 13 D). *Governmental Affairs* (4th of 8 D). Subcommittees: Federal Services, Post Office, and Civil Service; General Services, Federalism, and the District of Columbia (Chairman); Permanent Subcommittee on Investigations.

Group Ratings

	ADA	ACLU	COPE	CFA	LCV	ACU	NTLC	NSI	COC	CEI
1988	75	64	80	92	50	9	4	10	43	9
1987	80	—	79	83	—	12	—	—	28	17

National Journal Ratings

	1988 LIB	—	1988 CONS	1987 LIB	—	1987 CONS
Economic	61%	—	37%	74%	—	0%
Social	69%	—	30%	53%	—	42%
Foreign	84%	—	15%	69%	—	27%

Key Votes

1) Cut Aged Housing $	FOR	5) Bork Nomination	AGN	9) SDI Funding	AGN
2) Override Hwy Veto	FOR	6) Ban Plastic Guns	FOR	10) Ban Chem Weaps	AGN
3) Kill Plnt Clsng Notice	AGN	7) Deny Abortions	AGN	11) Aid To Contras	AGN
4) Min Wage Increase	FOR	8) Japanese Reparations	FOR	12) Reagan Defense $	AGN

Election Results

1988 general	James R. (Jim) Sasser (D)	1,020,061	(65%)	($3,069,615)
	Bill Andersen (R)	541,033	(35%)	($612,421)
1988 primary	James R. (Jim) Sasser (D), unopposed			
1982 general	James R. (Jim) Sasser (D)	780,113	(62%)	($2,091,872)
	Robin L. Beard (R).	479,642	(38%)	($1,639,858)

Sen. Albert Gore, Jr. (D)

Elected 1984, seat up 1990; b. Mar. 31, 1948, Washington, DC; home, Carthage; Harvard U., B.A. 1969; Baptist; married (Tipper).

Career: Army, Vietnam; Homebuilding business; Reporter, *Nashville Tennessean*, 1973–76; U.S. House of Reps., 1976–84.

Offices: 393 RSOB 20510, 202-224-4944. Also 530 Church St., Nashville 37219, 615-736-5129; 313 P.O. Bldg., Knoxville 37901, 615-673-4595; 9 E. Broad St., Cookeville 38501, 615-528-6475; Smith Cnty. Crthse., Carthage 37030, 615-735-0173; 403 Fed. Bldg., Memphis 38103, 901-521-4224; and 256 Fed. Bldg., Chattanooga 37402, 615-756-1328.

Committees: *Armed Services* (8th of 11 D). Subcommittees: Defense Industry and Technology; Projection Forces and Regional Defense; Strategic Forces and Nuclear Deterrence. *Commerce, Science and Transportation* (5th of 11 D). Subcommittees: Communications; Consumer; Science, Technology, and Space (Chairman); Surface Transportation; National Ocean Policy Study. *Rules and Administration* (6th of 9 D). *Joint Economic Committee.* Subcommittees: Economic Resources and Competitiveness; Education and Health; Investment, Jobs, and Prices. *Joint Committee on Printing.*

Group Ratings

	ADA	ACLU	COPE	CFA	LCV	ACU	NTLC	NSI	COC	CEI
1988	60	85	87	50	50	9	20	38	45	15
1987	60	—	88	67	—	6	—	—	10	14

National Journal Ratings

	1988 LIB — 1988 CONS		1987 LIB — 1987 CONS	
Economic	64%	— 35%	74%	— 0%
Social	86%	— 0%	*	— *
Foreign	63%	— 36%	81%	— 0%

Key Votes

1) Cut Aged Housing $	FOR	5) Bork Nomination	AGN	9) SDI Funding	AGN
2) Override Hwy Veto	FOR	6) Ban Plastic Guns	—	10) Ban Chem Weaps	—
3) Kill Plnt Clsng Notice	AGN	7) Deny Abortions	—	11) Aid To Contras	AGN
4) Min Wage Increase	FOR	8) Japanese Reparations	—	12) Reagan Defense $	AGN

Election Results

1984 general	Albert Gore, Jr. (D)	1,000,607	(61%)	($3,035,498)
	Victor Ashe (R)	557,016	(34%)	($1,777,581)
	Ed McAteer (I)	87,234	(5%)	
1984 primary	Albert Gore, Jr. (D)	345,527	(100%)	
1978 general	Howard H. Baker, Jr. (R)	642,644	(56%)	($1,922,945)
	Jane Eskind (D)	673,231	(42%)	($1,903,352)

FIRST DISTRICT

Between the corduroy-like ridges of the Appalachian chains, as they bend west and then south is an extension of the great valley of Virginia into far northeastern Tennessee. Two great movements have made its history. The first, right after the Revolution, was the rush of settlers over the mountains and through these valleys; this is where early settlers momentarily established the free state of Franklin and where Tennessee's first capital was, and you can still see some 18th and 19th century buildings here. The second movement was the building of the railroads through these valleys in the 1850s. Other Appalachian areas are cut off from the rest of America, and if they have railroads they are only branch lines to coal mines. But the little industrial cities that have grown up here—Johnson City, Kingsport, Bristol—are on the main lines of national commerce, and have been since before the Civil War. The war itself was not as formative an event here as in the rest of the South, or not in the same way. With few slaves, and with a connection to northern industry, this was Union territory and heavily Republican, as it has remained to this day.

The continuity in politics is all the more surprising because this area has had continuous economic growth and has developed the sort of industrial economy which produced unions and Democrats in the North. Its growth has been helped by modest wage levels, a skilled and hard-working labor force, low electric power rates (because of the TVA) and good transportation routes (it's on all major rail lines); its small cities boast major paper and printing plants, and have the look of comfortable, clean, 1920s factory towns. This is a part of America where things seem to work, and where the cultural trends of the 1960s and 1970s seem far away or altogether alien.

The far northeastern end of the state forms the 1st Congressional District of Tennessee, a district so heavily Republican that it has not elected a Democrat to the House for more than 100 years. Nonetheless, it has had turbulent politics on occasion. For almost 40 years (1921–61, with one two-year hiatus) the seat was held by B. Carroll Reece, a fierce mountain politician who was once Republican national chairman. After Reece died in 1961 and his widow was elected to fill out his term, there was a fierce primary here, the winner of which, Jimmy Quillen, has held the seat ever since. Quillen is one of those locally rooted Burkean conservatives—a poor boy from a family of 10 who made money publishing weekly newspapers and running an insurance business—who for years provided the backbone for the outnumbered Republicans in the House. For theories of the convergence of high-tech and traditional values, for free market economics or long-range political strategies, he has no interest at all. This is a bread-and-butter politician, interested in doing things for his district, and concerned with protecting and strengthening his own position as its representative.

All those things he has done. Quillen is the ranking Republican on the Rules Committee and, because of retirements, the only carryover on the Republican side in 1989. Yet he is not a man who sets party strategy or tries to build majorities on most national issues. Nor is he an obdurate partisan like his colleague Delbert Latta or a wily coalition-builder like now Senator Trent Lott. Instead, Quillen devotes most of his attention to local issues, such as getting the Tennessee Wilderness Act passed in 1986 and persuading the EPA to approve a sewage treatment plant for Bristol, and he has a more liberal voting record on economic issues than many Republicans; this is a working-class district and it has some use for federal money. Quillen takes great pride in the establishment of what now is the Quillen-Dishner Medical School in Johnson City, where a chair has been endowed in honor of his wife. He has little in common with the aggressive, brash crackling-with-ideas young Republicans who have dominated their party's ranks in the 1980s.

In fact, Quillen's partisan instincts are so weak that he can claim some credit for the election of two of Tennessee's top three Democrats. In 1986, he remembered that Winfield Dunn, the Republican gubernatorial nominee, had vetoed the Johnson City medical center when he was governor in the early 1970s. Quillen and much of east Tennessee remembered, and Democrat Ned McWherter carried the 1st District on his way to a 54% statewide victory. The 1988 Republican candidate for Senator, young Kingsport lawyer Bill Andersen, had earlier talked publicly about running against Quillen and may run again for this seat if Quillen should retire. During the campaign, Quillen spoke out strongly in praise of Democratic Senator Jim Sasser's work for east Tennessee; Sasser carried every county but one in that part of the state.

Quillen himself is routinely reelected by large margins and without significant opposition.

The People: Est. Pop. 1986: 532,700, up 3.9% 1980–86; Pop. 1980: 512,702, up 18.9% 1970–80. Households (1980): 80% family, 43% with children, 68% married couples; 24.8% housing units rented; median monthly rent: $128; median house value: $33,300. Voting age pop. (1980): 371,177; 2% Black.

1988 Presidential Vote: Bush (R) 117,511   (68%)
                                Dukakis (D)..................... 54,455   (31%)

Rep. James H. (Jimmy) Quillen (R)

Elected 1962; b. Jan. 11, 1916, Wayland, VA; home, Kingsport; United Methodist; married (Cecile).

Career: Kingsport Press, 1934–35; *Kingsport Times*, 1935–36; Founder, Publisher, *Johnson City Times*, 1939–44; Navy, WWII; TN House of Reps., 1955–62, Min. Ldr., 1959–60.

Offices: 102 CHOB 20515, 202-225-6356. Also Fed. P.O. Bldg., Rm. 157, Kingsport 37662, 615-247-8161.

Committees: *Rules* (Ranking Member of 4 R).

Group Ratings

	ADA	ACLU	COPE	CFA	LCV	ACU	NTLC	NSI	COC	CEI
1988	15	35	18	27	19	91	44	100	100	47
1987	16	—	17	14	—	76	—	—	64	48

National Journal Ratings

	1988 LIB — 1988 CONS	1987 LIB — 1987 CONS
Economic	29% — 70%	31% — 69%
Social	5% — 91%	28% — 71%
Foreign	22% — 76%	20% — 76%

Key Votes

1) Homeless $	FOR	5) Ban Drug Test	AGN	9) SDI Research	FOR
2) Gephardt Amdt	AGN	6) Drug Death Pen	FOR	10) Ban Chem Weaps	AGN
3) Deficit Reduc	AGN	7) Handgun Sales	FOR	11) Aid to Contras	FOR
4) Kill Plnt Clsng Notice	FOR	8) Ban D.C. Abort $	FOR	12) Nuclear Testing	AGN

Election Results

1988 general	James H. (Jimmy) Quillen (R)..........	119,526	(80%)	($227,503)
	Sidney S. Smith (D)...................	29,469	(20%)	
1988 primary	James H. (Jimmy) Quillen (R), unopposed			
1986 general	James H. (Jimmy) Quillen (R)..........	80,289	(69%)	($459,119)
	John B. Russell (D)...................	36,278	(31%)	($8,044)

SECOND DISTRICT

The ancestral tug of Tennessee politics is nowhere more apparent than in Knoxville, the largest city in east Tennessee, nestled between mountain ridges where the Holston and French Broad Rivers join to form the Tennessee. Knoxville was established not long after the first wave of pioneers came through the gaps and down between the mountains of the Appalachian chain; in the Civil War it was Union territory, and has remained Republican ever since. This has been the case even though its major institutions might be thought to bias it in other directions. Knoxville is an industrial, blue-collar town. It is the headquarters of the Tennessee Valley Authority, a venture in government enterprise which has proved remarkably durable for more than 50 years now, and is the home of the University of Tennessee. It was host to a World's Fair in 1982, a financially successful enterprise promoted by the likes of Democrat Jake Butcher, his party's 1978 candidate for governor whose own banking business came unraveled the next year and who went to prison not long after.

But for all these Democratic ties, Knoxville has remained strongly Republican in almost every election, except in 1984 when Senator Albert Gore Jr., carried both Knoxville and its surrounding counties. The 2d Congressional District of Tennessee, which includes Knoxville and several counties to the south, is one of the most reliably Republican districts in the nation. And if there was any doubt of that, it was dispelled by the results of the 1988 special and regular congressional elections.

The occasion for the special was the death in office of John Duncan, congressman from the 2d District for nearly 25 years. First elected in the Democratic year of 1964 (when Howard Baker could have had the nomination, but passed it up to run for the Senate), Duncan was reelected without incident and rose to be ranking Republican on the House Ways and Means Committee. However, he paid more attention to district projects than to national issues and was not a serious player in the tax reform bill of 1986. When he died, the obvious candidate to succeed him was his son, John J. Duncan Jr., generally known as Jimmy, who had been a criminal court judge in Knox County.

But Jimmy Duncan's election was not uncontested. He got spirited opposition from Democrat Dudley Taylor, possessor of a last name long prominent in east Tennessee politics, and a former revenue commissioner for Governor Ned McWherter. In a hard-hitting ad campaign, Taylor, a wounded Vietnam veteran, attacked Jimmy Duncan, a contemporary of Dan Quayle, for signing up in the National Guard after drawing a low draft number. He also pointed out that Duncan's brother Joe was tried for tax fraud and that Jimmy was named as an unindicted co-conspirator, and he recalled that Duncan withdrew his name for consideration as a federal judge in 1985 because he had had business connections with Jake Butcher. He challenged Duncan to debate and forced him to wage more than a quiet campaign. In the end, Duncan won with 57% for the special election to fill out his father's term and 56% in the election to the House seat for the 101st Congress. This percentage was far below the usual Republican level in this district (George Bush was winning 64% at the same time), but enough to get him safely to Congress where he has a slight advantage in tenure over his fellow freshmen who took office in January. There he promises to tend primarily to local matters rather than national issues and is not likely to make any big splash soon.

The People: Est. Pop. 1986: 530,600, up 4.0% 1980–86; Pop. 1980: 510,197, up 17.3% 1970–80. Households (1980): 75% family, 39% with children, 63% married couples; 31.8% housing units rented; median monthly rent: $152; median house value: $37,000. Voting age pop. (1980): 375,709; 6% Black, 1% Spanish origin.

1988 Presidential Vote: Bush (R) 117,355   (64%)
                             Dukakis (D). 65,552   (36%)

Rep. John J. (Jimmy) Duncan, Jr. (R)

Elected Nov. 1988; b. July 21, 1947, Lebanon; home, Knoxville; U. of TN, B.S. 1969, Geo. Wash. U., J.D. 1973; Presbyterian; married (Lynn).

Career: Practicing atty., 1973–81; St. Trial Judge, 1981–88.

Offices: 506 CHOB 20515, 202-225-5435. Also 318 P.O. Bldg., Knoxville 37902, 615-523-3772; 419 First American Bank Bldg., Maryville 37801, 615-984-5464; and Cthse., Athens 37303, 615-745-4671.

Committees: *Public Works and Transportation* (17th of 20 R). Subcommittees: Aviation; Investigations and Oversight; Public Buildings and Grounds; Surface Transportation. *Interior and Insular Affairs* (14th of 15 R). Subcommittees: General Oversight and Investigations; National Parks and Public Lands. *Select Committee On Aging* (25th of 27 R). Subcommittees: Housing and Consumer Interests; Human Services.

Group Ratings and Key Votes: Newly Elected

Election Results

1988 general	John J. (Jimmy) Duncan, Jr. (R)	99,631	(56%)	($435,567)
	Dudley W. Taylor (D).	77,540	(44%)	($381,980)
1988 special	John J. (Jimmy) Duncan, Jr. (R)	92,929	(57%)	
	Dudley W. Taylor (D).	70,576	(43%)	
1988 primary	John J. (Jimmy) Duncan, Jr. (R)	99,631	(87%)	
	Robert D. Profitt (R)	5,015	(13%)	
1986 general	John J. Duncan Sr. (R).	96,396	(76%)	($408,092)
	John F. Bowen (D)	30,088	(24%)	

THIRD DISTRICT

Through some of the most vivid scenery of the Appalachian chain, etching its way through the serrated ridges of east Tennessee, is the river that gave Tennessee—and the Tennessee Valley Authority—their names. From Knoxville, the river cuts through a ridge and then plunges down a long valley to the city of Chattanooga. There it switches course again, winding around the table-top Lookout Mountain and then moving into northern Alabama. This is the land of the 3d Congressional District of Tennessee. Chattanooga, the largest city, was a village when it was a Civil War battlefield; it grew into an industrial city during the New South years after the Civil War. The 3d District, spreading out on either side of the city, is split between Civil War Democrats and Republicans. Democratic for years, it was marginal enough to elect Bill Brock, a fire-breathing conservative then, in 1962; for most of the 1970s and 1980s, it has elected Democrat Marilyn Lloyd. Yet in national and even state elections, it has been trending Republican; it was a solid 62% for George Bush in 1988.

The 3d District is a part of Tennessee which has been profoundly affected by the federal government. First by the TVA, which dammed the river, controlled its flooding, generated cheap electricity, and attracted high-energy-consuming industry to the area; and then by the atomic energy laboratories at the Oak Ridge, built in secrecy during World War II, which have been promoting nuclear power ever since, including the controversial Clinch River breeder reactor. The care and tending of these federal facilities has been the main work of Congresswoman Marilyn Lloyd. She is on the Science, Space and Technology Committee and chairs the Energy Research and Production Subcommittee. But she has not had the success she might have hoped for. TVA rates have risen and its nuclear power plants have proven impractical. She promoted coal gasification and synfuels projects that would use east Tennessee coal, but they fell victim to low energy prices and budget cuts in the early 1980s. For years, she defended the breeder reactor every year against its critics, who included both environmentalist opponents of nuclear power and fiscal conservatives who argued that the project would never pay off. But support dwindled and opposition grew. In 1982, the House voted 217–196 to kill the Clinch River breeder reactor; it survived a little longer thanks to Howard Baker, but by 1983 it was gone.

Since then Lloyd, comfortably reelected from 1976 to 1982, has had tough races. In 1984, she won only 52% of the vote against little-known John Davis, a Howard Baker Republican. In 1986, though she prepared much better for the campaign, she won only 54% against Jim Golden, an evangelical Christian and Pat Robertson fan. Only Lloyd's big margins in Oak Ridge and a couple of rural counties carried her through. In 1988, Chattanooga tire retailer and county commissioner Harold Coker attacked her for accepting honoraria from defense contractors while serving on the Armed Services Committee and twitted her for announcing in 1987 that she was retiring and then changing her mind and running in 1988. But Lloyd did slightly better, winning 57%–43%.

In the House, Lloyd has a record somewhat liberal on economics and conservative on foreign policy; she has been one of the swing votes on close issues like the MX missile and contra aid, though she generally supports hawkish positions on Armed Services. She continues to urge more spending on alternative energy research and in 1989 was elected Chair of the Textile Caucus. Whether she will run for reelection in 1990 is not clear; if she doesn't, this seat will certainly be up for grabs.

The People: Est. Pop. 1986: 521,900, up 1.0% 1980–86; Pop. 1980: 516,692, up 17.1% 1970–80. Households (1980): 78% family, 42% with children, 64% married couples; 31.3% housing units rented; median monthly rent: $149; median house value: $35,400. Voting age pop. (1980): 370,457; 11% Black, 1% Spanish origin.

1988 Presidential Vote:

Bush (R)	117,220	(62%)
Dukakis (D)	70,874	(37%)

Rep. Marilyn Lloyd (D)

Elected 1974; b. Jan. 3, 1929, Ft. Smith, AR; home, Chattanooga; Shorter Col.; Church of Christ; divorced.

Career: Co-owner and Mgr., WTTI Radio, Dalton, GA.

Offices: 2266 RHOB 20515, 202-225-3271. Also 253 Jay Solomon Fed. Bldg., Chattanooga 37401, 615-267-9108; and 1211 Joe L. Evins Fed. Bldg., Oak Ridge 37830, 615-576-1977.

Committees: *Armed Services* (15th of 31 D). Subcommittees: Military Personnel and Compensation; Procurement and Military Nuclear Systems. *Science, Space and Technology* (4th of 30 D). Subcommittees: Energy Research and Production (Chairman); Space Science and Applications. *Select Committee on Aging* (6th of 39 D). Subcommittees: Housing and Consumer Interests; Retirement Income and Employment.

Group Ratings

	ADA	ACLU	COPE	CFA	LCV	ACU	NTLC	NSI	COC	CEI
1988	50	52	59	64	25	54	30	89	46	29
1987	32	—	57	36	—	32	—	—	42	26

National Journal Ratings

	1988 LIB — 1988 CONS	1987 LIB — 1987 CONS
Economic	56% — 44%	46% — 54%
Social	40% — 58%	48% — 52%
Foreign	35% — 64%	43% — 57%

Key Votes

1) Homeless $	—	5) Ban Drug Test	AGN	9) SDI Research	AGN
2) Gephardt Amdt	FOR	6) Drug Death Pen	FOR	10) Ban Chem Weaps	AGN
3) Deficit Reduc	FOR	7) Handgun Sales	FOR	11) Aid to Contras	FOR
4) Kill Plnt Clsng Notice	AGN	8) Ban D.C. Abort $	FOR	12) Nuclear Testing	AGN

Election Results

1988 general	Marilyn Lloyd (D)	108,264	(57%)	($618,173)
	Harold L. Coker (R)	80,372	(43%)	($626,945)
1988 primary	Marilyn Lloyd (D)	31,007	(89%)	
	Walter Ward (D)	2,168	(6%)	
	Lamar Lasley (D)	1,815	(5%)	
1986 general	Marilyn Lloyd (D)	75,034	(54%)	($637,887)
	Jim Golden (R)	64,084	(46%)	($445,298)

FOURTH DISTRICT

Passing over the invisible line between Civil War Republican and Civil War Democratic territory, criss-crossing Tennessee from northeast to southwest, following roughly the corduroy-like lines of the western Appalachian ridges and spilling over onto the verdant Cumberland Plateau, is the 4th Congressional District of Tennessee. This seat was newly created after the 1980 Census, the first new district entirely in rural Tennessee in many years. Reaching from Virginia almost all the way to Mississippi, it is more than 250 miles long, yet seldom more than 20 miles wide.

The congressman here, Jim Cooper, is one of several Tennessee politicians who come from successful political families. His father, Prentice Cooper, was elected governor of Tennessee in 1938, 1940 and 1942. But such lineage gives a candidate only a mild head start. It's a long time since 1942, after all, and Jim Cooper was born 10 years after his father left the governor's office. Not every famous child wins: Cooper won the seat in 1982 by beating Cissy Baker, daughter of former Senator Howard Baker and granddaughter of former Senate Majority Leader Everett Dirksen, even running ahead of party lines to win by a stunning 66%–34% margin, and raising $905,000 in the process. He was the youngest Member of Congress in 1983 and 1984.

In Cooper's first terms, he quietly bucked conventional wisdom, speaking against tobacco use and opposing the National Rifle Association. He has campaigned against illiteracy and would require teenagers to pass reading tests before getting drivers' licenses. He is ready to step in with regulations about high-price pay phones and about "lite" foods. He championed the Tennessee walking horse industry, centered in his home town of Shelbyville, against Agriculture Department regulations, and he has worked hard on rescuing TVA's nuclear program from its problems. In 1987, he won a seat on the Energy and Commerce Committee, the most sought after assignment in Congress, with the support of chairman John Dingell, but he has not been afraid to buck Dingell when they disagree. In 1988 and 1989, he was part of a "group of nine" Members seeking a compromise on Clean Air legislation that would be acceptable both to coal-producing states like Tennessee and states concerned about heavy air pollution or acid rain like California or New York; they sought to bridge the gap between full committee chairman Dingell and Health Subcommittee chairman Henry Waxman.

Cooper is an impressive political performer at home as well as in Washington. Despite his out-of-state schooling (University of North Carolina, Rhodes Scholar at Oxford, Harvard Law) and a Nashville law practice, he gets along easily with voters in courthouse towns and hollows, and he has been reelected without serious challenge. He might well have been a contender for Albert Gore's Senate seat if Gore had been elected president; in the meantime he appears to have a long and productive career ahead of him in the House.

The People: Est. Pop. 1986: 534,200, up 4.6% 1980–86; Pop. 1980: 510,732, up 22.2% 1970–80. Households (1980): 81% family, 45% with children, 70% married couples; 24.5% housing units rented; median monthly rent: $109; median house value: $29,000. Voting age pop. (1980): 359,160; 4% Black, 1% Spanish origin.

1988 Presidential Vote:

Bush (R)	91,186	(57%)
Dukakis (D)	66,656	(42%)

Rep. Jim Cooper (D)

Elected 1982; b. June 19, 1954, Nashville; home, Shelbyville; U. of NC, B.A. 1975, Rhodes Scholar, Oxford U., M.A. 1977, Harvard U., J.D. 1980; Episcopalian; married (Martha).

Career: Practicing atty., 1980–82.

Offices: 125 CHOB 20515, 202-225-6831. Also 116 Depot St., P.O. Box 725, Shelbyville 37160, 615-684-1114; City Hall, 7 S. High St., Winchester 37398, 615-967-4150; 208 E. 1st North St., Ste. 1, Morristown 37814, 615-587-9000; and 311 S. Main St., P.O. Box 845, Crossville 38555, 615-484-1864.

Committees: *Energy and Commerce* (23d of 26 D). Subcommittees: Energy and Power; Telecommunications and Finance. *Small Business* (13th of 27 D). Subcommittees: Antitrust, Impact of Deregulation, and Privatization; Environment and Labor; SBA, the General Economy and Minority Enterprise Development.

Group Ratings

	ADA	ACLU	COPE	CFA	LCV	ACU	NTLC	NSI	COC	CEI
1988	70	73	69	73	75	28	26	30	69	27
1987	68	—	67	71	—	9	—	—	43	23

National Journal Ratings

	1988 LIB — 1988 CONS			1987 LIB — 1987 CONS		
Economic	40%	—	58%	51%	—	48%
Social	66%	—	32%	65%	—	34%
Foreign	50%	—	50%	63%	—	37%

Key Votes

1) Homeless $	AGN	5) Ban Drug Test	AGN	9) SDI Research	AGN
2) Gephardt Amdt	FOR	6) Drug Death Pen	FOR	10) Ban Chem Weaps	FOR
3) Deficit Reduc	FOR	7) Handgun Sales	AGN	11) Aid to Contras	AGN
4) Kill Plnt Clsng Notice	FOR	8) Ban D.C. Abort $	AGN	12) Nuclear Testing	AGN

Election Results

1988 general	Jim Cooper (D)........................ 94,129	(100%)	($234,375)
1988 primary	Jim Cooper (D), unopposed		
1986 general	Jim Cooper (D)........................ 86,997	(100%)	($128,007)

FIFTH DISTRICT

Fifty years ago, most of the things that make it distinctive were already in place in Nashville. It was one of the first American cities established west of the Appalachian; Andrew Jackson built his Hermitage nearby on the banks of the Cumberland, and this was always his political home base—and it has remained Democratic ever since. It was the capital of Tennessee early on, just as it was—and still is—the center of its political life and discourse: the *Tennesseean* and the *Nashville Banner* still present Democratic and Republican views of Tennessee politics, and Nashville is the biggest television market in the state. Nashville was proud of its universities and of its very own Parthenon; it was firmly established as the religious publishing center of the country, producing more Bibles probably than any city in the world ever has—the buckle on the Bible Belt. And Nashville was also already well-known as the home of country music. The Grand Ole Opry was first aired on the radio in 1925, and the big stars of country music already hung out here.

Today, Nashville is still mostly Democratic, and it remains the capital, with its universities, Bible publishing businesses and country music industry stronger than ever before. But it has also been enormously changed, by the 50 years of prosperity and economic growth whose effects have been so especially pronounced in the South. People whose grandparents were surprised to encounter electric lights and indoor plumbing in homes are now taking for granted a living standard enjoyed previously by only the very richest in society—of spacious homes air-conditioned all summer, of shopping malls and supermarkets overflowing with affordable goods. Nashville in the 1980s has become the center of one of the boom areas of the interior South. The countryside around is dotted with big Japanese factories, most notably the Nissan plant in Smyrna; General Motors is building its Saturn facility in Spring Hill; Ingram, America's biggest wholesaler of trade books, is headquartered in Nashville itself; the Goo-Goo Cluster candy factory is here too. An agreeable quality of life, plenty of medium-wage high-skill labor, a central location, and an absence of urban strife and militant unions have all helped make Nashville a boom town.

The 5th Congressional District of Tennessee includes all of Nashville and Davidson County and one partly suburban county to the north—but this is only part of the Nashville metropolitan area now that development is spreading into the once rural countryside. The 5th is usually a reliable Democratic district in statewide elections, and it has long elected pretty liberal Democrats, who vote with most of their co-partisans from the North on most issues. Racial divisions have played less of a part in voting here than in most southern cities; blacks are 22% of the population, but even in the 1960s Nashville's congressman (and later mayor), Richard Fulton, voted for civil rights laws and had no trouble winning votes from Nashville whites.

The current congressman from Nashville is Bob Clement, a Democrat whose father was three times elected governor of Tennessee. He won the seat in 1988 after some of the most expensive and tumultuous politicking in the country. His predecessor, Bill Boner, while under investigation by the House Ethics Committee, was elected mayor of Nashville with 53% in a multi-million dollar contest; he quickly resigned his House seat, which conveniently terminated the investigation. That set up a multi-candidate Democratic primary, plus a candidacy by Republican Terry Holcomb who had won 40% against Boner in 1986. Among the competitors were Phil Bredesen, a businessman who was Boner's chief rival for mayor; Jane Eskind, public service commissioner and candidate for Senator in 1978 and governor in 1986; and Clement, former public service commissioner and candidate for governor in 1978 and for the 7th district House seat in 1982. Bredesen and Eskind each spent over $1 million, but Clement won the December 1987 primary by 40%–36% over Bredesen. In the January 1988 special election, Clement beat Holcomb 62%–36%. Clement's unopposed reelection is an example of what he can expect in future elections unless he makes some serious mistake.

In the House, Clement has made a point of emphasizing drug law enforcement by the Coast Guard and other agencies; he got through a bill to make it easier to prosecutor car dealers' odometer fraud. He serves on Public Works and Merchant Marine.

The People: Est. Pop. 1986: 537,900, up 4.5% 1980–86; Pop. 1980: 514,832, up 7.9% 1970–80. Households (1980): 71% family, 37% with children, 56% married couples; 41.5% housing units rented; median monthly rent: $193; median house value: $44,300. Voting age pop. (1980): 384,057; 20% Black, 1% Spanish origin.

1988 Presidential Vote:

Bush (R)	104,313	(52%)
Dukakis (D)	95,154	(47%)

Rep. Bob Clement (D)

Elected January 1988; b. Sept. 23, 1943, Nashville; home, Nashville; U. of TN, B.S. 1967, Memphis St. U., M.B.A. 1968; United Methodist; married (Mary).

Career: Army 1969–71; Founder and owner, Bob Clement & Assoc. 1981–83; Owner and Ptnr., Charter Equities real estate, 1981–83; Pres., Cumberland U., 1983–87.

Offices: 325 CHOB 20515, 202-225-4311. Also 552 U.S. Crthse., Nashville 37303, 615-736-5295; 2701 Jefferson St., N. Nashville 37208, 615-320-1363; and 510B Main St., Springfield 37122, 615-384-6600.

Committees: *Merchant Marine and Fisheries* (21 of 26 D). Subcommittees: Coast Guard and Navigation; Oceanography. *Public Works and Transportation* (24th of 31 D). Subcommittees: Aviation; Water Resources; Surface Transportation.

Group Ratings

	ADA	ACLU	COPE	CFA	LCV	ACU	NTLC	NSI	COC	CEI
1988	75	32	93	90	50	20	17	40	36	20
1987	*	—	*	*	—	*	—	—	*	*

National Journal Ratings

	1988 LIB — 1988 CONS		1987 LIB — 1987 CONS	
Economic	67% —	30%	* —	*
Social	52% —	48%	* —	*
Foreign	53% —	47%	* —	*

Key Votes

1) Homeless $	—	5) Ban Drug Test	—	9) SDI Research	—
2) Gephardt Amdt	—	6) Drug Death Pen	FOR	10) Ban Chem Weaps	—
3) Deficit Reduc	—	7) Handgun Sales	AGN	11) Aid to Contras	AGN
4) Kill Plnt Clsng Notice	AGN	8) Ban D.C. Abort $	—	12) Nuclear Testing	FOR

Election Results

1988 general	Bob Clement (D).....................	155,068	(100%)	($291,818)
1988 primary	Bob Clement (D), unopposed			
1987 special	Bob Clement (D).....................	56,090	(62%)	($645,000)
	Terry Holcomb (R)...................	32,765	(36%)	($247,958)
1986 general	William Hill (Bill) Boner (D)...........	78,658	(58%)	($909,521)
	Terry Holcomb (R)...................	58,701	(40%)	($189,566)

SIXTH DISTRICT

The 6th Congressional District of Tennessee is part of the Cumberland Plateau, the hilly and fertile land just west of the Appalachian chains, inside the U formed by the Tennessee River as it begins in the mountains, flows through northern Alabama, and then goes back up north again through Tennessee to meet the Ohio River near Paducah, Kentucky. Middle Tennessee, as this area is called, is one of the heartlands of the Democratic Party. It was the political home base of Andrew Jackson and supported him nearly unanimously; during the Civil War, though it had precious few slaves, it resented the invading Union armies, and has voted solidly Democratic ever since. It is neither particularly rich nor particularly poor; its farmers suffered during the Depression and 50 years ago the standard of living was rather low. But in the last half century, economic growth has fanned out into the farmland from Nashville—symbolized most vividly by the big Nissan plant in Smyrna and General Motors's Saturn plant in Spring Hill. These have in turn produced all manner of subsidiary jobs, and meanwhile thousands of affluent suburbanites have been moving beyond the limits of Nashville-Davidson County into formerly rural counties, most of which are in the 6th District.

This is having some political effect in a district long loyal to the party of Jackson, and which has elected such House Members as James K. Polk (1825–39), Speaker of the House and later President; Cordell Hull (1907–21, 1923–31), later Senator and Secretary of State; Albert Gore Sr., (1939–53), later Senator; and Albert Gore Jr., (1977–85), later senator and 1988 presidential candidate. In 1976, the counties that made up the 6th District voted 65% for Jimmy Carter; he won them again easily in 1980. But increasing numbers of Republicans have lowered the Democratic percentage, to 41% for Walter Mondale in 1984 and 39% for Michael Dukakis in 1988.

This trend means a lot of hard work, keeping in touch with voters and forestalling opposition, for the current Democratic congressman, Bart Gordon. Gordon's background is almost entirely political. He was Democratic state chairman in 1984 when Albert Gore Jr., decided to run for the Senate; Gordon quickly entered the race. Traditionally in this district, voters in the dusty courthouse towns of middle Tennessee expected to meet and talk several minutes with their political candidates. But new forms of campaigning are more important in the shopping center crossroads that are springing up in the countryside within 50 miles of Nashville. Gordon ran a computerized fundraising operation and voter contact system, and a sophisticated ad campaign; he boasted that, as state Democratic chairman, he had put the state party back in the black. He talked convincingly of aiding local development and spoke out against unfair tax loopholes and for a verifiable arms control agreement. He won a multicandidate primary with 28% of the vote—there is no runoff in Tennessee—and won the general election 63%–37%.

In the House, Gordon has not made a name on any specific issue. His close relationship with Jim Wright paid off in early 1987 when he was chosen to fill the late Sala Burton's seat on the House Rules Committee. This is a good platform for a Member from a safe district to undertake a variety of projects, and one the leadership fills with Members it is sure will be faithful. Gordon evidently qualifies. He was reelected easily and surely has a safe seat.

The People: Est. Pop. 1986: 573,000, up 12.0% 1980–86; Pop. 1980: 511,805, up 37.0% 1970–80. Households (1980): 81% family, 46% with children, 70% married couples; 25.1% housing units rented; median monthly rent: $151; median house value: $40,400. Voting age pop. (1980): 362,322; 7% Black, 1% Spanish origin.

1988 Presidential Vote:

Bush (R)	111,548	(60%)
Dukakis (D).	72,992	(39%)

Rep. Bart Gordon (D)

Elected 1984; b. Jan 24, 1949, Murfreesboro; home, Murfreesboro; Middle TN St. U., B.S. 1971, U. of TN, J.D. 1973; United Methodist; single.

Career: Practicing atty., 1974–84; Chmn., TN Dem. Party, 1981–83.

Offices: 103 CHOB 20515, 202-225-4231. Also P.O. Box 1986, 106 S. Maple St. Murfreesboro 37133, 615-896-1986; 102 W. 7th St., Columbia 38401, 615-388-8808; and P.O. Box 1140, Cookeville 38503, 615-528-5907.

Committees: *Rules* (8th of 9 D). Subcommittee: Legislative Process. *Select Committee on Aging* (26th of 39 D). Subcommittee: Housing and Consumer Interests.

Group Ratings

	ADA	ACLU	COPE	CFA	LCV	ACU	NTLC	NSI	COC	CEI
1988	80	68	81	73	63	12	18	30	36	16
1987	68	—	78	43	—	0	—	—	29	16

National Journal Ratings

	1988 LIB — 1988 CONS		1987 LIB — 1987 CONS	
Economic	67% —	30%	66% —	33%
Social	53% —	46%	57% —	43%
Foreign	74% —	23%	57% —	42%

Key Votes

1) Homeless $	AGN	5) Ban Drug Test	AGN	9) SDI Research	FOR
2) Gephardt Amdt	FOR	6) Drug Death Pen	AGN	10) Ban Chem Weaps	AGN
3) Deficit Reduc	FOR	7) Handgun Sales	FOR	11) Aid to Contras	AGN
4) Kill Plnt Clsng Notice	AGN	8) Ban D.C. Abort $	—	12) Nuclear Testing	FOR

1142 TENNESSEE

SEVENTH DISTRICT

From the city limits of Nashville to inside the city limits of Memphis, from the heart of middle Tennessee to the heart of west Tennessee, stretches the 7th Congressional District of Tennessee. Politically, it contains several distinct areas. The counties near Nashville and along the lower Tennessee River are part of the heavily Democratic bloc which has existed in this part of the state in almost uninterrupted fashion since the time of Andrew Jackson. In the southern part of the district, just across the Tennessee River, are several rural counties just north of Mississippi with black majorities—just about the only heavily black rural part of Tennessee. The district also includes nearly 200,000 people in Memphis's Shelby County, 92% of them white, the large majority of them affluent.

In political analysis, these sections of the district are usually collapsed into two: the rural counties, with about half the population, generally preferring country-based Democratic candidates; and Shelby County, with about 40% and growing, strongly preferring conservative Republicans. Voting in the Memphis area is heavily polarized by race: blacks are almost unanimously Democratic; whites, especially affluent whites, go Republican by percentages nearly as high.

The congressman from the 7th District is Republican Don Sundquist, a former Howard Baker aide active in politics since he beat Frank Fahrenkopf for president of the Young Republicans in 1971 and became acquainted with a young national party chairman named George Bush. Sundquist won this district in a very close race in 1982, beating Bob Clement 51%–49% by winning 75% in Shelby County and 35% in the rural counties. Since then he has made a point of keeping up with the rural areas with 100 "community days" a year, and he has had the additional advantage of Republican voters moving into new subdivisions in the counties nearest Nashville. He won 72% of the vote in 1986 and 80% in 1988—excellent showings, considering that he carried some of the most partisan Democratic parts of the United States.

Sundquist has also made some difference as a Republican in the House. He has criticized TVA officials harshly and has seen some of his criticisms vindicated as TVA's nuclear program has gotten into more and more trouble; his plan to increase the size of the TVA board was fought by Democratic Senators Sasser and Gore and Congressman Jim Cooper, but he claims that the new TVA head, Marvin Runyon, has made some of the changes he called for. He sponsored an amendment that stopped Japanese contractors from bidding on the Washington area subway so long as Japan excludes American contractors from working on construction jobs there and he worked with TVA to get a rocket booster plant for Yellow Creek in Iuka, Mississippi, just south of the district.

Sundquist has also shown some good in-house political skills. After making a skilled feint at Guy Vander Jagt's job as campaign committee chairman, Sundquist won a seat on the Budget Committee after the 1986 elections and one on the Ethics Committee as well. After the 1988 elections, he dropped those for the plum of a seat on Ways and Means. He got some notoriety—and support from Democrats—in the House when a federal appeals court ruled that he could be sued by a legal services lawyer he had criticized; both Democrats and Republicans think this should be barred by the speech and debate clause. It seems fitting that Sundquist should be involved in such a case: he seems aggressive, even feisty, often effective. He is about the strongest candidate his party has in Tennessee, although he says he has no interest in running for governor or Senator in 1990.

The People: Est. Pop. 1986: 559,800, up 11.2% 1980–86; Pop. 1980: 503,611, up 47.4% 1970–80. Households (1980): 81% family, 47% with children, 70% married couples; 26.4% housing units rented; median monthly rent: $184; median house value: $42,200. Voting age pop. (1980): 351,201; 11% Black, 1% Spanish origin, 1% Asian origin.

1988 Presidential Vote:

Bush (R)	138,246	(67%)
Dukakis (D)	67,200	(33%)

Rep. Don Sundquist (R)

Elected 1982; b. Mar. 15, 1936, Moline, IL; home, Memphis; Augustana Col., B.A. 1957; Lutheran; married (Martha).

Career: Navy, 1957–59; Jostens, Inc., 1961–72; Ptnr., Graphic Sales of Amer., 1972, Pres., 1973–82.

Offices: 230 CHOB 20515, 202-225-2811. Also 5909 Shelby Oaks Dr., Ste. 112, Memphis 38134, 901-382-5811; and 117 S. 2d St., Clarksville 37040, 615-552-4406.

Committees: *Ways and Means* (12th of 13 R). Subcommittees: Human Resources; Select Revenue Measures.

Group Ratings

	ADA	ACLU	COPE	CFA	LCV	ACU	NTLC	NSI	COC	CEI
1988	10	26	18	36	19	96	75	100	100	59
1987	4	—	18	21	—	82	—	—	80	68

National Journal Ratings

	1988 LIB — 1988 CONS		1987 LIB — 1987 CONS	
Economic	13% —	85%	11% —	83%
Social	0% —	95%	28% —	71%
Foreign	0% —	84%	25% —	74%

Key Votes

1) Homeless $	FOR	5) Ban Drug Test	AGN	9) SDI Research	FOR
2) Gephardt Amdt	AGN	6) Drug Death Pen	FOR	10) Ban Chem Weaps	AGN
3) Deficit Reduc	AGN	7) Handgun Sales	FOR	11) Aid to Contras	FOR
4) Kill Plnt Clsng Notice	FOR	8) Ban D.C. Abort $	FOR	12) Nuclear Testing	AGN

Election Results

1988 general	Don Sundquist (R)	142,025	(80%)	($307,656)
	Kenneth Bloodworth (D)	35,237	(20%)	($1,110)
1988 primary	Don Sundquist (R), unopposed			
1986 general	Don Sundquist (R)	93,902	(72%)	($281,817)
	M. Lloyd Hiler (D)	35,966	(28%)	($4,183)

EIGHTH DISTRICT

It could almost be the northern end of Mississippi, the flat land between the Mississippi River and the TVA lakes on the lower Tennessee River in west Tennessee. West of Nashville, north of Memphis, the rivers roll lazily through flat or only gently rolling land; cotton and, increasingly, soybeans are the main crops; many of the blacks who worked these fields before mechanization have long since left, but enough remain to give this district the highest black percentage of any rural district in Tennessee. This is the land of the 8th Congressional District of Tennessee, which dips into the north side of the Memphis area, but whose biggest city otherwise is Jackson, with 50,000 people.

This is part of the Democratic heartland of Tennessee (although there are a few Republican counties, which favored the Union in the Civil War) that trended Republican in national races in the 1960s and 1970s but has turned back towards the Democrats, with the help of some smart local politicians. One of them is Ned McWherter, who was first elected to the legislature from Weakley County in 1968 and served as speaker from 1973 to 1986 (one of the few to have made the transition from speaker to governor). Another was Congressman Ed Jones, former Agriculture Commissioner in Tennessee, who was first elected to the House in a three-way race in 1969, when George Wallace backed an independent candidate; Jones became a high-ranking member of the Agriculture Committee and a major policymaker on farm credit and soil conservation (he pioneered the "sodbuster" and "conservation reserve" laws). A third name needs to be added to the list: Congressman John Tanner, who won the seat when Jones retired in 1988 with a whopping 66% in a four-candidate primary and 62% against a Republican Pat Robertson backer in the general election.

Tanner is a banker and lawyer from Obion County, exactly the sort of notable who traditionally runs things in southern politics; after law school and service in the Judge Advocates Corps, he came back to west Tennessee, was elected to the legislature in 1976 and became chairman of the commerce committee. Like McWherter and Jones (who was a good friend of his grandfather), he seems to combine political shrewdness with a country demeanor; he campaigned in 338 communities in the district, with many stops listed on his schedule as "Tanner handshakin' and goodol' boyin'." At the same time, he raised over $800,000 and spent it shrewdly. When his Republican opponent said he would be a liberal national Democrat, his reply was, "Bull. Ed Jones has been his own man and John Tanner will be his own man." He supported the line-item veto, was dubious about a big minimum wage increase and opposes national health insurance.

In the House, Tanner got seats on the Armed Services Committee—there's a big Air Force Base in Millington, just north of Memphis—and on Science, Space and Technology. He seems set for a long House career.

The People: Est. Pop. 1986: 523,300, up 3.6% 1980–86; Pop. 1980: 504,957, up 12.2% 1970–80. Households (1980): 78% family, 43% with children, 65% married couples; 30.2% housing units rented; median monthly rent: $119; median house value: $30,400. Voting age pop. (1980): 358,805; 18% Black, 1% Spanish origin.

1988 Presidential Vote:

Bush (R)	89,899	(56%)
Dukakis (D)	69,420	(43%)

Rep. John S. Tanner (D)

Elected 1988; b. Sept. 22, 1944, Halls; home, Union City; U. of TN, B.S. 1966, J.D. 1969; Disciples of Christ; married (Betty).

Career: Navy, 1969–73; Practicing atty., 1973–88; Dir., Sr. Vice Pres., Metro. Federal Savings & Loan; TN House of Reps., 1977–88.

Offices: 512 CHOB 20515, 202-225-4714. Also 345 Harrison St., Union City 38261 901-885-7070; Federal Bldg., Rm. B-7, Jackson 38301, 901-423-4848; and 3179 N. Watkins, Memphis 38127, 901-358-4094.

Committees: *Armed Services* (30th of 31 D). Subcommittees: Investigations; Readiness. *Science, Space and Technology* (29th of 30 D). Subcommittees: Investigations and Oversight; Natural Resources, Agriculture Research and Environment; Space Science and Applications.

Group Ratings and Key Votes: Newly Elected

Election Results

1988 general	John Tanner (D)	94,571	(62%)	($863,425)
	Ed Bryant (R)	56,983	(38%)	($106,028)
1988 primary	John Tanner (D)	45,271	(66%)	
	Bob Conger (D)	10,468	(15%)	
	Ray Blanton (D)	7,202	(11%)	
	Ivy Scarborough (D)	5,311	(8%)	
1986 general	Ed Jones (D)	101,699	(80%)	($108,957)
	Dan H. Campbell (R)	24,792	(20%)	

NINTH DISTRICT

Memphis, the largest city in Tennessee, is smack in the far southwestern corner of the state; the financial and commercial center of much of the lower Mississippi Valley, it looks as much south to Mississippi and west to Arkansas as it does east to Tennessee. You are 500 miles here from the Appalachian border with Virginia, and only 20 miles from a Mississippi cotton field. Memphis' separateness is symbolized by its musical tradition: Beale Street, near downtown Memphis, gave birth to jazz in the 1920s; jazz, in turn, came from the blues music which is the product of the lower Mississippi Valley, particularly the Delta; and Elvis Presley, Mississippi-born but living in his Memphis mansion Graceland most of his adult life, drew on the blues and black music generally to produce the rock-and-roll which made him a star in his lifetime and a seemingly living presence a dozen years after his premature death.

Memphis has been one of the capitals of the Cotton Kingdom for many years, and today, as the home of the world's largest spot cotton market, still bears the imprint of the cotton culture. Black slaves and field hands were used to pick cotton, and Memphis continues to have a large black population—one of the largest, as a percentage of metropolitan area, in the country. For some years Memphis tried to live this heritage down, redeveloping Beale Street; now it recognizes its history as an asset, and is proud of its old fountains and the courtyard of the Peabody Hotel where you can get a sense of the days when big Mississippi planters came north to sell their one season's crop and make their financial arrangements for the next. It has other historical distinctions as well: it is the site of the first supermarket (Piggly Wiggly) in the 1920s, the first Holiday Inn in the 1950s and the beginning of Federal Express in the 1970s—each on the leading edge of American commercial innovation.

But Memphis doesn't live on just nostalgia. It is the nation's second largest soybean processor, the third largest meat processor, and the third largest food processor generally; it is proud of Elvis Presley and happy with the tourist dollars Graceland brings in, but proud as well of the success of Federal Express, all of whose packages change planes every night in Memphis; and it likes to boast of its four million trees, nurtured by the hot, humid climate.

Politically, Memphis has not been an entirely happy city. This is, after all, the place where Martin Luther King Jr., was murdered, while he was in town supporting a garbage workers' strike. And it is a city where voting patterns are still racially polarized. Blacks, as they do almost everywhere in the United States, vote almost unanimously Democratic. Whites vote by percentages almost as high for Republicans, at least in seriously contested races. The hard edge of racial animosity seems to have worn off these days, but the polarization, to most people's discomfort, remains. That separatism coexists with a tradition of almost authoritarian bossism. For 39 years, the political machine run by Ed Crump ruled the city government and could deliver Memphis's votes *en bloc*, particularly in the Democratic primary, making Crump the effective political boss of the state and a master of invective. In 1948, he attacked Estes Kefauver as "a pet coon that puts its foot in an open drawer in your room, but invariably turns its head while its foot is feeling around in the drawer. The coon hopes, through its cunning by turning its head, he will deceive any onlookers as to where his foot is and what it is into." Kefauver donned a coonskin cap, saying "At least I'm not Mr. Crump's pet coon," won the primary and ended Crump's control. But Crump governed efficiently, honestly, with the support of blacks who were allowed to vote in Memphis (unlike most southern cities)—and who voted almost unanimously for Mr. Crump's candidates.

The 9th Congressional District of Tennessee consists of most of the city of Memphis; most of its residents are black, and the district is solidly Democratic. Its congressman, Harold Ford, first elected in 1974, has gained more substantive power over major legislation than Crump ever did, but he appears also to have gotten into more trouble than Memphis's old boss ever experienced.

Ford sits on the Ways and Means Committee, and his power comes on the Human Resources Subcommittee of which he became chairman in 1981. (He had to step down from his chairmanship in April of 1987, however, pending the outcome of ethics charges against him. Tom Downey is now acting chairman.) Ford's major causes have been to get the government to aid workers after their unemployment benefits have been were exhausted and to extend AFDC to benefits to two-parent families if both parents otherwise qualify. Ford says this is a way of keeping families together; opponents say it is subsidizing idleness. The two-parent law got through the House but didn't become law in 1986; he tried again to get it in the welfare reform measure he was advancing in early 1987, and succeeded. In April 1987 the subcommittee reported out a welfare reform bill, authorizing and paying 60% of the cost for new state job training, education and work programs for welfare recipients; requiring welfare mothers with children over three to participate in them; adding the 1986 welfare-for-unemployed-fathers provision (already the law in half the states); and encouraging higher benefits in low-benefit states. Republicans opposed the bill as too costly (perhaps $5.5 billion a year) and on other grounds, but it looked like a good first step toward the workfare bill that Members of both parties were longing to pass. Ford's measure became law as part of the Family Support Act of 1988.

Then, less than a month later, Ford was indicted by a federal grand jury on charges of bank and tax fraud stemming from moneys he received from C. H. Butcher Jr., a Tennessee banker and brother and partner of Jake Butcher, the 1982 Democratic candidate for governor whose banking empire collapsed in 1983 and who was sentenced to 20 years in jail in 1985 for defrauding depositors of $20 million. The indictment said that a $350,000 "loan" from one of C. H. Butcher's firms to a corporation controlled by Ford was used by Ford, not for his family funeral home business, but to pay personal debts and buy personal belongings. A spokesman for Ford said he did not know all the details and that he had loaned the funeral home personal funds so that any moneys advanced were repayments; Ford charged that the U.S. attorney bringing the case was politically motivated. The trial judge in Knoxville imposed a gag order on Ford, because of his criticisms of the prosecutor; in September 1987, an appeals court ruled that the gag order was "blatantly unconstitutional" and the case was ordered transferred to Memphis.

After the indictment, Ford lost control of the welfare measure, and ultimately something much more like the rather different bill passed by the Senate was signed into law in 1988. Ford seems to have kept the confidence of his constituents, winning 80% in the 1988 primary and winning the 1988 general election with 82%. As of June 1989 his case had not come to trial; obviously, on its result hinges his career in Congress. If the seat is vacated, a successor will effectively be chosen in the Democratic primary. The seat will have to be enlarged after the 1990 Census, but will still likely have a large black majority.

The People: Est. Pop. 1986: 489,400, dn. 3.2% 1980–86; Pop. 1980: 505,592, dn. 9.4% 1970–80. Households (1980): 69% family, 38% with children, 46% married couples; 46.0% housing units rented; median monthly rent: $136; median house value: $32,300. Voting age pop. (1980): 359,672; 51% Black, 1% Spanish origin.

1988 Presidential Vote:			
	Dukakis (D)	117,491	(66%)
	Bush (R)	59,955	(34%)

Rep. Harold E. Ford (D)

Elected 1974; b. May 20, 1945, Memphis; home, Memphis; TN St. U., B.S. 1967, John Gupten Col., A.A. 1969; Howard U., M.B.A. 1982; Baptist; married (Dorothy).

Career: Mortician, 1969–75; TN House of Reps., 1971–75.

Offices: 2305 RHOB 20515, 202-225-3265. Also Fed. Office Bldg., Ste. 369, 167 N. Main St., Memphis 38103, 901-521-4131.

Committees: *Ways and Means* (7th of 23 D). Subcommittees: Human Resources; Oversight. *Select Committee on Aging* (4th of 39 D). Subcommittee: Health and Long-Term Care.

Group Ratings

	ADA	ACLU	COPE	CFA	LCV	ACU	NTLC	NSI	COC	CEI
1988	85	87	92	55	50	0	0	0	36	12
1987	68	—	92	64	—	0	—	—	0	3

National Journal Ratings

	1988 LIB — 1988 CONS			1987 LIB — 1987 CONS		
Economic	79%	—	17%	73%	—	0%
Social	86%	—	0%	60%	—	40%
Foreign	84%	—	0%	81%	—	0%

Key Votes

1) Homeless $	AGN	5) Ban Drug Test	—	9) SDI Research	—
2) Gephardt Amdt	FOR	6) Drug Death Pen	AGN	10) Ban Chem Weaps	—
3) Deficit Reduc	FOR	7) Handgun Sales	AGN	11) Aid to Contras	AGN
4) Kill Plnt Clsng Notice	AGN	8) Ban D.C. Abort $	AGN	12) Nuclear Testing	FOR

Election Results

1988 general	Harold E. Ford (D)................. 126,280	(82%)	($364,330)
	Isaac Richmond (I).................. 28,522	(18%)	
1988 primary	Harold E. Ford (D)................. 35,589	(80%)	
	Mark Flanagan (D)................. 8,720	(20%)	
1986 general	Harold E. Ford (D)................. 83,006	(83%)	($320,227)
	Isaac Richmond (R)................. 16,221	(16%)	

TEXAS

On the inaugural platform in front of the Capitol in the cold sunlight of January 1989 was a scene that would have been unthinkable 50 years before: a Texan was about to be sworn in as President of the United States and standing in his inaugural party were Texans who had been nominated to be Secretary of State and Secretary of Defense, a concentration of power in politicians who were all from a state unheard of even in the early 1800s in the days of the House of Virginia. Standing also on that platform were important Texans in Congress: the Speaker of the House, the chairman of the Senate Finance Committee, and three House committee chairmen.

To the Americans of half a century ago, powerful congressional Democrats were a familiar sight: Sam Rayburn was about to begin his long tenure as Speaker, and Texans had recently or would soon chair Foreign Relations and Armed Services in the Senate and Appropriations, Judiciary and Agriculture in the House. But in the America on the brink of World War II it seemed quite unlikely that a politician from Texas could be elected President—no candidate from a Confederate state had been elected to the presidency since before the Civil War—and it was utterly unthinkable that a Republican from Texas could be elected to anything or implausible that Texans would be entrusted with high executive offices with control over foreign and military policy.

But the sun-parched, wind-blown, dirt-poor Texas of 1940 in which Lyndon Johnson was a young scrambling politician was very different from the air-conditioned, sleek, stylish Texas of 1988 which chose between a ticket headed by incumbent Vice President George Bush and one that included incumbent Senator Lloyd Bentsen. In the days before air-conditioning, there were some six million Texans, with incomes well below the national average, three-quarters of them living outside the metropolitan orbit of the state's medium-sized cities, most of them still poor dirt farmers.

Texas had a proud history, remembering always the Alamo and its nine years as an independent Republic, assertive still in its commemoration of Confederate veterans (mention of whom could still bring a tear to Sam Rayburn's usually piercing eyes), resentful of the Wall Street bankers and financiers who, it believed, kept Texas as a colonial economy. To be sure, Texas was a major oil-producing state beginning with the Spindletop well of 1901; but oil prices had plummeted in the 1930s and were propped up only by the efforts of Democratic politicians, whose "hot oil" act forbade the sale of interstate oil at prices below that determined by production levels set by the Texas Railroad Commission. Texas's most influential money man at the time, Jesse Jones, was not an oil man at all, but a Houston cotton broker and newspaper publisher who was Franklin Roosevelt's Secretary of Commerce and who, as head of the Reconstruction Finance Corporation, controlled a pool of government capital that was one of the nation's major sources of financing for business in the 1930s and war industries in the 1940s. Texas's economic power was based on politics; and political power, in turn, was closely held in a system with only one functioning political party, with primaries closed to blacks, with voter turnout held down by a poll tax, and with local bankers, courthouse lawyers and big landowners who held sway through informal influence and, in some counties, ballot-box stuffing.

More than 50 years separate this Texas from the overly air-conditioned Texas of today, with its glittering galleries and its smooth sophistication. This empire state of nearly 17 million still depends on oil and gas—which gave it a roller coaster economy in the 1980s—and is not averse to accepting government largesse, like the huge defense contracts of the Dallas-Fort Worth metroplex and the super collider to be built at its south edge. But this Texas also has an economy that generates, rather than begs for capital, and a private sector that is technologically and economically innovative, rather than slavishly envious of others back east. The state has a vigorous two-party system which has more in common with the rest of the nation than the one-party system of pre-air-conditioned Texas; and if its dependence on the clout of its politicians is far less than it once was, it has succeeded in producing a set of officeholders at least as talented and enterprising as those from any other state.

Yet for all its successes, economic and political, Texas still sometimes seems to be tottering on the edge of disaster. The collapse of oil prices in the early 1980s not only hurt the oil and gas business but, because it resulted in an implosion of real estate values, has resulted in a crash of the high-flying Texas savings and loan business—one that may end up costing federal taxpayers billions of dollars. And for all the victories of Texas politicians, their hold on power is not utterly secure. John Tower, who in that golden moment in January 1989 expected to be Defense Secretary, was denied confirmation two months later by the same Senate of which he had been a member for 23 years. And Speaker Jim Wright, for all his large Democratic House majority was soon spending all his time fighting the Ethics Committee's charges that he violated House rules—and finally in June 1989 had to resign as speaker and leave the House. For all of Texas's advances, it still sits on the only land border between the First and Third Worlds, and its income levels, despite all the millionaires and the growth during the years of high oil prices, topped out at the national average and then fell back in the 1980s. Texans do not need to be reminded of the possibility of defeat; it is an integral part of their history: the Alamo was not a victory, the Republic did not last, the Confederacy was extinguished, and Texas's only President before George Bush, Lyndon Johnson, left office a defeated and bitter man.

But just as integral a part of Texas history is the confidence that defeats are never final, and that it is always worth making a fight. The Alamo is remembered as the beginning of a war that resulted in victory, Johnson's defeat did not prevent other Democrats of similar politics—Lloyd Bentsen and Jim Wright—from rising, even as Texas trended Republican in most elections, and George Bush carried Texas three times on national tickets after having lost the state twice in races for the U.S. Senate.

The bridge between the Texas to which George Bush moved as a young man in 1948 and the Texas which gave him a solid majority for President in 1988 is what Texans still call the "awl bidness". For oil is not just a windfall: finding it and getting it out of the ground is high-skill work. Oil made instant millionaires out of some lucky Texas farmers, but more importantly, it created a business which rewarded sophistication and placed a premium on knowledge. The men you'll see over scotch and steaks at the Petroleum Club in Fort Worth or Tyler or Midland may not look sophisticated to habitues of Ivy League faculty clubs, but beneath their bravado are

1150   TEXAS

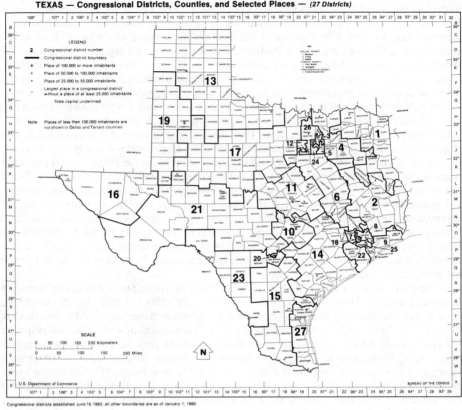
plenty of brains. By the 1970s, Texas was not so much the place where oil was found as the place where you found people who could find, drill, store and refine oil and natural gas. These skills led Texas naturally into technology. And starting in the 1960s, Texas was building the critical mass of knowledge and financing to produce firms like Texas Instruments and H. Ross Perot's EDS. At the same time, the University of Texas and, as time went on, Texas A&M—both helped by the huge income from their oil lands—were providing a superb university infrastructure to go with the highway system that this huge state built to tie itself together.

The benefits of a developing economy are never evenly distributed, and much of the tension in Texas politics comes from the wide disparities in wealth and the vast cultural variety in this huge state. Conservative Democrats led rebellions against their national ticket as early as 1944, and Texas voted Republican as Governor Allan Shivers endorsed Dwight Eisenhower in 1952. Republican professor John Tower surprised everyone when he got 41% against Lyndon Johnson in the 1960 Senate race (when Johnson was also on the Democratic ticket as Vice President), and even more when he won the 1961 special election to take Johnson's place (some liberals voted for Tower because his opponent was a conservative Democrat and they thought he'd be easier to get rid of). But Tory Democrats remained Texas's most successful politicians through the 1960s and 1970s, winning Democratic primaries (there is no party registration, so conservatives can vote in the Democratic primary and then for Republicans in November) and then overwhelming hapless Republicans. But in 1978, a more liberal Democrat won the gubernatorial primary and then lost the general election by a hair to Republican Bill Clements, while John Tower was getting reelected over the winner of a turbulent Democratic contest by a similarly thin margin. Just as oil prices were about to peak, Texas had developed a genuine two-party politics.

The years since have been something of a roller coaster for Texas's economy—and for its politicians. Clements was beaten by Democrat Mark White in 1982, a year when Lloyd Bentsen, up for reelection, organized a Democratic registration and turnout drive that, together with the downturn in the economy, helped to produce an across-the-board statewide victory for the ticket, including liberals like Attorney General Jim Mattox and Treasurer Ann Richards. Then, in 1984, Ronald Reagan swept the state overwhelmingly, and party-switcher and free market aficionado Phil Gramm beat, by nearly as much, the liberal the Democrats nominated for the Senate. In 1986, Clements came back and beat White, but Republican Judge Roy Barrera Jr., unaccountably underfinanced, failed to win the attorney general job. In 1988, Michael Dukakis's choice of Lloyd Bentsen helped to make Texas closer in the presidential race, but it still remained out of reach: Bush-Quayle beat Dukakis-Bentsen 56%–43%. Bentsen was reelected to the Senate easily against weak opposition (Democrats in 1984 passed a law saying that if a nominee resigned his nomination, the slot went unfilled; hence Bentsen had to run for Senate or his party would have forfeited the seat), but Republican Kent Hance won a statewide race for railroad commissioner—the first time a Republican has won a down-the-ballot race—by a 55%–45% margin that looks something like a straight ticket victory.

In these seemingly contradictory or at least fluctuating results, you can see Texas torn between faith in the free market and a desire for government safety nets, between the traditional culture of the rural South and the self-consciously modern culture of the rapidly growing cities, between Texas's traditional image of ethnic uniformity and suspicion of outsiders and its increasingly heterogeneous population and its natural friendliness. Some of the contradictions may be resolved in 1990, when Gramm comes up for reelection and when, with Clements's retirement, the governorship will be up for grabs.

In Texas's growing cities—in the Dallas-Fort Worth Metroplex, in greater Houston, in San Antonio and the once tiny capital, Austin, now spreading out into the hill country—politics tends to divide people along income lines. The divisions can be stark: you can drive just a few minutes on the freeway from the west side of Houston or north Dallas, where house sales of $750,000 are routine, and find neighborhoods of tiny, drafty frame houses which are little better than tarpaper shacks. Texas, for all its millionaires, has a substantial low-wage economy and, as the largest state with a right-to-work law, almost no union members; most of its blacks (12% of the population) and Hispanics (21%) are part of this low-wage economy, as are many whites of rural origin. All tend to vote Democratic, but they are not a homogeneous proletariat, and are seldom found together: there are few Mexicans in Dallas and almost no blacks in San Antonio or west of Fort Worth. Hispanics are sliding away from the Democrats in some elections, while blacks cast almost no Republican votes at all. The affluent neighborhoods, by contrast, are politically homogeneous, as heavily Republican as any in the United States. There is no apology or guilt about wealth; people here, like the rich in developing countries, do not feel defensive because others are still poor; they have grown up in a society in which most people are poor, and they realize that not everyone can get rich all at once.

All this leaves the metropolitan areas more divided than tradition would have it. The biggest cities have mayors who are Democrats and women: Houston's Kathy Whitmire, Dallas's Annette Strauss, San Antonio's Lila Cockrell and in 1989 El Paso's Suzie Azar. Dallas is well known as one of America's most Republican cities, and Fort Worth has been trending Republican too; yet in the closest recent major race, the 1986 governor's contest, Bill Clements carried the Metroplex by the solid but not overwhelming margin of 56%–42%. Greater Houston, always a little more Democratic, voted 51%–48% for Mark White, as did the combined San

Antonio-Austin areas (50%–48%). The heavily Mexican-American Border counties were a shade less Democratic than usual, 59%–40%.

The balance politically is in the rest of Texas, the smaller counties away from the Border where, after decades of metropolitan growth, more than one-third of the state's votes are still cast. Parts of this nonmetropolitan Texas are still exporting young people to the cities: around Lubbock, where the aquifers are giving out and irrigated cotton fields are going back to desert, in the wheat-growing country of the High Plains, and in cattle-ranching counties in the west, people are still moving out. But in central, east, and south Texas there has been growth through most of the 1980s, some seeping out of the big metropolitan areas, some as factories are built and jobs created off freeway interchanges in piney woods or cotton fields. And just as Texas has not, as many easterners predicted, moved to the heavy-industry-big-unions economy of the Great Lakes (the movement has been the other way around), so the small town values and cultural conservatism of the countryside has not withered away any more than the towns have died. Some things have changed: county option liquor by the drink came in 1970, divorce has grown more common. But there is still a vivid contrast between the big metropolitan areas, where the percentage of women working out of the home is among the highest in the country, and the smaller counties, where it is among the lowest.

Rural Texas, though decreasing as a percentage of the state, remains politically pivotal. A Democrat cannot carry Texas without carrying rural Texas. Mark White got 55% in rural Texas in 1982 and won, and got 41% in 1986 and lost—even though his percentage declined only 3% in the metropolitan and Border areas. Lloyd Bentsen got 59% in rural counties in 1982 and 58% in 1988, on his way to 59% statewide victories. In presidential contests, Jimmy Carter carried Texas in 1976 when he won the rural counties with 53% and lost it in 1980 when he won 42% there. In 1984, Walter Mondale, having conspicuously rejected Lloyd Bentsen for Geraldine Ferraro, got only 34% in rural Texas; in 1988, Michael Dukakis, having even more conspicuously embraced Bentsen, got 42% in the rural counties—as much as Carter—but still lost the state. All of which may sound like arcana, except for one little fact: no Democrat since James K. Polk has been elected President without carrying Texas. Unless Democrats can win electoral votes on the Pacific Coast or in the Great Plains, which have not been reliably theirs in the past, rural Texas remains the key to winning the presidency. James Farley and William Randolph Hearst, who brokered the Roosevelt-Garner ticket in 1932, and Joseph Kennedy and *Washington Post* publisher Philip Graham, who cobbled together the Kennedy-Johnson ticket in 1960, understood that; so too perhaps did Michael Dukakis, except that by 1988 it was not enough to put a Texan in second place.

Republicans have made slogging progress at making Texas bipartisan at other levels. In 1984, even as rural Texas was voting more Republican than the state as a whole, Republicans were electing countywide officials in Tarrant and Bexar Counties (Fort Worth and San Antonio); in 1988, they elected Hance and three Supreme Court justices (in races that were really contests between trial lawyers and insurance companies; the court now has three Republicans, four pro-plaintiff Democrats and two swing Democrats). Another index of Republican strength is the increasing number of Texans who choose, in a state without party registration, to vote in its primary. In 1978, when Clements first ran, 1.8 million Texans voted in the Democratic primary and only 158,000 in the Republican contest. In 1982, some 1.3 million Democratic votes were cast and 265,000 Republican. In 1986, the Democratic vote was down to 1.1 million and the Republican vote up to 544,000. In the 1988 presidential primary, Democratic turnout was 1.7 million and Republican turnout one million: George Bush won more votes than the total ever cast in a Republican primary before. The Republican primary electorate is still tilted toward the affluent, but it is much broader and more diverse than it used to be; the Democratic turnout is becoming more heavily Hispanic and black in the metropolitan areas and sparser in rural Texas.

Yet this trend toward the Republicans occurred in a decade of economic turmoil in much of

Texas, at times when unemployment in much of the state was rising. The Oil Patch in the 1980s seems to have developed political reflexes the opposite of those the industrial belt developed in the 1930s. In those days, industrial voters supported theory-minded Democrats to stimulate the economy in hard times, but otherwise were pleased to let experienced and practical-minded Republicans deal with the nuts and bolts of everyday government. In Texas in the 1980s, the voters have tended to call the Republicans in to deal with a weak economy; they see the free market, not government intervention, as more likely to produce economic growth. In other times, or when they are looking for practical men of action to run the everyday business of government, they may still indulge their historic preference and call in the Democrats. These tendencies were apparent in the metropolitan half of the state by the 1970s and in the 1980s in rural Texas.

The bulwark of the Texas Democrats now is Lloyd Bentsen. As Senate Finance chairman, he is a national power who is in a marvelous position to do things for the state. As a Texas politician, he is the leader of his own organization with workers on the ground in all 254 counties and topnotch organizers in all the big and medium-sized counties. Bentsen's career, since his first election to the Congress in 1948 and his defeat of George Bush in the 1970 Senate race, has been based on his ties with two different segments of the electorate: Hispanics who are the majority in his home area in the Lower Rio Grande Valley, and rural whites who provided key votes for him in 1970 and have stayed with him in every election since, despite their trend otherwise to the Republicans. Bentsen has made it his business to strengthen the state's Democratic Party, especially when he is running, and the fact is that the Democrats' only robust statewide victories in the last 12 years have been in 1982 and 1988, when he was on the ballot. He has responded sharply to Republicans' appeals to his two key groups of the electorate. He has cultivated Hispanic voters, and the Dukakis-Bentsen ticket—the first American presidential ticket with both members fluent in Spanish—carried solid margins on the Border and in Hispanic neighborhoods in San Antonio and Houston. And when Phil Gramm engineered a vacancy in the 1st District and ran a former Texas A&M quarterback for the seat in 1985, Bentsen quietly and behind the scenes set about raising money for the eventual Democratic nominee and bringing forward into public view the trade issue which became the deciding factor in the Democrat's 51%–49% victory.

Even as Texans like Bush, Bentsen, and Baker wield great authority in Washington, the underpinnings of power of their political allies in Texas are not entirely firm, and Texans on all sides are uneasily aware that the economic and political roller coaster rides of the 1980s may not yet be over.

Governor. For most of the past dozen years Bill Clements has been governor of Texas. Yet the legacy he leaves behind is not what you would have predicted when he came to office in 1978—and indeed its most distinctive features are more the product of the one-term hiatus of Mark White's governorship than of the two terms Clements has been in office. Clements is a gruff, tactless man with the angry streak apparent for years in many Dallas Republicans; he had to leave college to support his family when his father went broke in the 1930s, and in the half a century since he has made hundreds of millions building an offshore drilling service company. Clements wanted to keep taxes and spending down, he wanted to appoint procedural reformers rather than political hacks to high state jobs and judgeships, and he has had some success on both counts. But as oil prices plummeted and the high-tech economy boomed, it became apparent that Texas needed to do more to provide a high-skill work force and high-tech infrastructure in the 1980s and 1990s, just as it had had to provide roads, geological engineering education and tight regulation of production and prices to enable the oil business to grow in the 1940s and 1950s.

To those problems, the solution offered by Ross Perot, appointed by White to head a commission, was an education reform plan which included a no-pass-no-play rule, requiring high school students to make passing grades in all their courses before they could play football and other sports. In a state where towns charter 727s to fly fans to see state playoff football games, this was audacious stuff, but White stuck by it and—while saying little in the 1986 campaign— so did Clements. What Clements also had to do, once he took office again, was to raise taxes substantially. That, plus revelations that, as chairman of the SMU board of trustees, he approved payments to football players, left him with low job ratings in most of 1987 and 1988, and seemingly weakened enough to prevent his exerting much influence on the choice of his successor. Yet he was successful in the affecting the outcome of the railroad commissioner race and several of the Supreme Court races..

In early 1989, two Democrats seemed to be running for governor, while the Republican field was unclear. State Treasurer Ann Richards, famed nationally and in Texas for her ripping keynote speech at the 1988 Democratic National Convention, was eager to run; she is in many ways an attractive candidate, though her jibes against Bush did not sound as convincing as he was inaugurated in January 1989 as they had in Atlanta in July 1988, and her hard-line criticism of Ronald Reagan goes against the grain in a state that gave him 64% of its votes. The other Democrat is Attorney General Jim Mattox; he starts off better financed, but he showed weakness at the polls in 1986, he is identified as at least as liberal as Richards and, although he was acquitted in a criminal trial many retain doubts about his integrity.

Among Republicans, the best known name to be making the rounds in early 1989 was George W. Bush, the son of the President, often (and inaccurately) referred to as Junior; of all the Bush children he is the one who did most of his growing up in west Texas and has the strongest Texas accent. He is an oil man from Midland who ran for Congress in 1978 and lost to Kent Hance; his efforts in his father's 1988 campaign were more successful. Another possibility is Kent Hance himself, who won only 20% against Clements in the 1986 primary but was appointed by him to the Railroad Commission and then won that office with 55% in 1988. Hance was once a Democrat and, as a Boll Weevil, was a lead sponsor of the 1981 Reagan tax cut package, and in 1984 won 49% in the runoff for Senate. Absent from the field by their own decisions are two men who might have made stronger candidates than any of those running: Lieutenant Governor Bill Hobby, a moderate Democrat with nearly 20 years' experience running the state senate, and Democratic former San Antonio Mayor Henry Cisneros, Hispanic and intellectual, a graduate of Harvard and Texas A&M, a reformer and an ethnic hero, who in 1987 said he was leaving politics because of his infant son's illness and in 1988 revealed that he had a long-standing affair with a rich Anglo San Antonio woman.

The Texas governorship race will be watched in media markets far beyond Austin because of redistricting. Texas stands to gain three or four House seats after the 1990 Census—the exact number depends on the count—and how the district lines are drawn can determine which party holds not only those seats but some others as well. If the Republicans hold the governorship in 1990 and continue to hold enough state legislative seats to keep the Democrats from overriding a veto (when Clements was first elected Democrats had a 130–20 edge in the House—for the 1989 session it was 91–59), Republicans will have at least a say in the bargaining. But a Democratic governor able to amass a majority in the legislature can redraw the lines pretty much at will. So not only the governor's office, but three or four U.S. House seats may be at stake in the 1990 gubernatorial race.

Senators. Texas has two of the most powerful and effective Senators in Washington. But they are powerful and effective in entirely different ways and are certainly not friends; in fact Phil Gramm ran in the Democratic primary against Lloyd Bentsen in 1976. Gramm won 28% of the vote to Bentsen's 64%, but don't think that either of them has forgotten. Another struggle between them was the 1985 1st District special election, which Gramm hoped to make a precedent for Republican gains in the rural South and Bentsen hoped would protect his base among rural white Texans (Democrat Jim Chapman won that seat). A third struggle was the 1988 presidential race, in which Gramm nominated Bush (though it was not apparent in the first two pages of the speech text which Texas Republican he was nominating) and Bentsen was chosen for Vice President by Dukakis. These are tough politicians, betting big stakes and playing for keeps.

Lloyd Bentsen is one of two or three American politicians who is plainly of presidential stature. In breadth of experience, in depth of knowledge, in traits of character—a steely self-discipline and the capacity to rebound after setbacks—he is far and away the superior of most of the candidates who ran for the office in 1984 and 1988 and of some who have held it in the past. The conventional wisdom in Washington has long been that he is a dull politician. Certainly he is not a spellbinder, but he is operating in an era when voters are not looking for oratory; and he is anything but self-revealing in the manner of the Hollywood starlets or minor politicos who babble on about how they have finally gotten in touch with themselves. But on the campaign trail in 1988 he came up with the single best one-line response any Democrat has had to the Republican claim to have produced a strong economy ("If you let me write $200 billion dollars worth of hot checks every year, I'd give you an illusion of prosperity too" and he delivered the single most devastating putdown (of vice presidential nominee Dan Quayle) of the entire 1987–88 campaign ("Senator, you're no Jack Kennedy"). He emerged in some polls the strongest of the four men on the two national tickets, and there are many who think that if the Democrats had had the wisdom to nominate their ticket in alphabetical order it would have won.

Bentsen lacks the spontaneous charm that political reporters like in their politicians, and his careful preparation and calm discipline for every political task he takes on is difficult to dramatize or simply to appreciate. Yet he comes from a background that can only be called romantic and has shown aggressiveness to the point of daring in his career. His father—who was on the podium when his son was nominated in Atlanta and died in a car crash in 1989 at age 95—moved from the Dakotas to the Lower Rio Grande Valley in 1921 with five dollars in his pocket and became one of the great Texas landowners. Back in those days, the border was not patrolled, most of the people spoke Spanish, and business was done with people who toted guns. Bentsen grew up in a bungalow on a dirt road, speaking Spanish as fluently as English; he went off to war, came back and was elected to Congress in 1948 at age 27. After six years, he left to start an insurance business in Houston and make his millions; then in 1970 he ran for the Senate. In the primary, against liberal incumbent Ralph Yarborough, he raised Tory Democratic money and ran ads featuring footage of the riots outside the Democratic National Convention in Chicago in 1968; in the general election he ran with labor and black endorsements and many white rural votes and beat a Houston congressman named George Bush.

As chairman of the Senate Finance Committee, he is one of the most powerful Democrats in Washington, and beautifully placed to help Texas's oil industry. He already has, in the 1986 tax reform battle. As the leader of the oil state bloc on Finance, he insisted on retaining the intangible drilling allowance and other favorable tax treatments in the bill as his price for supporting chairman Bob Packwood's reform package; Packwood and reform author Bill Bradley had to go along. But Bentsen also has broader-gauged interests. In his first 18 months as Finance chairman, he steered to passage the 1988 trade legislation, the catastrophic health care bill, and two tax bills—detailed, difficult legislation, plus the Democrats' plant closing bill as well. It was this record of superb legislating which evidently influenced Michael Dukakis more than anything else in his choice of Bentsen, and it has also commended him to members of both houses and both parties. Cool and businesslike in his demeanor, he is willing to listen to colleagues and work with them on their projects; he is not a dictatorial chairman and spends time and effort coming up with solutions that can win majorities.

In the 101st Congress, he is one of two senators who, by their position and because of the respect in which they are held, can determine the outcome of an issue by his say-so alone. An example is the catastrophic health insurance plan, passed by Congress in 1988 after long debate; after the election, many Members started hearing complaints from the social security recipients who have to pay the tax the act imposed, and agitated for some kind of relief. To this attempt to welsh on a deal and play cheap shot politics, Bentsen in December 1988 just said no: Finance would not consider any such measure, he said, and it was promptly killed. Bentsen will, however, guide proceedings on any technical changes needed in the tax law, though he doesn't want to monkey with the 1986 reform; and he will have much to say about any medicare or medicaid repairs.

Bentsen is almost sure to be the Senate's major legislator on what could be the foremost issue of the 101st Congress, trade. In 1985, he came forward with a tough retaliatory trade bill, co-sponsored by Dan Rostenkowski and Richard Gephardt, which became the cornerstone of the Democrats' political thrust on the issue. The 1988 bill he sponsored and pushed to passage was considerably more moderate. On trade bills Bentsen seems to be playing several complicated games. On policy, he is keenly aware of the dangers of protectionism and wants to forestall it, but he also seems to believe that he sometimes has a responsibility to act as bad cop while the Administration acts as good cop in negotiations with Japan and other trading partners. On party politics, he sees trade as one issue on which the Democrats can take an assertive, even chauvinistic posture—this was how he framed the issue for the politically pivotal 1985 Texas 1st District race—but he probably also sees the dangers of splitting the party geographically between a protectionist bloc anchored in Ohio, Michigan and Pennsylvania, and a free trade bloc anchored on the West Coast. On presidential politics, trade is an issue on which Bentsen can show leadership but on which he may be accused of demagoguery—where he may make some Democratic friends but risk losing others. On all three dimensions, Bentsen has incentives to oscillate between policies and shift ground: watching him do so, and maintaining, as he almost invariably does, not just an intellectually defensible position but usually an intellectually elegant one, is surely as fascinating a spectacle as American politics offers.

Bentsen was embarrassed in early 1987 by one of his campaign tactics, a breakfast-with-Bentsen program for $10,000 a head—"Eggs McBentsen," it was called—and the furor helped spur demands for campaign finance reform. But it was just Bentsen operating with typical efficiency, admitting "a doozy" of a mistake, disbanding the breakfast group, and returning the money (much of which was contributed right back). Despite that setback, his fundraising for his 1988 Senate campaign was so efficient you could set a clock by it, and his organization for the general election left nothing significant undone. With his strong and deep support from Texas business interests—why on earth would you want to defeat a Texan who was chairman of Senate Finance?—he deterred any strong opponent from entering the race. The congressman who ran, Beau Boulter from the panhandle, was so weak that he had to face a runoff before winning; Bentsen, in his telegram to contributors just after his selection for the VP slot asking for their support in his Senate race regardless of their position on the national ticket, noted contemptuously, "My opponent is simply not qualified." Bentsen won the election 59%–40%, precisely the same as his margin in 1982; he ran slightly stronger in the metropolitan areas and 1% weaker in rural Texas, carrying even the Dallas-Fort Worth metroplex comfortably.

Will Bentsen run for President in 1992? He will be 71 then, but his father was entirely active until his death at age 95, he is in fine health, and he is only three years older than George Bush—whom he has beaten before. The Democratic selection process remains unfriendly to candidates of his moderate stripe, but less so perhaps than it used to be; the Democratic convention of 1988 accepted him much more meekly than the convention of 1984 would have, and by the strength of his campaigning and the steadfastness of his support of Dukakis—never once did his major differences with the presidential nominee cause either of them any problem—he made many friends and created new admirers among Democrats who used to think of him, if they thought of him at all, as a dull, gray, middle-aged white male. Now many of them are thinking of him as a nominee, or a President. In early 1989, Bentsen was not making any obvious preparations to run, but he was doing nothing ostentatious to disclaim interest either. Perhaps he is waiting to see if the flow of events and his health make a candidacy possible.

Phil Gramm, first elected to Congress in 1978, has made himself a major national politician and has changed the American fiscal firmament not once but twice. He started off as a Democrat in College Station, Texas, an economics professor at Texas A&M, which was founded as a military school and has Aggie jokes told about its students, but which can claim academic achievements to rival those of the vastly rich and much more famous University of Texas. He was politically unknown, unconnected to the great wealth and power brokers of Texas (he is a native of Georgia), armed with little but his belief in free market economics, a gift for making his political case pithily, and plenty of nerve. These have taken him a long way. He ran against Lloyd Bentsen in 1976 at age 34 and avoided humiliation. He was elected to Congress two years later after squeaking into second place in the primary by 115 votes out of 81,000 votes cast (just ahead of Chet Edwards, now one of the smartest Texas state senators) and winning the runoff 53%–47%.

In his second term, after Jim Wright helped him onto the House Budget Committee, he was the Democratic co-sponsor of the 1981 Reagan budget cuts, attending Democrats' strategy meetings and then reporting the results to Republican strategists; and so made the biggest dents in the domestic budget since the 1940s. Expelled from the Democratic Caucus after the 1982 election, he resigned, switched parties, and ran as a Republican in a special election quickly called by outgoing Governor Clements. It was both an honorable move (voters should be able to say whether they want a congressman of a different party) and a shrewd one (his district ran from the Houston to the Fort Worth suburbs, allowing him to campaign heavily in media markets covering almost half the state). His gift for aphorism did not fail him ("I had to choose between Tip O'Neill and y'all, and I decided to stand with y'all") and he won with 55% against nine Democrats and a Libertarian.

That set the stage for his 1984 Senate race. When John Tower surprised everyone by announcing his retirement in 1983, just after a big fundraiser, Gramm immediately jumped in. His Republican rivals had little chance. The Democrats were caught in an epic three-way race and the winner was Lloyd Doggett, a highly competent and liberal state senator from Austin. But Doggett was too close on the issues to Walter Mondale and it didn't help that Gramm kept attacking Doggett for receiving some $500 raised at a gay male strip joint in San Antonio.

Then, in his first year in the Senate, Gramm came forth with two bold initiatives: contriving the 1st District special election and, the week after that came up short, Gramm-Rudman. This idea—an orderly ratcheting down of the federal deficit—had appeal on all sides: conservatives thought it would force down domestic spending, liberals hoped it would squeeze defense, deficit-cutters of both parties figured it might force Ronald Reagan to allow a tax increase. Gramm surely hoped it would forestall any new spending initiatives, as it mostly has. It passed, it should be added, despite and not because of Phil Gramm's personal appeal. He is among the least popular of Senators. Colleagues will admit that he is true to his principles, but add that he is ready to be untrue to his colleagues or his word. Some think he has his eye on the presidency, and he does not deny that he might some day be interested. In the meantime, he has been the subject of some grumbling in Texas for his willingness to let the market drive down oil prices, his opposition to pork barrel projects, and his lack of interest in local issues: principle over politics again.

But, for this breathtakingly bold politician, principle seems to be paying off. He is the prohibitive favorite approaching the 1990 Senate election. Henry Cisneros took himself out of the race in September 1987. Agriculture Commissioner Jim Hightower, a populist with a marvelous wit, started to run and then left the race in January 1989. Congressman John Bryant of Dallas, a possible entrant, is also eyeing the race for attorney general; Congressman Mickey Leland may run. Lieutenant Governor Bill Hobby seems to have little interest in running.

Gramm, despite his occasionally impolitic stands on economic issues, is expected to raise $20 million and will be running in a state that seems comfortable with the positions he has long held and with the party he recently joined and of which he is now a national leader. Nor do Gramm's ambitions stop there. He sees himself as a man who has a mission to change the role of government in American life and, as a party-switcher and a Texan, the logical successor to party-switcher Ronald Reagan and Texan George Bush. It is a long way from the economics department at A&M to the White House, but Gramm has already traveled a good part of the distance. Incidentally his wife, Wendy Lee Gramm, also a free market economist, became chairman of the Commodities Futures Trading Commission in 1988.

Presidential politics. Texas is now the nation's third biggest prize in presidential elections, with 29 electoral votes. It is also a major source of funds and at least has been a major source of candidates, from Lyndon and John Connally to Lloyd Bentsen and George Bush, though all have been embarrassed on their home turf from time to time (Bush lost two Senate races, in 1964 and 1970, and narrowly lost the 1980 presidential primary to Ronald Reagan). It was part, the biggest single part, of the Super Tuesday southern regional primary March 8, 1988, but the southern regional candidate it promoted turned out not to be the Democrat contemplated by Super Tuesday enthusiasts, but Republican George Bush. Michael Dukakis won the Democratic primary with heavy support from Hispanics: he had 43% in San Antonio-Austin and 46% in the Border. But it's worth noting that his television advertising netted him 29% in the rest of the state—more than Jesse Jackson (25%, mainly from urban blacks), Albert Gore (22%) and Richard Gephardt (15%, despite running his trade ads in some media markets).

But Texas isn't up for grabs in presidential general elections, unless a southerner or a candidate with appeal to southern whites is on the top of the Democratic ticket. The 1988 election proved that about as conclusively as anything can be proved in politics. When Lloyd Bentsen was chosen by Michael Dukakis to be his running mate, the Democrats had hopes of carrying Texas and, buoyed by polls showing their ticket competitive (though never ahead), they poured money and time into the state. It was futile. Bentsen raised Dukakis's percentage from the 38% or so he would have won without him, but only to 43%, and the evidence suggests that for a Dukakis-like candidate that represents something close to a ceiling. It's hard to conceive of a liberal Democrat carrying rural Texas, the Dallas-Fort Worth Metroplex, or greater Houston, and those three areas account for 78% of Texas's votes; even the San Antonio-Austin corridor, with its increasing high-tech population, is trending Republican. That leaves a liberal Democrat with the Border counties, which cast 8% of the state's votes.

Congressional districting. In the 1980s Texas has had the largest—and the most bipartisan—House delegation in its history. Its population gains have raised it to 27 members. But gone are the days when a solidly Democratic delegation met regularly under the superintendency of Speaker John Nance Garner or Speaker Sam Rayburn and worked together on national issues and local projects. There is still cohesion among Texas Democrats—they rallied early and in some cases vociferously around Jim Wright when the Ethics Committee decided there was reason to believe he violated House rules—but there is also a wide range of views on the Democratic side, from Ralph Hall who seems temperamentally very close to a Republican to Mickey Leland who has one of the most liberal voting records in the House. Texas continues to have its powerful Democrats: Chairmen Jack Brooks of Judiciary and Kika de la Garza of Agriculture, Charles Wilson on Appropriations and Martin Frost on Rules and others as well. But some Texas Democrats have to fight hard for their seats, and some win fortuitously. The Democrats won a 19–8 edge on the delegation in the 1988 elections. But that is only because a locally popular Democrat won an open Republican seat in the High Plains and another Democrat beat a pathetically weak Republican incumbent.

For the 1990s the outlook is not entirely clear. If Texas gains 4 seats, there might be pressure to use state Senate seats, fixed in number at 31, for House elections; but that surely would be resisted by incumbents in both bodies, who would want to fashion districts for themselves. The slowdown in the Texas economy in the later 1980s suggests that the state may gain only 2 or 3 new seats, and demography suggests that all or most of them will be Republican. But if Democrats win the governorship in 1990, they will have the votes to redistrict, while if the Republicans win it they will still be in a strong position to protect their incumbents and pick up at least one new seat.

The People: Est. Pop. 1988: 16,780,000; Pop. 1980: 14,229,191, up 17.9% 1980–88 and 27.1% 1970–80; 6.92% of U.S. total, 3d largest. 17% with 1–3 yrs. col., 16% with 4+ yrs. col.; 14.7% below poverty level. Single ancestry: 12% English, 5% German, 4% Irish, 1% French, Italian. Households (1980): 75% family, 43% with children, 63% married couples; 35.7% housing units rented; median monthly rent: $213; median house value: $39,100. Voting age pop. (1980): 9,923,085; 18% Spanish origin, 11% Black, 1% Asian origin. Registered voters (1988): 8,201,856; no party registration.

1988 Share of Federal Tax Burden: $54,847,000,000; 6.20% of U.S. total, 3d largest.

1988 Share of Federal Expenditures

	Total		Non-Defense		Defense	
Total Expend	$49,485m	(5.60%)	$33,753m	(5.15%)	$17,320m	(7.58%)
St/Lcl Grants	5,168m	(4.51%)	5,163m	(4.51%)	5m	(4.08%)
Salary/Wages	8,600m	(6.40%)	3,729m	(5.57%)	4,871m	(5.57%)
Pymnts to Indiv	23,118m	(5.65%)	21,257m	(5.44%)	1,860m	(9.98%)
Procurement	10,564m	(5.60%)	1,588m	(3.42%)	10,564m	(5.60%)
Research/Other	2,035m	(5.45%)	2,015m	(5.44%)	20m	(5.44%)

Political Lineup: Governor, William (Bill) Clements (R); Lt. Gov., William P. Hobby (D); Secy. of State, Jack Rains (R); Atty. Gen., Jim Mattox (D); Treasurer, Ann Richards (D); Comptroller of Public Accounts, Robert Bullock (D). State Senate, 31 (23 D and 8 R); State House of Representatives, 150 (91 D and 59 R). Senators, Lloyd Bentsen (D) and Phil Gramm (R). Representatives, 27 (19 D and 8 R).

1988 Presidential Vote

Bush (R)	3,036,829	(56%)
Dukakis (D)	2,352,748	(43%)

1984 Presidential Vote

Reagan (R)	3,433,428	(64%)
Mondale (D)	1,949,276	(36%)

1988 Democratic Presidential Primary

Dukakis	579,533	(33%)
Jackson	433,259	(25%)
Gore	356,772	(20%)
Gephardt	240,033	(14%)
Hart	82,202	(5%)
Simon	34,690	(2%)
Babbitt	11,568	(1%)

1988 Republican Presidential Primary

Bush	648,178	(64%)
Robertson	155,449	(15%)
Dole	140,795	(14%)
Kemp	50,546	(5%)

1160   TEXAS

GOVERNOR

Gov. William (Bill) Clements (R)

Elected 1986, term expries Jan. 1991; b. Apr. 13, 1917, Dallas; home, Dallas; Southern Methodist U., B.A. 1939; Episcopalian; married (Rita).

Career: Founder and Chmn., Southeastern Drilling Co.; Dpty. Secy., U.S. Dept. of Defense, 1973–77; Gov. of TX, 1979–83.

Office: State Capitol, P.O. Box 12428, Austin 78711, 512-463-2000.

Election Results

1986 gen.	William (Bill) Clements (R)....	1,813,779	(53%)
	Mark W. White (D)...........	1,584,515	(46%)
1986 prim.	William (Bill) Clements (R)....	318,938	(58%)
	Tom Loeffler (R)	118,224	(22%)
	Kent Hance (R).............	108,583	(20%)
1982 gen.	Mark W. White, Jr. (D).......	1,697,527	(53%)
	William (Bill) Clements (R) ...	1,465,952	(46%)

SENATORS

Sen. Lloyd Bentsen (D)

Elected 1970, seat up 1994; b. Feb. 11, 1921, Mission; home, Starr Cnty.; U. of TX, LL.B. 1942; Presbyterian; married (Beryl Ann).

Career: Army Air Corps, WWII; Practicing atty., 1945–46; Judge, Hidalgo Cnty., 1946–48; U.S. House of Reps., 1948–54; Pres., Lincoln Consolidated, Inc., 1955–71; Dem. Nominee for Vice Pres., 1988.

Offices: 703 HSOB 20510, 202-224-5922. Also 961 Fed. Ofc. Bldg., Austin 78701, 512-482-5834; 515 Rusk, Ste. 4026, Houston 77002, 713-229-2595; and Earle Cabell Bldg., Rm. 7C14, Dallas 75242, 214-767-0577.

Committees: *Commerce, Science and Transportation* (7th of 11 D). Subcommittees: Aviation; Communications; Merchant Marine; Science, Technology, and Space. *Finance* (Chairman of 11 D) Subcommittees: Medicare and Long-Term Care; Taxation and Debt Management; International Trade. *Joint Economic Committee* (2d of 10 D). Subcommittees: Economic Goals and Intergovernmental Policy; Economic Growth, Trade and Taxes (Chairman); Education and Health. *Joint Committee on Taxation* (Vice Chairman).

Group Ratings

	ADA	ACLU	COPE	CFA	LCV	ACU	NTLC	NSI	COC	CEI
1988	40	53	53	83	40	42	27	70	25	19
1987	60	—	51	75	—	31	—	—	44	33

National Journal Ratings

	1988 LIB — 1988 CONS		1987 LIB — 1987 CONS	
Economic	55% —	44%	57% —	42%
Social	46% —	53%	45% —	52%
Foreign	44% —	54%	51% —	45%

Key Votes

1) Cut Aged Housing $	AGN	5) Bork Nomination	AGN	9) SDI Funding	FOR
2) Override Hwy Veto	FOR	6) Ban Plastic Guns	FOR	10) Ban Chem Weaps	FOR
3) Kill Plnt Clsng Notice	AGN	7) Deny Abortions	FOR	11) Aid To Contras	FOR
4) Min Wage Increase	—	8) Japanese Reparations	FOR	12) Reagan Defense $	AGN

Election Results

1988 general	Lloyd Bentsen (D).................	3,149,806	(59%)	($8,829,361)
	Beau Boulter (R)...................	2,129,228	(40%)	($1,353,345)
1988 primary	Lloyd Bentsen (D).................	1,365,736	(85%)	
	Joe Sullivan (D)	244,805	(15%)	
1982 general	Lloyd Bentsen (D).................	1,818,223	(59%)	($5,097,445)
	James M. Collins (R)	1,256,759	(40%)	($4,285,377)

Sen. Phil Gramm (R)

Elected 1984, seat up 1990; b. July 8, 1942, Ft. Benning, GA; home, College Station; U. of GA, B.A. 1964, Ph.D. 1967; Episcopalian; married (Wendy).

Career: Prof., TX A&M U., 1967–78; U.S. House of Reps., 1978–84.

Offices: 370 RSOB 20510, 202-224-2934. Also 900 Jackson, Ste. 570, Dallas 75202, 214-767-3000; 222 E. Van Buren., Ste. 404, Harlingen 78550, 512-423-6118; 515 Rusk, Houston 77002, 713-229-2766; 113 Fed. Bldg., 1205 Texas Ave., Lubbock 79401, 806-743-7533; 123 Pioneer Plaza, 6th Fl., Rm. 665, El Paso 79901, 915-534-6896; and InterFirst Plaza, 102 N. College St., Rm. 201, Tyler 75701, 214-593-0902.

Committees: *Appropriations* (13th of 13 R). Subcommittees: Commerce, Justice, State and Judiciary; District of Columbia (Ranking Member); Labor, Health and Human Services, Education; VA, HUD, and Independent Agencies. *Banking, Housing, and Urban Affairs* (4th of 9 R). Subcommittees: Consumer and Regulatory Affairs; Housing and Urban Affairs; International Finance and Monetary Policy (Ranking Member); Securities. *Budget* (9th of 10 R).

Group Ratings

	ADA	ACLU	COPE	CFA	LCV	ACU	NTLC	NSI	COC	CEI
1988	0	4	2	8	20	95	98	100	92	87
1987	5	—	2	8	—	100	—	—	89	91

National Journal Ratings

	1988 LIB — 1988 CONS		1987 LIB — 1987 CONS	
Economic	0% —	95%	0% —	94%
Social	0% —	89%	6% —	89%
Foreign	11% —	88%	0% —	76%

Key Votes

1) Cut Aged Housing $	AGN	5) Bork Nomination	FOR	9) SDI Funding	FOR
2) Override Hwy Veto	AGN	6) Ban Plastic Guns	FOR	10) Ban Chem Weaps	FOR
3) Kill Plnt Clsng Notice	FOR	7) Deny Abortions	FOR	11) Aid To Contras	FOR
4) Min Wage Increase	—	8) Japanese Reparations	AGN	12) Reagan Defense $	FOR

Election Results

1984 general	Phil Gramm (R)	3,111,348	(59%)	($9,452,360)
	Lloyd Doggett (D)	2,202,557	(41%)	($5,887,858)
1984 primary	Phil Gramm (R)	246,716	(73%)	
	Ron Paul (R)	55,431	(16%)	
	Rob Mosbacher (R)	26,279	(8%)	
1978 general	John G. Tower (R)	1,151,376	(50%)	($4,359,365)
	Robert Krueger (D)	1,139,149	(49%)	($2,428,666)

FIRST DISTRICT

Fifty years ago a traveler in the northeast corner of Texas would see "a rolling, forested region where shortleaf pine clothes the uplands, with white, red and burr oak, sweet gum, and wild magnolia trees along the streams. Sawmills dot timber areas. Dogwood blooms profusely in the spring, and the wild rose, shame vine, Virginia creeper and swamp pink are among the plants that ornament the roadside. Ponds have white and yellow lilies. In dense woods along creeks, small animals are hunted and trapped for their fur; mink and muskrat pelts are most valued." To the careless eye today, this scene described by the WPA writer has not changed much. People in east Texas—said in tones that make you think it is a separate state—are tradition-minded, and the great metropolitan areas have not grown out to these counties. But living standards have risen even as traditional values have mostly remained intact. If you still find sawmills and ponds, you also find Wal-Marts and Holiday Inns and new churches—signs of prosperity and widespread affluence which would have astonished the east Texans of two generations ago.

About half of east Texas—the northeastern corner of the state, but with jagged boundaries to exclude the oil towns of Tyler and Longview—forms the 1st Congressional District. The largest city here is Texarkana, with its city hall so squarely on the Texas-Arkansas line that different wings serve Texarkana, Texas, and Texarkana, Arkansas. This is part of the historic Democratic heartland: Bonham, the home of former Speaker Sam Rayburn, is just one county west of the district; the district that elected former Speaker Carl Albert is just across the Red River in Oklahoma. The 1st District was represented for nearly 50 years by Wright Patman, an old-fashioned populist, who began his career by moving the impeachment of Treasury Secretary Andrew Mellon (forcing him to resign to become Ambassador to Britain) and who ultimately became chairman of the Banking Committee; a gentle and good-humored man, he was voted out of his chairmanship at 81 in 1974, died in 1976, and was replaced by a much more conservative Democrat, Sam Hall.

In the summer of 1985, the 1st District was the scene of one the pivotal political battles of the 1980s. To shake the Democrats' hold on rural southern districts and encourage challengers to run in 1986 and 1988, Phil Gramm contrived a special election in the Texas 1st by getting Hall appointed to a federal judgeship and recruiting former Texas A&M and pro quarterback Edd Hargett, an authentic resident of the 1st, to run as the Republican candidate. Money and topflight consultants poured in, while the Democrats were handicapped because they had more than one serious candidate. Gramm claimed, plausibly, that if a Republican could win in the 1st in a nonpresidential year, Republicans could win in any southern district.

But this particular Republican didn't win. Even before the primary, Democratic Congressional Campaign Committee chairman Tony Coelho was raising money, much of it from Texas savings and loan operators, to oppose Hargett. He fell short of the 50% needed to win without a runoff, and Democrat Jim Chapman, a former district attorney, proved to be an adept candidate. Hargett stumbled on the trade issue—being raised simultaneously, and surely not coincidentally, in Washington by Senator Lloyd Bentsen—saying "I don't know what trade policies have to do with bringing jobs to east Texas," despite the recent closing of the Lone Star Steel plant in Morris County. That and a relentless emphasis on social security helped Chapman to a 51%–49% win. Gramm's gambit lost, and Republicans actually lost southern House seats in 1988 while George Bush was sweeping the region. Yet the Democrats paid a price. It was only after the S&L operators made their crucial contributions here that Jim Wright began intervening with federal regulatory agencies and bottling up reform bills on their behalf, at an ultimate cost to the taxpayer that may total tens of billions of dollars.

In the House, Chapman proved, over time, to be the most slavish of followers of Jim Wright and was been duly rewarded: with a seat on Steering and Policy in 1987 and a seat on Appropriations in 1989. His greatest moment in the spotlight came in October 1987, when Wright was about to be beaten on a $12 billion tax vote, former Wright aide John Mack physically carried Chapman to the floor, where Chapman changed his vote and gave Wright a 206–205 victory. This was in line with Chapman's general practice of compiling a moderate voting record but giving the leadership votes when they are really needed—it was the second time that day and the sixth time that session Chapman had switched his vote—and it enraged Republicans, who went out looking for a candidate. But Hargett did not want to run, and neither did former state Senator Ed Howard; broadcaster Horace McQueen raised very little money, and Chapman, in a district yellow-doggedly Democratic enough to have nearly voted for Michael Dukakis, won 62%–38%. For Chapman this looks like a safe seat.

The People: Est. Pop. 1986: 571,900, up 8.5% 1980–86; Pop. 1980: 527,016, up 20.4% 1970–80. Households (1980): 76% family, 39% with children, 65% married couples; 24.9% housing units rented; median monthly rent: $123; median house value: $26,300. Voting age pop. (1980): 376,964; 17% Black, 1% Spanish origin.

1988 Presidential Vote:

Bush (R)	107,949	(52%)
Dukakis (D)	97,014	(47%)

Rep. Jim Chapman, Jr. (D)

Elected 1985; b. Mar. 8, 1945, Washington, D.C.; home, Sulphur Springs; U. of TX, B.A. 1968, Southern Methodist U., J.D. 1970; United Methodist; married (Betty).

Career: Practicing atty.; D.A., 8th Judicial Dist. of TX, 1976–84.

Offices: 429 CHOB, 202-225-3035. Also P.O. Box 538, Sulphur Springs 75482, 214-885-8682; Fed. Bldg., G-15, 100 E. Houston, Marshall 75670, 214-938-8386; 210 U.S.P.O. & Fed. Bldg., Paris 75460, 214-785-0723; and 401 U.S.P.O. & Fed. Bldg., Texarkana 75504, 214-793-6728.

Committees: *Appropriations* (35th of 35 D). Subcommittees: Energy and Water Development; VA, HUD and Independent Agencies.

Group Ratings

	ADA	ACLU	COPE	CFA	LCV	ACU	NTLC	NSI	COC	CEI
1988	50	43	58	73	31	52	29	80	64	28
1987	48	—	54	57	—	9	—	—	47	22

National Journal Ratings

	1988 LIB — 1988 CONS	1987 LIB — 1987 CONS
Economic	49% — 50%	52% — 48%
Social	40% — 58%	39% — 61%
Foreign	47% — 53%	47% — 52%

Key Votes

1) Homeless $	—	5) Ban Drug Test	AGN	9) SDI Research	AGN
2) Gephardt Amdt	FOR	6) Drug Death Pen	FOR	10) Ban Chem Weaps	AGN
3) Deficit Reduc	FOR	7) Handgun Sales	FOR	11) Aid to Contras	FOR
4) Kill Plnt Clsng Notice	AGN	8) Ban D.C. Abort $	FOR	12) Nuclear Testing	FOR

Election Results

1988 general	Jim Chapman (D).....................	122,566	(62%)	($505,611)
	Horace McQueen (R)..................	74,357	(38%)	($94,477)
1988 primary	Jim Chapman (D), unopposed			
1986 general	Jim Chapman (D).....................	84,445	(100%)	($894,772)

SECOND DISTRICT

In east Texas, you can see many landmarks of Lone Star history. There's still an Indian reservation in Polk County, and the Big Thicket National Preserve, to remind you of what this land looked like when the first Texans came through. Over near Beaumont is the site of Spindletop, the world's first gusher that was also the first major oil find in the state in 1901; not far away is the huge oil field that wildcatter H. L. Hunt found in 1931 and made the foundation of his billion dollar fortune. To the uneducated eye, east Texas looks little different from the wildcat days of 50 years ago: the town squares with courthouses and churches, the stands of cheap, quick-growing pine are still there, plus the strip highway culture of the 1950s. Yet in many ways, things have changed. Real incomes have tripled over 50 years, endemic diseases have been wiped out, racial segregation has been abolished, and the isolation of the small town has been ended by television and the interstate highway.

The 2d Congressional District of Texas includes all or part of 16 counties in east Texas, most of them still seemingly rural, all of them more imbued with traditional values than most parts of America these days. It includes the oil port of Orange (but not nearby Beaumont or Port Arthur), the Big Thicket and the Alabama Coushatta Indian reservation, and goes past Lufkin and Nacogodoches to Palestine. Politically, it remains one of the most Democratic parts of rural Texas; it cast more votes for Michael Dukakis than George Bush in 1988.

Charles Wilson, the 2d District's congressman, is one of the most distinctive figures in the House—tall, almost spectrally thin, flamboyant, pleasure-loving—yet he is also serious-minded when he wants to be, and even idealistic. He is always ready with a wisecrack or quip; after President Carter fired HEW Secretary Joseph Califano and others in 1979 he said, "Good grief! He's cut down the tall trees and left the monkeys." He has represented east Texas in Austin and Washington since 1960, and with a voting record that got him classified with the liberals in the Texas Senate and a record in the House that on economics and cultural issues is often liberal today. In early 1989 he was one of the most articulate and determined defenders of Jim Wright.

The common thread in all this is aggressiveness. Wilson is a graduate of the Naval Academy and served four years in the Navy. He got himself elected to the legislature the year he returned to east Texas. He won the House seat of a scandal-plagued conservative in the 1972 Democratic primary; a term later he shoved aside a fellow Texan for a seat on Appropriations. Always a feisty liberal on economic issues, he is a hawk on matters military. He now sits on the Defense Appropriations Subcommittee, the small and mostly hawkish panel that gives the defense budget as close a combing as it usually gets on Capitol Hill; he also sits on the subcommittee that handles foreign aid, which gives him a potentially broad view of the whole range of foreign policy. As might be expected, he aggressively promotes the interests of Texas defense contractors.

Wilson's number one cause in the 1980s has been aiding the Afghan rebels, and probably more than any other member of the House, he is responsible for the American aid to the *mujaheddin* which enabled them to force the Soviets out of their country. He traveled 14 times to Afghanistan, Pakistan or South Asia in the 1980s, and in 1982 began working in secret Appropriations hearings to put lots of money into the Afghan cause. In 1987, he also got a seat on the Intelligence Committee, where he was able to further the Afghan cause. In 1988, Wilson got in a bit of a flap when it was learned that he put into an appropriation bill a cut in the Defense Intelligence Agency's budget apparently because a local DIA official had not allowed a woman accompanying Wilson, a former Miss World, to fly in a plane over Afghanistan; that would have violated the rules, but the local DIA official might have been wise to overlook that for the man who was, more than anyone else, the patron of the Afghan rebel movement the United States was trying to aid.

Wilson's voting record has never been a great problem for him in his district—though he has been criticized for his favorable attitude toward increasing the size of the Big Thicket Preserve. Rumors about drug use caused him problems in 1984, when he was held to 55% of the vote by four primary opponents (though the strongest got only 29%) and 59% in the general election; but he was cleared in all investigations and has not had serious opposition since.

The People: Est. Pop. 1986: 590,500, up 12.1% 1980–86; Pop. 1980: 526,772, up 35.4% 1970–80. Households (1980): 78% family, 43% with children, 67% married couples; 25.3% housing units rented; median monthly rent: $155; median house value: $31,300. Voting age pop. (1980): 372,792; 14% Black, 3% Spanish origin.

1988 Presidential Vote:

Dukakis (D).	99,074	(50%)
Bush (R)	98,720	(50%)

Rep. Charles Wilson (D)

Elected 1972; b. June 1, 1933, Trinity; home, Lufkin; U.S. Naval Acad., B.S. 1956; United Methodist; divorced.

Career: Navy, 1956–60; Mgr., retail lumber store, 1961–72; TX House of Reps., 1960–66; TX Senate, 1966–72.

Offices: 2256 RHOB 20515, 202-225-2401. Also 701 N. 1st St., Rm. 201, Lufkin 75901, 409-637-1770.

Committees: *Appropriations* (13th of 35 D). Subcommittees: Defense; Foreign Operations, Export Financing and Related Programs. *Permanent Select Committee on Intelligence* (7th of 12 D). Subcommittee: Program and Budget Authorization.

Group Ratings

	ADA	ACLU	COPE	CFA	LCV	ACU	NTLC	NSI	COC	CEI
1988	35	72	68	55	25	55	13	100	46	19
1987	52	—	67	57	—	43	—	—	8	13

National Journal Ratings

	1988 LIB — 1988 CONS	1987 LIB — 1987 CONS
Economic	64% — 36%	62% — 35%
Social	66% — 34%	50% — 50%
Foreign	33% — 66%	30% — 69%

Key Votes

1) Homeless $	AGN	5) Ban Drug Test	—	9) SDI Research	FOR
2) Gephardt Amdt	FOR	6) Drug Death Pen	FOR	10) Ban Chem Weaps	AGN
3) Deficit Reduc	FOR	7) Handgun Sales	FOR	11) Aid to Contras	FOR
4) Kill Plnt Clsng Notice	AGN	8) Ban D.C. Abort $	AGN	12) Nuclear Testing	AGN

Election Results

1988 general	Charles Wilson (D)...................	145,614	(88%)	($309,355)
	Gary W. Nelson (Lib.)	20,475	(12%)	
1988 primary	Charles Wilson (D), unopposed			
1986 general	Charles Wilson (D)...................	78,529	(57%)	($339,873)
	Julian Gordon (R)....................	55,986	(40%)	($47,660)

THIRD DISTRICT

All over the world it is one of the fabled parts of America, the locus of a novel about football players and one of the most popular TV shows of the 1980s, the place where J. R. Ewing lives on Southfork and H. L. Hunt lived in a replica of Mount Vernon and where insurance heir John Post bought a new $3 million, 19,000-square foot mansion and then tore it down because he didn't like it: north Dallas. Here in humid, heat-choked summers affluent people live in huge shuttered houses, and the 3d Congressional District, which is basically coincident with north Dallas, is one of the nation's richest, best educated, and most Republican congressional districts in the nation. The 3d begins, as affluent Dallas does, in the old suburbs of University Park and Highland Park, where most of the houses date back to the 1950s and where many of the elite, like Governor Bill Clements, still live, north through dozens of different half-a-million dollar neighborhoods, north through rich suburbs like Farmers Branch, Addison, Carrollton and Richardson—which together call themselves the Metrocrest—into the Collin County suburb of Plano. Four decades ago you would have found here little but mildly rolling hillsides with occasional trees and a little scrub; today you see huge office buildings and glittering shopping malls, high-walled condominiums and sprawling singles apartment complexes, neighborhoods full of schoolchildren farther out, neighborhoods for affluent empty nesters closer in.

Where does all of Dallas's wealth come from? And why is this city so especially strongly Republican? To the first question, the answer is that the wealth comes from a variety of things; that is why, when dropping oil prices choked off growth in Houston, Dallas still grew. Dallas was where the first railroad in Texas stopped at the three forks of the Trinity River. "Its wealth," wrote John Gunther in the 1940s, "originally came from cotton, and until recently it was the largest internal cotton market in the country; but primarily it is a banking and jobbing and distributing center, the headquarters of railroads and utilities; it is the second city in the United States in Railway Express business, the fourth in insurance, the fifth in number of telegrams." It has built, steadily and sometimes spectacularly, on that base for five decades, with special emphasis on high-tech and defense industries.

As to its Republicanism, affluent Dallas had soured on national Democrats by the 1940s, and by the 1950s there was a bitter, angry tone to its conservative politics seldom heard elsewhere. It was a tone that reverberated across the nation in the 1960 campaign when Republican Representative Bruce Alger led a group that shoved Lyndon and Lady Bird Johnson in the Adolphus Hotel lobby and was echoed sickeningly three years later when John Kennedy was murdered in Dallas, even though the killer was a left-wing fanatic. Dallas has sobered up since 1963, but the faith of affluent Dallas in free enterprise has grown, if anything, stronger. Unlike many rich people back East, they don't feel that they have done something evil by getting rich; they have the 1950s optimism that technology and free enterprise can produce a better life for all, and they have transformed the small provincial Dallas of the 1950s into a world capital of industry and finance of the 1980s. The role government has played in this—by providing education, infrastructure, defense contracts, a secure world market, and a very large consumer class—is largely invisible from their perspective; what they have seen instead is entrepreneurs going out and fighting against the forces of inertia, mishap, regulation and bureaucracy which keep most enterprises from succeeding.

The 3d District is represented in the House by one of its smarter and harder-working young Republicans, Steve Bartlett. He will take second place to no one as a champion of conservative principles and, as a former head of a company building custom knobs and molded plastic gears, he personifies the entrepreneurial ethic strong in Dallas. But unlike many other young conservatives, he is a busy and successful legislator. Operating from the unlikely precincts of the Banking Committee, he got the House to shift public housing programs from new construction to repair of existing units. He has cooperated with Democrats in making changes in the medicaid law and repealing a law interpreted by the Supreme Court as requiring overtime for state and local employees, and he played key roles on the "equal access" bill allowing religious groups in public schools and in creating bigger secondary mortgage markets. He worked on rewriting disability law so that disabled people could take jobs without losing government medical benefits and is working on a bill so that they would not lose benefits because their parents left money for their care. He worked on a $15 billion recapitalization of FSLIC, opposed by Jim Wright and many high-flying Texas savings and loans. He has something unusual for a free market conservative: an interest in how government actually works.

Bartlett won the seat in the 1982 Republican primary, when he was a 35-year-old Dallas councilman, beating former state legislator Kay Hutchinson by emphasizing gun control and abortion. There is no conceivable threat to his tenure in the House except an ambition to run for statewide office, but so far he seems to enjoy legislating too much to give that any thought.

The People: Est. Pop. 1986: 648,400, up 23.0% 1980–86; Pop. 1980: 527,023, up 66.5% 1970–80. Households (1980): 66% family, 36% with children, 57% married couples; 40.4% housing units rented; median monthly rent: $296; median house value: $82,100. Voting age pop. (1980): 389,627; 3% Black, 3% Spanish origin, 1% Asian origin.

1988 Presidential Vote:

Bush (R)	....	215,204	(74%)
Dukakis (D)	....	72,929	(25%)

Rep. Steve Bartlett (R)

Elected 1982; b. Sept. 19, 1947, Los Angeles, CA; home, Dallas; U. of TX, B.A. 1971; Presbyterian; married (Gail).

Career: Real estate broker, 1971–76; Pres. and Founder, Meridian Products Corp., 1976–82; Dallas City Cncl., 1977–81.

Offices: 1113 LHOB 20515, 202-225-4201. Also 6600 LBJ Freeway, Ste. 4190, Dallas 75240, 214-767-4848.

Committees: *Banking, Finance and Urban Affairs* (11th of 20 R). Subcommittees: Financial Institutions Supervision, Regulation and Insurance; General Oversight and Investigations; Housing and Community Development. *Education and Labor* (6th of 13 R). Subcommittees: Elementary, Secondary and Vocational Education; Labor Standards; Select Education (Ranking Member).

Group Ratings

	ADA	ACLU	COPE	CFA	LCV	ACU	NTLC	NSI	COC	CEI
1988	10	9	3	27	13	96	88	100	100	83
1987	4	—	4	21	—	100	—	—	100	91

National Journal Ratings

	1988 LIB — 1988 CONS		1987 LIB — 1987 CONS	
Economic	7%	— 91%	19%	— 81%
Social	18%	— 81%	0%	— 90%
Foreign	0%	— 84%	0%	— 80%

Key Votes

1) Homeless $	FOR	5) Ban Drug Test	—	9) SDI Research	FOR
2) Gephardt Amdt	AGN	6) Drug Death Pen	FOR	10) Ban Chem Weaps	AGN
3) Deficit Reduc	AGN	7) Handgun Sales	FOR	11) Aid to Contras	FOR
4) Kill Plnt Clsng Notice	FOR	8) Ban D.C. Abort $	FOR	12) Nuclear Testing	AGN

Election Results

1988 general	Steve Bartlett (R)	227,882	(82%)	($1,000,894)
	Blake Cowden (D).	50,627	(18%)	($17,757)
1988 primary	Steve Bartlett (R), unopposed			
1986 general	Steve Bartlett (R)	143,381	(94%)	($592,304)
	Brent Barnes (I)	6,268	(4%)	
	Don Gough (Libert.).	2,736	(2%)	

FOURTH DISTRICT

Rural east Texas 50 years ago, wrote the *WPA Guide,* "fosters folk music: singing conventions and festivals are held regularly, and public schools emphasize musical training. The social customs of rural folk are those of their pioneer ancestors, who developed a cooperative system in order that all might survive: new houses and barns are erected at 'raisings,' there are shucking and quilting bees, and graveyard workings. Square dances are popular; in the Gingham and Overall Dances, everyone wears work clothes. Hay rides and moonlight picnics are held. Signs govern many of the actions of farmers: cotton is planted when the whippoorwill cries; the worm (or bottom rail) of a log fence is laid when the moon is waning, so that it will not sink or rot; and it is believed by many that there will be a frost in four weeks from the time of the first cricket-chirp overheard by a farmer in the fall." This was the rural Texas that was represented for nearly 50 years in the House by Speaker Sam Rayburn, a place where despite the automobile and even after the rural electrification of the 1930s and 1940s, daily life in most respects resembled more closely the way people's ancestors had lived when they settled the territory a century before, than the way their descendants would live half a century later.

For in today's 4th Congressional District of Texas, the descendant of the district Rayburn represented, fewer than 10% of the people are farmers and not many more would describe themselves as poor. In their newly built evangelical churches they may pay respect to traditional values, but as they head for work on the interstate, listen to country music on their Walkmans, or shop at Wal-Marts, the customs of 50 years ago are not even memories.

Neither, increasingly, are the political attitudes. The east Texas counties of the Red River Valley were for years among the most heavily Democratic in the United States, united in their sentimental regard for Confederate veterans and their seething hatred for Wall Street bankers; in 1940, the first election in which he was Speaker, Rayburn's district voted 90% for Franklin Roosevelt. In 1988, the 4th District, its population swelled by overspill from the Dallas-Fort Worth Metroplex and growth over the years in the oil towns of Tyler and Longview, voted 61% for George Bush.

The congressman from the 4th, Ralph Hall, came to the House after a long career in business and local politics; he is a nominal Democrat, but one independent of the leadership enough to have once declined to vote for Tip O'Neill for Speaker. He got good committee assignments in his first term—Energy and Commerce and Science and Technology—and promptly proceeded to vote with the Republicans on the budget and tax cuts in 1985 and was also one of only five Democrats to vote in favor of seating the Republican rather than the Democrat in the hotly contested Indiana 8th District election. His voting record is one of the most conservative of Texas Democrats.

The People: Est. Pop. 1986: 628,700, up 19.3% 1980–86; Pop. 1980: 526,991, up 25.8% 1970–80. Households (1980): 76% family, 40% with children, 66% married couples; 28.0% housing units rented; median monthly rent: $159; median house value: $32,500. Voting age pop. (1980): 377,899; 13% Black, 2% Spanish origin.

1988 Presidential Vote:

Bush (R)	131,134	(61%)
Dukakis (D)	83,578	(39%)

Rep. Ralph M. Hall (D)

Elected 1980; b. May 3, 1923, Fate; home, Rockwall; U. of TX, TX Christian U., Southern Methodist U., LL.B. 1951; United Methodist; married (Mary Ellen).

Career: Navy, WWII; Rockwall Cnty. Judge, 1950–62; TX Senate, 1962–72; Pres. and CEO, Texas Aluminum Corp.; Gen. Cnsl., Texas Extrusion Co., Inc.; Practicing atty.

Offices: 236 CHOB 20515, 202-225-6673. Also 104 N. San Jacinto St., Rockwall 75087, 214-771-9118; 119 N. Fed. Bldg., Sherman 75090, 214-892-1112; and 211 Fed. Bldg., Tyler 75702, 214-597-3729.

Committees: *Energy and Commerce* (15th of 26 D). Subcommittees: Energy and Power; Health and the Environment; Telecommunications and Finance. *Science, Space and Technology* (10th of 29 D). Subcommittees: International Scientific Cooperation (Chairman); Space Science and Applications.

Group Ratings

	ADA	ACLU	COPE	CFA	LCV	ACU	NTLC	NSI	COC	CEI
1988	15	17	39	45	31	92	55	100	86	50
1987	28	—	38	36	—	70	—	—	73	51

National Journal Ratings

	1988 LIB — 1988 CONS	1987 LIB — 1987 CONS
Economic	27% — 72%	42% — 56%
Social	5% — 91%	10% — 85%
Foreign	16% — 78%	0% — 80%

Key Votes

1) Homeless $	FOR	5) Ban Drug Test	FOR	9) SDI Research	FOR
2) Gephardt Amdt	FOR	6) Drug Death Pen	FOR	10) Ban Chem Weaps	AGN
3) Deficit Reduc	AGN	7) Handgun Sales	FOR	11) Aid to Contras	FOR
4) Kill Plnt Clsng Notice	FOR	8) Ban D.C. Abort $	FOR	12) Nuclear Testing	AGN

Election Results

1988 general	Ralph H. Hall (D)	139,379	(66%)	($316,846)
	Randy Sutton (R)	67,337	(32%)	($65,068)
1988 primary	Ralph M. Hall (D), unopposed			
1986 general	Ralph M. Hall (D)	97,540	(72%)	($269,235)
	Thomas Blow (R)	38,578	(28%)	($20,000)

FIFTH DISTRICT

Dallas, wrote the *WPA Guide* 50 years ago, "has no tradition of invasions or battles, or of wild days when cattlemen, gamblers, and outlaws participated in lurid scenes of violence. It came into existence as a serious community with citizens of a peaceable and cultured type." Or so Dallas would have you believe: the city that is the home of the oldest Neiman-Marcus and the nation's newest major art museum has long been proud of its gentility and culture, and does not mind it at all if you mistake it for some sophisticated metropolis back east. The corollary of this is that Dallas, like eastern cities, has its funky and slummy sides as well. As the affluent north side of Dallas grows farther north through Plano, past the Dallas city and county lines, the nearly one million people within the Dallas city limits include numbers of poor people and blacks, singles and gays and Hispanics that you would expect in an eastern city.

This has political consequences: Dallas, long known as a Republican city, and still a very Republican metropolitan area, nonetheless has a lot of Democratic territory—enough to make up two Democratic congressional districts, the 5th and 24th. The 5th takes in Dallas's booming downtown, the singles and apartment neighborhood of Oak Lawn just to the north, and the Trinity River bottomlands to the northwest, which developer Trammell Crow has converted from marshland to prime commercial property, with not only warehouses and factories, but Dallas's huge furniture and apparel marts and the cathedral-like Anatole Hotel. It takes in the south Dallas black ghetto around the State Fair grounds. And it includes most of east Dallas, with its renovated prairie houses near downtown and the middle-class neighborhoods farther out and in the modest suburbs of Garland and Mesquite. Here people live in small frame houses, commute to unexciting office and factory jobs, try to make ends meet and keep their neighborhoods up. About one-fifth of the people here are black and one-eighth Mexican-American; but, as Representative John Bryant puts it, "Generally speaking, what you have in the 5th District are regular, red-blooded working Americans."

"Working" is the clue that this is an old-fashioned Democratic District in newly glitzy

Republican Dallas. The 5th District went for Michael Dukakis over George Bush, though only barely, and it almost always votes Democratic in Texas elections; its boundaries were drawn by a Democratic legislature determined to put as many Republican precincts as possible into the north Dallas 3d District and to leave just enough Democrats to keep the 5th and the 24th safely Democratic. There is enough resentment of north Dallas here for Bryant to denounce "Republican moneybags in north Dallas who want to have two congressmen and to control this district also." But it should be added that most east Dallas residents are currently upwardly mobile and hope to keep moving.

Bryant is one of the most politically talented of the young Democratic congressmen. He won this district in 1982; after the district lines were set, Republican Steve Bartlett left the race here and ran in the 3d—a gain for the republic since both these young men, born the same year but of very different views, have proved to be skilled legislators. Bryant, a minister's son and a rebellious liberal in high school, was elected to the Texas legislature in 1974, a year after finishing SMU Law School; he performed skillfully in Austin and won the endorsement of his predecessor, Jim Mattox (now Texas's attorney general) and 65% of the vote against a well-known opponent in the Democratic primary; he won the general election by a 2 to 1 margin. In his first term, he won the plum of a seat on the most coveted legislative committee, Energy and Commerce. There he has worked ably to represent oil interests, but he has been busy on other matters as well: a measure allowing utilities to produce energy through cogeneration, a children's television bill, a bill to revive the fairness doctrine in broadcasting. Bryant is a believer in regulation, and when he sees a problem his first impulse seems to be to write a law about it. He is proud of sponsoring a Texas wilderness bill that passed in his first term. He is proud also of his bill that would require foreign owners of American companies to make disclosure of assets—a bill attacked as a know-nothing attempt to discourage foreign investment but which has passed the House twice. He has a fairly solid liberal voting record, and is something of a workhorse, serving on Judiciary and Veterans' Affairs in the 100th Congress and Judiciary and Budget in the 101st, as well as Energy and Commerce, where he is one of John Dingell's aggressive interrogators on the Oversight and Investigations Subcommittee.

But Bryant may not remain in the House where he has done so well. He had raised prodigious sums of money with the help of his Energy and Commerce seat, and he has won handily against the challengers Republicans have touted. But redistricting could easily wipe the 5th District out by splitting it between a black-majority and a Republican district, neither of which Bryant could win. So in early 1989 he was considering running for lieutenant governor or attorney general in 1990; he would have liked to run for Lloyd Bentsen's Senate seat if Bentsen had been elected Vice President in 1988.

The People: Est. Pop. 1986: 608,600, up 15.6% 1980–86; Pop. 1980: 526,633, up 0.8% 1970–80. Households (1980): 68% family, 39% with children, 53% married couples; 46.8% housing units rented; median monthly rent: $222; median house value: $35,500. Voting age pop. (1980): 374,926; 18% Black, 10% Spanish origin, 1% Asian origin.

1988 Presidential Vote:

Dukakis (D)		80,731	(50%)
Bush (R)		80,275	(49%)

Rep. John Bryant (D)

Elected 1982; b. Feb. 22, 1947, Lake Jackson; home, Dallas; Southern Methodist U., B.A. 1969, J.D. 1972; United Methodist; married (Janet).

Career: Practicing atty., 1972–82; Chief counsel, TX Sen. Scmtee. on Consumer Affairs, 1973; TX House of Reps., 1974–83.

Offices: 208 CHOB 20515, 202-225-2231. Also 8035 East R. L. Thornton Freeway, Ste. 518, Dallas 75228, 214-767-6554.

Committees: *Budget* (21st of 21 D). Task Forces: Defense, Foreign Policy and Space; Urgent Fiscal Issues. *Energy and Commerce* (20th of of 26 D). Subcommittees: Energy and Power; Oversight and Investigations; Telecommunications and Finance. *Judiciary* (19th of 21 D). Subcommittees: Courts, Intellectual Property and the Administration of Justice; Criminal Justice; Immigration, Refugees, and International Law.

Group Ratings

	ADA	ACLU	COPE	CFA	LCV	ACU	NTLC	NSI	COC	CEI
1988	85	71	94	82	56	9	8	30	27	12
1987	80	—	93	71	—	4	—	—	14	4

National Journal Ratings

	1988 LIB — 1988 CONS		1987 LIB — 1987 CONS	
Economic	85%	— 15%	73%	— 0%
Social	60%	— 39%	73%	— 22%
Foreign	84%	— 0%	62%	— 37%

Key Votes

1) Homeless $	AGN	5) Ban Drug Test	AGN	9) SDI Research	AGN
2) Gephardt Amdt	FOR	6) Drug Death Pen	FOR	10) Ban Chem Weaps	AGN
3) Deficit Reduc	FOR	7) Handgun Sales	AGN	11) Aid to Contras	AGN
4) Kill Plnt Clsng Notice	AGN	8) Ban D.C. Abort $	AGN	12) Nuclear Testing	FOR

Election Results

1988 general	John Bryant (D)	95,376	(61%)	($646,218)
	Lon Williams (R)	59,877	(38%)	($179,201)
1988 primary	John Bryant (D), unopposed			
1986 general	John Bryant (D)	57,410	(59%)	($994,285)
	Tom Carter (R)......................	39,945	(41%)	($349,937)

SIXTH DISTRICT

Fifty years ago Waxahachie, Texas was, according to the *WPA Guide*, "densely wooded, with sycamores predominating. It is one of the largest primary cotton markets in Texas, in the heart of an agricultural region noted for its heavy production of the crop. A textile mill utilizes the lower grades of locally produced cotton in the manufacture of duck and other heavy materials. The town's industries also include two large cottonseed oil mills and a cotton compress." Waxahachie in the 1940s, was at the low end of the national economy, with most of the people in the countryside working in back-breaking drudgery under the broiling Texas sun and people in town concentrated in low-tech, low-skill operations. Waxahachie in the 1990s, will be at the other end of the national economy, for it is slated to be literally at the center of the superconducting super collider being built by the Energy Department—"the greatest basic science facility," in one booster's words, "of the latter 20th century." The accelerator, designed to probe the material origins of the universe, is being built like a race track more than 10 miles across, centered on Waxahachie; it will cost $4 to $6 billion to build and $270 million a year to run. More than 30 states competed for the SSC; Texas won, in an announcement made shortly after the 1988 election; and if politics played a role in giving Texas a major high-tech facility, this was not the first time: remember the Johnson Space Center south of Houston.

Perhaps the most enthusiastic political booster of the Texas site was Congressman Joe Barton, whose 6th District includes Waxahachie and has a history that reflects the changes in this town and in Texas that have transformed a low-income, low-skill state into one of the nation's technological leaders over the last 50 years. Two decades ago the 6th District was mostly a rural and small town seat, running almost from Houston to Dallas and Fort Worth; its largest town was College Station, the home of Texas A&M University. Politically, it was ancestrally Democratic, and for 32 years elected Olin (Tiger) Teague, who ended up as chairman of the Veterans Committee. But as Texas's metropolitan areas grew, the 6th District's boundaries were expanded to include what was overspill from Fort Worth, Houston and Dallas. These were not elite areas, but they were affluent; they contained not ancient farmers, but young families interested in honoring traditional values; they wanted not to preserve a pristine environment, but to build a high-tech economy in what had been pretty grubby areas.

Politically, this once Democratic district became Republican. So did its congressman. Phil Gramm, elected as a conservative Democrat in 1978, switched parties, resigned and won reelection as a Republican in early 1983, then he went on to win a Senate seat in 1984. He was succeeded by Republican Joe Barton who, like Gramm, won one of his early contests by a narrow margin—in Barton's case, the 1984 Republican runoff, which he won by 10 votes. In the general that year, he beat a Democratic legislator from College Station with 57%; two years later, against a protégé of Senator Lloyd Bentsen, he won with 56%. These were both million dollar contests. In 1988, he won with 68%. The race was still pretty marginal in the still rural counties in the center of the district. But the Dallas-Fort Worth Metroplex (including now Waxahachie) casts 41% of the vote and greater Houston 20%; with 18% more in Texas A&M's home county, there isn't much rural vote left.

Barton spent his first term as a sort of bomb thrower, organizing a picketing of a Jim Wright press conference in Fort Worth. In his second term he got a seat on Energy and Commerce and spent much of his time promoting the super collider, and pursuing other causes such as removing restrictions of offshore natural gas contracts and requiring manufacturers to give refunds to anyone whose children are injured while using three-wheeled all-terrain vehicles.

The People: Est. Pop. 1986: 659,200, up 25.1% 1980–86; Pop. 1980: 526,765, up 48.1% 1970–80. Households (1980): 75% family, 40% with children, 65% married couples; 28.4% housing units rented; median monthly rent: $192; median house value: $42,500. Voting age pop. (1980): 379,330; 10% Black, 5% Spanish origin.

1988 Presidential Vote: Bush (R) 158,954   (62%)

Dukakis (D). 95,403   (37%)

Rep. Joe L. Barton (R)

Elected 1984; b. Sept. 15, 1949, Waco; home, Ennis; Texas A&M U., B.S. 1972, Purdue U., M.S. 1973; United Methodist; married (Janet).

Career: Asst. to Vice Pres., Ennis Business Forms, 1973–81; White House Fellow, U.S. Dept. of Energy, 1981–82; Consultant, Atlantic Richfield Co., 1982–84.

Offices: 1225 LHOB 20515, 202-225-2002. Also InterFirst Tower, Ste. 507, Conroe 77301, 409-760-2291; 809 University Ave., Rm. 222, Creekwide Plaza, Bryan 77840, 409-846-9791; InterFirst Bank Bldg., Ste. 101, Ennis 75119, 214-875-8488; and 3509 Hulen, Ste. 110, Ft. Worth 76107, 817-737-7737.

Committees: *Energy and Commerce* (15th of 17 R). Subcommittees: Commerce, Consumer Protection and Competitiveness; Energy and Power.

Group Ratings

	ADA	ACLU	COPE	CFA	LCV	ACU	NTLC	NSI	COC	CEI
1988	5	4	3	9	6	96	87	100	100	83
1987	4	—	4	14	—	100	—	—	93	82

National Journal Ratings

	1988 LIB — 1988 CONS		1987 LIB — 1987 CONS	
Economic	13% —	85%	0% —	89%
Social	19% —	81%	18% —	81%
Foreign	30% —	70%	0% —	80%

Key Votes

1) Homeless $	FOR	5) Ban Drug Test	FOR	9) SDI Research	FOR
2) Gephardt Amdt	AGN	6) Drug Death Pen	FOR	10) Ban Chem Weaps	AGN
3) Deficit Reduc	AGN	7) Handgun Sales	FOR	11) Aid to Contras	FOR
4) Kill Plnt Clsng Notice	FOR	8) Ban D.C. Abort $	FOR	12) Nuclear Testing	AGN

Election Results

1988 general	Joe L. Barton (R)	164,692	(68%)	($654,260)
	Pat Kendrick (D)	78,786	(32%)	($17,414)
1988 primary	Joe L. Barton (R), unopposed			
1986 general	Joe L. Barton (R)	86,190	(56%)	($1,034,515)
	Preston Geren (D).	68,270	(44%)	($895,746)

SEVENTH DISTRICT

To the short list of congressional districts once represented in the House by a President of the United States you can add the 7th District of Texas. This is especially notable since the district in anything like its present form did not exist until the 1966 redistricting: this was a brand new part of America when it elected George Bush as its first congressman. Fifty years ago the *WPA Guide* described the rich subdivision of River Oaks as the "outlying" part of Houston; River Oaks is now about as close to downtown as you get in the 7th District whose 650,000 people live west and northwest in affluent and air-conditioned comfort on land that a half century ago housed perhaps 20,000, mostly in leaky-frame shotgun houses propped up to keep the swamp water out. The gas stations where you could buy food and bait have been replaced by gallery/

shopping malls full of Swiss chocolates and French furs and restaurants where you can get saltimbocca and sushi. Postmodern skyscrapers tower over clogged freeways and at odd intersections are side-by-side with a tiny gas station or U-Tote-M. Houston is America's only large city without zoning.

For much of the 1980s, Houston's economy has been sagging: home prices were down sharply, a lot of office space was going vacant, onetime high rollers were counting nickels and dimes. But the west side of Houston remained, by any national standard, affluent and prosperous. It remains the nation's center of expertise in the oil business. Its huge petrochemical complexes create ever higher technology. It has the Johnson Space Center (saved from cuts by the area's congressional delegation). It has a highly skilled, ambitious, resourceful work force. And the traffic congestion, probably the worst in the country, about which Houstonians complain bitterly, may be a harbinger of better times.

The key question is whether Houston, with a metropolitan population over three million, can diversify its economy, as Los Angeles did in the 1950s and Chicago in the 1880s, or whether it will stay tied to oil as Detroit was to the automobile or Pittsburgh to steel, remaining vulnerable to the declines that will come sooner or later. One good sign: bad times have spurred tens of thousands of Houstonians, who were once happy to rise upward on oil prices and regular corporate paychecks and bonuses, to go out and start their own businesses.

The 7th District remains also one of the most Republican districts in the United States in election after election—and number one in particular in 1988, when it cast 77% of its votes for its former congressman George Bush. The conservatism here is more economic than cultural; many of these people, after all, have moved far from their original roots and they are not much interested in changing other people's lifestyles. But few voters here are aggressive liberals on cultural issues, and very few dissent from the hawkish consensus on foreign policy.

The district's current congressman is Bill Archer, Bush's successor and one of the senior Republicans in the House. Born and brought up in Texas, Archer was elected to the legislature as a Democrat and then became a Republican. He is now the ranking Republican on the House Ways and Means Committee—a position which, as Dan Rostenkowski has pointed out, Bush could have had if he had stayed in the House. Unsurprisingly, he has been a vigorous advocate for positions on tax issues backed by the oil industry, especially independent producers. He has been a staunch opponent over the years of increases in social security benefits and coverage, and he opposed as well the 1983 social security refinancing. He has favored lower tax rates for years, but is proud of having opposed the 1986 tax reform and was one of the House Republicans who came close to scuttling it in December 1985. Up until 1989, anyway, Archer seemed almost entirely negative in his approach to legislation.

But on becoming the committee's ranking Republican after the death of John Duncan in 1988, and with his 7th District predecessor in the White House in January 1989, Archer started sounding much more disposed toward positive legislation and bipartisan compromise—and even possibly, if it comes to that, tax increases, though his first priorities are to cut capital gains and oil drilling taxes. He worked with Rostenkowski on a technical changes bill and has a better relationship with him than any previous ranking Republican had. With an utterly safe district, Archer is sure to be around; the interesting question is what impact he will have.

The People: Est. Pop. 1986: 651,000, up 23.5% 1980–86; Pop. 1980: 527,083, up 103.6% 1970–80. Households (1980): 72% family, 42% with children, 62% married couples; 37.9% housing units rented; median monthly rent: $302; median house value: $79,200. Voting age pop. (1980): 375,483; 6% Spanish origin, 3% Black, 2% Asian origin.

1988 Presidential Vote:

Bush (R)	194,529	(77%)
Dukakis (D)	56,781	(22%)

Rep. Bill Archer (R)

Elected 1970; b. Mar. 22, 1928, Houston; home, Houston; Rice U., 1945–46, U. of TX, B.B.A. 1949, LL.B. 1951; Roman Catholic; married (Sharon).

Career: Air Force, 1951–53; Pres., Uncle Johnny Mills, Inc., 1953–61; Hunters Creek Village Cncl. and Mayor Pro Tem, 1955–62; TX House of Reps., 1966–70; Dir., Heights St. Bank, Houston, 1967–70; Practicing atty., 1968–71.

Offices: 1135 LHOB 20515, 202-225-2571. Also 7501 Fed. Bldg., 515 Rusk St., Houston 77002, 713-229-2763.

Committees: *Ways and Means* (Ranking Member of 13 R). *Joint Committee on Taxation.*

Group Ratings

	ADA	ACLU	COPE	CFA	LCV	ACU	NTLC	NSI	COC	CEI
1988	0	9	4	18	25	100	87	100	100	90
1987	0	—	5	21	—	95	—	—	100	85

National Journal Ratings

	1988 LIB — 1988 CONS		1987 LIB — 1987 CONS	
Economic	0% —	93%	0% —	89%
Social	0% —	95%	0% —	90%
Foreign	0% —	84%	0% —	80%

Key Votes

1) Homeless $	FOR	5) Ban Drug Test	FOR	9) SDI Research	FOR
2) Gephardt Amdt	AGN	6) Drug Death Pen	FOR	10) Ban Chem Weaps	AGN
3) Deficit Reduc	AGN	7) Handgun Sales	FOR	11) Aid to Contras	FOR
4) Kill Plnt Clsng Notice	FOR	8) Ban D.C. Abort $	FOR	12) Nuclear Testing	AGN

Election Results

1988 general	Bill Archer (R)	185,203	(79%)	($180,255)
	Diane Richards (D)	48,824	(21%)	($11,090)
1988 primary	Bill Archer (R), unopposed			
1986 general	Bill Archer (R)	129,673	(87%)	($152,779)
	Harry Kniffen (D)	17,635	(12%)	

EIGHTH DISTRICT

"What built Houston," wrote John Gunther in the 1940s, "was a combination of cotton, oil, and the ship canal." The cotton and oil were the gifts of nature, though they require much human effort and ingenuity to produce in commercial quantities; the ship canal was almost totally man's creation. After the sand-spit port of Galveston was destroyed by a hurricane and tidal wave in 1900, Houston's town fathers decided to dredge out Buffalo Bayou and make their inland city a seaport, and they succeeded. By 1940, Houston had a "port district, a teeming, noisy place where the Neptune Shore, the Port Cafe, and the Seven Seas Store are part of a salty atmosphere that is authentic even though inland from the coast so many miles. Here a beer sign announces that a certain brand 'steadies your nerves'; a seamen's institute beckons passing sailors, and a maritime supply company offers merchandise dear to the hearts of seafaring men." On the west side of Houston, you might be forgiven for thinking this is entirely a white-collar, office-bound city; but on the east and north, around the turning basin in the port and through the maze of refinery towers and tubing, you can see clearly that Houston is also a blue-collar town, with blacks and Mexican-Americans and large numbers also of whites from the rural South and even Michigan and California who came here to move up in the world.

Politically, Houston is as polarized as a steel town in the 1930s. In 1988, the west side 7th District voted 77% for George Bush, while the inner city 18th District, with its large black population, went 75% for Michael Dukakis. They were watching the same TV ads and news from the same city, they depend on the same economy—but they vote as if they lived in different countries. In between politically, and off to the north and east geographically, is the 8th Congressional District of Texas, which gave 54% of its votes to Bush and 45% to Dukakis—two points off the national average. About one-third of the people in the 8th live in Houston, about a third are black; there are modest working-class precincts on the city's east side. To the north, the district includes what was once countryside, dotted by roadside stores and jerry-built houses, and what is now the home of Houston's Intercontinental Airport, and the glass high-rise office buildings and glittery subdivisions that were built nearby. At the far eastern end of the district is Baytown, an industrial refinery town where the Ship Channel empties out into the bay. People here believe in traditional cultural values, perhaps a little more fervently than their neighbors on the west side; they believe also in free enterprise, though their faith has been tested as the 1980s have gone on, and they are not averse to some government intervention here and there and a little tighter mesh in the safety net.

In the 1970s, this was a Democratic congressional constituency; in the 1980s, it was Republican, thanks largely to the talents and vote-getting abilities of Congressman Jack Fields. In Washington, Fields was at first seen as a blow-dried Reagan robot swept into office in 1980 and swept to reelection on billows of PAC money. The reality seems a little different. Fields won in 1980 in a district closer to the central city and more Democratic, and he beat a veteran and accomplished liberal, incumbent Bob Eckhardt—even while Jimmy Carter was beating Ronald Reagan in the district. Fields was helped by redistricting, but not overwhelmingly: the 8th is not much more Republican than the 5th District in Dallas that elects Democrat John Bryant or the 12th in Fort Worth that used to elect Jim Wright. Fields won with 57% in 1982 against a weak opponent; he got well over 60% in 1984 and 1986 and was unopposed in 1988.

His political assets seem to be these. He has genuine roots in the district, in the old Exxon company town of Humble out near Intercontinental Airport. He won a seat on the Energy and Commerce Committee in his second term—a valuable political asset in energy-dependent Houston. He is not enough of a free market ideologue to pass up chances to help the district, fighting efforts to move space station work away from the nearby Johnson Space Center, getting $38 million for flood control on White Oak Bayou and $3.3 million to clean up toxic wastes in the Highlands Acid Pit, and trying to block the sales of USX's Texas Works at Baytown to the government of Iraq. On the powerful Energy committee, he supports oil industry positions on various issues and is an adversary of Health Subcommittee Chairman Henry Waxman on issues like clean air and AIDS policy. All these have helped Fields gain a solid hold on what might otherwise be a Democratic district—a formidable political achievement for someone the Democrats have tried to dismiss as just another pretty face.

The People: Est. Pop. 1986: 685,500, up 29.9% 1980–86; Pop. 1980: 527,531, up 65.7% 1970–80. Households (1980): 81% family, 52% with children, 69% married couples; 30.4% housing units rented; median monthly rent: $256; median house value: $46,700. Voting age pop. (1980): 347,798; 15% Black, 11% Spanish origin, 1% Asian origin.

1178   TEXAS

1988 Presidential Vote: Bush (R) 89,941   (54%)
Dukakis (D). 74,588   (45%)

Rep. Jack Fields (R)

Elected 1980; b. Feb. 3, 1952, Humble; home, Humble; Baylor U., B.A. 1974, J.D. 1977; Baptist; married (Lynn).

Career: Practicing atty.; Vice Pres., Rosewood Mem. Funeral Home and Cemetery. 1977–80.

Offices: 108 CHOB 20515, 202-225-4901. Also 12605 E. Freeway, Ste. 320, Houston 77015, 713-451-6334.

Committees: *Energy and Commerce* (10th of 17 R). Subcommittees: Energy and Power; Health and the Environment; Telecommunications and Finance. *Merchant Marine and Fisheries* (5th of 17 R). Subcommittees: Merchant Marine; Panama Canal and Outer Continental Shelf (Ranking Member).

Group Ratings

	ADA	ACLU	COPE	CFA	LCV	ACU	NTLC	NSI	COC	CEI
1988	0	9	6	18	19	100	87	100	100	87
1987	0	—	7	29	—	86	—	—	93	75

National Journal Ratings

	1988 LIB — 1988 CONS		1987 LIB — 1987 CONS	
Economic	0%	93%	11%	83%
Social	0%	95%	15%	84%
Foreign	0%	84%	0%	80%

Key Votes

1) Homeless $	FOR	5) Ban Drug Test	FOR	9) SDI Research	FOR
2) Gephardt Amdt	AGN	6) Drug Death Pen	FOR	10) Ban Chem Weaps	AGN
3) Deficit Reduc	AGN	7) Handgun Sales	FOR	11) Aid to Contras	FOR
4) Kill Plnt Clsng Notice	FOR	8) Ban D.C. Abort $	FOR	12) Nuclear Testing	AGN

Election Results

1988 general	Jack Fields (R), unopposed			($226,581)
1988 primary	Jack Fields (R), unopposed			
1986 general	Jack Fields (R)	66,280	(68%)	($574,657)
	Blaine Mann (D).	30,617	(32%)	($19,666)

NINTH DISTRICT

From Spindletop park in Beaumont, where Texas's oil industry began, to the Lyndon B. Johnson Space Center south of Houston, where America's probes into space are planned, stretches the 9th Congressional District of Texas. It has two concentrations of population. One is around Beaumont and Port Arthur, near the border with Cajun Louisiana, an area of refineries, petrochemical plants, and other big processing operations. Heavily blue-collar and dependent on oil, this area had one of the highest levels of unemployment in Texas in the middle 1980s. The other populated area is around Galveston, built on a sand spit and rebuilt after 6,000 died in the devastating hurricane of 1900 (at which point even venturesome Texans decided it was better to build the big city which became Houston on swamps inland rather than on sand scarcely above sea level) and Texas City, just inland where more than 500 perished in a huge liquefied natural gas tanker explosion in 1947. This is not gentle country. Nonetheless, the Space Center was located here, under pressure from Vice President Johnson and longtime Houston Congressman Albert Thomas; and when NASA threatened to move space station operations out, they were stymied by the area delegation led by 9th District Representative Jack Brooks.

The delegation could hardly have picked a more aggressive or astute champion. Brooks worked his way through school as a reporter, was a Marine in the South Pacific in World War II, was elected to the legislature from the Beaumont area at age 23, politicked astutely enough to chair the Banks and Banking Committee in his mid-20s, and was elected to Congress in 1952, just before turning 30. He is undeniably brainy and even more undeniably forceful; an old-fashioned man's man who likes to hunt and fish with no evident interest in introspection but an impressive ability to figure out how to get things done and then the temperament to see that they are done his way. He is probably the current Member of Congress who most closely resembles Lyndon Johnson, in both his virtues and his faults, in his accent and even a bit in his craggy appearance. Brooks is extremely partisan, profane, knowledgeable, witty, effective. A story that may be apocryphal has it that he was charged with being pro-Communist in his 1952 House campaign. "I fought the fascists for five years in World War II," he is supposed to have told a political meeting; "I own an eight-inch revolver back at home and I'll *shoot* any man who calls me a Communist."

Whether that happened or not, it is clear that Brooks is fearless. Representing a district that reached far into rural east Texas in the 1950s and early 1960s, he compiled (and has now) a liberal record on economic issues and on many non-economic issues as well. While most southern congressmen postured in opposition to civil rights legislation, Brooks voted for the Civil Rights Act of 1964, something that took real guts—and he didn't show a tremor of hesitation. More recently, he was an ally and adviser and the strongest and most vocal defender of Jim Wright during the investigation that led to Wright's resignation. Brooks's position has been that Wright violated no rules, that charges were brought against him as they have been brought against liberal leaders in the past for political reasons only, and that the Ethics Committee has misunderstood the facts and the law. Only four days apart from Wright in age, a friend since they were both combat veterans elected to the Texas legislature in 1946 at age 23, Brooks made a point of renominating Wright for speaker in the Democratic Caucus, declaring "Jim Wright and I have worked together for two-thirds of our lives, and I know him as well as my brother," and defending his as faithfully as a brother could.

After 14 years of chairing Government Operations, Brooks became Chairman of Judiciary in 1989. At Gov Ops he was known as an aggressive investigator of agencies and a stickler on some big government procurement issues—the telephone contract, for example. On Judiciary, where he had been less active, he is expected to be a more aggressive and partisan chairman than Peter Rodino, and some think he will try to expand the committee's jurisdiction as John Dingell has with Energy and Commerce. But his differences with Rodino are limited: Brooks favors capital punishment, for example (but not for agency heads who displease him), and he is not a believer in Rodino's old-fashioned trust-buster approach to antitrust.

Brooks served on the special committee investigating the Iran-contra scandal, just as he served on Judiciary's impeachment hearings a dozen years ago. On both he was a prosecutorial-minded critic of Republican administration personnel; Nixon called him "the executioner" after Brooks tracked down all the public money spent on Nixon's San Clemente house. Brooks himself says, "I never thought being a congressman was supposed to be an easy job, and it doesn't bother me a bit to be in a good fight."

Brooks had some electoral problems in the early 1980s, in 1980 edging a primary challenger by an uncomfortably narrow 50%–43% margin and beating him two years later, after spending over $700,000, with just 53%. He has not had primary opposition since, but has won general elections with 59% in 1984 and 62% in 1986—a little lower than most congressmen with his seniority usually get, but not in the danger zone. The 9th District, with its blacks and Cajuns, union members and unemployed oil workers, is in any case pretty solidly Democratic; it went for Michael Dukakis over Texas's George Bush in 1988. Brooks seems likely to be an even more important congressman as the 1980s turn into 1990s.

The People: Est. Pop. 1986: 560,200, up 6.4% 1980–86; Pop. 1980: 526,443, up 17.5% 1970–80. Households (1980): 76% family, 43% with children, 63% married couples; 32.0% housing units rented; median monthly rent: $209; median house value: $39,300. Voting age pop. (1980): 370,362; 20% Black, 7% Spanish origin, 1% Asian origin.

1988 Presidential Vote:

Dukakis (D)...................... 105,562	(53%)
Bush (R) 94,083	(47%)

Rep. Jack Brooks (D)

Elected 1952; b. Dec. 18, 1922, Crowley, LA; home, Beaumont; Lamar Col., 1939–41, U. of TX, B.J. 1943, J.D. 1949; United Methodist; married (Charlotte).

Career: USMC, WWII; TX House of Reps., 1946–50; Practicing atty., 1949–52.

Offices: 2449 RHOB 20515, 202-225-6565. Also 230 Jack Brooks Fed. Bldg., Beaumont 77701, 409-839-2508; and 601 25th St., Galveston 77550, 409-766-3608.

Committees: *Judiciary* (Chairman of 21 D) Subcommittee: Economic and Commercial Law (Chairman). *Select Committee on Narcotics Abuse and Control* (2d of 18 D).

Group Ratings

	ADA	ACLU	COPE	CFA	LCV	ACU	NTLC	NSI	COC	CEI
1988	75	81	77	82	25	9	6	13	23	9
1987	88	—	76	64	—	0	—	—	13	8

National Journal Ratings

	1988 LIB — 1988 CONS		1987 LIB — 1987 CONS	
Economic	87% —	8%	73% —	0%
Social	75% —	24%	59% —	40%
Foreign	60% —	37%	68% —	30%

Key Votes

1) Homeless $	—	5) Ban Drug Test	AGN	9) SDI Research	AGN
2) Gephardt Amdt	FOR	6) Drug Death Pen	FOR	10) Ban Chem Weaps	FOR
3) Deficit Reduc	FOR	7) Handgun Sales	FOR	11) Aid to Contras	AGN
4) Kill Plnt Clsng Notice	AGN	8) Ban D.C. Abort $	—	12) Nuclear Testing	—

Election Results

1988 general	Jack Brooks (D), unopposed		($226,581)
1988 primary	Jack Brooks (D), unopposed		
1986 general	Jack Brooks (D) 73,285	(62%)	($400,038)
	Lisa D. Duperier (R) 45,834	(38%)	($237,179)

TENTH DISTRICT

In the 1940s, world traveler John Gunther found Austin "one of the pleasantest small cities I've ever seen. The street signs are colored orange, and the lamps, uniquely in the world I imagine, shine from towers 165 feet high, thus softly floodlighting the whole town. And Austin is fantastically full of fantastically pretty girls." Austin remains pleasant and the women are still attractive, but this southernmost state capital in the continental 48 states is scarcely small any more: it is one of the boom towns of America and one of its major centers of high-tech innovation and economic growth.

There is an irony here, for Austin was not established for economic reasons. It has been through most of its history a city with only a limited interest in commerce, its skies almost totally untainted with the smoke of industry, its ground not pocked with pumping oil rigs. Nor has state government been a major employer during most of Austin's history: the dome on the pink granite Capitol is just a tad higher than its counterpart in Washington, but Texas has always believed in minimalist government. The real secret behind Austin's growth and vitality, the public sector sparkplug that has produced the private sector combustion, is the University of Texas. Endowed with thousands of west Texas acres that turned out to sit on top of oil, it has the nation's largest single university campus here in Austin and has become one of the great institutions of higher learning in America.

But since the middle 1970s Austin has changed, almost doubling in size, bursting with outsiders, spreading shopping centers and condominiums willy-nilly into the surrounding hills. The catalyst again is the University, plus Austin's selection in 1983 as the site of the Microelectronics and Computer Technology Corporation research consortium headed by Admiral Bobby Inman. Austin in the 1980s has become not exactly yuppified, but more affluent, less of a college town and more a place where families with technical-minded breadwinners live ordered and disciplined lives. Its attitudes are now closer to those of the *Texas Monthly,* probably the most successful—editorially and financially—of the nation's regional magazines, which eyes Texas critically but usually affectionately; less the adolescent eager to overthrow all the older generation's pieties and more the adult interested in understanding and appreciating the society around him.

Politically, Austin has become more Republican. Austin and the surrounding 10th Congressional District voted for Ronald Reagan twice, and the high-tech and UT ticket of Michael Dukakis and Lloyd Bentsen won just 53% in the district once represented in the House by Lyndon Johnson. The city's blacks remain unanimously Democratic, and Democrats' percentages among Mexican-Americans and students have not fallen too much (conservative young people in Texas today tend to choose A&M, SMU or Baylor over UT). But the new affluent neighborhoods spreading all over the countryside are Republican, though not quite so heavily so as affluent neighborhoods in Dallas or Houston, of course (no place else in America is that Republican), but Republican enough to give a different tilt to Austin politics.

But congressional politics here remains in the LBJ mode, thanks to Congressman Jake Pickle. There is an old tradition here, going back to Lyndon Johnson's victory in the 1937 special election, of fairly liberal Democratic congressmen, who are fairly generous with public funds (especially for central Texas), tolerant on civil rights, hawkish on military affairs, and politically

1182   TEXAS

able—a tradition upheld by LBJ ("the best congressman ever," in the words of his unadmiring biographer Robert Caro), his successor Homer Thornberry, and the man who succeeded Thornberry when Johnson made him a federal judge in 1963, the current congressman, Jake Pickle. All three were contemporaries, born between 1908 and 1913; the 10th has been represented by politicians of the same generation for more than 50 years.

Pickle gives the impression of being a kindly man; he is conscientious about his work; on the Ways and Means Committee on which he ranks third and on the Social Security Subcommittee he used to chair, he has taken seriously his responsibilities for programs which affect all Americans and cut to the heart of the lives of a great many. He is not one to promise what he believes cannot be delivered, and while other Democrats go out and demagogue the social security issue on the campaign trail, Pickle has worked hard in the committee room and on the floor to make sure the system does not go bankrupt. He was the architect of the social security rescue of 1983, when benefits were in effect cut by raising the normal retirement age over the years to 67 in the next century; he now chairs the Oversight Subcommittee. He was a serious player on tax reform and on trade; he has come forward with well thought out amendments to help rural hospitals, to strengthen the Caribbean Basin Initiative, and to let owners of rental real estate deduct cash expenses. He is not the kind to challenge Chairman Dan Rostenkowski idly, but he knows how to get what he wants.

He knows how to win elections, too. It struck some Republicans that changes in Austin were making the old-fashioned Pickle vulnerable and in 1986 Carole Keeton Rylander, mayor of Austin in the 1970s and daughter of a dean of UT Law School, a family friend of Pickle's and a longtime Democrat, switched to the Republican Party and ran against him. Pickle showed energy, aggressiveness, tenacity and won 72% of the vote. For the 1990s, the outlook for Pickle is even better. The 10th was, according to the Census's 1986 estimate, the second most populous in the country (after the Texas 26th) and stands to be split up after the 1990 Census; one possibility is that Republican north Austin will become the nucleus of a new Republican district, leaving the 10th more Democratic and more pro-Pickle.

The People: Est. Pop. 1986: 702,400, up 33.2% 1980–86; Pop. 1980: 527,181, up 41.0% 1970–80. Households (1980): 65% family, 35% with children, 53% married couples; 45.4% housing units rented; median monthly rent: $222; median house value: $47,800. Voting age pop. (1980): 390,909; 15% Spanish origin, 9% Black, 1% Asian origin.

1988 Presidential Vote: Dukakis (D)....................... 156,015   (53%)
Bush (R) 132,984   (46%)

Rep. J. J. (Jake) Pickle (D)

Elected Dec. 17, 1963; b. Oct. 11, 1913, Roscoe; home, Austin; U. of TX, B.A. 1938; United Methodist; married (Beryl).

Career: Area Dir., Natl. Youth Admin., 1938–41; Navy, WWII; Co-organizer, KVET Radio, Austin; Adv. and pub. rel. business; Dir., TX St. Dem. Exec. Cmtee., 1957–60; Mbr., TX Employment Comm., 1961–63.

Offices: 242 CHOB 20515, 202-225-4865. Also 763 Fed. Bldg., Austin 78701, 512-482-5921.

Committees: *Ways and Means* (3d of 23 D). Subcommittees: Health; Oversight (Chairman). *Joint Committee on Taxation.*

Group Ratings

	ADA	ACLU	COPE	CFA	LCV	ACU	NTLC	NSI	COC	CEI
1988	80	70	54	64	63	16	14	40	38	19
1987	60	—	52	50	—	22	—	—	43	14

National Journal Ratings

	1988 LIB — 1988 CONS		1987 LIB — 1987 CONS	
Economic	67%	— 33%	54%	— 45%
Social	70%	— 28%	42%	— 57%
Foreign	50%	— 49%	50%	— 48%

Key Votes

1) Homeless $	AGN	5) Ban Drug Test	AGN	9) SDI Research	AGN
2) Gephardt Amdt	AGN	6) Drug Death Pen	FOR	10) Ban Chem Weaps	FOR
3) Deficit Reduc	FOR	7) Handgun Sales	FOR	11) Aid to Contras	AGN
4) Kill Plnt Clsng Notice	AGN	8) Ban D.C. Abort $	AGN	12) Nuclear Testing	FOR

Election Results

1988 general	J. J. (Jake) Pickle (D)................	232,213	(93%)	($172,921)
	Vincent J. May (Lib.)..................	16,281	(7%)	
1988 primary	J. J. (Jake) Pickle (D), unopposed			
1986 general	J. J. (Jake) Pickle (D)................	135,863	(72%)	($1,369,912)
	Carole Rylander (R)..................	52,000	(28%)	($316,175)

ELEVENTH DISTRICT

The heart of Texas, just off the geographic center of the state but the center of its traditional rural culture, is not in greater Houston or the Dallas-Fort Worth Metroplex, or even in the state capital of Austin. It is betwixt and between, a part of Texas whose farm fields and small towns recall the state as it was half a century ago, before the growth of the oil industry transformed Texas, once a rural backwater, into one of the centers of western capitalism. This is the Texas around Waco, which since its founding, wrote the *WPA Guide* in 1940, "has grown steadily and without spectacular boom periods. Negroes still sing and sweat in broad outlying cotton fields, and cowmen frequent Waco's elm-shaded streets, but false-fronted saloons have been replaced by tall hotels; old cattle trails are boulevards. River-bank slums, locally called Rat Row, have grown into an industrial zone." Waco has continued its steady growth since, fortified by the growth of the Army's huge Fort Hood, which occupies most of one of the counties next door, by the 1970s surge in the "awl bidness," and perhaps in the 1990s, by the high-tech influence radiating out of Dallas-Fort Worth on one side and Austin on the other.

Waco and the still mostly rural counties around it make up Texas's 11th Congressional District. Politically, this was long one of the most Democratic parts of what was the very Democratic state of Texas, not so much because of blacks and Hispanics (their numbers are not so high here) as because of the ancestral loyalties of rural and small city whites. As late as 1968, while Hubert Humphrey was carrying almost nothing but black precincts in the South, he won an absolute majority here against Richard Nixon and George Wallace. But in the two decades since, national Democratic loyalties have, if not evaporated, at least diminished: George Bush carried this district with 58% of the vote.

The congressman from the 11th District, Marvin Leath, in his first decade in the House became one of the leaders of the Democrats—and not just of the conservative Democrats: he has been one of the Members who has held the Democratic majority together. He came to the House with experience in business as a small Texas banker and after working two years for his predecessor, Bob Poage, a conservative and farm policy expert first elected in 1936 who chaired the Agriculture Committee until he was ousted by the Democratic Caucus after the election of 1974. Leath ran for the seat in 1978 and won after two tough struggles, against liberal Lane Denton in the primary and against a well-financed Republican in the general; in his first three years he compiled a conservative voting record. He even looked the part of a rural conservative: with his deep drawl, his tanned weatherbeaten look, his guitar and country music, he looks like the kind of Texan who keeps a shotgun mounted on his pickup truck.

But from the 1970s, he also gained an understanding that the road upward for a Democrat—unless he was to switch altogether to the Republicans, as the 6th District's Phil Gramm did in 1983—was to get along with the Democratic Caucus. He worked on the veterans' training and G.I. bills in 1983 and 1984—which have turned out to be one of the unsung public policy successes of the 1980s. He championed military spending and protected Fort Hood from his seat on Armed Services. In 1985, he got a seat on the Budget Committee, where he found his forum, advanced his own budget alternatives, saw them rejected by other Democrats (though they have gotten more votes than you might think), and then went on to support his fellow Democrats' alternative with force and vigor as the best available solution. He proved himself over and over again a good team player.

So when liberals were casting around for someone to run against Armed Services Chairman Les Aspin after he voted for the MX missile in 1985 and contra aid in 1986, they went down the committee list to number 14 in seniority and came to Leath. He was more hawkish than Aspin by any measure, but also they thought more candid and more of a team player, and he ran for the job in the Democratic Caucus, with support ranging from Ron Dellums to Sonny Montgomery. Eventually the move failed: Aspin was rejected in Caucus in January 1987, but the Leath forces came up short after leading liberals passed a letter backing Aspin and pointing to Leath's defense record. This is not the only setback Leath has suffered. He wanted to become chairman of the Budget Committee. But in July 1987, it became apparent that Leon Panetta of California had the votes, and Leath took himself out of the race.

Leath has taken these setbacks with characteristic good humor and found other worthwhile work to do. After the death of Dan Daniel in 1988, he became Chairman of the Armed Services Panel on Morale, Welfare, and Recreation; this handles over $16 billion worth of non-appropriated funds that may not have a direct bearing of defense capabilities but are important to military men and women—in, among other places, Fort Hood, Texas. Leath supported Richard Gephardt's presidential candidacy actively, as did many of his fellow House Democrats. He remains on Budget and in 1989 chaired its Task Force on Defense, Foreign Policy, and Space—all areas on which he is inclined to spend more than most other Democrats, but on which he presumably will work to find common ground with them. When his six-year stint on Budget ends, he will return to Veterans' Affairs as its number four Democrat.

At home, Leath has not had a serious opponent since his tough races in 1978, nor is he likely to in this district he fits like a glove.

The People: Est. Pop. 1986: 580,200, up 10.0% 1980–86; Pop. 1980: 527,382, up 25.3% 1970–80. Households (1980): 75% family, 41% with children, 65% married couples; 36.6% housing units rented; median monthly rent: $162; median house value: $30,400. Voting age pop. (1980): 381,013; 13% Black, 8% Spanish origin, 1% Asian origin.

1988 Presidential Vote:

Bush (R)	....	106,061	(58%)
Dukakis (D)	....	75,985	(41%)

Rep. J. Marvin Leath (D)

Elected 1978; b. May 6, 1931, Henderson; home, Waco; U. of TX, B.B.A. 1954; Presbyterian; married (Alta).

Career: Army, 1954–56; High sch. teacher and coach, 1957–59; Salesman, 1959–62; Banker, 1962–68; Spec. Asst. to U.S. Rep. W. R. Poage, 1972–74.

Offices: 336 CHOB 20515, 202-225-6105. Also 206 Fed. Bldg., Waco 76701, 817-752-9600.

Committees: *Armed Services* (10th of 31 D). Subcommittees: Procurement and Military Nuclear Systems; Readiness. *Budget* (5th of 21 D). Task Force: Defense, Foreign Policy and Space (Chairman).

Group Ratings

	ADA	ACLU	COPE	CFA	LCV	ACU	NTLC	NSI	COC	CEI
1988	15	22	30	45	38	71	44	90	77	41
1987	28	—	28	29	—	41	—	—	50	47

National Journal Ratings

	1988 LIB — 1988 CONS		1987 LIB — 1987 CONS	
Economic	40% —	58%	42% —	58%
Social	32% —	68%	35% —	65%
Foreign	38% —	62%	40% —	60%

Key Votes

1) Homeless $	FOR	5) Ban Drug Test	AGN	9) SDI Research	FOR
2) Gephardt Amdt	FOR	6) Drug Death Pen	FOR	10) Ban Chem Weaps	AGN
3) Deficit Reduc	FOR	7) Handgun Sales	FOR	11) Aid to Contras	FOR
4) Kill Plnt Clsng Notice	AGN	8) Ban D.C. Abort $	AGN	12) Nuclear Testing	FOR

Election Results

1988 general	J. Marvin Leath (D)	134,207	(95%)	($87,626)
	Frederick M. King (Lib.)	6,533	(5%)	
1988 primary	J. Marvin Leath (D), unopposed			
1986 general	J. Marvin Leath (D)	84,201	(100%)	($83,069)

TWELFTH DISTRICT

Fort Worth, Texas, has a fair claim to being the quintessential mid-American city. Halfway across the continent, midway between the oceans, it is where the East ends and the West begins, just west of the Balcones Escarpment that divides the dry treeless grazing lands of west Texas from the humid green croplands of east Texas. It is southern in its hell-of-a-fellow heritage and northern in its advanced post-industrial economy. It has the nation's biggest row of Western wear shops and in the redeveloped Stockyards the nation's largest honkytonk, Billy Bob's Texas; it has the nation's richest family, the Basses, who have put up the steel-sheen skyscrapers that dominate the skyline from hills miles away and at whose base is the Sundance Square dreamworld built by the eccentric Bass brother.

Half a century ago the *WPA Guide* said it was "as thoroughly representative of the Southwest as a long-horned steer. Its metropolitan aspects—towering business buildings, noisy traffic—vividly exemplify the modern city; but its people typify the spirit and atmosphere of the Old West. There is still time for a cordial 'Howdy, stranger,' and a nice disregard of the city's uproar in the easy pause for conversation that is definitely reminiscent of the top rail of a corral fence, with boot heels hooked for balance and plenty of time for talk."

Yet Fort Worth has become a center of America's high-tech and defense industries. Fort Worth is the place where an eight-engine B-52 bomber rolled off the runway and, circling lazily in the wide treeless sky, broke the United States out of the SALT II treaty in 1986, as it together with the new B-1 exceeded the treaty's limits. It took off from Carswell Air Force Base, right across the street from where General Dynamics built it in the nation's largest defense plant; not far away than Bell Helicopter Textron's almost equally huge plant. Fort Worth has some of the nation's premier small museums (better, it likes you to know, than Dallas's) and the definitive museum of Western art; it will also be the site of the second Bureau of Engraving and Printing plant to make paper money. Fort Worth had its beginning as a cow town, where stockmen drove their herds to the railhead, when it pushed west from Dallas; today it has a high-tech economy, with big employers like General Dynamics and Texas Instruments and Tandy Radio Shack. It has long been seen as a defensive rival looking over its shoulder at Dallas; now it is entitled to stand up on its own. Other cities have their claims, but the visitor from abroad who wants to see as much as possible of what is quintessentially American would be well advised to fly to the Dallas-Fort Worth Regional Airport and head west to Fort Worth.

Fort Worth's political heritage is Democratic, and for 34 years by the man who became the 48th Speaker of the House of Representatives, Jim Wright. In 1954, when Wright was first elected to Congress after a primary victory over anti-labor Democrat Wingate Lucas (who died the week before Wright announced his resignation), this was still a dusty blue-collar town, in contrast to white-collar Dallas, which was electing its first Republican congressman the same year. Much of Fort Worth still has that air, as sympathetic legislatures have shorn some of the more Republican parts of Tarrant County away from Wright's 12th District; currently Arlington and some affluent suburbs to the north are in the 26th District, and some of the heavily Republican neighborhoods in southwest Fort Worth are in the 6th District which stretches south all the way to Houston. That leaves the 12th District with almost all of Fort Worth's blacks and Hispanics, with most of its blue-collar voters, and with ordinary white Texans living in neighborhoods sprinkled with shopping centers, small Mexican and barbecue restaurants, and Southern Baptist and fundamentalist churches.

As Speaker and before, Wright was a man of tense ambition and mellifluous charm, a politician of mostly unchanging principles over a 40-year public career but with a tendency sometimes to flinch under pressure. For years, he seemed to shift because the world shifted around him: in the 1950s, this admirer of Franklin Roosevelt was the most liberal member of the Texas delegation, a young national Democrat among a group of old and mostly conservative nominal members of the party; by the late 1960s, he was being scorned by party liberals for his support of public works projects and the Vietnam war. But public works and an interventionist foreign policy had been the heart of Roosevelt's policies. On his way up, as well as on the way down, Wright had some severe political setbacks. He lost renomination to the legislature in 1948 when his opponent was murdered days before the primary. He ran for Lyndon Johnson's Senate seat in 1961 and came in third—tantalyzingly close to the second place which would have put him in a runoff with John Tower which he probably would have won. He tried for the Senate again in 1966, going on television to ask for $10 contributions, but he didn't get enough to make a statewide race. By the early 1970s, this Texan who surely hoped he might follow Lyndon Johnson to the White House was reduced to hoping that he might eradicate his 1961 campaign debt and succeed some day to the chairmanship of the House Public Works Committee.

Then in 1976, he ran for House Majority Leader. He began the race with support from the

Texas delegation and many but not all southerners. On the second of the secret ballots, he edged out Richard Bolling by two votes; on the third, he beat Phillip Burton 148–147. A reform-minded group of Democrats elected the one candidate without distinguished reform credentials. Suddenly Wright was a national leader, spokesman for the Democratic Party, in line for the speakership. His relationship with Speaker Tip O'Neill turned out to be good; he made peace eventually with his 1976 opponents; he worked hard and often effectively to find common ground with the majority of House Democrats on issues like energy and foreign policy that tended to separate them. He made his share of missteps along the way, championing and spotlighting the synfuels program which most Democrats eventually voted to kill, switching positions on the MX missile, putting Phil Gramm on the Budget Committee where he ended up sponsoring the Reagan budget cuts. Back home in Fort Worth, he seemed stronger than ever; even in the conservative climate of 1980, when challenged by then Mayor Jim Bradshaw, Wright raised $1.2 million and won with 60%. In the House he steadily consolidated his position until, by the middle 1980s, it seemed highly unlikely that anyone else would succeed O'Neill. By 1985, when O'Neill announced his retirement, Wright was able to announce that he had a majority of votes; Dan Rostenkowski and John Dingell, aggressive and ambitious men who admitted they'd like the job themselves, declined to run, knowing the vote count.

In his first term as Speaker, Wright showed a command over the technical content of legislation and he worked capably with committee and subcommittee chairmen to schedule legislation in a way that gave the Democratic House a chance to make a strong positive record. Working as O'Neill did only with Democrats, uninterested in the votes across the aisle, Wright put together clean water and highway bills which were quickly passed over President Reagan's veto. He helped fashion a responsible trade bill and attached the ultimately successful (and politically useful) factory closing notice provision to it. The House he led passed a catastrophic health insurance program, drug and homelessness laws, a farm credit bill, and a welfare reform bill that all represented constructive approaches to nagging national problems. Under his leadership Congress for the first time in nearly 40 years passed every appropriations bill in time for the new fiscal year. Technically, politically, in legislative substance, it was a fine, perhaps a dazzling, record.

On foreign policy, an area he had not been involved in previously, he literally took over U.S. Central American policy. Wright speaks Spanish, he has long travelled in Central America, and like most House Democrats he voted against opposed military aid to the Nicaraguan contras. After contra aid was ended in 1987, he began negotiating directly with the Sandinistas, the Reagan Administration, and Central American leaders like Costa Rica President Arias. The result was that the United States accepted the Arias plan, which produced an end to contra activities and called for, though it threatened no sanctions to obtain, freedoms of expression and free elections in Nicaragua. The young Democrats who had come to office in the 1970s had felt then that Congress should have ended the Vietnam war by denying the Johnson and Nixon Administration funds to fight it. Now, under Wright's leadership and with the votes of most House Democrats, Congress was ending the contra war by denying the Reagan and then the Bush Administrations funds to fight it. For many younger House members, notably David Bonior of Michigan, whom Wright appointed Chief Deputy Whip, this was a noble cause and one which cemented them to their leader. For everyone, pro or con, it was a sign of Wright's effectiveness.

Yet Wright's work also showed some of his characteristic defects. He was temperamentally a loner in an institution which places a premium on camaraderie and, though his yeomen efforts to consult his colleagues often resulted in legislative success, his occasional failures to do so resulted in political setbacks. His proposal for a tax rate increase in the 100th Congress embarrassed his fellow Democrats; his flinching on the pay raise issue at the beginning of the 101st Congress infuriated them. He infuriated the Republicans even more by his aggressive partisan tactics and increasing resort to steamroller tactics. Some of the Republican complaints were disingenuous: majorities always employ procedural devices in ways minorities always find unfair. But Wright, through his usually ironclad control of the Rules Committee, did use closed rules preventing amendments much more often than Tip O'Neill did; he did contrive to keep Republicans from having an up-or-down vote on their alternatives on major issues like contra aid; he did declare the House adjourned and then open up what he called a new legislative day one afternoon; he did have his key aide John Mack, convicted in 1973 of beating a young woman with hammer blows to the head, escort Texas Congressman Jim Chapman to the floor in October 1987 to switch his vote and give Wright a 206–205 victory on a budget issue. One must go back at least to the 1920s to see such hard-nosed partisan tactics employed habitually by a Speaker of the House.

One must go back even farther also to find a speaker embroiled with the kind of ethical problems facing Wright in early 1989. In fact, he is the first Speaker ever to resign because of such problems. In 1988, when Newt Gingrich filed charges against Wright before the Ethics Committee, Gingrich was a Republican backbencher with a reputation as a not very reliable gadfly and Wright was at the peak of his power as speaker. Democratic members could not imagine any more dire result than a partisan tussle that would be little noticed outside their chamber and on which they would win as they had won most partisan tussles within the House in the 1980s. But in March 1989 the Ethics Committee announced it found reason to believe Wright violated the rules of the House by taking gifts from his longtime business associate, George Mallick, on the grounds that Mallick had an interest in legislation, and that his unusual royalty and marketing arrangements for his book *The Reflections of a Public Man* was an attempt to evade the House limits on outside earned income.

Against both these charges Wright had defenses which were not frivolous: that Mallick had no interest in legislation beyond what any citizen has and that royalty income, which is allowed by the rules, is royalty income even if the arrangement is unusual. And the Ethics Committee refused to charge him with violations for his frequent and vehement interventions with federal regulators on behalf of Texas savings and loan operators—interventions which, together with his effective opposition to FSLIC recapitalization bills, may end up costing the taxpayers $100 billion to bail out the S&Ls bankrupted by improvident and crooked owners. But as the elaborate ethics process dragged on, and as more charges and facts surfaced (including a graphic *Washington Post* article on the story of the woman John Mack attacked in 1973), Wright's position became politically untenable. Jack Brooks, Charles Wilson, and other Texans tried to rally members behind him; Majority Leader Thomas Foley and Whip Tony Coelho defended him publicly and privately. But few Democrats felt for this competent but personally distant man the loyalty they felt, for instance, to the warm and gregarious O'Neill; and, while Democrats were ready to take seriously Wright's arguments that he hadn't violated the rules, very few relished the prospect of defending on the stump in 1990 all the things he had done.

As the early months of 1989 dragged on, Wright fought bravely, smiling and maintaining his innocence. Complaints were heard from many quarters that little legislation was being passed, but in fact the budget resolutions and appropriations bills were moving forward, committees were marking up legislation, and Wright himself during all his troubles continued to play the pivotal role on Central American policy, negotiating the Bush Administration's total surrender on contra aid. The sad irony is that genuine legislative competence which he always wanted to be the hallmark of his speakership seemed likely to be obscured by controversy over matters which Wright surely believes are at most peripheral to his public duties. But by May 1989 it was clear even to Wright that he could not prevail, and, after Tony Coelho abruptly announced his own resignation following charges that seemed far less serious, Wright spoke emotionally to the House, defending himself, and announcing his resignation.

Republicans looking ahead to the special election to replace him had some reason for optimism. Like the rural Texas from which many Fort Worth citizens come, Fort Worth has been shifting towards Republicans in the 1980s: Fort Worth's Tarrant County was actually 1% more for Ronald Reagan than Dallas County in 1984, and that same year Tarrant joined Dallas in electing the Republican slate to county-wide offices—a revolution in local politics. In 1986 Tarrant was only 2% less for Republican Governor Bill Clements than Dallas, and in 1988 not only Tarrant County but also the 12th district voted for George Bush over Michael Dukakis. But Bush's margin in the 12th was small, and as Wright announced his resignation, the Republicans were searching for a candidate and the major Democratic contenders appeared to be state Senator Hugh Parmer of Fort Worth and Pete Geren, a lawyer who ran against 6th District Congressman Joe Barton in 1986.

The People: Est. Pop. 1986: 631,500, up 19.4% 1980–86; Pop. 1980: 527,715, up 4.7% 1970–80. Households (1980): 73% family, 41% with children, 59% married couples; 36.0% housing units rented; median monthly rent: $204; median house value: $33,500. Voting age pop. (1980): 374,842; 15% Black, 9% Spanish origin.

1988 Presidential Vote:

Bush (R)	....	98,449	(53%)
Dukakis (D)	....	87,316	(47%)

Rep. Jim Wright (D)

Elected 1954; resigned June, 1989; b. Dec. 22, 1922, Ft. Worth; home, Ft. Worth; Weatherford Col., U. of TX; Presbyterian; married (Betty).

Career: Army Air Corps, WWII; Partner, trade extension and adv. firm; TX House of Reps., 1947–49; Mayor of Weatherford, 1950–54; Pres., TX League of Municipalities, 1953.

Offices: 1236 LHOB 20515, 202-225-5071. Also 9A10 Lanham Fed. Bldg., 819 Taylor St., Ft. Worth 76102, 817-334-3212; and 536 B Seminary Dr., Ft. Worth 76115, 817-334-4845.

Election Results

1988 general	Jim Wright (D)	135,459	(99%)	($940,760)
1988 primary	Jim Wright (D), unopposed			
1986 general	Jim Wright (D)	84,831	(69%)	($1,098,252)
	Don McNiel (R)	38,620	(31%)	($269,946)

THIRTEENTH DISTRICT

Heading west in Texas, the population thins out, the land becomes browner, till you can travel through a whole county where only a few hundred people—plus quite a few more head of cattle—live. And then you go up nearly 1,000 feet of elevation, up the steep gullies that surround the rivers which are most of the year just a tiny trickle, till you come to the tilted tableland that is the High Plains of west Texas. The winds here sweep down from the Rockies, the land is barren except where it is irrigated, often with the now dangerously depleted waters of the Ogallala Aquifer, but here and there in this demanding environment—sticky-hot in the summer, swept by north winds from Canada in much of the winter—comfortable cities have been built to house the people and businesses that bring forth oil and natural gas and helium and other elements from the earth.

The 13th Congressional District of Texas, the northernmost district in the state, spans all this territory. Its easternmost part, around Wichita Falls, is part of the agricultural land of the Red River Valley. It is dusty land, with empty skylines, afflicted with the woes—low crop and land prices, worse export markets, banks failing because of bad loans—characteristic in the middle 1980s of the Farm Belt. This is white Anglo Texas: few blacks got this far west and few Mexican-Americans go this far north. Population has been declining here not only in the rural counties, but also in the district's second largest city, Wichita Falls, whose population fell below 100,000 in 1980. Wichita Falls was the home base of John Tower, but historically this area, like the entire Red River Valley, has been one of the heartlands of the Democratic Party, and some of the sparsely populated counties to the west still vote heavily Democratic.

Up on the High Plains, the economy is different: it is based on minerals. The 13th District's largest city is Amarillo, the home of former oilman and now corporate raider T. Boone Pickens, the helium capital of the world, and just 15 miles west of the Pantex plant that builds America's nuclear bombs. It has churches whose members believe that the end of the world is near and nuclear destruction will come soon, and Stanley Marsh III who planted a row of 10 Cadillacs nose down in his "Cadillac ranch." Settled partly by people from neighboring northwest Oklahoma and western Kansas, the Panhandle has always been one of the most Republican parts of Texas. Opposition to energy price regulation has strengthened this area's Republicanism, and in national elections it almost seethes hostility toward the Democrats.

Politically, this is a split constituency, cobbled together from two districts after the 1980 Census: the Democratic Red River Valley and the Republican High Plains. It has shifted between the parties twice, in 1984 and 1988. The first time, Democratic Congressman Jack Hightower was beaten by Beau Boulter, a Republican of the religious right, and beaten 53%–47%. Boulter was reelected in 1986, partly because a month before he had tacked onto the $560 billion continuing resolution $700,000 for the Lake Wichita-Holliday Creek flood control project. In 1988, he gave up what was looking like a safe seat for a predictably uphill race against Senator Lloyd Bentsen, who not only won, but held Boulter to a 51%–49% margin in his home district.

The new congressman is Democrat Bill Sarpalius, who has beaten both of the leading Republicans who ran against him. One was Bob Price, elected congressman from the High Plains in 1966 and defeated by Hightower in 1974; Sarpalius beat him for the Amarillo state Senate district in 1980. This time Price lost the Republican nomination to Amarillo businessman Larry Milner, whom Sarpalius also beat. Sarpalius has a gripping personal history: he came to the High Plains as a child, stricken with polio, abandoned by his father, sent with his brothers by his alcoholic mother to Cal Farley's Boys Ranch near Amarillo. He went to Texas Tech, taught agriculture, went into the farm business, and ran for office. In Austin, he was a crusader against drunk driving; back home he broke his back while driving an all-terrain vehicle in 1986, and was beaten and had his jaw broken in an Amarillo bar in January 1988, but in neither case was he drinking. Milner charged Sarpalius with being a liberal and talked taxes and gun control; Sarpalius talked agriculture and natural gas, topics more adapted to the district. Milner won 54% in the High Plains; Sarpalius won 62% in the Red River Valley and the grazing counties to the west, and was elected with 52%.

With a seat on the Agriculture Committee as a new farm bill is being written, an arresting biography and considerable political acumen, Sarpalius seems to have a good chance to make this once Republican district a safe Democratic seat.

The People: Est. Pop. 1986: 551,700, up 4.7% 1980–86; Pop. 1980: 526,840, up 7.7% 1970–80. Households (1980): 75% family, 39% with children, 66% married couples; 30.0% housing units rented; median monthly rent: $166; median house value: $28,800. Voting age pop. (1980): 376,878; 7% Spanish origin, 5% Black, 1% Asian origin.

1988 Presidential Vote:

Bush (R) 121,111	(63%)
Dukakis (D)........................ 68,739	(36%)

Rep. William C. Sarpalius (D)

Elected 1988; b. Jan. 10, 1948, Los Angeles, CA; home, Amarillo; TX Tech. U., B.A. 1972, W. TX St. U., M.A. 1978; Methodist; divorced.

Career: Agribusiness; Teacher, 1976–79; TX state Senate, 1981–88.

Offices: 1223 LHOB 20515, 202-225-3706. Also 817 S. Polk, Amarillo 79109, 806-371-8844; 1000 Lamar, Ste. 208, Witchita Falls 76301, 817-767-0541.

Committees: *Agriculture* (23d of 27 D). Subcommittees: Conservation, Credit, and Rural Development; Cotton, Rice and Sugar; Domestic Marketing, Consumer Relations, and Nutrition; Wheat, Soybeans and Feed Grains. *Small Business* (23d of 27 D). Subcommittee: Procurement, Tourism, and Rural Development. *Select Committee on Children, Youth, and Families* (18th of 18 D).

Group Ratings and Key Votes: Newly Elected

Election Results

1988 general	William C. Sarpalius (D)	98,345	(52%)	($384,738)
	Larry S. Milner (R)	89,105	(48%)	($476,220)
1988 primary	William C. Sarpalius (D)	37,745	(58%)	
	Ed Lehman (D).......................	16,629	(26%)	
1986 general	Beau Boulter (R).....................	84,980	(65%)	($744,332)
	Doug Seal (D)........................	45,907	(35%)	($52,914)

FOURTEENTH DISTRICT

Going south from Houston, on the flat coastal plains along the Gulf of Mexico, you come to some of the hottest and most humid places in the United States. These cottonlands were settled well after the more temperate-climated northeast Texas, and they have always been dedicated to market-oriented rather than subsistence farming; the lifeline here is the railroad, with the cotton gin beside it. The coastline, though it has plenty of inlets, never had any important ports in the stretch between Houston and Corpus Christi, until the discovery of oil in this part of Texas made it worthwhile to build channels to ship the oil out. "A curious mixture of cultures lingers here," says the *WPA Guide*: "traces of the plantation era with its tangible evidences—rambling white houses set in groves of moss-draped oaks, old-time Negroes, and cotton; some of the glamour of the days of the cattle kings, who erected mansions; and combined with this, the thrift and customs of descendants of European immigrants. In this region of canebrakes, oil wells, rice, pecans, and hump-backed Brahmas, the land is black, rolling and open except along streams and where small groves of oaks make islands of darker green in a usually verdant picture."

This is the land of the 14th Congressional District of Texas, an area made up of rural countrysides, small towns and a couple of small cities, along the Gulf coast and inland toward the old Texas German country, which includes just the outer edges of the sprawling metropolitan areas of Houston, Austin, San Antonio and Corpus Christi. These cotton lands, settled well after the Civil War, don't have many blacks (11% districtwide); the percentage of Mexican-Americans (20% districtwide) is about average for Texas. You don't find many Mexicans until you get down to Victoria and the south. This is mostly white Anglo country, ancestrally Democratic except for a couple of counties settled by Texas Germans, who were pro-Union in the Civil War and have remained Republican ever since.

The 14th District has been represented by some odd congressmen: one was beaten in 1978 after a woman staffer charged him with sexual improprieties; his conservative successor retired after he was arrested on homosexual charges in 1979; Bill Patman, son of the longtime populist chairman of the House Banking Committee, won in 1980 and 1982 but was beaten in 1984 by the oddest of the lot, Republican Mac Sweeney. Sweeney, who had held some position on the Reagan White House staff, was guilty of resume inflation, of making inaccurate charges against Patman, of mailing out campaign literature under the frank after criticizing Patman for doing so, of claiming to have co-sponsored bills he hadn't yet co-sponsored, of being almost invisible in the House and in committees on which he was nominally serving. Sweeney won the seat by blindsiding Patman and held it in 1986 against a politically inexperienced opponent, Democrat Greg Laughlin. But voters catch on to this kind of thing, and in 1988, Laughlin came back and won the seat with 53% of the vote—more than either of Sweeney's two winning percentages.

Laughlin won in the Democratic heart of the district; his percentages were lower, and he lost a couple of counties, at the edges in places with metropolitan overspill. He has committee assignments—Public Works, Merchant Marine—that suggest he will be a nuts and bolts politician. But it's possible that the Republicans will try to win this one back, in which case it would be seriously contested in 1990 as it has been in each election of the 1980s.

The People: Est. Pop. 1986: 604,200, up 14.7% 1980–86; Pop. 1980: 526,920, up 26.0% 1970–80. Households (1980): 77% family, 42% with children, 67% married couples; 28.0% housing units rented; median monthly rent: $153; median house value: $34,900. Voting age pop. (1980): 368,619; 17% Spanish origin, 11% Black.

1988 Presidential Vote:

Bush (R)	121,903	(57%)
Dukakis (D)	90,108	(42%)

Rep. Gregory H. Laughlin (D)

Elected 1988; b. Jan. 21, 1942, Bay City; home, W. Columbia; TX A&M U., B.A. 1964, U. of TX, LL.B. 1967; Methodist; married (Ginger).

Career: Asst. Dist. Atty., Harris Cnty., 1970–74; Atty., Bd. of Dir., St. Bar of TX, 1981–84; Pres., TX Aggie Bar Assoc., 1984–85.

Offices: 1022 LHOB 20515, 202-225-2831. Also 312 S. Main St., Victoria 77901, 512-576-1231; and 221 E. Main St., Ste. 203, Round Rock 78664, 512-244-3765.

Committees: *Merchant Marine and Fisheries* (24th of 26 D). Subcommittees: Coast Guard and Navigation; Merchant Marine; Panama Canal and Outer Continental Shelf. *Public Works and Transportation* (30th of 31 D). Subcommittees: Aviation; Surface Transportation; Water Resources.

Group Ratings and Key Votes: Newly Elected

Election Results

1988 general	Gregory H. Laughlin (D)	111,395	(53%)	($600,114)
	Mac Sweeney (R)....................	96,042	(46%)	($645,988)
1988 primary	Gregory H. Laughlin (D)	59,213	(72%)	
	Michael L. Herzik (D)	22,770	(28%)	
1986 general	Mac Sweeney (R)....................	74,471	(52%)	($883,081)
	Gregory H. Laughlin (D)	67,852	(48%)	($429,672)

FIFTEENTH DISTRICT

"Starting virtually as a wilderness at the turn of the century," the *WPA Guide* wrote 50 years ago about the Lower Rio Grande Valley of Texas, it "has experienced an almost phenomenal development. Along this fertile plain, at intervals approximating seven miles, are thoroughly modern towns whose populations range from 3,000 to 12,000. Between them vast citrus groves crowd close to the highway. Along the main roads the glossy fronds of date palms, frequently so luxuriant that they serve as windbreaks for citrus groves, contrast with the lighter green of the orchards, the dusty emerald of salt cedars, and the duller tones of the unusually tall, slender *Washingtonia robusta* palms; the latter are strung out in long lines across the landscape, often marking the boundaries of property or the windings of irrigation canals." To this valley pioneers came, like Lloyd Bentsen Sr., who arrived after World War I with five dollars in his pocket and became one of the biggest Valley landowners, remaining active in his business until he died in an auto accident in 1989 at age 95.

But the neat towns settled by migrants from the North did not supply most of the labor in this southernmost part of the United States mainland; the workers mostly came from Mexico, or were from Hispanic families settled on the north side of the Rio Grande for generations. Off the paved streets, and in settlements in the counties to which the big citrus developments had not penetrated, "Mexicans here cling to the customs of their homeland across the river. One- and two-room *jacales* made of willow branches, daubed with mud or thatch, make rooms for the humbler folk; milk goats, dogs and cats, chickens and children swarm over these *casitas*. The border in those days was a porous thing, with no patrolling or border stations to speak of; and the Valley was a kind of border zone between the underdeveloped Mexican economy and the advanced economy of the United States."

It still is, with the proviso that all three economies have grown and produce levels of affluence today unforeseen by all but a few visionaries 50 years ago. It is still possible to find some backward dwellings in the Valley, but most residents live an air-conditioned life, and if wage levels are the lowest in the United States, so is the cost of living. People and money still ebb and flow across the border, depending on currency exchange rates; when the peso collapsed in 1982, Valley retail sales plummeted and Valley bank deposits surged to record levels. Population figures have bounced all around, rising sharply in the late 1980s.

Once upon a time in the small counties of south Texas local ranchers and oil men wielded absolute political power. The Parr family of Duval County, for example, held back their returns in the 1948 Senate runoff and then reported 4,622 votes for Lyndon Johnson and 40 votes for his opponent—a margin similar to that by which Johnson had been trailing in the first primary. But those days are pretty much gone. The Hispanic voters in small counties are heavily Democratic: Starr County voted 85% for Michael Dukakis and Lloyd Bentsen (his official Texas residence is here) in 1988. But in the larger counties there is more two-party voting these days, and Dukakis swept the Valley in the 1988 presidential primary not because of connections with local bosses but because he spoke Spanish and ran TV ads heavily on local stations.

The 15th Congressional District of Texas includes much of the Lower Rio Grande Valley, including Hidalgo, Starr and Zapata Counties along the river. It goes north almost as far as San Antonio, although most of its population is along the border. This is the descendant of a district that in 1948, 1950 and 1952 elected Lloyd Bentsen Jr., to the House, before he went to Houston to make his fortune and got elected to the Senate in 1970. The current congressman from the 15th District is Eligio (Kika) de la Garza. He came up from poverty, served 12 years in the legislature and was a favorite of the big landowners who was sometimes attacked by Austin-based liberals and militants. His voting record for years was rather conservative; he is somewhat liberal on economic issues and always supported civil rights, but he tends to be hawkish on foreign policy and rather conservative on cultural issues. This is out of line with many professional Hispanics but meshes well with the views of Mexican-American voters, who tend to be pro-military and culturally traditional. Generally, de la Garza is an earnest, pleasant man, who takes the trouble constantly to learn new languages and to surprise foreign visitors by speaking to them in their native tongue.

De la Garza has been chairman of the House Agriculture Committee since 1981—a troubled time for that assignment. He got the chair when Thomas Foley moved up in the leadership. As chairman, de la Garza has superintended the committee's work on two major farm bills, in 1981 and 1985. These have been melancholy duties: even as spending on farm programs went up to unprecedented heights, crop prices, land values and farm exports were declining disastrously. For years the Democratic Party has knitted together Farm Belt politicians who want to use government to bolster the family farmer and urban politicians who want to use government for other purposes, and they have voted for each others' programs. Now, on both sides, they know that government must pay less. The 1981 farm bill, in a way quite unanticipated by anyone, boosted costs enormously, so much so that de la Garza and everyone else knew that the 1985 bill would have to skin them back, and it did. In the years since, he has done craftsmanlike work, as on the 1988 drought relief bill and a 1988 pesticide bill which, characteristically, did not include provisions sought by lobbies on either extreme. De la Garza will be working on yet another farm bill in 1989; his expectation early in the year was that it would result in still further cuts in spending. No opposition has arisen to his chairmanship, and he has been reelected by overwhelming margins in the 15th District.

The People: Est. Pop. 1986: 638,100, up 21.0% 1980–86; Pop. 1980: 527,203, up 38.4% 1970–80. Households (1980): 84% family, 54% with children, 71% married couples; 27.8% housing units rented; median monthly rent: $126; median house value: $23,100. Voting age pop. (1980): 329,023; 66% Spanish origin, 1% Black.

1988 Presidential Vote: Dukakis (D)...................... 108,744   (63%)
Bush (R) 64,034   (37%)

Rep. E (Kika) de la Garza (D)

Elected 1964; b. Sept. 22, 1927, Mercedes; home, Mission; Edinburg Jr. Col., St. Mary's U., LL.B. 1952; Roman Catholic; married (Lucille).

Career: Navy, WWII, Army, Korea; Practicing atty., 1952–64; TX House of Reps., 1952–64.

Offices: 1401 LHOB 20515, 202-225-2531. Also 1418 Beech St., McAllen 78501, 512-682-5545; and Alice Fed. Bldg., Rm. 210, 401 E. 2d St., Alice 78332, 512-664-2215.

Committees: *Agriculture* (Chairman of 27 D).

Group Ratings

	ADA	ACLU	COPE	CFA	LCV	ACU	NTLC	NSI	COC	CEI
1988	50	55	61	45	38	20	10	63	50	16
1987	56	—	60	57	—	5	—	—	27	11

National Journal Ratings

	1988 LIB — 1988 CONS		1987 LIB — 1987 CONS	
Economic	56%	— 44%	73%	— 0%
Social	60%	— 39%	45%	— 54%
Foreign	72%	— 28%	49%	— 51%

Key Votes

1) Homeless $	AGN	5) Ban Drug Test	AGN	9) SDI Research	AGN
2) Gephardt Amdt	FOR	6) Drug Death Pen	FOR	10) Ban Chem Weaps	AGN
3) Deficit Reduc	FOR	7) Handgun Sales	—	11) Aid to Contras	AGN
4) Kill Plnt Clsng Notice	—	8) Ban D.C. Abort $	AGN	12) Nuclear Testing	—

Election Results

1988 general	E (Kika) de la Garza (D)	93,672	(94%)	($219,469)
	Gloria Joyce Hendrix (Lib.)	6,133	(6%)	
1988 primary	E (Kika) de la Garza (D), unopposed			
1986 general	E (Kika) de la Garza (D)	70,777	(100%)	($141,973)

SIXTEENTH DISTRICT

North America's largest border city, perhaps the largest border city in the world, is the city known as El Paso in Texas and Juarez in Mexico. "El Paso lies directly under the crumbling face of Comanche Peak," the *WPA Guide* wrote 50 years ago, "spreading out fan-shaped around the foot of the mountain. In some directions, irrigation has made bright green gardens of the residential section; in others, as in the Chihuahuita district and toward the west, the scene consists chiefly of brick and adobe houses. Fashionable residences, largely of a modified Spanish or Pueblo architecture, lie near the mountains, their roofs bright against gray rocks. The city's international tone is evident everywhere; on the streets, which bear English and Spanish names, and where fluent Spanish is spoken by Texans as well as Mexicans; in the schools, which face the problem of teaching more than 900 children who daily cross the bridge from Juarez by special arrangement with the immigrant authorities; in such segregated districts as Chihuahuita, where the sights and sounds, manners and folkways of Mexico are found." Today El Paso still is a bicultural, bilingual city, but it is vastly larger. In 1940, there were 97,000 people in El Paso and 39,000 in Juarez; in the late 1980s there were over a half million people in El Paso and more than—no one really knows how much more than—one million in Juarez.

Other American border cities owe their prominence to factors other than their position on a dotted line on the map: San Diego to the Navy, Detroit to autos, Buffalo to grain-shipping and steel. El Paso and Juarez would be little more than a crossroads, a pass through the mountains, without the border. What has grown up here is a huge metro area that lives off labor that is very low-wage by United States standards and attracts workers with wages that are very high by Mexican standards. They live in physical isolation—a kind of heavily populated island in the midst of a vast sea of sand: it is more than 600 miles east to Dallas-Fort Worth and 400 miles west to Phoenix; Albuquerque and Chihuahua are 260 miles north and 230 miles south, respectively. Government puts in some money in El Paso—there are big military bases here—while Juarez's economy increasingly depends on the *maquiladora* plants which enable U.S. and foreign (especially Japanese) firms to assemble products in Mexico but sell them duty-free in the U.S. market. To a north-of-the-border eye, life for most people in El Paso and Juarez looks pretty mean. Yet the huge migration from other parts of Mexico is mute evidence that this represents a significant improvement for these people.

The 16th Congressional District of Texas is made up of El Paso and several desert counties to the east; 90% of the 16th's votes are in El Paso County, while Loving County, out in the desert, is America's lowest populated county with only 91 people in 1980 (but 108 registered voters in 1988: it's growing), and the town of Langtry, where Judge Roy Bean once held court as the only law west of the Pecos. Politics here is very much divided on ethnic lines: most Anglos vote Republican in any contested race, most Mexican-Americans vote Democratic. The census-takers say there is an Hispanic majority here, but many are not citizens. For years, the border has been porous, and many workers cross it every day to go to work, in both directions.

The congressman from the 16th District is Ron Coleman, a Democrat with an aggressive personality, an old-fashioned Texas Anglo personal style, and a voting record which means that most of his votes come from Hispanics. In a House where Members try to please everyone in their districts, Coleman is not afraid to antagonize some in his—which may just be good politics, since the district is polarized anyway. He was the attorney for the strikers in the big Farah strike of the 1970s, and he served 10 years in the legislature, where he didn't mind tangling with the conservative House speaker. He gets along better with the Democratic leadership in Washington, though he's not always a reliable vote for them. In his first term, Coleman had a seat on the Armed Services Committee and he now serves on the Military Construction Appropriations subcommittee, where he has been able to funnel projects to the Fort Bliss Military Reservation, one of the mainstays of El Paso's economy. He competed with Mike Andrews of Houston to be the Texas candidate for a vacant Democratic seat on Ways and Means after the 1984 election, but the seat ultimately went to someone else. But Coleman converted the loss to a victory, by getting a seat on Appropriations instead; his first subcommittee assignment there was Military Construction, whose potential for district service need not be explained.

With his rather controversial politics, Coleman had some difficulty winning this seat when conservative Democrat Richard White retired in 1982; his task was complicated by the presence of a Mexican-American candidate in the initial Democratic primary. But Coleman had a strong enough base to lead with 33% in the first primary, and he had enough Mexican-American turnout to beat a conservative Democrat in the runoff and to get 54% against a Republican heavily supported by the national party in the general. The trajectory of his electoral performance has been upward, to 57% in 1984 when Ronald Reagan was carrying the district, 66% in 1986 and an unopposed 100% in 1988, when the 16th went for Michael Dukakis.

The People: Est. Pop. 1986: 610,900, up 15.8% 1980–86; Pop. 1980: 527,401, up 29.9% 1970–80. Households (1980): 81% family, 53% with children, 66% married couples; 39.3% housing units rented; median monthly rent: $158; median house value: $36,800. Voting age pop. (1980): 341,560; 55% Spanish origin, 4% Black, 1% Asian origin.

1988 Presidential Vote:

Dukakis (D)	69,550	(52%)
Bush (R)	63,062	(47%)

Rep. Ronald D. Coleman (D)

Elected 1982; b. Nov. 19, 1941, El Paso; home, El Paso; U. of TX, B.A. 1963, J.D. 1967; U. of Kent, England, 1981; Presbyterian; divorced.

Career: Army, 1967–69; Teacher, El Paso pub. schs., TX Schl. for the Deaf; Asst. El Paso Cnty. Atty., 1969; First Asst. El Paso Cnty. Atty., 1971; TX House of Reps., 1973–82.

Offices: 416 CHOB 20515, 202-225-4831. Also Fed. Bldg., 700 E. San Antonio St., El Paso 79901, 915-534-6200; and U.S.P.O. Bldg., Rm. 304, Pecos 79772, 915-445-6218.

Committees: *Appropriations* (31st of 35 D). Subcommittees: Foreign Operations, Export Financing and Related Programs; Military Construction.

Group Ratings

	ADA	ACLU	COPE	CFA	LCV	ACU	NTLC	NSI	COC	CEI
1988	80	81	88	73	44	17	3	50	29	7
1987	84	—	87	71	—	4	—	—	13	8

National Journal Ratings

	1988 LIB — 1988 CONS		1987 LIB — 1987 CONS	
Economic	67% —	33%	73% —	0%
Social	81% —	19%	66% —	32%
Foreign	51% —	48%	57% —	42%

Key Votes

1) Homeless $	AGN	5) Ban Drug Test	AGN	9) SDI Research	AGN
2) Gephardt Amdt	FOR	6) Drug Death Pen	FOR	10) Ban Chem Weaps	AGN
3) Deficit Reduc	FOR	7) Handgun Sales	—	11) Aid to Contras	AGN
4) Kill Plnt Clsng Notice	AGN	8) Ban D.C. Abort $	AGN	12) Nuclear Testing	FOR

Election Results

1988 general	Ronald D. Coleman (D), unopposed			($317,444)
1988 primary	Ronald D. Coleman (D), unopposed			
1986 general	Ronald D. Coleman (D)	50,590	(66%)	($511,094)
	Roy Gillia (R)	26,421	(34%)	($538,622)

SEVENTEENTH DISTRICT

Stretching endlessly from Fort Worth west to the horizon and beyond are the west Texas plains, thousands and thousands of acres of rolling grazing land punctuated occasionally by oases of irrigated farmland (often in those circles that show the reach of the sprinklers). This is primarily cattle country, although there is some oil here and some raising of cotton and grain. On the interstate straight west of Fort Worth the largest town is Abilene, with a high concentration of bankers, lawyers and professionals. Settled by Confederate veterans always suspicious of eastern bankers and Yankee businessmen, never much concerned about civil rights one way or the other (for there are very few blacks this far west), this was one of the Democratic heartlands of America for many years, right up through the 1970s. Right now, the 36 mostly sparsely populated counties west of Fort Worth that make up Texas's 17th Congressional District are fought-over political territory: still mostly Democratic in local and congressional elections (thanks to the popularity of Congressman Charles Stenholm) and Republican typically in presidential contests and increasingly in statewide races.

Stenholm is one of several conservative Texas Democrats first elected in 1978 who have made their mark in different ways—Phil Gramm is now a Republican senator, Kent Hance a Republican member of the Railroad Commission and Marvin Leath, who nearly got elected chairman of House Armed Services Committee. Stenholm has no taste for self-promotion and has made less of a splash in the outside world. Inside the House, he has made a difference in a variety of ways. Immediately on coming to Washington after working in Democratic Party affairs in Stamford (the home town also of Democratic mega-leader Robert Strauss) and running the Rolling Plains Cotton Growers Association, he complained correctly that conservative Democrats weren't getting good committee assignments and that Democratic leaders, used to 2 to 1 majorities, didn't care much about them. After the Democrats' big losses in 1980, Stenholm and others got Jim Wright to put Phil Gramm on the Budget Committee, supported Gramm and voted for the Reagan budget and tax cuts (they became known as the Boll Weevils) and formed a group called the Conservative Democratic Forum, which Stenholm still serves as chairman. After the Democrats' rebound in 1982, the Boll Weevils had to decide whether to stay Democrats or leave the party; Stenholm was one of those who stayed. He threatened momentarily to run against Speaker O'Neill in 1985, then desisted and got O'Neill to promise to give Democrats like him full representation in the Caucus. Since then Stenholm, with his pleasant personality and straightforwardness, has managed to find at least a little common ground with the Democratic leadership which had, by this time, great incentive to get along with him.

He has also managed to do some constructive legislative work. On the Agriculture Committee, he has worked on farm credit, disaster relief and animal product safety; he chairs the Livestock, Dairy and Poultry Subcommittee. A staunch supporter of rural health care, he has been crusading to keep small town doctors in the medicare program and to get small defense contractors relieved of the requirements of the Davis-Bacon Act. He favors a balanced budget constitutional amendment and an expanded Earned Income Tax Credit. He is not just trucking to district sentiment: he voted in 1988 for the Brady Amendment, the seven-day waiting period to buy handguns vociferously opposed by the National Rifle Association.

Stenholm seems temperamentally comfortable with being a Democrat, even as one who dissents so often from the party's majority. It is an affiliation that has worn well on the plains of Texas. A Republican congressman here might have vigorous competition from the Democrats. Stenholm has not had a Republican opponent since 1978 and he dispatched his only Democratic primary opponent, in 1984, by an 88%–12% margin.

The People: Est. Pop. 1986: 580,900, up 10.2% 1980–86; Pop. 1980: 526,913, up 9.3% 1970–80. Households (1980): 76% family, 38% with children, 67% married couples; 27.3% housing units rented; median monthly rent: $144; median house value: $25,900. Voting age pop. (1980): 380,499; 9% Spanish origin, 3% Black.

1988 Presidential Vote:

Bush (R)	118,173	(58%)
Dukakis (D)	85,322	(42%)

Rep. Charles W. Stenholm (D)

Elected 1978; b. Oct. 26, 1938, Stamford; home, Avoca; TX Tech. U., B.S. 1961; M.S. 1962; Lutheran; married (Cynthia).

Career: Teacher, vocational educ., 1962–65; Exec. Vice Pres., Rolling Plaines Cotton Growers, 1965–68; Mgr., Stamford Electric Coop., 1968–76; Farmer, 1976–78.

Offices: 1226 LHOB 20515, 202-225-6605. Also 903 E. Hamilton St., Stamford 79553, 915-773-3623; and 341 Pine St., Abilene 79604, 915-673-7221.

Committees: *Agriculture* (9th of 27 D). Subcommittees: Cotton, Rice, and Sugar; Department Operations, Research, and Foreign Agriculture; Livestock, Dairy, and Poultry (Chairman); Tobacco and Peanuts. *Veterans' Affairs* (10th of 21 D). Subcommittee: Hospitals and Health Care.

Group Ratings

	ADA	ACLU	COPE	CFA	LCV	ACU	NTLC	NSI	COC	CEI
1988	20	17	19	27	31	78	58	100	77	54
1987	12	—	17	50	—	74	—	—	80	59

National Journal Ratings

	1988 LIB — 1988 CONS		1987 LIB — 1987 CONS	
Economic	31% —	67%	36% —	63%
Social	12% —	87%	18% —	81%
Foreign	27% —	71%	24% —	76%

Key Votes

1) Homeless $	FOR	5) Ban Drug Test	FOR	9) SDI Research	FOR
2) Gephardt Amdt	AGN	6) Drug Death Pen	FOR	10) Ban Chem Weaps	AGN
3) Deficit Reduc	AGN	7) Handgun Sales	AGN	11) Aid to Contras	FOR
4) Kill Plnt Clsng Notice	AGN	8) Ban D.C. Abort $	FOR	12) Nuclear Testing	AGN

Election Results

1988 general	Charles W. Stenholm (D), unopposed		($342,766)
1988 primary	Charles W. Stenholm (D), unopposed		
1986 general	Charles W. Stenholm (D)	97,791 (100%)	($217,744)

EIGHTEENTH DISTRICT

What you see in Houston depends on your perspective. The gushing writer of the *WPA Guide* 50 years ago saw "towering above the lush green prairie where its suburbs multiply like ripples in a pond, Houston's sky line is that of a lusty growing giant; its factory smokestacks are as thick as are the oil derricks in the fields nearby; its office buildings are more those of the North and East than the usual product of a Texas city." But John Gunther a few years later found Houston, in those days before the windows were sealed shut to keep in the air-conditioning, "the noisiest city I have ever visited, with a residential section mostly ugly and barren, a city without a single good restaurant, and of hotels with cockroaches." Central Houston today remains a place of contrast, between the showy architecture of the downtown buildings, whose affluent daytime tenants escape home each night out Memorial Drive or the always-clogged Katy or Southwest Freeways. But in the neighborhoods just to the south and east, blacks and Mexican-Americans live in unpainted frame houses full of cracks wide enough to let in Houston's humid, smoggy air. The Houston slums look like something out of the sharecropper 1930s, and they remind us that although this was until recently one of our fastest-growing cities, its growth is based in large part on the availability of cheap labor; there are income disparities here as vast as there are in developing countries. Yet there is also upward mobility. Moving north from downtown, you find solid working and middle-class neighborhoods, some even with a touch of grandeur from when their houses were built many years ago.

Central Houston makes up the 18th Congressional District of Texas, which goes east beyond the Houston Ship Channel's Turning Basin, south to Loop 610, west to the edge of ultra-rich River Oaks and Memorial Park and far north, in some places past the city limits, toward Houston Intercontinental Airport. The 18th is Houston's minority district. It was created after the 1970 Census for then state Senator Barbara Jordan, famed later for her performance in the House Judiciary Committee impeachment hearings and as one of the 1976 Democratic Convention's keynoters; within its current boundaries, in 1980, 41% of its residents were black and 31% of Spanish origin, with very little overlap. The number of Mexican-Americans has been rising in the inner-city neighborhoods, as a result of heavy immigration in the 1970s; blacks have been moving outward, mostly to the north. Politically it is the most heavily Democratic district in Texas.

The congressman from the 18th District since 1978 has been Mickey Leland, who has turned out, contrary to expectations, to be an active legislator. Leland started off in politics as a dashiki-clad militant; now he is a Giorgio Armani-clad committee chairman. In his first term, he snagged a seat on the Energy and Commerce Committee, the hot committee during most of the 1980s because of all the regulatory work it handles. He serves on the Telecommunications and Health Subcommittees, where he has pushed for pet causes like getting more blacks on TV programs and lifeline phone rates for senior citizens. Leland also serves on the Post Office and Civil Service Committee, where he chairs the subcommittee on Postal Operations and Services. He was one of the few black politicians with the inclination and nerve to have backed Walter Mondale over Jesse Jackson in the 1984 presidential primaries; in 1988 he backed Jesse Jackson, but he helped to smooth things over at the convention when he seconded the vice-presidential nomination of Lloyd Bentsen.

His most visible assignment in this and the last Congress was as chairman of the Select Committee on Hunger which he helped create. He got it in place just as Americans began focusing on famine in Ethiopia and other African countries, and got Congress to spend $800 million for aid to sub-Saharan nations. But like most congressmen, he has been slow to criticize the Marxist government of Ethiopia whose policies helped create the famine and exacerbated it; maybe he remained silent prudently, to get as much food as possible to the starving. He criticized the Reagan Administration harshly for not providing aid to the hungry in Sandinista-held Nicaragua. He has worked on hunger at home too, passing a bill giving better tax treatment to companies that contribute to food banks and establishing grants to study pediatric undernutrition; he has also tried to provide more help for runaways and the mentally ill homeless.

Leland is an individual, even an eccentric, Congress's closest personal acquaintance of Fidel Castro and a booster of the Houston economy. As a young man, he ran into the barriers of segregation. Now, he not only serves but also exercises power in Congress. Incidentally, he is a licensed pharmacist, the most prominent in American politics since Hubert Humphrey. He has been mentioned as a possible candidate against Senator Phil Gramm in 1990, but that would seem to be a long shot; he would begin little-known statewide and without a large base, and his virtues are not ones that are easily communicated in 30-second spots—while in the 18th District he can be reelected indefinitely.

The People: Est. Pop. 1986: 541,600, up 2.7% 1980–86; Pop. 1980: 527,393, dn. 5.9% 1970–80. Households (1980): 65% family, 39% with children, 46% married couples; 57.2% housing units rented; median monthly rent: $185; median house value: $31,900. Voting age pop. (1980): 366,424; 39% Black, 27% Spanish origin, 1% Asian origin.

1988 Presidential Vote:

Dukakis (D)	92,191	(74%)
Bush (R)	30,408	(25%)

Rep. Mickey Leland (D)

Elected 1978; b. Nov. 27, 1944, Lubbock; home, Houston; TX Southern U., B.S. 1970; Roman Catholic; married (Alison).

Career: Instructor, TX St. U., 1970–71; Dir. of Spec. Dev. Proj., Hermann Hosp., 1971–78; TX House of Reps., 1973–78.

Offices: 2236 RHOB 20515, 202-225-3816. Also 1919 Smith St., Ste. 820, Houston 77002, 713-739-7339.

Committees: *Energy and Commerce* (10th of 26 D). Subcommittees: Energy and Power; Health and the Environment; Telecommunications and Finance. *Post Office and Civil Service* (5th of 15 D). Subcommittees: Compensation and Employee Benefits; Postal Operations and Services (Chairman). *Select Committee on Hunger* (Chairman of 19 D).

Group Ratings

	ADA	ACLU	COPE	CFA	LCV	ACU	NTLC	NSI	COC	CEI
1988	100	95	96	91	75	0	9	0	27	6
1987	96	—	95	93	—	0	—	—	0	6

National Journal Ratings

	1988 LIB — 1988 CONS			1987 LIB — 1987 CONS		
Economic	92%	—	0%	73%	—	0%
Social	86%	—	0%	78%	—	0%
Foreign	84%	—	0%	81%	—	0%

Key Votes

1) Homeless $	AGN	5) Ban Drug Test	AGN	9) SDI Research	AGN
2) Gephardt Amdt	FOR	6) Drug Death Pen	AGN	10) Ban Chem Weaps	FOR
3) Deficit Reduc	FOR	7) Handgun Sales	AGN	11) Aid to Contras	AGN
4) Kill Plnt Clsng Notice	AGN	8) Ban D.C. Abort $	AGN	12) Nuclear Testing	FOR

Election Results

1988 general	Mickey Leland (D)	94,408	(93%)	($534,732)
	J. Alejandro Senad (Lib.)	7,235	(7%)	
1988 primary	Mickey Leland (D)	38,963	(82%)	
	Elizabeth Spates (D)	8,321	(18%)	
1986 general	Mickey Leland (D)	63,335	(90%)	($207,419)
	Joanne Kuniansky (I)	6,884	(10%)	

NINETEENTH DISTRICT

Up on the High Plains of Texas, on land separated from the dusty cattlelands further east by rising gullies astride wide river courses, is some of the most productive cotton and wheat land in the United States, centered around the city of Lubbock. This fertility is a triumphant work of man: for this is irrigated land, which gets its water from the giant Ogallala Aquifer that undergirds so much of the western Great Plains, making this part of Texas a sort of green island in a vast brown sea of arid grazing land, to the east, west, north and south. It was settled relatively late, with most of the growth after World War II; Lubbock grew from 31,000 in 1940 to 128,000 in 1960 and 173,000 in 1980 and by 1988 was estimated to be at 190,000. In the 1980s, there have been signs that the aquifer is going dry, and populations in the rural counties have declined. But Lubbock, with an economy that includes Texas Tech University as well as agribusiness, and which has one of Texas's lowest unemployment rates, has continued to thrive.

Lubbock also entered the national political lexicon in March 1989 when President George Bush, asked to comment on the drumbeat of press criticism in Washington, said, "I talked to a fellow in Lubbock, Texas, the other day, and he said all the people in Lubbock think things are going just great." In this Texan's administration, Lubbock has replaced Peoria (a victim in the 1980s of the decline in farm prices and heavy manufacturing) as the metaphor for Middle America, and not altogether unfittingly. It is, like the country, ancestrally Democratic, and was happy to be the beneficiary of federal largesse for years, especially when its congressman, George Mahon, was chairman of the House Appropriations Committee (1964–79). But by the 1950s Lubbock was voting Republican in national elections and by 1970, in state contests as well.

The 19th Congressional District of Texas includes Lubbock and most of the agricultural counties around it, just east of the New Mexican border. It also stretches north to Deaf Smith County, where the government wanted to dispose of nuclear waste in a cavern 2,600 feet deep in the Palo Duro Basin, and south to the Permian Basin, where oil and gas reserves were first developed in the 1950s. The 19th includes Odessa, the more roughneck of the two main Permian Basin towns, which houses many of the technically skilled men who do the gritty, sweaty work of making the oil rigs work and getting the oil to the surface; George Bush lived here briefly in 1948 and 1949, when it emerged from World War II with just 3,000 people but was suddenly bursting with oil rig workers.

The 19th District, despite its Republican leanings, did not elect a Republican congressman until 1984; Mahon retired in 1978, and his successor was Kent Hance, then a Democrat from Lubbock, who beat George W. Bush, the President's oldest son, who was then an oilman from Midland, 53%–47%. (Both men in early 1989 were thinking about running for governor in 1990 as Republicans.) When Hance ran for the Senate in 1984, the 19th had another riproaring race, and the winner of a tough primary, runoff and general election was Republican Larry Combest. Combest worked on farm issues for seven years on Senator John Tower's staff, and specializes in them in the House (though professionally he was an electronics distributor rather than a farmer). There he started off with a good knowledge of farm programs and opposed Reagan Administration policy on occasion; otherwise he voted a pretty straight conservative line. In early 1989, he played an apparently unintentional role in defeating Tower's nomination to be Secretary of Defense by testifying privately that Tower was frequently incapacitated by alcohol in the 1970s; Combest's point was that he had improved and was not drinking so heavily in the 1980s, but Sam Nunn and other Democrats took this as a sign that Tower was unfit for the office.

In 1986, despite opposition from a veteran of the 1970s farmers' tractorcade to Washington, queasiness about the proposed nuclear dump in Deaf Smith County, and the general nationwide Democratic trend, Combest increased his percentage from 58% to 62%; in 1988, he raised it to 68%, with 70% in Lubbock.

The People: Est. Pop. 1986: 562,500, up 6.6% 1980–86; Pop. 1980: 527,805, up 15.2% 1970–80. Households (1980): 77% family, 45% with children, 68% married couples; 34.7% housing units rented; median monthly rent: $191; median house value: $33,200. Voting age pop. (1980): 360,942; 20% Spanish origin, 5% Black.

1988 Presidential Vote:

Bush (R)	110,148	(67%)
Dukakis (D)	54,551	(33%)

Rep. Larry Combest (R)

Elected 1984; b. Mar. 20, 1945, Memphis; home, Lubbock; W. TX St. U., B.B.A. 1969; United Methodist; married (Sharon).

Career: Farmer; teacher, 1970–71; Dir., U.S. Agric. Stabilization and Conserv. Svc., Graham, TX, 1971; Aide to U.S. Sen. John Tower, 1971–78; Founder and Pres., Combest Distributing Co., 1978–1985.

Offices: 1527 LHOB 20515, 202-225-4005. Also 613 Fed. Bldg., 1205 Texas Ave., Lubbock 79401, 806-763-1611; and 419 W. 4th St., Rm. 601, Odessa 79761, 915-337-1669.

Committees: *Agriculture* (12th of 18 R). Subcommittees: Conservation, Credit, and Rural Development; Cotton, Rice, and Sugar; Tobacco and Peanuts. *District of Columbia* (3d of 4 R). Subcommittees: Fiscal Affairs and Health; Government Operations and Metropolitan Affairs (Ranking Member). *Small Business* (9th of 17 R). Subcommittees: Environment and Labor; SBA, the General Economy and Minority Enterprise Development. *Select Committee on Intelligence* (4th of 7 R). Subcommittees: Oversight and Investigations; Program and Budget Authorization.

Group Ratings

	ADA	ACLU	COPE	CFA	LCV	ACU	NTLC	NSI	COC	CEI
1988	0	4	13	18	25	92	83	100	93	73
1987	0	—	11	7	—	89	—	—	93	73

National Journal Ratings

	1988 LIB — 1988 CONS		1987 LIB — 1987 CONS	
Economic	21% —	77%	11% —	83%
Social	0% —	95%	10% —	85%
Foreign	0% —	84%	0% —	80%

Key Votes

1) Homeless $	FOR	5) Ban Drug Test	FOR	9) SDI Research	—
2) Gephardt Amdt	AGN	6) Drug Death Pen	FOR	10) Ban Chem Weaps	AGN
3) Deficit Reduc	AGN	7) Handgun Sales	FOR	11) Aid to Contras	FOR
4) Kill Plnt Clsng Notice	FOR	8) Ban D.C. Abort $	FOR	12) Nuclear Testing	AGN

Election Results

1988 general	Larry Combest (R)...................	113,068	(68%)	($244,821)
	Gerald McCathern (D)................	53,932	(32%)	($44,082)
1988 primary	Larry Combest (R), unopposed			
1986 general	Larry Combest (R)...................	68,695	(62%)	($317,265)
	Gerald McCathern (D)................	42,129	(38%)	($112,732)

TWENTIETH DISTRICT

San Antonio sits at the frontier: not on the banks of the Rio Grande, but on that invisible line separating territory that is on the one side mostly Hispanic and on the other mostly Anglo. It has been at the frontier for a long time: San Antonio was the most important town in Texas when it was part of Mexico, and it was here that Santa Ana and his troops wiped out Davy Crockett, Jim Bowie and 184 others at the Alamo in 1836. (Crockett was a Tennessee congressman from 1827–31 and 1833–35; if he had not lost his bid for reelection in 1835, he never would have left Tennessee for Texas.) Today, San Antonio is Texas's third largest city, with more than 900,000 people and a metropolitan population over one million. That's only one-third the size of metropolitan Dallas-Fort Worth or Houston, but San Antonio in the 1980s has been a boom town in its own right. The local economy is based not on oil but on government: this is one of America's prime military towns, with Kelly Air Force Base, Fort Sam Houston, Brooke Army Medical Center and two other Air Force bases, with tens of thousands of military personnel and employees. Behind them as a local employer is the medical complex centered on the Health Science Center. In the 1980s, Mayor Henry Cisneros tried to build on that base by linking San Antonio with Austin, 70 miles north, and promoting them together as high-tech centers; at the same time San Antonio has the advantages of the low wages of a border city.

It also has the advantage of having its own special atmosphere. A block from the Alamo the Riverwalk along the little San Antonio River is lined with overhanging trees and with pleasant shops and restaurants below street traffic. Nearby is the HemisFair, preserved from the 1968 World's Fair here. San Antonio has ancient buildings from its Spanish days and old neighborhoods redolent of the Texas Germans who were its chief Anglo citizens for many years. On the west side, beginning with the bare-tabled Mexican restaurants in the market area, San Antonio is a Mexican-American city with an Hispanic majority. There is all the potential here for angry clashes between Hispanics and Anglos, and in partisan elections they vote quite differently.

Yet the level of animosity between the two groups seems low, the range of opportunities open now to Hispanics seems great, and such differences as do exist do not seem to end up as zero-sum games in which one side or the other (or both) must lose. For that some credit should go to political leaders, most notably Henry B. Gonzalez, congressman from the 20th District of Texas since 1961, and Henry Cisneros, mayor of San Antonio from 1981 to 1989. Cisneros has attracted the greater attention, as a Texas A&M and Harvard educated innovator who has stimulated economic development and started such projects as the Westover Hills development, where Pope John Paul II appeared in 1987, and Sea World that opened in 1988. He served on the Kissinger Commission on Central America in 1983 and was on the short list of possible Democratic vice-presidential candidates in 1984. But in 1987, Cisneros announced his retirement from politics after the birth of a son with serious health problems, and in 1988, it was revealed that Cisneros was having an affair with a rich Anglo woman. Still, even as he was leaving office, he remained widely popular and admired for his public record and for his demonstration that a politician proud of his Mexican-American heritage could operate successfully in mainstream politics and advance policies that would gain widespread support.

In many ways, Gonzalez has been doing that too, sometimes in a less tactful way, but over a longer period of time and beginning when there were much greater obstacles. The 20th District that he represents today, thanks to the equal-population standard, includes only the central part of San Antonio, leaving the mostly Anglo northern fringes and suburbs as part of the 21st District and the southern fringes and suburbs on three sides as part of the 23d; more than 60% of the 20th District's residents in 1980 were Mexican-American. But when Gonzalez first ran for Congress in 1961, the 20th was all of Bexar County, including the then less heavily populated but nonetheless conservative and rather anti-Mexican-American Anglo north side. It is hard to summon back now the prejudice against Mexican-Americans that existed in Texas then, or to imagine how it affected Gonzalez, who began serving on the San Antonio Council in 1953 and was elected to the Texas Senate in 1956—especially when he had the nerve to run for governor in 1958 and in the special election (against John Tower and Jim Wright, among others) for the Senate in 1961. Gonzalez ran poorly in those races, but later in 1961, when Congressman Paul Kilday, part of a long-successful San Antonio machine, was appointed to a federal judgeship, he got into the race for Congress—and won.

In his early days in Congress, Gonzalez was the patron saint of Texas liberalism, as he compiled a record of support for the national administration and for civil rights. Later, in the late 1960s and early 1970s, he alienated some liberals because he did not share their scorn for American foreign policy and heartily disagreed with the efforts of a few Hispanics to set up a separate La Raza Unida party. Gonzalez's stubbornness—or adherence to principle—seems vindicated now; his refusal to campaign on ethnic appeals and insistence that Mexican-Americans seek opportunity within the general framework of American society—assimilation rather than polarization—is now clearly the wave of the future.

Over the years Gonzalez developed a reputation of being prickly and quick to take offense, though he can argue persuasively that his judgment has been vindicated over time. He made his biggest headlines when he resigned as chairman of the House committee investigating the Kennedy and King assassinations, because he disagreed with the approach of the lead investigator, who himself was later discharged. He has had his successes: the poll tax, which he opposed early, is long gone, and several housing programs which he backed early were passed. But he also has a temper. In 1963, he took a swing at Texas Republican Congressman Ed Foreman who accused him of being a Communist; in 1986 he punched a 40-year-old man in a San Antonio restaurant for the same offense—one which must particularly rankle a man who has served his country loyally for many years. In 1983 and 1987, he called for the impeachment of President Reagan because of Grenada and Iran-contra respectively.

In 1989 Gonzalez became chairman of the Banking, Finance and Urban Affairs Committee, thanks to the defeat of Fernand St Germain in 1988. At first there was some nervous talk among Democrats about the prospect of his chairmanship, particularly since the committee was confronted with the vast savings and loan crisis and Gonzalez has spent most of his efforts on the committee on housing rather than banking issues (though he did a workmanlike job of chairing a subcommittee on international banking agencies); on banking he simply denounced the big banks and high interest rates in old-fashioned populist language. His legislative output even on housing was not great in the 1980s, primarily because of the adamant opposition of the Reagan Administration to new subsidy and public housing programs (though he did push through a bill lowering some mortgage interest rates and continues to support generous federal housing programs). But as time went on, Gonzalez began to seem a better choice. He clearly was utterly independent of the savings and loan lobby (and of the Texas S&Ls) in contrast to St Germain. He is independent, as well, of the lobbies of the big banks, the securities industry, the investment bankers—who have been lobbying furiously on banking issues. He is far less autocratic than St Germain and scrupulous about letting other committee members have their chance to speak and be heard. Even his detractors concede that his intellectual abilities are high. Much of the savings and loan crisis can be traced to laws that were pushed through to the benefit of sharp operators and crooks. No such law would ever be allowed through knowingly by Henry Gonzalez.

Gonzalez has become something of a civic institution in San Antonio and has no trouble winning reelection.

The People: Est. Pop. 1986: 546,100, up 3.8% 1980–86; Pop. 1980: 526,333, dn. 5.8% 1970–80. Households (1980): 75% family, 45% with children, 56% married couples; 42.5% housing units rented; median monthly rent: $142; median house value: $23,500. Voting age pop. (1980): 358,798; 56% Spanish origin, 9% Black, 1% Asian origin.

1988 Presidential Vote:

Dukakis (D)......................	92,584	(67%)
Bush (R)	44,444	(32%)

Rep. Henry B. Gonzalez (D)

Elected 1961; b. May 3, 1916, San Antonio; home, San Antonio; San Antonio Col., U. of TX, St. Mary's U., LL.B. 1943; Roman Catholic; married (Bertha).

Career: Army, Navy Intelligence, WWII; Bexar Cnty. Chf. Probation Officer, 1946; Dpty. Dir., San Antonio Housing Authority, 1950–51; Mbr., San Antonio City Cncl., 1953–56, San Antonio Mayor Pro Tem, 1955–56; TX Senate, 1956–61.

Offices: 2413 RHOB 20515, 202-225-3236. Also B-124 Fed. Bldg., 727 E. Durango St., San Antonio 78206, 512-229-6195.

Committees: *Banking, Finance and Urban Affairs* (Chairman of 31 D). Subcommittees: Consumer Affairs and Coinage; Domestic Monetary Policy; Financial Institutions Supervision, Regulation and Insurance.

Group Ratings

	ADA	ACLU	COPE	CFA	LCV	ACU	NTLC	NSI	COC	CEI
1988	100	96	90	82	88	0	10	0	15	7
1987	96	—	90	86	—	9	—	—	7	9

National Journal Ratings

	1988 LIB — 1988 CONS			1987 LIB — 1987 CONS		
Economic	87%	—	8%	68%	—	27%
Social	86%	—	0%	73%	—	22%
Foreign	84%	—	0%	81%	—	0%

Key Votes

1) Homeless $	AGN	5) Ban Drug Test	AGN	9) SDI Research	AGN
2) Gephardt Amdt	AGN	6) Drug Death Pen	AGN	10) Ban Chem Weaps	FOR
3) Deficit Reduc	FOR	7) Handgun Sales	AGN	11) Aid to Contras	AGN
4) Kill Plnt Clsng Notice	AGN	8) Ban D.C. Abort $	AGN	12) Nuclear Testing	FOR

Election Results

1988 general	Henry B. Gonzalez (D)...............	94,527	(71%)	($174,470)
	Lee Travino (R).....................	36,801	(28%)	($58,217)
1988 primary	Henry B. Gonzalez (D), unopposed			
1986 general	Henry B. Gonzalez (D)...............	55,363	(100%)	($133,055)

TWENTY-FIRST DISTRICT

Slightly larger than Ohio, with a single county that is larger than Connecticut, 500 miles from end to end, the 21st Congressional District is a Texas-sized chunk of the landscape, geographically the largest district in the state. It includes most of Texas's sheep and goat ranching country and 200 miles of its border with Mexico. Demographically, it is a series of modern urban settlements across ranges of arid hills and miles of rugged desert. It begins in the Anglo neighborhoods on the north side of San Antonio and goes all the way to the Big Bend territory, where 7,000-foot peaks tower up over stony desert where the Rio Grande in fact makes a big bend. About half the people live in and around San Antonio: the 21st has the north side, where few Mexican-Americans and most of the city's affluent Anglos live. Voters here in Bexar County (pronounced as a drawn-out bear) cast 41% of the district's votes in 1988. Affluent Anglos in San Antonio have voted heavily Republican since 1961, when Representative Henry Gonzalez was elected to replace Paul Kilday, the conservative Democrat whose machine controlled city politics. Then Bexar was Democratic; now the impact of the north side is great enough that the county has gone Republican in the last three presidential races and has even elected a Republican sheriff in 1984.

Just north and west of San Antonio you get into the Texas hill country, much of it first settled by refugees from the failed German revolutions of 1848. They made good livings, even off barren soil, but they disliked slavery, instinctively favored the Union, and when Texas became one of the most heavily Democratic states in the Union after the Civil War they insisted on voting Republican in every election. They still do. The hill country around Fredericksburg and Kerrville got electricity back in the 1930s thanks to Lyndon Johnson, whose LBJ Ranch is just at the edge of German country; the hill country now is the site of condominium developments for prosperous Texans who want a second home in a pleasant, quiet environment.

Beyond the hill country is flat plateau: ranch lands, oil fields, blank desert. Actually few people live out on the land, and their cities are distinctive. One is Midland, the headquarters of the people who run the Permian Basin, the rich oil and gas terrain where George Bush made his fortune in the 1950s and which, until the crash in oil prices, gave Midland one of the highest income levels in the country. Midland remains one of the most Republican cities in America. More typical is San Angelo, a center of sheep and cattle ranching as well as oil, one of the nation's biggest producers of mohair, which is ancestrally Democratic, but in current practice Republican.

The 21st District has been Republican in presidential elections for nearly 40 years and Republican in House elections for a dozen. The current congressman, Lamar Smith, won the seat in 1986 when his predecessor, Tom Loeffler, gave up seats on three plum committees (Energy and Commerce, Appropriations, Budget) and the post of chief deputy whip to run for governor; he got only 22% of the vote, a distant second behind 69-year-old William Clements, but remains active in Texas and national politics. Smith, who had served both in the legislature and on the Bexar County Commission, and who is from an old San Antonio and south Texas ranching family, had to win a tough primary race here, beating two other San Antonio-based candidates 31%–25%–20%. In the runoff, in which Senator Phil Gramm took the unusual step of endorsing him over a religious right conservative, he won 54%–46%. Smith had serious opposition in the general election as well, from Pete Snelson, an 18-year state senator from Midland. The Democrat did win a solid margin west of the German counties. But Smith won 67% in the German counties and 74% in Bexar County for a convincing 61% victory. He had minimal opposition in 1988 and seems to have a safe seat for as long as he wants it.

Smith seems to have been unusually busy in the House for a junior Republican. He pushed to passage a bill adding 100,000 acres to the Big Bend National Park in the western part of the district—one of the few freshmen to see his bill passed into law. He took part in the drug bill negotiations and worked to protect funding for local drug task forces. He pushed successfully for $18 million for gas and oil recovery research. He was one of the chief Republicans pushing to apply various ethics restrictions to Members of Congress. In 1989, he became ranking Republican on the subcommittee handling immigration, just as the Democrats dumped chairman Romano Mazzoli for Bruce Morrison of Connecticut.

The People: Est. Pop. 1986: 661,900, up 25.6% 1980–86; Pop. 1980: 526,846, up 38.0% 1970–80. Households (1980): 74% family, 39% with children, 65% married couples; 31.1% housing units rented; median monthly rent: $221; median house value: $47,700. Voting age pop. (1980): 381,130; 16% Spanish origin, 3% Black, 1% Asian origin.

1988 Presidential Vote:

Bush (R)	192,335	(70%)
Dukakis (D)	78,961	(29%)

Rep. Lamar S. Smith (R)

Elected 1986; b. Nov. 1, 1947, San Antonio; home, San Antonio; Yale U., B.A., 1969, Southern Methodist U., J.D., 1975; Christian Scientist; married (Jane).

Career: Small Bus. Admin. official, 1969–70; Bus. and Fin. reporter, *Christian Science Monitor*, 1971–72; Practicing atty., 1975–76; TX House of Reps., 1981–82; Bexar Cnty. Commissioner, 1982–85.

Offices: 422 CHOB 20515, 202-225-4236. Also 10010 San Pedro, Ste. 530, San Antonio 78216, 512-229-5880; 201 W. Wall St., Ste. 104, Midland 79701, 915-687-5232; 1006 Junction Hwy., Kerrville 78028, 512-895-1414; and 33 E. Twohig, Ste. 302, San Angelo 76903, 915-653-3971.

Committees: *Judiciary* (11th of 14 R). Subcommittees: Administrative Law and Governmental Relations; Crime; Immigration, Refugees, and International Law (Ranking Member). *Science, Space and Technology* (13th of 19 R). Subcommittees: Energy Research and Development; Natural Resources, Agriculture Research and Environment; Space Science and Applications. *Select Committee on Children, Youth, and Families* (9th of 12 R).

Group Ratings

	ADA	ACLU	COPE	CFA	LCV	ACU	NTLC	NSI	COC	CEI
1988	5	9	14	27	19	100	78	100	92	65
1987	4	—	6	21	—	96	—	—	93	75

National Journal Ratings

	1988 LIB — 1988 CONS		1987 LIB — 1987 CONS	
Economic	18% —	81%	0% —	89%
Social	0% —	95%	0% —	90%
Foreign	0% —	84%	0% —	80%

Key Votes

1) Homeless $	FOR	5) Ban Drug Test	FOR	9) SDI Research	FOR
2) Gephardt Amdt	AGN	6) Drug Death Pen	FOR	10) Ban Chem Weaps	AGN
3) Deficit Reduc	AGN	7) Handgun Sales	FOR	11) Aid to Contras	FOR
4) Kill Plnt Clsng Notice	—	8) Ban D.C. Abort $	FOR	12) Nuclear Testing	AGN

Election Results

1988 general	Lamar Smith (R)	203,989	(93%)	($418,989)
	James A. Robinson (Lib.)..............	14,801	(7%)	
1988 primary	Lamar Smith (R), unopposed			
1986 general	Lamar Smith (R)	100,346	(61%)	($1,062,154)
	Pete Snelson (D).....................	63,779	(39%)	($345,117)

TWENTY-SECOND DISTRICT

Just three or four miles from downtown Houston, the Gulf plains began 50 years ago: "flat, open prairies unbroken except for the outline of timber on the horizon, and occasional clumps of live oaks which make small green islands called mottes in Texas. Farming is diversified, although cotton is the largest crop. Beef cattle are raised, and dairy farms are frequent. Well-wooded sections are found along the river bottoms, and in the early spring, when rainfall is abundant, bluebonnets cover the prairies." That was the scene where today you will find, at Post Oak and Westheimer, the glitzy shopping centers that are the Fifth Avenue and 57th Street of the oil kingdom. Along the Southwest Freeway, 30 and 60-story high-rises tower over the traffic jams, and out into Fort Bend and Brazoria counties which are now choked with new subdivisions and office clusters, fields were once planted in the cotton that made the fortunes of the great Houston cotton traders and political operators Jesse Jones and Will Clayton, with the sun beating down mercilessly, the humidity fierce, the ground thick with bugs.

On this unforgiving environment was built the urban civilization that includes what is now the 22d Congressional District of Texas. It includes monuments of greater Houston's development: the high-rises airily flanking the Southwest Freeway near the Galleria, the Sharpstown shopping center and subdivision put up by a local wheeler-dealer whose financial collapse and political dealings brought down a governor in 1972, the newly-sprouted suburban towns of Sugar Land and Missouri City in Fort Bend County, the steamy Brazosport oil shipping complex around Freeport and Lake Jackson on the Gulf of Mexico. Air-conditioning—in malls, cars and homes—has made this civilization possible; insecticides have helped; the automobile ties it together (if the traffic would ever clear up). There were fewer than 100,000 people as World War II ended, in what now is the 22d District, less than 200,000 in 1960; as the Sharpstown scandal was breaking, there were 300,000 and, by the Census's 1986 estimate, there were 632,000.

This is a heavily Republican district: you will be hard put to find many national Democrats among the people who have come from other parts of Houston and Texas, the South and North and even foreign countries, and live now in the new and affluent subdivisions of Houston or Sugar Land or in the more widely-spaced subdivisions scattered farther out in Fort Bend and Brazoria; and even in local elections the historic Democratic leanings of the rural areas are usually overwhelmed by the strong Republican allegiance of the newcomers. In the 1970s, the 22d, then mostly in Houston and with more black neighborhoods, had a series of turbulent elections, in large part because of Republican Congressman Ron Paul, a libertarian so pure that he was an isolationist abroad and Congress's foremost champion of the gold standard. But Paul ran for the Senate in 1984, coming in second behind Phil Gramm in the Republican primary, and for President as the Libertarian party candidate in 1988, running a very distant third behind George Bush and Michael Dukakis; the current congressman, Republican Tom DeLay, fits the preferences of the newcomer majority here more easily.

Even so, DeLay has an interesting background. He was born in the border town of Laredo and spent much of his childhood in Venezuela, where his father drilled oil wells. In Sugar Land, the son built a pest control business—environmentalists might not like that, but in Houston people would rather control the bugs than preserve the environment—and was elected to the state legislature in 1978, the first Republican from Fort Bend County. When Paul retired in 1984, DeLay easily won the Republican primary and the general election: this is a safe seat for him. DeLay's voting record is solidly conservative on practically every issue, but he seems also to have traditional political instincts. In his first term he was the freshman representative on the Republican Committee on Committees, and in his second term he got a seat on the Appropriations Committee. He defends the indemnification of chemical companies when pesticides are banned. He is proud of helping Houston get $64 million to build a busway on the Southwest Freeway, $50 million for Houston Metro Rail, Rice University got $1.6 million to study how to improve mass transit, and Freeport, $15 million for harbor development and designation as a foreign trade zone. In 1989, DeLay served as campaign manager for Ed Madigan's unsuccessful run for minority whip.

The People: Est. Pop. 1986: 632,700, up 20.1% 1980–86; Pop. 1980: 526,602, up 76.9% 1970–80. Households (1980): 67% family, 38% with children, 57% married couples; 46.8% housing units rented; median monthly rent: $271; median house value: $64,200. Voting age pop. (1980): 381,492; 12% Spanish origin, 9% Black, 3% Asian origin.

1988 Presidential Vote:

Bush (R)	....	120,066	(62%)
Dukakis (D).	....	70,739	(37%)

Rep. Tom DeLay (R)

Elected 1984; b. Apr. 8, 1947, Laredo; home, Sugar Land; U. of Houston, B.S. 1970; Baptist; married (Christine).

Career: Owner, Albo Pest Control; TX House of Reps., 1979–85.

Offices: 308 CHOB 20515, 202-225-5951. Also 9000 S.W. Freeway, Ste. 205, Houston, 77074, 713-270-4000; and 500 N. Shenango, Ste. 310, Angleton 77515, 409-849-4446.

Committees: *Appropriations* (20th of 22 R). Subcommittees: Military Construction; Transportation.

Group Ratings

	ADA	ACLU	COPE	CFA	LCV	ACU	NTLC	NSI	COC	CEI
1988	0	5	2	18	6	100	77	100	92	90
1987	0	—	2	7	—	100	—	—	93	86

National Journal Ratings

	1988 LIB — 1988 CONS			1987 LIB — 1987 CONS		
Economic	0%	—	93%	0%	—	89%
Social	9%	—	89%	0%	—	90%
Foreign	0%	—	84%	0%	—	80%

Key Votes

1) Homeless $	FOR	5) Ban Drug Test	FOR	9) SDI Research	FOR
2) Gephardt Amdt	AGN	6) Drug Death Pen	FOR	10) Ban Chem Weaps	AGN
3) Deficit Reduc	AGN	7) Handgun Sales	FOR	11) Aid to Contras	FOR
4) Kill Plnt Clsng Notice	FOR	8) Ban D.C. Abort $	FOR	12) Nuclear Testing	AGN

Election Results

1988 general	Thomas D. (Tom) DeLay (R)	125,733	(67%)	($361,255)
	Wayne Walker (D)	58,471	(31%)	($109,004)
1988 primary	Thomas D. (Tom) DeLay (R), unopposed			
1986 general	Thomas D. (Tom) DeLay (R)	76,459	(72%)	($294,850)
	Susan Director (D)	30,079	(28%)	

TWENTY-THIRD DISTRICT

Texas is border country from San Antonio south: a part of the United States which is culturally neither entirely Anglo nor entirely Mexican, but a mixture—a volatile and constantly changing mixture—of the two. Historically the picture here has been of desert-like rural counties where big landowners rule the lives—and cast the votes—of their Mexican-American field hands. But these small counties have no economic future and few resources, as the "brown power" militants found out when they took over local government. The real economic growth comes in cities, through the growth of metropolises like San Antonio and Austin and through the special advantages of the towns on the land border with the greatest economic disparities in the world. Here the exchange rate, labor costs and flow of immigration change constantly. Laredo, down on the border, had chain stores with some of the highest sales in the U.S. before the peso devaluation of 1982; by 1986, most were closed and others were quiet. But those developments also made U.S. wages all the more attractive to residents of Mexico, stimulating twin-plant development here and there.

The 23d Congressional District of Texas extends from the south side of San Antonio south to Laredo and west to Eagle Pass, both on the Rio Grande. Most of the land area is in the border counties, which in most elections are among the most heavily Democratic counties in the nation. But some 64% of the votes are in San Antonio and surrounding Bexar County (pronounced with something like the soft Spanish X, which sounds like an H to English-speakers). The district includes the southern fringes of San Antonio, working-class neighborhoods near big military bases where nearly half the residents are Mexican-Americans. But the district also includes suburban territory east, west and north of the city. This takes in some of the most affluent precincts in Bexar County, where, historically, mistrust of Mexicans and Democrats is high.

The congressman from the 23d grew up in a small Mexican-American town, but he has made his political career in San Antonio. He is Albert Bustamante, who served a few years on Representative Henry B. Gonzalez's San Antonio staff and then proceeded to make his political fortune. He was elected to the Bexar County Commission in 1972 and was elected county judge in 1978. In 1984, he decided to run for Congress in the 23d, and challenged the incumbent, Abraham Kazen, who had 18 years of seniority but little in the way of accomplishments to show for it. There was an ethnic contrast—Kazen is Lebanese-American—but a more aggressive incumbent could have held this seat, or would never have been seriously challenged. In the 23d, Bustamante won what will probably remain his crucial contest by a 59%–37% margin. This is a pretty solidly Democratic district, although George Bush carried it 50%–49%, and Bustamante should have no difficulty winning reelection.

Bustamante has a seat on the Armed Services Committee, the second south Texas Hispanic on that body; he has looked after San Antonio's military bases and after military personnel and retirees, promising that no user fee for use of military medical facilities will be imposed on them. On economic issues he is liberal and an ally of organized labor; on cultural and economic issues he is more moderate. He was a swing vote on contra aid, opposing it in 1985 and voting for it in 1986, and he supported the immigration reform bill. He has been pushing hard and early for drug interdiction funds for the border. But he has also gone farther afield, getting interested in the issue of nuclear plant safety before it got hot in 1988.

The People: Est. Pop. 1986: 669,800, up 27.2% 1980–86; Pop. 1980: 526,746, up 50.0% 1970–80. Households (1980): 84% family, 56% with children, 70% married couples; 30.2% housing units rented; median monthly rent: $163; median house value: $33,100. Voting age pop. (1980): 332,851; 51% Spanish origin, 4% Black, 1% Asian origin.

1988 Presidential Vote:	Bush (R)	94,826	(50%)
	Dukakis (D)	93,074	(49%)

Rep. Albert G. Bustamante (D)

Elected 1984; b. Apr. 8, 1935, Asherton; home, San Antonio; San Antonio Col., Sul Ross St. U., B.A. 1961; Roman Catholic; married (Rebecca).

Career: Army, 1954–56; High sch. teacher and coach, 1961–68; Aide to U.S. Rep. Henry B. Gonzalez, 1968–71; Bexar Cnty. Commissioner, 1973–78, Judge, 1979–84.

Offices: 1116 LHOB 20515, 202-225-4511. Also Fed. Bldg., 727 E. Durango St., Rm. B-146, San Antonio 78206, 512-229-6191; 1300 Matamoros St., Rm. 115, Laredo 78040, 512-724-7774; Uvalde Cnty. Cthse., Uvalde 78801, 512-278-5021; Fed. Cthse. Bldg., Rm. 103, 100 E. Broadway, Del Rio 78841, 512-774-6549; 101 E. Dimmit, W. Annex, Crystal City 78839, 512-374-5200; Dimmit Cnty. Cthse., Carrizo Springs 78834, 512-876-2323; and Maverick Cnty. Cthse., P.O. Box 995, Eagle Pass 78852, 512-773-4110.

Committees: *Armed Services* (23d of 31 D). Subcommittees: Military Personnel and Compensation; Procurement and Military Nuclear Systems. *Government Operations* (19th of 24 D). Subcommittees: Commerce, Consumer, and Monetary Affairs; Environment, Energy, and Natural Resources. *Select Committee on Hunger* (14th of 19 D).

Group Ratings

	ADA	ACLU	COPE	CFA	LCV	ACU	NTLC	NSI	COC	CEI
1988	70	81	95	82	50	8	5	40	21	11
1987	76	—	93	50	—	0	—	—	14	8

National Journal Ratings

	1988 LIB — 1988 CONS		1987 LIB — 1987 CONS	
Economic	84% —	16%	73% —	0%
Social	70% —	30%	62% —	38%
Foreign	60% —	37%	59% —	40%

Key Votes

1) Homeless $	AGN	5) Ban Drug Test	AGN	9) SDI Research	AGN
2) Gephardt Amdt	FOR	6) Drug Death Pen	FOR	10) Ban Chem Weaps	AGN
3) Deficit Reduc	FOR	7) Handgun Sales	FOR	11) Aid to Contras	AGN
4) Kill Plnt Clsng Notice	AGN	8) Ban D.C. Abort $	AGN	12) Nuclear Testing	FOR

Election Results

1988 general	Albert G. Bustamante (D)	116,423	(65%)	($187,302)
	Jerome L. (Jerry) Gonzales (R)	60,559	(34%)	($6,365)
1988 primary	Albert G. Bustamante (D), unopposed			
1986 general	Albert G. Bustamante (D)	68,131	(91%)	($199,090)
	Ken Hendrix (L)......................	7,001	(9%)	

TWENTY-FOURTH DISTRICT

Dallas is built on two sides of the Trinity River; on the southwest side, overlooking downtown across the cement-lined river bed, is Oak Cliff. This is a kind of separate Dallas, just about as old as the city, with some fine old Victorian gingerbread houses; there is more evidence here than on the other side of the river of the kind of city Dallas was before steel-and-glass skyscrapers towered over downtown and were scattered around freeway interchanges on the north side of the city. The south side of Dallas, beyond Oak Cliff, is where most of the city's black residents live and almost half of its much smaller number of Mexican-Americans. There is a feeling of apartness here that became apparent in 1988 with criticism from blacks that Dallas police use force too readily, and from police supporters who criticize blacks for condoning violent attacks on policemen.

Oak Cliff is the heart of the 24th Congressional District of Texas, the strongest national Democratic district in the Dallas-Fort Worth Metroplex. Its population was 32% black and 13% Hispanic in 1980, its income rather low; its housing prices are relatively inexpensive. It does include some suburban territory, however: the modest suburb of Grand Prairie and somewhat higher-income Irving, the home of the Dallas Cowboys' stadium. The 24th District's boundaries were the key issue in the partisan fights over Texas's redistricting; the current lines were drawn by Democrats in 1983 after a federal court intervened.

The congressman from the 24th District is Martin Frost, who started his political career by challenging an incumbent congressman and became one of the young congressmen closest to the Democratic leadership of the House. In 1974 he ran against and in 1978 finally beat conservative Democrat and former TV weathercaster Dale Milford, with the help of large majorities from blacks. His rapport with black voters helped him again in 1982, enabling him to face down black primary opposition, when it looked like the district would have a black majority, and then to beat a black Dallas councilwoman running as a Republican by a 73%–26% margin. He has been easily reelected since.

Frost's House career took off when then Majority Leader Jim Wright got him a seat on the Rules Committee in 1979, making him only the second Democratic freshman in the 20th century to get a seat on Rules. Frost has generally not disappointed the Democratic leadership, voting often but not always on the liberal side. He was disappointed, however, in his run for the chairmanship of the Budget Committee after the 1984 elections. He led the move to deny waivers of the three-term rule to Jim Jones and Leon Panetta, thus barring them from the leadership; on this he was serving not just himself, but also Tip O'Neill and Jim Wright, who mistrusted both men. But it was apparent that William Gray of Pennsylvania had the votes sewn up to be chairman, and so Frost withdrew.

On Rules, he was a close ally of Jim Wright and of the beleaguered Texas savings and loan industry. On the committee in 1986, he helped kill a non-bank banks bill that would have tightened lending and investment requirements on S&Ls, and in 1988, he helped kill a bill that would have increased FSLIC capitalization $5 billion at the expense of the S&Ls. At the time presumably Frost had no idea of the huge amount of money—estimated in 1989 at $100 billion plus—that improvident and crooked S&Ls would cost the taxpayer.

The People: Est. Pop. 1986: 626,700, up 18.9% 1980–86; Pop. 1980: 527,267, up 14.2% 1970–80. Households (1980): 77% family, 48% with children, 60% married couples; 40.9% housing units rented; median monthly rent: $217; median house value: $37,900. Voting age pop. (1980): 352,993; 29% Black, 11% Spanish origin, 1% Asian origin, 1% American Indian.

1988 Presidential Vote:

Dukakis (D)	97,357	(52%)
Bush (R)	87,616	(47%)

Rep. Martin Frost (D)

Elected 1978; b. Jan. 1, 1942, Glendale, CA; home, Dallas; U. of MO, B.A., B.J. 1964, Georgetown U., J.D. 1970; Jewish; married (Valerie).

Career: Legal commentator, KERA-TV, Dallas, 1971–72; Practicing atty., 1972–78.

Offices: 2459 RHOB 20515, 202-225-3605. Also 400 S. Zang Blvd., Ste. 1319, Dallas 75208, 214-948-3401; and 801 W. Freeway, Ste. 720 Grand Prairie 75051, 214-262-1503.

Committees: *House Administration* (12th of 13 D). Subcommittees: Elections; Libraries and Memorials; Procurement and Printing. *Rules* (4th of 9 D). Subcommittee: The Legislative Process.

Group Ratings

	ADA	ACLU	COPE	CFA	LCV	ACU	NTLC	NSI	COC	CEI
1988	70	74	79	82	44	9	4	40	23	13
1987	88	—	81	57	—	0	—	—	29	6

National Journal Ratings

	1988 LIB — 1988 CONS		1987 LIB — 1987 CONS	
Economic	87% —	8%	73% —	0%
Social	63% —	36%	60% —	39%
Foreign	55% —	44%	55% —	44%

Key Votes

1) Homeless $	AGN	5) Ban Drug Test	AGN	9) SDI Research	AGN
2) Gephardt Amdt	FOR	6) Drug Death Pen	FOR	10) Ban Chem Weaps	FOR
3) Deficit Reduc	FOR	7) Handgun Sales	—	11) Aid to Contras	AGN
4) Kill Plnt Clsng Notice	AGN	8) Ban D.C. Abort $	AGN	12) Nuclear Testing	FOR

Election Results

1988 general	Martin Frost (D)	10,841	(93%)	($438,949)
	Leo Sadovy (Lib.)	10,841	(7%)	
1988 primary	Martin Frost (D), unopposed			
1986 general	Martin Frost (D)	69,368	(67%)	($709,864)
	Bob Burk (R)	33,819	(33%)	($23,676)

TWENTY-FIFTH DISTRICT

West from the scruffy towns where the Houston Ship Channel empties out into the bay near the giant San Jacinto Battle Monument, through Pasadena where the now defunct country music honkytonk Gilley's, with its mechanical bulls used to sit on Spencer Highway, out past the black neighborhoods near Houston's (comparatively) close-in Hobby Airport, to the Astrodome: this is working-class Houston. Some of the neighborhoods here are black, some are heavily Mexican, but most are white, and the cultural tone is down home and southwestern. These areas, plus the more affluent, and in some cases Jewish, neighborhoods west of Main near Rice University and the giant Texas Medical Center—out in territory where James Baker can remember his grandfather shooting quail on his acreage—make up Texas's 25th Congressional District.

This was one of the three new Texas districts created after the 1980 Census, a political bonus to the Houston area for the demographic gains it made from the oil price rises of the 1970s, with the partisan benefit going, as the legislature intended, to the Democrats. Working-class Houston, not only in black and Mexican neighborhoods, but in white as well, votes pretty faithfully Democratic—this was a Dukakis, not a Bush, district in 1988—and if one of the effects of the new district lines was to strengthen Republican Jack Fields in the 8th District and make the 22d District safely Republican, the other was to open up the 25th to an ambitious young Democrat named Mike Andrews.

Andrews had already run for Congress once, in 1980, in the 22d District against gold bug Ron Paul (and 1988 Libertarian presidential candidate), where he won 49% of the vote after spending $750,000. But he didn't capture the 22d without a fight. He was challenged by a former Pasadena mayor in the primary who charged he was too liberal and then by a Republican in the general who said he'd be a better supporter of President Reagan; Andrews spent $647,000 and won those races with 58% and 60%. As the size of his campaign treasury suggests, Andrews knows how to raise money from Houston's downtown business community even as he was winning the primary endorsement of the 18th district's black congressman Mickey Leland.

In the House, Andrews has shown considerable political adroitness and has an impressive list of accomplishments. He first won a seat on the Science and Technology Committee, where of course he looked after the interests of the Johnson Space Center in Clear Lake City, just at the southern edge of the district. He kept NASA from transferring several thousand jobs from there to Huntsville, Alabama, and he helped to keep alive the often beleaguered space station program. In 1986, he moved to the Ways and Means Committee, a place on which he had lost the year before by one vote.

On Ways and Means he has forged a reasonable working relationship with Chairman Dan Rostenkowski despite their differing regional interests. Andrews naturally lobbies heavily for lower energy taxes and claims credit for the repeal of the windfall profit tax (which had ceased to produce any revenue, but would have been reimposed if oil prices went back up). He took a part in the welfare reform bill, successfully moving at one point to cut its cost by $500 million and pushing for mandatory withholding of child support from wages. At Rostenkowski's request, he headed a task force working against Claude Pepper's long-term health care bill, opposing it because of its huge cost, and prevailing on the floor 243–169; this was not a particularly pleasant duty. Andrews may have had a better time working successfully with Robert Mrazek of New York to preserve part of the Manassas, Virginia Battlefield from a proposed shopping center. He also found time to become co-chairman of the Sunbelt Caucus.

After fighting through two tough election seasons before he finally won the seat, Andrews seems to have a secure hold on it: he was reelected without difficulty in 1984, 1986 and 1988. Given greater Houston's robust population growth, redistricting probably doesn't pose a serious threat to him.

The People: Est. Pop. 1986: 580,500, up 10.2% 1980–86; Pop. 1980: 526,801, up 20.4% 1970–80. Households (1980): 74% family, 44% with children, 60% married couples; 41.6% housing units rented; median monthly rent: $261; median house value: $46,700. Voting age pop. (1980): 366,175; 23% Black, 12% Spanish origin, 1% Asian origin.

1988 Presidential Vote:

Dukakis (D).....................	84,886	(51%)
Bush (R)	80,566	(48%)

Rep. Michael A. (Mike) Andrews (D)

Elected 1982; b. Feb. 4, 1944, Houston; home, Houston; U. of TX, B.A. 1967, Southern Methodist U., J.D. 1970; Episcopalian; married (Ann).

Career: Law clerk, U.S. Dist. Judge, Houston, 1970–72; Asst. Dist. Atty., Harris Cnty., 1972–76; Practicing atty., 1976–82.

Offices: 322 CHOB 20515, 202-225-7508. Also 1001 E. Southmore, Ste. 810, Pasadena 77503, 713-473-4334; and Fed. Bldg., 515 Rusk, Houston 77002, 713-229-2244.

Committees: *Ways and Means* (21st of 23 D). Subcommittees: Human Resources; Select Revenue Measures.

Group Ratings

	ADA	ACLU	COPE	CFA	LCV	ACU	NTLC	NSI	COC	CEI
1988	75	70	66	73	31	29	34	70	62	30
1987	58	—	62	57	—	0	—	—	47	25

National Journal Ratings

	1988 LIB — 1988 CONS		1987 LIB — 1987 CONS	
Economic	50% —	48%	60% —	39%
Social	58% —	40%	50% —	49%
Foreign	50% —	50%	46% —	53%

Key Votes

1) Homeless $	AGN	5) Ban Drug Test	AGN	9) SDI Research	AGN
2) Gephardt Amdt	FOR	6) Drug Death Pen	FOR	10) Ban Chem Weaps	AGN
3) Deficit Reduc	FOR	7) Handgun Sales	FOR	11) Aid to Contras	AGN
4) Kill Plnt Clsng Notice	AGN	8) Ban D.C. Abort $	AGN	12) Nuclear Testing	FOR

Election Results

1988 general	Michael A. (Mike) Andrews (D)	113,499	(71%)	($318,970)
	George Loeffler (R)...................	44,043	(28%)	
1988 primary	Michael A. (Mike) Andrews (D), unopposed			
1986 general	Michael A. (Mike) Andrews (D)	67,435	(100%)	($133,817)

TWENTY-SIXTH DISTRICT

It is almost invisible as you drive the freeways amidst construction cranes and newly built offices, shopping centers and apartment complexes, but it was one of the major geographical barriers in American history—the Balcones Escarpment, the rim of higher west Texas land that passes between Dallas and Fort Worth and extends southwest to Waco and Austin. East of the escarpment the land is low and green, often forested and sometimes swampy; west it is high and brown, with little water and few trees. This is the boundary between East and West, the reason why the first railroads here stopped at Dallas. It is still crucial territory today, the site, just west of the huge Dallas-Fort Worth Regional Airport, of the fastest population growth in the country in the 1980s.

This growth is all the more extraordinary because it has not been generated by the oil business; more important in this area have been defense industries and DFW Airport and a certain entrepreneurial drive. They have come together in Arlington, southwest of the Airport, which thirty years ago was almost entirely vacant land: rolling hills with scrubby vegetation, and long views from the escarpment over the plains to the skyscrapers of Fort Worth and Dallas. Now it is a city of more than 250,000 people, and not just a bedroom suburb of Fort Worth: it is the home of the Texas Rangers, of Six Flags Over Texas and of a branch of the University of Texas. Arlington is full of the people whose talents and skills have made the Dallas-Fort Worth Metroplex a ranking center of high tech and defense industries; it is progressive, with clean new streets and commodious public services; it seems safe and secure against the urban ills that afflict so many neighborhoods in so many of America's other major metropolitan areas. In national politics, Arlington is heavily Republican, receptive to the message of free enterprise and traditional moral values. It seems difficult, in this pleasant, hard-working America, to under-stand that there are other parts of the country (and even a few whole states) which disagree.

Arlington forms almost half of Texas's 26th Congressional District, a new seat created after the 1980 Census and made up of incipient or quasi-Arlingtons to the north, including several suburbs of north Dallas and going up through formerly rural territory and the county seat of Denton almost to the Red River. Its first congressman, fittingly, was former Arlington mayor of 26 years Tom Vandergriff, who ran as a conservative Democrat. But even with his local fame and in a Democratic year, it took him $700,000 of his own money to win a 344-vote victory in 1982; and it is not too surprising that he lost by 6,000 votes in the Republican year of 1984.

The current congressman, Dick Armey, has made a surprisingly strong impression on public policy in his few years in Washington. Like Senator Phil Gramm, he was an economics professor at a Texas public university who believed fervently in private free markets; unlike Gramm, he seems not to have been always ambitious for political office, but ran in 1984 only after his interest was piqued by watching House sessions on C-SPAN. Even at North Texas State in Denton, he was the odd man out as a free market advocate in a Keynesian department; in the House he served on the liberal-dominated Education and Labor and Government Operations Committees. He spent his first years in the House as a "budget commando," staying on the floor and offering budget-cutting amendments to almost all spending bills, a few of which actually passed; to save money, he slept the nights he was in Washington in the House gym and, when he was forced to stop that, on his office couch.

Yet unlike some of his conservative allies Armey, a cheerful man originally from North Dakota, seems to have genuine political skills. He can analyze not only issues but colleagues, figuring out what formulation of his principles he can sell to them. He has championed causes which have gone farther than conventional wisdom at first expected, such as selling public housing to tenants, privatization of government operations like Amtrak's Northeast Corridor and the sale of government loan assets, and has opposed parental leave bills as "yuppie welfare."

He won a seat on the Budget Committee in 1987 and supported the first bipartisan budget resolution in many years.

But his greatest achievement was the 1988 military base closing bill. In 1987 Armey pursued the well-trodden route of reformers of various ideologies by proposing an apolitical base closing commission. But Congress, as well as former Defense Secretary Caspar Weinberger, were not ready to delegate power in this way, and Armey's plan was narrowly defeated in 1987. In 1988 he came back again. After resolving disputes over the size and makeup of the commission—its 12-member composition was eventually agreed upon by senior members of the House and Senate Armed Services Committees and the Pentagon—Armey's bill passed the House 223–186, with the co-sponsorship not of some other bomb-thrower, but of Armed Services chairman Les Aspin. The bill's success lay in the fact that the commission's list of recommended closings had to be approved or vetoed by the Congress all at once, with no changes or suggestions, with any congressional actions vetoable by the President. The commission did draw up the list and Congress didn't veto it, producing the first base closings since 1977, and an advertised savings of nearly $700 million a year.

This may not be the last of Armey's achievements. He seems to suit this fast-growing district even better every two years, his ebullience matching its mood and his faith in market economics reflecting its settled conviction based on observations of the bounteous world on either side of the Escarpment. Armey won reelection in 1986 and 1988 by better than 2 to 1 margins, and with Arlington about to eclipse nearby Fort Worth in number of voters he seems politically safe no matter what happens in redistricting.

The People: Est. Pop. 1986: 746,000, up 41.7% 1980–86; Pop. 1980: 526,598, up 62.2% 1970–80. Households (1980): 76% family, 45% with children, 67% married couples; 33.7% housing units rented; median monthly rent: $251; median house value: $57,400. Voting age pop. (1980): 372,244; 4% Spanish origin, 3% Black, 1% Asian origin.

1988 Presidential Vote:
Bush (R)	203,541	(68%)
Dukakis (D)	92,508	(31%)

Rep. Richard K. (Dick) Armey (R)

Elected 1984; b. July 7, 1940, Cando, ND; home, Cooper Canyon; Jamestown Col., B.A. 1963, U. of ND, M.A. 1964, U. of OK, Ph.D. 1969; Presbyterian; married (Susan).

Career: Prof., W. TX St. U., 1967–68, Austin Col., 1968–72, N. TX St. U., 1972–77; Chmn., Dept. of Economics, N. TX St. U., 1977–83.

Offices: 130 CHOB 20515, 202-225-7772. Also 1301 S. Bowen Rd., Ste. 422, Arlington 76013, 817-461-2555; and 250 S. Stemmons, Ste. 210, Lewisville 75067, 214-221-4527.

Committees: *Budget* (7th of 14 R). Task Forces: Budget Process, Reconciliation and Enforcement; Economic Policy, Projections and Revenues; Urgent Fiscal Issues. *Education and Labor* (8th of 13 R). Subcommittees: Labor-Management Relations; Labor Standards.

Group Ratings

	ADA	ACLU	COPE	CFA	LCV	ACU	NTLC	NSI	COC	CEI
1988	0	4	2	18	19	100	89	100	100	90
1987	0	—	2	14	—	96	—	—	100	95

National Journal Ratings

	1988 LIB — 1988 CONS		1987 LIB — 1987 CONS	
Economic	7% —	91%	0% —	89%
Social	0% —	95%	0% —	90%
Foreign	0% —	84%	0% —	80%

Key Votes

1) Homeless $	FOR	5) Ban Drug Test	FOR	9) SDI Research	FOR
2) Gephardt Amdt	AGN	6) Drug Death Pen	FOR	10) Ban Chem Weaps	AGN
3) Deficit Reduc	AGN	7) Handgun Sales	FOR	11) Aid to Contras	FOR
4) Kill Plnt Clsng Notice	FOR	8) Ban D.C. Abort $	FOR	12) Nuclear Testing	AGN

Election Results

1988 general	Richard K. (Dick) Armey (R)	194,944	(69%)	($314,903)
	Jo Ann Reyes (D)	86,490	(31%)	($189,780)
1988 primary	Richard K. (Dick) Armey (R), unopposed			
1986 general	Richard K. (Dick) Armey (R)	101,735	(68%)	($541,542)
	George Richardson (D)................	47,651	(32%)	($133,785)

TWENTY-SEVENTH DISTRICT

Along the Gulf of Mexico from the port and industrial city of Corpus Christi down past the King Ranch and along Padre Island to the Mexican border is the 27th Congressional District of Texas. This is part of south Texas between the Nueces and the Rio Grande, the land in contention in the Mexican war, which despite the U.S. victory is still inhabited mostly by people of Mexican ancestry. There is, however, plenty of variety here. Corpus Christi is an oil port, the most important one south of Houston, with big petrochemical plants and a causeway to the beach. About half its citizens are Mexican-American, but they are less segregated and set apart than was once the case. Overall, they seem to fit in with the city's blue-collar, roughneck tone. Half the 27th's people live in and around Corpus Christi.

Most of the other half live in and around Brownsville and Harlingen in the Lower Rio Grande Valley. Harlingen became a figure of fun for many when backers of Ronald Reagan's Central American policy suggested it would be the next place to be invaded. But the fun is less apparent when you're there: Harlingen is not about to be overrun by Nicaraguans, of course, but its position down on the border could be an uncomfortable one if a government hostile to the United States should come to power in Mexico. Any Mexican development—the devaluation of the peso, unemployment in the northern Mexico states, the success or failure of *maquiladora* plants—changes life on the border, and a hostile Mexico could do more to damage the quality of American life, especially here, than any other foreign development short of war.

In between these two nodes are Texan versions of dreamland. Fronting the Gulf is the sandspit of Padre Island, for most of its length a national seashore, where the hot sands meet the almost steamy waters of the summertime Gulf. At its south end, there are extensive high-rise developments, where residents can sit high in air conditioning and watch the beach shimmer in the heat. Inland are the vast grazing and oil lands of the King Ranch, long America's largest.

This is a solidly Democratic district, and the congressman, Solomon Ortiz, was chosen in the Democratic primary in 1982. There were five main candidates, and in the first primary their votes fell in the narrow range between 14% and 26%. The high figure was won by Ortiz, then sheriff of Nueces County, known as a tough law enforcer. His major opponent was former Corpus Christi legislator Joe Salem. But Ortiz out-maneuvered him for support in the Brownsville area; by making a local alliance there, he cinched the runoff. The general election was anticlimactic: the Republican candidate had been mayor of Corpus Christi some time before, but had little personal support.

Ortiz's voting record is liberal on economics, moderate on cultural and military issues—like Kika de la Garza's in the 15th. Many in Washington assume that a Mexican-American will vote on the left wing of the Democratic Party, but Mexican-American voters are vociferously patriotic and culturally traditional; and Ortiz seems to share their attitudes. He is a member of Merchant Marine and Fisheries and the Armed Services Committee, where he seems to fit in well with the generally hawkish majority. The successful legislation he has sponsored has local angles: a technical bill on determining the taxes owed by oil refineries in foreign trade zones, delaying for a year the Endangered Species requirement that shrimpers use Turtle Excluding Devices, protecting the Flower Garden coral reefs 220 miles east of Corpus Christi in the Gulf. Ortiz is reelected easily and has a safe seat.

The People: Est. Pop. 1986: 609,600, up 15.7% 1980–86; Pop. 1980: 526,988, up 23.7% 1970–80. Households (1980): 80% family, 50% with children, 66% married couples; 37.8% housing units rented; median monthly rent: $171; median house value: $31,000. Voting age pop. (1980): 341,512; 55% Spanish origin, 3% Black.

1988 Presidential Vote:

Bush (R)	76,313	(46%)
Dukakis (D).	88,458	(53%)

Rep. Solomon P. Ortiz (D)

Elected 1982; b. June 3, 1937, Robstown; home, Corpus Christi; Del Mar Col., Natl. Sheriffs' Training Inst., 1977; United Methodist; divorced.

Career: Army, 1960–62; Nueces Cnty. Constable, 1965–68, Commissioner, 1969–76, Sheriff, 1977–82.

Offices: 1524 LHOB 20515, 202-225-7742. Also 3649 Leopard, Ste. 510, Corpus Christi 78408, 512-883-5868; and 3505 Boca Chica Blvd., Ste. 438, Brownsville 78521, 512-541-1242.

Committees: *Armed Services* (20th of 31 D). Subcommittees: Military Installations and Facilities; Readiness; Seapower and Strategic and Critical Materials. *Merchant Marine and Fisheries* (15th of 26 D). Subcommittees: Coast Guard and Navigation; Fisheries and Wildlife Conservation and the Environment. *Select Committee on Narcotics Abuse and Control* (12th of 18 D).

Group Ratings

	ADA	ACLU	COPE	CFA	LCV	ACU	NTLC	NSI	COC	CEI
1988	55	38	87	55	44	26	5	70	29	14
1987	60	—	85	43	—	17	—	—	33	14

National Journal Ratings

	1988 LIB — 1988 CONS			1987 LIB — 1987 CONS		
Economic	84%	—	15%	66%	—	33%
Social	43%	—	55%	42%	—	57%
Foreign	54%	—	46%	54%	—	45%

Key Votes

1) Homeless $	AGN	5) Ban Drug Test	AGN	9) SDI Research	AGN
2) Gephardt Amdt	FOR	6) Drug Death Pen	FOR	10) Ban Chem Weaps	AGN
3) Deficit Reduc	FOR	7) Handgun Sales	—	11) Aid to Contras	FOR
4) Kill Plnt Clsng Notice	AGN	8) Ban D.C. Abort $	FOR	12) Nuclear Testing	FOR

Election Results

1988 general	Solomon P. Ortiz (D), unopposed			($142,651)
1988 primary	Solomon P. Ortiz (D), unopposed			
1986 general	Solomon P. Ortiz (D).................	64,165	(100%)	($138,793)

UTAH

"Mormon Utah," wrote the *WPA Guide* 50 years ago (Utah has been mostly Mormon since 1847), "is primarily that fertile strip of occupied land, down through the north-central part of the state, lying at the foot of the Wasatch Mountain rampart. Four-fifths of the population lives here, in towns that vary from metropolitan Salt Lake City to humble villages that are distinguishable as towns only by their general store and sturdy 'meeting house.' Even in this richest and oldest-settled area, the stamp of a pioneer culture is everywhere manifest. Grandsires built too sturdily, albeit of such materials as wood and mud, for the pioneer period to have lost its substance. And these houses almost always are shadowed by trees. If houses could not stand as monuments to a culture, trees, gardens, and sheer greenness could. The cities themselves, almost universally set four-square to the directions, reflect an ideal of spacious and noble planning." Fifty years later, having grown from 550,000 people to 1.7 million, Utah's basic character remains stamped as firmly as ever on the desert, mountain-shadowed, often surrealistic landscape of what would have been, without the Mormons, an uninhabited wasteland.

Utah and Mormonism had their roots in a very different landscape more than 150 years ago, in a wave of religious enthusiasm, prophecy and utopianism that swept across the "burnt-over district" of Upstate New York in the 1820s and 1830s. There Joseph Smith, a young farmer, experienced a vision in which the Angel Moroni, a prophet of the lost tribe of Israel (the American Indians), appeared and told him where to unearth several golden tablets inscribed with hieroglyphic writings. (So important is this revelation to the religion that forged documents showing that Smith was directed by a "white salamander" to the tablets resulted in extortions, car-bombings, and finally the confession of forger Mark Hofmann in 1987.) With the aid of special spectacles, Smith translated the tablets and published them as the Book of Mormon in 1831. He later declared himself a prophet and founded the Church of Jesus Christ of Latter Day Saints. His Mormons, as they were called, attracted thousands of converts and created their own communities; persecuted for their beliefs, they moved west to Ohio, Missouri, and then Illinois. In 1844, the Mormon colony at Nauvoo, Illinois, had some 15,000 members, all living under the strict theocratic rule of Joseph Smith. In secular Illinois politics, Nauvoo—then the largest city in the state—held the balance of power between contending Democrats and Whigs. It was here that Smith received a revelation sanctioning the practice of polygamy, which led to his death at the hands of a mob in 1844.

After the murder, the new president of the church, Brigham Young, decided to move the faithful, "the saints," farther west into territory that was still part of Mexico and far beyond the pale of white settlement. Young led a well-organized march across the Great Plains and into the

Rocky Mountains. In 1847, the prophet and his followers stopped on the western slope of the Wasatch Range and, as Brigham Young gazed over the valley of the Great Salt Lake spread out below, he uttered the now famous words, "This is the place."

The place was Utah. Young was governor of the territory for many years, and it is the only state that continues to live by the teachings of the church responsible for its founding. Throughout the 19th century and even today "Zion" has attracted thousands of converts from the Midwest, the north of England, and Scandinavia. The object of religious fear, prejudice and perhaps some repressed envy, Utah was not granted statehood until 1896, after the church renounced polygamy.

The Church remains distinctive in many ways. It cares deeply about its past: in caves in the mountains of Utah the Church preserves America's most complete genealogical records. It tries to spread the faith: many young Mormons spend missionary years abroad. It prohibits the consumption of tobacco, alcohol, caffeine; it encourages large families and hard work; its members are healthier than the average American, better educated and more affluent. And while American mainline denominations are losing members, the Mormon Church is growing. Mormons, long derided by coastal sophisticates as old-fashioned, have the satisfaction in the late 1980s of seeing their respect for tradition and discipline accepted more and more in an America grown weary and wary of liberation from traditional cultural standards.

The Church's influence in Utah is great—it owns one of the two leading Salt Lake City newspapers and a TV station, it has holdings in an insurance company, several banks, real estate and owns ZCMI, the largest department store in Salt Lake City—and it is sometimes resented. But this influence is only occasionally exerted on political issues. The embarrassment of the Church's ban against blacks becoming full members was removed thanks to a revelation to LDS president Spencer Kimball in 1978. In the early 1980s, the Church opposed the racetrack basing mode for the MX missile which would have required laying tracks down over much of Utah and Nevada. And the Church itself, financed by the tradition of tithing, runs its own high-quality welfare programs: this is a society that favors market economics and free enterprise, but also has a lively tradition of communal effort and responsibility. In Utah, it is the community, not the individual, that is paramount and many of George Bush's thousand points of light are blazing brightly here.

But if the moral underpinnings of life in Utah have not changed in 50 years, Utah's view of its place in the nation has. Before World War II, Utah saw itself as a colonial victim of East Coast bankers and financiers and Mormons saw themselves as sufferers from religious discrimination and bigotry—and all with some cause. Its income levels were well below the national average, its cost of living was higher, the prices paid for the things it produced seemed to be controlled elsewhere. Politically, this perspective translated into a Democratic allegiance: in 1940, Utah was represented by staunch New Dealers in Congress and cast 62% of its votes for Franklin Roosevelt. Today, Utah is more likely to see itself as a busy—beehive, in the Mormon image—generator of wealth and to see its religion not as distinctive but as representing the traditional values that a majority of Americans share even though they are under attack in liberal media and intellectual circles. In Utah, the 1950s American ideal is still alive—and thriving, with as many intact families, as many children, and much higher income levels than average Americans had at the peak of the baby boom. Politically, this perspective translates into a strong Republican preference. Utah changed from a Democratic state in the Roosevelt-Truman years to a pretty solidly Republican state by the middle 1960s. In the last 20 years, as traditional values under attack elsewhere have thrived in Utah, it has become the most Republican of states—standing out in the national statistics politically just as it does demographically. In 1960, Richard Nixon carried Utah with 55% of the vote; by 1972, he won with 72%. Ronald Reagan won 73% and 75% of Utah's votes; George Bush won here 66%–32%. For four presidential elections in a row, Utah has been the nation's most Republican state.

Governor. The key event in recent state politics in Utah was the tax increase obtained by

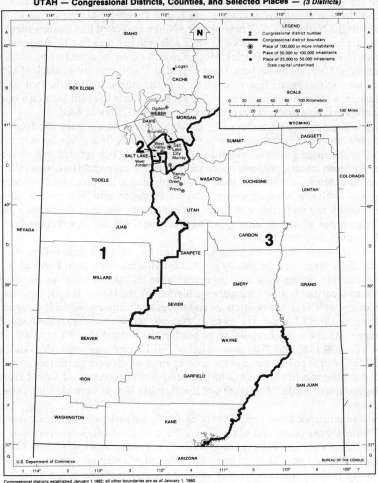

UTAH — Congressional Districts, Counties, and Selected Places — *(3 Districts)*

LEGEND

2 Congressional district number
Congressional district boundary
Place of 100,000 or more inhabitants
Place of 50,000 to 100,000 inhabitants
Place of 25,000 to 50,000 inhabitants
State capital underlined

SCALE

0 20 40 60 80 100 Kilometers
0 20 40 60 80 100 Miles

U.S. Department of Commerce

BUREAU OF THE CENSUS

Congressional districts established January 1, 1982; all other boundaries are as of January 1, 1980.

Governor Norman Bangerter in 1987. A tax revolt movement immediately arose, fueled by frustration, for Bangerter was the first Republican governor elected in 20 years and the Democrat then poised to run against him, former Salt Lake City Mayor Ted Wilson, wasn't denouncing the tax increase himself. The result was several anti-tax measures on the ballot in 1988 and the independent candidacy of tax protester Merrill Cook. Bangerter argued that the state needed the money for education and infrastructure, but in 1988, he sponsored a rebate and the state sent out checks by Labor Day. That may have been enough to make the difference, as Bangerter beat Wilson by a narrow 40%–38% margin, with a strong 21% going to Cook; and in early 1989, Bangerter and the legislature were grappling with ways to lower taxes further.

Senators. Utah has two Republican Senators both of whom chaired important committees for six years, and who are both back, but not necessarily quietly, on the minority side.

Of Senator Jake Garn's personal courage, there can be no doubt. He was a Navy pilot and a general in the National Guard; he went up in the space shuttle *Discovery* in April 1985 and was monitored for seven days for, among other things, motion sickness; in September 1986, he donated a kidney to one of his daughters. He is also known for his explosions of temper. He exploded at Ralph Nader in a 1979 hearing when Nader suggested that a safety regulation Garn opposed would have saved the life of Garn's late wife who had died in a 1976 accident. In 1984, when Barry Goldwater, Daniel Patrick Moynihan and others professed to be outraged at the CIA's mining of Nicaraguan harbors, Garn exploded, "You guys are a bunch of assholes;" he apologized later to Goldwater but, pointedly, not to the others. In 1988, he took to the Senate floor to denounce "sanctimonious attempts" of other members to avoid their own responsibility for the savings and loan crisis, though he has some responsibility himself.

Behind the courage and the temper lie some fierce convictions—and some frustrations with the legislative process. Garn was chairman of the Senate's Space Subcommittee and is an enthusiast for the space program, which has been politically beleaguered and threatened with cuts since the moon landing program ended more than a decade ago. Garn wants the maximum of manned exploration—the space station, a manned mission to Mars, and a permanent colony on the moon—which is very expensive, and he seems to give less priority to unmanned exploration which can go farther and faster but which may not seize the public's imagination. He is an advocate of greater defense spending also, and of tougher export control on American high-tech products and processes.

Garn was chairman of the Banking Committee for six years and had to deal with his philosophically different and personally unpleasant House counterpart, Fernand St Germain. Garn did succeed in getting some banking deregulation bills through, but his measures allowing banks into the securities business were always blocked by the House. He put together the Garn-St Germain law which relaxed restrictions on savings and loans, and so must be accorded some of the blame for the S&L crisis; the more so, because his chief staffer on the issue, M. Danny Wall, became one of the chief regulators as head of the Federal Home Loan Bank Board. But Garn was willing in 1985 and 1986 to recapitalize FSLIC generously enough to stifle losses and recognized the need to change some of the lending rules which were generating more losses, but he was stymied because St Germain (who was being lavishly entertained almost every night by S&L lobbyist James "Snake" Freeman) and Speaker Jim Wright were blocking these measures in the House.

Garn was an insurance agent and mayor of Salt Lake City who won his Senate seat in 1974 by beating Wayne Owens (then, and again since 1986, Salt Lake City's congressman) by a 50%–44% margin. Garn's position in Utah seems solid: he was reelected with 74% and 72% of the vote in 1980 and 1986, and he is likely to be easily reelected when his seat comes up again in 1992.

Orrin Hatch is also a conservative, but with a different temperament and different career. In 1981, after only four years in the Senate, he became chairman of the Labor and Human Resources Committee, the spawning ground of many Great Society measures, and the place where Hatch was expected to bury them again. But that is not exactly what happened. One reason was that Hatch never had a reliable conservative majority on the committee: Republicans Robert Stafford and Lowell Weicker often voted with the Democrats. Another is that some of Hatch's anti-labor causes got overtaken by events. He gained fame in the Carter years by filibustering the AFL-CIO's labor law reform, and for the 1980s, his agenda included the subminimum wage and repeal of the Davis-Bacon Act. Meanwhile, the building trades unions, which are the beneficiaries of Davis-Bacon, were undermined by the high interest rates and deunionization of the early 1980s.

And finally, Hatch did not dismantle the Great Society because he became a workhorse, taking seriously his responsibilities of superintending these programs and working hard to get the details right. He did push the Reagan Administration's block grants early on. But he approached the remaining programs as you might expect a bishop to in a church which runs a wide array of social welfare programs itself: he looked to see who was helped or hurt, if money was spent efficiently, if there were better ways to do it, or if more federal help was needed. So while he continued to staunchly oppose federal funding of abortion, he became one of the biggest boosters of the Job Corps. He supported the Japanese American redress legislation. He opposed the Civil Rights Restoration Act and supported the Danforth amendment that would prevent Catholic and other religious hospitals from being required to insure their employees for abortions. But he worked with Edward Kennedy—and against Jesse Helms—on the AIDS education and treatment bill in 1988, insisting that the government must help homosexuals even if it disapproves of their practices. He led the opposition on committee to mandated health insurance in 1988 and 1989, but at the same time he proposed his own child care bill and supported the ABC child care bill (that incorporated many of the proposals from his own child care bill) which many Republicans, including the Bush Administration, oppose. Yet at the same time he led the charge for the Administration's approach to the minimum wage.

This is not quite what was expected of Hatch after his surprise win in 1976. He had only gotten into the Senate race at the last minute when, as a Reagan backer and a newcomer to the state, he felt the other Republicans running for liberal Democrat Frank Moss's seat were too moderate; he ran a tough negative issues campaign against Moss and won an upset victory. Hatch had a tough race again in 1982, when he was closely pressed by Democrat Ted Wilson, then the mayor of Salt Lake City, a man with moderate views and a pleasant, modest personality; but this strong Republican finally won in Republican Utah by a 58%–41% majority. In 1988, he faced the son of the Senator he beat in 1976, but Brian Moss raised little money and Hatch won 67%–32%. There has been talk at various times that Hatch, a member of the Judiciary Committee, might be appointed to the Supreme Court, partly on the theory—obsolete now after the Tower nomination—that Senators will not deny confirmation to one of their own. In the meantime, he seems to have a safe Senate seat and plenty of work to do.

Presidential politics. The most Republican state in the nation is not likely to see any presidential candidates any time soon, unless their planes need refueling on the way to the West Coast. For the national conventions its relatively few delegates are chosen by party officials.

Congressional districting. In 1982, Utah got its third congressional district; the lines were drawn as predicted and little adjustment will be needed for 1992. The 2d District, which includes most of Salt Lake County, is the least Republican of the three, and went Democratic in 1986, when Wayne Owens won it—the first Democratic victory in a federal election here in the 1980s. The 1st District in Western Utah produced the fourth highest Bush percentage in 1988, surpassed only by west Houston, north Dallas and the Florida panhandle.

The People: Est. Pop. 1988: 1,691,000; Pop. 1980: 1,461,037, up 15.7% 1980–88 and 37.9% 1970–80; 0.69% of U.S. total, 35th largest. 24% with 1–3 yrs. col., 20% with 4+ yrs. col.; 10.3% below poverty level. Single ancestry: 28% English, 4% German, 2% Irish, 1% Swedish, Scottish, Dutch, Italian, French, Norwegian. Households (1980): 78% family, 50% with children, 69% married couples; 29.3% housing units rented; median monthly rent: $190; median house value: $60,000. Voting age pop. (1980): 920,932; 4% Spanish origin, 1% Asian origin, 1% American Indian, 1% Black. Registered voters (1988): 806,934; no party registration.

1988 Share of Federal Tax Burden: $4,095,000,000; 0.46% of U.S. total, 37th largest.

1226   UTAH

Political Lineup: Governor, Norman H. Bangerter (R); Lt. Gov., W. Val Oveson (R); Atty. Gen., Paul Van Dam (D); Treasurer, Edward T. Alter (R); Auditor, Tom L. Allen (R). State Senate, 29 (22 R and 7 D); State House of Representatives, 75 (48 R and 27 D). Senators, Edwin Jacob (Jake) Garn (R) and Orrin G. Hatch (R). Representatives, 3 (2 R and 1 D).

1988 Presidential Vote

Bush (R)	428,442	(66%)
Dukakis (D)	207,343	(32%)

1984 Presidential Vote

Reagan (R)	469,105	(75%)
Mondale (D)	155,369	(25%)

GOVERNOR

Gov. Norman H. Bangerter (R)

Elected 1984, term expires Jan. 1993; b. Jan. 4, 1933, Granger; home, West Valley City; Brigham Young U., U. of UT; Mormon; married (Colleen).

Career: Bldg. contractor; UT House of Reps., 1974–84, Speaker 1980–84.

Office: 210 State Capitol, Salt Lake City 84114, 801-538-1000.

Election Results

1988 gen.	Norman H. Bangerter (R)	260,462	(40%)
	Ted Wilson (D)	249,321	(38%)
	Merrill Cook (I)	136,651	(21%)
1988 prim.	Norman H. Bangerter (R), unopposed		
1984 gen.	Norman H. Bangerter (R)	351,792	(56%)
	Wayne Owens (D)	275,669	(44%)

SENATORS

Sen. Edwin Jacob (Jake) Garn (R)

Elected 1974, seat up 1992; b. Oct. 12, 1932, Richfield; home, Salt Lake City; U. of UT, B.S. 1955; Mormon; married (Kathleen).

Career: Navy, 1956–60; Insur. exec., 1960–68; Salt Lake City Commissioner, 1968–72; Mayor of Salt Lake City, 1972–74.

Offices: 505 DSOB 20510, 202-224-5444. Also 4225 Fed. Bldg., Salt Lake City 84138, 801-524-5933; 1010 Fed. Bldg., Ogden 84401, 801-625-5676; 88 W. 100 N., Rm. 111, Provo 84601, 801-374-2929; P.O. Box 99, Cedar City 84720, 801-586-8435; and Energy Bldg., Ste. 1, Moab 84532, 801-259-7188.

Committees: *Appropriations* (4th of 13 R). Subcommittees: Defense; Energy and Water Development; Interior; Military Construction; VA, HUD and Independent Agencies (Ranking Member). *Banking, Housing, and Urban Affairs* (Ranking Member of 9 R). *Energy and Natural Resources* (8th of 9 R). Subcommittees: Energy Research and Development; Public Lands, National Parks and Forests; Water and Power. *Rules and Administration* (6th of 7 R).

Group Ratings

	ADA	ACLU	COPE	CFA	LCV	ACU	NTLC	NSI	COC	CEI
1988	0	4	10	17	10	96	78	100	92	78
1987	5	—	10	17	—	96	—	—	94	82

National Journal Ratings

	1988 LIB — 1988 CONS		1987 LIB — 1987 CONS	
Economic	0%	— 95%	0%	— 94%
Social	0%	— 89%	0%	— 94%
Foreign	9%	— 89%	0%	— 76%

Key Votes

1) Cut Aged Housing $	AGN	5) Bork Nomination	FOR	9) SDI Funding	FOR
2) Override Hwy Veto	AGN	6) Ban Plastic Guns	FOR	10) Ban Chem Weaps	FOR
3) Kill Plnt Clsng Notice	FOR	7) Deny Abortions	FOR	11) Aid To Contras	FOR
4) Min Wage Increase	AGN	8) Japanese Reparations	AGN	12) Reagan Defense $	FOR

Election Results

1986 general	Edwin Jacob (Jake) Garn (R)............	314,608	(72%)	($752,944)
	Craig S. Oliver (D)..................	115,523	(27%)	($24,508)
1986 primary	Edwin Jacob (Jake) Garn (R), unopposed			
1980 general	Edwin Jacob (Jake) Garn (R)............	434,675	(74%)	($1,113,061)
	Dan Berman (D).....................	151,454	(26%)	($237,882)

Sen. Orrin G. Hatch (R)

Elected 1976, seat up 1994; b. Mar. 22, 1934, Pittsburgh, PA; home, Salt Lake City; Brigham Young U., B.S. 1959, U. of Pittsburgh, J.D. 1962; Mormon; married (Elaine).

Career: Practicing atty., 1962–76.

Offices: 135 RSOB 20510, 202-224-5251. Also 3438 Fed. Bldg., 125 S. State St., Salt Lake City 84138, 801-524-4380; 109 Fed. Bldg., 88 W. 100 N., Provo 84601, 801-375-7881; 1410 Fed. Bldg., 325 25th St., Ogden 84401, 801-625-5672; and 10 N. Main St., P.O. Box 99, Cedar City 84720, 801-586-8435.

Committees: *Judiciary* (2d of 6 R). Subcommittees: Antitrust, Monopolies and Business Rights; Constitution; Patents, Copyrights and Trademarks (Ranking Member). *Labor and Human Resources* (Ranking Member of 7 R). Subcommittees: Children, Family, Drugs, and Alcoholism; Education, Arts and Humanities; Handicapped. *Select Committtee on Intelligence* (2d of 7 R).

Group Ratings

	ADA	ACLU	COPE	CFA	LCV	ACU	NTLC	NSI	COC	CEI
1988	5	19	12	42	20	96	77	100	86	55
1987	5	—	11	33	—	92	—	—	100	73

National Journal Ratings

	1988 LIB — 1988 CONS	1987 LIB — 1987 CONS
Economic	9% — 81%	21% — 74%
Social	32% — 67%	11% — 87%
Foreign	0% — 92%	0% — 76%

Key Votes

1) Cut Aged Housing $	FOR	5) Bork Nomination	FOR	9) SDI Funding	FOR
2) Override Hwy Veto	AGN	6) Ban Plastic Guns	FOR	10) Ban Chem Weaps	FOR
3) Kill Plnt Clsng Notice	FOR	7) Deny Abortions	FOR	11) Aid To Contras	FOR
4) Min Wage Increase	AGN	8) Japanese Reparations	FOR	12) Reagan Defense $	FOR

Election Results

1988 general	Orrin G. Hatch (R)...................	430,089	(67%)	($3,706,381)
	Brian H. Moss (D)	203,364	(32%)	($153,475)
1988 primary	Orrin G. Hatch (R), unopposed			
1982 general	Orrin G. Hatch (R)...................	309,547	(58%)	($3,838,335)
	Ted Wilson (D).....................	218,895	(41%)	($1,703,170)

FIRST DISTRICT

In May 1869, a motley crowd of Irish and Chinese laborers, teamsters, engineers, train crews, officials and guests from California and Salt Lake City gathered in Promontory Point, Utah, to watch the opening of the transcontinental railroad. The Union Pacific train was late and Leland Stanford raised his hammer and totally missed the golden spike, but an alert telegrapher mimicked the sound over the wire and a photographer recorded the scene for posterity: united at last were the settled and civilized East with the mostly unsettled and untamed West. Here, beyond sight of the snow-capped mountains the Mormon pioneers crossed to reach Zion, the salt flats stretch out endlessly even today; the rail lines now pass north of here, and Promontory Point lies on uninhabited flat land beside the rising Great Salt Lake. The lake itself kept rising in the middle 1980s, despite state legislation forbidding it to get above a certain level. The local county commissioners called for a day of prayer for drought in May 1986, the lake finally obeyed the law, and the state didn't have to pump water through canals to form a vast new lake in the salt flats to the west.

The 1st Congressional District of Utah is the western half of Utah, from Promontory Point down to where the Colorado River flows south through Glen Canyon into Arizona; there are national parks (Zion, Bryce Canyon) in the south, mining country in the center, and the desert (as it still is at this writing) west of the lake. But 75% of the people of the 1st District live along the Wasatch Front, the thin strip of land between the Wasatch Mountains and the lowlands along the lake. The largest city is Ogden, an old working-class town on the Union Pacific line, the nearest station stop to Promontory Point. North of Ogden, the land is agricultural, and the towns—Brigham City and Logan—are mainly farm centers, almost entirely Mormon and heavily conservative. To the south is Davis County, with some high-income spillover from Salt Lake City. Ogden has a Democratic past, but any Democratic votes it casts today are overcome by Davis's Republican majorities. The rest of the voters live in small communities, many almost unanimously Mormon in central and southern Utah.

The congressman from this district is James Hansen, who despite his conservative and Republican record has not held it without challenge. He won the seat in 1980 by beating incumbent Gunn McKay 52%–48%; McKay, after several years heading an LDS mission overseas ran again in 1986 and 1988, losing 52%–48% and 60%–40%. McKay argued that he would provide "balance" for Utah and would have clout as he once was a majority member of the Appropriations Committee, where he helped protect Ogden's Hill Air Force Base. But that argument was undercut in summer 1986 when Hansen won a vacant seat on the Armed Services Committee. A former speaker of the Utah House, garrulous and fair-minded, he was respected enough to have been named to Standards of Official Conduct, the House's Ethics Committee, in his first term; in his second term, serving on Interior as well, he helped pass a compromise Utah Wilderness bill. He seems now to have a safe seat.

The People: Est. Pop. 1986: 574,000, up 17.7% 1980–86; Pop. 1980: 487,833, up 31.0% 1970–80. Households (1980): 81% family, 51% with children, 72% married couples; 25.8% housing units rented; median monthly rent: $177; median house value: $58,200. Voting age pop. (1980): 303,406; 3% Spanish origin, 1% Black, 1% Asian origin, 1% American Indian.

1988 Presidential Vote:
Bush (R)	162,713	(72%)
Dukakis (D)	60,984	(27%)

Rep. James V. Hansen (R)

Elected 1980; b. Aug. 14, 1932, Salt Lake City; home, Farmington; U. of UT, B.A. 1960; Mormon; married (Ann).

Career: Navy, Korea; Farmington City Cncl., 1962–72; UT House of Reps., 1972–80, Speaker, 1978–80.

Offices: 2421 RHOB 20515, 202-225-0453. Also 1017 Fed. Bldg., 324 25th St., Ogden 84401, 801-625-5677; and 435 E. Tabernacle, Ste. 105, St. George 84770, 801-628-1071.

Committees: *Armed Services* (13th of 21 R). Subcommittees: Military Installations and Facilities; Procurement and Military Nuclear Systems. *Interior and Insular Affairs* (6th of 15 R). Subcommittees: Energy and the Environment (Ranking Member); National Parks and Public Lands; Water, Power and Offshore Energy Resources. *Standards of Official Conduct* (2d of 6 R).

Group Ratings

	ADA	ACLU	COPE	CFA	LCV	ACU	NTLC	NSI	COC	CEI
1988	0	4	3	18	6	100	84	100	100	81
1987	4	—	4	14	—	95	—	—	100	86

National Journal Ratings

	1988 LIB — 1988 CONS		1987 LIB — 1987 CONS	
Economic	0%	— 93%	0%	— 89%
Social	0%	— 95%	0%	— 90%
Foreign	22%	— 76%	0%	— 80%

Key Votes

1) Homeless $	FOR	5) Ban Drug Test	FOR	9) SDI Research	FOR
2) Gephardt Amdt	AGN	6) Drug Death Pen	FOR	10) Ban Chem Weaps	AGN
3) Deficit Reduc	AGN	7) Handgun Sales	FOR	11) Aid to Contras	FOR
4) Kill Plnt Clsng Notice	FOR	8) Ban D.C. Abort $	FOR	12) Nuclear Testing	AGN

Election Results

1988 general	James V. Hansen (R)	130,893	(60%)	($426,902)
	Gunn McKay (D)	87,976	(40%)	($391,928)
1988 primary	James V. Hansen (R), unopposed			
1986 general	James V. Hansen (R)	82,151	(52%)	($419,959)
	Gunn McKay (D)	77,180	(48%)	($244,261)

SECOND DISTRICT

The center of Utah and of the Mormon Church is Temple Square, nestled beneath the towering mountains that flank Salt Lake City. Here you can find the Mormon Tabernacle, home of the famous choir, and the Temple itself, which is entered only by Church members. Two long blocks north is the state Capitol, four blocks south is City Hall, all around are Salt Lake City's impressive array of skyscrapers. Everywhere the snow-capped mountains can be seen towering in the east and the Great Salt Lake to the west shimmering in the waning light of day. Ironically, Salt Lake City is the least Mormon and most cosmopolitan part of Utah: with the state university and businesses bringing in outsiders, some think it now has a gentile (i.e., non-Mormon) majority. Salt Lake City, wrote the *WPA Guide* 50 years ago, "has probably more briefcases per capita than any other city in the state. In spite of these habiliments of importance, however, the tempo is relatively unhurried, with time enough to chat beside the parking meters about crops and precipitation, Church news and the price of copper, and to read the news bulletins in front of the newspaper offices. Men's headgear runs more to the stetson than in the East, and a cowboy in a ten-gallon hat, copper-riveted Levis, and high-heeled boots arouses no comments." Much larger today, Salt Lake City still has some of this laid-back western atmosphere.

Utah's 2d Congressional District, which includes most of Salt Lake County, has lower percentages of families, children and married couples per household than the other two Utah districts. The 2d District also includes most of Utah's most affluent people living in Salt Lake City and suburbs like East Millcreek, Holladay and Cottonwood, right next to the Wasatch Mountains which rise, at that point, to 9,000 feet. It is just an easy drive up or over the mountains, as recruiters for businesses here like to tell prospects, to the ski slopes at Park City and Alta. The district also includes some of the more modest suburbs on the flat land just south of Salt Lake City and east toward the Lake.

Politically the 2d District is relatively marginal, and has had volatile congressional politics, with close races in most years since 1972. That year, 35-year-old Democrat Wayne Owens attracted attention by walking the district (it went all the way down to the Arizona border then) and beat the incumbent Republican; he went on to vote against Richard Nixon in the Judiciary Committee impeachment hearings, to lose the Senate race to Jake Garn later that year, to be sent on an LDS mission to Montreal, and to lose the 1984 governor's race. In 1986, after three other men had served, he ran in the 2d district again and won 55%–44% over county commissioner Tom Shimizu, whose family came here as refugees from the removal of Japanese Americans from the West Coast in World War II.

In the House, Owens serves on the Foreign Affairs and Interior Committees. He has a moderately liberal voting record, but not what one might expect of a man who was once, as Republicans like to recall, a top aide to then Senate Democratic Whip Edward Kennedy. He has made a name for himself as an economizer, supporting the balanced budget constitutional amendment, joining the Grace Caucus, asking the Administration to cancel the C-17 cargo plane, and calling for repeal of Section 89 of the tax law that requires small companies to give all employees the same health care plans. In 1988, his Republican opponent, local ice cream magnate Richard Snelgrove, put on a spirited campaign, but Owens won 57%–41%. He says he is cured of any desire for statewide office and obviously hopes for a long career in what has been, for others, a somewhat shaky seat in the House.

The People: Est. Pop. 1986: 532,900, up 9.3% 1980–86; Pop. 1980: 487,475, up 21.3% 1970–80. Households (1980): 72% family, 43% with children, 61% married couples; 35.8% housing units rented; median monthly rent: $200; median house value: $63,100. Voting age pop. (1980): 325,863; 4% Spanish origin, 1% Asian origin, 1% Black, 1% American Indian.

1988 Presidential Vote:

Bush (R)	....	125,619	(58%)
Dukakis (D)	....	86,241	(40%)

Rep. Wayne Owens (D)

Elected 1986; b. May 2, 1937, Panquitch; home, Salt Lake City; U. of UT, B.A. 1961, J.D. 1964; Mormon; married (Marlene).

Career: Aide to Sen. Frank Moss, 1965–68; A.A. to Sen. Edward Kennedy, 1969–72; U.S. House of Reps., 1972–74; Pres., Mormon Church Mission, Montreal, Canada, 1975–78; Practicing atty.

Offices: 1728 LHOB 20515, 202-225-3011. Also 125 S. State St., Salt Lake City 84138, 801-524-4394.

Committees: *Foreign Affairs* (22d of 28 D). Subcommittees: Europe and the Middle East; Human Rights and International Organizations. *Interior and Insular Affairs* (20th of 26 D). Subcommittees: General Oversight and Investigations; Mining and Natural Resources; National Parks and Public Lands; Water, Power and Energy Resources.

Group Ratings

	ADA	ACLU	COPE	CFA	LCV	ACU	NTLC	NSI	COC	CEI
1988	75	78	94	91	81	16	17	0	36	18
1987	76	—	93	79	—	0	—	—	31	16

National Journal Ratings

	1988 LIB — 1988 CONS		1987 LIB — 1987 CONS	
Economic	65%	— 34%	62%	— 35%
Social	64%	— 34%	78%	— 0%
Foreign	67%	— 32%	60%	— 40%

Key Votes

1) Homeless $	AGN	5) Ban Drug Test	AGN	9) SDI Research	FOR
2) Gephardt Amdt	FOR	6) Drug Death Pen	AGN	10) Ban Chem Weaps	FOR
3) Deficit Reduc	FOR	7) Handgun Sales	FOR	11) Aid to Contras	AGN
4) Kill Plnt Clsng Notice	AGN	8) Ban D.C. Abort $	FOR	12) Nuclear Testing	FOR

Election Results

1988 general	Wayne Owens (D)...................	112,129	(57%)	($676,472)
	Richard Snelgrove (R)	80,212	(41%)	($254,823)
1988 primary	Wayne Owens (D), unopposed			
1986 general	Wayne Owens (D)....................	76,921	(55%)	($704,609)
	Tom Shimizu (R)	60,967	(44%)	($373,077)

THIRD DISTRICT

The heartland of the Mormon Church in America is in a geographically isolated valley between 11,000-foot peaks of the Wasatch Range and the shores of Utah Lake. Here is Provo, the home of Brigham Young University, an institution long known for the rigorous and conservative views of its faculty, the old-fashioned moral standards of its students, and the throwing skills of its quarterbacks. Mormonism has always welcomed, and not been hostile to, technological innovation. The Mormon commonwealth, after all, started off with a terrific shortage of both labor and water and was eager to use technology to replace physical labor and to preserve water in order to prosper. This is an optimistic area, and one with an historical warrant for its optimism: you have only to look at the beautiful but forbidding terrain to understand how much the early

Mormon settlers here banked on their own efforts and how much they accomplished.

Utah's 3d Congressional District includes Provo and Utah County and a strip of land about 10 miles wide and less than 40 miles long that runs up along the Jordan River to the modest southwestern suburbs of Salt Lake City. These two urban areas cast about two-thirds of the district's votes; the rest are cast in towns scattered amid huge mountains, florid rock formations and deep canyons from Wyoming down to the Arizona border. Its northernmost point is near Wyoming's Overthrust Belt, site of great oil and gas strikes in the late 1970s, and it includes the depressed uranium country in the eastern part of the state around Moab. This was the nation's most Republican congressional district in the 1980 presidential election, and was among the most Republican in 1984 and 1988.

The 3d District was created when Utah gained a third seat in the 1980 Census. Its only congressman, former Utah House Speaker Howard Nielson, has also been a professor of statistics at Brigham Young. He got a seat on the House Energy and Commerce Committee—a coveted post—and on the Health and the Environment Subcommittee, where he can be expected to resolve conflicts in favor of encouraging economic growth and taking some risks. In 1985, Nielson took a seat on Government Operations as well, and now serves as ranking Republican on the Government Activities and Transportation Subcommittee. Nielson is hard-working and has an eye for detail; he was the driving force behind the long-overdue measure extending daylight savings time three weeks earlier in April. He pushed successfully to have the FTC consider restrictions on what hours potential consumers can be contacted by phone. An early skeptic of the successful effort to upgrade the Veterans' Administration to cabinet status, he felt that veterans have been given ample attention without such a move.

Neilson won the seat in the Republican primary of 1982, and has had no significant electoral problem since. He has said that he expects his current term to be his last one. If he does carry out his threat to retire, his successor will surely be chosen in the 1990 Republican primary.

The People: Est. Pop. 1986: 558,400, up 15.0% 1980–86; Pop. 1980: 485,729, up 70.3% 1970–80. Households (1980): 83% family, 57% with children, 75% married couples; 25.1% housing units rented; median monthly rent: $183; median house value: $58,600. Voting age pop. (1980): 291,663; 3% Spanish origin, 2% American Indian, 1% Asian origin.

1988 Presidential Vote:

Bush (R)	140,110	(69%)
Dukakis (D)	60,118	(29%)

Rep. Howard C. Nielson (R)

Elected 1982; b. Sept. 12, 1924, Richfield; home, Provo; U. of UT, B.S. 1947; U. of OR, M.S. 1949, Stanford U., M.B.A. 1956, Ph.D. 1958; Mormon; married (Julie).

Career: Army, 1943–46; Statistician, 1949–51; Res. economist, Stanford Res. Inst., 1951–57; Prof., Brigham Young U., 1957–76, 1978–82, Chmn., Dept. of Statistics, 1960–63; UT House of Reps., 1967–74, Major. Ldr., 1969–70, Spkr., 1973–74.

Offices: 1122 LHOB 20515, 202-225-7751. Also 105 Fed. Bldg., 88 W. 100 N., Provo 84601, 801-377-1776; 92 E. Center St., Ste. 1, Moab 84532, 801-259-7188; and 2207 Fed. Bldg., 125 S. State, Salt Lake City 84138, 801-524-5301.

Committees: *Energy and Commerce* (12th of 17 R). Subcommittees: Commerce, Consumer Protection, and Competitiveness; Energy and Power; Health and the Environment. *Government Operations* (4th of 15 R). Subcommittee: Government Activities and Transportation (Ranking Member).

Group Ratings

	ADA	ACLU	COPE	CFA	LCV	ACU	NTLC	NSI	COC	CEI
1988	5	22	10	27	19	92	87	100	100	83
1987	8	—	8	29	—	87	—	—	87	84

National Journal Ratings

	1988 LIB — 1988 CONS	1987 LIB — 1987 CONS
Economic	10% — 88%	11% — 83%
Social	13% — 84%	23% — 76%
Foreign	26% — 73%	0% — 80%

Key Votes

1) Homeless $	FOR	5) Ban Drug Test	FOR	9) SDI Research	FOR
2) Gephardt Amdt	AGN	6) Drug Death Pen	FOR	10) Ban Chem Weaps	AGN
3) Deficit Reduc	AGN	7) Handgun Sales	FOR	11) Aid to Contras	FOR
4) Kill Plnt Clsng Notice	FOR	8) Ban D.C. Abort $	FOR	12) Nuclear Testing	AGN

Election Results

1988 general	Howard C. Nielson (R).................	129,951	(67%)	($102,055)
	Robert W. Stringham (D)...............	60,018	(31%)	($20,092)
1988 primary	Howard C. Neilson (R), unopposed			
1986 general	Howard C. Nielson (R).................	86,599	(67%)	($104,151)
	Dale F. Gardiner (D)...................	42,582	(33%)	($37,279)

VERMONT

"Vermont represents the past, is a piece of the past in the midst of the present and future," wrote Vermonter Dorothy Canfield Fisher in the *WPA Guide* 50 years ago. "We still live in small units where personal relations are almost the invariable rule of daily life, not the exception. On our streets, it is the sight of a totally unknown face or figure which arrests the attention, rather than, as in big cities, the strangeness of occasionally seeing somebody you know. Everybody in Vermont is still in a situation close enough to the primitive and natural to be not wholly conditioned by the amount of cash in his pockets." The needy could grow their own vegetables and chop their own firewood and depend upon "the tradition among us of indefatigable neighborliness and personal responsibility for help to the needy who are personally known to us. We realize that we are laggards from the past century, still living in what Marx kindly calls 'the idiocy of rural life,' and we know that our rural life is like that of the past, not like that of much of the present. We know that our ignorance of, our lack of instinctive 'feeling' for those modern industrial and mass-life problems make us seem to you like your great-aunt in curl papers, but we are helpless before our tradition of not pretending to know more than we do, of not being other than what we are."

It is a tradition, it has turned out, that has served to make Vermont over the intervening 50 years one of the growth areas of eastern America. In an era when Americans are increasingly ill-served by the rigidities of big organizations and repelled by the congestion of big cities, places like Vermont have become popular and *au courant*, not just as vacation places but as places to live year-round and work. As the industrial factories that Fisher professed not to understand shut down, and the computer makes it possible for increasing numbers of Americans to make their livings where they want, Vermont, a half-century after it looked like "a piece of the past," now increasingly, with its clapboard villages and ski condominiums, dairy cows and computer cottages, covered bridges and town greens, its Yankee farmers tapping sugar maples and its metropolitan visitors watching the changing of the leaves in October, looks like a forecast of the future.

Vermont began as an agricultural state, a target of America's northward and eastward migration (as important, for a while, as westward movement), a place where second sons and daughters from small New England farms, starting in the 1790s, went to scratch out livings from the rocky soil. Agriculture has remained important, especially dairy farming, but Vermont has commerce as well and, with its legendary thriftiness, accumulated capital that, invested wisely, was used to build the solid stone office buildings and courthouses, the thick-timbered houses and gold-topped state Capitol that have remained long after the ticky-tack, ramshackle buildings of the 1880s have crumbled into dust.

But Vermont never developed labor-intensive industry, and so over the years it exported people, and aged. Today millions of Americans have Vermont blood—far more than the half million who live here now, many of whom have no Vermont roots at all. Two Presidents were born here, but both made their careers elsewhere, Chester Arthur in New York, Calvin Coolidge in Massachusetts.

As a result of continuous outmigration, Vermont's population hovered between 300,000 and 400,000 from 1850 to 1960. Since then—perhaps the key date was 1963, when people started outnumbering cows—Vermont has been changing rapidly. Its economy has been booming, led by the leisure time industries—ski resorts, summer homes—and IBM, with several big and technologically important installations around booming Burlington, now the state's biggest employer. Vermont's tradition of cottage industries continues, with women knitters seeking to overturn union-inspired federal bans on home production. As more Americans get to live where they choose, more choose to live in Vermont. The 1960 population of 390,000 rose to 444,000 by 1970, 511,000 in 1980 and 548,000 by 1988.

Demographic change has produced political change. Nineteenth century Vermont was long the most Republican state in the nation; in 1936 Vermont and Maine were the only states to resist Franklin Roosevelt's landslide. Twenty-first century Vermont now has two-party, sometimes three-party, politics. Vermont today has one Democratic Senator—the first in its history—and for most of the last generation it has elected Democratic governors. Before 1960, the only areas of Democratic strength were the small Irish and French Canadian communities in Burlington and other towns near the Canadian border; it was almost as if the entire Catholic minority were Democrats and the entire Protestant majority Republicans. Today, the old Yankee and Catholic blocs don't always hold together, and the newcomers have increased the environmentalist, generally liberal vote that has helped not only Democrats, but also liberal Republicans and left-wingers like Bernard Sanders, the socialist mayor of Burlington, who received 36% of the vote for congressman-at-large in 1988.

Vermont has taken precisely the opposite path of its next-door neighbor New Hampshire. In the 1950s, they both had low taxes and small government; but New Hampshire has never passed a sales or income tax, while Vermont has raised taxes and spent money on education and environmental protection. Both strategies have been successful, since both states have attracted lots of migrants; increasingly they seem to self-select themselves to fit the state's images and policies and thus reinforce their existing differences. New Hampshire, with most of its population concentrated in the south and a heritage of heavy industry, would seem to have been the likelier candidate for a big-government strategy, but has set itself up as an alternative to nearby Massachusetts. Vermont, on the other hand, has its population scattered all over the state and its largest town up on Lake Champlain is nearer to Montreal than to any significant U.S. city; it has succeeded in attracting people from farther afield.

Governor. Governor Madeleine Kunin is a symbol of the new Vermont. Born in Switzerland,

**VERMONT — Congressional District, Counties,
County Subdivisions (Towns), and Places —** *(1 At Large)*

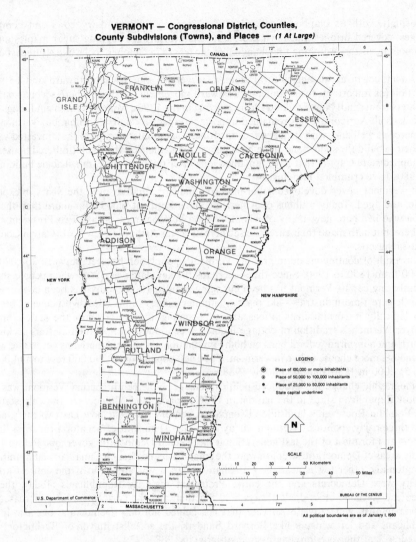

she grew up in the Berkshires of Massachusetts, moved to Vermont with her husband, and as she raised her four children was a teacher and journalist and got elected to the legislature in 1972. She thus came into government when concern for the environment was sweeping all before it in Vermont politics. In 1978, she was elected lieutenant governor, in 1982 she ran against popular businessman-Governor Richard Snelling and lost, but not badly (55%–44%). When Snelling retired in 1984 she ran and won. None of her victories has been overwhelming—50%–48% in 1984, 47%–38% in 1986 (when Bernie Sanders won 14%), 55%–43% in 1988. Vermont is one of the last three states to elect its governor every two years; in early 1989 it was mulling repealing the rule that a governor must win 50% of the vote or be elected by the legislature (this is how Kunin won in 1986) and requiring only 40% instead.

Kunin has been in the luxury position of running a state government whose revenues have been growing so fast as to produce unexpected surpluses and to allow spending increases of as much as 25% over two years. She had been helped as well by the fact that Democrats have often controlled the legislature, although now it's divided. Her chief program in 1987 was to equalize education spending across the state by redistributing local property tax revenues from cities and towns with large great lists (the great list is the property tax roll) to those with little money; in 1988, she presented a program for state and local planning and an increased property transfer tax; her chief goal for 1989 was to provide medical insurance for the 31,000 Vermonters who lack coverage while preserving an income tax cut voted in 1988. Her chief setbacks have been the defeat of the Equal Rights Amendment in a 1986 referendum and the criticism of the state's "house arrest" policy (now rescinded) for letting Geraldine Ferraro's son John Zacarro live in a $1,500-a-month apartment after being convicted of selling cocaine.

Senators. To those who can remember the Vermont of 50 years ago, it is unthinkable that Vermont's senior Senator should be a Democrat, but to those who know the Vermont of the 1980s, it seems plausible and even to be expected. Patrick Leahy was first elected in 1974, at 34; that makes him one of the more senior senators now, one who has held some important posts—and sat on some hot seats—in the Senate.

One of those was on the Intelligence Committee, where he served as vice-chairman while David Durenberger was chairman in 1985 and 1986. Leahy's impulses on foreign policy are dovish and, like Durenberger, he was critical of the Reagan Administration on both substance and procedure of foreign policy. But Leahy himself got in trouble for leaking a classified document to NBC News in January 1986; when the story came out, and after an Ethics Committee investigation, Leahy took the unusual—as well as humiliating but honorable—step of resigning from the committee in August 1987.

He has fared better in his other committee assignments. He became chairman of the Agriculture Committee when the Democrats took over the Senate in 1987 and, in that capacity, worked on the technically demanding and, in certain states, politically highly sensitive issues that are generated by farm problems and programs: the farm credit bill of 1987, the drought bill of 1988, the attempt to update federal pesticide laws in 1988. In early 1989, he faced the even more daunting prospect of putting together the latest quadrennial farm bill. Leahy brings to the chairmanship a greater attention to detail and civility to colleagues than his predecessor, Jesse Helms of North Carolina, and he has the advantage as well that Vermont does not have a vested interest in commodity programs, with the single exception of the *sui generis* dairy programs, which Leahy has spent years carefully tending. Leahy serves also on Appropriations, where he has been moving up in seniority, and on Judiciary, where he joined the other Democrats and some Republicans in opposing Robert Bork and supporting the Civil Rights Restoration Act.

Leahy has a record on other issues that is generally liberal, but one which he also argues plausibly is parsimonious. His dovishness is not out of line with state sentiments nor is his liberal stand on most cultural issues; his pro-choice stance on abortion has not hurt him in a state where Democrats' historic base was almost entirely Catholic, perhaps because he is an Irish and Italian Catholic himself. But he has the kind of quiet, thoughtful temperament, combined with a certain zest for life and puckish sense of humor, that seems to be part of the Yankee heritage in Vermont.

Leahy was the prosecutor in Burlington when he won by the narrowest of margins the seat held by that quintessential Vermont Yankee George Aiken for 34 years; he won again by a narrow margin in 1980 in a year when most other vulnerable Democrats lost. But in 1986, against his strongest opponent, former Governor Richard Snelling—a businessman who had been one of the nation's leading authorities on federalism and a thoughtful but sometimes angry critic of the Reagan Administration—Leahy won a solid 63%-35% margin. He was helped by Snelling's initial reluctance to run, by a backlash against his harsh and implausible negative campaign against Leahy, and by Leahy's argument that he could become Agriculture chairman. In a race in which voters began with positive feelings about both candidates, a consensus developed quickly for Leahy, and he carried every county and all but 10 of Vermont's towns. It looks like this Democrat has a safe Senate seat in historically Republican Vermont.

In April 1987, Robert Stafford, Senator since 1971, statewide officeholder since he was elected governor in 1958, announced his retirement, and the succession to his seat was effectively settled within days. Stafford was one of the liberal eastern Republicans who cast key votes and framed key legislation in the Reagan years; as chairman of the Environment and Public Works Committee, he helped to save the Clean Air Act and the Superfund from relaxation and then worked to increase their stringency. Less than a week after Stafford's announcement, Richard Snelling took himself out of the race for his seat; Governor Madeleine Kunin said she would decide by summer, but seemed to be leaning against it; while Congressman-at-Large Jim Jeffords had already announced that he would run for the Senate if Stafford didn't, and moved to put his campaign into gear.

It did not have to travel far uphill. By most measures Jeffords, a Republican with one of the most liberal records in the House (although not always on economics), from a modest but respected Yankee background, was the most popular politician in the state. Jeffords was the only House Republican to vote against the Reagan tax cut; he was a vocal critic of Reagan budget cuts; he was elbowed aside from the position as ranking Republican on the Agriculture Committee (where he was an expert on dairy issues) in 1982 by Edward Madigan of Illinois, because he was distrusted by his fellow party members. He did become the ranking Republican on Education and Labor, but there he was often closer on issues to Democrats than to Republicans. With an utterly safe seat, he was still in an uncomfortable position in the House, out of line with his fellow Republicans, not consulted by the Democratic leadership which, since 1977, has tried to amass its majorities from Democrats alone. In the Senate, where there is more bipartisanship and the partisan split is closer, he stood to start off in a position of high leverage and possible power. He has Stafford's seat on Environment plus one on Labor and Human Resources and Veterans' Affairs.

Jeffords's main obstacle was the Republican primary, where he was attacked fiercely by conservative Mike Griffes on gun control, abortion and church and family issues, and also for accepting $5,000 from the Teamsters' PAC after asking the Justice Department not to take over the union. Jeffords won, but by a 61%–39% margin—not impressive for a popular incumbent. Against Democrat Bill Gray in the general, he did better, winning with 70%

Congressman-at-large. Vermont's prosperity and its attraction to veterans of the counterculture and others with liberal cultural values, have spawned some of the oddest politics in the nation. Burlington, with the nation's lowest unemployment record and a booming private sector, elected socialist Bernard Sanders as its mayor by 10 votes in 1981, when the Democrats split, and kept him in office until 1989. Sanders himself, with long curly hair and an effervescence that recalls the late 1960s on campus, ran for governor in 1986 and won 14% of the vote and then, when Jim Jeffords ran for the Senate in 1988, ran for congressman-at-large. He campaigned for gay and lesbian rights, against "the illegal, immoral war against the people of Nicaragua." In the home state of Ethan Allen, he was explicitly Marxist: "I'll be putting emphasis on the class issue in my campaign. I'm going to talk about who really owns this country and the injustices of the present economic setup, which is something none of my potential opponents are going to do." He elbowed aside the Democratic nominee, legislative leader Paul Poirier, to emerge as the chief opponent of Republican Peter Smith, and in the process disproved the central tenet of Marxism, that people vote their economic interests, by winning 36% of the vote in prosperous Vermont.

But that was not enough to beat Peter Smith, who had 41%, and so Smith continues the Republican hold on Vermont's House seat which has been maintained with one exception (1958) since the Republican Party was founded. Smith seems to be a moderate, possibly a liberal Republican; he made a name as founder of the Community College of Vermont, was elected lieutenant governor in 1982 and 1984, and lost to Kunin in the 1986 governor's race. By most traditional standards he would seem to have a safe House seat. But given Vermont's oddball three-party politics, who can say for sure?

Presidential politics. James A. Farley had a good laugh on Vermont in 1936 when he updated an adage to say "As goes Maine, so goes Vermont." Vermont still has voted Democratic for President only once, in 1964. But, liberal on cultural and foreign issues, not tremendously conservative on economics, Vermont is not attracted to conservative Republicans and kind of prefers liberal Democrats. John Anderson got 15% here in 1980, his best showing in any state, and Ronald Reagan's 44% plurality was his seventh lowest percentage. In 1984, Reagan carried Vermont by almost precisely his national percentages. In 1988, Massachusetts neighbor Michael Dukakis ran 2% ahead of his national showing in Vermont—a vivid contrast with New Hampshire, where he ran 13% behind.

Vermont's presidential primary is early in the season, but it is after New Hampshire's and non-binding, so it gets far less attention.

The People: Est. Pop. 1988: 556,000; Pop. 1980: 511,456, up 8.8% 1980–88 and 15.0% 1970–80; 0.22% of U.S. total, 49th largest. 15% with 1–3 yrs. col., 20% with 4+ yrs. col.; 12.1% below poverty level. Single ancestry: 15% English, 11% French, 5% Irish, 2% German, Italian, 1% Scottish, Polish. Households (1980): 72% family, 40% with children, 61% married couples; 31.3% housing units rented; median monthly rent: $176; median house value: $42,300. Voting age pop. (1980): 366,138; 1% Spanish origin. Registered voters (1988): 348,312; no party registration.

1988 Share of Federal Tax Burden: $1,775,000,000; 0.20% of U.S. total, 49th largest.

1988 Share of Federal Expenditures

	Total		Non-Defense		Defense	
Total Expend	$1,550m	(0.18%)	$1,362m	(0.21%)	$221m	(0.10%)
St/Lcl Grants	324m	(0.28%)	324m	(0.28%)	0m	(0.17%)
Salary/Wages	181m	(0.13%)	143m	(0.21%)	38m	(0.21%)
Pymnts to Indiv	843m	(0.21%)	814m	(0.21%)	29m	(0.16%)
Procurement	154m	(0.08%)	33m	(0.07%)	154m	(0.08%)
Research/Other	48m	(0.13%)	48m	(0.13%)	0m	(0.13%)

Political Lineup: Governor, Madeleine M. Kunin (D); Lt. Gov., Howard Dean (D); Secy. of State, James H. Douglas (R); Atty. Gen., Jeffrey L. Amestoy (R); Treasurer, Paul Ruse (R); Auditor, Alexander V. Acebo (R). State Senate, 30 (16 D and 14 R); State House of Representatives, 150 (76 R and 74 D). Senators, Patrick J. Leahy (D) and James M. Jeffords (R). Representative, 1 R at-large.

1988 Presidential Vote

Bush (R) 124,331 (51%)
Dukakis (D). 115,775 (48%)

1984 Presidential Vote

Reagan (R) 135,865 (58%)
Mondale (D) 95,730 (41%)

GOVERNOR

Gov. Madeleine M. Kunin (D)

Elected 1984, term expires Jan. 1991; b. Sept. 28, 1933, Zurich, Switzerland; home, Burlington; U. of MA, B.A. 1956, Columbia U., M.S. 1957, U. of VT, M.A. 1967; Jewish; married (Arthur).

Career: Journalist, col. instructor; VT House of Reps., 1973–78; Lt. Gov. of VT, 1979–82; Radio interviewer and talk show host, WJOY, Burlington, 1982–83.

Office: 109 State St., 5th Fl., Montpelier 05602, 802-828-3333.

Election Results

1988 gen.	Madeleine M. Kunin (D)	134,438	(55%)
	Mike Bernhardt (R)	105,191	(43%)
1988 prim.	Madeleine M. Kunin (D)	28,125	(100%)
1986 gen.	Madeleine M. Kunin (D)	92,379	(47%)
	Peter Smith (R)	75,162	(38%)
	Bernard Sanders (I)	28,430	(14%)

SENATORS

Sen. Patrick J. Leahy (D)

Elected 1974, seat up 1992; b. Mar. 31, 1940, Montpelier; home, Burlington; St. Michael's Col., B.A. 1961, Georgetown U., J.D. 1964; Roman Catholic; married (Marcelle).

Career: Practicing atty., 1964–74; Chittenden Cnty. State's Atty., 1966–74.

Offices: 433 RSOB 20510, 202-224-4242. Also 199 Main St., Burlington 05401, 802-863-2525; and Fed. Bldg., Box 933, Montpelier 05602, 802-229-0569.

Committees: *Agriculture, Nutrition, and Forestry* (Chairman of 10 D). *Appropriations* (6th of 16 D). Subcommittees: Defense; Foreign Operations (Chairman); Interior; VA, HUD, and Independent Agencies. *Judiciary* (5th of 8 D). Subcommittees: Patents, Copyrights and Trademarks; Technology and the Law (Chairman).

Group Ratings

	ADA	ACLU	COPE	CFA	LCV	ACU	NTLC	NSI	COC	CEI
1988	100	85	84	100	100	0	14	0	36	13
1987	90	—	84	83	—	4	—	—	31	23

National Journal Ratings

	1988 LIB	—	1988 CONS	1987 LIB	—	1987 CONS
Economic	86%	—	0%	74%	—	0%
Social	86%	—	0%	88%	—	10%
Foreign	86%	—	0%	74%	—	19%

VERMONT 1241

Key Votes

1) Cut Aged Housing $	FOR	5) Bork Nomination	AGN	9) SDI Funding	AGN
2) Override Hwy Veto	FOR	6) Ban Plastic Guns	AGN	10) Ban Chem Weaps	AGN
3) Kill Plnt Clsng Notice	AGN	7) Deny Abortions	AGN	11) Aid To Contras	AGN
4) Min Wage Increase	FOR	8) Japanese Reparations	FOR	12) Reagan Defense $	AGN

Election Results

1986 general	Patrick J. Leahy (D).................	124,123	(63%)	($1,705,099)
	Richard Snelling (R)..................	67,798	(35%)	($1,502,304)
1986 primary	Patrick J. Leahy (D), unopposed			
1980 general	Patrick J. Leahy (D).................	104,176	(50%)	($434,644)
	Stewart M. Ledbetter (R).............	101,421	(49%)	($532,904)

Sen. James M. Jeffords (R)

Elected 1988, seat up 1994; b. May 11, 1934, Rutland; home, Shrewsbury; Yale U., B.S. 1956, Harvard U., LL.B. 1962; Congregationalist; married (Elizabeth Daley).

Career: Navy, 1956–59; Practicing atty.; Repub. Town Chmn., Shrewsbury, 1963–72; Town Agent, Grand Juror, 1964; VT Senate, 1967–68; VT Atty. Gen., 1969–73; U.S. House of Reps. 1975–1988.

Offices: 530 DSOB 20515, 202-224-5141. Also P.O. Box 676, 138 Main St., Montpelier 05602, 802-223-5273; 30 Airport Rd., Ste. 7, S. Burlington 05403; and P.O. Box 397, 2 South St., Rutland 05701, 802-773-3875.

Committees: *Environment and Public Works* (6th of 7 R). Subcommittees: Environmental Protection; Toxic Substances, Environmental Oversight, Research and Development; Water Resources, Transportation, and Infrastructure. *Labor and Human Resources* (3d of 7 R). Subcommittees: Education, Arts, and Humanities; Handicapped; Labor (Ranking Member). *Veterans Affairs* (5th of 5 R).

Group Ratings (as Member of the U.S. House of Representatives)

	ADA	ACLU	COPE	CFA	LCV	ACU	NTLC	NSI	COC	CEI
1988	70	83	50	64	94	21	50	0	54	19
1987	68	—	48	57	—	26	—	—	67	41

National Journal Ratings (as Member of the U.S. House of Representatives)

	1988 LIB — 1988 CONS			1987 LIB — 1987 CONS		
Economic	46%	—	54%	38%	—	62%
Social	64%	—	34%	56%	—	43%
Foreign	73%	—	26%	76%	—	19%

Key Votes (as Member of the U.S. House of Representatives)

1) Homeless $	FOR	5) Ban Drug Test	AGN	9) SDI Research	AGN
2) Gephardt Amdt	AGN	6) Drug Death Pen	FOR	10) Ban Chem Weaps	FOR
3) Deficit Reduc	FOR	7) Handgun Sales	FOR	11) Aid to Contras	AGN
4) Kill Plnt Clsng Notice	AGN	8) Ban D.C. Abort $	AGN	12) Nuclear Testing	FOR

1242　　VERMONT

Election Results

1988 general	James M. Jeffords (R)	163,183	(70%)	($876,877)
	Bill Gray (D).........................	71,460	(30%)	($549,908)
1988 primary	James M. Jeffords (R)	30,555	(61%)	
	Mike Griffes (R).....................	19,593	(39%)	
1982 general	Robert T. Stafford (R)	82,259	(51%)	($407,340)
	James A. Guest (D)	78,447	(48%)	($282,600)

REPRESENTATIVE

Rep. Peter P. Smith (R)

Elected 1988; b. Oct. 31, 1945, Boston, MA; home, Montpelier; Princeton U., B.A. 1968, Harvard U., M.A. 1970, Ph.D. 1984; Protestant; married (Sarah).

Career: Founder, Pres., Community Col. of VT, 1970–80; Vice Pres., Norwich U., 1987–88; Lt. Gov. of VT, 1982–86; VT Senate, 1980–82.

Offices: 1020 LHOB 20515, 202-225-4115. Also P.O. Box 676, Montpelier 05602, 802-223-5273; Champlain Mill, 1 Main St., Winooski 05404, 802-951-6732; and P.O. Box 397, 121 West St., Rutland 05701, 802-773-3875.

Committees: *Education and Labor* (13th of 13 R). Subcommittees: Elementary, Secondary, and Vocational Education; Employment Opportunities; Select Education. *Government Operations* (9th of 15 R). Subcommittees: Legislation and National Security; Human Resources and Intergovernmental Relations. *Select Committee on Children, Youth, and Families* (10th of 12 R).

Group Ratings and Key Votes: Newly Elected
Election Results

1988 general	Peter Smith (R)	98,937	(41%)	($450,162)
	Bernard Sanders (I)	90,026	(36%)	($331,284)
	Paul Poirier (D)......................	45,330	(19%)	($260,535)
	Three others	5,535	(4%)	
1988 primary	Peter Smith (R)	37,211	(79%)	
	David Gates (R)......................	9,954	(21%)	
1986 general	James M. Jeffords (R)	168,403	(89%)	($86,917)
	Three others	20,314	(11%)	

VIRGINIA

"Incontestably, what runs Virginia is the Byrd machine," wrote John Gunther nearly 50 years ago, though he would have said the same thing any time between 1925 and 1965, adding, as he did, "the most urbane and genteel dictatorship in America." But to the men who ran it, this was certainly not a dictatorship and not really a machine at all. Harry Byrd was a country boy with no money and fine lineage—his ancestor William Byrd was governor of Virginia in the 17th century and his uncle and namesake Hal Flood served in Congress. Byrd himself was elected governor in 1925 and, with an insistence on propriety and a flair for efficiency, imposed a rational structure over what, in Virginia, always had been the natural order of things.

For from the first, this was a commonwealth ruled by its landed gentry. As young men they were taken measure of by their neighbors and, if they were found up to it, were made officers in the local militia and members of the House of Burgesses. From these tobacco-growing counties emerged in the 1770s a group of leaders—George Washington, Patrick Henry, Thomas Jefferson, Richard Henry Lee, James Madison, James Monroe—who in learning, wisdom and strength of character equalled any such group from any similar-sized polity since Periclean Athens. The Virginia they led into the American Revolution was not only the most populous and richest of the 13 colonies, it was also the indispensable creator of the Republic and the Constitution that held together what has become the greatest nation in the world.

After the Revolution, gentry control continued even as Virginia was eclipsed in population and wealth by Pennsylvania and New York and, its tobacco fields exhausted, the commonwealth became a breeding ground for slaves. The dazzling brilliance of the generation of Revolutionary leaders gave way to the eccentricity of John Randolph of Roanoke and the unbridled selfishness and general mediocrity of the generation that followed. Virginia had only two more great heroes, Robert E. Lee and Stonewall Jackson, both of whom reluctantly and brilliantly fought for their state rather than their country; the state's leadership class was impoverished and embittered by the great war, so much of which was fought on Virginia soil. Industrialization came here and there to Virginia: railroads were built across the state to ship cotton up from the South and coal to the seaports; textile mills were built in Southside towns and tobacco factories in Richmond; the giant Newport News Shipbuilding & Dry Dock Company was built by railroad magnate Collis Huntington.

But most of the state remained agricultural, sunk in a low-wage economy, and ruled by the local gentry, by then a small class of landowners and bankers and lawyers who worshipped their Revolutionary past and were filled with bitterness over the failure of their Lost Cause. They were pessimists, looking not for economic growth but for stability, bent on maintaining Virginia's segregation and content with its second-class economy, determined to see that the poor masses did not use government to pillage the rich as Yankee troops once had. Organized county courthouse by county courthouse, required to provide honest, efficient, pay-as-you-go local and state government, this natural elite became the Byrd machine.

Nationally, the machine lost political battles more often than Lee lost military battles, and less gallantly. But it succeeded in keeping most vestiges of the welfare state and racial equality outside Virginia, even to the point of closing public schools in the late 1950s rather than obey federal court integration orders. But this massive resistance collapsed in the late 1950s. Governor Mills Godwin—a Byrd loyalist—accepted integration and upgraded state government in the late 1960s. Most important, demographics changed the Old Dominion. As the 20th century went on, the peripheral parts of the state grew: the coal-mining counties of the far

VIRGINIA — Congressional Districts, Counties, Independent Cities, and Other Selected Places — (10 Districts)

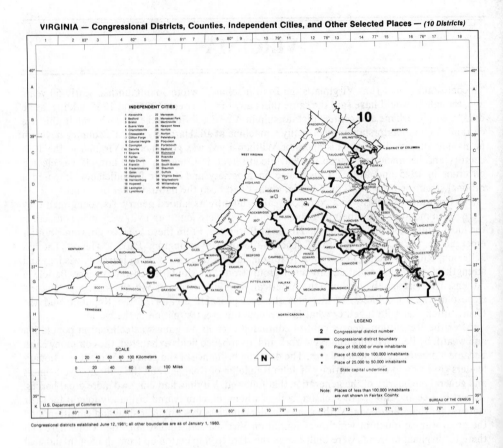

INDEPENDENT CITIES

1 Alexandria
2 Bedford
3 Bristol
4 Buena Vista
5 Charlottesville
6 Chesapeake
7 Clifton Forge
8 Colonial Heights
9 Covington
10 Danville
11 Emporia
12 Fairfax
13 Falls Church
14 Franklin
15 Fredericksburg
16 Galax
17 Hampton
18 Harrisonburg
19 Hopewell
20 Lexington
21 Lynchburg
22 Manassas
23 Manassas Park
24 Martinsville
25 Newport News
26 Norfolk
27 Norton
28 Petersburg
29 Poquoson
30 Portsmouth
31 Radford
32 Richmond
33 Roanoke
34 Salem
35 South Boston
36 Staunton
37 Suffolk
38 Virginia Beach
39 Waynesboro
40 Williamsburg
41 Winchester

LEGEND

2   Congressional district number
    Congressional district boundary
⊛   Place of 100,000 or more inhabitants
⊙   Place of 50,000 to 100,000 inhabitants
•   Place of 25,000 to 50,000 inhabitants
    State capital underlined

Note: Places of less than 100,000 inhabitants are not shown in Fairfax County.

SCALE
0 20 40 60 80 100 Kilometers
0 20 40 60 80 100 Miles

N

U.S. Department of Commerce   BUREAU OF THE CENSUS

Congressional districts established June 12, 1981; all other boundaries are as of January 1, 1980.

southwest, the Tidewater area around the Navy bases in Norfolk and the shipbuilding yards in Newport News, and the government employee-filled suburbs across the Potomac from Washington, D.C. Courthouse politicians here could no longer carry the vote for the Byrd machine by the middle 1960s: Harry Byrd Jr., appointed to his father's Senate seat, was nearly beaten in the 1966 Senate primary, and A. Willis Robertson, 20-year veteran of the Senate—and father of televangelist and 1988 presidential candidate Pat Robertson—was beaten in his primary. Linwood Holton, a Republican and a believer in integration, was elected in 1969. But over the next decade, most of the victories were won by conservatives, some of them Byrd stalwarts turned Republican (like Mills Godwin, who returned to the governorship in 1973), some the sons of former insurgent Republicans (like John Dalton, elected governor in 1977) or Republicans with no deep local roots (like John Warner, elected Senator in 1978). The conservatives, using busing, right-to-work, race or whatever issue came to hand, shrewdly outmaneuvered the liberals; Harry Byrd Jr., for example, avoided perilous primaries by running as an Independent in 1970 and 1976.

Then suddenly in the early 1980s, things began going the other way. The Democrats, shut out in all Virginia presidential elections but one since Byrd Sr.'s "golden silence" in 1952, won the governorship in 1981 after a 16-year political drought and proceeded to not only to hold onto it four years later, but to elect a black lieutenant governor and a woman attorney general. These

Democrats had strong black support, they carried the Washington suburbs, the Tidewater and the far western mountains; more important, they carried or ran even in the Richmond area and the rural counties that are geographically and historically the heart of the state. The Democrats won not because they no longer represented an attempt to impose a labor-liberal agenda on an unwilling Virginia, but they argued that they could use government effectively to improve education, build Virginia's economy, and (with bonds, not pay-as-you-go) build roads and improve transportation in boom and coal bust areas alike.

The catalyst in this change was Governor Charles Robb, elected rather narrowly in 1981, but so popular in 1985 that he would have won near-unanimously if Virginia allowed consecutive terms and had he run. He has impeccable military and Democratic credentials: he is the Marine who married Lynda Bird Johnson and then served in combat in Vietnam. Serious, quiet, he has a demeanor that tradition-minded Virginians trust, even when he promoted blacks and women to leadership positions and spent more money on education. After leaving office, Robb became a national figure as head of the Democratic Leadership Council, was mentioned as a possible presidential candidate for 1988, and was easily elected to the Senate in 1988.

Governor. Robb's successor as governor, Gerald Baliles, is a Democrat who benefited from Robb's strengths, but has considerable strengths of his own. On the surface he looks grey, quiet, even bookish (he is one of the more voracious readers in American politics today), but he has also proved to be a politician who gets what he wants. In 1981, that was the office of attorney general, for which he won upset victories at the state Democratic convention and in the general election; in 1985, it was the governorship. There he outmaneuvered Lieutenant Governor Richard Davis for convention delegates, by combining support from rural areas (he is from a rural county in the shadow of the Blue Ridge) with votes in northern Virginia (where his pro-choice position on abortion was critical). In the general election, he outcampaigned an attractive Republican, Wyatt Durrette. In office, Baliles was almost completely successful with the legislature. He pushed through a transportation program, sorely needed in Virginia's explosively growing suburban areas, including a gas tax and bonds for highway construction—unheard of in the Virginia of Byrd's pay-as-you-go tradition. He beefed up Virginia's already impressive system of higher education and promoted international trade. Baliles did encounter some problems in his last year in office, namely a strike by coal workers in Pittston, where he sent in state troopers to stabilize the situation. He also faced defeat at the hands of the legislature on a proposal to tax pensions over $16,000 a year. Still, he is often mentioned as a possible challenger to Republican Senator John Warner in 1990.

The race to succeed Baliles seems likely to be an historic one. The Democratic nomination went to Lieutenant Governor L. Douglas Wilder, who combined years of experience in the state Senate with a record a bit more conservative on some issues than Baliles's; what is remarkable about his candidacy is that he is black. He won the number two job by personally campaigning in dozens of once segregationist rural counties, shaking hands and winning support, and running an endorsement ad showing a white Southside state trooper endorsing him. Widely popular, not outside the consensus on the issues, articulate and knowledgeable, Wilder had an excellent chance in early 1989 to become the first black elected governor of an American state—and a state which, 25 years ago, any observer would have thought would be the last to do so.

To win, however, Wilder will have to beat the Republican nominee in a state which in national politics is solidly Republican. The Republicans, in 1989, decided to jettison the state convention they have used to choose candidates (the 1978 convention, with some 9,000 delegates, may have been the largest elected deliberative body in world history) and to have a June primary instead. The winner was former attorney general Marshall Coleman, who defeated former U.S. Senator Paul Trible, 37%-35%, with 8th District Congressman Stan Parris receiving 28% of the vote. The three candidates spent almost $10 million total (mostly on media) in the first Virginia statewide Republican primary since 1949.

Senators. Virginia is represented in the Senate by two residents of the greater Washington area, neither of whom comes from the local gentry that manned the Byrd machine, and both of whom first came to public notice because of whom they married; both have since shown more talent and accomplished more than most observers expected.

John Warner is now one of the senior Republicans in the Senate, ranking Republican on the Armed Services Committee, the winner of a second term by an impressive margin. Warner's secret in the Senate has been hard work. He does not have the Senate's strongest intellect; he is prone to cliches and pomposity; his service as Secretary of the Navy in the Nixon Administration prompted Nixon, perhaps in one of his bibulous moods, to say that proved anyone could do the job. His next appointment, to head the Bicentennial Commission, was not considered a promotion. But Warner does plug away at his homework. Elizabeth Taylor, his wife during his first campaign, complained during divorce proceedings that he spent too much time on dull things. A man who neglects one of the greatest movie stars for his briefing books is obviously bent on doing his duty.

This does not mean that Warner has pleased everyone on the Armed Services Committee and off. He is, as almost every Member of Congress from Virginia must be, a Navy man; Virginia's Tidewater region is the East Coast headquarters of the Navy. But, after first opposing it and then skipping a critical vote, Warner supported Navy Secretary John Lehman's homeporting plan to disperse the Navy's big vessels from its major ports at Norfolk and San Diego, casting the vote that got it through Armed Services 10–9. His statement that he did it because he thought it was in the national interest rings true; it certainly did him no good in Tidewater Virginia.

Nor does he always line up with his party. In 1987, after not announcing his position during the debate, Warner cast his vote against the nomination of Judge Robert Bork; it was not critical in the outcome, but he was the only southern Republican to vote against Bork. In early 1989, he tottered on the brink of voting against the nomination of John Tower, and only after last-minute requests from President Bush did he vote in favor. That probably hurt him with Senate Republicans, all but one of whom voted for Tower in the end; it surely undermines their confidence in him and diminishes their inclination to follow his lead on Armed Services issues, particularly when he takes a bipartisan approach supporting chairman Sam Nunn. On issues generally, Warner has a conservative record. But obviously he does not see himself as a die-hard partisan, and he wants to be known as a supporter of civil rights.

Warner started the 1978 Senate race with few political assets, other than Elizabeth Taylor at his side and a well-stocked campaign treasury. But he fought hard for the Senate nomination at the Republicans' huge convention that year, and when he came in second to longtime party chairman Richard Obenshain he cheerfully and actively supported his candidacy. Then in August Obenshain was killed in a plane crash, and Republican leaders, though reluctant, had no alternative but to give the nomination to Warner. In November, in a year that turned out to be more conservative than pundits expected, Warner won a hairsbreadth victory in the general election over Democrat Andrew Miller. He seemed at first to have an unsteady hold on that seat, but the rise in Republican fortunes in the 1980s and his own hard work on national issues and with local Virginians put him in strong shape for 1984. His Democratic opponent, former Delegate Edythe Harrison, was denigrated by state Democratic leaders just as she was announcing her candidacy against a man they shrank from challenging; she was labelled as an ultraliberal and failed even to carry her home city of Norfolk. For 1990, Warner looks strong on paper—depending on who opposes him. Gerald Baliles, who leaves the governorship at the end of 1989 because of the one-term limit and seems headed for a lucrative Richmond law practice, would certainly give him a hard time; and it's possible that some other Democrat could be a serious candidate. But Warner's hard work may well pay off with another weak opponent and a third Senate term.

Virginia's junior Senator, Charles Robb, has been in the public eye for more than 20 years. As a young Marine officer, he had duty in the White House, where he met Lynda Bird Johnson and married her in a White House wedding; then he went off to combat in Vietnam. In 1977, as a Washington lawyer, he ran for lieutenant governor and won, while Republicans were carrying the state otherwise; in 1981, he ran for governor and beat Marshall Coleman 54%–46%—the first Democrat to win in 16 years. As governor, he was widely popular and was given credit, rightly or wrongly, for much of Virginia's dynamic growth and the confidence and pride that has accompanied it. He added $1 billion to the education budget and worked to boost Virginia's coal export industry. He appointed blacks and women to top positions in large numbers.

Even as Robb was succeeding in Virginia, he was branching out into national politics; with Sam Nunn, he was one of the sparkplugs behind the Democratic Leadership Council beginning in 1985, combining an innovative approach to domestic policy—like the DLC community service bill sponsored by Nunn in the Senate—with support for a strong defense. The experience of combat certainly has been central to Robb's life, and he retains an interest in military tactics and strategy as well as foreign policy generally. He began eyeing the 1988 Senate race from afar and was far ahead of Trible in the polls when the incumbent bowed out; at that point, Robb was effectively presented with a Senate seat for the asking. The Republicans found a candidate in black minister Maurice Dawkins, and newspapers repeatedly printed stories of how Robb had attended parties in Virginia Beach at which drugs were used. But no evidence of any misconduct by Robb was ever presented, and Dawkins made no breakthrough: Robb won with 71% of the vote. In the Senate, he is a member of the Foreign Relations, Commerce and Budget Committees, but he is also watched by many for his stands on issues generally: his record and sense of command, despite a somewhat wooden speaking style, make him one politician who is seriously mentioned for national office. Robb made something of a splash in March of 1989 at a DLC meeting in Philadelphia by stating, while standing next to Jesse Jackson, that Jackson had encouraged perceptions "not conducive to the electoral success we are looking for"—a statement which Jackson countered.

Presidential politics. Virginia, prompted for years by Harry Byrd's 1952 "golden silence," has voted Republican in every presidential election since except 1964, when it went for Lyndon Johnson (who courted Byrd shamelessly); it was almost as solidly for George Bush in 1988 as for Ronald Reagan in 1984. Its biggest urban areas, which once seemed headed toward the national Democratic Party, no longer are: the northern Virginia suburbs of Washington seem increasingly caught up in a free enterprise boom, the Tidewater area is pro-military, and the Richmond area is dominated by conservative suburbanites. Virginia selected its 1988 delegates in the Super Tuesday primary. George Bush won easily among Republicans, while Jesse Jackson surprised many by winning the low-turnout Democratic contest.

Congressional districting. When Charles Robb was elected governor in 1981, Republicans held 9 of Virginia's 10 House seats; this was the most conservative delegation in the nation. Today 5 of the 10 are Democrats. Reapportionment may give Virginia an 11th seat, probably in the farther suburbs of Washington; this would probably be Republican, but adjustments to the other suburban districts by the Democratic legislature could throw one of them to the Democrats. Districts elsewhere in the state are not likely to be changed drastically.

The People: Est. Pop. 1988: 5,996,000; Pop. 1980: 5,346,818, up 12.1% 1980–88 and 14.9% 1970–80; 2.40% of U.S. total, 13th largest. 15% with 1–3 yrs. col., 19% with 4+ yrs. col.; 11.8% below poverty level. Single ancestry: 15% English, 5% German, 4% Irish, 1% Italian, French, Scottish, Polish. Households (1980): 75% family, 42% with children, 62% married couples; 34.4% housing units rented; median monthly rent: $207; median house value: $48,100. Voting age pop. (1980): 3,872,484; 17% Black, 1% Spanish origin, 1% Asian origin. Registered voters (1988): 2,878,718; no party registration.

1988 Share of Federal Tax Burden: $22,428,000,000; 2.54% of U.S. total, 11th largest.

1248   VIRGINIA

1988 Share of Federal Expenditures

	Total		Non-Defense		Defense	
Total Expend	$35,698m	(4.04%)	$16,277m	(2.48%)	$21,493m	(9.41%)
St/Lcl Grants	1,961m	(1.71%)	1,955m	(1.71%)	6m	(5.09%)
Salary/Wages	9,841m	(7.33%)	2,043m	(3.05%)	7,798m	(3.05%)
Pymnts to Indiv	10,597m	(2.59%)	9,208m	(2.36%)	1,389m	(7.45%)
Procurement	12,288m	(6.51%)	2,071m	(4.46%)	12,288m	(6.51%)
Research/Other	1,011m	(2.71%)	999m	(2.70%)	12m	(2.70%)

Political Lineup: Governor, Gerald L. (Jerry) Baliles (D); Lt. Gov., L. Douglas Wilder (D); Secy. of Commonwealth, Sandy Bowen (D); Atty. Gen., Mary Sue Terry (D); Treasurer, Alice W. Handy (D); Controller, Edward J. Mazur (D). State Senate, 40 (30 D and 10 R); State House of Delegates, 100 (64 D, 35 R, and 1 I). Senators, John W. Warner (R) and Charles S. Robb (D). Representatives, 10 (5 R and 5 D).

1988 Presidential Vote

Bush (R)	1,309,162	(60%)
Dukakis (D)	859,799	(39%)

1988 Democratic Presidential Primary

Jackson	164,709	(45%)
Gore	81,419	(22%)
Dukakis	80,183	(22%)
Gephardt	15,935	(4%)
Simon	7,045	(2%)
Hart	6,266	(2%)
Babbitt	2,454	(1%)

1984 Presidential Vote

Reagan (R)	1,337,078	(62%)
Mondale (D)	796,250	(37%)

1988 Republican Presidential Primary

Bush	124,738	(53%)
Dole	60,921	(26%)
Robertson	32,173	(14%)
Kemp	10,809	(5%)

GOVERNOR

Gov. Gerald L. (Jerry) Baliles (D)

Elected 1985, term expires Jan. 1990; b. July 8, 1940, Patrick Cnty.; home, Richmond; Wesleyan U., B.A. 1963; U. of VA, J.D. 1967; Episcopalian; married (Jeannie).

Career: VA Asst. Atty. Gen., 1967–72; VA Dpty. Atty. Gen., 1972–75; VA House of Del., 1976–82; VA Atty. Gen., 1982–86.

Office: State Capitol, Richmond 23219, 804-786-2211.

Election Results

1985 gen.	Gerald L. (Jerry) Baliles (D) ...	741,438	(55%)
	Wyatt B. Durette, Jr. (R)	601,652	(44%)
1981 prim.	Gerald L. (Jerry) Baliles (D), nominated by convention		
1981 gen.	Charles S. Robb (D)	760,357	(54%)
	J. Marshall Coleman (R)	659,398	(46%)

SENATORS
Sen. John W. Warner (R)

Elected 1978, seat up 1990; b. Feb. 18, 1927, Washington, D.C.; home, Middleburg; Wash. and Lee U., B.S., 1949, U. of VA, LL.B. 1953; Episcopalian; divorced.

Career: Navy, WWII, USMC, Korea; Law Clerk to U.S. Crt. of Appeals Chf. Judge E. Barrett Prettyman, 1953–54; Practicing atty., 1954–56, 1960–69; Asst. U.S. Atty., 1956–60; Undersecy. of the U.S. Navy, 1969–72, Secy., 1972–74; Dir., Amer. Rev. Bicentennial Comm., 1974–76.

Offices: 225 RSOB 20510, 202-224-2023. Also 1100 E. Main St., Richmond 23219, 804-771-2579; 805 Fed. Bldg., 200 Granby Mall, Norfolk 23570, 804-441-3079; 235 Fed. Bldg., 180 E. Main St., Abingdon 24210, 703-628-8158; and 1003 Dominion Bank Bldg., 213 S. Jefferson St., Roanoke 24011, 703-832-4676.

Committees: *Armed Services* (Ranking Member of 9 R). *Environment and Public Works* (5th of 7 R). Subcommittees: Environmental Protection; Toxic Substances, Environmental Oversight, Research and Development (Ranking Member); Water Resources, Transportation, and Infrastructure. *Special Committee on Aging* (8th of 9 R). *Select Committee on Intelligence* (5th of 7 R).

Group Ratings

	ADA	ACLU	COPE	CFA	LCV	ACU	NTLC	NSI	COC	CEI
1988	5	31	17	50	40	87	85	100	86	42
1987	25	—	15	50	—	60	—	—	94	61

National Journal Ratings

	1988 LIB — 1988 CONS		1987 LIB — 1987 CONS	
Economic	9%	81%	21%	74%
Social	14%	85%	39%	59%
Foreign	26%	72%	25%	73%

Key Votes

1) Cut Aged Housing $	AGN	5) Bork Nomination	AGN
2) Override Hwy Veto	AGN	6) Ban Plastic Guns	FOR
3) Kill Plnt Clsng Notice	FOR	7) Deny Abortions	FOR
4) Min Wage Increase	AGN	8) Japanese Reparations	—

9) SDI Funding	FOR
10) Ban Chem Weaps	FOR
11) Aid To Contras	FOR
12) Reagan Defense $	AGN

Election Results

1984 general	John W. Warner (R)	1,406,194	(70%)	($2,974,498)
	Edythe C. Harrison (D)	601,142	(30%)	($492,201)
1984 primary	John W. Warner (R), nominated by convention			
1978 general	John W. Warner (R)	613,232	(50%)	($2,897,237)
	Andrew P. Miller (D)	608,511	(50%)	($832,773)

Sen. Charles S. Robb (D)

Elected 1988, seat up 1994; b. June 26, 1939, Phoenix, AZ; home, McLean; U. of WI, B.B.A. 1961, U.of VA, J.D. 1973; Episcopalian; married, (Lynda).

Career: USMC, 1961–1970; Law Clerk to Judge John D. Butzner Jr., U.S. Crt. of Appeals, 1973–74; Practicing atty. 1974–77, 1986–88; VA Lt. Gov. 1978–82; Gov. of VA, 1982–86.

Offices: 493 RSOB, 20515, 202-224-4024. Also 1001 E. Broad St., Richmond, 23219, 804-771-2221.

Committees: *Budget* (13th of 13 D). *Commerce, Science, and Transportation* (11th of 11 D). Subcommittees: Consumer; National Ocean Policy Study; Science, Technology, and Space; Surface Transportation. *Foreign Relations* (10th of 10 D). Subcommittees: Near Eastern and South Asian Affairs; Terrorism, Narcotics and International Operations; Western Hemisphere and Peace Corps Affairs.

Group Ratings and Key Votes: Newly Elected

Election Results

1988 general	Charles S. Robb (D)	1,474,086	(71%)	($2,881,666)
	Maurice A. Dawkins (R)	593,652	(29%)	($282,229)
1988 primary	Charles S. Robb (D), nominated by convention			
1982 general	Paul S. Trible, Jr. (R)	724,571	(51%)	($2,170,961)
	Richard J. Davis (D)	690,839	(49%)	($1,192,203)

FIRST DISTRICT

When the first British settlers sailed up the sunken estuaries that are the rivers flowing into Chesapeake Bay, they were searching for gold, hoping to sail back soon with their fortunes. But they couldn't help noticing that the spot where the James River feeds into the Bay, Hampton Roads, was a fine natural harbor, with calm, deep water and good anchorages for the tiny wooden vessels that had made it across the Atlantic. There they established a civilization whose elegance is recalled in the craftsmanship of restored Williamsburg and whose coarseness and brutality is brought to life by any narrative of the story of Jamestown or the other beleaguered settlements. Tidewater Virginia brought slavery to America and tobacco to the world, and slave-raised tobacco was the center of its economy in the colonial era and in the years afterward, when its most talented sons left its depleted soil for better opportunities elsewhere.

Now the economy of Tidewater Virginia is based, and the tone of its life is set, by the American military. Fifty years ago, as America was on the brink of world war, the Navy base at Norfolk and the Newport News Shipbuilding and Drydock Company across Hampton Roads became the center of American naval might in the Atlantic. Just before World War II, there were some 369,000 people living on both sides of Hampton Roads. Today, after the huge expansion of the fleet in the war and after, there are 1.2 million—a population collected not just from the local rural hinterland but from all over the country, making this a metropolitan area that is not so much southern in atmosphere as it is, in the manner of our military bases abroad, national. But you can still see what has made this area what is by looking at the Shipbuilding and Drydock Company that lies over the flat neighborhoods lining the baysides, with its huge ships looming larger than life, their turrets and superstructures bristling with armored might. This is, among other things, the biggest private employer in Virginia. At the height of the naval expansion of the 1980s, 30,000 people worked here, and the Defense Department spent $1.2

billion a year.

Virginia's 1st Congressional District includes Newport News, Hampton, and their Peninsula suburbs, plus Williamsburg and Jamestown, and then goes farther north on both sides of Chesapeake Bay. On the east it includes the southern tip of the Delmarva Peninsula, site of the annual roundup of wild Chincoteague ponies; on the west are the rural Northern Neck counties where George Washington and Robert E. Lee were born and which, in recent years, have shown significant population and economic growth for the first time in decades. There is a large black population in all parts of this district, 31% overall; there were big plantations here before the Civil War, and many blacks moved into the industrial Tidewater to find good jobs. Today there is significant integration, the influence of slavery and segregation having been overcome by life in the integrated military.

Historically Democratic, this is now a Republican district in many contests; the national Democrats' anti-military leanings have moved voters away from them. The current congressman, Herbert Bateman, won the seat in 1982 when Paul Trible, after six vote-winning years, went on to the Senate. Bateman has deep roots in an area where many voters and politicians are newcomers, and his career goes back many years: he was a sometime opponent, sometime ally of the Byrd Democrats who represented Newport News in the Virginia Senate for 15 years and switched parties in 1976. He was outmaneuvered by Trible for the congressional nomination in 1976 and failed to get the Republican lieutenant governor nomination in 1981. But Bateman had the congressional nomination locked up in 1982 and won fairly easily after his first Democratic opponent withdrew from the race in June and another was substituted in his place.

In his second term, Bateman got a seat on the Armed Services Committee—a virtual must for this district—and he also has a helpful seat on Merchant Marine. He is a staunch supporter of high defense spending, in the 1st District and out, and is a detail man, working hard on measures that may or may not be of national importance but on which he often makes a difference. He is, of course, a strong believer in building aircraft carriers, and he has also moved to restrict the pollutant TBT that threatens local waters. To the military base closing bill he attached an amendment requiring the commission making recommendations to take into account historical preservation and environmental costs; this was obviously an attempt to save Fort Monroe, an antique fortress at the entrance of Hampton Roads (Jefferson Davis was held prisoner here after the Civil War), which is often held up as the paradigmatic example of an outmoded base, but which does have genuine historical value. Bateman has been successful: it didn't get on the final list of closings.

The military forces are the least segregated and probably the least racial-minded part of American life, and the attitudes they inculcate are apparent in the election returns in this district where so many voters are or were in the military or work as civilians in military installations. Bateman's toughest opponent since he was elected was Newport News state Senator Robert Scott, who in 1986 held him to 56% of the vote; Scott, a black, is elected to the legislature from a city that is 70% white. Against weaker opposition in 1988, Bateman won with 73% of the vote, and appears to have won between 15% and 25% of votes from blacks.

The People: Est. Pop. 1986: 584,500, up 9.2% 1980–86; Pop. 1980: 535,092, up 11.3% 1970–80. Households (1980): 76% family, 43% with children, 62% married couples; 33.8% housing units rented; median monthly rent: $180; median house value: $41,600. Voting age pop. (1980): 384,328; 29% Black, 1% Spanish origin, 1% Asian origin.

1988 Presidential Vote:

Bush (R)	131,341	(60%)
Dukakis (D)	83,291	(38%)

Rep. Herbert H. Bateman (R)

Elected 1982; b. Aug. 7, 1928, Elizabeth City, NC; home, Newport News; Col. of William and Mary, B.A. 1949, Georgetown U., LL.B. 1956; Presbyterian; married (Laura).

Career: Teacher, Hampton Sch., 1949–51; USAF, 1951–53; Law Clerk to Judge W. Bastian, 1956–57; Practicing atty., 1957–82; VA Senate, 1968–82.

Offices: 1230 LHOB 20515, 202-225-4261. Also 739 Thimble Shoals Blvd., Newport News 23606, 804-873-1132; P.O. Box 1183, Tappahannock 22560, 804-443-4740; and P.O. Box 447, Accomac, 23301, 804-787-7836.

Committees: *Armed Services* (10th of 21 R). Subcommittees: Military Personnel and Compensation (Ranking Member); Seapower and Strategic and Critical Materials. *Merchant Marine and Fisheries* (7th of 17 R). Subcommittees: Coast Guard and Navigation; Fisheries and Wildlife Conservation and the Environment; Merchant Marine.

Group Ratings

	ADA	ACLU	COPE	CFA	LCV	ACU	NTLC	NSI	COC	CEI
1988	20	22	10	27	44	84	54	100	85	56
1987	12	—	9	23	—	74	—	—	79	53

National Journal Ratings

	1988 LIB — 1988 CONS		1987 LIB — 1987 CONS	
Economic	24%	— 74%	23%	— 76%
Social	5%	— 95%	19%	— 78%
Foreign	0%	— 84%	25%	— 74%

Key Votes

1) Homeless $	AGN	5) Ban Drug Test	FOR	9) SDI Research	FOR
2) Gephardt Amdt	AGN	6) Drug Death Pen	FOR	10) Ban Chem Weaps	AGN
3) Deficit Reduc	AGN	7) Handgun Sales	AGN	11) Aid to Contras	FOR
4) Kill Plnt Clsng Notice	FOR	8) Ban D.C. Abort $	FOR	12) Nuclear Testing	AGN

Election Results

1988 general	Herbert H. Bateman (R)	135,937	(73%)	($284,702)
	James S. Ellenson (D).................	49,614	(27%)	($30,302)
1988 primary	Herbert H. Bateman (R), nominated by convention			
1986 general	Herbert H. Bateman (R)	80,713	(56%)	($602,251)
	Robert C. Scott (D)	63,365	(44%)	($348,485)

SECOND DISTRICT

In the quiet days before World War II, the Norfolk waterfront was, according to the *WPA Guide,* "a jumble of boats, wharves, warehouses, and industries extracting life from the sea. Plowing through the oily surface of the harbor are powerful little tugs with barges in tow, gleaming white coastal and Bay passenger steamers, rusty-hull coastal freighters, tramp steamers, battleships, trawlers and oyster boats, and less frequently transatlantic steamships. In narrow, tree-lined streets are old brick houses, some in large yards kept green and damp by sheltering boxwood, magnolia and crepe myrtle, and others shoulder to shoulder, flush with the sidewalk. East Main Street, its elegant old brick houses of the colonial elite now in decay, unrolls its wares in curio shops, wienie bars, tattoo clinics, shooting galleries, beer gardens and cheap rooming houses. Nightly, this quarter is patrolled by paired M.P.s, whose brassards and billies come most into play when Saturday shore leave spills recruits from the naval base, sailors from ships, and a goodly number of Marines into downtown Norfolk." As America was girding up to fight the war it wanted to avoid, Norfolk was its main Atlantic naval base, a small southern city whose history was already being overwhelmed by the forces stationed here and the growth they brought.

Today Norfolk is the center of the largest naval installations in the world, with more than 125 warships, 100,000 sailors and Marines and $2 billion in annual spending. Norfolk is also the center of a metropolitan area, on both sides of Hampton Roads, with over 1.2 million people— four times as many as 50 years ago. Norfolk preserves its antique past more carefully now, but the growth and development that has spilled out beyond the city limits into Virginia Beach on the ocean and the Chesapeake toward the Dismal Swamp has little regional or historic distinctiveness. Even the Christian Broadcasting Network complex built by 1988 presidential candidate Pat Robertson, with its Georgian buildings far bigger than any original Georgian buildings, could be almost anywhere, although in fact it is near a freeway interchange on the Norfolk-Virginia Beach border.

To the Hampton Roads area, the military buildup and economic growth of the last 45 years have brought a population drawn from a wider cross-section of the nation than is usually found in the South. There is no heavy accent here: the brothy Tidewater accent is heard more often farther up the rivers, toward Richmond. Parts of Norfolk have the look and feel of a working-class town, with shipyard workers and many blacks (35% of the total), but most of it is securely white middle-class, as is almost all of Virginia Beach except perhaps for the strip of motels along the ocean front. Norfolk and Virginia Beach together make up Virginia's 2d Congressional District. Once it was solidly Democratic; it voted for Hubert Humphrey in 1968. But that was when Norfolk cast 65,000 votes and Virginia Beach 37,000. After 20 years of metropolitan growth, Norfolk in 1988 cast 69,000 votes and Virginia Beach 111,000, leaving the 2d District solidly for former Navy pilot George Bush and against aircraft carrier critic Michael Dukakis.

Congressional elections have gone the other way, however: in 1986 the 2d district elected Democrat Owen Pickett, when the Republican who had held the seat sine 1968 retired. Pickett, though an accountant with little personal magnetism (the kind of guy who gets up at 4 a.m.) had a number of assets. A legislator since 1972, he was known as a fiscal conservative and a hard worker, the man who restructured the state retirement system. He was Democratic state chairman in 1981, when Charles Robb won the governorship and began a string of Democratic victories. He had a setback in 1982, when he was Robb's choice for the Senate but withdrew after Douglas Wilder, then state senator and now lieutenant governor, threatened to run as an independent against him. But by the time he ran for Congress in 1986, the quiet and methodical Pickett had Wilder's support and that of Jesse Jackson's Norfolk coordinator. He also had a Republican opponent plagued by his close relationship with the head of a bankrupt second mortgage company and his partnership with a Richmond stockbroker sentenced to 25 years in jail for embezzlement and business fraud. Pickett carried Norfolk heavily, lost Virginia Beach narrowly, and won 49%–42%.

In the House, Pickett showed his political acumen by getting a new seat created for him on the Armed Services Committee and getting a seat on Merchant Marine as well—the two crucial committees for any Norfolk congressman. There he worked unsuccessfully to let former military spouses into commissaries, helped increase military health benefits, restored $213 million to the Seawolf submarine program, and helped get approval for two new aircraft carriers. He was a swing vote on contra aid, and on issues generally stood at about the middle of the House. In 1988, he had an interesting opponent, retired General Jerry Curry, a black fundamentalist

Christian who had worked on the early stages of Pat Robertson's campaign, who attacked Pickett as insufficiently conservative. But this time Pickett carried Virginia Beach as well as Norfolk and won 61%–36%. He seems to have a safe seat.

The People: Est. Pop. 1986: 608,200, up 14.9% 1980–86; Pop. 1980: 529,178, up 10.2% 1970–80. Households (1980): 74% family, 44% with children, 58% married couples; 46.1% housing units rented; median monthly rent: $202; median house value: $50,000. Voting age pop. (1980): 383,036; 21% Black, 2% Asian origin, 2% Spanish origin.

1988 Presidential Vote:

Bush (R)	107,019	(59%)
Dukakis (D)	71,558	(40%)

Rep. Owen B. Pickett (D)

Elected 1986; b. Aug. 31, 1930, Richmond; home, Virginia Beach; VA Polytechnic Inst. and St. U., B.S. 1952, U. of Richmond, J.D. 1955; Baptist; married (Sybil).

Career: Practicing atty., CPA; VA House of Del., 1972–86.

Offices: 1429 LHOB 20515, 202-225-4215. Also Fed. Bldg., Rm. 815, Norfolk 23510, 804-624-9124; and 2710 VA Beach Blvd., Virginia Beach 23452, 804-486-3710.

Committees: *Armed Services* (26th of 31 D). Subcommittees: Military Personnel and Compensation; Research and Development; Seapower and Strategic and Critical Materials. *Merchant Marine and Fisheries* (18th of 26 D). Subcommittees: Coast Guard and Navigation; Merchant Marine; Oversight and Investigations.

Group Ratings

	ADA	ACLU	COPE	CFA	LCV	ACU	NTLC	NSI	COC	CEI
1988	50	57	83	73	50	40	22	60	50	25
1987	72	—	81	57	—	22	—	—	40	17

National Journal Ratings

	1988 LIB — 1988 CONS			1987 LIB — 1987 CONS		
Economic	60%	—	37%	57%	—	40%
Social	57%	—	42%	50%	—	49%
Foreign	48%	—	52%	50%	—	50%

Key Votes

1) Homeless $	AGN	5) Ban Drug Test	AGN	9) SDI Research	AGN
2) Gephardt Amdt	AGN	6) Drug Death Pen	FOR	10) Ban Chem Weaps	AGN
3) Deficit Reduc	FOR	7) Handgun Sales	FOR	11) Aid to Contras	FOR
4) Kill Plnt Clsng Notice	AGN	8) Ban D.C. Abort $	AGN	12) Nuclear Testing	AGN

Election Results

1988 general	Owen B. Pickett (D)	106,666	(61%)	($414,011)
	Jerry R. Curry (R)	62,567	(36%)	($189,391)
1988 primary	Owen B. Pickett (D), nominated by convention			
1986 general	Owen B. Pickett (D)	54,491	(49%)	($607,558)
	A.J. (Joe) Canada, Jr. (R)	46,137	(42%)	($639,598)
	Stephen P. Shao (I)	9,492	(9%)	

THIRD DISTRICT

Richmond remains, as it has been since Thomas Jefferson designed its chaste Roman Capitol, the center of Virginia. For years the elite that ran its great institutions—the Virginia Electric and Power Company, the big banks on Main Street and the big law firms like the one that produced Supreme Court Justice Lewis Powell, the Philip Morris tobacco company and the Richmond newspapers—operating from the capital of the Confederacy, maintained a way of life highly conscious of Virginia's traditions. "The city's social season, from late fall to Ash Wednesday," the WPA Guide noted 50 years ago in a description not rendered entirely obsolete today, "retains its old ritual, with the Monday germans as highlights. Tea in darkened drawing rooms, dinners served by tradition-trained butlers, frosted mint juleps in ancient goblets, and Smithfield ham and beaten biscuits are party of the ceremony that has continued with no deviation. It is still proper in old Richmond to refer to a guest as So-and-So's granddaughter or the descendant of a founding father. The very broad a and the added y are indispensable to good breeding. Guests come by street and motor cyar to have tea in the gyarden at hahlf pahst five, and no tomaytoes are served in Richmond." Yet underneath this genteel veneer, the city's economic life depended on the same commodity that had given that brilliant founding generation the time for intellectual reflection and public service. "Tobacco is the staple product. Downtown Richmond is fragrant with the odor of the cured leaves being converted into cigars, cigarettes, and smoking and chewing tobacco."

Many of Richmond's old traditions are maintained still and its heritage honored, but racial segregation is not among them: Douglas Wilder, who started working in a hotel where he could not take a room or get a meal is now Lieutenant Governor and may be elected governor in 1989. Yet the Byrd-Democrats-turned-Republicans who have run Richmond's affairs for so many years have seen some of their ideas prevail over their liberal critics: the economic boom has occurred without the labor unions and without the expensive welfare programs the liberals wanted.

Richmond and most of its suburbs in surrounding Henrico and Chesterfield Counties form Virginia's 3d Congressional District. The city itself has a black majority these days, even though the elite still lives in the Fanlight District around Monument Avenue, while the suburbs are heavily white. Overall the metropolitan area has been solidly Republican in presidential elections since Harry Byrd's first "golden silence" in 1952, and easily elects a Republican congressman, Thomas Bliley. Bliley, unusual for Richmond, is a Catholic whose family runs a funeral home. He was mayor (as a nominal Democrat) between 1970 and 1977. First elected to Congress in 1980, he has been something of a workhorse, snaring a seat on the coveted Energy and Commerce Committee by promising to serve on District of Columbia too. On Energy and Commerce and its Health Subcommittee he is predictably a supporter of the tobacco industry and has opposed restrictions on cigarette advertising. But he has also been able to work with Chairman John Dingell on overseeing generic drug regulation. He was the lead sponsor of the law banning dial-a-porn phone calls. Bliley casts occasional liberal votes on cultural and foreign issues favoring, for example, sanctions on South Africa. He is co-chairman of the Congressional Adoption Caucus, and one of those conservatives who seems genuinely concerned about those in need; as an opponent of abortion, he also favors infant health care and nutrition programs. And he keeps up with local Richmond issues, like getting funds to construct a flood wall in Richmond, which has been seriously flooded many times within the last 25 years.

In the old days, Richmond's conservatives seemed inert in national government; Bliley, while conservative, seems an activist. He is reelected without difficulty.

The People: Est. Pop. 1986: 575,300, up 8.0% 1980–86; Pop. 1980: 533,668, up 12.0% 1970–80. Households (1980): 71% family, 38% with children, 55% married couples; 39.5% housing units rented; median monthly rent: $203; median house value: $47,000. Voting age pop. (1980): 394,810; 26% Black, 1% Spanish origin, 1% Asian origin.

1988 Presidential Vote:
Bush (R) 151,033   (63%)
Dukakis (D). 86,678   (36%)

Rep. Thomas J. Bliley, Jr. (R)

Elected 1980; b. Jan. 28, 1932, Chesterfield Cnty.; home, Richmond; Georgetown U., B.A. 1952; Roman Catholic; married (Mary Virginia).

Career: Navy, 1952–55; Owner, funeral home, 1955–80; Richmond City Cncl., Vice Mayor, 1968–70, Mayor, 1970–77.

Offices: 213 CHOB 20515, 202-225-2815. Also 4914 Fitzhugh Ave., Ste. 101, Richmond 23230, 804-771-2809.

Committees: *District of Columbia* (2d of 4 R). Subcommittees: Fiscal Affairs and Health (Ranking Member); Judiciary and Education. *Energy and Commerce* (9th of 17 R). Subcommittees: Health and the Environment; Oversight and Investigations (Ranking Member); Telecommunications and Finance. *Select Committee on Children, Youth, and Families* (Ranking Member of 12 R).

Group Ratings

	ADA	ACLU	COPE	CFA	LCV	ACU	NTLC	NSI	COC	CEI
1988	10	17	12	36	31	96	67	100	93	56
1987	0	—	11	21	—	96	—	—	100	73

National Journal Ratings

	1988 LIB — 1988 CONS		1987 LIB — 1987 CONS	
Economic	13%	85%	0%	89%
Social	20%	78%	15%	84%
Foreign	30%	67%	0%	80%

Key Votes

1) Homeless $	FOR	5) Ban Drug Test	FOR	9) SDI Research	FOR
2) Gephardt Amdt	AGN	6) Drug Death Pen	FOR	10) Ban Chem Weaps	AGN
3) Deficit Reduc	AGN	7) Handgun Sales	FOR	11) Aid to Contras	FOR
4) Kill Plnt Clsng Notice	FOR	8) Ban D.C. Abort $	FOR	12) Nuclear Testing	AGN

Election Results

1988 general	Thomas J. Bliley, Jr. (R)	187,354	(100%)	($366,816)
1988 primary	Thomas J. Bliley, Jr. (R), nominated by convention			
1986 general	Thomas J. Bliley, Jr. (R)	74,525	(67%)	($816,159)
	Kenneth E. Powell (D)	32,961	(30%)	($214,498)
	J. Stephen Hodges (I)	3,675	(3%)	($13,545)

FOURTH DISTRICT

It took English settlers the better part of a century to explore, clear and cultivate the stretch of mostly rural Virginia from the Tidewater cities on Hampton Roads to rural counties up above the fall line that, politically, is the 4th Congressional District of Virginia. This was the scene of some of America's first settlements and of its first revolution, Bacon's Rebellion in 1676; it was the scene also of bitter fighting in the Civil War, as Union troops invested the battlements of the small industrial city of Petersburg, 25 miles south of Richmond. In between Tidewater and Petersburg are the flat lands of Southside Virginia fanning south from the James River—tobacco lands when the English first settled them; today they produce Virginia's peanut crop and its Smithfield hams. Today's 4th District has more than half its population in Portsmouth, a Navy port and industrial town with a charming old town section, and the newly developing suburbs of Chesapeake and Suffolk; one-third of the rest is concentrated around Petersburg; the remaining population is in rural counties, a few of which are attracting Richmond suburbanites.

More than 300 years ago, planters were bringing in African slaves to work these fields. Today the population of the 4th District is 40% black—the highest percentage of any district in Virginia. Portsmouth has a large and well-established black community, as does Petersburg and many of the tobacco and peanut counties. Politics here for years was run by big landowners, small town bankers, and the like. These people saw themselves as having paternal responsibilities to the community—to help people who are in trouble and, more important to many in Virginia, to keep the community from changing. More recently there has been a kind of plebiscitary democracy which here, in the most Democratic congressional district in Virginia tends to favor the Democrats.

At least it does when they are as shrewd and politically competent as Representative Norman Sisisky. A Pepsi-Cola distributor from Petersburg, as well as a state legislator from a majority black district, he had the money to finance a big campaign plus a base with black voters to prevent the kind of Independent black candidacies which had sunk some Democratic candidates in the past. All that enabled him in 1982 to beat a landowner-type Republican who had held on for 10 years mostly with pluralities. Since then, Sisisky has not had Republican opposition, and doesn't seem likely to given the record he has made in office and the resources he has shown he can bring to a campaign.

In the House, Sisisky began by getting himself assigned to the Armed Services Committee, which is of obvious importance in this base-laden district, and Sisisky is making sure there is no reduction (from 15 to 14) in the Navy's carrier requirements. He has been critical of the military for spending too much and has asked pointed questions about why the different services pay different amounts for the same items. He has come forward with procurement reforms; but he is also a strong challenger of the Navy's "homeporting" plan which would take some installations from Hampton Roads and scatter them to other ports. Overall, his record is rather middle-of-the-road on most issues—a good fit for the 4th District.

The People: Est. Pop. 1986: 567,600, up 5.9% 1980–86; Pop. 1980: 535,703, up 7.1% 1970–80. Households (1980): 79% family, 45% with children, 62% married couples; 32.7% housing units rented; median monthly rent: $145; median house value: $38,900. Voting age pop. (1980): 377,071; 37% Black, 1% Spanish origin, 1% Asian origin.

1988 Presidential Vote:

Bush (R)	110,155	(55%)
Dukakis (D)	89,094	(44%)

Rep. Norman Sisisky (D)

Elected 1982; b. June 9, 1927, Baltimore, MD; home, Petersburg; VA Commonwealth U., B.S. 1949; Jewish; married (Rhoda).

Career: Navy, 1945–46; Pres., Pepsi-Cola Bottling Co. of Petersburg, 1949–82; VA House of Del., 1973–82.

Offices: 426 CHOB 20515, 202-225-6365. Also Emporia Exec. Ctr., 425-H S. Main St., Emporia 23847, 804-634-5575; VA First Savings and Loan Bldg., Franklin and Adams St., Rm. 607, Petersburg 23803, 804-732-2544; and 801 Water St., Portsmouth 23704, 804-393-2068.

Committees: *Armed Services* (16th of 31 D). Subcommittees: Investigations; Procurement and Military Nuclear Systems; Seapower and Strategic and Critical Materials. *Small Business* (11th of 27 D). Subcommittees: Exports, Tax Policy and Special Problems (Chairman); Regulation, Business Opportunities, and Energy. *Select Committee on Aging* (22d of 39 D). Subcommittee: Health and Long-Term Care.

Group Ratings

	ADA	ACLU	COPE	CFA	LCV	ACU	NTLC	NSI	COC	CEI
1988	55	55	65	73	56	40	27	90	50	21
1987	52	—	61	69	—	39	—	—	60	18

National Journal Ratings

	1988 LIB — 1988 CONS		1987 LIB — 1987 CONS	
Economic	57%	— 41%	52%	— 48%
Social	50%	— 48%	47%	— 53%
Foreign	40%	— 59%	40%	— 60%

Key Votes

1) Homeless $	AGN	5) Ban Drug Test	AGN	9) SDI Research	FOR
2) Gephardt Amdt	AGN	6) Drug Death Pen	FOR	10) Ban Chem Weaps	AGN
3) Deficit Reduc	FOR	7) Handgun Sales	FOR	11) Aid to Contras	FOR
4) Kill Plnt Clsng Notice	AGN	8) Ban D.C. Abort $	AGN	12) Nuclear Testing	AGN

Election Results

1988 general	Norman Sisisky (D) 134,786	(100%)	($93,232)
1988 primary	Norman Sisisky (D), nominated by convention		
1986 general	Norman Sisisky (D) 64,699	(100%)	($53,807)

FIFTH DISTRICT

Southside Virginia is a geographic name which is also shorthand for a state of mind. Here is Appomattox Court House, the small town where Robert E. Lee surrendered to his onetime subordinate Ulysses S. Grant, who then allowed Confederate troops to keep their horses for spring plowing; here also is Prince Edward County, where Harry Byrd's massive resistance shut down the public schools in 1957 rather than obey a federal court desegregation order. The 5th Congressional District of Virginia includes most of the Southside region, from just past Richmond south to the dividing line Colonel William Byrd surveyed in 1728, and from the Tidewater west to the Blue Ridge. Its eastern counties, those nearest Richmond, are flat and humid; they were the frontier in the late colonial period and were plantation country by 1800.

Currently about 40% of their residents are black. As you go west into the Piedmont, slowly the land gets hillier. Here you find the textile and furniture manufacturing centers of Danville and Martinsville. Farther west, getting nearer the mountains, you find more livestock and less tobacco, more whites with mountain accents and fewer blacks; the black population is about 10%. Altogether, the 5th District is 25% black—significantly less than the 40% in the 4th District just to the east.

Politics here has changed utterly since the days of massive resistance. It has become biracial and bipartisan, and while local bankers and courthouse lawyers continue to play important roles—personified here by the figure of Virginia Speaker A. L. Philpott of Henry County—they have nothing like the monopoly of political power they exercised up through the middle 1960s. That became apparent in the June 1988 special election held to fill the vacancy caused by the death of Congressman Dan Daniel. A conservative Democrat first elected in 1968 after a career in Danville's Dan River Mills, he served on the Armed Services and Intelligence Committees and voted a solid conservative record: the last of the Byrd Democrats. Daniel died just after he announced his retirement, and after a Republican had entered the race. Following his death, a rather different Democrat ran, and won.

The Republican, Linda Arey, was a native of Danville and a Reagan White House staffer who came back to Southside and won the nomination in a convention against state Senator Onico Barker; she campaigned against drugs, against liberals, against the Civil Rights Restoration Act. The Democrat, chosen with the support of Governor Gerald Baliles, a 5th District native himself, was L. F. Payne, the developer of the Wintergreen ski resort which, after 15 years, accounts for half the payrolls in rural Nelson County. "Before you ask someone what they will do, ask them what they have done," Payne argued, stressing his experience, biography and work in the district; he was able to finance much of his campaign, and even got Barker, embittered at his rejection, to stand beside him at an appearance. The result wasn't even close: Payne won the special election with 59% of the votes. Arey, in a huff, resigned the nomination for the general election and moved back to Washington. Payne won again in November, this time by a narrower margin; but then this was a district where Michael Dukakis was winning only 37%. With seats on Veterans' Affairs and Public Works, this new kind of Southside politician seems on his way to a long House career.

The People: Est. Pop. 1986: 538,800, up 1.4% 1980–86; Pop. 1980: 531,308, up 13.7% 1970–80. Households (1980): 80% family, 43% with children, 67% married couples; 24.0% housing units rented; median monthly rent: $109; median house value: $32,600. Voting age pop. (1980): 382,312; 22% Black, 1% Spanish origin.

1988 Presidential Vote:

Bush (R)	119,560	(62%)
Dukakis (D)	71,107	(37%)

Rep. Lewis F. Payne, Jr. (D)

Elected June 1988; b. July 9, 1945, Amherst; home, Nellysford; VA Military Inst., B.S. 1967, U. of VA, M.B.A. 1973; Presbyterian; married (Susan).

Career: Engineering Assoc., C&P Telephone, 1970–71; Wintergreen Development Inc., Mgr., 1973–75, Pres., 1976–85, Chmn. 1985–88.

Offices: 1118 LHOB 20515, 202-225-4711. Also 301 P.O. Bldg., Danville 24541, 804-792-1280; and Abbitt Fed. Bldg., 103 S. Main St., Farmville 23901, 804-392-8331.

Committees: *Public Works and Transportation* (25th of 31 D). Subcommittees: Aviation; Economic Development; Surface Transportation. *Veterans' Affairs* (16th of 21 D). Subcommittees: Hospitals and Health Care; Housing and Memorial Affairs.

Group Ratings and Key Votes: Newly Elected

Election Results

1988 general	Lewis F. Payne, Jr. (D)	97,242	(54%)	($274,442)
	Charles R. Hawkins (R)	78,396	(44%)	($105,872)
1988 primary	Lewis F. Payne, Jr. (D), nominated by convention			
1988 special	Lewis F. Payne, Jr. (D)	55,406	(59%)	($563,422)
	Linda Arey (R)	38,086	(41%)	($404,468)
1986 general	W. C. (Dan) Daniel (D)	73,085	(82%)	($130,231)
	J. F. (Frank) Cole (I)	16,551	(18%)	

SIXTH DISTRICT

West of the Blue Ridge the settlers came down the Valley of Virginia on the great Wagon Road from Pennsylvania, and they included not only Englishmen but Highland and Lowland Scots, German Protestants and Mennonites and Moravians, with nary a slave. In the years before the Revolution, while Jefferson was still designing Monticello east of the Blue Ridge, this heterogeneous lot were streaming down the Wagon Road. East of the Blue Ridge, lands were planted in tobacco, which required lots of labor and exhausted the soil; west, the lands were planted in wheat and corn and hay, crops which could be rotated and which an individual farmer and his family could handle. East of the Blue Ridge, there was little industry outside Richmond; west, Roanoke grew from nothing in 1880 to a significant industrial center by 1940, a town, the *WPA Guide* sniffs, built in an "era of architectural ugliness," with "unsightly areas of houses quickly built and poorly kept, and junk heaps near historic places."

The casual traveler today must look carefully to discern the differences between these two Virginias, noting the different crops and the greater neatness in rural landscape west of the Blue Ridge, looking past the pleasantly renovated cities to see what struck others as ugly 50 years ago. In the election returns of the 1980s, you can trace the route of the old Wagon Road in the Republican majorities that are cast, even in elections the Democrats win, in the upper part of the Valley around Winchester, down through Harrisonburg and Staunton, and then going over the Blue Ridge in Roanoke down to the still Republican-voting cities of Winston-Salem and Charlotte, North Carolina. For much of the 20th century, Valley Republicanism was an insurgent faith, a credo hospitable to economic assistance to the little guy, and Valley Republicans ran brave campaigns against Harry Byrd's Democrats from time to time; some of them became federal judges during Republican administrations. For 30 years beginning in 1952, the 6th Congressional District, which has included within different boundaries most of the Valley counties, was represented by Republicans.

Now that district, which extends from Roanoke north to Harrisonburg and west to the West Virginia border, and which includes one county and most of the city of Lynchburg east of the Blue Ridge, is represented by a Democrat. He is James Olin, a retired vice president of General Electric, elected in 1982. In that year Olin was a kind of insurgent: Republicans had held the seat for 30 years and the Virginia governorship for 12 of the preceding 13. The Republicans, like southern Democrats of old, were divided; the Democrats united around Olin. He is particularly strong in the Roanoke area, but he has lost or carried only barely the upper Valley around Harrisonburg, where the Byrd family still owns the local newspaper.

Olin began his congressional career after a full life of achievement in business, and without the skittishness of some younger members who quiver in fear of their constituents. Olin seems to vote his conscience, which turns out to be pretty liberal on non-economic issues, and does just fine politically. His committees—Agriculture, Small Business—sound like a good match of district concerns. In fact, Agriculture has been a panel of great importance, especially when the farm bill is rewritten every four years, while Small Business is legislatively almost totally unimportant, bloated in size by politicians who seek a credential useful for reelection but supervising only the most minor of federal programs. Olin has been strengthened politically by his vigorous action in speeding flood relief funds to small businesses after the disastrous Roanoke flood of 1985; he also initiated a disaster relief program for southeastern farmers hurt by the 1986 drought. He is proud of his work on the passage of the Virginia Wilderness Act, which covers 81,000 acres of land, and he worked to secure funding for Lynchburg's airport. Opposition and age just seem to make him stronger: in 1988 Olin won 64% against a former executive director of Jerry Falwell's (now defunct) Moral Majority whom Olin called "mean-spirited" and a "liar."

The People: Est. Pop. 1986: 545,900, up 1.4% 1980–86; Pop. 1980: 538,360, up 8.6% 1970–80. Households (1980): 75% family, 39% with children, 62% married couples; 30.5% housing units rented; median monthly rent: $153; median house value: $38,600. Voting age pop. (1980): 401,356; 10% Black, 1% Spanish origin.

1988 Presidential Vote:

Bush (R)	121,107	(61%)
Dukakis (D)	74,602	(38%)

Rep. James R. (Jim) Olin (D)

Elected 1982; b. Feb. 28, 1920, Chicago, IL; home, Roanoke; Deep Springs Col., Cornell U., B.E.E. 1943; Unitarian; married (Phyllis).

Career: U.S. Army Signal Corps., WWII; Plant Mgr., Vice Pres. and Gen. Mgr., Industrial Electronics Div., General Electric, 1946–82.

Offices: 1314 LHOB 20515, 202-225-5431. Also 406 First St., Rm. 706, Roanoke 24011, 703-982-4672; 925 Main St., 3d Fl., Lynchburg 24504, 804-845-6546; 13 W. Beverly St., 2d Fl., Staunton 24401, 703-885-8178; and Sovran Bank Bldg., Rm. 415, Harrisonburg 22801, 703-433-9433.

Committees: *Agriculture* (14th of 27 D). Subcommittees: Department Operations, Research, and Foreign Agriculture; Forests, Family Farms, and Energy; Livestock, Dairy, and Poultry. *Small Business* (14th of 27 D). Subcommittees: Regulation, Business Opportunities, and Energy; SBA, the General Economy and Minority Enterprise Development.

Group Ratings

	ADA	ACLU	COPE	CFA	LCV	ACU	NTLC	NSI	COC	CEI
1988	70	65	57	64	44	28	43	10	64	38
1987	64	—	54	57	—	26	—	—	47	38

National Journal Ratings

	1988 LIB — 1988 CONS		1987 LIB — 1987 CONS	
Economic	31%	67%	40%	59%
Social	54%	45%	54%	45%
Foreign	68%	28%	64%	35%

Key Votes

1) Homeless $	FOR	5) Ban Drug Test	AGN	9) SDI Research	AGN
2) Gephardt Amdt	AGN	6) Drug Death Pen	FOR	10) Ban Chem Weaps	FOR
3) Deficit Reduc	FOR	7) Handgun Sales	FOR	11) Aid to Contras	AGN
4) Kill Plnt Clsng Notice	AGN	8) Ban D.C. Abort $	AGN	12) Nuclear Testing	FOR

Election Results

1988 general	James R. Olin (D)...................	118,369	(64%)	($322,160)
	Charles E. Judd (R)	66,935	(36%)	($110,756)
1988 primary	James R. Olin (D), nominated by convention			
1986 general	James R. (Jim) Olin (D)...............	88,230	(70%)	($356,857)
	Flo Neher Traywick (R)	38,051	(30%)	($199,880)

SEVENTH DISTRICT

Even as the Constitution was being hammered out in Philadelphia, the rolling green Piedmont of northern Virginia and the fertile mountain-bound lands of the Shenandoah Valley were buzzing with new settlers. From the Piedmont they were coming up the rivers that flow into the Chesapeake, into the Valley from the great Wagon Road south from Pennsylvania, moving onto lands which had been speculated by George Washington and his peers. For the four years of the Civil War, this was some of the most heavily contested land on the continent; afterwards, the surge of movement having propelled new settlers much farther west, this part of Virginia became well-settled and long ago was established as prime fox hunting country. In Warrenton 50 years ago, "in the foothills of the Blue Ridge Mountains, old and new Virginia meet. 'Horsey' folk in breeches share the crowded little business street with farmers in jeans. Old buildings stand beside newer ones in the few steep streets that are liberally shaded by trees."

Today these Virginians are less likely to meet in old Warrenton than in the Safeway on the four-lane bypass outside, that carries horse feed and Brie as well as disposable diapers and milk in gallon cartons. Metropolitan Washington is rapidly moving out to what was pristine countryside. Subdivisions are growing up on old fields, and the horse farms of the Piedmont, long the first or second homes of some of the richest people in America, have begun to attract a growing population of commuters and weekend residents. What looked like marginal farmlands to the settlers of the early 19th century now looks like something close to heaven for city-dwellers: rolling green hills, with views of the Blue Ridge and other mountains; antique houses and tiny crossroads communities. The region's major towns—Winchester in the valley, Charlottesville and Fredericksburg in the Piedmont, none with a population as large as 45,000—still retain an old-fashioned air at least in the narrow streets of their downtowns, although a McDonald's culture has developed on the bypass roads of their outskirts.

This is the land of the 7th Congressional District of Virginia, which stretches from the outermost Washington suburbs through much of northern Virginia, including Winchester at the northern end of the Shenandoah Valley and Charlottesville, home of the University of Virginia. It was the home of three Presidents (Jefferson, Madison, and Monroe) and, more recently, the home turf of Virginia's Byrd dynasty. In congressional and national elections, the 7th District has moved steadily from Byrd Democrats to conservative Republicans—a switch made easier because often they are the same people.

A case in point is the current 7th District congressman, who sports one of those uneuphonious names with which the men who run things in small Virginia towns seem to get saddled, D. French Slaughter Jr. He was first elected to Congress after a lifetime in and out of politics. He spent 20 years in the state legislature, and there sponsored bills creating Virginia's community college system; he also promoted Virginia's massive resistance to integration, in which the state ordered local school systems to close down rather than obey federal court desegregation orders. Asked to comment on that in the 1984 campaign, he allowed that the time for such measures had passed, but that he had no regrets about having supported them back then.

Slaughter won the seat in that campaign by a 56%–40% vote. He serves on the Science, Space and Technology Committee, but he seems to have spent much of his legislative energy on another project, a proposal for health care savings accounts—IRAs for health care, in effect, into which people could put tax-free money which they could use after 65 for health care—and he wants to encourage separate long-term care policies for federal employees. He prides himself on his constituency service, but steered largely clear of involvement over the bill to stop a shopping center from being built at the edge of the Manassas battlefield in his district. He has been reelected twice without opposition. Redistricting may very well create a new district combining large parts of the further-in Washington suburbs with much of the 7th. But given the strong Republican preference of all the territory involved, Slaughter is likely to retain a safe seat.

The People: Est. Pop. 1986: 592,500, up 10.7% 1980–86; Pop. 1980: 535,147, up 31.1% 1970–80. Households (1980): 77% family, 43% with children, 65% married couples; 30.4% housing units rented; median monthly rent: $190; median house value: $48,700. Voting age pop. (1980): 383,878; 11% Black, 1% Spanish origin.

1988 Presidential Vote:

Bush (R)	149,725	(66%)
Dukakis (D)	76,202	(33%)

Rep. D. French Slaughter, Jr. (R)

Elected 1984; b. May 20, 1925, Culpeper Cnty.; home, Culpeper; VA Military Inst., 1942–43, U. of VA, B.A. 1949, LL.B. 1953; Episcopalian; widowed.

Career: Army, WWII; VA House of Del., 1958–78; Practicing atty., 1978–84.

Offices: 1404 LHOB 20515, 202-225-6561. Also 100 Crt. Annex Sq., Charlottesville 22902, 804-296-2105; 110 South West St., Culpeper 22701, 703-825-3495; 904 Princess Anne St., Fredericksburg 22401, 703-373-0536; and 112 N. Cameron St., Winchester 22601, 703-667-0990.

Committees: *Judiciary* (10th of 14 R). Subcommittees: Courts, Intellectual Property and the Administration of Justice; Immigration, Refugees and International Law. *Science, Space and Technology* (12th of 19 R). Subcommittees: Science Research and Technology; Space Science and Applications. *Small Business* (7th of 17 R). Subcommittees: Antitrust, Impact of Deregulation, and Privatization; Exports, Tax Policy and Special Problems.

Group Ratings

	ADA	ACLU	COPE	CFA	LCV	ACU	NTLC	NSI	COC	CEI
1988	10	22	15	36	25	92	70	100	93	61
1987	0	—	15	29	—	91	—	—	93	68

National Journal Ratings

	1988 LIB — 1988 CONS	1987 LIB — 1987 CONS
Economic	19% — 80%	0% — 89%
Social	5% — 91%	23% — 76%
Foreign	0% — 84%	0% — 80%

Key Votes

1) Homeless $	FOR	5) Ban Drug Test	AGN	9) SDI Research	FOR
2) Gephardt Amdt	AGN	6) Drug Death Pen	FOR	10) Ban Chem Weaps	AGN
3) Deficit Reduc	AGN	7) Handgun Sales	FOR	11) Aid to Contras	FOR
4) Kill Plnt Clsng Notice	FOR	8) Ban D.C. Abort $	FOR	12) Nuclear Testing	AGN

Election Results

1988 general	D. French Slaughter, Jr. (R)............ 136,988	(100%)	($87,195)
1988 primary	D. French Slaughter, Jr. (R), nominated by convention		
1986 general	D. French Slaughter, Jr. (R)............ 58,927	(98%)	($212,026)

EIGHTH DISTRICT

Two hundred years ago, when George Washington trod the brick sidewalks of Alexandria, Virginia, on his way to market or court or church, this was the largest city in this part of Virginia, dwarfing Georgetown, Maryland, just up the Potomac River; what is now Capitol Hill and downtown Washington were just hills above the river's mud flats. As Washington grew, northern Virginia just across the river seemed left behind; the District of Columbia retroceded its land south of the Potomac—what is now Alexandria and Arlington—to Virginia in 1846 because it was obvious that the federal government would never need it. It was 97 years before the first federal building was built on the Virginia side, the Pentagon; Franklin Roosevelt wondered out loud what they would do with all that space after the war. When the Pentagon was built, Alexandria and all of the rural countryside of northern Virginia were represented in Congress by Judge Howard W. Smith, a Byrd Democrat, who saw his mission as the maintenance of the standards of Washington, Jefferson and Robert E. Lee.

Yet by the 1960s, even as Judge Smith kept his law offices in Old Town, Alexandria, northern Virginia was changing around him. New subdivision-dwellers, with white-collar jobs and lots of children, wanted schools with good academic programs—not the segregated eighth-grade schoolhouses Judge Smith's friends were willing to finance. They wanted freeways built and traffic lights installed, planning instituted to put limits on sprawl, parks and playgrounds and recreation facilities set aside. Smith's district was moved farther out into the countryside (although even there he was beaten in the 1966 primary), two-party politics came to the suburbs, and local governments got to work.

Today, the northern Virginia suburbs of Washington have two congressional districts. The 8th, which is technically the descendant of the district Smith represented for 36 years, begins in Alexandria, and includes not only Old Town but the city's large black population and the two-thirds of its households who live in apartments: this is now a national Democratic city. Beyond Alexandria, in Fairfax County, are the suburbs of Springfield, Annandale and Mount Vernon, affluent places, with large colonial or, occasionally, contemporary houses built for large families, and with newer townhouse clusters spotting the rolling landscape; voters here are wary both of new developments and higher taxes, and they have the cautious and sometimes reactionary impulses you find in parents of teenage children. South of Fairfax is Prince William County, where zoning restrictions are less stringent and incomes tend to be lower; and the 8th dips farther south into once rural Stafford County. Growth has occasionally slowed here, but then picks up apace, and has been at high levels in the late 1980s, especially as real estate prices in the closer Washington suburbs have skyrocketed. Its affluence is powered by the federal government, whose paychecks have more than doubled since 1960; in the 8th District, about 30% of all wage earners take home each payday the familiar green government check.

The congressman from the 8th District is Stanford Parris, a Republican who has proved one of the more resilient if not one of the more accomplished politicians in northern Virginia. He won the district in 1972 when William Scott (once named the dumbest man in Congress) was elected Senator, lost it to Democrat Herb Harris in 1974, came back and beat Harris in 1980, and has held on since. Parris's stock in trade has been to suggest that he shares all the prejudices many suburban residents harbor, particularly against the government of the District of Columbia—which gives Parris plenty of fodder. He is now ranking Republican on the District of Columbia Committee where he has helped to force repeal of the District's residency requirement for city employees, and has called for the District's public safety director to be appointed by the federal government rather than the mayor. What Parris has not done is to follow up his denunciations, or his professions of affection for government workers, with much work. Much of the job of a congressman from the D.C. suburbs comes down to handling constituent complaints and serving the parochial interests of government employees and local communities. Most of the current congressmen, of both parties, work hard at these chores. Parris, however, is known generally as one who dogs it.

Parris has won reelection easily in the 1980s but had also set his sights on being governor; he believed his knowledge of northern Virginia's transportation problems, his experience at various levels of government and in business, and the steadfastness of his convictions over the years made him a plausible candidate. They didn't succeed in doing that in 1985, but in 1989 he was running again, and hailing his fellow Republicans for deciding to choose their nominee in a primary (in which northern Virginians might cast more than a third of the votes, as they did in the 1988 presidential contest) rather than in a convention (where he would not have had much

1266 VIRGINIA

chance against former Senator Paul Trible). Many wondered whether Parris's constituents and those who see him frequently on the news think he has the qualities needed in a governor, in addition to his generally acknowledged ability to heckle the sometimes deserving-to-be-heckled D.C. government. His constituents did—he won the 8th District, but lost to winner Marshall Coleman and second place Paul Trible in the rest of the state, for a total of about 28% vote. He seems to have a safe seat going into 1990.

The People: Est. Pop. 1986: 623,500, up 16.7% 1980–86; Pop. 1980: 534,366, up 25.6% 1970–80. Households (1980): 73% family, 45% with children, 63% married couples; 36.8% housing units rented; median monthly rent: $312; median house value: $86,000. Voting age pop. (1980): 376,074; 10% Black, 3% Spanish origin, 3% Asian origin.

1988 Presidential Vote:

Bush (R)	157,228	(60%)
Dukakis (D)	102,516	(39%)

Rep. Stanford E. Parris (R)

Elected 1980; b. Sept. 9, 1929, Champaign, IL; home, Fairfax Cnty.; U. of IL, B.S. 1950, Geo. Wash. U., J.D. 1958; Episcopalian; married (Marlie).

Career: Air Force, Korea; Commercial pilot; Practicing atty.; Fairfax Cnty. Bd. of Spvsrs., 1964–67; VA House of Del., 1969–72; U.S. House of Reps., 1972–74; Secy., Commonwealth of VA, 1978; Dir., VA Fed. Liaison Ofc., 1978–80.

Offices: 2434 RHOB 20515, 202-225-4376. Also 6901 Old Keene Mill Rd., Ste. 101, Springfield 22150, 703-644-0004; and 14546 Jefferson Davis Hwy., Woodbridge 22191, 703-494-8199.

Committees: *Banking, Finance and Urban Affairs* (4th of 20 R). Subcommittees: Financial Institutions Supervision, Regulation and Insurance; General Oversight and Investigations (Ranking Member); Housing and Community Development. *District of Columbia* (Ranking Member of 4 R). Subcommittees: Fiscal Affairs and Health; Government Operations and Metropolitan Affairs. *Select Committee on Narcotics Abuse and Control* (4th of 12 R).

Group Ratings

	ADA	ACLU	COPE	CFA	LCV	ACU	NTLC	NSI	COC	CEI
1988	15	26	26	55	38	96	46	100	93	46
1987	8	—	25	29	—	82	—	—	73	52

National Journal Ratings

	1988 LIB — 1988 CONS			1987 LIB — 1987 CONS		
Economic	24%	—	74%	24%	—	74%
Social	11%	—	89%	29%	—	70%
Foreign	0%	—	84%	0%	—	80%

Key Votes

1) Homeless $	FOR	5) Ban Drug Test	AGN	9) SDI Research	FOR
2) Gephardt Amdt	AGN	6) Drug Death Pen	FOR	10) Ban Chem Weaps	AGN
3) Deficit Reduc	AGN	7) Handgun Sales	FOR	11) Aid to Contras	FOR
4) Kill Plnt Clsng Notice	FOR	8) Ban D.C. Abort $	FOR	12) Nuclear Testing	AGN

Election Results

1988 general	Stanford E. Parris (R)................	154,761	(62%)	($689,035)
	David G. Brickley (D)	93,561	(38%)	($273,203)
1988 primary	Stanford E. Parris (R), nominated by convention			
1986 general	Stanford E. Parris (R)................	72,670	(61%)	($428,788)
	James H. Boren (D)	44,965	(38%)	($73,981)

NINTH DISTRICT

Abingdon, in southwest Virginia, "radiates from shady Courthouse Square," wrote the *WPA Guide* 50 years ago. "Old houses, chiefly of brick, wall in undulating Main Street, which is crowded on Saturday with townspeople, 'Knobites' in for the day, and Negroes from the King's Mountain quarter. Chemical factories, wagon works, lumber mills, a milk condensory, and a cigar factory are the chief support of the town, though burley tobacco is shipped in quantities." This was one of the first settlements, dating to 1765, in the great valley of Virginia as it bends westward and south toward Tennessee and the Cumberland Gap. The old houses and the tobacco have something in common with the rest of Virginia, but most of these settlers were Scots-Irish rather than English, from the northern colonies rather than Virginia; and the mountainous region where they settled has been a region apart from Virginia since that time. Economically, it has depended more on coal mines and heavy industry, like neighboring West Virginia; politically, it was antislavery territory, skeptical about, if not hostile to, the cause of the Confederacy. The cultural traditions are different too: the federal government here can still mean the hated revenuers, and the local music is what you hear from bluegrass banjo pickers and the participants at the Galax Old Time Fiddlers' Convention.

Split between secessionists and unionists, southwest Virginia developed a vigorous two-party politics after the Civil War and has had one most of the years since, with both parties resembling their national counterparts more closely than they do in the rest of Virginia. The 9th Congressional District of Virginia covers all of southwest Virginia west of Roanoke. Over the years it became known as the Fighting Ninth, because of its taste for raucous, noisy politics, both conservative and populist; it is getting somewhat more like the rest of Virginia now, with development moving down Interstate 81 to and past Blacksburg, home of Virginia Tech; but its politics still has its own special tang. It has also changed partisan hands four times in 30 years— in 1952 and 1954, in 1966, and again in 1982—electing and then ousting Republican William Wampler, "the bald eagle of the Cumberlands." The current congressman, Democrat Rick Boucher, won in a recession year and has held on handily since.

Boucher, like other Fighting Ninth Democrats, has a record on issues basically in line with national Democratic positions. He is, however, not likely to get way out of line with his district; he is as quick to oppose gun control as he is to champion the interests of coal. In the House, he has seats on the Energy and Commerce, Science and Technology, and Judiciary Committees—a full load. He has done useful work on issues ranging from vocational education to criminal statutes. He has spent much time trying to rewrite the RICO statute whose overbroad definition of "racketeering" has caused it to be used by almost any aggrieved party to a business transaction and by federal prosecutors otherwise lacking much of a case. He also wants to amend the antitrust laws to allow firms to be built for high-definition TV, robotics and superconductors, and he has written a bill to guarantee satellite dish owners access to network TV signals. He is pushing also for federal protection of caves as worthy natural ecosystems.

In this competitive two-party district, Boucher has had tough races in presidential years. In 1984, Republican Jeff Stafford held him to 52% of the vote. In 1988, state Delegate John Brown, forced to give up his teaching and coaching job to run, waged a positive campaign, but was unable to make much headway outside his home area of Bristol on the Tennessee border and surrounding Washington County, and Boucher won with an impressive 63%. There was talk that he might run for the Senate in 1988, before it was clear that Charles Robb was in the race; but with his good committee assignments and strong position in the Fighting Ninth, Boucher is likely to work to stay in the House.

The People: Est. Pop. 1986: 541,300, up 0.4% 1980–86; Pop. 1980: 538,871, up 19.2% 1970–80. Households (1980): 79% family, 44% with children, 68% married couples; 24.9% housing units rented; median monthly rent: $137; median house value: $32,700. Voting age pop. (1980): 388,333; 2% Black, 1% Spanish origin.

1988 Presidential Vote:

Bush (R)	98,783	(54%)
Dukakis (D)	82,873	(45%)

Rep. Rick Boucher (D)

Elected 1982; b. Aug. 1, 1946, Abingdon; home, Abingdon; Roanoke Col., B.A. 1968, U. of VA, J.D. 1971; United Methodist; single.

Career: Practicing atty., 1971–83; VA Senate, 1975–1983.

Offices: 428 CHOB 20515, 202-225-3861. Also 180 E. Main St., Abingdon 24210, 703-628-1145; 321 Shawnee Ave. E., Big Stone Gap 24319, 703-523-5450; and 112 N. Washington Ave., Pulaski 24301, 703-980-4310.

Committees: *Energy and Commerce* (22d of 26 D). Subcommittees: Oversight and Investigations; Telecommunications and Finance; Transportation and Hazardous Materials. *Judiciary* (17th of 21 D). Subcommittees: Courts, Intellectual Property and the Administration of Justice; Crime. *Science, Space and Technology* (15th of 30 D). Subcommittee: Energy Research and Development.

Group Ratings

	ADA	ACLU	COPE	CFA	LCV	ACU	NTLC	NSI	COC	CEI
1988	75	85	82	64	56	9	9	10	29	12
1987	76	—	79	71	—	0	—	—	7	13

National Journal Ratings

	1988 LIB — 1988 CONS		1987 LIB — 1987 CONS	
Economic	71% —	23%	73% —	0%
Social	85% —	14%	65% —	34%
Foreign	60% —	37%	70% —	30%

Key Votes

1) Homeless $	—	5) Ban Drug Test	AGN	9) SDI Research	AGN
2) Gephardt Amdt	FOR	6) Drug Death Pen	AGN	10) Ban Chem Weaps	FOR
3) Deficit Reduc	FOR	7) Handgun Sales	FOR	11) Aid to Contras	AGN
4) Kill Plnt Clsng Notice	AGN	8) Ban D.C. Abort $	AGN	12) Nuclear Testing	FOR

Election Results

1988 general	Rick Boucher (D)	113,309	(63%)	($606,420)
	John C. Brown (R)	65,410	(37%)	($154,515)
1988 primary	Rick Boucher (D), nominated by convention			
1986 general	Rick Boucher (D)	59,864	(100%)	($262,606)

TENTH DISTRICT

The biggest center of office space between downtown Washington and Atlanta—or, for that matter, beyond downtown Atlanta—is not in Richmond or one of North Carolina's Piedmont cities, but in the cluster of office buildings around Tysons Corner, Virginia. Rising on a hill west of Washington and Arlington, Tysons Corner was a back country intersection 50 years ago and a junction of several suburban roads 25 years ago; none of Washington's cadre of metropolitan experts nor the designers of its Metro system expected office development here. They assumed that office work would still be centralized, and that if Washington's robust downtown needed to be supplemented it would happen in Crystal City near the Pentagon or Rosslyn just across the river from Georgetown, both in Arlington County. It did, but Crystal City and Rosslyn together are overshadowed by Tysons Corner.

This emergence of "edge cities," as *Nine Nations of North America* author Joel Garreau calls them, is a new chapter in the history of the northern Virginia counties just across the river from the nation's capital. Fifty years ago, the atmosphere here was rural: pleasant subdivisions had sprouted up in parts of Arlington, but schools and county services were of the rudimentary sort you'd find in rural Virginia. Then in the years after World War II, Arlington and parts of nearby Fairfax County filled up with suburbanites, young marrieds with large families and whites fleeing the increasingly black District of Columbia. With rising government salaries and local economic growth, they began to live in affluence that many had never anticipated. Politically, this was reflected by the demise of Byrd Democrats, first in Arlington and then in Fairfax, and the emergence of robust competition between two parties which resembled their national counterparts. The congressional seat here, though often bitterly contested, was held from 1952 to 1974 by Republican Joel Broyhill, a real estate developer hostile to D.C. home rule who ran a fine constituency service operation in a district more than one-third of whose residents were federal employees.

In the 1970s, Arlington began to change: families were outnumbered by apartment-dwellers, and Vietnamese and other Asians moved into close-in neighborhoods. The office space in the new "edge cities" was rented mostly not to government agencies but to private firms (some of them, to be sure, government contractors, known locally as "Beltway bandits"); Fairfax grew rapidly, overshadowing Arlington and inhabited less and less by the government employees who used to give the Washington suburbs their tone.

Since 1972, there have been enough people in the northern Virginia suburbs for two congressional districts; by 1992 there may be enough for three. Currently, the 10th district includes Arlington, the northern and western half of Fairfax, the tiny cities of Fairfax and Falls Church, and Loudoun County, once rural and still with estates on rolling hills around Leesburg, but also with some modest, crowded subdivisions, filled with young families and tradition-minded churches. This is a heavily Republican jurisdiction now, in contrast to the Maryland 8th just across the Potomac River, where income levels are almost identical. One difference seems to be that Montgomery County, Maryland attracts many people in health fields (the National Institutes of Health are in Bethesda), while Fairfax County attracts many people in defense businesses. And it may also be that these two areas, with their different mixes of shopping and churches, have taken on personalities that attract people of differing political attitudes.

The congressman from the 10th District is Frank Wolf, a Republican first elected in 1980, whose politics give some insight into the district's. He is a serious man whose personal attitudes are those of a churchgoing family man; he has a conservative record on national issues generally; but he reserves most of his fervor for local matters. He started off on Post Office and Civil Service, then moved to Appropriations in 1985; federal employees are less numerous here than they used to be, but he does not neglect their causes. He has worked to fund Washington's Metro subway lines, which now go far out into Virginia, and to build more highways; he has worked to get the federal government to unload National and Dulles Airports to a local authority. He has also gone far afield to become, with Queens Democrat Gary Ackerman, the House's leading backer of stern measures to feed starving people in the Sudan (making two trips in the first few months of 1989) despite the often uncooperative attitude of its government.

The Democrats do not give Wolf a free ride at election time, but as this district has changed, he has proved unbeatable. In 1986, he beat John Milliken, head of the Arlington County Board and the Metro Board, with 60% of the vote; in 1988, against Williams & Connolly lawyer Robert Weinberg, he won with 68%. With hard work, Wolf seems to have converted what has been a marginal district for most of the last 30 years into a safe seat.

The People: Est. Pop. 1986: 608,700, up 13.5% 1980–86; Pop. 1980: 535,125, up 15.1% 1970–80. Households (1980): 66% family, 35% with children, 55% married couples; 44.6% housing units rented; median monthly rent: $317; median house value: $92,900. Voting age pop. (1980): 401,286; 6% Black, 4% Spanish origin, 4% Asian origin.

1988 Presidential Vote:

Bush (R) 163,211	(57%)
Dukakis (D)....................... 121,878	(42%)

Rep. Frank R. Wolf (R)

Elected 1980; b. Jan. 30, 1939, Philadelphia, PA; home, Vienna; PA St. U., B.A. 1961; Georgetown U., J.D. 1965; Presbyterian; married (Carolyn).

Career: Army (Reserves), 1962–67; Legis. Asst. to U.S. Rep. Edward Biester, 1968–71; Asst. to U.S. Secy. of Interior Rogers Morton, 1971–74; Dpty. Asst. Secy., U.S. Dept. of Interior, 1974–75; Practicing atty., 1975–80.

Offices: 104 CHOB 20515, 202-225-5136. Also 1651 Old Meadow Rd., Ste. 115, McLean 22102, 703-734-1500; and 19 E. Market St., Rm. 4B, Leesburg 22075, 703-777-4422.

Committees: *Appropriations* (17th of 22 R). Subcommittees: Transportation; Treasury, Postal Service and General Government. *Select Committee on Children, Youth, and Families* (2d of 12 R). *Select Committee on Hunger* (10th of 12 R).

Group Ratings

	ADA	ACLU	COPE	CFA	LCV	ACU	NTLC	NSI	COC	CEI
1988	25	39	18	45	56	88	51	100	86	40
1987	12	—	15	43	—	87	—	—	73	55

National Journal Ratings

	1988 LIB — 1988 CONS		1987 LIB — 1987 CONS	
Economic	24% —	74%	23% —	76%
Social	29% —	70%	23% —	76%
Foreign	16% —	78%	0% —	80%

Key Votes

1) Homeless $	FOR	5) Ban Drug Test	AGN	9) SDI Research	FOR
2) Gephardt Amdt	AGN	6) Drug Death Pen	FOR	10) Ban Chem Weaps	AGN
3) Deficit Reduc	AGN	7) Handgun Sales	AGN	11) Aid to Contras	FOR
4) Kill Plnt Clsng Notice	FOR	8) Ban D.C. Abort $	FOR	12) Nuclear Testing	AGN

Election Results

1988 general	Frank R. Wolf (R) 188,550	(68%)	($758,365)
	Robert L. Weinberg (D) 88,284	(32%)	($241,445)
1988 primary	Frank R. Wolf (R), nominated by convention		
1986 general	Frank R. Wolf (R) 95,724	(60%)	($1,124,866)
	John G. Milliken (D) 63,292	(40%)	($748,918)

WASHINGTON

The state of Washington, half a century ago, as Americans faced the threat of war in the Pacific, was still being built. Its great ports on Puget Sound, its wheat-processing city of Spokane in the inland empire, its orchard towns and fishing ports had been settled and civilized in the two decades after 1890, when the first Northern Pacific locomotive steamed into Seattle. This fine natural port, shielded from the heavy rains and storms of the Pacific by the Olympic Mountains and the sinuous channels of Puget Sound, became in two decades a serious American city, our outpost on the northern Pacific Rim. It was a lusty town full of lumbermen and railroad workers and, when gold was struck in the Klondike and Alaska, a metropolis of miners and prospectors and get-rich-quick operators—a town where Yesler Way, a street heading down one of Seattle's steep hills to the harborfront area now known as Pioneer Square, became known as Skid Row. In that booming, young, lusty Seattle there developed a turbulent class warfare politics, pitting the Industrial Workers of the World (the IWW or Wobblies) against the city's business and civic leaders in the years before World War I; the businessmen, brutally, prevailed. Adding to the distinctiveness of the area were its large numbers of Scandinavian immigrants, who were more favorable to cooperative enterprises (Washington has more businesses owned by workers than any other part of the country) and government ownership than any other Americans.

But with the nation's economy collapsed and the war looming, this Washington of 1.7 million people, almost half of them within 50 miles of Seattle on the Sound, tucked away in the northwest corner of the country, was transformed by a series of national decisions which set the course of its development for decades. One was the decision by the government to develop hydroelectric power. The Columbia River and its tributary the Snake, falling thousands of feet in a relatively short distance, had far greater hydroelectric potential than any other American river system, and Franklin Roosevelt was always specially interested in river valley projects. In 1937, Bonneville Dam was completed on the lower Columbia; in 1940, Grand Coulee Dam, the largest man-made structure in the world at the time, was opened where the Columbia cuts through the arid, surrealistically contoured plains of eastern Washington. At the same time, Washington was proving hospitable to the industrial union movement of the 1930s, and by the 1940s became one of the most heavily unionized states in the nation. When war came, Washington's hydroelectric power—the cheapest electricity in the country—made it the natural site for huge plants to make aluminum, which requires vast amounts of electricity, and the Seattle area became the home not only of shipbuilders, but of the biggest aircraft manufacturer in the country, Boeing. After the war, the Hanford plant on the Columbia was one of the government's main nuclear weapons manufacturing sites. Cheap power, aluminum, aircraft, nuclear weapons and high unionized wages: these became the foundations of Washington's self-sustaining and growing economy in the post-World War II years.

After three decades, that economy faced problems in the 1970s, and Washington had an uncomfortable pause in its growth. With a shortage of orders—standard practice in the unstable airframe industry—and the cancellation of the government's supersonic transport, Boeing cut its employment from 101,000 to 38,000 in 1970. The Columbia's hydroelectric capacity was just about used up, and unwise decisions to build nuclear plants essentially bankrupted the Washington Public Power Supply System (WPPSS) in the early 1980s; electricity prices rose to at or above the national average. The aluminum industry had its problems in these years, and the Hanford Works were under attack and in 1988 failed to get the government to transform an idle WPPSS plant into a nuclear weapons plant. The percentage of workers in unions in Washington, as in the nation, plummeted sharply in the 1980s. The foundations of Washington's good life seemed to be crumbling.

But after a pause, Washington seems to be growing again. For this it has to thank geography most of all. Seattle, which within a 50 mile territory now contains over half of Washington's 4.5 million residents, is the closest major American city to the Orient, Middle America's outpost on the Pacific Rim. You can see clearly why on a relief and population map. On both sides of the Pacific, vast numbers of people are squeezed into small margins of level land between the steeply rising volcanic mountains and the sea, or tucked into valleys that are sometimes contained within the eye's sight and sometimes extend beyond the horizon far up between crevasses of mountains. These islands of settlement are surrounded by vast oceanic wildernesses: desert and mountains, open sea and Arctic vastness—and in another sense by the wildernesses of the totalitarian autarchies of China, Vietnam and the Soviet Union. Yet the peoples packed into these populated pockets of the Pacific Rim have over the past two or three decades produced more economic growth than anywhere else in the world. This has happened even though these are widely diverse, sometimes hostile, ethnic groups: the Japanese and Koreans, the Chinese of Taiwan, Hong Kong and Singapore, the Malays and Filipinos, and Washington's ethnic mix of Scandinavians, Yankees and new migrants attracted by the picturesque hills and outdoorsy atmosphere of Seattle and the communities along island-strewn, ferry-crisscrossed Puget Sound. Seattle, like Singapore and Hong Kong, Los Angeles and Tokyo, has spawned an innovative, white-collar economy whose growth is driven not only by the big enterprises that grew in the past—the aluminum companies, Boeing—but also by small companies only a few of which, like Bill Gates's Microsoft, have grown big enough to become nationally visible. But added together they provide a critical mass for economic growth—and have a vested interest, more than any other part of the country, in free trade. Washington's growth has also been helped by the physical attractions which have made Seattle and Washington for years a favorite of the environment-minded: the snow-capped volcanic peaks and the lush green valleys, the picturesque, steep streets of Seattle and the flannel shirted ambiance of little lumber and fishing towns, the sparkling array of merchandise in shopping malls and the ripple of the state-owned ferries as they ply through the deep waters of Puget Sound. Washington's position on the Pacific Rim, its lifestyle, its high competence and high tech type businesses will likely turn out to be more critical in the 1990s. At one time, a state full of apple farmers, fishermen, and dock hands needed cheap power to compensate for high freight costs. Now Washington is full of high-skilled people used to a higher standard of living and productive enough to sustain it.

The Washington of 50 years ago was liberal on economic issues: its IWW heritage was echoed in the big majorities Puget Sound cast for Franklin Roosevelt. It had some left-wing and even pro-Communist politicians, prompting FDR campaign manager James Farley to refer to "the 47 states and the Soviet of Washington." Its mainstream Democrats, notably Warren Magnuson and Henry Jackson who represented the state in Congress for a total of 87 years, believed in an active and compassionate federal government that built dams, aluminum plants and the Hanford Works at home and pursued an internationalist anti-Communist foreign policy abroad. Their political strength was built on a blue-collar base, augmented by the respect the leaders of the state's big businesses had for their clout in the capital. In today's Washington, the fulcrum of the electorate has moved from the blue-collar to the white-collar segment. The government is

WASHINGTON — Congressional Districts, Counties, and Selected Places — *(8 Districts)*

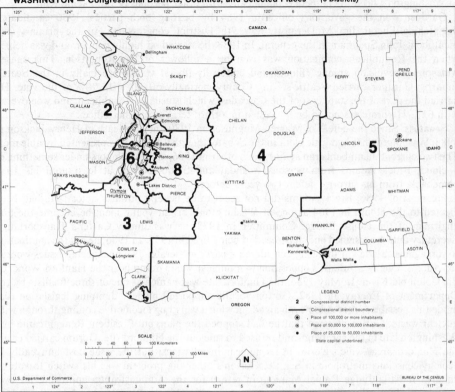

Congressional districts established March 29, 1983; all other boundaries are as of January 1, 1980.

seen no longer as the molder or even creator of the state's economy, but in some cases as an impediment to its growth, and the issue focus has moved from bread and butter economic issues to environmental and cultural issues which reflect an affluent electorate's desire to preserve and improve the quality of their lives. In the late 1980s, these impulses have moved Washington toward Democrats whose liberalism is more concentrated on cultural than economic issues: this state, which voted for Hubert Humphrey's liberalism in 1968, voted for Michael Dukakis's rather different liberalism 20 years later. But it is also a state with close partisan competition in which either party can win—Republicans have won three of the four Senate races here in the 1980s—and in which neither party has a lock on the electorate, where the candidate's particular positions, and the cultural cues their personality and character send, end up making the most difference.

Governor. Washington's current governor, Booth Gardner, is the first to establish command over state government since Daniel Evans retired in 1976. Gardner is a Democrat, an heir to a big lumber fortune and a former county executive in Tacoma. He pushed through one of the nation's more interesting workfare bills, providing mothers with child care but pestering them to go to work, and a number of education reforms. He failed to get the legislature to increase taxes—Washington is one of the few states without an income tax and is as averse to income taxes as next-door Oregon is to sales taxes—but that probably was to his advantage; by early

1989 the state's economy was generating enough revenue for surpluses. All this seems responsive to Washington's need to compete economically with other portions of the Pacific Rim.

Gardner won the governor's office in 1984 by beating both parties' 1980 candidates, dispatching liberal Jim McDermott, now 7th District congressman, in the primary and incumbent John Spellman in the general. In 1988, he started off highly popular and was helped when the Republican nomination was won by a follower of Pat Robertson. This caused widespread revulsion among affluent and culturally liberal voters, especially in the Seattle suburbs; Gardner carried Seattle's King County, normally 50–50, with 70% of the vote. He carried the part of the state east of the Cascades, which is usually Republican, and won overall with 62%. He professes not to be interested in a third term or in other office.

Senators. Since the defeat of Warren Magnuson in 1980 and the death of Henry Jackson in 1983, Washington has had little clout in the Senate, though it has been represented by able men. The two current incumbents ran against each other in 1986, and each labors under something of a cloud, Brock Adams from personal scandal and Slade Gorton, at least until his 1988 comeback, from his surprise defeat two years before.

For most of 1986, Brock Adams did not seem to be heading toward victory. He had been elected to the House in 1964 as one of Washington's bright young men; he became the first chairman of the House Budget Committee in 1975; he was Jimmy Carter's Transportation Secretary until he resigned one step ahead of being fired in 1979. In 1986, he got the nomination to run against Slade Gorton, long considered a party moderate. Two unexpected issues worked for Adams. One was Adams's opposition to a nuclear waste dump near the Hanford Works on the Columbia River. In May 1986, the Hanford site was named as one of three finalists by the Department of Energy; in 1982, Gorton vocally supported nuclear dumping legislation that made this possible. After Adams ran an ad showing a whistling locomotive coming through with nuclear waste, Gorton claimed that he had stopped the plan, but President Reagan came into Washington late in the campaign and refused to rule out the Hanford site. Gorton carried easily the Hanford area, which glories in its nuclear installations; but the issue cost him badly in ecology-conscious metropolitan Seattle. Gorton's other big problem was his switch to vote to confirm Indiana Judge Daniel Manion, in return for the Administration approving his own appointee—ironically a liberal Democrat—to a judgeship in Washington. Adams defeated Gorton 51%–49%.

In the Senate, Adams has a liberal record on most issues and seats on the Appropriations, Labor and Rules Committees. He authored a truck safety act, a bill to improve medical testing standards, and a trade amendment aimed at Boeing's competitor, Airbus. He conducted a filibuster of a nuclear waste bill and unavailingly sought to condemn the U.S. reflagging operation in the Persian Gulf. But in the fall of 1988, he was hurt by a story alleging that he had made sexual advances 18 months before to a 23-year-old woman, the daughter of longtime friends, while she was spending the night at his Washington, D.C., house while Mrs. Adams was out of town. Her allegations were found "meritless" by a Washington prosecutor, and Adams denied the charges; but obviously he was preoccupied by this unpleasant episode, and speculation is heavy in both Washingtons that Adams will retire when his seat is up in 1992.

The 1988 Senate race was something of a surprise. Daniel Evans, governor from 1964 to 1976, winner by a 55%–45% margin of a special election to succeed Jackson in 1983, seemed like a strong bet for a full term. But, never enthusiastic about the job, he decided to retire instead. Several Democratic congressmen had been eyeing the race, and two ran—liberal Mike Lowry from Seattle, who had lost the 1983 special, and Don Bonker from Olympia, who had been working hard on trade issues. Gorton, who had said he was through with politics, changed his mind and decided to run. He could point to serious accomplishments in his term—on the budget and a wilderness act—but he also seemed less arrogant and self-assured on the stump and ran ads that showed him with his granddaughter. Lowry changed his image, shaving his beard and looking less rumpled, but he remained clearly the most liberal of Washington politicians; that helped him win the Democratic primary but caused him problems outside Seattle in the general. Gorton, long known as a moderate, took a more conservative approach; in trouble for backing the nuclear waste dump in Hanford two years before, this time he called for converting a WPPSS nuclear plant in the Hanford complex to weapons manufacture. This was unpopular in some circles, but wildly popular in Hanford, a county Gorton carried with 81%. Statewide, Lowry ran well in Seattle and King County, but he failed to carry the counties heavy with traditional blue-collar Democrats in and around Tacoma, Everett and Bremerton. Gorton won 51%–49% and has his second chance in the Senate, this time, he says, as the voice of people outside the Seattle metropolitan area. Gorton is only the 15th U.S. Senator in history who has been defeated at the polls, and then has gone on to win back a seat in a later year.

Presidential politics. Washington moved from the economic liberalism of the 1930s to the cultural liberalism of the 1980s, on the way taking some contrarian stands in presidential elections: it voted for the losers in the close 1960, 1968 and 1976 contests. It cast an above average vote (43%) for Walter Mondale in 1984 and—despite those early evening network projections that George Bush would win—voted for Michael Dukakis in 1988.

Washington has a caucus system rather than a presidential primary. The 1988 contests, held on Super Tuesday, resulted in a victory for Michael Dukakis that enabled him to label his showing that day a four-cornered national triumph (Washington, Massachusetts, Florida, Texas); Jesse Jackson, however, was a close second in a state with few blacks but a good number of liberal activists. Among the Republicans, the winner was Pat Robertson, though more regular Republicans prevented his followers from taking over the party apparatus later in the year.

Congressional districting. Washington's clout in Washington used to be wielded mainly by its senators. These days its clout is strongest in the House. There it has Speaker Thomas Foley, who while unwilling to heavyhandedly favor his home state and district is not wholly aloof to their interests, plus effective legislators like Al Swift, who chairs the subcommittee with jurisdiction over campaign finance, and Norman Dicks, who serves on the Defense Appropriations Subcommittee. The clout of the Washington House delegation was apparent as long ago as 1981, when it helped to save the Export-Import Bank program that financed many of Boeing's foreign aircraft sales; the Democrats, citing this work, forced the Republican governor and legislature not to adopt a Republican redistricting plan. Washington will probably not gain a seat out of the 1990 Census and its districts will probably not be much changed.

The People: Est. Pop. 1988: 4,619,000; Pop. 1980: 4,132,156, up 11.8% 1980–88 and 21.1% 1970–80; 1.85% of U.S. total, 20th largest (tied with Maryland). 20% with 1–3 yrs. col., 19% with 4+ yrs. col.; 9.8% below poverty level. Single ancestry: 9% English, 8% German, 3% Irish, Norwegian, 2% Swedish, 1% French, Italian, Dutch, Scottish, Polish. Households (1980): 70% family, 38% with children, 59% married couples; 34.4% housing units rented; median monthly rent: $220; median house value: $60,700. Voting age pop. (1980): 2,992,796; 2% Asian origin, 2% Black, 2% Spanish origin, 1% American Indian. Registered voters (1988): 2,499,309; no party registration.

1988 Share of Federal Tax Burden: $16,431,000,000; 1.86% of U.S. total, 18th largest.

1988 Share of Federal Expenditures

	Total		Non-Defense		Defense	
Total Expend	$18,306m	(2.07%)	$12,811m	(1.95%)	$7,080m	(3.10%)
St/Lcl Grants	2,170m	(1.89%)	2,170m	(1.90%)	1m	(0.57%)
Salary/Wages	3,427m	(2.55%)	1,212m	(1.81%)	2,215m	(1.81%)
Pymnts to Indiv	7,669m	(1.87%)	7,013m	(1.80%)	656m	(3.52%)
Procurement	4,204m	(2.23%)	1,585m	(3.41%)	4,204m	(2.23%)
Research/Other	836m	(2.24%)	832m	(2.24%)	5m	(2.24%)

Political Lineup: Governor, William Booth Gardner (D); Lt. Gov., Joel Pritchard (R); Secy. of State, Ralph Munro (R); Atty. Gen., Kenneth Eikenberry (R); Treasurer, Dan Grimm (D); Auditor, Robert V. Graham (D). State Senate, 49 (25 R and 24 D); State House of Representatives, 98 (63 D and 35 R). Senators, Brock Adams (D) and Slade Gorton (R). Representatives, 8 (5 D and 3 R).

1988 Presidential Vote			1984 Presidential Vote		
Dukakis (D)	933,516	(50%)	Reagan (R)	1,051,670	(56%)
Bush (R)	903,835	(48%)	Mondale (D)	807,352	(43%)

GOVERNOR

Gov. William Booth Gardner (D)

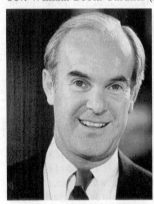

Elected 1984, term expires Jan. 1993; b. Aug. 21, 1936, Tacoma; home, Olympia; U. of WA, B.A. 1958, Harvard U., M.B.A. 1963; Protestant; married (Jean).

Career: Asst. to Dean, Harvard Sch. of Bus., 1966; Dir., Sch. of Bus. and Econ., U. of Puget Sound, 1967–72; WA Senate, 1970–73; Pres., bldg. and supply firm, 1972–80; Pierce Cnty. Exec., 1981–84.

Office: Office of the Governor, Olympia 98504, 206-753-6780.

Election Results

1988 gen.	William Booth Gardner (D)	1,166,448	(62%)
	Bob Williams (R)	708,481	(38%)
1988 prim.	William Booth Gardner (D)	539,243	(58%)
	Bob Williams (R)	187,797	(19%)
	Norm Maleng (R)	139,274	(15%)
	Five Others	69,189	(8%)
1984 gen.	William Booth Gardner (D)	1,006,993	(53%)
	John D. Spellman (R)	881,994	(47%)

SENATORS

Sen. Brock Adams (D)

Elected 1986, seat up 1992; b. Jan. 13, 1927, Atlanta, GA; home, Seattle; U. of WA, B.A. 1949, Harvard U., LL.B. 1952; Episcopalian; married (Betty).

Career: Navy, 1944–46; Practicing atty., 1952–61, 1979–86; U.S. Atty., Western Dist. of WA, 1961–64; U.S. House of Reps., 1964–76; U.S. Secy. of Transportation, 1977–79.

Offices: 513 HSOB 20510, 202-224-2621. Also 2988 Jackson Fed. Bldg., 915 2d Ave., Seattle 98174, 206-442-5545; and 770 U.S. Crthse., W. 920 Riverside Ave., Spokane 99201, 509-456-6816.

Committees: *Appropriations* (14th of 16 D). Subcommittees: Agriculture, Rural Development and Related Agencies; Commerce, Justice, State, and Judiciary; Legislative Branch. *Labor and Human Resources* (8th of 9 D). Subcommittees: Children, Family, Drugs, and Alcoholism; Employment and Productivity; Handicapped. *Rules and Administration* (9th of 9 D).

Group Ratings

	ADA	ACLU	COPE	CFA	LCV	ACU	NTLC	NSI	COC	CEI
1988	90	83	83	100	80	0	9	0	36	20
1987	95	—	90	100	—	4	—	—	38	20

National Journal Ratings

	1988 LIB	—	1988 CONS	1987 LIB	—	1987 CONS
Economic	83%	—	14%	65%	—	26%
Social	86%	—	0%	96%	—	0%
Foreign	79%	—	16%	74%	—	19%

Key Votes

1) Cut Aged Housing $	FOR	5) Bork Nomination	AGN	9) SDI Funding	AGN
2) Override Hwy Veto	FOR	6) Ban Plastic Guns	AGN	10) Ban Chem Weaps	AGN
3) Kill Plnt Clsng Notice	AGN	7) Deny Abortions	AGN	11) Aid To Contras	AGN
4) Min Wage Increase	FOR	8) Japanese Reparations	FOR	12) Reagan Defense $	AGN

Election Results

1986 general	Brock Adams (D)	677,471	(51%)	($1,912,307)
	Slade Gorton (R)	650,937	(49%)	($3,290,072)
1986 primary	Brock Adams (D)	287,258	(92%)	
	Five others.........................	26,027	(8%)	
1980 general	Slade Gorton (R)	936,317	(54%)	($896,532)
	Warren G. Magnuson (D).............	792,052	(46%)	($1,614,999)

Sen. Slade Gorton (R)

Elected 1988, seat up 1994; b. Jan. 8, 1928, Chicago, IL; home, Seattle; Dartmouth Col., A.B. 1950, Columbia U., LL.B. 1953; Episcopalian; married (Sally).

Career: WA House of Reps., 1959–69, Major. Ldr., 1967–69; WA Atty. Gen., 1969–80. U.S. Senator, 1980–86.

Offices: 730 HSOB, 20510, 202-224-3441; 3206 Jackson Fed. Bldg., 915 2d Ave., Seattle 98174, 206-442-0350; and U.S. Crthse., Rm. 697, Spokane 99201, 509-456-2507.

Committees: *Agriculture, Nutrition, and Forestry* (9th of 9 R). Subcommittees: Agricultural Credit (Ranking Member); Conservation and Forestry; Domestic and Foreign Marketing and Product Promotion. *Armed Services* (7th of 9 R). Subcommittees: Projection Forces and Regional Defense; Readiness, Sustainability and Support (Ranking Member); Strategic Forces and Nuclear Deterrence. *Commerce, Science, and Transportation* (8th of 9 R). Subcommittees: Communications; Consumer (Ranking Member); National Ocean Policy Study.

Group Ratings and Key Votes: Newly Elected

Election Results

1988 general	Slade Gorton (R)	944,359	(51%)	($2,851,591)
	Michael E. (Mike) Lowry (D)	904,183	(49%)	($2,191,187)
1988 primary	Slade Gorton (R)	335,846	(36%)	
	Michael E. (Mike) Lowry (D)	297,399	(32%)	
	Don Bonker (D)	241,170	(26%)	
	Three Others........................	61,048	(6%)	
1983 special	Daniel J. Evans (R).................	672,326	(55%)	($1,792,038)
	Michael E. (Mike) Lowry (D)	540,981	(45%)	($1,007,973)
1982 general	Henry M. (Scoop) Jackson (D).........	870,307	(69%)	($1,379,110)
	Doug Jewett (R)....................	306,522	(24%)	($241,695)

FIRST DISTRICT

Just a few miles north of Seattle, 50 years ago you were out in open country, where, "U.S. 99 runs between fruit and vegetable stands, scattered houses, and suburban beer parlors, road-houses, and skating rinks catering to those seeking out-of-town amusements." The *WPA Guide* went on to describe the area as, "Tawdry during the day, the establishments at night are brilliant with the blaze of red, white, green, and blue neon signs. On Saturday night, especially, business flourishes. From the dance floors come the throb of drums, the wail of saxophone, and the blare of trumpet and clarinet. In the early morning hours the music ceases, the lights are extinguished, and the traffic flows back to the city." The days of roadhouses are long over, and metropolitan growth has moved north from Seattle along Puget Sound all the way to Everett and farther. White-collar families who used to live in small houses in cramped neighborhoods in Seattle have seen their incomes rise and have moved out to more spacious quarters or to a bluff with a view of the Sound or Lake Washington. Inland you can find subdivisions amid the Washington state vineyards and wineries. Roadhouses and vegetable stands have been replaced by shopping centers and supermarkets, and the communal enjoyment of dance music by the different sounds adults and teenagers play on their Walkmans.

The 1st Congressional District of Washington includes most of this territory between Seattle and the much smaller port of Everett. It hugs both sides of Puget Sound and Lake Washington, taking in Bainbridge Island (where you can commute by ferry to downtown Seattle each day and then return to your flannel shirts and L.L. Bean shoes) and part of Kitsap County west of Puget Sound and the comfortable towns of Kirkland and Bothell east of Lake Washington. Although it contains quite a few of Seattle's comfortable neighborhoods and some rural countrysides, it is essentially the northern Seattle suburban district. Its boundaries are rather tortuous, designed to take in most of the Republican precincts in this part of Washington and to exclude most of the Democratic territory. Yet it is only tenuously Republican; its leanings on cultural issues, the environment and foreign policy leave it pretty close to even in statewide races and vulnerable to Democrats in the House contest.

That accounts for the fact that this district has seen several close elections. Republican Congressman John Miller, elected in 1984 with 56%, had a close call in 1986 when Democrat Reese Lindquist held him to 51%; and Lindquist ran again in 1988. Miller's problem was mainly foreign policy. He had a liberal record on the environment on the Seattle Council and in Washington, and he is liberal on cultural issues. But he is an adamant anti-Communist and strong supporter of aid to the Nicaraguan contras, for which he was roundly attacked. Lindquist, former president of the state teachers' union, attacked him on budget issues as well, and for putting his district office downtown.

Miller did not entirely back down in 1988: he took a seat on Foreign Affairs and continued to support the contras. But he also pointed out that he opposed the MX missile and voted for South African sanctions, and he opened district offices in the suburbs. He spent some of his own money in what became one of the country's more costly races. The TV ads got rough, maybe too rough. Lindquist ran a spot showing a dead body in a morgue while attacking Miller for voting against a Coast Guard appropriation. Miller ran an ad attacking Lindquist for having violated the law in leading a teachers' strike. Washington's peculiar primary system, in which voters are allowed to vote for candidates of different parties, often provides a preview of general election results. In the 1st in September Miller led Lindquist 51%–47%; in November Miller won 55%–45%. That is a decisive result, but scarcely an overwhelming one, and this could continue to be a seriously contested district.

The People: Est. Pop. 1986: 567,900, up 10.0% 1980–86; Pop. 1980: 516,378, up 20.5% 1970–80. Households: 73% family, 38% with children, 63% married couples; 27.2% housing units rented; median monthly rent: $287; median house value: $74,900. Voting age pop. (1980): 378,407; 3% Asian origin, 1% Spanish origin, 1% Black, 1% American Indian.

1988 Presidential Vote:

Dukakis (D)	141,024	(50%)
Bush (R)	139,138	(49%)

Rep. John R. Miller (R)

Elected 1984; b. May 23, 1938, New York, NY; home, Seattle; Bucknell U., B.A. 1959, Yale U., M.A., J.D. 1964; Jewish; married (June).

Career: Asst. Atty. Gen. of WA, 1965–68; Practicing atty., 1968–72, 1981–84; Seattle City Cncl., 1972–80; Commentator, KIRO-TV, KIRO and KSEA Radio, 1981–84.

Offices: 1406 LHOB 20515, 202-225-6311. Also 145 South Third Ave., Edmonds, 98020, 206-672-4224.

Committees: *Foreign Affairs* (13th of 18 R). Subcommittees: International Economic Policy and Trade; Human Rights and International Organizations. *Merchant Marine and Fisheries* (9th of 17 R). Subcommittees: Fisheries and Wildlife Conservation and the Environment; Merchant Marine.

Group Ratings

	ADA	ACLU	COPE	CFA	LCV	ACU	NTLC	NSI	COC	CEI
1988	60	78	41	82	75	38	76	90	79	43
1987	44	—	34	50	—	41	—	—	73	60

National Journal Ratings

	1988 LIB — 1988 CONS		1987 LIB — 1987 CONS	
Economic	31% —	67%	34% —	65%
Social	73% —	25%	55% —	45%
Foreign	36% —	64%	37% —	63%

Key Votes

1) Homeless $	AGN	5) Ban Drug Test	AGN	9) SDI Research	FOR
2) Gephardt Amdt	AGN	6) Drug Death Pen	AGN	10) Ban Chem Weaps	FOR
3) Deficit Reduc	AGN	7) Handgun Sales	AGN	11) Aid to Contras	FOR
4) Kill Plnt Clsng Notice	FOR	8) Ban D.C. Abort $	AGN	12) Nuclear Testing	AGN

Election Results

1988 general	John R. Miller (R)	152,265	(55%)	($1,321,021)
	Reese Lindquist (D)	122,646	(45%)	($625,926)
1988 primary	John R. Miller (R)	69,516	(51%)	
	Reese Lindquist (D)	62,941	(47%)	
1986 general	John R. Miller (R)	97,969	(51%)	($592,313)
	Reese Lindquist (D)	92,697	(49%)	($397,226)

SECOND DISTRICT

At the far northwest corner of the 48 continental states is the rainiest part of the United States (a small patch of Hawaii excepted). The cold waters of the Pacific evaporate, condense and then mist or rain down on the hills and mountains that jut up from the ocean or the sides of Puget Sound. The mountains here are always green, the trees that line the inlets towering and the evenness of the climate makes the way of life here steadier and less subject to violent surprise than it can be on the tornado-swept plains of Kansas or the hurricane coasts of Florida.

Most of this land is vacant of people; settlement in the 2d Congressional District of Washington, which covers the Olympic Peninsula and both sides of Puget Sound, is concentrated in a narrow strip of land just east of the Sound, in or near Bellingham, Everett with its paper mills and giant Boeing plant, and the agricultural Skagit Valley. Small numbers live on the islands in Puget Sound and the Strait of Juan de Fuca, and more live along the coast of the Olympic Peninsula and down the Pacific to the lumber mill and fishing town of Hoquiam. This land has attracted some counterculture veterans and young people looking for a more natural, less metropolitan life; there is little hint here of the sophistication of downtown Seattle. This is blue-collar country, where men go out to work at 6 a.m. in air cold enough to see your breath year round, and where there remains a certain surly independence and suspicion of authority. Convicted spy Robert Boyce spent several months here in Port Angeles after escaping from jail and, although some people suspected he was a fugitive, no one turned him in; writer and poet Raymond Carver, who lived in Port Angeles until his death in 1988, captured the atmosphere.

The political tradition in most of the lumbering and fishing areas here is Democratic; in the agricultural areas it is sometimes more Republican. For most of the last 50 years the 2d has elected Democratic congressmen. The current incumbent is among the ablest of the bunch—which is saying a lot, since one former representative was Henry Jackson. Congressman Al Swift, the only Washington Member on the Energy and Commerce Committee, has become one of the busiest and most knowledgeable of House members, a workhorse with considerable accomplishments. In the early 1980s, when the Washington Public Power Supply System (WPPSS) was going bankrupt, Swift had to frame the Northwest Power Act, a task which took constant negotiations with regional interests and politicians, and was fraught with political peril: the Northwest was losing its historically low power rates, and many young voters here hate and fear nuclear power. On the Telecommunications Subcommittee, Swift worked on broadcasting deregulation and he attacked the television network news divisions for projecting the results of presidential elections when the polls were still open on the West Coast; Swift—a former newscaster himself—wrote a uniform national poll closing law which would close all polling places in the continental United States at 9 p.m. EST, and got it passed by the House in 1986 and 1989.

On other broadcast issues, Swift is involved in reviving the fairness doctrine, regulating children's television, and license reform. He has also come forward with his own approaches to breaking the impasse over the Clean Air Act. But his most important work in the 101st Congress could come in the House Administration Committee on the issue of campaign finance reform.

After the 1984 election, he became chairman of the new House Administration Subcommittee on Elections which, in addition to election day matters, has jurisdiction over campaign finance reform. Swift has been favorable toward public financing of congressional elections and toward changing the rules on PACs, but he is also a practical politician who is not interested in reporting out a measure that can't pass on the floor. All the action in the 100th Congress on this issue took place in the Senate, which was ultimately stymied by a Republican filibuster. But some House Democrats, including Swift, would like to make a record and produce a genuine reform, so the action will this time be on the House side.

Swift has also paid attention to Washington state issues. One is nuclear waste disposal; on a 1988 conference committee he inserted a key amendment removing any chance that Hanford, Washington, would be used as a nuclear dump. He was also one of those who worked hard to secure the Navy homeport for Everett (scheduled now for 1992). It was a local issue after all—Indian fishing rights—which nearly beat his Democratic predecessor, Lloyd Meeds. Swift was a Bellingham TV newscaster and former aide to Meeds when Meeds retired in 1978; he ran for the seat, beating a Jackson staffer in the primary and an opponent of Indian fishing rights in the general. Since then he has been reelected easily. Swift gave some thought to running for the Senate in 1988, but decided that Mike Lowry's liberal views gave him a lock on the primary. That and the fact that he has a great deal of interesting work in the House, pretty much eliminates any chance he'll run for statewide office.

The People: Est. Pop. 1986: 574,500, up 11.2% 1980–86; Pop. 1980: 516,568, up 33.3% 1970–80. Households (1980): 72% family, 37% with children, 62% married couples; 30.7% housing units rented; median monthly rent: $211; median house value: $58,700. Voting age pop. (1980): 373,304; 2% American Indian, 1% Spanish origin, 1% Asian origin.

1988 Presidential Vote:

Dukakis (D)	120,954	(49%)
Bush (R)	119,362	(49%)

Rep. Al Swift (D)

Elected 1978; b. Sept. 12, 1935, Tacoma; home, Bellingham; Whitman Col., 1953–55, Central WA St. Col., B.A. 1957; Unitarian; married (Paula).

Career: Broadcaster and Dir. of Pub. Affairs, KVOS-TV, Bellingham, 1957–62, 1969–77; A. A. to U.S. Rep. Lloyd Meeds, 1965–69, 1977.

Offices: 1502 LHOB 20515, 202-225-2605. Also Fed. Bldg., Rm. 201, 3002 Colby, Everett 98201, 206-252-3188; Fed. Bldg., Rm. 308, 104 W. Magnolia, Bellingham 98225, 206-733-4500; and 138 W. First St., Port Angeles 98362, 206-452-3211.

Committees: *Energy and Commerce* (9th of 26 D). Subcommittees: Energy and Power; Telecommunications and Finance; Transportation and Hazardous Materials. *House Administration* (5th of 13 D). Subcommittees: Accounts; Elections (Chairman).

Group Ratings

	ADA	ACLU	COPE	CFA	LCV	ACU	NTLC	NSI	COC	CEI
1988	90	95	83	64	75	0	9	10	36	19
1987	92	—	83	71	—	9	—	—	23	10

National Journal Ratings

	1988 LIB	—	1988 CONS		1987 LIB	—	1987 CONS
Economic	65%	—	34%		68%	—	27%
Social	86%	—	0%		78%	—	0%
Foreign	77%	—	21%		76%	—	19%

Key Votes

1) Homeless $	AGN	5) Ban Drug Test	AGN	9) SDI Research	AGN
2) Gephardt Amdt	AGN	6) Drug Death Pen	—	10) Ban Chem Weaps	FOR
3) Deficit Reduc	FOR	7) Handgun Sales	AGN	11) Aid to Contras	AGN
4) Kill Plnt Clsng Notice	AGN	8) Ban D.C. Abort $	AGN	12) Nuclear Testing	FOR

Election Results

1988 general	Al Swift (D), unopposed			($301,229)
1988 primary	Al Swift (D), unopposed			
1986 general	Al Swift (D)	124,840	(72%)	($239,341)
	Thomas S. Talman (R)	48,077	(28%)	($5,926)

THIRD DISTRICT

From the Pacific Ocean to the row of volcanoes, active and inactive, from Mount Rainier to Mount St. Helens to Oregon's Mount Hood, the 3d District is one of America's most productive lumber areas. The moist air and almost constant rains that are blown in from the Pacific keep the trees on the coast growing rapidly; in the valleys just past the Coast Range there is still plenty of precipitation and fast-growing forests. Then come the high mountains, their snow-capped peaks looking majestically down on the plains—when there aren't clouds in the way. These Cascades are a genuine divide, wrenching almost all the precipitation out of the air, so that the climate eastward for a thousand miles is arid.

The land between the ocean and the Cascades, from the state capital of Olympia on an inlet of Puget Sound south to Vancouver, just across the Columbia River from Portland, Oregon forms the 3d Congressional District of Washington. Lumber is the biggest industry here, and there are always ferocious demands to stop the export of unfinished timber to East Asia; fishing is also important, and responsible for much export; the port of Portland is America's biggest unloader of Japanese cars. In all, this is one of the United States' biggest exporting congressional districts and perhaps the one most oriented to free trade. But its politics has little of the theoretical about it. The political atmosphere here has not changed much since the turn of the century, when the lumberjacks first attacked the firs and sawmill towns sprang up along rivers and in bays off Puget Sound and the ocean; there is still a rough-hewn populism, reminiscent of the days when the Industrial Workers of the World were trying to organize the lumber camps. Most voters here are Democrats, and if they are interested in trade issues it is for practical reasons, and their views are typically pugnacious.

The 3d District was the scene of the closest House race of 1988, as Congressman Don Bonker ran for the Senate (he lost in the Democratic primary) and both parties tried to pick up this seat. Neither of the two major party nominees was a standard politician. Jolene Unsoeld was a citizen activist in the 1970s who was elected to the legislature in 1984; the widow of a mountain climber, she lived in Nepal for five years in the 1960s and was the first woman to climb the North Face of Mount Teton. Unsoeld had a busy 1988; not only did she run for Congress but she also sponsored Initiative 97, mandating a state toxic waste cleanup, which passed by a wide margin. She was attacked as too liberal in the primary, but won nonetheless. In the general, however, her liberal reputation may have hurt; in most counties she ran behind rather than, as most Democrats do, ahead of her national ticket.

The Republican nominee, Bill Wight, was a Vietnam veteran and career military officer who only just returned to the district in 1988. He claimed in an ad to have channeled some aid after Mount St. Helens erupted in 1980, while working for Senator John Warner, but seems to have done little else. Wight argued that Unsoeld was too liberal on environmental issues and said he would do more for economic development. It was a winning message in Republican-leaning Lewis County and in usually Democratic Vancouver as well. But Unsoeld was ahead in Olympia and along the Columbia River and the coast, and won by 618 votes.

In the House, she has seats on the Merchant Marine and Education and Labor Committees and joined Oregon Democrat Peter DeFazio's fight against log exports and has come out against offshore oil drilling. Given the close margin, this could easily be a seriously contested seat in 1990.

The People: Est. Pop. 1986: 556,200, up 7.7% 1980–86; Pop. 1980: 516,473, up 35.4% 1970–80. Households (1980): 73% family, 41% with children, 63% married couples; 32.1% housing units rented; median monthly rent: $202; median house value: $54,500. Voting age pop. (1980): 360,673; 1% Spanish origin, 1% Asian origin, 1% American Indian, 1% Black.

1988 Presidential Vote:

Dukakis (D)	113,785	(51%)
Bush (R)	104,641	(47%)

Rep. Jolene Unsoeld (D)

Elected 1988; b. Dec. 3, 1931, Corvallis, OR; home, Olympia; U. of OR; no religious affil.; widowed.

Career: Dir., English Language Inst., Nepal, 1965–67; Lobbyist, consult., 1971–84; Author; WA House of Reps., 1984–88.

Offices: 1508 LHOB 20515, 202-225-3536. Also 207 Fed. Bldg., Olympia 98501, 206-753-9528; and 601 Main St., Ste. 505, Vancouver 98660, 206-696-7942.

Committees: *Education and Labor* (17th of 22 D). Subcommittees: Elementary, Secondary, and Vocational Education; Health and Safety; Human Resources. *Merchant Marine and Fisheries* (26th of 26 D). Subcommittees: Fisheries and Wildlife Conservation and the Environment; Merchant Marine. *Select Committee on Aging* (38th of 39 D). Subcommittee: Human Services.

Group Ratings and Key Votes: Newly Elected

Election Results

1988 general	Jolene Unsoeld (D)	109,412	(50%)	($684,206)
	Bill Wight (R)	108,794	(50%)	($354,142)
1988 primary	Jolene Unsoeld (D)	44,838	(40%)	
	John McKibbin (D)	30,112	(26%)	
	Bill Wight (R)	21,509	(19%)	
	Bill Hughes (R)	12,532	(11%)	
	John Libby, Sr. (D)	4,112	(4%)	
1986 general	Donald L. (Don) Bonker (D)	114,775	(74%)	($195,212)
	Joe Illing (R)	41,275	(26%)	

FOURTH DISTRICT

Fifty years ago, the towns of Richland, Kennewick and Pasco on the Columbia in eastern Washington were known as the center of a cherry and grape growing valley and as home of the Twin Cities Creamery; all around was an "area of sagebrush and coulee, [where] geese and ducks remain all winter, offering excellent sport for hunters. Cottontails, jack rabbits, Chinese pheasants and the sage hen are elusive targets." In this out-of-the-way place described by the *WPA Guide* in 1943, the DuPont company, working on the top-secret Manhattan Project, built the Hanford Works for housing the first nuclear reactors; and here still today, where the Columbia River etches its way through the arid plateau of eastern Washington, is one of the major nuclear manufacturing facilities in the country. The Hanford site provided plentiful water, rail transportation and, thanks to another great government engineering project, cheap electric power: for through it traversed power lines from Grand Coulee and Bonneville Dams, just recently completed by the government.

About half of eastern Washington, from Grand Coulee through the Hanford Works down to Bonneville Dam, makes up the 4th Congressional District of Washington. Sheltered from the coastal rains by the Cascades, this is mostly arid land, with wide extremes of temperature; around Richland it can go as high as 114 degrees in the summer and down to minus 27 in the winter. But here and there the valleys sheltered by mountains, blessed with running streams that can provide irrigation water, or with water from Grand Coulee's reservoirs, are some of America's major fruit producing land, most notably around Yakima. Most of this is by now stable, long-settled land; even Hanford and Grand Coulee, once sparkling new or covered with construction dust, are now places that have been there a long time.

The 4th District has been one of the great beneficiaries of government programs: without Grand Coulee, the Hanford Works, water and agricultural subsidies and aid, it would be unrecognizable. Yet its attitude toward the federal government is more often resentment than gratitude. It grouses as electric power becomes more expensive, partly because the Washington state public power system bungled a huge nuclear plant construction program and partly just because the Columbia's hydroelectric capacity is used up; but the blame goes to the feds. It is angry when farm prices go down or production is low. It is upset at the prospect of reducing the flow of migrant fruitpickers. It is angry when the federal government wants to cut back on nuclear power. It got mad when the federal government put Hanford on its list of three possible nuclear waste disposal sites in 1983 and when the government decided not to convert a nuclear power plant there to weapons production in 1988.

The job of articulating these angers and assuaging them belongs to the 4th District's congressman, Sid Morrison. He is a Republican first elected in 1980, a fruitgrower and veteran of the Washington legislature, but he is neither a free market ideologue nor a New Right cultural conservative. Morrison has also been a solid supporter of the nuclear industry and has welcomed most expansions of the Hanford Works because of the jobs they bring to the Tri-Cities. But in the mid-1980s, he was vociferously opposing the nuclear waste dump proposal and insisting that it made much more sense to put the stuff in Nevada's Yucca Mountains, and he succeeded in 1986 in getting funds cut off for study of the Hanford site. He was also co-sponsoring with Al Swift a bill that would make the federal government fully liable for damages from nuclear waste—a different approach from that used for nuclear plants, whose liability has been limited by federal statute. Morrison is not a dazzlingly articulate legislator, but he has been effective in advancing the interests of his district on the issues it cares about the most. Since he beat Democratic incumbent Mike McCormack in 1980, he has been reelected by wide margins in a district which is, in many elections, the most Republican in the state.

The People: Est. Pop. 1986: 546,000, up 5.7% 1980–86; Pop. 1980: 516,426, up 26.5% 1970–80. Households (1980): 74% family, 41% with children, 64% married couples; 33.0% housing units rented; median monthly rent: $186; median house value: $48,100. Voting age pop. (1980): 359,287; 7% Spanish origin, 2% American Indian, 1% Black, 1% Asian origin.

1988 Presidential Vote:
Bush (R)	109,085	(57%)
Dukakis (D)	78,786	(41%)

Rep. Sid Morrison (R)

Elected 1980; b. May 13, 1933, Yakima; home, Zillah; WA St. U., B.S. 1954; United Methodist; married (Marcella).

Career: Army, 1954–56; Orchardist, Morrison Fruit Co., Inc., 1956–81; WA House of Reps., 1966–74; WA Senate, 1974–80.

Offices: 1434 LHOB 20515, 202-225-5816. Also 212 E. E St., Yakima 98901, 509-575-5891; 3311 W. Clearwater, Ste. 105, Kennewick 99336, 509-376-9702; and Morris Bldg., 23 S. Wenatchee Ave., Ste. 210, Wenatchee 98801, 509-662-4294.

Committees: *Agriculture* (8th of 17 R). Subcommittees: Conservation, Credit, and Rural Development; Department Operations, Research, and Foreign Agriculture; Forests, Family Farms, and Energy (Ranking Member). *Science, Space and Technology* (7th of 19 R). Subcommittees: Energy Research and Development (Ranking Member); Natural Resources, Agriculture Research and Environment. *Select Committee on Hunger* (3d of 12 R).

Group Ratings

	ADA	ACLU	COPE	CFA	LCV	ACU	NTLC	NSI	COC	CEI
1988	55	52	26	45	50	64	55	100	93	46
1987	36	—	25	29	—	52	—	—	67	47

National Journal Ratings

	1988 LIB — 1988 CONS			1987 LIB — 1987 CONS		
Economic	21%	—	77%	29%	—	69%
Social	54%	—	45%	34%	—	65%
Foreign	41%	—	58%	39%	—	60%

Key Votes

1) Homeless $	FOR	5) Ban Drug Test	FOR	9) SDI Research	FOR
2) Gephardt Amdt	AGN	6) Drug Death Pen	FOR	10) Ban Chem Weaps	AGN
3) Deficit Reduc	AGN	7) Handgun Sales	FOR	11) Aid to Contras	FOR
4) Kill Plnt Clsng Notice	FOR	8) Ban D.C. Abort $	AGN	12) Nuclear Testing	AGN

Election Results

1988 general	Sid Morrison (R)	142,938	(75%)	($194,505)
	J. Richard Golob (D)	48,850	(25%)	($58,574)
1988 primary	Sid Morrison (R)	72,633	(73%)	
	J. Richard Golob (D)	26,638	(27%)	
1986 general	Sid Morrison (R)	107,593	(72%)	($105,513)
	Robert Goedecke (D)	41,709	(28%)	($5,142)

FIFTH DISTRICT

The 5th Congressional District of Washington is the easternmost part of the state. Centered on Spokane, Washington's second largest city, this has been called the Inland Empire. Here the Columbia, Spokane and Snake Rivers wind through and beneath vast plateaus, bringing vast amounts of water from the American and Canadian Rockies to this land of low rainfall. Irrigation systems divert great quantities of the water that lead to the production of some bountiful crop fields, but areas like the Palouse in the southeast corner of the state are so fertile (the topsoil is said to be 200 feet deep) that huge harvests issue just from the rainfall. These rivers are not hospitable streams; they are fast flowing, and in some places lie in great clefts, far below the rest of the landscape. Getting the water out to where it would be useful was a major task—achieved in large part by New Deal projects like the Grand Coulee Dam.

Historically and today, voting habits in eastern Washington are in between those of the urbanized Puget Sound area and those in neighboring Rocky Mountain states—which makes some sense, since this part of Washington is physically and economically much more a part of the intermountain basin than of the Pacific coast. In the late 1970s and early 1980s it veered very much toward the Republicans, as did the Rocky Mountain states generally, with their disgust at federal intervention and anger at lack of American assertiveness abroad. But in the late 1980s, like much of the West, it moved back toward the Democrats, and the 5th District nearly went for Michael Dukakis over George Bush.

One reason for that shift may be the increasing prominence of the 5th District's Democratic congressman, Thomas Foley. Well known in the Spokane area since he was first elected as a young lawyer in 1964, he became one of the more powerful members of the House when he was elected Majority Leader in January 1987, and he became one of the most nationally prominent members of Congress when he was elected Speaker, after Jim Wright's resignation, in June 1989. Foley came to the office in particularly unpleasant circumstances, with characteristic grace and aplomb, hailed on all sides as a man of fairness and integrity. Yet he emphasized that he was "proud to be a Democrat" and his record as majority leader and whip was one of a committed and effective Democratic partisan. Foley is a good listener and willing to accommodate himself to others. But he also insists on doing things his own way. In a town where offices are filled with massive desks and walls with inscribed photographs, Foley has a coffee table in front of his chairs, pictures of two Speakers on his wall (Henry Clay and Theodore Sedgewick), and mammoth stereo equipment so that he can listen to his classical music.

Foley's path upward has taken an unusual course, running not quite according to the form that was traditional in the days of Sam Rayburn and John McCormack, and not quite according to the folkways that have developed in the House. He is the product of both seniority and insurgency, of patronage from old leaders and support from younger members of the Democratic Caucus. Thus he was chosen chairman of the Democratic Study Group (DSG) just after the 1972 election, and just before the Democrats' Watergate surge, when the DSG was an insurgent group dominated by Phillip Burton. Yet by then the DSG was supplanting the leadership under Speaker Carl Albert in important ways, setting the legislative agenda, taking positions on issues, making head counts and whip calls. In the House membership elected in 1974, controlled by Watergate Democrats, Foley was a natural leader.

So much so that he did not seek leadership positions, but had them thrust upon him. He was voted in, over incumbent Bob Poage, as chairman of the House Agriculture Committee. This was a startling reversal of fortune, since four years before, in 1970, he ranked only eighth in seniority on the committee; but in 1972 three senior Democrats retired and two more were defeated; another was beaten in his 1974 primary; and Poage, though an expert on agricultural legislation, was such a bleak reactionary on every other issue that the post-1974 Democratic

Caucus was unwilling to back him, even though Foley himself supported him.

Foley's next elevation came after an election in 1980 which was as disastrous for the Democrats as 1974 was propitious. The House majority whip, John Brademas, had lost his seat in Indiana, and Foley, by this time long an ally of the leadership, was chosen for the post by then Speaker O'Neill and Majority Leader Jim Wright. Oddly, the post was still appointive (the Democratic Caucus later decided to make it elective), and so Foley was climbing up the leadership ladder in the same way O'Neill and others had before him. But if Foley was not any faction's first choice, he was widely popular and respected among Democrats (and for that matter among Republicans). The previous time the Democrats had chosen a majority leader, in 1976, there was a bitter fight. In 1986, Foley won the position unopposed.

Foley's fairmindedness and almost judicial temperament leave some of the more partisan Democrats frustrated sometimes, but his unwillingness to take positions unless he can justify both policy and procedure, and his ability to see the other side of issues even as he argues his own, make him uniquely respected on both sides of the aisle. Calmly, carefully, lucidly, he can explain the most complicated parliamentary tangle clearly enough for any member to understand and fairly enough to permit anyone to rely on it in making up his own mind. Even aggressively partisan Republicans like Newt Gingrich and Ed Rollins saluted Foley's fairness and integrity as he became Speaker.

Foley appears now to be one of those national leaders of the Democratic Party with no problems in his own, not always Democratic, constituency. That was not always so. Thrust suddenly into national prominence in the middle 1970s, he was hard pressed in 1976, 1978 and 1980; it's a tough transition from being the pleasant congressman who sends out all the literature and is identified with only the popular side of issues to the national leader of his party who is saddled with all its locally unpopular stands, and Foley, like others (notably Morris Udall, John Brademas, Jim Corman, Al Ullman), had trouble making the transition. But he has done so. In the 5th District he has raised his percentage from 52% in 1980, to 64% in 1982, 70% in 1984, 75% in 1986 and 76% in 1988. Evidently he has persuaded eastern Washington voters that they're fortunate to have a congressman as nationally prominent and competent as Foley has proven himself to be.

The People: Est. Pop. 1986: 536,700, up 3.9% 1980–86; Pop. 1980: 516,719, up 18.2% 1970–80. Households (1980): 70% family, 37% with children, 59% married couples; 33.4% housing units rented; median monthly rent: $181; median house value: $46,200. Voting age pop. (1980): 373,789; 2% Spanish origin, 1% American Indian, 1% Asian origin, 1% Black.

1988 Presidential Vote:

Bush (R)	105,193	(51%)
Dukakis (D)	99,301	(48%)

Rep. Thomas S. Foley (D)

Elected 1964; b. Mar. 6, 1929, Spokane; home, Spokane; U. of WA, B.A. 1951, LL.B. 1957; Roman Catholic; married (Heather).

Career: Practicing atty., 1957; Spokane Cnty. Dpty. Prosecuting Atty., 1958–60; Instructor, Gonzaga U. Sch. of Law, 1958–60; Asst. Atty. Gen. of WA, 1960–61; Asst. Chf. Clerk and Spec. Counsel, U.S. Sen. Cmtee. on Interior and Insular Affairs, 1961–63.

Offices: 1201 LHOB 20515, 202-225-2006. Also W. 601 First Ave., 2d Fl. W., Spokane 99204, 509-456-4680; 12929 E. Sprague, Spokane 99216, 509-926-4434; and 28 W. Main, Walla Walla 99362, 509-522-6370.

Committees: *Speaker of the House.*

Group Ratings

	ADA	ACLU	COPE	CFA	LCV	ACU	NTLC	NSI	COC	CEI
1988	85	91	80	55	50	4	8	11	38	14
1987	80	—	80	79	—	9	—	—	27	13

National Journal Ratings

	1988 LIB — 1988 CONS		1987 LIB — 1987 CONS	
Economic	65%	— 34%	68%	— 27%
Social	86%	— 14%	78%	— 0%
Foreign	67%	— 32%	66%	— 34%

Key Votes

1) Homeless $	AGN	5) Ban Drug Test	AGN	9) SDI Research	AGN
2) Gephardt Amdt	AGN	6) Drug Death Pen	AGN	10) Ban Chem Weaps	FOR
3) Deficit Reduc	FOR	7) Handgun Sales	FOR	11) Aid to Contras	AGN
4) Kill Plnt Clsng Notice	AGN	8) Ban D.C. Abort $	AGN	12) Nuclear Testing	FOR

Election Results

1988 general	Thomas S. Foley (D).................	160,654	(76%)	($476,460)
	Marlyn A. Derby (R)	49,657	(24%)	($13,534)
1988 primary	Thomas S. Foley (D).................	81,223	(76%)	
	Marlyn A. Derby (R)	25,300	(24%)	
1986 general	Thomas S. Foley (D).................	121,732	(75%)	($481,477)
	Floyd Wakefield (R)	41,179	(25%)	($56,502)

SIXTH DISTRICT

Looking down from snow-clad Mount Rainier to the cool blue waters of Puget Sound and Commencement Bay, the city you see first is not Seattle, far to the north, but Tacoma. This is the second largest city on Puget Sound, which has always been overshadowed by Seattle. In 1900, just before the state's most explosive decade of growth, Tacoma was still a credible rival—it had 37,000 people to Seattle's 80,000. But in the years that followed, Seattle's growth continued, while Tacoma got itself embroiled in an unsuccessful attempt to rewrite history and change the name of Mount Rainier to Mount Tacoma. While Seattle has a large and growing white-collar sector, Tacoma has been more of an industrial town. The *WPA Guide* 50 years ago, after noting its beautiful natural setting, noted "Along the bay and on the flats are sawmills, factories for lumber products, railroad shops and other industrial establishments, including two important electrochemical plants. Railroad tracks are lined with freight cars and noisy switch engines. The acrid odor of coal smoke and the penetrating smell of tideflats mingle with the resinous fragrance from piles of newly cut timber. Beyond the sluggish river, smoke rises from burning piles of refuse. Sometimes the air is heavy with the biting, choking smell of sulphur from the pulp mills. To the northwest is the towering smokestack of the Tacoma Smelter, one of the two highest stacks in the world and visible for miles, with its drifting trail of light, lemon-colored smoke."

Tacoma is shifting toward a more white-collar economy now, aided by the fact that the Seattle suburbs have grown southward right up to the edge of its city limits, and the city has always had its comfortable and high-income neighborhoods. But it retains its blue collar atmosphere, and so does the 6th Congressional District, which includes the city and virtually all of its suburbs. The 6th also crosses the Puget Sound Narrows (where the Tacoma Straits Bridge collapsed in 1940 and the new bridge, the 5th longest suspension bridge in the world, was opened in 1950) to include most of Kitsap County and its major city, Bremerton, which lies across the Sound from Seattle. Kitsap is bristling with several Navy installations and, as the home port of several nuclear submarines, it is one of the major military bases on the West Coast.

The congressman from the 6th is Democrat Norman Dicks. He is a product of the staff of Senator Warren Magnuson, which may have been one of the most competent staffs ever seen on Capitol Hill. He returned back home to Kitsap County to run for Congress in 1976, when the 6th District incumbent finally got the judgeship he had been hankering after for 12 years. Dicks was elected easily that year and reelected easily four times; only in 1980 was the election close, when he was held to 54% of the vote.

In the House, Dicks has shown the aggressiveness and political shrewdness that were the hallmarks of the Magnuson staff in its golden days. He won a seat on the Appropriations Committee and is on both the Defense and Military Construction Subcommittees—vital posts for Kitsap County where most workers depend on Pentagon payrolls. Deaths and defeats have made him second in seniority on Defense, just behind chairman John Murtha. In the early 1980s, Dicks took the lead on restoring Export-Import Bank loan authority—Boeing is America's biggest exporter and biggest user of the loans—when the Reagan Administration wanted to cut it, and led a campaign that switched 80 House votes overnight. With Les Aspin and Albert Gore Jr., he was one of the key House Members that lined up support for the MX missile in return for arms control commitments from the Reagan Administration, and felt vindicated when the United States got to the bargaining table. But he also pressed the Administration in 1986 by sponsoring an amendment requiring compliance with the unratified SALT II treaty—a measure that was put aside before the Reykjavik summit when Reagan complained it tied his hands. He is unblushing about obtaining defense spending for Washington, whether it's getting the military to use Boeing 747s rather than Lockheed C-5s for transport, securing funds for the Puget Sound Naval Shipyard in Brementon, keeping C-130s stationed at McChord Air Force Base near Tacoma, or getting the Navy home port for Everett.

Having passed by the Senate races of 1983, 1986 and 1988, Dicks now seems firmly committed to his career in the House, where he has the potential to be one of the real powers in the chamber.

The People: Est. Pop. 1986: 564,900, up 9.4% 1980–86; Pop. 1980: 516,561, up 13.9% 1970–80. Households (1980): 71% family, 39% with children, 59% married couples; 38.9% housing units rented; median monthly rent: $208; median house value: $53,900. Voting age pop. (1980): 374,063; 6% Black, 3% Asian origin, 2% Spanish origin, 1% American Indian.

1988 Presidential Vote: Dukakis (D)..................... 101,782 (50%)
                            Bush (R) 97,396   (48%)

Rep. Norman D. Dicks (D)

Elected 1976; b. Dec. 16, 1940, Bremerton; home, Bremerton; U. of WA, B.A. 1963, J.D. 1968; Lutheran; married (Suzanne).

Career: Ofc. of U.S. Sen. Warren G. Magnuson, Legis. Asst., 1968–73, A. A., 1973–76.

Offices: 2429 RHOB 20515, 202-225-5916. Also One Pacific Bldg., Ste. 201, Tacoma 98402, 206-593-6536; and Great Northwest Bldg., Ste. 307, Bremerton 98310, 206-479-4011.

Committees: *Appropriations* (15th of 35 D). Subcommittees: Defense; Interior; Military Construction.

Group Ratings

	ADA	ACLU	COPE	CFA	LCV	ACU	NTLC	NSI	COC	CEI
1988	85	73	84	73	69	9	8	40	39	17
1987	76	—	84	79	—	9	—	—	13	9

National Journal Ratings

	1988 LIB — 1988 CONS		1987 LIB — 1987 CONS	
Economic	63%	— 36%	68%	— 27%
Social	68%	— 31%	78%	— 0%
Foreign	59%	— 40%	59%	— 40%

Key Votes

1) Homeless $	AGN	5) Ban Drug Test	AGN	9) SDI Research	FOR
2) Gephardt Amdt	AGN	6) Drug Death Pen	FOR	10) Ban Chem Weaps	AGN
3) Deficit Reduc	FOR	7) Handgun Sales	AGN	11) Aid to Contras	AGN
4) Kill Plnt Clsng Notice	AGN	8) Ban D.C. Abort $	AGN	12) Nuclear Testing	FOR

Election Results

1988 general	Norman D. Dicks (D).................	125,904	(68%)	($288,168)
	Kevin P. Cook (R)....................	60,346	(32%)	($37,620)
1988 primary	Norman D. Dicks (D).................	62,833	(69%)	
	Kevin P. Cook (R)....................	28,640	(31%)	
1986 general	Norman D. Dicks (D).................	90,063	(71%)	($229,634)
	Ken Braaten (R)......................	36,140	(29%)	($57,166)

SEVENTH DISTRICT

Few American cities—maybe none—are more attractive than Seattle. It rises on steep hills, almost as precipitous as San Francisco's, from crescent-shaped Elliott Bay, an inlet on Puget Sound; and behind the city you can see on a clear day, from almost anywhere, the nimbus of Mount Rainier. Right on the waterfront, below the gleaming high-rises, is the Pike Place market, where you can get fresh salmon and Dungenesse crab; nearby is Pioneer Square, where stores and warehouses from the turn of the century have been restored and renovated. Seattle's vistas, the *WPA Guide* reported 50 years ago, "seem constantly shifting, as its streets move swiftly from one plane to another. Here, one sees automobiles parked on the roofs of houses built on the avenue below. Board sidewalks climb the older sections of the town, where the fragile frame dwellings cling to the streets above Lake Union and gaze down upon the towers of tall apartment hotels." Seattle's upper class, like San Francisco's, continues to be anchored downtown and has kept residential quarters not too far away; but people here are less obsessed with their aristocracy, and many may not realize it exists at all. Seattle's working class has maintained many comfortable neighborhoods of frame houses on steep hillsides. The old ethnic groups are not very distinctive to the untrained eye, because so many people are of Scandinavian ancestry; but Seattle is now getting a significant, although not huge, influx of newcomers of Asian and Mexican background.

Like every city, Seattle is divided into neighborhoods. Its topography—with lots of hills, bays and lakes—prevents it from having the huge miles-long expanses of homogeneous neighborhoods you find in such cities as Detroit or Houston; there is plenty of variety in almost every mile of Seattle. Generally blue-collar workers live on the south side of the city and in valleys, or midway between Puget Sound and Lake Washington; the factories, warehouses and railroad yards are concentrated in a flat plain near Puget Sound and south of downtown. The big Boeing factories are located in the plain farther south, and younger blue-collar workers have followed them into the suburban areas directly south of the city: Burien, Tukwila, Kent and Renton, which lie at the southern end of Lake Washington. More affluent, white-collar workers and better-educated people tend to live on hills and near the water, and are more likely to be found on the north than the south side.

The 7th Congressional District of Washington includes most of the city of Seattle and many of its suburbs directly to the south. Its boundaries were drawn artfully, however, to corral most of its Democratic voters into this district, and to keep them out of the Republican 1st and 8th Districts. So the 7th District doesn't include the north Seattle shores of Puget Sound or Lake Washington, nor the high-income suburb of Mercer Island; it does include the city's small black community (the only significant concentration of blacks in the state) and some of its recent communities of Asian immigrants. Overall, this is a solidly Democratic district and has been the most Democratic district in the state in most elections in the 1980s.

The 7th district seat became open in 1988 when Congressman Mike Lowry, the 55%–45% loser in the 1983 special Senate election, ran for the full term in 1988, winning the primary but losing the general 51%–49% to Slade Gorton. It was obvious that the congressional race would be decided in the Democratic primary, and the first two serious contenders were King County Assessor Ruthe Ridder and Seattle Councilman Norm Rice, who is black. But then a third, better-known candidate entered the race—from Zaire. This was Jim McDermott, who had resigned his state senate seat in 1987 after 16 years in the legislature and three unsuccessful gubernatorial bids in order to practice his profession of psychiatry (he is a psychiatrist and one of only two M.D.'s in Congress—Roy Rowland of Georgia is the other) to American diplomats and Peace Corps personnel in central Africa.

This was not entirely uncharacteristic for a man whose whole political career seems to be a combination of visionary liberal projects and political hustling; and if McDermott has not been successful in persuading voters in the whole state to give him the most important state office as their gift, he was successful in passing a mandated health benefits law in Olympia. McDermott's issue in the congressional race was health care, but he has also come to symbolize liberal attitudes on a wide range of issues, and in the primary, despite the odd provenance of his campaign, he won with 39% of all votes cast (a sensible way to compute in Washington, where you can vote for candidates of different parties in primaries) to 29% for Rice, 19% for Ridder, and 12% all together for the two competing Republicans. The general election was anticlimactic:

McDermott won with 76% of the vote. That leaves him with a safe seat and the difficult assignment of getting the House to move in a rather different way than it has been moving on the issues he knows and cares most about.

The People: Est. Pop. 1986: 531,800, up 3.0% 1980–86; Pop. 1980: 516,531, dn. 5.9% 1970–80. Households (1980): 53% family, 24% with children, 41% married couples; 50.0% housing units rented; median monthly rent: $232; median house value: $62,800. Voting age pop. (1980): 414,472; 8% Black, 7% Asian origin, 2% Spanish origin, 1% American Indian.

1988 Presidential Vote:	Dukakis (D)	162,541	(66%)
	Bush (R)	78,238	(32%)

Rep. James A. McDermott (D)

Elected 1988; b. Dec. 28, 1936, Chicago, IL; home, Seattle; Wheaton Col., B.S. 1958; U. of IL, M.D. 1963; Episcopalian; married (Virginia).

Career: WA House of Reps., 1971–72; WA Senate, 1975–87; Asst. Prof., U. of WA, psychiatric practice, 1970–83; Medical Officer, U.S. Foreign Service, Zaire, 1987–88.

Offices: 1107 LHOB 20515, 202-225-3106. Also 1212 Tower Bldg., 1809 7th Ave., Seattle 98101, 206-442-7170.

Committees: *Banking, Finance and Urban Affairs* (29th of 31 D). Subcommittees: Financial Institutions Supervision, Regulation and Insurance; Housing and Community Authority; International Development, Finance, Trade and Monetary Policy. *Interior and Insular Affairs* (25th of 26 D). Subcommittees: National Parks and Public Lands; Water, Power and Offshore Energy Resources.

Group Ratings and Key Votes: Newly Elected

Election Results

1988 general	James A. McDermott (D)	173,809	(76%)	($348,082)
	Robert Edwards (R)	53,902	(24%)	($5,265)
1988 primary	James A. McDermott (D)	47,026	(39%)	
	Norm Rice (D)	35,046	(29%)	
	Ruthe Ridder (D)	23,149	(19%)	
	Robert Edwards (R)	7,815	(6%)	
	Robert Blake (R)	7,675	(6%)	
1986 general	Michael E. (Mike) Lowry (D)	124,317	(73%)	($170,979)
	Don MacDonald (R)	46,831	(27%)	($66,103)

EIGHTH DISTRICT

In the five decades since the outbreak of World War II, Seattle has spilled out across the hills to the north and south, through the valleys lined with railroads and Boeing plants and airstrips, over Puget Sound and across the pontoon bridge over Lake Washington. What was rural territory when the troop ships steamed into Puget Sound after the war is now well-settled suburbia. The 8th Congressional District of Washington, newly created after the 1980 Census, collects some of this suburban territory. It includes essentially two geographically separate suburban sections of Seattle. One, which accounts for more than half the district's population, consists of the suburbs on the ridges and valleys that run up and down the land just east of Puget Sound, south of Seattle from Tacoma. The latter part includes hilly suburbs starting with Burien and Normandy Park in the north, near Sea-Tac Airport, down to the city limits of Tacoma. This is pleasant middle-income territory, on the average. Politically, Republican and Democratic suburbs seem to alternate, leaving a fairly even balance overall.

Connecting the two parts of the district, almost as a land bridge, is the industrial suburb of Auburn. Running north and east from there, up to and along the east side of Lake Washington, is the second part of the district, with about one-third of its population. The other 10% live in mostly agricultural country, which rises up to Mount Rainier National Park. The largest city here is Bellevue, a high-income suburb; the most prominent suburb is Mercer Island, where contemporary homes are set among the woods on hills overlooking Lake Washington, which is connected to Seattle by a once-famous pontoon bridge across the lake. This part of the district is heavily Republican. People here are solidly conservative on economic issues; on cultural matters, particularly environmental issues, they may be more liberal.

The current congressman from this district is Rod Chandler, a former television anchorman and state legislator. He ran in 1982 as a self-described centrist Republican in a multi-candidate primary, and was fortunate enough to have the conservative vote split between two significant opponents; he had little trouble in the general election. In the House, Chandler has proved to be rather conservative on economics and rather liberal on cultural issues; in the climate of the early 1980s, when cultural conservatives really thought they could wipe out abortions, they saw Republicans like Chandler as the enemy. They were angry as well when he voted against aid to the Nicaraguan contras and the MX missile; and perhaps they were not entirely pleased as he supported and obtained a Washington wilderness bill. But as the 1980s have gone on, the conservatives have grown more comfortable with Chandler and he with them. The cultural issues became less important to them; they were settled, one way or the other. Chandler turned out to support conservative positions more often than anticipated, even to the point of switching on contra aid and working out a position he and other moderate Republicans could support.

After the 1986 election, Chandler pulled off a great coup, in the Republican Committee on Committees, when he won a seat on the Ways and Means Committee. He had help from 92 Group moderates, but also from some conservatives; he argued that western Republicans were underrepresented on major committees, and he benefited from a small state alliance on the committee. It helped also that on economic issues he's not so different from the conservatives. For the 101st Congress, he wants to see that American consumers be allowed access to discount foreign products and "gray market" imports, and he seeks postponement of implementation of much of the Medicare Catastrophic Coverage Act approved by Congress in 1988.

Chandler's success in getting on Ways and Means and his reelection by wide margins suggest he has a long House career ahead of him—unless he should get into his head the not totally implausible idea of running for Brock Adams's Senate seat in 1992.

The People: Est. Pop. 1986: 584,700, up 13.2% 1980–86; Pop. 1980: 516,500, up 40.5% 1970–80. Households (1980): 77% family, 45% with children, 67% married couples; 26.5% housing units rented; median monthly rent: $288; median house value: $75,900. Voting age pop. (1980): 358,801; 2% Asian origin, 1% Spanish origin, 1% Black, 1% American Indian.

1988 Presidential Vote: Bush (R) 150,782   (56%)
Dukakis (D). 115,343   (43%)

Rep. Rod Chandler (R)

Elected 1982; b. July 13, 1942, La Grande, OR; home, Bellevue; OR St. U., B.S. 1968; Protestant; married (Joyce).

Career: Correspondent and anchorman, KOMO-TV, 1968–73; Asst. Vice Pres. for Mktg., WA Mutual Savings Bank, 1973–77; WA House of Reps., 1975–82; Partner, pub. rel. firm, 1977–83.

Offices: 223 CHOB 20515, 202-225-7761. Also 3326 160st Ave. S.E., Bellevue 98006, 206-442-0116; and 1025 S. 320th, Federal Way 98003, 206-593-6371.

Committees: *Ways and Means* (10th of 13 R). Subcommittees: Health; Oversight.

Group Ratings

	ADA	ACLU	COPE	CFA	LCV	ACU	NTLC	NSI	COC	CEI
1988	45	43	19	45	50	56	77	80	93	54
1987	32	—	17	29	—	61	—	—	93	70

National Journal Ratings

	1988 LIB — 1988 CONS		1987 LIB — 1987 CONS	
Economic	10%	— 88%	23%	— 76%
Social	46%	— 53%	34%	— 65%
Foreign	41%	— 58%	45%	— 55%

Key Votes

1) Homeless $	FOR	5) Ban Drug Test	FOR	9) SDI Research	AGN
2) Gephardt Amdt	AGN	6) Drug Death Pen	FOR	10) Ban Chem Weaps	AGN
3) Deficit Reduc	AGN	7) Handgun Sales	AGN	11) Aid to Contras	FOR
4) Kill Plnt Clsng Notice	FOR	8) Ban D.C. Abort $	AGN	12) Nuclear Testing	AGN

Election Results

1988 general	Rod Chandler (R)	174,942	(71%)	($300,048)
	Jim Kean (D)	71,920	(29%)	($12,601)
1988 primary	Rod Chandler (R)	76,861	(70%)	
	Jim Kean (D)	16,418	(15%)	
	Ray Kennedy (D)	12,625	(11%)	
	DeMilt Morse (D)	3,972	(4%)	
1986 general	Rod Chandler (R)	107,824	(65%)	($210,373)
	David Giles (D)	57,545	(35%)	($109,411)

WEST VIRGINIA

Half a century ago, coal was king in West Virginia, as it had been half a century before that, and as it is still to an uncomfortably large extent today. This state owes its separate existence to politics—it was created during the Civil War from 55 counties that never had many slaves and always had very little to do with lowland Virginia—but its economy, almost since that time, has been based on the fuel and energy source of which it has arguably the world's most plentiful supply: coal. Coal is what kept the sons of large mountaineer families here for much of the 20th century, men who would otherwise have left for big cities; coal is what brought immigrants in, a few from odd corners of Europe, but more from adjacent areas of the South where the local farming economies were stagnant when West Virginia's coal economy was booming. Coal helped to bring in the chemical plants of the Kanawha Valley around Charleston, one of the biggest chemical concentrations in the United States 50 years ago and today as well, and to build the steel mills in the panhandle and the Monongahela River valley, which are within the orbit of Pittsburgh.

The years around World War II were a turning point for West Virginia. The state's population was 1.9 million in 1940, just below its 2.0 million peak of 1950—and the same as the figure for the late 1980s. Coal was still the nation's premier industrial fuel at the time of Pearl Harbor, coal mining employment was at or near its peak and John L. Lewis's United Mine Workers, strong even before the labor laws were changed in the 1930s, had organized most of the mines in the state. Politically, West Virginia's heritage from the Civil War days was Republican, though some counties tilted toward the Confederacy and the Democrats; John L. Lewis helped to lead the coal miners and the state toward the Democrats in the 1930s. In 1940 Lewis, an isolationist, deserted Roosevelt on foreign policy, but West Virginia stuck with the Democrats and it has remained one of the most Democratic states ever since. It has gone Republican only in landslide years (1956, 1972, 1984) and was a Dukakis state in 1988 by a 52%–48% margin.

During those years, the coal-steel-petrochemicals economy of the state has gone boom and bust several times. In the 1940s, Lewis staged titanic miners' strikes during the war and just after, but his postwar goal was not more jobs but medical benefits and pensions for existing miners and cuts in jobs to adjust for increasing mechanization and strip mining. He was criticized for selling out his members, but the old days in mining were dangerous and often deadly, a past to which no one who knew it would want to return. Nor were conditions pleasant in old coal mining communities, often literally up a creek or a hollow, connected to the rest of the world by a rail line that carried only coal cars, with no local business but the company store. West Virginia's population bottomed out at 1.7 million in 1970, then started back up when higher energy prices revived the coal industry in the 1970s. But by the middle 1980s, after energy prices collapsed, population was declining again, at the fastest rate in the nation. Coal mines, which in 1950 employed 22% of West Virginia's work force, employed 5% in 1988. For at least two generations, West Virginia has had an aging population, wary of the future and bitter about the past.

In the process, old West Virginia institutions and customs have been dying out. The big coal companies have been replaced in importance by small operators; the United Mine Workers, rent by violent faction in the 1970s, represents far fewer workers far less aggressively; the old Democratic machine politicians that produced most of the state's leaders since the days of Franklin D. Roosevelt have not elected a governor in more than 20 years. Men it did not control—Republican Arch Moore, Democrats Jay Rockefeller and Gaston Caperton—have

WEST VIRGINIA — Congressional Districts, Counties, and Selected Places — *(4 Districts)*

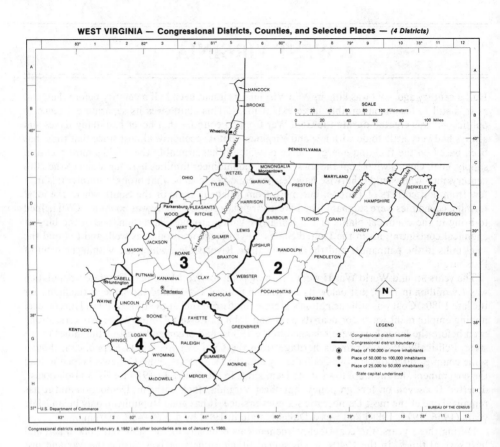

Congressional districts established February 8, 1982 ; all other boundaries are as of January 1, 1980.

been elected governor now for terms totalling 24 years, and insurgents won a variety of other elections. Faraway liberals like to imagine that leaders springing from poor people will represent poor people's interests altruistically, but the reality is there is often corruption: in the late 1980s 62 local officials were convicted of crimes in Mingo County, where the local school board president and poverty program head controlled 2,400 jobs personally in a county with only 8,700 total jobs.

Will West Virginia rebound as it has before? Its exports were at record high levels in 1988, it had attracted some $1 billion in investment after a 1986 tax change, it was using its resources of natural beauty and a location near huge population centers to attract tourism. But the number of jobs stubbornly refused to rise much, and none of West Virginia's small cities became the kind of thriving urban center that has kept many states growing. West Virginia remains vulnerable: its high-sulfur, remote coal can be hurt by acid rain legislation or by a coal slurry pipeline or by another sustained period of low energy prices. West Virginians have a strong attachment to their unique state, where the accent sounds southern and the early 20th century factories and houses look northern, where the landscape is rural and the economy industrial. But they are not always able to make their livings there.

Governor. The governorship, held for 20 years by bitter rivals Arch Moore and Jay Rockefeller, is in different hands now: Democrat Gaston Caperton, an insurance brokerage millionaire without previous elective experience, beat Moore by a convincing 59%–41% margin in 1988. The 1980s have not been good to West Virginia's governors. Jay Rockefeller, who left the office in 1984, only barely beat Republican John Raese for the Senate that year, and saw the governorship turned over to Republican Moore. Then Moore, an instinctive politician who has thrived in this Democratic state since he was first elected to Congress in 1956, who came back from scandal (he was indicted in 1975, but acquitted) and defeat (he lost to Senator Jennings Randolph in 1978 and to Jay Rockefeller, whom he beat in 1972, in 1980), ran into trouble in several significant areas. The 1985 tax reform turned out to be a mess, his 1986 year of education programs had to be slashed and he had a bruising session with the legislature in December 1987. Raese, a steel and limestone millionaire given to a playboy lifestyle, ran against him in the primary and in April was 24% ahead in one poll; Moore rallied with an old-fashioned display of personal campaigning and new job announcements and won—but by only 53%–47%, a disastrous result for an incumbent.

Gaston Caperton meanwhile was putting together a winning combination of a $2 million media campaign plus support from the United Mine Workers and other unions that enabled him to win 38% in a seven-candidate field. Moore's air of omniscience and unapproachability was working against him, while Caperton was insisting he would bring businesslike methods, not politics, to the office. He won 59%–41%, and went on to show considerable political skill. He steered a big program through the legislature, including a $392 million tax hike (restoring the sales tax on food Rockefeller had repealed), a reorganization bill, an ethics bill in often unethical West Virginia and a constitutional amendment making appointive rather than elective the treasurer (the incumbent lost $279 million in bad state investments), the secretary of state (a brilliant but impolitic 75-year-old former congressman), and the agricultural commissioner (a Republican former congressman who once ran against Senator Robert Byrd). The question is whether Caperton's program will provide needed infrastructure or drive business from the state.

Senators. When the large Democratic class of 1958 assembled in the Senate, it's possible that Robert Byrd was the least noticed by the press and even Senate insiders. Today he is the last surviving member of that class, the President Pro Tempore of the Senate. He was Senate Majority Leader for six years and Minority Leader for six years, and now he has taken the post he hoped for originally, the chair of the powerful and sought after Senate Appropriations Committee. Byrd comes from a background as grindingly and bitterly poor as any American politician, and the persistence he has shown in the Senate is evidence of his determination, the combination of hard work and ambition which have propelled this coal miner's son to the top ranks of the American Congress.

If you go back to the beginning of his career, his rise seems most improbable. He was a meatcutter in a coal town and a former welder in wartime shipyards, when he won his seat in the state House of Delegates in 1946; he campaigned in every hollow in the county, playing his fiddle and even going to the length of joining the Ku Klux Klan (which he quickly quit and has ever since regretted joining) to win votes. He worked hard in the legislature, and won a House seat when the incumbent retired in 1952; he made such a name for himself in West Virginia that by 1958, when he was 40, he was elected to the Senate even though the United Mine Workers had been against him and the coal companies were never for him.

The secrets behind his success are hard work and mastery of detail. He has cultivated constituents in West Virginia assiduously, keeping card files with thousands of names and telephone numbers, and calls constituents every night to ask their opinions on issues and to find out what is happening back home. He cultivated Senators just as assiduously, and when Edward Kennedy was neglecting his duties as majority whip in 1969 and 1970, after Chappaquiddick, Byrd quietly lined up support and, with Richard Russell's deathbed proxy, won the job himself in 1971. By 1976, when Majority Leader Mike Mansfield was retiring, Byrd was the natural choice for majority leader; Hubert Humphrey ran a quixotic campaign against him, but Byrd had the votes. He was never too busy to attend to the petty details that can make the lives of Senators easier: keeping them informed of the pace of floor debate and the scheduling of upcoming votes, helping them to get amendments before the Senate, arranging paired votes, and even getting taxis. This is not mindless work: it means understanding the political situations of each Senator, their strengths and weaknesses, and it means mastering the details of substantive legislation and parliamentary procedure.

By the middle 1980s, however, after the Democrats were in the minority, Byrd was the subject of grumbling and open rebellion. He was too much the technician, it was said; he did not project an attractive image on television; he did not lead the party on issues. After the 1984 election, Byrd was challenged by Lawton Chiles of Florida, who was soundly beaten. Before the 1986 election, Bennett Johnston of Louisiana announced he would challenge Byrd; but well before the election his nose-counting persuaded him to withdraw. In fact, as Minority Leader, Byrd was in an impossible position—the leader of a minority temperamentally disinclined to unite, with each member eager to demonstrate his independence and uniqueness. What was striking was that Byrd, back as Majority Leader in 1987 and 1988—the first man in history to return to that job— came back with an agenda and a schedule for united Democratic action. He helped make the way for the 1988 trade bill, including its plant closing notice provision; he worked with Sam Nunn and others on amending the War Powers Act; he pushed hard for his campaign finance reform bill. None of these was a risk-free position, and all required the mastery of detail he showed, for example, in unraveling the Watergate scandal: it was Byrd who got L. Patrick Gray to admit that John Dean "probably lied" about the affair, an admission that sparked Dean's determination to tell the truth.

Byrd's voting record has changed over the years; his popularity with West Virginia voters has not. In his early years in the Senate, dominated by Lyndon Johnson and Richard Russell, he was almost a Dixiecrat, opposing civil rights laws and conducting vitriolic investigations of D.C. welfare cheaters. He concentrated on bringing government spending to West Virginia, and succeeded. Later, as an elected leader serving younger and more liberal Democratic Senates, he had by the early 1980s one of the Senate's most liberal records, especially on economic issues. In the late 1980s, his voting record was somewhat more conservative. Byrd's popularity was tested in 1982, after NCPAC ran TV ads against him and Republican Representative Cleveland Benedict spent $1 million on a harshly negative campaign. Byrd raised and spent plenty himself but, more importantly, carried 54 of 55 counties and 69% of the vote. In 1988, he carried 53 counties and 65% against a weak candidate—minor slippage, but the fifth time that Byrd has been reelected with a higher percentage than any other West Virginia Senator in history. As Appropriations Chairman, he will certainly spend much time and effort on West Virginia projects, but he can also be expected to be punctilious about meeting budget deadlines and assertive about the committee's powers; and he is likely to take the initiative on other issues, and quite possibly to prevail.

The junior colleague of this coal miner's son is the scion of one of the richest families in the United States, John D. Rockefeller IV. The fourth in the direct line of eldest sons from the original John D. Rockefeller, Jay Rockefeller was an expert in Asian affairs when he moved to West Virginia in 1964 to work in an antipoverty program. He decided to stay and to enter politics but—unlike his uncles, the governors of New York and Arkansas—as a Democrat rather than as a Republican. He was elected to the legislature in 1966 and to statewide office in 1968. Moore beat him for the governorship in 1972, when the state was prosperous and his roadbuilding program was humming, and Rockefeller became president of West Virginia Wesleyan College for two years. He was elected governor easily in 1976, calling for economic development and—inevitably in this mountainous state—better roads; he promoted coal and removed the sales tax on food. In 1980, he faced Moore again, ran on his record and spent $9 million, and won. His second term was more difficult, as the state's economy plunged into recession and West Virginia had the nation's highest unemployment rate.

In 1984, barred from a third consecutive term, he ran for the Senate seat Jennings Randolph was vacating. The state's ailing economy made him vulnerable to Republican John Raese, who was originally spurred into the race by what he said was government harassment of his small business and who thought he could match Rockefeller's campaign spending. He couldn't: Rockefeller spent $12 million, and won a close race while Walter Mondale was losing the state. Rockefeller was snickered at in some quarters for spending hundreds of thousands on Pittsburgh and Washington media to reach a few counties in West Virginia's panhandles. But that may have made the difference. In most counties in the state, Rockefeller ran between 1% and 7% ahead of Mondale's 45% showing—not enough on balance to win. But in the northern panhandle and in the eastern counties between Maryland and Virginia, in the Pittsburgh and Washington media markets, he ran (with one exception) between 12% and 18% ahead of Mondale—votes vital to his 52%–48% victory over Raese.

In the Senate, Rockefeller has tried hard to avoid the national media limelight and to work on becoming an influential Senator. After the 1986 election, he got a seat on the Finance Committee, which will help him make his mark on trade laws. With his experience in Japan, he is less automatically interested in barring foreign imports and more interested in spurring American exports than most politicians from the coal-and-steel region; he was in early 1989, however, sponsoring a five-year extension of the voluntary restraint agreements on steel on the grounds that other countries subsidize their steel industries. He also worked on the alternative fuels legislation which passed and has struggled to fund Appalachian regional programs. He chairs the Subcommittee on Medicare and Long-Term Care—two hot potatoes in early 1989— and is a co-sponsor of a measure to allow payments for home care, as well as hospital care, in long-term illnesses. He has spent much time trying to get lower railroad freight rates for West Virginia coal. He has been careful not to thrust himself forward as a presidential candidate (though he did address the annual New Hampshire Democratic Party dinner in April 1989) and seems, as he passes age 50, to be settling in for what could be a long and productive career in the Senate, focused heavily on West Virginia issues.

Rockefeller's seat comes up in 1990, and on the basis of previous performances, it could be argued that he is not unbeatable. But his West Virginia orientation is a clear advantage, and an even greater one is his ability and willingness to spend whatever it takes to win. That tends to deter competition, except from venturesome types like Raese, and with the apparent political demise of Arch Moore, the best-known possible opponent might be Agriculture Commissioner Cleveland Benedict, who already lost lopsidedly to Byrd in 1982.

Presidential politics. For 50 years, West Virginia's partisan preferences have been the legacy of two searing decades, the 1860s and 1930s; the question now is whether those preferences still prevail. Although West Virginia stayed with the Union, parts of the state were more sympathetic to it than others, and there are Republican strongholds today—sparsely populated counties in the mountains, cities and towns along the Ohio River—dating from that period. There are rural Democratic counties as well, like the one around Harpers Ferry, where John Brown was convicted and hanged for storming the arsenal and trying to incite a local slave rebellion in what was then of course still part of Virginia. The 1930s saw the coal-mining counties not only unionized, but become heavily Democratic, to the point that the coal counties south of Charleston make up one of the most Democratic parts of the nation. But Charleston and Kanawha County, a heavily industrialized area and the most populous part of the state, still go Republican as often as they do Democratic—the Civil War legacy lives on.

On balance, that leaves West Virginia as one of the most Democratic of states. In 1980, it was Jimmy Carter's best state after Georgia; it was solidly Democratic in the close elections of 1948, 1960, 1968 and 1976; it was 6% more Democratic than the nation in 1988.

West Virginia's presidential primary was important here only once, in 1960, when John

Kennedy seized it as an opportunity to prove he could beat Hubert Humphrey in a virtually all-Protestant state, spending money freely and in ways that would not be legal today. The 1988 primary was notable only because Dukakis got his best percentage of any state here: 75%–13% over Jesse Jackson.

Congressional districting. The 1990 Census is going to make West Virginia's four-man Democratic House delegation play musical chairs. The state seems bound to lose a seat for 1992, and so one of these four scions—two are sons of congressmen, one the son of a successful broadcasting entrepreneur, one the son of a successful lawyer—must go.

The People: Est. Pop. 1988: 1,884,000; Pop. 1980: 1,949,644, down 3.4% 1980–88 and up 11.8% 1970–80; 0.80% of U.S. total, 34th largest. 10% with 1–3 yrs. col., 10% with 4+ yrs. col.; 15% below poverty level. Single ancestry: 20% English, 7% German, 5% Irish, 2% Italian, 1% Dutch, Polish, French. Households (1980): 77% family, 42% with children, 65% married couples; 26.4% housing units rented; median monthly rent: $137; median house value: $38,500. Voting age pop. (1980): 1,390,008; 3% Black, 1% Spanish origin. Registered voters (1988): 968,619; 640,255 D (66%); 303,061 R (31%); 25,303 unaffiliated and minor parties (3%).

1988 Share of Federal Tax Burden $4,524,000,000; 0.51% of U.S. total, 36th largest.

1988 Share of Federal Expenditures

	Total		Non-Defense		Defense	
Total Expend	$5,861m	(0.66%)	$5,473m	(0.83%)	$541m	(0.24%)
St/Lcl Grants	1,056m	(0.92%)	1,056m	(0.92%)	0m	(0.33%)
Salary/Wages	530m	(0.39%)	442m	(0.66%)	88m	(0.66%)
Pymnts to Indiv	3,838m	(0.94%)	3,757m	(0.96%)	81m	(0.43%)
Procurement	372m	(0.20%)	154m	(0.33%)	372m	(0.20%)
Research/Other	65m	(0.17%)	65m	(0.17%)	0m	(0.17%)

Political Lineup: Governor, Gaston Caperton (D); Secy. of State, Ken Hechler (D); Atty. Gen., Charlie Brown (D); Treasurer, A. James Manchin (D); Auditor, Glen B. Gainer (D). State Senate, 34 (30 D and 4 R); State House of Delegates, 100 (80 D and 20 R). Senators, Robert C. Byrd (D) and John D. (Jay) Rockefeller, IV (D). Representatives, 4 D.

1988 Presidential Vote

Dukakis (D)	341,016	(52%)
Bush (R)	310,065	(48%)

1984 Presidential Vote

Reagan (R)	405,483	(55%)
Mondale (D)	328,125	(45%)

1988 Democratic Presidential Primary

Dukakis	254,289	(75%)
Jackson	45,788	(13%)
Gore	11,573	(3%)
Hart	9,284	(3%)
Gephardt	6,130	(2%)
Simon	2,280	(1%)
Babbitt	1,978	(1%)

1988 Republican Presidential Primary

Bush	110,705	(77%)
Dole	15,600	(11%)
Robertson	10,417	(7%)
Kemp	3,820	(3%)

GOVERNOR

Gov. Gaston Caperton (D)

Elected 1988, term expires Jan. 1993; b. Feb. 21, 1940, Charleston; home, Charleston; U. of NC, B.A. 1963; Episcopalian; separated.

Career: Pres., McDonough Caperton Ins. Group, 1963-88.

Office: State Capitol, Charleston 25305, 304-340-1600.

Election Results:

1988 gen.	Gaston Caperton (D)	382,421	(59%)
	Arch A. Moore, Jr. (R)	267,172	(41%)
1988 prim.	Gaston Caperton (D)	132,435	(38%)
	Clyde See (D)	94,364	(27%)
	Mario J. Palumbo (D)	51,722	(15%)
	Gus R. Douglass (D)	48,748	(14%)
	Others	21,617	(6%)
1984 gen.	Arch A. Moore, Jr. (R)	394,937	(53%)
	Clyde See (D)	346,565	(47%)

SENATORS

Sen. Robert C. Byrd (D)

Elected 1958, seat up 1994; b. Nov. 20, 1917, North Wilkesboro, NC; home, Sophia; American U., J.D. 1963; Baptist; married (Erma).

Career: WV House of Del., 1946–50; WV Senate, 1950–52; U.S. House of Reps., 1953–58; U.S. Sen. Major. Whip, 1971–76, Minor. Ldr., 1981–86; Major. Ldr. 1977–80, 1987–88.

Offices: 311 HSOB 20510, 202-224-3954. Also Fed. Bldg., 500 Quarrier St., Rm. 1006, Charleston 25305, 304-342-5855.

Committees: *Appropriations* (Chairman of 16 D). Subcommittees: Defense; Energy and Water Development; Interior (Chairman); Labor, Health and Human Services, Education; Transportation. *Armed Services* (11th of 11 D). Subcommittees: Conventional Forces and Alliance Defense; Defense Industry and Technology; Manpower and Personnel. *Rules and Administration* (3d of 9 D).

Group Ratings

	ADA	ACLU	COPE	CFA	LCV	ACU	NTLC	NSI	COC	CEI
1988	55	48	73	100	60	36	22	60	29	16
1987	70	—	73	92	—	23	—	—	28	24

National Journal Ratings

	1988 LIB — 1988 CONS		1987 LIB — 1987 CONS	
Economic	57% —	40%	74% —	0%
Social	41% —	57%	53% —	42%
Foreign	57% —	42%	56% —	43%

1302   WEST VIRGINIA

Key Votes

1) Cut Aged Housing $	FOR	5) Bork Nomination	AGN	9) SDI Funding	FOR
2) Override Hwy Veto	FOR	6) Ban Plastic Guns	AGN	10) Ban Chem Weaps	AGN
3) Kill Plnt Clsng Notice	AGN	7) Deny Abortions	AGN	11) Aid To Contras	AGN
4) Min Wage Increase	FOR	8) Japanese Reparations	FOR	12) Reagan Defense $	AGN

Election Results

1988 general	Robert C. Byrd (D)...................	410,983	(65%)	($1,282,746)
	M. Jay Wolfe (R)	223,564	(35%)	($115,284)
1988 primary	Robert D. Byrd (D)..................	252,767	(81%)	
	Bobby Myers (D)	60,186	(19%)	
1982 general	Robert C. Byrd (D)..................	387,170	(69%)	($1,792,573)
	Cleveland K. (Cleve) Benedict (R).......	173,910	(31%)	($1,098,218)

Sen. John D. (Jay) Rockefeller IV (D)

Elected 1984, seat up 1990; b. June 18, 1937, New York, NY; home, Charleston; Harvard U., B.A. 1961, Intl. Christian U., Tokyo, 1957–60; Presbyterian; married (Sharon).

Career: Natl. Advisory Cncl. of Peace Corps, 1961; Asst. to Peace Corps Dir. Sargent Shriver, 1962–63; VISTA worker, 1964–66; WV House of Del., 1966–68; WV Secy. of State, 1968–72; Pres., WV Wesleyan Col., 1973–75; Gov. of WV, 1977–84.

Offices: 724 HSOB 20510, 202-224-6472. Also L&S Bldg., Ste. 200, 812 Quarrier St., Charleston 25301, 304-347-5372; 115 S. Kanawha St., Ste. 1, Beckley 25801, 304-253-9704; and 200 Adams St., Ste. A, Fairmont 26554, 304-367-0122.

Committees: *Commerce, Science, and Transportation* (6th of 11 D). Subcommittees: Foreign Commerce and Tourism (Chairman); Science, Technology, and Space; Surface Transportation. *Energy and Natural Resources* (10th of 10 D). Subcommittees: Energy Research and Development (Vice Chairman); Public Lands, National Parks and Forests. *Finance* (10th of 11 D). Subcommittees: Health for Families and the Uninsured; International Trade; Medicare and Long-Term Care (Chairman). *Veterans Affairs* (5th of 6 D).

Group Ratings

	ADA	ACLU	COPE	CFA	LCV	ACU	NTLC	NSI	COC	CEI
1988	70	59	92	91	70	16	9	10	36	11
1987	90	—	93	92	—	8	—	—	24	14

National Journal Ratings

	1988 LIB — 1988 CONS			1987 LIB — 1987 CONS		
Economic	74%	—	19%	74%	—	0%
Social	56%	—	41%	78%	—	17%
Foreign	86%	—	0%	58%	—	41%

Key Votes

1) Cut Aged Housing $	FOR	5) Bork Nomination	AGN	9) SDI Funding	AGN
2) Override Hwy Veto	FOR	6) Ban Plastic Guns	AGN	10) Ban Chem Weaps	FOR
3) Kill Plnt Clsng Notice	AGN	7) Deny Abortions	AGN	11) Aid To Contras	AGN
4) Min Wage Increase	FOR	8) Japanese Reparations	FOR	12) Reagan Defense $	AGN

Election Results

1984 general	John D. (Jay) Rockefeller, IV (D)	374,233	(52%)	($12,055,043)
	John R. Raese (R)....................	344,680	(48%)	($1,147,123)
1984 primary	John D. (Jay) Rockefeller, IV (D)	240,559	(66%)	
	Lacy Wright (D).....................	51,591	(14%)	
	Ken Auvil (D).......................	41,408	(11%)	
	Homer L. Harris (D)	29,138	(8%)	
1978 general	Jennings Randolph (D)................	249,034	(50%)	($684,605)
	Arch A. Moore, Jr. (R)...............	244,317	(50%)	($458,823)

FIRST DISTRICT

In the heart of America's steel country is West Virginia's northern panhandle, sticking up between western Pennsylvania and the Ohio River: a geographic anomaly created by boundary-drawers who never ventured west of the Appalachians. Geographically, this is the least isolated part of West Virginia. It is part of the Pittsburgh media market, and the terrain is comparatively gentle, enough for main line railroads and interstate highways. Along the Ohio River is Wheeling, once one of the richest cities in the country with its steel company investors and executives, and Weirton, a company town that literally spans the state run 50 years ago by Weirton Steel's E. T. Weir. Weirton is now the site of one of the most successful experiments with employee ownership, and in Weir's place are committees of steelworkers who have decided to cut their own pay in order to produce profits. In the early 1970s, people here worried about pollution; the air by some measures was the dirtiest in the country. In the early 1980s, they worried about the economy, and what they were going to do for a living; many factories were quiet, and it began to appear to people that the props under their communities and their personal lives had been kicked out.

The panhandle forms about one-third of West Virginia's 1st Congressional District. Another third is in the industrialized Monongahela valley, directly south of Pittsburgh, around Clarksburg and Fairmont. For years this was also coal, steel and glassmaking country. Finally, about one-third live in the more rural and less industrial hills along the Ohio River, or in the city of Parkersburg. The Panhandle and the Monongahela valley are ordinarily Democratic, though vestiges of Civil War Republicanism remain; the area along the Ohio tends to be Republican.

The incumbent congressman here, Alan Mollohan, is one of two sons of West Virginia congressmen who won seats themselves in 1982. His father, Robert Mollohan, was elected in 1952 and 1954, defeated by Arch Moore in 1956, then won the seat again when Moore was elected governor in 1968, and kept it until his retirement at age 73 in 1982. He was an old-time Democrat with a liberal record on economic issues and as a supporter of military spending increases on the House Armed Services Committee. Alan Mollohan did not win the seat automatically. His main problem was that from 1973 to 1982 he was a Washington, D.C. lawyer working for, among others, Consolidation Coal. He returned to Fairmont and established a base in the Monongahela valley, but his connection with the district was little closer than that of a British M.P. to a seat to which his party had assigned him.

The son of a rough-hewn old politico, Alan Mollohan looks something like Clark Kent, but has proved to be, if not Superman, then at least a pretty tough politician. In the 1st District, he won two races against serious Republican opponents, beating a former Republican state chairman who had some support from the United Mine Workers in 1982 and a former legislator and decorated Vietnam war veteran in 1984. In Washington, he worked to protect Weirton Steel from changes in ESOP taxation, debated Ralph Nader on the Clean Air Act, won a seat on the Appropriations Committee where he can work on local issues, and bucked his fellow Democrats to support contra aid and Persian Gulf reflagging. On the House Ethics Committee, he did not initially vote to find reasonable cause that Jim Wright broke House rules.

Mollohan may have another tough fight ahead, when West Virginia redistricts after the 1990 Census. One Democratic congressman will lose his seat, and while this panhandle-based district is a little hard to combine with others, he could still find himself in a primary fight with a colleague.

The People: Est. Pop. 1986: 473,700, dn. 3.1% 1980–86; Pop. 1980: 488,568, up 6.1% 1970–80. Households (1980): 76% family, 40% with children, 65% married couples; 26.3% housing units rented; median monthly rent: $137; median house value: $38,200. Voting age pop. (1980): 353,283; 2% Black, 1% Spanish origin.

1988 Presidential Vote:

Dukakis (D)	89,128	(51%)
Bush (R)	84,142	(48%)

Rep. Alan B. Mollohan (D)

Elected 1982; b. May 14, 1943, Fairmont; home, Fairmont; Col. of William and Mary, A.B. 1966, WV U., J.D. 1970; Baptist; married (Barbara).

Career: Practicing atty., 1970–82.

Offices: 229 CHOB 20515, 202-225-4172. Also 102 City-Cnty. Complex, Fairmont 26554, 304-363-3356; 1117 Fed. Bldg., Parkersburg 26101, 304-428-0493; 316 Fed. Bldg., Wheeling 26003, 304-232-5390; and 209 P.O. Bldg., Clarksburg 26301, 304-623-4422.

Committees: *Appropriations* (32d of 35 D). Subcommittees: Commerce, Justice, State, and Judiciary; VA, HUD and Independent Agencies. *Standards of Official Conduct* (4th of 6 D).

Group Ratings

	ADA	ACLU	COPE	CFA	LCV	ACU	NTLC	NSI	COC	CEI
1988	50	61	93	73	31	48	9	90	23	14
1987	68	—	92	64	—	17	—	—	13	7

National Journal Ratings

	1988 LIB — 1988 CONS		1987 LIB — 1987 CONS	
Economic	67% —	30%	73% —	0%
Social	48% —	51%	54% —	45%
Foreign	34% —	66%	46% —	53%

Key Votes

1) Homeless $	AGN	5) Ban Drug Test	AGN	9) SDI Research	AGN
2) Gephardt Amdt	FOR	6) Drug Death Pen	AGN	10) Ban Chem Weaps	AGN
3) Deficit Reduc	FOR	7) Handgun Sales	FOR	11) Aid to Contras	FOR
4) Kill Plnt Clsng Notice	AGN	8) Ban D.C. Abort $	FOR	12) Nuclear Testing	AGN

Election Results

1988 general	Alan B. Mollohan (D)	119,256	(75%)	($103,154)
	Howard K. Tuck (R)	40,732	(25%)	($15,220)
1988 primary	Alan B. Mollohan (D), unopposed			
1986 general	Alan B. Mollohan (D)	90,715	(100%)	($216,378)

SECOND DISTRICT

Fifty years ago, eastern West Virginia combined industrial landscape with some of the loveliest scenery in the country. For miles you could see gentle hills and rugged mountains, stands of green trees and vistas that stretched to far horizons—"almost heaven," in the words of the song. Yet over another hill you would find, amid scenery primeval and rural, sudden evidence of industrialization: a pulp mill or charcoal factory in a clearing scraped out of the forest; a small factory town, built close to a river in a cleft bordered with hills, its houses built in the same 1910s style as in the factory towns of Pittsburgh; the entrance to an underground coal mine or the exposed brown earth of a strip mine scar. This scenery is, if anything, better today, as forests are reseeded and grow, but the combination of industry and hills is old, going back to Harper's Ferry, where the government had one of its arsenals which before the Civil War produced most of America's weapons. This concentration of guns was the reason John Brown chose Harper's Ferry for what he hoped would be the center of a slave rebellion, and it was for military reasons that West Virginia's boundaries were extended so far eastward. But this is not the only part of eastern West Virginia that is remote from the state's major population centers. Practically all of it is, because of the continuous chains of mountains and the steep valleys sometimes swept by raging floodwaters.

The 2d Congressional District of West Virginia includes most of the mountainous and sparsely populated eastern part of the state. The district extends from Harper's Ferry south and west to Fayette County, near the state capital of Charleston, and not all that far from the Kentucky line. In the northwestern part of the district, not far from Pittsburgh, is the 2d's largest city, Morgantown, with a population of just 27,000—part of the industrial Monongahela valley and home of West Virginia University. Politically, the 2d Congressional District is a patchwork quilt of partisan preferences. Coal counties have generally been Democratic since the 1930s; counties with relatively few miners trace their partisan ancestry back to the Civil War. The balance generally favors the Democrats, but not overwhelmingly; this is typically the least Democratic of West Virginia's four districts, and the only one to go for George Bush in 1988.

The current congressman, Harley Staggers Jr., is the son of the man who represented this district from 1948 to 1980, and who, for more than a decade, chaired what now is the House Energy and Commerce Committee. Staggers lost the primary to succeed his father and was later appointed to a state Senate seat. The victor of the 1980 primary, in turn, lost to Republican Cleveland Benedict, who ran for the Senate in 1982, opening up the way for young Staggers. He had no primary opponent and won the general in that recession year handily. Benedict himself came back and tried to win the House seat again in 1984. But the response to his negative campaign against Robert Byrd has been a personal repudiation of such proportions that Staggers won with 56%.

Staggers has not gotten on his father's old committee, which has become the most sought after committee assignment in the House; he serves on Agriculture and Judiciary. He is a pleasant man, who keeps in close touch with his constituency, and seems earnest and determined to do what he thinks is right; he pushed an amendment to let the Forest Service enforce drug laws on National Forest land and led Select Committee on Hunger members to see hunger in a West Virginia hollow. After his first two tough races, he was reelected by an impressive margin in 1986 and without opposition in 1988. But he faces a formidable hurdle in 1992, when redistricting will cost one of West Virginia's four Democratic congressmen his seat.

The People: Est. Pop. 1986: 495,000, up 1.5% 1980–86; Pop. 1980: 487,438, up 20.5% 1970–80. Households (1980): 76% family, 41% with children, 64% married couples; 25.8% housing units rented; median monthly rent: $134; median house value: $36,600. Voting age pop. (1980): 350,168; 3% Black, 1% Spanish origin.

1988 Presidential Vote:
Bush (R)	86,633	(51%)
Dukakis (D)	81,178	(48%)

Rep. Harley O. Staggers, Jr. (D)

Elected 1982; b. Feb. 22, 1951, Washington, D.C.; home, Keyser; Harvard U., B.A. 1974, WV U., J.D. 1977; Roman Catholic; married (Leslie).

Career: Asst. Atty. Gen., Charleston, 1977–80; WV Senate, 1980–82.

Offices: 1504 LHOB 20515, 202-225-4331. Also 370 S. Main St., Keyser 26726, 304-788-6311; Harley O. Staggers Fed. Bldg., Morgantown 26507, 304-291-6001; 101 N. Court St., Lewisburg 24901, 304-645-3188; and 102 E. Martin St., Martinsburg 25401, 304-267-2144.

Committees: *Agriculture* (13th of 27 D). Subcommittees: Conservation, Credit, and Rural Development; Domestic Marketing, Consumer Relations, and Nutrition. *Judiciary* (18th of 21 D). Subcommittees: Administrative Law and Government Relations; Economic and Commercial Law. *Veterans' Affairs* (6th of 21 D). Subcommittee: Housing and Memorial Affairs (Chairman). *Select Committee on Aging* (36th of 39 D). Subcommittee: Human Services.

Group Ratings

	ADA	ACLU	COPE	CFA	LCV	ACU	NTLC	NSI	COC	CEI
1988	80	70	93	82	63	12	11	0	21	15
1987	96	—	92	79	—	4	—	—	13	8

National Journal Ratings

	1988 LIB — 1988 CONS		1987 LIB — 1987 CONS	
Economic	87% —	8%	73% —	0%
Social	58% —	40%	73% —	22%
Foreign	68% —	28%	76% —	19%

Key Votes

1) Homeless $	AGN	5) Ban Drug Test	AGN	9) SDI Research	AGN
2) Gephardt Amdt	FOR	6) Drug Death Pen	AGN	10) Ban Chem Weaps	FOR
3) Deficit Reduc	FOR	7) Handgun Sales	FOR	11) Aid to Contras	AGN
4) Kill Plnt Clsng Notice	AGN	8) Ban D.C. Abort $	FOR	12) Nuclear Testing	FOR

Election Results

1988 general	Harley O. Staggers, Jr. (D), unopposed			($90,537)
1988 primary	Harley O. Staggers, Jr. (D), unopposed			
1986 general	Harley O. Staggers, Jr. (D)	76,355	(69%)	($136,766)
	Michele Golden (R)	33,554	(31%)	($67,232)

THIRD DISTRICT

West Virginia almost was called Kanawha, and the valley of the Kanawha River (pronounced kanAW locally) where the city of Charleston sits on its banks is in every way but geographically the center of this mountain state. Along the Kanawha rises West Virginia's Capitol, one of the largest and most beautiful in the country; this is the center of West Virginia's state government and with its two partisan newspapers, the Democratic *Gazette* and the Republican *Daily Mail*, Charleston is the center of West Virginia politics, as well. It is also the center of an important part of the economy. In the hills above Charleston are many of West Virginia's coal mines; below, on the banks of the Kanawha in the industrial suburbs, are the large chemical plants that convert coal tar and other feedstocks into products Americans use every day. They were a center of American high technology in the 1940s, when they produced all the nation's lucite and polyethylenes and nylon as well as much of its artificial rubber and antifreeze. More recently, they are seen as heavy polluters in a valley that has well above average rates of cancer. Yet Charleston is also West Virginia's white-collar and professional center, with a few downtown skyscrapers and some pleasant affluent residential districts. But the overall atmosphere here is more raw than polished, more tradition-minded than culturally advanced.

Charleston and surrounding Kanawha County make up almost half of West Virginia's 3d Congressional District. To the south and west are mining counties, heavily Democratic; to the north and east, toward the Ohio River, are quieter rural counties, with few mine shafts in their hollows, where Civil War loyalties are still very much alive, and which often vote Republican. Kanawha County itself is often (though not in 1988) more Republican than the rest of the state.

The congressman from the 3d District is Bob Wise, a Democrat whose background is a bit unusual for a West Virginia politician—or would have been two generations ago. He is from an affluent Charleston family, went to elite schools, then returned to town to start a law practice geared to low- and middle-income clients; he led a movement to force coal companies to pay higher taxes; in a state where past politicians got ahead by relying on ancestral loyalties and smoothing relations with big economic institutions, he has made his way by emphasizing issues on which he opposes the big interests. Wise won the seat after veteran representative John Slack died and two successors fumbled the chance to hold it. Wise was shrewd and popular enough to beat the House of Delegates majority leader and a former Kanawha County sheriff in the 1982 primary and then to beat the incumbent soundly in November. He has been reelected easily, seems to have a safe seat, provided he can get through the 1992 redistricting (his Charleston base should help), and has been mentioned as a possible candidate for statewide office at some future date when there is a vacancy.

In the House, Wise started off as an insurgent, taking to the floor in 1983 to oppose a dam favored by the rest of the West Virginia delegation. But since then he has used his seat to promote his district. He does some of the standard things—getting government projects for local areas, calling for beefed up enforcement of reclamation laws. But he also travels to the Far East every year to market West Virginia. When he does take on an external issue, like getting oil companies out of South Africa, his solution of stopping foreign companies who operate there from bidding on U.S. oil leases here has the additional advantage of helping West Virginia's coal industry. He is a strong West Virginia booster, urging students to make their careers in their native state, and is Congress's best and most enthusiastic clog dancer. He retains a populist bias against luxury, declining to accept pay increases and using the money for $1,000-a-year scholarships at 3d District colleges. Yet in 1989 he had enough clout to become West Virginia's first member to sit on the House Budget Committee.

1308   WEST VIRGINIA

The People: Est. Pop. 1986: 479,600, dn. 1.3% 1980–86; Pop. 1980: 486,112, up 10.0% 1970–80. Households (1980): 78% family, 42% with children, 67% married couples; 26.8% housing units rented; median monthly rent: $150; median house value: $43,500. Voting age pop. (1980): 347,147; 3% Black, 1% Spanish origin.

1988 Presidential Vote:

Dukakis (D).		90,179	(52%)
Bush (R)		81,235	(47%)

Rep. Robert E. (Bob) Wise, Jr. (D)

Elected 1982; b. Jan. 6, 1948, Washington, D.C.; home, Clendenin; Duke U., B.A. 1970, Tulane, J.D. 1975; Episcopalian; married (Sandy).

Career: Practicing atty., 1975–80; Dir., WV for Fair and Equitable Assessment of Taxes, Inc., 1977–80; WV Senate, 1980–82.

Offices: 1421 LHOB 20515, 202-225-2711. Also 107 Pennsylvania Ave., Charleston 25302, 304-342-7170.

Committees: *Budget* (19th of 21 D). Task Forces: Community Development and Natural Resources; Human Resources. *Government Operations* (11th of 24 D). Subcommittees: Government Information, Justice, and Agriculture (Chairman); Employment and Housing. *Select Committee on Aging* (23d of 39 D). Subcommittees: Health and Long-Term Care; Retirement Income and Employment.

Group Ratings

	ADA	ACLU	COPE	CFA	LCV	ACU	NTLC	NSI	COC	CEI
1988	75	81	92	73	63	12	13	20	36	15
1987	84	—	91	79	—	0	—	—	7	7

National Journal Ratings

	1988 LIB — 1988 CONS		1987 LIB — 1987 CONS	
Economic	71% —	23%	73% —	0%
Social	70% —	28%	78% —	0%
Foreign	60% —	37%	64% —	35%

Key Votes

1) Homeless $	AGN	5) Ban Drug Test	AGN	9) SDI Research	FOR
2) Gephardt Amdt	FOR	6) Drug Death Pen	AGN	10) Ban Chem Weaps	FOR
3) Deficit Reduc	FOR	7) Handgun Sales	FOR	11) Aid to Contras	AGN
4) Kill Plnt Clsng Notice	AGN	8) Ban D.C. Abort $	AGN	12) Nuclear Testing	FOR

Election Results

1988 general	Robert E. (Bob) Wise, Jr. (D).	120,192	(74%)	($165,957)
	Paul W. Hart (R)	41,478	(26%)	($4,249)
1988 primary	Robert E. (Bob) Wise, Jr. (D), unopposed			
1986 general	Robert E. (Bob) Wise, Jr. (D).	73,669	(65%)	($138,732)
	Tim Sharp (R)	39,820	(35%)	($20,411)

FOURTH DISTRICT

As America geared up for war in 1940, one of the industrially critical places—and especially critical because of the propensity of the biggest union there to strike—was the coalfields of southern West Virginia. Early in the century, this was one of America's boom areas. Into rural farmland and hollows inhabited by the same families since they first came into the mountains a century or so before, came coal company lawyers with minerals rights' leases to sign, coal company engineers to design and sink the mineshafts, and men from other mountain counties and fresh from boats coming from Europe as well to work the mines. Company houses were built, company stores stocked with goods as the company dictated and company paymasters kept close tabs on the finances of every employee.

These conditions bred dull discontent, ignited into the fire of industrial unionism by the tongue of John L. Lewis, president of the United Mine Workers, and by 1940, the mines were mostly unionized. This made Lewis—bitterly opposed to Franklin Roosevelt's war policy, unapproachable and often unappeasable—a key to the war effort, which his strikes several times came close to stopping. Today, Lewis's Mine Workers organization is much smaller; underground mines by the dozens have been closed and strip mines, using far fewer men working under much safer conditions, have become the norm. The old underground mines are remembered by landscape that was spoiled by abandoned mineshafts and piles of tailings and in lives that were snuffed out in America's deadliest industry by cave-ins or simple carelessness.

West Virginia's 4th Congressional District includes several of the leading coal counties of southern West Virginia plus the city of Huntington on the Ohio River. Over the years, the eight counties of the 4th District have produced more bituminous coal than any other single congressional district in the United States. The ups and downs of the population of these eight counties tell the story of the industry. In 1940, there were 520,000 people here (more than enough for two districts in those days), and in 1950, after the wartime boom and as oil was just beginning to replace coal, there were 579,000. Then in 1970, after two decades of declining mine employment there were only 437,000. The rebound of the 1970s, as coal prices rose and strip mining boomed, raised the population to 487,000 in 1980; but it sagged back down in the hard times here of the 1980s to 470,000 in 1986.

The politics of this sometimes poverty-stricken area has little of the altruism that some liberal reformers expected in the 1960s when they called for the maximum feasible participation of the poor. In places like southern West Virginia, there are few ways for a bright young man to make money except by owning a coal mine or winning public or union office. In the struggle to get ahead, many politicians here are little concerned with unsafe mine conditions, black lung disease, or air and water pollution, and very concerned with enriching themselves. Mingo County, legendary for corruption was cleaned up between 1986 and 1988, exposing a fire chief who headed a drug ring, a sheriff who bought his job for $100,000 and politicoes who bought votes for $2 or a half-pint of bourbon.

The current congressman, Nick Joe Rahall II, did not use politics as a way up from poverty: he is part of a family that owns radio and television stations in such widely dispersed locales as Beckley, West Virginia and St. Petersburg, Florida, and he has been able and willing to spend his own money in campaigns. This helped him win, at age 27, a decisive 1976 Democratic primary, when incumbent Ken Hechler, a crusader against Tony Boyle's UMW leadership, was running for governor; the 1976 general election, when Hechler came back and ran as an independent; and the 1978 primary, when Hechler tried again to regain the seat.

In the House Rahall, is a member of Interior and Public Works—you could not find coalier assignments—and Education and Labor. He chairs the Mining and Natural Resources Subcommittee and concentrates heavily on promoting the cause of West Virginia coal. He works against legislation restricting use of eastern coal or encouraging use of its competition (oil, natural gas, western coal) for reregulating coal-hauling railroad rates, and against the coal slurry pipeline which would bring western coal east. He urged the establishment of a Federal Coal Export Commission and he resisted Administration efforts to increase the coal excise tax that replenishes the Black Lung Trust Fund. He has worked on Interior on bills to protect the scenic Gauley, Meadows and Bluestone Rivers and for a development act for the New River (which is actually one of the continent's oldest). He is solidly liberal on economic and foreign issues; on cultural matters, and particularly on environmental issues, his record is mixed. Of Arab descent, he is interested in Middle East issues and critical of Israel.

With important committee posts for this heavily Democratic (58% for Michael Dukakis) district, Rahall would seem to have a seat for life. But he has been hurt by incidents that made his lifestyle seem unattractive—a 1984 suit by a Nevada casino for $60,000 in debts, a divorce and a driving under the influence arrest in California in 1988. His percentage of the vote fell to 61% in November 1988—his lowest since he was elected—when with the most Democratic district in the state, he finished with the lowest percentage of the four Democratic incumbents. Whether this spells trouble for 1990 or after redistricting for 1992 is unclear. If legislators tried to split Rahall's district or put him in with another incumbent, he might have some trouble, though his primary showing in May 1988 (72% against two elderly candidates) indicates some strength.

The People: Est. Pop. 1986: 470,700, dn. 3.4% 1980–86; Pop. 1980: 487,526, up 11.4% 1970–80. Households (1980): 79% family, 45% with children, 66% married couples; 26.8% housing units rented; median monthly rent: $135; median house value: $36,000. Voting age pop. (1980): 339,410; 6% Black, 1% Spanish origin.

1988 Presidential Vote:

Dukakis (D)	80,531	(58%)
Bush (R)	58,055	(42%)

Rep. Nick Joe Rahall II (D)

Elected 1976; b. May 20, 1949, Beckley; home, Beckley; Duke U., A.B. 1971; Presbyterian; divorced.

Career: Aide to U.S. Sen. Robert C. Byrd, 1971–74; Pres., Mountaineer Tour and Travel Agency, 1975; Pres., WV Broadcasting Corp.

Offices: 343 CHOB 20515, 202-225-3452. Also 110½ Main St., Beckley 25801, 304-252-5000, 304-252-6507; 815 5th Ave., Huntington 25701, 304-522-6425, 304-529-1716; 1005 Fed. Bldg., Bluefield 24701, 304-325-6222; and R.K. Bldg., Logan 25601, 304-752-4934.

Committees: *Education and Labor* (18th of 22 D). Subcommittee: Elementary, Secondary, and Vocational Education. *Interior and Insular Affairs* (6th of 26 D). Subcommittees: Mining and Natural Resources (Chairman); National Parks and Public Lands. *Public Works and Transportation* (6th of 31 D). Subcommittees: Economic Development; Surface Transportation.

Group Ratings

	ADA	ACLU	COPE	CFA	LCV	ACU	NTLC	NSI	COC	CEI
1988	70	64	88	91	50	22	12	0	29	14
1987	76	—	87	69	—	4	—	—	7	13

National Journal Ratings

	1988 LIB — 1988 CONS		1987 LIB — 1987 CONS	
Economic	71% —	23%	55% —	43%
Social	54% —	45%	65% —	34%
Foreign	72% —	28%	68% —	30%

Key Votes

1) Homeless $	FOR	5) Ban Drug Test	AGN	9) SDI Research	AGN
2) Gephardt Amdt	FOR	6) Drug Death Pen	AGN	10) Ban Chem Weaps	FOR
3) Deficit Reduc	FOR	7) Handgun Sales	FOR	11) Aid to Contras	AGN
4) Kill Plnt Clsng Notice	AGN	8) Ban D.C. Abort $	FOR	12) Nuclear Testing	FOR

Election Results

1988 general	Nick Joe Rahall II (D)	78,812	(61%)	($152,271)
	Marianne R. Brewster (R)	49,753	(39%)	($32,039)
1988 primary	Nick Joe Rahall (D)	56,996	(73%)	
	William Sanders (D)	12,920	(16%)	
	Ted T. Stacy (D)	8,503	(11%)	
1986 general	Nick Joe Rahall II (D)	58,217	(71%)	($68,970)
	Martin Miller, Sr. (R)	23,490	(29%)	

WISCONSIN

Half a century ago, Wisconsin—the picture of ordinariness on a frost-bitten morning in its rolling dairylands—was politically one of the most distinctive of states. With next-door Minnesota, it was one of two states with a genuine three-party politics, a state that, in between the four times it voted for Democrat Franklin Roosevelt, cast most of its votes in gubernatorial elections for Progressives and Republicans. Wisconsin owes this distinction to the German heritage of most of its citizens and to the political genius—and peculiarities—of Robert LaFollette and his sons.

North of Chicago, west of the Great Lakes, Wisconsin is the first state of the Northwest—that vast stretch of the United States all the way to the Pacific settled more by immigrants from Germany and Scandinavia, than by descendants of the Middle Atlantic and New England Yankees who populated the states just to the south. The German language is seldom heard any more, the once plainly German beer brands now seem quintessentially American, and not many ties exist with the old country after two world wars. But in the 19th and early 20th centuries, Germans were among our most numerous immigrants and until the 1880s probably the most distinctive. They often kept their old language, maintained their separate religion, kept old customs from country weddings to drinking beer (a source of friction in temperance-minded America); they established, on the vast empty prairies or in crowded neighborhoods of growing cities, German communities.

Politically, they were never an entirely monolithic group; their origins were too diverse, and they were spread too widely across the nation. But where they were concentrated, you can see the growth of a distinctive politics, basically American, but with echoes of the ideas and movements also seen in German-speaking countries in Europe. Nowhere was the politics of German-Americans more apparent than in Wisconsin. This is one of the states that gave birth to the Republican Party in 1854, and German-Americans, then arriving in vast numbers, heavily preferred its free soil politics to the doughface stands of the Democrats. The German-Americans abhorred slavery; they welcomed the free lands the Republicans were advocating in the Homestead Act, the free educations they were promising by setting up land grant colleges, the transportation routes they were constructing by subsidizing railroad builders.

Then came Robert LaFollette and his Progressive movement, which can be dated conveniently from his election as governor in 1900. Up to that time, a conventional Republican politician, LaFollette completely revamped the state government before going to the Senate in 1906. At a time when Germany was Europe's leader in graduate education and the application of science to government, LaFollette brought in professors from the University of Wisconsin, across town in Madison, to develop the state's workmen's compensation system and income tax. The Progressive movement favored the rational use of government to improve the lot of the ordinary citizen—an idea borrowed, perhaps, from German liberals and adopted by the New Dealers a generation later. LaFollette himself became a national figure, and tried to run for President in 1912 as a Progressive, but was shoved aside by Theodore Roosevelt; in 1924 he finally did run for President as a Progressive and won 18% of the nation's votes. Making the best third-party showing of the last 65 years, he was strongest in the northern tier from Wisconsin to Washington, along the West Coast, and in some hitherto Republican factory towns like Cleveland.

After the elder La Follette's death in 1925, his sons maintained the traditions of Wisconsin's progressivism. Robert LaFollette Jr. served in the Senate from 1925 to 1947, and was one of the leaders of the liberal, pro-labor bloc. Philip LaFollette was elected governor of Wisconsin in 1930, 1934 and 1936, and in 1934 formed the separate Progressive party. His movement took on ominous tones later in the decade, with a Cross in Circle symbol his critics called a circumcised swastika, huge rally-like parades that were reminiscent of some in Europe at the time, and his call for the governor to propose all legislation. Philip LaFollette's dream of forming a national party was never achieved. At home, he was beaten badly in 1938 and did not run for office again. Robert LaFollette Jr. was reelected to the Senate by only 45%–41% over a Republican in 1940; the Progressives won the governorship once more in 1942, but won only 6% in statewide contests in 1944 and voted to disband their party before the 1946 election. Senator LaFollette, who decided to run for reelection as a Republican but didn't campaign much because he was busy passing congressional reorganization in Washington, was defeated in the 1946 primary by one Joseph McCarthy.

McCarthy's national prominence and other Republican victories made Wisconsin seem like a Republican state in the 1950s; and McCarthy's charges that Communists were influencing American foreign policy fed on the inarticulate convictions of many in Wisconsin and elsewhere that we should have been fighting Russia as much as Germany in World War II. But actually, McCarthy and other Republicans often won by narrow margins, and the energies of the old Progressive movement, centered in Madison somewhere between the State Capitol and the University of Wisconsin, were transferred largely to a Democratic Party led by the likes of William Proxmire and Gaylord Nelson.

But even with a two-party, liberal-conservative politics, Wisconsin remains distinctive, moving counter to national political cycles. While the nation mostly voted Democratic from 1944 to 1964, Wisconsin was voting mostly Republican. When the nation voted mostly Republican for President starting in 1968, Wisconsin has moved toward the Democrats, giving George McGovern and Walter Mondale some of their best percentages, providing 11 crucial electoral votes for Jimmy Carter in 1976 and coming close to voting for him in 1980 too, and voting for Michael Dukakis in 1988. It has become one of the most dovish states, as if a large number of Wisconsin voters were hit by the same impulse that has led so many voters in West Germany, suddenly in the early 1980s, to start fearing the presence of nuclear weapons and favoring unilateral disarmament. Yet during those same years, when most states were electing Demo-

WISCONSIN — Congressional Districts, Counties, and Selected Places — *(9 Districts)*

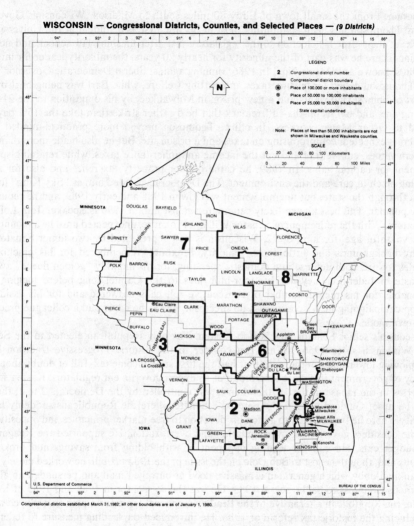

LEGEND

2 Congressional district number

Congressional district boundary

Place of 100,000 or more inhabitants

Place of 50,000 to 100,000 inhabitants

Place of 25,000 to 50,000 inhabitants

State capital underlined

Note: Places of less than 50,000 inhabitants are not shown in Milwaukee and Waukesha counties.

SCALE

0 20 40 60 80 100 Kilometers

0 20 40 60 80 100 Miles

U.S. Department of Commerce

BUREAU OF THE CENSUS

Congressional districts established March 31, 1982; all other boundaries are as of January 1, 1980.

cratic governors, Wisconsin was electing Republicans— in 1968, 1978 and 1986. That last year also saw the reelection of conservative Republican Senator Robert Kasten and the defeat of longtime Democratic attorney general Bronson LaFollette.

Environmental issues and cultural liberalism may work for Democrats in national contests, but in Wisconsin the sense is that the state's high taxes are stifling economic growth. The openness to forms of cultural liberation so apparent here in the past, seemed replaced by concern about the consequences: Wisconsin passed a trailblazing law making parents, not the state, responsible for supporting the illegitimate children of unmarried teenagers. Yet it's not clear that Wisconsin has moved heavily to the right. The Democrats beefed up their margins in the legislature and do well in congressional elections. If Wisconsin seems unlikely to extend the LaFollette version of the welfare state any further just now, it's not clear that it wants to do away with large parts of it either.

Governor. From the small town of Elroy 80 miles south to Madison, Wisconsin's Governor Tommy Thompson has been commuting most of his life, first as a student at the University of Wisconsin, then after his election to the legislature just after finishing law school, and now as governor. There he was part of the minority for nearly 20 years, the minority leader for most of the 1980s, known as "Doctor No." In 1986, running against liberal Democratic Governor Tony Earl, Thompson called for cutting taxes and cutting welfare, while Earl was being hurt by his support of homosexual rights and a new prison in Milwaukee, by his opposition to the 21-year drinking age, and by his off-the-cuff remark that he'd rather strike than take the 15% pay cut offered to Oscar Mayer workers. In office, Thompson proved more practical-minded than Democrats expected, compromising on taxes and a prison site. But he also made more than 290 line item vetoes, cut welfare and cut the income and inheritance taxes, while retaining special treatment for capital gains. In 1989, he came out for property tax relief and also for more spending on child care and the environment. The Democrats derided him as "Sky King" for his travels through the state, but unemployment was low in 1988 and early 1989, and he remained widely popular. The best known likely candidate against him in 1990 is Speaker Tom Loftus.

Senators. With the retirement of Senator William Proxmire, unexpected until he announced it at the youthful age, for him, of 72. Wisconsin is now represented by two junior Senators of wealthy backgrounds and little or no seniority. Proxmire, remembered for his pinchpenny attitudes toward both defense and domestic spending, for his monthly "golden fleece" awards for waste of federal money, for his four-mile jogs to the Capitol long before jogging was fashionable, for his record number of consecutive roll calls answered and for his assiduous nonstop campaigning in Wisconsin, has no successor, just as he never had a colleague precisely in his own mode.

Wisconsin's senior Senator now is Bob Kasten. The only Republican elected to the Senate from Wisconsin since 1956, he has run counter to the historic Progressive tradition here, championing lower taxes in the state that had the first state income tax, full of doubt about the efficacy of government in a state long proud of its expert government regulators. Kasten served two terms in the House in the 1970s, when it was controlled by the Democrats 2 to 1; then in 1980, he upset Gaylord Nelson and entered a Senate where the Republicans suddenly had a majority. There he translated into action his devotion to free-market principles and opposition to what he considers government overregulation and overtaxation. He supported the Reagan tax and budget cuts. He was the leading opponent of withholding from savings and brokerage accounts and, though he lost to Bob Dole on the issue in the 1982 tax bill, he worked closely with the banking lobby which generated a massive flood of outraged mail and persuaded an almost unanimous Congress to backtrack in 1983. He was the co-sponsor in 1984 and 1985 of Kemp-Kasten, the Republican alternative to the Bradley-Gephardt tax reform plan that played a role in producing the historic tax reform of 1986. He introduced the leading measure to federalize liability suits so as to reduce awards to plaintiffs and, presumably, insurance costs.

Over some time now, Kasten has shown the ability to stick to his guns under heavy pressure. But he lost badly to Alan Simpson in the 1984 race for Republican whip. For Wisconsin, he worked on local aid projects and fought to label pizzas made with casein "non-cheese" and to protect dairy subsidies. He chaired the Appropriations Subcommittee on Foreign Operations, supporting aid to Israel and Egypt and Administration policy in Central America.

In Wisconsin, he has had a splotchy electoral record. After being elected to the House in 1974 and 1976, he lost the gubernatorial primary in 1978; then he came back and won his Senate seat. In his first term, he got involved in a civil suit involving partnerships he had with a bankrupt real estate speculator who went to jail; in 1985, he was arrested for drunk driving; in 1986, he was the winner of one of the year's least edifying brawls. For that much blame must go to Democrat Ed Garvey, the onetime attorney for the National Football League players association who got them involved in a long and not very successful strike: Garvey attacked Kasten for being remote from the public and for "drinking on the job" and hired a detective who posed as a reporter to snoop into Kasten's financial affairs; Kasten ran ads opposing those tactics and attacking Garvey's stewardship of the football players' funds. The result was a narrow but decisive Kasten victory; Kasten lost Madison, Kenosha, Milwaukee County, but carried the broad Milwaukee metropolitan area, and won everywhere else for his second straight narrow victory.

The result was also close in the race for Proxmire's seat. Both parties had primaries, with results opposite to national trends: the most conservative candidate did not win the Republican primary and the most liberal candidate did not win the Democratic nomination. Among the Republicans, state Senator Susan Engeleiter, labeled a moderate because of her pro-choice views on abortion, beat former state party chairman Steve King 57%–40%. Among the Democrats, the leading event was the entry of Milwaukee businessman and Milwaukee Bucks owner Herb Kohl into the race. Congressman Jim Moody, reasoning that Kohl's local celebrity and ability to spend huge sums on ads would preempt his Milwaukee base, got out of the race. Garvey, though the 1986 nominee, was overshadowed and won only 10% of the vote. Former Governor Tony Earl, still well-liked by Democrats and with a statewide network of supporters, complained about Kohl's spending and attacked him for unfamiliarity with the issues. But Kohl's theme of "nobody's Senator but yours" enabled him to beat Earl 47%–38%. A millionaire grocery store scion, Kohl took no PAC contributions and contributed heavily to his own race. In the general, Kohl stressed his support of defense cuts—popular in dovish Wisconsin—and for requiring businesses to provide medical insurance; Engeleiter stressed her environmental stands, her legislative experience, and her status as a wife and mother—a contrast with Kohl, a bachelor. This turned out to be one of the closest Senate races in the country, with Kohl winning 52%–48%. Engeleiter also came to Washington as the head of Bush's Small Business Administration. In the Senate, where Kohl has seats on the Judiciary and Governmental Affairs Committees, he is not a prepossessing figure.

Presidential politics. Wisconsin was once one of the most influential states in presidential contests. Its presidential primary knocked Wendell Willkie out of the race in 1944 and helped John Kennedy establish his lead over Hubert Humphrey in 1960; Eugene McCarthy was all set to win heavily here in 1968 when Lyndon Johnson withdrew on the Sunday night before the election. More recently, Wisconsin was the scene of one of Morris Udall's agonizingly close second place finishes to Jimmy Carter in 1976.

In 1988, it was the first big contest after Jesse Jackson's surprise win in the Michigan caucuses. Jackson made a point of campaigning for blue-collar workers' votes, and there was much speculation that here would finally emerge the populist alliance of blacks and working class whites which some Democratic strategists and many members of the press have been longing to see for years. But it did not materialize in Wisconsin any more than anywhere else. Dukakis won the primary easily, and extinguished any doubts that he would be the Democratic nominee. The national Democrats, incidentally, have allowed Wisconsin to continue its open primary, one of Bob LaFollette's reforms.

Wisconsin has often had close races in the general elections. In 1960 and 1968 it voted for Richard Nixon. Countercyclically, it has become more Democratic, voting for Jimmy Carter in 1976 and Michael Dukakis in 1988, and giving Ronald Reagan only modest margins in 1980 and 1984.

Congressional districting. Wisconsin's congressional district lines were drawn according to a bipartisan plan agreed to by Democrat David Obey and Republican James Sensenbrenner. Something like that will probably happen after the 1990 Census. Population growth in the state has been modest, but it's not likely to lose a seat, and the district lines need to be modified only marginally.

1316   WISCONSIN

The People: Est. Pop. 1988: 4,858,000; Pop. 1980: 4,705,767, up 3.2% 1980–88 and 6.5% 1970–80; 1.99% of U.S. total, 17th largest. 15% with 1–3 yrs. col., 15% with 4+ yrs. col.; 8.7% below poverty level. Single ancestry: 24% German, 4% Polish, 3% English, Norwegian, 2% Irish, 1% Italian, Swedish, Dutch, French. Households (1980): 73% family, 40% with children, 63% married couples; 31.8% housing units rented; median monthly rent: $186; median house value: $48,600. Voting age pop. (1980): 3,347,947; 3% Black, 1% Spanish origin, 1% American Indian. No state voter registration.

1988 Share of Federal Tax Burden: $15,957,000,000; 1.80% of U.S. total, 19th largest.

1988 Share of Federal Expenditures

	Total		Non-Defense		Defense	
Total Expend	$13,127m	(1.48%)	$11,852m	(1.81%)	$1,569m	(0.69%)
St/Lcl Grants	2,228m	(1.94%)	2,226m	(1.94%)	2m	(1.59%)
Salary/Wages	1,049m	(0.78%)	793m	(1.18%)	256m	(1.18%)
Pymnts to Indiv	7,794m	(1.90%)	7,681m	(1.97%)	114m	(0.61%)
Procurement	1,192m	(0.63%)	294m	(0.63%)	1,192m	(0.63%)
Research/Other	864m	(2.31%)	858m	(2.32%)	5m	(2.32%)

Political Lineup: Governor, Tommy G. Thompson (R); Lt. Gov., Scott McCallum (R); Secy. of State, Douglas LaFollette (D); Atty. Gen., Donald Hanaway (R); Treasurer, Charles P. Smith (D). State Senate, 33 (20 D and 13 R). State House of Representatives, 99 (55 D and 44 R). Senators, Robert W. Kasten, Jr. (R) and Herbert H. Kohl (D). Representatives, 9 (5 D and 4 R).

1988 Presidential Vote

Dukakis (D)	1,126,794	(51%)
Bush (R)	1,047,499	(47%)

1984 Presidential Vote

Reagan (R)	1,198,584	(54%)
Mondale (D)	995,740	(45%)

1988 Democratic Presidential Primary

Dukakis	483,172	(48%)
Jackson	285,995	(28%)
Gore	176,712	(17%)
Simon	48,419	(5%)
Gephardt	7,996	(1%)
Hart	7,068	(1%)

1988 Republican Presidential Primary

Bush	295,295	(82%)
Dole	28,460	(8%)
Robertson	24,798	(7%)
Kemp	4,915	(1%)

GOVERNOR

Gov. Tommy G. Thompson (R)

Elected 1986, term expires Jan. 1991; b. Nov. 19, 1941, Elroy; home, Elroy; U. of WI, B.A. 1963, J.D. 1966; Roman Catholic; married (Sue Anne).

Career: Practicing atty; WI Assembly, 1966–86, Asst. Min. Ldr., 1973–81, Flr. Ldr., 1981–86.

Office: State Capitol, 115 E. State Capitol, Madison 53702, 608-266-1212.

Election Results

1986 gen.	Tommy G. Thompson (R)	805,090	(53%)
	Anthony S. Earl (D)	705,578	(46%)
1986 prim.	Tommy G. Thompson (R)	156,875	(52%)
	Jonathan B. Barry (R)	67,114	(22%)
	George Watts (R)	58,424	(19%)
	Albert Wiley (R)	15,233	(5%)
1982 gen.	Anthony S. Earl (D)	896,812	(57%)
	Terry J. Kohler (R)	662,838	(42%)

SENATORS

Sen. Robert W. Kasten, Jr. (R)

Elected 1980, seat up 1992; b. June 19, 1942, Milwaukee; home, Mequon; U. of AZ, B.A. 1964, Columbia U., M.B.A. 1966; Episcopalian; married (Eva).

Career: Air Force, 1967–72; Vice Pres. and Dir., shoe mftg. co.; WI Senate, 1972–74; U.S. House of Reps., 1974–78.

Offices: 110 HSOB 20510, 202-224-5323. Also 517 E. WI Ave., Milwaukee 53202, 414-291-4160; 6516 Watts Rd., Ste. 203, Madison 53719, 608-264-5366; and Fed. Bldg., Rm. 107, Wausau 54401, 715-842-3307.

Committees: *Appropriations* (6th of 13 R). Subcommittees: Agriculture and Related Agencies; Commerce, Justice, State, and Judiciary; Defense; Foreign Operations (Ranking Member); Transportation. *Budget* (6th of 10 R). *Commerce, Science, and Transportation* (5th of 9 R). Subcommittees: Aviation; Consumer; Science, Technology, and Space; Surface Transportation (Ranking Member). *Small Business* (2d of 9 R). Subcommittee: Government Contracting and Paperwork Reduction; Rural Economy and Family Farming (Ranking Member).

Group Ratings

	ADA	ACLU	COPE	CFA	LCV	ACU	NTLC	NSI	COC	CEI
1988	10	19	24	50	40	84	67	100	71	38
1987	20	—	21	33	—	92	—	—	83	63

National Journal Ratings

	1988 LIB — 1988 CONS		1987 LIB — 1987 CONS	
Economic	27%	70%	30%	68%
Social	19%	78%	16%	78%
Foreign	17%	81%	0%	76%

Key Votes

1) Cut Aged Housing $	AGN	5) Bork Nomination	FOR	9) SDI Funding	FOR
2) Override Hwy Veto	AGN	6) Ban Plastic Guns	FOR	10) Ban Chem Weaps	FOR
3) Kill Plnt Clsng Notice	FOR	7) Deny Abortions	FOR	11) Aid To Contras	FOR
4) Min Wage Increase	AGN	8) Japanese Reparations	FOR	12) Reagan Defense $	FOR

Election Results

1986 general	Robert W. Kasten, Jr. (R)	1,754,537	(51%)	($3,433,870)
	Edward Garvey (D)	1,702,963	(47%)	($1,702,963)
1986 primary	Robert W. Kasten, Jr. (R)	1,248,333	(100%)	
1980 general	Robert W. Kasten, Jr. (R)	1,106,311	(50%)	($686,758)
	Gaylord A. Nelson (D)	1,065,487	(48%)	($897,774)

Sen. Herbert H. Kohl (D)

Elected 1988, seat up 1994; b. Feb. 7, 1935, Milwaukee; home, Milwaukee; U. of WI, B.A. 1956, Harvard U., M.B.A. 1958; Jewish; single.

Career: Pres., Kohl Corp., 1970-79; Pres., Herbert Kohl Investments 1979–88; Owner, Milwaukee Bucks pro basketball team.

Offices: 702 HSOB 20510, 202-224-5653. Also 205 E. Wisconsin Ave., Milwaukee 53202, 414-291-4451; and 14 W. Mifflin St., Ste. 312, Madison, 53703, 608-264-5338.

Committees: *Governmental Affairs* (7th of 8 D). Subcommittees: Federal Services, Post Office, and Civil Service; Government Information and Regulation; Oversight of Government Management; Investigations. *Judiciary* (8th of 8 D). Subcommittees: Antitrust, Monopolies and Business Rights; Courts and Administrative Practice; Technology and the Law. *Special Committee on Aging* (10th of 10 D).

Group Ratings and Key Votes: Newly Elected

Election Results

1988 general	Herbert H. Kohl (D)	1,128,625	(52%)	($7,491,600)
	Susan Engeleiter (R)	1,030,440	(48%)	($2,853,842)
1988 primary	Herbert H. Kohl (D)	249,226	(47%)	
	Anthony S. Earl (D)	203,479	(38%)	
	Ed Garvey (D)	55,225	(10%)	
	Douglas J. LaFollete (D)	19,819	(4%)	
1982 general	William Proxmire (D)	983,311	(64%)	
	Scott McCallum (R)	527,355	(34%)	($119,924)

FIRST DISTRICT

It is one of those invisible dotted lines, marked by no natural feature, that makes so much difference in American politics, the boundary between the corruption-prone machine politics of Illinois and squeaky-clean progressive politics of Wisconsin. South on the shore of Lake Michigan is Chicago and its carefully landscaped North Shore suburbs; north of the line are the tidy small industrial cities of Kenosha, where the old Nash plant (and later Chrysler) closed down, and Racine, still the proud home of Johnson's Wax. Inland, along the Rock River, there is little to distinguish the industrial city of Rockford, Illinois from Beloit and Janesville, Wisconsin. Nor is there much difference from the little towns and dairy farms and lakes in between on the Illinois side and around prosperous Lake Geneva, Wisconsin. This is the land of the 1st District of Wisconsin, which politically has about the same balance as the state as a whole. In 1984 and 1986, it voted for Republicans Ronald Reagan, Senator Robert Kasten and Governor Tommy Thompson. In 1988, it voted for Democrats Michael Dukakis and Herbert Kohl.

In the 1960s, this was one of the more marginal of congressional districts. Now it is the home of Les Aspin, chairman of the House Armed Services Committee. Aspin, initially elected in 1970, was one of the first of the young generation of anti-Vietnam war Democrats elected to the House, and one of the first to rise to a position of power, when he upset aging chairman Mel Price in the Democratic Caucus after the 1984 election. As chairman, and even before on the MX missile issue, Aspin has been one of the most powerful Members of the House, negotiating with the Administration, influencing policy at the Pentagon, determining, because he is typically at the fulcrum of opinion, which way the House will vote on major issues. But Aspin's position is not totally solid. It depends on the support of the Democratic Caucus, which can be withdrawn as it was in January 1987 when many liberals were unhappy with him for casting a quiet vote against contra aid and for his support of the MX-Midgetman compromise. Early in the month the Caucus voted 130–124 against reconfirming him as chairman; only three weeks later did he win his chairmanship back, 133–116, with the understanding that he would consult with his fellow Democrats more and go off the reservation less.

Aspin's difficulties with the Caucus came because, while skeptical about much Pentagon spending, he does not share the almost religious opposition of many younger Democrats to Pentagon initiatives. He is of another generation: far younger than those who came of age in World War II, but decisively older and more experienced at a higher level than most of those who came to age in Vietnam. He finished college and studied at Oxford long before the days of student protest. He worked on Senator Proxmire's staff while Eisenhower was still President and for Council of Economic Advisers Chairman Walter Heller in the Kennedy years. When he served in the Vietnam-era Army, it was as a high-level staffer for Robert McNamara in the Pentagon, and he was detailed in 1968 to go back home to Wisconsin to manage Lyndon Johnson's hopeless primary campaign against Eugene McCarthy. From these experiences Aspin brings an intellectual curiosity that sometimes verges on playfulness, an Oxford common room debater's habit of understanding and being able to take any side of an argument, a knowledge of the size and heft of the military establishment and an appreciation that most of it is going to keep on operating as it has been, whatever Congress does.

Like so many Democratic policymakers then, Aspin had already turned against the Vietnam war when Johnson pulled out of the race two days before the Wisconsin primary. He returned to Wisconsin, moved to Racine, which was represented by an obviously vulnerable Republican congressman and, without difficulty, campaigned as an opponent of the war and an advocate of stronger policies against unemployment which was high then. He was sharp enough politically to beat a LaFollette in the primary and to win 61% against an incumbent in the general. In the House of the early 1970s, Aspin was clearly an outsider, and even more so on the Armed Services Committee. Aspin specialized in legislating by press release, attacking high Pentagon spending and wasteful projects and getting plenty of ink in the process.

By the late 1970s, this gadfly posture was obsolete, and Aspin was setting forth his own military strategy. He operated from an odd political position: he was far more critical of the military than almost all his fellow members of Armed Services, but far less adolescently negative about his country than many of his Democratic colleagues. By 1983, well before anyone thought he would become chairman, Aspin was the *de facto* leader of the House on military issues, supporting the nuclear freeze resolution and leading the debate when others stumbled, then becoming a leading supporter of the Scowcroft Commission recommendations for the MX missile. These performances made him a natural choice for the chair, even though he was only 7th in seniority, in 1984. House Democrats understand that they are represented on national TV by their leading chairmen and may be held responsible by their constituents for how well the chairmen do. Not all of them trusted Aspin, but most figured he would make a better appearance than Price, who was clearly beyond his best years, and they preferred him by a 124–103 vote over the emotional Charles Bennett, even though Bennett led the opposition to the MX.

Aspin's trouble in his first term as chairman came partly for institutional reasons, because he had to straddle the divide between Armed Services, which has a large hawkish majority, and the Democratic Caucus, which is overwhelmingly dovish. Keeping both happy is a difficult chore for a chairman who is temperamentally soothing and consultative, which Aspin is not. So he ended up opposed by a hawkish conservative, Marvin Leath of Texas, who was supported by none less than ultra-liberal Ron Dellums of Berkeley, California. Aspin's backers finally argued conclusively that his record was liberal, and he himself promised more consultation.

Since then, Aspin has voted an orthodox line against contra aid, but has spent most of his time and energy on Pentagon issues. He has boosted certain weapons systems, notably the Midgetman, and must have been mightily pleased to see President Bush keep it as part of his mix in April 1989; if it had been killed, Aspin would have been in trouble with anti-MX colleagues. He has also been a booster of the B-2 Stealth bomber and a critic of the trouble-plagued B-1. There remains a basic difference in attitude between Aspin and the liberal Democrats who think he should be their natural ally and resent it when he isn't. Like rebellious teenagers who take for granted the roof over their head, many of Aspin's critics take American security for granted and treat the Pentagon as a major threat to peace; Aspin takes the more adult view, well supported by 20th century history, that the forces of good have no guarantee of surviving, and that sometimes aggressive decisions and serious risks must be taken to maintain peace and freedom. Aspin may well be able to find common ground with most Democrats on weapons systems for the next few years. But he may have a harder time papering over this basic difference in attitude.

Aspin's performance as chairman may not have impressed all his colleagues; it did impress his constituents. His performance at the polls sagged in the late 1970s and was no higher than 56% in 1984. But in 1986 and 1988, he won 74% and 76% of the vote, the best showings of his career. There was once talk that he would run for the Senate, but that is history now.

The People: Est. Pop. 1986: 517,500, dn. 1.0% 1980–86; Pop. 1980: 522,838, up 5.1% 1970–80. Households (1980): 75% family, 43% with children, 64% married couples; 30.2% housing units rented; median monthly rent: $188; median house value: $47,900. Voting age pop. (1980): 366,924; 3% Black, 2% Spanish origin.

1988 Presidential Vote:

Dukakis (D)	114,078	(51%)
Bush (R)	107,375	(48%)

Rep. Les Aspin (D)

Elected 1970; b. July 21, 1938, Milwaukee; home, East Troy; Yale U., B.A. 1960, Oxford U., M.A. 1962, M.I.T., Ph.D. 1965; Episcopalian; divorced.

Career: Staff Asst. to U.S. Sen. William Proxmire, 1960; Staff Asst. to Walter Heller, Pres. Cncl. of Econ. Advisers, 1963; Army, 1966–68; Asst. Prof. of Econ., Marquette U., 1969–70.

Offices: 2336 RHOB 20515, 202-225-3031. Also 210 Dodge St., Janesville 53545, 608-752-9074; and 1661 Douglas Ave., Racine 53404, 414-632-4446.

Committees: *Armed Services* (Chairman of 31 D).

Group Ratings

	ADA	ACLU	COPE	CFA	LCV	ACU	NTLC	NSI	COC	CEI
1988	75	85	86	64	75	4	7	20	27	17
1987	76	—	85	79	—	0	—	—	8	9

National Journal Ratings

	1988 LIB — 1988 CONS			1987 LIB — 1987 CONS		
Economic	77%	—	23%	67%	—	32%
Social	69%	—	30%	78%	—	0%
Foreign	59%	—	40%	59%	—	41%

Key Votes

1) Homeless $	AGN	5) Ban Drug Test	—	9) SDI Research	AGN
2) Gephardt Amdt	FOR	6) Drug Death Pen	FOR	10) Ban Chem Weaps	AGN
3) Deficit Reduc	FOR	7) Handgun Sales	AGN	11) Aid to Contras	AGN
4) Kill Plnt Clsng Notice	AGN	8) Ban D.C. Abort $	AGN	12) Nuclear Testing	FOR

Election Results

1988 general	Les Aspin (D)	158,552	(76%)	($631,941)
	Bernard J. Weaver (R)	49,620	(24%)	($17,760)
1988 primary	Les Aspin (D), unopposed			
1986 general	Les Aspin (D)	106,288	(74%)	($497,588)
	Iris Peterson (R)	34,495	(24%)	($9,635)

SECOND DISTRICT

"The seven crowded commercial blocks of State Street link the Capitol to the University of Wisconsin in the western part of Madison," wrote the *WPA Guide* 50 years ago. "Partly wild, partly landscaped, the irregular beauty of the 200-acre campus runs nearly a mile along the ridge crests and slopes of Lake Mendota's southern shore. Though town and gown tend to form two distinct societies, at times they overlap. The Madison Literary Society allows a few from both groups to attend its solemnities; and the exclusive Town and Gown Club mingles the men of both sets. Members of the faculty, devoted to the 'Wisconsin Idea,' serve sometimes as public officials, sometimes as trade unionists, sometimes as advisers in the Capitol. There is a floating population of students, famous visitors, and legislators." This was still the LaFollette era, and the center of LaFollette progressivism was always Madison. Robert LaFollette Sr. was from Madison and, when elected governor in 1900, he called on the university to set up the Wisconsin Tax Commission and to draft a workmen's compensation law—both firsts in the nation. The *Progressive* magazine is still published in Madison, and the *Madison Capital-Times* continues to be one of the nation's most explicitly liberal newspapers, though it has a Republican rival, the *Wisconsin State Journal*, which has a much larger circulation.

LaFollette was originally a Republican, and he and his sons ran sometimes as Progressives. Their descendants, familial and ideological, have all been Democrats since the early 1950s. Madison produced the state's most successful Democrats—former Senators William Proxmire and Gaylord Nelson, and former governor Patrick Lucey who ended his electoral career as John Anderson's running mate in the 1980 presidential election. In the early 1970s, the student vote made Madison and Dane County an especially liberal constituency, but their long tradition has always been progressive, and in the 1980s Dane County has been casting higher percentages of votes than the Milwaukee metropolitan area.

Madison is the center of Wisconsin's 2d Congressional District; Madison and surrounding Dane County cast two-thirds of the district's votes. The rest are in several rural dairy counties which are all more Republican and conservative; but they've never been enough to outvote Madison. Since 1958, the congressman from the 2d District has been Robert Kastenmeier, and for most of that time he has been one of the most liberal members of the House. But he is not one of the most voluble or flamboyant; quite the contrary. Temperamentally, Kastenmeier is deliberate, quiet, careful, almost plodding. Legislatively, he has specialized in the arcane issue of copyright law which, like so many things, is more important than it sounds: just a few words or even a comma in a statute can make millions of dollars of difference for moviemakers or novelists, composers or computer program writers.

Kastenmeier's one moment in the national spotlight came in the 1974 hearings on the impeachment of Richard Nixon. As the fourth-ranking Democrat on Judiciary, Kastenmeier was considered the most senior member absolutely sure to vote for impeachment. He made an important contribution to the proceedings by insisting that each article of impeachment be voted on separately, after evidence pertaining to it was discussed. Some of the Republicans and conservative Democrats favoring impeachment wanted to wait and hold all the roll calls at the end, as if somehow people wouldn't notice then. But Kastenmeier's role ensured an orderly procedure and kept the evidence and the voting closely tied together in people's minds.

Kastenmeier is now the second ranking Democrat on Judiciary, just behind Chairman Jack Brooks. But Brooks, who just ascended to the seat in 1989, has shown no propensity to retire. In the meantime, Kastenmeier has shouldered responsibilities accordingly. In 1983 and 1984, he helped solve the problem caused by the elevation of bankruptcy referees to the status of federal judges. In 1986, he framed the impeachment resolution against Harry Claiborne, the imprisoned federal judge who refused to resign; Claiborne was impeached by the House and convicted by the Senate. Also in 1986, he got Congress to extend wiretap protections to cellular phone and electronic mail communications. Kastenmeier has successfully pushed for the U.S. to become a signatory to the Berne Convention, the international copyright treaty, and he favored the Satellite Home Viewer Copyright Act which would increase viewer access to television signals in rural areas.

Kastenmeier's long tenure suggests that he has a safe district. Actually, his percentages in the 2d are sometimes small, well below 60% in 1980 and 1986, 59% in 1988. The district is very polarized between liberal Dane County and the Republican rural counties. But the balance has always been in Kastenmeier's favor: he may lose the rural counties, as he did 52%–48% in 1988, but he usually carries Dane County by a bigger margin—64%–36% in this case. This is, after all, a nationally Democratic district, voting not only for Carter in 1976 and Dukakis in 1988, but for Mondale in 1984 and McGovern in 1972. So it seems likely that Kastenmeier will be able to continue his workmanlike and constructive career in the House.

The People: Est. Pop. 1986: 549,100, up 5.0% 1980–86; Pop. 1980: 523,011, up 9.8% 1970–80. Households (1980): 68% family, 37% with children, 59% married couples; 37.4% housing units rented; median monthly rent: $211; median house value: $53,900. Voting age pop. (1980): 383,086; 1% Black, 1% Asian origin, 1% Spanish origin.

1988 Presidential Vote:

Dukakis (D)	145,141	(55%)
Bush (R)	114,114	(44%)

Rep. Robert W. Kastenmeier (D)

Elected 1958; b. Jan. 24, 1924, Beaver Dam; home, Sun Prairie; U. of WI, LL.B. 1952; No religious affil.; married (Dorothy).

Career: Practicing atty., 1952–58.

Offices: 2328 RHOB 20515, 202-225-2906. Also 119 Martin Luther King Blvd., Ste. 505, Madison 53703, 608-264-5206.

Committees: *Judiciary* (2d of 21 D). Subcommittees: Civil and Constitutional Rights; Courts, Intellectual Property, and the Administration of Justice (Chairman). *Permanent Select Committee on Intelligence* (3d of 12 D). Subcommittees: Legislation; Program and Budget Authorization.

Group Ratings

	ADA	ACLU	COPE	CFA	LCV	ACU	NTLC	NSI	COC	CEI
1988	100	91	90	100	94	4	15	0	36	14
1987	100	—	90	79	—	0	—	—	0	12

National Journal Ratings

	1988 LIB — 1988 CONS		1987 LIB — 1987 CONS	
Economic	71% —	23%	73% —	0%
Social	86% —	0%	73% —	22%
Foreign	84% —	0%	73% —	26%

Key Votes

1) Homeless $	AGN	5) Ban Drug Test	AGN	9) SDI Research	AGN
2) Gephardt Amdt	FOR	6) Drug Death Pen	AGN	10) Ban Chem Weaps	FOR
3) Deficit Reduc	FOR	7) Handgun Sales	AGN	11) Aid to Contras	AGN
4) Kill Plnt Clsng Notice	AGN	8) Ban D.C. Abort $	AGN	12) Nuclear Testing	FOR

Election Results

1988 general	Robert W. Kastenmeier (D)	151,501	(59%)	($440,574)
	Ann Haney (R)......................	107,457	(41%)	($380,785)
1988 primary	Robert W. Kastenmeier (D), unopposed			
1986 general	Robert W. Kastenmeier (D)	106,919	(56%)	($385,947)
	Ann Haney (R)......................	85,156	(44%)	($271,007)

THIRD DISTRICT

On the rolling land of western Wisconsin, in the knobby hills just east of the Mississippi River, near some of the nation's most beautiful river landscape, is the site where Laura Ingalls Wilder's family's "little house in the big woods" was built in the 1870s, before the first railroad came steaming up on the narrow floodplain alongside the Mississippi River below. Today, it is hard to imagine the big woods: the trees have long since been cut down, and the hillsides are covered with green grass and grazed on by placid dairy cows. Where the pioneers tried to scratch out diversified crops, farmers today in western Wisconsin have made this the premier dairying region in America, a place where the minerals in the soil produce such good milk and butter and especially cheese. It is hard to think of another industry as benign. Dairy products are healthful, carefully regulated to guard against spoilage and are necessities for most babies and growing children. Its waste products are nontoxic and biodegradable; its business is conducted in pleasant surroundings, away from crowded cities; it does not withdraw land from other productive activities. Who can complain?

The taxpayers and the dairy farmers, and not necessarily in that order. For the dairy industry in America is in terrible trouble. First, because there's less demand for milk: there are fewer children in this country today than in the 1950s; more adults worry about cholesterol; and it is likely that a lower proportion of Americans are descended from the northern European stock that carries the genes for the enzymes needed for adults to digest milk. Second, affluence has reduced the demand for powdered milk and other dairy solids, which used to be one of the country's major products of the dairy industry. The final problem is that the industry has become too productive. It takes fewer cows, which thanks to selective breeding can produce torrents of milk, and fewer farmers to create the same amount of total output as dairy farms did in the 1950s. In these circumstances, dairy farmers have done what any group of American entrepreneurs would do: they have gone to the government for aid. Dairy farmers and processors have long been organized in cooperatives, and these co-ops became brilliant lobbyists and campaign contributors by the 1970s; they worked Democrats and Republicans alike to increase dairy subsidies and price supports. As a result, by the early 1980s the government had mountains of cheese and powdered milk it literally could not give away.

The politics of dairy subsidies is nowhere of greater concern than in the 3d Congressional District of Wisconsin, which hugs the eastern bank of the Mississippi River from the Illinois border to the outskirts of Minneapolis-St. Paul. This is probably the nation's number one dairy district. It was settled largely by German and Scandinavian immigrants (Laura's Yankee family may have moved west to get away from the Swedes), and it used to vote for LaFollette Progressives. More recently, it has been sharply contested partisan territory, Democratic in the Watergate years, Republican in the years around 1980, Democratic again in 1988, when 14 of the 16 counties wholly or partially in the 3d district voted for Michael Dukakis over George Bush.

After two partisan changes in 1974 and 1980, however, the 3d District remains Republican in the House, thanks to the popularity and ingenuity of Congressman Steve Gunderson. First elected in 1980 at 29, Gunderson supported the Reagan budget and tax cuts, but very quickly distanced himself from any proposals to cut dairy price supports. He got a seat on the Agriculture Committee and is now ranking member on the Livestock, Dairy and Poultry Subcommittee, a body stocked with dairy program lovers. When he went into the Oval Office after voting against the Reagan tax bill in December 1985, he started talking dairy cows and got the President's assurance that he would sign the farm bill before the congressman agreed to support the tax bill. He became an activist on other issues as well, sponsoring the law to make the federal telecommunication system accessible to the deaf, sponsoring an environmental management system for the upper Mississippi and championing the causes of rural hospitals and growth in western Wisconsin.

Gunderson is hard-working and hard-charging, partisan but not uniformly conservative, flexible enough to have consolidated his hold on a district whose depressed economy has led it to trend toward the Democrats, much like neighboring Iowa, in the 1980s. He carried a Dukakis district by more than 2 to 1 in 1988. Yet in March 1989, after Newt Gingrich was elected Republican whip, Gunderson was selected as one of two chief deputy whips. Mentioned earlier as a candidate for the Senate, Gunderson is now one of the leading Republicans in the House, with a vested interest in expanding Republican ranks toward a majority.

The People: Est. Pop. 1986: 539,800, up 3.2% 1980–86; Pop. 1980: 522,909, up 13.4% 1970–80. Households (1980): 73% family, 40% with children, 64% married couples; 27.3% housing units rented; median monthly rent: $162; median house value: $41,700. Voting age pop. (1980): 374,265.

1988 Presidential Vote:

Dukakis (D).............	126,354	(52%)
Bush (R).............	112,830	(47%)

Rep. Steve Gunderson (R)

Elected 1980; b. May 10, 1951, Eau Claire; home, Osseo; U. of WI, B.A. 1973, Brown Sch. of Broadcasting, 1974; Lutheran; single.

Career: WI Assembly, 1974–79.

Offices: 227 CHOB 20515, 202-225-5506. Also 438 N. Water St., Black River Falls 54615, 715-284-7431.

Committees: *Agriculture* (9th of 18 R). Subcommittees: Conservation, Credit, and Rural Development; Livestock, Dairy, and Poultry (Ranking Member); Tobacco and Peanuts. *Education and Labor* (5th of 13 R). Subcommittees: Elementary, Secondary, and Vocational Education; Employment Opportunities (Ranking Member); Postsecondary Education.

Group Ratings

	ADA	ACLU	COPE	CFA	LCV	ACU	NTLC	NSI	COC	CEI
1988	45	35	31	55	56	54	76	90	71	41
1987	20	—	25	29	—	65	—	—	86	62

National Journal Ratings

	1988 LIB — 1988 CONS		1987 LIB — 1987 CONS	
Economic	38%	62%	11%	83%
Social	40%	58%	34%	65%
Foreign	35%	64%	33%	65%

Key Votes

1) Homeless $	FOR	5) Ban Drug Test	FOR	9) SDI Research	FOR
2) Gephardt Amdt	AGN	6) Drug Death Pen	FOR	10) Ban Chem Weaps	AGN
3) Deficit Reduc	AGN	7) Handgun Sales	FOR	11) Aid to Contras	FOR
4) Kill Plnt Clsng Notice	AGN	8) Ban D.C. Abort $	FOR	12) Nuclear Testing	AGN

Election Results

1988 general	Steve Gunderson (R)	157,513	(68%)	($359,801)
	Karl Krueger (D)	72,935	(32%)	($22,626)
1988 primary	Steve Gunderson, unopposed			
1986 general	Steve Gunderson (R)	104,393	(64%)	($311,707)
	Leland E. Mulder (D)	58,445	(36%)	($62,459)

FOURTH DISTRICT

The south side of Milwaukee, criss-crossed by railroads, bounded by the factory zone around the Menomonee River that goes through the center of town and the harbor facing Lake Michigan to the east, has always been the city's blue-collar side. In outward appearance, it has changed little in a half-century: it is full of massive factories which require precision work and neighborhoods with sturdy houses that withstand northern winters and streets lined with bars emblazoned with beer signs. Here you can find Milwaukee's prototypical Polish neighborhoods, but they are not the whole south side: more people here claim German ancestry than Polish, and for decades younger families have spread out from the old neighborhoods into the suburbs of Milwaukee County and Waukesha County to the west. The 4th Congressional District of Wisconsin, which has been the south side district since 1892, has also spread out, matching the geographic spread and socioeconomic rise of the children of the south side, to the point where 60% of the people here live outside Milwaukee now. This was long the only securely Democratic part of Wisconsin, and has retained its Democratic preference, though sometimes narrowly in presidential races.

The congressman from the 4th District is a product of the south side, Gerald Kleczka. He seems to be one of those House members to whom politics comes naturally. He was elected to the Wisconsin Assembly in 1967 at age 24, was elected to the state Senate in 1974 and was co-chairman of the Joint Committee on Finance from 1979 to 1984. When Clement Zablocki, an old-style big city Democrat who served for 35 years and chaired the Foreign Affairs Committee, died suddenly in 1983, Kleczka was an obvious candidate to succeed him. In the April 1984 special election primary, he had serious competition from Clerk of Court Gary Barczak, a former Zablocki aide running as a conservative, from suburban state Senator Lynn Adelman who had run strong races against Bob Kasten in the 1974 general and Zablocki in the 1982 primary, and from Michael McCann, Milwaukee County District Attorney since 1968. Kleczka won the primary with 31% of the vote and has won easily ever since.

In the House, he has emerged, since an initial learning period, as a serious legislator, even though he failed to get a seat on Energy and Commerce in 1987. He is one of the sponsors of the bill to allow IRA funds to be used for down payments on homes for first time home buyers, and he is a staunch backer of a higher minimum wage. On the Banking subcommittee which considered the savings and loan crisis, he bucked chairman Frank Annunzio and voted to tighten regulation. After the accord between the government of Poland and Solidarity in April 1989, he urged the Overseas Private Investment Corporation to insure investments in Poland. In his third decade as a legislator, he seems headed for a long House career.

The People: Est. Pop. 1986: 518,800, dn. 0.8% 1980–86; Pop. 1980: 522,880, dn. 1.0% 1970–80. Households (1980): 73% family, 38% with children, 61% married couples; 38.5% housing units rented; median monthly rent: $210; median house value: $59,900. Voting age pop. (1980): 381,822; 3% Spanish origin.

1988 Presidential Vote: Dukakis (D). 140,826   (56%)
Bush (R) 108,994   (43%)

Rep. Gerald D. Kleczka (D)

Elected April, 1984; b. Nov. 26, 1943, Milwaukee; home, Milwaukee; U. of WI; Roman Catholic; married (Bonnie).

Career: Medic, WI Air Nat'l Guard, 1963–69; WI Assembly, 1968–72; WI Senate, 1974–84, Asst. Major. Ldr., 1977–82.

Offices: 226 CHOB 20515, 202-225-4572. Also 5032 W. Forest Home Ave., Milwaukee 53219, 414-291-1140; and 817 Clinton St., Waukesha 53186, 414-549-6360.

Committees: *Banking, Finance and Urban Affairs* (19th of 31 D). Subcommittees: Financial Institutions Supervision, Regulation and Insurance; Housing and Community Development; International Development, Finance, Trade and Monetary Policy. *Government Operations* (18th of 24 D). Subcommittees: Government Activities and Transportation; Legislation and National Security.

Group Ratings

	ADA	ACLU	COPE	CFA	LCV	ACU	NTLC	NSI	COC	CEI
1988	95	82	84	91	75	4	8	0	36	14
1987	84	—	81	93	—	5	—	—	13	7

National Journal Ratings

	1988 LIB — 1988 CONS	1987 LIB — 1987 CONS
Economic	87% — 8%	73% — 0%
Social	68% — 31%	66% — 32%
Foreign	84% — 0%	81% — 0%

Key Votes

1) Homeless $	AGN	5) Ban Drug Test	AGN	9) SDI Research	AGN
2) Gephardt Amdt	FOR	6) Drug Death Pen	AGN	10) Ban Chem Weaps	FOR
3) Deficit Reduc	FOR	7) Handgun Sales	AGN	11) Aid to Contras	AGN
4) Kill Plnt Clsng Notice	AGN	8) Ban D.C. Abort $	FOR	12) Nuclear Testing	FOR

Election Results

1988 general	Gerald D. Kleczka (D)	177,283	(100%)	($144,925)
1988 primary	Gerald D. Kleczka (D), unopposed			
1986 general	Gerald D. Kleczka (D)	120,354	(100%)	($93,749)

FIFTH DISTRICT

Fifty years ago, Milwaukee still was the German-American capital of the United States. In City Hall a Socialist mayor governed, elected by solid German-American blue and white-collar workers who believe in efficient, honest, and active government. German was still spoken on the streets and read in newspapers, German beer was brewed in dozens of breweries big and small and German cultural traditions breathed in churches, union halls and parlors. Today, the German heritage is more subtle. But you can see it in the names of beers and in signs over stores; you can enjoy it in the remaining German restaurants; there is a hint of it in the solidity of the buildings and the order of its streets.

For most Americans in the late 20th century, mention of German traditions summons up memories of Hitler and *junker* generals; but there were other German traditions which thrived in Milwaukee and Wisconsin. Germans in the late 19th century pioneered university education, scientific disciplines, technologically advanced industries like chemicals and electric engineering; they also pioneered in social insurance and income taxation, the growth of a humane and vigorous welfare state. These traditions helped to inspire the Wisconsin progressivism of Robert LaFollette; and they reached their most notable form in Milwaukee's Socialist tradition and in the politics of the 5th congressional district of Wisconsin which, since 1892, has been Milwaukee's north side district. One of the most heavily German districts in the United States, it elected Socialist Victor Berger to the House in 1910 and in every election from 1918 to 1926. Berger was denied his seat in Congress after the 1918 and 1920 elections because of his opposition to World War I; in 1919, he was sentenced to 20 years in prison for writing antiwar articles. Berger, like the LaFollettes and many German-origin Wisconsin voters, did not want the United States to intervene on the side of Britain and France against Germany, and opposition to wars with Germany was a major feature of Wisconsin politics—the root of its isolationism—from 1916 until at least 1946. Feeling in the 5th District was strong enough that Berger was reelected to Congress while his case was on appeal and after he had been denied his seat.

Today, some of the north side neighborhoods are black; 28% of 5th District residents were black in 1980, and they made up 81% of Wisconsin's black population. But most of the 5th District, which includes the pleasant, 1950s-ish subdivisions in the far northwest part of Milwaukee, the suburb of Wauwatosa and a couple of affluent suburbs near the lake shore, are white and middle-class. From the city's Socialist and the state's Progressive traditions, it has drawn its current Democratic preference.

The 5th District's congressman, Jim Moody, does not have roots in old German Milwaukee. He came to the city as a professor in 1973, was elected to the legislature in 1976, and when Representative Henry Reuss, chairman of the Banking and Joint Economic Committees, retired after 28 years of service in 1982, Moody was one of 11 candidates who ran in the Democratic primary. A loner in Madison, without much support from local politicos, he campaigned hard door to door and, among the six candidates who finished close together, ran ahead with 19% of the vote.

Moody entered the House with a reputation as a maverick, and sometimes lived up to it, voting against farm programs and for cost-sharing on water projects. But he has more often taken stands on issues pleasing to leading Democrats. Although never on the Foreign Affairs Committee, he has maintained a lively interest in foreign policy. He was one of three Democrats who visited the Soviet radar station in Krasnoyarsk, and said he found no evidence that it was violating the ABM treaty. He has peppered Republican administrations with demands for more progress in getting arms control agreements. He hailed Chester Crocker's success in Southwest Africa negotiations, and called for a bipartisan Africa policy. He pleased Ways and Means chairman Rostenkowski enough by his support of tax reform in 1985 and 1986 to get a seat on that committee in 1987. In 1988, he was the only Democratic member of the Ways and Means Committee to vote for the Pepper long-term health care bill. And in 1989, he was loudly proclaiming his support of the much-attacked congressional pay raise.

In between, Moody made some feints at running for the Senate. He passed up the 1986 race against Bob Kasten, and then entered the race for William Proxmire's seat in 1987. But when Herb Kohl's multi-million dollar media campaign and his local celebrity gave him a clear lead in Milwaukee, Moody realized that he had lost his base and jumped out of the Senate race and back into the contest for the House. He won handily enough, with 64%, and seems to have a lifetime seat in the House.

The People: Est. Pop. 1986: 499,600, dn. 4.4% 1980–86; Pop. 1980: 522,854, dn. 10.0% 1970–80. Households (1980): 64% family, 34% with children, 46% married couples; 52.1% housing units rented; median monthly rent: $190; median house value: $50,700. Voting age pop. (1980): 381,248; 22% Black, 2% Spanish origin, 1% Asian origin.

1988 Presidential Vote:

Dukakis (D)	145,028	(64%)
Bush (R)	80,649	(35%)

Rep. Jim Moody (D)

Elected 1982; b. Sept. 2, 1935, Richlands, VA; home, Milwaukee; Haverford Col., B.A. 1957, JFK Sch. of Govt., Harvard U., M.P.A. 1967, U. of CA at Berkeley, Ph.D. 1973; Protestant; divorced.

Career: Field Rep., CARE, Yugoslavia, 1958–59, Iran, 1960; Peace Corps, Pakistan and Wash., D.C., 1961–64; A.I.D., 1965–67; Economist, U.S. Dept. of Transportation, 1967–1969; Asst. Prof., U. of WI, 1973–77; WI Assembly, 1977–78; WI Senate, 1979–82.

Offices: 1019 LHOB 20515, 202-225-3571. Also 135 W. Wells St., Ste. 618, Milwaukee 53202, 414-291-1331.

Committees: *Ways and Means* (23d of 23 D). Subcommittees: Health; Social Security.

Group Ratings

	ADA	ACLU	COPE	CFA	LCV	ACU	NTLC	NSI	COC	CEI
1988	80	89	92	73	81	5	21	0	23	10
1987	84	—	90	85	—	0	—	—	27	14

National Journal Ratings

	1988 LIB — 1988 CONS		1987 LIB — 1987 CONS	
Economic	79%	— 17%	73%	— 0%
Social	81%	— 19%	72%	— 27%
Foreign	84%	— 0%	81%	— 0%

Key Votes

1) Homeless $	—	5) Ban Drug Test		9) SDI Research	AGN
2) Gephardt Amdt	FOR	6) Drug Death Pen	AGN	10) Ban Chem Weaps	FOR
3) Deficit Reduc	FOR	7) Handgun Sales	AGN	11) Aid to Contras	AGN
4) Kill Plnt Clsng Notice	AGN	8) Ban D.C. Abort $	AGN	12) Nuclear Testing	—

Election Results

1988 general	Jim Moody (D)	140,518	(64%)	($1,278,526)
	Helen I. Barnhill (R)	78,307	(36%)	($197,460)
1988 primary	Jim Moody (D)	47,789	(59%)	
	Matthew J. Flynn (D)	19,906	(25%)	
	Donald Sykes (D)	5,314	(7%)	
	Terrence Pitts (D)	4,966	(6%)	
	Two others	3,067	(4%)	
1986 general	Jim Moody (D)	109,506	(99%)	($302,442)

SIXTH DISTRICT

Fifty years ago, central Wisconsin was one of the most solidly prosperous and self-sufficient parts of a nation that was just emerging from depression. It produced basic commodities: milk, butter and other dairy products, paper and paper products, overalls and other clothing, machinery and other solid factory products. Settled first by Yankee Protestants, it was one of the birthplaces of the Republican Party in 1854, when a group of Whigs, Free Soilers and Democrats, meeting in a small white schoolhouse in Ripon, Wisconsin, proclaimed themselves

Republicans. Jackson, Michigan also claims to be the birthplace of the party; whichever is right, its growth was phenomenal: Republicans had success in the congressional elections of 1854 and nominated their first presidential ticket in 1856.

But Republicanism's roots here are not just Yankee. The 1850s was the decade of the first surge of German migration into the United States, and central Wisconsin became one of the favorite German destinations. Here they built the dairy farms and factory towns that seemed so solidly prosperous 50 years ago, though they have not grown as fast as the nation, and though dairy farming has become heavily subsidized, remain solidly prosperous today. The 6th Congressional District of Wisconsin, which cuts a swath across the state from Manitowoc through Oshkosh and Ripon west almost to the Mississippi River, includes country which has voted Republican almost uninterruptedly since that meeting in Ripon in March 1854.

It has also elected Republican congressmen who have come up with thoughtful and original solutions to problems. One was William Steiger, first elected in 1966, whose chief monuments are the all-volunteer military and the 1978 Steiger amendment cutting capital gains tax rates—considerable accomplishments for a member of the minority party, and for one who died young. Another is Thomas Petri, who won the 1979 special election to succeed Steiger by a narrow margin and has held the seat easily ever since. He specializes in thoughtful original proposals which cut across the usual ideological and party lines.

On Public Works and on the floor, he has argued for a more rational water projects policy. He pushed through a cost-sharing provision requiring local governments to pay part of the cost of federal water projects. He spoke out against special provisions on a water bill mandating low flood insurance rates for Sacramento. With George Miller of California, he opposed the Animas-La Plata compromise settlement which would have given Colorado Indians more water to produce crops already in surplus.

Petri's major cause in the 101st Congress is strengthening the Earned Income Tax Credit. This is a device that cuts the taxes of the working poor, and Petri argues that it targets aid to needy family heads far better than a higher minimum wage, most of whose beneficiaries are teenagers and young adults who are not heads of families. He has attracted support from Democrats as well as Republicans, and this may be an idea whose time has come. But he was also preoccupied, as one who agreed to take an Ethics Committee seat in 1987, with the case against Jim Wright.

The People: Est. Pop. 1986: 542,000, up 3.7% 1980–86; Pop. 1980: 522,477, up 7.5% 1970–80. Households (1980): 75% family, 40% with children, 67% married couples; 25.1% housing units rented; median monthly rent: $158; median house value: $41,100. Voting age pop. (1980): 370,486; 1% Spanish origin.

1988 Presidential Vote:　　Bush (R) . . . . 127,820　　(54%)

　　　　　　　　　　　　　　　Dukakis (D). . . . . 106,953　　(45%)

Rep. Thomas E. Petri (R)

Elected Apr. 3, 1979; b. May 28, 1940, Marinette; home, Fond du Lac; Harvard U., B.A. 1962, J.D. 1965; Lutheran; married (Anne).

Career: Law Clerk to Fed. Judge James Doyle, 1965–66; Peace Corps, Somalia, 1966–67; White House aide, 1969; WI Senate, 1973–79; Practicing atty., 1970–79.

Offices: 2443 RHOB 20515, 202-225-2476. Also 14 Western Ave., Fond du Lac, 54935, 414-922-1180; and 105 Washington Ave., Oshkosh 54901, 414-231-6333.

Committees: *Education and Labor* (3d of 13 R). Subcommittees: Elementary, Secondary and Vocational Education; Labor–Management Relations; Labor Standards (Ranking Member). *Public Works and Transportation* (7th of 20 R). Subcommittees: Aviation; Public Buildings and Grounds (Ranking Member); Water Resources. *Standards of Official Conduct* (4th of 6 R).

Group Ratings

	ADA	ACLU	COPE	CFA	LCV	ACU	NTLC	NSI	COC	CEI
1988	35	35	26	36	56	75	85	90	79	68
1987	16	—	23	21	—	61	—	—	80	73

National Journal Ratings

	1988 LIB	—	1988 CONS	1987 LIB	—	1987 CONS
Economic	26%	—	73%	19%	—	78%
Social	26%	—	73%	36%	—	64%
Foreign	38%	—	61%	38%	—	62%

Key Votes

1) Homeless $	FOR	5) Ban Drug Test	AGN	9) SDI Research	FOR
2) Gephardt Amdt	AGN	6) Drug Death Pen	FOR	10) Ban Chem Weaps	AGN
3) Deficit Reduc	AGN	7) Handgun Sales	FOR	11) Aid to Contras	FOR
4) Kill Plnt Clsng Notice	AGN	8) Ban D.C. Abort $	FOR	12) Nuclear Testing	AGN

Election Results

1988 general	Thomas E. Petri (R)	165,923	(74%)	($187,714)
	Joseph Garrett (D)	57,552	(26%)	($17,815)
1988 primary	Thomas E. Petri (R), unopposed			
1986 general	Thomas E. Petri (R)	124,328	(97%)	($106,394)
	John Richard Daggett (I)	4,268	(3%)	

SEVENTH DISTRICT

On the rail lines radiating northwest from Chicago and Milwaukee in the late 19th century, came thousands of migrants whose ancestors have made the northern reaches of Wisconsin the most thickly settled land this far north in the United States east of the Mississippi. What brought people up so far was not farmland—there are no acres of industrial-sized wheat farms as in the Red River Valley of Minnesota and North Dakota—but trees. This was one of America's largest virgin timberlands, and the towns on the rivers are dotted with paper mills still. Then it was iron, in the far north near Lake Superior, that brought people to the port of Superior, Wisconsin, right next to Duluth, Minnesota and to smaller towns on the chilly lake. And finally, there are dairy cows: properly cared for, they can thrive in these northern uplands, and it was natural for the sons of Wisconsin dairymen, many of them immigrants from Germany or Norway, to move their dairy herds farther north. On this base, small cities grew up, and even some big enterprises. The town of Wausau, for example, is the home of the Wausau insurance company, while the entrepreneur who designed the Cray supercomputers for years lived and worked in Chippewa Falls. Uncommon ethnic groups came here, like the Finns of Superior and the Poles of Stevens Point.

All these places are in Wisconsin's 7th Congressional District, which stretches from a point not far from Green Bay or Madison in the south up to Lake Superior in the north. The politics of northern Wisconsin and the 7th District has always had a rough-hewn quality about it, a certain populist flavor; although this is an ancestrally Republican area, it is also part of the state that always favored the progressivism of the LaFollettes. Superior and Stevens Point are heavily Democratic, while much of the country in between leans Republican.

The congressman from the 7th District is David Obey, one of the most accomplished and effective of his generation of legislators in the House. He is one of those natural politicians who won a seat in the legislature the year he finished graduate school, in 1962 at age 24. He was elected to the House in something of an upset in a 1969 special election, in the seat vacated by Defense Secretary Melvin Laird. By 1972, when he was placed in the same district as a 30-year incumbent Republican with a liberal record, he won with 63% of the vote. Obey is reelected every two years by wide margins, and seems to be widely popular in this district.

Not all of Obey's work has made him popular in the House, however. He has a prickly personality and a vigorous temper and does not suffer those he considers fools or knaves gladly: when Congressman Robert Walker was attaching his unenforceable "drug-free workplace" amendment to bills in 1988, Obey proposed adding to it zero tolerance for bribery, tax evasion, graft and price fixing—a bitter response to a measure Obey considered "a laughable piece of garbage." Some of the causes he champions are almost guaranteed to be unpopular. In 1977 and 1978, he chaired a special committee on ethics and came up with a new code that was backed by reformers and passed by the House, requiring detailed disclosure of personal finances and limiting outside income to a percentage of the congressional salary. This hit luxury-loving and tuition-paying Members where it hurt, and miffed a lot of his colleagues; but he got it through. Yet in 1989, he insisted that the House Ethics Committee counsel misinterpreted these rules in making his case against Jim Wright. Starting in 1979, he was the chief sponsor of bills to change the campaign finance laws to limit PAC contributions, and he actually got a bill through the House in the Carter years, only to see it killed in the Senate. For most of the 1980s, Members have been more interested in collecting PAC funds than in restricting them, but Obey persisted and, in the late 1980s, was still pressing this cause.

Obey has also been a leader in promoting traditional Democratic economic policies in years when they have been under fierce and often effective attack. In 1979, he was elected head of the liberal Democratic Study Group, just as the tax revolt was beginning and the demand for new domestic spending programs disappearing. After the 1980 elections, he came within one vote of becoming Budget Committee chairman; he tied James Jones of Oklahoma twice and finally lost to him on the third ballot by a 121–116 margin. Jones tried to concoct budget resolutions that could pass the House with virtually unanimous Democratic support, a course his successor William Gray has followed. Obey's course, suggested by the budget proposal he presented in 1982, would have been to advance a Democratic plan that contrasted sharply with the Republicans' proposal, to risk losing in the House but having a platform to take before the voters.

In 1985, after Gillis Long died on inauguration day, Obey succeeded to the chair of the Joint Economic Committee, and used it as a platform for disseminating his views on how the economy is working. Two of the studies he commissioned were cited and used again and again by Democratic leaders: one depicting the decline in family (as opposed to per capita) income since the early 1970s and the other describing what it called a "bicoastal economy," in which the East and West Coasts of America have grown smartly in the 1980s while the vast heartland in between has lagged behind or seen its economy contract. Some of Obey's studies have been attacked sharply by conservative economists, and one—a study purporting to show an increased concentration of wealth—was withdrawn by the committee. Another argued that the economy is creating too many low-wage and not enough middle-income jobs, but this was criticized for using as end points two years which present a picture different from those of any other two end-point years. The Obey JEC did not settle the raging argument over whether the economy of the Reagan years was producing enough growth evenly across the economic strata and geographic regions of the country; but it was a vigorous participant in the debate.

Obey brings similar attitudes to his major ongoing committee assignment, the chairmanship of the Foreign Operations Subcommittee of the Appropriations Committee. The foreign aid budget which it superintends had, by the time Obey became chairman in 1985, become dominated by huge amounts of aid for Israel and Egypt, and by military aid which increased rapidly in the first Reagan term. Humanitarian aid to poor countries had long been caught in a squeeze. Obey believes that military aid tends to be counterproductive and favors greater humanitarian aid; and he has not been afraid to cut into the Israel and Egypt requests, which have a strong American constituency, in order to preserve more for programs which he thinks do more good, like the Peace Corps, UNICEF and the Vitamin A deficiency program. Obey has also inserted some provisions that help Wisconsin, like an amendment selling surplus dairy products to China.

On the full Appropriations Committee Obey is now the fifth ranking Democrat, and much younger than those who are senior members: he turns 52 in 1990, and they turn 80, 81, 70 and 81. He has every chance to be chairman some day, and for a long time. In that role he can be expected to be punctilious about detail, scornful of cheap shots, tough, sometimes angry and often effective in negotiations.

Republicans have sometimes talked of giving Obey serious opposition, but they have not done so since 1972. His 1986 and 1988 opponent was Kevin Hermening who, as a Marine guard, was one of the hostages at the Tehran embassy. Obey won easily, and in his third decade as a legislator, he is still angered by what he regards as foolishness but doesn't seem fazed by the battering some of his ideas have taken in the political marketplace in the 1980s. Instead, he seems to look forward to a more propitious 1990s.

The People: Est. Pop. 1986: 533,000, up 2.0% 1980–86; Pop. 1980: 522,623, up 11.9% 1970–80. Households (1980): 75% family, 41% with children, 66% married couples; 24.0% housing units rented; median monthly rent: $158; median house value: $38,100. Voting age pop. (1980): 366,683; 1% American Indian.

1988 Presidential Vote: Dukakis (D)......................128,849   (54%)
Bush (R).........................108,341   (45%)

Rep. David R. Obey (D)

Elected Apr. 1, 1969; b. Oct. 3, 1938, Okmulgee, OK; home, Wausau; U. WI, B.S. 1960, M.A. 1962; Roman Catholic; married (Joan).

Career: Real estate broker; Family supper club and motel; WI Assembly, 1963–69.

Offices: 2462 RHOB 20515, 202-225-3365. Also Fed. Bldg., 317 First St., Wausau 54401, 715-842-5606.

Committees: *Appropriations* (5th of 35 D). Subcommittees: Foreign Operations, Export Financing and Related Programs (Chairman); Labor–Health and Human Services–Education; Legislative. *Joint Economic Committee.* Task Forces: Economic Resources and Competitiveness (Chairman); Fiscal and Monetary Policy; National Security Economics.

Group Ratings

	ADA	ACLU	COPE	CFA	LCV	ACU	NTLC	NSI	COC	CEI
1988	90	91	87	91	94	4	6	0	9	9
1987	100	—	87	79	—	0	—	—	0	10

National Journal Ratings

	1988 LIB — 1988 CONS		1987 LIB — 1987 CONS	
Economic	79%	— 17%	73%	— 0%
Social	86%	— 14%	78%	— 0%
Foreign	84%	— 0%	81%	— 0%

Key Votes

1) Homeless $	AGN	5) Ban Drug Test	AGN	9) SDI Research	AGN
2) Gephardt Amdt	FOR	6) Drug Death Pen	AGN	10) Ban Chem Weaps	FOR
3) Deficit Reduc	FOR	7) Handgun Sales	FOR	11) Aid to Contras	AGN
4) Kill Plnt Clsng Notice	AGN	8) Ban D.C. Abort $	AGN	12) Nuclear Testing	FOR

Election Results

1988 general	David R. Obey (D)	142,197	(62%)	($450,716)
	Kevin J. Hermening (R)	86,077	(37%)	($202,591)
1988 primary	David R. Obey (D), unopposed			
1986 general	David R. Obey (D)	106,700	(62%)	($462,535)
	Kevin J. Hermening (R)	63,408	(37%)	($124,210)

EIGHTH DISTRICT

In 1673, the French explorer and priest Father Marquette sailed from the open waters of Lake Michigan into what is now Green Bay, Wisconsin. He hoped he had come upon the Northwest Passage to the Pacific; actually, what he found was the Fox River, which leads to Lake Winnebago and, after a not-too-difficult portage, the Wisconsin River that flows into the Mississippi. Green Bay and the Fox River Valley remained mostly wilderness and Indian country for more than 150 years. But since they have been settled, the Fox River Valley and Green Bay have been, as surely Father Marquette would like, one of the most heavily Catholic parts of the United States. Economically, Green Bay and the towns clustered around Appleton live off the paper mills and high-skill manufacturing; psychically, they live for the triumphs, present and past, of the Green Bay Packers, America's only municipally owned National Football League franchise.

Green Bay and the Fox River Valley make up most of the 8th Congressional District of Wisconsin. It includes also several north woods and dairy counties inland, plus the Door County peninsula that juts out into Lake Michigan and is a favorite summer vacation spot for Chicago and Milwaukee families. Politically, this has often been malleable country. Democrats, especially those with Catholic credentials, can win here: John Kennedy carried the Fox River Valley in the primary and general election in 1960, and the most recent Democratic congressman was Robert Cornell, a priest elected in 1974 and 1976. But the 8th District can go almost ferociously Republican: Appleton was the home of Senator Joseph McCarthy, who did so much to tar the good names of politics, Congress, conservatism and the Republican Party in the early 1950s.

The congressman from the 8th district is Toby Roth, a Republican whose first victory in 1978 was one of the less well-known harbingers of the conservative tide that swept the country in 1980. Roth has played a major role on one important piece of legislation; as ranking Republican on the Subcommittee on International Economic Policy and Trade, he helped frame export control legislation, and he has been the leading congressional advocate for the Pentagon position that severe restrictions are needed on the export of strategic products to the Soviet Union and Eastern Europe. He was successful in frustrating efforts to soften the law. He portrays himself as a trade expert and a supporter of free trade and holds an annual export conference in Green Bay. He has also been not only a critic of the totalitarian Mengistu regime in Ethiopia but a leader in trying to make sure that food aid does get through to the starving despite Mengistu's attempts to use it for political advantage.

Roth supports conservative and Administration positions on most issues but, in line with Wisconsin's longstanding skepticism about foreign military involvement, he criticized the stationing of U.S. troops in Lebanon in 1983 and the bombing of Libya in 1986. On the Banking Committee, which he joined in 1985, he favors deregulation of banks in several respects and has been harshly critical of the lenience toward savings and loans of former chairman Fernand St Germain and other members.

Roth won the seat in 1978 by beating Robert Cornell, a Catholic priest who won it in the Watergate year of 1974. Except for 1982, when former League of Women Voters president Ruth Clusen held him to 57% of the vote, Roth has won by large margins and, barring yet another political turnaround in the Fox River Valley, has a safe seat.

The People: Est. Pop. 1986: 549,800, up 5.1% 1980–86; Pop. 1980: 523,225, up 12.3% 1970–80. Households (1980): 76% family, 42% with children, 67% married couples; 25.0% housing units rented; median monthly rent: $169; median house value: $43,800. Voting age pop. (1980): 362,554; 2% American Indian.

1988 Presidential Vote: Bush (R) 132,358   (53%)
                              Dukakis (D). 117,238   (47%)

Rep. Toby Roth (R)

Elected 1978; b. Oct. 10, 1938, Strasburg, ND; home, Appleton; Marquette U., B.A. 1961; Roman Catholic; married (Barbara).

Career: Realtor; WI House of Reps., 1973–79.

Offices: 2352 RHOB 20515, 202-225-5665. Also 333 Main St. Ste. 505, Green Bay 54301, 414-433-3931; and 126 N. Oneida St., Appleton 54911, 414-739-4167.

Committees: *Banking, Finance and Urban Affairs* (12th of 20 R). Subcommittees: Economic Stabilization; Financial Institutions Supervision, Regulation and Insurance; Housing and Community Development; Policy Research and Insurance. *Foreign Affairs* (5th of 18 R). Subcommittees: Asian and Pacific Affairs; International Economic Policy and Trade (Ranking Member).

Group Ratings

	ADA	ACLU	COPE	CFA	LCV	ACU	NTLC	NSI	COC	CEI
1988	10	13	15	36	31	83	83	90	92	61
1987	4	—	13	29	—	91	—	—	100	69

National Journal Ratings

	1988 LIB — 1988 CONS	1987 LIB — 1987 CONS
Economic	26% — 73%	0% — 89%
Social	19% — 80%	0% — 90%
Foreign	30% — 67%	31% — 68%

Key Votes

1) Homeless $	FOR	5) Ban Drug Test	FOR	9) SDI Research	FOR
2) Gephardt Amdt	AGN	6) Drug Death Pen	FOR	10) Ban Chem Weaps	AGN
3) Deficit Reduc	AGN	7) Handgun Sales	FOR	11) Aid to Contras	FOR
4) Kill Plnt Clsng Notice	FOR	8) Ban D.C. Abort $	FOR	12) Nuclear Testing	AGN

Election Results

1988 general	Toby Roth (R)......................	167,275	(70%)	($227,823)
	Robert A. Baron (D)...................	72,708	(30%)	($14,421)
1988 primary	Toby Roth (R),unopposed			
1986 general	Toby Roth (R)......................	118,162	(67%)	($284,287)
	Paul Willems (D)	57,265	(33%)	($84,037)

NINTH DISTRICT

Fifty years ago, most of the land that is now the suburban and exurban ring around Milwaukee was dairy farmlands. Out into land once dotted only with dairy cows, past small tiny towns and small cities with long-established high-skill factories, several hundred thousand Milwaukeeans have moved over the past five decades. The standard explanations for suburbanization—white flight, escape from apartments—don't apply much here: there never have been all that many blacks in Milwaukee and there has always been space around its single-family homes. The better explanation is that suburbanization is just the latest form of urbanization, that in a growing city, young families will tend to move to the newest subdivisions, where most of the housing is available, and which tend to be built to their specifications. Moving out in disproportionate numbers will be the affluent. But the subdivisions and garden apartments of Mequon and Brookfield, of Germantown and Menomonee Falls and Pewaukee and Oconomowoc, are by no means entirely filled with the top stratum of society.

They are filled disproportionately, however, with Republicans, as any glance at the election results from the 9th Congressional District of Wisconsin will show. The 9th District is a kind of ring around Milwaukee, including most of its suburbs on the north, northwest and west sides, proceeding out past the latest developments a county or two further into small town and dairying country, and including factory towns like West Bend and Sheboygan. About two-thirds of the population is technically within the Milwaukee metropolitan area; but its actual boundary is hazy, and probably a larger percentage than one-third of the residents of this district think of themselves as residents of rural and small-town Wisconsin. This is Wisconsin's most Republican congressional district, the descendant of a seat first created in 1964.

The current congressman, James Sensenbrenner, was first elected in the conservative upsurge year of 1978. He started off spending much time on the floor objecting to Democratic moves and measures for his party; he has worked hard on the Judiciary Committee, usually, though not always, objecting to the Democrats' and the civil rights lobby's arguments. He is now the ranking minority member of the Judiciary subcommittee on Civil and Constitutional Rights—a frustrating assignment since chairman Don Edwards holds a rock-solid majority.

Sensenbrenner's abrasive personality and stickiness over details have sometimes limited his effectiveness. But he perseveres—and takes interesting stands on some issues. It was he who insisted on impeachment action against federal Judges Walter Nixon and Harry Claiborne after they were convicted of crimes. He is an opponent of the MX missile and a backer of the Strategic Defense Initiative. He long supported the National Rifle Association, but backed the "Brady amendment" calling for a seven-day waiting period for handgun sales. He has written a redistricting bill which would require states to set up bipartisan commissions to redraw congressional district lines. In response to the Chilean grape scare of 1989, he favors labeling produce with the country of origin.

Sensenbrenner was mentioned as a possible candidate for the Senate in 1988, when William Proxmire retired; but with a decade of seniority and a safe seat, he declined to make the race. His only tough race was the 1978 primary, in which he barely beat moderate Susan Engeleiter, who won the Republican nomination for the Senate herself in 1988, and then just barely lost the general, while Sensenbrenner was reelected easily.

The People: Est. Pop. 1986: 534,600, up 2.2% 1980–86; Pop. 1980: 522,950, up 14.8% 1970–80. Households (1980): 81% family, 46% with children, 73% married couples; 23.2% housing units rented; median monthly rent: $206; median house value: $66,900. Voting age pop. (1980): 360,879; 1% Spanish origin.

1988 Presidential Vote:

Bush (R)	155,018	(60%)
Dukakis (D)	102,327	(39%)

Rep. F. James Sensenbrenner, Jr. (R)

Elected 1978; b. June 14, 1943, Chicago, IL; home, Menomonee Falls; Stanford U., B.A. 1965, U. of WI, J.D. 1968; Episcopalian; married (Cheryl).

Career: Practicing atty.; Staff of U.S. Rep. Arthur Younger, 1965; WI Assembly, 1969–75; WI Senate, 1975–78.

Offices: 2444 RHOB 20515, 202-225-5101. Also 120 Bishops Way, Brookfield 53005, 414-784-1111.

Committees: *Judiciary* (4th of 14 R). Subcommittees: Civil and Constitutional Rights (Ranking Member); Courts, Intellectual Property, and the Administration of Justice. *Science, Space and Technology* (2d of 19 R). Subcommittees: International Scientific Cooperation; Space Science and Applications (Ranking Member). *Select Committee on Narcotics Abuse and Control* (5th of 12 R).

Group Ratings

	ADA	ACLU	COPE	CFA	LCV	ACU	NTLC	NSI	COC	CEI
1988	15	13	10	27	56	88	92	70	100	82
1987	8	—	9	29	—	91	—	—	93	82

National Journal Ratings

	1988 LIB — 1988 CONS	1987 LIB — 1987 CONS
Economic	10% — 88%	0% — 89%
Social	18% — 81%	10% — 85%
Foreign	36% — 63%	36% — 63%

Key Votes

1) Homeless $	FOR	5) Ban Drug Test	FOR	9) SDI Research	FOR
2) Gephardt Amdt	AGN	6) Drug Death Pen	FOR	10) Ban Chem Weaps	FOR
3) Deficit Reduc	—	7) Handgun Sales	AGN	11) Aid to Contras	FOR
4) Kill Plnt Clsng Notice	FOR	8) Ban D.C. Abort $	FOR	12) Nuclear Testing	AGN

Election Results

1988 general	F. James Sensenbrenner, Jr. (R)	185,093	(75%)	($288,505)
	Thomas J. Hickey (D)	62,003	(25%)	($14,686)
1988 primary	F. James Sensenbrenner, Jr. (R), unopposed			
1986 general	F. James Sensenbrenner, Jr. (R)	138,766	(78%)	($178,698)
	Thomas G. Popp (D)................	38,636	(22%)	($10,753)

WYOMING

"Wyoming was, and continues to be," wrote the *WPA Guide* 50 years ago, "the land of the cowboy. Its mountains, plains, and valleys are essentially livestock country. A cowboy astride a bucking bronco greets the visitor from enameled license plates, from automobile guest stickers, from newspapers, magazines and painted signs. The cowboy and the Indian provide decorative motifs for Wyoming stores, hotel stationery, home-woven blankets, rugs, neckerchiefs, shirts and all sorts of advertising matter. Six-gallon hats, leather vests and high-heeled boots, as well as the latest styles in dress, are seen on the streets of every city, town and village in Wyoming."

The atmosphere on the surface is much the same 50 years later: Wyoming in many ways is the most western of states. Yet beneath the neat cowboy motifs, Wyoming is still largely unsettled, a thin veneer of civilization stretched over a forbidding and beautiful land. "Wyoming seems to be the doing of a mad architect," writes Gretel Ehrlich, who moved here from California, "tumbled and twisted, ribboned with faded, deathbed colors, thrust up and pulled down as if the place had been startled out of a deep sleep and thrown into a pure light." Wyoming "has a 'lean-to' look," says Ehrlich. "Instead of big, roomy barns and Victorian houses, there are dugouts, low sheds, log cabins, sheep camps and fence lines that look like driftwood blown haphazardly into place. People here still feel pride because they live in such a harsh place, part of the glamorous cowboy past, and they are determined not to be the victims of a mining-dominated future." The trailers and ore tailings left behind by the mining boom of 1973–83 seem to be making no greater imprint than the relics of earlier booms: in this improbable place, buildings are only small specks on the landscape, small towns and tiny settlements are just quick blips on the highway. Wyoming was one of leading energy states in the boom years after the two oil shocks of the 1970s. But it remained then, and still is, the closest state we have to the Old West.

Ironically, it is only high technology that makes that civilization in this Old West possible. After the passing of the open range, the West of cattle ranches was made possible only by the barbed wire that could fence in roaming herds of beef and the steam locomotives that could carry them to market back east. This 19th century high-tech was brought to Wyoming by some large capitalist operators, like the onetime Texas cowhands ("Lonesome Dovers") and second sons of English landed gentry who started the first big operations and consolidated their power in the Johnson County land war of 1890. The recent oil boom brought the big operators in again: Amoco and other big oil companies planted drilling rigs in the Overthrust belt near Evanston, while coal companies mined great quantities of surface coal up north.

The boom also brought in others, increasing Wyoming's population more in the 12 years after 1970 than in the 50 years before; then the bust drove them out, as Wyoming's population has leveled off during the rest of the 1980s. Both boom and bust left scars. Workers who flocked here live in grimy trailers, linked precariously to civilization's utilities and unprotected against the winds and snows that come out of the enormous sky. Wyoming simply does not have the infrastructure to protect itself against the pollution that even a small influx of people brings. There is another kind of pollution as well: the mining-camp atmosphere that developed around suddenly sprung-up camps near drilling rigs or mines. Wyoming is one of the few states that has always had more men than women—a sure sign that it never got far from a frontier atmosphere (and also the reason it was the first part of the United States, back in territorial 1869, to give women the vote). In the 1970s, around towns like Rock Springs there grew a subculture of prostitution, gambling and violent crime, which would have been familiar to anyone acquainted with the history of Virginia City, Nevada or Deadwood, South Dakota.

WYOMING — Congressional District, Counties, and Selected Places — *(1 At Large)*

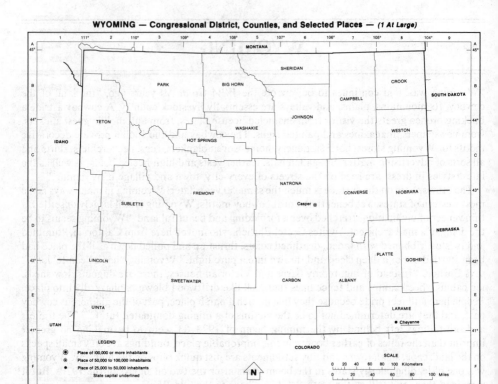

But there is a settled part of Wyoming as well, in the medium-sized towns that are regarded as the state's largest cities, and among sheep and cattle ranches, sugar beet farmers and denizens of tiny settlements. This is a small state, one community really, where people remember who played what position, when and how well, for what high school football team; where because all locals know who your father's cousins married, you mostly live pretty straight. "Wyoming for many years resembled a huge family; everyone of importance seemed to be personally known throughout the state," the *WPA Guide* said. That is still so.

Yet there is a sharp economic and regional split in Wyoming which traditionally has been reflected in partisan politics. The big economic interests—cattle ranchers, organized in the Wyoming Stock Growers' Association, and the Union Pacific Railroad—always favored the Republicans, as do the diminishing band of wildcatters, independent producers and oil company geologists, who want their industry liberated from government controls (except those which prop up prices); the ranching folks in the north and the oil people around Casper tend to vote Republican. The mainstay for the Democrats, on the other hand, were the Union Pacific railroad workers who built the first transcontinental line across southern Wyoming in the 1860s and have maintained it ever since; that southern tier of counties, from Cheyenne through Laramie to Evanston, tends to vote Democratic. Historically, the Republicans have been more numerous, though the state was closely contested from the New Deal days through the 1960s.

In the 1980s, this has been mostly a Republican state, regardless of local economic problems, except in governor's races, where it hasn't voted Republican since 1970. But personal campaigning plays the major role in Wyoming politics. Even today, there are no cities with as many as 50,000 people, and Wyoming voters expect to talk with—not just shake hands with, but actually exchange views with—their governor, Senators and congressman every few years. There is a general agreement that Wyoming needs to build a more diverse economy, and that government should play some role in that. But state government is small and its powers limited; while the federal government, distant, domineering, insensitive to the feel of daily life here, is mistrusted. Wyomingites, with their high tech sophistication in their vast, empty lands, will have to rely mostly on themselves for a solution, as usual.

Governor. Wyoming is one of those Rocky Mountain states which votes Republican for President and elects nothing, it seems, but Democratic governors. Mike Sullivan, elected in 1986, extended the string of Democratic victories established by Ed Herschler in 1974, 1978 and 1982. Campaigning in a trademark Stetson with a hole in it, Sullivan beat Pete Simpson, the Senator's brother. In office, he seemed the least pompous or pampered of governors—he has no bodyguard and answers his own phone. He wants to diversify Wyoming's economy—tough for a state so isolated and cut off from major markets. He also moved to allow three-trailer trucks in the state, to put a cap on tort verdicts and to stop the introduction of gray wolves into Yellowstone Park. Possible opponents for 1990 include Auditor Jack Sidi and state Senators Diemer True and John Turner.

Senators. The senior member of Wyoming's congressional delegation is Malcolm Wallop, first elected in 1976 and reelected in 1982 and by the narrowest of margins in 1988. Wallop is descended from one of those 19th century English toffs who came to Wyoming to ranch, and in both his physical appearance and some of his attitudes he resembles those 19th century imperial adventurers who penetrated the remotest corners of the world. He is proud of having roughed it for many years but he also takes a broad world view of public problems, stating his views incisively and sometimes with contempt for his opponents. And his English origin was underlined in October 1984, when he hosted Queen Elizabeth II at his ranch near Sheridan, on a private visit to see horses; for Wallop, who styles himself, and is in fact, a working rancher, is also the brother of Lady Jean Porchester, wife of Lord Henry Porchester, the Queen's racing manager. Wallop's grandfather was the Earl of Portsmouth.

In the Senate, Wallop is counted on the right, although in the 1970s he was something of an environmentalist in Wyoming. He is a strong believer in the free market as an allocator of resources, and opposes what he sees as intrusive federal regulations. While on the Finance Committee, he worked to lower or end energy taxes, like the windfall profits tax, and he voted against the 1988 welfare reform bill. On the Energy and Natural Resources Committee and as ranking Republican on the Subcommittee on Public Lands, National Parks and Forests, he opposes federal intrusion and bossiness from the Bureau of Land Management and the Forest Service in places like Wyoming. He has also performed his share of unpleasant duties. In 1981 and 1982, he chaired the Senate Ethics Committee, and was the leading advocate of the expulsion of convicted Abscam defendant Harrison Williams; that post was one he happily relinquished. He wanted the chair of the Republican Senate Campaign Committee for 1985 and 1986, but lost to John Heinz in the Republican Conference.

Once an English major at Yale, Wallop is now most interested in defense and foreign policy. He has been, since the late 1970s, one of the most ardent backers of the Strategic Defense Initiative, and wants the earliest possible deployment. Skeptical of arms control agreements with the Soviets, he wrote a 1987 book on the subject, *The Arms Control Delusion*. He was one of the handful of Senators who voted against the INF Treaty. When the Senate rejected one of his INF amendments 68–26, he blasted his colleagues for "sleepwalking" and said Senators "cannot walk out of the chamber with their heads held high." After the Senate rejected the Bork nomination, voted for its own interpretation of the ABM treaty, and refused to assert what he considered were important U.S. rights under the Panama Canal treaty, he told a Casper audience that in the Senate, "Consistency, integrity, common sense are just out the window."

This vehemence comes from a certainty that he is right, and is based on a considerable knowledge of the issues. Yet he often comes across, in Washington and Wyoming, as possessing an arrogance bordering on solipsism. Wallop's deep interest in international issues has left many Wyoming voters feeling that he doesn't return to the state often enough and simply isn't willing to talk their language. In fact, his cadences are those of a think tank policy intellectual, with whom a rancher has no acquaintance whatsoever.

In 1976, when he won his first term by upsetting Democrat Gale McGee, he portrayed himself as a rancher concerned about Wyoming's environment and about federal overregulation (one TV ad showed a cowboy carrying a portable toilet on his saddlebag). In 1982, he beat 34-year-old Edward Kennedy Democrat Rodger McDaniel 57%–43%, running under national Republican levels. In 1988, state Senator John Vinich, a restauranteur and barkeeper from the rough-and-ready town of Hudson, started off far behind Wallop but made great headway as he claimed the Senator was out of touch. In the end Wallop won, but with only 50% of the vote, losing not only the Union Pacific counties, but the Wind River country and Casper, where the Casper *Star-Tribune*, the state's largest paper, delights in baiting him. Unless Wallop can strengthen his popularity in Wyoming, he is probably serving his last term in the Senate.

Alan Simpson, Wyoming's junior Senator, first elected in 1978, is the Republican whip in the Senate, and was considered at least briefly for the vice presidential nomination in 1988. He has passed major legislation and taken a lead role in dozens of major debates. But he is known best as the possessor of one of the best senses of humor in American politics. This slim, 6'7" giant— taller than fellow Senators Jay Rockefeller or Bill Bradley—has brilliant timing, droll delivery and a repertoire of jokes that include some that will not find their way into a family almanac. But he is not just a joketeller; he is one of the better extemporaneous speakers in the Senate, one of its sharper debaters, and one of the more aggressive advocates of his positions. Get in his way, and see how funny he is.

Simpson made his reputation in the Senate by taking on some tough fights, and sticking with them. One was immigration. Unexpectedly saddled with the chairmanship of the Immigration and Refugee Affairs Subcommittee in 1981, Simpson took his assignment seriously, mastering the facts, deciding where he wanted to go on policy, and figuring out what he could get through the Senate. The major features of his bills were sanctions on employers who hire illegal immigrants, which were naturally unpopular with mostly conservative small businessmen and growers; an amnesty for immigrants who arrived here illegally prior to a certain date, unpopular with those who want previous laws sternly enforced; and limits on the numbers who can come in now, which are unpopular both with those who want more and those who want fewer immigrants. Simpson immigration bills passed the Senate in three successive Congresses and, almost miraculously, a bill passed the House and cleared the conference committee in the last moments of the 99th Congress in October 1986.

But the immigration issue is never really over. Edward Kennedy and others concerned about the low numbers of Irish immigrants allowed in under the 1986 law sought changes and in 1988 Simpson worked out a new bill to accommodate them. Other changes may be needed. Simpson's law is a constructive attempt to place some high limits on the numbers of immigrants but also to prevent the emergence of a separate and unequal body of illegal aliens, cut off from contact with and the benefits of American society generally.

Another tough issue Simpson has taken on is veterans' benefits. He was chairman of the Veterans' Affairs Committee in the Reagan years, and opposed strongly many of the demands of veterans' groups for new benefits. He insisted on requiring veterans to kick in $1,200 of their own money before becoming eligible for the educational benefits in Congressman Sonny Montgomery's 1984 G.I. Bill, and he opposed bills compensating Vietnam veterans supposedly injured by contact with Agent Orange on the grounds that there was no scientific evidence that the defoliant was harmful. Simpson has been point man on other controversial issues, championing the use of nuclear power, fighting the Endangered Species Act because it prevents Wyoming ranchers from protecting their animals against grizzly bears and wolves, defending Judge Robert Bork and vitriolically attacking the intellectual dishonesty of many of his detractors.

For all his good humor and good fellowship, Simpson is a strong, old-fashioned Republican partisan. He is skeptical of the ability of government to find real solutions, cautious about spending public money, respectful of local authorities. He is also decidedly out of sympathy with much of the cultural conservatism of the New Right: in 1982, he leveled a famous outburst at Jesse Helms, in a classic confrontation between the conservative as complainer and the conservative as doer. But the New Right had its revenge. In the weeks leading up to the 1988 Republican National Convention, opponents of abortion insisted that the pro-choice Simpson was unacceptable for the vice presidential nomination, and Simpson, an old friend of George Bush, took himself out of the running for the nomination.

Simpson's standing in Wyoming is strong. He is a member of one of Wyoming's leading political families. His grandfather, a gritty 19th century oldtimer, was one of the state's most influential Democrats. His father, Milward Simpson, served as Republican governor and Senator; always a conservative, he lost one governor's race, in Al Simpson's view, because of his opposition to capital punishment. His brother Pete ran for governor in 1986 and lost. Al jumped from the state House of Representatives to the U.S. Senate in 1978 with wonderfully little competition when Senator Clifford Hansen retired. Simpson was reelected with 78% of the vote in 1984, running well ahead of President Reagan in this Reagan Republican state. Although Democrat John Vinich seriously contested the other Senate seat and the state's sole House seat in 1988 and 1989, Simpson is expected to face no serious competition for his seat in 1990.

Presidential politics. Wyoming became one of the most Republican states in presidential elections by the early 1970s, when its residents reacted against federal energy price controls and city-based environmentalists. It remains so, despite the continuing problems of the local economy.

Wyoming Democrats held their caucuses three days before Super Tuesday and attracted some attention though they did not set any precedents: the winner was Albert Gore, followed by Michael Dukakis and Richard Gephardt. The Republicans met later and endorsed the by-then victor, George Bush.

Congressman-at-large. For a decade Wyoming's only congressman was Richard Cheney, White House Chief of Staff under President Ford, House Republican Whip and heir apparent to the party leadership in 1989 and, after the rejection of John Tower's nomination, President Bush's Secretary of Defense. Admired by both Washington insiders and by Republican rebels in the House, possessed of a strong intellect and intellectual honesty, aggressive, politically adroit and increasingly conservative in his views, Cheney is also popular in Wyoming and could have been reelected for life.

The contest to succeed him, as often happens in special elections early in a President's term, gave the minority party a chance to pick up a surprise victory. The Democrats had an obvious candidate in John Vinich, who had nearly beaten Malcolm Wallop just months before, and they found themselves with an obvious and powerful Wyoming theme—don't let outsiders make decisions for Wyoming—when the House Republicans' campaign committee chief honcho Ed Rollins said that, after the party's losses in special elections in Indiana and Alabama, he couldn't afford to lose Wyoming. That put the Republican nominee, state Rural Electric Association head Craig Thomas, on the defensive. Republicans were further hurt when campaigning was suspended after Vinich was in an auto accident and when they authorized a poll question implying that a national Democratic official was with Vinich in the car.

But the Republicans had their points as well. One was that Vinich's campaign was financed almost entirely by organized labor, which is unpopular with most voters in this right-to-work state. Another was the reaction to a Vinich TV ad suggesting that Thomas had voted in the legislature against an anti-crime measure. This was evidently an attempt to use a 1988 Bush issue against a 1989 Republican, just as Democratic candidate and now Congresswoman Jill Long used a no-new-taxes pledge against Republican Dan Heath in the Indiana special election. But the ad was denounced by the Casper *Star-Tribune*, as well as by Republicans. Thomas won with 53% of the vote, well below George Bush's showing here, but a comfortable margin nevertheless. Thomas is a Main Street Republican. He grew up in Cody with Al Simpson; he worked for the Farm Bureau and the Wyoming Rural Electric Association, organizations with conservative political leanings that kept him in touch with hundreds of people active in their communities; he served five years in the legislature. Thomas is likely to be a practical-minded, not theory-minded Republican, who opposes the federal government staunchly when it does things like reintroduce wolves into Yellowstone but who also appreciates the benefits and community-building potential of federal farm and reclamation programs. He was given Cheney's seat on the Interior Committee and seems likely to have a long House career ahead of him.

The People: Est. Pop. 1988: 471,000; Pop. 1980: 469,557, up 0.2% 1980–88 and 41.3% 1970–80; 0.21% of U.S. total, 51st largest. 20% with 1–3 yrs. col., 17% with 4+ yrs. col.; 7.9% below poverty level. Single ancestry: 13% German, 11% English, 5% Irish, 2% Swedish, 1% Norwegian, French, Scottish, Italian, Dutch, Polish. Households (1980): 73% family, 43% with children, 65% married couples; 30.8% housing units rented; median monthly rent: $220; median house value: $60,400. Voting age pop. (1980): 324,004; 4% Spanish origin; 1% American Indian, 1% Black. Registered voters (1988): 226,189; 80,889 D (36%), 124,194 R (55%), 21,106 unaffiliated and minor parties (9%).

1988 Share of Federal Tax Burden: $1,420,000,000; 0.16% of U.S. total, 50th largest.

1988 Share of Federal Expenditures

	Total		Non-Defense		Defense	
Total Expend	$1,626m	(0.18%)	$1,421m	(0.22%)	$350m	(0.15%)
St/Lcl Grants	448m	(0.39%)	447m	(0.39%)	1m	(0.80%)
Salary/Wages	281m	(0.21%)	164m	(0.25%)	116m	(0.25%)
Pymnts to Indiv	640m	(0.16%)	607m	(0.16%)	33m	(0.18%)
Procurement	199m	(0.11%)	145m	(0.31%)	199m	(0.11%)
Research/Other	59m	(0.16%)	58m	(0.16%)	0m	(0.16%)

Political Lineup: Governor, Michael (Mike) J. Sullivan (D); Secy. of State, Kathy Karpan (D); Atty. Gen., Joseph B. Meyer (R); Treasurer, Stan Smith (R); Auditor, Jack Sidi (R). State Senate, 30 (19 R and 11 D), State House of Representatives, 64 (41 R and 23 D). Senators, Malcolm Wallop (R) and Alan K. Simpson (R). Representatives, 1 R at large.

1988 Presidential Vote			1984 Presidential Vote		
Bush (R)	106,867	(61%)	Reagan (R)	133,241	(71%)
Dukakis (D)	67,113	(38%)	Mondale (D)	53,370	(28%)

GOVERNOR

Gov. Michael J. (Mike) Sullivan (D)

Elected 1986, term expires Jan. 1991; b. Sept. 22, 1939, Omaha, NE; home, Casper; U. of WY, B.S. 1961, J.D. 1964; Roman Catholic; married (Jane).

Career: Practicing atty, 1964–86.

Office: State Capitol Bldg., Cheyenne 82002, 307-777-7434.

Election Results

1986 gen.	Michael J. (Mike) Sullivan (D)	88,879	(54%)
	Pete Simpson (R)	75,841	(46%)
1986 prim.	Michael J. (Mike) Sullivan (D)	29,266	(71%)
	Pat McGuire (D)	5,406	(13%)
	Keith Brian (D)	4,039	(10%)
	Al Hamburg (D).	2,554	(6%)
1982 gen.	Ed Herschler (D)	106,424	(63%)
	Warren A. Morton (R)	62,119	(37%)

SENATORS

Sen. Malcolm Wallop (R)

Elected 1976, seat up 1994; b. Feb. 27, 1933, New York, NY; home, Big Horn; Yale U., B.A. 1954; Episcopalian; married (French).

Career: Rancher; Army, 1955–57; WY House of Reps., 1969–72; WY Senate, 1973–76.

Offices: 237 RSOB 20510, 202-224-6441. Also 2201 Fed. Bldg., Casper 82601, 307-261-5098; 2009 Fed. Ctr., Cheyenne 82001, 307-634-0626; P.O. Box 1014, Lander 82520, 307-332-2293; 2515 Foothill Blvd., Rock Springs 82901, 307-382-5127; and 40 S. Main, Sheridan 82801, 307-672-6456.

Committees: *Armed Services* (6th of 9 R). Subcommittees: Defense Industry and Technology (Ranking Member); Readiness, Sustainability and Support; Strategic Forces and Nuclear Deterrence. *Energy and Natural Resources* (4th of 9 R). Subcommittees: Mineral Resources Development and Production; Public Lands, National Parks and Forests (Ranking Member); Water and Power. *Small Business* (4th of 9 R). Subcommittees: Export and Expansion; Rural Economy and Family Farming.

Group Ratings

	ADA	ACLU	COPE	CFA	LCV	ACU	NTU	NSI	COC	CEI
1988	0	6	8	17	0	100	95	100	91	76
1987	0	—	8	0	—	96	—	—	80	84

National Journal Ratings

	1988 LIB — 1988 CONS		1987 LIB — 1987 CONS	
Economic	8% —	91%	0% —	94%
Social	0% —	89%	0% —	94%
Foreign	0% —	92%	0% —	76%

Key Votes

1) Cut Aged Housing $	AGN	5) Bork Nomination	FOR	9) SDI Funding	FOR
2) Override Hwy Veto	AGN	6) Ban Plastic Guns	FOR	10) Ban Chem Weaps	FOR
3) Plant Clsng Notice	FOR	7) Deny Abortions	—	11) Aid To Contras	FOR
4) Min Wage Increase	—	8) Japanese Reparations	AGN	12) Reagan Defense $	FOR

Election Results

1988 general	Malcolm Wallop (R)...................	91,143	(50%)	($1,344,185)
	John P. Vinich (D).....................	89,821	(50%)	($490,230)
1988 primary	Malcolm Wallop (R)...................	55,752	(83%)	
	Nora Marie Louis (R)..................	3,933	(6%)	
	Brad Kinney (R)......................	3,716	(6%)	
	Two others...........................	3,600	(5%)	
1982 general	Malcolm Wallop (R)...................	94,690	(57%)	($1,139,082)
	Rodger McDaniel (D).................	72,453	(43%)	($389,511)

Sen. Alan K. Simpson (R)

Elected 1978, seat up 1990; b. Sept. 2, 1931, Denver, CO; home, Cody; U. of WY, B.S. 1954, J.D. 1958; Episcopalian; married (Ann).

Career: Practicing atty., 1959–78; WY Asst. Atty. Gen., 1959; Cody City Atty., 1959–69; WY House of Reps., 1964–77, Major. Flr. Ldr. 1975–76, Speaker Pro-Tem, 1977.

Offices: 261 DSOB 20510, 202-224-3424. Also P.O. Box 430, Cody 82414, 307-527-7121; Fed. Ctr., Ste. 3201, Casper 82601, 307-261-5172; Fed. Ctr., Ste. 2007, Cheyenne 82001, 307-772-2477; 2201 S. Douglas Hwy., P.O. Box 3155, Gillette 82716, 307-682-7091; 2020 Grand Ave., Rm. 411, Laramie 82070, 307-745-5303; 2515 Foothills Blvd., Ste. 220, Rock Springs 82901, 307-382-5097; and 1731 Sheridan Ave., Ste. 1, Cody 82414, 307-527-7121.

Committees: *Environment and Public Works* (2d of 7 R). Subcommittees: Environmental Protection; Nuclear Regulation (Ranking Member); Superfund, Ocean and Water Protection. *Judiciary* (3d of 6 R). Subcommittees: Immigration and Refugee Affairs (Ranking Member); Patents, Copyrights and Trademarks. *Veterans' Affairs* (2d of 5 R). *Special Committee on Aging* (2d of 9 R).

Group Ratings

	ADA	ACLU	COPE	CFA	LCV	ACU	NTU	NSI	COC	CEI
1988	15	40	7	58	20	92	80	100	86	55
1987	10	—	6	33	—	79	—	—	71	68

National Journal Ratings

	1988 LIB — 1988 CONS			1987 LIB — 1987 CONS		
Economic	5%	—	93%	6%	—	87%
Social	30%	—	69%	16%	—	78%
Foreign	21%	—	77%	29%	—	68%

Key Votes

1) Cut Aged Housing $	AGN	5) Bork Nomination	FOR	9) SDI Funding	FOR
2) Override Hwy Veto	AGN	6) Ban Plastic Guns	FOR	10) Ban Chem Weaps	FOR
3) Plant Clsng Notice	FOR	7) Deny Abortions	FOR	11) Aid To Contras	FOR
4) Min Wage Increase	AGN	8) Japanese Reparations	FOR	12) Reagan Defense $	FOR

Election Results

1984 general	Alan K. Simpson (R)	146,373	(78%)	($862,039)
	Victor A. Ryan (D)....................	40,525	(22%)	
1984 primary	Alan K. Simpson (R)	66,178	(88%)	
	Stephen C. Tarver (R)	9,137	(12%)	
1978 general	Alan K. Simpson (R)	82,908	(62%)	($439,805)
	Raymond B. Whitaker (D).............	50,456	(38%)	($142,749)

REPRESENTATIVE

Rep. Craig Thomas (R)

Elected April, 1989; b. Feb. 13, 1933, Cody; home, Casper; U. of WY, B.A. 1955, LaSalle, L.L.B. 1959; Methodist; married (Susan).

Career: USMC, 1955–59; Vice Pres., WY Farm Bureau, 1959–66; Legis. Staff, Amer. Farm Bureau, 1966–75; Gen. Mngr., WY Rural Electric Assn., 1975–89; WY House of Reps., 1985–89.

Offices: 1631 LHOB 20515, 202-225-2311. Also Rm. 2015 Fed. Bldg., Cheyenne 82001, 307-772-2451; and Rm. 4003 Fed. Bldg., Casper 82601, 307-261-5413.

Committees: *Interior and Insular Affairs* (14th of 14 R). Subcommittees: Parks and Public Lands; Water and Power. *Government Operations* (14th of 15 R). Subcommittees: Environment, Energy and Natural Resources; Government Information, Justice and Agriculture.

Group Ratings and Key Votes: Newly Elected

Election Results

1989 special	Craig Thomas (R)....................	74,384	(53%)	($527,148)
	John Vinich (D)	60,845	(43%)	($479,705)
	Craig McCune (I).....................	5,825	(4%)	
1989 primary	Craig Thomas (R), nominated by convention			
1988 general	Richard B. (Dick) Cheney (R)..........	118,350	(67%)	($161,591)
	Bryan Sharratt (D)	56,527	(32%)	

PUERTO RICO, VIRGIN ISLANDS, GUAM, AMERICAN SAMOA

Four American insular territories are represented in Congress by elected delegates who, like the District of Columbia's representative, have floor privileges and votes on committees but may not vote on the floor of the House. They are Puerto Rico, the Virgin Islands, Guam and American Samoa, and they are a diverse lot.

Puerto Rico.   The largest by far is Puerto Rico, a Caribbean island with about 3.5 million people—about the same population as Connecticut, South Carolina or Oklahoma. Puerto Rico was one of Spain's last colonial possessions; the United States gained it in the Spanish-American War of 1898. Fifty years ago it was "the poorhouse of the Caribbean," heavily populated, devoted almost entirely to sugar cultivation. Then in the 1940s, 1950s and early 1960s, Puerto Rico was transformed by Governor Luis Muñoz Marin and his Popular Democratic Party. Muñoz initiated Operation Bootstrap, to lure businesses to Puerto Rico with promises of low-wage labor and government assistance; Puerto Rico is within the United States for trade purposes but is not subject to federal income taxes. Muñoz also developed the commonwealth form of government (in Spanish, Estado Libre Asociado (ELA): Free Associated State), which became effective in 1952. Under commonwealth, Puerto Rico is part of the United States for purposes of international trade, foreign policy and war, but has its own separate laws, taxes and representative government. Puerto Rico has also developed its own political parties: Muñoz's Popular Democrats, the New Progressives who favor statehood, and two Independence parties. Muñoz could have been reelected governor for life, but retired in 1964. His death in 1980 was an occasion for an islandwide outpouring of emotion for the man who was almost universally recognized as the father of his country.

In his first month in office, President George Bush reopened what has been for 50 years the central issue of Puerto Rican politics: status. Bush, like many Republicans, has long supported statehood, but in a speech to Congress he called for a plebiscite on the issue, which has been the subject of two referenda in the past. In both of those, commonwealth prevailed, with statehood, which would deprive Puerto Rico of its tax exemptions and threaten the official recognition of Spanish, a decided second choice. Independence, which some outsiders suppose Puerto Ricans long for, was the choice of fewer than 10% of the voters. Nor is there any large number of independence-minded abstentions. Voter turnout is much higher in the poorest parts of Puerto Rico than in the richest neighborhoods of the U. S. mainland.

Governor Rafael Hernandez Colón, a Popular Democrat elected in 1972, beaten in 1976 and 1980, then elected again in 1984 and 1988, favors ELA with some modifications of current arrangements; but he has supported the idea of holding another referendum, as has Resident Commissioner (the title of the non-voting delegate) Jaime Fuster. So in early 1989, it was widely anticipated that Congress would approve a referendum bill by November 1989 and that the plebiscite would probably be held in 1990. The Popular Democrats' recent victories suggest that the advantage would go again to commonwealth, crafted artfully by Muñoz to preserve Puerto Rico's Hispanic culture while using the island's ties with the United States and its exemption from U.S. taxes to achieve the phenomenal growth that followed 1952 and gives Puerto Rico today the highest income in Latin America. This achievement is all the more striking because it represents an enthusiastic endorsement of a position which is essentially a compromise in a society with a politics of enthusiasm. That enthusiasm has its positive aspects, like high voter turnout, but it also means that voters are slavishly uncritical of their own party's candidates and scathingly contemptuous of the opposition's.

But within that politics of enthusiasm, Puerto Ricans have developed an impressive appreciation of civil liberties. Carlos Romero Barcelo, the pro-statehood head of the New Progressive Party, after winning the elections of 1976 and 1980, lost in 1984 because of the unraveling of the coverup within the police of a scandal in which police undercover agents shot two terrorists on a hill called Cerro Maravilla. Few voters shared the terrorists' goals or doubted that their means were wrong, but many were prepared to vote against the authorities who wrongly killed them.

Once in office, Hernandez Colón and the Popular Democrats were faced with a different crisis: preventing Section 936 of the Internal Revenue Code—which exempts Puerto Rico manufacturing operations from U.S. taxes but allows their products within the U.S. duty-free—from being abolished by what became the 1986 tax reform bill. Hernandez responded brilliantly. He tied Section 936 to the Reagan Administration's flagging Caribbean Basin Initiative—which on its own at first seemed to threaten Puerto Rico with more competition—by proposing to use funds that U.S. banks are required by 936 to hold in Puerto Rico to finance "twin plants," with the more complex work done in Puerto Rico and simpler assembly work in Caribbean basin countries. While the tax bill was pending, Hernandez got the first agreement with Grenada; Dominica, whose Prime Minister Eugenia Charles had called for the U.S. to intervene in Grenada, added its support. In the past, Hernandez was identified with policies of the left, and he once went to the United Nations to testify before the anti-colonialism hearings that Fidel Castro uses to try to embarrass the United States (even though more Puerto Ricans want to be part of the U.S. than Cubans want Communism in Cuba). But in 1987, Hernandez skillfully lobbied both the Democrats on the House Ways and Means Committee and Republicans in the Administration, the Heritage Foundation, and points right. He had concocted a policy that appealed to both sides, and which strengthened Puerto Ricans' allegiance to the United States and to commonwealth even while it strengthened their own pride as Puerto Ricans. It emphasized the fact that they are the most economically sophisticated people in the Caribbean, the natural economic leaders of part of the hemisphere. Now his task in his third term seems to be to adjust ELA to increase Puerto Ricans' enthusiasm for it, to build Puerto Rican pride without jeopardizing the island's allegiance to the United States.

Some of the credit also belong to Jaime Fuster, the only member of Congress with a four-year term. Elected in his early 40s, he already had a distinguished career as a lawyer and educator and is part of that class of Puerto Rican leaders familiar with politics and government both on the mainland and in Puerto Rico. He sits in Congress as a Democrat, and has a seat on Interior and Insular Affairs, as representatives of the territories typically do; he also sits on the Foreign Affairs and Education and Labor Committees and was chosen head of the Hispanic Caucus. Much of his time is spent on the clauses that adjust U.S. legislation to the rather different economy of Puerto Rico: he is proud of having raised or eliminated the federal ceilings on medicaid and AFDC, of getting non-earmarked money for highways and airports and of getting some $550 million for federal water projects.

Fuster was reelected by a narrow margin in straight ticket Puerto Rico: in 1984 when Hernandez Colón won 48%–45%, Fuster won 49%–46%; in 1988, the corresponding numbers were 49%–46% and 49%–47%.

Puerto Rico does not vote for President in November, but it does choose delegates to the parties' national conventions. It elects only a few Republicans, but its Democratic delegation is larger than that of 25 states and since it is invariably made up of backers of a single candidate, it casts a bigger margin for its man than all but a few of the larger states. The Democratic delegates for 1988 were chosen in a contest with a huge turnout in which Hernandez Colón's Popular Democrats beat Romero Barcelo's New Progressives and swept all the seats; Hernandez Colón controlled the whole delegation and committed it to Michael Dukakis in April. This antagonized Jesse Jackson, who had won a much lower turnout, meaningless "beauty contest" primary with a small plurality; Hernandez Colón eventually agreed to release a half dozen votes to Jackson.

Virgin Islands. The United States' other insular area in the Caribbean is the Virgin Islands, a very different sort of place. It is much smaller than Puerto Rico, with a population under 100,000. Puerto Rico is multiracial and not self-conscious about it; most of the Virgin Islanders are black, and there is a pretty clear divide between the races, much resented by the blacks. While Puerto Rico has attracted all kinds of light industry, the Virgin Islands has lived off tourism and refineries, industries that have produced higher income levels for its few citizens but have not provided the basis for a mature economy. For years, the governor of the Virgin Islands was appointed by the President; more recently, contests have had some nasty racial overtones and produced Governor Alexander Farrelly, who cooperated with the questionable project under which District of Columbia officials went down to the Islands for months supposedly to assist in job reclassifications. The Virgins Islands' Democratic primary voters went 85% for Jesse Jackson.

The delegate from the Virgin Islands is Ron de Lugo, who votes with the Democrats. Like Ronald Reagan, he got his start in radio, inventing a character called Mango Jones on the first Virgin Island radio station in 1950; in 1952, he revived the Virgin Islands' carnival. First elected to Congress in 1968, he lost a race for governor in 1978, then came back to Washington in 1980: he is now the senior member from the territories. He serves on the Interior and Insular Affairs Committee, Post Office and Civil Service, and Public Works and Transportation; importantly, he chairs the Interior Subcommittee on Insular and International Affairs. In that capacity, he must work on other insular matters, like Puerto Rico's status referendum, the Palau Compact of Free Association, and Guam's commonwealth proposal. But he also found time in 1988 for Post Office hearings on Islands' mail service, focusing on a Virgin Islands-bound mail trailer that was lost in Puerto Rico for 2½ years. He worked to get General Education Assistance for the Virgin Islands and to frame special amendments to the drug bill for the insular areas.

Guam. It takes some 19 hours to fly from Washington, D.C., to Guam, the place where, as viewers of political conventions for years were informed, America's day begins. Guam lies just west of the International Date Line, and it is indeed the early hours of Tuesday there when the rest of us are just trying to get through Monday afternoon. Guam is geographically in the center of the Marianas, but judicially it is separate; Guam is an integral part of the United States, while the Marianas and the islands around them were for years United Nations territories administered by the United States, and became a Commonwealth in 1976. With a population of 125,000, Guam is a more advanced society than the Marianas, but economically it is not yet self-supporting. More than two-thirds of the workers are employed by the Guamanian or federal government (there are big defense bases here). The people are of mixed ethnic stock (Spanish and Pacific Islander), their religion is almost always Catholic, and they speak English, Spanish and a local language called Chamorro.

In Congress, Guam's major cause is a commonwealth bill introduced by Delegate Ben Blaz. It would not only grant commonwealth status, but would allow Guam's government to control immigration (preventing the Chamorros from becoming a minority), exempt Guam from federal tax laws and regulations, and give Guam the right of approval over treaties that affect it. Some of these are demands which, an Interior Department official tartly noted, Congress would never grant a state, much less a territory. It reflects, nonetheless, a desire by Guamanians to improve their island and upgrade their society.

Blaz is the product of Guam's two-party politics which is vibrant to the point of turbulent. The 1986 gubernatorial election saw Democratic incumbent Ricardo Bordallo indicted just before the election, defeated by Republican Joseph Ada, and then convicted in February 1987 of bribery and extortion. The party labels seem to matter less than personal reputations and alliances in a community that is small enough for almost everyone to know almost everyone else's business. Blaz is a Republican, a former Marine Corps general who in 1984 upset veteran Democrat Antonio Borja Won Pat by 354 votes. Blaz has seats on Armed Services, Foreign Affairs and, of course, Interior. He seems to have blended in well in the Republican Conference: he was named chairman of the small group of Republican freshmen after being elected in 1984.

American Samoa.   In the 1980s, for the first time, American Samoa had representation in Congress. That has not been an entirely happy experience for this Southern Pacific island which, unlike Guam, has been little influenced by western settlers and remains almost as Polynesian as it was when the United States took possession in 1900. Delegate Fofo I.F. Sunia, elected in 1982, 1984 and 1986, pleaded guilty in August 1988 to $130,000 in payroll fraud, resigned from Congress in September, and his administrative assistant was sent to jail. Elected to succeed him in the November 22, 1988, runoff was lieutenant governor Eni F. H. Faleomavaega, a Democrat, who beat former lieutenant governor Tufele Li'a. Faleomavaega serves on the Foreign Affairs and Interior Committees.

American Samoa staged a Democratic presidential primary in 1988, and it was gravely reported that Michael Dukakis beat Richard Gephardt by a 39%–22% margin. The significance of this result must be discounted, however, by the fact that exactly 36 votes were cast in the contest. None of the candidates campaigned in person.

PUERTO RICO
Gov. Rafael Hernandez Colon (D)   **Rep. Jaime B. Fuster (D)**

VIRGIN ISLANDS
Rep. Ron de Lugo (D)

GUAM
Rep. Ben Blaz (R)

AMERICAN SAMOA
Rep. Eni F. H. Faleomavaega (D)

DEMOGRAPHICS CHARTS

Population. All population figures are from the Bureau of the Census, U.S. Department of Commerce, Washington, D.C. 20233, 301-763-4040. Publications used for this section include: Congressional Districts of the 98th Congress, the 99th Congress, and the 100th Congress; and Provisional Estimates of Social, Economic and Housing Characteristics. Figures for 1970 and 1980 are final Census Bureau population counts as of April 1 of those years; 1988 figures are interim estimates as of July 1, 1988. (The District of Columbia is included as a state in all the following charts.)

Voting Age Population. This figure indicates all persons at least 18 years of age who are eligible to vote, including the Armed Forces, aliens and institutional members.

Congressional District Population. Figures for the 1986 congressional district populations are provisional estimates as of July 1, 1986. Congressional district population figures are not updated on a yearly basis.

Chart I shows the total U.S. population and total U.S. voting age population for 1988 (interim estimate), 1980, and 1970.

Chart I

Total U.S. Population		Total U.S. Voting Age Population	
July 1, 1988	245,807,000 (est.)	November 1, 1988	182,628,000 (est.)
April 1, 1980	226,545,805	April 1, 1980	163,997,000
April 1, 1970	203,302,031	April 1, 1970	135,290,000

Chart II indicates the range of highest and lowest state population changes in percentage growth and absolute change for 1970–80.

Chart II

1970–80 Population Change
(National Avg.: up 11.4%)

State	Highest		State	Lowest	
Nevada	63.8%	311,755	District of Columbia	−15.6%	−118,355
Arizona	53.1	942,816	New York	−3.7	−683,319
Florida	43.5	2,954,906	Rhode Island	−0.3	−2,569
Wyoming	41.3	137,141			
Utah	37.9	401,764			

Chart III illustrates the highest net in-migration and out-migration for the years 1980 through 1988.

Chart III

1980–88 Population Change
(National Avg.: 8.5%)

State	Highest		State	Lowest	
Nevada	32.5%	260,000	Iowa	−18.2%	(530,000)
Alaska	27.6	111,000	West Virginia	−3.4	(66,000)
Arizona	27.5	748,000	District of Columbia	−2.8	(18,000)
Florida	27.0	2,631,000	Wyoming	0.2	1,000
New Hampshire	19.1	176,000	Michigan	0.4	38,000

Chart IV shows the ten highest and the ten lowest state populations.

Chart IV

1988 U.S. Population: Ten Highest and Lowest States

State	Highest	State	Lowest
California	28,168,000	Wyoming	471,000
New York	17,898,000	Alaska	513,000
Texas	16,780,000	Vermont	556,000
Florida	12,377,000	District of Columbia	620,000
Pennsylvania	12,027,000	Delaware	660,000
Illinois	11,544,000	North Dakota	663,000
Ohio	10,872,000	South Dakota	715,000
Michigan	9,300,000	Montana	804,000
New Jersey	7,720,000	Rhode Island	995,000
North Carolina	6,526,000	Idaho	999,000

Chart V illustrates the highest and lowest average state congressional district population for states with three or more congressional districts. The average population size for a congressional district in 1986 was 553,000, up 6.4% from 519,000 as shown in the 1980 census.

Chart V

1986 Congressional District Population: Highest and Lowest States

State	Highest	State	Lowest
Arizona	649,000	Iowa	475,000
Texas	617,000	West Virginia	480,000
Florida	614,000	Kansas	492,000
Georgia	610,000	Michigan	509,000
California	600,000	Ohio	512,000

Chart VI indicates the highest gains and losses for congressional district population growth from 1980–1986.

Chart VI

1980–86 Congressional District Population Gains and Losses

State	Gain	Pop.	State	Loss	Pop.
Texas 26th	41.7%	746,000	Michigan 13th	−13.6%	444,600
Florida 11th	33.4	683,900	Pennsylvania 14th	−8.1	474,700
Texas 10th	33.2	702,400	New York 33rd	−7.6	477,300
California 37th	33.1	700,000	Michigan 1st	−6.3	482,000
Alaska at-large	32.8	534,000	New York 18th	−6.2	485,200
Arizona 1st	32.7	721,800	Michigan 17th	−5.9	484,400
Florida 6th	32.5	679,800	Illinois 17th	−5.8	489,200
Florida 12th	32.3	678,700	Indiana 1st	−5.8	515,600
Florida 14th	31.5	674,200	Illinois 18th	−5.4	490,700
Florida 13th	31.4	674,300			

Chart VII shows the distribution of the congressional district population growth by geographic region. The average population increase for a congressional district from 1980 to 1986 was 6.4%.

Chart VII

1980–86 Population Change of Congressional Districts by Region

Region	Total Districts	Population Loss	Under 6.4%	Population Increase 6.4–19.9%	20% or more
U.S.	435	94	163	144	34
Northwest	95	31	54	10	—
Midwest	113	52	49	12	—
South	142	10	47	65	20
West	85	1	13	57	14

Chart VIII indicates the spread of highest and lowest state percentages of persons living below the poverty level.

Chart VIII

Persons Living Below Poverty Level (1979)
(National Avg.: 12.4%)

State	Highest	State	Lowest
Mississippi	23.9%	Wyoming	7.9%
Arkansas	19.0	Connecticut	8.0
Alabama	18.9	New Hampshire	8.5
District of Columbia	18.6	Wisconsin	8.7
Louisiana	18.6	Nevada	8.7
Kentucky	17.6	Minnesota	9.5
New Mexico	17.6	New Jersey	9.5

Chart IX lists the states with the highest and lowest average percentages of family households.

Chart IX

1980 Family Households
(National Avg.: 73%)

State	Highest	State	Lowest
Kentucky, South Carolina,	78%	District of Columbia	53%
Utah		Nevada	68
Alabama, Arkansas, Hawaii,	77	California	69
North Carolina, Tennessee,		Colorado, New York,	70
West Virginia		Oregon, Washington	

Chart X illustrates the states with the highest and lowest average percentages of households with children.

Chart X

1980 Households with Children
(National Avg.: 40%)

State	Highest	State	Lowest
Utah	50%	District of Columbia	29%
Alaska	49	Florida	33
South Carolina	46	Nevada, Massachusetts	36
Hawaii, Louisiana,	45	California, New York,	37
New Mexico		Oregon	

Chart XI illustrates the states with the highest and lowest average percentages of married-couple households.

Chart XI

Married-Couple Households
(National Avg.: 60%)

State	Highest	State	Lowest
Utah	69%	District of Columbia	30%
Idaho	67	New York	54
Arkansas, Kentucky, North	65	California	55
Dakota, West Virginia,		Nevada	56
Wyoming		Massachusetts	57

Ethnic Breakdown. The ethnic breakdown illustrates the potential ethnic vote as opposed to the overall population. The concept of race as defined by the Census Bureau reflects self-identification and not clear-cut biological or scientific definitions.

Chart XII lists states with black voting age populations well above the national average of 10.9% in 1980. Black ethnic classification refers to those persons who indicated their race as Black or Negro on the Census questionnaire, and includes entries such as Jamaican, Black Puerto Rican, West Indian, Haitian or Nigerian. The total black population also illustrates the relative amount of black voters-to-be, children under eighteen years of age.

Chart XII

1980 Black Population: Total State and Voting Age Population

State	% of voting age pop.	% of total state pop.	State	% of voting age pop.	% of total state pop.
District of Columbia	66%	70.3%	Arkansas	14%	16.3%
Mississippi	31	35.2	Delaware	14	16.1
South Carolina	27	30.4	Tennessee	14	15.8
Louisiana	27	29.4	Illinois	13	14.7
Georgia	24	26.8	New York	12	13.7
Alabama	23	25.6	Michigan	12	12.9
Maryland	21	22.7	Florida	11	13.8
North Carolina	20	22.4	Texas	11	12.0
Virginia	17	18.9			

Chart XIII illustrates voting age and total state population figures for the ten states with the highest Spanish concentrations. The Spanish classification includes three specific categories—Mexican, Puerto Rican and Cuban, as well as those persons from Spain or the Spanish speaking countries of Central or South America. Persons of Spanish origin may be of any race.

Chart XIII

1980 Spanish Origin: Total State and Voting Age Population

State	% of voting age pop.	% of total state pop.
New Mexico	33%	36.6%
Texas	18	21.0
California	16	19.2
Arizona	13	16.2
Colorado	10	11.8
Florida	9	8.8
New York	8	9.5
New Jersey	6	7.4
Nevada	6	6.7
Hawaii	6	6.7

Share of Federal Tax Burden. The federal tax burden indicates federal-fund taxes (individual, corporate, alcohol, tobacco, etc.) and trust fund taxes rather than the Treasure Department tax collection data.

Chart XIV shows the overall national averages for total and per capita federal tax burdens.

Chart XIV

Total and Per Capita Federal Tax Burdens
(Fiscal Years 1985–88)

Total burden (in millions)					Per capita burden			
1985	1986	1987	1988		1985	1986	1987	1988
$709,400	$752,178	$822,386	$884,364		$2,982	$3,133	$3,395	$3,598

Chart XV shows the states with the highest and lowest federal tax burden; predictably, states with the highest populations pay the most.

Chart XV

1988 Total Federal Tax Burden
(in billions)

Highest		Lowest	
California	$113.2	Wyoming	$1.4
New York	77.9	Vermont	1.8
Texas	54.9	South Dakota	1.8
Illinois	46.2	North Dakota	1.9
Florida	45.7	Montana	2.1
Pennsylvania	42.9	Alaska	2.3
New Jersey	40.5	Idaho	2.5
Ohio	37.2	Delaware	2.8
Michigan	34.1	D.C.	3.1
Massachusetts	27.4	Maine	3.7

Chart XVI shows the states with the highest and lowest per capita federal tax burden.

Chart XVI

1988 Per Capita Federal Tax Burden

Highest		Lowest	
Connecticut	$5,575	Mississippi	$2,096
New Jersey	5,252	Kansas	2,282
D.C.	4,995	Utah	2,392
Massachusetts	4,668	West Virginia	2,395
New York	4,360	Arkansas	2,446
New Hampshire	4,356	Idaho	2,509
Maryland	4,325	Louisiana	2,520
Delaware	4,283	New Mexico	2,553
Alaska	4,163	South Dakota	2,583
California	4,006	Kentucky	2,612

Chart XVII shows the states with the highest and lowest per capita income.

Chart XVII

1988 Per Capita Income
(National Average: $16,444)

State	Highest	State	Lowest
Connecticut	$22,761	Mississippi	$10,992
New Jersey	21,882	West Virginia	11,658
District of Columbia	21,667	Utah	12,013
Massachusetts	20,701	Arkansas	12,172
Alaska	19,514	Louisiana	12,193
Maryland	19,314	South Dakota	12,475
New York	19,299	New Mexico	12,481
New Hampshire	19,016	Alabama	12,604
California	18,855	Idaho	12,657
Delaware	17,699	Montana	12,670

Federal Expenditures by State. For fiscal year 1988, the Census Bureau compiled statistics on federal expenditures amounting to $884 billion. Not included in this figure is interest on federal debts, international payments and foreign aid, and expenditures for selected federal agencies (*i.e.*, CIA and National Security Agency). *Federal Expenditures by State for Fiscal Year 1988* (March 1989) by the Department of Commerce contains an in-depth discussion of the categories composing the total federal expenditure. The raw numbers are in millions of dollars.

Defense numbers reflect amounts earmarked for the Department of Defense only. All other programs, including Veterans Administration benefits, are included in non-defense totals. (Defense and non-defense numbers, in some cases, do not equal the total since all numbers are rounded into millions of dollars.)

Chart XVIII shows the highest and lowest federal expenditures for defense by state.

Chart XVIII

Federal Expenditures for Defense

State	Highest $ (in millions)	% distribution	State	Lowest $ (in millions)	% distribution
California	42,398	18.56%	Vermont	221	0.10%
Virginia	21,493	9.41%	Montana	334	0.15%
Texas	17,320	7.58%	Wyoming	350	0.15%
Florida	11,585	5.07%	South Dakota	350	0.15%
New York	10,899	4.77%	North Dakota	459	0.20%

Chart XIX shows the highest and lowest federal expenditures for all other agencies by state.

Chart XIX

Federal Expenditures for All Other Agencies

| | Highest | | | Lowest | |
State	$ (in millions)	% distribution	State	$ (in millions)	% distribution
California	66,020	10.07%	Vermont	1,362	0.21%
New York	51,331	17.83%	Wyoming	1,421	0.22%
Texas	33,753	5.15%	Alaska	1,528	0.23%
Pennsylvania	33,719	5.14%	Delaware	1,644	0.25%
Florida	32,679	4.98%	New Hampshire	2,229	0.34%

Chart XX shows the highest and lowest per capita federal expenditures for defense by state.

Chart XX

Per Capita Federal Expenditures for Defense
(U.S. Median: $914.56)

| | Highest | | Lowest | |
State	$ per capita	State	$ per capita
District of Columbia	$3,386.98	West Virginia	$205.48
Virginia	3,326.09	Michigan	226.23
Hawaii	2,343.69	Wisconsin	261.15
Alaska	2,209.95	Illinois	280.63
Connecticut	1,695.90	Oregon	296.77

Chart XXI shows the highest and lowest per capita federal expenditures for all other agencies by state.

Chart XXI

Per Capita Federal Expenditures for All Other Agencies
(U.S. Median: $2,630.59)

| | Highest | | Lowest | |
State	$ per capita	State	$ per capita
District of Columbia	$21,220.97	Texas	$2,013.00
New Mexico	4,738.96	North Carolina	2,023.88
North Dakota	3,730.05	New Hampshire	2,034.61
Maryland	3,598.47	Georgia	2,142.45
South Dakota	3,380.50	Hawaii	2,191.47

CAMPAIGN FINANCE CHARTS

All data is derived from candidate and party reports as well as other official studies available from the Federal Election Commission (FEC) located at 999 E Street, N.W., Washington, DC 20463. Telephone 202-376-5140 (or toll-free 800-424-9530).

Chart XXII shows contributions from Political Action Committees (PACs), total receipts, expenditures and cash-on-hand (unspent) for all 1987–88 congressional candidates.

Chart XXII

1987–88 Total Senate Financial Activity: Winners/Losers

	No. of Cand.	Total PAC Contrib.	Total Receipts	Total Expenditures	Latest Cash-on-Hand
Senate	**210**	**$ 46,138,779**	**$199,056,261**	**$201,153,209**	**$ 9,844,411**
Democrats	**79**	24,590,128	107,414,413	107,596,186	5,912,035
Incumbents	15	15,376,208	51,005,078	51,857,179	5,025,168
Challengers	43	4,821,457	28,533,752	28,181,261	292,259
Open Seats	21	4,392,463	27,875,583	28,557,746	594,608
Republicans	**79**	21,543,451	91,315,371	93,248,748	3,914,079
Incumbents	12	13,397,761	47,268,625	49,410,978	2,909,519
Challengers	51	3,328,074	27,308,569	27,403,710	325,050
Open Seats	16	4,817,616	16,738,177	16,434,060	629,510
Others	**52**	5,200	326,477	308,275	18,297
Challenger	43	5,200	321,344	303,092	18,280
Open	9	0	5,133	5,183	17

1987–88 Total House Financial Activity: Winners/Losers

	No. of Cand.	Total PAC Contrib.	Total Receipts	Total Expenditures	Latest Cash-on-Hand
House	**1581**	**$101,946,237**	**$277,427,592**	**$256,540,203**	**$65,104,795**
Democrats	**745**	66,944,721	159,845,985	145,102,388	41,635,351
Incumbents	248	52,722,425	102,450,755	88,836,460	40,587,051
Challengers	368	7,798,605	29,447,048	28,881,669	534,147
Open Seats	129	6,423,691	27,948,182	27,384,259	514,153
Republicans	**624**	34,992,016	116,601,666	110,467,093	23,453,862
Incumbents	165	28,897,631	73,025,117	67,637,754	22,747,007
Challengers	336	2,280,881	22,017,798	21,628,100	325,307
Open Seats	123	3,813,504	21,558,751	21,201,239	381,548
Others	**212**	9,500	979,941	970,722	15,582
Challenger	179	9,400	530,220	525,508	11,470
Open	33	100	449,721	445,214	4,112
Total					
Senate/House	**1791**	**$148,085,016**	**$476,483,853**	**$457,693,412**	**$74,949,206**

Chart XXIII shows the total financial activity for Senate and House winners since 1977.

Chart XXIII

1987–88 Senate/House Winners: Financial Activity
(in millions)

Senate

	1987–88	1985–86	1983–84	1981–82	1979–80	1977–78
Receipts	$121.7	$106.8	$100.9	$70.7	$41.7	$43.0
Expend.	123.6	104.3	97.5	68.2	40.0	42.3
PAC Contrib.	31.9	28.4	20.0	15.6	10.2	6.0

House

	1987–88	1985–86	1983–84	1981–82	1979–80	1977–78
Receipts	$190.8	$172.7	$144.8	$123.1	$86.0	$60.0
Expend.	170.8	154.9	127.0	114.7	78.0	55.6
PAC Contrib.	86.1	72.8	59.5	42.7	27.0	17.0

Chart XXIV shows the top ten Senate Members and top twenty House Members elected in 1988 in terms of the highest cash-on-hand (unspent) during the 1987–88 election cycle.

Chart XXIV

1988 Senate Winners: Top Ten Cash-on-Hand

1. H. John Heinz III (R-PA) $924,534
2. Donald W. Riegle, Jr. (D-MI) 855,659
3. Edward M. Kennedy (D-MA) 708,350
4. John C. Danforth (R-MO) 645,784
5. Spark M. Matsunaga (D-HI) 639,844
6. Dennis DeConcini (D-AZ) 509,972
7. Robert C. Byrd (D-WV) 482,690
8. George J. Mitchell (D-ME) 480,728
9. Daniel P. Moynihan (D-NY) 460,075
10. Orrin G. Hatch (R-UT) 443,171

1988 House Winners: Top Twenty Cash-on-Hand

1. David Dreier (R-CA) $1,251,053
2. Stephen J. Solarz (D-NY) 1,158,484
3. Dan Rostenkowski (D-IL) 1,034,438
4. Charles E. Schumer (D-NY) 854,385
5. Ronnie G. Flippo (D-AL) 810,958
6. Mel Levine (D-CA) 805,977
7. Matthew J. Rinaldo (R-NJ) 746,181
8. James H. (Jimmy) Quillen (R-TN) 711,012
9. Robert T. Matsui (D-CA) 653,798
10. Bill Archer (R-TX) 629,908
11. Carlos J.Moorhead (R-CA) 622,634
12. Sam M.Gibbons (D-FL) 612,241
13. Larry J. Hopkins (R-KY) 608,792
14. William S. Broomfield (R-MI) 589,023
15. Thomas S. Foley (D-WA) 587,378
16. Dante B. Fascell (D-FL) 586,920
17. Michael A. (Mike) Andrews (D-TX) 565,626
18. Doug Barnard, Jr. (D-GA) 519,193
19. Tom Bevill (D-AL) 513,647
20. Thomas J. Downey (D-NY) 509,072

Chart XXV shows the top ten Senate Members and top twenty House Members elected in 1988 in terms of total receipts and expenditures during the 1987–88 election cycle.

Chart XXV

1988 Senate Winners: Top Ten Raisers

1.	Pete Wilson (R-CA)	$11,384,736
2.	Lloyd Bentsen (D-TX)	8,280,013
3.	Herbert H. Kohl (D-WI)	7,576,540
4.	Howard Metzenbaum (D-OH)	7,312,533
5.	Frank Lautenberg (D-NJ)	7,087,476
6.	H. John Heinz III (R-PA)	5,280,540
7.	Connie Mack III (R-FL)	5,224,061
8.	Dave Durenberger (R-MN)	4,969,448
9.	Daniel P. Moynihan (D-NY)	4,350,271
10.	John C. Danforth (R-MO)	4,077,855

1988 Senate Winners: Top Ten Spenders

1.	Pete Wilson (R-CA)	$12,969,294
2.	Lloyd Bentsen (D-TX)	8,829,361
3.	Howard Metzenbaum (D-OH)	8,547,545
4.	Herbert H. Kohl (D-WI)	7,491,600
5.	Frank Lautenberg (D-NJ)	7,298,663
6.	Dave Durenberger (R-MN)	5,410,783
7.	Connie Mack III (R-FL)	5,181,639
8.	H. John Heinz III (R-PA)	5,151,512
9.	Daniel P. Moynihan (D-NY)	4,809,810
10.	John C. Danforth (R-MO)	3,992,995

1988 House Winners: Top Twenty Raisers

1.	Robert K. (Bob) Dornan (R-CA)	$1,731,883
2.	Tom Campbell (R-CA)	1,445,770
3.	Jospeh P. Kennedy II (D-MA)	1,419,819
4.	Nita M. Lowey (D-NY)	1,338,147
5.	John R. Miller (R-WA)	1,328,979
6.	Jim Moody (D-WI)	1,291,564
7.	Robert J. Lagomarsino (R-CA)	1,226,229
8.	James A. (Jim) Courter (R-NJ)	1,211,060
9.	Nancy Pelosi (D-CA)	1,209,746
10.	Elizabeth J. Patterson (D-SC)	1,119,822
11.	C. Christopher Cox (R-CA)	1,111,321
12.	Peter H. Kostmayer (D-PA)	1,110,419
13.	David E. Price (D-NC)	1,031,004
14.	Harry A. Johnston (D-FL)	974,743
15.	John P. Hiler (R-IN)	971,929
16.	Bob Clement (D-TN)	941,940
17.	John S. Tanner (D-TN)	931,539
18.	Robert T. Matsui (D-CA)	916,025
19.	Stephen J. Solarz (D-NY)	899,313
20.	Thomas J. Downey (D-NY)	896,625

1988 House Winners: Top Twenty Spenders

1.	Robert K. (Bob) Dornan (R-CA)	$1,755,892
2.	Robert J. Lagomarsino (R-CA)	1,470,674
3.	Tom Campbell (R-CA)	1,440,639
4.	James A. (Jim) Courter (R-NJ)	1,333,882
5.	John R. Miller (R-WA)	1,321,021
6.	Nita M. Lowey (D-NY)	1,309,873
7.	Jim Moody (D-WI)	1,278,526
8.	Jospeh P. Kennedy II (D-MA)	1,186,852
9.	Nancy Pelosi (D-CA)	1,182,491
10.	Elizabeth J. Patterson (D-SC)	1,143,351
11.	C. Christopher Cox (R-CA)	1,110,126
12.	Peter H. Kostmayer (D-PA)	1,089,612
13.	John P. Hiler (R-IN)	1,085,140
14.	David E. Price (D-NC)	1,006,641
15.	Steve Bartlett (D-TX)	1,000,894
16.	Tony Coelho (D-CA)	972,235
17.	Harry A. Johnston (D-FL)	971,883
18.	Jim Wright (D-TX)	940,760
19.	Bob Clement (D-TN)	938,492
20.	James J. Florio (D-NJ)	924,427

Chart XXVI illustrates the Democratic and Republican Party financial activity for the 1987–88 election cycle.

Chart XXVI

1987–88 Party Financial Activity: Democratic/Republican

Democratic	Net Receipts	Net Expenditures	C.O.H. (12-31-88)	Debt Owed By	Contrib. To Cand.	Coordinated Expenditures
DNC Services	$ 52,295,783	$ 47,036,799	$5,414,658	$ 163,110	$ 137,998	$ 8,107,044
Senatorial	16,297,386	16,289,589	86,709	1,010,143	420,579	6,206,137
Congressional	12,469,354	12,481,532	46,676	2,117,760	666,637	2,425,603
Assn. of State Dem. Chair	9,669,282	9,725,339	527,804	0	0	0
Convention	9,495,119	9,426,792	0	0	0	0
State and Local	27,696,663	26,967,036	1,240,518	255,441	507,092	1,177,205
Totals	**$127,923,587**	**$121,927,087**	**$7,316,365**	**$3,546,454**	**$1,732,306**	**$17,915,989**

Republican	Net Receipts	Net Expenditures	C.O.H. (12-31-88)	Debt Owed By	Contrib. To Cand.	Coordinated Expenditures
RNC	$ 90,980,761	$ 89,893,536	$ 2,328,072	$ 0	$ 325,440	$ 8,291,273
Senatorial	65,896,691	63,350,247	2,731,779	135,668	760,488	10,250,538
Congressional	34,483,260	33,569,320	1,189,556	706,883	1,583,503	4,107,689
Other Natl. Repub.	6,329	6,421	0	0	0	0
Convention	9,640,356	9,604,159	38,243	0	0	0
State and Local	62,249,430	60,532,621	3,125,046	1,353,851	718,487	64,853
Totals	**$263,256,827**	**$256,956,304**	**$9,412,696**	**$2,196,402**	**$3,387,918**	**$22,714,353**

| **Grand Total** | **$391,180,414** | **$378,883,391** | **$16,729,061** | **$5,742,856** | **$5,120,224** | **$40,630,342** |

Chart XXVIII shows the top ten Senate Members and top twenty House Members elected in 1988 in terms of total PAC receipts during the 1987–88 election cycle.

Chart XXVIII

1988 Senate Winners: PAC $ Recipients

1.	Lloyd Bentsen (D-TX)	$2,320,541
2.	Pete Wilson (R-CA)	$1,837,925
3.	Dave Durenberger (R-MN)	$1,499,382
4.	H. John Heinz III (R-PA)	$1,441,438
5.	Frank Lautenberg (D-NJ)	$1,410,360
6.	James R. Sasser (D-TN)	$1,379,817
7.	Donald W. Riegle, Jr. (D-MI)	$1,281,641
8.	Orrin G. Hatch (R-UT)	$1,173,764
9.	John C. Danforth (R-MO)	$1,149,207
10.	Trent Lott (R-MS)	$1,118,111

1988 House Winners:
Top Twenty PAC $ Recipients

1.	Robert H. Michel (R-IL)	$555,417
2.	Thomas S. Foley (D-WA)	$555,140
3.	Jim Moody (D-WI)	$524,503
4.	David E. Price (D-NC)	$489,658
5.	Mike Espy (D-MS)	$480,490
6.	Robert T. Matsui (D-CA)	$475,366
7.	James Jontz (D-IN)	$471,725
8.	Thomas A. Luken (D-OH)	$468,685
9.	Byron L. Dorgan (D-ND)	$462,346
10.	John D. Dingell (D-MI)	$459,242
11.	Wayne Owens (D-UT)	$455,310
12.	David E. Skaggs (D-CO)	$452,772
13.	Ronnie G. Flippo (D-AL)	$445,960
14.	Dan Rostenkowski (D-IL)	$444,698
15.	Frank Pallone, Jr. (D-NJ)	$437,739
16.	Bill Emerson (R-MO)	$421,852
17.	Peter H. Kostmayer (D-PA)	$418,821
18.	George Hockbrueckner, Jr. (D-NY)	$417,961
19.	Tony Coehlo (D-CA)	$415,666
20.	James H. Quillen (R-TN)	$413,800

CAMPAIGN FINANCE BY MEMBER

ALABAMA

Sen. Howell Heflin (D)

1979-84		Direct Cont. 1979-84	
Receipts	$2,391,192	Indiv.	$1,315,791
Expend.	$2,001,386	PACS	$945,293
C.O.H.	$484,533		

Sen. Richard C. Shelby (D)

1985-86		Direct Cont. 1985-86	
Receipts	$2,400,488	Indiv.	$686,727
Expend.	$2,259,167	Party	$17,499
C.O.H.	$141,319	PACS	$891,434
		Cand.	$696,104

1st District, Rep. H. L. (Sonny) Callahan (R)

1987-88		Direct Cont. 1987-88	
Receipts	$596,631	Indiv.	$314,219
Expend.	$651,127	Party	$5,881
C.O.H.	$101,741	PACS	$253,301

2d District, Rep. William L. Dickinson (R)

1987-88		Direct Cont. 1987-88	
Receipts	$304,708	Indiv.	$117,145
Expend.	$234,923	Party	$2,978
C.O.H.	$421,368	PACS	$168,639

3d District, Rep. Glen Browder (D)

1987-88		Direct Cont. 1987-88	
Receipts	$720,808	Indiv.	$406,370
Expend.	$679,297	Party	$35,389
C.O.H.	$16,226	PACS	$440,300
Debts	$78,143	Cand.	$33,000

4th District, Rep. Tom Bevill (D)

1987-88		Direct Cont. 1987-88	
Receipts	$206,806	Indiv.	$53,440
Expend.	$130,642	PACS	$94,850
C.O.H.	$513,647		

5th District, Rep. Ronnie G. Flippo (D)

1987-88		Direct Cont. 1987-88	
Receipts	$711,580	Indiv.	$177,157
Expend.	$504,570	PACS	$445,960
C.O.H.	$810,958	Cand.	$6,000

6th District, Rep. Ben Erdreich (D)

1987-88		Direct Cont. 1987-88	
Receipts	$251,841	Indiv.	$52,641
Expend.	$159,323	PACS	$173,850
C.O.H.	$239,472		

7th District, Rep. Claude Harris, Jr. (D)

1987-88		Direct Cont. 1987-88	
Receipts	$405,426	Indiv.	$143,626
Expend.	$328,296	Party	$1,511
C.O.H.	$78,631	PACS	$257,205
Debts	$5,000		

ALASKA

Sen. Ted Stevens (R)

1979-84		Direct Cont. 1979-84	
Receipts	$1,418,819	Indiv.	$650,846
Expend.	$1,323,218	Party	$15,981
C.O.H.	$184,289	PACS	$660,019

Sen. Frank H. Murkowski (R)

1985-86		Direct Cont. 1985-86	
Receipts	$1,425,261	Indiv.	$738,750
Expend.	$1,389,056	Party	$17,885
C.O.H.	$53,848	PACS	$594,206
		Cand.	$15,853

At-Large, Rep. Don Young (R)

1987-88		Direct Cont. 1987-88	
Receipts	$623,760	Indiv.	$297,321
Expend.	$626,377	Party	$19,337
C.O.H.	$9,394	PACS	$296,950
Debts	$36,349		

ARIZONA

Sen. Dennis DeConcini (D)

1987-88		Direct Cont. 1987-88	
Receipts	$2,818,427	Indiv.	$1,603,419
Expend.	$2,640,650	PACS	$968,495
C.O.H.	$509,972		
Debts	$23,951		

Sen. John McCain (R)

1985-86		Direct Cont. 1985-86	
Receipts	$2,549,080	Indiv.	$1,441,759
Expend.	$2,228,498	Party	$23,107
C.O.H.	$287,217	PACS	$765,678
		Cand.	$214,406

1st District, Rep. John J. Rhodes III (R)

1987-88		Direct Cont. 1987-88	
Receipts	$293,044	Indiv.	$156,187
Expend.	$291,961	Party	$21
C.O.H.	$6,309	PACS	$135,419

2d District, Rep. Morris K. Udall (D)

1987-88		Direct Cont. 1987-88	
Receipts	$119,497	Indiv.	$32,199
Expend.	$99,607	PACS	$84,605
C.O.H.	$32,804		

3d District, Rep. Bob Stump (R)

1987-88		Direct Cont. 1987-88	
Receipts	$257,184	Indiv.	$94,670
Expend.	$319,690	Party	$2,000
C.O.H.	$107,674	PACS	$115,046

4th District, Rep. Jon L. Kyl (R)

1987-88		Direct Cont. 1987-88	
Receipts	$497,313	Indiv.	$302,381
Expend.	$316,476	Party	$4,239
C.O.H.	$189,890	PACS	$178,114
Debts	$4,196		

5th District, Rep. Jim Kolbe (R)

1987-88		Direct Cont. 1987-88	
Receipts	$419,090	Indiv.	$240,729
Expend.	$434,665	Party	$8,048
C.O.H.	$6,272	PACS	$158,738
Debts	$21,040		

ARKANSAS

Sen. Dale Bumpers (D)

1985-86		Direct Cont. 1985-86	
Receipts	$1,726,383	Indiv.	$1,132,857
Expend.	$1,672,432	Party	$3,250
C.O.H.	$124,978	PACS	$503,831

Sen. David Pryor (D)

1979-84		Direct Cont. 1979-84	
Receipts	$1,981,197	Indiv.	$1,162,696
Expend.	$1,838,352	Party	$24,030
C.O.H.	$174,188	PACS	$685,982

1st District, Rep. Bill Alexander (D)

1987-88		Direct Cont. 1987-88	
Receipts	$657,122	Indiv.	$263,058
Expend.	$640,427	PACS	$304,699
C.O.H.	$25,233	Cand.	$85,000
Debts	$28,830		

2d District, Rep. Tommy F. Robinson (D)

1987-88		Direct Cont. 1987-88	
Receipts	$503,328	Indiv.	$319,683
Expend.	$459,876	Party	$835
C.O.H.	$92,815	PACS	$182,980

3d District, Rep. John Paul Hammerschmidt (R)

1987-88		Direct Cont. 1987-88	
Receipts	$330,387	Indiv.	$128,112
Expend.	$159,221	Party	$7,108
C.O.H.	$339,600	PACS	$166,700

4th District, Rep. Beryl F. Anthony, Jr. (D)

1987-88		Direct Cont. 1987-88	
Receipts	$547,244	Indiv.	$52,269
Expend.	$570,155	PACS	$353,042
C.O.H.	$314,855	Cand.	$40,000
Debts	$40,000		

CALIFORNIA

Sen. Alan Cranston (D)

1985-86		Direct Cont. 1985-86	
Receipts	$10,851,596	Indiv.	$8,874,482
Expend.	$11,037,707	Party	$19,523
C.O.H.	$11,593	PACS	$1,373,466
		Cand.	$375,250

Sen. Pete Wilson (R)

1987-88		Direct Cont. 1987-88	
Receipts	$11,384,736	Indiv.	$9,187,165
Expend.	$12,969,294	Party	$30,499
C.O.H.	$54,088	PACS	$1,837,925
Debts	$289,022		

1st District, Rep. Douglas H. Bosco (D)

1987-88		Direct Cont. 1987-88	
Receipts	$252,328	Indiv.	$93,228
Expend.	$247,779	PACS	$119,638
C.O.H.	$5,198	Cand.	$38,000

2d District, Rep. Wally Herger (R)

1987-88		Direct Cont. 1987-88	
Receipts	$691,969	Indiv.	$407,753
Expend.	$696,748	Party	$6,575
C.O.H.	$13,809	PACs	$258,675
Debts	$10,602	Cand.	$1,000

3d District, Rep. Robert T. Matsui (D)

1987-88		Direct Cont. 1987-88	
Receipts	$916,025	Indiv.	$348,347
Expend.	$638,688	Party	$221
C.O.H.	$653,798	PACS	$475,366
		Cand.	$5,000

4th District, Rep. Vic Fazio (D)

1987-88		Direct Cont. 1987-88	
Receipts	$622,357	Indiv.	$222,795
Expend.	$529,334	PACS	$378,783
C.O.H.	$378,618		

5th District, Rep. Nancy Pelosi (D)

1987-88		Direct Cont. 1987-88	
Receipts	$655,522	Indiv.	$354,925
Expend.	$616,936	Party	$219
C.O.H.	$65,838	PACS	$279,300
		Cand.	$335,000

6th District, Rep. Barbara Boxer (D)

1987-88		Direct Cont. 1987-88	
Receipts	$450,306	Indiv.	$247,591
Expend.	$351,687	PACS	$185,330
C.O.H.	$233,086		

7th District, Rep. George Miller (D)

1987-88		Direct Cont. 1987-88	
Receipts	$429,305	Indiv.	$208,914
Expend.	$269,887	PACS	$179,984
C.O.H.	$416,855		

8th District, Rep. Ronald V. Dellums (D)

1987-88		Direct Cont. 1987-88	
Receipts	$1,153,750	Indiv.	$848,795
Expend.	$1,174,676	PACS	$87,299
C.O.H.	$132,270	Cand.	$183,425

9th District, Rep. Fortney H. (Pete) Stark (D)

1987-88		Direct Cont. 1987-88	
Receipts	$504,708	Indiv.	$159,985
Expend.	$410,540	PACS	$325,428
C.O.H.	$131,730		

10th District, Rep. Don Edwards (D)

1987-88		Direct Cont. 1987-88	
Receipts	$166,689	Indiv.	$41,438
Expend.	$173,537	Party	$221
C.O.H.	$39,708	PACS	$117,256

11th District, Rep. Tom Lantos (D)

1987-88		Direct Cont. 1987-88	
Receipts	$386,453	Indiv.	$223,034
Expend.	$269,510	Party	$601
C.O.H.	$470,219	PACS	$111,267

12th District, Rep. Tom Campbell (R)

1987-88		Direct Cont. 1987-88	
Receipts	$1,445,770	Indiv.	$1,176,961
Expend.	$1,440,639	Party	$9,998
C.O.H.	$5,132	PACS	$239,382
Debts	$101,059	Cand.	$17,221

13th District, Rep. Norman Y. Mineta (D)

1987-88		Direct Cont. 1987-88	
Receipts	$577,164	Indiv.	$256,899
Expend.	$521,674	PACS	$277,450
C.O.H.	$320,749		

14th District, Rep. Norman D. Shumway (R)

1987-88		Direct Cont. 1987-88	
Receipts	$390,233	Indiv.	$213,551
Expend.	$492,349	Party	$3,258
C.O.H.	$36,984	PACS	$151,635

15th District, Rep. Tony Coelho (D)

1987-88		Direct Cont. 1987-88	
Receipts	$837,955	Indiv.	$392,979
Expend.	$972,235	Party	$133
C.O.H.	$79,049	PACS	$415,666

16th District, Rep. Leon E. Panetta (D)

1987-88		Direct Cont. 1987-88	
Receipts	$318,076	Indiv.	$140,820
Expend.	$252,336	Party	$170
C.O.H.	$181,908	PACS	$112,600

17th District, Rep. Chip Pashayan, Jr. (R)

1987-88		Direct Cont. 1987-88	
Receipts	$216,479	Indiv.	$89,162
Expend.	$206,677	Party	$3,410
C.O.H.	$70,242	PACS	$117,170

18th District, Rep. Richard H. Lehman (D)

1987-88		Direct Cont. 1987-88	
Receipts	$279,981	Indiv.	$108,423
Expend.	$193,681	Party	$1,157
C.O.H.	$93,399	PACS	$131,276

19th District, Rep. Robert J. Lagomarsino (R)

1987-88		Direct Cont. 1987-88	
Receipts	$1,226,229	Indiv.	$809,074
Expend.	$1,470,674	Party	$18,284
C.O.H.	$28,043	PACS	$338,996

20th District, Rep. William M. Thomas (R)

1987-88		Direct Cont. 1987-88	
Receipts	$335,586	Indiv.	$79,654
Expend.	$329,354	Party	$2,010
C.O.H.	$200,913	PACS	$215,150

21st District, Rep. Elton Gallegly (R)

1987-88		Direct Cont. 1987-88	
Receipts	$506,391	Indiv.	$331,764
Expend.	$465,310	Party	$9,010
C.O.H.	$81,485	PACS	$163,825
Debts	$33,565		

22d District, Rep. Carlos J. Moorhead (R)

1987-88		Direct Cont. 1987-88	
Receipts	$397,417	Indiv.	$105,260
Expend.	$234,920	Party	$2,000
C.O.H.	$622,634	PACS	$215,165

23d District, Rep. Anthony C. Beilenson (D)

1987-88		Direct Cont. 1987-88	
Receipts	$150,275	Indiv.	$139,382
Expend.	$140,486	Cand.	$10,000
C.O.H.	$15,467		

24th District, Rep. Henry A. Waxman (D)

1987-88		Direct Cont. 1987-88	
Receipts	$345,006	Indiv.	$63,550
Expend.	$191,334	Party	$242
C.O.H.	$255,551	PACS	$257,841
		Cand.	$1,000

25th District, Rep. Edward R. Roybal (D)

1987-88		Direct Cont. 1987-88	
Receipts	$86,724	Indiv.	$5,805
Expend.	$67,957	Party	$170
C.O.H.	$243,294	PACS	$46,800

26th District, Rep. Howard L. Berman (D)

1987-88		Direct Cont. 1987-88	
Receipts	$528,296	Indiv.	$283,838
Expend.	$409,233	Party	$158
Debts	$140,335	PACS	$209,317
		Cand.	$20,000

27th District, Rep. Mel Levine (D)

1987-88		Direct Cont. 1987-88	
Receipts	$893,810	Indiv.	$575,866
Expend.	$398,597	Party	$3,000
C.O.H.	$805,977	PACS	$153,500

28th District, Rep. Julian C. Dixon (D)

1987-88		Direct Cont. 1987-88	
Receipts	$120,740	Indiv.	$45,098
Expend.	$114,523	PACS	$70,980
C.O.H.	$86,741		

29th District, Rep. Augustus F. Hawkins (D)

1987-88		Direct Cont. 1987-88	
Receipts	$109,450	Indiv.	$3,900
Expend.	$65,833	PACS	$105,550
C.O.H.	$155,055		

30th District, Rep. Matthew G. Martinez (D)

1987-88		Direct Cont. 1987-88	
Receipts	$437,775	Indiv.	$172,543
Expend.	$460,622	Party	$20,157
C.O.H.	$19,677	PACS	$226,400
Debts	$20,000	Cand.	$16,000

31st District, Rep. Mervyn M. Dymally (D)

1987-88		Direct Cont. 1987-88	
Receipts	$488,149	Indiv.	$307,281
Expend.	$481,799	Party	$154
C.O.H.	$10,136	PACS	$156,449
		Cand.	$13,000

32d District, Rep. Glenn M. Anderson (D)

1987-88		Direct Cont. 1987-88	
Receipts	$493,296	Indiv.	$197,948
Expend.	$457,410	PACS	$276,785
Debts	$82,442	Cand.	$3,000

33d District, Rep. David Dreier (R)

1987-88		Direct Cont. 1987-88	
Receipts	$487,407	Indiv.	$211,982
Expend.	$186,183	Party	$2,082
C.O.H.	$1,251,053	PACS	$101,850

34th District, Rep. Esteban E. Torres (D)

1987-88		Direct Cont. 1987-88	
Receipts	$226,964	Indiv.	$91,920
Expend.	$227,098	PACS	$108,280
C.O.H.	$124,561		

35th District, Rep. Jerry Lewis (R)

1987-88		Direct Cont. 1987-88	
Receipts	$212,905	Indiv.	$31,366
Expend.	$337,814	Party	$2,250
C.O.H.	$98,359	PACS	$156,400

36th District, Rep. George E. Brown, Jr. (D)

1987-88		Direct Cont. 1987-88	
Receipts	$504,361	Indiv.	$197,195
Expend.	$532,897	Party	$12,493
C.O.H.	$8,852	PACS	$276,543
Debts	$3,000	Cand.	$6,000

37th District, Rep. Al McCandless (R)

1987-88		Direct Cont. 1987-88	
Receipts	$129,505	Indiv.	$51,104
Expend.	$122,839	Party	$2,011
C.O.H.	$58,257	PACS	$75,500

38th District, Rep. Bob Dornan (R)

1987-88		Direct Cont. 1987-88	
Receipts	$1,731,883	Indiv.	$1,555,928
Expend.	$1,755,892	Party	$2,782
C.O.H.	$8,352	PACS	$83,231
Debts	$302,609	Cand.	$57,500

39th District, Rep. William E. Dannemeyer (R)

1987-88		Direct Cont. 1987-88	
Receipts	$300,156	Indiv.	$142,556
Expend.	$250,737	Party	$2,165
C.O.H.	$130,893	PACS	$144,472
		Cand.	$1,200

40th District, Rep. C. Christopher Cox (R)

1987-88		Direct Cont. 1987-88	
Receipts	$1,111,321	Indiv.	$787,770
Expend.	$1,110,126	Party	$10,497
C.O.H.	$703	PACS	$198,786
Debts	$300,395	Cand.	$121,450

41st District, Rep. Bill Lowery (R)

1987-88		Direct Cont. 1987-88	
Receipts	$453,289	Indiv.	$256,422
Expend.	$407,025	Party	$1,000
C.O.H.	$118,172	PACS	$182,415

42d District, Rep. Dana Rohrabacher (R)

1987-88		Direct Cont. 1987-88	
Receipts	$521,565	Indiv.	$279,194
Expend.	$494,487	Party	$9,999
C.O.H.	$27,077	PACS	$186,427
Debts	$73,651	Cand.	$41,471

43d District, Rep. Ronald C. Packard (R)

1987-88		Direct Cont. 1987-88	
Receipts	$215,956	Indiv.	$79,259
Expend.	$160,267	Party	$2,006
C.O.H.	$154,821	PACS	$114,538

44th District, Rep. Jim Bates (D)

1987-88		Direct Cont. 1987-88	
Receipts	$480,384	Indiv.	$213,909
Expend.	$480,679	Party	$12,253
C.O.H.	$80	PACS	$246,105
Debts	$14,256	Cand.	$3,000

45th District, Rep. Duncan L. Hunter (R)

1987-88		Direct Cont. 1987-88	
Receipts	$392,229	Indiv.	$214,988
Expend.	$489,395	Party	$2,339
C.O.H.	$24,864	PACS	$150,718

COLORADO

Sen. William L. Armstrong (R)

1979-84		Direct Cont. 1979-84	
Receipts	$3,169,764	Indiv.	$2,134,536
Expend.	$3,098,129	Party	$15,418
C.O.H.	$173,373	PACS	$837,784
		Cand.	$10,000

Sen. Timothy E. Wirth (D)

1985-86		Direct Cont. 1985-86	
Receipts	$3,819,308	Indiv.	$2,613,318
Expend.	$3,787,202	Party	$17,500
C.O.H.	$32,106	PACS	$842,038
		Cand.	$319,946

1st District, Rep. Patricia Schroeder (D)

1987-88		Direct Cont. 1987-88	
Receipts	$275,795	Indiv.	$114,101
Expend.	$217,503	Party	$457
C.O.H.	$262,049	PACS	$131,785
Debts	$3,614		

2d District, Rep. David E. Skaggs (D)

1987-88		Direct Cont. 1987-88	
Receipts	$730,990	Indiv.	$256,699
Expend.	$721,647	Party	$14,065
C.O.H.	$12,411	PACS	$452,772
Debts	$17,141	Cand.	$5,168

3d District, Rep. Ben Nighthorse Campbell (D)

1987-88		Direct Cont. 1987-88	
Receipts	$513,212	Indiv.	$183,120
Expend.	$482,789	Party	$5,000
C.O.H.	$39,099	PACS	$302,590

4th District, Rep. Hank Brown (R)

1987-88		Direct Cont. 1987-88	
Receipts	$287,187	Indiv.	$78,384
Expend.	$109,146	Party	$2,235
C.O.H.	$287,762	PACS	$190,891

5th District, Rep. Joel Hefley (R)

1987-88		Direct Cont. 1987-88	
Receipts	$228,896	Indiv.	$105,486
Expend.	$183,229	Party	$5,718
C.O.H.	$60,949	PACS	$112,827

6th District, Rep. Dan L. Schaefer (R)

1987-88		Direct Cont. 1987-88	
Receipts	$618,607	Indiv.	$236,865
Expend.	$636,204	Party	$14,913
C.O.H.	$26,832	PACS	$335,747

CONNECTICUT

Sen. Christopher J. Dodd (D)

1985-86		Direct Cont. 1985-86	
Receipts	$2,395,798	Indiv.	$1,551,211
Expend.	$2,276,764	Party	$14,973
C.O.H.	$266,781	PACS	$721,289

Sen. Joseph I. Lieberman (D)

1987-88		Direct Cont. 1987-88	
Receipts	$2,647,603	Indiv.	$2,309,193
Expend.	$2,570,779	Party	$17,050
C.O.H.	$76,824	PACS	$175,566
Debts	$100,637	Cand.	$50,000

1st District, Rep. Barbara B. Kennelly (D)

1987-88		Direct Cont. 1987-88	
Receipts	$448,010	Indiv.	$158,450
Expend.	$471,530	Party	$389
C.O.H.	$100,078	PACS	$269,603

2d District, Rep. Samuel Gejdenson (D)

1987-88		Direct Cont. 1987-88	
Receipts	$731,513	Indiv.	$435,249
Expend.	$727,919	PACS	$208,800
C.O.H.	$10,177	Cand.	$64,567

3d District, Rep. Bruce A. Morrison (D)

1987-88		Direct Cont. 1987-88	
Receipts	$490,274	Indiv.	$245,361
Expend.	$506,799	PACS	$224,533
C.O.H.	$30,721		

4th District, Rep. Christopher H. Shays (R)

1987-88		Direct Cont. 1987-88	
Receipts	$359,551	Indiv.	$236,202
Expend.	$372,680	Party	$11,254
C.O.H.	$23,361	PACS	$93,202
Debts	$2,158	Cand.	$9,000

5th District, Rep. John G. Rowland (R)

1987-88		Direct Cont. 1987-88	
Receipts	$440,111	Indiv.	$265,906
Expend.	$375,660	Party	$6,019
C.O.H.	$68,203	PACS	$148,135

6th District, Rep. Nancy L. Johnson (R)

1987-88		Direct Cont. 1987-88	
Receipts	$527,164	Indiv.	$375,787
Expend.	$399,370	Party	$5,788
C.O.H.	$156,660	PACS	$135,322

DELAWARE

Sen. William V. Roth, Jr. (R)

1987-88		Direct Cont. 1987-88	
Receipts	$1,887,995	Indiv.	$1,037,362
Expend.	$1,942,119	Party	$15,000
C.O.H.	$89,031	PACS	$794,191

Sen. Joe Biden (D)

1979-84		Direct Cont. 1979-84	
Receipts	$1,627,215	Indiv.	$1,101,130
Expend.	$1,602,052	Party	$22,500
C.O.H.	$24,489	PACS	$433,947

At-Large, Rep. Thomas R. Carper (D)

1987-88		Direct Cont. 1987-88	
Receipts	$365,432	Indiv.	$190,059
Expend.	$371,747	Party	$5,000
C.O.H.	$26,468	PACS	$161,235
Debts	$10,000		

DISTRICT OF COLUMBIA

Rep. Walter E. Fauntroy (D)

1987-88		Direct Cont. 1987-88	
Receipts	$68,018	Indiv.	$27,480
Expend.	$68,523	Party	$176
C.O.H.	$13,660	PACS	$31,446

FLORIDA

Sen. Robert Graham (D)

1985-86		Direct Cont. 1985-86	
Receipts	$6,215,914	Indiv.	$5,226,130
Expend.	$6,173,663	Party	$19,619
C.O.H.	$42,247	PACS	$926,157

Sen. Connie Mack, III (R)

1987-88		Direct Cont. 1987-88	
Receipts	$5,224,061	Indiv.	$3,834,016
Expend.	$5,181,639	Party	$34,428
C.O.H.	$42,420	PACS	$1,018,745
Debts	$388,611		

1st District, Rep. Earl Dewitt Hutto (D)

1987-88		Direct Cont. 1987-88	
Receipts	$212,973	Indiv.	$83,833
Expend.	$210,940	PACS	$109,186
C.O.H.	$55,834	Cand.	$15,000

2d District, Rep. Bill Grant (R)

1987-88		Direct Cont. 1987-88	
Receipts	$264,955	Indiv.	$123,214
Expend.	$223,117	Party	$712
C.O.H.	$42,345	PACS	$102,100
		Cand.	$14,977

3d District, Rep. Charles E. Bennett (D)

1987-88		Direct Cont. 1987-88	
Receipts	$104,518	Indiv.	$15,636
Expend.	$19,500	Party	$245
C.O.H.	$302,363	PACS	$53,861
Debts	$3,549		

4th District, Rep. Craig James (R)

1987-88		Direct Cont. 1987-88	
Receipts	$314,634	Indiv.	$59,994
Expend.	$313,415	Party	$40,540
C.O.H.	$1,218	PACS	$7,295
Debts	$171,700		

5th District, Rep. Bill McCollum (R)

1987-88		Direct Cont. 1987-88	
Receipts	$321,887	Indiv.	$126,144
Expend.	$304,853	Party	$2,000
C.O.H.	$239,063	PACS	$117,835

6th District, Rep. Clifford D. Stearns (R)

1987-88		Direct Cont. 1987-88	
Receipts	$421,198	Indiv.	$121,194
Expend.	$408,292	Party	$59,999
C.O.H.	$12,885	PACS	$52,270
Debts	$145,024	Cand.	$191,456

7th District, Rep. Sam M. Gibbons (D)

1987-88		Direct Cont. 1987-88	
Receipts	$604,570	Indiv.	$201,003
Expend.	$382,889	PACS	$345,387
C.O.H.	$612,241		

8th District, Rep. Bill Young (R)

1987-88		Direct Cont. 1987-88	
Receipts	$212,972	Indiv.	$57,233
Expend.	$208,320	Party	$2,961
C.O.H.	$311,561	PACS	$109,600

9th District, Rep. Michael Bilirakis (R)

1987-88		Direct Cont. 1987-88	
Receipts	$399,150	Indiv.	$237,819
Expend.	$193,901	Party	$2,773
C.O.H.	$217,312	PACS	$149,975

10th District, Rep. Andy Ireland (R)

1987-88		Direct Cont. 1987-88	
Receipts	$405,000	Indiv.	$217,558
Expend.	$460,468	Party	$4,821
C.O.H.	$72,351	PACS	$164,389

11th District, Rep. Bill Nelson (D)

1987-88		Direct Cont. 1987-88	
Receipts	$456,878	Indiv.	$177,308
Expend.	$565,632	Party	$772
C.O.H.	$4,983	PACS	$213,956
Debts	$38,042	Cand.	$46,089

12th District, Rep. Tom Lewis (R)

1987-88		Direct Cont. 1987-88	
Receipts	$288,963	Indiv.	$199,214
Expend.	$256,081	PACS	$64,465
C.O.H.	$186,252		

13th. District, Rep. Porter J. Goss (R)

1987-88		Direct Cont. 1987-88	
Receipts	$878,439	Indiv.	$640,991
Expend.	$836,224	Party	$6,075
C.O.H.	$42,215	PACS	$141,976
Debts	$73,308	Cand.	$81,908

14th District, Rep. Harry A. Johnston (D)

1987-88		Direct Cont. 1987-88	
Receipts	$974,743	Indiv.	$594,408
Expend.	$971,883	Party	$15,000
C.O.H.	$2,860	PACS	$296,636
Debts	$36,314	Cand.	$52,104

15th District, Rep. E. Clay Shaw, Jr. (R)

1987-88		Direct Cont. 1987-88	
Receipts	$348,233	Indiv.	$180,700
Expend.	$455,578	Party	$2,004
C.O.H.	$13,467	PACS	$153,750

16th District, Rep. Larry Smith (D)

1987-88		Direct Cont. 1987-88	
Receipts	$649,689	Indiv.	$346,229
Expend.	$555,473	Party	$332
C.O.H.	$151,246	PACS	$280,493

17th District, Rep. William Lehman (D)

1987-88		Direct Cont. 1987-88	
Receipts	$324,062	Indiv.	$171,758
Expend.	$257,487	PACS	$132,250
C.O.H.	$220,429		

18th District, Rep. Claude Pepper (D)

1987-88		Direct Cont. 1987-88	
Receipts	$434,858	Indiv.	$186,773
Expend.	$405,551	Party	$242
C.O.H.	$82,079	PACS	$243,565

19th District, Rep. Dante B. Fascell (D)

1987-88		Direct Cont. 1987-88	
Receipts	$490,976	Indiv.	$240,807
Expend.	$337,596	Party	$215
C.O.H.	$586,920	PACS	$176,934

GEORGIA

Sen. Sam Nunn (D)

1979-84		Direct Cont. 1979-84	
Receipts	$1,360,247	Indiv.	$760,453
Expend.	$843,891	Party	$850
C.O.H.	$676,199	PACS	$386,546

Sen. Wyche Fowler (D)

1985-86		Direct Cont. 1985-86	
Receipts	$2,912,638	Indiv.	$1,423,393
Expend.	$2,779,297	Party	$24,400
C.O.H.	$133,342	PACS	$596,601
		Cand.	$50,000

1st District, Rep. Robert Lindsay Thomas (D)

1987-88		Direct Cont. 1987-88	
Receipts	$339,987	Indiv.	$169,406
Expend.	$337,048	Party	$384
C.O.H.	$88,518	PACS	$149,969

2d District, Rep. Charles F. Hatcher (D)

1987-88		Direct Cont. 1987-88	
Receipts	$348,158	Indiv.	$110,111
Expend.	$368,470	Party	$651
C.O.H.	$6,673	PACS	$200,450
Debts	$85,829	Cand.	$30,000

3d District, Rep. Richard B. Ray (D)

1987-88		Direct Cont. 1987-88	
Receipts	$281,295	Indiv.	$103,069
Expend.	$256,751	PACS	$131,117
C.O.H.	$190,165	Cand.	$20,006
Debts	$13,006		

4th District, Rep. Ben Jones (D)

1987-88		Direct Cont. 1987-88	
Receipts	$522,594	Indiv.	$234,282
Expend.	$516,737	Party	$14,999
C.O.H.	$5,937	PACS	$265,606
Debts	$24,771	Cand.	$3,750

5th District, Rep. John R. Lewis (D)

1987-88		Direct Cont. 1987-88	
Receipts	$193,584	Indiv.	$46,607
Expend.	$101,540	Party	$242
C.O.H.	$92,401	PACS	$142,915

6th District, Rep. Newt Gingrich (R)

1987-88		Direct Cont. 1987-88	
Receipts	$851,786	Indiv.	$554,318
Expend.	$838,708	Party	$9,300
C.O.H.	$24,858	PACS	$262,976
Debts	$57,130	Cand.	$20,000

7th District, Rep. Buddy Darden (D)

1987-88		Direct Cont. 1987-88	
Receipts	$448,399	Indiv.	$185,540
Expend.	$382,281	Party	$574
C.O.H.	$115,951	PACS	$241,375
Debts	$12,000		

8th District, Rep. Roy Rowland (D)

1987-88		Direct Cont. 1987-88	
Receipts	$261,545	Indiv.	$113,992
Expend.	$195,895	Party	$506
C.O.H.	$207,955	PACS	$129,637

9th District, Rep. Ed Jenkins (D)

1987-88		Direct Cont. 1987-88	
Receipts	$453,174	Indiv.	$81,543
Expend.	$405,040	Party	$158
C.O.H.	$464,486	PACS	$310,897

10th District, Rep. Doug Barnard (D)

1987-88		Direct Cont. 1987-88	
Receipts	$285,060	Indiv.	$35,470
Expend.	$193,123	Party	$2,000
C.O.H.	$519,193	PACS	$176,171

HAWAII

Sen. Daniel K. Inouye (D)

1985-86		Direct Cont. 1985-86	
Receipts	$1,173,721	Indiv.	$484,097
Expend.	$1,039,418	Party	$17,500
C.O.H.	$598,388	PACS	$573,277

Sen. Spark M. Matsunaga (D)

1987-88		Direct Cont. 1987-88	
Receipts	$834,722	Indiv.	$359,666
Expend.	$494,580	PACS	$413,325
C.O.H.	$639,844		

1st District, Rep. Patricia Saiki (R)

1987-88		Direct Cont. 1987-88	
Receipts	$708,391	Indiv.	$424,401
Expend.	$686,165	Party	$6,934
C.O.H.	$30,825	PACS	$261,834

2d District, Rep. Daniel K. Akaka (D)

1987-88		Direct Cont. 1987-88	
Receipts	$255,470	Indiv.	$159,819
Expend.	$153,163	Party	$170
C.O.H.	$157,098	PACS	$81,372

IDAHO

Sen. James A. McClure (R)

1979-84		Direct Cont. 1979-84	
Receipts	$1,310,902	Indiv.	$615,391
Expend.	$1,016,944	Party	$16,072
C.O.H.	$305,402	PACS	$599,928

Sen. Steven D. Symms (R)

1985-86		Direct Cont. 1985-86	
Receipts	$3,387,726	Indiv.	$1,860,953
Expend.	$3,229,939	Party	$22,485
C.O.H.	$157,787	PACS	$1,371,618

1st District, Rep. Larry E. Craig (R)

1987-88		Direct Cont. 1987-88	
Receipts	$356,033	Indiv.	$189,097
Expend.	$361,113	Party	$2,376
C.O.H.	$9,748	PACS	$159,060

2d District, Rep. Richard H. Stallings (D)

1987-88		Direct Cont. 1987-88	
Receipts	$498,997	Indiv.	$205,481
Expend.	$502,083	Party	$14,998
C.O.H.	$1,687	PACS	$266,739
Debts	$9,570		

ILLINOIS

Sen. Alan J. Dixon (D)

1985-86		Direct Cont. 1985-86	
Receipts	$2,219,982	Indiv.	$1,172,681
Expend.	$1,928,750	Party	$17,500
C.O.H.	$408,427	PACS	$958,697

Sen. Paul Simon (D)

1983-84		Direct Cont. 1983-84	
Receipts	$4,550,571	Indiv.	$3,436,607
Expend.	$4,545,786	Party	$61,537
Debts	$408,966	PACS	$905,054
		Cand.	$50,000

1st District, Rep. Charles A. Hayes (D)

1987-88		Direct Cont. 1987-88	
Receipts	$150,960	Indiv.	$33,290
Expend.	$145,905	PACS	$115,634
C.O.H.	$40,381		
Debts	$6,572		

2d District, Rep. Gus Savage (D)

1987-88		Direct Cont. 1987-88	
Receipts	$240,244	Indiv.	$95,620
Expend.	$242,487	Party	$168
C.O.H.	$702	PACS	$116,218
Debts	$47,012	Cand.	$28,306

3d District, Rep. Marty Russo (D)

1987-88		Direct Cont. 1987-88	
Receipts	$558,458	Indiv.	$179,890
Expend.	$558,273	PACS	$357,996
C.O.H.	$2,289	Cand.	$20,000
Debts	$6,219		

4th District, Rep. George E. Sangmeister (D)

1987-88		Direct Cont. 1987-88	
Receipts	$378,294	Indiv.	$102,549
Expend.	$359,942	Party	$14,050
C.O.H.	$18,349	PACS	$144,294
Debts	$65,301	Cand.	$98,000

5th District, Rep. William O. Lipinski (D)

1987-88		Direct Cont. 1987-88	
Receipts	$154,568	Indiv.	$48,000
Expend.	$165,144	Party	$364
C.O.H.	$7,646	PACS	$96,464
		Cand.	$7,500

6th District, Rep. Henry J. Hyde (R)

1987-88		Direct Cont. 1987-88	
Receipts	$303,395	Indiv.	$164,681
Expend.	$281,229	Party	$3,037
C.O.H.	$155,663	PACS	$121,453

7th District, Rep. Cardiss Collins (D)

1987-88		Direct Cont. 1987-88	
Receipts	$235,058	Indiv.	$22,655
Expend.	$127,487	Party	$245
C.O.H.	$211,451	PACS	$199,043
Debts	$25,000		

8th District, Rep. Dan Rostenkowski (D)

1987-88		Direct Cont. 1987-88	
Receipts	$866,341	Indiv.	$345,096
Expend.	$428,607	Party	$242
C.O.H.	$1,034,438	PACS	$444,698

9th District, Rep. Sidney R. Yates (D)

1987-88		Direct Cont. 1987-88	
Receipts	$126,705	Indiv.	$101,455
Expend.	$122,900	PACS	$25,250
C.O.H.	$113,811		

10th District, Rep. John E. Porter (R)

1987-88		Direct Cont. 1987-88	
Receipts	$245,366	Indiv.	$110,577
Expend.	$212,630	Party	$2,000
C.O.H.	$129,521	PACS	$115,321

11th District, Rep. Frank Annunzio (D)

1987-88		Direct Cont. 1987-88	
Receipts	$260,514	Indiv.	$79,150
Expend.	$239,158	PACS	$158,200
C.O.H.	$168,512		

12th District, Rep. Philip M. Crane (R)

1987-88		Direct Cont. 1987-88	
Receipts	$466,894	Indiv.	$445,289
Expend.	$480,460	Party	$2,000
C.O.H.	$115,804		

13th District, Rep. Harris W. Fawell (R)

1987-88		Direct Cont. 1987-88	
Receipts	$292,896	Indiv.	$186,556
Expend.	$289,190	Party	$2,000
C.O.H.	$38,935	PACS	$98,171

14th District, Rep. J. Dennis Hastert (R)

1987-88		Direct Cont. 1987-88	
Receipts	$373,879	Indiv.	$190,552
Expend.	$346,785	Party	$8,836
C.O.H.	$42,612	PACS	$148,608

15th District, Rep. Edward R. Madigan (R)

1987-88		Direct Cont. 1987-88	
Receipts	$500,508	Indiv.	$111,401
Expend.	$374,760	Party	$3,039
C.O.H.	$388,122	PACS	$334,315

16th District, Rep. Lynn Martin (R)

1987-88		Direct Cont. 1987-88	
Receipts	$456,255	Indiv.	$251,403
Expend.	$329,598	Party	$2,918
C.O.H.	$273,268	PACS	$186,532

17th District, Rep. Lane Evans (D)

1987-88		Direct Cont. 1987-88	
Receipts	$461,211	Indiv.	$209,123
Expend.	$471,233	PACS	$211,218
C.O.H.	$3,686	Cand.	$20,000
Debts	$49,086		

18th District, Rep. Robert H. Michel (R)

1987-88		Direct Cont. 1987-88	
Receipts	$874,026	Indiv.	$271,691
Expend.	$861,969	Party	$6,310
C.O.H.	$115,375	PACS	$555,417

19th District, Rep. Terry L. Bruce (D)

1987-88		Direct Cont. 1987-88	
Receipts	$457,955	Indiv.	$76,677
Expend.	$193,205	Party	$252
C.O.H.	$360,770	PACS	$276,182
Debts	$50,000	Cand.	$75,000

20th District, Rep. Richard J. Durbin (D)

1987-88		Direct Cont. 1987-88	
Receipts	$367,468	Indiv.	$130,124
Expend.	$251,634	Party	$686
C.O.H.	$178,667	PACS	$220,605
Debts	$5,015		

21st District, Rep. Jerry F. Costello, Jr. (D)

1987-88		Direct Cont. 1987-88	
Receipts	$285,503	Indiv.	$59,995
Expend.	$394,412	Party	$10,000
C.O.H.	$260	PACS	$137,855
Debts	$75,000	Cand.	$75,000

22d District, Rep. Glenn W. Poshard (D)

1987-88		Direct Cont. 1987-88	
Receipts	$430,248	Indiv.	$174,056
Expend.	$392,791	Party	$9,999
C.O.H.	$37,457	PACS	$248,970

INDIANA

Sen. Richard Lugar (R)

1987-88		Direct Cont. 1987-88	
Receipts	$3,029,708	Indiv.	$2,110,438
Expend.	$3,022,597	Party	$17,189
C.O.H.	$417,309	PACS	$775,836

Sen. Daniel R. Coats (R)

1987-88		Direct Cont. 1987-88	
Receipts	$351,827	Indiv.	$137,761
Expend.	$266,016	Party	$2,651
C.O.H.	$233,253	PACS	$190,152

1st District, Rep. Peter J. Visclosky (D)

1987-88		Direct Cont. 1987-88	
Receipts	$222,620	Indiv.	$60,457
Expend.	$141,855	PACS	$157,250
C.O.H.	$95,066		

2d District, Rep. Philip R. Sharp (D)

1987-88		Direct Cont. 1987-88	
Receipts	$465,414	Indiv.	$129,167
Expend.	$444,422	Party	$5,000
C.O.H.	$88,631	PACS	$311,581

3d District, Rep. John Hiler (R)

1987-88		Direct Cont. 1987-88	
Receipts	$971,929	Indiv.	$496,625
Expend.	$1,085,140	Party	$11,543
C.O.H.	$2,617	PACS	$346,741
Debts	$11,577	Cand.	$60,000

4th District, Rep. Jill Long (D)

1987-88		Direct Cont. 1987-88	
Receipts	$326,025	Indiv.	$245,164
Expend.	$313,724	Party	$20,680
C.O.H.	$12,736	PACS	$182,763
Debts	$100,807		

5th District, Rep. James Jontz (D)

1987-88		Direct Cont. 1987-88	
Receipts	$721,637	Indiv.	$219,771
Expend.	$689,086	Party	$5,590
C.O.H.	$33,315	PACS	$471,725
Debts	$2,276		

6th District, Rep. Dan Burton (R)

1987-88		Direct Cont. 1987-88	
Receipts	$383,170	Indiv.	$224,210
Expend.	$333,723	Party	$3,011
C.O.H.	$193,617	PACS	$141,170

7th District, Rep. John T. Myers (R)

1987-88		Direct Cont. 1987-88	
Receipts	$165,678	Indiv.	$38,860
Expend.	$157,671	Party	$2,000
C.O.H.	$132,552	PACS	$96,500

8th District, Rep. Frank X. McCloskey (D)

1987-88		Direct Cont. 1987-88	
Receipts	$549,096	Indiv.	$172,748
Expend.	$551,484	Party	$12,499
C.O.H.	$1,441	PACS	$342,058
Debts	$6,126		

9th District, Rep. Lee H. Hamilton (D)

1987-88		Direct Cont. 1987-88	
Receipts	$369,547	Indiv.	$192,351
Expend.	$333,957	PACS	$152,066
C.O.H.	$51,442		

10th District, Rep. Andrew Jacobs, Jr (D).

1987-88		Direct Cont. 1987-88	
Receipts	$35,731	Indiv.	$33,004
Expend.	$35,786		
C.O.H.	$18,293		

IOWA

Sen. Charles E. Grassley (R)

1985-86		Direct Cont. 1985-86	
Receipts	$2,749,564	Indiv.	$1,586,655
Expend.	$2,513,319	Party	$15,642
C.O.H.	$487,347	PACS	$959,431

Sen. Tom Harkin (D)

1983-84		Direct Cont. 1983-84	
Receipts	$2,842,333	Indiv.	$1,935,255
Expend.	$2,838,277	Party	$52,054
C.O.H.	$1,537	PACS	$799,060

1st District, Rep. Jim Leach (R)

1987-88		Direct Cont. 1987-88	
Receipts	$206,618	Indiv.	$188,089
Expend.	$218,707	Party	$6,327
C.O.H.	$19,354		

2d District, Rep. Thomas J. Tauke (R)

1987-88		Direct Cont. 1987-88	
Receipts	$601,558	Indiv.	$290,552
Expend.	$581,514	Party	$4,117
C.O.H.	$123,620	PACS	$290,210

3d District, Rep. David R. Nagle (D)

1987-88		Direct Cont. 1987-88	
Receipts	$608,264	Indiv.	$147,337
Expend.	$595,977	Party	$15,003
C.O.H.	$14,930	PACS	$406,018
Debts.	$42,896	Cand.	$20,000

4th District, Rep. Neal Smith (D)

1987-88		Direct Cont. 1987-88	
Receipts	$205,035	Indiv.	$22,506
Expend.	$83,474	Party	$511
C.O.H.	$264,580	PACS	$162,585

5th District, Rep. Jim Ross Lightfoot (R)

1987-88		Direct Cont. 1987-88	
Receipts	$478,842	Indiv.	$297,197
Expend.	$420,730	Party	$5,234
C.O.H.	$61,580	PACS	$166,077

6th District, Rep. Fred Grandy (R)

1987-88		Direct Cont. 1987-88	
Receipts	$528,287	Indiv.	$196,482
Expend.	$523,108	Party	$13,965
C.O.H.	$245	PACS	$294,944
Debts.	$124,480		

KANSAS

Sen. Robert Dole (R)

1985-86		Direct Cont. 1985-86	
Receipts	$2,640,050	Indiv.	$1,298,106
Expend.	$1,517,585	Party	$15,275
C.O.H.	$2,166,732	PACS	$1,036,433

Sen. Nancy L. Kassebaum (R)

1979-84		Direct Cont. 1979-84	
Receipts	$570,629	Indiv.	$288,952
Expend.	$355,077	Party	$19,845
C.O.H.	$217,804	PACS	$214,269

1st District, Rep. Pat Roberts (R)

1987-88		Direct Cont. 1987-88	
Receipts	$191,584	Indiv.	$59,377
Expend.	$81,140	Party	$2,088
C.O.H.	$330,315	PACS	$99,600

2d District, Rep. Jim Slattery (D)

1987-88		Direct Cont. 1987-88	
Receipts	$453,832	Indiv.	$177,062
Expend.	$388,866	Party	$97
C.O.H.	$90,853	PACS	$266,122

3d District, Rep. Jan Meyers (R)

1987-88		Direct Cont. 1987-88	
Receipts	$201,229	Indiv.	$84,725
Expend.	$234,583	Party	$2,000
C.O.H.	$561	PACS	$110,395
Debts.	$2,478		

4th District, Rep. Dan Glickman (D)

1987-88		Direct Cont. 1987-88	
Receipts	$562,266	Indiv.	$265,276
Expend.	$545,755	PACS	$280,540
C.O.H.	$26,900		

5th District, Rep. Bob Whittaker (R)

1987-88		Direct Cont. 1987-88	
Receipts	$222,261	Indiv.	$25,063
Expend.	$117,312	Party	$2,468
C.O.H.	$446,218	PACS	$155,056

KENTUCKY

Sen. Wendell H. Ford (D)

1985-86		Direct Cont. 1985-86	
Receipts	$1,519,672	Indiv.	$606,323
Expend.	$1,201,624	Party	$1,146
C.O.H.	$360,775	PACS	$831,618

Sen. Mitch McConnell (R)

1983-84		Direct Cont. 1983-84	
Receipts	$1,582,289	Indiv.	$1,257,157
Expend.	$1,767,114	Party	$23,934
Debts	$8,935	PACS	$204,056
		Cand.	$40,000

1st District, Rep. Carroll Hubbard (D)

1987-88		Direct Cont. 1987-88	
Receipts	$518,338	Indiv.	$117,879
Expend.	$546,908	Party	$5,000
C.O.H.	$223,129	PACS	$356,663

2d District, Rep. William H. Natcher (D)

1987-88		Direct Cont. 1987-88	
Receipts	$8,397	Cand.	$8,204
Expend.	$8,397		

3d District, Rep. Romano L. Mazzoli (D)

1987-88		Direct Cont. 1987-88	
Receipts	$378,438	Indiv.	$157,267
Expend.	$371,431	Party	$221
C.O.H.	$30,687	PACS	$196,650
		Cand.	$10,000

4th District, Rep. Jim Bunning (R)

1987-88		Direct Cont. 1987-88	
Receipts	$593,585	Indiv.	$337,148
Expend.	$468,870	Party	$2,138
C.O.H.	$127,653	PACS	$236,184

5th District, Rep. Harold Rogers (R)

1987-88		Direct Cont. 1987-88	
Receipts	$177,242	Indiv.	$83,160
Expend.	$119,720	Party	$4,349
C.O.H.	$193,172	PACS	$69,566

6th District, Rep. Larry J. Hopkins (R)

1987-88		Direct Cont. 1987-88	
Receipts	$356,281	Indiv.	$135,376
Expend.	$295,333	Party	$2,382
C.O.H.	$608,792	PACS	$134,335

7th District, Rep. Carl C. (Chris) Perkins (D)

1987-88		Direct Cont. 1987-88	
Receipts	$418,749	Indiv.	$153,123
Expend.	$411,699	PACS	$264,300
C.O.H.	$8,161		
Debts.	$72,358		

LOUISIANA

Sen. J. Bennett Johnston, Jr. (D)

1979-84		Direct Cont. 1979-84	
Receipts	$2,312,701	Indiv.	$1,298,263
Expend.	$1,046,293	Party	$4,300
C.O.H.	$1,387,880	PACS	$645,358

Sen. John B. Breaux (D)

1985-86		Direct Cont. 1985-86	
Receipts	$3,000,614	Indiv.	$1,752,188
Expend.	$2,958,313	Party	$20,502
C.O.H.	$42,301	PACS	$875,717

1st District, Rep. Robert L. Livingston (R)

1987-88		Direct Cont. 1987-88	
Receipts	$262,408	Indiv.	$119,975
Expend.	$555,058	Party	$1,484
C.O.H.	$111,115	PACS	$127,834

2d District, Rep. Lindy Boggs (D)

1987-88		Direct Cont. 1987-88	
Receipts	$266,033	Indiv.	$109,400
Expend.	$252,835	PACS	$144,300

3d District, Rep. Billy Tauzin (D)

1987-88		Direct Cont. 1987-88	
Receipts	$347,890	Indiv.	$45,660
Expend.	$707,085	PACS	$263,228
C.O.H.	$61,804		

4th District, Rep. Jim McCrery (R)

1987-88		Direct Cont. 1987-88	
Receipts	$334,893	Indiv.	$160,682
Expend.	$286,813	Party	$10,222
C.O.H.	$49,429	PACS	$158,446
Debts	$34,866		

5th District, Rep. Jerry Huckaby (D)

1987-88		Direct Cont. 1987-88	
Receipts	$266,854	Indiv.	$106,425
Expend.	$194,021	PACS	$131,650
C.O.H.	$295,390		

6th District, Rep. Richard H. Baker (R)

1987-88		Direct Cont. 1987-88	
Receipts	$287,230	Indiv.	$150,043
Expend.	$270,899	Party	$1,450
C.O.H.	$17,341	PACS	$124,525

7th District, Rep. James A. Hayes (D)

1987-88		Direct Cont. 1987-88	
Receipts	$304,917	Indiv.	$90,560
Expend.	$268,116	PACS	$206,100
C.O.H.	$40,784		
Debts	$269,449		

8th District, Rep. Clyde C. Holloway (R)

1987-88		Direct Cont. 1987-88	
Receipts	$690,080	Indiv.	$360,761
Expend.	$629,950	Party	$27,071
C.O.H.	$64,285	PACS	$315,886
Debts	$2,400		

MAINE

Sen. William S. Cohen (R)

1979-84		Direct Cont. 1979-84	
Receipts	$1,193,674	Indiv.	$687,793
Expend.	$1,063,188	Party	$19,402
C.O.H.	$139,971	PACS	$419,637

Sen. George Mitchell (D)

1987-88		Direct Cont. 1987-88	
Receipts	$1,810,602	Indiv.	$970,159
Expend.	$1,340,157	Party	$5,241
C.O.H.	$480,728	PACS	$724,547

1st District, Rep. Joseph E. Brennan (D)

1987-88		Direct Cont. 1987-88	
Receipts	$496,668	Indiv.	$187,836
Expend.	$464,541	Party	$4,999
C.O.H.	$26,584	PACS	$280,229
Debts	$24,811		

2d District, Rep. Olympia J. Snowe (R)

1987-88		Direct Cont. 1987-88	
Receipts	$229,929	Indiv.	$142,917
Expend.	$202,317	Party	$2,183
C.O.H.	$31,404	PACS	$72,300
		Cand.	$5,000

MARYLAND

Sen. Paul S. Sarbanes (D)

1987-88		Direct Cont. 1987-88	
Receipts	$1,477,516	Indiv.	$796,276
Expend.	$1,466,477	Party	$25,000
C.O.H.	$11,394	PACS	$604,799
Debts	$24,279		

Sen. Barbara A. Mikulski (D)

1985-86		Direct Cont. 1985-86	
Receipts	$2,160,812	Indiv.	$1,251,938
Expend.	$2,097,216	Party	$1,000
C.O.H.	$103,596	PACS	$651,818
		Cand.	$204,146

1st District, Rep. Roy Dyson (D)

1987-88		Direct Cont. 1987-88	
Receipts	$691,251	Indiv.	$221,296
Expend.	$684,204	Party	$10,500
Debts	$13,867	PACS	$403,647
Debts	$87,759	Cand.	$25,000

2d District, Rep. Helen Delich Bentley (R)

1987-88		Direct Cont. 1987-88	
Receipts	$847,422	**Indiv.**	$531,975
Expend.	$779,318	Party	$8,276
Debts	$81,681	PACS	$293,984
Debts	$4,152		

3d District, Rep. Benjamin L. Cardin (D)

1987-88		Direct Cont. 1987-88	
Receipts	$405,789	Indiv.	$183,581
Expend.	$354,701	Party	$265
C.O.H.	$81,819	PACS	$208,148

4th District, Rep. Thomas McMillen (D)

1987-88		Direct Cont. 1987-88	
Receipts	$730,652	Indiv.	$267,246
Expend.	$599,881	PACS	$392,892
C.O.H.	$132,049	Cand.	$60,000
Debts	$42,503		

5th District, Rep. Steny H. Hoyer (D)

1987-88		Direct Cont. 1987-88	
Receipts	$490,736	Indiv.	$208,969
Expend.	$416,187	PACS	$239,828
C.O.H.	$312,458		

6th District, Rep. Beverly B. Byron (D)

1987-88		Direct Cont. 1987-88	
Receipts	$218,098	Indiv.	$63,434
Expend.	$213,554	PACS	$142,722
C.O.H.	$77,397		

7th District, Rep. Kweisi Mfume (D)

1987-88		Direct Cont. 1987-88	
Receipts	$130,466	Indiv.	$44,485
Expend.	$110,565	Party	$170
C.O.H.	$65,234	PACS	$72,250

8th District, Rep. Constance A. Morella (R)

1987-88		Direct Cont. 1987-88	
Receipts	$829,437	Indiv.	$496,408
Expend.	$821,574	Party	$9,998
C.O.H.	$11,454	PACS	$305,374
Debts	$12,705	Cand.	$7,500

MASSACHUSETTS

Sen. Edward M. Kennedy (D)

1987-88		Direct Cont. 1987-88	
Receipts	$3,304,580	Indiv.	$2,865,868
Expend.	$2,702,865	Party	$17,500
C.O.H.	$708,350	PACS	$322,972

Sen. John F. Kerry (D)

1983-84		Direct Cont. 1983-84	
Receipts	$2,169,775	Indiv.	$1,826,936
Expend.	$2,070,004	Party	$17,500
Debts	$367,994	Cand.	$309,000

1st District, Rep. Silvio O. Conte (R)

1987-88		Direct Cont. 1987-88	
Receipts	$142,186	Indiv.	$28,420
Expend.	$131,566	Party	$2,000
C.O.H.	$278,946	PACS	$72,624

2d District, Rep. Richard E. Neal (D)

1987-88		Direct Cont. 1987-88	
Receipts	$352,265	Indiv.	$151,311
Expend.	$268,094	PACS	$87,000
C.O.H.	$84,169		

3d District, Rep. Joseph D. Early (D)

1987-88		Direct Cont. 1987-88	
Receipts	$222,053	Indiv.	$128,603
Expend.	$205,989	PACS	$93,250
C.O.H.	$111,500		

4th District, Rep. Barney Frank (D)

1987-88		Direct Cont. 1987-88	
Receipts	$431,299	Indiv.	$284,351
Expend.	$343,097	Party	$158
C.O.H.	$125,724	PACS	$141,635
Debts	$4,068		

5th District, Rep. Chester G. Atkins (D)

1987-88		Direct Cont. 1987-88	
Receipts	$359,460	Indiv.	$356,308
Expend.	$344,930	PACS	$300
C.O.H.	$19,889		
Debts	$5,220		

6th District, Rep. Nicholas Mavroules (D)

1987-88		Direct Cont. 1987-88	
Receipts	$349,184	Indiv.	$238,831
Expend.	$337,199	PACS	$107,360
C.O.H.	$105,693		
Debts	$14,140		

7th District, Rep. Edward J. Markey (D)

1987-88		Direct Cont. 1987-88	
Receipts	$484,319	Indiv.	$443,311
Expend.	$134,388		
C.O.H.	$451,058		

8th District, Rep. Joseph P. Kennedy, II (D)

1987-88		Direct Cont. 1987-88	
Receipts	$1,419,819	Indiv.	$1,110,943
Expend.	$1,186,852	Party	$547
C.O.H.	$253,264	PACS	$272,840

9th District, Rep. Joe Moakley (D)

1987-88		Direct Cont. 1987-88	
Receipts	$385,654	Indiv.	$177,005
Expend.	$273,488	Party	$221
C.O.H.	$290,806	PACS	$180,830

10th District, Rep. Gerry E. Studds (D)

1987-88		Direct Cont. 1987-88	
Receipts	$243,095	Indiv.	$155,286
Expend.	$235,946	PACS	$83,545
C.O.H.	$41,973		

11th District, Rep. Brian J. Donnelly (D)

1987-88		Direct Cont. 1987-88	
Receipts	$264,323	Indiv.	$82,237
Expend.	$167,960	PACS	$131,300
C.O.H.	$461,743		

MICHIGAN

Sen. Donald W. Riegle, Jr. (D)

1987-88		Direct Cont. 1987-88	
Receipts	$3,289,327	Indiv.	$1,695,507
Expend.	$3,383,849	Party	$5,250
C.O.H.	$855,659	PACS	$1,281,641

Sen. Carl Levin (D)

1979-84		Direct Cont. 1979-84	
Receipts	$3,646,298	Indiv.	$2,734,684
Expend.	$3,569,330	Party	$32,545
C.O.H.	$55,177	PACS	$719,154

1st District, Rep. John Conyers, Jr. (D)

1987-88		Direct Cont. 1987-88	
Receipts	$151,676	Indiv.	$38,888
Expend.	$124,823	Party	$375
C.O.H.	$34,832	PACS	$82,614

2d District, Rep. Carl D. Pursell (R)

1987-88		Direct Cont. 1987-88	
Receipts	$811,384	Indiv.	$497,451
Expend.	$876,779	Party	$12,629
C.O.H.	$90,037	PACS	$264,993

3d District, Rep. Howard Wolpe (D)

1987-88		Direct Cont. 1987-88	
Receipts	$576,393	Indiv.	$254,348
Expend.	$600,940	Party	$18,219
C.O.H.	$82,880	PACS	$263,224

4th District, Rep. Frederick S. Upton (R)

1987-88		Direct Cont. 1987-88	
Receipts	$422,884	Indiv.	$255,317
Expend.	$323,829	Party	$7,721
C.O.H.	$99,428	PACS	$117,465
Debts	$38,789	Cand.	$41,286

5th District, Rep. Paul B. Henry (R)

1987-88		Direct Cont. 1987-88	
Receipts	$387,878	Indiv.	$275,959
Expend.	$309,436	Party	$5,103
C.O.H.	$118,046	PACS	$97,425

6th District, Rep. Bob Carr (D)

1987-88		Direct Cont. 1987-88	
Receipts	$534,741	Indiv.	$216,010
Expend.	$504,217	Party	$14,999
C.O.H.	$83,069	PACS	$277,823

7th District, Rep. Dale E. Kildee (D)

1987-88		Direct Cont. 1987-88	
Receipts	$152,246	Indiv.	$42,128
Expend.	$150,595	PACS	$103,770
C.O.H.	$2,634		

8th District, Rep. Bob Traxler (D)

1987-88		Direct Cont. 1987-88	
Receipts	$238,000	Indiv.	$67,988
Expend.	$128,400	Party	$3,502
C.O.H.	$239,742	PACS	$148,987

9th District, Rep. Guy Vander Jagt (R)

1987-88		Direct Cont. 1987-88	
Receipts	$456,634	Indiv.	$206,923
Expend.	$450,801	Party	$4,574
C.O.H.	$108,182	PACS	$238,725

10th District, Rep. Bill Schuette (R)

1987-88		Direct Cont. 1987-88	
Receipts	$782,377	Indiv.	$455,134
Expend.	$728,533	Party	$10,034
C.O.H.	$71,503	PACS	$292,987
Debts	$71,078		

11th District, Rep. Robert W. Davis (R)

1987-88		Direct Cont. 1987-88	
Receipts	$582,616	Indiv.	$217,926
Expend.	$680,819	Party	$12,677
C.O.H.	$99,789	PACS	$310,359

12th District, Rep. David E. Bonior (D)

1987-88		Direct Cont. 1987-88	
Receipts	$475,462	Indiv.	$111,648
Expend.	$434,200	Party	$355
C.O.H.	$89,628	PACS	$328,317

13th District, Rep. George W. Crockett, Jr. (D)

1987-88		Direct Cont. 1987-88	
Receipts	$97,827	Indiv.	$27,829
Expend.	$84,024	PACS	$63,822
C.O.H.	$64,161		

14th District, Rep. Dennis M. Hertel (D)

1987-88		Direct Cont. 1987-88	
Receipts	$251,004	Indiv.	$67,435
Expend.	$137,560	Party	$1,080
C.O.H.	$162,005	PACS	$154,565
		Cand.	$3,200

15th District, Rep. William D. Ford (D)

1987-88		Direct Cont. 1987-88	
Receipts	$335,331	Indiv.	$62,355
Expend.	$234,435	Party	$221
C.O.H.	$158,221	PACS	$267,901

16th District, Rep. John D. Dingell (D)

1987-88		Direct Cont. 1987-88	
Receipts	$613,770	Indiv.	$130,180
Expend.	$462,180	Party	$200
C.O.H.	$252,240	PACS	$459,242

17th District, Rep. Sander M. Levin (D)

1987-88		Direct Cont. 1987-88	
Receipts	$300,654	Indiv.	$89,819
Expend.	$233,421	Party	$150
C.O.H.	$170,048	PACS	$193,430

18th District, Rep. William S. Broomfield (R)

1987-88		Direct Cont. 1987-88	
Receipts	$235,699	Indiv.	$104,605
Expend.	$77,103	Party	$5,585
C.O.H.	$589,023	PACS	$57,700

MINNESOTA

Sen. David Durenberger (IR)

1987-88		Direct Cont. 1987-88	
Receipts	$4,969,448	Indiv.	$3,262,541
Expend.	$5,410,783	Party	$21,037
C.O.H.	$27,478	PACS	$1,499,382
Debts	$85,408		

Sen. Rudy Boschwitz (IR)

1979-84		Direct Cont. 1979-84	
Receipts	$6,843,489	Indiv.	$5,314,501
Expend.	$6,657,484	Party	$24,030
Unspent	$207,032	PACS	$1,099,767
		Cand.	$3,989

1st District, Rep. Timothy J. Penny (DFL)

1987-88		Direct Cont. 1987-88	
Receipts	$284,554	Indiv.	$133,759
Expend.	$165,016	PACS	$125,377
C.O.H.	$223,595		

2d District, Rep. Vin Weber (IR)

1987-88		Direct Cont. 1987-88	
Receipts	$728,427	Indiv.	$453,259
Expend.	$623,776	Party	$4,735
C.O.H.	$270,539	PACS	$232,704
		Cand.	$1,325

3d District, Rep. Bill Frenzel (IR)

1987-88		Direct Cont. 1987-88	
Receipts	$497,281	Indiv.	$148,660
Expend.	$381,646	Party	$1,229
C.O.H.	$429,576	PACS	$301,578

4th District, Rep. Bruce F. Vento (DFL)

1987-88		Direct Cont. 1987-88	
Receipts	$268,237	Indiv.	$58,556
Expend.	$216,172	Party	$404
C.O.H.	$162,421	PACS	$189,759

5th District, Rep. Martin Olav Sabo (DFL)

1987-88		Direct Cont. 1987-88	
Receipts	$363,965	Indiv.	$91,756
Expend.	$281,455	Party	$608
C.O.H.	$182,181	PACS	$237,550

6th District, Rep. Gerry Sikorski (DFL)

1987-88		Direct Cont. 1987-88	
Receipts	$547,198	Indiv.	$166,768
Expend.	$320,437	PACS	$358,582
C.O.H.	$243,181		
Debts	$3,714		

7th District, Rep. Arlan Stangeland (IR)

1987-88		Direct Cont. 1987-88	
Receipts	$658,882	Indiv.	$283,842
Expend.	$693,429	Party	$10,037
C.O.H.	$15,031	PACS	$344,281

8th District, Rep. James L. Oberstar (DFL)

1987-88		Direct Cont. 1987-88	
Receipts	$281,331	Indiv.	$52,408
Expend.	$157,802	PACS	$206,320
C.O.H.	$258,235	Cand.	$125

MISSISSIPPI

Sen. Thad Cochran (R)

1979-84		Direct Cont. 1979-84	
Receipts	$2,860,815	Indiv.	$1,664,711
Expend.	$2,870,894	Party	$12,917
C.O.H.	$138,875	PACS	$998,918
		Cand.	$50,000

Sen. Trent Lott (R)

1987-88		Direct Cont. 1987-88	
Receipts	$3,602,481	Indiv.	$1,991,671
Expend.	$3,405,242	Party	$22,422
C.O.H.	$197,239	PACS	$1,118,111

1st District, Rep. Jamie L. Whitten (D)

1987-88		Direct Cont. 1987-88	
Receipts	$175,925	Indiv.	$7,300
Expend.	$58,370	PACS	$135,400
C.O.H.	$348,365	Cand.	$500

2d District, Rep. Mike Espy (D)

1987-88		Direct Cont. 1987-88	
Receipts	$880,227	Indiv.	$367,041
Expend.	$886,540	Party	$4,999
C.O.H.	$3,060	PACS	$480,490
Debts	$89,278	Cand.	$31,250

3d District, Rep. Sonny Montgomery (D)

1987-88		Direct Cont. 1987-88	
Receipts	$148,077	Indiv.	$65,652
Expend.	$116,761	PACS	$71,650
C.O.H.	$130,311		

4th District, Rep. Mike Parker (D)

1987-88		Direct Cont. 1987-88	
Receipts	$844,541	Indiv.	$204,220
Expend.	$843,142	Party	$15,999
C.O.H.	$1,398	PACS	$234,164
Debts	$298,012	Cand.	$393,200

5th District, Rep. Larkin Smith (R)

1987-88		Direct Cont. 1987-88	
Receipts	$588,552	Indiv.	$391,554
Expend.	$569,830	Party	$17,499
C.O.H.	$18,723	PACS	$135,150
		Cand.	$43,000

MISSOURI

Sen. John C. Danforth (R)

1987-88		Direct Cont. 1987-88	
Receipts	$4,077,855	Indiv.	$2,651,190
Expend.	$3,992,995	Party	$16,028
C.O.H.	$645,784	PACS	$1,149,207

Sen. Christopher S. (Kit) Bond (R)

1985-86		Direct Cont. 1985-86	
Receipts	$5,444,030	Indiv.	$3,969,756
Expend.	$5,376,255	Party	$31,615
C.O.H.	$67,773	PACS	$1,334,222
		Cand.	$41,589

1st District, Rep. William Clay (D)

1987-88		Direct Cont. 1987-88	
Receipts	$178,594	Indiv.	$25,250
Expend.	$134,200	PACS	$141,830
C.O.H.	$102,620	Cand.	$3,660

2d District, Rep. Jack Buechner (R)

1987-88		Direct Cont. 1987-88	
Receipts	$721,239	Indiv.	$329,709
Expend.	$693,066	Party	$9,209
C.O.H.	$31,571	PACS	$280,111
Debts	$2,069		

3d District, Rep. Richard A. Gephardt (D)

1987-88		Direct Cont. 1987-88	
Receipts	$513,893	Indiv.	$53,927
Expend.	$512,206	Party	$219
C.O.H.	$1,866	PACS	$183,196

4th District, Rep. Ike Skelton (D)

1987-88		Direct Cont. 1987-88	
Receipts	$314,323	Indiv.	$118,241
Expend.	$273,316	Party	$157
C.O.H.	$228,021	PACS	$195,725

5th District, Rep. Alan Wheat (D)

1987-88		Direct Cont. 1987-88	
Receipts	$303,515	Indiv.	$80,549
Expend.	$240,623	PACS	$205,500
C.O.H.	$197,465	Cand.	$2,750
Debts	$2,750		

6th District, Rep. E. Thomas Coleman (R)

1987-88		Direct Cont. 1987-88	
Receipts	$305,961	Indiv.	$102,467
Expend.	$341,344	Party	$5,800
C.O.H.	$67,494	PACS	$175,134

7th District, Rep. Mel Hancock (R)

1987-88		Direct Cont. 1987-88	
Receipts	$373,434	Indiv.	$243,662
Expend.	$338,125	Party	$14,998
C.O.H.	$35,308	PACS	$79,913
Debts	$18,920	Cand.	$17,500

8th District, Rep. Bill Emerson (R)

1987-88		Direct Cont. 1987-88	
Receipts	$850,739	Indiv.	$396,850
Expend.	$768,792	Party	$19,922
C.O.H.	$87,454	PACS	$421,852

9th District, Rep. Harold L. Volkmer (D)

1987-88		Direct Cont. 1987-88	
Receipts	$300,348	Indiv.	$76,410
Expend.	$210,841	PACS	$218,185
C.O.H.	$89,968	Cand.	$2,004

MONTANA

Sen. Max Baucus (D)

1979-84		Direct Cont. 1979-84	
Receipts	$1,418,534	Indiv.	$599,890
Expend.	$1,386,561	Party	$17,845
C.O.H.	$29,910	PACS	$775,794

Sen. Conrad Burns (R)

1987-88		Direct Cont. 1987-88	
Receipts	$1,099,488	Indiv.	$540,479
Expend.	$1,076,010	Party	$27,316
C.O.H.	$23,477	PACS	$315,387
Debts	$38,921		

1st District, Rep. Pat Williams (D)

1987-88		Direct Cont. 1987-88	
Receipts	$279,856	Indiv.	$82,764
Expend.	$250,276	PACS	$185,656
C.O.H.	$104,412		

2d District, Rep. Ron Marlenee (R)

1987-88		Direct Cont. 1987-88	
Receipts	$416,031	Indiv.	$217,570
Expend.	$380,928	Party	$8,903
C.O.H.	$86,742	PACS	$171,992

NEBRASKA

Sen. J. James Exon (D)

1979-84		Direct Cont. 1979-84	
Receipts	$893,539	Indiv.	$325,745
Expend.	$866,760	Party	$23,391
C.O.H.	$51,762	PACS	$519,307

Sen. Robert Kerrey (D)

1987-88		Direct Cont. 1987-88	
Receipts	$3,485,728	Indiv.	$2,511,001
Expend.	$3,461,148	Party	$25,600
C.O.H.	$24,580	PACS	$799,279
Debts	$116,193	Cand.	$102,500

1st District, Rep. Doug Bereuter (R)

1987-88		Direct Cont. 1987-88	
Receipts	$215,704	Indiv.	$102,664
Expend.	$221,530	Party	$8,591
C.O.H.	$24,008	PACS	$99,120

2d District, Rep. Peter Hoagland (D)

1987-88		Direct Cont. 1987-88	
Receipts	$860,865	Indiv.	$232,482
Expend.	$858,762	Party	$14,499
C.O.H.	$2,045	PACS	$325,900
Debts	$276,929	Cand.	$286,000

3d District, Rep. Virginia Smith (R)

1987-88		Direct Cont. 1987-88	
Receipts	$271,730	Indiv.	$90,988
Expend.	$229,109	Party	$8,473
C.O.H.	$53,726	PACS	$138,715
Debts	$16,700		

NEVADA

Sen. Harry Reid (D)

1987-88		Direct Cont. 1987-88	
Receipts	$2,089,246	Indiv.	$1,084,711
Expend.	$2,055,756	Party	$40,000
C.O.H.	$33,490	PACS	$796,742
		Cand.	$30,000

Sen. Richard H. Bryan (D)

1987-88		Direct Cont. 1987-88	
Receipts	$2,986,727	Indiv.	$2,018,410
Expend.	$2,957,789	Party	$20,500
C.O.H.	$28,939	PACS	$802,792
Debts	$50,135	Cand.	$100,135

1st District, Rep. James Bilbray (D)

1987-88		Direct Cont. 1987-88	
Receipts	$669,014	Indiv.	$212,259
Expend.	$652,199	Party	$11,000
C.O.H.	$20,136	PACS	$300,116
Debts	$90,000	Cand.	$147,700

2d District, Rep. Barbara F. Vucanovich (R)

1987-88		Direct Cont. 1987-88	
Receipts	$608,009	Indiv.	$384,260
Expend.	$614,853	Party	$19,393
C.O.H.	$1,315	PACS	$201,719
Debts	$10,355		

NEW HAMPSHIRE

Sen. Gordon J. Humphrey (R)

1979-84		Direct Cont. 1979-84	
Receipts	$1,825,940	Indiv.	$906,761
Expend.	$1,806,653	Party	$35,874
Debts	$36,272	PACS	$742,004
		Cand.	$50,000

Sen. Warren Rudman (R)

1985-86		Direct Cont. 1985-86	
Receipts	$852,877	Indiv.	$803,674
Expend.	$831,098	Party	$15,970
Unspent	$57,085	PACS	$15,662

1st District, Rep. Robert C. Smith (R)

1987-88		Direct Cont. 1987-88	
Receipts	$364,164	Indiv.	$233,622
Expend.	$333,695	Party	$10,102
C.O.H.	$30,504	PACS	$109,500

2d District, Rep. Chuck Douglass III (R)

1987-88		Direct Cont. 1987-88	
Receipts	$735,185	Indiv.	$464,367
Expend.	$730,803	Party	$30,003
C.O.H.	$4,382	PACS	$169,555
Debts	$26,462	Cand.	$34,000

NEW JERSEY

Sen. Bill Bradley (D)

1979-84		Direct Cont. 1979-84	
Receipts	$5,497,613	Indiv.	$4,276,333
Expend.	$5,142,316	Party	$5,480
C.O.H.	$283,675	PACS	$869,400
		Cand.	$2,526

Sen. Frank R. Lautenberg (D)

1987-88		Direct Cont. 1987-88	
Receipts	$7,087,476	Indiv.	$5,060,472
Expend.	$7,298,663	Party	$18,500
C.O.H.	$40,146	PACS	$1,410,360
Debts	$3,759,000	Cand.	$330,000

1st District, Rep. James J. Florio (D)

1987-88		Direct Cont. 1987-88	
Receipts	$790,850	Indiv.	$425,946
Expend.	$924,427	Party	$158
C.O.H.	$24,272	PACS	$359,310
Debts	$80,531		

2d District, Rep. William J. Hughes (D)

1987-88		Direct Cont. 1987-88	
Receipts	$283,532	Indiv.	$155,537
Expend.	$235,629	PACS	$112,150
C.O.H.	$137,215		

3d District, Rep. Frank Pallone, Jr. (D)

1987-88		Direct Cont. 1987-88	
Receipts	$679,073	Indiv.	$204,840
Expend.	$678,647	Party	$14,999
		PACS	$437,739
		Cand.	$3,025

4th District, Rep. Christopher H. Smith (R)

1987-88		Direct Cont. 1987-88	
Receipts	$329,835	Indiv.	$189,319
Expend.	$252,823	Party	$6,000
C.O.H.	$77,641	PACS	$124,781
Debts	$6,494		

5th District, Rep. Margaret S. Roukema (R)

1987-88		Direct Cont. 1987-88	
Receipts	$406,469	Indiv.	$204,017
Expend.	$400,555	Party	$2,000
C.O.H.	$95,241	PACS	$181,513
Debts	$2,000		

6th District, Rep. Bernard J. Dwyer (D)

1987-88		Direct Cont. 1987-88	
Receipts	$136,330	Indiv.	$13,210
Expend.	$123,632	PACS	$113,000
C.O.H.	$71,449		

7th District, Rep. Matthew J. Rinaldo (R)

1987-88		Direct Cont. 1987-88	
Receipts	$607,728	Indiv.	$260,047
Expend.	$370,387	Party	$2,141
C.O.H.	$746,181	PACS	$271,527

8th District, Rep. Robert A. Roe (D)

1987-88		Direct Cont. 1987-88	
Receipts	$490,884	Indiv.	$175,605
Expend.	$267,609	Party	$625
C.O.H.	$484,615	PACS	$273,100

9th District, Rep. Robert G. Torricelli (D)

1987-88		Direct Cont. 1987-88	
Receipts	$631,151	Indiv.	$400,758
Expend.	$403,059	PACS	$177,488
C.O.H.	$484,447	Cand.	$22,508
Debts	$3,477		

10th District, Rep. Donald M. Payne (D)

1987-88		Direct Cont. 1987-88	
Receipts	$545,049	Indiv.	$228,154
Expend.	$413,338	Party	$5,056
C.O.H.	$132,152	PACS	$205,177
Debts	$5,000	Cand.	$100,000

11th District, Rep. Dean A. Gallo (R)

1987-88		Direct Cont. 1987-88	
Receipts	$531,548	Indiv.	$367,758
Expend.	$490,751	Party	$2,055
C.O.H.	$114,241	PACS	$151,245

12th District, Rep. Jim Courter (R)

1987-88		Direct Cont. 1987-88	
Receipts	$1,211,060	Indiv.	$1,015,008
Expend.	$1,333,882	Party	$2,000
C.O.H.	$971	PACS	$167,173

13th District, Rep. H. James Saxton (R)

1987-88		Direct Cont. 1987-88	
Receipts	$491,036	Indiv.	$270,183
Expend.	$411,620	Party	$2,039
C.O.H.	$151,707	PACS	$195,430

14th District, Rep. Frank J. Guarini (D)

1987-88		Direct Cont. 1987-88	
Receipts	$552,280	Indiv.	$182,082
Expend.	$369,578	Party	$157
C.O.H.	$182,701	PACS	$213,835

NEW MEXICO

Sen. Peter V. Domenici (R)

1979-84		Direct Cont. 1979-84	
Receipts	$2,675,819	Indiv.	$1,669,980
Expend.	$2,658,008	Party	$21,579
Debts	$88,215	PACS	$825,368

Sen. Jeff Bingaman (D)

1987-88		Direct Cont. 1987-88	
Receipts	$2,820,479	Indiv.	$1,635,859
Expend.	$2,808,659	PACS	$1,100,451
C.O.H.	$163,315		
Debts	$3,681		

1st District, Rep. Stephen Schiff (R)

1987-88		Direct Cont. 1987-88	
Receipts	$563,429	Indiv.	$320,980
Expend.	$559,134	Party	$29,999
C.O.H.	$4,292	PACS	$158,911
Debts	$40,615	Cand.	$33,500

2d District, Rep. Joseph R. Skeen (R)

1987-88		Direct Cont. 1987-88	
Receipts	$143,944	Indiv.	$45,927
Expend.	$67,727	Party	$3,307
C.O.H.	$79,810	PACS	$87,050
Debts	$2,750	Cand.	$2,500

3d District, Rep. Bill Richardson (D)

1987-88		Direct Cont. 1987-88	
Receipts	$456,787	Indiv.	$138,569
Expend.	$267,633	PACS	$297,898
C.O.H.	$219,713		
Debts	$34,000		

NEW YORK

Sen. Daniel Patrick Moynihan (D)

1987-88		Direct Cont. 1987-88	
Receipts	$4,350,271	Indiv.	$3,270,664
Expend.	$4,809,810	Party	$18,500
C.O.H.	$460,075	PACS	$892,773

Sen. Alfonse D'Amato (R)

1985-86		Direct Cont. 1985-86	
Receipts	$11,333,629	Indiv.	$4,825,412
Expend.	$12,914,822	Party	$18,113
C.O.H.	$456,293	PACS	$885,668
		Cand.	$885,668

1st District, Rep. George Hochbrueckner (D)

1987-88		Direct Cont. 1987-88	
Receipts	$736,474	Indiv.	$273,341
Expend.	$732,956	Party	$9,998
C.O.H.	$2,598	PACS	$417,961
Debts	$11,622	Cand.	$4,000

2d District, Rep. Thomas J. Downey (D)

1987-88		Direct Cont. 1987-88	
Receipts	$896,625	Indiv.	$480,011
Expend.	$627,584	Party	$660
C.O.H.	$509,072	PACS	$360,011

3d District, Rep. Robert J. Mrazek (D)

1987-88		Direct Cont. 1987-88	
Receipts	$447,902	Indiv.	$248,151
Expend.	$364,087	Party	$1,120
C.O.H.	$207,331	PACS	$176,931

4th District, Rep. Norman F. Lent (R)

1987-88		Direct Cont. 1987-88	
Receipts	$589,323	Indiv.	$182,978
Expend.	$436,310	Party	$2,000
C.O.H.	$489,416	PACS	$358,299

5th District, Rep. Raymond J. McGrath (R)

1987-88		Direct Cont. 1987-88	
Receipts	$502,509	Indiv.	$176,099
Expend.	$337,792	Party	$3,508
C.O.H.	$326,731	PACS	$251,324
Debts	$6,876		

6th District, Rep. Floyd H. Flake (D)

1987-88		Direct Cont. 1987-88	
Receipts	$344,391	Indiv.	$183,136
Expend.	$370,236	Party	$158
C.O.H.	$16,034	PACS	$150,681
Debts	$48,244		

7th District, Rep. Gary L. Ackerman (D)

1987-88		Direct Cont. 1987-88	
Receipts	$280,467	Indiv.	$80,011
Expend.	$142,041	Party	$664
C.O.H.	$252,498	PACS	$196,120

8th District, Rep. James H. Scheuer (D)

1987-88		Direct Cont. 1987-88	
Receipts	$77,854	Indiv.	$9,000
Expend.	$98,919	Party	$219
C.O.H.	$1,459	PACS	$55,600
Debts	$164,250	Cand.	$13,000

9th District, Rep. Thomas J. Manton (D)

1987-88		Direct Cont. 1987-88	
Receipts	$424,381	Indiv.	$101,190
Expend.	$256,832	PACS	$263,545
C.O.H.	$174,474		

10th District, Rep. Charles E. Schumer (D)

1987-88		Direct Cont. 1987-88	
Receipts	$437,574	Indiv.	$213,480
Expend.	$87,129	Party	$219
C.O.H.	$854,385	PACS	$137,325

11th District, Rep. Edolphus Towns (D)

1987-88		Direct Cont. 1987-88	
Receipts	$327,722	Indiv.	$172,226
Expend.	$278,709	PACS	$129,291
C.O.H.	$88,047	Cand.	$4,000

12th District, Rep. Major R. Owens (D)

1987-88		Direct Cont. 1987-88	
Receipts	$198,529	Indiv.	$56,771
Expend.	$189,684	Party	$462
C.O.H.	$9,107	PACS	$125,085
Debts	$26,891		

13th District, Rep. Stephen J. Solarz (D)

1987-88		Direct Cont. 1987-88	
Receipts	$899,313	Indiv.	$760,802
Expend.	$553,532	PACS	$60,605
C.O.H.	$1,158,484		

14th District, Rep. Guy V. Molinari (R)

1987-88		Direct Cont. 1987-88	
Receipts	$212,952	Indiv.	$98,715
Expend.	$206,796	Party	$14,000
C.O.H.	$143,489	PACS	$77,006

15th District, Rep. Bill Green (R)

1987-88		Direct Cont. 1987-88	
Receipts	$656,289	Indiv.	$466,422
Expend.	$602,942	Party	$19,000
C.O.H.	$63,211	PACS	$154,233
Debts	$237,000		

16th District, Rep. Charles B. Rangel (D)

1987-88		Direct Cont. 1987-88	
Receipts	$583,012	Indiv.	$204,059
Expend.	$479,427	Party	$125
C.O.H.	$362,997	PACS	$358,875

17th District, Rep. Ted Weiss (D)

1987-88		Direct Cont. 1987-88	
Receipts	$171,815	Indiv.	$103,792
Expend.	$170,567	PACS	$64,890
C.O.H.	$48,808		

18th District, Rep. Robert Garcia (D)

1987-88		Direct Cont. 1987-88	
Receipts	$306,376	Indiv.	$99,930
Expend.	$448,391	PACS	$187,075
C.O.H.	$4,430	Cand.	$1,013
Debts	$33,272		

19th District, Rep. Elliot L. Engel (D)

1987-88		Direct Cont. 1987-88	
Receipts	$187,088	Indiv.	$35,721
Expend.	$183,145	PACS	$99,600
C.O.H.	$1,935	Cand.	$36,817
Debts	$112,778		

20th District, Rep. Nita M. Lowey (D)

1987-88		Direct Cont. 1987-88	
Receipts	$1,338,147	Indiv.	$505,458
Expend.	$1,309,873	Party	$20,000
C.O.H.	$28,273	PACS	$164,175
Debts	$606,461	Cand.	$657,840

21st District, Rep. Hamilton Fish, Jr. (R)

1987-88		Direct Cont. 1987-88	
Receipts	$357,841	Indiv.	$145,767
Expend.	$277,680	Party	$3,486
C.O.H.	$168,252	PACS	$196,388
Debts	$1,000		

22d District, Rep. Benjamin A. Gilman (R)

1987-88		Direct Cont. 1987-88	
Receipts	$428,176	Indiv.	$220,764
Expend.	$411,056	Party	$2,755
C.O.H.	$120,413	PACS	$166,797
Debts	$11,533		

23d District, Rep. Michael R. McNulty (D)

1987-88		Direct Cont. 1987-88	
Receipts	$282,373	Indiv.	$114,908
Expend.	$273,505	PACS	$141,975
C.O.H.	$8,866		
Debts	$10,356		

24th District, Rep. Gerald B.H. Solomon (R)

1987-88		Direct Cont. 1987-88	
Receipts	$195,033	Indiv.	$107,157
Expend.	$151,276	Party	$9,000
C.O.H.	$97,294	PACS	$74,650

25th District, Rep. Sherwood L. Boehlert (R)

1987-88		Direct Cont. 1987-88	
Receipts	$235,512	Indiv.	$70,016
Expend.	$145,883	Party	$2,980
C.O.H.	$158,439	PACS	$90,173
		Cand.	$26,450

26th District, Rep. David O'B. Martin (R)

1987-88		Direct Cont. 1987-88	
Receipts	$133,256	Indiv.	$39,024
Expend.	$120,423	Party	$2,055
C.O.H.	$68,561	PACS	$84,316

27th District, Rep. James T. Walsh (R)

1987-88		Direct Cont. 1987-88	
Receipts	$610,935	Indiv.	$396,341
Expend.	$594,965	Party	$9,998
C.O.H.	$15,970	PACS	$202,620

28th District, Rep. Matthew F. McHugh (D)

1987-88		Direct Cont. 1987-88	
Receipts	$276,595	Indiv.	$134,161
Expend.	$172,905	PACS	$129,633
C.O.H.	$109,852	Cand.	$8,000

29th District, Rep. Frank Horton (D)

1987-88		Direct Cont. 1987-88	
Receipts	$163,751	Indiv.	$22,525
Expend.	$130,597	Party	$2,060
C.O.H.	$142,721	PACS	$126,560

30th District, Rep. Louise M. Slaughter (D)

1987-88		Direct Cont. 1987-88	
Receipts	$778,946	Indiv.	$342,876
Expend.	$802,886	Party	$4,996
C.O.H.	$4,851	PACS	$388,273
Debts	$20,306		

31st District, Rep. L. William Paxon (R)

1987-88		Direct Cont. 1987-88	
Receipts	$688,480	Indiv.	$398,627
Expend.	$688,382	Party	$24,998
C.O.H.	$95	PACS	$242,558
Debts	$13,349		

32d District, Rep. John J. LaFalce (D)

1987-88		Direct Cont. 1987-88	
Receipts	$241,784	Indiv.	$56,754
Expend.	$133,738	Party	$167
C.O.H.	$450,300	PACS	$141,022

33d District, Rep. Henry J. Nowak (D)

1987-88		Direct Cont. 1987-88	
Receipts	$122,306	Indiv.	$15,460
Expend.	$94,042	Party	$463
C.O.H.	$180,518	PACS	$91,225

34th District, Rep. Amory Houghton, Jr. (R)

1987-88		Direct Cont. 1987-88	
Receipts	$468,327	Indiv.	$344,856
Expend.	$319,098	Party	$3,457
C.O.H.	$151,219	PACS	$101,550
Debts	$2,944	Cand.	$1,754

NORTH CAROLINA

Sen. Jesse A. Helms (R)

1979-84		Direct Cont. 1979-84	
Receipts	$17,180,720	Indiv.	$16,200,119
Expend.	$16,917,559	Party	$20,517
Debt	$429,549	PACS	$865,528

Sen. Terry Sanford (D)

1985-86		Direct Cont. 1985-86	
Receipts	$4,181,701	Indiv.	$2,478,344
Expend.	$4,168,509	Party	$22,300
C.O.H.	$13,190	PACS	$658,632
		Cand.	$1,082,000

1st District, Rep. Walter Jones (D)

1987-88		Direct Cont. 1987-88	
Receipts	$141,476	Indiv.	$9,965
Expend.	$82,147	PACS	$96,550
C.O.H.	$312,342		

2d District, Rep. Tim Valentine (D)

1987-88		Direct Cont. 1987-88	
Receipts	$78,527	Indiv.	$15,551
Expend.	$84,671	PACS	$58,650
C.O.H.	$44,954		

3d District, Rep. H. Martin Lancaster (D)

1987-88		Direct Cont. 1987-88	
Receipts	$195,992	Indiv.	$61,467
Expend.	$98,956	PACS	$132,249
C.O.H.	$98,735		

4th District, Rep. David E. Price (D)

1987-88		Direct Cont. 1987-88	
Receipts	$1,031,004	Indiv.	$518,564
Expend.	$1,006,641	Party	$10,999
C.O.H.	$33,568	PACS	$489,658

5th District, Rep. Stephen L. Neal (D)

1987-88		Direct Cont. 87-88	
Receipts	$715,578	Indiv.	$230,967
Expend.	$756,115	Party	$9,999
C.O.H.	$3,113	PACS	$411,180
Debts	$29,419	Cand.	$27,000

6th District, Rep. Howard Coble (R)

1987-88		Direct Cont. 1987-88	
Receipts	$736,254	Indiv.	$420,782
Expend.	$738,088	Party	$18,807
C.O.H.	$16,650	PACS	$282,524
		Cand.	$2,303

7th District, Rep. Charlie Rose (D)

1987-88		Direct Cont. 1987-88	
Receipts	$293,187	Indiv.	$60,505
Expend.	$185,039	PACS	$177,500
C.O.H.	$365,916		
Debts	$50,000		

8th District, Rep. Bill Hefner (D)

1987-88		Direct Cont. 1987-88	
Receipts	$432,432	Indiv.	$96,080
Expend.	$581,888	PACS	$272,625
C.O.H.	$107,543	Cand.	$23,500
Debts	$4,238		

9th District, Rep. J. Alex McMillan, III (R)

1987-88		Direct Cont. 1987-88	
Receipts	$509,524	Indiv.	$287,646
Expend.	$440,082	Party	$2,494
C.O.H.	$89,508	PACS	$214,455
		Cand.	$11,500

10th District, Rep. T. Cass Ballenger (R)

1987-88		Direct Cont. 1987-88	
Receipts	$322,903	Indiv.	$130,068
Expend.	$302,215	Party	$3,501
C.O.H.	$26,135	PACS	$153,375
Debts	$62,000	Cand.	$34,000

11th District, Rep. James McClure Clarke (D)

1987-88		Direct Cont. 1987-88	
Receipts	$507,787	Indiv.	$160,135
Expend.	$494,092	Party	$11,000
C.O.H.	$14,259	PACS	$278,867
Debts	$43,000	Cand.	$43,000

NORTH DAKOTA

Sen. Quentin N. Burdick (D)

1987-88		Direct Cont. 1987-88	
Receipts	$1,755,318	Indiv.	$617,777
Expend.	$2,026,617	Party	$17,500
C.O.H.	$25,228	PACS	$1,059,524

Sen. Kent Conrad (D)

1985-86		Direct Cont. 1985-86	
Receipts	$993,040	Indiv.	$507,904
Expend.	$908,374	Party	$16,500
C.O.H.	$85,667	PACS	$500,387
		Cand.	$2,196

At-Large, Rep. Byron L. Dorgan (D)

1987-88		Direct Cont. 1987-88	
Receipts	$687,234	Indiv.	$183,963
Expend.	$747,594	Party	$1,657
C.O.H.	$143,210	PACS	$462,346

OHIO

Sen. John H. Glenn, Jr. (D)

1985-86		Direct Cont. 1985-86	
Receipts	$2,088,191	Indiv.	$1,345,763
Expend.	$1,319,026	Party	$17,749
C.O.H.	$818,910	PACS	$625,803
		Cand.	$47,872

Sen. Howard Metzenbaum (D)

1987-88		Direct Cont. 1987-88	
Receipts	$7,312,533	Indiv.	$5,838,248
Expend.	$8,547,545	Party	$18,500
C.O.H.	$221,751	PACS	$1,028,183
Debts	$9,798		

1st District, Rep. Thomas A. Luken (D)

1987-88		Direct Cont. 1987-88	
Receipts	$774,952	Indiv.	$258,615
Expend.	$908,765	Party	$5,245
C.O.H.	$1,814	PACS	$468,685
Debts	$16,951	Cand.	$18,000

2d District, Rep. Bill Gradison, Jr. (R)

1987-88		Direct Cont. 1987-88	
Receipts	$197,743	Indiv.	$158,617
Expend.	$125,682	Party	$2,000
C.O.H.	$364,822		

3d District, Rep. Tony P. Hall (D)

1987-88		Direct Cont. 1987-88	
Receipts	$216,111	Indiv.	$46,340
Expend.	$182,889	PACS	$140,160
C.O.H.	$272,692		

4th District, Rep. Michael G. Oxley (R)

1987-88		Direct Cont. 1987-88	
Receipts	$251,619	Indiv.	$35,313
Expend.	$207,157	Party	$2,242
C.O.H.	$220,485	PACS	$170,850

5th District, Rep. Paul E. Gillmor (R)

1987-88		Direct Cont. 1987-88	
Receipts	$742,123	Indiv.	$332,747
Expend.	$769,548	Party	$21,986
C.O.H.	$12,984	PACS	$319,120
Debts	$69,000	Cand.	$70,000

6th District, Rep. Bob McEwen (R)

1987-88		Direct Cont. 1987-88	
Receipts	$787,103	Indiv.	$606,456
Expend.	$884,754	Party	$9,184
C.O.H.	$22,951	PACS	$147,066

7th District, Rep. Michael DeWine (R)

1987-88		Direct Cont. 1987-88	
Receipts	$312,200	Indiv.	$186,011
Expend.	$299,553	Party	$1,234
C.O.H.	$64,484	PACS	$112,860

8th District, Rep. Donald E. (Buz) Lukens (R)

1987-88		Direct Cont. 1987-88	
Receipts	$151,231	Indiv.	$53,769
Expend.	$147,712	Party	$3,011
C.O.H.	$7,191	PACS	$84,880

9th District, Rep. Marcy Kaptur (D)

1987-88		Direct Cont. 1987-88	
Receipts	$277,724	Indiv.	$70,174
Expend.	$244,030	PACS	$201,740
C.O.H.	$35,833		
Debts	$5,000		

10th District, Rep. Clarence E. Miller (R)

1987-88		Direct Cont. 1987-88	
Receipts	$129,695	Indiv.	$14,040
Expend.	$99,247	Party	$5,597
C.O.H.	$102,113	PACS	$99,436

11th District, Rep. Dennis E. Eckart (D)

1987-88		Direct Cont. 1987-88	
Receipts	$569,638	Indiv.	$162,788
Expend.	$561,070	Party	$5,000
C.O.H.	$102,623	PACS	$382,928
Debts	$11,933		

12th District, Rep. John R. Kasich (R)

1987-88		Direct Cont. 1987-88	
Receipts	$370,579	Indiv.	$215,972
Expend.	$351,517	Party	$2,115
C.O.H.	$43,897	PACS	$130,686

13th District, Rep. Donald J. Pease (D)

1987-88		Direct Cont. 1987-88	
Receipts	$292,904	Indiv.	$81,588
Expend.	$157,632	PACS	$189,677
C.O.H.	$257,811		

14th District, Rep. Thomas C. Sawyer (D)

1987-88		Direct Cont. 1987-88	
Receipts	$447,420	Indiv.	$101,718
Expend.	$419,005	Party	$3,099
C.O.H.	$50,303	PACS	$314,754
Debts	$1,628		

15th District, Rep. Chalmers Wylie (R)

1987-88		Direct Cont. 1987-88	
Receipts	$231,063	Indiv.	$68,871
Expend.	$211,963	Party	$2,064
C.O.H.	$32,910	PACS	$158,415

16th District, Rep. Ralph S. Regula (R)

1987-88		Direct Cont. 1987-88	
Receipts	$108,672	Indiv.	$92,679
Expend.	$94,492	Party	$2,060
C.O.H.	$98,528		

17th District, Rep. James Traficant, Jr. (D)

1987-88		Direct Cont. 1987-88	
Receipts	$100,063	Indiv.	$41,483
Expend.	$96,003	PACS	$54,500
C.O.H.	$55,682		

18th District, Rep. Douglas Applegate (D)

1987-88		Direct Cont. 1987-88	
Receipts	$120,435	Indiv.	$23,026
Expend.	$86,061	Party	$169
C.O.H.	$130,506	PACS	$66,751
		Cand.	$11,650

19th District, Rep. Edward F. Feighan (D)

1987-88		Direct Cont. 1987-88	
Receipts	$391,199	Indiv.	$177,010
Expend.	$226,086	Party	$260
C.O.H.	$196,227	PACS	$205,414
Debts	$12,212		

20th District, Rep. Mary Rose Oakar (D)

1987-88		Direct Cont. 1987-88	
Receipts	$691,256	Indiv.	$252,852
Expend.	$783,180	Party	$3,952
C.O.H.	$3,640	PACS	$392,918
Debts	$16,360	Cand.	$28,000

21st District, Rep. Louis Stokes (D)

1987-88		Direct Cont. 1987-88	
Receipts	$241,646	Indiv.	$59,441
Expend.	$173,534	PACS	$147,800
C.O.H.	$190,827		

OKLAHOMA

Sen. David Lyle Boren (D)

1979-84		Direct Cont. 1979-84	
Receipts	$1,218,068	Indiv.	$1,139,519
Expend.	$1,192,026	Party	$12,803
C.O.H.	$52,468	PACS	$5,700

Sen. Don Nickles (R)

1985-86		Direct Cont. 1985-86	
Receipts	$2,995,708	Indiv.	$1,866,044
Expend.	$3,252,964	Party	$17,153
C.O.H.	$375,674	PACS	$859,335
		Cand.	$16,616

1st District, Rep. James M. Inhofe (R)

1987-88		Direct Cont. 1987-88	
Receipts	$482,552	Indiv.	$194,210
Expend.	$484,585	Party	$27,220
C.O.H.	$3,452	PACS	$263,222
Debts	$56,001	Cand.	$2,000

2d District, Rep. Michael L. Synar (D)

1987-88		Direct Cont. 1987-88	
Receipts	$310,865	Indiv.	$298,514
Expend.	$358,705		
C.O.H.	$34,269		

3d District, Rep. Wes Watkins (D)

1987-88		Direct Cont. 1987-88	
Receipts	$241,418	Indiv.	$149,324
Expend.	$174,437	PACS	$73,900
C.O.H.	$184,817		

4th District, Rep. Dave McCurdy (D)

1987-88		Direct Cont. 1987-88	
Receipts	$273,015	Indiv.	$107,910
Expend.	$251,956	PACS	$142,272
Debts	$96,779	Cand.	$10,392
Debts	$8,808		

5th District, Rep. Mickey Edwards (R)

1987-88		Direct Cont. 1987-88	
Receipts	$340,142	Indiv.	$211,625
Expend.	$318,822	Party	$4,124
C.O.H.	$60,504	PACS	$122,430

6th District, Rep. Glenn English (D)

1987-88		Direct Cont. 1987-88	
Receipts	$385,373	Indiv.	$165,368
Expend.	$306,600	Party	$466
C.O.H.	$243,324	PACS	$183,408
Debts	$1,777	Cand.	$14,750

OREGON

Sen. Mark O. Hatfield (R)

1979-84		Direct Cont. 1979-84	
Receipts	$860,361	Indiv.	$400,173
Expend.	$671,167	Party	$23,235
C.O.H.	$243,511	PACS	$376,194

Sen. Robert W. Packwood (R)

1985-86		Direct Cont. 1985-86	
Receipts	$6,725,027	Indiv.	$5,194,632
Expend.	$6,523,492	Party	$16,282
C.O.H.	$692,290	PACS	$936,759

1st District, Rep. Les AuCoin (D)

1987-88		Direct Cont. 1987-88	
Receipts	$724,149	Indiv.	$292,017
Expend.	$542,224	Party	$3,218
C.O.H.	$207,624	PACS	$340,550
Debts	$10,500	Cand.	$75,500

2d District, Rep. Robert F. (Bob) Smith (R)

1987-88		Direct Cont. 1987-88	
Receipts	$381,363	Indiv.	$204,319
Expend.	$340,643	Party	$9,311
C.O.H.	$90,322	PACS	$153,366

3d District, Rep. Ron Wyden (D)

1987-88		Direct Cont. 1987-88	
Receipts	$596,224	Indiv.	$253,749
Expend.	$287,996	Party	$321
C.O.H.	$437,007	PACS	$316,772

4th District, Rep. Peter DeFazio (D)

1987-88		Direct Cont. 1987-88	
Receipts	$327,640	Indiv.	$75,273
Expend.	$279,809	Party	$4,747
C.O.H.	$55,774	PACS	$235,589

5th District, Rep. Denny Smith (R)

1987-88		Direct Cont. 1987-88	
Receipts	$476,246	Indiv.	$234,854
Expend.	$559,616	Party	$5,931
C.O.H.	$48,597	PACS	$211,227

PENNSYLVANIA

Sen. H. John Heinz, III (R)

1987-88		Direct Cont. 1987-88	
Receipts	$5,280,540	Indiv.	$3,605,924
Expend.	$5,151,512	Party	$18,476
C.O.H.	$924,534	PACS	$1,441,438

Sen. Arlen Specter (R)

1985-86		Direct Cont. 1985-86	
Receipts	$5,450,763	Indiv.	$3,909,191
Expend.	$5,993,230	Party	$20,464
C.O.H.	$64,461	PACS	$1,313,401
		Cand.	$29,741

1st District, Rep. Thomas M. Foglietta (D)

1987-88		Direct Cont. 1987-88	
Receipts	$334,147	Indiv.	$159,993
Expend.	$234,957	Party	$283
C.O.H.	$135,520	PACS	$172,700

2d District, Rep. William H. Gray, III (D)

1987-88		Direct Cont. 1987-88	
Receipts	$656,859	Indiv.	$231,788
Expend.	$660,456	Party	$572
C.O.H.	$145,970	PACS	$377,752
Debts	$1,562	Cand.	$44,000

3d District, Rep. Robert A. Borski (D)

1987-88		Direct Cont. 1987-88	
Receipts	$337,723	Indiv.	$138,857
Expend.	$250,480	PACS	$189,654
C.O.H.	$107,024		

4th District, Rep. Joseph P. Kolter (D)

1987-88		Direct Cont. 1987-88	
Receipts	$175,980	Indiv.	$27,250
Expend.	$90,710	PACS	$146,606
C.O.H.	$149,083		

5th District, Rep. Richard T. Schulze (R)

1987-88		Direct Cont. 1987-88	
Receipts	$428,745	Indiv.	$129,575
Expend.	$444,205	Party	$2,212
C.O.H.	$275,895	PACS	$258,420

6th District, Rep. Gus Yatron (D)

1987-88		Direct Cont. 1987-88	
Receipts	$145,914	Indiv.	$23,970
Expend.	$121,435	Party	$409
C.O.H.	$135,923	PACS	$109,700

7th District, Rep. Curt Weldon (R)

1987-88		Direct Cont. 1987-88	
Receipts	$564,109	Indiv.	$325,514
Expend.	$507,360	Party	$2,013
C.O.H.	$110,936	PACS	$215,617
Debts	$47,982		

8th District, Rep. Peter H. Kostmayer (D)

1987-88		Direct Cont. 1987-88	
Receipts	$1,110,419	Indiv.	$657,411
Expend.	$1,089,612	Party	$128
C.O.H.	$38,957	PACS	$418,821
Debts	$50,509		

9th District, Rep. E.G.(Bud) Shuster (R)

1987-88		Direct Cont. 1987-88	
Receipts	$402,210	Indiv.	$237,290
Expend.	$332,647	Party	$2,118
C.O.H.	$114,385	PACS	$153,665

10th District, Rep. Joseph M. McDade (R)

1987-88		Direct Cont. 1987-88	
Receipts	$442,808	Indiv.	$128,825
Expend.	$430,322	Party	$3,477
C.O.H.	$326,216	PACS	$271,620

11th District, Rep. Paul E. Kanjorski (D)

1987-88		Direct Cont. 1987-88	
Receipts	$429,603	Indiv.	$128,668
Expend.	$310,305	PACS	$286,370
C.O.H.	$192,089	Cand.	$1,900
Debts	$106,917		

12th District, Rep. John P. Murtha (D)

1987-88		Direct Cont. 1987-88	
Receipts	$447,087	Indiv.	$107,612
Expend.	$401,945	Party	$138
C.O.H.	$251,340	PACS	$310,815

13th District, Rep. Lawrence Coughlin (R)

1987-88		Direct Cont. 1987-88	
Receipts	$396,262	Indiv.	$225,836
Expend.	$225,412	Party	$3,816
C.O.H.	$219,081	PACS	$150,851

14th District, Rep. William J. Coyne (D)

1987-88		Direct Cont. 1987-88	
Receipts	$168,698	Indiv.	$12,570
Expend.	$80,730	PACS	$156,075
C.O.H.	$191,524		

15th District, Rep. Don Ritter (R)

1987-88		Direct Cont. 1987-88	
Receipts	$759,713	Indiv.	$421,074
Expend.	$752,332	Party	$12,047
C.O.H.	$42,883	PACS	$293,454
		Cand.	$71,400

16th District, Rep. Robert S. Walker (R)

1987-88		Direct Cont. 1987-88	
Receipts	$106,318	Indiv.	$56,514
Expend.	$91,950	Party	$3,028
C.O.H.	$36,953	PACS	$44,375

17th District, Rep. George W. Gekas (R)

1987-88		Direct Cont. 1987-88	
Receipts	$95,878	Indiv.	$22,529
Expend.	$97,611	Party	$2,577
C.O.H.	$106,439	PACS	$46,750

18th District, Rep. Doug Walgren (D)

1987-88		Direct Cont. 1987-88	
Receipts	$389,537	Indiv.	$87,338
Expend.	$321,074	Party	$682
C.O.H.	$120,260	PACS	$232,214

19th District, Rep. William F. Goodling (R)

1987-88		Direct Cont. 1987-88	
Receipts	$54,123	Indiv.	$49,914
Expend.	$57,091	Party	$2,441
C.O.H.	$5,938		

20th District, Rep. Joseph M. Gaydos (D)

1987-88		Direct Cont. 1987-88	
Receipts	$184,634	Indiv.	$25,985
Expend.	$137,023	Party	$188
C.O.H.	$90,358	PACS	$143,850

21st District, Rep. Thomas J. Ridge (R)

1987-88		Direct Cont. 1987-88	
Receipts	$419,770	Indiv.	$172,212
Expend.	$370,619	Party	$4,484
C.O.H.	$134,081	PACS	$211,711

22d District, Rep. Austin J. Murphy (D)

1987-88		Direct Cont. 1987-88	
Receipts	$173,164	Indiv.	$35,656
Expend.	$183,335	PACS	$128,218
C.O.H.	$103,193		

23d District, Rep. William F. Clinger, Jr. (R)

1987-88		Direct Cont. 1987-88	
Receipts	$405,537	Indiv.	$203,654
Expend.	$336,675	Party	$3,148
C.O.H.	$73,800	PACS	$189,036
Debts	$11,000		

RHODE ISLAND

Sen. Claiborne Pell (D)

1979-84		Direct Cont. 1979-84	
Receipts	$740,729	Indiv.	$464,835
Expend.	$444,283	PACS	$213,030
C.O.H.	$338,004		

Sen. John H. Chafee (R)

1987-88		Direct Cont. 1987-88	
Receipts	$2,455,215	Indiv.	$1,267,565
Expend.	$2,841,985	Party	$17,500
C.O.H.	$50,360	PACS	$1,045,319

1st District, Rep. Ron Machtley (R)

1987-88		Direct Cont. 1987-88	
Receipts	$417,449	Indiv.	$198,366
Expend.	$385,402	Party	$29,998
C.O.H.	$32,046	PACS	$81,524
Debts	$99,093	Cand.	$125,809

2d District, Rep. Claudine Schneider (R)

1987-88		Direct Cont. 1987-88	
Receipts	$419,633	Indiv.	$197,484
Expend.	$443,267	Party	$5,967
C.O.H.	$96,586	PACS	$193,656
Debts	$1,675		

SOUTH CAROLINA

Sen. Strom Thurmond (R)

1979-84		Direct Cont. 1979-84	
Receipts	$2,038,457	Indiv.	$1,346,556
Expend.	$1,682,962	Party	$15,457
C.O.H.	$364,686	PACS	$596,785

Sen. Ernest F. (Fritz) Hollings (D)

1985-86		Direct Cont. 1985-86	
Receipts	$2,395,632	Indiv.	$1,329,904
Expend.	$2,233,843	Party	$17,223
C.O.H.	$197,854	PACS	$913,697

1st District, Rep. Arthur Ravenel, Jr. (R)

1987-88		Direct Cont. 1987-88	
Receipts	$273,828	Indiv.	$123,555
Expend.	$118,702	Party	$2,508
C.O.H.	$162,109	PACS	$141,080

2d District, Rep. Floyd Spence (R)

1987-88		Direct Cont. 1987-88	
Receipts	$363,171	Indiv.	$157,707
Expend.	$369,698	Party	$11,535
C.O.H.	$3,378	PACS	$191,268

3d District, Rep. Butler Derrick (D)

1987-88		Direct Cont. 1987-88	
Receipts	$579,468	Indiv.	$171,763
Expend.	$641,429	PACS	$370,841
C.O.H.	$166,031		

4th District, Rep. Elizabeth J. Patterson (D)

1987-88		Direct Cont. 1987-88	
Receipts	$1,119,822	Indiv.	$223,693
Expend.	$1,143,351	Party	$14,999
C.O.H.	$2,453	PACS	$412,855
Debts	$150,557	Cand.	$455,155

5th District, Rep. John M. Spratt, Jr. (D)

1987-88		Direct Cont. 1987-88	
Receipts	$203,552	Indiv.	$46,866
Expend.	$105,620	Party	$170
C.O.H.	$216,023	PACS	$140,970
Debts	$181,500		

6th District, Rep. Robin M. Tallon (D)

1987-88		Direct Cont. 1987-88	
Receipts	$381,464	Indiv.	$110,713
Expend.	$243,559	PACS	$203,958
C.O.H.	$214,838		
Debts	$3,333		

SOUTH DAKOTA

Sen. Larry Pressler (R)

1979-84		Direct Cont. 1979-84	
Receipts	$1,440,880	Indiv.	$671,725
Expend.	$1,155,683	Party	$29,376
C.O.H.	$325,441	PACS	$610,476
		Cand.	$30,000

Sen. Thomas A. Daschle (D)

1985-86		Direct Cont. 1985-86	
Receipts	$3,515,482	Indiv.	$2,241,772
Expend.	$3,485,870	Party	$19,724
C.O.H.	$40,245	PACS	$1,205,400
		Cand.	$72,740

At-Large, Rep. Tim Johnson (D)

1987-88		Direct Cont. 1987-88	
Receipts	$676,225	Indiv.	$296,996
Expend.	$632,105	Party	$7,499
C.O.H.	$51,452	PACS	$329,446
		Cand.	$6,793

TENNESSEE

Sen. James R. Sasser (D)

1987-88		Direct Cont. 1987-88	
Receipts	$3,218,986	Indiv.	$1,710,031
Expend.	$3,069,615	Party	$18,500
C.O.H.	$328,064	PACS	$1,379,817

Sen. Albert Gore, Jr. (D)

1983-84		Direct Cont. 1983-84	
Receipts	$3,101,546	Indiv.	$2,082,417
Expend.	$3,035,498	Party	$29,927
Debts	$19,335	PACS	$843,026

1st District, Rep. James H. Quillen (R)

1987-88		Direct Cont. 1987-88	
Receipts	$617,030	Indiv.	$121,373
Expend.	$227,503	Party	$2,159
C.O.H.	$711,012	PACS	$413,800

2d District, Rep. John J. Duncan, Jr. (R)

1987-88		Direct Cont. 1987-88	
Receipts	$448,530	Indiv.	$273,103
Expend.	$435,567	Party	$8,970
C.O.H.	$12,961	PACS	$161,675

3d District, Rep. Marilyn Lloyd (D)

1987-88		Direct Cont. 1987-88	
Receipts	$621,520	Indiv.	$259,730
Expend.	$618,173	Party	$6,157
C.O.H.	$3,670	PACS	$320,387
Debts	$16,334	Cand.	$10,000

4th District, Rep. Jim Cooper (D)

1987-88		Direct Cont. 1987-88	
Receipts	$292,770	Indiv.	$40,679
Expend.	$234,375	Party	$326
C.O.H.	$79,044	PACS	$244,977

5th District, Rep. Robert Clement (D)

1987-88		Direct Cont. 1987-88	
Receipts	$325,537	Indiv.	$135,895
Expend.	$291,818	Party	$992
C.O.H.	$37,164	PACS	$149,200
		Cand.	$224,500

6th District, Rep. Bart Gordon (D)

1987-88		Direct Cont. 1987-88	
Receipts	$587,878	Indiv.	$267,723
Expend.	$454,346	Party	$1,094
C.O.H.	$282,110	PACS	$256,095
		Cand.	$10,000

7th District, Rep. Don Sundquist (R)

1987-88		Direct Cont. 1987-88	
Receipts	$393,171	Indiv.	$183,625
Expend.	$307,656	Party	$2,672
C.O.H.	$275,374	PACS	$182,103

8th District, Rep. John S. Tanner (D)

1987-88		Direct Cont. 1987-88	
Receipts	$931,539	Indiv.	$630,468
Expend.	$863,425	Party	$6,669
C.O.H.	$68,113	PACS	$283,961
		Cand.	$2,000

9th District, Rep. Harold E. Ford (D)

1987-88		Direct Cont. 1987-88	
Receipts	$298,096	Indiv.	$57,258
Expend.	$364,330	Party	$391
C.O.H.	$824	PACS	$211,500
		Cand.	$17,900

TEXAS

Sen. Lloyd Bentsen (D)

1987-88		Direct Cont. 1987-88	
Receipts	$8,280,013	Indiv.	$5,406,218
Expend.	$8,829,361	Party	$5,341
C.O.H.	$86,737	PACS	$2,320,541
Debts	$118,652		

Sen. Phil Gramm (R)

1983-84		Direct Cont. 1983-84	
Receipts	$9,785,936	Indiv.	$7,947,011
Expend.	$9,452,360	Party	$30,180
C.O.H.	$250,355	PACS	$1,397,224

1st District, Rep. Jim Chapman, Jr. (D)

1987-88		Direct Cont. 1987-88	
Receipts	$541,159	Indiv.	$264,874
Expend.	$505,611	Party	$219
C.O.H.	$55,829	PACS	$270,430
Debts	$40,718		

2d District, Rep. Charles Wilson (D)

1987-88		Direct Cont. 1987-88	
Receipts	$338,839	Indiv.	$84,404
Expend.	$309,355	PACS	$254,350
C.O.H.	$77,702		

3d District, Rep. Steve Bartlett (R)

1987-88		Direct Cont. 1987-88	
Receipts	$769,201	Indiv.	$475,845
Expend.	$1,000,894	Party	$1,045
C.O.H.	$206,713	PACS	$230,678
Debts	$1,576		

4th District, Rep. Ralph M. Hall (D)

1987-88		Direct Cont. 1987-88	
Receipts	$350,284	Indiv.	$81,875
Expend.	$316,846	PACS	$242,743
C.O.H.	$201,630		

5th District, Rep. John Bryant (D)

1987-88		Direct Cont. 1987-88	
Receipts	$889,511	Indiv.	$321,277
Expend.	$646,218	PACS	$393,057
C.O.H.	$353,031	Cand.	$150,000

6th District, Rep. Joe L. Barton (R)

1987-88		Direct Cont. 1987-88	
Receipts	$750,559	Indiv.	$441,135
Expend.	$654,260	Party	$2,899
C.O.H.	$99,460	PACS	$288,083
		Cand.	$10,000

7th District, Rep. Bill Archer (R)

1987-88		Direct Cont. 1987-88	
Receipts	$269,695	Indiv.	$190,338
Expend.	$180,255	Party	$2,061
C.O.H.	$629,908		

8th District, Rep. Jack Fields (R)

1987-88		Direct Cont. 1987-88	
Receipts	$510,950	Indiv.	$228,089
Expend.	$483,544	Party	$2,000
C.O.H.	$69,460	PACS	$271,825

9th District, Rep. Jack Brooks (D)

1987-88		Direct Cont. 1987-88	
Receipts	$424,773	Indiv.	$104,025
Expend.	$226,581	Party	$245
C.O.H.	$440,347	PACS	$276,562

10th District, Rep. Jake J. Pickle (D)

1987-88		Direct Cont. 1987-88	
Receipts	$172,746	Indiv.	$97,787
Expend.	$172,921	PACS	$46,463
C.O.H.	$137,760		

11th District, Rep. Marvin Leath (D)

1987-88		Direct Cont. 1987-88	
Receipts	$178,312	Indiv.	$27,579
Expend.	$87,626	PACS	$95,150
C.O.H.	$488,621		

12th District, Rep. Jim Wright (D)

1987-88		Direct Cont. 1987-88	
Receipts	$776,295	Indiv.	$297,569
Expend.	$940,760	PACS	$179,603
C.O.H.	$83,843		

13th District, Rep. William C. Sarpalius (D)

1987-88		Direct Cont. 1987-88	
Receipts	$387,092	Indiv.	$91,224
Expend.	$384,738	Party	$11,999
C.O.H.	$2,454	PACS	$233,950
Debts	$77,455	Cand.	$36,581

14th District, Rep. Gregory H. Laughlin (D)

1987-88		Direct Cont. 1987-88	
Receipts	$623,491	Indiv.	$270,371
Expend.	$600,114	Party	$14,999
C.O.H.	$23,964	PACS	$240,699
Debts	$176,128	Cand.	$108,748

15th District, Rep. E. (Kika) de la Garza (D)

1987-88		Direct Cont. 1987-88	
Receipts	$263,843	Indiv.	$132,998
Expend.	$219,469	Party	$252
C.O.H.	$172,103	PACS	$127,452

16th District, Rep. Ronald D. Coleman (D)

1987-88		Direct Cont. 1987-88	
Receipts	$322,822	Indiv.	$95,635
Expend.	$317,444	PACS	$175,670
C.O.H.	$16,498	Cand.	$50,000
Debts	$22,500		

17th District, Rep. Charles W. Stenholm (D)

1987-88		Direct Cont. 1987-88	
Receipts	$289,551	Indiv.	$121,493
Expend.	$342,766	PACS	$111,716
C.O.H.	$146,938		

18th District, Rep. Mickey Leland (D)

1987-88		Direct Cont. 1987-88	
Receipts	$532,832	Indiv.	$160,893
Expend.	$534,732	PACS	$347,025
C.O.H.	$18,684		
Debts	$34,902		

19th District, Rep. Larry Combest (R)

1987-88		Direct Cont. 1987-88	
Receipts	$272,401	Indiv.	$139,252
Expend.	$244,821	Party	$4,593
C.O.H.	$34,187	PACS	$119,800

20th District, Rep. Henry B. Gonzalez (D)

1987-88		Direct Cont. 1987-88	
Receipts	$171,284	Indiv.	$64,872
Expend.	$174,470	PACS	$100,387
C.O.H.	$12,137	Cand.	$4,000

21st District, Rep. Lamar S. Smith (R)

1987-88		Direct Cont. 1987-88	
Receipts	$567,801	Indiv.	$382,551
Expend.	$418,989	Party	$2,919
C.O.H.	$152,944	PACS	$97,832
		Cand.	$37,151

22d District, Rep. Tom D. DeLay (R)

1987-88		Direct Cont. 1987-88	
Receipts	$364,837	Indiv.	$187,728
Expend.	$361,255	Party	$2,277
C.O.H.	$48,978	PACS	$171,650
Debts	$11,448		

23d District, Rep. Albert G. Bustamante (D)

1987-88		Direct Cont. 1987-88	
Receipts	$280,485	Indiv.	$114,605
Expend.	$187,302	PACS	$155,786
C.O.H.	$159,640		
Debts	$11,732		

24th District, Rep. Martin Frost (D)

1987-88		Direct Cont. 1987-88	
Receipts	$590,973	Indiv.	$262,037
Expend.	$438,949	PACS	$298,373
C.O.H.	$233,591		

25th District, Rep. Michael A. Andrews (D)

1987-88		Direct Cont. 1987-88	
Receipts	$638,035	Indiv.	$192,973
Expend.	$318,970	PACS	$403,635
C.O.H.	$565,626		

26th District, Rep. Richard K. Armey (D)

1987-88		Direct Cont. 1987-88	
Receipts	$419,632	Indiv.	$263,618
Expend.	$314,903	Party	$2,258
C.O.H.	$118,993	PACS	$150,800

27th District, Rep. Solomon P. Ortiz (D)

1987-88		Direct Cont. 1987-88	
Receipts	$198,217	Indiv.	$78,553
Expend.	$142,651	PACS	$100,383
C.O.H.	$150,139		

UTAH

Sen. Edwin Jacob (Jake) Garn (R)

1985-86		Direct Cont. 1985-86	
Receipts	$1,025,447	Indiv.	$393,653
Expend.	$752,944	Party	$16,234
C.O.H.	$285,275	PACS	$593,742
		Cand.	$2,498

Sen. Orrin G. Hatch (R)

1987-88		Direct Cont. 1987-88	
Receipts	$3,839,955	Indiv.	$2,522,983
Expend.	$3,706,381	Party	$15,000
C.O.H.	$443,171	PACS	$1,173,764
Debts	$176,188		

1st District, Rep. James V. Hansen (R)

1987-88		Direct Cont. 1987-88	
Receipts	$411,486	Indiv.	$127,312
Expend.	$426,902	Party	$12,499
C.O.H.	$8,144	PACS	$258,859
Debts	$10,000	Cand.	$10,000

2d District, Rep. Wayne Owens (D)

1987-88		Direct Cont. 1987-88	
Receipts	$736,198	Indiv.	$270,413
Expend.	$676,472	Party	$15,999
C.O.H.	$83,684	PACS	$455,310
Debts	$34,159	Cand.	$1,000

3d District, Rep. Howard C. Nielson (R)

1987-88		Direct Cont. 1987-88	
Receipts	$132,528	Indiv.	$17,782
Expend.	$102,055	Party	$2,319
C.O.H.	$61,328	PACS	$112,800

VERMONT

Sen. Patrick J. Leahy (D)

1985-86		Direct Cont. 1985-86	
Receipts	$1,919,740	Indiv.	$1,024,990
Expend.	$1,705,099	Party	$17,137
C.O.H.	$327,768	PACS	$833,356

Sen. James M. Jeffords (R)

1987-88		Direct Cont. 1987-88	
Receipts	$976,451	Indiv.	$223,170
Expend.	$876,877	Party	$15,733
C.O.H.	$312,249	PACS	$650,393

At-Large, Rep. Peter P. Smith (R)

1987-88		Direct Cont. 1987-88	
Receipts	$457,737	Indiv.	$278,049
Expend.	$450,162	Party	$12,500
C.O.H.	$7,574	PACS	$159,111
Debts	$17,794		

VIRGINIA

Sen. John W. Warner (R)

1979-84		Direct Cont. 1979-84	
Receipts	$3,108,607	Indiv.	$1,974,658
Expend.	$2,974,498	Party	$21,422
C.O.H.	$44,416	PACS	$883,952
		Cand.	$14,000

Sen. Charles S. (Chuck) Robb (D)

1987-88		Direct Cont. 1987-88	
Receipts	$3,198,630	Indiv.	$2,201,806
Expend.	$2,881,666	Party	$17,500
C.O.H.	$316,962	PACS	$914,763

1st District, Rep. Herbert H. Bateman (R)

1987-88		Direct Cont. 1987-88	
Receipts	$293,109	Indiv.	$129,262
Expend.	$284,702	Party	$2,015
C.O.H.	$39,534	PACS	$162,640
Debts	$1,137		

2d District, Rep. Owen B. Pickett (D)

1987-88		Direct Cont. 1987-88	
Receipts	$437,439	Indiv.	$209,294
Expend.	$414,011	Party	$9,999
C.O.H.	$28,550	PACS	$215,810
Debts	$6,711		

3d District, Rep. Thomas J. Bliley, Jr. (R)

1987-88		Direct Cont. 1987-88	
Receipts	$467,449	Indiv.	$168,715
Expend.	$366,816	Party	$2,000
C.O.H.	$108,636	PACS	$270,550
		Cand.	$20,000

4th District, Rep. Norman Sisisky (D)

1987-88		Direct Cont. 1987-88	
Receipts	$185,555	Indiv.	$32,260
Expend.	$93,232	PACS	$102,636
C.O.H.	$316,592		
Debts	$349,183		

5th District, Rep. L. F. Payne, Jr. (D)

1987-88		Direct Cont. 1987-88	
Receipts	$280,435	Indiv.	$134,979
Expend.	$274,442	Party	$3,033
C.O.H.	$9,041	PACS	$127,850
Debts	$275,000	Cand.	$279,662

6th District, Rep. James R. Olin (D)

1987-88		Direct Cont. 1987-88	
Receipts	$321,705	Indiv.	$161,600
Expend.	$322,160	Party	$3,000
C.O.H.	$11,751	PACS	$140,400
Debts	$22,000		

7th District, Rep. D. French Slaughter, Jr. (R)

1987-88		Direct Cont. 1987-88	
Receipts	$219,559	Indiv.	$104,469
Expend.	$87,195	Party	$4,000
C.O.H.	$180,208	PACS	$94,496
Debts	$2,500		

8th District, Rep. Stanford E. Parris (R)

1987-88		Direct Cont. 1987-88	
Receipts	$632,755	Indiv.	$405,411
Expend.	$689,035	Party	$9,897
C.O.H.	$157,957	PACS	$184,452
Debts	$2,261		

9th District, Rep. Frederick C. Boucher (D)

1987-88		Direct Cont. 1987-88	
Receipts	$616,821	Indiv.	$225,122
Expend.	$606,420	PACS	$367,600
C.O.H.	$130,299		

10th District, Rep. Frank R. Wolf (R)

1987-88		Direct Cont. 1987-88	
Receipts	$803,080	Indiv.	$519,889
Expend.	$758,365	Party	$2,038
C.O.H.	$57,022	PACS	$237,490

WASHINGTON

Sen. Brock Adams (D)

1985-86		Direct Cont. 1985-86	
Receipts	$1,973,142	Indiv.	$1,183,317
Expend.	$1,912,307	Party	$96,569
C.O.H.	$86,797	PACS	$718,771

Sen. Slade Gorton (R)

1987-88		Direct Cont. 1987-88	
Receipts	$2,736,101	Indiv.	$1,631,373
Expend.	$2,851,591	Party	$24,495
C.O.H.	$45,958	PACS	$939,406
Debts	$114,209	Cand.	$90,000

1st District, Rep. John R. Miller (R)

1987-88		Direct Cont. 1987-88	
Receipts	$1,328,979	Indiv.	$520,608
Expend.	$1,321,021	Party	$28,349
C.O.H.	$10,758	PACS	$333,860
Debts	$332,760	Cand.	$400,000

2d District, Rep. Al Swift (D)

1987-88		Direct Cont. 1987-88	
Receipts	$376,189	Indiv.	$75,044
Expend.	$301,229	Party	$2,058
C.O.H.	$131,488	PACS	$286,312

3d District, Rep. Jolene Unsoeld (D)

1987-88		Direct Cont. 1987-88	
Receipts	$687,800	Indiv.	$304,115
Expend.	$684,206	Party	$19,191
C.O.H.	$8,530	PACS	$282,082
Debts	$36,709	Cand.	$36,586

4th District, Rep. Sid Morrison (R)

1987-88		Direct Cont. 1987-88	
Receipts	$202,637	Indiv.	$99,773
Expend.	$194,505	Party	$3,202
C.O.H.	$156,996	PACS	$82,558

5th District, Rep. Thomas S. Foley (D)

1987-88		Direct Cont. 1987-88	
Receipts	$781,195	Indiv.	$176,701
Expend.	$476,460	PACS	$555,140
C.O.H.	$587,378		

6th District, Rep. Norman D. Dicks (D)

1987-88		Direct Cont. 1987-88	
Receipts	$366,934	Indiv.	$126,383
Expend.	$288,168	Party	$1,758
C.O.H.	$277,497	PACS	$213,239

7th District, Rep. James A. McDermott (D)

1987-88		Direct Cont. 1987-88	
Receipts	$366,810	Indiv.	$127,685
Expend.	$348,082	Party	$131
C.O.H.	$18,727	PACS	$233,226
		Cand.	$5,769

8th District, Rep. Rodney Chandler (R)

1987-88		Direct Cont. 1987-88	
Receipts	$333,019	Indiv.	$125,490
Expend.	$300,048	Party	$2,025
C.O.H.	$106,227	PACS	$191,478

WEST VIRGINIA

Sen. Robert C. Byrd (D)

1987-88		Direct Cont. 1987-88	
Receipts	$1,407,167	Indiv.	$351,092
Expend.	$1,099,709	PACS	$938,720
C.O.H.	$482,690		

Sen. John D. (Jay) Rockefeller, IV (D)

1983-84		Direct Cont. 1983-84	
Receipts	$12,091,551	Indiv.	$1,271,400
Expend.	$12,055,043	Party	$17,500
Debts	$10,241,457	PACS	$541,875
		Cand.	$10,250,000

1st District, Rep. Alan B. Mollohan (D)

1987-88		Direct Cont. 1987-88	
Receipts	$168,219	Indiv.	$53,873
Expend.	$103,154	PACS	$112,890
Debts	$95,346		

2d District, Rep. Harley O. Staggers, Jr. (D)

1987-88		Direct Cont. 1987-88	
Receipts	$146,928	Indiv.	$14,875
Expend.	$90,537	Party	$221
C.O.H.	$81,923	PACS	$131,953
Debts	$5,000		

3d District, Rep. Robert E. Wise, Jr. (D)

1987-88		Direct Cont. 1987-88	
Receipts	$173,893	Indiv.	$46,414
Expend.	$165,957	Party	$242
C.O.H.	$49,454	PACS	$122,952

4th District, Rep. Nick Joe Rahall, II (D)

1987-88		Direct Cont. 1987-88	
Receipts	$333,159	Indiv.	$97,206
Expend.	$152,271	PACS	$175,442
C.O.H.	$395,005		

WISCONSIN

Sen. Robert W. Kasten, Jr. (R)

1985-86		Direct Cont. 1985-86	
Receipts	$3,196,099	Indiv.	$1,855,680
Expend.	$3,433,870	Party	$16,958
C.O.H.	$125,579	PACS	$1,092,897
		Cand.	$42,420

Sen. Herbert H. Kohl (D)

1987-88		Direct Cont. 1987-88	
Receipts	$7,576,540	Indiv.	$642,927
Expend.	$7,491,600	Cand.	$6,920,071
C.O.H.	$84,938		
Debts	$881,095		

1st District, Rep. Les Aspin (D)

1987-88		Direct Cont. 1987-88	
Receipts	$618,045	Indiv.	$274,469
Expend.	$631,941	Party	$451
C.O.H.	$66,324	PACS	$265,249

2d District, Rep. Robert W. Kastenmeier (D)

1987-88		Direct Cont. 1987-88	
Receipts	$439,848	Indiv.	$244,142
Expend.	$440,574	Party	$500
C.O.H.	$31,507	PACS	$177,484

3d District, Rep. Steve Gunderson (R)

1987-88		Direct Cont. 1987-88	
Receipts	$404,942	Indiv.	$256,825
Expend.	$359,801	Party	$3,095
C.O.H.	$51,317	PACS	$133,235

4th District, Rep. Gerald D. Kleczka (D)

1987-88		Direct Cont. 1987-88	
Receipts	$210,781	Indiv.	$57,936
Expend.	$144,925	Party	$96
C.O.H.	$177,484	PACS	$128,783

5th District, Rep. Jim Moody (D)

1987-88		Direct Cont. 1987-88	
Receipts	$1,081,320	Indiv.	$542,416
Expend.	$1,060,125	Party	$1,302
C.O.H.	$17,588	PACS	$524,503
Debts	$76,250	Cand.	$194,000

6th District, Rep. Thomas E. Petri (R)

1987-88		Direct Cont. 1987-88	
Receipts	$258,876	Indiv.	$96,668
Expend.	$187,714	Party	$2,796
C.O.H.	$288,323	PACS	$120,980

7th District, Rep. David R. Obey (D)

1987-88		Direct Cont. 1987-88	
Receipts	$530,385	Indiv.	$192,719
Expend.	$450,716	PACS	$308,399
C.O.H.	$181,692		

8th District, Rep. Toby Roth (R)

1987-88		Direct Cont. 1987-88	
Receipts	$339,852	Indiv.	$131,840
Expend.	$227,823	Party	$2,989
C.O.H.	$203,375	PACS	$180,814

9th District, Rep. James Sensenbrenner, Jr. (R)

1987-88		Direct Cont. 1987-88	
Receipts	$309,612	Indiv.	$169,761
Expend.	$288,505	Party	$6,997
C.O.H.	$144,801	PACS	$109,839

WYOMING

Sen. Malcolm Wallop (R)

1987-88		Direct Cont. 1987-88	
Receipts	$1,492,048	Indiv.	$473,729
Expend.	$1,344,185	Party	$19,493
C.O.H.	$166,344	PACS	$872,664

Sen. Alan K. Simpson (R)

1979-84		Direct Cont. 1979-84	
Receipts	$1,071,830	Indiv.	$494,646
Expend.	$862,039	Party	$15,470
C.O.H.	$205,615	PACS	$491,437

At-Large, Rep. Craig Thomas (R)

1987-88		Direct Cont. 1987-88	
Receipts	$100,585	Indiv.	$86,070
Expend.	$89,022	Party	$25,000
C.O.H.	$11,562	PACS	$35,050

SENATE COMMITTEES

STANDING COMMITTEES

AGRICULTURE, NUTRITION AND FORESTRY

328A RSOB
202-224-2035

Majority (10 D): Leahy (VT), Chmn.; Pryor (AR), Boren (OK), Heflin (AL), Harkin (IA), Conrad (ND), Fowler (GA), Daschle (SD), Baucus (MT), Kerrey (NE).
Minority (9 R): Lugar (IN), Dole (KS), Helms (NC), Cochran (MS), Boschwitz (MN), McConnell (KY), Bond (MO), Wilson (CA), Gorton (WA).

SUBCOMMITTEES

AGRICULTURAL CREDIT

Majority (3 D): Conrad, Chmn.; Boren, Daschle.
Minority (2 R): Gorton, Boschwitz.

AGRICULTURAL PRODUCTION AND STABILIZATION OF PRICES

Majority (7 D): Pryor, Chmn.; Baucus, Kerrey, Boren, Heflin, Harkin, Conrad.
Minority (6 R): Helms, Dole, Cochran, McConnell, Boschwitz, Wilson.

AGRICULTURAL RESEARCH AND GENERAL LEGISLATION

Majority (2 D): Daschle, Chmn.; Kerrey.
Minority (2 R): Wilson, Bond.

CONSERVATION AND FORESTRY

Majority (3 D): Fowler, Chmn.; Heflin, Baucus.
Minority (2 R): Bond, Gorton.

DOMESTIC AND FOREIGN MARKETING AND PRODUCT PROMOTION

Majority (6 D): Boren, Chmn., Pryor, Fowler, Baucus, Harkin, Conrad.
Minority (6 R): Cochran, Helms, Bond, Wilson, Gorton, McConnell.

NUTRITION AND INVESTIGATIONS

Majority (4 D): Harkin, Chmn.; Fowler, Kerrey, Pryor.
Minority (3 R): Boschwitz, Dole, Helms.

RURAL DEVELOPMENT AND RURAL ELECTRIFICATION

Majority (3 D): Heflin, Chmn.; Daschle, Pryor.
Minority (2 R): McConnell, Cochran.

APPROPRIATIONS

S128 Capitol, 202-224-3471

Majority (16 D): Byrd (WV) Chmn.; Inouye (HI), Hollings (SC), Johnston (LA), Burdick (ND), Leahy (VT), Sasser (TN), DeConcini (AZ), Bumpers (AR), Lautenberg (NJ), Harkin (IA), Mikulski (MD), Reid (NV), Adams (WA), Fowler (GA), Kerrey (NE).

Minority (13 R): Hatfield (OR); Stevens (AK), McClure (ID), Garn (UT), Cochran (MS), Kasten (WI), D'Amato (NY), Rudman (NH), Specter (PA), Domenici (NM), Grassley (IA), Nickles (OK), Gramm (TX).

SUBCOMMITTEES

AGRICULTURE AND RELATED AGENCIES
Majority (6 D): Burdick, Chmn.; Bumpers, Harkin, Adams, Fowler, Kerrey.
Minority (5 R): Cochran, McClure, Kasten, Specter, Grassley.

COMMERCE, JUSTICE, STATE AND JUDICIARY
Majority (6 D): Hollings, Chmn.; Inouye, Bumpers, Lautenberg, Sasser, Adams.
Minority (5 R): Rudman, Stevens, Hatfield, Kasten, Gramm.

DEFENSE
Majority (10 D): Inouye, Chmn., Hollings, Johnston, Byrd, Leahy, Sasser, DeConcini, Bumpers, Lautenberg, Harkin.
Minority (8 R): Stevens, Garn, McClure, Kasten, D'Amato, Rudman, Cochran, Specter.

DISTRICT OF COLUMBIA
Majority (3 D): Adams, Chmn.; Fowler, Kerrey.
Minority (2 R): Gramm, Domenici.

ENERGY AND WATER DEVELOPMENT
Majority (7 D): Johnston, Chmn.; Byrd, Hollings, Burdick, Sasser, DeConcini, Reid.
Minority (6 R): Hatfield, McClure, Garn, Cochran, Domenici, Specter.

FOREIGN OPERATIONS
Majority (7 D): Leahy, Chmn.; Inouye, Johnston, DeConcini, Lautenberg, Harkin, Mikulski.
Minority (6 R): Kasten, Hatfield, D'Amato, Rudman, Specter, Nickles.

INTERIOR
Majority (8 D): Byrd, Chmn.; Johnston, Leahy, DeConcini, Burdick, Bumpers, Hollings, Reid.
Minority (7 R): McClure, Stevens, Garn, Cochran, Rudman, Nickles, Domenici.

LABOR, HEALTH AND HUMAN SERVICES, EDUCATION
Majority (8 D): Harkin, Chmn.; Byrd, Hollings, Burdick, Inouye, Bumpers, Reid, Adams.
Minority (7 R): Specter, Hatfield, Stevens, Rudman, McClure, Cochran, Gramm.

LEGISLATIVE BRANCH
Majority (3 D): Reid, Chmn.; Mikulski, Adams.
Minority (2 R): Nickles, Hatfield.

MILITARY CONSTRUCTION
Majority (4 D): Sasser, Chmn.; Inouye, Reid, Fowler.
Minority (3 R): Grassley, Garn, Stevens.

TRANSPORTATION
Majority (5 D): Lautenberg, Chmn.; Byrd, Harkin, Sasser, Mikulski.
Minority (4 R): D'Amato, Kasten, Domenici, Grassley.

TREASURY, POSTAL SERVICE AND GENERAL GOVERNMENT
Majority (3 D): DeConcini, Chmn.; Mikulski, Kerrey.
Minority (2 R): Domenici, D'Amato.

VA, HUD AND INDEPENDENT AGENCIES
Majority (6 D): Mikulski, Chmn.; Leahy, Johnston, Lautenberg, Fowler, Kerrey.
Minority (5 R): Garn, D'Amato, Grassley, Nickles, Gramm.

ARMED SERVICES   228 RSOB, 202-224-3871

Majority (11 D): Nunn (GA), Chmn.; Exon (NE), Levin (MI), Kennedy (MA), Bingaman
  (NM), Dixon (IL), Glenn (OH), Gore (TN), Wirth (CO), Shelby (AL), Byrd (WV).
Minority (9 R): Warner (VA), Thurmond (SC), Cohen (ME), Wilson (CA), McCain (AZ),
  Wallop (WY), Gorton (WA), Lott (MS), Coats (IN).

SUBCOMMITTEES

CONVENTIONAL FORCES AND ALLIANCE DEFENSE
Majority (6 D): Levin, Chmn.; Dixon, Glenn, Wirth, Shelby, Byrd.
Minority (5 R): Wilson, Thurmond, Cohen, McCain, Coats.

DEFENSE INDUSTRY AND TECHNOLOGY
Majority (4 D): Bingaman, Chmn.; Gore, Wirth, Byrd.
Minority (3 R): Wallop, Lott, Coats.

MANPOWER AND PERSONNEL
Majority (4 D): Glenn, Chmn.; Exon, Kennedy, Byrd.
Minority (3 R): McCain, Wilson, Lott.

PROJECTION FORCES AND REGIONAL DEFENSE
Majority (5 D): Kennedy, Chmn.; Exon, Dixon, Gore, Shelby.
Minority (4 R): Cohen, McCain, Gorton, Lott.

READINESS, SUSTAINABILITY AND SUPPORT
Majority (5 D): Dixon, Chmn.; Levin, Bingaman, Wirth, Shelby.
Minority (4 R): Gorton, Thurmond, Wallop, Coats.

STRATEGIC FORCES AND NUCLEAR DETERRENCE
Majority (6 D): Exon, Chmn.; Levin, Kennedy, Bingaman, Glenn, Gore.
Minority (5 R): Thurmond, Cohen, Wilson, Wallop, Gorton.

BANKING, HOUSING AND URBAN AFFAIRS   534 DSOB, 202-224-7391

Majority (12 D): Riegle (MI), Chmn.; Cranston (CA), Sarbanes (MD), Dodd (CT), Dixon (IL),
  Sasser (TN), Sanford (NC), Shelby (AL), Graham (FL), Wirth (CO), Kerry (MA), Bryan
  (NV).
Minority (9 R): Garn (UT), Heinz (PA), D'Amato (NY), Gramm (TX), Bond (MO), Mack
  (FL), Roth (DE), Kassebaum (KS), Pressler (SD).

SUBCOMMITTEES

CONSUMER AND REGULATORY AFFAIRS
Majority (4 D): Dixon, Chmn.; Graham, Kerry, Bryan.
Minority (3 R): Bond, D'Amato, Gramm.

HOUSING AND URBAN AFFAIRS

Majority (6 D): Cranston, Chmn.; Sarbanes, Dodd, Sasser, Kerry, Bryan.
Minority (5 R): D'Amato, Mack, Kassebaum, Pressler, Gramm.

INTERNATIONAL FINANCE AND MONETARY POLICY

Majority (6 D): Sarbanes, Chmn.; Dixon, Sanford, Shelby, Graham, Wirth.
Minority (5 R): Gramm, Roth, Heinz, Bond, Mack.

SECURITIES

Majority (6 D): Dodd, Chmn.; Cranston, Sasser, Sanford, Shelby, Wirth.
Minority (5 R): Heinz, Kassebaum, Pressler, D'Amato, Gramm.

BUDGET   621 DSOB, 202-224-0642

Majority (13 D): Sasser (TN), Chmn.; Hollings (SC), Johnston (LA), Riegle (MI), Exon (NE), Lautenberg (NJ), Simon (IL), Sanford (NC), Wirth (CO), Fowler (GA), Conrad (ND), Dodd (CT), Robb (VA).
Minority (10 R): Domenici (NM), Armstrong (CO), Boschwitz (MN), Symms (ID), Grassley (IA), Kasten (WI), Nickles (OK), Rudman (NH), Gramm (TX), Bond (MO).

NO SUBCOMMITTEES

COMMERCE, SCIENCE AND TRANSPORTATION   508 DSOB
202-224-5115

Majority (11 D): Hollings (SC), Chmn.; Inouye (HI), Ford (KY), Exon (NE), Gore (TN), Rockefeller (WV), Bentsen (TX), Kerry (MA), Breaux (LA), Bryan (NE), Robb (VA).
Minority (9 R): Danforth (MO), Packwood (OR), Pressler (SD), Stevens (AK), Kasten (WI), McCain (AZ), Burns (MT), Gorton (WA), Lott (MS).

SUBCOMMITTEES

AVIATION

Majority (5 D): Ford, Chmn.; Exon, Inouye, Kerry, Bentsen.
Minority (3 R): McCain, Stevens, Kasten.

COMMUNICATIONS

Majority (8 D): Inouye, Chmn.; Hollings, Ford, Gore, Exon, Kerry, Bentsen, Breaux.
Minority (6 R): Packwood, Pressler, Stevens, McCain, Burns, Gorton.

CONSUMER

Majority (4 D): Bryan, Chmn.; Gore, Ford, Robb.
Minority (3 R): Gorton, McCain, Kasten.

FOREIGN COMMERCE AND TOURISM

Majority (3 D): Rockefeller, Chmn.; Hollings, Bryan.
Minority (2 R): Burns, Packwood.

MERCHANT MARINE

Majority (4 D): Breaux, Chmn.; Inouye, Bentsen.
Minority (2 R): Lott, Stevens.

SCIENCE, TECHNOLOGY AND SPACE

Majority (6 D): Gore, Chmn.; Rockefeller, Bentsen, Kerry, Bryan, Robb.
Minority (4 R): Pressler, Stevens, Kasten, Lott.

SURFACE TRANSPORTATION

Majority (7 D): Exon, Chmn.; Rockefeller, Hollings, Inouye, Gore, Breaux, Robb.
Minority (6 R): Kasten, Packwood, Pressler, Burns, Gorton, Lott.

ENERGY AND NATURAL RESOURCES 364 DSOB, 202-224-4971

Majority (10 D): Johnston (LA), Chmn.; Bumpers (AR), Ford (KY), Metzenbaum (OH), Bradley (NJ), Bingaman (NM), Wirth (CO), Conrad (ND), Heflin (AL), Rockefeller (WV).
Minority (9 R): McClure (ID), Hatfield (OR), Domenici (NM), Wallop (WY), Murkowski (AK), Nickles (OK), Burns (MT), Garn (UT), McConnell (KY).

SUBCOMMITTEES

ENERGY, REGULATION AND CONSERVATION

Majority (4 D): Metzenbaum, Chmn.; Bradley, Bingaman, Wirth.
Minority (3 R): Nickles, Murkowski, Domenici.

ENERGY RESEARCH AND DEVELOPMENT

Majority (6 D): Ford, Chmn.; Rockefeller, Bumpers, Metzenbaum, Wirth, Heflin.
Minority (5 R): Domenici, McConnell, Nickles, Burns, Garn.

MINERAL RESOURCES DEVELOPMENT AND PRODUCTION

Majority (5 D): Bingaman, Chmn.; Heflin, Bumpers, Ford, Conrad.
Minority (4 R): Murkowski, McConnell, Wallop, Nickles.

PUBLIC LANDS, NATIONAL PARKS AND FORESTS

Majority (6 D): Bumpers, Chmn.; Wirth, Bradley, Bingaman, Conrad, Rockefeller.
Minority (5 R): Wallop, Hatfield, Burns, Garn, Domenici.

WATER AND POWER

Majority (5 D): Bradley, Chmn.; Conrad, Ford, Metzenbaum, Heflin.
Minority (4 R): Burns, Hatfield, Garn, Wallop.

ENVIRONMENT AND PUBLIC WORKS 458 DSOB, 202-224-6176

Majority (9 D): Burdick (ND), Chmn.; Moynihan (NY), Mitchell (ME), Baucus (MT), Lautenberg (NJ), Breaux (LA), Reid (NV), Graham (FL), Lieberman (CT).
Minority (7 R): Chafee (RI), Simpson (WY), Symms (ID), Durenberger (MN), Warner (VA), Jeffords (VT), Humphrey (NH).

SUBCOMMITTEES

ENVIRONMENTAL PROTECTION

Majority (7 D): Baucus, Chmn.; Moynihan, Mitchell, Lautenberg, Breaux, Graham, Lieberman.
Minority (6 R): Chafee, Simpson, Durenberger, Warner, Jeffords, Humphrey.

NUCLEAR REGULATION
Majority (3 D): Breaux, Chmn.; Moynihan, Reid.
Minority (2 R): Simpson, Symms.

SUPERFUND, OCEAN AND WATER PROTECTION
Majority (4 D): Lautenberg, Chmn.; Mitchell, Baucus, Graham.
Minority (3 R): Durenberger, Simpson, Symms.

TOXIC SUBSTANCES, ENVIRONMENTAL OVERSIGHT, RESEARCH AND DEVELOPMENT
Majority (3 D): Reid, Chmn.; Baucus, Lieberman.
Minority (2 R): Warner, Jeffords.

WATER RESOURCES, TRANSPORTATION AND INFRASTRUCTURE
Majority (7 D): Moynihan, Chmn.; Mitchell, Lautenberg, Breaux, Reid, Graham, Lieberman.
Minority (6 R): Symms, Warner, Jeffords, Humphrey, Durenberger, Chafee.

FINANCE   205 DSOB, 202-224-4515

Majority (11 D): Bentsen (TX), Chmn.; Matsunaga (HI), Moynihan (NY), Baucus (MT), Boren (OK), Bradley (NJ), Mitchell (ME), Pryor (AR), Riegle (MI), Rockefeller (WV), Daschle (SD).
Minority (9 R): Packwood (OR), Dole (KS), Roth (DE), Danforth (MO), Chafee (RI), Heinz (PA), Durenberger (MN), Armstrong (CO), Symms (ID).

SUBCOMMITTEES

ENERGY AND AGRICULTURAL TAXATION
Majority (2 D): Boren, Chmn.; Matsunaga.
Minority (2 R): Armstrong, Symms.

HEALTH FOR FAMILIES AND THE UNINSURED
Majority (4 D): Reigle, Chmn.; Bradley, Mitchell, Rockefeller.
Minority (3 R): Chafee, Roth, Durenberger.

INTERNATIONAL DEBT
Majority (2 D): Bradley, Chmn.; Riegle.
Minority (2 R): Dole, Armstrong.

INTERNATIONAL TRADE
Majority (10 D): Baucus, Chmn.; Bentsen, Matsunaga, Moynihan, Boren, Bradley, Mitchell, Riegle, Rockefeller, Daschle.
Minority (7 R): Danforth, Roth, Chafee, Heinz, Armstrong, Packwood, Symms.

MEDICARE AND LONG-TERM CARE
Majority (6 D): Rockefeller, Chmn.; Bentsen, Baucus, Mitchell, Pryor, Daschle.
Minority (6 R): Durenberger, Dole, Packwood, Heinz, Chafee, Danforth.

PRIVATE RETIREMENT PLANS AND OVERSIGHT OF THE INTERNAL REVENUE SERVICE
Majority (2 D): Pryor, Chmn.; Moynihan.
Minority (1 R): Heinz.

SOCIAL SECURITY AND FAMILY POLICY

Majority (2 D): Moynihan, Chmn.; Daschle.
Minority (2 R): Dole, Durenberger.

TAXATION AND DEBT MANAGEMENT

Majority (5 D): Matsunaga, Chmn.; Bentsen, Baucus, Boren, Pryor.
Minority (3 R): Roth, Danforth, Symms.

FOREIGN RELATIONS 446 DSOB, 202-224-4651

Majority (10 D): Pell (RI), Chmn.; Biden (DE), Sarbanes (MD), Cranston (CA), Dodd (CT), Kerry (MA), Simon (IL), Sanford (NC), Moynihan (NY), Robb (VA).
Minority (9 R): Helms (NC), Lugar (IN), Kassebaum (KS), Boschwitz (MN), Pressler (SD), Murkowski (AK), McConnell (KY), Humphrey (NH), Mack (FL).

SUBCOMMITTEES

AFRICAN AFFAIRS

Majority (3 D): Simon, Chmn.; Cranston, Moynihan.
Minority (2 R): Kassebaum, Mack.

EAST ASIAN AND PACIFIC AFFAIRS

Majority (4 D): Cranston, Chmn.; Pell, Biden, Dodd.
Minority (3 R): Murkowski, Lugar, McConnell.

EUROPEAN AFFAIRS

Majority (3 D): Biden, Chmn.; Sarbanes, Simon.
Minority (2 R): Pressler, Boschwitz.

INTERNATIONAL ECONOMIC POLICY, TRADE, OCEANS AND ENVIRONMENT

Majority (5 D): Sarbanes, Chmn.; Pell, Dodd, Kerry, Sanford.
Minority (4 R): Humphrey, Lugar, Boschwitz, Murkowski.

NEAR EASTERN AND SOUTH ASIAN AFFAIRS

Majority (4 D): Moynihan, Chmn.; Pell, Sarbanes, Robb.
Minority (3 R): Boschwitz, Kassebaum, Pressler.

TERRORISM, NARCOTICS AND INTERNATIONAL OPERATIONS

Majority (4 D): Kerry, Chmn.; Sanford, Moynihan, Robb.
Minority (3 R): McConnell, Murkowski, Humphrey.

WESTERN HEMISPHERE AND PEACE CORPS AFFAIRS

Majority (5 D): Dodd, Chmn.; Cranston, Kerry, Sanford, Robb.
Minority (4 R): Lugar, Kassebaum, McConnell, Mack.

GOVERNMENTAL AFFAIRS 340 DSOB, 202-224-4751

Majority (8 D): Glenn (OH), Chmn.; Nunn (GA), Levin (MI), Sasser (TN), Pryor (AK), Bingaman (NM), Kohl (WI), Lieberman (CT).
Minority (6 R): Roth (DE), Stevens (AK), Cohen (ME), Rudman (NH), Heinz (PA), Wilson (CA).

FEDERAL SERVICES, POST OFFICE, AND CIVIL SERVICE

Majority (3 D): Pryor, Chmn.; Sasser, Kohl.
Minority (2 R): Stevens, Wilson.

GENERAL SERVICES, FEDERALISM AND THE DISTRICT OF COLUMBIA

Majority (3 D): Sasser, Chmn.; Bingaman, Lieberman.
Minority (2 R): Heinz, Stevens.

GOVERNMENT INFORMATION AND REGULATION

Majority (4 D): Bingaman, Chmn.; Nunn, Levin, Kohl.
Minority (3 R): Rudman, Cohen, Heinz.

OVERSIGHT OF GOVERNMENT MANAGEMENT

Majority (5 D): Levin, Chmn.; Pryor, Bingaman, Kohl, Lieberman.
Minority (4 R): Cohen, Rudman, Heinz, Wilson.

PERMANENT SUBCOMMITTEE ON INVESTIGATIONS

Majority (7 D): Nunn, Chmn.; Glenn, Levin, Sasser, Pryor, Kohl, Lieberman.
Minority (5 R): Roth, Stevens, Cohen, Rudman, Wilson.

JUDICIARY   224 DSOB, 202-224-5225

Majority (8 D): Biden (DE), Chmn.; Kennedy (MA), Metzenbaum (OH), DeConcini (AZ), Leahy (VT), Heflin (AL), Simon (IL), Kohl (WI).
Minority (6 R): Thurmond (SC), Hatch (UT), Simpson (WY), Grassley (IA), Specter (PA), Humphrey (NH).

ANTITRUST, MONOPOLIES AND BUSINESS RIGHTS

Majority (5 D): Metzenbaum, Chmn.; DeConcini, Heflin, Simon, Kohl.
Minority (4 R): Thurmond, Specter, Humphrey, Hatch.

CONSTITUTION

Majority (4 D): Simon, Chmn.; Metzenbaum, DeConcini, Kennedy.
Minority (2 R): Specter, Hatch.

COURTS AND ADMINISTRATIVE PRACTICE

Majority (3 D): Heflin, Chmn.; Metzenbaum, Kohl.
Minority (2 R): Grassley, Thurmond.

IMMIGRATION AND REFUGEE AFFAIRS

Majority (2 D): Kennedy, Chmn.; Simon.
Minority (1 R): Simpson.

PATENTS, COPYRIGHTS AND TRADEMARKS

Majority (4 D): DeConcini, Chmn.; Kennedy, Leahy, Heflin.
Minority (3 R): Hatch, Simpson, Grassley.

TECHNOLOGY AND THE LAW

Majority (2 D): Leahy, Chmn.; Kohl.
Minority (1 R): Humphrey.

"The only way you get along in Washington is to know how all the pieces fit together. National Journal is the only publication that describes all the pieces."

James P. Mooney
President and CEO
National Cable Television Association

"...I rely on National Journal for its expertise and facts...the Journal is virtually required reading for my staff."

Senator Pete V. Domenici
New Mexico (R)

"American public policy cannot be understood without the aid of National Journal. It is as simple, and as complicated, as that."

Robert Reich
John F. Kennedy School of Government
Harvard University

NO POSTAGE
NECESSARY
IF MAILED
IN THE
UNITED STATES

1990 Almanac Extra Copy Order Form

	QUANTITY	ITEM	AMOUNT
YES! Send me:	_____	Hardcover ALMANAC(s) @ $56.95	_____
	_____	Softcover ALMANAC(s) @ $44.95	_____
		D.C. orders add 6% sales tax	_____
		Shipping & Handling @ $2.50 per book	_____
		TOTAL	_____

☐ I enclose a check (payable to National Journal)

☐ Charge my: ☐ Visa ☐ MasterCard ☐ American Express

Acct. # [　][　][　][　][　][　][　][　][　][　][　][　][　][　][　][　]   Exp. Date [　][　][　][　]

Signature _____

Name _____ Phone _____

Organization _____ Title _____

Address _____

City _____ State _____ Zip _____

Discounts begin with 4 copies! For more information call 1-800-424-2921. (In D.C. call 857-1448)
MAIL TO: National Journal • P.O. Box 7247-8621 • Philadelphia, PA 19170-8621   IN90

- -
▲ DETACH HERE AND MAIL ▲

▼ DETACH HERE AND MAIL ▼
- -

1990 Almanac Extra Copy Order Form

	QUANTITY	ITEM	AMOUNT
YES! Send me:	_____	Hardcover ALMANAC(s) @ $56.95	_____
	_____	Softcover ALMANAC(s) @ $44.95	_____
		D.C. orders add 6% sales tax	_____
		Shipping & Handling @ $2.50 per book	_____
		TOTAL	_____

☐ I enclose a check (payable to National Journal)

☐ Charge my: ☐ Visa ☐ MasterCard ☐ American Express

Acct. # [　][　][　][　][　][　][　][　][　][　][　][　][　][　][　][　]   Exp. Date [　][　][　][　]

Signature _____

Name _____ Phone _____

Organization _____ Title _____

Address _____

City _____ State _____ Zip _____

Discounts begin with 4 copies! For more information call 1-800-424-2921. (In D.C. call 857-1448)
MAIL TO: National Journal • P.O. Box 7247-8621 • Philadelphia, PA 19170-8621   IN90

BUSINESS REPLY MAIL

FIRST CLASS   PERMIT NO. 34354   PHILADELPHIA, PA

POSTAGE WILL BE PAID BY ADDRESSEE

NATIONAL JOURNAL
LB 8621
P.O. Box 7247
Philadelphia, PA 19101-9654

NO POSTAGE
NECESSARY
IF MAILED
IN THE
UNITED STATES

BUSINESS REPLY MAIL

FIRST CLASS   PERMIT NO. 34354   PHILADELPHIA, PA

POSTAGE WILL BE PAID BY ADDRESSEE

NATIONAL JOURNAL
LB 8621
P.O. Box 7247
Philadelphia, PA 19101-9654

LABOR AND HUMAN RESOURCES 428 DSOB, 202-244-5375

Majority (9 D): Kennedy (MA), Chmn.; Pell (RI), Metzenbaum (OH), Matsunaga (HI), Dodd (CT), Simon (IL), Harkin (IA), Adams (WA), Mikulski (MD).
Minority (7 R): Hatch (UT), Kassebaum (KS), Jeffords (VT), Coats (IN), Thurmond (SC), Durenberger (MN), Cochran (MS).

SUBCOMMITTEES

AGING
Majority (4 D): Matsunaga, Chmn.; Pell, Metzenbaum, Dodd.
Minority (3 R): Cochran, Durenberger, Coats.

CHILDREN, FAMILY, DRUGS AND ALCOHOLISM
Majority (4 D): Dodd, Chmn.; Pell, Harkin, Adams.
Minority (3 R): Coats, Hatch, Kassebaum.

EDUCATION, ARTS AND HUMANITIES
Majority (6 D): Pell, Chmn.; Metzenbaum, Matsunaga, Dodd, Simon, Mikulski.
Minority (5 R): Kassebaum, Cochran, Hatch, Jeffords, Thurmond.

EMPLOYMENT AND PRODUCTIVITY
Majority (4 D): Simon, Chmn.; Harkin, Adams, Mikulski.
Minority (3 R): Thurmond, Durenberger, Kassebaum.

HANDICAPPED
Majority (4 D): Harkin, Chmn.; Metzenbaum, Simon, Adams.
Minority (3 R): Durenberger, Hatch, Jeffords.

LABOR
Majority (4 D): Metzenbaum, Chmn.; Matsunaga, Harkin, Mikulski.
Minority (3 R): Jeffords, Cochran, Thurmond.

RULES AND ADMINISTRATION 305 RSOB, 202-224-6352

Majority (9 D): Ford (KY), Chmn.; Pell (RI), Byrd (WV), Inouye (HI), DeConcini (AZ), Gore (TN), Moynihan (NY), Dodd (CT), Adams (WA).
Minority (7 R): Stevens (AK), Hatfield (OR), McClure (ID), Helms (NC), Dole (KS), Garn (UT), McConnell (KY).

NO SUBCOMMITTEES

SMALL BUSINESS 428A RSOB, 202-224-5175

Majority (10 D): Bumpers (AR), Chmn.; Nunn (GA), Baucus (MT), Levin (MI), Dixon (IL), Boren (OK), Harkin (IA), Kerry (MA), Mikulski (MD), Lieberman (CT).
Minority (9 R): Boschwitz (MN), Kasten (WI), Pressler (SD), Wallop (WY), Bond (MO), Grassley (IA), Lott (MS), Burns (MT), Stevens (AK).

SUBCOMMITTEES

COMPETITION AND ANTITRUST ENFORCEMENT
Majority (2 D): Harkin, Chmn.; Lieberman.
Minority (1 R): Stevens.

EXPORT EXPANSION
Majority (4 D): Mikulski, Chmn.; Harkin, Lieberman, Bumpers.
Minority (3 R): Pressler, Wallop, Bond.

GOVERNMENT CONTRACTING AND PAPERWORK REDUCTION
Majority (3 D): Dixon, Chmn.; Boren, Lieberman.
Minority (2 R): Grassley, Kasten.

INNOVATION, TECHNOLOGY AND PRODUCTIVITY
Majority (3 D): Levin, Chmn.; Baucus, Kerry.
Minority (4 R): Lott, Stevens.

RURAL ECONOMY AND FAMILY FARMING
Majority (7 D): Baucus, Chmn.; Nunn, Levin, Dixon, Boren, Kerry, Bumpers.
Minority (6 R): Kasten, Pressler, Wallop, Bond, Grassley, Burns.

URBAN AND MINORITY-OWNED BUSINESS DEVELOPMENT
Majority (2 D): Kerry, Chmn.; Nunn, Mikulski.
Minority (1 R): Burns, Lott.

VETERANS' AFFAIRS   414 RSOB, 202-224-9126

Majority (6 D): Cranston (CA), Chmn.; Matsunaga (HI), DeConcini (AZ), Mitchell (ME), Rockefeller (WV), Graham (FL).
Minority (5 R): Murkowski (AK), Simpson (WY), Thurmond (SC), Specter (PA), Jeffords (VT).

NO SUBCOMMITTEES

SELECT COMMITTEES

SELECT COMMITTEE ON ETHICS   220 HSOB, 202-224-2981

Majority (3 D): Heflin (AL), Chmn.; Pryor (AR), Sanford (NC).
Minority (3 R): Rudman (NH), Helms (NC), Lott (MS).

NO SUBCOMMITTEES

SELECT COMMITTEE ON INDIAN AFFAIRS   838 HSOB, 202-224-2251

Majority (5 D): Inouye (HI), Chmn.; DeConcini (AZ), Burdick (ND), Daschle (SD), Conrad (ND).
Minority (3 R): McCain (AZ), Murkowski (AK), Cochran (MS).

SUBCOMMITTEE

SPECIAL COMMITTEE ON INVESTIGATIONS
Majority (2 D): DeConcini (AZ), Chmn.; Daschle (SD).
Minority (1 R): McCain (AZ).

SELECT COMMITTEE ON INTELLIGENCE   211 HSOB, 202-224-1700

Majority (8 D): Boren (OK), Chmn.; Nunn (GA), Hollings (SC), Bradley (NJ), Cranston (CA), DeConcini (AZ), Metzenbaum (OH), Glenn (OH).
Minority (7 R): Cohen (ME), V. Chmn.; Hatch (UT), Murkowski (AK), Specter (PA), Warner (VA), D'Amato (NY), Danforth (MO).

NO SUBCOMMITTEES

SPECIAL COMMITTEE

SPECIAL COMMITTEE ON AGING   G31 DSOB, 202-224-5364

Majority (10 D): Pryor (AR), Chmn.; Glenn (OH), Bradley (NJ), Burdick (ND), Johnston (LA), Breaux (LA), Shelby (AL), Reid (NV), Graham (FL), Kohl (WI).
Minority (9 R): Heinz (PA), Cohen (ME), Pressler (SD), Grassley (IA), Wilson (CA), Domenici (NM), Simpson (WY), Warner (VA), Kassebaum (KS).

NO SUBCOMMITTEES

JOINT COMMITTEES OF THE CONGRESS

JOINT ECONOMIC COMMITTEE   G01 DSOB, 202-224-5171

Senate (10): Sarbanes (MD), V. Chmn.; Bentsen (TX), Kennedy (MA), Bingaman (NM), Gore (TN), Bryan (NV), Roth (DE), Symms (ID), Wilson (CA), Mack (FL).
House (10): Hamilton (IN), Chmn.; Hawkins (CA), Obey (WI), Scheuer (NY), Stark (CA), Solarz (NY), Wylie (OH), Snowe (ME), Fish (NY), Upton (MI).

SUBCOMMITTEES

ECONOMIC GOALS AND INTERGOVERNMENTAL POLICY
Senate (4): Bentsen, Kennedy, Roth, Wilson.
House (4): Hamilton, Chmn.; Hawkins, Wylie, Snowe.

ECONOMIC GROWTH, TRADE AND TAXES
Senate (3): Bentsen, Chmn.; Roth, Mack.
House (5): Hamilton, Stark, Solarz, Wylie, Upton.

ECONOMIC RESOURCES AND COMPETITIVENESS
Senate (5): Sarbanes, Bingaman, Gore, Bryan, Symms.
House (3): Obey, Chmn.; Solarz, Upton.

EDUCATION AND HEALTH
Senate (4): Bentsen, Bingaman, Gore, Wilson.
House (4): Scheuer, Chmn.; Hawkins, Snowe, Fish.

FISCAL AND MONETARY POLICY
Senate (2): Kennedy, Chmn.; Symms.
House (3): Obey, Stark, Upton.

INTERNATIONAL ECONOMIC POLICY
Senate (4): Sarbanes, Chmn.; Kennedy, Roth, Mack.
House (4): Hamilton, Solarz, Wylie, Snowe.

INVESTMENT, JOBS AND PRICES
Senate (3): Gore, Bryan, Symms.
House (5): Hawkins, Chmn.; Scheuer, Solarz, Stark, Fish.

NATIONAL SECURITY ECONOMICS
Senate (5): Bingaman, Chmn.; Sarbanes, Bryan, Wilson, Mack.
House (3): Obey, Scheuer, Fish.

JOINT COMMITTEE ON THE LIBRARY   103 House Annex 1
202-226-7633

Senate (5): Pell (RI), V. Chmn.; DeConcini (AZ), Moynihan (NY), Hatfield (OR), Stevens (AK).
House (5): Annunzio (IL), Chmn.; Oakar (OH), Clay (MO), Gillmor (OH), Walsh (NY).

NO SUBCOMMITTEES

JOINT COMMITTEE ON PRINTING   818 HSOB, 202-224-5241

Senate (5): Ford (KY), Chmn.; DeConcini (AZ), Gore (TN), Stevens (AK), Hatfield (OR).
House (5): Annunzio (IL), V. Chmn.; Gaydos (PA), Bates (CA), Roberts (KS), Gingrich (GA).

NO SUBCOMMITTEES

JOINT COMMITTEE ON TAXATION   1015 LHOB, 202-225-3621

Senate (5): Bentsen (TX), V. Chmn.; Matsunaga (HI), Moynihan (NY), Packwood (OR), Dole (KS).
House (5): Rostenkowski (IL), Chmn.; Gibbons (FL), Pickle (TX), Archer (TX), Vander Jagt (MI).

NO SUBCOMMITTEES

HOUSE COMMITTEES

STANDING COMMITTEES

AGRICULTURE   1301 LHOB, 202-225-2171

Majority (27 D): de la Garza (TX), Chmn.; Jones (NC), Brown (CA), Rose (NC), English (OK), Panetta (CA), Huckaby (LA), Glickman (KS), Stenholm (TX), Volkmer (MO), Hatcher (GA), Tallon (SC), Staggers (WV), Olin (VA), Penny (MN), Stallings (ID), Nagle (IA), Jontz (IN), Johnson (SD), Harris (AL), Campbell (CO), Espy (MS), Sarpalius (TX), Long (IN), Dyson (MD), Lancaster (NC), one vacancy.

Minority (18 R): Madigan (IL), Coleman (MO), Marlenee (MT), Hopkins (KY), Stangeland (MN), Roberts (KS), Emerson (MO), Morrison (WA), Gunderson (WI), Lewis (FL), R. Smith (OR), Combest (TX), Schuette (MI), Grandy (IA), Herger (CA), Holloway (LA), Walsh (NY), Grant (FL).

SUBCOMMITTEES

CONSERVATION, CREDIT AND RURAL DEVELOPMENT

Majority (10 D): English, Chmn.; Tallon, Penny, Stallings, Nagle, Harris, Staggers, Espy, Sarpalius, Long.
Minority (6 R): Coleman, Morrison, Gunderson, Combest, Grandy, Holloway.

COTTON, RICE AND SUGAR

Majority (9 D): Huckaby, Chmn.; Tallon, Espy, Stenholm, Stallings, Sarpalius, Jones, Hatcher, one vacancy.
Minority (6 R): Stangeland, Emerson, Lewis, Combest, Herger, Holloway.

DEPARTMENT OPERATIONS, RESEARCH AND FOREIGN AGRICULTURE

Majority (9 D): Brown, Chmn.; Rose, Panetta, Stenholm, Glickman, Hatcher, Olin, Volkmer, Jontz.
Minority (5 R): Roberts, Coleman, Morrison, Grandy, Walsh.

DOMESTIC MARKETING, CONSUMER RELATIONS AND NUTRITION

Majority (6 D): Hatcher, Chmn.; Panetta, Glickman, Staggers, Espy, Sarpalius.
Minority (3 R): Emerson, Lewis, Herger.

FORESTS, FAMILY FARMS AND ENERGY

Majority (8 D): Volkmer, Chmn.; Huckaby, Olin, Stallings, Jontz, Panetta, Johnson, Harris.
Minority (5 R): Morrison, Marlenee, R. Smith (OR), Schuette, Herger.

LIVESTOCK, DAIRY AND POULTRY

Majority (11 D): Stenholm, Chmn.; Olin, Campbell, Johnson, Harris, Rose, Volkmer, Penny, Nagle, Long, one vacancy.
Minority (7 R): Gunderson, Hopkins, Stangeland, Lewis, R. Smith (OR), Walsh, Grant.

TOBACCO AND PEANUTS

Majority (7 D): Rose, Chmn.; Jones, Hatcher, English, Tallon, Stenholm, Lancaster.
Minority (4 R): Hopkins, Combest, Gunderson, Grant.

WHEAT, SOYBEANS AND FEED GRAINS

Majority (11 D): Glickman, Chmn.; Johnson, English, Volkmer, Penny, Nagle, Sarpalius, Jontz, Campbell, Dyson, Long.
Minority (7 R): Marlenee, Stangeland, Roberts, Emerson, R. Smith (OR), Schuette, Grandy.

APPROPRIATIONS   H 218 Capitol, 202-225-2771

Majority (35 D): Whitten (MS), Chmn.; Natcher (KY), Smith (IA), Yates (IL), Obey (WI), Roybal (CA), Stokes (OH), Bevill (AL), Alexander (AR), Murtha (PA), Traxler (MI), Early (MA), Wilson (TX), Boggs (LA), Dicks (WA), McHugh (NY), Lehman (FL), Sabo (MN), Dixon (CA), Fazio (CA), Hefner (NC), AuCoin (OR), Akaka (HI), Watkins (OK), Gray (PA), Dwyer (NJ), Hoyer (MD), Carr (MI), Mrazek (NY), Durbin (IL), Coleman (TX), Mollohan (WV), Thomas (GA), Atkins (MA), Chapman (TX).
Minority (22 R): Conte (MA), McDade (PA), Myers (IN), Miller (OH), Coughlin (PA), Young (FL), Regula (OH), Smith (NE), Pursell (MI), Edwards (OK), Livingston (LA), Green (NY), Lewis (CA), Porter (IL), Rogers (KY), Skeen (NM), Wolf (VA), Lowery (CA), Weber (MN), DeLay (TX), Kolbe (AZ), Gallo (NJ).

SUBCOMMITTEES

COMMERCE, JUSTICE, STATE AND JUDICIARY

Majority (6 D): Smith (IA), Chmn.; Alexander, Early, Dwyer, Carr, Mollohan.
Minority (3 R): Rogers, Regula, Kolbe.

DEFENSE

Majority (7 D): Murtha, Chmn.; Dicks, Wilson, Hefner, AuCoin, Sabo, Dixon.
Minority (4 R): McDade, Young, Miller, Livingston.

DISTRICT OF COLUMBIA

Majority (6 D): Dixon, Chmn.; Natcher, Stokes, AuCoin, Hoyer, Carr.
Minority (3 R): Gallo, Green, Regula.

ENERGY AND WATER DEVELOPMENT

Majority (6 D): Bevill, Chmn.; Boggs, Fazio, Watkins, Thomas, Chapman.
Minority (3 R): Myers, Smith (NE), Pursell.

FOREIGN OPERATIONS, EXPORT FINANCING AND RELATED PROGRAMS

Majority (8 D): Obey, Chmn.; Yates, McHugh, Lehman, Wilson, Gray, Mrazek, Coleman.
Minority (4 R): Edwards, Lewis, Porter, Gallo.

INTERIOR

Majority (6 D): Yates, Chmn.; Murtha, Dicks, AuCoin, Bevill, Atkins.
Minority (3 R): Regula, McDade, Lowery.

LABOR—HEALTH AND HUMAN SERVICES—EDUCATION

Majority (8 D): Natcher, Chmn.; Smith (IA), Obey, Roybal, Stokes, Early, Dwyer, Hoyer.
Minority (5 R): Conte, Pursell, Porter, Young, Weber.

LEGISLATIVE BRANCH

Majority (6 D): Fazio, Chmn.; Yates, Obey, Murtha, Traxler, Boggs.
Minority (4 R): Lewis, Conte, Myers, Porter.

MILITARY CONSTRUCTION

Majority (8 D): Hefner, Chmn.; Alexander, Thomas, Coleman, Bevill, Dicks, Dixon, Fazio.
Minority (4 R): Lowery, Edwards, Kolbe, DeLay.

RURAL DEVELOPMENT, AGRICULTURE AND RELATED AGENCIES

Majority (8 D): Whitten, Chmn.; Traxler, McHugh, Natcher, Akaka, Watkins, Durbin, Smith (IA).
Minority (4 R): Smith (NE), Myers, Skeen, Weber.

TRANSPORTATION

Majority (6 D): Lehman, Chmn.; Gray, Carr, Durbin, Mrazek, Sabo.
Minority (4 R): Coughlin, Conte, Wolf, DeLay.

TREASURY, POSTAL SERVICE, AND GENERAL GOVERNMENT

Majority (6 D): Roybal, Chmn.; Akaka, Hoyer, Alexander, Early, Sabo.
Minority (3 R): Skeen, Lowery, Wolf.

VA, HUD AND INDEPENDENT AGENCIES

Majority (6 D): Traxler, Chmn.; Stokes, Boggs, Mollohan, Chapman, Atkins.
Minority (3 R): Green, Coughlin, Lewis.

ARMED SERVICES   2120 RHOB, 202-225-4151

Majority (31 D): Aspin (WI), Chmn.; Bennett (FL), Montgomery (MS), Dellums (CA), Schroeder (CO), Byron (MD), Mavroules (MA), Hutto (FL), Skelton (MO), Leath (TX), McCurdy (OK), Foglietta (PA), Dyson (MD), Hertel (MI), Lloyd (TN), Sisisky (VA), Ray (GA), Spratt (SC), McCloskey (IN), Ortiz (TX), Darden (GA), Robinson (AR), Bustamante (TX), Hochbrueckner (NY), Brennan (ME), Pickett (VA), Lancaster (NC), Evans (IL), Bilbray (NV), Tanner (TN), McNulty (NY).
Minority (21 R): Dickinson (AL), Spence (SC), Stump (AZ), Courter (NJ), Hopkins (KY), Davis (MI), Hunter (CA), Martin (NY), Kasich (OH), Bateman (VA), Blaz (GU), Ireland (FL), Hansen (UT), Rowland (CT), Weldon (PA), Kyl (AZ), Ravenel (SC), Dornan (CA), Hefley (CO), McCrery (LA), Machtley (RI).

SUBCOMMITTEES

INVESTIGATIONS

Majority (10 D): Mavroules, Chmn.; Hertel, Sisisky, Spratt, McCloskey, Darden, Brennan, Evans, Tanner, Dellums.
Minority (6 R): Hopkins, Stump, Kyl, Ireland, Hefley, McCrery.

MILITARY INSTALLATIONS AND FACILITIES

Majority (10 D): Schroeder, Chmn.; Montgomery, Skelton, McCurdy, Foglietta, Ortiz, Robinson, Bilbray, Mavroules, Hutto.
Minority (7 R): Martin, Dickinson, Blaz, Spence, Ravenel, Courter, Hansen.

MILITARY PERSONNEL AND COMPENSATION

Majority (10 D): Byron, Chmn.; Montgomery, Skelton, Hertel, Lloyd, Robinson, Bustamante, Hochbrueckner, Pickett, Lancaster.
Minority (6 R): Bateman, Ravenel, Hefley, McCrery, Machtley, Dornan.

PROCUREMENT AND MILITARY NUCLEAR SYSTEMS

Majority (11 D): Aspin, Chmn.; Skelton, Leath, Dyson, Lloyd, Sisisky, Ray, Spratt, McCloskey, Bustamante, Evans.
Minority (8 R): Courter, Davis, Hopkins, Blaz, Ireland, Hansen, Rowland, Kasich.

READINESS

Majority (9 D): Hutto, Chmn.; Leath, Dyson, Ray, Ortiz, Lancaster, Bilbray, Tanner, McNulty.
Minority (5 R): Kasich, Martin, Dornan, Hefley, Machtley.

RESEARCH AND DEVELOPMENT

Majority (11 D): Dellums, Chmn.; McCurdy, Foglietta, Hertel, Darden, Hochbrueckner, Pickett, McNulty, Bennett, Schroeder, Byron.
Minority (7 R): Dickinson, Davis, Stump, Hunter, Weldon, Kyl, Dornan.

SEAPOWER AND STRATEGIC AND CRITICAL MATERIALS

Majority (9 D): Bennett, Chmn.; Foglietta, Sisisky, Ortiz, Robinson, Hochbrueckner, Brennan, Pickett, Hutto.
Minority (6 R): Spence, Hunter, Bateman, Weldon, Rowland, Blaz.

BANKING, FINANCE AND URBAN AFFAIRS   2129 RHOB, 202-225-4247

Majority (31 D): Gonzalez (TX), Chmn.; Annunzio (IL), Fauntroy (DC), Neal (NC), Hubbard (KY), LaFalce (NY), Oakar (OH), Vento (MN), Barnard (GA), Garcia (NY), Schumer (NY), Frank (MA), Lehman (CA), Morrison (CT), Kaptur (OH), Erdreich (AL), Carper (DE), Torres (CA), Kleczka (WI), Nelson (FL), Kanjorski (PA), Patterson (SC), McMillen (MD), Kennedy (MA), Flake (NY), Mfume (MD), Price (NC), Pelosi (CA), McDermott (WA), Hoagland (NE), Neal (MA).
Minority (20 R): Wylie (OH), Leach (IA), Shumway (CA), Parris (VA), McCollum (FL), Roukema (NJ), Bereuter (NE), Dreier (CA), Hiler (IN), Ridge (PA), Bartlett (TX), Roth (WI), McCandless (CA), Saxton (NJ), Saiki (HI), Bunning (KY), Baker (LA), Stearns (FL), Gillmor (OH), Paxon (NY).

SUBCOMMITTEES

CONSUMER AFFAIRS AND COINAGE

Majority (9 D): Lehman, Chmn.; Gonzalez, Pelosi, Hubbard, Barnard, Schumer, Kaptur, Erdreich, Price.
Minority (6 R): Hiler, Wylie, Ridge, Dreier, Bartlett, Saxton.

DOMESTIC MONETARY POLICY

Majority (5 D): Neal (NC), Chmn.; Barnard, Gonzalez, Annunzio, Hoagland.
Minority (3 R): McCollum, Leach, Bunning.

ECONOMIC STABILIZATION

Majority (9 D): Oakar, Chmn.; LaFalce, Vento, Kaptur, Kanjorski, Garcia, Patterson, Neal (MA), one vacancy.
Minority (6 R): Shumway, Roth, Saiki, Roukema, Gillmor, Paxon.

FINANCIAL INSTITUTIONS SUPERVISION, REGULATION AND INSURANCE

Majority (28 D): Annunzio, Chmn.; Hubbard, Barnard, LaFalce, Oakar, Vento, Schumer, Frank, Lehman, Kaptur, Nelson, Kanjorski, Gonzalez, Neal (NC), Erdreich, Carper, Torres, Kleczka, Patterson, McMillen, Price, Kennedy, Fauntroy, Flake, Mfume, Pelosi, McDermott, Hoagland.
Minority (19 R): Wylie, Leach, Shumway, McCollum, Dreier, Parris, Roukema, Bereuter, Bartlett, Roth, Hiler, Ridge, McCandless, Saxton, Saiki, Bunning, Baker, Stearns, Gillmor.

GENERAL OVERSIGHT AND INVESTIGATIONS

Majority (8 D): Hubbard, Chmn.; Gonzalez, Barnard, Flake, Annunzio, Hoagland, Neal (MA), one vacancy.
Minority (5 R): Parris, Dreier, Bartlett, McCandless, Gillmor.

HOUSING AND COMMUNITY DEVELOPMENT

Majority (27 D): Gonzalez, Chmn.; Fauntroy, Oakar, Vento, Garcia, Schumer, Frank, Lehman, Morrison, Kaptur, Erdreich, Carper, Torres, Kleczka, Kanjorski, Neal (NC), Hubbard, Kennedy, Flake, Mfume, Pelosi, LaFalce, Patterson, Price, McDermott, Hoagland, Neal (MA).
Minority (18 R): Roukema, Wylie, McCollum, Bereuter, Dreier, Hiler, Ridge, Bartlett, Roth, Saxton, Saiki, Bunning, Parris, McCandless, Baker, Paxon, Stearns, Gillmor.

INTERNATIONAL DEVELOPMENT, FINANCE, TRADE AND MONETARY POLICY

Majority (15 D): Fauntroy, Chmn.; Neal (NC), LaFalce, Torres, Morrison, Schumer, Kleczka, Carper, Kennedy, Pelosi, Frank, McMillen, Flake, McDermott, Hoagland.
Minority (10 R): Leach, Bereuter, Shumway, McCandless, Saxton, Saiki, Bunning, Baker, Stearns, Paxon.

POLICY RESEARCH AND INSURANCE

Majority (5 D): Erdreich, Actg. Chmn.; Garcia, Morrison, Kanjorski, one vacancy.
Minority (3 R): Bereuter, Roth, Paxon.

BUDGET   214 House Annex 1, 202-226-7200

Majority (21 D): Panetta (CA), Chmn.; Russo (IL), Jenkins (GA), Leath (TX), Schumer (NY), Boxer (CA), Slattery (KS), Oberstar (MN), Guarini (NJ), Durbin (IL), Espy (MS), Kildee (MI), Beilenson (CA), Huckaby (LA), Sabo (MN), Dwyer (NJ), Berman (CA), Wise (WV), Kaptur (OH), Bryant (TX), one vacancy.
Minority (14 R): Frenzel (MN), Gradison (OH), Goodling (PA), D. Smith (OR), Thomas (CA), Rogers (KY), Armey (TX), Buechner (MO), Houghton (NY), McCrery (LA), Kasich (OH), Gallo (NJ), Schuette (MI), Bentley (MD).

TASK FORCES

BUDGET PROCESS, RECONCILIATION AND ENFORCEMENT

Majority (8 D): Russo, Chmn.; Schumer, Oberstar, Beilenson, Huckaby, Sabo, Dwyer, Berman.
Minority (5 R): Buechner, Armey, Houghton, Gallo, Schuette.

COMMUNITY DEVELOPMENT AND NATURAL RESOURCES

Majority (6 D): Jenkins, Chmn.; Espy, Kildee, Huckaby, Dwyer, Wise.
Minority (4 R): Rogers, Goodling, D. Smith (OR), Houghton.

DEFENSE, FOREIGN POLICY AND SPACE

Majority (7 D): Leath, Chmn; Russo, Oberstar, Guarini, Berman, Kaptur, Bryant.
Minority (4 R): D. Smith (OR), McCrery, Kasich, Bentley.

ECONOMIC POLICY, PROJECTIONS AND REVENUES

Majority (5 D): Slattery, Chmn.; Jenkins, Guarini, Durbin, Beilenson.
Minority (4 R): Thomas, D. Smith (OR), Rogers, Armey.

HUMAN RESOURCES

Majority (7 D): Boxer, Chmn.; Durbin, Espy, Kildee, Sabo, Wise, Kaptur.
Minority (4 R): Goodling, Buechner, Kasich, Bentley.

URGENT FISCAL ISSUES

Majority (4 D): Schumer, Chmn.; Boxer, Slattery, Bryant.
Minority (4 R): Armey, Thomas, McCrery, Schuette.

DISTRICT OF COLUMBIA   1310 LHOB, 202-225-4457

Majority (8 D): Dellums (CA) Chmn.; Fauntroy (DC), Stark (CA), Gray (PA), Dymally (CA), Wheat (MO), Morrison (CT), one vacancy.
Minority (4 R): Parris (VA), Bliley (VA), Combest (TX), Rohrabacher (CA).

SUBCOMMITTEES

FISCAL AFFAIRS AND HEALTH

Majority (5 D): Fauntroy, Chmn.; Dellums, Gray, Dymally, one vacancy.
Minority (3 R): Bliley, Parris, Combest.

GOVERNMENT OPERATIONS AND METROPOLITAN AFFAIRS

Majority (5 D): Wheat, Chmn.; Fauntroy, Stark, Gray, one vacancy.
Minority (3 R): Combest, Parris, Rohrabacher.

JUDICIARY AND EDUCATION

Majority (5 D): Dymally, Chmn.; Stark, Dellums, Wheat, one vacancy.
Minority (3 R): Rohrabacher, Bliley, Parris.

EDUCATION AND LABOR   2181 RHOB, 202-225-4527

Majority (22 D): Hawkins (CA), Chmn.; Ford (MI), Gaydos (PA), Clay (MO), Miller (CA), Murphy (PA), Kildee (MI), Williams (MT), Martinez (CA), Owens (NY), Hayes (IL), Perkins (KY), Sawyer (OH), Payne (NJ), Lowey (NY), Poshard (IL), Unsoeld (WA), Rahall (WV), Fuster (PR), Visclosky (IN), Jontz (IN), Mfume (MD).

Minority (13 R): Goodling (PA), Coleman (MO), Petri (WI), Roukema (NJ), Gunderson (WI), Bartlett (TX), Tauke (IA), Armey (TX), Fawell (IL), Henry (MI), Grandy (IA), Ballenger (NC), Smith (VT).

SUBCOMMITTEES

ELEMENTARY, SECONDARY AND VOCATIONAL EDUCATION

Majority (15 D): Hawkins, Chmn.; Ford, Miller, Kildee, Williams, Martinez, Perkins, Hayes, Sawyer, Owens, Payne, Lowey, Poshard, Unsoeld, Rahall.
Minority (9 R): Goodling, Fawell, Grandy, Smith, Bartlett, Gunderson, Petri, Roukema, Coleman.

EMPLOYMENT OPPORTUNITIES

Majority (4 D): Martinez, Chmn.; Williams, Fuster, Mfume.
Minority (3 R): Gunderson, Henry, Smith.

HEALTH AND SAFETY

Majority (4 D): Gaydos, Chmn.; Ford, Unsoeld, one vacancy.
Minority (2 R): Henry, Ballenger.

HUMAN RESOURCES

Majority (5 D): Kildee, Chmn.; Sawyer, Unsoeld, Lowey, Poshard.
Minority (3 R): Tauke, Coleman, Grandy.

LABOR–MANAGEMENT RELATIONS

Majority (9 D): Clay, Chmn.; Ford, Kildee, Miller, Hayes, Owens, Sawyer, Murphy, Visclosky.
Minority (6 R): Roukema, Armey, Fawell, Ballenger, Petri, Grandy.

LABOR STANDARDS

Majority (6 D): Murphy, Chmn.; Williams, Clay, Hayes, Perkins, Payne.
Minority (4 R): Petri, Bartlett, Armey, Fawell.

POSTSECONDARY EDUCATION

Majority (9 D): Williams, Chmn.; Ford, Owens, Hayes, Perkins, Gaydos, Miller, Lowey, Poshard.
Minority (6 R): Coleman, Goodling, Roukema, Tauke, Gunderson, Henry.

SELECT EDUCATION

Majority (4 D): Owens, Chmn.; Martinez, Payne, Jontz.
Minority (3 R): Bartlett, Ballenger, Smith.

ENERGY AND COMMERCE   2125 RHOB, 202-225-2927

Majority (26 D): Dingell (MI), Chmn.; Scheuer (NY), Waxman (CA), Sharp (IN), Florio (NJ), Markey (MA), Luken (OH), Walgren (PA), Swift (WA), Leland (TX), Collins (IL), Synar (OK), Tauzin (LA), Wyden (OR), Hall (TX), Eckart (OH), Richardson (NM), Slattery (KS), Sikorski (MN), Bryant (TX), Bates (CA), Boucher (VA), Cooper (TN), Bruce (IL), Rowland (GA), Manton (NY).
Minority (17 R): Lent (NY), Madigan (IL), Moorhead (CA), Rinaldo (NJ), Dannemeyer (CA), Whittaker (KS), Tauke (IA), Ritter (PA), Bliley (VA), Fields (TX), Oxley (OH), Nielson (UT), Bilirakis (FL), Schaefer (CO), Barton (TX), Callahan (AL), McMillan (NC).

SUBCOMMITTEES

COMMERCE, CONSUMER PROTECTION AND COMPETITIVENESS
Majority (7 D): Florio, Chmn.; Scheuer, Rowland, Waxman, Sharp, Luken, Slattery.
Minority (4 R): Ritter, Dannemeyer, Nielson, Barton.

ENERGY AND POWER
Majority (13 D): Sharp, Chmn.; Walgren, Swift, Tauzin, Bates, Cooper, Bruce, Markey, Leland, Synar, Hall, Richardson, Bryant.
Minority (8 R): Moorhead, Dannemeyer, Fields, Oxley, Nielson, Bilirakis, Barton, Callahan.

HEALTH AND THE ENVIRONMENT
Majority (13 D): Waxman, Chmn.; Scheuer, Walgren, Wyden, Sikorski, Bates, Bruce, Rowland, Leland, Collins, Synar, Hall, Richardson.
Minority (8 R): Madigan, Dannemeyer, Whittaker, Tauke, Bliley, Fields, Nielson, Bilirakis.

OVERSIGHT AND INVESTIGATIONS
Majority (8 D): Dingell, Chmn.; Sikorski, Bryant, Walgren, Collins, Wyden, Eckart, Boucher.
Minority (5 R): Bliley, Lent, Oxley, Bilirakis, McMillan.

TELECOMMUNICATIONS AND FINANCE
Majority (15 D): Markey, Chmn.; Swift, Leland, Collins, Synar, Tauzin, Hall, Eckart, Richardson, Slattery, Bryant, Boucher, Cooper, Manton, Wyden.
Minority (9 R): Rinaldo, Madigan, Moorhead, Tauke, Ritter, Bliley, Fields, Oxley, Schaefer.

TRANSPORTATION AND HAZARDOUS MATERIALS
Majority (10 D): Luken, Chmn.; Eckart, Slattery, Boucher, Manton, Florio, Swift, Tauzin, Sikorski, Bates.
Minority (6 R): Whittaker, Rinaldo, Tauke, Schaefer, Callahan, McMillan.

FOREIGN AFFAIRS   2170 RHOB, 202-225-5021

Majority (28 D): Fascell (FL), Chmn.; Hamilton (IN), Yatron (PA), Solarz (NY), Studds (MA), Wolpe (MI), Crockett (MI), Gejdenson (CT), Dymally (CA), Lantos (CA), Kostmayer (PA), Torricelli (NJ), Smith (FL), Berman (CA), Levine (CA), Feighan (OH), Weiss (NY), Ackerman (NY), Udall (AZ), Clarke (NC), Fuster (PR), Owens (UT), Johnston (FL), Engel (NY), Faleomavaega (Am. Samoa), Bosco (CA), McCloskey (IN), Payne (NJ).
Minority (18 R): Broomfield (MI), Gilman (NY), Lagomarsino (CA), Leach (IA), Roth (WI), Snowe (ME), Hyde (IL), Bereuter (NE), Smith (NJ), DeWine (OH), Burton (IN), Meyers (KS), Miller (WA), Lukens (OH), Blaz (Guam), Gallegly (CA), Houghton (NY), Goss (FL).

SUBCOMMITTEES

AFRICA
Majority (6 D): Wolpe, Chmn.; Crockett, Dymally, Payne, Engel, McCloskey.
Minority (4 R): Burton, Lukens, Houghton, Blaz.

ARMS CONTROL, INTERNATIONAL SECURITY AND SCIENCE
Majority (8 D): Fascell, Chmn.; Berman, Udall, Clarke, Engel, Studds, Solarz, Bosco.
Minority (5 R): Broomfield, Gallegly, Snowe, Hyde, Goss.

ASIAN AND PACIFIC AFFAIRS

Majority (6 D): Solarz, Chmn.; Faleomavaega, Lantos, Torricelli, Ackerman, Clarke.
Minority (4 R): Leach, Blaz, Lagomarsino, Roth.

EUROPE AND THE MIDDLE EAST

Majority (8 D): Hamilton, Chmn.; Lantos, Torricelli, Smith (FL), Levine, Feighan, Ackerman, Owens.
Minority (5 R): Gilman, Meyers, Lukens, Leach, Smith (NJ).

HUMAN RIGHTS AND INTERNATIONAL ORGANIZATIONS

Majority (6 D): Yatron, Chmn.; Owens, Lantos, Feighan, Weiss, Ackerman.
Minority (4 R): Bereuter, Smith (NJ), Meyers, Miller.

INTERNATIONAL ECONOMIC POLICY AND TRADE

Majority (8 D): Gejdenson, Chmn.; Wolpe, Kostmayer, Levine, Feighan, Johnston, Engel, Faleomavaega.
Minority (5 R): Roth, Miller, Houghton, Bereuter, DeWine.

INTERNATIONAL OPERATIONS

Majority (6 D): Dymally, Chmn.; Yatron, Smith (FL), Berman, Weiss, Faleomavaega.
Minority (4 R): Snowe, Gilman, Blaz, Gallegly.

WESTERN HEMISPHERE AFFAIRS

Majority (8 D): Crockett, Chmn.; Studds, Kostmayer, Weiss, Fuster, Johnston, Solarz, Gejdenson.
Minority (5 R): Lagomarsino, Hyde, DeWine, Goss, Burton.

GOVERNMENT OPERATIONS   2157 RHOB, 202-225-5051

Majority (24 D): Conyers (MI), Chmn.; Collins (IL), English (OK), Waxman (CA), Weiss (NY), Synar (OK), Neal (NC), Barnard (GA), Frank (MA), Lantos (CA), Wise (WV), Boxer (CA), Owens (NY), Towns (NY), Spratt (SC), Kolter (PA), Erdreich (AL), Kleczka (WI), Bustamante (TX), Martinez (CA), Pelosi (CA), Payne (NJ), Bates (CA), one vacancy.
Minority (15 R): Horton (NY), Clinger (PA), McCandless (CA), Nielson (UT), Lukens (OH), Hastert (IL), Kyl (AZ), Shays (CT), Smith (VT), Schiff (NM), Douglas (NH), Smith (MS), Cox (CA), Thomas (WY), one vacancy.

SUBCOMMITTEES

COMMERCE, CONSUMER AND MONETARY AFFAIRS

Majority (6 D): Barnard, Chmn.; Spratt, Martinez, Kolter, Bustamante, Waxman.
Minority (4 R): Hastert, Schiff, Douglas, Cox.

EMPLOYMENT AND HOUSING

Majority (5 D): Lantos, Chmn.; Frank, Martinez, Weiss, Wise.
Minority (3 R): Lukens, Kyl, Shays.

ENVIRONMENT, ENERGY AND NATURAL RESOURCES

Majority (6 D): Synar, Chmn.; Towns, Bustamante, Kolter, Waxman, one vacancy.
Minority (3 R): Clinger, Douglas, Thomas.

GOVERNMENT ACTIVITIES AND TRANSPORTATION

Majority (5 D): Collins, Chmn.; Owens, Boxer, Kleczka, Lantos.
Minority (3 R): Nielson, Cox, one vacancy.

GOVERNMENT INFORMATION, JUSTICE AND AGRICULTURE

Majority (6 D): Wise, Chmn.; English, Towns, Spratt, two vacancies.
Minority (3 R): McCandless, Schiff, Thomas.

HUMAN RESOURCES AND INTERGOVERNMENTAL RELATIONS

Majority (6 D): Weiss, Chmn.; Waxman, Pelosi, Payne, two vacancies.
Minority (3 R): Smith (MS), Smith (VT), one vacancy.

LEGISLATION AND NATIONAL SECURITY

Majority (7 D): Conyers, Chmn.; Neal, Erdreich, Kleczka, English, Boxer, one vacancy.
Minority (4 R): Horton, Shays, Kyl, Smith (VT).

HOUSE ADMINISTRATION   H 326 Capitol, 202-225-2061

Majority (13 D): Annunzio (IL), Chmn.; Gaydos (PA), Rose (NC), Panetta (CA), Swift (WA), Oakar (OH), Bates (CA), Clay (MO), Gejdenson (CT), Kolter (PA), Flippo (AL), Frost (TX), one vacancy.
Minority (8 R): Thomas (CA), Dickinson (AL), Gingrich (GA), Vucanovich (NV), Roberts (KS), Gillmor (OH), Hiler (IN), Walsh (NY).

SUBCOMMITTEES

ACCOUNTS

Majority (7 D): Gaydos, Chmn.; Swift, Oakar, Gejdenson, Kolter, Flippo, one vacancy.
Minority (4 R): Vucanovich, Gingrich, Gillmor, Hiler.

ELECTIONS

Majority (7 D): Swift, Chmn.; Rose, Panetta, Bates, Clay, Frost, one vacancy.
Minority (4 R): Thomas, Roberts, Hiler, Walsh.

LIBRARIES AND MEMORIALS

Majority (3 D): Clay, Chmn.; Flippo, Frost.
Minority (2 R): Gillmor, Walsh.

OFFICE SYSTEMS

Majority (3 D): Rose, Chmn.; Kolter, Frost.
Minority (2 R): Walsh, Dickinson.

PERSONNEL AND POLICE

Majority (3 D): Oakar, Chmn.; Gaydos, Panetta.
Minority (2 R): Roberts, Dickinson.

PROCUREMENT AND PRINTING

Majority (3 D): Bates, Chmn.; Flippo, Frost.
Minority (2 R): Roberts, Gingrich.

INTERIOR AND INSULAR AFFAIRS   1324 LHOB, 202-225-2761

Majority (26 D): Udall (AZ), Chmn.; Miller (CA), Sharp (IN), Markey (MA), Murphy (PA), Rahall (WV), Vento (MN), Williams (MT), Byron (MD), de Lugo (VI), Gejdenson (CT), Kostmayer (PA), Lehman (CA), Richardson (NM), Darden (GA), Visclosky (IN), Fuster (PR), Levine (CA), Clarke (NC), Owens (UT), Lewis (GA), Campbell (CO), DeFazio (OR), Faleomavaega (Am. Samoa), McDermott (WA), one vacancy.

Minority (15 R): Young (AK), Lagomarsino (CA), Marlenee (MT), Craig (ID), D. Smith (OR), Hansen (UT), Vucanovich (NV), Blaz (Guam), Rhodes (AZ), Gallegly (CA), Parris (VA), R. Smith (OR), Lightfoot (IA), Thomas (WY), Duncan (TN).

SUBCOMMITTEES

ENERGY AND THE ENVIRONMENT

Majority (10 D): Udall, Chmn.; Miller, Sharp, Markey, Murphy, Vento, Gejdenson, Richardson, Darden, Clarke.

Minority (7 R): Hansen, D. Smith (OR), Vucanovich, Blaz, Rhodes, Parris, Lightfoot.

GENERAL OVERSIGHT AND INVESTIGATIONS

Majority (6 D): Kostmayer, Chmn.; Markey, Gejdenson, Levine, Owens, Faleomavaega.

Minority (3 R): Vucanovich, Rhodes, Duncan.

INSULAR AND INTERNATIONAL AFFAIRS

Majority (7 D): de Lugo, Chmn.; Udall, Darden, Fuster, Clarke, Lewis, Faleomavaega.

Minority (3 R): Lagomarsino, Blaz, Gallegly.

MINING AND NATURAL RESOURCES

Majority (5 D): Rahall, Chmn.; Udall, Murphy, Campbell, DeFazio.

Minority (3 R): Craig, Vucanovich, Marlenee.

NATIONAL PARKS AND PUBLIC LANDS

Majority (20 D): Vento, Chmn.; Murphy, Rahall, Williams, Byron, de Lugo, Kostmayer, Lehman, Richardson, Darden, Visclosky, Fuster, Levine, Clarke, Owens, Lewis, Campbell, DeFazio, McDermott, one vacancy.

Minority (12 R): Marlenee, Lagomarsino, Craig, Hansen, Blaz, Rhodes, Gallegly, Parris, R. Smith (OR), Lightfoot, Thomas, Duncan.

WATER, POWER AND OFFSHORE ENERGY RESOURCES

Majority (14 D): Miller, Chmn.; Udall, Sharp, Markey, Byron, Gejdenson, Kostmayer, Lehman, Levine, Owens, Campbell, DeFazio, McDermott, one vacancy.

Minority (9 R): D. Smith (OR), Young, Marlenee, Craig, Hansen, Blaz, Rhodes, R. Smith (OR), Thomas.

JUDICIARY   2138 RHOB, 202-225-3951

Majority (21 D): Brooks (TX), Chmn.; Kastenmeier (WI), Edwards (CA), Conyers (MI), Mazzoli (KY), Hughes (NJ), Synar (OK), Schroeder (CO), Glickman (KS), Frank (MA), Crockett (MI), Schumer (NY), Morrison (CT), Feighan (OH), Smith (FL), Berman (CA), Boucher (VA), Staggers (WV), Bryant (TX), Cardin (MD), Sangmeister (IL).

Minority (14 R): Fish (NY), Moorhead (CA), Hyde (IL), Sensenbrenner (WI), McCollum (FL), Gekas (PA), DeWine (OH), Dannemeyer (CA), Coble (NC), Slaughter (VA), Smith (TX), Smith (MS), Douglas (NH), James (FL).

SUBCOMMITTEES

ADMINISTRATIVE LAW AND GOVERNMENTAL RELATIONS

Majority (6 D): Frank, Chmn.; Glickman, Morrison, Staggers, Cardin, Edwards.
Minority (4 R): James, Smith (TX), Douglas, Smith (MS).

CIVIL AND CONSTITUTIONAL RIGHTS

Majority (5 D): Edwards, Chmn.; Kastenmeier, Conyers, Schroeder, Crockett.
Minority (3 R): Sensenbrenner, Dannemeyer, James.

COURTS, INTELLECTUAL PROPERTY AND THE ADMINISTRATION OF JUSTICE

Majority (9 D): Kastenmeier, Chmn.; Crockett, Berman, Bryant, Cardin, Boucher,
Sangmeister, Hughes, Synar.
Minority (6 R): Moorhead, Hyde, Coble, Slaughter, Fish, Sensenbrenner.

CRIME

Majority (6 D): Hughes, Chmn.; Mazzoli, Feighan, Smith (FL), Boucher, Conyers.
Minority (4 R): McCollum, Smith (MS), Gekas, DeWine.

CRIMINAL JUSTICE

Majority (5 D): Schumer, Chmn.; Sangmeister, Conyers, Smith (FL), Bryant.
Minority (3 R): Gekas, Coble, Smith (MS).

ECONOMIC AND COMMERCIAL LAW

Majority (9 D): Brooks, Chmn.; Mazzoli, Glickman, Feighan, Smith (FL), Staggers, Synar,
Schroeder, Edwards.
Minority (6 R): Fish, DeWine, Dannemeyer, Douglas, Moorhead, Hyde.

IMMIGRATION, REFUGEES AND INTERNATIONAL LAW

Majority (6 D): Morrison, Chmn.; Frank, Schumer, Berman, Bryant, Mazzoli.
Minority (4 R): Smith (TX), McCollum, Slaughter, Fish.

MERCHANT MARINE AND FISHERIES   1334 LHOB, 202-225-4047

Majority (26 D): Jones (NC), Chmn.; Studds (MA), Hubbard (KY), Hughes (NJ), Hutto (FL),
Tauzin (LA), Foglietta (PA), Hertel (MI), Dyson (MD), Lipinski (IL), Borski (PA), Carper
(DE), Bosco (CA), Tallon (SC), Ortiz (TX), Bennett (FL), Manton (NY), Pickett (VA),
Brennan (ME), Hochbrueckner (NY), Clement (TN), Solarz (NY), Pallone (NJ), Laughlin
(TX), Lowey (NY), Unsoeld (WA).
Minority (17 R): Davis (MI), Young (AK), Lent (NY), Shumway (CA), Fields (TX), Schneider
(RI), Bateman (VA), Saxton (NJ), Miller (WA), Bentley (MD), Coble (NC), Weldon (PA),
Saiki (HI), Herger (CA), Bunning (KY), Inhofe (OK), Goss (FL).

SUBCOMMITTEES

COAST GUARD AND NAVIGATION

Majority (14 D): Tauzin, Chmn.; Hutto, Clement, Laughlin, Lowey, Studds, Hughes, Carper,
Ortiz, Bennett, Manton, Pickett, Brennan, Hockbrueckner.
Minority (9 R): Davis, Young, Shumway, Bateman, Bentley, Coble, Bunning, Inhofe, Goss.

FISHERIES AND WILDLIFE CONSERVATION AND THE ENVIRONMENT

Majority (14 D): Studds, Chmn.; Hughes, Carper, Bosco, Ortiz, Manton, Tallon, Hochbrueckner, Solarz, Pallone, Unsoeld, Hutto, Tauzin, Dyson.
Minority (9 R): Young, Schneider, Bateman, Saxton, Miller, Coble, Weldon, Saiki, Herger.

MERCHANT MARINE

Majority (14 D): Jones, Chmn.; Hubbard, Lipinski, Borski, Bennett, Pickett, Brennan, Foglietta, Hertel, Tallon, Solarz, Pallone, Laughlin, Unsoeld.
Minority (9 R): Lent, Young, Shumway, Fields, Bateman, Miller, Bentley, Bunning, Inhofe.

OCEANOGRAPHY

Majority (9 D): Hertel, Chmn.; Borski, Clement, Lowey, Studds, Hughes, Bennett, Manton, Brennan.
Minority (6 R): Shumway, Saxton, Weldon, Saiki, Herger, Goss.

OVERSIGHT AND INVESTIGATIONS

Majority (3 D): Foglietta, Chmn.; Pickett, Pallone.
Minority (2 R): Schneider, Saxton.

PANAMA CANAL AND OUTER CONTINENTAL SHELF

Majority (3 D): Dyson, Chmn.; Lipinski, Laughlin.
Minority (2 R): Fields, Bentley.

POST OFFICE AND CIVIL SERVICE   309 CHOB, 202-225-4054

Majority (15 D): Ford (MI), Chmn.; Clay (MO), Schroeder (CO), Garcia (NY), Leland (TX), Yatron (PA), Oakar (OH), Sikorski (MN), McCloskey (IN), Ackerman (NY), Dymally (CA), Sawyer (OH), Kanjorski (PA), Udall (AZ), de Lugo (VI).
Minority (9 R): Gilman (NY), Horton (NY), Myers (IN), Young (AK), Burton (IN), Morella (MD), Ridge (PA), Chandler (WA), one vacancy.

SUBCOMMITTEES

CENSUS AND POPULATION

Majority (3 D): Sawyer, Chmn.; Garcia, Dymally.
Minority (2 R): Ridge, Chandler.

CIVIL SERVICE

Majority (3 D): Sikorski, Chmn.; Schroeder, McCloskey.
Minority (2 R): Morella, Ridge.

COMPENSATION AND EMPLOYEE BENEFITS

Majority (3 D): Ackerman, Chmn.; Oakar, Leland.
Minority (2 R): Myers, Morella.

HUMAN RESOURCES

Majority (3 D): Kanjorski, Chmn.; Yatron, Sikorski.
Minority (2 R): Burton, one vacancy.

INVESTIGATIONS

Majority (3 D): Ford, Chmn.; Yatron, Clay.
Minority (2 R): Chandler, Gilman.

POSTAL OPERATIONS AND SERVICES
Majority (4 D): Leland, Chmn.; Clay, Garcia, Ackerman.
Minority (3 R): Horton, Young, one vacancy.

POSTAL PERSONNEL AND MODERNIZATION
Majority (3 D): McCloskey, Chmn.; Sawyer, de Lugo.
Minority (2 R): Young, Myers.

PUBLIC WORKS AND TRANSPORTATION   2165 RHOB, 202-225-4472

Majority (31 D): Anderson (CA), Chmn.; Roe (NJ), Mineta (CA), Oberstar (MN), Nowak (NY), Rahall (WV), Applegate (OH), de Lugo (VI), Savage (IL), Bosco (CA), Borski (PA), Kolter (PA), Valentine (NC), Towns (NY), Lipinski (IL), Visclosky (IN), Traficant (OH), Lewis (GA), DeFazio (OR), Cardin (MD), Skaggs (CO), Hayes (LA), Clement (TN), Payne (VA), Costello (IL), Pallone (NJ), Jones (GA), Parker (MS), Laughlin (TX), Perkins (KY), Browder (AL), one vacancy.
Minority (20 R): Hammerschmidt (AR), Shuster (PA), Stangeland (MN), Clinger (PA), Molinari (NY), McEwen (OH), Petri (WI), Packard (CA), Boehlert (NY), Lightfoot (IA), Hastert (IL), Inhofe (OK), Ballenger (NC), Upton (MI), Emerson (MO), Craig (ID), Duncan (TN), Hancock (MO), Cox (CA), Grant (FL).

SUBCOMMITTEES

AVIATION
Majority (21 D): Oberstar, Chmn.; Kolter, de Lugo, DeFazio, Hayes, Laughlin, Mineta, Bosco, Valentine, Towns, Lipinski, Visclosky, Traficant, Skaggs, Clement, Payne, Costello, Jones, Nowak, Lewis, one vacancy.
Minority (13 R): Clinger, Shuster, Stangeland, Molinari, McEwen, Petri, Packard, Boehlert, Lightfoot, Inhofe, Ballenger, Duncan, Hancock.

ECONOMIC DEVELOPMENT
Majority (11 D): Savage, Chmn.; Rahall, Applegate, Borski, Kolter, Towns, Payne, Browder, three vacancies.
Minority (7 R): McEwen, Clinger, Hastert, Ballenger, Emerson, Craig, Cox, Grant.

INVESTIGATIONS AND OVERSIGHT
Majority (15 D): Anderson, Chmn.; Borski, Roe, Mineta, Oberstar, Applegate, Lipinski, Visclosky, Bosco, six vacancies.
Minority (8 R): Molinari, Clinger, Shuster, Boehlert, Hastert, Inhofe, Upton, Duncan.

PUBLIC BUILDINGS AND GROUNDS
Majority (7 D): Bosco, Chmn.; Lewis, Cardin, Parker, Nowak, Savage, one vacancy.
Minority (4 R): Petri, Lightfoot, Duncan, Cox.

SURFACE TRANSPORTATION
Majority (23 D): Mineta, Chmn.; Rahall, Applegate, Valentine, Towns, Lipinski, Visclosky, Traficant, Lewis, Cardin, Skaggs, Clement, Payne, Costello, Pallone, Jones, Parker, Roe, Nowak, de Lugo, Savage, Laughlin, one vacancy.
Minority (14 R): Shuster, Stangeland, Clinger, McEwen, Packard, Boehlert, Hastert, Upton, Emerson, Craig, Duncan, Hancock, Cox, Grant.

WATER RESOURCES

Majority (20 D): Nowak, Chmn.; Roe, Oberstar, Borski, Kolter, DeFazio, Cardin, Hayes, Pallone, Parker, Laughlin, Savage, Clement, Costello, Jones, Traficant, Browder, three vacancies.

Minority (13 R): Stangeland, Molinari, Petri, Packard, Lightfoot, Hastert, Inhofe, Ballenger, Upton, Emerson, Craig, Hancock, Cox.

RULES H 312 Capitol, 202-225-9486

Majority (9 D): Moakley (MA), Chmn.; Derrick (SC), Beilenson (CA), Frost (TX), Bonior (MI), Hall (OH), Wheat (MO), Gordon (TN), Slaughter (NY).

Minority (4 R): Quillen (TN), Solomon (NY), Martin (IL), Pashayan (CA).

SUBCOMMITTEES

THE LEGISLATIVE PROCESS

Majority (5 D): Derrick, Chmn.; Frost, Wheat, Gordon, one vacancy.
Minority (2 R): Martin, Pashayan.

RULES OF THE HOUSE

Majority (5 D): Moakley, Chmn.; Beilenson, Bonior, Hall, Slaughter.
Minority (2 R): Solomon, Pashayan.

SCIENCE, SPACE AND TECHNOLOGY 2321 RHOB, 202-225-6371

Majority (30 D): Roe (NJ), Chmn.; Brown (CA), Scheuer (NY), Lloyd (TN), Walgren (PA), Glickman (KS), Volkmer (MO), Wolpe (MI), Nelson (FL), Hall (TX), McCurdy (OK), Mineta (CA), Valentine (NC), Torricelli (NJ), Boucher (VA), Bruce (IL), Stallings (ID), Traficant (OH), Hamilton (IN), Nowak (NY), Perkins (KY), McMillen (MD), Price (NC), Nagle (IA), Hayes (LA), Skaggs (CO), Costello, (IL), Johnston (FL), Tanner (TN), Browder (AL).

Minority (19 R): Walker (PA), Sensenbrenner (WI), Schneider (RI), Boehlert (NY), Lewis (FL), Ritter (PA), Morrison (WA), Packard (CA), Smith (NH), Henry (MI), Fawell (IL), Slaughter (VA), Smith (TX), Buechner (MO), Morella (MD), Shays (CT), Rohrabacher (CA), Schiff (NM), Campbell (CA).

SUBCOMMITTEES

ENERGY RESEARCH AND DEVELOPMENT

Majority (9 D): Lloyd, Chmn.; Boucher, Bruce, Costello, Walgren, Stallings, Traficant, Wolpe, Valentine.
Minority (5 R): Morrison, Fawell, Schiff, Smith (TX), Henry.

INTERNATIONAL SCIENTIFIC COOPERATION

Majority (5 D): Hall, Chmn.; Torricelli, Hamilton, Brown, Scheuer.
Minority (3 R): Packard, Sensenbrenner, Fawell.

INVESTIGATIONS AND OVERSIGHT

Majority (5 D): Roe, Chmn.; Tanner, Hayes, Johnston, Bruce.
Minority (2 R): Ritter, Boehlert.

NATURAL RESOURCES, AGRICULTURE RESEARCH AND ENVIRONMENT

Majority (10 D): Scheuer, Chmn.; Nowak, Tanner, Brown, Wolpe, McCurdy, Valentine, McMillen, Price, Skaggs.
Minority (6 R): Schneider, Morrison, Shays, Smith (NH), Henry, Smith (TX).

SCIENCE, RESEARCH AND TECHNOLOGY

Majority (13 D): Walgren, Chmn.; Brown, Wolpe, Hamilton, Price, Mineta, Bruce, Nagle, Skaggs, Costello, Johnston, Hayes, Browder.
Minority (8 R): Boehlert, Schneider, Ritter, Henry, Morella, Campbell, Slaughter, Buechner.

SPACE SCIENCE AND APPLICATIONS

Majority (16 D): Nelson, Chmn.; Volkmer, Mineta, Torricelli, Stallings, Traficant, Perkins, McMillen, Nagle, Hayes, Skaggs, Johnston, Scheuer, Lloyd, Hall, Tanner.
Minority (10 R): Sensenbrenner, Lewis, Packard, Smith (NH), Slaughter, Smith (TX), Buechner, Rohrabacher, Morella, Schiff.

TRANSPORTATION, AVIATION AND MATERIALS

Majority (7 D): Valentine, Chmn.; Glickman, McCurdy, Nelson, McMillen, Brown, one vacancy.
Minority (4 R): Lewis, Shays, Rohrabacher, Campbell.

SMALL BUSINESS   2361 RHOB, 202-225-5821

Majority (27 D): LaFalce (NY), Chmn.; Smith (IA), Luken (OH), Skelton (MO), Mazzoli (KY), Mavroules (MA), Hatcher (GA), Wyden (OR), Eckart (OH), Savage (IL), Sisisky (VA), Torres (CA), Cooper (TN), Olin (VA), Ray (GA), Hayes (IL), Conyers (MI), Bilbray (NV), Mfume (MD), Flake (NY), Lancaster (NC), McNulty (NY), Sarpalius (TX), Hoagland (NE), Neal (MA), Poshard (IL), Engel (NY).
Minority (17 R): McDade (PA), Conte (MA), Broomfield (MI), Ireland (FL), Hiler (IN), Dreier (CA), Slaughter (VA), Meyers (KS), Combest (TX), Baker (LA), Rhodes (AZ), Hefley (CO), Upton (MI), Holloway (LA), Hancock (MO), Campbell (CA), one vacancy.

SUBCOMMITTEES

ANTITRUST, IMPACT OF DEREGULATION AND PRIVATIZATION

Majority (5 D): Eckart, Chmn.; Luken, Cooper, Bilbray, Neal.
Minority (3 R): Dreier, Campbell, Slaughter.

ENVIRONMENT AND LABOR

Majority (5 D): Torres, Chmn.; Poshard, Engel, Cooper, one vacancy.
Minority (3 R): Hiler, Combest, Upton.

EXPORTS, TAX POLICY AND SPECIAL PROBLEMS

Majority (7 D): Sisisky, Chmn.; Ray, Hoagland, Mazzoli, Lancaster, McNulty, Bilbray.
Minority (4 R): Ireland, Slaughter, Meyers, Rhodes.

PROCUREMENT, TOURISM AND RURAL DEVELOPMENT

Majority (10 D): Skelton, Chmn.; Hatcher, Bilbray, Lancaster, McNulty, Sarpalius, Neal, Poshard, Torres, Mfume.
Minority (6 R): Conte, Baker, Rhodes, Hefley, Upton, Holloway.

REGULATION, BUSINESS OPPORTUNITIES AND ENERGY

Majority (5 D): Wyden, Chmn.; Engel, Sisisky, Olin, McNulty.
Minority (3 R): Broomfield, Combest, Hancock.

SBA, THE GENERAL ECONOMY AND MINORITY ENTERPRISE DEVELOPMENT

Majority (11 D): LaFalce, Chmn.; Smith, Mazzoli, Mavroules, Savage, Cooper, Olin, Hayes, Conyers, Mfume, Flake.
Minority (7 R): McDade, Meyers, Combest, Baker, Holloway, Hancock, Campbell.

STANDARDS OF OFFICIAL CONDUCT   House Terrace 2, Capitol Bldg.
202-225-7103

Majority (6 D): Dixon (CA), Chmn.; Fazio (CA), Dwyer (NJ), Mollohan (WV), Gaydos (PA), Atkins (MA).
Minority (6 R): Myers (IN), Hansen (UT), Pashayan (CA), Petri (WI), Craig (ID), Brown (CO).

NO SUBCOMMITTEES

VETERANS' AFFAIRS   335 CHOB, 202-225-3527

Majority (21 D): Montgomery (MS), Chmn.; Edwards (CA), Applegate (OH), Evans (IL), Penny (MN), Staggers (WV), Rowland (GA), Florio (NJ), Robinson (AR), Stenholm (TX), Harris (AL), Kennedy (MA), Patterson (SC), Johnson (SD), Jontz (IN), Payne (VA), Morrison (CT), Sangmeister (IL), Parker (MS), Jones (GA), Long (IN).
Minority (13 R): Stump (AR), Hammerschmidt (AR), Wylie (OH), McEwen (OH), Smith (NJ), Burton (IN), Bilirakis (FL), Ridge (PA), Rowland (CT), Smith (NH), James (FL), Stearns (FL), Paxon (NY).

SUBCOMMITTEES

COMPENSATION, PENSION AND INSURANCE

Majority (6 D): Applegate, Chmn.; Sangmeister, Parker, Evans, Penny, Jones.
Minority (3 R): McEwen, Wylie, Bilirakis.

EDUCATION, TRAINING AND EMPLOYMENT

Majority (5 D): Penny, Chmn.; Robinson, Patterson, Sangmeister, Evans.
Minority (3 R): Smith (NJ), Wylie, Ridge.

HOSPITALS AND HEALTH CARE

Majority (12 D): Montgomery, Chmn.; Rowland (GA), Florio, Robinson, Stenholm, Harris, Kennedy, Patterson, Johnson, Jontz, Payne, Morrison.
Minority (8 R): Hammerschmidt, Stump, McEwen, Smith (NJ), Burton, Bilirakis, Ridge, Rowland (CT).

HOUSING AND MEMORIAL AFFAIRS

Majority (7 D): Staggers, Chmn.; Jones, Rowland (GA), Harris, Payne, Parker, Florio.
Minority (4 R): Burton, Rowland (CT), Smith (NH), Paxon.

OVERSIGHT AND INVESTIGATIONS

Majority (5 D): Evans, Chmn.; Applegate, Florio, Kennedy, Long.
Minority (4 R): Stump, Smith (NH), James, Stearns.

WAYS AND MEANS   1102 LHOB, 202-225-3625

Majority (23 D): Rostenkowski (IL), Chmn.; Gibbons (FL), Pickle (TX), Rangel (NY), Stark (CA), Jacobs (IN), Ford (TN), Jenkins (GA), Gephardt (MO), Downey (NY), Guarini (NJ), Russo (IL), Pease (OH), Matsui (CA), Anthony (AR), Flippo (AL), Dorgan (ND), Kennelly (CT), Donnelly (MA), Coyne (PA), Andrews (TX), Levin (MI), Moody (WI).
Minority (13 R): Archer (TX), Vander Jagt (MI), Crane (IL), Frenzel (MN), Schulze (PA), Gradison (OH), Thomas (CA), McGrath (NY), Brown (CO), Chandler (WA), Shaw (FL), Sundquist (TN), Johnson (CT).

SUBCOMMITTEES

HEALTH

Majority (7 D): Stark, Chmn.; Donnelly, Coyne, Pickle, Anthony, Levin, Moody.
Minority (4 R): Gradison, Chandler, Crane, Johnson.

OVERSIGHT

Majority (7 D): Pickle, Chmn.; Anthony, Flippo, Dorgan, Ford, Rangel, Jacobs.
Minority (4 R): Schulze, McGrath, Chandler, Shaw.

HUMAN RESOURCES

Majority (7 D): Downey, Actg. Chmn.; Ford, Pease, Matsui, Kennelly, Andrews, Coyne.
Minority (4 R): Shaw, Brown, Sundquist, Johnson.

SELECT REVENUE MEASURES

Majority (7 D): Rangel, Chmn.; Flippo, Dorgan, Kennelly, Andrews, Stark, Donnelly.
Minority (4 R): Vander Jagt, McGrath, Brown, Sundquist.

SOCIAL SECURITY

Majority (5 D): Jacobs, Chmn.; Gephardt, Gibbons, Levin, Moody.
Minority (3 R): Brown, Schulze, Gradison.

TRADE

Majority (9 D): Gibbons, Chmn.; Rostenkowski, Jenkins, Downey, Pease, Russo, Gephardt, Guarini, Matsui.
Minority (5 R): Crane, Vander Jagt, Frenzel, Schulze, Thomas.

SELECT COMMITTEES

SELECT COMMITTEE ON AGING   712 House Annex 1, 202-226-3375

Majority (39 D): Roybal (CA), Chmn.; Downey (NY), Florio (NJ), Ford (TN), Hughes (NJ), Lloyd (TN), Oakar (OH), Luken (OH), Byron (MD), Waxman (CA), Synar (OK), Derrick (SC), Vento (MN), Frank (MA), Lantos (CA), Wyden (OR), Crockett (MI), Skelton (MO), Hertel (MI), Borski (PA), Erdreich (AL), Sisisky (VA), Wise (WV), Richardson (NM), Volkmer (MO), Gordon (TN), Manton (NY), Robinson (AR), Stallings (ID), Clarke (NC), Kennedy (MA), Slaughter (NY), Bilbray (NV), Jontz (IN), Costello (IL), Staggers (WV), Pallone (NJ), Unsoeld (WA), one vacancy.

Minority (27 R): Rinaldo (NJ), Hammerschmidt (AR), Regula (OH), Shumway (CA), Snowe (ME), Tauke (IA), Courter (NJ), Schneider (RI), Ridge (PA), Smith (NJ), Boehlert (NY), Saxton (NJ), Bentley (MD), Lightfoot (IA), Fawell (IL), Meyers (KS), Blaz (GU), Henry (MI), Schuette (MI), Spence (SC), Clinger (PA), Morella (MD), Saiki (HI), Porter (IL), Duncan (TN), Stearns (FL), James (FL).

SUBCOMMITTEES

HEALTH AND LONG-TERM CARE

Majority (18 D): Florio, Chmn.; Ford, Oakar, Luken, Waxman, Synar, Derrick, Vento, Frank, Wyden, Skelton, Hertel, Borski, Erdreich, Sisisky, Wise, Richardson, one vacancy.
Minority (12 R): Regula, Rinaldo, Schneider, Ridge, Smith, Boehlert, Saxton, Bentley, Lightfoot, Fawell, Henry, Clinger.

HOUSING AND CONSUMER INTERESTS

Majority (10 D): Florio, Chmn.; Lloyd, Byron, Lantos, Richardson, Volkmer, Gordon, Manton, Bilbray, Pallone.
Minority (8 R): Courter, Hammerschmidt, Ridge, Fawell, Saiki, Schuette, Duncan, James.

HUMAN SERVICES

Majority (10 D): Downey, Chmn.; Hughes, Lantos, Robinson, Clarke, Kennedy, Slaughter, Staggers, Pallone, Unsoeld.
Minority (8 R): Snowe, Shumway, Blaz, Spence, Clinger, Morella, Saiki, Duncan.

RETIREMENT INCOME AND EMPLOYMENT

Majority (12 D): Roybal, Chmn.; Downey, Lloyd, Oakar, Synar, Crockett, Wise, Volkmer, Manton, Stallings, Jontz, Costello.
Minority (8 R): Tauke, Shumway, Meyers, Schuette, Spence, Porter, Stearns, James.

SELECT COMMITTEE ON CHILDREN, YOUTH AND FAMILIES

385 House Annex 2
202-226-7660

Majority (18 D): Miller (CA), Chmn; Lehman (FL), Schroeder (CO), Boggs (LA), McHugh (NY), Weiss (NY), Anthony (AR), Boxer (CA), Levin (MI), Morrison (CT), Rowland (GA), Sikorski (MN), Wheat (MO), Martinez (CA), Evans (IL), Durbin (IL), Skaggs (CO), Sarpalius (TX).
Minority (12 R): Bliley (VA), Wolf (VA), Vucanovich (NV), Packard (CA), Hastert (IL), Holloway (LA), Grandy (IA), Weldon (PA), Smith (TX), Smith (VT), Walsh (NY), Machtley (RI).

NO SUBCOMMITTEES

SELECT COMMITTEE ON HUNGER 507 House Annex 2, 202-226-5470

Majority (18 D): Leland (TX), Chmn.; Hall (OH), Panetta (CA), Fazio (CA), Kostmayer (PA), Dorgan (ND), Carr (MI), Penny (MN), Ackerman (NY), Espy (MS), Flake (NY), Patterson (SC), Foglietta (PA), Bustamante (TX), McNulty (NY), Faleomavaega (Am. Samoa), Engel (NY), AuCoin (OR).

Minority (12 R): Emerson (MO), Roukema (NJ), Morrison (WA), Gilman (NY), R. Smith (OR), Bereuter (NE), Upton (MI), Herger (CA), Hunter (CA), Wolf (VA), Smith (NJ), one vacancy.

NO SUBCOMMITTEES

PERMANENT SELECT COMMITTEE ON INTELLIGENCE

H 405
202-225-4121

Majority (12 D): Beilenson (CA), Chmn.; McCurdy (OK), Kastenmeier (WI), Roe (NJ), McHugh (NY), Dwyer (NJ), Wilson (TX), Kennelly (CT), Glickman (KS), Mavroules (MA), Richardson (NM), Solarz (NY).
Minority (7 R): Hyde (IL), Livingston (LA), Schuster (PA), Combest (TX), Bereuter (NE), Rowland (CT), Dornan (CA).

SUBCOMMITTEES

LEGISLATION

Majority (6 D): McHugh, Chmn.; Kastenmeier, Kennelly, Glickman, Richardson, Solarz.
Minority (3 R): Livingston, Rowland, Dornan.

OVERSIGHT AND EVALUATION

Majority (6 D): McCurdy, Chmn.; Roe, Kennelly, Mavroules, McHugh, Dwyer.
Minority (3 R): Schuster, Combest, Bereuter.

PROGRAM AND BUDGET AUTHORIZATION

Majority (8 D): Beilenson, Chmn.; Kastenmeier, Dwyer, Wilson, Glickman, Richardson, Solarz, McCurdy.
Minority (4 R): Hyde, Shuster, Livingston, Combest.

SELECT COMMITTEE ON NARCOTICS ABUSE AND CONTROL

234 House Annex 2
202-226-3040

Majority (18 D): Rangel (NY), Chmn.; Brooks (TX), Stark (CA), Scheuer (NY), Collins (IL), Akaka (HI), Guarini (NJ), Fascell (FL), Fauntroy (DC), Hughes (NJ), Levine (CA), Ortiz (TX), Smith (FL), Towns (NY), Traficant (OH), Mfume (MD), Brennan (ME), Lowey (NY).
Minority (12 R): Coughlin (PA), Gilman (NY), Oxley (OH), Parris (VA), Sensenbrenner (WI), Dornan (CA), Lewis (FL), Inhofe (OK), Herger (CA), Shays (CT), Paxon (NY), Grant (FL).

NO SUBCOMMITTEES

METROPOLITAN MAPS

The maps on the following pages illustrate congressional districts in the metropolitan areas of (in order) San Francisco and Los Angeles, California; Miami, Florida; Chicago, Illinois; Detroit, Michigan; and New York, New York.

CALIFORNIA — Congressional Districts, Counties, and Selected Places

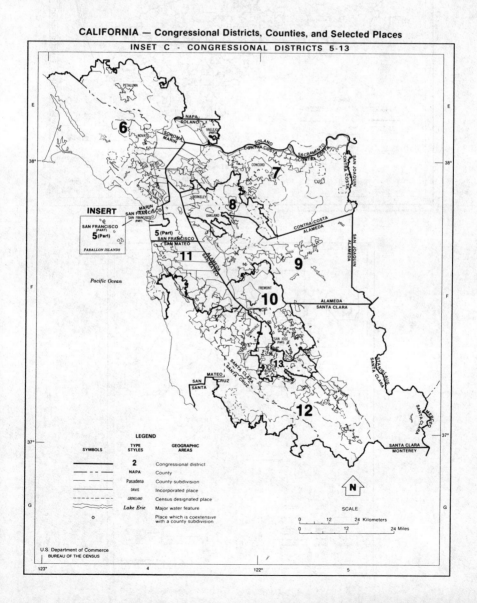

INSET C - CONGRESSIONAL DISTRICTS 5-13

LEGEND

SYMBOLS	TYPE STYLES	GEOGRAPHIC AREAS
	2	Congressional district
	NAPA	County
	Pasadena	County subdivision
	DAVIS	Incorporated place
	GROVELAND	Census designated place
	Lake Erie	Major water feature
○		Place which is coextensive with a county subdivision

SCALE

U.S. Department of Commerce
BUREAU OF THE CENSUS

CALIFORNIA — Congressional Districts, Counties, and Selected Places

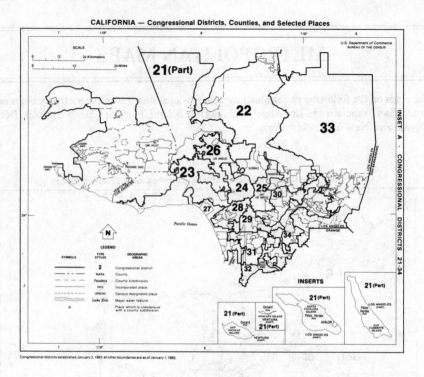

Congressional districts established January 2, 1983; all other boundaries are as of January 1, 1980.

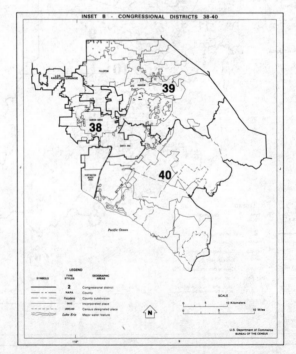

FLORIDA — Congressional Districts, Counties, and Selected Places

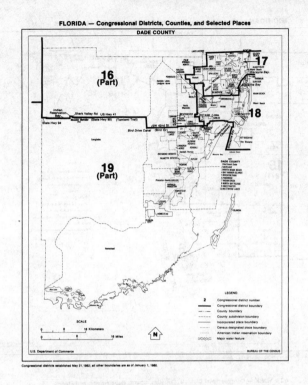

DADE COUNTY

Congressional districts established May 21, 1982; all other boundaries are as of January 1, 1980.

ILLINOIS — Congressional Districts, Counties, and Selected Places

INSET D—COOK, DU PAGE, AND WILL COUNTIES

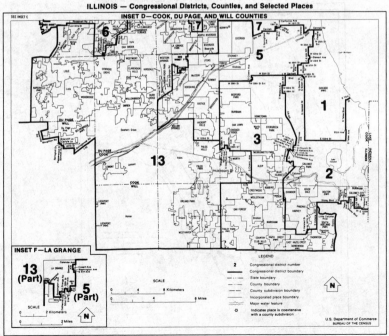

INSET F—LA GRANGE

Congressional districts established November 23, 1981; all other boundaries are as of January 1, 1980.

MICHIGAN — Congressional Districts, Counties, and Selected Places

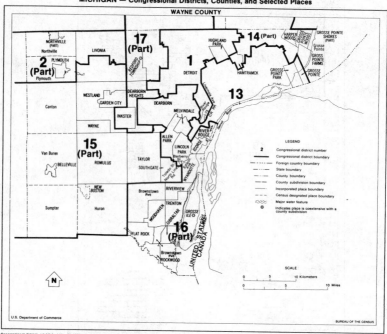

Congressional districts established May 24, 1962; all other boundaries are as of January 1, 1980.

NEW YORK — Congressional Districts, Counties, County Subdivisions, and Places

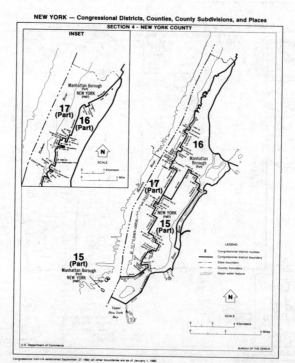

Congressional districts established September 27, 1962; all other boundaries are as of January 1, 1980.

NEW YORK — Congressional Districts, Counties, County Subdivisions, and Places

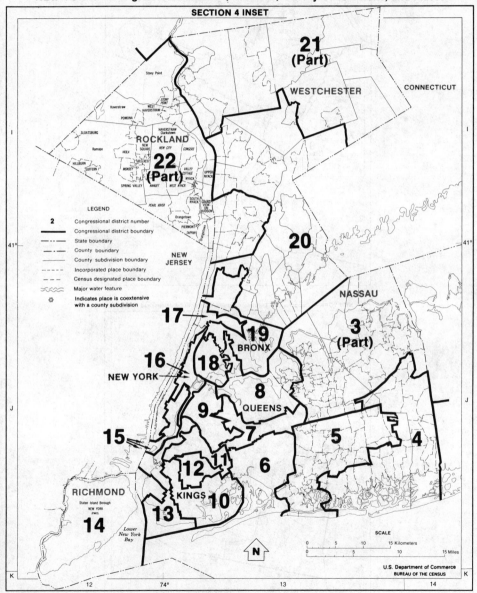

SECTION 4 INSET

21 (Part)

WESTCHESTER

CONNECTICUT

Stony Point

WEST HAVERSTRAW

STONY POINT

Haverstraw

POMONA

HAVERSTRAW
Clarkstown

SLOATSBURG

ROCKLAND

NEW CITY

CONGERS

22 (Part)

Ramapo

VIOLA

NEW SQUARE

HILLBURN

SUFFERN

MONSEY

SPRING VALLEY

HILLCREST

NANUET

WEST NYACK

VALLEY COTTAGE

UPPER NYACK

PEARL RIVER

SOUTH NYACK

GRAND VIEW ON HUDSON

Orangetown

PIERMONT

TAPPAN

LEGEND

2   Congressional district number
       Congressional district boundary
       State boundary
       County boundary
       County subdivision boundary
       Incorporated place boundary
       Census designated place boundary
       Major water feature
✿   Indicates place is coextensive
       with a county subdivision

NEW JERSEY

20

NASSAU

17

3 (Part)

19

BRONX

16

18

NEW YORK

8

QUEENS

9

15

7

5

4

12

11

6

RICHMOND

Staten Island Borough
NEW YORK
(PART)

KINGS

10

14

13

Lower New York Bay

SCALE

0   5   10   15 Kilometers
0   5   10   15 Miles

N

U.S. Department of Commerce
BUREAU OF THE CENSUS

12   74°   13   14

Congressional districts established September 27, 1983; all other boundaries are as of January 1, 1980.

NEW YORK — Congressional Districts, Counties, County Subdivisions, and Places

SECTION 4 - QUEENS COUNTY

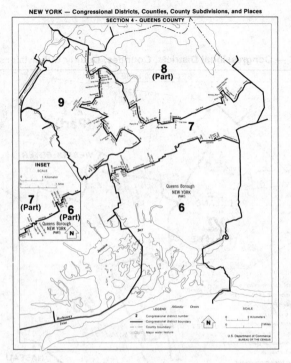

NEW YORK — Congressional Districts, Counties, County Subdivisions, and Places

SECTION 4 - KINGS COUNTY

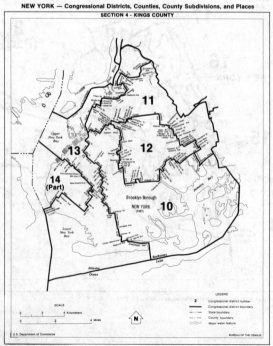

INDEX

The names of Governors, Senators and Representatives appear in boldface type. The number of the page that includes their corresponding biographical, voting and campaign finance information also appears in bold.

1472   INDEX

THE AUTHORS

MICHAEL BARONE is a graduate of Harvard College and Yale Law School. He has been affiliated with the polling group of Peter D. Hart Research Associates, Inc. and has been an editorial writer and columnist for *The Washington Post*. Barone is currently senior writer for *U.S. News and World Report*. He lives with his daughter Sarah in Washington, DC.

GRANT UJIFUSA is a senior editor at *Reader's Digest* magazine in Pleasantville, New York. Ujifusa, a native of Worland, Wyoming and a graduate of Harvard College, lives with his wife Amy and sons Steven and Andrew in Chappaqua, New York. He is also the Strategy Chair for a group associated with the Japanese American Citizens League.

THE PUBLISHER

"The nation's most respected nonpartisan source of information about how Washington policymaking machinery really works."

That's how *Newsweek* described *National Journal*. For 20 years, *National Journal* has reached subscribers with an award-winning weekly magazine noted for its dedication to "facts only" reporting. *National Journal* speaks to people who make it their business to know what's going on in the world's largest business—the United States Government.

Only *National Journal* is exclusively devoted to the coverage and analysis of what the government is doing today, what it's going to do tomorrow, and how its actions affect every facet of our lives.

This 1990 edition of *The Almanac of American Politics* marks the fourth volume to be published by National Journal Inc. In addition to the *Almanac* and *National Journal*, National Journal Inc. publishes the monthly *Government Executive* and *Military Forum* magazines, the semi-annual directory *The Capital Source* and the *National Journal Convention Daily*, in conjunction with the Democratic and Republican Conventions.

National Journal Inc. is a wholly-owned subsidiary of the Los Angeles-based Times Mirror Company.

1730 M Street, NW, Washington, DC 20036 Telephone (202) 857-1400